Brill Encyclopedia of Early Christianity

Brill Encyclopedia of Early Christianity
Authors, Texts, and Ideas

Volume I:
Aba – Bib

General Editors:
David G. Hunter, Boston College, United States
Paul J.J. van Geest, Tilburg University / Erasmus University Rotterdam, The Netherlands,
Bert Jan Lietaert Peerbolte, Vrije Universiteit Amsterdam, The Netherlands

Consultant Editor:
Angelo di Berardino, Augustinianum, Italy

Section Editors:
Juliette Day, University of Helsinki, Finland
Maria Doerfler, Yale University, United States
David Eastman, Ohio Wesleyan University, United States
Robin M. Jensen, University of Notre Dame, United States
Robert Kitchen, Sankt Ignatios Theological Academy, Sweden
Rebecca Krawiec, Canisius College, Buffalo, New York, United States
Jacob Abraham Latham, University of Tennessee, United States
Outi Lehtipuu, University of Helsinki, Finland
Christoph Markschies, Humboldt University of Berlin, Germany
Bronwen Neil, Macquarie University, Australia
Karin Berber Neutel, Umeå University, Sweden
Geert van Oyen, University of Louvain, Belgium
Karla Pollmann, University of Tübingen, Germany
Joshua Schwartz, Bar-Ilan University, Israel
Kristina Sessa, Ohio State University, United States
Tarmo Toom, Tartu University, Estonia

BRILL

LEIDEN | BOSTON
2024

The Library of Congress Cataloging-in-Publication Data is available online at https://catalog.loc.gov

Typeface for the Latin, Greek, and Cyrillic scripts: "Brill". See and download: brill.com/brill-typeface.

ISSN 2589-7993
ISBN 978-90-04-28892-8 (vol. I)
ISBN 978-90-04-28893-5 (vol. II)
ISBN 978-90-04-28894-2 (vol. III)
ISBN 978-90-04-28895-9 (vol. IV)
ISBN 978-90-04-28896-6 (vol. V)
ISBN 978-90-04-70061-1 (vol. VI)
ISBN 978-90-04-70449-7 (set)

Copyright 2024 by Koninklijke Brill BV, Leiden, The Netherlands.
Koninklijke Brill BV incorporates the imprints Brill, Brill Nijhoff, Brill Schöningh, Brill Fink, Brill mentis, Brill Wageningen Academic, Vandenhoeck & Ruprecht, Böhlau and V&R unipress.
All rights reserved. No part of this publication may be reproduced, translated, stored in a retrieval system, or transmitted in any form or by any means, electronic, mechanical, photocopying, recording or otherwise, without prior written permission from the publisher. Requests for re-use and/or translations must be addressed to Koninklijke Brill BV via brill.com or copyright.com.

This book is printed on acid-free paper and produced in a sustainable manner.

PRINTED BY DRUKKERIJ WILCO B.V. - AMERSFOORT, THE NETHERLANDS

Table of Contents

Preface	I: xxxv
List of Contributors	I: xxxvii
Biblical and Extrabiblical Abbreviations	I: l
Rabbinic Literature	I: lx
Nag Hammadi	I: lxii
Ancient Authors and Primary Sources	I: lxiii
Journals, Series, Encyclopedias, and Lexicons	I: cxi
General Abbreviations	I: cliv
Introduction	I: clvi

A

Aba (Disciple of Ephrem the Syrian)	I: 1
Abdon and Sennen	I: 3
Abelites	I: 4
Abercius	I: 6
Abgarids	I: 8
Ablutions	I: 13
Abortion	I: 16
Abraham	I: 20
Abraham of Pbou	I: 28
Abraham, Testament of	I: 30
Abrasax	I: 33
Abstinence → Fasting/Abstinence	I: 36
Acacian Schism	I: 36
Acacius of Constantinople	I: 39
Acedia	I: 44
Acheiropoietai	I: 48
Acilius Glabrio	I: 52
Acoumeti	I: 54
Acolyte	I: 56
Acts, Book of	I: 58
Ad Metalla (*Damnatio*)	I: 67
Ad Novatianum	I: 72
Ad Sanctos	I: 74
Adam and Eve	I: 77
I. Adam	I: 77
II. Adam and Eve	I: 81
III. *Adam and Eve, Life of*	I: 85
IV. *Adam, Testament of*	I: 89
Adamites	I: 91
Addai	I: 93
Adiabene	I: 98
Adimantus	I: 100

Adoption	I: 103
Adoptionists	I: 110
Adrian	I: 112
Adultery	I: 114
Advent	I: 117
Aelius Donatus	I: 119
Aeon	I: 121
Aërius	I: 123
Aëtius, Flavius	I: 124
Aetheria → Egeria	I: 126
Africa	I: 126
Afterlife	I: 133
Agape	I: 141
Agatha	I: 149
Agathangelos	I: 153
Agathangelus of Rome	I: 156
Age → Aeon	I: 157
Agilulf	I: 157
Agnes	I: 159
Agnus Dei	I: 162
Agrapha → Logia/Agrapha	I: 166
Agraphon	I: 166
Agrestius	I: 173
Agrippa Castor	I: 175
Agrippa II	I: 178
Akathistos	I: 180
Aksum	I: 184
Alaric I	I: 185
Alexander I (Bishop of Rome)	I: 187
Alexander I of Alexandria	I: 189
Alexander of Aphrodisias	I: 193
Alexander of Constantinople	I: 196
Alexander of Jerusalem	I: 198
Alexander Severus	I: 199
Alexandria	I: 202
I. City	I: 202
II. School of	I: 208
III. Councils of	I: 210
IV. Libraries of	I: 213
Alexandrians, Epistle to the	I: 218
Allegory	I: 219
Allogenes, Book of	I: 228
Alms/Almsgiving	I: 232
Altar	I: 237
Altar of Victory	I: 239
Altercatio Heracliani	I: 243
Amandus	I: 245
Amasea	I: 246

Amastris	I: 246
Ambrose (Disciple of Didymus)	I: 247
Ambrose (Friend of Origen)	I: 249
Ambrose of Milan	I: 251
Ambrosian Liturgy	I: 259
Ambrosiaster	I: 270
Ammianus Marcellinus	I: 275
Ammon	I: 279
Ammonius Saccas	I: 281
Amphilochius	I: 286
Amphipolis	I: 289
Anacletus (Bishop of Rome)	I: 291
Ananias and Sapphira	I: 293
Anaphora	I: 295
Anastasia Pharmacolitria	I: 304
Anastasius (Emperor)	I: 307
Anastasius of Thessalonica	I: 309
Anatolius of Constantinople	I: 310
Anazarbus	I: 313
Anchorites	I: 315
Ancyra	I: 322
Andrew the Apostle	I: 324
I. Andrew (Apostle)	I: 324
II. *Andrew, Acts of*	I: 325
Andrew of Samosata	I: 333
Anemius	I: 335
Angers	I: 336
Anianus of Orléans	I: 338
Anicetus	I: 341
Animals	I: 343
Annunciation → Mary	I: 348
Anointing	I: 348
Anonymous Apollinarist/Apollinarian Forgeries	I: 353
Anthony (Poet)	I: 353
Anthropology	I: 358
Anthropomorphism	I: 367
Antichrist	I: 376
Antidicomarianites	I: 380
Anti-Judaism	I: 384
Antioch, Councils of	I: 390
Antioch of Caria, Synods of	I: 399
Antony the Great	I: 400
Apatheia	I: 406
Apelles	I: 410
Aphrahat	I: 413
Apocalypse/Apocalypticism/Eschatology	I: 416
Apocrisarius	I: 429
Apocriticus	I: 431

Apocrypha → Bible: III. Apocrypha and Pseudepigrapha	I: 435
Apokatastasis	I: 435
Apollinarian Forgeries → Anonymous Appolinarist/Apollinarian Forgeries	I: 438
Apollinaris of Hierapolis	I: 438
Apollinaris of Laodicea	I: 440
Apollinaris of Valence	I: 445
Apollonius of Tyana	I: 447
Apologetics	I: 453
Aponius	I: 461
Apophthegmata Patrum	I: 463
Apostasy/Apostates	I: 472
Apostle(s)	I: 480
I. Apostle/Disciple	I: 480
II. Apostles, Apocryphal Acts of the	I: 487
III. Apostles' Creed	I: 491
IV. *Apostles, Epistle of the*	I: 496
Apostolic Canons	I: 499
Apostolic Church Order	I: 502
Apostolic Constitutions	I: 504
Apostolic Fathers	I: 508
Apostolic History → Arator	I: 515
Apostolic Tradition	I: 515
Apostolicity	I: 519
Apothetic Theology → Negative Theology	I: 523
Arabic Bible → Bible: XVI. Arabic Versions	I: 523
Arator	I: 523
Arbogast	I: 525
Archaeus	I: 527
Archbishop	I: 528
Archelaus, Acts of	I: 530
Archimandrite	I: 533
Archpriest	I: 535
Arian Sermons	I: 537
Arianism	I: 538
Ariminian Churches in the Germanic Kingdoms	I: 548
Aristides of Athens	I: 553
Aristo of Pella	I: 557
Aristotelianism	I: 559
Arius → Arianism	I: 568
Arles	I: 568
Armageddon	I: 570
Armenium Bible → Bible: XIV. Armenian	I: 575
Arnobius of Sicca	I: 575
Asarbus	I: 580
Ascension of Jesus Christ	I: 581
Asceticism	I: 585
Ascitae	I: 593
Asia, Central	I: 594

Assembly/Meeting	I: 599
Asterius the Sophist	I: 607
Asterius Turcius Rufus	I: 609
Astrology	I: 611
Asylum	I: 620
Asylum, Right of	I: 625
Ataraxia	I: 627
Athanasius of Alexandria	I: 632
Atheism/Atheist	I: 640
Athenagoras	I: 644
Athens	I: 649
Atonement	I: 653
Atonement, Day of	I: 658
Atticus	I: 661
Attila	I: 663
Audentius	I: 667
Augustine of Hippo	I: 667
Augustus	I: 683
Ausonius of Bordeaux	I: 688
Auspicius of Toul	I: 693
Autobiography	I: 695
Auxentius of Milan	I: 702
Axiopolis	I: 704

B

Baetica	I: 706
Balai	I: 711
Baleares	I: 712
Baptism	I: 716
Barbarians	I: 724
Barbarus Scaligeri → *Excerpta Latina Barbari*	I: 728
Barbelo	I: 728
Barcelona	I: 730
Bardaisan	I: 735
Barnabas	I: 738
I. Barnabas	I: 738
II. *Barnabas, Epistle of*	I: 742
Bartholomew the Apostle	I: 749
I. Bartholomew (Apostle)	I: 749
II. *Bartholomew, Questions of*	I: 757
Basil of Caesarea	I: 759
Basileiad	I: 766
Basilides	I: 768
Basiliscus	I: 773
Bath/Mikveh	I: 775
Beatitudes	I: 780

Belisarius (Scholasticus)	I: 785
Benedict I	I: 786
Benedict of Nursia	I: 786
Bethany	I: 789
Bethlehem	I: 791
Bethphage	I: 794
Bethsaida	I: 795
Bibiana	I: 799
Bible	II: 1
I. Hebrew Bible/Old Testament	II: 1
II. New Testament	II: 4
III. Apocrypha and Pseudepigrapha	II: 7
IV. Formation of Canons	II: 9
V. Hebrew Bible Translations	II: 15
VI. Septuagint/Old Greek	II: 15
VII. Targums	II: 20
VIII. Vetus Syra	II: 25
IX. Vetus Latina	II: 28
X. Recentiores and Hexapla	II: 31
XI. Peshitta	II: 34
XII. Vulgate	II: 38
XIII. Coptic	II: 41
XIV. Armenian	II: 43
XV. Georgian	II: 46
XVI. Arabic Versions	II: 51
XVII. Ethiopic	II: 53
XVIII. Christian Worship	II: 55
Biblical Interpretation	II: 58
Biography	II: 66
Birds	II: 74
Bishop (Episcopus)	II: 78
Bishops of Rome, Pre-Constantinian	II: 86
Blandina	II: 95
Blessing	II: 97
Bnay/Bnat Qyama	II: 105
Bodmer Papyri	II: 106
Body	II: 111
Boethius, Anicius Manlius	II: 121
Boniface I	II: 133
Boniface II	II: 136
Bonosus	II: 137
Book of Life	II: 140
Book of Steps	II: 143
Borboriani	II: 147
Braga	II: 149
Breviarium Hipponense	II: 152
Bride of Christ	II: 154
Brigid of Kildare	II: 158

Burgundy	II: 159
Byzantine Liturgy	II: 162
Byzantium	II: 167

C

Caecilian	II: 172
Caesarea in Cappadocia	II: 174
Caesarea in Palestine	II: 175
Caesaropapism	II: 180
Cairo Genizah	II: 182
Calcidius	II: 184
Calendar → Liturgical Year	II: 187
Canaan	II: 187
Candidus	II: 191
Cannibalism, Accusation of	II: 191
Canon Muratori	II: 195
Canon Romanus	II: 199
Canon Tables, Eusebian	II: 203
Canons, Formation of → Bible: IV. Formation of Canons	II: 207
Canons (of Councils)	II: 207
Canons of Hippolytus	II: 216
Capernaum	II: 218
Cappadocians	II: 223
Capreolus	II: 232
Carmen de Sodoma/Carmen de Iona	II: 233
Carpocrates	II: 236
Carthage	II: 239
I. City	II: 239
II. Councils of	II: 248
Cassiodorus	II: 263
Cataphrygians	II: 272
Catechesis	II: 276
Catenae	II: 284
Cathedra	II: 287
Celibacy of Clergy	II: 289
Celsus	II: 298
Celtic Liturgy	II: 302
Cemetery	II: 305
Central Asia → Asia, Central	II: 314
Cerdo	II: 314
Cerealis	II: 315
Cerinthus	II: 317
Chalcedon	II: 321
Charismata → Spiritual Gifts (*Charismata*)	II: 329
Charm	II: 329

Cherubs	II: 332
Chiliasm	II: 336
China	II: 341
Chorbishop	II: 345
Christ, Jesus	II: 347
I. Introduction	II: 347
II. Birth and Infancy Narratives	II: 348
III. Descent into Hell	II: 356
IV. Genealogy of Genealogy of Jesus Christ	II: 360
V. Quests for the Historical Jesus Christ	II: 364
Christianity and Classical Culture	II: 367
Christians and Jews	II: 377
Christmas	II: 383
Christology	II: 390
I. 1st–2nd Century CE	II: 390
II. 3rd Century CE	II: 395
III. 4th Century CE and Later	II: 399
Chromatius of Aquileia	II: 403
Chronograph of 354	II: 405
Church and Empire	II: 408
Church Authority	II: 418
Church Buildings	II: 420
I. Survey and Development	II: 420
II. Basilica and Baptistery	II: 424
Church of Rome	II: 429
Church Organization	II: 439
Churches of Lyons and Vienne, Letter of the	II: 441
Circumcelliones → Donatism/Donatists	II: 445
Circumcision	II: 445
Claudian	II: 449
Claudius	II: 452
Cleanthes	II: 454
Clement	II: 457
I. *1 Clement*	II: 457
II. *2 Clement*	II: 462
Clement of Alexandria	II: 465
Clementine Literature, Pseudo-	II: 469
Clovis	II: 474
Codex	II: 476
Codex Justinianus	II: 484
Codex Theodosianus	II: 489
Coenobia → Monasticism: II. Palestinian Monasticism	II: 493
Collatio Alexandri et Dindimi	II: 493
Collatio cum Donatistis	II: 494
Collatio Legum	II: 497
Collects	II: 499
Columba of Iona	II: 502
Columbanus	II: 503

Comfort	II: 507
Comma Johanneum	II: 514
Community Letters	II: 517
Complaint	II: 522
Confession → Penitence/Penance	II: 524
Conon	II: 524
Conon of Bidana	II: 526
Conscience, Freedom of	II: 528
Constantia (Flavia Iulia Constantia)	II: 532
Constantine I	II: 535
Constantine II	II: 544
Constantinople	II: 547
I. Council of 359/360 CE	II: 547
II. First Council (Second Ecumenical Council) of 381 CE	II: 550
III. Second Council (Fifth Ecumenical Council) of 553 CE	II: 553
Constantius I	II: 555
Constantius II	II: 557
Constantius III	II: 561
Constitutions of Hippolytus	II: 562
Continentes	II: 565
Contra Origenem de Visione Isaiae	II: 568
Coptic Bible → Bible: XIII. Coptic	II: 570
Córdoba	II: 570
Corinth	II: 574
Corinthians, Third Epistle to the	II: 580
Cornelius (Bishop of Rome)	II: 583
Cornelius (Centurion)	II: 585
Corsica	II: 587
Cosmas and Damian	II: 592
Cosmos/Cosmology	II: 594
I. In Second Temple Judaism and the New Testament	II: 594
II. In the Greek Philosophical Tradition	II: 598
Councils/Synods	II: 604
Creation	II: 613
Creation (Double)	II: 623
Creeds	II: 631
Cresconius	II: 642
Crispina	II: 644
Crispinus and Crispinianus	II: 646
Cross/Crucifixion	II: 648
Cryptography	II: 656
Cubicularius	II: 659
Cyprian of Carthage	II: 660
Cyprus	II: 668
Cyril of Alexandria	II: 673
Cyril of Jerusalem	II: 681
Cyrillona	II: 688

D

Dadisho' I	II: 690
Dalmatia	II: 691
Damasus (Bishop of Rome)	II: 694
Daniel	II: 699
David	II: 702
De bono pudicitiae	II: 705
De excidio Hierosolymitano	II: 707
De gentibus Indiae et Bragmanibus	II: 712
De recta in Deum fide	II: 714
Deacon/Deaconess	II: 716
Dead	II: 721
I. Care of the Dead	II: 721
II. Cult of the Dead	II: 730
III. Realm of the Dead	II: 739
Dead Sea Scrolls	II: 744
Death	II: 749
Decalogue → Law/Decalogue/Torah	II: 754
Decapolis	II: 754
Decius	II: 758
Decretum Gelasianum	II: 762
Dedication, Council of the	II: 764
Deer	II: 766
Delphinus of Bordeaux	II: 768
Demetrian of Antioch	II: 769
Demetrias	II: 770
Demonology/Demons	II: 773
Deo laudes	II: 779
Deogratias	II: 781
Deportation/Exile	II: 783
Depositio episcoporum	II: 788
Depositio martyrum	II: 789
Desert Fathers	II: 791
Devil	II: 794
Dexter	II: 802
Diakonia	II: 803
Dialogue	II: 808
Diaspora	II: 814
Diatesseron (Syriac)	II: 819
Diatribe	II: 822
Didache	II: 824
Didascalia Apostolorum	II: 829
Didaskalos	II: 831
Diocletian	II: 835
Diodore of Tarsus	II: 841
Diognetus, Epistle to	II: 846

Dionysius the Areopagite, Pseudo-	II: 848
Dionysius Exiguus	II: 855
Diptych	II: 857
Disciple → Apostle/Disciple	II: 861
Disciplina arcani	II: 861
Divination	II: 864
Divorce	III: 1
Docetism	III: 9
Doctrina Apostolorum	III: 14
Domitilla	III: 19
Donatism/Donatists	III: 21
Donatus the Great	III: 29
Dormition and Assumption Apocrypha	III: 34
Dorotheus of Gaza	III: 39
Dream	III: 41
Dumium	III: 46
Dura-Europos	III: 48

E

Early Christian Churches of the Holy Land	III: 52
Easter	III: 58
Ebionites/Ebionitism	III: 66
Ebionites, Gospel of the	III: 68
Ecclesiology	III: 69
Edessa	III: 77
Edict of Claudius	III: 83
Egeria (Aetheria)	III: 88
Egypt	III: 90
Egyptians, Gospel of the (Greek)	III: 97
Elchasaites	III: 104
Elements (*Stoicheia*)	III: 108
Eleusinian Mysteries	III: 110
Elijah	III: 114
Emilia	III: 118
Emotion	III: 120
Emperor/Imperial Cult	III: 129
Encratism/Encratites	III: 133
Energeia	III: 135
Enhypostasis	III: 139
Ennodius	III: 141
Ephebeia	III: 144
Ephesus	III: 146
I. City	III: 146
II. First Ecumenical Council	III: 151
Ephrem the Syrian	III: 158
Epictetus	III: 162

Epicurus/Epicureans	III: 164
Epiphanius of Salamis	III: 174
Epiphany	III: 178
Episcopus → Bishop (Episcopus)	III: 183
Eschatology → Apocalypse/Apocalypticism/Eschatology	III: 183
Essenes	III: 183
Ethiopic Bible → Bible: XVII. Ethiopic	III: 188
Etimasia/Hetoimasia	III: 188
Eucharist	III: 193
Eucherius of Lyon	III: 203
Euchites → Messalians/Euchites	III: 208
Eudocia	III: 208
Eudoxius of Antioch	III: 210
Eugenius	III: 212
Eugenius of Ancyra	III: 214
Eugenius of Carthage	III: 215
Eugippius	III: 216
Eugnostos the Blessed	III: 218
Eulalius → Boniface I	III: 222
Eunomianism	III: 222
Eunomius of Cyzicus	III: 226
Euphemia of Chalcedon	III: 230
Eusebians	III: 232
Eusebius of Alexandria	III: 237
Eusebius of Caesarea (Cappadocia)	III: 238
Eusebius of Caesarea (Palestine)	III: 240
Eusebius of Vercelli	III: 249
Eustochium	III: 250
Eutyches	III: 251
Evagrius of Antioch	III: 253
Evagrius of Pontus	III: 257
Evagrius the Monk	III: 262
Eve → Adam and Eve	III: 265
Evil	III: 265
Excerpta Latina Barbari	III: 274
Excommunication	III: 277
Exegesis → Biblical Interpretation	III: 280
Exile → Deportation/Exile	III: 280
Exorcism/Exorcist → Demonology/Demons	III: 280
Ezana	III: 280
Ezekiel	III: 282

F

Faith	III: 288
I. New Testament and Apostolic Fathers	III: 288
II. Apologists	III: 301
Faithfulness	III: 308

Fall	III: 313
Fan	III: 318
Fasting/Abstinence	III: 320
Faustinus	III: 325
Faustus of Riez	III: 327
Felicity	III: 331
Festal Letters	III: 333
Festus	III: 337
Fire	III: 339
Firmicus Maternus	III: 343
Firmilian of Caesarea	III: 346
First Thought, Three Forms of	III: 348
Fish	III: 351
Flavianus	III: 356
Flavius Clemens	III: 358
Flavius Josephus	III: 360
Foolishness	III: 370
Forgiveness of Sins	III: 375
Fortuna	III: 381
Fortunatianus of Aquileia	III: 383
Forty Martyrs of Sebaste	III: 385
Franks	III: 388
Friendship	III: 390
Fructuosus of Braga	III: 395
Frumentius	III: 398
Fulfillment	III: 399
Fulgentius of Ruspe	III: 407
Funeral	III: 412

G

Gaius	III: 420
Galatia	III: 423
Galen	III: 427
Galerius (Emperor)	III: 430
Galicia	III: 433
Galilee	III: 437
Galla Placidia	III: 443
Gallican Liturgy	III: 447
Gallienus	III: 451
Gamaliel	III: 456
Gangra	III: 459
Gaudentius of Brescia	III: 461
Gaul	III: 465
Gehenna	III: 475
Gelasius I (Bishop of Rome)	III: 479
Gender	III: 482
Gennadius of Marseilles	III: 492

Gennesareth	III: 496
Genovefa (Genevieve) of Paris	III: 500
George, Bishop of the Arabs	III: 502
Georgia	III: 504
Georgian Bible → Bible: XV. Georgian	III: 510
Gerontius	III: 510
Gervasius and Protasius	III: 512
Gesta martyrum	III: 515
Gildas the Wise	III: 518
Glossolalia	III: 520
Gnomologia	III: 525
Gnosis/Gnosticism	III: 529
Gnosis/Knowledge	III: 537
God	III: 546
I. Doctrine of God	III: 546
II. Knowledge of God	III: 558
Gog and Magog	III: 566
Golgotha	III: 571
Gordius	III: 574
Goths	III: 576
Grace	III: 581
Great Invisible Spirit, Holy Book of the	III: 587
Gregory of Nazianzus	III: 590
Gregory of Nyssa	III: 595
Gregory of Tours	III: 604
Gregory Thaumaturgus	III: 608
Gregory the Great	III: 609
Guilt → Forgiveness of Sins	III: 613

H

Hades	III: 614
Hadrian's *Rescript*	III: 618
Hagiography	III: 619
Halakhah	III: 622
Health Care → Medicine and Health Care	III: 628
Hebrew Bible → Bible: I. Hebrew Bible	III: 628
Hebrew Bible Translations → Bible: V. Hebrew Bible Translations	III: 628
Hebrews, Epistle to the	III: 628
Hegesippus	III: 635
Helena Augusta	III: 639
Hell → Hades	III: 641
Hellenism and Christianity	III: 641
Helvidius	III: 647
Heresy	III: 649
Hermas	III: 653
Hermenegild	III: 659

Hermeneutics → Biblical Interpretation	III: 662
Hermes Trismegistus	III: 662
Hermetism	III: 665
Hermias	III: 668
Herod	III: 669
Herodians	III: 671
Hexaemeron	III: 674
Hexapla → Bible: X. Recentiores and Hexapla	III: 677
Hilary of Arles	III: 677
Hilary of Poitiers	III: 681
Hippo	III: 689
Hippolytus → Bishops of Rome, Pre-Constantinian	III: 692
Hippolytus, *Canon* of	III: 692
Historia monachorum	III: 697
Holiness	III: 700
Holy Spirit	III: 710
Holy Week → Easter	III: 717
Homily → Sermon/Homiletics	III: 717
Honoratus Antoninus	III: 717
Hope	III: 719
Hospitality	III: 725
Humility	III: 730
Huns	III: 737
Hymnography (Greek)	III: 743
Hymnography (Latin)	III: 747
Hypatia	III: 752
Hypostasis/Hypostatic Union	III: 754

I

Iamblichus of Chalcis	III: 759
Ibas of Edessa	III: 766
Iberia of the Caucasus	III: 767
Iconoclasm	III: 773
Iconology/Icons/Iconicity	III: 780
Ignatians, Pseudo-	III: 786
Ignatius, Epistles of	III: 790
Immortality	III: 798
Imperial Cult → Emperor/Imperial Cult	III: 802
Incarnation	III: 802
Incense	III: 804
Infancy Gospels → Christ, Jesus: II. Birth and Infancy Narratives	III: 807
Initiation → Baptism	III: 807
Innocent I	III: 807
Ioca monachorum	III: 810
Ireland	III: 815
Irenaeus of Lyon	III: 824

Isaac of Nineveh	III: 829
Isaiah	III: 830
I. In the New Testament	III: 830
II. In the Fathers	III: 842
III. *Isaiah, Ascension of*	III: 847
IV. Iconography	III: 854
Isauria	III: 858
Isidore of Pelusium	III: 861
Isidore of Seville	IV: 1
Isidore (the Gnostic) → Basilides	IV: 7
Israel	IV: 7
Italy	IV: 14
I. Origins	IV: 14
II. Archaeology	IV: 17

J

Jacob of Serugh	IV: 23
Jairus	IV: 26
James the Apostle	IV: 29
I. James the Great	IV: 29
II. James the Less	IV: 33
III. James, Epistle of	IV: 38
IV. *James, First Apocalypse of*	IV: 46
V. *James, Second Apocalypse of*	IV: 48
VI. *James, Protevangelium of → Protevangelium Jacobi*	IV: 50
VII. *James, Secret Book of*	IV: 50
Jerome	IV: 52
Jerusalem	IV: 60
Jesus Christ → Christ, Jesus	IV: 69
Jews → Judaism	IV: 69
John the Apostle	IV: 69
I. *John, Acts of*	IV: 69
II. John, Epistles of	IV: 74
III. John, Gospel of	IV: 82
IV. *John, Secret Revelation of*	IV: 92
John Arkaph	IV: 98
John Cassian	IV: 99
John Chrysostom	IV: 109
John Mark	IV: 112
John the Baptist	IV: 115
Jonah	IV: 120
Joppa/Jaffa	IV: 124
Joseph of Arimathea on Demas, Narrative of	IV: 127
Judaea → Palestine	IV: 131
Judaeo-Hellenism	IV: 131
Judaism	IV: 135

Judaizers	IV: 144
Judas Thaddaeus	IV: 148
Judas, Gospel of	IV: 151
Jude, Epistle of	IV: 155
Judgment, Biblical Concept	IV: 157
Julian of Eclanum	IV: 161
Julian Romance	IV: 168
Julian the Apostate	IV: 170
Justice/Justification → Righteousness/Justice/Justification	IV: 175
Justin	IV: 175
I. Justin Martyr	IV: 175
II. *Justin, Acts of*	IV: 180
III. Justin, Pseudo-	IV: 182
Justin II	IV: 184
Justina of Padua	IV: 186
Justinian	IV: 188
Juvencus	IV: 191

K

King/Kingdom	IV: 196
Kingdom of God	IV: 204
Kiss	IV: 212
Knowledge, Interpretation of	IV: 216
Kyrie Eleison	IV: 218

L

Labor	IV: 221
Lactantius	IV: 225
Lamb of God → *Agnus Dei*	IV: 232
Laodicea, Councils of	IV: 232
Laurentian Schism	IV: 235
Law/Decalogue/Torah	IV: 237
Lawrence	IV: 244
Lazarus	IV: 248
Lectio divina	IV: 251
Lent	IV: 255
Leo I (Bishop of Rome)	IV: 258
Leontius	IV: 262
Lérins	IV: 264
Libelli pacis (*libellatici*)	IV: 266
Liber diurnus	IV: 268
Liber monstrorum de diversis generibus	IV: 269
Liber orationum psalmographus	IV: 271
Liber pontificalis	IV: 272

Liberius (Bishop of Rome)	IV: 277
Libya	IV: 279
Life, Tree of	IV: 284
Liturgical Language	IV: 288
Liturgical Year	IV: 290
Logia/Agrapha	IV: 296
Lord	IV: 300
Lord, Day of the (Judgment)	IV: 307
Lord's Prayer	IV: 311
Love (Biblical Concept)	IV: 316
Luciferians	IV: 324
Luke, Gospel of	IV: 326
Lying	IV: 335

M

Macarius the Egyptian/the Great → Desert Fathers	IV: 340
Maccabees	IV: 340
Macedonius/Macedonians → Pneumatomachi	IV: 348
Macedonius (Vicarius Africae)	IV: 348
Macrina, the Elder and the Younger	IV: 349
Magic	IV: 353
Magnificat	IV: 358
Mandaeans/Mandaeism	IV: 359
Mani/Manichaeism	IV: 362
Manumissio in ecclesia	IV: 365
Maranatha	IV: 367
Marcella	IV: 371
Marcellina	IV: 375
Marcellus of Ancyra	IV: 378
Marcian	IV: 386
Marcion/Marcionites/Marcionism	IV: 388
Marculus	IV: 394
Marcus Gnosticus/Marcosians	IV: 397
Marius Claudius Victorius	IV: 398
Marius Victorinus	IV: 401
Mark, Gospel of	IV: 407
Marriage	IV: 417
Marseille	IV: 427
Martin of Braga	IV: 429
Martin of Tours	IV: 433
Martyrium Polycarpi	IV: 437
Martyrologium Hieronymianum	IV: 441
Martyrs	IV: 443
I. Martyrs	IV: 443
II. Martyrs, Acts of the	IV: 450
Mary	IV: 455

Mary, Gospel of	IV: 463
Masculinity	IV: 468
Masona of Mérida	IV: 476
Mathematici → Astrology	IV: 479
Matthew the Apostle	IV: 479
I. Matthew, Gospel of	IV: 479
II. *Matthew, Pseudo-*	IV: 489
Mauricius	IV: 493
Maxentius (Emperor)	IV: 495
Maximian (Emperor) → Diocletian	IV: 498
Maximinus Thrax	IV: 498
Medical Ethics	IV: 502
Medicine and Health Care	IV: 508
Melania Junior	IV: 515
Melania Senior	IV: 517
Melchizedek/Melchizedekians	IV: 518
Meletian Schism	IV: 521
Melito of Sardis	IV: 522
Memnon of Ephesus	IV: 527
Mensa	IV: 530
Merobaudes	IV: 534
Mesrop (Maštoc‘)	IV: 537
Messalians/Euchites	IV: 540
Messiah → Christ, Jesus	IV: 544
Messianism/Messianic Movements	IV: 544
Metropolitan	IV: 550
Miaphysites/Miaphysitism	IV: 553
Micah	IV: 562
Middle Platonism	IV: 564
Midrash	IV: 568
Mikveh → Bath/Mikveh	IV: 573
Milan	IV: 573
Milevis	IV: 582
Military	IV: 584
Militia	IV: 587
Millenarianism → Chiliasm	IV: 591
Minucius Felix	IV: 591
Miracles	IV: 599
Mithras/Cult of Mithras	IV: 603
Modalism	IV: 607
Monarchianism	IV: 616
Monarchians	IV: 621
Monastery, Double	IV: 626
Monastic Prayer	IV: 629
Monastic Rules	IV: 638
Monasticism	IV: 646
I. Egyptian	IV: 646
II. Palestinian	IV: 654

Monophysites/Monophysitism → Miaphysites/Miaphysitism .... IV: 659
Monotheism .... IV: 659
Montanism/Montanists .... IV: 668
Montanus, Lucius, and Companions .... IV: 672
Mopsuestia, Council of .... IV: 674
Moses .... IV: 676
Muirchú .... IV: 686
Music .... IV: 687
Mystagogy .... IV: 692
Mystery Cults .... IV: 699

N

Naassenes → Ophites/Naassenes .... IV: 706
Nag Hammadi Writings .... IV: 706
Name, Divine .... IV: 714
Narsai .... IV: 722
Nazarenes, Gospel of the .... IV: 725
Nazarenes, Sect of .... IV: 729
Nazareth .... IV: 733
Nazirite .... IV: 736
Negative Theology .... IV: 738
Nemesius of Emesa .... IV: 744
Neocaesarea .... IV: 746
Neonicaeanism .... IV: 750
Neoplatonism .... IV: 753
Nero → Emperor/Imperial Cult .... IV: 760
Nestorianism/Nestorius .... IV: 760
New Testament → Bible: II. New Testament .... IV: 764
Nicaea, First Council of .... IV: 764
Nicodemus .... IV: 773
Nicodemus, Gospel of → Pilate, Acts of .... IV: 775
Nicolaitans .... IV: 775
Nimbus .... IV: 779
Nîmes, Council of .... IV: 783
Nomina sacra .... IV: 785
Norea, Thought of .... IV: 787
Nous .... IV: 790
Novatian .... IV: 798
Numenius of Apamea .... IV: 802
Numidia .... IV: 805

O

Oath .... IV: 809
Odilia .... IV: 809
Ogdoas .... IV: 811

Old Syriac	IV: 816
Olympias	IV: 820
Onesimos	IV: 823
Ophites/Naassenes	IV: 825
Optatus of Milevis	IV: 828
Optatus of Thamugadi	IV: 837
Oracles	IV: 840
Orange	IV: 848
Orant	IV: 852
Ordination	IV: 855
Origen	IV: 862
Origenism/Origenist Controversy	V: 1
Original Sin → Sin	V: 3
Orosius	V: 3
Orpheus	V: 6
Orthodoxy	V: 9
Ousia	V: 21
Oxyrhynchus Papyri	V: 29

P

Pachomius of Tabennese	V: 53
Pacian of Barcelona	V: 59
Pagan/Paganism	V: 61
Paideia	V: 66
Palestine	V: 72
Pammachius	V: 77
Pancras	V: 79
Panthera	V: 82
Papacy → Church of Rome	V: 84
Papal Letters and Archives	V: 84
Papal Schism	V: 93
Papias of Hierapolis	V: 98
Parable	V: 102
Paradise	V: 112
Parousia	V: 119
Parrhesía	V: 125
Passio Martyrum Scillitanorum	V: 130
Passion of Perpetua and Felicity	V: 133
Passover	V: 138
Patrick	V: 144
Patripassians	V: 151
Patrology/Patristics	V: 153
Paul the Apostle	V: 163
I. Paul (Apostle)	V: 163
II. Paul, 1 Thessalonians	V: 171
III. Paul, 2 Thessalonians	V: 176
IV. *Paul, Acts of*	V: 179

V. *Paul, Apocalypse of*	V: 186
VI. Paul, Colossians	V: 190
VII. Paul, Corinthian Correspondence	V: 195
VIII. Paul, Ephesians	V: 213
IX. Paul, Galatians	V: 218
X. *Paul, Life of*	V: 225
XI. Paul, Pastoral Epistles	V: 227
XII. Paul, Philemon	V: 243
XIII. Paul, Philippians	V: 247
XIV. *Paul, Prayer of the Apostle*	V: 255
XV. *Paul, Revelation of* (Nag Hammadi)	V: 257
XVI. Paul, Romans	V: 258
Paul and Thecla, Acts of	V: 268
Paul of Mérida	V: 273
Paul of Samosata	V: 274
Paula	V: 276
Paulinus of Nola	V: 278
Paulinus of Pella	V: 282
Pelagia	V: 285
Pelagians/Pelagianism	V: 287
Pelagius	V: 295
Pelagius I	V: 303
Pella, Flight to	V: 305
Penitence/Penance	V: 308
Pentecost	V: 319
Perfect Discourse, Excerpt from the	V: 323
Perichōrēsis	V: 325
Persecution of Christians	V: 327
Persona	V: 336
Peshitta → Bible: XI. Peshitta	V: 342
Peter the Apostle	V: 342
I. Peter (Apostle)	V: 342
II. 1 Peter	V: 351
III. 2 Peter	V: 355
IV. *Peter, Acts of*	V: 358
V. *Peter, Apocalypse of*	V: 360
VI. *Peter, Gospel of*	V: 364
VII. *Peter to Philip, Letter of*	V: 368
VIII. *Peter and the Twelve Apostles, Acts of*	V: 370
Peter (Patriarch of Jerusalem)	V: 375
Peter Chrysologus	V: 377
Pharisees → Judaism	V: 379
Philip the Apostle	V: 379
I. Philip (Apostle)	V: 379
II. *Philip, Gospel of*	V: 382
Philippi	V: 386
Philo of Alexandria	V: 390

Philosophical Opposition to Early Christianity	V: 399
Philostorgius	V: 410
Philosophy	V: 412
Philoxenos of Mabbug	V: 424
Phoenix	V: 428
Phōs Hilaron	V: 431
Photinus of Sirmium	V: 434
Physiologus	V: 439
Pilate	V: 443
I. Pilate, Pontius	V: 443
II. Pilate Cycle	V: 450
III. *Pilate, Acts of*	V: 452
IV. *Anaphora Pilati*	V: 454
V. *Mors Pilati*	V: 455
VI. *Paradosis Pilati*	V: 457
VII. *Pilate to Claudius, Letter of*	V: 459
VIII. *Pilate to Herod, Letters of*	V: 460
IX. *Pilate to Tiberius, Letters of*	V: 461
Pimenius	V: 462
Pisidia	V: 463
Pistis Sophia	V: 464
Plērōma	V: 469
Plotinus	V: 475
Pneumatomachi	V: 479
Polemon (Polemios)	V: 485
Polycarp of Smyrna	V: 486
Pomerius, Julianus	V: 491
Pontianus	V: 495
Pontifex Maximus	V: 496
Pontius Pilate → Pilate	V: 497
Pope/Father	V: 497
Porphyry of Tyre	V: 504
Possidius of Calama	V: 512
Potamius of Lisbon	V: 516
Poverty → Wealth	V: 519
Prayer	V: 519
Praxedis → Pudens/Pudentiana/Praxedis	V: 528
Predestination, Doctrine of	V: 528
Priest/Presbyter	V: 538
Priesthood of Believers	V: 543
Priscillian of Avila	V: 547
Priscillianism	V: 551
Processions	V: 559
Procopius of Caesarea	V: 566
Prophecy/Prophet	V: 568
Protevangelium Jacobi	V: 573
Protology	V: 578

TABLE OF CONTENTS

Proverbia Graecorum	V: 586
Providence	V: 588
Pseudepigraphy	V: 593
Pudens/Pudentiana/Praxedis	V: 599
Pulcheria	V: 602

Q

Q (Quelle)/Two Source Hypothesis	V: 606
Quadratus	V: 615
Quercia, Council of	V: 618
Quintus Aurelius Symmachus	V: 618
Quirinius	V: 622
Quodvultdeus of Carthage	V: 623

R

Rabbi	V: 627
Rabbula of Edessa	V: 629
Rapture	V: 631
Ravenna	V: 635
Recapitulation	V: 640
Recentiores → Bible: X. Recentiores and Hexapla	V: 641
Redemption	V: 641
Refrigerium	V: 646
Relics	V: 653
Remembrance and Commemoration	V: 658
Resurrection	V: 663
I. Resurrection (General)	V: 663
II. Resurrection of Jesus Christ	V: 670
III. *Resurrection, Treatise on the*	V: 679
Revelation, Book of	V: 680
Rhetoric	V: 688
Riez, Council of	V: 698
Righteousness/Justice/Justification	V: 700
Rimini, Council of	V: 710
Romanos the Melodist	V: 712
Rome	V: 717
Rufinus of Aquileia	V: 726
Ruricius of Limoges	V: 728

S

Sabbath/Sabbatical Year	V: 732
Sabellians/Sabellianism	V: 741
Sacramentarium Gelasianum	V: 744

Sacramentum	V: 746
Sacrifice	V: 748
Sadducees → Judaism	V: 757
Saint Catherine's Monastery	V: 757
Samson	V: 759
Sanctus	V: 760
Saragossa	V: 763
Sarcophagi, Christian	V: 765
Sardica	V: 770
Sarepta	V: 774
Satan → Devil	V: 777
Savior, Dialogue of the	V: 777
Scala Coeli	V: 779
Scapula	V: 781
Schism/Schismatics	V: 782
School, Difference Christianity and Pagan Schools	V: 792
Scillitani (Scillitan Martyrs) → *Passio Martyrum Scillitanorum*	V: 802
Scribes	V: 802
Sebastian	V: 806
Sect → Heresy	V: 810
Sedulius	V: 810
Seneca, Correspondence of Paul and	V: 813
Septuagint → Bible: VI. Septuagint, Old Greek	V: 815
Sermon on the Mount	V: 815
Sermon/Homiletics	V: 825
Servatius of Tongres and Maastricht	V: 833
Seth, Second Discourse of the Great	V: 835
Seth, Three Steles of	V: 837
Sethians	V: 840
Severus of Antioch	V: 847
Seville, Councils of	V: 851
Sextus, Sentences of	V: 853
Sexuality	V: 855
Shem, Paraphrase of	V: 864
Shenoute of Atripe	VI: 1
Sheol → Hades	VI: 4
Shepherd, The Good	VI: 4
Sibylline Oracles → Oracles	VI: 8
Sidonius Apollinaris	VI: 8
Simeon Stylites	VI: 14
Simon (Apostle) → Peter the Apostle	VI: 16
Simon Magus	VI: 16
Simplician of Milan	VI: 20
Sin	VI: 23
Singer(s)	VI: 32
Siricius (Bishop of Rome)	VI: 36
Sirmium	VI: 39
Slave/Slavery	VI: 42

Smyrna	VI: 47
Socrates	VI: 52
Socrates Scholasticus	VI: 55
Solomon, Odes of	VI: 59
Son of Man	VI: 64
Son(s) of God	VI: 71
Soteriology	VI: 75
Soul	VI: 85
Sozomen	VI: 94
Spain	VI: 96
Spirits → Demonology/Demons	VI: 99
Spiritual Gifts (*Charismata*)	VI: 99
State → State and Empire	VI: 102
Statuta ecclesiae antiqua	VI: 102
Stephen I → Bishops of Rome, Pre-Constantinian	VI: 106
Stephen the Martyr	VI: 106
Stilicho	VI: 109
Stoicheia → Elements (*Stoicheia*)	VI: 111
Stoicism and the Fathers	VI: 111
Stylite/Stylitism	VI: 120
Subordinatianists	VI: 124
Suetonius	VI: 126
Suicide	VI: 129
Sunday	VI: 133
Superstition	VI: 136
Syagrius	VI: 142
Sylvester I	VI: 143
Symmachians	VI: 148
Symmachus (Bishop of Rome)	VI: 150
Synagogue	VI: 152
Syncletica	VI: 156
Syncretism	VI: 159
Synesius of Cyrene	VI: 164
Synods → Councils/Synods	VI: 168

T

Tabernacle	VI: 169
Tabitha	VI: 177
Tacitus	VI: 179
Talmud	VI: 182
Tannaim	VI: 187
Targums → Bible: VII. Targums	VI: 190
Tarraconensis	VI: 190
Tarsus	VI: 193
Tatian	VI: 198

Te Deum	VI: 208
Teacher → Didaskalos	VI: 209
Tefillin → Tzitzit/Tefillin	VI: 209
Temple, Jerusalem	VI: 209
Tertullian	VI: 218
Testamentum Domini	VI: 226
Thamugadi	VI: 229
Theatre	VI: 231
Thecla	VI: 234
Theodore of Heraclea	VI: 239
Theodore of Mopsuestia	VI: 241
Theodore of Raith	VI: 245
Theodoret of Cyrrhus	VI: 251
Theodoric the Great	VI: 255
Theodosius I	VI: 259
Theodotion	VI: 261
Theopaschites	VI: 270
Theophilus of Alexandria	VI: 272
Theōsis	VI: 276
Thomas the Apostle	VI: 286
I. Thomas (Apostle)	VI: 286
II. *Thomas, Acts of*	VI: 290
III. *Thomas, Apocalypse of*	VI: 295
IV. *Thomas, Gospel of*	VI: 299
V. *Thomas, Infancy Gospel of* Christ, Jesus: II. Birth and Infancy Narratives	VI: 306
Thomas Christians	VI: 306
Thomas the Contender, Book of	VI: 308
Tiberius	VI: 310
Timotheus of Beirut	VI: 314
Tithing	VI: 316
Titulus	VI: 321
Titus	VI: 324
Toledo	VI: 328
Tonsure	VI: 332
Torah → Law/Decalogue/Torah	VI: 334
Tosefta	VI: 334
Toulouse	VI: 337
Tours	VI: 339
Trade	VI: 344
Tradition	VI: 348
Traditor	VI: 356
Traducianism	VI: 359
Trajan	VI: 366
Transcendence	VI: 370
Translatio imperii	VI: 374
Trinity	VI: 382
Tripartite Tractate	VI: 398

Truth	VI: 401
I. *Truth, Gospel of*	VI: 401
II. *Truth, Testimony of*	VI: 403
Turin, Council of	VI: 405
Two-Source Hypothesis → Q (Quelle)/Two-Source Hypothesis	VI: 408
Two Ways Doctrine	VI: 408
Tyconius	VI: 410
Tzitzit/Tefillin	VI: 415

U

Ursinus → Damasus	VI: 418
Usury	VI: 418

V

Vaison	VI: 423
Valens	VI: 425
Valentinus/Valentinians	VI: 427
I. Valentinus the Gnostic	VI: 427
II. Valentinians	VI: 433
III. *Valentinian Exposition*	VI: 438
Valentinus (the Apolliniarist)	VI: 440
Vandals	VI: 442
Vannes	VI: 449
Vatican	VI: 450
Velatio	VI: 461
Venantius Fortunatus	VI: 462
Verona Sacramentary	VI: 466
Vespasian	VI: 468
Vetus Latina → Bible: IX. Vetus Latina	VI: 472
Vetus Syra → Bible: VIII. Vetus Syra	VI: 472
Victor I → Bishops of Rome, Pre-Constantinian	VI: 472
Victor of Vita	VI: 472
Victorinus of Petovium (Pettau)	VI: 475
Vigilius (Bishop of Rome)	VI: 477
Vincent of Lérins	VI: 481
Vindicta Salvatoris	VI: 484
Virga	VI: 485
Virgil	VI: 490
Virgin/Virginity	VI: 496
Vita Antonii → Antony the Great	VI: 504
Vulgate → Bible: XII. Vulgate	VI: 504

W

Water, in the Bible	VI: 505
Wealth	VI: 510
Wedding → Marriage	VI: 518
White Monastery Federation	VI: 518
Wisdom of Jesus Christ	VI: 521
Witness	VI: 524
Word	VI: 527
Works of Relief and Charity	VI: 534
World, On the Origin of the	VI: 543
Writing Materials	VI: 547
Wulfila	VI: 550

Z

Zacchaeus	VI: 553
Zealots	VI: 557
Zion	VI: 560
Zosimus (Bishop of Rome)	VI: 568
Zosimus (Historian)	VI: 570
Index	VI: 577

Preface

Early Christianity is a multi-faceted and complex phenomenon – if we can even refer to it as a single phenomenon at all. Since the publication of W. Bauer's groundbreaking study *Rechtgläubigkeit und Ketzerei im frühesten Christentum* in 1934, the scholarly world has come increasingly to the conclusion that the variety of early Christian groups was not the result of the disintegration of a single, original form of Christianity over the course of several centuries but rather that variety has always been at the heart of what we call early Christianity. By sheer coincidence, several texts from which this pluriformity can be deduced were discovered in the Egyptian desert: texts including the *Gospel of Thomas*, *Gospel of Philip*, *Gospel of Judas*, *Gospel of Mary* as well as the *Secret Revelation of John*, a *Apocalypse of Peter*, and the *First* and *Second Revelation of James*. Pluriformity can be also inferred, for example, from the *Acts of Andrew*. The text has been preserved in different languages and versions. Thus, there is no definitive "text"; there is a transmission of manuscripts in which an open, dynamic, and thus never-ending story is told in different versions and finally put in writing in different versions. The same probably applies to an early orthodox text rediscovered in a library in the 19th century, the *Didache*. "Orthodox" texts were also partially rewritten in the early 2nd century CE according to the insights a particular early orthodox community developed regarding liturgy, prayer, and order of life. It is only after the first centuries that the pluriformity of Christian community and beliefs decreased, giving way to a less varied mainstream Christianity. Renewed study of proto-orthodox authors, such as Irenaeus of Lyon (c. 140–200 CE), proved that they were still familiar with the pluralistic Christianity of the first centuries.

And, in all its variety, early Christianity did not originate in a vacuum. It started as an intra-Jewish reform movement in Palestine, led by Jesus of Nazareth. Within one generation after Jesus' ministry, it had spread over large parts of the Roman Empire, reaching Rome even before Paul. As more and more non-Jews joined the movement, Greco-Roman customs and ideas also came to play an important role. For this reason, early Christianity is just as connected with the Greco-Roman context within which it grew as with its Jewish roots.

Therefore, the label "Christianity" is itself not unproblematic. Although the term naturally has a long history in the tradition of the Christian movement, its use, for example, to refer to 1st-century CE followers of Jesus is nevertheless an anachronism given that the term is first mentioned in the epistles of Ignatius of Antioch (*Magn.* 10.1; 10.13; *Rom.* 3.3; *Phld.* 6.1), dated to the early 2nd century CE. One can also question the appropriateness of its use for a number of groups that are currently seen as belonging to the extended family of early Christianity. Far from implying that "early Christianity" was a unified or monolithic movement, therefore, this encyclopedia uses the term as an umbrella covering a wide variety of historical phenomena.

In creating the *Brill Encyclopedia of Early Christianity*, the editors have made a number of decisions with regard to its subject matter, scope, and structure. The first choice made was to focus on the most significant topics concerning early Christianity: the most important authors, texts, ideas, and places that played a role in the history of the development of Christianity. The articles included in the *Brill Encyclopedia of Early Christianity* are based on exhaustive research, using both primary and secondary sources. While it is impossible to provide the user with a comprehensive survey of every detail in the growth of the Christian movement, an effort was made to cover the topics that would best provide the reader with a reliable map of the early Christian movement in its pluriformity and in its Jewish and Greco-Roman contexts.

A second decision made was related to the time period. Any periodization is bound to be arbitrary to some extent, and thus prone to criticism. For the purposes of this encyclopedia, the editors decided that the end of the 6th century CE should be the cut-off point, as by that time Christianity was established as the orthodox, Catholic Church in both the West as well as in the East. The formative debates on the nature of God and Christ had been more or less settled, and the biblical canon had been selected and approved by church councils. In the West, the demise of the Roman Empire had led to a new political constellation, and in the East, the rise of the Byzantine Empire ushered in a new era. Late antiquity may not have a clear beginning nor a well-defined end, but it is clear that the 6th century CE belongs to late antiquity and ushered in the start of the Middle Ages. These terms are also modern labels, of course, and subject to debate. And yet the 6th century CE has the characteristics of a transitional age in the history of early Christianity and, as such, the editors decided to include it within the scope of the encyclopedia.

Two other choices were also important for the scope and form of the *Brill Encyclopedia of Early Christianity*: the choice to bridge the divide between the fields of New Testament studies and patristics, and the choice to add the history of scholarship of the entries. The fields of New Testament studies and patristics have, over the years, grown into two separate specializations, organized into two different disciplines with their own methodologies and scholarly traditions. This makes collaboration on a project such as this a complicated task. And yet, there is no logical reason to divide early Christianity into these two separate fields. For this encyclopedia, the period covered is seen as an organic whole in which a large number of developments took place that led to the formation of the Christian church as a recognizable entity, and to the formulation of the orthodox Christian creeds as guidelines for the faith tradition.

Writings from the Old Testament are only listed if their reception has been of fundamental importance in works of the Fathers in general. As a result, the book of Genesis is dealt with in entries on authors who wrote about the creation accounts it contains. The influence of Isaiah is so prominent that it warrants inclusion of the entry, but Jeremiah can, for the same reason, be left out. Jonah is included, since the prophet influenced patristic ideas on Christ, but Job is left out. The books that are not included as entries do, after all, occur in contributions on authors and writings that deal with them (see Augustine of Hippo, *Adnotationes in Hiob*). The editors decided as a rule not to include entries on genres and to leave the material side of early Christianity largely out of consideration. Obviously, material religion is important, but the focus of this encyclopedia is first and foremost on authors, texts, and ideas. Similarly, geography is not covered to the full – only the most prominent geographic entries are included, and regions that produced prominent authors or texts feature in the entries on those authors or texts.

The last decision was to include in each entry some discussion of the modern history of scholarship. Often, this historiographical discussion is included as a separate paragraph; sometimes it is interwoven with the description of the topic of the entry. Wherever relevant, we also include an overview of the historiography of the subject of a particular entry. If the subject of an entry has been extensively studied in the past, its historiography is included in a separate paragraph. In all other cases, the historiography is referred to where necessary. In several cases, no historiography was required, as only one or two studies on the particular subject have been published. Every effort has been made to reflect as objectively as possible the different positions scholars took on a text or theme.

It is impossible, even in a work as extensive as this, to cover all topics that could have been included. The electronic version of this encyclopedia will have more entries than the printed version, so if the reader needs information that is not available here, it may be found online.

A word of thanks to all those who contributed to the success of this work is most appropriate. The editors-in-chief are immensely indebted to all authors, section editors, and editors, just as they are at least as indebted to the Brill staff: André Haacke, Giulia Buriola, Jean-Louis Ruijters, Mariya Mitova, Ruud van der Helm, and especially Louise Schouten.

The editors of the *Brill Encyclopedia of Early Christianity* hope that this encyclopedia will find its way into the libraries of universities, colleges, religious, and other institutions, as well as the studies of many individual scholars. It is our hope is that students of early Christianity who intend to research a particular subject will find their first information in the *Brill Encyclopedia of Early Christianity* and will be able to proceed with their research on the basis of the information found here. The easily accessible digital version of the encyclopedia offers numerous options for browsing its content. May it prove to be a useful and inspiring tool for the study and further understanding of early Christianity.

Paul van Geest
David G. Hunter
Bert Jan Lietaert Peerbolte

Contributors and Affiliations
(at the Time of Writing)

Aasgaard, Reidar — University of Oslo, Norway

Abrams Rebillard, Suzanne — Cornell University, US

Adamiak, Stanislaw — University of Warsaw, Poland

Adams Petrin, Anna — University of Notre Dame, US

Alçada Cardoso, Isabel Maria — Catholic University of Portugal, Portugal

Aleksidze, Nicholas — Central European University, Austria/ Hungary

Alwis, Anne P. — University of Kent, UK

Amparo Mateo Donet, María — University of Valencia, Spain

Amundsen, Darrel W. — Western Washington University, US

Anđelović, Aleksandar — University of Vienna, Austria

Anderson, Sonja — Carleton College, US

Andrade, Nathanail — Binghamton University, US

Andrews, Margaret A. — University of Chicago, US

Angel, Joseph — Yeshiva University, Israel

Arblaster, John — University of Antwerp, Belgium

Arfuch, Diego — Bollandist Society, Belgium

Argondizza-Moberg, Sean — University of St. Michael's College, Canada

Ashkenazi, Jacob — Kinneret College, Israel

Aspesi, Cara — University of Notre Dame, US

Attridge, Harry — Yale University, US

Auvinen, Risto — Church Institute for Research and Advanced Training, Evangelical Lutheran Church, Finland

Auwers, Jean-Marie — Catholic University of Louvain, Belgium

Awes Freeman, Jennifer — United Theological Seminary of the Twin Cities, US

Bailey, Lisa Kaaren — University of Auckland, New Zealand

Baker, Matthew — University of Tennessee, US

Bakker, Henk — Vrije Universiteit Amsterdam, The Netherlands

Banev, Krastu — Durham University, UK

Bar-Ashe Siegal, Michal — Ben-Gurion University of the Negev, Israel

Barclay Lloyd, Joan — La Trobe University, Australia

Barrier, Jeremy W. — Heritage Christian University, US

Barry, Jennifer — University of Mary, US

Bass, Alden — Oklahoma Christian University, US

Batten, Alicia — University of Waterloo, Canada

Bauer, Thomas Johann — University of Erfurt, Germany

Becker, Matthias — University of Goettingen, Germany

Beduhn, Jason D. — Northern Arizona University, US

Beek, Bram van de — Vrije Universiteit Amsterdam, The Netherlands

Behr, John — University of Aberdeen, Scotland

Bell, Brigidda — Moravian University, US

Benga, Daniel — University of Munich Ludwig Maximilian, Germany

Benjamins, Rick — Protestant Theological University, Utrecht, The Netherlands

Bergermann, Marc — Humboldt University of Berlin, Germany

Bergjan, Silke-Petra — University of Zürich, Switzerland

Berndt, Guido M. — Free University of Berlin, Germany

Bernett, Monika — Bavarian Academy of Sciences and Humanities, Germany

Berzon, Todd S. — Bowdoin College, US

Beshay, Michael — Stanford University, US

Beutler, Johannes	Independent researcher, based in Germany	Brennecke, Hanns Christof	University of Erlangen-Nürnberg Friedrich Alexander, Germany
Bick, Shraga	Yale University, US		
Bieberstein, Sabine	Catholic University of Eichstätt-Ingolstadt, Germany	Brent, Allen	King's College London, UK
		Broadhead, Edwin Keith	Berea College, US
		Brooke, George	University of Manchester, UK
Bilby, Mark G.	University of Virginia, US		
Binder, Stéphanie	Bar-Ilan University, Israel	Brooks Hedstrom, Darlene	Brandeis University, US
Bland Simmons†, Michael	Auburn University, US		
		Brown, Andrew J.	Melbourne School of Theology, Australia
Blaudeau, Philippe	University of Angers, France		
		Brugarolas, Miguel	University of Navarra, Spain
Bloemendal, Jan	Huygens Institute, The Netherlands		
		Buchinger, Harald	University of Regensburg, Germany
Blowers, Paul M.	Milligan University, US		
Boddens Hosang, FJ Elisabeth	University of Tilburg, The Netherlands	Buckner, Candace	Virginia Tech, US
		Buenacasa Pérez, Carles	University of Barcelona, Spain
Bolman, Elizabeth	Case Western Reserve University, US		
		Burgess, Richard	University of Ottawa, Canada
Bonar, Chance E.	Harvard University, US		
Bond, Helen	University of Edinburgh, UK	Burnet, Régis	University of Louvain, Belgium
Bonnie, Rick	University of Helsinki, Finland	Burns, Dylan Michael	University of Amsterdam, The Netherlands
Boodts, Shari	Radboud University, The Netherlands	Burrow, Andrew	Samford University, US
		Burz-Tropper, Veronika	University of Vienna, Austria
Borri, Francesco	Austrian Academy of Sciences, Austria		
		Butticaz, Simon	University of Lausanne, Switzerland
Bos, Annemarie	Radboud University, The Netherlands		
		Butts, Aaron Michael	Catholic University of America, US
Boter, Gerard	Vrije Universiteit Amsterdam, The Netherlands		
		Cabrera, Juan Antonio	Pontifical Patristic Augustinian Institute, Italy
Bradshaw, David	University of Kentucky, US	Cain, Andrew J.	University of Colorado, US
Bradshaw, Paul F.	University of Notre Dame, US	Canella, Tessa	University of Rome La Sapienza, Italy
Brakke, David	Ohio State University, US	Canellis, Aline	Université Jean Monnet, France
Brand, Mattias	University of Zürich, Switzerland		
		Capone, Alessandro	University of Salento, Italy
Brandt, Hartwin	University of Bamberg, Germany	Carleton Paget, James	University of Cambridge, UK
Brankaer, Johanna	University of Mainz Johannes Gutenberg, Germany	Caruso, Matteo	independent researcher based in Italy
		Casey, Damien	Australian Catholic University, Australia
Braun, Willi	University of Alberta, Canada		
		Casey, Michael	Order of Cistercians of the Strict Observance, Italy
Bray, Gerald L.	Samford University, US		

Casper, Charles M.A.	Radboud University, The Netherlands	Crislip, Andrew	Virginia Commonwealth University, US
Cassis, Marica	University of Calgary, Canada	Cruz Ryan, Jordan J.	Wheaton College, US
Celia, Francesco	University of Padua, Italy	Czachesz, István	Arctic University of Norway, Norway
Cesar Dias Chaves, Julio	Our Lady of Fatima Archdiocesan Major Seminary, Brasil	Daugherty, Bradley J.	Vanderbilt University, US
		D'Auria, Isabella	University of Naples Federico II, Italy
Chapman, David W.	Coventant Theological Seminary, US	Davidson, J. Ryan	Tyndale Theological Seminary, The Netherlands
Charles-Murray, Mary	Sisters of Notre Dame de Namur, US	Davis, Jamie P.	Trinity College Bristol, UK
Chase, Nathan	University of Notre Dame, US	Day, Juliette	University of Helsinki, Finland
Chavarria Arnau, Alexandra	University of Padua, Italy	De Blaauw, Sible	Radboud University, The Netherlands
Cheung Salisbury, Matthew	University of Oxford, UK	De la Haye, Régis	Major Seminary of Rolduc, The Netherlands
Childers, Jeff	Australian Catholic University, Australia	De Nie, Giselle	University of Utrecht, The Netherlands
Chiriatti, Matteo	University of Barcelona, Spain	de Wet, Chris	University of South Africa, South Africa
Clifton Ward, H	Tusculum University, US	Decker, Michael J.	University of South Florida, US
Cohen, Samuel	Sonoma State University, US	Deconick, April	Rice University, US
		Demacopoulos, George	Fordham University, US
Colautti, Federico	University of Mainz Johannes Gutenberg, Germany	Den Hengst, Daniël	University of Amsterdam, The Netherlands
Collins, John	City University of New York, US	Denzey Lewis, Nicola	Claremont Graduate University, US
Collins, Roger	University of Edinburgh, UK	Despotis, Athanasios	University of Bonn, Germany
Conti, Marco	University of Bologna, Italy	di Berardino, Angelo	Pontifical Patristic Augustinian Institute, Italy
Conway-Jones, Ann	University of Birmingham, UK	Di Segni, Leah	Hebrew University, Israel
		Di Serio, Chiara	Cyprus University, Cyprus
Cooper, Stephen	Franklin & Marshall College, US	Diem, Albrecht	Syracuse University, US
		Djuth, Marianne	Canisius University, US
Corcoran, Simon	Newcastle University, UK	Doane, Sébastien	Laval University, Canada
Costache, Doru	St Cyril's Coptic Orthodox Theological College, Australia	Döpp, Siegmar	Georg August University of Göttingen, Germany
		Doran, Robert	University of Massachusetts Amherst, US
Cox, Claude	McMaster Divinity College, Canada		
Crawford, Matthew R.	Abilene Christian University, US	Dorfbauer, Lukas J.	Paris Lodron University of Salzburg, Austria
Crégheur, Eric	Laval University, Canada	Dowden, Ken	University of Birmingham, UK

Drake, Susanna	Macalester College, US	Fatti, Federico	independent researcher based in Italy
Dresken-Weiland, Jutta	University of Goettingen, Germany	Ferguson, Everett	Abilene Christian University, US
Drijvers, Jan Willem	University of Groningen, The Netherlands	Férnandez, Samuel	Pontifical Catholic University of Chile, Chile
Dunkle, Brian	Boston College, US		
Dunn, Geoffrey D.	Abilene Christian University, US	Ferngren, Gary B.	Oregon State University, US
Dunn†, James G.	Durham University, UK	Ferreiro, Alberto	Seattle Pacific University, US
Dunning, Benjamin	Harvard University, US		
Dzino, Danijel	Macquarie University, Australia	Field, John Graham	independent researcher based in the UK
Eastman, David	University of Regensburg, Germany	Filipová, Alžběta	Tbilisi State University, Georgia
Eckhardt, Benedikt	University of Edinburgh, UK	Finamore, John F.	University of Iowa, US
		Finn, Richard	University of Oxford, UK
Edelmann-Singer, Babett	University of Regensburg, Germany	Firey, Abigail	University of Kentucky, US
		Fischer, Jens	University of Potsdam, Germany
Edsall, Benjamin	Regent College, Canada		
Edwards, Mark	University of Oxford, UK	Fitzgerald, Allan	Villanova University, US
Egmond, Peter van	Protestant Theological University, The Netherland	Flores Arcas, Juan Javier (Fr., OSB)	Pontificio Ateneo di S. Anselmo, Italia
Ehlen, Oliver	Friedrich Schiller University Jena, Germany	Flower, Richard	University of Exeter, UK
		Focant, Camille	University of Louvain, Belgium
Eklund, Rebekah	Loyola University, US		
Elliott†, J. Keith	University of Leeds, UK	Förster, Hans	University of Vienna, Austria
Elliott, Mark W.	University of St Andrews, UK		
		Fournier, Éric	West Chester University, US
Ellison, Mark D.	Vanderbilt University, US		
Elowsky, Joel	Concordia Seminary, St. Louis, US	Fox, Yaniv	Bar-Ilan University, Israel
		Frakes, Robert	California State University, Bakersfield, US
Enzor, Dunstan (Br Noah)	Boston College, US		
		Franchi, Roberta	University of Florence, Italy
Eriksen, Uffe Holmsgaard	University of Southern Denmark, Denmark	Francis, James A.	University of Kentucky, US
Erlemann, Kurt	University of Wuppertal, Germany	Franek, Juraj	Masaryk University, Czech Republic
Estes, Douglas	Friends University, US	Frankfurter, David T.M.	Boston University, US
Evans, Craig A.	Houston Christian University, US	Franklin, Carmela V.	Columbia University, US
		Frassetto, Michael	University of Delaware, US
Evers, Alexander W.	Loyola University, US	Freeman, Philip	Pepperdine University, US
Faesen, Rob	Catholic University of Leuven, Belgium	Freiseis, Fabian	Albert Ludwig University of Freiburg, Germany
Falkenberg, René	Aarhus University, Denmark	Frenkel, Luise Marion	University of São Paulo, Brasil
Fallica, Maria	University of Rome La Sapienza, Italy	Freund, Stefan	University of Wuppertal, Germany

CONTRIBUTORS AND AFFILIATIONS

Frisius, Mark	University of Olivet, US	Grabau, Joseph	Catholic University of Leuven, Belgium
Fuhrer, Therese	University of Munich Ludwig Maximilian, Germany	Gracanin, Hrvoje	University of Zagreb, Croatia
Fundic, Leonela	Australian Catholic University, Australia	Graf, Fritz	Ohio State University, US
		Granger Cook, John	LaGrange College, US
Furlong, Dean	University of Colorado, US	Greatrex, Geoffrey	University of Ottawa, Canada
Gador-Whyte, Sarah	Australian Catholic University, Australia	Green, Roger	University of Glasgow, UK
Garroway, Joshua D.	Hebrew Union College, US	Greschat, Katharina	Ruhr University Bochum, Germany
Garstad, Benjamin	MacEwan University, Canada	Griffin, Carl	Payson High School, UT, US
Gaytán, Antonio	Pontifical Patristic Augustinian Institute, Italy	Gruen, Erich	University of California, Berkeley, US
Geest, Paul van	Tilburg University, The Netherlands / Erasmus University Rotterdam	Grundeken, Mark	Catholic University of Leuven, Belgium
		Grünstäudl, Wolfgang	University of Muenster, Germany
Gemeinhardt, Peter	University of Goettingen, Germany	Grypeou, Emmanouela	Stockholm University, Sweden
Gentry, Peter J.	Southern Baptist Theological Seminary, US	Guignard, Christophe	University of Lausanne, Switzerland
Georges, Tobias	University of Goettingen, Germany	Gurry, Peter	Phoenix Seminary, US
		Gutsfeld, Andreas	University of Lorraine, France
Gerber, Simon	Berlin-Brandenburg Academy of Sciences and Humanities, Germany	Gwynn, David M.	University of London, UK
		Haarer , Fiona	King's College London, UK
Gerstenberger, Erhard S.	University of Marburg, Germany	Haitsma Kotva, Alyssa van	Ohio State University, US
Ghattas, Michael	St. Vincent Seminary, US	Häkkinen, Sakari	Evangelical Lutheran Church of Finland, Finland
Gieschen, Charles	Concordia Theological Seminary, US		
Gignac, Alain	University of Montreal, Canada	Halfond, Gregory I.	Framingham State University, US
Gili, Luca	University of Quebec in Montreal, Canada	Hallebeek, Jan	Vrije Universiteit Amsterdam, The Netherlands
Gilliam III, Paul R.	Chowan University, US		
Gleede, Benjamin	University of Tuebingen, Germany	Han, Jin H.	New York Theological Seminary, US
Goehring, James	University of Mary Washington, US	Handl, András	Catholic University of Leuven, Belgium
Gopalakrishnan, Pratima	University of Texas, US	Hannah, Darrell D.	rector of an Anglican parish in Ascot Heath, UK
Goudriaan, Aza	Evangelical University, Belgium	Hansen, Benjamin Harl Sellew	University of Maryland, US University of Maryland, US
Gounelle, Rémi	University of Strasbourg, France	(née Philip Sellew), Melissa	

Harrak, Amir	University of Toronto, US	Huber, Konrad	Johannes Gutenberg University Mainz, Germany
Harrill, J. Albert	Ohio State University, US		
Hartl, Martina	University of Regensburg, Germany	Huebenthal, Sandra	University of Passau, Germany
Hartog, Paul	Carolina University, US	Huebner, Ulrich	Christian-Albrecht University of Kiel, Germany
Heffernan, Thomas	University of Tennessee, Knoxville, US		
Heffron, Robert	University of Sheffield, UK	Humphries, Mark	Swansea University, UK
Heil, Uta	University of Vienna, Austria	Humphries, Thomas	Saint Leo University, US
		Hunink, Vincent	Radboud University, The Netherlands
Heintz, Michael	Mount St. Mary's University, US		
Hengstmengel, Joost	Vrije Universiteit Amsterdam, The Netherlands	Hunt, Hannah	Open University, UK
		Hunter, David	Boston College, US
		Hurtado†, Larry W.	University of Edinburgh, UK
Henten, Jan Willem van	University of Amsterdam, The Netherlands		
		Izydorczyk, Zbigniew	University of Winnipeg, Canada
Hermanowicz, Erika T.	University of Georgia, US		
Herrero, Miguel	Complutense University of Madrid, Spain	Jacobi, Christine	Humboldt University of Berlin, Germany
Hervik Bull, Christian	University of Oslo, Norway	Jacobs, Andrew S.	Harvard University, US
Heydemann, Gerda	Free University of Berlin, Germany	Jacobsen, Anders-Christian	Aarhus University, Denmark
Hezser, Catherine	School of Oriental and African Studies, University of London, UK	Jefferson, Lee M.	Centre College, US
		Jensen, Robin	Vanderbilt University, US; University of Notre Dame, US
Hildebrand, Stephen M.	ranciscan University of Steubenville, US	Johnson, Aaron	Lee University, US
Hillner, Julia	University of Sheffield, UK	Johnson, Benjamin J.M.	LeTourneau University, US
Hixson, Elijah	University of Edinburgh, UK	Johnson, Lee A.	East Carolina University, US
Hofer, Andrew	Dominican House of Studies, US	Johnston, Jeremiah	independent researcher, Dallas, US
Hoglund, Jonathan	Bethlehem College & Seminary, US	Jöris, Steffen	RWTH Aachen University, Germany
Holman, Susan	Harvard University, US	Judge-Mulhall, Julia	Harvard University, US
Hoof, Lieve van	University of Gent, Belgium	Jurgasch, Thomas	University of Tuebingen, Germany
Hoover, Jesse	Baylor University, US	Kahlos, Maijastina	University of Helsinki, Finland
Hope Griffin, Mary	Oakton College, US		
Hornung, Christian	University of Bonn, Germany	Kaiser, Martin	independent researcher based in Germany
Horst, Pieter W. van der	University of Utrecht, The Netherlands	Kalb, Herbert	Juliana King University, US
		Kalvesmaki, Joel	Catholic University of America, US
Hovorun, Serhiy	Loyola Marymount University, US		
		Kang Hoon Lee, James	Southern Methodist University, US

Kantzer Komline, Han-luen	Western Theological Seminary, US
Karamanolis, George	University of Crete, Greece
Kasumi Clements, Niki	Rice University, US
Keener, Craig	Asbury Theological Seminary, US
Khoperia, Lela	St Andrew Georgian University, Georgia
King, Justin D.	Baylor University, US
King, Karen	Harvard University, US
Kingreen, Sarah M.	Humboldt University of Berlin, Germany
Kinzig, Wolfram	University of Bonn, Germany
Kitchen, Robert A.	retired minister living in Saskatchewan, Canada
Kitzler, Petr	Palacký University, Czech Republic
Kleinkopf, Kathryn	University of Tennessee, Knoxville, US
Kloppenborg, John S.	University of Toronto, CA
Knöppler, Thomas	Ludwig Maximilian University of Munich, Germany
Kobets, Svitlana	University of Toronto, US
Kochańczyk-Bonińska, Karolina	University of Warsaw, Poland
Koet, Bart J.	Tilburg University, The Netherlands
Koltun-Fromm, Naomi	Haverford College, US
Konstan, David	New York University, US
Kooi, Kees van der	Vrije Universiteit Amsterdam, The Netherlands
Kooten, George van	University of Cambridge, UK
Koperski, Andrew	Ohio State University, US
Korak, Carol A.	Central Baptist Theological Seminary, US
Koziol, Geoffrey	University of California, Berkeley, US
Kraus, Thomas J.	University of Zurich, Switzerland
Kulikowski, Michael	Pennsylvania State University, US
Kuper, Charles	University of Rome La Sapienza, Italy
Kurek-Chomycz, Dominika	Liverpool Hope University, UK
Labarre, Sylvie	Le Mans University, France
Lamberigts, Mathijs	Catholic University of Leuven, Belgium
Lang, Michael	Diocese of Westminster, UK
Langbroek, Erika	Independent researcher, based in The Netherlands
Lans, Birgit van der	University of Groningen, The Netherlands
Latham, Jacob	University of Tennessee, Knoxville, US
Lecerf, Adrien	French National Centre for Scientific Research, France
Ledegang, Fred	Vrije Universiteit Amsterdam, The Netherlands
Lee, Doug	University of Nottingham, UK
Leemans, Johan	Catholic University of Leuven, Belgium
Leppin, Hartmut	Goethe University Frankfurt, Germany
Lettieri , Gaetano	University of Rome La Sapienza, Italy
Lichtenberger, Achim	Ruhr University Bochum, Germany
Lietaert Lietaert Peerbolte, Bert Jan	Vrije Universiteit Amsterdam, The Netherlands
Lightfoot, Jane L.	University of Oxford, UK
Lillo Botella, Carles	University of Alicante, Spain
Lincicum, David	University of Notre Dame, US
Litfin, Bryan	Liberty University, US
Litwa, David	Australian Catholic University, Australia
Liverani , Paolo	University of Florence, Italy
Livneh, Atar	Ben Gurion University, Isreal
Löhr, Winrich A.	University of Heidelberg, Germany

Longacre, Drew G.	University of Groningen, The Netherlands	Mauskopf Deliyannis, Deborah	Indiana University Bloomington, US
Loon, Hans van	Tilburg University, The Netherlands	Mawdsley, Harry E.	Durham University, UK; University of Sheffield, UK
Lovell, Graham	University of Adelaide, Australia	Maxwell-Stuart, Peter	University of St Andrews, UK
Lovell, Michael	University of Tennessee, Knoxville, US	Maynard, Matthew	Ohio State University, US
Löx, Markus	State Collections of Antiquities, Germany	Mc Carthy, Daniel	Trinity College Dublin, Ireland
Lunn-Rockliffe, Sophie	University of Cambridge, UK	McCarthy Spoerl, Kelley	Saint Anselm College, US
Luomanen, Petri	University of Helsinki, Finland	McConaughy, Daniel L.	California State University, Northridge, US
Lupieri, Edmondo	Loyola University, US	McDonald, Lee Martin	Fuller Theological Seminary Southwest, US
Luttikhuizen, Gerard	University of Groningen, The Netherlands	McGowan, Andrew	Yale University, US
Mace, Hannah	University of St Andrews, UK	McGrath, James F.	Butler University, US
		McGuckin, John	Columbia University, US
MacLeod†, Frederick	Saint Louis University, US	McIntyre, Gwynaeth	University of Otago, New Zealand
Mader, Heidrun	University of Cologne, Germany	Mein, Andrew	Queen's University Belfast, UK
Maier, Harry O.	Vancouver School of Theology, Canada	Meiser, Martin	Saarland University, Germany
Malavasi, Giulio	independent researcher based in Italy	Menze, Volker	Central European University, US
Marguerat, Daniel	University of Lausanne, Switzerland	Mercer, Jared	University of Oxford, UK
		Merdinger, Jane	Catholic University of America, US
Marinis, Vasileios	Yale University, US	Merz, Annette	Protestant Theological University, Utrecht, The Netherlands
Maritano, Mario	Salesian Pontifical University, Italy		
Marjanen, Antti	University of Helsinki, Finland	Meyer, Eric	Fordham University, US
		Milazzo, Vincenza	University of Catania, Italy
Markschies, Christoph	Berlin-Brandenburg Academy of Sciences and Humanities, Germany	Mimouni, Simon	Sorbonne University, Paris
		Mitsiou, Ekaterini	University of Vienna, Austria
Martens, John W.	St. Mark's College, Canada	Moffitt, David	University of St Andrews, UK
Martens, Peter	Saint Louis University, US		
Martin, Céline	Université Bordeaux Montaigne, France	Moloney, Francis J.	Salesian Community Rupertswood, Australia
Maskarinec, Maya	University of Southern California, US	Moorhead, John	University of Queensland, Australia
Mason, Steve	University of Groningen, The Netherlands	Morales, Xavier	Pontifical Catholic University of Chile, Chile
Maspero, Giulio	Pontifical University of the Holy Cross, Italy	Moreschini, Claudio	University of Pisa, Italy
		Moss, Candida	University of Birmingham, UK
Mathisen, Ralph W.	University of Illinois Urbana-Champaign, US		

Müller, Mogens	University of Copenhagen, Denmark	Papandrea, James	Garrett-Evangelical Theological Seminary, US
Mulligan, Bret	Haverford College, US	Parani, Maria G.	University of Cyprus, Cyprus
Murcia, Thierry	Aix-Marseille University, France	Pardue, Stephen T.	International Graduate School of Leadership, Philippines
Myllikoski, Matti	University of Helsinki, Finland		
Natal, David	Royal Holloway, University of London, UK	Patrich, Joseph	Hebrew University, Israel
Navoni, Marco	Amborisan Library, Italy	Pedersen, Nils Arne	Aarhus University, Denmark
Neil, Bronwen	Macquarie University, Australia	Peppard, Michael	Fordham University, US
Nesselrath, Heinz-Günther	University of Goettingen, Germany	Pergola, Philippe	Pontifical Institute of Christian Archeaology, Italy
Neubert, Luke	University of Munich Ludwig Maximilian, Germany	Petrey, Taylor	Kalamazoo College, US
		Peursen, Willem van	Vrije Universiteit Amsterdam, The Netherlands
Neuhoff, Klaus Heinrich	priest based in Cologne, Germany	Pfeiffer, Henrik	University of Erlangen-Nurenberg Friedrich Alexander, Germany
Nicak, Maros	Comenius University Bratislava, Slovakia		
Nichols, Bridget	Durham University, UK	Pierce, Alexander H.	Trinity Anglican Seminar, US
Norelli, Enrico	Université de Genève, Switzerland	Pietruschka, Ute	Martin Luther University of Halle-Wittenberg, Germany
Nuffelen, Peter van	University of Gent, Belgium		
Oefele, Christine	University of Bern, Switzerland	Pignot, Matthieu	University of Namur, Belgium
Oegema, Gerbern S.	McGill University, Canada	Pigott, Justin	University of Auckland, New Zealand
Økland, Jorunn	University of Oslo, Norway		
O'Loughlin, Thomas	University of Nottingham, UK	Pilhofer, Philipp	University of Rostock, Germany
Op de Coul, Michiel	Tilburg University, The Netherlands	Platte, Elizabeth	Valparaiso University, US
Orchard, Andy	University of Oxford, UK	Pollard, Richard M.	University of Quebec in Montreal, Canada
Orton, Robin	visiting research fellow, King's College London, UK	Poorthuis, Marcel	Tilburg University, The Netherlands
Os, Arjan van den	Theological University of Apeldoorn, The Netherlands	Popkes, Enno Edzard	Christian-Albrecht University of Kiel, Germany
Osiek, Carolyn	Texas Christian University, US	Porter, Nathan	Duke University, US
		Pouderon, Bernard	University of Tours, France
Ottenheijm, Eric	Utrecht University, The Netherlands	Price, Richard M.	Heythrop College, University of London, UK
Oyen, Geert van	University of Louvain, Belgium	Prinzivalli, Emanuela	University of Rome La Sapienza, Italy
Page, Christopher	University of Cambridge, UK	Ramelli, Ilaria	Sacred Heart Major Seminary, US

Rampton, Martha	Pacific University, US	Safrai, Zeev	Bar-Ilan University, Israel
Rasimus, Tuomas	University of Helsinki, Finland	Safranski, Ben	University of Steubenville, US
Reinhartz, Adele	University of Ottawa, Canada	Sághy†, Marianne	Eötvös Loránd University, Hungary
Ritari, Katja	University of Helsinki, Finland	Saint Laurent, Jeanne Nicole	Marquette University, US
Roberts, Michael	Wesleyan University, US	Sakvarelidze, Nino	University of Salzburg, Austria
Robinson, Gesine	Claremont School of Theology, US	Salazar Ortiz, Natalia	University of Lleida, Spain
Roddy, Nicolae	Creighton University, US	Sales Carbonel, Jordina	University of Barcelona, Spain
Roesch, Laura	University of Tennessee, Knoxville, US	Salminen, Joona	University of Eastern Finland, Finland
Rohrman, Dirk	University of Wuppertal, Germany	Salway, Benet	University College London, England
Roig Lanzillotta, Lautaro	University of Groningen, The Netherlands	Salzman, Michele R.	University of California, Riverside, US
Rollens, Sarah	Rhodes College, US		
Romano, John	Benedictine College, US	Sanchez, Christian	Baylor University, US
Rompay, Luc van	Duke University, US	Sanchez, Sylvain Jean Gabriel	Université Paris-Sorbonne, France
Ronzani, Rocco	Pontifical Patristic Augustinian Institute, Italy	Sandt, Huub van de	Tilburg University, The Netherlands
Rose, Els	Utrecht University, The Netherlands	Sarot, Marcel	Tilburg University, The Netherlands
Roth, Dieter T.	Boston College, US		
Rotman, Marco	Christelijke Hogeschool Ede, The Netherlands	Sarti, Laury	University of Freiburg Albert Ludwig, Germany
Roukema, Riemer	Protestant Theological University, Utrecht, The Netherlands	Sato, Makiko	Tilburg University, The Netherlands
		Sawyer†, John F.A.	Durham University, UK
Rouwhorst, Gerard	Tilburg University, The Netherlands	Schironi, Francesca	University of Michigan, US
		Schliesser, Benjamin	University of Bern, Switzerland
Rowland, Christopher	University of Oxford, UK		
Rubenson, Samuel	University of Lund, Sweden	Schmidt, Gleb	Radboud University, The Netherlands
Runia, David T.	University of Melbourne, Australia	Schmidt, Thomas C.	Yale University, US
		Schoenberger, Axel	University of Bremen, Germany
Russel Christman, Angela	Loyola University, US	Schöllgen, Georg	University of Bonn, Germany
Russell, Norman	University of Oxford, UK		
Russell, Paul	University of Lund, Sweden	Schreiber, Stefan	University of Augsburg, Germany
Russo, Nicholas	University of Notre Dame, US	Schultheiss, Jochen	Julius Maximilian University of Würzburg, Germany
Ruzer, Serge	Hebrew University, Israel		
Sadowski, Sydney	Pontifical University of John Paul II, Poland	Schulthess, Sara	University of Lausanne, Switzerland
		Schwartz, Daniel R.	Hebrew University, Israel

Schwartz, Joshua — Bar-Ilan University, Israel

Scopello, Madeleine — French National Centre for Scientific Research, France

Sears, Gareth — University of Birmingham, UK

Secord, Jared — University of Calgary, Canada

Serra, Simonetta — independent researcher based in Rome, Italy

Shannon-Henderson, Kelly E. — University of Cincinnati, US

Shean, John F. — LaGuardia Community College, US

Shoemaker, Stephen — University of Oregon, US

Shuve, Karl — University of Virginia, US

Siecienski, Anthony Edward — Stockton University, US

Simić, Kosta — Australian Catholic University, Australia

Simón, Francisco Marco — University of Zaragoza, Spain

Skinner, Christopher — Loyola University, US

Slootjes, Daniëlle — University of Amsterdam, The Netherlands

Smalbrugge, Matthias — Vrije Universiteit Amsterdam, The Netherlands

Smit, Peter-Ben — Vrije Universiteit Amsterdam, The Netherlands

Smith, Eric C. — Iliff School of Theology, US

Smith, Geoffrey S. — University of Texas, US

Smith, Zachary B. — Creighton University, US

Somov, Alexey — Vrije Universiteit Amsterdam, The Netherlands

Sotinel, Claire — Université Paris-Est Créteil, France

Spigel, Chad — Trinity University, US

Spittler, Janet E. — University of Virginia, US

Springer, Carl — University of Tennessee, US

Spronk, Klaas — Protestant Theological University, Utrecht, The Netherlands

Staalduine-Sulman, Eveline van — Vrije Universiteit Amsterdam, The Netherlands

Standhartinger, Angela — University of Marburg, Germany

Starling, David — Morling College, Australia

Stephens, Christopher — University of Roehampton, London

Stephens Falcasantos, Rebecca — University of Massachusetts Amherst, US

Stępień, Tomasz — Cardinal Stefan Wyszyński University, Poland

Stettner, Johannes — RWTH Aachen University, Germany

Stevenson, Walt — University of Richmond, US

Stewart, Alistair C. — Codrington College, Barbados

Stewart, Bryan A. — McMurry University, US

Stewart, Columba — College of Saint Benedict and Saint John's University, US

Steyn, Gert J. — University of Pretoria, South Africa

Strickler, Ryan — Newcastle University, UK

Svigel, Michael J. — Dallas Theological Seminary, US

Swain, Brian — Kennesaw State University, US

Tang, Li — Kazakhstan Academy of Sciences, Kazakhstan

Taormina, Daniela P. — University of Rome Tor Vergata, Italy

Te Velde, J.B. — St. Willibrords Abbey, Doetinchem, The Netherlands

Teepe, Ramona — Yale University, US

Teitler, Hans — independent researcher based in Germany

Testa, Rita Lizzi — University of Perugia, Italy

Thomassen, Einar — University of Bergen, Norway

Thomson†, Robert W. — Oxford University, UK

Tiersch, Claudia — Humboldt University of Berlin, Germany

Tilley†, Maureen — Fordham University, UK

Timbie, Janet	Catholic University of America, US
Timmermann, Josh	University of British Columbia, Canada
Tiwald, Markus	University of Vienna, Austria
Toca, Madalina	Catholic University of Leuven, Belgium
Tollefsen, Torstein Theodor	University of Oslo, Norway
Tolmie, Donald Francois	University of the Free State, South Africa
Tomson, Peter J.	Catholic University of Leuven, Belgium
Toom, Tarmo	University of Tartu, Estonia
Topalilov, Ivo	Bulgarian academy of Sciences, Bulgaria
Trebilco, Paul	University of Otago, New Zealand
Tripaldi, Daniele	University of Bologna, Italy
Trout, Dennis	University of Missouri, US
Tuckett, Christopher	University of Oxford, UK
Turner†, John D.	University of Nebraska, US
Twigg, Matthew	University of Oxford, UK
Tymister, Markus	Pontifical University of Sant'Anselmo, Italy
Uhalde, Kevin	Ohio University, US
Ullucci, Daniel	Stonehill College, US
Undheim, Sissel	University of Bergen, Norway
Urbano, Arthur P.	University of Providence, US
Vaggione†, Richard Paul	St. Matthias Anglican Church
Vahrenhorst, Martin	Saarland University, Germany
Vercruysse, Jean-Marc	Université Artois, France
Verde, Francesco	University of Rome La Sapienza, Italy
Verhoef, Eduard	University of Pretoria, South Africa
Veronese, Maria	University of Padua, Italy
Viezure, Iuliana	Georgia Institute of Technology, US
Villa, Massimo	University of Naples L'Orientale, Italy
Villegas Marín, Raúl	University of Barcelona, Spain
Vinzent, Markus	King's College London, UK
Vitiello, Massimiliano	University of Missouri-Kansas City, US
Vleugels, Gie	Evangelical Theological Faculty, Belgium
Volp, Ulrich	Johannes Gutenberg University Mainz, Germany
Vuong, Lily	Central Washington University, US
Waarden, Joop van	Radboud University, The Netherlands
Waers, Stephen	Milligan University, US
Walker White, Andrew	George Mason University, US
Walsh, David	University of Kent, UK
Wardle , Timothy	Furman University, US
Watson, Francis	Durham University, UK
Watt, John W.	Cardiff University, UK
Weckwerth, Andreas	Catholic University of Eichstätt-Ingolstadt, Germany
Weidmann, Clemens	Paris Lodron University of Salzburg, Austria
Weigel, Richard	Western Kentucky University, US
Werline, Rodney a.	Barton College, US
West, Christopher	Theology of the Body Institute, US
Whately, Conor	University of Winnipeg, Canada
White, Carolinne	University of Oxford, UK
Whiting, Colin	Dumbarton Oaks, US
Wiegels, Rainer	Osnabrück University, Germany
Wienand, Johannes	Technical University of Braunschweig, Germany
Wijnendaele, Jeroen	University of Gent, Belgium
Wilhite, David	Baylor University, US
Williams, Catrin H.	University of Wales Trinity Saint David, UK
Williams, Daniel H.	Baylor University, US
Williams, Michael	Maynooth University, Ireland
Williams, Travis B.	Tusculum University, US

Williams III, Drake	Evangelical Theological Institute, Leuven	Yates, Benedict	Taff Wenallt Ministry, US
Willigen, Marten van	Theological University of Apeldoorn, The Netherlands	Yirga, Felege-Selam	Ohio State University, US
		Young, Frances M.	University of Birmingham, UK
Wilson, Mark	Asia Minor Research Center, Türkiye	Young, Genevieve	Macquarie University, Australia
Wingerden, Ruben van	Tilburg University, The Netherlands	Zakarian, David	University of Oxford, UK
		Zangenberg, Jürgen	University of Leiden, The Netherlands
Winkler, Dietmar	Paris Lodron University of Salzburg, Austria	Zhyrkova, Anna	Ignatianum University, Poland
Wiśniewski, Robert	University of Warsaw, Poland	Zimmermann, Ruben	Johannes Gutenberg University Mainz, Germany
Wisse, Maarten	Protestant Theological University, Utrecht, The Netherlands	Zwiep, Arie W.	Vrije Universiteit Amsterdam, The Netherlands
Witulski, Thomas	Bielefeld University, Germany	Zwollo, Laela	Tilburg University, The Netherlands
Wortley†, John	University of Manitoba, US		
Wright, Charles D.	University of Illinois Urbana-Champaign, US		

Biblical and Extrabiblical Abbreviations

1. Old Testament

Gen	Genesis
Exod	Exodus
Lev	Leviticus
Num	Numbers
Deut	Deuteronomy
Josh	Joshua
Judg	Judges
1 Sam	1 Samuel (LXX: 1 Kgdm = 1 Kingdoms)
2 Sam	2 Samuel (LXX: 2 Kgdm = 2 Kingdoms)
1 Kgs	1 Kings (LXX: 3 Kgdm = 3 Kingdoms)
2 Kgs	2 Kings (LXX: 4 Kgdm = 4 Kingdoms)
Isa	Isaiah
Jer	Jeremiah
Ezek	Ezekiel
Hos	Hosea
Joel	Joel
Amos	Amos
Obad	Obadiah
Jonah	Jonah
Mic	Micah
Nah	Nahum
Hab	Habakkuk
Zeph	Zephaniah
Hag	Haggai
Zech	Zechariah
Mal	Malachi
Ps(s)	Psalm(s)
Prov	Proverbs
Job	Job
Song	Song of Songs
Ruth	Ruth
Lam	Lamentations
Qoh	Ecclesiastes (or Qohelet)
Esth	Esther
Dan	Daniel
Ezra	Ezra
Neh	Nehemiah
1 Chr	1 Chronicles
2 Chr	2 Chronicles

2. OT Apocrypha and Pseudepigrapha

Bar.	Baruch+B67
2 Bar.	*2 Baruch* (Syriac Apocalypse)
3 Bar.	*3 Baruch* (Greek Apocalypse)
4 Bar.	*4 Baruch* (Paraleipomena Jeremiou)
1 En.	*1 Enoch* (Ethiopic Apocalypse)
2 En.	*2 Enoch* (Slavonic Apocalypse)
3 En.	*3 Enoch* (Hebrew Apocalypse)
1–2 Esd	1–2 Esdras
1 Macc	1 Maccabees
2 Macc	2 Maccabees
3 Macc	3 Maccabees
4 Macc	4 Maccabees
4 Ezra	*4 Ezra*
5 Apoc. Syr. Pss.	*Five Apocryphal Syriac Psalms*
Add Dan	Additions to Daniel
Add Esth	Additions to Esther
Ant. bib.	see *L.A.B.*
Aḥiq(ar)	*Aḥiqar*
Apoc. Ab.	*Apocalypse of Abraham*
Apoc. Adam	*Apocalypse of Adam*
Apoc. Dan.	*Apocalypse of Daniel*
Apoc. El.	*Apocalypse of Elijah*
Apoc. Ezra	*Apocalypse of Ezra (also 4 Ezra)*
Apoc. Mos.	*Apocalypse of Moses (also L.A.E.)*
Apoc. Sedr.	*Apocalypse of Sedrach*
Apoc. Zeph.	*Apocalypse of Zephaniah*
Apocr. Ezek.	*Apocryphon of Ezekiel*
Aris. Ex.	Aristeas the Exegete
Aristob.	Aristobulos
Artap.	Artapanos
As. Mos.	*Assumption of Moses*
Ascen. Isa.	*Ascension of Isaiah*
Bk. Noah	*Book of Noah*
Cav. Tr.	*Cave of Treasures*
Cl. Mal.	*Cleodemus Malchus*
Dem.	Demetrius (the Chronographer)

BIBLICAL AND EXTRABIBLICAL ABBREVIATIONS

El. Mod.	*Eldad and Modad*	*T. Adam*	*Testament of Adam*
Ep Jer	Epistle of Jeremiah	*T. Ash.*	*Testament of Asher*
Eup.	*Eupolemos*	*T. Benj.*	*Testament of Benjamin*
Ezek. Trag.	*Ezekiel the Tragedian*	*T. Dan*	*Testament of Dan*
Gk. Apoc. Ezra	*Greek Apocalypse of Ezra*	*T. Gad*	*Testament of Gad*
Hec. AB	Hecataeus of Abdera	*T. Isaac*	*Testament of Isaac*
Hel. Syn. Pr.	*Hellenistic Synagogal Prayers*	*T. Iss.*	*Testament of Issachar*
Hist. Jos.	*History of Joseph*	*T. Jac.*	*Testament of Jacob*
Hist. Rech.	*History of the Rechabites*	*T. Job*	*Testament of Job*
Jan. Jam.	*Jannes and Jambres*	*T. Jos.*	*Testament of Joseph*
Jos. Asen.	*Joseph and Aseneth*	*T. Jud.*	*Testament of Judah*
Jub.	*Jubilees*	*T. Levi*	*Testament of Levi*
L.A.B.	*Liber Antiquitatum*	*T. Mos.*	*Testament Moses* (= *As. Mos.*)
	Biblicarum (Pseudo-Philo)	*T. Naph.*	*Testament of Naphtali*
L.A.E.	*Life of Adam and Eve*	*T. Reu.*	*Testament of Reuben*
	(= *Apoc. Mos.*)	*T. Sim.*	*Testament of Simeon*
Lad. Jac.	*Ladder of Jacob*	*T. Sol.*	*Testament of Solomon*
Let. Aris.	*Letter of Aristeas*	*T. Zeb.*	*Testament of Zebulun*
Liv. Pro.	*Lives of the Prophets*	*Treat. Shem*	*Treatise of Shem*
Lost Tr.	*The Lost Tribes*	Tob	Tobit
Mart. Ascen. Isa.	*Martyrdom and Ascension*	*Vis. Ezra*	*Vision of Ezra*
	of Isaiah	Wis	Wisdom of Solomon
Mart. Isa.	*Martyrdom of Isaiah* (in		
	Mart. Ascen. Isa.)		

3. Qumran

Par. Jer.	*Paraleipomena Jeremiou*
	(= *4 Bar.*)

a. Caves

Ph. E. Poet	Philo the Epic Poet
Pr. Jac.	*Prayer of Jacob*

(1Q from Cave 1; 2Q from Cave 2; etc.)

Pr. Jos.	*Prayer of Joseph*	1Q1	Genesis
Pr. Man.	*Prayer of Manasseh*	1Q2	Exodus
Pr. Mos.	*Prayer of Moses*	1Q3	Paleo-Leviticus
Ps.-Eup.	Pseudo-Eupolemus	1Q4–5	Deuteronomy
Ps.-Hec.	Pseudo-Hecataeus	1Q6	Judges
Ps.-Orph.	Pseudo-Orpheus	1Q7	Samuel
Ps.-Philo	Pseudo-Philo (*L.A.B.*)	1Q8	Isaiah
Ps.-Phoc.	Pseudo-Phocylides	1Q9	Ezekiel
Pss. Sol.	*Psalms of Solomon*	1Q10–12	Psalms
Ques. Ezra	*Questions of Ezra*	1Q13	Phylacteryies
Rev. Ezra	*Revelation of Ezra*	1Q14	*Pesher Micah*
Sib. Or.	*Sibylline Oracles*	1Q15	*Pesher Zephaniah*
Sir	Sirach/Ecclesiasticus	1Q16	*Pesher Psalms*
Syr. Men.	*Sentences of the Syriac*	1Q17–18	*Jubilees*
	Menander	1Q19	Noah
T. 3 Patr.	*Testaments of the Three*	1Q20	*Genesis Apocryphon*
	Patriarchs	1Q21	Levi
T. 12 Patr.	*Testaments of the Twelve*	1Q22	Moses
	Patriarchs:	1Q23–24	*Enoch, Book of Giants*
T. Ab.	*Testament of Abraham*	1Q25	*Apocryphal Prophecy*

1Q26	Instruction	3Q15	*Copper Scroll*
1Q27	*Mysteries*	4Q1	Genesis/Exodus
1Q28	*Rule of the Congregation*	4Q2–10	Genesis
1Q28	*Rule of the Blessings*	4Q11	Paleo-Genesis/Exodus
1Q29	Liturgy of 3 Tongues of Fire	4Q12	Paleo-Genesis
1Q30–31	Liturgical Text	4Q13–21	Exodus
1Q32	*New Jerusalem*	4Q22	Paleo-Exodus
1Q33	*War Scroll*	4Q23	Leviticus/Numbers
1Q34	*Liturgical Prayers*	4Q24–26b	Leviticus
1Q35	*Hodāyot*	4Q27	Numbers
1Q36	Hymns	4Q28–44	Deuteronomy
1Q37–40	Hymnic Compositions?	4Q45–46	Paleo-Deuteronomy
1Q41–70	Unclassified	4Q47–48	Joshua
1Q71–72	Daniel	4Q49–50	Judges
1QapGen	*Apocryphon of Genesis*	4Q51–53	Samuel
1QH	*Hodāyot*	4Q54	Kings
1QIsa	Isaiah	4Q55–69	Isaiah
1QM	*War Scroll*	4Q70–72	Jeremiah
1QpHab	*Pesher Habakkuk*	4Q73–75	Ezekiel
1QS	*Rule of the Community*	4Q76–82	Minor Prophets
2Q1	Genesis	4Q83–98	Psalms
2Q2–4	Exodus	4Q99–100	Job
2Q5–9	Paleo-Leviticus	4Q101	Paleo-Job
2Q10–12	Deuteronomy	4Q102–103	Proverbs
2Q13	Jeremiah	4Q104–105	Ruth
2Q14	Psalms	4Q106–108	Song of Songs
2Q15	Job	4Q109–110	Ecclesiastes
2Q16–17	Ruth	4Q111	Lamentations
2Q18	Sirach	4Q112–116	Daniel
2Q19–20	*Jubilees*	4Q117	Ezra
2Q21	*Apocryphon of Moses*	4Q118	Chronicles
2Q22	*Aprocryphon of David*	4Q119–120	Septuagint Leviticus
2Q23	Apocyrphal Prophecy	4Q121	Septuagint Numbers
2Q24	*New Jerusalem*	4Q122	Septuagint Deuteronomy
2Q25	Legal Documents	4Q123	Paleo-Joshua
2Q26	*Enoch, Book of Giants*	4Q124–126	Unclassified
2Q27–33	Unclassified	4Q127	Greek Paraphrase Exodus
3Q1	Ezekiel	4Q128–148	Phylacteries
3Q2	Psalms	4Q149–155	*Mezuzah*
3Q3	Lamentations	4Q156	*Targum of Leviticus*
3Q4	*Pesher Isaiah*	4Q157	*Targum of Job*
3Q5	*Jubilees*	4Q158	Paraphrases
3Q6	Hymn	4Q159	*Ordinances*
3Q7	*Testament of Judah*	4Q160	*Vision of Samuel*
3Q8	Unclassified (mentions Angel of Peace)	4Q161–165	*Pesher Isaiah*
		4Q166–167	*Pesher Hosiah*
3Q9	Sectarian Tekst	4Q168	*Pesher Micah*
3Q10–14	Unclassified	4Q169	*Pesher Nahum*

BIBLICAL AND EXTRABIBLICAL ABBREVIATIONS

4Q170	*Pesher Zephaniah*	4Q265–273	*Damascus Document*
4Q171	*Pesher Psalms*	4Q274	Purification Rules
4Q172	Unidentified *Pesher*	4Q275	Communal Ceremony
4Q173	*Pesher Psalms*	4Q276–278	Rule of Menstruating
4Q174	Florilegium		Women
4Q175	*Testimonia*	4Q279	Four Lots
4Q176	*Tanhumim*	4Q280	Curses
4Q177	Catena	4Q281–282	Unidentified Arguments
4Q178	Unclassified	4Q283	Cancelled
4Q179	*Apocryphal Lamentations*	4Q284	Purification Liturgy
4Q180–181	*Ages of Creation*	4Q284a	Harvesting
4Q182	*Catena*	4Q285	*Sefer ha-Milhamah*
4Q183	Historical Work	4Q286–290	*Berakhot*
4Q184	*Wiles of the Wicked Woman*	4Q291–293	*Prayers*
4Q185	Sapiential Work	4Q294	Sapiential-Didactic Work
4Q186	Horoscope	4Q295–297	Cancelled
4Q196–200	Tobit	4Q298	*Words of a Sage*
4Q201–2012	Several *Enoch* (also Enoch,	4Q299–301	*Mysteries*
	Giants)	4Q302	Admonitory Parable
4Q213–214	Levi	4Q303–305	Creation Meditation
4Q215	*Time of Righteousness*	4Q306	People Who Err
4Q216–228	(several) *Jubilees*	4Q307	Text Mentioning Temple
4Q229	Pseudo-Graphic Work	4Q308	Sapiential Fragments?
4Q230–231	Catalog of Spirits	4Q309	Cursive Work
4Q232	*New Jerusalem*	4Q310–311	Unclassified
4Q233	Fragments (with Place	4Q312	Hebrew Text
	Names)	4Q313	Cryptical
4Q234	Exercitium Calami	4Q314–316	Cancelled
4Q235	Unidentified Text	4Q317	Phases of the Moon
4Q236	Cancelled	4Q318	Zodiology
4Q237	Cancelled	4Q319	*Otot*
4Q238	Habakuk	4Q320–330	*Calendrical Document*
4Q239	*Pesher True Israel*	4Q331–333	Historical Work
4Q240	*Pesher Song of Songs?*	4Q334	*Ordinances*
4Q241	Cancelled	4Q335–336	Astronomical Fragments
4Q242	*Prayers of Nabonidus*	4Q337	*Calendrical Documents*
4Q243–245	*Pseudo-Daniel*	4Q338	Geneaology
4Q246	*Apocryphon of Daniel*	4Q339	List of False Prophets
4Q247	*Pesher Apocalypse of Weeks*	4Q340	List of *Netinim*
4Q248	Historical Text	4Q341	Exercitium Calami
4Q249–250	Papyri (several Texts)	4Q342–343	Letter
4Q251	Halakhah	4Q344	Acknowledgement of Debt
4Q252–253	*Commentary on Genesis*	4Q345–346	Bill of Sale
4Q253a	*Commentary on Malachi*	4Q347	Aramaic Papyrus
4Q254	*Commentary on Genesis*	4Q348–358	Accounting Documents
4Q255–264	*Rule of the Community*	4Q359	List of Names
4Q265	*Serekh Damascus*	4Q360	Exercitium Calami

4Q361	Scribbles on Papyrus	4Q426	Sapiential-Hymnic Work
4Q362–363	Undeciphered	4Q427–433	*Hodāyot*
4Q364–365	*Reworked Pentateuch*	4Q434–438	*Barkhi Nafshia*
4Q365a	*Temple Scroll?*	4Q439	*Lament by a Leader*
4Q366–367	Pentateuch Reworked	4Q440	*Hodayot* kind of text
4Q368	*Apocryphal Pentateuch*	4Q441–444	*Prayers*
4Q369	*Prayer of Enosh*	4Q445–447	Poetics
4Q370	*Apocryphon of the Flood*	4Q448	*Apocryphal Psalms and Prayer*
4Q371–373	*Apocryphon of Joseph*		
4Q374	*Commentary on Exodus*	4Q449–454	Prayers
4Q375–377	*Apocryphon of Moses*	4Q455	Didactic Work
4Q378–379	*Apocryphon of Joshua*	4Q456	Halleluyah
4Q380–381	Noncanonical Psalms	4Q457a	Creation?
4Q382	Paraphases of Kings	4Q457b	Eschatological Hymn
4Q383–384	*Apocryphon of Jeremiah*	4Q458	Narrative
4Q385	*Pseudo-Ezekiel*	4Q459–460	Pseudo-Graphical Work
4Q385a	*Apocryphon of Jeremiah*	4Q461–463	Narrative
4Q385b–386	*Pseudo-Ezekiel*	4Q464	*Exposition on the Patriarchs*
4Q387	Jeremiah	4Q464a	Narrative
4Q387a	*Apocryphon of Jeremiah*	4Q464b	Unclassifed Fragments
4Q388	*Pseudo-Ezekiel*	4Q465	Papyrus (mentions Samson?)
4Q388a–389	Jeremiah		
4Q389a	*Apocryphon of Jeremiah*	4Q466	Text (mentions *Congregation of the Lord*)
4Q390	*Pseudo-Moses*		
4Q391	*Pseudo-Ezekiel*	4Q467	Text (mentions *Light to Jacob*)
4Q392	Works of God		
4Q393	Communal Confession	4Q468a–d	Unidentified Fragments
4Q394	Some Precepts of the Law	4Q468e–f	Historical Text
4Q394a	*Calendrical Document*	4Q468g	Eschatological Work
4Q395–399	Some Precepts of the Law	4Q468h	Hymnic Text
4Q400–407	*Songs of the Sabbath Sacrifice*	4Q468i	Sectarian Text
		4Q468j	Unclassifed Fragments
4Q408	*Apocryphon of Moses*	4Q468k	Hymnic Text
4Q409	Liturgical Work	4Q468l	Fragment (mentions Qoh 1:8–9)
4Q410	Vision and Interpretation		
4Q411	Sapiential Hymn	4Q468m	Unidentified Fragments
4Q412	Sapiential-Didactic Work	4Q469	Narrative
4Q13	Composition Concerning Divine Providence	4Q470	Zedekiah
		4Q471	*War Scroll* kind of text
4Q414	*Ritual Purity*	4Q471a	Polemics
4Q415–418	Instruction	4Q471b	Self-Glorification Hymn
4Q419	Sapiential Work	4Q471c	*Prayer Concerning Godand Israel*
4Q420–421	Ways of Righteousness		
4Q422	Paraphrase of Genesis/ Exodus	4Q472	Eschatological Work
		4Q472a	Halakhah
4Q423–24	Instruction	4Q473	The Two Ways
4Q425	Sapiential-Didactic Work		

BIBLICAL AND EXTRABIBLICAL ABBREVIATIONS

4Q474	Text Concerning Rachel and Joseph	4Q529	*Words of Michael*
		4Q530–533	*Enoch, Book of Giants*
4Q475	Renewed Earth	4Q534–536	Noah
4Q476	Liturgical Work	4Q537	*Apocryphon of Jacob*
4Q477	*Rebukes of the Overseer*	4Q538	*Apocryphon of Judah*
4Q478	Fragment (mentions Festivals)	4Q539	*Apocryphon of Joseph*
		4Q540–441	Levi?
4Q479	Text Mentioning Descendants of David	4Q542	*Testament of Qahat*
		4Q543–549	*Visions of Amram*
4Q480	Narrative	4Q550	Ester?
4Q481	Text Mentioning Mixed Kinds	4Q551	Daniel Susanna
		4Q552–553	Four Kingdoms
4Q481a	*Apocryphon of Elisha*	4Q554–555	*New Jerusalem*
4Q481b	Narrative	4Q556–558	*Visions of Amram*
4Q481c	*Prayer for Mercy*	4Q559	Biblical Chronology
4Q481d	Fragments with Red Ink	4Q560	Proverbs
4Q481e	Narrative	4Q561	Horoscope
4Q481f	Unclassified Fragments	4Q562–575	Aramaic Texts
4Q482	*Jubilees?*	4Q576	Genesis
4Q483	Genesis or *Jubilees?*	4Q577	Text Mentioning the Flood
4Q484	Judah?	4Q578	Historical Text
4Q485	Prophets?	4Q579	Hymnic Work?
4Q486–487	Sapiential Work	5Q1	Deuteronomy
4Q488	Apocryphon	5Q2	Kings
4Q489	Apocalypse	5Q3	Isaiah
4Q490	Fragments	5Q4	Amos
4Q491–497	*War Scroll*	5Q5	Psalms
4Q498	Sapiential Work	5Q6	Lamentations
4Q499	Hymns	5Q7	Lamentations
4Q500	Benediction	5Q8	Phylacteries
4Q501	*Apocryphal Lamentations*	5Q9	Place Names
4Q502	*Ritual of Marriage*	5Q10	*Apocryphon of Malachi*
4Q503	*Daily Prayers*	5Q11	*Rule of the Community*
4Q504–506	*Words of the Luminaries*	5Q12	*Damascus Document*
4Q507–509	*Festival Prayers*	5Q13	Rule
4Q510–511	*Songs of the Sage*	5Q14	Curses
4Q512	*Ritual of Purification*	5Q15	*New Jerusalem*
4Q513–514	*Ordinances*	5Q16–25	Unclassified
4Q515–520	Unclassified	5QX1	Leather Fragment
4Q521	*Messianic Apocalypse*	6Q1	Paleo-Genesis
4Q522	Prophecy of Joshua	6Q2	Paleo-Leviticus
4Q523	Jonathan	6Q3	Deuteronomy
4Q524	*Temple Scroll*	6Q4	Kings
4Q525	Beautitudes	6Q6	Song of Songs
4Q526	Testament?	6Q7	Daniel
4Q527	Liturgical Work	6Q8	*Enoch, Book of Giants*
4Q528	Hymnic or Sapiential Work	6Q9	Samuel-Kings

6Q10	Prophecy
6Q11	Allegory of the Vine
6Q12	Apocryphal Prophecy
6Q13	Priestly Prophet
6Q14	Apocalypse
6Q15	*Damascus Document*
6Q16	Benediction
6Q17	*Calendrical Document*
6Q18	Hymn
6Q19	Genesis
6Q20	Deuteronomy
6Q21	Prophetic Text?
6Q22–6QX2	Unclassified
7Q1	Septuagint Exodus
7Q2	*Epistle of Jeremiah*
7Q3–5	Biblical Text?
7Q6–14	Unclassified
7Q15–18	Unclassified
7Q19	Imprint
8Q1	Genesis
8Q2	Psalms
8Q3	Phylacteries
8Q4	*Mezuzah*
8Q5	Hymn
8QX1	Tabs
8QX2–3	Thongs
9Q1	Unclassified Fragments
10Q1	Ostracon
11Q1	Paleo-Leviticus
11Q2	Leviticus
11Q3	Deuteronomy
11Q4	Ezekiel
11Q4–9	Psalms
11Q10	*Targum of Job*
11Q11	*Apocryphal Psalms*
11Q12	*Jubilees*
11Q13	Melchizedek
11Q14	*Sefer ha-Milhamah*
11Q15–16	Hymns
11Q17	*Songs of the Sabbath Sacrifice*
11Q18–20	*Temple Scroll*
11Q21	Hebrew Text
11Q22–28	Unclassified
11Q29	(related to) *Serekh ha-Yahad*
11Q30	Unclassified
11Q31	Unclassified
XQ1–4	Phylacteries

XQ5	Fragments
XQ6	Offering

b. General Abbreviations

1QS	*Serekh Hayahad* (*Rule of the Community*)
1QJub	*Jubilees*
1QLevi	see ALD
1QSa	*Rule of the Congregation*
1QSb	*Rule of the Blessings*
2QJub	*Jubilees*
3Q15	*Copper Scroll*
3QJub	*Jubilees*
4Q285	*Sefer Hamilhamah*
4QAgesCreat	*Ages of Creation*
4QapocrDan	*Apocryphon of Daniel*
4QapocrJosh	*Apocryphon of Joshua*
4QBarki Nafshi	*Barkhi Nafshi*
4QBeat	*Beatitudes*
4QCalDoc	*Calendrical Document*
4QCatena	*Catena*
4QCommGen	*Commentary on Genesis*
4QD	*Damascus Document*
4QDibHam	*Dibre Hame'orot* (*Words of the Luminaries*)
4QEn	Enoch (*1 Enoch* texts)
4QEnastr	*1 Enoch* (72–82)
4QExod–Lev	
4QFlor	*Florilegium*
4QInstruction	*Instruction*
4QJub	*Jubilees*
4Qlevia	see ALD
4QMessAp	*Messianic Apocalypse*
4QMMT	*Miqsat Ma'asê ha-Torah*
4QMyst	*Mysteries*
4QpaleoExod	Manuscript (Palaeo-Hebrew)
4QpapLXXLev	(pap = papyrus)
4QpapParaExod	*ParaExodus*
4QpapPrQuot	*Prières quotidiennes* (*Daily Prayers*)
4QpapRitMar	*Ritual of Marriage*
4QpapRitPur	*Ritual Purity*
4QPrFêtes	*Prières pour les fêtes* (*Festival Prayers*)
4QPrNab	*Prayer of Nabonidus*
4QRitPur	*Ritual Purity*
4QRP	*Reworked Pentateuch*
4QSD	*Serekh Damascus*

BIBLICAL AND EXTRABIBLICAL ABBREVIATIONS

4QShir	*Shirot* (*Songs of the Sage*)	MMT	*miqṣat maʿaśe hattorāh*
4QShirShabb	*Songs of the Sabbath Sacrifice*		("Some Precepts of the
4QTest	*Testimonia*		Law")
4QTob	Tobit	MSM	*Midrash Sefer Moshe*
4QToḥorot	*Toḥorot*	Myst	*Book of Mysteries*
4QXII	*Greek Minor Prophets Scroll*	NJ	*New Jerusalem*
11QApPs	*Apocryphal Psalms*	NPC	*Narrative and Poetic*
11QJub	*Jubilees*		*Composition*
11QMelch	*Melchizedek*	Ord	*Ordinances*
11QNJ	*New Jerusalem*	Ordo	*Ordo*
11QpaleoLev	Leviticus (Palaeo-Hebrew)	Otot	*Otot*
11QPs	*Psalms Scroll*	PB	*Patriarchal Blessings*
11QT	*Temple Scroll*	pGen	*Pesher Genesis*
11QtgJob	*Targum of Job*	pHab	*Pesher Habakkuk*
1QIsa	Isaiah	pHos	*Pesher Hosea*
ALD	*Aramaic Levi Document*	pIsa	*Pesher Isaiah*
apGen	*Genesis Apocryphon*	pMi	*Pesher Micah*
apocrDan	*Apocryphon of Daniel*	pNah	*Pesher Nahum*
apocrJer	*Apocryphon of Jeremiah*	PP	*Pentateuchal Paraphrase*
apocrJoseph	*Apocryphon of Joseph*	pPs	*Pesher Psalms*
apocrJosh	*Apocryphon of Joshua*	prEsther	*Proto-Esther*
apocrLevi	*Apocryphon of Levi*	PrNab	*Prayer of Nabonidus*
apocrMos	*Apocryphon of Moses*	psDan	*Pseudo-Daniel*
apocrPent A–B	*Apocryphal Pentateuch* A–B	psEzek	*Pseudo-Ezekiel*
ApPs	*Apocryphal Psalms*	PsJosh	*Psalms of Joshua*
Barki Nafshi	*Barki Napši*	psMos	*Pseudo-Moses*
Ber	*Berakhot*	pZeph	*Pesher Zephaniah*
BibPar	*Biblical Paraphrase*	RP	*Reworked Pentateuch*
CalDoc A–G	*Calendrical Document*	S	*Community Rule* (*serekh*
CalDoc/Mish	*Calendrical Document/*		*hayyahad*)
	Mišmārot A–D	Sa	*Rule of the Congregation*
Cat A	Catena A		(*serekh haʿedāh*)
CD	*Damascus Document*	Sap Work A	*Sapiential Work* A
CommGen	*Commentary on Genesis*	Sb	*Rule of the Blessings* (*dibre*
CTLevi	see ALD		*habbĕrākot*)
DibHam	*dibre hammĕ ʾorot*	SD	*serekh damešeq*
DM	*Words of Moses*	Shir	*Songs of the maśkil*
EnGiants	*Book of Giants*	ShirShabb	*Sabbath Songs* (*širot ʿolat*
Flor	Florilegium		*haššabbat*)
H	*Hodāyot*	SM	*serekk hammilhāmāh/sefer*
Inst	Instruction		*hammilhāmāh*
M	*War Rule* (*Scroll*)	T	*Temple Scroll*
Melch	*Melkiṣedeq Pesher*	Test	*Testimonia*
MidrEschat	*Midrash on Eschatology*	tgJob	*Targum of Job*
Misc. Rul.	*Miscellaneous Rules*	TLevi	*Testament of Levi*
Mish A–J	*Mišmārot* A-J	TQahat	*Testament of Qahat*
MLM	*musār lĕmebin* ("Discipline	VisAmram	*Vision of Amram*
	for an Instructor")		

4. New Testament

Matt	Matthew
Mark	Mark
Luke	Luke
John	John
Acts	Acts of the Apostles
Rom	Romans
1 Cor	1 Corinthians
2 Cor	2 Corinthians
Gal	Galatians
Eph	Ephesians
Phil	Philippians
Col	Colossians
1 Thess	1 Thessalonians
2 Thess	2 Thessalonians
1 Tim	1 Timothy
2 Tim	2 Timothy
Tit	Titus
Phlm	Philemon
Heb	Hebrews
Jas	James
1 Pet	1 Peter
2 Pet	2 Peter
1 John	1 John
2 John	2 John
3 John	3 John
Jude	Jude
Rev	Revelation

5. NT Apocrypha, Pseudepigrapha and Early Christian Literature

1 Clem	*1 Clement*
2 Clem	*2 Clement*
3 Clem	*3 Clement*
3 Cor.	*3 Corinthians*
Acts Andr.	*Acts of Andrew*
Acts Andr. Mth.	*Acts of Andrew and Matthias*
Acts Andr. Paul	*Acts of Andrew and Paul*
Acts Barn.	*Acts of Barnabas*
Acts Jas.	*Acts of James the Great*
Acts John	*Acts of John*
Acts Paul	*Acts of Paul*
Acts Pet.	*Acts of Peter* (not identical to *Acts Pet. 12 Apos.*, NHC VI,*1*)
Acts Pet. Andr.	*Acts of Peter and Andrew*
Acts Pet. Paul	*Acts of Peter and Paul*

Acts Phil.	*Acts of Philip*
Acts Pil.	*Acts of Pilate*
Acts Thad.	*Acts of Thaddaeus*
Acts Thom.	*Acts of Thomas*
Ap. John	*Apocryphon of John*
Apoc. Dosith.	*Apocalypse of Dositheus*
Apoc. Messos	*Apocalypse of Messos*
Apoc. Paul	*(Greek) Apocalypse of Paul (= Vision of Paul)*
Apoc. Pet. (Gk)	*(Greek) Apocalypse of Peter* (not identical to NHC VII,*3*)
Apoc. Thom.	*Apocalypse of Thomas*
Apoc. Vir.	*Apocalypse of the Virgin*
Apos. Con.	*Apostolic Constitutions and Canons*
Asc. Jas.	*Ascents of James*
Assum. Vir.	*Assumption of the Virgin*
Barn.	*Barnabas*
Cerinthus	*Cerinthus*
Desc. Chr.	*Descent of Christ*
Did.	*Didache*
Diogn.	*Diognetus*
Ep. Alex.	*Epistle to the Alexandrians*
Ep. Apos.	*Epistle to the Apostles*
Ep. Chr. Abg.	*Epistle of Christ and Abgar*
Ep. Chr. Heav.	*Epistle of Christ from Heaven*
Ep. Lao.	*Epistle to the Laodiceans*
Ep. Lent.	*Epistle of Lentulus*
Ep. Paul Sen.	*Epistles of Paul and Seneca*
Ep. Tit.	*Pseudo-Titus*
Gos. Barn.	*Gospel of Barnabas*
Gos. Bart.	*Gospel of Bartholomew*
Gos. Bas.	*Gospel of Basilides*
Gos. Bir. Mary	*Gospel of the Birth of Mary*
Gos. Eb.	*Gospel of the Ebionites*
Gos. Eg. (Gk)	*Gospel of the Egyptians* (Gk; not the same as the Coptic *Gos. Eg.* NHC III,*2*; IV,*2*)
Gos. Eve	*Gospel of Eve*
Gos. Gam.	*Gospel of Gamaliel*
Gos. Heb.	*Gospel of the Hebrews*
Gos. Marcion	*Gospel of Marcion*
Gos. Mary	*Gospel of Mary*
Gos. Naass.	*Gospel of the Naassenes*
Gos. Naz.	*Gospel of the Nazarenes*
Gos. Nic.	*Gospel of Nicodemus*
Gos. Pet.	*Gospel of Peter*

BIBLICAL AND EXTRABIBLICAL ABBREVIATIONS

Gos. Phil. — *Gospel of Philip* (= NHC II,3)

Gos. Thom. — *Gospel of Thomas* (= NHC II,2)

Herm. *Mand.* — Hermas, *Shepherd of Hermas: Mandate*

Herm. *Sim.* — Hermas, *Shepherd of Hermas: Similitude*

Herm. *Vis.* — Hermas, *Shepherd of Hermas: Vision*

Hist. Jos. Carp. — *History of Joseph the Carpenter*

Hymn Dance — *Hymn of the Dance*

Hymn Pearl — *Hymn of the Pearl*

Ign. *Eph.* — Ignatius, *To the Ephesians*

Ign. *Magn.* — Ignatius, *To the Magnesians*

Ign. *Phld.* — Ignatius, *To the Philadelphians*

Ign. *Pol.* — Ignatius, *To Polycarp*

Ign. *Rom.* — Ignatius, *To the Romans*

Ign. *Smyrn.* — Ignatius, *To the Smyrnians*

Ign. *Trall.* — Ignatius, *To the Trallians*

Inf. Gos. Thom. — *Infancy Gospel of Thomas*

Mart. Bart. — *Martyrdom of Bartholomew*

Mart. Mt. — *Martyrdom of Matthew*

Mart. Paul — *Martyrdom of Paul*

Mart. Pet. — *Martyrdom of Peter*

Mart. Pet. Paul — *Martyrdom of Peter and Paul*

Mart. Phil. — *Martyrdom of Philip*

Mart. Pol. — *Martyrdom of Polycarp*

Melkon — *Melkon*

Mem. Apos. — *Memoria of Apostles*

Odes Sol. — *Odes of Solomon*

Pap. — Fragments of Papias

Pol. *Phil.* — Polycarp, *To the Philippians*

Pre. Pet. — *Preaching of Peter*

Prot. Jas. — *Protevangelium of James*

Ps.-Abd. — *Apostolic History of Pseudo-Abdias*

Ps.-Clem. — *Pseudo-Clementines*

Ps.-Clem. H — Pseudo-Clementines *Homilia*

Ps.-Clem. R — Pseudo-Clementines *Recognitiones*

Ps.-Mt. — *Gospel of Pseudo-Matthew*

Rev. Steph. — *Revelation of Stephen*

Sec. Gos. Mk. — *Secret Gospel of Mark*

Sib. — *Sibyllines*

UBG — Unknown Berlin Gospel

Vis. Paul — *Vision of Paul* (= *Apoc. Paul* [Gk])

Rabbinic Literature

1. Mishnah, Talmud, and other Rabbinic Literature

ʾAbad.	ʾAbadim
ʾAbod. Zar.	ʾAbodah Zarah
ʾAbot	ʾAbot
ʾAbot R. Nat.	ʾAbot de Rabbi Nathan
Ag. Ag.	Aggadat Aggadot
ʾAg. Ber.	ʾAggadat Berešit
Ag. Esth.	Aggadat Esther
Ag. Shir.	Aggadat Shir HaShirim
ʾArak.	ʾArakin
ARN	Abot deRabbi Nathan
b.	Babylonian Talmud
B. Bat.	Baba Batra
B. Meṣiʿa	Baba Meṣiʿa
B. Qam.	Baba Qamma
Bat. M.	Bate Midrashot
Bek.	Bekhorot
Ber.	Berakhot
Beṣah	Beṣah Beṣah
BHM	Beth Ha-Midrash
Bik.	Bikkurim
Demai	Demai
DER (Der. Er. Rab.)	Derek Ereṣ Rabbah
Der. Er. Zuṭ.	Derek Ereṣ Zuṭa
Deut. R.	Deuteronomy Rabbah
DEZ	Derek Ereṣ Zuta
Ebel Rabbati	see Sem. (Semahot)
ʿEd.	ʿEduyyot
ʿErub.	ʿErubin
Esth. R.	Esther Rabbah
Exod. R.	Shemot Rabbah
Gem.	Gemara
Gen. R.	Genesis Rabbah (= Bereshit Rabbah)
Gen. Rab.	Genesis Rabbati
Gen. Z.	Bereshit Zutah
Gerim	Gerim
Giṭ.	Giṭṭin
Ḥag.	Ḥagigah
Ḥal.	Ḥallah
Hor.	Horayot
Ḥul.	Ḥullin
ISG	Iggeret Rab Sherira Gaʾon
Kallah	Kallah
Kallah	Kallah
Kallah Rab.	Kallah Rabbati
Kelim	Kelim
Ker.	Kerithot
Ketub.	Ketubbot
Kil.	Kilʾayim
Kutim	Kutim
Lam. Rab.	Lamentations Rabbati
Lam. Z.	Lamentations Zuta
Leq. Ṭ.	Lekah Ṭov
Lev. R.	Wayyiqra Rabbah
m.	Mishnah
Maʿaś.	Maʿaśerot
Maʿaś. Š.	Maʿaśer Šeni
Mak.	Makkot
Makš.	Makširin
Mas. Qeṭ.	Massektot Qeṭannot
Meg.	Megillah
Meg. Taʿan.	Megillat Taʿanit
Meʿil.	Meʿilah
Mek.	Mekilta
Mek.	Mekhilta deRabbi Ishmaʿel
Mek. SbY	Mekilta dʾRabbi Shimʿon ben Yoḥai
Menaḥ.	Menaḥot
Mez.	Mezuzah
Mid.	Middot
Midr. Deut.	Deuteronomy Rabbah
Midr. Exod.	Exodus Rabbah
Midr. Gen.	Genesis Rabbah
Midr. Lev.	Leviticus Rabbah
Midr. Mishle	Midrash Mishle
Midr. Num.	Numbers Rabbah
Midr. Rab.	Midrash Rabbah
Midr. Sam.	Midrash Shemuʾel
Midr. Song	Midrash Shir HaShirim
Midr. Tann.	Midrash Tannaʾim
Midr. Teh.	Midrash Tehillim
Miqw.	Miqwȧot
Moʾed	Moʾed
Moʾed Qaṭ.	Moʾed Qaṭan
Naš.	Našim
Naz	Nazir
Ned.	Nedarim
Neg.	Negaʿim
Nez.	Neziqin

RABBINIC LITERATURE

Nid.	*Niddah*	*Song R.*	*Shir HaShirim Rabbah*
Num. R.	*Numbers Rabbah*	*Song Z.*	*Shir HaShirim Zuta*
'Ohal.	*'Ohalot*	*Sop.*	*Soperim*
'Or.	*'Orlah*	*Soṭah*	*Soṭah*
OzM	*Ozar Midrashim*	*Sukkah*	*Sukkah*
Parah	*Parah*	*t*	*Tosefta*
Pe'ah	*Pe'ah*	*Ṭ. Yom.*	*Ṭebul Yom*
Pesaḥ.	*Pesaḥim*	*Ta'an.*	*Ta'anit*
Pesiq. Rab.	*Pesiqta Rabbati*	*Tamid*	*Tamid*
Pesiq. Rab Kah.	*Pesiqta de Rab Kahana*	*Tanḥ.*	*Tanḥuma*
Pirqe R. El.	*Pirqe Rabbi Eliezer*	*Tanḥ.*	*Tanhuma*
Pirqe R. El.	*Pirqe Rabbi Eliezer*	*Tanḥ. B.*	*Tanḥuma (Buber)*
Qidd.	*Qiddušin*	*Tanna d'be Eliyahu*	see *S. Eli. Rab.*, *S. Eli. Zut.*
Qinnim	*Qinnim*		(*Seder Eliyahu Rabbah/*
Qod.	*Qodašim*		*Zuta*)
Qoh. R.	*Qohelet Rabba*	*Tẹ har.*	*Tẹ harot*
Qoh. Z.	*Qohelet Zuta*	*Tem.*	*Temurah*
Rab.	*Rabbah* (plus biblical book:	*Tep.*	*Tepillin*
	Lev. Rab.= *Leviticus*	*Ter.*	*Terumot*
	Rabbah)	*'Uq.*	*'Uqsin*
Roš Haš.	*Roš Haššanah*	*y.*	*Yerushalmi Talmud*
Ruth R.	*Ruth Rabbah*	*Yad.*	*Yadayim*
Ruth Z.	*Ruth Zuta*	*Yal.*	*Yalquṭ*
S. Eli. Rab.	*Seder Eliyahu Rabbah*	*Yalq.*	*Yalquṭ Šim'oni*
S. Eli. Zut.	*Seder Eliyahu Zuta*	*Yalq. M.*	*Yalquṭ Makhiri*
S. Olam Rab.	*Seder Olam Rabbah*	*Yebam.*	*Yebamot*
S. 'Olam Rab.	*Seder 'Olam Rabbah*	*Yoma*	*Yoma* (= *Kippurim*)
S. Olam Z.	*Seder Olam Zuta*	*Zabim*	*Zabim*
S. Tan. Am.	*Seder Tanna'im we Amora'im*	*Zebaḥ.*	*Zebaḥim*
Šabb.	*Šabbat*	*Zera.*	*Zera'im*
SAME	*Sifre deAggadta Megillat*		
	Esther		

2. Targums

Sanh.	*Sanhedrin*		
Šeb.	*Šebi'it*	*Frg. Tg.*	*Fragmentary Targum*
Šebu.	*Šebu'ot*	*Pal. Tg.*	*Palestinian Targum*
Seder	*Seder*	*Sam. Tg.*	*Samaritan Targum*
Sek. T.	*Sekhel Tov*	*Tg. Esth. I*	*First Targum of Esther*
Sem.	*Semahot (Evel Rabbati)*	*Tg. Esth. II*	*Second Targum of Esther*
Sep. Torah	*Seper Torah*	*Tg. Isa.*	*Targum Isaiah*
Šeqal.	*Šeqalim*	*Tg. Jon.*	*Targum Jonathan*
Shocher Tov	see *Midr. Teh.* (*Midrash*	*Tg. Ket.*	*Targum of the Writings*
	Tehillim)	*Tg. Neb.*	*Targum of the Prophets*
Siddur	*Sidur Sefat Emet*	*Tg. Neof.*	*Targum Neofiti*
Sifra	*Sifra*	*Tg. Onq.*	*Targum Onqelos*
Sifre Deut.	*Sifre Devarim*	*Tg. Ps.-J.*	*Targum Pseudo-Jonathan*
Sifre Num.	*Sifre Bemidbar*	*Tg. Yer. I*	*Targum Yerušalmi I*
Sifre Z.	*Sifre Zuta*		(see *Tg. Ps.-J.*)
Sipra	*Sipra*	*Tg. Yer. II*	*Targum Yerušalmi II*
Sipre	*Sipre*		(see *Frg. Tg.*)
Ṣiṣit	*Ṣîṣit*	*Yem. Tg.*	*Yemenite Targum*
Sof.	*Soferim*		

Nag Hammadi Codices
(NHC; BG = Berolinensis Gnosticus)

1 Apoc. Jas.	*(First) Apocalypse of James*	NHC V,3		*Interp. Know.*	*Interpretation of Knowledge*	NHC XI,1
2 Apoc. Jas.	*(Second) Apocalypse of James*	NHC V,4		*Jeû*	*The Books of Jeû*	
				Marsanes	*Marsanes*	NHC X
				Melch.	*Melchizedek*	NHC IX,1
Act Pet.	*Act of Peter*	NHC XI,3; BG 4		*Norea*	*Thought of Norea*	NHC VI,5
Acts Pet. 12 Apos.	*Acts of Peter and the Twelve Apostles*	NHC VI,1		*On Anointing*	*On the Anointing*	NHC XI,2a
				On Bap. A	*On Baptism A*	NHC XI,2b
				On Bap. B	*On Baptism B*	NHC XI,2c
Allogenes	*Allogenes*	NHC XI,3		*On Euch. A*	*On the Eucharist A*	NHC XI,2d
Ap. Jas.	*Apocryphon of James*	NHC I,2		*On Euch. B*	*On the Eucharist B*	NHC XI,2e
Ap. John	*Apocryphon of John*	NHC III,1; IV,1; BG 1		*Orig. World*	*On the Origin of the World*	NHC II,5; XIII,2
Apoc. Adam	*Apocalypse of Adam*	NHC V,5		*Paraph. Shem*	*Paraphrase of Shem*	NHC VII,1
Apoc. Paul	*Apocalypse of Paul*	NHC V,3		*Plato Rep.*	*Plato, Republic 588B–589B*	NHC VI,5
Apoc. Pet.	*Apocalypse of Peter*	NHC VII,2		*Pr. Paul*	*Prayer of the Apostle Paul*	NHC 1,1
Asclepius	*Asclepius 21–29*	NHC VI,8				
Auth. Teach.	*Authoritative Teaching*	NHC VI,3		*Pr. Thanks.*	*Prayer of Thanksgiving*	NHC VI,7
Dial. Sav.	*Dialogue of the Savior*	NHC III,5		*Sent. Sextus*	*Sentences of Sextus*	NHC XII,1
				Soph. Jes. Chr.	*Sophia of Jesus Christ*	NHC III,4; BG 3
Disc. 8–9	*Discourse on the Eighth and Ninth*	NHC VI,6		*Steles Seth*	*Three Steles of Seth*	NHC XIII,1
Ep. Pet. Phil.	*Letter of Peter to Philip*	NHC VIII,2		*Teach. Silv.*	*Teachings of Silvanus*	NHC VII,4
Eugnostos	*Eugnostos the Blessed*	NHC III,3; V,1		*Testim. Truth*	*Testimony of Truth*	NHC IX,3
				Thom. Cont.	*Book of Thomas the Contender*	NHC II,7
Exeg. Soul	*Exegesis of the Soul (Exegesis de anima)*	NHC II,6		*Thund.*	*Thunder: Perfect Mind*	NHC VI,2
Frm.	*Fragments*	NHC XII,3		*Treat. Res.*	*Treatise on the Resurrection*	NHC I,4
Gos. Eg.	*Gospel of the Egyptians*	NHC III,2; IV,2		*Treat. Seth*	*Second Treatise of the Great Seth*	NHC VII,2
Gos. Mary	*Gospel of Mary*	BG 1				
Gos. Phil.	*Gospel of Philip*	NHC II,3		*Tri. Trac.*	*Tripartite Tractate*	NHC I,5
Gos. Thom.	*Gospel of Thomas*	NHC II,2		*Trim. Prot.*	*Trimorphic Protennoia*	NHC XIII,1
Gos. Truth	*Gospel of Truth*	NHC I,3; XII,2				
Great Pow.	*The Concept of our Great Power*	NHC VI,4		*Val. Exp.*	*A Valentinian Exposition*	NHC XI,2
Hyp. Arch.	*Hypostasis of the Archons*	NHC II,4		*Zost.*	*Zostrianos*	NHC XI,2e
Hypsiph.	*Hypsiphrone*	NHC XI,4				

Ancient Authors and Primary Sources

Acta Crisp.	Acta Crispinae	Aet. *Plac. rel.*	Aetius (Doxographus), *De placitis reliquiae*
Acta Cyp.	Acta Cypriani		
Acta Gal.	Acta Gallonii	Afric.	Julius Africanus
Acta Just.	Acta Justini	Afric. *Chron.*	Julius Africanus, *Chronographia*
Acta Luc. Mont.	Acta et Visio Martyrum Luci Montani et Cetorum Comitum	Afric. *Kes.*	Julius Africanus, *Kestoi*
		Agath. *Hist.*	Agathias Myrin, *Agathiae Myrinaei Historiarum* (*The Histories*)
Acta Mart. Apoll.	Acta et Martyrium Apollonii		
Acta Mart. Scil.	Acta Martyrum Scillitanorum		
Acta Paul. Thec.	Acta Pauli et Theclae	Agnel. *LPR*	Agnellus of Ravenna, *Liber pontificalis ecclesiae Ravennatis*
Acts Arch.	Acts of Archelaus		
Acts Phil.	Acts of Phileas		
Ad. *Intro.*	Adriani Isagoge, *Sacrarum literarum et antiquissimorum graecorum in prophetas fragmenta* (*Introduction to the Divine Scriptures*)	Alb.	Albinus
		Alb. *Epit.*	Albinus, *Epitome doctrinae platonicae* (*Didaskalikos*)
		Alb. *Intr.*	Albinus, *Introductio in Platonem* (*Prologus or Eisagogē; Introduction to Plato*)
Ad. Fulg.	Adversus Fulgentium Donatistam (*Against Fulgentius, the Donatist*)	Alc.	Alcinous
		Alc. *Didask.*	Alcinous, *Didaskalikos*
		Alc. *Epit.*	Alcinous, *Epitome doctrinae platonicae*
Ado *Mart.*	Ado of Vienne, *Martyrologium*		
Ael. *Var. hist.*	Aelian, *Varia historia*	Alcip. *Court.*	Alciphron, *Letters of the Courtesans*
Ael. Arist.	Aelius Aristides		
Ael. Arist. *El. Disc.*	Aelius Aristides, *Eleusinian Discourse*	Alex. Abon.	Alexander of Abonuteichus
		Alex. Alex.	Alexander of Alexandria
Ael. Arist. *Or.*	Aelius Aristides, *Orationes*	Alex. Alex. *Ep. Alex.*	Alexander of Alexandria, *Letter to Alexander of Byzantium*
Ael. Arist. *Pan.*	Aelius Aristides, *The Panathenaic Oration*		
Aen. Gaz. *Theophr.*	Aeneas of Gaza, *Theophrastus*	Alex. Alex. *Ep. encycl.*	Alexander of Alexandria, *Encyclical Letter*
Aesch.	Aeschylus	Alex. Alex. *Frgm(s).*	Alexander of Alexandria, *Fragmenta historica*
Aesch. *Ag.*	Aeschylus, *Agamemnon*		
Aesch. *Eum.*	Aeschylus, *Eumenides* (*Eumenides*)	Alex. Aphr.	Alexander of Aphrodisias
		Alex. Aphr. *Comm. Metaph.*	Alexander of Aphrodisias, *In Aristotelis Metaphysica commentaria* (*Commentaries on the methaphysics of Aristotle*)
Aesch. *Pers.*	Aeschylus, *Persae* (*Persians*)		
Aesch. *Sept.*	Aeschylus, *Septem contra Thebas* (*Seven Against Thebes*)		
Aet.	Aetius (Doxographus)	Alex. Aphr. *De an. lib. mantissa*	Alexander of Aphrodisias, *De Anima Libri Mantissa* (*Supplement to On the Soul* [*Mantissa*])
Aet. *Plac.*	Aetius (Doxographus), *Placita Philosophorum* (*Opinions of the Philosophers*)		

Alex. Aphr. *Fat.*	Alexander of Aphrodisias, *De fato* (*On Fate*)	Ambr. *Exh. virginit.*	Ambrose of Milan, *Exhortatio virginitatis* (*Exhortation to Virginity*)
Alex. Aphr. *Mixt.*	Alexander of Aphrodisias, *De mixtione* (*On Mixture and Growth*)	Ambr. *Exp. Apoc.*	Ambrose of Milan, *Expositio in Apocalypsim* (*Exposition of the Apocalypse*)
Alex. Lyc. *Manich.*	Alexander of Lycopolis, *Contra Manichaeos* (*Against the Manichaeans*)	Ambr. *Exp. Luc.*	Ambrose of Milan, *Expositio Evangelii secundum Lucam* (*Exposition of the Gospel according to Luke*)
Alex. Gr. *Ep.*	Alexander the Great, *Epistulae*	Ambr. *Exp. Ps. 118*	Ambrose of Milan, *Expositio Psalmi CXVIII* (*Exposition of Psalm 118*)
Alter. Sim. Theo.	*Altercatio Simonis et Theophili* (*The Dialogue of Simon and Theophilus*)	Ambr. *Expl. symb.*	Ambrose of Milan, *Explanatio symboli ad initiandos* (*An Explanation of the Creed for Those About to Be Baptised*)
Alyp. *Ordo monas.*	Alypius of Thagaste, *Ordo monasterii* (*Regulations for a Monastery*)	Ambr. *Fid.*	Ambrose of Milan, *De fide* (*On Faith*)
Am.	Ammianus Marcellinus, *Res Gestae*	Ambr. *Fug.*	Ambrose of Milan, *De fuga saeculi* (*Flight from the World*)
Amal. *Lib. offic.*	Amalar of Metz, *Liber officialis*	Ambr. *Hel.*	Ambrose of Milan, *De Helia et Jejunio* (*On Elijah and Fasting*)
Ambr.	Ambrose of Milan		
Ambr. *Abr.*	Ambrose of Milan, *De Abraham* (*On Abraham*)	Ambr. *Hex.*	Ambrose of Milan, *Hexaemeron libri sex* (*Six Days of Creation*)
Ambr. *Apol. Dav.*	Ambrose of Milan, *Apologia prophetae David* (*Apology for David*)	Ambr. *Hom. in Ps.* (etc.)	Ambrose of Milan, *Homiliae in Psalmos* (*Homilies on Psalms* [*etc.*])
Ambr. *Aux.*	Ambrose of Milan, *Sermo contra Auxentium de basilicis tradendis* (*Sermon Against Auxentius on the Giving Up of the Basilicas*)	Ambr. *Hymn.*	Ambrose of Milan, *Hymni* (*Hymns*)
Ambr. *Bon. mort.*	Ambrose of Milan, *De bono mortis* (*Death as a Good*)	Ambr. *Incarn.*	Ambrose of Milan, *De incarnationis dominicae sacramento* (*The Sacrament of the Incarnation of the Lord*)
Ambr. *Cain*	Ambrose of Milan, *De Cain et Abel* (*On Cain and Abel*)		
Ambr. *Enarrat. Ps.*	Ambrose of Milan, *Enarrationes in XII Psalmos davidicos* (*Explanations of Twelve Psalms of David*)	Ambr. *Instit.*	Ambrose of Milan, *De institutione virginis* (*An Instruction for a Virgin*)
Ambr. *Epist.*	Ambrose of Milan, *Epistulae*		
Ambr. *Epist. EC*	Ambrose of Milan, *Epistula Extra Collectionem*	Ambr. *Isaac*	Ambrose of Milan, *De Isaac vel anima* (*Isaac, or The Soul*)
Ambr. *Exc.*	Ambrose of Milan, *De excessu fratris sui Satyri* (*On the Decease of his Brother Satyrus*)	Ambr. *Jac.*	Ambrose of Milan, *De Jacob et vita beata* (*Jacob and the Happy Life*)

Ambr. *Job*	Ambrose of Milan, *De interpellatione Job et David* (*The Prayer of Job and David*)	Ambrosi. *Quaest.*	Ambrosiaster, *Quaestiones*
		Ambrosi. *Quaest. VNT*	Ambrosiaster, *Quaestiones veteris et novi testamenti CXXVI*
Ambr. *Jos.*	Ambrose of Milan, *De Joseph patriarcha* (*On Joseph*) (*On Naboth*)	Amp. *Lib. mem.*	Ampelius, *Liber memorialis*
		AN	*Ad Novatianum*
		An. Flor.	Annaeus Florus
Ambr. *Myst.*	Ambrose of Milan, *De mysteriis* (*The Mysteries*)	An. Flor. *Epit.*	Annaeus Florus, *Epitome Rerum Romanorum*
Ambr. *Nab.*	Ambrose of Milan, *De Nabuthae historia*	An. Flor. *Epit. T.L.Bell.*	Annaeus Florus, *Epitome de Tito Livio Bellorum omnium annorum*
Ambr. *Noe*	Ambrose of Milan, *De Noe et arca* (*On Noah and the Ark*)		
Ambr. *Ob. Theo.*	Ambrose of Milan, *De obitu Theodosii* (*On the Death of Theodosius*)	Anast.	Anastasius Sinaita
		Anast. *Quaest.*	Anastasius Sinaita, *Quaestiones et responsiones*
Ambr. *Ob. Val.*	Ambrose of Milan, *De obitu Valentianiani consolatio* (*On the Death of Valentinian*)	Anast. *Serm. duo*	*Anastasius Sinaita, Sermones duo in constitutionem hominis secundum imaginem Dei*
		Anat. *Rat. pasch.*	Anatolius of Laodicea, *De ratione paschali* (*The Paschal Tract*)
Ambr. *Off.*	Ambrose of Milan, *De officiis ministrorum* (*On the Duties of Ministers*)	Anax. *Rhet. Alex.*	Anaximenes of Lampsacus, *Rhetorica ad Alexandrum* (*Ars rhetorica*) (*Rhetoric to Alexander*)
Ambr. *Paen.*	Ambrose of Milan, *De paenitentia* (*On Repentance*)		
Ambr. *Parad.*	Ambrose of Milan, *De paradiso* (*Paradise*)	Anaxag. *Frgm(s).*	Anaxagoras, *Fragmenta*
Ambr. *Patr.*	Ambrose of Milan, *De benedictionibus patriarcharum* (*The Patriarchs*)	*AnHo*	*Anecdoton Holderi*
		Anon. *Val.*	*Anonymus Valesianus*
		AnPi	*Anaphora Pilati*
		Ant. *Hist. mir.*	Antigonus of Carystus, *Historiarum mirabilium collectio*
Ambr. *Sacr.*	Ambrose of Milan, *De sacramentis* (*The Sacraments*)	Ant. Gr. *Ep.*	Antony the Great, *Epistulae*
Ambr. *Spir.*	Ambrose of Milan, *De Spiritu Sancto* (*The Holy Spirit*)	Ant. *Plac. It.*	*Antonini Placentini Itinerarium*
Ambr. *Tob.*	Ambrose of Milan, *De Tobia* (*On Tobias*)	Anth. *Lat.*	*Anthologia Latina*
		Anth. *pal.*	*Anthologia palatina* (*Palatine Anthology*)
Ambr. *Vid.*	Ambrose of Milan, *De viduis* (*On Widows*)	Antip. *Or.*	Antiphon, *Orationes* (*Speeches*)
Ambr. *Virg.*	Ambrose of Milan, *De virginibus* (*On Virgins*)	Anton. *Vita Sim. Styl.*	Antonius, *Vita Simeonis Stylitae*
Ambr. *Virginit.*	Ambrose of Milan, *De virginitate* (*On Virginity*)	Apam.	John of Apamea
Ambrosi.	Ambrosiaster	Apam. *Ep.*	John of Apamea, *Epistulae*
Ambrosi. *Comm. in Rom.* (etc.)	Ambrosiaster, *Commentarius in xiii epistulas Paulinas: ad Romanos* (etc.)	Apam. *Ep. Hes.*	John of Apamea, *Letter to Hesychius*
		Apam. *Pray.*	John of Apamea, *On Prayer*

Apam. *Still.*	John of Apamea, *On Stillness*	Apul. *Flor.*	Apuleius, *Florida*
Aphr. *Dem.*	Aphrahat, *Demonstratio* (*Demonstrations*)	Apul. *Metam.*	Apuleius, *Metamorphoses* (*The Golden Ass*)
Apht. *Prog.*	Aphthonius, *Progymnasmata*	Ar.	Arius
Apol.	Apollinarius of Laodicea	Ar. *Ep. Alex.*	Arius, *Letter to Alexander of Alexandria*
Apol. *Corp. div.*	Apollinarius of Laodicea, *De unione corporis et divinitatis in Christo* (*On the Unity of Humanity and Divinity in Christ*)	Ar. *Ep. Eus.*	Arius, *Letter to Eusebius of Nicomedia*
		Arat. *Phaen.*	Aratus, *Phaenomena*
		Arist.	Aristotle
Apol. *Ep. Dion.*	Apollinarius of Laodicea, *Epistula ad Dionysium*	Arist. *An. post.*	Aristotle, *Analytica posteriora*
		Arist. *Ath. pol.*	Aristotle, *Athēnaīn politeia* (*Constitution of Athens*)
Apol. *Fid.*	Apollinarius of Laodicea, *De fide et incarnatione* (*On Faith and Incarnation*)	Arist. *Cael.*	Aristotle, *De caelo* (*Heavens*)
		Arist. *Cat.*	Aristotle, *Categoriae* (*Categories*)
Apol. *Frgm.*	Apollinarius of Laodicea, *Fragment*	Arist. *De an.*	Aristotle, *De anima* (*On the Soul*)
Apol. *Kat.*	Apollinarius of Laodicea, *Kata meros pistis*	Arist. *Div. somn.*	Aristotle, *De divinatio per somnum* (*Prophesying by Dreams*)
Apol. *Recap.*	Apollinarius of Laodicea, *Recapitulatio*		
Apol. Tyana *Ep.*	Apollonius of Tyana, *Epistulae*	Arist. *Eth. eud.*	Aristotle, *Ethica eudemia* (*Eudemian Ethics*)
Apollod. *Bib.*	Apollodorus, *Bibliotheca*	Arist. *Eth. Nic.*	Aristotle, *Ethica Nicomachea* (*Nicomachean Ethics*)
Apophth. Patr. (*anom. coll.*)	*Apophthegmata Patrum* (*anonymous collection*)	Arist. *Frag.*	Aristotle, *Fragmenta* (*Fragments*)
Apophth. Patr. (*coll. alph.*)	*Apophthegmata Patrum* (*collectio alphabetica*)	Arist. *Gen. an.*	Aristotle, *De generatione anamalium* (*Generation of Animals*)
Apophth. Patr. (*coll. syst.*)	*Apophthegmata Patrum* (*collectio systematica*)		
Apos. Ch. Ord.	*Apostolic Church Order* (*Canones patrum apostolorum*)	Arist. *Hist. an.*	Aristotle, *Historia animalium* (*History of Animals*)
		Arist. *Metaph.*	Aristotle, *Metaphysica* (*Metaphysics*)
Apos. Trad.	*Traditio Apostolica* (*Apostolic Tradition*)	Arist. *Mete.*	Aristotle, *Meteorologica* (*Meteorology*)
App.	Appian	Arist. *Phys.*	Aristotle, *Physica* (*Physics*)
App. *Bell. civ.*	Appian, *Bella civilia* (*Civil Wars*)	Arist. *Pol.*	Aristotle, *Politica* (*Politics*)
App. *Hist. rom.*	Appian, *Historia romana* (*Roman History*)	Arist. *Protr.*	Aristotle, *Protrepticus*
		Arist. *Rhet.*	Aristotle, *Rhetorica* (*Rhetoric*)
App. *Mithrid.*	Appian, *Mithridatic Wars*	Arist. *Soph. elench.*	Aristotle, *Sophistici elenchi* (*Top. 9*) (*Sophistical Refutations*)
App. *Syr.*	Appian, *Syriacus Liber*		
Apul.	Apuleius		
Apul. *Apol.*	Apuleius, *Apologia* (*Pro se de magia*)	Aristid. *Apol.*	Aristides of Athens, *Apologia* (*Apology*)
Apul. *De deo Socr.*	Apuleius, *De deo Socratico* (*God of Socrates*)	Aristoph.	Aristophanes
Apul. *Dogm. Plat.*	Apuleius, *De dogmate Platonis* (*On Plato and his Doctrine*)	Aristoph. *Av.*	Aristophanes, *Aves* (*Birds*)
		Aristoph. *Nub.*	Aristophanes, *Nubes* (*Clouds*)

Aristoph. *Pax* — Aristophanes, *Pax* (*Peace*)

Aristoph. *Ran.* — Aristophanes, *Ranae* (*Frogs*)

Aristoph. *Vesp.* — Aristophanes, *Vespae* (*Wasps*)

Aristoph. *Eccl.* — Aristophanes, *Ecclesiazusae* (*Women of the Assembly*)

Aristox. *El. Har.* — Aristoxenus, *Elementa harmonica* (*Elements of Harmony*)

Arn. — Arnobius of Sicca

Arn. *Adv. gen.* — Arnobius of Sicca, *Adversus gentes* (*Against the Heathen*)

Arn. *Adv. nat.* — Arnobius of Sicca, *Adversus nationes* (*Against the Pagans*)

Arn. Jr. *Praed. Haer.* — Arnobius Junior, *Praedestinatorum haeresis*

Arrian *Anab.* — Arrian of Nicomedia, *The Anabasis of Alexander*

Artem. *Onir.* — Artemidorus Daldianus, *Oneirocritica* (*The Interpretation of Dreams*)

AShR — *Acta Synhodorum habitarum Romae*

Ast. Amas. — Asterius of Amasea

Ast. Amas. *Hom.* — Asterius of Amasea, *Homiliae*

Ast. Amas. *Serm.* — Asterius of Amasea, *Sermones*

Ath. — Athenagoras

Ath. *Res.* — Athenagoras, *De resurrectione* (*On the Resurrection*)

Ath. *Leg.* — Athenagoras, *Legatio pro Christianis* (also known as *Supplicatio pro Christianis*; *Apology*)

Athan. — Athanasius of Alexandria

Athan. *Apol. Const.* — Athanasius of Alexandria, *Apologia ad Constantium*

Athan. *Apol. sec.* — Athanasius of Alexandria, *Apologia secunda* (= *Apologia contra Arianos*; *Defense against the Arians*)

Athan. *Ar.* — Athanasius of Alexandria, *Orationes contra Arianos* (*Orations against the Arians*)

Athan. *C. Gent.* — Athanasius of Alexandria, *Contra gentes* (*Against the Pagans*)

Athan. *Comm. Ps.* — Athanasius of Alexandria, *Commentarii in Psalmos*

Athan. *Decr.* — Athanasius of Alexandria, *De decretis Nicaenae synodi* (*Defense of the Nicene Definition*)

Athan. *Dion.* — Athanasius of Alexandria, *De sententia Dionysii* (*On the Opinion of Dionysius*)

Athan. *Ep. Adelph.* — Athanasius of Alexandria, *Epistula ad Adelphium* (*Letter to Adelphius*)

Athan. *Ep. Aeg. Lib.* — Athanasius of Alexandria, *Epistula ad episcopos Aegypti et Libyae* (*Letter to the Bishops of Egypt and Libya*)

Athan. *Ep. Afr.* — Athanasius of Alexandria, *Epistula ad Afros episcopos* (*Letter to the Bishops of Africa*)

Athan. *Ep. encycl.* — Athanasius of Alexandria, *Epistula encyclica* (*Circular Letter*)

Athan. *Ep. Epict.* — Athanasius of Alexandria, *Epistula ad Epictetum* (*Letter to Epictetus*)

Athan. *Ep. fest.* — Athanasius of Alexandria, *Epistulae festales* (*Festal Letters*)

Athan. *Ep. Marcell.* — Athanasius of Alexandria, *Epistula ad Marcellinum de interpretatione Psalmorum* (*Letter to Marcellinus on the Interpretation of the Psalms*)

Athan. *Ep. mon. 1* — Athanasius of Alexandria, *Epistula ad monachos i* (*First Letter to Monks*)

Athan. *Ep. mon. 2* — Athanasius of Alexandria, *Epistula ad monachos ii* (*Second Letter to Monks*)

Athan. *Ep. mort. Ar.* — Athanasius of Alexandria, *Epistula ad Serapionem de more Arii* (*Letter to Serapion Concerning the Death of Arius*)

Athan. *Ep. Ors.* 2	Athanasius of Alexandria, *Epistula ad Orsisium ii* (*Second Letter to Orsisius*)
Athan. *Ep. Serap.*	Athanasius of Alexandria, *Epistulae ad Serapionem* (*Letters to Serapion Concerning the Holy Spirit*)
Athan. *Ep. virg.* (*Copt.*)	Athanasius of Alexandria, *Epistula ad virgines* (*Coptice*) (*First* [*Coptic*] *Letter to Virgins*)
Athan. *Exp. Ps.*	Athanasius of Alexandria, *Expositiones in Psalmos* (*Expositions of the Psalms*)
Athan. *Fug.*	Athanasius of Alexandria, *Apologia de fuga sua* (*Defense of His Flight*)
Athan. *Hist. Ar.*	Athanasius of Alexandria, *Historia Arianorum ad monachos* (*History of the Arians*)
Athan. *Inc.*	Athanasius of Alexandria, *De incarnatione* (*On the Incarnation*)
Athan. *Syn.*	Athanasius of Alexandria, *De synodis* (*On the Councils of Ariminum and Seleucia*)
Athan. *Tom.*	Athanasius of Alexandria, *Tomus ad Antiochenos*
Athan. *Trin.*	Athanasius of Alexandria, *De sancta trinitate* (*On the Most Holy Trinity*)
Athan. *Vit. Ant.*	Athanasius of Alexandria, *Vita Antonii* (*Life of Antony*)
Athen. *Deipn.*	Athenaeus, *Deipnosophistae*
Auct. Haun.	*Auctarium Hauniense*
Aug.	Augustine of Hippo
Aug. *Cat. rud.* (*Catech.*)	Augustine of Hippo, *De catechizandis rudibus* (*Catechizing the Uninstructed*)
Aug. *Acad.*	Augustine of Hippo, *Contra Academicos* (*Against the Academics*)
Aug. *Adim.*	Augustine of Hippo, *Contra Adimantum* (*Against Adimantus*)

Aug. *Adult. coniug.*	Augustine of Hippo, *De adulterinis coniugiis* (*Adulterous Marriages*)
Aug. *Agon.*	Augustine of Hippo, *De agone christiano* (*Christian Combat*)
Aug. *An. orig.*	Augustine of Hippo, *De anima et eius origine* (*The Soul and Its Origin*)
Aug. *Arian.*	Augustine of Hippo, *Contra sermonem Arianorum* (*Against a Sermon of the Arians*)
Aug. *Bapt.*	Augustine of Hippo, *De baptismo contra Donatistas* (*Baptism*)
Aug. *Beat.*	Augustine of Hippo, *De vita beata* (*The Happy Life*)
Aug. *Bon. conj.*	Augustine of Hippo, *De bono conjugali* (*The Good of Marriage*)
Aug. *Brev. coll.*	Augustine of Hippo, *Breviculus collationis cum Donatistis* (*Summary of the Proceedings of the Conference with the Donatists*)
Aug. *C. du. ep. Pelag.*	Augustine of Hippo, *Contra duas epistulas Pelagianorum ad Bonifatium* (*Against the Two Letters of the Pelagians*)
Aug. *C. Jul.*	Augustine of Hippo, *Contra Julianum* (*Against Julian*)
Aug. *C. Jul. op. imp.*	Augustine of Hippo, *Contra secundam Juliani responsionem imperfectum opus* (*Against Julian: Opus Imperfectum*)
Aug. *C. litt. Petil.*	Augustine of Hippo, *Contra litteras Petiliani* (*Against the Book of Petilian*)
Aug. *C. mend.*	Augustine of Hippo, *Contra mendacium* (*Against Lying* [*to Consentius*])
Aug. *Cath. fr.*	Augustine of Hippo, *Ad catholicos fratres*

ANCIENT AUTHORS AND PRIMARY SOURCES

Aug. *Civ.* — Augustine of Hippo, *De civitate Dei* (*The City of God*)

Aug. *Coll. Max.* — Augustine of Hippo, *Collatio cum Maximino Arianorum episcopo* (*Debate with Maximinus, Bishop of the Arians*)

Aug. *Conf.* — Augustine of Hippo, *Confessionum libri XIII* (*Confessions*)

Aug. *Cons.* — Augustine of Hippo, *De consensu evangelistarum* (*Harmony of the Gospels*)

Aug. *Contin.* — Augustine of Hippo, *De continentia* (*Continence*)

Aug. *Corrept.* — Augustine of Hippo, *De correptione et gratia* (*Admonition and Grace*)

Aug. *Cresc.* — Augustine of Hippo, *Contra Cresconium grammaticum (et) Donatistam libri quatuor* (*Against the Donatist Grammarian, Cresconius*)

Aug. *Cur.* — Augustine of Hippo, *De cura pro mortuis gerenda* (*The Care to Be Taken for the Dead*)

Aug. *De mend.* — Augustine of Hippo, *De mendacio* (*On Lying*)

Aug. *Disc.* — Augustine of Hippo, *De disciplina christiana* (*Christian Discipline*)

Aug. *Div.* — Augustine of Hippo, *De divinitate daemonum* (*The Divination of Demons*)

Aug. *Div. quaest. LXXXIII* — Augustine of Hippo, *De diversis quaestionibus LXXXIII* (*Eighty-Three Different Questions*)

Aug. *Div. quaest. Simpl.* — Augustine of Hippo, *De diversis quaestionibus ad Simplicianum* (*Various Questions for Simplicianus*)

Aug. *Doctr. chr.* — Augustine of Hippo, *De doctrina Christiana* (*Christian Instruction*)

Aug. *Don.* — Augustine of Hippo, *Post collationem adversus Donatistas*

Aug. *Duab.* — Augustine of Hippo, *De duabus animabus* (*Two Souls*)

Aug. *Dulc.* — Augustine of Hippo, *De octo Dulcitii quaestionibus* (*The Eight Questions of Dulcitius*)

Aug. *Emer.* — Augustine of Hippo, *De gestis cum Emerito* (*Debate with Emeritus*)

Aug. *Enarrat. Ps.* — Augustine of Hippo, *Enarrationes in Psalmos* (*Enarrations on the Psalms*)

Aug. *Enchir.* — Augustine of Hippo, *Enchiridion de fide, spe, et caritate* (*Enchiridion on Faith, Hope, and Love*)

Aug. *Ep.* — Augustine of Hippo, *Epistulae* (*Letters*)

Aug. *Ep.* (*Div.*) — Augustine of Hippo, *Epistulae* (*Letters; Divjak*)

Aug. *Ep.* (*Erf.*) — Augustine of Hippo, *Epistulae* (*Letters; Erfurt*)

Aug. *Exp. Gal.* — Augustine of Hippo, *Expositio in epistulam ad Galatas* (*Commentary on the Letter to the Galatians*)

Aug. *Exp. quaest. Rom.* — Augustine of Hippo, *Expositio quarumdam quaestionum in epistula ad Romanos* (*Commentary on Statements in the Letter of Paul to the Romans*)

Aug. *Faust.* — Augustine of Hippo, *Contra Faustum Manichaeum* (*Against Faustus the Manichaean*)

Aug. *Fel.* — Augustine of Hippo, *Contra Felicem Manichaeum* (*Against Felix the Manichaean*)

Aug. *Fid.* — Augustine of Hippo, *De fide rerum quae non videntur* (*Faith in Things Unseen*)

Aug. *Fid. op.* — Augustine of Hippo, *De fide et operibus* (*Faith and Works*)

Aug. *Fid. symb.*	Augustine of Hippo, *De fide et symbolo* (*Faith and the Creed*)	Aug. *Jud.*	Augustine of Hippo, *Tractatus adversus Judaeos* (*In Answer to the Jews*)
Aug. *Fund.*	Augustine of Hippo, *Contra epistulam Manichaei quam vocant Fundamenti* (*Against the Letter of the Manichaeans That They Call "The Basics"*)	Aug. *Leg.*	Augustine of Hippo, *Contra adversarium legis et prophetarum* (*Against the Opponent of the Law and the Prophets*)
Aug. *Gaud.*	Augustine of Hippo, *Contra Gaudentium Donatistarum episcopum* (*Against Gaudentius the Donatist Bishop*)	Aug. *Lib.*	Augustine of Hippo, *De libero arbitrio* (*On Free Will*)
		Aug. *Mag.*	Augustine of Hippo, *De magistro* (*The Teacher*)
Aug. *Gen. imp.*	Augustine of Hippo, *De Genesi ad litteram imperfectus liber* (*On the Literal Interpretation of Genesis: An Unfinished Book*)	Aug. *Maxim.*	Augustine of Hippo, *Contra Maximinum Arianum* (*Against Maximinus the Arian*)
Aug. *Gen. lit.*	Augustine of Hippo, *De Genesi ad litteram* (*On Genesis Litarally Interpreted*)	Aug. *Mor. eccl.*	Augustine of Hippo, *De moribus ecclesiae catholicae* (*The Way of Life of the Catholic Church*)
Aug. *Gen. Man.*	Augustine of Hippo, *De Genesi contra Manichaeos* (*On Genesis Against the Manicheans*)	Aug. *Mor. Manich.*	Augustine of Hippo, *De moribus Manichaeorum* (*The Way of Life of the Manichaeans*)
		Aug. *Mus.*	Augustine of Hippo, *De musica* (*Music*)
Aug. *Gest. Pelag.*	Augustine of Hippo, *De gestis Pelagii* (*Proceedings of Pelagius*)	Aug. *Nat. bon.*	Augustinus of Hippo, *De natura boni* (*The Nature of the Good*)
Aug. *Grat.*	Augustine of Hippo, *De gratia et libero arbitrio* (*Grace and Free Will*)	Aug. *Nat. grat.*	Augustine of Hippo, *De natura et gratia* (*Nature and Grace*)
Aug. *Grat. Chr.*	Augustine of Hippo, *De gratia Christi, et de peccato originali* (*The Grace of Christ and Original Sin*)	Aug. *Nat. orig.*	Augustine of Hippo, *De natura et origine animae* (*The Nature and Origin of the Soul*)
Aug. *Grat. N. Test.*	Augustine of Hippo, *De Gratia Novi Testamenti* (*The Grace of the New Testament*)	Aug. *Nupt.*	Augustine of Hippo, *De nuptiis et concupiscentia ad Valerium comitem* (*Marriage and Concupiscence*)
Aug. *Haer.*	Augustine of Hippo, *De haeresibus* (*On Heresies*)	Aug. *Oct. quaest. Vet. Test.*	Augustine of Hippo, *De octo quaestionibus ex Veteri Testamento* (*Eight Questions from the Old Testament*)
Aug. *Immort. an.*	Augustine of Hippo, *De immortalitate animae* (*The Immortality of the Soul*)	Aug. *Op. mon.*	Augustine of Hippo, *De opere monachorum* (*The Work of Monks*)

Aug. *Ord.*	Augustine of Hippo, *De ordine* (*On Order*)	Aug. *Quant. an.*	Augustine of Hippo, *De quantitate animae* (*The Magnitude of the Soul*)
Aug. *Parm.*	Augustine of Hippo, *Contra epistulam Parmeniani* (*Against the Letter of Parmenian*)	Aug. *Reg.*	Augustine of Hippo, *Regula ad servos Dei* (*Rule*)
Aug. *Pat.*	Augustine of Hippo, *De patientia* (*Patience*)	Aug. *Retract.*	Augustine of Hippo, *Retractationum libri II* (*Retractations*)
Aug. *Pecc. merit.*	Augustine of Hippo, *De peccatorum meritis et remissione* (*Guilt and Remission of Sins*)	Aug. *Secund.*	Augustine of Hippo, *Contra Secundinum Manichaeum* (*Against Secundinus the Manichee*)
Aug. *Perf.*	Augustine of Hippo, *De perfectione justitiae hominis* (*Perfection in Human Righteousness*)	Aug. *Serm.*	Augustine of Hippo, *Sermones* (*Sermons*)
		Aug. *Serm.* (*Dol.*)	Augustine of Hippo, *Sermones* (*Dolbeau*)
Aug. *Persev.*	Augustine of Hippo, *De dono perseverantiae* (*The Gift of Perseverance*)	Aug. *Serm. Dom.*	Augustine of Hippo, *De sermone Domini in monte* (*Sermon on the Mount*)
Aug. *Praed.*	Augustine of Hippo, *De praedestinatione sanctorum* (*The Predestination of the Saints*)	Aug. *Solil.*	Augustine of Hippo, *Soliloquiorum libri II* (*Soliloquies*)
Aug. *Praes.*	Augustine of Hippo, *De praesentia Dei* (*On the Presence of God*)	Aug. *Spec.*	Augustine of Hippo, *Speculum de scriptura sancta* (*Mirror*)
Aug. *Priscill.*	Augustine of Hippo, *Ad Orosium contra Priscillianistas et Origenistas* (*To Orosius Against the Priscillianists and the Origenists*)	Aug. *Spir. et litt.*	Augustine of Hippo, *De spiritu et littera* (*The Spirit and the Letter*)
		Aug. *Symb.*	Augustine of Hippo, *De symbolo ad catechumenos* (*The Creed: For Catechumens*)
Aug. *Prob.*	Augustine of Hippo, *Epistula ad Probam*	Aug. *Tract. ep. Jo.*	Augustine of Hippo, *In epistulam Johannis ad Parthos tractatus* (*Tractate on the First Epistle of John*)
Aug. *Psal. Don.*	Augustine of Hippo, *Psalmus contra partem Donati* (*Psalm against the Donatists*)	Aug. *Tract. Ev. Jo.*	Augustine of Hippo, *In Evangelium Johannis tractatus* (*Tractates on the Gospel of John*)
Aug. *Quaest. ev.*	Augustine of Hippo, *Quaestionum evangelicarum libri II*	Aug. *Trin.*	Augustine of Hippo, *De Trinitate* (*The Trinity*)
Aug. *Quaest. Exod.*	Augustine of Hippo, *Quaestiones in Exodum* (*Questions on Exodus*)	Aug. *Unic. bapt.*	Augustine of Hippo, *De unico baptismo* (*Single Baptism*)
Aug. *Quaest. Hept.*	Augustine of Hippo, *Quaestiones in Heptateuchum* (*Questions on the Heptateuch*)	Aug. *Unit. eccl.*	Augustine of Hippo, *De unitate ecclesiae* (*The Unity of the Church*)

Aug. *Util. cred.*	Augustine of Hippo, *De utilitate credendi* (*The Usefulness of Believing*)	Barsan.	Barsanuphius of Palestine
		Barsan. *C. Or.*	Barsanuphius of Palestine, *Contra opiniones Origenistarum* (*Against the Opinions of the Origenists*)
Aug. *Util. jej.*	Augustine of Hippo, *De utilitate jejunii* (*The Usefulness of Fasting*)		
		Barsan. *Ep.*	Barsanuphius of Palestine, *Epistulae*
Aug. *Ver. rel.*	Augustine of Hippo, *De vera religione* (*True Religion*)	Barsan. John *Q&A*	Barsanuphius and John, *Questions and Answers*
Aug. *Vid.*	Augustine of Hippo, *De bono viduitatis* (*The Excellence of Widowhood*)	Bas.	Basil of Caesarea (Basil the Great)
Aug. *Virginit.*	Augustine of Hippo, *De sancta virginitate* (*Holy Virginity*)	Bas. *Ad adolesc.*	Basil of Caesarea, *Oratio ad adolescentes* (*Address to Young Men*)
Aur. Vict.	Aurelius Victor	Bas. *Ca.*	Basil of Caesarea, *Constitutiones asceticae*
Aur. Vict. *Epit.*	Aurelius Victor, *Epitome de Caesaribus* (*Epitome of Emperors*)		
		Bas. *Comm. Isa.*	Basil of Caesarea, see Bas. *Isa.*
		Bas. *Ep.*	Basil of Caesarea, *Epistulae*
Aur. Vict. *Lib. Caes.*	Aurelius Victor, *Liber de Caesaribus* (*Biographies of Emperors*)	Bas. *Eun.*	Basil of Caesarea, *Adversus Eunomium* (*Against Eunomius*)
Aur. Vict. *Vir. ill.*	Aurelius Victor, *De Viris Illustribus Romae* (*The Lives of the Illustrious Romans*)	Bas. *Hex.*	Basil of Caesarea, *Homiliae hexaemeron* (*On Hexaemeron*)
Aus.	Ausonius of Bordeaux	Bas. *Hom.*	Basil of Caesarea, *Homiliae*
Aus. *Ep.*	Ausonius of Bordeaux, *Epistulae*	Bas. *Hom. ex. Bapt.*	Basil of Caesarea, *Homilia exhortatoria ad sanctum baptisma* (*Exhortation to Baptism*)
Aus. *Ephem.*	Ausonius of Bordeaux, *Ephemeris*		
Aus. *Epit.*	Ausonius of Bordeaux, *Epitaphia*	Bas. *Hom. grat. act.*	Basil of Caesarea, *Homilia de gratiarum actione* (*Sermon on Gratefulness*)
Aus. *Parent.*	Ausonius of Bordeaux, *Parentalia*		
		Bas. *Hom. II Ps. XIV*	Basil of Caesarea, *Homilia 2 in Psalm 14*
Aus. *Pasch.*	Ausonius of Bordeaux, *Versus Paschales*	Bas. *Hom. Ps.*	Basil of Caesarea, *Homiliae super psalmos* (*Homilies on Psalms*)
Aus. *Prof.*	Ausonius of Bordeaux, *Commemoratio professorum Burdigalensium*		
		Bas. *Isa.*	Basil of Caesarea, *Enarratio in prophetam Isaiam* (*Commentary on the Prophet Isaiah*)
Aus. *Urb. nob.*	Ausonius of Bordeaux, *Ordo urbium nobilium*		
Avit.	Avitus of Vienne	Bas. *Reg.*	Basil of Caesarea, *Regulae* (*Rules*)
Avit. *Ep.*	Avitus of Vienne, *Epistulae*		
Avit. *Serm.*	Avitus of Vienne, *Sermones*	Bas. *Reg. Brev.*	Basil of Caesarea, *Regulae Brevius* (*Shorter Rules*)
AXP	*Acts of Xanthippe and Polyxena*		
Barb. lat.	Barbarinus latinus	Bas. *Reg. Fus.*	Basil of Caesarea, *Regulae Fusius* (*Greater Monastic Rules*)
Barhad. *Found.*	Barhadbeshabba, *Cause of the Foundation of the Schools*		

Bas. *Reg. Long.*	Basil of Caesarea, *Regulae Longior* (*Longer Rules*)
Bas. Sel. *Hom.*	Basil of Seleucia, *Homiliae*
Bas. *Spir.*	Basil of Caesarea, *De Spiritu Sancto* (*On Holy Spirit*)
Bas. Anc. *Virg.*	Basil of Ancyra, *De Virginitate* (*On True Chastity in Virginity*)
Bede	The Venerable Bede
Bede *Gen.*	The Venerable Bede, *In Genesim* (*On Genesis*)
Bede *Hist. eccl.*	The Venerable Bede, *Historia ecclesiastica gentis Anglorum* (*Ecclesiastical History of the English People*)
Bede *Vita Cuth.*	The Venerable Bede, *Vita Cuthberti*
Ben. *Reg.*	Benedict of Nursia, *Regula* (*Rule of St. Benedict*)
Besa *Vita Shen.*	Besa, *Vita Shenoute*
BG	Berolinensis Gnosticus
BLC	*Book of the Laws of Countries*
BoC	*Book of the Cock*
Bodl. MS Gr.Th.	Bodleian Library, Oxford, Manuscript Graecus Theologicus
Boethius	Boethius
Boethius *Arithm.*	Boethius, *Institutio arithmetica* (*On Arithmetic*)
Boethius *Cic. Top.*	Boethius, *Commentarii in Ciceronis Topica* (*Topics*)
Boethius *Cons.*	Boethius, *De consolatione philosophiae* (*Consolation of Philosophy*)
Boethius *Eut. Nest.*	Boethius, *Contra Eutychen et Nestorium* (*Against Eutyches and Nestorius*)
Boethius *Fid.*	Boethius, *De fide catholica* (*On the Catholic Faith*)
Boethius *Isag. comm. alt*	Boethius, *Isagoge commentum alterum* (*The Second Commentary on Porphyry, based on Boethius' own translation*)
Boethius *Mus.*	Boethius, *Institutio Musica* (*On Music*)
Boethius *Top.*	Boethius, see Boethius *Cic. Top.*
Boethius *Trin.*	Boethius, *De sancta Trinitate* (*On the Holy Trinity*)
Boethius *Utrum Pater*	Boethius, *Utrum Pater et Filius et Spiritus Sanctus de divinitate substantialter praedicentur* (*Whether Father and Son and Holy Spirit Are Substantially Predicated of the Divinity*)
Boh. Pach.	*Bohairic Life of Pachomius*
Bon. *Ep.*	Boniface I, *Epistulae*
Bordeaux Pilgrim	see *Itin. Burd.* (*Itinerarium Burdigalense*)
BoSt	*Book of Steps*
Braul. Sarag.	Braulio of Saragossa
Braul. Sarag. *Ep.*	Braulio of Saragossa, *Epistulae*
Braul. *Vita Aemil.*	Braulio of Saragossa, *Vita Aemiliani*
Brev.	*Brevarius*
Brev. Al.	*Breviary of Alaric*
Brev. apost.	*Breviarium apostolorum*
Brev. Hipp.	*Breviarium Hipponense*
Caes. *Bell. gall.*	Julius Caesar, *Bellum gallicum* (*Gallic War*)
Caesar.	Caesarius of Arles
Caesar. *Ep.*	Caesarius of Arles, *Epistulae*
Caesar. *Hom.*	Caesarius of Arles, *Homily*
Caesar. *Serm.*	Caesarius of Arles, *Sermones*
Cal. *Tim.*	Calcidius, *In Timaeum* (*On Timaeus*)
Call. *Cog.*	Callistratus, *Libri VI de cognitionibus* (*Six Books on Imperial Judicial Hearings*)
Callim. *Epigr.*	Callimachus, *Epigrammata* (*Epigrams*)
Callin. *Vita Hyp.*	Callinicus, *Vita Hypatii* (*Life of St. Hypatius*)
Can. ap.	*Canones apostolicae* (*Apostolic Canons*)
Can. Hipp.	*Canones Hippolyti* (*Canons of Hippolytus*)
Can. Mur.	*Canon Muratori*
Cap. *Nupt.*	Martianus Capella, *De Nuptiis Philologiae et Mercurii* (*The Marriage of Philology and Mercury*)
Carm. de Sod.	*Carmen de Sodoma*
Cass.	John Cassian

Cass. *Con.*	John Cassian, *Conlationes* (*Conferences*)	Chron. Gal. 511	*Chronica Gallica of 511* (*Gallic Chronicle of 511*)
Cass. *Incarn.*	John Cassian, *De incarnatione Domini contra Nestorium* (*On the Incarnation of the Lord Against Nestorius*)	Chron. Pasch.	*Chronicon Paschale*
		Chrys.	John Chrysostom (Ioannes Chrysostomus)
Cass. *Inst.*	John Cassian, *De institutis coenobiorum* (*On the Institutes of the Coenobia*)	Chrys. *Anna*	John Chrysostom, *De Anna* (*On Anna*)
		Chrys. *Ascens.*	John Chrysostom, *In ascensionem domini nostri Jesu Christi* (*On the Ascension of our Lord Jesus Christ*)
Cassio.	Cassiodorus		
Cassio. *An.*	Cassiodorus, *De Anima* (*On the Soul*)		
Cassio. *Chron.*	Cassiodorus, *Chronica*	Chrys. *Bab.*	John Chrysostom, *De sancto hieromartyre Babyla* (*Babylas the Martyr*)
Cassio. *Exp. Ps.*	Cassiodorus, *Expositio psalmorum* (*Exposition of the Psalms*)		
		Chrys. *Bab. Jul.*	John Chrysostom, *De Babyla contra Julianum et gentiles* (*On Saint Babylas, Against Julian and the Gentiles*)
Cassio. *Hist. eccl.*	Cassiodorus, *Historia ecclesiastica tripartita* (*Tripartite History*)		
Cassio. *Inst.*	Cassiodorus, *Institutiones Divinarum et Saecularium Litterarum* (*Institutions of Divine and Secular Learning*)	Chrys. *Bapt.*	John Chrysostom, *De baptismo Christi* (*On the Baptism of Christ*)
		Chrys. *Bapt. Instr.*	John Chrysostom, *Catecheses baptismales* (*Baptismal Instructions*)
Cassio. Orat. *Frgm*(s).	Cassiodorus, *Orationum Fragmenta*	Chrys. *Bern.*	John Chrysostom, *De sanctis Bernice et Prosdoce* (*On St. Bernice and St. Prosdoce*)
Cassio. *Ord.*	Cassiodorus, *Ordo generis Cassiodorum*		
Cassio. *Var.*	Cassiodorus, *Variae*	Chrys. *Catech. illum.*	John Chrysostom, *Catecheses ad illuminandos* (*Instructions to Catechumens*)
Cat. *Agr.*	Cato the Elder, *De agricultura* (*De re rustica*) (*On Agriculture*)		
Catul. *Carm.*	Catullus, *Carmina*	Chrys. *Catech. ult.*	John Chrysostom, *Catechesis ultima ad baptizandos* (*The Last Instruction for Those About to be Baptized*)
CDL	Codice Diplomatico Longobardo		
Cel. *Med.*	Celsus, *De Medicina*		
Celes. *Ep.*	Celestine I, *Epistulae*	Chrys. *Comm. Job*	John Chrysostom, *Commentarius in Job* (*A Commentary on Job*)
Ch.Fr.	*Chronicle of Fredegar*		
Char. *Gram.*	Charisius, *Ars Grammatica*		
Chris. Cop. *Anth. Graec.*	Christodoros of Coptos, *Anthologia Graeca*	Chrys. *Compunct. Stel.*	John Chrysostom, *Ad Stelechium de compunctione* (*On Compuction. To Stelechius*)
Chrom.	Chromatius of Aquileia		
Chrom. *Serm.*	Chromatius of Aquileia, *Sermones*		
		Chrys. De coem. et cruc.	John Chrysostom, *De coemeterio et cruce* (*On the Cemetery and the Cross*)
Chrom. *Tract. Matt.*	Chromatius of Aquileia, *Tractatus in Matthaeum* (*Treatise on Matthew*)		
		Chrys. De prod. Judae	John Chrysostom, *De proditione Judae* (*Homily on the Betrayal of Judas*)
Chron. Gal.	*Chronica Gallica of 452* (*Gallic Chronicle of 452*)		

Chrys. *Dros.* — John Chrysostom, *De sancta Droside martyre (On St. Drosis)*

Chrys. *Ep.* — John Chrysostom, *Epistulae*

Chrys. *Ep. Olymp.* — John Chrysostom, *Epistulae ad Olympiadem (Letters to Olympias)*

Chrys. *Eutrop.* — John Chrysostom, *In Eutropium (On Eutropius)*

Chrys. *Exp. Ps.* — John Chrysostom, *Expositiones in Psalmos (Expositions on Psalms)*

Chrys. *Fem. reg.* — John Chrysostom, *Quod regulares feminae viris cohabitare non (That Women Under Ascetic Rule Ought Not Live Together)*

Chrys. *Hom 1 Thess.* — John Chrysostom, *Homiliae in epistulam i ad Thessalonicenses (Homilies on the First Epistle to the Tessalonians)*

Chrys. *Hom 2 Thess.* — John Chrysostom, *Homiliae in epistulam ii ad Thessalonicenses (Homilies on the Second Epistle to the Tessalonians)*

Chrys. *Hom. 1 Cor.* — John Chrysostom, *Homiliae in epistulam i ad Corinthios (Homilies on the First Epistle to the Corinthians)*

Chrys. *Hom. 1 Cor. 11:19* — John Chrysostom, *In dictum Pauli: Oportet haereses esse*

Chrys. *Hom. 1 Cor. 7:2* — John Chrysostom, *In illud: Propter fornicationes autem unusquisque suam uxorem habeat*

Chrys. *Hom. 1 Tim.* — John Chrysostom, *Homiliae in epistulam i ad Timotheum (Homilies on the First Epistle to Timothy)*

Chrys. *Hom. 2 Cor.* — John Chrysostom, *Homiliae in epistulam ii ad Corinthios (Homilies on the Second Epistle to the Corinthians)*

Chrys. *Hom. 2 Tim.* — John Chrysostom, *Homiliae in epistulam ii ad Timotheum (Homilies on the Second Epistle to Timothy)*

Chrys. *Hom. Act.* — John Chrysostom, *Homiliae in Acta apostolorum (Homilies on the Acts of the Apostles)*

Chrys. *Hom. Col.* — John Chrysostom, *Homiliae in epistulam ad Colossenses (Homilies on the Epistle to the Collossians)*

Chrys. *Hom. Dia.* — John Chrysostom, *Homiliae de imbecillitate diaboli (Homilies on the Weakness of the Devil)*

Chrys. *Hom. Eph.* — John Chrysostom, *Homiliae in epistulam ad Ephesios (Homilies on the Epistle to the Ephesians)*

Chrys. *Hom. Eutrop. Div. Van.* — John Chrysostom, *Homilia de capto Eutropia et de divitiarum vanitate (Homily Two on Eutropius)*

Chrys. *Hom. Gal.* — John Chrysostom, *Homiliae in epistulam ad Galatas commentarius (Homilies on the Epistle to the Galatians)*

Chrys. *Hom. Gen.* — John Chrysostom, *Homiliae in Genesim (Homilies on Genesis)*

Chrys. *Hom. Heb.* — John Chrysostom, *Homiliae in epistulam ad Hebraeos (Homilies on the Epistle to the Hebrews)*

Chrys. *Hom. Isa. 45:7* — John Chrysostom, *In illud Isaiae: Ego Dominus Deus feci lumen*

Chrys. *Hom. Isa. 6:1* — John Chrysostom, *In illud: Vidi Dominum*

Chrys. *Hom. Jo.* — John Chrysostom, *Homiliae in Joannem (Homilies on the Gospel of John)*

Chrys. *Hom. Matt.* — John Chrysostom, *Homiliae in Matthaeum (Homilies on the Gospel of Matthew)*

Chrys. *Hom. Natal.* — John Chrysostom, *Homilia in Natale Christi (Homily on the Birth of the Lord)*

Chrys. *Hom. Pent.*	John Chrysostom, *Homiliae in Pentecosten* (*Homily on Pentecost*)	Chrys. *Pecc.*	John Chrysostom, *Peccata fratrum non evulganda* (*Against Publicly Exposing the Sins of the Brethren*)
Chrys. *Hom. perf. car.*	John Chrysostom, *Homilia de perfecta caritate*	Chrys. *Pelag.*	John Chrysostom, *De sancta Pelagia virgine et martyre* (*On St. Pelagia, the Virgin and Martyr*)
Chrys. *Hom. Phil.*	John Chrysostom, *Homiliae in epistulam ad Philippenses* (*Homilies on the First Epistle to the Tessalonians*)		
		Chrys. *Pent.*	John Chrysostom, *De sancta pentecoste* (*On Holy Pentecost*)
Chrys. *Hom. princ. Act.*	John Chrysostom, *Homiliae in principium Actorum* (*Homilies on the Beginnings of Acts*)	Chrys. *Phoc.*	John Chrysostom, *De sancto hieromartyre Phoca* (*Homily on St. Phocas*)
Chrys. *Hom. Rom.*	John Chrysostom, *Homiliae in epistulam ad Romanos* (*Homilies on the First Epistle to the Romans*)	Chrys. *Ps. 50*	John Chrysostom, *In Psalmum 50* (*On Psalm 50*)
Chrys. *Hom. Tit.*	John Chrysostom, *Homiliae in epistulam ad Titum* (*Homilies on the Epistle to Titus*)	Chrys. *Sac.*	John Chrysostom, *De sacerdotio* (*Priesthood*)
		Chrys. *Serm. Gen.*	John Chrysostom, *Sermones in Genesim* (*Homilies on Genesis*)
Chrys. *Inan. glor.*	John Chrysostom, *De inani gloria* (*Concerning Vainglory and the Education of Children*)	Chrys. *Stag.*	John Chrysostom, *Ad Stagirium a daemone vexatum* (*Exhortatory Treatise to the Ascetic Stageirios, Being Harassed by a Demon*)
Chrys. *Incomp.*	John Chrysostom, *De incomprehensibili dei natura* (*On the Incomprehensible Nature of God*)		
		Chrys. *Stat.*	John Chrysostom, *Ad populum Antiochenum de statuis* (*On the Statues. To the People of Antioch*)
Chrys. *Jud.*	John Chrysostom, *Adversus Judaeos* (*Against the Jews*)		
Chrys. *Kal.*	John Chrysostom, *In Kalendas* (*On the Kalends*)	Chrys. *Theatr.*	John Chrysostom, *Contra ludos et theatra* (*Against the Circuses and the Theatre*)
Chrys. *Laz.*	John Chrysostom, *De Lazaro* (*Concerning Lazarus*)	Chrys. *Theod. laps.*	John Chrysostom, *Ad Theodorum lapsum* (*Exhortation to Theodore after His Fall*)
Chrys. *Mart.*	John Chrysostom, *De sanctis martyribus; Homilia in martyres*		
Chrys. *Natal.*	John Chrysostom, *In diem natalem Christi* (*Homily on the Date of Christmas*)	Chrys. *Turt.*	John Chrysostom, *De turture seu de ecclesia sermo*
		Chrys. *Virg.*	John Chrysostom, *De virginitate* (*On Virginity*)
Chrys. *Oppugn.*	John Chrysostom, *Adversus oppugnatores vitae monasticae* (*Against the Opponents of the Monastic Life*)	Chrysol. *Serm.*	Petrus Chrysologus, *Sermones*
		Cic.	Cicero
		Cic. *Acad.*	Cicero, *Academicae quaestiones*

ANCIENT AUTHORS AND PRIMARY SOURCES

Cic. *Acad. post.* — Cicero, *Academica posteriora* (*Lucullus*)

Cic. *Amic.* — Cicero, *De amicitia* (*On Friendship*)

Cic. *Att.* — Cicero, *Epistulae ad Atticum* (*Letters to Atticus*)

Cic. *Brut.* — Cicero, *Brutus* or *De claris oratoribus*

Cic. *Caecin.* — Cicero, *Pro Caecina*

Cic. *Cael.* — Cicero, *Pro Caelio*

Cic. *Cat.* — Cicero, *In Catalinam*

Cic. *Clu.* — Cicero, *Pro Cluentio*

Cic. *De or.* — Cicero, *De oratore* (*On the Orator*)

Cic. *Div.* — Cicero, *De divinatione* (*Concerning Divination*)

Cic. *Dom.* — Cicero, *De domo suo*

Cic. *Fam.* — Cicero, *Epistulae ad familiares* (*Letters to Friends*)

Cic. *Fin.* — Cicero, *De finibus bonorum et malorum* (*On the Ends of Good and Evil*)

Cic. *Flac.* — Cicero, *Pro Flacco*

Cic. *Har. resp.* — Cicero, *De haruspicum responso* (*On the Responses of the Haruspices*)

Cic. *Inv.* — Cicero, *De inventione rhetorica* (*On Invention*)

Cic. *Lael.* — Cicero, *Laelius de amicitia* (*Laelius on Friendship*)

Cic. *Leg.* — Cicero, *De legibus* (*On the Laws*)

Cic. *Lig.* — Cicero, *Pro Ligario* (*For Ligarius*)

Cic. *Nat. d.* — Cicero, *De natura deorum* (*On the Nature of the Gods*)

Cic. *Off.* — Cicero, *De officiis* (*On Moral Duties*)

Cic. *Pis.* — Cicero, *In Pisonem* (*Against Piso*)

Cic. *Quint. fratr.* — Cicero, *Epistulae ad Quintum fratrem* (*Letters to Brother Quintus*)

Cic. *Rab. Perd.* — Cicero, *Pro Rabirio Perduellionis Reo* (*For Rabirius on a Charge of Treason*)

Cic. *Rep.* — Cicero, *De republica* (*On the Republic*)

Cic. *Rosc. Amer.* — Cicero, *Pro Sexto Roscio Amerino*

Cic. *Rosc. com.* — Cicero, *Pro Roscio comoedo*

Cic. *Tusc.* — Cicero, *Tusculanae disputationes* (*Tusculan Disputations*)

Cic. *Verr.* — Cicero, *In Verrem* (*Against Verres; Verrine Orations*)

Claud. — Claudian

Claud. *Bell. Goth.* — Claudian, *De Bello Gothico* (*On the Gothic War of 402–403 CE*)

Claud. *Carm.* — Claudian, *Carmen*

Claud. *Carm. min.* — Claudian, *Carmina minora*

Claud. *Cons. Stil.* — Claudian, *De Consulatu Stilichonis* (*On the Consulship of Stilicho*)

Claud. *Epith.* — Claudian, *Epithalamium*

Claud. *Eutr.* — Claudian, *In Eutropium* (*Against Eutropius*)

Claud. *L. Ser.* — Claudian, *Laus Serenae*

Claud. *Pan. Quarto* — Claudian, *Panegyricus de Quarto Consulatu Honorii Augusti* (*The Fourth Consulship of the Emperor Honorius*)

Claud. *Pan. Sexto* — Claudian, *Panegyricus de Sexto Consulatu Honorii Augusti* (*The Sixth Consulship of the Emperor Honorius*)

Claud. *Pan. Tertio* — Claudian, *Panegyricus de Tertio Consulatu Honorii Augusti* (*The Third Consulship of the Emperor Honorius*)

Claud. *Ruf.* — Claudian, *In Rufinum* (*Against Rufinus*)

Claud. *Stil.* — Claudian, see Claud. *Cons. Stil.*

Claud. Ael. *Nat. an.* — Claudius Aelianus, *De natura animalium* (*On the Nature of Animals*)

Claud. Mam. *Stat. Anim.*	Claudianus Mamertus, *De statu animae* (*The Standing of the Soul*)	Cod. Par. Graec.	Codex Parisinus Graecus
		Cod. Par. Syr.	Codex Parisinus Syriacus
		Cod. Sang.	Codex Sangallensis
Clem.	Clement of Alexandria	Cod. Tchac.	Codex Tchacos
Clem. *Ecl.*	Clement of Alexandria, *Eclogae propheticae* (*Extracts from the Prophets*)	Cod. Theod.	Codex Theodosianus
		Cod. Vat.	Codex Vaticanus
		Cod. Ver.	Codex Veronensis
Clem. *Exc.*	Clement of Alexandria, *Excerpta ex Theodoto* (*Excerpts from Theodotus*)	Col.	Columbanus
		Col. *Ep.*	Columbanus, *Epistulae*
		Col. *Serm.*	Columbanus, *Sermones vel Instructiones*
Clem. *Frgm.*	Clement of Alexandria, *Fragmenta*	*Coll. Arel.*	*Collectio Arelatensis*
Clem. *Hyp.*	Clement of Alexandria, *Hypotyposes*	*Coll. Avell.*	*Collectio Avellana*
		Coll. Quesn.	*Collectio Quesnelliana*
Clem. *Paed.*	Clement of Alexandria, *Paedagogus* (*Christ the Educator*)	*Coll. Sirm.*	*Collectio Sirmondiana*
		Coll. Leg.	*Collatio Legum Mosaicarum et Romanarum*
Clem. *Protok.*	Clement of Alexandria, *Protokatechesis*	Colum. *Rust.*	Columella, *De re rustica* (*On Agriculture*)
Clem. *Protr.*	Clement of Alexandria, *Protrepticus* (*Exhortation to the Greeks*)	Columb. *Reg. Mon.*	Columban, *Regula Monachorum* (*Rule of Monks*)
Clem. *Quis div.*	Clement of Alexandria, *Quis dives salvetur* (*Salvation of the Rich*)	Comm. *Instr.*	Commodian(us), *Instructiones*
		Con. *Caes.*	*Consularia Caesaraugustana*
		Con. *Ovet.*	*Continuatio codicis Ovetensis*
Clem. *Strom.*	Clement of Alexandria, *Stromata* (*Miscellanies*)	Con. *vet. c. iur.*	*Consultatio veteris cuiusdam iurisconsulti*
Clim. *Scala par.*	Joannes Climacus, *Scala paradisi* (*The Ladder of Divine Ascent or Ladder of Paradise*)	Con. *Zac. Apol.*	*Consultationes Zacchaei et Apollonii*
		Conc. Cartag. Grato	*Concilium Carthaginense sub Grato* (348 CE)
CLMR	*Collatio legum Mosaicarum et Romanarum*	Cons. *Const.*	*Consularia Constantinopolitana*
Clod. Lic. *Hist.*	Clodius Licinus, *Historiae*	Cons. *Ep.*	Consentius, *Epistula*
Cod. Ambr.	Codex Ambrosianus	Cons. *Ital.*	*Consularia Italica*
Cod. Baroc.	Codex Baroccianus	Cons. *Zacch. Apoll.*	see Con. *Zac. Apol.*
Cod. Can. Eccl. Afr.	Codex Canonum Ecclesiasticorum Africanae	ConSir	*Constitutio Sirmondiana*
Cod. Clar.	Codex Claromontanus	Const. *ap.*	*Constitutiones apostolicae* (*Apostolic Constitutions*)
Cod. Farf.	Codex Farfensis		
Cod. Fuld.	Codex Fuldensis	Const. *Vita Ger.*	Constantius of Lyon, *Vita Germani*
Cod. Guel.	Codex Guelferbytanus		
Cod. Justin.	Codex Justinianus	Const. Porphyr. *Cerem.*	Constantine Porphyrogennetos, *De cerimoniis aulae Byzantinae* (*Book of Ceremonies*)
Cod. lat. monac.	Codices latini monacenses		
Cod. Manich. Col.	Codex Manichaicus Coloniensis		
Cod. Ottob. Lat.	Codex Ottobonianus Latinus	Constant.	Constantinus
Cod. Pal. germ.	Codices Palatini germanici		

Constant. *Ep. Alex. Ar.*	Constantinus, *Epistula ad Alexandrum et Arium*	Cyp. *Test.*	Cyprian of Carthage, *Ad Quirinum testimonia adversus Judaeos* (*To Quirinius: Testomonies against the Jews*)
Constant. *Ep. eccl. Alex.*	Constantinus, *Epistula ad ecclesiam Alexandrinam*		
Constant. *Ep. om. eccl.*	Constantinus, *Epistula ad omnes ecclesias*	Cyp. *Unit. eccl.*	Cyprian of Carthage, *De catholicae ecclesiae unitate* (*On the Unity of the Catholic Church*)
Contra Const.	*Contra Constantinopolitanos*		
Corip. *Iust.*	Corippus, *In laudem Iustini Augusti*		
Corp. herm.	*Corpus hermeticum*	Cyp. *Zel. liv.*	Cyprian of Carthage, *De zelo et livore* (*On Jealousy and Envy*)
Cosmas *Top. Chris.*	Cosmas Indicopleustes, *Topographia christiana* (*Christian Topography*)		
		Cyprian (Gaul) *Vita Caes. Arel.*	Cyprian (Gaul), *Vita Caesarii Arelatensis* (*Life of Caesarius of Arles*)
Crates *Ep.*	Crates, *Epistulae*		
CSP	*Confessio seu paenitentia*	Cyr.Alex.	Cyril of Alexandria
Cyp.	Cyprian of Carthage	Cyr.Alex. *Ador. spr. ver.*	Cyril of Alexandria, *De adoratione in spiritu et veritate* (*On Adoration and Worship in Spirit and Truth*)
Cyp. *Demetr.*	Cyprian of Carthage, *Ad Demetrianum* (*To Demetrianus*)		
Cyp. *Dom. or.*	Cyprian of Carthage, *De dominica oratione* (*The Lord's Prayer*)	Cyr.Alex. *Apol.*	Cyril of Alexandria, *Apologeticus ad imperatorem Theodosium* (*Apologia to Emperor Theodosius*)
Cyp. *Don.*	Cyprian of Carthage, *Ad Donatum* (*To Donatus*)		
Cyp. *Eleem.*	Cyprian of Carthage, *De opere et eleemosynis* (*On Works and Alms*)	Cyr.Alex. *C. Jul.*	Cyril of Alexandria, *Contra Julianum* (*Against Julian*)
Cyp. *Ep.*	Cyprian of Carthage, *Epistulae*	Cyr.Alex. *Comm. Joh.*	Cyril of Alexandria, *Commentarius in Johannem* (*Commentary on the Gospel of John*)
Cyp. *Fort.*	Cyprian of Carthage, *Ad Fortunatum* (*To Fortunatus: Exhortation to Martyrdom*)		
		Cyr.Alex. *Duod. proph.*	Cyril of Alexandria, *In duodecim prophetas*
Cyp. *Hab. virg.*	Cyprian of Carthage, *De habitu virginum* (*On the Dress of Virgins*)	Cyr.Alex. *Ep.*	Cyril of Alexandria, *Epistulae*
		Cyr.Alex. *Ep. ad Rom.*	Cyril of Alexandria, *Explanatio in Epistulam ad Romanos* (*Commentary on Romans*)
Cyp. *Idol.*	Cyprian of Carthage, *Quod idola dii non sint* (*That Idols Are Not Gods*)		
Cyp. *Laps.*	Cyprian of Carthage, *De lapsis* (*On the Lapsed*)	Cyr.Alex. *Ep. fest.*	Cyril of Alexandria, *Epistulae festales*
Cyp. *Mort.*	Cyprian of Carthage, *De mortalitate* (*Mortality*)	Cyr.Alex. *Frgm(s). Heb.*	Cyril of Alexandria, *Fragmenta In Epistulam Ad Hebraeos*
Cyp. *Pat.*	Cyprian of Carthage, *De bono patientiae* (*The Advantage of Patience*)	Cyr.Alex. *Glaph.*	Cyril of Alexandria, *Glaphyra on Leviticus* (*Elegant Comments on Leviticus*)
Cyp. *Sent.*	Cyprian of Carthage, *Sententiae episcoporum de haereticis baptizandis*		

Cyr.Alex. *Hom. Luc.*	Cyril of Alexandria, *Homiliae in Lucam* (*Commentary on Luke*)	Cyrillona	Cyrillona
		Cyrillona *Euch.*	Cyrillona, *On the Institution of the Eucharist*
Cyr.Alex. *Incarn.*	Cyril of Alexandria, *De incarnatione Unigeniti* (*On the Incarnation of the Word*)	Cyrillona *Pasch*	Cyrillona, *On the Pasch of Our Lord*
		Cyrillona *Zacch.*	Cyrillona, *On Zacchaeus*
Cyr.Alex. *Isa.*	Cyril of Alexandria, *In Isaiam* (*Commentary on Isaiah*)	Cyz. *Hist eccl.*	Anonymus Cyzicenus, *Historia ecclesiastica*
Cyr.Alex. *Nest.*	Cyril of Alexandria, *Adversus Nestorii blasphemies contradictionum libri quinque* (*Five Tomes Against the Blasphemies of Nestorius*)	D.L.	Diogenes Laertius, *Vitae philosophorum*
		Dam.	John of Damascus
		Dam. *Comm. 1 Cor*	John of Damascus, *Commentarium In Epistulam 1 ad Corinthios*
Cyr.Alex. *Recta fid.*	Cyril of Alexandria, *De recta fide ad reginas*	Dam. *Dial. Cap.*	John of Damascus, *Dialectica sive Capita philosophica*
Cyr.Alex. *Sanc trin. dial.*	Cyril of Alexandria, *De sancta trinitate dialogi* (*Dialogues on the Trinity*)	Dam. *Dial. fus.*	John of Damascus, *Dialectica fusior*
		Dam. *Dua.*	John of Damascus, *De duabus in Christo voluntatibus* (*The Two Wills in Christ*)
Cyr.Alex. *Trin.*	Cyril of Alexandria, *De Trinitate* (*On the Trinity*)		
Cyr.Jer.	Cyril of Jerusalem	Dam. *Expos. Fid*	John of Damascus, *Expositio fidei* (*Exposition of the Faith*)
Cyr.Jer. *Cat.*	Cyril of Jerusalem, *Cathechesis*		
Cyr.Jer. *Cat. Myst.*	Cyril of Jerusalem, *Catecheses Mystagogicae* (*Mystagogical Cateches*) (could also be attributed to John of Jerusalem)	Dam. *Fid.*	John of Damascus, *De fide orthodoxa* (*On the Orthodox Faith*)
		Dam. *Haer.*	John of Damascus, *Liber de haeresibus* (*On Heresies*)
Cyr.Jer. *Catech.*	Cyril of Jerusalem, *Catecheses illuminandorum*	Dam. *Hom.*	John of Damascus, *Homiliae*
Cyr.Jer. *Comm. Joh.*	Cyril of Jerusalem, *Commentarii in Joannem*	Dam. *Imag.*	John of Damascus, *De Imaginibus* (*On the Divine Images*)
Cyr.Jer. *Cons.*	Cyril of Jerusalem, *Epistula ad Constantium* (*Letter to Constantius*)	Dam. *Jac.*	John of Damascus, *Contra Jacobitas* (*Against the Jacobites*)
Cyr.Jer. *Prebap.* (= *Proc.*)	Cyril of Jerusalem, *Prebaptismal Catecheses*	Dam. *Or. Imag.*	John of Damascus, *Orationes de imaginibus tres* (*Three Treatises on the Divine Images*)
Cyr.Jer. *Proc.*	Cyril of Jerusalem, *Procatechesis*		
Cyr.Scyt.	Cyril of Scythopolis	Damas.	Damasus (Bishop of Rome)
Cyr.Scyt. *Vita Cyr.*	Cyril of Scythopolis, *Vita Cyriaci*	Damas. *Ad Gall. Ep.*	Damasus (Bishop of Rome), *Ad Gallos Episcopos*
Cyr.Scyt. *Vita Euth.*	Cyril of Scythopolis, *Vita Euthymii* (*Life of Euthymius*)	Damas. *Epigr.*	Damasus (Bishop of Rome), *Epigram*
Cyr.Scyt. *Vita Sab.*	Cyril of Scythopolis, *Vita sancti Sabae* (*Life of Saint Sabbas*)	Damasc.	Damascius
		Damasc. *Isid.*	Damascius, *Vita Isidori* (*Life of Isidore*)

Damasc. *Parm.*	Damascius, *In Parmenidem*	Dio. Chrys. *Alex.*	Dio Chrysostom, *Ad Alexandrinos* (*Or. 32*) (*To the People of Alexandria*)
Damasc. *Phaed.*	Damascius, *In Phaedonem*		
Decr. *Dam.*	*Decretum Damasi*		
Decr. *Gel.*	*Decretum Gelasianum*		
Decr. *Grat.*	*Decretum Gratiani*	Dio. Chrys. *Or.*	Dio Chrysostom, *Oratio*
Dem.	Demosthenes	Diod.	Diodore of Tarsus
Dem. *Cor.*	Demosthenes, *De corona* (*On the Crown*)	Diod. *Com. Ps.*	Diodore of Tarsus, *Commentarii in Psalmos* (*Commentary on the Psalms*)
Dem. *Ep.*	Demosthenes, *Epistulae*		
Dem. *Halon.*	Demosthenes, *De Halonneso* (*On the Halonnesus*)	Diod. *Prov.*	Diodore of Tarsus, *De providentia* (*On Providence*)
Dem. *Or.*	Demosthenes, *Orationes*	Diod. Sic. *Bib. hist.*	Diodorus Siculus, *Bibliotheca historica*
Des. *Ep.*	Desiderius of Cahors, *Epistulae*		
Diad.	Diadochus of Photike	Diog. *Ep.*	Diogenes of Sinope, *Epistulae*
Diad. *Perf.*	Diadochus of Photike, see Diad. *Spir. fer.*	Diog. Oen. *Frgm(s).*	Diogenes of Oenoanda, *Fragment(s)*
Diad. *Spir. per.*	Diadochus of Photike, *Capita centum de perfectione spirituali* (*Spiritual Perfection*)	Dion. Alex.	Dionysius of Alexandria
		Dion. Alex. *Ep.*	Dionysius of Alexandria, *Epistulae*
		Dion. Alex. *Ep. Basil.*	Dionysius of Alexandria, *Epistula ad Basilidem* (*Letter to Basilides*)
Dial. *Adam.*	*De recta in Deum fide* (*Dialogue of Adamantius on the Orthodox Faith in God*)	Dion. Alex. *Ep. can.*	Dionysius of Alexandria, *Epistula canonica*
Did. *Apost.*	*Didascalia Apostolorum*	Dion. Ant. *Frgm(s).*	Dionysius of Antioch, *Fragmenta*
Did. *Syr.*	*Didascalia Syriaca*		
Didy.	Didymus the Blind	Dion. Ar.	Dionysius Areopagita
Didy. *Comm. Eccl.*	Didymus the Blind, *Commentarii in Ecclesiasten*	Dion. Ar. *Cael. hier.*	Dionysius Areopagita, *De caelesti hierarchia* (*The Celestial Hierarchy*)
Didy. *Comm. Job*	Didymus the Blind, *Commentarii in Job*		
Didy. *Comm. Ps.*	Didymus the Blind, *Commentarii in Psalmos*	Dion. Ar. *Eccl. hier.*	Dionysius Areopagita, *De ecclesiastica hierarchia* (*Ecclesiastical Hierarchy*)
Didy. *Comm. Zach.*	Didymus the Blind, *Commentarii in Zachariam*	Dion. Ar. *Myst.*	Dionysius Areopagita, *De mystica theologia* (*Mystical Theology*)
Didy. *Spir.*	Didymus the Blind, *De spiritu sancto*		
Didy. *Trin.*	Didymus the Blind, *De Trinitate*	Dion. Ex.	Dionysius Exiguus
Didym. *Epit.*	Arius Didymus, *Epitome of Stoic Ethics*	Dion. Ex. *Vita Pac.*	Dionysius Exiguus, *Vita Pachomii* (*Life of Pachomius*)
Dig.	*Digesta*	Dion. Ex. *Praefatio*	Dionysius Exiguus, *Praefatio ad Petrum episcopum in epistulam encyclicam Cyrilli Alexandrini*
Dinarchus	Dinarchus, *Orationes* (*Speeches*)		
Dio *Hist. rom.*	Dio Lucius Cassius, *Historiae romanae* (*Roman History*)	Dion. Hali.	Dionysius of Halicarnassus
Dio. Chrys.	Dio Chrysostom	Dion. Hali. *Ant. rom.*	Dionysius of Halicarnassus, *Antiquitates romanae*

Dion. Hali. *Dem.*	Dionysius of Halicarnassus, *De Demosthene*	Ephr. *Comm. Gen.*	Ephrem the Syrian, *Commentary on Genesis*
Disc. Seth	see *Treat. Seth* (*Second Treatise of the Great Seth*)	Ephr. *Comm. Rom.*	Ephrem the Syrian, *Commentary on Romans*
Disp. Bizyae	*Disputatio Bizyae*	Ephr. *Epiph.*	Ephrem the Syrian, *Epiphany*
Doctr. Apost.	*Doctrina Apostolorum*	Ephr. *Hom. Lord*	Ephrem the Syrian, *Homily on Our Lord*
Dor.	Dorotheus of Gaza		
Dor. *Disc.*	Dorotheus of Gaza, *Discourses and Sayings*	Ephr. *Hym. Cruc.*	Ephrem the Syrian, *Hymns on the Crucifixion*
Dor. *Doctr. div.*	Dorotheus of Gaza, *Doctrinae diversae*	Ephr. *Hym. Fid.*	Ephrem the Syrian, *De Fide, adversus Scrutatores Hymni* (*Hymns on Faith*)
Dor. *Instr.*	Dorotheus of Gaza, *Instructions Beneficial to the Soul*	Ephr. *Hym. Haer.*	Ephrem the Syrian, *Hymni Contra Haereses* (*Hymns against Heresies*)
Ed. *Theod.*	*Edictum Theodorici* (*Edict of Theoderic*)	Ephr. *Hym. Jul.*	Ephrem the Syrian, *Hymni Contra Julianum*
Eger. *It.*	Egeria, *Itinerarium Egeriae* (*Travels of Egeria*)	Ephr. *Hym. Nat.*	Ephrem the Syrian, *Hymni de Nativitate* (*Hymns on the Nativity of Christ*)
Ekth. Makros.	*Ekthesis Makrostichos*		
Ennod.	Ennodius		
Ennod. *Carm.*	Ennodius, *Carmina*	Ephr. *Hym. Par.*	Ephrem the Syrian, *Hymni de Paradiso* (*Hymns on Paradise*)
Ennod. *Ep.*	Ennodius, *Epistulae*		
Ennod. *Lib. adv. syn.*	Ennodius, *Liber adversus eos qui contra synodum scribere praesumpserunt*	Ephr. *Hym. Vir.*	Ephrem the Syrian, *Hymni de virginitate* (*Hymns on Virginity*)
Ennod. *Lib. syn.*	Ennodius, *Libellus pro synodo*		
Ennod. *Opusc.*	Ennodius, *Opusculum*	Ephr. *Nis. Hym.*	Ephrem the Syrian, Carmina Nisibena (*Nisibene Hymns*)
Ennod. *Pan.*	Ennodius, *Panegyricus Regi Theodorico* (*The Panegyric of Theodoric*)	Ephr. *Ref.*	Ephrem the Syrian, *Prose Refutations of Mani, Marcion, and Bardaisan*
Ep. Anast. Apoc.	*Epistola Anastasii Apocrisiarii*		
Ep. Apos.	*Epistula Apostolorum* (*Epistle to the Apostles*)	Ephr. *Or.*	Ephrem the Syrian, *Oratio*
		Epic.	Epicurus
Ep. Arel. gen.	*Epistolae Arelatensis genuinae*	Epic. *Her.*	Epicurus, *Epistula prima ad Herodotum* (*Letter to Herodotus*)
Ep. Avell.	*Epistulae Avellana*		
Ep. Cath. Donat.	*Epistula ad Catholicos de secta Donatistarum*	Epic. *Men.*	Epicurus, *Epistula ad Menoeceum* (*Letter to Menoeceus*)
Ephr.	Ephrem the Syrian		
Ephr. *Carm.*	Ephrem the Syrian, *Carmina Nisibena*	Epic. *Pyt.*	Epicurus, *Epistula ad Pythoclem* (*Letter to Pythocles*)
Ephr. *Comm. Acts*	Ephrem the Syrian, *Commentary on Acts*	Epic. *Rat.*	Epicurus, *Ratae Sententiae*
		Epict.	Epictetus
Ephr. *Comm. Diat.*	Ephrem the Syrian, *Commentary on the Diatessaron*	Epict. *Diatr.*	Epictetus, *Diatribai* (*Dissertationes*)
Ephr. *Comm. Exod.*	Ephrem the Syrian, *Commentary on Exodus*	Epict. *Ench.*	Epictetus, *Enchiridion* (*Handbook* or *Manual*)

Epiph.	Epiphanius of Salamis	Euch. *Instr. Sal.*	Eucherius of Lyon, *Instructiones ad Salonium*
Epiph. *Anac.*	Epiphanius of Salamis, *Anacephalaiosis*	Eud. *Simpl. Arist.*	Eudorus of Alexandria, *Simplicius, In Aristotelis physicorum*
Epiph. *Anc.*	Epiphanius of Salamis, *Ancoratus*	Eug. *Carm.*	Eugenius of Toledo, *Carmina*
Epiph. *Ep.*	Epiphanius of Salamis, *Epistola*	Eugip.	Eugippius
Epiph. *Fid.*	Epiphanius of Salamis, *De Fide (On Faith)*	Eugip. *Ep. Pas.*	Eugippius, *Epistula ad Paschasius*
Epiph. *Haer.*	Epiphanius of Salamis, see Epiph. *Pan.*	Eugip. *Ep. Prob.*	Eugippius, *Epistula ad Probam virginem*
Epiph. *Hom. Mar.*	Epiphanius of Salamis, *Homilia in laudes Mariae deiparae (Homily in Praise of Mary, Mother of God)*	Eugip. *Vita Sev.*	Eugippius, *Vita Sancti Severini (Life of St. Severinus)*
		Eun.	Eunapius
		Eun. *Frgm(s).*	Eunapius, *Fragmenta (Fragments)*
Epiph. *Mens.*	Epiphanius of Salamis, *De mensuris et ponderibus (On Weights and Measures)*	Eun. *Vitae phil.*	Eunapius, *Vitae philosophorum*
Epiph. *Pan.*	Epiphanius of Salamis, *Panarion (Adversus haereses; Refutation of All Heresies)*	Eun. *Vitae soph.*	Eunapius, *Vitae sophistarum*
		Eunom. *Apol.*	Eunomius, *Liber Apologeticus*
		Eurip.	Euripides
		Eurip. *Alc.*	Euripides, *Alcestis*
Epiph. *Phryg.*	Epiphanius of Salamis, see Epiph. *Pan.*	Eurip. *Frgm(s).*	Euripides, *Fragment(s)*
		Eurip. *Hel.*	Euripides, *Helena (Helen)*
Epit. Caes.	*Epitome de Caesaribus (Epitome on Emperors)*	Eurip. *Heracl.*	Euripides, *Heraclidae (Children of Hercules)*
Epit. Con.	*Epitome Cononiana*	Eurip. *Hipp.*	Euripides, *Hippolytus*
Epit. Const. ap.	*Epitome Constitutiones apostolicae*	Eurip. *Ion*	Euripides, *Ion*
		Eurip. *Iph. aul.*	Euripides, *Iphigenia aulidensis (Iphigeneia at Aulis)*
Epp. Apoll.	*Epistula Apollonii (Letters of Apollonius)*	Eurip. *Iph. taur.*	Euripides, *Iphigenia taurica (Iphigeneia at Tauris)*
Erch. *Hist. Langob. Benev.*	Erchempertus, *Historia Langobardorum Beneventanorum degentium (The History of the Lombards living in Benevento)*	Eurip. *Orest.*	Euripides, *Orestes*
		Eurip. *Suppl.*	Euripides, *Supplices (Suppliants)*
		Eus.	Eusebius of Caesarea
		Eus. *Chron.*	Eusebius of Caesarea, *Chronicon (Chronicle)*
Eriug.	Eriugena	Eus. *Chron. Olym.*	Eusebius of Caesarea, *Chronicon ad Olympiades*
Eriug. *Ann. Mart.*	Eriugena, *Annotationes in Martianum (Annotations on Martianus Capella)*	Eus. *Coet. sanct.*	Eusebius of Caesarea, *Ad coetum sanctorum (Oration of the Emperor Constantine Which He Addressed to the Assembly of the Saints)*
Eriug. *Periph.*	Eriugena, *Periphyseon*		
Euch.	Eucherius of Lyon		
Euch. *Faust.*	Eucherius of Lyon, *Epistula ad Faustum presbyterum (Letter to Faustus)*		
		Eus. *Comm. Isa.*	Eusebius of Caesarea, *Commentarius in Isaiam (Commentary on Isaiah)*
Euch. *Instr.*	Eucherius of Lyon, *Instructiones*		

Eus. *Comm. Ps.*	Eusebius of Caesarea, *Commentarius in Psalmos* (*Commentary on the Psalms*)	Eus. *Theoph.*	Eusebius of Caesarea, *Theophania* (*Divine Manifestation*)
Eus. *Dem. ev.*	Eusebius of Caesarea, *Demonstratio evangelica* (*Demonstration of the Gospel*)	Eus. *Vita Const.*	Eusebius of Caesarea, *De vita Constantini* (*Life of Constantine*)
Eus. *Eccl. theol.*	Eusebius of Caesarea, *De ecclesiastica theologica* (*Ecclesiastical Theology*)	Eus.Alex. *Hom.*	Eusebius of Alexandria *Homiliae*
		Eus.Em. *Hom. Mart.*	Eusebius of Emesa, *Homilia de Martyribus*
Eus. *Ecl. proph.*	Eusebius of Caesarea, *Eclogae propheticae* (*Extracts from the Prophets*)	Eus. Nic. *Ep. Paul.*	Eusebius of Nicomedia, *Epistula ad Paulinum* (*Letter to Paulinus of Tyre*)
Eus. *Ep. Caes.*	Eusebius of Caesarea, *Epistula ad Caesarienses* (*Epistle to his diocese in Caesarea*)	Eus.Ver. *Ep.*	Eusebius of Vercelli, *Epistulae*
		Euseb. Gall.	Eusebius Gallicanus Collection
Eus. *Ep. Alex.*	Eusebius of Caesarea, *Epistula ad Alexandrum Alexandrinum* (*Epistle to Alexander of Alexandria*)	Eust. *Frgm(s).*	Eustathius of Antioch, *Fragment(s)*
		Eut.	Eutropius
		Eut. *Brev.*	Eutropius, *Breviarum ab urbe condita* (*Short History of the Roman Empire*)
Eus. *Hier.*	Eusebius of Caesarea, *Contra Hieroclem* (*Against Hierocles*)	Eut. *Frgm(s).*	Eutropius, *Fragment(s)*
Eus. *Hist. eccl.*	Eusebius of Caesarea, *Historia ecclesiastica* (*Ecclesiastical History*)	Eva. Pon.	Evagrius of Pontus
		Eva. Pon. *An.*	Evagrius of Pontus, *Epistula ad Anatolium* (*Letter to Anatolius*)
Eus. *Laud. Const.*	Eusebius of Caesarea, *De laudibus Constantini* (*Praise of Constantine*)	Eva. Pon. *Antirr.*	Evagrius of Pontus, *Antirrhetikos* (*Talking Back*)
Eus. *Marc.*	Eusebius of Caesarea, *Contra Marcellum* (*Against Marcellus*)	Eva. Pon. *Cog.*	Evagrius of Pontus, *De malignis cogitationibus* (*Treatise on Various Evil Thoughts*)
Eus. *Mart. Pal.*	Eusebius of Caesarea, *De martyribus Palaestinae* (*The Martyrs of Palestine*)	Eva. Pon. *Ep.*	Evagrius of Pontus, *Epistulae*
		Eva. Pon. *Eul.*	Evagrius of Pontus, *Ad Eulogium* (*To Eulogius*)
Eus. *Onom.*	Eusebius of Caesarea, *Onomasticon*	Eva Pon. *Exh. mon.*	Evagrius of Pontus, *Institutio ad monachos* (*Exhortations to Monks*)
Eus. *Pasch.*	Eusebius of Caesarea, *De sollemnitate paschali* (*On the Celebration of Easter*)	Eva. Pon. *Gnos.*	Evagrius of Pontus, *Gnostikos*
		Eva. Pon. *KG*	Evagrius of Pontus, *Kephalaia Gnostika* (*Propositions on Knowledge*)
Eus. *Praep.*	Eusebius of Caesarea, *Praeparatio evangelica* (*Preparation for the Gospel*)	Eva. Pon. *Mel.*	Evagrius of Pontus, *Epistula ad Melaniam* (*Letter to Melania*)
Eus. *Sep. Chr.*	Eusebius of Caesarea, *De sepulchro Christi* (*On Christ's Sepulchre*)	Eva. Pon. *Mon.*	Evagrius of Pontus, *Ad monachos* (*To the Monks*)

ANCIENT AUTHORS AND PRIMARY SOURCES

Eva. Pon. *Octo* — Evagrius of Pontus, *De octo spiritibus malitiae (The Eight Spirits of Evil)*

Eva. Pon. *Orat.* — Evagrius of Pontus, *De oratione (De oratione caputula; Chapters on Prayer)*

Eva. Pon. *Prak.* — Evagrius of Pontus, *Praktikos*

Eva. Pon. *Refl.* — Evagrius of Pontus, *Reflections*

Eva. Pon. *Schol. in Eccl.* — Evagrius of Pontus, *Scholia in Ecclesiasten (Scholia on Ecclesiastes)*

Eva. Pon. *Schol. in Prov.* — Evagrius of Pontus, *Scholia in Proverbs (Scholia on Proverbs)*

Eva. Pon. *Skem.* — Evagrius of Pontus, *Skemmata*

Eva. Pon. *Th.* — Evagrius of Pontus, *De cognitionibus (On Thoughts)*

Eva. Pon. *Virg.* — Evagrius of Pontus, *Sententiae ad Virginem (To a Virgin)*

Eva. Schol. *Hist. eccl.* — Evagrius Scholasticus, *Historia ecclesiastica (Ecclesiastical History)*

Evang. Ver. — *Evangelium Veritatis*

Evod. *Fid. Manich.* — Evodius of Uzalis, *De fide contra Manichaeos (On Faith Against the Manicheans)*

Excid. — *De excidio Hierosolymitano (On the Ruin of Jerusalem)*

Expos. Tot. — *Expositio Totius Mundi et gentium*

Ezek. *Exag.* — Ezekiel the Tragedian, *Exagoge*

Fac. — Facundus of Hermiane

Fac. *Def.* — Facundus of Hermiane, *Pro defensione trium capitulorum concilii Calchedonensis libri XII, ad Juslinianum imperatorem (Defense of the Three Chapters. To Justinian)*

Fac. *Moc.* — Facundus of Hermiane, *Liber contra Mocianum Scholasticum*

Fasti Vind. priores — *Fasti Vindobonenses Priores*

Faus. — Faustus of Riez

Faus. *Ep.* — Faustus of Riez, *Epistulae*

Faus. *Grat.* — Faustus of Riez, *De gratia dei et libero arbitrio (On the Grace of God and Free Will)*

Faust. — Faustinus

Faust. *Conf.* — Faustinus, *Confessio verae fidei (Confession of the True Faith)*

Faust. *Libel.* — Faustinus, *Libellus Precum (Booklet of Petitions)*

Faust. *Trin.* — Faustinus, *De trinitate (On the Trinity)*

FeIn — *Festal Index*

Felix II *Ep.* — Felix II of Rome, *Epistulae*

Felix III *Ep.* — Felix III of Rome, *Epistulae*

Ferr. *Ep.* — Ferrandus, *Epistulae*

Fest. *Brev.* — Festus, *Breviarium Rerum gestarum populi Romani (Summary of the Accomplishments of the Romans)*

Filas. *Haer.* — Filastrius of Brescia, *Diversarum haereseon liber (Book of Various Heresies)*

Firm. — Firmicus Maternus

Firm. *Err. prof. rel.* — Firmicus Maternus, *De Errore Profanarum Religionum (The Error of the Pagan Religions)*

Firm. *Math.* — Firmicus Maternus, *Mathesis*

Firm. Caes. *Ep.* — Firmus of Caesarea, *Epistolae*

Flor. *Ant.* — Florentius, *Anthologia Latina*

For. — Venantius Fortunatus

For. *Carm.* — Venantius Fortunatus, *Carmina*

For. *Vita Germ.* — Venantius Fortunatus, *Vita Germani (Life of St. Germanus)*

For. *Vita Hil.* — Venantius Fortunatus, *Vita Hilarii (Life of St. Hilarius)*

For. *Vita Mart.* — Venantius Fortunatus, *Vita Sancti Martin (Life of St. Martin)*

For. *Vita Radeg.* — Venantius Fortunatus, *Vita Radegundis (Life of St. Radeguna)*

For. *Vita Sev.* — Venantius Fortunatus, *Vita Severini (Life of St. Severinus)*

Ful.	Fulgentius of Ruspe
Ful. *Ep.*	Fulgentius of Ruspe, *Epistulae*
Ful. *Fast.*	Fulgentius of Ruspe, *Contra sermonem Fastidiosi Ariani (Against a Sermon of the Arian Fastidiosus)*
Ful. *Mon.*	Fulgentius of Ruspe, *Ad Monimum (To Monimus)*
Ful. *Petr.*	Fulgentius of Ruspe, *De fide ad Petrum (To Peter on Faith)*
Ful. *Praed. Grat.*	Fulgentius of Ruspe, *De veritate praedestinationis et gratiae Dei (On the Truth about Predestination and God's Grace)*
Ful. *Tras.*	Fulgentius of Ruspe, *Ad Thrasamundum regem (To King Thrasamundus)*
Gai. *Inst.*	Gaius, *Institutiones*
Gal.	Galen
Gal. *Aff. dign.*	Galen, *De propriorum animi cuiuslibet affectuum et peccatorum dignotione et curatione (The Passions of the Soul)*
Gal. *Avoid.*	Galen, *Peri Alupias (Avoidance of Grief)*
Gal. *Diff. puls.*	Galen, *De differentiis pulsuum (Differences of Pulses)*
Gal. *Hipp. art.*	Galen, *In Hippocratis De articulis (Commentary on Hippocrates' Joints)*
Gal. *Hipp. Epid.*	Galen, *In Hippocratis librum tertium epidemiarum commentarii (Commentary on Hippocrates' Third Epidemics Book)*
Gal. *Lib.*	Galen, *De Libris Propriis (On My [His] Own Books)*
Gal. *Praen.*	Galen, *De praenotione (On Prognosis)*
Gal. *San. tuen.*	Galen, *De sanitate tuenda (On the Preservation of Health)*
Gal. *Simpl.*	Galen, *De Simplicium Medicamentorum Temperamentis ac Facultatibus (On the Powers [and Mixtures] of Simple Remedies [Drugs])*
Gal. *Symp.*	Galen, *De Symptomatum Causis Simplicium Medicamentorum Temperamentis (Of [On] the Causes of Symptoms)*
Gal. *Us. Part.*	Galen, *De usu partium (The Usefulness of the Parts of the Body)*
Gaud.	Gaudentius of Brescia
Gaud. *Serm.*	Gaudentius of Brescia, *Sermo*
Gaud. *Tract.*	Gaudentius of Brescia, *Tractatus*
Gel. *Hist. eccl.*	Gelasius of Caesarea, *Historia ecclesiastica*
Gel. Cyz. *Hist. eccl.*	Gelasius Cyzicenus, *Historia ecclesiastica*
Gelas. *Ep.*	Gelasius I (Bishop of Rome), *Epistulae*
Gell. *Noct. att.*	Aulus Gellius, *Noctes atticae (Attic Nights)*
Gennad.	Gennadius of Massilia (Marseilles)
Gennad. *Eccl. Dogm.*	Gennadius of Massilia, *De Ecclesiasticis Dogmatibus*
Gennad. *Vir. ill.*	Gennadius of Massilia, *De viris illustribus*
Georg.Alex. *Vit.Chr.*	Georgius Alexandrinus, *Vita S. Chrysostomi*
Georg.Cyp. *Descr.*	Georgias Cyprius, *Descriptio Orbis Romani*
Georg. Sync. *Chron.*	George Syncellus, *Chronicle*
Ges. Col. Carth.	*Gesta Collationis Carthaginensis*
Gesta Zenoph.	*Gesta apud Zenophilum*
Gil. *Excid.*	Gildas the Wise, *De excidio Britanniae (On the Ruin and Conquest of Britain)*
Gk.Anth.	*Greek Anthology*
Greg. VII *Ep.*	Gregory VII (Bishop of Rome), *Epistulae*

Greg. M.	Gregorius Magnus (Gregory the Great)	Greg. Naz. *Sel.*	Gregory of Nazianzus, *Ad Seleucum*
Greg. M. *Dial.*	Gregorius Magnus, *Dialogi*	Greg. Naz. *Theol. Or.*	Gregory of Nazianzus, *The*
Greg. M. *Ep.*	Gregorius Magnus, *Epistulae*		*Five Theological Orations*
Greg. M. *Ezech. hom.*	Gregorius Magnus, *In Ezechielem homiliae*	Greg. Naz. *Vita*	Gregory of Nazianzus, *De vita sua*
Greg. M. *Hom. Evan.*	Gregorius Magnus, *Homeliae in Evangelium*	Greg. Nyss.	Gregory of Nyssa
		Greg. Nyss. *Abl.*	Gregory of Nyssa, *To Ablabius*
Greg. M. *Mor.*	Gregorius Magnus, *De mortuis*	Greg. Nyss. *Anim. et res.*	Gregory of Nyssa, *De anima et resurrectione* (*On the Soul and Resurrection*)
Greg. M. *Moral.*	Gregorius Magnus, *Expositio in Librum Job, sive Moralium libri xxv* (*Moralia*)	Greg. Nyss. *Bas.*	Gregory of Nyssa, *In laudem fratris Basilii*
Greg. M. *Past.*	Gregorius Magnus, *Regula pastoralis* (*The Book of Pastoral Rule*)	Greg. Nyss. *Beat.*	Gregory of Nyssa, *De beatitudinibus* (*On the Beatitudes*)
Greg. M. *Reg.*	Gregorius Magnus, *Registrum* (*Register*)	Greg. Nyss. *Enc. Steph.*	Gregory of Nyssa, *Encomium in sanctum Stephanum protomartyrem*
Greg. M. *Reg. Ep.*	Gregorius Magnus, *Registrum Epistolarum*	Greg. Nyss. *Ep.*	Gregory of Nyssa, *Epistulae*
Greg. Naz.	Gregory of Nazianzus	Greg. Nyss. *Ep. can.*	Gregory of Nyssa, *Epistula canonica*
Greg. Naz. *Bap.*	Gregory of Nazianzus, *On Baptism*	Greg. Nyss. *Eun.*	Gregory of Nyssa, *Contra Eunomium* (*Against Eunomius*)
Greg. Naz. *C.Eun.*	Gregory of Nazianzus, *Contra Eunomium oratio prodialis*		
Greg. Naz. *C.Jul*	Gregory of Nazianzus, *Contra Julianum*	Greg. Nyss. *Fate*	Gregory of Nyssa, *Against Fate*
		Greg. Nyss. *Graec.*	Gregory of Nyssa, *Ad Graecos ex communibus notionibus*
Greg. Naz. *Carm.*	Gregory of Nazianzus, *Carmina*	Greg. Nyss. *Hex.*	Gregory of Nyssa, *Apologia in Hexaemeron* (*Apology for Hexaemeron*)
Greg. Naz. *Carm. dogm.*	Gregory of Nazianzus, *Carmina dogmatica*		
Greg. Naz. *Carm. ipso*	Gregory of Nazianzus, *Carmina de se ipso*	Greg. Nyss. *Hom. Eccl.*	Gregory of Nyssa, *In Ecclesiasten homiliae*
Greg. Naz. *Carm. mor.*	Gregory of Nazianzus, *Carmina moralia*	Greg. Nyss. *Hom. opif.*	Gregory of Nyssa, *De hominis opificio* (*On the Making of Man*)
Greg. Naz. *Ep.*	Gregory of Nazianzus, *Epistulae*	Greg. Nyss. *Hom. Theod.*	Gregory of Nyssa, *Homilia in Theodoro Martyre*
Greg. Naz. *Epigr.*	Gregory of Nazianzus, *Epigrams*	Greg. Nyss. *Icc.*	Gregory of Nyssa, *In canticum canticorum*
Greg. Naz. *Ir.*	Gregory of Nazianzus, *Contra iram*	Greg. Nyss. *In illud*	Gregory of Nyssa, *In illud: Tunc et ipse Filius*
Greg. Naz. *Or.*	Gregory of Nazianzus, *Orationes*	Greg. Nyss. *Inscrip.*	Gregory of Nyssa, *On the Inscriptions*
Greg. Naz. *P.Arc.*	Gregory of Nazianzus, *Poemata arcana*	Greg. Nyss. *Inscrip. Ps.*	Gregory of Nyssa, *In inscriptions psalmorum*
Greg. Naz. *Parth.*	Gregory of Nazianzus, *Parthenies epainos*	Greg. Nyss. *Lum.*	Gregory of Nyssa, *In Diem Luminum*

Greg. Nyss. *Maced.*	Gregory of Nyssa, *Adversus Macedonianos*
Greg. Nyss. *Mart. II*	Gregory of Nyssa, *In XL Martyres II*
Greg. Nyss. *Mort.*	Gregory of Nyssa, *De Mortuis*
Greg. Nyss. *N. Thr. Gods*	Gregory of Nyssa, *Not Three Gods*
Greg. Nyss. *Not.*	Gregory of Nyssa, *From Common Notions*
Greg. Nyss. *Or. catech. magna*	Gregory of Nyssa, *Oratio catechetica magna*
Greg. Nyss. *Or. dom.*	Gregory of Nyssa, *De oratione dominica*
Greg. Nyss. *Or. usur.*	Gregory of Nyssa, *Oratio contra usurarios*
Greg. Nyss. *Pascha*	Gregory of Nyssa, *In sanctum Pascha* (*On the Holy Passover*)
Greg. Nyss. *Perf.*	Gregory of Nyssa, *On Perfection*
Greg. Nyss. *Song*	Gregory of Nyssa, *On the Song of Songs*
Greg. Nyss. *Virg.*	Gregory of Nyssa, *De virginitate* (*On Virginity*)
Greg. Nyss. *Vita Greg. Thaum.*	Gregory of Nyssa, *Vita Gregorii Thaumathurgi*
Greg. Nyss. *Vita Mac.*	Gregory of Nyssa, *Vita Sanctae Macrinae* (*Life of Macrina*)
Greg. Nyss. *Vita Moy.*	Gregory of Nyssa, *De Vita Moysis* (*Life of Moses*)
Greg. Presb. *Vita Greg.*	Gregorius Presbyter, *Vita Sancti Gregorii Theologi*
Greg. T.	Gregory of Tours
Greg. T. *Glor. con.*	Gregory of Tours, *Liber in Gloria confessorum*
Greg. T. *Glor. Mart.*	Gregory of Tours, *In Gloria Martyrorum*
Greg. T. *Hist.*	Gregory of Tours, *Historiae* (*Histories*)
Greg. T. *Hist. Fr.*	Gregory of Tours, *Historia Francorum*
Greg. T. *Mir. Mar.*	Gregory of Tours, *Miracula Sancti Martini*
Greg. T. *Pass. Iul. mart.*	Gregory of Tours, *Liber de passione et virtutibus sancti Iuliani martyris*

Greg. T. *SDE*	Gregory of Tours, *Passio sanctorum septem dormientium apud Ephesum*
Greg. T. *Stell.*	Gregory of Tours, *De cursu stellarum ratio*
Greg. T. *Vit. Patr.*	Gregory of Tours, *Liber vitae Patrum*
Greg. T. *VSM*	Gregory of Tours, *De virtutibus sancti Martini* (*On the virtues of Saint Martin*)
Greg. Thaum.	Gregory Thaumaturgus
Greg. Thaum. *Ep. can.*	Gregory Thaumaturgus, *Epistula canonica*
Greg. Thaum. *Or. pan.*	Gregory Thaumaturgus, *Oratio panegyrica in Originem* (*Address of Thanksgiving to Origen*)
Guel.	*Guelferbytanis*
H.A.	*Historia Augusta*
H.A. Carus	*Historia Augusta, Carus*
H.A. Elag.	*Historia Augusta, Vita Elagabali*
H.A. Hadr.	*Historia Augusta, Vita Hadrianus*
H.A. Sev.Alex.	*Historia Augusta, Vita Severus Alexander*
Hdn.	Herodianus, *Historia ab excessu divi Marci*
Hdt.	Herodotus, *Historiae*
Her. *Hist.*	see Hdn.
Herac. *Nov.*	Heraclius, *Novellae*
Heraclit. *All.*	Heraclitus, *Allegoriae* (*Quaestiones homericae*)
Hermias *Sat.*	Hermias, *Satire on the Profane Philosophers*
Herod. *Hero.*	Aelius Herodian, *Herodiani technici reliquiae*
Hes.	Hesiod (Hesiodus)
Hes. *Op.*	Hesiod, *Opera et dies*
Hes. *Theog.*	Hesiod, *Theogonia*
Hesych. Jer. *Hom.*	Hesychius of Jerusalem, *Homiliae*
Hier. *Syn.*	Hierocles, *Synecdemus*
Hil. *Coll.*	Hilarius, *Collectana antiariana Parisiana*
Hil. Arl. *Serm. Vita Hon.*	Hilary of Arles, *Sermo de Vita S. Honorati* (*Sermon on the Life of St. Honoratus*)

ANCIENT AUTHORS AND PRIMARY SOURCES

Hil. Poit.	Hilary of Poitiers
Hil. Poit. *Adv. Val. Urs.*	Hilary of Poitiers, *Liber adversus Valentem et Ursacium*
Hil. Poit. *Arian.*	Hilary of Poitiers, *Contra Arianos*
Hil. Poit. *CAP*	Hilary of Poitiers, *Collectanea Antiariana Parisina* (*Fragmenta historica*)
Hil. Poit. *Comm. Matt.*	Hilary of Poitiers, *Commentarius in Evangelium Matthaei*
Hil. Poit. *Comm. Ps.*	Hilary of Poitiers, *Commentarii in Psalmos*
Hil. Poit. *Contra Aux.*	Hilary of Poitiers, *Contra Auxentium*
Hil. Poit. *Contra Const.*	Hilary of Poitiers, *Contra Constantium*
Hil. Poit. *Lib. (I) Const.*	Hilary of Poitiers, *Liber (I) ad Constantium*
Hil. Poit. *Syn.*	Hilary of Poitiers, *De synodis*
Hil. Poit. *Tract. 51 Ps*	Hilary of Poitiers, *Tractatus in LI Psalmum*
Hil. Poit. *Tract. Ps.*	Hilary of Poitiers, *Tractatus in Psalmum*
Hil. Poit. *Trin.*	Hilary of Poitiers, *De trinitate*
Hilary *Ep.*	Hilary (Bishop of Rome), *Epistulae*
Hipp.	Hippolytus of Rome
Hipp. *Antichr.*	Hippolytus of Rome, *De antichristo*
Hipp. *Can.*	Hippolytus of Rome, *Canones*
Hipp. *Chron.*	Hippolytus of Rome, *Chronicon*
Hipp. *Comm. Dan.*	Hippolytus of Rome, *Commentarium in Danielem*
Hipp. *El.*	Hippolytus of Rome, *Elenchos*
Hipp. *Haer.*	Hippolytus of Rome, *Refutatio omnium haeresium* (*Philosophoumena*; *Refutation of All Heresies*)
Hipp. *Jud.*	Hippolytus of Rome, *Adversus Judaeos*
Hipp. *Noet.*	Hippolytus of Rome, *Contra haeresin Noeti* (*Contra Noëtum*)
Hipp. *Trad. ap.*	Hippolytus of Rome, *Traditio apostolica* (*The Apostolic Tradition*)
Hipp. *Univ.*	Hippolytus of Rome, *De universo*
Hist. Aceph.	Historia Acephela
Hist. Aug. Hadr.	see H.A. Hadr.
Hist. Aug. Alex. Sev.	see H.A. Sev.Alex.
Hist. mon. Aeg.	Historia monachorum in Aegypto
Hom.	Homer (Homerus)
Hom. *Il.*	Homer, *Ilias* (*Iliad*)
Hom. *Od.*	Homer, *Odyssea* (*Odyssey*)
Hom. *Hym.*	Hymni Homerici
Homeri H. Cer.	Hom(eri) H(ymnus in) Cer(erem) (*Homeric Hymn to Demeter*)
Honor. *Ep.*	Honorius (Emperor), *Epistulae*
Hor.	Horace (Horatius)
Hor. *Ars.*	Horace, *Ars poetica*
Hor. *Carm.*	Horace, *Carmina* (*Odes*)
Hor. *Epod.*	Horace, *Epodi* (*Epodes*)
Hor. *Saec.*	Horace, *Carmen saeculare*
Hor. *Sat.*	Horace, *Satirae*
Hord. *Hist. Eccl.*	Hordericus Vitalis, *Historia Ecclesiastica*
Huc. *Vita Amati*	Hucbald, *Vita Amati*
Hyd.	Hydatius
Hyd. *Chron.*	Hydatius,*Chronicon*
Hyd. *Con. ch.*	Hydatius, *Continuatio chronicorum Hieronymianorum*
Hyg. *Fab.*	Hyginus, *Fabulae*
Hypomn.	Hypomnesticon
Iamb.	Iamblichus of Chalcis
Iamb. *An.*	Iamblichus of Chalcis, *De Anima* (*On the Soul*)
Iamb. *Comm. Math.*	Iamblichus of Chalcis, *De communi mathematica scientia* (*On the General Science of Mathematics*)
Iamb. *Myst.* (= *Reply*)	Iamblichus of Chalchis, *De mysteriis* (*On the Mysteries*)
Iamb. *Protr.*	Iamblichus of Chalcis, *Protrepticus in philosophiam* (*Exhortation to Philosophy*)

Iamb. *Reply* (= *Myst.*)	Iamblichus of Chalcis, *Reply of Master Abamon to the Letter of Porphyry to Anebo, and Solutions to the Questions it Contains*	Isid. Pelus. *Ep.*	Isidorus Pelusianus, *Epistulae*
		Isoc. *Or.*	Isocrates, *Orationes*
		Itin. Burd.	*Itinerarium Burdigalense* (Bordeaux Pilgrim)
Iamb. *Tim.*	Iamblichus of Chalcis, *In Timaeum*	J.R.	John Rufus
		J.R. *Pleroph.*	John Rufus, *Plerophoria*
		J.R. *Vita Pet.*	John Rufus, *Vita Petri Iberi*
Iamb. *Vita Pyth.*	Iamblichus of Chalcis, *De vita Pythagorica* (*On the Pythagorean Life*)	Jac. *Hom.*	Jacob of Serugh, *Homiliae*
		Jer.	Jerome (Hieronymus)
		Jer. *Adv. Jo. Hier.*	Jerome, *Adversus Johannem Hierosolymitanum*
Ild. *Vir. Ill.*	Ildefonsus, *De viris illustribus*		
Inn. *Ep.*	Innocent I, *Epistulae*	Jer. *Chron.*	Jerome, *Chronicon Eusebii a Graeco Latine redditum et continuatum*
Iren.	Irenaeus of Lyon		
Iren. *Epid.*	Irenaeus of Lyon, *Epideixis tou apostolikou kērygmatos* (*Demonstration of the Apostolic Preaching*)		
		Jer. *Comm.*	Jerome, *Commentarii*
		Jer. *Comm. Abd.*	Jerome, *Commentariorum in Abdiam liber*
		Jer. *Comm. Agg.*	Jerome, *Commentariorum in Aggaeum liber*
Iren. *Haer.*	Irenaeus of Lyon, *Adversus haereses* (*Against Heresies*)	Jer. *Comm. Am.*	Jerome, *Commentariorum in Amos libri III*
Iren. *Trad. ap.*	Irenaeus of Lyon, *Traditio apostolica*	Jer. *Comm. Dan.*	Jerome, *Commentarii in Danielem*
IRT	*Inscriptions of Roman Tripolitania*	Jer. *Comm. Eccl.*	Jerome, *Commentarii in Ecclesiasten*
Isaac *Second Part*	Isaac of Nineveh, *Second Part*	Jer. *Comm. Eph.*	Jerome, *Commentariorum in Epistulam ad Ephesios libri III*
Isid.	Isidore of Seville		
Isid. *Chron. Mai.*	Isidore of Seville, *Chronica Maiora*		
Isid. *De Nat. rer.*	Isidore of Seville, *De Natura Rerum*	Jer. *Comm. Ezech.*	Jerome, *Commentariorum in Ezechielem libri XVI*
Isid. *De Ortu*	Isidore of Seville, *De ortu et obitu patrum*	Jer. *Comm. Gal.*	Jerome, *Commentariorum in Epistulam ad Galatas libri III*
Isid. *Diff. rer.*	Isidore of Seville, *De differentiis rerum*		
Isid. *Etym.*	Isidore of Seville, *Etymologiae*	Jer. *Comm. Habac.*	Jerome, *Commentariorum in Habacuc libri II*
Isid. *Expos.*	Isidore of Seville, *Expositiones sacramentorum seu quaestiones in Vetus Testamentum*	Jer. *Comm. Isa.*	Jerome, *Commentariorum in Isaiam libri XVIII*
		Jer. *Comm. Jer.*	Jerome, *Commentariorum in Jeremiam libri VI*
Isid. *Hist.*	Isidore of Seville, *Historia de regibus Gothorum, Vandalorum et Suevorum*	Jer. *Comm. Joel.*	Jerome, *Commentariorum in Joelem liber*
		Jer. *Comm. Jon.*	Jerome, *Commentariorum in Jonam liber*
Isid. *In Num.*	Isidore of Seville, *In Numeros* (*Commentary on Numbers*)		
		Jer. *Comm. Mal.*	Jerome, *Commentariorum in Malachiam liber*
Isid. *Quaest.*	Isidore of Seville, *Quaestiones in III Regum*		
		Jer. *Comm. Matt.*	Jerome, *Commentariorum in Matthaeum libri IV*
Isid. *Sent.*	Isidore of Seville, *Sententiae*		
Isid. *Vir. ill.*	Isidore of Seville, *De viris illustribus*		

Jer. *Comm. Mich.*	Jerome, *Commentariorum in Michaeum libri II*	Jer. *Tract. Ps II*	Jerome, *Tractatuum in psalmos series altera*
Jer. *Comm. Phlm.*	Jerome, *Commentariorum in Epistulam ad Philemonem liber*	Jer. *Tract. Ps.*	Jerome, *Tractatus in Psalmos*
		Jer. *Vigil.*	Jerome, *Adversus Vigilantium*
Jer. *Comm. Ps.*	Jerome, *Commentarioli in Psalmos*	Jer. *Vir. ill.*	Jerome, *De viris illustribus*
		Jer. *Vit. Hil.*	Jerome, *Vita S. Hilarionis eremitae*
Jer. *Comm. Tit.*	Jerome, *Commentariorum in Epistulam ad Titum liber*	Jer. *Vit. Paul.*	Jerome, *Vita S. Pauli, primi eremitae*
Jer. *Comm. Zach.*	Jerome, *Commentariorum in Zachariam libri III*	John Ant. *Frgm(s).*	John of Antioch, *Fragment(s)*
		John Bicl. *Chron.*	John of Biclaro, *Chronicle*
Jer. *Dard.*	Jerome, *Ad Dardanum*	John Eph.	John of Ephesus
Jer. *Ep.*	Jerome, *Epistulae*	John Eph. *Hist eccl*	John of Ephesus, *Historia ecclesiastica*
Jer. *Expl. Dan.*	Jerome, *Explanatio in Danielem*	John Eph. *Vitae*	John of Ephesus, *Vitae sanctorum orientalium*
Jer. *Helv.*	Jerome, *Adversus Helvidium de Mariae virginitate perpetua*	John Eph. *Vitae Beat.*	John of Ephesus, *Vitae Beatorum Orientalium*
Jer. *Hom. in Eph.*	Jer. *Homiliae in Ephesios*	John Gram. *Apol.*	John the Grammarian, *Apologia concilii Chalcedonensis*
Jer. *Hom. Nat. Dom.*	Jerome, *Homily on the Birth of the Lord*	John Max.	John Maxentius
Jer. *Jo. Hier.*	Jerome, *Adversus Joannem Hierosolymitanum liber*	John Max. *Nes.*	John Maxentius, *Dialogus contra Nestorianos (libri duo)*
Jer. *Jov.*	Jerome, *Adversus Jovinianum libri II*	John Max. *Nest. Pelag.*	John Maxentius, *Capitula edita contra Nestorianos et Pelagianos ad satisfactionem fratrum*
Jer. *Lucif.*	Jerome, *Altercatio Luciferiani et orthodoxi seu dialogus contra Luciferianos*	John Max. *Prof. brev.*	John Maxentius, *Item eiusdem professio brevissima catholicae fidei*
Jer. *Nom. hebr.*	Jerome, *De nominibus hebraicis (Liber nominum)*	John Mos. *Prat. Spir.*	John Moschus, *Pratum Spirituale*
Jer. *Pelag.*	Jerome, *Adversus Pelagianos dialogi III*	John Nik. *Chron.*	John of Nikiu, *Chronicle*
Jer. *Qu. hebr. Gen.*	Jerome, *Quaestionum hebraicarum liber in Genesim*	Jon. *Vita Col.*	Jonas of Bobbio, *Vita Columbani*
		Jor.	Jordanes
Jer. *Reg. Pachom.*	Jerome, *Regula S. Pachomii, e Graeco*	Jor. *Get.*	Jordanes, *Getica*
		Jor. *Rom.*	Jordanes, *Romana*
Jer. *Ruf.*	Jerome, *Adversus Rufinum libri III (Apology against Rufinus)*	Jos.	Flavius Josephus
		Jos. *Ant.*	Flavius Josephus, *Antiquitates Judaicae (Jewish Antiquities)*
Jer. *Sit.*	Jerome, *De situ et nominibus locorum Hebraicorum (Liber locorum)*	Jos. *Apion.*	Flavius Josephus, *Contra Apionem (Against Apion)*
Jer. *Tract. Marc.*	Jerome, *Tractatus in Evangelium Marci*	Jos. *Bell.*	Flavius Josephus, *Bellum Judaicum (Jewish War)*

Jos. *Vita*	Flavius Josephus, *Vita* (*Life*)	Juv. *Sat.*	Juvenal, *Satirae*
Jos. Asen.	*Joseph and Aseneth*	Juven. *ELQ*	Juvencus, *Evangeliorum libri*
JSZ	*History of John Son of Zebedee*		*quattuor*
Jul.	Julian the Apostate (Emperor)	Kor. *Mes.*	Koriun, *Life of Mesrop*
Jul. *Caes.*	Julian the Apostate, *Caesares*	Lact.	Lactantius
Jul. *Deo.*	Julian the Apostate, *Ad*	Lact. *Epit.*	Lactantius, *Epitome*
	deorum Matrem		*divinarum institutionum*
Jul. *Ep.*	Julian the Apostate, *Epistulae*		(*Epitome of the Divine*
Jul. *Gal.*	Julian the Apostate, *Contra*		*Institutes*)
	Galileos (*Against the*	Lact. *Inst.*	Lactantius, *Divinae*
	Galileans)		*institutiones* (*The Divine*
Jul. *Hel.*	Julian the Apostate, *Hymn to*		*Institutes*)
	King Helios	Lact. *Ir.*	Lactantius, *De ira Dei*
Jul. *Or.*	Julian the Apostate, *Orationes*		(*The Wrath of God*)
Jul. *Aecl.*	Julian of Aeclanum	Lact. *Mort.*	Lactantius, *De mortibus*
Jul. Aecl. *Ep. Valer.*	Julian of Aeclanum, *Epistula*		*persecutorum* (*The Deaths*
	ad Valerium comitem		*of the Persecutors*)
Jul. Aecl. *Flor.*	Julian of Aeclanum,	Lact. *Opif.*	Lactantius, *De opificio Dei*
	Ad Florum		(*The Workmanship of God*)
Jul. Aecl. *Ruf.*	Julian of Aeclanum, *Epistula*	*Laur. Frgm.*	*Laurentian Fragment*
	ad Rufum	Leo M.	Leo the Great (Leo Magnus)
Jul. Aecl.	Julian of Aeclanum,	Leo M. *Ep.*	Leo the Great, *Epistulae*
Tract. Proph.	*Tractatus Prophetarum*	Leo M. *Serm.*	Leo the Great, *Sermones*
	Osee, Iohel et Amos	Leo M. *Tom.*	Leo the Great, *Tomus*
Jul. Aecl. *Turb.*	Julian of Aeclanum,	Leo M. *Tract.*	Leo the Great, *Tractatus*
	Ad Turbantium	Leon. Byz.	Leontius of Byzantium
Jul. Hal. *Anath.*	Julian of Halicarnassus,	Leon. Byz.	Leontius of Byzantium,
	Anathema	*Depr. Nest.*	*Deprehensio et Triumphus*
Jul. Pom.	Julian Pomerius, *De vita*		*super Nestorianos*
Vita cont.	*contemplativa*	Leon. Byz. *Epap.*	Leontius of Byzantium,
Just.	Justin Martyr		*Epaporemata*
Just. 1 *Apol.*	Justin Martyr, *Apologia i*	Leon. Byz. *Epil.*	Leontius of Byzantium,
	(*First Apology*)		*Epilyseis*
Just. 2 *Apol.*	Justin Martyr, *Apologia ii*	Leon. Byz.	Leontius of Byzantium,
	(*Second Apology*)	*Nest. Eut.*	*Contra Nestorianos*
Just. *Dial.*	Justin Martyr, *Dialogus cum*		*et Eutychianos*
	Tryphone Judaeo (*Dialogue*	Leon. Con. *Hom.*	Leontius of Constantinople,
	with Trypho)		*Homiliae*
Justin, *Epit.*	Justin, *Epitome*	*Let. Ly. Vie.*	*Letter of the Churches of Lyons*
Justin.	Justinian		*and Vienne*
Justin. *Ed. Or.*	Justinian, *Edictum contra*	*lex Put.*	*lex Puteolana*
	Origenem	*Lib. Gen.*	*Liber Genealogus*
Justin. *Ep. Tria Cap.*	Justinian, *Epistula contra Tria*	*Lib. Grad.*	*Liber Graduum*
	Capitula	*Lib. moz.*	*Liber mozarabicus*
Justin. *Inst.*	Justinian, *The Institutes of*	*Lib. ord.*	*Liber ordinum*
	Justinian	*Lib. prec.*	*Libellus precum*
Justin. *Nov.*	Justinian, *Novellae*	*Lib. S. Steph.*	*Liber de miraculis sancti*
Justin. *Nov. App.*	Justinian, *Novellae Appendix*		*Stephani*

LibCar. *Brev.*	Liberatus of Carthage, *Breviarium causae Nestorianorum et Eutcyhianorum*	Luc. *Jupp. trag.*	Lucian of Samosata, *Juppiter tragoedus* (*Zeus Rants*)
		Luc. *Laps.*	Lucian of Samosata, *Pro lapsu inter salutandum* (*A Slip of the Tongue in Greeting*)
Liber. *Ep.*	Liberius of Rome, *Epistulae*		
Libian.	Libianius of Antioch	Luc. *Luct.*	Lucian of Samosata, *De luctu* (*Funerals*)
Libian. *Ep.*	Libianius of Antioch, *Epistulae*		
		Luc. *Musc. laud.*	Lucian of Samosata, *Muscae laudatio* (*The Fly*)
Libian. *Or.*	Libianius of Antioch, *Orationes*		
		Luc. *Nigr.*	Lucian of Samosata, *Nigrinus*
Lic. Car. *Ep.*	Licinianus Carthagensis, *Epistula*	Luc. *Par.*	Lucian of Samosata, *De parasito* (*The Parasite*)
LiCo	*Liber Comicus*	Luc. *Peregr.*	Lucian of Samosata, *De morte Peregrini* (*The Passing of Peregrinus*)
Livy	Livy (Livius), *Ab urbe condita* (*From the Founding of the City*)		
		Luc. *Philops.*	Lucian of Samosata, *Philopseudes* (*The Lover of Lies*)
Loc. sanc.	*De locis sanctis martyrum quae sunt foris civitatis Romae*		
		Luc. *Pisc.*	Lucian of Samosata, *Piscator* (*The Dead Come to Life, or The Fisherman*)
Lol. *Phoin.*	Lollianos, *Phoinikika*		
Longus *Daphn.*	Longus, *Daphnis and Chloe*		
LP	*Le liber pontificalis*	Luc. *Prom.*B1329	Lucian of Samosata, *Prometheus*
Luc.	Lucian of Samosata		
Luc. *Alex.*	Lucian of Samosata, *Alexander* (*Pseudomantis*)	Luc. *Symp.*	Lucian of Samosata, *Symposium* (*The Carousal, or The Lapiths*)
Luc. *Bis acc.*	Lucian of Samosata, *Bis accusatus* (*The Double Indictment*)		
		Luc. *Syr. d.*	Lucian of Samosata, *De syria dea* (*On the Syrian Goddess*)
Luc. *Char.*	Lucian of Samosata, *Charon*	Luc. *Vit. Auct.*	Lucian of Samosata, *Vitarum auctio* (*Philosophies for Sale*)
Luc. *Dial. mort.*	Lucian of Samosata, *Diologi mortuorum* (*Dialogues of the Dead*)		
		Lucan, *Phar.*	Lucan, *Pharsalia*
Luc. *Eunuch.*	Lucian of Samosata, *Eunuchus* (*The Eunuch*)	Lucif.	Lucifer of Cagliari
		Lucif. *Athan.*	Lucifer of Cagliari, *De Athanasio*
Luc. *Fug.*	Lucian of Samosata, *Fugitivi* (*The Runaways*)		
		Lucif. *Conv. haer.*	Lucifer of Cagliari, *De non conveniendo cum haereticis*
Luc. *Hermot.*	Lucian of Samosata, *Hermotimus* (*De sectis*) (*Hermotimus, or Sects*)		
		Lucif. *Morien.*	Lucifer of Cagliari, *Moriendum esse pro dei filio*
Luc. *Icar.*	Lucian of Samosata, *Icaromenippus*	Lucif. *Par. deliq.*	Lucifer of Cagliari, *De non parcendo in deum deliquentibus*
Luc. *Jud. voc.*	Lucian of Samosata, *Judicium vocalium* (*The Consonants at Law*)		
		Lucr. *Rer.*	Lucretius, *De rerum natura*
		LV	*Leges Visigothorum* (*Visigothic Code*)
Luc. *Jupp. conf.*	Lucian of Samosata, *Juppiter confutatus* (*Zeus Catechized*)		
		Lyc. *Adv. Leo.*	Lycurgus, *Against Leocrates*
		Lyd.	John Lydus

Lyd. *Mag.*	John Lydus, *De magistratibus*	Marc.Aur. *Med.*	Marcus Aurelius, *Meditationes*
Lyd. *Men.*	John Lydus, *De Mensibus*	Marc. Diac. *Vita Porph.*	Marcus Diaconus (Mark the Deacon), *Vita Porphyrii (Life of Porphyry)*
Lysias	Lysias, *Speeches*		
Mac. *Apoc.*	Macarius of Magnesia, *Apocriticus*	Marcel. *Chron.*	Marcellinus, *Chronicon*
Maced. *Ep.*	Macedonius (Vicarius Africae), *Epistulae*	Mark M. *Spir.*	Mark the Monk, *On the Spiritual Law*
Macr.	Macrobius	Mart. Apol. Sak.	Martyrdom of Apollonios Sakkeas
Macr. *Sat.*	Macrobius, *Saturnalia*		
Macr. *Som.*	Macrobius, *In Somnium Scipionis*	Mart. Brag. *Corr. rust.*	Martin of Braga, *De correctione rusticorum (On the Reform of Rustics)*
Mal. *Frgm(s).*	Malchus of Philadelphia, *Fragmenta*	Mart. Carp. Pap. Aga.	Martyrdom of Carpus, Papylus, Agathonice
Malalas *Chron.*	John Malalas, *Chronographia*		
Man. *Astro.*	Marcus Manilius, *Astronomica*	Mart. Con.	Martyrdom of Saint Conon
Mandak. *Hom.*	Johannes Mandakuni, *Homiliae*	Mart. Fel.	Martyrdom of Felix the Bishop
		Mart. Fruc.	Martyrdom of Fructuosus
Mar. *Vita Proc.*	Marinus of Neapolis, *Vita Procli (Life of Proclus)*	Mart. Hier.	Martyriologium Hieronymianum
Mar. Aven. *Chron.*	Marius of Avenches, *Chronicle*	Mart. Iren. Sir.	Martyrdom of Irenaeus Bishop of Sirmium
Mar. Com. *Chron.*	Marcellinus Comes, *Chronicon*	Mart. Iust.	Martyrium Sancti Iustini et Sociorum
Mar. Rep.	*Book of Mary's Repose*	Mart. Jul.	Martyrdom of Julius the Veteran
Mar. Vic.	Marius Victorinus		
Mar. Vic. Ar.	Marius Victorinus, *Adversus Arium (Against Arius)*	Mart. Lugd	Martyrium Lugdunensium
Mar. Vic. Ad Cand.	Marius Victorinus, *Ad Candidum Arrianum*	Mart. Mar. Jam.	Martyrdom of Marian and James
Mar. Vic. *Comm. Cic.*	Marius Victorinus, *Commenta in Ciceronis Rhetorica*	Mart. Mont. Luc.	The Martyrdom of Montanus, Lucius, and Their Companions
Mar. Vic. *Hom. Rec.*	Marius Victorinus, *De homoousio recipiendo*	Mart. Perp.	Martyrium vel Passio Perpetuae et Felicitatis (or Passio Sanctarum Perpetuae et Felicitatis; Passion of Perpetua and Felicitas)
Mar. Vic. *In Eph.*	Marius Victorinus, *In epistolam Pauli ad Ephesios libri duo*		
Mar. Vic. *In Gal.*	Marius Victorinus, *In epistolam Pauli ad Galatas libri duo*	Mart. Pet.	Martyrdom of Peter
		Mart. Pion.	Martyrium Pionii (Martyrdom of Pionius)
Mar. Vic. *In Phil.*	Marius Victorinus, *In epistolam Pauli ad Philippenses liber unicus*	Mart. S. Crisp.	Martyrium Sanctae Crispinae
		Martial	Martial
		Martial *Epigr.*	Martial, *Epigrammata*
Marc. Anc.	Marcellus of Ancyra	Martial *Spec.*	Martial, *De spectaculis*
Marc. Anc. *Ep.*	Marcellus of Ancyra, *Epistula*	Maur.	Maurists' Collection of Letters
Marc. Anc. *Frgm.(s)*	Marcellus of Ancyra, *Fragment(s)*	Max.	Maximus the Confessor
Marc. Anc. *Sanc. eccl.*	Marcellus of Ancyra, *De sancta ecclesia*	Max. *Amb. lib.*	Maximus the Confessor, *Ambiguorum liber*

Max. *Car.*	Maximus the Confessor, *De caritate*	Mod. *Dig.*	Herennius Modestinus, *Digest*
Max. *Ep.*	Maximus the Confessor, *Epistulae*	Mont. Tol. *Ep.*	Montanus of Toledo, *Epistulae*
Max. *Myst.*	Maximus the Confessor, *Mystagogia*	Mos. *PH*	Moses of Chorene, *Patmut'iwn Hayoc'* (*History of Armenia*)
Max. *Opus. theol. pol.*	Maximus the Confessor, *Opuscula theologica et polemica*	*MRLC*	*Mosaicarum et Romanarum Legum Collatio*
Max. *Quaest. dub.*	Maximus the Confessor, *Quaestiones et dubia*	Muir. *Vita Pat.*	Muirchú, *Vita sancti Patricii*
Max. *Thal.*	Maximus the Confessor, *Quaestiones ad Thalassium*	Mur.Frgm.	Muratorian Fragment
		Narsai	Narsai
Max. *Var. def.*	Maximus the Confessor, *Variae definitiones*	Narsai, *Hom.*	Narsai, *Homily*
		Narsai, *Hom. Ascen.*	Narsai, *Homily on the Feast Day of the Ascension*
Max. Taur. *Serm.*	Maxiumus Taurinensis (Maximus of Turin), *Sermones*	Nem. *Nat. hom.*	Nemesius of Emesa, *De natura hominis* (*On the Nature of Man*)
Max. Tyre *Or.*	Maximus of Tyre, *The Philosophical Orations*	Nest.	Nestorius
		Nest. *Bazaar*	Nestorius, *The Bazaar of Heracleides*
Maxim. *Eleg.*	Maximianus, *Elegies*		
Mel.	Melito of Sardis	Nest. *Ep. Cael.*	Nestorius, *Epistula ad Caelestinum papam*
Mel. *An. Cor.*	Melito of Sardis, *De anima et corpore fragmentum*	Nest. *Ep. Cyril.*	Nestorius, *Epistulae ad Cyrillum*
Mel. *Pascha*	Melito of Sardis, *Peri Pascha* (*On the Passover*)	Nest. *Heracl.*	Nestorius, *Liber Heraclidis*
		Nic.	Nicephorus
Men.	Menander	Nic. *Antir.*	Nicephorus, *Antirrhetici tres adversus Constantinum Copronymum*
Men. *Epitr.*	Menander, *Epitrepontes*		
Men. Prot. *Hist.*	Menander Protector, *Historia*	Nic. *Epik*	Nicephorus, *Epikrisis*
Merc.	Marius Mercator	Nic. *Vita*	Nicephorus, *Vita*
Merc. *Com. Coel.*	Marius Mercator, *Commonitorium de Coelestio imperatori oblatum*	Nic.Cal. *Hist. eccl.*	Nicephorus Callistus, *Historia ecclesiastica*
Merc. *Diss. haer.*	Marius Mercator, *Dissertatio prima de haeresi et Libris Nestorii*	Nich. *Ep.*	Nicholas I (Bishop of Rome), *Epistulae*
		Nicom. *Introd.*	Nicomachus of Gerasa, *Introductio arithmetica*
Merob.	Merobaudes	Nik. *Chron.*	John of Nikiu, *Chronicle*
Merob. *Carm.*	Merobaudes, *Carmina*	Nil. Anc. *Com. Cant.*	Nilus of Ancyra, *Commentarii in canticum canticorum*
Merob. *Pan.*	Merobaudes, *Panegyricus*		
Meth.	Methodius of Olympus	*Not. Dign.*	*Notitia dignitatum*
Meth. *Res.*	Methodius of Olympus, *De resurrectione*	*Not. Dign. Occ.*	*Notitia dignitatum, Occidentalis*
Meth. *Symp.*	Methodius of Olympus, *Symposium* (*Convivium decem virginum*)	Nov.	Novatian
		Nov. *Spec.*	Novatian, *De spectaculis*
		Nov. *Trin.*	Novatian, *De Trinitate* (*On Trinity*)
Min.Fel. *Oct.*	Minucius Felix, *Octavius*	*Nov. Val.*	*Novellae Valentiniani*
Mir. Art.	*Miracula Artemii*		

NPCA	*Notitia provinciarum et civitatum Africae*	Or. *Comm. Jo.*	Origen, *Commentarii in evangelium Joannis*
NPCA.Num.	*– Numidiae*	Or. *Comm. Matt.*	Origen, *Commentarium in evangelium Matthaei*
Num. *Frgm(s).*	Numenius of Apamea, *Fragment(s)*	Or. *Comm. Ps.*	Origen, *Commentarii in Psalmos*
Obseq. *Prod.*	Julius Obsequens, *De prodigiis*	Or. *Comm. Rom.*	Origen, *Commentarii in Romanos*
Oecum.	Oecumenius	Or. *Comm. ser. Matt.*	Origen, *Commentarium series in evangelium Matthaei*
Oecum. Comm. 1 Cor.	Oecumenius, *Commentarium In Epistulam 1 ad Corinthios*	Or. *Comm. Tit.*	Or. *Commentarius in Titum*
Oecum. Comm. Rev.	Oecumenius, *Commentary on Revelation*	Or. *Dial.*	Origen, *Dialogus cum Heraclide (Dialogue with Heraclides)*
Oecum. Frgms. Heb.	Oecumenius, *Fragments in Hebrews*	Or. *Ep. Afr.*	Origen, *Epistula ad Africanum*
Olymp. *Frag.*	Olympiodorus of Thebes, *Fragmenta*	Or. *Ep. Greg.*	Origen, *Epistula ad Gregorium Thaumaturgum (Letter to Gregory Thaumaturgus)*
Olymp. Y.	Olympiodorus the Younger		
Olymp. Y. Phaed.	Olympiodorus the Younger, *In Phaedonem*	Or. *Exc. Lat.*	Origen, *Excerpta Latina Barbari*
Olymp. Y. Proleg. Arist. Cat.	Olympiodorus the Younger, *Prolegomena in Aristotelis Categorias*	Or. *Fr. 1 Cor.*	Origen, *Fragmenta ex commentariis in epistulam i ad Corinthios*
Op. Imp. Matt.	*Opus Imperfectum in Matthaeum (incomplete Commentary on Matthew)*	Or. *Fr. Cat. Cor.*	Origen, *Fragments from the Catenae on 1 Corinthians*
Opt.	Optatus of Milevis	Or. *Fr. Gen.*	Origen, *Fragmenta in Genesim*
Opt. *App.*	Optatus of Milevis, *Appendix*	Or. *Fr. Jer.*	Origen, *Fragmenta in Jeremiam*
Opt. *Parm.*	Optatus of Milevis, *Contra Parmenianum Donastistam (Against Parmenian the Donatist)*	Or. *Fr. Lam.*	Origen, *Fragmenta in Lamentationes*
		Or. *Fr. Luc.*	Origen, *Fragmenta in Lucam*
Opt. Por. *Carm.*	Optatianus Porphyrius, *Carmina*	Or. *Fr. Ps.*	Origen, *Fragmenta in Psalmos 1–150*
Or.	Origen (Origenes)	Or. *Hom. 1 Reg.*	Origen, *Homiliae in I Reges*
Or. *Adnot. Gen.*	Origen, *Adnotationes in Genesim*	Or. *Hom. 1 Sam*	Origen, *Homilies on 1 Samuel*
		Or. *Hom. Cant.*	Origen, *Homiliae in Canticum*
Or. *Adnot. Lev.*	Origen, *Adnotationes in Leviticum*	Or. *Hom. Exod.*	Origen, *Homiliae in Exodum*
		Or. *Hom. Ezech.*	Origen, *Homiliae in Ezechielem*
Or. *Ap.*	Origen, *Apologies*		
Or. *Cant. (Adulesc.)*	Origen, *In Canticum canticorum (libri duo quos scripsit in adulescentia)*	Or. *Hom. Gen.*	Origen, *Homiliae in Genesim*
		Or. *Hom. Isa.*	Origen, *Homiliae in Isaiam*
		Or. *Hom. Jer.*	Origen, *Homiliae in Jeremiam*
Or. *Cels.*	Origen, *Contra Celsum*	Or. *Hom. Jes. Nav.*	Origen, *In Jesu Nave homiliae xxvi*
Or. *Comm. Cant.*	Origen, *Commentarius in Canticum*		
		Or. *Hom. Job*	Origen, *Homiliae in Job*
Or. *Comm. Gen.*	Origen, *Commentarii in Genesim*	Or. *Hom. Jos.*	Origen, *Homiliae in Josuam*
		Or. *Hom. Judic.*	Origen, *Homiliae in Judices*
		Or. *Hom. Lev.*	Origen, *Homiliae in Leviticum*

Or. *Hom. Luc.*	Origen, *Homiliae in Lucam*	P.Beatty	Chester Beatty Biblical Papyri
Or. *Hom. Num.*	Origen, *Homiliae in Numeros*	P.Ber.	Papyrus Berolinensis (see BG)
Or. *Hom. Ps.*	Origen, *Homiliae in Psalmos*	P.Bodmer	Bodmer Papyri
Or. *Hom. Sam.*	Origen, *Homiliae in Samuelem*	P.Cair.	Papyrus Cairo
Or. *Mart.*	Origen, *Exhortatio ad martyrium* (*Exhortation to Martyrdom*)	P.CtYBR	Papyri, Beinecke Library, Yale University
		P.Fack.	Papyrus Fackelmann
Or. *Or.*	Origen, *De oratione* (*Peri proseuchēs*; *On Prayer*)	P.g.l.	Papiri greci e latini
		P.GrM	Papyri Graecae magicae (Greek Magical Papyri)
Or. *Pasch.*	Origen, *De pascha*		
Or. *Philoc.*	Origen, *Philocalia*	P.Hamb.	Papyrus Hamburg
Or. *Princ.*	Origen, *De principiis* (*On First Principles*)	P.Hanna	Papyrus Hanna
		P.Heid.	Papyrus Heidelberg
Or. *Res.*	Origen, *De resurrectione libri ii*	P.Herc.	Papyrus Herculaneum
Or. *Sel. Gen.*	Origen, *Selecta in Genesim*	P.Ital.	Ppapyri Italian
Or. *Sel. Num.*	Origen, *Selecta in Numeros*	P.Lond.	Greek Papyri in the British Museum, London
Or. *Sel. Ps.*	Origen, *Selecta in Psalmos*		
Orac. chald.	*De oraculis chaldaicis* (*Chaldaean Oracles*)	P.Lond.Lit.	Catalogue of the Literary Papyri in the British Museum
Oratio fun. Chrys.	*Oratio in funebris Iohannis Chrysostomi*		
		P.Mich.	Papyrus Michigan
Ordo R.	*Ordo Romanus*	P.Oxy.	Papyrus Oxyrhynchus
Orie. *Com.*	Orientius, *Commonitorium*	P.Pet.	Papyrus Petaus
Oros.	Orosius	P.Ryl.	Papyri Rylands
Oros. *Adv. pag.*	Orosius, *Historiae adversus Paganos libri septem* (*History Against the Pagans*)	P.Saint Sabas	Papyrus of the Monastery of Saint-Sabas
		P.Schøy.	Papyrus Schøyen
Oros. *Lib. apol.*	Orosius, *Liber apologeticus contra Pelagium de arbitrii libertate*	P.Vindob.G.	Papyrus Vindobonensis Graecus
		P.Vindobonensis hist. gr.	Papyrus of Vienne
Ovid	Ovid (Ovidius)	P.Deac.	Paul the Deacon
Ovid, *Am.*	Ovid, *Amores*	P.Deac. *Hist. Lang.*	Paul the Deacon, *Historia gentis Langobardorum*
Ovid, *Ars*	Ovid, *Ars amatoria*		
Ovid, *Fast.*	Ovid, *Fasti*	P.Deac. *Vita Ambr.*	Paul the Deacon, *Vita di sancti Ambrogio* = Paulus Diaconus, *Vita Sancti Ambrosii*
Ovid, *Met.*	Ovid, *Metamorphoses*		
Ovid, *Rem.*	Ovid, *Remedia Amoris*		
Ovid, *Trist.*	Ovid, *Tristia*		
Ovid., *Ep. Pon.*	Ovid, *Epistulae ex Ponto*		
P.Alex.	Greek papyri Greco-Roman Museum, Alexandria, Egypt	Pac. *Pan.*	Pacatus, *Panegyric*
		Pach.	Pachomius of Tabennese
P.Amherst	Papyrus Amherst	Pach. *Ep.*	Pachomius of Tabennese, *Epistulae*
P.Ant.	Antinoopolis Papyri		
P.Athos	Papyri Athos	Pach. *Instr.*	Pachomius of Tabennese, *Instruction on the Six Days of the Passover*
P.Bad.	Veröffentlichungen aus den badischen Papyrus-Sammlungen		
		Pach. *Instr. Spit.*	Pachomius of Tabennese, *Instruction Concerning a Spiteful Monk*
P.Bas.	Basel Papyri		
P.Beat. Panop.	Papyrus Beatty Panopolis		

Pach. *Pr.*	Pachomius of Tabennese, *Pachomian Precepts*	Pass. Maxim. et Isa.	*Passio Martyrum Maximiani et Isaac*
Pacian	Pacian	Pass. Pim.	*Passio Pimenii*
Pacian *Ep.*	Pacian, *Epistola*	Pass. Praei.	*Passio Praeiecti*
Pacian *Novat.*	Pacian, *Contra tractatus Novatianorum*	Pass. Sat.	*Passion of Saturnini*
		Pass. Scil.	*Passion of the Scillitan Martyrs*
Pacian *Paen.*	Pacian, *De paenitentibus*	Pass. Seb.	*Passio Sebastiani*
Pall.	Palladius of Helenopolis	PaSu	*Parochiale Suevum*
Pall. *Dial.*	Palladius of Helenopolis, *Dialogus de vita Johannis Chrysostomi* (*Dialogue on the Life of St. John Chrysostom*)	Pat.	Patrick (Saint)
		Pat. *Conf.*	Patrick, *Confessio*
		Pat. *Ep.*	Patrick, *Epistula*
		Pau. Sent.	Paulus, *Sententiae*
		Paul Mér. *VSPE*	Paul of Mérida, *Vitas Sanctorum Patrum Emeretensium*
Pall. *Dial.H.*	Palladius of Helenopolis, *Dialogus Historicus Palladii*		
Pall. *Hist. Laus.*	Palladius of Helenopolis, *Historia Lausiaca*	Paul.	Paulinus of Nola
		Paul. *Carm.*	Paulinus of Nola, *Carmina*
Pall. *Par. Fath.*	Palladius of Helenopolis, *Paradise of the Fathers*	Paul. *Ep.*	Paulinus of Nola, *Epistulae*
		Paul. Mil. *Vita Ambr.*	Paulinus of Milan, *Vita sancti Ambrosii*
Pamp.	Pamphilus		
Pamp. *Ap.*	Pamphilus, *Apology*	Paul. Pel.	Paulinus of Pella
Pamp. *Apol. Or.*	Pamphilus, *Apologia pro Origene*	Paul. Pel. *Euch.*	Paulinus of Pella, *Eucharisticos*
Pan. *Frgm*(*s*).	Pantaenus, *Fragment*(*s*)	Paul. Pel. *Or.*	Paulinus of Pella, *Oratio*
Paph.	Paphnutius	Paul. Pér. *Vita Mar.*	Paulinus of Périgueux, *Vita Martini*
Paph. *Hist. Monks*	Paphnutius, *Histories of the Monks of Upper Egypt*	Paus. *Descr.*	Pausanias, *Graeciae description* (*Description of Greece*)
Paph. *Onup.*	Paphnutius, *Vita Sancti Onuphrii*		
Papias *Frgm*(*s*).	Papias of Hieropolis, *Fragment*(*s*)	P'aws.	*P'awstos Buzand*
		Pel.	Pelagius
Pasch. *Partu*	Paschasius Radbertus, *De partu virginis*	Pel. *Dem.*	Pelagius, *Epistula ad Demetriadem*
Paschas. *Ep. Eugip.*	Paschasius, *Epistula ad Eugippus*	Pel. *Exp. Ep. Pauli*	Pelagius, *Expositiones XIII epistularum Pauli*
Pass.	*Passiones*	Pel. *Lib. fid.*	Pelagius, *Libellus fidei*
Pass. Art.	*Passio Artemii*	Pel. *Rom.*	Pelagius, *Expositiones XIII epistularum Pauli: In Romanos*
Pass. Cris.	*Passion of Crispina*		
Pass. Cucuf.	*Passio Cucuphatis*		
Pass. Cyp.	*Passio Cypriani*	Pelag. *Ep.*	Pelagius I (Bishop of Rome), *Epistulae*
Pass. Dat. et Sat.	*Passio Dativi et Saturnini*		
Pass. Don.	*Passio Donati*	Per. Eg.	*Peregrinatio Egeriae*
Pass. Fel.	*Passio Felicis*	Pers. Sat.	Persius, *Satirae*
Pass. Marc.	*Passio Marculi*	Pet. Alex. *Ep. can.*	Peter I of Alexandria, *Epistula canonica* (*Canonical Letter*)
Pass. Max.	*Passion of Maxima*		
Pass. Maxim.	*Passio Maximiani*	Pet. Chr. *Serm.*	Peter Chrysologus, *Sermons*
Pass. Maxim. Don. et. Sec.	*Passio Maximae, Donatillae et Secundae*	Petr. Sat.	Petronius, *Satyricon*
		Phil.	Philodemus of Gadara

Phil. *De oec.*	Philodemus of Gadara, *De oeconomia* (*On Property Management*)
Phil. *Frank*	Philodemus of Gadara, *On Frank Criticism*
Phil. *Ind. Stoic.*	Philodemus of Gadara, *Index Stoicorum*
Phil. *Mort.*	Philodemus of Gadara, *De morte*
Phil. *Piet.*	Philodemus of Gadara, *De pietate*
Phil. *Rhet.*	Philodemus of Gadara, *Volumina rhetorica*
Philo	Philo of Alexandria
Philo *Abr.*	Philo of Alexandria, *De Abrahamo* (*On the Life of Abraham*)
Philo *Aet.*	Philo of Alexandria, *De aeternitate mundi* (*On the Eternity of the World*)
Philo *Agr.*	Philo of Alexandria, *De agricultura* (*On Agriculture*)
Philo *Anim.*	Philo of Alexandria, *De animalibus* (*Whether Animals Have Reason*)
Philo *Apol.*	Philo of Alexandria, *Apologia pro Judaeis*
Philo *Cher.*	Philo of Alexandria, *De cherubim* (*On the Cherubim*)
Philo *Conf.*	Philo of Alexandria, *De confusione linguarum* (*On the Confusion of Tongues*)
Philo *Congr.*	Philo of Alexandria, *De congressu eruditionis gratia* (*On the Preliminary Studies*)
Philo *Cont.* (or *Contempl.*)	Philo of Alexandria, *De vita contemplativa*
Philo *Decal.*	Philo of Alexandria, *De decalogo* (*On the Decalogue*)
Philo *Det.*	Philo of Alexandria, *Quod deterius potiori insidari soleat* (*That the Worse Attacks the Better*)
Philo *Deus*	Philo of Alexandria, *Quod Deus sit immutabilis* (*That God Is Unchangeable*)
Philo *Ebr.*	Philo of Alexandria, *De ebrietate* (*On Drunkenness*)
Philo *Flacc.*	Philo of Alexandria, *In Flaccum* (*Against Flaccus*)
Philo *Fug.*	Philo of Alexandria, *De fuga et inventione* (*On Flight and Finding*)
Philo *Gig.*	Philo of Alexandria, *De gigantibus* (*On Giants*)
Philo *Her.*	Philo of Alexandria, *Quis rerum divinarum heres sit* (*Who Is the Heir?*)
Philo *Hypoth.*	Philo of Alexandria, *Hypothetica* (*Hypothetica*)
Philo *Jos.*	Philo of Alexandria, *De Josepho* (*On the Life of Joseph*)
Philo *Leg.* 1, 2, 3	Philo of Alexandria, *Legum allegoriae* I, II, III (*Allegorical Interpretation 1, 2, 3*)
Philo *Legat.*	Philo of Alexandria, *Legatio ad Gaium* (*On the Embassy to Gaius*)
Philo *Migr.*	Philo of Alexandria, *De migratione Abrahami* (*On the Migration of Abraham*)
Philo *Mos.*	Philo of Alexandria, *De vita Mosis* I, I (*On the Life of Moses 1, 2*)
Philo *Mut.*	Philo of Alexandria, *De mutatione nominum* (*On the Change of Names*)
Philo *Opif.*	Philo of Alexandria, *De opificio mundi* (*On the Creation of the World*)
Philo *Plant.*	Philo of Alexandria, *De plantatione* (*On Planting*)
Philo *Post.*	Philo of Alexandria, *De posteritate Caini* (*On the Posterity of Cain*)
Philo *Praem.*	Philo of Alexandria, *De praemiis et poenis* (*Rewards On Rewards and Punishments*)

Philo *Prob.*	Philo of Alexandria, *Quod omnis probus liber sit* (*That Every Good Person Is Free*)
Philo *Prov.*	*De providentia* (*On Providence*)
Philo *Quaest. Ex.*	Philo of Alexandria, *Quaestiones in Exodum* I, II (*Questions and Answers on Exodus* 1, 2)
Philo *Quaest. Gen.*	Philo of Alexandria, *Quaestiones in Genesin* I, II, III, IV (*Questions and Answers on Genesis* 1, 2, 3, 4)
Philo *Sacr.*	Philo of Alexandria, *De sacrificiis Abelis et Caini* (*On the Sacrifices of Cain and Abel*)
Philo *Sobr.*	Philo of Alexandria, *De sobrietate* (*On Sobriety*)
Philo *Somn.*	Philo of Alexandria, *De somniis* I, II (*On Dreams* 1, 2)
Philo *Spec.*	Philo of Alexandria, *De specialibus legibus* I, II, III, IV (*On the Special Laws* 1, 2, 3, 4)
Philo *Virt.*	Philo of Alexandria, *De virtutibus* (*On the Virtues*)
Philost. *Hist. eccl.*	Philostorgius, *Historia ecclesiastica*
Philostr.	Philostratus
Philostr. *Apoll.*	Philostratus, *Letters of Apollonius*
Philostr. *Vita Ap.*	Philostratus, *Vita apollonii* (*Life of Apollonius of Tyana*)
Philostr. *Vitae soph.*	Philostratus, *Vitae sophistarum*
Philox. *Comm. Matt. Luc.*	Philoxenus, *Commentarii in Matthaeum et Lucam*
Phoeb. *Arian.*	Phoebadius of Agen, *Liber contra Arianos*
Phot. *Bibl.*	Photius, *Bibliotheca* (*Library*)
Physiol.	*Physiologos*
Pin.	Pindar
Pin. *Frgm(s).*	Pindar, *Fragments*
Pin. *Ol.*	Pindar, *Olympionikai* (*Olympian Odes*)
Pin. *Pyth.*	Pindar, *Pythionikai* (*Pythian Odes*)
Pist. Soph.	*Pistis Sophia*
Plato	Plato
Plato *Alc.*	Plato, *Alcibiades*
Plato *Apol.*	Plato, *Apologia* (*Apology of Socrates*)
Plato *Crit.*	Plato, *Criton*
Plato *Critias*	Plato, *Critias*
Plato *Ep.*	Plato, *Epistulae*
Plato *Euthyphr.*	Plato, *Euthyphro*
Plato *Gorg.*	Plato, *Gorgias*
Plato *Lach.*	Plato, *Laches*
Plato *Leg.*	Plato, *Leges* (*Laws*)
Plato *Lys.*	Plato, *Lysis*
Plato *Meno*	Plato, *Meno*
Plato *Parm.*	Plato, *Parmenides*
Plato *Phaed.*	Plato, *Phaedo*
Plato *Phaedr.*	Plato, *Phaedrus*
Plato *Pol.*	Plato, *Politicus* (*Statesman*)
Plato *Prot.*	Plato, *Protagoras*
Plato *Rep.*	Plato, *De republica*
Plato *Soph.*	Plato, *Sophista* (*Sophist*)
Plato *Symp.*	Plato, *Symposium*
Plato *Theaet.*	Plato, *Theaetetus*
Plato *Tim.*	Plato, *Timaeus*
Plaut.	Plautus
Plaut. *Asin.*	Plautus, *Asinaria*
Plaut. *Capt.*	Plautus, *Captivi*
Plaut. *Carb.*	Plautus, *Carbonaria*
Plaut. *Curc.*	Plautus, *Curculio*
Plaut. *Mil. glor.*	Plautus, *Miles gloriosus*
Plaut. *Most.*	Plautus, *Mostellaria*
Plaut. *Stic.*	Plautus, *Sticus*
Plin. *Nat.*	Pliny the Elder, *Naturalis historia*
Plin. Y.	Pliny the Younger
Plin. Y. *Ep.*	Pliny the Younger, *Epistulae*
Plin. Y. *Ep. Tra.*	Pliny the Younger, *Epistulae ad Trajanum*
Plin. Y. *Pan.*	Pliny the Younger, *Panegyricus*
Plot. *Enn.*	Plotinus, *Enneades* (*Enneads*)
Plut.	Plutarch (Plutarchus)
Plut. *Adol. poet. aud.*	Plutarch, *Quomodo adolescens poetas audire debeat* (*How the Young Man Should Study Poetry*)

Plut. *Adv. Col.*	Plutarch, *Adversus Colotem* (*Reply to Colotes*)	Plut. *Sol.*	Plutarch, *Solon*
Plut. *Aem.*	Plutarch, *Aemilius Paullus*	Plut. *Stoic. rep.*	Plutarch, *De Stoicorum repugnantiis*
Plut. *Alc.*	Plutarch, *Alcibiades*	Plut. *Suav. viv.*	Plutarch, *Non posse suaviter vivi secundum Epicurum* (*That Epicurus Actually Makes a Pleasant Life Impossible*)
Plut. *Alex.*	Plutarch, *Alexander*		
Plut. *An. procr.*	Plutarch, *De animae procreatione in Timaeo*		
Plut. *Ant.*	Plutarch, *Antonius*		
Plut. *Arat.*	Plutarch, *Aratus*	Plut. *Sull.*	Plutarch, *Sulla*
Plut. *Brut.*	Plutarch, *Brutus*	Plut. *Superst.*	Plutarch, *De superstitione*
Plut. *Caes.*	Plutarch, *Caesar*	Plut. *Thes.*	Plutarch, *Theseus*
Plut. *Cam.*	Plutarch, *Camillus*	Plut. *Tranq. an.*	Plutarch, *De tranquillitate animi*
Plut. *Cat. Maj.*	Plutarch, *Cato Major*		
Plut. *Cic.*	Plutarch, *Cicero*	Plut. *Virt. mor.*	Plutarch, *De virtute morali*
Plut. *Comp. Thes. Rom.*	Plutarch, *Comparatio Thesei et Romuli*	Plut. *Vit. aere al.*	Plutarch, *De vitando aere alieno*
Plut. *Conj. praec.*	Plutarch, *Conjugalia Praecepta*	Plut. *Vita Ant.*	Plutarch, *Vita Antonii*
		Pol. Silv.	Polemius Silvius
Plut. *Cor.*	Plutarch, *Marcius Coriolanus*	Pol. Silv. *Chron.*	Polemius Silvius, *Chronicon*
Plut. *De esu*	Plutarch, *De esu carnium*	Pol. Silv. *Fasti*	Polemius Silvius, *Fasti*
Plut. *Def. orac.*	Plutarch, *De defectu oraculorum*	Pol. Silv. *Lat.*	Polemius Silvius, *Laterculus*
		Polyb. *Hist.*	Polybius, *Historiae*
Plut. *Demetr.*	Plutarch, *Demetrius* (*Life of Demetrius*)	Pom.	Pomponius Mela
		Pom. *Chor.*	Pomponius Mela, *De Chorographia*
Plut. *E Delph.*	Plutarch, *De E apud Delphos*		
Plut. *Frgm(s).*	Plutarch, *Fragment(s)*	Pom. *Situ orb.*	Pomponius Mela, *De situ orbis* (*Description of the World*)
Plut. *Galb.*	Plutarch, *Galba*		
Plut. *Gen. Socr.*	Plutarch, *De genio Socratis*	Pomer. *Vita cont.*	Pomerius (Julianus), *De vita contemplativa*
Plut. *Is. Os.*	Plutarch, *De Iside et Osiride*		
Plut. *Luc.*	Plutarch, *Lucullus* (*Life of Lucullus*)	Pon. *Vita Cyp.*	Pontius, *Vita Cypriani* (*Life of Cyprian*)
Plut. *Mar.*	Plutarch, *Marius*	Por. *Hor.*	Pomponius Porphyrio, *In Horatii Sermones*
Plut. *Mor.*	Plutarch, *Moralia*		
Plut. *Num.*	Plutarch, *Numa*	Porph.	Porphyry of Tyre (Porphyrius)
Plut. *Per.*	Plutarch, *Pericles*	Porph. *Abst.*	Porphyry of Tyre, *De abstinentia*
Plut. *Phoc.*	Plutarch, *Phocion*		
Plut. *Plac. philos.*	Plutarch, *De placita philosophorum*	Porph. *Aneb.*	Porphyry of Tyre, *Epistula ad Anebonem*
Plut. *Quaest. conv.*	Plutarch, *Quaestionum convivialum libri IX*	Porph. *Antr. nymph.*	Porphyry of Tyre, *De antro nympharum*
Plut. *Quaest. plat.*	Plutarch, *Quaestiones platonicae*	Porph. *Christ.*	Porphyry of Tyre, *Contra Christianos* (*Against the Christians*)
Plut. *Quaest. rom.*	Plutarch, *Quaestiones romanae et graecae* (*Aetia romana et graeca*)	Porph. *Frgm(s).*	Porphyry of Tyre, *Fragment(s)*
		Porph. *Gau.*	Porphyry of Tyre, *Ad Gaurum*
Plut. *Rom.*	Plutarch, *Romulus*	Porph. *Isag.*	Porphyry of Tyre, *Isagoge sive quinque voces*
Plut. *Sera*	Plutarch, *De sera numinis vindicta*		

Porph. *Know.*	Porphyry of Tyre, *On Knowing Yourself*	*Profh. ex om.*	*Prophetiae ex omnibus*
		Pros.	Prosper of Aquitaine
Porph. *Marc.*	Porphyry of Tyre, *Ad Marcellam*	Pros. *Cap.*	Prosper of Aquitaine, *Capitula*
Porph. *Sent.*	Porphyry of Tyre, *Sententiae ad intelligibilia ducentes (Sentences)*	Pros. *Epit. chron.*	Prosper of Aquitaine, *Epitoma chronicorum*
		Pros. *Omn. gent.*	Prosper of Aquitaine, *De vocatione omnium gentium (Call of All Nations)*
Porph. *Sym.*	Porphyry of Tyre, *Symmikta zêtêmata*		
Porph. *Vita Plot.*	Porphyry of Tyre, *Vita Plotini (Life of Plotinus)*	Prot. *Frgm(s).*	Protagoras of Abdera, *Fragment(s)*
Pos. *Vita Aug.*	Possidius of Calama, *Vita S. Augustini (Life of Augustine)*	Prud.	Prudentius
		Prud. *Apoth.*	Prudentius, *Apotheosis*
Praed.	*Praedestinatus*	Prud. *Carm.*	Prudentius, *Carmina*
Pris.	Priscillian of Avila	Prud. *Cath.*	Prudentius, *Liber cathemerinon*
Pris. *Can.*	Priscillian of Avila, *Canones epistularum Pauli apostoli*		
		Prud. *Ham.*	Prudentius, *Hamartigenia*
Pris. *Tract.*	Priscillian of Avila, *Tractates*	Prud. *Peri.*	Prudentius, *Peristephanon*
Priscus, *Frgm(s).*	Priscus of Panion, *Fragment(s)*	Prud. *Psychom.*	Prudentius, *Psychomachia*
		Prud. *Sym.*	Prudentius, *Contra Symmachum*
Pro.	Procopius of Caesarea		
Pro. *Anec.*	Procopius of Caesarea, *Anecdota (Secret History)*	Ps. iux. Hebr.	Psalterium iuxta Hebraeos
		Ps.-Ambr.	Pseudo-Ambrose of Milan
Pro. *Bel.*	Procopius of Caesarea, *Bella (Wars)*	Ps.-Ambr. De *laps. Sus.*	Pseudo-Ambrose of Milan, *De lapsu Susannae: Ad lapsam virginem libellus*
Pro. *Bell. Goth.*	Procopius of Caesarea, *De bello gothico*		
		Ps.-Ambr. *Ep.*	Pseudo-Ambrose of Milan, *Epistulae*
Pro. *Bell. Pers.*	Procopius of Caesarea, *Bellum Persianum (Persian War)*	Ps.-Ambrosi. *Quaest.*	Pseudo-Ambrosiaster, *Quaestiones*
Pro. *Bell. Van.*	Procopius of Caesarea, *De bello vandalico (Vandal War)*	Ps.-Amph. *Vita Bas.*	Pseudo-Amphilochian, *Vita Basilii*
Pro. *Comm. Gen.*	Procopius of Caesarea, *Commentary on Genesis*	Ps.-Athan.	Pseudo-Athanasius of Alexandria
Pro. *De aedif.*	Procopius of Caesarea, *De aedificiis (On Buildings)*	Ps.-Athan. Ar.	Pseudo-Athanasius of Alexandria, *Oratione contra Arianos*
Pro. *In. Gen.*	Procopius of Caesarea, *In Genesim*		
Proc.	Proclus	Ps.-Athan. Quaest. Ant.	Pseudo-Athanasius of Alexandria, *Quaestiones ad Antiochum ducem*
Proc. *Alcib.*	Proclus, *In Alcibiadem*		
Proc. *In Tim.*	Proclus, *In Platonis Timaeum Commentaria*	Ps.-Athan. *Syncl.*	Pseudo-Athanasius of Alexandria, *The Life and Regimen of the Blessed and Holy Teacher Syncletica*
Proc. *Parm.*	Proclus, *In Parmenidem*		
Proc. *Poet.*	Proclus, *Poetics*		
Proc. *Rem publ.*	Proclus, *In rem publicam commentarii*	Ps.-Aug.	Pseudo-Augustine of Hippo
		Ps.-Aug. Alter. Pas.	Pseudo-Augustine of Hippo, *Altercatio cum Pascentio Ariano*
Proc. *Theol. Plat.*	Proclus, *Theologia Platonica*		
Proc. *Elem. Theol.*	Proclus, *Elements of Theology*		

Ps.-Aug. *Jud.*	Pseudo-Augustine of Hippo, *Contra Judaeos, Paganos, et Arianos*	Ps.-Dion.	Pseudo-Dionysius the Areopagite
Ps.-Aug. *Serm.*	Pseudo-Augustine of Hippo, *Sermones*	Ps.-Dion. Myst. theo.	Pseudo-Dionysius the Areopagite, *De mystica theologia*
Ps.-Aug. *Ver. fals. poenit.*	Pseudo-Augustine of Hippo, *De vera et falsa poenitentia ad Christi devotam*	Ps.-Dion. Cael. Hier.	Pseudo-Dionysius the Areopagite, *De Caelesti Hierarchia*
Ps.-Aur. Vict. *Epit. Caes.*	Pseudo-Aurelius Victor, *Epitome de Caesaribus* (*Epitome on Emperors*)	Ps.-Dion. *Div.*	Pseudo-Dionysius the Areopagite, *De divinis nominibus*
Ps.-Bas.	Pseudo-Basil of Caesarea	Ps.-Dion. Eccl. hier.	Pseudo-Dionysius the Areopagite, *De Ecclesiastica hierarchia*
Ps.-Bas. *Can.*	Pseudo-Basil of Caesarea, *Canones*		
Ps.-Bas. *Comm. Isa*	Pseudo-Basil of Caesarea, *Commentary on the Prophet Isaiah*	Ps.-Epiph.	Pseudo-Epiphanius of Salamis
		Ps.-Epiph. *Anac.*	Pseudo-Epiphanius of Salamis, *Anacephalaiosis*
Ps.-Bas. *Eun.*	Pseudo-Basil of Caesarea, *Adversus Eunomium* (*Against Eunomius*)	Ps.-Epiph. *Not.*	Pseudo-Epiphanius of Salamis, *Notitiae*
Ps.-Chrys.	Pseudo-John Chrysostom	Ps.-Faus. *Serm.*	Pseudo-Faustus of Riez, *Sermones*
Ps.-Chrys. *Eliam*	Pseudo-John Chrysostom, *In Eliam prophetam sermo*	Ps.-Ful. *Serm.*	Pseudo-Fulgentius of Ruspe, *Sermones*
Ps.-Chrys. *Op. imp. Matt.*	Pseudo-John Chrysostom, *Opus imperfectum in Matthaeum*	Ps.-Hipp.	Pseudo-Hippolytus of Rome
		Ps.-Hipp. *Haer.*	Pseudo-Hippolytus of Rome, *Refutatio omnium haeresium* (*Refutation of All Heresies*)
Ps.-Chrys. *Pascha*	Pseudo-John Chrysostom, *In sanctum Pascha sermo*		
Ps.-Chrys. *Perf.*	Pseudo-John Chrysostom, *De perfecta charitate*	Ps.-Hipp. *Trad. ap.*	Pseudo-Hippolytus of Rome, *Traditio Apostolica*
Ps.-Chrys. *Qoud*	Pseudo-John Chrysostom, *Quod Mari*	Ps.-Ign.	Pseudo-Ignatius of Antioch
Ps.-Clem.	*Pseudo-Clementines*	Ps.-Ign. *Antioch.*	Pseudo-Ignatius of Antioch, *Epistula ad Antiochenses*
Ps.-Clem. 1 Ep. virg	*Pseudo-Clementines, Epistola I ad virgines*	Ps.-Ign. *Hero.*	Pseudo-Ignatius of Antioch, *Epistula ad Heronem*
Ps.-Clem. 2 Ep. virg	*Pseudo-Clementines, Epistola II ad virgines*	Ps.-Ign. *Mar.*	Pseudo-Ignatius of Antioch, *Epistula ad Mariam*
Ps.-Clem. Ep. Iac.	Pseudo-Clementines, *Epistula Clementis ad Iacobum*	Ps.-Ign. *Mar. Ign.*	Pseudo-Ignatius of Antioch, *Maria ad Ignatium*
Ps.-Clem. Ep. Pet.	Pseudo-Clementines, *Epistula Petri*	Ps.-Ign. *Philip.*	Pseudo-Ignatius of Antioch, *Epistula ad Philippenses*
Ps.-Cyp.	Pseudo-Cyprian of Carthage	Ps.-Ign. *Phld.*	Pseudo-Ignatius of Antioch, *To the Philadelphians*
Ps.-Cyp. *Pas. Comp.*	Pseudo-Cyprian of Carthage, *De Pascha Computus*		
Ps.-Cyp. *Rebap.*	Pseudo-Cyprian of Carthage, *De rebaptismate*	Ps.-Ign. *Smyrn.*	Pseudo-Ignatius of Antioch, *To the Smyrnaeans*
Ps.-Didy. *Trin.*	Pseudo-Didymus the Blind, *De Trinitate*	Ps.-Ign. *Tars.*	Pseudo-Ignatius of Antioch, *Epistula ad Tarsenses*

Ps.-Ign. *Trall.*	Pseudo-Ignatius of Antioch, *To the Trallians*
Ps.-Ild. *Serm.*	Pseudo-Ildefonsus, *Sermones*
Ps.-Iren. *Frgm(s).*	Pseudo-Irenaeus of Lyon, *Fragment(s)*
Ps.-Jer. *Ind. haer.*	Pseudo-Jerome, *Indiculus de haeresibus*
Ps.-Josh. Styl. *Chron.*	Pseudo-Joshua the Stylite, *Chronicle*
Ps.-Just.	Pseudo-Justin Martyr
Ps.-Just. *Coh.*	Pseudo-Justin Martyr, *Cohortatio ad Graecos* (*Exhortation to the Greeks*)
Ps.-Just. *Quaest.*	Pseudo-Justin Martyr, *Quaestiones et responsiones ad orthodoxos*
Ps.-Just. *Res.*	Pseudo-Justin Martyr, *De resurrectione*
Ps.-Liban. *Epist. char.*	Pseudo-Libanius, *Epistolimaioi charakteres* (*Epistolary Styles* or *Characteres epistolici*)
Ps.-Linus *Mart. Petr.*	Pseudo-Linus, *Martyrium beati Petri apostoli*
Ps.-Lucian *Cyn.*	Pseudo-Lucian, *Cynicus*
Ps.-Mac.	Pseudo-Macarius
Ps.-Mac. *Ep. Mag.*	Pseudo-Macarius, *Epistula Magna*
Ps.-Mac. *Hom.*	Pseudo-Macarius, *Homiliae*
Ps.-Mac. *Log.*	Pseudo-Macarius, *Logos*
Ps.-Marc. *Mart. Petr. et Paul.*	Peudo-Marcellus, *Passio Sanctorum apostolorum Petri et Pauli*
Ps.-Max. *Sol.*	Pseudo-Maximinus, *De solemnitatibus*
Ps.-Max. Taur. *Serm.*	Pseudo-Maxiumus Taurinensis (Maximus of Turin), *Sermones*
Ps.-Paul. *Sent.*	Pseudo-Paulus, *Sententiae*
Ps.-Pel. *Div.*	Pseudo-Pelagius, *De divitiis*
Ps.-Plut. *Plac. philos.*	Pseudo-Plutarch, *De placita philosophorum.*
Ps.-Quint. *Decl. Min.*	Pseudo-Quintilian, *Declamationes Minores* (*Minor Declamations*)
Ps.-Tert. *Haer.*	Pseudo-Tertullian, *Adversus omnes haereses*
Ps.-Zach. *Hist. eccl.*	Pseudo-Zachariah, *Historia ecclesiastica Zachariae Rhetori vulgo adscripta*
Ps.-Zach. Mit. *Chron.*	Pseudo-Zachariah of Mitylene, *Chronicle*
Ps.-Zal. *Pro. Nom.*	Pseudo-Zaleucus, *Prooimia Nomōn*
Ptol. *Geo.*	Claudius Ptolemaeus, *Geographia*
Ptolem. *Tetr.*	Ptolemy, *Tetrabiblos*
Ptolemy *Flor.*	Ptolemy (the Gnostic), *Epistula ad Floram* (*Letter to Flora*)
Pyth. Sent.	*Pythagorean Sentences*
Quint.	Quintilian
Quint. *Ep. Tryph.*	Quintilian, *Epistula ad Tryphonem*
Quint. *Inst.*	Quintilian, *Institutio oratoria*
Quod.	Quodvultdeus of Carthage
Quod. *Adv. quin. haer.*	Quodvultdeus of Carthage, *Adversus quinque haereses*
Quod. *Prom. praed.*	Quodvultdeus of Carthage, *Liber promissionum et praedictorum Dei*
Quod. *Sym.*	Quodvultdeus of Carthage, *De symbolo*
Rab. Maur. *Cler. Inst.*	Rabanus Maurus, *De clericorum institutione*
Rebapt.	Anonymous, *De rebaptismate* (*On Rebaptism*)
Ref.	Anonymous, *Refutation of All Heresies* (previously, but incorrectly attributed to Hippolytus of Rome)
Reg. Bas.	*Regula Basilii*
Reg. Eccl. Car. Exc.	*Registri Ecclesiae Carthaginensis Excerpta*
Reg. mag.	*Regula magistri*
Reg. Pach.	*Regula Pachomii*
Rel. mot.	*Relatio motionis*
Res gest. divi Aug.	*Res gestae divi Augusti*
RM	*Regula Magistri* (*Rule of the Master*)
Roma. *Kon.*	Romanos the Melodist, *Kontakia*
Ruf.	Rufinus of Aquileia
Ruf. *Exp. symb. Apost.*	Rufinus of Aquileia, *Expositio in symbolum apostolorum*

Ruf. *Adul. Orig.*	Rufinus of Aquileia, *De adulteratione librorum Origenis*	Sen. *Apol.*	Seneca, *Apolocyntosis*
		Sen. *Ben.*	Seneca, *De beneficiis*
		Sen. *Brev.*	Seneca, *De brevitate vitae*
Ruf. *Anast.*	Rufinus of Aquileia, *Apologia ad Anastasium papam*	Sen. *Clem.*	Seneca, *De clementia*
		Sen. *Dial.*	Seneca, *Dialogi*
Ruf. *Apol. Hier.*	Rufinus of Aquileia, *Apologia adversus Hieronymum*	Sen. *Ep.*	Seneca, *Epistulae morales*
		Sen. *Ira*	Seneca, *De ira*
Ruf. *Clem. Rec.*	Rufinus of Aquileia, *In Clementis recognitiones*	Sen. *Lucil.*	Seneca, *Ad Lucilium*
		Sen. *Nat.*	Seneca, *Naturales quaestiones*
Ruf. *Exp. Symb.*	Rufinus of Aquileia, *Expositio Symboli*	Sen. *Tranq.*	Seneca, *De tranquillitate animi*
Ruf. *Hist.*	Rufinus of Aquileia, *Eusebii Historia ecclesiastica a Rufino translata et continuata*	Sen. *Tro.*	Seneca, *Troades*
		Sen. *Vit. beat.*	Seneca, *De vita beata*
		Sen. El. *Contr.*	Seneca the Elder, *Controversiae*
Ruf. *Hist. eccl.*	Rufinus of Aquileia, *Historia ecclesiastica*	Ser. *Sacr.*	Serapion of Thmuis, *Sacramentary*
Ruf. *Hist. mon.*	Rufinus of Aquileia, *Historia monachorum in Aegypto*	Ser. Alex. *Frgm(s).*	Serapion of Alexandria, *Fragment(s)*
Ruf. *Princ.*	Rufinus of Aquileia, *De principiis*	Serv. *Verg.*	Servius, *In Vergilii Aeneidem commentarii*
Ruf. *Symb.*	Rufinus of Aquileia, *Commentarius in symbolum apostolorum*	Sev.	Severian of Gabala
		Sev. *Hom. creat.*	Severian of Gabala, *Homiliae VI in mundi creationem*
Rufus	Musonius Rufus	Sev. *Joh. 1:13 hom.*	Severian of Gabala, *In Joh. 1:13 homiliae*
Rufus *Diat.*	Musonius Rufus, *Diatribe*		
Rufus *Dis.*	Musonius Rufus, *Discourse*	Sev. Ant.	Severus of Antioch
Rufus *Frgm(s).*	Musonius Rufus, *Fragments*	Sev. Ant. *Hom.*	Severus of Antioch, *Homilia*
Rup. *Com. Ion.*	Rupert of Deutz, *Commentarius in Ioannem*	Sev. Ant. *Hom. cath.*	Severus of Antioch, *Homiliae cathedrales*
Ruric. *Ep.*	Ruricius of Limoges, *Epistulae*	Sev. Ant. *Neph.*	Severus of Antioch, *Ad Nephalium*
Rut. Nam. *Red. suo*	Rutilius Namatianus, *De reditu suo*	Sev. Ant. *Oecum.*	Severus of Antioch, *Ad Oecumenium*
Sacram. Gel. Vet.	*Sacramentarium Gelasianum Vetus*	Sev. Ant. *Serg.*	Severus of Antioch, *Ad Sergium*
Sacram. Greg. Hadr.	*Sacramentarium Gregorianum Hadrianum*	Sex.Emp.	Sextus Empiricus
		Sex.Emp. *Math.*	Sextus Empiricus, *Adversus mathematicos* (*Against the mathematicians*)
Sacram. Ver.	*Sacramentarium Veronese*		
Sal.	Salvian of Marseille		
Sal. *Eccl.*	Salvian of Marseille, *Ad ecclesiam*	Sex.Emp. *Pyr.*	Sextus Empiricus, *Pyrrhoniae hypotyposes*
Sal. *Gub.*	Salvian of Marseille, *De gubernatione Dei*	SHA	*Scriptores Historiae Augustae* (*The Writers of the Historia Augusta; also known as Historia Augusta, see H.A.*)
Sall. *Bell. Cat.*	Sallust, *Bellum catalinae*		
Sallus. *Diis*	Sallustius, *De diis et mundo*		
Sch. *Sin.*	*Scholia Sinaitica*		
Sed. *Pasch.*	Sedulius, *Paschale carmen*	SHA *Alex.*	*Scriptores Historiae Augustae Alexander Severus*
Sen.	Seneca		

SHA M. Ant.	Scriptores Historiae Augustae Marcus Aurelius Antoninus	Suet. Dom.	Suetonius, Domitianus
SHA Max	Scriptores Historiae Augustae	Suet. Gramm.	Suetonius, De grammaticis
SHA Max. duo	Scriptores Historiae Augustae Maximini duo	Suet. Jul.	Suetonius, Divus Julius
		Suet. Nero	Suetonius, Nero
		Suet. Otho	Suetonius, Otho
SHA Max. et Balb.	Scriptores Historiae Augustae Maximi et Balbini	Suet. Tib.	Suetonius, Tiberius
		Suet. Tit.	Suetonius, Divus Titus
Shen. Opus	Shenoute of Atripe, Opus	Suet. Vesp.	Suetonius, Vespasianus
Sid.	Sidonius Apollinaris	Suet. Vit.	Suetonius, Vitellius
Sid. Carm.	Sidonius Apollinaris, Carmen	Sul.	Sulpicius Severus
Sid. Ep.	Sidonius Apollinaris, Epistulae	Sul. Chron.	Sulpicius Severus, Chronicorum libri ii
Simpl.	Simplicius	Sul. Dial.	Sulpicius Severus, Dialogi (Dialogues)
Simpl. Arist. caelo comm.	Simplicius, In Aristotelis de caelo commentaria	Sul. Ep.	Sulpicius Severus, Epistulae
Simpl. Arist. phys.	Simplicius, In Aristotelis physicorum	Sul. Vita Mart.	Sulpicius Severus, Vita sancti Martini
Sinai syr.	Sinai syriac	Sul. Ep. ded.	Sulpicius Severus, Epistula dedicatoria
Sir. Ep.	Siricius Romanus, Epistulae		
Smar. Crown	Smaragdus of Saint-Mihiel, The Crown of Monks	Sum. Per.	Summa Perusina
		Sym.	Quintus Aurelius Symmachus
Socr. Hist. eccl.	Socrates (of Constantinople) Scholasticus, Historia ecclesiastica	Sym. Ep.	Quintus Aurelius Symmachus, Epistulae
		Sym. Or.	Quintus Aurelius Symmachus, Orationes
Soli. Coll.	Solinus, Collectanea Rerum Memorabilium	Sym. Rel.	Quintus Aurelius Symmachus, Relatio
Sophoc. Frgm(s).	Sophocles, Fragment(s)	Syme. Hymn	Symeon the New Theologian, Hymn
Sor. Gyn.	Soranos, Gynecology		
Soz. Hist. eccl.	Sozomen, Historia ecclesiastica	Symmac. Ep.	Symmachus (Bishop of Rome), Epistulae
Stat.	Statius	Syn.	Synesius of Cyrene
Stat. Sil.	Statius, Silvae	Syn. Dio	Synesius of Cyrene, Dio, sive de suo ipsius instituto
Stat. Theb.	Statius, Thebaid		
Stob.	Stobaeus	Syn. Ep.	Synesius of Cyrene, Epistulae
Stob. Anth.	Stobaeus, Anthology	Syn. Hym.	Synesius of Cyrene, Hymni (Hymns)
Stob. Ecl.	Stobaeus, Eclogae		
Stob. Exc.	Stobaeus, Excerpta	Syn. Orient.	Synodicon Orientale
Stob. herm.	Stobaean (Fragments of) Hermetica	Sync. Chron.	Georgius Syncellus, Chronographia
Stra. Geogr.	Strabo, Geographica	Syr. Chr.	The Syriac Chronicle Known as that of Zacharias of Mitylene
Suda	Suda		
Suet.	Suetonius		
Suet. Aug.	Suetonius, Divus Augustus (Life of Augustus)	T. 40 Mart.	Testament of the Forty Martyrs of Sebaste
Suet. Caes.	Suetonius, Ceasar	T. Dom.	Testamentum Domini
Suet. Cal.	Suetonius, Caligula	Tac.	Tacitus
Suet. Claud.	Suetonius, Divus Claudius (Life of Claudius)	Tac. Agr.	Tacitus, Agricola

Tac. *An.*	Tacitus, *Annales*	Tert. *Mon.*	Tertullian, *De monogamia* (*On Monogamy*)
Tac. *Dial.*	Tacitus, *Dialogus de oratoribus*	Tert. *Nat.*	Tertullian, *Ad nationes* (*To the Heathen*)
Tac. *Hist.*	Tacitus, *Historiae*		
Tac.*Germ.*	Tacitus, *Germania*	Tert. *Or.*	Tertullian, *De oratione* (*Prayer*)
Tat. *Orat.*	Tatian, *Oratio ad Graecos* (*Oration to/against the Greeks*)	Tert. *Paen.*	Tertullian, *De paenitentia* (*Repentance*)
Tatius *Leuc. Clit.*	Achilles Tatius, *Leucippe et Clitophon* (*The Adventures of Leucippe and Cleitophon*)	Tert. *Pall.*	Tertullian, *De pallio* (*The Pallium*)
		Tert. *Pat.*	Tertullian, *De patientia* (*Patience*)
Taur.	*Taurinensis*		
Tert.	Tertullian	Tert. *Praesc.*	Tertullian, *De praescriptione haereticorum* (*Prescription against Heretics*)
Tert. *Adv. Jud.*	Tertullian, *Adversus Judaeos* (*Against the Jews*)		
Tert. *An.*	Tertullian, *De anima* (*The Soul*)	Tert. *Prax.*	Tertullian, *Adversus Praxean* (*Against Praxeas*)
Tert. *Apol.*	Tertullian, *Apologeticus* (*Apology*)	Tert. *Pud.*	Tertullian, *De pudicitia* (*Modesty*)
Tert. *Bapt.*	Tertullian, *De baptismo* (*Baptism*)	Tert. *Res.*	Tertullian, *De resurrectione carnis* (*The Resurrection of the Flesh*)
Tert. *Carn. chr.*	Tertullian, *De carne Christi* (*The Flesh of Christ*)		
Tert. *Cor.*	Tertullian, *De corona* (*The Crown*)	Tert. *Scap.*	Tertullian, *Ad Scapulam* (*To Scapula*)
Tert. *Cult. fem.*	Tertullian, *De cultu feminarum* (*The Apparel of Women*)	Tert. *Scorp.*	Tertullian, *Scorpiace* (*Antidote for the Scorpion's Sting*)
		Tert. *Spect.*	Tertullian, *De spectaculis* (*The Shows*)
Tert. *Exh. cast.*	Tertullian, *De exhortatione castitatis* (*Exhortation to Chastity*)	Tert. *Test.*	Tertullian, *De testimonio animae* (*The Soul's Testimony*)
Tert. *Fug.*	Tertullian, *De fuga in persecutione* (*Flight in Persecution*)	Tert. *Ux.*	Tertullian, *Ad uxorem* (*To His Wife*)
Tert. *Herm.*	Tertullian, *Adversus Hermogenem* (*Against Hermogenes*)	Tert. *Val.*	Tertullian, *Adversus Valentinianos* (*Against the Valentinians*)
Tert. *Idol.*	Tertullian, *De idololatria* (*Idolatry*)	Tert. *Virg.*	Tertullian, *De virginibus velandis* (*The Veiling of Virgins*)
Tert. *Jejun.*	Tertullian, *De jejunio adversus psychicos* (*On Fasting, against the Psychics*)	Th. Her. *Frag. Joh.*	Theodore of Heraclea, *Fragmenta in Joannem*
Tert. *Marc.*	Tertullian, *Adversus Marcionem* (*Against Marcion*)	Th. Lec.	Theodore Lector
		Th. Lec. *Epit.*	Theodore Lector, *Epitome*
		Th. Lec. *Hist. eccl.*	Theodore Lector, *Historia ecclesiastica*
Tert. *Mart.*	Tertullian, *Ad martyras* (*To the Martyrs*)	Th. Mop.	Theodore of Mopsuestia

Th. Mop. *Bapt.*	Theodore of Mopsuestia, *Liber ad Baptizandos*	Thdt. *Int. Rom.*	Theodoret of Cyrrhus, *Interpretatio epistolae ad Romanos*
Th. Mop. *Com. 1 Tim.*	Theodore of Mopsuestia, *Commentary on 1 Timothy*	Thdt. *Int. XIV Epp. Paul*	Theodoret of Cyrrhus, *Interpretatio in quatuordecim epistolas S. Pauli*
Th. Mop. *Com. Gal.*	Theodore of Mopsuestia, *Commentary on Galatians*		
Th. Mop. *Com. Jon.*	Theodore of Mopsuestia, *Commentary on Jonah*	Thdt. *Prov.*	Theodoret of Cyrrhus, *De providentia (Ten Discourses on Providence)*
Th. Mop. *Com. LP*	Theodore of Mopsuestia, *Commentary on the Lord's Prayer*	Thdt. *Quaest.*	Theodoret of Cyrrhus, *Quaestiones in libros Regnorum et Paralipomenon*
Th. Mop. *Com. Tit.*	Theodore of Mopsuestia, *Commentary on Titus*		
Th. Mop. *Frgms. Heb.*	Theodore of Mopsuestia, *Fragments of the Commentary on Hebrews*	Thdt. *Quaest. Exod.*	Theodoret of Cyrrhus, *Quaestiones in Exodum*
		Thdt. *Quaest. Lev.*	Theodoret of Cyrrhus, *Quaestiones in Leviticum*
Th. Mop. *Hom.*	Theodore of Mopsuestia, *Homily*	Them. *Or.*	Themistius, *Orationes*
Th. Mop. Hom. Cat.	Theodore of Mopsuestia, *Catechetical Homilies*	Theo. *Comm. Ps.*	Theodore, *Commentary on the Psalms*
Th. Mop. *Rom.*	Theodore of Mospsuestia, *On Romans*	Theod. *Nov.*	Theodosius II, *Novella*
Th. Stud. *Antir.*	Theodore the Studite, *Antirrhetici tres adversus iconomachos*	Theodos. *Sit. ter. sanc.*	Theodosius, *De situ terrae sanctae (Topography of the Holy Land)*
Thal. *Lib.Th.*	Thalassius of Constantinople, *Libellus ad Theodosium*	Theog. *Eleg.*	Theognis of Megara, *Elegiae*
		Theon *Prog.*	Aelius Theon, *Progymnasmata*
Thdt.	Theodoret of Cyrrhus	Theon Smyr.	Theon of Smyrna, *Expositio rerum mathematicorum*
Thdt. *Affect.*	Theodoret of Cyrrhus, *De Graecarum affectionum curatione (Therapeia of the Greek Maladies)*	Theon Smyr. *Expos. math.*	
		Theop. Ohr. *Expos. ep. 1 Cor.*	Theophylact of Ohrid, *Expositio in epistolam 1 ad Corinthios*
Thdt. *Comm. in...*	Theodoret of Cyrrhus, *Commentarii* etc. (On Books of the Bible)	Theoph. Conf.	Theophanes the Confessor
		Theoph. Conf. *AM*	Theophanes the Confessor, *Anno Mundi*
Thdt. *Ep.*	Theodoret of Cyrrhus, *Epistulae*	Theoph. Conf. *Chron.*	Theophanes the Confessor, *Chronographia*
Thdt. *Eran.*	Theodoret of Cyrrhus, *Eranistes*	Theophil. Alex. *Ep.*	Theophilus of Alexandria, *Epistulae*
Thdt. *Haer. fab.*	Theodoret of Cyrrhus, *Haereticarum fabularum compendium*	Theophil. *Autol.*	Theophilus of Antioch, *Ad Autolycum (To Autolycus)*
		Theophr. *Char.*	Theophrastus, *Characteres*
Thdt. *Hist. eccl.*	Theodoret of Cyrrhus, *Historia ecclesiastica*	Theophyl. *Hist.*	Theophylact of Simocatta, *Historiae*
Thdt. *Hist. rel.*	Theodoret of Cyrrhus, *Historia religiosa*	*Theos. Sib.*	*Sibylline Theosophy*
Thdt. *Inc.*	Theodoret of Cyrrhus, *De incarnatione*	Thom. *De Nav.*	Thomas of Edessa, *De nativitate*

Thphyl. *Hist.*	Theophylaktos Simokattes, *Historiae*	Vic. Pet. *Apoc*	Victorinus of Pettau (Petovium), *In Apocalypsin*
Thuc.	Thucydides	Vic. Pet. *Comm.*	Victorinus of Pettau
Thuc. *Hist.*	Thucydides, *Historiae*	*apoc.*	(Petovium), *Commentarius*
Thuc. *Pelop.*	Thucydides, *Peloponnesian War*		*in apocalypsin*
Thuyc.	Thuycidides, *History of the Peloponnesian War*	Vic. Tun. *Chron.*	Victor of Tunnuna, *Chronicon (Chronicle)*
Tibul. *Poems*	Tibullus, *Poems*	Vic. Vit.	Victor Vitensis (Victor of Vita)
Tim. *Frgm(s)*	Timotheos, *Fragment(s)*	Vic. Vit. *Hist.*	Victor Vitensis, *Historia Vandalae persecutionis*
Tír. *Collec.*	Tírechán, *Collectanea*	Vic. Vit. *Hist. Afr.*	Victor Vitensis, *Historia*
Tit. *Manich.*	Titus of Bostra, *Contra Manichaeos*		*persecutionis Africanae provinciae*
Trad. Ap.	Traditio Apostolica (Apostolic Tradition)	Vig. *Ep.*	Vigilius (Bishop of Rome), *Epistulae*
Treb.	Trebellius Pollio	Vin. *Com.*	Vincent (Vincentius) of Lérins, *Commonitorium*
Treb. *Thir. Pret.*	Trebellius Pollio, *Thirty Pretenders*	Virg.	Virgil
Treb. *Two Gal.*	Trebellius Pollio, *Two Gallieni*	Virg. *Aen.*	Virgil, *Aeneis*
Tur. *Ep. Id. Cep.*	Turibius of Astorga, *Epistula ad Idatium et Ceponium*	Virg. *Catal.*	Virgil, *Catalepton*
		Virg. *Ecl.*	Virgil, *Eclogae*
Tyc.	Tyconius	Virg. *Georg.*	Virgil, *Georgica*
Tyc. *Exp. Apoc.*	Tyconius, *Exposition of the Apocalypse*	Vita	Vita Euth.
		Vita Alb.	Vita Albini
Tyc. *Reg.*	Tyconius, *Liber regularum*	Vita Alex.	Vita Alexandri
Ulp. *Off. pro.*	Ulpian, *De officio proconsulis*	Vita Amati	Vita Amati abbatis Habendensis
Unt. Cod. Bruc.	Untitled Treatise in the Bruce Codex	Vita Ani.	Vita Aniani episcopi Aurelianensis
Val. Bier *Van.*	Valerius of Bierzo, *De vana saeculi sapientia*	Vita Anth.	Vita Anthusae
Val. Max.	Valerius Maximus, *Facta et dicta memorabilia (Memorable Deeds and Sayings)*	Vita Apoll.	Vita Apollinaris Valentinensis
		Vita Aug.	Vita Augustini
		Vita Caes.	Vita Caesarii (Life of Caesarius)
Valen. *Nov.*	Valentinian III, *Novella*	Vita Caes. Arel.	Vita Caesarii Arelatensis
Varro	Varro	Vita Dan.	Vita Danieli
Varro *Ling. Lat.*	Varro, *De Lingua Latina*	Vita Dan. Styl.	Vita Danielis Stylitae
Varro *Rust.*	Varro, *De re rustica*	Vita Eleem.	Vita Ioannis Eleemosynarii
Vat. gr.	Vaticanus graecus	Vita Epiph.	Vita Epiphanii
Vat. Reg.	Papyrus of the Vatican	Vita Eup.	Vita Eupraxiae
Vell. Pat. *Hist. rom.*	Velleius Paterculus, *Historiae romanae (Roman History)*	Vita Fulg.	Vita Fulgentii
		Vita Heliog.	Vita Heliogabali
Vic. *Laud.*	Victricius of Rouen, *De laude sanctorum (On the Praise of the Saints)*	Vita Hil.	Vita Hilarii
		Vita Isa.	Vita Isaaci
		Vita Lup.	Vita Lupi episcopi Trecensis
Vic. Pet.	Victorinus of Petovium (Pettau)	Vita Marcel.	Vita Marcelli
		Vita Mel.	Vita Melaniae Junioris

Vita Olym.	*Vita Olympiadis*	Xenoph. *Frgm(s).*	Xenophanes of Colophon, *Fragment(s)*
Vita Pach.	*Vita Pachomii*		
Vita Pach. Iun.	*Vita Pachomii Iunioris*	*XII Pan. lat.*	*XII Panegyrici latini*
Vita Patr. Iur.	*Vita Patrum Iurensium*	Yda. *CC Hier.*	Ydatius, *Continuatio Chronicorum Hieronymianorum*
Vita Pet. Ib.	*Vita Petri Iberi*		
Vita Pol.	*Vita Polycarpi*		
Vita Sym. Styl Iun.	*Vita Symeonis Stylitae Iunioris*	Zach. Rhet.	Zachariah Rhetor
Vita Syn.	*Vita Syncletica*	Zach. Rhet. *Hist. eccl.*	Zachariah Rhetor, *Historia ecclesiastica*
Vita. Or.	*Vita Orientii*		
Vitr. *Arch.*	Vitruvius, *De architectura*	Zach. Rhet. *Vita Sev.*	Zachariah Rhetor, *Vita Severi*
VPJ	*Vitae partum Iurensium*	Zeno	Zeno of Verona
Wis. Jes. Chr.	see *Soph. Jes. Chr.* (*Sophia of Jesus Christ*)	Zeno, *Hom.*	Zeno of Verona, *Homilies*
		Zeno, *Tract.*	Zeno of Verona, *Tractatus*
Xen.	Xenophon	Zeno, *Tract. Ion.*	Zeno of Verona, *Tractatus in Ionam*
Xen. *Ages.*	Xenophon, *Agesilaus*		
Xen. *Anab.*	Xenophon, *Anabasis*	Zon. *Epit. Hist.*	Zonaras, *Epitome historiarum*
Xen. *Cyr.*	Xenophon, *Cyropaedia*	Zos. *Hist.*	Zosimus, *Historia nova* (*New History*)
Xen. *Hell.*	Xenophon, *Hellenica*		
Xen. *Mem.*	Xenophon, *Memorabilia*	Zosi. *Ep.*	Zosimus (Bishop of Rome), *Epistulae*
Xen. *Oec.*	Xenophon, *Oeconomicus*		

Journals, Series, Encyclopedias, and Lexicons

21CGT	21st Century Greek Theologians	ÄAT	Ägypten und Altes Testament
30Days	30 Days	AAWB	Abhandlungen der königlichen Akademie der Wissenschaften zu Berlin
A&R	Ancient Philosophy & Religion		
AA	Archäologischer Anzeiger		
AAA	Annals of Archaeology and Anthropology	AAWG	Abhandlungen der Akademie der Wissenschaften in Göttingen
AAA	Archaiologika analecta ex Athenon	AAWG.PH	– Philologisch-historische Klasse
AAAbo	Acta Academiae Aboensis, Åbo	AB	Anchor Bible
AAAbo.H	– Series A: Humaniora	ABAW	Abhandlungen der (königlich-) bayerischen Akademie der Wissenschaften
AAAHP	Acta ad archaeologiam et artium historiam pertinentia		
AAAp	Acta Apostolorum Apocrypha	ABAW.PH	– Philosophisch-historische Abteilung
AAASH	Acta Antiqua Academiae Scientiarum Hungaricae	ABAW.PPH	– Philosophisch-philologische und historische Klasse
AaAT	Astronomical and Astrophysical Transactions	ABC	Anchor Bible Commentary
AAC	Anales de arqueología cordobesa	ABD	Anchor Bible Dictionary
AAH	Arte, Arqueologia e Historia	ABG	Arbeiten zur Bibel und ihrer Geschichte
AAM	Advances in Applied Mathematics		
AANL	Atti della accademia nazionale die lincei	ABR	Australian Biblical Review
		ABRL	Anchor Bible Reference Library
AANL.M	– Memorie: Classe di scienze morali, storiche e filologiche	AbrN	Abr-Nahrain
		AbSa	Abba Salama
AANLM	Atti della accademia nazionale dei Lincei; Memorie: Classe di scienze morali storiche e filologiche	ABSAth	The Annual of the British School at Athens
		ACA	Ancient Commentators on Aristotle
AARAS	American Academy of Religion Academy Series	ACADEMIA	ACADEMIA
		ACADÜ	Antike christliche Apokryphen in deutscher Übersetzung
AARC	Atti dell'accademia romanistica costantiniana		
		AcAn	Acta antique
AARSU	Acta academiae regiæ scientiarum Upsaliensis	ACBI	Academia biblica
		ACC	Alcuin Club Collections
AARTTS	American Academy of Religion Texts and Translations Series	AcCL	Acta classica
		ACCS	Ancient Christian Commentary on Scripture
AASc	Archaeological and Anthropological Sciences		
		ACCS.NT	Ancient Christian Commentary on Scripture: New Testament
AASF	Annales academiae scientiarum fennicae		
		AcHi	Acta histriae
AASF.B	– Series B	Acme	Acme
AASS	Acta sanctorum quotquot toto orbe coluntur	AcNoTe	Apocryphes du Nouveau Testament
		ACO	Acta conciliorum oecomenicorum
AAST	Atti dell'(a R.)accademia delle scienze di Torino (from 1933 Acta R. Academiae Scientiarum Taurinensis)	AcOr	Acta orientalia
		ACQR	American Catholic Quarterly Review
		AcRC	Accademia romanistica costantiniana

ACS	American Classical Studies	*Aethiopica*	*Aethiopica: International Journal of Ethiopian and Eritrean Studies*
ACT	Ancient Christian Texts		
ActaSS	*Acta sanctorum*	*Æthiops*	*Æthiops*
AcTSL	Accademia Toscana di scienze e lettere	*Aevum*	*Aevum: Rassegna di scienze storiche, linguistiche e filologiche*
ActTheo	*Acta Theologica*	*AevumA*	*Aevum Antiquum*
AcUG	Acta universitatis Gothoburgensis	AFCS	Apostolic Fathers Commentary Series
AcUG.SGLG	– Studia Graeca et Latina Gothoburgensia		
		AFECS	Ad Fontes: Early Christian Sources
ACUSD	*Acta classica universitatis scientiarum debreceniensis*	*AFP*	*Archivum fratrum praedicatorum*
		Africa	*Africa: Journal of the International African Institute*
ACW	Ancient Christian Writers		
AdAC	*Anejos de Antiguedad y Cristianismo*	AFSBSS	American Folklore Society Bibliographical and Special Series
ADADL	*Anzeiger für deutsches Altertum und deutsche Literatur*		
		AG	Archivum Gregorianum
ADAIK	Abhandlungen des deutschen archäologischen Instituts Kairo	AGJU	Arbeiten zur Geschichte des antiken Judentums und des Urchristentums
ADAIK.KR	– Koptische Reihe		
ADAJ	*Annual of the Department of Antiquities of Jordan*	AGLB	Aus der Geschichte der lateinischen Bibel
Adam.	Adamantiana	AGP	Arbeiten zur Geschichte des Pietismus: Im Auftrag der historischen Kommission zur Erforschung des Pietismus
Adamantius	*Adamantius: Newsletter of the Italian Research Group on "Origen and the Alexandrian Tradition"*		
ADB	*Allgemeine deutsche Biographie*	AGWG	Abhandlungen der (königlichen) Gesellschaft der Wissenschaften zu Göttingen
ADCA	*A Dictionary of Christian Antiquities*		
AdI	*Annali d'italianistica*		
Adnot.	Adnotationes	AGWG.PH	– Philologisch-historische Klasse
ADPV	Abhandlungen des deutschen Palästina-Vereins	*AHB*	*Ancient History Bulletin*
		AHC	*Annuarium historiae conciliorum*
ADRAL	Atti della reale accademia dei Lince	*AHDL*	*Archives d'histoire doctrinale et littéraire du moyen âge*
AduM	*Annales du midi: Revue archéologique, historique et philologique de la France méridionale*		
		AHI	*Anuario de historia de la iglesia*
		AHP	*Archivum historiae pontificae*
		AHR	*American Historical Review*
AdV	Anejos de Veleia: Series minor	AHRO	Archéologie et Histoire Romaine
AE	*L'année épigraphique*	*AHRE*	*Anuario de historia del derecho espanol*
AEA	*Archivo Español de arqueología*		
AeFo	Aethiopische Forschungen	*AHSS*	*Annales, histoire, sciences sociales*
Aeg.	*Aegyptus: Rivista italiana di egittologia e di papirologia*	*AIIGSS*	*Annali dell'istituto italiano per gli studi storici*
AeH	*Artibus et historiae*	*AION*	*Annali dell'istituto universitario orientale di Napoli*
AEPHE	*Annuaire de l'école pratique des hautes études*		
		AIRF	Acta Instituti Romani Finlandiae
AEPHE.R	*– Section des sciences religieuses*	Aisth.	Aisthema: International Journal
AeS	*Anthropologie et sociétés*	*AITIA*	*AITIA: Regards sur la culture hellénistique*
AESC	*Annales: Économies, sociétés, civilisations*		

AIVS	*Atti dell'istituto Veneto di scienze, lettere e arti*	AmUSt	American University Studies
AJA	*American Journal of Archaeology*	AmUSt.TR	– Series 7: Theology and Religion
AJEC	Ancient Judaism and Early Christianity	*AN*	*Auctores nostri: Studi e testi di letteratura cristiana antica*
AJP	*American Journal of Philology*	*AN*	*Ancient Narrative*
AJPA	*American Journal of Physical Anthropology*	*AnAf*	*Antiquités africaines*
		AnAl	*Antichità altoadriatiche*
AJS	*American Journal of Sociology*	*Anám*	*Anámnesis*
AJS Review	*Association for Jewish Studies Review*	*Anaphora*	*Anaphora*
AJSLL	*The American Journal of Semitic Languages and Literatures*	*AnAra*	*Anadolu Araştırmaları*
		AnArt	*Ancient Art*
AJT	*The American Journal of Theology*	*Anastasis*	*Anastasis: Research in Medieval Culture and Art*
AKathKR	*Archiv für katholisches Kirchenrecht*	*Anat*	*Anatolica*
AKG	Arbeiten zur Kirchengeschichte	*AnBib*	*Analecta biblica*
AkR	Die aktuelle Reihe	*AnBoll*	*Analecta Bollandiana*
AKThG	Arbeiten zur Kirchen- und Theologiegeschichte	AncB	Anchor Bible
		ANCL	Ante-Nicene Christian Library
AKuG	*Archiv für Kulturgeschichte*	*AnCr*	*Antigüedad y cristianismo*
ALGHJ	Arbeiten zur Literatur und Geschichte des hellenistischen Judentums	*AncSoc*	*Ancient Society*
		ANCTRTBS	Ashgate New Critical Thinking in Religion, Theology, and Biblical Studies
AlKo	Altertumswissenschaftliches Kolloquium		
		AncW	*The Ancient World*
ALMA	*Archivum latinitatis medii aevi: Bulletin du change*	*ANES*	*Ancient Near Eastern Studies*
		ANES.S.	– Supplement
ALW	*Archiv für Liturgiewissenschaft*	*ANET*	*Ancient Near Eastern Texts Relating to the Old Testament*
AmA	*American Anthropologist*		
AmBR	*The American Benedictine Review*	*AnÉt*	*Annales d'Éthiopie*
Ambr.	*Ambrosius*	ANETS	Ancient Near Eastern Texts and Studies
AMG	Annales du Musée Guimet		
AMGL	Abhandlungen der Marburger Gelehrten Gesellschaft	*ANF*	*The Ante-Nicene Fathers*
		AnFo	Anglistische Forschungen
AMH	*Annals of Medical History*	*Ang.*	*Angelicum: Periodicum trimester Pontificiae Studiorum Universitatis a Sancto Thoma Aquinate in Urbe*
AmJAH	*American Journal of Ancient History*		
AMLTL	Ancient and Modern Library of Theological Literature		
		AnGr	Analecta Gregoriana
AMMTC	Ancient Mediterranean and Medieval Texts and Contexts	*AnHe*	*Analecta Hermeneutica*
		AnHu	Analecta humanitatis
AMNSU	Arbeiten und Mitteilungen aus dem neutestamentlichen Seminar zu Uppsala	ANL	Annua Nuntia Lovaniensia
		AnQu	Antenor Quaderni
		ANRW	*Aufstieg und Niedergang der römischen Welt*
AMRhKG	*Archiv für mittelrheinische Kirchengeschichte*		– I: *Von den Anfängen Roms bis zum Ausgang der Republik*
AMS	*American Numismatic Society: Museum Notes*		– II: *Principat*
			– III: *Spätantike und Nachleben*
AMSL	*Archives des missions scientifiques et littéraires*		– IV: *Indexes*

ANS	Ancient Narrative: Supplementum	APSM	American Philological Association Monograph Series
ANS	*Anglo-Norman Studies*		
AnSt	*Anatolian Studies: Journal of the British Institute of Archaeology at Ankara*	*Aquitania*	*Aquitania*
		ARAM	*ARAM: Periodical*
		ArBib	Aramaic Bible
AnTa	*Antiquité tardive: Revue internationale d'histoire et d'archéologie*	*ArBo*	*Archivum Bobiense*
		ARC	*ARC: The Journal of the Faculty of Religious Studies*
ANTC	Abingdon New Testament Commentaries	*Arch.*	*Archaeology*
		Archaeus	*Archaeus: Studies in the History of Religions*
AntClass	*L'antiquité classique: Revue semestrielle*		
		Archéopages	*Archéopages*
Anth. Gr.	*Anthologia Graeca*	*Arctos*	*Arctos: Acta Philologica Fennica*
Antichthon	*Antichthon*	*ARelG*	*Archiv für Religionsgeschichte*
Antiphon	*Antiphon*	*Aret.*	*Arethusa*
Antiquitas	Antiquitas	*ArFi*	*Archivio di filosofia*
Antiquity	*Antiquity*	*ARG*	*Archiv für Reformationsgeschichte: Internationale Zeitschrift zur Erforschung der Reformation und ihrer Weltwirkungen: Archive for Reformation History*
Anton.	Antonianum		
ANTT	Arbeiten zur neutestamentlichen Textforschung		
ANWAW	Abhandlungen der Nordrhein-Westfälischen Akademie der Wissenschaften		
		ARGU	Arbeiten zur Religion und Geschichte des Urchristentums/ Studies in the Religion and History of Early Christianity
ANWAW.PC	– Papyrologica Coloniensia		
AoAa	Anaphorae orientales/Anaphorae armeniacae		
		ArHi	*Art History*
AOAT	Alter Orient und Altes Testament	*Aries*	*Aries: Journal for the Study of Western Esotericism*
AOB	Acta Orientalia Belgica		
AOC	Archives de l'orient chrétien	*ARIV*	*Atti del reale istituto Veneto*
AoF	*Altorientalische Forschungen*	*ArJo*	*The Archaeological Journal*
AP	*Ancient Philosophy*	*ArLa*	*Archeologia laziale*
APAW	Abhandlungen der (königlichen) preußischen Akademie der Wissenschaften	*ArLo*	*Arte Lombarda*
		Armarium	*Armarium*
		ArMe	*Archéologie médiévale*
APAW.PH	– Philosophisch-historische Klasse	*ArsD*	*Ars disputandi*
APB	*Acta patristica et byzantina*	*ArtB*	*The Art Bulletin*
Apeir.	*Apeiron*	*AruCr*	*Arzt und Christ*
Apeliotes	Apeliotes	*ArUT*	*Archeologia uomo territorio*
APF	*Archiv für Papyrusforschung und verwandte Gebiete*	*ArVe*	*Arheološki vestnik*
		ARW	*Archiv für Religionswissenschaft*
ApFa	The Apostolic Fathers	AS	Assyriological Studies
APGa	*Antiquity Project Gallery*	*AS*	*Aramaic Studies* (previously *Journal for the Aramaic Bible*)
Apocrypha	*Apocrypha: Revue internationale des littératures apocryphes*		
		AS.S.	– Supplement
Apocryphes	Apocryphes: Collection de poche de l'AELAC	*ASAA*	*Annuario della scuola archeologica di Atene e delle missioni italiane in oriente*
Apoll.	*Apollinaris: Quaderni di Apollinaris*		

ASCAM	Archäologische Studien zum christlichen Altertum und Mittelalter		*AuC*	*Antike und Christentum*
			AucNos	*Auctores Nostri*
ASCBT	Archivio storico civico e biblioteca trivulziana		*AUF*	*Archiv für Urkundenforschung und Quellenkunde des Mittelalters*
ASE	*Anglo-Saxon England*		*Aug(L)*	*Augustiniana: Tijdschrift voor de studie van Sint Augustinus en de Augustijnenorde*
ASEs	*Annali di storia dell'esegesi*			
ASGW	Abhandlungen der königlich-sächsischen Gesellschaft der Wissenschaften			
			Aug.	*Augustinianum: Periodicum quadrimestre instituti patristici "Augustinianum"*
ASGW.PH	– Philologisch-historische Klasse			
ASL	*Accademia di scienze e lettere*		AUGG	Acta universitatis Gotoburgensis Göteborgs högskolas Arsskrift
ASNSP	*Annali della scuola normale superiore di Pisa: Classe di lettere e filosofia*			
			AugL	*Augustinus-Lexikon*
ASoc	*L'année sociologique*		*AugS*	*Augustinian Studies*
AsP	*Archiv für slavische Philologie*		*Augustinus*	*Augustinus*
ASP	American Studies in Papyrology		*AUSS*	*Andrews University Seminary Studies*
ASPTLA	Ashgate Studies in Philosophy and Theology in Late Antiquity		AUU	Acta universitatis Upsaliensis
			AUU.HR	– Historia religionum
ASR	*American Sociological Review: Official Journal of the American Sociological Association*		AUU.SBU	– Studia Byzantina Upsaliensia
			AUU.SGU	– Studia Graeca Upsaliensia
			AvS	*Arkeoloji ve sanat*
ASRSP	*Archivio della società romana di storia patria*		*AW*	*Antike Welt: Zeitschrift für Archäologie und Kulturgeschichte*
ASSO	*Archivio storico per la Sicilia orientale*		AWE.FCB	Ausgewählte Werke in Einzelausgaben: F.C. Baur
AST	*Analecta sacra tarraconensia*			
ASTI	*Annual of the Swedish Theological Institute*		AWH	Heidelberger Akademie der Wissenschaften
			AWH.PH	– Philosophisch-Historische Klasse
ATAE	*Augustine Through the Ages: An Encyclopedia*		AWR	Aus der Welt der Religion: Forschungen und Berichte
ATD	Das Alte Testament deutsch: Neues Göttinger Bibelwerk			
			AYBC	Anchor Yale Bible Commentaries
Ath.	*Athenaeum*		AYBRL	Anchor Yale Bible Reference Library
AThANT	Abhandlungen zur Theologie des Alten und Neuen Testaments		*Azania*	*Azania*
			B&O	Byzantina & orientalia: Studia 1
AThD	Acta theologica Danica		*BA*	*The Biblical Archaeologist*
ÄthF	*Äthiopistische Forschungen*		*BAAT*	*Bulletin de l'association pour l'antiquité tardive*
AtiqEn	*'Atiqot: English Series*			
ATLA	American Theological Library Association		*BAB*	*Bulletin Antieke Beschaving*
			BABELAO	*Bulletin de l'académie Belge pour l'étude des langues anciennes et orientales*
ATLA.BS	– ATLA Bibliography Series			
ATR	*Anglican Theological Review*			
ATSAT	Arbeiten zu Text und Sprache im Alten Testament		*Babesch*	*Babesch*
			Babesch.S	– Supplements
AuA	Asien und Afrika: Beiträge des Zentrums für Asiatische und Afrikanische Studien		BAC	Biblioteca de autores cristianos
			BAC	*Bullettino di archeologia cristiana*
			BACTHS	*Bulletin archéologique du comité des travaux historiques et scientifiques*
AuA	*Antike und Abendland*			

BAGB	*Bulletin de l'association Guillaume Budé*
BAH	*Bulletin de l'Académie d'Hippone*
BAIAS	*Bulletin of the Anglo-Israel Archeological Society*
BALAC	*Bulletin d'ancienne littérature et d'archéologie chrétiennes*
BaLe	Bampton Lectures
BAR	*Biblical Archaeology Review*
BARCE	*Bulletin of the American Research Center in Egypt*
BARIS	British Archaeological Reports International Series
BASOR	*Bulletin of the American Schools of Oriental Research*
BASOR.S.	– Supplement Series
BASP	*Bulletin of the American Society of Papyrologists*
BASP.S	– Supplement
BASS	*Bulletin de l'académie impériale des sciences de Saint-Petersbourg*
BATa	Bibliothèque de l'antiquite tardive
Baug	Bibliothèque augustinienne
BAug	*Bibliothèque augustinenne*
BAW	Bibliothek der alten Welt
BAW.AC	– Series Antike und Christentum
BBA	Berliner byzantinistische Arbeiten
BBB	Bonner biblische Beiträge
BBC	Blackwell Bible Commentaries
BBGG	*Bollettino della Badia Greca di Grottaferrata*
BBKL	*Biographisch-bibliographisches Kirchenlexikon*
Bbod	Bibliotheca bodmeriana
BBOM	Birmingham Byzantine and Ottoman Monographs
BBR	*Bulletin for Biblical Research*
BBR.S	– Supplement
BBS	Berliner byzantinistische Studien
BCACR	*Bullettino della commissione archeologica comunale di Roma*
BCCR	*Brill's Companions to Classical Reception*
BCCT	*Brill's Companions to the Christian Tradition*
BCH	*Bulletin de correspondance hellénique*
BCH.S	– Supplement

BCHADP	*Bulletin du comité d'histoire et d'archéologie du diocèse de Paris*
BCNH	Bibliothèque copte de Nag Hammadi
BCNH.C	– Section Concordances
BCNH.É	– Section Études
BCNH.T	– Section Textes
BCRA	*Brill's Companion to the Reception of Homer from the Hellenistic Age to Late Antiquity*
BCRL	*Bulletin du centre de romanistique et de latinité tardive*
BCT	*Bible and Critical Theory*
BCtR	*Blackwell Companions to Religion*
Bd'A	La Bible d'Alexandrie
BDAG	W. Bauer, F.W. Danker, W.F. Arndt & and F.W. Gingrich: *Greek-English Lexicon of the New Testament and Other Early Christian Literature*
BDAIR	Bilderhefte des deutschen archäologischen Instituts Rom
BDB	*A Hebrew and English Lexicon of the Old Testament* (ed. *Brown–Driver–Briggs*)
BdByz	Bibliothèque de Byzantion
BDC	*Bollettino dei classici*
BDC.S	– Supplement
BDGN	*The Brill Dictionary of Gregory of Nyssa*
BDIA	*Bulletin of the Detroit Institute of Arts*
BdL	Bibliothèque de Liturgie
BdSm	Biblioteca degli "Studi medievali"
BE	*Biblische Enzyklopädie*
BEAH	*Blackwell Encyclopedia of Ancient History*
BEC	Bibliothèque d'études coptes
BEC	*Bibliothèque de l'école des Chartes*
BECNT	Baker Exegetical Commentary on the New Testament
BEEC	*Brill Encyclopedia of Early Christianity*
BEFAR	Bibliothèque des écoles françaises d'Athènes et de Rome
BegChr	*The Beginnings of Christianity*
BÉHÉ	Bibliothèque de l'école des hautes études
BÉHÉ.QS.SHP	– Quatrième section: Sciences historiques et philologiques

JOURNALS, SERIES, ENCYCLOPEDIAS, AND LEXICONS

BÉHÉ.SR	– Sciences religieuses	BHR	Bibliotheca helvetica romana
BEIFA	Bibliothèque d'étude: Institut français d'archéologie	BHTh	Beiträge zur historischen Theologie
		BIA	*Bulletin of the institute of archaeology*
BeKa	*Bedi K'art'lisa: Recueil historique, scientifique et littéraire géorgien: Le destin de la Géorgie*	BiAd	Biblioteca Adelphi
		BiAr	Biblia arabica
		BiArm	Bibliotheca Armeniaca
BELS	Bibliotheca "Ephemerides liturgicae subsidia"	BiAT	Bibliothèque de l'antiquité tardive
		BiAth	Biblioteca di athenaeum
Ber.	*Berytus: Archeological Studies*	*Bib.*	*Biblica: Commentarii periodici ad rem biblicam scientifice investigandam*
Bes.	*Bessarione*		
BEThL	Bibliotheca Ephemeridum theologicarum Lovaniensium	*Bib.Int.*	*Biblical Interpretation: A Journal of Contemporary Approaches*
BEvTh	Beiträge zur evangelischen Theologie	Bib.Int.S	Biblical Interpretation Series
		Bibl. Apost. Vat. Cod.	*Bibliothecae apostolicae vaticanae codicum [...]*
BGAMD	Beiträge zur Geschichte des alten Mönchtums und des Benediktinertums		
		BiblCas	*Bibliotheca casinensis*
		BibOr	Biblica et orientalia
BGBE	Beiträge zur Geschichte der biblischen Exegese	BibSem	The Biblical Semina
		BICS	*Bulletin of the Institute of Classical Studies*
BGK	Biblische Gestalten bei den Kirchenvätern		
		BICS.S	– Supplement
BGQM	Beiträge zur Geschichte und Quellenkunde des Mittelalters	BIDC	Bibliothèque de l'institut de droit canonique de l'université de Strasbourg
BGrL	Bibliothek der griechischen Literatur		
		BIDR	*Bullettino dell'istituto di diritto romano*
BGU	*Aegyptische Urkunden aus den königlichen staatlichen Museen zu Berlin, Griechische Urkunden*		
		BIE	*Bulletin de l'institut d'Egypte*
		BIEJ	*Boletín del instituto de estudios helénicos*
BH.TF	Biblioteca Herder: Sección de teología y filosofía		
		BIFAO	*Bulletin de l'institut français d'archéologie orientale*
BHCMA	Bibliothèque d'histoire culturelle du Moyen-Âge		
		BiGe	Biblische Gestalten
BHDL	*Bulletin historique du diocèse de Lyon*	*BIHBR*	*Bulletin de l'institut historique belge de Rome*
BHF	Bonner historische Forschungen	*Bijdr.*	*Bijdragen: Tijdschrift voor filosofie en theologie*
BHG	Bibliotheca hagiographica graeca		
BHG NAuct	Novum auctarium bibliothecae hagiographicae graecae	BiIC	Biblioteca internazionale di cultura
		BiLit	Biblioteca litúrgica
BHGNT	Baylor Handbook on the Greek New Testament	Bill.	H.L. Strack & P. Billerbeck: Kommentar zum Neuen Testament aus Talmud und Midrasch
BHH	*Biblisch-historisches Handwörterbuch*		
BHL	Bibliotheca hagiographica Latina antiquae et mediae aetatis and Supplement; new suppl.: *Novum Supplementum Bibliothecae hagiographicae latinae*		
		Bilychnis	*Bilychnis*
		Biogr.	*Biography*
		BiOr	*Bibliotheca orientalis*
		BIOSCS	*Bulletin of the International Organization for Septuagint and Cognate Studies*
BHMed	*Bulletin of the History of Medicine*		
BHO	Bibliotheca hagiographica orientalis		

BiPl	Bibliothèque de la pléiade	*BoAv*	*Boletín Avriense*
BiRL	Bibliotheca Romanica et Latina	*BOCV*	*Bibliotheca orientalis Clementino-Vaticana*
BiSe	The Biblical Seminar		
BISI	*Bullettino dell'istituto storico italiano per il medio evo*	*BoJ*	*Bonner Jahrbücher des rheinischen Landesmuseums in Bonn und des Vereins von Altertumsfreunden im Rheinlande*
BiTeu	Bibliotheca scriptorum Graecorum et Romanorum Teubneriana		
BiTh	Bibliothèque de théologie	*BoJ.B*	– Beihefte
BiToTe	*Bible de tous les temps*	*BoMo*	*Bollettino dei monumenti, musei e gallerie pontificie*
BiWo	BibleWorld		
BJHP	*British Journal for the History of Philosophy*	*Boreas*	*Boreas: Münsterische Beiträge zur Archäologie*
BJRL	*Bulletin of the John Rylands Library* (1972ff.: *Bulletin of the John Rylands University Library*)	BoSe	Bollingen series
		BPat	Biblioteca patristica
		BPC	Biblical Performance Criticism
BJS	Brown Judaic Studies	*BPhWS*	*Berliner philologische Wochenschrift*
BKAW	Bibliothek der klassischen Altertumswissenschaften	*BR*	*Biblical Research*
		BRABLB	*Boletín de la real academia de buenas letras de Barcelona*
BKENTC	Bibliothek für Kritik und Exegese des Neuen Testaments und ältesten Christengeschichte	*BRAH*	*Boletín de la real academia de la historia*
BKMR	Beiträge zur Kulturgeschichte des Mittelalters und der Renaissance	BrAR	British Archaeological Reports: International Series
BKP	Beiträge zur klassischen Philologie	*BRev*	*Bible Review change*
BKV	Bibliothek der Kirchenväter	BRHE	Bibliothèque de la revue d'histoire ecclésiastique
BL Add.	British Library Additional Manuscripts		
		Brit. Lib. Or.	British Library Oriental Manuscripts
BLCS	Brepols Library of Christian Sources	*Britannia*	*Britannia*
BLE	*Bulletin de littérature ecclésiastique*	BRPBS	Brill Research Perspectives in Biblical Studies
BMB	*Bulletin du musée de Beyrouth*		
BMC	*The Burlington Magazine for Connoisseurs*	*BS*	*Bibliotheca sacra: A Theological Quarterly*
BMCC	*The British Museum Catalogue of Coins*	*BSAC*	*Bulletin de la société d'archéologie copte*
BMCL	*Bulletin of Medieval Canon Law*	*BSAHL*	*Bulletin de la société archéologique et historique du Limousin*
BMCR	*Bryn Mawr Classical Review*		
BMGS	*Byzantine and Modern Greek Studies*	*BSAHO*	*Bulletin de la société archéologique et historique de l'Orléanais*
BMus	Bibliothèque du Muséon		
BMW	The Bible in the Modern World	BSCR	Bloomsbury Studies in Classical Reception
BN	*Biblische Notizen: Beiträge zur exegetischen Diskussion*		
		BSCT	Brill's Studies in Catholic Theology
BNF	Bibliothèque nationale de France	*BSELS*	*Bulletin de la sociéte des études littéraires: Scientifiques et artistiques du Lot*
BNF.NAL	– Nouvelle Acquisition Latine		
BNP	Bibliothèque nationale de Paris		
BNP	*Brill's New Pauly: Encyclopaedia of the Ancient World*	BSEMA	Brill's Series on the Early Middle Ages
BNTC	Black's New Testament Commentaries	*BSER*	*Bulletin de là société Ernest Renan*

BSGR	Bibliothek der Symbole und Glaubensregeln der alten Kirche	BzA	Beiträge zur Altertumskunde
BSK	Bonner Studien zur Kunstgeschichte	BZAW	Beihefte zur Zeitschrift für die alttestamentliche Wissenschaft
BSMAT	Bibliotheca scriptorum medii aevi teubneriana	BzK	Beiträge zur Kontroverstheologie
BSNAF	*Bulletin de la société nationale des antiquaires de France*	BZNW	Beihefte zur Zeitschrift für die neutestamentliche Wissenschaft und die Kunde der älteren Kirche
BSOAS	*Bulletin of the School of Oriental and African Studies*	BzR	Beiträge zur Religionsgeschichte
BSP	*Bullettino storico pistoiese*	*BKM*	*Βυζαντινά Κείμενα και Μελέται*
BSR	*Bulletin for the Study of Religion*	CAAM	College Art Association Monographs
BSS	*Bibliotheca sanctorum istituto Giovanni XXIII*	*CaAr*	*Cadernos de arqueologia*
		CaBi	*Calwer Bibellexikon*
BSSR	*Bollettino di studi storico-religiosi*	CaCL	California Classical Library
BSt	Biblische Studien	CaCS	Cambridge Classical Studies
BTA	The Bible Through the Ages	*CaE*	*Cahiers évangile*
BTB	*Biblical Theology Bulletin: A Journal of Bible and Theology*	CaE.S.	– Supplement
		CAEC	Critical Approaches to Early Christianity
BTCP	Biblical Theology for Christian Proclamation	*Caes. (Caesarod.)*	*Caesarodunum*
BThSt	Biblisch-theologische Studien	*CAH*	*The Cambridge Ancient History*
BThZ	*Berliner theologische Zeitschrift*	*CAH2/3*	*The Cambridge Ancient History*, 2nd and 3rd ed.
BTM	*Brittisches theologisches Magazin*		
BTS	Beiruter Texte und Studien	CAHS	Clarendon Ancient History Series
BTSt	Biblical Tools and Studies	*CaMCS*	*Cambrian Medieval Celtic Studies*
BU	Biblische Untersuchungen	*CANT*	*Clavis apocryphorum Novi Testamenti*
BUAC	*Bullettino di archeologia Christiana*	*CAr*	*Cahiers archéologiques*
Budé	Collection Budé	CASS	*Canadian-American Slavic Studies*
BuL	*Bibel und Liturgie*	*Cass.*	*Cassiodorus: Rivista di studi sulla tarda antichità*
BUSEK	Bibliothèque de l'université Saint-Esprit de Kaslik		
BVPA	Bibliotheca veterum patrum antiquorum que scriptorum ecclesiasticorum graeco-latina	CatBrux	Catalogus codicum hagiographicorum bibliothecae regiae Bruxellensis
BvS	Bronnen van Spiritualiteit	*Cath(M)*	*Catholica: Jahrbuch für Kontroverstheologie*
BVSAW	Berichte über die Verhandlungen der Sächsischen Akademie der Wissenschaften zu Leipzig	*Cath.*	*Catholicisme: Hier, aujourd'hui, demain*
		CATIR	*Cristianismo y aculturación en tiempos del imperio romano*
BWANT	Beiträge zur Wissenschaft vom Alten und Neuen Testament	CATR	Classical Armenian Text Reprint Series
ByAu	Byzantina australiensia	CB	Coniectanea biblica
ByF	*Byzantinische Forschungen*	CB.NT	– New Testament Series
BySl	*Byzantinoslavica: International Journal of Byzantine Studies*	CB.OT	– Old Testament Series
		CBCo	Cahiers de la bibliothèque copte
ByZ	*Byzantinische Zeitschrift*	CBCR	Corpus Basilicarum Christianarum Romae
Byz.	*Byzantion: Revue internationale des études byzantines*		
BZ	*Biblische Zeitschrift*		

CBET	Contributions to Biblical Exegesis and Theology	CCSR	Canadian Corporation for Studies in Religion Dissertation Series
CBL	Collectanea Biblica Latina	CD	Cairo Genizah: copy of the *Damascus Document*
CBM	Chester Beatty Monographs		
CBMLC	Catalogue of Byzantine Manuscripts in Their Liturgical Context	*CDCT*	*The Cambridge Dictionary of Christian Theology*
CBMLC.Sub	– Subsidia I	*CDH*	*The Canterbury Dictionary of Hymnology*
CBP	Collection bibliothèque de la pléiade		
CBPa	*Cahiers de biblica patristica*	*CDM*	*Il calamo della memoria*
CBQ	*Catholic Biblical Quarterly*	*CDSAJ*	*City of David Studies of Ancient Jerusalem*
CBQ.MS	– Monograph Series		
CBQMS	Catholic Biblical Quarterly Monograph Series	*CdT*	*Cuadernos de teología*
		CEC	Collection les études carmélitaines
CBR	*Currents in Biblical Research*	*CÉC*	*Cahiers d'études cathares*
CC	*Collectanea cisterciensia*	CEFR	Collection de l'école française de Rom
CCA	*The Cambridge Companion to Augustine*		
		CEG	*Cuadernos de estudios gallegos*
CCARB	Corsi di cultura sull'arte ravennate e bizantina	CEJL	Commentaries on Early Jewish Literature
CCAthe	*The Cambridge Companion to Atheism*	CELAMA	Cultural Encounters in Late Antiquity and the Middle Ages
CCC	Collection civilisations et cultures	*Celtica*	*Celtica*
CCCM	Corpus Christianorum: Continuatio mediaevalis	*CENM*	*Cahiers Égypte nilotique et méditerranéenne*
CCF	Commentaries for Christian Formation	*CEOC*	*The Concise Encyclopedia of Orthodox Christianity*
CCHPS	Caucasus Christianus, Historical and Philological Studies	*CEtA*	*Cahiers des études anciennes*
		CEUMS	Central European University Medieval Studies
CChr	Corpus Christianorum		
CChr.CS	– Claves, Subsidia	CF	Collectanea Friburgensia
CChr.ILL	– Instrumenta Lexicologica Latina	*CF*	*Classical Folia* (former title *Folia*)
CChr.SA	– Series apocryphorum	CFM	Corpus Fontium Manichaeorum
CChr.SG	– Series Graeca	CFM.Cop.	– Series Coptica
CChr.SL	– Series Latina	CFM.Lat.	– Series Latina
CChr.Trans.	– In Translation	CFM.Sin.	– Series Sinica
CCJ	*Cambridge Classical Journal*	CFM.Sub.	– Series Subsidia
CCL	Corpus christianorum seu nova Patrum collectio series Latina	CFM.Syr.	– Series Syriaca
		CGLC	Cambridge Greek and Latin Classics
CClCr	*Civiltà classica e cristiana*	*CGR*	*Conrad Grebel Review*
CCMéd	*Cahiers de civilisation médiévale, Xe–XIIe siècles*	CGS	Collection Gratianus Series
		CHAC	*The Cambridge History of Ancient Christianity*
CCO	*Collectanea christiana orientalia*		
CCR	*Comparative Civilizations Review*	*CHAfr*	*The Cambridge History of Africa*
CCRev	*Coptic Church Review*	CHAN	Christianismes antiques
CCS	Classical Culture and Society	*CHAP*	*Clavis historicorum antiquitatis posterioris*
CCSL	Corpus Christianorum: Series latina, Turnhout, 1953–		
		CHB	*The Cambridge History of the Bible*
		CHC	*The Cambridge History of Christianity*

JOURNALS, SERIES, ENCYCLOPEDIAS, AND LEXICONS

ChCa	*Chartae Caritatis*	CitRom	*Città romane*
CHECL	*The Cambridge History of Early Christian Literature*	*CJ*	*Classical Journal*
ChH	*Church History: American Society of Church History*	CJA	Christianity and Judaism in Antiquity
		CJS	Congress of Jewish Studies
ChHi	Christianity and History: Series of the John XXIII Foundation for Religious Studies in Bologna	CL	Collection Latomus
		CLA	Codices Latini antiquiores
		ClaIr	*Classics Ireland*
CHI	Le chiese di Roma illustrate	*ClAn*	*Classical Antiquity*
Chiron	*Chiron: Mitteilungen der Kommission für alte Geschichte und Epigraphik des deutschen archäologischen Instituts*	*ClBu*	*The Classical Bulletin: A Journal of International Scholarship and Special Topics*
		ClCh	*Classica et christiana*
CHJud	*The Cambridge History of Judaism*	*ClCr*	*Classica cracoviensia*
ChKo	*Chaos e kosmos*	*CleRev*	*The Clergy Review*
CHL	Commentationes humanarum litterarum	*ClMed*	*Clio Medica: Studies in the History of Medicine and Health*
CHLLL	*The Cambridge History of Later Latin Literature*	*ClRe*	*The Classical Review*
		CLSt	Canon Law Studies
CHMWW	*The Cambridge History of Magic and Witchcraft in the West*	*ClWe*	*The Classical Weekly*
		CM	*Classica et mediaevalia*
Chôra	*Chôra*	CMCS	*Cambridge Medieval Celtic Studies*
CHR	*Catholic Historical Review*	CMG	Corpus Medicorum Graecorum
CHRA	Christianisme antique	*CMH*	*Cambridge Medieval History* (new version = *NCMH*)
CHRAW	*The Cambridge History of Religions in the Ancient World*		
		CMR	*Christian-Muslim Relations: A Bibliographical History*
CHRC	*Church History and Religious Culture*		
ChRe	*The Chaucer Review*	CNP	Corpus Nummorum Palaestinensium
ChVo	*Christianskii Vostok*		
CHWME	*The Cambridge Handbook of Western Mysticism and Esotericism*	CNT(N)	Commentaire du Nouveau Testament
CICNRS	Colloques internationaux du centre national de la recherche scientifique	*CoAq*	*Codex Aquilarensis*
		CoAu	Collectanea Augustiniana
		CoBi.NT	Commentaire biblique: Nouveau Testament
CIG	Corpus inscriptionum Graecarum		
CIIP	Corpus Inscriptionum Judaeae/ Palaestinae: A Multi-Lingual Corpus of the Inscriptions from Alexander to Muhammad	CoCom	Concordia Commentary
		CODCC	*The Concise Oxford Dictionary of the Christian Church*
		CODO	Convivium domenicum: Studi sull'eucarestia nei padri della chiesa antica e miscellanea patristica
CIJ	Corpus inscriptionum Judaicarum		
CIL	Corpus inscriptionum Latinarum		
CIS	Corpus inscriptionum Semiticarum		
CISA	Contributi dell'istituto di storia antica	CoLa	Corona lateranensis
		CoLat	Collection Latomus
CistSQ	*Cisterian Studies Quarterly: An International Review of Monastic and Contemplative Spirituality*	*Colloquium*	*Colloquium: The Australian and New Zealand Theological Review*
		Comitatus	*Comitatus: A Journal of Medieval and Renaissance Studies*
CistSS	Cistercian Studies Series		

CoMo	Collection monastica	CRS	Classics in Religious Studies
Comp.	*Compostellanum*	*CrSt*	*Cristianesimo nella storia*
COMS	Civitatum orbis mediterranei studia	CRThPh	Cahiers de la revue de théologie et de philosophie
COMSt	*Comparative Oriental Manuscript Studies*	CSANAY	Celtic Studies Association of North America Yearbook
Conc(D)	*Concilium: Internationale Zeitschrift für Theologie*	CSASE	Cambridge Studies in Anglo-Saxon England
Concept	*Concept: An Interdisciplinary Journal of Graduate Studies*	CSB.SSB	Commenti e studi biblici: Sezione studi biblici
ConSup	Convivium Supplementum	CSCO	Corpus scriptorum Christianorum
COP	Colloquium oecumenicum paulinum		orientalium
		CSCO.Ae	– Scriptores Aethiopici
Cop.	*Coptica*	CSCO.Ar	– Scriptores Armeniaci
CoPo	Collection portugaise	CSCO.Arab.	– Scriptores Arabici
CorTrop	Corpus Troporum	CSCO.C	– Scriptores Coptici
CP	*Classical Philology*	CSCO.S	– Scriptores Syri
CPC	*Clavis patrum Copticorum (Clavis Coptica)*	CSCO.Sub	– Subsidia
CPE	*Connaissance des pères de l'église*	CSCT	Columbia Studies in the Classical Tradition
CPG	*Clavis patrum Graecorum*	CSEL	Corpus scriptorum ecclesiasticorum Latinorum
CPHi	Corpus patristicum Hispanum		
CPJ	Corpus papyrorum Judaicarum	CSeP	Collana studi e proposte
CPL	Clavis patrum Latinorum	CSIC	Consejo superior de investigaciones científicas
CPMA	Corpus Platonicum Medii Aevi		
CPPMA	Clavis patristica pseudepigraphorum mediiaevi	CSML	Cambridge Studies in Medieval Literature
CPS	Corona patrum Salesiana, Sanctorum patrum Graecorum et Latinorum opera selecta	CSMLT	Cambridge Studies in Medieval Life and Thought
		CSMSF	Classe di science morali, storiche e filosofiche
CQ	*The Classical Quarterly*		
CQR	*Church Quarterly Review*	CSP	Celtic Studies Publications
CQS	*Companion to the Qumran Scrolls*	*CSP*	*Canadian Slavonic Papers*
CRAI	*Comptes rendus des séances de l'académie des inscriptions et belles lettres*	CSPC	Cambridge Studies in Palaeography and Codicology
		CSQ	*Cistercian Studies Quarterly*
CRB	Cahiers de la revue biblique	*CSSH*	*Comparative Studies in Society and History*
CRBR	*Critical Review of Books in Religion*		
CRBS	*Currents in Research, Biblical Studies*	CStS	Collected Studies Series
CRDAC	Centro ricerche e documentazione sull'antichità classica: Monografie	CTC	Christian Theology in Context
		CTCR	*Codice topografico della città di Roma*
CrEr	*Cronache Ercolanesi*	*CTG*	*Compendium theologiae graecae*
CRHCB	Centre de recherche d'histoire et civilisation de Byzance: Monographies	*CTh*	*Cahiers théologiques*
		CTM	*Concordia Theological Monthly*
CRiBS	Critical Readings in Biblical Studies	CTP	Collana di testi patristici
CRINT	Compendia rerum iudaicarum ad Novum Testamentum	*CTR*	*Criswell Theological Review*
		CUFr	Collection des universités de France
CrQu	*Crozer Quarterly*	CUFr.SG	– Série grecque

CuMu	Cursor Mundi		DELC	*Dictionnaire étyologique de la langue copte*
CurBS	*Currents in Research: Biblical Studies*			
CurTM	*Currents in Theology and Mission*		DELL	*Dictionnare étymologique de la langue latine*
CV	*Communio viatorum*			
CW	*Classical World*		DEP	*Dizionario enciclopedico dei papi*
CWHV	*The Cambridge World History of Violence*		DeRu	*Deutsche Rundschau*
			Deutsche Gaue	*Deutsche Gaue: Zeitschrift für Gesellschaftswissenschaft und Landeskunde*
CWS	Classics of Western Spirituality			
DAC	*Dictionnaire des antiquités chrétiennes*			
			DGAS	*Dokumente zur Geschichte des arianischen Streites*
DACB	*Dictionary of African Christian Biography*			
			DGE	*Diccionario griego–español*
Dacia	*Dacia: Revue d'archéologie et d'histoire ancienne*		DGRBM	*Dictionary of Greek and Roman Biography and Mythology*
DACL	*Dictionnaire d'archéologie chrétienne et de liturgie*		DGWE	*Dictionary of Gnosis & Western Esotericism*
DAGR	*Dictionnaire des antiquités grecques et romaines*		DHA	*Dialogues d'histoire ancienne*
			DHCCGLB	*Dictionnaire historique, critique, chronologique, géographique et littéral de la Bible*
DAn	*Dictionnaire de l'antiquité*			
Davar	*Davar Logos*			
DB(V)	*Dictionnaire de la Bible*			
DB(V).Sup.	– Supplement		DHEE	*Diccionario de historia eclesiástica de España*
DBI	*Dizionario biografico degli Italiani*			
DBM	*Deltio Biblikōn Meletōn*		DHGE	*Dictionnaire d'histoire et de géographie ecclésiastiques*
DBS	*Dictionnaire de la bible: Supplément*			
DBT	Discovering Biblical Texts		DHRP	*Diccionário de história religiosa de Portugal*
DCB	*Dictionary of Christian Biography: Literature, Sects and Doctrines*			
			Diacritics	*Diacritics: A Review of Contemporary Criticism*
DCBL	*A Dictionary of Christian Biography and Literature to the End of the Sixth Century AD, with an Account of the Principal Sects and Heresies*			
			Diakonia	*Diakonia*
			Dialog	*Dialog: A Journal of Theology*
			Diaspora	*Diaspora: A Journal of Transnational Studies*
DCBLCD	*A Dictionary of Christian Biography, Literature, Sects and Doctrines; During the First Eight Centuries*		DicEL	*Dictionnaire encyclopédique de la liturgie*
			Did	*Didaskalia*
DCL	Deuterocanonical and Cognate Literature Yearbook		*Didas.*	*Didaskaleion*
			DiEc	*Dialogo ecumenico*
DCLS	Deuterocanonical and Cognate Literature Studies		*DiEc*	*Dizionario di ecclesiologia*
			Diff.	*Differences*
DCS	*A Dictionary of Christian Spirituality*		*Dionys.*	*Dionysius*
DCT	*Dictionnaire critique de théologie*		*DIP*	*Dizionario degli istituti di perfezione*
DdA	*Dictionnaire des apocryphes*		*Discentes*	*Discentes: The Undergraduate Magazine for the Department of Classical Studies at the University of Pennsylvania*
DDC	*Dictionnaire de droit canonique*			
DDD	*Dictionary of Deities and Demons in the Bible*			
			DissAb	Dissertation Abstracts
DECA	*Dictionnaire encyclopédique du christianisme ancien*		Divinations	Divinations: Rereading Late Ancient Religion

Divinitas	*Divinitas*	*DSD*	*Dead Sea Discoveries*
DivThom	*Divus Thomas*	*DSHCE*	*Documents pour servir à l'histoire des civilisation éthiopiennes*
Dixon	*Dixon*		
DJD	Discoveries in the Judaean Desert	DSI	De Septuaginta investigationes
DJG	*Dictionary of Jesus and the Gospels*	*DSp*	*Dictionnaire de spiritualité ascétique et mystique, doctrine et histoire*
DK	*Die Fragmente der Vorsokratiker*		
DKKS	Dzveli kartuli enis k'atedris shromebi	*DSP*	*Dizionario storico del papato*
DLCA	*Dizionario di letteratura cristiana antica*	DSR	Dissertatio series romana
		DSSTFM	*Documenti e studi sulla tradizione filosofica medievale*
DLNTD	*Dictionary of the Later New Testament and Its Developments*	*DTC* (*DThC*)	*Dictionnaire de théologie chrétienne: Par une équipe internationale de théologiens*
DLP	Dutch Lectures in Patristics		
DNP	*Der Neue Pauly: Enzyklopädie der Antike* (ET: see *BNP*)		
		DuG	Dogma und Geschichte
DNTB	*Dictionary of New Testament Background: A Compendium of Contemporary Biblical Scholarship*	EAA	Collection des études augustiniennes: Série antiquité
		EAA	*Enciclopedia dell' arte antica*
DoAr	*Les dossiers de l'archéologie*	*EAB*	*The Encyclopedia of Ancient Battles*
DoArch	Documenti di archeologia	*EAC*	*Encyclopedia of Ancient Christianity*
DOML	Dumbarton Oaks Medieval Library	*EaCA*	*Eastern Christian Art*
DOO	Donne d'Oriente e d'Occidente	*EAH*	*The Encyclopedia of Ancient History*
DOOTBS	Dumbarton Oaks Other Titles in Byzantine Studies	*EAJT*	*East Asia Journal of Theology*
		EAM	*Enciclopedia dell'arte medieval*
DOP	Dumbarton Oaks Papers	*EaMu*	*Early Music*
DORLC	Dumbarton Oaks Research Library and Collection	EAsh	Excavations at el-Ashmunein
		Éaug	Études augustiniennes
DOS	Dumbarton Oaks Studies	*EBib*	*Études bibliques*
DoSt	*Dominican Studies*	EBR	*Encyclopedia of the Bible and its Reception*
DPA	*Dictionnaire des philosophes antiques*		
DPAC	*Dizionario patristico e di antichità cristiane*	*EBrit*	*Encyclopaedia Britannica*
		EC	*Enciclopedia cattolica*
DPARA	*Dissertazioni della pontificia accademia romana di archeologia*	ECAp	Early Christian Apocrypha
		ECCA	Early Christianity in the Context of Antiquity
DPEB	Documents pour l'étude de la bible		
DR	*The Downside Review*	ECF	The Early Church Fathers
Dreaming	*Dreaming: Journal of the Association for the Study of Dreams*	*Echr*	*Early Christianity*
		ECI.TDWA	*Encyclopedia of Comparative Iconography: Themes Depicted in Works of Art*
DS	H. Denzinger, *Enchiridion symbolorum definitionum et declarationum de rebus fidei et morumi* = *Kompendium der Glaubensbekenntnisse und kirchlichen Lehrentscheidungen, verbessert*		
		ECJ	*Eastern Churches Journal*
		ECL	Early Christianity and Its Literature
		EClás	*Estudios clásicos*
		ECLS	Early Christian Literature Series
		ECO	*Encyclopedia of Christianity Online*
DSBP	*Dizionario di spiritualità biblico patristica*	*EcOra*	*Ecclesia orans zur Einführung in den Geist der Liturgie*
DSCM	*Dizionario dei santi della chiesa di Milano*	*Ecr*	see *Echr*
		ECR	*Eastern Churches Review*

ECS	Eastern Christian Studies	*EMS*	*Early Medieval Studies*
ECSt	Early Christian Studies	EMSAEL	Extrait des mémoires de la société archéologique d'Eure-et-Loir
ECTe	España Cristiana Textos		
EDEJ	*The Eerdmans Dictionary of Early Judaism*	EnAC	Entretiens sur l'antiquité classique: De la Fondation Hardt pour l'étude de l'antiquité classique
EdF	Erträge der Forschung		
EdP	*Enciclopedia dei papi*		
EDSH	*Encyclopedic Dictionary of the Syriac Heritage*	*EnAe*	*Encyclopaedia Aethiopica*
		EnAp	*The Encyclopedia of Apocalypticism*
EE	*Estudios eclesiásticos*	EncDSS	*Encyclopedia of the Dead Sea Scrolls*
EEC	*Encyclopedia of the Early Church*	*Enchoria*	*Enchoria: Zeitschrift für Demotistik und Koptologie*
EEECAA	*The Eerdmans Encyclopedia of Early Christian Art and Archaeology*		
		EnChr	*The Encyclopedia of Christianity*
		EncIS	*Encyclopedia of Islam*
EEM	*En la España medieval*	*EncRel (E)*	*The Encyclopedia of Religion*
EEOC	*The Encyclopedia of Eastern Orthodox Christianity*	*EnIT*	*Enciclopedia italiana Treccani*
		EnJu	*Encyclopedia judaica*
EHE	Études d'histoire de l'exégèse	*EO*	*Ecclesia orans: Periodica de scientiis liturgicis*
EHPR	Études d'histoire et de philosophie religieuses		
		EOEC	*Encyclopedia of Early Christianity*
EHR	*The English Historical Review*	EOMIA	Ecclesiae occidentalis monumenta iuris antiquissima
EHS	Europäische Hochschulschriften		
EHS.T	– Series 23: Theologie	*EOr*	*Échos d'orient*
EichPhuTh	Eichstätter Beiträge: Abteilung Philosophie und Theologie	*Eos*	*Eos: Commentarii societatis philologae polonorum*
Eikasmós	*Eikasmós*	EPAHA	Études de philologie, d'archéologie et d'histoire anciennes
EIr	*Encyclopaedia Iranica*		
Eirene	*Eirene*	*Epig.*	*Epigraphica*
EJA	*European Journal of Archaeology*	*EpigrAnat*	*Epigraphica Anatolica: Zeitschrift für Epigraphik und historische Geographie Anatoliens*
EJCR	*Encyclopedia of Jewish-Christian Relations*		
EJMS	*Electronic Journal of Mithraic Studies*	*EPLBHC*	*Encyclopedic Prosopographical Lexicon of Byzantine History and Civilization*
EKK	Evangelisch-katholischer Kommentar zum Neuen Testament		
		EpPa	Epifania della parola
Ekstasis	Ekstasis	EpPa.TE	– Testi ermeneutici
EL	*Ephemerides liturgicae*	EPRO	Études préliminaires aux religions orientales dans l'empire romain
Electrum	*Electrum: Journal of Ancient History*		
Elenchos	*Elenchos*	*ER*	*Ecumenical Review*
EMC	*Echos du monde classique/Classical Views*	*ErAn*	*Eruditio antiqua*
		Eranos	*Eranos: Yearbook*
EMCr	*Encyclopedia of the Medieval Chronicle*	*ERE*	*Encyclopedia of Religion and Ethics*
		EREra	*Encyclopedia of the Romantic Era 1760–1850*
EME	*Early Medieval Europe*		
Emerita	*Emerita*	*Erga-Logoi*	*Erga-Logoi*
EMH	*Encyclopedia of Mediterranean Humanism*	*ERHis*	*European Review of History*
		ErIs	*Ereṣ-Yiśrāʾēl; Eretz-Israel*
EMH	*Early Music History*	*Ériu*	*Ériu*
Empúries	*Empúries*	*ErJb*	*Eranos-Jahrbuch*

EsBi	*Estudios bizantinos*	*Expositor*	*The Expositor*
ESI	Excavations and Surveys in Israel	FAB	Frankfurter althistorische Beiträge
EstBib	*Estudios bíblicos*	FaCh	Fathers of the Church
ESTJ	*(T & T Clark) Encyclopaedia of Second Temple Judaism*	FaiCu	Faith and Cultures
EsVi	*Esprit et Vie*	*FaPh*	*Faith and Philosophy: Journal of the Society of Christian Philosophers*
ET	*The Expository Times*	FARG	Forschungen zur Anthropologie und Religionsgeschichte
ÉtAu	Études augustiennes		
EtB	Études bibliques	FAT	Forschungen zum Alten Testament
EtCa	Études carmelitaines	FBRG	Forschungen zur byzantinischen Rechtsgeschichte
ÉtCe	*Études celtiques*		
EtCl	*Les études classiques*	FChr	Fontes Christiani: Zweisprachige Neuausgabe christlicher Quellentexte aus Altertum und Mittelalter
Etco	*Etudes corses*		
ETCSL	The Electronic Text Corpus of Sumerian Literature		
ETCSM	*Encyclopedia of Theology: The Concise Sacramentum Mundi*	FCNTECW	Feminist Companion to the New Testament and Early Christian Writings
ÉtÉp	Études épigraphiques		
ETF	*Espacio, tiempo y forma*	FCT	The Formation of Christian Theology
ÉtF	Études franques		
EtGr	*Études grégoriennes*	*FeH*	*Fides et Historia*
EThL	*Ephemerides theologicae Lovanienses*	*FeT*	*Filosofia e teologia*
EThSt	Erfurter theologische Studien	*FeTh*	*Feminist Theology*
ÉtPh	*Les études philosophiques*	*FGH*	*Die Fragmente der griechischen Historiker*
EtPl	*Études platoniciennes*		
EtPr	Études prosopographiques	FGM	Forschungen zur Geschichte des Mittelalters
ETR	*Études théologiques et religieuses*		
ETSE	Estonian Theological Society in Exile	FHG	Fragmenta Historicorum Graecorum
EtSy	Études syriaques	FIFGWS	Forschungsgespräche des internationalen Forschungszentrums für Grundfragen der Wissenschaften Salzburg
EtTr	*Étude et travaux*		
Études	*Études: Revue catholique d'intérêt général*		
EU	Egyptologische Uitgaven		
EuGeStA	*Eugesta: Journal of Gender Studies in Antiquity*	*FiMe*	*Filologia mediolatina*
		FJB	*Frankfurter judaistische Beiträge*
Euph.	*Euphrosyne*	FKDG	Forschungen zur Kirchen- und Dogmengeschichte
EVK	Exegetische Verantwortung in der Kirche: Aufsätze		
		FKTh	*Forum katholische Theologie*
EvQ	*The Evangelical Quarterly: A Theological Review*	*Flor.*	*Florentia iliberritana*
		Floril.	*Florilegium*
EvTh	*Evangelische Theologie*	FMAG	Forschungen zur mittelalterlichen Geschichte
EWNT	*Exegetisches Wörterbuch zum Neuen Testament*		
		FMSt	*Frühmittelalterliche Studien*
Exchange	*Exchange: Bulletin de la littérature des églises du Tiers monde: Bulletin of Third World Christian Literature*	*FoBr*	*Forma breve*
		FoFa	Forum fascicles
		FoPh	*Forum philosophicum*
ExCl	*Exemplaria classica*	FOTL	The Forms of the Old Testament Literature
Exem.	*Exemplaria*		

Francia	*Francia: Forschungen zur westeuropäischen Geschichte*	*GEDSH*	*Gorgias Encyclopedic Dictionary of the Syriac Heritage*
Francia.B	– Supplement series	*GeLe*	*Geist und Leben: Studien zur Verwirklichung der christlichen Botschaft*
FRC	The Family, Religion, and Culture		
FRLANT	Forschungen zur Religion und Literatur des Alten und Neuen Testaments	*Geríon*	*Geríon: Revista de Historia Antigua*
		Gesta	*Gesta: International Center of Medieval Art*
FrNe	Frühe Neuzeit		
FrSt	*Frühmittelalterlichen Studien*	*GeV*	*Geloof en Vrijheid*
FTECS	Foundations of Theological Exegesis and Christian Spirituality	*GFA*	*Göttinger Forum für Altertumswissenschaft*
FTS	Frankfurter theologische Studien	*GHA*	*Göteborgs högskolas årsskrift*
Fund.	*Fundamina*	*GJRT*	*Ghana Journal of Religion and Theology*
FuPa	Fuentes patrísticas		
FV	*Foi et vie*	*GK*	*Gestalten der Kirchengeschichte*
FyL	Filosofia y letras	*GLAJJ*	*Greek and Latin Authors on Jews and Judaism*
FzB	Forschung zur Bibel		
FZPhTh	*Freiburger Zeitschrift für Philosophie und Theologie*	*GLB*	*Graeco-Latina Brunensia*
		GLH	*Great Lives from History: Ancient and Medieval Series*
G&H	*Gender & History*		
G&RNSC	Greece & Rome: New Surveys in the Classics	*GLS*	*Il grande libro dei santi: Dizionario enciclopedico*
GABR	Guides to Advanced Biblical Research	*GMO*	*Grove Music Online*
		GMT	Great Medieval Thinkers
GaHi	Galicia histórica	*GNO*	*Gregorii Nysseni Opera*
Gaia	*Gaia: Revue interdisciplinaire sur la Grèce archaïque*	*Gnomon*	*Gnomon: Kritische Zeitschrift für die gesamte klassische Altertumswissenschaft*
GAP	Guides to the Apocrypha and Pseudepigrapha		
		Gnosis	*Gnosis: Journal of Gnostic Studies*
GAT	*Gaza dans l'antiquité tardive: Archéologie, rhétorique et histoire*	GNS	Good News Studies
		GnVa	*Gnomologium Vaticanum*
GBA	*Gazette des beaux-arts*	GOHA	Gorgias Handbooks
GBS	Guides to Biblical Scholarship	GoPe	Gospel Perspectives
GCh	*Die Geschichte des Christentums: Religion, Politik, Kultur*	*GOTR*	*The Greek Orthodox Theological Review*
GCS	Die griechischen christlichen Schriftsteller der ersten drei Jahrhunderte	*GPAHW*	*Geschichte des Papstums von den Anfängen bis zur Höhe der Weltherrschaft*
GCS.NF	Die griechischen christlichen Schriftsteller der ersten Jahrhunderte	*GPMB*	*Greek Papyri in the British Museum*
		GR	*Greece and Rome*
		Graphè	*Graphè*
GDECS	Gorgias Dissertations in Early Christian Studies	GRBS	Greek, Roman and Byzantine Studies
		GREC	Graeco-romanae religionis electa collectio
GDIP	*Grande dizionario illustrato dei papi*		
GDK	Gottesdienst der Kirche: Handbuch der Liturgiewissenschaft	*Greg*	*Gregorianum*
		Gregoriana	Gregoriana
GECS	Gorgias Eastern Christian Studies	GRL	Gesellschaft für romanische Literatur

GRM (GrRoM)	Graeco-Roman Memoirs	HDRG	*Handwörterbuch zur deutschen Rechtsgeschichte*
GSECP	Gorgias Studies in Early Christianity and Patristics	HDSB	*Harvard Divinity School Bulletin*
GTA	Göttinger theologische Arbeiten	HDThG	*Handbuch der Dogmen- und Theologiegeschichte*
GTR	Gender, Theory, and Religion	Hel.	*Helmántica*
Gymnasium	*Gymnasium: Zeitschrift für Kultur der Antike und humanistische Bildung*	HeLa	*Das Heilige Land*
		Helikon	Helikon
		Hellenika	Hellenika
HaAr	*Hadashot arkheologiyot*	Henoch	*Henoch: Studi storicofilologici sull'ebraismo*
HABES	Heidelberger althistorische Beiträge und epigraphische Studien	Hereditas	Hereditas: Studien zur alten Kirchengeschichte
Habis	*Habis*	*Heritage*	*Heritage: Journal of Multidisciplinary Studies in Archaeology*
HagSSH	Hagiologia: Études sur la sainteté et l'hagiographie/Studies on Sanctity and Hagiography	*HerKorr*	*Herder-Korrespondenz: Orbis catholicus*
Hallel	*Hallel: A Review of Monastic Spirituality and Liturgy*	*Herma.*	*Hermathena*
		Hermeneia	Hermeneia: A Critical and Historical Commentary on the Bible
HALOT	*The Hebrew and Aramaic Lexicon of the Old Testament*	*Hermeneutica*	*Hermeneutica*
HAM	*Hortus Artium Medievalium*	*Hermes*	*Hermes: Zeitschrift für klassische Philologie*
Harp	*The Harp*		
HATS	Harvard Armenian Texts and Studies	Hermes.E.	– Einzelschriften
HAW	*Handbuch der Altertumswissenschaft*	*Hesp.*	*Hesperia: Journal of the American School of Classical Studies at Athens*
HBE	History of Biblical Exegesis		
HBO	Hallesche Beiträge zur Orientwissenschaft		
		HeSt	Herkulanische Studien
HBS	Herders biblische Studien	HeSts	Hellenic Studies
HBSo	Henry Bradshaw Society	*HeyJ*	*Heythrop Journal: A Quarterly Review of Philosophy and Theology*
HBSo.Sub	– Subsidia		
HBT	*Horizons in Biblical Theology*	HeyM	Heythrop Monographs
HBzO	*Hallesche Beiträge zur Orientwissenschaft*	HGF	Hermaea Germanistische Forschungen
HCMR	The History of Christian-Muslim Relations	*HHR*	*Hungarian Historical Review*
		HiAn	*Hispania antiqua*
HCO	Histoire des conciles oecuméniques	*HiJo*	*The Hibbert Journal*
HCS	Hellenistic Culture and Society	*HiRe*	*Historical Reflections/Réflexions historiques*
HCSPTH	Holy Cross Studies in Patristic Theology and History		
		Hirundo	*Hirundo: The McGill Journal of Classical Studies*
HD	*Handbuch der Dogmatik*		
HDAC	Histoire des doctrines de l'antiquité classique	*HiSa*	*Hispania sacra*
		Hist.	*Historia: Zeitschrift für alte Geschichte*
HDG	*Handbuch der Dogmengeschichte*		
HDIEO	Histoire du droit et des institutions de l'église en occident	Hist.E	– Einzelschriften
		HistJ	*Historical Journal*
HDR	Harvard Dissertations in Religion	Historica	Historica

Histos	*Histos*	HUTh	Hermeneutische Untersuchungen zur Theologie
Histos.S	– Supplements	*HWR*	*Historisches Wörterbuch der Rhetorik*
HiTh	Histoire de la théologie	*Hymn*	*The Hymn*
HJb	*Historisches Jahrbuch*	Hyp.	Hypomnemata: Untersuchungen zur Antike und zu ihrem Nachleben
HJSS	*Hugoye: Journal of Syriac Studies*		
HKG(J)	*Handbuch der Kirchengeschichte*	*Hyperboreus*	*Hyperboreus*
HLL	*Handbuch der lateinischen Literatur der Antike (= Handbuch der Altertumswissenschaft)*	*HZ*	*Historische Zeitschrift*
		HzS	Handbuch zur Septuagint
		IAA	Israel Antiquities Authority
HLV	Hans-Lietzmann-Vorlesungen	IbFa	Iberian Fathers
HMA	Haute moyen âge	IBMFN	Interdisziplinäre Beiträge zu Mittelalter und früher Neuzeit
HMCL	History of Medieval Canon Law		
HNB	*Herders Neues Bibellexikon*	ICC	International Critical Commentary of the Holy Scriptures of the Old and New Testaments
HNT	Handbuch zum Neuen Testament		
HO	Handbuch der Orientalistik		
HoRe	Homo religiosus	ICHA	Acts of the International Congress of the History of Art
HOS	Handbook of Oriental Studies		
HPBl	*Historisch-politische Blätter für das katholische Deutschland*	*ICIS*	*Inscriptiones christianae Italiae septimo saeculo antiquiores*
HPE	*History of Political Economy*	*Iconogra-phica*	*Iconographica*
HPTh	*Handbuch der Pastoraltheologie: Praktische Theologie der Kirche in ihrer Gegenwart*	*ICQ*	*Irish Church Quarterly*
		ICS (*ICST*)	Illinois Classical Studies
HR	*History of Religions*	*ICS*	*Encyclopedia of the Bible and its Reception*
HSCP	*Harvard Studies in Classical Philology*		
HSem	Horae Semiticae	*ICUR*	*Inscriptiones christianae urbis Romae septimo saeculo antiquiores*
HSJ	*Haskins Society Journal*		
HSM	Harvard Semitic Monographs	*IDS*	*In die Skriflig*
HSSC	*Histoire des saints et de la sainteté chrétienne*	*IEJ*	*Israel Exploration Journal*
		IELOA	Instruments pour l'étude des langues de l'orient ancien
HTGANT	*Handbuch theologischer Grundbegriffe zum Alten und Neuen Testament*		
		IEPA	*Internet Encyclopedia of Philosophy and its Authors*
HThK	Herders theologischer Kommentar zum Neuen Testament		
		IFAO	Institut francais d'archéologie orientale
HThKAT	Herders theologischer Kommentar zum Alten Testament		
		IG	*Inscriptiones graecae*
HThR	*The Harvard Theological Review*	*IGRR*	*Inscriptiones graecae ad res romanas pertinentes*
HThS	Harvard Theological Studies		
HTS	*Hervormde theologiese studies*	IGSK	Inschriften griechischer Städte aus Kleinasien
HTSt	Hamburger theologische Studien		
HTSTS	*HTS Teologiese Studies*	*IGUR*	*Inscriptiones graecae urbis Romae*
HUCA	*Hebrew Union College Annual*	*IHA*	*L'Information d'histoire de l'art*
HUDCL	Harvard University Department of Comparative Literature	*IJCT*	*International Journal of the Classical Tradition*
Hug.	see *HJSS*	*IJHS*	*International Journal of the History of Sport*
HuNa	*Human Nature*		
HUS	*Harvard Ukrainian Studies*	*IJM*	*International Journal of Musicology*

IJO	*Inscriptiones Judaicae Orientis*	IPM	Instrumenta Patristica et Mediaevalia
IJPlT	*International Journal of the Platonic Tradition*	IPS	International Plato Studies
IJPT	*International Journal of Practical Theology*	*Iran*	*Iran: Journal of the British Institute of Persian Studies*
IJSCC	*International Journal for the Study of the Christian Church*	*Iraq*	*Iraq: British School of Archaeology in Iraq*
IJSL	*International Journal for the Semiotics of Law*	*Irén.*	*Irénikon: Revue des moines de Chevetogne*
IJST	*International Journal of Systematic Theology*	IRT	Issues in Religion and Theology
IKZ	*Internationale kirchliche Zeitschrift/ Revue internationale ecclésiastique/ International Church Review*	ISACR	Interdisciplinary Studies in Ancient Culture and Religion
		ISBE	*International Standard Bible Encyclopedia*
IL	*Invigilata lucernis*	ISCAB	Istituto di cultura e archeologia delle terre bibliche
I-L	*Intus-legere*		
ILCV	Inscriptiones latinae christianae veteres	ISCAB.Arch.	– Serie archeologia
		Isis	*Isis*
ILD'A	Inscriptions latines d'Algérie	ISLL	Illinois Studies in Language and Literature
IliffRev	*Iliff Review*		
ILLPRON	*Inscriptionum lapidariarum Latinarum provinciae Norici*	*ISSQ*	*Indiana Social Studies Quarterly*
		Ist.	*Istina: Publication avec le concours du centre national de la recherche scientifique*
Illum.	Illuminations		
ILQ	Instrumenta liturgica quarreriensa		
ILS	Inscriptiones Latinae selectae	*IstMitt*	*Istanbuler Mitteilungen*
Ilu	*Ilu: Revista de ciencias de las religiones*	*ItBur*	*Itinerarium burdigalense*
		IThS	Innsbrucker theologische Studien
Imm	*Immanuel*	*ITQ*	*The Irish Theological Quarterly*
IMR	International Medieval Research	*ITS*	*Indian Theological Studies*
IMSA	*Israel Museum Studies in Archaeology*	*IWJRS*	*Intermountain West Journal of Religious Studies*
IMU	*Italia medioevale e umanistica*	*JA*	*Journal asiatique*
InArch	Internationale Archäologie	*JaAj*	*Judaïsme ancien/Ancient Judaism*
InBS	Innsbrucker Beiträge zur Sprachwissenschaft	*JAAR*	*Journal of the American Academy of Religion*
InChr	Inventing Christianity	*JAAS*	*Journal of Assyrian Academic Studies*
IndoBib	Indogermanische Bibliothek	*JAB*	*Journal for the Aramaic Bible*
InFr	*Inter fratres*	*JAC*	*Journal of Ancient Civilizations*
Initiations	Initiations	*JACS*	*Journal of the American College of Surgeons*
InLi	*Information littéraire*		
INR	Israel Numismatic Research	*JAEMA*	*Journal of the Australian Early Medieval Association*
InSo	*International Sociology*		
Interfaces	*Interfaces: A Journal of Medieval European Literatures*	*JAH*	*Journal of Ancient History*
		JAJ	*Journal of Ancient Judaism*
Interp.	*Interpretation: A Journal of Bible and Theology*	*JAJ.S*	*– Supplements*
		JAMSt	*Journal of Ancient and Medieval Studies*
IOS	*Israel Oriental Studies*		
IP	Instrumenta patristica		

JANER	Journal of Ancient Near Eastern Religions	JEI	Jerusalem and Eretz-Israel: A Journal for Land of Israel Studies and Archaeology
JAOC	Judaïsme ancien et origines du christianisme	JePa	Jerash Papers
JAOS	Journal of the American Oriental Society	JerCat	The Jerusalem Cathedra
		JES	Journal of Ecumenical Studies
JArS	Journal of Archaeological Science	JETS	Journal of the Evangelical Theological Society
JaSt	Jakobus-Studien		
JBAA	Journal of the British Archaeological Association	JewHis	Jewish History
		JfR	Jahrbuch für Religionsphilosophie
JbAC	Jahrbuch für Antike und Christentum	JFSR	Journal of Feminist Studies in Religion
JbAC.KR	– Kleine Reihe	JGRCJ	Journal of Greco-Roman Christianity and Judaism
JbAC.Sup.	– Supplement		
JBL	Journal of Biblical Literature	JHA	Journal for the History of Astronomy
JBQ	The Jewish Bible Quarterly	JHC	Journal of Higher Criticism
JBRec	Journal of the Bible and its Reception	JHI	Journal of the History of Ideas
JBTh	Jahrbuch für biblische Theologie	JHMAS	Journal of the History of Medicine and Allied Sciences
JCH	Journal of Cultural Heritage		
JCMAMW	Jews, Christians, and Muslims from the Ancient to the Modern World	JHP	Journal of the History of Philosophy
		JHS	Journal of Hellenic Studies
JCP	Jahrbücher für classische Philologie	JHSX	Journal of the History of Sexuality
JCP.S	– Supplement	JIATA	Journal of the Institute of Archaeology of Tel Aviv University
JCPS	Jewish and Christian Perspective Series		
		JIBS	Journal for Interdisciplinary Biblical Studies
JCRR	Journal of the Council for Research on Religion	JIG	Jahrbuch für internationale Germanistik
JCRT	Journal for Cultural and Religious Theory		
		JIGRE	Jewish Inscriptions of Graeco-Roman Egypt
JCSCoS	Journal of the Canadian Society for Coptic Studies		
		JiTR	Jinling Theological Review
JCSSS	Journal of the Canadian Society for Syriac Studies	JJA	Journal of Jewish Art
		JJMJS	Journal of the Jesus Movement in Its Jewish Setting
JCST	Journal of Coptic Studies		
JCT	Jesus Christ Today	JJP	Journal of Juristic Papyrology
JDAI	Jahrbuch des deutschen archäologischen Instituts	JJP.S	– Supplement
		JJS	Journal of Jewish Studies
JDS	Judean Desert Studies	JJTP	Journal of Jewish Thought and Philosophy
JDT	Jahrbücher für deutsche Theologie		
JE	Jewish Encyclopedia	JK	Regesta pontificum Romanorum (Jaffé &Kaltenbrunner)
JEaCS	Journal of Eastern Christian Studies		
JECH	Journal of Early Christian History	JLAn	Journal of Late Antiquity
JECS	Journal of Early Christian Studies: Journal of the North American Patristic Society	JLARC	Journal of Late Antique Religion and Culture
		JLH	Jahrbuch für Liturgik und Hymnologie
JEGP	Journal of English and Germanic Philology	JLL	The James Lydon Lectures in Medieval History and Culture
JEH	Journal of Ecclesiastical History	JLS	Joint Liturgical Studies
		JLW	Jahrbuch für Liturgiewissenschaft

JMA	*Journal of Mediterranean Archaeology*	*JRVDL*	*Jahrbuch des rheinischen Vereins für Denkmalpflege und Landschaftsschutz*
JMEMS	*Journal of Medieval and Early Modern Studies*	*JS*	*Journal des savants*
JMES	*Journal of Middle Eastern Studies*	*JSAS*	*Journal of the Society for Armenian Studies*
JML	*Journal of Medieval Latin*		
JMMH	*Journal of Medieval Military History*	*JSCS*	*Journal of Septuagint and Cognate Studies*
JMMS	*Journal of Men, Masculinities and Spirituality*	*JSHJ*	*Journal for the Study of the Historical Jesus*
JNeoS	*Journal of Neoplatonic Studies*		
JNES	*Journal of Near Eastern Studies*	JSHRZ	Jüdische Schriften aus hellenistisch-römischer Zeit
JNG	*Jahrbuch für Numismatik und Geldgeschichte*	JSHRZ.S	– Supplementa
JNSL	*Journal of Northwest Semitic Languages*	*JSIJ*	*Jewish Studies Internet Journal*
JÖB	*Jahrbuch der österreichischen Byzantinistik*	*JSJ*	*Journal for the Study of Judaism in the Persian, Hellenistic, and Roman Period*
JÖB	*Journal of Northwest Semitic Languages*	*JSJ.S*	*– Supplement Series*
JoCS	*Journal of Classical Studies*	*JSL*	*Journal of Sacred Literature*
JP	*Journal of Philology*	*JSLBR*	*Journal of Sacred Literature and Biblical Record*
JPMMS	*Journal of the Plainsong & Mediaeval Music Society*	*JSNT*	*Journal for the Study of the New Testament*
JPS	Jewish Publication Society	*JSNT.S*	*– Supplement Series*
JPsT	*Journal of Psychology and Theology: An Evangelical Forum for the Integration of Psychology and Theology*	*JSOT*	*Journal for the Study of the Old Testament*
		JSOT.S	*– Supplement Series*
		JSP	Judea and Samaria Publications
JQR	*Jewish Quarterly Review*	*JSP*	*Journal for the Study of the Pseudepigrapha*
JR	*Journal of Religion*		
JRA	*Journal of Religion in Africa; Religion en Afrique*	*JSP.S*	*– Supplement Series*
		JSPL	*Journal for the Study of Paul and his Letters*
JRAr	*Journal of Roman Archeology*		
JRAr.S	*– Supplementary Series*	*JSQ*	*Jewish Studies Quarterly*
JRDH	*Journal of Religion, Disability & Health*	JSRC	Jerusalem Studies in Religion and Culture
JRE	*Journal of Religious Ethics*	*JSSt*	*Journal of Semitic Studies*
JRelS	*Journal of Religious Studies*	JTC	Journal for Theology and the Church
JRH	*Journal of Religious History*	JThF	Jerusalemer theologisches Forum
JRS	*Journal of Roman Studies*	JThS	Journal of Theological Studies
JRSAI	*Journal of the Royal Society of Antiquaries of Ireland*	JTI	Journal of Theological Interpretation
		JTI.S	– Supplements
JRSoc	*Journal of Religion and Society*	JTS	see *JThS*
JRSoc.S.	– Supplement	*JTSR*	*Journal for Theology and the Study of Religion*
JRSt	*Journal of Refugee Studies*		
JRV	*Journal of Religion and Violence*	Jud.	Judaica: Beiträge zum Verständnis des jüdischen Schicksals in Vergangenheit und Gegenwart

JudChr	Judaica et christiana
Jurist	*The Jurist: Studies in Church Law and Ministry*
JWAG	*The Journal of the Walters Art Gallery*
JWCI	*Journal of the Warburg and Courtauld Institutes*
JWH	*Journal of World History*
JZWL	*Jüdische Zeitschrift für Wissenschaft und Leben*
KAANT	Kleinere Arbeiten zum Alten und Neuen Testament
Kairos	*Kairos: Zeitschrift für Religionswissenschaft und Theologie*
Kanon	*Kanon: Jahrbuch der Gesellschaft für das Recht der Ostkirchen*
KaR	Kulturtopographie des alemannischen Raums
Kart.	*Kartvelologi*
Katholik	*Der Katholik*
KAV	Kommentar zu den apostolischen Vätern (= KEK supplement series)
KAW	Kulturgeschichte der antiken Welt
KAWW	Kaiserliche Akademie der Wissenschaften in Wien
KAWW.PH.D	– Philosophisch-historische Klasse: Denkschriften
KEK	Kritisch-exegetischer Kommentar über das Neue Testament
Kentron	*Kentron*
Kernos	*Kernos*
KfA	Kommentar zu frühchristlichen Apologeten
KG.A	Konziliengeschichte: Reihe A: Darstellungen
KG.B	Konziliengeschichte: Reihe B: Untersuchungen
KGQS	Kirchengeschichtliche Quellen und Studien
Kleronomia	*Kleronomia*
Klio	*Klio: Beiträge zur alten Geschichte*
KlT	Kleine Texte für Vorlesungen und Übungen
KMJ	*Kirchenmusikalisches Jahrbuch*
KOiL	Kunst en Oudheden in Limburg
Koin.	*Koinonia*
KöJa	*Kölner Jahrbuch*
Kokalos	*Kokalos*
KRB	Kleine Reihe zur Bible
KRR	Klostermann RoteReihe
KStTh	Kohlhammer Studienbücher Theologie
Ktèma	*Ktèma*
KTVU	Kleine Texte für theologische und philologische Vorlesungen und Übungen
KuD	*Kerygma und Dogma*
KuI	*Kirche und Israel: Neukirchener theologische Zeitschrift*
Kyrios	*Kyrios: Vierteljahresschrift für Kirchen- und Geistesgeschichte Osteuropas*
LAA	Late Antique Archaeology
L'AC	*L'année canonique*
LACL	*Lexikon der antiken christlichen Literatur*
LAEMI	Late Antique and Early Medieval Iberia
LAHR	Late Antique History and Religion
LAMon	Leicester Archaeology Monographs
Lampas	*Lampas*
LaO	*Limnology and Oceanography*
L'AS	L'Art et les saints
LASBF	*Liber annuus: Studium biblicum franciscanum*
Lat.	Lateres
Later.	*Lateranum*
Latinitas	*Latinitas*
Latomus	*Latomus*
Laur	*Laurentianum*
Laverna	*Laverna*
LB	*Linguistica biblica*
LBS	Linguistic Biblical Studies
LC	Law and Christianity
LCA	Letteratura cristiana antica
LCA.NS	– Nuova serie
LCA.S	– Studi
LCC	The Library of Christian Classics
LCCA	*La civiltà cattolica*
LCI	*Lexikon der christlichen Ikonographie*
LCL	Loeb Classical Library
LCP	Latinitas christianorum primaeva
LCPM	Letture cristiane del primo millennio
LDAB	Leuven Database of the Ancient Books
LDD	Linguistica delle differenze

LEC	Library of Early Christianity	LSAWS	Linguistic Studies in Ancient West Semitic
LeCRI	Le chiese di Roma illustrate		
Lectio	*Lectio difficilior*	*LSJ*	see Liddell/Scott
LeDiv	Lectio divina	LSTS	Library of Second Temple Studies
LeDiv. Comm.	– Commentaires	*LThK*	*Lexikon für Theologie und Kirche*
		LTP	*Laval théologique et philosophique*
LEGC	Letteratura egiziana gnostica e cristiana	LTPM	Louvain Theological and Pastoral Monographs
Leit.	*Leiturgia: Handbuch des evangelischen Gottesdienstes*	*LTUR*	*Lexicon topographicum urbis Romae*
		LTUR.Sub	– Suburbium
Levant	*Levant: Journal of the British School of Archaeology in Jerusalem*	*LumVit*	*Lumen Vitae*
		LV	*Lumen et Vita*
Lexis	*Lexis*	LWQF	Liturgiewissenschaftliche Quellen und Forschungen
LHBOTS	Library of Hebrew Bible/Old Testament Studies		
		LyFi	*Lysty filologické*
Libitina	Libitina	*M&L*	*Music & Letters*
Libri	*Libri*	MA	Monumenta archaeologica
Libyca	*Libyca*	*MAAR*	*Memoirs of the American Academy in Rome*
Liddell/ Scott	*A Greek-English Lexicon*, compiled by H.G. Liddell & R. Scott-Jones		
		Maasgouw	*De Maasgouw*
LIMC	*Lexicon iconographicum mythologiae classicae*	*MAB*	*Miscellanea academica berolinensia*
		MAH	*Mélanges d'archéologie et d'histoire*
LiPo	Litografica pontificia	*Maia*	*Maia*
LiRo	Le livre et le rouleau	*Main.*	*Mainake*
LiRu	*Literarische Rundschau*	*MaJaKu*	*Marburger Jahrbuch für Kunstwissenschaft*
LiSt	*Libyan Studies*		
LitCon	Liturgia condenda	MAMA	Monumenta asiae minoris antiqua
Literator	*Literator: Journal of Literary Criticism, Comparative Linguistics and Literary Studies*	*MaMi*	*Madrider Mitteilungen*
		Mansi	J.D. Mansi, *Sacrorum conciliorum nova et amplissima collectio*
LiTh	*Literature and Theology*	*Manu.*	*Manuscripta*
LitOen	Liturgica Oenipontana	*MaRE*	*Material Religion*
LitWo	*Liturgisch woordenboek*	MARep	Medieval Academy Reprints
LJNLA	*Lexicon of Jewish Names in Late Antiquity*	*Maria*	*Maria*
		MartHieron	*Commentarius in Martyrologium Hieronymianum*
LLT	Library of Latin Texts		
LMA	*Lexikon des Mittelalters*	*Marturia*	*Marturia: E-magazine over de betekenis van de vroege kerk voor vandaag*
LNTS	Library of New Testament Studies		
LNTS.ISCO	– International Studies in Christian Origins		
		Matsne	*Matsne: Archaeology, Ethnography and Art History Series*
LO	*Lex Orandi*		
LoGa	Land of Galilee	*MBAHWS*	*Marburger Beiträge zur Antiken Handels-, Wirtschafts- und Sozialgeschichte*
Logos	*Logos*		
LouvSt	*Louvain Studies*		
LPTB	Linzer philosophisch-theologische Beiträge	MBPR	Münchener Beiträge zur Papyrusforschung und antiken Rechtsgeschichte
LQF	Liturgiegeschichtliche Quellen und Forschungen		
		MBTh	Münsterische Beiträge zur Theologie

MChA	*Mitteilungen zur christlichen Archäologie*	*MeSc*	*Medieval Scandinavia*
		MeSo	*Mediaeval Sophia*
MCJP	Mémoires du centre Jean Palerne	*Méth.*	*Méthexis*
MCPL	*Meddelanden från collegium patristicum Lundense*	METI	Middle Eastern Texts Initiative
		METis	*Mélanges Eugène Tisserant*
MCSMS	*Memorie della classe di scienze morali e storiche dell'accademia dei Lincei*	*MeWo*	*Medieval Worlds: Comparative and Interdisciplinary Studies*
		MFC	Message of the Fathers of the Church
McTS	McMaster Theological Studies		
MD	La maison-dieu: Cahiers de pastorale liturgique	*MGDTM*	*Mélanges Gilbert Dagron: Travaux et mémoires*
MD	*La maison-dieu: Revue pastorale liturgique*	*MGG2*	*Die Musik in Geschichte und Gegenwart*
MDAI	*Mitteilungen des deutschen archäologischen Instituts*	MGH	Monumenta Germaniae historica inde ab a. C. 500 usque ad a. 1500
MDAI.K	*– Kairo Abteilung*	MGH.AA	– Auctores antiquissimi
MDAI.R	*– Römische Abteilung*	MGH.Cap	– Capitularia regum Francorum
MDATC	*Materiali e discussioni per l'analisi dei testi classici*	MGH.Conc	– Concilia
		MGH.D	– Diplomata
MEAH	*Miscelánea de estudios arabes y hebraicos*	MGH.Ep	– Epistolae
		MGH.ES	– Epistolae selectae
MeAn	*Mediterraneo Antico*	MGH.GPR	– Gesta pontificum Romanorum
MeAr	*Medieval Archaeology*	MGH.H	– Hilfsmittel
MeCl	Medieval Classics	MGH.OCC	– Ordines de celebrando concilio
Med.	*Médiévales*	MGH.PL	– Poetae latini aevi carolini
MedChr	*Mediterranean Chronicles*	MGH.SRM	– Scriptores rerum Merovingicarum
Medieval Encounters	*Medieval Encounters: Jewish, Christian and Muslim Culture in Confluence and Dialogue*	MGH.SS	– Scriptores
		MGH.ST	– Studien und Texte
		MGMA	Monographien zur Geschichte des Mittelalters
Medievalia	Medievalia		
Medioevo	*Medioevo: Rivista di storia della filosofia medievale*	*MGWJ*	*Monatschrift für Geschichte und Wissenschaft des Judentums*
MeditArch	*Mediterranean Archaeology*	*MH*	*Museum Helveticum: Schweizerische Zeitschrift für klassische Altertumswissenschaft*
MEFR	*Mélanges d'archéologie et d'histoire de l'école française de Rome*		
MEFR.A	– Série Antiquité	Mha	Monografías de historia antigua
MEFR.M	– Série Moyen âge	*MHA*	*Memorias de historia antigua*
Megh.	*Meghillot*	*MHE*	*Miscellanea historiae ecclesiasticae*
MeHi	Medievalia Hispanica	*MHJ*	*The Medieval History Journal*
MeHu	*Medievalia et humanistica*	*MHR*	*Mediterranean IIistorical Review*
MeJo	*The Mediaeval Journal*	MHS	Monumenta Hispaniae Sacra
MEL	Monumenta ecclesiae liturgica	MHS.Lit.	– Serie litúrgica
MeNu	*Metallurgy in Numismatics*	MIH	Macmillan Interdisciplinary Handbooks
Meqorot	*Meqorot: The University of Chicago Journal of Jewish Studies*		
		Mill.	*Millennium*
MeRe	*The Medieval Review*		

Mill.Y.	Millennium: Yearbook on the Culture and History of the First Millennium CE/Jahrbuch zu Kultur und Geschichte des ersten Jahrtausends n. Chr.	MNTC	Moffatt New Testament Commentary
		MoBi	Le monde de la Bible
		MoBi	Le monde de la Bible
		MOEST	McMaster Old English Studies and Texts
Mils	Milltown Studies		
MIPWMU	Mediaeval Institute Publications	Month	Month
Mishkan	Mishkan	Mortality	Mortality
Miss.	Missiology: American Society of Missiology	MoTh	Modern Theology
		Mous.	Mouseion
MiSt	Millennium-Studien/Millennium Studies	MP	Medieval Prosopography
		MPARA	Memorie della pontificia accademia romana di archeologia
MiStud	Mittelalter-Studien		
MITS	Mittellateinische Studien und Texte	MPh	Modern Philology
MitStud	Mittelalter Studien	MPIL	Monographs of the Peshitta Institute
MJS	Münsteraner judaistische Studien	MRABLB	Memorias de la real academai de buenas letras de Barcelona
MJTh	Marburger Jahrbuch Theologie		
ML.T	Museum Lessianum. Section théologique	Mrav.	Mravaltavi: Pilologiur-ist'oriuli dziebani
MLC	Miscellània litúrgica catalana	MRTS	Medieval and Renaissance Texts and Studies
MLJb	Mittellateinisches Jahrbuch: Internationale Zeitschrift für Mediävistik		
		MS	Mediaeval Studies: Pontifical Institute of Mediaeval Studies
MLLM	Mediae Latinitatis Lexicon Minus	MS Laur.	Manuscript in the Biblioteca Laurenziana
MLTT	Medieval Latin Texts and Their Transmission		
		MSAMF	Mémoires de la société archéologique du midi de la France
MMAA	Monographs of the Mediaeval Academy of America		
		MSDB	Memorie storiche della diocesi di Brescia
MMAFC	Mémoires publiés par les membres de la mission archéologique française au Caire		
		MSiT	Mediaeval Sources in Translation
		MSR	Mélanges de science religieuse
MMBT	Monumenta musicae Byzantinae transcripta	MSRa	Medioevo: Saggi e rassegne
		MSU	Mitteilungen des Septuaginta-Unternehmens
MMFEP	Monuments et memoires de la Fondation Eugene Piot		
		MTal	Monumenta talmudica
MMIF	Mémoirs publiés par les membres de l'institut français d'archéologie orientale du Caire	MTB	Münchener theologische Beiträge
		MThSt	Marburger theologische Studien
		MThZ	Münchener theologische Zeitschrift
MMJ	Metropolitan Museum Journal	MTSR	Method and Theory in the Study of Religion: Journal of the North American Association for the Study of Religion
MMPEC	The Medieval Mediterranean: Peoples, Economies and Cultures		
Mn.	Mnemosyne: Bibliotheca classica/ Philologica batava		
		MuHe	Musem Helvetium: Schweizerische Zeitschrift für klassische Altertumswissenschaft
Mn.S	– Supplement		
MNIR	Mededelingen van het Nederlands Instituut te Rome (Papers of the Dutch Institute in Rome)		
		Muséon	Le Muséon: Revue d'études orientales
		Musiktheorie	Musiktheorie
		MUSJ	Mélanges de l'université Saint-Joseph

MVB	Mainzer Veröffentlichung zur Byzantinik	NEB	Neue Echter Bibel
Myrtia	*Myrtia: Revista de Filología clásica*	NEB.AT	– Kommentar zum Alten Testament mit der Einheitsübersetzung
NA	*Neues Archiv der Gesellschaft für ältere deutsche Geschichtskunde zur Beförderung einer Gesamtausgabe der Quellen deutscher Geschichte des Mittelalters*	NEB.AT.E	– Ergänzungsband zum Alten Testament
		NEB.NT	– Kommentar zum Neuen Testament mit der Einheitsübersetzung
		NEB.NT.E	– Ergänzungsband zum Neuen Testament
NABHC	New Approaches to Byzantine History and Culture	NEB. Themen	– Main Themes of the Bible
NAC	New American Commentary	*NedThT*	*Nederlands theologisch tijdschrift*
NaCo	*Nature Communications*	NeHiSe	A New History of the Sermon
NAKG	*Nederlands(ch) archief voor kerkgeschiedenis*	*Neotest.*	*Neotestamentica: Annual Publication of the New Testament Society of South Africa*
NAWG	*Nachrichten der Akademie der Wissenschaften in Göttingen* (until 1940: *NGWG*)		
		NES	Near Eastern Studies
NAWG.PH	– Philologisch-historische Klasse	Nestle-Aland	Nestle-Aland Novum testamentum Graece
NBAC	*Nuovo bullettino di archeologia cristiana*	*New Grove*	*The New Grove Dictionary of Music and Musicians*
NBL	*Neues Bibel-Lexikon*	NHC	Nag Hammadi Codices
NBMA	Nouvelle bibliothèque du moyen âge	NHiS	New History of the Sermon
NBS	Numen Book Series	NHLE	Nag Hammadi Library in English
NBST	Neukirchener Beiträge zur systematischen Theologie	*NHLi*	*Neues Handbuch der Literaturwissenschaft*
NC	*Nouvelle Clio: Revue mensuelle de la découverte historique*	*NHLL*	*Nouvelle histoire de la littérature latine*
NCBC	The New Century Bible Commentary	NHMS	Nag Hammadi and Manichaean Studies
NCBCo	New Cambridge Bible Commentary		
NCC	New Covenant Commentary	NHRF	National Hellenic Research Foundation Centre for Greek and Roman Antiquity
NCE	*New Catholic Encyclopedia*		
NCHB	*The New Cambridge History of the Bible*		
		NHS	Nag Hammadi Studies (from 1991 continued as NHMS)
NCMH	*The New Cambridge Medieval History*	NIBC	New International Biblical Commentary
NCTh	New Century Theology		
NDBT	*New Dictionary of Biblical Theology*	NICNT	New International Commentary on the New Testament
NDIEC	*New Documents Illustrating Early Christianity*	NICOT	New International Commentary on the Old Testament
NDPAC	*Nuovo dizionario patristico e di antichità cristiane*		
		NIDNTTE	*New International Dictionary of New Testament Theology and Exegesis*
NDT	*New Dictionary of Theology*		
NEA	*Near Eastern Archaeology: A Publication of the American Schools of Oriental Research*	*NIDOT*	*New International Dictionary for Old Testament Theology and Exegesis*
		NIGTC	The New International Greek Testament Commentary
NEAEHL	*The New Encyclopedia of Archaeological Excavations in the Holy Land*		

NInDB	*The New Interpreter's Dictionary of the Bible*		NTOA	Novum Testamentum et orbis antiquus
NKZ	*Neue kirchliche Zeitschrift*		NTOA.SA	– Series archaeologica
NLR	*Newcastle Law Review*		NTP	Novum Testamentum patristicum
NMS	*Nottingham Medieval Studies*		NTR	New Testament Readings
Not. Eccl.	*Notitia ecclesiarum urbis Romae*		NTS	New Testament Studies
NoTe	*Nova Tellus*		*NTS*	*New Testament Studies: An International Journal Published Under the Auspices of Studiorum Novi Testamenti Societas*
NovTSup	Novum Testamentum Supplements			
NPNF1	*Nicene and Post-Nicene Fathers, Series 1*			
NPNF2	*Nicene and Post-Nicene Fathers, Series 2*		NTSer	New Testament Series
			NTT	*Norsk Teologisk Tidskrift*
NQ	*Notes and Queries*		NTTS	New Testament Tools and Studies
NRS	*Nuova rivista storica*		NTTSD	New Testament Tools, Studies and Documents
NRTh	*La nouvelle revue théologique*			
NSA	*Notizie degli scavi di antichità*		*Nubica (et Aethiopica)*	*Nubica (from 1999: et Aethiopica): Internationales Jahrbuch für äthiopische, meroitische und nubische Studien (from 1999: Internationales Jahrbuch für koptische, meroitisch-nubische, äthiopische und verwandte Studien)*
NSAJR	*New Studies in the Archaeology of Jerusalem and its Region*			
NSCMDLW	*The New SCM Dictionary of Liturgy and Worship*			
NSHERK	*The New Schaff-Herzog Encyclopedia of Religious Knowledge*			
NSK	Neuer Stuttgarter Kommentar			
NSK.AT	– Altes Testament		*NUDI*	*Nuovo Didaskaleion*
NSMH	New Studies in Medieval History		*NumC*	*Numismatic Chronicle*
NSS	Nuovi Studi Storici		*Numen*	*Numen: International Review for the History of Religions*
NStJ	*New Studies on Jerusalem*			
NT	*Novum Testamentum: An International Quarterly for New Testament and Related Studies*		Numen.S	– Supplements
			NWDLW	*The New Westminster Dictionary of Liturgy & Worship*
NT.S	– Supplements		*NZSTh*	*Neue Zeitschrift für systematische Theologie und Religionsphilosophie*
NTA	Neutestamentliche Abhandlungen			
NTAF	The New Testament and the Apostolic Fathers		OAF	Oxford Apostolic Fathers
			ÖAKR	*Österreichisches Archiv für Kirchenrecht*
NTAK	*Neues Testament und antike Kultur*			
NTApo	*Neutestamentliche Apokryphen in deutscher Übersetzung*		OBC	Orientalia biblica et christiana
			OBO	Orbis biblicus et orientalis
NTApoc	*New Testament Apocrypha*		ÖBS	Österreichische biblische Studien
NTC	The New Testament in Context		OBSO	Oxford Biblical Studies Online
NTD	Das Neue Testament Deutsch: Neues Göttinger Bibelwerk; supplementary series: GNT		OCA	Orientalia christiana analecta
			OCD	*Oxford Classical Dictionary*
			OCM	Oxford Classical Monographs
NTG	New Testament Guides		*OCP*	*Orientalia christiana periodica*
NTL	New Testament Library		*ODB*	*Oxford Dictionary of Byzantium*
NTL.C	New Testament Library Commentary		*ODCC*	*Oxford Dictionary of the Christian Church*
NTM	New Testament Message			

ODNB	Oxford Dictionary of National Biography in Association with the British Academy: From the Earliest Times to the Year 2000	OHES	Oxford Handbook of Eschatology
		OHGRC	Oxford Handbook of Greek and Roman Coinage
		OHGRM	Oxford Handbook of Greek and Roman Mythography
ODP	Oxford Dictionary of Popes	OHJDL	Oxford Handbook of Jewish Daily Life in Roman Palestine
ODS	Oxford Dictionary of Saints		
OEAGR	Oxford Encyclopedia of Ancient Greece and Rome	OHJS	Oxford Handbook of Jewish Studies
OEBA	The Oxford Encyclopedia of the Bible and Archaeology	OHLA	Oxford Handbook of Late Antiquity
		OHMC	Oxford Handbook to Maximus Confessor
OEBB	Oxford Encyclopedia of the Books of the Bible	OHMT	Oxford Handbook of Mystical Theology
OEBGS	Oxford Encyclopedia of the Bible and Gender Studies	OHNTGS	Oxford Handbook of New Testament, Gender, and Sexuality
OECS	Oxford Early Christian Studies	OHP	Oxford Handbook of Plato
OECT	Oxford Early Christian Texts	OHPa	Oxford Handbook of Papyrology
OeO	Oriens et Occidens: Studien zu antiken Kulturkontakten und zu ihrem Nachleben	OHPs	Oxford Handbook of Psalms
		OHRS	Oxford Handbook of Roman Studies
		OHSR	Oxford Handbook for Study of Religion
OGHRA	Oxford Guide to the Historical Reception of Augustine		
		OHST	Oxford Handbook of Sacramental Theology
OGIS	Orientis Graecae Inscriptiones Selectae		
		OHT	Oxford Handbook of Trinity
OHAB	Oxford Handbook of Ancient Biography	Oikonomia	Oikonomia: Quellen und Studien zur orthodoxen Theologie
OHACTL	Oxford Handbook of Animals in Classical Thought and Life		
		OIR	Orbis iuris romani
OHAGR	Oxford Handbook of Ancient Greek Religion	OJP	Open Journal of Philosophy
		OLA	Orientalia Lovaniensia analecta
OHAthe	Oxford Handbook of Atheism	OLB	Orte und Landschaften der Bibel
OHCE	Oxford Handbook of Christianity and Economics	Olba	Olba
		OLD	Oxford Latin Dictionary
OHCM	Oxford Handbook of Christian Monasticism	OLoP	Orientalia lovaniensia periodica
		OLZ	Orientalische Literaturzeitung
OHCW	Oxford History of Christian Worship	OPEP	Opuscula epigraphica
OHDA	Oxford Handbook of Dionysius the Areopagite	OPRO	Opuscula romana
		OpTh	Open Theology
OHE	Oxford Handbook of Epicureanism	Opus.	Opuscula
OHECA	Oxford Handbook of Early Christian Apocrypha	Or.	Oriental Collection of the Library of the University of Leiden
OHECArch	Oxford Handbook of Early Christian Archaeology		
		Or.	Orientalia
		ORA	Orientalische Religionen in der Antike
OHECBI	Oxford Handbook of Early Christian Biblical Interpretation		
		OrAnt	Oriens antiquus
OHECR	Oxford Handbook of Early Christian Ritual	Or-AR	Orient-Archaeologie
		OrChr	Oriens christianus
OHECS	Oxford Handbook of Early Christian Studies	OrEx	Oriens extremus

Oriens	*Oriens: Zeitschrift der Internationalen Gesellschaft für Orientforschung*
Origen.	*Origeniana*
Orph.	*Orpheus: Rivista di umanità classica e cristiana*
OrSuec	*Orientalia Suecana*
OrSyr	*Orient Syrien*
Ortod.	*Ortodoksia*
OS	*Ostkirchliche Studien*
OSA	Oeuvres de saint Augustin
OSAP	Oxford Studies in Ancient Philosophy
OSB	Oxford Studies in Byzantium
OSHT	Oxford Studies in Historical Theology
OSLA	Oxford Studies in Late Antiquity
OSLS	Österreichische Studien zur Liturgiewissenschaft und Sakramententheologie
ÖTBK	Ökumenischer Taschenbuchkommentar zum Neuen Testament
OTM	Oxford Theological Monographs
OTP	*Old Testament Pseudepigrapha*
OTS	Oudtestamentische studiën
PA	*Philosophie antique*
PAAJR	*Proceedings of the American Academy for Jewish Research*
PAB	Postdamer altertumswissenschaftliche Beiträge
PaBi	see PatSor
PaBo	*Pastor bonus*
PaBr	Papyrologica Bruxellensia: Études de papyrologie et édition de sources
PAC	*Prosopographie de l' Afrique chrétienne (303–533)*
PACA	*The Proceedings of the African Classical Associations*
Pacifica	*Pacifica*
PAE	*The Papacy: An Encyclopedia*
PaKeSe	Papadopoulos-Kerameus series
PaLi	Paroisse et liturgie: Collection de pastorale liturgique
Palilia	Palilia
Palingenesia	Palingenesia: Schriftenreihe für Klassische Altertumswissenschaft
Pall	*Palladio*

Pallas	*Pallas*
PaMe	*Patristica et mediaevalia*
PaNT.C	Paideia NT Commentary
PaP	*Past and Present: A Journal of Scientific History*
PAPS	*Proceedings of the American Philosophical Society*
PapyCol	Papyrologica Coloniensia
PAR	*La parola del passato: Rivista di studi antichi*
Par.	Paradosis: Études de littérature et de théologie ancienne
ParD	Parole de Dieu
ParOr	*Parole de l'orient*
PaSt	Pauline Studies
PATH	*Rivista semestrale della pontificia accademia di teologia*
PaThSt	Paderborner theologische Studien
PatMS	Patristic Monograph Series
Patr.	Patristica
Patr.	*Patrology*
Patrologia	Patrologia
PatSor	Patristica Sorbonensia
PatST	Patristic Studies
Pazisi	*Pazisi: Journal for Greek and Roman Studies*
PBA	Proceedings of the British Academy
PBM	Paternoster Biblical Monographs
PBSK	Patrologia: Beiträge zum Studium der Kirchenväter
PBSR	*Papers of the British School at Rome*
PC	Patrimoines Christianisme
PCA	Post-Classical Archaeologies Studies
PCBE	*Prosopographie chrétienne du Bas-Empire*
PCC	Paul in Critical Contexts
PCPS	*Proceedings of the Cambridge Philological Society*
PCPS.S	– Supplement
PCRCDCO	Pontificia commissione per la redazione del codice di diritto canonico orientale
PDAR	*Pictorial Dictionary of Ancient Rome*
PdO	Pliegos de oriente
PECS	*Princeton Encyclopedia of Classical Sites*
PeEu	The Peoples of Europe

JOURNALS, SERIES, ENCYCLOPEDIAS, AND LEXICONS

PEFR	Publications de l'école française de Rome	*PJT*	*Pharos Journal of Theology*
Pègaso	*Pègaso*	*PKKW*	*Programm des königlichen Kaiser Wilhelm-Gymnasiums zu Köln*
PEID	Pathways for Ecumenical and Interreligious Dialogue	PKNT	Papyrologische Kommentare zum Neuen Testament
PEQ	*Palestine Exploration Quarterly*	PL	Patrologiae cursus completus: Series Latina
Perich.	*Perichoresis*		
Peritia	*Peritia*	PLB	Papyrologica Lugduno-Batava
PETSE	Papers of the Estonian Theological Society in Exile	PLECA	Pictorial Library of Eastern Church Art
PFLFP	Pubblicazioni della facoltà di lettere e filosofia dell'università di Pavia	PlHy	Plutarchea Hypomnemata
		PLO.NS	Porta Linguarum Orientalium. New Series
PFLSHUM	Publications de la faculté des lettres et sciences humaines de l'université de Montpellier	*PLRE*	*The Prosopography of the Later Roman Empire*
PG	Patrologiae cursus completus: Series Graeca	PLS	Patrologiae Latinae supplementum
		PMAAR	Papers and Monographs of the American Academy in Rome
PGL	*A Patristic Greek Lexicon: With Addenda et Corrigenda*	*PMASAL*	*Papers of the Michigan Academy of Science, Arts and Letters*
PGP	*Pastoraltheologie mit Göttinger Predigtmeditationen*	PmE	Papsttum im mittelalterlichen Europa
Ph.	*Philologus: Zeitschrift für klassische Philologie*	PMS	Publications in Mediaeval Studies
Ph.S	– Supplement	PNTC	Pillar New Testament Commentary
PhAb	Philosophische Abhandlungen	PNTC	Pelican New Testament Commentaries
PhAnt	Philosophia antiqua: A Series of Monographs on Ancient Philosophy	PO	Patrologia orientalis
		POC	*Proche-orient chrétien*
Phasis	*Phasis*	*PoKn*	*Polata knigopisnaja*
PHC	A People's History of Christianity	*Polis*	*Polis: Revista de ideas y formas politicas de la antiguedad clásica*
PHCr	Problèmes d'histoire du christianisme	*Pomoer.*	*Pomoerium*
Philosophia	*Philosophia*	*Pontica*	*Pontica*
Philot.	*Philotheos*	*Postmed.*	*Postmedieval: A Journal of Medieval Cultural Studies*
Phoe.	*Phoenix*		
PhPa	Philosophia patrum	PPS	Popular Patristics Series
Phrasis	*Phrasis*	PPSD	Pauline and Patristic Scholars in Debate
Phro.	*Phronema*		
Phron.	*Phronesis: A Journal for Ancient Philosophy*	*PRE*	*Paulys Real-Encyclopädie der classischen Alterthumswissenschaft*
PHTF	Philologiae et historiae Turcicae fundamenta	PRE.S	– Supplement
		PrEu	Prex eucharistica
PiLi	Pietas liturgica	*PRIA*	*Proceedings of the Royal Irish Academy*
PIR	*Prosopographia imperii Romani saeculi I–III*		
		PrJ	*Preußische Jahrbücher*
PIRSB	Publications de l'institut romand des sciences bibliques	PrMS	Princeton Monograph Series
		ProEccl	*Pro ecclesia*
PJBR	*Pacific Journal of Baptist Research*	*Proverbium*	*Proverbium*

PRSA	Problemi e ricerche di storia antica	*QuAm*	*Quaderni di Ambrosius*
PrTMS	Princeton Theological Monograph Series	*QUCC*	*Quaderni urbinati di cultura classica*
		QuLi	*Questions liturgiques (formerly QLP)*
Prud.	*Prudentia*	QULPM	Quellen und Untersuchungen
PrViSo	*Proceedings of the Virgil Society*		zur lateinischen Philologie des
PS	Patrologia syriaca		Mittelalters
PSAS	*Proceedings of the Society of Antiquaries of Scotland*	*QuUt*	*Quaderni utinensi*
		QVC	Quaderni di vetera christianorum
PSB	*The Princeton Seminary Bulletin*	*R&T*	*Recherches & travaux*
PSBF	Pubblicazioni dello studium biblicum franciscanum	*RA*	*Revue d'assyriologie et d'archéologie orientale*
PSHAL	Publications de la société historique et archéologique dans le Limbourg	*Rabinowitz*	*Louis M. Rabinowitz Fund for the Exploration of Ancient Synagogues Bulletin*
PSI	Papiri della società italiana		
PSIRPE	Pubblicazioni della aocietà italiana per la ricerca dei papiri greci e latini in Egitto	*RAC*	*Reallexikon für Antike und Christentum*
		RAC.S.	– Supplement
PTA	Papyrologische Texte und Abhandlungen	*RACF*	*Revue archéologique du centre de la France*
PTh	*Pastoraltheologie: Wissenschaft und Praxis*	RACF.S	– Supplement
		RAL	*Rendiconti dell'accademia dei Lincei*
PTHe	Praktische Theologie heute	*RAL.CSMSF*	*– Classe di Scienze Morali, Storiche e Filologiche*
PTS	Patristische Texte und Studien		
PTW	Praktische Theologie im Wissenschaftsdiskurs	*RAM*	*Revue d'ascétique et de mystique*
		RAP	*Revista d'arqueologia de Ponent*
PuP	Päpste und Papsttum	*RAr*	*Revue archéologique*
PUPCM	Publicaciones de la universidad pontificia comillas Madrid	*RB*	*Revue biblique*
		RBen	*Revue bénédictine de critique, d'histoire et de littérature religieuses*
PVTG	Pseudepigrapha Veteris Testamenti Graece		
PWCJS	*Proceedings of the World Congress of Jewish Studies*	*RBK*	*Reallexikon zur byzantinischen Kunst*
		RBPH	*Revue belge de philologie et d'histoire/ Belgisch tijdschrift voor filologie en geschiedenis*
PzB	*Protokolle zur Bibel*		
QaDi	*Quaestiones Disputatae*		
QAHB	*Quaderns d'arqueologia i història de la ciutat de Barcelona*	*RBS*	*Regulae benedicti studia*
		RBS.S	– Supplement
QAL	*Quaderni di archeologia della Libia*	*RCCM*	*Rivista di cultura classica e medievale*
QCSCM	*Quaderni Catanesi di studi classici e medievali*	RCT	Routledge Classical Translations
		RCT	*Revista catalana de teología*
QD	Quaestiones disputatae	*RdA*	*Revue de l'art*
QDAP	*Quarterly of the Department of Antiquities in Palestine*	*RDC*	*Revue de droit canonique*
		RddM	*Revue des deux mondes*
QdH	Quaderni di "hagiographica"	*RDM*	*Revista Diálogos Mediterrânicos*
Qedem	Qedem: Monographs of the Institute of Archaeology	*RdQ*	*Revue de Qumrân*
		RDSO	*Rivista degli studi orientali*
QFRG	Quellen und Forschungen zur Reformationsgeschichte	*RE*	*Realencyklopädie für protestantische Theologie und Kirche*
QLP	*Questions liturgiques et paroissiales*	*Re&Th*	*Religion & Theology*

REA	Revue des études anciennes
REAC	Revista de estudios de antiguedad classica
Reaf	Revue africaine
ReAn	Revealing Antiquity
ReAp	Revue apologétique
REAP	Revue d'études augustiniennes et patristiques
REArm	Revue des études arméniennes
REAug	Revue des études augustiniennes
REAugP	Recherches augustiniennes et patristiques
ReAugus	Recherches augustiniennes
ReBL	Review of Biblical Literature
ReBo	Revue Bossuet
ReBo.S	– Supplements
REByz	Revue des études byzantines
RECA	Real-Encyclopädie der classischen Alterthumswissenschaft in alphabetischer Ordnung
RECA.S	– Supplement
ReCat	Revista de Catalunya
RechAug	Recherches augustiniennes (= Supplement to REAug)
RECM	Routledge Early Church Monographs
RED	Rerum ecclesiasticarum documenta
RED.F	– Series maior: Fontes
RED.SM	– Series minor: Subsidia studiorum
REDC	Revista española de derecho canónico
REG	Revue des études grecques: Publication de l'association pour l'encouragement des études grecques
ReHy	Repertorium hymnologicum
REJ	Revue des études juives
REL	Revue des études latines
RELat	Revista de Estudios Latinos
Religion	Religion: A Journal of Religion and Religions
Religions	Religions: Open Access Theology Journal
RelSoc	Religion and Society
RelSoc	Religion and Society: Advances in Research
RelSt	Religious Studies
ReMe	Reti medievali
ReOr	Res orientales

Rep.	Repertorium der christlich-antiken Sarkophage
Repr.	Representations
ReQu	Restauration Quarterly
ReRe	Reading Religion
RES	RES: Anthropology and Aesthetics
RESl	Revue des études slaves
RESS	Review of Ecumenical Studies Sibiu
RestQ	Restoration Quarterly
ReStud	Renaissance Studies
RET	Revista española de teología
RETA	Revue des études tardo-antiques
RevQ	Revue de Qumran
RevSR	Revue des sciences religieuses: Faculté catholique de théologie
RevTeo	Revista Teologica
Rexp	Review and Expositor: A Baptist Theological Quarterly
RFIC	Rivista di filologia e di istruzione classica
RFIF	Review of Faith & International Affairs
RFNS	Rivista di filosofia neo-scolastica
RfR	Review for Religious
RGG	Die Religion in Geschichte und Gegenwart
RGI	Revue germanique internationale
RGRW	Religions in the Graeco-Roman World
RGSL	Rassegna gregoriana per gli studi liturgici e per il canto sacro
RGVV	Religionsgeschichtliche Versuche und Vorarbeiten
RH	Revue historique
RHDFE	Revue historique de droit français et étranger
RHE	Revue d'histoire ecclésiastique
RHECA	The Routledge Handbook of Early Christian Art
RHEF	Revue d'histoire de l'église de France
Rhetoric	Rhetorica: A Journal of the History of Rhetoric
Rhizai	Rhizai: A Journal for Ancient Philosophy and Science
RHL	Revue d'histoire de Lyon
RHLR	Revue d'histoire et de littérature religieuse

RHPhR	Revue d'histoire et de philosophie religieuses	RPh	Revue de philologie, de littérature et d'histoire anciennes
RHR	Revue de l'histoire des religions	RPL	Res publica litterarum
RHS	Revue d'histoire de spritualité	RPP	Religion Past and Present
RHT	Revue d'histoire des textes	RPR(J)	Regesta pontificum Romanorum; Ab condita ecclesia ad annum post Christum natum 1198
RIC	The Roman Imperial Coinage		
Ricerca Papirologica	Ricerca papirologica: Università degli studi di Messina: Facoltà di lettere e filosofia	RQ	Römische Quartalschrift für christliche Altertumskunde und Kirchengeschichte
RIDA	Revue internationale des droits de l'antiquité	RQ.S	– Supplement issue
RIEV	Revista internacional de los estudios vasco	RQH	Revue des questions historiques
		RR&T	Reviews in Religion & Theology
RIK	Römische und italienische Katakomben	RRE	Religion in the Roman Empire
		RRH	Regions and Regionalism in History
RIL	Rendiconti. (R.) Istituto lombardo (up to 91,1957:) di scienze e lettere	RRJ	Review of Rabbinic Judaism
		RSA	Revista storica dell'antichità
RIP	Revue internationale de philosophie	RSAC	Recherches suisses d'archéologie copte
RiPa	Ricerca papirologica		
RiRe	Ricerche religiose	RSBN	Rivista di studi bizantini e neoellenici
RiSI	Rivista storica italiana	RSC	Rivista di studi classici
RivAC	Rivista di archeologia cristiana	RSCI	Rivista di storia della chiesa in Italia
RivBib	Rivista biblica	RSCr	Roma sotterranea cristiana
RJ	Römisches Jahrbuch für Kunstgeschichte	RSCri	Rivista di storia del cristianesimo
		RSE	Revue des sciences ecclésiastiques
RKA	Realenzclopädie der klassischen Altertumswissenschaft	RSECW	Routledge Studies in the Early Christian World
RLS	Recherches en littérature et spiritualité	RSER	Revue de la société Ernest-Renan
		RSEt	Rassegna di studi etiopici
RLT	Roman Legal Tradition	RSJ	Roma Subterranea Judaica
RMAL	Revue du moyen âge latin	RSLR	Rivista di storia e letteratura religiosa
RMP	Rheinisches Museum für Philologie	RSPhTh	Revue des sciences philosophiques et théologiques
RNT	Regensburger Neues Testament		
RO	Res orientales: Groupe pour l'étude de la civilisation du moyen-orient	RSR	Recherches de science religieuse
		RSSS	Research in the Social Scientific Study of Religion
ROC	Revue de l'orient chrétien		
RoHu	Roczniki humanistyczne: Annales de letters et sciences humaines	RStB	Ricerche storico-bibliche
		RSTh	Regensburger Studien zur Theologie
Roma	Roma	RThAM	Recherches de théologie ancienne et médiévale
Romania	Romania		
RomBarb	Romanobarbarica	RThom	Revue thomiste: Revue doctrinale de théologie et de philosophie
Romula	Romula		
RoOr	Rocznik Orientalistyczny/Yearbook of Oriental Studies	RThPh	Revue de théologie et de philosophie
		RTL	Revue théologique de Louvain
RPARA	Rendiconti della pontificia accademia romana di archeologia	RUSCH	Rutgers University Studies in Classical Humanities
RPFE	Revue philosophique de la France et de l'étranger	RVV	Religionsgeschichtliche Versuche und Vorarbeiten

SA.SE	Studi africanisti: Serie etiopica		SBL.SP	– Seminar Papers: Annual Meeting
SAAA	Studies on the Apocryphal Acts of the Apostles		SBL.SS	– Symposium Series
SAAu	Studia antiqua Australiensia		SBL.TCS	– Text-Critical Studies
SAC	Studies in Antiquity and Christianity		SBL.TT	– Texts and Translations

SA.SE — Studi africanisti: Serie etiopica
SAAA — Studies on the Apocryphal Acts of the Apostles
SAAu — Studia antiqua Australiensia
SAC — Studies in Antiquity and Christianity
SAG — Studien zur alten Geschichte
SAIS — Studies in the Aramaic interpretation of Scripture
Sal. — *Salesianum: Pontificio atheneo salesiano*
Salm. — *Salmanticensis: Commentarius de sacris disciplinis*
Salt. — *Salternum*
SANT — Studien zum Alten und Neuen Testaments
SapCr — *Sapientia Crucis*
Sapere — Sapere
SaTu — Sammlung Tusculum
SAW — Studienhefte zur Altertumswissenschaft
SAWW — *Sitzungsberichte der Akademie der Wissenschaften in Wien*
SAWW.PH — – Philosophisch-historische Klasse
SB — Sammelbuch griechischer Urkunden aus Aegypten
SBA — Schweizerische Beiträge zur Altertumswissenschaft
SBAB — Stuttgarter biblische Aufsatzbände
SBAW — *Sitzungsberichte der Bayerischen Akademie der Wissenschaften in München*
SBAW.PH — – Philosophisch-historische Klasse
SBB — Stuttgarter biblische Beiträge
SBE — *Studia biblica et ecclesiastica*
SBF — Studium biblicum franciscanum
SBF.CMa — – Collectio major
SBHC — Studies in Byzantine History and Civilization
SBL — Society of Biblical Literature
SBL.CA — – Christian Apocrypha
SBL.DS — – Dissertation Series
SBL.ECL — – Early Christianity and its Literature
SBL.EJL — – Early Judaism and its Literature
SBL.MS — – Monograph Series
SBL.RBS — – Resources for Biblical Study
SBL.SBS — – Sources for Biblical Study
SBL.SCSt — – Septuagint and Cognate Studies

SBL.SP — – Seminar Papers: Annual Meeting
SBL.SS — – Symposium Series
SBL.TCS — – Text-Critical Studies
SBL.TT — – Texts and Translations
SBL.WGRW — – Writings from the Greco-Roman World
SBL.WGRW.SS — – Supplement Series
SBL.WLAW — – Wisdom Literature from the Ancient World
SBR — Studies of the Bible and its Reception
SBS — Stuttgarter Bibelstudien
SBT — Studies in Biblical Theology
SC — Sources chrétiennes
SCA — Studies in Christian Antiquity
ScBi — Scholars Bible
ScC — *La scuola cattolica*
SCCB — Studies in Cultural Context of the Bible
ScEccl — *Sciences ecclésiastiques*
ScEs — *Science et esprit: Revue théologique et philosophique*
SCH — Studies in Church History
SCH(L) — *Studies in Church History: Ecclesiastical History Society*
SCHNT — Studia ad corpus hellenisticum Novi Testamenti
Scholastik — *Scholastik: Vierteljahresschrift für Theologie und Philosophie*
Schweich Lectures — The Schweich Lectures of the British Academy
SCI — *Scripta classica israelica*
SCJ — Studies in Christianity and Judaism
S-CJ — *Stone-Campbell Journal*
SCJR — *Studies in Christian-Jewish Relations*
SCL — Sather Classical Lectures
ScMi — *Scripta minora*
SCN — *Studii si cercetari de numismatica*
SCO — *Studi classici e orientali*
ScOr — Script Oralia or Scripta Orientalia
ScPa — Scrittori padovani
Scr. — *Scripture*
Scr.&e-Scr. — *Scripta & e-Scripta: The Journal of Interdisciplinary Medieval Studies*
ScrHier — *Scripta hierosolymitana*
ScRi — Scavi e ricerche
Scrinium — *Scrinium*

Script.	Scriptorium: Revue internationale des études relatives aux manuscrits médiévaux		SEP	Stanford Encyclopedia of Philosophy
Scrit.	Scritture		SERAPHIM	Studies in Education and Religion in Ancient and Pre-Modern History in the Mediterranean and Its Environs
ScrTh	Scripta theologica			
SCS	Septuagint Commentary Series			
SCSt	Septuagint and Cognate Studies		SERep	Salvage Excavation Reports
SdCdA	Scrittori della chiesa di Aquileia		SESJ	Suomen eksegeettisen seuran julkaisuja/Publications of the Finnish Exegetical Society
SdiE	La scuola di Epicuro			
SdiE.S	– Supplement			
SdOC	Scritti delle origini cristiane		SF	Spicilegium Friburgense
SdR	Storia di Roma		SFA	Studies in Funerary Archaeology
SdS	Settimane di studio		SFCB	Spätantike–Frühes Christentum–Byzanz
SDSD	Studi e documenti di storia e diritto			
SDWG	Schriften der deutschen wasserhistorischen Gesellschaft		SFCB.B	– Reihe B: Studien und Perspektiven
			SFCB.KeJ	– Kunst im ersten Jahrtausend
SE	Sacris erudiri: Jaarboek voor godsdienstwetenschappen		SFCT	Series on Formative Contemporary Thinkers
SEAug	Studia ephemerides "Augustinianum"		SFG	Spanische Forschungen der Gorresgesellschaft
SEC	Studies in Early Christianity		SFS	Spicilegii Friburgensis Subsidia
SECA	Studies on Early Christian Apocrypha		SFSHJ	South Florida Studies in the History of Judaism
SecCen	The Second Century: A Journal of Early Christian Studies		SG	Siculorum Gymnasium
SECH	Studies in Early Church History		SGKA	Studien zur Geschichte und Kultur des Altertums
SECL	Studies in Eastern Christian Liturgies		SGKAO	Schriften zur Geschichte und Kultur des Alten Orients: Berliner Turfan Texte
SeCl	Semitica et Classica			
SECT	Sources of Early Christian Thought		SGKIO	Studien zur Geschichte und Kultur des islamischen Orients
SeD	Scripta et documenta			
SEFP	Studies in Eucharistic Faith and Practice		SGTK	Studien zur Geschichte der Theologie und der Kirche
SEG	Supplementum epigraphicum Graecum		SHAR	Studies in the History and Anthropology of Religion
SEHEM	Studies in the Early History of Ecclesiastical Music		SHAW	Sitzungsberichte der Heidelberger Akademie der Wissenschaften
			SHAW.PH	– Philosophisch-historische Klasse
Sehepunkte	Sehepunkte		SHBC	The Smyth & Helwys Bible Commentary
Seia	Seia			
SEL	Studi epigrafici e linguistici		SHCT	Studies in the History of Christian Thought
Sem.	Semitica			
SEMA	Studies in the Early Middle Ages		SHCTr	Studies in the History of Christian Traditions
Semeia	Semeia: An Experimental Journal for Biblical Criticism			
Semeia Studies	Semeia Studies		SHG	Subsidia hagiographica
			SHHA	Studia historica: Historia antigua
Semi.	Semiotica			

SHPH	Publicaciones del seminario de historia primitiva del hombre: Monografías	SO	*Symbolae osloenses*
		SoAN	*Society for Ancient Numismatics*
		SÖAW	Sitzungsberichte der Österreichischen Akademie der Wissenschaften
SHR	Studies in the History of Religions (supplement to *Numen*)		
SHRP	Studies in Hellenistic and Roman Philosophy	SÖAW.PH	– Philosophisch-Historische Klasse
		SoCA	Sources canoniques
SHT	*Studia Humaniora Tartuensia*	*SOEL*	*Studies in Old English Literature*
SiAp	Silentium apophthegmata	SOK	Studien zur orientalischen Kirchengeschichte
SIFC	*Studi italiani di filologia classica*		
SIG	Sylloge inscriptionum Graecarum	*SOPJ*	*Syriac Orthodox Patriarchal Journal*
SiLA	*Studies in Late Antiquity*	SOR	Serie orientale Roma
Sileno	*Sileno*	SOVM	Spiritualité orientale et vie monastique
SiS	*Studies in Spirituality*		
SJ	Studia Judaica: Forschungen zur Wissenschaft des Judentums+C1284	SP	Sacra pagina
		SP	*Studia patristica*
		SPap	*Studia papyrologica*
SJC	*Scripta judaica cracoviensia: Studia z historii, kultury i religii żydów*	SPAW	Sitzungsberichte der preußischen Akademie der Wissenschaften zu Berlin
SJLA	Studies in Judaism in Late Antiquity		
SJOT	*Scandinavian Journal of the Old Testament*	SPAW.PH	– Philosophisch-historische Klasse
		SpCh	*Spes christiana*
SJRS	*The Scottish Journal of Religious Studies*	*Spec.*	*Speculum: A Journal of Mediaeval Studies*
SJTh	*Scottish Journal of Theology*	*SPhilo*	*Studia Philonica Annual*
SLH	Scriptores Latini Hiberniae	SPIB	Scripta pontificii instituti biblici
SLiS	The Society for Libyan Studies	SPL	Scrinium patristicum lateranense
SLNPNCF	A Select Library of Nicene and Post-Nicene Church Fathers	SPM	Studia philonica monographs
		SPMe(d)	Studia patristica mediolanensia
SlPr	Slavische Propyläen	SPNPT	Studies in Platonism, Neoplatonism, and the Platonic Tradition
SLRST	Storia e letteratura, raccolta di studi e testi		
		SPNT	Studies on Personalities of the New Testament
SLS	The Sacred Literature Series		
SMA	Studia mediterrana archaeologica	SpOr	Spiritualité orientale
SMGH	Schriften der Monumenta Germaniae Historica	*SPQ*	*Social Psychology Quarterly*
		SPS	Sacra Pagina Series
SMH	The Catholic University of America: Studies in Medieval History	SPS	Studia Patristica Supplements
		Spudasmata	Spudasmata
SMSR	*Studi e materiali di storia delle religioni*	*SpWi*	*Sprachwissenschaft*
		SR	*Studies in Religion/Sciences religieuses*
SNAM	Studies in Neoplatonism: Ancient and Modern		
		SRB	Studies in Rewritten Bible
SNTA	Studiorum Novi Testamenti Auxilia	SrBi	Scripta biblica
SNTR	*Saint Nersess Theological Review*	SrHAW	Schriften der Heidelberger Akademie der Wissenschaften, Heidelberg
SNTSMS	Society for New Testament Studies Monograph Series		
SNTU	Studien zum Neuen Testament und seiner Umwelt	SrHAW.PH	– Philosophisch-historische Klasse
		SROC	*Studi e ricerche sull'oriente cristiano*

SSA	Schriften der Sektion für Altertumswissenschaft	*StFi*	*Studi filosofici*
SSAC	Sussidi allo studio delle antichità cristiane	*StGen*	*Studium generale*
		StGra	*Studia gratiana*
SSAM	*Settimana di studio del centro italiano di studi sull'alto medioevo*	StHa	Studia hagiographica
		StHib	*Studia hibernica/Coláiste phádraig*
SSAW	Sitzungsberichte der sächsischen Akademie der Wissenschaften	*StIc*	*Studies in Iconography*
		StIm	Studia imagologica: Amsterdam Studies on Cultural Identity
SSEJC	Studies in Scripture in Early Judaism and Christianity	*STK*	*Svensk Teologisk Kvartalskrift*
SSF	Studien zu Spätantike und Frühmittelalter	STKSJ	Suomalaisen teologisen kirjallisuusseuran julkaisuja
		STL	Studia theologica Lundensia
SSH	Social Sciences and History	*StLi*	*Studia Liturgica: An International Ecumenical Quarterly for Liturgical Research and Renewal*
SSL	Spicilegium sacrum lovaniense		
SsOC	*Studi sull'oriente cristiano*		
SSR	*Studi storico-religiosi*	*StMC*	*Studies in Medieval Culture*
SSRH	Sociological Studies in Roman History	*StMed*	*Studi medievali*
		StMon	*Studia monastica*
SST	Studies in Sacred Theology	StNT	Studien zum Neuen Testament
SSTar	Studi sulla tardoantichità	StOR	Studies in Oriental Religions
SStHe	*Studia hellenistica*	Storia	Storia
SSW	*Studies in Social Work*	*StoRu*	*Studie o rukopisech*
StAaNe	Studia aarhusiana Neotestamentica	*StPat*	*Studia patavina*
STAC	Studien und Texte zu Antike und Christentum	StPatr	Studia patristica: Papers Presented to [...] the International Conference of Patristic Studies held at Christ Church
StACr	Studi di antichità cristiana		
StAcSu	*Studia academia šumenensia*		
StAm(br)	*Studia ambrosiana*	StPB	Studia post-biblica
StAnCh	Standorte in Antike und Christentum	*StPh*	*Studia philonica*
		StPiAl	Studies in Philo of Alexandria
StAns	Studia Anselmiana: Philosophica, theologica	STPIMS	Studies and Texts: Pontifical Institute of Mediaeval Studies
StANT	Studien zum Alten und Neuen Testament	*STR*	*Southeastern Theological Review*
		StRe	Studies in Religion
STAR	Studies in Theology and Religion	*STRev*	*Sewanee Theological Review*
STAR	*STVDIA ARCHÆVS*	*StRo*	*Studi romani*
StArTe	La storia dell'arte: Temi	STRT	Studia theologica Rheno-Traiectina
StAug	*Studia ephemerides augustinianum*	StSe	Stavronikita series
StBi	Studi biblici	StSin	Studia sinaitica
StBiAn	*Studies in the Bible and Antiquity*	STSt	Strassburger theologische Studien
StBL	Studies in Biblical Literature	*StStor*	*Studi storici: Rivista trimestrale*
StC	*Studia catholica*	StT	Studi e testi: Biblioteca apostolica Vaticana
StCe	*Studia celtica*		
StCl	*Studii clasice*	*StTh*	*Studia theologica: Scandinavian Journal of Theology*
StD	Studies and Documents		
STDJ	Studies on the Texts of the Desert of Judah	StTrTh	Studia traditionis theologiae
		StudBib	*Studia biblica*
StEL	*Studi epigrafici e linguistici*		

Studia Archaeologica	Studia Archaeologica		*TAM*	*Tituli asiae minoris*
			TAM.S	– Supplement
Studies	*Studies*		TANZ	Texte und Arbeiten zum neutestamentlichen Zeitalter
StuMiss	*Studia missionalia*		*TAPhA*	*Transactions of the American Philological Association*
StUNT	Studien zur Umwelt des Neuen Testaments		*TAPhS*	*Transactions of the American Philosophical Society*
StUP	*Studi Umanistici Piceni*		*Tarb.*	*Tarbiz: A Quarterly Review of the Humanities*
StuSt	Studi storici			
Stylos	*Stylos*		TaS	Texts and Studies: Contributions to Biblical and Patristic Literature
SUBBP	*Studia UBB Philosophia*			
SUC	Schriften des Urchristentums		TAT	Treasures of the Armenian Tradition
SuGr	*Subseciva groningana*		TAzB	Texte und Arbeiten zur Bibel
SUHV	Skrifter utgifna af humanistiska vetenskapssamfundet i Uppsala		TB	Theologische Bücherei: Neudrucke und Berichte aus dem 20. Jahrhundert
SUNT	Studien zur Umwelt des Neuen Testaments			
			TBL	Tübinger Beiträge zur Linguistik
SVF	*Stoicorum veterum fragmenta*		TBN	Themes in Biblical Narrative
SVigChr	Supplements to Vigiliae Christianae: Review of Early Christian Life and Language		TBT	Theologische Bibliothek Töpelmann
			TC	Traditio Christiana: Texte und Kommentare zur patristischen Theologie
SVRG	Schriften des Vereins für Reformationsgeschichte			
SVSL	Skrifter utgivna av vetenskaps-societeten i Lund		*TCE*	*The Coptic Encyclopedia*
			TCHS	The Transformation of the Classical Heritage Series
SVTP	Studia in veteris testamenti pseudepigrapha			
			TCJ	*The Classical Journal*
SVTQ	*St. Vladimir's Theological Quarterly*		TCLA	Texts from Christian Late Antiquity
SWGS	Schriften der wissenschaftlichen Gesellschaft zu Straßburg		TCoL.GK	Translations of Christian Literature, series 1: Greek Texts
SwJT	*Southwestern Journal of Theology*		TCoL.LAT	Translations of Christian Literature, series 2: Latin Texts
SWLAEMA	Social Worlds of Late Antiquity and the Early Middle Ages		TDMAM	Textes et documents de le méditerrané antique et médiévale
SWR	Studies in Women and Religion		*TDNT*	*Theological Dictionary of the New Testament*
SyCS	The Syrian Churches Series			
Syn.	*Synaxis*		*TDOT*	*Theological Dictionary of the Old Testament*
Syr.	*Syria: Revue d'art oriental et d'archéologie*			
			TdS	*Teología del sacerdocio*
SZRK	*Schweizerische Zeitschrift für Religions– und Kulturgeschichte*		Te. Tra.	Mediaeval Latin Texts and their Transmission
T&E	Universidad de Buenos Aires: Textos & Estudios		*TeCu*	*Technology and Culture*
			TEG	Traditio exegetica graeca
T&T	Texts and Translations		TEL	Textes et études liturgiques
T&T CSST	T&T Clark Studies in Systematic Theology		TeLi	Testimonis liturgicis
			TeM	*Travaux et mémoires*
TaF	Testi a fronte		*Temis*	*Temis*
TAF	Tübinger archäologische Forschungen			

TENT	Texts and Editions for New Testament Study
TENTS	Textes et études liturgiques
TePo	Temas Portugueses
TerInc	*Terrae Incognitae*
TeSI	*Temporis signa: Archeologia della tarda antichità e del medioevo*
TeT	Textes et traditions
TeTe	Texte und Textgeschichte
Textus	*Textus*
TH	Théologie historique
THB	Textual History of the Bible
ThBeitr	*Theologische Beiträge*
ThCE	*The Catholic Encyclopedia*
Thean.	*Theandros: An Online Journal of Orthodox Christian Theology and Philosophy*
Theoforum	*Theoforum*
Theol(P)	Théologie: Études publiées sous la direction de la faculté de théologie s.j. de Lyon-Fourvière
Theologia	*Theologia*
Théologiques	*Théologiques: Revue de la faculté de théologie de l'université de Montréal*
Theology	*Theology*
Theoph.	Theophaneia: Beiträge zur Religions- und Kirchengeschichte des Altertums
ThF	Theologische Forschung: Wissenschaftliche Beiträge zur kirchlich-evangelischen Lehre
ThGl	*Theologie und Glaube: Zeitschrift für den katholischen Klerus*
ThH	Théologie historique
ThIn	*Theological Investigations*
ThJb	*Theologisches Jahrbuch*
THKNT	Theologischer Handkommentar zum Neuen Testament
ThKomNT	Theologischer Kommentar zum Neuen Testament
ThLi	Theologie der Liturgie
ThLZ	*Theologische Literaturzeitung*
Thom.	*The Thomist: A Speculative Quarterly Review of Theology and Philosophy*
Thought	*Thought*
ThPh	*Theologie und Philosophie*

ThQ	*Theologische Quartalschrift*
ThR	*Theologische Rundschau*
ThRv	*Theologische Revue*
ThSGW	*Theoria: Studies over de Griekse wijsbegeerte*
ThSp	Theologie der Spiritualität
ThSt	Theologische Studien
ThSt	*Theologische Studiën*
ThTo	*Theology Today*
ThWAT	*Theologisches Wörterbuch zum Alten Testament*
ThZ	*Theologische Zeitschrift: Theologische Fakultät der Universität Basel*
TIB	Tabula imperii byzantini
TilTS	Tilburg Theological Studies/ Tilburger Theologische Studien
Times LitSupp	*Times Literary Supplement*
TIP	*Temi di iconografia paleocristiana*
TIR	Tabula imperii romani: Iudaeae Palaestina, Maps and Gazetteer
Tituli	*Tituli*
TJ	*Trinity Journal*
TJT	*Toronto Journal of Theology*
Tjurunga	*Tjurunga*
TK	Texte und Kommentare: Eine altertumswissenschaftliche Reihe
TLG	*Thesaurus linguae graecae: Canon of Greek Authors and Works*
TLL	*Thesaurus linguae latinae*
TLT	Two Liturgical Traditions
TMCB	Travaux et mémoires: Centre de Recherche d'Histoire et Civilisation Byzantines
TMLT	Toronto Medieval Latin Texts
TMWC	Theology and Mission in World Christianity
Topoi	Topoi orient-occident
Topoi	*Topoi*
TPAPA	*Transactions and Proceedings of the American Philological Association*
TPL	Textus patristici et liturgici
TPSS	Theologische Perspectieven Supplement Series
TQ	*Theologische Quartalschrift*
Tr.	*Traditio: Studies in Ancient and Medieval History, Thought and Religion*

JOURNALS, SERIES, ENCYCLOPEDIAS, AND LEXICONS

TrAn	Transformationen der Antike
Trans.	*Transformation*
Transc UlturAl	*TranscUlturAl: A Journal of Translation and Cultural Studies*
TrCo	Tria corda
TRE	*Theologische Realenzyklopädie*
TRHS	*Transactions of the Royal Historical Society*
TRSR	Testi e ricerche di scienze religiose
TrVi	Tradizione e vita
TRW	The Transformation of the Roman World
TS	*Theological Studies*
TSAJ	Texts and Studies in Ancient Judaism (= Texte und Studien zum antiken Judentum)
TSBA	*Transactions of the Society of Biblical Archaeology*
TSHP	Texts and Studies in the History of Philosophy
TSMAO	Typologie des sources du moyen âge occidental
TSR	Toronto Studies in Religion
TTH	Translated Texts for Historians
TTH.C	– Contexts
TThZ	*Trierer theologische Zeitschrift*
TTKY	Türk Tarih Kurumu yayinlarindan
TTQ	*Tübinger theologische Quartalschrift*
TU	Texte und Untersuchungen zur Geschichte der altchristlichen Literatur
TUAT	Texte aus der Umwelt des Alten Testaments
TUAT.NS	– New Series
TUGAL	see TU
Turchia	Turchia: La chiesa e la sua storia
TV	*Teología y vida*
TVOA	Testi del vicino oriente antico
TWNT	*Theologisches Wörterbuch zum Neuen Testament*
TWQ	*Theologisches Wörterbuch zu den Qumrantexten*
Tyche	*Tyche: Beiträge zur alten Geschichte, Papyrologie und Epigraphik*
TynB	*Tyndale Bulletin*
TZ	*Theologische Zeitschrift*
TzF	Texte zur Forschung

TZS	*Theologische Zeitschrift aus der Schweiz*
TZTh	*Tübinger Zeitschrift für Theologie*
UALG	Untersuchungen zur antiken Literatur und Geschichte
UBL	Ugaritisch-biblische Literatur
UCL	Universitas catholica lovaniensis: Dissertationes ad gradum doctoris in facultate theologica consequendum conscriptae
UCOP	University of Cambridge Oriental Publications
Ueberweg	Grundriß der Geschichte der Philosophie
Ueberweg AntF	– Die Philosophie der Antike
UJA	*Ulster Journal of Archaeology*
ULB.FPL	Université libre de Bruxelles: Faculté de philosophie et lettres
UMS	University of Michigan Studies
UMS.H	– Humanistic series
UnSa	Unam sanctam
UNT	Untersuchungen zum Neuen Testament
UPATS	University of Pennsylvania Armenian Texts and Studies
UrTa	Urban-Taschenbücher
USML	Utrecht Studies in Medieval Literacy
UTB	Uni-Taschenbücher
VAFLNW	[Veröffentlichungen der] Arbeitsgemeinschaft für Forschung des Landes Nordrhein-Westfalen
VAMZ	*Vjesnik arheološkoga muzeja u Zagrebu*
VAPD	*Vjesnik za arheologiju i povijest dalmatinsku*
VC	*Verbum caro: Revue théologique et ecclésiastique oecuménique*
VCS	Veterum et coaevorum sapientia
VeEC	*Verbum et Ecclesia*
Vergentis	*Vergentis*
Vergilius	*Vergilius*
VerSen	Verba seniorum
Vestigia	Vestigia
VetChr	*Vetera Christianorum*
VeVi	*Verbum Vitae*

Viator	*Viator: Medieval and Renaissance Studies*	VT.S	– Supplements
Vich.	*Vichiana: Rassegna internazionale di studi filologici e storici*	VVAW	Verhandelingen van de Koninklijke Vlaamse Academie voor Wetenschappen, Letteren en Schone Kunsten van België
VIEG	Veröffentlichungen des Instituts für europäische Geschichte		
VIEG.B	– Beiheft	VVAW.L	– Klasse der Letteren
VigChr	*Vigiliae Christianae: Review of Early Christian Life and Language*	VWGTh	Veröffentlichungen der wissenschaftlichen Gesellschaft für Theologie
VIGGP	*Veröffentlichungen der Internationalen Gesellschaft für Geschichte der Pharmazie*	*W&I*	*Word & Image*
		WA	M. Luther, Werke: Kritische Gesamtausgabe (Weimarer Ausgabe)
ViLa	*Vita latina*	WBC	Word Biblical Commentary
VIÖG	Veröffentlichungen des Instituts für österreichische Geschichtsforschung	WBJG	Wissenschaftliche Beilage zum Jahresbericht des herzoglichen Gymnasiums zu Wolfenbüttel
ViOr	*Vicinio oriente*	WBLI	Das wissenschaftliche Bibellexikon im Internet
Vivarium	*Vivarium*		
ViVr	*Vizantijskij vremennik*	WBS	Wiener byzantinistische Studien
VKAMAG	Vorträge und Forschungen: konstanzer Arbeitskreis für mittelalterliche Geschichte	WBT	Wiener Beiträge zur Theologie
		WCJS	*World Congress of Jewish Studies*
		WdF	Wege der Forschung
VKHCLK	Veröffentlichungen der Kommission zur Herausgabe des Corpus der lateinischen Kirchenväter	WEC	The Worlds of Eastern Christianity, 300–1500
		WGRW	see SBL.WGRW
VKNAW	Verhandelingen der Koninklijke Nederlandse Akademie van Wetenschappen	WGRW.S	see SBL.WGRW.SS
		WHB	*Wiener humanistische Blätter*
		WiBiLex	*Das Wissenschaftliche Bibellexikon im Internet*
VKNAW.ALA	– Afdeling Letterkunde Amsterdam		
VKSM	Veröffentlichungen aus dem kirchenhistorischen Seminar München	WisCom	Wisdom Commentary
		WisWei	*Wissenschaft und Weisheit*
VL	Vetus Latina: Die Reste der altlateinischen Bibel	*WJA*	*Würzburger Jahrbücher für die Altertumswissenschaft*
VL.GLB	Vetus Latina: Aus der Geschichte der lateinischen Bibel	*WJT*	*Wiener Jahrbuch für Theologie*
		WMANT	Wissenschaftliche Monographien zum Alten und Neuen Testament
VMPIG	Veröffentlichungen des Max-Planck-Instituts für Geschichte	WoAn	Women in Antiquity
		WoAr	*World Archaeology*
VMStA	Veröffentlichungen des Missionspriesterseminars St. Augustin	*Worship*	*Worship*
		WR	Wissenschaft und Religion
VolBla	*Volynskyi blahovisnyk*	WSA	Wolfenbütteler Studien zur Aufklärung
VoxL	*Vox Latina: Commentarii periodici*	WSAMA	Walberberger Studien der Albertus-Magnus-Akademie
VoxP	*Vox patrum*		
VSpir	*La vie spirituelle*	WSAMA.TR	– Theologische Reihe
VT	*Vetus Testamentum*	WST	Warszawskie studia teologiczne

WSt	*Wiener Studien: Zeitschrift für klassische Philologie und Patristik*	*ZDMG*	*Zeitschrift des deutschen morgenländischen Gesellschaft*
WTS	Wijsgerige teksten en studies	*ZDPV*	*Zeitschrift des deutschen Palästina-Vereins*
WuBi	Württembergische Bibelanstalt		
WUNT	Wissenschaftliche Untersuchungen zum Neuen Testament	ZECNT	Zondervan Exegetical Commentary on the New Testament
WW	*Word and World*	*ZEE*	*Zeitschrift für evangelische Ethik*
WWKL	*Wetzer und Welte's Kirchenlexikon oder Encyklopädie der katholischen Theologie und ihrer Hülfswissenschaften*	Zet.	Zetemata: Monographien zur klassischen Altertumswissenschaft,
WZ(H)	*Wissenschaftliche Zeitschrift der Martin-Luther-Universität Halle-Wittenberg*	*ZGR*	*Zeitschrift für geschichtliche Rechtswissenschaft*
		ZHTh	*Zeitschrift für die historische Theologie*
WZ(H).GS	– Gesellschafts- und sprachwissenschaftliche Reihe	*Zion*	*Zion*
		ZKG	*Zeitschrift für Kirchengeschichte*
XeAn	*Xenia antiqua*	*ZKTh*	*Zeitschrift für katholische Theologie*
YaCL	Yale Classical Studies	*Zmanim*	*Zmanim*
YARL	Yale Anchor Reference Library	*ZNW*	*Zeitschrift für die neutestamentliche Wissenschaft und die Kunde der älteren Kirche*
YCS	*Yale Classical Studies*		
ZA	*Zeitschrift für Assyriologie*		
ZAC	*Zeitschrift für antikes Christentum: Journal of Ancient Christianity*	*ZPE*	*Zeitschrift für Papyrologie und Epigraphik*
ZAMit	*Zeitschrift für Archäologie des Mittelalters*	*ZRGG*	*Zeitschrift für Religions- und Geistesgeschichte*
ZAr	*Zona arqueológica*	*ZS*	*Zeitschrift für Semitistik und verwandte Gebiete*
ZÄS	*Zeitschrift für ägyptische Sprache und Altertumskunde*		
		ZSP	*Zeitschrift für slavische Philologie*
ZAW	*Zeitschrift für die alttestamentliche Wissenschaft*	*ZSRG*	*Zeitschrift der Savigny-Stiftung für Rechtsgeschichte*
ZBK	Zürcher Bibelkommentare	ZSRG.K	– Kanonistische Abteilung
ZBK.AT	– Altes Testament	ZSRG.R	– Romanistische Abteilung
ZBK.NT	– Neues Testament	*ZThK*	*Zeitschrift für Theologie und Kirche*
ZCINT	Zondervan Critical Introductions to the New Testament	*ZVS*	*Zeitschrift für vergleichende Sprachforschung*
ZDA	*Zeitschrift für deutsches Altertum und deutsche Literatur*	*ZWTh*	*Zeitschrift für wissenschaftliche Theologie*
		ZZ	*Zwischen den Zeiten*

General Abbreviations

*	denotes variant manuscript tradition or discrepancy, or corresponding LXX verse, or newly discovered letters
→	on a fragment, the section with horizontal fibers
//	and parallel/parrallels
ad loc.	there, at the specified location
ad v.	see the verse
Akkad.	Akkadian
ap.	in the writings of/as quoted in
approx.	approximately
Arab.	Arabic
Aram.	Aramaic
Armen.	Armenian
b.	Babylonian (prefix)
b.	born
bibl.	biblical, bibliographic, bibliography
Bul.	Bulgarian
c.	circa
c./cc.	canon/canons
cap./capa.	capitulum/capitula (chapter/chapters)
cent./cents.	century/centuries
ch./chs.	chapter/chapters
cm	centimeter(s)
col./cols.	column/columns
comm.	commentaded by
Comm.	Commentary
coni.	coniecit ("conjectured by"; terminus technicus of textual criticism)
Cop.	Coptic
crit.	critical(ly)
d.	died
diff.	different from
diss.	dissertation
doc.	document
DOI	Digital Object Identifier
e.g.	for example/for instance
ed.	edition, edited, edited by, editor
Egyp.	Egyptian
Eng.	English
Ep(p).	Letter(s)
esp.	especially
ESV	English Standard Version
ET	English translation
et al.	and others
etc.	and so on
Eth.	Ethiopic
Ethiop.	Ethiopian
f./ff.	following
facs.	facsimile
fasc.	fascicle
fig(s).	figure(s)
fl.	flourished
fol./fols.	folio/folios
Fr.	French
frgm./frgms.	fragment/fragments
FS	Festschrift
Georg.	Georgian
Ger.	German
Gk	Greek
Goth.	Gothic
Habil.	Habilitation
HB	Hebrew Bible
Heb.	Hebrew
Hell.	Hellenistic
Hung.	Hungarian
i.e.	that is/in other words
idem	the same
illus./illuss.	illustration/illustrations
incipit	inc.
inscr. no.	inscription number
inscrip.	introductory paragraph to a letter
introd.	introduced by
Ital.	Italian
KJV	King James Version
km	kilometer(s)
l./ll.	line/lines
Lat.	Latin
lib.	liber (book)
lit.	literal, literary, literature
LXX	Septuagint
m	meter(s)
MA	Middle Ages
ms./mss.	manuscript/manuscripts
MT	Masoretic Text (of the OT)
Mt.	mount

n(n)	note(s)	rev.	revised (by)
n.s.	new series	RSV	Revised Standard Version
NETS	A New English Translation of the Septuagint	Russ.	Russian
		s.a.	under the year
NIV	New International Version	s.l.	place of publication unknown
NKJV	King James Version	s.v.	under the heading
no./nos.	number/numbers	Sah.	Sahidic
NRSV	New Revised Standard Version	sc.	namely, that is to say
NRSVue	New Revised Standard Version Updated Edition	ser.	series
		sg.	singular
NRSV-CE	New Revised Standard Version-Catholic Edition	sic	thus it was written
		Slav.	Slavonic
NT	New Testament	Slov.	Slovenian
orig.	original(ly)	Span.	Spanish
OT	Old Testament	St.	Saint
P.	Papyrus manuscript	suppl(s).	supplement(s), supplementary issue, supplemented
p./pp.	page/pages		
par./parr.	and parallel/parrallels	Syr.	Syriac/Syrian
para.	paragraph	*t.*	Tosefta (prefix)
passim	here and there, everywhere	trans.	translated (by/translator)
per se	through itself	u.c./a.u.c.	years reckoned from the foundation of Rome
Pers.	Persian		
pl./pls.	plural or plate/plates	unpubl.	unpublished
pr.	printed	v (superscript)	verso
publ./publs.	publication, published (by)/ publications	v./vv.	vers/verses
		Vg.	Vulgate
Q	Logia/Sayings Source Q	vis-à-vis	in relation to, in comparison with
r (superscript)	recto	viz.	namely, that is to say, as follows
r.	ruled	vol./vols.	volume/volumes
rec(s).	recension(s)	vs.	versus
repr./reprs.	reprint/reprints	*y.*	Jerusalem (prefix)
resp.	respectively		

Introduction: The status of an encyclopedia and the history of survey works in the area of early Christianity studies

It is due to Quintilian's translation and explanation of the Greek ἐγκύκλιος παιδεία/*enkýklios paideía* ("all-around education") that our current word "encyclopedia" contains the pretense of presenting a collection of general knowledge expressed in articles or, also in lemmata, an exhaustive overview of history, of persons and of themes crucial in a particular field of science. He translated the Greek expression with *orbis ille doctrinae* and added: *quem Graeci encyclion paedian vocant* ("the course of learning which the Greeks call *enkyklios paideia*"; Quint. Inst. 1.10.1) Monumental examples of the first kind of "universal" encyclopedia are the *Brockhaus Encyclopedia* (from 1808) or the *Encyclopedia Britannica* (from 1768). In these, an attempt was made to provide an exhaustive overview of the historical, religious, political, economic, medical, and cultural developments in the world as we construct and know it (i.e. *mundus*), as well as the findings of research on nature, its flora and fauna (i.e. *creatio*). A good example of the second kind of encyclopedia is *Paulys Realencyclopädie der classischen Altertumswissenschaft* (1837–1864; 1890–1978). At universities, thirdly, the encyclopedia of a particular discipline (i.e. an encyclopedia of legal science) means the course that introduces that discipline of science, explains its theoretical foundations, and clarifies its relationship to other disciplines of science. In the first type of encyclopedia, the emphasis is on comprehensiveness. In the latter two on thematic arrangement of articles, so that there emerges not only an overview of but also an understanding of a particular discipline. Accessibility of the material offered is crucial in each of the three types of encyclopedias. And paradoxically, with each of the three, its representation of the material entails both an end point and a beginning. After all, the knowledge hitherto acquired in a science discipline is tailored to the level of a student, who needs to be introduced to the discipline in question.

The Greek word ἐγκύκλιος means both "going around in a circle" and "general"; "all-encompassing." The word παιδεία stands for "teaching." Unlike Pliny the Elder (d. c. 79 CE) and Quintilian (d. c. 96 CE), Vitruvius (d. c. 15 BCE) translated the first term and, in his sample books of architecture, *De architectura libri decem*, indicated by *encyclios disciplina* ("the circle of arts and sciences") that the universal science, like a body, consists of limbs; of parts (Vitr. *Arch.* 1.1; see 6.4: *encyclioque doctrinarum omnium disciplina*; "knowledge of letters, and of the 'liberal arts'"). As mentioned, Quintilian translated the Greek phrase with *orbis ille doctrinae*. He used it to summarize the formation of young rhetoricians that preceded specialization in, say, geometry or music. He thus laid the foundation for the meaning of the word encyclopedia as expressed in the first and third types of encyclopedias.

The word encyclopedia only really came into vogue when the word group *tas encyclopaedias* in editions of Pliny the Elder's *Naturalis historia* from 1497 onwards was understood as a Greek translation of *orbis doctrinae*. In 37 books, comprising a total of 2,493 chapters, Pliny set out the *mirabilia* of *creatio* ("wonders [of] creation") based on the work of more than 500 authors before him: the course of the heavens, the monsters said to live at the far corners of the earth, the hidden powers of plants and rocks. He also dealt with the *mirabilia* created in the *mundus*: the works of art, instruments, and technology that humans had produced. Almost all early modern naturalists drew on Pliny's work: his encyclopedia, or one of its many concise editions, was the beginning of their research (Labarre, 1973; Nauert, 1979; Stahl, 1962). In his commission letter to Emperor Titus, Pliny explicitly says:

> My object is to treat of all those things which the Greeks include in the Encyclopædia [τῆς ἐγκυκλίου παιδείας], which, however, are either not generally known or are rendered dubious from our ingenious conceits. And there are other matters which many writers have given so much in detail that we quite loathe them. (Plin. *Nat.* 1, preface 14)

The work had already been completed in the year 77 CE, when Pliny dedicated it to Titus; however, the author continued to work on it until his death. It was published posthumously by Pliny the Younger, who appreciatively qualified 37 books by his namesake as "a work of great compass and learning, and as full of variety as nature herself/itself" (Plin. Y. *Ep.* 3.5.6). Pliny the Elder continually pointed out the admirable structure of all that exists and explicitly speculated about the higher power that would be responsible for it. He thought it miraculous how nature could bring together all bodily functions in even the tiniest of insects and described the eyesight possessed by a flea as a form of unfathomable perfection. Augustine of Hippo would speak in similar terms as he elaborated on the *ordo naturae, casu quo* ("order of nature, especially") the sections in the flea (Plin. *Nat.* 11.1; see Aug. *Enarrat. Ps.* 148.8).

Pliny would not be the last, in whose survey work, besides striving for completeness and coherence, another intention would also shine through. Indeed: in his *Institutiones divinarum et saecularium litterarum*, statesman and monastic founder Cassiodorus (d. 560 CE) appears to have arranged the encyclopedic survey of all the books of the Bible, the early Christian exegetes, and the *artes liberales*. His aim was to produce a hermeneutical handbook as an introduction to Bible exegesis for the spiritual growth of Christians who read the Scriptures and partly through this would attain the *aeterna salus* ("eternal salvation"; Cassio. *Inst.* 1, preface 1; Bürsgens, 2003; Schultheiß, 2016). Centuries later, Melchor Cano (d. 1560) still followed his lead. In his posthumously published and in the Roman Catholic Church highly authoritative *De locis theologicis libri duodecim* (1563), this Dominican had presented a list in which the sources of knowledge about God were ordered according to relevance. The canonical books of Holy Scripture occupied the most authoritative "place" (*locus*), the non-scriptural sources like reason, philosophy, and history the last (Colombo, 1979). In his encyclopedic survey, written in the spirit of Cassiodorus, reason was thus, paradoxically, greatly undervalued. The intention with which he had crafted this was also to emphasize revelation as recorded in Scripture as the highest source of knowledge.

Isidore of Seville (d. 636 CE) drew inspiration from Cassiodorus' *Institutiones* when producing his *Etymologiarum sive originum libri XX* (*Etymologiae* or *Origines* for short). Still, this is a different kind of work. The *Etymologiae* is an immense compilation in 20 volumes with a total of 448 chapters of "everything one needs to know" (*quaecunque fere sciri debentur*), as Isidore's pupil Braulio wrote in the *Elogium* of Isidore that he wrote in Isidore's *De viris illustribus*. Isidore wrote an encyclopedia of the first kind: all secular knowledge useful to the Christian scholar was summarized in it. Not only did Isidore list the notions relevant in the literary *trivium* (grammar, rhetoric, and dialectics) or the mathematical *quadrivium* (arithmetic, geometry, astronomy, and music) based on his study of many classical works. He also summarized the basic concepts in medicine and philosophy – interdisciplinary before this word even was invented, he saw these sciences together as disciplines that covered the whole of man. In addition, Isidore summarized legal theories, Catholic doctrine, heresies; classical philosophy have been discussed as well as matters related to food, geography, roads, agriculture, buildings, metals, rocks, war, ships, clothing, and tools. It has been argued that Isidore's work consisted of recapitulating, and sometimes simply transliterating both data and theories from Roman manuals, *compendia* and *miscellanea* and his work lacked research and originality (D'Onofrio, 2011). Nevertheless, Book XV on cities had a lasting influence on medieval cartography. Isidore's work is a good example of the first kind of encyclopedia, except that he arranged his "survey articles" thematically, as in a handbook. Thus, the strength of his work lay not in originality but in synthesis. Evidently, there was already a great need for this in the early Middle Ages. Now, before the invention of printing, copying manuscripts was an extremely expensive business. Apart from the fact that the preparation methods of calf's, goat's or sheep's skin were time-consuming, only about three sheets of parchment could be extracted from the skin of one calf: only six bifolia in other words. That Isidore's work has thus been handed down to us in as many as 1,000 manuscripts – and many will have been lost – indicates that the work was immensely popular in the monastic communities where it could be consulted in the library. But consulting Isidore's *Etymologiae* reveals that many encyclopedic works, which he could still use as sources, have been lost (Collison, 1966). Here a problem arises that was evidently inherent in the production of survey works in his time. It may well be that because Isidore had already summarized the insights presented in classical works, the original works were not copied because of the high cost. Of course, works are more likely to be lost when they have been little handed down than when they have been copied frequently. On the other hand, it is equally true that it is thanks to Isidore's *Etymologiae* that to this day we not only have fragments of lost works at our disposal but also realize that as long as humankind thinks and writes, there is a need for an encyclopedic overview.

However, on the basis of Isidore's work in particular, in the period between his abbacy in Fulda and his appointment as archbishop of Mainz, Rabanus Maurus (d. 856 CE) compiled a kind of encyclopedia which he titled *De rerum naturis*. In a letter to Bishop Haimo of Halberstadt, he wrote that he was striving to put together a work about the nature of things and particular attributes of words, but also about their mystical meaning: "Thus you might find, placed contiguously, each historical and allegorical explanation"(Throop, 2009, xviii; Kössinger, 2008). His craving for overview, and his gift for crafting it, is equally evident in his treatise on the training of clergy, a manual on *computus paschalis* (i.e. the calculation of the date of Easter), a martyrology, and many tracts on specific topics such as penance, child oblation, and the virtues and vices. Like Isidore's *Etymologiae*, his main source, Rabanus' *De rerum naturis* was characterized as a work that demonstrated erudition rather than original thought (Throop, 2009, xii). Yet in the arrangement of the themata, which he brought together in 22 books, the synthetic spirit of Scholasticism already seems to present itself to some extent. Indeed, Rabanus discusses successively those themata related to God, angels, nature, in this case the stars and the plant kingdom in the cosmos as a whole, before describing man, his anatomy, diseases and works and his domestic/domesticated animals (Heyse, 1969).

The pursuit of encyclopedic overview did not only define scholars in the Occident. In Byzantium, a group of scholars produced the *Suda* in Greek, a work with 30,000 keywords arranged, for the first time, according to the (Greek) alphabet (Adler, 1928–1938). It is likely that the lemmata were first written on file cards after depositing the sources before being recorded in quires (Mazzucchi, 2020). The fact that several authors worked on this first lexicon could explain the varying quality of the lemmata. The *Suda* contains relatively many articles on biblical characters, starting with Abimelech and, curiously, under the lemma "Abraham," a short chronology of biblical vicissitudes is published. Also included are life and works of authors from antiquity and the early Middle Ages, of political, ecclesiastical, and literary figures from the Byzantine Empire to the 10th century CE. Because many works were used to compile the *Suda*, which later were lost, as was the case with Isidore's *Etymologiae*, the work remains important as a source for classical philology because of its preservation of literary history, despite the quality of some of the lemmata in this lexicographical compilation itself. It was also given importance in the West: the *Suda* was quickly translated into Latin and a printed version appeared in the 15th century.

The scholastic period saw a certain departure from the precursors of encyclopedias in which a collection of general knowledge contained in articles was presented: encyclopedias of the first kind, in other words. It was during this period that encyclopedias of the second kind mainly appeared in the form of *summae*, which attempted to provide an exhaustive overview of history, people, and themes that are crucial in a particular field of science. A *summa* or a more concise *summula* involved a synthesis and compendium of insights within a discipline of science such as philosophy, canon law, or theology. For canonists, decretal collections such as the *Decretum Gratiani* or *Decretales Gregorii IX* became indispensable reference works and *Fundgruben* at the same time. The *Summa de vitiis* and the *Summa de virtutibus* by Guilielmus Peraldus (William Perault) count as the most important medieval encyclopedias on the virtues and vices; the latter work comprises an average of 250 folia, of which the cardinal virtues fill 90 to 100. "Prudentia" comes to about ten, "Iustitia" to about 40 folia. In keeping with its intention to be serviceable rather than original, the text itself is mainly a succession of quotations and definitions that are themselves often quotations. It was written in any case before 1248 and it has survived in no fewer than 400 surviving manuscripts, after which printed editions appeared for two more centuries (Dondaine, 1948; Verweij, 2007).

For the nurturing mother of all sciences in the Middle Ages, theology, the four *Libri sententiarum* (*Books of Sentences*) by the scholastic theologian and later bishop of Paris, Peter Lombard, became foundational. The first version of this work must have originated between 1142 and 1158. Precursor to the second form of encyclopedia, the "statements" (*sententiae*) he included in it from Scripture and the work of church fathers and other early Christian authors formed the building blocks for equally synthetic and systematic treatises on the main themes in theology of his day. These were the doctrine of God and the doctrine of the Trinity (Book I), creation including anthropology and the doctrine of sin (Book 2), Christology and doctrine concerning God's incarnation (Book III), and the sacraments (Book IV). And because the production of a commentary on Lombard's *Libri sententiarum* from the 13th to the 16th century was an important part of the study of theology leading to the title of magister, numerous other *summae* arose on the basis of this work. The commentaries of *doctor universalis*, Dominican and Bishop Albertus Magnus, William of Auxerre's *Summa Aurea*, Alexander of Hales' *Summa Theologiae*, or also the works of John Duns Scotus, William of Ockham and especially the *Summa Theologiae* of Albertus' fellow brother Thomas Aquinas were the most influential (Rosemann, 2002).

It is due to Albertus' synthetic mind that Aristotle's "physics" survey work was no longer considered controversial in the Christian world because of its pagan origins. Albertus edited and commented, for example, on the *Physica*, *De generatione et corruptione*, and the *Meteorologica*; his own *De mineralibus* shows how much he also sought overview in subjects other than just theology. Thomas' *Summa*, which he started in the Convent of Santa Sabina on the Aventine Hill in Rome, is considered the most perfect example of this form of scholastic survey literature. Here Thomas follows the route of the realists (see www.corpusthomisticum.org/iopera.html). The *Collectorium* of Gabriel Biel, the first professor of theology at the University of Tübingen and the last significant representative of scholasticism and influential supporter of nominalism, counts as the last example of such a scholastic-theological synthesis, although he was certainly not the last scholastic.

It should be noted, however, that knowledge accumulation among scholastics as precursors of the makers of the second type of encyclopedia, whether they were realists or nominalists, was achieved in a different way from the encyclopedists avant la lettre like Pliny, Isidore or the producers of the *Suda*. When Peter Abelard in his *Sic et Non* adopted the method of the 10th-century CE logician Gerbert of Aurillac's *De Rationali et Ratione Uti*, he laid the foundations for a mode of knowledge accumulation in which knowledge was established by systematically explaining the apparent contradiction between the opinions presented on certain subjects. Realists such as Thomas Aquinas assumed here that general concepts exist in themselves before things (i.e. *universalia ante res*). In contrast, influenced by Abelard's terminist thinking, nominalist William of Ockham and his followers argued that these *universalia* are merely names that people have construed and thus come into existence only after things (i.e. *universalia post res*). Thus, Ockham and his followers emphasized that only the *realia*, the concrete descriptions of reality, are valid. They are given on the basis of experience of reality, of empirical knowledge. The *universalia*, on the other hand, in their view, are abstract creations of the human mind.

This form of thinking that Ockham developed would have repercussions on the principles that would underlie later encyclopedias. Ockham was convinced that humans have no experiential knowledge of God and God cannot be "grasped" in abstract and reasonable concepts. Only faith leads to insights about God. Human intellect speaking on the basis of empirical testing, measuring, and verifying leads to insights about the world. More than in the *summae* of the realists, the commentaries on Lombard and other works of the nominalists foreshadowed a separatist thinking in which knowledge of faith became/was to be separated from reasonable knowledge. The nominalists' sharp attacks on Thomas Aquinas' thinking had led to a strict separation between the religious and the natural order. This met with resistance. Fifty-one propositions from Ockham's writings were condemned in 1326 by Pope John XXII, who was residing in Avignon at the time. This French pope gave strong support to Thomism.

But this did not detract from the fact that the separatist thinking inherent in nominalism persisted in the Anglo-Saxon world of thought, especially after the universities had freed themselves from papal control since the English Reformation. The early foundations of the British tradition of empirical philosophy lay in the medieval problem of universals. There was debate between the rationalists, who grounded true knowledge, some way in the spirit of Abelard, in their reliance on human reason and mathematical logic, and the empiricists who argued that true knowledge was based on experience and experiment. Thinkers like Francis Bacon and Thomas Hobbes dominated this debate. Francis Bacon's approach in particular was indebted to

Ockham's. He separated the empirical method, which was to arrive at natural knowledge through research, from theology in an extremely strict manner. The latter discipline was indebted to another source of knowledge, Scripture, which in turn was the written record of revelation. The title of one of his works was certainly symbolic: the *Novum Organum*. This work of 1620 was part of a new encyclopedia in which all accumulated knowledge was arranged as harmoniously as possible with a practical and operational purpose in mind. Crucial in his idea was testable and measurable experiential knowledge as a ground for true science and as a source of nourishment for (his) empirical philosophy. This conviction of Francis Bacon, incidentally, also resonated with his *Of the Proficience and Advancement of Learning, Divine and Human* (1605), from which, much later, Jean le Rond d'Alembert and Denis Diderot, would take the arrangement and subdivisions in their highly influential *Encyclopédie, ou dictionnaire raisonné des sciences, des arts et des métiers*.

A new form of encyclopedia was born: an encyclopedia, no longer based on Pliny's or Augustine's wonderment at the unfathomable perfection of the natural order and at the higher power in which it was embedded but describing the dynamisms in *mundus* and *creatio* "etsi deus non daretur" ("as if God did not exist"). The formula is attributed to Hugo Grotius (1583–1645) to mark the advent of a secular worldview, according to which the world and man are autonomous and independent from God. But paradoxically, this formula was already in use in, nota bene, the scholastic *summae* as early as the 14th century and repeatedly occurred in works of Catholic scholastics such as Gabriel Biel, Domingo de Soto, Francisco Suárez (Appolonov, 2018). But this did not take away from the fact that later not their *summae*, but the *Novum Organum* became the new form of encyclopedia.

There was yet another reason why the *summae* lost authority as an exponent of the second kind of encyclopedia. To trace this, it is important to recall Erasmus' view of scholasticism. Like the Greek and Latin classical writers, *patres* ("fathers") in the Renaissance were not regarded as *auctoritates* ("authorities") as in scholasticism but as *fontes* ("sources"). These had to be read in their entirety because they could contain answers to religious or moral questions. The penchant for manuscripts and integral texts led the humanist, classicist, and bibliophile Tomasso Parentucelli (d. 1455), for example, to search monastic libraries across Europe in the retinue of Cardinal Niccolò Albergati. Elected pope in 1447, Parentucelli, as Nicholas V, made the papal court the leading center of humanism-inspired scholarship. He and his followers continued to collect Greek texts from around the world and had them translated into Latin. It is striking that he described the fall of Constantinople in 1453 as the "second death" of Homer and Plato. Renewing the study of classical writers was evidently at least as important as that of early Christian authors. Nevertheless, the *Decretum Gratiani* was almost always present in Renaissance libraries because it was considered of great value as a sourcebook (Rutherford, 1997).

At this time, Desiderius Erasmus (d. 1536) also saw the importance of the critical edition of the works of the church fathers for his program of church reform and inner renewal at the same time. Corrected as accurately as possible and kept in public libraries as much as possible, the integral works of the early Christian authors in his idea could be read by many. He considered the constant increase of laws, ceremonies, forged documents and of falsely attributed documents in the church of the West to be signs of decay as were the scholastic *summae* and commentaries, which were increasingly laced with barbarism. In his view, the bishops had been asleep when a "sullied and morose group of fabricators of sickening *summae*" caused the "lights" (*lumina*, the fathers) "eminent in writings, renowned in eloquence" to be forgotten (Brady & Olin, 1992). It is true that he confessed in letters to the very much-admired Pope Adrian VI that he also saw advantages of the scholastic method for the reform of church and individuals, at least, in the way Adrian practiced the scholastic method to this end (Allen & Allen, 1923). But that does not alter the fact that, in his view, the study of early Christian authors needed to restore the former splendor and dignity of theology. It is typical of Erasmus that, in his introductions to their works, he expresses appreciation not only for their literary and exegetical qualities, but also for their piety and moderation. For him, scholarly practice and knowledge forging went hand in hand with personal formation and reformation. He had studied Cassiodorus.

Erasmus proved his full commitment to this humanistic reverence for the integral text as well as his desire to make the *fontes* accessible for the sake of (re)formations by producing the first edition of the Greek New

Testament based on several ancient manuscripts, followed by four revisions His new edition formed the basis for his new Latin translation of the New Testament. But also, his paraphrasing of books of the Bible – retellings of all the books of the New Testament (except the book of Revelation; Bloemendal, 2019) – and his editions of the works of several church fathers as sources of knowledge did not take away from the fact that even in the Renaissance there remained a need for works to be classified under encyclopedias of the first and third types.

In 1502, for example, Ambrogio Calepino published a *Dictionarium latinum*, in which Latin keywords were also given in other languages (Greek, sometimes Hebrew, or modern languages; *AA.VV.*, 2005; Lazcano González, 2014). His *Septem Linguarum Calepinus* was not a Latin dictionary in the modern sense of the word, but had a certain encyclopedic character, as it discussed people and places and Calepino frequently elaborated/expanded, for example in a treatise on the letter A. The work had a tremendous dissemination throughout Europe and was translated into many languages. There are 211 known editions; the Bayerische Staatsbibliothek München alone has 81 editions.

From the mid-16th century, the term "encyclopedia" was applied without further explanation in book titles to works "in which the totality of the sciences is presented according to a certain order" (Dierse, 1977; Blom, 2005). Johann Georg Turmair (d. 1534) first used the term in the title of one of his works *Encyclopedia orbisque doctrinarum, hoc est omnium artium, scientiarum, ipsius philosophiae index ac divisio*. The work was published in 1517. In 1538, the Dutch pedagogue Joachim Sterck of Ringelbergh published his *Lucubrationes, vel potius absolutissima κυκλοπαίδεια, nempe liber de ratione studii*. He used the term encyclopedia in the title of his work, although in this book he was more concerned with a method of learning. All the more so since the priest, humanist, and encyclopedist Paul Skalich (Paulus Scalichius de Lika) did produce an encyclopedia of the first type in his *Encyclopaediae, seu orbis disciplinarum* in 1559, it seems as if the exact meaning of the term encyclopedia was still subject to variation (Yeo, 2001). Yet nothing could be further from the truth. The Capuchin father Lawrence of Brindisi (1559–1619) uses the term twice in his work against Luther, arguing that it should encompass all sciences, human and divine (Centre Traditio Litterarum Occidentalium = Laurentius a Brindisio, 2010, 325; Drenas, 2018). And from the early 1600s, the term is used in modern European languages to denote general encyclopedias as well as encyclopedias for a particular field of knowledge. Some are huge in size, others only a few volumes. The most comprehensive encyclopedia of this period is the *Encyclopaedia septem tomis distincta*, published in 1630 in Herborn. It is credited to Johannes Henricus Alstedius (Johann Heinrich Alsted, d. 1638; Valbusa, 2008).

In the English world, from the 18th century onwards, the word "cyclopedia" (or cyclopædia) was adopted: an edited transcription of the original Greek expression ἐγκύκλιος παιδεία/*encyklios paideia*. Ephraim Chambers, for example, titled his encyclopedia *Cyclopædia: or, An Universal Dictionary of Arts and Sciences*. The work was published in London in 1728 in two volumes. The work was reprinted many times and many times also expanded with numerous keywords. It was also translated into other European languages. The term cyclopedia is still widely used in the Anglo-Saxon world but not in other European languages. One reason may be that the term ciclopedia in Italian refers to information about cycling.

Encyclopedias, in which knowledge was systematically set out by means of keywords in alphabetical order – the form we know today – appeared on the market from 1674 onwards. *Le grand dictionaire historique* by Louis Moréri, published in Lyon in 1674 is considered the first encyclopedia in this form. Louis Moréri compiled a one-volume dictionary on mythology and history and conceived of history as genealogy. The first edition was expanded and improved by other authors; the 20th and best edition, was published in 1759 in ten volumes. In fact, this work is considered the forerunner of the encyclopedia in which the knowledge of a subfield in science is deepened. Of the all-encompassing encyclopedias, the most famous in these times is the already mentioned *Encyclopédie, ou dictionnaire raisonné des sciences, des arts et des métiers*, edited by Jean le Rond d'Alembert and Denis Diderot and first published in 17 volumes with notes (1751–1765) and 11 volumes with illustrations (1762–1772). Five volumes with supplementary material and two volumes with indexes were distributed from 1776 to 1780, under the supervision of other publishers, by Charles-Joseph Panckoucke of Paris. The 35 volumes eventually contained 71,818 articles, and 3,129 plates.

Gaetano Moroni (1802–1883) single-handedly compiled an immense encyclopedia on ecclesiastical subjects: his *Dizionario di erudizione storico-ecclesiastica da san Pietro fino ai nostri giorni*. Published in Venice from 1840–1861, the work eventually numbered 103 volumes; six more volumes with indices were added. Jacques-Paul Migne (1800–1875), who, in the vein of Erasmus, also had the works of Greek and Latin church fathers published in his *Patrologia Graeca* (161 vols.) and *Patrologia Latina* (221 vols.), also showed a commitment to encyclopedism, sometimes republishing earlier encyclopedic works but sometimes having new ones compiled. His words, penned in an introduction to one of his encyclopedias, proved to be a prophetic for any encyclopedist. For he argued that a complete course of Christian literature was missing but he did not pretend to fill this gap and had only carefully, patiently, and conscientiously collected material to fill the gap to some extent (Migne, 1851). As part of his huge project of a *Bibliothèque universelle du clergé* in which he commissioned nearly 500 works, Abbé Migne also published a theological encyclopedia: the *Nouvelle encyclopédie théologique, ou nouvelle série de dictionnaires sur toutes le parties de la science religieuse* (171 vols., 1844–1875). It was a series of special lexicons covering the various disciplines of theology and history: Scripture, liturgy, canon law, ecclesiastical geography, philology, apocryphal texts, councils, archaeology, symbolism, dogma, and heresies. For instance, in this context, Alain Sevestre provided a four-volumes lexicon in the field of patrology, the *Dictionnaire de patrologie* (1851–1895). To Jacques-Paul Mignes' name came a two-volumes *Dictionnaire des apocryphes, ou, Collection de tous les livres apocryphes relatifs à l'Ancien et au Nouveau Testament* (1856–1858). He also published the *Dictionnaire d'iconographie* (1850), the *Dictionnaire d'épigraphie chrétienne* (1851), the two-volumes *Dictionnaire de persécutions* (1851), and the two-volumes *Dictionnaire d'archéologie sacré* (1862), as well as a four-volumes *Dictionnaire de la bible* (1860).

At the same time as Jacques-Paul Migne, the Swiss Protestant theologian Johann Jakob Herzog, in collaboration with other scholars, published his 22-volumes *Real-Encyklopädie für protestantische Theologie und Kirche* (1854–1868), which under the editorship of Albert Hauck had a third edition with two later supplements. Philip Schaff, a Protestant theologian, who taught most of his life in the United States, showed himself to be a minor counterpart of Jacques-Paul Migne. He not only initiated the production of *A Select Library of the Nicene and Post-Nicene Fathers of the Christian Church*, usually known as the *Nicene and Post-Nicene Fathers* (1886–1900). He also edited a slightly reduced translation of Johann Jakob Herzog's work into English: *The New Schaff-Herzog Encyclopedia of Religious Knowledge* (1882–1884).

The *Theologische Realenzyklopädie*, which would eventually have 36 volumes and four indices and was published at Berlin and New York in the years 1977–2007, is considered the follow-up to the aforementioned *Real-Encyklopädie*. The absence of the adjective "Protestant" in the title indicates that the encyclopedia pursued a more ecumenical approach; non-Protestant authors also contributed. Theological topics are covered in a historically comprehensive way. Many lemmata relate to Christian antiquity. The same applies to two other German reference works. The first is *Die Religion in Geschichte und Gegenwart* (1909–1913), a work that emerged from the Protestant tradition and has had four editions, the last of which appeared in the years 1998–2005 under the editorship of Kurt Galling. *Religion Past and Present* is the English translation of the fourth edition of *Die Religion in Geschichte und Gegenwart*. This edition was more international in scope. The other is the *Lexikon für Theologie und Kirche*. The first edition was published at Freiburg by Konrad Hofman and Michael Buchberger in the period 1930–1938 and had ten volumes. Leaving aside the fact that Michael Buchberger was bishop of Regensburg, the papal keys and tiara printed on the cover leave nothing to be desired regarding the catholicity of this lexicon. The second edition of this work also appeared in Freiburg from 1957–1965 and was edited by Josef Höfer and Karl Rahner. The ten volumes (excluding volume XI: *Register*) were edited under the direction of Herbert Vorgrimler from 1966–1968 with three volumes in which the genesis of the constitutions and decrees of the Second Vatican Council was analyzed, and these constitutions and decrees (in Latin and German) were included and commented on. The third edition of the *Lexikon für Theologie und Kirche* edited by Walter Kasper appeared in the years 1993–2001, also in ten volumes excluding register. Remarkably, in this edition, lemmata relevant to scholars focusing on modernity are more prominently featured than those covering a theme of early Christianity.

It was not only in Germany that numerous encyclopedias were published from the beginning of the last century, covering theology, its history, and the ecclesiastical sciences, and thus also addressing themes and authors that concerned early Christianity. We limit ourselves here to a brief discussion of those most relevant to the study of early Christianity.

The first edition of the *Dictionnaire de la bible* edited by Fulcran Vigouroux was published in Paris in the years 1895–1912; the last supplement appeared in 2015. The *Dictionnaire de théologie catholique* was initiated in 1898 under the direction of Abbé Jean Michel Alfred Vacant (1852–1901) and continued under the direction of Eugène Mangenot (1856–1922) and then Émile Amann. From 1899 to 1950 30 volumes would eventually appear with excellent indices. What is true of this encyclopedia of the second type is also true of the *Dictionnaire di spiritualité ascétique et mystique, doctrine et histoire*, published in 16 volumes (excluding register binding) in Paris from 1932 to 1995. Started under the editorship of Marcel Viller SJ, numerous scholars from all over the world have for decades discussed those themes and authors relevant to the history of spirituality, and thus also to history and spirituality of early Christianity. Like the lemmata in the *Dictionnaire de théologie catholique* that deal with a theme, person or developments in early Christianity, the similar articles in the *Dictionnaire di spiritualité* also differ from similar lemmata in the aforementioned German encyclopedias in two respects. First, in the French lemmata, the early Christian authors themselves are given much more of a say in extensive quotations that are sometimes barely commented on or summarized, so that it is not the author of the lemma but the author of the primary source who shines his light on a particular theme. As a result, the reader does not perceive the focal points of a theme or the broad outlines of a development as quickly as in the German encyclopedias. On the other hand, and second, the developmental progress of an author or the developments in (dogma) history are almost perceptible from the chronologically ordered, crucial texts.

Finally, worth mentioning among the French-language encyclopedias are the *Dictionnaire d'histoire et de géographie ecclésiastique*, begun in 1912 and of which volume XXXI was published in 2015. However, the work is not yet complete. The seven-volumes *Dictionnaire de droit canonique* edited by Raoul Naz and published at Paris in the years 1935–1965 also contains many lemmata relevant to scholars in the field of early Christianity. It is true that The *Catholic Encyclopedia*, published in New York in the years 1905–1918 and partly replaced by the *New Catholic Encyclopedia* (2nd ed., 2003), like the Italian *Enciclopedia cattolica* (1949–1954) is in general a encyclopedia of the first type, albeit with Catholic teaching and history as its main focus. However, this does not take away from the fact that most of its lemmata relating to early Christian archaeology, patrology, and patristics are very adequate.

Scottish clergyman James Hastings (1852–1922) may be considered the editor of works that can be described as precursors to the *Brill Encyclopedia of Early Christianity*. With the collaboration of numerous English scholars, he compiled *A Dictionary of the Bible* (5 vols., 1898–1904), the *Encyclopaedia of Religion and Ethics* (13 vols., 1908–1926), *A Dictionary of Christ and the Gospels* (2 vols., 1906–1908). With John Selbie and John Lambert, he additionally prepared the two-volumes *Dictionary of the Apostolic Church* (1915–1918; repr. 2015). This work was reprinted several times, including in New York in 1915–1918. As many as 99 scholars – almost all English-speaking and all Protestant except one French Catholic (Pierre Batiffol) – collaborated in the work. It was William Smith's intention that the *A Dictionary of Christ and the Gospels* and the *Dictionary of the Apostolic Church* should be complementary. In the preface to the second work, James Hastings writes that this book carries the history of the church as far as the end of the 1st century CE and that together with the *Dictionary of Christ and the Gospels*, it forms a complete and independent *Dictionary of the New Testament*. But this did not mean that many keywords were not repeated. As the mostly comprehensive lemmata on languages, persons, texts archaeological sites, theological terms, as well as on, for example, Anger; Dissentery; Gravity (*gravitas*); Groaning; Hair, Hearth; Mourning; Roads and Journeys, are very expertly written, this is by no means disturbing. It is noteworthy that James Hastings used the term "church" and not "Christianity." The keyword "persecution" could be the chapter of a book and extends to modern times.

During the years when James Hastings published his works, no less than three encyclopedias on Christian antiquities were also published. They all consisted of two volumes and the quality varied. The first was Joseph-Alexandre Martigny's *Dictionnaire des antiquites chretiennes* (1865; repr. 1877). Although Joseph-Alexandre Martigny lacked libraries as a chaplain in the province and, as a result, many keywords were treated superficially, his work did provide the breeding ground for an English- and German-language encyclopedia.

The first one was prepared by William Smith and Samuel Cheetham. These scholars managed to attract many scholars from Oxford and Cambridge to produce their *Dictionary of Christian Antiquities* (1875–1880). They structured their dictionary like the *Dictionary of Christian Biography, Literature, and Doctrines* (4 vols., 1877–1879) and the *Dictionary of the Bible* (1870). The *Dictionary of Greek and Roman Geography* (1854), all of which are to William Smith's credit. He also edited the *Dictionary of Greek and Roman Antiquities* (1842) and the *Dictionary of Greek and Roman Biography and Mythology* (1844). All these sectional encyclopedias complemented each other well. The *Dictionary of Christian Antiquities* is a reference work of considerable scholarly value because of its accuracy of information and soundness of judgement. It covers many topics from Christian antiquity: saints and martyrs, the history of the church and its organization, worship services, liturgical vestments, symbolism, prayer buildings, early Christian art, tombs, the Christian calendar, and so on. Some lemmas, such as Alienation of Church Property, Antiphon, Appeal, Apostolic Canons, Contract of Marriage, Canon in Music, Bishop, Marriage, and so on, are more like a chapter in book than a compact lemma. Many keywords are not readily found in other encyclopedias (e.g. Asinarii; Authentic [Music]; Balance; Campanarius, Calliculae; Canister; Caracalla [Vestiment]; Caupona; etc.) The expertise of the scholars who contributed to William Smith's *Dictionary of Christian Antiquities* were almost without exception of global stature and provided a variety of judgements, sometimes bordering on opposition to the opinion of another contributor to the dictionary. William Smith did not redact the polemic away, so his work is still interesting because the *status quaestionis* regarding the study of the plethora of material on the ancient, pagan, and Christian world also remained visible.

The German-language encyclopedia is the *Real-Encyklopädie der christlichen Alterthümer* by Franz Kraus, published in two volumes in Freiburg in the years 1882–1886. Franz Kraus, knowledgeable about early Christianity and very meticulous, wrote almost all lemmata himself about Christian antiquities known to him, but did not treat characters, doctrines, and geography because this was beyond the scope of his *Real-Encyklopädie*.

At the beginning of the last century the era arrived in which the great encyclopedias on Christianity and its history were created. Some are general in nature and include many topics related to early Christianity. Others, however, are sectoral; these specifically deal with church history, theology, spirituality, or persons in this era. To this day, the voluminous work begun by Fernand Cabrol and continued by Henri Leclercq, the *Dictionnaire d'archéologie chrétienne et de liturgie* (1903–1953), remains a rich source of information. The main themes of this comprehensive work are archaeology, respectively architecture, early Christian art, symbols and figures, palaeography, epigraphy, numismatics, as well as liturgical themata. Compared to earlier works, the approach to the many aspects and facets of the (history of) liturgy is new. The various rites, liturgical books, formulas, and documents, which became common from the Carolingian periods onwards, are valued mainly through a method of comparison. The contributions are almost all written by French-speaking researchers; one researcher, Henri Leclercq (d. 1945), did take the lion's share. He wrote very extensive articles; some, such as "Afrique Chrétienne," have the length of more than 150 columns, with Fernand Cabrol adding to Henri Leclercq's lemma another 50 columns on the liturgy in Africa (see vol. I, cols. 576–775). Although the bibliographies at the end of the lemmata are particularly abundant, as are the notes, Henri Leclercq deliberately does not cite certain standard works. For example, Ernst Diehl, *Inscriptiones latinae christianae ueteres* (3 vols., 1924–1931), is not mentioned. Precisely because certain lemmata in the *Dictionnaire d'archéologie chrétienne et de liturgie* seems to paraphrase far too extensively complete monographs, certain keywords are unnecessarily inflated, and imbalances arise between the respective lemmas. Some keywords, even important ones, are very short, others, less important ones, very long. Moreover, the disproportionate and unnecessary length has led to many errors of all kinds. Henri-Irénée Marrou edited the missing volumes after Henri Leclercq's death.

The *Reallexikon für Antike und Christentum* initiated by Theodor Klauser is then of much greater value. Theodor Klauser headed the editorial board until his death in 1984. The first volume appeared in Stuttgart in 1950; volume XXIX has since been published. The *Reallexikon* is the outcome of an ambitious interdisciplinary project for which Theodor Klauser founded the Franz Joseph Dölger Institute at the University of Bonn in 1955. In the spirit of Franz Joseph Dölger, the starting point in the respective lemmata is consistently the study of the relationship between classical antiquity and Christianity, and the aim is to describe the transformation process of ancient cultures by Christianity and its influences. It also describes the interactions between Christianity of the first centuries of our era and the Jewish world. The articles are written by experts of different nationalities, but German experts are most in demand. A wide range of topics is covered: personalities, geography, law, art, science, liturgy, material culture, festivals, daily life, theological ideas, and so on. Each topic is studied, sometimes by different authors, taking into account the context provided by the ancient world for developments in early Christianity.

Although the topics did not initially concern early Christianity as such, more than worth mentioning is the *Realencyclopädie der classischen Altertumswissenschaft* (1893–1980), commonly called *Pauly-Wissowa*. The history of this work begins with the initiative of a teacher, August Pauly (d. 1845), who in 1839 began work on a six-volumes encyclopedia (now 7 vols.) for the benefit of grammar school students and which was completed in 1852. New editions were published from 1861 to 1866. In 1890, Georg Wissowa began work on a new edition, one that culminated in *Paulys Realencyclopädie der classischen Altertumswissenschaft: Neue Bearbeitung*. Initially, Georg Wissowa planned to complete his work within ten years. He obtained cooperation from the best German scholars of his time. However, the last volume, volume LXXXIII, was not published until 1978. Volumes with indexes followed in the years 1997–2000. In 1996, work began on the publication of a new 15-volumes encyclopedia of the ancient world, *Der Neue Pauly*. The 15th volume was published in three volumes. An updated English translation, *The New Pauly*, was published in 2002–2011.

In contrast to his *Realencyclopädie*, the authors of the contributions in *Der Neue Pauly* as those of the *Reallexikon für Antike und Christentum* also paid much more attention to the influence of ancient Oriental and Egyptian influences on the Greco-Roman world as well as to its interaction with neighboring peoples and cultures. Also, the fruits of Byzantine studies were considered, as was the interchange between Judaism, early Christianity, and emerging Islam.

Launched by Angelo Di Berardino in 1980, the *Dizionario patristico e di antichità cristiane* (2 vols., 1982) is a work that was midway between a dictionary and a compact encyclopedia on patristics and Christian antiquity. In this project 167 people of 17 different nationalities, different religious denominations and of many cultural interests collaborated. The *dizionario* was created because there appeared to be a great need for an immediately usable tool for any person of any culture, looking for quick and precise information on a person, development or subject related to the first eight centuries of Christian history. Two major volumes were published in four years, followed by a volume with maps and illustrations. The work has an interdisciplinary character and has had numerous translations. The *dizionario* was thoroughly revised and expanded into three volumes (2006–2008) and translated into English under the title *Encyclopedia of Ancient Christianity* (2014). The English edition also had numerous additions. Finally, Everett Ferguson edited the *Encyclopedia of Early Christianity* (1990); the second edition was expanded and published in 1998, in two volumes. The contributors are almost all Americans.

To conclude. The very recent *Encyclopedia of the Bible and Its Reception*, which is being prepared over these decades by 38 editors and almost 4,000 authors from more than 55 countries – the 26th and final volume is expected in 2025 – has been proof, as it has been since the publication of the first volume in 2009, that major developments in the study of Scripture and tradition are taking place. In the field of research concerning the origin and development of the Bible in the canons of Judaism and Christianity and into the ways in which biblical texts have been interpreted and integrated into thought and culture in Judaism, Christianity, Islam and other non-Western religious traditions over the centuries, developments are rapidly following. The lemmata in the *Encyclopedia of the Bible and Its Reception*, which covers the most recent scholarly enquiries into the reception of the Bible in academic disciplines and cultural-social domains such as literature, visual arts, or music, reveal that there is now a particular emphasis on interdisciplinary approaches that transcend the purely theological and theology-historical far-flung (Furey et al., 2009–).

The exhaustive survey of textbooks in the field of patrology and patristics, as recently established by Angelo Di Berardino, shows that a similar movement is taking place in patristics (Di Berardino, 2015; see Van Geest, 2014, for the differences between patrology and patristics). Since the publication of Simon de Voyon's *Catalogue des docteurs de l'église de Dieu* (1607) and Robertus Bellarminus' *De scriptoribus ecclesiasticis* (also in the editions of Labbe, Casimir Oudin & A. de Saussy), early Christian writers appear to have been mainly put in position by Protestant and Catholic scholars to squeeze their work into the Procrustes bed of their own theological rightness. This despite the fact that the French Huguenot Jean Daillé (Johannes Dallaeus, 1594–1670), in his *De usu Patrum ad ea definienda religionis capita quae hodie sunt controversa*, already wrote that it was impossible to know exactly and precisely what the thoughts of the church fathers encompassed (Daillé, 1632, 1). He therefore argued that the church fathers were dealing with very different issues from those of his own time (Daillé, 1632, 8). Biographical, literary-critical, dogma-historical studies, and studies on the life and work of the church fathers were, as the Gallicanist Louis Dupin (or Du Pin; d. 1719) also proves in his *De antiqua ecclesiae disciplina dissertationes historicae*, for example, completed from a particular agenda. Louis Dupin wanted to adduce the insight that the pope's power could not be deduced from either the Bible or the works of the church fathers (the book therefore remained on the index until 1948, when the index was abolished; Du Pin, 1691; Denzinger, 1991). But the above-mentioned overview shows that from the publication of Wilhelm Wilhelmus, *Patrologia adusus academicos* (1775) at universities in Germany, England, France, Spain Italy, Greece, and Romania, the textbooks were also produced more interdisciplinary in nature and gradually demanded more attention to other cultures and languages (Coptic, Syriac, Armenian). The question of added value of patristics to profane sciences such as economics is raised (Di Berardino, 2015; Van Geest, 2021).

The *Brill Encyclopedia of Early Christianity* focuses on the history of early Christian texts, authors, geography, ideas, doctrines, communities, and institutions. It aims to provide a critical review of the methods used in early Christian studies and to update the historiography. In doing so it intends to offer the most significant knowledge accumulated in relation to early Christianity to a vast range of readers between the fields of New Testament studies and patristics, covering the whole period of early Christianity up to 600 CE. In this very long period, many incredible changes had happened in the Roman Empire: in religion, in society, in politics, in the spread and accepted values, in the social and religious public life, and in the way of living. In the 4th century CE, caring for the poor, giving alms, and helping the needy was institutionalized and formed the core of early Christian preaching and church activity. This changed society as the building of church in cities and in the countryside changed the look of the landscape. The rise of monasticism in its various forms, the spread of Christian values through it, the growth of the church as an institution in which clerics of different hierarchical and social rank and file caused a radical transformation of all regions around the Mediterranean. The rise and spread of Christian feasts as well as the organization of public, social, political, and religious time changed profoundly with the conversion of many people to Christianity. By the end of the 6th century CE, theologians and councils had solved the main theological problems, and ecclesiastical institutions were largely definitively developed and the system in which parishes formed the last organizational unit also gave the church its prestige (Di Berardino, 2021). In short, by the 6th century CE, churches were organized nationally, and liturgical "families" were functioning. Catechumenate declined with the spread of infant baptism. The way penance was finished underwent a radical transformation. Everything had been subject to change but by the 6th century CE there was relative calm.

A citizen of the 2nd century CE, who had participated intensively in the cultural and religious life of his city, would have felt somewhat lost if he had been walking around the same city at the end of the 5th century CE

INTRODUCTION

(see Liebeschuetz, 2003, for some aspects). He had probably imagined himself one of the seven sleepers who, in one of the Christian versions of the legend – there is also a variant included in the Qur'an – had been walled up in a cave near Ephesus on the orders of Emperor Decius because of their being a Christian. They were found alive exactly 196 years later in 447 CE under the impression that they had only slept one night. The sleeper sent out to buy bread could not believe his eyes: the whole of Ephesus had been Christianized and in Ephesus the name of Christ was allowed to be mentioned just like that.

Whether the users of the *Brill Encyclopedia of Early Christianity* also experience themselves as one of the seven sleepers of Ephesus when taking in the overview provided of the history or persons, subjects, and developments that were crucial in early Christianity is quite possible. And yet: it is highly probable that in all the discontinuity that centuries bring about between the different periods, traces of continuity also light up, becoming concrete in, for example, laws and practices for which the foundations were laid in early Christianity.

Bibliography

AA.VV.: *Società, cultura, luoghi al tempo di Ambrogio di Calepio*, Bergamo, 2005.

Adler, A., ed., *Suidae Lexicon*, 5 vols., Leipzig, 1928–1938; repr. Leipzig, 1994–2001; Suda online.

Allen, H.M., & P.S. Allen, *Opus epistolarum des Erasmi Roterdami*, vol. V: *1522–1524*, Oxford, 1923; *Ep.* 1304; 1310; 1329; 1352.

Appolonov, A., "Etsi Deus non daretur" ("as if God does not exist"): Hugo Grotius and Scholastic Theology," *STUR* 77, 2018, 63–71.

Bloemendal, J., "Erasmus and His Paraphrases on the New Testament: What Kind of Enterprise?" *Erasmus Studies* 40, 2019, 34–54.

Blom, P., *Enlightening the World: Encyclopédie: The Book that Changed the Course of History*, New York, 2005.

Brady, J.F., & J.C. Olin, eds., *Collected Works of Erasmus*, Toronto, 1991, vol. LXI: *Patristic Scholarship: The Edition of St. Jerome*, Toronto, 1992, vol. I, 196.

Bürsgens, W., ed., *Flavius Magnus Aurelius Cassiodorus: Institutiones divinarum et saecularium litterarum: Einführung in die geistlichen und weltlichen Wissenschaften*, FChr 39, Freiburg, 2003.

Centre Traditio Litterarum Occidentalium, = Laurentius a Brindisio. *Lutheranismi hypotyposis*, part 2: *Hypotyposis ecclesiae et doctrinae Lutheranae*, Turnhout, 2010, 325.

Collison, R.L., *Encyclopaedias: Their History Throughout the Ages: A Bibliographical Guide with Extensive Historical Notes to the General Encyclopedias Issued Throughout the World from 250 BC to the Present Day*, New York, ²1966, passim.

Colombo, G., "La teologia manualistica," in: G. Colombo, ed., *La teologia italiana oggi*, Milan, 1979, 25–56, esp. 40–51.

D'Onofrio, S., "Isidore of Seville," in: H. Legerlund, ed., *Encyclopedia of Medieval Philosophy, 500–1500*, Dordrecht, 2011, 574.

Daillé, J., *De usu Patrum ad ea definienda religionis capita quae hodie sunt controversa*, Geneva, 1632, 1.

Denzinger, H., *Kompendium der Glaubensbekenntnisse und kirchlichen Lehrentscheidungen: Verbessert, erweitert, ins Deutsche übertragen und unter Mitarbeit von Helmut Hoping herausgegeben von Peter Hünermann*, Freiburg, ³⁷1991, 2281–2284, 2285.

Di Berardino, A., "Chapter 3: Modern Patrologies," in: K. Parry, ed., *The Wiley Blackwell Companion to Patristics*, Chichester, 2015, 51–67.

Di Berardino, A., *Istituzioni della chiesa antica*, Rome, 2019; ET: *Ancient Christianity: The Development of Its Institutions and Practices*, New Haven, 2021.

Dierse, U., *Enzyklopädie: Zur Geschichte eines philosophischen und wissenschaftlichen Begriffs*, Bonn, 1977, 7–8.

Dondaine, A., "Guillaume Peyraut: Vie et oeuvres," *AFP* 18, 1948, 162–236.

Drenas, A.J.G., *The Standard Bearer of the Roman Church: Lawrence of Brindisi and Capuchin Missions in the Holy Roman Empire (1599–1613)*, Washington DC, 2018.

Du Pin, L.E., *De antiqua ecclesiae disciplina dissertationes historicae, excerptae ex conciliis oecumenicis & sanctorum Patrum ac auctorum ecclesiasticorum scriptis*, Paris, 1691.

Furey, C.M., P. Gemeinhardt, J.M. LeMon, T. Römer, J. Schröter, B. Dov Walfish & E. Ziolkowski, eds., *Encyclopedia of the Bible and Its Reception*, 21 vols., Berlin, 2009–.

Heyse, E., *Hrabanus Maurus' Enzyklopädie* De rerum naturis: *Untersuchungen zu den Quellen und zur Methode der Kompilation*, Munich, 1969.

Kössinger, N., ed., *Hrabanus Maurus: Profil eines europäischen Gelehrten*, Sankt Ottilien, 2008.

Labarre, A., "Diffusion de l'*Historia naturalis* de Pline au temps de la Renaissance," in: J. Benzing et. al., *FS für Claus Nissen: Zum siebzigsten Geburtstag*, Wiesbaden, 1973, 451–470.

Lazcano González, R., "Ambrosio Calepino (1440–1510), y su dictionarium latino del saber clásico," *AAug* 77, 2014, 193–220.

Liebeschuetz, J.H.W.G., *The Decline and Fall of the Roman City*, rev. ed, Oxford, 2003.

Mazzucchi, C.M., "De compositione et nomine lexici Sudae," *Aevum* 94/2, 2020, 291–296.

Migne, J.-P., ed., *Dictionnaire de littérature chrétienne*, Paris, 1851, 1.

Nauert, C.G., "Humanists, Scientists and Pliny: Changing Approaches to a Classical Author," *AHR* 84, 1979, 72–85.

Rosemann, P.W., ed., *Mediaeval Commentaries on the Sentences of Peter Lombard*, 3 vols., Leiden, 2002–; vol. II, 2009, passim.

Rutherford, D., "Gratian's *Decretum* as a Source of Patristic Knowledge in the Italian Renaissance: The Example of Timoteo Maffei's *In sanctam rusticitatem* (1454)," in: I. Backus, ed., *The Reception of the Church Fathers in the West: From the Carolingians to the Maurists*, vol. I, Leiden, 1997, 473–510.

Schultheiß, J., "Cassiodor: *Institutiones divinarum et saecularium litterarum*," in: M.H.G. Durst, ed., *Handbuch der Bibelhermeneutiken: Von Origenes bis zur Gegenwart*, Berlin, 2016, 97–110, esp. 97, 109–110.

Stahl, W.H., Roman *Science: Origins, Development and Influence to the Later Middle Ages*, Madison, 1962, ch. 6.

Throop, P., trans., *Hrabanus Maurus: De Universo: The Peculiar Properties of Words and Their Mystical Significance*, 2 vols., Charlotte, 2009, vol. I: *Books I–XI*, xviii.

Valbusa, I, *La forma dell'enciclopedia: Una valutazione della prospettiva di J.H. Alsted*, Trento, 2008.

Van Geest, P., "Patristics Among the Tulips: Interdisciplinarity as a Chance for Theology and Patristics," *Greg* 95, 2014, 73–94; see also his *BEEC*-article "Patrology/Patristics."

Van Geest, P., *Morality in the Marketplace: Reconciling Theology and Economics*, Leiden, 2021.

Verweij, M., "Vierhonderd handschriften in tweeënhalve eeuw: Het geval van Peraldus," *De Gulden Passer* 85, 2007, 21–41 (Dutch).

Yeo, R., *Encyclopaedic Visions: Scientific Dictionaries and Enlightenment Culture*, Cambridge MA, 2001.

ANGELO DI BERARDINO
PAUL VAN GEEST

A

Aba (Disciple of Ephrem the Syrian)

That → Ephrem the Syrian (d. 373 CE) had a disciple by the name of Aba is attested in the Syriac text known as the *Testament of Ephrem* (Beck, 1973). "Aba, man of wonder [*gabrā d-tedmurtā*]" is listed as the first among seven disciples (Beck, 1973, 56, l. 441), and one manuscript of the Testament (BL Add. 14.582), dated 816 CE, calls him "the head [*rēshā*] of all my disciples." The author of the Testament (only part of which may go back to Ephrem himself) must have in mind the same Aba to whom Syriac literary works of theological and exegetical content are attributed. Whenever the author's name is mentioned, he is presented as "Aba, the disciple [*talmidā*] of Mar Ephrem." Unfortunately, we mostly have short extracts and isolated pieces by Aba, which do not allow us to draw an overall picture of his work. No details of his life are known, and Aba largely remains in the shadow of his master.

A 9th-century CE Syriac florilegium (BL Add. 17.194) with extracts from several Greek and six Syriac authors (the latter include: Aba "the disciple of Mar Ephrem," the "Teaching of Addai," Ephrem, → Jacob of Serugh, and John the Solitary) has five fragments under Aba's name: three fragments from a commentary on the gospel, one fragment from a Psalm commentary, and one from a *mēmrā* (treatise) on Job "the [Old Testament] athlete" (Wright, vol. II, 1871, 1002–1003). The fragments from the gospel commentary were published by J. Rendel Harris (1895, 92–95), and the five fragments together by F. Nau (1912).

Another 9th-century Syriac manuscript, Sinai Syr. 67, contains a long extract (240 ll. of seven syllables each) from a poem attributed to "Mar Aba, the disciple of the holy Mar Ephrem." It was published by E. Beck (1975) and deals with God's immeasurable power and mercy, to which humanity should respond with praise and thankfulness, albeit according to our limited ability. As creatures of the "Existing Creator," we are given existence, while God is master of the existent and the nonexistent alike and is able to turn the latter into a treasure house full of the former. This is the longest text securely attributed to Aba giving us insight into his thought world.

The Syriac author Anṭun of Tagrit (9th cent. CE), in his as yet unpublished work "On the Holy Myron" (preserved in one 10th-cent. CE ms. [BL Add. 14.726, f. 72r–85r]), quotes "Mar Aba, the disciple of Ephrem" twice, on ff. 75r and 81r (Wright, vol. II, 1871, 831a).

In the *Gannat Bussāmē*, an extensive commentary on the East Syriac lectionary, the final redaction of which may be dated between the 10th and 13th centuries, 40 fragments attributed to Ephrem may belong to Aba's writings. While the other quotations from Ephrem in the *Gannat Bussāmē* are attested in the Syriac *Commentary on the Diatessaron* attributed to Ephrem, these 40 fragments have no parallel in this commentary. Similarities with the fragments published by F. Nau led G. Reinink (1980) to propose Aba's authorship. The fragments show the author's familiarity with the *Diatessaron* as well as with the four separate Gospels. Along with the three fragments in BL Add. 17.194, the 40 fragments may have been taken from a *Commentary on the Diatessaron* authored by Aba, which must have coexisted with Ephrem's commentary on the same work.

Questions about the existence of two distinct commentaries on the *Diatessaron* and their mutual relationship have become even more acute due to recent scholarship that raises doubts about Ephrem's authorship of the commentary transmitted under his name. Rather than Ephrem himself, some of his students are seen as the compilers of the work, in the decades following Ephrem's death (Lange, 2005, 162–173; 2008, 75–81). Since Aba is the most well known among Ephrem's disciples and the one most securely associated with literary works (Baumstark, 1922, 66–67), it is difficult to imagine how he would have authored his own commentary without being involved in some way in the redaction of the commentary preserved under Ephrem's name as well.

Finally, the name of "Aba, the disciple of Mar Ephrem" is found three times in the margin of a large Syriac composition that has only recently come to light in manuscript Deir al-Surian Syr. 20, ff. 76–194, datable to the 7th or 8th century CE (Brock & Van Rompay, 2014, 105–110). The work is incomplete at the end. Its title at the beginning is [*Mēmr*]*ā on Faith*, or *Book* ([*Ktāb*]*ā*) *on Faith*. Three marginal notes, on ff. 145v, 154v, and 165v, all written by the same hand, which is slightly later than the hand of the main text, identify the work as "Book of Understanding (or: Book of the Mind – *Ktābā d-reʿyānā*) of Mar Aba, the disciple of Mar Ephrem." Scholars would love to know whether the threefold annotator made a learned guess or whether he based himself on the now lost end title or colophon, or had other information at his disposal. Extracts from a work with the title *Ktābā d-reʿyānē* (plur.) "Book of Thoughts [or: senses]" are preserved on ff. 293v–298v of BL Add. 12.167, an anthology of ascetic writings, dated 876 CE (Wright, vol. II, 1871, 774ab – the title is translated here as "Book of Sentences"). This work is said to be by Ephrem, but it is not otherwise attested as one of Ephrem's works. Further research will be needed to determine whether the as yet unpublished extracts of BL Add. 12.167 are from the same work that is transmitted in manuscript Deir al-Surian Syr. 20.

The new prose composition of manuscript Deir al-Surian Syr. 20 may, for reasons of content and style, safely be dated to the period around 400 CE or to the early 5th century CE. Written in a rich poetic language, it provides spiritual guidance for a readership that does not seem to be limited to monks or solitaries. Using many of the images, parallelisms, and paradoxes known from Ephrem's works, it is inspired by a theology of spiritual unification and reconciliation, transcending the brokenness and the composite nature of the visible world and finding its fullest expression in the love between God and humanity, and in humanity's faithful acceptance of its Creator. If future scholarship would find arguments for corroborating the claim of the annotator of manuscript Deir al-Surian Syr. 20 and thereby for attributing the work to Aba, the disciple would finally emerge from his master's shadow and be granted his rightful place in Syriac literature.

Bibliography

Baumstark, A., *Geschichte der syrischen Literatur mit Ausschluss der christlich-palästinensischen Texte*, Bonn, 1922.

Beck, E., *Des heiligen Ephraem des Syrers Sermones*, vol. IV, CSCO.S 334–335, 148–149, Louvain, 1973, 43–69 ("Testament," Syr.), 53–80 (trans.).

Beck, E., *Nachträge zu Ephraem Syrus*, CSCO.S 363–364, 159–160, Louvain, 1975, 72–76 (Mar Aba, Syr.), 98–104 (trans.).

Brock, S.P., & L. Van Rompay, *Catalogue of the Syriac Manuscripts and Fragments in the Library of Deir al-Surian, Wadi al-Natrun (Egypt)*, OLA 227, Louvain, 2014.

Harris, J. Rendel, *Fragments of the Commentary of Ephrem Syrus upon the Diatessaron*, London, 1895.

Lange, C., *The Portrayal of Christ in the Syriac Commentary on the Diatessaron*, CSCO.Sub 616, 118, Louvain, 2005.

Lange, C., *Ephraem der Syrer: Kommentar zum Diatessaron*, vols. I & II, FChr 54, Turnhout, 2008.

Nau, F., "Fragments de Mar Aba, disciple de Saint Ephrem," *ROC* 7/17, 1912, 69–73.

Poiani, M., "Le notizie erudite di Giuseppe Simonio Assemani sulla 'Scuola di Efrem' nella Bibliotheca Orientalis," *ParOr* 48, 2022.

Reinink, G.J., "Neue Fragmente zum Diatessaronkommentar des Ephraemschülers Aba," *OLoP* 11, 1980, 117–133.

Van Rompay, L., "Aba (c. 400)," in: S.P. Brock, A.M. Butts, G.A. Kiraz, & L. Van Rompay, eds., *GEDSH*, Piscataway, 2011, 2.

Wright, W., *Catalogue of Syriac Manuscripts in the British Museum Acquired since the Year 1838*, vols. I–III, London, 1870–1872.

LUCAS VAN ROMPAY

Abdon and Sennen

Abdon and Sennen are among the first martyrs who came to be venerated by the Roman church. The most ancient information we have regarding the devotion to them comes from the → *Depositio martyrum* of around 336 CE, included in the → *Chronograph of 354* by Philocalus. On Jul 29 it contains the following notices: *III kal. Aug. Abdos et Semnes in Pontiani, quod est ad ursum piliatum* (*MGH Chronica Minora*, vol. I, 1892, 71). The notice of the *Depositio* was taken up by the *Martyrologium Hieronymianum* for Jul 30. They were known and venerated, since their names are also found in the *Marble Calendar of Naples* (on Jul 30 and not on Jul 29), and in the Gelasian and Gregorian sacramentaries. The catacomb of Pontian(us) is located at approximately the 3rd km of the Via Portuense, which today is in the region of the Gianicolense in Monteverde (Via Alessandro Poerio/Via Pisacane). In ancient sources it was called *Cymiterium Pontiani ad ursum pileatum Via Portuensi* (the cemetery located next to the bear with the Phrygian beret along the Via Portuense). Pontian was perhaps the owner of the terrain or the founder of the cemetery. This is not the pope Pontian. The *ursus pileatus* was the name of the locale, perhaps deriving from the emblem of a bear with a Phrygian beret or cap – there remains little from the ancient catacomb. The *Index coemeteriorum vetus*, a catalogue raisonné of the 7th century CE, defined the place of the burial of the two martyrs *Cymiterium Pontiani ad ursum pileatum Abdon et Sennen Via Portuensi*. The two martyrs described and defined the cemetery and the church. The *Itinerarium Salisburgense* (= *Notitia ecclesiarum urbis Romae*), a guide for pilgrims that was composed around midpoint of the 7th century CE by some competent Roman, writes thus: *invenies ecclesiam Sanctae Candidae virginis et martyris. Discendis in antrum et invenies. Ascendis et pervenies ad Sanctum Anastasium. Deinde intrabis in ecclesiam magnam: ibi sancti martyres Abdo et Sennes quiescunt.* Along the (Via) Portuense there was a church of Saint Candida, where her body rested, and underneath the church was a catacomb where innumerable → martyrs had been buried (Pigmenius, Miles, Pollion, Quirinus, Abdon, and Sennen). It sloped up again from that area, and there was the Church of Saint Anastasius, where Pope Anastasius I (399–401 CE) had been buried. Thus it followed the "great church," that of Abdon and Sennen, and it was restored several times during the High Middle Ages, by the Popes Hadrian I (772–795 CE) and Nicholas I (856–867 CE). Close by was the tomb of Pope → Innocent I (401–417 CE). There remains nothing left from the "great church." From the Middle Ages until the Renaissance, many pilgrims made their way to the church to venerate Abdon and Sennen, despite the fact that their bodies had been transferred to the Church of Saint Mark. The entire area remained a place often visited by devotees of the two martyrs.

The remains of the two martyrs had been taken outside of the catacomb and had been placed inside the great church, perhaps during the 6th century CE, because the (pilgrims') itineraries by that point place them within the "great church." Their tomb was at first located in the underground cemetery, in a sarcophagus made of bricks. In fact, inside the crypt at the foot of the ascending stairs – which may be the place of their burial – there is the representation of two people, in a fresco from the 6th century CE or later (Lefort), who have clothed themselves with a buttoned-up cape on the chest upon a tunic and with a hood folded in the form of the Phrygian beret, accompanied by the halo. Abdon seems older with his rounded beard, while Sennen would be younger with his tapered beard. Christ, in the middle of the illustration, above a cloud, places the crown of victory upon the two martyrs. (Wilpert, 1903, 79–80 e tav. 258). Their names were written vertically upon the fresco (*SCS ABDO* and *SCS SENNE*). On the sides of the fresco, there are two figures who are praying, two other saints, with their names at the bottom of the fresco: to the left there is *SCS BI (n)CENTIVS*, while on the right we find *SCSM (ilix)*. In the upper part there is something that says that Gaudiosus had this fresco made (*de donis fecit*). At the Colosseum there was a church dedicated to the two martyrs (Marucchi, 1905, 69).

The remains of Abdon and Sennen were transported by Pope Gregory IV (827–844 CE) to the Basilica of Saint Mark the Evangelist in Rome, beside Piazza Venezia, in the crypt (Ferrua, 1948, 503–513). Different cities claimed to have the bones of the two martyrs, but they were never carried outside Rome. Even today the two martyrs are venerated in many places, for example, at Pescia (Tuscany), Brescia and Perpignan (France), and Sahagún (León, Spain). Nothing else is known of the two martyrs, except based on their clothes, which come from the east. Their *Passio* is too late to contain any sure and certain facts. This *Passio* is an expanded version of the story that is found in the *Passio Polychronii*, wherein the events regarding Pope Xystus and Lawrence are recounted; but before the account of this *Passio*, there was another that is more ancient, the so-called *Passio vetus* (*Passio sanctorum Xysti, Laurentii et Yppoliti*), edita ora dal Verrando. This last version was composed after the first half of the 5th century CE and before the beginning of the 6th century CE. A brief paragraph narrates the affairs of Abdon and Sennen: the most impious Decius returns to Rome carrying two Persian citizens – who were at this point Christians – bound in chains; he forces them to undergo torture and consigns them to the ferocious beasts, which had been let free. These beasts do not touch the martyrs. Then the emperor orders that they be killed by the gladiators and that their bodies be thrown from the Colosseum so as to leave their corpses at the mercy of the dogs. Their bodies were taken up by the Christians and they were buried in the cemetery of Pontian[us] on Jul 29. These few pieces of information are expanded upon in the *Passio* from the 9th century CE. The first mention of these martyrs, in the Laurentian Cycle, is found in the hymn of Pseudo-Ambrose "De Sancto Sixto" (hymn 72; PL 17.1254). The first three strophes of this hymn speak of Pope Xystus, the fourth is dedicated to Abdon and Sennen, and the other strophes speak of the martyrdom of Xystus and Lawrence. There is no mention of the emperor who persecuted them.

In the expectation of other sources and other information, one might advance some hypotheses. The author of the hymn and the author of the *Passio vetus* probably knew only the names of the two martyrs, who were so venerated in Rome, but they did not know anything about who they were and when they were killed. On account of their exotic names, they were thought to have been Persians, and certainly their origins were eastern. Due to the fact that their liturgical celebration was very close, through time they were associated with the martyrdom of Xystus and Lawrence, during the reign of Decius, who was considered the terrible persecutor

of the Christians in the Christian popular imagination. The image from the cemetery of Pontian[us] (Christ who crowns the two martyrs) took its inspiration from the *Passio* and not vice versa (Farioli, 1963, 25–27, fig. 9).

Bibliography

Delehay, H., "Recherches sur le légendier romain," *AnBoll* 51, 1933, 34–98.
Farioli, R., *Pitture di epoca tarda nelle catacombe romane*, Ravenna, 1963.
Ferrua, A., "La basilica di papa Marco," *LCCA* 99, 1948, 503–513.
Fornari, F., "Via Portuense: Scoperte nella regione sopra terra del cimitero cristiano di Ponziano," *NSA*, 1917, 227–288.
Kirsch, G.P., *Der stadtrömische christliche Festkalender im Altertum*, Aschendorff, 1924.
Manna, B., "Contributi allo studio del cimitero di Ponziano sulla Via Portuense," *BCACR* 52, 1924, 163–224.
Marucchi, O., *Le catacombe romane*, Rome, ²1905.
Marucchi, O., "Scoperte nel cimitero di Ponziano sulla via Portuense," *NBAC* 23, 1917, 111–115.
Matthiae, G., *Pittura romana del medioevo: Secoli IV–X*, Rome, 1987.
Ricciardi, M., "Gli edifici di culto del sopratterra della catacomba di Abdon e Sennen sulla Via Portuense," in: *Ecclesiae Urbis Romae*, vol. I, Vatican City, 2002, 661–676.
Valentini, H., & G. Zucchetti, *CTCR*, vol. II, Rome, 1942.
Verrando, N., "Alla base e intorno alla più antica Passio dei SS Abdon, Sennen, Sisto, Lorenzo ed Ippolito," *Aug.* 30, 1990, 144–187.
Verrando, G.N., *Passio SS. Xysti, Laurentii et Yppoliti: La trasmissione manoscritta delle varie recensioni della cosiddetta passio vetus*, RechAug 25, Turnhout, 1991.
Wilpert, J., *Die römischen Mosaiken und Malereien der kirchlichen Bauten vom IV bis XIII Jahrhundert*, vol. II, Freiburg, 1917.

ANGELO DI BERARDINO

Abelites

The group depicted as a → heresy only known from two short accounts, that is, from Aug. *Haer.* 87 (in epilogue 2 of *De haeresibus*, → Augustine of Hippo also mentioned them briefly), and the so-called *Praedestinatus* (1.87) whose authorship is not entirely certain. The latter extensively reproduced the former, often even following its wording exactly, which means that our information about this sect is reduced almost completely to a single short source.

According to Augustine's account (and its different versions in the manuscripts), the adherents of that group were called "Abeloitae," "Abelonii"/"Abeloim" (Plaetse & Beukers, 1969, 339 – "punica declinatione") or "Abeliani"; hence, there are different names to be found in literature, too: "Abelites," "Abeloites," "Abelonians," "Abeloim," "Abelians." The name Augustine used most frequently was "Abeloitae" (Oort, 1991, 382). Some said that this name was referring to the biblical Abel, son of Adam (→ Adam and Eve). From Augustine's words, it cannot even be deduced whether the so-called Abelites had a preferred name for themselves. However, what becomes clear from Augustine's account is a specific feature in their way of life that contrasted with their environment: they were not allowed to remain unmarried and had to get married to a member of the other sex, yet the marital partners did not have sexual intercourse with each other. At the moment of promising chastity, the partners also adopted a boy and a girl as their children and their heirs. When one of the children died, it was substituted by another one of the same sex. The intention was to ensure that, in each household, two persons of different sex succeeded the adoptive parents. If either of the parents died and the other lived, the adoptive children served the latter until their death. Once both parents had died, the children took their place and likewise adopted a boy and a girl.

Augustine testifies to the presence of Abelites among the rural population of the district of Hippo in North Africa. According to him, it was easy for them to find children they could adopt because there were many impoverished families living around them that willingly surrendered their children hoping to make them profit from the inheritance.

Concerning the time and duration of their existence, Augustine only informs us that by his own time, they had just ceased to exist: after gradually dying out, they had lasted on in one little village, but finally, all its members were "merged into" the "Catholic" church (Oort, 1991, 382).

The so-called *Praedestinatus* adds two interesting pieces of information (according to Schubert, 1903, 70, *Praed*. 1.87 only reproduces Aug. *Haer*. 87; against

this view, see Wermelinger, 1986, 5): according to him, the Abeloitae had predated most of the other heresies, and the only difference between them and the Catholic church actually was their conviction that they had to keep chastity within marriage. Of course, the *Praedestinatus* is a problematic source, and we do not know where its author had that information from. If his pieces of information were reliable, they would point to the early beginnings of the Abelites and to the fact that it was rather a special feature in their way of life than profound dogmatic differences that made them be qualified as a heresy – and from Augustine's point of view, even the ethical peculiarity might have been of secondary importance: according to what G. Ackermans (2011, 123–138) assumes, it was rather his resistance to their schismatic position that made Augustine group them among the heresies. As a → bishop, he felt responsible for his diocese's contested unity and could not stand the Abelites' ascetic elitism.

It is tempting to situate this group within the context of gnostic movements or of African Manichaeism (e.g. Guilloreau, 1930, 55; → Mani/Manichaeism) or to explain its name by their adherents' sticking to the biblical Abel as their model of life (e.g. Ermoni, 1912, 92). But seeing the reduced textual evidence, those scholarly approaches cannot be more than speculations. Even the attempts to place the group within the context of → Judaism or of Jewish-Christian tendencies (Simon, 1962, 55–57; Oort, 1991, 382; Chadwick, 1962, 348, only referred to the parallel that the → Essenes shall also have recommended celibacy and adopted children) cannot really be substantiated, in the end. On the other hand, to call the existence of the Abelites absolutely into doubt (e.g. Walch, 1762, 608) seems to be exaggerated, too.

Seeing the reduced information we get on the Abelites, it stands at hand that, in research, they never became a topic on their own and that they were treated within other, bigger issues.

Bibliography

"Abeliten," in: J. Hergenröther & F. Kaulen, eds., *WWKL*, vol. I, Freiburg im Breisgau, 1882, 33.

"Abelites," in: F.L. Cross & E.A. Livingstone, eds., *ODCC*, Oxford, [3]1997, 4–5.

Ackermans, G., "Einige rechtliche und theologische Fragen zu den Abeloitae in Augustins *De haeresibus*," in: J.A. van den Berg et. al., eds., *"In Search of Truth": Augustine, Manichaeism and other Gnosticism: Studies for Johannes van Oort at Sixty*, Leiden, 2011, 123–138.

Chadwick, H., "Enkrateia," in: *RAC*, vol. V, Stuttgart, 1962, 343–365.

Ermoni, V., "Abéliens, Abéloites ou Abéloniens," in: *DHGE*, vol. I, Paris, 1912, 92–93.

Geest, P. van, "Augustine's Approach of Heresies as Eye-Opener to his Ideas of Interaction between Religious Traditions," in: M. Frederiks, ed., *The Study of World Christianity: Approaches, Methods, Cases* Leiden, 2018.

Gori, F., ed., *Arnobii Ivnioris: Praedestinatvs qvi dicitvr*, CCSL 25B, Turnhout, 2000.

Guilloreau, L., "Abéliens, Abéloites ou Abéloniens," in: *DTC*, vol. I, Paris, 1930, 55.

Müller, L.G., *The De Haeresibus of Saint Augustine: A Translation with an Introduction and Commentary*, Washington DC, 1956.

Oort, J. van, "The 'Augustinus-Lexikon'," (review), *VigChr* 45, 1991, 376–387.

Plaetse, R. van der, & C. Beukers, eds., "Augustine of Hippo, *De haeresibus 87*," in: *Sancti Avrelii Avgvstini De fide rervm invisibilivm; Enchiridion ad Lavrentivm de fide et spe et caritate; De catechizandis rvdibvs; Sermo ad catechvmenos de symbolo; Sermo de disciplina Christiana; Sermo de vtilitate ievnii; Sermo de excidio vrbis Romae; De haeresibvs*, CCSL 46, Turnhout, 1969, 283–343.

Schubert, H. von, *Der sogenannte* Praedestinatus*: Ein Beitrag zur Geschichte des Pelagianismus*, Leipzig, 1903.

Simon, M., "Le Judaïsme berbère dans l'Afrique chrétienne," in: M. Simon, *Recherches d'histoire judéo-chrétienne*, Paris, 1962, 30–87.

Walch, C.W.F., *Entwurf einer vollständigen Historie der Ketzereien, Spaltungen und Religionsstreitigkeiten, bis auf die Zeiten der Reformation*, vol. I, Leipzig, 1762.

Wermelinger, O., "Abeloim," in: C. Mayer, ed., *AugL*, vol. I, Basel, 1986, 5–6.

Tobias Georges

Abercius

The Abercius Inscription (*SEG*, vol. XXX, no. 1479; Lüdtke & Nissen, 1910; Wischmeyer, 1980) is a 22-line funerary epigram of Abercius of Hieropolis, Phrygia, from about 170–180 CE. It can be reconstructed partially epigraphically (through two marble fragments found by W.M. Ramsay, now at the Museo Pio Cristiano, Vatican, and a stele from 216 CE that was inspired by the Abercius epigram and provides a *terminus ante quem*), and partially on a literary basis

(from the later *Vita Abercii*, which reproduces the epitaph at the end).

A Christian reading of this inscription is prevalent, although the text is often ambiguous and allows for multiple interpretations of its symbolism (Mitchell, 2011). So, already at the end of the 19th century, debate was open whether this inscription was Christian at all. The 19th-century Italian archaeologist G.B. De' Rossi called this "an epitaph that is the queen of Christian inscriptions" (*epitaphium Christianarum inscriptionum regina*):

[1] A citizen of a select city, I made this, [2] while living, so that I might have a visible place of deposition for my body here. [3] Abercius is my name, one who is a disciple of a holy shepherd, [4] who pastures flocks of sheep on mountains and plains, [5] who has huge eyes which oversee everything. [6] For this one taught me trustworthy texts. [7] To Rome he sent me to look upon a kingdom [8] and to see a queen, golden-stoled, golden-sandaled. [9] I saw a people there, having a resplendent seal. [10] And I saw the land of Syria and all the towns, [even] Nisibis [11] after crossing the Euphrates. Everywhere I had fellow-? [12] having Paul [...] Faith everywhere led the way, [13] and served up food everywhere, fish from a fountain [14] utterly huge and pure, which a holy virgin grasped [15] and she freely distributed this to friends to eat at all times, [16] having good wine/Christ-wine, giving it mixed, with bread. [17] When standing here, I, Abercius, said these things should be written just so. [18] Seventy-two years was I, in truth. [19] May the one who understands these things pray for Abercius, everyone in tune. [20] Nevertheless, no one will deposit another in my tomb. [21] But if anyone does, he will deposit 2,000 gold pieces in the Roman treasury [22] and 1,000 gold pieces in my good home-city, Hieropolis. (trans. Mitchell, 2011)

Abercius introduces himself as a "citizen of a select city" and a "disciple of a pure/holy shepherd," μαθητὴς ποιμένος ἁγνοῦ (1.3), which on a Christian interpretation would be identifiable with Christ. At 1.14 a "pure/holy virgin," παρθένος ἁγνή, (→ Virgin/Virginity) appears, which on a Christian reading would symbolize the church, who takes a big "pure" (καθαρός) fish from a fountain. This will be served with bread and wine, which in a Christian exegesis would be a eucharistic banquet. Due to the mention of the fountain, the eucharistic and the baptismal symbology would merge in 2.12–16. The wine is described as "good wine," and/or perhaps also "Christ-wine," οἶνον χρηστόν, with a possible double entendre on the meaning of χρηστός.

There is little ambivalence around Abercius' visit to Rome and what he saw there. At 1.9, Abercius says that he went to Rome and saw there a people provided with a resplendent seal: λαὸν [...] λαμπρὰν σφραγῖδαν ἔχοντα. On a Christian interpretation, these would be the members of the Roman church, and the seal would be their → baptism. Likewise, indeed, in the *Odes of Solomon* (→ *Solomon, Odes of*), which were discovered in 1905 in a Syriac codex (but as it seems were originally written in Greek toward the end of the 2nd century CE, and would therefore be contemporary with the Abercius Inscription), in 8.16 baptism is connected with a seal (σφραγίς). But Abercius could also have referred – alternatively, or maybe at the same time – to the Roman people as masters of the world, and the seal might be that of the senators. In Rome Abercius saw also a βασίλεια, a queen or a princess, or else a βασιλεία, a kingdom, depending on the accent's place – the inscription, in capitals, has no accents – and a βασίλισσα χρυσόστολος χρυσοπέδιλος, a queen with a golden stole and golden sandals. According to M. Guarducci (1978; 2014), this passage from the inscription was meant to have two levels of meaning: the "reign" was both that of Marcus Aurelius and that of Christ, the queen was both the empress, or Rome as queen, and the Christian Church, and the "people" was both that of Rome, who ruled over the world with the seal of imperial authority, and that of the Christians with the "seal" of baptism. According to M. Mitchell (2011), who follows the hypothesis that a double level of meaning was intended, Abercius wanted to assimilate his identity as a Christ disciple with his identity as a faithful citizen of his polis and of the Roman Empire, to which he expresses loyalty, as the apologists of his day did (see also Ramelli, 2000).

It is probable that Abercius was familiar with the *Shepherd of Hermas* (Volante, 1987; → Hermas). Historically, the Abercius Inscription is a valuable document, in that it attests the diffusion of Christianity in the regions to the east of the Euphrates in the second half of the 2nd century CE: there Abercius found everywhere "fellows," probably fellow believers (the last letters of the noun are difficult to read; a συνομαίμους has been proposed, "siblings, brothers and sisters"). Abercius was probably a Christian, albeit it is uncertain whether he was the Avircius Marcellus mentioned by → Eusebius of Caesarea (*Hist. eccl.* 5.16) who healed Phrygilla – an allegory of Montanism, from Phrygia – from blindness. Thus, it is probable that his "fellows" or "siblings" were Christians too. And he found them in all the Syrian cities he saw, including Nisibis, and when he crossed the Euphrates: "everywhere" he "met fellows/siblings." During these travels, Abercius was always keeping "Paul" with him, in other words probably Paul's letters (2.10–12; → Paul the Apostle). It was "faith" (πίστις) that led Abercius on his long journeys. So, his visits to Rome and the Middle East had to do with his faith. The *Chronicle of Edessa*, from the 6th century CE but based on older documents, under 202 CE testifies to the presence of a "church of the Christians" in Edessa, certainly with King Abgar the Great's permission. The same *Chronicle* also registers the activity of → Bardaisan, who had a school of Christian philosophy in Edessa between the end of the 2nd and the early 3rd century CE (Ramelli, 2009; 2019). Interestingly enough, it does not present him as a heretic, while it does portray Marcionites, in the 2nd century CE, as heretics.

Now, Bardaisan has a connection with Abercius. The *Vita Abercii* is about a century later than the inscription, and it reveals a sure knowledge of the *Liber Legum Regionum* (by Bardaisan's school, and featuring Bardaisan as the main speaker). The discussion between Abercius and Euxinianus in the *Vita* is partially modeled on the *Liber*. Euxinianus' questions to Abercius correspond exactly, in content and sequence, to Awida's questions to Bardaisan in the *Liber*. In the *Vita* Euxinianus represents Marcionism (his very name probably alludes to Marcion, who was from Pontus Euxinus). This is particularly clear at the beginning of the conversation, when Euxinianus asks Abercius how God can be good and just at the same time. This was a foundational issue of Marcionism (→ Marcion/Marcionites/Marcionism), which, deeming it impossible to reconcile these two attributes of God, distinguished the Hebrew Bible God, the Creator, seen as an evil demiurge (→ Gnosis/Gnosticism), from the New Testament God, the Father of Christ.

P. Thonemann has no doubts concerning the Christian nature of the inscription. He shows that the *Vita* includes parts of genuine 2nd-century CE documents and "is a uniquely valuable document of the processes by which the Christians of late antique Asia Minor refashioned their (pagan) Roman past in their own image" (Thonemann, 2012, 277).

Historiography

Already at the end of the 19th century it was debated whether the epitaph of Abercius was Christian or not. The critical study of this text was promoted by G. Lüdtke and T. Nissen (1910), W. Wischmeyer (1980), and R.A. Kearsley (1992). M. Mitchell (2011) rightly emphasized the ambiguity of many expressions in this text; P. Thonemann (2012) has no doubts concerning the Christian nature of the inscription. I Ramelli (2000) has offered a critical edition, with study and full commentary received by M. Guarducci (2014). N. Andrade (2018, 151) supports the historical value of the inscription.

Bibliography

Andrade, N., *The Journey of Christianity to India in Late Antiquity*, Cambridge UK, 2018.

Bundy, G., "The Life of Abercius: Its Significance for Early Syriac Christianity," *SecCen* 7, 1989–1990, 163–176.

Guarducci, M., *Epigrafia greca IV: Epigrafi sacre, pagane e cristiane*, Rome, 1978, 377–388.

Guarducci, M., "Abercius," in: A. Di Berardino, ed., *EAC*, Downers Grove, 2014, 8.

Hirschmann, V., "Untersuchungen zur Grabschrift des Aberkios," *ZPE* 129, 2000, 109–116.

Kearsley, R.A., "The Epitaph of Aberkios: The Earliest Christian Inscription?" in: S.R. Llewelyn, ed., *NDIEC* 6, Liverpool, 1992, 177–181.

Lüdtke, G., & T. Nissen, eds., *Abercii Titulus Sepulcralis*, Leipzig, 1910, 36–43.

Merkelbach, R., "Grabepigramm und Vita des Aberkios von Hierapolis," *EpigrAnat* 28, 1997, 125–139.

Mitchell, M., "The Poetics and Politics of Christian Baptism in the Abercius Monument," in: D. Hellholm et al., eds., *Ablution, Initiation, and Baptism*, Berlin, 2011, 1743–1777.

Ramelli, I., "L'epitafio di Abercio," *Aevum* 74, 2000, 191–206.

Ramelli, I., *Bardaisan of Edessa*, Piscataway, 2009.

Ramelli, I., ed., *Bardaisan on Free Will, Fate, and Human Nature*, Tübingen, 2019.

Ramelli, I., "Review of Andrade, *The Journey of Christianity to India*," *Sehepunkte* 20, 2020, no. 5; http://www.sehepunkte.de/2020/05/druckfassung/32184.html.

Ramelli, I., "Review of Vinzent, *Writing the History of Early Christianity*," *JThS*, 2022; https://doi.org/10.1093/jts/flab136.

Thonemann, P., "Abercius of Hierapolis: Christianization and Social Memory in Late Antique Asia Minor," in: B. Dignas & R. Smith, eds., *Historical and Religious Memory in the Ancient World*, Oxford, 2012.

Vinzent, M., *Writing the History of Early Christianity: From Reception to Retrospection*, Cambridge UK, 2019.

Volante, M., "Il 'casto pastore' dell' Iscrizione di Abercio e il Pastore di Erma," *Orph.* 8, 1987, 355–365.

Wischmeyer, W., ed., "Die Aberkiosinschrift als Grabepigram," *JbAC* 23, 1980, 24–26.

ILARIA L.E. RAMELLI

Abgarids

The Abgarids were a Nabatean dynasty who reigned between 134 and 242 CE over the city of Edessa and the northern Mesopotamian region of Osrhoene, first a buffer state between Rome and the Parthians and later a vassal state of Rome (Ramelli, 1999). Recent research (see Ramelli, 2004) has demonstrated that the Abgarid monarchy endured in Edessa still for some decades after Caracalla, contrary to what was assumed earlier on the basis of the *Chronicle* of Pseudo-Dionysius of Tell-Maḥre or *Chronicle of Zuqnîn*. This fixed the end of the Abgarids' reign to 220/221 CE, because Pseudo-Dionysius, like Elias of Nisibis, ignored the reign of Aelius Septimius Abgar (see below). A. Luther (1999) and other studies such as S. Ross (2001) have modified our perspective on the end of the Edessan dynasty, thanks to the discovery of papyrus and parchment Mesopotamian documents of the first half of the 3rd century CE and thanks to a reconsideration of the "list of the kings of Edessa" inserted in Elias of Nisibis' *Chronicle*. M. Gawlikowski (1998) studied the last king of Edessa, and J. Teixidor (1989; 1990) concentrated on the Abgarids who came after Abgar the Great.

A parchment, P. Mesopotamia A, has revealed the existence of Aelius Septimius Abgar, formerly unknown. He was "honored with the consulate in Orhāy," in other words Edessa, in 239/240 CE. After the foundation of a Roman colony in Edessa, a Ma'nu, son of Abgar, ruled, according to Pseudo-Dionysius, for 26 years. The title he had is attested by P. Mesopotamia A: *paṣgribā*, "crown prince," "hereditary prince." After these 26 years, in 239/240 CE, Ma'nu's son, the aforementioned Aelius Septimius Abgar, is attested by the same source. The Roman emperor Gordian III deposed him in 242 CE, according to P. Mesopotamia B (Teixidor, 1993). Rome handed the rule, for some time, to Abgar the Fair and Aelius Septimius Abgar, and to others who are indicated as "those who succeeded each other in the consulate." These were governors of knightly order, mentioned in four official documents of the Mesopotamian dossier: Pomponius Letianus, Marcellus, and Julius Priscus, governor (ὕπαρχος) of Mesopotamia. He was the brother of Philip the Arab, who might have been the first Christian emperor of Rome – just as Abgar the Great was possibly the first Christian king of Edessa. Under Diocletian (284–305 CE), Edessa became the capital of the Roman province of Osrhoene, protected to the east by the province of Mesopotamia.

The most common names in the Abgarid dynasty are those of Abgar and Ma'nu. And the most famous sovereigns of the whole dynasty were Abgar Ukkama ("the Black"), from the 1st century CE, and Abgar the Great or VIII (sometimes counted also as IX), around 200 CE. Both the Abgar-Jesus correspondence (see below) and the Abgar legend (see below) have as protagonist Abgar Ukkama, but are likely to have developed later, under the Great. The Abgar-Tiberius correspondence, instead, is probably historical.

1. The Abgar Ukkama-Tiberius Correspondence and Its Historical Setting

Two epistolary exchanges are handed down under the name of Abgar Ukkama: the Abgar-Tiberius short correspondence, which likely goes back to a historical document, and the longer Abgar-Jesus correspondence, which is entirely fictional. Both are reported in the Syriac apostolic novel *Doctrina Addai* and in the Abgar legend as transmitted by the Armenian historian Moses of Chorene; → Eusebius of Caesarea, and other sources report only the Abgar-Jesus letters.

The Abgar-Tiberius correspondence contains historical details that perfectly fit in the historical situation of the mid-thirties of the 1st century CE, when Tiberius was engaging in clever maneuvers in the Near East against the Parthians (Ramelli, 2009b). These letters did not come down through the same tradition as the Abgar-Jesus letters, and their source was early enough to be well informed about the details of Tiberius' reign. They may derive from a historical exchange, dictated for purely political reasons, from which the legend of Abgar's conversion later arose, probably in the Severan age, when the story of Abgar and → Addai may have been first written down in a literary work. This formed the source of the first extant account of the Abgar story: that of Eusebius.

Historically, Abgar wrote to → Tiberius about Jesus' condemnation to death by Pontius Pilate (→ Pilate) and some Jews, not because Abgar had "converted to Christianity," as the later legend goes, but for political interests. In the mid-thirties, Tiberius was maneuvering against the Parthians, just as Abgar was re-enthroned after being previously usurped. Abgar needed Tiberius' support against his opponents, and Tiberius needed the allegiance of kings of vassal states close to Parthia (Tac. *An.* 6.31–37; 41–44) such as Abgar. This is precisely what emerges from the Abgar-Tiberius correspondence. Abgar in his letter to Tiberius ascribes to some Jews the responsibility for Jesus' execution. These mainly were Caiaphas, his circle, Pilate, and Herod. The deposition of Pilate, to which the correspondence refers, historically took place by order of Tiberius and by means of his *legatus* Vitellius (Jos. *Ant.* 18.89–90; 122). Tiberius in the letters also promises to "take legal steps against those who acted against the law." Historically, indeed, through Vitellius, Tiberius also deposed Caiaphas (*Ant.* 18.4.3). Abgar had just participated in the war between Aretas IV of Nabatea and Herod Antipas, as an ally of Aretas (Mos. *PH* 2.29), between 29 CE and 35/36 CE, the time of the correspondence (*PH* 2.34). The war continued until 34 CE (*Ant.* 18.109–150) and ended during Vitellius' mission in the Near East in 35–37 CE (*Ant.* 18.106; 120–124). The war, with its possible negative consequences for Abgar as an ally of Aretas, was just before Abgar's epistolary exchange with Tiberius. At that time, according to Moses, Abgar's display of faithfulness was not believed by the Romans because Herod, Philip the Tetrarch, and Pilate were hostile to him. Hence Abgar's emphasis on his own loyalty and an attempt to put Herod, Pilate, and Caiaphas in a bad light before the emperor as those responsible for the death of an innocent. Tiberius' mention, in the correspondence, of a conflict in which the Iberians were involved with him is usually deemed an anachronism because it is interpreted as a reference to the Iberian Peninsula, but in fact it confirms the accuracy and antiquity of the source of the Abgar-Tiberius correspondence. For these are the Iberians of Caucasian Iberia, and this is a precise historical detail: the Caucasian Iberians were used by Tiberius against the Parthians, precisely in 35–37 CE (Tac. *An.* 6.32–36), the very years of the Abgar-Tiberius letters.

In the Abgar-Tiberius correspondence there is no trace of a "conversion" of either Abgar or Tiberius, but their letters do deal with Jesus, his execution, and the situation in Palestine and the Near East in 35–36 CE, with exact historical details. In the correspondence nothing indicates a religious conversion of Abgar, but everything shows that he knew something about Jesus' ministry and crucifixion (→ Cross/Crucifixion), what was also known to Mara bar Serapion in Samosata in the early seventies of the 1st century CE and to → Flavius Josephus toward the end of that century, and what was probably made known to Tiberius by Pilate in an official report. Abgar's letter displays indignation at the unjust execution of a benefactor; it does not present Jesus as the Messiah, let alone the Son of God or God. The same indignation at the unjust execution of Jesus as a wise benefactor is shown by Mara, who likewise was neither a Christian nor a Jew, but a "pagan" Stoicizing philosopher. Abgar's letter to Tiberius was not dictated by his alleged conversion, but by political reasons. Abgar had excellent reasons to put those responsible for Jesus' death in a bad light before Tiberius. Caiaphas was an ally of Pilate and Herod Antipas; the latter's brother, Herod Agrippa, conferred the high priesthood to a son of Caiaphas. Pilate never deposed Caiaphas; they were allies and were deposed together in 36 CE by Vitellius by Tiberius' order. After Jesus' trial, Herod and Pilate became friends (Luke 23:12). Abgar fought against Herod as an ally of Aretas, and both Pilate and Herod were hostile to him and tried to discredit him before the Romans (Mos. *PH* 2.39). Therefore, for Abgar, the Jesus affair was a chance to attack both Pilate and Herod, as well as their ally Caiaphas, putting them in a bad light before Tiberius as involved in an unjust execution. Abgar's letter to Tiberius about Jesus and those responsible for his execution was not dictated by any conversion to Christianity, or by other religious concerns, or by anti-Semitism, but by precise political reasons.

Later, this correspondence in which Abgar wrote positively about Jesus favored the birth of the legend of Abgar's conversion, probably under Abgar the Great, possibly a Christian himself, or certainly not hostile to a growing Christianity in Osrhoene. It contributed to exalting, and defending, Abgar the Great by celebrating Abgar the Black.

The Abgar-Jesus forged letters appear in Eusebius, the *Doctrina Addai*, and Moses of Chorene, who all claim to have drawn these letters and the narrative that surrounded them from Edessan archival materials. In these letters, set in 30 CE, Abgar Ukkama, having learned of Jesus' miracles from his envoys, invited Jesus to come to Edessa, to escape from those Jews who wanted to kill him, and to heal him, Abgar, who was severely ill. Jesus did not go, but promised by letter to send a disciple to Abgar after his own ascension. In some versions of these letters, there was Jesus' promise to Abgar that his city, Edessa, would be blessed and would never be conquered by its enemies. The narrative in which these letters were embedded, and which is also found in Eusebius, the *Doctrina*, and Moses, recounts how Addai, after Jesus' ascension, went indeed to Edessa, healed Abgar and other people, and converted both the king and all of his family and subjects.

2. Abgar Legend

The Abgar-Addai legend probably originated from the Abgar-Tiberius historical exchange. For a thorough account of the development of this legend through different literary forms and religious agendas, see here the entry Addai. → Bardaisan of Edessa, who was close to the royal court and friends with Abgar the Great, could use the royal archive and read the correspondence of the kings. He, or some other courtier or official, may have read the correspondence of Abgar Ukkama with Tiberius, creating from there the legend of Ukkama's conversion to Christianity. Thence, this legend passed on to Eusebius' history, enriched with the alleged Abgar-Jesus letters that will be found again in the *Doctrina*, Moses, and other documents.

The first layer of the Abgar legend, incorporated by Eusebius in his *Church History*, included the "conversion" of Abgar to Christianity thanks to the miracles of Addai, a figure absent from the earlier Abgar-Tiberius letters. As demonstrated by I. Ramelli (2010; 2015), Eusebius' narrative consists of three layers. The most recent layer is Eusebius' final summary. Another, the middle one, derives from a document from Edessa's archives and contains the letters purportedly exchanged between Jesus and Abgar Ukkama, plus the Addai narrative section that accompanied them. The most ancient layer (Eus. *Hist. eccl.* 1.13.1–4), instead, includes neither letters nor speeches nor dialogues, and narrates the key events of the Addai story. This section reveals an exaggeratedly encomiastic tone and the intention to extol the ancient king of Edessa; it must go back to an Edessan source, possibly Bardaisan (Ramelli, 2015). This section focuses on Abgar Ukkama, his celebration as a great monarch, his illness, his learning of Jesus' miracles, and the latter's promise to heal him, which also resulted in Abgar's spiritual salvation and the Edessans' conversion to Christianity, thanks to the apostle Addai. Bardaisan's account, if it is Bardaisan's, lies behind Eusebius' first four paragraphs; the following paragraphs derive from a different source. They quote the Abgar-Jesus letters and narrate the story of Addai's healing of Abgar, the latter's conversion, and that of the entire Edessan people. The evident, heavy repetitions are obviously due to Eusebius' use of two different sources.

The Syriac *Doctrina Addai*, a historical novel from the early 5th century CE, built on the Edessan lore already used by Eusebius, adding to it doctrinal and narrative expansions. It tells the story of the first evangelization of Edessa by Addai. He was sent to Edessa by Thomas, one of the Twelve, healed Abgar and others and preached the gospel before all the inhabitants. The result was the conversion of both the king and all the Edessan people to Christianity. A further stage of the Abgar narrative is found in the *Acts of Mari*, another Syriac apostolic novel with historical nuggets and fictional material, completed in the late 6th or 7th century CE (Ramelli, 2008; Brock, 2008; Perkins, 2009). In its first part, it condenses the Abgar legend and connects it to that of Mari, the apostle of Mesopotamia.

Moses of Chorene in his *History of Armenia*, whose date is controversial, used the same archival source as that of the *Doctrina* for the Abgar legend. Moses claims that he visited Edessa's archives (Mos. *PH* 3.62). Eusebius and the Armenian version of the *Doctrina* probably were among Moses' sources, but his report sometimes differs from those sources, for example when he makes a connection between the Abgar-Tiberius letters and the *senatus consultum* that under Tiberius outlawed Christianity. Another historian who spoke of Abgar Ukkama is → Procopius of Caesarea, who in the 6th century CE, speaking of Chosroes' attempt to capture Edessa, recounts how the miracles of Christ induced Abgar to ask Jesus to come to Edessa and heal him (Pro. *Bell. Pers.* 2.12). Jesus did not go, but promised by letter to heal the toparch (as Procopius, like Eusebius' second source, calls him, moreover describing his kingdom as "small," again like Eusebius' second source). Abgar recovered after reading Jesus' letter, and not after Addai's arrival, as in Eusebius, the *Doctrina*, the *Acts of Mari*, and Moses. Procopius does not even mention Addai. He was more interested in the clause that Jesus purportedly added to his reply to Abgar, that no barbarian would be able to conquer Edessa, since Procopius intended to explain how Chosroes was induced by that fame of impregnability to try its reliability, by sieging Edessa – and failed. The clause was inscribed in the walls of the city as a protection, the same that, in a parallel tradition, was granted to Edessa by Jesus' image (→ Acheiropoietai). The gist of Procopius' version of the Abgar story is the Abgar-Jesus correspondence already known to Eusebius, but the emphasis is placed on the healing and protective power of Jesus' letter, and not on Addai as the guarantor of the apostolic origin of Edessa's Christianity, unlike in the *Doctrina*, the *Acts of Mari*, and Moses (Ramelli, 2015).

Historiography

The study of the Abgarid dynasty began in the 19th century, with research into the history of Edessa (Duval, 1892; Segal, 1970); more recent contributions include S.K. Ross (2001), P. Wood (2010), and shortly T.S. Wardl (2011), as well as, on the inscriptions of Edessa, H.J.W. Drijvers (1999a). I. Ramelli (1999; 2009a) has investigated the reigns of Abgar Ukkama and Abgar the Great and found historical traces in the Abgar-Tiberius correspondence, and has studied the historical attestations of the Abgar legend, Eusebius and possibly Bardaisan or a local Edessan source (Ramelli, 2010; 2015). She has pointed out possible historical traces in the *Doctrina Addai* and the *Acts of Mari*, which both speak of the Abgarids (Ramelli, 2008; 2009a). Recent studies, also on the basis of new evidence, have changed our perspective on the end of the Edessan dynasty, which now seems to have endured longer than previously thought (Gawlikowski, 1998; Teixidor, 1989; 1990; 1993; Luther, 1999; Ross, 2001).

Bibliography

Brock, S.P., "Review of Ramelli, 2008," *AN* 7, 2008, 123–130; http://www.ancientnarrative.com; http://www.thefree library.com/I.+Ramelli:+Atti+di+Mar+Mari.-a019 7420329.

Desreumaux, A., ed., *Histoire du roi Abgar et de Jésus*, Turnhout, 1993.

Drijvers, H.J.W., "Rabbula, Bishop of Edessa: Spiritual Authority and Secular Power," in: H.J.W. Drijvers & J.W. Watt, *Portraits of Spiritual Authority: Religious Power in Early Christianity, Byzantium, and the Christian Orient*, Leiden, 1999a, 130–154.

Drijvers, H.J.W., *The Old Syriac Inscriptions of Edessa and Osrhoene*, Leiden, 1999b, 237–248.

Duval, R., *Histoire politique, religieuse et littéraire d'Édesse*, Paris, 1892.

Edwell, P.M., *Between Rome and Persia: The Middle Euphrates, Mesopotamia and Palmyra under Roman Control*, London, 2008.

Feissel, D., & J. Gascou, "Documents d'archive romains inédits du Moyen Euphrate (IIIème siècle après J.-C.)," *CRAI*, 1989, 535–561.

Gawlikowski, M., "The Last Kings of Edessa," in: R. Lavenant, ed., *Symposium Syriacum VII, Uppsala University, 11–14 August, 1996*, OCA 256, Rome, 1998, 421–429.

Griffith, S.H., "The *Doctrina Addai* as a Paradigm of Christian Thought in Edessa in the Fifth Century," *HJSS* 6/2, 2003, §§1–46.

Howard, G., trans., *The Teaching of Addai*, Chico, 1981.

Luther, A., "Elias von Nisibis und die Chronologie der edessenischen Könige," *Klio* 81, 1999, 180–198.

Mirkovic, A., *Prelude to Constantine*, Frankfurt am Main, 2004.

Perkins, J., "Review of Ramelli, 2008," *Aevum* 83, 2009, 269–271.

Ramelli, I., "Edessa e i Romani tra Augusto e i Severi: Aspetti del regno di Abgar V e di Abgar IX," *Aevum* 73, 1999, 107–143.

Ramelli, I., "Un tribute dei Parti a Roma agli inizi del I sec. a.C.?" *RIL* 134, 2000, 321–330.

Ramelli, I., "Abgar Ukkama e Abgar il Grande alla luce di recenti apporti storiografici," *Aevum* 78, 2004, 103–108.

Ramelli, I., "Il *Chronicon di Arbela*: Una messa a punto storiografica," *Aevum* 80, 2006, 145–164.

Ramelli, I., trans., comm., *Atti di Mar Mari*, Brescia, 2008.

Ramelli, I., *Bardaisan of Edessa: A Reassessment of the Evidence and a New Interpretation*, Piscataway, 2009a; Berlin, 2019.

Ramelli, I., *Possible Historical Traces in the DoctrinaAddai?* Piscataway, 2009b.

Ramelli, I., "The Biography of Addai: Its Development Between Fictionality and History," *Phrasis* 51, 2010, 83–105.

Ramelli, I., "The Possible Origin of the Abgar-Addai Legend: Abgar the Black and Emperor Tiberius," *HJSS* 16, 2013, 325–341.

Ramelli, I., "The Addai-Abgar Narrative: Its Development Through Literary Genres and Religious Agendas," in: I. Ramelli & J. Perkins, eds., *Early Christian and Jewish Narrative: The Role of Religion in Shaping Narrative Forms*, Tübingen, 2015, 205–245.

Ramelli, I., "The Spacial, Literary, and Linguistic Translations of the Mandylion of Edessa," in: J. Spittler, ed., *The Narrative Self in Early Christianity: FS J. Perkins*, Atlanta, 2019, 171–192.

Ross, S.K., *Roman Edessa*, London, 2001.

Segal, J.B., *Edessa: The Blessed City*, Oxford, 1970.

Teixidor, J., "Les derniers rois d'Édesse d'après deux nouveaux documents syriaques," *ZPE* 76, 1989, 219–222.

Teixidor, J., "Deux documents syriaques du IIIème siècle après J.-C., provenant du moyen Euphrate," *CRAI*, 1990, 144–166.

Teixidor, J., "Un document syriaque de fermage de 242 après J.-C.," *Sem.* 41/42, 1993, 195–208.

Wardle, T.S., "Abgarids of Edessa," in: S.P. Brock, ed., *GEDSH*, Piscataway, 2011, 5–7.

Wood, P., *"We Have No King but Christ": Christian Political Thought in Greater Syria on the Eve of the Arab Conquest*, Oxford, 2010.

Wood, P., "Syriac and the 'Syrians'," in: *OHLA*, Oxford, 2012; online ed. DOI: 10.1093/oxfordhb/9780195336931.013 .0006.

ILARIA L.E. RAMELLI

Ablutions

Use of water assumed many forms during the formative centuries of Christianity. Alongside wheat, wine, and oil, water became one of the key elements of Christians' worship and way of life. This article is focused on the use of water in Christian life and rituals, excluding baptism. Ritual use and ablutions can encompass various practices, both domestic and public (see also respective entries in Bradshaw, 2002; Fernand & Leclercq, 1924). In the examples chosen, the use of water includes a special meaning that distinguishes it from other daily washing. One may cleanse oneself to prepare for a ritual or as a reminder or enactment of one's moral and spiritual purity. Biblical imagery such as "living water" (John 4:10) or "living fountains of waters" (Rev 7:17) has served as a powerful resource for preachers and prayers through the ages. In early Christian practices, water – in Hebrew *majim*, in Greek *hydôr*, and in Latin *aqua* – is often related to great events of salvation history, and remembered and reenacted in Christian rituals.

1. Baths of Initiation and Purification

Ancient Christians understood water as medium used in initiation and for purification (Hellholm, 2011). A. McGowan notes tension between these two ways of using water: the Greek word for Christian baptism, *baptisma*, refers to immersion and bathing. Though ancient religious traditions used various kinds of washing, regarding early Christianity those in Second Temple Judaism and within the Qumran community are particularly interesting. Pseudo-Clementine homilies (→ Clementine Literature, Pseudo-) contain material on a Christian branch close to → Judaism in favor of purification by repeated washing. While initiation happened through immersion, the majority of Christians did not adopt ritual baths as part of their way of life, though there were Christian groups that recommended repeated washing (e.g. Hipp. *Haer.* 9.13–16). In Heb 6:2 *baptismôn didakhê* ("instruction on immersions") may refer to the use of water in Jewish rituals and in Qumran, possibly also to the baptism of → John the Baptist. These examples are at least

somewhat at odds with the uniqueness of baptism (McGowan, 2014, 166; see also Heb 9:10). One of the peculiarities of early Christian baptism was that the person baptized was immersed by a baptizer. R. Uro (2016, 71–98) has emphasized the role of John the Baptist as an "innovator" from the perspective of ritual and cognitive studies. This Christian innovation differed from washing and ritual baths (*miqva'ot*) known from Qumran and other Jewish groups, for example, the → Essenes (→ Bath/Mikveh).

Though there is no evidence of early Christian use of *miqveh* pools, public bathing – central to ancient Mediterranean city life – emerges as a hot topic in early Christian literature. By the end of the 2nd century CE, several Christian authors discussed immersion in water in relation to moral purity.

In the *Shepherd of Hermas* (→ Hermas), the ex-slave protagonist admires the beauty of his former owner Rhoda when helping her out of the bath (Herm. *Vis.* 1). After rising from the river, Rhoda is taken up to heaven and she makes Hermas confess his sins. Seeing Rhoda naked after her bath makes Hermas insist that he thought of "nothing else" than how happy he would be having such a virtuous lady as his wife.

Thus, the opening scene of *Hermas* should be read in the context of ancient bathing culture to see how it anticipates Christian discussions on public bathing. The nudity in the context of *balnea mixta* evoked strong reactions among Christian authors who were bothered by both sexes being naked in public. In his educational manual *Paedagogus* (finished c. 195 CE) → Clement of Alexandria gives a very graphic description of what happens in public baths and how those who spend time in those facilities endanger their chastity. Clement would not have approved the incident such as the one in the beginning of *Hermas* where a slave sees her or his owner bathing naked (Clem. *Paed.* 3.5). Clement's view on public bathing seems similar to Stoic philosopher → Epictetus' discussion of public bathing in his *Encheiridion* (e.g. 4; 45) a few decades earlier (Pujiula, 2006, 213–215; Salminen, 2017, 166–170). Clement is aware that washing hands before prayer is a Jewish custom (Hammerling, 2008, 51). When it comes to bathing, the most important thing to remember is to "wash one's soul" (*Paed.* 3.9) and wash away the "dirt of wealth" – not to indulge one's body by taking long, luxurious baths (*Paed.* 3.5).

Clement was not the only 2nd-century CE North African author to discuss bathing before attending Christian rituals. According to → Tertullian, too, Christians can use public baths (Tert. *Apol.* 42) but in the first place, cleansing before prayers should be a spiritual act. Tertullian makes critical remarks on those who wash their hands before prayers even if they have just come out of a bath (Tert. *Or.* 13); in his view, excessive bodily washing is superstitious and may even distract someone from spiritual cleansing. Both Clement and Tertullian, however, discuss bathing from a male perspective. It is important to note that Christian women had special issues to deal with in terms of purity and cultic practices, such as menstruation. J. Day (2018) has emphasized the gender aspect in relation to ablutions in ancient Christianity. It should also be noted that the Qu'ran (Surah 5:6) recommends repeated "partial washings" (*wudu*) and "full baths" (*ghusl*) in certain situations for ritual purity (see Zellentin, 2022, 8–10, 23, 32, passim for more details).

In the ancient world, public bathing was an integral part of life (Fagan, 2002). Ancients regarded bathing as a therapeutic practice (Squatriti, 2002, 54). The practice was related to personal hygiene and considered as a good way of taking care of one's health. Christian authors, such as Clement and Tertullian, approved this practice though they were critical of how people behaved in public baths. Though they expressed their worries about nakedness in relation to one's chastity, they had to deal with the popularity of public bathing. Their strategy was to remind Christians about spiritual purity and make pedagogical use of bathing water by linking bodily immersions to Christian ritual and to moral and spiritual exercises, thus giving ordinary washing an almost ritualistic meaning (Salminen, 2017, 169–170). It is worth noting that they viewed immersion within the Greco-Roman context rather than in relation to Jewish practices. Clement's definition of baptism as a bath (*Paed.* 1.6.26) should be understood from this perspective, though the same way of defining baptism also appears later, in Diadochus of Photike's ascetic literature *Discourses* (ch. 78).

As Clement and Tertullian emphasized, the spiritual and moral dimensions of bathing in the following centuries show that new perspectives were on the rise. It has been argued that the 6th century CE marks a change in how Christian attitudes to bathing in public changed. For example, → Gregory the Great emphasized virtuous bathing only "on account of the needs of body" (Squatriti, 2002, 54). This kind of ascetic argumentation was present earlier, in both Stoic teaching and pre-Constantinian authors such as Clement of Alexandria who thought that immersing oneself into the waters of public baths should not have been done out of pleasure and socializing but rather for hygiene (of body) and purity (of soul). M. Thurlkill notes that Christian authors "could not easily dissuade the baths' practical popularity, however; popes continued to build baths situated within church basilicas and monasteries throughout the early medieval period" (Thurlkill, 2016, 6–11).

2. Liturgical Use of Water: Hands and Feet

Let us now turn to a more liturgical context of water use in ancient Christianity. In addition to Tertullian, the washing of hands before prayer is also mentioned by Hippolytus of Rome (*Trad. ap.* 41). This notion is not restricted to clerical activities during the liturgy. The "cleric" (*hieros*, a priest or more likely a bishop in this case) washing his hands is first mentioned by Cyril (or John) of Jerusalem (→ Cyril of Jerusalem) in the *Mystagogical Catecheses* where the → deacon gives the water to the presider of the ceremony. The act of washing of hands is related to purity received in baptism and blamelessness from sin (Cyr.Jer. *Cat. Myst.* 5.2). A similar account is found in the → *Apostolic Constitutions* (8.9). Later manuals, too, mention ritual ablutions. The biblical basis for ablution is vast. In the Hebrew Bible (→ Bible), for instance, washing hands is mentioned (alongside bathing) in laws regarding legal purity (e.g. Lev 15:11–14) and in the Psalms (e.g. 26:6). In the New Testament the most famous hand washing is that of Pontius Pilate (Matt 27:24 parr.; → Pilate), but in Matt 15:2 Jesus' disciples are criticized for not washing their hands before eating (see Luke 11:38). However, Christ washing the feet of the apostles (as depicted in John 13:1–17) was to affect Christian worship perhaps even more greatly.

Like the Johannine scene, the ritual of foot washing was understood and performed in various ways in the ancient church – though it is difficult to say whether the custom was actually based on John 13 (McGowan, 2014, 175–176). → Ambrose of Milan mentions the ritual of foot washing after baptism in *De Sacramentis* (3.5) (see also his preface to Ambr. *Spir.* 1.12), and → Aphrahat the Persian regarded the scene of John 13 as the "institution of baptism" in *Demonstrations* (12.10). As a communal and baptism-related ritual the washing of the feet seems to have originated in the West, for instance, Spain, Gaul, and Italy. African authors mention various foot washings, for example, washing the feet of the martyrs and caressing the feet of the newly baptized. In Spain, the Council of Elvira discussed the matter in the beginning of the 4th century CE. (McGowan, 2016, 177–179.) It remains obscure when exactly the ritual became part of Holy Week celebrations (→ Easter).

3. Blessing of Water, Asceticism, and Ablutions

Various ways of using water can be found in ascetic literature and practices (→ Asceticism), yet the lack of water is one of the key elements of desert Christianity. W. Harmless has described the idea of building cities in the desert as "an absurdity." Finding and carrying water to where monks lived took a lot of effort (Harmless, 2004, 65, 174, 204; for later monastic developments concerning water and hygiene, see Classen, 2017). When Palladius of Helenopolis visits the cell of → Evagrius of Pontus in Kellia around 392 CE, he reports how Evagrius was standing naked in a well to vanquish the demon of fornication with cold water (Pall. *Hist. Laus.* 38.11). Otherwise, bathing was not part of desert life. Ascetics were expected to be pure in spirit, not paying too much attention to the cleanliness of the body. → Athanasius of Alexandria mentions that he learned of → Antony the Great from a monk who "poured water" over Antony's hands (thus referencing 2 Kgs 3:11, maybe not meant to be taken literally; Harmless, 2004, 70). In the desert ascetics, both women and men, did not bathe. M. Pujiula (2006, 215) notes how different the asceticism in Clement of Alexandria is when considering the later ascetics' relationship to water and bathing.

In the West, the *Rule of Saint Benedict* (→ Benedict of Nursia) insists on washing the hands and the feet of visitors to the monastery (Ben. *Reg.* 53.12–14). Also, those assigned to serve in the kitchen should wash the feet of all the brethren (*Reg.* 35.9). Benedictine customs of hospitality derive (in part, at least) from the ascetic instructions of → Basil of Caesarea, who on one occasion depicts washing the feet as an act of humble service toward one's neighbors (Harmless, 2004, 429). In Benedictine spirituality receiving and washing the guests of their monastery is Christologically inspired (*Reg.* 53.1–2).

Within the Bible, Ezek 36:25–27 uses the image of sprinkling water to describe how God will make God's people clean. But when did Christians start to use blessed water for liturgical and other purposes? According to Basil of Caesarea the blessing of water is a mystical tradition handed down to the church (Bas. *Spir.* 27.66), and Ambrose emphasizes the role of the → Holy Spirit together with the prayers of the priest in blessing of water (Ambr. *Spir.* 7.88). However, there is no evidence of sprinkling or asperges in the early centuries; when discussing baptism, the → *Didache* (7.3) and → Eusebius of Caesarea (*Hist. eccl.* 6.43) comment on sprinkling with reservations. Also, we learn from Palladius that Abba Macarius the Egyptian (→ Desert Fathers) blessed some water to heal a woman cursed by a sorcerer. The curse was removed when Macarius poured the water over the naked woman (Pall. *Hist. Laus.* 17.9; Harmless, 2004, 297). In addition to this incident, miraculous healings start to emerge during the 4th century CE in relation to shrines, relics, cults of saints, holy men and women of the desert, etc. We know of medieval pilgrims who washed themselves in the River Jordan (Hill, Ryan & Wilkinson, 1988, 269, 304). The so-called Piacenza Pilgrim from circa 570 CE informs us of earlier accounts regarding healing baths in the Jordan area, the river itself, and the Salt Sea. The Piacenza Pilgrim also reports a priest blessing water of the River Jordan at Epiphany. Before the baptisms take place, men working on Alexandrian ships fill jars with holy water "they use for sprinkling their ships when they are about to set sail" (Wilkinson, 2002, 135–137). It is intriguing to note how water attracted pilgrims, the sick, and other people to holy places for ablutions.

Historiography

In scholarship, ablution has been approached from various perspectives. For general studies in Roman history and culture, see, for instance, G. Fagan (2002) and P. Squatriti (2002); for history of Christian worship and rituals, see A. McGowan (2014), D. Hellholm (2011), and R. Uro (2016); for early Christian lifestyle and ascetic practices, see M. Pujiula (2012), J. Salminen (2017). For entries covering the same topic, see P. Bradshaw (2002) and C. Fernand and H. Leclercq (1924).

Bibliography

Bradshaw, P., ed., *The New SCM Dictionary of Liturgy and Worship*, London, 2002.

Classen, A., ed., *Bodily and Spiritual Hygiene in Medieval and Early Modern Literature: Explorations of Textual Presentations of Filth and Water*, Berlin, 2017.

Day, J., "Women's Rituals and Women's Ritualizing," in: R. Uro, J. Day, R. Roitto & R. De Maris, eds., *Oxford Handbook of Early Christian Ritual*, Oxford, 2018, 644–660.

Fagan, G., *Bathing in Public in the Roman World*, Michigan, 2002.

Fernand, C., & H. Leclercq, *Dictionnaire d'archéologie chrétienne et de liturgie*, vol. I, Paris, 1924, col. 103 ff.

Hammerling, R., *A History of Prayer: The First to the Fifteenth Century*, Leiden, 2008.

Harmless, W., *Desert Christians: An Introduction to the Literature of Early Monasticism*, Oxford, 2004.

Hellholm, D., *Ablution, Initiation, and Baptism: Late Antiquity, Early Judaism, and Early Christianity/Waschungen, Initiation und Taufe: Spätantike, frühes Judentum und frühes Christentum*, Berlin, 2011.

Hill, J., W.F. Ryan & J. Wilkinson, *Jerusalem Pilgrimage, 1099–1185*, London, 1988.

Johnson, M., *The Rites of Christian Initiation: Their Evolution and Interpretation*, Collegeville, 2007.

McGowan, A., *Ancient Christian Worship: Early Church Practices in Social, Historical, and Theological Perspective*, Grand Rapids, 2014.

Pujiula, M., *Körper und christliche Lebensweise: Clemens von Alexandreia und sein Paidagogos*, Berlin, 2012.

Salminen, J., "Asceticism and Early Christian Lifestyle," diss., Helsinki, 2017.

Squatriti, P., *Water and Society in Early Medieval Italy AD 400–1000*, Cambridge UK, 2002.

Thurlkill, M., *Sacred Scents in Early Christianity and Islam*, Lanham, 2016.

Uro, R., *Ritual and Christian Beginnings*, Oxford, 2016.

Wilkinson, J., *Jerusalem Pilgrims Before the Crusades*, ²2002.

Zellentin, H.M., *Law Beyond Israel: From the Bible to the Qur'an*, Oxford, 2022.

JOONA SALMINEN

Abortion

Abortion is the deliberate ending of a pregnancy prior to birth wherein the unborn fetus or baby is terminated. The practice has regularly been considered controversial, and was clearly so, even prohibited, among the paraenesis of the early Christian movement. Associated with the topic are the concepts of when life begins, the question of whether the practice is murder, the human constitution regarding the soul, and the human being as made in the *Imago Dei* ("Image of God"). In the patristic period, the practice was most often viewed with concern and in many cases considered murderous.

1. Background of Antiquity

The practice of abortion or chemically induced miscarriage can be seen in the earliest parts of ancient civilization. It existed almost completely as an attempted remedy for unwanted children, which were often produced by sexual encounters where the production of offspring was not desired. On a tablet from ancient Sumer there appears to be a recipe for inducing abortion and Egyptian papyri as early as BCE 1500 have references to chemicals being used as abortifacients (Riddle, 1997, 35, 68; see also Davidson, 2012). Middle Assyrian laws, which were a collection of the legal codes of Babylon, exist and speak to abortion from the first part of the 11th century BCE (Tetlow, 2004, 126; see also Davidson, 2012). The practice moved into the Greek world and Aristotle speaks of it as a part of society (Kapparis, 2002, 40, 50–51) and indeed Aristotle (*Pol.* 7.14.10) and Plato before him (*Rep.* 5.9) spoke of the possible necessity of family planning through abortion (Gorman, 1982, 15).

Ancient abortive practices varied and although certainly not limited to the following, often included: the ingestion of certain chemicals to induce a miscarriage (some of which → Galen appears to have had knowledge); the binding of the womb of the woman from the outside; a strong blow to the abdomen of the pregnant woman (Soranus appears to advocate this); or the prescription of vigorous movement by the pregnant woman (Jones, 2004, 37).

There were a variety of changing realities when it came to how the practice of abortion fared within the Roman world. The *Twelve Tables* (c. 450 BCE) required a demonstrably good reason for a husband to permit his wife to have an abortion, yet the practice was widespread by the 1st century BCE. The practice was often associated with prostitution wherein pregnancies could often result, and therefore the open sexual practices of many within the culture provided a regular foundation for abortion and infanticide. And while remaining widespread, by the 3rd century CE, attitudes regarding the practice were changing such that the *Digest* considered the practice to be offensive (Gorman, 1982, 24–25, 31). With the growth of the Christian movement into the 4th century CE, attitudes regarding the practice became more clearly enshrined.

2. Early Christian Sources

The New Testament does not explicitly mention abortion. However, its prohibition of murder, following on the Hebrew Bible (→ Bible), provides the main foundation of the Christian sources where abortion is discussed. One key passage for various groups was Exod 21:22–25 which reads:

> When people who are fighting injure a pregnant woman so that there is a miscarriage and yet no further harm follows, the one responsible shall be fined what the woman's husband demands, paying as much as the judges determine. If any harm follows, then you shall give life for life, eye for eye, tooth for tooth, hand for hand, foot for foot, burn for burn, wound for wound, stripe for stripe.

M.J. Gorman argues that the Alexandrian Jewish school viewed this as a significant passage in their view that abortion was immoral (Gorman, 1982, 34–38). This example of Hebrew Bible text would have been in the background in early Christian thought on the issue. There is a steady stream of non-New Testament sources within early Christianity that decry the practice of abortion. In the → *Didache* (2:1), the practice is envisaged as the killing of a

child. There, the word used is φθορά (meaning "ruin, destruction [...] in specific senses – a destruction by abortion," BDAG 858). Crucial to understanding the placement of abortion within this early Christian document is the larger context of the work where the "two paths" approach is the foundation of all the paraenesis given. The path of life was that which the Christian adherent was to practice, and part of that "path" was avoiding the practice of abortion. This practice was clearly part of the larger prohibition against murder or killing and thus, abortion was envisaged within that larger framework. The same is true in the *Epistle of Barnabas* (19:5; → Barnabas) where the destruction of an unborn child was considered murder. In both of those early Christian works, the prohibition of abortion comes in a list of certain practices that Christians were to avoid. Christian morality was envisaged as including an opposition to abortion. Early Christians would have some connections to Jewish thoughts on morality and thus related to Christian concepts of morality on the issue would be the general Jewish belief that abortion (and similarly child exposure) was not to be practiced (Gorman, 1982, 33).

One noteworthy statement in *Diognetus* (5.6–7; → *Diognetus, Epistle to*) speaks to the general perceived outlook of Christians regarding children. The author states that Christians are like everyone else in the world, but they do not "murder" or "expose" their children. It is unclear if this is a reference only to *expositio* (i.e. the practice of killing or abandoning children already born) or if this includes under "murder" a general prohibition of abortive practice. In either case, there is an envisioned ideal regarding early Christians and their progeny and when combined with other writings on abortion specifically, there is a clearly recognizable narrative that develops.

Athenagoras simply states that it was almost a proverbial statement that women who use substances or chemicals to induce abortion were committing murder (→ Athenagoras). It was apparent in his mind that this was the standard view of Christian paraenesis (Ath. *Leg.* 35; see Gorman, 1982, 53–54). → Tertullian in similar fashion demonstrates a clear aversion to the practice of abortion. He states that since murder is prohibited, destroying a fetus in the womb is equated with committing murder (Tert. *Apol.* 9).

Elsewhere, he pleads with readers to pursue → marriage to have offspring, and makes the argument that the "gentiles," the outside world, is plagued by abortion (Tert. *Ux.* Book 1.5). In these sources, and in other writings (Tert. *An.* 37.2; *Apol.* 9.8; see Gorman, 1982, 53–59), Tertullian clearly condemns abortion (Elsakkers, 2010, 377). Yet, M.D. Kamitsuka argues for a nuanced interpretation of Tertullian's writings on the matter particularly regarding how modern-day readers utilize his writings on the topic for their own purposes (Kamitsuka, 2019, 40). This concern aside, Tertullian clearly expresses a distaste for the practice as does Athenagoras (*Leg.* 35) who also speaks against the practice. Both the works *Apocalypse of Paul* (→ Paul the Apostle) and *Apocalypse of Peter* (→ Peter the Apostle) paint a picture of individuals having to face the children one day that they had aborted or caused to be aborted in the present (Jones, 2004, 60). This clearly demonstrates that a thoughtful consideration regarding the practice of abortion should be given with a view towards avoiding guilt.

Moving into the 3rd century CE, → Minucius Felix speaks of the practice negatively when he addresses the idea of women ingesting certain substances to commit an abortion. This, he says, is an extinguishing of a future man who could have been a parent of another. Thus, for him, abortion is "parricide" (Min. Fel. *Oct.* ch. 30). Hippolytus of Rome, → Cyprian of Carthage, and perhaps even → Origen (depending on how he is interpreted) appear to have concerns about the practice and the influence of the larger culture on the Christian Church (Gorman, 1982, 59). Cyprian reports in one letter that a particular father he had in mind was guilty of murder because of his foot kicking the womb of his wife (Cyp. *Ep.* 48). Hippolytus (*Haer.* 9.7; see also Gorman, 1982, 60) decries that practice of self-induced chemical abortions among purported Christian women with a particular note tying the practice with pregnancy out of wedlock. His concern is the outstanding "double" immorality of both → adultery and abortion.

With the progression of the Christian movement, early 4th-century CE councils dealt with the practice. The Council of Elvira (305 CE) in canons 63 and 68, while not initially focused on abortion, speaks to the practice in terms that clearly demonstrate that the practice would have been viewed as sinful. The Council of Ancyra (314 CE) in canon 21 speaks to the previous excommunication of women prostitutes who abort children resulting from their sexual practices being softened in some ways to allow for a decade of penance (Gorman, 1982, 64–65). These 4th-century CE councils provide a helpful look at aspects of Christian views regarding the practice at the time, but also provide a glimpse of the unfolding development of Christian thought regarding abortion throughout the early Christian period.

M.J. Elsakkers (2010) argues that there were two main expressions of Christian thought on abortion within the early Christian movement: those that held a "strict" prohibitive view, and those who mainly condemned it as murder only when it was practiced in the late term of pregnancy. Early term abortion was, in their view, a less serious crime (Elsakkers, 2010, 377). However, in the examples cited (Augustine of Hippo, Jerome) there is a range of interpretation applicable to their various statements. The *Apostolic Constitutions and Canons* (→ Apostolic Constitutions), → Basil of Caesarea, → Ambrose of Milan, and → Jerome all argue in varying ways against the practice of abortion, and Jerome states that the practice is the "murder" of an unborn child (Jer. *Ep.* 22.13; see Gorman, 1982, 68). Lastly, → John Chrysostom reveals a strong rhetoric against the practice of abortion. M.J. Gorman writes,

> [...] he associates abortion with sexual immorality, calls it murder, makes known the punishment it deserves and sees the fetus as an object of God's care. In fact, Chrysostom's profound abhorrence of abortion leads him to classify it as "something even worse than murder. (Gorman, 1982, 73)

Chrysostom demonstrates an example of early homiletics touching on abortion as → evil (Chrys. *Hom. Rom.* 24) wherein he bemoans turning the "chamber of procreation" into a place of murder. Thus, up to the time of Augustine, there is a clear picture of Christian expectations regarding abortion with a fairly uniform approach to the issue.

3. Augustine of Hippo

Augustine also frequently spoke against abortion (Bakke, 2005, 133), and it has been argued that he was the patristic author (→ Patrology/Patristics) to address the topic the most extensively (Mistry, 2015,

48). His writings however would have taken a less strict view in some sense given his view of when, in his developing thoughts, a fetus is fully "alive." Yet there is a common connection between infanticide, abortion, and contraception (Noonan, 1986, 136). In *Enchiridion* he engages the question both of when life begins (Aug. *Enchir.* 85) and has a discussion of an abortion procedure (*Enchir.* 86). He ultimately includes the argument that children or fetuses dying in the womb will be included in the resurrection (→ Resurrection) if they were fully formed (Stensvold, 2015, 18–39). In fact, while arguing against the practice of abortion, → Augustine of Hippo is not clear on when an unborn child, or fetus, is ensouled by God. Thus, his writings against abortion are not tied only to his view of personhood (Kamitsuka, 2019, 38–39). In *On Marriage and Concupiscence* (1.17) he bemoans that certain sins of sexual lust end up leading to the practice of seeking to rid oneself of a life conceived by those sexual acts. Part of the concern for Augustine was not only the practice, but the connection of the practice to other sins. When all his writings are considered, the picture becomes clear that Augustine disapproved of the practice, but in terms of related issues and concerns, (i.e. when a fetus receives a soul) he was less dogmatic.

4. Later Development 450–600 CE

In the years following Augustine, it is more difficult to demonstrate strong discussion on the topic of abortion. Z. Mistry (2015, 4) argues that from Aristotle to Augustine, there is more literature concerning the topic and related themes (i.e. contraception) but that from 500–1000 CE, the picture is less clear. There are some scant references in late ancient Christian sources such as a commentary on a Pauline Letter (Titus; → Paul the Apostle) from the 6th century CE, and early medieval Christian poetry (Mistry, 2015, 1–2). Yet, the development of thought on the issue clearly continued as, for instance, there is evidence to suggest that formal criminality of the practice occurred at least as early as 1140 in Gratian's canonistic textbook (Müller, 2012, 1).

5. Reception

The practice of abortion has fluctuated throughout history and has been a regular source of controversy within the parts of the world influenced by Christianity, with a regular aversion to the practice by most Christians. However, the regular rejection of the practice by Christians is due in large measure to the usual association of the practice with that of committing murder, and this association was cradled in the early Christian view of the practice. In the modern West, abortion as a practice came to foreground in the 20th century in connection with both the feminist movement(s), as well as with ideas of sexual revolution or changing sexual ideals. Even though there was a growth in the practice during that century, exceptions notwithstanding (i.e. Dombrowski & Deltete, 2000), many major Christian bodies and denominations have largely spoken against the practice and a majority continue to do so, in varying degrees, to the present time.

Historiography

M.J. Gorman (1982) and O.M. Bakke (2005) have detailed aspects of the early Christian outlook on abortion. In fact, B.M. Metzger, in the foreword to M.J. Gorman's work (1982, 10) summarizes the work by stating:

> Especially noteworthy [...] was the opposition of the early church to contemporary practices of abortion. It is really remarkable how uniform and how pronounced was the early Christian opposition to abortion.

J.M. Riddle (1992; 1997) and K. Kapparis (2002) have detailed the history of the practice from antiquity thus demonstrating that it predates the early Christian period. There are others like M.D. Kamitsuka (2019) who in more recent times have sought to argue for nuance in interpretation of the sources regarding the practice. E.M. Tetlow (2004) and D.A. Jones (2004) have also detailed the related legalities of the practice within the ancient Near Eastern background. M.J. Elsakkers (2010) has written a doctoral thesis with a chapter detailing early

Christian views on abortion. On a related concept, J.T. Noonan (1986) has written a helpful background on contraception. The data from the patristics sources is fairly clear in expressing opposition to the practice of abortion.

Bibliography

Bakke, O.M., *When Children Became People: The Birth of Childhood in Early Christianity*, Minneapolis, 2005; ET: Brian McNeil.

Bauer, W., W.F. Arndt, F. Wilbur Gingrich & F.W. Danker, *Greek-English Lexicon of the New Testament and Other Early Christian Literature.* 2nd ed., Chicago, 1979.

Davidson, J.R., "Abortion," in: J.D. Barry, ed., *Lexham Bible Dictionary*, Logos, 2012.

Dombrowski, D.A., & R.J. Deltete, *A Brief, Liberal, Catholic Defense of Abortion*, Champaign, 2000.

Elsakkers, M.J., "Reading Between the Lines: Old Germanic and Early Christian Views on Abortion," diss., Amsterdam, 2010; https://hdl.handle.net/11245/1.327030.

Gorman, M.J., *Abortion & the Early Church*, Downers Grove, 1982.

Jones, D.A., *Soul of the Embryo: Christianity and the Human Embryo*, London, 2004.

Kamitsuka, M.D., *Abortion and the Christian Tradition: A Pro-Choice Theological Ethic*, Louisville, 2019.

Kapparis, K., *Abortion in the Ancient World*, London, 2002.

Mistry, Z., *Abortion in the Early Middle Ages c. 500–900*, Rochester, 2015.

Müller, W.P., *The Criminalization of Abortion in the West: Its Origins in Medieval Law*, Ithaca, 2012.

Noonan Jr., J.T., *Contraception: A History of its Treatment by the Catholic Theologians and Canonists*, enlarged ed., Cambridge MA, 1986.

Riddle, J.H., *Contraception and Abortion from the Ancient World to the Renaissance*, Cambridge MA, 1992.

Riddle, J.M., *Eve's Herbs: A History of Contraception and Abortion in the West*, Cambridge MA, 1997.

Stensvold, A., *A History of Pregnancy in Christianity: From Original Sin to Contemporary Abortion Debates*, London, 2015.

Tetlow, E.M., *Women, Crime, and Punishment in Ancient Law and Society*, vol. I: *The Ancient Near East*, New York, 2004.

J. RYAN DAVIDSON

Abraham

Abraham holds a unique place within the history of Christianity, deriving his central status and authority from the contexts in which he is found. He appears in the biblical sources and their dependent traditions from the book of Genesis, through the New Testament, and into the continuous theological tradition of the church. Because Matthew's Gospel depicts him as the ancestor of Christ, and Christ himself refers to Abraham on several occasions, his meaning and significance become fundamental. They are made the subject of discussion in the Epistles of Paul and the Epistle to the Hebrews. Outside the literary tradition, he is found repeatedly in the iconographical tradition up to the present day. Finally, he is one of those extraordinary figures whose life and activities are meaningful for the other great monotheistic traditions (→ Monotheism).

The continuous popularity is due largely to the fact that his adventurous life is not only interesting but above all dramatic – with the leading protagonist in his story as none other than God himself. The account is also very long, stretching from Gen 11:26 to 25:10. Since the purpose of this story is to chronicle the relationship of God to human beings, Abraham is chosen as the outstanding example of this divine and human partnership.

The salient points of the narrative can be outlined briefly. After considering the general view of the actions of God and those of the human race as a whole, Genesis devotes itself to discussing the origins of the single people of → Israel, whose progenitors are given as Abraham, his wife Sarah, and their son Isaac, and his descendants. From now on the divine–human partnership is changed from an earlier antagonistic stage to a close covenant relationship, in which God is shown as highly favorable to Abraham because of the obedience of his servant. Abraham's name was originally Abram, and he is referred to by that name for much of the biblical account, until he and his wife, Sarai, are renamed by God in Gen 17:5, where the Bible explains the name as meaning "father of a multitude."

According to the biblical chronology, his story takes place in the largely agricultural and polytheistic period of the Middle Bronze Age, circa 1813–1638 BCE, when God calls to Abram to go into a land that he would show him. It is not clear why Abram is chosen, but in answering God's call, he seems to understand and accept monolotry. In return for leaving his home and country, God promises Abram three things: a relationship or covenant with God himself, numerous descendants, and a land (Gen 12:1–3). And to show that there is no human evidence that would support such claims, the text emphasizes Abrams's old age and his wife's childlessness. The action proceeds through a series of journeys made by Abram and his family that geographically cover the whole biblical world, including its major cities, and that anticipate the later historical movements of the Israelite people.

Abram and his nephew Lot are portrayed as wealthy people with large flocks in need of grazing, and on returning to → Canaan, they agree to separate, with Lot settling in the land around Sodom, while Abram remains in Canaan on the plain of Mamre. In a local war, Sodom falls and Lot is captured. So in addition to his characterization as a man of status and wealth, the text now introduces Abram as a warrior chieftain with his own trained force, and as a militarily strategic thinker. Abram defeats the local kings and celebrates his victory with Melchizedek, the king of Salem, whom Genesis calls a priest of the most high God. Abram gives him a tithe of the booty, and Melchizedek in his turn makes an offering of bread and wine (Gen 17:18–20).

When God next appears to Abram, he ratifies his covenant with him and all humankind. Four different versions of this covenant are given in Genesis, but in essence it is a solemn contract by which God pledges to make Abram the father of nations, and to give to him and his innumerable descendants the land of Canaan, and to be their God forever. In chapter 17 is introduced the cultural requirement of → circumcision as the physical sign of Abrahamic descent, and at this point the names are changed.

Because she was barren, and presumably in an effort to achieve the fulfilment of God's promise by the normal human means, Sarah gives her servant, Hagar, to Abraham to bear a son, Ishmael. But when Abraham reaches the age of 99, God appears to him again under the oak trees of Mamre (Gen 18:1). The theophany takes the form of three visitors who enjoy Abraham's hospitality and then promise him a son by Sarah. The name change, making them almost different people, is a sign of this divinely planned event, and the following year Isaac is born.

Having been told by God that he intends to destroy Sodom and Gomorrah because of their wickedness, Abraham respectfully pleads for the salvation of the cities, and God rescues Lot. After further journeys the text then moves to clarify Isaac's birthright. After Hagar had slighted her, and in order that Isaac's inheritance might be secure, Sarah demands that Hagar and Ishmael should be sent away. God permits this but promises that Ishmael too would become a great nation. Then at some point in his life that is not clear, Abraham's faith is subjected to its greatest test when God orders him to sacrifice Isaac in the land of Moriah. After three days of travel, they arrive, and Abraham is on the point of killing Isaac when an angel intervenes and a ram is provided instead. For his complete trust, God reiterates his promises to Abraham (Gen 22:19). The narrative then ends swiftly.

1. Exegesis

For earliest Christianity, as for → Judaism, the authority of the whole of the Hebrew Bible was accepted as the historical revelation of God. But within the general Christian tradition, although it contained many differing approaches, there was a fundamental agreement that among the various stories and figures found there, some were of such an outstanding nature and importance that they could be neither ignored nor dispensed with. Accordingly a principle of selectivity was employed, first within the New Testament, by which those figures and their associated themes considered best suited to answering current theological problems were chosen for emphasis. This became the standard theological approach.

Within this methodology a further refinement of principle operated, in which the chosen themes were placed in a kind of hierarchical order of importance. So the stories, detached from their original narrative histories, came to be treated as free-standing representations of new contexts. As a story that functions on so many levels, it is unsurprising that the Abrahamic narrative lent itself particularly to this kind of treatment and has since become one of the most fruitful stories of the Bible. He figured in the actual construction of the text as we know it, composed of the Hebrew Bible and New Testament, because he was considered as the link connecting both. This continual stream of exegesis, first created within the New Testament, is still a matter of importance to modern philosophical and theological thought, as evidenced in the work of I. Kant, S. Kierkegaard, J. Derrida, and J.-L. Marion.

2. New Testament Approaches

References to Abraham in the New Testament are numerous and diverse. But they are grouped mainly around the two great theological themes of promise and faith. These are the two aspects of Abraham's story that dominate the exegesis of the evangelists and of the writers of the Epistles. One of the purposes of the New Testament was to show that the life, message, and significance of Christ are the culmination of the religious history of Israel as it is described in the Hebrew Bible. Thus the theological problem it faced was to explain the internal relationship of the new Christian community to the Judaism within which it was formed, and also its external relationship to the non-Jewish world. The figure of Abraham was ideally placed to serve these two objectives. As the father of Hebrew Bible religion, Abraham forms the obvious bond between Judaism and Christianity, but in view of his role as the representative of humanity in its covenant with God, the texts can then offer him in terms of his continuity with all peoples.

In the teaching of Christ as given in the Gospels, God is the God of Abraham, Isaac, and Jacob (Matt 22:31–32; see also Acts 7:32). With this exegesis, the identity of the God of Israel as the object of Jewish worship, who revealed himself to Abraham, is preserved as the God of the New Testament. Once this common theology of God is established, the theological themes with which Abraham is associated come into prominence in order to describe and legitimate the person and work of Christ. Since the promises of God required Abrahamic descent for their fulfilment, for the Synoptic Gospels, the question of the genealogy of Christ is important. Matthew opens his Gospel (→ Matthew the Apostle) by tracing the bloodline of Christ back to Abraham.

The Gospel of John (→ John the Apostle), however, takes the claim of descent further, to the idea of supercession. John relates a controversy with the Pharisees (John 8:33) in which the whole dispute turns entirely on Jewish pride in descent from Abraham. He points out that carnal descent is not enough, and the report has for its climax the claim that in Christ is present a greater than Abraham (John 3:9). → John the Baptist likewise claims that God is able to create children of Abraham out of mere stones (Matt 3:9); conversion to God requires imitation of the virtues of Abraham.

An unusual use of Abraham in connection with the afterlife is made in Luke (16:19–31; → Luke, Gospel of). In the parable of Dives and → Lazarus, Luke expands the idea of the bosom of Abraham into an entire → parable, the only one that links the earthly and heavenly spheres, and the only one in which a character has a name. Here the elements of the Abrahamic story are abstracted to teach the lesson that behavior in this life has consequences for the next, and by the 3rd century CE, the bosom of Abraham generally becomes a metaphor for → paradise. In this way the Hebrew Bible account of Abraham becomes only a prefiguration of Christ, whose person and work are unique. The story becomes solidified as the explanation of the fulfilment in Christ of the promises made to Abraham, and the establishment of the new Israel in the church.

The relationship of the new community to the Gentile world required a different exegesis. Here the problem was to explain the universal application of the meaning of Christ, and the application of salvation not merely to the people of Israel but to the whole world. While importance was attached to all the promises, as far as the New Testament is concerned, everything depends on Gen 12, the assertion that in Abraham's seed all people would be blessed. The main element in the story of the promises, as isolated by the New Testament, is its universality. With this emphasis the theme of promise achieves complete theological dominance, and its possibilities become fully exploited.

The promises had been explained partly as a response to the faith that Abraham as an individual had placed in God, so the counterpart to the theme of promise was the theme of faith. For the Epistles, primarily concerned with the nature of discipleship, Abraham not only is the representative of the community in its faith, but also provides a model for the faith of the individual. Just as Abraham had proved useful as a means of explaining Christ, the content and the object of the faith, so in the Epistles, particularly the Epistle to the Hebrews, he is also useful as the model for the psychology of the faith: how faith works. Because of the nature of the writings, letters addressed to specific groups and individuals, the theology of faith, found in the gospel in narrative form, is here greatly expanded. For the Epistles the personal attitude of the believer becomes important, with Abraham as its inspiration. An analysis of the personal character of Abraham fuses together theology and psychology in an account that becomes archetypal, especially in the Epistles of Paul and in the Epistle to the Hebrews.

In the Hebrew Bible the psychology of faith was shown to be a firm and trusting dependence on the power and the will of God to keep his word. Throughout the narrative, whenever God spoke Abraham listened and responded. He put in God a faith that counted as trust and that had justified him. Since Christians count Abraham as their father in faith, he provides a template for the faith of his children. The life in faith of the Christian becomes a reproduction of that of Abraham, as in Paul's letter to the Galatians (3:6–9).

Paul develops a very personal view of faith based on his intimacy with Christ; he puts forward the idea of absorption or identification with him. He initiates a kind of Christian mysticism in which the nature of discipleship is identified with the new way of faith and love taught by Christ, whom he had encountered personally. The identity of Christianity for Paul consists in faith, which he sees as the organizing principle of the Hebrew Bible, because it is the appropriate response to the gracious activity of God. According to him this principle is set out in the example of Abraham, the patriarch of the Jewish nation. He quotes Gen 15:6 in Rom 4:8 and Gal 3:6, and with this quotation he transfers the Hebrew Bible principle and its key figure to the Christian context.

As the chief representative in the New Testament of the theology of conversion, Paul is proud of his descent from Abraham, but the new element in his life is his faith in Christ, and in him crucified (1 Cor 1:18; Gal 3:1). Since Abraham predates the giving of the law (→ Law/Decalogue/Torah) to → Moses, Paul is able to make him his criterion of justification by faith. Abraham underlies the main arguments of one of his earliest letters, that to the Galatians, and his greatest, that to the Romans; the various arguments to be found there revolve around this contrast of faith and law. He exploits the various aspects of the story, with the exception of the sacrifice of Isaac. Hagar and Sarah represent the two covenants,

one of the bondage to the old law and the other the liberty of the covenant of Christ. Abraham had lived before the giving of the law to Moses and so was not dependent on it: justification by faith alone is sufficient (Rom 4:3). While Abraham is the father of the circumcised, he is the father of the multitude with regard to his descendants in faith. Although the whole of the New Testament sees Abraham as obedient to God, faith and obedience are so closely related for Paul that he can speak of the obedience of faith (Rom 1). For the Christian then the unlimited faith of Abraham and his self-abandonment to God become the exemplar for the Christian when making his or her decision for Christ. It is the description of the entire surrender and existential commitment of the believer of the person of Christ (Gal 2:20).

The Epistle to the Hebrews adds to the general lines of thought in a manner entirely its own. It contains in chapters 11 and 12 a lengthy discussion of faith that it presents with great clarity and that includes what is arguably the most quoted definition of faith in the whole theological tradition. "Now faith is the assurance of things hoped for, the conviction of things not seen" (Heb 11:1). The author is particularly anxious to convey to his readers the marks that distinguish this attitude of faith; in his view it is characterized by the twin aspects of the conviction of invisible reality and a confident assurance. This attitude of confidence in what is hoped for is exemplified by a cloud of witnesses, who are also noteworthy for their perseverance and patience in faith (Heb 10:36; 12:1). These figures testified by faith and not by sight to the reality that they lived. All the salient points in Abraham's story are alluded to, and especial emphasis is laid on the episode of Melchizedek, who, for the writer, is the expression of the great high priesthood of Christ, one of the major themes of his work (Heb 4–8). Without being named, Abraham's courageous frankness in his dealings with regard to God underlies the essential attitude of faith necessary for the confidence by which the Christian has access to God (Heb 4:16; 10:19).

3. Patristic Exegesis

The importance of Abraham to patristic exegesis is very clear. He appears repeatedly in the texts dating from the 2nd to the 6th century CE. While the earliest

Christians had encountered Abraham as a living figure within their own Jewish inheritance, for the postbiblical writers, who regarded themselves primarily as biblical expositors, he was a figure encountered in texts. So for the patristic tradition his person and history became the subject of commentary, adapted to their particular theological and ethical interests. Conformity to Christ according to Paul had led to what he called "sanctification" (Rom 6:17–22; 1 Thess 4:3): faith applied to the everyday situations of life as lived out in society. It was this strain of mysticism, originating in Paul and Hebrews, and its pastoral consequences that the church fathers developed. They developed a mystical theology of holiness in which morality and the spiritual life became important. Since the essence of mysticism is its particularity and its idea of unimpeded vision, they used Abraham as a figure typifying these qualities (Cyp. *Pat.* 10; Ambr. *Off.* 1.24). Abraham had communed with God directly, through personal experience, and so he could well serve as a model for the Christian life and prayer. He now became the pattern of the virtuous man.

Patristic scholarship, intellectual and wide in perception and spirituality, with a large space made for ethics, understood the mysteries of the Christian faith in terms influenced by Greek philosophy and Hellenistic Jewish mysticism. Abraham appears throughout the bulk of Hellenistic Jewish literature, but the main ideas of that type of Judaism, as inherited by Christianity, came from the works of → Philo of Alexandria (c. 20 BCE–50 CE), whose writings display the most extreme example of the integration of Greek and Jewish thought. He had elaborated a method of explaining the biblical material by → allegory. Since for him it was axiomatic that nothing in Scripture could fail to be in line with God, allegory proved helpful in disposing of those parts of revelation that appeared to be theologically or ethically difficult to accept.

Further as a philosopher within the platonic tradition, he was always interested in the universal rather than the particular and had written several allegorical books on Abraham from this point of view. Inevitably Abraham lost any individuality and became an example of a universal proposition: the acquisition of wisdom. His allegories became very influential from the 3rd century CE onward, especially that of

Hagar and Sarah, which had very little in common with that of the Epistle to the Galatians. The protagonists became timeless concepts totally divorced from history: Abraham is mind seeking wisdom, which makes use of the Greek academic curriculum (Hagar) until it passes through virtue (Sarah) and reaches wisdom (Philo *Congr.* 23–24). The figurative meaning of the text totally eclipses the historical story and serves as a template for later thinking, particularly in the Christian school of Alexandria (→ Alexandria).

Until the prevalence of allegory in the 3rd century CE, the stories of Abraham had reached the postcanonical writers as typological exegesis, an inheritance from the tradition of testimonia – cases of witnesses giving confirmatory evidence of events. This Christian adaptation was in keeping with the norms of ancient rhetoric, which provided lists of examples to be used in the demonstration of cases. The earliest community seems to have made collections of the most important Hebrew Bible texts, which were interpreted as witnessing to Christ. The New Testament considered testimony based on fact to be fundamental, and these texts appear to have formed the substructure for its theology. The promises made to Abraham figured in these collections, and Abraham passed into what the Epistle to the Hebrews call the "cloud of witnesses." These collections were followed later by lists of "types," foreshadowings of Christian events in the persons and events of the Hebrew Bible. The commonest of these was the willingness of Abraham to sacrifice Isaac as foreshadowing the passion and death of Christ. This became so frequently used and for so long a time that → Augustine of Hippo later remarked that it recurred to the mind automatically, because it had been repeated so often in different languages and portrayed in so many places that no one could shut it out of one's eyes or ears (Aug. *Faust.* 22.73).

This typological kind of exegesis of the Abraham stories is well illustrated in the collection of the oldest texts of the postapostolic period, conventionally referred to as the → Apostolic Fathers. This generation of Christians had inherited the problem not merely of the interpretation of Scripture, but also the question of its application to matters of authority in the church and judgment in theological debate. The *First Epistle of Clement* (→ Clement) addresses this issue, which had caused strife in the church of Corinth. For Clement Abraham is an example of saints who have ministered to God's glory by obedience. The obedient do not create discord, which is abhorrent to God, and Abraham is offered as an example of the kind of ethics required of the Christian community. The *Epistle of Barnabas* (→ Barnabas) in the same collection extends the reference to Abraham in a bizarre way. In chapter 9 the writer expounds the story of Abraham's circumcision of his 318 servants as showing, by allegory, that God had revealed to Abraham the → redemption of the world through Christ's crucifixion (→ Cross/Crucifixion).

The allusions to Abraham in the Apostolic Fathers are more or less random, and by now largely traditional, confined in their reference to the Christian community. But with the 2nd century CE, Christianity enters the domain of culture and science in the work of the apologists (→ Apologetics). It is exemplified particularly in that of → Justin Martyr. Converted from paganism (→ Pagan/Paganism) and trained in the Greek philosophical tradition, he addresses himself to the outside world, Jewish and pagan, and his work begins to show the formal presentation of Christian doctrine as theology.

In the 2nd century CE, the debate with Judaism no longer concerned itself with the problem of justifying the existence of Christianity, but with the question of the retention of the Hebrew Scriptures as Christian books, and with the issue of offering worship to Christ as God. It was to be expected that Abraham would figure largely in these debates. For Justin Christianity is primarily the religion of truth, and in his *Dialogue with Trypho the Jew*, he uses the figure of Abraham as one by means of which he can reach an understanding with his opponent (Just. *Dial.* 45–46). Though unsystematic and in places erratic, the dialogue falls basically in two parts: the first explaining the Christian reinterpretation of the Hebrew Bible, and the second justifying Christian adoration of Christ. The conclusion shows Christ to be the king of Israel and Christians to be the true chosen people of God. What is noteworthy here is the use of Abraham in connection with the divinity of Christ. Justin takes the story of Abraham's hospitality to the three angels as a demonstration of the fact that God is more than a simple unity.

Once introduced by Justin into the context of the → Trinity and the question of the nature of Christ, the → hospitality becomes a constant reference in the Trinitarian and Christological debates of the succeeding centuries. The dogmatic exploitation of Abraham continued within the Greek patristic tradition long after the empire had become Christian and the nature of theology had moved from the apologetic to the dogmatic sphere.

Toward 200 CE a shift occurred in Christian thinking. The more the new religion entered the social world, the more a need was felt for something structured and comprehensive concerning the church and its beliefs. Theological schools were established, where interest focused on problems of an abstract nature, and in which the Bible was expounded not merely in homilies in the liturgy but also in the form of written commentaries, particularly on the book of Genesis. The most famous school was that of Alexandria and its most famous director was → Origen, the most controversial theologian of the Greek Church. The greatest part of his output was devoted to the Bible. His main interest was in the mystical application of the text, and under the influence of Philo, he adopted the allegorical method. Though most of his work was destroyed by → Justinian, 16 of his homilies on Genesis survive, and Or. *Hom. Gen.* 3–11 deal with Abraham, beginning with his circumcision and ending with his marriage to Cetura. Of the 13 books of the commentary on Genesis, written to provide a more scholarly exegesis, only fragments remain. But in the *Contra Celsum*, an important document for the history of religion, he introduces a new approach. In this book, a conversation between two educated exponents of religion, the pagan → Celsus, who had read Genesis, and the Christian Origen, they have an exchange of views about Abraham's well at Ascalon, to the extraordinary style and construction of which Origen draws attention (Or. *Cels.* 4.33–44). As part of the argument, Origen introduces the idea of the importance of personal engagement with the historical evidence for biblical events.

This requirement for historical and archaeological evidence appears most strongly in his devoted disciple, → Eusebius of Caesarea in Palestine, (c. 265–339 CE?). The notion of the demonstration of the gospel as historical preparation is made explicit by Eusebius, the first church historian to whom accurate evidence matters. The journeys of Abraham had become influential on the Christian mind not merely as an allegory for the crucial inward journey of faith, but in the idea of physical journeying for religious purposes. Under the influence of Constantine's family, pilgrimages to the Holy Land became fashionable. Eusebius had begun his *Chronicon* with Abraham rather than Adam (→ Adam and Eve), since he regarded Adam's date as unverifiable. In the *Life of Constantine* he records the oak of Mamre as still standing and refers to the basilica erected there by Constantine to crush a syncretistic cult of Abraham taking place at the site (Eus. *Vita Const.* 3.51–53).

The Syriac tradition as exemplified in the theological poems of → Ephrem the Syrian (c.307–373 CE) being more directly biblical and Semitic, stands in contrast to much of the eastern and western philosophical theology. Intending to show the inherent link between the spiritual and the material worlds through symbolism and poetic imagery, Ephrem refers to Abraham in cycle of his 15 *Hymns on Paradise*. These are theological syntheses organized round the book of Genesis, on which he had also written a commentary, and in which Abraham forms a link.

However, the most important example of the use of Abraham for public exegesis is found in the West, in what is by far the most extended treatment, that of Ambrose, the 4th-century CE bishop of Milan (→ Ambrose of Milan). Heavily influenced by Origen, his two books *On Abraham* make use of all the elements of the story. The first, which may have originated in sermon form, addressed to the catechumens (→ Catechesis), explains the entire narrative from Abraham's vocation to his death, as presented in Gen 12–25. The second, a written allegorical treatise, very erudite in character, is thought to have been intended for the baptized. Its purpose is to inculcate the principles and practice of the faith understood as the moral life.

This kind of public exegesis continues throughout the later centuries and becomes the norm. It focuses particularly on the episode of Hagar and Sarah, especially in the debates concerning virginity and → marriage, which dominated much of the 4th and 5th centuries CE and influences current feminist theology.

4. Iconography

Along with the literary idiom, the early church developed a cultural trust in the visual as a means of theological expression. Paul had foreseen the future of Christianity as a means of cultural accessibility, and from the 3rd century CE onward, art became one of the most successful tools for its achievement. Because the symbol, like the allegory, facilitates the intuitive transfer of knowledge and is of its nature open to varied interpretation, Christian iconography became a distinctive form of discourse in its own right. On the initiative of the laity, the biblical stories were translated into a visual language of instruction and devotion with certain constantly repeated symbols coming to stand for the ideas and ideals found in the literary tradition.

Among the symbols Abraham was one of the earliest adopted, and one of the most easily understood. Abraham is ubiquitous and appears in different artistic genres and on different kinds of monuments throughout the patristic period, and the images like the texts are commentaries. Scholarly research in recent years and the publication of some outstanding exhibition catalogues, for example *Picturing the Bible: The Earliest Christian Art* (Spier, 2007) have offered a wide range of new information about these monuments, and those of early Christianity in general. And although we have only accidental survivals, we have enough material to understand the popularity of the figure of Abraham and its development.

The earliest Christian representations, from the 3rd century CE, are found in funerary contexts in the Roman catacombs (→ Cemetery) and on their related → sarcophagi. Abraham can appear as a single figure, in cycles that tell the whole story, and especially in the episodes highlighted in the literary tradition, the sacrifice of Isaac and the hospitality to the angels.

The most popular representation is the sacrifice of Isaac, of which more than 20 are recorded in the catacombs alone. Although the formulation of the image is never completely fixed, even from the earliest times, there are basically two types of rendition. The pre-Constantinian images are unconcerned with the dramatic aspects of the story. The symbolic character of the scenes predominates, as the images typify perfectly in visual form the divine work of salvation. Forming part of a range of symbols that emphasize the idea of deliverance, they are usually associated with the figure of the good shepherd (→ Shepherd, The Good). A depiction in the chapel of the sacraments in the catacomb of Callixtus, in an unusual formulation, shows Abraham and Isaac as *orans* (praying) figures, offering thanks for deliverance. This image illustrates the multilayered nature of early Christian art as a form of visual exegesis. By typology, Isaac had referred to the passion and resurrection of Christ (→ Resurrection); and since according to Hebrews (11:17–19) Abraham's faith was in the resurrection, here he also represents the general concept of resurrection; finally in the funerary context, he points to the resurrection of the individual soul.

On the sarcophagi the scene has a more fixed form. The earliest known is that of Le Mas d'Aire (France). Of the Constantinian sarcophagi, the most well-known example is probably that of the sarcophagus of Junius Bassus in Saint Peter's Basilica, Rome. On the upper-left register is one of the most beautifully executed and most economically presented of all the representations. It shows the angel staying the hand of Abraham, resting on the head of Isaac. The angel and Abraham are turned to face the substitute ram.

What appears to have been the earliest representation of the hospitality of Abraham is lost. It is the one recorded by Eusebius in the basilica at Mamre, where apparently the middle angel had a halo. If this is so, it perhaps introduces the idea of the Trinity and the status of the Son. The earliest known extant image is that of the catacomb of the Via Latina. In the mid-4th century CE, after the Constantinian settlement, a transition of iconographic themes took place. While some earlier images like the sacrifice of Isaac continued, because of their importance, others disappeared and new themes replaced them. Many occur for the first time in the Via Latina.

These extraordinary paintings are very wide in scope and are an admixture of pagan and Christian iconography. Dating from the 4th century CE, in cubiculum B Abraham is shown seated under a tree, a calf beside him, welcoming three men, who are placed higher and appear to be standing on a ledge. The reason for the introduction of the iconography here is not clear. The same catacomb also has two dramatic renderings of the sacrifice of Isaac.

The hospitality scene became important in Christian mosaic art. Unconnected with any funerary context, it appears in the 5th-century CE nave mosaics of Santa Maria Maggiore, where scenes from the Hebrew Bible on one side are paralleled by those from the New Testament on the other. The reference here is clearly still to the history of salvation, but in the 6th-century CE mosaics of San Vitale in Ravenna, the reference becomes eucharistic (→ Eucharist). Along with the sacrifices of Abel and Melchizedek and the sacrifice of Isaac, the figure of Abraham in these scenes brings together the idea of hospitality, eating, and offering, in a kind of shorthand form. This is the primordial visual link of Abraham to the liturgy, where in the textual tradition the connection is made in the Roman Canon of the Mass. A presentation in old Saint Peter's (5th cent. CE), said to have depicted the hospitality and surviving in a baroque copy, appears to be the first representation of Abraham kneeling before the angels, which in the eastern iconographic tradition translates into *proskynesis* (prostration). If this is the case, it presumably introduces an iconographical development of the iconography of the Trinity. By the 15th century with the Trinity of Rublev, Abraham is missing altogether.

Models and visual ideas are easily transferred, and Abraham features on lamps, on gold glasses, and in the earliest extant manuscript illustrations of Genesis from the 6th century CE. The manuscript tradition added other details to the story, culminating in the famous 13th-century Abraham cupola of Saint Marco in Venice, and the paradise door of the baptistery of Florence (15th cent.). An interesting example of the minor arts, witnessing to the story's universal popularity, is the mold for a die stamp in Cologne showing the sacrifice of Isaac (Credo II, no. 38; see Stiegemann, Kroker & Walter, 2013).

The patristic pattern of literary and visual reinterpretation became normative for the succeeding centuries. There was no paradigm shift in exegesis until the Enlightenment, where the perspectives arose from different preoccupations.

Bibliography

Deichmann, F.W., ed., *Repertorium der Christlich-Antiken Sarcophage*, 2 vols., Wiesbaden, 1967.

Dodd, C.H., *According to the Scriptures*, London, 1965.

Ferrua, A., ed., *Le pitture della catacomba di Via Latina*, Vatican City, 1960.

Hanson, R.P.C., *Allegory and Event*, Richmond, 1959.

Hunt, E.D., *Holy Land Pilgrimage in the Later Roman Empire AD 312–460*, Oxford, 1982.

James, M.R., *Illustrations of the Book of Genesis*, Oxford, 1921.

Lucchesi-Palli, E., "Abraham," in: E. Kirschbaum, ed., *LCI: Allgemeine Ikonographie A–E*, vol. I, Herder, 1994, 19–35.

Malbon, E.S. *The Iconography of the Sarcophagus of Junius Bassus*, Princeton, 1990.

Nestori, A., ed., *Repertorio topografico delle pitture delle catacombe romane*, Vatican, 1975.

Spier, J., ed., *Picturing the Bible: The Earliest Christian Art*, New Haven, 2007.

Stiegemann, C., M. Kroker & W. Walter, eds., *Credo Christianisierung Europas im Mittelalter*, 2 vols., Petersberg, 2013.

Thompson, T., *The Historicity of the Patriarchal Narratives: The Quest for the Historical Abraham*, Valley Forge, 2002.

MARY CHARLES-MURRAY

Abraham of Pbou

Abraham of Pbou (or Pbow) served as the last Coptic Orthodox abbot of the Pachomian monastic federation. His tenure during the 6th-century CE reign of Justinian I (527–565 CE) was marked by sharp divisions within the federation over the Council of → Chalcedon, political intrigue undertaken by the pro-Chalcedonian elements within it to remove him, and the resulting loss of the Pachomian movement to Coptic Orthodoxy. Forced out of the federation, Abraham returned to his native Farshut, where he established and led a new monastery. His origin from Farshut and his tenure as head of the monastery that he founded there have led to the use of the alternative title "Abraham of Farshut" in some modern sources.

Abraham of Pbou appears in only five texts from late antiquity. Two panegyrics composed in his honor for his feast day (Jan 19) survive in fragmentary form in a single 10th–11th-century CE parchment codex from the → White Monastery in Upper Egypt (Codex GC, according to the classification of White Monastery codices established by Tito Orlandi). A second codex from the same monastery (Codex GB) adds an extensive excerpt on Abraham, again fragmentary, within a panegyric on the closely related monastic saint Manasse. In addition, a brief account dependent on the above panegyrics appears in the Copto-Arabic Synaxarion, and he is mentioned in a literary attack on the Byzantine emperor Justinian I contained in the *Panegyric on Apollo*. The sources, replete with pre- and postmortem miracles stories, conform their accounts of history to the dictates of the sharply polemical non-Chalcedonian Coptic discourse that emerged in the mid- to late 6th century CE. The hagiographical nature and ideological function of the stories raise serious questions with respect to the portrayal of history contained within them. While the three primary panegyrics are fragmentary and diverge on the details of the story, together they supply a fairly complete account of Abraham's life.

Born to a family of note in the village of Tbercot (Farshut), Abraham enrolled in school at age 12, where he proved to be an exceptional student. Upon completing his education, God called him to the monastic life. He delayed acceptance for a year, however, due to the death of his parents. Left alone with his sister, he attempted to persuade her to follow him in his ascetic calling. When she refused, he departed for the monastery of Pachomius, where he was received into the monastic life by the archimandrite Pshintbahse. He embarked there on a difficult ascetic regimen, inspired by the example of the movement's founding figures.

Upon Pshintbahse's death, Abraham became archimandrite, shepherding the community in accordance with the rules. During the course of his tenure, a crisis arose within the federation over its stance with respect to the Council of Chalcedon. The sources link the crisis to the religious policies of Justinian I, whom they style as Abraham's primary antagonist. While the various panegyrics diverge on the initial cause of the crisis, it appears that pro-Chalcedonian elements from within the federation brought charges against Abraham, which resulted in his summons to appear before Justinian in Constantinople. One source reports that the duke of Antinoë, following orders from Justinian, had Abraham arrested and taken on a difficult journey overland to the imperial court. Once in Constantinople, Abraham appeared before Justinian. The emperor demanded his loyalty, which included adherence to the decrees of Chalcedon, under threat of his removal as archimandrite.

As the drama unfolds, the empress Theodora (not mentioned by name) attempts to intercede on Abraham's behalf. When her efforts fail, Abraham has no choice but to refuse the emperor's demand, which leads to his removal as archimandrite of the Pachomian federation. He reports the outcome in a letter sent from the capitol to his former monastery in Upper Egypt. Eventually, aided by the empress, he is allowed to return to Egypt.

Back in Egypt, soldiers effect the installment of Pancharis, one of Abraham's original accusers, as the Pachomian federation's new pro-Chalcedonian archimandrite. The non-Chalcedonian monks respond by dispersing to the desert and other monasteries. Abraham went first to the White Monastery of Shenoute (→ Shenoute of Atripe), where he made a copy of the rules. Then, following a revelation, he proceeded to Farshut and, with the rule in hand, founded a small monastery with two brothers. Under Abraham's leadership, the monastery grew, building projects were undertaken, and a women's community was added. The Synaxarion reports that Abraham was ordained as a priest. Eventually he learned through revelation of his impending death, which he reported to his disciples. On three separate occasions as he grew weaker through the following months, he called the community together to encourage the monks to keep the rules. He celebrated the → Eucharist one final time on the Feast of the Nativity, so weakened that the monks Theophilus and John had to hold him upright. He then entered the infirmary and did not arise from bed again. He died in old age on Jan 19 (Tuba 24, in the Coptic calendar).

The texts on Abraham, as one would expect, are filled with revelations and miracle stories attributed to him. The latter occur both during his life and after his death, a fact supported by Scripture (Ps 115:6; 2 Kgs 13:20–21). Among those that survive, one finds the multiplication of loaves during a famine, the destruction of crop-destroying worms, the cure of a man with dropsy and another with gout, an exorcism, the revelation of a monastic farmer who stole lemons, and the revelation of a local man and his wife who hid their own bread while drawing on the monastery's stores during a famine. The fluidity of the tradition is marked by the fact that the last story in the above list occurs during Abraham's life in the Synaxarion and after his death in one of the panegyrics.

The hagiographical nature of the sources calls the historical details of Abraham's life into question. The prominence of his parents and the details of his monastic call, for example, appear to be modeled on the account of Antony the Great in → Athanasius of Alexandria's *Life of Antony*. The sharp antagonism toward Justinian I developed in the story likewise reflects common themes, as does the sympathetic role of the empress. Nonetheless, while the authors fashioned a good story, certain elements within the account suggest a connection, however distant, with actual events. The emergence of Abraham's accusers from within the federation, for example, an event at odds with the sharp duality separating the pro- and non-Chalcedonian players elsewhere in the drama, suggests a basis in reality. It is hard to imagine an author creating Pachomians who betrayed their archimandrite to the evil emperor. So too the disappearance of the Pachomian movement from the plane of history after this period, coupled with the parallel rise of Shenoute within the Coptic Church, suggests that something dramatic took place to effect this change. The accounts of Abraham supply the only evidence we have to explain it.

It seems in fact likely that Abraham's place in history and the hagiographic construction of his life resulted from the fact of his undoing by pro-Chalcedonian elements centered in the federation's Lower Egyptian Monastery of Metanoia. They sought to gain control of the entire federation and found in Justinian's religious policies motivation to act. However the subsequent events unfolded, memory of them drove the production of Abraham's story, which eventually required an account of his early life and led to the accumulation of miracle stories. Had the political intrigue that led to the demise of the Pachomian movement not occurred, Abraham would likely have lost his place in history, as have most of the later Pachomian archimandrites.

Historiography

Abraham of Pbou appears initially in the scholarly world through the identification, editing, and publication of fragmentary remains of two Coptic codices from the White Monastery of Shenoute. A history of this process, which began in the late 19th century, can be found in the critical edition of the texts published in 2012 (Goehring). Initial accounts of Abraham, based on the fragments available at the time and his story in the Copto-Arabic Synaxarion were primarily descriptive (Cauwenbergh, 1914; Coquin, 1991). Later work by J.E. Goehring, who produced a critical edition of the texts, deepened the analysis, arguing that the efforts against Abraham of Pbou in post-Chalcedonian Egypt led to the ultimate demise of the Pachomian movement and the reshaping of the Coptic memory of Upper Egyptian monasticism (Goehring, 2006; 2010; 2012).

Bibliography

Cauwenbergh, P. van, *Étude sur les moines d'Égypte depuis le concile de Chalcédoine (451) jusqu'à l'invasion arabe (640)*, Paris, 1914.

Coquin, R.-G., "Abraham of Farshut," in: A.S. Atiya, ed., *TCE*, vol. I, New York, 1991, 11–12.

Goehring, J.E., "Remembering Abraham of Farshut: History, Hagiography, and the Fate of the Pachomian Tradition," *JECS* 14, 2006, 1–26.

Goehring, J.E., "Abraham of Farshut's Dying Words: Reflections on a Literary Motif in the Ascetic Literature of Early Christian Egypt," *Cop.* 8, 2009, 21–39.

Goehring, J.E., "The Life and Miracles of Abraham of Farshut: Community Disaster and the Making of a Saint," in: G. Gabra & H.N. Takla, eds., *Christianity and Monasticism in Upper Egypt*, vol. II: *Nag Hammadi-Esna*, Cairo, 2010, 49–61.

Goehring, J.E., *Politics, Monasticism, and Miracles in Sixth Century Upper Egypt: A Critical Edition and Translation of the Coptic Texts on Abraham of Farshut*, STAC 69, Tübingen, 2012.

JAMES E. GOEHRING

Abraham, Testament of

By most accounts, the *Testament of Abraham* is an originally Alexandrian Jewish text, composed in Greek sometime around the turn of the Common Era. An engaging narrative, the *Testament of Abraham* recounts the final days of the patriarch's long, righteous, and hospitable life but defies the testamentary genre with its uncharacteristic humor, irony, and lack of a testament. In the longer, more coherent version (see the recension issue below), God sends his archangel Michael to remind → Abraham of his mortality so that he might set his affairs in order. Michael visits Abraham in disguise, but when his identity and mission are revealed, the

patriarch cleverly resists expropriation of his soul. Eventually, he agrees to yield on condition that he first be allowed to view the inhabited world. During his chariot ride above the earth, righteous Abraham calls death upon everyone he sees in the act of sinning. Concerned that Abraham would eventually expunge the earth of its inhabitants, God commands Michael to divert the chariot to the gates of heaven, where Abraham witnesses Abel's weighing of souls before the merciful judgment of God, leading him to acquire an appreciation for mercy as well. Returning home, Abraham surprisingly reneges on his agreement with Michael, which prompts God to summon Death and dispatch him to Abraham's home to complete the task. Death offers his hand to Abraham, who lies fatigued and resting upon his bed. Surrounded by his family, Abraham kisses the hand of Death, whereupon his soul clings to it, as Michael and his delivering angels await nearby.

1. Manuscript Tradition

The *Testament of Abraham* emerged into the light of scholarship with M. Gaster's presentation of the Romanian version at a meeting of the Biblical Archaeology Society in 1887 (Gaster, 1893), followed by M.R. James' publication of a critical edition of the Greek text in 1892. Of the nine manuscripts known to M.R. James, three represent a complete albeit somewhat less coherent version roughly half the length of the other, raising the question of recensional priority, which has occupied scholars up to recent times. It is almost certainly the case that both recensions derive from a common source, but the parting of the ways occurred early on, so that each developed its own distinct tradition, this obscuring any obvious trajectory of dependence of one upon the other. M.R. James held that the longer recension (Rec. A) was more complete, hence original, although he fell short of calling the shorter recension (Rec. B) a direct abridgment. Several decades later, F. Schmidt (1986) cataloged an additional 16 manuscripts witnessing to the longer recension but argued for the priority of the shorter recension, best represented by 11th-century Gr. MS E and Slavonic versions. G.W.E. Nickelsburg (1976) maintained the priority of Rec. A on the basis of a structural analysis of the heavenly journey and the judgment scene. In general, scholars who have favored the priority of the shorter recension (e.g. Schmidt, 1986; Turner, 1955) have usually done so on the basis of discrete elements such as terminology and syntax, whereas scholars who have favored the priority of the longer recension have argued on the basis of aesthetical considerations, such as narrative logic and coherence (e.g. James, 1892; Nickelsburg, 1976). In the decades following R.A. Kraft's (1976) call for reassessing the recensional issue, the dominant scholarly view favors the longer recension (Rec. A) without identifying the proverbial smoking gun of direct dependence on the part of the shorter (Rec. B). This popular tale spread to several cultures around the Mediterranean basin and into southeastern Europe, surviving in Coptic (Bohairic and Sahadic), Arabic, Ethiopic (Falasha and Christian), Slavonic, and Romanian manuscripts.

2. Provenance

Discussion over the *Testament of Abraham*'s provenance revolves around the following binaries, with all possible combinations represented: whether the text was composed

1. in Egypt or Palestine,
2. in Greek or Hebrew, and
3. by a Jew or Jewish-Christian.

M.R. James (1892) maintained that the *Testament of Abraham* was originally written in Greek by a Jewish-Christian writer living in northern Egypt during the 2nd century CE. A.-M. Denis (1970) accepted a 1st- or 2nd-century CE Egyptian provenance but posited a Hebrew original. Other scholars (e.g. Ginsberg, 1904; Kohler, 1895; Janssen, 1975; Schmidt, 1986) posited a Hebrew original, some citing Palestine as the likely place of origin. These conflicting conclusions are based on each scholar's assessment of the text's Semiticisms and ancient Near Eastern (esp. Egyptian) motifs, as well as structural and other literary elements. The leading arguments assert that the *Testament of Abraham* was originally written in Greek by a Jewish author living in northern Egypt sometime around the turn of the Common Era (Schmidt, 1986; Nickelsburg, 1976; Delcor, 1973), a position supported by the text's many affinities with other Hellenistic Jewish texts thought to be of that provenance, most notably the *Testament of Job, 3 and 4 Maccabees*, and *3 Baruch*.

The date of composition is bracketed by circulation of the Septuagint (→ Bible) in the 2nd century BCE, upon which the *Testament of Abraham*'s Semiticized Greek vocabulary and style obviously depends, and as *terminus ad quem*, the purge of Jewish lives and literature following the Alexandrian revolt of 115–117 CE (Allison, 2003, 38–39). Most scholars narrow the date of composition more tightly to within a century before or after the turn of the Common Era. Finally, D. Allison provides invaluable discussion over the extent to which known versions of the *Testament of Abraham* have their origins within a Christian milieu (Allison, 2003, 28–31).

3. Other Versions

Given its likely Alexandrian provenance, it is not surprising that the oldest translation of the *Testament of Abraham* would be in Coptic (Sahidic). Later Bohairic manuscripts show affinities with both recensions. The Arabic version derives from the Coptic, which itself is the source of the Ethiopic, with the Falasha version following upon an earlier Christian version. The Slavonic version witnesses to the shorter recension (Turdeanu, 1981), while the Romanian version is represented by manuscripts of both recensions: the shorter a direct translation of the Slavonic, the longer copied from Greek Rec. A, with significant contemporizing reflecting Romanian society of the Phanariot period (Roddy, 2001).

4. Genre

The testamentary genre, as modeled most notably by the *Testaments of the Twelve Patriarchs*, is typically characterized by a deathbed setting in which a biblical character accepts his own mortality and uses the occasion to offer sage retrospective paraenesis and an occasional glimpse into the future. By contrast, Abraham's humorous attempts to forestall the inevitability of → death preclude any opportunity for somber reflection let alone the making of any sort of testament. This fact has led some scholars (e.g. Nickelsburg, 1976, 4; Allison, 2003, 42) to assert that the *Testament of Abraham* offers a parody of the genre. This ambiguity is reflected in the manuscript tradition, in which the descriptor "testament" (διαθήκη) is sometimes replaced by titles like *Life of*, or perhaps more appropriately *Death of Abraham*. The text's revelatory elements, including its heavenly chariot ride, otherworldly judgment scene, and angelology (Kolenkow, 1976), have led some monastic copyists (Slavonic, Romanian), and hence a few modern scholars (Kohler, 1895; Gaster, 1893), to refer to the text as an apocalypse, thus risking confusion with the other apocryphon of that name. While testaments often contain apocalyptic motifs, the fact remains that Abraham dies without consent, offering neither paranaesis nor any sort of testament. Resisting facile identification with any particular genre, it was noted as far back as M.R. James (1892) that the *Testament of Abraham* shares many thematic parallels with rabbinic traditions associated with the death of → Moses, a subject thoroughly explored by S.E. Lowenstamm (1976). Others as far back as L. Ginsberg (1904) have noted the narrative's universalizing ethic, which found no apparent need for mentioning the Torah. Still others find in the *Testament of Abraham* a delightful moral tale, perhaps along the lines of Tobit. It is the case that the *Testament of Abraham* draws upon all of these, leaving the typical categorization of the text as a testament largely a matter of convenience.

Historiography

The *Testament of Abraham* was first introduced to the scholarly world at a meeting of the Biblical Archaeology Society in December 1887, where M. Gaster presented a critical edition of the Romanian version, based on three manuscripts he discovered and later published under the title *Apocalypse of Abraham* (Gaster, 1893). About the same time, M.R. James published the first critical edition of the Greek text, extant in two recensions of differing length (James, 1892). The debate over recensional priority has dominated *Testament of Abraham* scholarship into recent times. Major 20th-century text and tradition studies include those by G.H. Box (1927), N. Turner (1955), É. Turdeanu (1957), M. Delcor (1973); A.-M. Denis (1970) and M.E. Stone (1972). A summative culmination of *Testament of Abraham*-studies – its texts, recensions, versions, and traditions – occurred with the publication of papers delivered at the 1972 SBL Pseudepigrapha Seminar (Nickelsburg, 1976), by which time known

manuscripts in Coptic (Bohairic and Sahadic), Arabic, Ethiopic (Falasha and Christian), and Slavonic were represented. Since that time, significant works by É. Turdeanu (1981), E.P. Sanders (1983) and F. Schmidt (1986) have appeared. As of today, the definitive work on the *Testament of Abraham* remains that of D. Allison (2003).

Bibliography

Allison, D., *Testament of Abraham*, Berlin, 2003.

Box, G.H., *The Testament of Abraham: Translated from the Greek Text with Introduction and Notes*, London, 1927.

Delcor, M., *Le testament d'Abraham*, Leiden, 1973.

Denis, A.-M., *Introduction aux pseudépigraphes grecs d'Ancien Testament*, Leiden, 1970.

Gaster, M., "The Apocalypse of Abraham: From the Roumanian Text, Discovered and Translated," *TSBA* 9, 1893, 196–226.

Ginsberg, L., "Abraham, Testament of," in: *JE*, vol. I, New York, 1904, 93–96.

Janssen, E., "Testament Abrahams," in: W.G. Kümmel & H. Lichtenberger, JSHRZ, vol. III: *Unterweisung in lehrhafter Form*, Gütersloh, 1975, 192–256.

James, M.R., *The Testament of Abraham: The Greek Text Now First Edited with Notes and Translation*, Cambridge MA, 1892.

Kohler, K., "The Pre-Talmudic Haggadah II C: The Apocalypse of Abraham and Its Kindred," *JQR* 7, 1895, 581–606.

Kolenkow, A., "The Angelology of the Testament of Abraham," in: G.W.E. Nickelsburg, ed., *Studies on the Testament of Abraham*, Missoula, 1976, 153–162.

Kraft, R.A., "Reassessing the 'Recensional Problem' in Testament of Abraham," in: G.W.E. Nickelsburg, ed., *Studies on the Testament of Abraham*, Missoula, 1976, 121–137.

Lowenstamm, S.E., "The Testament of Abraham and the Texts Concerning Moses' Death," in: G.W.E. Nickelsburg, ed., *Studies on the Testament of Abraham*, Missoula, 1976, 219–226.

Nickelsburg, G.W.E., ed., *Studies on the Testament of Abraham*, Missoula, 1976.

Roddy, N., *The Romanian Version of the Testament of Abraham*, Atlanta, 2001.

Sanders, E.P., "Testament of Abraham," in: J. Charlesworth, ed., *Old Testament Pseudepigrapha*, 2 vols., Garden City, 1983, vol. I, 871–904.

Schmidt, F., *Le testament grec l'Abraham*, Tübingen, 1986.

Stone, M.E., *The Testament of Abraham*, Missoula, 1972.

Turdeanu, É., "Notes sur la tradition littéraire du Testament d'Abraham," *RSBN* 9, 1957, 405–409.

Turdeanu, É., *Apocryphes slaves et roumains de l'Ancien Testament*, Leiden, 1981.

Turner, N., "The Testament of Abraham: Problems in Biblical Greek," *NTS* 1, 1955, 219–223.

NICOLAE RODDY

Abrasax

Abrasax (Ἀβρασάξ; the Latin fathers spell it Abraxas, probably due to confusion between σ, sigma, and ξ, xi) is a term that appears in a large and unequal quantity of material: the heresiologists' works, three texts from the Nag Hammadi library, the Greek magical papyri (*Papyri Graecae magicae*), magical gems, and *tabellae*. The links among these various sources are widely debated and not yet clarified. The problem of this term and the figure to whom it is connected intertwines with the problem of the status and the interconnections between Gnosis (→ Gnosis/Gnosticism) and → magic. At first, we have to say that the numeric value of the word Abrasax according to the Greek alphabet is 365 (α [a] = 1, β [b] = 2, ρ [r] = 100, σ [s] = 200, ξ [xi] = 60).

1. Abrasax and Basilides

The term Abrasax appears in the works against heresy of the church fathers, related to the figure of the gnostic → Basilides.

Irenaeus of Lyon's *Adversus haereses* (1.24.7; → Irenaeus of Lyon) presents Basilides' system as an evolution from the thought of Simon Magus and Menander. From an "Unbegotten Father" there were successive emanations until the first angels, who created the first heaven. In a decreasing order, other angels and other heavens were created up to the sum of 365 heavens. The angels of the last heavens created the world and the nations. Abrasax is the ruler of the 365 heavens, the second world, possessing as his own the number 365. Abrasax coincides with the Jewish God. It should be noted that Irenaeus, speaking about Abrasax, says that Basilides and his sect drew this sort of principle from astrologists (*mathematici*) and introduced them into their doctrine.

Hippolytus of Rome's presentation of Basilides is more complex and profound, very different from Irenaeus' account. Given the impossibility of a full representation of Hippolytus' account, let us see only the cosmogony of Basilides according to Hippolytus. He makes a distinction between the Ogdoad, which is the heaven of the fixed stars and the planets, where the "Great Archon" and his son lie, and the Hebdomad, the sublunary world. Abrasax (Hipp. *Haer.* 7.26.6) is the archont of the Hebdomad. He has this name because it corresponds to 365, like the 365 heavens, so that this figure embraces all things, and for this reason, the year has this number of days.

In Pseudo-Tertullian (*Haer.* 1) Abraxas is Basilides' supreme divinity, who created "Mind," who in turn created the "Word," and so in a progressive way the heavenly powers and the world were created. The mission of Christ is also the work of Abrasax, and not of the God of the Jews, who is an angel distinguished by the supreme god Abraxas.

Epiphanius of Salamis (*Pan.* 24. 7.2–4; 24.8.2–4; *Anc.* 2.24.1–2; → Epiphanius of Salamis) describes Abrasax as the supreme power, above powers and angels, according to Basilides' system. The number 365, concealed in the word Abrasax, is a reference to the 365 heavens, the 365 days of the year, and the 365 parts of a person. Abrasax is the holy name, τὸ ἅγιον ὄνομα.

Also → Jerome in many works (Jer. *Comm. Am.*1.3.3/8; *Comm. Abd.* 7; *Ep.* 75.3; *Lucif.* 23; *Vir. ill.* 21) identifies Abraxas with the supreme God in Basilides' system. He explains the numerical value of this name; besides, he comments that this is the same system used by pagans with the name Mithras, spelled Meithras, the letters of whose name total 365. The origin of the name is speciously traced back to the Hebrew language by heretics who used them for scaring ignorant people and weak women.

Theodoret of Cyrrhus (*Haer. fab.* 349.37), who describes Abrasax in connection with his numerical value, mentions him briefly.

Augustine of Hippo quotes Abrasax in his *De haeresibus ad Quodvultdeus* (*Haer.* 1.4; → Augustine of Hippo) in the chapter about the Basilidians. He mentions the expression "sanctum nomen" (holy name) in connection with Abrasax; Augustine also explains as usual the numerical value of the name.

One should note (see Pearson, 2005, 16n62) that it is only with Pseudo-Tertullian, Epiphanius, and then Jerome that Abrasax is the supreme deity in Basilides' account, but it is probably a misunderstanding. In Ireneus' report about Basilides, it is clear that Abrasax is the chief of the 365 heavens and is very well distinguished from the Unbegotten Father. The same is found in Hippolytus' account, which places great emphasis on the transcendence of the first principle.

2. The Nag Hammadi Texts

The name Abrasax appears in three Coptic texts from the Nag Hammadi library; → Nag Hammadi Writings: the *Gospel of the Egyptians*, the *Apocalypse of Adam*, and *Zostrianos*. All these texts are considered as belonging to so-called Sethian Gnosticism (→ Sethians). In this type of Gnosis, not yet well clarified and classified by scholars, Seth, son of Adam, and his race play an important role.

The so-called *Gospel of the Egyptians* is a mythological treatise, that speaks about the origin of the world and of the race of Seth, son of Adamas, the incorruptible man, and a transcendental version of the biblical Adam. This seed of Seth struggles with demonic powers until the final coming of Jesus, a form of the great Seth (see Williams, 2005, 37–39). In the first section of the text, in which the origin of the heavenly world is described (see Böhlig, Wisse & Labib, 1975, 27), Adamas prays for a son; answering his prayer, the great light manifestation begets Seth with the four great lights, Harmozel, Oroiael, Davithe, Eleleth, and their consorts, who together form an Ogdoad. Then the ministers of the four lights come: Gamaliel, Gabriel, Samlo, Abrasax, with their consorts; they are a second Ogdoad. Thus, Abrasax is the minister of Eleleth and has as consort the "Eternal Life." Each of the four lights is assigned to one of the eternal realms: Eleleth and his assistant are the location for the souls of the race of Seth.

The redeeming action of the great Seth, sent by the four great "Lights," includes the knowledge of the "bringers of salvation" (see Böhlig, Wisse & Labib, 1975, 148). He reveals to the saints (the race of Seth) the powers who give salvation; among them Abrasax is enumerated with the other ministers. The ministers have the role of "receivers" (see Böhlig, Wisse & Labib's trans., 1975) of the great race of Seth. A.J. Welburn qualifies these ministers as a gnostic version of the four archangels (see Welburn, 1981, 267).

The *Apocalypse of Adam* is a revelation received by Adam from three angelic visitors and then shared with his son Seth. The revelation concerns the destiny of the seed of Seth and their struggle against the creator god. In an attack against this gnostic race, made with fire, Abrasax, Sablo, and Gamaliel will descend and rescue them. Finally, a savior will come and triumph.

Finally, there is a briefer quotation of Abrasax in *Zostrianos*. This revelation narrates an afterlife journey made by Zostrianos and also his mystical experiences. The purpose of the narration is the salvation of the race of Seth through Gnosis (see Layton & Sieber, 1991, 10–12). Zostrianos ascends among the otherworldly realms and is baptized several times.

In a description of the souls destined to salvation, Ephesech, one of the revealers of Zostrianos' journey, lists many heavenly beings, "conceptual patterns of salvation available as helpers to anyone who wishes to transcend this world" (see Barry, Funk, Poirier & Turner, 2000, 558). They "act to preserve and confirm that which is worthy and precious" (Barry, Funk, Poirier & Turner, 2000, 558). Abrasax is quoted here and is counted among the "attendants" with Isauel and Adauel.

The existence of a triad or a tetrad of ministers/attendants of the four Lights has been recognized by scholars as one of the recurrent mythological features of the so-called Sethian tradition (Barry, Funk, Poirier & Turner, 2000, 134–135). The role of Abrasax in the three texts analyzed is not always the same, but his positive and auxiliary function is clear.

3. The Magical World

The name of Abrasax appears several times in the Greek Magical Papyri (*Papyri Graecae magicae*), the body of papyri from Greco-Roman Egypt containing magical spells, hymns, and rituals, from the 2nd century BCE to the 5th century CE (see Betz, 1986, xli). It also appears in a great number of magical objects such as gems, tablets, amulets, and *lamellae* (plates of metal). The antiquaries of the 17th and 18th centuries studied and classified the engraved stones with names such as Iao, Sabaoth, Abrasax, and so on, giving to the whole body of gems the name of "Abraxas" or "gnostic gems" and crediting their production to gnostic teachers. This univocal attribution was sometimes rejected, and in the last two centuries the close connection between magical gems and magical papyri, both attributed to magicians, has been affirmed. However, the problem of the connection between these gems and their use in gnostic circles remains (see Mastrocinque, 2003, 66–67).

The context of spells and incantations in which Abrasax appears is very wide and very often related to the sun and its worship. The use of the name Abrasax in the love spells (P.GrM 4; 11c; 19; 32; 36; 61; 67; 68) is also typical. The memory of the numerical value of the figure is often preserved. In P.GrM 8; 49, an invocation to Hermes, the author writes,

> and the second name [of the deity] with the number 7, corresponding to those who rule the world, with the exact number 365 corresponding to the days of the year. Truly: ABRASAX. (trans. E.N. O'Neil, in: Betz, 1986, 146)

Therefore, Abrasax is the encrypted name of a deity that reveals the planets ("those who rule the world", trans. E.N. O'Neil, in: Betz, 1986, 146) and the days of the year (see Michel, 2004, 481).

P.GrM 61 prescribes the pronouncement of a love spell having an iron ring, on "which has been engraved Harpokrates, sitting on a lotus, and his name is ABRASAX" (trans E.N. O'Neil, in: Betz, 1986, 291). In P.GrM 13, a hymn in which the rising sun is greeted by the sacred animals making their distinctive noises (M. Smith, in: Betz, 1986, 174), the god is called Abrasax in "baboonic" (after the manner of the dog-headed animal). The invocation further says:

> Now he who appears on the boat rising together with you is a clever / baboon; he greets you in his own language, saying "You are the number of [the days of] the year, ABRASAX. (trans. M. Smith, in: Betz, 1986, 176)

In the scene C. Sfameni (Sanzi & Sfameni, 2009, 135) identifies a representation of a subject, which is very often depicted on the magical gems: the child on the lotus flower, namely Harpokrates, the son of Isis and Osiris, surrounded by animals, which are maybe adoring him. The connection between Abrasax and the scene of the young Egyptian god Harpokrates sitting on a lotus, a typical syncretistic solar figure of late antiquity (see Mastrocinque, 2003, 154), is well attested on magical gems.

The name of Abrasax on the magical gems is very often associated with a composite figure, the cock-headed monster with serpentine legs. The monster (see Bonner, 1950, 123) usually has human arms and trunk and holds a whip in its right hand and a round shield in its left hand. A military kilt covers its trunk. About this figure and its meaning there is widespread debate; usually it was considered a representation of Abrasax, because the name of Abrasax very

often appears on the gems with the cock-headed anguipede. Alternatively, he was called Iao, another name often appearing in association with the figure, usually inscribed on the shield. Iao is a Greek term, derived from the Hebrew Tetragrammaton, to indicate the Jewish God. Iao is also a term very often used in association with Abrasax in the papyri, along with Adonai or Sabaoth, other Jewish titles for God, which are very much used in magical practice. The connections between the cock-headed monster and Abrasax or Iao are now sometimes rejected (see Mastrocinque, 2005, 274–275). Scholars have not yet given a fully and entirely convincing explanation of the depiction of the monster, although many attempts have been made (see e.g. Bonner, 1950, 123; Nilsson, 1951, 61–64; Philonenko, 1979, 297–303, etc.).

Another attestation of the connection between Abrasax and the magical world is the account coming from Iulius Africanus' *Cesti*, (frgms. 10; 30), circa 230 CE. The account about Abrasax is included in an invocation of demonic powers, the incantation of Odysseus in the pseudo-Homeric citation. This text presents many analogies with Greek magical papyri, such as the simultaneous presence of Greek, Hebrew, and Egyptian deities, the sun and names such as Ablanatho and our Abraxas (Ogden, 2002, 183). Abraxas is presented as a demon with a cosmic name, ruling the earth's axis.

4. The Solar Context

In the magical world, the figure of Abrasax is very often connected with the sun. I have already pointed out this theme when speaking about the Egyptian Harpokrates. This connection is also shown in the usual association with Mithras, as Jerome pointed out in Jer. *Comm. Am.*1.3.3/8. Another text that can support this solar character of the figure is the *Fabulae* of Hyginus (*Fab.* 183.3), in which Abrasax is one of the horses of the sun, according to Homer. This is the only account that mentions Homer, but it confirms the solar context of the name.

Furthermore, the cock-headed monster, which is often associated with Abrasax, has a solar component in his head: the cock is a typical solar animal. Besides, sometimes the cock-headed monster on magical gems drives the chariot of the sun.

Finally, we can say that the name Abrasax itself is solar, representing the solar year of 365 days.

Historiography

Many scholars nowadays (see e.g. Bonner, 1950, 134; Mastrocinque, 2005, 203) doubt that the origin of the figure or the name of Abrasax is to be sought in Basilides' teaching. The already quoted account by Irenaeus, who presupposes an influence of magicians or astrologers in Basilides' system, speaking about Abrasax, appears to be indicative. Probably the numerical value of the name, already known and used by astrologers, induces Basilides to use it. He may have got it from the knowledge of magicians (perhaps the Chaldeans).

The use of the name in the magical papyri has not been entirely clarified. Some scholars think that it is used not as a proper noun of a deity but as a "word of power" (see Bonner, 1950, 134). Other scholars emphasize the personal character of the deity, often invoked in the papyri explicitly as a god (e.g. P.GrM 3; 150; P.GrM 69; 2). Others (see Sanzi & Sfameni, 2009, 129–138) underline the typical henotheism of the papyri, in which all the deities are manifestations of a unique and supreme, divine, and solar power. S. Michel says (Michel, 2004, 487) that the gems use the name Abrasax as an overall denomination of a solar deity, with whom the cock-headed monster is often associated.

The fact that both in Irenaeus' account and in the magical papyri Abrasax is associated with the Jewish God also appears to be interesting. Finally, for a correct understanding of the figure, we must refer to a typical gnostic notion: "Knowing the magic names of the heavenly powers is indispensable to any ascent to the highest regions of the divine world." (Broek, 2013) Thus, the role of Abrasax in the gnostic texts of Nag Hammadi appears compatible with the role that he plays in the magical texts and object: a mediator between the divine world, to which he belongs, and the material world.

In conclusion, for a real and overall comprehension of the figure of Abrasax, a profound and wide view of all the contexts in which he appears, without neglecting the massive magical setting, is necessary.

Bibliography

Barry, C., W.P. Funk, P.H. Poirier & J.D. Turner, eds., *Zostrien*, BCNH.T 8/1, Québec, 2000.

Böhlig, A., F. Wisse & P. Labib, eds., trans., *Gospel of the Egyptians* (actually: *Egyptian Gospel*), NHC 3.2; 4.2, NHS 4, Leiden, 1975.

Bonner, C., *Studies in Magical Amulets, Chiefly Graeco-Egyptian*, Ann Arbor, 1950.

Betz, H.D., *The Greek Magical Papyri in Translation: Including the Demotic Spells*, Chicago, 1986.

Broek, R. van den, *Gnostic Religion in Antiquity*, Cambridge MA, 2013.

Delatte, A., & P. Derchain, *Les intailles magicques gréco-ègyptiennes*, Paris, 1964.

King, C.W., *The Gnostics and Their Remains*, London, 1887.

Layton, B., & J. Sieber, eds., *Zostrianos*, NHC 8.1, NHS 31, Leiden, 1991, 7–225.

Mastrocinque, A., *Sylloge gemmarum gnosticarum*, Rome, 2003.

Mastrocinque, A., *From Jewish Magic to Gnosticism*, Tübingen, 2005.

Michel, S., *Die magischen Gemmen: Zu Bildern und Zauberformeln auf geschnittenen Steinen der Antike und Neuzeit*, Berlin, 2004.

Nilsson, M.P., "The Anguipede of the Magical Amulets," *HThR* 44, 1951, 61–64.

Ogden, D., *Magic, Witchcraft, and Ghosts in the Greek and Roman Worlds: A Sourcebook*, Oxford, 2002.

Pearson, B.A., "Basilides the Gnostic," in: A. Marjanen & P. Luomanen, eds., *A Companion to Second-Century Christian "Heretics"*, Boston, 2005.

Philonenko, M., "L'anguipède alectorocéphale et le dieu Iaô," *CRAI* 123/2, 1979, 297–304.

Rasimus, T., *Paradise Reconsidered in Gnostic Mythmaking: Rethinking Sethianism in Light of the Ophite Evidence*, Boston, 2009.

Sanzi, E., & C. Sfameni, *Magia e culti orientali: Studi storico-comparativi su due fenomeni religiosi della tarda antichità*, Cosenza, 2009.

Welburn, A.J., "Reconstructing the Ophite Diagram," *NT* 23/3, 1981.

Williams, M.A., "Sethianism," in: A. Marjanen & P. Luomanen, eds., *A Companion to Second-Century Christian "Heretics"*, Boston, 2005.

MARIA FALLICA

Abstinence → Fasting/Abstinence

Acacian Schism

The Acacian schism is a late antique split between Rome and the eastern patriarchates over issues of Christological orthodoxy. The schism, which lasted from 484 to 518 CE, takes its name from Acacius, the patriarch of Constantinople from 471 to 489 CE and one of the main ecclesiastical actors of this period. The primary point of contention was the status of the Council of → Chalcedon (451 CE), which had approved the definition of Christ as being "in two natures." Additionally, the schism was deepened by a conflict between Rome and the eastern patriarchates over the inscription on the diptychs and liturgical recitation of names of ecclesiastical actors, both deceased and alive, who were known anti-Chalcedonians or had demonstrated some amount of support for the anti-Chalcedonian movement.

1. The Period Leading to the Schism: Contested Episcopal Election in Alexandria

A contested episcopal election in Alexandria in 481–482 CE reinforced three decades of Roman concern over the state of ecclesiastical affairs and Christological → orthodoxy in the East, especially in Alexandria. Developments surrounding this election ultimately triggered the beginning of the Acacian schism in the summer of 484 CE.

In 481 CE, John Talaia, a Tabennesiote monk, traveled to Constantinople in order to obtain assurance on behalf of Chalcedonian patriarch of Alexandria Timothy Salophaciolus that, upon the latter's death, a Chalcedonian → bishop would be appointed to replace him on the see of Alexandria. Once in Constantinople, John Talaia was, it seems, asked to take an oath and sign a document in which he vowed not to seek ordination for himself (Eva. Schol. *Hist. eccl.* 3.12; Ps.-Zach. *Hist. eccl.* 5.7). This arrangement, however, failed to secure a smooth episcopal succession in Alexandria upon the death of Timothy Salophaciolus in February of 482 CE. The Chalcedonian party appointed John Talaia, with little regard for the imperial arrangement presumably set in place only months earlier. The anti-Chalcedonians rallied around Timothy Aelurus' companion Peter Mongus, the leading figure of the anti-Chalcedonian movement in Alexandria at this time. Both Chalcedonians and anti-Chalcedonians carried out intense lobbying for support, papal or imperial.

2. The Publication of the Henoticon

It was in response to the conflict in Alexandria, according to Evagrius Scholasticus, that Emperor Zeno undertook the publication of the edict known as the Henoticon – or the "Unitive" – in 482 CE. Patriarch Acacius was likely the mastermind and possibly even the author of this decree (Eva. Schol. *Hist. eccl.* 3.13; Theoph. Conf. *AM* 5976). Inspiration for the document likely came from petitions brought to Constantinople by Alexandrian anti-Chalcedonian monks at this time. E. Schwartz (1934), followed by A. Grillmeier (1987) and P. Gray (1979), has also argued for similarities with, and therefore possible influence from, a unitive document produced by Patriarch Martyrius of Jerusalem (478–486 CE). The Henoticon (text in Eva. Schol. *Hist. eccl.* 3.14; LibCar. *Brev.* 17; and Ps.-Zach. *Hist. eccl.* 5.8) was originally addressed to the Churches of Alexandria, Egypt, Lybia, and Pentapolis, and was intended as a basis for fostering peace in this region, which, since 451 CE, had been the most affected by tension and open conflicts between Chalcedonians and anti-Chalcedonians. The highlights of this document include a reaffirmation of the faith of → Nicaea as the foundation of orthodox belief, emphatic support for the title *Theotokos* ("Mother of God") for → Mary, the affirmation of the unity of subject in Christ, approval for → Cyril of Alexandria's Twelve Anathemas (a document upheld by anti-Chalcedonians as an important source for Christological orthodoxy, but which had not been officially endorsed, neither at the Council of → Ephesus in 431 CE nor at the Council of Chalcedon in 451 CE), the rejection of a passage from the *Tome* of Pope Leo (one of the documents sanctioned for orthodoxy at the Council of Chalcedon and upheld by Rome as an epitome of correct Christological belief), and, finally, close to the end of the document, a somewhat discreet and vague, but ultimately very consequential, rejection of errors that may have been allowed "either in Chalcedon or in any synod whatever." An official imperial legation to Alexandria sought and obtained Peter Mongus' approval of this document. After accepting the Henoticon, Peter was confirmed as patriarch of Alexandria, while John Talaia fled his see and eventually went to Rome to plead his case. (Ps.-Zach. *Hist. eccl.* 5.7; LibCar. *Brev.* 17)

3. Roman Reactions to the Situation in the East and the Beginning of the Schism

The confirmation of Peter Mongus as patriarch of Alexandria caused a severe deterioration in the relations between Rome and Constantinople. In correspondence with Constantinople, Pope Simplicius (468–483 CE) deplored the inability of Emperor Zeno and Patriarch Acacius of Constantinople to handle the situation in an appropriate manner and the concessions made to a known anti-Chalcedonian, over whose lack of orthodoxy Rome and Constantinople had previously been in agreement. The pope also complained about the eastern refusal to provide detailed information about the situation in Alexandria. (Thiel, 1867, Simplicius, *Ep.* 18) Arriving in Rome soon after the accession of Pope Felix III in 483 CE, John Talaia stirred further discontent, presenting the results of the election in Alexandria and the confirmation of Peter Mongus as an outright rejection of Chalcedon in the East and a triumph of heresy. His credibility was strengthened by the support of Chalcedonian Constantinopolitan monks, the Acoimetai (LibCar. *Brev.* 17).

A legation sent by Pope Felix III to Constantinople in 483 CE was entrusted with the mission to obtain the condemnation of Peter Mongus, to enforce support for Chalcedon in the eastern capital, and to summon Patriarch Acacius of Constantinople to Rome to defend himself before the pope against accusations laid by John Talaia. (Thiel, 1867, Felix, *Ep.* 3) The papal legates, Misenus of Cumae and Vitalis of Truentinum, failed on all three counts. What is more, they entered into communion with the Constantinopolitan patriarch and the emperor, despite the pope's explicit prohibition. Upon their return to Rome, the two were condemned in a Roman synod in July 484 CE (Eva. Schol. *Hist. eccl.* 3.18–21). The same synod pronounced the excommunication of Acacius of Constantinople (Thiel, 1867, Felix, *Ep.* 6). Acacius responded, in his turn, by removing the name of Pope Felix from the diptychs (Theoph. Conf. *AM* 5980). This marked the beginning of the Acacian schism proper.

4. Negotiations for Resumption of Communion

As far as Rome was concerned, the healing of the schism required eastern acceptance of the Council of Chalcedon, as well as the removal from the → diptychs of easterners who either were or were perceived in Rome as being opponents of the Council of Chalcedon. Papal correspondence sent to Constantinople in the 480s and 490s CE emphasizes, time and time again, the condemnation of Peter Mongus and Acacius of Constantinople. After their deaths, in 487 or 488 and 489 CE, respectively, successive popes requested with increasing insistence the erasure of their names from the diptychs, as well as the condemnations of those who had been in communion with them and/or continued to adhere to the Henoticon. This unrelenting request, which, over time, triggered eastern accusations that the popes were stubborn, behaved arrogantly and did not have the unity of the church at heart, became, starting in the 490s CE, the main stumbling block to the healing of the Acacian schism (Thiel, 1867, Felix, *Ep.* 14; Gelasius, *Ep.* 3; Anastasius *Ep.* 2.1; Symmachus, *Ep.* 10). The Constantinopolitan refusal to remove from the diptychs the name of Patriarch Acacius prevented fruitful discussions between the two capitals even at a time when the patriarchal see in Constantinople was occupied by pro-Chalcedonians like Euphemius (490–496 CE) and Macedonius (496–511 CE).

Roman legations sent to Constantinople in the 490s CE to secure imperial recognition for the title *rex* on behalf of the new political leader of Italy, the Ostrogoth Theoderic, who came to power in 493 CE after having ousted Odoacer, the first Ostrogothic king of Italy, were also entrusted with the task of negotiating an end to the Acacian schism (Collectio Veronensis 7–8, see Schwartz, 1934). A brief moment of hope is recorded in the sources for the year 497 CE, when reactions in Constantinople to the presence of the Roman senator Faustus and the western bishops Cresconius and Germanus, the latter two representing the newly elected pope Anastasius II (496–498 CE), indicate a perceived papal openness to negotiate issues that had previously been presented as nonnegotiable, including the issue of the erasure of names from the diptychs (Th. Lec. *Epit.* 461, see Hansen, 1971; Theoph. Conf.

AM 5993; Collectio Avellana 102, see Gunther, 1895). Whether this perceived papal flexibility was real or not, the negotiations failed.

From 491 to 518 CE, the presence on the imperial throne in Constantinople of Anastasius I, an emperor who was considerably more interested in uniting the eastern churches (even if this involved further compromises on the status of the Council of Chalcedon) than in negotiating a healing of the schism with the papacy, further increased the alienation between Rome and Constantinople. Papal pressure, as well as pressure from pro-Chalcedonian parties in Constantinople and in the East, failed to increase Emperor Anastasius' desire to prioritize peace with Rome. Equally unsuccessful in this respect, despite some strong initial expectations of success, was the pressure exerted by the powerful Scythian general Vitalian, a supporter of the Council of Chalcedon, who organized three rebellions against Emperor Anastasius I (513–515 CE; Malalas *Chron.* 402–406; Eva. Schol. *Hist. eccl.* 3.43).

5. Healing of the Schism

Upon his accession to the imperial throne in 518 CE, Justin I openly pronounced the validity of the Council of Chalcedon, which was almost immediately confirmed by a Constantinopolitan synod. The new emperor also sent letters to Rome announcing his accession and the Constantinopolitan willingness to heal the schism through full support for the Council of Chalcedon. In response, Pope Hormisdas sent to the East a *Libellus*, a statement of faith originally produced in 515 CE (Collectio Avellana 116a and b, see Gunther, 1895), intended to form the basis for reconciliation. In addition to unreserved acceptance of the Council of Chalcedon, the statement required the erasure from the diptychs of Acacius of Constantinople, as well as various anti-Chalcedonian leaders, and declared the unchallengeable authority of the papacy in matters of orthodox belief. Patriarch John II of Constantinople (518–520 CE) signed the papal statement in approval in the spring of 519 CE, after what seems to have been some moderate initial resistance. The *Libellus* was then sent for approval throughout the eastern patriarchates. This marked the end of the Acacian schism and the resumption of communion between Rome and Constantinople, even though tensions regarding both doctrinal issues and issues of ecclesiastical practice and discipline did not disappear. In the East, the imperially required acceptance of the papal *Libellus* caused renewed conflict between Chalcedonians and anti-Chalcedonians, a situation that would eventually result in the separation of the Syrian and Egyptian churches from the imperial church.

Bibliography

Blaudeau, P., *Alexandrie et Constantinople (451–491): De l'histoire à la géo-ecclésiologie*, Rome, 2006.

Blaudeau, P., *Le siège de Rome et l'Orient (448–536): Étude géo-ecclésiologique*, Rome, 2012.

Frend, W.H.C., *The Rise of the Monophysite Movement*, Cambridge UK, 1979.

Gray, P.T.R., *The Defense of Chalcedon in the East (451–553)*, Leiden, 1979.

Grillmeier, A., *Christ in Christian Tradition*, vol. II: *From the Council of Chalcedon (451) to Gregory the Great (590–604)*, ET: P. Allen & J. Cawte, Atlanta, 1987.

Gunther, O., ed., *Collectio Avellana*, CSEL 35.1–2, Vienna, 1895, 1898.

Hansen, G.C., ed., *Theodore Lector: Kirchengeschichte*, Berlin, 1971.

Kötter, J.-M., *Zwischen Kaisern und Aposteln: Das Akakianische Schisma (484–519) als kirchlicher Ordnungskonflikt der Spätantike*, Stuttgart, 2013.

Schwartz, E., *Publizistische Sammlungen zum acacianischen Schisma*, Munich, 1934.

Thiel, A., ed., *Epistolae Romanorum pontificum genuinae et quae ad eos scriptae sunt a S. Hilaro usque ad Pelagium II*, vol. I, Braunsberg, 1867.

DANA IULIANA VIEZURE

Acacius of Constantinople

Acacius (d. 489 CE) was patriarch of Constantinople from 471 CE until 489 CE. Previously a presbyter (→ Priest/Presbyter) and head of an orphanage (ὀρφανότροφος), his competence caught the attention of Emperor Leo I. After the death of Patriarch Gennadius in 471 CE, Acacius was selected bishop of Constantinople and soon got involved in the post-Chalcedonian struggles. The politically able → bishop endured three changes of government, tried to restore unity among the eastern patriarchates, and caused the first great schism between eastern and western Christianity, which lasted 35 years.

On the one hand, he was not attracted by the theological decision of the Council of → Chalcedon (451 CE), while on the other hand, he favored the council's canon 28, which promoted privileges for the see of Constantinople. When he opposed the anti-Chalcedonian politics of the usurper → Basiliscus (474–476 CE), Acacius earned the approval of Pope Simplicius (468–483 CE). When Emperor Zeno returned to power, pope, patriarch, and emperor were agreed on the necessity of affirming the decrees of Chalcedon and for a time acted in concert. Because of the anti-Chalcedonian patriarch of Alexandria, Peter Mongos, a theological compromise had been necessary to restore union in the East. Acacius drafted the famous formula of union called *Henoticon*, which neglected to mention the Council of Chalcedon. The document was promulgated by Emperor Zeno in 482 CE and united the eastern patriarchates; more extreme anti-Chalcedonian parties did not accept the *Henoticon* though. For Rome too the *Henoticon* was not acceptable, since the West stood fast to the decrees of Chalcedon. Pope Felix III excommunicated Acacius at a synod in 484 CE. As a reaction Acacius deleted the name of Pope Felix from the → diptychs and continued as a powerful patriarch until his death in 489 CE. The Acacian schism was ended only under Emperor Justin and at the times of Pope Hormisdas in 519 CE.

1. Controversies After Chalcedon

When Emperor Leo I died in 474 CE, his grandson Leo II was still a child. Therefore the Isaurian Zeno was promoted as augustus by Empress Verina. Both Zeno and Patriarch Acacius appeared publicly to be loyal to the Council of Chalcedon (451 CE), and there was no change in imperial church policy. However, in 475 CE Zeno was put out of office by the brother of Verina, Basiliscus (475–476 CE). The usurper was in need of support and tried to gain it among the anti-Chalcedonians. The anti-Chalcedonian patriarch of Alexandria, Timothy Aelurus (457–460 CE, 475–477 CE), returned triumphant from exile. He had succeeded in becoming the only bishop of Alexandria after the assassination of the Chalcedonian patriarch Proterios in 457 CE and was deposed by Emperor Leo I in late 459 CE or early 460 CE. At Timothy's suggestion, the Egyptian monk Paul the

Sophist composed an imperial circular, which confirmed the faith of → Nicaea (325 CE) but anathematized the faith of Chalcedon and the *Tome* of Pope Leo. The usurper Basiliscus publicly released this encyclical and by that practically reinstalled the Second Council of Ephesus (449 CE), which had been called a robber-synod by Pope Leo the Great. On his way back to Alexandria, Timothy Aelurus participated in a synod for the province of Asia in Ephesus (457 CE), which cut the patriarchal rights of the see of Constantinople as confirmed by canon 3 of the Council of Constantinople (381 CE) and canon 28 of the Council of Chalcedon (451 CE). Also the anti-Chalcedonian patriarch, Peter the Fuller (471 CE, 475–477 CE, 485–488 CE), who was detained by Emperor Leo I, regained his see, and patriarch Anastasius of Jerusalem (458–478 CE) signed the encyclical of Basiliscus (*Encyclicon*). Now all the eastern patriarchs, despite Constantinople, as well as the bishop's sees of the provinces of Asia, Syria, and Egypt were anti-Chalcedonian.

It was Acacius who mobilized Chalcedonian monks and the populace against Basiliscus. Definitively Acacius was ready to make dogmatic compromises, but he needed the Council of Chalcedon to protect the patriarchal rights of Constantinople. When in 476 CE the Isaurian Zeno and his army marched against Constantinople, the political situation for Basiliscus was hopeless. Monks and the populace demonstrated against the usurper. In his trouble he revoked the encyclical by an antencyclical (*Antencyclicon*), which condemned Eutyches and Nestorius. Furthermore, an imperial synod planned by Timothy Aelurus was prohibited, and the privileges of the see of Constantinople were confirmed. However, it was too late: Basiliscus was deposed, the anti-Chalcedonian movement collapsed for the time being, and Acacius had consolidated the power of his see. In 479 CE he even ordained a patriarch of Antioch, Calendion, and thus exceeded the limits of his jurisdiction. Pope Simplicius' protest was slight; he accepted the procedure on the plea of necessity.

2. Theological Compromise on Political Grounds: The Henoticon (482 CE)

Emperor Zeno (474–475 CE, 476–491 CE) started a Chalcedonian restoration that encountered strong resistance, especially in Egypt. Hence, the emperor decided not to depose the aged Timothy Aelurus and let him die in peace. However, the heavy pressure of Zeno's politics allowed the anti-Chalcedonian movement in Egypt to select a successor for Timothy Aelurus only in secret, and Peter Mongus was clandestinely ordained. The official Chalcedonian patriarch of the imperial church became again the modest Timothy Salophakiolos (460–475 CE, 477–481 CE). He had been in office already when Timothy Aelurus had been expelled, but returned to the Tabennesiot monastery at Canopos when the anti-Chalcedonian patriarch was installed by the rebellion of the usurper Basiliscus. Emperor Zeno now restored Salophakiolos to his see, which he kept until his death in 481 CE.

Since Timothy Salophakiolos did not succeed in reconciling the anti-Chalcedonians with the imperial church and inaugurating stability, a delegation guided by the *oikonomos* of the Alexandrian Church, John Talaia, arrived in Constantinople to ensure the election of a Chalcedonian patriarch after the death of Salophakiolos. Emperor Zeno agreed, but he compelled John Talaia to take an oath in front of Patriarch Acacius and the senate, that he himself would not assume this office. The emperor was suspicious of John Talaia, who had connections with the *magister officiorum* and *patricius* Illos, a mighty Isaurian general who once fought with Zeno and later wanted to overthrow him. An alliance between a powerful patriarch and a renegade commander in turbulent Egypt could not be a matter of particular interest for the emperor. Shortly after the return of the delegation, Timothy Salophakiolos died, and the perjured John Talaia was ordained patriarch. Emperor Zeno became frantic and saw his suspicions of traitorous plans confirmed. Talaia was deposed immediately and had to flee to Rome, where he, as a convinced Chalcedonian, was welcomed by Pope Simplicius. At the same time, partisans of Peter Mongus called on Zeno and vouched for him as the sole patriarch.

For Patriarch Acacius it was now time to act, because he could not tolerate Peter Mongus becoming patriarch of Alexandria without any concessions, as was the case with Timothy Aelurus in the time of Basiliscus. Acacius feared that again Chalcedon's canon 28 would disappear and, together with it, the privileges of the see of Constantinople. Although the Council of Constantinople (381 CE) had formulated in its canon 3 that the bishop of the New Rome should have the prerogative of honor after the bishop of Rome, Alexandria tried to oppose this decision. Three bishops of Alexandria in a row were able to depose their colleagues from the see of the new capital: Theophilos (384–412 CE) managed to get → John Chrysostom deposed as patriarch at the Synod of the Oak (402 CE), his nephew Cyril (412–444 CE) condemned Nestorius (→ Nestorianism/Nestorius) at the First Council of Ephesus (431 CE), and his successor Dioscoros (444–454 CE) defeated Flavian at the Second Council of Ephesus (449 CE), the so-called robber-synod. The political circumstances and the conflicts of rank among the patriarchates established the substrate for the theological controversies.

Since Peter Mongus wanted to be confirmed by the emperor as bishop of Alexandria and as successor not only of Timothy Aelurus but also of Timothy Salophakiolos, it was up to Zeno to define the conditions. Therefore, in autumn 482 CE, Emperor Zeno submitted a declaration for signature to Peter Mongus drafted by Acacius. For the emperor, this document, called the *Henoticon* or formula of union, was an attempt to reconcile the supporters and opponents of the Council of Chalcedon. The *Henoticon* anathematized Eutyches and Nestorius and confirmed the unique authority of the Nicene Creed (→ Nicaea) as well as the Councils of Constantinople (381 CE) and Ephesus (431 CE). It also canonized the third letter of Cyril to Nestorius with its 12 anathemas, which was not approved at the Council of Ephesus. However, the *Henoticon* did not condemn the *Tome* of Leo and the Council of Chalcedon. Hence the necessary canons for the primacy of the see of Constantinople were intact. To consolidate his influence in the East, Acacius had no problems with a theological compromise and abstained from the formula of faith of Chalcedon. The *Henoticon* could likewise be accepted by Chalcedonians and anti-Chalcedonians. Nevertheless it held the germ of future conflicts, since it slid over the Council of Chalcedon and neglected the *Tome* of Leo.

Peter Mongus signed the *Henoticon*, and communion between Alexandria and Constantinople was reinstated. Patriarch Calendion of Antioch refused to agree with the document, because he considered it a veiled attempt to abolish the Council of Chalcedon. At the same time he made the mistake of supporting the rebellion of the Isaurian *patricius* Illus in 484 CE and thus was deposed and exiled. Again Peter the Fuller regained the see of Antioch, and patriarch Martyrius of Jerusalem (478–486 CE) too accepted the *Henoticon*.

Thus, Acacius managed to get all the patriarchates of the East into agreement with his initiative on the theological basis of a document drafted by him. However, the attempt to resolve the heavy conflicts between Chalcedonians and anti-Chalcedonians remained unsuccessful for several reasons. First, extremist groups on both sides, for whom the theological substance of the *Henoticon* was too watered down, contributed to its failure. Second, the unity was too underpinned by the attempt of Acacius to secure his primacy among the patriarchates in the East. And finally, Rome had no appreciation at all for Acacius' procedure. The promulgation of the *Henoticon* was followed by the first main separation between the churches of East and West, the "Acacian schism."

3. The Acacian Schism (484–519 CE)

When Peter Mongus was pushed into the Alexandrian see against the Chalcedonian John Talaia, the latter took refuge in Rome. Pope Simplicius supported Talaia – probably without knowing that he had committed perjury – and objected to the pronounced opponent of Chalcedon, Peter Mongus. The pope, who previously was in concord with the patriarch of Constantinople, now wrote letters of protest to Acacius, since for Rome, Peter Mongus was a condemned heretic. The letters remained without effect, and Simplicius died soon afterward (483 CE). His successor Felix III (483–492 CE) sent a delegation of two bishops to Constantinople, with letters to Emperor Zeno and Patriarch Acacius, to solve the problem. Since the mission failed, a synod held in Rome in 484 CE, chaired by Pope Felix III, anathematized Peter Mongus and excommunicated Acacius of Constantinople for his connection with him (but not because of heretical opinions). At the same time, Pope Felix wrote to Emperor Zeno and the Church of Constantinople threatening that everybody who would not separate from the deposed patriarch would be excommunicated. A delegate was sent to Constantinople to communicate the decrees in person. Acacius' reaction was the deletion of the pope's name from the diptychs. The actions of the western synod remained without effect in the East, and the eastern patriarchs remained in communion with Acacius. However, Peter the Fuller of Antioch was excommunicated by a Roman synod one year later.

At this point, questions of faith and theological disputes did not come to the fore. The schism was caused more by personal controversies and questions of politics. Since the popes got their information only from John Talaia, they had only one perspective, and secondhand information about the situation in the East. In the West, there was no understanding of the eastern situation about the controversies after Chalcedon. This lack of understanding was also due to their respective and specific political circumstances.

Already when the Council of Chalcedon was convoked, the western Roman Empire was confronted by the Huns. Pope Simplicius witnessed plundering attacks of Bavarian invaders, the deposition of the last western Roman emperor (Romulus Augustulus), and the proclamation of Odoacer as king of Italy (476 CE). There was a deepening divide between the eastern and western Roman Empire. From 493 CE onward, the court of the Ostrogoths was established by → Theodoric the Great in Ravenna. Although the Ostrogothic kings were officially subordinate to Constantinople and wanted their rule to be recognized by the emperor, they did not care too much about Constantinople.

In the East, the religious controversies between Chalcedonians and anti-Chalcedonians were shaking the provinces and weakening the imperial borders. For the emperor it was a necessity to calm the conflicts and to find theological compromises. The politics of the *Henoticon* have to be seen mainly from an eastern perspective and not from the point of view of papal polemics. Although Acacius certainly had his own agenda concerning the see of Constantinople, the faith of the *Henoticon* certainly was orthodox, though pre-Chalcedonian. Furthermore, he succeeded in uniting the church in the East and contributed to the restoration of peace in the eastern provinces.

The West stood firmly with the Council of Chalcedon. Pope Felix III and his successors even extended the → Acacian schism after the death of Acacius in 489 CE for another unnecessary 20 years, although the patriarchs of Constantinople, Fravitas (489–490 CE), and Euphemios (490–496 CE), had deleted Peter Mongus from the diptychs. But Zeno's successor, Anastasius (491–518 CE), continued his religious policy with the *Henoticon*. Pope Gelasius (492–496 CE) even requested the eastern patriarchs to delete Acacius from the diptychs.

Only Pope Anastasius (496–498 CE) made efforts for reconciliation and got in contact with patriarch Makedonios of Constantinople (459–511 CE). This was in the context of a delegation sent by Theodoric to request the emperor for official recognition as king. But when the delegation returned to Rome, Anastasius had died, and all peace efforts ceased since two popes were elected simultaneously. Pope Symmachus (498–514 CE) continued the policy of Pope Gelasius, while his opponent, the anti-pope Laurentius, seemed to hold a more appeasing position. Until 506 CE, the "Laurentian Schism" in the West made any political overtures toward the East impossible.

The Acacian schism lasted until the death of Emperor Anastasius, and the situation only changed after 518 CE. In the late 5th and early 6th century CE, the eastern Roman Empire was dominated by the anti-Chalcedonians.

With the accession to power of Emperor Justin (518–527 CE) and his nephew → Justinian (527–565 CE), a Chalcedonian restoration took place, and opponents of the council began to be persecuted. Because of their attempts to revive the whole Roman Empire to its ancient glory, restoring ecclesial unity was on the agenda of the emperors. Therefore not only the eastern patriarchates were in their focus, but also the powerful see of Rome. Justin started negotiations with Pope Hormisdas (514–523 CE). Already Emperor Anastasius had tried to resolve the schism by contacting Hormisdas, but the negotiations failed. The pope had drafted a confession of faith, called the formula of Hormisdas, requesting the emperor and the eastern bishops to officially accept the Council of Chalcedon and the letters of Pope Leo (esp. the *Tome* of Leo), as well as condemning Nestorius, Eutyches and Disocorus, Timothy Aelurus, Peter Mongus, Peter the Fuller, and Acacius with all their followers.

Now Emperor Justin adopted a hard Chalcedonian line and forced patriarch John of Constantinople to accept the formula of Hormisdas and to delete the names of Acacius and others from the diptychs. On Mar 28, 519 CE, the end of the Acacian schism and the reunion were solemnly celebrated in the cathedral of Constantinople.

Though officially condemned in the Chalcedonian churches, Acacius remains a saint in eastern Orthodoxy, as he succeeded in reconciling opponents and supporters of the Council of Chalcedon in the East. He is commemorated in the Coptic Orthodox Church on Nov 26, which is 30th Hatour in the Coptic Calendar.

Bibliography

Bacht, H., "Die Rolle des orientalischen Mönchtums in den kirchlichen Auseinandersetzungen um Chalkedon (431–519)," in: A. Grillmeier & H. Bacht, eds., *Das Konzil von Chalkedon: Geschichte und Gegenwart*, vol. II, Würzburg 1962, 193–314.

Beck, H.-G., "Die frühbyzantinische Kirche," in: K. Baus, ed., *Die Reichskirche nach Konstantin dem Großen*, vol. II: *Die Kirche in Ost und West von Chalkedon bis zum Frühmittelalter (451–700)*, HKG(J) 2/2, Freiburg, 1975, 3–92.

Beyschlag, K., *Grundriß der Dogmengeschichte*, vol. II: *Gott und Mensch*, part 1: *Das christologische Dogma*, Darmstadt, 1991.

Frend, W.H.C., "Eastern Attitudes to Rome during the Acacian Schism," in: W.H.C. Frend, *Town and Country in the Early Christian Centuries*, vol. XI, London, 1980, 69–81.

Gray, P.T.R., *The Defense of Chalcedon in the East (451–553)*, Leiden, 1979.

Grillmeier, A., *Christ in Christian Tradition*, vol II/1: *From Chalcedon to Justinian I*, Atlanta, 1987.

Schwartz, E., *Codex Vaticanus gr. 1431: Eine antichalkedonische Sammlung aus der Zeit Kaiser Zenos*, ABAW.PPH 30, Munich, 1927.

Schwartz, E., *Publizistische Sammlungen zum Acacianischen Schisma*, ABAW.PH, 10, Munich, 1934.

Winkler, D.W., *Koptische Kirche und Reichskirche: Altes Schisma und neuer Dialog*, IThS 48, Innsbruck, 1997.

Winkler, D.W., "Monophysitism," in: G.W. Bowersock, P. Brown & O. Grabar, eds., *Late Antiquity: A Guide to the Postclassical World*, Cambridge MA, 1999, 586–588.

DIETMAR W. WINKLER

Acedia

Acedia (from Gk ἀκηδία, through Lat. *acedia*) basically means "carelessness, indifference, torpor, apathy, listlessness, weariness, boredom, or sloth" (see also Wenzel, 1963). The Greek noun appears in the Septuagint in Isa 61:3,

> so that to those who mourn for Sion be given glory instead of ashes, oil of joy to those who mourn, a garment of glory instead of a spirit of weariness [ἀντὶ πνεύματος ἀκηδίας]. They will be called generations of righteousness, a plant of the Lord for glory. (NETS trans.)

It also appears in Ps 118(119):28: "My soul was drowsy from exhaustion [ἀπὸ ἀκηδίας]; confirm me in your words" (NETS); *Bar.* 3:1: "O Lord Almighty, God of Israel, a soul in straits and a weary spirit [πνεῦμα ἀκηδιῶν] calls out to you" (NETS); Sir 29:5: "he will pay back words of apathy [λόγους ἀκηδίας]" (NETS). The corresponding verb, ἀκηδιάζω, is also used in the Septuagint, in Pss 60(61):2; 101(102):1; 142(143):4; Sir 22:14). In patristic literature acedia designates a state of boredom, spiritual sloth, or sluggishness, lack of attention, dissatisfaction, and tedium, which is similar to depression – also with physical symptoms such as sleepiness or sickness and debility – but for which the moral subject is responsible, as a result of yielding to a temptation.

For → Evagrius of Pontus, the ascetic author of the late 4th century CE, ἀκηδία is one of the eight evil thoughts (λογισμοί, *logismoi*) that tempt the moral subject. If one yields to them, this yielding will result in sin. For Evagrius, acedia is even the most troublesome of all the *logismoi*. Indeed it pushes back the soul that is making progress in asceticism (πρακτική, *praktikê*), in other words the struggle against passions. Acedia takes away the willingness and engagement from the ascetic. In *KG*1.49, Evagrius observes that "the intellect, out of carelessness, turns its own face away from it," namely from the unity or unification, "and, due to the privation of it, gives birth to ignorance." Evagrius traces here a descending hierarchy from the "One" to the intellect or *nous* and explains how intellects fell away from an initial state of unity. This account reflects Origen's ideas on the fall of intellectual creatures from the initial unity.

It is not the original unity that is the principle of movements (a term that, in the Origenian language followed by Evagrius also in *Schol. in Eccl.* 10.1–2 on Eccl 2:11 and *Schol. in Prov.* 23.1 on Prov 2:17, means acts of will, volitions, implying choices between good and evil), but it is the will of some intellectual creatures who directed themselves elsewhere than the good, which constitutes the unity (this was essentially a unity of will rather than a unity of substance: all intellects' wills were directed toward one and the same object, God–the good). The intellect is somehow distracted away from the true good and led astray by lesser or apparent goods, which become the new objects of its deviating will. What is most important, Evagrius describes the defection of intellectual creatures from the blessed unity as a result of their "carelessness," exactly as Origen had done. Now carelessness in the Syriac version of the *Kephalaia Gnostika* either translates ἀκηδία or can be seen as a direct factor in acedia.

According to Origen, when their ardent love for God, who is Good itself, and their zeal diminish, rational creatures experience a fall, which Origen described as a ψύξις, a cooling off that transforms intellects into souls (ψυχαί – note the etymological wordplay with ψύξις). Origen explicitly mentioned neglect, the very basis of acedia, in connection with the fall in Or. *Princ.* 2.9.2: "Every intellectual being, neglecting the Good to a greater or lesser extent due to its own movements, was dragged to the opposite of the Good, that is, evil." Origen depicted those rational creatures who do not care for their own spiritual progress and salvation as careless in *Princ.* 3.5.8, and in 2.9.6 neglectfulness is said to be the cause of the fall of the rational creatures who fell; here these are opposed to those who used their free will to progress in their loving imitation of God, instead of detaching themselves from the good: "Freedom of will dragged each one either to progress by means of the imitation of God or to deficiency due to neglectfulness [*ad defectum per neglegentiam*]." Neglectfulness is so serious a fault that it can make human beings rank among irrational animals (from the moral, and not the ontological, point of view):

> Human wisdom, if it turns uncultivated and neglected due to much carelessness in life,

becomes like an irrational animal due to incompetence or neglectfulness [*per imperitiam uel per neglegentiam*] although not by nature. (*ap.* Pamp. *Ap.* 180)

Origen, intellectually minded and hard worker as he was, insisted everywhere on the gravity of neglectfulness (ἀμέλεια), lack of attention (ἀπροσεξία), and laziness (ῥαθυμία, ἀργία). This is no small fault, but is the very cause of the fall, qua opposite of the ardent love for God-the good and attachment to it. Origen's above-mentioned notion of "cooling off" is but another metaphor for the same concept. In the same passage Origen is adamant that "turning away from the better and neglecting it gave rise to the detachment from the Good." The same is stressed in Or. *Cels.* 45: those who adhere to evil are said to do so "due to neglect of the Good," δι' ἀμέλειαν τοῦ καλοῦ.

Against this background it is not surprising that Origen indicates laziness as the very factor that opens up the door to the action of demons on one's soul in *Princ.* 3.3.6, which proved immensely influential on Evagrius. Evagrius himself, in *KG* 3.28, described the soul as an intellect that, due to neglectfulness, has fallen down from unity and, because of its lack of vigilance, has descended to the level of the *praktikē*, in other words from the level of intellect to that of soul that must struggle with passions. Directly related to neglectfulness is acedia, one of the aforementioned "evil thoughts" or *logismoi* that Evagrius systematized (see e.g. Sorabji, 2000; Ramelli, 2003; Corrigan, 2009, ch. 5; Tobon, 2023, ch. 2; also Augst, 1990; Joest, 1993; Maier, 1994, and Bunge, 1995; for developments Wenzel, 2012). The gravity of this sin was pointed out to Evagrius by Origen. Consistently with this set of ideas, Evagrius, like Origen, places a great emphasis on hard work, effort, and πόνος, which he identifies especially with ascetic labor (see e.g. Eva. Pon. *Eul.* 32.34).

John Chrysostom associated acedia with ἀθυμία, inaction, lassitude, despondency, discouragement, dejection, and disheartenment, in his Letters to Olympia and Stagyrius, and ῥαθυμία, slothfulness, which keeps humans from virtue – just as according to Origen. Disheartenment, sadness and sorrow (ἀθυμία, λύπη) are "the will of the devil" (*Ep.*9.4b SChr 13bis.232).

Cassian, who followed in the footsteps of Origen and Evagrius (whatever his exact identity, the traditional one being doubted by Tzamalikos, 2012; 2012a, and reinstated by others scholars), studied acedia in depth. In *Con.* 5.9 Cassian describes acedia as affecting especially monastics, and particularly hermits: dejection and acedia generally arise without any external provocation; they often harass solitaries, and those who have settled themselves in the desert without any intercourse with other people. What is more, Cassian devoted the whole tenth book of his *Institutiones* to acedia, not in general, but specifically in ascetics:

> Our sixth combat is with what the Greeks call ἀκηδία, which we may term weariness or distress of heart. This is akin to dejection, and is especially trying to solitaries, and a dangerous and frequent foe to dwellers in the desert; and especially disturbing to a monk about the sixth hour [i.e. noon], like some fever which seizes him at stated times, bringing the burning heat of its attacks on the sick man at usual and regular hours. Lastly, there are some of the elders who declare that this is the 'midday demon' spoken of in the ninetieth Psalm. (*Inst.*10.1; see Ps 90(91):6 LXX: δαιμονίου μεσημβρινοῦ).

Cassian follows Evagrius' reflections on the noonday demon (Clark, forthcoming). In *Inst.* 10.2 Cassian explains how acedia produces in the monk dislike of the place, disgust with the cell, and disdain and contempt of the brothers who dwell with him or at a little distance. It also makes the monk lazy and sluggish about work. The monk is unable to stay in his cell, or to read, and he often groans because he can do no good while he stays there, and complains and sighs because he can bear no spiritual fruit in ascetic life. He thinks that monasteries far away are better than his own, and the like. At 11 am or at noon he feels exhausted and extremely hungry. In general, he is restless, prey of "a kind of unreasonable confusion of mind, like some foul darkness." The effect of such attacks of acedia over the monk are well described in *Inst.* 10.3: the monk sinks into slumber, or else continually leaves his cell to visit some brothers, abandoning "meditation and contemplation of that divine purity which excels all things, and which can only be gained by silence and continually remaining in the cell, and by reflection." Cassian quotes the above-mentioned Ps 118(119):28 as to how acedia puts the soul to sleep, while it should be active in the contemplation of the virtues (*Inst.* 10.4).

The person attacked by the *logismos* of acedia, then, "should hasten to expel this disease also from the recesses of his soul," so as to neither fall into slumber and stay in his cell idle and lazy, without making any spiritual progress, nor be driven out from the monastic cloister in search of company and distraction (*Inst.* 10.5–6). Cassian also cites 1 Thess 4:9, 10 as a remedy to acedia: to abound more in charity, be quiet, and work with their own hands, without coveting other people's goods. Cassian applies this to monks, who should remain in their cells, without being disturbed by rumors, and do their own business. Manual work is recommended as a means to avoid laziness, which opens up the door to acedia. It is also necessary for the monk to stay away from the brothers who behave disorderly (*Inst.* 10.7). Cassian sets up the example of Paul, who was not restless, and worked with his own hands, night and day (2 Thess 3:8); so he was the opposite of the monk affected with acedia (*Inst.* 10.8). Not only Paul, but also those who were with him, Silvanus and Timothy, worked with their own hands, in order to set an example of laboriousness for all, and Paul overtly declared that "if a man will not work, neither should he eat" (*Inst.* 10.9–12). Paul reproached those who did not work at all and curiously meddled around, rather recommending that, "working with silence, they would eat their own bread." Instead of stealing, Paul in Eph 4:28 recommended work, so as to have something to give to those in need, and, according to Cassian, he associated himself with Prisca and Aquila, because they were tentmakers like him (Acts 18:1–3; *Inst.*10.13–14.17–20).

Cassian recounts, with disapproval, that a monk affected by acedia tried to persuade others to leave the monastery (*Inst.* 10.20), and collects quotations from biblical writings attributed to Solomon (e.g. Prov 31:25; 15:19; 13:4) and, again, from Paul against acedia or, more properly, against idleness and sluggishness, which were so heavily blemished already by Origen (*Inst.* 10.21). Cassian sets as an example the desert fathers in Egypt, his contemporaries, who

never allow monks, and especially the younger ones, to be idle, estimating the purpose of their hearts and their growth in patience ... Therefore, this saying has been handed down from the old fathers in Egypt: that a monk who works is attacked by but one devil; but an idler is tormented by countless spirits. (*Inst.* 10.22–23)

This praise of Egyptian monks as immune to acedia through hard work is common to other patristic authors from the 4th and 5th centuries. Jerome, in a letter to Rusticus (Jer. *Ep.* 125), states that no one is received in a monastery in Egypt unless he will work, and that this rule is made for the good of the soul rather than for the sake of providing food. Sozomen (*Hist. eccl.* 6.28) attests that Serapion and his followers, who lived in the desert close to Arsinöe,

> live on humility by their diligence in work; and they not only do not allow them to receive anything from another to supply their own wants, but further, they not merely refresh pilgrims and brethren who come to visit them by means of their labors, but actually collect an enormous store of provisions and food, and distribute it in the parts of Libya which suffer from famine and barrenness, and also in the cities, to those who are pining away in the squalor of prison; as they believe that by such an offering of the fruit of their hands they offer a reasonable and true sacrifice to the Lord.

This is also one of the ways in which Patristic ascetics contributed to social justice (Ramelli 2016). Cassian offers Abba Paul as an example of repelling acedia in *Inst.* 10.24. Paul lived in the Porphyrian Desert and worked even if he had no need to do so, because he was supported by fruits. But he collected the leaves of the palms there, and when his cave had been filled with a whole year's work, each year he would burn everything with fire,

> thus proving that without manual labor a monk cannot stop in a place nor rise to the heights of perfection: so that, although the need for food did not require this to be done, yet he performed it simply for the sake of purifying his heart, and strengthening his thoughts, and persisting in his cell, and gaining a victory over acedia and driving it away.

Finally, Cassian reports his own experience of battling acedia in *Inst.* 10.25. When he was beginning his stay in the desert, and had said to Abba Moses, the chief of all the saints, that he had been terribly troubled the day before by an attack of acedia, and that he could only be freed from it by running at once to Abba Paul, Abba Moses replied that actually Cassian had not freed himself from that attack, but rather had given himself up to it

> as its slave and subject. For the enemy will henceforth attack you more strongly as a deserter and runaway, since it has seen that you fled at once when overcome in the conflict: unless on a second occasion when you join battle with it you make up your mind not to dispel its attacks and heats for the moment by deserting your cell, or by the inactivity of sleep, but rather learn to triumph over it by endurance and conflict.

Cassian concluded that this episode taught that a fit of acedia should not be evaded by running away from it, but should be overcome by resisting it.

Acedia continued to worry monastic authors. According to the *Regula Benedicti* or *Rule of Saint Benedict*, a monk affected by acedia "should be reproved a first and a second time. If he does not amend, he must be subjected to the punishment of the rule, so that the others may fear this." This is also why in the same rule, 48, it is stated that "since idleness is the enemy of the soul, the brothers are to be employed alternately in manual labor and pious reading."

Historiography

S. Wenzel (1963; 2012) has given a strong impulse to studies on acedia. I. Ramelli (2015) has pointed out the importance of acedia within Evagrius' doctrine of the *logismoi* (studied, e.g. by August, 1990; Joest, 1993/2004; Maier, 1994; Bunge, 1995; Sorabji, 2000; Ramelli, 2003; Corrigan, 2009, ch. 5; Tobon, 2023; Clark, forthcoming) and its dependence on Origen's repeated attacks on neglectfulness and laziness and their moral and metaphysical consequences. This is one of the many points in which Evagrius' thought (metaphysical, spiritual, and ascetic) derives from Origen, as well as from Gregory of Nyssa, in addition

to the other Cappadocians (Ramelli, 2017). Further research is needed in this direction, as well as on the influence of Greek philosophical ethics on Christian thought.

Bibliography

Augst, R., *Lebensverwirklichung und christlicher Glaube, Acedia, religiöse Gleichgültigkeit als Problem der Spiritualität bei Evagrius Ponticus*, Frankfurt, 1990.

Bunge, G., *Akedia: Die geistliche Lehre des Evagrios Pontikos vom Überdruss*, 5th ed., Würzburg, 1995.

Clark, S. "Evagrius and the Noonday Demon," in *Human and Divine Nous from Ancient to Renaissance Philosophy and Religion: Key Themes, Intersections, and Developments*, forthcoming.

Chryssavgis, J. *In the Heart of the Desert. The Spirituality of the Desert Fathers and Mothers*, Bloomington, 2003.

Corrigan, K., *Evagrius and Gregory: Mind, Soul and Body in the 4th Century*, Farnham, 2009.

Edwards, R.G.T., "Healing Despondency with Biblical Narrative in John Chrysostom's Letters to Olympias," *JECS* 28.2, 2020, 203–231.

Joest, C., "Die Bedeutung von Akedia und Apatheia bei Evagrios Pontikos," *StMon* 35, 1993, 7–53; ET: *AmBR* 55, 2004, 121–50, 273–307.

Leyerle, B. "Animal Passions: Chrysostom's Use of Animal Imagery," *SP* 83, 2017, 185–202.

Maier, B., "Ἀπάθεια bei den Stoikern und ἀκηδία bei Evagrios Pontikos: Ein Ideal und die Kehrseite seiner Realität," *OrChr* 78, 1994, 230–249.

Ramelli, I., "Review of Sorabji, 2000," *Aevum* 77/1, 2003, 217–221.

Ramelli, I., "Harmony between *arkhē* and *telos* in Patristic Platonism and the Imagery of Astronomical Harmony Applied to the Apokatastasis Theory," *IJPlT* 7, 2013, 1–49.

Ramelli, I., *The Christian Doctrine of Apokatastasis: A Critical Assessment from the New Testament to Eriugena*, Leiden, 2013.

Ramelli, I., *Evagrius' Kephalaia Gnostika: Propositions on Knowledge*, Leiden, 2015.

Ramelli, I., *Social Justice and the Legitimacy of Slavery: The Role of Philosophical Asceticism from Ancient Judaism to Late Antiquity*, Oxford, 2016.

Ramelli, I., "Gregory Nyssen's and Evagrius's Biographical and Theological Relations: Origen's Heritage and Neoplatonism," in: I. Ramelli, ed., *Evagrius between Origen, the Cappadocians, and Neoplatonism*, Leuven, 2017, 165–231.

Ramelli, I., "Origen on the Unity of Soul and Body in the Earthly Life and Afterwards and His Impact," in: J. Ulrich, A. Usachev & S. Bhayro, eds., *The Unity of Soul and Body in Patristic and Byzantine Thought*, Leiden-Paderborn, 2021, 38–77.

Ramelli, I., "Matter in the Dialogue of Adamantius: Origen's Heritage and Hylomorphism," in: J. Zachhuber & A. Schiavoni, eds., *Platonism and Christianity in Late Ancient Cosmology: God, Soul, Matter*, Ancient Philosophy and Religion 9, Leiden, 2022, 74–124.

Ramelli, I., "Origen, Evagrius, and Dionysius," in M. Edwards, D. Pallis & G. Steiris, eds., *Oxford Handbook of Dionysius the Areopagite*, Oxford, 2022, 94–108.

Sorabji, R., *Emotion and Peace of Mind: From Stoic Agitation to Christian Temptation*, Oxford, 2000.

Tobon, M., *Apatheia in the Teachings of Evagrius Ponticus: The Health of the Soul*, London, 2023.

Tzamalikos, P., *The Real Cassian Revisited: Monastic Life, Greek Paideia, and Origenism in the 6th Century*, Leiden, 2012.

Tzamalikos, P., *A Newly Discovered Greek Father, Cassian the Sabaite Eclipsed by John Cassian of Marseilles*, Leiden, 2012a.

Wenzel, S., "Ακηδία. Additions to Lampe's *Patristic Greek Lexicon*," *VigChr* 17, 1963, 173–176.

Wenzel, S., *The Sin of Sloth: Acedia in Medieval Thought and Literature*, Chapel Hill, 2012.

Wright, J. "Between Despondency and the Demon," *JLA* 8.2, 2015, 352–367.

ILARIA L.E. RAMELLI

Acheiropoietai

Acheiropoietai (ἀχειροποίηται) are images "not made by (human) hand," a category first attested in the 6th century CE. The term, however, is more ancient: it was used by Paul in 2 Cor 5:1 in reference to Christ's risen body, and shortly afterward it appears again in Mark 14:58 and Col 2:11. Thus, acheiropoietai are especially images that are considered to be direct impressions of Christ's face: the Mandylion of Edessa; the Veronica of Rome; the Camuliana image, which Heraclius and other emperors carried into battle for protection and victory; the veil of Manoppello; and the Turin shroud, which besides the face reproduces also the whole body, front and back (see below). Other such images represent the Virgin → Mary, for example the Hodegetria and the later Virgin of Guadalupe (1531, Mexico). By the end of the 6th century CE, both the Mandylion and the image of Camuliana in Cappadocia (which Pfeiffer, 2000, identifies with both the Roman Veronica and the Manoppello Veil, as a single object known under different names) were famous; especially the Mandylion was adduced against iconoclasm.

The Mandylion (μανδύλιον, "towel") was preserved in Edessa and connected with the legend of → Addai. It showed the head of Christ and his beard, as is clear from its reproductions. The earliest extant of these is a 10th-century CE icon at Saint Catherine's monastery, Sinai, which refers to the Abgar-Addai story. → Eusebius of Caesarea's account of this story does not mention the portrait of Jesus, probably due to Eusebius' own aversion to representations of the divinity of Christ. But shortly after Eusebius, *Per. Eg.* 19.6, from 381/384 CE, seems to offer the first allusion to the Mandylion. Egeria, probably a Spanish abbess, does not report having seen the Mandylion herself in her pilgrimage to Edessa, perhaps because it was still kept in the ancient royal palace of Edessa and was not visible to the public, or because it was hidden (according to the legend: see below), but the words that the local bishop addressed to her clearly allude to the Edessan image:

> Here is (the portrait of) King Abgar, who, before seeing the Lord, believed that he was truly the Son of God" [*Ecce rex Aggarus, qui antequam videret Dominum credidit ei, quia esset vere filius Dei*].

Abgar, in the Abgar legend, believed in Jesus on the basis of his envoys' reports concerning his miracles, before seeing his portrait. The bishop of Edessa knew that Abgar never saw Jesus in person on earth, but he did see him in the image that, as the story goes, was brought to him. Thus, his words "*before seeing the Lord*" (and not, "*without* seeing the Lord") obviously allude to the portrait. In the second half of the 4th century CE, in Egeria's day, just as at the time of the redaction of the *Doctrina Addai* in the early 5th century CE, the image was still in the old royal palace, long after the extinction of the dynasty of the → Abgarids. In the late 6th–7th centuries CE, at the time of the *Acts of Mari*, the Mandylion was in the Great Church of Edessa. Obviously because of the association of the image of Christ with Edessa already in the late 4th century CE – as suggested by the *Peregrinatio Egeriae* – Macarius of Magnesia at the same epoch described Berenice/Veronica, traditionally associated with Christ's Calvary image, as a woman from Edessa (Mac. *Apoc.* 1). This indicates that at least a part of the tradition knew that the Edessa image represented a suffering Christ.

In the early 5th century CE, the *Doctrina Addai* instead identifies the Edessa image as a portrait painted before Jesus' passion by Hannan, Abgar's archivist and emissary. The portrait, says the *Doctrina*, was brought to Edessa and kept in one of the royal palaces (13). Moses of Chorene, the 5th-century CE Armenian historian, whose Abgar narrative is parallel to that of the *Doctrina Addai* and seems to be based on it and on Eusebius (translated into Armenian), also includes this story of the image of Christ and adds that it was still in Edessa in his day, or in the day of his source: "The image of the Savior, which is still found today in the city of Edessa" (Mos. *PH* 2.32). The church historian Evagrius Scholasticus, about 593 CE, reports that an image of Christ, here "divinely made" (θεότευκτος), miraculously defended Edessa against the Persians in Chosroes' siege of 544 CE. The historian → Procopius of Caesarea attributed the same miraculous protection of Edessa in 544 CE to Jesus' letter to Abgar and his promise that Edessa would never be conquered by enemies. This is Evagrius' account:

> They had reached a point in which they did not know what to do. Then they brought out the image produced by God, not made by human hands [τὴν θεότευκτον εἰκόνα, ἣν ἀνθρώπου μὲν χεῖρες οὐκ εἰργάσαντο]. Christ-God had sent it to Abgar, because Abgar wished to see him. (Eva. Schol. *Hist. eccl.* 4.27)

Note this last explanation, which throws further light onto the earlier *Peregrinatio Egeriae*'s remark that Abgar believed "before seeing Christ," namely in his image. After the failed siege, Justinian devoted a special chapel in Edessa's Great Church to the image, which was kept there from then on. A Syriac hymn of praise was composed on the image, which was translated into Latin by Smera from Constantinople in the 9th century CE.

In the 6th–7th centuries CE, the first sections of the Syriac *Acts of Mar Mari* offer a short version of the story narrated in the *Doctrina* concerning Abgar. In section 3, the detail of the image is prominent: Abgar, after receiving Jesus' letter, sent painters to Jerusalem to make a portrait of Jesus, but they were unable to reproduce his features ("the portrait of the humanity of our venerable Lord"). Jesus then pressed

a cloth (in Syr. *seddona*, from Gk σινδών) on his face and gave them his portrait to bring to their king. It was put in the church of Edessa and remained there "until today." The latter is the same assertion that is found in Moses of Chorene's account. Thus, in the *Acts of Mari* what was a portrait of Jesus becomes an acheiropoieta image proper, and its location in the church of Edessa reflects the Mandylion's historical location after Justinian.

In the *Acts of Thaddeus*, also from the 7th century CE, the Addai story is applied to Thaddeus, and, differently from what happens in Eusebius, the *Doctrina*, and Moses, the healing of Abgar is due to the very portrait of Christ on a σινδών. This is described as a τετράδιπλον, which was brought to Abgar by Ananias before Thaddeus' arrival. Thus, by the time of the redaction of these Acts it was known that the image of Christ preserved in Edessa was on a fabric "folded four times/fourfold." This fits very well with the hypothesis that the Edessa picture was a full sheet folded up four times, so that only the face of the person portrayed thereon was visible. The face area was therefore on a fraction of the full sheet, which in its size would be therefore comparable with that of the Turin shroud.

John of Damascus in the 8th century CE repeated the Abgar legend in terms close to those of Evagrius and attested that the image was still preserved in Edessa. He called it ἱμάτιον, ῥάκος, and ἀπεικόνισμα on which Jesus impressed his traits (Dam. *Fid.* 4.281; PG 94.1173; *Imag.* 1.320A; PG 94.1261.B). Under 787 CE, in the documents concerning the Second Council of Nicaea (*Mansi*, vol. XIII, 192C), Leo Anagnostes from Constantinople was quoted, who saw in Edessa this "holy acheiropoieta [τὴν ἱερὰν τὴν ἀχειροποίητον εἰκόνα], honored and venerated by believers." The noun μανδύλιον was used when the image was transported from Edessa to Constantinople in 944 CE. The Syriac parallel term was *mandili*. In a passage in the *Chronicle to the Year 1234*, which probably derives from the early 8th-century CE Chronicle of Dionysius of Tel-Mahre or *Chronicle of Zuqnîn*, the cloth is described as a *šušeppa*, "veil." In 944 CE, General John Kourkouas besieged Edessa, which had been under the Arabs from 637 CE, and obtained the Mandylion in exchange for its safety. The image was thus transported in a triumphal procession to the

Pharos Chapel in the imperial palace, and presented to Emperor Romanus I Lecapenus. Its arrival is described in the *Narratio de imagine Edessena* (*Story of the Image of Edessa*; PG 113.421–54) attributed to Constantine VII Porphyrogenitus, a successor of Romanus. The translation was celebrated annually on Aug 16 from then on, and a copy of the Mandylion, the painted "holy face of Genoa" in the Church of San Bartolomeo degli Armeni, has the translation represented among the scenes on its frame (and in the most ancient layer of painting the face had its eyes closed, as in the Turin shroud).

I. Ramelli (1999a) demonstrated that the Abgar account in the *Narratio* – whose Greek title calls the Mandylion ἀχειροποίητος θεία εἰκών ("divine image not made by human hand") – includes some interesting details that are unknown from other sources and likely historical, such as the friendship between Abgar and the prefect of Egypt. In this narrative an alternative explanation of the origin of the Mandylion appears, which reminds one of Macarius' association of Edessa with the image of the suffering Christ. According to the *Narratio* (11–13; PG 113.434.A–435.A) the image of Christ was impressed on a cloth through his blood in Gethsemane, and it was brought to Edessa, not by Abgar's emissary-painter Hannan before the death of Jesus, but by his apostle Thaddeus after Jesus' death and resurrection. The story was incorporated into the μηνολόγιον of Symeon Metaphrastes and, interestingly, not only associates the Mandylion with Christ's passion, but also explains that in Constantinople it was laid to sit on the imperial throne, possibly unfolded (*Narratio* 30; PG 113.452.C). This would be easily explained if originally it had been a long funeral shroud. Also Germanus of Constantinople, speaking of the translation of the Mandylion to Constantinople, called it σουδάριον, thus referring to its sepulchral nature (Dobschütz, 1899, 135).

A 10th-century CE codex, Vossianus Latinus Q 69, found by G. Zaninotto in the Vatican Library (codex 5696, fol. 35), contains an 8th/9th-century CE account saying that an imprint of Christ's whole body was left on a canvas kept in a church in Edessa: it quotes Smera from Constantinople: according to the story it recounts, King Abgar wanted to see Jesus, who, instead of going to Edessa, promised to send him

a linen on which you will be able to see not only the image of my face, but the full length, miraculously transposed, of the whole of my body" [*linteum, in quo non solum faciei mee figuram, sed totius corporis mei figuram cernere poteris statum divinitus transformatum*]. (Biblioteca Apostolica Vaticana, Codex 5696, fol. 350)

Jesus "lay down with the whole of his body on a linen that had been whitened like snow" (*supra quodam linteum ad instar nivis candidatum toto se corpore stravit*). Thus, on the linen there remained impressed both "the glorious image of the Lord's face and the most noble length/state of the whole of his body" (*dominice faciei figura gloriosa et totius corporis nobilissimus status*). The text goes on to detail that this linen, which despite its venerable age remained incorrupt, "was kept in the city of Edessa in Mesopotamia of Syria, stored in the Great Church." But on some specific feasts dedicated to the Savior, the linen was "extracted from its golden box with hymns, psalms, and special canticles, and venerated by all people with great reverence and honour." Smera therefore confirms that the Mandylion of Edessa could be unfolded and actually was unfolded every year – at least for a certain period in the 8th century CE – and that it contained a full figure impressed on it, like the Turin shroud. Smera's statement that the image of Edessa included not only Christ's face, but his whole body, is found again, repeated almost literally, in Gervase of Tilbury's *Otia imperialia* (111).

Pseudo-Simeon Metaphrastes in the 10th century CE reports that on its arrival in Constantinople the emperor's children had a hard time distinguishing the face on the Mandylion, the same as anybody has looking at the Turin shroud. The Edessan acheiropoieta is still mentioned in the Greek *Epistula Abgari* (11th cent. CE?) and later documents. It may have been one of the relics purchased by King Louis IX in 1247 and taken to the Sainte-Chapelle in Paris. Or else, as an increasing number of clues suggests, the Mandylion might be, in its unfolded form, the Turin shroud (Ramelli, 1999b; forthcoming). This shroud, now the property of the Roman Catholic Church and kept in the Turin Cathedral in Italy, after being held for centuries in France and Piedmont as the property of the Savoy family, is a linen cloth with the full image of a man killed by crucifixion impressed on it, back and front. The image, formed by the oxidation of the most superficial linen fibrils, is faint, but well visible as a photographic negative. Besides the likeness between the head of the shrouded man and the various extant copies of the Mandylion, and the fact that the history of the Turin shroud begins when that of the Mandylion ends, another of the many elements that suggest the identity between the two acheiropoietai, is the pollens of plants typical of the Edessan area found on the Turin shroud. Moreover, the initial description of the Mandylion in the aforementioned *Narratio* concerning its translation to Constantinople, "the face left its shape on the linen texture from a humid vapor, without colors, without any art of painting" (ἐξ ἰκμάδος ὑγρᾶς, δίχα χρωμάτων καὶ τέχνης τῆς γραφικῆς ἐναπεμορφώθη), perfectly corresponds to the image on the linen shroud: monochromatic, without colors, without traces of pigments, similar to an exhalation.

Veronica's veil, the Volto Santo ("Holy Face"), is now in the Vatican, but while in the late Middle Ages it was perfectly visible, very famous, and the object of pilgrimage, today no image is discernible on it. This raises suspicions that the original image disappeared from the Vatican, probably in the 16th century. According to tradition, Veronica (from *veraicona*, "true image") followed Jesus on his way to Calvary and wiped the sweat off his face with her veil. Jesus' image was left imprinted there. In a late version of the *Acts Pil.* 7, Veronica is identified the woman with a blood flux in Matt 9:20–22 (Tischendorf, 1876, 239) and is said to have healed Emperor Tiberius' illness with the image of Christ. The Vatican Veronica seems to have been in Rome since the 8th century CE and was translated by Boniface VIII to Saint Peter's Basilica in 1297.

H. Pfeiffer (2000) in 1999 identified the lost Vatican Veronica with the veil of Manoppello, now preserved in a church of the Capuchin monastery in the small village of Manoppello, in central Italy, not very far from Rome, where it had been in the custody of the Capuchin Friars since 1660. The image is mentioned by Donato da Bomba in his *Relatione historica (Historical Relation)*, tracing back to 1640. Recent studies by B.P. Schlömer and others have revealed a perfect superimposability of the Manoppello face with that on the Turin shroud (Bianchi, 2009). The veil's size is now 17. 5 × 24 cm, but originally – as results from Bomba's *Relatione historica* – it was bigger, and it has an extremely fine texture. The image appears in a specular way on both sides of the veil, front and back, with the same intensity of color. The face is asymmetric, as in the Turin shroud, with one cheek more swollen than the other; there are stains, apparently of blood, close to the mouth and the nose, which also looks swollen. H. Pfeiffer (2000) hypothesizes that the Manoppello veil, formerly the Roman Veronica, and formerly the Camuliana image, was the σουδάριον placed on the face of Jesus for burial, while the Turin shroud, formerly the Mandylion (when it was folded up four times), was the full shroud that was placed over the σουδάριον to cover the whole corpse of Jesus, front and back.

Historiography

Research into the Acheiropoietai is centuries old, but their scientific study is relatively recent. The first systematic study regarded images of Christ, including the Mandylion of Edessa (Dobschütz, 1899). R. Warland (1993) offered a *status quaestionis*, and H. Pfeiffer (2000) identified the lost Vatican Veronica with the veil of Manoppello (see also Bianchi, 2009). The Mandylion of Edessa has been investigated historically by a number of scholars after E. von Dobschütz, especially M. Illert (2007) and I. Ramelli (1999a; 2015; 2016), who has traced the various developments of the legend throughout a range of texts, particularly Greek, Latin, Syriac, and Armenian. K. Dietz, C. Hannick and C. Lutzka (2016) provide a recent continuation to the groundbreaking study by E. von Dobschütz (1899), with many important new discoveries and arguments.

Bibliography

Bianchi, L., "The Veil of Manoppello," *30Days* 4, 2009, 75–81.

Brock, S.P., "Review of I. Ramelli, *Atti di Mar Mari* (Brescia, 2008)," *AN* 7, 2008, 123–130; http://www.ancient narrative.com; http://www.thefreelibrary.com/I.+Ramelli :+Atti+di+Mar+Mari.-a0197420329.

Cormack, R., *Writing in Gold: Byzantine Society and Its Icons*, London, 1985.

Devos, P., "Égérie à Édesse: St. Thomas l'apôtre: Le roi Abgar," *AnBoll* 85, 1967, 381–400.

Dietz, K., C. Hannick & C. Lutzka, *Das Christusbild: Zu Herkunft und Entwicklung in Ost und West*, Würzburg, 2016.

Dobschütz, E. von, *Christusbilder: Untersuchungen zur Christlichen Legende*, Leipzig, 1899.

Fiey, J.M., "Image d'Edesse ou Linceul de Turin," *RHE* 82, 1987, 271–277.

Florowsky, G., "Origen, Eusebius and the Iconoclastic Controversy," *ChH* 19, 1950, 3–22.

Frale, B., *La sindone di Gesù Nazareno*, Bologna, 2009.

Guscin, M., ed., *Recent Studies on the Image of Edessa – Iconography, History and Theology*, Newcastle, 2022.

Illert, M., trans., *Doctrina Addai/De imagine Edessena*, Turnhout, 2007.

Perkins, J., "Review of I. Ramelli, Atti di Mar Mari (Brescia, 2008)," *Aevum* 83, 2009, 269–271.

Pfeiffer, H., "The Veronica is at Manoppello," *30Days* 5, 2000, 78–79.

Ramelli, I., "Edessa e i Romani tra Augusto e i Severi," *Aevum* 73, 1999a, 107–143.

Ramelli, I., "Dal Mandylion di Edessa alla Sindone? Alcune note sulle testimonianze antiche," *Ilu* 4, 1999b, 173–193.

Ramelli, I., "Abgar Ukkama e Abgar il Grande alla luce di recenti apporti storiografici," *Aevum* 78, 2004, 103–108.

Ramelli, I., "Review of Illert, 2007," *ReBL*, 2009a; http://www.bookreviews.org/BookDetail.asp?TitleId=6797.

Ramelli, I., *Possible Historical Traces in the Doctrina Addai?* Piscataway, 2009b.

Ramelli, I., "Review of Frale, 2009c," *Aevum* 86, 2012, 39–42.

Ramelli, I., "The Addai-Abgar Narrative: Its Development Through Literary Genres and Religious Agendas," in: I. Ramelli & J. Perkins, eds., *Early Christian and Jewish Narrative: The Role of Religion in Shaping Narrative Forms*, Tübingen, 2015, 205–245.

Ramelli, I., "Sindōn-Mandylion-Turin Shroud? The Long Development of the Abgar Legend and the Emergence of the Image of Jesus," in: K. Dietz, C. Hannick, C. Lutzka & E. Maier, eds., *Das Christusbild: Zu Herkunft und Entwicklung in Ost und West – The Image of Christ: Provenance and Origin in East and West*, Würzburg, 2016, 499–535.

Schiller, G., *Ikonographie der Christlichen Kunst*, Gütersloh, 1976.

Warland, R., "Acheiropoieta," in: *LThK*, vol. I, Freiburg, 1993, 112–113.

Weitzmann, K., "The *Mandylion* and Constantine Porphyrogennetos," *CAr* 11, 1960, 163–184.

ILARIA L.E. RAMELLI

Acilius Glabrio

Manius Acilius Glabrio was a Roman consul in the year 91 CE, together with the later emperor → Trajan

(Espérandieu, 1929, inscription no. 350; Dessau, 1916, inscription no. 9245). His family was of plebeian origin, but several family members held high positions (Leclercq, 1907, 2854–2860). According to the poet Juvenal, "Acilius (the elder) [...] and his young relative (the later consul)" were part of the council of the emperor Domitian (Juv. *Sat.* 4.94–95). It has been suggested that the father (or grandfather) was Manius Acilius Aviola, the consul of 54 CE (Syme, 1970, 98; Ferguson, 1979, 166n94), but this cannot be substantiated. Some time after his consulship, Acilius Glabrio was put to death by Domitian (Juv. *Sat.* 4.95–96; Suet. *Dom.* 10.2; Dio *Hist. rom.* 67.14.3).

1. A Christian Martyr?

It has been assumed that Acilius Glabrio was a Christian martyr (see already Baronius, 1601, 936–937 [anno 94, no. 1]; and more recently Ramelli, 2001, passim). A first argument that has been used is that the main literary sources that refer to Acilius Glabrio's death would imply that he was accused of being a Christian. However, most of these sources do not say anything about Acilius Glabrio's religion. According to Juvenal, the death of Acilius the younger had to do with Domitian's suspicions of the nobility ("It has long been a miracle to survive to old age among the nobility") and with the fact that Acilius had been successful as a gladiator in fighting with bears at the emperor's Alban arena (Juv. *Sat.* 4.96–97, 99–101). Suetonius stated that Domitian

> put to death many senators, including several (ex-)consuls; among them [...] Acilius Glabrio while he was in exile – these for allegedly having subversive plans, the others on any charge, however trivial. (Suet. *Dom.* 10.2)

Dio Cassius wrote that the consul roused the emperor's "jealousy" because he managed to kill a lion in the emperor's Alban arena at the Juvenalia (Dio *Hist. rom.* 67.14.3). Only Dio hinted (much later than Juvenal and Suetonius) at Acilius Glabrio's religion: he linked him with people who were charged with "atheism" (ἀθεότης) and inclinations to "Jewish customs" (τὰ τῶν Ἰουδαίων ἤθη; *Hist. rom.* 67.14.2).

None of these sources proves that Acilius Glabrio was a Christian. Suetonius does not seem to refer to Christians (*pace* Leclercq, 1924, 1272) but to political opponents (Sordi, 1983, 50). And Dio may well mean Jewish sympathizers rather than Christians (Smallwood, 1981, 382). All three sources suggest that Acilius Glabrio was a victim of Domitian's suspicions (Cross & Livingstone, 1997, 679). The reliability of the accounts is disputable, because they intend to denigrate the emperor (Courtney, 1980, 218; Braund, 2004, 194–195; Pagán, 2012, 114; Murison, 1999, 26, 261) by suggesting that he was paranoid (fearing conspiracies, sects, and skilled fighters). Furthermore, in early Christian writings, Acilius Glabrio is not referred to as a martyr. Finally, it is questionable whether an anti-Christian → persecution under Domitian ever took place.

A second argument that has been used to assert that Acilius Glabrio was a Christian martyr (→ Martyrs) is based on archeological evidence. With the discovery in 1888 of the so-called hypogeum of the Acilii in the catacomb of Priscilla in Rome, it was claimed that some of Acilius Glabrio's family members died as Christians (De Rossi, 1888–1889, passim; Wilpert, 1888, 295–297; Leclercq, 1907, 2858). However, the crypt dates from the late 2nd century CE at the earliest (Jonckheere, 2006, 283). For this early period, there is no Christian evidence in the crypt (Styger, 1933, 103–104; Jonckheere, 2006, 283; Brink & Green, 2008, 188n21). The earliest inscriptions attesting to persons named Acilius were not found in situ but in the material that was used in later times to fill up the corridors of this catacomb region, and most likely come from the burial place above the ground (Styger, 1933, 109–111). These inscriptions cannot be taken as Christian (e.g. CIL 6.31679–31681); the idea that they are "crypto-Christian" (Kaufmann, 1917, 102; Sordi, 1983, 53; Ramelli, 2001, 390n6) is unfounded. The earliest Christian Acilii inscriptions date from the 3rd or 4th century CE (Lampe, 2003, 35; Jonckheere, 2006, 282). These inscriptions do not prove that the (ex-)consul was a Christian (Saxer, 1983, 36; *pace* Highet, 1954, 260). The claim that Acilius Glabrio was a Christian martyr cannot be proved or refuted (Griffith, 1969, 140).

Historiography

The earliest known historiography of Manius Acilius Glabrio is found in *The Twelve Caesars* written in the 2nd century CE by the Roman historian → Suetonius, who mentions Acilius Glabrio as one of the (ex-)consuls who had been executed under emperor Domitian (Suet. *Dom.* 10.2). The first historian commenting on Acilius Glabrio's religion is Dio Cassius in the 3rd century CE, who links him with people who had been charged with "atheism" and inclinations to "Jewish customs" (Dio *Hist. rom.* 67.14.2). Some historians have interpreted this charge as evidence that Acilius Glabrio was a Christian (see already Baronius, 1601). When at the end of the 19th century the hypogeum of the Acilii was found in the catacomb of Priscilla in Rome, some historians took this archeological evidence as proof that Acilius Glabrio was indeed a Christian (De Rossi, 1888–1889; Wilpert, 1888; but see e.g. Styger, 1933). Short introductions to Manius Acilius Glabrio that differ in their interpretations of the literary and archeological evidence include P. von Rhoden (1894), H. Leclercq (1924), V. Saxer (1983), S. Keil (1995), W. Eck (1996), A. Momigliano & B.M. Levick (1996), F.L. Cross and E.A Livingstone (1997), and I.L.E. Ramelli (2001).

Bibliography

Baronius, C., *Annales ecclesiastici*, vol. I, Mainz, ²1601.

Braund, S.M., ed., *Juvenal and Persius*, LCL 91, Cambridge MA, 2004.

Brink, L., & D. Green, eds., *Commemorating the Dead: Texts and Artifacts in Context*, Berlin, 2008.

Cary, E., & H.B. Foster, eds., *Dio's Roman History*, vol. VIII, LCL 176, London, 1925.

Courtney, E., *A Commentary on the Satires of Juvenal*, London, 1980.

Cross, F.L., & E.A. Livingstone, eds., s.v. "Glabrio, Manius Acilius," in: *ODCC*, Peabody, ³1997, 679.

De Rossi, G.B., "L'ipogeo degli Acilii Glabrioni nel cimitero di Priscilla," *BUAC* 6, 1888–1889, 15–66, 103–133.

Dessau, H., ed., *Inscriptiones latinae selectae*, vol. III/2, Berlin, 1916.

Eck, W., "Acilius Glabrio, M.," in: H. Cancik & H. Schneider, eds., *DNP*, vol. I, Leiden, 1996, 88.

Elvers, K. L. et al., "Acilius," in: H. Cancik, H. Schneider & M. Landfester, eds., *BNP*, BrillOnline, Jan 4, 2022, http://dx.doi.org/10.1163/1574-9347_bnp_e102460.

Espérandieu, M.E., ed., *Inscriptions latines de Gaule (Narbonnaise)*, vol. I, Paris, 1929.

Ferguson, J., ed., *Juvenal: The Satires*, New York, 1979.

Griffith, J.G., "Juvenal, Statius and the Flavian Establishment," *GR* n.s. 16, 1969, 134–150.

Groag, E., & A. Stein, *PIR*, vol. I, Berlin, 1933, 9–10, A 67.

Highet, G., *Juvenal the Satirist*, Oxford, 1954.

Jonckheere, R.M.G., "Christenen en de dood: Een studie naar het ontstaan van de christelijke catacomben te Rome," diss., Utrecht, 2006 (Dutch).

Jones, B.W., *Suetonius: Domitian*, London, 1996.

Jory, E.J., & D.W. Moore, eds., *CIL*, vol. VI/7/3, 1975.

Kaufmann, C.M., *Handbuch der altchristlichen Epigraphik*, Freiburg, 1917.

Keil, S., "Glabrio (*Manlius Acilius G.*)," in: M. Buchberger, W. Kasper & K. Baumgartner, eds., *LThK*, vol. IV, Freiburg, ³1995, 661.

Keresztes, P., "The Jews, the Christians and the Emperor Domitian," *VigChr* 27, 1973, 1–28.

Lampe, P., *From Paul to Valentinus: Christians at Rome in the First Two Centuries*, trans. M. Steinhauser, Minneapolis, 2003.

Leclercq, H., "Aristocratiques (Classes), VI: Les Acili Glabrions," in: F. Cabrol, ed., *DACL*, vol. IV/2, Paris, 1907, 2854–2860.

Leclercq, H., "Glabrion (Manius Acilius)," in: F. Cabrol, ed., *DACL*, vol. VI, Paris, 1924, 1259–1274.

Mooney, G.W., ed., *Caius Suetonius Tranquillus: De vita Caesarum libri VII–VIII*, New York, 1979.

Momigliano, A., & B.M. Levick, "Acilius Glabrio, Manius," in: S. Hornblower & A. Spawforth, eds., *OCD*, Oxford, ³1996, 8.

Murison, C.L., *Rebellion and Reconstruction: Galba to Domitian: An Historical Commentary on Cassius Dio's Roman History*, vol. IX: *Books 64–67 (AD 68–96)*, APSM 37, Atlanta, 1999.

Pagán, V.E., *Conspiracy Theory in Latin Literature*, Austin, 2012.

Ramelli, I.L.E., "L'omen per Acilio Glabrione e per Traiano: Una corona?" *RSCI* 55, 2001, 389–394.

Rhoden, P. von, "M.' Acilius Glabrio," in: A.F. Pauly & G. Wissowa, eds., *PRE*, vol. I, Stuttgart, 1894, 257.

Rolfe, J.C., ed., *Suetonius*, vol. II, LCL 38, Cambridge MA, 1997.

Santorelli, B., *Giovenale, Satira*, vol. IV: *Introduzione, traduzione e commento*, TK 40, Berlin, 2012.

Saxer, V., "Acilio Glabrione," in: A. di Berardino, ed., *DPAC*, vol. I, Casale Monferrato, 1983, 36.

Smallwood, E.M., *The Jews Under Roman Rule: From Pompey to Diocletian: A Study in Political Relations*, Leiden, ²1981.

Sordi, M., *The Christians and the Roman Empire*, trans. A. Bedini, London, 1983.

Styger, P., *Die römischen Katakomben: Archäologische Forschungen über den Ursprung und die Bedeutung der altchristlichen Grabstätten*, Berlin, 1933.

Syme, R., *Ten Studies in Tacitus*, Oxford, 1970.

Wilpert, J., "Sitzungsberichte der Akademie für christliche Altertumskunde," *RQ* 2, 1888, 281–297.

MARK GRUNDEKEN

Acoumeti

Acoumeti (Gk ἀκοίμητοι), or the "sleepless ones," was an epithet given to a group of monks near Constantinople based on the unique monastic rule of their founder, Alexander the Sleepless. Alexander's rule was based on strict adherence to a life of voluntary poverty (→ Wealth) and freedom from care as interpreted from the Gospels. The label "sleepless" came from the practice devised by Alexander of dividing his monks into liturgical shifts who continually performed hymns and doxology (Caner, 2002, 131). This strict ascetic discipline made the Acoumeti both controversial and highly influential, at times accused of → heresy, and at others playing major roles in theological controversies. As W.B. Sweetser has shown, the unique discipline of the Acoumeti would go on to influence western monastics in the form of the *laus perennis* ("continual prayer"; Sweetser, 2000).

Their founding abbot, Alexander the Sleepless, was most likely born on Samos or an island in the vicinity (Baguenard, 1988, 42). According to his *Vita*, Alexander was educated in Constantinople and had a successful career as a civil servant (*Vita Alex.* 5). After a short period, Alexander is said to have abandoned civil service to study the Scriptures, where he first encountered the injunction of Matt 19:21, to sell one's possessions and give them to the poor to achieve perfection (*Vita Alex.* 6).

Alexander abandoned his friends and family for the cenobitic monasteries of Syria. Here, the monk was influenced by the unique ascesis of Syrian monasticism which rejected manual labor for a life of → prayer. D. Caner has suggested that Alexander likely was influenced by the 4th-century CE Syriac → *Book of Steps*, which prescribes a life of continual prayer, and a complete rejection of manual labor, even "righteous labor," such as gardening, as a distraction (Caner, 2002, 136).

Alexander quickly drew a following of monks, whom he initially divided into 50-man choruses based on languages, including "Romans, Greeks, Syrians, and Egyptians," who would pray in shifts according to the seven apostolic hours (*Vita Alex.* 26–27; Caner, 2002, 131). With time, this was expanded into an ambitious 24-hour, ceaseless cycle of prostrations, hymns, psalter reading, and other prayers.

Alexander soon felt called to return to Roman territory to spread his ascetic calling and to minister to the poor. He forced his followers to reject → hospitality and to rely on begging, while giving the rest of their possessions and donations, beyond those which were necessary for survival, to the poor (Caner, 2002, 134). Alexander and his followers first entered Antioch, where their presence became precarious. The bishop Theodosius had them driven out of the city (Caner, 2002, 132). They then entered Constantinople, where Alexander founded a several monasteries, including one at Irenaeon which would become the most prominent.

Alexander's rule and rejection of episcopal oversight made his monks controversial within the city and led to clashes of authority. Alexander was condemned as a Messalian (→ Messalians/Euchites) based on his strict rejection of manual labor and emphasis on prayer (Caner, 2002, 137). There has been some debate concerning when this took place, but D. Caner locates the condemnation during the episcopal synod of 426 CE, perhaps giving the gathering, which had been assembled for the sole purpose of electing a → bishop, a reason to go into doctrinal concerns (Caner, 2002, 137).

Alexander's condemnation was not applied to his followers, who continued to flourish in and around Constantinople, founding several satellite communities. The most influential community remained the Irenaeon. The spiritual rigor of the Acoumeti secured many important patrons, including Pulcheria, the sister and regent of the emperor Theodosius II during his minority (Sweetser, 2000, 110).

We have little information about Alexander's immediate successor John; however, the community flourished under John's successor and fellow disciple of Alexander, Marcellus, who became abbot in 448 CE (Sweetser, 2000, 111). Under Marcellus' leadership, the sleepless ones earned a reputation for strict opposition to miaphysitism (→ Miaphysites/ Miaphysitism) and for ascetic rigor. By the time of Marcellus' ascent, the Acoumeti had gained enough clout to weather the exile of Pulcheria and the subsequent attack on her allies.

The Acoumeti used their spiritual capital to exert influence in religious affairs of the empire and were highly influential during major controversies of the 5th and 6th centuries CE. The monks vocally opposed the Henotikon of Zeno, and supported Rome during the → Acacian schism, a position which harmed their popularity in Constantinople while gaining powerful allies within the papacy (Sweetser, 2000, 124).

The influence of the Acoumeti in imperial doctrinal controversies reached its apex during the reigns of Anastasius I through Justinian I (c. 491–565 CE). Perhaps the most infamous example can be found in their role in the so-called Trisagion controversy of 511 CE (Maxwell, 2003, 72). The Trisagion prayer, "Holy God, Holy Mighty, Holy Immortal, have mercy on us," became popular during the episcopate of Proclus of Constantinople (434–446 CE), and became closely associated with Chalcedonian orthodoxy due to its use in the first session of the Council of → Chalcedon on Oct 8, 451 CE (Grillmeier, 1975, 254). Peter the Fuller, during his episcopacy in Antioch, added the phrase "who was crucified for us" to the Antiochene liturgy, which caused controversy when it was encountered in Constantinople (Maxwell, 2003, 72).

Peter had spent some time at the Acoumeti monastery in Constantinople, where he was expelled under the charge of Eutychianism (Maxwell, 2003, 73; → Eutyches). Upon his addition of the phrase "who was crucified for us," in order to further undermine Peter's reputation, the Acoumeti forged a series of letters from various bishops accusing him of patripassianism (→ Patripassians), the doctrine that God the Father suffered during the crucifixion (Grillmeier, 1975, 257; → Cross/Crucifixion). The controversy reached a head when Peter's successor, Severus, arranged for the Trisagion with the addition to be chanted in Constantinople, and when Timothy, the patriarch of Constantinople, ordered the addition of the phrase in the capital. Riots broke out as a result, and in 518 CE the addition was removed (Maxwell, 2003, 73).

The Acoumeti continued their forgery activity in opposition to the Scythian monks, who came to Constantinople in 518 or 519 CE to appeal their treatment by the bishop of Paternus (Maxwell, 2003, 78). The Scythian monks advocated a formula "One of the Trinity was crucified in the flesh," which bore strong similarity to the Trisagion addition recently removed in 518 CE. In response, the Acoumeti forged three further letters addressed to Peter the Fuller directly addressing the formula, and thereby associating the Scythian monks with Peter by proxy (Maxwell, 2003, 80).

With the ascent of Justinian I, who saw theopaschitism (→ Theopaschites) as a mechanism for unity, the Acoumeti quickly fell out of favor (Sweetser, 2000, 130). On Mar 25, 534 CE, Pope John II excommunicated the Acoumeti as Nestorians (→ Nestorianism/Nestorius), at which point the Acoumeti disappeared from the historical record (Sweetser, 2000, 133). Although the Acoumeti ceased to be a force of political influence, the influence of their spirituality lived on, influencing the famous Studios Monastery in Constantinople, and carried on in the *laus perennis* tradition in the West, particularly Merovingian Gaul (Sweetser, 2000, 140–235).

Historiography

With the exception of a flurry of scholarship in the early 2000s, the Acoumeti remain largely neglected in recent scholarship. To date, D. Caner's monograph (2002), based on his 1998 PhD thesis, remains the starting point for scholarship on the topic, placing the Acoumeti in the context of eastern itinerant monasticism of the 6th century CE. D. Caner helpfully provides a new English translation of the *Vita Alexandri* with commentary (Caner, 2002, 249–280). Unpublished dissertations by W.B. Sweetser (2000) and D.R. Maxwell (2003) address the influence of the Acoumeti in Merovingian traditions of perpetual prayer and the theopaschite controversies respectively, though the sleepless monks are not the focus of either work. Considering the influence of Alexander and his monks in 5th-century CE Constantinople, there is plenty of room for future scholars to extend the field.

Bibliography

Baguenard, J.-M., *Les moines acémètes: Vies des saint Alexandre, Marcel, et Jean Calybite*, Bégrolles-en-Mauges, 1988.

Caner, D., *Wandering, Begging Monks: Spiritual Authority and the Promotion of Monasticism in Late Antiquity*, Berkeley, 2002.

Grillmeier, A., *Christ in Christian Tradition*, vol. II: *From the Council of Chalcedon (451) to Gregory the Great (590–604)*, part 1: *From Chalcedon to Justinian*, Atlanta, 1975; ET: P. Allen & J. Cawte.

Maxwell, D.R., "Christology and Grace in The Sixth-Century Latin West: The Theopaschite Controversy," unpubl. diss., South Bend, 2003.

Stroop, E. de, ed., *La vie d'Alexandre l'Acemete*, PO 6, Paris, 1911, 645–704.

Sweetser, W.B., "A Dynasty of Prayer: The Perpetual Praise (*Laus Perennis*) in Merovingian Gaul (515–816)," unpub. diss., Richmond, 2000.

RYAN W. STRICKLER

Acolyte

Acolyte (ἀκόλουθος) indicates "he who follows," and in the Latin *sequens* is found in the *Liber pontificalis*. In Latin there are orthographical variations: *acolythus, acoluthus, acoluthos, acolytus, acolitus*. We find it for the first time in a letter by the bishop of Rome, Cornelius, to Fabius of Antioch (Eus. *Hist. eccl.* 6.43.11). Cornelius wrote that at Rome there were 42 acolytes, a significant group. The order of acolyte (*akolytatus*) is a minor ministry, or order, that already had a history. The institution of it took place somewhat earlier, according to the → *Liber pontificalis*, and hails from the time of Pope Victor (189–199 CE): *Hic fecit sequentes cleros* (*LP*, vol. I, 173). Their number and the fact that the acolytes were present in Carthage, too, show that their institution could not be more recent, that is, from the time of Pope Fabian (236–250 CE), who reorganized the Roman church locally. In the community of the *Traditio Apostolica* (→ *Apostolic Tradition*), which is not a Roman text, they were not present. → Tertullian does not mention acolytes, but his silence does not signify that they did not exist. → Cyprian of Carthage spoke of the acolytes several times (see Cyp. *Ep.* 7.2; 34.4.1; 45.4.3; 49.3.1; 52.1.1; 59.1), functioning as letter carriers; they were those who distributed alms to prisoners (*Ep.* 77.3.2; 78.1). They were members of the clergy, and therefore they had a right to be sustained by the community. Their function was not as specific and precise as that of the lectors, but it had the general character of working together with the bishops, and of being in the number of the superior clergy. In the western churches, where the usage was prevalent of having only seven deacons, other ministries were necessary. Meanwhile, in those churches where the number of deacons could be greater, they themselves fulfilled more roles, and therefore it was unnecessary to have the ministry of the order of acolytes.

Eusebius of Caesarea (→ Eusebius of Caesarea [Palestine]) gives witness that at the Council of → Nicaea in 325 CE there were present some of the "collaborators" at the service of the bishops (Eus. *Vita Const.* 3.8), but he does not say that they were acolytes. The acolytes, who were members of the clergy, were the coworkers of the higher clergy, and especially in the service of the altar, but they also had different functions: some of them were couriers, who carried letters; in Rome they carried the *fermentum* (the → Eucharist) consecrated by the bishop to the presbyters of the titular churches (Innocent, *Ep. ad Decentium* 5: *I canoni dei concili*, 148). An inscription of the cemetery of Mark and Marcellinus attests that the acolyte Annius Innocentius had been in the service of two popes, Julius (d. 352 CE) and Liberius (d. 366 CE), twice going to Macedonia and several times to Campania, Puglia, and Calabria for ecclesiastical reasons, and finally to Sardinia, where he died at 26 years of age (ICUR 4.11805; Carletti, 1986, 129, 138–139). His body was carried back to Rome. His tomb was built by his priest brother, Annius Vincentius, who died in 366 CE and was buried in the same cemetery. The acolyte Innocentius must have spoken Greek in order to have gone into Macedonia and had diplomatic capabilities. He was not a simple carrier of a letter. → Augustine of Hippo makes use of an acolyte from Rome in order to respond to Marius Mercator (Aug. *Ep.* 193.1.1).

Pope Siricius speaks of a clerical *cursus*, wherefore only he who has lived well and has only once been married to a virgin may be ordained an acolyte or a subdeacon, and then – after five years – he can be promoted to the deaconate (*Ep. ad Him.* 9: *I canoni dei concili*, 72; 10, 74; Zosimus, *to Hesychius*, can 2). Gelasius decreed that, in the absence of clergy, some monks can be ordained exorcists and acolytes (*To the bishops of Lucania* 3.3). According to the *Statuta Ecclesiae antiqua*, from the 5th century CE, the ordination took place in the following manner:

> Whenever an acolyte is ordained, the bishop shall instruct him regarding how he ought to carry out his duties, while the archdeacon will consign to him a candle holder with a candle so that he might learn to light the lamps of the church; he will also receive an empty cruet/

ampulla in which to keep the wine [destined] for the Eucharist of the blood of Christ" (c. 94).

The service is connected with that which transpires at the altar. The anonymous text, attributed to → Jerome, but in reality from the Gaul of the 5th century CE, the *De septem ordinibus ecclesiae*, does not list the acolyte among the minor ministers (PL 30.162–163). On the other hand, the text attributed to the Venerable Bede is worded thus: *Acolythi et ceroferarii, in veteri testamento lumen praeparabant; modo in Ecclesia lumen veritatis debent praeparare mentibus fidelium* (PL 94.554).

At the time of → Gregory the Great, the acolytes worked together with the deacons, they accompanied the bishops, and they were at their disposition for ambassadorial needs; they collected the *pensiones* from the various Roman "domus," and they dedicated themselves to the care of the titular churches at which they worked (see TTL s.v. *Acolythus*). They also carried out pastoral activities in *lucrandis animabus* (Greg. M. *Reg. Ep.* 8.1). The ministry of the acolyte was unknown in the Gallican Rite (→ Gallican Liturgy), and yet an inscription certifies that a certain Desiderius was an acolyte at Lyon (Le Blant, 1864, 77). Such a ministry did not exist in all of the East, except in the Armenian Church. In the 8th century CE, → Isidore of Seville (d. 636 CE) described the function of the acolyte in this manner: *Acolythi Graece, Latine ceroferarii dicuntur, a deportandis cereis, quando legendum est Evangelium, aut sacrificium offerendum* (Isid. *Etym.* 7.12). Many Latin inscriptions commemorate the acolytes (see index Diehl, 1924–1931).

Bibliography

Andrieu, M., "Les ordres mineurs dans l'ancien rituel romain," *RevSR* 5, 1925, 232–274.

Carletti, C., *Iscrizioni cristiane a Roma*, Florence, 1986.

Carluccio, C., *The Seven Steps to Spiritual Perfection According to St. Gregory the Great*, Ottawa, 1949.

Casagrande, G., "On the Origin of the Spelling Acolytus," *JThS* 28, 1977, 112–113.

Cattaneo, E., *I ministeri nella chiesa antica*, Milan, 1997, 179–180.

Croce, W., "Die niederen Weihen und ihre hierarchische Wertung," *ZKTh* 70, 257–314.

DACL, vol. I, Paris, 348–356 (the acolytes in the inscriptions).

Davis, J.G., "Deacons, Diaconesses and the Minor Orders in the Patristic Period," *JEH* 14, 1963, 1–15.

Diehl, E., *Inscriptiones latinae christianae ueteres*, 3 vols., Berlin, 1924–1931.

EC, vol. I, Vatican City, 198–199.

Fischer, B., "Esquise historique sur les ordres mineurs," *MD* 16, 1960, 58–69.

Harnack, A. von, *Untersuchung des Lektorates und der anderen niederen Weihen*, TU, vol. II/5, Leipzig, 1886.

Lungkofler, J., "Die Vorstufen zu den höheren Wiehen nach dem Liber pontificalis," *ZKTh* 66, 1–19.

Pellegrini, P., *Militia clericatus monachici ordines*, Rome, 2008, 100f.

Righetti, M., *Manuale di storia liturgica*, Milan, 1953, 276ff.

Seagraves, R., *A Lexical Study of the Clergy in the Cyprianic Correspondence*, Fribourg, 1993, 133–176.

Snijders, A., "Acolytus cum ordinatur," *SE* 9, 1957, 163–198.

ANGELO DI BERARDINO

Acts, Book of

The book of Acts is unique of its type in the New Testament: neither gospel, nor letter, nor prophetic writing, it describes the first expansion of Christianity after the death and resurrection of Jesus. Writing an apostles' (→ Apostle) story after that of Jesus is a unique act in Christian antiquity: no one did it before Luke, and no one was to repeat it after him.

1. Luke's Second Volume

The Gospel of Luke (→ Luke, Gospel of) and the book of Acts form a literary unit with two components whose literary and theological homogeneity is evidenced.

a. A Sequel to the Gospel

Internal data attest to the literary homogeneity of Luke–Acts. The common vocabulary is significant (of 143 terms familiar to the third Gospel, i.e. used more than four times, 108 are found in Acts). Vocabulary specific to Luke–Acts but absent from the remainder of the New Testament is substantial (130 words or expressions unique to Luke–Acts). Luke's stylistic particularities abound in Acts (use of verbs with prefix; participle formed with neutral article; use of tou + infinitive, in order to;

participle placed at the start of a sentence, etc.). Sentences from the Gospel are found in whole or partially in Acts (compare Luke 1:66 and Acts 11:21; Luke 12:14 and Acts 7:27; Luke 24:19 and Acts 7:22; Luke 15:20 and Acts 20:37, etc.). Moreover, Luke's prologue (Luke 1:1–4) is taken up in Acts 1:1; this is a sure indication that Acts presents itself as a continuation of the Gospel.

The two components of the Lucan work articulate on the ascension of Jesus, narrated in two different formats (Luke 24:50–53; Acts 1:6–11). This divergence has raised the question as to whether Luke's text may not have been split into two afterward, the break being concealed by means of interpolations. The opposite is true: the separation of a long text into two books is a practice known in antiquity, as evidenced by the Septuagint (books of Kings, Chronicles, and → Maccabees) and numerous Greco-Roman writings. For practical reasons of manuscript length and in order to facilitate the production and distribution of his work, the author has split his writing into two parts of equal length.

The choice of the caesura was not fortuitous. Repeating the story of the ascension, which joins the two parts of the work, allows the author to offer a double reading for it: Luke 24:50–53 considers the ascension as the conclusion of Jesus' activity, while Acts 1:6–11 sees it as the start of the Jesus' movement after his resurrection (→ Resurrection).

However, it is a fact that no ancient manuscript has transmitted the text of Acts immediately after Luke. This anomaly is explainable: the split occurred very early. In the canonization process (canon) of the New Testament in the 2nd century CE, Luke was separated from Acts to constitute the corpus of the Gospels; the latter were regrouped and copied together. Dividing Luke's work into two halves was therefore a doctrinal decision resulting from the greater authority which the ancient church attached to the Gospels; the apostolic and canonical authority of Acts was to be recognized at a later date, thanks especially to the efforts of → Irenaeus of Lyon (c. 180 CE). Acts was then placed after the four Gospels in the canon, sometimes with the Catholic Epistles in the process of their regrouping. The position given to Acts at the head of the Pauline Epistles provided them with a narrative framework. The → Holy

Spirit's authorship of Scriptures mattered more than the human author's desire to see the two parts of his work joined together. Ancient tradition has not questioned the single authorship of Luke–Acts; Muratori's fragment (c. 190 CE), as much as Irenaeus, → Tertullian, or → John Chrysostom, attributes both writings to Luke the physician, companion of Paul.

b. Title

The title "Acts of the Apostles" (Πράξεις Ἀποστόλων) was popularized from the late 2nd century CE with Irenaeus (Iren. *Haer.* 3.13.3), along with variant titles (Acts of the Apostles, Acts of the Saint Apostles, etc.). This title likened the narrative to Greco-Roman writings glorifying the career of famous men (*Acta*). These suggested titles do not come from Luke, who would certainly not have subscribed to the addition of "apostles"; in fact, to his mind, only the twelve are honored with the title reserved for the companions of the earthly Jesus (Acts 1:21–22); Paul was deprived of it (except Acts 14:4, 14), even though he became the main hero of the story from chapter 13 onward. The suspended title reflects the usage of the term "apostle" as it became common in the postapostolic church, appropriate for Peter (→ Peter the Apostle) as much as for Paul (→ Paul the Apostle), the two main figures of the book.

c. Literary Genre

Identifying the literary genre of Luke–Acts is a difficult task, for which research offers no definite solution. Some have proposed to see Luke and Acts as a biography modeled on the *Lives of Philosophers*, followed by the story of their successors, but antiquity really has no known narrative displaying the activities of a master's successors (if the apostles can be described as such). Acts were moved closer to the apologetic historiography of the Hellenistic period (→ Hellenism and Christianity), as illustrated by the works of Manetho, Berossos, and especially → Flavius Josephus, who aim to communicate the history of a people or culture in order to defend their memory. In any case, Luke is the first in antiquity to present a religious movement by means of a historical narrative. Equal emphasis has been placed on the literary devices which Luke's Acts and the apocryphal *Acts of* the apostles have in common with the Greek novel, though the author's resolve to produce a historiographical work is hardly questionable.

It seems obvious that Gospel and Acts are not issued from the same literary genre. By binding the history of the apostles to that of Jesus, Luke produced a writing that resembles both biographical (Gospel) and historical (Acts) books. Jewish and Hellenistic literature displays no equivalence to this mixed genre, but it is true that the boundary between biography and history was becoming fluid at the time. One must therefore acknowledge that Luke's intention shatters the then available literary genres. His "Acts of Apostles" tells a story (historiographical aim) in order to present the Christian movement (apologetic aim), and does so with a strong taste for novelistic writing. That is why the broad label of "historical monograph" is most appropriate. Historical books of the Septuagint offer the closest analogy. In its aims, Acts rejoins stories of primordial history contained in the Hebrew Bible: the story of → Adam and Eve (Gen 2–3), of Cain and Abel (Gen 4), or → Abraham's call (Gen 12), the crossing of the Sea of Reeds (Exod 14), and so on. Through his work, Luke means to offer the Christian community of his time a *story of origins* that allows it to determine its identity.

2. Plot of the Book

Like the Gospel, Acts presents a series of narrative scenes (healing, speech, dispute, travelling, etc.). But unlike the Gospel, which sets small literary units side by side, Acts is characterized by long episodes, sizeable speeches, and meticulous transitions. Efforts in literary composition are evident.

a. Structure

The episodic style of Acts likens the narrative to a succession of pictures; but how do these interconnect? The narration avoids a schematic organization that would divide it into two parts articulated around the Jerusalem Council (15:1–35) or distinguish a cycle of Peter (Acts 1–12) from a cycle of Paul (Acts 13–28). However, the story itself holds the key to its organization. In Acts 1:8, the risen Christ commissions his disciples to be his "witnesses in Jerusalem, in all Judea and Samaria and to the ends of the earth." This statement formulates the program of Acts in condensed form. The book tells how, under the impetus of the Holy Spirit, the word of the Gospel is spread in the Roman Empire through the Christian mission; this expansion is gradual, starting from Jerusalem to reach Judea, Samaria (Acts 8), and finally Rome, where Paul arrives as a prisoner (Acts 28). This geographical movement simultaneously conveys a theological value: the word breaks away from Jerusalem, the setting of Jesus' story, to reach the capital of the pagan world, thereby opening the door to the God of Israel for non-Jews. The narrative is thus structured along the lines of a geographical plan in which six stages can be discerned.

b. Six Stages

First Stage: Waiting for the Spirit (1:1–26)
The preface (1:1–3) is followed by the story of the ascension and the reconstitution of the college of the twelve with the election of Matthias.

Second Stage: The Community Around the Twelve Apostles (2:1–8:1a)
The coming of the Holy Spirit at → Pentecost (2:1–13) triggers the growth of the community. Three summaries (2:42–47; 4:32–35; 5:12–16) emphasize the unanimity of the group, its exemplary communion, and the effectiveness of its healing practices. But this church growth goes hand in hand with a rise in hostility on the part of the Jewish authorities: the arrest of the apostles and the hearings before the Sanhedrin (high court) reach their climax in the trial and stoning of → Stephen (the Martyr), the Hellenist (6:7–8:1a).

Third Stage: From Jerusalem to Antioch (8:1b–12, 25)
The crisis triggered by the murder of Stephen causes the dispersion of the Church of Jerusalem (8:1b–4). The word spreads throughout Samaria thanks to Philip's evangelization (8:5–40), then along the Mediterranean coast with the apostle Peter (9:32–11:18). The meeting between Peter and → Cornelius (Centurion) in Caesarea (10:1–48) is a high point of the book because Peter is driven by divine force to admit a non-Jew into the church.

Fourth Stage: The First Missionary Journey to the Gentiles (13:1–15:35)
Barnabas (person) and Paul, sent from the Church of Antioch, concretize the openness of Peter toward non-Jews in a missionary journey to Cyprus and Asia Minor (chs. 13–14). A turning point occurs in the Jerusalem assembly (15:1–35), where the unity of the church is preserved: salvation as preached by Paul and → Barnabas without requiring obedience to the law is confirmed as a work of the Holy Spirit, and the observance of minimal rules of purity is the sole requirement.

Fifth Stage: Paul the Missionary (15:36–21:14)
Paul takes center stage as the model missionary. The new journey takes him to Greece and Ephesus, where the gospel comes across Greek philosophy and Greco-Roman syncretism. Paul's preaching does not stop incurring the hostility of Jews or the dislike of crowds, but each time the witness of Christ bounces back: Philippi (16:16–40), Thessalonica and Berea (17:1–15), Athens (17:16–34), Corinth (18:12–17), Ephesus (19:21–40). One last trip of Paul to Jerusalem (20:1–21:14) gives the occasion for the farewell address to the Ephesian elders.

Sixth Stage: From Jerusalem to Rome, the Martyrdom of Paul (21:15–28:31)
Arrest of Paul in the → Temple (21:15–36), imprisonment in Caesarea (23:11–26:32), transfer to Rome to be tried by the emperor (chs. 27–28). This final stage is marked by speeches in which Paul proclaims the gospel by justifying his conversion and defending himself against the grievance of infidelity to the law: before the people of Jerusalem (22:1–21), before the Sanhedrin (23:1–6), before Governor Felix (24:10–21), and before King Agrippa I (26:2–29). The book ends with a final interview with the Jews in Rome (28:17–31).

3. The Author and His Audience

a. Traditional Attribution

The first attestations of the name Luke, Greek diminutive of a Latin name (Lucius?), stem from the manuscript P[75] (c. 175–225) and from Irenaeus' roughly contemporary commentary: "And Luke,

Paul's companion, recorded in a book the gospel which Paul preached" (Iren. *Haer.* 3.1.1). Twenty years later, Muratori's fragment confirms that "Luke, the physician, after the → ascension of Jesus Christ, as Paul had taken him along, in the manner of someone who studies law, wrote under his own name, as he saw fit." Henceforth, the attribution of the Gospel to "Luke the physician," Paul's collaborator, does not change (Col 4:14; 2 Tim 4:11; Phlm 24). The reason is as follows: according to 2 Tim 4:11, Luke was the last associate who remained faithful to the apostle; yet this epistle, written at the dictation of the author in Rome (2 Tim 1:17), fits precisely where the narrative of Acts ends (28:30–31). As a result, the combination of these two texts designates Luke as the author of Luke–Acts. The anti-Marcionite prologues to the Gospel describe Luke as a Syrian of Antioch, a physician, a disciple of the apostles and of Paul, deceased at age 84 in Boeotia after writing Gospel and Acts in Achaia; but do these prologues date from the 2nd or 4th century CE? We do not know.

Can one infer the medical training of the author from the text of Luke–Acts? Diseases are sometimes described accurately (Luke 4:38; 5:12; 8:44; 13:11; Acts 28:9–10). But the description of diseases does not go beyond what is found in the Greek and Roman literature of the time. Moreover, antiquity does not know of an established medical language. In short, the medical expertise of the author of Luke–Acts cannot be proven. As to the connection of Luke–Acts with Pauline theology, the Lucan portrait of the apostle does not make a case in favor of a chronological proximity of the author with the apostle to the Gentiles, but rather of a reception of Pauline theology through tradition.

b. A Third-Generation Christian, Disciple of Paul

Four factors play a role in dating the book.
1. The insistence of Acts on the rejection of the gospel by the synagogue is hardly conceivable if the dialogue between Christians and Jews is still open at the time of the book's writing; yet, the Judaism–Christianity conflict escalates after 70 CE;

2. The frequent use of the label the Jews in a pejorative sense (from 9:23) implies that Judaism and Christianity are in the process of separating;
3. The significant gap between the Lucan portrait of Paul and the apostle's own manner of thinking as set out in his Epistles makes it difficult to accept the hypothesis of a companionship, unless Luke had misunderstood the apostle;
4. The image of Christianity conveyed by the story is a third-generation Christianity, close to the pastoral letters; the farewell speech of Paul provides confirmation of this advanced state of Christianity (Acts 20:25–32).

What image of the author does the book give? Although his "I" stands out (Luke 1:3), his name is unknown; however, it is the custom among biblical authors to retire behind the word they proclaim, except in the case of letters. Luke's excellence in the use of the Koine Greek and his good knowledge of → rhetoric (construction of discourses in Acts) leads one to imagine a writer of good formation endowed with a superior education background. But we must add to that his profound familiarity with Jewish Scriptures (OT), inconceivable from someone who would not have used them for a long time. Luke effectively writes in "biblical style," borrowing phrases and stylistic effects from the Septuagint. From his closeness to Jewish tradition, one can conclude that before his conversion to Christianity, Luke, a Gentile, approached the synagogue to the point of becoming a proselyte or a Godfearer. That he may have been a Jew of the → Diaspora is fairly unlikely given his lack of interest in details of the Torah's commandments. His christological interpretation of the Law rather points to the theology of Gentile Christianity. He belongs to the Pauline sphere of influence, which, in the 80s CE, regroups believers attached to the memory of the apostle to the Gentiles who preserve his tradition and perpetuate his evangelizing activity. A great traveler, he is very familiar with the topography of the empire and its institutions.

c. Dating the Book

The book of Acts was written at the same time or shortly after the Gospel of Luke. As the latter dates from soon after the destruction of the Temple of Jerusalem in 70 CE, the writing of Acts can be set between 80 and 90 CE: the author's silence on the Pauline correspondence makes a dating in the early 2nd century CE unlikely. At that time, the break between church and synagogue is advanced and Roman persecutions intensify, but Acts bears no trace of it.

d. The Recipients

Where did the author write his work? Ephesus has been proposed, Antioch (because of a reference of the *Ps.-Clem. R* 10:71), Achaia (because of the anti-Marcionite prologues), Macedonia (because the first of the "we" passages in Acts begins here; see below), and Rome (because Acts end there). This indecision is indicative of a certain universality of the author and his work.

The audience for which his work is intended consists of churches in the eastern Mediterranean basin as well as readers eager to learn about Christianity. The clear trend in Luke to be both presenter and apologist (→ Apologetics) of the Christian faith denotes an ambition to aim for a wide audience. Noting the cross-culture-oriented effort perceptible in the rewriting of the tradition, his audience is clearly of Greek culture.

4. The Text and Its Sources

a. The Enigma of the Text of Acts

The Greek text of Acts puts textual criticism in a very peculiar situation: the manuscripts are separated into two distinctly dissimilar families. The Alexandrian text (*receptus textus* adopted by tradition) is represented by two important papyri of the 3rd century CE (P.45, P.53) and three large uncials: Vaticanus (B), Sinaiticus (a), Alexandrinus (A). Another textual form, 8.5% longer, is identifiable in some manuscripts of the Latin version (hence its name "Western text"), but also in the Syriac version, preserved on papyri of the late 3rd century CE (P.38, P.48) and in the Codex Bezae (D). In total, more than 600 variants differentiate between the two versions. These variants consist of
a. an effort at stylistic improvement (see Acts 12:4–5),

b. providing more detailed information (see 16:10–11; 18:2), and
c. increased readability of the text through the elimination of apparent contradictions (see 3:11; 10:25; 15:34; 16:35–40). The additional material sometimes fills whole verses (see 8:37; 9:5; 10:25; 11:2; 19:1, 14; 23:24–25; 24:7; 25:24; 28:29).

The hypothesis of two editions of the text of Acts has been advanced; it relies on the latitude which antiquity granted to an author by allowing him to modify his text after a scribe had copied it for the first distribution. Four variants are conceivable:
a. Luke wrote both versions, thus implying that he subsequently shortened a long text (hence the Alexandrian variant) or amplified a more concise text (hence the western variant);
b. secretary annotated the short original text on the basis of notes left by the author;
c. the Western text is the original edition, from which an abridged version was made in the 2nd century CE in order to facilitate dissemination;
d. both versions of Acts are the result of two revisions, independently of each other, and the original text of Luke is now lost.

One thing is clear: each of the two texts can claim high antiquity, but the theory of a double edition of Acts runs into two difficulties. Firstly, all variations of the Western text can be explained as a desire to annotate the short text, while a reduction of the long text is less understandable. Secondly, annotations of the Western text bear the mark of a theology subsequent to Luke, notably when pertaining to the rise of anti-Judaism, the primacy of Peter, and the exaltation of the power of the Holy Spirit.

The evolution of the manuscript tradition seems to lead from the Alexandrian text to the Western text, and not the reverse. The break between Acts and the Gospel of Luke in the 2nd century CE, inherent to the process of canonization, has afforded the text of Acts a lesser protection than that given to the text of the Gospel. The liberalization of the text that followed was not necessarily channeled into a single variant because we now wonder if the so-called Western text does not rather cover a nebula of variations of Luke's (short) original text. Irenaeus, the first to quote Acts (c. 180), seemingly bases himself on a text that includes only certain features of the so-called Western text. The annotated text could have appeared as early as the 2nd century CE in the east of the empire, for example Syria; that would explain its very rapid dissemination in the Syriac tradition and in Egypt.

b. Documentary Sources

From which sources did the author of Acts draw his information? Obviously, the situation is not the same as that of the Gospel, where the small traditional literary units inherited by Luke can be easily identified. Here, the author works differently, writing long narrative sequences where it is difficult to unravel the traditional from the editorial.

In the early 20th century, critics attempted to distinguish a Palestinian source (Jerusalem), an Antiochian source, and a Pauline source. The difficulty arises from the criteria used to reconstruct these sources: a geographical affiliation is not enough to identify a source, a stylistic criterion must be added. One could invoke the strongly Semitic style of the first 12 chapters of Acts, but the argument is not convincing: the author excels at varying styles. A comparison of Peter's speech at Pentecost (2:14–36), saturated with Septuagint traits, with Paul's refined Greek before philosophers in Athens (17:22–31) or before King Agrippa (26:2–29) may suffice. Actually, all sections of Acts bear the marks of Lucan style and vocabulary. Conclusion: Luke uses sources, but he has completely rewritten them. The definite identification of these sources still escapes us today.

The failure of the documentary hypothesis speaks for the excellence of Luke's literary work, who, like any good writer, camouflages his borrowings – as recommended by Lucian of Samosata, author of the handbook *Quomodo Historia conscribenda sit* (c. 166–168 CE). Lucian advises the historian to record his information in a "memoire" like a notebook, then to sketch a draft, and finally to write the final text (§48). Luke has clearly complied with Lucian's codified usage: notes taken by the historian from his source already bear the mark of his style, and when he writes, after the draft, the literary characteristics of the source have been absorbed by these successive filters.

If the firm identification of documents prior to the text of Luke escapes us, fragments let us glimpse preexisting traditions:

a. lists of names (1:13; 6:5; 13:1; 20:4);
b. isolated episodes such as the death of Judas (1:16–20), the healing of the lame man at the Beautiful Gate (3:1–10), Ananias and Sapphira (5:1–11), the election of the seven (6:1–6), and so on;
c. a narrative cycle of Peter (9:32–11:18; 12:1–17);
d. an itinerary of the Pauline mission involving travel notices and stages of information discernible in the background of chapters 16–21; a traveling logbook or "diary" has been suggested; and
e. a kerygmatic scheme present in the speeches of Peter (2:22–24, 32–36; 3:13–15; 4:10–11; 5:29–32;, 10:37–43) as much as in Paul (13:23–33): "Jesus, whom you put to death – he has been raised by God – it is the God of Israel who exalted him – of this we are witnesses."

Moreover, the widely traveled Luke certainly collected local oral traditions, such as the conversion of the Ethiopian eunuch in Samaria (8:26–39) or the story of Elymas, the magician in Cyprus (12:4–12). If it turns out that he was actually Macedonian, the figure of Lydia, the seller of purple goods (16:13–15, 40), and the wonderful deliverance of Paul and Silas from prison (16:16–39) must have been living memories in his community.

c. The "We" Passages

The origin of the "we" passages remains a mystery. On four occasions and without transition, the narrator shifts to the first-person plural and leaves it just as abruptly. Each time, it refers to a sea voyage: from Troas to Philippi (16:10–17), from Philippi to Miletus (20:1–15), from Miletus to Jerusalem (21:1–18), and from Caesarea to Rome (27:1–28:16). Proposed hypotheses are the following:

a. "Luke the physician," companion of Paul and author of Acts, recounts his own experiences (but such an early dating of Acts does not fit);
b. Luke rewrites a source: the journal of the sea passage of a companion of Paul (but why such an awkwardness in transitions?); or
c. Luke uses a literary device known to Greco-Roman writers (Homer, Virgil, Varro, Josephus, Lucian) to enliven his story (but why reserve it for Paul's crossings?).

Note that these breaks in style by a narrator as careful as Luke are not due to negligence – albeit dictated by a source. It is therefore important to distinguish between the question of origin (the resumption of a travel diary is quite plausible) and the desired effect on the reader. In this regard, the "we" of the travels is not to be confused with the "I" of the author's preface (Luke 1:1–4; Acts 1:1). The use of "we" is a narrative process for the credibility of the story, aiming to indicate its origin from a group to which the narrator belongs. On four crucial occasions in Paul's itinerary, the narrator wanted to declare his attachment to a theological tradition dating back to the close circle of the grand apostle.

5. A Literary Art

As a pastor committed to enlightening Theophilus with his account of Christian origins, Luke knows that messing up his story could lose his reader – or rather his listener – along the way. He integrated what the poet Horace said of the need to join pleasure and usefulness when teaching: "He who mixes what is pleasant with what is useful (*qui miscuit utile dulci*), and both charms and instructs the reader, gets all the votes" (Hor. *Ars.* 343). The care with which he chooses to communicate leads the author of Acts to embellish his story: dramatization, art of suspense, burlesque, theatrical bombshell, irony – no narrative tool escapes him. The scene of Ananias and Sapphira's death (5:1–11) or the riot of silversmiths in Ephesus (19.23–40) are models of the genre. When he must repeat, he avoids tiring the reader by varying the wording; one realizes this when comparing the three versions of the conversion of Paul in Damascus in Acts 9, 22, 26.

a. An Episodic Style

To present a story, Luke has adopted the episodic style of his colleagues in Greco-Roman historiography. This means that instead of presenting long procedures, he condenses an atmosphere or an evolving event into a scene that acquires symbolic value. Thus, the smoldering crisis between Hebrews and Hellenists in the Jerusalem Church crystallizes into one scene, the election of the seven (6:1–6), while the first mission to the nations unfolds in the course of a few selected scenes (chs. 13–14). In some scenes, the narrator provides a programmatic value for the rest of the story: the event of Pentecost (2:1–13), the meeting of Peter and Cornelius (10:1–48), and Paul's sermon in Pisidian Antioch (13:13–52) fill that programmatic role. Summaries and brief reports on the condition of the community guide the reading by reminding the reader of the common thread that runs throughout the narrative: the spread of the word (2:42–47; 4:32–35; 5:12–16; 6:7, see also 9:31; 12:24; 16:5; 19:20; 28:30–31).

b. Evidence of Continuity

Luke is bound to illustrate the theological continuity that connects both the acts of God in Israel with the story of Jesus and the activity of Jesus with that of his disciples. To make this clear, he uses three narrative processes: repeated scenarios, narrative chains, and *syncrisis*.

a. *Repeated scenarios*: the most stereotyped is the Pauline mission, based on the recurring pattern: preaching in the synagogue/rejection by the majority/conversion of some (13:42–52; 14:1–7; 17:1–9; 17:10–14; 18:1–10; 19:8–10);

b. *Narrative chains* run through the whole of Luke–Acts: the chain of centurions whose exemplary faith legitimizes access to salvation for the Gentiles (Luke 7:1–10; Luke 23:47; Acts 10); the Pentecostal chain links the first Pentecost (Acts 2:1–13) to collective resurgences of the Holy Spirit (Acts 10:44–46; 19:6); the chain of Paul's conversions reinterprets the event (Acts 9) at the end of the story (Acts 22 and 26);

c. The *process of syncrisis* consists in modeling the staging of a character on another in order to establish a correlation between the two. Thus, Stephen's martyrdom is modeled on the death of Jesus (compare Acts 7:55–60 and Luke 23:34–46). The most spectacular example of *syncrisis* is the parallel Jesus-Peter-Paul: Peter and Paul heal as Jesus healed (Luke 5:18–25; Acts 3:1–8; 14:8–10); like Jesus at his baptism, they receive an ecstatic vision at the highest moment of their ministry (Acts 9:3–9; 10:10–16); like Jesus, they preach and endure the hostility of sections of the Jews, as Jesus they suffer and are threatened with death (Acts 12 and 21); Paul is on trial as Jesus was

(Acts 21–26), and as their master, Peter and Paul are the subject of a miraculous deliverance at the end of their lives (Acts 12:6–17; 24:24–28:6). One realizes that these editorial processes not only betray Luke's aesthetic concern but also embody a theological strategy.

c. Speeches

Speeches occupy more than a third of the book of Acts: 24 in total, attributed to Peter, Stephen, Paul, James, or Alexander. Speeches by Peter: 1:16–22; 2:14–36; 3:12–26; 4:9–12; 5:29–32; 10:34–43; 11:5–17; 15:7–11. Speech of Stephen: 7:2–53. Speech of James: 15:13–21. Speech of Alexander: 19:35–40. Paul's speeches: 13:16–41; 14:15–17; 17:22–31; 20:18–35; 22:1–21; 23:1–6; 24:10–21; 26:2–23; 27:21–26; 28:17–20, 25–28. Speeches play an important role in the story as they interpret current events, showing how they relate to God's plan. It is easily comprehensible that in the formative days of Christianity, when the church was no more than a small group, no secretary took note of the apostles' words. Ancient historians, who loved to put speeches on the lips of their heroes, faced the same difficulty. Luke followed the principle adopted by Thucydides: "I expressed what I thought they could have said that better corresponded to the situation" (Thuc. *Pelop.* 1.22.1). This principle legitimizes the reconstruction of speeches, while subjecting it to a double conformity: the reconstructed speech must agree with what is known of the speaker and be appropriate to the situation. Through his choice of style and oratory comments, Luke followed Thucydides' rule. By adopting for each of his heroes the language that suits him, he excels in the art of *imitatio*, the popular stylistic imitation of Hellenistic writers. The Septuagint provided the author with the expressions he sought.

6. Luke the Historian

From a historical perspective, the book of Acts is valuable as it constitutes our only direct source of information on early Christianity apart from the Pauline correspondence. But to what extent is this source reliable? The debate on the historical reliability of Acts is wide open.

a. An Oriented History

Any historiography, either ancient or modern, is the result of a narrative construction. Like any historian, Luke tells the story from a specific viewpoint, and it is according to this view that he selects data and puts them into perspective. The Lucan point of view depends on three factors.

Firstly, like the Deuteronomist or the Chronicler, Luke offers a faithful reading of history; only elements capable of serving his theological reading, which is to show how God leads his own, are retained. The way Luke looks at history rests on the conviction that time belongs to God.

Secondly, Luke wants to explain how the gospel has left its native cradle, → Judaism, to reach the Gentiles; the route from Jerusalem (Acts 1) to Rome (Acts 28) symbolizes this opening of the word to the world. That is why the author has focused his story on Christian evangelization in the Near East, Asia Minor, Greece, and Italy, ignoring Egypt and the western part of the empire; the rise of Johannine Christianity equally remains outside the scope of his concern.

Thirdly, Luke is convinced that Paul was the special instrument by which the offer of salvation came to the Gentiles; it matters to him to show that the irresistible thrust of Paul's mission to the nations is the culmination of a divine plan announced by the "risen one" (Acts 1:8) and gradually realized by Philip (Acts 8), followed by Peter (Acts 10–11).

To sum up, Luke's historiography is theological; it does not purport to summarize all that is to be known about Christian origins but illustrates a theological position, namely the universalization of Christianity through the vector of Paul's mission. Therefore, Acts present a partial and oriented history of the origins of Christianity, viewed from a Pauline point of view and intended to perpetuate the memory of the apostle to the Gentiles.

b. Concern for Accuracy

Luke the historian's concern for accuracy is remarkable. The care with which he describes the itineraries is the result of this concern; his meticulous knowledge of the empire's institutions and of the titles of imperial officials points to accurate and verified information. The author knows the titles of political officials (16:20; 18:12; 19:35; 25:13) and the legal procedures in the empire (16:19–21; 19:35–40; 22:25–29; 25:10–11). His description of the itineraries taken by the Pauline mission matches what we know of Roman road networks. It clearly matters to the author that his work should provide an accurate picture of that *imperium romanum* in which Christianity is to live and grow in the future.

c. Idealization of the Past?

The flattering portrait of the first community in Jerusalem – of its unanimity (2:46; 4:32; 5:12), its community of goods (2:44–45; 4:32–37), and its meteoric rise in numbers (2:41; 4:4; 5:14; 6:7) – raises a hint of idealization in Luke. There is no doubt that in the eyes of the author, the first Christian community grouped around the twelve constitutes an exceptional golden age and as such a model for readers. Following the example of Gen 1–11, the "story of origins" in Acts 1–6 serves as a founding myth for a Christendom that, at the time of Luke, is divided and in the process of breaking away from Judaism. The impressive numbers of conversions have a symbolic value; they indicate that the growth of the church enjoys divine blessing.

However, it should be noted that in this model state, neither internal crises (5:1–11; 6:1–6) nor aggression from the outside world spared the first church (4:1–21; 5:17–40; 6:11–15). The practice of sharing goods described in 4:34–35 was not as widespread as suggested by the author, yet the proof of similar conventions among the → Essenes (1QS 1.11–13; 6.16–22) does support this notion, which Luke picked up as a fact of tradition and generalized for the first Christians.

7. Luke the Theologian

a. A History of Salvation Driven by the Spirit

The fundamental aim of Luke's theology is to show that the access of non-Jews to salvation fits into the rationale of the salvation history that began with Israel. Between Judaism and Christianity, the book of Acts creates an indestructible theological continuity. One after another, speeches repeat it as they keep reviewing salvation history: the God of Israel raised Jesus from the dead and calls for conversion to the gospel today (2:22–36; 3:13–26; 4:9–12; 7:2–53; 13:17–41; 24:14–15). Israel's precedence in the order of salvation is fully upheld, but now the grace given by Jesus extends to everyone who believes (13:39–40). The people of God assembled around the name of Jesus Christ are composed of Jews and non-Jews.

Luke is adamant that despite the efforts of missionaries, Judaism is largely against this proclamation. Yet God has given clear signs of his approval to this extension of Israel's holiness to the world. The irruption of the Holy Spirit is the divine seal given to the apostles' mission when it opens to universality. The miracle of Pentecost foreshadows the proclamation of the word to all nations (2:5–11), the Holy Spirit provokes the baptism of the Ethiopian eunuch in Samaria (8:26–40), and the millennium barrier between pure and impure falls in the encounter between Peter and Cornelius (10:1–48). The Holy Spirit is the instrument by which God precedes his own and takes the initiative in history.

Christian identity as configured in Acts places Christianity between Jerusalem and Rome. Jerusalem is the place of origin, the guarantor of the inviolable faithfulness of God to his people; Rome symbolizes the future where the ancient promise of God's salvation sent to all nations will be realized (see Luke 3:6 and Acts 28:28 quoting Isaiah 40:5). Regarding the empire, the author adopts a notoriously favorable outlook: imperial officials adopt benevolent neutrality toward Christianity (18:12–17; 19:21–40; 21:30–24:23). On many occasions, Luke seeks to demonstrate that the new faith is politically harmless (18:14–15; 19:35–40; 23:29; 26:2–8). Is the author seeking to defend the cause of Christianity in Roman society, to demonstrate its political innocence and intellectual dignity? Given the largely Christian readership Luke–Acts is intended for, it is likely that the generally favorable portrait of Roman institutions aims at facilitating the establishment of the church in imperial society.

b. The Image of Paul

The difference between the portrait of Paul drawn by Luke in Acts and the discourse of the apostle in his letters is no less than striking. In addition to differences regarding his theological positions (compare Gal 2:1–10 and Acts 15:19–21; Gal 6:12–15 and Acts 16:3; Phil 3:7–8 and Acts 22:6), the apostle's struggle in favor of the validity of the Torah (→ Law/Decalogue/Torah) disappears in Acts. There is no trace in it of the conflicts that pitted Paul against his opponents (esp. Gal and 1–2 Cor), or of his epistolary activity.

The considerable timespan that lies between Paul (50s CE) and Luke (80s CE) must be taken into account. The author of Acts, a generation away, belongs to a milieu that manages the legacy of the apostle. His intention is not to repeat what the apostle has said, but to preserve his memory by highlighting the role he played in the birth of Christianity. Since the time of Paul, the conflict over the Torah has lost its relevance. On the other hand, Luke wishes to emphasize the coherence and the spirit of unity that drive the various streams of Christianity. Perhaps the author also wants to defend Paul from a reproach of anti-Judaism. The absence of any quotation of the epistles rests on the fact that for Luke, the memory of the apostle is not mediated through his writings but through the story of his missionary activity. It is the memory of this missionary epic that Luke wants to glorify.

c. A Theology of Providence

Among the shifts of Lucan theology *vis-à-vis* Paul's thought, the abandonment of the centrality of the → cross is particularly noteworthy: the death of Jesus embodies the human error before God, but the offer of salvation is based on the certainty of the resurrection (2:23–24; 3:14–15; 7:52; 13:27–31). In → soteriology, the resurrection takes the place occupied by the cross in Paul: it is no longer the death of Jesus that is the object of scandal (see 1 Cor 1:18–25), but the news that God has raised him from the dead. Consequently, the assertion of → Easter, and no longer the law, is the point at issue between church and synagogue in Acts.

Yet for all that, no theology of glory was to be attributed to Luke. For if the spread of the word in the empire is unstoppable, the bearers of the gospel are constantly harassed, insulted, brought to justice, beaten, and stoned (4:1–3; 5:17–18; 7:54–60; 8:1; 9:23,

29; 12:1–4; 13:50; 14:5, 19–20, 16:19–24; 17:5, 13; 18:12; etc.). Despite these difficulties and sufferings, the word spreads and evangelization advances. The mission bounces back because God protects his envoys and transforms their distress into opportunities for witnessing. The concept that imposes itself is that of providential failure: witnesses of Christ are by no means immune to suffering, following the example of Jesus (Luke 12:4–12); but within their frailty, God looks after the fertility of the word.

Bibliography

Alexander, L.C.A., *Acts in Its Ancient Literary Context*, LNTS 298, London, 2005.

Dibelius, M., *Studies in the Acts of the Apostles*, London, 1956 (ET).

Dupont, J., *Nouvelles études sur les actes des apôtres*, LeDiv 118, Paris, 1984.

Keener, C.S., *Acts: An Exegetical Commentary*, 4 vols., Grand Rapids, 2012–2015.

Marguerat, D., *The First Christian Historian: Writing the "Acts of the Apostles,"* SNTSMS 121, Cambridge UK, 2002.

Marguerat, D., *Paul in Acts and Paul in His Letters*, WUNT 310, Tübingen, 2013.

Plümacher, E., *Lukas als hellenistischer Schriftsteller*, StUNT 9, Göttingen, 1972.

Roloff, J., „Die Apostelgeschichte," *NTD* 5, Göttingen, 1981.

Squires, J.T., *The Plan of God in Luke–Acts*, SNTSMS 76, Cambridge UK, 1993.

Strange, W.A., *The Problem of the Text of Acts*, SNTSMS 71, Cambridge UK, 1992.

Winter, B.W., I.H. Marshall & D.W.J. Gill, eds., *The Book of Acts in Its First Century Setting*, 5 vols., Grand Rapids, 1993–1996.

DANIEL MARGUERAT

Ad Metalla (*Damnatio*)

The sentence *ad metalla* ("to the mines"), included among the *poenae mediocres* ("minor punishments") according to Roman law, along with the sentencing to public works (*opus publicum*), consists in making criminals work in the places where minerals are extracted or marble is cut into blocks. This was a commonly adopted measure for penalizing criminals in the ancient world, especially those of low social origin.

1. Antecedents in Ancient Egypt

Already in Egypt, prisoners of war and certain common-law delinquents who had committed crimes such as stealing, tomb robbery, and sacrilege were condemned to this punishment. The most ancient document bearing witness to this penalty is a decree issued by the Fifth Dynasty pharaoh Nefirirkare (c. 2450 BCE), which prescribes compulsory work in certain granite quarries for captured fugitives and those condemned to services, as also for men of the *nome* who had attempted to distract the priests and servants of the temple of Abydos from their functions (Husson & Valbelle, 1998, 156–157). Another testimony from Hellenistic Egypt is provided by Diodorus Siculus (*Bib. hist.* 3.12–14), who quotes Agatharchides' description of convicts working in the gold mines of southern Egypt in the late 2nd century BCE. He indicates that those sent there, without distinction of age or of sex, are persons who have been unjustly accused and imprisoned as a result of the king's displeasure. The conditions were very hard, since they were permanently chained up, overseen by guards or foreign soldiers, and forced to work day and night, most of the time inside tunnels, and at times even tortured, thus causing many of them to die.

2. Development in Roman Times

In Rome, the sentence to the mines seems to have been in use since the time of the Roman Republic. Strabo says that those in charge – vested with authority, without direct intervention by the state – of the red sulphate mine of Pimolysene in Pontus used slaves who had been sold off by rogues (Stra. *Geogr.* 562).

It is the harshest penalty after that of death; in fact, it could only be inflicted in Rome by the *praefectus Urbis* (the governor of the city) and in the provinces by the proconsul (*Dig.* 1.18.6.8; 48.19.8.5). It could be indefinite, although it was usually limited to ten years if no precise duration was stipulated by the judge (*Dig.* 48.19.23). Apart from this, the convicts who became unfit for work over the course of time, as a result of either illness or age, could be removed at the completion of ten years, in case the limit was longer (*Dig.* 48.19.22). Thus, Trajan's answer to Pliny

the Younger, written in response to his question of what to do with convicts at the end of such a period, suggests that they should be employed in tasks that are commensurate with their punishment and adds that they are commonly made to work in the baths or used to clean out drainage channels and to repair the Roman roads and streets (Plin. Y. *Ep.* 10.31–32).

No consideration was shown for age or sex (*Dig.* 48.19.8.8; 48.19.28.6; 49.15.6; Cod. Justin. 9.47.9); nevertheless, a passage from → Eusebius of Caesarea tells us that in the wake of the sentences passed by the governor of Palestine Firmilian (at the time of Diocletian), some had obtained exemption from such works on account of old age, mutilations, or other physical defects; these included Silvanus, the bishop of Gaza (Eus. *Mart. Pal.* 13.4). In Roman law, this punishment was reserved for the *humiliores* ("low-ranking persons"; see Cod. Theod. 7.18.1; *Dig.* 47.20.3.2; 48.19.9.11; 50.13.5.3; Pau. *Sent.* 5.22.2) and for slaves (*Sent.* 5.4.22; 5.30B.2; *Dig.* 48.18.17.3; 48.19.8.12; Cod. Theod. 8.5.17; 9.10.4; 9.17.1; 12.1.6; Cod. Justin. 9.47.11; Hipp. *Haer.* 9.12). Exemptions were granted to *honestiores* ("high-ranking persons"), soldiers, veterans, and their children (Cod. Justin. 9.47.5; *Dig.* 49.16.3.1). However, all of this does not mean that exceptions to the rule could not be made in accordance with the interests of the emperors or even through bad use of the rule (Suet. *Cal.* 27; Plin. Y. *Ep.* 10.58–60; Pau. *Sent.* 5.19). Likewise, in certain cases, leniency could be shown to this type of convict, as for instance when → Constantine I granted freedom to all Christians sentenced to the mines or to hard labor (Cassio. *Hist. eccl.* 1.9.3; Eus. *Vita Const.* 2.30–32).

The main crimes punishable by sentencing to the mines were: for slaves, grave offenses and usurpation of freedom (Pau. *Sent.* 5.4.22; 5.22.6); and for free men, assassination, violation of tombs, falsification of coins, plagiarism, stealing of livestock or of sacred objects or metals belonging to the emperor, stealing at the baths, setting fire to crops, the kidnapping of children, and inducing to gamble, above all by the use of force (Pau. *Sent.* 5.3.5; 5.18.2; 5.19; 5.20.5; 5.23.4, 12; 5.25.1; 5.30B.1; Cod. Theod. 9.18; 7.18.1; *Dig.* 11.5.1.4; 48.13.6; 48.19.38; Plin. Y. *Ep.* 10.58). It was also contemplated appropriate for plebeians who failed to denounce a deserter, for those offering love potions or helping to procure an abortion (if not resulting in murder), and for those who opened or read the testament of a person who was still alive.

The jurisconsults distinguish two degrees of the punishment *metallum* and *opus metallic* ("work at the mines"), the latter of which was a little less harsh since the chains were not so wide and rigid (*Dig.* 48.19.8.4, 6, 12; 48.19.17; 48.19.28.6; 50.13.5.3). A third category consists of the *ministerium metallicorum* (also "work at the mines"), seemingly reserved for women, which could be lifelong or temporary (*Dig.* 48.19.8.8). In any case, at least from the time of → Tiberius, the person sentenced to the death penalty, to public works, or to gladiatorial games suffered the *servitus poenae* ("penal servitude"), that is to say, civil death with all its consequences (Cod. Theod. 9.40; *Dig.* 28.1.8.4; 28.3.6.6; 48.19.8.11–12; 48.19.12, 29; 48.20.5; Pau. *Sent.* 4.8.22(24); Tert. *Apol.* 27), except for those women with a temporary sentence, who retained their citizenship (Pau. *Sent.* 3.6.29; *Dig.* 28.1.8.4; 34.8.3; 48.9.8.4, 8; 48.19.8.8; 48.19.17, 36; Tert. *Apol.* 27.7). Hadrian established by rescript (→ Hadrian's Rescript) that these women continued to be free, as well as any children born of female convicts (*Dig.* 48.19.28.6). Immediately after pronouncement of the sentence and up to the time of its implementation (if he had been condemned to death), or of his death (if he was condemned to the games), the free man was reduced to the status of a slave and became the property of the state, losing his civil and political rights as well as his family rights (he was removed from his family and his marriage was annulled). Moreover, his property devolved upon the state treasury so that he might no longer possess, dispose of, or benefit from it, while even his prior will was considered null and void. However, servitude was excluded from the penalty by Justinian, since the emperor declared that it was intolerable for anyone born free to become a slave as a result of criminal punishment (Justin. *Nov.* 22.8; 536).

Furthermore, these convicts had to undergo a series of physical hardships. Half of their head was shaved, and they were branded with a red-hot iron (Jones, 1987), although a law promulgated by Constantine in 316 CE stipulated that this branding was not permitted on the face (Cod. Theod. 9.40.2). Thereafter, they were secured with irons on the feet (Cyp. *Ep.* 76.2; 77.3; *Dig.* 4.6.9; Ovid *Ep.* 1.6.31; Plaut.

Capt. 3.650–655): this device consisted of several links in the case of a short chain, sometimes tied at the waist, which enabled them to walk but prevented them from escaping. All of this was in addition to the already difficult conditions of daily work: ten hours a days, at times in underground tunnels where breathing was difficult and the space so cramped that the convicts even had to work on their knees. In Egypt, they were tortured inside the mines (Eus. *Mart. Pal.* 8.13; 13.6), meaning that in certain places, death ensued after a few days. In this regard, the mines of Palestine seem to have been the worst.

The *damnatio ad metalla* ("condemnation to the mines") included all types of extraction, since the removal of salt from limestone and the extraction of sulfur may be assimilated to work in the mines (*Dig.* 48.19.8.8, 10; 49.15.6; Isid. *Etym.* 5.27.31). In fact, a papyrus has been preserved that documents an order issued in the year 139 CE by the prefect of Egypt, Avidius Heliodorus, to the effect that a prisoner who had completed the five years of his sentence *ad alabastronem* was to be freed: in this case, it was a punishment in the alabaster quarries (Bastianini, 1988, 351–356). And finally, another form of punishment was the obligation to serve the miners, generally inflicted on women (*Dig.* 48.19.8.8; 48.19.28.6). In Republican Rome, the sentence was served in the ancient quarries situated on the slopes of the capitol, which supplied the city with tuff, a kind of limestone used above all in the buildings of Republican times. In Egypt, Aelius Aristides describes a porphyry quarry that was worked by convicts, which was presumably the same as the one mentioned by Eusebius when speaking of the Christians condemned in the Thebais in the year 308 CE (Eus. *Mart. Pal.* 8.1). This was the Mons Porphyrites, situated in the desert to the east of the region, close to Myos Hormos. As indicated in the Digest, some provinces had no mines to which sentenced prisoners could be sent, so that these were transferred to other provinces where there were mines (*Dig.* 48.19.8.4).

Nevertheless, all of this does not imply that work in the mines or quarries was carried out exclusively by criminals; in fact, reports may be found of other places at which minerals were apparently not extracted by convicts but rather by employees working on the basis of a contract. This is the case, for example, for the mines in Dacia, Lusitania, or Phrygia. However, it is difficult to ascertain the conditions under which the administration of these mines might have taken place and to determine the ownership of these sites within the empire; what is certain is that there were as many private mines as imperial ones and that the labor force of both types consisted of both free men and slaves. As far as convicts are concerned, it is possible that these may also have been used in the privately owned mines, but this is mere conjecture. Apart from that, some authors assume that the increased number of criminals who were sentenced to work in the mines during the empire may be due to the decreased availability of slave labor for these works following the cessation of the wars of conquest, that is to say, the prisoners who had formerly been used as slaves may have been replaced by judicial convicts (Täckholm, 1937).

3. Application against Christians

During the persecutions, Christians were often sentenced to the mines (Eus. *Hist. eccl.* 4.23.10; Tert. *Apol.* 12; Cyp. *Ep.* 76–79; *Passio Quattor Coronati*), where they were forced to work on the extraction of stone, marble, and porphyry, or also of gold, silver, and copper, an activity that was managed by the state in different parts of the empire. Persons sentenced on confessional grounds were also sent to the mines, above all in the reign of Constans and Valens (Vaillé, 1898/1899, 66–70; Lagrange, 1898, 114). One of them was the subdeacon Euthychius, although he already belongs to a late stage (356 CE) and was sent there by the Arians (→ Arianism). Others were also sent to Palestine, Proconnesus (quarries of Marmara), Tunis, Numidia, Algeria, and so on. However, it is very curious that there are no historical juridical documents that speak of Christians being condemned to the extraction of lime or sulfur. Neither is this reflected in any of the acts of martyrdom (→ Martyrs), though we dispose of another type of testimony provided to us by various Christian authors. In one of his letters (*Ep.* 76), → Cyprian of Carthage praises the martyrs who had been exiled and condemned to the mines of Siga in central Numidia (Millar, 1984, 140). In doing so, he describes all the details of this punishment (Cyp. *Fort.* 76.2.1–5; 77.3.1): after having been beaten with rods, irons and chains were then fastened onto

them and their heads were shaved; moreover, the conditions were atrocious: it is mentioned that they had no milk nor a mattress on which to rest, but slept on the ground; that it was filthy in that place; and that the food provided was insufficient, as were the clothes, an especially painful circumstance when the weather was cold.

Hippolytus of Rome also mentions the martyrs condemned to the mines in Sardinia in his account of the punishment of Callistus, a former slave of Carpophorus who was accused of theft and violence by the prefect of Rome in 180 CE (Hipp. *Haer.* 9.11–12). Later on, Martia, concubine of Commodus, orders the readying of a list of Christians sentenced to be sent there, for the purpose of setting them free (*Haer.* 9.2.12). In the martyrdom of Clement, we read that at the beginning of the 2nd century CE, the bishop of Rome was deported to a city beyond the Euxinian Chersonesus (Cotelier, 1672, 828–836; Leclercq, 1924, 467). On his arrival, he encountered 2,000 Christians condemned some time earlier to the quarrying of marble.

Moreover, Eusebius reports that at the order of the emperor Maximinus, 130 convicted persons from Egypt were again sent to the mines, some to Palestine and others to Cilicia (Eus. *Hist. eccl.* 8.13). On this occasion, Aedesius died from exposure at sea after having previously spent some time working off a sentence in the mines of Palestine (Eus. *Mart. Pal.* 5.2). But his fullest testimony deals with the Christians of Caesarea in Palestine who had been condemned to the mines (*Mart. Pal.* 7.2–4), first by the governor Urban, who sent them to the copper mines of Phaeno in Palestine. Concretely, speaking of the companions of Silvanus, he indicates that they had been previously branded with red-hot irons and that the tendons of one of their legs had been severed. He then goes on to speak of those sent (97 men, women, and children) by Firmilian (Urban's successor) to the porphyry quarries of the Thebais, who suffered the cutting of the tendons of their left foot with red-hot irons down to the very nerves, after which they were blinded in the right eye with red-hot irons down to the root (*Mart. Pal.* 8.1). Sometime later, at the emperor's behest, the governor decided to divide up the multitude of confessional prisoners in the mines of Palestine by sending some to Cyprus and others to Lebanon, while yet others were dispersed in the different regions of Palestine, ordering them to carry out various types of work (*Mart. Pal.* 13.2).

The same punishment is likewise documented in a papyrus relating to the transportation of certain convicts deported to the mines during the period of the persecutions carried out by → Diocletian, although it is by no means certain that these were Christians (Wessely, 1907, 38; Leclercq, 1933, 1213–1225).

Despite the fact that no act of martyrdom is preserved in which those found guilty were sentenced to punishment in the mines, we cannot overlook the extremely complete and detailed information provided by Christian authors. One should perhaps be cautious about accepting the figures relative to the number of condemned persons, as they do seem excessive in certain cases; however, it cannot be denied that Christians were sent to this torment in the course of the persecutions. In fact, this was a mechanism so firmly rooted and accepted by society that no one doubted its necessity or denounced the ill treatment implied by the recourse to this form of punishment. Accordingly, it is normal that the Roman authorities, who considered the Christians a dangerous element in society and viewed them as delinquents guilty of grave crimes against the emperor and the state, should have decided that this was one more way of punishing them.

4. Archeological Testimonies

One inscription relative to punishment has been preserved (Bruzza, 1889, 83). Further evidence is provided by the representation of an individual identified as a convict of this type, found on the bottom of a vase representing a man condemned *ad metalla* who later becomes a chariot driver in the circus (Dölger, 1929, 229–235; Rossi, 1868, 25). He has a shaven head and a rope around his neck. Along with this testimony, one may also cite the bas-relief of the miners of Linares, which depicts the work carried out at one of these mining operations (see Daubrée, 1882; Rodríguez, 2001). But apart from these two pictorial documents, no other ancient representation is known of anyone who had been condemned to the mines. The only monuments that may be considered as such belong to the Middle Ages (Wey, 1875, 127).

Historiography

The subject of *damnatio ad metalla* in Christian antiquity has not been specifically studied as such in ancient historiography, except for the work of J.B. De Rossi (1868), but it is not very extensive. This first research is completed with those encyclopaedical works that contain specific concepts from the classical world. So, for example, we can find the "metalla" entry in: *Dictionnaire des antiquités grecques et romaines* (Ardaillon, 1910); and the "Ad metalla" and "Mines" entries in: *Dictionnaire d'archéologie chrétienne et de liturgie* (Leclercq, 1924; 1933). From about the same time, there are more specific studies which analyze aspects related to epigraphical findings (Bruzza, 1889; Lagrange, 1898; Vaillé, 1898).

In more recent historiography we have reference to contributions about Roman Criminal Law, such as P. Garnsey (1970) or R.A. Bauman (1996), and about the persecutions of Christians, such as M.-F. Baslez (2007) or T.D. Barnes (2010) that contain interesting information. It is from this point onwards that more specific studies appear, such as F. Millar (1984) and P.A. Brunt (1980) about this punishment in Roman world, and M.A. Mateo (2016) where specifically the punishment of mines in relation to early Christians has been analyzed in a part of the contribution. Finally, we know of specific individuals from Christian communities that have been condemned *ad metalla* in antiquity due to the publication of the *Acts of the Martyrs* (such as those edited in the journal *Analecta Bollandiana*).

Bibliography

Ardaillon, E., "Metalla," in: C. Daremberg & E. Saglio, eds., *DAGR*, vol. III/2, Paris, 1910, 1840–1873.

Barnes, T.D., *Early Christian Hagiography and Roman History*, Tübingen, 2010.

Baslez, M.-F., *Les persécutions dans l'antiquité: Victimes, héros, martyrs*, Paris, 2007.

Bastianini, G., "Un ordine di scarcerazione: PBerol. inv. 8997 (ChLA X 421)," in: *Proceedings of the XVIII International Congress of Papyrology*, vol. II, Athens, 1988, 351–356.

Bauman, R.A., *Crime and Punishment in Ancient Rome*, London, 1996.

Brunt, P.A., "Free Labour and Public Works at Rome," *JRS* 70, 1980, 81–100.

Bruzza, L., "Di un'epigrafe cristiana scoperta nelle cave di marmo giallo in Numidia," *SDSD* 10, 1889, 83.

Cotelier, J.-B., *Sanct. Barnabae et aliorum Patrum Apostolicorum scripta*, Paris, 1672.

Daubrée, F.A., "Bas-relief trouvé à Linarés (Espagne): Des mineurs antiques en tenue de travail," *RAr* 43, 1882, 193–196.

De Rossi, J.B., "Dei Cristiani condannati alle cave dei marmi nei secoli delle persecuzioni e della cura, ch'ebbe di loro la chiesa romana," *NBAC* 6/2, 1868, 17–25.

Dölger, F.I., "Der Rennfahrer Liber mit der Kreuztätowierung auf einem Goldglass aus der Kallistkatakombe," *AuC* 1, 1929, 229–235.

Garnsey, P., *Social Status and Legal Privilege in the Roman Empire*, Oxford, 1970.

Husson, G., & D. Valbelle, *Instituciones de Egipto: De los primeros faraones a los emperadores romanos*, Madrid, 1998.

Jones, C.P., "Stigma: Tattooing and Branding in Graeco-Roman Antiquity," *JRS* 77, 1987, 139–155.

Lagrange, M.J., "Phounon," *RB* 7, 1898, 112–115.

Leclercq, H., "Ad metalla," in: *DACL*, vol. I/1, Paris, 1924, 467.

Leclercq, H., "Mines," in: *DACL*, vol. XI/1, Paris, 1933, 1213–1225.

Mateo, M.A., *La ejecución de los mártires cristianos en el Imperio Romano*, Murcia, 2016.

Millar, F., "Condemnation to Hard Labour in the Roman Empire, from the Julio-Claudians to Constantine," *PBSR* 52, 1984, 124–147.

Noeske, H.C., "Studien zur Verwaltung und Bevölkerung der dakischen Goldbergwerke in römischer Zeit," *BoJ* 177, 1977, 373–426.

Rodríguez, O.P., "El relieve de los mineros de Linares (Jaén) del Deutsches Bergbau-Museum de Bochum," *Main.* 23, 2001, 197–206

Täckholm, U., *Studien über den Bergbau der römischen Kaiserzeit*, Uppsala, 1937.

Vaillé, S., "Les martyrs de Phounon," *EOr*, 1898, 66–70.

Wessely, C., *Les plus anciens monuments du christianisme écrits sur papyrus*, Paris, 1907.

Wey, F., *Rome: Descriptions et souvenirs*, Paris, 1875.

M. AMPARO MATEO DONET

Ad Novatianum

The *Ad Novatianum* (*To Novatian*) is an anonymous letter (or a treatise in the form of a letter) addressed to the schismatic leader Novatian, likely written between 250 and 260 CE, during Novatian's active years. It is a rebuke of → schism and of the rigorism that set Novatian apart from his prominent contemporaries, particularly Cornelius of Rome (→ Cornelius [Bishop of Rome]) and → Cyprian of Carthage. This rebuke takes the form largely of arguments from Scripture in favor of the mercy of God, the unity of the church, and the possibility of repentance after all sins, including idolatry.

The author, who writes as a → bishop might, emphasizing his paternal care for his flock and the danger of further dissolution to which Novatian subjects the church, compares that danger to the danger the church faces from → persecution. He also turns about Novatian's accusations of defilement in the Catholic Church, writing that Novatian's willingness to leave the church makes him "defiled with the filth of sacrilege" (*AN* 1.4). Among the Scriptures interpreted against Novatian, the most remarkable is perhaps an extended treatment of Noah and the flood (*AN* 2.9–6.5). The ark is the church, which contains both clean and unclean animals, and the flood is the Decian → persecution (*AN* 6.5). The author identifies the two sendings of the dove from the ark as representing two persecutions, in the second of which the church is victorious. This tells Novatian that, though the one ark contains both sinners and saints, its legitimacy is proven by its victory in the second persecution. The identity of this second persecution is important for establishing the date of the *Ad Novatianum*, as will be shown below.

Overall, the themes and rhetoric are well in line with what we see in Cyprian's anti-Novatian (and more generally anti-schismatic) writings, especially *De catholicae ecclesiae unitate* and Cyp. *Ep.* 44, 45, 55, and 68. The *Ad Novatianum* interprets Noah's Ark as a type of the church (*AN* 2.9), as does Cyprian (Cyp. *Unit. eccl.* 6). Both see the dove sent out from the Ark as representing the → Holy Spirit, which resides in the Catholic Church and not with the Novatianists (*AN* 3.2; Cyp. *Unit. eccl.* 9). According to Cyprian, Novatian came "charging in and seize[d]" the office of bishop, "swollen and bloated with [...] conceit and arrogance" (Cyp. *Ep.* 55.8.3). The writer of the *Ad Novatianum* laments that, among the Novatianists, "shamelessly, and without any law of ordination, the episcopate is sought after" (*AN* 2.6). Novatian "is placed in such great guilt of dissension and schism, and is separated from the Church" (*AN* 1.3), and now "offer[s] up sacrilegious sacrifices in opposition to the true bishop" (Cyp. *Ep.* 68.2.1). The concerns of the

Ad Novatianum appear North African and display a likely contemporaneity with Novatian and Cyprian.

1. Manuscripts and Editions

Ad Novatianum comes to us via seven manuscripts of Novatian's opuscule *De Bono Pudicitiae* (*In Praise of Purity*), all of which represent a fairly homogenous branch in the transmission history of that work (Diercks, 1971, 130). As Novatian was a condemned heretic, *De Bono Pudicitiae* was transmitted under Cyprian's name. This could explain the attachment of the *Ad Novatianum* if it was also believed to have been authored by Cyprian. Within the text, it is anonymous and untitled. The *editio princeps* is the *Daventria* (c. 1477); it was popularized in the 1520 edition of Erasmus, who included it among the works of Cyprian, though he did not think Cyprian to be the author. Editions were produced regularly throughout the 16th and 17th centuries, mostly derived from Erasmus; one in the 18th century; and W. Hartel in 1871 (PL, vol. III). The most recent edition is by G.F. Diercks in CChr.SL (vol. IV, 1972).

2. Reception

First, one must be careful not to confuse *Ad Novatianum* with another anonymous anti-Novatianist work that is known as *Contra Novatianum* (*Against Novatian*). The latter has a more convoluted history of dating and attribution and is now generally thought to be a work of Ambrosiaster from the late 4th century CE. Confusion of these works is aided by the fact that the translation of the *Ad Novatianum* in *ANF* (vol. V) is titled "Anonymous Treatise Against the Heretic Novatian."

The style and tone of the *Ad Novatianum*, as well as references to seemingly past and present persecutions, have led to general acceptance of its contemporaneity with Novatian. The author refers to *Deciana persecutione* (*AN* 6.5) as a past event, and a *secundum proelium* that is either past or present. The author states that some of those who lapsed in the Decian → persecution admirably redeemed themselves in the *secundum proelium*. Most have taken this *secundum proelium* to refer to the persecution under Gallus (r. 251–253 CE) since there is no reference to the next persecution, that of Valerian

(r. 253–260 CE, issued his first edict against Christians in 257 CE). Cyprian and his fellow North Africans were anticipating the advent of persecution by Gallus in 252 or 253 CE (Cyp. *Ep.* 57), but there is no evidence that it had a major impact on either North Africa or Rome in actuality (Clarke, 1986, 4–17). Therefore, it is reasonable to suggest that the *secundum proelium* refers either to the persecution under Valerian or simply to a second opportunity for the lapsed (→ Apostasy/Apostates) to prove themselves under the Decian persecution. Given that the author nowhere mentions the martyrdom of Cyprian, one can reasonably place the letter in the period between the end of the Decian persecution, which had died down by spring of 251 CE, and Cyprian's martyrdom in September of 258 CE.

This date range means that the letter is potentially contemporaneous, not only with Novatian but with several of the possible authors. While Cyprian has been suggested by a few, more famous attributions include Popes Sixtus II (Harnack. 1895; 1964; D'Alès, 1924) and Cornelius (Erasmus). E.W. Benson (2004) attributes it to a bishop in or around Rome, roughly contemporaneous with Cornelius. P. Monceaux believed that the author had to be North African, since he wrote that only the church could administer baptism, a statement seemingly incompatible with Italian belief and practice (Monceaux, 1902, 89). Among the few more recent scholars who have written on the authorship of the *Ad Novatianum*, J.L. Papandrea (2011) thinks it was written either by Cornelius or Sixtus, while G.W. Clarke (1986) considers it an open question. Based on style and theological concerns, North Africa is the most likely provenance. However, barring the discovery of new manuscripts or other ancient evidence, the identity of the anonymous author will likely remain up for debate.

Historiography

There are no full book-length studies of the *Ad Novatianum*, though there are several shorter studies worth consulting. The seminal modern work is A. von Harnack's lengthy investigation (Harnack & Gebhardt, 1895, 1–70) in which he argues for the authorship of Pope Sixtus II. E.W. Benson (2004) challenges A. von Harnack in an appendix of his work on Cyprian. A. von Harnack was not convinced, but E.W. Benson raises key objections to A. von Harnack. Besides A. von Harnack and E.W. Benson, G.F. Diercks (1971) provides a thorough history of the manuscripts and of the authorship question in the Series Latina of the Corpus Christianorum, in the introductions to both *Ad Novatianum* and Novatian's *De Bono Pudicitiae* in the same volume. Finally, G.W. Clarke (1984b; 1986; 1989) examines many relevant questions surrounding the document in his notes on the epistles of Cyprian, frequently through comparison of the language of *Ad Novatianum* with that of Cyprian.

Bibliography

"Anonymous: *Ad Novatianum*," in: G.F. Diercks, ed., CChr. SL, vol. III, Turnhout, 1972, 129–152; ET: "Anonymous Treatise Against the Heretic Novatian," in: R.E. Wallis, trans., A. Roberts, J. Donaldson & A.C. Coxe, eds., *ANF*, vol. V, Buffalo, 1886, 656–663.

Benson, E.W., *Cyprian: His Life, His Times, His Work*, Eugene, 2004.

Clarke, G.W., *The Letters of St. Cyprian of Carthage*, ACW 43, vol. I, New York, 1984a.

Clarke, G.W., *The Letters of St. Cyprian of Carthage*, ACW 44, vol. II, New York, 1984b.

Clarke, G.W., *The Letters of St. Cyprian of Carthage*, ACW 46, vol. III, New York, 1986.

Clarke, G.W., *The Letters of St. Cyprian of Carthage*, ACW 47, vol. IV, New York, 1989.

D'Alès, A., *Novatien: Étude sur la théologie Romaine zu milieu du IIIe siècle*, Paris, 1924.

Diercks, G.F., "Some Critical Notes on Novatian's De Bono Pudicitiae and the Anonymous Ad Novatianum," *VigChr* 25/2, 1971, 121–130.

Harnack, A. von, "Über eine bisher nicht erkannte Schrift des Papstes Sixtus II. vom Jahre 257/8," in: A. von Harnack & O. von Gebhardt, eds., TU, vol. 8/1, Leipzig, 1895, 1–70.

Harnack, A. von, "Novatian, Novatianism," in: S.M. Jackson, ed., *NSHERK*, vol. VIII, Grand Rapids, 1964, 197–202.

Heine, R.E., "Articulating identity," in: F. Young, L. Ayres & A. Louth, eds., *CHECL*, Cambridge UK, 2004, 200–221.

Monceaux, P., *Histoire litteraire de l'Afrique chretienne depuis les origines jusqu'a l'invasion arabe*, vol.II, Paris, 1902.

Papandrea, J.L., *Novatian of Rome and the Culmination of Pre-Nicene Orthodoxy*, Eugene, 2011.

BENJAMIN SAFRANSKI

Ad Sanctos

In the 3rd century CE, there was a development in the devotion to the → martyrs. Close to their tombs the *cultus* took place. There was born a desire to be buried close to the martyrs – as close as was possible. In the 4th century CE, after the period of the persecutions, burial inside the catacombs developed as a practice. One would want a burial as close as possible to the → relics of the martyrs. This idea was expressed with different terminology: *ad sanctos, retro sanctos, ad sanctum Cornelium, ad dominum Caium,* and so on. An inscription, preserved at Velletri, but from the Rome of the year 319 CE, synthesizes this praxis and the vivid desire for a nice place for one's burial ground: the deceased lady, who had been an *amatrix pauperum* according to her means, *quae pro tanta merita accepit sepulchrum intra limina sanctorum quod multi cupiunt et rari accipiunt* (*ICUR*, vol. I, 3127; see Carletti, 2008, Quod multi cupiunt et rari accipiunt. *A proposito di una nuova iscrizione dell'ex vigna Chiaraviglio*, in: *Historiam pictura refert*, Veganzones, Vatican City, 1994, 111–126). The observation that many desired it, but that few were able to obtain this privilege, which the deceased woman had obtained by her merits, reflects the then current mentality. The author of the inscription makes a point to highlight for us that the privileged spot had been granted to her not with any payment and by corruption, but rather by the conduct of her life. Furthermore, this expressed the conviction that a similar spot was not always obtainable; many had hoped for it, but few were able to obtain it. → Constantia too – also called *Bonifatia* – had merited to be buried "beside the place of the saints" (Diehl 2156). These were privileged tombs and privileged persons, economically and socially. The clergy enjoyed an advantage by its position. Naturally, the bishops were given quite decent burials, and their deacons shared the surroundings of the depositions. In Saint Peter's Basilica, the subdeacon Marcellus obtained this from Pope John for himself and for his descendants (*ICUR*, vol. II, 4186). In Rome the choice of a cemetery also depended upon its prestige and on its characteristics as a monument. For example, the basilicas that were dedicated to the apostles (→ Apostle) on the Appian Way, along the Via Ostiense, and by the Via Cornelia were preferred by the ecclesiastical hierarchy and by the laity who had means. In certain places an obstruction of the tombs came to be; they were laid down in every direction, in order to be close to the saint, even with one upon another. Pope → Damasus, in an epigram, speaks of the situation at the tomb of Peter (→ Peter the Apostle), in the → Vatican, where the tombs of the faithful crowded (*cingebant*) the space (Ferrua 3); in another places he speaks of the *turba piorum* in the crypt of the popes at the catacombs of Callistus (Ferrua 16).

The first known example comes from Africa; in the *Passio Maximiliani* we find mention of two burials beside the tomb of → Cyprian of Carthage at Mappalia (*iuxta Cyprianum*), near Carthage, where → Augustine of Hippo would then preach several times. The greatest development of the devotion to the martyrs in the collective catacombs came about beginning with Pope Damasus (d. 384 CE), who promoted the *cultus* effectively. Concomitantly there was a diffusion of the phenomenon of the burial beside the most venerated tombs – and therefore also the most costly (ICVR 2.6077; 3.8669; 4.9441, 9924, 12748; 6.17192; 8.23546; 10.27034, 27060). The *fossores*, among their other activities, also managed and oversaw their sales. As the number of Christians increased, there was an ever greater solicitation by people who would be permitted to buy a similar tomb. In Rome there are epigraphical testimonies of these sales. In the cemetery of Ciriaca, Lucilius Pelio – while living – bought a sepulcher with two spots in the *basilica maior* close to Lawrence's in the presbytery (*ICUR*, vol. VII, 17912), while Flavius Eurialus, a very important person, had purchased a tomb from the *fossor* Faustinus, actually beside that of the blessed martyr Lawrence (7.1735). In the cemetery of Callistus, Serpentius purchased a tomb from *fossor* Quintus in the crypt of Cornelius (*ICUR*, vol. IV, 9441), Iovina bought an *arcosolium* beside Gaius (*ICUR*, vol. IV, 9924) and beside Quirinus (*ICUR*, vol. V, 14270), and Dracontius Pelagius had his daughter laid down beside Hippolytus of Rome (*ICUR*, vol. VII, 20059). In the inscriptions of the sepulchers *ad sanctos*, the name of the martyr is recalled, which itself gives importance to the choice. In order to satisfy the great demands, places were also created behind the tombs of the martyrs (*retro sanctos*). Victor was content to have acquired a tomb

for himself and for his two relatives that was close to the tomb of Pope Damasus and to his family (*ICUR*, vol. IV, 12502.). In the cemetery of Priscilla, Felicissimus and Leoparda had purchased a *loculus* with two places, close to the martyr Crescentio (*ICUR*, vol. IX, 25165).

The more that the tombs were prestigious, so much more difficult was it to obtain a place beside the tomb of the martyr. Two people were unique to Rome, relative to the two most famous tombs, those of Peter and Paul (→ Paul the Apostle). A certain Verus "after his death, merited to lay inside the sanctuary of Peter" (*ICUR*, vol. II, 4226); even someone such as Felix, who was *primiscrinarius sedis apostolicae*, merited that his remains repose within the sanctuary of Paul (*ICUR*, vol. II, 5745; ILCV 1310).

In Germany, the city of Xanten (*ad sanctos*), the ancient Colonia Ulpia Traiana, took its name from this practice of the burial beside a *memoria*. In the neighboring city of Cologne, an inscription of a little girl was discovered, Rudu[f])ula, from 5th–6th centuries CE, which contained the expression *SOCIATA MS*, which perhaps stands for *sociata m[artyribu]s* "associated with the tombs of the martyrs" and may allude to a tomb. At Regensburg (Castra Regina), too, a commemorative gravestone of a deceased woman was discovered (from the end of the 4th cent. CE) with a Christological monogram and the inscription *martiribus sociatae* (*CIL*, vol. III, 5972).

So, too, when the practice of above-ground burial became widespread, this (previous) practice continued. For example, to the east of the city of Tipasa (also, Tipaza), a basilica was built for the martyr Salsa, around which a large concentration of tombs developed. Likewise did this happen at Tarragona surrounding the basilica of Fructuosus and his two deacon companions, safeguarded in the cemetery's basilica. At times it is noted that the deceased was placed inside the basilica of a cemetery.

Hagiographical stories and inscriptions emphasize the importance of the proximity of the deceased's body to the body of a saint: the closeness created an association and a relationship of a familial sort, which then also leads to the benefit of the soul. The conviction had spread that from the relics of the martyrs gushes forth a salvific and beneficent power. Their sanctity benefited the bodies too (as well as the souls) of the people who were buried in their proximity. This explains the origin of the so-called circiform basilicas, in the form of a circus, that is, with blanketing naves that surrounded the one in the center; there were some extensive communal cemeteries that were covered. The presence of the relics of a martyr guaranteed the martyr's protection. → Paulinus of Nola constructed an edifice around the tomb of the martyr Felix, with funereal basilicas, so as to satisfy the demand for burial *ad sanctos*.

What was the attitude of the clergy toward this? They were favorable and promoted it. Ambrose, in Milan (→ Ambrose of Milan), had his brother Satyrus buried close to the tomb of the martyr Victor in the *basilica apostolorum*, because he firmly believed in the benefit of a burial beside his tomb. He placed this inscription on it:

> This extreme honor did Ambrose, his brother, confer upon Uranius Satyrus, (by placing him) to the left of the martyr. This is the reward for his merit: may the waves of his holy blood – by seeping within – soak the remains which lie close by. (Carletti, 2008, 286)

He also had the consecrated virgin Manlia Dedalia buried in the same basilica adjacent to the martyr (ILCU 1700). Ambrose also expressed this conviction in the commemoration of his brother (*De excessu fratris*).

Paulinus of Nola wrote to Augustine to ask his opinion of this practice and about the widespread certainty of the benefit from this type of burial. Paulinus forwarded to Augustine the question that Flora – a pious widow – had addressed to him. He was convinced that, just as with the prayers for the deceased, so too their burial near the body of the martyrs would be for their benefit. Augustine sent back to him a full response (*De cura pro mortuis gerenda*), composed during the years 420/421 CE, in which he discusses all of the aspects of the attention given to the deceased. To bury their bodies near the *Memoriae* of saints is a beautiful manifestation of the human connections in the relationships with one's own loved ones; it is a religious act, as is all the attention shown to them (Aug. *Cur.* 18.22). Yet, everything is for the consolation of the survivors (*Cur.* 4.6). For this reason, the church prays for the deceased. All that is done for them is beneficial, only if they are in the condition to receive the fruits on the basis of their conduct in this life, prior to death.

> Everyone shall receive the recompense for their works, done while they were in the body, be it for good or for evil, because the Lord will render to each one according to his works. (Aug. *Cur.* 1.1)

These ideas are found in a succinct manner in an epitaph for a Roman archdeacon by the name of Sabinus, in a complete countertrend in regard to the clergy and the faithful of the Roman church. Had he read the work written by Augustine? We do not know. On his epitaph, which is located at the entrance to the Basilica of Saint Lawrence, he says,

> He gains no benefit, nay what is more, he increases the weight (of his responsibility), by resting beside the sepulchers of the pious ones [in other words, of the martyrs]; a well-lived life is close to the merits of the saints. There is no usefulness in the body; we turn to them with our soul, which – if it is saved – can (also) become the salvation of the body. (*ICUR*, vol. VII, 18017)

He had "chosen to be the doorkeeper of this holy place" (*elegi sancti ianitor esse loci*: *ICUR*, vol. VII, 18017; Diehl 1194). The opinion of Augustine and of Sabinus did not enjoy success, inasmuch as during the Middle Ages the burial *ad sanctos* continued, be it beside the body or relics of martyrs, but also beside those people who were popularly considered to be saints, or in otherwise holy places.

Bibliography

Carletti, C., *Epigrafia dei cristiani in occidente dal III al VII secolo, Ideologia e prassi*, Bari, 2008.

DACL, vol. I, Paris, 1953, 479–509.

Duval, Y., *Loca Sanctorum Africae: Le culte des martyrs en Afrique du IVe au VIe siècle*, vol. II, Rome, 1982.

Duval, Y., *Auprès des saints, corps et âme: L'inhumation "ad sanctos" dans la chrétienté d'Orient et d'Occident du IIIe au VIIe siècle*, Paris, 1988.

Duval, Y., & J.C. Picard, eds., *L'inhumation privilégiée du IVe au VIIIe siècle en Occident: Actes du Colloque tenu à Créteil le 16–18 mars 1984*, Paris, 1986.

Picard, J.C., *Le souvenir des évêques: Sépultures, listes épis-copales et culte des évêques en Italie du Nord des origines au Xe siècle*, Rome, 1988.

ANGELO DI BERARDINO

Adam and Eve

I. Adam ◆ II. Adam and Eve ◆ III. *Adam and Eve, Life of* ◆ IV. *Adam, Testament of*

I. Adam

Adam does not feature often in the biblical texts, but the references and allusions to him indicate a figure who provided an explanation of human character and destiny. Paul's Adam theology and its influence thereafter indicate how important the figure of Adam was in early Christian theology.

1. Adam in Genesis and Other Jewish Scriptures

The most famous passage in the Hebrew Bible is the → creation account in Gen 1–3, in which several features become fundamental to early Christian Adam (and Eve) references. *Adam* is widely used throughout the Hebrew Scriptures in the sense of "humankind, human being" (*BDB*, s.v. *adam* 2). The same is true in Gen 1–2, where *adam* is best translated as "man/humankind" (Gen 1:26–28; 2:7). The ambivalence between *adam* as an individual and *adam* representing humankind as a whole only really begins at Gen 2:18 (LXX translates *adam* as *anthrōpos* up to Gen 2:18, but thereafter, and including Gen 2:16, translates *adam* as *Adam*). In Gen 2:23–24 the Hebrew shows awareness of the ambivalence by using *'ish* ("man") with *'ishah* ("woman, wife"). It is not unimportant to note the deliberate play in the Hebrew of Gen 2:7 between *adam* and the material from which *adam* was made, *adamah* ("ground, earth") – "the Lord God formed the *adam*, dust from the *adamah*." The tie-in was no doubt deliberate: the *adam* was formed to till the *adamah* (Gen 2:5–9), and subsequently the *adamah* is caught up in *adam*'s penalty for his disobedience (the ground cursed and its produce necessitating hard labor), a penalty that shall last until *adam* returns to the *adamah* (Gen 3:17–19; note also Gen 4:11–12; 5:29; 8:21–22).

"The tree of the knowledge of good and evil" (Gen 2:9), from which the *adam* was sternly ordered not to eat (Gen 2:17; → Life, Tree of), has prompted endless discussion. The most obvious understanding is not that the fruit would give Adam an awareness of right and wrong that he would otherwise have totally lacked; the command itself presupposes Adam already knew the difference between obedience and disobedience. Rather what seems to be in view is the issue of moral autonomy. The order is followed by a warning that disobedience on this point will result in → death (Gen 2:17 – "in the day that you eat of it you shall die"). In the event the result is exclusion from the other named tree, "the tree of life" (Gen 2:9; 2:22; 2:24), and by implication from the presence of God in the garden. Since only the tree of the knowledge of good and evil was forbidden to *Adam*/man (Gen 2:17), the implication is that eating from the tree of life was permitted (Gen 2:16). So presumably in Gen 2–3 the divine intention was that humankind should "live forever" (Gen 3:22), presumably by regularly eating from that tree. The implication is that by being debarred from the tree, death would be the consequence (Gen 3:19).

Outside of the creation account, the Hebrew Scriptures take little notice of the Adam story, although there are allusions in a number of places (1 Chr 1:1; Deut 4:32; Ezek 28:12–15; Hos 6:7; see Callender, 2000).

2. Adam in Early Jewish Texts

In the Septuagint, most references to Adam are in the book of Wisdom (2:23–24; 7:1; 9:2–3; 15:8; 15:11; also Tob 8:6). In other early postbiblical Jewish texts, the role of Adam's disobedience becomes a major factor in generating explanations for the human condition. We may simply note the retelling of the story of Adam's disobedience and expulsion in *Jub.* 3:7–25, with its striking though also characteristic elaboration in *Jub.* 3:26–31.

For → Philo of Alexandria, the two creation stories speak of two kinds of humans; those who live by reason granted to them by the divine inbreathing, and those who live by the pleasure of the flesh. The latter remain a molded clod of earth while the former are the faithful impress of the divine image. (Philo *Her.* 56–57) Philo relates that God did not take just any clay to form Adam, but he selected the best, pure clay, and the most refined in order to fashion Adam (Philo *Opif.* 137). Philo does not state where this took place, but *2 En.* 71:35 places Adam's creation on the Temple Mount, the center of the earth and the place that will be his final grave. Thus, Adam and Abel were buried in the place from where Adam was created (*Apoc. Mos.* 40:6) and near the place of the future altar (*Apoc. Mos.* 33:4). These motifs will also appear in rabbinic literature (Gafni, 2019, 36).

Knowledge of the nakedness of Adam (and Eve) after having eaten from the forbidden fruit was "the beginning of evil" (Philo *Quaest. Gen.* 1.40). Zeal for pleasure brings about spiritual death, by causing the earth-born creature to give himself over to the earth from which he was created and to turn away from heaven (the soul) back to the earth (physical death; *Quaest. Gen.* 1.51; see further Levison, 1988, 63–88).

The *Life of Adam and Eve* (*Vita Adae et Evae*) presents the theme of "death gaining rule over all our race" as a result of Adam and Eve's transgression (*Apoc. Mos.* 14). The consequence is Adam's estrangement from the glory with which he had been clothed (*Apoc. Mos.* 20:2; 21:6), whereas his share in the image of God seems to be unaffected (*Apoc. Mos.* 10:3; 12:1–2; 33:5; 35:2; *L.A.E.* 37.3; 39.2–3). Notable also was the promise to a faithful Adam of → resurrection and renewed access to the tree of life, "and you shall be immortal forever" (*Apoc. Mos.* 28.4).

The two classic Jewish apocalypses, *4 Ezra* and *2 Baruch*, emerged in the period following the destruction of → Jerusalem in 70 CE. Both texts discuss the question of human responsibility and blame human sinfulness for the disaster. According to *4 Ezra*, Adam transgressed the commandment "and immediately you (God) appointed death for him and his descendants" (*4 Ezra* 3:7). More striking is Ezra's attribution of Adam's → sin to his "evil heart" (*4 Ezra* 3:21–26). There is no "original sin"; the "evil heart" is an unexplained part of humanity. If anyone is to be blamed, it is God, for failing to take away the evil heart (*4 Ezra* 3:20). At the same time, the angel Uriel's alternative image speaks of a grain of evil seed that was sown in Adam's heart from the beginning from where all ungodliness derives (*4 Ezra* 4:30).

Both "the evil heart" and the "grain of evil seed" are presumably equivalent to the "inclination" of Gen 6:5 and 8:21, the rabbis' evil "inclination" (*yetzer*). Most striking of all is Ezra's lament in *4 Ezra* 7:118: "O Adam, what have you done? For though it was you who sinned, the fall [*casus*] was not yours alone, but ours also who are your descendants."

2 Baruch reflects a similar agonizing about responsibility for the disaster that befell Jerusalem in 70 CE. The question of responsibility is explicitly posed:

> O Adam, what did you do to all who were born after you? And what will be said of the first Eve who obeyed the serpent, so that this whole multitude is going to corruption? (*2 Bar.* 48:42–43)

It is, however, answered in terms of individuals being repaid for their own transgressions (*2 Bar.* 48:47); "Adam is, therefore, not the cause, except only for himself, but each of us has become our own Adam" (*2 Bar.* 54:19).

Thus, the Adam traditions based on Genesis present two different perspectives on Adam. On the one hand, the Gen 1–3 Adam traditions invite an interpretation that takes seriously the play between Adam and *adam* ("humankind"). On the other hand, Gen 2–3 provides an explanation for the reality of death in human experience (see further Scroggs, 1966, 19).

3. Adam in Paul's Theology

In the New Testament it is mostly the Pauline corpus that relates to Adam (otherwise only Luke 3:38 and Jude 1:14). In speaking of or alluding to "Adam," Paul (→ Paul the Apostle) refers to humankind as a whole. He builds a contrast between Adam and Christ, between the first Adam and the last Adam, between the one responsible for the death of humankind and the one who became a life-giving spirit (1 Cor 15:22; 15:45). Paul speaks of "man" (*anēr*, not *anthrōpos*) as the "image and glory of God," whereas "the woman/wife is the glory of man/husband" (1 Cor 11:7). Moreover, he implies that the initial failure in Eden was that of Eve (2 Cor 11:3; much starker in the later 1 Tim 2:13–14). Still more striking is the broader trend that Paul no doubt influenced, to merge Ps 8:6 and Ps 110:1, so that Christ's exaltation is seen as the fulfillment of the divine initiative in creating humankind (1 Cor 15:25–27; but also Eph 1:20–22; Heb 1:13–2.8; and reflected in Mark 12:36 and 1 Pet 3:22; Dunn, 1998, §14).

However, it is particularly in Romans that Paul repeatedly calls upon the Adam references in Gen 1–3 to explain the human condition (Dunn, 1998, §4). Inexplicit but integral to Paul's indictment of humankind is the figure of Adam as portrayed in Gen 1–3. It was Adam who had failed to glorify God as God or to give him thanks (Rom 1:21) by refusing to obey his one command (Gen 2:17). Hence, as in Wis 13:8–9, they are without excuse (Rom 1:20). The consequence, again as in Wis 13:1, is futility of thinking, and foolish heart darkened (Rom 1:21). In Rom 1:22, the echo becomes stronger. The claim to be wise, which actually plunged into folly, recalls the current understanding of the tree of the knowledge of good and evil. The implication is that humankind is dependent for wisdom from on high. If it claims such wisdom in itself or in its own resources, that is simply a recipe for folly, darkened counsel, and disaster. Rom 3:23 echoes the thought of *Apoc. Mos.* 20:2 and 21:6 that Adam's sin resulted in his being deprived of the glory of God, with the implication that in the age to come the original glory would be restored or enhanced (*Apoc. Mos.* 39:2–3).

The first explicit reference to Adam appears at the conclusion to the first complete section of Paul's argument in Romans (5:12–21). In these verses Paul encapsulates all human history under the two archetypal figures (note the double "all" of Rom 5:18) – Adam and Christ. Whether Paul also thought of Adam as a historical individual and the act of disobedience as a historical event is less clear.

The use that Paul makes of Gen 1–3 is entirely in concert with the tradition of Jewish theologizing on Adam, in using the Genesis account to make sense of the human experience of sin and death. Paul's concern and point is not dependent on the resolution of any tension between questions of history or myth.

Paul draws the obvious implication from the function of the tree of life in Gen 2–3, that death was not part of the original divine intention in creation.

Paul's more distinctive ideas become evident in his emphasis that death is not simply the natural consequence of the created state but the consequence of sin (Rom 5:12; 5:21), including sins unlike those of Adam (Rom 5:14). Moreover, Paul seems to distinguish death of humanity as an *outcome* of Adam's first transgression, and death as a *consequence* or even penalty for one's own individual transgressions.

In Rom 7:7–13, Paul reverts to the Adam narrative, without referring explicitly to Adam. The echo is clearest in Paul's attributing the root of sin to "covetousness" (as in *Apoc. Mos.* 19:3 and 24:9; also Jas 1:15). The command not to eat of the tree of the knowledge of good and evil (Gen 2:17) is read as a particular expression of the commandment "you shall not covet" (Exod 20:17). The serpent is identified as the representation of "sin." And the "I" is an existential self-identification with Adam, *adam*, "everyman, humankind" (see 2 *Bar.* 54:19).

Rom 8:19–22 forms Paul's final allusion in Romans to the Gen 3 narrative. What is striking is the way he includes creation within the hope of final salvation. When he says that "creation was subjected to futility [*mataiotēs*]" (Rom 8:20), the allusion is clearly to Gen 3:17–18 (see Rom 1:22 where the equivalent verb is used). As creation shares in humankind's futility, so it will share in humankind's liberation from "the slavery of corruption" (Rom 8:21). The point to be underlined here is the solidarity of humankind with the rest of creation, of *adam* with the *adamah* from which *adam* was made.

4. Adam in Early Christian Tradition: Engagement with Paul in Irenaeus of Lyon

Adam is little mentioned in the 2nd century CE, and the few early references are of little significance (as in *1 Clem.* 6:3; 29:2; 50:3). But → Irenaeus of Lyon marks the beginning of serious engagement with Paul (Osborn, 2001, 189). This is nowhere as clear as in his thesis of recapitulation: that Christ, the Word, the Son of God, recapitulated Adam in himself (Iren. *Haer.* 3.21.10–23.8; 4.24.1; 6.1.2; 14.1–3; 20.2; 21.1–3). Irenaeus builds particularly on Rom 5:14 and 1 Cor 15:20–22 (*Haer.* 3.22.3; 4); in Christ the one God "re-formed the human race" (*Haer.* 4.24.1);

the → Word, having become united with the ancient substance of Adam's formation, rendered man living and perfect, receptive of the perfect Father, in order that as in the natural [Adam] we all were dead, so in the spiritual we may all be made alive. (Iren. *Haer.* 5.1.2; see 5.14.2)

This enabled Irenaeus to refute those who denied Adam's salvation (*Haer.* 3.23.2; 5; 7). His recapitulation thesis was at the heart of his refutation of the soteriologies of the Valentinians (→ Valentinus/ Valentinians) and → Marcion: it was one and the same God who made Adam and sent his Son; salvation has been achieved by the Word combining with flesh; it is the Son's assumption of flesh which ensures the resurrection of the flesh (*Haer.* 5.14.1).

It was not least the genius of Irenaeus that in his theology of recapitulation he managed to blend the Adam Christology of Paul and the incarnation Christology of John to provide a truly biblical theology.

5. The Tomb of Adam: Creation and Burial in Christian Tradition

The *Brevarius*, the Jerusalem guide to Christian holy sites (c. 400 CE), states that Adam was formed or created at → Golgotha (*Brev.* 2; Wilkinson, 2002, 93). As the buildings on Golgotha and the tomb complex of Jesus corresponded to the Jerusalem Temple (→ Temple, Jerusalem) and the Temple Mount (Eus. *Vita Const.*3.33; Wilkinson, 2002, 363), Jesus created at Golgotha would correspond to the Second Temple period Jewish traditions cited above that Adam was created on the Temple Mount, and as also mentioned above, this idea will also appear in rabbinic literature (below) and Christian tradition might also have been aware of the Jewish traditions.

Creation in Golgotha would eventually morph into the Tomb of Adam located under Golgotha. The first to mention this was → Origen (*Comm. Matt.* 27.33) who quotes 1 Cor 15:22, "As in Adam all die, even in Christ shall all be made alive," and adds, that Christ's death on the → cross brought life to Adam who was buried beneath the place of the crucifixion. The redemptive blood of Jesus, shed at the crucifixion, flowed onto the grave of the original Adam (Jeremias, 1958; Wilkinson, 2002, 363). As stated above, Second Temple period Jewish tradition also had Adam buried on the Temple Mount

and Origen's statement would seem to be a similar transfer of Jewish tradition from the Temple Mount to Golgotha (Aptowitzer, 1924).

The tradition of Adam being buried in Golgotha was not accepted by all. → Jerome, for instance, states that although it might have been pleasing to some to think that Adam was under Golgotha, he was actually buried in Hebron (Jer. *Comm. Matt.* 27.33), a view that was also found in rabbinic literature (below). In Jerome's description of the pilgrimage of → Paula in the late 4th century CE, she encountered in Hebron what the Hebrews described as the grave of Adam (Jer. *Ep.* 108.11.3; Gafni, 2019, 39n44). While some stood steadfast by the Hebron identification, eventually the Golgotha became the more accepted view with the tomb and skull of Adam being there. This even became an accepted explanation for the term Golgotha (Epiph. *Pan.* 46).

6. Adam in Rabbinic Literature and the Polemics of Burial

It is impossible to know to what extent the → rabbis were familiar with the Adam traditions of the Second Temple period, if at all. They do, however, repeat some of the prominent motifs from that time. Adam, according to Palestinian rabbinic tradition was created at the site of the future Temple altar, the place of atonement (*y. Naz.* 7.2.56b). Adam achieved the status of a prophet (*S. Olam Rab.* 21) and had his own altar on the Temple Mount, which David later found (*Pesiq. Rab.* 43). The Babylonian → Talmud (*b. Sanh.* 38a–b) took a more expansive view of the creation of Adam. One opinion states that Adam was gathered from dust from all over the world. Other views state that the dust was gathered from particular countries such as Babylonia or the land of Israel (Gafni, 2019, 41).

Rabbinic tradition was less insistent on the burial of Adam in Jerusalem and for good reason. A Palestinian tradition possibly hints at the skull of Adam buried under the altar (*y. Sotah* 5.2.20b and parallels). Most rabbinic traditions have Adam buried in Hebron in the Cave of the Doubles (*Gen. Rab.* 58:8; *b. 'Erub.* 53a; *b. Soṭah* 13a; *b. Bat.* 58a). The Jewish Hebron identification was possibly a response to the Christian tradition of seeking the tomb of Adam under Golgotha. Rabbinic tradition sought to cut any ties that Adam traditions may have developed to Christianity and to strengthen an independent Jewish tradition in Hebron (Gafni, 2019, 40). It was unlikely, though, that Jewish tradition was aware of Jerome's placing Adam's grave in Hebron.

Only one extremely worthy could merit burial in Hebron in the Cave of the Doubles with the patriarchs and matriarchs (except for Rachel). Thus, Adam spoke Hebrew (*Gen. Rab.* 17.4), kept the → Sabbath (*Gen. Rab.* 16.5) celebrated → Passover (*Pirqe R. El.* 21), studied Torah (*Sifre Deut.* 41; → Law/Decalogue/Torah), and even composed a chapter of Psalms (*Gen. Rab* 22.13). In addition to all this, Adam was celebrated for being monogamous, which the rabbis preferred, as opposed to the biblical patriarchs (*ʾAbot R. Nat.*, recension B, ch. 2; Gafni, 2019, 353). The same argument is also used by some Christian writers in their promotion of monogamy (see Tert. *Ux.* 2).

Historiography

Adam has been studied within the context of the Hebrew Bible and the ancient Near East (Callender, 2000). This served as the basis for continued scholarship on portraits of Adam in Second Temple and early Jewish literature (Levison, 1988). Both of these were the springboard for Adam studies in early Christianity and particularly in Paul, whether in general (e.g. Barrett, 1962; Dunn, 1998; Jervell, 1960; Scroggs, 1966) or in relation to specific works (Wedderburn, 1980). The best works on the burial of Adam are still the classic study of V. Aptowitzer (1924) and J. Jeremias (1958) and are summarized by J. Wilkinson (2002). I. Gafni (2019) has examined the relevant Jewish material in relation to Christian Adam traditions.

Bibliography

Aptowitzer, V., "Les élément juifs dans la légende du Golgotha," *REJ* 79, 1924, 145–162.
Barrett, C.K., *From First Adam to Last: A Study in Pauline Theology*, London, 1962.
Brandenburger, E., *Adam und Christus: Exegetisch-religionsgeschichtliche Untersuchungen zu Röm. 5.12–21 (1 Kor. 15)*, WMANT 7, Neukirchen, 1962.
Callender, D.E., *Adam in Myth and History: Ancient Israelite Perspectives on the Primal Human*, Leiden, 2000.

Dunn, J.G., *The Theology of Paul the Apostle*, Grand Rapids, 1998.
Gafni, I., *Jews and Judaism in the Rabbinic Era: Image and Reality-History and Historiography*, Tübingen, 2019.
Jeremias, J., *Golgotha*, Leipzig, 1958.
Jervell, J., *Imago Dei: Gen. 1.26f. im Spätjudentum, in der Gnosis und in den paulinischen Briefen*, FRLANT 76, Göttingen, 1960.
Levison, J.R., *Portraits of Adam in Early Judaism: From Sirach to 2 Baruch*, JSP.S 1, Sheffield, 1988.
Merklein, H., "Paulus und die Sünde," in: H. Frankemölle, ed., *Sünde und Erlösung im Neuen Testament*, Freiburg, 1991, 123–163.
Osborn, E., *Irenaeus of Lyons*, Cambridge UK, 2001.
Scroggs, R., *The Last Adam: A Study in Pauline Anthropology*, Philadelphia, 1966.
Wedderburn, A.J.M., "Adam in Paul's Letter to the Romans," in: E.A. Livingstone, ed., *Studia Biblica*, vol. III, JSOT.S, Sheffield, 1980, 413–430.
Wilkinson, J., *Jerusalem Pilgrims Before the Crusades*, Warminster, 2002.

JAMES D.G. DUNN (†)

II. Adam and Eve

Concerning the story of Adam and Eve in the Bible, there are some topics that attracted interest within both exegesis and art. Within exegesis, these main topics are "image and likeness" (Gen 1:26–27), breath of life (Gen 2:7), Adam and Eve in paradise (Gen 2:8–14), God's command (Gen 2:16, 17), human free will (Gen 3), seduction and sin (Gen 3:1–7), mortality and immortality (Gen 3:19), and repentance of Adam and consequences for humankind. Within art, the creation of Adam, paradise, the creation of Eve, Adam's fall, and Adam's and Eve's pain after the fall are the main issues.

1. Exegesis

Typologies between Adam and Jesus Christ have been part of Christian thinking on → Adam since Paul (see 1 Cor 15:45–47; Rom 5:12–21; see *Gos. Phil.* 70:9–13; 71:18–21; 73:15–19; 74:2–12), and subsequently also typologies between Eve and → Mary (Just. *Dial.* 100.4; Iren. *Haer.* 19.1).

Interpreting Gen 1:26–27, some authors distinguish between εἰκών (image) and ὁμοίωσις (likeness); others do not. For Origen, only our immaterial, inner human is the image of God. Origen seeks to avoid any anthropomorphic theology (Or. *Hom. Gen.* 1.13). According to → Novatian, God imparted mind, reason, and foresight to the human being made in his image, that he might imitate God (Nov. *Trin.* 1.8). → Gregory of Nyssa similarly states the mind, but also the αὐτεξούσιον, as likeness: the αὐτεξούσιον is the liberty of decision with regard to the orientation of our προαίρεσις to good or bad (Streck, 2005, 131). According to Severian of Gabala, holiness, righteousness, and mercy are characteristics of being εἰκών of God (Sev. *Hom. creat.* 5.4). Other authors follow a tradition shaped by both Platonic philosophy and biblical exegesis:

1. Plato has formulated the idea of human perfection by using the formula ὁμοίωσις τῷ θεῷ κατὰ δύνατον (Plato *Theaet.* 176b).
2. God announces Adam to be εἰκών and ὁμοίωσις, but he created Adam only as εἰκών (Gen 1:27).

Some ancient theologians combine these two views: God had created Adam as εἰκών; it is, however, an obligation for Adam himself to achieve the ὁμοίωσις by his own virtue, by imitation of God (Or. *Princ.* 3.6.1; referring on 1 John 3:2; Chrys. *Hom. Gen.* 9.3, referring to Matt 5:45 [ὅπως γένεσθε]; Anast. *Quaest.* 24).

The "breath of life" (Gen 2:7) is sometimes identified with the → soul (Philo *Opif.* 135; Tert. *An.* 11.3). Due to God's breathing, the soul is immortal (Philo *Opif.* 135; Iren. *Haer.* 5.7.1; Chrys. *Hom. Gen.* 12.5).

The topic of Adam and Eve in → paradise implies a debate about whether they had sexual intercourse in paradise. Jewish texts (see Anderson, 1989, 123–128 on *b. Yebam.* 63a; *Gen. Rab.* 18.6; 19:3; *Jub.* 3:2–6 et al.) suppose sexual intercourse, similarly Ambrosiaster (*Quaest. VNT* 127.28, based on Gen 1:28). Only birth-giving "in tristitia," not the birth-giving as such, is the consequence of the → fall. According to → Irenaeus of Lyon (*Haer.* 3.23.4), however, Adam and Eve lived without the knowledge of procreation. This notion is sometimes part of an angelic concept of the supra-lapsarian state of life, sometimes part of motivating an ascetic lifestyle (see e.g. Greg. Nyss. *Virg.* 12; Aug. *Civ.* 14.21).

God's Command (Gen 2:16–17) implies problems concerning the notion of God. In gnostic exegesis (→ Gnosis/Gnosticism), Gen 2:16–17 is sometimes regarded as the result of God's or the archon's ignorance (*Nat. Rulers* 88.24–89.3) or envy (*Nat. Rulers* 89.31–90.19; *Testim. Truth* 47). Adversely, the so-called orthodox authors emphasized the necessity of this command: Adam should learn to distinguish between God and himself (Iren. *Epid.* 15) and to learn freedom (Theophil. *Autol.* 2.27.4; Greg. Nyss. *Or. catech. magna* 5.10; Bas. Sel. *Hom.* 3.2).

But how to understand seduction and sin? The author of the *Gospel of Philip* (→ Philip the Apostle) interprets the seduction of Eve as sexual seduction by the masculine serpent (*Gos. Phil.* 61:5–10). Other authors name the desire for coequality (Chrys. *Hom. Gen.* 16.3), disobedience (Theophil. *Autol.* 2.25), sexual impatience (Clem. *Protr.* , 111.1; Tert. *Pat.* 5.13, but see Aug. *Gen. lit.* 11.41), love of self (*Gen. lit.* 11.30), or pride (Chrys. *Hom. Matt.* 15.1; Paul. *Ep.* 38.3) as rationale for being seduced.

Sin, however, is not an inevitable consequence of being affected by desire. Gen 3 in Jewish literature is often read not as aetiology of human existence inevitably being under sin but as an admonition to avoid sinfulness (Sir 15:11–20; Philo *Plant.* 45; *2 Bar.* 54:15; *4 Ezra* 7:118–131; *L.A.E.* [Gk] 30.1; → Sin). The possibly Manichean (→ Mani/Manichaeism) *Epistula ad Menoch* uses Gal 5:17 in order to describe the antagonism between the soul, created by God, and the body, whose powers enslave the soul due to the influence of → devil (Meiser, 2007, 266). So-called orthodox authors defended the concept of free will against presupposed (see, however, Aland, 1977 passim) gnostic determinism (see e.g. Bas. *Hom.* 15.7). → Augustine of Hippo's renunciation of the concept of free will is an implication of the so-called Pelagian controversy (→ Pelagians/Pelagianism). Before this controversy, Augustine emphasized the fundamental goodness of Adam's nature as God's creation: he was free to choose the higher instead of the lower objects of will, but he freely decided to indulge the serpent's seduction (Aug. *Lib.* 3.74). In later times, Augustine's theory is based on Rom 9:16: due to the *peccatum originale*, the freedom of choice is by no means a possibility of a created being but only a possibility by support of God's grace (Aug. *Div. quaest. Simpl.* 1.2.12).

The debate on the issue of mortality versus immortality is a result of Gen 3:19. Theophilus of Antioch's argumentation reveals the very theological problem: if Adam were created as mortal, creation would not be good (see Gen 1:31); if, however, Adam were created as immortal, he would live in an inconvenient similarity to God, and this would be a confirmation not of God's plan but (see Gen 3:5) of the devil's proposal (Heither & Reemts, 2007, 100). Some authors state immortality for the supralapsarian Adam (Tert. *Adv. Jud.* 2.2; Thdt. *Int. Rom.* 117; Aug. *Pecc. merit.* 2); they understand the punishment by → death, announced in Gen 3:19, as a new, hitherto unknown condition of human life (Bas. *Hom.* 15.7). → Nemesius of Emesa, however, seizes → Philo of Alexandria's theory: the human being is created neither mortal nor immortal but in potentiality to both. If God had created him mortal from the beginning, he would not have punished him by death; if he had created him immortal, he would have not changed this state of immortality in such a short time (Nem. *Nat. hom.* 1). Procopius of Gaza also denies the immortality of the supralapsarian Adam – it is impossible that God who is free from all affects should change his mind due to his wrath (Procopius of Gaza, *Commentarii in Genesin*).

The Pauline reading of Gen 3 as part of salvation history is by no means the predominating one in Jewish or Christian thought. Adam and Eve are negative examples for ethical admonition as well. Such a reading is the basis also for the issue of Adam's and Eve's repentance. In Jewish (see *Midr. Lev.* 4.1) and early Christian tradition (Iren. *Haer.* 3.23.5; Tert. *Paen.* 12.9), Adam is represented also as penitent, mostly for the sake of ethical admonition. The different versions of the *Life of Adam and Eve* include a story of Adam's repentance in the Jordan, Eve's repentance in the Tigris, where the devil anew seduces her (*L.A.E.* [Armen.] 44[6.1–10.3]; *L.A.E.* [Lat.] 6.1.–10.3). In *L.A.E.* (Slav.) she resists.

Consequences for humankind are an issue of debate as well. According to *2 Bar.* 54:15, 19, and *4 Ezra* 7:118–131, Adam's sin had consequences only for himself; our death, however, is the consequence not of Adam's sin but our own. Both apocalyptic texts, written in a challenging situation, admonish the reader to live according to the divine law. The catastrophe concerning Israel as a whole does not have consequences for salvation of the individual, which presupposes obedience to the Torah (→ Law/Decalogue/Torah).

The gnostic *Interpretation of Knowledge* (→ *Knowledge, Interpretation of*) names the consequence of Adam's sin in a general way as slavery (*Interp. Know.* 11.1). According to → Melito of Sardis, our sinning is the heritage (κληρονομία) of Adam's sin (Mel. *Pascha* 49). Later authors were more sophisticated. → John Chrysostom distinguishes: the consequence of Adam's sin for humankind was the slavery described in Gen 3:14–19; the sinners after Adam, however, confirm this slavery by their own sinning (Chrys. *Serm. Gen.* 7.2).

There was a long debate in New Testament exegesis whether in Rom 5:12 ἐφ' ᾧ πάντες ἥμαρτον (*in quo omnes peccaverunt*) the beginning ἐφ' ᾧ (*in quo*) is to be understood masculine or neutral. → Theodoret of Cyrrhus reads the clause as neutral: due to the exaggeration of the effects, human beings sin (Thdt. *Int. Rom.* 100a–b). The decision for a masculine reading of ἐφ' ᾧ (*in quo*) by no means includes the abrogation of the free will. We are generated as sinners but deserve the second death in hell by our own sinning (Ambrosi. *Comm. in Rom.* 5.12.3). We are imitators (Cyr.Alex. *Ep. ad Rom.* 5.12.) of Adam's sin.

2. Iconography

Scenes of Gen 2 and 3 have been part of Christian art from the very beginning (→ Dura-Europos, 3rd cent. CE; Naples, catacomb San Gennaro dei Poveri; Rome, Santi Pietro e Marcellino, 3rd/4th cent. CE; sarcophagus of the bishop Agritius, Trier, 314–336 CE; → Sarcophagi, Christian). The sarcophagus of Iunius Bassus (359 CE, Vatican Museums, no. 104) also includes a typological interpretation: side by side, Adam's creation stands over against Jesus' resurrection (→ Resurrection); the → fall and Jesus' cross, expulsion from paradise and Jesus' presentation in the → Temple (Luke 2), and so on (see e.g. St. Michael, Hildesheim, bronze door, 1015 CE). Some typological interpretations share the concept that not God the Father, but God the Son (see John 1:1; Col 1:15; Prov 8:22–31), interacts with Adam and Eve, for example, the mosaic sequence of Monreale cathedral (Sicily, c. 1180) or the Genesis sculptures within the cathedral of Orvieto (Italy). Within the so-called *Biblia pauperum* (see e.g. Cod. Pal. germ. 148 Heidelberg, University Library), texts from Gen 2 and 3 are relevant for the annunciation of Jesus' birth according to Luke 1:26–38 (Gen 3:15), Jesus' temptation (Gen 3:1–7), and the opening of Jesus' side according to John 19:33–34 (Gen 2:21–22; in exegesis see Aug. *Tract. Ev. Jo.* 120.2; Bede *Gen.* 2.20–22).

Michelangelo's *Creation of Adam* (Rome, Sistine Chapel 1511) illustrates the Genesis story of God breathing life into Adam. The harmonious beauty of the nude Adam refers to the harmony of creation in general. God is horizontally floating (for the first time in art history!) amid a cluster of angels. Rather than wearing royal garments and depicted as an all-powerful ruler, he wears only a light tunic that leaves much of his arms and legs exposed. The similarity between God's and Adam's bodies refers on Gen 1:26 (creation in the image and likeness of God). He extends his right hand toward Adam in order to discharge the spark of life.

In William Blake's (1757–1827) *Elohim Creating Adam* (1795), a gnostic worldview is visible. The painting, part of the illustration of John Milton's inspiring poem *Paradise Lost* (publ. 1667), depicts Elohim as a winged angel, "hovered malevolently above the tormented man" (Hoagwood, 2004, 316), Adam lying on the earth, pressed and enrolled by a worm signifying Adam's mortality. The so-called fall is identical with the free spirit of humankind, enslaved into materiality.

The paradise mostly is presented as *locus amoenus*; Adam and Eve are nude, surrounded by animals (see e.g. Jan Brueghel the Elder, *The Garden of Eden*, 1613).

The creation of Eve from Adam's rib is sometimes expressed very naturally: the lower part of Eve's body is emerging from the sleeping husband (Orvieto, cathedral, c. 1290; Munich, Bayerische Staatsbibliothek Cod. lat. monac.835, fol. 8r, scene 6, 1190–1210; Ghiberti, 1425–1452), at the *Door of Paradise* (Florence, Baptistery; Michelangelo; Orvieto, cathedral, c. 1290; Munich, Bayerische Staatsbibliothek Cod. lat. monac. 835, fol. 8r, scene 6, 1190–1210; Ghiberti, 1425–1452). Sometimes Eve represents one of the seven deadly sins, the lust (Blöcker, 1993, 115–116). Sometimes the iconography of Eve is conflated with the iconography of Venus.

The iconography of Adam's fall sometimes includes the portrait of the snake as a young girl (see also Petrus Comestor, *Historia Scholastica, Genesis*, 21). This is seen at first in Amiens (1270), but is also visible, for example, in Master Bertram's *Grabow Altar* (Hamburg, 1379–1383), in Paul of Limburg' *Les très riches heures du Duc De Berry* (1413–1416), and in Paolo Uccello's fresco in Florence, Santa Maria Novella, Green Cloister (c. 1430), Raffael (Rome/Vatican).

Albrecht Dürer's engraving from 1504 also shows the theory of the four temperaments: the cat (foreground) is choleric, the rabbit (behind the cat) is sanguine, the ox (behind Eve) stands for phlegmatic, the elk (behind the tree) stands for melancholia. Whereas Albrecht Dürer presented the ideal of the human body (human beings are understood as the image of God) and characterizes Adam and Eve as lovers (Bark, 1994, 24), Hans Baldung (Strasbourg, 1511) interprets the fall as sexual sinning: Eve grasps the forbidden fruit, and Adams grasps Eve's breast (Bark, 1994, 47f.). Adam can be portrayed as uncertain, perhaps due to 1 Tim 2:14 (Master Bertram), or as willingly participating in the fall (Baldung; Michelangelo, Bark, 1994, 47f.): both, Eve and Adam, reach into the branches of the tree of life. Peter Paul Rubens portrays Eve as a seductive nude (Boeckl, 1998, 836). Peter Paul Rubens interprets the fall as the moment of erotic awaking (1628/1629, Madrid, Prado), whereas Titian (1550, Madrid, Prado) emphasizes Adam's warning to Eve concerning sin (Büttner & Gottdang, 2006, 18). In Rembrandt's painting from 1638, Adam appears doubting between rebuking Eve and having a bite. Rembrandt shows the snake as a dragon. The contrast between the light background and the dank foreground symbolizes the contrast between the radiant paradise and the world after the fall (Sluijter, 2006, 290). In more recent times, different evaluations of sexuality are present; Franz von Stuck (*Temptation, Adam and Eve*, c. 1920–1928) presents Eve, without interest in biblical issues, as glamorous seductress; Emil Nolde's *Paradise Lost* (1921) symbolizes anew the horrifying aspects of human desire.

Gen 3:19 sparked presentations on Adam's work *in sudore*; see the presentation of the digging Adam at the north choir clerestory of the cathedral in Canterbury, circa 1180. Sometimes Eve is also portrayed working as a farmer (Cathedral Modena, c. 1184) or spinning (Master Bertram). Sometimes Adam and Eve are also represented as penitents (Bamberg, cathedral; Nuremberg, St. Laurence).

Bibliography

Aland, B., "Erwählungstheologie und Menschenklassenlehre: Die Theologie des Herakleon als Schlüssel zum Verständnis der christlichen Gnosis?" in: M. Krause, ed., *Gnosis and Gnosticism*, NHS 8, Leiden, 1977, 148–181.

Anderson, G., "Celibacy or Consummation in the Garden? Reflections on Early Jewish and Christian Interpretations of the Garden of Eden," *HThR* 82, 1989, 121–148.

Bark, S., *Auf der Suche nach dem verlorenen Paradies: Das Thema des Sündenfalls in der altdeutschen Kunst, 1495–1545*, Frankfurt am Main, 1994.

Blöcker, S., *Studien zur Ikonographie der sieben Todsünden in der niederländischen und deutschen Malerei und Graphik von 1450–1560*, BSK 8, Muenster, 1993.

Boeckl, C.M., "Article Sin/Sinning," in: H.E. Roberts, ed., *ECI.TDWA*, Chicago, 1998, 835–838.

Büttner, F., & A. Gottdang, *Einführung in die Ikonographie: Wege zur Deutung von Bildinhalten*, Münster, 2006.

Cook, J.G., *The Interpretation of the Old Testament in Greco-Roman Paganism*, STAC 23, Tübingen, 2004.

Heither, T., & C. Reemts, *Adam*, BGK, Münster, 2007.

Hoagwood, T.A., "Article Elohim Creating Adam 1795: Colour Print of William Blake," in: C.J. Murray, ed., *ERERa 1760–1850*, vol. I, New York, 2004, 315–317.

https://www.alamy.com/stock-photo/adam-and-eve-painting.html.

Kirchner, J., *Die Darstellung des Ersten Menschenpaares in der bildenden Kunst von der ältesten Zeit bis auf unsere Tage*, Stuttgart, 1903.

Meiser, M., *Galater*, NTP 9, Göttingen, 2007.

Mittelrheinisches Landesmuseum Mainz, *Adam- und Eva-Darstellungen aus eigenem Museumsbesitz*, Mainz, 1983.

Sluijter, E.J., *Rembrandt and the Female Nude*, Amsterdam, 2006.

Streck, M., *Das schönste Gut: Der menschliche Wille nach Nemesius von Emesa und Gregor von Nyssa*, FKDG 88, Göttingen, 2005.

MARTIN MEISER

III. *Adam and Eve, Life of*

The *Life of Adam and Eve*, originally written in Greek (former title "Apocalypse of Moses"), was translated in Armenian ("Penitence of Adam"), Georgian, Latin ("Vita Adae et Evae"), and Slavonian; its thoroughgoing reception history in the medieval age includes widespread traditions in France, England, Ireland,

and Denmark (see Murdoch, 2009). G. Anderson and M.E. Stone present in the second edition of their *Synopsis of the Books of Adam and Eve* (1999) the versions in their original languages and translations of these version on the facing page. It is uncertain whether the ancient Christian testimonies of an Adam book (Epiph. *Pan.* 26.8; *Apos. Con.* 6.16.3; *Decretum Gelasianum*) refer to this text. The text attempts to fill the gaps of the biblical narrative by integrating new ideas.

1. Content

The starting point for the Armenian "Penitence" and the other versions, with the exception of the Greek "Apocalypse" in its original form, is the poverty and repentance of the first human beings immediately after their expulsion from → paradise. Whereas Adam, staying in the Jordan, is not disturbed during his stay, the devil, taking on the form of an angel, deceives Eve anew during her stay in the Tigris. Only Adam recognizes this deceit when Eve and the devil come to meet him. The devil explains to Adam why he deceived them: after Adam's creation, the archangel Michael demanded all angels to worship the image of God, but as the devil and his angels refused it, they were expelled from paradise. Eve gives birth to Cain under severe pain, and angels come to help her, but only after Adam's prayer. Later, she gives birth to Abel. In a dream, Eve foresees the murder of Abel.

After a short description of Adam's life, the story continues with the report of Adam's last days (*L.A.E.* 5–14). He falls ill but refuses Seth's suggestion to bring him fruit from paradise. Adam retells the story of his transgression as rationale for his sickness, underlining Eve's responsibility. In the next scene, he demands Eve and Seth to wander to paradise in order to bring the "oil of mercy" to him. During this wandering, a beast attacks Seth. The beast explains this by referring to Eve's sin, a narrative dramatization of Gen 3:15. The archangel Michael refuses to give the requested oil but gives promises for the last days of humankind (the versions offer different variants concerning the content of his promise).

The next great section (*L.A.E.* 15–30) is Eve's exhaustive testament speech retelling the story of Gen 3 with clarifying additions. When Eve was guarding the animals in the south and the west of the paradise, the → devil manipulated the serpent by the speaking of the fruit of paradise, and they seduced Eve. She refused to eat at first, but the serpent succeeded in tempting her and demanded an oath that she give fruit to her husband. The versions differ in their characterization of the fruit (Armenian "Penitence of Adam": desires of sins, harlotries, adulteries, greed; Greek "Life": poison of covetousness). Some other motifs are also added to the biblical text, for example God's appearance on a chariot of cherubim, Adam's hunger and bitterness, and his plea of pardon and his offering. Eve concludes her speech by admonishing her children not to forsake the good.

The "Finale" (*L.A.E.* 31–43) recounts Adam's death and his postmortem fate. God grants him mercy, and he is washed in the Acherusian Lake and deported to paradise. In the next subsections, God promises Adam the reversal of his state and his resurrection, angels bury Adam and Abel in paradise, and God seals the grave with a triangular seal. Eve also dies, and Seth buries her at Adam's side.

2. Original Language and Manuscripts

The archetype of this tale was written in Greek fashioned by a moderate biblical style. Theories on a Hebrew *Vorlage* have failed; the formerly supposed Hebraisms (parataxis, redundant personal pronouns, word order) can be explained as Septuagintisms.

D.A. Bertrand (1987, 40–47), J. Dochhorn (2005, 21–26), and J. Tromp (2005, 17–27, 67–111) offer descriptions of the available Greek manuscripts, which number nearly 30. There is a consensus concerning subgroups of the Greek manuscripts (on differences in theology, see Levison, 2000, 21–46), but there is no consensus concerning an appropriate stemma visualizing connections between these subgroups (see Dochhorn, 2008, 316).

For the Armenian "Penitence of Adam," M.E. Stone, the editor, used three manuscripts (Stone, 1981), while the editions of the Georgian *Life of Adam and Eve* are based on five manuscripts (for details, see Dochhorn, 2005, 40).

The Latin version of the *Life of Adam and Eve* is transmitted in more than a hundred manuscripts that can be divided in at least three groups.

Recently, the Latin transmission process has been highly debated, due to two newly edited manuscripts (Pettorelli, 1998; 1999).

The oldest Greek manuscripts are to be dated to the 11th century, the oldest Armenian and Georgian manuscripts to the 15th century, and the oldest Latin manuscript to the 8th century CE. The text-critical value of different manuscripts, however, does not simply correlate with the dating.

3. Literary Development and Genre

The text is a composed unit where some parts only appear in some versions, and some parts are also known independently of the context of the *Life of Adam and Eve*. There are also other features that point to the composite nature of the text, such as minor points of disagreement (e.g. concerning the setting of paradise) and awkward transitions (e.g. *L.A.E.* 9:2/9:3; 14:2/14:3; 37:6/38:1; 38:4/39:1). Moreover, there are several themes that are not prepared or developed further. For example, the terms ἀρχή, θρόνος, ἀπατάω in *L.A.E.* 39:2 are not prepared in the story of the devil's fall (*L.A.E.* 12:1–16:4); the concept of the "holy people" (λαὸς ἅγιος) in *L.A.E.* 13:3–5 is not taken up later in the text; the motifs of Eve's righteousness (*L.A.E.* 20:1) and her glory (*L.A.E.* 20:2) are not developed in the "Finale" (*L.A.E.* 31–43); in *L.A.E.* 41:3 only the motif of resurrection is mentioned, but not the motif of tree of life (*L.A.E.* 28:4; → Life, Tree of).

There is a relative scholarly consensus according to which some traditions were originally independent. These include the devil's fall at the beginning, Eve's testament speech *L.A.E.* 15–30. Adam's death and reprieve *L.A.E.* 31*–37*, and Adam's burial * *L.A.E.* 38–43. There is also a relative consensus according to which the "Finale" in the Latin *Life of Adam and Eve* (*L.A.E.* 45.1–48.6) has been secondarily shortened. Formerly, the tales of Adam's and Eve's repentance and of the devil's fall were evaluated as secondary additions to a corpus that already included Eve's testament speech and the finale. New insights concerning the relevance of the Armenian "Penitence of Adam," however, have challenged this view. This is confirmed by two hitherto unknown Latin manuscripts, edited by J.-P. Pettorelli (1999). This points to a relatively early stage of redaction preserved in

Armenian, Georgian, and Latin, including the tale of Adam's and Eve's repentance and of the devil's fall at the beginning, Eve's testament speech in the middle, and the expanded version of the "Finale" at the end. The differences between the Latin "Life" and the other versions are the result of an inner-Latin transmission process. In other cases, however, there is no certainty. It is uncertain whether *L.A.E.* 5–14 can be taken as a redactional whole (Dochhorn, 2005, 133–135) or rather as a mélange of divergent traditions. Some elements only make sense as part of a thoroughgoing tale: the remark of the "throne of him who deceived you" (i.e. Adam) in *L.A.E.* 39:2 presupposes a story of the devil's fall. The clumsiness of some transitions suggests a redaction, intended simply to collect all available material on Adam and Eve within one text. Other redactional elements are more sophisticated. The lack of interest concerning minor points of disagreement suggests "popular religion" as the milieu of origin (Tromp, 1997, 32). There are, however, also exegetical issues that suggest a milieu of scribes familiar with both Hebrew and Greek text of Genesis (Dochhorn, 2005; see below). The narrative is "concerned with large questions posed by the biblical text" (Eldridge, 2001, 171, who on p. 172 suggests "midrashic novella" as a designation of its genre). Any theory of literary development must be balanced with this coexistence of awkward and sophisticated elements. Some scholars, therefore, are skeptical with regard to reconstruction of any preliminary stages (Niebuhr, 2011, 63).

4. Jewish or Christian Origin: Date and Place

In former times, Jewish, Christian, and gnostic origin (→ Gnosis/Gnosticism) was supposed for the text. The theory of a gnostic origin was based on the special role of Seth as mediator of revelation to his mother Eve. This theory is now outdated, and rightly so, for it is the archangel of God, who demands the angels to venerate Adam, not an inferior being, and mercy on Adam is based on his status as a created being (*L.A.E.* 33:5; 37:2). The question of Jewish or Christian origin, however, is highly debated (see de Jonge & Tromp, 1997, 65–75; Knittel, 2002, 31–74; Dochhorn, 2005, 149–172; Merk & Meiser, 2005, 170–177).

The theory of a Jewish origin was based on several facts. First, there are no specific Christian elements where they would be expected (*L.A.E.* 13:3D; 37:2; 43:4D). The only exception is *L.A.E.* 13:3–6 (in most of its versions), but this was explained as a Christian addition, in analogy to similar additions within the *Testament of the Twelve Patriarchs*. Second, the motif of Adam's offering after the expulsion (*L.A.E.* 29:3) and after the birth of Seth (*L.A.E.* 4:2, see Lev 12:6–8) points to a milieu that is not hostile to traditional cult (Bertrand, 1987, 36). Third, while the motif of Adam's and Eve's penitence was popular in Christian literature of the 2nd and 3rd century CE, it did not appear in later Christian writings, but it occurs in rabbinic Jewish texts. Nevertheless, an increasing number of scholars favor the theory of a Christian origin, due to several factors. First, the text is transmitted only in Christian manuscripts. Second, there are elements that are best explained as Christian tendencies: the motif of the Acherusian Lake in the Greek *L.A.E.* 37:3 occurs only in Christian and not in Jewish texts; the triangular seal symbolizes Christian → baptism (de Jonge & Tromp, 1997, 72); *L.A.E.* 40–41 has its closest parallels in John 19:38–40 (Nir, 2004, 35–38); the analogies to the *Journey of Zosimos* suggest a monastic milieu of origin (Nikolsky, 2004, 356). Third, there is nothing that would reveal a specific Jewish interest in these writings, comparable with the halachic interests, for example, in *Jubilees*.

There are, however, also arguments supporting a Jewish origin: the mentioning of → Sabbath instead of → Sunday (*L.A.E.* 43:3; see Niebuhr, 2011, 49n1), the lack of Christian elements in the description of God's mercy on Adam (*L.A.E.* 37:2; see Eldridge, 2001, 259–260), and the coexistence of the Greek and the Hebrew text of Gen 3 (Dochhorn, 2002;, 2005, see below).

5. Intention

At its final stage, the *Life of Adam and Eve* is a sapiential narrative text (for narrative analyses see Levison, 1988, 163–190; Eldridge, 2001, 137–230; Knittel, 2002; Dochhorn, 2005, 105–124; Meiser, 2010).

Creation and primordial history are seen as both etiology and admonition. The work seeks answers to a number of questions. Why is human life constrained by illness and premature death; why is the relation between humankind and animals disturbed; why is the relationship between man and woman disturbed by sexual desire (which Eve cannot escape), leading to the experience of man's dominion? J. Tromp (1997) also underlines the importance of the motif of consolation. On the other hand, the primordial history offers an etiology of cult: God's mercy grants this favor in order to sustain the relation with humankind. Creation and primordial history also express an admonition to the readers to guard themselves from sin in the present life in order to obtain mercy after death.

The narrative strictly observes its temporal frame; there are no allusions to post-Adamic events in real history, and references to past and future are only given in some speeches. Gen 3 is interpreted in terms of etiology of ethical endangering (*L.A.E.* 44[1–21]) and of illness (*L.A.E.* 7:1–8:2); the fall of the first humans is a warning example (*L.A.E.* 30) but not the precondition for human sinning. Terms like ἐντολή, φυλάττειν, ἐπιθυμία, and παρανομία (*L.A.E.* 21:2) allow the readers to recognize their own experiences in Jewish or Christian piety. The woman's sexual desire is evaluated negatively as sin of the flesh (*L.A.E.* 25:4); however, it is not part of her condemnation by God but the result of Satan's mixing the poison of ἐπιθυμία (Loader, 2014, 387). God's judgment provides the deliverance from this poison. This pessimistic view of sexuality has many parallels in ancient Christian literature. However, there were also ascetic tendencies in ancient → Judaism, shaped by the desire of distinguishing from Gentiles.

6. Exegetical Issues

Some details of the text are not only the result of pious fantasy, but they fill gaps of the biblical text. The Greek *Life of Adam and Eve* often presupposes both the Greek and the Hebrew text of Genesis (or even *Jubilees*, see Greek *L.A.E.* 4:2 and *Jub* 4:7), concerning for example the location of paradise in the East (*L.A.E.* 1:2 presupposes the Hebrew text of Gen 3:24) or the division of paradise (*L.A.E.* 15:2 presupposes the Hebrew text of Gen 2:18, 20). God's command (Gen 2:16) is directed to Adam and Eve (*L.A.E.* 7:1; see Gen 2:17, where the Greek text differs),

for otherwise Eve could not be guilty. *L.A.E.* 24:2 presupposes Gen 3:17 in both Hebrew and Greek, which is comparable with 4Q423 which combines Gen 3:17–19 and Gen 4:11–12 (Dochhorn, 2002). The motif of Eve's oath to the serpent (*L.A.E.* 19.2) can be a narrative reference to Gen 3:13 with different Hebrew vocalization; J. Dochhorn (2005, 118). The setting of Abel's voice ἀπὸ τῆς γῆς "from the earth" (*L.A.E.* 40:4–5) is a correction of Gen 4:10 (the Septuagint ἐκ τῆς γῆς is in full accordance with the Hebrew text; Dochhorn, 2005, 532f.). Also in other cases, the Greek *Life of Adam and Eve* fills gaps of the biblical text. *L.A.E.* 7:2 gives the reason why the serpent spoke with Eve alone (Gen 3:1–7). *L.A.E.* 10–12, the story of the beast's attack against Eve, is a narrative realization of Gen 3:15. *L.A.E.* 19:1 explains why Eve offers the forbidden fruit also to Adam. *L.A.E.* 22:4 avoids the impression of God's walking for nothing (Gen 3:8). God's question (Gen 3:9) is reformulated in order to avoid the association of God's ignorance (*L.A.E.* 8:1; 23:1), which was an obstacle in gnostic anti-orthodox literature (NHC IX, 3, p. 47). The order of God's condemnations is rearranged according to the preceding inquiries (*L.A.E.* 24:1–5).

Bibliography

Anderson, G.A., & M.E. Stone, *A Synopsis of the Books of Adam and Eve*, 2nd rev. ed., SBL.EJL 17, Atlanta, 1999.

Anderson, G.A., M.E. Stone & J. Tromp, eds., *Literature on Adam and Eve, Collected Essays*, SVTP 15, Leiden, 2000.

Bertrand, D.A., *La vie grecque d'Adam et Ève: Introduction, texte, traduction et commentaire*, Paris, 1987.

Dochhorn, J., "'Sie wird dir nicht ihre Kraft geben': Adam, Kain und der Ackerbau in 4Q423 2 3 und Apc Mos 24," in: C. Hempel, A. Lange & H. Lichtenberger, eds., *The Wisdom Texts from Qumran and the Development of Sapiential Thought*, Louvain, 2002, 351–364.

Dochhorn, J., *Die Apokalypse des Mose*, TSAJ 106, Tübingen, 2005.

Dochhorn, J., "Review of J. Tromp, The Life of Adam and Eve in Greek," *JSP* 17, 2008, 313–319.

Eldridge, M., *Dying Adam with his Multiethnic Family: Understanding the Greek Life of Adam and Eve*, SVTP 6, Leiden, 2001.

Jonge, M. de, & J. Tromp, *The Life of Adam and Eve and Related Literature*, Sheffield, 1997.

Knittel, T., *Das griechische "Leben Adams und Evas": Studien zu einer narrativen Anthropologie im frühen Judentum*, TSAJ 88, Tübingen, 2002.

Levison, J.R., *Portraits of Adam in Early Judaism: From Sirach to 2 Baruch*, JSP.S, Sheffield, 1988.

Levison, J.R., *Texts in Transition: The Greek Life of Adam and Eve*, SBL.EJL 16, Atlanta, 2000.

Loader, W., "Genesis 3,16–19 LXX in Reception: Observations on its Use in Early Judaism and Christianity to ca. 100 CE," in: W. Kraus & S. Kreuzer, eds., *Die Septuaginta – Text, Wirkung, Rezeption*, WUNT 325, Tübingen, 2014, 381–391.

Meiser, M., "Ätiologie und Paränese: Schöpfung und Urgeschichte im *Leben Adams und Evas*," in: T. Nicklas & K. Zamfir, eds., *Theologies of Creation in Early Judaism and Ancient Christianity: In Honour of Hans Klein*, DCLS 6, Berlin, 2010, 201–223.

Merk, O., & M. Meiser, *Das Leben Adams und Evas*, JSHRZ, vol. II/5, Gütersloh, 1998.

Merk, O., & M. Meiser, "Das Leben Adams und Evas," in: G.S. Oegema, ed., *Unterweisung in erzählender Form*, JSHRZ, vol. VI/2, Gütersloh, 2005, 151–194.

Murdoch, B.O., *The Apocryphal Adam and Eve in Medieval Europe: Vernacular Translations and Adaptations of the Vita Adae et Evae*, Oxford, 2009.

Nagel, M., "La vie grecque d'Adam et Ève, Apocalypse de Moïse," 3 vols., diss., Lille, 1974.

Niebuhr, K.-W., "Auf der Suche nach dem Paradies: Zur Topographie des Jenseits im griechischen Leben Adams und Evas," in: W. Ameling, ed., *Topographie des Jenseits: Studien zur Geschichte des Todes in Kaiserzeit und Spätantike*, AlKo 21, Würzburg 2011, 49–67.

Nikolsky, R., "The Adam and Eve Traditions in the Journey of Zosimos," in: E.E. Chazon, D. Satran & R. Clements, eds., *Things Revealed: Studies in Early Jewish and Christian Literature in Honor of Michael E. Stone*, JSJ.S 89, Leiden, 2004, 345–356.

Nir, R., "The Aromatic Fragrances of Paradise in the Greek Life of Adam and Eve and the Christian Origin of the Composition," *NT* 46, 2004, 20–45.

Pettorelli, J.-P., "La Vie latine d'Adam et Ève," *ALMA* 56, 1998, 5–104.

Pettorelli, J.-P., "Vie latine d'Adam et Ève, La recension de Paris, BNF, lat. 3832," *ALMA* 57, 1999, 5–52.

Stone, M.E., ed., *The Penitence of Adam Edited*, CSCO.Ar 13–14, Louvain, 1981.

Stone, M.E., *A History of the Literature of Adam and Eve*, SBL.EJL 3, Atlanta, 1992.

Tromp, J., "Literary and Exegetical Issues in the Story of Adam's Death and Burial (GLAE 31–42)," in: J. Frishman & L. van Rompay, eds., *The Book of Genesis in Jewish and Oriental Christian Interpretation: A Collection of Essays*, TEG 5, Louvain, 1997, 25–41.

Tromp, J., *The Life of Adam and Eve in Greek: A Critical Edition*, PVTG 6, Leiden, 2005.

MARTIN MEISER

IV. *Adam, Testament of*

The *Testament of Adam* belongs to the extensive postbiblical literature on the first human being, together with the *Life of Adam and Eve* (*Vita Adae et Evae*), the (gnostic) *Apocalypse of Adam*, the Syriac *Cave of Treasures*, the Arabic *Book of the Rolls*, the *Combat of Adam and Eve with Satan*, and the Syriac *Book of the Bee*. All these texts belong to the genre of the so-called retold Bible, in which an explicit reference to the biblical text or to a spokesman is generally lacking. From a methodological point of view, and in order to avoid confusion, the *Testament of Adam* should be treated as an independent work and not as a part of other documents. One should also ignore earlier labels of the *Testament of Adam* such as "gnostic" or "pagan" (→ Gnosis/Gnosticism; → Pagan/Paganism).

If we take the division of the hours of the day and the hours of the night as one section, called the Horarium, the *Testament of Adam* consist of three sections: the Horarium, the Prophecy of Adam to Seth, and the Celestial Hierarchy. The latter is present in only one of the three Syriac recensions, and it is an addition, but not arbitrarily: the first hour of the night in which demons are present corresponds with the angels controlling those demons (Robinson, 1983, 147). Here is the beginning of the Hierarchy (4:1):

> The heavenly powers, what they are like, and how each of their orders is occupied in the service and in the plan which concerns this world. Listen, my beloved, while they are set in array one order after another, from the bottom until we reach those who carry our Lord Jesus the Messiah and bear him up. The lowest order is that of the angels.

After that the archangels, the archons, the authorities, and so on follow, each with their function, In this case the *Testament of Adam* has been modeled after the Letter to the Ephesians (1:19; 3:10; → Paul the Apostle), rather than after the hierarchy according to Pseudo-Dionysius (Brannon, 2011, 212).

In spite of opinions in the past, the first two sections of the *Testament of Adam* seem to form a unit, in which Adam reveals secrets to his son Seth. The Horarium begins with the night, which may point to a Jewish original (see Gen 1 and the discussion in *b. Ber.* 2a). The possible affinity of the *Testament of Adam* with Jewish → Midrash has been obscured somewhat, due to the tendency of rabbinic literature (→ Rabbi) to integrate stories of the retold Bible into a framework of midrashic commentary. Still, an independent narrative of Adam and Eve can be distinguished quite clearly in the midrashic account of the 12 hours of the day in which Adam and Eve were created and they transgressed and were expelled (*Pirqe R. El.* 11; *'Abot R. Nat.* ch. 1, recensions A and B). Even God spends his time according to the 12 hours of the day (*b 'Abod. Zar.* 3b). In the division of the 12 hours in the *Testament of Adam*, the emphasis lies upon the creatures, birds, and quadrupeds, and upon the angelic forces: cherubim and seraphim:

> The first hour of the night: the praise of the demons. And in that hour they neither harm nor injure nor harm a human being.
> The second hour: the praise of the doves.
> The third hour: the praise of the fish and of fire and of all the depths below.
> The fourth hour: the Trishagion of the seraphim.
> (First Syriac recension)

In this way, all 12 hours of the night and of the day receive their characteristics, probably in correspondence with certain liturgical rituals, such as the priests burning incense and mixing water with oil to anoint the afflicted. In one of the four Greek recensions (Paris 2419), the character of the hours – here starting with the day hours – is transformed into a theurgic manual by changing the role of the priests to that of "man" and by the adding of specific names of each hour, written in Hebrew characters to enhance the magical power:

> The names of the hours of the day
> "The first hour is called איאהכ in which it is good to pray."

It is impossible to transcribe this word into English. The Hebrew word may be connected to the Greek εὐχή ("prayer").
After 12 hours, the document continues:

> The names of the hours of the night
> "The first hour is called שוכולום/*sokolom* in which the demons, praising God, neither injure nor punish."

The meaning of "Sokolom" is unclear, like most of the other names for the hours, but the few recognizable names refer to a Greek word rather than a Hebrew word. One is reminded of magical amulets in which Hebrew words enhance the power, in spite of (or because of) their incomprehensibility. A magical division of the day into 12 hours, each with a specific characteristic and using (pseudo-)Hebrew words, can be found in the Greek Magical Papyri (111.494–611; Betz, 1986, 31). This use of the *Testament of Adam* should be considered a secondary adaptation, as is the attribution to → Apollonius of Tyana.

The second section, Prophecy, contains predictions of the future birth of the Redeemer, "born from a virgin," as told by Adam to Seth. In spite of the obviously Christian character, many Jewish motifs can be detected, such as the fig as the forbidden fruit (*Gen. Rab.* 15.7; 19.6); the Aramaic wordplay on Eve (*hawa*) and the serpent (*hiwya, Gen. Rab.* 20.11), which remains a wordplay in Syriac; the age of the world at 6,000 years; and Cain having a sister, here called Lebuda. All these themes may, however, have been part and parcel of Syriac Christian tradition; hence, the Prophecy document does not need to be a reworking of a Jewish *Vorlage*. The Horarium shows more traces of a Jewish original.

The original language of the *Testament of Adam* is most probably Syriac, as the Greek is dependent upon the third Syriac recension. The *Testament of Adam* in other languages are all later.

The *Testament of Adam* is quoted in the *Transitus Mariae* from the end of the 4th century CE. Some characteristics of the Messiah are transposed to the → antichrist by the *Apocalypse of Elijah*, generally dated to the 3rd century CE. We may assume that this has been a reworking of motifs in the *Testament of Adam*; hence, a date in the 3rd century CE is plausible.

Historiography

J.B. Frey (1928) offers a careful treatment of the *Testament of Adam* in his article about Adam in apocryphal literature. A.M. Denis (1970) is a general a concise update of J.B. Frey. Because of the magical elements, some passing references to the *Testament of Adam* may be found in H.D. Betz (1986). Both studies of S.E. Robinson are indispensable. S.E.

Robinson (1978) offers several versions of the Syriac text, whereas S.E. Robinson (1983) offers an extensive treatment of previous studies and includes the text of the *Testament of Adam* in English.

Bibliography

Betz, H.D., *The Greek Magical Papyri in Translation: Including the Demotic Spells*, Chicago, 1986.
Brannon, M.J., *The Heavenlies in Ephesians: A Lexical, Exegetical and Conceptual Analysis*, London, 2011.
Charlesworth, J.C., *The Pseudepigrapha and Modern Research with a Supplement*, Michigan, 1981, 91–92.
Denis, A.M., *Introduction aux Pseudepigraphes Grecs de l'Ancien Testament*, Leiden, 1970, 9–12.
Frey, J.B., "Adam (Livres apocryphes sous son nom)," in: *DB(V)*, suppl. 1, Paris, 1928, cols. 117–125.
Kmosko, M., *Testamentum Adae*, PS 2, Paris, 1907, 1309–1360.
Robinson, S.E., *The Testament of Adam*, Chico, 1978.
Robinson, S.E., "Testament of Adam," in: J.C. Charlesworth, ed., *OTP*, vol. I, New York, 1983, 989–995.

M.J.H.M. POORTHUIS

Adamites

The Adamites (Adamians, Ἀδαμιανοί, *Adamitae, Adamiani*) were an ancient Christian sect first referred to by → Epiphanius of Salamis in 374 CE. Its members allegedly identified their church with → paradise as it was before the fall, calling themselves → Adam and Eve, convening in the nude for their worship services, and considering sexuality to be the result of sin. The sect is known only from descriptions in heresiological collections. Yet, even if its precise nature and origins remain uncertain, some historical nucleus may be accepted.

1. As an Ancient Christian Sect

a. Primary Sources

Apart from the heresiological records there are no extant primary sources on the Adamites. Moreover, the existing records are at odds with each other. This necessitates a critical evaluation of the source material and its value.

Epiphanius of Salamis is the first to mention the Adamites, in a list of 60 → heresies that "falsely adopted the name of Christ" (Epiph. *Anc.* 13; written 374 CE). A year later, he describes the sect at greater length (Epiph. *Pan.* 52). Employing his usual strategy of connecting heresies to harmful creatures (Verheyden, 2008), he compares the sect to a mole: hidden and damaging, but also blind and the object of ridicule. Though relying entirely on oral sources (which he emphasized were manifold), Epiphanius of Salamis gives a consistent and, in its factual details, relatively cautious description (*Pan.* 52.1.6 and 52.2.1–4). His account makes clear that the Adamites ascribed a central place to the paradise narrative (Gen 2–3) in their rituals, language, and theology. They called their church "paradise" and each other "Adam" and "Eve," celebrating their worship services entirely unclothed, in heated rooms. Emphasis on rank and class was avoided: men and women, teachers, leaders, and laypeople all sat together in no particular order. Continence was norm; sexuality was seen as a consequence of the first → sin: those who "fell into transgression" were considered as "Adam after eating from the tree" and expelled from church as though from paradise. Epiphanius' subsequent refutation mainly consists in highlighting how ridiculous and inconsistent in his view the Adamian ideas and practices were (*Pan.* 52.2.5–52.3.8).

Epiphanius' account influenced many authors of both East and West, especially through the summary in Epiph. *Anac.* 4.52, which was used by → Augustine of Hippo (*Haer.* 31) and John of Damascus (*Haer.* 52). Most western accounts depend on Augustine (Arn. Jr. *Praed. haer.* 1.31; Isid. *Etym.* 8.5 [no. 14]; the latter is used in: Rab. Maur. *Cler. inst.* 2.58; Honorius of Autun, *Liber de haeresibus* 29; *Decr. Grat.* 2.24.3 [39.13]). Ps.-Jer. *Ind. haer.* 13 may derive directly from Epiph. *Pan.* 52 (both quote Gen 2:25). Pseudo-Jerome and Arnobius Junior add some details of uncertain reliability (i.e. a dual concept of the → soul, and the mention of a certain *presbyter Polycarpus* as opposing the sect).

Another account, independent from and at odds with the Epiphanius tradition, is found in the work of → Theodoret of Cyrrhus (*Haer. fab.* 1.6 [c. 453 CE]). Theodoret claims that "the heresy of those called Adamites" was established by a certain Prodicus, who set out a doctrine that encouraged and even sacralized promiscuity. Not only were wives considered common property and was sexual intercourse openly practiced, but, as Theodoret writes, all this was also construed as a "mystical experience" or "communion." He quotes → Clement of Alexandria three times (from Clem. *Strom.* 3.27–30), but the latter does not himself mention the Adamites.

There is no evidence that Theodoret used or knew Epiphanius' work (contra Holl, 1980, 311n; repeated in Williams, 2013, 68n). The bishop of Cyrus makes no mention of paradise, the fall, or naked worshipping, nor does he explain the name "Adamites." The only common element in both accounts is the name: *Adamianoi* (Epiphanius), *Adamitoi* (Theodoret). Moreover, the sacralized promiscuity described by Theodoret is at odds with the strict ascetic views in Epiphanius' version. Our two main sources, then, should be distinguished carefully, more than some scholars have done (e.g. Blunt, 1874; Bareille, 1930).

Of the two accounts, Epiphanius' seems the more prudent and reliable. Stripped of the rhetoric, it is consistent and factual, and it clearly points out the biblical-theological background of sect's practices. Despite his evident misgivings, especially regarding claims of continence, Epiphanius kept these separated from his factual claims. Theodoret on the other hand seems less careful, as becomes clear from the way he uses his main source. Several of the characteristics he ascribes to Prodicus had been ascribed to others by Clement (e.g. wives as common property; *Strom.* 3.5, 3.8). This also contaminates his claim of a link between Prodicus and the Adamites (see also Oulton & Chadwick, 1954, 30; Theodoret's claim is ignored in Broek, 2005).

The discrepancy between Epiphanius and Theodoret is best explained by assuming that the Adamian practices provoked malicious rumors, which in turn inspired Theodoret to connect the sect with what he read in Clement's work. The inverse scenario, in other words that reports of promiscuity would evolve into an account emphasizing continence, is improbable.

b. Date and Geographical Origins

The sources do not provide conclusive evidence on date or geography. Epiphanius' account sets the *terminus ante quem* at 374 CE, but he himself was uncertain whether the sect still existed (Epiph. *Pan.* 52.1.6–9). The reluctant and consistent claims of his sources may indicate chronological (mid-4th cent. CE) and geographical proximity (Cyprus/Cilicia/Syria/Iudaea). The sect's literal reading of Genesis suggests Antiochene influence (see Reuling, 2006, ch. 4). Similarly, the fact that Theodoret had heard of the sect points to the region of Antioch.

c. Theological Emphases

First, it is worth noting that the Adamites were explicitly listed among the Christian sects, and that the extant records suggest that much of their liturgy (readings, prayers, etc.) resembled that of other churches (perhaps "Christians groups," for there was no church of Adamites).

Further, their theological emphasis was on returning to a pre-fall state of purity, *not* on nudity as such. Nude worship was related to purity, not sexuality. In Greco-Roman cults "ritual nudity" mostly occurred in specific rites such as sacrifices or initiation (Heckenbach, 1911; Weiler, 2000). The Adamian practice, however, was not restricted to a single rite (e.g. baptism, as in Hipp. *Trad. ap.* 21) but rather connected to the overall theology and self-perception of the community.

Other known aspects should be explained from the perspective of paradise and fall as well. Sexuality was considered to be a consequence of the first sin and therefore rejected. The egalitarian character of the services may have had a similar background. In parallel manner, → John Chrysostom connects the submission of Eve in Gen 3:16b to various other kinds of submission, all the result of sin (Chrys. *Hom. Gen.* 4; Reuling, 2006, 134). The importance of the paradise account is further confirmed by the name *Adamianoi* (and cognates). Reports that the sect was named "after a certain contemporary Adam" (ἀπό τινος Ἀδὰμ ζῶντος) seem based on an inferior manuscript variant (Epiph. *Anac.* 4.52; Holl, 1980, 212, *apparatus criticus*; edited text: Ἀδαμίζοντες, "Adamizers").

Apart from the Genesis account, Jesus' saying on the disappearance of sexual differences in the resurrection may have played an important role (Matt 22:30; Mark 12:25; Luke 20:34–36; for noncanonical parallels see Schneemelcher, 1987, vol. I, 174–179). For the Adamites, however, this was present reality, which points to a soteriology in which the *eschaton* plays no part. All consequences of sin are treated as abolished, at least in the church: they *are* Adam and Eve and their church *is* paradise (Epiph. *Pan.* 52.2.4).

The often presumed connection between the sect and Gnosticism (→ Gnosis/Gnosticism) is uncertain. The sources do not reveal whether the ascetic practices were inspired by dualistic worldviews: there are no references to rejection of food and drink or material possessions. Theodoret's remark on gnostics is doubtful, as argued above (Thdt. *Haer. fab.* 1.6: "The followers of Prodicus who falsely call themselves gnostics"; quoted from Clement). According to A.D. Nock (1964, 265), gnostic speculation was often related to the early chapters of Genesis, including the future restoration of paradise, but as noted, the Adamites believed that this was realized in the present.

2. As a Heresiological Topos

During the Middle Ages, the term "Adamites" developed into a polemical epithet for the discrediting of a wide variety of sects. As such, it referred to nude, mixed worship. This use is well documented for movements in Bohemia (Büttner & Werner, 1959, 73–141), England (Cressy, 2000), France (Ginzburg, 1996), Austria, Italy, and the Netherlands (Schütte, 1993; Selge, 1998). The accusations may well be questionable from a historical perspective, and in so far true, the underlying theological frameworks differed significantly from one another and from that of ancient Christian Adamites (e.g. mysticism, chiliasm).

The transformation into a heresiological *topos* was probably facilitated by the recurrent appearance of the Adamites in medieval heresiology (e.g. → Isidore of Seville; *Decretum Gratiani*). In these works, the ancient descriptions of the sect were reduced to a few core elements, for the purpose of applying them to contemporary movements.

Bibliography

Bareille, G., "Adamites," in: *DThC*, vol. I, Paris, ³1930, 391–392.

Blunt, J.H., *Dictionary of Sects, Heresies, Ecclesiastical Parties, and Schools of Religious Thought*, London, 1874.

Broek, R. van den, "Prodicus," in: W.J. Hanegraaff, ed., *DGWE*, vol. II, Leiden, 2005, 974–975.

Büttner, T., & E. Werner, *Circumcellionen und Adamiten: Zwei Formen mittelalterlicher Haeresie*, FMAG 2, Berlin, 1959.

Cressy, D., *Travesties and Transgressions in Tudor and Stuart England: Tales of Discord and Dissension*, Oxford, 2000.

Ginzburg, L., "Adamiti, nuovi adamiti nella morale del Seicento francese," *ASEs* 13/2, 1996, 583–596.

Heckenbach, J., *De nuditate sacra sacrisque vinculis*, RGVV 9.3, Gießen, 1911.

Holl, K., & J. Dummer, eds., *Epiphanius II: Panarion haer. 34–64*, GCS 31, Berlin, ²1980.

Nock, A.D., "Gnosticism," *HThR* 57/4, 1964, 255–279.

Oulton, J.E., & H. Chadwick, eds., *Alexandrian Christianity*, LCC 2, Philadelphia, 1954.

Reuling, H., *After Eden: Church Fathers and Rabbis on Genesis 3:16–21*, JCPS 10, Leiden, 2006.

Schneemelcher, W., *Neutestamentliche Apokryphen in deutscher Übersetzung*, vol. I, Tübingen, ⁵1987.

Schütte, H., "Adamiten, Adamianer," in: *LThK*, vol. I, Freiburg, 1993, 142–143.

Selge, K.-V., "Adamiten (Adamianer)," in: *RGG*, vol. I, Tübingen, ⁴1998, 111–112.

Verheyden, J., "Epiphanius of Salamis on Beasts and Heretics: Some Introductory Comments," *JEaCS* 60.1, 2008, 143–173.

Weiler, I., "Nacktheit: B. Kult," in: H. Cancik & H. Schneider, eds., *DNP*, vol. VIII, Stuttgart, 2000, 674–678.

Williams, F., ed., *The Panarion of Epiphanius of Salamis, Books II and III: De Fide*, NHMS 79, Leiden, ²2013.

PETER VAN EGMOND

Addai

Addai was a Christian → apostle who, according to tradition, in the 1st century CE evangelized the city of Edessa and the region of Osrhoene in northern Mesopotamia. His name seems to be the Syriac form of Greek Θαδδαῖος and Latin *Thaddaeus*. His legend is related to that of the purported conversion of King Abgar Ukkama ("the Black") of Edessa to Christianity. I. Ramelli (2015) investigates how the superimposition of different religious discourses and agendas over the centuries shaped the complex development of the Addai narrative through different literary genres, such as epistles and epistolary novels, history, hagiography, biography, acts of apostles, and historical novels. Indeed, the narratives containing the Addai legend developed through a number of literary forms, each shaped by the almost always religious, and religious-political, motivations of their authors or redactors.

The historical point of departure is likely to have been the letters exchanged in the thirties of the 1st century CE, for purely political reasons, between Abgar Ukkama and the Roman emperor Tiberius. These letters, which originally had arguably nothing to do with a "conversion" of Abgar to the Jesus movement, were later incorporated into the Syriac apostolic novel *Doctrina Addai* (*Teaching of Addai*), where they form a nugget isolated from the rest, as well as into the Armenian version of the Addai legend found in the historian Moses of Chorene, and in some Syriac *Transitus Mariae*. The first extant account of the Addai legend, that of → Eusebius of Caesarea in the early 4th century CE, reports the fictional Abgar-Jesus correspondence, but not the Abgar-Tiberius letters. This suggests that the source of the Abgar-Tiberius letters is different from that of the pseudepigraphical Abgar-Jesus letters and is surely very ancient, since the Abgar-Tiberius letters include historical details that perfectly fit in the political panorama of the mid-thirties, when the emperor was maneuvering against the Parthians, very few years after Jesus' death and Abgar Ukkama's reestablishment in 31 CE from a usurpation (Ramelli, 2009a; 2015). At that time, Abgar needed the emperor's support against his opponents, and the latter needed the faithfulness of vassal kings close to the Parthian border, such as Abgar. The Abgar-Tiberius letters perfectly reflect this historical situation, and it is for these political reasons that, historically, Abgar probably wrote to Tiberius about Jesus' condemnation to death by Pontius Pilate (→ Pilate) and Caiaphas' party, and not as a consequence of a "conversion to Christianity." Abgar wanted to take advantage of the Jesus incident and those responsible for it to put his adversaries in a bad light before the emperor and the Roman Empire (Ramelli, 2013).

The legend of Abgar Ukkama's Christianity arose later, under Abgar the Great (177/179–212/214 CE), when Christianity began to appear in Edessa. A Christian church is attested at that time in Edessa by the *Chronicle of Edessa* (1). Other sources also indicate that Christianity had spread in Osrhoene by that time, and the education of Abgar's son, Ma'nu, was handed to Christian intellectuals such as Julius Africanus and → Bardaisan of Edessa. The letters in

which Abgar Ukkama denounced the unjust killing of Jesus favored the birth of the legend of his and his kingdom's conversion, which seems to have shaped during the reign of Abgar the Great, who probably became a Christian himself, as both Bardaisan in the *Book of the Laws of Countries* and Africanus indicate (Ramelli, 2017). This legend was likely meant to exalt Abgar the Great by celebrating Ukkama. Bardaisan, the Syriac Christian Middle Platonist, philosopher, theologian, historian, and polymath, who was close to the royal court of Osrhoene and friends with Abgar the Great, could use the royal archive and read the letters of the Edessan kings. He or some other courtier or official may have read the correspondence of Abgar Ukkama with Tiberius concerning Jesus and the situation in Palestine in the thirties of the 1st century CE, creating from there the legend of Ukkama's "conversion." Bardaisan may have incorporated a first representation of Addai in his history, which probably included an account of the evangelization of Edessa. Bardaisan must have seen the incorporation of the Addai story in his own history as a celebration of the early Christianization of Edessa and in homage to Abgar the Great through his earlier namesake. From Bardaisan's historical work, then, or whatever other Edessan historical work representing Eusebius' first source (see below), this legend passed on to Eusebius' *Church History*, where it is found enriched with the purported Abgar-Jesus letters that will appear again in the *Doctrina*, Moses, and other documents.

The first layer of the Addai legend, absorbed by Eusebius in his *Church History*, included the "conversion" of Abgar to Christianity thanks to the miracles of Addai, a figure significantly absent from the earlier Abgar-Tiberius letters. As demonstrated by I. Ramelli (2010; 2015), Eusebius' narrative consists of three layers. Two come from earlier sources, the earliest of which might be Bardaisan' historical work. Eusebius knew Bardaisan's oeuvre well and in *Praeparatio Evangelica* preserves two excerpts from his work against fate; he also provides information about his historical figure and literary production. He had good, direct documentation on Bardaisan available and read his works, which were likely already translated into Greek. That Bardaisan wrote a history of the Near East where the Addai story was found is attested by Moses of Chorene, a favorable and informed source on Bardaisan. Moses, who in the 5th century CE used materials from the Edessan archives and offers information unavailable from other sources on the kings of Edessa and the relationship between the Roman Empire and the Parthians, was also acquainted with the historical work of the aforementioned friend of → Origen's, Africanus, who was in Edessa with Bardaisan. Moses read Bardaisan's history of the Near East and used it for his own historical work. Moses presents Bardaisan as a reliable historian (Mos. *PH* 2.66), who composed a history using archival materials and recording his own day's events. Moses declares that he based himself on Bardaisan's history for what happened in the period to which Abgar Ukkama belongs.

Within the story of Addai in Eusebius, the most recent layer is Eusebius' final summary. Another layer, the middle one, derives from a document kept in the archives of Edessa and contains the letters purportedly exchanged between Jesus and Abgar Ukkama, plus the Addai narrative section that accompanied them. The most ancient of Eusebius' layers (Eus. *Hist. eccl.* 1.13.1–4) includes neither letters nor speeches nor dialogues, and narrates the key events of what became the Addai story. This section reveals an exaggeratedly encomiastic tone and the manifest intention to extol the ancient king of Edessa; it must therefore go back to an Edessan source, which may be Bardaisan's history (Ramelli, 2015). This section focuses on Abgar Ukkama, his celebration as a great monarch, his illness, his learning of Jesus' miracles, and the latter's promise to heal him, which also resulted in Abgar's spiritual salvation and the Edessans' conversion to Christianity, thanks to the apostle Addai. This may have been the first outline of the Addai legend in Bardaisan, possibly a development from the Abgar-Tiberius correspondence about Jesus and the situation in Palestine and the Near East in 35–37 CE. The Addai story was apt both to celebrate Abgar the Great and to create a precedent for his benevolent attitude toward Christianity, or even his conversion to Christianity, which probably put him in a difficult situation. If Bardaisan included the Addai story in his history, he intended to celebrate both Abgar the Great, at whose court he was honored, and the introduction of Christianity to various peoples, and especially in his own, the Edessan people. This celebration was magnificent, since

Ukkama was described not only, hyperbolically, as a great dynast who reigned over whole peoples, but also and above all as the first Christian king; this was clearly meant to be a unique distinction, long before Constantine.

Another argument supports the hypothesis that Bardaisan or someone from his circle elaborated the first version of the Addai narrative: in the 4th century CE, orthodoxy established itself at the expense of those labeled as heresies: in Edessa, Manichaeism (→ Mani/Manichaeism), Gnosticism, (→ Gnosis/Gnosticism) and Marcionism (→ Marcion/Marcionites/Marcionism). In the 3rd and 4th centuries CE, Bardaisan was precisely misrepresented as a gnostic, a Manichaean, and even a Marcionite. At the same time, the figure of the apostle Addai was appropriated by Syrian orthodoxy, whose expression was the *Doctrina Addai*, concluded in the early 5th century CE. Addai's theological speeches and doctrinal teachings therein serve the purpose of ascribing a perfectly orthodox thought to him. This insistence on the orthodoxy of the apostle of Edessa would be very well understandable if the Addai legend had been first fixed and spread by an author who had meanwhile come to be regarded as a heretic, such as Bardaisan. Eusebius, on the contrary, did not consider Bardaisan to be a heretic – he even quoted his arguments against fate as authoritative along with those of Origen, his hero – and was not concerned about Addai's orthodoxy either. Thus, he includes no orthodox speech of this apostle.

The subsequent layer of the Addai story is the Edessan lore revolving around the letters purportedly exchanged by Abgar and Jesus, which represents a common source of both Eusebius and the later *Doctrina Addai*. Bardaisan's account, if it is Bardaisan's, lies behind Eusebius' first four paragraphs; the following paragraphs derive from a different source. They quote the Abgar-Jesus pseudepigraphic epistolary exchange and narrate the subsequent story of Addai's healing of Abgar, the latter's conversion, and that of the entire Edessan people.

The *Doctrina Addai*, an apostolic historical novel, about a century after Eusebius built on the Edessan lore that was already used by Eusebius, adding to it doctrinal and narrative expansions. The doctrinal additions are Addai's long doctrinal speeches, so important that the author calls his work "teaching" (*Doctrina*), and not "history." The narrative expansions include the Protonike legend, a reworking of Helena's *inventio Crucis* (Drijvers, 1997). These expansions responded to the religious agenda of the Edessan "official" church in the early 5th century CE (Mirkovic, 2004). The author of the *Doctrina* proposed:

A paradigm of normative Edessan Christianity, supported by the local ecclesiastical and historical lore, which he hoped would play an authoritative role in the largely Christological controversies of his own days. (Griffith, 2003, 3)

This narrative was composed from preexisting material to promote Rabbula's program for the Edessan "Church of the Empire" (Griffith, 2003, 46). P. Wood (2010, 82–116) considers the *Doctrina* and the later *Acts of Mari* to be aimed at constructing a picture of a distinct Edessene or Syriac ethnic identity, with Edessa as a Christian center, protected by a promise of Christ, occupying a not insignificant place in a Christian Roman Empire. P. Wood (2012, ch.4) plausibly dates the *Doctrina* to the 440s CE, but as a composite of earlier traditions and documents, and correctly notes that it is ten times longer than the Addai legend in Eusebius.

The whole narrative of the *Doctrina* was in the service of the strategic needs of the religious group that promoted its redaction and diffusion. Indeed, the religious political agenda that shaped this narrative is clear: the newly established Syriac orthodoxy wanted to reappropriate Edessa and its apostle Addai, who was first celebrated by heretics such as Bardaisan and his entourage. This is why Addai in the *Doctrina* is attributed doctrinal homilies that shine with orthodoxy and were absent from Eusebius and his two Edessan sources (the celebratory source possibly identifiable with Bardaisan and the source of the Abgar-Jesus fictional letters and the narrative revolving around them). This is also why the *Doctrina* presents Palut as the successor of Aggai, in turn Addai's successor, whereas in fact, as the first bishop of Edessa, he was ordained by Serapion of Antioch around 190 CE. Such a chronological telescoping between the apostolic age and the Severan age was intended to stress the apostolic origins of the church of Edessa. Palut in Edessa presented himself as a true heir of the apostles, in opposition to heretical groups such as that of Bardaisan.

Like Eusebius' second section encompassing the Abgar-Jesus letters, the *Doctrina* declares to be based on a Syriac document from the archives of Edessa. It was written by the king's scribe, Labubna, and checked by the king's archivist (Howard, 1981, lii–liii, 105–107). The *Doctrina* narrates that Abgar Ukkama sent two Edessan nobles and his archivist on a diplomatic mission to the Roman official in Eleutheropolis. On their way back, they passed by Jerusalem and came to know Jesus and his → miracles. Abgar, informed, sent a letter to Jesus, inviting him to come to Edessa, escape from "the Jews," and heal him, as he had long been ill. Jesus in a letter promised that a disciple would arrive at Edessa after his ascension. He also let Abgar's archivist paint his portrait, which Abgar then enshrined in one of his palaces. In fulfilment of Jesus' promise, after his resurrection (→ Resurrection) one of the Twelve, Thomas, actually sent to Edessa "one of the 72," Addai, who immediately began to work miracles and thus was introduced to Abgar, who was healed by him and converted, along with all of his people. The last sections narrate the establishment of the church in Osrhoene after Addai's death.

A further stage of the Addai narrative is found in the *Acts of Mar Mari*, another Syriac apostolic novel with both historical nuggets and fictional material, composed in its final shape in the late 6th or 7th century CE (Ramelli, 2008). In its first part it condenses the Addai legend and connects it to the legend of Mari, the apostle of Mesopotamia. Again, as with the previous layers of the Addai story, political-ecclesiastical reasons shaped this narrative. The *Acts of Mari* provided evidence for the apostolic origins of the church in Seleucia-Ctesiphon, thus justifying, at the time of their composition, the hegemonic plans of the καθολικός, the eastern Syriac patriarch whose see was Seleucia-Ctesiphon. The apostolic origins were guaranteed by Mari, via his link with Addai and, through Addai, to Thomas and the apostles. The redactor of the *Acts of Mari* is interested in the *Doctrina* not so much for Addai's doctrinal sermons in it, which are linked to the time and place of the composition of the *Doctrina* itself, as for its narrative sections, which provided the Mari story with a valuable connection with Edessa and the apostles.

A different development of the Addai narrative, shaped by different motivations, is found in a historical work, like Eusebius': Moses of Chorene's *History of Armenia* (*Patmut'iwn Hayoc'*). Moses' source was Lebubna (Mos. *PH* 2.36), the alleged source of the *Doctrina* too. Moses claims that he visited Edessa and its archives (*PH* 3.62). Both Eusebius and the Armenian version of the *Doctrina* probably were among Moses' sources, but in several details his report differs from those sources. Moses introduces Abgar as an Armenian king and offers an Armenian etymology of his name, to trace back to him the very origin of Christianity in "Armenia" (Moses tends to incorporate many territories in his idea of "Armenia"). At the beginning of the 4th century CE, thanks to Gregory the Illuminator, Armenia was the first kingdom to adopt Christianity as a state religion, while the Roman Empire did so only under Theodosius. But Moses, by representing Abgar Ukkama as Armenian and reporting the legend of his and his subjects' conversion to Christianity, suggested that already in the 1st century CE an Armenian kingdom adopted Christianity as state religion.

Historiography

The study of the Addai legend begun relatively early, especially among scholars of Eusebian and Syriac studies. G. Howard (1981) and A. Desreumaux (1993) favored the spread of the knowledge of the *Doctrina Addai*, which has been examined by many scholars, among whom H.J.W. Drijvers (1997), S.H. Griffith (2003), P. Wood (2012, ch. 4), and A. Mirkovic (2004). I. Ramelli (2015) offered a systematic examination of the complex development of the Addai narrative through different authors and literary genres and in response to various religious agendas, from the Abgar-Tiberius correspondence (the focus of Ramelli, 2013) to Bardaisan (studied in his complexity in Ramelli, 2009), Eusebius, the *Doctrina Addai*, the *Acts of Mari* (fully commented on in Ramelli, 2008, reviewed by Brock, 2008; Perkins, 2009), Moses of Chorene, Procopius, and so on. (On the relation between the Addai story and the Mandylion of Edessa, see "Acheiropoietai" and the relevant historiography.)

Bibliography

Andrade, N., *The Journey of Christianity to India in Late Antiquity: Networks and the Movement of Culture*, Cambridge UK, 2018.

Brock, S.P., "Review of Ramelli, 2008," *AN* 7, 2008, 123–130; http://www.ancientnarrative.com; http://www.thefreelibrary.com/I.+Ramelli:+Atti+di+Mar+Mari.-a0197420329.

Desreumaux, A., ed., *Histoire du roi Abgar et de Jésus*, Turnhout, 1993.

Drijvers, H.J.W., "The Protonike Legend, the *Doctrina Addai*, and Bishop Rabbula of Edessa," *VigChr* 51, 1997, 288–315.

Drijvers, H.J.W., "Rabbula, Bishop of Edessa: Spiritual Authority and Secular Power," in: H.J.W. Drijvers & J.W. Watt, eds., *Portraits of Spiritual Authority: Religious Power in Early Christianity, Byzantium, and the Christian Orient*, Leiden, 1999, 130–154.

Griffith, S.H., "The *Doctrina Addai* as a Paradigm of Christian Thought in Edessa in the Fifth Century," *HJSS* 6/2, 2003, §§1–46.

Howard, G., trans., *The Teaching of Addai*, Chico, 1981.

Mirkovic, A., *Prelude to Constantine*, Frankfurt an Main, 2004.

Perkins, J., "Review of Ramelli, 2008," *Aevum* 83, 2009, 269–271.

Ramelli, I., "Edessa e i Romani tra Augusto e i Severi: Aspetti del regno di Abgar V e di Abgar IX," *Aevum* 73, 1999, 107–143.

Ramelli, I., trans., comm., *Il Chronicon di Arbela*, Madrid, 2003.

Ramelli, I., "Abgar Ukkama e Abgar il Grande alla luce di recenti apporti storiografici," *Aevum* 78, 2004, 103–108.

Ramelli, I., "La *Doctrina Addai* e gli *Acta Maris*: Note storico-letterarie," *AION* 65, 2005, 75–102.

Ramelli, I., "*Il Chronicon di Arbela*: Una messa a punto storiografica," *Aevum* 80, 2006, 145–164.

Ramelli, I., trans., comm., *Atti di Mar Mari*, Brescia, 2008.

Ramelli, I., *Bardaisan of Edessa: A Reassessment of the Evidence and a New Interpretation*, Piscataway, 2009.

Ramelli, I., *Possible Historical Traces in the Doctrina Addai?* Piscataway, 2009a.

Ramelli, I., "The Narrative Continuity between the *Teaching of Addai* and the *Acts of Mari*," *OLA* 189, 2009b, 411–450.

Ramelli, I., "Bardesane, l'apologia siriaca 'di Melitone' e la *Doctrina Addai*," *Aevum* 83, 2009c, 141–168.

Ramelli, I., "The Biography of Addai: Its Development Between Fictionality and History," *Phrasis* 51, 2010, 83–105.

Ramelli, I., "The Possible Origin of the Abgar-Addai Legend: Abgar the Black and Emperor Tiberius," *HJSS* 16, 2013, 325–341.

Ramelli, I., "The Addai-Abgar Narrative: Its Development Through Literary Genres and Religious Agendas," in: J. Perkins & I. Ramelli, eds., *Early Christian and Jewish*

Narrative: The Role of Religion in Shaping Narrative Forms, Tübingen, 2015, 205–245.

Ramelli, I., ed., trans., comm., *Bardaisan on Free Will, Fate, and Human Nature: The Book of the Laws of Countries*, Tübingen, 2017.

Ramelli, I., "The Spacial, Literary, and Linguistic Translations of the Mandylion of Edessa," in: J. Spittler, *The Narrative Self in Early Christianity: Essays in Honor of J. Perkins*, Atlanta, 2019, 171–192.

Ramelli, I., "Review of Andrade, *The Journey of Christianity*," *Sehepunkte* 20, 2020, no. 5; http://www.sehe punkte.de/2020/05/druckfassung/32184.html.

Wood, P., *"We Have No King but Christ": Christian Political Thought in Greater Syria*, Oxford, 2010.

Wood, P., "Syriac and the 'Syrians'," in: *OHLA*, Oxford, 2012; online ed. DOI: 10.1093/oxfordhb/9780195336931 .013.0006.

ILARIA L.E. RAMELLI

Adiabene

Adiabene is a geographical name that refers to the heartland of ancient Assyria, the region confined between the Upper and Lower Zāb Rivers, with Erbil, Assyrian Arba'ilu, as its capital. The name Adiabene or Adiabena occurs in Greek and Latin sources dated to the first centuries of our era, while the forms *Ḥadyab* and *Ḥdayyab* in reference to the same region are encountered in Jewish Aramaic and Syriac sources during the same time period and beyond. In Arabic sources dated after the 9th century CE, Adiabene or rather *Ḥadyab* was replaced by *Ḥazzā*, after the name of the most important city in its region, located some 12 km northeast of Erbil.

The etymology of Adiabene, or *Ḥadyab* and *Ḥdayyab*, is obscure. → Ammianus Marcellinus (Am. 6.21) derives the name of Adiabene from the two Zāb Rivers, which he calls Diabas and Adiabas. The etymology is doubtful since the Roman author gives other names to the Zāb, for example Anzaba (Am. 6.19; 7.1), while Diabas and Adiabas are not the native river names and are thus unlikely to have generated the name for the land in which they run. Pliny the Elder (*Nat.* 16) mentions that during the Hellenistic period Adiabene was called Mygdonia "on account of the resemblance it bore to Mygdonia in Europe." The toponym Adiabene, and probably its counterpart *Ḥadyab* or *Ḥdayyab*, must have also been coined during that period, replacing the Athurâ of the Achaemenid royal inscriptions (King, 1907, col. 1:14–15); the latter name is a rendering of the native name Aššur, given as Ator or Athor in Aramaic. The name Adiabene continued to be used throughout the Parthian period, while its counterpart *Ḥadyab* is attested in Syriac sources for a long time after the advent of Islam.

The history of Adiabene is relatively well known thanks to several ancient and multilingual sources. During the Achaemenid period, the capital Erbil was an important trade center. It is mentioned in a letter written by the satrap of Egypt, Arshama, which traces a long trade route linking Elam and Babylonia with northern Syria and Egypt, via Erbil and Damascus (Porten, 1986). During the Hellenistic period, Adiabene seems to have been part of a vast province whose center was Seleucia on the Tigris. Strabo (*Geogr.* 16.1.3–4), writing before 25 CE, describes Adiabene as a small district separated from Nineveh and forming "part of Babylonia," although it had its own king who was probably a governor. Pliny the Elder (*Nat.* 14.42), writing some 50 years later, describes Arbelitis, the main city of Adiabene, in more impressive terms. It is a district that not only includes Nineveh, located slightly to its northwest, but also extends as far as Nisibis in the Khabur region of Upper Syria, an expansion due to its active involvement in trade and international politics. The contrasting descriptions of Adiabene in Strabo and Pliny the Elder suggest that Strabo's information, most probably drawn on Hellenistic sources, fits the Hellenistic period much better.

Around the first half of the 1st century CE, Adiabene rose to power under the leadership of its king Izates. When the latter was still young, his father, King Monobazes, who married his own sister Helena, sent him to Spasinou Charax (Syr. Karka d-Meshan near the mouth of the Persian Gulf) in order to protect him from "the hatred of his brothers" (Jos. *Ant.* 20.22). There, the crown prince was raised at the court of the local king Abennerigos and eventually converted to → Judaism at the hand of a merchant named Ananias. Upon his return to Adiabene to succeed his father, he found out that his mother had also converted to Judaism, undoubtedly under the influence of the important Jewish community, the "inhabitants of Adiabene," as they are referred to by → Flavius Josephus (*Bell.* 1.6). Both mother and son remained in their new faith until they died and were buried in Jerusalem, having showered it during their lives with donations and gifts (Jos. *Ant.* 20.17–48).

Izates enjoyed quite a remarkable reign, during which Adiabene expanded as far as Nisibis, and perhaps even beyond. He lent great support to Artabanus II in regaining his throne after the latter sought refuge in Adiabene in the year 36 CE (Jos. *Ant.* 20.66–68). Pliny the Elder's description of this small kingdom (*Nat.* 6.42) corroborates its geographical expansion under Izates, as he includes in it Nineveh and Nisibis, while Strabo, using late sources, writes that Adiabene reached the frontiers of Armenia (Stra. *Geogr.* 16.1.19). It is possible that Izates left his statue in one of the shrines of Hatra under the name of '*tlw* "the Assyrian" (Teixidor, 1967). The inscribed statue, which does not resemble those of Hatra, calls him the "worshipper of '*lh*', blessed by '*lh*'," without specifying the divine identity (Aggoula, 1991).

International trade added to the fortunes of Adiabene before and after the Common Era, as was the case for other caravan cities such as Hatra to the southwest, Edessa near the upper Euphrates, Palmyra in Syria, and Petra in Arabia. These trade centers formed semi-autonomous kingdoms ruled by leaders called *marya* (lord) and *malka* (king), used the Aramaic language, and were dotted with monumental buildings and sculptures of Hellenistic-Semitic design. Adiabene has not yielded visible signs of material wealth as the other kingdoms have, probably because this wealth is still buried in the impressive citadel of modern Erbil, which remains untouched by archaeologists.

After the era of Izates, the history of Adiabene reflects tense relations between the Romans and the Parthians, as Dio Cassius (*Hist. rom.* 26.1–4) and Ammianus Marcellinus (Am. vol. VI/9, 20–22) relate. Monobazes II succeeded his younger brother Izates, continuing the latter's favorable policy toward Parthia. In the year 61 CE, he assisted the Parthian crown prince Tiridates against the Armenian Tigranes, who had invaded the land of Adiabene and was defeated by the invading army. By the time → Trajan invaded northern Mesopotamia in 115 CE, Adiabene was still an independent kingdom ruled by Meharaspes, but not for long. Trajan, whose siege of Hatra ended in failure, managed to annex Adiabene to Roman

territory, naming it the province of Assyria. In 117 CE, Hadrian gave up Assyria, Armenia, and Mesopotamia altogether, but in 196 CE Adiabene once again fell into Roman hands. Ardashir, founder of the Sassanian dynasty, began to rule over Mesopotamia in 224 CE, and sometime after this date, Adiabene lost its semi-independence, as did Hatra and Parthian Aššur.

As was almost certainly the case with Edessa and Nisibis, it is likely that Christianity first spread to Adiabene among its Jewish community. It has been argued that the unsophisticated Judaism known to the 4th-centuryCE Syriac author → Aphrahat (the so-called Persian sage) probably reflected that of "the descendants of the first century converts to Judaism of Adiabene" (Neusner, 1971; 1986; Murray, 1975), though this claim remains in the realm of speculation given our ignorance of Aphrahat's location. It has even been suggested that the earliest Syriac version of the Bible was produced in Adiabene "as an adaptation of the Palestinian Targum for the new converts" (Kahle, 1951), but while there are some affinities between the two versions of the Bible, nothing suggests that the Syriac version originated there. The Syriac *Chronicle of Arbela* (Kawerau, 1985), which traces the history of Christianity in Adiabene, depicts a triumphal entry of the new faith in Arbela and gives a long list of bishops with remarkable detail. But this source has been judged to be unreliable for at least the first two centuries of the Common Era.

Adiabene became a metropolitan seat possibly as early as 310 CE in the person of Papa (Fiey, 1993), and by the time the synod of 410 CE was held in Seleucia-Ctesiphon, the seat was occupied by metropolitan Daniel. Thereafter, Adiabene grew into an extensive province of the church of the East, led by a long line of metropolitans, eight among them attested in the acts of synods (Chabot, 1902). The jurisdiction of the metropolitan of Adiabene was not limited to his own province but extended at one point to include Azerbaijan and Nineveh, and was divided into as many as 19 suffragan dioceses led by bishops. The Christians of Adiabene, like many other ecclesiastical provinces, suffered several persecutions at the hands of the Zoroastrian Sassanians, the harshest under Shapur II (309–379 CE). Several members of the clergy, including → metropolitans, → bishops, → priests , and laypeople, some known by name, fell victim to this 40-year-long persecution. Most famous among the martyrs is Qardagh of Adiabene, and although his story is legendary, it nevertheless reflects the culture of the late Sassanian period (Walker, 2006).

The vast domain of Adiabene led to its separation from Mosul when this city grew in political and economic importance early 9th century CE, but it continued to be a metropolitan seat until the early 17th century. Late 18th century, most of Adiabene joined the Catholic Uniate movement, and Erbil fell under the jurisdiction of the Chaldean archbishop of Kirkuk.

Historiography

The conflict between ancient authors in naming the region of ancient Assyria and in assessing its political entity emanates from the fact that this region did not have the same borders in all historical periods. Strabo (*Geogr.* 16.1.3–4) calls it Adiabene and portrays it as a small district, but Pliny the Elder (*Nat.* 14.42) names it Arbelitis and describes it as a large and influential state. The contrasting descriptions suggest that Strabo's information, most probably drawn on Hellenistic sources, fits the Hellenistic rather than the Parthian period.

The Syriac *Chronicle of Arbela* (Kawerau, 1985) dates the history of Christianity in Adiabene to the apostolic age and traces the lineage of its bishops to the apostles themselves. These claims are not corroborated by archaeology and or epigraphy, and the *Acts of Synods* (Chabot, 1902) indicate that the first metropolitan of Adiabene was established two centuries after the time of the apostles.

Bibliography

Aggoula, B., *Inventaire des inscriptions hatréennes*, Paris, 1991.
Chabot, J.-B., trans., *Synodicon orientale ou recueil des synodes nestoriens*, Paris, 1902; trans. from Syr.
Fiey, J.M., *Pour un oriens christianus novus: Répertoire des diocèses syriaques orientaux et occidentaux*, BTS 49, Stuttgart, 1993.
Kahle, P., *The Cairo Geniza*, Oxford, 1951, 265–273.
Kawerau, P., trans., *Die Chronik von Arbela*, Louvain, 1985; trans. from Syr..

King, W.L., et al., trans., *The Sculptures and Inscription of Darius the Great on the Rock of Behistûn in Persia*, London, 1907; trans from Pers.
Murray, R., *Symbols of Church and Kingdom: A Study in Early Syriac Tradition*, London, 1975.
Neusner, J., *Aphrahat and Judaism*, Leiden, 1971.
Neusner, J., *Judaism, Christianity, and Zoroastrianism in Talmudic Babylonia*, Lanham, 1986.
Porten, B., & A. Yardeni, *Textbook of Aramaic Documents from Ancient Egypt*, vol. I: *Letters*, Jerusalem, 1986, 114.
Teixidor, J., "The Kingdom of Adiabene and Hatra," *Ber.* 17, 1967, 1–11.
Walker, J.T., *Christianity in Late Antique Iraq and the Legend of Mar Qardagh*, Berkeley, 2006.

AMIR HARRAK

Adimantus

Adimantus is known as the author of "some disputations" that have been refuted by Augustine of Hippo in *Contra Adimantum* and in some of his sermons. In the extensive corpus of Augustine's writings, the proper name "Adimantus" is found nearly 40 times. More than half of Augustine's references to Adimantus are in *Contra Adimantum*. Furthermore, Augustine also mentions Adimantus in Aug. *Retract.* 1.22.1 and in Aug. *Leg.* 2.12.42. In *Contra Faustum Manichaeum*, both Faustus and Augustine refer to Adimantus.

Augustine provides us with two important biographical details. The first is his description of Adimantus as "a disciple of Mani" (*Retract.* 1.22.1; *Leg.* 2.12.42). The second is his claim that Adimantus was actually Addas. This identification is very important, because Addas is well known in both Manichaean and anti-Manichaean writings, namely as one of the first missionaries of → Mani.

1. Is Adimantus Identical with Addas?

Because of the far-reaching implications of this claim, it is important to discuss in some detail whether Augustine's claim should be regarded as probable. Scholars of Manichaeism do not all agree on the question of whether Augustine is right in his identification of Adimantus with Addas (Drijvers, 1983, 176, versus Merkelbach, 1984, 52; 1985, 57; and Tubach, 1995, 165–174). In scholarly discussion, the most important argument has to do with the Greek abjuration formulas. The documents originated in the Byzantine period when authorities unleashed a vigorous campaign against heresies (→ Heresy). Three of these tractates were dedicated to the abandonment of Manichaeism: the so-called *Short Formula for the Renunciation of Manichaeism* (mid-5th cent. CE), the *Long Formula for the Renunciation of Manichaeism* (c. 10th cent. CE), and the *Seven Chapters Against the Manichaeans* (6th cent. CE; Lieu, 1999, 210f.).

In these *Formulae* the proper names Addas and Adimantus appear alongside each other and seem to refer to two different persons. This made scholars believe that Augustine erred in his identification of Adimantus with Addas. This view was especially based on J.-P. Migne's edition of the *Short Formula*. However, this edition has turned out to contain a crucial error. J.-P. Migne's text, reproduced by A. Adam in his collection of Manichaean sources, reads (Adam, 1969, 94, l. 35ff.):

Eti anathematizoo [...] kai Addanton kai Adimanton, hon apesteilen ho auto ho dussebès Manès eis diaphora klimata.

(Further I anathematise [...] and Addantos and Adimantos, who was sent by the wicked Mani himself to the various regions of the world).

J.-P. Migne's text missed a word marker in *Addanton*, which should be read as *Addan ton kai Adeimanton* (Ficker, 1906, 443–464). The corrected text supports Augustine's observation, because it says, "Addas, who is also called Adeimantos." The *Seven Chapters* contains a sentence against Adimantus and Addas, who wrote a book "against Moses and the other prophets" (Lieu, 1999, 236). Evidently, the book against which Augustine wrote is meant here. As a consequence, this reference to Adimantus and Addas seems to support Augustine's remark, rather than undermining it. It furthermore demonstrates that the author of this document was not well informed about Adimantus and Addas. The other two instances in which both names are mentioned demonstrate at least that the names "Addas" and "Adimantus" were closely associated in the *Seven Chapters*: they do not appear independently of each other. The same goes for the references to both names in the *Long Formula*. Furthermore, the *Long Formula* may well

have been influenced by the *Seven Chapters* (Lieu, 1999, 210–223).

Hence, the occurrence of the names "Addas" and "Adeimantos" in the Greek abjuration formulas does not necessarily undermine Augustine's opinion on the identity of Adimantus. They can even be read in support of it. Furthermore, Adimantus (Gk *Adeimantos*) can well be seen as an epithet of Addas given by his followers (Alfaric, 1919, 104; Tubach, 1995, 172–174).

2. Biographical Remarks

The name of Addas was as widespread as Manichaeism itself and is found in both Manichaean and anti-Manichaean sources. These sources describe him as a key figure in the early Manichaean Church.

From a fragment in the Cologne Mani Codex, we may conclude that Addas encountered Mani on the occasion of Mani's visit to Shâpûr's palace (Römer, 1994, 159f.) By then, Mani was 25 years old, and therefore Addas seems to have been one of the first followers of Mani (Koenen & Römer, 1988, 113). Manichaean sources found on the Silk Road contain information about Addas' position in Mani's church. In the Parthian text M216 and the Sogdian text 13941/14285, Addas is called a → bishop. This means that he was at the third level of the Manichaean hierarchy. In Latin and Greek sources (see above), Addas-Adimantus was designated a disciple, which might imply that he later received a higher rank, namely of a teacher (Oort, 2004, 275–285, on the Manichaean hierarchy).

Addas plays a major role in the Manichaean mission. The sources present us with a missionary who is active and very successful. He is reported as a founder of monasteries (monastery), an effective debater, and a prolific author. Addas seems to have traveled very much, which brought him across the eastern boarders of the Roman Empire and possibly even to Egypt (Berg, 2010, ch. 2).

3. Writings and Theological Opinions

Concerning the contents of Adimantus' writings and his theological opinions, → Augustine of Hippo is the most important source. In *Contra Adimantum* and in some sermons, Augustine quoted directly from

Adimantus' work, in order to refute his opponent's views. Augustine calls Adimantus' work *Disputations*.

The subject matter of the *Disputations* are the contradictions between the Hebrew Bible and the New Testament. One or more texts from both parts of the canon were put in opposite of each other by Adimantus. Some 30 contradictions can be found in Augustine's writings, such as Gen 1:1–5 against John 1:10 and Col 1:15b–16a; Gen 2:1f. against John 5:17; Gen 2:18–24 against Matt 19:29, and so on. In most cases, Augustine only cited the biblical texts quoted by Adimantus.

Contra Faustum Manichaeum is also to be mentioned as an important document to establish the contents of Adimantus' writings. The Manichaean bishop Faustus, whose work Augustine quotes in full before discussing it chapter by chapter, honors Adimantus as one of his most important teachers (Aug *Faust.* 1.2). Therefore, Faustus' work in all likelihood reflects much of Adimantus' thoughts (Berg, 2013).

Although its historical value cannot easily be estimated, the *Acta Archelai* are to be mentioned as well in this connection. The author of the *Acta* portrays Addas as a theologian who used much of Marcion's *Antitheses* (BeDuhn, 2007).

Some other traces of Addas-Adimantus literary activity can be found in Photius of Constantinople's *Bibliotheca*. In this work, Photius (d. 895 CE) quoted among other things from an anti-Manichaean work of a certain Heraclianus of Chalcedon (supposedly 5th cent. CE), whose references demonstrate that Addas' writings were attacked by Christian authors (Photius, 1960, 85, 6ff.):

> [...] *kai Titon hos edoxe mèn kata Manichaioon grapsai egrapse de mallon kata Addou suggrammatoon* [...]

> ([...] and Titus, who thought to write against the works of Manichaeans, actually wrote against the treatises of Addas [...])

Diodore of Tarsus (d. 390 CE; → Diodore of Tarsus) supposed that he was refuting the *Living Gospel* of Mani. Actually, however, he was fulminating against a writing of Addas, called *Modion* (Photius, 1960, 85, 11–16):

> [...] *Kai to Diodooron, en k' kai e' bibliois ton kata Manichaioon agoona agoonisamenon, hos dia*

> *men toon prootoon biblioon hepta oietai men to tou Manichaiou zoon euaggelion anatrepein, ou tugchanei de ekeinou, alla anatrepei to hupo Adda gegrammenon, ho kaleitao Modion.*

> ([...] And Diodoros, disputing Manichaeans in a collection of 25 books, thought to reject the Living Gospel of Manichaeus in the first seven books, but he actually dealt with the writing of Adda, which is called Modion.)

From these quotes, as well as from the position in the *Abjuration Formulae*, it can be concluded that Addas-Adimantus was rather prolific and influential: he urged the Catholic Church to respond to his writings.

The contents of Adimantus' writings make it highly probable that he was influenced by Marcion's *Antitheses*. It is possible that Adimantus was a Marcionite (→ Marcion/Marcionites/Marcionism) before he adhered Mani's church.

Bibliography

Adam, A., *Texte zum Manichäismus*, Berlin, ²1969, 1954.

Alfaric, P., *Les écritures manichéennes*, vol. I: *Vue générale*, Paris, 1918; vol. II: *Étude analytique*, Paris, 1919.

BeDuhn, J.D. et al., eds., *Frontiers of Faith: The Christian Encounter with Manichaeism in the Acts of Archelaus*, Leiden, 2007.

Berg, J.A. van den, *Biblical Argument in Manichaean Missionary Practice: The Case of Adimantus and Augustine*, Leiden, 2010.

Berg, J.A. van den, "Biblical Quotations in Faustus' *Capitula*," in: J. van Oort, ed., *Augustine and Manichaean Christianity: Selected Papers from the First South African Conference on Augustine of Hippo*, Leiden, 2013, 19–36.

Decret, F., *Aspects du Manichéisme dans l'afrique romaine: Les controversies de Fortunatus, Faustus et Felix avec saint Augustin*, Paris, 1970.

Decret, F., *L'Afrique manichéenne (IVe–Ve siècles): Étude historique et doctrinale*, vols. I–II, Paris, 1987.

Decret, F., "Adimantum Manichei discipulum (Contra-)," in: *AugL*, vol. I, Basel, 1994, 91–93.

Decret, F., "Adimantus," in: *AugL*, vol. I, Basel, 1994, 94–95.

Drijvers, H.J.W., *Addai und Mani: Christentum und Manichäismus im dritten Jahrhundert in Syrien*, OCA 221, Rome, 1983.

Ficker, G., "Eine Sammlung von Abschwörungsformeln," *ZKG* 27, 1906, 443–464.

Henry, R., ed., *Photius: Bibliotheca*, vol. II, Paris, 1960.

Koenen, L., & C. Römer, eds., *Der Kölner Mani-Kodex: Über das Werden seines Leibes: Kritische Edition auf Grund der von A. Henrichs und L. Koenen besorgten Erstedition,* Opladen, 1988.

Lieu, S.N.C., *Manichaeism in the Later Roman Empire and Medieval China,* Tübingen, [2]1992.

Lieu, S.N.C., "An Early Byzantine Formula for the Renunciation of Manichaeism: The 'Capita VII contra Manichaeos' of <Zacharias of Mitylene>: Introduction, Text, Translation and Commentary," in: S.N.C. Lieu, *Manichaeism in Mesopotamia and the Roman East,* Leiden, [2]1999, 210f.

Lieu, S.N.C., & D.A.S. Montserrat, "From Mesopotamia to the Roman East: The Diffusion of Manichaeism in the Eastern Roman Empire," in: S.N.C. Lieu, *Manichaeism in Mesopotamia and the Roman East,* Leiden, [2]1999, 22–131.

Merkelbach, R., "Manichaica (1–3)," *ZPE* 56, 1984, 45–53.

Merkelbach, R., "Manichaica (5–6)," *ZPE* 58, 1985, 55–58.

Oort, J. van, "The Emergence of Gnostic-Manichaean Christianity as a Case of Religious Identity in the Making," in: J. Frishman et al., eds., *Religious Identity and the Problem of Historical Foundation,* Leiden, 2004, 275–285.

Römer, C., *Manis frühe Missionsreisen nach der Kölner Manibiographie: Textkritscher Kommentar und Erläuterungen zu p.121–p.192 des Kölner Mani-Kodex,* Opladen, 1994.

Tubach, J., "Nochmals Addas-Adeimantos," *ZPE* 106, 1995, 165–174.

JACOB ALBERT VAN DEN BERG

Adoption

Adoption refers both to the cultural practice of adoption of children or adults into a new family and the spiritual understanding prevalent in early Christianity that Christians are adopted into the family of God through the son Jesus Christ. The influences on both notions of adoption, physical and spiritual, range from the ancient Near East and Israel to Greece and the Roman Empire. The Hebrew Bible speaks of both the king and the people of Israel as God's children in language that mimics that of adoption. The individual sense of spiritual adoption found in the Hebrew Bible influences the discussions in the New Testament with respect to Jesus as Son of God. At the same time, the concept of physical adoption became relevant for early Christianity due to the supposed adoption of Jesus into the Davidic line as son of Joseph, based primarily on the Roman notion of adoption. The corporate notion of the adoption of the people of Israel by God found in the Hebrew Bible was maintained in the New Testament with

the sense that Christians as a whole were adopted children of God. Yet, the Greek and Roman conceptions of adoption retained their relevance in early Christianity through Paul's notion that Christians have been adopted as true sons and daughters in the family of God. Spiritual adoption remained significant for early Christianity throughout the Patristic period.

1. Adoption in the Hebrew Bible: Physical and Spiritual

Mesopotamian and Egyptian sources attest to the fact that adoption was practiced in the ancient Near East. Ancient modes of adoption varied significantly from our modern conceptions, since the adoptee could range from infant to adult. Claims that there is a formal process of adoption in the Hebrew Bible have often been disputed due to the fact that the incidents that seem to reflect adoption do not actually bring the child or adult into the lineage or bloodline of a new family, but incorporate them into the existing family (Donner, 1969, 87–119). In addition, many scholars dispute that technical language for adoption exists in Hebrew. Part of the problem with these arguments is a narrow focus on specific technical language or a particular process of adoption, and when specific notions or language are missing from the Hebrew Bible, the reality of adoption itself is said not to exist. This is too narrow a definition of adoption, though, and when the scope is broadened, many passages in the Hebrew Bible reflect practices of adoption.

Some of the incidences that have been considered to reflect adoption in the Hebrew Bible include the accounts of Eliezer (the slave of Abraham) being chosen as his heir (Gen 15:2), Ephraim and Manasseh by Jacob (Gen 48:5), → Moses by Pharaoh's daughter (Exod 2:10), Ruth's child by Naomi (Ruth 4:16–17), and Esther by Mordecai (Esth 2:7, 15). In Gen 15:2, → Abraham laments to God that his heir will be his slave Eliezer of Damascus since he did not have a son. This practice is substantiated in ancient Nuzi law, where a childless man is allowed to adopt a male slave as heir and guardian. What is more, Nuzi and Hammurabi law both permit the adoption as legal heir of a child born from a slave–master relationship. These same laws also made allowances for the extraction of these rights upon the birth of a son to the primary wife of the master; a vivid example of this practice is detailed in the story of Isaac and Ishmael. Scholars have noted that in many of these cases, the process of adoption takes place with foreign adopters, such as Moses by Pharaoh's daughter, and according to the laws of other lands. J.M. Scott, however, argues that Gen 48:5–6, Exod 2:10, and Esth 2:7 and 15 share a Hebrew adoption formula (Scott, 1992, 75). Similarly, M. Malul has argued that the foundling imagery in Ezek 16:1–7 offers technical language for adoption, based upon Babylonian and Akkadian legal precedents for the adoption of foundlings (Malul, 1990, 99). It is important to note as well that later Jewish authors in antiquity understood many of the Hebrew Bible passaged just discussed, such as Exod 2:10, as reflecting the practices of adoption (Philo *Mos.* 1.19, 32–33; Jos. *Ant.* 2.263; Acts 7:21). Spiritual adoption in the Hebrew Bible designates the sonship of the king in an individual sense and the sonship of the nation of Israel in a corporate sense with respect to God. Such metaphors only make sense for their readers if there is some preexisting understanding of adoption as a social practice, from either Israelite culture or its neighbors. In the corporate sense, Israel is called the Lord's "firstborn son" (Exod 4:22), and the people of Israel are referred to as God's children (Isa 1:2, 4). An individual, usually the king, can also be chosen apart from the corporate body of Israel. The basis for this election is found in a number of royal Psalms and Davidic passages. In Ps 2:7, God says to the king, "You are my son; today I have begotten you." In Ps 89:27–29, the king is described as the "firstborn" and told that his line will be "established forever." Ps 110:1 refers to the king as "lord," to whom God will give sovereignty. Most important, however, is 2 Sam 7:14, in which God says of → David's heir, "I will be a father to him, and he shall be a son to me." Both corporate and individual spiritual adoption, and these specific passages, will be central to New Testament and early Christian theological presentations and discussions of adoption. Foundationally, adoption is the result of divine election, for both the king and the people of Israel. In addition, neither individual nor corporate adoption is based upon the merits of its recipients, but the notion of individual adoption of the king will be radically transformed in the New Testament

and early Christianity. Finally, discussions of both individual and corporate adoption are clearly based on Hebrew Bible precedents, but will be altered by the influences of Greek and Roman conceptions of physical and spiritual adoption.

2. Adoption in Greece: Physical and Spiritual

While the Septuagint never uses the word, the technical term used to designate adoption in Greek, and the word used most commonly for adoption in the New Testament, is υἱοθεσία. There were, though, a number of words and phrases in common usage that described adoption, including εἰσποιεῖν, ἐκποιεῖν, ποιεῖσθαι, υἱοποιεῖσθαι, and τίθεσθαι. In Greece the process of adoption was not always formal, but it almost always accounted for the lack of a male heir and was designed to maintain and continue the family lineage and cultus. Adoption was usually of a male and by a male, since women did not have the authority of a male and only a male perpetuated the family lineage. Adoption served the needs of the adopter, who would maintain his family line, though it was not without benefit for the adoptee. There were three forms of adoption known in Greece, *inter vivos*, testamentary, and posthumous. *Inter vivos* adoption took place during the lives of both the adopter and adoptee, and was accompanied by the public presentation of the adopted son into the family, while both testamentary and posthumous adoption took place after the death of the adopter. Both the adopter and adoptee had to be Greek citizens, and while it was not necessary, it was often the case that a relative was adopted. The name of the adopted person would change, often to the name of the paternal grandfather, so the family lineage into which the new heir was being adopted was being preserved. The adopted son had the same status as a natural-born son and would receive his inheritance upon the death of the father. Adoption was found in Greco-Roman Egypt, as well, though M. Kurylowicz's research on papyri suggests that a "common law" situation attained there, which means that the formal language and the formal and public processes for adoption were often lacking (Kurylowicz, 1983, 72–75). Spiritual adoption was also found in Greece with respect to the king, and authors utilized the wide range of technical terminology noted above. In Greece, the general view of the divinity of the ruler was not attributed to adoption, but to descent, and yet there are a number of significant accounts of rulers who are considered to have been adopted by the gods. Alexander the Great is presented as having divine origin and being adopted by Ammon-Zeus (Plut. *Alex.* 50.1–52.7). In a famous account in Diod. Sic. *Bib. hist.* 4.39.2, after Heracles was deified, Zeus convinced Hera to adopt him (υἱοποιεῖσθαι). What is unique about this situation is that it is the mother who is adopting the son, and although there were times when adoption was seen as a way to solve female childlessness, in this case it is Zeus' attempt to reconcile Hera and Heracles, and it is clear that a type of adoptive divinity is on display.

3. Adoption in Rome: Physical and Spiritual

In Rome, adoption was the process by which a child or adult adoptee was brought into the lineage or bloodline of the adopting family through the father. The Roman practice of adoption took three forms: *adrogatio, adoptio,* and *adoptio testamentaria* (Kunst, 2005, 13–34; Lindsay, 1998, 63–77). In *adrogatio* an adult who was either a *paterfamilias* (father of the family) or *sui iuris* (an independent person) came under the *potestas* (authority) of another male citizen. This was a serious step to take since adrogation resulted in the disappearance of the adoptee's family of origin, and he would take on "the role and status of a natural child" (Lindsay, 1998, 63). *Adoptio* was the second form of adoption, and the person adopted was not *sui iuris,* but *alieni iuris* (under the authority of the natural *paterfamilias*). By the process of *adoptio,* the one adopted came under the *potestas* of his adopted father. The third form of adoption, *adoptio testamentaria* (testamentary adoption) is similar to *adrogatio,* except that the heir was designated in the will of the adoptive father and became heir only after the death of the testator. A motivation for adoption in Rome was the need for a legitimate male heir. Every Roman family needed a son to carry on the family name (the adoptive father's name, plus a *cognomen* designating the family of origin) and inherit the estate. For this reason, adoption remained a normative practice during the

days of the republic and beyond. In the first two centuries of the Roman Empire, adoption became a way of selecting the next successor to the throne. Octavian was adopted by Julius Caesar, and Octavian, in turn, adopted Tiberius, initiating the informal yet standard practice in which succeeding emperors adopted their heirs (e.g. Augustus, Tiberius, Caligula, Nero, Trajan, Hadrian, Antoninus Pius, and Lucius Verus all ascended to the throne through adoption). Some adopted sons, such as Nero, were adopted even when a natural son was present.

Divine sonship or spiritual adoption in the Roman emperor cult was based upon the practices of physical adoption in Rome. Caesar's adoption of Octavian was by means of testamentary adoption. Beginning with Julius Caesar and his worship as *divi Iulius* (divine Julius), the son of an emperor, such as Octavian, would be considered a *divi filius* (son of God). In the emperor cult it did not matter that the adopted son was not an actual son by birth of the adoptive father, for by virtue of adoption the adopted son became a *divi filius.* Octavian, however, claimed not only an adoptive divinity through Julius Caesar but a divine begetting from Apollo.

4. Adoption in the New Testament: Physical and Spiritual

a. Adoption in the Gospels

It is the Roman process of adoption, specifically *adoptio,* that seems to lie behind the implicit adoption of Jesus into the Davidic line through Joseph, as described in the infancy narratives of Matthew and Luke → Christ, Jesus: II. Birth and Infancy Narratives). None of the practices of adoption found in the Hebrew Bible brings the adoptee into the new bloodline of the adoptive father as does the Roman practice, so Y. Levin argues that the Roman conception of adoption in which the adopted son inherits the adopter's legal status must lie behind these accounts (Levin, 2006, 429). The key Hebrew Bible text for the necessity of Jesus sharing this Davidic lineage as messianic claimant would be 2 Sam 7:14, which itself speaks of the adoption of the king by God. In the Gospel of Mark (→ Mark, Gospel of), there is an assumption of Davidic lineage (Mark 10:47), though how Jesus is a part of this line is unexplored.

The Gospel of John (7:42; John the Apostle) is the least clear in terms of Jesus' relationship to the Davidic lineage. Indeed, apart from John's basic silence, all of the Synoptic Gospels contain a scene in which Jesus challenges the centrality of the Davidic status of the Messiah (Matt 22:45; Mark 12:37; Luke 20:44). This raises the question of the relationship of the Davidic son to the broader designation as "Son of God." At the beginning of Mark 1:1, Jesus is called "Son of God," while in the baptism scene (1:11), reliant on Ps 2:7, God calls him "my son," which will be repeated at the Transfiguration (Mark 9:7). → Baptism in all of the Gospels could be seen as the adoption of Jesus as divine son (Matt 3:16–17; Luke 3:21–22; John 1:32–34; Horn & Martens, 2009, 48). It is possible to understand Ps 2:7 ("you are my son; today I have begotten you") as indicative of Jesus' begottenness and his adoption, in light of the use of the word "today," an issue that will be considered again in the Nicene period. M. Peppard has argued that such adoptive divine sonship might be better seen through the lens of the divine adoption of the Roman emperor, but it is possible for this to fit with both the language of the emperor cult and the language of the Hebrew Bible (Peppard, 2011, 107). It is the case, though, that the baptism scenes and allusions to them, such as Matt 12:18, include the language of being "chosen." In the same way, Acts 2:36, in which it is said that "God has made him both Lord and Messiah," and Heb 1:1–14, which cites Ps 2:7, point to a process of adoption. It seems likely, therefore, that both Hebrew and Roman conceptions of adoption influence the Gospel portrait of Jesus as Son of God. In the Gospel of John, Jesus is "begotten," a natural son of God the Father, and the notion of adoption does not seem to enter into consideration with respect to the divine origin of Jesus (1:1–5; 5:17–47). Yet there is one significant way in which adoption imagery and conceptions enter into the discussion in John. It is through Jesus' sonship, for instance, that Christians can be called children Τὰ τέκνα of God (John 3:16–18, 35–36; 8:34–38), which echoes the Hebrew Bible notion of the people of Israel as God's children. It is possible to see the idea of adoption in all of the gospels used to explain how followers of Jesus are in a familial relationship with God and each other. Significantly, the New Testament conception carries over many of the same assumptions and themes from the Hebrew Bible, such as election and grace, combined with the expanded and inclusive agenda of Christian eschatology. All three Synoptic Gospels recount that in the early phases of his ministry, Jesus' biological family went to "take hold" of him since it was being said of him that "he is out of his mind" (Mark 3:20–21, 31–34; Matt 12:46–50; Luke 8:19–21). In response, Jesus is recorded as asking, "'who are my mother and my brothers?" and then pointing to his disciples, those who are obedient to the Father, as his mother and siblings. Becoming a follower of Jesus was tantamount to being adopted into a new family of God (Horn & Martens, 2009, 54–56).

5. Adoption in the Letters of Paul

The term υἱοθεσία occurs only in Paul (→ Paul the Apostle) in the New Testament. The use of υἱοθεσία demonstrates that the followers of Jesus have been adopted through divine initiative by God. There are a number of aspects to this adoption that must be stressed. Though adoption was of sons almost without fail in Greece and Rome, the language in Paul refers to both males and females and helps to make sense of Gal 3:27 that there is no longer male or female, slave or free, Jew or Greek in the church, for all are equal members of God's family. Second, adoption in Paul's letters, especially Galatians and Romans, must be seen to have two levels, namely, adoption into the family and lineage of Abraham and, as a result, the adoption of this covenantal family into God's family. Third, such adoption is due to the son Jesus Christ, though it is not clear from Greek, Roman, or Jewish precedents how the natural son would be the means by which others were adopted into a family. Most often it is the lack of a natural son that leads to adoption, but in Paul's understanding, Jesus' natural sonship is what allows others to become sons and daughters of the father and heirs to his promises. It is not clear what historical precedent, if any, there is for this conception of adoption, apart from the covenantal language of Gen 15 and 17 in which all one's heirs are received into the covenantal lineage. Paul speaks, however, of the "Spirit" as significant for such adoption, and J.M. Scott stresses that in Hellenistic Judaism 2 Sam 7:14 was applied not just eschatologically to the Messiah

(4QFlor. 1.11), but also to the corporate Israel (*Jub.* 1:24) or both (*T. Jud.* 24:3; Scott, 1992, 104). *Jub.* 1:24 seems to provide the precedent for the application of the promises to the whole corporate body and not just the Davidic king. Whatever the influences, Paul will present a situation in which Christians receive the Spirit and become heirs to the Abrahamic promise and the Davidic promise, which originally focused on the son of David alone. Rom 1:3–6 describes the gospel of God's Son, descended from David according to the flesh, but established as Son of God in power, and the participation of his followers who have been called to belong to him (Rom. 1:6).

In Rom 8:14–17, Paul writes that "all who are led by the Spirit of God are children of God" and "have received a spirit of adoption," allowing them to cry, "Abba! Father!" This cry has its source in the Spirit, which bears witness that Christians are "children of God, and if children, then heirs, heirs of God and joint heirs with Christ." All of the language of Roman adoption – and its result, inheritance – is present here, but Paul uniquely talks of the Spirit of God as the means by which Christians become children of God. Later in Rom 8:23, Paul speaks of adoption as a reality that will only be completed with the resurrection (→ Resurrection), as now "we wait for adoption, the → redemption of our bodies." Christians share in this adoption because they are "conformed to the image of his Son, in order that he might be the firstborn within a large family" (Rom 8:29). The use of "firstborn" in Rom 8:29 connects this passage with Ps 89:28, where God promises to adopt the Messiah as the "firstborn" son, while Rom 8:34 denotes Ps 110:1 in which the Davidic king would be the world ruler, similar to Ps 2:7–8. It is this conformation to the Son, through the Spirit, a transformation only completed at the eschaton, that allows Christians to be adoptive members of God's family. For Paul, believers already participate in the adoptive sonship, and they already share the Spirit as "firstfruits" of their adoption (Rom 8:23).

This fits with the use of adoption in Gal 4:5. Paul, after the use of the Παιδαγωγός (disciplinarian) image in Gal 3, speaks of the followers of Christ as heirs when they come to maturity. As long as they were minors, they were not able to inherit, but God sent his son in order that Christians would receive "adoption as children" and because the Spirit of his Son has been sent to these newly adopted children, they can cry, "Abba! Father!" and are heirs (Gal 4:4–7). In this case, it is the "Spirit of his Son" that is transformative and allows all those who are Christians to claim the membership as adopted children in God's family. It is the cry of Abba that points to the participation of Christians in the sonship of Jesus Christ, since the phrase "Abba! Father!" is elsewhere found only in Mark 14:36 on the lips of Jesus. This is related to the fact that all those who are adopted as children of God are also children of Abraham. In fact, Gal 3:7 speaks of "those who believe" as "the sons of Abraham." So, too, does Rom 4 speak of Abraham as the father of "all who believe." The significant issue here is that adoption as sons of God is linked to the adoption into the family of Abraham. This helps to make sense of the complex usage of adoption in Rom 9:4, where Paul says that "adoption, the glory, the covenants, the giving of the law, the worship, and the promises" belong to the Israelites. Coming as it does so soon after the discussion of the adoption of the Christians as a whole in Rom 8, who have been brought into the familial line, it seems possible that this refers to the adoption of the Israelites by God through the covenantal promises given to Abraham and his descendants. The Israelite adoption by God, in the divine sense, is no more or less natural, than the adoption of the nations, promised to Abraham in the establishment of the covenant.

The deuteropauline Ephesians maintains the same lines of thought found in Romans and Galatians. Eph 1:5 says, "He destined us for adoption as his children through Jesus Christ, according to the good pleasure of his will." Eph 2, however, creates the broader context of one humanity and one family created through and by Christ. Those who were once estranged and separated from God, foreigners and aliens, are now members of the οἰκεῖοι (household) of God (2:19).

6. Spiritual Adoption in Early Christianity

The early Christian church would focus on two aspects in particular of the New Testament discussion regarding adoption. First, the focus on Jesus' as → Son of God, whether he was "made" (adopted) or "begotten" (a natural son), continued through the 4th century CE, based on the mixed evidence of the New Testament, until the issue was brought to a head with the Council of → Nicaea and the language that definitively stated that Jesus was "begotten not made." Second, the church fathers concentrated their attention on the spiritual sonship or adoption of Christians, although Christians themselves could be described as "begotten" or "made" as adopted children of God. Though Jewish and Roman conceptions and practices of adoption influenced these continuing discussions, the Christian focus derived its impetus from the internal discourse of the church and interpretation of the relevant biblical passages in light of Christological and soteriological debates.

a. Adoption in the 2nd and 3rd Centuries CE

Due to the high view of adoption in the Roman Empire, and the language of adoption that appeared in the New Testament, it was possible to speak of both Jesus and Christians as adopted in their divine sonship. It is also the case that adoption as a theological idea moved from being the strictly soteriological idea (→ Soteriology) it had been in the New Testament, connected to a constellation of others (e.g. baptism, the giving of the Spirit, spiritual inheritance), to an idea with Christological, soteriological, and ecclesiological implications (→ Ecclesiology).

While we are used to hearing of the "adoptionism" of the → Ebionites and Theodotus of Byzantium (both the cobbler and the banker), it is not clear that these two groups did use such language to describe themselves. The focus of the Ebionites and Theodotus was on the → baptism of Jesus and the language of Ps 2:7, but this is also the case for many other early Christians. More than adoptionism, the Ebionites and Theodotus and his followers focused on Jesus as a "mere man" (Alexander of Alexandria's *Letter to Alexander of Constantinople* 9, see Thdt. *Hist. eccl.* 1.3; Eus. *Hist. eccl.* 5.28.3–6).

Clement of Alexandria speaks of the adoption of Christians into divine sonship (Clem. *Paed.* 1.5.21; 1.6.26; *Strom.* 2.23.137; 6.8.68). → Clement of Alexandria also defines Christians as "legitimate children of light," but their sonship is grounded in their adoption through Christ (*Protr.* 10.92.5). Still, Clement can also describe Christians as "begotten again" into adoption as their first begetting was through baptism. Clement

is, therefore, a proponent of "exemplarist" Christology, in which Jesus is the model for both begotten and adoptive sonship (Peppard, 2011, 154–55).

Irenaeus of Lyon distinguishes clearly between the begotten nature of Jesus and the adoptive nature of the sons of God. → Irenaeus of Lyon, first of all, states that Jesus was not begotten by Joseph or he would not be able to give the gift of eternal life (→ Immortality) and to make human beings like him in incorruptibility and immortality. Irenaeus cites Ps 82:6.7, in which people are both described as gods, and destined to die. Those who die, says Irenaeus, are those who do not have "the gift of adoption, but who despise the incarnation of the pure generation of the Word of God." Adoption as sons of God derives from Jesus' distinct being as "son of the living God" (Iren. *Haer.* 3.19.2). It is still possible at this time to see the "begotten" and "made" metaphors used of the divine sonship of Christians, that is, Christians are begotten into faith in order to receive adoption from God (*Haer.* 4.33.4). Even though language of "begottenness" is used to describe Christian baptism in Irenaeus, there is a clear distinction between Jesus as begotten son and the adoption of Christians as sons. We become partakers in the divine nature only because Jesus took on human flesh, and it is through Jesus becoming a human that we can share in adoption to divine sonship (*Haer.* 3.16.3; 3.18.7; 3.19.1; 3.20.2). Irenaeus places emphasis on the Pauline notion of "recapitulation," but extends the meaning in a unique fashion to include spiritual adoption. Recapitulation speaks of restitution as a kind of "fresh start," in which the effects of the → fall are reversed and the reproduction of the original features are restored through the → incarnation. For Irenaeus, this "fresh start" is not merely reconciliation – in the sense of alleviating the wrath of God – but a readmission to the privileged status of Adam as friend. Recapitulation opens up the possibility for communion with God the Father and qualifies humanity for adoption and subsequently incorruptibility.

Tertullian uses language that clearly distinguishes between the son of God who was begotten when he proceeded from God the Father and Christians who share in his divine sonship (Tert. *Prax.* 7). → Tertullian does not shy away from Ps 82:6, "I say, 'You are gods, children of the Most High, all of you,'" for this speaks of Christians who have become sons of God by faith, but he stresses that there is only one true Son of God (*Prax.* 13). In *Praesc.* 2.27, Tertullian speaks of God having made his son by emitting him from himself. Further, he says that if Jesus had a human father, he could not be Son of God, but if he was made through a divine father also, he is reduced to Hercules of fable (*Praescr.* 3.10).

Origen also stresses that Jesus is son by nature not adoption, that he is not created, has no beginning and cannot be compared to any human being – such comparisons are "monstrous," says → Origen (Or. *Princ.* 1.2.2–4). Origen also makes sense of a sticky issue in Ps 2:7 that the son is said to be made "today," a possible argument for creation and adoption, by saying that every day is "today" for God so one cannot by this means suggest that Jesus the Son is "created" (Or. *Comm. Jo.* 1.28–29). In *Comm. Rom.* 7.9.3, Origen also defines Jesus on the basis of Rom 8:32 as God's "own" (ἴδιος) son, which means there can be none other like him. Christians are simply adopted brothers of the only son of God (*Comm. Jo.* 20.24–34; *Pasch.* 41).

b. Adoption to Nicaea and Beyond

Christian discussion of adoption continued along the same lines that were sketched in the work of Origen, and increasingly certain positions on adoption, especially with respect to the distinction between Jesus being a "begotten" or a "made" Son of God, were out of bounds in orthodox circles. At the same time, though, it became problematic to speak of Christians as "begotten" children or sons of God; adoption was the only language that could apply to the other sons of God. The primary issue for the Council of Nicaea was not whether Jesus was the begotten Son of God, but when this begetting occurred. Whether Arius actually preferred the language of adoption is not obvious, though › Athanasius of Alexandria attributed such teachings to him (Athan. *Syn.* 15; *Ar.* 1.38; 2.64; 3.9). It is clear throughout all of Athanasius' writing that Jesus is the unique Son of God (Athan. *Dion.* 18.79), whose eternal divinity allowed others, in the past and today, to become adopted sons of God (*Ar.* 1.39, 2.64). The language and imagery of John 1:12–13, however, caused trouble for this reading since the language of begetting appears here in the context of the sons of God. Athanasius explains that all of us can be said to have been born of God, but there is a difference between the son by nature and those of us who have been adopted by God. Elsewhere he says that when Christians are baptized, we do truly become sons, but it is not a natural sonship, but an adoptive sonship (*Decr.* 31).

It is in the Letter of Alexander of Alexandria to → Alexander of Constantinople (Thdt. *Hist. eccl.* 1.3) where a new word emerges to make the clear distinction that Jesus' natural sonship is utterly different from the adopted sonship of Christians. Alexander uses the word υἱότης, "sonship," to describe Jesus' sonship, while using υἱοθεσία to describe the sonship of Christians. This neologism will occur some 91 times in the subsequent writings of the church fathers, setting Jesus' sonship apart entirely from the adoptive sonship of Christians. This is strengthened by his interpretation of Rom 8:32, in which Jesus as God's ἴδιος son is stressed. → Cyril of Jerusalem also draws this sharp distinction between the sonship of Christ and the sonship of Christians. In Cyr.Jer. *Cat. Myst.* 3, *On Baptism*, he says that Jesus is always and has always been God's son, but Christians receive adoptive sonship. He, too, uses the word υἱότης to distinguish between adoptive sons and the one natural Son.

Didascalia Apostolorum retains a quotation in the baptismal formula from Ps 2:7, which intended to indicate the divine sonship of Christians, but the text goes on to describe how one becomes a son of God through the parentage of the bishop (→ *Didascalia Apostolorum*). The usage of the image of the believer as a "son of God" was transformed so that the Christian was now called to love the → bishop and view him as father and mother. The son of God was now increasingly viewed as a "child of Mother Church" and under the authority of the bishop as father (Horn & Martens, 2009, 67–68). The *Apostolic Constitutions* maintains this language, saying, "Through your bishop, God adopts you, O human" (Peppard, 2011, 170).

When we get to → Jerome and → Augustine of Hippo in the 4th and 5th centuries CE, discussion about adoption and sonship still takes place, though often against an apologetic backdrop. In his *Commentary on Galatians*, Jerome begins his discussion about adoption with a refutation of Marcionite and gnostic ideals (Jer. *Comm. Gal.* 2.4.4–5; → Marcion/Marcionites/Marcionism; → Gnosis/Gnosticism). He goes on to follow the Pauline line of thinking that adoption is closely connected with reception of the → Holy Spirit. What is more, Jerome's language may reflect the influence of both Greco-Roman as well as Jewish conceptions of adoption, as he says in *Comm. Gal.* 2.4.4–5, "We therefore receive the *full rights* of [adopted] sons." In *Enarrationes in Psalmos*, in his comment on Ps 89(88):6, Augustine emphasizes Christian adoption as distinct from the uniqueness of Jesus as Son of God, declaring that Christians are indeed sons of God, but Jesus is the Son of God in another sense. By the 5th century CE, the lines of the discussion, vague and obscure in some ways in the New Testament, had become sharply and clearly drawn.

Bibliography

Bartlett, D.L., "Adoption in the Bible," in: M.J. Bunge, ed., *The Child in the Bible*, Grand Rapids, 2008, 375–398.

Burke, T.J., *Adopted into God's Family: Exploring a Pauline Metaphor*, Downers Grove, 2006.

Collins, A.Y., & J.J. Collins, *King and Messiah As Son of God: Divine, Human, and Angelic Messianic Figures in Biblical and Related Literature*, Grand Rapids, 2008.

Corbier, M., "Constructing Kinship in Rome: Marriage and Divorce, Filiation and Adoption," in: D.I. Kertzer & R.P. Saller, eds., *The Family in Italy from Antiquity to the Present*, New Haven, 1991, 127–44; also in: M. Corbier, "Divorce and Adoption as Roman Familial Strategies," in: B. Rawson, ed., *Marriage, Divorce and Children in Ancient Rome*, 1991, 47–78; see also M. Corbier, "Adoptés et nourris," in: M. Corbier, ed., *Adoption et fosterage*, Paris, 2000, 6–41.

Donner, H., *OrAnt* 8, 1969, 87–119.

Gardner, J.F., "Status, Sentiment and Strategy in Roman Adoption" in: M. Corbier, ed., *Adoption et fosterage*, Paris, 2000, 63–80.

Horn, C.B., & J.W. Martens, *Let the Little Children Come to Me: Childhood and Children in Early Christianity*, Washington DC, 2009.

Jüssen, B., *Patenschaft und Adoption im fruhën Mittelalter*, Göttingen, 1991; ET: *Spiritual Kinship as Social Practice: Godparenthood and Adoption in the Early Middle Ages*, trans. P. Selwyn, Newark, 2000.

Kunst, C., *Römische Adoption: Zur Strategie einer Familienorganisation*, FAB 10, Hennef, 2005.

Kurylowicz, M., "Adoption on the Evidence of the Papyri," *JJP* 19, 1983, 61–75.

Lallemand, S., "Adoption, fosterage et alliance," *AeS*, 12/2, 1988, 25–40.

Leduc, C., "L'adoption dans la cité des Athéniens, VIe siècle–IVe siècle av. J.-C.," *Pallas* 48, 1998, 175–202.

Levin, Y., "Jesus, 'Son of God' and 'Son of David': The 'Adoption' of Jesus into the Davidic Line," *JSNT* 28/4, 2006, 415–442.

Lindsay, H., "Adoption and Succession in Roman Law," *NLR* 3/1, 1998, 57–81; also in: H. Lindsay, "Adoption in Greek Law and Society: Some Comparison with the Roman World," *NLR* 3/2, 1998, 91–110; also in: H. Lindsay, "Adoption and Its Function in Cross-Cultural Contexts,"; in: S. Dixon, ed. *Childhood, Class and Kin in the Roman World*, Oxford, 2001, 190–204.

Malul, M., "Adoption of Foundlings in the Bible and Mesopotamian Legal Documents: A Study of Some Legal Metaphors in Ezekiel 16:1–7," *JSOT* 46, 1990, 97–126.

Mosser, C., "The Earliest Patristic Interpretations of Psalm 82, Jewish Antecedents, and the Origin of Deification," *JThS* 26, 2005, 20–74.

Nielsen, H.S., "Quasi-kin, Quasi-adoption and the Roman Family," in: M. Corbier, ed., *Adoption et fosterage*, Paris, 2000, 249–262.

Orbe, A., "¿San Ireneo adopcionista?" *Greg* 65, 1984, 5–52.

Peppard, M., *The Son of God in the Roman World: Divine Sonship in Its Social and Political Context*, Oxford, 2011.

Rubinstein, L. et al., "Adoption in Hellenistic and Roman Athens," *CM* 42, 1991, 139–151; also in: L. Rubinstein, *Adoption in Fourth-Century Athens*, Copenhagen, 1993; see also: L. Rubinstein, "Adoption in Classical Athens," in: M. Corbier, ed., *Adoption et fosterage*, Paris, 2000, 45–62.

Salomies, O., "Names and Adoption in Ancient Rome," in: M. Corbier, ed., *Adoption et fosterage*, Paris, 2000, 141–56.

Scott, J.M., *Adoption as Sons of God*, WUNT 48, 2nd ser., Tübingen,1992.

Syme, R., "Clues to Testamentary Adoption," *Tituli* 4, 1982, 397–410.

Taubenschlag, R., *The Law of Greco-Roman Egypt in the Light of the Papyri, 332 BC–640 AD*, Milan, 1972.

Widdicombe, P., *The Fatherhood of God from Origen to Athanasius*, Oxford, 1994.

JOHN W. MARTENS

Adoptionists

The term "Adoptionism" emerged in the context of an 8th-century CE Spanish controversy. Its semantic scope was extended to denote what may be seen more as a Christological tendency acknowledging Jesus' ontological character than as a heresy that might have served to define a group.

Adoptionism is indeed a religious doctrine according to which Jesus only became the Son of God through → adoption, in other words, after having been baptized in the Jordan by → John the Baptist – a baptism that conferred him the status of *Filius adoptivus* ("adopted son") following a symbolic struggle against the forces of → evil and from which Jesus emerged as the man whom this adoption designated as the Messiah.

It was first formulated in the 2nd century CE by Theodotus the Elder (or the Tanner), whose concern was to return to divine unity by distinguishing the Son from the Father.

Paul of Samosata, bishop of Antioch (→ Paul of Samosata), took it up again in 268 CE. The very same year, he was condemned by a synod held in a political context that cannot be ignored, that of Zenobia's Palmyrene Empire, which sought to restore the unity of the eastern Roman Empire for its own benefit. Paul of Samosata's condemnation remained unenforceable until 272 CE, when imperial legality was reestablished by Aurelian.

Adoptionism resurfaced in 8th-century CE Spain, where it was championed by Archbishop Elipandus of Toledo and Felix of Urzel, the bishop of Urgell. It was repeatedly condemned in the name of orthodoxy, first by Pope Adrian I, then by the Council of Frankfurt, which was convoked in 794 CE by Charlemagne (counseled by Paulinus of Aquileia, Alcuin, Benedict of Aniane, and Leidrad of Lyon), and finally by the Synod of Rome in 799 CE. In 792 CE, Felix of Urzel recanted under pressure at the Council of Ratisbon in Bavaria. Subsequently arrested and condemned for relapse by Pope Leo III, he died in prison in Lyon in 818 CE. However, it was not until the 12th century that Pope Alexander III finally succeeded in quelling Adoptionism, which was now definitely considered a → heresy.

The reasoning of this school of thought, with its multifaceted ramifications, is roughly as follows: there is only one God, Creator and Lord of the universe; accordingly, Jesus cannot be God and is merely an ordinary human being born from the union of → Mary and Joseph; he simply lived in greater holiness than others, and he spoke and acted more extraordinarily than all others, having been specially "chosen" by God.

In short, the privileges enjoyed by Jesus did not make him a divine being, but a privileged adoptive

son of the sole God (whence the designation "Adoptionism"). His mission is that of a prophet and his salvific role reducible to that of a paradigm.

Adoptionism and → Monarchianism have in common that they both reevaluate the oneness of God in such a manner that the divinity of the Son is denied as such. But while Adoptionism denies the divinity of the Son (Christ is merely a human being), Monarchianism denies it within a clearly "Trinitarian" perspective (Christ is considered a god, though not as one who is really distinct from the Father).

Adoptionism is believed to owe more to Aramean than to Greek culture, notably on account of its proximity to Ebionite beliefs. It nevertheless characterized Paul of Samosata's Christological thinking in the 3rd century CE.

The → Ebionites assign a certain transcendent quality to Jesus and do not merely consider him an "ordinary man." In their eyes, Jesus is the "chosen one of God" and, above all, the "true prophet," although they do deny the virgin birth and Jesus' divine filiation, and at the same time also his preexistence. Thus, according to them, when the → Holy Spirit descends upon Jesus during → baptism, when it enters into him, and when the Father's voice calls him "Son," all of this should be understood neither as a divine filiation nor as a divine adoption, but much rather as the union of a celestial being with the human Jesus, which transforms the latter into Christ and Son of God.

For this reason, it seems somewhat erroneous to view the Ebionites as Adoptionists, as the heresiologists are in the habit of doing.

Toward the end of the 2nd century CE, the first true exponents of Adoptionism – at least according to the heresiologists of the "Great Church" (means the [later] majority church) – are Theodotus the Elder and Theodotus the Younger (or the Banker).

In Rome, Theodotus the Elder was accused of having claimed that he had not rejected God in Jesus but merely a man, using textual passages from the Hebrew Bible and New Testament in order to prove that Jesus was an "ordinary human being" who nevertheless received a special vocation from God (Epiph. *Pan.* 54.1). Theodotus the Elder is considered the founder of a hypothetical group known as the "Melchisedechians"; according to certain critics, he based himself on the *Epistle to the Hebrews*, already attributed to → Paul the Apostle, and on its messianic doctrine, which goes back to Melchizedek (*Pan.* 54.35).

Again in Rome, during the pontificate of Victor or of Zephyrinus, Theodotus the Younger – who alludes specifically to Gen 14:1–24; Ps 110(109):4; and Heb 7 – was accused of placing Melchizedek over Christ as "the greatest power of God." In his opinion, Christ was indeed not a human being, in spite of having been conceived and born by the Holy Spirit and Mary (Hipp. *El.* 7.36; Epiph. *Pan.* 55).

While Theodotus the Elder's position may be qualified as truly Adoptionist, this does not really hold true for Theodotus the Younger – in spite of the fact that the latter was condemned as such in 190 CE by Pope Victor I.

It is thus advisable not to confuse Adoptionists and Ebionites, or to attribute texts to the latter that should perhaps be attributed to the former, as recently proposed with regard to certain versions of the *Infancy Gospel of Thomas* or to the *Acts of Pilate* (→ Pilate) in Greek.

However this may be, the impact of Adoptionism remains difficult to assess, this tendency having elicited the interest of those whose understanding of divinity did not allow them to accept that it could be imparted to a human creature.

Bibliography

Bardy, G., "Melchisédech dans la tradition patristique," *RB* 35, 1926, 496–505; 36, 1927, 24–45.

Bardy, G., "Paul de Samosate," in: *DThC*, vol. XII/1, Paris, 1933, cols. 46–61.

Grillmeier, A., *Le Christ dans la tradition chrétienne: De l'âge apostolique au concile de Chalcédoine (451)*, Paris, 2003.

Portalié, E., "Adoptianisme," in: *DThC*, vol. I/1, Paris, 1902, cols. 403–421.

SIMON C. MIMOUNI

Adrian

Scholars customarily date Adrian to the early 5th century CE and regard him as a representative of the so-called Antiochene approach to → biblical interpretation. There are striking verbal and thematic parallels between his εἰσαγωγὴ εἰς τὰς θείας γραφάς (*Introduction to the Divine Scriptures*) and the exegetical writings of → Diodore of Tarsus (d. 394 CE) and → Theodore of Mopsuestia (c. 350–428 CE). We know very little of Adrian. → Cassiodorus is the first author who unambiguously mentions him, thereby providing us with a *terminus ante quem*. In the *Institutiones Divinarum et Saecularium Litterarum (Institutions of Divine and Secular Learning)*, composed in the 560s CE, he writes,

> After reading this work [i.e. *Institutions*], our first concern should be to consider introductory manuals to Divine Scripture that I previously found, that is, Tyconius the Donatist, St. Augustine *On Christian Learning*, Adrian, Eucherius, and Junilius [...]. By arranging the rules of usage to elucidate the text, and by comparisons of various examples, they have clarified what was hitherto obscure. (Cassio. *Inst.* 1.10.1; see Halporn & Vessey, 2004, 133)

Photius is the first author who specifically names Adrian's treatise: "Read an *Introduction to Scripture* by Adrian. This book is useful for beginners" (Phot. *Bibl.*, codex 2).

Adrian's only known work is the *Introduction*. He opens this treatise with an announcement of its overarching theme and structure:

> There are three kinds of peculiarities of the Hebrew literary style: one will find that the first of these pertains to its message, the second to its diction, and the third to its syntax. (Ad. *Intro.* 1)

By "peculiarities" (ἰδιώματα) Adrian means uses of language in the Bible that frequently occur and are unconventional. While the reference to the peculiarities of the "Hebrew" literary style might suggest Adrian's familiarity with the original language of the Hebrew Bible, his interest rests primarily with the Septuagint, the church's official Greek translation of the Hebrew Bible (→ Bible). The Septuagint often obscures because it has kept very close to the wording of the original Hebrew, transparently conveying peculiarities into its Greek translation that cause its readers difficulties.

The *Introduction* is a handbook on the peculiar stylistic features of Scripture, which Adrian subdivides into three categories: thought, diction, and word arrangement. This tripartite classification system of style had precedent in Greco-Roman rhetorical theory (→ Rhetoric; see Demetrius, *On Style*; Longinus, *On Sublimity;* Pseudo-Aristides, *On Political Discourse* and *On Simple Discourse*; and Hermogenes, *On the Types of Style*; Martens, 2013, 201–210). This threefold classification of style also informs the general structure of the treatise. In the first section of the *Introduction*, Adrian adopts a modified problems-and-solutions format. He first catalogues his problems – the anthropomorphic (→ Anthropomorphism) ways in which God is portrayed in Scripture, the Psalms in particular – and then explains how such expressions ought properly to be understood. For example, one of the problems identified by Adrian is the portrayal of God exercising his wrath or anger (*Intro.* 2.3). The corresponding solution, several paragraphs later, runs as follows:

> It [that is Scripture] calls the opposition of God's will to evil his "anger" and "wrath," since enmity toward hostile forces occurs among us. For example, [Scripture says] "from then is your wrath" (Ps 75:8[76:7]), instead of, "from the beginning, and always, you have been disposed to oppose evil." (Ad. *Intro.* 5)

The second section on diction identifies difficult word usages and syntax, offers lexicographical analyses of semantically rich terms, and discusses a handful of tropes. For instance, "Using the term ἐκεῖ not only with respect to place ('there'), but also conduct" (*Intro.* 24). Or, "It expresses things wished for in the imperative mood. For example [...]" (*Intro.* 63). Again,

> Scripture often speaks about God as if making a change of person. For example, [...] "Your arrows are sharp, O Mighty one [...] in the heart of the king's enemies" (Ps 44:6[45:5]), that is, "[in the heart of the enemies] of you, the powerful king." (Ad. *Intro.* 51)

The third section on word arrangement lists and illustrates a handful of figures of speech, including ellipsis and tautology. Throughout the treatise, Adrian's interpretations of biblical peculiarities amount to glosses or paraphrases designed to help the neophyte reader with stylistic obscurities.

There are noticeable parallels between Adrian's *Introduction* and Theodore's *Commentary on the Psalms*. For instance, in *Intro.* 32 Adrian glosses the term "bosom" as a term that indicates something "inseparable." He then lists five passages where the term has this signification: Ps 78[79]:12; Ps 88:51[89:50]; Ps 34[35]:13; Ps 73[74]:11; John 1:18. In Theodore's *Commentary on the Psalms*, we find the very same interpretation of "bosom":

> It is customary with the divine Scripture to mention the "bosom" not when referring to the actual thing called "bosom" by us, but when wanting to suggest something inseparable and indivisible. (Theo. *Comm. Ps.* 34[35]:13)

Theodore then provides a nearly identical catalogue of verses that illustrate this use, listing four of the five verses mentioned by Adrian above (minus Ps 73[74]:11).

The treatise concludes with a series of appendices: a catalogue of 22 tropes (most of which are defined and illustrated from Scripture), a twofold classification of Scripture into prophetic and narratival (or historical) literature, an extended excursus on how to interpret the Bible, and, finally, another classification of Scripture into prose and poetry. The *Introduction* provides an excellent entrée into Antiochene, and especially Theodoran, biblical scholarship: see especially *Intro.* 75–78, where Adrian announces several exegetical guidelines for teachers of Scripture. In this section he discusses important technical exegetical terms, including ὑπόθεσις ("purpose"), ἀκολουθία ("sequence"), θεωρία ("speculative sense"), and τὸ πρέπον ("fitting sense").

1. Manuscript Tradition, Editions, and Translations

In addition to a number of fragments from the catenae (see Pitra, 1884; Mercati, 1914), this treatise survives in two recensions in the direct manuscript tradition. The oldest manuscript that transmits the commonly-received text is *Conventi Soppressi 39* (Florence, Laurenziana). Its last folios were excised and are now in Hamburg under the designation *In Scrinio* 221 (Staats- und Universitätsbibliothek). This manuscript dates from 1095 or 1105. There was a heightened interest in the *Introduction* in the 16th century, as almost all the other manuscripts date to this period.

The other recension is not transmitted in its entirety and was only recently edited. Three manuscripts transmit two large fragments: Vaticanus Graecus 1862 (16th cent.), Vaticanus Graecus 1447 (1534 CE), and Iviron, Ms. Gr. *1333* (Lambros 5453; 17th cent.). These fragments correspond to

1. P.W. Martens, 2017, §§26–55; and
2. P.W. Martens, 2017, §§72–74.3.3.

A few items are of particular interest in this longer recension: it refers to the treatise anonymously under the heading ἐκ τοῦ περὶ τῶν ἰδιωμάτων τῆς θείας γραφῆς (From the treatise about the peculiarities of Divine Scripture), it contains an extended discussion of → allegory that is not in the commonly-received text, and it makes open use of Symmachus' translation to help clarify obscurities in the Septuagint.

There have been three editions of the main text. The editio princeps was published by D. Höschel in Augsburg in 1602 (this edition was reprinted with minor corrections in PG 98.1273–1312). F. Goessling's edition (1887) drew upon a wider, though still incomplete, manuscript base and did not call attention to the catenae fragments already known in his day, nor the second recension. A comprehensive new edition of both recensions was recently produced by P.W. Martens (2017).

Cassiodorus either discovered a Latin translation of the *Introduction* or had one made at his monastery in Scyllacium. Traces of the reception of Adrian's *Introduction* occur in Cassiodorus' *Institutes* (1.15.4) and perhaps in his *Explanation of the Psalms*, which reflects a strong interest in scriptural *proprietates* (ἰδιώματα). There have been at least two modern Latin translations of the *Introduction*: one was made by Bishop Aloysius Lollin (in *Lollini characters*, [1630], 257–273) and the other is printed in PG 98.1273–1312. F. Goessling (1887) offered a facing German translation to his critical edition. P.W. Martens (2017) provides an annotated English translation of both recensions and prefaces his text and translation with a study that orients readers to Adrian and his treatise.

Historiography

The editors of Adrian's *Introduction* are responsible for most of the scholarship on this treatise (Goessling, 1887; Mercati, 1914; Martens, 2013; 2017). Except for A. Léonas (2005), there are only scattered remarks.

Bibliography

Goessling, F., *Adrians* ΕΙΣΑΓΩΓΉ ΕΙΣ ΤΑΣ ΘΕΙΑΣ ΓΡΑΦΑΣ aus Neu Aufgefundenen Handschriften, Berlin, 1887.

Halporn, J.W., & M. Vessey, *Cassiodorus: Institutions of Divine and Secular Learning and On the Soul*, TTH 42, Liverpool, 2004.

Henry, R., *Photius: Bibliothèque*, vol. I, Paris, 1959.

Léonas, A., *Recherches sur le langage de la Septante*, Göttingen, 2005, 132–249.

Martens, P.W., "Adrian's Introduction to the Divine Scriptures and Greco-Roman Rhetorical Theory on Style," *JR* 93, 2013, 197–217.

Martens, P.W., *Adrian's Introduction to the Divine Scriptures: An Antiochene Handbook on Biblical Interpretation*, Oxford, 2017.

Mercati, G., "Pro Adriano," *RB* 11, 1914, 246–55.

Pitra, J.B., *Analecta Sacra*, vol. I: *Patres Antenicaeni*, Paris, 1884, 130–136.

PETER MARTENS

Adultery

In the Hebrew Bible (→ Bible) and in Roman law, the term "adultery" (Lat. *adulteria*; Gk *moicheia*) was defined as sexual relations between a married woman or a betrothed woman and a man who was not her husband. In this case, both the man and the woman were considered guilty of adultery. If a married man engaged in sexual relations with an unmarried woman (slave or free), however, this was not considered adultery, although it might be considered *stuprum* (i.e. illicit intercourse), if it occurred with a woman of high status. Strictly speaking, adultery could be committed only by or with a married woman. It constituted a violation of a husband's right to have sole sexual possession of his wife and presented the risk of corrupting the family line with illegitimate offspring.

Jewish law and Roman law instituted harsh penalties for both men and women found guilty of adultery. Leviticus (20:10) and Deuteronomy (22:22) prescribed the death penalty for adulterers, although it is unclear how frequently it was imposed. In Roman law a husband could execute his wife and her lover if he caught the adulterous couple in flagrante delicto. At the beginning of the early Christian era Emperor → Augustus initiated legislation to suppress adultery as part of a broader initiative to strengthen the institution of legitimate marriage. Under the *lex Julia de adulteriis* (18 BCE) adultery became a criminal offense punishable by exile and confiscation of property; husbands were also required to divorce their adulterous wives or risk prosecution for "pimping" (*lenocinium*).

Against the background of these Jewish and Roman traditions, the teachings of Jesus and Paul (→ Paul the Apostle) preserved in the New Testament created some difficulties for early Christians. The problem lay in the legacy of the New Testament on → divorce and remarriage. Unlike the Hebrew Bible and Roman law, which permitted divorce and remarriage, teachings attributed to Jesus in the New Testament expressly forbade both men and women to divorce and remarry (Mark 10:11–12; Luke 16:18). This new and radical prohibition of divorce and remarriage led to a reinterpretation of what was meant by adultery. But the situation was further complicated by Matthew (19:19), which included an exception in the case of a wife's "sexual misconduct" (*porneia*): "Whoever divorces his wife, except for sexual misconduct, and marries another commits adultery" (Matt 5:32). The precise meaning of *porneia*, however, is disputed (see Harper, 2011; Glancy, 2015; Wheeler-Reed, Glancy & Martin, 2018).

The most obvious reading of the Matthean exception is that a man who divorced his wife because of her unfaithfulness was allowed to remarry, although a similar exception was not explicitly stated in the case of a woman whose husband engaged in extramarital relations. In 1 Corinthians (7:10 11) Paul had repeated as a command of the Lord:

> That the wife should not separate from her husband, but if she does separate, let her remain unmarried or else be reconciled to her husband, and that the husband should not divorce his wife.

Since Paul did not explicitly forbid a man to remarry after divorcing his wife, as he did the woman, some Christians believed this supported the Matthean exception and allowed remarriage to a man whose wife was guilty of sexual misconduct, but not to the wife whose husband was unchaste (e.g. Ambrosi. *Comm. in 1 Cor* 7:11).

But many early Christians were troubled by the apparent double standard enshrined in the biblical texts, as well as by the fact that adultery was customarily defined as a crime committed by or with a married woman and did not necessarily apply to a man's extramarital affairs. Early in the 4th century CE the Latin apologist → Lactantius argued that any extramarital activity, even on the part of the husband, constituted adultery (Lact. *Inst.* 6.23). By the late 4th century CE western Christians, such as → Ambrose of Milan and → Augustine of Hippo, applied the same principle to remarriage after divorce: even after divorce for a legitimate reason (i.e. adultery), remarriage was forbidden and considered adultery, both for men and for women (Ambr. *Exp. Luc.* 8.5; 8.7; Augustine, *De coniugiis adulterinis*). By thus defining a Christian → marriage as indissoluble, these western theologians simultaneously redefined adultery to include remarriage after divorce. Eastern Christian tradition eventually solved the problem of inequality by allowing remarriage after divorce to both men and women (L'Huillier, 1988).

Another issue around the problem of adultery that was raised by specifically Christian teaching was the question of whether a person guilty of adultery could be granted → forgiveness of the sin and remain a member of the church. Although the example of Jesus offering forgiveness to the woman caught in adultery (John 8:1–11, a passage missing from many manuscripts and unknown to the Greek Fathers) might have encouraged a generous attitude toward sinners, early Christians took adultery very seriously as a moral failure. The earliest discussion is found in the *Shepherd of Hermas* (→ Hermas), written in Rome early in the 2nd century CE. According to Hermas, if a Christian discovered his wife in adultery, he had to separate from her as long as she refused to repent. But the man was not allowed to marry another woman after the divorce or else he would be guilty of adultery. He had to remain unmarried and be prepared to take back his wife if she repented; but repentance was allowed only once. Hermas applied this ruling to the wife as well as to the husband (Herm. *Mand.* 4.29).

By the early 3rd century CE a more rigorous discipline was in place in many churches. In the mid-3rd century CE, Cyprian, bishop of Carthage (→ Cyprian of Carthage), observed that some of his episcopal colleagues in North Africa refused to grant "peace" (*pax*; i.e. ecclesiastical penance or forgiveness of sins) to adulterers, but he clearly supported the practice of allowing penance (→ Penitence/Penance) and reconciliation to adulterers who underwent public penance (Cyp. *Ep.* 55.21). The more rigorous position was supported by → Origen (*Or.* 28) and by → Tertullian (*Pud.* 2.14; 19.27), who argued that adultery was one of the mortal sins or "sins unto death" (*hamartia pros thanaton*) mentioned in 1 John (5:16); both Tertullian and Origen acknowledged, however, that some bishops were granting absolution for adultery. At the same time in Rome, Bishop Callistus caused scandal among the rigorists by claiming the authority to remit the sin of adultery (Hipp. *Haer.* 9.12).

But the rigorist position was slow to die out. For example, around the year 305 CE a canon attributed to the Spanish Council of Elvira (c. 8) decreed lifelong → excommunication for a woman who committed adultery; not even deathbed penance was allowed. Other councils took a laxer position, however; the Council of Ancyra (314 CE), perhaps in direct response to Elvira, offered a more lenient penalty that applied both to men and women:

> If the wife of anyone has committed adultery or if any man commit adultery, it seems fit that he shall be restored to full communion after seven years passed in the prescribed degrees [of ecclesiastical penance]. (Council of Ancyra, c. 20)

By the end of the 4th century CE, however, it was common practice for bishops to grant absolution to adulterous men and women after a requisite period of penance (e.g. Bas. *Ep.* 199.34). Augustine, however, observed that a double standard often persisted and that men usually found it more difficult than women to forgive their wives for adultery (Aug. *Adult. coniug.* 2.8.7).

Historiography

The most comprehensive overview of Roman perspectives and traditions on marriage can be found in S. Treggiari (1991). For a survey of the continuity and change with the rise of Christianity, especially after Constantine I, see J. Evans Grubbs (1995). H. Crouzel (1970) offers a reliable account of Christian perspectives on divorce and remarriage, although on the question of Ambrosiaster and the normativity of Augustine's views on divorce and remarriage, see D.G. Hunter (2017). P.L. Reynolds provides a magisterial account of the rise and development of western Christian legal traditions on marriage and divorce (Reynolds, 1994) and on the development of a sacramental theology of marriage (Reynolds, 2016). The eastern Christian traditions are helpfully summarized in P. L'Huillier (1988).

Bibliography

Crouzel, H., *L'Église primitive face au divorce: Du premier au cinquième siècle*, Paris, 1970.

Evans Grubbs, J., *Law and Family in Late Antiquity: The Emperor Constantine's Marriage Legislation*, Oxford, 1995.

Evans Grubbs, J., *Women and Law in the Roman Empire: A Sourcebook on Marriage, Divorce, and Widowhood*, London, 2002.

Glancy, J., "The Sexual Use of Slaves: A Response to Kyle Harper on Jewish and Christian *Porneia*," *JBL* 134, 2015, 215–229.

Harper, K., "*Porneia*: The Making of a Christian Sexual Norm," *JBL* 131, 2011, 363–383.

Hunter, D.G., "Augustine's Doubts on Divorce: Reconsiderations on Remarriage," *AugS* 48, 2017, 161–182.

L'Huillier, P., "The Indissolubility of Marriage in Orthodox Law and Practice," *SVTQ* 32, 1988, 199–221.

Reynolds, P.L., *Marriage in the Western Church: The Christianization of Marriage During the Patristic and Early Medieval* Periods, Leiden, 1994.

Reynolds, P.L., *How Marriage Became One of the Sacraments: The Sacramental Theology of Marriage from its Medieval Origins to the Council of Trent*, Cambridge UK, 2016.

Treggiari, S., *Roman Marriage: Iusti Coniuges from the Time of Cicero to the Time of Ulpian*, Oxford, 1991.

Wheeler-Reed, D., J. Glancy & D. Martin, "Can a Man Commit πορνεία with His Wife?" *JBL* 137, 2018, 383–398.

DAVID G. HUNTER

Advent

The word is derived from a Latin root meaning "coming, "arriving." In classical non-Christian texts, the substantive *adventus* can have the connotation of the arrival of a godhead in a temple or the first visit of a ruler to his territory. In the Roman → *Chronograph of 354*, the term refers to the enthronement of the emperor → Constantine I. In early Christian texts, it is a common term for the "coming" of Christ, both the second coming in glory at the end of times (thus several times in the Vulgate; → Bible) and the first coming (incarnation). After the introduction of → Christmas as the commemoration of the birth of Christ, in Rome the Latin word was first used to designate that feast, but from the 7th century CE onward it became a common term for the preceding period of preparation. This custom subsequently became widely accepted in western Christianity (Augé, 2000, 201; Righetti, 1955, 39).

1. Origins

There is no general consensus about the earliest origins of the Advent (see for the various views, Talley, 1986, 147–155; Bradshaw & Johnson, 2011, 158–168). The discussion on this question centers on the interpretation of two sources: a passage from a writing called *Liber officiorum*, which is quoted by Berno of Reichenau (11th cent.) in a sermon about Advent and ascribed by the latter to → Hilary of Poitiers (PL 142.1066), and canon 4 of the Spanish Council of → Saragossa (380 CE). The former passage points to a three-week period of fasting (during Advent), while the latter prescribes that for a total of 21 days, from Dec 17 to → Epiphany, one should not stay at home or escape to the countryside or the mountains or run around barefoot (?) but "go every day to Church." It has been assumed by some scholars that both passages could refer to a three-week period of preparation for the feast of Epiphany, which would have been celebrated on Jan 6 in commemoration of the → baptism of Jesus in the Jordan and on which people would also have been baptized (Bradshaw & Johnson, 2011, 160–164). Starting from these assumptions, it has been suggested that the Advent would have originated as a period of preparation for baptism and baptismal → catechesis. However,

this hypothesis is highly speculative: the authorship of the passage from the *Liber officiorum* has been seriously questioned and the text in question makes no mention of Epiphany. Furthermore, the canons of Saragossa say nothing about the character of Epiphany and its festal theme(s), or about Epiphany baptism, or about baptismal catechesis. T. Talley has advanced another interpretation of the canons of the Council of Saragossa that is at least not less plausible (Talley, 1986, 150–152). He points to the fact that the period from Dec 17 to Jan 6 was marked by very popular pagan midwinter festivals, beginning with the Saturnalia on Dec 17 and including the feast of Calends at the beginning of January. The exhortation to go to church during this period may have been at least partly motivated by the wish to prevent the faithful from participating in these feasts. Further corroboration of T. Talley's hypothesis is provided by the polemics of leading Spanish authors against the practices connected with the feast of Calends. → Pacian of Barcelona, for instance, states in his *Paraenesis* (1; PL 13; 1081–1082) that he had written a tractate called *Cervulus* – which is now lost – against all sorts of pagan practices, including those connected with the feast of Calends (see also Isid. *Eccl. Offic.* 1.41).

2. Fasting Before Christmas

The earliest unambiguous evidence for the existence of a period of preparation for the feast of Nativity (on Dec 25 and not on Jan 6) comes from northern Italy and Gaul. It emerges from the sources available that the preparation had the character of a fast (as was also the case with Easter and would become current for other feasts; → Fasting/Abstinence). The earliest author known to have made reference to such a preparatory fast is Filastrius of Brescia (around 385 CE; see Filas. *Haer.* 6). Subsequently, the Synod of → Tours (567 CE), canon 17, prescribed that monks should fast every day from December till Christmas. Somewhat later, canon 9 of the Council of Mâcon (581 CE) ordered that everybody – monks and laypeople – should fast from Saint Martin's Day (Nov 11; → Martin of Tours) to Christmas on Mondays, Wednesdays, and Fridays, which means that the Monday was added to the two older weekly fast days of Wednesday and Friday. This Martin's fast is also mentioned by → Gregory of Tours who attributed its introduction to his predecessor Perpetuus (Greg. T. *Hist. Fr.* 10.31).

3. Traces of a Liturgical Celebration of the Advent (Northern Italy)

The earliest indications of the existence of a *liturgical* celebration of the Advent – through biblical lectures and readings specifically intended for specific days falling into this period – are found in sources that originate from northern Italy. The fact that → Peter Chrysologus, bishop of Ravenna, has preached on the two Sundays before Christmas about the annunciation to Zechariah (Luke 1:5–25) and the annunciation to Mary (Luke 1: 26–38) might suggest (Pet. Chr. *Serm.* 86–92; 140–144; see Benz, 1967, 228–235) that it had been customary to read these two pericopes on these Sundays (Bradshaw &Johnson, 2011, 164). Furthermore, the so-called *Rotulus of Ravenna* (mid-7th cent. CE) contains a collection of 40 liturgical prayers compiled for the period of the Advent (Benz, 1967). Most of the prayers date from the 5th and 6th centuries CE and appear to have originated in Ravenna or at least in northern Italy (some of them may have been written by Peter Chrysologus). The prayer texts vary considerably in theological content. Yet, a considerable number of them explicitly deal with the birth of Christ and the → incarnation. This proves that some sort of liturgical preparation of Christmas existed in Ravenna – and probably elsewhere in northern Italy. Unfortunately, nothing can be said with certainty about the character or the length of the preparation. It is very doubtful that a longer or shorter period was reserved for it. Most scholars assume that it was limited to a feast, or two Sundays, preceding Christmas, with the festal theme of the annunciation of Christ (or that of John the Baptist and Christ). It may be added that in the 5th and 6th centuries CE, such a practice did not exist in Rome since Leo the Great (→ Leo I [Bishop of Rome]) does not refer to it in any of his sermons for the liturgical year.

4. Liturgical Celebration of the Advent in Rome

A liturgical Advent proper – which involved a shorter or longer period – is only attested in liturgical sources that date from the 7th century CE onward, the earliest one having preserved traditions that are one or two centuries older (see Chavasse, 1957, 412–426). Here, some noteworthy differences can be observed between the non-Roman (Milanese, northern Italian, Spanish) sources and the Roman ones (see *Sacram. Gel. Vet.* 2.80–84 = nos. 1120–1156; *Sacram. Greg. Hadr.* 778–781; the oldest Roman lectionaries; see esp. Klauser, 1935, and the 8th-century CE collection of liturgical readings, mostly called the *Comes* of Murbach; see Wilmart, 1913). These differences are related to the following three items:

a. Length

The length of the Advent attested by the former sources spans six weeks (probably coinciding with a period of fasting). This practice also existed in Rome until the 12th century in the so-called presbyteral liturgy (which was presided over by the presbyters), but in the papal liturgy, the period was shortened to four weeks in the 6th or 7th century CE (see Augé, 2000, 202).

b. Position Within the Liturgical Year

In the non-Roman liturgical books, the period of the Advent is placed right at the beginning, before Christmas. In the Roman sources, material for the Sundays of Advent is found at the end of the book. The reason is that Christmas, and not the Advent, is considered to mark the beginning of the liturgical year. It also implies that there is no direct link between Advent and Christmas.

c. Theological Content

The non-Roman sources refer to the second coming of Christ at the end of times (→ *Parousia*), but also explicitly to the themes that are specific to Christmas, that is, to the birth of Christ and the incarnation. By contrast, the Roman sources feature a more multivocal and future-oriented interpretation of the coming of Christ. The emphasis is on the expectation of the coming of Christ as described at various places in the Gospels (remarkable is the reading of Jesus' entry into Jerusalem narrated in Matt 21:1–9 on the fifth Sunday before Christmas) and on the second coming. By contrast, there are very few (explicit) references to the birth of Christ or the incarnation. This means that the content of the texts and readings is more attuned to the end of the year (December being the last month) than to the feast of the Nativity. It was only in the 8th and 9th centuries CE, when the liturgical material of the Advent was placed before Christmas and other texts were added that referred to the incarnation, that the link between Advent and Christmas was made more explicit.

5. The Eastern Churches

Most eastern churches have some sort of preparation for the feast of Nativity, celebrated either on Dec 25 or Jan 6 (Armenian tradition). Mention should be made here in particular of the Syrian and Armenian traditions, where the feast is preceded by a period called Annunciation, which spans four or six weeks. The character of these periods differs fundamentally from that of the Roman liturgy, and their origins do not go back to early Christianity but to the early Middle Ages.

Historiography

Research has mainly been focused on the question of the origins of the Advent and on the reconstruction of the development of its liturgical celebration in Rome. Of primary and lasting importance for these purposes are the seminal studies of A. Chavasse (1957) on the *Sacramentarium Gelasianum Vetus*, early Roman lectionaries, and the thorough analysis of the *Rotulus of Ravenna* by S. Benz (1967).

Bibliography

Augé, M., "The Liturgical Year in the Roman Rite," in: A. Chupungco, ed., *Handbook of Liturgical Studies*, vol. V: *Liturgical Time and Space*, Collegeville, 2000, 177–210.

Benz, S., *Der Rotulus von Ravenna nach seiner Herkunft und seiner Bedeutung für die Liturgiegeschichte kritisch untersucht*, LQF 45, Münster, 1967.

Bradshaw, P., & M.E. Johnson, *The Origins of Feasts, Fasts and Seasons in Early Christianity*, ACC 86, Collegeville, 2011.

Chavasse, A., *Le sacramentaire gélasien* (*Vaticanus Reginensis 316*), Paris, 1957.

Klauser, T., *Das römische Capitulare Evangeliorum*, vol. I, Münster, 1935.

Righetti, M., *Storia liturgica*, vol. II: *L'Anno liturgico, il breviario*, 2nd ed., Milan, 1955.

Talley, T., *The Origins of the Liturgical Year*, New York, 1986.

Wilmart, A., "Le Comes de Murbach," *Rben* 30, 1913, 25–69.

GERARD ROUWHORST

Aelius Donatus

Aelius Donatus is considered one of the most influential grammarians of the Latin language. He lived in the 4th century CE. The year of his birth and death are unknown. The only date that is considered certain is that Donatus taught in Rome in 354 CE, according to the testimony of his student → Jerome. He probably taught grammar and literature there for several decades (Holtz, 2005, 109). He wrote a short outline of Latin grammar, which was used as a textbook until the 19th century. Grammar lessons also included the reading and interpretation of important works. The most important authors of classical Latin in imperial times were → Virgil and Terence, on whose works Donatus wrote commentaries, which in turn were commented on. Only small parts of his commentary on Virgil, which was in turn commented on by Servius, have come down to us (Herzog, 1989, 148–154), while his commentary on Terence has survived in a version that apparently combines several strands of tradition (Herzog, 1989, 154–158). He may also have written a lost treatise on the metrical clauses in prose (Herzog, 1989, 148).

The subject of his *Ars grammatica*, originally conceived as a four-part work, is not the Latin language of his time, but the classical Latin, long since no longer spoken in this form by the native speakers. All of his examples come from classical literature, mostly from the works of Virgil; the view that his grammar contains evidence from the vernacular Latin of his time is wrong. He describes and teaches the "classical language" of the upper class, like the other grammarians of the imperial period, whose subject matter is always only the older classical written

Latin (2nd cent. BCE to the beginning of the 2nd cent. CE), never the spoken Latin of their own time, which became increasingly differentiated during the imperial period. In doing so, he shortens the content of earlier grammars to a minimum, which is why his grammar already required extensive oral and written explanation in antiquity and was commented on several times. His model may be the equally minimalist grammar of the classical Greek language that has come down to us under the name of Dionysius Thrax, which in the version we know is probably from the imperial period, even if it may go back in parts to an older version.

The first book contains the basics in dialogue form, presumably intended for memorization. Ancient grammarians analyzed the basic elements of every linguistic enunciation on the basis of a binary feature system of accidentals. Each "part of a sentence" (Lat. *pars ōrātiōnis*) had to differ from all other parts of a sentence in at least one *accidēns* in order to be distinguished as a separate "part of a sentence" – nowadays we usually say, "part of speech," but the ancient term means more than that. Some grammarians distinguished fewer *partēs ōrātiōnis* than Donatus – who follows the majority opinion for Latin and gives eight "parts of the sentence," four of which are inflectional, four invariable – others more, depending on their approach to the *accidentia*, than Donatus, who follows the majority opinion for Latin and gives eight "parts of the sentence," four of which are inflectional, four invariable. The teaching of the inflection of the noun, pronoun, verb, and participle familiarizes the reader with the basic features of Latin declensions and conjugations but does not include a complete morphology. For example, for the nouns, five paradigms are declined according to the five genera of ancient Latin grammar – masculine, feminine, neuter, *genus commūne*, and *genus omne* – excluding the special cases of *genus prōmiscuum* and *genus incertum*, with the Latin declension article *hic, haec, hoc*; thus, the aim is to set out the grammatical categories of genus, numerus and case, but not to convey all possible forms of all declensions. According to the paradigms, Donatus gives a rule for the formation of certain, but not all, *cāsūs*. As was customary at the time, he distinguishes between the optative in the main clause and the subjunctive in the subordinate clause; understands the perfect

future as the subjunctive future; and, in the passive of the perfect stem, distinguishes between a continuous and a completed series of verbal forms in the indicative and subjunctive of perfect and plusquamperfect tenses, as well as in the "subjunctive future tense." Like other grammarians, he regards the consonantal and i-declension as short- and long-vowel third conjugation and distinguishes purely "medial verbs" (Lat. *verba dēpōnentia*) from "mediopassive verbs" (Lat. *verba commūnia*). This analysis of the "types of words" and not entirely detailed inflection theory was later handed down as a supposedly independent *Ars minor*, the remaining three as *Ars maior*.

The second book deals with phonetics (sounds and syllables), the binary doctrine of verse feet, prosody and punctuation, while the third deals with the eight *partēs ōrātiōnis* in a more detailed but still condensed presentation. Some manuscripts also contain a chapter on the final syllables, which is probably not genuine. The third book contains his syntax, which fits entirely in the tradition of the older grammatical teaching preceding Apollonios Dyskolos. It is a casuistic deviation syntax, which on the one hand gives the different types of "barbarisms" (i.e. errors in only one word) and "solecisms" (i.e. morphosyntactic errors in the use of at least two words) for all possible deviations from a linguistically correct Latin expression, and on the other hand lists 12 other types of errors. Finally, the 14 types of metaplasm serving stylistic variance, 17 figures of speech (the figures of thought belong to rhetoric), and 13 tropes are presented with examples from classical literature. If one is accustomed to a "modern" syntax based on Apollonios Dyskolos and Priscian, it is only at second glance that one realizes that the last of the four books is a syntax in a different form, by no means merely a "stylistics," aimed at the most error-free syntactic use possible of the standard language, classical Latin, which was no longer a native language at the time of Donatus.

Historiography

Donatus' grammar was very intensively received, often commented on (e.g. by Servius, *Explanationes in Donatum*) and introduced to the Middle Ages especially by Irish monks. Throughout Europe, it served as the first textbook for learning Latin, especially for many clergy. Donatus' name became synonymous with "grammar" and the first vernacular grammars of Romance languages, such as the *Donatz proensals* by U. Faidit (c. 1240). His *Ars minor* was still used as a school textbook in parts of Europe until the 19th century. Although he can justifiably be called the "most superficial" of the ancient Latin grammarians, and some of his abbreviated rules have led to erroneous statements in modern late Latin grammars to this day, of all Latin grammarians he has probably had the greatest and most lasting impact. The sparse medieval and extensive early modern grammatical tradition of the modern languages of Europe draws fundamentally on him (Holtz, 1981). A translated and annotated study edition of the grammar is available in German (Schönberger, 2008, 2009).

Bibliography

Beck, J.-W., *Zur Zuverlässigkeit der bedeutendsten lateinischen Grammatik: Die Ars des Aelius Donatus*, Stuttgart, 1996.

Chase, W.J., *The Ars Minor of Donatus: For One Thousand Years the Leading Textbook of Grammar, Translated from the Latin, with Introductory Sketch*, SSH 11, Madison, 1926.

Gatti, P., "Aelius Donatus," in: H. Cancik & H. Schneider, eds., *DNP*, vol. III, Stuttgart, 1997, col. 775.

Herzog, R., ed., "Restauration und Erneuerung: Die lateinische Literatur von 284 bis 374 n. Chr.," in: *HLL*, vol. V, Munich, 1989.

Holtz, L., *Donat et la tradition de l'enseignement grammatical: Étude sur l'Ars Donati et sa diffusion (IVe–IXe siècle) et édition critique*, Paris, 1981.

Holtz, L., "Aelius Donatus (um die Mitte des 4. Jahrhunderts n. Chr.)," in: W. Ax, ed., *Lateinische Lehrer Europas: Fünfzehn Portraits von Varro bis Erasmus von Rotterdam*, Köln, 2005, 109–131.

Ising, E., *Die Herausbildung der Grammatik der Volkssprachen in Mittel- und Osteuropa: Studien über den Einfluß der lateinischen Elementargrammatik des Aelius Donatus De octo partibus orationis ars minor*, Berlin, 1970.

Keil, H., ed., *Grammatici Latini*, vol. IV: *Probi Donati Seruii qui ferunter de arte grammatica libri*, Leipzig, 1864; repr. H. Hagen, Hildesheim, 1961.

Schindel, U., *Die lateinischen Figurenlehren des 5. bis 7. Jahrhunderts und Donats Vergilkommentar (mit zwei Editionen)*, AAWG.PH, part 3/91, Göttingen, 1975.

Schönberger, A., *Die Ars minor des Aelius Donatus: Lateinischer Text und kommentierte deutsche Übersetzung einer antiken Elementargrammatik aus dem 4. Jahrhundert*, BiRL, vol. VI, Frankfurt am Main, 2008.

Schönberger, A., *Die* Ars maior *des Aelius Donatus: Lateinischer Text und kommentierte deutsche Übersetzung einer antiken Lateingrammatik des 4. Jahrhunderts für den fortgeschrittenen Anfängerunterricht*, BiRL, vol. VII, Frankfurt am Main, 2009.

Stock, C., *Sergius (Ps.-Cassiodorus): Commentarium de oratione et de octo partibus orationis artis secundae Donati: Überlieferung, Text und Kommentar*, Munich, 2005.

Uhl, A., *Servius als Sprachlehrer: Zur Sprachrichtigkeit in der exegetischen Praxis des spätantiken Grammatikerunterrichts*, Hyp. 117, Göttingen, 1996.

Uhlig, G., ed., *Dionysios Thrax: Dionysii Thracis ars grammatica*, Leipzig, 1883.

AXEL SCHÖNBERGER

Aeon

An aeon (αἰών; *aevum*) in patristic authors is a long period, an age, or this world or the world to come, according to the biblical usage. Only in reference to God does αἰών mean "eternity." Aeon is divine life or a divine being or emanation only in gnostic writings (→ Gnosis/Gnosticism).

Origen, Didymus the Blind, the → Cappadocians, the Antiochenes, and Pseudo-Dionysius are the patristic thinkers who most reflected on the meaning of αἰών and its cognate adjective, αἰώνιος. → Origen provided the Christian definition of αἰών: "The time coextensive with the constitution of this world, from the beginning to the end." Unlike the Stoic aeons, identical to one another and infinitely succeeding one another, Christian aeons, as Origen emphasized, differ from each other, depending on rational creatures' free choices; their succession is not infinite, but terminates in the eventual → *apokatastasis*. While postmortem retribution is commensurate to sins and limited to one or more aeons, blessed life after purification is God's gift (Or. *Comm. Rom.* 22.11) and absolutely eternal (ἀΐδιος). Ἀΐδιος, unlike αἰώνιος, means "eternal" proper, and Origen uses "ἀΐδιος life" when stressing that it is endless rather than that it is in the next world. Life αἰώνιος is that which will occur in the future αἰών (Or. *Philoc.* 1.30.21–3). According to biblical usage, Origen and many patristic authors use αἰώνιος to designate → death, punishment, and → fire in the next world, but never ἀΐδιος, which is reserved for life, beatitude, God, and divine attributes (Ramelli & Konstan, 2013).

Origen maintained an ethical conception of the aeons: their succession and organization is not necessary and repetitive, but depends on rational creatures' free choices. This opposed not only Stoicism, but also gnostic predestinationism, against which Origen constructed his → protology and eschatology (→ Apocalypse); Ramelli, in preparation. An aeon must finish because the evil in it must be eliminated, but the λογικά survive into the next, whose structure depends on their past choices, and this until the end of aeons. Aeons are the diastematic dimensions where rational creatures use their free will, and they experience the consequences of this, with the assistance of divine providence. At the end of the aeons and of purification, they will experience divine grace and participate in divine eternity. Origen rejected the gnostic, Valentinian concept of αἰών (aeon, each component of the *pleroma*). P. Tzamalikos (1991) rightly noticed that Origen refused to call αἰών the divine life, but according to P. Tzamalikos this choice is due to Origen's refusal to adopt Plato's terminology (in which αἰών is the technical term for atemporal eternity, transcending all time: Ramelli & Konstan, 2013). I suspect that Origen rather refused to appropriate *gnostic* terminology: he wanted to oppose the "Valentinian" system of Aeons. The Valentinians (→ Valentinus/Valentinians) in turn drew on Plato's definition of αἰών, but they developed it into the notion of "Aeon" as divine and living. Origen, who spent his life fighting Valentinian determinism, and elaborated his philosophy of history and *apokatastasis* doctrine against Valentinian predestinationism, refused to reproduce gnostic terminology, in which every αἰών is a deity of the → *pleroma*. This is why Origen considers an αἰών to be not divine life, but a span of time; it does not belong to the divine sphere, which transcends time, but to the diastematic sphere of time, space, dimensions, and extension (Ramelli, 2013a). So Origen scorns the gnostic "mythopoiesis concerning the Aeons" which existed prior to the *logos* (Or. *Comm. Jo.* 2.14; *Comm. Matt.* 17.33). For Origen, on the contrary, the *logos* preexists all aeons and is their creator: "Before any time [χρόνος] and aeon [αἰών] existed, in the beginning was the Logos" (*Comm. Jo.* 2.1). Heb 1:2 declares that the αἰών was created by Christ, so aeons are creatures, made through the Son-*logos* (*Comm. Jo.*

2.10.72). "The whole aeon [αἰών] is long in relation to us, but very short in relation to the life of God" (*Comm. Matt.* 15.31).

Eternity pertains only to God-Trinity; whatever else can become eternal can do so only by grace and as a participation in God's life (θέωσις). In Origen's works, ἀΐδιος is the technical term for what is eternal, and as such it is only found in reference to God or eternal life. Origen often uses ἀΐδιος while commenting on, or glossing, scriptural passages with αἰών and αἰώνιος in reference to God: he prefers to elucidate the biblical polysemic term αἰώνιος with ἀΐδιος as a marker of eternity in the strict sense. Origen and the Cappadocians use ἀΐδιος, in its technical meaning, in the theological discussion on the coeternity and consubstantiality of the hypostases of the → Trinity.

Didymus also shows awareness of the multiple meanings of αἰών and αἰώνιος (Didy. *Comm. Job* 76.11ff.): if αἰώνιος refers to God, it means "absolutely eternal," beginningless and endless; when it refers to humans it indicates this life or its continuation in the life to come, "for the time that extends over the life of a human is also called an αἰών." The eternal life, which lasts beyond all aeons, is "ὑπεραιώνιος salvation" (Didy *Comm. Zach.* 2.370). Salvation, unlike punishment and death, which can only be αἰώνιοι, does not come to an end with the end of aeons.

Gregory of Nyssa, who depends on Origen, abundantly uses the philosophical adjective ἀΐδιος, in reference to the Trinity, its attributes, the Son – against Neo-Arianism (→ Arianism) – and eternal life (→ Immortality), which awaits all humans by Christ's grace (Gregory of Nyssa, *De tridui spatio*; *GNO* 9.278.10). Eternal life is God's life, in which humans will participate (Gregory of Nyssa, *In Canticum canticorum*; *GNO* 6.69.3) after the end of times and aeons. Like many fathers, → Gregory of Nyssa never refers ἀΐδιος to otherworldly punishment, death, or evil, which is not from eternity, ἐξ ἀϊδίου, and cannot subsist eternally (Gregory of Nyssa, *In inscriptiones Psalmorum*; *GNO* 5.100.21–5; 101.3). Αἰώνιος is used mostly in biblical reminiscences and means "eternal" only in reference to God. It is often employed in reference to life in the world to come. Death, fire, and punishment are merely αἰώνια, for they will be commensurate to sins and will cease either earlier or at the end of the αἰών, with *apokatastasis*, in eternity.

Gregory of Nazianzus used αἰών in the sense of the whole of history, like Origen (e.g. Greg. Naz. *Theol. Or.* 5.25.136; PG 36.160.D). The Antiochene → Diodore of Tarsus (*ap.* Solomon of Bostra, *Book of the Bee* 60) was likewise aware that αἰών does not mean "eternity" in Scripture and adduces the expressions "These shall go away into αἰώνιος [*l-ʿôlām*] punishment, the righteous into αἰώνιος life" (Matt 25:46), "You shall not wash my feet *l-ʿôlām*" (John 13:8), and "No man shall dwell in Babylon *l-ʿôlām*" (Isa 13:20), while many generations have dwelled there. Conclusion: "In the New Testament *l-ʿôlām* (αἰώνιος) does not mean 'without end'."

Diodore's disciple, → Theodore of Mopsuestia, in the prologue to his commentary on Ps 2 interprets "αἰώνιος condemnation" as "future condemnation" (*damnatio futura*), not "eternal" (*aeterna*). That of the two aeons of divine economy is a main characteristic of his thought. The present aeon is a training place for souls; due to Adam's sin God made humans mortal (→ Adam and Eve), but providentially (Th. Mop. *Com. Gal.* 1:4). Very close to Origen's is Theodore's definition of αἰών (*Com. Gal.* 1:4), not as "eternity," but as "an interval of time," διάστημα χρόνου, from the short interval of a person's life to the longest, from the foundation of the world to the second coming of Christ. Even in reference to Christ, Theodore refuses to understand αἰώνιος as "eternal" (Th. Mop. *Frgms. Heb.* 207.1): Christ is "the αἰώνιος high priest" (Heb 6:20) because all the aeons or generations (αἰῶνες), believing in him, will be led by him to God. In Theodore, ἀΐδιος never refers to future punishment, fire, or death in the next world (modified only by αἰώνιος), but is applied to the future life, as in many patristic authors. Likewise Maximus the Confessor used only αἰώνιος, never ἀΐδιος, to describe otherworldly punishment, death, or fire (Ramelli & Konstan, 2013).

Pseudo-Dionysius also alerts readers that in Scripture αἰών does not mean eternity: "In Scripture sometimes there is mention of an αἰών that is in time and of an αἰώνιος time," to denote a distant time, remote, or indeterminate, long, but not eternal: "Therefore, one must not consider things called αἰώνια in Scripture to be coeternal with God [συναΐδια θεῷ], who is rather prior to every αἰών" (Ps.-Dion. *Div.* 216.14).

Historiography

The notion of aeon in the whole of Patristics and the connected adjective αἰώνιος have been studied systematically by I. Ramelli and D. Konstan (2013). The concept of aeons in Origen should be seen within his anti-gnostic polemic has been analysed by I. Ramelli (2013; and a monograph on Origen, in preparation, ch. 2), and P. Tzamalikos (1991).

Bibliography

Ramelli, I., "Christian Soteriology and Christian Platonism," *VigChr* 61, 2007, 313–356.

Ramelli, I., "Origen, Bardaisan, and the Origin of Universal Salvation," *HThR* 10, 2009, 135–168.

Ramelli, I., "Αἰώνιος and αἰών in Origen and Gregory of Nyssa," *SP* 47, 2010, 57–62.

Ramelli, I., "Gregory of Nyssa's Trinitarian Theology in *Tunc et ipse*," in: M. Berghaus & V. Drecoll, eds., *Gregory of Nyssa: The Minor Treatises on Trinitarian Theology and Apollinarism*, Leiden, 2011, 445–478.

Ramelli, I., "Apokatastasis in Coptic Gnostic Texts," *JCST* 14, 2012a, 33–45.

Ramelli, I., "*Stromateis* VII and Clement's Hints of the Theory of Apokatastasis," in: M. Havrda et al., eds., *The Seventh Book of the Stromateis*, Leiden, 2012b, 239–257.

Ramelli, I., *The Christian Doctrine of Apokatastasis*, Leiden, 2013a.

Ramelli, I., "Origen and Augustine," *Numen* 60, 2013b, 280–307.

Ramelli, I., *Tempo ed eternità in età antica e patristica: Filosofia greca, ebraismo e cristianesimo*, Assisi, 2015.

Ramelli, I., "Time and Eternity," in: *The Routledge Companion to Early Christian Philosophy*, London, 2021, 41–54.

Ramelli, I., *Origen of Alexandria: His Identity and Philosophy*, in preparation.

Ramelli, I., & D. Konstan, *Terms for Eternity*, Piscataway, 2007; new ed. 2011, 2013.

Tzamalikos, P., *The Concept of Time in Origen*, Bern, 1991.

ILARIA L.E. RAMELLI

Aërius

According to → Epiphanius of Salamis (*Haer.* 75; see *Anc.* 13.8) Aërius was an ascetic in the circle around Eustathius of Sebaste. He was still alive when Epiphanius wrote the *Panarion* at the end of the 370s CE (*Haer.* 75.1.3); Filastrius, on the other hand (*Haer.* 72), appears to take his death for granted, so he must have died before 390 CE.

Epiphanius places Aërius among the followers of Eustathius of Sebaste. It is not known if he could already be counted among these disciples before the Synod of Gangra (c. 340 CE), where Eustathius or rather his radically ascetic followers were condemned. When Eustathius became bishop of Sebaste circa 355/356 CE, he made Aërius a presbyter (→ Priest/Presbyter) and principal of a ξενοδοχεῖον ("guesthouse, hospice"). Epiphanius notes that this generally meant a public poorhouse (πτωχοτροφεῖον), institutions in Pontus that in the Church of Sebaste clearly came under the charge of the bishop.

Soon after this there must have been a parting of the ways between Aërius and Eustathius. Epiphanius' polemical interpretation, that Aërius came into conflict with his bishop out of envy because Eustathius and not he himself had been elected bishop, is to be taken as a haeresiological topos. The conflict must rather be seen against the background of a contradiction between radical asceticism and the office of bishop. Epiphanius reports that Aërius withdrew from the position assigned to him. When he gathered an ascetic group of men and women around him, he and his followers were excommunicated (presumably by a synod in Sebaste of which we have no records). Filastrius names his followers "Aërians" and classifies them as "Encratites" ("Abstinentes"). According to Epiphanias, Aërius and his followers left towns and villages and lived as Anchorites, away from land cultivated by humans.

Epiphanius' polemical description – for which there was presumably a written source from which he quotes Aërius directly – portrays Aërius as a radically ascetic critic of the episcopally constituted church and its hierarchic structures of office. According to the quotations passed down by Epiphanius, he rejected any differentiation between the office of presbyter and that of bishop and stressed the one and the same order, honor, and dignity of both offices. Moreover, he rejected the prescribed forms of fasting and the celebration of the Christian *Pasch* (→ Easter), which he understood as an eschatological celebration. Probably his rejection of the intercession for the dead is also to be understood from eschatological conceptions in the monastic tradition.

Perhaps Epiphanius saw Aërius as an Arian simply because of his connection to Eustathius. After his parting from Eustathius, we cannot detect a personal position in the theological Trinitarian controversies of the 4th century CE; his original connection with Eustathius allows us for the moment to assume a link with the homoeousian monastic milieu.

However, for Filastrius, who is dependent upon Epiphanius, although he does not see Aërius in connection with Eustathius or as an Arian, Aërians are a phenomenon that still exists; he knows that they exist in Pamphylia but has little other knowledge of them. → Basil of Caesarea, also originally an ascetic follower of Eustathius, mentions neither Aërius nor Aërians as his followers. It seems doubtful whether Aërius' followers existed as an independent group for any considerable time after his death; according to Filastrius they were mentioned later only by → Augustine of Hippo (*Haer.* 53), but as he expressly emphasizes he is dependent upon Filastrius and Epiphanius and has no personal knowledge of them.

(A historiography for this topic is not applicable.)

Bibliography

Coccini, F., "Aërius," in: *EEC*, vol. I, Cambridge UK, 1992, 13.
Cocchini, F., "Aërius," in: *EAC*, vol. I, Downers Grove, 2014, 46.
Ermoni, V., "Aërius," in: *DHGE*, vol. I, Paris, 1912, 663.
Ulrich, J., "Aërius, Presbyter," in: *LACL*, Freiburg, ³2002, 9.

HANNS CHRISTOF BRENNECKE

Aëtius, Flavius

Aëtius, Flavius (Roman general, b. c. 390 BCE, Durostorum, Moesia Secunda–d. Sep 21/22, 454 CE, Ravenna, Italy) is the son of the high-ranking Roman officer Flavius Gaudentius (originally from the province of Scythia Minor) and an unnamed Italian lady from a noble and well-off family. He is sometimes claimed to have been of Thracian origin (Vlachopoulou, 2007, 69), but this is erroneous and refers to his and his father's origins from the diocese of Thrace. His father was a staunch orthodox Christian who is known from sources to have destroyed pagan temples when active as the *comes Africae* in 399 CE (Aug. *Civ.* 18.54; *Cons. Const.* s.a. 399 CE). Aëtius' rise in military ranks began only after the death of Emperor Honorius when he was appointed by the usurper emperor

Johannes as the *cura palatii* (423 CE), apparently one of the top officers within the imperial guard (*scholae palatinae*), while his father was promoted to the rank of *magister equitum praesentalis*, only to be killed in Gaul in 424 CE. Forcing the hand of the new regime of Galla Placidia and Valentinian III, Aëtius saw further advancements when he became the *comes et magister militum per Gallias* (425 CE) and later the junior *magister militum praesentalis* (429 CE). He lost the last post in 432 CE after his defeat by General Bonifatius in the struggle over influence at the Ravenna court, but returned to power in 433 CE, becoming the senior *magister militum praesentalis*, which was soon followed by his promotion to the rank of *patricius* (Sep 5, 435 CE). He held an ordinary consulship three times, in 432, 437, and 446 CE, which was an unparalleled honor among the late Roman dignitaries, with the exception of Flavius Constantius, who himself had been the *patricius et magister militum praesentalis* under the emperor Honorius. Aëtius enjoyed the supreme position and effectively ran the western Roman government until his murder in 454 CE. In the late Roman tradition, he was remembered as the "main salvation of the western [Roman] Empire" (Mar. Com. *Chron.* s.a. 454.2), "inferior (along with Bonifatius) to none of that time in experience of many wars" and Valentinian III's "right hand" (Pro. *Bel.* 3.3.13; 3.4.28), a man "whose counsel (Valentinian III) then followed in all things, because of his wisdom, and his glorious labours in the state" (Cassio. *Var.* 1.4.11), and on whom "the public affairs of the western realm depended" (Jord. *Get.* 191). His successes were undoubtedly due to his talents as both an energetic military commander and a shrewd politician. In his youth he spent several years as a hostage among barbarian groups, first the Alaric → Goths and later the Ruga → Huns. With the latter he forged close connections that proved instrumental in his acquiring and retaining the position of power, while enabling him to conduct successful military campaigns since he probably hired the Huns both as mercenaries and as his personal retainers (Wijnendaele, 2017, 474). His main area of operation was Gaul, where he campaigned against the Goths and → Franks (428–432 CE), the Burgundians (436–437 CE), the Bacaudae (437 CE), and the Goths again (438–439 CE), as well as pursued the policy of settlement of barbarian groups to achieve the region's inner stability (the Alans in 440 and in 442 CE, the Burgundians in 443 CE). He also led expeditions against the Iuthungi and the rebelled Noricans on the Danube (430–431 CE). One of his most notable military accomplishments was against the Attila Huns at the Catalaunian Plains in 451 CE, a hard victory won with the major help of the Goths with whom he concluded a *foedus* in 439 CE. However, he failed to prevent the Hun invasion of Italy in 452 CE, and he consented to the Vandal control of Africa in 442 CE. His occasionally brutal ambition is shown by his murderous elimination of a rival fellow general Flavius Felix in 430 CE. Aëtius himself was assassinated by Valentinian III as a consequence of a palace plot after he had arranged the betrothal of his younger son Gaudentius (by his second wife Pelagia, the widow of General Bonifatius; see Clover, 1971, 30–32) with the emperor's daughter. He was an orthodox Christian who was never engaged in religious strife. He had his son Gaudentius baptized (Merob. *Carm.* 4.23ff.) and is said to have entrusted himself to the apostle Peter (→ Peter the Apostle) before the battle against the Huns in Gaul (*Con. Ovet.* 18). He also had connections to eminent ecclesiastical personalities. He is potrayed as showing due reverence to the → bishop and future saint Orientius of Auch, who, ostensibly acting circa 439 CE as an envoy on behalf of the Gothic king Theoderic I, is said to have met with Aëtius (*Vita Or.* 1.3; Gillett, 2003, 138–143). In 440 CE, the deacon and future pope Leo intervened to reconcile Aëtius with the *praefectus praetorio* Albinus (Pros. *Epit. chron.* 1341 [s.a. 440 CE]). In 451 CE, the bishop and future saint Anianus of Orléans is said to have turned for help to Aëtius in the face of the attack by the Attila Huns and was honorably received (*Vita Ani.* 4; 7). Aëtius seems to have been active in the ecclesiastical affairs in Gaul, even though the evidence is scarce and mostly circumstantial (Zecchini, 1981; Stickler, 2002, 211–223). He is the addressee of Valentinian III's novel from Jul 8, 445 CE, which was directed against Bishop Hilary of Arles (*Nov. Val.* 17).

Historiography

Long since Aëtius and his role in political affairs have usually been accorded an overall positive appraisal by modern scholarship (for surveys, see Zecchini, 1983, 7ff.; Stickler, 2002, 2ff.). The 19th-and early 20th-century historians mainly regarded the general as a last bulwark against forces poised at destroying the crumbling western Roman Empire. Such a sentiment still resonates in G. Zecchini's monograph, who saw himself obliged to pay homage to the traditional view by titling his book *Aëtius: The Last Defense of the Roman West* (Zecchini, 1983), as well as in the favorable (and to some extent even exculpating) account by J.M. O'Flynn, who also titled the second of his book's two chapters on Äetius *Defending the Empire* (O'Flynn, 1983, 74ff.). Nevertheless, even early on there had been differing outlooks as well. T. Mommsen portrayed Aëtius' drive with which the general fought for and maintained his position of powerbroker at the Ravenna court (Mommsen, 1901), whereas E. Stein criticized Aëtius of having colluded with the aristocracy as a whole in an attempt to extract privileges from the central government and to obstruct the tax reform, thus weakening the imperial power (Stein, 1928, 501ff. = 1959, 337ff.), which, to be fair, cannot be substantiated. Moreover, one scholar even argued that Aëtius' policies had a rather adverse impact on the state of the western Roman Empire (Moss, 1973, 712, 729). Newly it has been concluded that Aëtius owed his success to his willingness to go to the extreme in protection of his interests, but that achievements of his policies or what was constructive in his dealings should not be overlooked (Stickler, 2002, 312, 315). On another balanced note, his actions have been explained as a result of a politically more narrow scope perception of the Roman West (Wijnendaele, 2017, 482). Recently it has been suggested, unconvincingly, that the well-known Monza consular diptych, usually taken to represent the *magister militum* Flavius Stilicho and his family, actually depicts Aëtius, his first wife (daughter of the *comes domesticorum* Carpilio), and their son Carpilio (Atanasov, 2014).

Bibliography

Atanasov, G., "The Portrait of Flavius Aetius (390–454) from Durostorum (Silistra) Inscribed on a Consular Diptych from Monza," *StAcSu* 1, 2014, 7–21.

Clover, F.M., "Flavius Merobaudes: A Translation and Historical Commentary," *TAPhS* n.s. 61, 1971, 1–78.

Gillett, A., *Envoys and Political Communication in the Late Antique West, 411–533*, Cambridge UK, 2003.

Martindale, J.R., "Aetius 7," in: *PLRE*, vol. II, Cambridge UK, 1980, 21–29.

Mommsen, T., "Aetius," *Hermes* 36, 1901, 516–547; also in: *Gesammelte Schriften*, vol. IV, Berlin, 1906, 531–560.

Moss, J.R., "The Effects of the Policies of Aetius on the History of Western Europe," *Hist.* 22, 1973, 711–731.

O'Flynn, J.M., *Generalissimos of the Western Roman Empire*, Edmonton, 1983.

Scharf, R., "Der Iuthungenfeldzug des Aëtius: Eine Neuinterpretation einer christlichen Grabinschrift aus Augsburg," *Tyche* 9, 1994, 131–145.

Stein, E., *Geschichte des spätrömischen Reiches*, vol. I: *Vom römischen zum byzantinischen Staate: (284–476 n. Chr.)*, Vienna, 1928; J.-R. Palanque, ed., *Histoire du Bas-Empire*, vol. I: *De l'état romain à l'état byzantin (284–476)*, Paris, 1959.

Stickler, T., *Aëtius: Gestaltungsspielräume eines Heermeisters im ausgehenden weströmischen Reich*, Vestigia 54, Munich, 2002.

Tackholm, U., "Aetius and the Battle on the Catalaunian Fields," *OPRO* 7, 1969, 259–276.

Vlachopoulous, P., "Aetius, Flavius," in: A.G. Savvides & B. Hendrickx, with A.J. Simpson & T. Sansaridou-Hendrickx, eds., *EPLBHC*, vol. I, Turnhout, 2007, 69–70.

Wijnendaele, J., "The Early Career of Aëtius and the Murder of Felix (c. 425–430 CE)," *Hist.* 66, 2017, 468–482.

Zecchini, G., "La politica religiosa di Aezio," in: M. Sordi, ed., *Religione e politica nel mondo antico*, CISA 7, Milano, 1981, 250–277.

Zecchini, G., *Aezio: L'ultima difesa dell'occidente romano*, CRDAC 8, Rome, 1983.

Hrvoje Gračanin

Aetheria → Egeria

Africa

By the Christian era, Africa was ruled by Rome. Christianity, however, outlasted the Roman era and witnessed multiple conquests of the region by foreign invaders (Fage, 1979). Whereas the Greek writers, like Herodotus, preferred to refer to the region as "Libya," the Romans named the province surrounding Carthage (*Africa Proconsularis*) after the *Afri* people who lived in the area and tended to call the whole region Africa (e.g. Livy). After Rome defeated Carthage in the Punic Wars (264–146 BCE), its control over the surrounding regions spread, resulting in the establishment of other provinces in the region west of Egypt and north of the Sahara, and yet these provinces could still be referred to collectively as "Africa." Aside from various developments in how these provinces were organized, Roman rule of the region remained relatively stable through the first four centuries of the Christian era. In 429 CE, however, the Vandals invaded Africa from Spain, and by 439 CE they had seized control of Carthage. They would rule Africa until 533 CE, when Justinian reclaimed control of the region. Byzantine rule then continued until 642 CE, when Arab forces began raiding west of Egypt. The exarch of Africa at the time, Gregory, was defeated in 648 CE. By 683 CE the Arab leader Uqba Ibn Nafi led a force all the way to the Atlantic, and the end of the 7th century CE witnessed the end of Byzantine control of the region for good. Throughout these political events, Christianity thrived in the region and left behind numerous sources.

1. Earliest Christian Sources

The earliest records for African Christianity date to the late 2nd century CE. Even so, because the extant sources point to a widespread and well-established Christian community by that time, scholars can safely assume that Christianity arrived in Africa by the mid- or even early 2nd century CE. Writing in 190 CE, → Irenaeus of Lyon speaks generically of churches in "Libya" (Iren. *Haer.* 1.10.2). Writing from Carthage a decade later, Tertullian refers to specific places where Christians experienced persecution, and these range as far as Byzacena, Numidia, and Mauretania (Tert. *Scap.* 3.4–5).

There are even sources that claim Christians were in Africa in the 1st century CE. The book of Acts (→ Acts, Book of) describes the crowd at → Pentecost as including those from "the parts of Libya belonging to Cyrene" (Acts 2:10). Pseudo-Hippolytus of Rome claims that a certain Epaenetus (see Rom 16:5), who was one of the 70 chosen by Jesus (see Luke 10:1), became bishop of Carthage (Pseudo-Hippolytus, *De LXX Apostolis/On the Seventy Apostles*; PG 10.953–958, see 955–956). These records, of course, must be read critically, and it must be admitted that there is no extant material from Africa itself that indicates a 1st-century CE Christian presence.

In 180 CE a group of 12 men and women were tried and beheaded for their claim to be Christians. In what is appears to be a court transcript, the *Acta Martyrum Scillitanorum* (→ *Passio Martyrum Scillitanorum*) records the exchange between the proconsul Saturninus and the Christians (Tert. *Scap.* 3.4). There is virtually no narrative, and their death is only described in the sentencing, which condemns them to die by the sword. The group's spokesperson, Speratus, holds "books and letters of a just man named Paul" (*Libri et epistulae Pauli, viri iusti*; *Acta Mart. Scil.* 12–13).

Another famous martyrdom occurred in 203 CE when Perpetua, Felicity, and other catechumens were arrested, tried, and condemned to the beasts. The *Passio Perpetuae et Felicitatis* (→ *Passion of Perpetua and Felicity*) weaves together the voice of the narrator, and what purports to be a diary from Perpetua herself recounting her time in prison and the extraordinary visions she experienced there. A certain Saturus also tells in the first person about his experience of a vision. These visions inspire the martyrs to go boldly into the arena and accept the suffering awaiting them.

The most bountiful source from the early period of African Christian history is the writings of → Tertullian of Carthage. Little is known about Tertullian's life, but he began writing in the late 190s CE, and his last datable work was completed by at least 220 CE (Barnes, 1985; Wilhite, 2007). He wrote over 30 treatises, some of which are non-extant. His surviving works are all in Latin (with a few Greek fragments also extant), and as the first significant Christian author to write in this language, Tertullian veritably crafted a new theological vocabulary for succeeding generations. Later Christian writers read and appreciated Tertullian's works (e.g. Eus. *Hist. eccl.* 2.2.4; Lact. *Inst.* 5.1; 5.4; Opt. *Parm.* 1.9; and even see Jer. *Chron.* 16.23–24; *Vir. ill.* 53.2) until the late 4th century CE, when → Jerome and those influenced by him deem him "Montanist" (Jer. *Vir. Ill.* 53.3; see Aug. *Vid.* 4.6, 5.6; *Leg.* 2.9.32; → Montanism/Montanists). However, in his own lifetime Tertullian never joined a schismatic group; instead, he defended those who continue to receive prophetic utterances, including those associated with "the New Prophecy" including Montanus, Priscilla, and Maximilla, as well as those in his Carthaginian congregation (Powell, 1975; Rankin, 1995).

2. 3rd-Century Writers and Developments

After Tertullian, many other writings survive from the 3rd century CE that offer insights into African Christianity. One of those influenced by Tertullian was → Minucius Felix. His apologetic (→ Apologetics) dialogue *Octavius* is of uncertain date but likely belongs to the mid- to late 3rd century CE. It is set in Ostia near Rome, where a certain Octavius, the protagonist, converses with a non-Christian about the futility of worshiping Serapis and other false gods (Schubert, 2014). Octavius represents the Christian viewpoint, all the while disparaging the pagan views and practices. The work, however, explicitly invokes ties to Africa, especially the city of Cirta.

The most significant writer from the 3rd century CE is Cyprian, who was bishop of Carthage (→ Cyprian of Carthage) from around 248 until his death in 258 CE (Brent, 2010). He wrote 12 different treatises, and a collection of 82 letters survives, including epistles written to Cyprian and those written by councils. Some of his works address Christian practice, while others address specific controversies that arose in the aftermath of the Decian → persecution (J.P. Burns, 2002; Dunn, 2007).

In 250 CE the emperor Decius required everyone to sacrifice to the Roman deities. While many Christians refused to do so and either fled or died from torture, many other Christians offered the sacrifice or obtained some certificate saying they had done so. Controversy arose over how to reconcile such "lapsed" Christians: on the one hand, the "Laxist" party welcomed the lapsed (→ Apostasy/Apostates) with little to no penance, while on the other hand, the "Rigorist" party (led in Rome by Novatian) refused to readmit the lapsed even after a lifetime of penance. Cyprian met in council with bishops throughout Africa, which offered a middle ground between these two parties and allowed the lapsed to be reconciled after an agreed-upon period of public penance. Further controversy emerged when some who had been baptized (→ Baptism) in the Laxist or Rigorist churches asked for entrance into Cyprian's church. Cyprian insisted that those individuals' baptisms were invalid because they had been administered in a false church. Cyprian's opponents called his practice "rebaptism," which conflicted with the tradition in Rome. Stephen, the bishop of Rome at the time, vehemently opposed Cyprian, and he summoned a synod of Italian bishops who supported his practice of accepting any into communion who had been baptized under the triune formula, even if said baptism had been performed by a schismatic group. Cyprian gathered with bishops in Africa, and that synod confirmed his practice, resulting in a conflict between the two regions. When both Stephen and Cyprian died as → martyrs in 258 CE, the controversy abated.

Cyprian's death occurred when Valerian renewed the requirement that everyone in the empire sacrifice to the Roman deities. The proconsul first exiled Cyprian, and then had him beheaded. Cyprian's legacy in Africa was vast. Two different *Acta* survive of his martyrdom; his deacon, Pontius, wrote the first Christian *Vita* about him, and numerous devotions to him survive in the archaeological record (Rebillard, 2012, 197–251; Bass, 2012). He will also figure prominently in the Donatist controversy (→ Donatism/Donatists), where both sides will claim to be heirs to his teachings (Gaumer, 2016).

Aside from Cyprian, several other writings from the mid- to late 3rd century CE testify to the ongoing tensions between Christians and non-Christians in Africa. A number of works survive from this time that were misattributed to Cyprian, such as a work entitled *Quod idola dii non sint*, which offers many of the same kinds of apologetic arguments found in Tertullian, Minucius Felix, and Cyprian (Heck, 1922). Other works from this period include a number of martyrdoms, such as the *Passio Mariani et Iacobi* and the *Passio Montani et Lucii*, which both discuss events from 259 CE. Martyrdoms from the end of the 3rd century and beginning of the 4th century CE include the *Acta Maximiliani*, the *Passio Felicis Episcopi*, and the *Passio Crispinae*. These texts, however, may represent later views stemming from the Donatist controversy, as is the case with the so-called *Acts of the Abitinian Martyrs*, which purports to describe events from 304 CE but is unknown in the historical record until 411 CE (Dearn, 2016). Another source that dates from either the 3rd or 4th, or perhaps even the 5th, century CE is the writer Commodianus, whose verse writings *Carmen de duobus populis* and *Instructiones* both survive (T.S. Burns, 1994, 365n33).

3. The 4th Century CE

In the early 4th century CE, Diocletian's rule came to an end, and Constantine rose to power. In Africa numerous sources survive from this period. Writers like → Arnobius of Sicca and → Lactantius left behind a number of treatises from the early decades of this century, and their works addressed both internal theological concerns of African Christians as well as matters pertaining to the developments occurring in the empire at large (Simmons, 1995; Digeser, 2000; Nicholson, 2004).

The reign of → Diocletian marked a decisive moment for African Christian history. Once again a requirement that everyone in the empire perform the sacrificial rituals to the Roman deities produced an internal controversy for Christians. In addition to the many who died for refusing the order and the many who lapsed, a new problem arose due to a number of clergy whose only compromise was to surrender the church's sacred items to the officials. Anyone who "handed over" the Scriptures or some other sacred relic came to be labeled a *traditor* (etymologically linked to "traitor"), and the act was deemed equal to the sin of idolatry itself since it was a submission to the demonic persecutors.

This view of a *traditor* impacted on the status of clergy in particular because the African Christians viewed the sin of idolatry as one that contracts a contagion from evil spirits. This contagion, moreover, could pollute sacraments, such as baptism, → Eucharist, and the laying on of hands. When the bishop of Carthage died, and his successor, Caecilius, was accused of being ordained by a *traditor*, many claimed that his ordination was polluted and therefore invalid. In his place, his opponents elected Majorinus, and this resulted in two rival parties. Majorinus soon died, and his successor, → Donatus the Great, presided as bishop for circa 40 years. Thus, those who sided with → Caecilian considered themselves "Catholic" and their rivals "Donatists" (Frend, 1952; Shaw, 2011).

The Catholic party, or the Caecilianists, won the approval of Constantine. They also gained approval from two ecclesial synods, one in Rome in 313 CE and one in Arles in 314 CE. The Donatist party, however, refused to acquiesce, and so Constantine intervened. In 317 CE he ordered that the Donatist basilicas be seized, and when some Donatists resisted, the soldiers removed them violently, even resulting in the death of some Donatists. The Donatists viewed Constantine's actions as identical to those of Diocletian, who had also seized the Christian basilicas. Therefore, the Donatists came to understand themselves as the church of the martyrs, while their opponents were the church of the *traditores* in league with the devil. In what was likely a common motto, the Donatists insisted that the true church always "endures persecution, it never persecutes" (*quae persecutionem patitur, non quae facit*; *Ges. Col. Carth.* 3.258, ll.3–4; CCL 149A.243). In 321 CE Constantine relented and allowed the Donatists to reclaim at least some of their basilicas (Frend, 1952, 161; Opt. *Parm.* appendix. 9).

In the mid-4th century CE, further violence erupted between the two parties in Africa. The emperor sent two envoys, Paul and Macarius, as "agents of unity" (*Parm.* 3.1.1), but they encountered a group known as the Circumcellions. Scholars today debate the exact nature of this group (Shaw, 2011, 828–839), but they were known to use brutal measures against the Caecilianists and the Roman officials who backed them. The conflict resulted in further deaths (see e.g. *Passio Maximiani et Isaac* and *Passio Marculi*). The intensity of the conflict again abated, and at this point it was the Donatists – not the Caecilianists – who earned the legal status as the Catholic party in the eyes of the local officials (Hermanowicz, 2008, 126–129).

The Donatist party began to decline in several ways in the late 4th century CE. They were accused of joining the revolts of Firmus (372–375 CE) and Gildo (398 CE), which made them suspect in the eyes of the empire. Furthermore, the party experienced its own internal schisms, most notably the Maximianist controversy, which began in 393 CE. Finally, when a series of violent attacks against the Caecilianists occurred, the victims appealed to Ravenna. The resulting legislation eventually treated the Donatists not merely as schismatics (→ Schism/ Schismatics) but as heretics (→ Heresy) who should be compelled into unity. The legal battle climaxed in the Conference of → Carthage (411 CE), wherein both sides appeared with their full entourage of bishops. Marcellinus, who presided over the proceedings, unsurprisingly upheld the emperor's support of the Caecilianist party, and so the Donatists were declared heretical and ordered to unite with the Catholic church. Although the Donatists mostly disappear from the historical record at this time, scholars assume that they continued as an underground movement (Brown, 1967, 335). Further Donatist sources can be found during later periods, and references to Donatists continue in the following centuries (Adamiak, 2014).

4. Augustine of Hippo

The most influential voice in the late 4th century CE, both in terms of the Donatist controversy and more generally regarding wider Christian concerns, was that of → Augustine of Hippo (Brown, 1967). Born in 354 CE in the small town of Thagaste, Augustine came from a family of moderate means. His father, Patricius, a pagan, served as a local official (Pos. *Vita Aug.* 1) and used his connections to secure a good education for his son. His mother, Monica, was a Christian. Augustine studied rhetoric in Madouros, and then went on to teach in Carthage, Rome, and Milan. Appointed *magister rhetoricae* by the emperor, Augustine's career had reached the highest levels of public acclaim.

It was while in Milan that he reconsidered the Christianity practiced by his mother. He had never been baptized, and as a young man he adhered to the Manichaean school for nine years. He eventually became disenchanted with Manichaeism (→ Mani/ Manichaeism) and instead began to follow the philosophy of the Platonists. The bishop of Milan, Ambrose (→ Ambrose of Milan), showed Augustine how the Christian Scriptures could be read allegorically so as to accommodate some of the tenets of Platonism, and so Augustine started to take seriously the Christian faith. By this time, Augustine lived with his second concubine, but his mother, Monica, was arranging for a proper, socially advantageous marriage. It seems that his reluctance to convert fully to Christianity had as much to do with his struggle to accept celibacy as with anything else. He famously narrated his internal struggle in his *Confessiones*, and after a dramatic scene where he was turned by an anonymous voice to Rom 13:13–14, Augustine relented and was baptized in 387 CE.

Augustine renounced his public career and returned to Africa. While attempting to recruit for his newly established monastic community at his family estate, he was enlisted as a priest in the city of Hippo Regius in 391 CE. In 395 CE his bishop, Valerius, made him co-bishop, and after his death Augustine became his successor. Because of his controversial stint with Manichaeism, Augustine had to defend himself against the charge of being a closet heretic brought especially by the Donatists in the area (Aug. *Cresc.* 4.64.79; *C. litt. Petil.* 3.16.19). During the early and middle part of his career, therefore, Augustine devoted many works to refuting both Manichaeism and Donatism. Later in his career the Pelagian controversy evoked many works from Augustine as well.

In addition to his writings against various internal disputes, Augustine also wrote works devoted to the wider political events of his day, especially in his famous *Civitas Dei*. He also penned numerous letters, and many of his sermons have been collected. In sum, by his death in 430 CE, Augustine had left an enormous amount of material that would influence later generations of Christianity (Pollman & Otten, 2013).

5. The Vandal, Byzantine, and Arab Periods

As Augustine lay dying in Hippo, the → Vandals were sweeping across Africa and seizing control of the region. They brought with them an Arian or subordinationist form of Christianity (→ Arianism) with them, and so the Catholics, or Christians supported by the Roman Empire, became targets. Writing in 488 CE several decades after the original events, → Victor of Vita described the events in graphic terms as a "persecution" (*Historia Vandalae persecutionis*), but historians have questioned whether this is an appropriate category (see esp. Fournier, 2008). The depictions found in other sources are more complex. These other sources include African writers, such as → Quodvultdeus, → Fulgentius of Ruspe, and the collection known as the *Anthologia Latina*, and they include non-Africans who discussed events in Africa at this time, such as Salvian of Marseille and → Procopius of Caesarea.

The Vandals ruled until 534 CE, when → Justinian reconquered the region, and this Byzantine era of

African history witnessed a series of controversies. Under Justinian's reign a conflict arose throughout the empire known as the Three Chapters Controversy. In this debate, African writers, such as Facundus and Ferrandus, offered staunch resistance to Justinian's decisions. In the late 6th and early 7th centuries CE, more conflict would be recorded in the letters of Pope Gregory I (r. 590–604 CE; → Gregory the Great). Gregory found that "Donatists" (or at least Africans exhibiting what were deemed to be Donatist characteristics) continued to defy his orders. Two years after Gregory's death, another controversy erupted in Africa when Maximus (later named "the Confessor" after he was tortured for his defense of orthodoxy; Maximus the Confessor) arrived in Carthage. Maximus had been embroiled in the ongoing Christological debates with the so-called Monophysites (→ Miaphysites/Miaphysitism) and Monothelites. With the support of the local African bishops, Maximus defied Emperor Heraclius, who supported these groups. For his resistance, and under the accusation of supporting the rebellion of the exarch of Africa at the time (Booth, 2014), Maximus was tortured and exiled. After Maximus, the literary sources from Africa fall silent.

We know very little about the Christian communities who continued in the area under the time of the Arab invasion. A number of sources from outside Africa along with a few details gleaned from the archaeological remains suggest that Christianity persisted in the region for centuries to follow (Handley, 2004; Kaegi, 2010, 29–40; Adamiak, 2014; Reynolds, 2016; Morrisson, 2016). Eventually, however, Christianity would disappear altogether from the region until modern times.

Historiography

During and after the modern French colonization of Africa, which began in 1830 and ended 1962, much interest arose in the pre-Arab history, which resulted in studies that still prove helpful for contemporary scholarship (e.g. Monceaux, 1901–1923; Gsell, 1913–1929). It deserves mention that many modern scholars of African Christianity mould their research within a colonialist framework (see Mattingly, 1996; Stern, 2007, 6–11). Those who conquered

North Africa assumed themselves to be heirs to the ancient Romans who had done the same, believing that both had a civilizing mission (see esp. the criticisms of Laroui, 1979, and Benabou, 1976). Modern historians and archaeologists viewed their "primitive" subjects as inferior in racial terms. This was especially applied to particular groups of African Christians, like the Donatists and their Circumcellions. Many scholars attempted to view them as representatives of a "nationalist" or indigenous sect that opposed Rome both militarily and culturally (e.g. Thümmel, 1893; Leclercq, 1914; Frend, 1952; Brisson, 1958). This view came under sharp criticism because of its Euro-centric and reductionistic commitments (Mandouze, 1960; Tengström, 1964; Brown, 1967). The Donatists and other African Christians need to be read as legitimate in their theological concerns and as sharing much with the Christianity of the wider empire.

Closely affiliated with the nationalist view of African Christian history, scholars like M. le Glay (1961; 1966a; 1966b) and G. Charles-Picard (1954), upon finding that Punic culture continued to persist throughout the Roman period through means of accommodation, believed that the Semitic/Canaanite background explained how easily Christianity spread throughout the region, since Christianity was itself a Semitic/Canaanite religion sharing many concepts with Punic thought. Furthermore, this same idea explained how easily Islam replaced Christianity in the region since the latter had steadily grown more affiliated with the foreign expression of Christianity centralized under the emperors. Such theories, of course, are difficult to establish, and so most recent scholars have abandoned the idea (however, see e.g. Simmons, 1995, 16, 196–197, 201, who still finds this theory helpful).

Most recent studies of Christianity in Africa focus on specific authors and periods of history, finding that locating Christian sources within the broader context of late antiquity provides fresh insights (e.g. Shaw, 1995; 2011; Dossey, 2010; Conant, 2012; Rebillard, 2012; Leone, 2013). Even so, some are finding the need to see African Christianity writ large as a "school" unto itself that passes on its own traditions and theological motifs (e.g. Burns & Jensen et al., 2014).

Bibliography

Adamiak, S., "When did Donatist Christianity End?" in: A. Dupont, M. Gaumer & M. Lamberigts, eds., *The Uniquely African Controversy: Studies on Donatist Christianity*, Louvain, 2014, 211–236.

Barnes, T.D., *Tertullian: An Historical and Literary Study*, rev. ed., Oxford, 1985.

Bass, A., "The *Passion of Cyprian* in the So-Called 'Donatist Dossier' of Würzburg *M. p. the. f. 33*," in: K. Steinhauser & S. Dermer, eds., *Text and Meaning: Textual Criticism and Theological Interpretation*, Lewiston, 2012, 2–23.

Benabou, M., *La résistance africaine à la romanisation*, Paris, 1976.

Booth, P., *Crisis of Empire: Doctrine and Dissent at the End of Late Antiquity*, Berkeley, 2014.

Brent, A., *Cyprian and Roman Carthage*, Cambridge MA, 2010.

Brisson, J.-P., *Autonomisme et christianime dans l'Afrique romaine: Dans l'Afrique romaine de Septime Sévère à l'invasion vandale*, Paris, 1958.

Brown, P., *Augustine of Hippo: A Biography*, London, 1967.

Burns, J.P., *Cyprian the Bishop*, London, 2002.

Burns, J.P. Jr., & R.M. Jensen et al., *Christianity in Roman Africa: The Development of Its Practices and Beliefs*, Grand Rapids, 2014.

Burns, T.S., *Barbarians Within the Gates of Rome: A Study of Roman Military Policy and the Barbarians, ca. 375–425 AD*, Bloomington, 1994.

Charles-Picard, G., *Les religions de l'Afrique antique*, Paris, 1954.

Charles-Picard, G., *La civilisation de l'Afrique romaine*, Paris, 1990.

Conant, J., *Staying Roman: Conquest and Identity in Africa and the Mediterranean, 439–700*, Cambridge MA, 2012.

Dearn, A., "Donatist Martyrs, Stories and Attitudes," in: Richard Miles, ed., *The Donatist Schism: Controversy and Contexts*, Liverpool, 2016, 70–100.

Decret, F., *Early Christianity in North Africa*, Eugene, 2009; Fr. orig., 1996, trans. E.L. Smither.

Digeser, E.D., *The Making of a Christian Empire: Lactantius & Rome*, Ithaca, 2000.

Dossey, L., *Peasant and Empire in Christian North Africa*, Berkeley, 2010.

Dunn, G.D., *Cyprian and the Bishops of Rome: Questions of Papal Primacy in the Early Church*, Strathfield, 2007.

Dupont, A., Gaumer, M., Lamberigts, M., (eds), *The Uniquely African Controversy: Studies on Donatist Christianity*, LaHR 9), Louvain, 2015.

Fage, J.D., *CHAfr*, vol. II: *From c. 500 BC to AD 1050*, Cambridge UK, 1979.

Fournier, É., "Victor of Vita and the Vandal 'Persecution': Interpreting Exile in Late Antiquity," diss., Santa Barbara, 2008.

Frend, W.H.C., *The Donatist Church*, Oxford, 1952.

Gaumer, M.A., *Augustine's Cyprian: Authority in Roman Africa*. Louvain, 2016.

Gsell, S., *Histoire ancienne de l'Afrique du Nord*, 8 vols., Paris, 1913–1929.

Handley, M., "Disputing the End of African Christianity," in: A.H. Merrills, ed., *Vandals, Romans, and Berbers: New Perspectives on Late Antique North Africa*, Aldershot, 2004, 291–310.

Heck, E., "Pseudo-Cyprian, *Quod idola dii non sint* und Laktanz, *Epitome diuinarum institutionum*," in: M. Wacht, ed., *Panchaia: FS für Klaus Thraede*, JbAC.S., vol. XXII, Münster, 1922, 148–155.

Hermanowicz, E.T., *Possidius of Calama: A Study of the North African Episcopate at the Time of Augustine*, Oxford, 2008.

Kaegi, W.E., *Muslim Expansion and Byzantine Collapse in North Africa*, Cambridge MA, 2010.

Laroui, A. *L'histoire du Maghreb: Un essai de synthèse*, Paris, 1970.

Leclercq, H., *L'Afrique chrétienne*, 2 vols., Paris, 1914.

Glay le, M., *Saturne africain: Monuments*, 2 vols., Paris, 1961, 1966a.

Glay le, M., *Saturne africain: Histoire*, Paris, 1966b.

Leone, A., *The End of the Pagan City: Religion, Economy, and Urbanism in Late Antique North Africa*, Oxford, 2013.

Lepelley, C., *Les cités de l'Afrique romaine au bas-empire*, Paris, 1979.

Maier, J.-L., *L'Episcopat de l'Afrique romaine, vandale et byzantine*, Rome, 1973.

Mandouze, A., "Encore le donatisme: Problèmes de méthode posés par la thèse de J.-P. Brisson: *Autonomisme et christianisme dans l'Afrique romaine de Septime Sévère à l'invasion vandale*," *AntClass* 29, 1960, 61–107.

Mandouze, A., *PCBE*, vol. I: *Prosopographie de l'Afrique chrétienne (303–533)*, Paris, 1982.

Mattingly, D.J., "From One Colonialism to Another: Imperialism and the Maghreb," in: J. Webster & N.J. Cooper, eds., *Roman Imperialism: Post-Colonial Perspectives*, LAMon 3, Leicester, 1996, 49–69.

Monceaux, P., *Histoire littéraire de l'Afrique chrétienne depuis les origines jusqu'a l'invasion arabe*, 7 vols., Paris, 1901–1923.

Morrisson, C., "*REGIO DIVES IN OMNIBUS BONIS ORNATA*: The African Economy from the Vandals to the Arab Conquests in the Light of Coin Evidence," in: S.T. Stevens & J.P. Conant, eds., *North Africa Under Byzantium and Early Islam*, Washington DC, 2016, 173–200.

Nicholson, O., "Arnobius and Lactantius," in: F.M. Young, L. Ayres & A. Louth, eds., *The Cambridge History of Early Christian Literature*, Cambridge UK, 2004, 259–265.

Pollmann, K., ed., *Oxford Guide to the Historical Reception of Augustine*, 3 vols. Oxford, 2013.

Powell, D., "Tertullianists and Cataphrygians," *VigChr* 29, 1975, 33–54.

Rankin, D., *Tertullian and the Church*, Cambridge MA, 1995.

Rebillard, É., *Christians and Their Many Identities in Late Antiquity, North Africa, 200–450 CE*, Ithaca, 2012.

Reynolds, P., "From Vandal *Africa* to Arab *Ifrīgiya*: Tracing Ceramic and Economic Trends through the Fifth to the Eleventh Centuries," in: S.T. Stevens & J.P. Conant, eds., *North Africa Under Byzantium and Early Islam*, Washington DC, 2016, 129–172.

Schubert, C., *Minucius Felix, Octavius*, KfA 12, Freiburg, 2014.

Shaw, B.D., *Rulers, Nomads, and Christians in Roman North Africa*, Aldershot, 1995.

Shaw, B.D., *Sacred Violence: African Christians and Sectarian Hatred in the Age of Augustine*, Cambridge MA, 2011.

Simmons, M.B., *Arnobius of Sicca: Religious Conflict and Competition in the Age of Diocletian*, Oxford, 1995.

Stern, K.B., *Inscribing Devotion and Death: Archaeological Evidence for Jewish Populations of North Africa*, Leiden, 2007.

Tengström, E., *Donatisten und Katholiken: Soziale, wirtschaftliche, und politische Aspekte einer nordafrikanischen Kirchenspaltung*, Götenborg, 1964.

Thümmel, W., *Zur Beurtheilung des Donatismus: Eine kirchengeschichtliche Untersuchung*, Halle, 1893.

Tilley, M.A., "North Africa," in: M. Mitchell & F. Young, eds., *Cambridge History of Early Christianity*, vol. I: *Origins to Constantine*, Cambridge MA, 2006, 380–396.

Wilhite, D.E., *Tertullian the African: An Anthropological Reading of Tertullian's Context and Identities*, Berlin, 2007.

Wilhite, D.E., *Ancient African Christianity: An Introduction to a Unique Context and Tradition*, London, 2017.

DAVID E. WILHITE

Afterlife

The afterlife is the continued existence of human beings after physical death, either in a specific realm or on the earth. It can also be called "life after death," "the hereafter," or "the postmortem existence." The early Christian belief in an afterlife is manifested in several aspects: various ideas of the abode of the dead, an intermediate state of the deceased between their death and their final destiny as well as their final eschatological state, and forms of afterlife existence.

1. Origins

Early Christian views on the afterlife mostly originated in the cultural-religious milieu of the ancient Mediterranean world, primarily in Jewish beliefs, which were often mixed and molded into more complex concepts, even within one text. Traditionally, the world of the dead is represented in the Hebrew Bible as שְׁאוֹל/*sheol*, a dark and gloomy underworld (Job 10:21–22) into which both the righteous and the wicked descend after → death and from which there is no possibility of returning. Due to the development of the idea of personal rewards and punishments for the dead, at a certain time the deepest parts of Sheol were regarded as designed for the wicked. In the Septuagint, ᾅδης becomes the regular translation of Sheol. In the archaic Greek view reflected in the Homeric epics, → Hades is a neutral place for the dead. However, in the Hellenistic and Roman periods, the concept of Hades was often associated with the place of punishment for the wicked. Nevertheless, the older concept of Sheol/Hades as the place or abode of the dead continued to exist.

In the *Book of Watchers* (*1 En.* 1–36), the souls of the deceased receive their preliminary rewards and punishments immediately after death: the righteous are separated from the wicked and put into various chambers in the underworld according to their ethical behavior, where they wait for the day of the great judgment (*1 En.* 22:1–4, 8–11). This idea of an intermediate state of the dead is found in some later texts (*4 Ezra* 7:79–87; see also *L.A.B.* 23:13; 32:13). At the end of time, Hades will give back the souls of the dead for the final judgment (*1 En.* 51:3; *4 Ezra* 4:42; 7:32; *2 Bar.* 42:8; 50:2; Ps.-Philo 3:10; 33:3).

Sometimes, the underworld was believed to be reserved exclusively for the wicked. In *1 En.* 108:3–4 it is described as a desolate and unseen place between heaven and earth, quaking like a mountain, enveloped by something like a cloud, and burning with flames of fire. The imagery of this fiery place is linked to → Gehenna, the final abode of the wicked assigned for their punishment, that is, to hell. Indeed, *4 Ezra* 7:36–38 indicates that those who are found guilty in the final judgment will be put into the fire of Gehenna and the pit of torment (see *1 En.* 26:4–27:2; *2 Bar.* 59:10; 85:13; *2 En.* 40:12–13; 42:1; *Sib. Or.* 1:101–103; 2:288–292; 4:183–186).

Next, Jewish literature often speaks about the special blessed realm reserved for the righteous, whether after their death or after the final judgment. Some early texts locate it in this world (see e.g. *1 En.* 25:5–6; 26:1–3), but later ones more explicitly refer to heaven (Wis 4:10–11; 5:5; *2 Bar.* 51:10). In addition, the abode of the righteous is sometimes associated with a → paradise located on the earth (*1 En.* 32:3–4; 70:3–4), in heaven (*2 Bar.* 51:11), or even both (*L.A.E.* 13:1–5; 37:2–6; 32:1–2; 25:3; 29:1; 45:2). In any case, paradise is never located in the underworld and is not seen as an interim location before transition to a final abode. Some texts attempt to harmonize all these ideas of preliminary and final judgment as well as of an intermediate state between death and the final destiny, and incorporate them into a single eschatological scenario (*4 Ezra*; *2 Baruch*).

Moreover, there was no single Jewish view on the form of afterlife existence. While some Jews believed in resurrection (→ Resurrection), others saw life after death as an incorporeal form of → immortality of the soul. It seems that in the Qumran community, in spite of their familiarity with the belief in resurrection (see e.g. 4Q521; 4Q385–388 [4QPseudo-Ezekiel]), resurrection itself was not dominant and central for them. In contrast, a few Jewish groups like the Sadducees, who were influenced by popular Epicurean philosophy (→ Epicurus/Epicureans), had no faith in any postmortem existence at all (see Jos. *Bell.* 2.165; *Ant.* 18.16; Mark 12:18; Matt 22:23; Luke 20:27; Acts 23:8; *b. Sanch.* 90b; '*Abot R. Nat.* 5).

The collective eschatological resurrection was perceived in two ways. Some texts argue that resurrection is a gift and reward for the righteous after the final judgment (see e.g. Isa 26:19; *1 En.* 22:13; 102:4–8; 103:4; 104:2–6; 108:9–12; *Pss. Sol.* 3:10–12; *Jub.* 23:30–31), while others deal with the general resurrection, which precedes the final judgment. In this scenario, both the righteous and the wicked will be restored to life and will be judged along with the living, either to be rewarded with eternal life or to be punished and to experience disgrace (see e.g. Dan 12:2–3; *1 En.* 51:1–2; *4 Ezra* 7:31–38; *2 Bar.* 30:1–5; 42:8; *Sib. Or.* 4:181–182; *L.A.B.* 3:10; *T. Benj.* 10:6–10; *T. Jud.* 25:1–2; *L.A.E.* 13:3b–6).

Some documents deal with forms of afterlife without direct reference to the end of time or to the issue of judgment. For instance, 2 Macc 7 speaks about the bodily resurrection of the martyrs (individual resurrection) functioning as recompense for losing their bodies because of their adherence to the Jewish Law. It is significant, however, that in its representation of the same story (see 2 Macc 7:4–9), 4 Maccabees

replaces bodily resurrection with a spiritual incorporeal existence (e.g. 9:22; 14:5).

In addition, in their final destiny the righteous would be transformed into a glorious state that is often depicted in astral imagery: shining like stars, enjoying celestial life, and in some way resembling angels (Dan 12:2–3; *1 En.* 104:2; *T. Levi* 18:3; *T. Jud* 24:1). The latter is connected with the belief that the transformed existence of the righteous is similar to the exalted human state at creation, which is likened to that of angels, especially in their immortality and glorious shape (see *1 En.* 69:11; *L.A.E.* 39:2). It can also be connected with the widespread view that the soul is composed of some celestial substance.

In the Wisdom of Solomon, the righteous are immortal, and their death in this world is seen as only an illusion (Wis 3:1–4). This text depicts their afterlife existence as the immortality of the soul (see Wis 3:4; 4:7, 10–11), which is not their intermediate state but the ultimate postmortem existence. In contrast to Plato's views on immortality as an inalienable feature of the human soul, this immortality is granted only to the righteous. Other Jewish texts go even further (e.g. Pseudo-Phocylides – esp. Ps.-Phoc. 115; → Philo of Alexandria; and → Flavius Josephus) and adopt the pagan view on the liberation of the immortal → soul from the perishable → body at death, and that of metempsychosis. All this indicates that for many Jews the character of resurrection remains ambiguous and sometimes seems to be that of the spirit or the soul rather than of the body, while for others, other forms of afterlife or more general ideas of the afterlife are implied.

2. The Afterlife in the Earliest Christian Tradition

Although the abode of the dead in the New Testament corpus is usually associated with the underworld, the various authors give it different characteristics. Hades, on the one hand, is seen as a neutral place where all the dead are located (Acts 2:27, 31; Rev 20:13), but also with gates (Matt 16:18), the keys of which are held by Jesus after his resurrection (Rev 1:18). However, in Luke 16:23–26 it is a place of punishment immediately after death, without reference to the final judgment. It is separated from the abode of the righteous by a great chasm (Luke

16:26). Nevertheless, in the book of Revelation, the character of Hades is temporal: it will be thrown into the fiery lake together with Death and the enemies of God (Rev 20:14).

In Mark (→ Mark, Gospel of) and Matthew (Matthew the Apostle), the place of eternal punishment is Gehenna, into which both the bodies and the souls of the wicked will be cast after the final judgment (Mark 9:43, 45, 47; Matt 5:29–30; 10:28; 18:9). The fiery lake in Rev 20:10, 14–15, with its eternal fire and torments, is implicitly related to the same idea. Luke (→ Luke, Gospel of), however, may use Hades and Gehenna (Luke 12:5) as rough equivalents of the place of punishment for the wicked immediately after death regardless of its interim or final character (Lehtipuu, 2007, 273–274). Moreover, 2 Pet 2:4 refers to Tartarus functioning as the place of the temporal imprisonment of the fallen angels until the judgment at the end of time (see also ἄβυσσος, abyss, with a similar meaning in Luke 8:31). This term (Τάρταρος) had been taken from Greek writings (Hom. *Il.* 8.13–15; Hes. *Theog.* 740–741) and was later used in Hellenistic Jewish texts (e.g. *1 En.* 20:2; *Sib. Or.* 4:186).

As with the fate of the rich man, Luke does not regard → Lazarus' abode as temporary (Luke 16:19–31). He was carried to → Abraham's bosom (κόλπος Ἀβραάμ). This expression, unique in the New Testament corpus and the Jewish literature of the period, does not necessarily relate to the special section of Hades reserved as a temporary place for the righteous. It metaphorically depicts a close relationship between Lazarus and Abraham in the honored and blessed reality of the abode of the righteous (Lehtipuu, 2007, 276), probably at the heavenly banquet (Somov & Voinov, 2017) This is often located in heaven, where Jesus was taken at his ascension (Acts 1:9–11; 7:55–56) and where the believers will be rewarded (Matt 5:12; Luke 6:23; Col 1:5; 1 Pet 1:4) and settled at the resurrection (Matt 22:30). However, this does not mean that the righteous will be physically transported to heaven in the afterlife. It rather indicates the belief that they will enter the divine realm that is metaphorically identified with heaven. Other representations of this blessed reality also do not indicate its exact locality (either heavenly or earthly), but it is certainly not underground. Thus, the Synoptics use the spatial aspect of the

concept of the → kingdom of God, which is opposed to Gehenna in Mark 9:47. Entering the kingdom is a reward (Matt 7:21) and a final destiny for believers (Lehtipuu, 2007, 291). However, it is not always clear whether entry to the kingdom of God is granted in the hereafter or already in this life. Nevertheless, the context of Luke 13:23–30 may imply that the metaphor of the kingdom as an eschatological banquet refers to the hereafter. In Luke 23:42–43 the kingdom is probably represented as → paradise, which designates its limited character in this age and the gift of eternal life for the righteous. Paradise also occurs in 2 Cor 12:2–4, where Paul identifies it with the present heavenly realm in the third heaven, and in Rev 2:7 (see also Rev 22:1–5) as the final reward of the righteous. In addition, Luke uses the imagery of "eternal habitations" (αἱ αἰώνιοι σκηναί) in Luke 16:9 as the place of salvation and joy for the righteous.

A principal form of afterlife existence in early Christianity is resurrection. Nevertheless, the New Testament authors sometimes prefer more general descriptions of the afterlife without reference to corporeal postmortem existence or to any other particular form of the afterlife (see Luke 13:28–30; 16:19–31; 23:42–43). Moreover, among Christians there were those who did not believe in resurrection at all (see 1 Cor 15:12), or who thought about the resurrection of the soul/spirit only (see Iren. *Haer.* 1.30.13; 5.31.1), or who argued that the resurrection had already taken place, probably as a metaphor of spiritual revival from a dead society or as a certain illumination of the soul (see 2 Tim 2:17–18). It might also have been perceived as the beginning of the new life in conversion, as the link between → baptism and → resurrection in Col 2:12 may be interpreted (see Rom 6:2–11).

Eschatological issues include both collective and individual aspects: although Paul talks about the eschatological resurrection in 1 Cor 15:51–52 and 1 Thess 4:14–17, in Phil 1:23–24 he speaks about his desire to be with Christ immediately after his death, with no reference to resurrection. Individual eschatology is also very important for Luke. Indeed, in certain passages that speak about the individual's afterlife, he interprets the traditional eschatological terminology in an "individual" way: the judgment with its reward or punishment explicitly or implicitly takes place immediately after one's death (see e.g. Luke 12:16–21; 16:9, 19–31; 23:42–43;

Acts 1:25). This eschatological dichotomy was supported by later authors. For instance, Ignatius of Antioch (→ Ignatius, Epistles of), while depicting the resurrection of Jesus as the prototype for the future resurrection of believers (Ign. *Trall.* 9.1–2), expects immediate access to heaven after death (Ign. *Rom.* 6.1–2).

Paul (→ Paul the Apostle) was probably the first who linked together the → resurrection of Jesus Christ and the eschatological resurrection (1 Cor 15:12–23; see also Rom 6:5; Holleman, 1996, 137.) He describes the eschatological resurrection as a two-stage process (1 Cor 15:20–23), with the two stages corresponding "to two categories of people to be raised" (Holleman, 1996, 52). As the firstfruits (ἀπαρχή) of those who have fallen asleep, Jesus belongs to the first category, while Christians belong to the second. His resurrection is the basis of the victory over death and the future resurrection of believers (1 Cor 15:57). While the resurrection of Jesus Christ is "a unique incidence of a full bodily resurrection" (Fletcher-Louis, 1997, 70), the nature of the collective eschatological resurrection was less clearly defined in this period. In his early accounts, Paul deals with it in very general terms (1 Thess 4:13–18), merely assuring the believers that the dead will be raised and taken up together with the living to meet the Lord. Then, in 1 Cor 15, he clarifies the nature of the resurrection body by making an analogy with heavenly bodies (σώματα ἐπουράνια; see 1 Cor 15:39–41) in order to distinguish the resurrection body (σῶμα) from earthly flesh (σάρξ): "flesh and blood cannot inherit the kingdom of God" (1 Cor 15:50 NRSV). For him, resurrection is a transformation of the physical body, which is subject to decay, into a new incorruptible, glorified, and "spiritual" (πνευματικόν) substance (1 Cor 15:42–44). Nevertheless, even this "spiritual" resurrection is expressed in bodily terms. The Synoptics metaphorically represent the transformed state of the resurrected as angel-like (ἰσάγγελοι in Luke 20:36), not as if they literally became angels, but because they are similar in their immortality and celestial life as well as in their splendid and glorious shape (Mark 12:18–27; Matt 22:23–33; Luke 20:29–40).

The general resurrection and that of the righteous only are often combined or mingled in the New Testament texts (Matt 12:41–42 and 22:30; Luke 14:14; 20:35 and Acts 24:15; Rev 20:4–6 and 20:12–13; John 5:29 and 6:39; 11:25). On the other hand, some texts are less ambivalent about the features of the resurrection: for instance, Mark speaks only about the resurrection of the righteous (Mark 12:25; see also 13:27) and so does Paul (see Rom 2:7–8; 6:20–23; 9:22–23; 1 Cor 1:18; 2 Cor 2:15; Phil 1:28; 3:19), while Q mentions general resurrection (Luke 11:31–32). However, those accounts that mention only the resurrection of the righteous may be dealing with the positive half of the general resurrection, which implies that only the righteous would be resurrected to eternal life.

Luke goes even further and speaks about the eschatological destiny of the righteous as if it were already accomplished (Luke 20:27–40; see also Luke 5:20–21; 7:8; 15:11–32). It is connected with his understanding of salvation: those who have repented already anticipate or even receive it and are somehow already granted eternal life while still living in this world. This tension between future and realized eschatology is attested even more strongly in John (→ John the Apostle). Those who believe in Jesus will not die (John 11:25–26) and already have eternal life without coming to the final judgment (John 5:24). However, other passages in John speak about future judgment and resurrection (John 6:39, 40, 44, 54; 5:27–29).

In the book of Revelation (→ Revelation, Book of), the righteous and the martyrs will be resurrected first to be God's priests and to reign with Christ for a 1,000 years ("the first resurrection"; Rev 20:4–6). In the later Christian tradition, this view was developed into the idea of → chiliasm. Then, after the defeat of Satan (Rev 20:7–10; → Devil), the general resurrection and the judgment with its rewards and punishments ("the second death") follow (Rev 20:11–15). However, this book also deals with a certain kind of immortality for the blameless (Rev 14:5, 13). Probably, the author tries to combine and even harmonize several eschatological scenarios, as *4 Ezra* and *2 Baruch* also do.

3. Further Developments in Early Christian Literature

A very detailed description of the otherworld is found in the *Apocalypse of Peter* (2nd cent. CE; → Peter the Apostle), which is probably the first

Christian account of postmortem destiny outside the New Testament (Bernstein, 1993, 282). This text synthesizes several views on the afterlife, attested not only in previous Christian and Jewish apocalyptic ideas (e.g. *4 Ezra*) and images, but also in some Greek traditions, such as the detailed description of the underworld (see Plato's myth of Er in Plato *Rep.* 10.614d–621d). It also uses some Greek terminology: Tartarus with the Acherusian Lake (see Hom. *Il.* 8.13–15; Hes. *Theog.* 740–741; Plato *Phaid.* 113–114) and Elysium (see Hom. *Od.* 4.561–569; Plato *Gorg.* 526c).

In the *Apocalypse of Peter*, the judgment follows the general resurrection at the end of time (*Apoc. Pet.* 4). Then the wicked will experience 21 different punishments in hell appointed for their specific sins. Their torments are depicted in a much more elaborate way than in the New Testament (see Mark 9:48). Moreover, the very image of this underworld is much more developed than that given in Luke 16:19–31. For instance, those who blasphemed the way of righteousness will be hung by their tongues, those who perverted justice will be put into the fiery lake, murderers will suffer from beasts and snakes, and so on (*Apoc. Pet.* 7–13). As this punishment takes place after the general resurrection, these people will be penalized in the flesh, and their torments are depicted in a very physical way. Repentance after death is impossible (see Luke 16:25–26). However, some of these people would be saved by washing in the Acherusian Lake with the intercession of the elect, which may even reverse their postmortem fate (*Apoc. Pet.* 14).

After the judgment, the elect will be given eternal life in the kingdom of God (*Apoc. Pet.* 14). This place is depicted as a beautiful paradise-like garden with fruit-bearing trees and fragrant spices, where the elect are clad in shining angelic garments (*Apoc. Pet.* 16). Similar accounts of the abode of the righteous as a garden full of light and with plenty of trees and flowers of all kinds, where the believers are dressed in white garments, are found in some other early Christian texts (e.g. *Mart. Perp.* 4.22–26; 11.11–15; see also Rev 22:2).

While the *Apocalypse of Peter* developed the Lucan image of Hades (Luke 16:19–31), some others tried to give an adequate interpretation of Abraham's bosom. They usually did not regard it as a type of relationship but represented it as a specific location in the otherworld to which they wanted to assign an appropriate place. For instance, criticizing → Marcion, who located Abraham's bosom in heaven, → Tertullian argues that it is not located in heaven while at the same time stating that is not as deep as hell. For him, it is a sort of temporal refuge for the souls of believers until the general resurrection, similar to the Greek Elysian fields (Tert. *Marc.* 4.34.11–14; see also Tert. *An.* 7.3). It is a higher region of Hades where the righteous already experience their consolation, while the lower one is designed for sinners who are already being punished there in anticipation of their final verdict (Tert. *An.* 57.11; 58.1–8). Hippolytus of Rome also regards Abraham's bosom as the abode of the righteous in Hades, where they await the final judgment that will bring them to eternal life in heaven (Hipp. *Univ.* 33).

In addition, according to Tertullian, the souls of the dead cannot escape Hades until the general resurrection, apart from the souls of the martyrs, who go to paradise in heaven immediately after death (Tert. *An.* 55.4). The idea that the destiny of a martyr is special appears already in Acts 7:54–60: → Stephen the Martyr certainly goes to heaven immediately after his death. This view is also supported by some martyr acts (→ Martyrs) of the 2nd–3rd centuries CE (e.g. *Mart. Pol.* 14.2). However, in the *Shepherd of Hermas* (→ Hermas), all Christians go to heaven immediately after death, but the martyrs sit at the right hand of Christ, while the rest are at his left (Herm. *Vis.* 3.2.1). In the *Passion of Perpetua*, this female martyr has a vision of thousands of people in heaven (*Mart. Perp.* 4.22–26) apart from martyrs (*Mart. Perp.* 13.17–19). Later, → Augustine of Hippo regards the souls of the wicked as being in Hades, where they suffer from an immaterial fire. After the general resurrection and the Last Judgment, they will be sent to Gehenna, where both their souls and bodies will be punished by eternal and material fire (Aug. *Civ.* 21.10).

The vagueness of Jewish and New Testament texts regarding the character of resurrection and its role in the future fate of believers became a matter of debate in early Christian thought, typically appearing in a polemical context. Given Paul's idea that Jesus' resurrection is an anticipation of the eschatological resurrection, its bodily character came to be closely associated with the general resurrection. Paul's claim that earthly flesh and blood are excluded from resurrection (1 Cor 15:50) was reinterpreted and developed into the idea of the "resurrection of the flesh," an expression introduced in the 2nd century CE by → Justin Martyr, which, as he argues, will follow the 1,000-year reign of Christ (Just. *Dial.* 80.5; see 1 *Apol.* 52.3). To prove his argument about bodily resurrection, he refers to Ezek 37:6–7 (Just. 1 *Apol.* 52.5). Some other works also indicate that the sins of the wicked will be punished in their flesh after the general resurrection (Herm. *Sim.* 5.7.1–4; 2 *Clem.* 9.1–5; *Barn.* 5.6–7; see also *Apoc. Pet.* 4; *Apoc. Paul* 14). The idea of the resurrection of the flesh was further developed by → Irenaeus of Lyon in the context of his thoughts on the involvement of the material world in salvation and his chiliastic picture of Christ's 1,000-year kingdom (Iren. *Haer.* 5.33–36). Tertullian also argued that the body will receive its reward or punishment along with the soul (Tert. *Res.* 14–17).

4. Later Developments

In the course of time, the picture of the otherworld reflected in the *Apocalypse of Peter* acquired a more detailed description and imagery. The *Apocalypse of Paul* (*Visio Pauli*; c. 388 CE; → Paul the Apostle), which depends on the *Apocalypse of Peter* as well as on some other earlier apocalyptic documents, became the main source in the spread of the popular ideas of heaven and hell in the western church. In this text, each soul has its guardian angel watching over it and defending it at the judgment (*Apoc. Paul* 11–12). After death, the deceased go to God to receive preliminary judgment. Then the souls of the righteous are handed over to the archangel Michael to go to heaven, while those of the sinners are handed over to the angel Tartaruchus to go to the underworld (Tartarus), there to be in torment until the general resurrection and the final judgment (*Apoc. Paul* 14–18). The heavens have further divisions within each, described in paradise-like terms (*Apoc. Paul* 19–21). Between them lies an intermediate region (Lake Acherusia) where repentant sinners are baptized by Michael so that they can join the righteous in the city of Christ (*Apoc. Paul* 22).

Further, the sinners are gathered into groups in hell, which is located in the dark region beyond the ocean (*Apoc. Paul* 31). In addition to classes of sinners similar to those in the *Apocalypse of Peter*, new classes are added in this text, such as false clergy and monastics that perverted the way of their calling (*Apoc. Paul* 36; 40). Moreover, the punishment of sinners for ethical crimes is seven times less than of those who denied the basic doctrines of Christianity (the incarnation, the resurrection, or the Eucharist; *Apoc. Paul* 41). However, this text stresses the importance of prayer for the wicked and attributes this practice to Christ himself (*Apoc. Paul* 43–44). Because of his mercy and his resurrection, he grants the sinners relief from their torments for a 24-hour period every Sunday in perpetuity.

The interest of Christians in the description of the otherworld as well as in postmortem rewards and punishments is also attested in the apocryphal literature ascribed to Ezra. The *Greek Apocalypse of Ezra*, dated from 150 to 850 CE, uses both Jewish (e.g. *4 Ezra*) and Christian sources (e.g. several NT documents; the *Syriac Apocalypse of Ezra;* Melito, *Paschal Homily*) and gives an extended picture of the afterlife. It contains a meticulous description of Tartarus with its lowest parts designed for sinners (esp. mentioning Herod in *Gk. Apoc. Ezra* 4:9–12) and various punishments according to their crimes (*Gk. Apoc. Ezra* 4:13–24; 5:1–6; 5:23–28). The righteous are rewarded in paradise in the East (*Gk. Apoc. Ezra* 1.12–15; 5.20–22). This text also speaks about the final judgment following the appearance of the → antichrist coming up from Tartarus (*Gk. Apoc. Ezra* 3.15). At the end of time, the dead will be raised up uncorrupted at the signal of a trumpet. Then the antichrist will hide himself in the deeps of the earth (*Gk. Apoc. Ezra* 4.36–37). Thereupon, the earth and the heavens along with the wicked will be burned and melted (*Gk. Apoc. Ezra* 4.38–39). Moreover, according to *Gk. Apoc. Ezra* 3.5–6, the wicked will be annihilated.

The *Vision of Ezra* (dated from the 4th to 7th cent. CE) offers an even fuller description of the underworld. The list of the sins according to which punishments are appointed in Tartarus corresponds to church teaching about almsgiving, fidelity in marriage, confession, hospitality, right instruction, and so on (*Vis. Ezra* 12–55). In contrast, the reward of the righteous in paradise, which is eternal rest and the kingdom of heaven, is granted for observing these norms (*Vis. Ezra* 64–66).

The further development of the issue of an intermediate state of the deceased and their final fate is found in the *Questions of Ezra*. This text contains the dualistic idea that the souls of the righteous and the wicked are taken by good and evil angels, respectively. According to it, there are seven heavenly levels: the lower ones are for those who are held by evil powers, while the upper are for the good. Hell is located in the third level; the throne of God is on the highest level (*Ques. Ezra* A19–21). The righteous are led into the upper atmosphere through these levels and allowed to see the throne of God, while the wicked are placed into the lower atmosphere held by evil spirits and are punished by demons and Satan (*Ques. Ezra* A31–33; B 12). At the end of time, at Gabriel's trumpet blast, the dead will be resurrected in their bodies and judged at Christ's second coming (*Ques. Ezra* B11–14).

Another spectacular description of the underworld is attested in the fictive *Acts of Pilate* (→ Pilate) containing the *Gospel of Nicodemus* (4th–6th cent. CE). The second part of this work, attributed to Nicodemus from the Gospel of John (3:1–15; 19:39), contains an account of Christ's descent into Hades prior to his resurrection and reflects earlier beliefs (see Acts 2:31; Eph 4:9; Tert. *An.* 55.1–2). In this story, the underworld (Hades) is seen as the abode of all the dead. Death, Hades, and Satan have been defeated. Satan has been bound in chains and cast into Tartarus (*Acts Pil.* 6–8). Thereafter, Jesus led Adam (→ Adam and Eve) by the hand from Hades (see the *Gk. Apoc. Ezra* 7.2) and delivered all the righteous to the archangel Michael to settle them in paradise, where Enoch, → Elijah, and the repentant criminal (see Luke 23:40–43) met them (*Acts Pil.* 9–10). Various details of this story were later visualized in medieval artworks, including the eastern iconography of Christ's descent to hell. Moreover, the picture of the otherworld with its division into several regions assigned to the different categories of the righteous and the wicked that the texts discussed above depict affected many medieval descriptions of heaven and hell, including such a prominent work as Dante Alighieri's *Divine Comedy*.

Further, although the corporeal character of the eschatological resurrection had more or less become the standard view from the 2nd century CE, it had not always been perceived as the resurrection of the physical body. Thus, linking resurrection to the Eucharist, the gnostic *Gospel of Philip* (3rd cent. CE; → Philip the Apostle) argues that the resurrected flesh and blood are not earthly but those of Jesus, which are associated with *logos* and the Spirit. The resurrected body is indeed connected with that of Jesus, who had been raised in the true spiritual flesh (*Gos. Phil.* 23). → Origen, following Paul's thought in 1 Cor 15:36–44, confirms that the body has to be transformed in resurrection because it is unworthy of God to raise untransformed matter. Accordingly, God transfigures the nature of the body and lifts humans up above nature, thus making them more divine in resurrection (Or. *Cels.* 5.22–23). In the even later writings of Augustine, the spiritual bodies of the righteous are different from those of the wicked because for the former, it is flesh that is joined to spirit, while for the latter it remained flesh, which will suffer from eternal fire (Aug. *Civ.* 21.9–10; 22.21).

The belief in the future eschatological judgment and resurrection found its place in the Nicene Creed (325 CE), while that of Christ's descent into Hell and of the resurrection of the flesh had been included in the Apostles' Creed (→ Apostle). However, the debates about the activity or inactivity of the souls in their intermediate state between death and the eschatological resurrection continued unabated. These debates were provoked by the development of the cult of the saints and of intercession for the dead. While it seems that Irenaeus saw the souls of the dead as dwelling in a certain allotted invisible place where they remain inactive and await their future resurrection (Iren. *Haer.* 5.31.2), Eustratius of Constantinople, writing around 582 CE, argued in his *On the State of the Souls* that the souls of the deceased retain their activity and that this feature enables the souls of the saints to intercede on behalf of the living and to perform miracles. In contrast, the souls of the sinners are also active in hell, where they experience remorse. According to this view, the souls of those who are neither saints nor unrepentant sinners also remain active. The western church resolved this problem by accepting the doctrine of purgatory at the Second Council of Lyons (1274 CE).

The eastern church also *de facto* assumed the post-mortem activity of souls, although their condition was not always certain (Dal Santo, 2009, 45).

Historiography

The study of early Christian views on the afterlife has always been a subject of particular scholarly interest. In contrast to the idea (held, e.g., by O. Cullmann) that the Christian view of the afterlife as well as the Jewish one (the resurrection of the body) has to be clearly distinguished from the pagan view (the immortality of the soul), modern scholarship emphasizes the great diversity of views of the hereafter in pagan, Jewish, and early Christian documents. In this regard, mention must first be made of the works of G.W.E. Nickelsburg (1972; 2006), G. Stemberger (1972), H.C.C. Cavallin (1974), and P. Figueras (2019), which present a multifaceted picture of the diversity of Jewish beliefs shared by early Christianity. Furthermore, A.E. Bernstein (1993) explores afterlife issues focusing on the origins of the idea of hell as far back as ancient Mediterranean views and then into early Christianity up until Augustine. A.F. Segal (2004) also examines the origins and the history of the development of the beliefs in afterlife and their interrelations, starting from Egypt, Mesopotamia, and Canaan, then moving to Greece and Rome, → Judaism and early Christianity, and finally to Islam. In his opinion, the various views on afterlife reflect the social identity of the religious communities.

C. Walker Bynum (1995) investigates the idea of the resurrection of the body in ancient and medieval western culture (the late 2nd–14th cents.) in the context of its social, cultural, and religious background, including the cult of saints, burial practices, and the visualization of afterlife issues in Christian art. She argues that modern attitudes toward the body, personal identity, and individuality are affected by the discussions of that period. In addition, C. Setzer makes an important contribution to the development of modern research about the idea of the resurrection of the body in Jewish and early Christian circles (Setzer, 2004). This idea has also been explored in the study of O. Lehtipuu (2015), who demonstrates that the issue of the resurrection of the dead was approached in different ways in early

Christianity. She shows that the belief in resurrection was used as both an identity marker and as a sign of inclusion in the community.

J. Clark-Soles (2006) discusses the questions of death and afterlife in the New Testament texts (mainly in Paul's writings, Matthew, John, and 1–2 Peter) and indicates that although they speak about resurrection, each author depicts the afterlife with his own unique language and imagery. However, J. Clark-Soles does not discuss the diversity of the views on afterlife in Luke–Acts, this gap has been filled by O. Lehtipuu's (2007) and A. Somov's (2017) integrated studies of Luke's afterlife ideas and imagery.

Analyzing the early Christian beliefs in the resurrection of the flesh D.Ø. Endsjø (2009) investigates the views of Greco-Roman paganism and argues that especially in popular circles, it often understood immortality as involving both body and soul, that is, it regarded human nature as a psychosomatic unity. The development and reception of the idea of physical incorruptibility in Christianity contributed to the success of this religion among the pagans.

Bibliography

Bernstein, A.E., *The Formation of Hell: Death and Retribution in the Ancient and Early Christian Worlds*, London, 1993.

Bynum, C.W., *The Resurrection of the Body in Western Christianity: 200–1336*, New York, 1995.

Cavallin, H.C.C., *Life after Death: Paul's Argument for the Resurrection of the Dead in 1 Cor 15*, part 1: *An Enquiry into the Jewish Background*, CB: New Testament Series, Lund, 1974.

Charlesworth, J.H., ed., *The Old Testament Pseudepigrapha*, 2 vols., ABRL, New York, 1983, 1985.

Clark-Soles, J., *Death and the Afterlife in the New Testament*, New York, 2006.

Cullmann, O., *Immortality of the Soul or Resurrection of the Dead? The Witness of the New Testament*, London, 1958.

Dal Santo, M.J., "Philosophy, Hagiology and the Early Byzantine Origins of Purgatory," in: P. Clarke & T. Claydon, eds., *The Church, The Afterlife and the Fate of the Soul*, SCH 45, Suffolk, 2009, 41–51.

Endsjø, D.Ø., *Greek Resurrection Beliefs and the Success of Christianity*, New York, 2009.

Figueras, P., *Death and Afterlife in Ancient Jewish and Christian Literature*, Piscataway, 2019.

Lehtipuu, O., *The Afterlife Imagery in Luke's Story of the Rich Man and Lazarus*, NovTSup 123, Leiden, 2007.

Lehtipuu, O., *Debates over the Resurrection of the Dead: Constructing Early Christian Identity*, OECS, Oxford, 2015.

Nickelsburg, G.W.E., *Resurrection, Immortality, and Eternal Life in Intertestamental Judaism*, HThS 26, Cambridge MA, 1972.

Nickelsburg, G.W.E., "Resurrection: Early Judaism and Christianity," in: D.N. Freedman, ed., *ABD*, 6 vols., vol. I, 1992, 684–691.

Nickelsburg, G.W.E., *Resurrection, Immortality, and Eternal Life in Intertestamental Judaism and Early Christianity*, HThS 56, Cambridge MA, 2006.

Fletcher-Louis, C.H.T., *Luke–Acts: Angels, Christology and Soteriology*, Tübingen, 1997.

Holleman, J., *Resurrection and Parousia: A Traditio-Historical Study of Paul's Eschatology in 1 Cor. 15:20–23*, Leiden, 1996.

Perkins, P., *Resurrection: New Testament Witness and Contemporary Reflection*, Garden City, 1984.

Segal, A.F., *Life After Death: A History of the Afterlife in the Religions of the West*, New York, 2004.

Setzer, C., *Resurrection of the Body in Early Judaism and Early Christianity: Doctrine, Community, and Self-Definition*, Leiden, 2004.

Somov, A., *Representations of the Afterlife in Luke–Acts*, LNTS 556, London, 2017.

Somov, A., & V. Voinov, "Translating 'Abraham's Bosom' (Luke 16:22–23) as a Key Metaphor in the Overall Composition of the Parable of the Rich Man and Lazarus," *CBQ* 79/4, 2017, 615–633.

Stemberger, G., *Der Leib der Auferstehung*, Rome, 1972.

ALEXEY B. SOMOV

Agape

In what follows some of the main lines of early Christian thought will be sketched, from the Palestinian setting of Jesus to the western Mediterranean one of Augustine of Hippo. This will follow an order for which the term "development" is not quite right. Given that the fathers of the 4th and 5th centuries CE were, not least in their consideration of the › Trinity and of the Christian life, very much *biblical* theologians, it should not come as a surprise to see strong continuities with the 1st-century CE expressions, albeit with forceful variations.

"Apart from the Great Commandment Jesus spoke nowhere explicitly about loving God" (Schnackenburg, 1965, 98). Love of God was inseparable from brotherly love; it was perhaps even defined by it, yet without exhausting it completely. For when Jesus speaks about serving God or Mammon in Matt 6:24, it is not directly about other people, but about trusting God the Father enough to love him

despite anxieties, so as to be free to serve him while resisting the → devil. Nevertheless the occurrences of *agape* or its cognates emphasize the "horizontal" aspect of love. Of course classical writers like Seneca could also write (Sen. *Ben.* 6.26.1), "If you want to imitate the gods, do favors even to the ungrateful; for the sun rises even over the wicked and the sea is open to the pirates." R. Hillel had the negative form of Jesus' Golden Rule (Matt 7:12; *b. Šabb.* 31a) as a summary of Torah, to lead the learner into it. Summaries of Torah with respect to love of God and neighbor are frequent (Philo *Spec.* 2.63; *Let. Aris.* 131; *Sifra Lev* 19.18): "love of neighbor" is already a "great comprehensive principle" in the Torah.

1. Gospels

New Testament Christology can be said to have "love" at its heart from early on: ἀγαπητὸς υἱός (Mark 1:11; see John 3:16 "only son").

> What is new is that Jesus provides a new motive and power for the love command [...] a response to how God is bringing in his reign through his deeds and words. (Burridge, 2007, 327)

One might want to add that Jesus also re-imagines love as something that emerges out of darkness. As V. Furnish (1973, 148) insisted, the Johannine love command does not exclude love for the other who is outside the community, and the theology as a whole is inclusive, although not indulgently so. In Luke 10:25–37, the Samaritan who disregarded the lines of conflict is the neighbor by his deeds, although possibly also by observing the Torah (→ Law/Decalogue/Torah) he is defined by loving the Jew as neighbor – and yet love for *enemy* is not spelled out in the New Testament much beyond a handful of texts (Sauer, 1985). The accent then is very much on loving the neighbor, to be understood as including "the other," and even the enemy.

If Jesus' main message was "the kingdom of God" inaugurated in his own person, in what sense then was *agape* part of some intensified interim ethics of preparation until his return? Love of God therefore can be viewed as a basis for radical love of others:

> It alone makes possible the self-conquest from which the most secret and powerful acts of

love spring. Only this love grounded in God, becomes *agape*, which surpasses every natural *eros* [...] in this Christian *agape* the urge towards union has quite receded in favor of pure benevolence and mercy. (Schnackenburg, 1965, 108)

It is something deeply felt in order to be active: more than "moved deep down" to the fore (Collange, 1980, 130). In this case it is not the perfection of the self-contained, and in Luke 6:36 the original reading is "merciful" since the Hebrew Bible calls God that, but never "perfect." Also at Matt 5:20 perfection is defined as "mercy" in terms of its radical and interior nature.

Covenantal theology plays a part here. One might even detect an echo of Deuteronomy and Jer 31/Ezek 36 in Jesus' farewell discourses (John 13:31–17:26), even though there is no direct citation of Deut 6:4 ("loving the Lord thy God") in John (Beutler, 1986). In John 15 love has a familial and as such egalitarian character. For Jesus, → love is not so much about simply obeying the command, but it is understanding and enacting the content of the love command through self-giving. The New Testament love commandment is something both old and new. The Fourth Gospel does not talk of human love for God, but makes the "horizontal," interhuman love warmly communitarian, even as Lev 19:18 ("love your neighbor as yourself") becomes realized in 1 John 2:7–8, which presupposes not something cozy, but a community as a place of the reconciliation of enemies and rivals. Behind that, both Hebrew Bible and New Testament passages presuppose the initiating love in action of the covenantal God. It is the Septuagint (→ Bible) usage of *agape*, not least in the later books, that offered a platform to its wide usage in the New Testament. This gets repeated in Matt 19:19, but the verb is also used to command love for God (Matt 22:37). Sinners (those turned away from God?) tend to love those who love them (Luke 6:32). Those who love enemies and the unloved have some "grace." Love does seem to have force of action rather than sentiment at its core, without the New Testament seeing these two things as mutually exclusive.

2. Pauline Letters

In the early church's Hellenistic context, it would seem that *agape* plays a role that comes second in order, this time to Christian freedom, in the light of → *parousia* expectation and faith. Compared with the Synoptic Gospels, love is much more dominant a theme in the Epistles, whatever verbal form is used: love is not a prisoner of language (Collange, 1980, 132). Jesus' self-giving → death "for us" is arguably also a Hellenistic notion. Paul's "love" is less forceful than Jesus' direct encounter, which contains conflict. Paul (→ Paul the Apostle) is more communitarian and constructively positive. If love was embodied in the Galilean, then it was at Antioch that Christian ἀγάπη became a world-transforming community project (Collange, 1980, 160–162; see Furnish, 1973, 96–102). Paul's conviction that love fulfills Torah (Gal 5:14: the whole law, meaning Torah, is fulfilled in "love thy neighbor") shows how closely connected law and love are. And Gal 6:2, that carrying another's burdens means fulfilling "the law of Christ," indicates that an ethical system that is much more than a list of "do's and don't's" (see Dunn, 2006, 631–658). Paul is best understood in his context of Greek-speaking Jewish piety, given that in Tobit truth, justice, and compassion are the hermeneutical lenses for the Torah (Tob 1:3; 14:9; 14:11; Schreiber, 2012) Through love Christians fulfill and overcome the creditor-debtor identities (Schreiber, 2012, 110n33). In other words, love is a constant obligation, not a one-off freeing one from debt. This should not promote a constant anxiety or Sisyphean despair, but a joyful sense that even Christ's work did not mean that the law was thenceforth redundant (Rom 10:2). "To fulfill" does not mean to supersede, replace, or fulfill completely. Likewise it is hardly a Jewish Paul, much less the Paul of his letters, who "reduces Torah to Greek-Roman thought and leaves Jewish behind" (Schnelle, 2003, 273) or lifts the law's demands by means of the law, in order to leave "love" standing (see Wolter, 2001). "Distinctively Pauline is the emphasis on love of neighbor according to Lev 19:18 as fulfilment of the (entire) Torah" (Schreiber, 2012, 116).

Rom 8:28 seems to indicate that those who love God are also those who are called: these things stand in apposition rather than in a relationship of cause and effect, although verse 37 does seem to give priority to the love of Christ. It would not be too inaccurate here to speak of moral identity formation. Rom 13:8–13 (along with Mark 12:29f.) is indebted to and identifies love with "walking in the light," serving the neighbor as a spirit that does not do less than the Ten Commandments, but includes them, yet wants more of the best for others. *Agape* is also quite dominant in 1 and 2 Corinthians and in Ephesians, where it concerns building up and unifying (see the five occurrences in Rom 12–15 and three in 1 Cor 16). It stands at the summit of that Pauline letter that deals with community tensions and the question of spiritual hierarchies within the church. The core of the ethic of mutual love in Philippians seems formed by the Christological kenosis principle of Phil 2:6.

3. New Testament Ethic of Love

One concern is that in some of the later ("deuteropauline") writings of the New Testament, love has been "relegated" to being one virtue among others: still important, but not central, compared with εὐσέβεια (Schrage, 1989, 366). Yet already it had left its mark by being an outward-looking eschatological principle of challenge to overly tight natural ties. In Paul it could be poured out in hearts; with John it was predicated of God himself. These convictions – especially that love is divine and powerful – set the tone for reception in the centuries immediately following.

It should be noted that in an influential work, R. Hays, with more than a nod to S. Hauerwas (1981), is dismissive of love as a central component for New Testament ethics, preferring categories of community, cross, and new creation as more fundamental. He regards Mark 12:28–24 as an isolated element in that Gospel.

> For Mark, however, the Torah has been eclipsed by the coming of Jesus; consequently, the call of Christian discipleship cannot be understood simply in terms of continuity with the commandment of the Law, even the greatest ones. Nowhere in Mark's Gospel does Jesus teach or command his disciples to love; discipleship is defined not by love but by taking up the cross and following Jesus. (Hays, 1996, 200)

Similarly, in Hebrews and Revelation it is about faithful endurance, and nowhere in Acts does "love" appear: "Acts is a book not about love but about power" (Hays, 1996, 201). However, given that any treatment of *agape* should not confine itself to occurrences of the word "*agape*," then love in action of course does seem to be the motor of community living in Acts, and to deny love its place at the heart of Pauline and Johannine ethics would be perverse. R. Hays' point is that the → cross, or Jesus laying down his life for others, defines love (see 1 John 3:16).

> The ethic of the Gospel is not a love ethic, but it is an ethic of adherence to this man Jesus as he has bound our destiny to his, as he makes the story of our life his story. As an ethic of love the Gospels would be an ethic at our disposal, since we would fill in the context of love by our wishes. (Hauerwas, 1981, 115)

One may concur with the particularism of R. Hays, who insists on Christ defining love and not vice versa, yet surely one's working definition of Christ needs no less care, not to be too restrictive. R. Hays seems happier to see love as the embodiment of nonviolence as a New Testament theme (Hays, 1996, 328), presumably because it is less prone to being colonized by sentimentality. Love for enemies is a general ethical principle, since τέλειος is held up as a possibility (Matt 5:44–45), given the power of the Lord – although this is of course not explicit in Matthew (see above for a plausible version of the τέλειος – ἀγάπη connection as "mercy"). One might note that the *agape* principle reminds Christians, as Paul would in Rom 14:17, that "the kingdom of God is" not about religious gatherings but about lifestyle. As T. Söding explains (1995, 290), it concerns a belief in the transcendental aspect (→ Transcendence) of humanity that drives benevolence in ἀγάπη, with the latter as organizing center and critical principle of the whole realm of ethics. Of course ἀγάπη itself is defined by Christ's death in the light of his resurrection and spirit whose power helps apply the concrete to the concrete now (Söding, 1995, 273). Love is the outworking of faith and hope: it is about love for other people (Söding, 1992, 140). All three "remain" in contrast to the gifts. Yet the "never fails" of verse 8 and "remains" need to be understood in terms of the Hebrew Bible concept of "everlasting" and God's ceaseless faithfulness, so that it is an eschatological power poured into hearts (Rom 5:5). Paul is contrasting the other-centeredness of love with the self-expression of gifts (Schrage, 1999, 100–105). In Rom 15:30 it is *agape of the spirit*, whereas in 1 Cor 13 it has no such association, nor does Paul relate it to the fulfilling of the Law, nor Christ nor God (Wischmeyer, 1981, 229–233). Nevertheless on closer inspection, verses 4–7 contain an implicit Christology, and the description of love as "working no evil" in Rom 13:10 bears a close connection with "Christlike virtue" as detailed in 1 Cor 13:4–7, which is arguably fuller and more universal than "Christian life," appealing also to pagan and Jews.

4. *Agape* Meals

If a practice sets the tone for an ethical and theological concept, then in the case of *agape* that was the practice of communal meals, which seemed related to Jesus' instructions in Luke 22:14–23 and parallels. Any idea that in the North Africa of → Tertullian *agape* was separate from the → Eucharist (Georges, 2013) should be disregarded. Likewise Tertullian was clear that the meal was part of a liturgy, and vice versa.

> Our dinner shows its purpose by its name: it is called what among the Greeks means affection (*dilectio*) [...] We do not recline until we have first tasted of prayer to God. So much is eaten as satisfies hunger; as much drunk as is fitting for the pure.
>
> Appetite is satisfied to the extent appropriate for those who are mindful that they have to worship God even at night; speech, as for those who know the Master is listening. After washing of hands, and lights, each is invited into the middle to sing to God as able, from knowledge of sacred writings or from their own mind; thus it can be tested how much has been drunk. Prayer again closes the feast. (Tert. *Apol.* 39.16–18)

By the time of → Cyprian of Carthage, a move to morning sacrifice to celebrate the resurrection (→ Resurrection) at a nonbanquet, nonprivate place had emerged (McGowan, 2004). So, "by the first quarter of the second century onwards at the latest, *agape* is a usual appellation for the eucharistic meal" (Tert. *Apol.* 39.2; see Jude 12; see Alikin, 2010, 142). But by the mid-3rd century CE, this seemed to be on the way out.

5. *Agape* in Christian Ethics After the New Testament

Justin Martyr seems to have ruled out any kinship between God and the → soul that would be necessary for a soul to love and know God. However, the close relationship between knowing and loving is accepted by → Justin Martyr. Since it is something that has been brought into being, the soul is not naturally akin to the eternal God; instead it must keep itself virtuous and not have fallen into "bestial" vice for there to be knowing and loving of God. In Justin's *Dialogue* love seems defined as something on the way to possession of full knowing, "especially when it has been set free from the body, and being apart by itself, it gets possession of that which it was wont continually and wholly to love" (Just. *Dial.* 4). There is something of the same spirit in the famous passage of Tertullian (*Apol.* 39.7):

> But it is mainly the deeds of a love so noble that lead many to put a brand upon us. *See*, they say, *how they love one another*, for themselves are animated by mutual hatred; how they are ready even to die for one another, for they themselves will sooner put to death.

Likewise with → Irenaeus of Lyon (*Haer.* 4.33.9), who asserts that that the church shows love to God the Father by sending him martyrs. Love is the active outworking of faith.

A. Nygren argued that despite De Faye's presentation of him, → Clement of Alexandria had no place for *agape*, as in Clem. *Strom.* 7.10.55–57: "to faith knowledge [shall be given]; and to knowledge, love and to love the possession." Even if *agape* is employed as a motor or a driver of ethical life, what Clement really means in Clem. *Paed.* 1.3.7–8 is *eros* toward "the Savior [who] fulfils much the same function as the beauty of the sensible world in Platonism." Even if that is true, it is only one side of the story. In Clem. *Quis div.* 28, Clement's interpretation of Luke 10:27–29 starts by affirming that loving one's neighbor as oneself is one thing, but God is to be loved *more* than oneself: for that is the implication of the exact language of the love command – as well as seeing Christ as the neighbor means (*Quis div.* 33), seeing the community as his body, and doing practical service for the weak, making friends with them with God's love and practical gifts, such that in *Quis div.* 38 he can comment on 1 Cor 13:13 for those who have let generous love into their souls: "but love enters together with us into fullness, and increases the more when the things that are perfect are given."

Origen could interpret 1 Cor 13:4 "Love never fails" in terms of the Hebrew Bible text that calls love a consuming fire (Song 8:7), since it bears all things (PG 87.2.1744; see the fuller Latin translation by Rufinus in GCS 33.74.3; 190.24). → Origen made sure to call *agape* the chief of the virtues, since it was what the *logos* gifted to the soul of Jesus (GCS 33.165). Origen saw the promise of John 14:23 as referring to that soul first and paradigmatically as the place of indwelling love, the condition for entry to a "meal" of peace, purity, and other virtues. It suited him to speak of the Song of Songs' message as epithalamic: love leads upward to higher things (see Plato *Symp.* 210–211), from the image to the likeness, which would seem to allow for a relationship of *eros* (love of likeness). However, as with Justin, this "erotic" love of God by creatures is not something given in created nature, but presupposes prior, divine action. It is not just that *eros* can have fleshly connotations (Or. *Comm. Cant.* 2.20, prologue) such that the Bible avoids it in favor of *agape*; it is also the case that *agape* (Lat. *caritas*) means divine love, which might also be human. For the church it seems that *agape* starts the process by seeking the unlovely and making "her" lovely, as in Song 1:7: "I am black but beautiful." As J.C.M. van Winden (1997, 297) observes, → Plotinus taught an ἔρως προνοητικός, which provokes an ἔρως ἐπιστρεπτικός, returning to Νοῦς (Plot. *Enn.* 6.8.(39].15.1). When it comes to the order of Christian salvation, Origen, writing on Romans (Book 4.4) asserts that hope advances the work that faith starts, yet it is love that completes (see GCS 33.112; also Or. *Hom. Cant.* 2; GCS 33.52). This love expands the → kingdom of God beyond where faith and hope would take it. So it is characteristic of the Alexandrian scheme to see *agape* as beginning things with God's initiative of the "crucified *eros*" (Origen, then Dionysius echoing Ign.

Rom. 7.2, in his *Homilies on Ezekiel*; GCS 33.319), even as Christ begins the upward ascent to God. God is called "lover of men," with the descent of divine *agape* as means to an end, as in Athan. *Inc.* 9 and 12, where it is God's φιλανθρωπία ἀγαθότης that is at work, with something like divine *eros* taking over in the ascent of humanity to God. Such descending love recognizes the created goodness but intends restoration where there is corruption. Origen and → Gregory of Nyssa used φιλανθρωπία – a flame that contrary to nature sinks downward, as Gregory put it (Greg. Nyss. *Or. catech. magna* 24). In Nyssa's *Commentary on the Song*, at Homily 5 (860A *belos tes agapes*) and at Homily 13 (1048C), there is *belos tou erôtos*, which shows a certain amount of interchangeability of terms.

> Thus *agape* means for him fundamentally love in the sense of desire; constitutive of it is its connection with the Beautiful and its ceaseless effort to win this for itself. (Nygren, 1953, 437)

True, God loves the beautiful, and the latter responds. Gregory seems to have been quite aware of the differences between *agape* and *eros*, yet he was happy to use the former both for God's love for humans and their response. One notes that for Gregory, participation is not preexistent to *agape*, as was the case with the Platonic *eros*. Freedom from necessity in Christian love was important for Nyssa, and one might think of *eros* as intensification of *agape*, even its ecstatic dimension (Maspero, 2010, 461; see Daniélou, 1944, 206). In his *De anima et resurrectione*, divine life is seen as energized through agape (PG 46.96.C). In God *eros* is the freely chosen passion between the divine persons. "One could then say, at the end, that the relationship between ἀγάπη and ἐρῶς is analogous to that between ζωή and βίος. The first term is more general than the second, can be applied to God, an for this very reason, becomes the foundation of the value of the second term, which can be understood only through the first" (Maspero, 2010, 265).

The Origenian priority of love among the virtues echoed in → John Chrysostom (Chrys. *Pent.* 2.3; PG 50.468, with reference to Rom 13:10), as he comments that love is the fullness of the law and the root, source, and mother of all goods, and that it enables us to enjoy the happiness of others as our own – although John then goes on to explain love as the removal and absence of strife. In his homily on Rom 16, Chrysostom sees how much Paul valued the nexus between love for God and love for neighbor. → Theodoret of Cyrrhus' *Treatise on Agape* stands as his conclusion to his *Historia religiosa*. It is *agape* that drives ascetical movements, he argues; a devoted and passionate *ascesis* is presented as the successor to martyrdom. The pain of schism was the context for an insistence on *agape*, a theme he shared with Augustine.

For Didymus the Blind (Heinrichs, 1968, vol. II, 134), Paul in 1 Cor. 13:4ff. is not talking about love itself, but about the one who has it: "Love does not [...]" For a virtue cannot be an agent, he argues. The righteous are the ones who love. Diadochus of Photike wrote that to know God means love (Diad. *Perf.*, ch. 14). Ardor and union, or cleaving (*kollesis*), need to be continual, and fixing the right direction matters, so as to be turned toward God (see Max. *Car.* 2.48), without any "Messalian" excess of intense emotion. Similarly, perfection as resemblance to God, with the restoring of the divine image as goal (Eva. Pon. *Prak.* 1.61), takes place without change of nature, but by love for God and obedience. Severian of Gabala (d. c. 420 CE; Staab, 1984, 266) interpreted 1 Cor. 13:8's "never fails" to mean "never slides into sin." Mercy is one thing and love another: love is *not* the same thing as giving all to the poor or showing a martyr's devotion to God. It is rather the intention that goes with these acts. Heartfelt, intentional, and sober action comes to the fore even in the usage in "spiritualizing" Christian circles around 400 CE.

6. Augustine of Hippo

Such is the significance of → Augustine of Hippo for western Christian thought that he deserves special treatment. In Aug. *Civ.* 15.22 he wrote,

> But if the Creator is truly loved, that is, if he himself is loved and not another thing in his stead, he cannot be evilly loved; for love itself is to be ordinately loved, because we do well to love that which, when we love it, makes us live well and virtuously. So that it seems to me that it is a brief but true definition of virtue to say, it is the order of love; and on this account, in the Canticles, the bride of Christ, the city of God,

> sings, *Order love within me.* [Song 2:4] This is how things are ordered, to the extent that love cannot be selfish, but "bows in obedient conformity to the order he finds. (O'Donovan, 1979, 14)

One can love wrongly, especially in "loving oneself" (*amor sui*). What matters is that which qualifies or is the target of *amor* or *dilectio*.

> Hence the love that is bent on obtaining the object of its love is desire [*cupiditas*], while the love that possesses and enjoys its object is joy [*laetitia*]; the love that avoids what confronts it is fear [*timor*], and the love that feels it when it strikes is grief [*tristitia*]. Accordingly, these emotions are bad if the love [*amor*] is bad, and good if it is good. (Aug. *Civ.* 14.7)

Hence love is more than just feeling but is intentional, yet pre-moral (good and bad). Love means a disposition toward something other. In Aug. *Grat. Chr.* 1.19, commenting on 1 Tim 6:10, Augustine writes that whereas *cupiditas* is the root of all bad things, *caritas* is the root of all good. *Caritas*, as the Latin form of *agape*, is always good, for *caritas* seems to begin in faith, which makes one pure in heart, even before there is knowing (Aug. *Trin.* 8.6). Desire to know a thing leads the mind toward that which is already the expression of mind, that is, a word. Love is that which moves outward with energy and allows a fuller kind of knowledge of things and people. It is its own reward (Aug. *Enarrat. Ps.* 149.4). Even Christ did not create the world for the sake of any reward (Aug. *Serm.* 340.1).

If → Pelagius argued, on the basis of 1 Cor 13:8, that only "love" (*caritas*) would remain in the future, since it belongs to heaven and so keeps growing into infinity when it arrives there (not unlike Clem. *Quis div.* 38.3; GCS 117.184f.), Augustine was more nuanced. In *Trin.* 14.2.4 he does admit that faith will once be no more, yet thinks that in this life love somehow includes faith and hope in it, analogously to how the work of each Trinitarian person (→ Trinity) included the other (Aug. *Tract. ep. Jo.* 83.3; see Schrage, 1999, 306). Yet this does not mean that anything other than love will survive in the life to come. For Augustine, love is not so much desire as it is power, not so much aiming toward something as keeping all exalted things exalted. It is even the power to lift the soul, through "two wings of love" (*duas alas caritatis*), that is, love of God and neighbor (*Enarrat. Ps.* 148.5) These two get the soul off the ground, where "feet" would keep it down (see Plot. *Enn.* 1.6.8; Dideberg, 1994, 298). That love had for Augustine primarily a divine character such that its presence in a created soul was a gift, can be seen in *Trin.* 15.17: the → Holy Spirit is first and "foremost" (*principaliter*) the gift of *caritas*, the spirit of their mutual love, whether Father and Son, God and saint, self and other. The operation of charity means that there is no living out the ethical life or law without radical grace. Rom 5:5 is one of the most crucial verses in Augustine's thought. At ground level this meant, the cardinal virtues were subsumed under love. Virtue consists in nothing else but in loving what is worthy of love (see 1 Tim 1:5). "Thus the end of every commandment is charity, that is, every commandment relates to charity" (Aug. *Enchir.* 121). Here one can see that what was distinctive in Augustine's treatment of "love" was the love of God for his own sake as loving God back (*redamare*), for even in loving one's neighbor one loved God through loving the one created in his image (Aug. *Ep.* 10.9.10; Maraval, 1991). Love for the image of God is joined to the other reason given: love because oneself is already loved by God in Christ (*Trin.* 8.8.12; *Tract. ep. Jo.* 7.10) Yet of course that love comes first from God. If Didymus had called it a gift of grace from the triune God (Didi. *Spir.* 16), Augustine would refer it to the Holy Spirit (Aug. *Serm.* 265, ch. 9.10). Love is so strong that it can change a nature: love kills what has been there before in order to change us (*Enarrat. Ps.* 121; CSEL 95.3); it is a desire that manifests human vocation toward God, as a gift of God that sweeps a person up (Bochet, 1982, 403).

The famous distinction between "enjoyment" and "use" was spelled out:

> I mean by charity that affection of the mind which aims at the enjoyment [*frui*] of God for his own sake and then enjoyment of one's self and the neighbor for God's sake. (Aug. *Doctr. chr.* 3.10; Forrell, 1979, 167)

The "use/enjoyment" (*uti/frui*) distinction is not adequate philosophically, but it would be wrong to call Augustine "corrupter of Christian morality," as did K. Holl in the 1930s (Forrell, 1979, 212n90). *Agape* is "fitted on to the framework of *eros*," yet surely *agape*

with its self-humbling God breaks and remakes *eros* (see Aug. *Conf.* 7.20.26). A. Nygren (1953, 553) was unconvinced:

> Love to neighbor thus occupies an insecure position in Augustine: in principle there is no place for it in his scheme of love, yet the influence of the New Testament compels him to include it.

All love is about our loving God, and, A. Nygren complained, it is hard to find a place within this scheme for God's *agape*, that is, God's spontaneous, unmotivated love. Augustine was just like Origen in identifying *eros* with *agape*, or in Latin terms, *amor* with *caritas*. According to A. Nygren's understanding, there could be nothing "given" in creation for grace to build on. But, contra A. Nygren, it is not a zero-sum game, in which humans lose and God wins. One loves once one knows one is loved and longs to be loved (O'Donovan, 1979, 125), such that it is not simply that we love because God first loved us, but also because we know this, as a revealed truth. Love for "neighbor" has become love for "everyman," as an advance of the New Testament on Leviticus, yet building on it, stretching it. One starts with loving one's own, but there is a pressure that is centrifugal, seeking the best for the enemy. (Aug. *Enarrat. Ps.* 25.[2].2). To be truly neighbor love, it must be directed to God, even as one directs oneself to that happiness in so doing (O'Donovan, 1979, 120). Self-love as contemplation leads to self-knowledge, patterned on the Trinity. One loves oneself properly only in loving God strongly (*Trin.* 8.6.9), with the possibility given by the converse suggested by Ps 10:6: to love injustice is to hate oneself.

Proper self-love leads to divine love. It is not the selfish *amor sui*, but the healthy working of the human mind. Neither self and other nor God and neighbor are in competition where love is concerned (Canning, 1993, 12). In orienting the neighbor toward God, one is hardly using him in a selfish way. In the space between neighbor and God as focus, there is less chance for worldly considerations. Love for one's neighbor should be that which stands in relation to our amount of self-love (Canning, 1993, 165), but both are to be checked by love for God. When it comes to love, one starts with God in theory and the neighbor in practice. Aug. *Civ.* 19.3 tells its readers that citizens are to become friends. In its motivation and outworking, the ecclesial context of believers (and Augustine himself) contributes greatly.

The importance of the Donatist (→ Donatism/Donatists) schism for his thinking should not be underestimated (Canning, 1993). In this long-running crisis, Augustine prayed for the *dilectio* of God to bind the church. However, Cyprian in the 250s CE had already spoken of ecclesial concord as founded in love and not just in believing alike: it was a love not of hypocritical smiles (Rom 12:9), but, as → Basil of Caesarea put it in *Ep.* 150 and *Hom.* 1 on Ps 14, it was action of Acts 4:32 quality, with Pseudo-John Chrysostomos (*Perf.* 2; PG 56.281) describing that love as a force (Bori, 1974, 105, 110). Thinking a little less positively, Augustine considered that life was made tolerable by community. "Mutual fraternal love, as it was, for instance, explicitly expressed in the Rule of Saint Augustine under the main idea 'with one heart and one soul' – a quotation from Acts 4:32, served the spiritual cohesion of the monastic community and, apart from this definitely also served the realization and the verification of exterior uniformity" (Melville, 2011, x) – similarly the Rule of Saint Benedict (4.1–2). Both those monastic rules were influenced by the transmission of the model in Acts 2 and 4 via the eastern fathers and then through Augustine. "This new social life, which is grounded in Christ, is defined by mutual love (*diligere invicem*), which replaces mutual dependence" (Arendt, 1998, 108, on *The City of God*): the common life is that of equals (Aug. *Enarrat.* 32.31). Yet it is also outward looking: "Extend your love [*caritas*] over the whole earth if you will love Christ [...] Pass beyond them and reach the stage of loving your enemies" (Aug. *Tract. ep. Jo.* 10.8.4; Arendt 1998, 107).

O. O'Donovan sums up how Augustine by aligning self-love and love of God was beginning to overcome the duality of these two things, as Thomas Aquinas would do in a much fuller way. Yet paradoxically this meant less mystical intensity since it is not a case of two distinct spheres of being or agencies, which might then come to absorb each other. There is less of a sense of a distinct self that might then choose to identify, even fuse, itself with God.

A true self-love, a self-love based on true self-knowledge, must coincide with love-of-God because it involves a love of the whole of which self is understood to be a part, the love of Being itself instead of love restricted to the self's artificially individuated being. (O'Donovan, 1979, 146–147)

Of course that comes only when love is perfect. Love is not part of human created being as things stand, but they are somehow "wired" for it.

Historiography

The modern study of C. Spicq (ET: 1963–1966) stuck very much with the biblical material as did the generous sections in R. Schnackenburg (1965). F. Watson (2000) was in some ways narrower ("Pauline"), and can be seen as complemented by T. Söding (1992; 1995). U. Schnelle (2003) in wider terms and S. Schreiber (2012) in narrower have advanced the theme. Recently O. Wischmeyer (2015; see her earlier sketch in *Biblische Zeitschrift*, 1986) has sought to move the object forward from the New Testament into early Christian reception.

The bold and vigorous contrast advanced over two volumes by A. Nygren (1953) which bases its thesis on the "patristic" merging of two distinct biblical categories. Significant as part of a treatment in theological ethics was G. Outka (1972), which responds to A. Nygren and development. A more nuanced account of patristic theory can be found at least as regards Augustine in O. O'Donovan (1979). C. Moreschini's (1993) is a wide-ranging treatment. P. Maraval (1991) shows the development from the earliest thinking up to medieval. J.C.M van Winden (1997) is an excellent attempt to bridge the apostolic and the post-apostolic.

On the specifics of the eucharistic love-feast, early religious concepts and practices have been integrated by A. McGowan (2004) and V.A. Alikin (2010).

Bibliography

Alikin, V.A., *The Earliest History of the Christian Gathering*, Leiden, 2010.

Arendt, H., *Love and Saint Augustine*, Chicago, 1998.

Beutler, J., "Das Hauptgebot im Johannesevangelium," in: K. Kertelge, *Das Gesetz im Neuen Testament*, QD 108, Freiburg, 1986, 222–236.

Bochet, I., *Saint Augustin et le désir de Dieu*, Paris, 1982.

Bori, P.C., *Chiesa primitiva: L'immagine della comunità delle origini: Atti 2, 42–47; 4, 32–27 nella storia della chiesa antica*, Brescia, 1974.

Burridge, R.A., *Imitating Jesus: An Inclusive Approach to New Testament Ethics*, Grand Rapids, 2007.

Canning, R., *The Unity of Love for God and Neighbour in St. Augustine*, Louvain, 1993.

Collange, J.-P., *De Jesus à Paul: L'ethique du Nouveau Testament*, Geneva, 1980.

Collins, R.F., "'A New Commandment I Give to You, That You Love One Another ...' (John 13: 34)," *LTP* 35, 1979, 235–261.

Daniélou, J., *Platonisme et théologie mystique*, Paris, 1953.

Dideberg, D., "Caritas," in: *AugL.*, vol. I, Würzburg, 1986–1994, 730–743.

Dideberg, D., "Amor," in: *AugL.*, vol. I, Würzburg, 1986–2004, 294–300.

Dideberg, D., "Dilectio," in: *AugL.*, vol. II, Würzburg, 1996–2002, 435–453.

Dunn, J.D.G., *The Theology of Paul the Apostle*, Grand Rapids, 2006.

Forell, G.W., *History of Christian Ethics*, vol. I: *From the New Testament to Augustine*, Minneapolis, 1979.

Furnish, V.P., *The Love Command in the New Testament*, London, 1973.

Georges, T., "The Communal Meal by Tertullian in *Apologeticum* 39: A Non-Sacramental Agape Celebration," *ZAC* 16, 2013, 279–291.

Hauerwas, S., *Vision and Virtue Essays in Christian Ethical Reflection*, Notre Dame, 1981.

Hays, R.B., *The Moral Vision of the New Testament*, San Francisco, 1996.

Heinrichs, A., *Didymos der Blinde: Kommentar zu Hiob (Tura-Papyrus)*, vols. I & II, Bonn, 1986.

Lattke, M., *Einheit im Wort*, StANT 41, Munich, 1975.

Maraval, P., "Liebe V: Alte Kirche und Mittelater," in: *TRE*, vol. XXI, Berlin, 1991, 146–152.

McGowan, A., "Rethinking Agape and Eucharist in Early North African Christianity," *StLi 34*, 2004, 165–176.

Melville. G., ed., *Aspects of Charity*, Berlin, 2011.

Moreschini, C., "L'amore nei padri Cappadoci'," in: *DSBP*, Rome, 1993, 274–293.

Nygren, A., *Agape and Eros*, London, 1953.

O'Donovan, O., *The Problem of Self-Love in St Augustine*, New Haven, 1979.

Outka, G., *Agape: An Ethical Analysis*, New Haven, 1972.

Perkins, P., *Love Commands in the New Testament*, New York, 1982.

Sauer, G., "Traditionsgeschichtliche Erwägungen zu den synoptischen und paulinischen Aussagen über Feindesliebe und Wiedervergeltungsverzicht," *ZNW* 76, 1985, 1–28.

Schlosser, J., "Les agapes et l'identité Chrétienne," *RHPhR* 93, 2013, 157–170.

Schnackenburg, R., *The Moral Teaching of the New Testament*, Freiburg, 1965.

Schnelle, U., *Paulus: Leben und Denken*, Berlin, 2003.

Schrage, W., *Grundrisse zum Neuen Testament*, vol. IV: *Ethik des Neuen Testaments*, Göttingen, 1989.

Schrage, W., *Evangelisch-katholischer Kommentar zum Neuen Testament*, vol. VII: *Der erste Brief an die Korinther*, Zürich, 1999.

Schreiber, S. "Law and Love in Romans 13:8–10," in: M. Meiser, ed., *The Torah in the Ethics of Paul*, LNTS 473, London, 2012, 100–119.

Söding, T., *Die Trias Glaube, Hoffnung, Liebe bei Paulus: Eine exegetische Studie*, SBS 150, Stuttgart, 1992.

Söding, T., *Das Liebesgebot bei Paulus: Die Mahnung zur Agape im Rahmen der paulinischen Ethik*, Münster, 1995.

Spicq, C., *Agape dans le Nouveau Testament*, 3 vols., Parijs, 1959–1966; ET: St. Louis, 1963–1966.

Staab, K., *Pauluskommentare aus der Griechischen Kirche*, Münster, ²1984.

Watson, F., *Agape, Eros, Gender: Towards a Pauline Sexual Ethic*, Cambridge UK, 2000.

Winden, J.C.M. van, "What Is Love? Eros and Agape in Early Christian Thought," in: J. den Boeft & D.T. Runia, eds., *Arche: A Collection of Patristic Studies by J.C.M. van Winden*, SVigChr 41, Leiden, 1997, 287–306.

Wischmeyer, O., "Das Gebot der Nächstenliebe bei Paulus: Eine traditionsgeschichtliche Untersuchung," *BZ* 30, 1986, 161–197.

Wischmeyer, O., *Der höchste Weg: Das 13. Kapitel des Korintherbriefes*, StNT 13, Gütersloh, 1981.

Wischmeyer, O., *Liebe als Agape: Das frühchristliche Konzept und der moderne Diskurs*, Tübingen, 2015.

Wolter, M., "Die ethische Identität christlicher Gemeinden in neutestamentlicher Zeit," *MJTh* 13, 2001, 61–90.

MARK W. ELLIOTT

Agatha

According to an ancient hagiographic tradition (*BHL* 133; *BHG* 36–37), Agatha suffered martyrdom (→ Martyrs) in Catania, Sicily, during the persecution of → Decius (250–251 CE). Less widespread is the ancient tradition (*BHL* 134) that places her martyrdom at the time of Diocletian's persecution (303–311 CE). She is celebrated in the liturgical sources on Feb 5, the day of her martyrdom. Her identification with the homonymous Agatha, protagonist of the *Symposium* by Methodius of Olympus (d. 311 CE), is uncertain.

The earliest testimonies of her cult seem to date back to the 4th century CE, with reference to a Latin epigraph of Iulia Florentina (*CIL* 10.7112; see Frasca & Soraci, 2021), discovered in a cemeterial area in Catania in the 18th century and now exhibited at the Louvre Museum, which does not directly mention Agatha but generically refers to the burial "before the tombs of Christian martyrs" (see Grasso, 1953; but see Rizzone, 2021, 78–81; Soraci, 2021). At the same burial site, a small early Christian basilica was unearthed in the 1950s, probably a place of worship of the martyrs of Catania: maybe Agatha and Euplus (Rizza, 1964). The cult of Agatha could be connected to two funerary inscriptions from Catania (Korhonen, 2004, 252n174; Rizzone, 2011, 280–281) and from Ustica (*IG* 14.592: Ferrua, 1941, 237–238). In Catania, however, there is no evidence of sites specifically dedicated to the martyr before the Norman conquest. In the 5th and 6th centuries CE, some basilicas were dedicated to her outside of Sicily: in Rome, along the Via Aurelia (*LP*, vol. I, 267 by Pope Symmacus [498–514 CE], see Sardella, 2005, 271–282); in Ravenna: Sant'Agata Maggiore (late 5th cent. CE; see Cirelli, 2007, 309); in Capua (by the bishop Germanus [516–541 CE], see Episcopo, 2007, 1025). She is depicted in the mosaics of Ravenna's Sant'Apollinare Nuovo and in those of the Euphrasian basilica in Poreč, in Istria (6th cent. CE).

The pope → Gregory the Great (594–604 CE) dedicated an Arian church (→ Arianism) to Agatha and Sebastian in Rome, in the Suburra, which he converted into a Catholic church (Greg. M. *Dial.* 3.30.2–6: see Zeiller, 1904; Fasoli, 1952; Scorza Barcellona, 2011), and the monastery called "Lucuscanum" to Agatha and Maxim (Greg. M. *Ep.* 9.67) in the vicinity of Palermo. The pope allowed Sabino, bishop in Capri, to place some relics of the martyr in the Monastery of Saint Stephan (Greg. M. *Ep.* 1.52).

Agatha's feast day is mentioned in the liturgical books of the western and eastern churches, ranging from the calendar of Carthage (early 6th cent. CE) and the *Martyrologium Hieronymianum* to historical martyrologies (Bede's, Adon's, and Usuard's), sacramentaries (already occurring in the Gregorian: Verbecke, 1938), antiphonaries, and the *Synassarium Costantinopolitanum* (see Magrì, 2011, vol. I, 105–131). Agatha is mentioned in the Ambrosian liturgical books (→ Ambrosian Liturgy) and in the *praefatio* to the Ambrosian Mass (5th–7th cents. CE; see Pasini, 1991, 382–396). Her name occurs in the canon of the Church of Ravenna and in that of the Church of Rome, where it was introduced, along with the name of Lucy, by Pope Gregory the Great.

The account of Agatha's martyrdom has been transmitted in Latin (*BHL* 133–140) and Greek

redactions (*BHG* 36–38b), which attests both to the late-antique bilingualism of Sicily (see Milazzo, 2018) and to the spread of the Sicilian martyr's cult within the universal church. The Latin redaction (*BHL* 133: Mombritius, 1477, 16–18; Caietanus, 1657, vol. I, 43–46; 50–53; *ActaSS Febr.* vol. I, 1658, 615–618; Zanghi & Isetta, 2014; and *BHL* 134: D'Arrigo, 1988, vol. I, 379–387) is essentially uniform with an exception in the *incipit* concerning the martyrdom, set in the time of the persecution of → Decius (250–251 CE) according to *BHL* 133 and that of → Diocletian (303–311 CE) according to *BHL* 134. The Latin redaction is transmitted by more than 200 manuscripts, the oldest ones dating from the 8th century CE (Lanéry, 2010, 280–282n597). The Greek redaction (*BHG* 36: Gk: Re, 2019, 278–289; Lat. trans: Caietanus, 1657, vol. I, 37–42; 47–50; but see Milazzo, 2018, 90–91n58; *ActaSS Febr.* vol. I, 1658, 618–620: see Milazzo, 2018, 97–98; Re, 2019, 276–277 and *BHG* 37, a pseudo-metaphrastic text: PG 114,1331–1346; Lat. trans. Surius, 1581, vol. I, 266–267; *ActaSS Febr.* vol. I, 1658, 620–624) is transmitted by 20 manuscripts, the oldest ones dating from the 10th century CE (Dörrie, 1950, 180; Stelladoro, 1995–1996; Re, 2019, 255–260, 270–277). Greek and Latin redactions, despite their strong similarities, display a significant difference in the opening: in the Greek redaction, the girl was arrested in Palermo and then taken to Catania, where she was martyred; in the Latin one, instead, all the action takes place in Catania. This philological issue fuels the centuries-old debate (very lively in 17th cent.: see *ActaSS Febr.* vol. I, 1658, 605–615; Motta, 2004, 76–80) on the martyr's hometown, and has accredited the Latin redaction in Catania's municipalistic historiography, which is flawed by clever falsifications and text forgeries (Crimi, 1985; Crimi, 2020, 56–60, about the Methodius' Encomium, *BHG* 38; Milazzo, 2018, 97–99, 109–110; Re, 2019, 260–270, about *BHG* 36). The debate over the precedence of the Greek or Latin redaction is still open (see Motta, 2004, 24–26; Milazzo, 2009, 254–258), although there is evidence that the oldest text we possess is the Latin one (first half of 5th cent. CE: see Lanéry, 2008, 486–489; 2010, 283–286; end 5th cent.–first half 6th cent. CE: see Milazzo, 2018, 100–108).

The plot is similar in both redactions: the protagonists are Agatha, the martyr, and Quintianus, the persecutor: she is young, beautiful, noble, rich, firm in her determination, a skillful debater, and brave; by contrast, he is brutal, rough, greedy, cowardly lascivious, and unable to face up to the girl's arguments. Quintianus entrusts the virgin to courtesan Aphrodisias to persuade her to surrender herself to him. The girl's firmness lies first in her ability to resist both the promises and threats of Aphrodisias, and the interrogations and terrible tortures to which she is subjected, notably the cutting off of her breast and the hot coals. After the interrogation, Agatha is sent to prison, where Peter appears to her and miraculously heals her. Agatha died in prison from torture; Quintianus dies overwhelmed by the flood of the river Simeto. While she is being entombed in her sepulcher, an angel lays a marble tablet beside her head that bears the following inscription: *Mentem Sanctam Spontaneum Honorem Deo et Patriae Liberationem*, "healthy mind, spontaneous honor to God and homeland freedom." According to the hagiographic texts, the year following her martyrdom, the saint's veil saves the city from one of Etna's eruptions. Since then, Agatha's veil has been carried in procession when particularly violent eruptions threaten Catania or the villages around Mount Etna. The aforementioned inscription or its initials *M.S.S.H.D.E.P.L.* were widely employed and carved onto church bells in medieval Europe (Favreau, 1995) as a protection against fires or storms, or written down on paper strips, the latter becoming a widespread tradition in Germany (Heinz, 2006, 169–172).

The *Passio* was known in West between the 5th and 6th centuries CE: see the Pseudo-Ambrosian hymn "Agathae sacrae virginis," the *praefatio* to the Mass of the Ambrosian liturgy (Pasini, 1991, 382–396; Lanéry, 2008, 490–494), and the *Passio* of Lucy of Syracuse, the Greek redaction of which dates from the 5th century CE (Rossi Taibbi, 1959); the Pseudo-Damasian hymn "Martyris ecce dies Agathae" (*ReHy* 11271–11272) is not older than the 5th century CE. Aldhelm of Malmesbury's (640–709) *Prosa de virginitate* (ch. 41) and *Carmen de virginitate* (vv. 1736–1778) as well as Bede's Martyrology (first half of 8th cent. CE) use *BHL* 134. The Latin *passio* is included in the Cistercensian *Liber de natalitiis* (12th cent.; Morini, 1991, 320–329) and in the *Legenda aurea* (ch. 39) by Jacobus de Varagine (13th cent.).

In Constantinople, Patriarch Methodius of Syracuse delivered an encomium to the martyr (*BHG* 38:

Crimi, 2020, 60–85) between 843 CE and 847 CE, in which he also referred to the annual miracle of the lamp oil overflowing (Mioni, 1950; Crimi, 2006). The Greek redaction was included in Metaphrastes' collection (10th–11th cents).

The *passio* is largely present in medieval Greek and Latin hymnology.

After the Norman conquest of Sicily and the re-establishment of the episcopal see of Catania (1091 CE), the cult of Agatha received a further boost in Catania and on the whole island, both as a sign of the re-Christianization of Sicily after Muslim leadership (Oldfield, 2011; 2014) and as as a symbol of local identity (Tramontana, 1995). The cathedral was dedicated to the martyr, and there her relics were translated in 1126 from Constantinople, where, according to a Norman tradition, the Byzantine commander George Maniakes had brought them from Catania sometime between 1030 and 1041 (Hord. *Hist. Eccl.* 5). Their journey from Constantinople is narrated in Bishop Mauritius' (1125–1131?) *Epistola* (*BHL* 139: see Scalia, 1928; Oldfield, 2011; 2014, 139–180), which was very probably written down in Catania, in the same monastery scriptorium where the monk Blandinus wrote a *Libellus miraculorum* (*BHL* 140) between 1140 and 1150. In the second half of the 12th century, moreover, the martyr was depicted in the mosaics of the Royal Chapel of the Norman kings of Sicily (Cappella Palatina) in Palermo and in those of the Cathedral of Monreale (in a remarkable position, in the central apse: see Brodbeck, 2010, 124, 314–317; Zito, 2014, 130–131). According to another tradition (Andrea Dandolo, *Chronica per extensum descripta*, composed between 1343 and 1352), Agatha's relics were brought to Constantinople by order of the emperors Basil II and Constantine VIII (976–1028), then carried off by Venetians during the Fourth Crusade (1204), and finally handed over to some Sicilian pilgrims by Doge Enrico Dandolo (c. 1107–1205). The relics of the martyr are now enshrined in a precious 14th-century reliquary bust, a work by Giovanni di Bartolo, a goldsmith from Siena, active in the papal court of Avignon, where the bust was made. The reliquary bust is carried in solemn → procession on the feast days, Feb 4 and 5 and Aug 17, when the translation is celebrated. The treasure of Agatha is huge and displays particularly precious items, both through their intrinsic and historical value. Among them is the crown which tradition claims to have been a gift of King Richard Lionheart, although it was actually made in the late 14th century, and Vincenzo Bellini's Knight's Cross of the Legion of Honor. Agatha's iconography is abundant and of high artistic merit (see Squarr, 1973, 44–48; *Agata santa*). Several hagiotoponyms in Italy, Europe, and the Americas attest the spread of the cult of the Sicilian martyr. Agatha is called upon to protect against fire, earthquakes, the plague, and women's ailments such as breast cancer.

Bibliography

Agata santa: Storia, arte, devozione, Milan, 2008.

Brodbeck, S., *Les saints de la cathédrale de Monreale en Sicile: Iconographie, hagiographie et pouvoir royal à la fin du 12e siècle*, Rome, 2010.

Brusa, L., "Gli Atti del martirio di S. Agata," *RCCM* 1/3, 1959, 342–367.

Caietanus, O., ed., *Vitae sanctorum Siculorum* [...] *Animadversionibus illustratae*, 2 vols., Panormi, 1657, vol. I, 50–63; 37–50.

Cirelli, E., "'Élites' civili ed ecclesiastiche nella Ravenna tardoantica," *HAM* 13/2, 2007, 301–318.

Crimi, C., "L'encomio 'lacerato'. A proposito di un apocrifo secentesco su s. Agata," *Syn.* 3, 1985, 387–412.

Crimi, C., "S. Agata a Bisanzio nel IX secolo: Rileggendo Metodio patriarca di Costantinopoli," in: T. Sardella & G. Zito, eds., *Euplo c Lucia: 304–2004: Agiografia e tradizioni cultuali in Sicilia: Atti del convegno di studi (Catania-Siracusa, Oct 1–2, 2004)*, Catania, 2006, 143–163.

Crimi, C., "Metodio, Patriarca di Costantinopoli, 'Encomio di s. Agata' (BHG 38): Introduzione, edizione critica, traduzione e note," *RSBN* n.s. 57, 2020, 25–128.

D'Arrigo, S., *Il martirio di Sant'Agata nel quadro storico del suo tempo*, 2 vols., Catania, 1988.

Dörrie, H., "Agatha (hl)," in: *RAC*, vol. I, Stuttgart, 1950, 179–184.

Episcopo, S., "La cristianizzazione di Capua: Nuove prospettive per una ricerca archeologica," in: R.M. Bonacasa Carra & E. Vitale, eds, *La cristianizzazione in Italia tra tardoantico ed altomedioevo: Atti del IX Congresso Nazionale di Archeologia Cristiana (Agrigento, 20–25 novembre 2004)*, vol. I, Palermo, 2007, 1017–1040.

Favreau, R., "'Mentem sanctam, spontaneam, honorem Deo et patriae liberationem': Épigraphie et mentalité," in: R. Favreau, *Études d'épigraphie médiévale*, Limoges, 1995, 127–137.

Fasoli, G., "Su la diffusione del culto di S. Agata nell'Italia del Nord," *ASSO* 48, 1952, 10–17.

Ferrua, A., "Epigrafia sicula pagana e cristiana," *RivAC* 18, 1941, 151–243.

François, G., ed., *Sant'Agata: Il reliquiario a busto: Contributi interdisciplinari*, Catania, 2010.

Frasca, E., & C. Soraci, eds., *Iulia Florentina e i martiri catanesi: Giornata interdisciplinare di studi in memoria di Mons. Gaetano Zito (Catania, 8 febbraio 2020)*, Acireale 2021.

Grasso, S., "'Martyrorum'? Intorno all'epigrafe di Iulia Florentina," *Epig.* 15, 1953, 151–153.

Heinz, A., "Agata, Lucia ed Euplo nella tradizione liturgica medievale," in: T. Sardella & G. Zito, eds., *Euplo e Lucia: 304–2004: Agiografia e tradizioni cultuali in Sicilia: Atti del Convegno di studi (Catania-Siracusa, Oct 1–2, 2004)*, Catania, 2006, 165–177.

Korhonen, K., *Le iscrizioni del Museo Civico di Catania: Storia delle collezioni, cultura epigrafica, edizione*, Helsinki, 2004.

Lanéry, C., *Ambroise de Milan hagiographe*, Paris, 2008.

Lanéry, C., "Hagiographie d'Italie (300–550): I. Les passions latines composées en Italie," in: G. Philippart, ed., *Hagiographies: Histoire internationale de la littérature hagiographique latine et vernaculaire en occident des origines à 1550*, vol. V, Turnhout, 2010, 15–369.

Magrì, S., *"Agathae, beatae virginis et martyris": La figura e l'ideale di santità di Agata nell'eucologia eucaristica romana e nei Propri regionali siciliani*, 2 vols., Troina, 2011.

Milazzo, V., "La Sicilia: Agata e Lucia: Note storiografiche," in: A. Tilatti & F.G.B. Trolese, eds., *Giustina e le altre: Sante e culti femminili in Italia settentrionale dalla prima età cristiana al secolo XII: Atti del VI convegno di studio dell'AISSCA (Padova, Oct 4–6, 2004)*, Rome, 2009, 243–270.

Milazzo, V., "Bilinguismo e agiografia siciliana: Alcune osservazioni sulle 'Passiones' di Agata e di Lucia," in: V. Milazzo & F. Scorza Barcellona, eds., *Bilinguismo e scrittura agiografiche: Raccolta di studi*, Rome 2018, 77–110.

Mioni, E., "L'encomio di S. Agata di Metodio patriarca di Costantinopoli," *AnBoll* 68/1, 1950, 58–93.

Mombritius, B., *Sanctuarium*, Mediolani (incunable without a title page, so without a date, but certainly before 1478).

Morini, C., "Una redazione sconosciuta della Passio s. Agathae: Ms. Auxerre, Bibl. Mun., 127 (s. XII in.), f. 17^r–19^r," *AnBoll* 109/2, 1991, 305–330.

Morini, C., *La passione di S. Agata di Ælfric di Eynsham*, Alessandria, 1993.

Motta, D., *Percorsi dell'agiografia: Società e cultura nella Sicilia tardoantica e bizantina*, Catania, 2004.

Oldfield, P., "The Medieval Cult of St. Agatha of Catania and the Consolidation of Christian Sicily," *JEH* 62/3, 2011, 439–456.

Oldfield, P., *Sanctity and Pilgrimage in Medieval Southern Italy, 1000–1200*, Cambridge UK, 2014.

Pasini, C., "Chiesa di Milano e Sicilia: Punti di contatto dal IV all'VIII secolo," in: S. Pricoco, F. Rizzo Nervo & T. Sardella, eds., *Sicilia e Italia suburbicaria tra IV e VIII secolo: Atti del Convegno di Studi (Catania, Oct 4–27, 1989)*, Soveria Mannelli, 1991, 367–398.

Peri, V., ed., *Agata: La santa di Catania*, Gorle, 1996.

Re, M., "La Passio' di s. Agata BHG e Nov. Auct. BHG 36: Introduzione, edizione del testo, traduzione," *RSBN* n.s. 56, 2019, 249–289.

Rizza, G., "Un martyrium paleocristiano di Catania e il sepolcro di Iulia Florentina," in: *Oikoumene: Studi paleocristiani pubblicati in onore del Concilio ecumenico Vaticano II*, Catania, 1964, 593–612.

Rizzone, V.G., *Opus Christi edificabit: Stati e funzioni dei cristiani di Sicilia attraverso l'apporto dell'epigrafia (secoli IV–VI)*, Troina, 2011.

Rizzone,V.G., "L'iscrizione di Iulia Florentina: Peculiarità linguistiche ed epigrafiche," in: E. Frasca & C. Soraci., eds., *Iulia Florentina e i martiri catanesi: Giornata interdisciplinare di studi in memoria di Mons. Gaetano Zito (Catania, 8 febbraio 2020)*, Acireale 2021, 75–87.

Rossi Taibbi, G., ed., *Martirio di Santa Lucia: Vita di Santa Marina: Testi greci e traduzioni*, Palermo, 1959.

Sardella, T., "Roma e la Sicilia nella promozione del culto dei santi siciliani: Il pontificato di Simmaco," in: T. Sardella & G. Zito, eds., *Euplo e Lucia: 304–2004: Agiografia e tradizioni cultuali in Sicilia: Atti del Convegno di studi (Catania-Siracusa, Oct 1–2, 2004)*, Catania, 2006, 267–282.

Scalia, G., "La traslazione del corpo di S. Agata e il suo valore storico," *ASSO*, ser. 2/3–4, 1927–1928, fasc. 1–3, 40–128.

Scorza Barcellona, F., "I Goti e sant'Agata," *BSP* 113, 2011, 25–42.

Soraci C., "Il luogo di sepoltura di Iulia Florentina: Ubicazione e caratteristiche del 'cimiterio'," in: E. Frasca & C. Soraci, eds., *Iulia Florentina e i martiri catanesi: Giornata interdisciplinare di studi in memoria di Mons. Gaetano Zito (Catania, 8 febbraio 2020)*, Acireale 2021, 89–105.

Stelladoro, M., "Ricerche sulla tradizione manoscritta degli atti greci del martirio di s. Agata," *BBGG* n.s. 49–50, 1995–1996, 63–89.

Studi su s: Agata e il suo culto nella ricorrenza del XVII centenario del martirio, Catania, 1953 = *ASSO* 48, 1952 (various authors: it is an entire number of the Historical Archive of Eastern Sicily dedicated to St. Agatha).

Squarr, C., "Agatha von Catania," in: *LCI*, vol. V, Freiburg, 1973, 44–48.

Surius, L., ed., *De probatis sanctorum vitis*, vol. I, Venice, 1581, 266–267.

Tixier, F., ed., *Sant'Agata: Il reliquiario a busto: Nuovi contributi interdisciplinari*, Catania, 2014.

Tramontana, S., "Sant'Agata e la religiosità della Catania normanna," in: G. Zito, ed., *Chiesa e società in Sicilia*, vol. I: *L'età normanna: Atti del I Convegno internazionale organizzato dall'arcidiocesi di Catania (Nov 25–27, 1992)*, Turin, 1995, 189 202.

Verbecke, G., "S. Grégoire et la messe de Sainte Agathe," *EL* 51/1, 1938, 67–76.

Zanghi, V., & S. Isetta, eds., "Passio Agathae BHL 133," in: M. Goullet & S. Isetta, eds., *Le Légendier de Turin: MS.D.V.3 de la Bibliothèque Nationale et Universitaire,*

Avec DVD réalisé par L. Tessarolo, Florence, 2014, 357–371.

Zeiller, J., "Les églises ariennes de Rome à l'époque de la domination gothique," *MEFR* 24/1, 1904, 17–33.

Zito, G., "Il contesto storico del martirio di Agata," in: V. Peri, ed., *Agata: La santa di Catania*," Gorle, 1996, 13–65.

Zito, G., "Su sant'Agata nuovi documenti medievali a Catania: Un lacerto di pergamena e un sigillo plumbeo," in: F. Tixier, ed., *Sant'Agata: Il reliquiario a busto: Nuovi contributi interdisciplinari*, Catania, 2014, 113–139.

VINCENZA MILAZZO

Agathangelos

Agathangelos (*Agat'angełos*) is the name given in Armenian tradition to the unknown editor of the story of the conversion of Armenia by Gregory the Illuminator in the early 4th century CE. Some aspects of the story are mentioned in the *Buzandaran*, a compilation of "Epic Tales" dating to the 460s CE (Thomson, 2010, 27–30). But not until late that century do a title and author's name appear: Ł. P'arpec'i states that "Agathangelos" composed the first written history of Armenia, which was called "The Book of Gregory" (Łazar, 1904, 2–3). "Agathangelos" himself claims that he was commissioned by King Trdat (Tiridates) to write down the course of events from the time of Trdat's father Xosrov, through the conversion of Trdat, down to the appointment of Gregory as first patriarch of Armenia.

The Armenian text of the story begins with the fall of the Iranian Arsacids to the Sasanian line soon after 224 CE, and ends with the death of Gregory at an unknown date after the Council of → Nicaea in 325 CE. The various episodes may have had different origins and motivations, but they are linked together through Trdat and Gregory in a more or less coherent fashion. According to Agathangelos the Armenian Arsacid king Xosrov did not submit to the Sasanians after the overthrow of the Parthian Arsacids circa 224 CE, and he was treacherously slain by the Parthian Anak. In vengeance Anak's family was put to death, but his infant son Gregory survived and was taken to Greek territory; he was raised in Caesarea of Cappadocia as a Christian. This points to the Iranian nature of Armenian society and Gregory's own background. The Persian king now occupied Armenia, but Xosrov's son, the infant Trdat, escaped and was brought up by a count Licinius. On growing up Gregory took service with Trdat, who was restored to his ancestral kingdom with the help of a Roman army. This was Tiridates IV, king of Armenia between 298 and 330 CE. After Gregory refused to participate in sacrifice to Anahit, King Trdat inflicted 12 tortures; on discovering his identity, he had Gregory cast into a deep prison to die. There he languished for 13 (or 15) years, miraculously preserved.

Meanwhile, Diocletian sought a wife. His designs fell on a beautiful nun in Rome named Rhipsimē, but she with her companions and their leader Gaianē fled to Armenia. Eventually they were discovered, and King Trdat tried to seize Rhipsimē for himself. His lust was thwarted, so he martyred all the Christian nuns. Agathangelos associates the martyrs with the persecutions of → Diocletian, but their names are Anatolian (Outtier & Thierry, 1990) and thus recall the persecution of Maximin Daia in Roman Armenia in 311 CE. Divine punishment fell upon Trdat, as he was changed into the form of a wild boar "in the likeness of Nebuchadnezzar," and many at court and in the city became demon possessed. The king's sister had a vision, and Gregory was rescued from the deep pit. He instructed the king and court, following which Trdat was cured. Gregory then related a vision, in which the burial places for the martyrs were pointed out and forebodings of future → apostasy adumbrated. Gregory's vision thus authenticated the placement of the shrines and of the cathedral in the old Arsacid capital of Vałaršapat, later known as Ejmiacin ("where the Only-begotten descended"). It also pointed to the rebellion of 450/451 CE against Sasanian Iran, later interpreted in heroic terms as the equivalent of the rebellion of the → Maccabees (Ełišē, 1957; Thomson, 1975). Gregory's elaborate "Teaching" summarizes the Armenian theological position of the early 6th century CE (Thomson, 2001), and later developments in liturgy and ecclesiastical tradition were anachronistically considered to be part of that legacy (Thomson, 2010, 24–108).

According to Agathangelos the Armenians now began to destroy their ancient pagan shrines, thus giving information about sites and rituals. Trdat then sent Gregory to Caesarea for consecration as Armenia's first → bishop, and on his return king and people were baptized. Gregory's own sons succeeded him as patriarch and were also consecrated

in Caesarea. Only in the 5th century CE was the hold of Gregory's direct descendants on the patriarchate broken and the link with Caesarea ended (Garsoïan, 1999, 65–66). On hearing of Constantine's conversion, Gregory and Trdat visited him in "Rome." This visit (with reminiscences of Trdat I's visit to Nero in 66 CE; Tac. *An.* 16.23) pointed to Armenia as a Christian nation of equal antiquity to the empire. Later, in times of invasion by Turks and Mongols, the pact confirmed in "Rome" was cited in apocalyptic expectations of salvation from the west (Pogossian, 2010).

Gregory's son Aristakes attended the Council of Nicaea, bringing back the canons to Armenia, to which Gregory made additions. This confirmed the place of that council as the basis of Armenian orthodoxy, for Armenia never accepted the definition of → Chalcedon (Garsoïan, 1999). Gregory spent his last days in eremitic retreat. Agathangelos does not mention the site of his tomb, though it was already known to the author of the *Buzandaran* as T'ordan in northwestern Armenia.

The surviving Armenian *History* is a carefully edited version of many episodes, brought together to create a foundation document for the Armenian church. It is not known whether a previous written text existed, but the existence of numerous variants in different languages not only points to a somewhat different Armenian text that did not survive, but also indicates the popularity of Gregory's fame throughout the Christian world. The diverse versions fall into two branches: those translations dependent on the surviving Armenian are known as the *A* recension, and those deriving from an unknown Armenian source as the *V* recension (Garitte, 1946). Two Greek versions of the *V* recension exist; these renderings of unknown date were made by Greek translators who did not understand numerous Armenian terms. According to the version in the manuscript at the Escorial dated to 1107, at Gregory's consecration in Caesarea a council of 20 bishops was convened. This reflects confusion in the canon lists, which mistakenly introduce such a council between Ancyra in 314 and Neocaesarea in 319 CE. Nonetheless, a date of 314 CE for Gregory's consecration fits all the other evidence and is widely accepted (Mahé, 2012, 79). A Syriac adaptation drew upon both traditions, adding new material of its own. It reflects a time of the early 7th century CE when there was a schism between pro- and anti-Byzantine patriarchs in the Armenian church (Esbroeck, 1977). The Arabic version is based on a Greek original, showing knowledge of traditions in both known texts of the *V* recension; it has Trdat and Gregory play a greater role in the wider Caucasus than the other texts. A plethora of secondary renderings and adaptations exists in many languages (Winkler, 1980).

The *History* of "Agathangelos" is closely associated with the patriarchal site of Vałaršapat. The Armenian text took its present form after the rebellion against Iran in 450/451 CE, but before the end of that century; the section known as the *Teaching* was probably added early 6th century CE (Thomson, 2001). However, the traditions concerning Gregory and his activities were in continuous flux. One cannot speak of an "author," but rather of successive editors.

Historiography

The Armenian account of the country's conversion by Gregory "the Illuminator" in the reign of King Tiridates was first published in 1709 in Constantinople, and the only critical edition exactly 200 years later, in Tiflis (Agathangelos, 1909, and in the series *Matenagirk' Hayoc'*, vol. II, Antelias, Lebanon, 2003). A Greek version was first published in 1762 in the *Acta Sanctorum*, and a critical edition by G. Lafontaine appeared in 1973 at Louvain-la-Neuve. In 1905 an Arabic rendering based on a different Greek text was published in Saint Petersburg by N. Marr. The most important work on this enigmatic "History" was done by G. Garitte (1946), who pointed out that two different versions of the story had given rise to a plethora of divergent texts in many different eastern Christian languages. The surviving Armenian text he called A, for *Agathangeli Historia*; from this derive the long-known Greek and numerous subsidiary versions. Other, more recently discovered Greek texts also have an Armenian origin, but the original text behind them is not extant. This version G. Garitte called V, for *Vita Gregorii*. Drawing on both versions, with its own idiosyncrasies, is a Syriac rendering (Esbroeck, 1977); one of the recently discovered Greek texts also draws on both recensions. On the other hand, later Armenian writers refer to the story of Gregory only in terms of the A recension. The variant V tradition was lost, or deliberately suppressed.

This complex picture points to a succession of rewritings and adaptations appropriate to the time and circumstances of each text, and indicates that the original was composed in Armenian -- therefore after the invention of that script at the beginning of the 5th century CE, two centuries after the events described (Winkler, 1980). Debate continues as to the identity of the various "editors" of the basic story (Thomson, 2010).

Bibliography

Agathangelos, *Agathangelos: Agat'angełay Patmut'iwn Hayoc'*, ed. G. Ter-Mkrtč'ean & S. Kanayeanc', Tiflis, 1909, repr. Delmar, 1980; trans. *History* §§1–258, 716–900: R.W. Thomson, *The Lives of Saint Gregory*, Ann Arbor, 2010 (Armen., Gk, Arab. & Syr. versions); *Teaching* §259–715: R.W. Thomson, *The Teaching of Saint Gregory*, TAT 1, New Rochelle, 2001.

Buzandaran, *Buzandaran: P'awstosi Buzandac'woy Patmut'iwn Hayoc'*, ed. K.' Patkanean, St. Petersburg, 1883, repr. Delmar, 1984; trans. N.G. Garsoïan, *The Epic Histories Attributed to P'awstos Buzand (Buzandaran Patmut'iwnk')*, HATS 8, Cambridge MA, 1989.

Ełišē, *Ełišē: Vasn Vardanay ew Hayoc' paterazmin*, ed. E. Ter-Minasyan, Erevan, 1957, repr. Delmar, 1993; trans. R.W. Thomson, *Elishē: History of Vardan and the Armenian WarI*, HATS 5, Cambridge MA, 1982.

Garitte, G., *Documents pour l'étude du livre d'Agathange*, StT, 127, Vatican City, 1946.

Garsoïan, N.G., *L'église arménienne et le grand schisme d'Orient*, CSCO 574, Subsidia 100, Louvain, 1999.

Łazar P'arpec'i, *Łazar P'arpec'i: Patmut'iwn Hayoc'*, ed. G. Ter-Mkrtč'ean & T. Malxasean, Tiflis, 1904, repr. Delmar, 1985; trans. R.W. Thomson, *The History of Łazar P'arpec'i*, Atlanta, 1991.

Mahé, A., & J.-P. Mahé, *Histoire de l'Arménie*, Paris 2012.

Outtier, B., & M. Thierry, "Histoire des saintes Hripsimiennes," *Syr.* 67, 1990, 695–733.

Pogossian, Z., *The Letter of Love and Concord*, Leiden, 2010.

Thomson, R.W., "The Maccabees in Early Armenian Historiography," *JThS* 26; repr. R.W. Thomson, *Studies in Armenian Literature and Christianity*, CStS 451, Aldershot, 1994, section VII.

Thomson, R.W, *The Lives of Saint Gregory: The Armenian, Greek, Arabic, and Syriac Versions of the History attributed to Agathangelos*, Ann Arbor, 2010.

Esbroeck, M. van, "Le résumé syriaque de l'Agathange," *AnBoll* 95, 1977, 291–358.

Winkler, G., "Our Present Knowledge of the History of Agat'angełos and Its Oriental Versions," *REArm* n.s. 14, 1980, 125–141.

ROBERT W. THOMSON

Agathangelus of Rome

Agathangelus of Rome (d. 312 CE) was a martyr in Ancyra in Galatia and is remembered together with Clement of Ancyra, the deacons Christopher and Carito, and other martyrs. Information on this martyr comes from the *Passio Clementis Ancyrani*, which is considered a reliable source by the Bollandists, but not by Baronio and Tillemont. Ever since his adolescence, Clement had displayed a propensity for hermitism and serving the poor and the sick. He joined the clergy in Ancyra and became → bishop at a very young age. After having been imprisoned in Ancyra, he was transferred to Rome, where, according to a popular hagiographical *topos*, he converted many pagans and baptized several fellow prisoners, among whom was Agathangelus, who then followed him until death. Agathangelus secretly boarded the ship on which Clement was supposed to be taken from Rome back to Ancyra. The trip took a staggering 28 years, during which the two saints stopped in Rhodes, Nicomedia, Ancyra, Amisus, Tarsus, and, finally, again in Ancyra. During their journey, they both suffered increasingly cruel tortures, always emerging unscathed.

Clement also received a revelation about the duration and quality of his tribulations. Back in Ancyra, they both received the crown of martyrdom: Agathangelus on Nov 5 and Clement two months later, on Jan 23. The year of martyrdom is placed between 304 and 309 CE. The martyrs' relics were translated to Constantinople, presumably during the 4th century CE. A church dedicated to the two martyrs, among the most revered saints in the Greek Church, was built on the European shore of the Bosphorus, and in Constantinople evidence of their veneration is also found in Saint Irene and in a small oratory built by Basil the Macedonian inside the imperial palace (*ActaSS* 2.458). In 907 CE, relics of Agathangelus, as well as Clement's *omophorion*, were donated by Gabriel of Ancyra to Euthymius of Constantinople, who placed them in the monastery of Psamathia, which he had founded (*Vita Euth.* 15.21). Clement's head, which had reached Paris at the time of the Crusades, was donated by Anne of Austria (1601–1666) to the Church of Notre-Dame de l'Hôpital du Val-de-Grâce. In Greek calendars, Agathangelus is celebrated on Nov 5; he is also celebrated on Jan 23 together with Clement, which is also the date on which both martyrs are remembered in Latin martyriologies.

See the bibliography for sources and studies of a more specialized nature and historiography on the theme.

Bibliography

Baronio, C., *Martyrologium Romanum*, Rome, 1630.

Baudot, J., & L. Chaussin, *Vies des saints et des bienheureux selon l'ordre du calendrier avec l'historique des fêtes*, vol. I, Paris, 1935.

Boyens, I., "Catalogus coducum hagiographicorum graecorum bibliothecae monasterii Deiparae in Chalce insula," *AnBoll* 20, 1901, 45–70.

Chabot, B., "Trois homélies de Proclus, évêque de Constantinople," *AnBoll* 22, 1903.

"Clemens ep. Ancyrae et Agathangelus," in: *BHG*, vol. I, SHG 8, Brussels, ³1957, nos. 352–354, 117–118.

Delehaye, H., *Propylaeum ad Acta sanctorum novembris: Synaxarium Ecclesiae Constantinopolitanae*, Brussels, 1902.

Delehaye, H., *étude sur le légendier romain: Les saints de novembre et de décembre*, Brussels, 1936.

Doukakis, K., Μέγας Συναξαριστής παντῶν τῶν ἁγιῶν (*The Great Synaxarium of All the Saints*), Athens, 1889.

Eldarov, G., "Agatangelo e Clemente," *BS* 1, 1961, 337–338.

Gédéon, M., Βυζαντινὸν Ἑορτολόγιον (Byzantine Calendar), Constantinople, 1899.

Halkin, F., "Manuscrits byzantins d'Ochrida en Macédoine yugoslave," *AnBoll* 80, 1962, 5–21

Halkin, F., ed., "Clemens Ancyranus," in: *BHG NAuct*, SHG 47, Brussels, 1969, 48–49.

Halkin, F., ed., "Clemens Ancyranus," in: *BHG NAuct*, SHG 65, Brussels, 1984.

Le Nain de Tillemont, L.-S., *Mémoires pour servir à l'histoire ecclésiastique*, vol. V, Paris, 1698.

Martinov, P.I., "Annus ecclesiasticus graeco-slavicus editus anno millenario ss. Cyrilli et Methodii slavicae gentis apostolorum, seu commentano et breviarium rerum gestarum eorum qui fastis sacris graecis et slavicis illati sunt," *ActaSS* 11, Brussels, 1863.

Morcelli, S.A., *Kalendarium Ecclesiae Constantinopolitanae*, vol. II, Rome, 1788.

Nilles, N., *Kalendarium manuale utriusque ecclesiae orientali set occidentalis*, vol. I, Innsbruck, 1896.

Pasini, C., *Inventario agiografico dei manoscritti greci dell'Ambrosiana*, SHG 84, Brussels, 2003.

Peeters, P., ed., *Bibliotheca Hagiographica Orientalis*, Brussels, 1910.

Salaville, S., "Agathange, Saint," in: *DHGE*, vol. I, Paris, 1912, 906.

Rocco Ronzani

Age → Aeon

Agilulf

Agilulf, king of the Lombards (590–616 CE), of the lineage of Anawas (*Edictum Rothari, Prologum*), was also called Ago (Greg. M. *Ep.* 4.2). The name shows similarities with the one of ducal Bavarian family Agiolfings, but a relationship seems improbable (Jarnut, 1986, 10–11). Before becoming king, Agilulf titled as duke, perhaps of the town Turin (Gasparri, 1978, 45–46). As king, he succeeded Authari and married his widow Theodelinda (Balzaretti, 1999). In the *Chronicles of Fredegar*, he became the son of Authari (*Ch.Fr.* 4.45). According to → Gregory of Tours, a certain Paul succeed Authari instead (Greg. T. *Hist.* 10.3). Two historical works are linked to King Agilulf and his wife Theodelinda: the history of Secundus of Trent, a narrative recorded only by Paul the Deacon; and a continuation of Prosper of Aquitaine's chronicle until 625 CE (Pohl, 2000; Borri, 2014; Everett, 2003, 85–87). In Agilulf's years, the Roman heritage of Italy strongly influenced the Lombard court (Delogu, 2010, 175–180; McCormick, 1986, 284–296). Agilulf ruled from Milan, a former imperial capital, crowning his son in the amphitheatre of the city (P.Deac. *Hist. Lang.* 4.30).

Agilulf fought the rebellious dukes of the kingdom: Mimulf of San Giulio Island, Gaidulf of Bergamo, Ulfari of Treviso (*Hist. Lang.* 4.3), Zagrulf of Verona, Maurisius of Perugia (*Hist. Lang.* 4.8), and a man called Warnecautius, located near Pavia (*Hist. Lang.* 4.13). Gaidoald of Trent and Giusulf II of Friuli eventually returned to the king's side (*Hist. Lang.* 4.27). Theodelinda's brother Gundoald, the duke of Asti, was killed by Agilulf (*Ch.Fr.* 4.34). The king secured the duchy of Benevento, traditionally autonomous, by putting in charge his man Arechi (*Hist. Lang.* 4.18).

The reign's opening years were characterized by war against the empire. Agilulf conquered Monselice (*Hist. Lang.* 4.25), Bagnoreggio, Orvieto (*Hist. Lang.* 4.35), Cremona, and Mantua (*Hist. Lang.* 4.28). He also pillaged and destroyed Padua (*Hist. Lang.* 4.23). Eventually, he sieged Rome in 593 CE. It was on this occasion that Gregory the Great saw the Romans brought away in chains by the Lombards to be sold into slavery, their hands cut off (Gasparri, 2012, 74–75; Markus, 1997, 102–103; Bertolini, 1941, 249–251). According to the Continuator of Prosper, Agilulf desisted from the siege of Rome after meeting Pope → Gregory the Great. The author was apparently echoing the episode of Pope Leo and → Attila narrated by Prosper of Aquitaine (*Auctari Havnensis Extrema* 17; Deliyannis, 2012). Agilulf also suffered setbacks, as the victorious campaigns of the patrician Romanus of Roso in 592 CE (*LP*, vol. I, 312), or when the patrician Gallicinus managed to capture a daughter of the king, eventually returned by Gallicinus' successor Smaragdus (*Hist. Lang.* 4.20, 28). Truces were signed in 592 CE (*Hist. Lang.* 4.12), 605 CE (*Hist. Lang.* 4.32), and 611 CE (*Hist. Lang.* 4.40). In 609 CE an embassy led by Stabilicianus reached Constantinople (*Hist. Lang.* 4.35).

Yet, the relationships with the neighboring barbarian polities were peaceful, although tense. Reconciliation with the → Franks, involving Bishop Agnellus of Trent and Duke Ewin, was a main concern of Agilul's (*Hist. Lang.* 4.1). A *pax perpetua* followed (*Hist. Lang.* 4.13). In 604 CE a marriage between Agilulf's son Adaloald and a daughter of the Frankish king Theudebert was planned (*Hist. Lang.* 4.30). It was together with Theudobert, Clothar, and the Visigothic king Witteric that Agilulf planned to attack and assassinate King Theodoric (*Ch.Fr.* 4.31). A further truce was signed in 611 CE (*Hist. Lang.* 4.40). It was perhaps in 616 CE that Agilulf managed to have the tribute cancelled to the Franks (*Ch.Fr.* 4.35).

Agilulf pursued alliance also with the Avars (Pohl, 1988, 149). A military alliance was established in 603 CE (*Hist. Lang.* 4.4). An embassy eventually reached Agilulf in Milan (*Hist. Lang.* 4.12). The king supported the Avars with ships and manpower, apparently used to conquer an island on the Black Sea (*Hist. Lang.* 4.12). Lombard envoys were sent to Avaria, signing there a *pax perpetua*. A joint attack of Lombards, Slavs, and Avars to Byzantine Istria followed (*Hist. Lang.* 4.24). Agilulf received military backing from the Avars at least in one further occasion (*Hist. Lang.* 4.28). Questionable is if King Agilulf was behind the devastating Avar attack of Friuli of 610 CE (*Hist. Lang.* 4.37; Bognetti, 1948, 103–104).

In religious matters Agilulf defended the Three Chapters (Pohl, 2007). After Patriarch Candidianus of Grado reconciled with Rome in 607 CE, King

Agilulf, together with Duke Gisulf II, promoted Abbot John to patriarch (*Hist. Lang.* 4.33). Agilulf's own faith is unknown, but Saint Columbanus was dissatisfied with his religious beliefs (Col. *Ep.* 5). His wife Theodelinda and his son Adaloald were Catholic. Under Agilulf relationships with the papacy grew better. Gregory the Great lamented the continuous raids of the Lombards, but he also exchanged amicable letters with royal court (Markus, 1997, 105–107). He corresponded with Saint Columbanus, granting the foundation of Bobbio in 613 CE (Richter, 2008, 13–14).

Agilulf is portrayed in the so-called *Lamina di Agilulfo*, a bronze artifact found in unclear circumstances close to Valdinievole, perhaps at the end of the 19th century. The plate was debatably a nose guard of a helmet or the decoration to a wooden casket. It represents the king sitting in his throne surrounded by winged victories and suppliants. Yet, due to the many shadows surrounding the object discovery and iconographic anomalies, the object is perhaps a modern falsification (Rocca & Gasparri, 2010).

After his death Agilulf was succeeded by his son Adaloald until 625 CE. By the reign of King Rothari (636–654 CE), it seems that Agilulf had become victim of a process of *damnatio memoriae*. In the *Origo gentis Langobardorum*, written in the 660s CE, but with a textual layer ascribable to King Rothari's reign, the bloodlines linking the house of Agilulf to the one of his successors are severed. Moreover, the king is remembered only for his wars against fellow Lombards, and a Thuringian origin is attributed to him (Borri, 2014).

Eventually the story of King Agilulf was largely enriched and dramatized. Paul the Deacon, besides reporting the romantic adventure of the king when he first met Theodelinda (*Hist Lang.* 3.35), narrated that, once attending the marriage of Theodelinda and Authari, Agilulf was approached by an *aruspex* who foresaw Agiluf's kingship and the death of Authari (*Hist. Lang.* 3.30). The sinister episode casts a grim shadow on the king's memory (Borri, 2011, 252–253).

As no real monograph has been published yet, a historiography is not applicable (see the Bibliography below).

Bibliography

Balzaretti, R., "Theodelinda, 'Most Glorious Queen': Gender and Power in Lombard Italy," *MHJ* 2, 1999, 183–207.

Bertolini, O., *Roma di fronte a Bisanzio e ai Longobardi*, SdR 9, Rome, 1941.

Bognetti, G.P., *S. Maria foris portas di Castelseprio e la storia religiosa dei Longobardi*, in: G.P. Bognetti, *L'età longobarda*, 4 vols, Milan, 1966–1968, vol. II, 13–673.

Borri, F., "Murder by Death: Alboin's Life, End(s), and Means," *Mill.* 8, 2011, 223–270.

Borri, F., "Romans Growing Beards: Identity and Historiography in Seventh-Century Italy," *Viator* 45, 2014, 39–71.

Everett, N., *Literacy in Lombard Italy, c. 568–774*, Cambridge UK, 2003, 69–72.

Deliyannis, D.M., "The Holy Man and the Conqueror: The Legend of Attila and Pope Leo I," in: M. Coumert, M.-C. Isaïa, K. Krönert & S. Shimahara, eds., *Rerum gestarum scriptor: Histoire et historiographie au Moyen Âge: Hommage à Michel Sot*, Paris, 2012, 239–248.

Delogu, P., *Le origini del Medioevo*, Storia 57, Rome, 2010.

Gasparri, S., *I duchi longobardi*, StuSt 109, Rome, 1978.

Gasparri, S., *Italia longobarda: Il regno, i Franchi, il papato*, Rome, 2012.

Jarnut, J., *Agilolfingerstudien: Untersuchungen zur Geschichte einer adligen Familie im 6. und 7. Jahrhundert*, MGMA 32, Stuttgart, 1986.

Markus, R.A., *Gregory the Great and His World*, Cambridge MA, 1997.

McCormick, M., *Eternal Victory: Triumphal Rulership in Late Antiquity, Byzantium and the Early Medieval West*, Harvard, 1986.

Pohl, W., "Memory, Identity and Power in Lombard Italy," in: Y. Hen & M. Innes, *The Uses of the Past in the Early Middle Ages*, Cambridge UK, 2000, 9–28.

Pohl, W., *Die Awaren: Ein Steppenvolk in Mitteleuropa, 567–822 n.Chr.*, Munich, 1988, [2]2002.

Pohl, W., "Heresy in Secundus and Paul the Deacon," in: C.M. Chazelle & C.R.E. Cubitt, *The Crisis of the Oikoumene: The Three Chapters and the Failed Quest for Unity in the Sixth-Century Mediterranean*, SEMA 14, Turnhout, 2007, 243–264.

Richter, M., *Bobbio in the Early Middle Ages: The Abiding Legacy of Columbanus*, Dublin, 2008.

Rocca, C. La, & S. Gasparri, "Forging an Early Medieval Royal Couple: Agilulf, Theodelinda and the 'Lombard Treasure' (1888 – 1932)," in: M. Mehofer & W. Pohl, eds., *Archaeology of Identity/Archäologie der Identität*, FGM 17, Vienna, 2010, 79–287.

FRANCESCO BORRI

Agnes

On Jan 21 the liturgical calendar celebrates Agnes, Roman virgin and martyr, whose cult is early attested to and veneration of whom is widespread in the whole Christian church. Agnes was martyred in Rome; the year is unknown, but it was most likely at the time of the persecutions of Decius (250–251 CE) or of Valerian (258–260 CE). There are no historical sources about her martyrdom, but there is considerable literary, archaeological, and liturgical evidence.

The hagiographic tradition (→ Hagiography), although diversified by type and content, presents some common elements: Agnes' young age, his choice of chastity, martyrdom faced with pride. Condemnation is rogue, decapitation, or a throat injury (*iugulatio*), depending on the texts.

A quick examination of the most significant literary sources will allow us to trace the lines of this character, who was widely viewed in the early church as a model of female consecrated virginity (→ Virgin/Virginity).

1. Literary Sources

The late antique hagiographic tradition includes firstly literary compositions: in poetry an epigram by Pope Damasus (305–c. 384 CE) and two hymns, one by Ambrose, bishop of Milan (340–c. 397 CE), and one by the Spanish poet Prudentius (348–after 405 CE); in prose, some extracts from Ambrose's *De virginibus* and four redactions of a *Passio*: one in Latin (*BHL* 156), two in Greek (*BHG* 45–46), and one in Syriac (*BHO* 34). The links among the various literary works are not well defined (see Lanéry, 2014; Milazzo, 2015), nor is the relation between them and the *Passio*. However, they all contribute to depicting the image of this very young martyr, who spontaneously seeks her martyrdom as if it were marriage.

Pope Damasus (366–384 CE), a great promoter of the cult of → martyrs (Saxer, 1986; Sághy, 2000; Reutter, 2009, 57–153), placed a marble slab on the tomb of the martyr, on which the engraver Furius Dionisius Philocalus (mid-late 4th cent. CE) carved in elegant capital letters an epigram composed by Damasus himself (Ihm, 1895, 43–45; Ferrua, 1942, 175–178). Today this epigraph is affixed on the wall of the staircase leading to the basilica on the Via Nomentana. In the epigram, Agnes is described as an extraordinarily brave girl. She is sentenced to the stake: ashamed to be seen naked, she lets her hair down so that no mortal eyes can glance at her body, "temple of the Lord" (1 Cor 3:16–17; 6:19; 2 Cor 6:16). → Ambrose of Milan is the author of the praise to Agnes (Ambr. *Virg.* 1.2.5–9), and of the hymn "Agnes, beatae virginis" (hymn 8: its attribution to Ambrose is "certain" according to G. Nauroy (1992, 363–374), and C. Lanéry (2008, 239–242); it is "probable" according to M. Simonetti (1952, 403). P. Franchi de' Cavalieri (1962, 296–301), on the contrary, attributes it to a possible imitator of Ambrose). In *De virginibus*, Agnes is "exemplum of virginity and martyrdom" as her name reveals, implicitly referring to Greek (ἀγνή, "chaste," *agna*, "lamb," then "sacrificial victim"). She thus wins the crown of a "dual martyrdom, of modesty and faith" (Ambrose) and at last dies, not by flames, as Damasus reports, but by the sword. Similarly, in hymn 8 (Nauroy, 1992, 361–403) the central theme is the link between martyrdom and virginity: Agnes escapes from home, where her parents have locked her up. She is proud and challenges her torturers; eventually, she wraps herself in her dress, before falling down from her executioner's blows (this description seems to be influenced by the literary pattern of the Euripidean Polissena; see P. Franchi de' Cavalieri (1908, 146–149); R. Braun (1983); G. Nauroy (2003, 624–6300); C. Lanéry, 2008, 239–240), and V. Milazzo (2015, 403–405).

Prudentius' hymn 14 of *Peristephanon* (Canningam, 1966, 386–402; Fux, 2003, 463–496, with commentary) was composed between the end of 4th century and the beginning of 5th century CE (Fux, 2003, 43–46). Here, the main core of the story is Agnes' condemnation to a brothel, the most terrible punishment for a virgin. The girl is stripped; nobody dares to look at her but an impudent passerby, who had looked at her, had been blinded. Finally, the girl dies by the sword of a soldier (on the sexual connotations of vv. 70–80, see Burrus, 1995). The poem ends with the apotheosis of Agnes treading upon Satan's head (see Gen 3:15).

The last text is the pseudo-epigraphical *Passio s. Agnetis* (*BHL* 156: *ActaSS Ian*, vol. II, 351–354; PL 17, 813–821) dated between the 5th and 7th century CE, whose author claims to be Ambrose. It is the most renowned and widespread text in the hagiographic dossier of the Roman martyr (more than 400 manuscripts across Europe; see Lanéry, 2008, 347–349). Here, the young girl attracts the son of Symphronius, the *praefectus* of the city, who asks her to marry, but she claims to have already been betrothed to Jesus Christ, her heavenly spouse. So, Agnes is arrested and dragged through the streets to a brothel; her hair spontaneously grows long and thick to cover her naked body as a dress; then a blinding light and a pure white tunic protect her from the glances of those who want to approach. The son of the *praefectus* tries to touch Agnes, but he is immediately struck to death by the light surrounding her. At his father's request, Agnes prays to God, and the young man revives, acknowledging the greatness of the Christian God. Nevertheless, the pagan crowd, demands Agnes' death. So, she is burned alive, and then beheaded and buried in a cemetery on the Via Nomentana. A few days later, a girl named Emerentiana is stoned to death near Agnes' tomb. One day, as her parents are praying by Agnes' sepulcher, she appears to them surrounded by a multitude of glorious virgins and with a white lamb at her side. The *Passio* also recounts the healing of Constantia/Constantina, Emperor Constantine's daughter. She is said to be sick with leprosy, and although a pagan, she prays to Agnes for healing her. Constantia is miraculously cured, converts to Christianity and builds a basilica in honor of Agnes with an attached mausoleum for herself; morever, she takes a vow of chastity and the veil, followed by several Roman virgins. P. Franchi de' Cavalieri (1962, 341–354) considers the final part of the text a later juxtaposition; C. Lanéry, conversely, an integral part of the original text, probably written by a a well-learned and skillful Roman forger of the early 6th century CE, who was close to Pope Symmachus and eager to increase the antiquity and imperial prestige of a Roman female monastery by attributing its foundation to Constantia, (Lanéry, 2008, 355–361, 371–376).

The several texts and verse rewritings and adaptations of the Latin text of the *Passio* (*BHL Novum Supplementum* 160–164e) were extremely successful from both a liturgical and literary point of view (on its legacy in the Middle Ages, see Thompson, 2001; Giovini, 2002; Lanéry 2008, 371–383; Tomea, 2010). The most noteworthy of them are the following:

1. Aldhelm of Malmesbury's *De virginitate* in prose (ch. 45) and verse (1925–1974), composed between 685 and 700 CE;
2. The Venerable Bede's (672–735 CE) hymn "Illuxit alma saeculis" (Williamson, 2012);
3. Hrotswita of Gandersheim's poem *Agnes* (10th cent. CE).

Moreover, the *Passio* became part of the most important medieval legendaries, like the *Legenda aurea* by Jacopo da Varazze (13th century), ch. 24.

The two Greek redactions *BHG* 45 and 46 present some differences among them: in *BHG* 45 Agnes is a well-read woman (not a girl) who teaches matrons and dares to argue with the judges; arrested and dragged to the brothel, she is then condemned to the stake. In contrast, *BHG* 46 is surely a translation of the Latin redaction (Franchi de' Cavalieri, 1962, 361–379). The Syriac version *BHO* 34 is a translation of *BHG* 45.

Agnes is mentioned by Ambrose in *Virg.* 1.4.19; *Ep.* 7.36; and *Off.* 1.41.204; by → Jerome (*Ep.* 130.5), by → Augustine of Hippo (*Serm.* 273.6, 286.2), and by → Gregory the Great (*Hom. Evan.* 11.3). Another sermon, the first text to employ the *Passio*, once attributed to Maximus of Turin (d. 420; *BHL* 158a; PL 57, 643–648; the same sermon is sometimes ascribed to Ambrose: PL 17, 701–705), is spurious and probably dates to the second half of the 6th century CE (Lanéry, 2008, 414–418).

2. Liturgical Sources

The name of Agnes recurs in several liturgical sources ranging from the oldest list of Roman martyrs: in the 336 CE → *Depositio martyrum* (Valentini & Zucchetti, 1942, 17), and in the calendars of Carthage (early 6th cent. CE) and of Naples (9th cent. CE; → Liturgical Year); in the *Hieronymian Martyrology* (6th cent. CE) and in the historical martyrologies by Bede (8th cent. CE) and by Usuard (9th cent. CE); in the *Synassarium Constantinopolitanum* and in the menologies; and in Gelasian and Gregorian sacramentaries and in the lectionaries for the Mass. She is listed among the martyrs in both the Ambrosian and Roman canons of the Mass.

3. Archeological Sources

The monumental complex of Agnes in Rome, erected over a preexisting cemetery along the Via Nomentana, was built during the pontificate of → Sylvester I (314–335 CE; Frutaz, 1960; Schirò, 2012, 141–145). The *Book of Pontiffs* (→ *Liber pontificalis*) records that Emperor Constantine the Great (306–337 CE; → Constantine I) built a basilica in honor of the martyr "at the request of his daughter" (*LP*, vol. I, 80). Next to the basilica, the Augusta had a splendid mausoleum built up between 338 and 350 CE, where she was entombed (it is nowadays known as the Mausoleum of Saint Constantia or Saint Constantina, see J. Rasch & A. Arbeiter (2007). It is very likely that Constantia is the author of the acrostic poem in honor of Agnes carved in the basilica's apse (*ICUR* n.s. 20752; Ihm, 1895, 87–88; Ferrua, 1942, 246–250). This epigraph, no longer legible in its original location, was transcribed in several manuscripts at the bottom of hymn 14 of Prudentius' *Liber Peristephanon*. The *Book of Pontiffs* also recounts that Pope Liberius (352–366 CE) adorned Agnes' sepulcher with a marble slab (*pluteus*: *LP*, vol. I, 208) depicting a very young Agnes praying. The slab is now placed over the walls at the bottom of the 16th-century entrance staircase to the "basilica Honoriana." Liberius' successor was Pope Damasus, the author of the above-mentioned epigraph. Moreover, the *Book of Pontiffs* records that Pope Symmachus (498–514 CE) restored the abandoned basilica (*LP*, vol. I, 263) and that Honorius (625–638 CE) rebuilt it over the shrine of the martyr (*LP*, vol. I, 323). The Byzantine mosaic on the apse of the "basilica Honoriana" displays a central standing figure of Agnes in sumptuous garments and jewelry, flanked by Symmachus and Honorius. The basilica was further embellished and repeatedly restored over the centuries and suffered from destructive interventions (e.g. the frescoes with scenes from the *Passion* had been destroyed by the end of the 16th cent.).

The place of worship, maybe an oratory, located near the stadium of Domitianus (a place related to the facts of the *Passion*) and mentioned by the Anonymous from Einsiedeln (Valentini & Zucchetti, 1942, 180–181) at the end of the 8th century CE, has an uncertain but probably earlier dating. Pope Callixtus II (1119–1124 CE) converted it into a small basilica, consecrated in 1123 CE. In 1652 Francesco Borromini received from Pope Innocent X (1644–1655) the commission to construct the new church, one of the masterpieces of Roman Baroque architecture "Saint Agnese in Agone," facing into the current Piazza Navona. Outside of Rome, in Ravenna, a church was dedicated to Agnes in the 5th century CE (Agnel. *LPR* 31; 33).

Several iconographic sources such as the 4th-century CE gold-stained glass (Morey & Ferrari, 1959, 75, 82–85, 121, 124, 221, 226, 246, 248, 265, 283, 412, 425) and Leo's cubicle fresco at the catacombs of Commodilla (dating to the last 20 years of the 4th cent. CE) display the praying martyr with a lamb (Ferrua, 1959; Proverbio, 2012, 429–430). The small fresco, unearthed in the 1950s only, represents today the first example of this successful iconographic pattern, long before it was displayed, at the end of the 6th century CE, in the mosaics depicting the procession of virgins in Ravenna's Sant'Apollinare Nuovo. Agnes is one of the most portrayed martyr in the European paintings of the Middle Ages and Renaissance.

Bibliography

Allard, P., "Agnès," in: *DACL*, vol. I/1, Paris, 1907, 906–918.

Braun, R., "'Honeste cadere': Un topos d'hagiographie antique," *BCRL* 1, 1983, 1–12.

Burrus, V., "Reading Agnes: The Rhetoric of Gender in Ambrose and Prudentius," *JECS* 3/1, 1995, 25–46.

Cunningam, M.P., ed., *Aurelii Prudentii Clementis Carmina*, CCSL 126, Turnholti, 1966.

Dreves, G.M, "Der Hymnus des hl. Ambrosius 'Agnes beatae virginis'," *ZKTh* 25, 1901, 356–365.

Ferrua, A., ed., *Epigrammata Damasiana*, Vatican City, 1942.

Ferrua, A., "S. Agnese e l'agnello," *LCCA* 110/1, 1959, 141–150.

Franchi de' Cavalieri, P., "S. Agnese nella tradizione e nella leggenda," *RQ.S* 10, 1899 = P. Franchi de' Cavalieri, *Scritti agiografici*, vol. I, Vatican City, ²1962, 293–381

Franchi de' Cavalieri, P., "Intorno ad alcune reminiscenze classiche nelle leggende agiografiche del IV secolo," in: P. Franchi de' Cavalieri, *Hagiographica*, Rome, 1908, 121–164.

Frutaz, A.P., *Il complesso monumentale di sant'Agnese e di santa Costanza*, Vatican City, 1960.

Fux, P.-Y., ed., *Les sept passions de Prudence (Peristephanon 2.5.9.11–14)*, Freiburg, 2003.

Giovini, M., "Come trasformare un bordello in una casa di preghiere: Il motivo della verginità redentrice nell'

Agnes di Rosvita di Gandersheim," *Maia* 54/3, 2002, 589–617.

Ihm, M., ed., *Anthologiae Latinae supplementa*, vol. I: *Damasi epigrammata*, Leipzig, 1895.

Jones, H., "Agnes and Constantia: Domesticity and Cult Patronage in the 'Passion of Agnes'," in: K. Cooper & J. Hillner, eds., *Religion, Dynasty, and Patronage in Early Christian Rome 300–900*, Cambridge UK, 2007, 115–139.

Josi, E., & R. Aprile, "Agnese," in: *BSS*, vol. I, Rome, 1961, 382–411.

Lanéry, C., *Ambroise de Milan hagiographe*, Paris, 2008.

Lanéry, C., "La légende de sainte Agnès: Quelques réflexions sur la genèse d'un dossier hagiographique (IVe–VIe s.)," in: *Le culte de sainte Agnès à place Navone entre Antiquité et Moyen Âge*, MEFR.M, [on line]126/1, 2014.

Milazzo, V., "Verginità e sacrificio: Agnese in Damaso, Ambrogio e Prudenzio," in: C. Giuffré Scibona & A. Mastrocinque, eds., *"Ex pluribus unum": Studi in onore di Giulia Sfameni Gasparro*, Rome, 2015, 397–413.

Morey, C.R., & G. Ferrari, *The Gold-Glass Collection of the Vatican Library: With Additional Catalogues of Other Gold-Glass Collections*, Vatican City, 1959.

Nauroy, G., ed. & comm., Hymne 8, "Agnes beatae virginis," in: J. Fontaine, ed., *Ambroise de Milan: Hymnes*, Paris 1992, 361–403.

Nauroy, G., "La courtisane au désert et la vierge sacrifiée: Ambroise de Milan, médiateur culturel entre Euripide et Anatole France?" in: G. Nauroy, *Ambroise de Milan: Écriture et esthétique d'une exégèse pastorale: Quatorze études*, Bern, 2003, 617–636.

Palmer, A.M., *Prudentius on the Martyrs*, Oxford, 1989.

Proverbio, C., "Martiri e potenti: A proposito del cubicolo di Leone in Commodilla," in: A. Coscarella & P. De Santis, eds., *Martiri, Santi, Patroni: Per una archeologia della devozione: Atti del X congresso nazionale di archeologia cristiana*, Cosenza, 2012, 425–436.

Rasch, J., & A. Arbeiter, *Das Mausoleum der Constantina in Rom*, Mainz, 2007.

Reutter, U., *Damasus, Bischof von Rom (366–384): Leben und Werk*, Tübingen, 2009.

Sághy, M., "'Scinditur in partes populus': Pope Damasus and the Martyrs of Rome," *EME* 9/3, 2000, 273–287.

Saxer, V., "Damase et le calendrier des fêtes de martyrs de l'église romaine," in: *Saecularia Damasiana: Atti del convegno internazionale per il XVI centenario della morte di papa Damaso I*, Vatican City, 1986, 59–88.

Schirò, G., "Sant'Agnese fuori le mura," in: S. Boesch Gajano, T. Caliò, F. Scorza Barcellona & L. Spera, eds., *Santuari d'Italia: Roma*, Rome, 2012, 141–145.

Simonetti, M., "Studi sull'innologia popolare cristiana dei primi secoli," *AANL.M*, 349 (1952), serie VIII 4/6, 342–484.

Thompson, A.B., "The Legend of St. Agnes: Improvisations and the Practice of Hagiography," *Exem.* 13/2, 2001, 355–397.

Tomea, P., "'Corpore quidem iuvencula sed animo cana': La 'Passio Agnetis' *BHL* 156 e il topos della 'puella senex' nell'agiografia mediolatina," *AnBoll* 128/1, 2010, 18–55.

Trout, D.E., "Damasus and the Invention of Early Christian Rome," *JMEMS* 33/3, 2003, 517–537.

Valentini, R., & G. Zucchetti, eds., *CTCR*, vol. II, Rome, 1942.

Williamson, C., "Bede's Hymn to St. Agnes of Rome: The Virgin Martyr as a Male Monastic 'exemplum'," *Viator* 43/1, 2012, 39–66.

Zimmermanns, K., "Agnes von Rom," in: *LCI*, vol. V, Freiburg, 1973, 58–63.

Zocca, E., "(Ri-)Scrivere di santi: Sulle tracce di Agnese," in: *'Acri Sanctorum Investigatori': Miscellanea di studi in memoria di Gennaro Luongo*, Rome, 2019, 261–284.

VINCENZA MILAZZO

Agnus Dei

The figure of the *agnus dei* ("Lamb of God"; Gk ἀμνός τοῦ Θεοῦ) is among the most striking and versatile images in biblical and early Christian sources. The identification of Christ as the lowly yet victorious lamb, which finds its scriptural inspiration primarily in the Gospel of John (John 1:29; 1:36; see Rev 5:1–7), came to exert profound influence on Christian theological, liturgical, musical, and artistic traditions. The figure appears frequently in sources ranging from the earliest Christian funerary art to congregational song, culminating in the insertion of the proclamation *agnus dei* into the Roman liturgy at the fraction rite. In its various iterations, *agnus dei* reflects an understanding of Jesus' humble sacrifice effecting victory over death and sin.

1. History and Scriptural Background

The motif of the *agnus dei* in biblical and early Christian material is deeply influenced by agrarian conceptions of a tribe or nation gathered as a flock under a shepherd. Ancient Egyptian, Persian, and Greek literary and epigraphic sources attest to the identification of the king as a good shepherd who guards the nation, his flock. At the same time, divinities, including Ammon among the Egyptians and Zeus among the Greeks, were often associated with ram horns, which signified their power and strength, an attribute incorporated into depictions of Alexander the Great (Lerdon, 2020, 72–74).

The Hebrew conception of the Lord as shepherd, especially in the Psalms (e.g. Ps 23; 79:13; 100:3), adopts the imagery to stress divine care and protection for both the nation of → Israel and the individual at prayer. At the same time, the lamb as object of the good shepherd's particular concern appears with some frequency throughout the Scriptures. Influenced by accounts of Abel's offering of the firstborn of his flock (Gen 4:4) and the ram that → Abraham offers as a holocaust in place of Isaac (Gen 22:13), the scriptural basis for the title is found in references to the lamb of sacrifice, eventually linked directly to the → Passover (see Exod 12:46) as well as to the daily offering of two lambs in the sanctuary (Exod 29:38–39; Num 28:4) and to sacrifices for special occasions (e.g. Lev 14:24–25; 22:18–19; Harrington, 2007, 513). Drawing links between the paschal lamb (Exod 12:1–4) and the "gentle lamb" of offering (Isa 53:7; Jer 11:19), the Hebrew accounts combine the connotations of the ram as a beast of strength with the meek submission of the humble lamb (Rusam, 2005, 67; Lerdon, 2020, 47–48). Jewish apocalyptic literature regularly draws on the image of a lamb, at times to signify the victory of the lowly over the exalted (*1 En.* 89–90), and other times to indicate the chosen of God. The *Targum Yerushalmi* on Exod 1:15 records a dream of Pharaoh where Moses appears as a lamb (Koch, 1966, 79). Likewise, the *Testamentum Josephus* (19:8) speaks of a vision of a "spotless lamb" (Gk ἀμνός ἄμωμος) who conquers all the other beasts (Lerdon, 2020, 81).

The Hebrew background inspired extensive reflection on Christ as the innocent or spotless lamb, whose life, passion, and death constitute an eternal sacrifice for the sins of the world. In reflections on the sacrifice of Christ (e.g. 1 Cor 5:7; Acts 8:32), early Christian sources explore the ritual and spiritual significance of the lamb (Nielsen, 2006, 225–226). The Gospel of John (→ John the Apostle) records → John the Baptist identifying Jesus by the proclamation, "behold the Lamb of God, who takes away the sin of the world" (John 1:29), a reference that exerted heavy influence on subsequent writings and congregational prayer. Other New Testament texts draw on the link to stress the expiatory power of Christ's suffering. The Lamb of the book of Revelation (→ Revelation, Book of) stands out as central to the visions of divine triumph in the apocalypse (Rev 5:6; Bieringer, 2007), where the diminutive ἀρνίον ("little lamb," from ἀρήν, or "lamb"), in contrast to the Gospel of John's preference for ἀμνός ("lamb"), may

stress the lamb's lowliness (Lerdon, 2020, 56), while his "seven horns" and "seven eyes" may signify his omnipotence and omniscience, offering the faithful a symbol of hope (Harrington, 2007, 515; Giesen, 2012, 175). The implications of the lamb for Christian life are expressed in 1 Peter, which exhorts the audience to recognize the blood of the lamb as the source of their salvation (1 Pet 1:18–19; Giesen, 2012, 186). Christ depicted as *agnus dei* therefore linked a range of basic themes central to the faith of the community, including purity, humility, and sacrifice.

2. Early Christian Treatments

Early Christian commentators explore the various connotations of *agnus dei* at length (Nikolasch, 1963). → Melito of Sardis links Christ typologically both to the ram sacrificed by Abraham and the slaughtered lamb of Isa 53 (frgm. 9; see Hall, 1979, 75). → Tertullian, perhaps influenced by Melito, takes the "horns" (Lat. *cornua*) of the ram as types for the extent of the → cross (Tert. *Adv. Jud.* 13.21). Later interpreters extend the specific correspondence between the lamb of sacrifice and the crucifixion in detail (Nikolasch, 1963, 25–40). The Greek patristic (→ Patrology/Patristics) interpretation of "passover" (Gk πάσχα) as "passion" or suffering (Gk πάσχω) reinforced the links (e.g. Iren. *Haer.* 4.10.1).

Christ as *agnus dei* has theological implications, both for the union of divinity and humanity in the Lord, as well as for his role in communal sacrifice. → Origen provides an early witness to an interpretation that took the biblical lamb who is sacrificed to refer specifically to Christ as human (Or. *Comm. Jo.* 6.273–274; Dickson, 2018, 32). In the 4th century CE, disputes over the union between God the → Word and human flesh were often related to the self-offering of the Lamb (Eus. *Pasch.* 3; Athan. *Ep. Aeg. Lib.* 17). Similar emphases on the humanity of Christ as precisely that which is offered appear in Syriac (e.g. Ephr. *Hym. Fid.* 18.13) and Latin sources (Ambr. *Exp. Ps. 118* 13.6).

At the same time, Christ as *agnus dei* embodies the meek self-offering that also victoriously reconciles God and fallen humanity. Christ as the "ram" of offering is occasionally seen to indicate the sacrifice of the leader of the herd (Ambr. *Abr.* 1.77; Thdt. *Prov.* 10.29–32; Nikolasch, 1963, 58–61). → Augustine of

Hippo, commenting on Isa 53:8, provides a series of reasons for the identification of Christ as both lamb and lion, the former signifying his humble offering and the latter signifying his divine victory over → death (Aug. *Serm.* 375A). At times Christ is identified simultaneously as shepherd and lamb, especially in reflections on Christ the good shepherd (see Matt 18:12–14; John 19:1–16; → Shepherd, The Good). → Ephrem the Syrian's hymn on the crucifixion summarizes: "O Hidden Lamb who slaughtered the visible lamb in the midst of Egypt [...] The Lamb was both shepherded and saw to the shepherding: He shepherds His shepherds." (Ephr. *Hym. Cruc.* 2; trans. Kiraz & Brock, 2006).

In addition to the Christological links, the Lamb of God comes to prominence in theological reflection on the → Eucharist. → Ambrose of Milan draws a direct connection between the title *agnus dei* and the eucharistic offering, where he notes the distinction between an "irrational" beast and the dignity of the divine Christ (Ambr. *Epist.* 1.2.10). → John Chrysostom makes the liturgical link explicit: "In the prayer of petition we approach the Lamb that lies before us" (Chrys. *Hom. 4 in 1 Cor.* 8). By the end of the 4th century CE, then, Christian authors implicitly associated the Lamb with the bread offered liturgically. Such references provide early evidence for the designation of the eucharistic host as the "Lamb," especially in the Byzantine tradition, as it is still known today (Craig, 2011, 109).

3. Liturgical Usage

While early doctrinal and sermonic material linked the Lamb and the eucharistic elements, the earliest evidence for a liturgical proclamation of *agnus dei* emerges only gradually. The *Gloria* includes a quotation of John 1:29 among its praises to Christ. The *Gelasian Sacramentary* (→ *Sacramentarium Gelasianum*) seems to allude to the formula in an instructional rubric for the Easter vigil. The first direct reference appears in the *Ordo Romanus* of the 7th–8th centuries CE, which includes the formula for the fraction rite, when the host would be divided for distribution among the faithful (Craig, 2011, 137–138).

The prompt for the insertion of *agnus dei* in the Roman liturgy remains the subject of some controversy. The earliest clear reference to its insertion appears in the → *Liber pontificalis*, which reports that Pope Sergius I (687–701 CE) ordered the invocation to be sung by clergy and laity throughout the fraction rite. The record includes early evidence for a trope appended to the title, combining the Johannine text and the *kyrie eleison*, "who take away the sins of the world, have mercy on us."

Scholars are divided on the motive for the insertion. Some speculate a link to the formulation of the *Gloria*, which appears much earlier in liturgical usage, and which invokes the *agnus dei* for forgiveness and peace (Iversen, 1980, 197–199). A 4th-century CE Alexandrian codex includes a Greek equivalent of the formula in a rendering of the proclamation. Some others note that the West Syrian liturgy includes a similar formula at the fraction rite; hence, Pope Sergius' Syrian origins and the migration of eastern clergy westward after the Muslim conquests may explain the insertion of an eastern formula into western practice (Iversen, 1980, 196; Taft, 2000, 515). The historical context, as discussed below under "Artistic History," may suggest some relationship to disputes over depicting Christ as a lamb in visual art.

Later developments particularly affect the variable tropes appended to the simple *agnus dei* (Iversen, 1980). These came to be multiplied, introducing an extended series of invocations in the model of earlier litanies, such as the → *kyrie eleison* (Iversen, 1980, 199). The original recitation, simply "have mercy on us" (Lat. *miserere nobis*), was expanded in the 10th century CE with the addition of "grant us peace" (Lat. *dona nobis pacem*). In Requiem Masses, the final request for the congregation, "grant us peace" (Lat. *dona nobis pacem*) became a request for eternal rest to the departed, "grant to them eternal rest" (Lat. *dona eis requiem sempiternam*). Later collections include nearly 100 tropes, often composed in classical meter or adopting rhyme or assonance, as well as rubrics indicating the beating of the breast. Some of these expansions may have weakened the link between *agnus dei* and the fraction rite, as the tropes came to be sung over the → kiss of peace and/ or over communion itself (Craig, 2011, 187–188).

Beginning in the early 9th century CE, the liturgical *agnus dei* itself becomes a subject in commentaries on the Mass. Authors including Amalarius of Metz and Rhabanus Maurus stressed the role the *agnus dei* played in effecting peace among the members of the congregation (Iversen, 1980, 207–209). Such theological interpretation may have further weakened the links between the *agnus dei* and the fraction and distribution of communion. The formula came to be considered an independent element of the liturgy.

The simple formula probably prompted the much later introduction of priest's proclamation of the words of John's Gospel before the reception of the Eucharist: "Behold the Lamb of God; behold the one who takes away the sins of the world" (Lat. *Ecce agnus dei, ecce qui tollit peccata mundi*). The expanded prayer serves as a humble preparation for communion and reflects a shift from the singular "sin" (Lat. *peccatum*) of the scriptural source to the plural.

Musical settings for the refrain and the tropes multiplied. The modern era compositions of *agnus dei* adopt a range of ornate and creative forms, relating it especially to the five classic parts of the Mass, along with *Kyrie, Gloria, Credo,* and *Sanctus.*

4. Artistic History

Along with depictions of Christ as shepherd, lambs are among the earliest images in Christian art, first appearing in catacomb remains from the 3rd and 4th centuries CE (Lerdon, 2020, 124–125). A lamb appears with a dove and a cross-anchor in the 3rd-century CE tombstone of Faustinian from the Crypt of Lucina (Catacombs of San Callisto). In similar depictions, the Lamb comes to be visually linked to the standard of victory, signifying Christ's conquest over evil and death. S. Lerdon has identified 26 distinct "image types" (*Bildtypen*) of the lamb in art history, most of which contain references to the "Lamb of Victory" celebrated in the book of Revelation.

Scholars often observe that the introduction of the *agnus dei* into the fraction rite occurs just at the time of nascent → iconoclasm, where there emerged public disputes over the production and ritual use of visual depictions of Christ. At least in Greek sources, there is some particular resistance to the use of the lamb in such imagery. Canon 82 of the council in Trullo (692 CE) states: "We decree that the figure in human form of the Lamb who takes away the sin of the world, Christ our God, be henceforth exhibited in images, instead of the ancient lamb." Given the anti-western sentiment of some of Trullo's canons, scholars have speculated that the formulary was introduced into the liturgy on account of an anti-eastern reaction (although the proposal is dubious; Taft, 2000, 353).

Accounts of the development of the title "agnus dei" refer also to the wax medallions, usually oval-shaped, made from the paschal candle and stamped with an image of a lamb. Initially given as tokens to the faithful and later blessed regularly by the → pope, the earliest record of such a practice appears in Amalarius of Metz (d. 850 CE). These medallions of the *agnus dei* came to be used as tokens of exchange in the Middle Ages (Snoek, 1995, 296).

Historiography

Scholars of the Hebrew Bible have examined the background and meaning of the lamb, especially in sacrifice, at great length (Schipper, 2013). Studies of Johannine literature have traced the Hebrew Bible's influences and the social and cultural connotations of the *agnus dei* to stress both its continuity and distinction from standard Mediterranean motifs (Hengel, 1966). Biblical scholarship has generally focused on the Hebrew significance of the lamb and its influence on traditions of the Lamb of God across religions (Caspi & Cohen, 1995). Proposals for the interpretation of the Lamb of Revelation range widely and included the claim that meaning itself is intentionally indeterminate (Rusam, 2005). Recent work has explored the symbolic resonance communicated especially through the intertextual links exploited through the metaphor of the lamb (Chan, 2015; Harrington, 2007). Scholars engaged with contemporary literary theory stress the construction of meaning achieved through the "conceptual blending" of the multivalence of the Lamb of God (Nielsen, 2006).

As a liturgical formula, *agnus dei* has received relatively little scholarly attention, at least in comparison with *Gloria* and *Kyrie* (but see Atkinson, 1991). G. Iversen (1980) focuses on the manuscript tradition of the tropes, offering a rare book-length treatment of the formula's origins and development. Historians of art, especially S. Lerdon (2020), who draws on contemporary theories of the metaphor, have studied the origins and interactions between textual and visual depictions of the *agnus dei*. Specialists focus on the image in coinage and wax medallions to examine the symbol in media of cultural and economic exchange (Snoek, 1995). In theological studies, classic treatments of the links between the Scripture and liturgy trace the influence of the Johannine texts on the liturgical celebration (Daniélou, 1956). The image of the lamb continues to inspire constructive theologies (Dickson, 2018).

Bibliography

Atkinson, C.M., "*O amnos tu theu:* The Greek Agnus Dei in the Roman Liturgy from the 8th to the 11th Century," *KMJ* 65, 1981, 7–30.

Bieringer, R., "Das Lamm Gottes, das die Sünde der Welt hinwegnimmt (Joh 1,29): Eine kontextorientierte und redaktionsgeschichtliche Untersuchung auf dem Hintergrund der Passatradition als Deutung des Todes Jesu im Johannesevangelium," in: G. van Belle, *The Death of Jesus in the Fourth Gospel*, Louvain, 2007, 199–232.

Caspi, M., & S. Cohen, *The Binding [Aqedah] and Its Transformation in Judaism and Islam: The Lamb of God*, Lewiston, 1995.

Chan, L.P.C., *Die Metapher des Lammes in der Johannesapokalypse: Eine sprach- und sozialgeschichtliche Analyse*, NTOA/StUNT, Göttingen, 2016.

Craig, B., *Fractio Panis: A History of the Breaking of Bread in the Roman Rite*, Rome, 2011.

Daniélou, J., *The Bible and the Liturgy*, Notre Dame, 1956.

Dickson, J.R., *The Humility and Glory of the Lamb: Toward a Robust Apocalyptic Christology*, Eugene, 2018.

Giesen, H., "Der Christustitel 'Lamm' in der Offenbarung des Johannes und sein religionsgeschichtlicher Hintergrund," in: M. Labahn, & M. Karrer, *Die Johannesoffenbarung: Ihr Text und ihre Auslegung*, Leipzig, 2012, 173–196.

Harrington, D., "The Slain Lamb (Rev 5 5,6.12; 13,8) as an Image of Christian Hope," in: J. Chiu, F. Manzi, F. Urso & C. Estrada, *"Il verbo di dio è vivo": Studi sul nuovo testamento in onore del cardinale Albert Vanhoye, S.I.*, Rome, 2007, 511–519.

Hall, S., *Melito of Sardis: On Pascha and Fragments*, Oxford, 1979.

Hengel, M., "Die Throngemeinschaft des Lammes mit Gott in der Johannes-Apokalypse," *ThBeitr* 27, 1996, 159–175.

Iversen, G., *Tropes de l'Agnus Dei*, CorTrop, vol. IV, Stockholm, 1980.

Kiraz, G., & S. Brock, *Ephrem the Syrian: Select Poems*, Provo, 2006.

Koch, K., "Das Lamm, das Ägypten vernichtet," *ZNW* 57, 1966, 579–593.

Lerdon, S., *Ecce agnus dei: Rezeptionsästhetische Untersuchung zum neutestamentlichen Gotteslamm in der bildenden Kunst*, Göttingen, 2020.

Nielsen, J., "The Lamb of God: The Cognitive Structure of a Johannine Metaphor," in: J. Frey, J. van der Watt & R. Zimmermann, *Imagery in the Gospel of John: Terms, Forms, Themes, and the Theology of Johannine Figurative Language*, Vienna, 2006.

Nikolasch, F., *Das Lamm als Christussymbol in den Schriften der Väter*, WBT 3, Vienna, 1963.

Rusam, D., "Das 'Lamm Gottes' (Joh 1,29.36) und die Deutung des Todes Jesu im Johannesevangelium," *BZ* 49, 2005, 60–74.

Schipper, J., "Interpreting the Lamb Imagery in Isaiah 53," *JBL* 132, 2013, 315–325.

Snoek, G., *Medieval Piety from Relics to the Eucharist*, Leiden, 1995.

Stuhlmacher, P., "Das Lamm Gottes–eine Skizze," in: H. Cancik & H. Lichtenberger, *Geschichte, Tradition, Reflexion: FS für Martin Hengel zum 70. Geburtstag*, Tübingen, 1996, 529–542.

Taft, R., *A History of the Liturgy of St. John Chrysostom*, vol. V: *The Precommunion Rites*, Rome, 2000.

BRIAN DUNKLE

Agrapha → Logia/Agrapha

Agraphon

Agraphon means "unwritten." So the reference is to the "unwritten" sayings of Jesus. This should immediately put us in an impossible position. Since all our knowledge of Jesus and the beginnings of Christianity depend on what was written down or transcribed, more or less by definition we have no access to, and therefore no knowledge, of *unwritten* tradition. Consequently, the common definition of Jesus' *agrapha* has been sayings attributed to Jesus, which were not recorded in the New Testament Gospels but have been referred to elsewhere in the history of earliest Christianity.

1. The Oral Tradition, Mark, and Q

Two important issues are immediately raised. One arises from the fact that, by common account, the records of Jesus' ministry and teaching did not begin to be substantially transcribed till the 60s or even later in the 1st century CE. In which case, assuming that Jesus was crucified (→ Cross/Crucifixion) in about 30 CE, and that the earliest Gospel (→ Mark, Gospel of) was not written before the late 60s CE, we have to envisage some 30 years in which the memory of and traditions of Jesus' teaching were formulated, used, and presumably passed on, in oral terms.

The → Q (Quelle)/two-source hypothesis alleviates the situation somewhat, since it infers from the material common to Matthew and Luke, but unknown in Mark (or unused by Mark?), that Matthew and Luke were able to draw on a collection of Jesus' sayings, where the collection had been made earlier. The problem is that while much of the common material is so close in wording that the hypothesis that it was drawn from a common text/ source in Greek makes good sense, about half of the shared material, while dealing with what seems to be the same material/tradition, is often quite different in wording. So, was there one further written source (Q) or several (Q^1, Q^2, Q^3 ...)?

This suggests that the variety of forms and wordings in which the sayings of Jesus were transmitted in the Synoptic Gospels must at least have reflected the diversity of wording and form in which the Jesus tradition was formulated and grouped, celebrated and taught in the growing range of churches in Israel and beyond. However, the fact that the great bulk of the Synoptic teaching has a striking consistency and indeed that a clear and consistent picture of the one who formulated the teaching emerges gives confidence that the circulation and transmission process of the Jesus tradition, while keeping the tradition alive, did not corrupt it or add significant other or interpretative material.

2. John and Thomas

A second issue arises from the fact that there are more documents known as "Gospels" than those of Mark, Matthew (→ Matthew the Apostle), and Luke (→ Luke, Gospel of). Notably, of course, there are the Gospels of John (→ John the Apostle) and of *Thomas*. In John it is almost as though a different Jesus was being recorded. The dilemma posed can be eased by the probability that the teaching attributed to Jesus by John is not so much a remembrance of what Jesus in the event taught, but more an extensive reflection

on who Jesus was and on the significance of his mission. For the Johannine discourses often seem to grow out of or to be based on more aphoristic teaching of Jesus as evidenced by the Synoptic tradition. Note, for example, the following comparisons:

John; *Synoptics* [] *John*; *Synoptics*
3:5; Matt 18:3 [] 10:1–18; Matt 18:12–13/Luke 15:4–7
3:29; Mark 3:29 [] 13:16; Matt 10:24/Luke 6:40
6:20; Mark 6:50 [] 13:20; Matt 10:40/Luke 10:16
6:26–58; Mark 14:22; 14:24 [] 15–26–27; Mark 13:11

In fact, what we see in John, then, are elements that were present but not prominent in the earlier tradition, brought into the spotlight and their significance spelled out at length, notably the call to faith and the promise of life eternal (→ Immortality). And we see elements which one or more of the earlier Gospels had already reflected on and developed, even if modestly, similarly brought to center stage and given a prominence that showed how much more light could be shed on the significance of Jesus' mission and teaching, notably the Father-Son imagery and the reinforcement of Jesus' divine authority. Because the roots of this can be clearly identified in the earlier Jesus tradition, this can be characterized as a development of the earlier Jesus tradition *from within*.

In contrast, in the case of the *Gospel of Thomas* (→ Thomas the Apostle), much of the teaching attributed to Jesus has the same character as the Synoptic tradition. Of the 114 *Thomas* logia, 42 contain close parallel material, and when less close parallels are included, the figure goes up to 63 or more. This assuredly indicates that *Thomas* shared a great deal of the Jesus tradition known to us from the Synoptics. Other material, however, seems to come from a different source, even though attributed to Jesus. For example,

- *Gos. Thom.* 28 – Jesus said: "I stood in the midst of the world, and I appeared to them in flesh. I found all of them drunk. I found none of them thirsty. And my soul suffered pain for the sons of men, because they are blind in their hearts and do not see that they have come into the world empty, seeking to go out of the world empty again. But now they are drunk. When they shake off (the effects of) their wine, then they will repent."

- *Gos. Thom.* 29 – Jesus said: "If the flesh existed for the sake of the Spirit, it would be a miracle. If the Spirit (existed) for the sake of the body, it would be a miracle of miracles! But I marvel at how this great wealth settled in this poverty."
- *Gos. Thom.* 49 – Jesus said: "Blessed are the celibate people, the chosen ones, because you will find the kingdom. For you are from it. You will return there again."
- *Gos. Thom.* 50 – Jesus said: "If they say to you: "Where did you come from?" say to them: "We came from the light" – the place where the light came into being of its own accord and established (itself) and became manifest through their image. If they say to you: "Is it you?" say: "We are its children, and we are the chosen people of the living Father." If they ask you: "What is the sign of your Father in you?" say to them: "It is movement and rest."
- *Gos. Thom.* 56 = *Gos. Thom.* 80 – Jesus said: "Whoever has come to know the world has found a corpse. And he who has found a corpse, of him the world is not worthy."
- *Gos. Thom.* 114 – Simon Peter said to them: "Mary should leave us because women are not worthy of life." Jesus said: "Look, I shall lead her, in order to make her male, so that she too may become a living spirit, resembling you males. For every woman who will make herself male will enter the kingdom of heaven."

In contrast to the Johannine tradition, the distinctive *Thomas* material does not appear to be an unfolding of the Synoptic material on which *Thomas* draws. The distinctive *Gospel of Thomas* is an add-on to the Synoptic-like tradition; it has another source. The Synoptic tradition could be read in the light of *Thomas'* analysis of the human condition, but the reading was not drawn from that tradition; it was imposed upon it. If John's can be characterized as a development of the earlier Jesus tradition *from within*, *Thomas'* would have to be described as a development *from without*, drawing on a very different understanding of the human situation and a very different understanding of the good news that it needed. In short, the distinctive *Thomas* teaching material should not be counted as *agrapha*, unrecorded sayings of Jesus only rediscovered with the discovery of the *Gospel of Thomas*. They were additions to the Jesus tradition, tacked on to increase its appeal, but not deriving from Jesus himself.

Even so, *Thomas* raises the question whether some of it has drawn on memories of Jesus' teaching that the Synoptists chose to pass over. Here the evidence of *agrapha* could play an important role in either confirming that the Synoptic portrayal was sufficiently complete (sufficient to give an accurate portrayal of Jesus and his ministry) or suggesting that the Synoptists had given a one-sided or curtailed presentation of Jesus and his teaching.

3. Other Streams of Jesus Tradition

It is already clear from the *Gospel of Thomas* that there were other streams of Jesus tradition than those preserved in the New Testament Gospels. So, what other attestation is available regarding the Jesus tradition? How valuable is the source material either as further testimony to the remembered Jesus or as testimony to the development and developing character of the Jesus tradition? The issues have become of substantially greater importance since in the later decades of the 20th century it became fashionable in some scholarly circles to find in these "other gospels" expressions of Jesus tradition that were *earlier* than the tradition of the New Testament Gospels. This was partly a follow-through from the great quest for the pre-Christian gnostic redeemer myth, which featured so strongly (and failed) in the middle decades of the 20th century. Partly also the effect of a weariness with a quest for the historical Jesus (→ Christ), which had become bogged down in endless debates about particular passages and features of the New Testament Gospels, and a dissatisfaction with having to depend so much on the traditional sources (particularly → Acts, Book of) for knowledge of Christianity's beginnings. So the possibility that other writings from the second or even later centuries could contain forms of tradition about Jesus that were earlier than the New Testament traditions, and could even provide a source for some of the New Testament Gospel material, became a great incentive for fresh investigation and speculation. The *Gospel of Thomas* posed the sharpest questions, but the discussion has embraced a good number of other gospels.

In fact, some of what has been casually referred to as "streams of Jesus tradition" would be better imaged as pools or puddles than rivers – *agrapha*, and fragmentary papyri particularly. But others are parts of more extensive writings, or the writings themselves, containing extensive teaching attributed to Jesus or further stories particularly of his birth and infancy and of his ministry and passion.

4. *Agrapha*

For more than a century, that is, from long before the discovery of the *Gospel of Thomas*, close attention has been paid to the fact that various sayings of Jesus or attributed to Jesus are attested in the variant textual traditions of the New Testament Gospels and in the church fathers, sayings that are without parallel in the New Testament Gospels and would otherwise be unknown. Their description as *agrapha* is a further reminder of the mindset that envisaged the transmission of Jesus' teaching almost exclusively in literary terms. The very few that have impressed or appealed to 20th-century scholars as probably "authentic" (teaching that Jesus himself gave) are a reminder of the richness, diversity, and durability of the oral Jesus tradition. But their credibility as sayings that Jesus was remembered as uttering depends largely on their compatibility with the more familiar Synoptic traditions, and that credibility is minimal. So while the *agrapha* attest the developing character of what can still be included under the title "Jesus tradition," their value lies in demonstration that the late Jesus tradition was a stream that was becoming more and more remote from the Jesus tradition of the 1st century CE.

Two of the most interesting *agrapha* occur in the New Testament itself:

- Luke 6:5 Codex Bezae – On the same day he (Jesus) saw a man working on the → Sabbath and said to him: "Man, if you know what you are doing, you are blessed; but if you do not know, you are accursed and a transgressor of the law";
- Acts 20:35 – Jesus is quoted as saying: "It is more blessed to give than to receive."

Both have a ring of the wisdom and priorities of Jesus as attested elsewhere in the Synoptic tradition. That the former is recorded no earlier than the Codex Bezae (5th cent. CE) makes it doubtful that

it can be traced back to Jesus himself, but if not, its formulation would probably have been attributed to (the exalted) Jesus or to the inspiration of his teaching.

The latter also lacks attestation elsewhere, but it is consistent with other teaching of Jesus, and John 21:25 alerts us to the probability that not all of Jesus' teaching was written down.

In short, the sayings cohere well with the teaching of Jesus recorded in the Synoptic Gospels, in both style and emphasis, and as such add very little to the Jesus tradition.

- In 1 Thess 4:15, Paul (→ Paul the Apostle) refers to "the word of the Lord, that we who are alive, who are left until the coming of the Lord, will by no means precede those who have died."

But this should not be counted as an *agraphon*.

It deals with an issue that only came up in the earliest days of the Christian mission, dealing with the problem of those believers who had died before the (second) coming of Christ, and should probably be attributed to a prophetic utterance given in a gathering of believers concerned at the unexpected death of fellow believers awaiting the → *parousia*.

A saying of Jesus drawn from *Thomas* (82) has attracted much support as probably authentic, even though → Origen, who says he read it somewhere (Or. *Hom. Jer.* 3.3), may show some uncertainty on the matter:

- He who is near me is near the fire. He who is far from me is far from the kingdom.

Beyond that, all that is necessary is to note that the most striking "unknown sayings" illustrate the character and potential value of the *agrapha* as a whole.

- Jer. *Comm. Eph.* 5.4, quotes from "the Hebrew Gospel" Jesus as saying to his disciples: "Never be glad unless you are in charity with your brother" (Elliott, 1933)/"Only then shall you be glad, when you look on your brother with love" (Hofius, in Schneemelcher & Wilson, 1991).
- Epiph. *Pan.* 30.16.5 quotes the *Gospel of the Ebionites* (→ *Ebionites, Gospel of the*) recording Jesus as saying: "I have come to abolish the sacrifices: if you do not cease from sacrificing, the wrath [of God] will not cease from weighing upon you."

The former can certainly be counted as consistent with Jesus' undisputed teaching. But the latter reflects too much the Ebionite (→ Ebionites/Ebionitism) reaction to the destruction of the Jerusalem Temple (→ Temple, Jerusalem) to provide any confidence that it can be traced back to Jesus himself.

Clement of Alexandria, *Stromata*, records two sayings from the *Kerygma Petri* that seem to be elaborations of the traditions of Jesus' (post-resurrection) missionary commissions:

- *Strom.* 6.5.43 notes that in the *Kerygma Petri*, Peter records Jesus saying to the disciples: "If then any of Israel will repent and believe in God through my name, his sins shall be forgiven him; and after 12 years go out into the world lest any say: 'We did not hear.'"
- *Strom.* 6.6.48 has a somewhat similar but more extensive missionary commission by the Lord after his resurrection. Also similar is the Freer logion preserved in Codex W (5th cent. CE) after Mark 16:14, that is, probably a scribal elaboration of the longer ending to Mark's Gospel, itself an addition to Mark's Gospel.

Clement seems also to draw on the more gnostically (→ Gnosis/Gnosticism) inclined teaching that came to be attributed to Jesus:

- *Strom.* 2.9.45 – As it is also written in the *Gospel of the Hebrews*: "He who wonders shall reign, and he who reigns shall rest."
- *Strom.* 3.9.1 – according to the *Gospel of the Egyptians*, Jesus said: "I have come to undo the works of the female," to which → Clement of Alexandria adds the note, "by the 'female' meaning lust, and by "the works" birth and decay."
- *Strom.* 3.13.92 also refers to the *Gospel of the Egyptians* quoting the Lord as saying: "When you tread under foot the covering of shame and when out of two is made one, and the male with the female, neither male nor female."
- *Strom.* 5.14.96 – "He that seeks will not rest until he finds; and he that has found shall marvel; and he that has marveled shall reign; and he that has reigned shall rest" (but not attributed to Jesus).

The first seems to echo and the last to quote *Gos. Thom.* 2, and the third echoes *Gos. Thom.* 37.2 and 22.4–5, as did 2 *Clem.* 12.2.

All in all, the evidence of *agrapha*, while interesting, adds little to our knowledge of tradition that can be traced back to Jesus. What is of interest, as especially in the *Gospel of Thomas*, is the readiness to attribute material to Jesus or to the tradition of his teaching. Whether this was the result of prophetic utterances, or a vagueness as to what could be attributed to Jesus, or reflection on earlier Jesus tradition (as with the Fourth Gospel) can hardly be decided now. We do not even have to assume contrivance or malfeasance, simply a concern to give the teaching offered the authority of Jesus. When the undisputed Jesus tradition is set alongside it, very little suggests that any more than one or two items should be attributed to Jesus during his life.

But it does confirm that Jesus was more widely seen as an authoritative teacher whose teaching should be cherished.

5. Fragmentary Papyri

The → Oxyrhynchus-papyri provide evidence that the *Gospel of Thomas* was known in Greek. But other papyri from Egypt indicate that the Jesus tradition was widely known and was being elaborated in different ways.

In Papyrus Egerton 2, the front and back of fragment 1 show clear evidence of the influence of John's Gospel – drawing on John 5:39, 45; 9:29; 5:46; 10:31; 7:30; 10:39. But fragment 1 recto also uses the story known from Luke 5:12–16 parr. Most interesting, however, is fragment 2 recto, which weaves together John 3:2, Mark 12:14–15 parr., Luke 6:46, and Matt 15:7–9 par. It is of interest that what we know as the content of three or even four written Gospels are thus interwoven, and that no *agrapha* are included or quoted.

These findings are confirmed by other papyri fragments; for example,

- The Fayyum Fragment (3rd cent. CE) is a briefer version of Mark 14:27, 29–30/Matt 26:31, 33–34.
- The Merton Papyrus 51 (P.Mert. 51; 3rd cent. CE) is a small fragment recounting response to → John the Baptist and a saying about a tree, its fruit, and the treasure of the heart (see Luke 6:43–45/Matt 7:17–20; 12:33–35).
- P.Oxy. 1224 (beginning of the 4th cent. CE) has fragments of two pages. One has a brief summary of the tradition attested in Mark 2:16–17 parr., and the second combines elements of the tradition attested in Matt 5:44/Luke 6:27–28 and Mark 9:40 parr.

Of particular interest is P.Oxy. 840 (4th or 5th cent. CE), which has a story of Jesus being criticized by a Pharisee for failing to perform the required ritual washing before entering the Temple. Jesus replies by contrasting the Pharisee's purity gained by washing in dirty water with himself and his disciples having bathed "in the living water which comes down from (heaven)." The story has no parallel in the New Testament Gospels, but could have been inspired by the awareness of the many confrontations they attest between Jesus and Pharisees, and particularly by a Jesus tradition such as Mark 7:1–23 par, Matt 23:25/Luke 11:39, and John 4:10, 14.

The best we can say, then, is that even in the later centuries, when the fourfold Gospels had become established Scripture, reference to and use made of the Gospel tradition in homily and reflection show little concern for precision of quotation or for the careful ordering of passages alluded to. These papyri also provide no substantive evidence of knowledge of or reliance on noncanonical gospels.

6. Jewish-Christian Gospels

The references to the so-called Jewish-Christian gospels in Clement of Alexandria, Origen, → Jerome, and other church fathers contain a fair number of passages that include versions of episodes or teaching of Jesus more familiar from the New Testament Gospels, particularly Matthew. Whether the passages come from one or more actual Gospels, perhaps even a Hebrew/Aramaic version of Matthew, is unknowable. But at least we can say with some confidence that they provide insufficient evidence of a pre-Matthean or proto-Matthean version of the Jesus tradition quoted, since the variations are well within the scope that could be expected in use made of Matthew itself. They thus provide further indications that the Jesus tradition as known to us in the Synoptic/Matthean tradition was more widely known, was packaged and repackaged in different ways, and was supplemented by further material. Interestingly, they provide no support for theories that there were many otherwise unrecorded sayings of Jesus being still circulated.

The most obvious variant parallel material is as follows:

The Gospel according to the Hebrews:
Clem. *Strom.* 2.9.45 [] Matt 7:7/Luke 11:9
Jer. *Comm. Isa.* 11.2 [] Mark 1:9–11 parr.
Jer. *Vir. ill.* 2 [] resurrection appearance to James
The Gospel of the Nazaraeans:
Or. *Comm. Matt.* 15.14 [] Matt 19:16–24/Mark 10:17–25
Eus. *Theoph.* 4.22 [] Matt 25:14–30
Jer. *Vir. ill.* 3 [] quotes Matt 2:15 and 23
Jer. *Comm. Matt.* 12.13 [] Matt 12:9–14 parr.
Jer. *Pelag.* 3.2 [] Matt 3:13–14; 18:21–22
The Gospel of the Ebionites:
Epiph. *Pan.* 30.13.2–3 [] Mark 1:16–20 par.; 3.13–19 parr.
Epiph. *Pan.* 30.13.4–5 [] Mark 1:4–6 par.
Epiph. *Pan.* 30.13.7–8 [] Matt 3:14–15
Epiph. Pan. 30.14.5 [] Mark 3:31–35 parr.
Epiph. *Pan.* 30.22.4–5 [] compare Mark 14:12–16 parr.

Such brief extracts make it impossible to build up a coherent picture of these gospels (or this gospel). But it does appear that the extracts are from versions of one or more of the New Testament Gospels, most likely the Gospel of Matthew, but versions that have drawn on elaborated Jesus tradition and have been adapted to express Ebionite views. They provide no evidence that unrecorded sayings were well known or used in the early oral tradition.

7. Gnostic Gospels

The issue here again is whether later apocryphal gospels have preserved an early Jesus tradition, earlier than (much of) the Synoptic tradition. This question has been posed by the → Nag Hammadi Codices in particular and has already been discussed in relation to the most plausible instance of such an early Jesus tradition (the *Gospel of Thomas*). But attempts have been made, by H. Koester (1990) in particular, to find evidence of other source material, in particular sources used by John's Gospel in two "dialogue gospels" in the Nag Hammadi codices, the *Dialogue of the Savior* (NHLE 3.5; → *Savior, Dialogue of the*) and the *Apocryphon of James* (NHLE 1.2; → James: VII. *James, Secret Book of*). However, the evidence H. Koester cites hardly supports his case; the links are at best tenuous and the supporting arguments tendentious.

a The *Dialogue of the Savior* certainly has parallels with the Gospel of John – reference to the Father's "only-begotten son" (2), and emphasis on light (14; 27; 34; 50). But so far as the *Dialogue of the Savior* is concerned, the stronger parallels are with the *Gospel of Thomas*. As with both John and *Thomas*, there are clear echoes of and influence from Jesus tradition as attested in the Synoptic Gospels. The most obvious examples are the following:

- *Dial. Sav.* 8 – "The lamp [of the body] is the mind"; compare Matt 6:22–23;
- *Dial.* Sav. 9–12, 20 – "He who seeks [...] reveals [...]"; compare Matt 7:7/Luke 11:9;
- *Dial. Sav.* 14 – "In that place [there will] be weeping and [gnashing] of teeth over the end of [all] these things"; compare Matt 8:12;
- *Dial.* Sav. 35 – "How will someone who does [not] know [the Son] know the [Father]?"; compare Matt 11:27/Luke 10:22; and
- *Dial. Sav.* 53 – Mary said. "[...] the laborer is worthy of his food" and "the disciple resembles his teacher"; compare Matt 10:10/Luke 6:40.

Much more striking, however, are the *Thomas*-like features that, as with *Thomas*, shift the line of thought into a quite different and gnostic-like narrative – talk of "this impoverished cosmos" (26), "carrying flesh around" (28), and "[Everyone] who has known himself" (30). The *Thomas*-like character of the *Dialogue of the Savior* is confirmed by further references to what can be referred to as a gnostic (or gnostic-like) narrative, usually in parallel to *Thomas*:

- *Dial. Sav.* 34 – "you are from [that] place"; compare *Gos. Thom.* 50;
- *Dial.* Sav. 37 – the Son of Man greeted them and said to them: "A seed from a power was deficient and it went down to [the] abyss of the earth. And the Greatness remembered [it] and he sent the [Word to] it. It brought it up into [his presence] so that the First Word might not fail";
- *Dial.* Sav. 50 – "[...] you will clothe yourselves in light and enter the bridal chamber"; compare *Gos. Thom.* 75;
- *Dial.* Sav. 55 – He said to them: "You are from the fullness and you dwell in the place where the deficiency is";

- *Dial.* Sav. 84–85 – Judas said to Matthew: "We [want] to understand the sort of garments we are to be [clothed] with, [when] we depart the decay of the [flesh]." The Lord said: "[...] you will become [blessed] when you strip [yourselves]"; compare *Gos. Thom.* 37; and
- *Dial.* Sav. 92, 95 – Matthew said: "Pray in the place where there is [no woman]," he tells us, meaning: "Destroy the works of womanhood," not because there is any other [manner of birth], but because they will cease [giving birth] [...]" Judas said [to Matthew]: "[The works] of [womanhood] will dissolve [...]"; compare *Gos. Thom.* 114.

In short, the most obvious way to interpret the *Dialogue of the Savior* is along the lines suggested for interpretation of the *Gospel of Thomas*. The association between the Synoptic-like Jesus tradition and the *Dialogue of the Savior* is much more flimsy than in the case of *Thomas*. But like *Thomas*, the *Dialogue of the Savior* has a gnostic-like perspective to which Jesus and his disciples have been recruited, but in the case of the *Dialogue*, with little to no purchase from the earlier Jesus tradition.

b With the *Apocryphon of James*, the case made by H. Koester for the Gospel of John evidencing some influence from or reaction to the *Apocryphon* is even less persuasive. There is certainly some evidence of knowledge of or influence from Jesus tradition:

- *Ap. Jas.* 2–3; 6–9; 12–14 – There are several references to "the kingdom of God/heaven," though in each case the link with the Synoptic material is at best tenuous.
- *Ap. Jas.* 4.23–30 – compare Mark 10:28–29 parr. and Matt 6:13.
- *Ap. Jas.* 8.16–23 is somewhat like the kingdom parable in Mark 4:26–29.
- *Ap. Jas.* 8–10; 13–15, parallels the Johannine descent/ascent of the Son of Man, but dependence on or derivation from one or other is hardly demonstrable.
- *Ap. Jas.* 12.41–13.1 – "Blessed will they be who have not seen, [yet have believed]!" may have been influenced by John 20.29, but the context is quite different.

That there are some connections here is evident, but they can best be described as remote, a connectedness at some remove from the Synoptic and Johannine Jesus tradition. Any argument that the *Apocryphon of James* is evidence of forms of the Jesus tradition earlier than the Synoptic and Johannine versions is again tendentious, even more so than in the case of the *Dialogue of the Savior*. Absence of Synoptic or redactional features, in particular echoes of Jesus tradition, is itself no evidence of pre-Synoptic/Johannine tradition, since the *Apocryphon of James* material is always bonded with traits at some remove from the Synoptic/Johannine parallels, and since the oral Jesus tradition must have been known and provided stimulus to different reflection in other circles. The impression given by the *Apocryphon of James* is rather of distant echoes and fading influence.

In short, if the hope is that *agrapha* – that is, otherwise unknown sayings attributed to Jesus that only appear in written material best dated to the 2nd CE or later centuries – either add significantly to what is known of Jesus from the four New Testament Gospels or provide a historically valid portrayal of Jesus and/or his teaching that extends or contradicts what can be known of Jesus from the Synoptic tradition in particular, then the hope remains unfulfilled. Instead what becomes evident is that the Synoptic Gospels provide the best evidence of how Jesus was remembered during the early decades of Christianity, and that the other material attributed to Jesus in later decades and centuries is best attributed to different views of the human condition interwoven with what had stemmed from Jesus.

Bibliography

Cameron, R., *The Other Gospels: Non-Canonical Gospel Texts*, Guildford, 1983.

Elliott, J.K., *The Apocryphal New Testament*, Oxford, 1993, esp. 26–30.

Foster, P., *The Non-Canonical Gospels*, London, 2008.

Frey, J., & J. Schröter, eds., *Jesus in apokryphen Evangelienüberlieferungen*, WUNT, series 1, 254, Tübingen, 2010.

Gathercole, S., *The Composition of the Gospel of Thomas: Original Language and Influences*, SNTSMS 151, Cambridge UK, 2012.

Goodacre, M., *Thomas and the Gospels: The Case for Thomas's Familiarity with the Synoptics*, Grand Rapids, 2012.

Jenkins, P., *Hidden Gospels: How the Search for Jesus Lost its Way*, Oxford, 2001.

Jeremias, J., *Unknown Sayings of Jesus*, London, 1958, ²1964.

Koester, H., *Ancient Christian Gospels: Their History and Development*, London, 1990.

Robinson, J. M., ed., *The Nag Hammadi Library in English*, Leiden, 1988.

Schneemelcher, W., & R.M. Wilson, *New Testament Apocrypha*, trans. J. Clarke, Cambridge UK, 1991, vol. I, esp. 88–91: O. Hofius, "Isolated Sayings of the Lord."

Stroker, W.D., *Extracanonical Sayings of Jesus*, Atlanta, 1989.

Tuckett, C., *Nag Hammadi and the Gospel Tradition*, Edinburgh, 1986.

JAMES D.G. DUNN (†)

Agrestius

The Codex Parisinus Latinus 8093 (9th cent. CE), which forms the first part of a collection of Visigothic poetry, comprises a fragmentary poem in dactylic hexameters entitled *Versus Agresti episcopi de fide ad Avitum episcopum in modum facetiae* ("Verses by the Bishop Agrestius on Faith to the Bishop Avitus in Pleasant Style"). This fragment contains the 49 initial verses. The length of the proem suggests that a large part of the poem has been lost.

1. Author and Addressee

While a certain consensus has been reached with regard to the identification of the author (Agrestius), research is still far from any agreement on the addressee, Avitus. As the fact that the poet describes his status within the title of the work and refers to himself later on as a "servant of the lord" (*domini famulus*, v. 3) clearly indicates, Agrestius (first half of the 5th cent. CE) was a → bishop. Researchers widely agree in considering the author to be identical to a bishop of the same name acting in Lucus Augusti (Lugo) in the Spanish province Gallaecia (Galicia). According to the *Chronicon* of Hydatius of Aquae Flaviae, in 433 CE Agrestius opposed two bishop candidates, Pastor and Syagrius, for reasons that cannot be clearly ascertained. Most likely, these candidates can be identified as two writers engaged for the orthodox side against → Priscillianism (Gennad. *Vir. ill.* 66; 77). Presumably, Agrestius belonged to a wing within the orthodox clergy that advocated a less rigid position towards the heretics (Cardelle de Hartmann, 1997, 88–89). In 441 CE, Agrestius took part in the First Council of → Orange, as can be inferred from the acts of this synod.

The dedicatee of the poem has been identified as Avitus of Braga, an outstanding ecclesiastical figure in contemporary → Galicia (Vega, 1966, 198–201). He was, however, not a bishop. Taking Avitus of Vienne (460–518 CE) as an alternative addressee presupposes abandoning the plausible Agrestius of Lugo as author for chronological reasons. Avitus has also been identified with Eparchius Avitus, the praetorian prefect of Gaul, and later emperor (Mathisen, 1994). Still, the idea that the work, with its confession of orthodoxy, was written in order to support a plea for political assistance in internal conflicts finds no textual support, as such an interpretation would require at least a partial rejection of the title and does not coincide with the relationship between the author and the addressee portrayed in the poem. Despite the frequent use of topoi in prefaces of the late antiquity, addressing a military and political leader as a spiritual teacher is hardly comprehensible.

2. *De Fide*

The poem starts with the topical *intitulatio* (intitulation, vv. 1–4), followed by a *prooemium* (proem, vv. 5–28). The *narratio* (narration, vv. 29–49) finally presents the subject matter of the poem, containing a confessional statement on the → Trinity (vv. 29–32) and a paraphrase of the creation narrative (vv. 33–49). Most likely, the title, which shows specific characteristics of the epoch, was penned by Agrestius himself. The words *de fide* assign the work to the contemporary confessions of faith. The speaker's intention to offer a creed becomes apparent through the fiction of a public confession of faith at the end of the proem (v. 28). He apostrophizes not only Avitus, but any interested reader as his imagined addressees. Like the Gallic poet → Hilary of Poitiers in his treatise on the Genesis, Agrestius begins the poem with a dedication in verse (vv. 1–4), which resembles the opening of a letter. Thus, he associates the poem with a popular genre of Latin poetry, the verse epistle. The introduction contains topical vocabulary, metaphors, and greeting formulas from pagan and Christian epistolography.

The proem directed toward Avitus (vv. 5–24) follows the tradition of sending literary works to obtain an assessment from the recipient. The speaker depicts the relationship between him and the addressee as the relationship between a pupil eager to learn and his teacher (vv. 5–6). He apologizes for potential shortcomings in his intellectual efforts, using metaphors of spiritual fertilization and growth. In so doing, he integrates traditional literary imagery into a Christian framing.

The *narratio* presents the contents of the Catholic faith. Agrestius subscribes to the tradition of the hymnic formulas of the creeds: stylistic devices support the Trinitarian predications (e.g. anaphor, asyndeton, and tricolon, vv. 29–30). In the contemporary controversies between heretics and orthodox Christians, the Trinity was a moot point. Referring the attribute *ingenitus* (unbegotten) only to the father, Agrestius takes up a decidedly orthodox stance, similar to the positions of Syagrius (see Gennadius' portrayal).

The succession of a Trinitarian confession and an account of the creation is a traditional feature in Christian poetry on Genesis (e.g. Hilary, Claudius Marius Victorius, *Cento Probae*). Agrestius' literary and theological formation becomes apparent: as can be derived from the disposition of the single events of the creation in his account, Agrestius can be numbered among the more recent exponents within the tradition of poetry on Genesis. The poet's ideas on the human soul show his familiarity with → Ambrose of Milan. The explanation of the → fall as a result of the linking of the soul with matter derives from the Platonic view of preexistence (see Smolak, 1973, 90–91).

The poem was composed in a time when an educated class that was receptive to an artful work rife with literary allusions still existed. Agrestius is familiar both with pagan (Virgil, Ovid, Lucan, Rutilius Namatianus) and Christian poetry (Juvencus; Prudentius). Nonetheless, the imitation of classical poetic models is of a strictly technical and stylistic kind. However, this should not be regarded as a purely formal, linguistic imitation (see Smolak, 1973, 18). By creating intertextuality late antique authors aim at inserting their texts into the literary tradition in order to establish them in an intellectual discourse with the past and the present.

3. Interpretations

The speaker of the poem shows his intention to deliver a confession of faith, expressing his wish to present the "secrets of a faithful Catholic heart" (*catholica recti cordis secreta fidelis*, v. 26). He develops the fictive illusion of making his confession in front of Avitus and any other reader. Confessions of faith had a literary tradition (they were often entitled *de fide*) and were composed to avert suspicions of heresy. Like the poem in question, they usually contained a section about creation. However, as the full title indicates, the attribution of the poem to a literary genre is more complex: it is written in the manner of a *facetia* (pleasant poem). K. Smolak, in a semantic analysis of this term, has convincingly shown that in late antiquity its meaning of "witticism" pales in favor of "elegance." The poem's classification as part of urbane and skillful literature intends to distance the work from dry theological prose writings (see Smolak, 1973, 26–27, 46–49). Distinctly orthodox positions within the poem have given rise to the interpretation that Agrestius may have tried to repel public suspicions that he was a Priscillianist. By contrast, the literary mode of the text does not support the idea of an urgent need to compose it for self-defense. For such aims, Agrestius would have chosen prose writing, because even at this late time there were reservations about poetry's reputedly doubtful aptitude for communicating reliable contents. The character of the poem suggests that the author must have had more general literary aims that exceeded a personal confessional, apologetic, or political goal. In employing the speaker's intention to deliver a creed as a literary device that also fulfilled other purposes, Agrestius drew on a tradition of confessions of faith that were taken as a basis for more general theological texts (e.g. → Augustine of Hippo, *Confessiones*).

K. Smolak (1973, 22–27) considered this work a didactic poem in the mode of a verse epistle (*Lehrepistel*). The presentation of Christian themes in didactic poems was very popular in late antiquity. Nevertheless, Agrestius' text lacks any clear hint of an educational intention. Most plausibly, it should be classified into the genre of biblical epic (Paniagua, 2010, 16). As is typical for this category, Agrestius paraphrases the genesis narrative, choosing this technique with the intention of providing an aesthetically pleasing presentation of the contents of the Bible. The original verse account must have exceeded by far the fragment that is still extant.

Bibliography

Cardelle de Hartmann, C., "Ortodoxos y priscilianistas en la época sueva," in: E. Koller & H. Laitenberger, eds., *Suevos–Schwaben*, TBL 426, Tübingen, 1997, 76–99.

Mathisen, R.W., "Agrestius of Lugo, Eparchius Avitus, and a Curious Fifth-Century Statement of Faith," *JECS* 2, 1994, 71–102.

Paniagua, D., "Agrestio de Lugo," in: C. Codoñer et al., eds., *La Hispania visigótica y mozárabe: Dos épocas en su literatura*, Salamanca, 2010, 15–17.

Smolak, K., ed., *Das Gedicht des Bischofs Agrestius: Eine theologische Lehrepistel aus der Spätantike (Einleitung, Text, Übersetzung und Kommentar)*, SAWW.PH 284/2, Vienna, 1973.

Vega, Á.C., ed., "Un poema inédito titulado 'De fide', de Agrestio, obispo de Lugo, siglo V," *BRAH* 159, 1966, 167–209.

JOCHEN SCHULTHEISS

Agrippa Castor

Agrippa Castor was a 2nd-century CE apologist (→ Apologetics), active around 130 CE, who was instrumental in refuting the heresy of → Basilides and other gnostic teachings. As with many of the heretics exposed and attacked by apologists and polemicists, nothing of Agrippa's own writing has survived. The extent to which his ideas and teachings were recorded by church historians and patristic writers is testament to his reputation at the time. It is not known why none of his works has survived. His writings expose the dualistic nature of gnostic heresies that were antithetical to the evolving Christological formulations of Jesus Christ's dual natures.

1. Identity and Dates

The name Agrippa Castor is wholly Latin in origin, but the associations of both names may reflect the author's standing; "Castor" may have been chosen to mark his rhetorical skills, in honor of Castor of Rhodes, a 1st-century BCE rhetorician. "Agrippa" as a cognomen may have been drawn from the two Roman officials mentioned in Acts, King Agrippa (Herod Agrippa II, ruler of Galilee, Acts 25:13–27), the son of Herod Agrippa I (referred to in Acts 2:1–23; → Agrippa II). Agrippa was therefore associated with Hellenized Palestinian → Judaism toward the end of the 1st century CE. Since Agrippa's main contribution was to refute Basilides, who is thought to have operated in Alexandria, it is likely Agrippa may also have been North African in origin.

Agrippa's dates may be inferred from book 21 of Jerome's *De Viris Illustribus* (*On Illustrious Men*) because of the adjoining entries; number 20 is on → Aristides of Athens, and Quadratus is referred to in entries 19 and 20 (Jer. *Vir. ill.* 19–22). Assuming a roughly chronological order in Jerome, this places Agrippa as being active during the rulership of the emperor Hadrian; this Quadratus is presented as being a direct disciple of the apostles, who presented proofs to Emperor Hadrian of the healing and other miracles of the apostles. The entry after Agrippa is devoted to Hegesippus, a prolific and learned historian, who is also described by Jerome as "a near contemporary of the apostles." Both Quadratus and Aristides came from Athens and were viewed as among the earliest Christian apologists alongside Hegesippus and → Justin Martyr. Since apologists and heretics wrote in response to one another and often both sides attracted large followings, it is possible that the texts of both were suppressed or destroyed by supporters in order to stifle the debate. Agrippa may have been the earliest recorded writer against such heresies and is believed to have written an entire book against Basilides. By juxtaposing Agrippa to these illustrious defenders of the faith, Jerome is asserting Agrippa's place in the canon of great apologists.

2. Christian Apologetics

Christian apologetics flourished as a genre of writing in the 2nd century CE, when no more apostles (→ Apostle) with firsthand knowledge of Christ's teachings remained alive and a new criterion of Christian orthodoxy evolved, often allied to martyrdom. The refutations of heresies contained in these texts paved the way for the doctrinal statements issued by ecumenical councils from the 4th century CE onward, by beginning to draw boundaries round what was acceptable Christian teaching, with heterodox teachings being condemned as heresy, their promulgators anathematized and sympathizers excommunicated. "Apologies," being the reverse of what their name suggests in common parlance, might be addressed to new converts, Jews, philosophers, and heretics. From the second quarter of the 2nd century CE, apologetics became one of the most dominant forms of Christian witness and often expressed critique of both religious and political practices. They were sometimes dedicated to emperors in the hope they would promote the Christian message and gain socially influential converts to the faith. Persecutions of Christians and others continued apace, however, until the Edict of Milan in 313 CE, when all religions became subject to imperial toleration and fewer instances of persecution took place. At this stage although exegesis of the Hebrew Bible was taking place, the Jewish faith was not acknowledged as forming a building block for Christianity but was seen rather as apostasy or heresy, and some Christian apologetics appear antisemitic today.

3. 4th-Century CE Responses to Agrippa Castor

Eusebius of Caesarea is the first writer to refer to Agrippa Castor, seeing him as contributing to the "brilliant lights" of the Christian churches of his day, which were pushing back the encroaching darkness of heresy (Eus. *Hist. eccl.* 4.7; 6.8; PG 25; LCL). While we can be sure that there are elements of hagiographical embellishment in → Eusebius of Caesarea's account (since the concept of "history" was rather different in his day from the modern one) we are dependent on his evidence for the context of apologetics and his attempts to provide a chronological frame of reference. Eusebius affirms the importance of providing written defense against deviant and erroneous teachings and notes especially Agrippa's focus on refuting Basilides, who by these datings would have been a contemporary of Agrippa. This refutation is presented as his key legacy to Christian apologetics. Eusebius records Agrippa as being "a most famous writer of that time, revealing the cleverness of the man's [Basilides'] deception." He praises Agrippa's thoroughness and method, which he sees as inspiration to subsequent writers, suggesting that he was among the first to take on this task.

From Eusebius' account we also learn more about the extent of Basildes' writings. He apparently compiled 24 exegetical texts on the Christian gospel, a thorough exposition, and in these Basilides named prophets of his own choosing, as well as others Eusebius insists never existed. According to Eusebius, Agrippa also castigates Basilides for suggesting it was acceptable to eat food offered to idols, being lax about maintaining the faith under persecution and insisting that secrecy be imposed on his disciples (like Pythagoras apparently he insisted that his followers kept silence for five years after receiving his teaching, a means of maintaining the elect inner circle associated with Gnosticism).

Jerome adds little to this account, stressing as Eusebius does the man's learning and effectiveness, suggesting that rhetorical method and thoroughness was his hallmark (Jer. *Vir. ill.* 21; PL 23; → Jerome). He adds to the refutation of Basilides' chosen prophets Bar Cochebas and Bar Coph the erroneous teaching about Abraxas, a supreme deity in the panoply of gods that figured in his cosmology. Referring to the numeric value of his name in Greek letters, he explains that Abraxas' name "occupies about the space of a year," a point picked up on by → Irenaeus of Lyon in his refutation of Basilides (Iren. *Haer* 1.24.7); the numeric value adds up to 365 according 1 for A, 2 for B, and so on. Neither author records the titles of Agrippa's apologetic works.

Since the Syrian writer → Theodoret of Cyrrhus' church history picks up where Eusebius ends, there is no mention of Agrippa here, but in his *Compendium of Heretical Fables*, he mentions briefly that in addition to refuting Basilides, Agrippa also equally condemned the writings of the heresiarch's son, Isidore (*Haer.* 1.4; PG 83).

4. Modern Reception of Apologetics and Agrippa Castor

M. Edwards' study (2009) of heresy and orthodoxy in the early church subverts the normal reception of Basilides as a heretical gnostic (→ Gnosis/Gnosticism), affirming instead that the church's response to his teachings is typical of the period. M. Edwards argues that some gnostics (including Valentinus the Gnostic and Marcion as well as Basilides) provided the seed corn for what became Catholic doctrine, although the original thinkers were condemned as heretics and condemned by the established church. At the time such gnostics were writing, the canon of the Bible was yet to be confirmed, and other boundaries between acceptable orthodoxy and heterodoxy were more porous than in later centuries. However, it is fair to say that many modern scholars would see Basilides' teachings as falling outside the canon of the church's accepted doctrines about the divine λόγος, and the nature of redemption through faith in Christ. The praise accorded by 3rd-/4th-century CE writers to Agrippa Castor as a refuter of gnostics is in line with → Clement of Alexandria's view that Basilides was fundamentally dualistic in his worldview; Irenaeus condemned him in *Haer.* 1.24. Agrippa Castor can therefore be regarded as a significant inspiration to subsequent apologetic writing, having been a close contemporary to his subjects, as well as possibly from a similar culture.

Bibliography

Altaner, B., *Patrologie: Leben, Schriften und Lehre der Kirchenväter*, Freiburg, 1978, 109–110.

Christie, A.J., "Agrippa Castor," in: W. Smith, ed., *DGRBM*, Boston, 1870, 77.

Dulles, A., *A History of Apologetics*, Eugene, 1999.

Edwards, M., *Catholicity and Heresy in the Early Church*, Farnham, 2009.

Ermoni, V., "Agrippa Castor," in: A. Baudrillart, ed., *DHGE*, vol. I, Paris, 1912, 1029–1030.

Frend, W.H.C., *The Archaeology of Early Christianity: A History*, London, 1996.

Grant, R.M., *Greek Apologists of the Second Century*, Philadelphia, 1988.

Löhr, W.A., *Basilides und seine Schule: Eine Studie zur Theologie und Kirchengeschichte des zeiten Jahrhunderts*, WUNT 83, Tübigen, 1996, 5–15.

Quasten, J., *Patrology*, 3 vols., vol. I, Utrecht, 1975.

Quispel, G. ,"Valentinus and the Gnostikoi," *Vigiliae Christiane* 50, 1996, 1–4.

Scholten, C., "Agrippa Castor," in: W. Kasper, ed., *LThK*, vol. I, Freiburg, 1993, 251.

DACB, www.dacb.org/stories/egypt/agrippa.castor.html accessed Jun 24, 2013.

HANNAH HUNT

Agrippa II

Agrippa II (c. 27/28–c. 93? 100? CE), → Herod the Great's great grandson and son of Agrippa I ("Herod" of Acts 12), who figures in the New Testament in the story of Paul's imprisonment (Acts 25–26), was the last of the dynasty to play an active role in the relations between Rome and Judaea. He was raised in Rome, with the advantages supplied by his father's close ties to Claudius (who is reported to have described himself as having raised Agrippa; Jos. *Ant.* 20.12), and where he acquired what → Flavius Josephus would characterize as his thorough familiarity with Greek culture (Jos. *Vita* 359). Upon his father's death, when he was 16 or 17 years old, Agrippa remained in Rome; Claudius' advisors are said (*Ant.* 19.362) to have used the excuse of Agrippa's young age in order to reinstate direct Roman rule in Judaea. However, by virtue of being in Rome, Agrippa was able successfully to intervene, on at least two occasions (*Ant.* 20.9; 20.135), in support of Judaean delegations to Rome, thus demonstrating his willingness and ability to undertake his family's traditional role of mediators, or buffers, between Judaea and Rome.

In 48 CE, upon the death of his uncle, King Herod of Chalcis (a small kingdom in Lebanon), Agrippa began his public career. Claudius appointed him king of Chalcis in his uncle's stead, and endowed Agrippa with "custodianship" of the → Temple (*Ant.* 20.15). The main expression of this was the right to appoint and depose high priests, and the rest of *Ant.* 20 is punctuated by Josephus' reports that he did so regularly over the next decades until the revolt of 66 CE. But the position also entailed a more general authority concerning the Temple, an authority that Agrippa exercised, for example, by convening a council that intervened in such details as allowing Levites who sang in the Temple to wear vestments previously reserved for priests (*Ant.* 20.216–218), and by demanding to be allowed literally to oversee, from his palace, the Temple cult (*Ant.* 20.189–196). Both measures aroused opposition from priests, who would have preferred to run the Temple without such a Roman-imposed supervisor and without his support for competition from Levites.

Rome, however, wanted the go-between, and in 53 CE Claudius gave further recognition to Agrippa's role in Judaean affairs: moving him closer to the center, Claudius took Chalcis from Agrippa, and in its stead gave him a larger kingdom in northern Palestine and southern Syria (*Ant.* 20.138). Similarly, a year or two later, Nero further expanded Agrippa's kingdom by adding to it a part of the Galilee, including the cities of Tiberias and Tarichaea next to the Sea of Galilee, along with some further territory in Transjordan (*Ant.* 20.159). Agrippa, and others, will certainly have remembered that his late father had begun his career as king of parts of northern Palestine, but moved on from them, within a few years, to rule of a larger and more central kingdom, including the Galilee and, eventually, Judaea proper.

Rome maintained direct rule in Judaea proper and never gave it to Agrippa. But he was increasingly involved in Jerusalem, maintained a "royal palace" (*basileion*; Jos. *Ant.* 20.189) there, and frequently exercised his authority as supervisor of the Temple and, to some extent, public works in Jerusalem (Jos. *Ant.* 20.219–223). The recurrent snippets in Josephus' *Antiquities* that record his appointments and depositions of high priests all refer to him as "King Agrippa" and, as in Acts 25–26, it sounds as if he were king of Judaea; apparently, he was often so considered, in a general way. It is on this background that Luke's report in Acts 25–26 should be understood; it begins with Agrippa's official visit – together with his sister Berenice – to the Roman governor in Caesarea and goes on to report the latter's willingness to enlist Agrippa to help with the investigation. That, apparently, reflects the same logic as that assumed by the same author when he reported that Pilate once asked Herod Antipas, the ruler of the Galilee, to intervene in the trial of Jesus, since Jesus was from the Galilee (Luke 23:7).

As Herod the Great and Agrippa I, so too Agrippa II walked the thin line between being a faithful vassal of Rome and being a king in his own right. Thus, on the one hand, → Tacitus reports (Tac. *An.* 13.7) that Nero asked Agrippa, in 54 CE, to prepare for a possible invasion of Parthia. Agrippa's coins, which portray all the Roman emperors from Claudius to Domitian and proclaim his loyalty to them, point in the same direction, as does his renaming of his capital, Caesarea Philippi, as Neronias. Likewise, when, in the case of James the Just (→ James: II. James the Less), the incumbent high priest tried and executed him and thus overstepped the bounds imposed by Rome, Agrippa stepped in and did his part, as Rome expected of him, by removing the high priest from office (Jos. *Ant.* 20.197–203). On the other hand, however, in his dynasty's tradition, he both took responsibility for building projects in Jerusalem and subsidized, as a Hellenistic "benefactor," projects in non-Jewish cities, even abroad, such as Beirut; a Latin inscription from Beirut (see Boffo, 1994), which was a Roman colony, dutifully acclaims him, in acknowledging one such donation, as a *rex magnus* ("great king").

But as opposed to his great grandfather and his father, who lived in times in which it was possible to mediate between Rome and Jerusalem and play a buffer role that served the needs of both sides, by the second decade of Agrippa II's rule, the 60s, relations between the Judaeans and Rome had deteriorated irretrievably into open rebellion. Josephus reports that aristocrats such as himself and Agrippa, who knew the power of Rome, did their best to dissuade the rebels, and he ascribes to Agrippa one of the great set speeches of his work, a long catena of arguments against rebellion (Jos. *Bell.* 2.345–404). Although Josephus' text may have played a role in preserving Agrippa's good standing with Rome, the speech, as other efforts by Agrippa, could not prevent the war. In the end, therefore, such aristocrats had to choose sides: Josephus chose, at first, to side with the rebels; Agrippa, with Rome. While we may suspect he hoped Rome might seek a compromise, giving up direct rule and reverting to Herodian (i.e. his) rule as a vassal king, as his father and great grandfather before him, his actions were clearly pro-Roman and only secondarily attempted to mitigate the Jews' suffering. His troops fought on Rome's side from the outset; his sister, Berenice, became Titus' best friend; and the slingshot wound Agrippa incurred when urging the defenders of Gamala to submit to the Roman besiegers (Jos. *Bell.* 4.14) indicates the degree of his success as a mediator and of the rebels' gratitude for his efforts. In the end, the war story is bracketed on the one hand by Agrippa's lavish hosting of Vespasian at his capital, Caesarea Philippi, when he first arrived in Palestine in 67 CE (*Bell.* 3.444), and on the other by → Titus' victory celebrations on his way back to Rome, again at Caesarea Philippi, after putting down the rebellion

and destroying Jerusalem (*Bell.* 7.23–24). Following the war, correspondingly, with Agrippa's coins now celebrating the Roman victory (*nikē*) and *Judaea capta* ("capture of Judaea"), → Vespasian confirmed Agrippa in his kingdom and expanded it, apparently northward. But at this point Agrippa starts to drop out of sight. It is difficult to know to what extent that is due merely to Josephus ending his *Jewish War* in the early 70s CE or, rather, to Agrippa having become something of a superfluous relic. For once Rome upgraded Judaea into a senatorial province, with a legion (the Tenth) of its own, and once Jerusalem was destroyed and the real basis for Jewish opposition to Rome was gone, there was, it may have seemed, no need for a middleman, certainly not for one who had not been able to deliver the goods and prevent the war. Therefore, although there are some post-70 CE glimpses of Agrippa visiting Rome – in 75 CE coming away with honorary praetorian insignia (Dio *Hist. rom.* 65.15) or corresponding with Josephus about details of the rebellion (Jos. *Vita* 364–367) – virtually all that remains of him from those years are his coins. Those continue down to the reign of Domitian, but there is some controversy about their eras and, therefore, about how to date them and what *terminus post quem* they give for his death. Indeed, the date of his death is unknown, for while the Byzantine writer Photius reports in his *Bibliotheca* (33) that he died in Trajan's third year (100 CE), the coins and such additional literary and epigraphic evidence as there is do not require a date later than the early 90s CE.

Similarly, very little of Agrippa as an individual can be gathered. He died unmarried and childless; the sources frequently report him as being accompanied by his sister Berenice, something that seems to have fostered scurrilous rumors (Jos. *Ant.* 20.145). Acts 26:28 reports that Agrippa told Paul (→ Paul the Apostle) that he might turn him into a Christian in short order, which seems to be ironic, but his Roman upbringing, iconic coins, and loyal support to Rome during the rebellion leave little room to imagine that he was very attached to → Judaism. Rather, he was a Roman Judaean, or a Judaean Roman, one whose time passed with the destruction of Jerusalem – whereupon, bereft of any real function, he faded away.

Historiography

There is, to date, no monograph on Agrippa II, in contrast to other Herodian rulers. This probably reflects both the relative paucity of sources relating to him and the relatively marginal role that he played. Among the topics that have attracted scholarly interest and imagination are his role in the Judaean rebellion against Rome (e.g. Baerwald, 1877; see Cohen, 1979, 13); Josephus' attitude toward him (e.g. D.R. Schwartz, 1981/1982; S. Schwartz, 1990, 110–160): rabbinic stories about "King Agrippa" (which do not differentiate between him and his father, Agrippa I; see D.R. Schwartz, 1990, 157–171; S. Schwartz, 1990, 160–169); and chronological issues of his reign, especially with regard to numismatic evidence (such as Kushnir-Stein, 2002; Kokkinos, 2003).

Bibliography

Baerwald, A., *Josephus in Galiläa: Sein Verhältniss zu den Parteien, insbesondere zu Justus von Tiberias und Agrippa II*, Breslau, 1877.

Boffo, L., *Iscrizioni greche e latine per lo studio della Bibbia*, Brescia, 1994.

Cohen, S.J.D., *Josephus in Galilee and Rome: His Vita and Development as a Historian*, CSCT 8, Leiden, 1979.

Ilan, T., *Queen Berenice: A Jewish Female Icon of the First Century* CE, STAR 39, Leiden, 2022.

Kokkinos, N., *The Herodian Dynasty: Origins, Role in Society and Eclipse*, JSP.S. 30, Sheffield, 1998, 317–341.

Kokkinos, N., "Josephus, Justus, Agrippa II and His Coins," *SCI* 22, 2003, 163–180.

Kushnir-Stein, A., "The Coinage of Agrippa II," *SCI* 21, 2002, 123–131.

Schürer, E., G. Vermes & F. Millar, eds., *The History of the Jewish People in the Age of Jesus Christ (175 BC–AD 135)*, vol. I, Edinburgh, 1973, 471–484.

Schwartz, D.R., "KATA TOYTON TON KAIPON: Josephus' Source on Agrippa II," *JQR* 72, 1981/1982, 241–268.

Schwartz, D.R., *Agrippa I: The Last King of Judaea*, TSAJ 23, Tübingen, 1990.

Schwartz, S., *Josephus and Judaean Politics*, CSCT 18, Leiden, 1990.

Wilker, J., *Für Rom und Jerusalem: Die herodianische Dynastie im 1. Jahrhundert n. Chr.*, SAG 5, Frankfurt am Main, 2007.

DANIEL R. SCHWARTZ

Akathistos

The *Akathistos hymnos*, a Byzantine hymn to the Virgin Mary still very popular in the Orthodox and the Catholic Churches today, goes back to late antiquity. The word means that the hymn was [to be] sung "unseated" (α privativum + καθίζομαι). The time of its composition and the identity of its author are controversial issues. According to the historical tradition, the *Akathistos* was first performed on the night of Aug 7, 626 CE, following the siege of Constantinople by the Persians and the Avars. Presumably, this event marked the first time it was sung standing. However, the hymn must reach back to an earlier date.

1. Structure and Content

The *Akathistos* is opened by three different proems followed by 24 strophes, whose initial letters form an alphabetical acrostic pursuant to the Greek alphabet (see Trypanis, 1968, for the metrical structure of the strophes). The three proems transmitted by the manuscripts vary in content and meter. The first proem is considered authentic, since it outlines the key issue of the hymn – the incarnation of the → Word – and uses identical vocabulary and a similar style to the main text. The second proem not only differs in meter, vocabulary, and style, but it also ignores the hymn's acrostic structure and lacks any mention of the incarnation. Furthermore, its praise of → Mary as "defender and commander" (prologue 2.1: τῇ ὑπερμάχῳ στρατηγῷ) suits the situation of defense during the siege in 626 CE and thus seems to be a later addition related to this event.

The stanzas, varying in length, close alternately with one of two refrains (ἐφύμνια) that were common in the church: the odd stanzas 1 to 23 are longer and consist of 18 lines including 12 "salutations" (χαιρετισμοί) directed toward the mother of God, with each verse beginning with χαῖρε ("hail"). They close with a refrain of one line: "Hail, bride unwedded" (Χαῖρε, νύμφη ἀνύμφευτε). The singers take up the words thought of as spoken by the archangel. The *Akathistos* owes its hymnic character in the first place to these 144 salutations. The even stanzas 2 to 24 are shorter and comprise 6 lines including a refrain of one line: "Alleluia" (Ἀλληλούϊα), directed toward Christ. In all strophes lines 1 to 5 have an identical metrical structure and melody.

The hymn can be divided into two sections of 12 strophes. Further subdivisions, however, are not convincing (against Wellesz, 1956, 156–157). The number of 12 derives from Rev 12:1 and is widespread in the early Christian literature dealing with Mary (Del Grande, 1948, 21–22). The first part (strophes 1–12) is narrative and historical, presenting the story of Jesus' birth according to Luke from the annunciation up to the presentation at the temple. In the opening annunciation scene (1–4), the angel declares to the Virgin that she will give birth to God (1); Mary asks how this could happen to a virgin (2); the angel refers to divine omnipotence (3); the annunciation ends with the conception (4). The following strophes cover the reactions of Elizabeth's child (5), Joseph (6), the shepherds (7), the magi (8–10), the Egyptian idols (11), and Simeon (12).

The second part (strophes 13–24) may be classified as a theological comment or meditation on the significance of the mystery of the → incarnation within the whole of creation. Formulated in a lyrical manner, this section praises the miracle: a new kind of creation and creature are brought forth by the Virgin (13). This unfamiliar birth shall effect alienation from the world and conversion toward God (14). A general laudation of the incarnation (15) is followed by the angels marveling at the mystery (16). In contrast to the uncomprehending scholars (17), the faithful do indeed understand the message (18). The following stanzas contain an appeal to all who seek Mary's protection and to virgins in particular to praise God and the "mother of God" (19.1: θεοτόκος), thereby emphasizing, however, the inadequacy of earthly singing (20). The Virgin is presented as life-giving light (21), the redeemer as born by the Virgin (22). An appeal to praise the mother of God (23) precedes a final laudation to her (24).

The original date of performance may have been the Feast of the Annunciation (Mar 25), as historical sources and the context of transmission in the collections (*kontakaria*) suggest. However, the focus being put on the incarnation and the Virgin's role in it as well as the biblical events referred to widely exceed the annunciation itself and rather imply the veneration of Mary in the context of the nativity as the original time of performance. The mother of God was also commemorated on Dec 26 (Trypanis, 1968, 17–20; Peltomaa, 2001, 28, 75–76).

The outstanding stylistic feature of the *Akathistos* is the use of parallelism, paronomasia, and rhyme in order to give expression to antithetical thoughts. When applying paronomasia, the poet presumably also forms neologisms (e.g. 7.9). Bold metaphors used as epitheta for Mary figure prominently in the hymn. Thus, she is called "stola for all who were deprived of their freedom of speech" (13.16: στολὴ τῶν γυμνῶν παρρησίας; see also 5.17). This imagery derives from the custom of wearing a stola in the assembly or at a law court as a sign of political and legal freedom. In the last judgment, the Virgin metaphorically makes self-defense possible for the unfree "slaves" of the sins (see Meersseman, 1958, vol. I, 117).

2. The *Akathistos* and the Kontakion

Though the hymnos, the solemn song of praise for a god or a hero on the occasion of a cultic festival, is a widespread genre in classical antiquity, Christian authors shaped their own tradition of this poetical form. The hymn was a choral or a monodic song or a responsory between the chorus and a single person. After some isolated forerunners of psalmody (→ *Apostolic Constitutions*, Book 8) and hymnody (e.g. the anapaestic Hymn on Christ by → Clement of Alexandria at the end of his *Paed.* 3), from the 4th century CE on, a new kind of poetry developed that was destined for liturgy. It had to be understood by all Christians, not just by those who had read Homer and lyric poets. The metrical system of that time was not quantitative anymore, but was based on regulated positions of the word accents (isotonia) and a fixed number of syllables (isosyllabism) without distinction by duration (isochrony).

The *Akathistos* can be assigned to the genre of the kontakion, the most popular form of the Byzantine hymn between the 4th and the 7th century CE, reaching its final form in the works of → Romanos the Melodist (d. between 551 and 565 CE). The kontakia are poetical homilies on saints and holidays. The development of these hymns from the origin to its heyday in the 9th century CE is difficult to retrace. Although there is no evidence determining an exact starting point of this genre, it is considered to build on Syriac poetical traditions. The kontakia consist of 18 to 24 strophes (*oikoi*) of identical metrical structure preceded by an allometrical proem (*koukoulion*). The proem and the stanzas are linked by a refrain they have in common. The kontakion is especially rich in rhetoric and poetic ornament. The stanzas are connected by an acrostic following the alphabet. All these features can be found in the *Akathistos*. Dating this hymn to the 5th century CE does not exclude it from the kontakion tradition, since this genre can be traced as far back as the 4th century CE (see Maas, 1910, 289–295).

3. Authorship, Date, and Theological Context

Due to its anonymous tradition, there has been much speculation on the authorship of the *Akathistos*. Some early scholars take the siege of Constantinople in 626 CE for its time of origin (see Del Grande, 1948, 9–31, for older research), citing historical sources. Accordingly, the *Akathistos* has been attributed to the poet George of Pisidia, a contemporary of this battle and the author of a laudatory poem referring to it. However, the idea that such an artful work containing 24 stanzas was composed spontaneously and delivered on the same day is hardly credible (Wellesz, 1956, 152).

Several other scholars who have proposed Romanus the Melodist to be the author (Del Grande 1948, 17–19; Wellesz, 1956, 148–156; Trypanis, 1968, 2122) base their arguments on general judgments of the hymn's literary quality, claiming that only Romanus at the time could have achieved this style with its expressiveness, bold similes, and artistry of composition. Taken from a different perspective, however, the correspondence of rare words found in both the *Akathistos* and the poems of Romanus Melodius (e.g. ἄφθαστος, χρεωλύτης) does not necessarily point to a common authorship; instead, it rather displays the contemporary familiarity with the *Akathistos*. Furthermore, though Romanus does have a certain predilection for stylistic devices underlining contrasting thoughts, paronomasia is not as strikingly evident in his poems as it is in the *Akathistos*. Nor should we ignore that other writers were also using the same devices at the time, such as Proclus of Alexandria. The theme of a quarrel with pagan culture is common to both Romanus and the *Akathistos*, but that, too, is insubstantial evidence to justify attributing the hymn to the Syrian, since it may simply indicate that both texts are taking part in the same cultural discourse. So, to conclude, the adduced and existing similarities have never been striking enough to prove the alleged authorship by Romanus (Grosdidier de Matons, 1977, 32–36).

Recent research has come to a more precise dating of the *Akathistos* by contextualizing its expressions of theological ideas. By this method, the period immediately following the Council of → Ephesus (431 CE) has convincingly been shown to be the time of composition: this synod founding the dogma of Mary as Theotokos offers the Mariological prerequisites for the metaphors and epithets used to describe the Virgin (Peltomaa, 2001, 113–114, 121–125, 145). The Christological concepts in the *Akathistos* also speak for an earlier date of production: the emphasis on the unchangeability and unity of God (*prooemium* 1.5: χωρεῖται ἀναλλοιώτως ὅλος ἐν σοί; 15.1–2: ὅλος ἦν ἐν τοῖς κάτω καὶ τῶν ἄνω οὐδ'ὅλως/ἀπῆν) reflects the topics of the Nestorian debate that were at issue in the years before and after Ephesus as they were becoming apparent in the homilies of the time (Trypanis, 1968, 22; Peltomaa, 2001, 77–85, on Basil of Seleucia, 95–102, on Cyril of Alexandria) or in the *Tomus ad Armenios* by Proclus of Constantinople (d. 446/447 CE). The Council of → Chalcedon (451 CE) should be considered the Christological landmark before which the *Akathistos* was written, since it led to changes in the dogmatic background that the hymn would have missed if composed at a later date (Peltomaa, 2001, 85–101). The point of interest after Ephesus lay in the explanation of the incarnation, the "how" (*Akathistos* 3.15: τὸ πῶς), as the *Akathistos* puts it in accordance with contemporary homilies. In the time closer to Chalcedon, the focus shifted away from the mother of God to Christ. The hymn, however, lacks any terminological traces of a concern with the central statements on the two natures – divine and human – in the one person of Christ, which the Council of Chalcedon had determined in order to settle debates on the issue. Furthermore, the typological contraposition of Eve and Mary and the figure of Mary as a model for female ascetical virtues (see 13.3–7 on ἀφθαρσία, "incorruption" implying "chastity," and ἐγκράτεια, "continence") point to the Mariological discourse of that time (see Peltomaa, 2001, 178–180, 191–195 on similarities with → Gregory of Nyssa).

4. The *Akathistos* and Its Late Antique Environment

The *Akathistos* and Romanus both reflect on the relationship between Christian belief and the traditional intellectual culture. Romanus criticizes pagan philosophy as well as → rhetoric (see Wellesz, 1956, 153 on the *Hymn on Pentecost*, stanza 18 and *Hymn* 72.7.1). In the *Akathistos*, Mary is praised for "having proven the philosophers as unwise" (17.8: φιλοσόφους ἀσόφους δεικνύουσα 3.16) and "having drawn asunder the contortions of the Athenians" (17.12: Χαῖρε, τῶν Ἀθηναίων τὰς πλοκὰς διασπῶσα). The hymn also cautions against rhetoric (17.1–2, 9) and rejects the value of mythological poetry (17.11). The reference to the Athenians and the contrasting of Christianity with philosophy, rhetoric, and poetry make these verses part of a distinctly late antique discourse (Kaldellis, 2008, 178–179) going back to Paul's speech on the Areopagus in Acts 17. This allusion to the Apostle is supported by the following mention of the fishing of men (*Akathistos* 17.13), the symbolic expression for the major task assigned by Jesus Christ to his disciples (Luke 5:1–11). At the same time, this stanza highlights Athens' enduring reputation as the center for pagan elite education in late antiquity. The *Akathistos* makes evident that the clash between Christianity and pagan culture had gone beyond the boundaries of intellectual debate, to penetrate the sphere of popular piety via a liturgical text.

Another reflex of the clash of different religious beliefs is found in the praise of Mary for "having freed the Christians from the barbarian worship" (9.12: ἡ τῆς βαρβάρου λυτρουμένη θρησκείας). "The veneration of the fire she brought to an end" (9.14: πυρὸς πρόσκυνησιν παύσασα) is considered a circumscription of the Zoroastrian cult of Persia serving as an example for pagan religion (Trypanis, 1968, 24). In this strophe the *Akathistos* also deals with the Virgin as a liberator from the "passions" (9.15: παθῶν) and as a guide to "moderation" (9.16: σωφροσύνη). By using terms fundamental to ancient philosophy

and referring them to the achievements of Mary, the hymn presents Christianity as the only true belief overcoming pagan thinking.

5. Development

The second proem, which praises the Virgin as "defender and commander," presumably was added in the course of a specific historical event. According to the Synaxarium, the *Akathistos* was sung during the night of Aug 7, 626 CE, after Constantinople was sieged. Under the direction of the patriarch Sergius, the people sang the hymn praising the Virgin for her intervention all night long without anybody sitting down. In all likelihood, the hymn was already popular at the time of this event, but it was given the name *Akathistos* only afterward. In later sieges of Constantinople, the victory was always assigned to the Virgin, and the *Akathistos* became a victory song and Byzantium's most famous hymn. The hymn has been transmitted broadly, the extant manuscripts dating from the 10th century CE onwards. A primary group of nine codices can be singled out (Trypanis, 1968, 11–12, 26 for a listing). The editio princeps was published by Aldus Manutius in Venice as early as 1501.

From an early date on, although not originally, the *Akathistos* was sung at the Feast of the Annunciation (Mar 25), in later times it was also performed on the Saturday in the middle of Lent or on the following Saturday. In the service, it was divided into four sections, and additional proems, psalms, chants, lectures, or doxologies were inserted. Singing all four sections probably took about one hour. It was to be sung during matins (ὄρθροι), which followed an established liturgical rite framing the hymn. Sitting down during the chant was only forbidden after 800 CE. The oldest extant manuscripts containing musical signs are very late (second half 13th/first half 14th cent.), but the neumes may go back to older manuscripts from the 10th century CE and thus to the earliest time of Byzantine notation. The melody was to a large extent melismatic (with several notes on one syllable of a word); in other words, it was sung slowly and in a highly expressive manner (Wellesz 1956, 143–145, 158–159).

6. Reception

The *Akathistos Hymn* is fundamental within the development of the imagery attributed to the mother of God in Byzantine literature (see Krueger, 2011, 37–38, on the metaphor of the gate). It was first translated into Latin around 800 CE, and from the 11th century onward, it also gained influence in western Marian poetry. From the 14th century onwards, the *Akathistos* is often represented in ecclesiastical wall and book paintings.

The *Akathistos* is the oldest hymn and the only kontakion that is still sung completely in eastern liturgy. In the Greek Orthodox Church, it is sung on the fifth Friday evening or Saturday morning of Lent in full length and in front of the standing congregation. Additionally, it can be performed in parts on the first four Friday evenings or Saturdays in Lent.

Historiography

Philological scholarship has struggled to determine precisely the *Akathistos'* date and authorship and the occasion for which it was originally composed. Historical events of a late date like the siege of Constantinople by the Persians and the Avars (626 CE), or even the siege by the Russians (860 CE), have been dismissed. After a long tendency to date the hymn in the 6th century CE and cautious attempts to determine Romanus the Melodist as the author (Maas, 1910; Wellesz, 1956; Trypanis, 1968), recent research analyzing the dogmatic contents has convincingly established an earlier date of composition in the time between the Councils of Ephesus (431 CE) and Chalcedon (451 CE) (Peltomaa, 2001). Latest studies have turned attention to the reception of the imagery of the Marian epithets (Krueger, 2011) and the position of the *Akathistos* within the cultural discourse of late antiquity (Kaldellis, 2008) – two promising fields for coming research.

Bibliography

Del Grande, C., ed., *L'Inno acatisto in onore della Madre di Dio*, Florence, 1948.
Grosdidier de Matons, J., *Romanos le Mélode et les origines de la poésie religieuse à Byzance*, Paris, 1977.

Kaldellis, A., *Hellenism in Byzantium: The Transformations of Greek Identity and the Reception of the Classical Tradition*, Cambridge UK, 2008.
Krueger, D., "Mary at the Threshold: The Mother of God as Guardian in Seventh-Century Palestinian Miracle Accounts," in: L. Brubaker & M.B. Cunningham, eds., *The Cult of the Mother of God in Byzantium: Texts and Images*, Farnham, 2011, 31–38.
Maas, P., "Das Kontaktion," *ByZ* 19, 1910, 285–306.
Meersseman, G.G., ed., *Der Hymnos Akathistos im Abendland*, 2 vols., SF 2/3, Freiburg, 1958.
Peltomaa, L.M., *The Image of the Virgin Mary in the Akathistos Hymn*, Leiden, 2001.
Trypanis, C.A., ed., *Fourteen Early Byzantine Cantica*, WBS 5, Vienna, 1968, 17–39.
Wellesz, E., "The 'Akathistos': A Study in Byzantine Hymnography," *DOP* 9/10, 1956, 141–174.
Wellesz, E., ed., *The Akathistos Hymn*, MMBT 9, Copenhagen, 1957.

JOCHEN SCHULTHEIß

Aksum

Aksum is a city located in the north of present-day Ethiopia. According to recent archaeological excavations, its origins date back to the second half of the 2nd century BCE, although its name is not attested until the 1st century CE, when it appears in the *Periplus of the Erythraean Sea*. Its greatest period of splendor was between the 1st and 6th centuries CE, when it became the capital of the Axumite kingdom and the major religious center after the adoption of Christianity as the official religion in the mid-4th century CE. Currently, Aksum is a small town with little administrative importance, although it retains significant archaeological sites and remains a holy city around the Church of Maryam Seyon, where Ethiopian tradition places the Ark of the Covenant, brought there from Jerusalem by the child who was conceived, according to legend, by King Solomon and the queen of Sheba.

The lack of literary sources, partly due to the excesses committed during the Somali Islamic invasion of the 16th century, makes the use of archaeological methods and numismatics even more necessary in the case of Aksum. Thus, thanks to so-called Monumentum Adulitanum – a bilingual inscription in Greek and Ge'ez that has come down to us through the 6th-century CE transcription of an anonymous source which tradition ascribes to Cosmas Indicopleustes (probably an Alexandrian Nestorian merchant) – some of the military campaigns conducted in various parts of Africa and the Arabian Peninsula in the late 3rd century CE are known and reveal an Aksumite expansion beyond the geographical boundaries of the African kingdom of Aksum at that time. The chronology of the Aksumite kings can be reconstructed with some assurance, though not for all of them, from the coins minted during their reigns. With its main seaport in Adulis, Aksum could join the main trade routes of the time, in both the Roman and Byzantine Mediterranean regions, the south of Arabia, and even India. The economic power attained by Aksum was reflected in the grandeur and magnificence of its monuments, among them the funerary complexes and, within these, the monolithic stelae that dominated them until the conversion of the kingdom to Christianity.

Mentions of the presence of Christianity in the area prior to the 4th century CE are quite vague and lack a firm historical basis. The first reliable data do not reach us until the reign of → Ezana, who adopted Christianity as the official religion of the Aksumite kingdom around the year 330 CE. Different epigraphic remains and the iconography used in the minting of his coins show how he dedicated his political achievements and military victories to the pagan deities during the first part of his reign, before shifting to to use Christian symbols and formulas in the latter part. Other information on the origins of Christianity in Aksum, such as the story of Aedesius and Frumentius in → Rufinus of Aquileia's *Ecclesiastical History*, suffers from enough historical inaccuracy to prohibit definitive conclusions, although it does suggest the existence of an ecclesiastical dependence on the Church of Alexandria from the earliest times.

The decline of Aksum began in the wake of the Muslim expansion during the 7th century CE. The impact of the first wave of Islamic expansion weakened the kingdom, but did not lead to its disappearance. At least during the early days of the Islamic era, Aksum enjoyed the recognition and appreciation of Muslim leaders for the protective policy which the Axumite kingdom had apparently adopted toward Muhammad.

Bibliography

Anderson, J.C., ed., *The Christian Topography of Kosmas Indikopleustes: Firenze, Biblioteca Medicea Laurenziana, Plut. 9.28: The Map of the Universe Redrawn in the Sixth Century with a Contribution on the Slavic Recensions*, Rome, 2013.

Bernard, E., A.J. Drewers & R. Schneider, *Recueil des inscriptions de l'Ethiopie des periodes pré-axoumite et axoumite: Introduction de Fr. Anfray*, vol. I: *Les documents*, vol. II: *Les planches*, vol. III: *Traductions et commentaires*, part A: *Les inscriptions grecques*, Paris, 1991–2000.

Bowersock, G.W., *The Throne of Adulis: Red Sea Wars on the Eve of Islam*, Oxford, 2013.

Brakmann, H., *Einwurzelung der Kirche im spätantiken Reich von Aksum*, Bonn, 1994.

Conti Rossini, C., "Axoum," in: *DHGE*, vol. V, Paris, 1931, 1257–1259.

Deutsche Aksum-Expedition, 4 vols., Berlin, 1913.

Fattovich, R., "Archaeology of Aksum," in: *EnAe*, vol. I, Wiesbaden, 2003, 179–183.

Fattovich, R. et al., *The Aksum Archaeological Area: A Preliminary Assessment*, Naples, 2000.

Fauvelle-Aymar, F.-X., "Les inscriptions d'Adoulis (Érythrée): Fragments d'un royaume hellénistique et gréco-romain sur la côte africaine de la mer Rouge," *BIFAO* 109, 2009, 135–160.

Meck, B., *Über die Stelen von Axum, Äthiopien: Ein Beitrag zur Astro-Archäologie*, Frankfurt, 1979.

Munro-Hay, S.C.H., *Aksum: An African Civilisation of Late Antiquity*, Edinburgh, 1991.

Munro-Hay, S.C.H., "Aksum," in: *EnAe*, vol. I, Wiesbaden, 2003, 173–179.

Pankhurst, R., "The Greek Coins of Aksum," *AbSa* 6, 1975, 70–83.

Phillipson, D.W., *Ancient Ethiopia: Aksum: Its Antecedents and Successors*, London, 1998.

Phillipson, D.W., *Archaeology at Aksum, Ethiopia, 1993–1997*, London, 2000.

Phillipson, D.W., *Ancient Churches of Ethiopia: Fourth-Fourteenth Century*, New Haven, 2009.

Voicu, S.J., "Aksum," in: *NDPAC*, Genova, 2006, 171.

JUAN ANTONIO CABRERA MONTERO

Alaric I

The greatest Germanic chieftain of the early 5th century CE, Alaric led the Gothic army that sacked Rome in 410 CE, a catastrophe that has become a symbol of the "decline and fall" of the western Roman Empire. He was born circa 370 CE north of the Danube River (the account of his noble ancestry in Jordanes – see Jor. *Get.* 29.146 – cannot be relied upon) and first appears in our sources as a Gothic war leader in the early 390s CE. The Tervingi and Greuthungi → Goths, who had defeated and killed the eastern Roman emperor → Valens at the Battle of Adrianople in 378 CE after crossing the Danube, had settled in the Balkans under the treaty of 382 CE with the new eastern emperor → Theodosius I. Alaric's rise to power is obscure, but in 394 CE he commanded Gothic federate troops who fought for Theodosius against the western usurper → Eugenius. The Goths suffered heavy casualties at the battle of the Frigidus, which fuelled their sense of grievance, and when Theodosius died in 395 CE, Alaric led them in revolt.

Alaric had united the majority of the Tervingi and Greuthungi Goths under his rule, and over time his following evolved into what have become known as the Visigoths. His own position remained unstable, however, and between 395 CE and 410 CE he faced an ongoing struggle to secure his authority and the successful settlement of his people. The division of the empire between Theodosius' sons Arcadius (East) and Honorius (West) allowed Alaric to play East and West against each other, but he also sought Roman recognition and a military title to reinforce his status. Alaric and his Goths ravaged Greece and Thrace from 395 CE to 397 CE, until Alaric received the title of *magister militum per Illyricum* in 397/398 CE. Yet tensions continued, and early 5th century CE Alaric turned his attention westward toward Italy.

Alaric began his first invasion in late 401 CE, possibly intending to pass through northern Italy and seek settlement in Gaul. The Goths were driven back by → Stilicho, the leading general of the western emperor Honorius, after battles at Pollentia and Verona in 402 CE. These two battles are presented as great Roman victories by the poet Claudian (*The Gothic War; On the Sixth Consulship of Honorius*), and Stilicho has been accused of deliberately allowing the Goths to escape. But Claudian was Stilicho's panegyricist and propagandist, and while Alaric withdrew to the Balkans his power was little reduced. The threat he posed contributed to the weakening of the Roman frontiers as troops were withdrawn to protect Italy, and as the pressure mounted in August 408 CE Stilicho was executed on Honorius' orders.

Alaric seized his opportunity. By late 408 CE he had Rome under siege, demanding land and food for his people and a military title for himself. Honorius, safe in Ravenna, refused all Alaric's demands and was further alienated by Alaric's election of a puppet emperor, Attalus, in December 409 CE. Finally, on Aug 24, 410 CE, the Goths entered Rome, and for three days they sacked the symbolic heart of the Roman Empire (Olymp. *Frag.* 11; Aug. *Civ.* 1.1; Oros. *Adv. pag.* 7.39).

News of the sack of Rome echoed across the Roman world. Far away in the Holy Land, → Jerome lamented that "the whole world perished in one city" (Jerome, preface *Commentary on Ezekiel*). Yet our sources agree that the Goths did relatively little physical damage and in particular that the Roman churches and those who took sanctuary within them were spared. According to Orosius, when Alaric entered the city,

> he first gave the order that whoever had fled to the holy places, above all to the basilicas of the holy apostles Peter and Paul, were to be left safe and unharmed. (Oros. *Adv. pag.* 7.39.1; see also Aug. *Civ.* 1.1–7)

Jerome recounted how two female ascetics, Principia and Marcella, were spared by the Goths and escorted to safety in the basilica of Paul (Jer. *Ep.* 127.13). None of these authors provides any detailed evidence for the personal religious beliefs of Alaric. Like his people, Alaric followed the Christian teachings of Ulfila, the apostle to the Goths. Ulfila had taught a Homoian doctrine of the → Trinity (that the Son was "like" the Father), a belief that had been imperial orthodoxy when the Goths first entered the empire but was regarded by most Roman Christians in 410 CE as heretical and Arian (→ Arianism). Nevertheless, Alaric and the Goths showed their Christian faith in their treatment of the churches and people of Rome.

The psychological impact of the sack of Rome far outweighed the event's practical significance. Rome was no longer the western imperial residence, while for Alaric the assault on the city in fact marked the failure of his hopes. There would be no agreement with Honorius, and Alaric and his followers remained without a secure homeland. Alaric marched south toward Sicily, and late in 410 CE he died of disease in Bruttium. Gothic rule passed to his brother-in-law Athaulf, beginning another decade of warfare and internal strife, until in 418 CE Alaric's people eventually settled in southern Gaul with the creation of the Visigothic kingdom of Aquitaine. It was Alaric who forged the Visigoths, the first independent Germanic people to create their own state within Western Europe, and through this achievement no less than the sack of Rome he played a key role in the unfolding story that culminated in the fall of the western Roman Empire.

(A historiography for this topic is not applicable).

Bibliography

Berndt, G.M., & R. Steinacher, eds., *Arianism: Roman Heresy and Barbarian Creed*, Farnham, 2014.

Burns, T.S., *Barbarians within the Gates of Rome: A Study of Roman Military Policy and the Barbarians, ca. 375–425 AD*, Bloomington, 1994.

Goffart, W., *Barbarian Tides: The Migration Age and the Later Roman Empire*, Philadelphia, 2006.

Gwynn, D.M., *The Goths: Lost Civilizations*, London, 2017.

Heather, P., *Goths and Romans, AD 332–489*, Oxford, 1991.

Kulikowski, M., *Rome's Gothic Wars From the Third Century to Alaric*, Cambridge UK, 2007.

„Alaricus I," in: *PLRE*, vol. II, Cambridge UK, 1980.

Thompson, E.A., *Romans and Barbarians: The Decline of the Western Empire*, Madison, 1982.

Wolfram, H., *The Roman Empire and its Germanic peoples*, Berkeley, 1997.

DAVID M. GWYNN

Alexander I (Bishop of Rome)

Alexander I was the sixth bishop in Rome (counting Peter as the first one) and held office between circa 109 and 116 CE. His identity is frequently confused with a martyr of the same name, but contemporary textual evidence suggests that this is hagiographic legend rather than fact. The concept of papacy (→ Pope/Father) at this early stage of the Christian church is contested; some contemporary records refer to him as "pope," but it might be more accurate to describe his status as "bishop of Rome." He is viewed retrospectively by the Roman Catholic Church as one in the succession of popes and is honored as such in the liturgy of the Mass. Contemporary sources are contaminated by hagiographical rhetoric.

1. Identity and Dates

There is a plethora of men named Alexander in the period under scrutiny, resulting in many opportunities for confused or conflated identities. This makes it especially challenging in confirming the facts about this early churchman, and the chief misattribution concerning Alexander I remains unresolvable due to lack of evidence from primary sources. The early church's hunger for inspiring → martyrs in support of the claims of orthodoxy in the face of persecution and heresy is another factor in the persistent romanticization of Alexander I.

The date of his birth is unknown, and the date of his death is cloaked in the uncertainty surrounding the duration of his period of office. Since he would have remained as pope until he died, this makes his death likely between 116 and 119 CE. There is no entry for the supposed date of his burial (which would be the normal date for celebrating his feast); that of May 3 is suppressed in *Butler's Lives of the Saints* presumably because of skepticism about his alleged martyrdom. What is confirmed from various sources is that he was pope for a period between 109 and 116 or 119 CE (according to the Liberian Catalogue, which is notoriously unreliable), holding office for seven years, two months, and a day according to the → *Liber pontificalis*. L. Duchesne's chart giving the variants among the Liberian Catalogue, a 5th-century CE catalogue, the 6th-century CE *Liber pontificalis*, *l'Abrégé Canonien*, and *Révision* shows a length of pontificate up to 12 years, seven months, and 11 days. He is described as being bishop of Rome during the time of → Trajan up to "the consulship of Aelianus and Vetus." This information from the *Liber pontificalis* is not the same as found in Eusebius, and these early confirmations of the dates of his episcopacy have been described by several modern commentators as no more than guesswork. He is variously described as the fifth or sixth pope in line from Peter (→ Peter the Apostle); this phrase causes confusion as it is not always clear whether Peter is included in this number, and → Anacletus is confusingly given a second entry in listings as Cletus. The consensus is the following succession: Peter, Linus, Anacletus, Clement, Evaristus, Alexander I, followed by Sixtus (also known as Xystus).

Eusebius of Caesarea mentions him twice; in the first reference, he places Alexander's death in the third year of Emperor Hadrian's reign "after completing the tenth year of his ministry" (Eus. *Hist. eccl.* 4.4; PG 25; LCL; → Eusebius of Caesarea). The second reference reports → Irenaeus of Lyon's account in *Adversus haereses*, which merely records the succession outlined above, denoting Xystus as "the sixth from the apostles," in other words not counting Peter as the first in line because he is the original → apostle (Eus. *Hist. eccl.* 5.6; PG 25; LCL). This would appear to make Alexander I the fifth successor to Peter and sixth bishop of Rome. His name is Greco-Roman one, and he was known by no qualifier indicating place of origin. The *Liber pontificalis* claims he was born in Rome and the son of an Alexander from the reign of Caput Tauri. However, since the *Liber pontificalis* only records Roman pontiffs, the author may have had a vested interest in describing Alexander as Roman by birth.

2. Key Events in His Life

The exact nature of his role as constitutional leader of the Christian community is unclear, as is the case for Anacletus and → Anicetus because the concept of monarchical episcopacy at Rome had not yet been established. He is, however, attributed as having performed December ordinations of six priests and two deacons as well as six bishops "for various places." December seems to be the standard period for ordinations; local ordinations of priests and deacons took place on ember days while consecration of bishops could occur at any time, planned to minimize the interregnum after the death of the previous incumbent. The *Liber pontificalis* gives the length of the "vacancy," often as short as two days. The interregnum after Alexander was 35 days.

He is also reputed to have converted the Romans, including senators, and the prefect of the city of Hermes whose wife was subsequently healed through his intercession, though this is more likely to be the Alexander who was held with Eventius and

Theodolus at Hermes and martyred with them, as discussed below.

3. Liturgical Innovations Associated with Alexander I

Two liturgical practices are attributed to Alexander, the first being that he was the first to insert the memorial of the Lord's passion (the *Qui pridie quam pateretur*; on the day before he suffered) into the narrative of the eucharistic celebration (→ Eucharist). This is now in the Roman canon of the Mass, though there is no evidence or agreement that Alexander was responsible for this innovation, and indeed, some commentators today condemn this attribution as "transparent anachronism." The other innovation associated with Alexander is the use of blessed salt and water for sanctifying private homes. This is also seen as a spurious attribution, being more probably adapted from pagan customs of the day. Three letters attributed to him in PG 5 are clearly apocryphal, as they deal with canonical, liturgical, and dogmatic matters that were not resolved before the Council of → Nicaea in 325 CE.

4. Arguments For and Against His Having Been Martyred

Alexander's death is the most contentious part of his history. Irenaeus clearly states that Telesphorus was the first martyred bishop, and the suppression of Alexander's feast day suggests lack of consensus about his martyrdom (Iren. *Haer.* 3.3.63). The legend states that he died along with the priest Eventius and deacon Theodulus, decapitated on the Via Nomentana, and buried at the seventh milestone. This legend was circulated for some time; William of Malmsbury the 12th-century English Chronicler perpetuates it. A tomb for a martyr named Alexander was indeed found here in 1855, but there is no evidence that he was our pope. Pope Eugene II (d. 827) transferred these relics to Rome, where they are buried beside Saints Seraphia and Sabina in the Church of Saint Sabina. At a similar period, the Church of Saint Pelino in Valva, Italy, erected a tomb inscribed "Here are buried the bones of Pope St. Alexander, fifth successor to Peter." Below the tomb a further inscription confirms that the bones were removed to Pelgni to be interred beneath the high altar. An unsubstantiated account dated 834 states that the bones were moved to Freising in Bavaria.

Bibliography

Altaner, B., *Patrologie: Leben, Schriften und Lehre der Kirchenväter*, Freiburg, 1978.

Barcellona, F.S., "Alessandro I," *EdP*, Rome, 2000, 213–215.

Bareille, G., "Alexander I," in: A. Vacant, ed., *DThC*, vol. I, Paris, 1923, 708–709.

Caspar, E., "Alexander I," in: *GPAHW*, vol. I, Tübingen, 1930, 8–13.

Davis, R., trans., *Liber Pontificalis* (*The Book of Pontifs*), Liverpool, 2000.

Doyle P., ed., *Butler's Lives of the Saints*, 12 vols., Chicago, 1999.

Dufourcq, A., "Alexander I (Pope)," in: A. Baudrillart, ed., *DHGE*, vol. II, Paris, 1914, 204–206.

Duffy, E., *Saints and Sinners: A History of the Popes*, New Haven, 1997.

Farmer, D.H., *ODS*, Oxford, 1978.

Goggi, P., "Alexander I," in: *EC*, vol. I, Vatican City, 1949–1954, 787.

Gontard, F., *The Popes*, trans. A.J. Peeler & E.F. Peeler, London, 1964.

Jaffé, P., *Regesta pontificum Romanorum ab Condita Ecclesia ad Annum post Christum Natum*, 2 vols., Leipzig, 1885–1888.

John, E., ed., *The Popes: A Concise Biographical History*, London, 1964.

Josi, E., "Alexander I," in: *BSS*, vol. I, Rome, 1961–1970, 792–798.

Kelly, J.N.D., & M.J. Walsh, *ODS*, Oxford, 2010.

Kirschbaum, E., *Tombs of St. Peter and St. Paul*, trans. E. Murray, New York, 1959.

Llewellyn, P.A.B., "The Passion of S. Alexander and his Companions, of S. Hermes and S. Quirinus: A Suggested Date and Author," *VetChr* 13, 1976, 289–296.

Maxwell-Stuart, P.G., *Chronicle of the Popes: The Reign-by-Reign Record of the Papacy from St. Peter to the Present*, London, 2002.

Reardon, W.J., *The Deaths of the Popes: Comprehensive Accounts, Including Funerals, Burial Places and Epitaphs*, Jefferson, 2004.

Salamito, J-M., "Alexander I," in: P. Levillain, ed., *PAE*, vol. I, New York, 2002, 39–40.

Schwaiger, G., "Alexander I," in: *LThK*, vol. I, Freiburg, 1995, 367.

Testini, P., *Archaeologia cristina*, Bari, 1980.

Vegliani, T., ed., "Alesandro I papa (Epistolae)," in: T. Veglianti, *Test I patristici sul sangue di Cristo 4*, Rome, 1996, 58–62.

Vogel, C., *Commentary to Duchesne Liber Pontificalis*, Paris, 1955–1957.

Weltin, E.G., "Alexander I," in: T. Carson & J. Cerrito, eds., *NCE*, vol. I, Washington DC, 2003, 253.

Williams, G.L., *Papal Genealogy: The Families and Descendants of the Popes*, Jefferson, 1998.

HANNAH HUNT

Alexander I of Alexandria

Alexander held the Alexandrian episcopate (312–328 CE) during the crucial formative years that witnessed the conversion of Constantine and the outbreak of what has become known as the Arian controversy. Primarily remembered today for his clash with the presbyter Arius, which sparked the 4th-century CE Trinitarian doctrinal debates, Alexander was one of the leading figures at the First Council of → Nicaea in 325 CE and laid the ecclesiastical (→ Ecclesiology) and theological foundations upon which his protégé and successor Athanasius of Alexandria would build.

We know almost nothing of Alexander's life before his election as bishop in 312 CE, but he must have witnessed the impact of the Great Persecution (→ Persecution of Christians) in which Peter I of Alexandria (bishop 300–311 CE) died. Peter's successor Achillas (312 CE) held office for barely six months, and Alexander's election came at a difficult time for the Alexandrian see. The Great Persecution was still drawing to a close, and Alexander found his position immediately threatened by the Meletian schism. → Meletius of Lycopolis had opposed the relatively mild terms that Peter had set for the re-admission of Christians who lapsed under the persecution, and his rival "Church of the Martyrs" challenged Alexandrian authority over the Egyptian church throughout Alexander's episcopate and beyond. It is against this tense background that the initial conflict between Alexander and Arius (→ Arianism) must be set.

Arius rose to prominence during the early years of Alexander's episcopate as the presbyter (→ Priest/Presbyter) of the Alexandrian parish church of "Baucalis." Alexandrian presbyters possessed unusual independence in this period (Epiph. *Haer.* 69.1.2), and Arius developed a considerable local following. His popularity presented another potential threat to Alexander's authority, particularly when Arius began to preach doctrines that others regarded as suspect. At a council of Alexandria, Alexander heard the different arguments and decided against Arius.

The presbyter refused to compromise his views, and Alexander expelled him and his followers from the Alexandrian church (Soz. *Hist. eccl.* 1.15).

The exact chronology of Arius' initial condemnation and the events that followed remains the subject of debate, which is important for our understanding of Alexander's thought and writings. The traditional interpretation, laid down by H.-G. Opitz (1934–1935), placed the beginning of the controversy in 318 CE. Arius appealed for support from other eastern churches, exchanging letters with Eusebius of Nicomedia, and in response Alexander circulated an *Encyclical Letter* in 319 CE. In circa 320 CE Alexander received a conciliatory letter from Arius, but tensions continued to simmer until September 324 CE, when Constantine defeated his eastern rival Licinius and united the empire under his rule. This allowed renewed debate, and to this period H.-G. Opitz assigned Alexander's other major surviving letter, written to his namesake Alexander (bishop of either Thessalonica or less probably Byzantium). Constantine himself was forced to intervene, and the Council of Nicaea met in May/June 325 CE.

An alternative chronology has been proposed more recently by R. Williams (2001), who argued that the traditional order of Alexander's two letters should be reversed. R. Williams placed the formal beginning of the controversy, the Council of Alexandria that condemned Arius, in circa 321 CE. Arius then began to rally support in the East, and this prompted Alexander to write to his namesake in circa 321/322 CE warning him of the danger. Debate continued to escalate over the following years, until Constantine's conquest of the East began a new phase of the controversy and provided the context for the *Encyclical Letter*, which Alexander circulated across the eastern churches in late 324 CE or early 325 CE. Only the *Encyclical Letter* attacks Eusebius of Nicomedia or shows any detailed knowledge of Arius' *Thalia*, suggesting that this letter should be dated later than Alexander's *Letter to Alexander*, and the revised chronology therefore offers a more natural interpretation of the development of Alexander's thought in the years after his condemnation of Arius.

The *Letter to Alexander of Thessalonica/Byzantium* (preserved in Thdt. *Hist. eccl.* 1.4), which on R. Williams' chronology is the earlier of the two letters, is a long and somewhat rambling document. Alexander denounces those who now disturb the churches and warns his namesake to guard against those who might deceive him. Arius and his followers imitate the Jews and fight against Christ.

> They deny his divinity, and declare him to be on a level with all [humankind]. They pick out every saying relative to his saving dispensation and to his humiliation for our sake, and try to compound from them the proclamation of their own impiety, by abandoning the words showing his divinity from the beginning and his ineffable glory with the Father.

Alexander's characterization of Arius' teachings in this letter immediately fixed upon the themes that would dominate all subsequent anti-Arian polemic. The heretics teach that the Son of God is a creature just like all other created beings and that there was a time when he was not. Therefore they teach that the Son is changeable and that we may be advanced as sons just as he was. The main body of the letter catalogues the scriptural verses that the Arians bring forward to support their views, many of which reappear among the Arian scriptural texts refuted in → Athanasius of Alexandria's *Orationes contra Arianos*. Alexander was also concerned to reject the charge that had been levelled against him, that because he maintained the eternity of the Son so he taught that Father and Son were two unbegotten beings. The Father alone is unbegotten, but the Son is only-begotten from the Father and so is perfect and immutable, the exact image of the Father.

Arius' *Letter to Eusebius of Nicomedia* (preserved in Thdt. *Hist. eccl.* 1.5), approximately contemporary to Alexander's *Letter to Alexander*, confirms from Arius' perspective the question that had divided the two men.

> The bishop makes great havoc of us and persecutes us severely, and is in full sail against us. He has driven us out of the city as atheists, because we do not concur in what he publicly preaches, namely "God always, the Son always; as the Father so the Son; the Son co-exists unbegotten with the Father; he is everlasting; neither by thought nor by any interval does God precede the Son; always God, always Son; the Son is from God himself."

In Arius' eyes, Alexander's insistence that the Son was eternal inevitably led to two unbegotten beings and denied the unique authority of the Father. Eusebius of Nicomedia's fragmentary reply to Arius (in Athan. *Syn.* 17) and his *Letter to Paulinus of Tyre* (in Thdt. *Hist. eccl.* 1.6) confirm that he shared the same concerns. Alexander had thus been correct to emphasize his distinction between the eternity of the only-begotten Son and the unbegotten Father. The underlying issue at stake was how to define the divinity of the Son and his relationship with the Father within the → Trinity, and it is hardly surprising that so fundamental an issue could not be easily resolved. With the arrival of Constantine in 324 CE, the eastern churches were ruled by a Christian emperor for the first time, and in his *Encyclical Letter* Alexander seized this opportunity to lay down more precisely his vision of the Arian heresy and of the traditional orthodox faith.

There has been some discussion of the authorship of the *Encyclical Letter*. In comparison to the *Letter to Alexander*, the *Encyclical Letter* is more concise, and in argument, style, and vocabulary there are notable similarities with the later writings of Athanasius. As Athanasius was Alexander's → deacon, it is possible that he drafted the text of the letter. However, the parallels with Athanasius' later works may equally reflect the influence of his mentor, and the *Encyclical Letter* remains the strongest surviving statement of Alexander's theology.

The *Encyclical Letter* (in Socr. *Hist. Eccl.* 1.6) opens with another condemnation of the *Christomachoi* (fighters against Christ) who have disturbed the Alexandrian church. Alexander then attacks Eusebius of Nicomedia as the man responsible for escalating the conflict, offering the earliest denunciation of the so-called Eusebians as an Arian party, before providing the first detailed polemical description of the Arian heresy:

What they have invented and assert, contrary to the Scriptures, are as follows: God was not always a father, but there was when God was not a father; the Word of God was not always, but came to be out of nothing; for the ever-existing God has made him who did not previously exist, out of the non-existent. Therefore indeed there was once when he was not. For the Son is a creature and a thing made. He is neither like the Father according to essence, nor true Word by nature of the Father, nor true Wisdom. He is one of the things made and one of the generated beings, being inaccurately called Word and Wisdom, since he came to be himself through the proper Word of God and the Wisdom in God, in which indeed God made everything and also him. Therefore indeed he is changeable and mutable by nature, as are all rational beings, [and] the Word is foreign and alien and separate from the essence of the Father. And the Father is unintelligible to the Son, for the Word neither perfectly and exactly knows the Father, nor is he able to see him perfectly.

Alexander's polemic cannot be taken as an accurate account of Arius' own teachings, for Arius did not describe the Son as "a thing made" (ποίημα) and consistently maintained that the Son was a perfect and immutable creature (κτίσμα), not one of the creatures. But the polemic does reveal clearly the dangers that Alexander and others saw in Arius' teachings. If the Son has a beginning, and is foreign to the essence (οὐσία) of the Father, then how can he be the Father's Word and the savior of humankind through the incarnation? Against the errors of Arius, Alexander contrasted his understanding of the scriptural faith of the church:

Who that has heard the words of John, "in the beginning was the Word" [John 1:1], will not denounce the saying of these men, that "there was a time when he was not"? Or who that has heard in the Gospel, "the only-begotten Son" [John 1:14], and "by him were all things made" [John 1:3], will not detest their declaration that he is "one of the things that were made"? For how can he be one of those things which were made by himself? Or how can he be the only-begotten when, according to them, he is counted as one among the rest, since he is himself a creature and a work? And how can he be "made of things that were not," when the Father says, "my heart has uttered a good Word" [Ps 45:1], and "out of the womb I have begotten you before the morning star" [Ps 110:3]? Or again, how is he "unlike in essence to the Father," who is "his perfect image" [Col 1:15] and "the brightness of his glory" [Heb 1:3], and says "he who has seen me has seen the Father" [John 14:9]? And if the Son is the Word and Wisdom of God, how was there "a time when he was not"? It is the same as if they should say that God was once without Word and without Wisdom.

And how is he "subject to change and mutable," who says of himself, "I am in the Father, and the Father in me" [John 14:10], and "I and the Father are one" [John 10:30]; and again by the prophet, "behold me, for I am, and I change not" [Mal 3:6]? For although one may refer this expression to the Father, yet it may now be more aptly spoken of the Word, because he was not changed by having become man, but as the apostle has said, "Jesus Christ is the same yesterday, today, and forever" [Heb 13:8]. And what can have persuaded them to say that he was made for us, when Paul has expressly declared that "all things are for him and by him" [Heb 2:10]. We need not wonder indeed at their blasphemous assertion that "the Son does not know the Father perfectly," for having once set themselves to fight against Christ, they reject even the words of the Lord himself, when he says, "As the Father knows me, so I know the Father" [John 10:15]. If therefore the Father knows the Son only in part, then it is evident that the Son also knows the Father only in part. But if it would be improper to affirm this, and it is admitted that the Father does know the Son perfectly, then it is evident that as the Father knows his own Word, so also does the Word know his own Father, whose Word he is.

By the standards of later orthodoxy, Alexander's emphasis upon the full divinity of the Son still left unresolved how to conceive of Father and Son as one God and yet distinct identities within the Trinity. Nevertheless, his *Encyclical Letter* laid down starkly the opposing theological alternatives as Alexander understood them. When Constantine arrived in the East, he was immediately confronted by the divisions within the eastern churches. His initial reaction was to encourage those involved to agree to reconcile (although the text known as Constantine's *Letter to Alexander and Arius*, quoted in Eus. *Vita Const.* 2.64–72, was actually sent to a council of bishops rather than to the two men themselves). The emperor soon realized, however, that the questions at stake were too important to dismiss in this way. Alexander answered the summons to attend the Council of Nicaea, accompanied by his deacon Athanasius. There are no formal acts surviving from the council, so we cannot reconstruct Alexander's role in the discussions with any certainty. But the council enforced his condemnation of Arius, and at least one later tradition attributed to Alexander the inclusion of the key term ὁμοούσιος in the original Nicene Creed (Philost. *Hist. eccl.* 1.7). While this term does not occur in any of Alexander's few extant writings, he certainly asserted that the Son was from the Father's οὐσία, and he was well placed to reassure those eastern bishops who distrusted ὁμοούσιος potentially Sabellian implications.

The Nicene Creed (→ Nicaea) upheld Alexander's vision of the orthodox faith and anathematized the tenets of Arius that he had particularly condemned. Yet theology was not Alexander's sole concern. The Meletian schism continued to divide the Egyptian church and was reexamined at Nicaea. The council ruled that Meletius and the clergy whom he had appointed should retain their positions, although inferior in status to the equivalent clergy of Alexander's church, and that properly elected Meletian bishops could succeed catholic bishops when the contested sees became vacant (Letter of the Council, in Socr. *Hist. eccl.* 1.9; Thdt. *Hist. eccl.* 1.9). The *Breviarium Melitii*, the list of Meletian clergy that Meletius submitted to Alexander at Nicaea, records a Meletian presence all along the Nile Valley and confirms the threat that the schismatic church posed. The status of the Alexandrian see was further reaffirmed by the sixth canon of Nicaea, which acknowledged the bishop of Alexandria's traditional authority over the churches of Egypt, Libya, and Pentapolis.

On his return to Egypt, Alexander could be well satisfied by the theological and ecclesiastical work done at Nicaea. But the final years of his episcopate were not peaceful ones. Supporters of Arius and his teachings still remained, particularly within Alexandria, and the coexistence of catholic and Meletian clergy was not always smooth. These tensions were inherited by Athanasius and divided the Egyptian church throughout the 4th century CE. Alexander also set another precedent for Athanasius, through his promotion of the nascent ascetic movement. Athanasius reports that a number of female ascetics once approached Alexander for guidance. Alexander instructed the virgins that to draw near to Christ, they had to understand the → incarnation, for

> if it used to be impossible for a human being to join with God, he has made it possible by having become human (quoted in Athan. *Ep. virg.* [*Copt.*] 40)

Alexander died on Apr 17, 328 CE. Athanasius, his protégé and chosen heir, was not elected until Jun 8, the delay an early indication of the challenges that Athanasius would face across his own long episcopate (328–373 CE). In the history of both Christian doctrine and the Egyptian church, Alexander has been overshadowed by his illustrious successor. Only two of his letters survive intact, the *Letter to Alexander* and the *Encyclical Letter*, together with scattered fragments of a letter to Sylvester of Rome and a sermon of highly dubious authenticity (the *Sermo de anima et corpore deque passione Domini*). But Alexander's achievement should not be underestimated. He preserved the authority and doctrinal traditions of the see of Alexandria through years of conflict, preparing the ground for Athanasius within Egypt and the wider church, and through his efforts he helped to shape the eventual triumph of Nicene orthodoxy.

(A historiography for this topic is not applicable.)

Bibliography

Ayres, L., *Nicaea and its Legacy: An Approach to Fourth-Century Trinitarian Theology*, Oxford, 2004.

Davis, S.J., *The Early Coptic Papacy: The Egyptian Church and Its Leadership in Late Antiquity*, Cairo, 2004.

Edwards, M., "Alexander of Alexandria and the 'Homoousion'," *VigChr* 66, 2012, 482–502.

Griggs, C.W., *Early Egyptian Christianity: From its Origins to 451 CE*, Leiden, 1990.

Hanson, R.P.C., *The Search for the Christian Doctrine of God: The Arian Controversy 318–381*, Edinburgh, 1988.

Opitz, H.-G., *Athanasius Werke II.1.*, vol. III, part 1: *Urkunden zur Geschichte des arianischen Streites 318–328*, Berlin, 1934–1935.

Schneemelcher, W., "Der Sermo 'De Anima et corpore': Ein Werk Alexanders von Alexandrien?" in: W. Schneemelcher, ed., *FS für Günther Dehn*, Neukirchen, 1957, 119–143.

Simonetti, M., *La crisi ariana nel quarto secolo*, Rome, 1975.

Stead, G.C., "Athanasius' Earliest Written Work," *JThS* n.s. 39, 1988, 76–91.

Williams, R.D., *Arius: Heresy and Tradition*, London, ²2001.

DAVID M. GWYNN

Alexander of Aphrodisias

Alexander of Aphrodisias was an Aristotelian philosopher active at the beginning of the 3rd century CE. Thanks to an inscription discovered in 2001 and published in A. Chaniotis (2004), it has been possible to establish that the native city was Aphrodisias in Caria and that his father, also a philosopher, was called Titus Aurelius Alexander. Our Alexander presents himself as one of *diadochoi* in Athens, that is, likely the holder of the chair in Aristotelian philosophy established in Athens by Marcus Aurelius in 176 CE. Alexander's *De fato* is dedicated to the co-emperors Septimius Severus and Caracalla, who ruled in 198–209 CE, but nothing more can be inferred about the chronological coordinates of his activity. In his writings, he refers to Sosigenes and Herminus as his masters, but it is safe to assume that he had his philosophical education at home from his father Titus Aurelius.

1. Alexander's Philosophy

Alexander is the main Greek commentator of Aristotle's works whose commentaries have been preserved. His philosophical production was vast and included a series of autonomous treatises. The extant commentaries include:

1. a commentary on Books I–V of the *Metaphysics* (Hayduck, 1891);
2. a commentary on Book I of the *Prior Analytics* (Wallies, 1883);
3. a commentary on the *Topics* (Wallies, 1891);
4. a commentary on the *De sensu* (Wendland, 1901);
5. a commentary on the *Meteorologica* (Hayduck, 1899).

He also wrote commentaries on other treatises and there are several editions of fragmentary works (see Moraux, 1979, for the *Posterior Analytics*, to be supplemented by Gili & Podolak, 2018; see Rashed, 2011, for the *Physics*; see Genequand, 2001, and Rescigno,

2004; 2008, for the *De coelo*; see Freudenthal, 1885, for the commentary on Arist. *Metaph.* 12). His autonomous works include:

1. a treatise *De anima*, that follow the structure of the homonymous Aristotelian treatise but is not a commentary thereof (edition in Bruns, 1887);
2. minor treatises that include the *De intellectu* (edition in Bruns, 1892);
3. *De fato* (edition in Sharples, 1983);
4. *De mixtione* (edition in Groisard, 2013).

Among the several general reconstructions of Alexander's philosophy, R.W. Sharples (1987) is to this date to be commended as an excellent overview, while M. Rashed (2007) presents Alexander's philosophy as centered around the core notion of form and essence against the nominalist Aristotelianism advanced in the 1st century BCE by Boethus of Sidon (for more references on Alexander and his philosophy, see the updated bibliography in Fazzo & Gili, 2018). On the basis of the extant evidence, Alexander's philosophical activity appears to focus on the systematic exposition of Aristotle's doctrine. In the wake of the recent interest in late antique philosophy, scholars have stressed that the effort to explain "Aristotle with Aristotle" has a philosophical pay-off, in that it forces Alexander to conceive of Aristotelianism as a "system" (see esp. Fazzo, 2002) and to choose a particular version thereof among the many possible interpretations (Rashed, 2007) in order to strive for consistency (Gili, 2011) while presenting each Aristotelian science along the model proposed in the *Posterior Analytics* (see e.g. Bonelli, 2001). Thanks to his systematic presentation of Aristotelian philosophy and to the clarity of his commentaries, Alexander became the leading exegetical authority on the Aristotelian text in late antiquity and beyond. There are, however, some genuinely new ideas in his writings. He stresses the unity of the substantial whole, where matter and form cannot be separate from each other in the physical world, against Stoic materialism and probably against rival versions of Aristotelianism (according to Boethus of Sidon, an Aristotelian of the 1st cent. BEC, forms are secondary qualities). In many of his treatises, Alexander criticizes several Stoic doctrines. The antagonistic attitude toward the Stoics and a more accommodating approach toward Platonism are very understandable for an Aristotelian

philosopher, who shares many tenets with Platonists and fewer with the Stoics. But it is important to notice at this stage that Alexander would not shy away from controversy when he deemed it necessary for philosophical reasons. His polemic against the Stoics centers around three major themes: the status of logic, the definition of fate, and that of mixture. While the Stoics maintained that logic is a *part* of philosophy, Alexander was resolute in arguing that it is a mere instrument thereof and he was criticizing Stoic propositional arguments as useless in a scientific context. In his treatise *On Fate*, Alexander challenges Stoic determinism and identifies fate with nature (including human nature). By stressing that many events happen outside of their natural course, that is, by chance, and that nature arrives at its end in most but not all cases, Alexander was laying the ground for a non-determinist philosophy of nature along the lines of Aristotle's *Physics* and for a non-determinist account of human action. In his treatise *On mixture*, Alexander rejects the idea that two different substances can mix while keeping their nature as two different substances – an idea that would be supported instead within the framework of a materialist account of the physical world, as it was the case for the Stoics. Next to the polemics with the Stoics, that helped him outline a more personal account of Aristotelianism, Alexander is best known for his idea that the higher intellect of human beings is identical with the unmoved mover of the universe. This claim has wide implications for his religious opinions as well, and it is worth focusing on it in more detail.

2. Alexander and Religion

Apart from the scanty information included in the dedication of his *De fato*, Alexander does not make any autobiographical remark in his extant writings. He does not state his own religious affiliation, but it seems safe to assume that he was pagan. As evidence of this claim, we could refer to the *Proemium* to his commentary on Aristotle's *Prior Analytics* (see Wallies, 1883, para. 5.21ff.), where Alexander approvingly quotes a phrase from Plato's *Laws* (5.730.c1–2) where it is stated that truth brings everything that is good to both gods and human beings. One would not expect from a believer in a monotheist religion such a quote without any cautionary limitation. But apart from sparse references to the "gods" in the plural, it is reasonable to hypothesize that Alexander was neither a Jew nor a Christian because of his understanding of the soul and of divinity. In both *Metaphysics* (12) and in *Physics* (8), Aristotle introduced his idea that all motions in the universe entail the existence of an "unmoved Mover" that would serve as an ultimate cause. In *Metaphysics* (12), Aristotle explicitly identifies this unmoved Mover with God and describes it as "thought of thought." Many scholars have been uncomfortable with the hypothesis that Aristotle might have been a monotheist. While R. Bodéüs (1992) maintained that Aristotle believed in the traditional pagan gods, B. Botter (2005) interpreted the reference to "god" in Arist. *Metaph.* 12 as having a predicative value, thereby implying that the "unmoved Mover" is divine but cannot be referred to as the only "God" of the Aristotelian universe. R. Bodéüs, however, is not able to convincingly reconcile the unique unmoved Mover with the many gods of pagan polytheism, and B. Botter's remarks on are grammatically questionable. It comes to nobody's surprise that the compatibility of Aristotle's "theology" with monotheist religions has been defended by a long tradition of philosophers in both the Muslim and the Christian world. Scholars have also debated the role of the unmoved Mover in the Aristotelian cosmos. While for most scholars it is unquestionable that the unmoved Mover is the final cause of all motions, E. Berti (2007) has suggested that it is the ultimate efficient Cause of motion, following in the footsteps of a long tradition that attributed this type of causality to the Mover. Against this backdrop, the issue of the compatibility of Aristotle's "theology" with the fast-spreading Christianity of the first centuries CE would have been a rather evident topic of philosophical discussion. → Justin Martyr (c. 100–c. 168 CE) and Theophilus of Antioch (second half of the 2nd cent. CE) were debating the compatibility of Platonism with Christianity (see e.g. Just. 1 *Apol.* ch. 59; Theophilus of Antioch, *Ad Autolycum*). Despite his love for debates, Alexander does not seem to have engaged with the topic of the (in)compatibility of Christianity with Greek philosophy in his extant writings. One can easily argue that his version of Aristotle's philosophy would not have been compatible with Christianity, since Alexander does not believe that individual human souls are

immortal (→ Immortality). The only immortal element in us, that is, the active intellect, is indeed the very unmoved Mover that supersedes at the motions of the whole cosmos. Alexander does not develop any further his ideas in his extant writings, but it seems legitimate to suppose that they would be open to both a version of immanentism, since God is in us if the intellect thinks of concepts in us, and to the negation of the immortality of the individual soul, in as much as all the individual traits die together with the → body. Both ideas are not compatible with biblical Christianity. The incomplete transmission of Alexander's works leaves us in the realm of hypotheses to explain why he did not feel the urge to criticize Christianity as he did criticize Stoic philosophy. It is possible to think that in Alexander's eyes Christianity as a body of doctrines did not have a philosophical significance and it was idle to confront it. After all, he does not discuss the pseudo-Aristotelian treatise *De mundo ad Alexandrum* either in his extant writings. We know that the *De mundo* was written before Alexander's activity, since Apuleius of Madaura (active in the 2nd cent. CE) translated it into Latin. While the treatise commonly attributed to Aristotle in antiquity, Alexander does not seem to take note of it either, presumably because its description of the universe is not philosophically acute and stresses the role of a transcendent God as the ultimate cause of motion. Alexander was probably not keen on discussing version of Aristotelianism that would challenge his own immanentism.

Bibliography

Berti, E., "Ancora sulla causalità del motore immobile," *Méth.* 20, 2007, 7–28.
Bodéüs, R., *Aristote et la théologie des vivants immortels*, Montreal, 1992.
Bonelli, M., *Alessandro di Afrodisia e la metafisica come scienza dimostrativa*, Naples, 2001.
Botter, B., *Dio e divino in Aristotele*, Sankt Augustin, 2005.
Bruns, I., ed., *Alexandri Aphrodisiensis praeter commentaria Scripta Minora*, vol. I, Berlin, 1887.
Bruns, I., ed., *Alexandri Aphrodisiensis praeter commentaria Scripta Minora*, vol. II, Berlin, 1892.
Chaniotis, A., "New Inscriptions from Aphrodisias (1995–2001)," *AJA*, 108/3, 2004, 377–416.
Fazzo, S., *La materia, la forma, il divino nelle Quaestiones di Alessandro di Afrodisia*, Pisa, 2002.
Fazzo, S., & L. Gili, *Alexander of Aphrodisias*, 2018; in Oxford Bibliographies Online.

Freudenthal, J., ed., *Die durch Averroes erhaltenen Fragmente Alexanders zur Metaphysik des Aristoteles*, Berlin, 1885.

Genequand, C., *Alexander of Aphrodisias: On the Cosmos*, Leiden, 2001.

Gili, L., *La sillogistica di Alessandro di Afrodisia: Sillogistica categorica e sillogistica modale nel commento agli Analitici Primi di Aristotele*, Hildesheim, 2011.

Gili, L., P. Podolak & H. Eterianus, "Alexander of Aphrodisias and Syllogistic Demonstrations: A Newly Discovered Fragment of Alexander of Aphrodisias' Commentary on Aristotle's Posterior Analytics," *DSSTFM*, 2018, 137–154.

Groisard, J., ed., *Sur la mixtion et la croissance d'Alexandre d'Aphrodise: Texte établi, traduit et commenté*, Paris, 2013.

Hayduck, M., ed., *Alexandri Aphrodisiensis in Aristotelis Metaphysicam commentaria*, Berlin, 1891.

Hayduck, M., ed., *Alexandri in Aristotelis Meteorologicorum libros commentaria*, Berlin, 1899.

Moraux, P., *Le commentaire d'Alexandre d'Aphrodise aux Secondes Analytiques d'Aristote*, Berlin, 1979.

Rashed, M., *Essentialisme: Alexandre d'Aphrodise entre logique, physique et cosmologie*, Berlin, 2007.

Rashed, M., ed., *Alexandre d'Aphrodise: Commentaire perdue à la Physique d'Aristote (livres IV–VIII): Les scholies byzantines*, Berlin, 2011.

Rescigno, A., ed., *Alessandro di Afrodisia: Commentario al De caelo di Aristotele: Frammenti del primo libro*, Amsterdam, 2004.

Rescigno, A., ed., *Alessandro di Afrodisia: Commentario al De caelo di Aristotele: Frammenti del secondo, terzo e quarto libro*, Amsterdam, 2008.

Sharples, R.W., ed., *Alexander of Aphrodisias On Fate*, London, 1983.

Sharples, R.W., "Alexander of Aphrodisias: Scholasticism and Innovation," in: W. Haase, ed., *ANRW*, vol. XXXVI/7, Berlin, 1987, 1176–1243.

Wallies, M., ed., *Alexandri Aphrodisiensis in Aristotelis Analyticorum Priorum librum primum commentarium*, Berlin, 1883.

Wallies, M., ed., *Alexandri Aphrodisiensis in Aristotelis Topicorum libros octo commentaria*, Berlin, 1891.

Wendland, P., ed., *Alexandri in librum De sensu commentarium*, Berlin, 1901.

LUCA GILI

Alexander of Constantinople

The date of Alexander's accession to the bishopric of the predecessor town of Constantinople, Byzantium, is as unclear as the date of his death. According to → Socrates Scholasticus, Alexander died in 340 CE, after a tenure of office of 23 years, at age 98, his predecessor being a certain Metrophanes (Socr. *Hist.*

Eccl. 1.37.3; 2.6.2). → Theodoret of Cyrrhus, however, seems to date the death of Alexander around the time of the foundation of Constantinople, that is, to 330 CE (*Hist. Eccl.* 1.19.1). Both dates are likely to be wrong: modern scholarship agrees that the correct dating of the death of Alexander depends on determining the date of the accession of his successor Paul. → Athanasius of Alexandria claims to have met with Paul and his priest Makedonios in Constantinople when Paul was under accusation (Athan. *Hist. Ar.* 7.1). This episode seems to be conceivable only after the controversial accession of Paul to his office. Athanasius was in Constantinople in the winter of 331/332 CE, then again from Oct 30 to Nov 7, 335 CE (Martin, 1985, 228–229, 232–235) and – as has been plausibly conjectured (Barnes, 1993, 213) – a third time in summer/autumn 337 CE. Of these three possibilities for the encounter of Paul, Makedonios, and Athanasius, the second is improbable because of the shortness of Athanasius' stay and its circumstances. The first and the third dates have each been advocated by modern scholars. If Athanasius met with Paul and Makedonios in 331/332 CE, Alexander must have died before, and it was as a bishop that Paul took part in the Council of Tyre (Hil. Poit. *CAP* A.4.1.3). However, according to Athanasius, Paul's predecessor Alexander was still alive at the time of Arius' death (→ Arianism), which cannot have occurred before 333 CE (Barnes, 2009). But Athanasius' story about the death of Arius is very dubious (see below). If, however, Athanasius met with Paul and Makedonios in 337 CE, Alexander must have died before 337 CE. In this case it is possible that he was still alive at the time of Arius' death and that his successor Paul acted at his deputy at the Council of Tyre. Athanasius also claims that Paul (presumably as a bishop) was first exiled by Constantine the Great (→ Constantine I), who died May 22, 337 CE (Athan. *Hist. Ar.* 7.3?). This would fit the earlier date of Alexander's death unless this notice rests on a mistake by Athanasius or, less likely, by a copyist (with respect to Barnes, 1993, 216).

1. The Arian Controversy

Alexander's tenure of office has left few traces. He is the addressee, probably in 324 CE (Opitz, 1935, *Urkunde* 15), of an anti-Arian encyclical that

Alexander of Alexandria had sent to him through his deacon Apis. Asked to subscribe, the encyclical he apparently did not reply (Schwartz, 1959, 132). Alexander of Alexandria sent a second anti-Arian missive (Opitz, 1935, *Urkunde* 14), urging him again to subscribe – apparently to no effect. Again, the synod in Antioch in early 325 CE, which was presided possibly by Ossius and which condemned → Eusebius of Caesarea, issued an anti-Arian encyclical that endorsed the theological position of Alexander of Alexandria. The copy sent to Alexander of Byzantium is extant in Syriac translation (Opitz, 1935, *Urkunde* 18). Again no reaction on the part of Alexander is known. Alexander's name is missing in the subscription lists of the Council of → Nicaea (summer 325 CE). If Paul succeeded him only in 337 CE, it is possible that Alexander took part in the Synod of Constantinople in 336 CE, which – in the presence of Constantine himself – condemned the teachings of Markellos of Ankyra (Hil. Poit. *CAP* A.4.1.3). But no source attests his presence at this council. If the impression is correct that Alexander remained studiously neutral during the Arian controversy, it may tell against the assumption that Paul acted as the aged Alexander's deputy when he condemned Athanasius at the Council of Tyre. However, Athanasius was not condemned for doctrinal reasons by the council. Although Alexander did not designate a successor, rumor credited him with a carefully worded opinion, which of two candidates – Paul and Makedonios – seems to recommend the first. Their respective orthodoxy was not an isssue (Soz. *Hist. eccl.* 3.3.2; Dagron, 1974, 422).

2. The Legend

The fact that during his lifetime Alexander of Byzantium refused to join the anti-Arian camp did not discourage Athanasius from turning him posthumously into a staunch anti-Arian. Athanasius relates in two slightly different versions (Athan. *Ep. mort. Ar.* 2.1–4; 3; *Ep. Aeg. Lib.* 18.6–19.4; see also Athan. *Hist. Ar.* 51.1; *Letter to the Monks* 3.2), a story that connects Alexander with the death of Arius: at the instigation of Eusebius of Nicomedia and his friends, Constantine grants Arius an audience. The Alexandrian presbyter (→ Priest/Presbyter) confirms the orthodoxy of his teaching with an oath and presents a written statement of faith. It is Saturday, and in order to put pressure on Alexander, the Eusebians threaten to enter the church together with Arius on the following Sunday. Alexander, however, is determined not to readmit Arius. Desperate to prevent Arius from entering the church, he goes there to pray for divine help. His prayer is granted: on the same day Arius dies under shameful circumstances in a public convenience in Constantinople (Acts 1:18 is quoted) thus "being deprived both of the communion of the church and of his life." This story is likely to be a pious fiction (for an analysis, see Seeck, 1897, 3–41; for its afterlife, see Leroy-Molinghen, 1968). Which of its two versions is chronologically prior remains controversial (Martin, 1989, 320–324). The version in *Letter to Serapion on the Death of Arius* is meant to assure the addressee Serapion of Thmuis and his monks that Arius died unreconciled (Winkelmann, 1966, 61). The factual kernel of the story is probably Arius' appearance before Constantine (Athan. *Syn.* 21.4) and the sudden death of Arius, which was interpreted as God's punishment of a perjurer (Socr. *Hist. Eccl.* 1.26.5; Martin, 1989, 333). The second part with its focus on the praying Alexander seems like an addition (Seeck, 1897, 37), intended for the credulous – only in *On the Death of Arius* (2.1 and 3.1) is the Alexandrian priest Makarios mentioned as the putative eyewitness of Alexander's prayer. Athanasius celebrates Alexander as a model for his own resistance against the Arians. Even if Athanasius had been aware that Arius died during the tenure of Paul, not Alexander, he would have clearly cast the latter rather than the former in the role of orthodox hero: not only had Paul remained a controversial figure, but he had agreed to the condemnation of Athanasius at the Council of Tyre. It seems, then, highly unlikely that Alexander of Constantinople, who had for so long managed to remain on the sidelines of the controversy, would, near the end of his life, change his attitude in order to prevent a reconciliation of Arius, risking the displeasure not only of Eusebius of Nicomedia and his friends, but also of the emperor himself. The Anonymus Cyzicenus claims that Alexander's predecessor Metrophanes sent him, at the time a presbyter, together with his successor Paul, at the time a reader, to the Council of Nicaea. There he fought together with Athanasius, at the time archdeacon of the Alexandrian church, against the

Arians (Cyz. *Hist. eccl.* 2.5.4; 2.7.44; 2.28.13). Another notice in Cyz. *Hist. eccl.* 3.10.20, which claims that Constantine urged Alexander to ordain a bishop for the Iberians, seems to rest on a chronological inference rather than on genuine information. For most of this the Anonymus Cyzicenus is possibly dependent on a lost work of Gelasius of Caesarea (Winkelmann, 1966, 58–59; *Gel. Hist. eccl.* T5a.3–7; F12a; F16b.247–252). Soz. *Hist. eccl.* 1.18.5–7 relates that on his arrival in Byzantium, Constantine ordered Bishop Alexander to enter into a debate with pagan philosophers. They had criticized the emperor for introducing a new religion. Alexander, devoid of dialectical skills, quickly decided the contest for himself by literally silencing in the name of Christ the spokesman selected by his opponents. The *Life of the Fathers Metrophanes and Alexander* (Phot. *Bibl.* codex 256) added the detail that after the close of the Nicene council, Alexander toured through Thrace, Illyricum, Greece, and Greek isles in order to preach the dogma of Nicaea. In the western churches, Alexander is commemorated as a saint on Aug 28, in the Greek churches on Aug 30 or 31.

Bibliography

Barnes, T.D., *Constantine and Eusebius*, Cambridge MA, 1993.

Barnes, T.D., "The Exile and Recalls of Arius," *JThS* 60, 2009, 109–129.

Dagron, G., *Naissance d'une capitale*, Paris, 1974.

Leroy-Molinghen, A., "La mort d'Arius," *Byz.* 38, 1968, 105–111.

Martin, A., ed., *Histoire acéphale et index syriaque des lettres festales d'Athanase d'Alexandrie*, SC 317, Paris, 1985.

Martin, A., "Le fil d'Arius: 325–335," *RHE* 84, 1989, 297–333.

Opitz, H.-G., *Athanasius Werke*, vol. III/1: *Urkunden zur Geschichte des arianischen Streites 318–328*, Berlin, 1935.

Schwartz, E., *Gesammelte Schriften*, vol. III, Berlin, 1959.

Seeck, O., "Untersuchungen zur Geschichte des Nicänischen Konzils," *ZKG* 17, 1897, 1–71.

Wallraff, M., J. Stutz & N. Marinides, *Gelasius of Caesarea: Ecclesiastical History. The Extant Fragments*, Berlin, 2018.

Winkelmann, F.W., "Die Bischöfe Metrophanes und Alexander von Byzanz," *ByZ* 59, 1966, 47–71.

WINRICH LÖHR

Alexander of Jerusalem

A prominent → bishop in the first half of the 3rd century CE, Alexander (d. 250/251 CE) is primarily remembered today through his relationship with → Origen as recorded in Book 6 of → Eusebius of Caesarea's *Historia ecclesiastica*. Little is known of Alexander's early life. In a letter to Origen (preserved in Eus. *Hist. eccl.* 6.14.8–9), he refers to Pantaenus and Clement of Alexandria as his past teachers through whom he came to know Origen himself. This statement has encouraged the belief that Alexander studied in Alexandria together with Origen, although there is no explicit indication that the pair were fellow students.

Alexander settled in Cappadocia, where he may have been born, and became bishop of an unspecified see (*Hist. eccl.* 6.11.1; possibly Cappadocian Caesarea). There he became a confessor during the reign of Septimius Severus, and somewhere between 202 CE and 204 CE he was imprisoned (*Hist. eccl.* 6.8.7). He was still in prison in early 211 CE, when he learned of the appointment of Asclepiades as bishop of Antioch. Alexander's letter to the Antiochenes congratulating them on their choice, quoted in *Hist. eccl.* 6.11.5–6, states that he heard the good news while in his cell but implies that his imprisonment is now in the past. He was probably released shortly after the accession of Emperor Caracalla in February 211 CE. The bearer of Alexander's letter to Antioch was → Clement of Alexandria, who had been living in Cappadocia and whom Alexander now commended to the Antiochenes. Clement dedicated one of his writings to Alexander, the *Canon ecclesiasticus* (also known as *Against the Judaizers*). The work itself is lost except for a single fragment, but may have been composed during Clement's stay in Cappadocia.

Soon after his release in 211/212 CE, Alexander departed Cappadocia and settled in Jerusalem (at this time still called Aelia). There he became coadjutor to the aged bishop Narcissus (of Jerusalem), and subsequently the sole bishop of Jerusalem after Narcissus' death. This is the first recorded instance of the translation of a bishop from one see to another, and also made Alexander the first coadjutor bishop. It is perhaps to justify the novelty of the situation that Eusebius repeatedly insists that both Alexander's departure from Cappadocia and his acceptance by the Jerusalem congregation were inspired by divine visions, as well as acknowledging Alexander's interest in the holy places (*Hist. eccl.* 6.11.1–2). Eusebius also declares that Alexander's appointment received approval from the surrounding bishops of Palestine (*Hist. eccl.* 6.11.2). Looking back from the 5th century CE, → Socrates Scholasticus omits any such reference and cites Alexander as an example of how easily such translations occurred in the early church (Socr. *Hist. eccl.* 7.36). Alexander himself does not seem to have felt any concern over his position, and in his letter to the Antinoites following his appointment, he merely states that he is now associated in office with Narcissus, who had reached 116 years of age (Eus. *Hist. eccl.* 6.11.3).

As bishop of Jerusalem, Alexander organized an influential library, which was later exploited by Eusebius among others (Eus. *Hist. eccl.* 6.20.1). Yet Alexander is best known for the support that he gave to Origen and his role in the tensions between Origen and Bishop Demetrius of Alexandria. Origen visited Palestine in circa 217 CE and although still a layman was invited by Alexander and Bishop Theoctistus of Caesarea to expound the Scriptures in the churches (*Hist. eccl.* 6.19.16). Demetrius reacted angrily, circulating a letter criticizing this presumption, and in response Alexander and Theoctistus circulated their own letter appealing to precedents to explain their actions (*Hist. eccl.* 6.19.17–18). A decade later, when Origen settled in Caesarea in circa 229/230 CE after his final departure from Alexandria, Alexander and Theoctistus again united in ordaining Origen as a presbyter (*Hist. eccl.* 6.8.4) and encouraged him once more to preach upon the Scriptures (*Hist. eccl.* 6.27.1). The majority of Origen's extant homilies derive from his time in Caesarea, but at least a few were preached in Jerusalem at Alexander's request. In his homily on the birth of Samuel, Origen warns his audience not to expect the sweetness and gentleness of their father Alexander (Or. *Hom. 1 Sam*).

No further evidence illuminates Alexander's long episcopate in Jerusalem until his final days. The emperor Decius' command that all should sacrifice to the traditional gods inspired the first empire-wide → persecution of Christians. Alexander and Origen were both imprisoned in Caesarea. Origen survived, but Alexander in his old age died in prison in 250 or 251 CE (*Hist. eccl.* 6.39.2–3). His death

was sufficiently important to be noted in a letter of Dionysius of Alexandria, possibly sent to Cornelius of Rome (*Hist. eccl.* 6.19.16; → Cornelius [Bishop of Rome]). Despite Alexander's influence in his own time, however, his only writings to survive are the short passages quoted by Eusebius from his letters to Antioch (*Hist. eccl.* 6.11.5–6), to the Antinoites (*Hist. eccl.* 6.11.3), to Origen (*Hist. eccl.* 6.14.8–9), and in defense of Origen as a lay preacher (*Hist. eccl.* 6.19.17–18).

(A historiography for this topic is not applicable.)

Bibliography

Heine, R., *Origen: Scholarship in the Service of the Church*, Oxford, 2010.

Holliday, L., "From Alexandria to Caesarea: Reassessing Origen's Appointment to the Presbyterate," *Numen* 58, 2011, 674–696.

Kannengiesser, C., & W.L. Petersen, eds., *Origen of Alexandria: His World and His Legacy*, Notre Dame, 1988.

Trigg, J.W., *Origen*, London, 1998.

Wilken, R.L., *The Land Called Holy: Palestine in Christian History and Thought*, New Haven, 1992.

DAVID M. GWYNN

Alexander Severus

Severus Alexander was born as (Gessius) Julius Bassianus Alexianus on Oct 1 in 208 CE in Arca, Caesarea (Phoenicia; *CIL*, vol. I, 255, 274; Hdn. 5.7.4; Aur. Vict. *Lib. Caes.* 24.1; *SHA Alex.* 1.2) as a member of the Severan dynasty. His parents were the procurator Gessius Marcianus and Julia Avita Mammaea, the niece of Septimius Severus and Julia Domna (*SHA Alex.* 1.2; Dio. *Hist. rom.* 78.30.3). He was a cousin of Elagabal, who was Roman emperor between 218 and 222 CE. Because of his cruelty and eccentric behavior, however, Elagabal soon lost acceptance within the wider circles of Roman society, in other words among the soldiers as well as in the Roman Senate. Fearing that this would cause the end of the Severan dynasty, his grandmother Julia Maesa forced Elagabal to adopt his cousin. Alexander was appointed Caesar in June 221 CE and took the name of Marcus Aurelius Alexander (Feriale Duranum; Dio. *Hist. rom.* 79.17). Elagabal's resistance against the adoption was suppressed by her, and Alexander became *princeps iuventutis* and *consul* for the first time in 222 CE (for the second time in 226 CE, and for the third time in 229 CE together with Cassius Dio). After Elagabal was assassinated during a mutiny, Alexander ascended the throne on Mar 13, 222 CE (Dio. *Hist. rom.* 79.19–21; *SHA Alex.* 1.1–3), now calling himself Severus Alexander, son of Divus Magnus Antoninus (Caracalla). The next day, he was proclaimed *Augustus, pater patriae* and *pontifex maximus* by the Senate. Because Alexander was only 13 years old at this time, his mother, → Julia Mammaea, after receiving the title of *Augusta*, had a decisive influence on official duties (Hdn. 6.1.2; Zon. 12.15), a fact that has been considered a sign of weakness of Alexander Severus' reign, since Julia Mammaea did not try to hide her dominant position. Several coins praise her as *Juno Conservatrix, Fecunditas Augustae, Venus Genetrix, Venus Victrix, Venus Felix, Vesta*, as mother of the emperor, of the camps, of the Senate, of the fatherland, and of the whole human race (*BMCC*, vol. VI., 119, no. 42; 203, no. 913; 128, no. 151; 184, no. 712; 132, no. 188; 151, no. 380; 160, no. 483; 196, no. 821; *AE* 1912.155; *ILS* 482; 484; 485; Campbell, 2005, 22–24). Moreover, she seems to have prevented close personal contacts between her son and members of the senatorial aristocracy. At least, unlike in the case of Elagabal or the other emperors of the Severan dynasty, sources have not preserved any evidence of close relationships with the exception of that between him and Ulpian (Schöpe, 2014, 162–174). When Ulpian, then prefect of the praetorians, was threatened by a conspiracy of his guard in 223 CE, Alexander was not able to protect him from being killed, although Ulpian had fled directly to the imperial palace (Dio. *Hist. rom.* 80.2.2–4; P.Oxy. 2565; *SHA Alex.* 51.4; Zos. *Hist.* 1.11.2–3; Zon. 12.15). A similar example that illustrates the limited power of Alexander is the case of Cassius Dio. Dio was elected *consul ordinarius* in 229 CE and was highly appreciated by the emperor. However, Alexander asked him to spend his year of office outside Rome, since Dio had a bad reputation among the soldiers because of the strict discipline he had demanded from them as former governor of Africa Proconsularis, Pannonia, and Dalmatia (Dio. *Hist. rom.* 80.4.2–5.1).

All in all, Alexander Severus has been judged positively in such authors as Herodian and Cassius Dio or in the *Historia Augusta* for having exercised a benevolent and effective regime and for having been respectful toward the Senate (Nasti, 1995, 67–99) and benevolent toward other groups of the population (Hdn. 6.1.2; Aur. Vict. *Lib. Caes.* 24.2; Eut. *Brev.* 8.23). From the beginning, Alexander and his advisers tried to set themselves apart from the odious regime of Elagabal by upholding Roman traditions instead. The Syrian god was banished from Rome, and statues of Roman gods like Jupiter were re-erected in their former places (Hdn. 6.1.3; Dio. *Hist. rom.* 80.21.2; *SHA Alex.* 6.2). Further indicators for this conservative ideology along Roman lines are the renovation and the repairing of buildings at this time (*RIC*, vol. IV/2, Severus Alexander 58–59, 449–451, 453 *thermae Alexandri*, 410–411 *Colosseum*, temple of Jupiter Ultor; see *SHA Alex. Sev.* 24.3–4; 25.3–9; 27.7–11; 28.6; 45.8). Moreover, the imperial coins propagated virtues like *aequitas, fides, spes, providentia, libertas,* and *liberalitas,* the silver types placing significant emphasis on Mars and Jupiter (Rowan, 2012, 221–223).

Alexander is furthermore known for his intensive legislative activities that took place especially during the first years of his reign. The → Codex Justinianus has preserved 427 of his *constitutiones* that were presumably issued during his reign, too (Nasti, 2006, 20). Alexander presented as the new moral guidelines the imperial *clementia* and a certain harshness that was necessary in order to keep under control the enemies of the just social order. He was particularly interested in regulating the *appellatio* in order to give everyone a better access to legal opportunities of appeal (Nasti, 2006, 25–107). Moreover, he stressed his intention to consolidate the central budget and to reduce the tax burdens (Cleve, 1982, 242–243). While it is a matter of debate how much direct influence Alexander actually possessed during his reign, it is clear that at least the attitudes of his advisers seem to have corresponded with his general wishes. This is suggested by several rescripts that contain the phrases "the purity of my times," "the demise of treason charges in my era," and "it is particularly appropriate in the exercise of power to abide by the laws" (rescripts: Cod. Justin. 6.23.3; 9.8.1; 9.9.9). Obviously, this approach received a positive response among groups like the provincial cities, the Roman *populus*, and the praetorians as well. The city of Rome had to suffer almost no popular unrest (the exceptions being described in: Dio. *Hist. rom.* 80.2.2–3; *SHA Alex.* 22.7–8), and when Seius Sallustius, Alexander's father-in-law, tried to instigate his guard against the emperor and his mother, his attempts were doomed to fail. In the end, Sallustius was executed, and his daughter Orbiana divorced and banished (Hdn. 6.1.9–10; *SHA Alex.* 49.3–4).

Alexander's essential failure can be seen in his unsatisfying relationship with the army, a group that was gaining importance continuously since the 3rd century CE and that had been therefore reorganized by the first Severan emperors. Although Alexander was supported by his troops when he succeeded to the throne, he did not manage to establish a sustainable relationship with his soldiers or to gather able generals around him who could have used their influence on the troops. The reasons for this failure are to be found in his lack of interest in military matters and the serious errors of his personnel policy (Handy, 2009, 162–167).

This poor relationship proved to be disastrous when the military situation at the borders deteriorated – thereby serving as a precursor to the migration period. An immediate consequence of the consolidation of the Sassanid dynasty instead of the Arsacids was a renewed expansion of the Persian Empire. In 230 or 231 CE, a Persian army invaded and devastated the Roman province of Mesopotamia and laid siege to Nisibis (Hdn. 6.2.3–5; 6.4.4–6; Sünskes Thompson, 1990, 80–91). After negotiations had failed, Alexander was forced to react. He ultimately left Rome and tried to attack the Persian cities of Seleuceia/Ctesiphon with the Roman army that marched in three separated contingents. However, the campaign turned into a disaster because the military command was unable to cope with the organization of this complicated strategy. One of the contingents was destroyed by the Persian king Ardashir, and the other two groups had to withdraw while suffering huge losses, because many of the starving soldiers could not endure the exhausting way that led back to Rome through the highland of Armenia (Hdn. 6.6.5–6). The soldiers put the blame for the failed campaign on Alexander, and the emperor could appease the uprising only by offering huge donations (Hdn. 6.6.1–4). Meanwhile, at the Rhine border in 235 CE, Germanic tribes, probably the Alamanni, used the opportunity to

invade unprotected Roman territory after some of the Roman troops had been relocated to the Euphrates for the Persian war. Upon hearing this bad news, many soldiers who were coming from the Rhine border were deeply enraged because they considered their families threatened by the Germans (Hdn. 6.7.2–5). Thus, Alexander immediately had to leave for the northern front. When he tried to take over the command together with his mother, he finally lost all authority over the soldiers. He and Mammaea, both willing to avoid the risk to fight against the Alamanni, initially tried to pay them subsidies (Hdn. 6.7.9–10). The soldiers, however, who were getting angry about the loss of donations and booty and who interpreted this behavior as a sign of weakness, began to revolt. They finally proclaimed Maximinus Thrax, who had been an officer responsible for training the recruits, their new emperor. Alexander, learning about the revolt, was not able to regain the loyalty of his troops and was slain by them in his tent together with his mother in March 235 CE near Mogontiacum (Hdn. 6.8.1–9.8; *SHA Alex.* 59.5–8; 63.5–6; 64.3; *SHA Max.* 7.4–5; Aur. Vict. *Lib. Caes.* 24.4; Pseud. Aur. Vict. Epit. de Caes. 24.3–4; Eut. *Brev.* 8.23.1; Jer. *Chron.* 253.13; Oros. *Adv. pag.* 7.18.8; Zos. *Hist.* 1.12.1–13.2; *Chron. Pasch.* 268.1–11; Jor. *Rom.* 280; Jordanes, *Getica*; Zon. 12.15). With Severus Alexander's death, the Severan dynasty ended, and the time of the imperial crisis commenced.

Historiography

The evaluation of Alexander Severus has shifted somewhat in recent research. While Alexander was considered a civilian and senate-friendly emperor until the 19th century on the basis of prosenatorial historiography (e.g. Burckhardt, 1853, 9), this view changed in the 20th century. Here, especially his dependence on his mother and grandmother was noted negatively, which severely damaged his acceptance, especially among the army (e.g. Heuß, 1960, 352). Current research places the personal specifics of Alexander's reign more firmly in the structural fabric of his time. Thus, his efforts to maintain a positive relationship with the Senate and special protection of senatorial officials continue to be emphasized (De Blois, 2006, 45–52). However, his defensive policy is now associated primarily with the precarious financial situation and the already overstretched tax power of the provinces (Campbell, 2005, 22–27). All this actually led to a low acceptance of Alexander by the army and the praetorians as well as to revolts. The glamorous highlighting of his victory in the Persian campaign is seen as an attempt to counter this acceptance problem (Haake, 2016, 359–364). However, the intensive legislative activity under his rule is also highlighted (Nasti, 2006), as well as the fact that, in contrast to the army, his mother's strong political position certainly met with a positive response in the epigraphy of the provinces (Nadolny, 2016). The assumption of the generally limited authority of the emperor, however, holds.

Bibliography

Burckhardt, J., *Die Zeit Constantins des Großen*, Basel 1853.

Campbell, B., "The Severan Dynasty," in: A.K. Bowman, P. Garnsey & A. Cameron, eds., *CAH²*, vol. XII, Cambridge UK, 2005, 1–27.

Cleve, R.L., *Severus Alexander and the Severan Women*, Los Angeles, 1982.

De Blois, L., "Administrative Strategies of the Emperor Severus Alexander and his Advisers," in: A. Kolb, ed., *Herrschaftsstrukturen und Herrschaftspraxis*, Berlin, 2006, 45–52.

Haake, M., "Zwischen Severus Alexanders Triumph über die Sasaniden im Jahre 233 und den Triumphfeierlichkeiten Diocletians und Maximians im Jahre 303: Zum römischen Triumph im dritten Jahrhundert n. Chr.," in: F. Goldbeck & J. Wienand, eds., *Der römische Triumph in Prinzipat und Spätantike*, Berlin 2016, 357–395.

Handy, M., *Die Severer und das Heer*, Berlin, 2009.

Heuß, A., *Römische Geschichte*, Braunschweig 1960.

Nadolny, S., *Die severischen Kaiserfrauen*, Palingenesia, vol. CIV, Stuttgart 2016.

Nasti, F., "Note sulla politica filosenatoria di Alessandro Severo con particolare riferimento alla Historia Augusta," *AIIGSS* 13, 1995/1996, 67–99.

Nasti, F., *L'attività normativa di Severo Alessandro*, vol. I: *Politica di governo, riforme amministrative e giudiziarie*, Naples, 2006.

Rowan, C., *Under Divine Auspices: Divine Ideology and the Visualisation of Imperial Power in the Severan Period*, Cambridge MA, 2012.

Schöpe, B., *Der römische Kaiserhof in severischer Zeit (193–235 n. Chr.)*, Stuttgart, 2014.

Sünskes Thompson, J., *Aufstände und Protestaktionen im Imperium Romanum: Die severischen Kaiser im Spannungsfeld innenpolitischer Konflikte*, Bonn, 1990.

CLAUDIA TIERSCH

Alexandria

I. City ◆ II. School of ◆ III. Councils of ◆ IV. Libraries of

I. City

Since its foundation in 331 BCE under Macedonian king Alexander III (356–323 BCE) and its completion under his immediate successors, Alexandria was for centuries one of largest, most economically potent, culturally vibrant, and socially diverse metropolises of the ancient world, second perhaps only to Rome. Alexandria's impact on the development of classical culture, art and religion, Hellenistic Judaism (as evidenced, above all, by the Septuagint (→ Bible) and nascent Christianity can hardly be overestimated (Bagnall & Rathbone, 2004, 51–73; Venit, 2012; McEvedy & Oles, 2019; Quertinmont & Amoroso, 2022).

Nevertheless, archaeological research on land and below sea level has only produced relatively limited data. Therefore, our perception of the city and its cultural life, as well as of many of its buildings, to a large extent still depends upon the relatively broad literary tradition on Alexandria (above all Pseudo-Callisthenes 1.31–33; Diod. Sic. *Bib. hist.* 17.52; Stra. *Geogr.* 17.1.6–11; Plin. *Nat.* 5.11.26; Arrian *Anab.* 3.1–2; Plut. *Alex.* 26). Today, Alexandria houses more than five million inhabitants and is the second-largest city in the modern Arab Republic of Egypt.

1. Location

Strategically located on the coastline of the northwestern Nile Delta, north of Lake Mareotis, Alexandria was the ideal connector between the vast Egyptian hinterland towards Nubia and Ethiopia far into east Africa via the Kanopus channel and the Nile, and the gate to sailing routes across the whole Mediterranean via two large harbors on the Mediterranean Sea. During its heyday, Alexandria's inhabited area measured circa 4–5 km east-west along the coast and around 2 km north-south, covering circa 10 km².

Alexandria's location continues a centuries-old Egyptian tradition of maritime trade. Minoan presence is attested at Avaris, a potentially Mycenean harbor was identified on Pharos Island, and the 7th-century BCE colony Naukratis 80 km east of later Alexandria made sure that the delta coast was known to and frequented by Greeks (Hdt. 2.178–179; see also Empereur, 2018, 6–7; Tallet, 2021, 7–26). Also, Homer mentions Pharos Island, harbors, and fertile lands (Hom. *Od.* 4.354–359), while Pseudo-Callisthenes (1.32.1) reveals that Proteus was venerated by indigenous inhabitants of Rhakotis, an important pharaonic trade hub (Goddio, 1998, 29–31) and center of several villages that later became a district of Alexandria with a very strong Egyptian profile (Grimm, 1998, 16f.; Chauveau, 2022).

2. Hellenistic Alexandria

Among the many other cities bearing the same name, the Egyptian Alexandria has always kept especially strong ties with Alexander the Great (see Pseudo-Callisthenes 1.31–33), the deified Macedonian king, son of Zeus-Ammon and new Egyptian pharaoh. According to Polybius, Alexander created it as an ideal city according to the ideas of his tutor Aristotle (Polyb. *Hist.* 7.5–6; 7.11–12; see Grimm, 1998, 18–30). Eventually, he was buried there, although perhaps against his will (see Diod. Sic. *Bib. hist.* 18.28.3–5, who says that Alexander's body was snatched by Ptolemy I when on route to Macedon). It is indeed likely that the initiative for and the early planning of the new eponymous city goes back to Alexander and his architect Cleomenes. The actual execution of these plans, however, was carried out after Ptolemy I son of Lagos assumed royal power was crowned king in Memphis in 306/305 BCE (Stadler, 2012, 59–94; Caneva, 2022). From the beginning, the city territory was organized according to the so-called Hippodamic plan, divided up by 13 m wide monumental east-west alleys intersected by narrower north-south roads into five checkerboard–like neighborhoods, each labelled with a Greek letter from A through E. In the city center lay the central civic areas and institutions.

Alexandria was designed as a Greek city and, from its foundation, constitutionally fashioned on the Greek polis, having the political machinery of a democracy concomitant with the autocratic reality of regal power. It had a citizen body [*demos*], a civic law code, an assembly [*ecclesia*], a council [*boule*], a board of magistrates [*prytaneis*], and a body of elders [*gerousia*]. (Venit, 2002, 9; 2012, 103f.)

Despite such formally democratic institutions, the Ptolemies preferred to keep the often-rebellious Alexandrian population under close control, and later the Romans even temporarily dissolved the *boule*. The city itself was subdivided into five districts named by the first five letters of the Greek alphabet (Philo *Flacc.* 55). Factually, the city was not considered part of Egypt, but emphasized its unique character and independence by the title *Alexandria ad Aegyptum*.

Though from the beginning populated by inhabitants of multiple ethnic and cultural backgrounds (about a third of them Greek-speaking Jews), the city's cultural profile was largely Greek, while both the Greek-speaking population and the Ptolemaic powers in various ways anchored their identities and practices in native cultural traditions. Like in all Egypt, only inhabitants able to claim Macedonian descent were considered full citizens who enjoyed legal and financial privileges over the rest of the Alexandrian population (e.g. exemption from poll tax), although certain outsiders like mercenaries or athletes could also have been granted Alexandrian citizenship in the Hellenistic period (Delia, 1991). Despite clear social layering, Ptolemaic kings actively promoted social cohesion in Alexandria. Ptolemy II Philadelphos (r. 285–246 BCE) ordered various legal traditions of ethnic groups resident in Alexandria – including those of the Jews (Kooij, 2007) – to be collected, translated, and studied. All relevant books were to be housed in the famous Museion, at the same time a sanctuary, a library, and an academy (Nesselrath, 2013; Haggag, 2022). Groundbreaking philological as well as exegetical and interpretive work based on textual critique, commentaries, and allegory as method by an unprecedented number of publicly paid scholars made Alexandria the center of classical learning and cultural transmission. At the same time, Alexandrian scholars excelled in natural sciences, medical studies, technology, and engineering, laying the foundations for many centuries to come (Engster, 2013). It was, therefore, a catastrophic blow for the intellectual cohesion of the Mediterranean world when the library (→ Alexandria) was partly destroyed in 48 BCE during Caesar's conquest of Alexandria and finally seems to have gone out of use in 391 CE by a decree of the local bishop.

As capital of Ptolemaic Egypt, "Alexander's own city" quickly adapted to the needs of a new, ambitious Greco-Egyptian royal dynasty (Caneva, 2022; Versluys, 2022). It rapidly developed into an "economically powerful, visually breathtaking, and intellectually vibrant" center (Venit, 2012, 118). The most prominent urban transformation was the expansion of the original palace on the Lochias peninsula into a grandiose royal quarter (*basileia*) directly on the northeastern shore, not only housing the grand royal palaces, but also featuring harbors, shipyards, magazines, barracks, gardens, and temples as well as representational and entertainment buildings. At the very northern end of the Lochias peninsula rose the Akra, from which a wall reached out towards the Pharos and its island. On the west, this island is again connected with the coast by a combined bridge/aqueduct (Heptastadion dam) on whose littoral side additional harbor and trade facilities were located. The eastern wall, the Pharos Island and the western dam together form a huge half-circle surrounding the Great Harbor basin that housed the largest merchant fleet of the Mediterranean and the mighty Ptolemaic navy which dominated the seas until Egypt came under Roman control during the latter part of the 1st century BCE (Khalil, 2022).

While the main enclosure of the Serapeion has been securely located in the southwest of Alexandria (today's Karmuz district; Sabottka, 2008), the lack of sufficient evidence does not allow the same for the Museion or the Mausoleion of Alexander (though Adriani, 2000, sees it integrated in a larger Ptolemaic funeral complex partly preserved as the "Alabaster tomb"). The only monumental building whose location is known, is the Pharos, the magnificent lighthouse built by Sostratos of Knidos under Ptolemy II Philadelphos to guide ships into the safe port during storms and darkness. Due to its height of between 120–160 m, its architectural grandeur and technical sophistication, the Pharos was often counted by some among the seven wonders of the ancient world (Plin. *Nat.* 36.18; Baebler, 2013, 13–16; Queyrel, 2022). Outside of texts, coins give us the best impression of how this magnificent building once had looked before it was destroyed between the 10th and 14th century by earthquakes and subsequent stone robbing. Its remains are now built over by Mamluk Fort Kait Bey.

At the end of the Hellenistic period, Diodorus reports that Alexandria had about 300,000 free citizens (Diod. Sic. *Bib. hist.* 17.52.6), to which perhaps more than double the number of free non-citizens and unfree inhabitants need to be added.

3. Roman Alexandria

A new era begun after the Battle of Actium in 31 BCE when Alexandria became the capital of the new Roman *provincia Aegyptus* in 30 BCE after the deaths of Cleopatra and Antonius, ruled by an equestrian *praefectus Aegypti*. Now, the city emphasized its new character and independence from the rest of Egypt with the formal name *Alexandria ad Aegyptum*. To keep control over the city and the delta, the Romans stationed the largest garrison of Egypt at Nikopolis (named to commemorate Actium) only 7 km east of Alexandria (Haensch, 2012, 69). As capital of Aegyptus, Alexandria was also the center of the emperor cult (as it had already been the center of the Ptolemaic royal cult). According to A. Abdo (2022), the famous Kaisareion stood in the northern district of Alexandria, in the area around the Ramleh railway station, and was dismantled in early Christian times.

Even after Alexandria had lost all political and military influence under the Romans, it remained one of the uncontested cultural, academic, and economic leaders of antiquity. Not only were countless goods such as papyrus, textiles, ivory, spices, or gemstones channeled from Africa and India into the wider Mediterranean basin via Alexandrian harbors, Alexandria itself was a bustling hub of arts and crafts that tremendously influenced the development of Hellenistic culture far into the Roman period. Sculpture, architectural forms, mosaic art, painting, coin and stone-cutting, textile processing (silk), luxurious vessels made of precious metal, glass, feldspar, or sardonyx (see the famous "Farnese cup") or more affordable pottery imitating them like the popular "Megarian bowls" were either invented or perfected in Alexandria. Examples of products made in or inspired by those from Alexandria can be found almost anywhere in the Hellenistic and Roman world and beyond. Alexandrian culture radiated out into suburbia via countless members of the rural elite who had property in the capital and imitated the Alexandrian lifestyle. Apart from its general function as a trade hub, the Romans retained a keen interest in Alexandria as a conduit to transport Egypt's grain to Italy. About 250,000 tons of wheat were transported annually to imperial Rome (Bagnall, 2015, 57).

Religion played an especially important role in multi-ethnic and multicultural Alexandria (Frankfurter, 1998). The Ptolemaic kings presented themselves not just as successors of the divine pharaohs but also experimented with their Greek heritage. In this way they connected their dynasty to Egyptian cults that had since time immemorial safeguarded the harmony between the divine *kosmos* and life on earth resulting in regular Nile inundations, and blended them with Greek practices into a "syncretistic" religion often emphasizing all-encompassing, healing, and saving functions of their "gods" (*soteres*). The most prominent examples of such Greco-Egyptian developments are the concept and cult of the all-goddess Isis with her consorts Osiris and Horus-the-child/Harpocrates (Bommas, 2012), and her male counterpart Sarapis whose image, commissioned by Ptolemy I or the very early reign of Ptolemy II and attributed by literary sources to a sculptor named Bryaxis, did not only resemble the Olympian Zeus with his beard and long, curly hair, but whose head is adorned with a "measuring cup" (*kalathos*/*modius*) symbolizing his function as bringer of grain and wealth. Especially in Roman times, Sarapis is also often accompanied by one or two hounds representing his power over the underworld and the elements of *kosmos* and time (Macr. *Sat.* 1.20.13; Bommas, 2012; Bricault & Veymiers, 2022).

Kom ed-Dikka, excavated by Polish archaeologists since the 1960s, offers insight into a luxurious domestic area with houses, workshops, and public buildings (Baebler, 2013, 23–27; general, see Nenna, 2022). The loss of much of the Alexandrian necropolises due to continuous changes of the water level and looting is particularly unfortunate. Alexander's tomb and those of his royal successors must have exerted a deep impact on architecture and decoration of the funeral culture of the city's Macedonian inspired elite, and from there on "Alexandrian" fashions trickled down to the city's lower social groups as well as radiated out across the Hellenistic world

(Venit, 2002; Baebler, 2013, 21–243; Abd El-Fattah & Seif el-Din, 2022). Good examples for this type are hypogea and mausolea at Mustafa Pasha, Gabbari, and Hadra. But Alexandrian cemeteries do not only bear witness to the creativity and traditionalism of the Greek elite milieu, but also to Alexandria's multicultural character. Very soon after Alexandria's foundation, we also find funeral stelae mentioning middle and lower-class individuals who had come from cities and regions across the entire eastern Mediterranean to find their fortune in Alexandria. They all brought elements of their specific traditions to the new melting pot (Hinge, Krasilnikoff & Jensen, 2009). Next to Greek and other Mediterranean funeral cultures we, of course, also see Egyptian funeral culture continue to flourish, some of it indicating a strong "Egyptian" presence (i.e. perhaps non-Greek-speaking inhabitants), and some also witnessing the blending of Greek funeral culture with Egyptian elements (Anfushi cemetery). Mummification was still widespread and even taken over by non-Egyptian elements of the population (see Dio *Hist. rom.* 51.15, claiming that both Marcus Antonius and Cleopatra were mummified). Usually, indigenous and overseas elements appear side by side, and in some cases intermingled, in Alexandrian necropolises.

Soon after the Roman take-over, social tensions rose in Alexandria since once privileged groups like the Alexandrian "Greeks" were now also subjected to Roman taxation and feared losing their privileged status, while others such as the widely assimilated Jewish community tried to improve their civic position (Honigman, 2021). Given Alexandria's multiculturalism and frequent internal frictions, speaking "a common cultural language" was therefore essential to create and maintain a minimum of social cohesion in the city despite all cultural barriers and legal divisions between different classes of inhabitants (Zangenberg, 2013). Many different "ethnically labelled" groups were therefore granted some sort of internal administration and jurisdiction, being called a *politeuma*. A good example is provided by the numerous Greek-speaking Jews who might represent up to a third of Alexandria's population. Jews had been present since the beginnings of Hellenistic Alexandria where they first lived spread out across the entire city. Being recognized as an independent ethnic group, the Ptolemies allowed the Jewish elite to self-administrate using their own laws (on the LXX Thora as law code, see Kooij, 2007; → Law/Decalogue/Torah). Many members of the Jewish elite assimilated and strove to be accepted as "equal" members of civic institutions like the gymnasium as ephebes (Paganini, 2021). The Jewish community had at least one large synagogue and was intellectually very productive and creative, as both the works of Philo of Alexandria as well as a large number of pseudepigraphical works (→ Pseudepigraphy) indicate (Niehoff, 2018; 2011; Sly, 1996; Zangenberg, 2009). After the Roman take-over, however, members of the Jewish community struggled for *isopoliteia* ("equal civic rights") and civic recognition (→ Philo of Alexandria, *Legatio ad Gaium*; *In Flaccum*) by referring to their own traditions about Alexander (Schwemer, 2013). Unrest broke out in 38 CE between the "Greeks" supported by the Roman governor Flaccus and Jews but was contained due to an appeal to Emperor Claudius (Horst, 2005; Harker, 2008; Gambetti, 2009). When another revolt erupted in Cyrenaica in 115/116 CE, it was so brutally put down by Trajan and his successor Hadrian that the once cosmopolitan Jewish community simply disappears from the records (Pucci Ben-Zeev, 2005).

Difficult times began in the later 3rd century CE. Large parts of Alexandria were destroyed in 272 CE when Aurelian had to conquer the city back from the Palmyrenes. It was devastated again when a tsunami hit it on Jul 21, 365 CE (Am. 26.10.15–19). Nevertheless, Alexandria quickly regained its importance as political and religious center under Christian influence (as attested, for example, by the influence of → Athanasius of Alexandria in the 4th cent. CE), marked by the destruction of the Serapeion in 391 CE.

Historiography

The history of western research on Alexandria started with Napoleon's Egyptian campaign of 1798–1801 that triggered tremendous public and academic interest and opened up ancient Egypt to the western world. During the Khedivate in the 19th century and especially after Egypt had come under British control in 1882, countless western scholars, learned societies, and museums entered a fierce competition to explore and display the most spectacular Egyptian antiquities, many of whom had come from

or were traded through Alexandria. Archaeological research in the city itself, however, remained very limited (Bagnall & Rathbone, 2004, 56–58; Baebler, 2013, 3–5; Fragaki, 2022). The first map documenting archeological remains was drawn in 1867 by M. Bay al-Falaki at the request of Napoleon III, and while it is notoriously problematic, it remains the basis of much topographical research until today. Especially during the latter part of the 20th century, research distanced itself from old-fashioned antiquarianism and greatly professionalized, systematically exploring Alexandrine necropolises, mosaics, the harbor, and Pharos. Nowadays, spectacular museums like the Alexandria National Museum, the Greco-Roman Museum and the new Bibliotheca Alexandrina document the city's place in the development of ancient Egyptian, classical and world cultures.

Bibliography

Abd El-Fattah, A., & M. Seif el-Din, "The Necropolis of Alexandria," in: A. Quertinmont & N. Amoroso, eds., *Alexandria: Past Futures*, New Haven, 2022, 188–197; exhibition at Mucem.

Abdo, A., *Alexandria Antiqua: A Topographical Catalogue and Reconstruction*, Oxford, 2022.

Adriani, A., *La tomba di Alessandro: Realtà ipothesi e fantasie*, Rome, 2000.

Bagnall, R., "Alexandria," in: C. Fluck, G. Helmecke & E.R. O'Connell, eds., *Ein Gott: Abrahams Erben am Nil: Juden, Christen und Muslime in Ägypten von der Antike bis zum Mittelalter*, Berlin, 2015, 48–63.

Bagnall, R., & D. Rathbone, eds., *Egypt from Alexander to the Copts: An Archaeological and Historical Guide*, London, 2004.

Baebler, B., "Zur Archäologie Alexandrias," in: T. Georges, F. Albrecht & R. Feldmeier, eds., *Alexandria: Stadt der Bildung und der Religion*, Tübingen, 2013, 3–27.

Bommas, M., "Isis, Osiris and Serapis," in: C. Riggs, ed., *The Oxford Handbook of Roman Egypt*, Oxford, 2012, 419–435.

Bricault, L., & R. Veymiers, "The Temple of Sarapis in Alexandria," in: A. Quertinmont & N. Amoroso, eds., *Alexandria: Past Futures*, New Haven, 2022, 126–135; exhibition at Mucem.

Caneva, S., "The Ptolemies, from a General to Gods," in: A. Quertinmont & N. Amoroso, eds., *Alexandria: Past Futures*, New Haven, 2022, 86–99; exhibition at Mucem.

Chauveau, M., "Alexandria before Alexandria: Rhakotis," in: A. Quertinmont & N. Amoroso, eds., *Alexandria: Past Futures*, New Haven, 2022, 24–31; exhibition at Mucem.

Czajkowski, K., "Jewish Associations at Alexandria?" in: B. Eckhardt, ed., *Private Associations and Jewish Com-*

munities in the Hellenistic and Roman Cities, Leiden, 2019, 76–96.

Delia, D., Alexandrian Citizenship During the Roman Principate, Atlanta, 1991.

Empereur, J.-Y., "New Data Concerning the Foundation of Alexandria," in: C.S. Zerefos & M.V. Vardinoyannis, eds., Hellenistic Alexandria: Celebrating 24 Centuries: Papers Presented at the Conference Held on December 13–15 2017 at Acropolis Museum, Athens, 2018, 3–12.

Engster, D., "Wissenschaftliche Forschung und technologischer Fortschritt in Alexandria," in: T. Georges, F. Albrecht & R. Feldmeier, eds., Alexandria: Stadt der Bildung und der Religion, Tübingen, 2013, 29–63.

Fragaki, H., "Beneath the Modern City: The Topography and Urban Landscape of Alexandria," in: A. Quertinmont & N. Amoroso, eds., Alexandria: Past Futures, New Haven, 2022, 34–41; exhibition at Mucem.

Frankfurter, D., Religion in Roman Egypt: Assimilation and Resistance, Princeton, 1998.

Gambetti, S., The Alexandrian Riots of 38 CE and the Persecution of the Jews: A Historical Assessment, Leiden, 2009.

Goddio, F., Alexandria: The Submerged Royal Quarters, London, 1998.

Grimm, G., Alexandria–Die erste Königsstadt der hellenistischen Welt: Bilder aus der Nilmetropole von Alexander dem Großen bis Kleopatra VII, Mainz, 1998.

Guimier-Sorbets, A.-M., A. Guimier, N. Morand & D. Weidman, Mosaïques d'Alexandrie: Pavements d'Égypte greque et romaine, Alexandria, 2019.

Haensch, R., "The Roman Army in Egypt," in: C. Riggs, ed., The Oxford Handbook of Roman Egypt, Oxford, 2012, 68–82.

Haggag, M., "The Ancient Library of Alexandria," in: A. Quertinmont & N. Amoroso, eds., Alexandria: Past Futures, New Haven, 2022, 100–113; exhibition at Mucem.

Harker, A., Loyalty and Dissidence in Roman Egypt: The Case of the Acta Alexandrinorum, Cambridge UK, 2008.

Hinge, G., J.A. Krasilnikoff & M.S. Jensen, eds., Alexandria: A Cultural and Religious Melting Pot, Aarhus, 2009.

Honigman, S., "The Shifting Definition of Greek Identity in Alexandria Through the Transition from Ptolemaic to Roman Rule," in: B. Schliesser, J. Rüggemeier, T.J. Kraus & J. Frey, eds., Alexandria: Hub of the Hellenistic World, Tübingen, 2021, 125–143.

Horst. P.W. van der, Philo's Flaccus: The First Pogrom: Introduction, Translation and Commentary, Leiden, 2005.

Khalil, E., "Ports and Trade: Ships of Alexandria," in: A. Quertinmont & N. Amoroso, eds., Alexandria: Past Futures, New Haven, 2022, 68–83; exhibition at Mucem.

Kooij, A. van der, "The Septuagint of the Pentateuch and Ptolemaic Rule," in: G.N. Knoppers & B. Levinson, eds., The Pentateuch as Torah: New Models for Understanding its Promulgation and Acceptance, Winona Lake, 2007, 289–300.

McEvedy, C., & D.S. Oles, Cities of the Classical World: An Atlas and Gazetteer of 120 Centres of Ancient Civilization, London, 2019.

McKenzie, J., The Architecture of Alexandria and Egypt 300 BC–AD 700, New Haven, 2007.

Nenna, M.-D., "The City of the Living: Homes and Mosaics," in: A. Quertinmont & N. Amoroso, eds., Alexandria: Past Futures, New Haven, 2022, 164–179; exhibition at Mucem.

Nesselrath, H.-G., "Das Museion und die Große Bibliothek von Alexandria," in: T. Georges, F. Albrecht & R. Feldmeier, eds., Alexandria: Stadt der Bildung und der Religion, Tübingen, 2013, 65–88.

Niehoff, M., Jewish Exegesis and Homeric Scholarship in Alexandria, Cambridge UK, 2011.

Niehoff, M., Philo of Alexandria: An Intellectual Biography, New Haven, 2018.

Paganini, M.C.D., Gymnasia and Greek Identity in Ptolemaic Egypt, Oxford, 2021.

Pucci Ben-Zeev, M., Diaspora Judaism in Turmoil 116/117 CE: Ancient Sources and Modern Insights, Louvain, 2005.

Queyrel, F., "From the Lighthouse of Alexandria to the City of Qaitbay," in: A. Quertinmont & N. Amoroso, eds., Alexandria: Past Futures, New Haven, 2022, 42–53; exhibition at Mucem.

Sabottka, M., Das Serapeum in Alexandria: Untersuchungen zur Architektur und Baugeschichte des Heiligtums von der frühen ptolemäischen Zeit bis zur Zerstörung 391 n.Chr., Cairo, 2008.

Schwemer, A.M., "Zur griechischen und jüdischen Gründungslegende Alexandriens," in: T. Georges, F. Albrecht & R. Feldmeier, eds., Alexandria: Stadt der Bildung und der Religion, Tübingen, 2013, 175–192.

Sly, D., Philo's Alexandria, London, 1996.

Stadler, M.A., "Die Krönung der Ptolemäer zu Pharaonen," WJA n.s. 2012, 59–94.

Tallet, G., La splendeur des dieux: Quatre études iconographiques sur l'hellénisme égyptien, Leiden, 2021.

Venit, M.S., Monumental Tombs of Ancient Alexandria: The Theater of the Dead, Cambridge UK, 2002.

Venit, M.S., "Alexandria," in: C. Riggs, ed., The Oxford Handbook of Roman Egypt, Oxford 2012, 103–121.

Versluys, M.J., "Hellenistic Alexandria: A Global Cosmopolis," in: A. Quertinmont & N. Amoroso, eds., Alexandria: Past Futures, New Haven, 2022, 114–123; exhibition at Mucem.

Quertinmont, A., & N. Amoroso, eds., Alexandria: Past Futures, New Haven, 2022; exhibition at Mucem.

Zangenberg, J.K., "Joseph und Aseneths Ägypten: Oder: Von der Domestikation einer gefährlichen Kultur," in: E. Reinmuth. ed., Joseph und Aseneth, Tübingen, 2009, 159–186.

Zangenberg, J.K., "Fragile Vielfalt: Beobachtungen zur Sozialgeschichte Alexandrias in hellenistisch-römischer Zeit," in: T. Georges, F. Albrecht & R. Feldmeier, eds., Alexandria: Stadt der Bildung und der Religion, Tübingen, 2013, 91–107.

JÜRGEN K. ZANGENBERG

II. School of

The school of Alexandria, the Didaskaleion (διδασκαλεῖον τῶν ἱερῶν λόγων, school of sacred learning; Eus. *Hist. eccl.* 5.10.1), was a Christian liberal arts, philosophical, theological, and exegetical "school" that was initially independent of ecclesiastical institutions, but later became dependent on the local bishop. Similar schools were those of → Justin Martyr in Rome and of → Bardaisan in Edessa between the 2nd and 3rd centuries CE. From Hellenistic times onward, Alexandria had been a prominent cultural center, not only for Greek παιδεία but also for Hellenistic Judaism; the Septuagint had originated here. The main exponents of the school of Alexandria were Pantaenus, Clement of Alexandria, Origen – who was a disciple of the "Socrates of Neoplatonism," → Ammonius Saccas, and who later, around 233 CE, moved his school to Caesarea – and some successors of Origen, among whom the most remarkable was Didymus in the 4th century CE, who was appointed by Bishop → Athanasius of Alexandria.

From its beginnings in the 2nd century CE, the school remained active until the 4th century CE. In the 2nd century CE, Alexandrian Christianity, whose origins are wrapped in mystery and legend and are traditionally traced back to Mark the evangelist (Ramelli, 2011), may have been prevalently "gnostic," but J. Chapa (2010, 349–352) and D. Brakke (2008, ch. 17, section 1) challenge the hypothesis of a predominantly heterodox Alexandrian Christianity in the first two centuries CE. → Basilides was based there, as was Valentinus, before moving to Rome (Thomassen, 2006). "Gnosticism" attracted intellectually demanding Christians, but with Pantaenus, → Clement of Alexandria, and especially → Origen such people could find an adequately refined theology, philosophy, and exegesis in the catholic church too (Ramelli, 2015). Origen was the first systematic theologian (with his De principiis/*On First Principles*) and biblical philologist (with his *Hexapla*) in Christianity. He also was one of the best Christian apologists (→ Apologetics), both against "paganism" (with his *Contra Celsum/ Against Celsus*, the Middle Platonist; → Celsis) and against Valentinian Gnosticism, wanting to build an orthodox Christian Platonism (Eus. *Hist. eccl.*

6.18 and 6.23). In this way, as an apologist against Valentinianism (→ Valentinus/Valentinians), Origen won Ambrose of Alexandria, a Valentinian, over to mainstream Christianity.

In the days of Pantaenus and Clement, the school was neither institutionalized nor controlled by the bishop; thus, Pantaenus' mission to India for the sake of teaching was not an episcopal initiative, unlike later Alexandrian missions (Ramelli, 2011a). Pantaenus' and Clement's seem to have been rather private schools, notwithstanding → Eusebius of Caesarea's tendency to describe the Didaskaleion as a formal ecclesiastical institution from the beginning, with a succession of leaders: Pantaenus succeeded by Clement succeeded by Origen (Eus. *Hist. eccl.*5.10; 6.6). In the 5th century CE, Philip of Side cites → Athenagoras as the first leader of the Alexandrian school before Pantaenus (PG 39.329), though his information is not confirmed by Eusebius or other sources. Philip also claims that during the directorship of Rhodon, the school moved from Alexandria to Side under → Theodosius I (379–395 CE).

Pantaenus is described by Eusebius as a Stoic; Clement, his disciple, who displays Middle Platonic and Stoic elements as well as a strong influence from → Philo of Alexandria, claims that most of his own works are based on Pantaenus' teaching. Clement called the most advanced Christians gnostics, insisting that this was the true → gnosis (knowledge), as opposed to the gnostics' false gnosis. For Clement, simple and advanced Christians were not distinguished by nature, but by education and a commitment to moral life and the study of Scripture. Origen, who also insisted on the distinction between simple and advanced Christians, surely knew Clement and his writings, but never mentions him, at least in his extant works. When Origen must adduce examples of philosophers who were also Christians and even presbyters in a letter (*ap.* Eus. *Hist. eccl.* 6.19.12–14), he cites Pantaenus, Clement's teacher, and Heraclas, a presbyter (→ Priest/Presbyter) in Alexandria who studied philosophy and wore philosophical attire even when he was a presbyter, but not Clement, although he would have been an excellent example of a philosopher-presbyter/Christian, all the more so if he had been his teacher.

If Eusebius can be taken at face value, Origen was only 18 when he became the head of the Catechetical

School (τῆς κατηχήσεως διδασκαλεῖον; *Eus. Hist. eccl.* 6.3.3). During the persecution in 202 CE, other teachers, including Clement, fled, and Origen took up the task of the instruction (κατήχησις) by decision of Bishop Demetrius (*Hist. eccl.* 6.3.8). Origen is credited with having divided the higher teaching courses at the school from the lower ones. According to Eusebius, Heraclas took on the less advanced courses, and Origen the more advanced; however, Origen states in a letter that Heraclas was five years ahead of him in the study of → philosophy; this may sound at odds with his teaching of less advanced courses than Origen (*ap.* Eus. *Hist. eccl.* 6.19.12–14; Ramelli, 2009a).

After Origen, the direction of the Didaskaleion passed on to Heraclas, Dionysius, Theognostus, Pierius, Achillas, Serapion, and Peter, over half of whom also became bishops of Alexandria: Heraclas, Dionysius, Achillas, and Peter. This is *per se* significant; after Origen, the Didaskaleion became more and more dependent on the episcopate. Didymus, a faithful follower, defender, and exegete of Origen (he wrote a commentary on his *On First Principles*), and a supporter of the → *apokatastasis* doctrine himself, was appointed head of the Didaskaleion by Athanasius, who was aware of his doctrines.

Rhodon succeeded Didymus as head of the school. During his term of office, however, the conflict with the Alexandrian bishop Theophilus arose, when the latter, for merely strategic and political reasons – and fearing the threats of the anti-Origenian ("Origenian" being followers of Origen's thought) monks – began to persecute the Origenian monks and the whole Origenian party, in a period in which → Epiphanius of Salamis had revived the polemics against Origen. The "zetetic" philosophical spirit in exegetical and theological investigation was no longer appreciated; authority tended to prevail over research. The Alexandrian school had represented a stronghold of the opening of Christianity to Hellenic philosophy and παιδεία and had formulated the main Christian dogmas (which are largely based on Origen's theology: Ramelli, 2011b; 2012; 2015). The emblematic end of this openness may be seen in the tragic killing of the "pagan" Neoplatonist Hypatia, philosopher, ascetic, and scientist, the teacher of → Synesius of Cyrene. She was massacred in Alexandria in 415 CE by the same anti-Origenian monks, hostile to philosophy and learning, who had scared Theophilus shortly beforehand and made him condemn learned Origenism. Socrates, Damascius, and the *Suda* ascribe this misdeed to "envy/hostility" against Hypatia for her learning – the opposite of the spirit of education and investigation that inspired the Didaskaleion at least until Origen and Didymus.

Historiography

The School of Alexandria was studied already in antiquity, starting from Eusebius, who strongly "institutionalised" it, but its modern scientific study owes much to the pioneering investigation by H. Chadwick (1954), M. Hornschuh (1960), F. Pericoli Ridolfini (1962), and R. Grant (1971). Further research into the origin and development of the school, through Pantaenus, Clement, Origen, and beyond, has been offered by R. van der Broek (1995), C. Scholten (1995), A. van den Hoek (1997), A. Boulluec (1999), and E. Prinzivalli (2003), who scrutinized the sources, specially Eusebius and Philip. I. Ramelli analyzed Heraclas' and Origen's contribution to the School of Alexandria (Ramelli, 2009a) and showed that the Alexandrian school represented the opening of Christianity to Hellenic philosophy and education and paved the way for the main Christian dogmas (Ramelli, 2011b; 2012; 2015; 2021; and a forthcoming monograph). I. Ramelli (2011) examined the tradition of the origin of Alexandrian Christianity and its school with Mark and the possible link between *Secret Mark* and Clement, and J. Chapa (2010) and D. Brakke (2008) challenged the hypothesis of a predominantly heterodox Alexandrian Christianity in the first two centuries CE. Further study is needed, especially on the relation between the main exponents of the Alexandrian school, Clement and Origen, their teachers Pantaenus and Ammonius Saccas, and the pagan side of Alexandrian Platonism, especially → Plotinus (and Porphyry, a disciple of both Origen and Plotinus). The legacy of Ammonius Saccas was negotiated among various strands of → Neoplatonism, as it was still clear to Proclus.

Bibliography

Boulluec, A. Le, "Aux origines, encore, de l'école d'Alexandrie," *Adamantius* 5, 1999, 8–36.

Brakke, D., "The East (2): Egypt and Palestine," in: S.A. Harvey & D. Hunter, eds., *OHECS*, Oxford, 2008, ch. 17; online version: DOI:10.1093/oxfordhb/9780199271566 .003.0018.

Broek, R. van der, "The Christian School at Alexandria in the Second and Third Centuries," in: J.W. Drijvers & A. MacDonald, eds., *Centers of Learning*, Leiden, 1995, 39–47.

Camelot, T., "Les chrétiens à Alexandrie," in: P. Geoltrain, ed., *Aux origines du christianisme*, Paris, 2000, 495–504.

Chadwick, H., *Alexandrian Christianity*, Philadelphia, 1954.

Chapa, J., "The Fortunes and Misfortunes of the Gospel of John," *VigChr* 64, 2010, 327–352.

Dorival, G., "Les débuts du christianisme à Alexandrie," in: J. Leclant, ed., *Alexandrie*, Paris, 1999, 157–174.

Grant, R., "Early Alexandrian Christianity," *ChH* 40, 1971, 133–144.

Griggs, C.W., *Early Egyptian Christianity*, Leiden, 1990.

Hoek, A. van den, "The 'Cathechetical School' of Early Christian Alexandria and Its Philonic Heritage," *HThR* 90, 1997, 59–87.

Hornschuh, M., "Das Leben des Origenes und die Entstehung der alexandrinischen Schule," *ZKG* 71, 1960, 1–25, 193–214.

Jakab, A., *Ecclesia Alexandrina*, Bern, 2004.

Jakab, A.,"Earliest Christianity in Egypt," in: J. Goehring & J. Timbie, eds., *The World of Early Egyptian Christianity*, Washington DC, 2007, 97–112.

McGuckin, J., "Christian Asceticism and the Early School of Alexandria," *SCH(L)* 22, 1985, 25–39.

Mimouni, S., "À la recherche de la communauté chré tienne d'Alexandrie," in: L. Perrone, ed., *Origeniana*, vol. VIII, Louvain, 2003, 137–163.

Neymeyr, U., *Die christliche Lehrer im zweiten Jahrhundert*, SVigChr 4, Leiden, 1989.

Osborn, E., *Clement of Alexandria*, Cambridge UK, 2005.

Pearson, B., *Gnosticism, Judaism, and Egyptian Christianity*, Minneapolis, 1990.

Pearson, B., "Earliest Christianity in Egypt," in: B. Pearson & J. Goehring, eds., *The Roots of Egyptian Christianity*, Philadelphia, 1990, 132–156.

Pericoli Ridolfini, F., "Le origini della chiesa d'Alessandria e la cronologia dei vescovi alessandrini," *RAL* 17, 1962, 308–343.

Plese, Z., & R. Hirsch-Luipoldt, eds., *Alexandrian Personae: Scholarly Culture and Religious Traditions in Ancient Alexandria*, Tübingen, forthcoming.

Prinzivalli, E., "La metamorfosi della scuola alessandrina da Eracla a Didimo," in: L. Perrone, ed., *Origeniana*, vol. VIII, Louvain, 2003, 911–937.

Ramelli, I., "Origen, Bardaisan, and the Origin of Universal Salvation," *HThR* 102, 2009, 135–168.

Ramelli, I., "Origen, Patristic Philosophy, and Christian Platonism," *VigChr* 63, 2009a, 217–263.

Ramelli, I., *Bardaisan of Edessa: A Reassessment of the Evidence and a New Interpretation*, Piscataway, 2009.

Ramelli, I., "The Birth of the Rome-Alexandria Connection: The Early Sources on Mark and Philo, and the Petrine Tradition," *SPhilo* 23, 2011, 69–95.

Ramelli, I., "Early Christian Missions from Alexandria to 'India': Institutional Transformations and Geographical Identification," *Aug.* 51, 2011a, 221–231.

Ramelli, I., "Origen's Anti-Subordinationism and Its Heritage in the Nicene and Cappadocian Line," *VigChr* 65, 2011b, 21–49.

Ramelli, I., "Origen, Greek Philosophy, and the Birth of the Trinitarian Meaning of Hypostasis," *HThR* 105, 2012, 302–350.

Ramelli, I., "Ethos and Logos: A Second-Century Apologetical Debate between 'Pagan' and Christian Philosophers," *VigChr* 69, 2015, 123–156.

Ramelli, I., "Christian Apokatastasis and Zoroastrian Frashegird: The Birth of Eschatological Universalism," *R&T* 24, 2017, 350–406.

Ramelli, I., "Clement and Origen of Alexandria," in: I. Ramelli, J. McGuckin & P. Ashwin, eds., *T&T Clark Handbook to the Early Church*, London, 2021, 191–223.

Ramelli, I., "Philosophy and Religion – 'Pagan' and Christian Platonism," in: S.S. Griffin & I. Ramelli, *Lovers of the Soul and Lovers of the Body: Philosophical and Religious Perspectives in Late Antiquity*, Cambridge MA, 2021, 397–402.

Scholten, C., "Die alexandrinische Katechetenschule," *JAC* 38, 1995, 16–37.

Simonetti, M., "Alessandria II: Scuola," in: A. Di Berardino, ed., *NDPAC*, vol. I, Genoa, 2006, 184–188.

Thomassen, E., *The Spiritual Seed: The Church of the "Valentinians"*, Leiden, 2006.

Tloka, J., *Griechische Christen, Christliche Griechen*, Tübingen, 2006.

ILARIA L.E. RAMELLI

III. Councils of

Alexandria in antiquity hosted many gatherings of ordained Christian clerics – bishops, presbyters, and deacons – who assembled in the city to address issues of ecclesial administration, church governance, or doctrinal matters (MacMullen, 2006). Such councils could consider local topics relevant to Alexandria, regional issues affecting Egypt, or Mediterranean-wide affairs. Some councils featured the bishop of Alexandria as the sole episcopal presider; others drew hundreds of bishops, from Egypt and from throughout the Roman Empire. Indeed, given that canon law mandated that regular synods take place annually in each province, many councils that left no historical record may have transpired in

Alexandria (MacMullen, 2006, 1–11). Alongside the six major Alexandrian councils surveyed here, others occurred which could also form objects of study.

These councils must be framed in their Alexandrian setting. As one of the Roman Empire's most populous and vibrant urban centers, Alexandria was an economic, political, and cultural powerhouse with a robust Christian life. The first two centuries of Christianity in the city prove difficult to reconstruct, including how the community might have been administered by church leaders or councils. Around 200 CE, however, a "monarchical episcopate" becomes visible in which Alexandria's bishops claimed authority over local Christians (Davis, 2004, 1–42). Moreover, the see soon oversaw suffragan bishops in Egypt, establishing Alexandria as a great patriarchate on the international stage as well. This trifold set of themes – the importance of Alexandria as a Roman city, the vibrancy of its ecclesial life, and the prestige of its bishops – undergirds its church councils.

The issue of the bishop of Alexandria's local authority takes center stage in the council of 231 CE. Dated scholarship rehearses that in that year Demetrius, Alexandria's bishop, led a council that excommunicated → Origen (Shahan, 1907). Historically, tensions over authority indeed emerged between Demetrius and Origen, leading to Origen's departure from the city. But none of the standard ancient sources for Origen's life (esp. Eus. *Hist. eccl.* 6) state that he was excommunicated by an Alexandrian *council*, per se, nor do most modern scholars note such an event (McGuckin, 2004b, 1–23; Heine, 2010). R.P.C. Hanson (1982) observes that the idea of Origen's expulsion via an Alexandrian synod possibly originates only with the 9th-century CE author Photius. The historicity of this supposed council thus stands on uncertain ground.

Later, a series of Alexandrian councils occurred during the first phase of the Trinitarian controversy (c. 319 and c. 324 CE). These councils prove historically opaque: major details, including number of councils, dates of councils, and number of attendees, remain conjectural. Events began with a theological dispute between Arius (→ Arianism), a presbyter of Alexandria, and his bishop, Alexander: Arius asserted a strict → monotheism recognizing the Father alone

as fully divine, whereas Alexander professed the divinity of the Son. Two alternate scholarly accounts of events exist, one proposed by H. Opitz (1934; Hanson, 2005, 133–138; Williams, 2001, 48–50, 58–59), the other by R. Williams (2001, 48–61; 251–256). H. Opitz dates the crisis' outbreak to 318 CE, with two Alexandrian councils thereafter, one in 319 CE, another in 324 CE. According to him, an extant document (Opitz, 1934, *Urkunde* 4b) condemning Arius was an encyclical issued by Alexander on behalf of an Alexandrian synod gathered in 319 CE which featured 100 bishops from Egypt and Libya. In 324 CE, when the crisis escalated, Alexander convoked a large Alexandrian council of bishops from Egypt and elsewhere in the east, as reflected by an anti-Arian encyclical from 324 CE allegedly signed by them (Opitz, 1934, *Urkunde* 15). Conversely, R. Williams' account delays the crisis' outbreak until 321 CE, with up to three Alexandrian councils afterward. The first, in 321 CE, assembled under Alexander and condemned Arius and his supporters (Williams, 2001, 56). In 323 CE, facing further controversy, Alexander possibly convoked a second Alexandrian council of 100 Egyptian and Libyan bishops; extant fragments (Opitz, 1934, *Urkunde* 15) might preserve its synodical letter (Williams, 2001, 57). Eventually, Alexander oversaw a third Alexandrian synod in late 324/early 325 CE, which restored communion with a shadowy Alexandrian priest, Colluthus, and deposed two of Arius' supporters, the Libyan bishops Secundus and Theonas (Williams, 2001, 57–58). R. Williams identifies an extant document (Opitz, 1934, *Urkunde* 4b) as the encyclical of this council, which he believes only Alexander and local clergy attended since it lists no episcopal subscriptions. Regardless of whether one prefers H. Opitz's or R. Williams' version of events, Alexander's church councils – despite difficulties in their reconstruction – surely played a key role in the early Trinitarian controversy.

As the Trinitarian controversy persisted, Alexander's successor as bishop, → Athanasius of Alexandria, assembled an Alexandrian council in 338 CE. In 335 CE, the Council of Tyre condemned Athanasius and deposed him from his see, citing charges of episcopal misconduct (illegitimate election, violence against enemies, misuse of funds). Athanasius rejected this verdict, later blaming an Arian conspiracy that targeted him due to his orthodoxy. The emperor → Constantine I nevertheless sent Athanasius into exile in Trier. After Constantine's death, Athanasius returned to Alexandria in 337 CE. Athanasius had maintained support at home, and a synod of Egyptian and Libyan bishops soon assembled in Alexandria. This was the Alexandrian council of 338 CE (Barnes, 2001, 34–41), which gathered for two purposes: to affirm Athanasius' legitimacy as → bishop, and to reject the machinations against him (Gwynn, 2012, 9, 25–26, 31–32). Athanasius preserves the council's encyclical (Athan. *Apol. sec.* 3–19), which defends Athanasius by lionizing his character, rejecting the accusations against him, and deprecating his enemies. The Alexandrian council of 338 CE shows the strong local support enjoyed by Athanasius at this time: it sought to vindicate him as the spiritual leader of Egypt amid his fierce struggles with rivals.

The Alexandrian council of 362 CE likewise supported Athanasius' agenda amid the Trinitarian controversy (Armstrong, 1921a; 1921b; Barnes, 2001, 156–159; Gwynn, 2012, 49–50; Fairbairn, 2015). It transpired between Athanasius' third (February 362 CE) and fourth exile (October 362 CE), perhaps in April or May of that year (Barnes, 2001, 156; Armstrong, 1921a, 214). Participants included bishops from Egypt, Libya, Arabia, and Italy, with Athanasius presiding. The council addressed two major issues:

1. conditions for admitting former Arians into communion;
2. a schism that had broken out in Antioch between two pro-Nicene groups there, one led by Paulinus (an arch-Nicene) and the other by Meletius, who was originally elected bishop of Antioch by an Arian faction, but who came to support pro-Nicene views.

Two documents survive from this council:

1. the *Epistula Catholica*, a fragmentary encyclical discovered by M. Tetz (1988) that recommended generous terms for admitting repentant Arians into communion;
2. the *Tomus ad Antiochenos* (written by Athanasius), a letter addressed by the council to Christians in Antioch. The *Tomus* urged the two pro-Nicene factions in Antioch to enter into communion, prescribing that all members of the community must simply abjure Arius'

heresy, confess the Nicene formula, and affirm the divinity of the Holy Spirit.

Further wrangles were to be avoided, especially those centering on correct usages in Trinitarian discourses of the (at the time) ill-defined terms ὑπόστασις/*hypostasis* ("person") and οὐσία/*ousia* ("essence"; → Trinity). Despite the council's efforts, schism persisted in Antioch. Nevertheless, the council's attempt to broker such a peace established a blueprint for the powerful alliance which developed at the end of the 300s CE that eventually united pro-Nicene Christians across the empire into a single dominant anti-Arian party gathered around the faith of Nicaea (Barnes, 2001, 158). Thus, the council stands as a watershed in light of the enduring political and theological outcomes which it helped forge.

Another major Alexandrian council took place in 430 CE, this time amid the Christological controversy that erupted between Nestorius of Constantinople → Nestorianism/Nestorius and → Cyril of Alexandria (McGuckin, 2004a, 44–45). The heart of the conflict was a fundamental disagreement over how divinity and humanity joined in Christ: Nestorius' Antiochene Christology emphasized division between the two, whereas Cyril's Alexandrian Christology stressed unity. From 428 to 430 CE, Cyril and Nestorius had become engaged in an increasingly bitter standoff over such issues (→ Christology). Nestorius had additionally provoked Pope Celestine of Rome, who objected not only to Nestorius' Christology, but also to the fact that Nestorius had harbored western Pelagian exiles previously condemned as heretics in Rome (→ Pelagians/Pelagianism). Cyril and Celestine had thus formed an alliance against Nestorius. As the conflict intensified, a future council at Ephesus was planned to settle the dispute. Meanwhile, in Rome, a synod had condemned Nestorius in August 430 CE. Celestine tasked Cyril with enforcing this decree in the east. When Cyril learned of the Roman verdict, in November he convoked a synod of Egyptian bishops: the Alexandrian council of 430 CE. Cyril's synod repeated Rome's condemnation of Nestorius. To accompany the Alexandrian council's decision, Cyril wrote his *Third Letter to Nestorius* (Cyr.Alex. *Ep.* 17), a Christological statement incorporating aggressive polemic against his rival; also appended were a series of 12 anathemas, the "Twelve Chapters," which articulated Cyril's Christology and condemned principles associated with Nestorius' in stark terms. Cyril's letter demanded Nestorius' recantation, demanding acceptance of the anathemas for readmission to communion. Nestorius refused these uncompromising conditions. The Alexandrian council of 430 CE thus inflamed a dispute that climaxed with Nestorius' defeat at the Council of → Ephesus in 431 CE.

Historiography

Ancient councils have been treated generally (MacMullen, 2006) and some Alexandrian councils specifically (Armstrong, 1921a; 1921b; Fairbairn, 2015). Apart from a very short, outdated encyclopedia entry (Shahan, 1907) no concentrated synthesis of Alexandrian councils exists. Treatments do appear in biographical studies of major associated figures (Barnes, 2001; Williams, 2001; McGuckin, 2004a; Gwynn, 2012) and in thematic surveys of related developments (Opitz, 1934; Hanson, 2005). Modern scholarship has shined light on the contextual complexity of councils by providing comprehensive narratives which reveal that these were not always two-party debates or single-issue affairs, but instead involved multiplex casts of agents operating according to diverse sets of interests, both religious and political (Barnes, 2001; McGuckin, 2004a; Hanson, 2005). Revisionist works have questioned older chronologies, proposing new sequential orderings (Williams, 2001). Scholarship has even queried the historicity of certain councils (Hanson, 1982).

Bibliography

Armstrong, C.B., "The Synod of Alexandria and the Schism at Antioch in AD 362," *JThS* 22, 1921a, 206–221.
Armstrong, C.B., "The Synod of Alexandria and the Schism at Antioch in AD 362 (continued)," *JThS* 22, 1921b, 347–355.
Barnes, T., *Athanasius and Constantius: Theology and Politics in the Constantinian Empire*, Cambridge MA, 2001.
Davis, S., *The Early Coptic Papacy: The Egyptian Church and Its Leadership in Late Antiquity*, Cairo, 2004.
Fairbairn, D., "The Sardican Paper, Antiochene Politics, and the Council of Alexandria (362): Developing the 'Faith of Nicaea'," *JThS* 66, 2015, 651–678.
Gwynn, D., *Athanasius of Alexandria: Bishop, Theologian, Ascetic, Father*, Oxford, 2012.

Hanson, R.P.C., "Was Origen Banished from Alexandria?" *SP* 17, 1982, 904–906.
Hanson, R.P.C., *The Search for the Christian Doctrine of God: The Arian Controversy, 318–381*, Grand Rapids, 2005.
Heine, R., *Origen: Scholarship in the Service of the Church*, Oxford, 2010.
MacMullen, R., *Voting About God in Early Church Councils*, New Haven, 2006.
McGuckin, J., *Saint Cyril of Alexandria and the Christological Controversy*, Crestwood, 2004a.
McGuckin, J., *Westminster Handbook to Origen*, Louisville, 2004b.
Opitz, H., "Die Zeitfolge des arianischen Streites von den Anfängen bis zum Jahr 328," *ZNW* 33, 1934, 131–159.
Shahan, T., "Alexandria, Councils of," in: C. Herbermann et al., eds., *ThCE*, vol. I, New York, 1907, 300.
Tetz, M., "Ein enzyklisches Schreiben der Synode von Alexandrien (362)," *ZNW* 79, 1988, 262–281.
Williams, R., *Arius: Heresy and Tradition*, rev. ed., Grand Rapids, 2001.

CHRISTOPHER T.M. WEST

IV. Libraries of

The most explicit testimony for the simultaneous existence of two substantial libraries in Alexandria for about 500 years is admittedly late: according to the Byzantine author John Tzetzes (12th cent.; *Prolegomena in Aristophanem*; see Koster, 1975), Ptolemy II established an "outer library" with 42,800 books and a library "inside the palace grounds" with 490,000 books; this inner library is usually identified with the Great Library, the outer library with the Serapeum Library. T. Hendrickson (2016, 454) argues that John Tzetzes must be wrong because the Ptolemaic foundation plaques found at the Serapeum indicate Ptolemy III and not II as the founder of the Serapeum. He does not take into account, however, that Ptolemy III integrated into his (re-)foundation (for which see below) of the Serapeum at least two older buildings, which might already have served as a library.

Other authors, too, indicate (or at least imply) that a library in the Serapeum was connected with Ptolemy II: the Italian bishop Filastrius of Brescia in his *Diversarum haereseon liber* (142.7–8), written in the 370s CE; → John Chrysostom in his *First Discourse Against the Jews* of 386 CE (Chrys. *Jud.* 1.6.1; PG 48, p. 851.46–53); the Cypriote bishop → Epiphanius of Salamis in his book on biblical measures and weights of 392 CE (Epiph. *Mens.* 11; see Moutsoulas, 1973, ll. 324–327), the Byzantine chronographer Georgius Syncellus (*Chron.* p. 327.17–21; see Mosshammer, 1984; later 8th or early 9th cent. CE), and the Alexandrian patriarch Eutychius (first half of the 10th cent. CE) in his *Annales* (§119). Already around 200 CE, Athenaeus of Naucratis (*Deipn.* 5.203e) remarked that all knowledgeable people of his time were well informed about Ptolemy II's establishment of the Alexandrian libraries (plural!). Athenaeus wrote only shortly after the time when, according to T. Hendrickson, the Serapeum library was first founded; if that really had been the case, he surely could not have attributed that foundation to an early Ptolemaic king.

Moreover, several sources called the library situated in the royal quarters of Alexandria the Great Library (*OGIS* 172/714 of 88 BC; Plut. *Caes.* 49.6; Gal. *Hipp. Epid.* 3.17a.606; CMG 5.10.2.1); this implies that there also was a smaller library at the same time.

The only source for a third library is the Jewish author → Philo of Alexandria (*Legat.* 151), who around 40 CE mentions a Sebasteum built 80 years before with libraries attached to it (Rico, 2017, 295), but nothing more is known.

1. The Founding and First Period of the Great Library

The founding of the Great Library is connected with the establishment of the famous Alexandrian Museum; both came into being by the initiative of King Ptolemy I (r. 323–285 BCE) and his adviser Demetrius of Phalerum, a pupil of Aristotle's master pupil Theophrastus (Nesselrath, 2013, 67–70). Ptolemy's role is attested by Plutarch (*Suav. viv.* 13, p. 1095D) and the Christian writer → Irenaeus of Lyon (*Haer.* 3.21.2/in Gk *Frgm.* 31). The *Letter of Aristeas* (written by an unknown Jewish-Greek author in the 2nd century BCE) also attests Demetrius' importance for the library, but wrongly associates him with Ptolemy II (*Let. Aris.* ch. 9–10.12): Ptolemy was an enemy of Demetrius, because Demetrius had favored another of Ptolemy's I sons as his successor. After Ptolemy II's accession, Demetrius was detained and died soon afterwards (D.L. 5.78); therefore, his

involvement in the foundation of the Great Library must have been earlier under Ptolemy I.

However, S. Johnstone (2014) has argued that there are no explicit sources for the invention of libraries before the early 2nd century BCE, but his methodology is questionable: he rejects late and apocryphal sources, but does not consider that in antiquity such sources may well reflect earlier but lost sources.

While the geographer Strabo (1st cent. BCE) described some facilities of the Museum (Stra. *Geogr.* 17.1.8), we have no specific information about the location of the Great Library; but as it was connected with the Museum – which was situated in the Bruchion quarter (near the harbor), inside the royal palace grounds – it was probably located in the same area. A papyrus (P.Oxy. 1241, col. ii) attests that famous poets and scholars (Apollonius Rhodius, Eratosthenes of Cyrene, Aristophanes of Byzantium, Aristarchus of Samothrace) were directors of the library in the first 150 years of its existence. Because of rather aggressive acquisition policies by the Ptolemaic kings (on which see e.g. Männlein-Robert, 2010, 164; Zdiarsky, 2011, 168), the book collections of the library grew rapidly; but how many books the library contained in its heyday, is a matter of debate: H.G. Nesselrath (2012, 69–73) has argued that we may reckon with much more than the 10,000–15,000 that R.S. Bagnall (2002, 353) thought probable. According to Livy (quoted by Sen. *Tranq.* 9.4–5), 40,000 books perished in the conflagration of 48 BCE; but according to the *Letter of Aristeas* (10), already Demetrius of Phalerum claimed to have collected 200,000 books and that he hoped to bring their number up to 500,000.

2. The Serapeum and Its Library in the First Period

When, after the death of Alexander the Great, Ptolemy son of Lagos established himself as ruler of Egypt, one of his means to consolidate his power over a mixed population of Egyptians, Macedonians, and Greeks was the establishment of the god Serapis (or Sarapis) as divine protector of the realm. Recent research has stressed important Egyptian origins of Serapis (Kleibl, 2015, 625). As site for a suitable sanctuary of the god, Ptolemy chose the most elevated spot of Alexandria, a rocky plateau in its south-west quarter called Rhacotis, where according to the Roman historian → Tacitus (*Hist.* 4.84) "an ancient shrine dedicated to Serapis and Isis" already existed, which then became the most important sanctuary of the city and the leading shrine of Serapis in the Mediterranean world. The first buildings were probably already erected by Ptolemy I (see McKenzie et al., 2004, 79–81; McKenzie, 2007, 32–41). → Clement of Alexandria (*Protr.* 4.48.2), however, connects the acquisition of the cult statue and its placing on the site in Rhacotis with Ptolemy II, so he, too, was probably involved in the development of the cult of Serapis in this place. Then, Ptolemy III (r. 246–221 BCE) undertook a major refoundation of the sanctuary, but preserved two already existing older buildings (the so-called T-shaped Building and the South Building), in which there may already have been space for a library; so, reports that associate Ptolemy II with the founding of the Serapeum Library (see above) may in fact not be mistaken (*pace* Hendrickson, 2016, 454).

In the course of the refounding by Ptolemy III, the Serapeum received impressive surrounding colonnades (with rooms on their west and south sides), a new Temple of Serapis in the north-eastern part of the courtyard, and, to the west of it, a "Stoa-like structure" with four rooms in it (McKenzie, 2004, 89). There also were the two older buildings already mentioned and some underground passages, the walls of which still exhibit some niches that might have served as spaces for books.

Thus, the early architectural history of the Serapeum shows that, at least in theory, facilities for library rooms were there since its earliest buildings. However, T. Hendrickson (2016) has asserted that the Serapeum Library did not exist much before its first explicit attestation around 200 CE; but he does not take sufficiently into account that the connection between the library and the sanctuary within which it was located may be so intimate (see below) that it is hardly conceivable that this library was established only 400 years after the foundation of the sanctuary. Moreover, T. Hendrickson (2016, 458–459) interpreted a passage from Strabo's *Geography* (17.1.10) as meaning that at the time of Strabo's visit to Alexandria (c. 20 BCE) the Serapeum was a rather neglected place; but the text of the Strabo passage

provides no secure evidence for this (see e.g. Rowe, 1946, 3n1). It is, in fact, hardly believable that the Alexandrians would have tolerated the decay of their most important sanctuary.

What might have been the reason(s) to establish a second substantial library in Alexandria, and why, of all places, in the Serapeum? According to M. El-Abbadi (1992, 91), the Serapeum Library started as a "branch library to accommodate the surplus books" of the Great Library, but this does not explain why this branch library was located in the Serapeum. If, however, this sanctuary was to appeal also to Egyptians (see above), equipping it with a library made good sense: traditional Egyptian temples used to have two institutional components that in appearance and function come at least close to what might be considered a library, the so-called House of Papyrus Rolls, which was "a small room inside the temple where a catalogue of the documents, and perhaps a copy of individual documents related to the temple's daily life [...] were kept" (Haikal, 2008, 45); and the so-called House of Life, which was "outside the temple and had a larger library and a more complex organization" (Haikal, 2008, 45). During the times of Late Period Egypt, the House of Life was "intimately related to the cult of Osiris" (Ryholt, 2019, 445), who was one of the "ideological ancestors" of Serapis. It has also been described as "partly a library, partly a centre of higher learning, partly a scriptorium, partly a centre for the editing of older texts and partly a cult centre" (Shubert, 1993, 165); the parallels to the functions of the two Alexandrian libraries are obvious.

Already Ptolemy I took considerable interest in Egyptian temple libraries: the so-called Satrap Stela from 312 BCE relates "how Ptolemy [...] returned to [...] Egypt [...] the sacred writings [...] abducted by the Persians" (Ryholt, 2019, 453). He thus was well aware of this Egyptian institution and its importance. So, if Ptolemy III (and perhaps already his predecessors) conceived Serapis and his sanctuary as something that was to appeal to Greeks and Egyptians alike, they had good reasons to include a library – as a "House of Life"-like institution – in the Alexandrian Serapeum from the very start. Other Egyptian temples of Ptolemaic times had library components, too: the Temple of Horus at Edfu (begun in 237 BCE by the same Ptolemy III who also undertook the first major refounding of the Alexandrian Serapeum) contained a library with liturgical texts (El-Abbadi, 1992, 74; Haikal, 2008, 46).

3. The Further History of the Great Library

Some scholars still assume that the already-mentioned outbreak of fire in the Alexandrian harbor caused by the fighting between Julius Caesar and hostile Egyptian factions in 48 BCE led to the destruction of the Great Library in the royal quarters near the burning harbor (El-Abbadi, 1992, 150–153; Rico, 2017, 308–320, 326). Others believe that this fire caused quite some damage but that the library as a whole survived (Nesselrath, 2012; Hatzimichali, 2013, 170–171; Hendrickson, 2016, 461, and Rico, 2017, 321, cite the epitaph [*AE* 78, 1924] of a certain Tiberius Claudius Balbillus, a leading official of the Alexandrine Museum and the Great Library during the times of the emperor Claudius). T. Hendrickson thinks that "the Great Library might have lasted into the reign of [...] perhaps even Domitian, but perhaps not all the way to Hadrian" (Hendrickson, 2016, 461); this assumption, however, is contradicted by evidence that "the post of palace librarian still existed at the end of the third century" (McKenzie et al., 2004, 100, with documentation in note 134). The most probable date for the demise of the Great Library is about 273 CE, when fighting between the forces of Emperor Aurelian and Empress Zenobia of Palmyra so much afflicted Alexandria that the former royal quarters (Bruchion), in which the library was housed, were laid waste (Barnes, 2000, 73; Bagnall, 2002, 357–358).

4. The Further History of the Serapeum Library After the 1st Century BCE

It has sometimes been assumed that the Serapeum suffered severe damage from an uprising of Jews in 115–116 CE (Horbury, 2014, 231–233); but no traces of a destruction of the Serapeum datable to this time have been found. However, in 181 CE, a major fire – recorded in → Eusebius of Caesarea's *Chronicle* (Helm, 1956, see p. 208, l. 19 & 423g) – apparently destroyed much of the Serapeum's substance and necessitated a major rebuilding. This not only restored the Serapeum, but also enlarged it (McKenzie et al., 2004, 93): the colonnades surrounding the *temenos* were extended to the north and east, so that the (also enlarged) Temple of Sarapis now lay squarely on the middle axis of the courtyard and dominated its northern half. The two Ptolemaic entrances on the eastern side were replaced by a single larger one, with a majestic stairway leading to it. The rooms at the back of the western and southern colonnades were retained, and at least some of them – according to the late 4th-century CE description of the Serapeum by Aphthonius (*Prog.* 12; see 40.3–6 in Rabe, 1913 – served as repositories for books. In 297 CE the last monumental part of the Serapeum (still remaining *in situ* today) was added: the triumphal column erected in honor of Emperor → Diocletian. In early 392 CE, the Serapeum and its library were destroyed by a Christian mob instigated by the Alexandrian patriarch Theophilus (Hahn, 2008; → Theophilus of Alexandria). C. Rico (2017, 305, 326) believes that the Serapeum library had already vanished earlier, namely during the fire of 181 CE, but no losses affecting the library at that time are recorded.

5. The Relationship Between the Serapeum Library and the Great Library

John Tzetzes (cited above) states that the number of books in the Serapeum Library was about ten times smaller than in the Great Library, but we do not know to which time these numbers refer; it is possible that before the final destruction of the Great Library in 273 CE (see above) at least some of its holdings were transferred to the Serapeum library.

One intriguing detail regarding the contents of the Serapeum Library has to be added. Several already-mentioned sources – Filastrius, John Chrysostom, Syncellus, Eutychius, and before them implicitly also → Tertullian (*Apol.* 18.5–8) – report that Ptolemy II, after commissioning the translation of the Hebrew Bible into Greek, had this new translation (i.e. the Septuagint; → Bible) stored in the Serapeum Library. It has been assumed that, in these sources, the Serapeum Library is confused with the Great Library, because at the time when most of these sources were written only the Serapeum Library was still in existence, and because the Serapeum Library was founded only after Ptolemy II. These assumptions, however, are doubtful, because the history of the Alexandrian Serapeum did not start with Ptolemy III and the alleged confusion of the two Alexandrian libraries is questionable (see above). Epiphanius (also mentioned above) reports that the Septuagint was originally deposited in the Great Library, while the later Greek translations of the Hebrew Bible were housed in the Serapeum Library.

It is, then, at least conceivable that the original Septuagint translation was actually kept in the Serapeum Library (Rajak, 2009, 44, has suggested that it went there after the Serapeum's Roman rebuilding). There, it would also have been more accessible to Alexandria's Greek-speaking Jewish (and later also Christian) population than if it had been in the Great Library, which was housed in the more restricted royal quarters.

If, then, the Serapeum Library really held the original Septuagint translation, the Christians, who in 392 CE smashed the Serapeum sanctuary and its library – as the Christian historiographer → Orosius, who visited the place in 415 CE and saw only "book-shelves emptied by our people" (Oros. *Adv. pag.* 6.15.32) attests – might actually have destroyed the oldest witness of their own Hebrew Bible in Greek.

Historiography

The interest in the history of the Alexandrian libraries is of long standing; already in the first half of the 19th century several major works were dedicated to them, especially to their origins (Ritschl, 1838) and in connection with the Museum of Alexandria (Klippel, 1838; Parthey, 1838). Already in these works, opinions diverged as to the later history of the libraries: while G.H. Klippel and G. Parthey agreed that the Great Library had suffered severe damage in 48 BCE and that the vanished books were massively replaced by acquiring the library from Pergamon, they disagreed about the alleged destruction of the library by the Arabs (in favor: Klippel; against: Parthey). The 20th and 21st centuries have witnessed the proposal of more divergent theses regarding the libraries' destruction: while E.A. Parsons (1952) assumed their continuation up to the end of antiquity (until the Muslim conquest) and L. Canfora (1989) denied the fiery end of the Great Library during Caesar's stay in Alexandria, P. Fraser (1972) argued for a major destruction in that time, and M. El-Abbadi (1992) and C. Rico (2017) were convinced that it was wholly destroyed in 48 BCE. More recent voices have again expressed widely diverging opinions regarding the origins and end of these libraries: that the Alexandrian Libraries were not founded before the 2nd century BCE (Johnstone, 2014); that the Great Library did last only until about Domitian's time (Hendrickson, 2016); that the Serapeum Library did not come into existence before circa 200 CE (Hendrickson, 2016), or that it had already vanished before the end of the 2nd century CE (Rico, 2017). Against these opinions, the article above has set out what its author believes to be the most probable view.

Bibliography

Bagnall, R.S., "Alexandria: Library of Dreams," *PAPS* 146, 2002, 348–362.

Barnes, R., "Cloistered Bookworms in the Chicken-Coop of the Muses: The Ancient Library of Alexandria," in: R.M. MacLeod, ed., *The Library of Alexandria: Centre of Learning in the Ancient World*, London, 2000, 61–77.

Canfora, L., *The Vanished Library*, Berkeley, 1989.

El-Abbadi, M., *The Life and Fate of the Ancient Library of Alexandria*, Paris, ²1992.

Fraser, P., *Ptolemaic Alexandria*, vols. I–III, Oxford, 1972.

Hahn, J., "The Conversion of the Cult Statues: The Destruction of the Serapeion 392 AD," in: J. Hahn & U. Gotter, eds., *From Temple to Church*, Leiden, 2008, 335–366.

Haikal, F.M., "Private Collections and Temple Libraries in Ancient Egypt," in: M. El-Abbadi, ed., *What Happened to the Ancient Library of Alexandria?* Leiden, 2008, 39–54.

Hatzimichali, M., "Ashes to Ashes? The Library of Alexandria After 24 BC," in: J. König et al., *Hellenistic and Roman Republican Libraries*, part 2, 2013, 167–182.

Helm, R., ed., *Eusebius Werke*, vol. VII: *Die Chronik des Hieronymus*, Leipzig, 1956.

Hendrickson, T., "The Serapeum: Dreams of the Daughter Library," *CP* 111, 2016, 453–464.

Horbury, W., *Jewish War Under Trajan and Hadrian*, Cambridge UK, 2014.

Johnstone, S., "A New History of Libraries and Books in the Hellenistic Period," *ClAn* 33, 2014, 347–393.

Kleibl, K., "Greco-Egyptian Religion," in: E. Eidinow & J. Kindt, eds., *OHAGR*, Oxford, 2015, 621–636.

Klippel, G.H., Ueber das alexandrinische Museum, Göttingen, 1838.

König, J. et al., eds., *Ancient Libraries*, Cambridge UK, 2013.

Koster, W.J.W., ed., *Prolegomena de Comoedia*, Groningen, 1975.

McKenzie, J.S., *The Architecture of Alexandria and Egypt, c. 300 BC to AD 700*, New Haven, 2007.

McKenzie, J.S. et al., "Reconstructing the Serapeum in Alexandria," *JRS* 94, 2004, 73–121.

Männlein-Robert, I., "Zwischen Musen und Museion oder: Die poetische (Er-) Findung Griechenlands in den *Aitien* des Kallimachos," in: G. Weber, ed., *Alexandreia und das ptolemäische Ägypten: Kulturbegegnungen in hellenistischer Zeit*, Berlin, 2010, 160–186.

Mosshammer, A.A., ed., *Georgii Syncelli Ecloga Chronographica*, Leipzig, 1984.

Moutsoulas, E.D., ed., "Epiphanius of Salamis, Concerning Weights and Measures," *Theologia* 44, 1973, 157–198.

Nesselrath, H.-G., "Did it Burn or Not? Caesar and the Great Library of Alexandria: A New Look at the Sources," in: I. Volt & J. Päll, eds., *Quattuor Lustra: Papers Celebrating the 20th Anniversary of the Re-Establishment of Classical Studies at the University of Tartu*, Tartu, 2012, 56–74.

Nesselrath, H.-G., "Das Museion und die Große Bibliothek von Alexandria," in: T. Georges et al., eds., *Alexandria*, Tübingen, 2013, 65–88.

Parsons, E.A., *The Alexandrian Library, Glory of the Hellenic World: Its Rise, Antiquities, and Destruction*, Amsterdam, 1952.

Parthey, G., *Das alexandrinische Museum*, Berlin, 1838.

Rabe, H., ed., *Aphthonii Progymnasmata*, Leipzig, 1913.

Rajak, T., *Translation and Survival: The Greek Bible of the Ancient Jewish Diaspora*, Oxford, 2009.

Rico, C., "The Destruction of the Library of Alexandria: A Reassessment," in: C. Rico & A. Dan, eds., *The Library of Alexandria: A Cultural Crossroads of the Ancient World*, Jerusalem, 2017, 293–329.

Ritschl, F.W., *Die alexandrinischen Bibliotheken unter den ersten Ptolemäern*, Breslau, 1838.

Rowe, A., *Discovery of the Famous Temple and Enclosure of Serapis at Alexandria*, Cairo, 1946.

Ryholt, K., "Libraries from Late Period and Graeco-Roman Egypt," in: K. Ryholt & G. Barjamovic, eds., *Libraries Before Alexandria: Ancient Near Eastern traditions*, New York, 2019, 390–472.

Shubert, S.B., "The Oriental Origins of the Alexandrian Library," *Libri* 43, 1993, 142–172.

Zdiarsky, A., "Bibliothekarische Überlegungen zur Bibliothek von Alexandria," in: E. Blumenthal & W. Schmitz, eds., *Bibliotheken im Altertum*, Wiesbaden, 2011, 161–172.

HEINZ-GÜNTHER NESSELRATH

Alexandrians, Epistle to the

The so-called *Muratorian Fragment* (→ *Canon Muratori*; a passage from Cod. Ambr. 1.101 suppl.; Bobbio, 8th cent. CE; see Leqlercq, 1934, 543–546], Muratori, 1740, 851–856) mentions and rejects a certain *Epistle to the Alexandrians* (2nd cent. CE?), together with an *Epistle to the Laodiceans*. The crucial passage of the fragment reads as follows:

> There is current also [an epistle] to the Laodiceans, [and] another to the Alexandrians, [both] forged in Paul's name to [further] the heresy of Marcion, and several others which cannot be received into the catholic Church – for it is not fitting that gall be mixed with honey. (2.63–68; Lietzmann, 1921, 8; Tregelles, 1867, 10–11, facs.; trans. Metzger, 1997, 307)

Like the whole text of the Muratorian Fragment, this passage does allow more than one reading. Most importantly, the phrase "forged in Paul's name to [further] the heresy of Marcion" (*pauli nomine fincte ad heresem marcionis*) "could refer either to *Alex* [*Ep. Alex.*] ('fincta') or to *Alex* and *Laod* [*Ep. Alex.* and to *Ep. Lao.*] ('finctae'), or, possibly even to a separate group of Marcionite letters" (Verheyden, 2003, 539). Under these circumstances, the common phrase that every translation is already an interpretation proves to be true to the full extent.

For the author of the fragment, the *Epistle to the Alexandrians* seems to be

a. written as a pseudepigraphical letter bearing Paul's name (*Pauli nomine*);

b. designed to foster Marcionite concepts (*ad haeresem Marcionis*), and;

c. relatively widely (i.e. not only in Marcionite circles) read (*fertur*).

Moreover, it is important to notice that this passage of the fragment does not describe the "canon" of → Marcion but rather discusses and, indeed, condemns the reception of Marcionite writings in its author's community, "into the catholic church" (*in catholicam ecclesiam*).

While numerous medieval manuscripts preserve copies of a certain *Epistle to the Laodiceans* (see Tite, 2012) – leading to the question of whether this text is already in view in the Muratorianum's statement or if it refers to canonical Ephesians, which was called by Marcion *Epistle to the Laodiceans* (see Tert. *Marc.* 5.11.12; 5.17.1) – no such textual evidence for the *Epistle to the Alexandrians* exists.

T. Zahn, however, cautiously identified a short passage (two pages) in the *Bobbio missal* (BNF, ms. Lat. 13246, fol. 212; palimpsest, likely to be composed in the south of France during the late 7th/early 8th cents.; see Hen & Meens, 2004) as stemming from our epistle (see Zahn, 1892, 586–592) but hardly convinced anyone (see e.g. Bardenhewer, 1913, 600f.; Tite, 2012, 21n8).

Others have assumed that the *Epistle to the Alexandrians* may be just another title of Hebrews, which is otherwise missing in the Muratorian Fragment (see Hahnemann, 1992, 196). Nevertheless, given the absence of any evidence for such an assumption within the textual witnesses and the reception history of Hebrews, this identification also remains a mere guess. Therefore, G.M. Hahnemann's statement is correct: "This remark in the [Muratorian] Fragment about the *Epistle to the Alexandrians* is all that is known about the work" (Hahnemann, 1992, 196).

Bibliography

Bardenhewer, O., *Geschichte der altchristlichen Literatur*, vol. I.: *Vom Ausgang des apostolischen Zeitalters bis zum Ende des zweiten Jahrhunderts*, Freiburg im Breisgau, ²1913.

Hahnemann, G.M., *The Muratorian Fragment and the Development of the Canon*, OTM, Oxford, 1992.

Hen, Y., & R. Meens, eds., *The Bobbio Missal: Liturgy and Religious Culture in Merovingian Gaul*, New York, 2004.

Leqlercq, H., "Muratorianum," in: F. Cabrol & H. Leqlercq, eds., *DACL*, vol. XII/1, Paris, 1934, 543–560.

Lietzmann, H., ed., *Das Muratorische Fragment und die monarchianischen Prologe zu den Evangelien*, KTVU 1, Bonn, 1921; repr. 1908.

Metzger, B.M., *The Canon of the New Testament: Its Origin, Development, and Significance*, Oxford, ²1997.

Muratori, L.-A., *Antiquitates italicae Medii Aevi*, Milan, 1740.

Tite, P.L., *The Apocryphal Epistle to the Laodiceans: An Epistolary and Rhetorical Analysis*, TENTS 7, Leiden, 2012.

Tregelles, S., *Canon Muratorianus: The Earliest Catalogue of the Books of the New Testament*, Oxford, 1867.

Verheyden, J., "The Canon Muratori: A Matter of Debate," in: J.-M. Auwers & H.J. de Jonge, eds., *The Biblical Canons*, BEThL 163, Louvain, 2003, 487–556.

Zahn, T., *Geschichte des Neutestamentlichen Kanons*, vol. II: *Urkunden und Belege zum ersten und dritten Band*, Erlangen, 1892.

WOLFGANG GRÜNSTÄUDL

Allegory

Allegory: in Greek Ἀλληγορία signifies "saying" (ἀγορεύειν) some things but meaning "others" (ἄλλα).

This definition of allegory was given in the early imperial age by Heraclitus the grammarian, or rhetor, in his *Homeric Allegories* (5), an allegorical interpretation of the Homeric poems. This definition covers mainly the first of the two principal meanings of allegory:

1. as a compositional method – writing an allegorical text, in which the literal level differs from its symbolic meaning(s);
2. as the allegorical interpretation of a text. The latter is also called allegoresis (from "allegorical" + "exegesis").

Allegory as a compositional method can be found both in classical literature, from its archaic phases onward, and in Jewish and Christian literature, from the Bible to gnostic (→ Gnosis/Gnosticism) myths. In the 7th century BCE, for example, the poet Alcaeus famously employed the ship as an allegory for the polis (Lobel & Page, 1955, frgm. 326). Pythagoras seems to have used symbolic language, and Plato's myths could be interpreted as allegories (Plato's Cave, *Rep.* 514a–520a). The Epicurean (→ Epicurus/Epicureans) poet Lucretius represented the torments of hell (→ Hades) as symbols of the insatiable desires of ignorant people (Lucr. *Rer. nat.* 3.978–1023). The *Cebetis Tabula* or *Tablet of Cebes*, probably from the 1st century CE or shortly afterward, joins allegory to ἔκφρασις, describing an allegorical picture ostensibly preserved in a temple. As in the Sophist Prodicus' tale of Heracles at the crossroad, virtues and vices are personified, and a road is said to lead to παιδεία, true education (Nesselrath, 2005; Konstan & Ramelli, 2009). In the 2nd century CE, Apuleius in his novel *Metamorphoses* narrates the story of Cupid and Psyche, possibly the allegory of the soul's desire for immortality, at least in Fulgentius' interpretation of the late 5th century CE. This is at least Fulgentius' interpretation in the late 5th century CE. In the same century, Martianus Capella composed a full allegorical narrative: *De nuptiis Philologiae et Mercurii* (*Marriage of Philology and Mercury*), a prosimeter, in which Mercury is a symbol of the λόγος, philology represents the love for the λόγος, and the liberal arts are personified as maidens. Capella's allegorical work was further allegorized by Eriugena, Bernardus Silvestris, and scholars of the Platonic school of Chartres (Ramelli, 2006).

In the Jewish world, in the Hebrew Bible, and in Qumran literature (→ Dead Sea Scrolls), there is some use of allegory. For example, in 2 Sam 12:1–4, the parable of the poor man who had a single lamb, which a wealthy neighbor stole, allegorizes King → David's sin, who stole Uriah's wife. In Isa 5:1–6, the vineyard that is taken care of but does not thrive allegorizes → Israel. 6Q.11.3–6 has the allegory of the vine, and both the Qumran community and the Johannine literature employ the imagery of light and darkness allegorically. In the New Testament, Jesus explains his messages in many → parables (παραβολαί, meaning "comparisons"). Parables such as that of the vineyard in Mark 12, are allegories. In some cases the Gospels portray Jesus explaining his allegories to his disciples, for instance the parable of the sower in Mark 4 and that of the wheat and tares in Matt 13. Jesus' declarations, especially in John, such as "I am the good shepherd," and "I am the gate," "I am the vine," are also allegorical. In Rev 17–18, Rome is symbolized by the "whore of Babylon." Christian authors, already in the 2nd century CE, composed allegories; for example, The *Shepherd of Hermas* (→ Hermas) features symbolic visions and similitudes, and the *Acts Thom.* 109–113 comprise the "Hymn of the Pearl." Gnostic mythopoiesis can also be considered a form of allegory.

Allegoresis – the second, hermeneutical meaning of allegory – was especially applied in antiquity to religiously authoritative texts: pagan philosophers such as Stoics and Middle and Neoplatonists (→ Middle Platonism; → Neoplatonism) allegorized myths concerning divinities, rituals, cultic epithets of deities, and the like, while Hellenistic Jewish and Christian exegetes, such as → Philo of Alexandria and → Origen, who read the Bible allegorically, reacted both against an exclusively literal reading of Scripture (advocated e.g. by the Marcionites, who rejected Hebrew Bible allegoresis, therefore deriving

a poor concept of God from the Hebrew Bible) and against extreme allegorists, who were present in Hellenistic → Judaism and early Christianity, especially among gnostics, particularly Valentinians (→ Valentinus/Valentinians). Origen explicitly appealed to the authority of Philo (Ramelli, 2012) to defend a biblical exegesis that valued both the literal level and the spiritual meanings (Ramelli, 2011a).

Both pagan and Christian allegorizers of theological texts aimed at finding deeper meanings and philosophical truths in traditional texts, thereby rescuing them from accusations of superficiality or impiety. The goal was to find in Homeric and other theological myths, as well as in the Septuagint, meaning "worthy of the divine." If we credit → Porphyry of Tyre, allegoresis of theological myths began as early as the 6th century BCE with Theagenes of Rhegium, who identified Homeric deities with physical qualities and ethical notions. The Derveni papyrus (4th cent. BCE) allegorizes a more ancient Orphic poem, and I. Ramelli (2007, 897–944) pointed out parallels with later Stoic allegoresis. The latter may have been prompted by Plato's ban on Homer, as well as by the purpose of finding worthy meanings in Homer's theological myths.

The *Homeric Problems*, by the aforementioned Heraclitus, opens with a defense of allegoresis (1–5) and concludes with a polemic against Plato (76–79). Pseudo-Plutarch's *Life and Poetry of Homer* ferreted many philosophical concepts out of Homer's text. These works, just like the scholia to Homer, drew on the tradition of Stoic allegoresis, on which more below. Plutarch's *De Daedalis Plataeensibus* is an example of Stoic allegoresis, although the author was a "Middle Platonist." Indeed, Middle and Neoplatonists abundantly cultivated allegoresis, deeming it – as did many Stoics – a constituent of philosophy. Porphyry in the 3rd century CE interpreted the Cave of the Nymphs, in Hom. *Od.* 13, as an allegory of the universe. In the 4th century CE the Neoplatonist Sallustius voiced the position of Platonic allegorists, that myths never happened historically, but are allegories of eternal truths (Sallus. *Diis* 4.9). His friend the emperor → Julian the Apostate similarly asserted that mythological events never happened, but are to be interpreted allegorically (Jul. *Deo.* 170–171). The late Neoplatonist Proclus in the 5th century CE writes that the inventors of myths "fashion likenesses of the indivisible by way of division, of the eternal by what moves in time, of the noetic by the perceptible" (Proc. *Rem publ.* 1.17).

In both Stoicism and Platonism, allegoresis was part and parcel of philosophy, rather than being a mere etymologizing device – although etymologies, especially of epithets of deities, were important in Stoicism (Ramelli, 2004, chs. 2 and 9; 2007; 2011a). Allegoresis had been used since the early Stoa, from Zeno's commentaries on Homer and Hesiod onward. Cleanthes also allegorized archaic poetry, even proposing textual emendations that supported it. In his view, poetry was the aptest way to express the sublimity of the divine (*SVF* 1.486; 1.538; 1.482). He distinguished between physics and theology, but at the same time coupled them; in Stoic immanentism, physics ended up coinciding with theology, but Cleanthes attached a special importance to the religious plane, from a "mystical" perspective. Chrysippus allegorized Orpheus, Musaeus, Homer, and Hesiod in Book 2 of *On Divinities* and above all theorized philosophical allegoresis in Book 1 of the same work (*SVF* 2.1009). He pointed out the relation of allegory to theology, as expressed in poetry, rituals, and tradition in general, including visual representations. He claimed that the expression of truth, of the λόγος, takes place through philosophers, poets, and "legislators," in other words institutors of norms and customs, including rituals. Poetry, expressing myth, and cultic traditions must therefore be interpreted allegorically to detect the truth hidden in them, in other words the philosophical truth of Stoicism. Chrysippus' theorization means that allegory is part of theology; allegory, to be precise, provides the very link between theology and physics (or sometimes ethics), which is the heart of Stoic immanentistic philosophy. It is remarkable that in *SVF* 2.1009 Chrysippus also offers a physical or ethical allegoresis of the deities and heroes of myths, thus programmatically conferring a systematic character to Stoic theological allegoresis. Allegory, according to Chrysippus, is in fact the main modality of the study of theology, in all of its traditional expressions, and connects it with physics and ethics, proving an important instrument of cultural unity. This was important for Chrysippus, given his extremely broad cultural interests, reflected in a great deal of works on a wide range of topics, many devoted to linguistics and logic.

Allegoresis of myths was carried out by many Stoics afterward, such as Diogenes of Babylonia, Apollodorus of Athens in *On Divinities* and a Homeric allegorical commentary, and Crates of Mallus, the author of commentaries on Homer, who coined the self-designation "critic" (κριτικός), meaning that he was well versed in philology, grammar, linguistics, and literature, but these competences were framed in a philosophical system, the Stoic one. Chrysippus' theorization was of such import that it was still reflected, alongside Apollodorus and Crates, in Varro's *theologia tripertita* and in Annaeus Cornutus, in the 1st century CE. In his handbook of allegoresis applied to the Greek gods, Cornutus declares,

> The ancients were not people of no account, but were both able to understand the nature of the cosmos and well capable of expressing philosophical truths on it through symbols and allusions. (*CTG* 35)

Allegoresis finds the philosophical truths under the veil of symbols; this is why it belongs to philosophy. For each divinity Cornutus provides an allegorical-etymological interpretation of its names and epithets, its attributes, aspects of its myths and rituals, and so on. Physical allegory (Zeus = aether, Hera = air, etc.) is prevalent; there are also examples of ethical and historical exegeses. From Cornutus' and Chrysippus' perspective, poetry and the other forms of transmission of ancient theology (rituals, cultic epithets, and visual representations), express truths in a symbolic way, which philosophical allegoresis must decrypt. Chaeremon of Alexandria, a contemporary of Cornutus, was another Stoic allegorist.

The role of allegory in Stoicism was not simply to "apologetically" support Stoic philosophy. This might have been the case at the beginning of the Stoa, but less so in the day of Chrysippus, and even less in that of Cornutus. Stoic interest in allegoresis and allegorical production *grew* over time. If allegoresis had merely been meant to prove the truth of Stoicism, one should expect a *decline* of Stoic interest in allegoresis of myth over time, when the Stoic system could stand by itself. In such a structured system, at a certain point the support of the allegoresis of

Homer and other mythological and cultic traditions would have proved too unsystematic. Rather, I suspect, Stoicism intended to serve the interpretation of theological poems and aimed at integrating into its philosophical system the traditional expressions of theology with a view to the creation of a broad cultural synthesis, including the traditional – but now philosophically legitimized – heritage. This meant a reevaluation of myth as bearer of truth, in its various traditional expressions: rituals, epithets, poetry, iconography. The Stoics, interested as they were in linguistics, etymology, poetry, and literature, intended to validate poetry and other expressions of myth and theology by means of allegoresis according to their own philosophical system. Such a validation was probably meant to construct a broad and organic cultural unity, systematic and comprehensive, based on the λόγος (Ramelli, 2014). The Stoics' insistence on Homer as the possessor of the truths of the various disciplines aimed at projecting onto the origins of culture that unity grounded in the λόγος that was the ideal of Stoicism.

Allegoresis in Hellenistic Judaism flourished with Philo, but he had precursors such as Aristobulus, the → Essenes, the Alexandrian Therapeutae, and others. Biblical allegoresis among Essenes and Therapeutae is attested by Philo *Prob.* 75–91 (esp. 82) and *De vita contemplativa*, devoted to the Therapeutae. Philo *Jos.* 151 attests that the episode of Joseph in Egypt was allegorized by thinkers who interpreted Egypt as the body and Pharaoh as the intellect. Aristobulus (2nd/1st cent. BCE), described as a Peripatetic by both → Clement of Alexandria and → Eusebius of Caesarea, applied philosophical allegoresis to Scripture, demonstrating that Aristotelianism derived from Scripture (Clem. *Strom.* 5.14.97.7). Orpheus, Pythagoras, Socrates, Plato, Aratus, and others also depended on Scripture and drew their philosophy from it (frgm. 4). Biblical allegoresis is particularly necessary for divine anthropomorphisms (frgm. 2). Aristobulus even allegorized an apocryphal Homeric verse on departing from Acheron in the sense of departure from vice and journeying towards the acquisition of true knowledge (frgm. 5).

Philo (d. c. 50 CE), who immensely influenced patristic allegoresis, applied a systematic allegoresis of Scripture in the light of Platonism, Stoicism, and Pythagoreanism. In the preface to his commentary on Ps 118, → Theodore of Mopsuestia, polemicizing against biblical allegoresis, claimed that Philo was the first who applied pagan allegoresis to Scripture. It is significant that a supplemental volume of *Biblia Patristica* is devoted to Philo. He believed that the Bible taught the doctrine of the ideas (Philo *Spec.* 1.41.45–48; *Quaest. Gen.* 2.82; *Mos.* 2.74–76, with an exegesis taken over by Origen). Thus, he read Scripture as an allegorical exposition of what were fundamentally Platonic doctrines. Philo (*Post.* 14; *Mut.* 7), and after him Clement, Origen, and → Gregory of Nyssa, buttressed apophatic theology by means of Exod 20:21 (Moses enters the darkness where God is), allegorized as a reference to God's unknowability. Philo's allegoresis, like Origen's, seems partially indebted to Stoic allegoresis and is deeply linked to philosophy, but in Philo it is applied to Scripture, not to Greek myths, and assumes a more systematic character. Moreover, the divinity that allegoresis reveals is transcendent for Philo, but immanent for the Stoics. Philo's scriptural exegesis influenced philosopher-exegetes such as Origen and Gregory of Nyssa, often in the tiniest details. And to allegoresis are attached important philosophical and theological concepts that passed on from Philo to these fathers. The result is that, both in Philo and in Origen and Gregory, philosophical materials are often inseparable from allegoresis (Ramelli, 2008).

In the New Testament, Paul (→ Paul the Apostle) is the great allegorizer and the only author to use a cognate term for "allegory." In Gal 4:24 he describes → Abraham, Hagar, Sarah, and their children as allegories (ἀλληγορούμενα). The two women are the two covenants. Paul also interpreted the rock from which the Hebrews drank in the desert as Christ (1 Cor 10:1–4). These passages were often invoked by patristic allegorists, as well as 2 Cor 3:6 was: "The letter kills, but the spirit vivifies." Among the first Christian supporters of the necessity of scriptural allegoresis are the author of the *Letter of Barnabas*, Justin Martyr, Valentinus, Ptolemy (the Gnostic), Irenaeus of Lyon, and Melito of Sardis. The early Christian terminology of allegory is varied: ἀλληγορία, ἀναγωγή (elevated sense), ὑπόνοια (under-sense), πνευματικά, and νοητά (spiritual and intelligible realities). Origen, however, used ἀλληγορία and cognates with circumspection, because they were linked with pagan allegorical traditions.

Origen, a Christian Middle/Neoplatonist, is certainly the greatest Christian allegorist. He was inspired by Philo, Paul, Clement, and Stoic and probably also Middle Platonic allegorists. The inclusion of allegoresis in philosophy, a typical Stoic feature, returned in Middle and Neoplatonism – which incorporated significant Stoic elements – not only on the pagan side, but also on the Christian: Origen included his theorization of biblical allegoresis not in an exegetical work, but in his philosophical masterpiece, *On First Principles* (Περὶ ἀρχῶν), since he too, like the Stoics, deemed allegory part and parcel of philosophy. He was very well acquainted with the works of Cornutus and Chaeremon. Porphyry considers Origen responsible for the transfer of the allegorical exegetical method from pagan myths to the Bible. He does not mention Clement, nor Philo or other Jewish allegorists. The same noteworthy, and likely intentional, omission is already found in Celsus (*ap.* Or. *Cels.* 4.51).

Besides the Stoics, Origen also knew Middle Platonic and Neo-Pythagorean allegorists, such as Numenius, who, apparently without being either Jew or Christian, allegorized the Septuagint and parts of what became the New Testament. Moreover, Origen was acquainted with gnostic allegorists, especially Valentinians, such as Heracleon, whose allegorical method he criticized, just as Philo had criticized the Hellenistic Jewish allegorists who preceded him: both these and the gnostics, in their extreme allegorizing, were said to have emptied the historical level of the Bible. This is also the main difference between Christian and pagan Platonic allegoresis: the Christians retained the historical plane of the Bible, while pagan Platonists thought that the stories in the myths never happened but are exclusively allegorical. In Origen's view the Bible has a literal meaning as well as an allegorical one, apart from only a few cases whose function is to show that deeper meanings must be sought out.

In Book 4 of *First Principles*, devoted to scriptural exegesis and also preserved in Greek in the *Philocalia*, Origen theorizes a threefold interpretation of Scripture, literal, moral, and spiritual, in which each level corresponds to a component of the human being (body, soul, and spirit) and to a degree of Christian perfection: *incipientes*, *progredientes*, and *perfecti*. In Or. *Princ.* 4.2.4 (*Philoc.* 1.11), Origen relies

on Prov 22:20, interpreted in the sense that one is invited to read the texts τρισσῶς, "in three ways" or "at three levels"; the aim of a correct reading of Scripture is the salvation of the human being in its three components and phases of development:

> It is necessary to write the meanings of the sacred Scriptures onto one's soul in a threefold way, that the simpler person may be edified by the flesh, so to say, of Scripture – I call so its most obvious meaning; the person who is advanced to some degree may be edified by its soul, as it were, and the perfect [...] by the spiritual law, which includes in itself "the shadow of the future goods." For, just as the human being consists of body, soul, and spirit, in the same way also Scripture does, which was given by the divinity in its providential economy for the salvation of humans.

In *Philoc.* 1.30 Origen considers these three stages of development from a historical perspective: the first phase is that of Jewish dispensation and corresponds to the *littera*, the "body" or "flesh" of Scripture (see also *Comm. Jo.* 6.227; *Hom. Lev.* 1.1); the second is that of the Christians at present; and the third is the spiritual one, in the eschatological dimension. Origen, however, in his exegesis did not always develop all three of these hermeneutical levels.

In *Princ.* 1, preface 8, Origen presents as a doctrine recognized by the church that the Scriptures have been written by means of God's Spirit and have a patent meaning and a hidden one, the latter eluding most people and including "the images of divine things." Origen assures that "the whole church entertains one and the same opinion: that all the Law is spiritual." This, which he presents as the orthodox position of the church, contrasts with both the "Jewish" and the Marcionite (→ Marcion/Marcionites/Marcionism) praxis of reading the Hebrew Bible only literally, and with the gnostic praxis of annihilating the historical level of Scripture by means of an exclusively allegorical meaning. This position is clear in Origen's polemic against Heracleon on the interpretation of John. For him, not only among the Jews – often just a rhetorical category – but among Christians, too, the spiritual sense escapes the majority, due to its difficulty. Since the Bible is full of enigmas and types (αἰνίγματα, τύποι), the simple (ἀπλούστεροι, *simpliciores*), actually most people (οἱ πολλοί, *quam plurimi*), interpret God's anthropomorphisms in the Hebrew Bible literally (πρὸς λέξιν, κατὰ τὸ ῥητόν, *Princ.* 4.2.1–3). Criticism of → anthropomorphisms ascribed to deities was precisely one of the main reasons that, in ancient Greece, first led to theological allegoresis.

For Origen, the most important scriptural sense is the spiritual, reserved for those to whom the Spirit communicates the meanings "no longer through letters, but through living words" (*Princ.* 4.2.4, reminiscent of Plato's "living speech" in *Phaedr.* 276A). As results from *Princ.* 4.3.6ff., the spiritual sense is divided into typology and allegory, but Origen does not draw a sharp and consistent distinction between the two. Hebrew Bible prophecies had their typological fulfillment in Christ. This reading was already found in Paul, as Origen notes in *Princ.* 4.2.6, describing Paul's exegesis as typological (τυπικῶς). But the facts of the Hebrew Bible cannot be just prefigurations of facts of the New Testamant; more broadly, they prefigure spiritual truths, because an elevation of level (ἀναγωγή) has to take place. Therefore, Origen speaks of multiple interpretations of the Bible: its spiritual meanings are inexhaustible.

Origen drew moral interpretation (*moralis interpretatio, moralis locus*: *Hom. Gen.* 2.6; *moralis doctrina vel ratio*: *Hom. Num.* 9.7) above all from Philo, who read the sacred text as an allegory of the troubles of the soul between good and evil. This "psychological" exegesis had already been Christianized by Clement. Origen, who uses it more systematically, considers this level – the "soul" of Scripture – useful for those who are making progress (*progredientes*), thanks to the moral teaching that they can find in it. Another source of Origen's allegoresis of Scripture, besides Stoics, Middle Platonists, and Philo, is Clement, who may not have been Origen's teacher, but was surely known to Origen and drew heavily on Stoic allegoresis. Clement remarked that in every people the expression of religious contents is characterized by hiddenness in the recess of the truth (Clem. *Strom.* 5.419.3–4). All those who spoke about God, barbarians and Greeks, hid the principles of being and expounded the truth only symbolically, through αἰνίγματα, σύμβολα, ἀλληγορίαι, μεταφοραί, and so on, like the Greeks' → oracles: for this reason, Apollo is called Loxias, "oblique" (*Strom.* 5.4.21). According to Clement, the Bible is pervaded by the principle of

intratextuality: each point in Scripture can be clarified thanks to similar points (*Strom.* 7.16.96.2–4). Likewise, Origen often speaks of "interrelation," "continuity," and "harmony" in all the parts of Scripture, and of "affinity" of the various exegetical readings to one another (Or. *Philoc.* 6; see 1.30). Therefore, he interprets the Bible with the Bible, relating a passage of Scripture to another in which similar concepts or terms occur, thus attaining the spiritual meaning of both. He does not take into consideration an isolated allegorical point, but a whole passage in its allegorical system. In *Philoc.* 2, from the commentary to Ps 1, Origen assimilates God's providence and power, which permeates everything, to the divine inspiration that pervades the whole Scripture, as far as the smallest details: "traces and hints" of God's wisdom are to be found everywhere, spread "in each letter"; for, as the Jewish masters asserted, the words of Scripture have been calculated "with the utmost accuracy"; not even one is superfluous. Therefore, it is necessary to "investigate Scripture down to its tiniest details" (Or. *Comm. Jo.* 32.6.68).

For Origen, the literal, historical level of Scripture maintains its full value in almost all cases. Whereas every scriptural passage has a spiritual sense, only very few are deprived of literal meaning (*Princ.* 4.2.5; 9) due to logical absurdities, paradoxes, or material impossibilities (*Princ.* 4.3.1–4). There are many more passages in Scripture that are endowed with a literal meaning (besides the spiritual) than those which are deprived of it and only have a spiritual sense (*ap.* Pamp. *Ap.* 123). Thus, for example, the whole story of the patriarchs is historical, and the miracle of Joshua really happened (*Ap.* 125). But God's anthropomorphisms, grammatical or factual incongruities, facts that did not really happen (*Princ.* 4.3.1), and legal prescriptions impossible to fulfill have "bare spiritual meanings," without a literal sense, which must send readers to seek a deeper meaning (*Princ.* 4.3.1), and legal prescriptions impossible to fulfill have "bare spiritual meanings" not wrapped in a literal sense, to have readers understand that it is necessary to seek for a deeper meaning (*Princ.* 4.2.9; *Philoc.* 1.16). For example,

> "The arms of the sinners will be shattered." How can this possibly be true in a literal sense, even in case one should try to force the meaning out of ineptitude? In Scripture there are many such

passages, which can induce, or better force, even one who is stupid like a beast and so asleep as to snore, to see that it is necessary to abandon the literal meaning and to ascend to the spiritual interpretation. (Or. *Hom. 3 Ps.* 36.7)

In a remarkable methodological passage, Origen observes:

But sometimes a useful discourse does not appear. And on other occasions, even impossible things are prescribed by the law, for the sake of those who are more expert and particularly fond of investigation, that, applying themselves to the toil of the examination of Scriptures, they may be persuaded by reason that in Scriptures it is necessary to look for a meaning *worthy of God.* (Or. *Princ.* 4.2.9)

Here Origen attaches to the study of Scripture the lexicon of philosophical investigation (ζητητικωτέρους, ἐξετάσεως, πεῖσμα ἀξιόλογον, ζητεῖν), because biblical allegoresis is an important part of *philosophy*; this is also why he included its theorization in his philosophical masterpiece. The very function of the few scriptural passages deprived of literal meaning is to have the exegete-philosopher realize that a philosophical scrutiny of Scripture is needed. This scrutiny seeks in the Bible meanings "worthy of God." Again, this was one of the very first factors that produced a search for allegorical meanings of myths whose literal sense sounded unworthy of the divine. But in Scripture, apart from few exceptions, "Even if these passages have a spiritual meaning, however their spiritual sense must be received only after first maintaining their historical truth" (*ap.* Pamp. *Ap.* 113). Thus, for instance, Jesus' → miracles, such as healing or resurrections, did take place historically, although they also mean spiritual healing and resurrections.

Within the Bible, however, there are narratives concerning the beginning (ἀρχή) and the end (τέλος) that escape this composite model of interpretation, literal and allegorical: the first sections of Genesis, with the account of the → creation of the world and of the human being, and Revelation. Their literal, historical meaning was the thinnest among all biblical books in Origen's eyes. In the prologue to his commentary on the Song of Songs, Origen ascribes a peculiar status to the first chapters of Genesis:

these must be studied only at the end of one's study plan, after the rest of Scripture, because the Genesis account of creation, just as the Song of Songs (and Revelation), must be entirely allegorized and cannot be taken literally. These biblical books are the δευτερώσεις, since they must be studied after the others. Therefore, they require a mature student. For the exclusively allegorical interpretation of the accounts of the *arkhē* and the *telos*, Origen was inspired, I surmise, by Plato's philosophical myths, which Origen explicitly praised as the only way of speaking of what is otherwise impossible to expound. He knew very well that Plato could use only a mythical, not theoretical, language when tackling the question of the *arkhē* – in his *Timaeus*, with which Origen was well acquainted – and the *telos*, in his eschatological myths such as that of Er and his other accounts of the underworld, with which Origen was also deeply familiar. To the *arkhē* and the *telos*, which lie before and after human historical experience, Scripture had to apply a mythical, and not historical, language, and this demands an allegorical interpretation. Origen declares that the *arkhē* and the *telos* have been left unclarified by the teaching of the church (Or. *Princ.* 1, preface 7) and are unknown even to angels (*Princ.* 4.3.14; Pamp. *Ap.* 82). This is why they are described only mythically and allegorically.

Origen included Genesis' whole account of the paradise and of creation among the scriptural passages deprived of literal meaning and susceptible only of allegoresis (*Princ.* 4.3.1), since no one endowed with intelligence will believe that three days, and an evening and a dawn, took place without sun, moon, and stars, and that the first day took place even without the sky:

Nobody can be so stupid as to believe that God, like a human farmer, planted a garden in Eden and put a visible and sense-perceptible tree of life therein, so that one, by eating its fruit with one's bodily teeth, could acquire life, and also could participate in good and evil after munching what is taken from that tree. If, then, God is said to stroll in the garden/Paradise in the evening, and Adam to hide under the tree, I do not think anybody will doubt that these things indicate *symbolical truths allegorically*, by means of what looks like a historical account, and yet has *never happened corporeally.*

One finds many examples of allegoresis of creation and the paradise in Origen's exegetical production, for instance "intelligible trees" (Or. *Hom. Gen.* 2.4), "intelligible rivers" and "intelligible woody valleys" in paradise (*Selecta in Numeros*; PG 12.581.B), and "Eden" etymologized as ἤδη, "once upon a time," to signify a primeval state (Or. *Fr. Gen.* 236). The first homily on Genesis bristles with passages from the creation story, of which only allegorical explanations are given. That the creation account must be allegorized emerges also from Or. *Hom.* 1 *Ps.* 36: "At the beginning, God is said to have planted a garden/ Paradise of delights, undoubtedly with the intention that in it we might enjoy *spiritual* delights."

By allegorizing the Hebrew Bible, Origen countered Marcionite claims that it was a product of an inferior God or evil demiurge and could not contain philosophical truths to be discovered through allegoresis. In *Hom.* 5 *Ps.* 36.5, Origen is thinking of Marcionites (and some gnostics) when denouncing their distinction between God the Creator and a superior God:

> The heretics imagine a certain other God superior to the Creator and deny that the God who created all things is the good God, in their impious preaching [...] if they are so mistaken in their thoughts it is because *they interpret the Law exclusively literally, and ignore that the Law is spiritual.*

Origen indicates the reason why, in his view, the Marcionites were so deceived: because they did not read the Hebrew Bible allegorically.

Yet Origen, like Philo, also blamed extreme biblical allegorists, who annihilated the historical plane of Scripture by exclusively applying allegoresis. In this way, these exegetes, such as some gnostics, transformed all the events narrated by Scripture into myths, which, as pagan Neoplatonists maintained, never happened historically. Instead Origen drawing inspiration from Plato's use of myths, distinguished the biblical accounts of the beginning and the end from the rest of Scripture: only these accounts are susceptible to an exclusively allegorical interpretation, since they are no historical narratives – and were compared by Origen to Plato's myths – while the rest of Scripture maintains its historical value along with many spiritual meanings.

Origen compared the Genesis story of the creation and fall of the human being to Plato's myths of Poros and Penia and the fall of the soul, claiming that they mythically expressed similar concepts and should be interpreted allegorically to get a philosophical truth out of them, whereas their literal expositions are laughable. His commentary on Genesis is lost, but from Or. *Cels.* 4.39 it is possible to grasp the terms of this comparison and Origen's own explanation of the reason why such striking similarities emerge between Plato's myth and the Genesis account of the ἀρχή:

> It is not quite clear whether this story [i.e. the myth of Poros] occurred to Plato's mind by chance or, as some believe, during his sojourn in Egypt Plato also ran into people who adhered to the philosophy of the Jews, learnt from them, and then retained some things and altered some others.

Origen mentions a Jewish *philosophy*, rather than religion, not only because from that philosophy stemmed what he wanted to present as *Christian philosophy* (Ramelli, 2015), but also because the allegorical interpretation of Scripture is a *philosophical* task, already performed by Jewish authors. In *Cels.* 4.51, after reporting Celsus' criticism of any allegoresis of the Bible, Origen observes that this is not only an attack on Christian, but also on Jewish, allegoresis of Scripture, as represented by Philo, Aristobulus, and others. Origen is creating for himself a non-Christian and pre-Christian ancestry in the philosophical allegoresis of Scripture. This ancestry seems to have been overlooked or intentionally obscured by Middle and Neoplatonists who opposed biblical allegoresis, such as Celsus and Porphyry.

The importance of the prerogative of correct interpretation of myths, in other words of the possession of the key to allegory, emerged in the dispute between pagan and Christian Middle and Neoplatonists on what myths were worthy of and susceptible to allegoresis. This was tantamount to asking what myths contained philosophical truths that had to be unveiled by allegoresis. The virulence of the debate betrays the cruciality of the question. Most pagan Platonists, apart from Numenius, denied that biblical myths hid philosophical truths; this is why Porphyry so sharply criticized the foremost Christian allegorist, Origen, for having applied the allegorical hermeneutics inherited from the Stoics to a text (Scripture) that, from his viewpoint, was not susceptible to it. Some pagan Middle and Neoplatonists such as → Celsus, Porphyry himself, and Julian – unlike Numenius – refused to recognize the Hebrew and Christian Bible, depriving it of a philosophical value and rejecting the principle, already supported by Philo, that this writing hid philosophical truths to be decoded by allegoresis. Celsus claimed,

> The more reasonable ones among both Jews and Christians interpret these stories allegorically [...] they have recourse to allegory because they are ashamed of them. [...] The more reasonable ones among Jews and Christians try to allegorize these stories someway; yet, they are not susceptible of any allegorical interpretation, but, on the contrary, they are bare myths, and of the most stupid kind. [...] However, the allegories that appear to be written on these myths are far more shameful and unlikely than the myths themselves, since, with astonishing and totally senseless madness, they link together things that are absolutely and completely incompatible with one another. (Or. *Cels.* 4.48; 4.50–51)

Indeed, Celsus believed "that in the Law and the prophets there is no deeper doctrine beyond the literal sense of the words" (*Cels.* 7.18).

Allegoresis was taken over by Origenian exegetes such as Gregory of Nyssa, who explicitly defended scriptural allegoresis in the prologue to his homilies on the Song of Songs (Ramelli, 2015); → Evagrius of Pontus (Ramelli, 2013); → Ambrose of Milan, who read both Philo and Origen in Greek; and Peter Chrysologus in Ravenna in the 5th century CE. Hearing Ambrose use 2 Cor 3:6 as a hermeneutical principle struck → Augustine of Hippo, because "he expounded spiritually, removing the mystical veil, texts which, taken literally, seemed to contain perverse teachings" (Aug. *Conf.* 6.4.6; 5.14.24). Augustine, however, later verged toward the literal and abandoned Origen's allegoresis as well as *apocatastasis* (see e.g. *De Genesi ad litteram* and Ramelli, 2013a).

Historiography

The study of ancient allegory and allegoresis (or allegorical exegesis) have been promoted by important monographs, commentaries, and collected works such as the works of J. Pépin (1958), D. Dawson (1992), P.T. Struck (2004), G. Dahan and Goulet (2005). The monograph by I. Ramelli (2004) is a systematic study of ancient allegoresis from the beginning of philosophy, especially on Ancient to Roman Stoicism; Ramelli (2007), Copeland and Struck (2010) and a Polet (2012) contain commented or translated editions of texts on Homeric myths, Stoic allegorises and allegories from classical antiquity own to the Renaissance. D.A. Russell and D. Konstan (2005) have offered a valuable commented translation of Heraclitus' *Homeric Problems* and H.-G. Nesselrath (2005) has done so with *Cebetis Tabula*; I. Ramelli (2001; 2006) has done so with M. Capella's allegorical work and his allegorical commentators, and in 2003 with the edition, translation, monographic study, and full commentary on Annaeus Cornutus' Handbook of Greek theological allegoresis. A concise investigation is provided by D. Konstan and I. Ramelli (2009).

Abundant literature is available on Jewish Christian and patristic allegoresis (mostly applied to Scripture, but also to Plato, as in the cases of Calcidius and Origen: see Ramelli, forthcoming), both as standalone and in its relation to Stoic and Platonic allegoresis. Philo's influence on patristic allegoresis makes the object of many studies (e.g. Geljon; Ramelli, 2008; 2012; 2018b; Runia). The philosophical value of allegory in Stoicism has been argued for by I. Ramelli (2016) and its reception in Platonism, pagan, and Christian (esp. Origen), has been investigated by I. Ramelli (2011a; 2014); for Evagrius alone see I. Ramelli (2013). Allegoresis in Origen has been explored by several scholars, from M. Simonetti to I. Ramelli to P. Martens (Martens, 2008; Ramelli, 2012). Further investigation is needed especially on the relations between "pagan" and Christian Platonism in the exegetical use of philosophical allegoresis.

Bibliography

Copeland, R., & P.T. Struck, eds., *The Cambridge Companion to Allegory*, Cambridge UK, 2010.

Dahan, G., & R. Goulet, eds., *Allégories des poètes, allégories des philosophes*, Paris, 2005.

Dawson, D., *Allegorical Readers and Cultural Revision in Ancient Alexandria*, Berkeley, 1992.

Konstan, D., & I. Ramelli, "Allegory I (Graeco-Roman Antiquity)," in: H.-J. Klauck et al., eds., *EBR*, vol. I: *Aaron–Aniconism*, Berlin, 2009, 780–785.

Lobel, E., & D.L. Page, *Poetarum Lesbiorum Fragmenta*, 1955.

Martens, P., "Revisiting the Allegory/Typology Distinction: The Case of Origen", *JECS* 16, 2008, 283–317.

Nesselrath, H.-G., ed., *Die Bildtafel des Kebes*, Darmstadt, 2005.

Pépin, J., *Mythe et allégorie: Les origines grecques et les contestations judéo-chrétiennes*, Paris, 1958.

Ramelli, I., ed., *Marziano Capella, nozze di Filologia e Mercurio*, Milan, 2001.

Ramelli, I., *Anneo Cornuto*, Milan, 2003.

Ramelli, I., *Allegoria*, Milan, 2004.

Ramelli, I., ed., *Tutti i commenti a Marziano Capella*, Milan, 2006.

Ramelli, I., *Allegoristi dell'età classica*, Milan, 2007.

Ramelli, I., "Philosophical Allegoresis of Scripture in Philo and Its Legacy in Gregory Nyssen," *SPhilo* 20, 2008, 55–99.

Ramelli, I., "Allegory II (Judaism)," in: H.-J. Klauck et al., eds., *EBR*, vol. I: *Aaron–Aniconism*, Berlin, 2009, 785–793.

Ramelli, I., "The Philosophical Stance of Allegory in Stoicism and its Reception in Platonism," *IJCT* 18, 2011a, 335–371.

Ramelli, I., "Ancient Allegory and its Reception throughout the Ages," *IJCT* 18, 2011b, 569–578.

Ramelli, I., "Philo as Origen's Declared Model," *SCJR* 7, 2012, 1–17.

Ramelli, I., "A Rhetorical Device in Evagrius: Allegory, the Bible, and Apokatastasis," in: A. Quiroga, ed., *The Purpose of Rhetoric in Late Antiquity: From Performance to Exegesis*, Tübingen, 2013, 55–70.

Ramelli, I., "Origen in Augustine: A Paradoxical Reception," *Numen* 60, 2013a, 280–307.

Ramelli, I., "Valuing Antiquity in Antiquity by Means of Allegoresis," in: J. Ker & C. Pieper, eds., *Valuing the Past in the Greco-Roman World*, Leiden, 2014, 485–507.

Ramelli, I., "*Ethos* and *Logos*: A Second-Century Apologetical Debate between 'Pagan' and Christian Philosophers," *VigChr* 69.2, 2015, 1–34.

Ramelli, I., "Stoic Homeric Allegoresis," in: C.P. Manolea, ed., *BCRA*, Leiden, 2021, 229–258.

Ramelli, I., "Annaeus Cornutus and the Stoic Allegorical Tradition: Meaning, Sources, and Impact," *AITIA* 8, 2018b.

Ramelli, I., "Apokatastasis and Epektasis in *Hom. in Cant.*: The Relation between Two Core Doctrines in Gregory and Roots in Origen," in: G. Maspero & M. Brugarolas, eds., *XIII International Colloquium on Gregory of Nyssa, Rome, 17–20 September 2014*, Leiden, 2018a, 312–339.

Ramelli, I., "Allegorizing and Philosophizing," in: R. Scott Smith & S. Trzaskoma, eds., *OHGRM*, Oxford, 2016.

Ramelli, I., "*Ethos and Logos*: A Second-Century Apologetical Debate between 'Pagan' and Christian Philosophers," *VigChr* 69.2, 2015, 1–34.

Ramelli, I., "Stoic Homeric Allegoresis," in: C.P. Manolea, ed., *BCRA*, Leiden, 2021, 229–258.

Ramelli, I., "The Reception of Paul in Origen: Allegoresis of Scripture, Apokatastasis, and Women's Ministry," in: S. Porter & D. Yoon, *The Pauline Mind*, New York, 2023.

Ramelli, I., "Secular and Christian Commentaries in Late Antiquity," in: G. Kelly & A. Pelttari, eds., *CHLLL*, Cambridge UK, forthcoming.

Rolet, A., ed., *Allégorie et symbole: Voies de dissidence? De l'antiquité à la renaissance*, Rennes, 2012.

Russell, D.A., & D. Konstan, eds., *Heraclitus, Homeric Problems*, Atlanta, 2005.

Struck, P.T., *Birth of the Symbol: Ancient Readers at the Limits of their Texts*, Oxford-Princeton, 2004

ILARIA L.E. RAMELLI

Allogenes, Book of

In nascent but already very complex discussions on the interpretation and religio-historical setting of the texts of the Codex Tchacos, the *Gospel of Judas* (→ *Judas, Gospel of*) attracted by far the utmost attention. One text of the Codex Tchacos that attracted less interest is the written witness that directly follows the *Gospel of Judas* in the chronological order of the Codex Tchacos, the *Book of Allogenes*, which was completely unknown before. That there were certain scripts that could be ascribed to a guarantor of tradition named Allogenes has already been known from evidence of late classic history of philosophy and theology. In chapter 16 of his *Vita Plotini* (*Life of Plotinus*), → Porphyry of Tyre mentions Christian marginal groups at the time of Plotinus who referred among other things to the apocalypses by Zoroaster, Zostrianos, Nekotheos, Allogenes, and Messos (for the philosophic and religio-historical setting of Plotinus' anti-gnostic explanation, see Alt, 1990, 15–20; Tornau, 2001, 394f.). According to Porphyry, the supporting groups of these scriptures courted the communication of Christian and Platonic ideas.

Nevertheless, they were strongly opposed by the representatives of contemporary Platonism. Plotinus already strived for a presentation of the inappropriateness of the gnostic recourses (→ Gnosis/Gnosticism) of Platonic traditions. Corresponding explanations by school-forming initiators of Neoplatonic reformulations of Platonic tradition of thought went down in a script that is today – as a consequence of its arrangement and editing by Porphyry – known as *Enneads* (2.9), it commonly carries the title *Against the Gnostics*. But even Porphyry himself emphasizes that he questions the claim of those gnostic revelatory scriptures. He proved that for example the apocalypse of Zoroaster was not hundreds-of-years-old Persian scripture. Rather, it was a fabrication that was written by that very Christian gnostic marginal group itself not long prior. These Neoplatonic explanations in turn correspond with heresiological explanations given by Epiphanius of Salamis, who additionally emphasizes that there had been a number of scriptures that refer to a figure named Allogenes (Epiph. *Pan.* 40.2.1).

The discovery of the → Nag Hammadi library showed that those anti-gnostic executions are not assumptions or defamations (for corresponding structures of argumentation in gnostic tracts as found in the Nag Hammadi library, see Koschorke, 1978, 242ff.; McLachlan Wilson, 1984, 535–550, 536; Popkes, 2007, 125–134).

With reference to its subscription, the first text of the eighth Nag Hammadi Codex is commonly referred to as *Zostrianos*. But this term falls short of the mark. In their current form, the last lines of this work appear in a cryptographically presented colophon, in which the last preceding lines are characterized as the revelation of Zostrianos and Zoroaster. Without entering a discourse about the naming of the tract, it can be stated that the eighth Nag Hammadi Codex is opened by a script that refers to Zostrianos and Zoroaster as guarantors of tradition and therefore parallels Plotinus' statements.

A corresponding affinity to → Plotinus' words can also be found in the 11th Nag Hammadi Codex, whose third script presents a figure called Allogenes as the protagonist. Information can be found in the end section of this document, which is insightful in its reference to the fourth text of the Codex Tchacos. In this context, the fictitious author claims to be the receiver and communicator of a secret revelation knowledge that he wrote down after careful deliberation and handed to his "son Messos." The text leads to the thesis that this document is the "seal for all the books of Allogenes." This information equals among other things a note by → Epiphanius of Salamis mentioned above, which claims that several writings exists that can be traced back to a guarantor of tradition named "Allogenes" (Epiph. *Pan.* 40.2.1). One of their writings apparently is the fourth text of the Codex Tchacos. The literary form and the religio-historical profile will be examined in more detail below. The beginning, which only survived in fragments, apparently reads "*The Book* [...]" (Cod. Tchac. 59.1). Based on the preceding explanation and the dominance of the figure of Allogenes, one can assume that the original superscriptio of this tract was simply named *The Book of Allogenes* (for that reason, tract Cod. Tchac. 4 is called *Book of Allogenes* in the following, while tract NHC XI,3 is referred to as *Apocalypse of Allogenes*).

Because of the absence of the end or the superscriptio of the fourth script of the Codex Tchacos, the genre has to be identified on the basis of content characteristics. The first preserved words directly address the reader with the expression paSh[re] ("My [son]," Cod. Tchac. 59.3). This detail is close to the outlined design of the *Apocalypse of Allogenes* (NHC XI,3) in which the also fictional author addresses the figure of Messos as his child and engages him to propagate the visions written down in this work (NHC XI,3 68.10ff.).

As the *Apocalypse of Allogenes*, the *Book of Allogenes* also has characteristics of a vision or audition report. More complicated is the answering of the question of who the subject of this vision report is. After the first lines of the *Book of Allogenes*, which are hardly text-critically reconstructable, starting in Cod. Tchac. 59.6ff. it is reported that a not specifically identified group prays for insight and revelation, which allows them to be saved. The prayer that they say is as follows:

> Lord God, you who are aboveall the great aeons, you who have no beginning and no end, grant us a spirit of knowledge for the revelation of your mysteries, so that we may know ourselves, namely, where we come from, where we are going, and what we should do in ordert hat we

may live. (Cod. Tchac. 59.17–25; Kasser & Wurst, 2007, 261)

These words are reminiscent of the seven fundamental questions of gnostic soteriology as referenced by → Clement of Alexandria (*Exc.* 78.2; GCS, vol. III, 131, 17–19), especially the first and fifth question ("Who were we?") and ("Where are we rushing to?"; concerning these questions referenced by Clement of Alexandria, see Foerster & Böhlig, 1979, 301f.). The importance of these questions for the intention of the message of the *Book of Allogenes* (Cod. Tchac. 4) may be recognized not least by the fact that they are repeated word for word once again in the following. According to the vision report, the not specifically identified group proceeds to a mountain called Thambor. The name "Thambor" evokes associations with the legendary design of synoptic narratives according to which a mountain called Tabor was the place of temptation or transfiguration of Jesus. This fact is even more remarkable when one considers that the following narrative flow of the *Book of Allogenes* (Cod. Tchac. 4) shows allusions to the temptation story as well as the story of transfiguration. Before these intertextual connections can be addressed, one has to visualize a literary circumstance that confronts the reader of this text with a peculiar phenomenon. According to this narration, the group says a second prayer on top of the mountain "Thambor" that, to the greatest extent, parallels the first prayer. In contrast to the first version, the addressed god is further identified and invoked with words that show a clear affinity to gnostic designations for God. In the first version the fragmentarily transmitted prayer is introduced by impersonally formulated words (Cod. Tchac. 59.10). In the second version the prayer is introduced by the direct address (Cod. Tchac. 59.17–20). A nearly word-by-word repetition of the previously formulated supplication for insight and revelation follows the detailed introduction (Cod. Tchac. 59.20–25). This impression is even heightened when looking at the further development in which a peculiar change concerning the description of the characters can be observed. Directly after this prayer follows the statement, "After Allogenes had spoken these words" (Cod. Tchac. 59.26). This information is surprising because beforehand a group is mentioned that prayed on a mountain called Thambor. Now only one person named Allogenes

is mentioned, whose identity apparently does not need to be explained to the reader and is now introduced as the main protagonist of the narrative. After Allogenes says his prayer, Satan (→ Devil) appears to him. In accordance with the narration of Jesus' temptation, Satan tries to win over Allogenes, and Allogenes resists the temptation. While the fictional narrative is told from the perspective of a third-person narrator until Cod. Tchac. 62.8, another abrupt change of the narrative text structure follows. Starting at Cod. Tchac. 62.9 the fictional figure Allogenes in first-person narration tells about his attempts to resist temptation by praying and that he received the vision of a luminous cloud. In the span of the preserved textual elements, this narrative level is maintained. Whether the *Book of Allogenes* (Cod. Tchac. 4) goes back to the level of direct communication between a fictional author and addressee at the end cannot – on the basis of the currently available evidential texts – be reconstructed.

The observations outlined here show that the *Book of Allogenes* (Cod. Tchac. 4) apparently attaches great importance to prayer practices. For a start, a nearly identical prayer, which thematizes insight and revelation, is repeated twice in a relatively small text area. The third prayer of Allogenes finally forms the condition for the praying individual to be granted the desired insight. These aspects suggest that the *Book of Allogenes* (Cod. Tchac. 4) portrays a liturgical prayer practice, for example a prayer practice within an initiation ceremony.

This assessment develops more profile when the traditio-historical reference values of the text are included in the discussion. As already mentioned, the first text passages show association with synoptic temptation and transfiguration stories. Under these circumstances one could assume that Allogenes is probably a name for Jesus. But this assumption does not fulfil the following narration. Instead, the name Allogenes seems to be – in my view – a generic term and a designation for those who belong to "another world," which means that they do not belong to the world of the maker of the given world but to the race of → *pleroma* of the world above.

The validity of this thesis becomes clear in the further development of the vision report in the *Book of Allogenes* (Cod. Tchac. 4), which shall be closer considered in the following. Differences within the

Book of Allogenes and the synoptic specifications are becoming apparent in the confrontation between Satan and Allogenes. These differences show the religio-historical profile of this script.

According to the story of temptations as found in the Sayings Source document, Jesus meets Satan after 40 days of → fasting. This tradition is based on Hebrew Bible and early Jewish ideas of creation according to whom the devil is a fallen creature of God that wants to lead humans astray from God's path. In the *Book of Allogenes*, Satan is no fallen angel but the creator of the given cosmos who wants to keep all "Allogenes" – that means all people of a foreign race – imprisoned in his world. The speech of Satan, which is unfortunately not preserved for the most part, ends with the demand: "And take for yourself what is in my world, and eat from my good things, and take yourself silver and gold and clothes" (Cod. Tchac. 60.9–13). The reaction of Allogenes corresponds with a gnostic reformulation of biblical stories. He vehemently emphasises that he does not belong to those whose existences are due to the lower maker. Instead, Allogenes addresses the higher maker of the world above in form of a prayer: "O God, you who are in the great aeons, hear my voice, have mercy on me, and save me from everything evil" (Cod. Tchac. 61.18–21; see Kasser & Wurst, 2007, 265).

As well as the introduction of the second prayer, the prayer of Allogenes is addressed to a God supposed to be living in "in the great aeons." The prayer leads to the situation that Allogenes receives a vision and an audition from the addressed world above. Although the length of the text cannot be defined precisely (the textual corpus is not reconstructable starting in Cod. Tchac. 62.26), the instructive text passage for the question posed reads as follows:

> Then Allogenes cried out with a loud voice, saying: "O God, you who are in the great aeons, hear my voice, have mercy on me, and save me from everything evil. Look at me and hear me in this forsaken place. Now let your ineffable light shine on me [...] Yea, Lord, help me, for I do not know [...] for ever and ever." And while I was saying this, look, a luminous cloud surrounded me I could not stare at the light around it, the way it was shining. (Cod. Tchac. 61.16–62.15; Kasser & Wurst, 2007, 265–267)

As already mentioned, this passage of the *Book of Allogenes* shows associations with synoptic narrations about the transfiguration of Jesus (Mark 9:2–10 parr.). The Matthean version is of particular importance. This can be especially demonstrated with the motif of a luminous cloud that is in the synoptic tradition forming only mentioned in Matt 17:5 (ἔτι αὐτοῦ λαλοῦντος ἰδοὺ νεφέλη φωτεινὴ ἐπεσκίασεν αὐτούς). However, the contental development of the luminous cloud motif in the *Book of Allogenes* is not close to New Testament traditions but to gnostic evidences that also contain the motif of a luminous cloud (concerning the historical linguistic classification of this text, it should be noted that the phrase *ouChpi Nouoiòn* is an example of middle and lower Egyptian insertions that characterize the Sahidic texts of the Codex Tchacos). The vision of the luminous cloud is paralleled by an addition that is realized on the textual level in first-person plural. A yet-unidentified figure from the world above assures Allogenes that his prayer has been heard and that he will return to his heavenly home in the higher eons.

> And I heard a word from the cloud and the light, and its shone over me, saying, "O Allogenes, the sound of your prayer has been heard, and I have been sent here to you to tell you the good news, before you leave this place." (Cod. Tchac. 62.15–24; Kasser & Wurst, 2007, 267)

As comforting as those words may be for Allogenes on an intertextual level, the external reader is left clueless. With these words, the preserved text of the *Book of Allogenes* ends. What further message the speech from the luminous cloud should provide and even how long this speech was are indistinguishable on the basis of the currently preserved textual evidences. Only few textual remains could be reconstructed from the following three pages of the Codex Tchacos. Nevertheless, the few preserved words of the introduction of the speech from the luminous cloud provide a basis of discussion for the definition of the religio-historical profile of the *Book of Allogenes* and its position in the Codex Tchacos. It can be noted that the motif of the knowledge conveying luminous cloud embodies an integral part of the message of this script. The prayers of the not-further-identified group and Allogenes are dominated by the request for redemption imparting knowledge from the world above. After all, the medium for conveying this knowledge is the luminous cloud. For this reason it is a good idea to look at further gnostic evidences that inherit such a motif as a next step. In view of the outlined aspects, one may conclude that the *Book of Allogenes* is a gem of gnostic history of literature that, despite its shortness and its poor state of preservation, enriches our knowledge of the imagination and composition of gnostic texts with some valuable details.

Historiography

The *Book of Allogenes* was unkown until the edition of Codex Tchacos. Because of this there is no such thing like a history of research or a history of discussion regarding the text yet. Nevertheless it is clear, that the text is another witness for pluriform spectrum of different systems within in the history of early Christianity.

Bibliography

Alt, K., *Philosophie gegen Gnosis: Plotins Polemik in seiner Schrift II 9*, Stuttgart, 1990, 15–20.

Foerster, W., & A. Böhlig, *Die Gnosis*, vol. I: *Zeugnisse der Kirchenväter*, BAW.AC, Zürich, ²1979, 301f.

Kasser, R., & G. Wurst, eds., *The Gospel of Judas, Critical Edition: Together with the Letter of Peter to Phillip, James, and a Book of Allogenes from Codex Tchacos*, Washington DC, 2007, 261.

Koschorke, K., *Die Polemik der Gnostiker gegen das kirchliche Christentum: Unter besonderer Berücksichtigung der Nag-Hammadi-Traktate "Apokalypse des Petrus" [NHC VII,3] und "Testimonium Veritatis" [NHC IX,3], NHS XII*, Leiden, 1978, 242ff.

McLachlan Wilson, R., "Gnosis II: Neues Testament/Judentum/Alten Kirche," in: *TRE*, vol. XIII, Berlin 1984, 535–550.

Popkes, E.E., *Das Menschenbild des Thomasevangeliums: Untersuchungen zu seiner religionshistorischen und chronologischen Verortung*, WUNT 206, Tübingen, 2007, 125–134.

Tornau, C., *Plotin: Ausgewählte Schriften*, Stuttgart, 2001, 394f.

ENNO EDZARD POPKES

Alms/Almsgiving

Gifts are always charged with significance, but what they mean is highly dependent on the cultural context in which they occur. The meaning of a gift may be determined in part by the pre-existing relationship between the donor(s) and the recipient(s), the nature of the gift, and the occasion of its bestowal set against a background of expectation, a community's conventional practices, and the discourses concerning them. Some gifts largely reinforce an earlier relationship; others form a radically new relationship between those involved. Almsgiving, gifts to the poor of money, food, clothing, or shelter because they are poor, was widely practiced in the ancient Near East and the Greco-Roman world where early Christianity developed; but the form such almsgiving took, and its significance, varied between communities which practiced polytheistic cults, Jewish communities, and early Christian churches. Furthermore, since these communities overlapped to some extent, and as early Christianity in particular was subject to rapid evolution, the significance of early Christian almsgiving must be established with careful attention to its form, time, and place.

One major element in shaping the significance of Christian almsgiving was the biblical canon. Numerous texts adopted from the Hebrew Scriptures either exhorted almsgiving (Deut 15:11; Isa 58:10), or valorized it as a mark of holiness (Job 29:15–16), or presented it as a source of divine reward (Ps 40:2). Several of the sacred texts found in the Septuagint (→ Bible) placed a high value first on almsgiving as effecting the → forgiveness of the donors' sins. This redemptive understanding of almsgiving which had developed in Hellenistic → Judaism was promoted, for example, in the citation by the 3rd-century CE African author, → Cyprian of Carthage, of Dan 4:27, Prov 15:27a, Sir 3:30 and 29:12, Tob 4:9–12 and 12:8–9, and Luke 11:41 (Cyp. *Eleem.* 2; 5; 20). Since this theology of post-baptismal forgiveness was later considered unorthodox by post-Reformation Protestants, its presence in the earliest strands of Christian thought was long downplayed by many historians, but has more recently received fuller recognition in the scholarship of R. Garrison (1993) and D.J. Downs (2012). Among the texts which were eventually revered as elements of the New Testament canon, the Gospel of Matthew (→ Matthew the Apostle) was of particular importance for its identification of the needy recipient of alms with the person of Jesus (Matt 25:31–46). Thus, → Augustine of Hippo made frequent reference to this passage in his advocacy of almsgiving (e.g. Aug. *Serm.* 9.21; 25.8; 38.8).

Continuity with Jewish almsgiving is also seen in the institutional forms of almsgiving practiced by some early churches. The corpus of letters attributed to Paul (→ Paul the Apostle) presented their hearers with the collection taken by the apostle from the Churches of Macedonia, Achaia, and Corinth for distribution among the Christians in Jerusalem (Rom 15:25–28; 2 Cor 8). Paul urged Christians in Galatia to "do good to all, but especially to those who belong to the household of faith" (Gal 6:10). Such gifts were thus analogous to the collections made among → Diaspora Jews for the Jerusalem Temple (→ Temple, Jerusalem) and articulated in similar fashion the desired religious unity of donors and recipients. For Paul, meeting "the needs of the saints" more generally expressed one's shared membership in Christ's body (Rom 12:13).

Chapters 4–6 of the Acts of the Apostles presented the role of the apostles and → deacons in the collection and daily distribution of alms to widows at Jerusalem. This may parallel the role of the synagogues in distributing alms among worshippers, and sanctioned the later role of church leaders, especially bishops and deacons, in the collection and distribution of alms to which the Christian poor, and widows in particular, had a privileged claim. Support for enlisted elderly Christian widows who were unsupported by their families was advocated at 1 Tim 5:1–16. The would-be martyr Ignatius of Antioch (→ Ignatius, Epistles of) urged Polycarp (a leading elder of the church at Smyrna in the first half of the 2nd century CE whom he addressed as its bishop; → Polycarp of Smyrna), to act as the φροντιστης/*phrontistes* ("guardian") of the church's widows (Ign. *Pol.* 4.1). At Rome, in the small church community to which → Justin Martyr belonged in the mid-2nd century CE, the head of the eucharistic assembly (→ Eucharist) was presented with a collection from the wealthier members for him to assist the needy (Just. 1 *Apol.* 67.6–8). We likewise hear from → Tertullian of a practice at Carthage at the end of the 2nd century CE when "on one day a month or when they wish each person contributes a modest sum in alms" to a fund which Tertullian terms a "sort of chest" (*arcae genus*), a term usually interpreted as referring to a poor box in which coins were dropped (Tert. *Apol.* 39). Tertullian does not reveal how these alms were then distributed. Some 50 years later, however, Cyprian's letters from hiding during persecution both express his dutiful concern as bishop, and assert his authority, to oversee the distribution of alms to the needy by his priests and deacons (Cyp. *Ep.* 5.1; 7.2). Christians were strongly encouraged to give as alms from what they saved in → fasting by the author of the *Shepherd of Hermas* (*Sim.* 5.3.7; → Hermas), a work perhaps originating at Rome in the early 2nd century CE, but much more widely read.

Gifts by the powerful to their clients in the Greco-Roman world were met with a corresponding bestowal of honor by the recipients who praised the virtues of their generous benefactors. Gifts to beggars who could make no such return traditionally fell outside this circle of virtuous giving. Seneca in the *De Beneficiis* (*On Favors*) had explicitly stated that odd gifts to beggars were too trivial to serve as benefactions (Sen. *Ben.* 4.29). However, the expectation of a proper return for favors granted led some Christians to portray widows and other recipients of alms within the church community as the altar on which the donor placed his or her gift. In return for alms, the recipients' prayers were offered up to God for their benefactor. Polycarp stressed the widows' responsibility to act as such altars in a manner acceptable to God (Pol. *Phil.* 4.3). A similar note was later struck in the church order we know as the → *Apostolic Constitutions*: a person in need of alms because orphaned at a young age, or old and infirm, weakened by illness, or raising a large family, is honored by God when he or she prays (→ Prayer) continually and zealously for benefactors "making a recompense as far as possible for the gift through prayer" (*Apos. Con.* 4.3.3). Where the church re-distributed large gifts from a wealthy donor, it might facilitate the recipients' prayers by advertising the donor's name. By the early 4th century CE it was expected that a donation by one wealthy Carthaginian would have been accompanied by the proclamation "Lucilla gives you this from her own belongings" (*Gesta Zenoph.* 18; 20; → Wealth).

The assertion that God honored the needy Christian who prayed for the almsgiver contrasts with older attitudes in which radical dependency rendered the beggar contemptible. → Clement of Alexandria's *Salvation of the Rich* (*Quis dives salvetur?*) urged would-be donors in the early 3rd century CE not to turn away from the Christian poor in repugnance at their appearance; and to lessen that repugnance he re-characterized them as a retinue of bodyguards whose prayers warded off danger (Clem. *Quis div.* 33–34). The residual weight of traditional attitudes may be measured, however, by how promoters of almsgiving interpreted Luke 16:9. Alms given to the poor were not generally understood to make the receivers their benefactors' friends. Ambrose, for example, in 4th-century CE Milan took the verse to mean that donors won friends among the saints and the angels by means of their gifts to the poor (Ambr. *Exp. Luc.* 7.245; → Ambrose of Milan). Clement may be the partial exception in that he urged the rich to become friends of God through their gifts to the Christian poor, among whom some one or more beneficiaries would be a friend of God; but Clement stops short of identifying the poor as the benefactors' friends (for a different emphasis, see O'Brien, 2004). Augustine drew on the biblical injunction to store up treasure in heaven to characterize the destitute as "porters, cargo- or baggage-handlers" (*laturarii*). They carried the bags of the wealthy to heaven when earthly goods given to them as alms were thereby transformed into spiritual wealth. The image, familiar to inhabitants of a busy port, turned passive recipients into active agents, but did not turn the poor into the social equals of their benefactors (e.g. Aug. *Serm.* 38.9; *Serm.* 53A.6).

By the early 4th century CE, re-characterization of the poor, together with large gifts for distribution among many recipients, facilitated the re-characterization of almsgiving as a virtuous benefaction practiced by better-off Christians. Almsgiving was thus incorporated within euergetism. This was the traditional practice of making public gifts by which an elite displayed their munificence and thereby reinforced their status within the civic community (Patlagean, 1977). → Lactantius attacked Cicero for advocating a counterfeit or spurious virtue of *liberalitas*, which was wrong precisely because it omitted almsgiving (Lact. *Inst.* 6.11). → Eusebius of Caesarea' *Ecclesiastical History* included a letter by Pope Cornelius (→ Cornelius [Bishop of Rome]) in which the Roman bishop described the recipients of Christian alms at Rome as fed by the Lord's favor and φιλανθροπια/ *philanthropia* ("love for humankind"), a virtue which the historian later applies to would-be charitable Christians: Licinius had decreed that no-one was to show *philanthropia* by their gifts of food to prisoners (Eus. *Hist. eccl.* 6.43.11; 10.8.11). → Basil of Caesarea similarly incorporated almsgiving within the virtue of *philanthropia*: the rich farmer in the Gospel of Luke (12:16–20; → Luke, Gospel of) should have imitated Joseph by his *philanthropia* in opening his granaries to the needy (PG 31.263a). The funeral orations delivered by → Gregory of Nazianzus for his sister Gorgonia and for his father, a local bishop, both present copious almsgiving as part of μεγαλοψυχια/ *megalopsuchia* ("greatness of heart"; Greg. Naz. *Or.* 8.13; 18.21). Both bishops and lay people proudly advertised their status in Christian circles as a "lover of the poor": a Roman epitaph of 341 CE praises both the deceased, Iunianus, as such an *amator pauperum*, and likewise styles his wife Victoria as *amatrix pauperum* (*ICUR*, vol. I, 1420).

The re-configuration of classical euergetism to include virtuous almsgiving facilitated the large-scale grant by Christian emperors of grain to the major churches for the bishops and their deacons to distribute to the needy (Delmaire, 1989). This replaced the imperial gifts which previously supported the temple cults of Greco-Roman cities and articulated the same piety – an emperor's responsibility to support worship which would secure the peace of the empire. Constantine, for example, had grain sent to the Alexandrian Church each year for redistribution to widows and possibly others among the poor. → Athanasius of Alexandria was accused of manipulating the grant for his own ends (Athan. *Apol. sec.* 18.2). The accusation suggests the degree to which imperial funds could raise the status of the bishop who distributed them.

High-ranking women in the imperial family were praised for a form of almsgiving which developed from the late 4th century CE: the foundation of hospitals or hostels where the sick and elderly poor could obtain shelter, food, and nursing. One of the earliest had been founded by Basil at Caesarea in 372 CE shortly after he became bishop there (Bas. *Ep.* 94). Eudocia, wife of Theodosius II, founded several such hostels, as did Theodosius' sister → Pulcheria (Constantelos, 1991; Theoph. Conf. *Chron.* 81). Monastic hostels in Judea, Syria, and elsewhere were often centers for the care of the sick (Choi, 2020).

The rise and spread of monasticism (→ Monasticism) from the late 3rd century CE involved almsgiving both to and by individual monks and monasteries (Brown, 2016). Lay donors were keen to win through alms the prayers of holy ascetics, whether male or female. The very wealthy sometimes founded monasteries on their estates. They might pressed gifts on famous monks whom they were anxious to visit. However, a monk in the semi-anchoretic tradition (→ Anchorite) was meant to earn his living by manual labor, and to practice almsgiving himself from the meager resources his labor had obtained. Reception of alms might tempt the monk to avarice. A letter on the anchoretic life ascribed to Basil but probably from a later hermit warned against acceptance of alms for redistribution precisely because it exposed the hermit to the charge of being "money-loving" (Bas. *Ep.* 42.3). Egyptian monastic literature (→ Monasticism), in particular the hagiography of sainted monks, distanced the latter from any receipt of alms. The literature probably hides the economic dependency of many monks on the alms of the lay faithful (Wipszycka, 1996). Gerontius in his *Life of Melania the Younger* (38; → Melania Junior) told how she and her husband hid gold in the cell of Abba Hephestion when he refused to accept it. When the monk discovered it on the pilgrims' departure, he first remonstrated with them, and finally flung it into the river.

On the other hand, suburban and remote monasteries might facilitate regular almsgiving through appointed officers. The *Historia monachorum* (18; Gk version) described a monastic federation comprising several houses, whose members gave a portion of their income for distribution to the needy. Grain was sent by boat to feed the poor of Alexandria, as there were not enough recipients in the vicinity of the monasteries to benefit. The author claimed that such gifts were made by almost all Egyptian monks.

A monastic leader such as → Shenoute of Atripe in 5th-century CE Egypt was able to redistribute vast sums of money and thereby cut a powerful figure in wider society. By describing the gifts received as "blessings," Shenoute distanced gifts from their lay donor, allowing him to maintain and advance his own status (López, 2013).

The self-dispossession of wealth through almsgiving on entry into a monastic or other ascetic life became a *topos* of Christian → hagiography. Thus, in the 4th-century CE *Life* of → Antony the Great, the future holy man was meditating on Acts, chapter 4, when he entered church and heard Matt 19:21 being read. At once, he left the church and organized the sale of the family estate, the proceeds of which he then gave to the poor after reserving a portion for his unmarried sister (Athan. *Vit. Ant.* 1). However, not all churchmen advocated just self-dispossession by the very rich, which risked rending the social fabric that bound slaves, tenants, and landowners in a stable common life (Allen, Neil & Mayer, 2009).

Almsgiving became associated with particular times and places. Although Christians were exhorted to give alms throughout the year, they were urged to do so especially in → Lent. Thus, Augustine's winter and Lenten preaching frequently promoted almsgiving as did sermons which he preached at designated times of fasting, such as the ember days around → Pentecost. While beggars were often found at the doors to baths as well as church doors, by late antiquity almsgiving featured in how many pilgrims approached a martyr's shrine or that of any saint whom they wished to intercede for them (Chrys. *Stat.* 1; PG 49.29).

The clergy, though not poor in comparison with the destitute, were generally entitled to a share in proportion to their rank of the offerings made to the church by the laity. While these offerings were not generally understood as forms of almsgiving, Augustine in *Sermon 3* found in Erfurt developed a theology of reciprocity in which such offerings featured alongside almsgiving. The church was the setting for exchanges in which the clergy and the destitute benefited from the material support of the laity, and the laity benefited both from the spiritual goods supplied by the clergy but also from the eternal life which rewards their almsgiving:

In return for these paltry, earthly and transitory things, for the food which is given to Christ hungering in his little ones, he will give not something of his own but his very self. What a champion will there be in that contest, the prize in which will be the judge himself! (Aug. *Ep.* [*Erf.*] 3.4)

The church is a school of mutual support:

God wants to teach his little ones through the stewardship of other men and wants to support his stewards through the ministration of other men, so that while each supplies what the other lacks, they grow heavy with good will and bring forth good deeds.

Finally, the belief that almsgiving expiated post-baptismal sin led by the 6th century CE in late antique Gaul to almsgiving as part of dutiful prayer for the dead. This came to be effected through gifts of land to the church for the feeding of the poor, a development which contributed to the belief that church property had been consecrated to God who would punish those who sought to alienate it for their own ends (Brown, 2015).

Historiography

Study of almsgiving in the first six centuries of the Common Era may be traced back to É. Chastel (1853). É. Chastel drew on sermons, treatises, *vitae*, and legal texts to describe Christian "charitable" care for the poor, but his definition of charity precluded consideration of pagan and Jewish almsgiving, while Christian sources were read without regard to their rhetorical strategies. This led to a misreading of developments in the post-Constantinian Churches as indicative of a decline in charitable ardour. G. Uhlhorn (1882) covered the same period, but interpreted changes through a Lutheran lens opposing faith to works. A breakthrough in understanding the continuity between Jewish and Christian almsgiving as expressive of virtue (unlike pagan almsgiving), came in H. Bolkestein (1939). Christians and Jews were now seen to share motives for giving, in particular, belief in the redemptive value of almsgiving, as explored by L.W. Countryman (1980) and R. Garrison (1993), who both focused on the early Roman Empire. Examination of almsgiving's

relationship to euergetism in the Greco-Roman world owes much to E. Patlagean (1977). Attention on the later Roman Empire begins in earnest with B. Ramsey (1982). P. Brown (1992) encouraged study of the relations between Christian discourse and practice in almsgiving, the topic of R. Finn (2006).

Bibliography

Allen, P., B. Neil & W. Mayer, *Preaching Poverty in Late Antiquity: Perceptions and Realities*, Leipzig, 2009.

Bolkestein, H., *Wohltätigkeit und Armenpflege in Vorchristlichen* Altertum, Utrecht, 1939.

Brown, P., *Power and Persuasion in Late Antiquity*, Madison, 1992.

Brown, P., *The Ransom of the Soul: Afterlife and Wealth in Early Western Christianity*, Cambridge MA, 2015.

Brown, P., *Treasure in Heaven: The Holy Poor in Early Christianity*, London, 2016.

Chastel, É., *Études historiques sur l'influence de la charité*, Paris, 1853.

Choi, H.G., *Between Ideals and Reality: Charity and the "Letters" of Barsanuphius and John of Gaza*, Macquarie, 2020.

Constantelos, D., *Byzantine Philanthropy and Social Welfare*, New York, ²1991.

Countryman, L. W., *The Rich Christian in the Church of the Early Empire*, New York, 1980.

Delmaire, R., *Largesses sacrées et res privata: L'aerarium impérial et son administration du IVᵉ au VIᵉ siècle*, Rome, 1989.

Downs, D.J., "Prosopological Exegesis in Cyprian's 'De opere et eleemosynis'," *JTI* 6/2, 2012, 279–293.

Finn, R., *Almsgiving in the Later Roman Empire*, Oxford, 2006.

Garrison, R., *Redemptive Almsgiving in Early Christianity*, Sheffield, 1993.

López, A.G., *Shenoute of Atripe and the Uses of Poverty: Rural Patronage, Religious Conflict, and Monasticism in Late Antique Egypt*, Berkeley, 2013.

O'Brien, D., "Rich Clients and Poor Patrons: Functions of Friendship in Clement of Alexandria's *Quis Dives Salvetur*," unpubl. diss., Oxford, 2004.

Osiek, C., "The Widow as Altar: The Rise and Fall of a Symbol," *SecCen* 3/3, 1983, 159–169.

Patlagean, E., *Pauvreté économique et pauvreté sociale à Byzance 4e–7e siècles*, Paris, 1977.

Ramsey, B., "Almsgiving in the Latin Church: The Late Fourth and Early Fifth Centuries", *Th. St.* 43, 1982, 226–259.

Uhlhorn, G., *Die christliche Liebestätigkeit in der alten Kirche*, Stuttgart, 1882.

Wipszycka, E., *Études sur le christianisme dans l'Égypte de l'antiquité tardive*, Rome, 1996.

RICHARD FINN

Altar

Throughout history, the meaning of the altar has been subject to change. The change in meaning was related to the change in concrete historical circumstances.

1. The Altar in the Hebrew Bible

The altars in the Hebrew Bible (→ Bible) were not only places of sacrifice, but also objects of remembrance and places of prayer. The book of Exodus shows a development in construction and use of the altars: on the one hand, the people in the desert still knew the crude stone altars of remembrance; on the other hand, the book also depicts an idealized situation, colored by the later → Temple in Jerusalem, with the construction of altars from precious materials that required much craftsmanship. It is unlikely that such altars were transported in the desert. That the people had a tent sanctuary as a place to meet God is plausible. In the time of the kings, Solomon builds the Temple in Jerusalem, place for the ark, and as a place for the sacrificial cult. The description of the first book of Kings twice mentions an altar lined with gold in the back hall where the ark also stood (1 Kgs 6:20; 6:22; see 1 Kgs 7:48). This probably refers to the altar of incense. At the dedication of the Temple, the ark is placed in it. In 1 Kgs 8:64, the bronze altar of burnt offering is mentioned. 1 Kgs 9:25 reports that Solomon offered a slaughter and burnt offering on the altar three times a year, and also burned incense before the face of the Lord. So even according to later sources, the Temple had two altars, a bronze altar of burnt offering and a golden altar of incense. The book of Ezra describes the returned exiles building an altar on the site of the destroyed Temple in Jerusalem and offering sacrifices, according to the law of Moses (→ Law/Decalogue/Torah; → Moses). In the book of Nehemiah, it is notable that the construction of the Temple takes place in ever-expanding circles, starting with the altar. Seventy years after the birth of Jesus, the Romans destroyed the Second Temple. Both altars disappeared and the centuries-old sacrificial service in the Jerusalem Temple came to an end.

a. The Altar in the New Testament

The New Testament has two different perspectives on the altars of the Temple in Jerusalem. On the one hand, it describes a situation in which the Temple was still in full operation and in which Jesus, his apostles, and his followers, also visited that Temple and participated in the sacrificial cult. On the other hand, the New Testament also has the situation of the destroyed Temple. For the nascent Christian movement, the destruction of the sanctuary influenced the reflection on the person of Jesus as the new Temple, his death as the new atonement sacrifice, and the → Eucharist as its remembrance. The Epistle to the Hebrews (→ Hebrews, Epistle to the) describes the new high priest as the one-time sacrifice that brings reconciliation between God and men and makes all sacrifices redundant. At the end of this letter, the concept of the altar also comes up: "We have an altar from which the priests of the tabernacle may not eat" (Heb 13:10). The Epistle to the Hebrews is a somewhat obscure text, which most interpreters believe to refer to the opposition between the old covenant and the new order of salvation. The altar referred to would then refer to Jesus himself: he sacrificed his life; he is the new altar with the new, one-time sacrifice of his own life. We thus find the later liturgical view of the altar as a symbol of Christ already in present in nuce in this New Testament text.

Many places in the New Testament mention "sacrifice" in connection with Christ's death (→ Sacrifice). However, in connection with the eucharistic meal, instituted to commemorate that death (Matt 26:20; Mark 14:18; Luke 22:14), the word "altar" is nowhere used in the New Testament. In the First Letter to the Corinthians, Paul (→ Paul the Apostle) does speak of "the Lord's table." There he sharply contrasts partaking of the Eucharist with partaking of sacrificial meals of idols (1 Cor 10:21). There is a substantive parallel between the pagan altars and the table of the Eucharist. In both cases, whoever eats from it has fellowship with the one to whom sacrifices were made. So, it was in the Temple cult of Israel (1 Cor 10:18), so it is with the sacrifices to idols, which according to Paul are actually sacrifices to demons (→ Demonology/Demons), and so it is with the sacrifice of Christ: whoever eats from it is in communion with his body (1 Cor 10:16).

2. Early Christianity

Depending on their background, early Christians knew the altars of the Jewish Temple and/or the many altars of the Greek, Roman, and Hellenistic religions. In their own liturgy of prayer, Scripture reading and Eucharist, as attested by the New Testament, the term "altar" did not yet play a role. Their meetings took place in private homes and for the celebration around bread and wine that Jesus had left them, they probably used a table or something similar from the furniture of the house in question. Soon, however, the word "altar" (*thusiasterion*) was used in connection with the Eucharist. Ignatius of Antioch (→ Ignatius, Epistles of) writes in his *Letter to the Philadelphians* (4.1):

> See to it that you maintain one Eucharist, for there is one body of our Lord Jesus Christ and one chalice for unity in his blood; there is one altar, just as there is one bishop, together with the presbytery and the deacons.

Even though he seems to be talking about an actual used object called altar, we must assume that he is using the word "altar" symbolically here. After all, there is no indication that even then people used altar for the piece of furniture on which bread and wine were placed. "We have no temples and no altars" was a self-evident expression in the 2nd century CE: people were distancing themselves from pagan religion.

No Christian altars have survived from the first three centuries CE. Wooden tables will often have been used, even when there were already church buildings. Second-century CE frescoes show a simple wooden table with three legs, on which the gifts of bread and wine are placed and where a priest says a prayer with his hands raised. There was not much focus on the object of the altar in those first centuries; the bishop's seat in the apse was considered a more important liturgical symbol than the table of the Eucharist. In the so-called papal crypt in the Catacomb of Saint Calixtus, one finds traces of a bishop's seat and of a base plate of an altar of 80 by 48 cm.

Gradually, the table of the Eucharist, fixed or movable, assumed an increasingly important role (Heid, 2019). Possibly it was in opposition to the all-spiritualizing tendency of Gnosticism (→ Gnosis/Gnosticism) that people began to emphasize the concrete and material of the gifts of bread and wine and of the physical sacrifice of the man Jesus Christ. Thus, the sacrificial walk develops with the gifts of the people brought to the altar, giving greater emphasis to the altar. → Irenaeus of Lyon (d. 202 CE) says that then also that → Word (Christ) gave his people the precept to offer sacrifices, not as if he needed them, but so that they might learn to serve God, just as he also wants us to offer the gift (namely of bread and wine) regularly and without interruption (Iren. *Haer.* 50.4.8.18, no 6 (PG, vol. VII, col. 1029).

The altar is explicitly so named and assumes a more important place when Christianity becomes from the Edict of Milan (313 CE) a permitted religion and gradually more and more the dominant religion. Constantinian altars were likely of the → *mensa* ("table") type, that is, open structures formed by a horizontal plate on associated supports. They could usually be used quite flexibly, were movable but had a fixed location, usually several meters from the wall of the apse. Stone altars were probably also placed in the large, richly decorated churches built from the 4th century CE onwards. A report is already known from the early 4th century CE that a Roman prefect ordered the destruction of church buildings with their altars, indicating an altar as a fixed structure. Based on archaeological research, it has been established that fixed altars were already common in North Africa by the end of the 4th century CE, while in the Middle East they only appeared during the 6th century CE (Duval, 2005, 13). → Augustine of Hippo mentions that people knew the custom of celebrating the Eucharist at the grave of a martyr (→ Martyrs) on the anniversary of his death (Aug. *Conf.* 9.11.27; see also *Serm.* 318).

Altars above a martyr's tomb and facilities to reach the tomb below the altar, called *confessio*, then gradually emerged (Gerhards, 2000, 273). Later, from the 6th century CE onwards, the conviction that a martyr's tomb belongs to every altar prevailed and → relics of witnesses of faith were placed under or in the altar. "This ultimately created, in reverse to the original intention, the assumption that relics are a necessary part of the altar" (Gerhards, 2000, 276). From this time, an altar was also considered consecrated only when relics were placed in it and the first Mass was celebrated on it. In the time of the church fathers, the altar was austere and empty; only in the Middle Ages is there a tendency to fill the altar with objects of devotion (see Fuchß, 1999, 17).

Historiography

J.B. te Velde (2013) summarizes theological and (art-historical) research. S. Heid (2019), draws on an impressive wealth of sources and literature, and provides a good critical discussion of theories concerning the absence of the sacred altar in the early Christian communities.

Bibliography

Braun, J., *Der christliche Altar in seiner geschichtlichen Entwicklung*, 2 vols., Munich, 1924.

Duval, N., "L'autel paléochrétien: Les progrès depuis le livre de Braun (1924) et les questions à résoudre," *HAM* 11, 2005, 7–17.

Fuchß, V., *Das Altarensemble: Eine Analyse des Kompositcharakters früh- und hochmittelalterlicher Altarausstattung*, Weimar, 1999.

Gerhards, A., "Der christliche Altar: Opferstätte oder Mahltisch?" in: A. Budde, *Das Opfer: Biblischer Anspruch und liturgische Gestalt*, Freiburg, 2000, 272–285.

Heid, S, *Altar und Kirche: Prinzipien christlicher Liturgie*, Regensburg, 2019.

Velde, J.B. te, *Het verhaal van het altaar: Een dynamisch fenomeen in de christelijke liturgie*, Nijmegen, 2013 (Dutch).

J.B. TE VELDE

Altar of Victory

The Altar of Victory was dedicated on Aug 28, 29 BCE, in the Senate House (*Curia Julia*) in Rome. Augustus encouraged this because, according to → Suetonius (*Aug.* 35), he wanted the Senate to perform their duties more conscientiously after the civil war. Next to the altar, → Augustus placed a statue of the goddess Victory brought from Taranto; this statue, according to Dio Cassius (*Hist. rom.* 51.22), signified that Augustus had received the empire through the divine support of the goddess. The Senate accepted the gift and, by a senatorial decree (*Senatus Consultum*), declared the day of the altar's dedication a holiday (Degrassi, 1963, 503–504).

By the 4th century CE, the statue and Altar of Victory were revered ornaments in the Senate, associated with the military success of the emperor and hence critical for the continued survival of the Roman Empire. To demonstrate their loyalty, senators swore oaths on this altar, most notably to the emperor on the day of his accession to power. Senators also traditionally burned incense and offered libations on this same altar before meetings of the Senate. Because of these pagan and sacrificial associations, however, the Christian emperor Constantius II removed the altar from the Senate House during his visit to Rome in 357 CE (Sym. *Rel.* 3.6–7; Am. 16.10.4–12). Most likely, the altar was returned after a successful appeal to the pagan emperor Julian (359–361 CE), and it was certainly back in the Senate House by 382 CE when the Christian emperor Gratian ordered its removal once again (Sym. *Rel.* 3.1). At this time, Gratian also took certain financial steps against the state cults (Sym. *Rel.* 3.11–15).

Gratian's actions met with protest; a delegation of senators headed by the pagan aristocrat Symmachus went to the imperial court in Milan to present their case but were denied access (Sym. *Rel. 3*; Liebeschuetz, 2005, 69–78). Two years later, under the newly elevated boy-emperor Valentinian II, the then urban prefect Symmachus went on a second delegation, for which he wrote a state paper (*Rel.* 3.1–2) requesting the restoration of the altar and a return to preexisting financial arrangements for the state cults. The bishop of Milan, Ambrose (→ Ambrose of Milan), got wind of this request and drafted a letter of protest to the emperor Valentinian II (Ambr. *Epist.* 72; [Maur. 17]; Zelzer, 1983); and after getting a copy of Symmachus' third state paper, Ambrose drafted a second letter (*Epist.* 73; [Maur. 18]; Zelzer, 1983), which was composed only after the emperor Valentinian II had turned down the pagan petition of 384 CE. Ambrose claimed in a later letter (Ambr. *Epist. EC* 10 [Maur. 57.2]; Zelzer, 1983) which he sent to the usurper Eugenius in 394 CE that his two earlier letters about the altar had been read aloud to the then emperor Valentinian.

These documents survive for reasons that will be discussed below, and they have subsequently taken on great significance for modern scholars because they present, in clear and articulate prose, the views of one eminent pagan senator and of one important Christian bishop about the religious transformation of the Roman state in the last decades of the 4th century CE. The letters also provide important information for historians seeking to better understand imperial policy *vis-à-vis* the pagan cults.

Although some modern scholars question how widespread the contemporary significance of the Altar of Victory controversy was, it is clear that later generations in the Latin West did see this as a key issue in the Christianization of the Roman Empire. Two decades later, in late 402/403 CE (Cameron, 2011, 337–341), the Spanish poet Prudentius (*Contra Symmachum*, Books 1 and 2) memorialized the controversy in epic poetry as part of his demonstration that Symmachus' arguments in his third state paper were wrong and hence that Christianity was the right religion for Rome. Paulinus, writing his *Life of Ambrose* in 412/413 CE, also saw the Altar of Victory controversy as an important demonstration of this bishop's character and rhetorical skills, consulting the bishop's own letters on this topic as evidence of Ambrose's faith and courage (P.Deac. *Vita Ambr.* 26–27).

1. The Altar of Victory and the Statue of Victory: The Physical Evidence

Before addressing the 4th-century CE controversy, it is of some importance to realize the historical and symbolic importance of the Altar of Victory and the statue of the goddess that had stood beside it for four centuries. In excavations from the 1930s inside the Curia that had been rebuilt by → Diocletian after a fire, there was found a concrete square base on the raised podium assumed to be for the head of the senate at the far end of the building (Tortorici, 1999, 150). The excavators hypothesized that this was where the statue of Victory stood, with the altar presumably in front of the statue, even though they found no physical remains of the altar or the statue. If this is the 4th-century CE location, then the position of both may have changed at some point in time. In the early 3rd century CE, as Herodian (*Hist.*

5.5) relates, the statue was then located in the center of the building, with senators "burning frankincense and pouring libations of wine," presumably on an altar in front of the statue. The space suggests that the altar was of modest proportions and quite traditional, something like the rectangular Augustan Belvedere Altar, which, not accidentally, was also dedicated by the Senate and people of Rome and depicts, on one face, a Victory inscribing a shield (De Rose Evans, 1992, 46–47).

2. The Controversy Over the Altar of Victory: The Evidence from the Manuscripts of the Letters of Symmachus and Ambrose

The manuscript traditions for the third state paper of Symmachus and for the letters of Ambrose shed important light on how contemporaries came to know about the protests over the Altar of Victory. Indeed, it was not because of Symmachus that we know about this controversy. Symmachus wrote his third state paper in his official capacity as urban prefect of Rome (Sym. *Rel.* 3.2). It seems, however, that he never intended to publish his state papers (Callu, 2009, LXV–LXVII; Seeck, 1883, xxii–xxxix). We can see this because, as D. Vera has observed (Vera, 1981, lxxxix; and 1977, 1003–1036), there are numerous errors in the headings of the state papers that specify the imperial addressees; errors of this sort indicate that these documents were Symmachus' private copies, which he never corrected. More likely, Symmachus' state papers were taken from family archives and have hence come down to us only in a later, posthumous edition.

Ambrose, however, made the third state paper of Symmachus widely available because he included a copy of it with his two letters (Ambr. *Epist.* 72 [Maur. 17]; *Epist.* 73 [Maur. 18]; Zelzer, 1983) on the Altar of Victory in Book 10 of his published correspondence. Ambrose himself most likely collected his letters for publication toward the end of his life, between 395 CE and 397 CE, following the death of → Theodosius I (*Epist.* 32 [Maur. 48]). Interestingly, *Epist.* 73.1 shows that only *Epist.* 72 was actually read in the consistory. Moreover, *Epist.* 73.1 also suggests that the emperor had decided not to return the altar before Ambrose delivered his first letter (*Epist.* 72

[Maur. 17]). Hence, what now stands as Ambrose's lengthy refutation of the third state paper in *Epist.* 73 (Maur. 18) was an academic exercise. Indeed, it is quite plausible that Ambrose circulated his letters with Symmachus' third state paper even before he published his whole collection of letters, though we cannot be certain of this.

Yet another letter of Ambrose about the Altar of Victory, *Epist.* 10 in the letters outside the collection (Ambr. *Epist. EC* 10 [Maur. 57]; Zelzer, 1983), was not included for publication by the bishop, though it was easily available when Ambrose's biographer, Paulinus, was looking for material for his *Life*, in 412/413 CE (P.Deac. *Vita Ambr.* 23–24, 27, 31). Perhaps Ambrose omitted this letter to the usurper Eugenius because it cast him in a somewhat suspect light. In any case, it was due to Ambrose that Symmachus' third state paper circulated widely, and for this reason it was attached to later manuscripts of Symmachus' private correspondence (Callu, 1972, 21; Salzman, 2011, lxii).

3. The Meaning of the Altar of Victory Controversy

Given the publication history noted above, we can see why Ambrose gets the last word in the Altar of Victory controversy. But one should begin with Symmachus' third state paper in order to gain some sense of what prompted the controversy. Although the Altar of Victory had been removed earlier in the century, this is the first time that we hear of a public embassy of senators taking an openly oppositional stand on the religious policy of Christianizing emperors. The reason is, in no small part, that Gratian took this step in conjunction with actions that undermined the financial status of the pagan cults. The two issues are artfully combined in the arguments made by Symmachus for a return to the *status quo ante.*

For Symmachus, the Altar of Victory represents the traditions of our fathers that have conserved the state for so long (Sym. *Rel.* 3.3). Clearly, it is in the light of the recent memory of the Roman disaster at Adrianople in 378 CE that Symmachus asked,

> Who is on such good terms with the barbarians as not to need the altar of Victory? We are

apprehensive about the future, and therefore avoid omens of that kind. (Sym. *Rel.* 3.3)

Indeed, the pagans senators saw the removal of the altar as a bad omen, foretelling defeat. And victory is something that the emperor needs:

> For your Eternity owes much to Victory, and will owe more still. Let those men shun this power, who have gained no benefits from her. But as for you, don't reject the patronage, which favors our triumphs. (Sym. *Rel.* 3.3)

It is surely indicative of Symmachus' rhetorical skill (→ Rhetoric) that he omits any mention of pagan rituals associated with the altar that Christians found offensive; only from Ambrose (*Epist.* 72 [Maur. 17.9]; *Epist.* 73 [Maur. 18.31]) do we get a graphic description of an incense-filled senate, forcing Christian senators' eyes to burn by simply attending the chamber. Symmachus focuses instead on the patriotic function of the Altar of Victory. "Where are we to swear to observe your laws and decrees? What religious sanction will deter the dishonest mind from lying when giving evidence?" (Sym. *Rel.* 3.5.). In a striking phrase about the omnipresence of the divine that sustains the "harmonious unity of all in the senate," Symmachus (*Rel.* 3.5) elevates the sanctity of the Senate and reminds the emperor of its importance.

Symmachus' third state paper advances a view of religious tolerance that has been justly praised, for it strikes the modern ear as quite liberal and progressive. In terms meant to appeal even to a Christian court, Symmachus claims: "For everyone's customs, everyone's cults are his own. The divine mind assigned different cults to different cities to be their protectors" (*Rel.* 3.9). Symmachus reinforces his plea for tolerance for different paths to the truth with a rhetorical trope, having the personified, elderly goddess Roma herself pleading for tolerance for her "ancestral ceremonies" (*Rel.* 3.9).

It is clever for Symmachus to have the goddess Roma raise the issue of financing the state cult: "What profit did your sacred treasury derive from withdrawing the privileges of the Vestal Virgins?" (*Rel.* 3.11). In addition, Roma continued: "The exchequer retains lands left to the Virgins and ministers of religion in accordance with the wishes of the dying" (*Rel.* 3.12). Symmachus chooses to focus, for rhetorical effect, on the damage done to the dying as a means of winning sympathy. However, this change in the finances of the state cult was a serious departure from past policy, for, as Symmachus notes, although Constantius II had removed the Altar of Victory in 357 CE, he "did not refuse funds for Roman rituals" (*Rel.* 3.7).

This has been generally read to mean that Gratian had also refused funding to the public cults because, as A. Cameron (2011, 41) observes, "the state cults were not funded directly from state funds, but rather from the income of estates willed to the temples over the course of the centuries." Recently, R. Lizzi Testa has challenged this interpretation and proposed that only the Vestal Virgins were defunded (Lizzi Testa, 2007, 251–262). The selective nature of Symmachus' third state paper indicates to this author that the issue at hand is public funding for the state ceremonies of all the pagan cults. These, according to Symmachus, must be financed with state monies and celebrated in public to be valid. The delegitimizing aspect of this new policy led the pagan senators to react publicly; this remained an issue, since we can count at least five embassies to the emperors in the years between 382 CE and 394 CE to protest the removal of the altar, and the changed policy (Cameron, 2011, 42–44, notes six embassies, including one presumably to Julian). This was seen, by a group of western pagans, as an issue worth protesting at the highest levels.

Ambrose's response takes on an aggressively assertive and highhanded tone. In his initial letter (Ambr. *Epist.* 72 [Maur. 17]), written before he has seen the text of Symmachus' state paper, Ambrose stresses the Christian faith of Valentinian I and family piety in order to persuade the emperor to keep the policy of his predecessor Gratian. Ambrose reveals that Gratian had taken these steps without the bishop's advice (*Epist.* 72.3) but argues that once in place, a good Christian like Valentinian should not act to support idolatry. Ambrose insists that the emperor should listen to him on this matter (*Epist.* 72.7; Maur. 10.13) because of his office as bishop. There can be no compromise, according to Ambrose, due to the sacrilegious nature of the Altar and its offensiveness to Christian senators (*Epist.* 72.9).

As noted above, Ambrose's *Epist.* 73 (Maur. 18) is a point-by-point refutation of the arguments raised by Symmachus. Ambrose mocks the notion that the Altar of Victory and the state cults brought victory by listing notable defeats suffered by the Romans under the pagan gods (*Epist.* 73.4–7). In response to Symmachus' request for tolerance for alternative "roads to the truth," Ambrose asserts, unequivocally, that this cannot be allowed because pagans and Christians are searching for different things:

> But what you do not know, we have learnt from the voice of God, and what you seek with misgivings, we know with certainty directly from the wisdom and truth of God. Our objective and yours are therefore not the same. (Ambr. *Epist.* 73.8)

This attack is a harbinger of the growing intolerance articulated by Christian bishops in the late 4th and 5th centuries CE.

In response to Symmachus' argument for the tolerance of custom, Ambrose crafts a novel argument which includes a positive view of change: just as men learned to farm, and children mature, and as the pagans themselves took in new, foreign cults, so too the changes brought by Christianity are good for Rome (Ambr. *Epist.* 73.26–30). Ambrose is one of the first ancient authors to argue that progress is positive. Indeed, he often sounds quite modern in making his case. For example, in response to the notion that famine took place due to the pagan gods being angry at changes in imperial policy, Ambrose talks instead about weather cycles (*Epist.* 73.17–18).

Responding directly to Symmachus, Ambrose devoted a good portion of his *Epist.* 73 to arguments in favor of changes in financing for the state cults. He dismisses any claims that this action is improper. He tells us that the temples were not taken away, only their properties, meaning the estates (*Epist.* 73.16). Indeed, the pagan temples were maintained for some time as public spaces by the Roman state. But, Ambrose adds, the pagan cults are not justified in having these properties because their priests do not exercise charity, as do Christian churches (*Epist.* 73.16). Ambrose again expresses intolerance for any alternative modes of religious life that do not fit his vision of a Christian empire.

Historiography

The letters of Symmachus and Ambrose on the Altar of Victory controversy provide invaluable testimony for the kinds of arguments pagans and Christians used in response to changes in society in the late 4th century. Modern scholars have consequently taken different positions on how best to interpret these as evidence for the state of late Roman paganism and for the Christianization of the Roman Empire. A. Cameron (2011, 31–55) sees these texts as evidence for the weak position of pagans, whose cults had now lost all public funding. R. Lizzi Testa (2007, 251–262), on the other hand, sees these letters as evidence for the vitality of late Roman paganism; in her view, only the cult of the Vestal Virgins was under financial attack by this new law. But both R. Lizzi Testa and A. Cameron represent what scholars have more recently done in interpreting this controversy in the light of the work of N.B. McLynn (1994, 151–152; 312–13; 344–445), who demonstrated that these letters were not the simple direct expressions of two opposing religious viewpoints but represent, instead, the contemporary political and rhetorical needs of both writers. Newer scholarship aims to read these letters with greater sensitivity to these factors (see e.g. Chenault, 2016, 46–63).

Bibliography

Callu, J.P., *Lettres [de] Symmaque1*, Books 1–2, Paris, 1972.
Callu, J.P., *Symmaque: Discours – Rapports*, Paris, 2009.
Cameron, A., *The Last Pagans of Rome*, Oxford, 2011.
Chenault, R., "Beyond Pagans and Christians: Politics and Intra-Christian Conflict in the Controversy over the Altar of Victory," in M.R. Salzman, M. Sághy & R. Lizzi Testa, *Pagans and Christians in Late Antique Rome*, New York, 2016, 46–63.
Degrassi, A., *Inscriptiones Italiae*, vol. XIII: *Fasti et elogia*, part 2: *Fasti anni Numani et Iuliani*, Rome, 1963.
De Rose Evans, J., *The Art of Persuasion: Political Propaganda from Aeneas to Brutus*, Ann Arbor, 1992.
Liebeschuetz, J.H.W.G., with C. Hill, *Ambrose of Milan: Political Letters and Speeches*, Liverpool, 2005.
Lizzi Testa, R., "Christian Emperor, Vestal Virgins and Priestly Colleges: Reconsidering the End of Roman Paganism," *AnTa* 15, 2007, 251–262.
McLynn, N.B., *Ambrose of Milan: Church and Court in a Christian Capital*, Berkeley, 1994.

"Prudentius: Contra Symmachum, Books 1–2," in: H.J. Thomas, *Prudentius*, 2 vols. Cambridge MA, 1949, 1953.
Salzman, M.R., with M. Roberts, *The Letters of Symmachus: Book 1*, Atlanta, 2011.
Seeck, O., "Q. Aur. Symmachi opera quae supersunt," in: *MGH.AA*, vol. VI/2, Berlin, 1883.
Tortorici, E., "Victoria, Ara," in: E.M. Steinby, ed., *LTUR*, vol. V, Ann Arbor, 1993–1999, 150.
Vera, D., *Commento storico alle "Relationes" di Q. Aurelius Symmachus*, Pisa, 1981.
Zelzer, M., *Sancti Ambrosii Opera 10.1–4*, CSEL 82, Vienna, 1983.

MICHELE RENEE SALZMAN

Altercatio Heracliani

The *Altercatio Heracliani cum Germinio* is a brief Latin dialogue, purportedly recounting a public debate that took place on Friday, Jan 13, 366 CE, in the Balkan city of Sirmium between the local bishop, Germinius, and a trio of Christian laymen, led by an otherwise obscure individual named Heraclianus. A critical edition was published in 1883 (Caspari, 1883, 133–147), based on two manuscripts from the 10th and 12th centuries, in which this text is preserved alongside a selection of the works of → Augustine of Hippo (Simonetti, 1967, 39n1). C.P. Caspari's text was reprinted in PLS 1 (at 345–350), and an English translation is available (Flower, 2013, 230–237, incorporating textual emendations proposed in Simonetti, 1967, 39n1). The text's transmitted introduction states that the dispute concerned the faith of the Council of → Nicaea (325 CE), as represented by Heraclianus, Firmianus, and Aurelianus, and that of the Homoian Council of Ariminum (359 CE), which was defended by Germinius and a number of his clergy, although the Christological views of Germinius appear to have differed from those of some of his Homoian contemporaries (see Simonetti, 1967, 46–49; Williams, 1996). Heraclianus is the only defender of Nicaea to speak in the dialogue, where he is depicted as triumphing in theological debate over the bishop himself, as well as the presbyter Theodorus and a certain Agrippinus of unknown rank.

At the opening of the text (Caspari, 1883, 133; PLS 1.345), Heraclianus is questioned about his use of the key Nicene term ὁμοούσιος, which was rejected by Homoian Christians along with all use of οὐσία (→ *Ousia*) terminology in Christological statements. Germinius says to Heraclianus, "The exiled Eusebius has taught this to you, as has Hilary, who has recently returned from exile" (Caspari, 1883, 134; PLS 1.345). This must refer to the bishops → Eusebius of Vercelli and → Hilary of Poitiers, both of whom had returned to the West from eastern exile in the early 360s CE. The majority of the discussion concerns not only the relationship between the Father and the Son, but also the divinity of the → Holy Spirit, which is defended by Heraclianus against the arguments of his opponents, with both sides making frequent reference to relevant scriptural passages. In its concern for expressing this Trinitarian doctrine (→ Trinity), the text moves beyond the Christological focus of the theological arguments of the 350s CE and the main issues discussed at the Council of Ariminum. Although it could be suggested that this might imply a later date than 366 CE for the text, the suggestion that the Holy Spirit was a creature had recently been anathematized at the Council of Alexandria in 362 CE, which had been attended by Eusebius of Vercelli before his return to Italy (Athan. *Tom.* 3; see also Hil. Poit. *Trin.* 12.55 for a similar statement from Hilary after his return from exile).

Toward the end of the treatise (Caspari, 1883, 143–145; PLS 1.350), in response to Germinius' invitation to explain his own faith, Heraclianus responds with a statement that repeats, almost verbatim, a passage from the *Apology* of → Tertullian on the unity of substance of the Father and the Son (Tert. *Apol.* 21.12–14). At this point, Germinius becomes enraged and condemns Heraclianus as a Homoousian heretic, before commanding that the three men should be sent into exile and that faithful Christians should not communicate with them. The angry crowd seeks to force the Nicene trio to subscribe to their creed (presumably the text approved at Ariminum in 359 CE) and even clamors for them to be dragged before the local governor and condemned to death, but Germinius intervenes to prevent this, allowing them to depart instead (Caspari, 1883, 147; PLS 1.350). He had, however, earlier sanctioned some violence toward Heraclianus, declaring, "See how much he speaks! Has no one knocked out his teeth?" – causing Jovinianus the deacon and Marinus the reader to beat the layman (Caspari, 1883, 134; PLS 1.345).

In response, Heraclianus declared that his suffering was salutary, proclaiming, "This leads to my good fortune and glory."

By celebrating the heroes' steadfast faith in the face of threats and cruel treatment, as well as their victory over their enemies in debate, this text presents Heraclianus and his colleagues as similar to earlier confessors and → martyrs who had refused to renounce their beliefs during persecution (see Simonetti, 1967, 42n11; Flower, 2013, 1–6). In particular, the beating of Heraclianus is reminiscent of Acts 23:2, where the high priest Ananias gives an order for Paul (→ Paul the Apostle) to be struck on the mouth, while the hostile crowd at the end of the text evokes the mob who petitioned Pontius Pilate (→ Pilate) to release Barabbas and execute Christ. Moreover, the opening of the text is structured like a formal record of judicial proceedings, providing precise details of the date and location of the events before introducing the dialogue with the statement,

> They led Heraclianus, Firmianus and Aurelianus out from custody in front of all the people, with the bishop sitting on his throne with the entire clergy before all the populace and the elders. (Caspari, 1883, 133; PLS 1.345)

Similar dating formulae and prefatory statements also appear in early martyr *acta* ("acts") from the Roman Empire (see e.g. *Acta Mart. Scil.* 1). These aspects of the text present the Nicene laymen not as disputants who challenged the theology and authority of their bishop, but rather as the latest in a long line of pious figures who suffered for their faith and who would be rewarded for their constancy, with Heraclianus declaring that

> God, who liberated Israel from the hand of the king of the Amorites and the king of Bashan, and Paul from the hand of the Samaritans, will liberate me from your hands also. (Caspari, 1883, 146; PLS 1.350)

In contrast, the Homoian Christians of Sirmium are presented as replaying the behavior of numerous enemies of the faithful.

The authenticity of the events described in this text is therefore difficult to assess. Many of the aspects of the work that evoke martyr literature, including the ease with which Heraclianus is able to defeat all his opponents in theological debate, suggest that it contains a degree of rhetorical embellishment at the very least. M. Simonetti has expressed this view, while suggesting that the more positive portrayal of Germinius at the end of the text, where he rescues the laymen from the angry crowd, lends a certain sense of authenticity to the central account, even if the work as a whole cannot be seen as an accurate representation of events in Sirmium on that day (Simonetti, 1967, 41–44). It is certainly possible that a confrontation of this sort occurred, but the *Altercatio* should not be relied upon as a verbatim record of any discussion that took place. Its value arguably lies more in what it reveals about the literary presentation of theological debate in the 4th century CE.

Historiography

The critical edition of the text is C.P. Caspari (1883, 133–147, repr. in PLS 1, 345–350). A number of important suggestions for emendations to this edition are provided in M. Simonetti (1967, 39n1). An English translation of the corrected text, together with limited commentary, is to be found in R. Flower (2013, 230–237). M. Simonetti (1967) remains fundamental for the study of this brief work, including questions concerning its content, date and authenticity.

Bibliography

Caspari, C.P., *Kirchenhistorische Anecdota*, Oslo, 1883.

Flower, R., *Emperors and Bishops in Late Roman Invective*, Cambridge UK, 2013.

Simonetti, M., "Osservationi sull' 'Altercatio Heracliani cum Germinio'," *VigChr* 21, 1967, 39–58.

Williams, D.H., "Another Exception to Later Fourth-Century 'Arian' Typologies: The Case of Germinius of Sirmium," *JECS* 4, 1996, 335–357.

RICHARD FLOWER

Amandus

Amandus (early 5th cent. CE) was a presbyter (→ Priest/Presbyter) in Bordeaux under Bishop Delphinus, after whose death around 404 CE he succeeded as → bishop in this city. He as a presbyter with close connections to Delphinus probably took part at the deposition of the Priscillianists (→ Priscillianism) at the synod in Bordeaux 384/385 CE (Sul. *Chron.* 2.48.1; 49.2–50.1; SC 441, 338–343; Prosper of Aquitaine, *Epitoma chronicorum* under year 385 CE and under year 389 CE; *MGH.AA* 9, 462; Hydatius, *Chronicle* under year 386 CE; OCM 76f.), but nothing is known about his activity. His successor as bishop in Bordeaux was Severinus. Later traditions that honor Severinus relate that Amandus voluntarily retreated from his office to defer it to the more holy Severinus but received it again after the death of this Severinus (see For. *Vita Sev.* 2–4; *MGH.SRM* 7.220–222; see Greg. T. *Glor. con.* 44; *MGH SRM* 1.2, 325). These events cannot be confirmed elsewhere, and therefore exact chronology remains unclear. A historiography for this topic is also not applicable

Amandus was one of the correspondents of → Paulinus of Nola, who praises him as an outstanding bishop (Greg. T. *Hist.* 2.13). His connections to Paulinus began during his time as presbyter in Bordeaux, because he was the teacher of the catechumen (→ Catechesis) Paulinus before his baptism through Bishop Delphinus, the predecessor of Amandus, in 389 CE. He is the recipient of six letters of Paulinus (*Ep.* 2; 9; 12; 15; 21; 36) which all stem from his time as presbyter. But none of the letters of Amandus to Paulinus have been preserved. This first letter Amandus had written was a short consolatory letter on the death of Paulinus' brother, which Paulinus answered with *Ep.* 36. *Ep.* 9 and 2 (392–395 CE), about Paulinus' ordination to the priesthood in which he expresses his wish for further support and spiritual nourishment by Amandus. *Ep.* 12 (397/398 CE) is an answer to Amandus' request for further exchange of theological and spiritual letters. It may be read as a kind of mirror of the catechesis of Amandus and contains a summary of salvation history and people's inclination to worldly matters and spiritual humility. In *Ep.* 15 (399 CE) Paulinus is happy to be informed about Bishop Desiderius' recovery from illness. This letter, together with *Ep.* 21 (401 CE), also deals with a person named Cardamas, who recovered from alcoholism.

Bibliography

Griffe, E., *La Gaule chrétienne à l'époque romaine*, 2nd ed., vol. I, Paris, 1964, 310–312, vol. II, Paris, 1966, 271–274.

Skeb, M., trans. & introduction, *Paulinus von Nola: Epistulae/Briefe*, 3 vols., FChr 25, Freiburg, 1998, esp. 82–84.

Wilson, D.R., "Amaseia," in: R. Stillwell, W.L. McDonald & M. Holland McAllister, eds., *PECS*, Princeton, 1976, 47.

UTA HEIL

JUAN ANTONIO CABRERA MONTERO

Amasea

Amasea is the capital of the current Turkish province of Amasya. It is associated with many legends and myths about its origins and foundation. Amasea became the capital of the kingdom of Pontus until the Roman conquest in 70 BCE. A detailed description of the city is owed to one of its most illustrious citizens, Strabo (*Geogr.* 12.3.39). Rich in archaeological remains as the seat of the royal dynasty of Pontus, Amasea always maintained its position as the largest city in the region even during the many administrative changes that were happening at that time in the region. It is difficult to indicate when Christianity came to Amasea. Ancient traditions tells us about the presence in the area of the apostle Peter (→ Peter the Apostle), by whom Nicetas of Remesiana would have been consecrated as the first → bishop of the city, and Andrew (→ Andrewthe Apostle). Also in the *Acta Sanctorum* appear numerous references to bishops and → martyrs from Amasea in the first decades of the expansion of Christianity. Among the early saints associated with the city are Basil, Philantia, → Gregory Thaumaturgus, Phocas of Sinope, Hesychius the homologete, Eutychius of Constantinople, and Theodore of Tyre. The period of splendor of the city during the early centuries of Christianity occurred during the conciliar period and its leading representatives were Asterius and Seleucus.

Bibliography

Beazley, J.D., "Amasea," *JHS*, 1931, 256–284.

Dalaison, J., *L'atelier d'Amaseia du Pont: Recherches historiques et numismatiques*, Paris, 2008.

Driver, L.D.M., "The Cult of Martyrs in Asterius of Amaseia's Vision of the Christian City," *ChH* 74, 2005, 236–254.

Leemans, J., "Christian Diversity in Amaseia: A Bishop's View," *Adamantius* 13, 2007, 247–257.

Stiernon, D., "Amasea del Ponto," in: *NDPAC*, Genova, 2006, 226–227.

Vailhé, S., "Amasea," in: *DHGE*, vol. II, Paris, 1914, 964–970.

Amastris

Amastris is a city of Greek origin (modern-day Amasra, Turkey) in the small peninsula along the coast of the Black Sea (Pontus Euxinus) and on a small adjacent island, which are now connected by a bridge. In Paphlagonia upon a creek of the same name. It had two ports at the two sides of the peninsula; the most important of these was the one to the east. The ancient Sesamus was renamed Amastris in honor of the wife of Dionysius (d. 335/336 BCE), the tyrant of Heraclea Pontica (today called Karadeniz Ereğli). It belonged to the kingdom of Pontus and was sacked first by Nicomedes and then by Lucullus in 70 BCE (App. *Mithrid.* 11). According to Strabo, the city was located about 15 km to the east of the river Parthenius (today's Bartın Çayı). Pompey included the city in the province of Bithynia and Pontus. It coined money until the time of Emperor → Maximinus Thrax (d. 238 CE). On one of the coins, from the time of → Trajan, there was the title of *metropolis* of the *ora Pontica*, and it continued to be important, even in later centuries. In the third year of his governorship in Bithynia and Pontus, Pliny the Younger was at Amastris. In one letter he wrote to Trajan,

> The city of Amastris, both elegant and lovely, possesses, among its most notable edifices, a street (*platea*) that is very long and magnificent, along one side of which – for all its length – extends beside that which is called a river, but which in reality is a very stinky and fetid sewer and not only is it embarrassing to look upon its filthy and grimy appearance, but it is also dangerous on account of its horrid stench.

He asked the emperor to cover it, which Trajan conceded and granted as asked (Plin. Y. *Ep.* 10.98, 99). That creek still flowed underneath the Roman vaults, which were built during the time of Pliny. The ancient ruins are under the fortifications that were built by the Genoese, underneath the house of the modern town. There are ruins from a large temple and from an enormous depository of three stories.

The Roman city was broader than the modern city. Along the eastern coast, at around 180 km, there was the city of Abonuteichus (then Ionopolis, modern-day Inebolu), famous in the 2nd century CE for the prophet Alexander, who was also against the Christians. Alexander of Abonuteichus said that

> the Pontus had become full of atheists and Christians, who dared to blaspheme against him – the most horrendous things; he gave the advice that they be stoned if they wanted to have their propitious god. (Alex. Abon. 25)

Alexander created a rite of banishment of the Christians, which began with the words "out with the Christians" (Alex. Abon. 38).

In the 2nd century CE it was part of a κοινὸν of the eastern part of the province (κοινὸν τοῦ Πόντου). With the multiplication of the provinces under → Diocletian, Amastris began to belong to Paphlagonia, whose capital city was Gangra (today Çankırı), which was also the see of the → metropolitan. We do not know when Christianity made its arrival in the city, but it was at least before the end of the 1st century CE. The city's first known → bishop was Palmas, to whom Dionysius of Corinth (c. 171 CE) wrote a letter, exhorting him "to receive [into the church] those who have converted from any sort of downfall, be it one of negligence or that of a heretical error" (Eus. *Hist. eccl.* 6.23.6). → Eusebius of Caesarea informs us that at the time of Pope Victor I (189–199 CE), the bishops of Pontus, too, convoked a council regarding the date of → Easter, a council that was presided over by Palmas "in his capacity as the eldest" (Eus. *Hist. eccl.* 5.23.3). This was a role attributed only to Palmas and not to the other bishops who presided at other councils, and Eusebius knew of the letter they had written in favor of the celebration of Easter on a Sunday. Bishop Eupsychius of Amastris was present at the First Council of → Nicaea (325 CE; *Patrum Nicaenorum nomina*, 82n116.). At the Council of → Chalcedon (451 CE), the city's bishop, Themistius, was represented by the presbyter (→ Priest/Presbyter) Philotimus (Mansi, vol. VII, 650B). Amastris was the first episcopal see that was a suffragan of Gangra (Darrouzès, 1963: *Notitia* 1.1.1, 228). In the 9th century CE, it became an autocephalous episcopal see and was no longer dependent on Gangra, per the request of the city's bishop, George (*AASS* febr.

3.21.277); it successively became a metropolis (10th cent. CE). At the Ecumenical Council of Constantinople in 680–681 CE, Bishop Cometas was represented by Deacon Irenarcus (Mansi, vol. IX, 677), and at the council in Trullo, Deacon George represented Bishop Zoilus (Mansi, vol. IX, 1000). At the Second Council of Nicaea in 787 CE, the bishop, Gregory, was present (Mansi, vol. XIII, 369).

The most representative figure of Amastris was George, who lived between the end of the 8th century CE and the beginning of the 9th century CE and was born at Kromna, a village outside the city. He received a good education; he gave himself to the monastic life. He was elected bishop of Amastris, where he carried out an intensive pastoral activity, full of charity. He defended his people against the Saracens; he died during the reign of Emperor Nicephorus I (802–811 CE). His feast day falls on Feb 21.

Bibliography

BHG 668, Brussels.

Brandes, W., *Die Städte Kleinasiens im 7. und 8. Jahrhundert*, Amsterdam, 1989.

Darrouzès, J., *Notitiae episcopatuum Ecclesiae Constantinopolitanae*, Paris, 1981.

DHGE, vol. II, Paris.

Fedalto, G., *Hierarchia ecclesiastica orientalis*, vol. I, Padua, 1988.

Laurent, V., *Le corpus des sceaux de l'empire byzantin*, vol. V/1, Paris, 1963, vol. V/2, Paris, 1965.

Matthews, R., & C. Glatz, eds., *At Empire's Edge: Project Paphlagonia: Regional Survey in North-Central Turkey*, London, 2009.

Nautin, P., *Lettres et écrivains chrétiens du IIe et IIIe siècles*, Paris, 1961.

ODB, vol. I, New York.

ANGELO DI BERARDINO

Ambrose (Disciple of Didymus)

Little is known about the life of Ambrose of Alexandria, thus making it difficult to establish a chronology of his literary activities. Most of what is known about him is based upon brief information given solely by → Jerome (347–419 CE) in chapter 126 of his book *De viris illustribus* (*Lives of Illustrious Men*) and upon few additional details found in J. Bollandus'

Acta sanctorum, Martii, Tomus Secundus (2nd vol. of March).

1. The Life of Ambrose of Alexandria

Ambrose was born in Alexandria in the 4th century CE, perhaps shortly before the outbreak of the Arian controversy (→ Arianism), which was to engross his mind and the minds of his contemporaries, and before the First Ecumenical Council of → Nicaea of 325 CE. He was probably born to Christian parents. Nothing definite is known about his family and about his early life and childhood. It is not known whether he was an ascetic like his teacher Didymus the Blind (313–398 CE), who lived an eremitical like life.

As a deacon in the Church of Alexandria, Ambrose must have attended the Catechetical School of that illustrious city, which owned in all probability no buildings. "Lectures" were most likely held in private homes, borrowed rooms, or even perhaps rented halls. When Ambrose joined this famous Christian school, Didymus the Blind, who was appointed by → Athanasius of Alexandria (295/300–373 CE), had already been at its head for over a half century, at a time when that city was, in a certain sense, the intellectual capital of the world.

The personality and teachings of Didymus must have made an impression on Ambrose and shaped his theological education. It could be for this reason that Jerome called him an "*auditor Didymi*" (disciple of Didymus) in his book *De viris illustribus*, or a rational way not to mistake him for Ambrose of Alexandria (before 212–c. 250 CE), the friend of → Origen. Jerome met Ambrose and was impressed by him during the former's visit to Alexandria in 389 CE, where he spent 30 days seeking Didymus' clarification on some difficult scriptural passages.

Ambrose lived his entire life in the midst of the theological controversies in Alexandria, but he took no active part in the great theological controversies of his epoch. Neither he nor any one of his generation could have escaped the influence of the theological atmosphere of Alexandria during the 4th century CE. Since the name Ambrose was closely associated with that of Didymus the Blind, whose name came to the forefront in connection with the Origenistic controversies (→ Origenism/Origenist

Controversy) in the 6th century CE, Ambrose of Alexandria might have been overlooked as a worthy theological writer of the 4th century CE.

The date of his death is unknown. However, G. Bardy maintains that Ambrose lived sometime after 392 CE (Bardy, 1910, 9), which could mean that he died at the beginning of the 5th century CE. According to the calendar of the eastern Orthodox Church (Orthodoxy), his feast day falls on Mar 17.

2. The Works of Ambrose of Alexandria

Jerome mentions that Ambrose authored two works, *Ambrosius Alexandrinus, auditor Didymi, scripsit adversum Apollinarium volumen multorum versuum de dogmatibus: et, ut ad me nuper quodam narrante relatum est, commentarios in Job. Qui usque hodie superset*("Ambrose of Alexandria, disciple of Didymus, wrote a doctrinal book of many verses against Apollinaris and a commentary on Job, of which I was recently informed; he [i.e. Ambrose] is still living"). Ambrose must have adhered in his commentary on Job to the rules of scriptural exegesis of the Catechetical School of Alexandria since he had been trained in it, in other words, the allegorical method of interpretation, which had become the standard exegetical tool in Alexandria.

The dogmatic work *De dogmatibus*written against → Apollinaris of Laodicea (315–392 CE) was perhaps composed after the Second Ecumenical Council of → Constantinople (381 CE). Up until the 19th century, this work was thought to have been authored by Athanasius of Alexandria. J. Dräseke, however, supposes in his study *Zwei Gegner des Apollinarios*(1889) that *De dogmatibus*against Apollinaris originated in Alexandria and was composed by Ambrose of Alexandria.

Historiography

Hieronymus is considered to be the only source on which the researchers of the history of the early church confirmed that Ambrose of Alexandria is a disciple of Didymus the Blind at the Catechetical School in Alexandria. Nevertheless G.D. Dragas (1985), pointed out that Ambrose was a disciple of Athanasius of Alexandria. The scholars also agreed that Ambrose had interpreted the book of Job. As for the controversy surrounding the author of the book of *Contra Apollinarem I & II*, whose Greek text was published as an *apologetic* book for the first time in the 17th century under the name of Athanasius of Alexandria. The opinion that *Contra Apollinarem* was written by Athanasius prevailed until 1889 when J. Dräseke pointed out that *Contra Apollinarem I* may have been written by Didymus the blind, and *Contra Apollinarem II* by Ambrose. This opinion was supported by U. Chevalier (1905), J. Leipoldt (1905), G. Bardy (1910) and S. Salaville (1914). In 1914 E. Weigel supported the old belief that Athanasius was the author of *Contra Apollinarem* and in 1985 G.D. Dragas supported him in this view. At the end of the 20th century, E. Prinzivalli (1992), W.A. Bienert (1993) and M. Ghattas (2001) based on Hieronymus, attributed to Ambrosius that he was the author of *Contra Apollinarem*

In fact, there are no other dogmatic tractate of Ambrose to identify his Christological doctrine, so that we can compare them to the Christological content of *Contra Apollinarem*. Generally it can be concluded that the Christological thought in *Contra Apollinarem* is undoubtedly coherent with that of the Christology of Alexandria of the 4th century CE.

Bibliography

Bardy, G., *Didyme L'Aveugle*, Paris, 1910.
Bienert, W.A., "Ambrosius," in: *LThK*, vol. I, Freiburg im Breisgau, 1993, 493.
Chevalier, U., *Repertoire des sources historiques du moyen-âge*, vol. I: *Bio-bibliographie*, Paris, 1877–1883, 1905, col. 185.
De S. Ambrosio Diacono Alexandriae in Aegypto, in: J. Bolland, G. Henschen, J.-B. Carnandet & D. van Papenbroeck, eds., *Actas*, Paris, 1865, col. 509.
Dragas, G.D., *St. Athanasius contra Apollinarem*, Athens, 1985.
Dräseke, J., "Zwei Gegner des Apollinarios," in: J. Dräseke, *Gesammelte patristische Untersuchungen*, Altona, 1889, 167–207.
Ghattas, M., *Die Christologie Didymus' des Blinden von Alexandria in den Schriften von Tura: Zur Entwicklung der Alexandrinischen Theologie des 4. Jahrhunderts*, Münster, 2001.
Leipoldt, J., *Didymus der Blinde von Alexandria*, Leipzig, 1905.
Prinzivalli, E., "Ambrose," in: *EEC*, vol. I, New York, 1992, 28.
Prinzivalli, E., *Magister ecclesiae: Il dibattito su Origene fra III e IV secolo*, SEAug 82, Rome, 2002.

Salaville, S., "Ambroise," in: *DHGE*, vol. II, Paris, 1914, 1108.
Tillemont, L.-S.N., *Mémoires pour servir à l'histoire ecclési-astique des six premiers siècles*, vol. X, Paris, 1705.
Weigl, E., *Untersuchungen zur Christologie des heiligen Athanasius*, Paderborn, 1914.

MICHAEL GHATTAS

Ambrose (Friend of Origen)

Ambrose flourished in the first half of the 3rd century CE. Our knowledge of him is based exclusively on the reports of others. Only one fragment of Ambrose's letters survives.

1. Family

From Origen we learn that Ambrose had a number of siblings, that he was married to Marcella, and that the couple had children (Or. *Ep. Afr.* 24; Or. *Mart.* 37). Ambrose was wealthy, owning multiple houses and several tracts of land (Or. *Mart.* 14–17). In language evocative of political position, Origen says that he was "honored and respected by a great many cities" (Or. *Mart.* 36). → Epiphanius of Salamis calls him a "prominent imperial official" (Epiph. *Haer.* 64.3.1).

2. Conversion

Our sources tell us nothing explicit of the early life of Ambrose. → Eusebius of Caesarea reports that he was an adherent of Valentinian (Valentinus/Valentinians) Christianity when he met Origen in Alexandria (Eus. *Hist. eccl.* 6.18.1). → Jerome, however, says that Ambrose was a follower of Marcion (Jer. *Vir. ill.* 56; 61.3), while Epiphanius says that he was either a Marcionite or Sabellian (Epiph. *Haer.* 64.3.1; → Marcion/Marcionites/Marcionism; → Sabellians). The *Suda* claims that he subscribed to the heresies of both Valentinus and Marcion, thus likely conflating earlier testimonies (Ω 183). Most scholars accept Eusebius' report. Valentinus, who had taught in Alexandria in the early 2nd century CE, still had followers in the city in Origen's day.

In response to Origen's teaching, Ambrose "accepted the orthodox doctrine of the church" (Eus. *Hist. eccl.* 6.18.1). This conversion probably happened during the reign of Caracalla (211–217 CE), though P. Nautin dates it later to the reign of Elagabalus (218–222 CE; Nautin, 1977, 409, 419–420). Origen also refers to this conversion, recalling that Ambrose was at one time devoted to the teachings of the heterodox before abandoning them in favor of those of "the holy church of Christ" (Or. *Comm. Jo.* 5.8). There is an oblique reference to Ambrose's catechetical instruction at Or. *Mart.* 17 where Origen is discussing the true worship of God.

3. Scriptorium

Sometime after his conversion, probably around the beginning of the reign of → Alexander Severus (222–235 CE), Ambrose urged Origen to begin writing commentaries on Scripture. Ambrose provided Origen the means to do so, establishing a scriptorium and providing him with seven stenographers to take dictation, at least seven → scribes for copying books, and an unspecified number of girls skilled in calligraphy (Eus. *Hist. eccl.* 6.23.1–2; Jer. *Vir. ill.* 56; 61.3; *Ep.* 43.1; Epiph. *Haer.* 64.3.4). Origen refers to "agreements" with Ambrose regarding the publication of his books (Or. *Comm. Jo.* 5.2). At least part of Ambrose's motivation for facilitating Origen's literary activity seems to have been apologetic (→ Apologetics): he saw in Origen an able spokesperson for the church's dispute with the heterodox (Or. *Comm. Jo.* 5.8). Even after Origen settled permanently in Caesarea Maritima circa 234 CE, Ambrose provided him with stenographers to encourage his literary production (Or. *Comm. Jo.* 6.9–10).

4. Relationship with Origen

Origen describes Ambrose as "most devout and zealous for learning in the Lord" (Or. *Comm. Jo.* 20.1). Other sources pass along similar reports: Ambrose had "an inexpressible earnestness in diligence and zeal for the divine oracles" (Eus. *Hist. eccl.* 6.23.2; see also Epiph. *Haer.* 64.3.2; 64.7.1). Sometimes → Origen complained about the onerous demands Ambrose placed upon him, calling him, for instance, a "taskmaster" (ἐργοδιώκτης at Or. *Comm. Jo.* 5.1; Jer. *Vir. ill.* 61.3). In a letter from Origen preserved in the *Suda*, he speaks vividly of Ambrose's demanding regimen:

Although he [Ambrose] thinks that I am industrious and exceedingly thirsty for the divine word, he has put [me] to shame with his own zeal and his love for the sacred disciplines [...] For it is neither possible to eat without conversation, nor, after having eaten, to take a walk and allow the body to rest awhile, but even during these times we are compelled to study and to correct the copies; nor indeed are we allowed to go to bed for the whole night in order to care for the body, since study extends deep into the night. (Nautin, 1961, 250.3–251.15)

This letter is strikingly similar in content to a letter Jerome claims Ambrose wrote to Origen (Jer. *Ep.* 43.1). The overlapping content led A. von Harnack to dispute Jerome's attribution, proposing that he had, in fact, the above letter preserved in the *Suda* in mind, and confused author and recipient (Harnack, 1904, 55n5). There is another report from Jerome of a letter sent from Origen to Fabian, bishop of Rome. According to this letter, Origen ostensibly "expresses penitence for having made erroneous statements, and charges Ambrose with over haste in making public what was meant only for private circulation" (Jer. *Ep.* 84.9; on this distinction between Origen's private and public writings, see Pamp. *Ap.*, 36). P. Nautin thinks that this letter is the same as the aforementioned letter preserved in the *Suda* (Nautin, 1977, 57–59, 172).

Scholars customarily describe Ambrose as Origen's "patron," but this designation can mislead. Ambrose certainly commissioned a number of writings (e.g. Or. *Comm. Jo.* 6.6; *Comm. Ps. 1–25* [Epiph. *Haer.* 64.7.1–4]; *Cels.* pref. 1). But his relationship to Origen's literary oeuvre is more complex. Some writings appear to be addressed, or even dedicated, to Ambrose (Or. *Comm. Jo.* 1.9; Or. *Mart.* 1, written on the occasion of the arrest of Ambrose and Protoctetus). *On Prayer* is Origen's direct response to a letter he received from Ambrose and Tatiana (perhaps his sister), in which they requested his answer to the objection that prayer was superfluous since God foreknows what will happen and everything that happens according to his will cannot be altered (Or. *Or.* 2.1). Note the citation of an excerpt from this letter at Or. *Or.* 5.6 (see also Jer. *Vir. ill.* 56.2). Finally, Ambrose travelled with Origen to Nicomedia, from which the *Epistula ad Africanum* was written; Origen credits Ambrose with collaborating and correcting parts of this letter (Or. *Ep. Afr.* 24).

Origen also calls Ambrose his "brother" (*Or.* 34; Or. *Cels.* 7.1; Or. *Comm. Jo.* 2.1; 28.6; 32.2) and "friend" (Epiph. *Haer.* 64.7.2) and requests that he pray for him (*Haer.* 64.7.4). Customarily, Origen describes Ambrose's piety. He is "God-fearing" (Or. *Mart.* 1), "God-loving" (Or. *Cels.* pref.1), "most Christian" (Or. *Cels.* 3.1), "pious" (Or. *Cels.* 6.1), "most religious and industrious" (Or. *Or.* 2.1), and a "man of God, and a man in Christ, and [...] eager to be spiritual, no longer being man" (Or. *Comm. Jo.* 1.9). The adjective that occurs most frequently, however, is "holy" (ἱερός; Or. *Mart.* 14; 36; Or. *Ep. Afric.* 24; Or. *Cels.* 4.1; 7.1; 8.76; Or. *Comm. Jo.* 2.1; 6.6; 28.6; 32.2; Epiph. *Haer.* 64.7.1). Jerome says Ambrose became a → deacon (Jer. *Vir. ill.* 56), a biographical detail perhaps obliquely attested by Origen at *Mart.* 42.

When → Maximinus Thrax became emperor, he initiated a → persecution of Christians, "commanding that only the rulers of churches should be put to death" (Eus. *Hist. eccl.* 6.28). Ambrose and a presbyter (→ Priest/Presbyter) in the Caesarean church, Protoctetus, were arrested and were "eminent in confession" during the three-year reign of Maximinus (who died in 238 CE; Eus. *Hist. eccl.* 6.28; Jer. *Vir. ill.* 56.1). Origen speaks of Ambrose facing the possibility of execution "in Germany [ἐν Γερμανίᾳ]" (Or. *Mart.* 41). A. von Harnack entertained the possibility that this was an authentic geographic reference (since Maximinus was in Germany in 235), but considered it likely a scribal error (Harnack, 1904, 56–57). R.E. Heine plausibly suggests that Ambrose might have been singled out for persecution because of his political status (Heine, 2010, 167–168).

Ambrose evidently survived the Maximinian persecution because he furnished Origen a copy of → Celsus' *The True Doctrine* and prompted Origen to write his *Against Celsus* (preface 4). This treatise was written circa 248 CE. Origen's last reference to Ambrose occurs at Or. *Cels.* 8.36. Jerome says Ambrose died "in the year prior to Origen's death" (Jer. *Vir. ill.* 56.3), thus circa 252 CE. There has been debate in the literature about whether the Ambrose of Alexandria mentioned in the ancient martyrologies (feast day: Mar 17) is our Ambrose, or the Ambrose who was a pupil of Didymus the Blind

(Jer. *Vir. ill.* 126; Bolland, 1668, 513–514; Salaville, 1914, 1089–1090).

Historiography

There is limited scholarly debate about Ambrose. The preceding entry has highlighted the few disagreements or alternative theories that have emerged about the surviving evidence.

Bibliography

Bolland, J., et al., *Acta Sanctoru: Martii,* vol. II, Antwerp, 1668.

Cadiou, R., *La jeunesse d'Origene: Histoire de l'école d'Alexandrie au début du IIIe siècle*, Paris, 1936.

Harnack, A. von, *Die Chronologie der altchristlichen Literatur bis Eusebius*, vol. II, Leipzig, 1904.

Harnack, A. von, *Geschichte der altchristlichen Literatur*, vol. I/1, Leipzig, ²1958.

Heine, R.E., *Origen: Scholarship in the Service of the Church*, Oxford, 2010.

Nautin, P., *Lettres et écrivains chrétiens des IIe et IIIe siècles*, Paris, 1961.

Nautin, P., *Origène: Sa vie et son oeuvre*, Paris, 1977.

Salaville, S., "3. Ambroise," in: *DHGE*, vol. II, Paris, 1914, 1086–1090.

PETER MARTENS

Ambrose of Milan

Ambrose of Milan (*Aurelius Ambrosius*) was born into a Christian family in Trier in about 340 CE (Visonà, 2004, 215–220), the son of Ambrosius, the praetorian prefect of Gaul (*Gallia Narbonensis*). After the death of his father, he went to Rome with his mother and two siblings, Marcellina and Satyrus, where he received a classical Roman education (Somenzi, 2009). His praise of his brother's education may reveal something about the education that he also received (Ambr. *Exc.* 49 and 58).He was a lawyer in Sirmium in about 365 CE and was chosen as governor of Liguria and Emilia in about 370 CE, but very little is known about that part of his life. In the autumn of 374 CE, after the death of Bishop Auxentius of Milan, Ambrose was chosen by the people of Milan as their bishop. While he initially resisted that appointment (Ambr. *Epist. EC* 14 [63 M], 65), the fact that Valerian I approved of his selection as bishop may have persuaded him to accept it. As the Catholic leader of an imperial city, he would use his Roman education and experience and his Christian upbringing to confront a raft of commitments and responsibilities. Even though it is not possible to know the specifics of his faith-knowledge before being baptized, it is likely that he was more prepared for being a Catholic bishop than is generally assumed (Savon, 1997, 79). He was baptized and, within a week, ordained as bishop (Dec 7, 374 CE). He used his previous experience to advocate effectively for unity both in the Christian community and in the society beyond at a time of significant transformations in the social, economic, religious, and political realities of that time.

1. His Life

Ambrose would come to be considered one of the great theologians of the early church, using his Roman education and his experience in Roman governance as significant dimensions of his Catholic ministry. He was known as an accomplished and passionate preacher and as an astute negotiator. As bishop of Milan, he served the needs of more than one community – both in Milan and beyond – building a "community featuring a diverse and complex blend of religion and philosophy, social networking, politics, patronage, and personal relationships" (Gannaway & Grant, 2021, 6). Relating the story of his life, therefore, is more than an accumulation of facts and dates. Whether tending to the needy or engaging emperors or working with other bishops, his influence was felt in areas well beyond the limits of Milan (Testa, 2021, 12–42). His consistent reliance on the word of God became the foundation for his preaching and pastoral efforts. Even though it is clear that he relied on the work of authors like Philo of Alexandria and Origen for his work, he carefully adapted his sources into preaching, writing, or actions that were significant for the spiritual life, the social engagement, and the theological vision of his listeners.

2. 374–387 CE

In his first years as bishop of Milan, Ambrose appears to have been sensitive to the practice of neutrality of Valentinian I toward the religious differences of that time. He kept, for example, the clergy ordained by his predecessor, Auxentius (Theophil. Alex. *Ep.* 2.2). Yet his insistence on being baptized by a minister who adhered to the Nicene faith shows that he attached significant importance to his adherence to that creed (Paul. Mil. *Vita Ambr.* 9). When he did begin to write in 377 CE, his initial focus was on virginity and on themes from the early books of the Hebrew Bible. His adherence to Nicene faith, however, is subtly evident in his early works (Ambr. *Virg.* 3.2–4; *Parad.* 58). At some point in 378 CE, he was asked by the emperor Gratian for an explanation of the relationship of the Father and the Son (Savon, 1997, 89). In response, Ambrose wrote the first two books of the *De fide* and gave them to Gratian later that year. Two years later, Ambrose will respond to a request by Gratian, writing the last three new books of the *De fide* and *De Spirito Sancto* as well, giving them to Gratian in March 381 CE. These works for the emperor Gratian, as well as his leadership at the Council of Aquileia (Sep 3, 381 CE) appear to have given him a way to give fuller expression to his Nicene convictions and to display his keen sense of how to use his administrative background to work with existing personalities and realities toward unity in faith. The murder of Gratian in Lyon in 383 CE led to a fear that Maximus – emperor of the western portion of the Roman Empire – would invade Italy. That appears to have been sufficient to motivate Valentinian II to send Ambrose as ambassador to Maximus so as to persuade him to remain in Trier and thus to maintain his existing sphere of influence: Britain, France, and Spain. Ambrose was again sent to Trier – probably in 385 CE (Visonà, 2004, 32–36) – for the same reason, as well as to ask for the remains of the emperor Gratian. Apparently believing that Ambrose had deceived him in the first encounter, Maximus told Ambrose to leave Trier – a sign of the failure of that mission. In 384 CE, Ambrose chose to argue against an effort by Symmachus – as president of the Roman Senate – to repeal the 382 CE law of Gratian that required the removal of the *ara victoriae* from the Senate. Symmachus also asked for the restoration of the pagan rites and the privileges that had been suppressed (Ambr. *Epist.* 72; 72a; 73). Ambrose's multifaceted arguments against the petition by Symmachus appear to have given Valentinian

II a rationale for denying the request – although it is likely that the emperor also wanted to avoid any provocation against the Nicene faith of the emperors Maximus and Theodosius I. In the autumn of that year, a new imperial rhetorician was appointed, thus bringing Augustine to Milan. A conflict over the use of the churches in Milan began in 385 CE. Valentinian II and his mother tried, unsuccessfully, to get Ambrose to allow them to use a Catholic basilica for Arian worship at Easter, 385 CE. The dispute reached its high point as Easter approached in 386 CE. Ambrose's opposition to that request was widely supported by the people of Milan (Kiely, 2013, 124). Even if there is no clear agreement on the precise succession of events or on the relationship of the descriptive documents to those events, most all agree that the discovery of the relics of Gervasius and Protasius in June 386 CE signaled the end of the conflict (Visonà, 2004, 37–44). Ambrose baptized Augustine of Hippo at the Easter vigil of 387 CE (Apr 24–25), along with his son, Adeodatus, and his friend, Alypius. In the spring of that year, Maximus invaded Italy. He would be defeated by Theodosius at Aquila in August 388 CE. 388–397 CE Events of 388 and 390 CE put Ambrose in direct conflict with the emperor Theodosius, both in relation to the burning of the synagogue at Callinicum (Ambr. *Epist. EC*1: 1a; *Epist.* 74) and in relation to the massacre at Thessalonica (Ambr. *Epist. EC*11; *Ob. Theo.* 34). In the first of these, Ambrose reacts to the decree that would have forced the bishop to rebuild the synagogue that was burned by his own order and another decree to punish the monks who burned the gathering space of a Valentinian gnostic sect. By refusing to continue with the eucharistic celebration which Theodosius attended unless those decrees were abrogated, Ambrose left no room for ongoing difference on this matter. Two years later, in spring 392 CE, Ambrose required that Theodosius do formal penance because of having called for the massacre at Thessalonica (*Epist. EC* 11; *Ob. Theo.* 34). It is possible that Ambrose learned of that massacre while meeting with other bishops of Italy (*Epist. EC* 11.6). In any case, Theodosius seems to have done penance for eight months and was reconciled at Christmas of that year (Visonà, 2004, 46–50). Ambrose presided over a council at Capua that dealt with the affair of Bonosus, probably at the beginning of 392 CE (*Epist.*

70). Another council would have been held in Milan at the beginning of 393 CE; it condemned the view of Jovinian that Mary ceased to be a virgin with the birth of Jesus (*Epist. EC* 15 to Pope Siricius) – a position confirmed by a synod in Milan that may have taken place in the early months of 393 CE. A sermon that Ambrose preached for the veiling of Ambrosia at Easter 392 CE led to his work, the *De institutione virginis* which was probably published at the end of 393 CE. The emperor Valentinian II was murdered on May 15, 392 CE, in Vienne in Gaul, while Ambrose was on the way there to respond to his request for baptism. His funeral was held in Milan – probably in September – and Ambrose preached the *De obitu Valentiniani* in the presence of his sisters, Justa and Grata. At about the same time, Eugenius was proclaimed emperor by Arborgast. He invaded Italy in 393 CE. As a result, Ambrose chose to flee to Bologna where he assisted with the finding of the relics of the martyr, Agricola and Vital. During this time of exile, he wrote a discreetly challenging letter to Eugenius (*Epist. EC* 10). In March of 394 CE, he went to Florence to consecrate a basilica, and – probably at Easter – he gave the sermon which would be the basis for his *Exhortatio virginitatis*. In August of that year, he returned to Milan. Shortly thereafter, Theodosius defeated and killed Eugenius and sent a letter to Ambrose announcing that victory. Theodosius would die in January 395 CE and Ambrose gave the funeral oration in the presence of his son, Honorius. There is little that can be said about the last year of Ambrose's life, other than that which Paulinus wrote in his biography – a recounting of deeds done by Ambrose that it is not possible to verify. Ambrose died in Milan on Easter eve in 397 CE.

3. Significant Writings

Formed by a classical education, Ambrose also became adept in biblical learning, leading him to affirm the Scriptures as the basis for life and for truth. His consistent criticism of philosophical ways of thinking and living was also a way of saying that the real origin of philosophy was from the Bible – providing a basis for explaining why so much of what Ambrose wrote was on people and themes from the Hebrew Bible. He composed works on virginity, on faith, on creation, on the patriarchs, on ethical matters, on some of the Psalms and on the Gospel of Luke. He wrote letters, composed hymns, and gave funeral orations for his brother and for two emperors. Rather than describe his method of interpreting these texts as merely rhetorical or spiritual, his approach also has a poetic (Kiely, 2013; Dunkle, 2016, 2) or rhythmic quality that is rhetorically engaging and spiritually moving. In other words, his writing of hymns for his people to sing was consistent with the way he thought about preaching and writing. The most important examples of his perspectives on the formation of his listeners or community members were his works on clerical ethics (*De officiis*), on the Gospel of Luke (*Expositio evangelii secundum Lucam*) and on the Psalms, especially on Ps 118 (*Expositio psalmi cxviii*). Historically speaking, his most important writings are those that were meant to strengthen the Christian community in its service of the common good. That includes the works of catechesis (*De sacramentis*; *De mysteriis*), as well as several works on the patriarchs (e.g. *De Isaac vel anima*; *De Iacob et beata vita*) who were proposed as *exempla* for his people to learn from. His doctrinally significant works include those on faith and penance (*De fide*; *De Spiritu Sancto*; *De Incarnatione Domini*; *De poenitentia*) as well as a commentary on the six days of creation (*Hexaëmeron*). The works on virginity, both at the beginning of his ministry (*De virginibus*; *De virginitate*) and in its final years (*Exhortatio uirginitatis*; *De Institutione virginis*) highlight the saving work of Christ.

4. Significant Ideas

A presentation of his significant ideas emphasizes the importance of belief in Christ as true God. Ambrose tends to place the focus of his efforts to affirm that belief on Christian virtue that is seen in the many biblical *exempla* that he explores. Scriptural wisdom, in other words, is the source and basis for all of his thinking. While it is clear that Ambrose's work was often inspired by other writers – whether classical or Christian – the adaptations required to adapt those ideas to his own time and circumstances testify to the creative originality of his work (Michel, 1996). It is also significant that he gave very much attention to the engagement of God with the world – a principle that is at the foundation of his actions – whether

personal, ecclesial, or political. Even if it is clear that Ambrose did not respond to situations in a fully consistent way, significant emphases can be identified.

5. *Omnia Christus Est Nobis*

"Christ is everything for us" (Ambr. *Virg.* 16.99) – this phrase was the focus of the article by G. Madec (1998), an article that developed its meaning as standing at the center of the life and preaching of Ambrose, whose focus from the very beginning of his time as the bishop of Milan was a gentle yet firm provocation in his time. As Ambrose said:

> When we speak about wisdom, it is Christ. When we speak about virtue, it is Christ. When we speak about justice, it is Christ. When we speak about peace, it is Christ. When we speak about truth and life and redemption, it is Christ. Open your mouth with the word of God, it is written. You say [it], he is the one speaking. (*Explanatio psalmorum xii* 36, 65)

Ambrose's language can insist on a focus on Christ, in the first place, because his written work had its origins in the liturgy where the building up of the faith was the primary concern. The theme, namely "Christ is everything for us," explains the depth and the breadth of Ambrose's work (Madec, 1998, 218) – a work of emotion-filled and rhetorically rhythmic images – perhaps rather pleasingly developed in relation to the Song of Songs (Kiely, 2013). More than one author recognizes that Ambrose's presentations abound with biblical citations, one of whom speaks of his "unceasing rumination of the Scriptures" (Nauroy, 1986, 371). His theology is biblical insofar as he says that it is Christ who is the one who is teaching: "We teach [*exponamus*] insofar as we can, but it is Christ who teaches" (Ambr. *Fid.* 4.10.122). Ambrose counts on the "auto-interpretation of Christ" (Markschies, 1997, 748) for Christ is a teacher in a special way because he teaches as God teaches (*Fid.* 2.9.79). There is, therefore, in Ambrose a reflex that not only places Christ at the center of every reflection – whether in relation to the spiritual life of his listeners or to the controversies of his time – but also relies on the word of God as the very basis for faith and for truth. It was, therefore, not necessary for Ambrose to engage in a debate about the spiritual value or philosophical truth of any one position. He lets the source of all wisdom, justice, and truth speak for himself. That also means that Ambrose's exegesis can appear to be haphazard and disorganized to modern interpreters. It has been noted, however, that – at least among those seeking to affirm a Homoean understanding of Christ – it was normal to use strings of biblical citations to make one's case (Markschies, 1997, 751). Confronted with those who spoke of Christ in Homoean terms, Ambrose proposed a reading of the Scriptures which was not limited to the interpretation of isolated passages. It was in that way that he could let Christ speak for himself: "We demonstrate this with the words of the Lord" (Ambr. *Fid.* 5.3.42; *Exp. Ps. 118* 20.10). In fact, it has barely been noticed that Ambrose did

> establish new and varied constellations of scriptural texts so as to respond to the doctrinal and cultural needs of his time [...] What may appear to be a gratuitous exercise of imagination at first sight, however, turns out to be a thoughtful and consistent pattern of addressing his listeners' interests and needs. (Fitzgerald, 2009, 959)

Ambrose's hymns were integral part of his pastoral and theological vision and practice – uniting faith with the beauty of its expression. Ambrose uses hymns to delight and fascinate his congregation with a Nicene understanding of the Scriptures (Dunkle, 2016, 217). His hymns do not simply sing of Christ as divine but also see creation as revealing Christ. His hymns also need to be seen as more than a way to protect Christians from heretics (Williams, 2013, 130–131). Ambrose was not trying to define the identity of his community in its opposition to others; he was affirming their experience of faith in Christ by "singing hymns and Psalms in the manner customary in regions of the East" (*Aug. Conf.* 9.7.15), thus affirming the link between faith and beauty (Springer, 2014). Hymns, therefore, are part of Ambrose's teaching (Gordley, 2011) and mystagogical agenda (Vopřada, 2016). Their singing was an expression of faith in Christ as truly God (Dunkle, 2016, 217).

6. *Pulchra Decore Virtutis*

The church is "beautiful with the beauty of virtue" (Ambr. *Exp. Ps. 118* 19.22). In his *De officiis*, Ambrose sets the tone for his work on clerical ethics by talking about humility at the very beginning, eliminating right away any question about the Christian dimensions of his work and demonstrating that this work is not a simple derivation from the *De officiis* of Cicero (Zelzer, 1996, 50). Humility, in fact, was the main Christian virtue since the time of Paul – a virtue that was foreign to pagan thought (Aug. *Conf.*7.18.24; 7.21.27). Ambrose sees humility as the foundation of this work. By using biblical figures to exemplify the cardinal virtues, Ambrose does much more than build upon roman heroic figures; he develops a distinctively appropriate Christian methodology (Fitzgerald, 2021, 176–177). Ambrose also sees virgins as examples that lead to Christ. Using the example of virgins, Ambrose proclaims Christ as the one who is in the work of encouraging his people to live up to the mystery that virgins manifest by their lives. For the divinizing work of Christ can be in every Christian. Virgins reveal Christ as come from heaven, teaching every Christian (Ambr. *Virg.* 1.8.42), to live with integrity (*Virg.* 1.2.5; 1.7.39; 1.11.66). The opening paragraphs of the *De officiis* describe David as a "master of humility." By placing his teaching in the care of David, Ambrose makes the relationship with the God of the Bible the basis for human searching for wisdom and happiness. "Just as the Stoics could only attain happiness through virtue, so was it that the Christian attained happiness only through a life of humility that accords with the will of God" (Zelzer, 1996, 51). Ambrose also uses David and other biblical figures to emphasize the antiquity of his teaching. In fact, however, those biblical *exempla* always give way to another reality:

> For [Christ] is the true David, truly humble and gentle, first and last, first in terms of eternity, last in terms of humility, through whose obedience the fault of the human race is deleted, and justice shines. (Ambr. *Apol. Dav.* 17.81)

Thus does David's life provide a connection to the humility of Christ – the true David (*Exp. Ps. 118* 14.4; 21.11; *Epist.* 39.11). In this way, Ambrose lays the foundation for that what he will say about virtue in the rest of this book and specifically in relation to the cardinal virtues, prudence, justice, courage, and temperance. David is also an exemplar in many other works, especially in the Psalms. Hence, Ambrose says in the introduction to the commentary on Ps 118:

Loud and clear as a trumpet the prophet David has proclaimed every mystery. But in this psalm, by its sheer beauty; he clearly sets forth the excellence of morality. All moral doctrine is sweet, but it becomes more so when to it are added the sweetness of song and the charm of psalmody. (Ambr. *Exp. Ps. 118*preface 1)

All of Ambrose's preaching, in fact, is about the mystery of Christ, no matter whether it is found in his works on the rites of initiation or on the Psalms or elsewhere. As a sustained reflection, its purpose is the formation of that community in the celebration and practice of the faith. His preaching, therefore, is more than a matter of moral exhortation. It is a "mystagogical method that aims to deepen the believers' knowledge of Christ and their union with him" (Vopřada, 2017, 87; 2021, 106), making connections between the saving events of the Hebrew Bible, the New Testament, and the life of the church. As a mystagogue (Vopřada, 2016, part 2), Ambrose introduces his community to their true teacher (Matthew 23:8). Also, in his commentary on Ps 118, he points to David's prayer that God make him a teacher in his Psalms (Vopřada, 2021, 113):

But no one can express a hymn with sincerity unless he has first learnt the statutes of God and learnt them from the Lord God himself. Therefore, David asks specially that God would teach him; for he had heard and known in spirit 'there is one master' and therefore he asked him to be his teacher (Vopřada, 2021, 114) everywhere, so that he might learn his statutes from God himself. (Ambr. *Exp. Ps. 118*22.18)

Ambrose's work is consistently focused on the mystery that completes the moral message, and on how to bring about actions that are truly Christian. This challenge of integrating the Christian with the human and the sacred with the secular could not have been limited to the well-educated (Fitzgerald, 2004, 133–134). "The four cardinal virtues, given Stoic definitions but informed by the Scriptures, as well as the Gifts of the Holy Spirit and the Theological Virtues, constitute the structure of his ethical thinking" (Grant, 2013, 306). Ambrose's appeals to Hebrew Bible *exempla* function as an appeal to antiquity, thus using a typical Roman practice to bring his community together in the formation of their identity in the life and experience of Christ (Mohrmann, 1995; Colish, 2005; Harmon, 2017).

7. *Deum Certum Est Omnibus Praeferendum*

Ambrose's interactions with others are guided by the idea that "God is certainly preferred to all" (Ambr. *Epist.* 72.6) – even if that ideal may not be immediately obvious or successful in every one of his experiences (Grant, 2013, 302). Yet, Ambrose acts as

a Christian ethicist who understands that human virtue is a response to one's intimate relationship with Christ and that it is this relationship, and the virtues that it generates, which influences the course of human events.

Hence,

it is through the Church that the Christian's ethical disposition is established toward emperors, the Church itself, the state, non-Christians, and civil society. (Grant, 2013, 307)

It cannot be a surprise that Ambrose – who was raised as a Roman patrician and classically educated – would have had principles which were at least implicit to guided him through the varied and even dangerous interactions with emperors. R. Grant suggests and then discusses in some detail several pairs of contrasting principles:

First, emperors are chosen by God, and yet are 'part of, not over, the Church'; secondly, bishops are mediators of God in the world while the Church remains autonomous in its innerworkings; further, the Church supports the state in its duties but the Church must non-violently resist the state in matters of moral duty; then, non-Christians have no rights that impinge on the Church's role but are entitled to civil justice; and finally, the poor have a claim on the Church and wealth should be offered in support the Church's mission. (Grant, 2013, 302)

What is significant about his efforts to interrelate the church and the world is that he does not separate one from the other. While a certain autonomy is given to the church, it is also clear that the church serves society. "The real issue is not how to keep faith apart, but how to exercise its demands within social, political, cultural, and economic realities" (Grant, 2013, 333). R. Grant described his enduring legacy as having framed the question of the relationship of the church to the world (Grant 2013, 333). He summarizes appropriately:

> Toward the Christians under his care, Ambrose used didactic and hortatory sermons [...] Toward priests and vowed religious women he used recruitment, instruction, and spiritual and sometimes financial support. Toward the rich he encouraged the cultivation of Roman and Christian virtues and particularly urged them to philanthropy. Toward the poor he offered shelter, food, and care. To the community at large he offered beautiful buildings, his own hymnic compositions, and, of course, the sacraments framed in the liturgy. In order to influence the Church as an institution, Ambrose called councils as at Aquileia, Rome, and Capua, where he exercised great skills as a barrister to gain the results he sought, though not always successfully. His influence was evident in the appointment of many bishops, though he was more successful within the sphere of his direct influence than he was, say, in Antioch. His third tool was the strategic "seeding" of churches with the relics of martyrs whose bodies he had exhumed. [...] Finally, and most generally, Ambrose's life influenced others. His personal asceticism, generous philanthropy, courageous defiance, theological output, artistic expressions, incisive intellect, masterful rhetoric, and spiritual expressions constitute the deepest extent of his "advice" to his generation and beyond. (Grant, 2013, 331–332)

8. Evaluation

It has been noted – perhaps especially in the case of the study of Ambrose – that the historical climate and the theological questions of the age that reads him have a significant influence on the research on him than on the study of other historical figures (Visonà, 1998, 31–32). His way of engaging the political, social, and religious issues of his time through personal interactions not only suggest that faith and life are interrelated, but also require that such concerns be addressed at other times. The description of Ambrose's most significant ideas in this article, therefore, did not portray him in merely political or polemical terms. He was a stateman turned pastor, whose life and work also had to deal with difficult and even dangerous situations. It is all too easy to forget that no Latin bishop before him had to deal so directly with emperors and success was far from certain (Brown, 2012, 121). This article, therefore, did not deal with specific successes or failures in any depth but chose to place the focus on his methods and motivations.

Historiography

The view of Ambrose held by those who were his contemporaries (Augustine, Rufinus, Paulinus, Basil, Gaudentius, and Jerome) shared three praiseworthy elements: his eloquence as the pastor of his people, his care for the faith of his people, and, most especially, his reliance on Scripture for all that he said. None of these contemporaries pay much attention to his role in relations with the political figures of his day – although his experience with the conflict over the use of the Milanese basilicas and his insistence that Theodosius do penance after the massacre at Thessalonica left an enduring impression, namely that such events gave a shape to the relations between religious and political power (Visonà, 2004, 46). Paulinus of Milan does describe Ambrose's journeys to Trier as an ambassador of the emperor, as well as the challenges of the decisions of Theodosius in rather hagiographic terms. Jerome's esteem for Ambrose's defense of virginity is also unique – as is his criticism of the commentary on the Holy Spirit (Hunter, 2009). Scholarly interest in Ambrose increased over the last century, especially since the celebration of the anniversary of his installation as bishop of Milan in 1974. G. Visonà (1998, 34) notes that the study of Ambrose has many possible dimensions: "Ecclesiastical politics and political theology [against the background of church-empire relations], theological controversies and anti-Arian struggle, biblical exegesis, liturgy and sacraments, literature, poetry, music, art, law" – leading to scholarship that has been richer and more varied than in previous times (Visonà, 1998, 31). In 1997, another conference on Ambrose took place in Milan (*Nec timeo mori*, 1998). The interest in Ambrose shifted from the person and his works to the social and religious context of his time (Visonà, 2004, 55–62), exploring the importance of his work across many disciplines. Thus is Ambrose seen as having had a significant role in the transformation of his time in several different ways. The criticism that his writings were an effort to gain political power or enhance his own image (McLynn, 1994) has been set against other studies that highlight "his episcopal responsibilities, his Nicene theology, and his asceticism" (Gannaway & Grant, 2021, 3). Another shift in the scholarship on Ambrose now recognizes Ambrose's originality as a thinker and writer (Markschies, 1997; Layton, 2002) and the centrality of Christ in all of his work (Madec, 1974; 1998). Even though his writings were influenced by Stoic ethics, platonic anthropology, and secular literature, it has become more evident that he was always adapting a fresh reading of the Scriptures to the spiritual life, social engagement, and theological vision of the Christian community (Nauroy, 1986; Markschies, 1997). That shift is confirmed in the papers of the conference at Saint Ambrose University (2018). In the words of the editors,

> Ambrose's biography permits modern scholars to apply, broadly speaking, historical and theological methodologies. As a patrician bishop of the imperial city of Milan, Ambrose stood at the crux of many different communities and, by his peculiar position and training and by his own initiative, influenced them profoundly. This context [...] provides a unique opportunity to seek the inner motivations of a late antique bishop regarding his delicate balance of various community commitments and responsibilities.
>
> (Gannaway & Grant, 2021, 3)

Bibliography

Braschi, F., "A Comprehensive Reading of Ambrose's *Explanatio psalmorum* XII," *SP* 46, 2010, 137–142.

Braschi, F., *L'explanatio psalmorum XII di Ambrogio: una proposta di lettura unitaria: Analisi tematica, contenuto teologico e contesto ecclesiale*, StAmbr 1, 2007, 29–44.

Brown, P., *Through the Eye of a Needle: Wealth, the Fall of Rome, and the Making of Christianity in the West, 350–550 AD*, Princeton, 2012.

Christman, A.R., "A Window into Biblical Culture: Virgil's Aeneid in Ambrose of Milan's *Expositio Psalmi cxviii*," in: E. Gannaway & R. Grant, eds., *Ambrose of Milan and Community Formation in Late Antiquity*, Cambridge UK, 2021, 120–1134.

Colish, M., *Ambrose's Patriarchs: Ethics for the Common Man*, Notre Dame, 2005.

Dassmann, E., *Die Frömmigkeit des Kirchenvaters Ambrosius von Mailand: Quellen und Entfaltung*, Münster, 1965; trans. *La sobria ebbrezza dello spirito: La spiritualità di S. Ambrogio, Vescovo di Milano*, Sacro Monte di Varese, 1975.

Dunkle, B., *Enchantment and Creed in the Hymns of Ambrose*, Oxford, 2016.

Duval, Y.-M., "Ambroise et l'Arianisme Occidental," in: Y.M. Duval, *L'extirpation de l'arianisme en Italie du nord et en occident*, Aldershot, 1998, 1–39.

Duval, Y.M., "Commenter Ambroise: Principes et application," in: G. Nauroy, ed., *Lire et éditer aujourd'hui Ambrose de Milan: Actes du colloque de l'université de Metz, 20–21 mai 2005*, RLS 13, New York, 2007, 125–164.

Fitzgerald, A., "Ambrose, Paul and *Expositio Psalmi CXVIII*," *Aug(L)* 54, 2004, 131–32.

Fitzgerald, A., "Ambrose of Milan: His Interpretive Method," in: H.J. Klauck et al., eds., *EBR*, New York, 2009, 958–960.

Fitzgerald, A., "Ambrose and Truth," in: E. Gannaway & R. Grant, eds., *Ambrose of Milan and Community Formation in Late Antiquity*, Cambridge UK, 2021, 172–183.

Fontiane, J., "Congrès internationale d'etudes ambrosiennes à l'occasion du XVIe centenaire de l'élection épiscopale (Milan, 2–7 décembre 1974)," *REAug* 21, 1975, 202–208.

Gannaway, E., & R. Grant, eds., *Ambrose of Milan and Community Formation in Late Antiquity*, Cambridge UK, 2021.

Gordley, M.E., *Teaching Through Song in Antiquity*, Tübingen, 2011.

Grant, R., "Weapons Strong for God: The Moral Theology of Ambrose of Milan Applied to War, Torture and Capital Punishment," *StAm* 5, 2011, 195–228.

Grant, R., "The Ambrose Doctrine," *StAm* 7, 2013 301–333.

Harmon, A.M., "History and Virtue: Contextualizing Exemplarity in Ambrose," *JECS* 25/2, 2017, 201–229.

Hunter, D.G., "The Raven Replies: Ambrose's *Letter to the Church at Vercelli* (*Ep.ex.coll. 14*) and the Criticisms of Jerome," in: A. Cain & J. Lössl, *Jerome of Stridon: His Life, Writings and Legacy*, Farnham, 2009, 175–189.

Kiely, M.M., "Ambrose the Pastor and the Image of the "Bride": Exegesis, Philosophy, and the Song of Songs," diss., Washington DC, 2013.

Layton, R.A., "Plagiarism and Lay Patronage of Ascetic Scholarship: Jerome, Ambrose and Rufinus," *JECS* 10/4, 2002, 489–522.

Lazzati, G., ed., "Ambrosius Episcopus: Atti del congresso internazionale di studi ambrosiani nel XVI centenario della elevazione di Sant'Ambrogio alla cattedra episcopale, 2–7 dicembre 1974," *SPMe* 6–7, 1976, 266–285.

Madec, G., *"L'homme intérieur selon saint Ambroise,"* Ambroise de Milan: XVIe centenaire de son élection épiscopale, Paris, 1974, 203–308.

Madec, G., "La centralité du Christ dans la spiritualité d'Ambroise," in: L.F. Pizzolato & M. Rizzi, eds., *Nec timeo mori: Atti del congresso internazionale di studi amborsiani nel XVI centenario della morte di sant'Ambrogio,* SPMed 21, Milan, 1998, 207–220.

Markschies, C., "Ambrogio Teologo Trinitario," *ScC* 125, 1997, 741–762.

Maschio, G., *La figura di Cristo nel* Commento al Salmo 118 *di Ambrogio di Milano,* Rome, 2003.

McLynn, N.B., *Ambrose of Milan: Church and Court in a Christian Capital,* Berkeley, 1994.

Michel, A., "Du *De Officiis* de Cicéron á Saint Ambroise: La théorie des devoirs," *StAug* 53, 1996, 39–46.

Mohrmann, M., Wisdom and the Moral Life: the Teachings of Ambrose of Milan, 8;, PhD diss., University of Virginia 1995.

Nauroy, G., "L'Écriture dans la pastorale d'Ambroise de Milan," in: J. ?Fontaine – C. Pietri (eds), *Bible de tous les temps,* vol. III: *Le monde latin et la Bible,* Paris, 1986, 371–408.

Pizzolato, L.F., & M. Rizzi, eds., *Nec timeo mori: Atti del congresso internazionale di studi amborsiani nel XVI centenario della morte di sant'Ambrogio,* SPMed 21, Milan, 1998.

Satterlee, C.A., *Ambrose of Milan's Method of Mystagogical Preaching,* Collegeville, 2002.

Savon, H., *Ambroise de Milan,* Paris, 1997.

Somenzi, C., *Egesippo-Ambrogio: Formazione scolastica e cristiana a Roma alla metà del IV secolo,* Milan, 2009.

Sordi, M., "I rapporti di Ambrogio con gli imperatori del suo tempo," in: L.F. Pizzolato & M. Rizzi, eds., *Nec timeo mori: Atti del congresso internazionale di studi ambrosiani nel XVI centenario della morte di Sant'Ambrogio (Milano 4–11 Aprile 1997),* SPMed 21, Milan, 1998, 117–118.

Springer, C.P.E., *"Of Roosters and repetitio: Ambrose's* Aeterne rerum conditor," *VigChr.* 68/2, 2014, 155–177.

Testa, R.L., "Ambrose and the Creation of a Christian Community," in: E. Gannaway & R. Grant, eds., *Ambrose of Milan and Community Formation in Late Antiquity,* Cambridge UK, 2021.

Visonà, G., "Lo 'status quaestionis' della ricerca ambrosiana, in: L.F. Pizzolato & M. Rizzi, eds., *Nec timeo mori: Atti del congresso internazionale di studi ambrosiani nel XVI centenario della morte di Sant'Ambrogio (Milano 4–11 Aprile 1997),* SPMed 21, Milan, 1998, 31–72.

Visonà, G., "Cronologia Ambrosiana: Bibliografia Ambrosiana (1900–2000)," *Tutte le Opere di Sant'Ambrogio,* Sussidi 25/26, Milan, 2004.

Vopřada, D., *La Mistagogia del Commento al Salmo 118 di Sant'Ambrogio,* Rome, 2016.

Vopřada, D., "Bonum mihi quod humiliasti me: Ambrose's Theology of Humility and Humiliation," *SP* 85, 2017, 87–94.

Vopřada, D., "Ambrose's Exegesis of the Psalms: A Bishop Forming the Community Around Christ the Teacher," in: E. Gannaway & R. Grant, eds., *Ambrose of Milan and Community Formation in Late Antiquity,* Cambridge UK, 2021, 106–119.

Williams, M.S., "Hymns as Acclamations: The Case of Ambrose of Milan," *JLAn* 6/1, 2013, 108–134.

Zelzer, K., "L'etica di sant'Ambrogio e la tradizione stoica delle virtù," Studia Epheremides Augustiniana 53: *L'etica cristiana nei secoli III e IV: Eredità e confronti: XXIV Incontro di studiosi dell'antichtà cristiana Roma, 4–6 maggio 1995,* Rome, 1996, 47–56.

ALLAN FITZGERALD

Ambrosian Liturgy

The Church of Milan's own liturgy, named after its patron saint Ambrose, is termed *Ambrosian*. It evolved and developed from the 4th century CE onward: first during the long tenure of the Arian bishop Auxentius of Milan (355–374 CE), a native of Cappadocia, and then under the episcopate of Ambrose.

Born into a noble Roman family in Trier in 340 CE, Ambrose became bishop of Milan on Dec 7, 374 CE (→ Ambrose of Milan), and was undoubtedly one of the major protagonists of the history of church and empire in the second half of the 4th century CE; owing to the clarity and orthodoxy of his teachings in times of antiheretical conflicts, he is venerated as a doctor of both the western and the eastern churches. He died on the dawn of Holy Saturday on Apr 4, 397 CE.

Most of Ambrose's works are more or less directly linked to his activities as a preacher and pastor, and their original *inspirational context* thus lies in the substratum of liturgical celebrations: in fact, his writings contain valuable information (sometimes explicit, sometimes allusive) that allows us to reconstruct, at least along general lines, the liturgy of the Church of Milan in the 4th century CE, which may be described as the Ambrosian liturgy in its founding moment. The treatise *De Sacramentis* preserves Ambrose's programmatic statement regarding the Milanese liturgical praxis of his time, and although it is true that the attribution of this work to Ambrose is still a matter of debate, numerous scholars argue convincingly in favor of its authenticity. Speaking of the rites of Christian initiation, the author notes that in Milan, the → bishop washes the feet of the neophytes immediately after having administered baptism, as opposed to what is practiced in Rome. He then comments,

> Non ignoramus quod ecclesia Romana hanc consuetudinem non habet, cuius typum in omnibus sequimur et formam. Hanc tamen consuetudinem non habet, ut pedes lavet [...] In omnibus cupio sequi ecclesiam Romanam, sed tamen et nos hominis sensum habemus. ["We are not ignorant that the Roman Church has not this custom. Her type and form we follow in all things; however, she has not this custom of washing the feet. (...) In all things I desire to follow the Roman Church. Yet we too are not without discernment."] (Ambr. *Sacr.* 3.5)

On the one hand, therefore, Ambrose professes to conform to the liturgical model of the Church of Rome, but on the other, he claims that any differences with respect to this model are legitimate. In fact, the liturgy of the Church of Milan at the time of Ambrose frequently and significantly deviates from the liturgical tradition of the Church of Rome while drawing closer to other traditions, especially eastern ones.

1. The Celebration of the Mass

Ambrose is one of the first church fathers to bear testimony to the daily celebration of the Mass; equally explicitly, he invites the faithful to receive Holy Communion every day, and not just once a year as the Greeks were believed to do (Ambr. *Hex.* 5.90; *Patr.* 38; *Sacr.* 5.25). Mass was celebrated around midday on days of half fasting, whereas it was moved to the evening on those of → fasting (Ambr. *Exp. Ps. 118* 8.48; *Jos.* 52).

The structure of the ritual is clearly bipartite: first the liturgy of the word, then the liturgy of the → Eucharist.

Regarding the order of the readings, Ambrose explicitly states: *Prius propheta legatur et apostolus et sic evangelium* (*Exp. Ps. 118* 17.10; "First be read the prophetic reading, then that of the apostle, and finally the gospel"). The liturgy of the word thus displayed a three-part structure, which the Ambrosian Church would retain without change (at least

for festive celebrations), even when the readings were reduced to two in the Roman liturgy due to the elimination of the passage from the Hebrew Bible (*propheta*). Moreover, when Ambrose states that the *apostolus* is read after the reading from the Prophets, this refers to the writings of the apostle Paul (→ Paul the Apostle), and in the subsequent Ambrosian tradition, the second reading would indeed not be concerned with the New Testament in general, but always with the Pauline corpus. The readings are followed by the bishop's homily, which is normally referred to as *tractatus*. At the conclusion of the liturgy of the word, the catechumens (→ Catechesis) were dismissed, as they were not allowed to attend the eucharistic liturgy. Ambrose mentions this explicitly in a letter to his sister Marcellina (Ambr. *Epist.* 76.4–5) and immediately adds: *Ego tamen mansi in munere, missam facere coepi* ("I instead continued the celebration and began the Mass [missa]"). In this case, the word *missa* is not to be taken as a reference to the dismissal of the catechumens, which has already taken place, but rather as a synonym of *oblatio*, a term that recurs a few lines later in the sense of "offertory (and consecratory) prayer." We would thus appear to be dealing with one of the first attestations of the word *missa* in the current sense of "Mass."

Prior to the consecratory prayers, prayers of intercession are addressed to God – as Ambrose himself states – *pro populo, pro regibus, pro ceteris* (Ambr. *Sacr.* 4.14; "for the people, for the kings, for everyone else"): most probably, he is alluding to the litany that is now known as *oratio fidelium* ("prayer of the faithfuls"). During the early Middle Ages, it disappeared in the Roman liturgy, except for a solemn recitation on Good Friday. The Ambrosian liturgy, however, not only retained the litany of Good Friday but at least two litanic formulas for Lenten Sundays (→ Lent) alone, which are known as *preces*: the latter are clearly of Byzantine origin (5th–6th cents. CE) but demonstrate a certain congruity with the words of Ambrose through their nature as prayers of intercession and through their content.

The offerings for the eucharistic celebration were presented by the faithful at the altar (Ambr. *Exp. Ps. 118*, prologue 2); furthermore, the use of implements dedicated exclusively to worship is clearly attested in the writings of Ambrose (the *vasa mystica, mysticum poculum*, and *sacer calyx* of Ambr. *Off.* 2.136.143; "sacred vessels, mystical chalice and sacred calyx"). Ambrose's fourth discourse on the sacraments (Ambr. *Sacr.* 4.21–29) is of fundamental importance here because it preserves the middle part of the true eucharistic prayer, the *canone*, as it would later be handed down, with some variation, in both the Roman and the Ambrosian liturgies. The most recent studies have demonstrated that the canon of *De Sacramentis* and the Roman canon represent two different developments that originated in an Alexandrian paleoanaphora, even though the text quoted by Ambrose is closer to the original source and thus constitutes the oldest form in the West.

It is of course also necessary to take a larger problem into account, namely that of the authorship of *De Sacramentis* in relation to the similar treatise entitled *De Mysteriis*, which is securely attributed to Ambrose but does not mention the canon. In reality, both treatises can be attributed to Ambrose, even if they are different in nature. The *De Sacramentis* exhibits a very direct style of "oral" character, almost as if it were a "stenographic recording" of Ambrose's sermons made right in the middle of his preaching: this explains the fragmentary form of the canon contained in it, as it is quoted from memory and not copied like a liturgical text. The *De Mysteriis*, however, is an independent treatise, even if it addresses the same topic and exhibits a very accurate literary development that is intended for publication: this would explain the omission of the eucharistic prayer, which, according to the so-called Discipline of the Secret (Lat. *disciplina arcani*), was to be kept hidden from the unbaptized, together with the text of the creed and of the → Lord's Prayer (see Ambr. *Instit.* 10; *Cain* 1.37).

Ambrose also testifies to the custom of remembering the dead during the eucharistic celebration (Ambr. *Ob. Val.* 78), even though it is difficult to determine exactly when such a remembrance took place during the ritual, be it within the canon or at another moment.

The eucharistic prayer was followed by the Lord's Prayer, which ended with a solemn doxology (Ambr. *Sacr.* 6.24). After this prayer the faithful received the eucharistic communion by coming directly to the altar (*Sacr.* 5.14; P.Dec. *Vita Ambr.* 44). Ambrose describes this moment in the following way:

Ergo non otiose dicis tu "Amen," iam in spiritu confitens quod accipias corpus Christi. Cum ergo tu petieris, dicit tibi sacerdos: "Corpus Christi," et tu dicis: "Amen," hoc est: "verum." ["Therefore, it is not superfluous that you say 'Amen,' already in spirit confessing that you receive the body of Christ. The bishop or the priest says to you: 'The body of Christ.' And you say: 'Amen,' that is: True." (Ambr. *Sacr.* 4.24)

In this regard, it may be noted that in the Ambrosian liturgy, according the testimony provided by Ambrose, it is always up to the faithful to personally respond to the communion with "Amen," even though the praxis of the Roman rite entrusts this directly to the celebrant or to the minister. Moreover, Ambrose's words concerning the human hand *per quam offerimus et sumimus sacramenta coelestia* (Ambr. *Hex.* 6.69; "the human hand through which we offer and receive the heavenly sacraments") may be interpreted as meaning that the faithful received the eucharistic bread directly from the bishop's hand.

Ps 22 was sung during communion: in fact, the allusions to the lavishly decked table and to the overflowing chalice could be interpreted in the eucharistic sense (Ambr. *Hel.* 34; *Sacr.* 5.13).

It is not certain whether the congregation was dismissed with a → blessing. Ambrose is clearly referring to a benediction of liturgical character, with subsequent acclamation by the people, when he states: *Cum sacerdos benedicit, populus respondet amen* (Ambr. *Enarrat. Ps.* 40 36; "When the bishop or priest blesses, the congregation answers 'Amen'"), but a precise reconstruction of the context is not possible.

Finally, Ambrose also mentions the positioning of the ministers around the altar during the performance of the ritual, namely in such a way that *non omnes vident alta mysteriorum quia operiuntur a levitis* (Ambr. *Off.* 1.251; not everyone can see the sublime mysteries, because they are hidden by the Levites").

2. The Christian Initiation and Baptismal Rites

The path of Christian initiation in 4th-century CE Milan can be easily reconstructed due to the fact that Ambrose himself describes it in the two parallel treatises *De Sacramentis* and *De Mysteriis*.

It seems likely that the catechumens were divided into two groups: the simple catechumens, who were probably admitted into this category with the simple ritual of tracing the sign of the → cross on the forehead (Ambr. *Myst.* 20), and the *competentes* or *electi*, the baptismal candidates who have already reached the end of their preparation (Ambr. *Epist.* 76.4). On the feast of Epiphany, the *competentes* had to supply the name for the baptismal preparation that was about to begin, probably by signing the registration in their own hand (Ambr. *Exp. Luc.* 4.76; *Hel.* 79; *Abr.* 1.23; *Sacr.* 3.12). On the Sunday before → Easter, following the dismissal of the catechumens at the end of the liturgy of the word, the ceremony of "delivery of the creed" (*traditio Symboli*) to the *competentes* was held so that they could learn the fundamental truths of the Christian faith.

The actual baptismal rites took place during the Easter Vigil; they can be reconstructed in accordance with the following sequence of events:

- the rite of *ephphatha* or the "mystery of the opening" (*apertionis mysterium*);
- entry into the baptistery;
- prebaptismal anointing;
- renunciations;
- exorcism and consecration of the water;
- triple profession of faith and triple immersion;
- post-baptismal anointing;
- washing of the feet;
- bestowal of the white garment,
- confirmation (*signaculum spiritale*);
- procession from the baptistery to the altar of the basilica for the eucharistic celebration.

This complex sequence of rites obviously presupposes a structured ritual space: in fact, Ambrose did have a large baptistery of octagonal shape built next to the main basilica of Milan; at its center was the font in which the catechumen immersed him- or herself as if buried there. *Fons quasi sepulturaest* ("Therefore the font is, as it were, a burial"), as Ambrose explicitly says (Ambr. *Sacr.* 2.19). But superimposed on the symbolism of the burial, that of the resurrection (→ Resurrection) is no less evident, being highlighted by the octagonal shape of the baptistery and of the same font. In Ambr. *Exp. Luc.* 7.173, we thus read that *in octavo numero resurrectionis est*

plenitudo ("the number eight indicates the fullness of the resurrection"). In this way, the celebration of the sacraments of Christian initiation were perceived as the actualization of the Paschal mystery on the catechumen's path toward the fullness of the life of faith.

More specifically, the following particularities can be noted:

> The rite of *ephphatha* called for the bishop to touch the catechumen's ears and nostrils, thereby repeating the gesture made by Jesus to heal the deaf-mute (according to Mark 7:32–35), in order to indicate the opening (*apertionis mysterium*) of the senses to the Word and to the grace of God. (Ambr. *Sacr.* 1.2)

Following the entry into the baptistery, the catechumen received the prebaptismal anointing, which made him an *athleta Christi* (*Sacr.* 1.4) ready to take up the struggle against the devil.

The renunciations of the → devil and of the world involved only two questions, as also attested at all times in the subsequent Ambrosian tradition, but unlike the Roman tradition, which included three questions. While making the renunciations, the catechumen symbolically stood facing the west, the place of darkness, and then turned toward the east, the symbolic place of light, as a sign of his own adherence and conversion to Christ: *Ad orientem converteris; qui enim renuntiat diabolo, ad Christum convertitur* (Ambr. *Myst.* 7; "You turned to the east. Who renounces to the devil, turns to Christ."

The blessing of the water comprises two aspects – the negative one of exorcism and the positive one of the actual benediction. A homiletic text written by Ambrose (*Exp. Luc.* 10.48) shows numerous congruities with the prayer of benediction that is handed down by the successive Ambrosian liturgical books of the medieval period. This circumstance suggests not only a direct dependence of the later liturgical texts from the Ambrosian passage in question but also the dependence of Ambrose's entire homiletic passage from the liturgical prayer that was used to bless the water in his day, and of which the homiletic passage would be nothing other than the paraphrase. Already in the 4th century CE, therefore, there probably existed an original text of the blessing, to which some scholars would like to assign a Syriac origin.

The custom of baptizing by having the three questions on the profession of faith in the → Trinity follow upon the three immersions, as attested in Ambr. *Sacr.* 2.20 and *Spir.* 2.105, is ancient. The immersion took place in the so-called horizontal fashion: with help, the catechumen stretched out completely under water and probably spread his arms in the form of a cross. In this way, the Paschal mystery was *quasi* reenacted through the rite: the catechumen, by immersing himself, was buried together with Christ and, by reemerging, was resurrected to the new Christian life, according to Rom 6:4–5.

The neophyte was finally led to the eastern edge of the baptismal font, where the bishop awaited him: he or she thus completed the *transitus*, the passage across the baptismal water from west to east, in what may be described as a kind of new exodus.

Whether the writings of Ambrose actually attest to the conferral of the confirmation after baptism is a much-debated issue. The explicit mention of the postbaptismal anointing (Ambr. *Myst.* 29–30; *Sacr.* 2.24) does not refer to the confirmation but denotes the assimilation of the Christian to Christ, the anointed one of God. A reference to the confirmation, however, may be seen in the subsequent allusions to the *signaculum spiritale* mentioned in *Myst.* 42 and in *Sacr.* 3.8: the bishop invoked the outpouring of the Holy Spirit with its seven gifts onto the neophytes, although the ritual does not appear to have included the anointing of the forehead.

This was followed by the washing of the feet (Ambr. *Myst.* 31–32; *Sacr.* 3.4–7), which, as we have already said, characterized the postbaptismal rites of Milan in Ambrosian times, in contrast to what was done in Rome. The Ambrosian liturgy of the Middle Ages would always remain true to this approach and, in accordance, never placed disproportionate emphasis on the washing of the feet in the ritual of Holy Thursday (as laid down in the Roman liturgy).

Regarding the wearing of the white garment by the newly baptized, it is worth noting that Ambrose, together with his contemporary Zeno of Verona, provides the earliest attestation of this custom in the West (Ambr. *Myst.* 34–35; *Exp. Luc.* 5.25).

The path of Christian initiation finally reached its conclusion with the procession from the baptistery to the altar of the basilica for the eucharistic celebration. Ambrose briefly summarizes the entire liturgy of the Easter Vigil in the following way: *Venit iam dies resurrectionis, baptizantur electi, veniunt ad altare, accipiunt sacramentum* (Ambr. *Hel.* 34; "The day of the resurrection has now come; the elected are baptized, they come to the altar and receive the sacrament").

During the Octave of Easter, the bishop instructed the neophytes in the mystagogic catecheses explaining the sacraments received in the preceding Easter Vigil: the invaluable tractates *De Sacramentis* and *De Mysteriis* are the result of the stenographic recording of these homilies and of their revision on the part of Ambrose.

3. The Ritual Aspects of the Other Sacraments

Only a few references have come down to us regarding the ritual aspects of the other sacraments. The reconciliation of the penitents took place on Holy Thursday, defined by Ambrose as the day *quo sese Dominus pro nobis tradidit, quo in Ecclesia poenitentia relaxatur* (Ambr. *Epist.* 76.26: "On which the Lord gave himself up for us, the day on which penance is granted in the Church"), a praxis that would remain unchanged even in the Middle Ages. In *Spir.* 3.139, furthermore, Ambrose states that the → priests remit sins in the name of the Father and of the Son and of the → Holy Spirit, perhaps alluding to a formula of reconciliation.

The ritual of laying on the hands is attested for the sick, but anointings do not appear to have taken place (Ambr. *Paen.* 1.36). Ambrose also speaks of the laying on of the hands and of the *benedictio in nomine Domini Iesu* in the context of the episcopal ordination (Ambr. *Epist.* 5.6.)

With regard to → marriage, finally, Ambrose states explicitly that the constitutive act of marriage consists in the exchange of mutual consent between the bride and the groom (Ambr. *Instit.* 41), but also adds that *ipsum coniugium velamine sacerdotali et benedictione sanctificari oportet* (Ambr. *Epist.* 62.7): the pagan custom of Roman origin provided that the bride was to be brought already veiled to the ceremony by the groom, whereas Ambrose assigned the laying on of the veil to the priest.

Fairly precise information is also provided regarding the veiling of the virgins (→ Virgin/Virginity), which was undoubtedly celebrated on Easter (Ambr. *Exh. Virginit.* 42) and in the context of the Christmas festivities (whether on Christmas, Dec 25, or on the feast of the Epiphany, Jan 6, remains a matter of debate). It seems likely that the rite included the following sequence of celebratory moments: the presentation of the virgin at the altar prior to the eucharistic liturgy and, following the allocution of the bishop, the public profession of virginity, the recitation of a ritual formula on the part of the bishop, the laying on of the veil with nuptial meaning, and the blessing (Ambr. *Virg.* 1.65). Ambrose also alludes to a change of clothes (*mutatio vestis*) and to the assumption of the *stola*, which was perhaps a distinctive dress of the virgins, even though the term could be interpreted in an allegorical sense (→ Allegory), namely as a new raiment of Christian virtue (Ambr. *Virg.* 3.1; *Instit.* 100).

4. The Liturgical Year

The writings of Ambrose enable us to reconstruct the structure of the → liturgical year in 4th-century CE Milan. Without any doubt, the Christmas cycle revolved around two feasts, → Christmas and the → Epiphany, for which two hymns by Ambrose have been preserved: *Intende qui regis Israel* and *Illuminans Altissimus*, respectively. From the second hymn, one can deduce that the Epiphany originally commemorated at least four *manifestations* of Christ as the Son of God: first the baptism in the Jordan, following the eastern tradition, then the adoration of the → Magi, the wedding at Cana, and the multiplication of the bread.

Regarding the time of preparation for Easter, Ambrose states literally: *Quadragesima totis praeter sabbatum et dominicam ieiunatur diebus; hoc ieiunium Domini pascha concludit* (Ambr. *Hel.* 34: "The day on which the Lord gave himself up for us, the day on which penance is granted in the Church"). With these words, he provides us with the oldest attestation of Lenten fasting in the West, but at the same time also testifies to the fact that in Milan, among

the days of the week, not only Sunday but also Saturday had preserved a distinctly festive character, so much so that even during Lent, fasting was not required on this day; this particular feature clearly deviates from the normal western praxis, although it does find an interesting parallel in some eastern liturgical traditions. The testimony of → Augustine of Hippo, who records the surprise of his mother Monica, is interesting in this respect: accustomed to Saturday fasting in Rome, she encountered a distinctly different praxis when she arrived in Milan. Augustine also records Ambrose's reaction to this problem: *Quando Romae sum, ieiuno sabbato; et ad quamcumque Ecclesiam veneritis, inquit, eius morem servate* (Aug. *Ep.* 36.32: "When I am in Rome, I fast on Saturdays; and in whichever Church you arrive – he said – observe its customs").

Furthermore, Ambrose's statement that *hoc ieiunium Domini pascha concludit* ("the Passover of the Lord closes this fast") is to be understood in the sense that the Lenten fasting ended on Good Friday, which is called *Domini pascha*: Lent thus lasted from the sixth Sunday before Resurrection Sunday until the evening of Holy Thursday, based on a computation to which the subsequent Ambrosian liturgical tradition would always remain faithful. The end of Lent – as Ambrose explicitly states in an important letter to the bishops of Emilia – was followed by the celebration of *triduum illud sacrum* [...] *intra quod* [*Dominus*] *et passus est et quievit et resurrexit* (Ambr. *Epist. EC* 13.13; "that sacred triduum during which [the Lord] suffered, slept and raised again"), a clear reference to the three days of the Paschal Triduum: Good Friday as the day of the passion, Holy Saturday as the day when Christ lay in the tomb, and Easter Sunday as the day of his resurrection (→ Resurrection). The profound unity of the mystery of → death and resurrection is apparent in Ambrose's Paschal hymn *Hic est dies verus Dei*, which expands on the scene of the Calvary to contemplate the salvific death of Christ as a victory over our death and thus as a source of eternal life.

Moreover, the aforementioned letter to the bishops of Emilia informs us that in Milan, the calculation of Easter dates according to the lunar phases followed the eastern tradition of Alexandria (with a cycle of 19 years) and not the western Roman one (with a cycle of 84 years): as in the case of the festive Saturday, this again confirms the presence of an eastern substratum that probably preceded Ambrose, who had declared that he wanted to follow the Roman model in all things.

The ensuing Paschal feast extended over a period of 50 days (→ Pentecost), each of which was considered to be as festive as → Sunday. Hence, there was no fasting on these days; instead, the Hallelujah was sung as a sign of joy (Ambr. *Exp. Luc.* 8.25; esp. *Apol. Dav.* 42).

It is also possible to reconstruct, at least in its basic outline, the sanctorale cycle of the Church of Milan at the time of Ambrose: in fact, his writings reveal the importance that was attached to the veneration of the martyrs and of some saints whose memorial liturgy was celebrated. It was above all Ambrose who, in Milan, introduced the custom of the translating the relics of martyrs from the site of their discovery to the basilica in which they were deposited: this practice, by the way, is not mirrored in the West and especially not in Rome but seems once again to come from the East. In Milan, Ambrose discovered the bodies of the saints Protasius and Gervasius in Jun 386 CE, as well as those of the saints Nazarius and Celsus, probably in 395 CE: he wrote the hymn *Grates tibi Iesu novas* in honor of the former. However, the veneration of the three martyrs Victor, Nabor, and Felix, all three of Mauritanian origin but Milanese by choice, may perhaps have preceded Ambrose, who calls them *martyres nostri* (Ambr. *Exp. Luc.* 7.178) and to whom he dedicated the hymn *Victor, Nabor, Felix pii*. There is also clear evidence for the veneration of the Roman martyrs Agnes and Lawrence, for whom he composed the hymns *Agnes, beatae virginis*, and *Apostolorum supparem*, as well as of Sebastian, for whom he claims a Milanese origin (Ambr. *Exp. Ps.* 118 20.44). The Feast of Saints Peter and Paul was undoubtedly celebrated, which was preceded by a vigil *tota nocte* (Ambr. *Virginit.* 125–126) and for which he wrote the hymn *Apostolorum passio*; the hymn *Amore Christi nobilis*, composed for John the evangelist, is also extant. Other saints are mentioned extensively in his works, and a liturgical remembrance may also be assumed for → John the Baptist, Stephen, Pope Sixtus, the martyr Thecla, and, obviously omitting the pro-Arian Auxentius, the bishops who immediately preceded him, Eustorgius and Dionysius.

With regard to the veneration of the martyrs, Ambrose specifically inaugurated the practice of linking the dedication of the basilicas to the deposition of their relics under the altar: he did so for the basilica of Porta Romana (which he built in cruciform shape; now called San Nazzaro Maggiore e Santi Apostoli) with the relics of the apostles and, in 386 CE, for the basilica known as *Ambrosiana* (now Sant'Ambrogio) with the bodies of the saints Gervasius and Protasius.

However, he purged the veneration of the martyrs of certain funerary customs that had a pagan origin, such as the funerary banquet that took place on their tombs and which often degenerated into abuse; he is abundantly clear in his condemnation of those *qui calices ad sepulcra martyrum deferunt atque illic in vesperum bibunt* [...] *O stultitia hominum qui ebrietatem sacrificium putant* (Ambr. *Hel.* 62; "those who carry the chalices on the sepulchres of the martyrs and there in vespers drink [...] What foolish men those who think that drunkenness is a sacrifice"). The strict prohibitions of such practices by Ambrose is also recorded by Augustine (*Conf.* 6.2). Finally, some ritual elements of the funerary liturgy can be detected: in the funeral oration for his brother Satyrus, Ambrose alludes to a threefold act of salutation and homage to the body of the deceased when he states: *Ultimum coram populo vale dico, pacem paedico, osculum solvo* (Ambr. *Exc.* 1.78; "In the presence of the people, I want to give you my last farewell, to wish you peace, to give you the homage of a kiss"). He also provides clear testimony for the transition from the pagan custom of remembering the dead on the day of their birth to the Christian one, which considers the true *dies natalis* to be that of the death in Christ: *Nos ipsi natales dies defunctorum obliviscimur et eum quo obierunt diem celebri solemnitate renovamus* (Ambr. *Exc.* 2.5; "We too do not remember the day of the birth of our deceased, but we commemorate with great solemnity the day they left this world").

5. The Liturgy of the Hours

Among the various hymns composed by Ambrose, there are four that make reference to certain specific moments of prayer during the day: *Aeterne rerum Conditor* when the cock crows, *Splendor paternae gloriae* at sunrise, *Iam surgit hora tertia* during the day, and *Deus creator omnium* at vespers.

In his writings, we also find specific attestations of a least three vigils *tota nocte*: the Easter Vigil, the vigil held on the occasion of the Feast of Saints Peter and Paul (with regard to which Ambrose deplored the poor participation of the people; Ambr. *Virginit.* 126: *Nox fuit: pauciores ad vigilias convenerunt*; "Night fell and few people came for the vigil"), and the vigil held on the occasion of the discovery of the bodies of the saints Protasius and Gervasius (Ambr. *Epist.* 77.2).

The custom of keeping vigil in prayer for the entire night has ancient origins: we may well ask ourselves if Ambrose found this practice already in force in the Church of Milan or if he introduced it there himself. In this regard, Augustine and Ambrose's biographer Paulinus the Deacon attribute an innovation to him: in the days preceding Easter 386 CE, the empress Justina planned to confiscate a basilica in order to hand it over the Arian faction, whereupon Ambrose and the people occupied it day and night to defend the bishop's right over the worship buildings of the Catholic community. Augustine relates that on this occasion *Hymni et psalmi ut canerentur secundum morem Orientalium partium, ne populus moeroris taedio contabesceret, institutum est* (Aug. *Conf.* 9.15; "This was the time that the custom began, after the manner of the eastern church, that hymns and Psalms should be sung, so that the people would not be worn out with the tedium of lamentation"). Paulinus confirms that:

> Hoc in tempore primum antiphonae, hymni ac vigiliae in ecclesia Mediolanensi celebrari coeperunt. Cuius celebritatis devotio usque in hodiernum diem non solum in eadem ecclesia, verum per omnes paene Occidentis provincias manet. ["At that time for the first time in the Milanese Church the vigils began to be celebrated with antiphoned singing and hymns and this liturgical use has persisted until today not only in that Church but in almost all provinces in the West."] (P.Deac. *Vita Ambr.* 23)

Both testimonies are normally not interpreted in the sense that no night offices were held in Milan prior to Ambrose but in the sense that Ambrose was the one who structured them, inasmuch as he issued

more precise rules regarding the timing of the celebrations, the Psalms that were to be used, and the chants that were to be performed. He probably also introduced the custom of daily vigils by following the example of the eastern praxis, although in this case, this would seem to refer less to the vigils *tota nocte* than to the nocturnal/early morning praying sessions, for which he wrote the hymn that was to be sung when the cock crows.

A more complex matter, however, is the interpretation of the information regarding the introduction of the antiphonal chanting of the Psalms. For some scholars, this would refer to the practice of having the people repeat the identical refrain following each Psalm verse or stanza sung by the soloist (the so-called responsorial psalmody); for others, however, it would allude to the genuine antiphonal psalmody, in which the congregation is divided into two choirs that alternate in the singing of the individual Psalm verses. With regard to the choral singing of the people during the liturgical celebration, Ambrose states: *In oratione totius plebis [...] cum responsoriis psalmorum cantus virorum, mulierum, virginum, parvulorum consonus [...] resultat* (Ambr. *Hex.* 3.23; "When the congregation prays in chorus, the singing of men, women and children echoes in the responsories of the Psalms").

The following statement provides clear evidence of the early-morning prayer session: *Mane festina ad ecclesiam [...] quam iucundum inchoare ab hymnis et canticis, a beatitudinibus quas in evangelio legis* (Ambr. *Exp. Ps. 118.* 19.32: "Hurry to the church early in the morning [...] How pleasant it is to start the day with the hymns, songs and beatitudes that we read in the gospel"). Ambrose mentions hymns and songs, but there is little doubt that certain Psalms were also sung, as evidenced by Ambr. *Hel.* 55.

Regarding the Beatitudes, some scholars have thought of something along the lines of the so-called μακαρισμοί, under the probable influence of the Liturgy of Jerusalem; it is nonetheless strange that the singing of the Beatitudes, which is clearly attested in the writings of Ambrose, should have totally disappeared from the Ambrosian rite of the Middle Ages.

Ambrose alludes to the evening Psalm prayer with the following words: *Qui enim sensum hominis gerens non erubescat sine psalmorum celebritate diem claudere?* (Ambr. *Hex.* 5.36; "Which sensitive man would not be ashamed to end the day without reciting the Psalms?"). Concerning Lent, the reference to the following sequence of liturgical events is more explicit: the afternoon psalmody, the eucharistic celebration, and finally an evening office that Ambrose calls the *sacrificum vespertinum* (Ambr. *Exp. Ps. 118* 8.48).

Speaking to the virgins, finally, the bishop sets out the details of a daily program of prayer that pretty much corresponds to the cycle of a regular liturgy of the hours:

> Oratio quoque nos Deo crebra commendet [...] Certe sollemnes orationes cum gratiarum actione sunt deferendae, cum e somno surgimus, cum prodimus, cum cibum paramus sumere, cum supserimus, et hora incensi, cum denique cubitum pergimus. ["Let us recommend ourselves to God with frequent prayers [...] Certainly, we must raise solemn prayers with thanksgiving when we wake up from sleep, when we go out, when we prepare to take food, after eating and in the evening, finally when we go to sleep."] (Ambr. *Virg.* 3.18)

A notable aspect is the link between the evening prayer and the moment at which the lamps are lit (*hora incensi*): in line with these remarks by Ambrose, the Ambrosian Liturgy always retained the so-called *lucernarium* at the beginning of vespers, a psalmodic chant that accompanied the ritual of the lighting of the candles.

6. The *Ordo lectionum*

Drawing on the writings of Ambrose, it is possible to reconstruct an incipient order of scriptural readings, at least as far as Lent and the Holy Week are concerned.

At the beginning of Ambr. *Myst.* 1, the bishop, while going back over the catechetical instructions dispensed to the catechumens during Lent, states the following: *De moralibus cotidianum sermonem habuimus, cum vel patriarcharum gesta vel proverbiorum legerentur paecepta* ("Every day we gave a talk on moral issues, when the lives of the patriarchs or the precepts of the Proverbs were being read"). On each day of Lent, Ambrose thus gave the catechumens a homily of moral content, based on the reading of a passage from Genesis (*patriarcharum*

gesta) and on a passage from the book of Proverbs. It is not known if this catechetical tradition must be attributed to Ambrose himself or to his predecessor; in fact, it is found in the 5th-century CE Liturgy of Jerusalem, in the church of the East, and in the rite of Constantinople and of the Hispanic Churches; in the Ambrosian Church, it was constantly retained throughout the centuries, albeit in various arrangements and with different selections of pericopes: even today, on Lenten weekdays, the Ambrosian lectionary advocates two readings from Genesis and Proverbs, in keeping with the testimony of Ambrose.

Ambrose also gives us a hint regarding the probable order of the gospels on Lenten Sundays and during the Holy Week; in *Exp. Luc. 7*, 182, he states:

> Audimus et legimus ieiunasse Dominum, sitisse Dominum, lacrimasse Dominum, vapulasse Dominum, vapulasse Dominum, dicentem Dominum: "Vigilate et orate ne intretis in tentationem." ["We hear and read that the Lord fasted, that the Lord was thirsty, that the Lord wept, that the Lord was beaten, that the Lord said: 'Watch and pray that you may not undergo the test.'"]

And indeed, the episodes of the temptations and of the fasting of Jesus in the desert, of his encounter with the Samaritan woman, and of the raising of → Lazarus are constantly found in the sequence of Sunday gospels of the Ambrosian Lent. However, Ambrose also alludes to the agony in Gethsemane with a quotation from Matthew, the exact same reading that the Ambrosian liturgical order reserves for Holy Thursday.

In the letter to his sister Marcellina, in which he retraces what had happened during the Holy Week of 386 CE, he recalls, among other things, that the book of Job had been read *ex usu* on Wednesday and the book of the prophet → Jonah *de more* on the following day (Ambr. *Epist.* 76.14 and 25). *Ex usu* and *de more* are practically synonymous and probably allude to a tradition that was even older than Ambrose; in fact, this custom has been admirably preserved up to the present day in the order of the Ambrosian lectionary, which prescribes the reading of the book of Job during the first three days of the Holy Week and of the book of Jonah during the *in cena domini* Mass on Holy Thursday. Moreover,

Ambrose also provides clear testimony that the book of Tobit was read in the liturgy of Milan of his day (Ambr. *Tob.* 1): although he does not say when this was done, the Ambrosian liturgy would always retain, along with the reading of the book of Job, that of the book of Tobit during the first three days of the Holy Week.

On a Holy Thursday between 386 and 390 CE, furthermore, Ambrose delivered a homily on the passion of the Lord and concluded it with a comment on the denial of Peter (→ Peter the Apostle) and the crowing of the cock (Ambr. *Hex.* 5.88–92): this is the very same gospel pericope that the Ambrosian liturgy always prescribed for the Thursday of the Holy Week and for which we have already found an allusion in *Exp. Luc.* 7.182.

It is, of course, difficult to determine exactly on which occasions Ambrose, for the drafting of his own homilies, drew on an order of biblical readings that had already existed before him and was thus, to some degree, already traditional in the Church of Milan, or in which cases the gradual fixing of such an order can be attributed to Ambrose himself: there is little doubt that the subsequent Ambrosian liturgical tradition, on a number of points such as Lent and the Holy Week, reveals a substantial continuity with the few but precious details that are present in his writings.

7. From Ambrose to the Ambrosian Liturgy

At the end of this brief overview, one may understand how difficult it is to establish a direct relationship between Ambrose and the Ambrosian liturgy: although he did not exactly devise the liturgy, as he would later (somewhat simplistically) come to believe, he did collect and carry on the ritual praxis that had already existed before him, introduced some new elements, confronted the liturgical tradition of Rome, and defended the autonomy of the local tradition. In the following centuries, the reference to Ambrose undoubtedly became an element of identity for the Church of Milan, and even the liturgical tradition that was proper to this church was gradually attributed to him.

One of the earliest explicit attestations of this attribution is found in the liturgical manual *De exordiis et incrementis quarundam in observationibus ecclesiasticis rerum* by Walafrid Strabo, abbot of Reichenau (d. 849 CE): *Ambrosius Mediolanensis episcopus tam missae quam ceterorum dispositionem officiorum suae Ecclesiae et aliis Liguribus ordinavit: quae usque hodie in Mediolanensi tenentur ecclesia* (PL 114.944; "Ambrose, bishop of Milan, ordered the rules of the Mass and of the whole liturgy for his church and for all the churches of northern Italy; and this liturgical order continues to this day in the Milanese Church").

The extreme outcome of this "ideological procedure" would reach its peak in Milan in the centuries after 1000 CE (see esp. the works of the so-called Landulf Senior and of Bonvesin de la Riva), when all that is proper to the church and city of Milan, especially the liturgical rites and the ecclesiastical institutions, would be attributed to Ambrose. This is obviously unacceptable from a critical point of view, but it does reveal the intention of finding the root of one's identity in the figure and in the works of the patron saint.

Indeed, Ambrose's episcopate would always remain paradigmatic for the Church of Milan and its liturgy, and it is a significant fact that during the Carolingian period, the adjective *ambrosiano* emerged as a qualifying term denoting either the Milanese Church (*Ambrosiana Ecclesia*) or its specific liturgy (*Ambrosianum mysterium*). In this manner, the Church of Milan, either erroneously or rightly on the historical level but with perfect consistency on the symbolic level, found the ideal origin of all of its distinctive features in the person of Ambrose.

Historiography

The first organic reconstruction of the liturgy of the Milanese Church at the time of Saint Ambrose as it results from his works is due to A. Paredi (1940b) and G. Nicodemi (1942); more recently, C. Alzati (2000), has proposed a rigorous and documented summary on this topic. However, as regards the liturgical year and the liturgy of the Christian initiation, with this reconstruction interferes the problem of the authenticity of some hymns and above all the treatise entitled *De Sacramentis*. For example, J. Fontaine (1994) raised doubts about the authenticity of the two hymns for the Epiphany and for Easter; but more recently A. Zerfass (2008) and B.P. Dunkle (2016) have confirmed that they are works by Ambrose. Similarly, it's known that since the 16th century the authenticity of *De Sacramentis* has been repeatedly questioned until recent contributions (e.g. Savon, 2012); however, currently most scholars, following the contributions of C. Mohrmann (1952; 1978), G. Lazzati (1955), and A. Paredi (1964), recognize in this treatise the tachygraphic transcription of the homilies offered by Ambrose to the neophytes (see a useful summary of the issue in Satterlee, 2002, 20–30).

Bibliography

Alzati, C., *Ambrosianum Mysterium: La chiesa di Milano e la sua tradizione liturgica*, Milan, 2000.

Auf Der Maur, H.J., *Das Psalmenverständnis des Ambrosius von Mailand: Ein Beitrag zum Deutunghintergrund der Psalmenverwendung im Gottesdienst der Alten Kirche*, Leiden, 1977.

Beumer, J., "Die ältesten Zeugnisse für die Römische Eucharistiefeier bei Ambrosius von Mailnad," *ZKTh* 95, 1973, 311–324.

Borella, P., "Le valeur de la messe ambrosienne et l'oeuvre de S. Ambroise," *QLP* 40, 1959, 127–138.

Borella, P., "Appunti sul Natale e l'Epifania a Milano al tempo di sant'Ambrogio," in: *Mélanges liturgiques offerts à dom B. Botte*, Abbaye du Mont-César, 1972, 49–70.

Braschi, F., "Luoghi e riti per la celebrazione del battesimo in epoca ambrosiana: un'ipotesi di ricostruzione," *StAm* 1, 2007, 131–146.

Cantù, D., "La modulazione salmodica ambrosiana: Origine–sviluppo–critica," *Ambr.* 8, 1932, 23–31.

Caprioli, A., "Battesimo e confermazione in S. Ambrogio," in: *Miscellanea Carlo Figini*, Venegono Inferiore, 1964, 49–57.

Caprioli, A., *Battesimo e confermazione: Studio storico sulla liturgia e catechesi in S. Ambrogio*, Venegono Inferiore, 1977.

Cattaneo, E., *La religione a Milano nell'età di sant'Ambrogio*, Milan, 1974.

Del Bo, L., "Riti ed usi funerari del IV secolo in Milano," *Ambr.* 15, 1939, 233–237; 16, 1940, 25–28.

Dunkle, B.P., *Enchantment and Creed in the Hymns of Ambrose of Milan*, Oxford, 2016.

Faller, O., "Das Taufelsanspeien im Mailänder Taufrituel (Zu Ambrosius, De Mysteriis 2,7)," *JLW* 9, 1929, 128–132.

Fontaine, J., *Ambroise de Milan: Hymnes: Texte établi, traduit et annoté*, Paris, 1994.

Frank, H., "La celebrazione della festa 'natalis Salvatoris' e 'Epiphania' in Milano ai tempi di S. Ambrosio," *ScC* 62, 1934, 683–695.

Frank, H., "Ambrosius und die Büsseraussöhnung in Mailand: Ein Beitrag zur Geschichte der mailändischen Gründonnerstagsliturgie," in: O. Casel, ed., *Heilige Überlieferung: Ausschnitte aus der Geschichte des Mönchtums und des hl. Kultes*, Münster, 1938, 136–173.

Frank, H., "Das mailändischen Kirchenjahr in den Werken des hl. Ambrosius," *PaBo* 51, 1940, 40–48, 79–90, 120–127; 52, 1941, 11–17.

Franz, A., "Die Tagzeitenliturgie der Mailänder Kirche im 4. Jahrhundert: Ein Beitrag zur Geschichte des Kathedraloffiziums im Westen," *ALW* 34, 1992, 22–83.

Franz, A., *Tageslauf und Heilsgeschichte: Untersuchungen zum literarischen Text und liturgischen Kontext der Tagseitenhymnen des Ambrosius von Mailand*, St. Ottilien, 1994.

Franz, A., "Gli inni di Ambrogio e la liturgia delle ore giornaliera," in: R. Passarella, ed., *Ambrogio e la liturgia*, Milan, 2012, 3–22.

Garavaglia, L., "I santi e le ragioni del loro culto negli scritti di sant'Ambrogio," in: *Ricerche storiche sulla chiesa ambrosiana*, vol. VI, Milan, 1976, 5–28.

Lazzati, G., "L'autenticità del De Sacramentis e la valutazione letteraria delle opere di S. Ambrogio," *Aevum* 29, 1955, 17–48.

Leeb, H., *Die Psalmodie bei Ambrosius*, Vienna, 1967.

Lemarié, J., "La liturgie d'Aquilée et de Milan au temps de Chromace et de Ambroise," in: M. Mirabella Roberti, ed., *Aquileia e Milano*, Udine, 1973, 249–270.

Magistretti, M., *La liturgia della chiesa milanese nel sec. IV*, Milan, 1899.

Marchioro, R., *La prassi penitenziale nel IV secolo a Milano secondo S. Ambrogio*, Rome, 1975.

Mazza, E., "Sul Canone della messa citato nel De Sacramentis di Ambrogio," in: R. Passarella, ed., *Ambrogio e la liturgia*, Milan, 2012, 47–68.

Mitchell, L., "Ambrosian Baptismal Rites," *StLi* 1, 1962, 241–253.

Mohrmann, C., "Le style oral du *De Sacramentis* de Saint Ambroise," *VigChr* 6, 1952, 168–177.

Mohrmann, C., "Observations sur le De Sacramentis et le De Mysteriis de Saint Ambroise," in: G. Lazzati ed., *Ambrosius Episcopus*, Milan, 1978, 107–123.

Monachino, V., *S. Ambrogio e la cura pastorale a Milano nel secolo IV*, Milan, 1973.

Moneta Caglio, E.T., "S. Ambrogio e l'ufficiatura," *Ambr.* 16, 1940, 113–127.

Monzio Compagnoni, G., *Sant'Ambrogio: La luce nel cuore: Catechesi sulla fede (Explanatio Symboli–De mysteriis–De sacramentis)*, Milan, 2013.

Navoni, M., ed., *Dizionario di Liturgia Ambrosiana*, Milan, 1996.

Nicodemi, G., "Sant'Ambrogio e la liturgia della sua Chiesa," in: *Ambrosiana: Scritti di storia, archeologia ed arte pubblicati nel XVI centenario della nascita di sant'Ambrogio CCCXL-MCMXL*, Milan, 1942, 273–284.

Paredi, A., "Influssi orientali sulla liturgia milanese antica," *ScC* 68, 1940a, 574–579.

Paredi, A., "La liturgia di Sant'Ambrogio," in: *Sant'Ambrogio nel XVI Centenario della nascita*, Milan, 1940b, 69–157.

Paredi, A., "La liturgia del 'De Sacramentis'," in: *Miscellanea Carlo Figini*, 1964, 59–72.

Payer, A., "Die Liturgie und die Hymnen des hl: Bischofs Ambrosius von Mailand," *Heiliger Dienst* 20, 1966, 26–31.

Saint-Laurent, G.E., *St. Ambrose's Contribution to latin liturgical Hymnography*, Washington DC, 1968.

Satterlee, C.A., *Ambrose of Milan's Method of Mystagogical Preaching*, Collegeville, 2002.

Savon, H., "Doit-on atribuer à Ambroise le De Sacramentis?," in: R. Passarella, ed., *Ambrogio e la liturgia*, Milan, 2012, 23–45.

Schmitz, J., *Christliche Initiation und Messfeier im Laufe des Jahres bei Ambrosius von Mailand*, Bonn, 1974.

Schmitz, J., *Gottesdienst im altchristlichen Mailand: Eine liturgiewissenschaftliche Untersuchung über Initiation und Messfeier während des Jahres zur Zeit des Bischofs Ambrosius († 397)*, Köln, 1975.

Trisoglio, F., "Stile ed efficacia artistica nel De Sacramentis e nel De Mysteriis di sant'Ambrogio," *StAm* 3, 2009, 267–283.

Yarnold, E.J., "The Ceremonies of Initiation in De Sacramentis and De Mysteriis of St. Ambrose," in: *StPat*, vol. X, Berlin, 1970, 453–463.

Zerfass, A., *Mysterium mirabile: Poesie, Theologie und Liturgie in den Hymnen des Ambrosius von Mailand zu den Christusfesten des Kirchenjahres*, Tübingen, 2008.

MARCO NAVONI

Ambrosiaster

"Ambrosiaster," that is, "would-be Ambrose," is the name coined in the late 16th century to refer to the author of the first complete Latin commentary on the letters of Paul. The name "Ambrosiaster" seems to have first appeared in 1580 in the *Notationes in sacra biblia* of Franciscus Lucas Brugensis, although earlier Desiderius Erasmus had raised questions about the attribution of the synopses in the commentary to Ambrose of Milan (Krans, 2013). The same author composed the *Questions on the Old and New Testaments* (*Quaestiones veteris et novi testament CXXVI*) generally transmitted in the Middle Ages under the name of Augustine of Hippo. Both works exist in multiple versions that scholars believe go back to the hand of the same author. The Corpus scriptorum ecclesiasticorum Latinorum edition of the Pauline commentary presents three versions of the commentary on Romans (α, β, and γ) and two versions of the other commentaries (α and γ). The

Questions exists in collections of 127 and 150 questions, which also underwent revision at the hands of the author. Fragments of several other works have been attributed to Ambrosiaster: a discussion of Matt 13:33 and Luke 13:21, a commentary on Matt 24, and a treatment of the arrest of Jesus in Gethsemane and Peter's denial (Mercati, 1903).

While the true identity of the Ambrosiaster has continued to elude scholars, important information is known about him. The author himself refers to his residence in Rome during the papacy of → Damasus (366–384 CE). He mentions the church in Rome "whose leader at present is Damasus" (Ambrosi. *Comm. in 1 Tim 3:15*), and in two places he refers to being "here in the city of Rome" (Ambrosi. *Quaest. VNT* 115.16) and "here, that is, in Rome" (Ambrosi. *Comm. in Rom 16:3–5*). Elsewhere the author gave special attention to problems affecting the church in Rome; for example, in *Quaest. VNT* 101, *The Boasting of the Roman Deacons* (*De iactantia Romanorum levitarum*), Ambrosiaster attacked a specific Roman deacon who had argued that deacons held a rank superior to that of presbyters (→ Priest/Presbyter). This deacon, Ambrosiaster argued, was "led by stupidity and by the boasting of the city of Rome" (*Quaest. VNT* 101.2) and thought that deacons in Rome were more honorable than those elsewhere "because of the eminence of the city of Rome, which seems to be the head of all cities" (*Quaest. VNT* 101.4; Hunter, 2017).

In addition to residing at Rome, it is virtually certain that Ambrosiaster was a member of the Roman clergy, probably a presbyter. As just noted, in *Quaest. VNT* 101 he defended the prerogatives of presbyters against the presumption of Roman deacons. His works also show detailed knowledge of ecclesiastical customs, especially pertaining to liturgy and church office. In one place he discussed at length the historical origins of the office of → bishop and the evolution of the distinction between presbyters and bishops (Ambrosi. *Comm. in Eph 4:11–12*). Ambrosiaster also was among the earliest Latin writers to refer to presbyters as "priests" (*sacerdotes*) and to claim that bishops and presbyters share the same "priesthood" (*sacerdotium*; Bévenot, 1997). In several places he explained the rationale for the practice of permanent sexual continence among the higher clergy (→ Celibacy of Clergy), a practice that was being legislated in his day by the bishops of Rome (*Quaest. VNT* 127.35–36; *Comm. in 1 Tim 12–13*). Some of the *Questions* seem to be sermons, and in one he refers to the speaker, almost certainly himself, as a *sacerdos* (*Quaest. VNT* 120.1). It has been plausibly suggested that Ambrosiaster was a presbyter attached to one of the great cemetery churches outside of the walls of Rome (Lunn-Rockliffe, 2007, 80–86). The cumulative arguments for his status as a Roman presbyter, therefore, are overwhelming.

1. Ambrosiaster and the Bible

As the author of the earliest complete Latin commentary on the epistles of Paul (→ Paul the Apostle), Ambrosiaster is an important source of information on a version of the Old Latin (Vetus Latina; → Bible) text of the Pauline Corpus, which can be reconstructed from the quotations in his commentary (Vogels, 1955; 1957). As a commentator Ambrosiaster was especially attentive to the historical and grammatical meaning of the text (Geerlings, 1996). In the Pauline commentary he would usually begin by citing a portion of the biblical text, sometimes just a few words, but more usually one or two sentences. This was followed by a paraphrase and application of the text to the moral life of the individual or the Christian community. Ambrosiaster prefaced his commentary on each Pauline Epistle with a synopsis (*argumentum*) that outlined the context of the letter and gave an overview of its arguments.

Similarly, in the *Questions* Ambrosiaster favored a literal interpretation, although he did not shy away from offering a moralizing interpretation that related the biblical text to the situation of his audience. At times this approached a form of typology and was akin to the *sensus plenior* ("fuller sense") discussed by modern scholars (Bussières, 2011). A large number of the *Questions* dealt with ambiguities or theological conundrums in the texts of Scripture. Questions about the justice of God are prominent: for example, "why was the sacrifice of Abel accepted, but that of Cain rejected?" (*Quaest. VNT* 5); "if God's judgment is just, why were infants burned to death at Sodom along with their parents?" (*Quaest. VNT* 13); "although we know that Abraham was forbidden to sacrifice his son, why was Jephthah not forbidden to

sacrifice his daughter?" (*Quaest. VNT* 43). Many of the *Questions*, however, were not questions at all, but rather mini treatises, such as *Against Arius* (*Quaest. VNT* 97), *Against Novatian* (*Quaest. VNT* 102), *Against the Pagans* (*Quaest. VNT* 114), and *Concerning Fate* (*Quaest. VNT* 115).

2. Ambrosiaster Revising Ambrosiaster

One of the advantages of having multiple extant versions of Ambrosiaster's commentaries and *Questions* is that it is possible to discern developments in his thought and responses to contemporary events. H. Vogels brought attention to this feature of Ambrosiaster's work in a brief, but important, article published in 1956. He noted that the multiple versions of the *Commentary on Romans* show Ambrosiaster interacting with a letter of Jerome to → Marcella (Jer. *Ep.* 27). In the letter → Jerome complained of certain "two-legged asses" who were criticizing his revision of the Gospels based on Greek manuscripts, and H. Vogel showed that Ambrosiaster was the source of these criticisms. Moreover, in the later versions of the *Commentary on Romans 5:14* (β and γ), Ambrosiaster provided a more developed argument for the superiority of the Latin versions over the Greek codices, and H. Vogels argued that these changes were a response to Jerome's letter. Ambrosiaster appealed to the authority of previous commentators, such as → Tertullian, → Victorinus of Pettau, and → Cyprian of Carthage, and argued that his version of the Latin Bible was based on earlier and more reliable Greek texts than the Greek texts circulating in his day.

Following H. Vogels' lead several scholars have now investigated Ambrosiaster's revision of his own writings and reached important conclusions about the impact of theological debates at Rome on Ambrosiaster's thought. M.-P. Bussières (2010) has shown that a Roman council of 382 CE, held in the wake of the Council of → Constantinople in 381 CE, influenced Ambrosiaster's account of the divinity of the → Holy Spirit in *Quaest. VNT* 41 of the collection of 127 questions, which was a revised version of *Quaest. VNT* 56 of the collection of 150 questions (see Bussières, 2006). Similarly, T. de Bruyn has argued that a long digression added in the γ recension of Ambrosiaster's comment on 1 Thess 3:9–10, which insisted on the unity of divine substance while distinguishing between the persons of the Trinity, "was almost certainly occasioned by deliberations about the status of the Holy Spirit in the years immediately before and after the Council of Constantinople in 381" (Bruyn, 2017, xl; citing Bruyn, 2010, 63–65). Likewise, S. Cooper and D.G. Hunter have suggested that Ambrosiaster's additions to the γ version of his comments on Gal 1:19 and 1 Cor 7:33–34 may reflect his reading of Jerome's *Against Helvidius* and debates about the perpetual virginity of Mary at Rome around 384 CE (Cooper & Hunter, 2010). It may also be the case that Ambrosiaster modified his comments on 1 Cor 7:5 to present a more moderate view of marriage in the face of recent papal legislation on clerical sexual continence (Hunter, 2013, 425–426).

3. Ambrosiaster and Christian Ethics

There are numerous aspects of Ambrosiaster's social and ethical thought that distinguish him from his contemporaries. He often employed legal language to discuss everything from the role of political authorities to gender relations to the persons of the → Trinity (Heggelbacher, 1959; Lunn-Rockliffe, 2006; 2007; Hunter, 2019). He had peculiar notions of male-female relations, insisting that only men, not women, bore the image of God; he based this view on the derivation of Eve from Adam (→ Adam and Eve) in the Genesis story, which he took as replicating the origin of all creation from one God as monarch (Hunter, 1992). Ambrosiaster used this double-standard to justify a man's remarriage if he divorced his wife for → adultery but did not grant the same right to the woman (Ambrosi. *Comm. in 1 Cor 7:10–11*). But compared to some of his contemporaries, such as → Ambrose of Milan or Jerome, he had a more moderate view of human sexual relations, arguing strongly for the goodness of creation and human reproduction and resisting efforts to characterize sexual relations as unclean (*Quaest. VNT* 127, *On the Sin of Adam and Eve*; Hunter, 1989; 2013). It has been suggested that Ambrosiaster's attitude toward sex and marriage was "less alarmist, more old-fashioned" than that of Jerome and a view more amenable to the Roman clergy (Brown, 1988,

378). The same moderate tendency is evident in Ambrosiaster's attitude toward wealth and poverty (Lunn-Rockliffe, 2009) and salaries for the clergy (Hunter, 2021).

4. Ambrosiaster and his Reception

While Ambrosiaster appears to have issued his works anonymously, they were read with interest by several of his contemporaries. Jerome clearly was aware of Ambrosiaster's work, although he declined to mention him in *De viris illustribus*. In addition to their conflict over the value of the Greek and Latin codices of the New Testament, both authors discussed the relative status of deacons and presbyters, and Jerome's *Ep.* 146 seems to draw directly from Ambrosi. *Quaest. VNT* 101 (Hunter, 2017). Jer. *Ep.* 73 also appears to respond to Ambrosiaster's idiosyncratic view that → Melchizedek was the Holy Spirit (*Quaest. VNT* 109). Whether or not Jerome was aware of Ambrosiaster's true identity, he must have perceived him as a rival in the field of biblical commentary (Cain, 2005). → Augustine of Hippo also cited Ambrosiaster on several occasions, once under the name of Ambrose and once under the name of → Hilary of Poitiers. In the course of his debate with Jerome over the interpretation of Gal 2, Augustine cited Ambrosiaster's comment on Gal 2:11 as Ambrose to counter Jerome's interpretation of the conflict between Peter and Paul at Antioch. Around 420 CE, in his treatise *Against Two Letters of the Pelagians* (4.4.7), Augustine also cited Ambrosiaster's interpretation of Rom 5:12, that is, that "all sinned in Adam as if in a lump," as the view of Hilary (Valero, 1990). Pelagius also used Ambrosiaster in his own commentary on Paul's epistle to the Romans, though without identifying the author (Smith, 1918).

During the Middle Ages, when the Pauline commentary was transmitted under the name of Ambrose and the *Questions* were thought to have been written by Augustine, the works of Ambrosiaster were widely distributed. Numerous 9th-century CE authors made use of the Pauline commentary, referring to it as the work of Ambrose, among them Claudius of Turin, Hatto of Vercelli, Amalarius of Metz, Sedulius Scottus, Hrabanus Maurus, and Hincmar of Reims. The influence of both the Pauline commentary and the *Questions* was especially strong on the medieval canon lawyers. For example, Ambrosiaster's interpretation of 1 Cor 7:15, the so-called Pauline Privilege, where he stated that "a marriage is not valid [*ratum*] if it lacks devotion to God, and therefore it is no sin if the person who divorces for the sake of God marries another," was cited and discussed by several 12th-century canonists and theologians, including Vacarius, Gratian, Hugh of Saint Victor, and Peter Lombard (Reynolds, 2016).

Historiography

Modern critical study of Ambrosiaster began early in the 20th century with the appearance of two seminal works by A. Souter. In 1905, he published *A Study of Ambrosiaster*, in which he demonstrated conclusively that the same author was responsible for both the *Commentary on the Pauline Epistles*, once attributed to Ambrose of Milan, and the *Questions on the Old and New Testaments*, transmitted in the Middle Ages under the name of Augustine of Hippo. Three years later A. Souter published a critical edition of the *Questions* in the series Corpus scriptorum ecclesiasticorum Latinorum (1908). Between 1966 and 1969 H. Vogels issued the Pauline Commentary in the Corpus scriptorum ecclesiasticorum Latinorum. A new and more complete edition of the *Questions* is in preparation by M.-P. Bussières, which will take account of the revisions of the *Questions* that A. Souter's edition did not. M.-P. Bussières (2007) has already edited *Quaest. VNT* 114 and 115 in the series Sources Chrétiennes. Much previous scholarship on Ambrosiaster has been devoted to identifying the anonymous author, which has been largely a fruitless task. Famously, D.G. Morin offered no less than five different hypotheses for Ambrosiaster's real name, none of which has gained general acceptance (Morin, 1899; 1903; 1914–1919; 1918; 1928). Several recent scholars have repeated the attempt, suggesting Maximus of Turin (Heggelbacher, 1994; decisively refuted by Merkt, 1996), or Simplicianus of Milan (Bielawski, 2003). None of these efforts has gained the approval of scholars, and, given that the treatises of Ambrosiaster were originally issued anonymously, it is unlikely that his true identity will ever be conclusively discerned (Bussières, 2007, 38). Ambrosiaster's theology has received increased attention in recent decades. The Christology of his *Commentary on Romans* has been examined by A. Pollastri (1976), as well as by D. Foley (1997a, b). On grace and soteriology, see V. Hušek (2014). It has long been recognized that Ambrosiaster provides important information about pagan practices in the late 4th century CE (Cumont, 1903; Courcelle, 1959), as well as arguments against astral fatalism. His significance as an apologist (→ Apologetics) is discussed by E. di Santo (2008). T. de Bruyn (2017) has published a critical English translation of Ambrosiaster's *Commentary on Romans* that takes account of all three recensions of the text. The volume by T. de Bruyn (2017) also contains a comprehensive introduction to Ambrosiaster's life, works, and theological significance by T. de Bruyn, S. Cooper and D.G. Hunter.

Bibliography

Bévenot, M., "Ambrosiaster's Thoughts on Christian Priesthood," *HeyJ* 18, 1977, 152–164.

Bielawski, M., "Simpliciano e Ambrosiaster: Potrebbero essere la stessa persona?" in: *Le "Confessioni" di Agostino: Bilancio e prospettive*, Rome, 2003, 533–539.

Brown, P., *The Body and Society: Men, Women, and Sexual Renunciation in Early Christianity*, New York, 1988.

Bruyn, T. de, "Ambrosiaster's Revisions of his *Commentary on Romans* and Roman Synodal Statements about the Holy Spirit," *REAug* 56, 2010, 45–68.

Bruyn, T. de, "Ambrosiaster's Interpretation of Romans 1:26–27," *VigChr* 65, 2011, 463–483.

Bruyn, T. de, trans., *Ambrosiaster's Commentary on the Pauline Epistles: Romans*, Atlanta, 2017.

Bussières, M.-P., "Les *quaestiones* 114 et 115 de l'Ambrosiaster ont-elles été influencées par l'apologétique de Tertullien," *REAug* 48, 2002, 101–130.

Bussières, M.-P., "L'influence du synode tenu à Rome en 382 sur l'exégèse de l'Ambrosiaster," *SE* 45, 2006, 107–124.

Bussières, M.-P., ed., *Ambrosiaster: Contre les païens (Question sur l'Ancien et le Nouveau Testament 114) et sur le destin (Question sur l'Ancien et le Nouveau Testament 115)*, SC 512, Paris, 2007.

Bussières, M.-P., "L'esprit de Dieu et l'Esprit Saint dans les 'Questions sur l'Ancien et Le Nouveau Testament' de l'Ambrosiaster," *REAug* 56, 2010, 25–44.

Bussières, M.-P., "Ambrosiaster's Method of Interpretation in the *Questions on the Old and New Testament*," in J. Lössl & J.Watt, eds., *Interpreting the Bible and Aristotle in Late Antiquity: The Alexandrian Commentary Tradition Between Rome and Baghdad*, Surrey, UK, 2011, 49–65.

Cain, A., "In Ambrosiaster's Shadow: A Critical Re-Evaluation of the Last Surviving Letter Exchange Between Pope Damasus and Jerome," *REAug* 51, 2005, 257–277.

Cooper, S., & D.G. Hunter, "Ambrosiaster *redactor sui*: The Commentaries on the Pauline Epistles (Excluding Romans)," *REAug* 56, 2010, 69–91.

Courcelle, P., "Critiques exégétiques et arguments anti-chrétiens rapportés par Ambrosiaster," *VigChr* 13, 1959, 133–169.

Cumont, F., "La polémique de l'Ambrosiaster contre les païens," *RHLR* 8, 1903, 417–440.

Di Santo, E., *L'Apologetica dell'Ambrosiaster: Cristiani, pagani et giudei nella Roma tardoantica*, Rome, 2008.

Foley, D., "The Christology of Ambrosiaster–I," *Mils* 39, 1997a, 27–47.

Foley, D., "The Christology of Ambrosiaster–II," *Mils* 40, 1997b, 31–52.

Geerlings, W., "Zur exegetischen Methode des Ambrosiaster," in: G. Schöllgen & C. Scholten, eds., *Stimuli: Exegese und ihre Hermeneutik in Antike und Christentum*, Münster, 1996, 444–449.

Heggelbacher, O., *Vom römischen zum christlichen Recht: Juristische Elemente in den Schriften des sogenannten Ambrosiaster*, Freiburg, 1959.

Heggelbacher, O., "Beziehungen zwischen Ambrosiaster und Maximus von Turin? Eine Gegenüberstellung," *FZPhTh* 41, 1994, 5–44.

Hušek, V., "*Duplex gratia*: Ambrosiaster and the Two Aspects of His Soteriology," in: T. Hainthaler, F. Mali, G. Emmenegger & M. Ostermann, eds., *Für uns und für unser Heil: Soteriologie in Ost und West*, Innsbruck, 2014, 151–159.

Hunter, D.G., "*On the Sin of Adam and Eve*: A Little-known Defense of Marriage and Childbearing by Ambrosiaster," *HThR* 82, 1989, 283–299.

Hunter, D.G., "The Paradise of Patriarchy: Ambrosiaster on Woman as (Not) God's Image," *JThS*, n.s. 43, 1992, 447–469.

Hunter, D.G., "The Significance of Ambrosiaster," *JECS* 17, 2009, 1–26.

Hunter, D.G., "Asceticism, Priesthood, and Exegesis: 1 Corinthians 7:5 in Jerome and his Contemporaries," in H.-U. Weidenmann, ed., *Asceticism and Exegesis in Early Christianity*, Göttingen, 2013, 413–427.

Hunter, D.G., "Rivalry Between Presbyters and Deacons in the Roman Church: Three Notes on Ambrosiaster, Jerome, and *The Boasting of the Roman Deacons*," *VigChr* 71, 2017, 495–510.

Hunter, D.G., "Ambrosiaster," in: P.L. Reynolds, ed., *Great Christian Jurists and Legal Collections in the First* Millennium, Cambridge UK, 2019, 252–265.

Hunter, D.G., "'Neither Poverty nor Riches': Ambrosiaster and the Problem of Clerical Compensation," *ZAC* 25, 2021, 93–107.

Krans, J., "Who Coined the Name 'Ambrosiaster'," in: J. Krans, B.J. Lietaert Peerbolte, P.-B. Smit & A. Zwiep,

eds., *Paul, John, and Apocalyptic Eschatology: Studies in Honour of Martinus C. de Boer*, Leiden, 2013, 274–281.

Lunn-Rockliffe, S., "Ambrosiaster's Political Diabology," *SP* 43, 2006, 423–428.

Lunn-Rockliffe, S., *Ambrosiaster's Political Theology*, Oxford, 2007.

Lunn-Rockliffe, S., "A Pragmatic Approach to Poverty and Riches: Ambrosiaster's *quaestio* 124," in: M. Atkins & R. Osborne, eds., *Poverty in the Roman World*, Cambridge UK, 2009, 115–129.

Lunn-Rockliffe, S., "Bishops on the Chair of Pestilence: Ambrosiaster's Polemical Exegesis of Psalm 1:1," *JECS* 19, 2011, 79–99.

Martini, C., *Ambrosiaster: De auctore, operibus, theologia*, Rome, 1944.

Mercati, G., "Il commentario latino d'un ignoto chiliasta su s. Matteo," in: G. Mercati, *Sacra*, vol. I, Rome, 1903, 3–22.

Merkt, A., "Wer war der Ambrosiaster? Zum Autor einer Quelle des Augustinus-Fragen auf eine neue Antwort," *WisWei* 59, 1996, 19–33.

Morin, G., "L'Ambrosiaster et le juif converti Isaac, contemporain de pape Damase," *RHR* 4, 1899, 97–121.

Morin, G., "Hilarius l'Ambrosiaster," *Rben* 20, 1903, 113–131.

Morin, G., "Qui est l'Ambrosiaster? Solution nouvelle," *Rben* 31, 1914–1919, 1–34.

Morin, G., "Una nuova possibilità a proposito dell'Ambrosiastro," *Ath*. 6, 1918, 62–71.

Morin, G., "La critique dans une impasse: À propos du cas de l'Ambrosiaster," *Rben* 40, 1928, 251–259.

Pollastri, A., *Ambrosiaster, Commento alla Lettera ai Romani: Aspetti cristologici*, L'Aquila, 1976.

Reynolds, P., *How Marriage Became One of the Sacraments: The Sacramental Theology of Marriage from its Medieval Origins to the Council of Trent*, Cambridge UK, 2016.

Smith, A., "The Latin Sources of the Commentary of Pelagius on St. Paul's Epistle to the Romans," *JThS* 19, 1918, 162–230.

Souter, A., *A Study of Ambrosiaster*, Cambridge UK, 1905.

Souter, A., ed., *Pseudo-Augustini Quaestiones Veteris et Novi Testamenti CXXVII*, CSEL 50, Vienna, 1908.

Valero, J., "Pecar en Adán según Ambrosiaster," *EE* 65, 1990, 147–191.

Vogels, H., *Untersuchungen zum Text paulinischer Briefe bei Rufin und Ambrosiaster*, Bonn, 1955.

Vogels, H., "Ambrosiaster und Hieronymus," *Rben* 66, 1956, 14–19.

Vogels, H., *Das Corpus Paulinum des Ambrosiaster*, Bonn, 1957.

Vogels, H., ed., *Ambrosiastri qui dicitur commentarii in epistulas paulinas*, CSEL 81.1–3, Vienna, 1966–1969.

DAVID G. HUNTER

Ammianus Marcellinus

The historian Ammianus Marcellinus (c. 330–c. 395 CE) was born in the eastern part of the empire, probably in Antioch. He served in the elite cavalry corps of the protectores domestici on the staff of general Ursicinus. In 355 CE he travelled in this capacity from the eastern part of the empire to the court of Constantius II Augustus at Milan, who sent Ursicinus on a mission to Cologne in order to liquidate the usurper Silvanus. Between 357 and 359 CE, Ammianus took part in the actions against the Persian king Sapor II in Mesopotamia. In 363 CE Ammianus followed the emperor Julian on his Persian campaign, in the course of which the emperor died near the site of Baghdad. For Ammianus, who was a great admirer of Julian, this was a personal tragedy. Ammianus probably left the army soon after Julian's death. He settled in Rome, where he wrote his *Res Gestae* (= Am. below) in Latin during the reign of Theodosius the Great (→ Theodosius I) in the 380s–390s CE.

In the final section of the *Res Gestae* (31.16.9), Ammianus writes,

> This is the history of events from the reign of the emperor Nerva to the death of Valens, which I, a former soldier and a Greek, have composed to the best of my ability. (trans. Hamilton, 1986)

The first 13 books are lost. Books 14–31 treat the period from 353 CE until 378 CE. The fact that Books 1–13 covered a period of 250 years, whereas the remaining 18 books deal with only 25 years, proves that Ammianus opened his work with a relatively short survey followed by a more detailed account of recent history. No historical work on this scale had appeared in Latin since → Tacitus wrote his *Annales* and *Historiae*, and the starting point chosen by Ammianus shows that he intended his work as a continuation of Tacitus' monumental work on the emperors of the 1st century CE.

Ammianus calls himself a Greek and reminds his readers repeatedly that Greek was his first language. His command of Latin, however, is impressive, and his numerous quotations from and allusions to Latin literature, especially Cicero and Virgil (Kelly, 2008, 180–181), show that Ammianus was widely read in Latin literature, far more so than in Greek (Fornara, 1992).

The central character in the *Res Gestae* is → Julian the Apostate, the last pagan emperor. He is introduced in Book 15, where Ammianus describes how the emperor Constantius appointed him as his Caesar to restore order in Gaul, large parts of which had been ravaged by Alamannic tribes. Julian, who up until then had led the life of a student, was a surprisingly successful commander in his campaigns against the barbarian intruders, crowned by the victory in the Battle of Strasbourg (359 CE). Books 15–19 are devoted to his activities as Caesar in Gaul. In Book 20 Ammianus reports how Julian was acclaimed as Augustus by his troops in Paris. A civil war against the legitimate emperor Constantius was averted by the latter's death, after which Julian was universally recognized as sole ruler (November 361 CE). Books 20–25 are devoted to Julian's short reign as Augustus, which ended in disaster, when he was killed during his Persian campaign. The last books (26–31) deal with the dual reign of Valentinian and his brother Valens. The former died in 375 CE, the latter was defeated and killed in the battle at Adrianople (378 CE). Although Julian is hardly mentioned in these last books, he is still present in the background as the standard against which his successors are measured and found wanting.

When Julian arrived in Constantinople in December of 361 CE, he openly declared his adherence to the traditional religion. Baptized and raised as a Christian, Julian had renounced Christianity at the age of 20 under the influence of Maximus of Ephesus. This Neoplatonist philosopher had introduced Julian to theurgy, the ritual means by which the → soul could be reunited with the divine principle from which it had descended, and divination to which Julian became addicted. During the life of his predecessor Constantius, who was a devout Christian, Julian kept his → apostasy a secret. Ammianus relates (Am. 21.2.5) that in 361 CE Julian, in order not to arouse suspicion, went to church in Vienna "on the holy-day which the Christians celebrate in January and call Epiphany," adding in studiously ambiguous terms "and departed after joining in their customary worship" (*sollemniter numine orato*). In Constantinople Julian made sacrifice to the gods on an unprecedented scale and started restoring temples to their former use.

There can be no doubt that Ammianus, too, was a pagan. Julian is not just the main character in the

Res Gestae, but he is also Ammianus' hero. At the beginning of Book 16 (1.3) about Julian's successes in Gaul, Ammianus admits that his narrative will be almost panegyrical in character. Almost, but not quite. In a real panegyric, criticism is absent, whereas in the *Res Gestae*, Ammianus condemns even central aspects of Julian's reign (such as his excessive sacrificing [25.4.17] and his *Grammatikerverbot* [25.4.20]). Still, it would be inconceivable for a Christian author to describe with such enthusiasm the arch enemy of the church. Of equal importance in this respect is the fundamental discussion of divination in Am. 21.1.7–14 with its Stoical and Neoplatonic arguments in favor of this "by no means unimportant branch of learning," which reads like a provocation of the Christian emperors, who threatened their subjects with decapitation if they tried to predict the future (Boeft et al., 1991, 11–23).

Specialists in the church history of the 4th century CE like T.D. Barnes have drawn attention to Ammianus' reticence in ecclesiastical matters (→ Ecclesiology), which were so important to 4th-century CE emperors like Constantius. The reason for this reticence was that historiography as a genre tended to ignore this subject since it belonged to the *res privata* (private matters). Other 4th-century CE historians like Eutropius and Aurelius Victor are silent about Christianity even when they describe the reign of Constantine the Great. Ammianus, too, keeps to the rules of the genre and concentrates on political and military history.

From several casual remarks it is clear that Ammianus was familiar with Christian terminology, but in many cases he prefers a periphrasis or adds an explanation. For → bishop he uses the technical term *episcopus* six times, alternating with a circumlocution like *Christianae legis antistes* (a priest of the Christian faith). In a similar fashion he refers to a priest as *Christiani ritus presbyter, ut ipsi appellant* (a Christian "presbyter," as they call him themselves; Am. 31.12.8) and to nuns as *virgines Christiano cultui divino sacratas* (virgins devoted to divine service according to the Christian custum; Am. 18.10.4). Such periphrastical designations do not betray unfamiliarity or disdain, but are part of the historiographical tradition to avoid technical terminology (Cameron & Cameron, 1964). Exactly the same tendency can be observed with regard to technical military and administrative vocabulary.

When Ammianus introduces a character, he never calls him either a Christian or a polytheist, nor does he mention different Christian denominations like Arians, Orthodox Christians, or Donatists (→ Arianism; → Donatism/Donatists). For instance, he does not tell his readers that Hypatius, consul in 359 CE and the only person Ammianus warmly calls "our Hypatius," was a Christian; the same applies to one of his *bêtes noires* (bugbears), Petronius Probus.

Ammianus has written extensive *elogia* or necrologies about the emperors Constantius, Julianus, and Valentinanus. As may be expected from a serious historian, he discusses their "virtues" (*bona*) as well as their "vices" (*mala*). In all three we find a short section concerning their religious policies. About Constantius he writes (Am. 21.16.18),

> The plain and simple religion of the Christians was bedeviled by Constantius with old wives' fancies. Instead of trying to settle matters he raised complicated issues which led to much dissension, and as this spread more widely he fed it with verbal argument.

The passage is part of the *mala*, and Ammianus' judgment of Constantius' attitude is clearly negative. As regards Christianity, this is Ammianus' only pronouncement on the Christian doctrine as such. The connotations of the adjectives Ammianus uses to qualify the Christian faith, "plain and simple" (*absoluta et simplex*), are positive, although *simplex*, as V. Neri (1992, 61) has argued, may be slightly condescending. The adjectives are in contrast with the casuistry introduced by Constantius. Ammianus' verdict may be paraphrased as follows:

> Constantius complicated the simple doctrine of the Christians by hairsplitting subtleties about the nature of Christ, and tried to impose his convictions on his fellow-believers. (21.16.18)

It is interesting to note that Constantius' Christian opponents reacted much more vehemently against the emperor's interventions and called him "archtyrant," "wild beast," and "horrible monster." Ammianus' "old wives' fancies" (*anilis superstitio*) sounds mild in comparison. The label *superstitio* is difficult to pinpoint exactly, but it implies in any case the notion of excess. Ammianus does not condemn Constantius' adherence to the Christian religion, but he does criticize his interference in dogmatic quibbles.

In the *elogium* on Julian (Am. 25.4) the section on his religious policy is also part of the *mala*:

> Julian was too much given to divination [...] He was superstitious rather than genuinely observant of the rites of religion, and he sacrificed innumerable victims regardless of expense.

Again the purport of the section is unmistakably negative. This alone suffices to demonstrate that Ammianus, in spite of his admiration for Julian's qualities in military and juridical matters, did not idealize his emperor, and that his judgment of a person's character and actions was not determined by his religious affiliation. Ammianus focuses on two points: Julian's obsession with divination and his exorbitant sacrifices.

In his criticism the notion of excess is a recurrent theme. As was the case with Constantius, Julian is accused of being superstitious. Ammianus certainly does not disapprove of Julian's reinstatement of the ancient cult forms, but he criticizes him for overstepping all bounds and for his extravagance in sacrificing on an almost daily basis, instead of on the days prescribed by tradition.

Of vital importance in the *elogium* on Julian is the section on justice. During his reign the goddess Iustitia, who had left the world, seemed to have returned from heaven. An exquisite compliment, but Ammianus roundly condemns Julian's notorious *Grammatikerverbot*, by which the emperor barred Christian teachers from the higher forms of education on the ground that they were not qualified to interpret the classical texts in which the ancient gods played a vital part. Ammianus calls this a "harsh act which should be buried in lasting oblivion" (Am. 22.10.7).

As mentioned before, Julian's religious policy is brought under the heading of his *mala*. Much more attention is given by Ammianus to his great qualities as an army commander. If he had been successful in Persia as he had been in Gaul, the borders of the empire would have been secured for a long time. Also, as a lawgiver, Ammianus judges him to be far superior to Constantius and his successors Valentinian and Valens. Since Ammianus is more critical of Julian's religious policy than of any other aspect of his reign, we may conclude that Ammianus admires the last pagan emperor not so much because of his religious policy, but rather in spite of it.

In the *elogium* of the Christian emperor Valentinian, the section on religion is, surprisingly, part of his *bona*:

> His reign was distinguished for religious tolerance. He took a neutral position between opposing faiths, and never troubled anyone by ordering him to adopt this or that mode of worship. (Am. 30.9.5)

In Ammianus' opinion this is clearly the right attitude vis-à-vis religious matters. The words "he never troubled anyone" are presumably an allusion to Julian's *Grammatikerverbot*, but it is highly plausible, as E.D. Hunt (1985) among others has argued, that Ammianus also intended to make Valentinian an example for the Christian emperor Theodosius, who in 391 CE had strictly forbidden sacrificing to the gods and even visiting their temples.

Ammianus has little to say about the Christian faith as such, but regularly comments on the behavior of individual Christians, especially bishops. Speaking of Georgius, bishop of Alexandria, he fiercely criticizes him for behaving in a manner unbecoming for his position, which prescribed only justice and mercy (Am. 22.11.5). Also the most famous Alexandrian bishop, Athanasius (→ Athanasius of Alexandria), comes under attack. Ammianus reports that he was condemned by an assembly of his peers ("a synod as they call it") for employing illicit divination and other practices inconsistent with his position (Am. 15.7.7–8). In both cases Ammianus signals the contrast between the high demands of the episcopate and the inability of the bishops to meet them. This does not imply a general condemnation of the Christian faith, but it signals the discrepancy between the position and the behavior of these dignitaries. Ammianus has a keen eye for false pretensions, regardless of the religion of those who do not meet the required standards.

The discrepancy between the demands of the Christian faith and the practice of its believers is also a major theme in Ammianus' report about the battle for the Roman episcopal see between Damasus and Ursinus in the year 366 (Am. 27.3.12–15), which led to savage fighting and the murder by Damasus' supporters of 137 men and women in the Basilica of Sicininus (*basilica Sicinini*). Ammianus pays no attention whatsoever to the theological background of the riots, but coolly proceeds to say that the see of Rome is well worth fighting for, since the bishop of Rome leads a life of luxury, rides in a carriage, dresses in splendor, and outdoes kings in the lavishness of his table. He adds – with a malicious allusion to the term of address of the bishop, *beatitudo tua* (your blessedness) – that they would be really fortunate (*beatus*) if they imitated the simple lifestyle of their provincial colleagues, whose humility commends them to the eternal deity (*perpetuum numen*) and his true servants. *Numen* is Ammianus' normal term for the godhead, which he uses in a henotheistic sense, suggesting in this oblique way that the god of the Christians is in fact the same god he venerates himself.

Again, it would be rash to interpret Ammianus' censure of the Roman clergy as condemnation of Christianity in general. Apart from the favorable judgment of the provincial bishops, there are striking resemblances with Ammianus' severe criticism of the senatorial aristocracy in Rome. In the digressions on Rome (Am. 14.6 and 28.4), these aristocrats are chided for the same extravagant luxury as the Roman clergy: flamboyant clothes, luxury carriages, and opulent meals. Just as the Roman clergy fails in comparison with their provincial colleagues, the Roman aristocrats fall short of the standards set by their Republican ancestors.

This last topos returns in Am. 31.5.10–14. When the Goths created havoc in the Balkans, many Romans felt that this was an unprecedented low point in Roman history. Ammianus disagrees and points to the invasions of the Cimbri and the Teutones in 100 BCE and to the wars against the Marcomanni during the reign of Marcus Aurelius. Rome, however, recovered, and the situation was restored

> because our old, sober morality had not yet been undermined by the temptations of a laxer and more effeminate way of life (*solutioris vitae mollities*); there was no craving for ostentatious banquets and ill-gotten gain. (Am. 31.5.14)

According to T.D. Barnes (1998, 176) the Latin words correspond to the Greek terms Τρυφή ("luxury") and Ἀσωτία ("wantonness"), whom Julian in his *Caesares*

had depicted as the boon companions of Jesus as he extended pardon to murderers and adulterers 329a, 336a). In this way Ammianus would intimate that the old Roman sobriety had been destroyed by Christianity. This seems far-fetched. It ignores the topical character of Ammianus' idealization of the past and is linguistically unconvincing. The combination of the words *solutus*, *vita*, and *mollities* is not uncommon in Latin, and the expression *solutioris vitae* is found in Valerius Maximus (6.9.2), an author often quoted in the *Res Gestae*.

E. Gibbon famously praised Ammianus as

> an accurate and faithful guide, who has composed the history of his own time without indulging the prejudices and passions which usually affect the mind of a contemporary. (Gibbon, 1776–1789, vol. I, 1073)

This praise seems well deserved, although at times Ammianus' personal convictions do come to the fore in subtle hints. Ammianus mentions the urban prefect Tertullus with respect, who during an imminent food shortage sacrificed in the temple of Castor and Pollux in Ostia, after which the cargo boats with corn safely entered the harbor "through the divine providence which has attended the growth of Rome from its cradle and guaranteed that it shall endure for ever" (Am. 19.10.4). Another prefect, Claudius, managed to provide the citizens of Rome with food when the Tiber had flooded large parts of the city. Ammianus reports that Claudius had erected a large colonnade, called "the colonnade of Good Success (*Bonus Eventus*)," after a temple to the same deity nearby. In both cases the implicit message is clear: honoring the gods leads to prosperity.

Ammianus was not an impartial historian. He does not conceal that he is attached to the traditional cults, but he refused to make religion a central issue in his *Res Gestae*.

Historiography

Modern scholarship begins with E.A. Thompson (1947). Other important studies are G. Sabbah (1978), J.F. Matthews (1989; repr. 2008), T.D. Barnes (1998) and G. Kelly (2008). P de Jonge (1935–1982) published philological and historical commentaries on Books 14–19. His work was continued and completed by J. den Boeft, J.W. Drijvers, D. den Hengst and H.C. Teitler (1987–2018). A Dutch translation was made by D. den Hengst (2013).

The basis for the philological and historical study of Ammianus Marcellinus has been laid by the 17th-century scholars Lindenbrog, the brothers De Valois and Gronovius. Their commentaries have been incorporated in J.A. Wagner (1808; repr. 1975). Twentieth-century text editions are C.U. Clark (1910–1915) and W. Seyfarth, L. Jacob-Karau and I. Ullmann (1978). Editions with translation and notes are J.C. Rolfe (1935–1938) en J. Fontaine et al. (1968–1999).

Modern scholarship begins with E.A. Thompson (1947). Other important studies are G. Sabbah (1978), J.F. Matthews (1989; repr. 2008), T.D. Barnes (1998) and G. Kelly (2008). P de Jonge (1935–1982) published philological and historical commentaries on Books 14–19. His work was continued and completed by J. den Boeft, J.W. Drijvers, D. den Hengst and H.C. Teitler (1987–2018). A Dutch translation was made by D. den Hengst (2013).

Bibliography

Barnes, T.D., *Athanasius and Constantius: Theology and Politics in the Constantinian Empire*, Cambridge MA, 1993.

Barnes, T.D., *Ammianus Marcellinus and the Representation of Historical Reality*, London, 1998.

Boeft den J., J.W. Drijvers, D. den Hengst & H.C. Teitler, *Philological and Historical Commentaries on Ammianus Marcellinus XX–XXXI*, 12 vols. Groningen, 1987–2018.

Cameron, A., & A. Cameron, "Christianity and Tradition in the Historiography of the Late Empire," *CQ* 14, 1964, 316–328.

Clark, C.U., *Ammiani Marcellini Rerum Gestarum libri qui supersunt: Recensuit rhythmiceque distinxit*, 2 vols. Berolini, 1910 – 1915.

Fontaine J. et al., *Ammien Marcellin Histoire*, 6 vols. Paris., 1968–1999.

Fornara, C.W., "Studies in Ammianus Marcellinus, II: Ammianus' Knowledge and Use of Greek and Latin Literature," *Hist.* 41, 1992, 420–438.

Gibbon, E., *The History of the Decline and Fall of the Roman Empire*, 6 vols., place of publication not identified, 1776–1789; many reprs.

Hamilton, W., *Ammianus Marcellinus: The Later Roman Empire*, Harmondsworth, 1986.

Hengst, D. den, trans. & comm., *Ammianus Marcellinus: Julianus, de laatste heidense keizer. Nadagen van een wereldrijk*, Amsterdam, 2013 (Dutch).

Hunt, E.D., "Christians and Christianity in Ammianus Marcellinus," *CQ* 35, 1985, 186–200.

Jonge, P. de, *Philological and Historical Commentaries on Ammianus Marcellinus XIV–XIX*, 6 vols., Groningen, 1935–1982.

Kelly, G., *Ammianus Marcellinus: The Allusive Historian*, Cambridge UK, 2008.

Matthews, J.F., *The Roman Empire of Ammianus*, London, 1989, repr. Ann Arbor, 2008.

Neri, V., "Ammianus' definition of Christianity as absoluta et simplex religio," in: J. den Boeft, D. den Hengst & H.C. Teitler, eds., *Cognitio Gestorum: The Historiographic Art of Ammianus Marcellinus*, Amsterdam, 1992, 59–65.

Pollmann, K., "Virtue, Vice and History in Ammianus Marcellinus' Obituaries on the Emperors Julian and Valentinian I," in: B.R. Suchla, ed., *Von Homer vis Landino: FS A. Wlosok*, Berlin, 2011, 355–384.

Rolfe, J.C., trans., *Ammianus Marcellinus*, 3 vols. Cambridge MA, 1935–1938.

Sabbah, G., *La méthode d'Ammien Marcellin*, Paris, 1978.

Seyfarth, W., L. Jacob-Karau & I. Ullmann, eds., *Ammiani Marcellini Rerum Gestarum libri qui supersunt*, 2 vols. Leipzig, 1978.

Thompson, E.A., *The Historical Work of Ammianus Marcellinus*, Cambridge UK, 1947, Groningen; repr. 1969.

Wagner, J.A., *Ammiani Marcellini quae supersunt, cum notis integris Frid. Lindenbrogii, Henr. et Hadr. Valesiorum et Iac. Gronovii, quibus Thom. Reinesii quasdam et suas adiecit, editionem absolvit Car. Gottl. Aug. Erfurdt*, 3 vols., Leipzig 1808, repr. in 2 vols., Hildesheim 1975.

DANIËL DEN HENGST

Ammon

Ammon of Alexandria is known solely through the letter that bears his name (*Epistula Ammonis*). Composed in response to a request from a certain Theophilus, likely the archbishop of Alexandria, the letter recounts Ammon's conversion, entry into the monastic life, three-year tenure in the Pachomian monastery of Pbow, and subsequent move to the mountain of Nitria. The information on Ammon is, however, incidental to the letter's primary focus on Theodore, the head of the Pachomian federation, about whom Theophilus had asked. Given that Ammon composed the letter much later in Lower

Egypt, where he lived for a time as a monk in Nitria and developed close connections with ecclesiastical authorities, the accuracy of his account of Pachomian life and practice remains suspect.

Ammon became a Christian at age 17 and upon hearing → Athanasius of Alexandria's praise of the ascetic life chose to embrace it. He initially planned to follow a Theban monk whom he met in Alexandria, but was steered away from him as heretical by his priest, who sent him instead to the Pachomian federation in Upper Egypt. The priest connected him with two Pachomian monks who were in Alexandria on business, and they took him with them back to the monastery of Pbow. When they arrived, Theodore met them at the gate and received Ammon into the community as a member of the Greek-speaking house. Ammon remained at Pbow for three years (352–355 CE), at which point he learned from a passing friend of the family of his parents' grief over his sudden unexplained departure from Alexandria. When he asked Theodore's permission to return for a visit to comfort his mother, he was told of his mother's conversion to the faith and encouraged to continue his ascetic life on the mountain of Nitria. Ammon accepted the advice and moved to Nitria, where he remained in contact with the Pachomians. Little is known about his time there beyond communications he received from and about Theodore. The duration of his tenure in Nitria is unknown. At some point, he became a → bishop, though when and in which diocese are not recorded. His connection with the Alexandrian hierarchy is, however, clear. He closes the letter with an account of Theodore delivered by Archbishop Athanasius in the great church in Alexandria and reports the archbishop's personal request to tell him what he knew about Theodore. The date of his death is unknown. The lack of evidence about Ammon's later life is to be expected, since the request from Theophilus had asked him for information on Theodore gleaned from his stay at Pbow.

The letter is in fact a hagiographic encomium on the saint. Ammon positions himself from the start as a favorite of Theodore in order to rhetorically lend support to his claims. He portrays Theodore throughout as an awe-inspiring man of God. He tells stories that underscore his miraculous power and clairvoyant ability. Theodore predicts the Arian

(→ Arianism) and pagan persecutions, receives a vision of the → Trinity, is fed by angels and declared worthy of revelation, reads hearts and minds, reveals hidden thoughts and behaviors, heals a villager's daughter, cures a monk bitten by an asp, foresees another monk's impending death, and predicts the emperor Julian's demise and the failure of his efforts against the church. Ammon established Theodore as Pachomius' successor through the introduction of secondary eyewitness accounts attributed to the monks Ausonius and Elourion. They report that Pachomius received Theodore at age 13 and brought him up as his own son. He rewarded Theodore when he stood his ground after an earthquake brought on by Pachomius' prayer and again when Theodore received a vision of the Trinity. A subsequent dream sequence in which Theodore is fed by an assembly of angels serves to crown him as Pachomius' clairvoyant heir apparent. When Theodore reports the dream to his master, the latter, knowing Theodore's secret thoughts through revelation, cites Scripture in support of Theodore's abilities and promise:

> The one who received two talents brought back four, and the one who received five returned ten (Matt 25:20–22). Therefore, gird up your loins and bear fruit for the one who has given you grace. [...] And from that day, [Theodore] was deemed worthy of frequent revelations from the Lord. (Pach. *Ep. Am.* 14)

There is no hint here of the rift recorded in the vita tradition between Pachomius and Theodore that occurred shortly before Pachomius' death.

While the focus on Theodore ostensibly fulfills the request for information on him that occasioned the writing of the letter, the nature of the information supplied suggests something more. The presentation of Theodore, cleansed of shortcomings apparent elsewhere in the Pachomian dossier, fits the production of a saint. In addition, the letter's systematic linkage of Theodore, Pachomius, and Ammon to the ecclesiastical hierarchy in Alexandria implies a role in cementing and/or affirming the relationship between the two. As such it may well have been composed in connection with Theodore's entry into the Alexandrian diptych or list of saints.

The reliability of the letter in terms of its information on the Pachomian period it purports to describe has been the subject of serious debate. Some episodes seem to be modeled on earlier sources, and its author seems unfamiliar with certain Pachomian terms and practices. Given the likely liturgical and clearly political intent of the letter, it should come as no surprise that accuracy in such historical details is wanting. Furthermore, if Ammon composed the letter years later, separated from his early sojourn at Pbow by a long tenure in a distinctly different type of monastic community in Lower Egypt and his entry into the episcopacy, one might naturally expect inaccuracies in matters of little relevance to the primary intent of the letter. In the end, whatever the case may be with respect to the letter's historical credentials as a source of mid-4th-century CE Pachomian monasticism, it offers a fascinating glimpse into the movement's growing impact in later 4th-century CE Egypt and its incorporation by the church into its understanding of itself.

Historiography

The Greek *Letter of Ammon*, the sole source of information about Ammon of Alexandria, has played a role in the historiography of Pachomian monasticism from the start. The letter was initially seen as a primitive source containing valuable facts (Tillemont, 1699), though later scholars cautioned in its use due to its numerous miracle stories and hagiographic orientation (Amélineau, 1889; Grützmacher, 1896; Ladeuze, 1898). A critical edition of the Greek Pachomian sources, including the *Letter of Ammon*, while maintaining this cautious orientation, noted the letter's invaluable chronological data and evidence for the Greek influence in Pachomian monasticism (Halkin, 1932). L.T. Lefort challenged to the letter's reliability in 1943, noting various examples that suggested its dependence on earlier sources (Lefort, 1943). His arguments were countered almost immediately (Peeters, 1946), and the letter continued to be used as a valuable early Pachomian source, particularly in the work of Derwas Chitty, who debated with L.T. Lefort over the primacy of the Greek or Coptic *Life of Pachomius* (Chitty, 1954). Subsequent discussions have treaded more cautiously between L.T. Lefort's rejection of the letter and its uncritical acceptance (Veilleux, 1968; Goehring, 1986).

Bibliography

Amélineau, E., *Monuments pour servir à l'histoire de l'Égypte chrétienne au IVe siècle: Histoire de saint Pachôme et de ses communautés*, AMG, vol. XVII, Paris, 1889.

Chitty, D.J., "Pachomian Sources Reconsidered," *JEH* 5, 1954, 39–45.

Goehring, J.E., *The Letter of Ammon and Pachomian Monasticism*, PTS 27, Berlin, 1986.

Grützmacher, G., *Pachomius und das älteste Klosterleben: Ein Beitrag zur Mönchsgeschichte*, Leipzig, 1986.

Halkin, F., *Sancti Pachomii Vitae Graecae*, SHG 19, Brussels, 1932.

Ladeuze, P., *Étude sur le cénobitisme pakhomien pendant le ive siècle et la première mointié di ve*, Louvain, 1898.

Lefort, L.T., *Les vies coptes de saint pachôme et de ses premiers successeurs*, BMus, 1943.

Peeters, P., "Le dossier copte de S. Pachôme et ses rapports avec la tradition grecque," *AnBoll* 64, 1946, 258–277.

Tillemont, M. Lenain de, *Mémoires pour server à l'histoire ecclésiastique des six premiers siècles*, Paris, 1699.

Veilleux, A., *La liturgie dans le cénobitisme pachômien au quatrième siècle*, Rome, 1968.

Veilleux, A., *Pachomian Koinonia*, vol. II: *Pachomian Chronicles and Rules*, CistSS 46, Kalamazoo, 1981.

JAMES E. GOEHRING

Ammonius Saccas

Ammonius Saccas (2nd–3rd cent. CE) was a philosopher, commonly regarded as the "Socrates" of → Neoplatonism. He was the teacher of both the pagan philosopher Plotinus and the Christian philosopher and theologian Origen. His life is very scarcely documented, and his precise philosophical ideas are not much better known. His byname Saccas is malignantly etymologized by → Theodoret of Cyrrhus of as a reference to the "sacks" that he purportedly carried in Alexandria's harbor (Thdt. *Affect.* 6.60–73). Theodoret also sets Ammonius historically under Commodus and presents both → Origen the Christian and → Plotinus as his disciples. An alternative, less denigrating etymology has his byname derive from Śakyas, an Indian noble clan (Seeberg, 1941 versus Hindley, 1964). This would also explain Plotinus' desire to become acquainted with the wisdom of the Indian sages as a result of his training in philosophy under Ammonius:

From that day on, he followed Ammonius continuously, and under his guidance made such progress in philosophy that he became eager to investigate the Persian methods and the system adopted among the Indians. It happened that the emperor Gordian was at that time preparing his campaign against Persia; Plotinus joined the army and went on the expedition. He was then 38, for he had passed 11 entire years under Ammonius. When Gordian was killed in Mesopotamia, it was only with great difficulty that Plotinus came off safe to Antioch. At 40, in the reign of Philip, he settled in Rome. (Porph. *Vit. Plot.*3)

In the late 2nd century CE, there were continual contacts between Alexandria and India, not only of commercial but also of intellectual nature: a semi-contemporary of Ammonius, the Christian philosopher Pantaenus, who was a teacher of both → Clement of Alexandria and Origen, traveled from Alexandria to India toward the end of the 2nd century CE, upon an explicit request from existing Indian Christian communities, to provide them with a doctrinally richer teaching (Ramelli, 2000; 2011a).

According to → Porphyry of Tyre (*ap.* Eus. *Hist. eccl.* 6.19.4–8), Ammonius was raised a Christian, but at a certain point, as a result of his study of → philosophy, he converted to paganism (→ Pagan/ Paganism) – or this is how Porphyry's words are commonly understood. More precisely, Porphyry was contrasting Ammonius with Origen: whereas Ammonius had Christian parents and was brought up as a Christian, but changed his way of life after he received philosophical instruction, Origen was a Greek and received a Greek education, but converted to Christianity. Porphyry does not state that Ammonius became a pagan or rejected Christianity, but that "when he adhered to philosophical wisdom, he immediately turned to the way of life according to the laws [πρὸς τὴν κατὰ νόμους πολιτείαν]," in other words, he began to behave according to the laws. Porphyry wrote when Christianity was still an illegal religion in the Roman Empire. Not accidentally, it is precisely Porphyry, or an author closely inspired by him, who attests, together with → Tertullian, the *senatus consultum* that outlawed Christianity (Ramelli, 2004; 2013b). In Mac. *Apoc.* 2.25, J. Schott (2015,

83–84) notes no connections with Tertullian's report about the senatus consultum of 35 CE, but only indicates a connection with Or. *Cels.* 2.63. However, Celsus does not mention the Senate's unanimous decision to condemn to death Jesus' followers as impious that both Macarius' Hellene and Tertullian mention. Porphyry's insistence on Christianity as illegal (ἄνομος) is clearly reflected at another point of the critique of Macarius' Hellene, in *Apoc.* 3.31.4: Paul behaves "at one time like an ἄνομος but at another like a Hellene." This is the same opposition we find in the Hellene's passage about the senatus consultum and in Porphyry's judgment on Origen (see below).

According to → Eusebius of Caesarea, Ammonius was a Christian all of his life and wrote a treatise on the agreement between Moses and Jesus (Eus. *Hist. eccl.* 6.19.10). This treatise should not surprise in a philosopher. Also the Middle Platonist and Neo-Pythagorean → Numenius of Apamea, who was no Christian and was held in highest esteem by both Plotinus and Origen, allegorized both the Old and the New Testaments, as Origen certifies in his polemic against → Celsus on biblical allegoresis (Or. *Cels.* 4.51 = Num. *Frgms.* 1c & 10a). Ammonius probably also wrote a gospel harmony, which inspired Origen's *Hexapla* (Crawford, 2015) and Eusebius' *Gospel Canons.* It is indeed Eusebius who, in his preface to these Canons, speaks of Ammonius' synoptic work. The idea that Christianity was "against the laws" appears again in Porphyry's intellectual profile of Origen in the same fragment in which he also speaks of Ammonius' life "according to the laws": according to Porphyry, Origen had Greek parents – which does not necessarily contrast with Eusebius' description of Leonides the martyr as Origen's "so-called father," λεγόμενος πατήρ, although Eusebius insists that Origen's parents were Christians (Eus. *Hist. eccl.* 6.19.10) – and was trained "in Greek culture," which is in line with Eusebius' biography of Origen, but then "he inclined toward the barbaric daring and shameless way of life [τόλμημα]."Porphyry introduces at this point a distinction between Origen's way of life, which was against the laws (of Rome and of the gods) in that it was Christian, and Origen's philosophy, which was Greek. Porphyry is saying that in metaphysics and theology Origen was a Greek philosopher, and indeed he studied these disciplines at Ammonius Saccas', and interpreted Scripture in the light of philosophy, which in Porphyry's eyes looked monstrous, but in fact was what → Philo of Alexandria had already done. As I. Ramelli (2009) has argued, Eusebius' and Porphyry's contrasting accounts of Ammonius' religious allegiance in fact arose from their different apologetic and ideological agendas.

Plotinus studied with Ammonius Saccas from 231 CE onward, for nine years. The same source, Porphyry, also testifies that Origen, the Christian philosopher, was a disciple of Ammonius Saccas (*ap. Eus. Hist. eccl.*6.19.6). Since Origen left Alexandria in 233 CE or later, and Plotinus began to attend Ammonius' classes at 28, around 231 CE, Origen and Plotinus may even have frequented Ammonius' school together for at least two years. Longinus too was a pupil of Ammonius. Longinus attests (*ap.* Porph. *Vit. Plot.* 20) that he visited both Ammonius and Origen for instruction for a long time. He presents them as Platonists who did not offer a written account of the philosophy they learned from Ammonius, apart from sparse works, among which he too, like Porphyry (see below), cites Origen's treatise *On Rational Beings* or *On Spirits/Demons* (→ Demonology/Demons). Longinus' admiration for Origen is great: he praises him and Ammonius as "by far superior to all their contemporaries in intelligence."

It is very probable that Ammonius was also the teacher of philosophy of Heraclas, the Christian philosopher and presbyter who was the friend and colleague of Origen and later became the bishop of Alexandria. Origen, in a letter reported by Eusebius (*Hist. eccl.* 6.19.12–14), attests that Heraclas, "who now sits in the πρεσβυτέριον of Alexandria," was first found by him in Alexandria "at the teacher of philosophical doctrines," who is almost certainly Ammonius. Heraclas had been studying philosophy with him for five years before Origen began to attend Ammonius' classes himself. This disciple of Ammonius, Heraclas, not only was a Christian philosopher, but even dressed as a philosopher when he was a presbyter, and was still wearing philosophical garb and studying the "books of the Greeks" when Origen wrote his letter. It is clear from this firsthand description that for Ammonius Christianity and philosophy, in particular Platonism, were thoroughly compatible, and precisely this attitude of his, which was

inherited by his disciples, such as Origen and Heraclas, may have given rise to divergent interpretations concerning his religious allegiance, as we have seen.

The 5th-century CE Neoplatonist Hierocles of Alexandria, who knew Origen as the brightest and most remarkable and illustrious student of Ammonius together with Plotinus (ἐπιφανέστατοι), reports that Ammonius was "divinely taught" (θεοδίδακτος), and his most distinctive doctrine was that Plato and Aristotle in fact were in agreement with respect to the most important doctrines; so, Ammonius traced their philosophies to one and the same intention or mind (νοῦς) and

> transmitted philosophy without conflicts (ἀστασίαστον) to all of his disciples, and especially to the best of those acquainted with him, Plotinus, Origen, and their successors. (*ap.* Phot. *Bibl.* codex 14.172ab; 251.461b).

Ammonius clearly was a "harmonizer." His interest in the harmonization of Plato and Aristotle (on which see Karamanolis, 2006,191–215) was shared by Porphyry, Plotinus' (and perhaps also Origen's) disciple: according to the *Suda*, under the heading Πορφύριος, Porphyry wrote a multivolume treatise entitled *The Philosophical School of Plato and that of Aristotle Were One and the Same.*

Similarities can be traced between Ammonius' thought and the few extant fragments of the aforementioned Pantaenus, who also taught in Alexandria during the reign of Commodus and later (Eus. *Hist. eccl.* 5.10.1–4), exactly when Ammonius too was teaching there. In particular, Ammonius' ideas as reported by Hierocles (*ap.* Phot. *Bibl.* codex 251.461b and 462b), concerning the → creation of beings by God's will (βούλημα, θέλημα), coincide with Pan. *Frgm.* 2, where he says that the λόγοι in God's mind are called by Scripture "God's wills" because the Godhead created everything by God's will (θέλημα) and knows all beings as its own wills. This train of thought was developed by Origen and especially by his follower → Gregory of Nyssa (Ramelli, 2016).

According to Porphyry, Plotinus in his classes expounded Ammonius' teachings, and in his own *Enneads* he developed the philosophy of Ammonius. He brought Ammonius' intelligence or mind (νοῦς) into his own research (Porph. *Vit. Plot.* 14). Origen, together with Plotinus and Erennius, had promised not to divulge their teacher Ammonius' doctrines, expounded in his classes, but then, when Erennius broke the promise, he did make them public; however, he did not write down these doctrines, apart from composing two treatises, *On Rational Creatures/Spirits* and *The King is the Only Creator* (*Vit. Plot.* 3). Porphyry is not stating that Origen wrote *only* these two treatises and nothing else, but that he did not expound Ammonius' philosophy in any written work apart from these. Plotinus, instead, did not write anything for ten years, limiting himself to teaching orally on the basis of Ammonius' classes (*Vit. Plot.* 3). For Origen, rational creatures are angels, humans, and demons (e.g. Or. *Princ.* 2.9.1), as for his teacher Ammonius (*ap.* Phot. *Bibl.* codex 251.461b–462a). Ammonius divided the incorporeal nature into heavenly beings or gods, intermediate rational beings, that is ethereal, good demons, interpreters, and angels, and the last rational beings, in other words terrestrial, human souls, the immortal parts of humans. In 462a the focus is again on the three classes of λογικά or νοερὰ γένη (see Origen's νόες and λογικά/λογικοί: the parallel extends even to their definition as εἰκὼν τοῦ νοητοῦ θεοῦ and, in 462b, their free will). The same is repeated almost verbatim in Ammonius' other fragment preserved by Hierocles (*ap.* Phot. *Bibl.* codex 214.172a).

The title of the other treatise in which Origen expounded Ammonius' doctrines, *The King Is the Only Creator*, probably refers to Plato's Second Letter, with the "three kings" indicating God, whom already Clement had interpreted in a Trinitarian sense (→ Trinity), and whom Origen cited and referred to God as universal king (Or. *Cels.* 6.18). Origen's teacher, Ammonius, likewise insisted that God is the creator of all, to the point that he ascribed to Plato a kind of doctrine of *creatio ex nihilo*, and attributed to God the creator (ποιητής) precisely the kingdom or royalty (βασιλεία) and the fact of being king (βασιλεύειν). This, in turn, manifests itself in God's providence (πρόνοια, *ap.* Hierocles, *ap.* Phot. *Bibl.* codex 251.461b; perfectly parallel is the fragment from Ammonius handed down by Hierocles via Phot. *Bibl.* codex 214.172ab). These ideas were definitely compatible with Origen's Christian thought. Indeed, both of Origen's tracts on rational creatures and on the creator-king are expressly said by Porphyry to reflect Ammonius' teaching. The latter

treatise, according to Porphyry, was composed under Gallienus, that is, in 253 CE or soon after, which fits in the chronology of Origen, who probably died in 255/256 CE (Ramelli, 2009; forthcoming). There is no compelling reason to affirm that the Christian philosopher Origen cannot have written these works on God, who created the universe – noetic and corporeal – and governs it, and on the λογικά, one of his favorite themes in his *On First Principles* and elsewhere. Indeed, this was one of the topics, as he says at the beginning of his masterpiece, that were still open to philosophical investigation, since they had been left undetermined by Scripture and tradition.

Porphyry in *Vit. Plot.* 14 recounts a significant episode:

> Once, when Origen turned up at a class of Plotinus', the latter was filled with embarrassment and wished to stand up and go away, but, since he was begged by Origen to speak, he replied that one's willingness lessens when the speaker realizes that he will address persons who already know what he is going to say. Thus he discussed a little and left.

It is not specified that the event took place in Rome, but even in this case there would be no obstacle to the identification of this Origen with the Christian philosopher. Plotinus went to Rome around 244 CE, when Origen was still alive: he lived for another decade, and it is perfectly possible that he went to Rome again. Porphyry was not yet a disciple of Plotinus' then, and indeed he does not report the fact as an eyewitness. Clearly, if Origen already knew what Plotinus had to teach, this is because they had the same teacher, Ammonius, and Plotinus elaborated on Ammonius' teaching in his own classes. It is even more probable that Origen in this episode is the Christian Platonist in that, shortly after, Porphyry affirms that "many Christians" attended Plotinus' classes (Porph. *Vit. Plot.* 16).

The above-mentioned Theodoret briefly outlines Ammonius' metaphysics: the first principles for him were the → *nous* and the *logos*, by which the universe was created and maintained in existence and harmony (Origen will identify the *nous* with God and the *logos* with Christ). Ammonius was a supporter of divine → providence and of the Stoic and Platonic ethical principle that only good and virtuous people are happy. It is noteworthy that the Christian Theodoret had no problem with Ammonius' mention of "gods," whereas Eusebius, against Porphyry's allegation that Ammonius shifted from Christianity to paganism, felt it necessary to claim that Ammonius remained a Christian throughout his life, as we have seen. The Christian Nemesius always describes Ammonius as the teacher of Plotinus. In Nem. *Nat. hom.* 2.19ff. he demonstrates that the soul is immaterial on the basis of the philosophy of Ammonius and the aforementioned Middle Platonist and Neo-Pythagorean Numenius. And in *Nat. hom.* 3.56–60 Nemesius quotes Ammonius about the union of → body and → soul, to the effect that the soul in its union with the body is not altered, because this is a union without confusion (ἀσυγχύτως ἥνωται: the same adverb was later used at Chalcedon to describe the union of the divine nature and the human nature in Christ).

Even the Origen cited by Proclus as a disciple of Ammonius Saccas in Proc. *Theol. Plat.* 2.4 may be none other than the Christian philosopher. Proclus wonders how Origen, who shared the same philosophical formation as Plotinus at Ammonius' – as he explicitly remarks – did not identify the supreme principle with the One, but with the Nous and the prime Being, while stopping here and leaving aside the One, which is beyond the Nous and beyond Being. Whereas Plotinus famously placed the One beyond the Nous and Being, Origen, according to Proclus, thought that the Nous is the first Being and the first One, which is alien to Plato's thinking and, in his view, rather depends on Peripatetic innovations. Of course, Origen also knew Peripatetic doctrines (also being the disciple of a harmonizer of Plato and Aristotle such as Ammonius himself), but he felt bound by Exod 3:14 – which he commented on philosophically in his *Comm. Jo.* 13.21.123 – and therefore he indeed identified God with the Nous and the οὐσία, although at the same time he also said that God may be considered to be superior to both νοῦς and οὐσία. In other passages Proclus pairs the exegeses of Plato offered by two prominent disciples of Ammonius', Origen and Longinus (Ramelli, 2009; 2011b). In light of Origen's discipleship of Ammonius' and of his probable identity with Origen the Neoplatonist (as argued with new proofs and discussion of objections in Ramelli, 2022), it is not surprising that

close relations have been detected, not only between Clement's and Plotinus' thinking, but also between Origen and Plotinus, which still deserve close and systematic investigation.

Ammonius Saccas was even identified by E. Elorduy (1944) with Pseudo-Dionysius the Areopagite (see Tovar, 1948). While this identification is doomed to remain extremely uncertain, deep affinities of thought can be pointed out between Pseudo-Dionysius and Pantaenus, Clement, Plotinus, Porphyry, and above all Origen (see Lilla, 1993; Sinnige, 2002, with comparison between Pseudo-Dionysius and Plot. *Enn.* 1.6.1 and 6.9.9 on psychology; Lilla, 1997, who argues for a dependency of Pseudo-Dionysius on Porphyry's and Damascius' commentaries on the *Parmenides*; Ramelli, 2013a, 694–721, who demonstrates Pseudo-Dionysius' dependence on Origen and probable references to Origen, e.g. in the treatment of love and *apokatastasis*).

Historiography

In the ancient world, Ammonius Saccas was the object of study by historians and philosophers such as Theodoret, Hierocles of Alexandria, and Proclus, as we have seen, but in the modern world he has been studied for a long time in history of philosophy as the "Socrates of Neoplatonism": the teacher of Plotinus, the founder of Neoplatonism, and also of Origen, the Christian Platonist. E. Seeberg (1941) and C. Hindley (1964) discussed the meaning of his surname, Saccas, and his identification with Dionysius the Areopagite was put forward by E. Elorduy (1944). Ammonius' "harmonization" of Plato and Aristotle is explored by G. Karamanolis (2006, 191–215). The question of the religious identity of Ammonius, about which Porphyry and Eusebius disagree, and the secrecy of (part of) his doctrines, on which two treatises by Origen were based, is discussed by I. Ramelli (2009; 2011a; a forthcoming monograph on Origen) and the relation between his thought and that of Pantaenus, especially on creation by God's will, is investigated by I. Ramelli (2015). Further investigation needs to be devoted to Ammonius, his ideas, as reported by later sources, and his school, on both the pagan and the Christian side: different strands of Neoplatonism were claiming the heritage of Ammonius. In particular, a systematic comparison of the philosophy of the two main disciples of Ammonius, Origen and Plotinus, even after the seminal study by H. Crouzel, is an important desideratum.

Bibliography

Beatrice, P.F., "Porphyry's Judgment on Origen," in: R.J. Daly, ed., *Origeniana V*, Louvain, 1992, 351–367.

Crawford, M., "Ammonius of Alexandria, Eusebius of Caesarea and the Origins of Gospels Scholarship," *NTS* 61, 2015, 1–29.

Elorduy, E., "Es Ammonio Sakkas el Pseudo-Areopagita?" *EE* 17, 1944, 501–557.

Hindley, C., "Ammonios Sakkas: His Name and Origin," *ZKG* 75, 1964, 332–336.

Karamanolis, G., *Plato and Aristotle in Agreement? Platonists on Aristotle from Antiochus to Porphyry*, Oxford, 2006.

Kettler, F.H., "Origenes, Ammonios Sakkas und Porphyrius," in: C. Andresen & A.M. Ritter, eds., *Kerygma und Logos: FS C. Andresen*, Göttingen, 1979, 322–328.

Lilla, S., "De pseudo-Dionysio Areopagita cum Clemente Alexandrino conspirante," *Latinitas* 41, 1993, 284–287.

Lilla, S., "Pseudo-Denys l'Aréopagite, Porphyre et Damascius," in: Y. de Andia, ed., *Denys l'Aréopagite et sa postérité*, Paris, 1997, 117–152.

Ramelli, I., "La missione di Panteno in India: Alcune osservazioni," in: C. Baffioni, ed., *La diffusione dell'eredità classica nell'età tardoantica e medievale*, Alessandria, 2000, 95–106.

Ramelli, I., "Il senatoconsulto del 35 contro i Cristiani in un frammento porfiriano," preface by M. Sordi, *Aevum* 78, 2004, 59–67.

Ramelli, I., "Origen, Patristic Philosophy, and Christian Platonism: Re-thinking the Christianisation of Hellenism," *VigChr* 63, 2009, 217–263.

Ramelli, I., "Early Christian Missions from Alexandria to 'India': Institutional Transformations and Geographical Identification," *Aug.* 51, 2011a, 221–231.

Ramelli, I., "Origen the Christian Middle/Neoplatonist," *JECH* 1, 2011b, 98–130.

Ramelli, I., *The Christian Doctrine of Apokatastasis: A Critical Assessment from the New Testament to Eriugena*, Leiden, 2013a.

Ramelli, I., "Constantine: The Legal Recognition of Christianity and its Antecedents," *AHI* 22, 2013b, 65–82.

Ramelli, I., "Divine Power in Origen of Alexandria: Sources and Aftermath," in: A. Marmodoro & I.F. Viltanioti, eds., *Divine Powers in Late Antiquity*, Oxford, 2017a, 177–198.

Ramelli, I., "Origen and the Platonic Tradition," in: J. Warren Smith, ed., *Plato and Christ*, 2017b, 1–20; doi:10.3390/rel8020021.

Ramelli, I., "The Study of Late Ancient Philosophy: Philosophy and Religion – 'Pagan' and Christian Platonism," in: S.S. Griffin & I.L.E. Ramelli, eds., *Lovers of the Soul and Lovers of the Body: Philosophical and Religious Perspectives in Late Antiquity*, Cambridge MA, 2022, 397–402.

Ramelli, I., "Matter in the *Dialogue of Adamantius*: Origen's Heritage and Hylomorphism," in: J. Zachhuber & A. Schiavoni, eds, *Late Antique Cosmologies*, Leiden, 2022, 74–124.

Ramelli, I., "Some Aspects of the Reception of the Platonic Tradition in Origen," in: K. parry & E. Anagnostou, eds., *Later Platonists and Their Heirs Among Christians, Jews, and Muslims*, Leiden, 2023.

Ramelli, I., *Origen of Alexandria as Philosopher and Theologian: A Chapter in the History of Platonism*, Cambridge, forthcoming.

Schott, J., "The Hellene," in: J. Schott & M. Edwards, trans., *Macarius, Apocriticus*, Liverpool, 2015.

Seeberg, E., "Ammonius Sakas," *ZKG* 60, 1941, 136–170.

Sinnige, T.G., "Plotinus on the Human Person and its Cosmic Identity," *VigChr* 56, 2002, 292–295.

Tovar, A., "El Pseudo-Dionisio y Ammonio Sakkas," *Emerita* 16, 1948, 277–281.

ILARIA L.E. RAMELLI

Amphilochius

Amphilochius (Ἀμφιλόχιος; 345[?]–404[?] CE) was bishop of Iconium (Ἰκόνιον, today Konya) from 373/374 CE to at least 394 CE. He had strong ties to the three Cappadocian fathers (→ Basil of Caesarea, → Gregory of Nazianzus, and → Gregory of Nyssa) whose church policy and theology he continued. Held in high regard by his contemporaries and posterity, nowadays he is commonly assumed to have been more of a practical churchman (active metropolitan and preacher) than an original theologian. This judgment, however, is difficult to assess, as a large part of his writings is apparently lost, and of the works preserved under his name, some are certainly spurious, while the authenticity of others is questioned.

With regard to the dates of Amphilochius' later life, and because he seems to have been considerably younger than Basil and Gregory of Nazianzus (see the fatherly tone in Bas. *Ep.* 161, 176; Greg. Naz. *Ep.* 22, 23, 184), his date of birth can be supposed to be somewhere between 340 CE and 345 CE. He was likely born in Diocaesarea (perhaps the same place as Nazianzus, the town) in Cappadocia where at least his father, Amphilochius the Elder (see *Anth. pal.* 8.131–138), was born. The family of Amphilochius belonged to the rich, Christian upper class; his father practiced oratory and law. His mother Livia (see *Anth. pal.* 8.118–120) and his brother Euphemius (see *Anth. pal.* 8.121–130) passed away early – Livia before Euphemius, who died soon after 361 CE at the age of 20. His sister Theodosia was probably married in Constantinople and there educated the wealthy Olympias (see Greg. Naz. *Carm.* 6.97–103; PG 37.1549f.), who later supported several bishops, especially → John Chrysostom. Amphilochius was a cousin to Gregory of Nazianzus – the paternal grandfather (Philtatius) of the former also being the maternal grandfather of the latter (see Clémencet, 1778; PG 35.81–92).

Amphilochius presumably had his first rhetorical training (→ Rhetoric) from his own father, from whom Gregory of Nazianzus also had his first lessons (see *Anth. pal.* 8.133.5f.). Around 361 CE, together with his brother Euphemius, Amphilochius studied in Antioch on the Orontes under the famous pagan orator, and school friend of Amphilochius the Elder, Libanius (see Libian. *Ep.* 634, 670, 671; Libanius praises the eloquence, talent, and promise of both brothers). Around 364 CE, Amphilochius – either in Constantinople or in Caesarea – started a public career as a lawyer (see Greg. Naz. *Ep.* 9 and 13, in which Gregory asks Amphilochius to support the deacon Euthalius and Nicobulus, the nephew of Gregory by marriage). After an unclear financial affair (see Greg. Naz. *Ep.* 22–24, in which Gregory asks three different people of high social standing – Sophronius, Caesarius, and Themistius – to help his cousin), Amphilochius finished his oratorical career and withdrew (around 370 CE) to his paternal estate in Ozizala (near Nazianzus), where he grew vegetables (see Greg. Naz. *Ep.* 25–28) and cared for his aged father (see Bas. *Ep.* 150: a letter of Heraclides, who is visiting Basil, to Amphilochius, written in 372/373 CE). At this time Amphilochius decided to dedicate his life to God and made his first personal contact with Basil (see Greg. Naz. *Ep.* 25; Bas. *Ep.* 150, and *Ep.* 50, which seems to be a letter of Amphilochius to Basil). His plans, however, to lead an anchoritic life were apparently never realized, contrary to the information given in the preserved lives (PG 39.13–26; *BHG* 73; PG 116.955–970; *BHG* 72: late works without great historical value).

After the death of Faustinus of Iconium (373 CE), who chose his own successor in correspondence with Basil (see Bas. *Ep.* 81, which seems to be a letter of Basil to Faustinus), Amphilochius – against his own will (see Bas. *Ep.* 161; Libian. *Ep.* 1543) and against the will of his father (see Greg. Naz. *Ep.* 63) – was made bishop of Iconium. The → ordination also made him → metropolitan of the newly formed (see Bas. *Ep.* 138) province of Lycaonia. In the first years of his episcopacy up to the death of Basil (379 CE or 377/378 CE), a lively correspondence between the two of them took place, of which unfortunately only Basil's letters are preserved. Amphilochius, who surely had not expected to become bishop, sought the assistance of the experienced Basil; subsequently, a close and trusting friendship arose between them. Basil wrote to Amphilochius about canonical (*Ep.* 188.1–14; 199; 217) and exegetical (*Ep.* 190.3; 188.15–16; 236.1–3) matters, about philosophical-theological problems (*Ep.* 233–235; 236.6), but also to give him practical advice or simply to inform him about certain circumstances (*Ep.* 190.1–2; 200–202; 218; 231; 232; 248). On several occasions these two neighboring metropolitan bishops also met in person (see Bas. *Ep.* 163; 176; 200–202; 216; 217). Amphilochius apparently not only heeded Basil's advice in regulating his diocese and metropolitan province, but also embraced his theological and church-political ideas. Basil wrote his treatise *De spiritu sancto* at the request of Amphilochius and dedicated it to him. But Amphilochius was himself also committed to the new Nicene theology. In 377/378 CE he presided over a synod in Iconium that defended the divinity of the → Holy Spirit against the Macedonians; the preserved synodical letter is probably written by Amphilochius. There also is a creed of Amphilochius, preserved in a Syriac translation, which perhaps is a sketch in preparation for the Council of → Constantinople (May–July 381 CE), in which Amphilochius participated (see e.g. Thdt. *Hist. eccl.* 5.8.4). Furthermore, Amphilochius himself wrote a treatise, *De spiritu sancto*, which, unfortunately – besides the short fragment *CPG* 3258 – is not preserved. This treatise is attested by → Jerome (*Vir. ill.* 133), who, furthermore, in *Ep.* 70.4.4, lists Amphilochius among Christian literary writers from Cappadocia.

Through a law given by the emperors Gratian, Valentinian I, and → Theodosius I on Jul 30, 381 CE, Amphilochius officially became an authority on the orthodox faith: he is named as one of the normative bishops whose doctrine the others had to follow (see Cod. Theod. 16.1.3). → Theodoret of Cyrrhus lists Amphilochius among the excellent bishops at this point in time (*Hist. eccl.* 4.30.3). His effort for orthodoxy is illustrated by the popular legend of Amphilochius moving Theodosius to take action against the Arians by refusing to salute the emperor's son Arcadius (*Hist. eccl.* 5.16.1–5). This episode, if historical, must have happened in 383 CE, when Arcadius was created Augustus (in January), and Theodosius issued two laws against heretics (July and December; Cod. Theod. 16.5.11–12). Between 383 and 394 CE, Amphilochius presided over a synod of 25 bishops in Side in Pamphylia against the → Messalians (see Phot. *Bibl.* 52; see also Thdt. *Hist. eccl.* 4.11.4). He wrote a treatise against the Encratites (→ Encratism/ Encratites) of which a long fragment (1,094 ll.) is preserved.

Amphilochius stayed in contact with Gregory of Nazianzus and Gregory of Nyssa (Greg. Naz. *Ep.* 171; 184; Greg. Nyss. *Ep.* 25; see also the testament of Gregory of Nazianzus [PG 37.393.C–D], which Amphilochius signed in 381 CE as first witness), and he was also part of the circle around Olympias in Constantinople (see Pall. *Dial.* 17 [110.10]; *Vita Olympiadis* 14; Georg.Alex. *Vit.Chr.* 50). The last notice of him – his participation in a synod held at Constantinople in 394 CE – testifies once more to the high esteem in which he was held: in the list of illustrious participants (see PG 119.821.C), he holds the seventh place, shortly after the patriarchs. Because he is not mentioned in the events surrounding the removal and banishment of John Chrysostom, Amphilochius is generally assumed to have died before 403/404 CE.

The following writings of Amphilochius are preserved:

A. the didactic poem *Iambi ad Seleucum* (*CPG* 3230);
B. several homilies (*CPG* 3231–3235, 3237–3239, 3240, 3241, 3249) whose authenticity, however, is disputed in part (notably 1–3 and 7):
  1. On the Nativity of the Lord;
  2. On the Purification of the Lord (Luke 2:21–40);
  3. On the Four-Day Dead Lazarus (John 11:17–44);
  4. On the Sinful Women (Luke 7:36–50);
  5. On the Holy Sabbath;
  6. On Matt 26:39;
  7. On the Newly Baptized and on the Resurrection of the Lord;
  8. On Zacchaeus (Luke 19:1–10);
  9. On John 5:19;
  10. On John 14:28, preserved in a Syriac translation;
  11. On the Patriarch Abraham (about the Sacrifice of Isaac: Gen 22:1–19), preserved in a Coptic (Bohairic) translation;
C. the already mentioned synodical letter (*CPG* 3243) and creed (*CPG* 3244; preserved in a Syriac version);
D. the letter to Basil (Bas. *Ep.* 50);
E. the fragment *Contra Haereticos* (*Against the Encratites*; *CPG* 3242; although the name of the author is not preserved, there is little doubt that Amphilochius wrote this treatise; see Ficker, 1906, 111–169);
F. several fragments (*CPG* 3245–3248, 3257–3258) that mainly come from homilies (e.g. on Prov 8:22; John 5:19; 5:24; 16:14; 20:17; On the Son [of God]; On the Fleshly Begetting; About the Day and the Hour).

Considered spurious are the following: a homily On the Feast of Mid-Pentecost (*CPG* 3236); a homily On the Resurrection of the Lord (*CPG* 3251); a homily On Circumcision and on Basil (*CPG* 3254); a homily On the Holy Mother of God and on Simeon (Combefis, 1644, 36–56); a collection of nine homilies (*CPG* 3250), of which only the first (On Penitence) is edited (Combefis, 1644, 91–115); an encomium (*CPG* 3252) and a life (*CPG* 3253) of Basil; a life of Athanasius (*CPG* 3256); a speech about the infertile trees (*CPG* 3255). (Holl, 1904, 59, also lists *De non desperando* and *Vita Ephrem Syri* as certainly spurious.)

Bibliography

Barkhuizen, J.H., "The Preaching of Amphilochius of Iconium: An Introduction to the Authentic (Greek) Homilies," *APB* 16, Pretoria, 2005, 132–156.

Bonnet, M., & S.J. Voicu, eds., *Amphiloque d'Iconium: Homélies*, vols. I–II, SC 552–553, Paris, 2012.

Clémencet, C., *Gregorii Theologi opera quae extant omnia*, vol. I, Paris, 1778, repr. in: PG 35.

Combefis, F., ed., *SS. PP. Amphilochii Iconiensis, Methodii Patarensis et Andreae Cretensis Opera Graeco-Latina*, Paris, 1644.

Datema, C., ed., *Amphilochii Iconiensis Opera: Orationes, pluraque alia quae supersunt, nonnulla etiam spuria*, CChr.SG 3, Turnhout, 1978.

Destephen, S., "Amphilochios 1," in: S. Destephen, *PCBE*, vol. III: *Diocèse d'Asie (325–641)*, Paris, 2008, 106–133.

Drobner, H.R., "Bibliographia Amphilochiana," *ThGl* 77, 1987, 14–35, 179–196.

Ficker, G., *Amphilochiana*, part 1, Leipzig, 1906.

Holl, K., *Amphilochius von Ikonium in seinem Verhältnis zu den großen Kappadoziern*, Tübingen, 1904 (= Darmstadt, 1969).

Lightfoot, J.B., "Amphilochius," in: W. Smith & H. Wace, eds., *DCB*, vol. I, London, 1877 (= New York, 1967), 103–107.

Oberg, E., ed., *Amphilochii Iconiensis Iambi ad Seleucum*, PTS 9, Berlin, 1969.

Pouchet, J.-R., "L'enigme des lettres 81 et 50 dans la correspondance de saint Basile: Un dossier inaugural sur Amphiloque d'Iconium?" *OCP* 54, 1988, 9–45.

MARTIN KAISER

Amphipolis

Amphipolis is an ancient city that was a conduit of eastern Macedonia and became an Athenian colony in the year 437 BCE. It was in a strategic position along the Strymon River and 8 km from the port at the Aegean Sea (Eion). On its sides were the gold mines of the Pangaion. Its name (meaning around the city), according to Thucydides, stems from the fact that the river ran around city. After the Battle of Pydna in 168 BCE, Lucius Aemilius Paulus made it the capital of one of the four districts of Macedonia (Macedonia prima). Pompey the Great took refuge at Amphipolis after his defeat suffered at Pharsalus in 48 BCE at the hands of Julius Caesar. After the Battle of Philippi in 42 BCE, it had the status of a *civitas libera* (free city) with the rights to coin bronze money. It was located along the Via Egnatia, which led from Thessalonica to Philippi, about 45 km prior to its arrival in the latter city, which was a Roman colony. Amphipolis was encompassed by two walls on the perimeter, one on the outside, which had five doors, and another within its interior, shorter by 2,200 m. The people lived inside the latter of these two surrounding perimeter walls. The walls had been begun at the time of the foundation of the Athenian colony (438–437 BCE) andwere restored during the Hellenistic period. The eastern part of the wallwas redone in the Roman period. Along the southern section, the honorary inscriptions praised Augustus as the "founder of the city" and the proconsul Calpurnius Piso as the "patron and benefactor of the city." This shows that by then the city had been rebuilt at least in part upon the acropolis. The E gate, situated along the eastern segment of the perimeter, belonged to the wall from the Roman phase, but it took the place of a more ancient port from the classic era.

The recent excavations, carried out by D.I. Lazaridis (1975), have brought to light many of the ancient remainswhich were found in situ, are held in the local museum and in that of Kavala (the ancient Neapolis). During the Roman period, until the Slavic invasion of the 6th century CE, the city was prosperous, since it found itself in a region rich with agricultural products and mined minerals on an important Roman road and was not far from the harbor for exportation. That period, of its entire history, was the best for Amphipolis. The wealth of the city in those centuries was vouched for by the abundance and by the wealth of the pagan monuments – numerous temples – and Christian buildings. In the Middle Ages it was also called Chrysopolis, from a Byzantine fortress with that name that had been built in its vicinity (Burckhardt, 1893). Before and during the Slavic invasion of the 6th century CE, the population diminished in number, occupying only the zone near and around the acropolis. The inhabited zone was thus reduced, and the material from previous edifices was reutilized. Parts of the wall were preserved; the cisterns from the tall zones were redeployed and used by small houses. At the beginning of the 7th century CE, during the second Avaro-Slavic invasion, the city again underwent a reduction in size and population, when the city of Philippi was destroyed. There remained few inhabitants closed up in a restricted space; the traditional urban life practically ceased to be. The population moved alongside the coast, at the ancient site of Eion, the small port, which sremained active. This place, too, was abandoned during the Ottoman period. In 1367 a guardian tower was constructed in order to protect the property of the monastery of the Pantokrator, which was located on Mount Athos.

Paul (→ Paul the Apostle) and Silas, chased away from Philippi, and following the Via Egnatia to Thessalonica, passed through Amphipolis, stopping there in order to rest (Acts 18:1), as it was the main city between those two centers. Perhaps even Ignatius of Antioch (→ Ignatius, Epistles of) passed through this city as he was being brought to Rome. Since there were important Christian centers such as Philippi and Thessalonica, Christianity developed and progressed in Macedonia (Arn. *Adv. gen.* 2.12; PL 5.828) and, we may also suppose, at Amphipolis. We do not know when an organized Christian community was constituted, because only at the council of 533 CE was a bishop, Alexander, mentioned as its suffragan (Mansi, vol. IX, 392). The text, however, speaks of Amphipolis Primae Armeniae, which ought to be Primae Macedoniae (Stein, 1949, 662–663). The area neighboring Philippi and its position along the Via Egnatia must have had an influence on the birth of a Christian community. According to the Synaxarion of the Church of Constantinople, the martyrs Auctus, Taurion, and Thessalonica would have died at Amphipolis (Delehaye, 1902, col. 202, 12; *BSS*, vol. II, 637). They are also remembered in the Roman martyrology. Presbyter (→ Priest/Presbyter) Mocius, then one of the patrons of Constantinople, was originally from Amphipolis, but he underwent martyrdom at Constantinople (Delehaye, 1912, 267–270; Halkin, 1965, 5–22; *BSS*, vol. IX, 512). The passion regarding the events of Mocius are legendary, but there is evidence of devotion to him in the capital in 402 CE, the year in which there is the notice of a church that was dedicated to him.

At the council in Trullo (691–692 CE), the bishop Andrew (Andreas) was present (Mansi, vol. XI, 993). In the council that Photius held at Constantinople in 878/879 CE, a bishop from Chrysopolis gave his signature (Mansi, vol. XVII, 376). Yet which Chrysopolis? The pilgrim from Bordeaux, around the year 333 CE, went through Amphipolis; there is mention of it also by the anonymous cleric from Ravenna in his *Cosmographia*. The city is recalled, too, by the *Synecdemos* of Hierocles in 527 CE as a city of Macedonia.

The ruins of five Christian churches have been found; they were built between the 5th and 6th centuries CE, and all of them are rich with mosaic floors. Four of these were churches with three naves. Archeological research has not found traces of Christian structures from before the 5th century CE. Given that their names are not known to us, in order to differentiate them one uses the letters of the

Greek alphabet. The first (called A) had three naves with two lines of ten columns, from the beginning of the 6th century CE. The second (called B), again a church with three naves, is from the second half of the 5th century CE. The third (called Γ), in the western part of the hill of the acropolis, came to find itself outside of the fortification from the 6th century CE; it had an abundance of marble, and initially it had three naves, but it was restructured to have only one nave. The fourth (called Δ) is the most ancient of all, in as much as it dates back to the first half of the 5th century CE; rising to the southwest and at a distance of nearly 30 m from the basilica A. The monolithic columns had been taken from preexisting monuments. The fifth basilica (called E) was discovered in 1976 at the southeastern offshoot of the acropolis; it was a building with a hexagonal central plan, located inside a structure that had an almost circular form. During its construction ample use was made of the preexisting material from other edifices. One may suppose that it was built in the first half of the 6th century CE. Why are there so many Christian edifices for worship in such a restricted area? Given the dimension of the city at that period, the constructed buildings were not carried out in order to satisfy the exigencies of the worship of their large population, but perhaps on account of the presence of some rich families or by the clergy who wished to leave a recorded memory of their name.

Bibliography

Burckhardt, A., ed., *Hieroclis synecdemus*, Leipzig, 1893, 62n15, 65n6

Delehaye, H., *Propylaeum ad Acta sanctorum novembris*, Brussels, 1902.

Delehaye, H., *Les origines du culte des martyrs*, Brussels, 1912.

Halkin, F., "Une passion de saint Mocius martyr à Byzance," *AnBoll* 83, 1965, 5–22.

Koukouli-Chrysanthaki, C., "Amphipolis," in: *EAA*, Rome, 1994.

Koukouli-Chrysanthaki, C., *Excavating Classical Amphipolis*, in: M. Stamatopoulou & M. Yeroulanou, eds., *Excavating Classical Culture*, BARIS 1031, Oxford, 2002.

Lazaridis, D.I., "The walls of Amphipolis," *AAA* 8, 1975, 56–76.

Lazaridis, D.I., "La cité d'Amphipolis et son système de défense," *CRAI*, 1977, 194–214.

Lorber, C.C., *Amphipolis: The Civic Coinage in Silver and Gold*, Los Angeles, 1990.

Pallas, D.I., *Les monuments paléochrétiens de Grèce décou-verts de 1959 à 1973*, Vatican City, 1977.

Stein, E., *Histoire du Bas-Empire*, vol. II, Paris, 1949.

Taddei, A., "I monumenti protobizantini dell'acropoli di Amphipolis," *ASAA* 3/8, Rome, 2008, 253–310.

Veymiers, R., "Les cultes isiaques à Amphipolis," *BCH* 133, 471–520.

ANGELO DI BERARDINO

Anacletus (Bishop of Rome)

Anacletus was the third bishop of Rome, second in line from Peter (→ Paul the Apostle). From the earliest days, a doubling of his name occurs, and he is also known as Cletus. The confusion was persistent; until Vatican II the Roman liturgy celebrated two popes (→ Pope/Father), Anacletus on Jul 13 and Cletus on Apr 26. Today only the July date is kept, Apr 26 being shared with Marcellinus (pope). The concept of papacy at this early stage of the Christian church is contested; some contemporary records refer to him a "pope," but it might be more accurate to describe his status as "bishop of Rome." He is viewed retrospectively by the Roman Catholic Church as one in the succession of popes and is honored as such in the liturgy of the Mass. Contemporary sources are contaminated by hagiographical rhetoric.

1. Identity and Dates

Two separate entries appear in the *Liber pontificalis* (entries 3 and 5). To compound the confusion, there is the variant spelling of Anencletus, for example in → Eusebius of Caesarea, who cites → Irenaeus of Lyon's sequence of apostolic ministry, placing Anencletus between Linus and Clement of Rome (Eus. *Hist. eccl.* 3.13, 21; 5.6; PG 25). The situation is complicated by a reference in Clement's writings on Clement having been Peter's original successor but deciding "for the sake of harmony" to relinquish the post to Linus, resuming it again after the death of Anacletus. The usual sequence given omits this earlier appearance of Clement and has him purely as Anacletus' successor. The *Liberian Catalogue*'s erroneous dating and doubling are unconvincing, and the duality of popes is assumed to be a copying error that was perpetuated.

The name Anacletus, meaning "blameless," would be an especially appropriate designation for a pope, following Paul's (→ Paul the Apostle) insistence on blamelessness in Tit 1:7 and 1 Tim 3:2. Since the term is a Greek adjective, this better fits the second of the entries in the → *Liber pontificalis*, which gives Anecletus as being born in Athens, whereas the entry for Cletus claims his birth in Rome. The name was often given to slaves, suggesting perhaps the pope's social origins; "Cletus" might be an abbreviation of either name. Attributing Roman birth to Anacletus may be a pious reading of events in order to affirm the primacy of Rome, contested as the chief city within Christendom until the ecumenical councils of the 4th and 5th centuries CE, rather than an accurate record. An image of Anacletus shows him bearded, with large ears.

Eusebius locates Anencletus' ministry by the reigns of the Roman emperor (Eus. *Hist. eccl.* 3.13). According to this, Anencletus (as he calls him) succeeded Linus in the second year of Titus' reign (i.e. 81 CE) and held his post until the 12th year of Emperor Domitian's reign, having been bishop for 12 years. This does not quite add up but suggests a period between 80 and 90 CE, though his dates are generally taken as between 79 and 91 CE (Eusebius' dates of imperial reigns are not infrequently unreliable). Eusebius is keen to stress the apostolicity of this succession, stressing that Linus is mentioned in 2 Tim 4:21, and presuming Clement to be the fellow worker referred to in Phlm 4:3. The identification of Anacletus with Cletus continues via Eusebius' recording of Irenaeus through → Optatus of Milevis to → Augustine of Hippo. However, both the *Liberian Catalogue* and the *Liber pontificalis* distinguish between them and give widely different facts. Cletus is presented as the son of Aemiliarus, from the region of Vicus Patricius, occupying the papal throne for 12 years, one month, and 11 days. The consulships of Vespasian, Domitian, and Rufus locate him as living during the reigns of Vespasian and Titus.

2. Key Events

As with other popes in the early centuries, it is impossible to be sure of the exact nature of the role, as monarchical episcopacy had not yet been established in Rome. The ambiguous phrase "on Peter's instruction he ordained [...]" must surely refer to the sense of apostolic succession being established (evoked from 180 CE by Irenaeus as a marker of orthodoxy) since if Peter had been succeeded by Linus, he would no longer have been alive to give direct instruction on this matter. The 25 priests he is reputed to have ordained fits rather too tidily with the number of parishes in Rome at the time, suggesting this may be hagiographic embellishment. By contrast the entry for Anecletus claims birth in Athens to one Antiochus, an episcopacy of nine years, two months, and ten days. The consulships mentioned seem to follow on from Cletus despite the interposition of Clement, with Cletus being bishop during the ninth consulship of Domitian and Anacletus from the tenth onward. His ordinations are listed as five → priests, three → deacons, and six → bishops.

3. Martyrdom and Burial

Although Cletus is designated a martyr, Anacletus is not (→ Martyrs). If he had been martyred, it would have been as part of the *Lex Julia Majestatis* of 48 CE. Dante places Cletus in heaven in *Paradiso* 28.40–42. Mention is made of the sepulcher constructed for Peter, close to whom he was buried on Jul 13. There are no contemporary sources extant to elucidate these contradictions; details from the → *Chronograph of 354* and the *Epitome of the First Edition of the Liber Pontif* (Davis, 2000, 97–98) only confound the issue by offering Apr 20 as a burial date. Other epitomes are even later. The *Liber pontificalis* creates further confusion by attributing to Anacletus the building of a memorial to Peter, which was more likely done by Anicetus, a later pope. Modern excavations on Vatican Hill provide evidence that the modestly sized tomb was too small to contain either Anacletus or his successors. Around 850 CE, Pseudo-Isiodorus forged three letters he attempted to pass under the name of Anecletus.

4. Reception during the Reformation

Anacletus was the subject of a significant dispute between Martin Luther and Johann Mayr von Eck, which took place in Pleissenburg in Leipzig on Jul 4, 1519. The basis of this is highly relevant to our discussion of the reliability of evidence. Roman Catholic dogma asserts the apostolicity of the bishops in succession from Peter, and the primacy of Rome as the home of the pope. Martin Luther's protestant argument asserts the primacy of Scripture, which he sees as supreme over human teaching. He challenged Johann Mayr von Eck on the very issues of the claims to apostolic succession in the papacy, stating that there is no biblical proof that Peter ever ordained an → apostle, while acknowledging his key ranking among the apostles. This Martin Luther saw as a primacy of honor not jurisdiction. For three days the men debated the issue, and when Johann Mayr von Eck excused the "scant learning" of Anacletus on account of his piety, Martin Luther responded, "whether a pope is holy or not, it is a scandal that he should not know the Gospels, for he is shepherd of the flock and a teacher of the gospel." In January 1521, Martin Luther was formally excommunicated by Pope Leo X for denying papal authority.

Bibliography

Altaner, B., *Patrologie: Leben, Schriften und Lehre der Kirchenväter*, Freiburg, 1978.

Barcellona, F.S., "Anacleto," *EdP*, Rome, 2000, 197–199.

Caspar, E., "Anacletus," in: *GPAHW*, vol. I, Tübingen, 1930, 8–15.

Cavatta, F., "Anacletus," in: E. Josi, ed., *BSS*, vol. I, Rome, 1961–1970, 1032–1036.

Cross, F.L., & E. Livingstone, *ODCC*, Oxford, 2005.

Davis, R., trans., *Liber pontificalis (The Book of Pontifs)*, Liverpool, 2000.

Doyle, P., ed., *Butler's Lives of the Saints*, 12 vols., Chicago, 1999.

Duchesne, L., ed., *Le Liber pontificalis, texte, introduction et commentaire*, 2 vols., Paris, 1886–1892.

Duffy, E., *Saints and Sinners: A History of the Popes*, New Haven, 1997.

Dufourcq, A., "Alexander I (Pope)," in: A. Baudrillart, ed., *DHGE*, vol. II, Paris, 1912, 204–206.

Farmer, D.H., *ODS*, Oxford, 1978.

Ferguson, E., *EOEC*, New York, 1997.

Frend, W.H.C., *The Archaeology of Early Christianity: A History*, London, 1996.

Gontard, F., *The Popes*, trans. A.J. Peeler & E.F. Peeler, London, 1964.

Goggi, P., *EC*, vol. I, Vatican City, 1948–1954.

Hemmer, H., "Anacletus," in: A. Vacant, ed., *DThC*, vol. I, Paris, 1923, 1141–1142.

Jaffé, P., *Regesta pontificum Romanorum ab Condita Ecclesia ad Annum post Christum Natum*, 2 vols., Leipzig, 1885–1888.

John, E., ed., *The Popes: A Concise Biographical History*, London, 1964.

Kelly, J.N.D., & M.J. Walsh, "Anacletus," in: *ODP*, Oxford, 2010, 3.

Kirsch, J.P., "Anacletus," in: A. Baudrillart, ed., *DHGE*, vol. II, Paris, 1407–1408.

Kirschbaum, E., *Tombs of St. Peter and St. Paul*, trans. E. Murray, New York, 1959.

Koep, L., "Anacletus," in: T. Klauser, *RAC*, vol. II, Stuttgart, 1950, 410–415.

Maxwell-Stuart, P.G., *Chronicle of the Popes: The Reign-by-Reign Record of the Papacy from St Peter to the Present*, London, 2002.

Quasten, J., *Patrology*, vol. I, Utrecht, 1975.

Reardon, W.J., *The Deaths of the Popes: Comprehensive Accounts, Including Funerals, Burial Places and Epitaphs*, Jefferson, 2004.

Salamito, J.-M., "Anacletus," in: P. Levillain, ed., *PAE*, vol. I, London, 2002, 41–42.

Walsh, M., ed., *DCB*, New York, 2001.

Weltin, E.G., "Anacletus," in: T. Carson & J. Cerrito, *NCE*, vol. I, Washington DC, 2003, 370.

Williams, G.L., *Papal Genealogy: The Families and Descendants of the Popes*, Jefferson, 1998.

HANNAH HUNT

Ananias and Sapphira

According to the Acts of the Apostles (→ Acts, Book of), Ananias and Sapphira were two members of the early church in Jerusalem. Their story, narrated in Acts 5:1–11, is perhaps one of the most famous and mysterious episodes of Luke's second book. In short: they sell their estate and put the earnings at the apostle's feet, but Ananias withholds part of the profits for himself, "with his wife colluding in it" (Acts 5:2). Summoned before Peter – first Ananias (Acts 5:3–6), then Sapphira (Acts 5:7–11) – who exposes their fraud, the sinful couple abruptly falls down and dies. The story ends with a "great fear" seizing everyone who hears of the incident, in particular the church (Acts 5:5b, 11).

The morally questionable violence of this story has disturbed the readers throughout history, generating a multitude of interpretations, including iconographic receptions. Paradoxically, the fame of the story contrasts with the scarcity of historical information about the episode. Apart from the narrative

of Luke (Acts 5:1), the name of Sapphira – which stems etymologically from the Aramaic term שפירא ("beautiful") – appears nowhere else in the New Testament literature. The situation is similar for her husband, Ananias, which is probably a transcription from the Hebrew חנניה and translatable as "God is gracious." In addition to Acts 5 (vv. 1, 3, 5), there are only two other people in the New Testament who bear the same name: Ananias from the church in Damascus (Acts 9:10, 12, 13, 17; 22:12) and Ananias, a great priest, who, according to Luke, presided over Paul's trial (Acts 23:2; 24:1). However, aside from their name, they have nothing in common with Sapphira's husband.

Scholars (Menoud, 1950, 147ff., 153f.; Roloff, 1981, 92–93; Lüdemann, 1989, 66; etc.) have attempted to reconstruct a literary source behind the Lucan narrative to establish its historical basis. Such an inquiry comes up against major difficulties, since in the case of Acts, Luke has systematically deleted the traces of traditions he incorporates (Dupont, 1960). Any attempt to ascertain the exact form and extent of Ananias and Sapphira's original narrative is therefore bound to be speculative (see e.g. Jervell, 1998, 197–199; Marguerat, 2007, 23, 164–165).

That said, given the Septuagint style of the story (the names of the characters are of Semitic origin; the feet as seat of authority and the theme of religious fear are common motifs in the OT), the commentators almost unanimously postulate an ancient Judeo-Christian tradition about Ananias and perhaps also his wife (the duplication of the story could also be a later development) (see e.g. Lüdemann, 1989, 64–66; Jervell, 1998, 195–199; Marguerat, 2007, 164).

1. Ancient History of Reception

The story about Ananias and Sapphira has received great attention via reception, in particular in the commentaries and readings of early patristic writers; precisely, two main avenues can be identified in the ancient history of its interpretation (see Brown, 1989, 51–92):

1. a doctrinal exegesis, particularly Trinitarian, which shows the divine nature of the Spirit and its equality with the Father, is exemplified

by → Ambrose of Milan (*Spir.* 3.9.55–58) and → Augustine of Hippo (*C. litt. Petil.* 3.48);

2. a moral reading of the story is attested by → John Chrysostom (*Hom. Act.* 12) and by → Jerome (*Ep.* 130.14; *Ep.* 14.5) – both of whom interpret the story as condemning the sin of greed. Alternatively, in the *De Officiis Ministrorum* treatise of Ambrose (*Off.* 3.11.74), the narrative aims to reject the sin of lying. Some Fathers also linked the punishment that fell upon the couple to their disrespect of a vow, applying this reading to the monastic way of life (e.g. Aug. *Serm.* 148).

2. Literary Context, Narrative Function, and Generic Form

As one deduces from this short review of scholarly views, the importance of the episode is linked less to the biography of its protagonists than to the ideological/theological thesis that Luke wants to illustrate through them. Here, we have a good example of the "dramatische Episodenstil," also encountered elsewhere in the Acts of the Apostles (Plümacher, 1972, esp. 109–110; the quoted formula comes originally from Haenchen, 1977, 117n1): through the narrative of the fraud committed by Ananias and Sapphira (Acts 5:1–11), a story contrasted with the positive paradigm of Josef called Barnabas (Acts 4:36–37), the author gives a counterexample of the practice in the Jerusalemite Church of the principle of sharing one's goods (Acts 4:32–35; see also 2:44–45). In this sense, Acts 4:32–5:11 should be read as a narrative unit in which the story about Ananias and Sapphira serves a specific function (see Marguerat, 2002, 158–164). Precisely, regarding the generic form of the text – a "punishment miracle" (Theissen, 1983, 109–110) – the goal of the Lucan account is probably pedagogic and hortatory: what is at stake is the reinforcement of a sacred norm and the punishment of its infringement (Marguerat, 2002, 168–169). At the beginning of the sequence, the first Christian community is said to be "of one heart and soul" (Acts 4:32; see also 2:44). This harmony, generated by the → Holy Spirit, is made tangible thanks to the sharing of possessions. The theological fate of the community and the demonstration of its economic communion are thus central to the literary sequence (Marguerat, 2007, 158–178; Puig i Tàrrech, 2010).

3. An Original Sin and the Final Judgment

The sin of Ananias and Sapphira is not merely an institutional or a moral one; it is ultimately an act against the Holy Spirit or God himself (Acts 5:3–4, 9), who has secured the communal integrity and the growth of the eschatological people since the → Pentecost event (see Acts 2:42–47). This also explains the violent reaction to Ananias and Sapphira's fraud: it anticipates within the scope of human history the final judgment, a view which, according to Luke, places decisive weight on the economic ethics of the early Christians (e.g. Butticaz, 2011, 149–156). For those reasons, according to D. Marguerat, *"the original sin in the Church is the sin of money"* (Marguerat, 2002, 158–178, quotation p. 176; italics original).

Historiography

In modern exegesis, five chief explanations (see Marguerat, 2007, 165–166, 173) have been formulated by scholars in order to interpret this episode of the Christian origins according to Luke.

1. An etiological explanation: this reading, first put forth by P.-H. Menoud (1950), considers Acts 5 to be a legend that addresses the problem of the first deaths in the early Christian community (see 1 Thess 4:13–18).

2. A socioeconomic reading: developed by scholars such as E. Trocmé (1957), B.J. Capper (1983), or J. Taylor (2001), this interpretation relates the episode of Acts 5 to the community discipline of the Qumran community that punished, as part of its politics of pooling resources, any attempt at escape (e.g. 1QS 6.24b–25; CD 14.20–21).

3. A legal reading: this interpretation, supported in particular by C. Perrot (1981), sees the text as legitimating the discipline of excommunication in the early church.

4. A typological exegesis: very popular since John Chrysostom until now (see e.g. Haenchen, 1971, 237, 239), this interpretation draws on the story related in Josh 7 – the rare verb νοσφίζεσθαι used at Josh 7:1 also appearing at Acts 5:2–3 – a story that is marked by a financial fraud: the theft of the booty of Jericho's conquest and, as a

consequence, the killing of Akan, author of this crime.

5. An ecclesiological reading: from this perspective, especially represented in the studies of D. Marguerat (2002; 2007) and C. Combet-Galland (2005), the nature of the fraud is theological rather than ethical, since it negatively affects the growth of the nascent church – a character that appears explicitly, for the first time in Luke's second book, at the end of this story (Acts 5:11; the occurrence of ἐκκλησία in Acts 2:47 is considered to be a gloss).

Bibliography

Barrett, C.K., *The Acts of the Apostles*, ICC, vol. I, Edinburg, 1994, 261–271.

Brown, P.B., "The Meaning and Function of Acts 5,1–11 in the Purpose of Luke–Acts," diss., Ann Arbor, 1989.

Butticaz, S.D., *L'identité de l'église dans les Actes des apôtres: De la restauration d'Israël à la conquête universelle*, BZNW 174, Berlin, 2011, 149–156.

Capper, B.J., "The Interpretation of Acts 5.4," *JSNT* 19, 1983, 117–131.

Combet–Galland, C., "L'expulsion du mal: Un acte de naissance de l'église (Pourquoi Satan a–t–il rempli ton cœur?)," *FV* 104, 2005, 43–61.

Dupont, J., *Les sources du livre des Actes: État de la question*, Bruges, 1960.

Dupont, J., "La communauté des biens aux premiers jours de l'église (Actes 2, 42.44–45; 4, 32.34–35)," in: J. Dupont, ed., *Études sur les Actes des apôtres*, LeDiv 45, Paris, 1967, 503–519.

Haenchen, E., *The Acts of the Apostles: A Commentary*, trans. B. Noble, G. Shinn, H. Anderson & R. McL. Wilson, Philadelphia, 1971, 236–241.

Haenchen, E., *Die Apostelgeschichte*, KEK 3.16, Göttingen, [7]1977.

Harrill, J.A., "Divine Judgment against Ananias and Sapphira (Acts 5:1–11): A Stock Scene of Perjury and Death," *JBL* 130, 2011, 351–369.

Havelaar, H., "Hellenistic Parallels to Acts 5.1–11 and the Problem of Conflicting Interpretations," *JSNT* 67, 1997, 63–82.

Jervell, J., *Die Apostelgeschichte*, KEK 3.17, Göttingen, 1998, 194–199.

Lüdemann, G., *Early Christianity According to the Traditions in Acts: A Commentary*, trans. J. Bowden, London, 1989, 63–66.

Mathieu, Y., *La figure de Pierre dans l'œuvre de Luc (Évangile et Actes des Apôtres)*, EtB 52, Paris, 2004, 211–221.

Marguerat, D., *The First Christian Historian: Writing the "Acts of the Apostles,"* trans. K. McKinney, G.J. Laughery & R. Bauckham, SNTSMS 121, Cambridge UK, 2002, 155–178.

Marguerat, D., *Les Actes des apôtres (1–12)*, CNT(N) 5a, Geneva, 2007, 23, 158–178.

McCabe, D.R., *How to Kill Things with Words: Ananias and Sapphira under the Prophetic Speech–Act of Divine Judgement (Acts 4.32–5.11)*, LNTS 454, London, 2011.

Menoud, P.-H., "La mort d'Ananias et de Sapphira (Actes 5,1–11)," in: *Aux sources de la tradition chrétienne: Mélanges offerts à Maurice Goguel à l'occasion de son soixante–dixième anniversaire*, Neuchâtel, 1950, 146–154.

Mineshige, K., *Besitzverzicht und Almosen bei Lukas: Wesen und Forderung des lukanischen Vermögensethos*, WUNT 163, 2nd series, Tübingen, 2003, 230–236.

Perrot, C. "Ananie et Sapphire: Le jugement ecclésial et la justice divine," *L'AC* 25, 1981, 109–124.

Plümacher, E., *Lukas als hellenistischer Schriftsteller: Studien zur Apostelgeschichte*, StUNT 9, Göttingen, 1972, 80–111.

Puig i Tàrrech, A., "Enganyar la comunitat i mentir a l'Esperit: L'episodi d'Ananies i Safira (Ac 5,1–11)," in: A. Puig i Tàrrech, ed., *La veritat i la mentida*, SrBi 10, Barcelona, 2010, 173–202.

Roloff, J., *Die Apostelgeschichte*, NTD 5, Göttingen, 1981, 91–96.

Strelan, R., *Strange Acts: Studies in the Cultural World of the Acts of the Apostles*, BZNW 126, Berlin, 2004, 199–208.

Taylor, J., "The Community of Goods among the First Christians and among the Essenes," in: D. Goodblatt et al., eds., *Historical Perspectives from the Hasmoneans to Bar Kokhba in Light of the Dead Sea Scrolls*, Leiden, 2001, 147–161.

Theissen, G., *The Miracle Stories of the Early Christian Tradition*, ed. J. Riches, trans. F. McDonagh, Philadelphia, 1983, 109–110.

Trocmé, E., *Le "Livre des Actes" et l'histoire*, EHPR 45, Paris, 1957, 197–199.

Witherington, B. III, *The Acts of the Apostles: A Socio-Rhetorical Commentary*, Grand Rapids, MI, Cambridge UK, 1998, 213–220.

SIMON DAVID BUTTICAZ

Anaphora

The term "anaphora" is derived from the Greek verb ἀναφέρειν, the basic meaning of which is "to lead, to carry up." Used in a religious context, it may designate the act of "bringing something before" God and, more specifically, the "offering up" of a → sacrifice or oblation. In the Septuagint, the verb and its derivatives are commonly employed to render the *hiph'il* of the Hebrew *'alah* and related verbs that have the meaning of "offering up." In line with the specific connotation of offering it could evoke, the noun anaphora is used from the 4th century CE onward in Greek Christian texts to designate either the second (sacrificial) part of the Eucharist – which begins when the eucharistic gifts are brought to the altar and concludes with the communion – or the eucharistic prayer. Employed in its specifically liturgical meaning, the term found its way into several oriental languages, in particular Syriac, Coptic, Arabic, and Ethiopic (Baumstark, 1950). Although the word only occurs in eastern liturgical sources and its precise meaning fluctuates, in liturgical science it has gained general acceptance as a technical term for the eucharistic prayer as it developed from the 4th century CE onward in a variety of forms in the eastern – and in the western – parts of the Mediterranean important selection of texts in Latin translation (Hänggi & Pahl, 1968).

1. Early Forms of Eucharistic Prayers

Fully developed anaphoras are only attested since the late 3rd century CE or the early or mid-4th century CE (depending on the period to which one dates the oldest examples). These texts presuppose the existence of a classical type of Eucharist, in which communion, the partaking of bread and wine, was preceded by a single (eucharistic) prayer (the anaphora) in which explicit reference was made to the death of Christ. This type of → Eucharist did not gain general acceptance until the 3rd or 4th century CE. However, the various forms of the anaphora did not originate from scratch. Several sources point to the existence of prayers that fulfilled a similar function in varying sorts of eucharistic meals held by the Christians in the first three centuries CE and may be considered as precursors of the anaphoras.

Chapters 9 and 10 of the → Didache contain the texts of a number of thanksgivings intended for a eucharistic meal, two of them being said before and one after the meal proper (ch. 10). The literary structure of the latter presents a remarkable similarity to that of the later anaphoras, even if it is situated after and not before the meal proper and if essential elements of these texts (reference to the death of Jesus and the Last Supper) are lacking (Bradshaw, 2004, 24–42).

Justin Martyr, in his description of Sunday Eucharist, makes mention of prayers and thanksgivings that are sent up by the president after bread and

wine and water have been brought and before these are given to those present (Just. 1 *Apol.* 65 and 67; → Justin Martyr). Remarkably, the prayers have the same position in the Eucharist as the later anaphoras (before the sharing of bread and wine), and, moreover, by the recitation of this prayer of thanksgiving, bread and wine are transformed into the body and blood of Christ (1 *Apol.* 66.2).

In the Apocryphal Acts of the Apostles, we find several descriptions of eucharistic meals that find their culmination point in the breaking and sharing of bread (which is called the "Eucharist"). In most of these eucharistic scenes, the gesture of the breaking of the bread is preceded by prayers. In the *Acts of John* (→ John the Apostle), these have the character of litany-like series of thanksgivings and praises addressed to Jesus (chs. 85 and 109). The most remarkable of the meal prayers given by the *Acts of Thomas* (→ Thomas the Apostle) is a long litany-like invocation (epiclesis) of the → Holy Spirit depicted as a mother (ch. 50). Compared to the later classical anaphoras, these texts appear rather idiosyncratic, but they certainly reflect real liturgical traditions (Rouwhorst, 1990). The evidence provided by other (later) sources confirms that the Spirit epiclesis had a prominent position in the Syriac-speaking communities from which the *Acts of Thomas* originated (Rouwhorst, 2013).

2. The Pre-Christian Roots of the Eucharistic Prayers and the Anaphoras

In various anaphoras and prayers recited during early Christian eucharistic meals, one finds striking parallels to non-Christian, especially Jewish, prayer traditions. One may first of all note that both the anaphoras themselves and some of their ancestors provide literary structures that are very similar to those of biblical and postbiblical Jewish prayers. Very frequent in both prayer traditions is the combination of an "opening" praise/thanksgiving section (addressed to God), an anamnetic part in which the → creation and the → redemption realized by God in the past are commemorated, and a petitionary (or: epicletic) part, containing one or more supplications (see Giraudo, 1981). Equally common in both prayer traditions is the insertion of narrative sections in which the grounds for the commemoration or the supplication are explained (Giraudo, 1981). Besides these more or less common patterns, some of the Christian prayers in question show a more precise similarity with specific Jewish prayer texts (Rouwhorst, 2007, 302). Thus, the prayers of thanksgiving of *Did.* 9 and 10 seem to be shaped after early (orally transmitted) forms of Jewish meal blessings, more specifically the bread- and the wine-*berakoth* (blessings) and the *birkat ha-mazon* (blessing after meal), the prayer of thanksgiving said after the meal, while they also have several motifs in common with them (see e.g. Mazza, 1992, 19–50). Likewise, some parts of the anaphora of → Addai and Mari offer parallels to the blessings preceding the recitation of the Shema during the Jewish morning prayer (Vellian, 1982). Recent research (Bradshaw, 1997, 9–10) has, however, rightly emphasized the impossibility of tracing the origins of all the Christian meal prayers and anaphoras back to one specific type of Jewish prayer or prayer form, for instance the *birkat ha-mazon* (Dix, 1945) or an Hebrew Bible prayer form that is often called *todah* (thanksgiving; thus Giraudo, 1981).

While the eucharistic prayers and anaphoras have preserved essential elements and motifs that are characteristic of Jewish prayers, there are fewer traces of non-Jewish prayer forms to be found in these texts. In spite of a recent tendency to emphasize the importance of customs connected with the Greco-Roman banquets called *symposia* (Leonhard, 2010), there is no evidence of Christian texts used in the context of eucharistic meals (→ Eucharist) that have specific characteristics in common with the *paean*, a hymn sung or recited at the end of the Greco-Roman banquet. One of the rare examples of a prayer spoken in the context of a Christian meal and exhibiting features characteristics of pagan Greek prayer texts – more specifically invocations and hymns addressed to gods – is provided by the repeated invocation of the Spirit in the eucharistic epiclesis of the *Acts of Thomas* (Rouwhorst, 2014, 207–208).

3. Early Examples of Christian Anaphoras

Most of the anaphoras that have been preserved date from the mid- or the late 4th century CE and are quite easy to classify into regional types or families, as is common usage in scientific publications. Some of them, however, date to an earlier period and, moreover, do not fit the commonly accepted classifications. That is why these much-debated and important texts may be best dealt with separately.

The Papyrus Strasbourg Gr. 254 contains a short version of the Egyptian anaphora of Mark, which just consists of three elements: a praise and thanksgiving addressed to God because of the creation and the salvation of mankind, a sentence referring to an offering of a spiritual sacrifice, and a series of intercession prayers. All the other elements that feature in the later, much more developed anaphora of Mark (Sanctus, institution narrative, epiclesis) are missing. It is generally accepted that this short text is not an incomplete prayer, but forms the oldest (3rd cent. CE?) nucleus of what later would become the anaphora of Mark (see Cuming, 1990; counterarguments by Zheltov, 2008, 500–501).

The fifth of the *Mystagogical Catecheses* (or *Mystagogic Catecheses*) that have traditionally been ascribed to → Cyril of Jerusalem contains an explanation of the second part of the Eucharist as celebrated in Jerusalem. The references made by the author to the anaphora make clear that it has the following peculiar structure (Burreson, 1997): an introductory dialogue followed by a prayer of thanksgiving and praise in which mention is made of the visible und invisible realities created by God and which culminates into the → *Sanctus*. Afterwards, God is asked to send the Holy Spirit, and next follow the prayers of intercessions for the living and the dead. No mention is made of an institution narrative that, in spite of attempts that have been made to prove the contrary, probably was not part of the anaphora. The general structure of the prayer shows remarkable parallels to that of the Egyptian anaphora of Mark (as it had developed in the course of the 4th cent. CE), but it remains difficult to decide whether the similarities can be explained in terms of literary dependency (whether, e.g., both anaphoras were derived from a common, Egyptian, ancestor as has been hypothesized by Cuming, 1990). A factor that complicates the study of this anaphora is that no general consensus has been reached regarding the authorship of the *Mystagogical Catecheses*, some scholars attributing the text not to Cyril but to his successor, Bishop John of Jerusalem. In that case, the fact that such an archaic anaphora would have been used in the late 4th century CE would become all the more remarkable but also puzzling.

The most debated of the anaphoras is probably the Syriac anaphora of Addai and Mari. It is the only early Christian eucharistic prayer preserved that was originally written in Syriac (text ed. Gelston). It is still used by the churches that follow the East Syrian rite. The Maronite anaphora of Peter (usually called "Sharrar," which is the word with which the text begins) is an elaborated version of Addai and Mari. The parts that Addai and Mari and the Maronite text have in common (see Gelston, 1992) represent an old stratum in the development of Addai and Mari that must have been composed in Edessa or its surroundings, possibly in the 3rd century CE. It comprises an introductory dialogue; a prayer of praise addressed to the → Trinity (or, to the Son, as is the case in Sharar), which is followed by the *Sanctus*; a prayer of thanksgiving in which thanks is given to God for the salvation of mankind, which was realized by his assuming humanity and conquering death by his descent into the underworld; a prayer of intercession for the fathers – the prophets and the apostles and the member of the church – who have died; and the invocation of the Holy Spirit, who is asked to come and to rest upon the offering of the church, with a concluding doxology. One of the most striking characteristics of the text is the absence of an institution narrative (see Giraudo, 2014). The sole reference to the Last Supper is to be found in the prayer of intercession, where just a brief allusion is made to it. None of the arguments that have been adduced to prove that the prayer would have once contained such a narrative – and that it would have disappeared afterwards for some reason – has proven convincing (see Giraudo, 2014). On the other hand, there is no solid basis for reconstructions of older or more original cores than the one underlying Addai and Mari and Sharrar. There is for instance no proof for the existence of supposedly earlier versions without *Sanctus* or epiclesis.

We find an equally early but different type of anaphora in the document that was long known as the → *Apostolic Tradition* and was attributed to a certain Hippolytus of Rome, who was supposed to have been active as a presbyter (→ Priest/Presbyter) in Rome in the early 2nd century CE. The prayer, found in the Latin and Ethiopic versions (ch. 4), has a rather simple structure. It begins with an introductory dialogue, which is followed by a thanksgiving for the salvation of humanity realized by Jesus Christ and, next, by a version of the institution narrative, the latter ending with Jesus Christ ordering to "do this in remembrance of him." In response to this call, the "anamnesis" takes place, which has the form of a remembrance of the death and → resurrection of Jesus Christ, in combination with an offering of bread and wine as an expression of thanksgiving. This is in turn followed by a Spirit epiclesis in which God is asked to send the Holy Spirit upon the offering (Lat. *oblatio*) of the church and by a final doxology. Particularly noticeable, on the one hand, is the absence of a *Sanctus* and on the other hand the presence of an institution narrative followed by an anamnesis consisting of an offering of thanksgiving, a feature that will play a prominent role in nearly all the full-blown anaphoras of the 4th and 5th centuries CE. As is the case with Addai and Mari, scholars have suggested that some part(s) of this prayer, for instance the Spirit epiclesis, might be later additions to an older core (Bradshaw, 1997, 13–14). Such hypotheses are, however, difficult to substantiate. A no less plausible explanation for the presence of elements characteristic of texts dating to the 4th and 5th centuries CE would be that the entire anaphora was incorporated into the *Apostolic Tradition* in a late phase of its complicated process of redaction (e.g. late 3rd or early 4th cent. CE; Rouwhorst, 2007). What makes it most difficult to situate this prayer in the development of early Christian anaphoras is that the longstanding view that the *Apostolic Tradition* was composed in Rome early 3rd century CE has now been abandoned by most scholars and that there is no consensus about the date or the provenance or authorship (Bradshaw, Johnson & Phillips, 2002). We do not know where, when, by whom, and for what sort of community this prayer was created. The only thing that can be said with certainty is that its structure shows some striking points of similarity with the 4th- and 5th-century CE anaphoras belonging to the "Antiochene" type (see further on).

4. Fully Developed Eastern Anaphoras (4th and 5th Centuries CE)

Whereas the relatively rare data pertaining to the development of the Christian meal prayers and anaphoras in the first three centuries CE leave a very fragmentary impression, the 4th century CE provides an abundance of fully developed prayer texts, the date and provenance of which can mostly be quite well determined (see Bradshaw, 1997). An analysis and comparison of the various prayer texts show that a process of standardization has taken place that resulted in the formation of specific types of anaphoras characterized by specific literary structures and combinations of theological themes and motifs. As far as the East is concerned, two major traditions of anaphora construction may be distinguished, the first one often being called "Antiochene" or West Syrian and the second one "Alexandrian" or "Egyptian" (Mazza, 1992; 2010, 35–120). Whereas the latter designation may be considered more or less adequate, since all of these texts had their origins in Egypt and were only used in this region, the former term is less appropriate because it might wrongly suggest that the province of Syria or the city of Antioch and its direct surroundings formed the cradle of this type of anaphora. However, texts belonging to this type were produced and used from the mid-4th century CE onward in a wider region stretching from Cappadocia to Jerusalem. No less importantly, they had an even wider radius of action, being in use in the entire eastern part of the Mediterranean, from Constantinople to Egypt (where they would practically overrule the Egyptian type). If the designation "Syrian" will be nonetheless used here, it is for lack of an adequate and practical alternative.

One of the most challenging aspects of the study of a great number of these texts – in particular some belonging to the Syrian type – lies in the fact that several versions in various languages (Greek as well as Syriac, Armenian, Coptic, Georgian, Ethiopic) have been preserved. The reason is that they were used by a great variety of Christian communities speaking various languages and belonging to different cultures. Liturgical scholars have concentrated much of their energies on reconstructing "original texts," or at least the earliest possible phases. This approach, however, risks underestimating the fact that anaphoras were examples of "living literature" that were possibly orally transmitted before they were written down and continuously adapted to the changing needs and traditions of the living communities in which they were employed. The focus should therefore not lie exclusively or primarily on the origins and on the earliest phases, but attention should also be paid to their further development, which deserves attention for its own sake, not just as a means to come as close as possible to the oldest or supposedly original strata (see Budde, 2004).

5. "Syrian" Traditions of Anaphoral Construction

Anaphoras belonging to the "Syrian" type have in common a peculiar basic structure that consists of the following elements (Mazza 1992; 2010, 35–120):

a. Introductory dialogue.
b. Praise addressed to God resulting in the *Sanctus* which is followed by the *Benedictus*.
c. An often very elaborated thanksgiving for the salvation of mankind, beginning with the sin of Adam and Eve, the history of the Jewish people prior to the coming of Christ, the incarnation and the death of Christ, and his victory in Sheol (see Addai and Mari). Sometimes this thanksgiving is combined with (b), but in several anaphoras an entire section following after the Sanctus is devoted to this theme. In that case, there is a natural and often smooth transition between the thanksgiving and the following part, the institution narrative.
d. This institution narrative is followed by an anamnesis (similar to the one found in the *Apostolic Tradition*).
e. An epiclesis in which God is asked to send the Spirit upon both bread and wine – and to transform them into the body and blood of Christ – and upon the faithful.
f. A prayer of intercession for the living and the dead.
g. A concluding doxology.

This family of anaphoras encompasses a large group of (more than 80) texts (see Feulner, 2000). Not all of them were employed on a large scale, and some were composed in a fairly late period (in the second half of the Middle Ages). The origins of the following texts, some of which are in use up to the present in one or more eastern rites, can certainly be traced to the early Christian period (exhaustiveness is impossible and is not intended here):

The anaphora of → Basil of Caesarea: redactions in several languages have been preserved (Greek, Armenian, Coptic Sahidic and Coptic Bohairic, Syriac, Georgian, and Ethiopic). Several of them belong to the same family as the (long) Greek version that has always been in use in the Byzantine tradition, but a short Sahidic Coptic redaction and one of the two Armenian recensions, which in Armenian tradition is attributed to Gregory the Illuminator, represent older stages in the development of the text (Budde, 2004; Winkler, 2005). There is no general consensus as to the precise provenance of the oldest Greek archetype – supposing there once was a written archetype – lying at the basis of the different versions (see McGowan, 2010). It is usually located in Syria (Antioch or its surroundings) or in Cappadocia. As for the role of Basil, it is generally agreed that he was not the author of the oldest core. However, the parts of the (longer) Greek version that are missing in the Sahidic and the Old Armenian redactions fit in remarkably well with the theological ideas of the Cappadocian father. He may therefore well have had a role in redacting the core text of that longer version (see Budde, 2004, 573–577).

The Greek anaphora of → John Chrysostom and the Syriac anaphora of the twelve apostles: the two texts have as their common ancestor a mid-4th-century CE Greek core that has been further developed and elaborated in two different communities (Taft, 1997). The additions to the common ancestor that are missing in the Syriac text show striking parallels to the authentic works of John Chrysostom and appear to date to the late 4th century CE. It is very likely that the church father was the author of these additions (Taft, 1997). The Greek anaphora of John Chrysostom has become the most common anaphora of the Byzantine rite.

The anaphora of James, which was composed for use in the Church of Jerusalem by the late 4th century CE, has been employed in several other eastern churches and still is, particularly in the Syriac-speaking Syrian Orthodox Church. Different versions are extant in Greek, Syriac, Armenian, Georgian, and Ethiopic (Tarby, 1972; Winkler, 2013). By comparing the various versions, especially textual witnesses of the Greek and Syriac ones, one may reconstruct the outlines of an ancient 4th-century CE common core that has many features in common with the anaphora underlying the *Mystagogical Catecheses* (Tarby, 1972) and equally with the oldest versions of the anaphora of Basil. Several hypotheses have been propounded to explain the material that the anaphora of James and the anaphora of Basil have in common, but it remains difficult to determine the precise relationships among the various versions of the anaphora of James and even more so between those of the anaphora of James and those of anaphoras of the same type, as for instance the anaphora of Basil. G. Winkler (2013) has convincingly shown that theories claiming to trace back the variety of (versions) of prayers to one original type do no justice to the complicated processes in which the (various redactions of) the anaphora of James and the anaphora of Basil have continuously interacted with one another (and possibly with other prayers).

An extremely long prayer, that of the → *Apostolic Constitutions* (8.12), is a source that was compiled in the neighborhood of Antioch (late 4th cent. CE). It is doubtful that the prayer as found in this document was actually used in the liturgy.

The Armenian anaphora of Athanasius that was composed in Armenian in the 5th/6th centuries CE, which has been the only eucharistic prayer to be used in the Armenian liturgy since the 9th/10th century CE. Dating roughly from the same period, three other Armenian anaphoras have an "Antiochene" structure and are attributed, respectively, to Sahak, → Gregory of Nazianzus, and → Cyril of Alexandria (Feulner, 2001).

The (originally Greek) anaphora of Gregory of Nazianzus that is still used in the Coptic Church (Gerhards, 1984) is, remarkably, entirely addressed to Christ.

One may also attribute two texts to the Antiochene family that are used in the East Syrian rite (besides Addai and Mari), namely those of → Theodore of Mopsuestia and of Nestorius (→ Nestorianism/ Nestorius). A characteristic feature of these prayers is that the prayers of intercession precede the epiclesis (like in Addai and Mari), and this is the main reason why they are often considered to form a singular East Syrian group (together with Addai and Mari and the anaphora underlying Theodore of Mopsuestia's 16th Cathechetical Homily). Yet they were originally written in Greek and, apart from the position of the intercessions, have the same structure as the so-called Antiochene anaphoras.

6. Egyptian Traditions of Anaphoral Construction

Compared to the large number of anaphoras produced in the Syrian region, relatively few texts are extant that originated in Egypt. The best-preserved and the most widely used representatives are the Greek anaphora of Mark and its Coptic translation, which is attributed to Cyril of Alexandria and (albeit rarely) used in the Coptic Church up to the present (Cuming, 1990). Beside Mark's anaphora and Cyril's translation, two other anaphoras that originated in Egypt have been preserved in part or in their entirety:
   a. an anaphora included in the 4th-century CE collection of prayers of Sarapion of Thmuis (see Johnson, 1995) and
   b. the anaphora fragments preserved in the so-called Deir Balyzeh Papyrus (c. 600).

Finally, an anaphora transmitted by the 4th-century CE Barcelona papyrus (P. Montserrat Roca) has many features in common with the purely Egyptian prayers (Zheltov, 2008).

The first three texts have the following features in common (most of which are also found in the Barcelona Papyrus):

The praise addressed to God that follows upon the introductory dialogue explicitly makes mention of the creation of the world (not only of the redemption of humankind).

The anamnesis recited after the institution narrative makes mention of the offering of the gifts of bread and wine as having already taken place prior to the anaphora or in its first part, where mention is made of a spiritual sacrifice (difference with the *Apostolic Tradition* and most Syr. anaphoras).

Apart from the text of Mark from the Strasbourg Papyrus, all the representatives have a *Sanctus* without *Benedictus* that is followed by a first Spirit epiclesis (in the case of the prayer of Sarapion of Thmuis, a *logos* epiclesis). Both elements form a coherent unit with the epiclesis and develop the idea, found in the *Sanctus*, that heaven and earth are full of God's glory.

The first epiclesis is followed by a unit consisting of the institution narrative, an anamnesis, and a second epiclesis that is more developed and more explicitly consecratory than the first one. After the second epiclesis, the prayer is concluded by a final doxology.

In the only anaphora in which intercessions have been incorporated (Mark's anaphora and Cyril's translation), they are connected with the theme of the spiritual sacrifice and located in the section preceding the *Sanctus* (not in the final part, as is the case in all the Syrian anaphoras).

The relatively complicated structure of this type of anaphora with its double epiclesis and the peculiar position of the oblation – and the intercession, at least in Mark's anaphora and Cyril's translation – may be best explained as being the result of a gradual growth by accumulation that must have taken place in two stages during the 4th century CE. The oldest core was constituted by a text roughly identical or similar to that of the Papyrus Strasbourg, which included a praise and thanksgiving, the offering of a spiritual sacrifice, and (sometimes) intercessions. To this nucleus, the *Sanctus*/first epiclesis unit was added. The process of accumulation was completed by the addition of the institution narrative, the anamnesis, and the second epiclesis.

7. The Roman Canon and the Non-Roman Western Eucharistic Prayers

Very little is known about the eucharistic prayers that were in use in Rome and Italy prior to the mid-4th century CE. Because the *Apostolic Tradition* was translated into Latin in the 4th century CE, it is very likely that the anaphora it contains was occasionally employed in this region (even if it would not have been composed there). It is, however, certain that in the 4th or 5th century CE, early versions of the so-called Roman and the Ambrosian canon (for the latter text, see Triacca, 2005) – the eucharistic prayers of the (later) Roman, respectively Ambrosian/Milanese rites – were in use. Large parts of an early version of this prayer are quoted by → Ambrose of Milan in his *De sacramentis* (see Mazza, 1992, 261–307). It emerges from his citations that the prayer he knew included at least the following elements (the corresponding elements of the later, fully developed version of the Roman and Ambrosian canon are indicated between brackets): a praise addressed to God (the so-called preface), a prayer for the "people, the kings and the others" (see the *Te igitur* and the *Memento* for the living), an ancient version of the *Quam oblationem*, in which God is asked to accept the gifts offered by the faithful, the institution narrative and the anamnesis (*Unde et memores*), and again a prayer for acceptance of the eucharistic gifts (*Supra quae*). The *Sanctus* is not mentioned by Ambrose and was probably inserted later. This also holds true for others parts of the Roman/Ambrosian canon that are lacking (the *Communicantes*, the *Hanc igitur*, and the *Memento* of the dead). Particularly noteworthy are two features that are equally characteristic of the later texts: the emphasis placed upon the offerings of the faithful and the lack of a Spirit epiclesis.

For information concerning the eucharistic prayers used in the 4th and 5th centuries CE in Gaul and Spain, we are dependent on liturgical sources that date to the (early) Middle Ages. They depict a great variety of prayers that included the following components (Smyth, 2003, 261–459; Mazza, 2010, 113–118):

a. an introduction dialogue and a thanksgiving called *contestatio* (supplication, invocation), *immolatio* (Gallican; sacrifice), or *inlatio* (Span.; offering);
b. *Sanctus* with introduction;
c. a brief post-*Sanctus* that connected the *Sanctus* with the following;
d. institution narrative and anamnesis;
e. a prayer called *Post mysteria/mysterium/post secreta* (Gallican) or *Post pridie* (Span.) that sometimes, especially in the Spanish texts, contains a Spirit epiclesis.

The *Sanctus*, the institution narrative, and the anamnesis were later additions. The oldest nucleus seems to have consisted of the *contestatio/inlatio* and the *Post mysterium/Post pridie*. A text called *Qui formam* refers to the institution of the Eucharist without citing the dominical words and may be considered an ancestor of the full-blown institution narrative. The *Post mysterium/Post pridie* is closely connected to the communion, and the epiclesis that is occasionally part of it was added later.

The structures of these western prayers show remarkable similarities to that of the Egyptian anaphoras. Like the latter, they give the impression of having grown through the expansion of an old nucleus that consisted of praise and thanksgiving (in Rome/Italy and Egypt also of prayers of intercession) and was interpreted as a (spiritual) sacrifice. The *Sanctus*, the institution narrative, and the anamnesis were in principle simply added to this ancient core (see esp. for the Roman canon and the Egyptian texts: Mazza, 1992).

8. 4th- and 5th-Century CE Developments and Unsolved Questions

In the great variety of prayer texts dating from the 4th and 5th centuries CE, the following general tendencies may be discerned.

A typical feature of the prayers of the "Syrian" group is that they culminate in a Spirit epiclesis. Insofar as they appear in the Egyptian and western texts, they have been added in a later phase. In most of the western texts – including the Roman and the Ambrosian canon – they are completely lacking.

The theme of a spiritual offering/sacrifice was an integral part of the oldest nucleus of the Egyptian and western prayers. In the Syrian texts, it appears only in the anamnesis that was inserted at the same time as the institution narrative (in the oldest forms of the anamnesis, the offering motif is still lacking; see Winkler, 2005, 722–741).

The institution narrative was originally not part of the eucharistic prayer and was only gradually inserted into it. In some texts (e.g. Addai and Mari), it was only briefly alluded to. Some early forms of the institution narratives (*Qui formam*) did not yet contain the dominical words that would become a central element in the full-blown versions.

There is no general consensus about the origins of the *Sanctus*. It remains difficult to determine how its insertion in the anaphora relates to the *qeduššā* contained in Jewish prayers. Another point of continuing debate is whether the *Sanctus* entered the anaphora first in Egypt (Taft, 1991, 192) or in Syria (Spinks, 1991). It seems more firmly anchored in the Syrian prayers than in the Egyptian ones. But however this may be, it is an integral part of practically all of the 4th- and 5th-century CE eastern and western eucharistic prayers.

In the earliest Spirit epicleses (Addai and Mari; the *Apostolic Tradition*; Egyp. Basil), the role of the Spirit with regard to the faithful and the gifts upon which it is invoked is not clearly defined. In later texts (e.g. John Chrysostom and the versions of James), one may discern a growing emphasis on the transformation of the gifts.

The texts of various parts of the eucharistic prayers (esp. those belonging to the Syriac type) clearly reflect the theological developments of the 4th and 5th centuries CE as formulated by councils and synods, creeds, and influential theologians like Basil and John Chrysostom (Tarby, 1972; Winkler, 2005; 2013).

Historiography

The beginning of a scholarly interest in the study of early Christian eucharistic prayers can be traced back to the 18th century when scholars like E. Renaudot (1716) and S.E Assemani (1749–1766) published scientific editions and Latin translations with introductions of the various eastern and western liturgies which also comprised the texts of eucharistic prayers. However, a more systematic study of these texts was inaugurated only in the 20th century. One of the most influential scholars in this field was G. Dix (1945). The scholarly interest in this topic reached a highpoint in the second part of the 20th century as being part of a widespread fascination for the liturgical traditions of early Christianity. This phenomenon was closely linked to the influence of liturgical movements in various western churches which sought inspiration for the liturgical reforms they strived at, in early Christian liturgy. The study of the texts was considerably facilitated and stimulated by critical editions of texts in various languages, in particular Syriac (Gelston, 1992), Coptic (Budde, 2004) and Armenian (Winkler, 2005; 2013; Feulner, 2001). Since G. Dix published his book, the search for the Jewish roots of the early Christian prayers, more specifically its relationship with Jewish meal blessings (Mazza, 1992; 2010) or other Jewish prayer types (Giraudo, 1981) has been a central issue and has remained so till the beginning of the 21st century. Quite a lot of debate has also been raised by the questions of the origins of the institution narrative

which is lacking in a number of eucharistic prayers, in particular in the East Syrian anaphora of Addai and Mari (Gelston, 1992). Contrary to earlier tendencies to reconstruct the historical development of the prayers starting from a common supposedly primitive pattern which itself was believed to go back to common pre-Christian (Jewish) roots, for instance, the *birkat ha-mazon*, that is the prayer of thanksgiving said after a meal, recent publications point to the great variety of prayer types and argue that they cannot be reduced neither to a primitive common pattern nor to one sort of pre-Christian tradition (Bradshaw, 1997; 2004).

Bibliography

Assemani, S.E., *Codex liturgicus Ecclesiae universae*, Rome, 1749–1766.

Baumstark, A., "Anaphora," in: *RAC*, vol. I, Stuttgart, 1950, 418–427.

Bradshaw, P., ed., *Essays on Early Eastern Eucharistic Prayers*, Collegeville, 1997.

Bradshaw, P., *Eucharistic Origins*, Oxford, 2004.

Bradshaw, P., & M.E. Johnson, *The Eucharistic Liturgies: Their Evolution and Interpretation*, Collegeville, 2012.

Bradshaw, P., E.J. Johnson & L. Phillips, *The Apostolic Tradition: A Commentary*, Minneapolis, 2002.

Budde, A., *Die ägyptische Basilios-Anaphora: Text-Kommentar-Geschichte*, JThF 7, Münster, 2004.

Burreson, K., "The Anaphora of the Mystagogical Catecheses," in: P. Bradshaw, ed., *Essays on Early Eastern Eucharistic Prayers*, Collegeville, 1997, 131–152.

Cuming, G.J., *The Liturgy of St. Mark Edited from the Manuscripts with a Commentary*, OCA 234, Rome, 1990.

Dix, G., *The Shape of the Liturgy*, London, 1945, many reprs.

Feulner, H.-J., "Zu den Editionen orientalischer Anaphoren," in: H.-J. Feulner, E. Velkovska & R. Taft, eds., *Crossroad of Cultures: Studies in Liturgy and Patristics in Honor of Gabriele Winkler*, OCA 260, Rome, 2000, 251–282.

Feulner, H.-J., *Die armenische Athanasius-Anaphora: Kritische Edition, Übersetzung und liturgievergleichender Kommentar*, AoAa 1, Rome, 2001.

Gelston, A., *The Eucharistic Prayer of Addai and Mari*, Oxford, 1992.

Gerhards, A., *Die griechische Gregoriosanaphora: Ein Beitrag zur Geschichte des Eucharistischen Hochgebets*, LWQF 65, Münster, 1984.

Gerhards, A., H. Brakmann & M. Klöckener, eds., *Prex eucharistica*, vol. III: *Studia*, part 1: *Ecclesia antiqua et occidentalis*, SF 42, Fribourg, 2005.

Giraudo, C., *La struttura letteraria della preghiera eucharistica*, AnBib 92, Rome, 1981.

Giraudo, C., ed., *The Anaphoral Genesis of the Institution Narrative in Light of the Anaphora of Addai and Mari:*

Acts of the International Liturgy Congress Rome, Oct 25–26, 2011, OCA 295, Rome, 2013.

Hänggi, A., & I. Pahl, *Prex eucharistica: Textus e variis liturgiis antiquoribus selecti*, SF 12, Fribourg, 1968; ³1998.

Johnson, M.E., *The Prayers of Sarapion of Thmuis: A Literary, Liturgical and Theological Analysis*, OCA 249, Rome, 1995.

Johnson, M.E., ed., *Issues in Eucharistic Praying in East and West: Essays in Liturgical and Theological Analysis*, Collegeville, 2010.

Leonhard, C., "Mahl V (Kultmahl)," in: *RAC*, vol. XXIII, Stuttgart, 2010, 1012–1105.

Mazza, E., *L'anafora eucaristica: Studi sulle origini*, BELS 62, Rome, 1992.

Mazza, E., *Rendere grazie: Miscellanea eucaristica per il 70° compleanno*, Bologna, 2010.

McGowan, A.V., "The Basilian Anaphoras: Rethinking the Question," in: M.E. Johnson, ed., *Issues in Eucharistic Praying in East and West: Essays in Liturgical and Theological Analysis*, Collegeville, 2010, 219–262.

Renaudot, R., *Liturgia orientalium collectio*, Paris, 1716.

Rouwhorst, G., "La célébration de l'eucharistie selon les Actes de Thomas," in: C. Caspers & M. Schneiders, eds., *Omnes circumdastantes: Contributions Towards a History of the Role of the People Presented to Herman Wegman*, Kampen, 1990, 51–77.

Rouwhorst, G., "The Roots of the Early Christian Eucharist: Jewish Blessings or Hellenistic Symposia?" in: A. Gerhards & C. Leonhard, eds., *Jewish and Christian Liturgy and Worship: New Insights into its History and Interaction*, JCPS 15, Leiden, 2007, 295–308.

Rouwhorst, G., "Eucharistic Meals East of Antioch," in: M. Vinzent, ed., *StPatr*, vol. LXIV, Louvain, 2013, 85–104.

Smyth, M., *La liturgie oubliée: La prière eucharistique en Gaule antique et dans l'occident non-romain*, PC, Paris, 2003.

Spinks, B., *The Sanctus in the Eucharistic Prayer*, Cambridge UK, 1991.

Taft, R., "The Interpolation of the Sanctus into the Anaphoras: When and Where? A Review of the Dossier," *OCP* 57, 1991, 281–308; *OCP* 58, 1992, 83–121.

Taft, R., "St. John Chrysostom and the Anaphora That Bears His Name," in: P. Bradshaw, ed., *Essays on Early Eastern Eucharistic Prayers*, Collegeville, 1997, 195–206.

Tarby, A., *La prière eucharistique de l'église de Jérusalem*, TH 17, Paris, 1972.

Triacca, A., "Le preghiere euccaristiche ambrosiane," in: A. Gerhards, H. Brakmann & M. Klöckener, eds., *Prex eucharistica*, vol. III: *Studia*, part 1: *Ecclesia antiqua et occidentalis*, SF 42, Fribourg, 2005, 145–202.

Vellian, J., "The Anaphoral Structure of Addai and Mari compared to the Berakoth Preceding the Shema in the Synagogue Morning Service contained in the Seder R. Amram Gaon," *Muséon* 85, 1982, 201–223.

Winkler, G., *Die Basilius-Anaphora: Edition der beiden armenischen Redaktionen und der relevanten Fragmente, Übersetzung und Zusammenschau aller Versio-nen im Lichte der orientalischen Überlieferungen*, AoAa 2, Rome, 2005.

Winkler, G., *Die Jakobus-Liturgie in ihren Überlieferungssträngen: Edition des Cod. arm. 17 von Lyon, Übersetzung und Liturgievergleich*, AoAa 4, Rome, 2013.

Zheltov, M., "The Anaphora and the Thanksgiving Prayer from the Barcelona Papyrus: An Underestimated Testimony to the Anaphoral History in the Fourth Century," *VigChr* 62, 2008, 467–504.

GERARD ROUWHORST

Anastasia Pharmacolitria

Anastasia φαρμακολύτρια (the poison curer/deliverer from spells) is also known as Anastasia of Sirmium or Anastasia the widow. She was purportedly martyred in Sirmium (Sremska Mitrovica, Serbia), in the era of → Diocletian (284–311 CE). The unknown author of her fictional Latin *passio* (*BHL* 400–401) gave her a Roman origin and inserted three other *passiones*, those of Chrysogonus, Agape and her companions, and Theodote and her children. Some or all of these other martyrdoms are omitted in the transmission of the Greek translations (*BHG* 81, 81a, 81e, 82a, 83, 83e). Anastasia was commemorated on Dec 22 in Constantinople and on Dec 25 in Rome. She is sometimes mistaken for Anastasia the Virgin/Roman, who was martyred under Diocletian and Valerian on Oct 12, 28, or 29 (*BHL* 404; *BHG* 76z, 77–78) or Anastasia the Patrician, martyred under → Justinian (*BHG* 79, 80, 80e).

1. Story

Anastasia is the daughter of Praetextatus and wife of Publius. Against her husband's wishes, she regularly visits incarcerated Christians and initiates a correspondence with Chrysogonus, a → priest. After Publius dies, his widow is at liberty to accompany Chrysogonus when Diocletian summons the priest to Aquileia. Anastasia is present during his interrogation and decapitation. His body is abandoned near the homes of three sisters, Agape, Chionia, and Irene, and their priest, Zoilus. Zoilus buries Chrysogonus, who then appears in a dream to foretell the sisters' capture. The women are duly apprehended, and Diocletian departs for Thessalonica with his prisoners. Anastasia follows. Once there, the sisters reject two prefects, Dulcitius and Sisinnius, and are killed. Anastasia takes care of the sisters' burials. Diocletian then travels to Sirmium, where Anastasia becomes involved with Theodote and her three children, who have escaped from Nicaea, Bithynia. The women minister to imprisoned Christians. Consequently, Theodote is taken back to her native city for interrogation by the prefect Probus. Anastasia again follows and confronts him. Diocletian's response is to force Anastasia to marry Ulpian, a high priest. After he attempts to embrace her, he is blinded and dies. Anastasia recounts her experiences to Theodote; however, soon afterwards, the mother and her children are burned to death. Anastasia is now taken to Illyria and detained without food, but at night Theodote appears, bringing sustenance. After 30 days, Lucius the prefect puts Anastasia on a ship, sabotaged with holes, along with criminals and another Christian called Euticianus. When the boat begins to sink, Theodote reappears and averts disaster while Anastasia converts the 120 men on board. The Christians reach the island of Palmaria, where they are given the choice between → apostasy and death. Choosing the latter, Anastasia is attached to four rocks by her hands and feet, and a fire is lit beneath her. She dies on Dec 25, and her remains are laid to rest on Sep 7 in a church that Apollonia, a Christian, has built.

2. Origins

The only Anastasia noted in the → *Martyrologium Hieronymianum* (Jerome's martyrology) is Anastasia of Sirmium, under Dec 25. Although Anastasia φαρμακολύτρια's *passio* states that she is from Rome, she does not feature in the lists of martyrs. Evidently, her hagiographer appropriated Anastasia of Sirmium to create his epic Roman passion and also wove in Chrysogonus, the three sisters, and Theodote. His inspiration probably stemmed from the existence of the churches of an Anastasia, near the Palatine, and of a Chrysogonus, in Trastevere. The titular churches of both Anastasia and Chrysogonus are first mentioned in the council of 499 CE and were later elevated to the Churches of Saint Anastasia and of Saint Chrysogonus, as they were known by the time of the council of 595 CE (see Rossi,

1857; Valentini & Zucchetti, 1940). The hagiographer acknowledges Anastasia φαρμακολύτρια's roots by introducing the convenient martyrdom of Theodote and her children, the main events of which take place in Sirmium, thus locating Anastasia's imprisonment there. However, a Roman martyr cannot die abroad, so that Palmaria (also Palmarola or Ponza), a traditional place of exile (→ Deportation/Exile), becomes a convenient location for her death. The hagiographer incorporated the acts of Chrysogonus (*BHL* 1795; *BHG* 2067), Agape and her companions (*BHL* 118; *BHG* 34), and of Theodote (*BHL* 8093; *BHG* 1781) into Anastasia's *passio* and amalgamated the stories of the foreign martyrs to create epic voyages with Anastasia as the link.

3. Later Versions

In 824 CE, while on an embassy to the → pope in Rome, Theodore Krithinos, an οἰκονόμος of the Great Church, translated the text into Greek with the help of "John" and brought it to Constantinople. Symeon Metaphrastes adapted the Greek version, which was subsequently translated by Lipomanus and added to Surius' collection, under Dec 25. The metaphrast changed the date of commemoration from Dec 25 to the 22, conforming to Greek custom. Thus, this is the date on which the Church of Saint Anastasia is dedicated in the *Vita* of Marcian (*BHG*² 1032, ch. 5).

4. Churches

Theodore Anagnostes confirms that Patriarch Gennadius of Constantinople (458–471 CE) visited Sirmium, not Palmaria, to view Anastasia's body (*Hist. trip.* 2.83–84). Her → relics were transferred to Constantinople and placed in the 4th-century CE Anastasis Church at the Portico of Domninus, northwest of Constantine's forum. They were subsequently moved to Rome in the 6th century CE and installed in Anastasia's titular church. Each church, originally dedicated to a different Anastasia, became known as Anastasia the Great Martyr (see Baun, 2007). L. Rydén (1974) notes that R. Janin (1953) locates four churches of Anastasia in Constantinople, but on reviewing the evidence, he believes that only the Anastasis church existed.

5. Pharmacolitria

The Greek epithet φαρμακολύτρια does not appear in her *passio*, nor does Anastasia perform any miracle that relates to poisoning or → magic. However, she and her church in Constantinople appear in this capacity in the *Vitae* of Andrew the Fool, Basil the Younger, and Irene of Chrysobalanton. Andrew is chained for four months inside Anastasia's church to cure him of his supposed demonic possession until she appears and comforts him. In Basil's *Vita*, the church is the destination for a possessed servant girl and a poisoned eunuch. In Irene's *Vita*, Anastasia, together with Basil the Great, heal "the possessed nun from Cappadocia" by producing the very "devices" that caused the possession. Once the nun is taken to Anastasia's tomb, located in her church, and anointed with lamp oil, a priest burns the devices, and the nun is exorcised. The *Vitae* provide a *terminus ante quem* of the 9th/10th century CE for her epithet, a period in which her churches begin to appear throughout the empire (see Buckton, 1994). In F. Halkin's Greek edition (1973), the earliest five of the seven manuscripts date from the 9th to the 11th century CE. Interestingly, the 10th-century CE *passio* of Anastasia the Virgin/Roman states that she performs cures (ch. 1), while a 14th-century version adds that she protects those who have been poisoned (ch. 8), confusing her with Anastasia φαρμακολύτρια. Furthermore, the *Apocalypse of Anastasia*, dated between the 10th and 12th century (although some parts may be earlier; see Beck, 1959), refers to a nun who "released those under the spell of sorcerers/ or who are poisoned" (Palermo version: ch. 5) and "freed those troubled by unclean spirits" (Milan version: ch. 5). L. Rydén (1974) notes that the Anastasis church in Constantinople had always been associated with the Virgin → Mary and miraculous healings (Soz. *Hist. eccl.* 7.5). It is possible that after the transference of her relics from Sirmium in the mid-5th century CE, the church's association with healing led to Anastasia being celebrated as a φαρμακολύτρια. In addition, her prominence in the 10th century CE, stimulated by the *passio*'s 9th-century CE Greek translation, led to confusion with the two Anastasias of the 10th century CE – the virgin/Roman and the nun – and thus to the diffusion of the idea.

6. Iconography

Anastasia is sometimes depicted holding a medicine bottle. She appears among the virgins in the mosaics of Saint Apollinare Nuovo, Ravenna, but without an accessory. L. Rodley lists four appearances in the rock-cut Cappadocian churches (see Rodley, 1985). The only instance where she is depicted with Chrysogonus, Agape, Irene, Chionia, and Theodote is in the "Pigeon House" Church at Çavuşin (see Rodley, 1983), which was decorated during the reign of Nikephoros II Phokas (963–969 CE), again attesting to her popularity in this period.

Bibliography

Baun, J., *Tales from Another Byzantium*, Cambridge UK, 2007.

Beck, H.-G., *Kirche und theologische Literatur im byzantinischen Reich*, Munich, 1959.

Brandi, M.V., & S. Orienti, "Anastasia," in: *BSS*, vol. I, Rome, 1960, 1042–1049.

Buckton, D., ed., *Byzantium: Treasures of Byzantine Art and Culture from British Collections*, London, 1994.

Delehaye, H., *Étude sur le légendier romain*, Brussels, 1936.

Devos, P., "Sainte Anastasie la vierge et la source de sa Passion (³*BHG* 76z)," *AnBoll* n.s. 80, 1962, 33–51.

Halkin, F., *Légendes grecques de "martyres romaines"*, Brussels, 1973.

Janin, R., *La géographie ecclésiastique de l'empire byzantine*, vol. III: *Les églises et les monastères*, Paris, 1953.

Lanéry, C., "Hagiographie d'Italie (300–550): I. Les Passions latines composées en Italie," in: G. Philippart, ed., *Hagiographies: Histoire internationale de la littérature hagiographique latine et vernaculaire en occident des origines à 1550*, vol. V, Turnhout, 2010, 15–369, esp. 45–60.

Lapidge, M., *The Roman Martyrs: Introduction, Translations, and Commentary*, Oxford, 2018, 54–63.

Moretti, P.F., *La Passio Anastasiae: Introduzione, testo critico, traduzione*, Rome, 2006.

Moretti, P.F., "L'edizione di un testo minore riccamente tràdito, la *Passione Anastasiae*: Problemi e vantaggi," in: A. Cadioli & P. Chiesa, eds., *Prassi ecdotiche: Esperienze editoriali su testi manoscritti e testi a stampa. Milano, 7 giugno e 31 ottobre 2007*, Milan, 2008, 65–93, esp. 90–91.

Rodley, L., "The Pigeon House Church, Çavuşin," JÖB n.s. 33, 1983, 301–339.

Rodley, L., *Cave Monasteries of Byzantine Cappadocia*, Cambridge UK, 1985.

Rossi, G.B. De, *Inscriptiones Christianae Urbis Romae*, vols. I–II, Rome, 1857.

Rydén, L., "A Note on Some References to the Church of St. Anastasia in Constantinople in the 10th Century," *Byz.* n.s. 44, 1974, 198–210.

Valentini, R., & Zucchetti, G., *CTCR*, vol. II, Rome, 1940.

ANNE P. ALWIS

Anastasius (Emperor)

Born in Dyrrachium in circa 430 CE, little is known about Anastasius' early life. He pursued a career at the imperial court and became one of the 30 silentiaries. His interest in theological matters is clear from his habit of preaching private sermons to a select congregation in the Great Church, an action that incurred the wrath of the patriarch, Euphemius of Constantinople. Anastasius, however, went on to become a candidate for the patriarchy of Antioch in 488 CE after the death of Peter the Fuller. When he was chosen by Ariadne, Emperor Zeno's widow, as the successor to the imperial throne, Euphemius was only persuaded to carry out his role in the coronation ceremony in return for a declaration of orthodoxy accepting the Council of Chalcedon signed by the new emperor.

On his accession, Anastasius inherited a number of problems from his unpopular Isaurian predecessor, including the Isaurian issue itself, a struggling state economy, and religious schisms. In addition to these, he later had to deal with issues of foreign policy on the eastern frontier (war with the Persians) and difficult diplomatic relations with the West (esp. the Ostrogoths) and security issues in the Balkans.

Anastasius got off to a good start by expelling the hated Isaurians from Constantinople, and, carrying the offensive to their native mountainous terrain, he had rounded up and executed the key Isaurian leaders by 498 CE. At the start of his reign, it was important for Anastasius to remove the threat of a coup masterminded by Zeno's brother, Longinus, and the Isaurians, characterized as bandits, had never been popular in the capital. Anastasius' victory was celebrated by his panegyricists, Procopius and Priscian, who likened him to Pompey the Great.

Anastasius was now free to turn his attention to financial and administrative matters. In an erratic reign troubled by three internal revolts and the depredations of the two Gothic Theoderics, there had

been no opportunity for Zeno to rebuild the treasury after the disastrously expensive (and unsuccessful) 468 CE naval expedition against the → Vandals. The empire Anastasius inherited was close to bankruptcy. That the treasury held 320,000 pounds of gold at the time of his death in 518 CE is a tribute to his successful reforms to taxation and monetary, agrarian, and military policy. He introduced improvements to bureaucratic procedures and the judicial system, and he took stringent measures to bring faction rioting under control. The smooth running of the state led to a stronger economy, allowing Anastasius to offer tax cuts and subsidies, and to fund a building program.

Concern for efficient economic governance is also apparent in his foreign policy: a fragmentary inscription found in several locations in Arabia records changes to army regulations and the administration of customs. Otherwise, defense and diplomacy were Anastasius' key weapons against external threats. In the East, he cultivated relations with the Arab tribes and made an important alliance with the Ghassanids, hoping to counter the Persians' Arab allies, the Lakhmids. Interestingly, doctrinal politics played a role in this maneuvering: Anastasius successfully encouraged the loyalty of the Ghassanids by their cultural and religious assimilation into his empire, while similar efforts by the monophysite patriarch, → Severus of Antioch, failed to wean the Lakhmids away from the Persians. When the Persians did invade Roman territory in 502 CE, they won several easy victories, but eventually the Romans began to hold their own and even conduct incursions into Persian territory. A peace treaty was negotiated in 506 CE, after which Anastasius took care to strengthen the defenses along the eastern frontier, most conspicuously at Dara.

Even greater diplomatic efforts were required in the West. As he was in no position to oust Theoderic, now ruling in Italy courtesy of an invitation from Zeno, Anastasius could only seek to control the Ostrogothic king's expansionist plans and secure the loyalty of the → Franks and Burgundians. To control the menace of the Bulgar incursions into Thrace, he built or restored the Long Walls to the west of Constantinople.

An exemplary ruler in many ways then, Anastasius has attracted criticism for his handling of the doctrinal dispute between the Chalcedonians and Monophysites (→ Miaphysites/Miaphysitism). The problem stemmed from the unresolved issues of the Council of → Chalcedon (451 CE), which Zeno had attempted to resolve with his *Henoticon*, a document that preserved an uneasy compromise among the eastern patriarchs but led to a split between Patriarch Acacius of Constantinople and Felix III. Anastasius failed to heal the → Acacian schism, which endured for 35 years, and apart from the short-lived papacy of the sympathetic Anastasius II, Popes Gelasius, Symmachus, and Hormisdas remained intransigent on any softening of the decisions taken at Chalcedon, and opposed to the notion that an emperor could formulate church policy. The attempt to install the pro-*Henoticon* Laurentius as successor to Anastasius II was thwarted by Theoderic, who gave recognition to the hard-line Symmachus.

While Anastasius could not dictate theological policy in the West, he could assert his authority much more easily over the eastern patriarchates. In Constantinople, Euphemius resolutely promoted the Chalcedonian cause, aligning himself closely with Pope Gelasius. When he refused to surrender the emperor's signed profession of faith, he found himself deposed on the charge of → Nestorianism and exiled to Euchaita. He was replaced by the compliant Macedonius, who adopted a flexible approach by signing the *Henoticon*, accepting communion with the monophysite patriarch of Alexandria, John II, and winning support from the pro-Chalcedonian Sleepless Monks in Constantinople. However, the rise of the extreme Monophysites, Severus of Antioch and Philoxenus, made his accommodating methods unacceptable, and in 511 CE he followed his predecessor in exile to Euchaita. Building on their success, they exerted pressure on the patriarch of Antioch, the moderate Flavian of Antioch. Despite some setbacks, Philoxenus and his disciples eventually succeeded in forcing him into exile at Petra. Severus was ready to succeed him (Nov 512 CE) and was consecrated at the Synod of Antioch in 513 CE, orchestrated by Philoxenus.

But even as the Monophysites celebrated their achievements, the tide began to turn in favor of the Chalcedonians. In Constantinople, the monophysite version of the Trishagion led to severe rioting until Anastasius was forced to appear in the hippodrome without his diadem and offer to resign. In the eastern provinces, the position of Severus proved too extreme for many of the clergy and monks who adhered to rather more moderate views. Anastasius continued to hope that communion among the four eastern patriarchates could be achieved and in July 516 CE agreed to the deposition of Elias, patriarch of Jerusalem, a pro-Chalcedonian who would not accept the ordination of Severus. However, the new incumbent, John, bowing to the pressure of the crowds inflamed by the monks Theodosius and Sabas, anathematized all those who did not accept the definition of Chalcedon, including Severus.

Meanwhile, in the Balkans, many bishops declared their loyalty to the pope, including Dorotheus, bishop of Thessalonica, who switched his allegiance from the Constantinopolitan patriarch to Hormisdas in January 515 CE. Far more serious was the rebellion of Vitalian, who used Anastasius' increasingly hard-line anti-Chalcedonian stance as a pretext for his uprising. After several military successes in 514 CE, he arrived on the outskirts of the capital, and – following negotiations in which a number of concessions were supposedly accepted, including the reinstatement of Patriarchs Macedonius and Flavian, and the healing of the Acacian schism – Vitalian retreated. Hostilities continued, however, with Vitalian enjoying the upper hand, and for a second time he brought his forces to the capital. This time the promise of a synod at Heraclea attended by all bishops was one of the concessions. A lengthy correspondence between Anastasius and Hormisdas followed, but ultimately the demands for the complete submission of the emperor to the pope, and acceptance of the Council of Chalcedon, were too great a price to pay for communion. For a third time, Vitalian brought his army to Constantinople, only to be defeated by the praetorian prefect, Marinus, who used Greek fire against the enemy ships at the Golden Horn. Vitalian was defeated and remained in exile until after the death of Anastasius. To his credit, the emperor continued to negotiate with the West, sending letters to Hormisdas and also the Roman Senate, but such was the distrust on both sides that no compromise could be reached. After his death, Justin (emperor) and → Justinian rapidly healed the schism but on terms scarcely acceptable to the East, and their attempts to impose unity among the eastern patriarchates were as unsuccessful as those of their predecessor. Indeed, a separate monophysite

(Jacobite) church developed, demonstrating that a compromise solution between Chalcedonians and Monophysites was no longer viable. Anastasius' support for the monophysite cause not only represented his personal belief but also was a pragmatic policy to retain the loyalty of the eastern provinces, crucial in the context of the Persian threat. And his methods in handling the crisis should be judged against the background of the ultimate impossibility of achieving unity among the four eastern patriarchates and with Rome.

Historiography

Basic accounts of Anastasius' reign are found in all the standard studies of the late Roman world (e.g. Bury, 1923; Stein, 1949–1959; Jones, 1964). However, there are now three monographs devoted to the reign of Anastasius (Capizzi, 1969; Haarer, 2006; Meier, 2009). There are also two studies on Anastasius' panegyricists, Priscian and Procopius (Chauvot, 1986; Coyne, 1991), and separate aspects of the reign have been covered in a number of books and articles, starting with G.A. Rose (1888) and E. Merten (1906), but these have obviously been superseded by P. Charanis' study on religious policy (Charanis, 1939) and G. Greatrex (1998) on the Persian wars; and there is also J. Prostko-Prostyński (1994) on western foreign policy. Of the proliferation of publications on all aspects of the late Roman world perhaps the most useful aspect to mention is the widening access to Anastasius' reign by the growing availability of translations of and commentaries on some of the key primary sources: for example, Theophanes (1997); Malalas (1986) and Marcellinus Comes (1995) published by the Australian Association for Byzantine Studies, and the *Chronicon Paschale* (1989), Pseudo-Dionysius of Tel-Mahre (1996), Evagrius (2000), Joshua the Stylite (2000) and Pseudo-Zachariah Rhetor (2011) published in the Translated Texts for Historians Series.

Bibliography

Bury, J.B., *History of the Later Roman Empire*, New York, 1923.
Cameron, A., "The House of Anastasius," *GRBS* 19, 1978, 259–276.

Capizzi, C., *L'imperatore Anastasio I*, Rome, 1969.
Charanis, P., *Church and State in the Later Roman Empire: The Religious Policy of Anastasius I: 491–518*, Thessaloniki, 1939, ²1974.
Chauvot, A., *Procope de Gaza, Priscien de Césarée: Panégyriques de l'empereur Anastase Ier*, Bonn, 1986.
Coyne, P., *Priscian of Caesarea's De Laude Anastasii Imperatoris*, Lampeter, 1991.
Greatrex, G., *Rome and Persia at War: 502–532*, Leeds, 1998.
Haarer, F.K., *Anastasius I: Politics and Empire in the Late Roman World*, Cambridge UK, 2006.
Jones, A.H.M., *The Later Roman Empire*, Oxford, 1964.
Meier, M., *Anastasios I: Die Entstehung des Byzantinischen Reiches*, Stuttgart, 2009.
Merten, E., *De bello Persico ab Anastasio gesto*, Leipzig, 1906.
Moorhead, J., *Theoderic in Italy*, Oxford, 1992.
Motta, D., "L'imperatore Anastasio: Tra storiografia ed agiografia," *MeAn* 6, 2003, 195–234.
Prostko-Prostyński, J., *Utraeque res publicae: The Emperor Anastasius I's Gothic Policy (491–518)*, Poznań, 1994.
Rose, G.A., *Die byzantinische kirchenpolitik unter Kaiser Anastasius I*, Wohlau, 1888.
Stein, E., *Histoire du bas-empire*, Bruges, 1949–1959.

F.K. HAARER

Anastasius of Thessalonica

Anastasius of Thessalonica was metropolitan bishop of Thessalonica (c. 431–452 CE) shortly after the Council of → Ephesus of 431 CE, in which he participated. He maintained an important epistolary correspondence with Popes Sixtus III (432–440 CE) and → Leo I (440–461 CE), which gives evidence of the ecclesiastical struggles over office and episcopal → ordination in others jurisdictions. From the time of Pope Damasus, the metropolitan of Thessalonica was the vicar of the bishop of Rome with jurisdiction over the region of eastern Illyricum (this region was civilly dependent on Constantinople but, in religious matters, dependent on the bishop of Rome).

Confronted with the desire of Perigenus, bishop of Corinth, for independence, Pope Sixtus wrote to the bishops who had come together for a synod in Thessalonica, reminding them of the subjugation to the see which Anastasius occupied as the legate of the bishop of Rome. (PL 50.611–612; Mansi, vol. VIII, 760–761). Likewise, in December of 437 CE, in a letter to Proclus of Constantinople, Pope Sixtus once again recalled the authority and rights when the bishop of Thessalonica enjoyed in the region of Illyricum (PL 50.612–613; Mansi, vol. VIII, 672).

The exchange of letters between Pope Leo and Anastasius shows us that the privilege that Anastasius enjoyed in ordaining the metropolitan bishops of Illyricum was at times resisted by the bishops of the territory. In July of 444 CE Leo specified in various letters Anastasius' powers, and he renewed his faculties. Since the time of the Council of → Nicaea in 325 CE, the authority to consecrate the bishops of the area belonged to the metropolitans, but, despite this privilege of the metropolitans, Anastasius could consecrate the bishops of Illyricum, and furthermore he could convoke synods in which they had to participate. Leo reminds them in his *Fifth Letter* that these ordinances ought to be observed given that, ultimately, Anastasius represented – in Illyricum – the apostle Peter's authority and pastoral solicitude over all the churches (PL 54.614–617; Mansi, vol. V, 1130, 1133).

On Jan 6, 446 CE, Leo responded to the complaint lodged by Anastasius: Peter of Corinth had appointed a bishop for the city of Thespies with the consent of the metropolitan of Thessalonica. The pope mentioned the rights of the vicar of Thessalonica and insisted upon the obligation of the suffragans (i.e. a bishop who heads a diocese, which is part of a larger ecclesiastical province, led by a metropolitan archbishop) to be present at provincial synods (PL 54.663; Mansi, vol. V, 1173).

In the correspondence from that era, we can see that attending synods was not always something to look forward to, and the bishops sometimes resisted. Anastasius showed himself to be quite harsh with the old bishop Atticus of Nicopolis, who did not attend the synod. Anastasius forced him to participate, with the help of the civil authorities. Atticus went to Rome to complain about Anastasius's authoritarian methods, with the result that Pope Leo wrote to the metropolitan of Thessalonica with an exhortation that he proceed with the sensibilities, prudence, and mildness about which Paul (→ Paul the Apostle) spoke (1 Tim 5:1). In the same letter Leo confirmed once again the powers of the bishop of Thessalonica as the representative of the bishop of Rome in the region. Nevertheless, in case problems should arise between the bishop of Thessalonica and another bishop of that region, both should have recourse to Rome in order to resolve the dispute (PL 54.666–677; Mansi, vol. V, 1178).

At the Second Council of Ephesus, in 449 CE (*latrocinium ephesinum*) and at → Chalcedon in 451 CE, Anastasius was represented by his suffragan, Quintillus of Heraclea (at Chalcedon Quintillus did not sign the canon regarding the privileges of the see of Constantinople, which represented a derogation from the authority of the other sees and, furthermore, of Rome's authority in view of the political prowess of the *New Rome*).

It is commonly accepted that Anastasius died before Sep 1, 457 CE, when Leo wrote to Euxiteus, naming him to the see of Thessalonica (Petit, 1900–1901, 142–143, however, places the date of Anastasius' death at the beginning of September 451 CE, during the Council of Chalcedon).

Bibliography

ACO, vol. I, part 7, Berlin, 1922–1930, 143–145.
Acta Romanorum Pontificum, vol. I, Vatican City, 1943, 172–183.
Aigrain, R., "Anastase, métropolitain de Thessalonique," in: *DHGE*, vol. II, Paris, 1914, 1444–1446.
Batifoll, P., *Le siège apostolique*, Paris, 1924, 406–407.
Hefele, K.J., &-H. Leclercq, *Histoire des conciles*, vol. II, Paris, 1952, 830.
Jaffé, P., & W. Wattenbach, *Regesta pontificum Romanorum*, Graz, 1956, 393–396, 403, 404, 409, 411, 440.
Petit, L., "Les évêques de Thessalonique," *EOr* 4, 1900–1901, 142–143.
Pietri, C., *Roma christiana: Recherches*, Rome, 1976, 1143–1147.
Silva Tarouca, C., *Epistolarum Romanorum Pontificum ad vicarios per Illyricum aliosque episcopos collectio Thessalonicensis*, Rome, 1937, 36–43, 53–65.
Stiernon, D., "Anastasio di Tessalonica," in: *NDPAC*, Rome, 2006, 279–280.

DIEGO E. ARFUCH

Anatolius of Constantinople

Anatolius was bishop of Constantinople (449–458 CE) during the Council of → Chalcedon (451 CE;) and one of the key figures responsible for drafting the Chalcedonian Definition. His role in the events surrounding the council brought him into conflict with Leo the Great of Rome (→ Leo

I [Bishop of Rome]), particularly concerning the controversial canon 28, which gave the see of Constantinople preeminence after → Rome, and Leo's frequently hostile letters are a crucial source for reconstructing Anatolius' career. His early life is unknown, although he was presumably born in Alexandria in or around 400 CE. A → deacon in the Egyptian church, Anatolius represented Dioscorus of Alexandria as his *apocrisiarius* ("emissary") in Constantinople during the tumultuous years leading up to the Second Council of Ephesus in 449 CE (Th. Lec. *Hist. eccl.* 351; LibCar. *Brev.* 12; Zon. *Epit. Hist.* 13.23). Flavian of Constantinople was deposed at that council through Dioscorus' influence and died shortly afterward. Anatolius was elected as Flavian's replacement by the Constantinopolitan clergy and consecrated by the bishops present in the city late in 449 CE (Anatolius' letter to Leo, recorded as Leo M. *Ep.* 53), bishops who were probably led by Dioscorus himself.

The circumstances of his consecration made Anatolius suspect in the eyes of those who opposed the Second Council of Ephesus, notably Leo. On learning of Anatolius' election, Leo wrote to both Theodosius II (Leo M. *Ep.* 69) and Pulcheria (*Ep.* 70) requiring that Anatolius prove his orthodoxy by upholding the First Council of Ephesus against Nestorius and Leo's own *Tome* against → Eutyches. The death of Theodosius II on Jul 28, 450 CE, and the accession of → Marcian (emperor) and Pulcheria altered the balance of power and gave Anatolius the opportunity to exert his independence from Dioscorus. He wrote to Leo confirming that he had endorsed Leo's *Tome* (Leo acknowledges this in *Ep.* 80 to Anatolius, dated Apr 13, 451), and the pair exchanged a number of letters in the following months that helped to prepare the ground for the new council that opened at Chalcedon on Oct 8, 451 CE.

In the *Acts* of Chalcedon, Anatolius is recorded in each session as second in precedence after the Roman representatives of Leo (the majority of sessions were chaired by the imperial officials led by his namesake, the patrician Anatolius), and he played a crucial role in a number of the council's most pivotal debates. After the reading of Leo's *Tome* (Leo M. *Ep.* 28 to Flavian) in the second session was disrupted by repeated interruptions (*Acts* 2.24–26), it was declared that Anatolius would hold an informal meeting of the bishops to reassure those who had objected (*Acts* 2.31). Although there are no recorded minutes from that meeting, Anatolius was evidently successful and at the fourth session the council approved the *Tome*. The need to condemn Dioscorus during the third session of Chalcedon was potentially a grave embarrassment for Anatolius, but his insistence that Dioscorus was being condemned for canonical misbehavior and not for → heresy (*Acts* 3.95; 5.14) helped to reassure Dioscorus' previous supporters, notably the Egyptian bishops who looked to their fellow countryman Anatolius for an understanding of their situation (*Acts* 4.56–58).

Most importantly for the subsequent history of Christian doctrine, Anatolius headed the committee that drafted the original version of what became the Chalcedonian Definition. The exact sequence of debate is impossible to reconstruct in full as the *Acts* for the fifth session of the council were extensively edited before their circulation. Nevertheless, it is clear that on the day before the fifth session met, a draft definition was discussed at an informal meeting and received approval from the bishops in attendance (*Acts* 5.7–8, 12). This draft had been prepared by Anatolius' committee, but was not recorded in the *Acts* (as is explicitly stated in *Acts* 5.3). The objections that were now raised reveal that the draft described Christ as being "from two natures," a Cyrilline expression acceptable to most eastern bishops but not to some Syrian bishops or the Roman legates. Under strong imperial pressure (*Acts* 5.22), a new committee that included Anatolius and the legates withdrew to make the required revisions (*Acts* 5.29). This committee presented the final Chalcedonian Definition, with Christ "acknowledged in two natures." It has sometimes been suggested that if Anatolius' original draft definition had been accepted, then the entire Chalcedonian-Miaphysite (→ Miaphysites/Miaphysitism) division might have been avoided. Yet the draft definition could not have received Roman approval and so would have opened a different East-West schism even earlier than otherwise occurred.

For Anatolius, the definition of the faith was not the only essential business that Chalcedon undertook. The council issued 27 official canons (→ Canons [of Councils]), at least three of which derived from imperial decrees that were then entrusted to Anatolius for final preparation (*Acts* 6.16–20). As the *Acts* do not record any discussion during which these canons were approved, they were probably confirmed at another informal session over which Anatolius presided. The most famous "canon" of Chalcedon, however, was the subject of heated debate in the 16th and last session of the council on Nov 1, 451 CE, and was then added to the original canons as "canon 28." Anatolius had an obvious vested interest in the debate, as this canon gave the see of Constantinople precedence second only to Rome and authority over Pontus, Asia, and Thrace. Again there is a reference to an earlier informal meeting under Anatolius, at which 182 bishops had already approved the canon (*Acts* 16.4–9). The Roman legates, who had not attended the informal meeting, rejected the canon and sought to impose a veto, at which point the *Acts* end.

In the aftermath of the council, Anatolius' immediate concern was to secure Leo's acceptance of both the Chalcedonian Definition and the disputed canon. His letter to Leo (preserved as Leo M. *Ep.* 101) in December 451 CE celebrated the confirmation of the true faith and then appealed to the precedent set by the Council of → Constantinople in 381 CE to justify the rights asserted in canon 28. Rather optimistically, he declared that:

> we embarked on this undertaking with a natural confidence in your beatitude that you would consider the honor of the see of Constantinople your own, since your apostolic see has from of old exhibited solicitude and accord in its regard. (Leo M. *Ep.* 101)

Therefore he asked Leo to correct the error of his legates and approve the canon.

Leo upheld the position taken by his legates. In his letter to Marcian (*Ep.* 104 on May 22, 452), Leo congratulated the emperor on the council's success, then denounced Anatolius. He recalled Anatolius' suspect antecedents, noting "my brother Anatolius appears to have had a necessary regard for his own interests in abandoning the error of those who ordained him and with a salutary amendment changing to an assent to the catholic faith," and condemned his pride in seeking to promote Constantinople by overturning the Nicene canons ("let

him not disdain an imperial city because he cannot make it an apostolic see"). Leo repeated the same arguments in an accompanying letter to Pulcheria (*Ep.* 105), and again to Anatolius himself (*Ep.* 106). With backhanded praise, Leo commended Anatolius for his services to the orthodox faith, acknowledging that God had allowed him "to make good use of bad beginnings." But now he has transgressed the Nicene canons and dishonored the apostolic authority of Alexandria (given by Peter through Mark) and Antioch (given through Peter directly). Leo repeated his support for his legates and dismissed Anatolius' appeal to the council of 381 CE, a council whose canons were never brought to the attention of Rome. The letter closed on a menacing note – "If you seek what is not permitted, you will by your own action and verdict deprive yourself of the peace of the universal church" – although this threat of excommunication was never carried out.

The remaining years of Anatolius' episcopate were dominated by ongoing disputes with Leo and the struggle for unity in the post-Chalcedonian eastern church. In addition to his condemnation of canon 28, Leo took issue with Anatolius' efforts to extend his authority into Illyricum (*Ep.* 117) and with his handling of his Constantinopolitan clergy, not all of whom were fully supportive of Chalcedonian theology. Anatolius' poor treatment of Archdeacon Aetius in favor of the allegedly Eutychian Andrew prompted Leo to complain to Marcian (*Ep.* 111) and Pulcheria (*Ep.* 112), and he memorably commented to his associate Julian of Cos that Anatolius "had no enthusiasm for the catholic faith and not much for the sacrament of salvation" (*Ep.* 113).

Eventually, however, the bishops of old and new Rome were reconciled. Anatolius and Leo continued to exchange letters (see Leo M. *Ep.* 132; 135; 136) and cooperated in their efforts to support Chalcedonian orthodoxy. When Marcian died, Leo urged Anatolius to ensure that the reign of a new emperor did not allow new outbreaks of heresy (*Ep.* 146), and he repeatedly encouraged Anatolius to show greater zeal against those in error, particularly within the Constantinople church (*Ep.* 151; 156). We see Anatolius' relationship with Leo almost entirely through Leo's eyes during these years, but although often critical, Leo seems to have developed a grudging respect for his Constantinopolitan counterpart and the pressures that Anatolius faced. Nevertheless, Leo was still prepared to warn Marcian's successor Leo I that there were heretical clergy in Constantinople whom Anatolius had failed to keep in check (*Ep.* 156).

Anatolius died on Jul 3, 458 CE. One of his last major acts may have been to preside at the coronation of Leo I in 457 CE (Th. Lec. *Hist. eccl.* 2.65; Theoph. Conf. *Chron.* 1.170), which would represent the earliest instance of an emperor crowned in an ecclesiastical ceremony by the bishop of Constantinople. Unfortunately, different sources give different accounts of Leo's coronation, and many do not refer to the bishop at all, so certainty on this point is not possible. Today, Anatolius is venerated as a saint of the Greek Orthodox Church, and a number of liturgical hymns known as Anatolian verses are sometimes ascribed to him (which were in fact composed several centuries after his death). Very few of Anatolius' genuine words do survive, almost entirely preserved in the *Acts* of Chalcedon and in Pope Leo's letters. Yet while Anatolius' clashes with Leo have damaged his reputation in the West, he deserves respect for his efforts to achieve Chalcedonian unity and he was an important figure in consolidating the authority of the patriarchate of Constantinople.

(A historiography for this topic is not applicable.)

Bibliography

Frend, W.H.C., *The Rise of the Monophysite Movement: Chapters in the History of the Church in the Fifth and Sixth Centuries*, Cambridge UK, 1972.

Grillmeier, A., *Christ in Christian Tradition*, 2 vols., rev. ed., London, 2013.

Meyendorff, J., *Imperial Unity and Christian Divisions: The Church 450–680 AD*, New York, 1989.

Neil, B., *Leo the Great*, London, 2009.

Price, R., & M. Gaddis, *The Acts of the Council of Chalcedon*, 3 vols., Liverpool, 2005.

Price, R., & M. Whitby, eds., *Chalcedon in Context: Church Councils 400–700*, Liverpool, 2009.

Wessel, S., *Leo the Great and the Spiritual Rebuilding of a Universal Rome*, Leiden, 2008.

DAVID M. GWYNN

Anazarbus

The abundant ruins of the ancient city of Anazarbus are found close to the modern Turkish village of Anavarza (Ayn Zarba, close to the current city of Kozan), about 75 km to the northeast of the city of Adana in Turkey, part of Cilicia Campestris, located 18 km from the Pyramus River (now called Ceyan) and close to its affluent Sumbas Çayı. It was founded on a preexisting habitat, used as a secure fortress in the 1st century BCE, as the coins that were found on site demonstrate. As a fortress it was used by the Romans, Byzantines, and then Armenians of the kingdom of Cilicia. The name may have been given first to the hill of chalky limestone and then to the town built on the spot. It belonged to a local prince who had been named Tarcondimotus by Pompey the Great (he was residing at Hierapolis Castabala), who was killed by Octavian in 31 BCE. The city was granted to his son, Tarcondimotus II, who renamed it Caesarea, or Caesarea near Anazarbus (see Plin. *Nat.* 5.93) on the occasion of the visit by → Augustus. The city's era began in 19 BCE, perhaps because it was then that it acquired a new name. After his death, Anazarbus passed under the direct control of Rome; at that time it became a prosperous city, rivaling the city of Tarsus, which was located to the southwest about 130 km away, for its political, cultural, and religious importance. An inscription from the time of Septimius Severus (d. 212 CE) attributes to the city the titles of *metropolis* and *neokoros* (guardian of the imperial cult of the province; Woodward, 1963, 5–10; → Emperor/Imperial Cult), during his visit to the city on the occasion of the war against Pescennius Niger. The city coined money, and from the beginning of the 3rd century CE, they were in abundance. In 260 CE the city was taken by the Sassanian Shapur I. The rivalry between the two cities was resolved, at the time of Arcadius, around the year 400 CE, when Cilicia was subdivided into two provinces: one of the capital, Tarsus (Cilicia Prima); the other included (Cilicia Secunda) Anazarbus, whose → bishop also became the → metropolitan. Anazarbus was the country of origin to the famous physician Dioscorides (d. c. 90 CE) and to the didactic poet Oppianus.

The ruins are many in number, among which there is an aqueduct dedicated to Domitian (there were three aqueducts), a part of an imposing Roman triumphal arch from the time of Septimius Severus, a very large stadium outside the walls (which are nearly 365 m in length), an amphitheater, a theater (which could hold about 700 people), thermal baths, tombs, and pagan and Christian inscriptions. The pagan cults flourished, above all those of Zeus and of Mithras. Different roads connected Anazarbus with other cities (e.g. Flaviopolis, Hierapolis Castabala, Tarsus). The city reached its greatest prosperity during the reign of Theodosius II (d. 450 CE); in 526 CE it was destroyed by an earthquake and rebuilt, with the name Iustinianopolis (Eva. Schol. *Hist. eccl.* 4.8). In the 8th century CE, Anazarbus passed under the dominion of the Arabs and was renamed Ayn Zarba; it was subsequently fortified again by Hārūn ar-Rashid in 796 CE. In the 11th century, Anazarbus passed under the power of the Armenian kingdom of Cilicia, and it again became prosperous. From this period there are also remains of an Armenian church and of the fortifications from the crusades. In 1375 the control of the territory passed into the hands of the Mamelucchi (Mamlūk) of Egypt, and the city was abandoned.

We do not know when the first organized Christian community at Anazarbus was established. During Diocletian's → persecution there were some → martyrs. The first was Marinus, already very old by that time, condemned, tortured, and killed at Tarsus in 285 CE (*Bibl. Sanct.*, vol. VIII, 1172–1173). Julianus was born of a pagan father and a Christian mother, but he was killed at Aegeae (Aigai), along the coast, which is modern-day Yumurtalık. According to the tradition, the relics were carried to Antioch, where a basilica was erected in his honor (*Anboll* 15, 1896, 73–76; an unedited portion of his *passio*). Two homilies have been preserved, one preached by → John Chrysostom (*BHG* 2n965) and the other by → Severus of Antioch (PO 12.112–132). A legendary account of a passion tells of the martyrdom of Theodula and companions (*Bibl. Sanct.*, vol. XII, 314–315; F. Halkin: AB 83(1965)420–421). The most famous martyrs from Anazarbus and of all Cilicia were Tarachus, Probus, and Andronicus (see Gough, 1974, 262–267). According to the *passio*, which is only partially reliable and worthy of credence, they were of diverse provenance: Tarachus was a Roman citizen of Claudiopolis and a

former soldier, Probus was from Side, and Andronicus was from Ephesus. They suffered through three interrogations, first at Tarsus, then at Mopsuestia, and finally at Anazarbus, where they were killed. Auxentius of Mopsuestia, toward the end of the 5th century CE, built a basilica outside the city in their honor. Another martyr is Zosimus (Halkin, 1952, 249–261). The legend recounts the story of Zosimus – whose memory is celebrated during January in the synaxaria – who was defended by a lion that had run to his aid in order to rebut the magistrate who was persecuting him. In the Byzantine synaxaria a certain Domnina of Anazarbus is also remembered (*Bibl. Sanct.*, vol. IV, 762).

Around the year 333 CE Aetius was teaching at Anazarbus, he who would later become a famous Arian (→ Arianism) theologian; he had been a hearerstudent of Paulinus of Antioch, and thereafter he taught in Cilicia (Kaster, 1997, 3–7). He was born in Syria, then ordained to the diaconate at Antioch by Leontius; he became a supporter of radical Arianism (anomeism; Vaggione, 2000).

The first known bishop was the Arian Athanasius, who was among the first of Arius' supporters, but he was not present at the Council of → Nicaea in 325 CE. He was recorded by Arius himself (see Thdt. *Hist. eccl.* 1.4: PG 82.912), but he was forced to accept the ὁμοούσιος, and he was Aetius' teacher (Bardy, 1936, 204–210). The other bishops who are known are Maximinus (the years 431–433 CE), who was the opponent of → Cyril of Alexandria; Valerius, who assisted at the Council of Antioch in 445 CE (Mansi, vol. VII, 325, 328, 335, 343); Stephanus (449 CE); Cyrus, who was present at the Council of → Chalcedon (Mansi, vol. VII, 137, 164, 357, 423, 429); Orestes (458 CE); Antarchius (who was exiled in 518 CE); John (550 CE); Aetherius (553 CE); Stephanus (580–581 CE); Isidorus (692 CE). Maximinus presided over a council of the bishops of Cilicia Secunda; the council, even though it showed itself to be contrary to Cyril of Alexandria, preferred the reconciliation between the Alexandrian and Antiochian churches (Mansi, vol. V, 1179), and so on. (Fedalto, 1988). According to the *Notitia episcopatuum* of Antioch (from the 6th cent. CE), there were eight suffragan sees: Epipahneia (Gözene), Alexandria ad Issum (Esentepe in İskenderun), Irenopolis (Düziçi [Haruniye]), Flaviopolis (Kadirli), Rhosus (Uluçınar [Arsuz]), Mopsuestia (Yakapınar, Misis), Hierapolis

Castabala (Bodrum Kalesi), and Aegeae (Yumurtalık, Ayas).

While the ruins of the city are abundant, there is a lack of remains of churches; from the proto-Byzantine period the ruins of two churches remain: one dedicated to the apostles (→ Apostle) and another called the Church on the Rocks (Kaya Kilises), which is decorated with mosaics.

Bibliography

Bardy, G., *Recherches sur S. Lucien d'Antioche et son école*, Paris, 1936, 204–210.

Dagron, G., & D. Feissel, *Inscriptions de Cilicie*, Paris, 1987, 157–202.

Fedalto, G., *Hierarchia orientalis*, vol. II, Padova, 1988, 761–763

Gascó, F., "Septimio Severo en Anazarbo," *Emerita* 60, 1992, 235–239.

Gough, M., "Anazarbus," *AnSt* 2, 1952, 85–150.

Gough, M., "Three Forgotten Martyrs of Anabarzus in Cilicia," in: J.R. O'Donnel, ed., *Essays in Honour of Anton Charles Pegis*, Toronto, 1974, 262–267.

Halkin, F., "Un émule d'Orphée: La légende grecque inédite de saint Zosime, martyr d'Anazarbe en Cilicie," *Anboll* 70, 1952, 249–261.

Halkin, F., "L'inscription métrique d'Anazarbe en l'honneur de saint Ménas," *Byz.* 23, 1953, 239–243.

Kaster, R.A., *Guardians of Language: The Grammarian and Society in Late Antiquity*, Berkeley, 1997.

Oberziner, M., "La leggenda di S. Giuliano il parricida," *AIVS* 93, 1933/1934, 253–309.

Ricci, A., "Alcune annotazioni sull'impianto difensivo di epoca pre-armena di Anazarbus (Cilicia)," in: C. Barsanti, A. Guiglia Guidobaldi & F. de' Maffei, eds., *Costantinopoli e l'arte delle province orientali*, Rome, 1990, 457–464.

Vaggione, R.P., *Eunomius of Cyzicus and the Nicene Revolution*, Oxford, 2000.

Verzone, P., "Città ellenistiche e romane dell' Asia minore: Anazarbus," *Pall* 7, 1957, 9–25.

Woodward, A.M., "The Neocorate at Aegeae and Anazarbus in Cilicia," *NumC* 3, 1963, 5–10.

ANGELO DI BERARDINO

Anchorites

Anchorites, also known sometimes as eremites, were early Christian and medieval monks who lived in isolation from society. While there were more specific rules for anchorites in the Middle Ages than there were in early Christianity – think of Julian of Norwich cloistered in her cell, the *Ancrene Wisse* rulebook for anchoresses, or rites of enclosure as a kind of funeral for the solitary attached to a church (as in e.g. Jones, 2012) – the origins of anchoritism are in the solitaries of the Egyptian and Syrian deserts of early Christianity. While anchorites in early Christianity were *written* as living apart from civil and religious institutions, this was more likely a trope than a geographical reality (see Brooks Hedstrom, 2009). The anchoritic way of life was reserved usually for those more advanced ascetic practitioners, though sometimes monks "accidentally" became anchorites. Moreover, some early Christians reportedly viewed anchoritism with suspicion. For many early Christian monastic authors, though, anchoritism was not only acceptable, but was, for some, the desirable end of the ascetic life.

A narrative of evolution from solitary to communal (and, subsequently, from perfect asceticism to imperfect) is a popular story in both later texts and in scholarship (see e.g. Rousseau, 1978, though tempered in Rousseau, 2010, and Dunn, 2003). It does not, however, match what appears to be the frequent early Christian monastic view of the eremite as the end of ascetic practice (→ Asceticism) instead of the beginning. Moreover, the common misperception of early Christian monasticism as primarily anchoritic and medieval monasticism as coenobitic, or communal, relies on such texts as the *Rule of the Master*, which prioritizes coenobitism.

There were a collection of words used to describe anchorites in the early Christian literature. Sometimes the descriptions of the monks' lifestyle sufficed to identify them as anchorites – retreat, withdraw, leave, and other similar verbs marked monks as anchorites. Other times they received Greek or Latin titles based on those verbs – such as *anachoretes/anachoreta* – or based on their location – such as *eremites/eremita* – marking them as anchorites. In this article, we will use "anchorite" and "eremite" (and their related terms) interchangeably.

1. Athanasius of Alexandria's *Vita Antonii* (Mid-4th Cent. CE)

Athanasius of Alexandria's *Vita Antonii* provides an early description of anchoritism. → Antony the

Great's call to the ascetic life from hearing Scripture requires that he learn the practices from a teacher; all of the early practitioners are *moneres* ("solitaries"). However, they all lived near civilization and at least some of them took on disciples. → Athanasius of Alexandria contrasts Antony's ascetic origins living "alone" with a master in the village next to his home village (Athan. *Vit. Ant.* 2–3) with the next phase of his development as a "true" enclosed anchorite. His training and his struggles with Satan (*Vit. Ant.* 2–7), mirroring in some ways Jesus' contest with Satan (→ Devil), prepared Antony, according to Athanasius, to withdraw completely and enclose himself in a tomb with some companions occasionally bringing him food (*Vit. Ant.* 8). At the end of *Vit. Ant.* 7, Athanasius writes that Antony explicitly mimicked the life of → Elijah, suggesting that for Athanasius at least, Elijah in 1 Kgs 17:2–6 was the inspiration for anchoritic living. Elijah hid himself in a valley and received food from birds; Antony hid himself in a tomb and received food from his companions. Elijah heard God's voice directly telling him to go into the wilderness; Antony heard God's voice through Scripture telling him to retreat from life (*Vit. Ant.* 2–3).

Within the tomb (*Vit. Ant.* 8), Satan brought demons (→ Demonology/Demons) to beat Antony, mirroring Jesus' beatings before his execution (see *Mart. Perp.* 18.9 for another example of the enthusiasm among some early Christian to receive beatings in order to suffer like Jesus). After his friends took him from the tomb thinking Antony dead from the beatings, Antony awoke from unconsciousness and had his friend lock him again in the tomb (*Vit. Ant.* 9). While he was again alone in the tomb fighting and being physically beaten by demons, Antony mocks Satan and the demons similarly to Elijah's mockery of the priests of Ba'al (1 Kgs 18:27). Antony's contest with the demons ends with a beam of light descending from heaven; Elijah's contest with the priests of Ba'al ended with fire from heaven (1 Kgs 18:38). Antony eventually leaves the tomb and heads to the mountains, finding an abandoned fortress and enclosing alone himself inside (*Vit. Ant.* 12). According to Athanasius, Antony spent two decades enclosed in the fortress, speaking to visitors through the closed door and receiving food through a hole in the roof until potential disciples forced open the locked door (*Vit. Ant.* 12–14).

In the *Vita Antonii*, Athanasius explicitly links anchoritism to an imitation of Elijah. Athanasius quotes Elijah (*Vit. Ant.* 7; 1 Kgs 17:1; 18:15), says that Antony claimed Elijah as his inspiration, and wrote Antony's retreat and struggles as a mirror of Elijah's. Antony's way of life is the evolved form of Antony's teacher's way of life, from the near-anchoritism of Antony's master to the full-anchoritism Antony pioneered in the tomb and mountain fortress in the model of Elijah. What is unclear is whether the two accounts of Antony's enclosures represent something that Antony tried in the late 3rd century CE or a practice in the 4th century CE about which Athanasius knew and that he then ascribed to Antony. In either case, we know that by the mid-4th century CE, anchoritism was established enough, at least as a theoretical concept as we will see below, to feature without comment in the *Vita Antonii*.

Athanasius provided two views of early Christian anchorites through the *Vita Antonii*. In the first place, Antony learned the solitary life from another solitary – they lived as anchorites, though near each other. Athanasius contrasts that with a stricter understanding of anchoritism, which finds the practitioner entirely alone with only a modicum of interaction with the outside world and taking on no disciples. This distinction between a teaching eremite and a self-oriented eremite, however, does not necessarily map onto other texts.

2. Jerome's Anchorites (Late 4th Cent. CE)

Jerome takes explicit aim at Athanasius in his *Vita Sancti Pauli primi eremitae*, written less than a decade after the *Vita Antonii* was translated into Latin. He writes that he wants to correct the record that it was Paul of Thebes, not Antony, who was the first eremite, and that those who look to either → John the Baptist or Elijah as the origins of the anchoritic way of life are mistaken (Jer. *Vit. Paul.* 1; see, however, Jer. *Ep.* 22.36, in which Jerome places John the Baptist as the first anchorite). The dueling accounts of the origins of anchoritism and the attempts to control the memory of how eremitism originated suggests the importance of this idea in early Christianity. → Jerome writes that Paul enclosed himself in a collapsed cave, hidden in the mountains, with only a spring and a palm tree for sustenance, and that Paul lived there his entire life (*Vit. Paul.* 5–6). However, his entry into the solitary life had less to do with a desire for monastic living and more to do with him fleeing persecution and his brother-in-law's desire to have him killed in order to take Pauls' (→ Paul the Apostle) inheritance, and he moved by measures further from civilization instead of seeking total isolation all at once (*Vit. Paul.* 4–5). That monks embraced the eremitic life as a way of escaping undesirable outcomes is not unheard of. In the *Apophthegmata Patrum* (*collectio alphabetica*), the famous monk Macarius of Egypt (→ Desert Fathers) left his original cell because the locals in the nearby village wished to ordain him. After being falsely accused by the residents of the village near his new cell, he fled again when the entire town tried to do penance and ask his forgiveness for believing the false accusation (Gk *Apophth. Patr.* (*coll. alph.*) Macarius of Egypt 1). On the other hand, monks could be encouraged to embrace a more distant anchoritic life if they were at risk of pridefulness because their ascetic life received excessive praise in local villages (*Hist. mon. Aeg.* 1.31).

In writing the story of the monk Paul, Jerome anticipates doubt that one could live an anchoritic way of life, so he swears by Jesus and the angels that he has seen other enclosed monks in Syria, including one at the bottom of a cistern (*Vit. Paul.* 6). That his readers may doubt the account may mean that it was an uncommon enough way of life to be suspicious to his readers. Jerome did not have to explain the eremitic way of life, so the idea must have sufficiently populated early Christian thought in the late 4th century CE. However, either it was not practiced at all or not practiced enough that some people viewed accounts of it with suspicion – and indeed, in his *Vita Sancti Hilarionis* written some decade and a half later, Jerome explicitly states that some people doubted Paul of Thebes' very existence because he was an anchorite and will probably also doubt Jerome's account of Hilarion (Jer. *Vit. Hil.* 1).

The *Vita Sancti Hilarionis* purports to record the life and deeds of the 4th-century CE Palestinian monk Hilarion. According to Jerome, Hilarion learned the ascetic life under Antony of Egypt, then went to live alone in the Gazan desert to escape the visitors who sought Antony, moving frequently to

avoid robbers (*Vit. Hil.* 3–4). He eventually settled into a small cell in the desert, and lived without visitors for over two decades, though Jerome says that his reputation was known throughout the entire region (*Vit. Hil.* 9; 13) and spread even to farther-flung regions of the empire (*Vit. Hil.* 22), and he soon had a steady stream of people wishing his help or instruction (*Vit. Hil.* 13–24). He was eventually head of a large group of monks and communities in the region, and part of his time was spent traveling throughout Gaza and Palestine meeting with his followers (*Vit. Hil.* 24–30). Jerome recounts, however, that the visitors and duties of leading coenobitic life overwhelmed Hilarion, who was at heart an anchorite, so he left Gaza with a dwindling retinue of fellow monks and traveled all over the Mediterranean basin seeking a return to the eremitic life as best he could (*Vit. Hil.* 30–38). Everywhere Hilarion went, however, his miracles or way of life garnered attention, and he was only able to stay unbothered for a month at most in any new place (*Vit. Hil.* 39–42). Finally, in Cyprus, he lived his final five years in relative isolation atop a mountain, with only a servant to help the aged Hilarion and occasional visits by his remaining disciple, and even rarer visits by others (*Vit. Hil.* 43–45). While Hilarion spent most of his first 25 years as a monk in isolation, he spent the remainder of his life seeking but never reattaining what he considered to be the true anchoritic life.

Jerome repeatedly emphasized in the *Vita Sancti Hilarionis* that Hilarion desired the eremitic life, but that it was out of his reach when his fame reached a certain point. Both Athanasius and Jerome extol the anchoritic way of life and wrote significance into that choice, and both wrote in attempts to exert influence on ascetics in their regions (Brakke, 1998; Rousseau, 2010). In all three of these near-contemporary writings, the monks Antony, Paul, and Hilarion are presented as progenitors of asceticism in a particular region, and more importantly as the progenitors of *anchoritism* in their region. For these monks, their movement into the eremitic way of life either started through training with another eremite (Antony and Hilarion) or accidentally (Paul fleeing persecution and betrayal). There was not a defined trajectory, moving from either the eremitism of earliest monasticism to the coenobitism of later monasticism, or training in a coenobium in order to later practice anchoritism, though John Cassian saw the latter as the standard trajectory, moving from being trained in the coenobium to practicing on one's own in isolation (Cass. *Con.* 18.4.2). It seems that the desires to live as an anchorite were as nuanced as the varied monks who practiced that way of life.

3. John Cassian's Anchorites (Late Fourth and Early 5th Cent. CE)

In his largest work on monastic living (*Conlationes/Conferences*), → John Cassian writes in his introduction to the first part that the greatest monks he met in Scetis were the anchorites, even greater than coenobites in the communities from which they originally came (Cass. *Con.* preface to the first part 2; 4; see also *Con.* preface to the third part 1–2). Similar to, and perhaps relying on, Jerome's tripartite classification of monks (Jer. *Ep.* 22.34–36), Cassian has the anchorite Piamun relate the three kinds of monks, two of them (coenobitic and anchoritic) being the desirable kind (*Con.* 18.4.2). The anchoritic life is considered the perfected form of the coenobitic life and is an imitation of John the Baptist, Elijah, and Elisha (*Con.* 18.6.1–2, 11.1), similar to Athanasius' view. But it is also a life that has its own challenges, and coenobitic life has its advantages.

The 19th conference recounts a conversation with a monk named John who left the coenobium for a life of anchoritism, only to return later to the coenobium. John's story and reasoning, as recorded or constructed by Cassian, mirror what we saw written by Athanasius and Jerome – that as the number of monks increased, the desert began to fill with both visiting monks who required hospitality and monks who wished to learn the anchoritic life (*Con.* 19.5.1–2). This, then, signals a trope in the literature, that the monks who embraced anchoritism earliest were able to perform that way of life best because the desert was emptier. Later adherents of the eremitic life found the practice less sustainable, and increasing numbers of monks overall wore deep ruts to the remotest cells of would-be monastic isolationists in order to learn from their wisdom enhanced through constant contemplation of the divine. Indeed, there is a longing throughout monastic literature for the former days, the early days of Christian asceticism

in the deserts, when it was almost easier to be a monk, and certainly it was less distracting (see e.g. Gk *Apophth. Patr.* (*coll. alph.*) Elias 2, in which the monk Elias unfavorably compares the best of the second monastic generation with the best of the first monastic generation).

In Cassian's account of John, Cassian's companion Germanus asks about the goal of both anchoritic and coenobitic monasticism (*Con.* 19.7). John answers them that the anchoritic life aims for complete concentration on and union with the divine (*Con.* 19.8.4). He further tells them that gaining the goals of either anchoritic or coenobitic monasticism are rare, and rarer still are those who are able to do both – he identifies but four monks who did (*Con.* 19.9.1–2). John also lays out a theory that monks who fail in the anchoritic way of life were insufficiently trained in their monasteries, leading them to fall short of the goals of both ways of living as a monk (*Con.* 19.10.1–2). For Cassian, then, there was a natural progression from advancement in the coenobium to contemplation in the wilds as an anchorite – communal living allowed one to grow in the virtues necessary for living as an eremite. The anchoritic life, thus, was open only to those who had advanced sufficiently through obedience in a coenobium. Those who just wished to live alone because of a desire for independence were doomed to failure.

4. Anchorites in Other Christian Literature

Anchorites appear by title or description throughout monastic and other early Christian literature, generally with no comment, reflecting common knowledge of what these terms meant as a way of life. The *Apophthegmata Patrum* (*collectio alphabetica*), the *Historia monachorum in Aegypto*, Palladius of Helenopolis' *Lausiac History*, and the Christian historians → Socrates Scholasticus and → Sozomen – all from the 5th century CE (with the *Historia monachorum in Aegypto* possibly coming from the very late 4th century CE and the *Apophthegmata Patrum* (*collectio alphabetica*)possibly coming from the very early 6th century CE) – mention anchoritic living, seemingly taking it as a fact of monastic life. Taking all the evidence together, it would seem that the late 4th century CE saw the concept of anchoritism become mainstream in Christianity. In the late 4th century CE, Jerome claims that some readers would disbelieve the possibility of anchoritic living, and his *Ep.* 22 to → Eustochium describes coenobitic and anchoritic ways of life using those terms. On the other hand, Athanasius' references to Antony's anchoritism without much comment are nearly contemporary to Jerome's writings, and the *Historia monachorum in Aegypto* coming roughly a decade after Jerome's life of Hilarion just offhandedly mentions monks' retreat from the world without explanatory comments (see e.g. *Hist. mon. Aeg.* 8.3). By the middle of the 5th century CE, the idea of anchoritism was established in the Christian imagination, at least in those Christians who were likely to read or hear read monastic works. Socrates and Sozomen, likewise, are able to mention anchorites and assume that their reader understands that way of living.

While the historical origins of the anchoritic life remain a mystery – and were a subject of 4th-century CE debate and dueling accounts – it is clear that the concept was solidly established by the early 5th century CE throughout the Mediterranean. A clear through-line exists in anchorites seeing themselves as the heirs of the prophets of Torah – especially Elijah (see e.g. in addition to the above, Soz. *Hist. eccl.* 3.14). Some also considered themselves continuations of John the Baptist or the apostle Paul, and the anchorite-turned-coenobite John in Cassian's *Conferences* saw it as the fulfillment of the words of the prophet Jeremiah (Cass. *Con.* 19.8.4), so the question of "origins" was less relevant to anchoritic practitioners than the construction of continuity.

5. Realities of Monastic Distance

While distance and retreat were important concepts in monastic literature, the realities of physical existence required most anchorites to be within traveling distance of towns to allow other monks to bring them food and water. As D.L. Brooks Hedstrom (2009) and J.E. Goehring (1999; 2003) have shown, the idea of retreat into the desert was important as a trope, but it was less a lived reality – and indeed, the many complaints in the literary sources from anchorites who received constant visitors demonstrate the tension between ideal and reality.

D.L. Brooks Hedstrom's (2009) interpretation of the cell, following M. Foucault, as a panopticon is significant to understand that anchoritism was more an idea of how to conduct one's life than a reality of actual distance from society. And indeed, often anchorites would affiliate in small groups, such that they all could observe each other – and particularly the elder practitioner could observe the newer anchorites. She demonstrates that there were many areas in which a large number of cells occupied a small geographic space, such that monks were alone only inside the cell, not alone because their cell was isolated far from others. Some coenobia, such as those of the Tabennesites following the way of Pachomius, even had anchorites as a part of their communities (see e.g. Pach. *Instr. Spit.* 1.22). In the deserts of Palestine, anchorites who lived under the direction of an advanced practitioner were known as *lavrae*. The reality of anchoritic living was less remoteness and more internality.

6. An Anchorite *Politeia*

There was a variety to the anchoritic life in early Christianity, from the complete solitaries who were entirely self-sufficient (rare) to individuals who lived in isolation from most people, receiving few visitors and/or having a few close disciples. They mainly lived in single room huts or "cells," owning little and eating little, either what they grew or gifts from visitors or disciples. Most of these cells were remote enough that they required intention to visit the inhabitants – one generally did not just stumble upon the cells of eremites – but were not so far as to be truly removed from all human contact. Different monks held different practices regarding manual labor (generally a feature), amount of sleep, reading Scripture or other theological works (or if they were even allowed to own books), whether they would speak to visitors or maintain total silence, if they would leave to participate in → Eucharist, among others.

This demonstrates an important distinction between coenobitic practices and eremitic practices – the former were highly regulated, and the latter were highly individualized. In the *Apophthegmata Patrum* (*collectio alphabetica*), there is the story of the monk Agathon who had two disciples living as anchorites, each with a different practice for eating – one fasted until sundown and then ate two small loaves of bread, and the other fasted for two days and then ate two small loaves (Gk *Apophth. Patr.* (*coll. alph.*) Agathon 20). Both practices were considered worthy, and they reflected the relative abilities of each anchorite. Individualized practices, however, sometimes led monks to a single-minded obsession with one aspect of their practice, a kind of mania that found reproach in the monastic literature (see e.g. Gk *Apophth. Patr.* (*coll. alph.*) Gelasius 5).

Undisputed, though, the central part of the anchoritic life was continual → prayer throughout the waking hours. Monks isolated themselves in order to focus on their perfected practices, especially on the mental practices of prayer and contemplation. Visitors distracted from this focus, leading anchorites to move locations when their cells became overrun with pilgrims and practitioners. However, some practitioners who demonstrated clear potential in the solitary life might be allowed to stay, living in a cell near the anchorite and becoming disciples of a particular monk and the eremitic path.

Anchorites, however, were not always static, remaining in a cell. The *Apophthegmata Patrum* (*collectio alphabetica*) contains stories about anchorites visiting other monks (e.g. Gk *Apophth. Patr.* (*coll. alph.*) Sarah 4; Macarius of Egypt 3; Poimen 6), and part of Hilarion's travels in search of solitude included him seeking out fellow practitioners. This supports the idea that anchoritism was more a mindset and less a single monk sitting, working, and praying alone for a period of his life. Eremites traveled, took disciples, had people who helped sell their wares or bring them food, received guests, went to churches to receive Eucharist, taught visiting monks – they were alone, but intimately a part of the fabric of late antique communities, known to both Christians and non-Christians for their way of life. The mindset of living an individualized practice that emphasized prayer and contemplation was what marked anchorites more than their actual (or, rather, fictional) retreat from the world around them.

Conclusion

Perhaps the best summary of the *idea* of anchoritism comes from the late-5th century CE, from a story in the *Apophthegmata Patrum* (*collectio alphabetica*): "A brother directed his course toward Scetis to ask Apa Moses for a teaching. The old man said to him, 'Go away! Sit in your cell! Your cell will teach you everything'" (Gk *Apophth. Patr.* [*coll. alph.*] Moses 6). The anchoritic cell was a space conceptually removed from everyday life, even (and perhaps especially) if it were surrounded by other cells or flooded with visitors oriented toward holiness or holidaying. Anchorites turned their minds toward contemplation of themselves and contemplation of the divine, toward constant prayer and meditation, in order to make themselves as close to God as possible.

As one of the two sanctioned modes of the ascetic life, anchoritism or eremitism was generally reserved for the most advanced monks, and even the most famous anchorites who started their practices young (e.g. Antony or Hilarion) studied with another monk before going out into the desert. In a change from the norm, Jerome's progenitor of monasticism, Paul, was an accidental convert to the anchoritic life, and in other instances anchoritism was the cure for potential pitfalls. Whatever one's reasons for entering eremitic practice, the way of life itself was intimately interiorly focused. This has its origins in early Christianity, if only in concept. While complete retreat from the world was functionally impossible, early Christian anchorites strove to attain the ideal of complete withdrawal. And, according to the monastic texts, a few even attained it.

Historiography

A historiography of anchorites is the history of monasticism itself, and a good starting-point bibliography for monasticism writ large can be found in W. Harmless (2008). Whereas scholars like D. Chitty (1966) and M. Dunn (2003) write the development of monasticism as linear from anchoritism to coenobitism, the reality is that anchoritism was considered the perfection of the monastic life (see e.g. Rousseau, 2010, a change from his view in the first edition of 1978). S. Rubenson (1995) and Z.B. Smith (2018) explore some of this idea of anchoritism as the final form, for certain monks, of ascetic life. As demonstrated by A. Vööbus (1958–1988), the developments of asceticism were independent in Syria from the activities in Egypt but followed a similar trajectory.

Useful here would also be the history of asceticism, with G.G. Harpham (1987), P. Brown (1988), E.A. Clark (1999), and the essays in V.I. Wimbush and R. Valantasis (1998) being the touchstones for such a study.

Bibliography

Bartelink, G., *Athanase d'Alexandrie: Vie d'Antoine*, SC 400, Paris, 2004.

Bidez, J., & G.C. Hansen, *Sozomène: Histoire ecclésiastique*, SC 306, 418, 495, 516, Paris, 1983–2008.

Binns, J., *Ascetics and Ambassadors of Christ: The Monasteries of Palestine, 314–631*. Oxford, 1994.

Brakke, D., *Athanasius and Asceticism*, Baltimore, 1998.

Brakke, D., "From Temple to Cell, from Gods to Demons: Pagan Temples in the Monastic Topography of Fourth-Century Egypt," in: J. Hann, S. Emmel & U. Gotter, eds., *From Temple to Church: Destruction and Renewal of Local Cultic Topography in Late Antiquity*, Leiden, 2008, 91–112.

Brooks Hedstrom, D.L. "The Geography of the Monastic Cell in Early Egyptian Monastic Literature," *ChH* 78, 2009, 756–791.

Brown, P., *The Body and Society: Men, Women, and Sexual Renunciation in Early Christianity*, New York, 1988; repr. 2008.

Butler, C., *The Lausiac History of Palladius*, TaS 6, 2 vols., Cambridge UK, 1904.

Caner, D. *Wandering, Begging Monks: Spiritual Authority and the Promotion of Monasticism in Late Antiquity*, TCHS 33, Berkeley, 2002.

Chitty, D., *The Desert a City*, Oxford, 1966, repr. Crestwood, NY, 1999.

Clark, E.A., *Reading Renunciation: Asceticism and Scripture in Early Christianity*, Princeton, 1999.

Dietz, M., *Wandering Monks, Virgins, and Pilgrims: Ascetic Travel in the Mediterranean World, AD 300–800*, University Park, 2005.

Dunn, M., *The Emergence of Monasticism: From the Desert Fathers to the Early Middle Ages*, Oxford, 2003.

Evelyn-White, H.G., *The Monasteries of the Wadi 'n Natrûn*, 3 vols., New York, 1926–1932.

Festugiére, A.-J., *Historia monachorum in Aegypto*, Brussels, 1971.

Gleason, M., "Visiting and News: Gossip and Reputation-Management in the Desert," *JECS* 6, 1998, 501–521.

Goehring, J.E. "The Encroaching Desert: Literary Production and Ascetic Space in Early Christian Egypt," in: J.E. Goehring, ed., *Ascetics, Society, and the Desert: Studies in Early Egyptian Monasticism*, Harrisburg, 1999, 73–88.

Goehring, J.E., "The Dark Side of Landscape: Ideology and Power in the Christian Myth of the Desert," *JMEMS* 33, 2003, 437–451.

Grote, A.E.J., *Anachorese und Zönobium: Der Rekurs des frühen westlichen Mönchtums auf monastische Konzepte des Ostens*, Stuttgart, 2001.

Han, J.H., "Mani the Anchorite, Mani the Apostle: The Cologne Mani Codex and Syrian Asceticism," *VC* 77, 2022, 47–68.

Hansen, G.C., *Socrate de Constantinople: Histoire ecclésiastique*, SC 477, 493, 505–506, Paris, 2004–2007.

Harmless, W., "Monasticism," in: S.A. Harvey & D.G. Hunter, eds., *The Oxford Handbook of Early Christian Studies*, Oxford, 2008, 493–517.

Harpham, G.G., *The Ascetic Imperative in Culture and Criticism*, Chicago, 1987.

Hilberg, I., *Sancti Eusebii Hieronymi Epistulae*, part 1: *Epistulae I–LXX*, CSEL 54, Vienna, 1910.

Jones, E.A., "Rites of Enclosure: The English *Ordines* for the Enclosing of Anchorites, S. XII–S. XVI," *Tr.* 67, 2012, 145–234.

Leclerc, P., E.M. Morales & A. de Vogüé, *Jerome: Trois vies de moines: Paul, Malchus, Hilarion*, SC 508, Paris, 2007.

Lefort, T., *Oeuvres de s. Pachôme et de ses disciples*, CSCO.C 23–24, Louvain, 1956.

Lloyd-Moffett, S.R., "The 'Anchorite Within': Basil of Caesarea's *Erotapokrisis* 7 and the Ascetic Challenge to Christian Identity," *Re&Th* 17, 2010, 268–288.

Migne, J.-P., *Apophthegmata Patrum*, PG 65: 71–440.

Neyt, F., P. de Angelis-Noah & L. Regnault, *Barsanuphe et Jean de Gaza: Correspondance*, SC 426–427, 450–451, 468, Paris, 1997–2002.

Pichery, E., *Jean Cassien: Conférences*, SC 42, 54, 64, Paris, 1955–1959.

Rousseau, P., *Ascetics, Authority, and the Church in the Age of Jerome and Cassian*, Oxford, 1978.

Rousseau, P., *Pachomius: The Making of a Community in Fourth-Century Egypt*, TCHS 6, Berkeley, 1999.

Rousseau, P., *Ascetics, Authority, and the Church in the Age of Jerome and Cassian*, 2nd ed., Notre Dame, 2010.

Rubenson, S., *The Letters of St. Antony: Monasticism and the Making of a Saint*, Minneapolis, 1995.

Schroeder, C.T., "Women in Anchoritic and Semi-Anchoritic Monasticism in Egypt: Rethinking the Landscape," *ChH* 83, 2014, 1–17.

Smith, Z.B., *Philosopher-Monks, Episcopal Authority, and the Care of the Self: The* Apophthegmata Patrum *in Fifth-Century Palestine*, Turnhout, 2018.

Vogüé, A. de, *Histoire littéraire du mouvement monastique dans l'antiquité*, 6 vols., Paris, 1991–2002.

Vööbus, A., *History of Asceticism in the Syrian Orient*, CSCO 184, 197, 500, Louvain, 1958–1988.

Wimbush, V.L., & R. Valantasis, eds., *Asceticism*, Oxford, 1998.

ZACHARY B. SMITH

Ancyra

Ancyra (modern-day Ankara, capital of Turkey) is located in the central high plains of Anatolia, at an altitude of more than 900 m; it is surrounded by steppes in a continental climate. The historical center is upon a hill along the right shore of the river (Ankara Çayı), tributary of the river Sangarius (Sakarya). Its legendary founder was supposedly King Midas; however, until the arrival of the Romans this center was of little importance. After the death of King Amyntas (25 BCE), his kingdom became a Roman province of Galatia, and it was governed by a *propraetor*. The region was inhabited, as was Ancyra too, by the Celtic tribes. With the Roman administrative system of creating cities as small states, partially independent, Ancyra grew in importance at the costs of Gordion (today Yassihöyök), the ancient capital of Frygia. It then became a city, since it had been refounded by → Augustus, thus making it the center of a Celtic tribe (the Tectosages of Sebaste or the Sebasteni Tectosages) together with a *boule* (*curia*), which made municipal decisions. This was now the *metropolis provinciae Galatiae*. He promoted the urbanization of Galatia with the foundation of new cities (e.g. Pessinus, Tavium). In the interior of → Galatia, a tribal system was widespread, both in the north and in the south. The Roman administration sought to transform Galatia by means of the spread of the Greek and Latin culture of urbanization. Initially it did not have the status of a *polis*, which it successively acquired; it was only later that the city was permitted to coin money. Since the most important people of Galatia came there, the *Res gestae divi Augusti* (*The Deeds of the Divine Augustus*) were written down there in Latin and in Greek. The political, cultural, and economic importance of the city grew throughout the entire Roman period.

The *Acts of Paul and Thecla* (→ Paul and Thecla, Acts of) speak of the Roman governor Castellius, who participated in Thecla's proceedings and in her condemnation at Iconium. At Antioch of Pisidia there was another governor who was in charge of the trials of her condemnation and of the liberation of the virgin (→ Virgin/Virginity). Actually, both during Paul's (→ Paul the Apostle) time and at the end of the 2nd century CE, the governor resided permanently at Ancyra (Ankara) and not at Iconium, nor at Antioch, which were only *conventus iuridici*, in the sense that the governor, a *legatus* – even if Pliny speaks of a *proconsul* – went there once during the year on the occasion of the feasts in order to administer justice. The unity of a province that was so varied in its population, languages, culture, and political forms was given by the Roman governor for administration, and by the *koinon* of the Galatians (or of Galatia) for its religious aspects. The latter of these had a reunion at Ancyra on Sep 23, the day of → Augustus' birthday, and the *galatarca* (*sacerdos provinciae*) presided over it.

With the → Diocletian reform Galatia's dimensions were reduced, and at the time of Arcadius it was subdivided into two provinces: Galatia (capital Ancyra), Galatia salutaris (capital Pessinus), of which both belonged to the *diocesis* Pontica. The road that was traveled by the pilgrims the virgin (→ Virgin/Virginity/Velatio). Actually and by the armies that came from the area of the Danube, passing through the Bosphorus, followed its way through Chalcedon, Nicomedia, (Nycaea), Iuliopolis (Sarılar), Mnizus (Ayaş), Ancyra, Colonia (Archelais), Aspona, and Sasima.

As the capital of Galatia, Ancyra assumed all the characteristics of a classical city, rich with public edifices for the system of civil, political, and religious life. Very little of that remains, because it was destroyed by the construction of the modern city. There remain part of the temple of Augustus with the great inscription, the column of Emperor → Julian the Apostate, part of the theater, and some of the baths from the time of Caracalla. The Byzantine citadel is preserved, of which there is a reconstructed part that is dated after the reconquest of Emperor Heraclius in 630 CE from Chosroes II.

Paul, according to the Acts of the Apostles (13:13–14:28; → Acts, Book of) evangelized four cities of the province of southern Galatia, whose inhabitants were not ethnically Gauls or Celts. Those cities were Antioch of Pisidia, Iconium, Lystra, and Derbe. The author of the 2 Timothy affirmed the very same thing (3:11). To whom was the letter to the Galatians sent? Some scholars think that the letter was directed to the inhabitants of these cities, called Galatians solely because they belonged to the Roman province of Galatia. Others, however, think that the letter was aimed at the Galatians of Celtic descent, and thus to the inhabitants of the northern part of the province, for example, to those of Pessinus (the modern Bala-hissar), where the Tolostobogi Celts dwelt, and the other two tribes, of the Trocmi (Tavium) and of the Tectosagi (Ancyra). Now, the Letter to the Galatians was sent "to the Churches of Galatia" (plural), and these were located in the north: are they the churches of one single city or of several cities? There are no definite answers to the query. Since every urban Christian community was likewise becoming mission oriented, we may correctly presume that Christianity was preached early at Ancyra, because it was the administrative and religious capital of Galatia, where the governor was in residence. In order to be judged, the Christians from the secondary cities had to be taken to Ancyra. It is perhaps on account of this that its martyrology is rich with names – about 30 of them – beginning with Crescentius, at the time of → Trajan, until the most famous Hypatius, from Diocletian's era, when Clement, too, was martyred (*Bibliotheca Sanct*, vol. I, 337). The first bishop would have been a martyr, Theodorus, but we are unable to give dates for him – assuming that he ever even existed.

At the beginning of the 4th century CE the see must have been important since a council was held there, after Easter in 314 CE, above all to resolve the problems that followed in the wake of the end of the persecution by Maximinus Daia. Twelve (or perhaps 18 bishops) participated in it, one who had come from Syria. The council published 25 canons, which are the first – in all of Christian antiquity – that have been preserved. Ten canons confronted the questions regarding the *lapsi* (the fallen; → Apostasy/Apostates), both clerics and laity, who had apostatized during the persecution, and it takes into account the depositions they had given. The other canons treated ecclesiastical discipline, adultery, prostitution, infanticide, bestiality, abortion, homicide, and magical practices. The tenth canon legislated a practice regarding the marriage of deacons, who were unable to marry after their ordination, if they had not requested it at the moment of the ceremony. In 358 and in 375 CE, two councils – of Arian tendencies – were celebrated (*DTC*, vol. I, 1173–1177). Bishop Marcellus was documented as having assisted, he who was perhaps present at the council of 314 CE and participated in the Council of → Nicaea, and who was in fierce opposition to every form of → Arianism, for which he was accused of being a follower

of Sabellius (→ Monarchianism). Deposed in 336 CE, he was replaced by Basil. Marcellus, who was rehabilitated by Pope Julius in 340 CE and then later by the Council of Sardica (343 CE) – a person who was cumbersome for the Nicenes who were seeking peace – was condemned by Macedonius of Constantinople and was definitively replaced by the Arian Basil (d. 362 CE). After him Athanasius was bishop till the year 373 CE. Theodotus, a defender of Nestorius, took part in the Council of → Ephesus (Mansi, vol. IV, 1124); Eusebius participated in the Council of → Chalcedon in 451 CE (Mansi, vol. VII, 404, 452); Dorotheus I was condemned to death in 513 CE by Emperor Anastasius for his faithfulness to the orthodox faith (Marcel. *Chron.*; PL 51.938). The complete list of the bishops is found in the *Dictionnaire d'histoire et de géographie ecclésiastiques* (vol. II, 1540–1541). Ancyra has always been the → metropolitan see of Galatia. After the division of the province into two, the suffragan bishoprics were Aspona (Sarıhüyük), which was only a *statio* in the 4th century CE; Cinna (Karahamzılı); Iuliopolis (Sarılar; founded at the time of Augustus); Lagania (Anastasiopolis from the time of Emperor Anastasius [491–518 CE; Beypazarı); and Mnizus (8 km to the west of modern-day Ayaş Balçiçek Çiftliği). There are no remains of Christian edifices at Ancyra.

Bibliography

Belke, K., *Galatien und Lykaonien*, TIB 4, Vienna, 1984, 126–130.

Bennett, J., "The Political and Physical Topography of Early Imperial Graeco-Roman Ancyra," *Anat* 32, 2006, 89–227.

Bosch, E., *Quellen zur Geschichte der Stadt Ankara im Altertum*, Ankara, 1967.

Darrouzès, J., *Notitiae episcopatuum Ecclesiae Constantinopolitanae*, Paris, 1981.

DHGE, vol. II, Paris, 1912ff.

Foss, C., *Late Antique and Byzantine Ankara*, DOP 31, 1977.

Laurent, V., *Le corpus des sceaux de l'empire byzantin*, vol. V/1, Paris, 1963; vol. V/2, Paris, 1965.

Leschhorn, W., "Die Anfänge der Provinz Galatia," *Chiron* 22, 1992, 315–336.

Mitchell, S., *Regional Epigraphic Catalogues of Asia Minor*, vol. II: *The Ankara District, the Inscriptions of North Galatia*, Oxford, 1982 (with the assistance of D. French & J. Greenhalgh).

Murphy, J., & P. O'Connor, *A Critical Life*, Oxford, 1996.

ANGELO DI BERARDINO

Andrew the Apostle

I. Andrew (Apostle) ◆ II. *Andrew, Acts of*

I. Andrew (Apostle)

Andrew is, in the Synoptic Gospels and the book of Acts (→ Acts, Book of), little more than a name in the lists of the apostles (Mark 3:18; Matt 10:2; Luke 6:14; Acts 1:13), which place him among either the first two or first four apostles.

According to Mark (and Matthew; → Mark, Gospel of; → Matthew the Apostle), Andrew was the brother of Simon Peter (→ Peter the Apostle), and both were Jesus' first disciples. While the brothers were fishing on the Sea of Galilee, Jesus called them to become "fishers of men" (Mark 1:16–18; Matt 4:18–20). The Second Gospel further adds that the brothers lived in → Capernaum, on the north shore of the Sea of Galilee, and offers other small details (Mark 1:29–31; Matt 8:14 and Luke 4:38 only refer to the house of Peter, while Andrew is not mentioned). Mark mentions Andrew one more time, namely as addressee – together with Peter, James, and John – of Jesus' speech concerning the end of times (Mark 13:3; in Matthew and Luke, Jesus addresses a larger group of followers). There is no further additional information: in contrast to his brother's important role as a leader of the apostles, Andrew's figure fades into the background. Matthew shows even less interest in his person, while Luke (→ Luke, Gospel of), other than in the lists of apostles, omits any reference to him. This is all we get to know about Andrew from the Synoptic Gospels.

By contrast, John (→ John the Apostle: III. John, Gospel of) shows a growing interest in the apostle. He adds some conflicting information, however. To begin with, the narration of how Andrew comes to know Jesus is different from in the Synoptic Gospels. Before becoming a follower of Jesus, the Fourth Gospel tells us that Andrew was a disciple of → John the Baptist. Moreover, the scene of his first meeting with Jesus is rather different: he was not fishing, as Mark tells us, but was together with the Baptist at → Bethany; after John the Baptist exclaims that Jesus is the "Lamb of God," he then decides to follow Jesus (John 1:35–40; → *Agnus Dei*). Andrew is therefore already presented in the Fourth Gospel as the first disciple Jesus called, which gave rise to the epithet πρωτόκλητος ("first called") that in later tradition frequently accompanies his name (Peterson, 1958, 5): it is Andrew who brings his brother Peter into contact with Jesus (John 1:41–42). Another striking point of disagreement is the place in which the brothers are said to live, which according to John is → Bethsaida, also on the north shore of the Sea of Galilee, and not Capernaum as in Mark. John further refers to Andrew on two other occasions: the first concerns the story about the feeding of the 5,000, since it is Andrew who tells Jesus about the boy with some bread (John 6:8–9); in the second, together with Philip, Andrew tells Jesus about the Greeks who want to meet him (John 12:20–22).

1. Andrew in Early Christian Literature

With the exception of the *Acts of Andrew* (Bonnet, 1898; Prieur, 1989; Roig Lanzillotta, 2007), early Christian literature offers very little information about the apostle Andrew. Noncanonical writings show the same lack of interest in this apostolic figure: the *Gospel of Peter* (14 [60]; → Peter the Apostle) and the *Gospel of the Ebionites* (2; → *Ebionites, Gospel of the*) refer to the apostle only in passing; the *Epistle of the Apostles* (2; 11; → Apostle: IV. *Apostles, Epistle of the*) also mentions Andrew, together with Peter and Thomas; and → Origen, besides indulging in the etymology of his name, goes on to attribute Scythia, as missionary region, to Andrew (in Eus. *Hist. eccl.* 3.1), which might also be echoed in the *Acts of Andrew and Matthias* (Elliott, 1993, 236; Roig Lanzillotta, 2006; Bonnet, 1898).

It is therefore plausible to think that the author of the *Acts of Andrew*, when focusing on the apostle, in fact intended to fill this gap in information. However, it is also true that the author of this 2nd-century CE text is not especially interested in narrating the wondrous acts and life of the apostle but rather in using him as an authoritative figure to spread his own ideas (Roig Lanzillotta, 2007). Together with the acts of John, Paul, Peter, and Thomas, the *Acts of Andrew* is one of five major Apocryphal Acts of Apostles. Just like the other acts, *Acts of Andrew* allegedly narrates Andrew's travels and martyrdom in Achaia. However, all the versions of the story that include both sections tend to be rather late sources whose relationship with the primitive text is not always easy to evaluate.

Later saint veneration provided an important impetus to the creation of new texts that, on the basis of old materials, was intended to suit the need for more detailed information concerning the life and the death of the apostles. First, we see the proliferation of later Christian compositions that have Andrew as protagonist and continue the story of the major *Acts of Andrew*, such as the *Acts of Peter and Andrew* (Bonnet, 1898), the *Acts of Andrew and Paul* (Jacques, 1969), and the *Acts of Andrew and Bartholomew* (Budge, 1899; Lucchesi & Prieur, 1978; 1980). Second, the 5th and 6th centuries CE saw a dramatic explosion of texts focused on Andrew's martyrdom, probably intended for the calendar observances of his death on Nov 30. Third, from the 8th century CE onward, new political interests provided a renewed impulse to Andrew literature: in its rivalry with Rome, Byzantium needed a founder whose stature could equate with that of Peter, founder of the Christian community in Rome (Dvornik, 1958). According to an old legend, Andrew's relics had been transported to Constantinople already in the 4th century CE (Jer. *Vigil.* 5); a new legend came to reinforce this view, stating that Byzantium had been an important station in Andrew's missionary peregrination, where he had appointed Stachys as first bishop (Epiphanius of Cyprus). By assuring the continuity between Andrew and its own medieval bishops, Byzantium successfully claimed the "first called" from among the apostles as its own foundational saint. The biographical genre (→ Biography) that develops in this period around Andrew's figure, as represented by later anonymous texts known as *Narratio* (Bonnet, 1894a) and *Laudatio* (Bonnet, 1894b), or the *Vita Andreae*, probably by Epiphanius the Monk (Dressel, 1843), was intended to nourish these claims (Roig Lanzillotta, 2007, 7–8, 77–80).

Bibliography

Bonnet, M., "Acta Andreae apostoli cum laudatione context," *AnBoll* 13, 1894a, 309–352.

Bonnet, M., "Martyrium sancti apostoli Andreae," *AnBoll* 13, 1894b, 353–372.

Bonnet, M., *Acta Apostolorum Apocrypha*, vol. II/1, Leipzig, 1898, 38–45.

Budge, E.A.W., *The Contendings of the Apostles*, vol. I: *Ethiopic Texts*, London, 1899.

Elliott, J.K., *The Apocryphal New Testament*, Oxford, 1993.

Dressel, A., "Epiphanii monachi et presbyteri de vita et actibus et morte sancti, et plane laudandi, et primi vocati inter alios apostolos Andreae," in: A. Dressel, *Epiphanii monachi et presbyteri edita et inedita*, Paris, 1843, 45–82, PG 120, cols. 216–260.

Dvornik, F., *The Idea of Apostolicity in Byzantium and the Legend of the Apostle Andrew*, Cambridge MA, 1958.

Jacques, X., "Les deux fragments conserves des 'Actes d'André et de Paul,'" *Or.* 38 n.s., 1969, 187–213.

Lucchesi, E., & J.M. Prieur, "Fragments coptes des Actes d'André et Matthias et d'André et Barthelémy," *AnBoll* 96, 1978, 339–350; 98, 1980, 75–98.

Peterson, M.P., *Andrew, Brother of Simon Peter: His History and His Legends*, Leiden, 1958.

Prieur, J.-M., *Acta Andreae*, Turnhout, 1989.

Roig Lanzillotta, L., "Cannibals, Myrmidonians, Sinopeans or Jews? The Five Versions of the Acts Andrew and Matthias (in the City of the Cannibals) and their Source(s)," in: M. Labahn & L.J. Lietaert Peerbolte, eds., *Wonders Never Cease*, London, 2006, 221–243.

Roig Lanzillotta, L., *Acta Andreae Apocrypha: A New Perspective on the Nature, Intention and Significance of the Primitive Text*, Geneva, 2007.

Roig Lanzillotta, L., *Diccionario de Personajes del Nuevo Testamento*, Córdoba, 2011; Barcelona, 2017.

LAUTARO ROIG LANZILLOTTA

II. *Andrew, Acts of*

The *Acts of Andrew* provides a unique opportunity to access a different sort of Christianity than the one we are used to from the New Testament and the fathers of the church. Behind the *Acts of Andrew* we see a strand of Christianity that was entrenched in Greco-Roman society. The worldview found in the text reveals an author and a readership facing the same problems, by and large, that confronted individuals in the ancient world, and seeking similar solutions for them. The ideas about the world, God, human beings, the individual's position within the group, women's status in ancient society, the value and character of → marriage, male-female relationships, and the emphasis on ethics that characterize the *Acts of Andrew* were all in fact hot issues in 2nd-century CE society and, as such, turn up in a wide range of ancient literary sources. In this sense the Christian character of the *Acts of Andrew* comes more from its marked Christian framework than from its addressing typically Christian issues.

1. The Textual Witnesses of the *Acts of Andrew* and the Reconstruction of the Earliest Version

From the five major Apocryphal Acts of the Apostles of Andrew, Peter, John, Paul, and Thomas, the *Acts of Andrew* no doubt presents the most complicated textual situation (→ Apostle: II. Apostles, Apocryphal Acts of the). The *Acts of Andrew* allegedly survives in a large number of texts of various types and provenances. Most of these versions are imperfect and only transmit the primitive *Acts of Andrew* in a fragmentary fashion. In the few cases where sources do seem to include the text in a complete way, these show clear traces of editorial intervention. The biggest problem, however, is the highly divergent nature of the accounts. For this reason, the literary genre, contents, length, thought, and intention of the *Acts of Andrew* are still a matter of conjecture.

On the basis of the available sources, it seems impossible to establish with certainty what the primitive *Acts* actually looked like. The textual evidence comes in a total of 16 versions, written in different periods and languages (Greek, Latin, Coptic, and Armenian) and including rather conflicting accounts (for a complete list of testimonies, see Roig Lanzillotta, 2007a, 3–9). The sources that include both the peregrinations and the martyrdom of the apostle are the following:

1. Gregory of Tours' Latin text *Liber de miraculis Beati Andreae apostoli* (*Epitome*), edited by M. Bonnet (1969, 371–396);
2. a Greek text known as *Narratio*, edited by M. Bonnet (1894b, 353–372);
3. a Greek text known as *Laudatio*, edited by M. Bonnet (1894a, 309–352);
4. *Vita Andreae* by the monk Epiphanius. There are three different versions of this Greek text but only one of them, based on an inferior manuscript (Vat. gr. 824), has been published (Dressel, 1843, 45–82). The other two manuscripts (Paris BN gr. 1510, and designated Escorial y II 6 [gr. 314]) are still unpublished.

According to other testimonies, however, the *Acts of Andrew* only included the martyrdom only with a couple of preliminary events. These are the following:

1. Fragment "ex actis Andreae" in Vat. gr. 808 (V), Greek text first edited by M Bonnet (1898, 38–45), collated by J.-M. Prieur (1989) and D.R. MacDonald (1990), and reedited by L. Roig Lanzillotta (2007a).
2. *Martyrdom of Saint Andrew* preserved in two manuscripts (Sinaiticus gr. 526 and Hierosolymitanus Sabbaiticus 103). This Greek text was first identified by A. Ehrhard (1912) and edited by T. Detorakis (1981–1982), both collated by J.-M. Prieur (1989, 441–549) with other testimonies for the martyrdom.
3. *Martyrdom of Saint Andrew* (manuscript Ann Arbor 36), Greek text collated by J.-M. Prieur (1989, 507–549).
4. *Martyrium alterum* A and B, Greek texts edited by M. Bonnet (1898, 58–64).
5. *Passio sancti Andreae apostoli* (= *Latin Epistle*), Latin text edited by M. Bonnet (1898, 1–37).
6. The so-called *Greek Epistle*, two independent Greek translations of the Latin *Passio sancti Andreae apostoli* (see above), edited by M. Bonnet (1898, 1–37).
7. *Passio altera sancti Andreae apostoli*, Latin text better known as *Conversante*, in M. Bonnet (1894c, 373–378).
8. *Armenian passion*, Armenian text first edited by C. Tchékarian (1904, 146–167); French translation by L. Leloir (1986, 232–257).
9. *Martyrium prius* (*Mpr*), in M. Bonnet (1898, 46–57); reedited by J.-M. Prieur (1989).

In their efforts to establish what the original *Acts* actually looked like, scholars up to the end of the 20th century ended up with two textual reconstructions of the primitive *Acts*: either it consisted of two parts, the peregrinations and the martyrdom (Hennecke, 1904a; 1924; Blumenthal, 1933; Quispel, 1956; Deeleman, 1946; Hornschuh, 1964; Söder, 1969; Erbetta, 1978; Plümacher, 1978; MacDonald, 1990), or it mainly consisted of the martyrdom (Flamion, 1911; Prieur, 1989). There are translations of these texts in most European languages (Eng.: James, 1924; Elliott, 1993; Ger.: Hennecke, 1904a, 1924; Schneemelcher, 1989; Dutch: Klijn, 1985; Fr.: Prieur, 1989; Ital.: Erbetta, 1978; Span.: Piñero, 2004).

Both approaches, however, are problematic. The witnesses that include two differentiated parts – the peregrinations and the martyrdom of the apostle – present three different versions of Andrew's itinerary. Moreover, some of them actually lack a martyrdom properly speaking and only include some short reference to Andrew's end.

As far as the view is concerned that the *Acts of Andrew* only included the martyrdom, it is clear that both the number and the homogeneity of testimonies are higher. However, the production of *new* martyrdom texts was a widespread phenomenon in the 4th and 5th centuries CE and it cannot be ruled out that some of the witnesses to Andrew's passion may have appeared in this period. Furthermore, the cohesion of these testimonies should not be overstated; the texts actually present rather divergent accounts of Andrew's passion.

However, there seems to be no doubt that the fragment in codex Vat. gr. 808 (V) represents the earliest textual stage of the *Acts of Andrew* (Roig Lanzillotta 2007a; 2001). According to general consensus (Bonnet, 1893, XIV; Liechtenhan, 1902, 295; Hennecke, 1904a, 544; 1924, 249; Flamion, 1911, 177; James, 1924, 337, 350; Blumenthal, 1933, 38; Hornschuh, 1964, 271; Junod & Kaestli, 1982, 65; Prieur & Schneemelcher, 1989, 97; Prieur, 1989, 2–3, 425), this text is the closest to, or even a genuine fragment of, the primitive *Acts*. This is supported by a thorough textual analysis and a comparison of V with the other extant documents (Roig Lanzillotta, 2007a, 53–10). The comparison shows, first, that the section of the *Acts of Andrew* preserved in V is also transmitted, albeit transformed, in six other important textual witnesses. Second, it is always V's version that seems to retain the most primitive account. Third, the later versions not only abridged the primitive account but they also always eliminated the same sections.

2. The Primitive *Acts of Andrew* According to the Vatican Manuscript

Given its prominent position in the many reworked texts, the *Acts of Andrew*'s fragment found in V should serve as the starting point for an analysis of the mentality, character, style, message, and intention of the primitive *Acts of Andrew* (Roig Lanzillotta, 2007a; 2011). V may also help to test the reliability of other witnesses and to evaluate other potentially primitive sections preserved in them.

a. Plot

As the fragment begins, Andrew is in Patras, where he has arrived in the course of his missionary travels to announce the gospel. Part of his message is that Christians should live a spiritual life detached from the influence of both the body and externals. The wife of proconsul Aegeates, Maximilla, finds his message appealing and decides to suspend all marital relations with her husband and follow the apostle. As a result, Aegeates first imprisons Andrew and subsequently sentences him to death.

This fragment mainly consists of Andrew's four speeches, one to the brethren, one to Maximilla, one to Aegeates' brother Stratocles, and another again to the brethren. The first incomplete speech to the brethren (1; chapters and line numbers [V^r] according to Roig Lanzillotta, 2007a), which establishes the conceptual framework of the whole fragment, takes place in prison, at a meeting between Andrew and his followers. The apostle here tells them about the superiority of God's community, and that they belong to the higher realm of the good, of justice, and of the light. This belonging to the transcendent realm provides them with complete insight into earthly matters.

With the exception of Stratocles, the ensuing narrative section (2–4) introduces all of the personas of the fragment: Andrew, Aegeates, Maximilla, her chambermaid Iphidama, and the brethren. The first half of this section focuses on the meetings in prison and the optimism of the followers during the days in which Aegeates seems to have forgotten Andrew's case. However, consistent with the tone of the first incomplete speech that stresses the flux of the realm of change, which deprives it of any stability, the brethren's joy is quickly curtailed. The second half of the narrative section introduces a sudden twist in the action as soon as Aegeates remembers Andrew's case. In a rage, the proconsul rushes out of the court and back to the praetorium in order to address his wife: if she agrees to resume their former conjugal life, he will free Andrew; if she refuses, the apostle will be punished. Dismayed by this new turn of events, the silent Maximilla returns to the prison to tell the apostle about her husband's ultimatum.

Andrew's answer to Maximilla takes the form of a long speech (5–9), in which he encourages her to reject Aegeates' proposition. She should accept the apostle's suffering, since that is the only way to attain a complete liberation from her husband. In order to reassure her, Andrew analyzes the consequences of both a negative and a positive answer to Aegeates. The plea for a negative answer is based on an interpretation of → Adam and Eve's "error" in the garden of Eden, in which Andrew and Maximilla are presented as the exact opposites of the first man and woman. Thanks to the awareness that Maximilla has gained and her knowing that she belongs to the divine realm, she and Andrew, as representatives of spiritual humankind, can correct the first couple's deficiency. After describing the positive results of such a correction (6), Andrew's speech praises the generic "nature that saves itself": at the end of the long process by means of which humankind ascends to its original nature, it will see the "Ungenerated" (God).

After some transitional lines (7), Andrew then evaluates the consequences if Maximilla were to accept her husband's terms (8). In Andrew's view, Maximilla's accepting them would have negative effects not only for her but also for Andrew himself. However, by rejecting her husband's threat, Maximilla would help the apostle to abandon his prison, by which he refers both to the jail in which he is imprisoned and to his physical body. The proconsul might think he is punishing him, but in fact he will be liberating him. Hence, Andrew concludes, his own perfection depends on the "clear sight" of Maximilla's intellect (9).

The next section, Andrew's speech to Stratocles (10–13), is the only one in pseudo-dialogue form. In it Andrew deals with the human soul, its rational and irrational parts, and the way the proclaimed words may help the soul restructure the inner balance between these parts. Realizing that Stratocles is now crying, Andrew asks him the reason for his grief. If his words have really reached the rational (or "thinking") part of his soul, Stratocles' expressions of acute suffering are inexcusable. In fact, grief might even be proof that they have not reached their goal and that the irrational part has taken control of Stratocles' soul. In his short answer (12), the proconsul's brother aims to allay the apostle's worries by affirming that the words have indeed reached his soul. He knows that Andrew's departure is a positive event; if he is crying, this is simply because he will not be able to

complete his process of education. An agricultural simile is then used to express the impending deprivation Stratocles is already feeling: while his soul is the soil, Andrew's words are the seeds; in order to grow and develop properly, however, the seeds need the constant care of the sower. Andrew, satisfied with this answer, changes the subject and announces that the next day he will be crucified (13).

There follows a short narrative section (14), in which Maximilla returns to the praetorium. Facing her husband, she announces her refusal, after which Aegeates decides to have Andrew crucified. When the Proconsul leaves, Maximilla and Iphidama return to the prison, where they meet Andrew and his followers. Immediately after this section, Andrew's gives his last speech to the brethren (15–18). The apostle declares that he has been sent by the Lord to remind everyone "akin to the words" that they are wasting their time in ephemeral evils. He praises those who "have become listeners to his words," attaining in this way the vision of their own true nature. Finally, Andrew warns them not to be overcome by his death. His martyrdom is not only necessary but also expected, since it is the final release from his last ties to the world. At this point, in the middle of a sentence, the text ends abruptly.

b. Message

Andrew's first discourse in V is essential for understanding the theology, cosmology, and anthropology of the fragment. In a rudiment of negative theology, God is described as the "One, the immutable supercelestial God abiding beyond the world. The "blessed race" (V^r 4, τὸ μακάριον γένος) is said to have originated in this transcendent realm and to have there its final destination. In spite of the current degraded human state in the world of nature (V^r 213, φύσις), God's recognition of his people, by means of the principle of "like knows like," allows them to know him and recover their pristine condition. Despite its strongly dualistic worldview, the *Acts of Andrew* is consequently basically a monistic text: both human beings and (probably) the totality of the physical world proceed from an original unity of being as a result of a process of devolution. However, the *Acts of Andrew*'s main interest is not in cosmology but in anthropology; the three speeches that follow provide a detailed description of how human beings ended up in the world of nature and how they may manage to recover their transcendent condition.

The anthropology of the fragment distinguishes three elements in the human being: intellect, soul, and body (Roig Lanzillotta, 2007b) and each addressee of the following three speeches – Maximilla, Stratocles, and the brethren – represent these human aspects, respectively. As such, they illustrate the involvement of intellect, soul, and body in prolonging human exile in the physical world (Vr 213–214, πλάνη): discursive thinking (intellect), immoderate affections (soul), and a combination of sensorial perception and representation (body) keep humanity in bondage (Vr 90, αἰχμαλωσία; Vr 97–98, τὰ δεσμά). Andrew's intervention by means of his "saving words" allows a reorganization of the three realms in such a way that these also provide for the beginning of human liberation. Listening to the words allows individuals to control the distortions inherent in the three aspects which opens the path to the process of self-knowledge. When human beings thus become conscious both of their origin and their current degraded condition, they take control of their being and despise the accretions acquired during the gradual process of devolution.

c. Background of the *Acts of Andrew*'s Thought

The comparison of *Acts of Andrew*'s thought with that of contemporary texts shows the extent to which it reflects the religious and philosophical world of late antiquity. The parallels to the text's cosmology, theology, anthropology, ethics, and epistemology are overwhelming and show a marked influence from → Middle Platonism, notably from those Middle Platonists who had incorporated Aristotelian thought into the common Platonic heritage (Roig Lanzillotta, 2007a, 191–265). The Platonic-Peripatetic background is, for example, clear in the text's theology: the *Acts of Andrew* shows the combination of the One beyond time, place, generation and corruption of Plato's *Parmenides* and the Aristotelian unmoved Mover (Vr 1–20). The *Acts of Andrew*'s cosmology, however, has a more distinct Aristotelian character, since it reflects a tripartite view of the universe that

distinguishes supercelestial, celestial, and earthly regions (Vr 16, τὰ ἐπίγεια). This seems also to be the case with the *Acts of Andrew*'s anthropological views. The tripartite conception of human, consisting of intellect, soul, and body, is distinctively Aristotelian, since it tends to elevate the status of the intellect, the only immortal element in a human being, and to oppose it to the complex soul-body (Roig Lanzillotta, 2015).

As far as ethics is concerned, the emphasis on virtue conceived of as a mean between excess and deficiency seems to imply the Platonic-Peripatetic background (Roig Lanzillotta, 2007a, 168–174). The same can be said about the text's epistemology. The epistemic tripartition that distinguishes the immediate apprehension of the intellect both from discursive thinking and from sensorial perception is also an Aristotelian echo; furthermore, distortion proceeds not from sense perception, which is always true, but from perceptual representation (Vr 209, φαντασία).

Acts of Andrew's philosophical echoes are not the result of a conscious use or adaptation of philosophical categories in order to suit its expository needs, however. The *Acts of Andrew* is not a philosophical text and has no philosophical intentions. Rather, philosophical views seem to proceed from indirect acquaintance with them. Of course, it might be argued that they result from the author's direct exposure to Middle Platonism, but it seems more plausible that the views had already been incorporated into the thought of the religious community he belonged to. Taking into account the *Acts of Andrew*'s close proximity to Hermetic and gnostic thought, this second possibility seems even more plausible.

Indeed the *Acts of Andrew*'s thought reveals conspicuous similarities with the Hermetic (→ Hermetism) and gnostic world of ideas. Gnosis (→ Gnosis/Knowledge) is a central idea in our text: whereas lack of knowledge or ignorance accounts for the current degraded state of humans, knowledge allows their restoration to the primal condition. Human degradation is the result of a process of devolution that follows three causally related stages – namely intellect, soul and physis – which shows obvious similarities with the realms described by gnostic cosmogonical myths. Also gnostic are the ideas of dispersion of the primal unity of the intellect and need to recollect the divine elements that appear scattered in the world of nature. Owing to Andrew's intervention, the intellect awakes from its lethargy and, after becoming aware humans begin their process of introspection that will further allow them to recover the lost condition. Also interesting is that the *Acts of Andrew* even seems to derive matter from a substantialization of affections (V[r] 71–82), as was customary in Valentinianism and as the *Gospel of Truth* (17.10ff.; → Truth) and other sources (Iren. *Haer.* 1.2.3; Markschies, 1992, 408–409; Jonas, 1970, 183–184) clearly transmit. This conceptual proximity with the world of *gnosis* is also stressed both by Andrew's role as a revealer, as a redeemer who comes to remind the blessed race of its true origin, and the strong dualistic view of reality opposing the transcendent world of light to that of the lower, material darkness (τὰ κλίματα ταῦτα) that governs the text (V[r] 7–9; 15–17).

d. Date and Place of Composition

The *Acts of Andrew* used to be dated either to the 2nd or to the 3rd century CE. The first reference to the *Acts of Andrew* in → Eusebius of Caesarea (*Historia ecclesiastica*; 4th cent. CE), indeed provides the *terminus ante quem*. The *terminus post quem* seems to be confirmed by the philosophical influences on the text, which are clearly Middle Platonic but do not imply → Plotinus' system. There is, however, an interesting literary echo that might help us to establish a more precise *terminus a quo*. I am referring to the *Acts of Andrew*'s (V[r] 55–56) almost literal echo of Achilles Tatius' *Leucippe and Cleitophon* (5.27.1), customarily dated circa 170 CE. Not only are both passages very close to one another; the *Acts of Andrew* also deliberately adapts Achilles Tatius's passage in order for it to fit the more pious relationship between Maximilla and Andrew. As regards the *Acts of Andrew*'s place of origin, the scanty textual evidence does not permit a definitive answer. Scholars have proposed three possible locations: Alexandria, Achaia, and Asia Minor or Bithynia.

3. The *Acts of Andrew* and the other Apocryphal Acts of the Apostles

Despite their specific stories, characters, and locations, it is indisputable that the five major Apocryphal Acts of the Apostles (*Acts of John*; *Acts of Peter*;

Acts of Paul; *Acts of Thomas*; → John the Apostle; → Peter the Apostle; Paul the Apostle; → Thomas the Apostle; and *Acts of Andrew*) share a number of common characteristics. In fact, they seem to have a similar origin, character, tenor, textual transmission, and reception during the Middle Ages.

Probably written in the second half of the 2nd century CE somewhere in the Mediterranean, the Apocryphal Acts of the Apostles properly reflect the "global" ancient Greco-Roman world in which Christians had to live: arrivals, departures, travels, separations, and reunions shape the lives and destinies of their protagonists.

As for their textual characteristics, the Apocryphal Acts of the Apostles also share some common tokens: narrative structure, style, vocabulary, and motifs are particularly similar, so much so that the Apocryphal Acts of the Apostles were traditionally attributed to the same legendary author, Leucius Charinus (Schäferdiek, 1989). Just like the other Acts do with the other apostles, the *Acts of Andrew* supposedly describes Andrew's adventures as he carries out his missionary activities around the world. As is also the case with the other Acts, these adventures normally include two major sections, namely the apostle's wanderings through the ancient world (or περίοδοι) and his martyrdom. We have seen above, however, that this internal dichotomy might be more the result of later textual transmission than of the primitive intention of the texts. In fact, the Apocryphal Acts of the Apostles do not seem to have originally had the devotional intent they acquired later on. Rather they were actually conceived as a Christian variety of the ancient novel, which as such intended to verbalize Christian ideals, incarnating them in certain typically Christian figures. Hero and heroine, traditionally represented in the Greek novel by the lovers, are in the Apocryphal Acts of the Apostles substituted by the Apostle and the wife of a dignitary, who typically converts to Christianity, provoking in this way the fury and revenge of her husband.

However, it is specially Apocryphal Acts of the Apostles' tenor that brings all five close to each other. The texts reflect a form of Christianity that was formed in, or was acquainted with, Greek philosophical thought patterns. Theological, anthropological, and ethical issues are approached from perspectives known from contemporaneous philosophical debates in Neo-Pythagorean and Middle Platonic circles. Albeit without philosophical intent, the numerous discussions and/or views that are exposed in the Apocryphal Acts of the Apostles imply philosophical positions and interschool polemics.

As far as their textual transmission is concerned, the Apocryphal Acts of the Apostles show common patterns as well. Given their clear heterodox character, the Apocryphal Acts of the Apostles were at an early stage condemned as "spurious" by ecclesiastical authorities. They were not completely eliminated, however. Thanks to the view that they had been used and falsified by the Manicheans, even if first stigmatized and relegated, the texts were in the long run expurgated and cleansed of "all possible error." The next step was the editing and adaption of the texts to suit the intentions and goals of a succession of editors throughout the Middle Ages. Consequently, even if not in their primitive form, they were thus "transmitted" to posterity.

4. Medieval Reception of the *Acts of Andrew*

The *Acts of Andrew*, as is also indeed the case with the Apocryphal Acts of the Apostles, enjoyed a prolific afterlife and reception. They were reworked and adapted to the needs of changing Christian readerships. There are at least three stages in the medieval reception of the Apocryphal Acts of the Apostles.

1. First of all, the ancient acts generated a very productive martyrdom literature. Following earlier examples of martyrdom texts based on court records, the last part of the acts was already reworked and adapted at an early stage (5th–6th cents. CE) for the calendar observance. Intended to be read on the anniversary of the saint's death, these texts were mainly focused on the last events of the apostle's life, as a result of which their lengths were dramatically reduced. This was also aided by their inclusion in menologia (Ehrhard, 1937–1952), or collections of saints' lives (initially in half-year and subsequently in whole-year versions), which could not surpass the 600-page material limit of a manuscript. In the case of the Apostle Andrew, this genre is very well represented by eleven textual testimonies.

2. A second stage is the one represented by the collection of wondrous acts and healings by the apostle and preserved in texts such as the Coptic fragment in Papyrus Copt. Utrecht 1, first edited by R. van den Broek in J.-M. Prieur (1989, 652–671, with Fr. trans. by Prieur), the Latin text of *Epitome*, and the *Acts of Andrew and Matthias among the Cannibals*, edited by M. Bonnet (1898, 65–127). In line with the Greek aretalogies, these texts focus on the apostle's healings and wondrous actions, leaving aside all "superfluous" sections, notably the discourses by the apostle (see the reference to the *Acts of Andrew*'s *verbositas* in *Epitome*, prol. 11–13).

3. A third stage is the biographical *Gattung* that develops between the 8th and 9th centuries. It includes *Narratio*, *Laudatio*, and *Vita*. In addition to the clear biographical intentions, all three texts pretend to have consulted local traditions and to have combined them with other written sources (*Narratio* 356.8; 356.24–25; 357.1; *Laudatio* 324.8; 341.30–342.2). Common to all of the texts is the attempt to provide an overview of Andrew's travels that is at the same time an outline of his apostolic career. Eventually, all three texts end with Andrew's death, even if their versions of the martyrdom, if they include one, differ considerably from one another.

5. The *Acts of Andrew* and the *Acts of Andrew and Matthias Among the Cannibals*

As far as the story of Andrew's and Matthias' adventures among the cannibals is concerned, Flamion (1911, 302) claimed that the *Acts of Andrew and Matthias* was a later composition that originated in Egypt. More recently, and on the basis of a thorough philological analysis, A. Hilhorst and P. Lalleman (2000) have demonstrated that, given their diverse stylistic characteristics, the *Acts of Andrew and Matthias* and the *Acts of Andrew* could not belong to the same text. In its present state, the *Acts of Andrew and Matthias* indeed does not seem to belong to the primitive textual core. This does not necessarily preclude the possibility that the story in a simpler form appeared in the primitive *Acts*, however. One should keep in mind that there are five versions of the story (in *Epitome* 377.21–378.24; *Laudatio* 317.13–20 and 330.20–331.25; *Vita*; *Narratio* 5–7; and *Acts of Andrew and Matthias*), and that they are all so different from one another that they cannot be explained as mutually interdependent (Blumenthal, 1933). However, they might go back to a common source, which "in a simpler and shorter form might very well have been one of the *Acts of Andrew* numerous episodes" (Roig Lanzillotta, 2006, 242–243).

Bibliography

Blumenthal, M., *Formen und Motive in den apokryphen Apostelgeschichten*, Leipzig, 1933.

Bonnet, M., "Georgii Florentii Gregorii Episcopi Turonensis liber de miraculis Beati Andreae Apostoli," in: B. Krusch, ed., *Monumenta Germaniae historica: Scriptores rerum merovingicarum*, vol. I/2, Hannover, 1969, 371–396; repr. Hannover, 1885.

Bonnet, M., "Acta Andreae apostoli cum laudatione contexta," *AnBoll* 13, 1894a, 309–352.

Bonnet, M., "Martyrium sancti apostoli Andreae," *AnBoll* 13, 1894b, 353–372.

Bonnet, M., "Passio sancti Andreae apostoli," *AnBoll* 13, 1894c, 373–378.

Bonnet, M., *Acta Apostolorum Apocrypha*, vol. II/1, Leipzig, 1898, 38–45.

Deeleman, C.F.M., "Acta Andreae," *GeV* 46, 1912, 541–577.

Detorakis, T., "Τὸ ἀνέκδοτο μαρτύριο τοῦ ἀποστόλου Ἀνδρέα," in: *Second International Congress of Peloponnesian Studies*, vol. I, Athens, 1981–1982, 325–352.

Dressel, A., "Epiphanii monachi et presbyteri de vita et actibus et morte sancti, et plane laudandi, et primi vocati inter alios apostolos Andreae," in: A. Dressel, *Epiphanii monachi et presbyteri edita et inedita*, Paris, 1843, 45–82; PG 120, cols. 216–260.

Elliott, J.K., *The Apocryphal New Testament*, Oxford, 1993.

Erbetta, M., *Gli apocrifi del Nuovo Testamento*, vol. II: *Atti e leggende: Versione e comment*, Turin, ²1978.

Ehrhard, A., "Review Flamion," *ByZ* 21, 1912, 516–518.

Ehrhard, A., *Überlieferung und Bestand der hagiographischen und homiletischen Literatur der griechischen Kirche von den Anfänge bis zum Ende des 16. Jahrhunderts*, Leipzig, 1937–1952.

Flamion, J., *Les Actes Apocryphes de l'apôtre André: Les Actes d'André et de Matthias, de Pierre et d'André et les textes apparentés*, Louvain, 1911.

Hennecke, E., "Review Bonnet," *ThLZ* 9, 1900, 271–276.

Hennecke, E., *Neutestamentliche Apokryphen*, Tübingen, 1904a.

Hennecke, E., *Handbuch zu den neutestamentlichen Apokryphen*, Tübingen, 1904b.

Hennecke, E., "Review Flamion," *ThLZ* 3, 1913, 73–74.

Hennecke, E., *Neutestamentliche Apokryphen*, 2nd ed., Tübingen, 1924.

Hennecke, E., "Zur christlichen Apokryphenliteratur," *ZKG* 45, 1926, 309–315.

Hilhorst, A., & P. Lalleman, "The Acts of Andrew and Matthias: Is It Part of the Original Acts of Andrew?" in: J.N. Bremmer, ed., *The Apocryphal Acts of Andrew*, Louvain, 2000, 1–14.

Hornschuh, M., "Andreasakten," in: E. Hennecke & W. Schneemelcher, eds., *Neutestamentliche Apokryphen*, vol. II: *Apostolisches: Apokalypsen und Verwandtes*, Tübingen, 1964, 270–296.

James, M.R., *The Apocryphal New Testament: Being the Apocryphal Gospels Acts, Epistles, and Apocalypses with Other Narrations and Fragments Newly Translated*, Oxford, 1924.

Jonas, H., *The Gnostic Religion*, Boston, ²1970, 1958.

Klijn, A.F.J., ed., *Apokriefen van het Nieuwe Testament*, vol. II, Kampen, 1985.

Leloir, L., *Écrits Apocryphes sur les Apôtres: Traduction de l'édition arménienne de Venise*, vol. I: *Pierre, Paul, André, Jacques, Jean*, Turnhout, 1986.

Liechtenhan, R., "Die pseudepigraphische Litteratur der Gnostiker," *ZNW* 3, 1902, 222–237, 286–299.

MacDonald, D.R., *The Acts of Andrew and the Acts of Andrew and Matthias in the City of Cannibals*, Atlanta, 1990.

Markschies, C., *Valentinus Gnosticus?*, Tübingen, 1992.

Piñero, A., & G. Del Cerro, *Hechos apócrifos de los Apóstoles*, vol. I: *Hechos de Andrés, Juan y Pedro*, Madrid, 2004.

Prieur, J.-M., *Acta Andreae*, Turnhout, 1989.

Prieur, J.M., & W. Schneemelcher, "Andreasakten," in: W. Schneemelcher, *Neutestamentliche Apokryphen in deutscher Übersetzung*, vol. II: *Apostolisches. Apokalypsen und Verwandtes*, Tübingen, ⁵1989, 93–137.

Plümacher, E., *Apokryphe Apostelakten*, PRE.S 15, 1978, cols. 11–70.

Quispel, G., "An Unknown Fragment of the Acts of Andrew," *VigChr* 10, 1956, 129–148.

Roig Lanzillotta, L., "Vaticanus Graecus 808 Revisited: A Re-evaluation of the Oldest Fragment of Acta Andreae," *Script.* 56, 2001, 126–140.

Roig Lanzillotta, L., "Cannibals, Myrmidonians, Sinopeans or Jews? The Five Versions of the Acts Andrew and Matthias (in the City of the Cannibals) and their Source(s)," in: M. Labahn & L.J. Lietaert Peerbolte, eds., *Wonders Never Cease*, London, 2006, 221–243.

Roig Lanzillotta, L., *Acta Andreae Apocrypha: A New Perspective on the Nature, Intention and Significance of the Primitive Text*, Geneva, 2007a.

Roig Lanzillotta, L., "One Human Being, Three Early Christian Anthropologies: An Assessment of Acta Andreae's Tenor on the Basis of its Anthropological Views," *VigChr* 61, 2007b, 414–444.

Roig Lanzillotta, L., "The Acts of Andrew," in: M. Coogan, ed., *OEBB*, Oxford, 2011, 34–39.

Roig Lanzillotta, L., "The Acts of Andrew and the New Testament: The Absence of Relevant References to the Canon in the Primitive Text," in: J.-M. Roessli & T. Nicklas, eds., *Christian Apocrypha: Receptions of the New Testament in Ancient Christian Apocrypha*, Göttingen, 2014, 173–188.

Roig Lanzillotta, L., "Plutarch's Anthropology and its Influence on His Cosmological Framework," in: M. Meeussen & L. Van der Stock, eds., *Aspects of Plutarch's Natural Philosophy*, PlHy, Louvain, 2015, 179–195.

Schneemelcher, W., *Neutestamentliche Apokryphen in deutscher Übersetzung*, vol. II: *Apostolisches. Apokalypsen und Verwandtes*, Tübingen, ⁵1989.

Söder, R., *Die apokryphen Apostelgeschichten und die romanhafte Literatur der Antike*, repr. Darmstadt, ²1969.

Tchékarian, C., *Ankanon girk' arak'elakank (Non-Canonical Apostolic Writings: Armenian Treasury of Ancient and Recent Texts 3)*, Venice, 1904.

LAUTARO ROIG LANZILLOTTA

Andrew of Samosata

Andrew of Samosata (fl. 423–444 CE) is mainly known for his initial opposition to Cyril of Alexandria's Twelve Anathemas and for his part in the reconciliation between Cyril and John of Antioch. Besides that, little is known of him. He was probably consecrated bishop of Samosata before 423 CE (Évieux, 1974, 261). Samosata was a town in the province of Euphratensis (present-day Samsat in southeast Turkey). The last thing we know about Andrew is that he was invited to a council in Antioch in 444 CE, but he was too ill to attend. At the time of the Robber Synod, Rufinus was bishop of Samosata. So, Andrew would have died between 444 and 449 CE, probably closer to 444 CE.

1. His Role in the Christological Controversy

Andrew of Samosata became actively involved in the Christological controversy, in which Nestorius of Constantinople (→ Nestorianism/Nestorius) and → Cyril of Alexandria were the key players, when in November 430 CE an Egyptian synod sent Cyril's *Third Letter to Nestorius*, to which were attached Twelve Anathemas (or Twelve Chapters), to Nestorius. Archbishop John of Antioch was outraged at the anathemas and asked both Andrew of Samosata

and → Theodoret of Cyrrhus to refute this document. Only part of Andrew's refutation has survived, in the defense that Cyril wrote in response to it in the spring of 431 CE.

Due to an illness, Andrew could not be present at the Council of → Ephesus in the summer of 431 CE. Briefly after the council, → Rabbula of Edessa defected from the oriental party and joined the Cyrillian party, and he accused Andrew of using the same language as Nestorius. Andrew's response, which has only survived in Syriac, gives us some insight into his Christological views.

In the summer of 432 CE, the emperor, Theodosius II, urged both parties to come to a solution of the Christological crisis. Cyril demanded that the oriental party accept the deposition of Nestorius and anathematize his teachings, but in a letter to Acacius of Beroea (Cyr.Alex. *Ep.* 33), he expressed his own views in such a way that they were acceptable to many eastern bishops. Cyril's position created disunity among the oriental party. The hardliners would only accept communion with Cyril if he condemned his Twelve Anathemas. Their leader was Alexander of Hierapolis, Andrew's → metropolitan in the province of Euphratensis. Andrew, however, joined the group that was in favor of the reunion. A number of letters between Andrew and Alexander have been preserved in Latin, in which they gradually move further apart.

In 433 CE, the negotiations resulted in the Formula of Reunion, and in Cyril's letter to John of Antioch, containing the text of this Formula (Cyr. Alex. *Ep.* 39). At a synod in Zeugma in 433 CE, the bishops of the province of Euphratensis, among whom were Andrew and Theodoret, agreed that the text of Cyril's letter with the Formula of Reunion was orthodox. Alexander of Hierapolis was absent. The last document we have from Andrew, a letter written somewhat later, implies that he accepted the deposition of Nestorius.

Anastasius Sinaïta's *Hodegos* (ch. 22, section 4) contains a passage from a second work that Andrew of Samosata must have written against Cyril's Christological views. Since it mentions Cyril's *Scholia*, this work of Andrew's would have been composed after the Council of Ephesus. It should, therefore, be dated between the summer of 431 CE and April 433 CE, when the union of the churches was restored.

2. His Christological Views

Andrew of Samosata's Christological views have to be gathered from the few writings of his that have survived, especially his refutation of the Twelve Anathemas, his letter to Rabbula of Edessa, and the passage quoted by Anastasius Sinaïta.

As for his refutation of the Twelve Anathemas, it seems that Andrew and Cyril were not far apart in their Christology, but that there were misunderstandings about terminology. Andrew defends the oriental party, stating that they do not confess two sons or two persons (πρόσωπα, "persons"), of which Cyril accused Nestorius. And just like Cyril, he declares that all the sayings should be applied to one Son and Lord and Christ, but that this one Son can be denoted by a name that suggests only one of the natures, such as "Son of Man" in John 3:13 and John 6:62 (→ Son of Man), verses to which Cyril also refers in this context. When Andrew attacks Cyril's formulations, it often is because he misinterprets the Alexandrian archbishop's intentions. When Cyril writes that the Virgin gave birth to the → Word of God incarnate "in a fleshly way" (σαρκικῶς, "in a fleshly way"), Andrew seems to imply that by this Cyril denies the divine nature of Christ. And he takes the archbishop's expression "natural union" to mean that the union of the Word with humanity took place out of necessity, as if the Word did not become man voluntarily.

Several times, he asserts that Cyril contradicts himself, but Andrew does not pay enough attention to the qualifying additions. When, for example, Cyril argues that Christ is not glorified by the → Holy Spirit, as if he were a mere man, but that it is his own Spirit who works through him, Andrew incorrectly infers that the archbishop denies that the Spirit is active through Christ. In the elaboration of this point, however, he teaches, just like Cyril, that the exterior works of the → Trinity are undivided.

Andrew of Samosata's preferred terminology in his refutation of the Twelve Anathemas seems to be one person (πρόσωπον, "person") and two natures. He only uses the word "hypostasis" because he has encountered it in Cyril's writings. When he denies two sons and two persons, he at times also adds "two hypostases." And one of the contradictions he

has observed in Cyril's works is that the archbishop speaks both of two hypostases and of one hypostasis in Christ.

In his reply to Rabbula of Edessa's accusations, Andrew explicitly condemns the view that there would be two sons or two persons. He repeats several times that in Christ there is a connection of two natures, which without confusion form one person. And he declares that the unity is not severed when we separate in the mind or in language the attributes that belong to the natures. Interestingly, like Cyril, he compares the union of divinity and humanity in Christ with that of → body and → soul in a human being. The word "hypostasis" occurs only twice in this letter. Once, Andrew writes that when the Word became man, the nature of his hypostasis was not changed. The second time, the term is part of a reference to Heb 1:3.

The quotation in the *Hodegos* is, according to Anastasius Sinaïta, a comment on Cyril's fourth anathema, which states that the sayings should not be attributed to two "persons" (πρόσωπα) or hypostases, regarded as two separate beings. From this and from the use of these terms in Trinitarian contexts, Andrew concludes that Cyril treats "person" and "hypostasis" as synonyms. He then cites a few instances in which the Alexandrian archbishop juxtaposes "nature" and "hypostasis" and concludes that here, "hypostasis" is synonymous with "nature." Andrew comes close to a solution of this problem, when he suggests that hypostases could be defined as "the real existence of substantial beings" (ὑπάρξεις τινὰς πραγμάτων ἐνουσίων), which is indeed the way in which Cyril usually understands "hypostasis." But Andrew dismisses this, since he incorrectly applies the view that juxtaposition implies synonymity.

Modern scholarship's most thoroughgoing publication on Andrew of Samosata is an article by the late P. Évieux (1974). He gives a detailed description of the history of the bishop's involvement in the Nestorian controversy and in the reunion of the churches that followed it. P. Évieux promised to write a separate paper on Andrew's theology, based on his refutation of the Twelve Anathemas and on his letter to Rabbula of Edessa, but this plan never materialized. Andrew's Christology, then, is still waiting to be investigated.

Bibliography

Abramowski, L., "Zum Brief des Andreas von Samosata an Rabbula von Edessa," *OrChr* 41, 1957, 51–64.

Abramowski, L., "Perpatetisches bei späten Antiochenern," *ZKG* 79, 1968, 358–362.

"Andrew of Samosata: Letters to Alexander of Hierapolis (7), to the oeconomi of Hierapolis (1), and to Theodoret of Cyrus (1)," in: ACO, vol. I/4, Berlin, 1922–1923, 276–295.

"Andrew of Samosata: Refutation of Cyril of Alexandria's 'Twelve Anathemas,'" in: *Cyril of Alexandria: Contra Orientales*, in: ACO, vol. I/1/7, Berlin, 1929, 33–65.

"Andrew of Samosata: Letter to Rabbula of Edessa," in: F. Pericoli-Ridolfini, "Lettera di Andrea di Samosata a Rabbula di Edessa," *RDSO* 28, 1953, 153–169.

"Andrew of Samosata: Fragment of a Text against the Fourth Anathema," in: K.-H. Uthemann, ed., *Anastasius Sinaïta: Viae dux 22.4*, CChr.SG 8, Turnhout, 1981, 300–303.

Baumstark, A., "Ein Brief des Andreas von Samosata an Rabblua von Edessa und eine verlorene dogmatische Katene," *OrChr* 1, 1901, 179–181.

Évieux, P., "André de Samosate: Un adversaire de Cyrille d'Alexandrie durant la crise nestorienne," *REByz* 32, 1974, 253–300.

Pericoli-Ridolfini, F., "La controversia tra Cirillo d'Alessandria e Giovanni di Antiochia nell'epistolario di Andrea di Samosata," *RDSO* 29, 1954, 187–217.

HANS VAN LOON

Anemius

Anemius (fl. 370s; d. 390–391 CE) was bishop of Sirmium in Pannonia from about 376 CE (according to others, 378 or 380 CE) until his death around 390 CE. Nothing is known about him prior to his ordination, which → Ambrose of Milan personally and skillfully maneuvered, in order to counteract Empress Iustina's plans to favor the anti-Nicene party and impose another Homoean bishop after the newly deceased Germinius (see Paulinus *Vita Ambr.* 11). Since then, working side by side with Ambrose, Anemius was deeply committed to imposing the Nicene Creed (→ Nicaea) in Illyricum and promoting imperial legislation against heretics: in 377–378 CE, a regional synod of Illyrian bishops was probably held in Sirmium, reaffirming the Trinitarian profession of faith (→ Trinity), perhaps even supporting the doctrine of the three hypostases in the form the Cappadocians had been divulgating it in the East

(see Thdt. *Hist. eccl.* 4.8–9); by 381 CE, Anemius had already successfully urged the emperor Gratian to forbid followers of → Photinus to gather in Sirmium. On Sep 3, 381 CE, Anemius counted among the about 30 bishops from northern Italy, Illyricum, Gaul, and Africa gathered together for the Council of Aquileia and introduced himself as bishop of Sirmium and → metropolitan of the whole Illyricum. As a matter of fact, the council turned into a doctrinal process against two Homoean bishops, Palladius of Ratiaria and Secondianus of Singidunum, and a former Catholic priest, Attalus. One copy of the acts was sent to the emperor Gratian, and three letters addressed to Gratian, Valentinian II, and Theodosius were attached: among other things, the convened bishops requested that Gratian enforce the resolutions of the council against the condemned Homoean bishops as well as wipe out the last Photinians still active in Sirmium (see Ambr. *Epist.* 10). In the summer of 382 CE, Anemius participated at the Council of Rome summoned by Pope → Damasus under Ambrose's pressure (see Thdt. *Hist. eccl.* 5.9.1), as contested episcopal elections that had taken place in Antioch and Constantinople were fueling dissensions in the West too. After 382 CE, Anemius disappears from historical records. In 391 CE we hear of a new bishop of Sirmio, Cornelius, which suggests that by that year Anemius had already died – probably not too long before.

Historiography

Although its narrative follows quite closely the canons of confessional ecclesiastical history, the standard work on Anemius and his action as bishop of Sirmio is still D. Farlati and J. Coleti (1817). It should be integrated by M. Simonetti (1975) and C. Pietri (1995), which both help profiling in a critical perspective Anemius' role against the broader context of the Arian controversy during the last quarter of the 4th century CE.

Bibliography

Farlati, D., & J. Coleti, *Illyricum Sacrum*, vol. VII, Venetiis, 1817, 538–539.

Pietri, C., "Les dernières résistances du subordinatianisme et le triomphe de l'orthodoxie nicéenne (361–385)," in: J.-M. Mayeur, C. Pietri, L. Pietri, A. Vauchéz &

M. Venard, eds., *Histoire du christianisme des origines à nos jours*, vol. II: *Naissance d'une chrétienté (250–430)*, Paris, 1995, 357–398.

Prinzivalli, E., "Anemio," in: A. Di Berardino, ed., *NDPAC*, vol. I, Genoa, ²2006, 290.

Simonetti, M., *La crisi ariana nel IV secolo*, Rome, 1975, 438–442; 542–551.

Wilmart, A., "1. Anemius," in: A. Baudrillart, P. Richard, U. Rouziés & A. Vogt, eds., *DHGE*, vol. II, Paris, 1914, cols. 1827–1828.

DANIELE TRIPALDI

Angers

Early October 453 CE, bishops from the province *Lugdunensis III* (Eustochius from Tours, Victorius from Le Mans, Charitton, Rumorides and Viventius) met together with Leo from Bourges in Angers to ordain a new → bishop, Thalasius, for this city and took the opportunity to enact 12 canons. Unfortunately, the transmission of this council's canons is obscure in two respects.

First, the critical edition can rely only on two codices of Saint-Maur-dés-Fossés that present a collection of canons from diverse councils, namely Codex Parisinus lat. 1451 (once Codex Fossatensis) from the 8th century CE, and Codex Vaticanus Reginen 1127 (once Codex Engolismensis Tilianus) from the 9th century CE. Both codices were already used by J. Sirmond in his publication *Concilia antiqua Galliae* volume I (Paris, 1629, 116–118), whose text is the basis for the new critical edition of the councils in Gaul in *Corpus Christianorum: Series Latina* (vol. CXLVIII, 137–139) by C. Munier. The Council of Angers is mentioned by F. Maassen (1870, 200f.), who described in detail Codex Parisinus lat. 1451 (613–624), where the council is listed under number 15 (*canones Andicavensis*).

Second, L. Duchesne (1910, 245–250) suggested that the 12 canons of the Council of Angers belong to a collection of five documents that were brought together by the bishop of Angers to consolidate ecclesiastical structures and episcopal authority in this far west region in France still under Roman rule before the Merovingian conquest under → Clovis in 486. L. Duchesne (249) identified this collection with the "annals of Angers" (*annales angevines*) which are supposed to be used by → Gregory of Tours in his *History* (Greg. T. *Hist.* 18.19). According to L. Duchesne, this collection included the 12 canons of the Council of Angers and four more documents that can be linked directly or indirectly with Bishop Thalasius:

- A letter of Leo (Bourges), Victurius (Le Mans), and Eustochius (Tours) to Sarmatio (?), Chariato (?), Desiderius (Nantes), and all clerics of the province *Lugdunensis III* (PL 54.1239f., transmitted among letters of Leo the Great). This letter, probably also from a council and to be dated a short time before the election of Thalasius, deals with the same item as canon 1 of Angers.
- A letter of Lupus of Troyes and Euphronius of Autun to Thalasius (CCSL, vol. CXLVIII, 140f.; Munier, 1963) about liturgical questions regarding the celebration of Easter and Christmas vigil and regarding the problem of a second marriage of clerics.
- The canons of the Council of Tours from Nov 18, 461 CE (CCSL, vol. CXLVIII, 142–149; Munier, 1963). Thalasius did not attend this council but obviously received these canons, because the text is transmitted with an additional agreement by him: *Thalasius peccator hanc definitionem domnorum meorum episcoporum ab ipsis ad me transmissam in ciuitatula mea relegi, subscripsi atque consensi* ("I, the sinner Thalasius, have read this definition of my colleagues, which was sent to me in my city, and subscribed and consented to it")
- The canons of the Council of Vannes (461–491 CE), which were also sent to Thalasius (CCSL, vol. CXLVIII, 150–158; Munier, 1963).

Already C. Munier (1963, 135) had doubts about the existence of this collection because of the diversity of the material (canons and letters) and because no manuscript had conveyed this collection as a whole. However, he nevertheless presented those five documents under the heading "Collection Andegavensis" (1963, 135). J. Gaudemet repeats this hesitation (1985, 86f.) as well as J. Limmer (2004, 126). In 2007 M.E. Moore accepted the thesis of L. Duchesne without discussing the difficulties and took this collection as a further example for the importance of canon collections in the history of canon law (Moore, 2007,

48f.). However, the problems regarding the existence of this collection remain. Against L. Duchesne, therefore, it cannot be taken as part of the annals of Angers (*annales angevines*).

1. Canons

Whether the 12 canons of Angers belong to a broader collection or not, the existence of a council at Angers should not be taken into question, even though only the manuscripts of Saint-Maur transmit those canons. The introductory remark states that the bishops Leo (Bourges), Eustochius (Tours), Chariaton (?), Rumoridus (?), Viventius (?), Victurius (Le Mans), were assembled to consecrate Thalasius as bishop of Angers and decided some rules that should become effective on this day (*ut ab hoc die [...] hae regulae ecclesiaticae servarentur*, p. 137, ll. 6–8; Munier, 1963), that is, Oct 4, 453.

Canon 1 emphasizes the episcopal authority and jurisdiction over the clerics: they have to accept the judgment of their bishops. They are not allowed to appeal to a secular court (see already the Council of → Chalcedon, 451 CE, c. 9; this point is also stated in the letter of Leo, Victurius, and Eustochius mentioned above, and adopted in Vannes (461–491 CE, c. 9); in the so-called Second Council of → Arles, c. 31[30]; and in Agde, 506 CE, c. 32) or to change their place of duty without authorization by a bishop ([...] *nec de loco ad alium sine episcopi permissione transire*, p. 137, l. 12f.; Munier, 1963; see already Arles, 314 CE, cc. 2 and 21). They even need a commendatory letter from their bishop for travelling (first stated in western councils here, repeated in Tours, 461 CE, c. 12; Vannes, 461–491 CE, c. 5; Agde, 506 CE, c. 38, perhaps inspired by the Council of Chalcedon in the East, c. 13). The possibility to appeal to a synod in disputed matters is not mentioned here (see Vaison, 442 CE, c. 5), but this is included in Vannes, 461–491 CE, c. 9 (see the differentiated stages of appeal in Chalcedon, c. 9).

Canon 2 admonishes the → deacons to encounter the presbyters in a humble manner (already in Arles, 314 CE, c. 18).

Canon 3 prohibits violence, crime, and carousals (probably *perpotationis*, "drinking bout" or "carousals," instead of for *perputationis*) for all clerics in general (see Tours, 461 CE, c. 2 about drunken clerics).

Canon 4 enforces the celibate status of the clerics. They have to keep away from contact with women besides family ties (*familiaritatem extranearum feminarum noverint esse vitandam*, p. 137, l. 18f.; Munier, 1963). This was an often iterated item since the Council of Elvira, 306 CE (c. 33) and heavily demanded in the 11th century in the West; it became a controversial point especially in the schism between the eastern and western churches in 1054 CE. In canon 4, however, the noncelibate cleric will just lose the possibility to achieve a higher degree of consecration (*nequaquam gradu altiore donabitur*, p. 138, l. 24f.; Munier, 1963; see Orange, 441 CE, cc. 21–23), so perhaps a lower status may still allow a → marriage (see c. 11 below and the letter of Lupus of Troyes and Euphronius of Autun to Thalasius mentioned above).

Interestingly this canon adds another quite different point, which hints at the political changes and military threat in those times: any cleric who is detected to have assisted in capturing and handing over cities (*tum si qui tradendis vel capiendis civitatibus fuerint interfuisse detecti*, p. 138, l. 26f.; Munier, 1963) has to be suspended from the community (see c. 7 below). It would be interesting to have more background information about this issue, especially because there is no other comparable canon in those times. There were some bishops in Gaul, however, who were engaged in defending their city and acted as mediators between the inhabitants and the invading or besieging troops, for example against the → Huns: Orientus of Auch in 439 CE, → Anianus of Orleans and Lupus of Troyes in 451 CE. Perhaps the canon demands loyalty of the clerics in this province, which was still under Roman rule.

Canon 5 deals with broken religious vows. Someone who ceases his public repentance ahead of time (see Tours, 461 CE, c. 8; Vannes, 461–491 CE, c. 3) and someone who breaks his vow of celibacy (see Valence, 374 CE, c. 2; Tours, 461 CE, c. 6; and Vannes, 461–491 CE, c. 4; also Chalcedon, 451 CE, c. 16) are to be punished in a comparable manner (see c. 12 below).

Canon 6 imposes a ban on those who live together with a second woman while their wife is still alive (see Vannes, 461–491 CE, c. 2).

Canon 7 forbids clerics to take part in military campaigns and secular matters (*ad saecularem militiam et ad laicos contulerint*, p. 138, l. 36f.; Munier, 1963; see Tours, 461 CE, c. 5; see for secular matters Chalcedon, 451 CE, c. 7). Since Constantine the clerics were relieved from military service (Cod. Theod. 16.2.2, from 313 CE, see also Cod. Theod. 7.20.12.2 from 400 CE), but this canon deals with the case that a cleric himself chooses to take part in military campaigns (see Latunense/Saint-Jean-de-Loisne, 673–675 CE, c. 2 and Burdegalense, 663–675 CE, c. 1: clerics are not allowed to wear weapons). Perhaps either due to the military threat of the Wisigoths and the → Franks (see c. 4 above) or due to a military career of some clerics before their → ordination, the bishops in Angers wanted to draw a line between secular and spiritual matters.

Canon 8 demands the monks to stay in obedience and not to travel around on their own without permission letters and concrete charges and duties (*absque epistolis et absque certis negotiis vel necessitatibus per regiones vagantur alienas*, p. 138, l. 40f.; Munier, 1963; see Chalcedon, 451 CE, c. 4; Vannes, 461–491 CE, cc. 6 and 7; Agde, 506 CE, cc. 27 and 38; see also one century later the *Regula Benedicti* 1.10–12 about the detested tramping monks, the Gyrophags). Perhaps this is directed against monks who chose a solitary life outside the cloister like an → anchorite, or maybe those monks are meant who leave the cloister to found a new one as criticized by the Councils of → Vannes and Agde.

Canon 9 adds an aspect to canon 1: no bishop can ordain a cleric to a higher degree who received already an ordination by another bishop (see Vannes, 461–491 CE, c. 10; Tours, 461 CE, c. 9).

Canon 10 deals with laymen and clerics who leave their ministry, but only the consequence for the laymen is mentioned: they are excluded from the community. Therefore the tradition of this canon seems to be incomplete and corrupted.

Canon 11 adds a detail to the theme of canon 4: only those can be ordained as presbyter (→ Priest/Presbyter) or deacon who have married just once, namely a virgin (see Valence, 374 CE, c. 1; Tours, 461 CE, c. 4; Agde, 506 CE, cc. 1 and 43). It is not sure if this means a celibate life as well, as demanded in Tours, 461 CE, canon 1, and Agde, 506 CE, canon 9, supported by a quotation of a letter of Innocentius I (402–417 CE) to Exsuperius of Toulouse from Feb 20, 405 CE.

Canon 12 complements canon 5 about public penitence: a bishop has to reconcile a sinner after his public penitence (see already Arles, 314 CE, c. 17[16]; Nimes, 394–396 CE, c. 3; Turin, 398 CE, c. 5; and Orange, 441 CE, c. 10[11]), but to decide about the form and time period of → penitence falls within the competence of the bishop.

In general, the 12 canons of the Council of Angers organize ecclesial affairs, especially the position of the bishop and the celibate life of the clerics. They suit to the discussion in those times as the parallel canons demonstrate; exceptions are canons 4 and 7 on political and military aspects.

Bibliography

Diefenbach, S., "'Bischofsherrschaft': Zur Transformation der politischen Kultur im spätantiken und frühmittelalterlichen Gallien," in: S. Diefenbach & G. M. Müller, eds., *Gallien in Spätantike und Frühmittelalter: Kulturgeschichte einer Region*, MiSt 43, Berlin, 2013, 91–149.

Duchesne, L., *Fastes épiscopaux de l'ancienne Gaule*, vol. II, Paris, 1910.

Gaudemet, J., *Les sources du droit de l'église en occident du IIe au VIIe siècle*, Paris, 1985.

Ferme, B.E., *Introduction to the History of the Sources of Canon Law: The Ancient Law Up To the Decretum of Gratiann*, CGS, Montreal, 2007.

Maassen, F., *Geschichte der Quellen und Literatur des canonischen Rechts im Abendlande bis zum Ausgang des Mittelalters*, vol. I, Graz, 1870.

Limmer, J., *Konzilien und Synoden im spätantiken Gallien von 314 bis 696 nach Christi Geburt*, WR 10, Frankfurt am Main, 2004.

Moore, M.E., "The Spirit of the Gallican Councils AD 314–506," *AHC* 39, 2007, 1–52.

Munier, C., ed., *Concilia Galliae A. 314–A. 506*, CCSL 148, Turnhout, 1963.

Sirmond, J., ed., *Concilia antiqua Galliae*, vol. I, Paris, 1629.

UTA HEIL

Anianus of Orléans

Anianus was (according to a late list of bishops of the 11th cent., the fifth; see Renaud, 1976, 83f.) bishop of Orléans in the mid-5th century CE and died in 454 CE. Only one important event was remembered about him, namely, his activities to retrieve the city of Orléans from the invading → Huns under → Attila in 451 CE. This incident is the main item in the *Vita*

Aniani Aurelianensis (*Vita I*), composed probably around 500 CE (Renaud, 1976, 86f.) in Orléans. The text, the "earliest extant hagiographic work from Orléannais" (Head, 1990, 20), is more a historical description of the siege of Orléans than a hagiographical vita, as the title already mentions (*Incipit virtus sancti Aniani episcopi, quemadmodum civitatem Aurelianus suis orationibus a Chunus liberavit*, "Beginning account of the virtue of the holy bishop Anianus how he liberated the city Orléans from the Huns with his prayers"), perhaps because the unknown author did not have more information about Anianus at hand (Elm, 2003, 209f.).

Already some time before 479 CE, → Sidonius Apollinaris was requested by Prosper of Orléans, the successor of Anianus, to compose a double work, namely to celebrate with highest praise the holy Anianus (*laudibus summis sanctum Annianum* [...] *vis celebrari*), and to write a history of the war of Attila and his assault of Orléans. Sidonius mentions in his reply Anianus' divinely fulfilled prophecy (*illa vulgata exauditi caelitus sacerdotis vaticinatio*, "the bishop's celebrated prophecy as divinely answered from above") that the city will be rescued (Sid. *Ep.* 8.15, 479 CE), but he declined to write the history and postponed the *Vita*. If Sidonius ever wrote his *enkomion* on Anianus it was not transmitted; some historical mistakes in *Vita I* exclude the possibility that Sidonius is its author (Loyen, 1969, 70; Beaujard, 1993, 296).

A century later → Gregory of Tours relates a successful threefold prayer of Anianus for divine help against Attila (Greg. T. *Hist.* 2.7) because he suspected (*suspicari*) the arrival of the troops of Aetius. In this context Gregory hints at a report of Anianus' wondrous deeds, which may be *Vita I*. However, different details in the report on the siege of Orléans may question this dependence.

A later *Vita* (*Vita II*) from the second half of the 9th century CE relates the events more wondrously and adds information on the choice of Anianus, his funerary, and translation; a third *Vita* (*Vita III*, 10th cent. CE) reports on his background and youth and omits the siege of Orléans (Head, 1990, 35–37). A collection of further *Miracula*, mainly after his death, stems from the 11th century (Renaud, 1976).

1. *Vita*

The battle at Orléans was a decisive turning point that marks the beginning of the defeat of the Huns under Attila in Gaul. Anianus as the bishop of the city played an important role for the defense of Orléans, although the details of his engagement are packed in hagiographic language in *Vita I*, while other historical sources neglect him (Jordanes, *De origine actibusque Getarum Getica*) and even the siege of Orléans (Prosper of Aquitaine, *Epitoma chronicorum*; Hydatius, *Continuatio chronicorum Hieronymianorum*). He seems to have been a person with good contact to the Roman elite in Gaul up to the *magister militum* and *patricius* Aetius. Thus Anianus supported the new alliance between Aetius in Arles and the Visigothic troops under Theoderich in Toulouse. *Vita I* does not give any information about his parents, youth, education, and career but just mentions, after a general description of the invading Huns (section 1), his assumption of the office (section 2).

Before the political engagement of Anianus is presented, the reader gets the sole information that the new bishop rebuilt, that is, heightened the ruined major church of the city (section 2 *fabricam ipsam altius sublimare*, "he began to heighten this building"approached Orléans. This menacing situation (section 4 per Attila re). The *Vita* describes Anianus right at the beginning as a powerful man of God with divine might at his hands and with the ability to work wonders, that is, the bishop reanimates the leading craftsman who fell from the scaffold.

Besides this he was involved in releasing captives, which was an important social engagement of the church in those days. The reader learns in section 3 that Anianus sought out Agrippinus, *vir inlustris* and *magister militum*, who was in an on-site inspection through the cities of Gaul, to free the prisoners of Orléans. Agrippinus refused, but a stone fell down from the church and injured him severely. Anianus was able to heal him, so Agippinus gave way to the request of the bishop. This typical hagiographic element of divine intervention nevertheless points at a historical context: in the late 440s CE, Orléans was a center of the riots of the "Bagaudes" who were sent to prison in great numbers. In the face of the invading Huns, one obviously sought in Orléans to pacify the region to close ranks (Stickler, 2002, 138f.).

In spring 451 CE, Attila marched west along the Danube toward Gaul, crossed the Rhine with his troops, and attacked Treves, Metz, and Reims, then approached Orléans. This menacing situation (section 4 *per Attila rege persecutio Galliarum*, "persecution in Gaul by king Attila") led Anianus to travel to Arles for a meeting with the Roman general and *patricius* Aetius. On his way he reanimated the nobleman Mamertus (in Vienne; section 5), again a demonstration of the almighty God. In addition he healed the blind abbot of the monastery Arnainum (section 6; Gabriel; 10 km ahead Arles; see Loyen, 1969, 71).

Anianus then reached Arles and was welcomed by Aetius with high respect. The report on the personal meeting between them is related in much detail and supplemented with dramatic direct speech. Anianus portrayed the destructiveness of the Huns and begged for military support as God's auxiliary forces to defend Gaul and rescue the population (*Id metuens, ne in hanc saevam tempestatem plebs mea cadat, potentiam gloriae vestrae exposco, ut ad defensandam Galliam post Deum cum omnem vestrorum falanges ad repellendas Chunorum insidias properitis, auxiliante Deo*, "In fear of this, lest the people die in this cruel onslaught, I demand the force of your Glory, haste to defend Gaul, following God, with all your phalanx to withdraw the ambush of the Huns"; section 7). The bishop was successful and achieved an agreement that Aetius will send a relief force to Orléans, Jun 14, the day prophesized by Anianus on which God will save the city. The *Vita* does not report the problematic negotiations between the Romans and the Visigoths to form a new alliance against the Huns, but mentions the danger of a broken Gallic contract. This may point to the *foedus* (treaty) between the Alans and Rome from 442 CE to settle in northern Gaul because meanwhile the Alans under Sangibanus had defected to the Huns (Loyen, 1969, 71).

Anianus hurried back to Orléans, locked the city, and called on the dwellers to trust in God who will rescue the city (section 8). Then the Huns arrived and besieged the city (section 9). The bishop was active in encouraging the people and hampering the Huns. He is described as praying and singing bravely on the wall. Another bishop, who was captivated by the Huns and mocked at Anianus' senseless behavior, died suddenly. Nevertheless, the Huns attacked the walls and were on the verge of entering the city. Thus, Anianus left the city with a small group to negotiate with Attila that he should spare the people, but without success. Back in the city, the bishop was able to evoke strong rain and wind, and this storm hindered the Huns for three days while taking the city.

The last hours before the turn of events are described in a dramatic way (section 10). On the same day, the auxiliary forces approached, and the Huns entered the city. But Aetius encamped not far away while the Huns started plundering the city and expulsing the inhabitants. Again the bishop was the person who urged the friendly troops to hurry up. Thus the Huns were cast out, and Orléans was rescued. The last deed of Anianus was to prevent Aetius' troops from slaying all Huns. The final paragraph of the *Vita* (section 11) relates the flourishing of the region and the death of Anianus three years later.

Vita I shows Anianus in a twofold way. First, he is a man of God the almighty and embodies his power on earth. Second, he is the leading head and protector of the city (no other person or institution is mentioned in the text) with best connections to the Roman elite in Gaul. So he seems to be a good example of the emerging *Bischofsherrschaft*, "episcopal reign" as a new spiritual force (Diefenbach, 2013) at this time. But of course one has to take into account that only this hagiographic text relates his engagement in detail:

- *Vita I*: "Vita Aniani episcopi Aurelianensis," *MGH.SRM* 3, 1896, 108–117;
- *Vita II*: Theiner, A., *Saint-Aignan, ou le siège d'Orléans par Attila: Notice historique, suivie de la vie de ce saint, tirée des manuscrits de la bibliothèque du roi*, Paris, 1832, 13–26;
- *Vita III*: Theiner, A., *Saint-Aignan, ou le siège d'Orléans par Attila: Notice historique, suivie de la vie de ce saint, tirée des manuscrits de la bibliothèque du roi*, Paris, 1832, 34–36;
- Miracles: Renaud, G., "Les miracles de saint Aignan d'Orléans (XIe siècle)," *AnBoll* 94, 1976, 256–274

Historiography

Besides some passing references to Anianus in publications dealing with the Huns in Gaul (Thompson, 1996; Wirth, 1999) or with the development of the episcopal offices (Beaujard, 1993; Elm, 2003; Loyen, 1969) or with hagiography in the Early Middle Ages (Renaud, 1976; 1978), there is almost no explicit research on him.

Bibliography

Beaujard, B., "Germain d'Auxerre, Aignan d'Orléans et Médard de Noyon: Trois évêques gaulois et la justice de leur temps," *BSNAF* 64, 1993, 295–303.

Diefenbach, S., "Bischofsherrschaft: Zur Transformation der politischen Kultur im spätantiken und frühmittelalterlichen Gallien, " in: S. Diefenbach & G. M. Müller, eds., *Gallien in Spätantike und Frühmittelalter: Kulturgeschichte einer Region*, MiSt 43, Berlin, 2013, 91–149.

Elm, S., *Die Macht der Weisheit: Das Bild des Bischofs in der Vita Augustini, des Possidius und anderen spätantiken und frühmittelalterlichen Viten*, SHCT 109, Leiden, 2003.

Head, T., *Hagiography and the Cult of Saints: The Diocese of Orléans, 800–1200*, Cambridge UK, 1990.

Loyen, A., "Le rôle de saint Aignan dans la défense d'Orléans," in: *Académie des Inscriptions et Belles-Lettres: Comptes-rendus de l'Academie des Inscriptions et Belles-Lettres*, Paris, 1969, 64–74.

Renaud, G., "Les miracles de saint Aignan d'Orléans (XIe siècle)," *AnBoll* 94, 1976, 245–274.

Renaud, G., "Saint Aignan et sa legend, les 'Vies' et les 'Miracles'," *BSAHO* 49, 1978, 83–113.

Stickler, T., *Aetius: Gestaltungsspielräume eines Heermeisters im ausgehenden weströmischen Reich*, Vestigia 54, Munich, 2002.

Thompson, E.A., *The Huns*, Oxford, ²1996.

Wirth, G., *Attila: Das Hunnenreich in Europa*, Stuttgart, 1999.

UTA HEIL

Anicetus

Anicetus was a Syrian-born bishop of Rome, the 11th including Peter (→ Peter the Apostle); his pontificate was probably between 150 and 166 CE. His most notable contribution to the development of the church was a discussion with Polycarp, bishop of Smyrna (→ Polycarp of Smyrna), about the date of Easter. The two churchmen took opposing positions on the matter but agreed to differ, and Polycarp was honored by being invited to celebrate Mass in Rome. The concept of papacy at this early stage of the Christian church is contested; some contemporary records, including Anicetus' epitaph, refer to him as "pope," but it might be more accurate to describe his status as "bishop of Rome." He is viewed retrospectively by the Roman Catholic Church as one in the succession of popes and is honored as such in the liturgy of the Mass. Contemporary sources are contaminated by hagiographical rhetoric.

1. Dates and Identity

According to the → *Liber pontificalis*, he was the son of John, and born in the Syrian city of Emesa (modern-day Homs); he held office during the reigns of Emperors Severus and Marcus Aurelius from the consulship of Gallicanus and Vetus through to those of Praesens and Rufinus. His length of pontificate is variously given in L. Duchesne's (1886–1892) chart as between four years (the *Liberian Catalogue*, clearly an incomplete entry as these entries normally include the number of weeks and days of a period of office) and 11 years, four months, and three days. The *Liberian Catalogue* replicates an error from a 3rd-century CE listing and is demonstrably unreliable; for example, it is alone in the early sources as placing Anicetus before Pius, which is clearly refuted by the evidence from → Irenaeus of Lyon and Hegesippus, who were contemporaries with the → pope. → Eusebius of Caesarea lists him as coming after Pius and before Soter. Anicetus' conversations with Polycarp about the date of → Easter help fix the start of his episcopacy at 155 CE at the latest (and probably 150 CE) as Polycarp was martyred on his return to Smyrna in 155 CE. This date is confirmed in turn by a letter from the church in Smyrna to the Christian community of Philomelium.

His name is taken from the Greek word meaning "invincible," and his feast day is usually taken as Apr 17, although *Butler's Lives of the Saints* has it as Apr 20. Eusebius' dating would place his death at 168 CE.

2. Discussions About the Date of Easter

As Polycarp is reputed to have sat at the feet of the apostle John, he was highly regarded by the Roman pontiff. During his visit, possibly with two disciples, Florinus and Irenaeus, the variant approaches to celebrating Easter were discussed (Eus. *Hist. eccl.* 4.14; PG 25). Christians in Asia Minor took a lead from John's Gospel (→ John, Gospel of), which commemorates the death of Jesus Christ on the 14th day of the Jewish month of Nissan (hence the title of Quartodecimans for those who follow this dating) regardless of whether that date is a → Sunday. The Roman church prior to Soter felt that every Sunday represented a resurrection experience and that this would be a more appropriate day to celebrate the passion and → resurrection of Jesus Christ. One theological issue behind the controversy was whether the death or resurrection of Christ was what should be commemorated. Neither Polycarp nor Anicetus was willing to concede, but in the face of such serious challenges to orthodoxy as posed by the gnostics (→ Gnosis/Gnosticism), the scheduling of paschal celebrations remained a topic on which they could agree to differ. The issue was raised again in around 190 CE, when Irenaeus was asked to mediate between Pope Victor I and the Quartodecimans (→ Melito of Sardis) from Asia Minor: the church did not finally decide on this matter of liturgical practice until the Council of → Nicaea in 325 CE. Irenaeus mentions Polycarp coming to Rome "in the time of Anicetus" and making many converts in the face of strong competition from the very active gnostics in Rome at the time. (Iren. *Haer.* 3.3.4) Eusebius mentions the influential Valentinus having arrived in Rome during the episcopacy of Hygenius and "flourishing" under Pius; he was likely still in Rome when Anicetus was on the papal throne (Eus. *Hist. eccl.* 4.11).

3. Other Visitors During Anicetus' Time

Justin Martyr, whose *Apology* dedicated to the emperor failed to save his life, suffered martyrdom in Rome during this period (→ Justin). He is mentioned in Jer. *Vir. ill.* 22.23 (PL 23), immediately after another crucial witness to the time, the historian → Hegesippus, who was sufficiently occupied in refuting heresy to remaining in Rome until Pope Eleutherus (174–189 CE). Eusebius lists no fewer than seven heresies actively circulating (*Hist. eccl.* 5.23). To Hegesippus we owe another debt: a list of bishops up to the time of Anicetus. The word Eusbius gives for this is διαδοχή, generally translated as teaching but at the time also having the meaning of transmission of knowledge, hence the sense of reception rather than instigation of a tradition. If we take this to mean that Hegesippus received a list (rather than made one), this suggests the succession of Roman pontiffs had already been recorded, in a source now lost to us.

4. Religious Practices Attributed to Anicetus

Anicetus is reputed to have issued instructions about the length of hair permitted to clergy. By the time the *Liber pontificalis* was written, tonsuring denoted episcopacy, but his injunction seems simply to mean that other clergy should not have long, "groomed" hair. → Jerome mentions it in *Comm. Ezech.* 44.20. Pseudo-Isidor in a letter spuriously attributed to Anicetus adds the implausible instruction to sport a tonsure *in modum sphaerae radant* ("in the shape of a sphere") suggesting the shape of a crown, but this is anachronistic. Anicetus is recorded as having ordained 19 priests and four deacons and nine bishops "for various places."

Also attributed to Anicetus is the building of a small tomb for Peter and an associated burial ground. This was also attributed to Anacletus (clearly an error of dating, as there is reference to the tropaion mentioned by the Roman priest Gaius in the 2nd cent. CE). Excavations between 1939 and 1949 revealed fresh evidence in the form of bricks dating to the time of Marcus Aurelius, which correlates to Anicetus' not Anacletus' dates. Also, it was not until 230 CE that bishops were routinely buried in the single papal crypt in the catacomb of Calixtus on the Appian Way, forming what E. Duffy calls "the architectural equivalent of the succession lists" (Duffy, 1997, 9). The discovered tomb would have been too small for the number of burials likely if Anicetus had placed the relics of Peter there. The second edition of the *Liber pontificalis* describes Anicetus as a → martyr, but the customary phrase *martyrio coronatur* (crowned with martyrdom) is not used. However he died, it is likely that Anicetus was buried in the cemetery of Calixtus on Apr 16 or 17. In 1604 Pope Clement VIII (1592–1605) moved the relics (then in an urn once used as a sepulcher for Emperor Alexander Severius) to the chapel of the Altemps Palace in the Piazza Navone, Rome. The epitaph refers to him as "pope and martyr."

Bibliography

Altaner, B., *Patrologie: Leben, Schriften und Lehre der Kirchenväter*, Freiburg, 1978.

Barcellona, F.S., "Aniceto," *EdP*, Rome, 2000, 222–224.

Bareille, G., "Anicetus," in: A. Vacant, ed., *DThC*, vol. I, Paris, 1923, 1302–1303.

Bardy, G., "L'église romaine sous le pontificat de saint Anicet," *RSR* 17, 1927, 481–511.

Caspar, E., "Anicetus," in: *GPAHW*, vol. I, Tübingen, 1930, 8–13.

Davis, R., trans., *Liber Pontificalis (The Book of Pontifs)*, Liverpool, 2000.

Doyle, P., ed., *Butler's Lives of the Saints*, 12 vols., Chicago, 1999–2000.

Duchesne, L., ed., *Le Liber Pontificalis, texte, introduction et commentaire*, 2 vols., Paris, 1886–1892.

Duffy, E., *Saints and Sinners: A History of the Popes*, New Haven, 1997

Dufourcq, A., "Anicetus (Pope)," in: A. Baudrillart, ed., *DHGE*, vol. II, Paris, 1912, 204–206.

Flamant, J., "Le Calendrier chrétien: Naissance du comput ecclésiastique," in: J.-M. Mayeur, C. Pietri, A. Vauchex & M. Vernard, eds., *Histoire du christianisme*, vol. I, Paris, 1992–2000, 493–508.

Frend, W.H.C., *The Archaeology of Early Christianity: A History*, London, 1996.

Goggi, P., "Anacletus," in: *EC*, vol. I, Vatican City, 1948–1954, 1126.

Gontard, F., *The Popes*, trans. A.J. Peeler & E.F. Peeler, London, 1964.

Jaffé, P., *Regesta pontificum Romanorum ab Condita Ecclesia ad Annum post Christum Natum*, 2 vols., Leipzig, 1885–1888.

John, E., ed., *The Popes: A Concise Biographical History*, London, 1964.

Kirsch, J.-P., "Anicet," in: A. Baudrillart, ed., *DHGE*, vol. I, Paris, 1912, 280–281.

Kirschbaum, E., *Tombs of St. Peter and St. Paul*, trans. E. Murray, New York, 1959.

Lampe, P., *From Paul to Valentinus*, London, 2003.

Maxwell-Stuart, P.G., *Chronicle of the Popes: The Reign-by-Reign Record of the Papacy from St Peter to the Present*, London, 2002.

Quasten, J.F., *Patrology*, 3 vols., Utrecht,1975.

Reardon, W.J., *The Deaths of the Popes: Comprehensive Accounts, Including Funerals, Burial Places and Epitaphs*, Jefferson, 2004.

Richard, M., "La Question Pascale au deuxieme siècle," *OrSyr* 6, 1961, 179–212.

Schwaiger, G., "Anicet," in: *LThK*, vol. I, Freiberg, 1995, 678.

Vogel, C., *Commentary to Duchesne Liber pontificalis*, Paris, 1955–1957.

Walsh, M., ed., *DCB*, New York, 2001.

Weltin, E.G., "Anicetus," in: *NCE*, vol. I, Washington DC, 2003, 455.

Williams, G.L., *Papal Genealogy: The Families and Descendants of the Popes*, Jefferson, 1998.

HANNAH HUNT

Animals

The reason why Christians were interested in animals and in nature in general is twofold. First, animals are all God's creatures. Second, some Christians adopted the scheme of macrocosm and microcosm: the human person is so integrated into the entire cosmos that a kind of parallelism exists between the macrocosm and the human person as microcosm. As a result of this parallelism, the macrocosm with animals, plants, and so on can teach us a lot about humanity, just as the creation can teach us about the creator (Rom 1:20). Looking at the natural world was a religious affair for Christians. They looked for the spiritual meaning of the physical world with its plants and animals.

1. The Hebrew Bible

The attitude toward animals in early Christian thought is grafted onto the Jewish tradition and the Greek and Latin classical authors.

In the biblical story of → creation (Gen 1:1–2:4a), nature is demythologized. It is stripped of its divine character. For instance, the sun and the moon are not gods, but are created by the one God. Several psalms are hymns to the creator (Pss 29; 104; 147; 148), in which nature is admired as his handiwork.

There is a certain structure or pattern in the created world that allows human beings to learn lessons from nature. Such an analogy or contrast between events in nature and human behavior is found in Prov 6:6–8 and 30:24–31. Small animals can be extremely wise. Therefore one must not be deceived by outward appearances.

According to Gen 1:26–28; 2:19–20; and 9:2–3 and Ps 8, human beings are in charge of the other creatures and must rule over tame and wild animals. Created in the image of God, they are the head of creation. → Philo of Alexandria points out that humans were created last, so that they should find the creation ready to receive them (Philo *Opif.* 77). While Gen 1:29–30 seems to point to a vegetarian diet for humankind, Gen 9.3–4 allows the consumption of flesh. The only exception is "flesh with its blood." Inhumane treatment of animals is forbidden (Deut 22:6–7, 10; 25:4).

The detailed descriptions of animals in the Hebrew Bible betray careful study of the animal kingdom. Different kinds of ruminants (Lev 11:3–7; Deut 14:3–8) and the stages of development of the grasshoppers (Amos 7:1; Nah 3:16–17) were known. Animals that scavenge were loathed. Animals were classified into clean and unclean animals (Lev 11; Deut 14:3–21). It was not allowed to offer or to eat unclean ones. For that matter, the sacrifice of animals was brought up for discussion by some prophets. They emphasized the attitude of mind of the person who sacrifices (Isa 1:11ff.; Jer 6:20; Hos 6:6; Mic 6:6ff.; see Pss 50:8–14; 51:18–19).

A symbolic meaning was ascribed to some animals. The lion is a symbol of power (Gen 49:9–10; Isa 31:4; Jer 49:19). Voluptuous women are compared with the cows of Bashan (Amos 4:1), and the beloved is likened to a dove (Song 2:14). The worm is an example of helplessness (Ps 22:7; Isa 41:14). A lamb symbolizes patience (Isa 53:7). Snake, dragon, and viper are symbols of evil (Gen 3:14f.; Ps 74:13; 91:13), and the eagle is the symbol of renewal (Ps 103:5). Animal imagery of God likens him to a lion, panther, or bear (Hos 5:14; 13:7–8; Lam 3:10; Henry, 1966, 1984–1987).

2. Classical Authors

In classical antiquity writers also tried to gain a better insight into the doings and goings of humankind by a close observation of animal life. We find in Greek epic in Homer already a keen observation of animal life (e.g. Hom. *Il.* 2.87ff.; 3.151f.; 6.506ff.; 17.133ff.; 18.318ff.; *Od.* 17.290ff.). He mentions about a

100 names of animals (Rahn, 1967, 91, 104). When he compares people with animals, it bears mostly upon their distinctive behavior (*Il.* 3.23ff.; 5.136ff.; 11.172ff.; 383). It results in distinguishing human types in the Greek fable and in the famous satire on women by Semonides (7th cent. BCE; Snell, 1955, 258–298).

Homer already points out that the human person has to subdue animal passions (Hom. *Od.* 20.13ff.). Plato agrees with him (Plato *Phaid.* 94d–e). Hesiod fundamentally opposes the reasonable person against animals, because animals do not have any consciousness of justice (Hes. *Op.* 274ff.). The sophist Archelaos (5th cent. BCE) was the first to take the view that civilization separates man from animals (DK 2.46; 60A.4.6).

Philosophers who held the view of metempsychosis turned against the eating of meat: → Porphyry of Tyre in his *De abstinentia*, the young Plutarch (*De esu* 996A), Xenokrates (frgm. 100), and the Pythagoreans. Porphyry also rejected the offering of animals (Porph. *Abst.* 2.5–7; 20–22; 27). Aristotle, however, did not consider the killing of animals as injustice, because there is no community of right between men and beasts (Arist. *Eth. Nic.* 8.11.1161b1–3) and because he considered animals to exist for the sake of man (*Pol.* 1.8.1256b15–22). Except for Xenophon (*Mem.* 4.3.10), this consideration was rarely found before him. However, it is a widespread thought in Hellenism within Stoicism and in Jewish and Christian circles. Lucretius (5.222ff.) and Pliny the Elder (*Nat.* 7.1ff.), on the contrary, opposed this anthropocentrism and thought that man is at a disadvantage in some respects with regard to animals.

Aristotle was the first author who in several writings extensively dealt with biology. It is for him a very integral part of his thought, because it serves to raise the consciousness of humankind of its identity in the whole of the living world. He (or his pupil Theophrastus) asked the question whether human characteristics are also to be found in animals. He thinks that some characteristics are comparable and that there is only a quantitative difference. For others it is a matter of analogy. Animals lack reason, but instead of human intelligence, they have other capabilities, which are identical in action (Arist. *Hist. an.* 7[8].588a17ff.).

In this period unscientific folktales about animals became common. The miraculous anthropomorphic animal tales written under the name of the Aristotelian Eudemos of Rhodos are probably wrongly attributed to him.

The Cynics advocated a natural way of life like that of animals. They criticized laws and civilization. The Epicureans (→ Epicurus/Epicureans) claimed that pleasure is the only thing that is good as an end, and they refer to animals. Therefore they incited to follow the voice of nature. The Stoa observes that any living being starts with self-love, looking for pleasure. Love for offspring to continue its own existence comes next. In this respect humans and animals are similar. But by virtue of intellect, humans are superior to the animals (Cic. *Off.* 1.30.105). In the 1st century CE, Plutarch argued in favor of a humane treatment of animals (Plut. *Cat. Maj.* 5.2.339a).

3. The Earliest Christian Texts

The New Testament frequently refers to animals, especially in comparisons between humans and animals. → John the Baptist and Jesus denounce the Pharisees as a brood of poisonous vipers (Matt 3:7; 12:34). False teachers are compared with irrational animals (Jude 10; 2 Pet 2:12). Men are called to be "wise as snakes and sincere as doves" (Matt 10:16). Elsewhere snakes express hostility, after Gen 3:14–15 (Matt 7:10; Luke 10:19). In Rev 12:9 the ancient snake is identified with the → devil. The devil is compared with a lion who seeks someone he can devour in 1 Pet 5:8. The dog and the swine are symbols of uncleanness (Matt 7:6; see 2 Pet 2:22; Rev 22:15), the fox of cunning and guile (Luke 13:32). Jesus is the Lamb of God (John 1:29; see Rev 5:6; → *Agnus Dei*) and the good shepherd (→ Shepherd, The Good) who lays down his life for the sheep (John 10:11). Christians are sheep, threatened by wolves (John 10:11–13; Matt 10:16; see Acts 20:29).

Philo of Alexandria already had testified that moral or philosophical lessons are taught by the distinction between clean and unclean animals (Philo *Spec.* 4.100ff.; → Philo of Alexandria). In the New Testament, the distinction between clean and unclean is wiped out (Acts 10:9–16). The difference between clean and unclean animals refers according to Barnabas to different types of men (*Barn.* 10; → Barnabas: *Barnabas, Epistle of*).

With regard to animal sacrifices, Jesus emphasizes the attitude of the person who sacrifices, just like the Hebrew Bible prophets did (Matt 5:23f.; 9:13). In Christianity sacrificial terminology was transferred from animals to humans and used to describe personal salvation (Rom 12:1; Ign. *Rom* 4.2; *Mart. Pol.* 14.1).

Paul (→ Paul the Apostle) denounces the worship of animals as inferior religion and opposes animal → sacrifice (1 Cor 10:19–22; Rom 1:23–25; see Wis 15:18–16:1). Christ has made the ultimate sacrifice and made all other sacrifices superfluous. The → Ebionites did not admit the offering of animals and the eating of meat (*Ps.-Clem. H* 3.45; 8.15–17; Schoeps, 1949, 188–196). Paul, however, calls vegetable eaters in Rome "weak in faith" (Rom 14:1–2), and he admits that even the eating of animals sacrificed to idols is not wrong (1 Cor 8:1–8).

4. Later Patristic Sources

The fathers display deep interest in nature, enjoyed it, and were quite well informed. → Basil of Caesarea describes with great devotion the aquatic animals (Bas. *Hex.* 7), the birds (*Hex.* 8), and the land animals (*Hex.* 9), and he gives an almost lyrical description of his rural estate (Bas. *Ep.* 14). His brother Gregory also betrays a remarkable power to describe nature, when he gives a vivid picture of spring after the vicissitudes of winter (*Ep.* 9) or of the loveliness of Vanote (*Ep.* 15). Natural beauty is often praised by the fathers, but it is almost invariably cultivated land, because God planted a garden in Eden as the culmination of his ordering of the chaos (Clem. *Strom.* 1.7.37.1ff.; 7.18.111.1f.). We find an echo of the Hebrew Bible Psalms in the hymns of → Synesius of Cyrene, who summons all creation to the praise of the creator (Syn. *Hym.* 3.190ff.; 4.170). In *Hym.* 3.341–356, we find associations with Ps 148. The contemplation of nature is important as a first stage by which the soul attains to the knowledge of God (Clem. *Strom.* 2.2.5; Or. *Comm. Cant.* 3.14.17; Greg. Nyss. *Beat.* 6).

Christians are of the opinion that nature forms a single divinely created and divinely maintained whole. → Origen points out that the universe is an immense, monstrous animal, held together by the power and reason of God as by one soul (Or. *Princ.* 2.1.3). According to → Nemesius of Emesa, there is a continuity running through the whole of creation: from the inanimate into the plant, from the plant into the irrational animal, from the animal into humankind, and from humankind into the unembodied spiritual beings. Every higher order is rooted in the lower (Nem. *Nat. hom.* 1.3). For this reason the human person was made last after the animals, as nature advanced in an orderly course to perfection (Greg. Nyss. *Hom. opif.* 8.5). Origen compared the human being and cosmos, and he considers the human person as a microcosm (Or. *Hom. Lev.* 5.2), as do → Clement of Alexandria (Clem. *Protr.* 1.5.3), → Gregory of Nyssa (*De anima et resurrectione*; PG 46.28.B), and → Ambrose of Milan (Ambr. *Hex.* 6.55; 75). This conception goes back to, among others, Democritus (frgm. 34) and Aristotle (Arist. *Phys.* 8.2.252b) and became an important part of Stoicism.

Origen and → Celsus were involved in a discussion about whether God has made all things for humankind. Celsus wanted to show that every thing was made just as much for animals as for humanity, but Origen opposed that idea (Or. *Cels.* 4.74–99). The → *Tripartite Tractate* (NHC I,5 104.26–30), Clement (Clem. *Paed.* 2.1.14.4), Ambrose (Ambr. *Hex.* 5.79), and Nemesius (*De natura hominis*) share Origen's view that nature had generated most things for the benefit of humanity.

Following in the footsteps of the Aristotelian and Stoic denial of rationality in animals, the fathers in general taught that animals do not possess reason (Or. *Cels.* 4.74). Origen, however, says also that the instinct comes close to reason itself (Or. *Princ.* 3.1.2–3; Bas. *Hex.* 8.5). Celsus argues that some of the animals have ideas of God. He is thinking, for example, of augury and divination. Origen does not believe any such thing, because God had forbidden omens and → divination (Lev 19:26; Deut 18:10–14; Or. *Cels.* 4.88–89; 95). → Lactantius, who allowed reason to animals, says, quoting Cicero, "what distinguishes humans from animals is the knowledge of God" (Lact. *Inst.* 3.10; see 7.9; Cic. *Leg.* 1.8.24). Like → Augustine of Hippo after him, he thinks that this knowledge does imply reason (Aug. *Enarrat. Ps.* 36.2.13). But it is only one type of reason, not possessed by all rational beings, namely perfect reason or wisdom (Sorabji, 1993, 7–96). The difference between humans and animals is indicated by the human person's erect posture, which enables him

or her to look up to heaven (Ambr. *Hex.* 6.10; 54; 74; Thdt. *Provid.* 3; PG 83.521.B; see Plato *Tim.* 90a).

On biblical and philosophical grounds, Augustine points out that humankind is not linked with animals by communion of law (*societas legis*; Aug. *Mor. Manich.* 2.17.54; 59; see Cic. *Fin.* 3.20.67). Because animals lack reason, they have no rational community with us (Sorabji, 1993, 116–169, 195–205). Therefore it is permitted to kill animals, and God is just in subordinating animals to us (Aug. *Civ.* 1.20; see Ambr. *Noe* 26.94).

However, Christian rituals no longer included any offering of animal flesh. In Christian thinking blood sacrifices were seen as serving the purpose of providing food for evil demons (Or. *Mart.* 45; *Cels.* 8.21, 31; Arn. *Adv. nat.* 7.3; see 1 Cor 10:19–21). → Arnobius of Sicca bases his opposition to animal sacrifice partly on pity for animals because of the cruelty and injustice done to them (*Adv. nat.* 7.9). Instead of animal sacrifices, God asks us the sacrifice of ourselves (Lact. *Inst.* 6.24). So the → martyrs became the new sacrificial victims.

Novatian thought that the only food for the first human beings was fruit and the produce of the trees (→ Novatian). Afterward, through Adam's sin (→ Adam and Eve), the need for the fruit trees was transferred to the produce of the earth. Finally, the use of flesh was added (Nov. *Cib.* 2). The idea that at the beginning humankind did not eat flesh occurs also in Plato (*Leg.* 782c), Ovid (*Metam.* 15.96ff.; *Fast.* 4.395ff.), and Porphyry (*Abst.* 2.5–7; 20–22; 27.5–7). Most Christians, however, ate flesh without scruples (Acts 10:10–15; Clem. *Paed.* 2.1.16.2–3). They relate the distinction between clean and unclean animals to different types of human persons, just like Barnabas did. But Clement of Alexandria forbids the eating of meat that has been offered to idols (*Paed.* 2.1.8.3–4; see Acts 15:29). Origen argues against Celsus that all the animals that are regarded as having prophetic powers by the Egyptians and others are unclean (Or. *Cels.* 4.93). The eating of meat was sometimes seen as fostering sexual drives. Therefore the desert father → Antony the Great did not eat meat (Athan. *Vit. Ant.* 7).

For many Christians nature had an allegorical meaning. A moral or theological lesson could be learned from nature. Basil's and Ambrose's homilies on the Hexaemeron are interspersed with moral lessons borrowed from the life of animals. They joined the moralizing tendency in Pliny and Aelian, who alleged that animals are sometimes better than humans. Origen for instance refers to the stork that returns affection and brings food to its parents. It puts human beings to shame in the matter of paying their debt of gratitude to their parents (Or. *Cels.* 4.98). On the other hand, the gnostic → Basilides spoke about spirits attached to the rational soul like wolves, apes, lions, and goats, whose properties assimilate the lusts of the soul to the likeness of the animals (Clem. *Strom.* 2.20.112.1). Base passions and irrational impulses are like wild, savage beasts (*Teachings of Silvanus* NHC VII,4 85.29–86.8; 87.27–88.6; 93.34–94.18). In the *Lives of the Desert Fathers*, internal passions and external powers like demons were conceived of in the shape of animals and animal hybrids. Other animals, however, behaved in a pious way, for instance when two lions assisted Antony to bury Paul of Thebes (Jer. *Vit. Paul.* 16; see *Acts of Paul and Thecla* 28, 33).

An anthology from the 2nd century CE that played an important part in the propagation of animal allegories was the *Physiologus*. It had its origin in Alexandria. The original text had 48 chapters, including some about plants and stones. The unknown author used the stock of animal stories from Greek literature. He included accounts of mythical animals (phoenix, ant-lion, unicorn, sirens, and centaurs), because they also have a message. By making statements about animals, he explains different aspects of Christian faith, especially about the struggle against the → devil and demons (→ Demonology/Demons). Important is the similarity between nature and the history of salvation. Therefore Augustine places also the knowledge of nature in the service of theology. Even when the saying is not true, it serves the truth (Aug. *Doctr. chr.* 2.16.24–18.28; *Enarrat. Ps.* 66.10).

5. Reception

In the 7th century CE, → Isidore of Seville made use of these classical sources and patristic authors in his writing *On the Nature of Things* and in his encyclopedia called *Etymologiae*. With regard to the animal metaphors, they played an important part in the allegorical exegesis from Philo until far into the

Middle Ages. The influence of the *Physiologus* has been very important in this history. It was a source of inspiration for Christian art, medieval bestiaries, and later literature.

Historiography

R. Sorabji (1993) has posed the question concerning the roles we conventionally assign to animals. The ancient debate seemed to be driven by an Aristotelian and Stoic view of the nature of humankind, that only humankind has reason or belief. According to him Augustine incorporated the Stoic view into Christianity. It accounts for the relative complacency of western Christian tradition about the killing of animals. But there were also many philosophers who defended animals. R. Sorabji rethinks in his book the origins of the western debate about animal minds and human morals.

I.S. Gilhus (2006) started her study of animals in ancient religion as part of a cross-disciplinary research project about the construction of Christian identity in antiquity. It led to her book about changing attitudes toward animals in Greek, Roman, and early Christian ideas.

Bibliography

Broek, R. van den, *The Myth of the Phoenix According to Classical and Early Christian Traditions*, Leiden, 1971.

Dierauer, U., *Tier und Mensch im Denken der Antike: Studien zur Tierpsychologie, Anthropologie und Ethik*, Amsterdam, 1977.

Fonck, L., "Hieronymi scientia naturalis exemplis illustratur," *Bib.* 1, 1920, 481–499.

French, R., *Ancient Natural History: Histories of Nature*, London, 1994.

Gilhus, I.S., *Animals, Gods and Humans: Changing Attitudes to Animals in Greek, Roman and Early Christian Ideas*, London, 2006.

Grant, R.M., *Early Christians and Animals*, London, 1999.

Hiechelheim, F.M., & T. Elliott, "Das Tier in der Vorstellungswelt der Griechen," *StGen* 20, 1967, 85–89.

Henry, M.-L., "Tier," in: B. Reicke & L. Rost, eds., *BHH*, vol. III, Göttingen, 1966, 1984–1987.

Murphy, M.G., *Nature Allusions in the Works of Clement of Alexandria*, PatST 65, Washington DC, 1941.

Rahn, H., "Das Tier in der homerischen Dichtung," *StGen* 20, 1967, 90–105.

Schoeps, H.J., *Theologie und Geschichte des Judenchristentums*, Tübingen, 1949.

Snell, B., *Die Entdeckung des Geistes: Studien zur Entstehung des europäischen Denkens bei den Griechen*, Hamburg, ³1955.

Sorabji, R., *Animal Minds and Human Morals: The Origins of the Western Debate*, London, 1993.

Wallace-Hadrill, D.S., *The Greek Patristic View of Nature*, Manchester, 1968.

FRED LEDEGANG

Annunciation → Mary

Anointing

Anointing is the application of oil to the body to effect a spiritual, social, or physical change. Early Christian use of oils was influenced by the biblical tradition, especially the Hebrew Bible, and by contemporary Greco-Roman practice; together these provided the theological and ritual models exploited by the Fathers. The principal Christian ritual use of oil was in connection with baptism, although the type of oil, its position in the ritual, and its effects are highly varied within and between regions. "Anointing" may also be used metaphorically to refer to the gift of the Holy Spirit or divine blessing without the application of oil. There is evidence of the blessing and use of oil for the anointing of the sick in the early church, and of the popular use of holy oils independently of the clergy. Later Christian use would add to this anointings of people at ordination and at coronations, and of churches as part of their consecration; these are unconnected to baptismal anointings.

1. Antecedents to Early Christian Practice

a. Greco-Roman Practice

Oil was used in connection with bathing practices and medicinally throughout the late antique world. For both men and women, the social practice of bathing involved a full body anointing prior to exercise, and then after bathing another anointing with perfumed oil (Yegül, 1992, 12–16). Oil was also widely used medicinally but could be ingested rather than applied externally.

b. The Bible

In the Hebrew Bible, the anointing of priests (Lev 8:11–12) and kings (1 Sam 10:1), as well as of objects and places (Exod 30:23–33, 40) signified a setting apart, divine approval, or sanctification, resulting in a new status or purpose. The practices are varied depending on the situation, but the anointings were performed by an authorized person in a ritual context. In some instances, a reference to anointing may be metaphorical (Isa 61:1–3). In the New Testament and early Christian apocryphal texts, we increasingly find anointing with oil as part of healing rituals for physical ailments and in connection with demonic expulsion (Mark 6:13; Jas 5:14–15). The term is also applied metaphorically to describe the descent of the → Holy Spirit on Jesus at his baptism, and to denote the relationship of Χριστιανοί to the Christ (see 2 Cor 1:21).

2. Baptismal Anointing

a. Pre-Nicene Christianity

The rather scant pre-Nicene evidence for baptismal anointings exhibits considerable ritual variety. The 3rd-century CE *Acts of Thomas* (→ Thomas the Apostle) refers to pre-baptismal anointings of the head alone, of the head and the whole body, to baptism without anointing, and to initiatory anointings without water baptism. This variety within the same text has been explained by stages in ritual evolution (Winkler, 1978), or that a double anointing was only applied to women (Meyers, 1988, 41), or that it reflects parallel traditions (Bradshaw, 2010). For the West, the limited 3rd-century CE evidence points to a post-baptismal anointing: in North Africa, → Tertullian attests to an anointing of the head alone with reference to Aaron (Tert. *Bapt.* 7), while the gift of the Holy Spirit is associated with a separate laying-on of hands (*Bapt.* 8). It must be said that the evidence is so patchy that it is not possible to say much more than that anointing was part of most baptismal rites, but there was no consistency in either ritual or significance.

b. Post-Nicene Christianity

In the post-Nicene period, the more abundant liturgical material testifies to the increased importance attached to the rituals of anointing amidst an elaboration of the baptismal rites more generally (see "Baptism"). We also find that, although anointing forms part of all rites, its position, significance, and ritual application was extremely diverse. In order to understand the precise role that a particular anointing played in the initiatory process; these factors should be taken into account:

- the number of anointings in the whole rite;
- the position of an anointing in relation to the water immersion and any other anointings;
- the location of its administration in the baptismal space;
- the type of oil used and how it was prepared for use (e.g. whether by a consecratory prayer or not);
- the location and manner of its administration on the body of the baptismal candidate;
- the prayers accompanying its administration;
- the status of the minister administering the oil;
- the function and theological interpretation of the anointing ritual within the whole initiatory process, and its dominant theology.

By such precise evaluation of each instance of anointing, subject to the comprehensiveness of the sources, it is possible to discern the distinctiveness of regional baptismal practices and to consider the influence of one region upon another (see Day, 2007, 3–10, 65–77, 105–119). Such attentiveness to the ritual pattern reveals that it is not possible to use one example as representative of all, nor is it so easy to categorize them, as the following examples indicate.

The baptismal liturgy of Jerusalem at the end of the 4th century CE had two anointings, according to the account of → Cyril of Jerusalem in *Mystagogical Catecheses* (2; 3; see Day, 2007, 66–68, 107–111; *Mystagogical Catecheses* could also be attributed to John of Jerusalem). The first occurred after the renunciation of Satan (→ Devil) and the confession of faith, after the candidates had entered the baptistery and removed their clothing. Olive oil that had been exorcized was applied to the whole body by an unknown minister (Cyr.Jer. *Cat. Myst.* 2.3); there was no provision for women deaconesses (→ Deacon/Deaconess) to anoint the women (Piédagnel, 2004, 107n5). The effect was to drive away all trace of Satan and → sin. A second anointing occurred after the water baptism using μύρον, a perfumed olive oil consecrated by an epiclesis of the Holy Spirit (*Cat. Myst.* 3.3) It was applied by an unspecified minister, to selected bodily organs only: the forehead; the ears; the nostrils; and the chest (*Cat. Myst.* 3.4). This anointing ritually conveyed the Holy Spirit, although the biblical verses that are applied to each location make no reference to this.

In Antioch, the rite described by → John Chrysostom has two anointings before the water baptism, and none after. The first occurred after the confession of faith and retains that position even when the preliminary rituals have been detached from the rest of the rite (Chrys. *Catech. illum.* 2.22; see Green, 1962; Wenger, 1970, 146n1). It was probably administered by the → bishop who signed the forehead with a cross and recited a Trinitarian formula. The "spiritual Myron" does not convey the Holy Spirit, but instead is prophylactic in the battle against Satan by the "athletes of Christ" (*Catech. illum.* 2.23). The second anointing immediately preceded entry into the font; it was a whole body anointing of naked candidates using the same oil by lesser clergy or even deaconesses (*Catech. illum.* 2.24; on deaconess see Wenger, 1970, 92–93; Piédagnel, 1990, 53; Bradshaw, 2012). This anointing also served as protection against "the enemy." It has been suggested that this double anointing resulted from a separation of the renunciation and confession of faith from the immersion, or that they had subtly different significance for immediate and future protection from Satan (see Finn, 1967, 119; Wenger, 1970, 147n1; Bradshaw, 2010; Day, 2007, 70–72).

In late 4th-century CE Milan, Ambrose also knew of two anointings (→ Ambrose of Milan). The first occurred on entering the baptistery and before the renunciation of Satan; it was administered by a "Levite" (deacon) and presbyter (→ Priest/Presbyter) and its purpose was to make the candidates athletes of Christ (Ambr. *Sacr.* 1.4) the assumption is that this was a whole body anointing and that it was not theologically significant (Bradshaw, 2010). The second immediately followed the water baptism; it was administered by the *sacerdos* (i.e. the bishop; *Sacr.* 3.4) who applied μύρον/chrism to the head only, the location of wisdom. Its purpose was for "everlasting life" (*Sacr.* 2.24), but it also imitated the priestly anointing of Aaron (Ambr. *Myst.* 6.29–30).

The Egyptian *Canons of Hippolytus* have one pre-immersion anointing and two post-immersion anointings using oils blessed by the bishop at the start of the rite (see Day, 2007, 74, 116–117, 128–129). A pre-immersion anointing with the oil of exorcism administered by a presbyter occurs after the renunciation of Satan and before the confession of faith; as the candidates had already removed their clothes by this stage it may have been a whole body anointing (*Can. Hipp.* 19). The first post-immersion anointing occurs when the candidate leaves the font; it is administered by a presbyter with the "oil of thanksgiving" who signs the forehead, mouth, and breast, and then anoints the whole body, face, and head accompanied by a Trinitarian formula (*Can. Hipp.* 19). The second occurs in church administered with a signing on the forehead only (with the cross?) by the bishop using the same oil of thanksgiving; it follows the laying on of hands and a prayer for the gift of the Holy Spirit (*Can. Hipp.* 19).

This variety has received a number of interpretations based upon ritual and theological evolution. G. Winkler suggested that the adoption of Pauline death-mystery typology caused the pre-immersion rituals to take on exorcistic, apotropaic, or prophylactic emphases which replaced earlier ideas of the anointing as imitation of Christ's anointing by the Holy Spirit in the Jordan and of Hebrew Bible priestly and kingly anointings. Consequently, a post-immersion anointing was required for the ritual gift of the Spirit (Winkler, 1978, 24–45). S.P. Brock, studying the Syrian evidence, suggested that the original meaning of the pre-immersion anointing was transferred first to the water and then to the post-immersion anointing, when in the 4th century CE

> Christ's baptism becomes the conceptual model for the baptismal rite *as a whole*, and attention is now paid to the fact that the Holy Spirit only appeared after Christ had gone up from the water. (Brock, 1981, 221)

Both in the New Testament and in patristic texts σφραγίς and its cognates are used with reference to the "seal with the Holy Spirit." The sealing is to be understood as a sign of ownership, setting apart or making complete (Lampe, 1967). In some cases sealing clearly refers to a physical anointing, even a signing with the cross using oil; however, in many more its use is metaphorical. Cyril of Jerusalem makes frequent references to sealing by the Holy Spirit in baptism in the *Catechetical Lectures* without once indicating any ritual form for doing that (see Day, 2011, 1192–1194).

c. Historiography

There has been extensive research into early Christian baptism since the 1960s, and except for L.L. Mitchell's monograph (1966), the study of baptismal anointings has been incorporated into these larger surveys. Earlier scholarship tended to harmonize the variant sources and/or attempt to provide justification for later liturgical practice, particularly the link between post-baptismal anointing in the West and the sacrament of confirmation (see Leclercq, 1935, vol. XII, 2116–2130; and later, Austin, 1985), or to provide background for the revised Roman Catholic initiation rites, especially that for adults (see Yarnold, 1994). Recent scholarship emphasizes the distinctiveness of the regional traditions represented in the sources and that within one region a variety of practices could co-exist (see Bradshaw, 2010; Day, 1999; 2007). The most significant surveys of early baptismal practices, including anointing, are D. Hellholm (2011), E. Ferguson (2009), M.E. Johnson (2007), and B.D. Spinks (2006), and to these should be added the monographs on individual texts and authors. Only the highly varied Syriac tradition has received focused studies of its baptismal anointings discussed extensively by S.P. Brock (1977), B. Varghese (1989), and G. Winkler (1978). The most useful discussion of the *status quaestionis* is by P.F. Bradshaw (2010).

3. Anointing for Healing

a. Early Christian Practice

The use of oil in healing among the earliest Christians followed its use more generally in late antique Mediterranean societies. The New Testament attests to the importance of healing activities among the followers of Jesus, but anointing is only mentioned explicitly in Mark 6:13 and Jas 5:14–16. In subsequent centuries the sources remain silent about whether anointing continued to be practiced, either because it was not ritually performed (Ferngren, 2009, 68), or because it was conducted in private and therefore not discussed (Ronzani, 2007, 44), or because it was too obvious to mention.

From the 4th century CE, evidence exists for the widespread ritual use of oil for healing which should be set in the context of many other healing rituals. The euchological sources indicate the range of theological and practical meanings attached to the oil and its administration, and elsewhere we find instructions about when and how it is to be administered. From Egypt in the first part of the 4th century CE, the *Sacramentary* of Serapion of Thmuis includes a prayer which refers to the types of malaise for which the blessed oil was to be efficacious:

> Father of our Lord and Savior Jesus Christ [...] we implore you that healing power of your only-begotten may be sent out from heaven upon this oil. May it become to those who are anointed [...] for a rejection of every disease and every sickness, for an amulet warding off every demon, for a departing of every unclean spirit, for a taking away of every evil spirit, for a driving away of all fever and shiverings and every weakness, for good grace and forgiveness of sins, for a medicine of life and salvation, for health and wholeness of soul, body, spirit, for perfect strength. (Ser. *Sacr.* 17; Johnson, 1995, 67).

The *Canons of Hippolytus*, also Egyptian from the early part of the 4th century CE, state that the anointing should take place in church unless the person is too sick, in which case the clergy are to visit the home (*Can. Hipp.* 21; see Bradshaw, 1987; Barrett-Lennard, 2005).

From the year 416 CE, → Innocent I, bishop of Rome, responding to liturgical questions from Decentius of Gubbio instructs that oils for the sick should be blessed by the bishop, although its administration can be left to priests and the laity (Inn. *Ep.* 25; see Connell, 2002, 46–47). One hunderd years later, Caesarius of Arles also insisted that the oil be obtained from the church:

> As soon as some infirmity overtakes him, a sick man should receive the Body and Blood of Christ, humbly and devoutly ask the presbyters for blessed oil, and anoint his body with it. (Caesar. *Hom.* 13.3; FaCh vol. XXXI, 77)

The laity might also anoint themselves with oil obtained from the holy places or by contact with → relics. There is considerable material evidence of ampullae from pilgrimage sites, and of reliquaries with spouts for pouring oil in and out via contact with the martyrs' bones. The oil was seen as a medium for divine power effected through contact with holy matter and thus it retained its sacral character even if self-administered.

b. Historiography

L. Larson-Miller's studies of Christian medicinal anointing as a distinct topic are somewhat unique (Larson-Miller, 2005); more commonly, anointing is referred to in historical surveys of general healing practices (Barrett-Lennard, 1994; Porterfield, 2005; Ferngren, 2009). Additionally, a number of studies place the early Christian historical material in the context of the development of rites for the sick in different ecclesial traditions: P. Meyendorff (2009) for the eastern orthodox church; J. Ziegler (1987) for the Roman Catholic; M. Dudley and G. Rowell (2008) produced a collection of essays surveying the historical and contemporary use of oils in a number of Christian traditions.

4. Consecratory Anointing

Although the Hebrew Bible provided models for the anointing of priests and kings, these are not in evidence in the early Christian church, even though the relevant biblical passages were applied metaphorically to all Christians. Christian Roman emperors were not anointed. The first evidence in the West is of the Pépin the Short in 750 CE (Minea, 2016, 129). In the Byzantine Empire, Basil I may have been anointed in 867 CE, although the *Book of Ceremonies* of Constantine Porphyrogenitus (945–959 CE) makes no mention of it (Minea, 2016, 132).

P.F. Bradshaw has shown that the anointing of the Jewish high priest, derived from the kingly anointing and following the model of Aaron's consecration as priest (Lev 8:12), was extended to other priests (see Bradshaw, 2014, 4). This priestly anointing was used metaphorically by early Christian writers in relation to the baptismal anointing, and there is no evidence for its use in ordination in the early centuries. Western liturgical evidence for the anointing of priests (their hands only) appears in the 9th-century CE *Missale Francorum*, and it became part of Roman practice only from the 10th century CE (Lindblad, 1984, 18–19; see also Ellard, 1933, 18); the eastern church never anointed bishops or presbyters at their ordination (see Bradshaw, 2014, 39–105).

Bibliography

Austin, G., *Anointing with the Spirit: The Rite of Confirmation, the Use of Oil and Chrism*, New York, 1985.

Barrett-Lennard, R.J.S., *Christian Healing After the New Testament: Some Approaches to Illness in the Second, Third, and Fourth Centuries*, Lanham, 1994.

Barrett-Lennard, R.J.S., "The Canons of Hippolytus and Christian Concern with Illness, Health, and Healing," *JECS* 13, 2005, 137–164.

Bradshaw, P.F., *The Canons of Hippolytus*, Bramcote, 1987.

Bradshaw, P.F., "Varieties of Early Christian Baptismal Anointing," in: M. Ross & S. Jones, eds., *The Serious Business of Worship: Essays in Honour of Bryan D. Spinks*, London, 2010, 65–76.

Bradshaw, P.F., "Women and Baptism in the Didascalia Apostolorum," *JECS* 20, 2012, 641–645.

Bradshaw, P.F., *Rites of Ordination: Their History and Theology*, London, 2014.

Brock, S.P., "Syrian Baptismal Ordines (with Special Reference to the Anointings)," *StLi* 12, 1977, 177–183.

Brock, S.P., "The Transition to a Post-Baptismal Anointing in the Antiochene Rite," in: B. Spinks, ed., *The Sacrifice of Praise: Studies on the Themes of Thanksgiving and Redemption in the Central Prayers of the Eucharistic and Baptismal Liturgies*, Rome, 1981, 215–225.

Connell, M., *Church and Worship in Fifth-Century Rome: The Letter of Innocent I to Decentius of Gubbio*, Cambridge UK, 2002.

Day, J., *Baptism in Early Byzantine Palestine 325–451*, 43, Cambridge UK, 1999.

Day, J., *The Baptismal Liturgy of Jerusalem: Fourth and Fifth Century Evidence from Palestine, Syria, and Egypt*, Aldershot, 2007.

Day, J., "The Catechetical Lectures of Cyril of Jerusalem: A Source for the Baptismal Liturgy of Mid-Fourth Century Jerusalem," in: D.Hellholm, ed., *Ablution, Initiation, and Baptism: Late Antiquity, Early Judaism, and Early Christianity*, BZNW 176, Berlin, 2011, 1179–1204.

Dudley, M., & G. Rowell, eds., *The Oil of Gladness: Anointing in the Christian Tradition*, London, ²2008.

Ellard, G., *Ordination Anointings in the Western Church before 1000 AD*, Cambridge MA, 1933.

Ferguson, E., *Baptism in the Early Church: History, Theology, and Liturgy in the First Five Centuries*, Grand Rapids, 2009.

Ferngren, G.B., *Medicine and Health Care in Early Christianity*, Baltimore, 2009.

Finn, T.M., *The Liturgy of Baptism in the Baptismal Instructions of St. John Chrysostom*, Washington DC, 1967.

Green, H.B., "The Significance of the Pre-Baptismal Seal in St John Chrysostom," *StPatr* 6, 1962, 84–90.

Hellholm, D., *Ablution, Initiation, and Baptism: Late Antiquity, Early Judaism, and Early Christianity*, BZNW 176, Berlin, 2011.

Johnson, M.E., *The Prayers of Sarapion of Thmuis: A Literary, Liturgical, and Theological Analysis*, OCA 249, Rome, 1995.

Johnson, M.E., *The Rites of Christian Initiation: Their Evolution and* Interpretation, Collegeville, ²2007.

Lampe, G.W.H., *The Seal of the Spirit: A Study in the Doctrine of Baptism and Confirmation in the New Testament and the Fathers*, London, ²1967.

Larson-Miller, L., *The Sacrament of the Anointing of the Sick*, Collegeville, 2005.

Leclercq, H., "Onction," in: *DACL*, vol. XII, Paris, 1935, 2116–2128.

Lindblad, N.H., *Anointing as an Ordination Problem*, Lund, 1984.

Meyendorff, P., *The Service of the Anointing of the Sick*, Crestwood, 2009.

Meyers, R., "The Structure of the Syrian Baptismal Rite," in: P.F. Bradshaw, ed., *Essays in Early Eastern Initiation*, Bramcote, 1988, 31–43.

Minea, R., "An Aspect of the Symbolism of the Political Power during the Middle Ages: The Anointment," *Anastasis* 2, 2016, 126–136.

Mitchell, L.L., *Baptismal Anointing*, London, 1966.

Piédagnel, A., *John Chrysostom: Trois catéchèses baptismales*, SC 366, Paris, 1990.

Piédagnel, A., *Cyrille de Jérusalem: Catéchèses mystagogiques*, SC 126 bis, Paris, ²2004.

Porterfield, A., *Healing in the History of Christianity*, New York, 2005.

Ronzani, R., *Christian Healing: The Anointing of the Sick*, Nairobi, 2007.

Spinks, B.D., *Early and Medieval Rituals and Theologies of Baptism: From the New Testament to the Council of Trent*, Aldershot, 2006.

Varghese, B., *Les onctions baptismales dans la tradition syrienne*, CSCO.Sub. 82, Louvain, 1989.

Wenger, A., *Jean Chrysostome: Huit catéchèses baptismales inédites*, SC 50, Paris, ²1970.

Winkler, G., "The Original Meaning and Implications of the Prebaptismal Anointing," *Worship* 52, 1978, 24–45.

Yarnold, E.J., *The Awe-Inspiring Rites of Initiation: The Origins of the RCIA*, Edinburgh, ²1994.

Yegül, F., *Baths and Bathing in Classical Antiquity*, New York, 1992.

Ziegler, J., *Let Them Anoint the Sick*, Collegeville, 1987.

JULIETTE J. DAY

Anonymous Apollinarist/ Apollinarian Forgeries

There is evidence going back to antiquity of the circulation of Apollinarian texts under the name of characters of proven faith, whose writings or biographical events could somehow justify this attribution (Leontius of Byzantium, *Adversus frauds Apollinaristarum*; PG 86b.1948.A–B; 1969.A–B; 1973.C; Caspari, 1879, 120–123; Voisin, 1901, 152–161; Capone, 2013, 315–317). Among them is Pope Julius I (337–352 CE), defender of → Athanasius of Alexandria against the party of Eusebius of Nicomedia (Studer, 2007, 2317–2318). The question of the attribution to Julius of *Encyclion* (*CPG* 3735) and of other Apollinarian documents has been discussed by H. Lietzmann (1904, 158–163), who offers two explanations: the orthodoxy of the pope and reasons of ecclesiastical policy that elude us.

Encyclion, addressed to the bishops of the Catholic Church, contains a brief profession of faith that in the first part is based on the quotation of Hos 11:9, in which God promises not to destroy Jacob (a rather rare textual variant, attested also in Eus. *Dem. ev.* 5.22.1, in place of the more common "Ephraim"), because he is God and not man. The biblical text is understood in a Christological way by the anonymous Apollinarists but it does not seem to be used in other Apollinarian texts, apart from in a fragment transmitted in Syriac under the name Felix, bishop of Rome (Caspari, 1879, 123; Lietzmann 1904, 319–321; Spinelli, 2007, 1926–1927). The fact that this text, which contains the same variant "Jacob" instead of "Ephraim," is attributed to a Roman pope may perhaps throw some light on the presence of Apollinarists in Rome (Capone, 2011, 462–469). In the second part of *Encyclion*, individual points of the profession of faith are listed. Among them is the expression μίαν ὑπόστασιν καὶ ἕν πρόσωπον τοῦ θεοῦ λόγου καὶ τῆς ἐκ Μαρίας σαρκός, ("one hypostasis and one prosopon of God the *logos* and of the flesh of Mary") which is a clear indication of Appollinarian Christology (Voisin, 1901, 212).

Historiography

The text, printed in the Patrologia Latina (8.876AB) and published by H. Lietzmann (1904, 292–293), is also known in a Latin version (Schwartz, 1937, 39), a Syrian one (Fleming & Lietzmann, 1904, 41–42), and an Armenian one by Timothy Aelurus (Ter-Mekerttschian & Ter-Minassiantz, 1908, 264–265), as well as in a fragment in Arabic (Achelis, 1897, 284–285).

Bibliography

Achelis, H., ed., *Hippolyt's kleinere exegetische und homiletische Schriften*, Leipzig, 1897.

Bellini, E., ed., *Su Cristo: Il grande dibattito nel quarto secolo*, Milan, 1977.

Capone, A., "Apollinarismo e geografia ecclesiastica: Luoghi e forme della polemica," in: *AN*, vol. IX, Bari, 2011, 457–473.

Capone, A., "Apollinaris, Basil and Gregory of Nyssa," *ZAC* 17/2, 2013, 315–331.

Caspari, C.P., *Alte und neue Quellen zur Geschichte des Taufsymbols und der Glaubensregel*, Christiania, 1879.

Cavalcanti, E., "Anonimo apollinarista (encyclion)," in: *NDPAC*, vol. I, Genoa, 2006, 325–326.

Fleming, J., & H. Lietzmann, *Apollinaristische Schriften syrisch*, AGWG 7/4, Berlin, 1904.

Geerard, M., *CPG*, vol. II, Turnhout, 1974.

Lietzmann, H., *Apollinaris von Laodicea und seine Schule*, Tübingen, 1904.

Schwartz, E., ed., ACO, vol. II/2/1, Berlin, 1937.

Spinelli, M., "Felice I papa," in: *NDPAC*, vol. II, Genoa, 2007, 1926–1927.

Studer, B., "Giulo I papa," in: *NDPAC*, vol. II, Genoa, 2007, 2317–2318.

Ter-Mekerttschian, K., & E. Ter-Minassiantz, eds., *Timotheus Älurus' des Patriarchen von Alexandrien Widerlegung der auf der Synode zu Chalcedon festgesetzten Lehre*, Leipzig, 1908.

Voisin, G., *L'apollinarisme: Étude historique, littéraire et dogmatique sur le début des controverses christologiques au IVe siècle*, Louvain, 1901.

ALESSANDRO CAPONE

Anthony (Poet)

The *Carmen Antonii* is a characteristic example of early Jewish-Christian apologetic literature (→ Apologetics), likely dating from the end of the 2nd century CE (in the zfollowing explanation of this poem the serial succession of lines has been followed). Anthony declares he examined "all sects" and "found nothing better than to believe in Christ" (*sed nihil inveni melius quam credere Christo*). Although well educated and instructed in classical literature and religion, Anthony chooses the style of Jewish wisdom literature. The poem provides an authentic example of early Christian apologetic poetry. Some elements of this poem are recognizable in Tertullian's *Apologeticum* (cap. 15) and in Minucius Felix' *Octavius*.

At the onset of the poem, Anthony imitates the biblical book of Ecclesiastes (Eccl. 1:13, 14) *plurima quaesivi, per singula quaeque cuccurri* (I have searched out many things, all I saw in detail in a rush), apparently with the intention of proving the verity of the Christian faith and imitating Solomon and Christ as teachers of wisdom. Through the use of the dactylic hexameter, which Anthony utilizes throughout Carmen, → David the king is presented as his example, although in reality Anthony makes use of classical poetry (ll. 6–7): *David ipse chelyn modulata voce rogavit, Quo nos exemplo pro magnis parva canemus* (David himself conducted a lyre to conduct his voice. He is an example for us. But we shall sing only small songs instead of great ones). The classical poet → Virgil, who frequently used dactylic hexameters, is only once quoted in the poem. Nevertheless, in his imitation of Virgil's style in this poem, Anthony demonstrates a great appreciation for this classical author. Implicit and explicit references to the Torah (→ Law/Decalogue/Torah) and the exhortation to follow the commandments at the beginning of this poem are remarkable (l. 8) *dicentes quae sunt fugienda, sequenda, colenda* (Saying what has to be fled from, followed and adored [Vergilian quotation?]). The history of the exodus is presented at the very beginning of the poem, and different episodes of the journey of the Jewish nation through the desert are briefly mentioned, such as the provision of manna and the water from the rock (ll. 14–15) *Et cui desertis nihilum quoque defuit agris, Manna cui e caelo et fons de rupe cucurrit* (And for him nothing was lacking in desert places, for him Manna descended from heaven and water from the rock). The way the Jewish people imitate pagan religion through the adoration of self-made simulacra, especially in the adoration of the golden calf, is used by Anthony as a bridge to start an attack on pagan religion. Pagan practices, such as making idols – intended for worship and healing –, the aimless sacrifice of people, and the consultation of oracles are criticized. Anthony's attack on the pagan gods is a serious one. At first Jupiter is criticized.

The consultation of gods, *calido in pulmone* (with a hot lung), the creation and the adoration of statues, and the images of coins are products of human fantasy. Philosophers are deprived of logic (l. 32). With etymological and rhetorical skills the philosophy of the "Cynici" is criticized. They are people who do not have logic and possess idle wisdom. Embarrassed by their inquiry into the substance of the → soul, the fanatic disciples of the uncertain dogma of Plato highly esteem his book about the soul. This book contains – according to Anthony – in contrast with the promising title, "nothing which is certain." In his criticism of the *Fysici*, (philosophers living a life close to nature), one of these men, equipped with a stick and a cup, is considered too extravagant. When seeing a farmer drinking water with his hands, this *fysicus* threw away his drinking vessel and broke his cup. The story has a parallel in Diogenes Laertius, in his *Vita Diogenis*, which does not speak, however, about a farmer but about a child.

After rhetorical questions concerning the relevance of different sanctuaries (l. 52 *Quid dicam diversa sacra? Et Dis atque Deabus condita templa loquar?* Why should I speak about different sanctuaries? And speak about the temples that are dedicated to the male and female deities?), Anthony continues the poem with an analysis of Jupiter's behavior. The negative evaluation of this behavior serves as a kind of gauge for the reliability of the pagan god. For Christians, the immoral behavior of Jupiter is unacceptable for a real god or goddess. For that reason, seen through the eyes of Christians, Jupiter is considered to be an improper and non-existent deity and no match for the threefold God (→ Trinity); however, seen through the eyes of the Pagans, Jupiter is an eternal deity who must be worshipped. A connection with the *Octavius* of → Minucius Felix is evident. Using Virgil as his source, Anthony characterizes especially Jupiter as an incestuous god. The given description of Juno as *Soror et Conjunx* accentuates the incestuous attitude of Jupiter, as illustrated in the following Virgilian-like passage:

> Esse volunt, quam Vergilius notat auctor eorum
> Dicendo: Et Soror, et Conjunx. Plus de Jove fertur,
> Et natam stuprasse suam, fratrique dedisse;
> Utque alias caperet, propriam variasse figuram;

Nunc serpens, nunc taurus erat nunc cygnus et
 arbos:
Seque immutando, qualis fuit indicat ipse,
Plus aliena sibi quam propria forma placebat.
Turpius his aquilam finxit, puerique nefandos
Venit in amplexus. Quid dicit turba colentum?

People like it that Hera is the spouse and Jupiter's
 own sister,
as Virgil, their author contends that she is.
And they tell still more about Jupiter himself.
That he assaulted his daughter and gave her to
 her brother,
that he had other women and changed his own
 shape.
What is more scandalous/ shameful than stories like these?
Sometimes he is a snake, sometimes a bull, at
 other times he is a swan or a tree.
By changing himself he shows what/how he
 himself is.
He preferred another shape to his own.
What is more shameful than this:
He created an eagle to secure an ungodly
 embrace of a boy?

People react with either negation or acceptance
(l. 63 *quid dicit turba colentum? Aut neget esse Jovem,
aut fateatur dedecus istud*. And what is the reaction
of the multitude of admirers? Either a negation or
an acknowledgement that this is a shame). Nevertheless, the adoration of Jupiter is not impeded by
his bad reputation (r. 66 *Sacra Jovi faciunt et Juppiter
optime dicunt*). Interestingly, for that very reason, the
kingdom is entrusted to Janus, the first king of Rome,
instead of Jupiter, who is adored (l. 67 *Huncque
rogent et Jane Pater primo ordine ponunt*, They pray
to Jupiter and they give you, father Janus, a place in
the first rang). In this verse, the Virgilian influence
can be seen in the apostrophic use of *Jane Pater*.

The mythological history of the first king Janus
contrasts with the mythological kingship of the second king, Jupiter himself. Jupiter's genealogy and the
cruelty of his mother change the subject and tone of
the poem; Anthony rigorously criticizes the mysteries of Cybele, the Magna Mater, and her priests, the
semiviri. The myth of Atys occurs in lines 80–86, as a
sample of the "just sentence" of the pagan gods.

Nam prior est pastor, quam Juppiter, aut Jovis
 ipse;
Sed melius pastor castum servare pudorem
Qui voluit, sprevitque deam, qui saeva viriles
Abscidit partes, ne quando tangeret ille
Alterius thalamum, qui noluit ejus adire.
Hoc tamen, hoc egit sententia justa deorum,
Ne fieret conjux, qui non est factus adulter?

Because he is either an earlier shepherd than
 Jupiter or he is Jupiter himself.
But it is best to preserve your shame as a
 shepherd,
as he wanted to do, because he condemned the
 goddess.
For that reason she deprived him of his virile
 parts in a cruel way,
 thus avoiding that he would arrange to marry
 another woman,
because he was not willing to go to her bedroom.
Nevertheless, do you think this is not the result
 of the righteous judgment of the deities?

In early Christian tradition, Minucius Felix refers to
the same story in his apologetic writing *Octavius*:
*Cybeles Dyndima, pudet dicere, quae adulterum suum
infeliciter placitum, quoniam et ipsa deformis et vetula,
ut mullorum deorum mater, ad stuprum illicere non
poterat, exsecuit, ut deum scilicet faceret eunuchum*
(It is a shame to speak about the twin sister, daughter of Cybele, who could not seduce her lover to
dishonor, a lover who charmed her in an unhappy
manner, because she herself was not beautiful and
an old wife, yes the mother of the red deities. So she
emasculated him, to make him the eunuch of the
gods).

Augustine of Hippo is also acquainted with this
myth (Aug. *Civ.* 6.7; → Augustine of Hippo): *Sacra
sunt matris deum, ubi Atys pulcher adolescens ab ea
dilectus, et muliebri zelo abscissus, etiam hominum
abscissorum, quos Gallos vocant, infelicitate deplora-
tur* ("There are sacred rites of the mother of the
gods, in which the beautiful youth Atys, loved by her,
and castrated by her through a woman's jealousy,
is deplored by men who have suffered the same
calamity, whom they call Galli"). → Lactantius states:
*Deum mater et amavit formosum adulescentem, et
eumdem cum pellice deprehensum exsectis virilibus
semivirum reddidit. Et ideo nunc sacra eius a Gallis*

sacerdotibus celebrantur (The mother of the gods fell in love with a beautiful young man; and when he was caught with his mistress she made him half-man, removing his virility. And for that reason now the sacred rituals are celebrated by the Galli priests). Minucius Felix disapproves of these mysteries and paints them as follows *Propter hanc fabulam Galli eam, et semiviri sui corporis supplicio colunt. Haec iam non sunt sacra; tormenta sunt* (For this story the Galli adore her; as they do the semiviri through the punishment of their own body. These rituals are not holy. They are in reality cruelties!). Anthony defines these mysteries as not only scandalous but also in sharp contrast with the Christian mysteries (l. 87 *Nunc quoque semiviri mysteria turpia plangunt*, Also in this time the semiviri are in sorrow about those shameful mysteries). Successively, other gods and goddesses are thoroughly criticized in lines 87–110ff.

Etymological explications, which can also be found in Augustine's *De Civitate Dei* (6.7–8: *Cur Forculus, qui foribus praeest, et Limentinus, qui limini, dii sunt masculini, atque inter hos Cardea femina est, quae cardinem servat?*, Why are Forculus, who leads the door, and Limentinus, who guides the limen, male gods and for what reason is Cardea, one of them, who takes care for the door-spill, a female god?), illustrate in Anthony's poem the for Christians abnormal practice of human sacrifices. The starting point of these etymological clarifications is Kronos, also called Chronos by Anthony and identified with Time, creating and annihilating everything. As Anthony explains, Kronos was thrown down from heaven to earth in the Latium region. There he was hidden in the fields of Italy (*latuisse per agros Italiae*). To Anthony this seems ludicrous, and he does not shy away from using sarcasm, saying (ll. 105–106), *Magnus uterque deus! Terris est abditus alter, alter non potuit terrarum scire latebras* (Beautiful gods, really! One of them is hidden in the earth, the other one was not able to know the hidden places of the earth). For him the myth how Kronos devoured his child, which precedes in the poem (ll. 94–98), and the following etymological clarifications as well, explains the origin of the human sacrifices for this god in Latium. Anthony thoroughly despises this practice (ll. 107–110):

Hinc Latiare malum prisci statuere Quirites,
Ut mactatus homo nomen satiaret inane.
Quae nox est animi? Quae sunt improvida corda?

Quod colitur nihil est, et sacra cruenta geruntur.

As a consequence the first Quirites put in operation "the evil of Latium."
I mean: that a slaughtered man would satisfy an idle expression,
without any significance. What a complete blindness of the mind!
How incapable are their hearts to see beyond tomorrow.
What is venerated is nothing and nevertheless bloody rituals are celebrated!

The mystery cults of Isis and Serapis are strongly criticized in lines 111–125. Adoring the light and the supreme star (*sidus supernum*), while simultaneously hiding this light in the deep darkness of the underworld, seems suspect (ll. 113–114). Serapis is divided into separate entities: a dog, a dead donkey, a human being, bread, and somebody with a sickness (ll. 121–124). Anthony considers the adoration of Vesta as both a goddess and fire to be ridiculous. Why is she, being fire, a goddess and not a god? Vesta's meal is also offered to Drako, who is – according to Anthony – either nothing or the devil himself. Ancient pagan customs, such as the hanging out of clothes for the sun, usually took place during the Vulcanalia (ll. 130–133). A reference to the mythological story about the adultery of Venus and Mars can be found in lines 134–137, illustrating the foolishness of the pagan belief. A next illustration of this foolishness is the carrying around of Adonis, and his being spread as manure (ll. 138–139; possibly the poem points to the Adonis-gardens, see *BNP*, vol. I), pp. 145–146: "The regeneration of Adonis was symbolized by the so-called Adonis gardens: baskets and jugs with sprouting grain (or vegetable seeds)." The remark of Murator is also interesting: *Sed cur Adonis stercora patiebatur? Causam invenisse mihi videor. Nonnulli Adonidem semen tritici esse statuerunt, inter quos Theocriti Scholiastes ita locutus est* (Adonis had to endure manure, but for what reason? I think we can know the reason. Some people profess that Adonis is the seed of wheat, one of them, Theokritus the Scholiast says: [*BNP*, vol.XIV, 433–437]) . See also for the interpretation of the Latin preposition *pro*: PL 5, col. 277, s.v. "commentarius." L.A. Muratori (1697) interprets *pro* as an exclamation.

A change of subject and tone occur in line 149 and on (l. 149). Being grateful for his own salvation is one of the themes. Anthony uses the image of a ship which, after a stormy journey, arrives at the right place, namely the peaceful of the church (ll. 150–153). The final part of his poem (ll. 149–253) is dedicated to the specific nature of the Christian belief. In Anthony's poetical speech, rich in imagery, he compares God with a steersman who never looses control, and diffuses the lights of → paradise (ll. 159–163). In a eulogy on the Father and the Son, Christ is depicted as the creator of the cosmos and mankind. The Word which removed "that idle chaos" was not a person being born, but someone coming out of the mouth of God the Father.

The unity between the Father and the Son and the wonderful power of the only God, demonstrated in the miracles of → creation, are strongly emphasized. It is the spirit keeping everything together (ll. 164–187). In the poem, the spirit of the mouth is also used as a definition of Christ (ll. 199–201). Anthony urges pagans to avoid idols and to adore the Father and the Son. Again, the necessity of adoring both persons as God is pointed out (l. 202ff.). God is invisible and incomprehensible, as is the Son.

The divine Word can neither be comprehended nor seen by anyone. Only his works are visible (ll. 206–209). Both persons are equal in their creative power and in their protection of creation (ll. 210–211).

The end of the poem focusses on both its climax and an eschatological perspective. Christ is the Savior who removed all sins and enables man to see things as they truly are. It is Christ who gave back a forlorn world to an appeased Father (ll. 212–214). It is also God's forgiveness which, for Anthony, is essential, as is evident in the following lines 218–224:

Quodque in carne fuit, carnis peccata remittit.
Cernit enim, fragilem faciles incurrere lapsus,
Corripiensque tamen veniam dabit omnibus
     unam,
(Remque novam dicam, nec me dixisse pigebit)
Plusque pius quam justus erit. Si denique justus
Esse velit, nullus fugiet sine crimine poenam:
justus enim mala condemnat, pius omnia donat.

Because He was in the flesh, He forgives also the
     sins of the flesh.
He is aware that a feeble person easily stumbles.
In saving such a person He will provide forgive-
     ness to all people.
I say something new and I feel not bad about it.

He will be more a pious man than a righteous
     person.
In short: When somebody wants to be righteous,
nobody will flee punishment without sin.
A righteous man condemns all bad things,
a pious man forgives all things.

At the very end of the poem, awareness of sin, repentance, and forgiveness are the recurrent themes. The *indulgentia Dei*, the merciful nature of God, is called upon, to give back what sin caused to disappear (l. 226).

In the last part of the poem, the unity between the Father and the Son strongly accentuated twice, although the author does not refer to the Gospel of John (→ John, the Apostle), chapter 17. The theological elaboration of the divine Trinity, which consists of the Father, the Son, and the Holy Spirit, is completely absent; the Holy Spirit is scarcely and tentatively mentioned.

The end of the poem lacks a doxology. Instead, the threatening thunder and lightning of God, which bring about fear, are expounded by the author as an important manifestation of God, which demands respect for the almighty. A remarkable, concluding parallel exists between Zeus/Jupiter and the Christian God, as an illustration of his unlimited power. Apparently this parallel was helpful to convince the pagans of the power and importance of the Christian God.

(A historiography for this topic is not applicable.)

Bibliography

DECA, vol. I: A–I. Genoa, 1983.
Dolveck, F., ed., *Paulini Nolani Carmina*, CCSL 21, Turnhout, 2015.
Gallandius, A., ed., *Antonius, Carmen adversus gentes*, BVPA, vol. III, Venice, 1767.
Migne, J.-P., ed., *Antonii Carmen adversus gentes*, PL, vol. V, Paris, 1844, 261–282.
Muratori, L.A., ed., *Anecdota, quae ex Ambrosianae Bibliothecae codicibus*, vol. I: *Quae Sancti Paulini Episcopi Nolani Poemata complectens*, Milan, 1ste ed., 1697.
PRE, 2nd half vol.: *Alexander-Apollokrates*, Stuttgart, 1894, 2576.
Sirna, F.G., "Sul. C.d.Poema ultimum Ps. Paoliniano," *Aevum* 35, 1961, 87–107.
WWKL, vol. I/2, Freiburg, 1882, s.v. *Antonius*.

MARIUS A. VAN WILLIGEN

Anthropology

Anthropology, from ἄνθρωπος ("human being") and λόγος ("discourse, theory"), in its classical sense is a branch of philosophy and theology that studies the human being. Patristic anthropology is rich and rooted in Scripture – for example the doctrines of creation, the fall, and redemption – and in Greek philosophy (esp. Platonism, but with Stoic and Aristotelian elements), for example the tripartition of the human soul, the human as a microcosm, or the composition of human bodies from the four elements. Other aspects, such as the notion of the human being as image and likeness of God, in other words the "theology of the image," and the relevant moral imperative of assimilation to God (Kooten, 2008), come from both Scripture and Greek philosophy.

The "theology of the image" is the heart of patristic anthropology (Harrison, 2010). Its foundations lie in Gen 1:26–27: the human being, created by God, is in God's image. Properly, Christ is God's image (Col 1:15, which Origen referred to the eternal Son, invisible image of the invisible God) and humans are Christ's image. This mediated notion of image was developed by → Origen after → Philo of Alexandria's *logos* theology: God's *logos* is the true image of God, and humans are in the *logos'* image. Origen interpreted the Philonian *logos* and wisdom of God as Christ. God's image in a human was often identified by patristic theologians with the "intellect" (νοῦς) – an identification already found in Philo – and freedom or free will (αὐτεξουσία, αὐτεξούσιον, ἐλευθερία, ἐξουσία αὐτοπραγίας). This depends on the intellect in ancient ethical intellectualism, which goes back to the Socratic-Platonic line and was taken over by many church fathers. A contemporary of → Clement of Alexandria, → Bardaisan, a Christian Middle Platonist, claimed that humans, "in respect to their bodies, keep to their nature, like animals, whereas in respect to their intellect they do whatever they want, as free and powerful, qua images of God" (*BLC* 560; Ramelli, 2009). Like many church fathers, Bardaisan associated God's image in humans with their intellect and free will.

For few patristic thinkers, God's image in humans resides in their power over the world, in their creative potential, or in their immortality. M. Steenberg (2009) stresses the importance of the theology of the image for understanding the anthropology of → Irenaeus of Lyon, → Tertullian, → Cyril of Jerusalem, and → Athanasius of Alexandria – to whom at least Origen, → Gregory of Nyssa, and Maximus the Confessor should be added on account of the core position that the theology of the image assumes in their anthropology. The → incarnation is central to Irenaeus' anthropological theology, and his eschatological doctrine of recapitulation, enabled by Christ's inhumanation (i.e. his taking up of humanity, also called incarnation), influenced Clement and Origen in the formulation of → *apokatastasis*, especially because recapitulation depends on all humans' being the image of God through Christ, on Irenaeus' idea of humanity as "one race" (which I think influenced Gregory of Nyssa's notion of humanity as "one lump," φύραμα), and on Christ's saving power as recapitulator. Also, Irenaeus' insistence on the universality indicated by the three dimensions of Christ's salvific cross, pointing to the whole cosmos, was further developed by Gregory of Nyssa.

Several patristic theologians, such as Origen, distinguished between "image" (εἰκών) of God and "likeness" (ὁμοίωσις) to God. Observing that in Gen 1:26 God announces: "Let us make the human being in our image, after our likeness," but in Gen 1:27 only the image is mentioned apropos of the newly created humanity, while the likeness is withheld, Origen concluded that the image was an initial datum, whereas likeness to God has to be achieved by each one through moral engagement and will reach perfection in the end, with deification (θέωσις: see below), in an image-likeness-unity progression. → Basil of Caesarea too identified likeness to God with deification, "becoming God" (Bas. *Spir.* 9.109C), and so did Pseudo-Dionysius, another admirer of Origen (Ps.-Dion. *Eccl. hier.* 1.3). Likeness to God thus comes close to the Platonic ideal of assimilation to God, ὁμοίωσις θεῷ, as far as possible to humans (Plato *Theaet.* 176AB; e.g. Merki, 1952). Origen's image/likeness distinction exerted a remarkable influence on patristic anthropology down to Symeon the New Theologian (*Hymn* 44).

The theology of the image had numerous ramifications in patristic anthropology, ethics, sociology, and theology at large. Here there is no room to explore all of them, but I will offer a couple of examples. Gregory of Nyssa, in an articulate way, grounded in the theology of the image the illegitimacy of slavery and of social injustice leading to the dire poverty of many (Ramelli, 2012; 2016), and the equality and equal dignity of women and men. Both are God's image in the same way; this principle from Gen 1:26–27 is reinforced by Paul (→ Paul the Apostle) in Gal 3:28: "In Christ there is neither slave nor free, neither Jew nor Greek, neither man nor woman." The term ὁμότιμος ("of equal dignity/worth/rank"), used by Gregory of Nyssa and Basil in reference to women and men, was also applied by their friend → Gregory of Nazianzus to Theosebia, Gregory of Nyssa's ordained sister: she was σύζυγος ("colleague") and ὁμότιμος ("equal in rank and ecclesiastical dignity") of a ἱερεύς, her brother – who was presbyter and bishop – and was worthy of the celebration of the great mysteries, that is, the eucharistic consecration (Ramelli, 2010a; Taylor & Ramelli, 2021; → Eucharist). Women's ecclesiastical ministry, already advocated by Origen (Paul "teaches with apostolic authority that women too are ordained in the ecclesiastical ministry, and must be ordained," Or. *Comm. Rom.* 10.17) and attested in the patristic age, is thus grounded in the theology of the image. Women are no less in the image of Christ, who is God's image, than men; so they can fully share in Christ's priestly ministry. Women are Christ's images like men because Christ's humanity is all humanity, not simply Jesus' gendered and racially connoted body. Origen, Gregory of Nyssa, and Gregory of Nazianzus were aware that, if women should be excluded from ecclesiastical ministry because Jesus was a man, black and yellow men for instance also should, because Jesus was neither black nor yellow, and all non-Jews should also be excluded, because Jesus was a Jew. The faulty logic of this anthropological argument did not escape these patristic theologians, who were adamant that Christ's humanity is all humanity, not only one gender, one race, one color, and so on. This is why Christ incorporates in his mystical body, and saves, all humans, not only white men and Jews like Jesus.

An essential part of patristic anthropology is the doctrine of the → soul (psychology, from ψυχή) and λόγος ("discourse, theory"), its origin, structure, and relation to the → body. The soul's Platonic tripartition into rational, irascible, and concupiscible/appetitive (λογιστικόν, θυμικόν, ἐπιθυμητικόν) was followed by patristic philosophers such as Bardaisan, Origen, Gregory of Nyssa, Evagrius, and others, down to Symeon (Alfeyev, 2000). Gregory also embraced another, Aristotelian division, finding in the Genesis → creation narrative support of the tripartition of the soul into vegetative (vital), sense-perceptive (animal), and rational parts (Greg. Nyss. *Hom. opif.* 8), which he superimposes to the body-soul-spirit tripartition, with the following equation: "body" = vegetative soul; "soul" = sense-perceptive soul; "spirit" = intellectual soul. Interestingly, in this equation the actual body disappears.

While Tertullian, for example, wrote a *De anima*, Origen wrote none, because this matter was uncertain and the apostles left the soul's origin unclarified (Pamp. *Ap.* 8). Though he expounded his psychology in many places and laid out the principles of psychological investigation in Or. *Comm. Jo.* 6.85, one must examine

> the soul's essence, the principle of its existence and its joining this earthly body [...] whether it can enter a body twice, whether this will happen during the same cosmic cycle and arrangement, in the same body or another, and, if the same, whether this will remain identical to itself in its substance, only acquiring different qualities, or will remain the same in both its substance and qualities, and whether the soul will always use the same body or it will change.

Origen's insightful follower, Gregory of Nyssa, wrote a dialogue *On the Soul and the Resurrection*, devoted to the demonstration of the soul's intelligible nature and role in the body's resurrection, which is the first step in the eventual restoration. Gregory Platonically upheld the immortality of the rational soul, immaterial, incorporeal, intelligible, adiastematic, divine, and distinct from the soul's inferior faculties. Origen and Gregory of Nyssa ruled out the body's preexistence, because souls would become subordinate to bodies, which would be worthier than souls. Souls would merely serve the vivification of bodies (Or. *Comm. Cant.* 2.5.23). Thus, either the disembodied soul existed before the body – the Platonic option, leading to metensomatosis – or soul and body were created together: the latter was Origen's and Gregory of Nyssa's option, provided that one understands soul as intellectual and body as spiritual, initially one with the intellect. Metensomatosis was repeatedly rejected by Origen as impious, although he was accused by misinformed people of supporting it (Ramelli, 2013c).

For Origen, rational creatures began to exist at a certain point (Or. *Princ.* 2.9.2) – albeit not in the time measured by sun and stars – as created independent substances, not coeternal with God (*Princ.* 1.4.4–5). They existed eternally only as projects in God's *logos*, but were created as substances at a certain point (Or. *Comm. Jo.* 1.19.114–115). They did not receive a body only after their → fall, which transformed their existing bodies. They were provided with a body from the beginning of their creation as substances: not heavy and corruptible, but similar to the spiritual, angelic body of resurrection (→ Resurrection). After the fall, humans had their fine, immortal bodies changed into perishable ones. They will recover a spiritual body at the resurrection-restoration. The "skin tunics" (Gen 3:21) are not the body, but mortality (Or. *Hom. Lev.* 6.2). The human had a body before receiving those tunics, which represent not the body tout court, but the heavy, mortal body given to humans after the fall (Or. *Fr. 1 Cor.* 29). Already Clement warned that the encratite Julius Cassian's identification of the "skin tunics" with the body was incorrect (Clem. *Strom.* 3.14.95.2). → Procopius of Caesarea (*In Gen.* 3.21; PG 87.1.221.A) attests to Origen's interpretation: the "skin tunics" are not the body, since, according to biblical allegorizers, the human in → paradise already had a body, "fine" (λεπτομερές), "suitable for life in paradise," "luminous" (αὐγοειδές) and immortal, which corresponds to the human "molded from the earth"; the human created "according to the image" is the soul. "Initially, the soul used the luminous body as a vehicle, and this body was later clothed in the skin tunics." Gobar (*ap.* Phot. *Bibl.* codex 232.287b–291b) also attests to Origen's identification of the "skin tunics" with mortality, heavy corporeality, and liability to passions, using αὐγοειδές, which indicates that Procopius, too, was referring to Origen. Origen indeed described the angels' bodies as ethereal and αὐγοειδές φῶς (Or. *Comm. Matt.* 17.30) and the risen body as "finest" = λεπτομερές and "brightest" = αὐγοειδές (Or. *Princ.* 3.6.4; 3.6.19). The depiction of this body as a suitable dwelling place for life in paradise also corresponds to Procopius' passage. Origen postulated a fine, luminous prelapsarian body; such will also be the risen body, "after shedding this thick shell" (Or. *Comm. Ps.* 6 *ap.* Pamp. *Ap.* 157). → Theodoret

of Cyrrhus (*Coll. Coisl. in Gen.* frgm. 121), probably from Origen's *Commentary on Genesis*, states that it is "unworthy of God" to think that God, like a leather cutter, sewed tunics, which some identified with "mortality," which covered Adam and Eve, "put to death due to sin."

Humans had a fine body from the beginning of their substantial existence. Only the → Trinity for Origen is incorporeal; creatures need a body to live: bodies can be separated from them only theoretically (Or. *Princ.* 2.2.2). If anyone could live without a body, all could do so, but then corporeal substance would be useless and would not exist (*Princ.* 2.3.2). Rational creatures always need a body (*Princ.* 4.4.8); thus, they had one at the beginning of their substantial existence, when God created them and matter (*Princ.* 2.9.1). The soul must always be in a body suited to the place in which it is according to its spiritual progress (Or. *Hom.* 2 *Ps.* 38.8.27; *Res.* 2 *ap.* Pamp. *Ap.* 134.28; *Comm. Ps.* 1 *ap.* Pamp. *Ap.* 141; *Res. ap.* Phot. *Bibl.* codex 234.301a). Origen rejected the preexistence of bare souls in his exegesis of Titus: "The doctrine that souls exist before bodies is justified neither by the apostles nor by ecclesiastical tradition [...] whoever maintains this doctrine is a heretic" (*ap.* Barsanuphius of Palestine, *Contra opinions Origenistarum*; PG 86.891–893). Souls are only anterior to *mortal, earthly* bodies (Or. *Comm. Cant.* 2.5.16; *Comm. Jo.* 6.85: "The reason for the soul's being clothed with the present earthly body"). Rational creatures exist neither before their bodies nor before the cosmos (*Comm. Cant.* 2.8.4). That they were endowed with fine bodies from the beginning explains how they diversified their wills, since "there cannot be diversity without bodies" (*Princ.* 2.1.4; 2.9.2).

The charge concerning the preexistence of bare souls circulated against Origen already in the 3rd century CE (Pamp. *Ap.* 159), but Gregory of Nyssa knew it was unfounded. In *De anima et resurrectione* he took over Origen's *De resurrectione*, also considering Methodius and the *Dialogue of Adamantius*. For Gregory, universal restoration will begin with resurrection. For him, as for Origen, the risen body is the same as the earthly as for individual identity, but spiritual and immortal, with a "more magnificent complexion" (Greg. Nyss. *Anim. et res.* 153C) and different qualities (Greg. Nyss. *Anim. et res.* 108; *Mort.*; *GNO* 9.62–63). Gregory highlights the soul's role in the resurrection (Greg. Nyss. *Hom. opif.* 27; *Anim. et res.* 76; 80A-88C9): after the return of the particles of one's body to their respective elements, the soul can still recognize and assemble them (see *Anim. et res.* 45C-48B; 85A), dragging to itself what is οἰκεῖον to itself. Gregory regards the resurrection as the soul's reappropriation (οἰκείωσις) of what belongs to her, which parallels his notion of *apokatastasis* as God's reappropriation (οἰκείωσις) of all creatures, belonging to God but alienated by evil (Ramelli, 2014a). The mortal body is restored to its prelapsarian state of spiritual body and the intellectual soul to its prelapsarian condition free from evil.

In *De anima* Gregory, like Origen (*Princ.* 2.8.2–3), treats the intellectual soul as the true human (Plato *Alc.* 1.129E-130C; *Rep.* 4.441E-442B, *Phaedr.* 246B) and God's image. The signs of the divine image are not in the corruptible body, but in wisdom, justice, moderation, knowledge, and all virtues, which are in God substantially and can be found in humans thanks to personal engagement and imitation of God (Or. *Princ.* 4.4.9–10). For what keeps the intellectual soul alive and truly God's image is sticking to the Good, God, who only is. Gregory and Origen also agreed that the soul will eschatologically be the intellect and not its inferior faculties, which are accessory and will disappear, since

> the intellect that fell from its original condition and dignity has become, and has been called, "soul," but if it has emended and corrected itself, it will become again an intellect. (Or. *Princ.* 4.8.4; Greg. Nyss. *Anim. et res.* 52–56; 64; *In illud* 3)

The "skin tunics" are identified by Gregory, as by Origen, with the heavy body and its passions (Greg. Nyss. *Icc.* 2; 11; *Virg.* 12–13; *De Vita Moysis*; *GNO* 7.1.39–40), "the form of the irrational nature we have been wrapped in after becoming familiar with passion" (Greg. Nyss. *Anim. et res.* 148). It will vanish at the resurrection. Those resurrected will have spiritual bodies; since this state is the restoration to the original condition (*Anim. et res.* 148), at the beginning, too, humans had spiritual bodies.

The material, earthly "load" of passions must be purified in the other world with a painful process, if one failed to discard them here (*Anim. et res.* 105). This purification will make it possible for God to achieve his purpose "to have all participate in the

goods that are in God," in other words θέωσις (*Anim. et res.* 152). Humans did not know → evil in the beginning and will not in the end: all will experience restoration to the Good (Greg. Nyss. *In illud* 13; 20.8–24). In *Anim. et res.* 101–104 and *In illud* 17.13–21, Gregory links 1 Cor 15:28 to the eventual disappearance of evil through Origen's syllogism: if God must be "all in all" in the end, then evil will be no more, lest God be found in evil. Gregory also takes from Origen (*Princ.* 1.6.1; 3.5.6) the equation between universal submission to Christ and universal salvation, and derives (Greg. Nyss. *Anim. et res.* 72B; 136A; *In illud* 20.8–24) the interpretation of Phil 2:10–11 in this light of universal salvific submission from Or. *Princ.* 1.2.10; 1.6.2. In his last homily on the Song of Songs, he stresses the final unity in God, basing it on John 17 and viewing it as a unity of will, like Origen.

The angelic nature of human prelapsarian life finds a perfect correspondence in the angelic life of *apokatastasis*, anticipated by ascetics on earth, and in the eschatological reunion of humans and angels in the dancing and singing feast of *apokatastasis*. Likewise, Origen claimed that all rational creatures share the same nature (so *Anim. et res.* 105) and before the fall formed one choir and enjoyed unity among themselves and with God; after the fall they were differentiated into angels, humans, and demons (→ Demonology/Demons), but will return to unity in *apokatastasis*. Like Origen, Gregory insists that the end will reproduce the beginning (*Anim. et res.* 156). Humans will become what they were before falling onto the earth. The original creation thus implies, like the resurrection, an intellectual soul with its spiritual body.

Gregory, like Origen, does not support the preexistence of bare souls. He declares each soul to be originated with its body: the ideas-*logos*-projects of intellects with their bodies were in God from eternity; then came their creation as substances, as Origen also maintained. Gregory never says that each rational soul is created with a *mortal* body. He says that humanity was created at the beginning, with a project anterior to the world and with a preparation of a "matter" that is likely the matter of the prelapsarian, immortal body, also in that its preparation is mentioned with the delineation of the human form as the image of God-*logos*' beauty. This refers to the prelapsarian state, before the assumption of mortal bodies. God's image is virtue, beatitude, impassivity, intelligence, *logos*, love (Greg. Nyss. *Hom. opif.* 5); it is the intellect, immaterial, and adiastematic, transcending place and time (*Hom. opif.* 11; 14–15).

In the human as God's image, there is neither male nor female (*Hom. opif.* 16); this division is "a departure from the prototype," since in Christ there is neither male nor female (Gal 3:28). The human proper, that is its intellect, is not like the cosmos, but like the creator, while in the part that is divided into genders, humans are like beasts. "The priority belongs to the intellectual component"; the association with irrationality came afterward. God made all humanity "once and for all," in "the first creation." This suggests that humans, intellectual souls and spiritual bodies, were created then. The intellect is in all humans; gender difference "was created after, as the last thing, in the molded human," due to the fall (*Hom. opif.* 17). Humans will be like angels in the resurrection, at "the restoration of those who have fallen to their original condition." Without the fall, humans would have multiplied like angels, with angelic bodies (which therefore they presumably had before the fall). In the resurrection too, they will have angelic bodies. In *Hom. Eccl.* 1, Gregory states that the risen body is the same as that of the first creation:

> The body was made and created by God's hands *exactly as the resurrection will reveal it* in due course. For, *just as you will see it after the resurrection, so was it created at the beginning.*

So, before the fall, humans had a spiritual body. Therefore, the body with which the soul is created is not the mortal body.

In *De anima* and *De hominis opificio*, Gregory criticizes metensomatosis or the transmigration of souls from body to body, and not – as is regularly assumed – Origen's purported doctrine of the preexistence of bare souls. Gregory did not believe in the preexistence of disembodied souls, but neither did Origen. In *Hom. opif.* 28 and and *Anim. et res.* 121, Gregory maintains that the soul does not exist before the body, nor the body before the soul, which works if understood in reference to the intellectual soul and the spiritual body. In both texts, this discussion comes after a rebuttal of metensomatosis, not of Origen. In *Anim. et res.* 108 the preexistence of souls is ascribed to those who supported metensomatosis, and the repeated reference to the loss of the soul's

wings points to Plato and pagan → Neoplatonism. The reference to the reincarnation of human souls into plants also excludes connections with Origen. Also, in *Anim. et res.* 116–117 the soul's fall into a material body as a combination of the soul's sin and the coupling of two humans or animals or the sowing of a plant cannot refer to Origen. The reference in *Hom. opif.* 28 to those who have discussed the principles (ἀρχαί) indicates philosophers who treated protology and metaphysics, not Origen. Even taking περὶ ἀρχῶν, "on principles," as a title, many other works were thusly entitled besides Origen's, for example Longinus' or Porphyry's. Gregory criticizes "one of those before us," τις τῶν πρὸ ἡμῶν, not "one of us" Christians; one who upheld metensomatosis and wrote on protology/metaphysics: besides Plato, it may be Plotinus who believed in reincarnations of human souls into animal bodies (Plot. *Enn.* 3.4.2.16– 24) and wrote on the ἀρχαί in his *Enneads* (περὶ τῶν τριῶν ἀρχικῶν ὑποστάσεων, "on the three hypostases that are the principles"), or Porphyry, who believed in metensomatosis, perhaps extended to animals (Eus. *Dem. ev.* 1.10.7) and wrote a Περὶ ἀρχῶν. Origen refers thrice to a non-Christian, Philo, as τις τῶν πρὸ ἡμῶν (Or. *Comm. Matt.* 17.17; *Hom. Num.* 9.5; *Cels.* 7.20). Gregory himself, also elsewhere, refers τῶν πρὸ ἡμῶν τινες, to a non-Christian, Philo, in a passage in which he disagrees with him (Greg. Nyss. *Vita Moy.* 2.191). The same expression will therefore indicate a non-Christian such as Porphyry, in the passage at stake, in which Gregory disagrees with him. The doctrine, attacked by Gregory, of the preexistence of souls "as a people in a State of their own" joined to a body on account of their demerits, is not Origen's. Beside (Neo)platonic, it can be gnostic (→ Gnosis/Gnosticism) or Manichaean: a critique of Manichaeism (→ Mani/Manichaeism) is probable in Greg. Nyss. *Anim. et res.* 108, where metensomatosis is attacked because it even prohibits the consumption of vegetables and fruit, and *Anim. et res.* 121, in a discussion of the anteriority of soul or body. To this position Gregory opposes that of some who thought that the body existed prior to the soul, which Gregory, like Origen and Pamphilus, abhors because it would make "flesh worthier than the soul." Gregory describes the theory of the preexistence of disembodied souls as a "myth," which fits gnostic and Manichaean mythology, besides Plato's myths. The transmigration of human souls into animal bodies was already rejected by Origen (*Comm. Matt.* 11.17), who also opposed the transmigration of human souls to human bodies, which would entail the eternity of the world, a pagan tenet denied by Scripture (*Comm. Matt.* 13.1–2; *Comm. Cant.* 2.5.24). Origen attests that some Christians, too, believed in metensomatosis of human souls even into animals (*Pamp. Ap.* 186). Gregory may have had in mind these too, though the mention of a work on the ἀρχαί rather points to Porphyry. Anyway, Gregory did not target Origen.

In *Hom. opif.* 29, Gregory observes that the cause of the constitution of each human's soul and body is the same, meaning the intellectual soul, since Gregory insists on the accessorial nature of the lower soul faculties. He defines the soul as "created, living, and intellectual substance" (Greg. Nyss. *Anim. et res.* 29B). This is tenable only if the soul is created before time. This dissolves a contradiction that would arise if the body with which the soul is originated were the mortal body: the contradiction raised by the "perishability axiom" (whatever had a beginning in time has an end in time). Gregory knew this axiom, deemed it grounded in Scripture (Wis 7:1–18; PG 45.796.B-C), and, like Origen, applied it to the world: if it is created in time, it will have an end (*Hom. opif.* 23). But when Gregory states that the soul is created with the body, if he means the *mortal* body, this would imply that the soul is created in time and thus mortal. But if the soul is adiastematic, it transcends the local and temporal dimension and was created not in time, but prior to time. Gregory never says that the body at stake is the mortal one, since he was aware of the perishability axiom and knew Origen's and Pamphilus' position on it. Pamphilus (*Ap.* 168–170) had deployed it in defense of Origen's doctrine of the origin of rational creatures. After observing that in the church there were different opinions on the soul's origin (*Ap.* 166), and after rejecting that of the simultaneous creation of soul and mortal body (*Ap.* 167), he rejected traducianism too and invoked the perishability axiom against both theories: the intellectual soul must die with the mortal body if it came into existence with it (*Ap.* 168; 170). But if Gregory is speaking of a spiritual body, the contradiction vanishes, and the perishability axiom stands: humans had spiritual bodies before the fall, transformed into mortal because of sin; after sin's disappearance, their bodies will become again angelic. This is confirmed

by Anastasius Sinaita (*Serm. duo* 3), according to whom Gregory of Nyssa and Gregory of Nazianzus believed that "Adam had a body that was incorruptible, immortal, and more immaterial" than the mortal body; this "was turned by God into a body that is liable to passion and denser."

Due to the composite nature of humans, body and soul (whose highest part is the intellect), patristic thinkers such as Gregory of Nazianzus described the human as "a double being" (Greg. Naz. *Or.* 40.8.1), "a single living being consisting of the visible and invisible nature [...] earthly and heavenly, temporal and immortal, visible and intellectual [...] spirit and flesh" (*Or.* 38.11.8–19). While the soul, specifically the intellectual soul, is the bearer of God's image, coming from God's breath (Greg. Naz. *Carm. dogm.* 8.1), being a part of God (*Or.* 14.7) and "a piece broken off the invisible divinity" (*Carm. dogm.* 8.73), as Gregory says with a metaphor already used by → Epictetus ("a piece broken off God," Epict. *Diatr.* 2.8.11), the mortal body comes from the mud of the visible earth (*Or.* 14.6–7). Likewise Maximus depicted the human as "a composite nature" (φύσις σύνθετος, Max. *Ep.* 12.488D), on account of its being both soul and body. Maximus also received from patristic thinkers such as Origen, Evagrius, and others the threefold division of the human into body, soul, and intellect (σῶμα, ψυχή, and νοῦς, e.g. Max. *Myst.* 4.678B), or a fourfold division into body, soul, intellect and spirit (πνεῦμα, *Myst.* 4.678BC). → Nemesius of Emesa, who provided a treatise of patristic anthropology (*De natura hominis, On the Nature of the Human Being*), in Nem. *Nat. hom.* 1.1 remarked upon the twofold or threefold structure of a human. Tert. *Test.* 4 is an example of Tertullian's bipartite anthropology: here the necessity that body and soul together appear before God-judge is an important point, recently explored by J. Perkins (2009; see Ramelli, 2009a). Tertullian seems to postulate no development of the soul alone – which is no human being – after one's death. This differs from Clement's view and Origen's and his followers' view, which is a premise for *apokatastasis*, not shared by Tertullian.

Another trait associated with humans' double nature in patristic anthropology is mediation between God and creation, or between the intelligible and the sense-perceptible world. This notion that the human is a mediator (μεσίτης, μεταξύ) was already in Philo (*Virt.* 9) and passed on to Clement

(*Strom.* 2.81.155), Origen, Gregory of Nazianzus (*Or.* 38.11), Gregory of Nyssa, Maximus (*Amb. Lib.* 4.1305A), and others, who applied it to humans and Christ. Patristic anthropology also took over the widespread Greek philosophical notion of the human as a microcosm, a "small cosmos", already used by Philo too. Macrina and Gregory of Nyssa in *De anima et resurrectione*, which deals a lot with theological anthropology, devote an entire section (3) to expounding the Greek idea of the human being as a microcosm. As Macrina explains, just as from the human body one can infer the existence of the soul – especially the intellect – which governs it, so also from the visible world one can infer the existence of the divinity, who created it and governs it providentially (commentary in Ramelli, 2007). Still Johannes Scotus Eriugena, in a way the last patristic philosopher, utilized this concept in Eriug. *Periph.* 4.5–6: humans are a compendium of the whole creation, animal and intellectual. This is why Christ, by assuming all humanity in the inhumanation, automatically saved the whole cosmos, which is summed up in humanity (*Periph.* 5.24).

A vital part of patristic anthropology, closely related to ethics, is the doctrine of free will – depending on the intellect – and its relation to providence, upheld in contrast to predestinationism, fatalism, and casualism. Clement and Origen strongly supported human free will against gnostics and Marcionites (→ Marcion/Marcionites/Marcionism), Diodore and → Augustine of Hippo against Manichaeans (when Augustine still embraced *apokatastasis*: Ramelli, 2013b). Through free will humans must choose virtues, which are Christ (Origen), so humans' being images of Christ must be substantiated by the practice of virtues. This is what Evagrius called πρακτική (ethics, asceticism), which, through the purification of the soul's inferior faculties, leads to contemplation (θεωρία), by means of the intellect. Πρακτική aims at → *apatheia*, θεωρία at knowledge (γνῶσις), which is ultimately apophatic in the case of the knowledge of God. This is also why the highest form of prayer is imageless prayer (→ Anthropomorphism).

Patristic anthropology embraces protology and eschatology, humanity's creation, the fall, life in history, → redemption, and eschatological destinies. As Eriugena puts it, humans were created to live in paradise, not to die on earth (*Periph.* 5.2). The fall, in other words the introduction of sin, which is "the

death of the soul" (Ramelli, 2010; 2011), produced also bodily death – which some church fathers, such as Origen, Methodius, or Gregory of Nyssa, saw as a blessing in disguise, a way to liberate humans from sinning, stopping the chain of sins, and to create them anew, in a re-creation that is a restoration to the ideal state of humanity according to God's plan (Ramelli, 2014). This restoration is needed not only at the level of bodies, which must be resuscitated from death, but also at the level of souls and intellects, which too have been affected by the fall. For Evagrius, the intellect, which was simple and undivided, descended to the level of soul and became divided into intellectual soul and inferior parts of the soul, subject to passions (πάθη, which are against human nature according to Gregory of Nyssa and Climacus) and in need of reconquering *apatheia* (a pivotal ideal in Gregory of Nyssa, Evagrius, and others), and further acquired a heavy body (Ramelli, 2015a). Already according to Origen, and later to Gregory of Nyssa, the fall implied for humans the acquisition of a heavy, mortal, and gendered body, subject to passions and corruption. Hence the need for a restoration of body, soul, and intellect, which must also be a restoration to harmony and unity within the human being, and unity among all rational creatures, and between all rational creatures and God (Ramelli, 2013a). Evagrius, after Origen and Gregory of Nyssa, depicted a protological movement from unity (union with God, unity among rational creatures, and unification within a single rational creature, being pure intellect) to multiplicity (a dispersion of volitions, multiplication of intellect-soul-body) and a glorious eschatological movement back to unity with God and the other rational creatures, and within oneself, with the body elevated to the rank of soul, and the soul to the rank of intellect. The intellect will be elevated to God in deification. These progressive subsumptions (or transforming elevations) of inferior elements into the superior ones will be developed by Eriugena.

The restoration of the whole human being was in the focus of the *apokatastasis* doctrine. This theory and that of eternal damnation confronted each other throughout the patristic period. Most patristic thinkers, from Origen to Gregory of Nyssa, from Macrina to Gregory of Nazianzus, from Didymus to Evagrius, from Melania to the Tall Brothers, from Pamphilus to Eusebius of Ceasarea, from Ambrose of Milan to the early Augustine, from Victorinus to Rufinus, from Bardaisan to Isaac of Nineveh, from Clement to Cassian, from Diodore of Tarsus to Theodore of Mopsuestia, probably from Pseudo-Dionysius to Maximus, and others, thought that all humans would eventually be restored. Others, such as Tertullian or the late Augustine, expected that most would be eternally damned. This view became dominant in the West mainly under Augustine's influence, but still in the 9th century, Eriugena opposed Origen's authority to Augustine's to support a strong doctrine of universal restoration and salvation. For Eriugena, as for the others who supported *apokatastasis*, this is enabled by Christ. All the above-mentioned patristic theologians display a christocentric notion of *apokatastasis* (demonstration in Ramelli, 2013).

Deification or theosis is the culmination of *apokatastasis* and of all of patristic theological anthropology. Maximus, giving voice to the precedent patristic tradition, remarks that the human being was created to "be deified" (Max. *Thal.* 22.28–30). This means participation in the divine nature, sharing God's eternity (Ramelli & Konstan, 2007; 2013), and "coming to be like God through deification by grace" (Max. *Myst.* 43.640BC). This, as Evagrius explained in his *Letter to Melania*, does not mean a confusion of substances between creatures and the transcendent creator, but a unity of will and a participation in divine life (Ramelli, 2015). Theosis, which is not by nature but by grace, is made possible by, and has its counterpart in, Christ's inhumanation (ἐνανθρώπησις), which is also entirely by grace and is the utmost manifestation of God's love together with Christ's sacrifice (Origen, Isaac of Nineveh). God's Son, *logos*-wisdom, became fully human, assuming all humanity – but without sin – for humans to become divine, as Athanasius has it: Christ "was made a human being, that we might be made God" (Athan. *Inc.* 54.3). Irenaeus anticipated this principle: Christ became what we are to bring us to be what Christ is (Iren. *Haer.* preface). For Irenaeus, Christ recapitulates all humanity in his own deified humanity. Augustine, of whom we have already spoken above, posited the human compound of soul and body as one of the wonders of the mystery of the human being (Aug. *Civ.* 21.10). Indeed, he saw Christian anthropology as a mystery, reflecting the mystery of God. Only God can fulfil the utmost need of the human being (Aug. *Conf.* 1.1.1.),

since God is the creator as well as the end of humanity. The anthropological structure itself reflects God the Trinity: human *mens* is in relation to the Father; *intelligentia-notitia* to the Son-*logos*-truth, and *amor-voluntas* to the Spirit (Aug. *Trin.* 15.3.5).

It should be noted that Augustine's *epp.* 92, 147, 148 express a form of "negative" anthropology. Augustine's denial of being able to adequately describe or think God's being – as later negative theology emphasized – goes hand in hand with Augustine's denial, from 407 onwards, of knowing how the human being, in his glorified body, will eventually "see" God. Augustine denies that this "seeing" can be compared to sensory perception on earth, because God is not physical and does not take up space like an object (*ep.* 92. 4; *ep.* 147.49–51). The awareness of not being able to adequately describe God goes hand in hand with the awareness of not knowing how man is after the resurrection. Negative theology, negative anthropology and negative eschatology go together in his work (van Geest, 2010).

Much of patristic theology can be argued to be grounded in anthropological tenets. For example, Athanasius' theology and eventual adhesion to the Nicene consubstantiality formula – the Son is ὁμοούσιος with the Father, possessing naturally the Father's attributes – derive from his anthropology (Steenberg, 2009). What he rejects in Arius' subordinationist Christology is indeed an *anthropological* impossibility: a created Son could be divine, and life, only by participation, but he does what no creature can: give life and not receive it. The soteriological implications of an Arian or anti-Arian Christology are clear.

Indeed, theology itself is necessarily also anthropology, since the ineffable deity chose to reveal itself most fully in the God-human, Christ, the Theanthropos, who reveals God's plan for humanity and humans' truest identity. Because Christ inhumanated (i.e. who has taken up humanity, as a human being) is perfectly sinless humanity, his death could produce the total elimination of evil:

A human being died, and his death not only constituted a model of death by devotion, but also produced the principle and advancement of the destruction of evil and the devil, who ruled upon the whole earth. (Or. *Cels.* 7.17)

Historiography

Patristic anthropology has been debated in ancient controversies, especially the Origenian one, but its scientific study (within philosophical, theological, and social studies of late antiquity) is rather recent. G. Giannini (1965) provided a synthesis from Greek philosophy to Aquinas, while E. Dinkler (1934) focused on Augustine and H. Karpp (1950) dealt with ancient Christian anthropology. D. Garrison (2012) has recently provided a rich cultural history of anthropology in antiquity, with the relevant bibliography. G.H. van Kooten (2008) examines Paul's anthropology in its philosophical context and is a basis for the study of its aftermath in patristics.

The "theology of the image" as the heart of patristic anthropology has been studied by N.V. Harrison (2010) and its importance especially in Origen, Gregory of Nyssa, and Evagrius has been pointed out by I. Ramelli (2013 for Origen; 2012 for Gregory; 2016 for Origen and Gregory; 2017 for Gregory and Evagrius; 2009 and forthcoming on Bardaisan) and in Irenaeus, Tertullian, Cyril of Jerusalem, and Athanasius by M. Steenberg (2009). Gregory of Nyssa's psychology as part and parcel of his anthropology has been explored and reassessed by I. Ramelli (2018a). Its relation to the notion of ὁμοίωσις θεῷ has been investigated from H. Merki (1952) to I. Ramelli (2013a; and in Origen against the backdrop of ancient philosophy, in a forthcoming monograph on Origen). Metensomatosis as a core anthropological doctrine was repeatedly rejected by Origen as impious, although he was accused by misinformed people of supporting it (Ramelli 2013c; forthcoming).

A recent reassessment of the issue of anthropology and of the soul-body relation in ancient philosophy and early Christianity is offered by S.S. Griffin and I. Ramelli (2022). This volume not only bridges the divide between pagan and Christian ideas on the body and its relation to the soul, but also challenges the widespread assumption that Platonists and Christians held opposite views on this score and that Platonists despised bodies. This must be nuanced, both on the pagan and on the Christian side. The meaning of asceticism in ancient and patristic thought and its relation to patristic anthropology and notions of justice has been thoroughly explored by I. Ramelli (2016), also in conversation with P. Brown and other scholarship.

The complex doctrine of anthropology, the body, its creation, its relation to the soul, and its resurrection in Origen of Alexandria has been studied, with innovative arguments and comparisons with Bardaisan, other Middle Platonists, and Plotinus by I. Ramelli (2013b; forthcoming), who also argues extensively that Gregory of Nyssa was not criticizing Origen's doctrine of the body, as is commonly assumed, and that Evagrius Ponticus' anthropology entertains a nuanced terminology of bodies, distinguishes between mortal and spiritual body, and is less hostile to bodies than is generally held in scholarship (Ramelli, 2015; 2017).

The anthropological grounds of Augustine's criticism of Origen are investigated by I. Ramelli (2013b), who also highlights the imprecision of the category of the "preexistence of souls" in many patristic Platonists (Ramelli, 2013c). Augustine's changing attitudes toward the body, analyzed, among others, by V. Grossi (1980), still need to be systematically examined against the backdrop of his relation to Origen – which still requires a methodical investigation, in the works. Patristic anthropology (or anthropologies) must continue to be explored, both against the backdrop of ancient philosophy, and in its relation to Patristic ideas on psychology, doctrine of bodies, asceticism, soteriology, and ecclesiology.

Bibliography

Alfeyev, H., *St. Symeon the New Theologian and Orthodox Tradition*, Oxford, 2000.

Dinkler, E., *Die Anthropologie Augustins*, Stuttgart, 1934.

Dusenbury, D.L., *Nemesius of Emesa on Human Nature: A Cosmopolitan Anthropology from Roman Syria*, Oxford, 2022.

Frey, J., & M. Nägele, eds., *Der νοῦς bei Paulus im Horizont griechischer und hellenistisch-jüdischer Anthropologie und Wirkungsgeschichte*, WUNT 464, 1st series, Tübingen, 2021.

Garrison, D., *A Cultural History of the Human Body in Antiquity*, London, 2012.

Geest, P. van, *The Incomprehensibility of God. Augustine as a Negative Theologian*, Louvain, 2010, 109–127.

Giannini, G., *Il problema antropologico: Linee dio sviluppo storico-speculativo dai presocratici a San Tommaso*, Rome, 1965.

Griffin, S.S., & I. Ramelli, eds., *Lovers of the Soul, Lovers of the Body: Philosophical and Religious Perspectives in Late Antiquity*, Harvard, 2022.

Grossi, V., "L'Antropologia cristiana negli scritti di Agostino," *SSR* 4, 1980, 89–113.

Harrison, N.V., *God's Many-Splendored Image*, Grand Rapids, 2010.

Karpp, H., *Probleme der altchristlichen Anthropologie*, Bad Godesberg, 1950.

Kooten, G.H. van, *Paul's Anthropology in Context*, Tübingen, 2008.

Merki, H., *Ὁμοίωσις Θεῷ*, Freiburg, 1952.

Perkins, J., *Roman Imperial Identities in the Early Christian Era*, London, 2009.

Ramelli, I., *Gregorio di Nissa sull'anima e la resurrezione*, Milan, 2007.

Ramelli, I., *Bardaisan of Edessa*, Piscataway, 2009; Berlin, 2019.

Ramelli, I., "Review of Perkins, 2009," *ReBL* 4, 2009a.

Ramelli, I., "1 Tim 5:6 and the Notion and Terminology of Spiritual Death," *Aevum* 84, 2010, 3–16.

Ramelli, I., "Theosebia: A Presbyter of the Catholic Church," *JFSR* 26/2, 2010a, 79–102.

Ramelli, I., "Spiritual Weakness, Illness, and Death in 1 Cor 11:30," *JBL* 130, 2011, 145–163.

Ramelli, I., "Gregory Nyssen's Position in Late-Antique Debates on Slavery & Poverty" *JLAn* 5, 2012, 87–118.

Ramelli, I., *The Christian Doctrine of Apokatastasis*, Leiden, 2013.

Ramelli, I., "Harmony between *arkhē* and *telos* in Patristic Platonism," *IJPlT* 7, 2013a, 1–49.

Ramelli, I., "Origen and Augustine: A Paradoxical Reception," *Numen* 60, 2013b, 280–307.

Ramelli, I., "Preexistence of Souls?" *SP* 56/4, 2013c, 167–226.

Ramelli, I., "Death," in: A. Di Berardino, ed., *EAC*, vol. I., Downers Grove, 2014, 673–681.

Ramelli, I., "Οἰκείωσις in Gregory of Nyssa's Theology," in: J. Leemans & M. Cassin, eds., *Gregory of Nyssa: Contra Eunomium III*, Leiden, 2014a, 643–659.

Ramelli, I., *Evagrius Ponticus' Kephalaia Gnostika*, Leiden, 2015a.

Ramelli, I., *Social Justice and the Legitimacy of Slavery: The Role of Philosophical Asceticism from Ancient Judaism to Late Antiquity*, Oxford, 2016.

Ramelli, I., "Gregory Nyssen's and Evagrius's Biographical and Theological Relations: Origen's Heritage and Neoplatonism," in: I. Ramelli, ed., *Evagrius between Origen, the Cappadocians, and Neoplatonism*; in collaboration with K. Corrigan, G. Maspero & M. Tobon, Louvain, 2017, 165–231.

Ramelli, I., "Gregory of Nyssa," in: S. Cartwright & A. Marmodoro, eds., *A History of Mind and Body in Late Antiquity*, Cambridge UK, 2018, 283–305.

Ramelli, I., "Gregory of Nyssa on the Soul (and the Restoration): From Plato to Origen," in: A. Marmodoro & N. McLynn, eds., *Exploring Gregory of Nyssa: Historical and Philosophical Perspectives*, Oxford, 2018a, 110–141.

Ramelli, I., "Origen on the Unity of Soul and Body in the Earthly Life and Afterwards and His Impact," in: J. Ulrich, A. Usacheva & S. Bhayro, eds., *The Unity of Soul and Body in Patristic and Byzantine Thought*, Leiden, 2021, 38–77.

Ramelli, I., "*Soma* (Σῶμα)," in: *RAC*, vol. XXX, Stuttgart: 2021, cols. 814–847.

Ramelli, I., "The Soul-Body Relation in Origen of Alexandria: Ensomatosis vs. Metensomatosis," in: P. van Geest & N. Vos, eds., *Early Christian Mystagogy and the Body*, Louvain, 2022, 97–119.

Ramelli, I., & D. Konstan, *Terms for Eternity*, Piscataway, 2007; Berlin, 2021.

Steenberg, M., *Of God and Man*, London, 2009.

Talor, J., & I.L.E. Ramelli, eds., *Patterns of Women's Leadership in Ancient Christianity*, Oxford, 2021.

Wallace-Hadrill, D.S., *The Greek Patristic View of Nature*, Manchester, 1968.

ILARIA L.E. RAMELLI

Anthropomorphism

Anthropomorphism, a term that first appears in the mid-18th century, comes from ἄνθρωπος, "human being," and μορφή, "form." It is the attribution of human forms or traits to whatever is not a human being, for example an animal, an object, and especially a divinity. Anthropomorphisms ascribed to → animals are typical of traditional fables that feature animals able to think and talk like humans. Examples in the classical world can be found in the Greek fables ascribed to Aesop, a historical or legendary figure from the 6th century BCE, and in the Latin Phaedrus, a contemporary of → Philo of Alexandria and of Jesus of Nazareth, a freedman who Latinized the Aesopic fables. Aesop's anthropomorphisms were very well known in the early imperial age, as → Apollonius of Tyana attests:t

> After being brought up from childhood with these stories [namely of talking animals, and so on], and after being as it were nursed by them from babyhood, we acquire certain opinions of the several animals and think of some of them as royal animals, of others as silly, of others as witty, and so on. (Philostr. *Vita Ap.* 11)

Apollonius emphasized that everybody knew that the events narrated in the Aesopic fables never took place historically, but are only allegorical fictions, unlike the myths concerning deities narrated by the poets, which were sometimes taken literally, but were mostly allegorized by philosophers, precisely in order to remove embarrassing anthropomorphisms from them (see discussion below).

Examples of anthropomorphisms applied to animals are also found in early Christian literature, for example in the *Acts of Philip* (Ramelli, 2007a; 2013, 81–87). These *Acts* have an encratite vein and seem to counter Ophite Gnosticism (→ Gnosis/Gnosticism) in their opposition to the veneration of a serpent. In *Acts* 8, the Lord, through Philip, converts a leopard from his "evil heart" to meekness, so that he renounces devouring a small kid. The leopard symbolizes evil people who convert to meekness and gentleness. In Isa 11:6–7, a prediction of the restoration of the people of the Lord and the eventual → *apokatastasis* brought about by the righteousness and faithfulness of the descendant of Jesse, it is stated that the leopard and the kid will lie down together, and the lion will eat straw like the ox. Mindful of Isaiah's prophecy, in the *Acts of Philip* the apostles pray to God that the animals may "attain meekness and eat no more flesh." Philip refers to the kid as "the wounded one who has recovered and cures the one who has wounded him," the latter being the leopard (in the Christological allegory, the wounded may represent Christ, God's lamb (→ *Agnus Dei*), who heals the human being who killed him). Both the leopard and the kid convert to the Lord and assume human *logos*, in other words word and reason, glorifying God for this. This is a sign of the divine grace that converts souls, even the most ferocious. This is why the apostles Philip (→ Philip the Apostle) and Bartholomew (→ Bartholomew the Apostle), before this miracle, declare: "Now we have really realized that there is nobody who surpasses your tender and compassionate mercy, o Jesus, you who love humanity!" The fact that Jesus is said to have mercy upon wild animals because he loves humanity further suggests that these animals represent fierce sinners, as it also happens in Theophil. *Autol.* 2.17. Jesus is declared to be able to convert and save even these. The assimilation of fierce sinners to ferocious beasts is also found in Origen's *Dialogue with Heraclides* (14), who too avers that Christ-*logos* can transform these ferocious beasts into humans:

Even if you were a ferocious beast, by listening to the Logos who tames and makes gentler, who transforms you into a human being, by the Logos you will never be addressed as "snake, race of vipers" any longer. For, if it were

impossible for these snakes – snakes in their souls because of sin – to be transformed into human beings, the Savior, o John, would not have said, "Make worthy fruits of repentance." After repenting, you will no more be a "snake, race of vipers."

Likewise Origen interpreted ferocious beasts as symbols of those people who are so beastly cruel that the sweetness of faith has not made them meek (Or. *Hom. Gen.* 2.3). Here in the *Acts of Philip*, too, the conversion of animals to faith and even to human form and speech may symbolize the transformative power of the *logos*.

After their "humanization," the animals stand like humans and glorify God: "You who have changed our bestial nature into meekness." In *Act* 12, when Philip gives the Eucharist to Mariamme and Bartholomew, the leopard and the kid, being excluded, cry, and the former protests with human eloquence:

My bestial nature has been modified and has transformed into goodness [...] The beauty of the figure of the Son has killed the dragon and the serpents, and has not forbidden us to accede to his mystery [...] we have experienced the glorious presence of your intercessory prayers and benedictions [...] Granted, I am a ferocious beast, but why has this kid here not merited the Eucharist? Is it not the case that we, too, have life secured with God? Thus, you be merciful with us, because the same God is in everyone and has given us the Logos with generosity [...] we have become like humans, and truly God dwells in us [...] Apostles of the good Savior, make this grace to us: let our bestial body be transformed, and may we abandon the animal appearance.

What transforms "animals" into humans, however, is not so much a bodily change, but it is the *logos* and the → *nous*, the intellect:

The *nous* that inhabits all thoughts/reasonings [λογισμοί] and even the heart. This *nous* has begun to dwell in us and has led us to lofty sentiments [...] It drags us out of the heavy torpor of bestiality and little by little transfers us to meekness, until we become complete human beings, in body and soul. (*Acts Phil.* 12.5)

God is said to take providential care of every nature, even those of ferocious creatures, on account of his great mercy, maternal and compassionate (πολλὴ εὐσπλαγχνία). If the anthropomorphic animals here are allegories of sinners, this means that God's → providence extends even to the worse sinners, who also are creatures of God, an idea that was developed by → Clement of Alexandria, → Origen, and → Diodore of Tarsus in their doctrine of *apokatastasis*.

The text insists that God has visited the universe by means of his Christ, including in his salvific economy not only human beings, but also animals. After receiving a human soul – which may symbolize the transformation of fierce sinners into meek persons, a spiritual resurrection – the animals also receive a human body, and the way in which they thank the Lord for this suggests that this is a metaphor of the resurrection, and possibly also of baptism, which in turn symbolized the resurrection: "We glorify you, o Lord, only-begotten Son, for the immortal birth in which we have now been born." Soon after, the animals profess to believe that there exists no living creature to which God does not extend providential care for its salvation. An interesting parallel to the conversion of savage beasts to meekness is found in the *Acts of Paul* (→ Paul the Apostle), where a lion experiences this same conversion and is baptized. After this, Paul glorifies God, "who has given the Logos/reason/speech to savage beasts and salvation to those who serve him." Savage beasts represent the worst sinners, those who are most removed from God and human nature.

But the most important kind of anthropomorphism, and the most relevant to early Christianity, is theological anthropomorphism, that is, the attribution of human characteristics to the divine. This anthropomorphism is found not only in Jewish and Christian Scriptures, but also, and even more prominently, in pagan theological myths. These often represented the divinities with human forms, features, and behaviors such as eating, drinking, falling in love, marrying, begetting children, being unfaithful to their spouses, waging wars, and falling prey to passions such as hatred, jealousy, greed, lust, and anger. Ancient philosophers, almost from the very beginning of Greek philosophy, criticized the anthropomorphic traits of the deities of myths. Xenophanes of Colophon (d. c. 480 BCE) attacked the traditional

depiction of deities as anthropomorphic in passages that were later cited with approval by Clement of Alexandria (*Strom.* 5.110 and 7.22):

> But if cattle and horses and lions had hands, or could paint with their hands and create works such as humans do, horses also would depict the gods' shapes like horses and cattle like cattle, and would make their bodies of such a sort as the form they themselves have. [...] Ethiopians say that their gods are snub-nosed and black, Thracians that they are pale and red-haired.

Xenophanes, instead, promoting an early kind of philosophical henotheism, averred that there is "one god, greatest among gods and humans, like mortals neither in form nor in thought/mind." Philosophical criticism continued throughout Greek and Roman philosophy, and earned thinkers like Seneca the denomination of *saepe noster* by Christians such as → Tertullian (*An.* 20). Even a philosopher who gained the undeserved fame of atheist such as → Epicurus insisted that the true piety is to entertain worthy notions of the gods, which excluded passions from them (Ramelli, 2012; 2020). It is significant that Judaism rejected an anthropomorphic representation of God precisely during the Hasmonean period (c. 300 BCE), that is, when it began to incorporate some Greek philosophy.

One prominent way in which philosophy, and especially Stoicism, sought to bypass the embarrassing problem of anthropomorphisms unworthy of the divine, was through → allegory, that is, through an allegorical exegesis of theological myths, also called "allegoresis." Allegorizers of theological texts aimed at finding deeper meanings and philosophical truths in traditional texts, thereby rescuing them from accusations of superficiality or impiety. The goal was to find in the Homeric poems, and in other theological myths, meanings "worthy of the divine." Particularly for Stoic allegorists, and later for Middle and Neoplatonic allegories, allegoresis was part and parcel of philosophy, the way to ennoble philosophical traditions, purging them from unbecoming elements, and integrating them into philosophy. The presupposition, as the Roman Stoic Annaeus Cornutus has it, was that the ancients were not people of no account, but they were able to express philosophical truths by means of symbols and allusions (*CTG* 35).

The Bible, too, and especially the Hebrew Bible, teems with theological anthropomorphisms. God has feet, arms and hands, even a back and shoulders, and a face; God speaks, breathes, sees, hears, strolls in the garden of Eden, sits in the heavens, and uses the earth as a footstool; what is worse, God gets angry and repents, thereby displaying human passions. Hence the application of allegoresis to Scripture as well, from Jewish Hellenistic allegorists such as Aristobulus and Philo of Alexandria to Christian allegorists such as Clement of Alexandria, Origen, → Gregory of Nyssa, → Evagrius of Pontus, → Ambrose of Milan, the young → Augustine of Hippo, and others. Aristobulus in fragment 2 explicitly made it clear that biblical allegoresis was necessary particularly for divine anthropomorphism. And the Christian allegorists whom I have just mentioned were all Christian Platonists who insisted on the spiritual nature of God, who is therefore deprived of any human shape, on divine → *apatheia* or absence of passions, and on apophatic theology. They agreed that human mind can grasp the existence of the divinity, but not its essence or nature, given God's → transcendence (Ramelli, 2014a). Scriptural anthropomorphisms were regularly allegorized by them and often seen as accommodations to the limited capacities of simple humans. Origen in his theorization of biblical exegesis in book 4 of his *On First Principles* remarked that God's anthropomorphisms, just as grammatical or factual incongruities, facts that did not really happen, and legal prescriptions impossible to fulfill, have "bare spiritual meanings" not wrapped in a literal sense, to have readers understand that it is necessary to seek a deeper meaning (Or. *Princ.* 4.2.9; 4.3.1; *Philoc.* 1.16). These are exceptions to Origen's general rule that all of Scripture has both a literal, historical meaning and a spiritual meaning, or better many spiritual meanings (Ramelli, 2011). But in the case of passages containing ἄλογα (illogicalities) and ἀδύνατα (impossibilities), Scripture only has a spiritual meaning, without a literal meaning. And God's anthropomorphisms were prominent among such passages. C.W. Griffin and D.N. Paulsen (2002) have indicated that, unlike the way Origen casts it, anthropomorphism was widespread not only among simple-minded, uneducated people, but also among learned people. But Origen and Victorinus were the

main promoters of the (Platonizing) doctrine of the incorporeality of God, and, like Augustine later, tended to associate anthropomorphism with the uneducated. D.A. Giulea (2015) has shown how the theory of the noetic form of God (as opposed to a sense-perceptible form) was elaborated by Origen and other intellectuals precisely as a reaction to anthropomorphism.

So-called Anthropomorphites are also recorded as a Christian heresy (→ Heresy), identified especially with the Syriac Audians – from their founder Audius or Audaeus – in the 3rd/4th century CE, but also present in 4th-century CE Egypt. Their argument, as reported in heresiological literature, was grounded in a literal, naïf interpretation of Gen 1:26–27 about the → creation of the human being in the image (εἰκών) of God. → Jerome in his *Ep.* 6, *Ad Pammachium*, heavily denounced the mistake of taking Gen 1:2–27 as evidence that God has human shape. This heresy is also attested among some African Christians. Epiphanius of Salamis also included the Audians in his *Panarion* or *Refutation of All Heresies*, as did also → Theodoret of Cyrrhus in *Hist. eccl.* 4.9, a chapter entirely devoted to "the heresy of the Audians." He traces them back to Audaeus, a Syrian by birth and by language, and to his literal interpretation of Gen 1:26–27, which led him to believe that God has "a human form" and "bodily parts." Instead,

> Scripture frequently describes the divine operations under the names of human parts, since by these means the providence of God is made more easily intelligible to minds incapable of perceiving any immaterial ideas. (Thdt. *Hist. eccl.* 4.9)

Epiphanius also accuses Audaeus of having adopted some of the Manichean doctrines (→ Mani/Manichaeism). → Cyril of Alexandria composed a brief treatise against some anthropomorphites among the Egyptian monks in his day (*Adversus Anthropomorphitas*; PG 76). These monks were obviously the heirs of the anthropomorphite monks who determined a sharp political change in Cyril's predecessor, → Theophilus of Alexandria.

Theophilus' anti-Origenian period was closely related to the anthropomorphite controversy. This period of his life was limited to a stretch of very few years, a good while after his election to the bishopric of Alexandria in 385 CE. First, during the outburst of the Origenistic controversy (→ Origenism/Origenist Controversy) in Palestine, he sided with the Origenists and against Epiphanius, as is attested by Palladius (*Dial.* 16), Socrates of Constantinople (*Hist. eccl.* 6.10; → Socrates Scholasticus), and → Sozomen (*Hist. eccl.* 8.14). In his letter to the pope, Theophilus even expressed his disdain for Epiphanius' theological arguments. It is significant that, when the controversy was ignited in 396 CE, Theophilus sent Isidore, an Origenian monk, to calm down the disagreement. Isidore wrote to John, the bishop of Jerusalem, another Origenian, advising him to resist Jerome, as we learn from Jerome himself (*Adv. Jo. Hier.* 37). Theophilus exhorted John and Jerome to be reconciled with each other, although he also invited John to adhere to orthodoxy, thus implying that John had been in some way unorthodox so far. This is why the bishop of Jerusalem in 396 CE produced an apologetic (→ Apologetics) response that was reconstructed by P. Nautin on the basis of Jerome's work *Adversus Johannem Hierosolymitanum*, against John of Jerusalem. In this apology John, the Origenian bishop, defended his own orthodoxy. At this stage, Theophilus could definitely not be regarded as an anti-Origenian. Indeed, in 397 CE Jerome wrote to Theophilus that "many people" considered him to be excessively indulgent with the Egyptian Origenists (Jer. *Ep.* 63.3). Theophilus wrote to Jerome as a pacifier (*Ep.* 82.1), but Jerome reproached him for the concord obtaining between him and the Origenian monks of the Egyptian desert (*Ep.* 82.3). Theophilus indeed invited these monks to serve in ecclesiastical ministries, as is attested by Socrates (*Hist. eccl.* 6.7) and Sozomen (*Hist. eccl.* 8.12). This concord was not appreciated by Jerome (after his U-turn against Origen), who can be deemed one of the concurring factors in Theophilus' short, ambiguous anti-Origenian activity.

But the main factor was the arrival of anthropomorphite, anti-Origenian monks from Scetis at Theophilus' seat in Alexandria. The link between anti-Origenism and anthropomorphism is clear: Origen has insisted a great deal on the spiritual and absolutely incorporeal nature of God (to the point of claiming that only the → Trinity is completely immaterial, while all creatures participate in corporeality, albeit to different extents). This was totally incompatible with the attribution of human forms and passions to the divinity. As I have mentioned, Origen even indicated theological anthropomorphism in Scripture as the main element that triggered the necessity of an exclusively allegorical interpretation of a given scriptural passage. The aim of the anthopomorphite and anti-Origenian monks was to vigorously protest, not even without threats, against Theophilus' festal letter on the incorporeal nature of God, which was issued in 399 CE and obviously followed Origen's anti-anthropomorphite line. Probably out of fear due to those threats, for a very political reason rather than a real theological change of mind, Theophilus suddenly admitted the anthropomorphism of God, thereby siding with the so-called anthropomorphite monks and against the Origenians. The following is Photius' account of the facts, gathered in turn from George of Alexandria, who blamed the anthropomorphite monks as inept and unlearned:

> At that time the controversy against the Anthropomorphites happened to burst out. The Egyptian monks, for the most part unlearned and rough, were in agitation. Theophilus was scared, as it seems, because they were attacking him, and had recourse to a sophism, so he said to them: "I saw your faces as the face of God!" But they insisted, adding a further request: that Origen be anathematised, because he claimed that the divine has no form/shape [ἀσχημάτιστον τὸ θεῖον]. Theophilus promised that he would do so, and thus escaped death. (Phot. *Bibl.* codex 96.82a)

Therefore, in 400 CE, in a letter to Jerome preserved in Jerome's epistolary correspondence (Jer. *Ep.* 87; see 90), Theophilus announced that he had chased away the "furious" Origenists from the monasteries of Nitria. Moreover, he exhorted Jerome to write against Origenism. He also wrote to Epiphanius, urging him to summon a synod in Cyprus in order to condemn Origen, and then to notify such a condemnation to Constantinople and in Asia Minor. Finally, Jerome wrote to Pope Anastasius as well, with the same concerns. According to the *Dialogue on the Life of John Chrysostom* attributed to Palladius (*Dial.* 7.24), Theophilus had recourse to drastic methods. The Origenian monks' cells were burned along with their books, and more than 300 hundred monks had to flee. The same is confirmed by George of

Alexandria: the Origenian monks called Tall Brothers, in open polemic against the Anthropomorphites and Theophilus, who had suddenly sided with them,

> insisted that the divinity has no form, and rightly so. Thus, Theophilus falsely accused them before the Egyptian monks and stirred that stupid mass against them [...] Finally, after many vexations and plots against them, and after the fire was set against their cells, they fled from there to Constantinople, where they were courageously received by Deaconess Olympia and Bishop John Chrysostom. (*ap.* Phot. *Bibl.* codex 96, 82a)

These sources, from the heresiologists to Palladius and John of Alexandria, display no sympathy whatsoever for the anthopomorphites, be these the Audians or the Egyptian monks of the time of Theophilus and Cyril of Alexandria. P.A. Patterson (2012) has endeavored to reassess what the anthropomorphites in the Egyptian desert believed, also in the light of the *Life of Apa Aphou of Pemdje*. This document defends the anthropomorphites, but does not uphold an anthropomorphic doctrine of the crude kind, such as one maintaining that "God has a body" or "bodily features" or the like. Some scholars then concluded that the anthropomorphites in Egypt were only claiming that it was legitimate to form images of the incarnate Christ in prayer. This position, though, fails to give account of the numerous anti-anthropomorphite writings by Theophilus, Cyril, Cassian (Ioannes Cassianus) – on whose criticism of anthropomorphism see below – Jerome, and Augustine. On this basis, P.A. Patterson (2012) has argued that the anthropomorphites in fact promoted an ancient tradition, seeking in prayer the vision, not of the Incarnate Christ, but of the eternal, divine body of Christ. As I will argue, this position was contrasted by Evagrius, whose milieu was precisely the Egyptian desert and whose friends were the Origenian monks dubbed Tall Brothers.

The Origenian → John Cassian, whose identity has been recently and provocatively (but not unproblematically) reassessed by P. Tzamalikos (2012a; 2012b), is the most interesting voice in the polemic against anthropomorphism. In his *Conlationes* or *Conferences*, book 10, the second conference is that of Abbot Isaac, and here the sections 2–5 are entirely devoted to a refutation of anthropomorphism. In section 2, Cassian illustrates the custom of the patriarch of Alexandria to send out letters every year to all the churches of Egypt, both in the cities and in the monasteries, to indicate the exact date of the beginning of Lent, and the day of Easter. These were the so-called festal letters. Cassian recounts that, a few days after the previous conference had been held with Abbot Isaac, there arrived among the Egyptian monks the festal letter of the aforementioned Theophilus of Alexandria, in which, together with the announcement of the date of the Easter that year, he considered as well "the foolish heresy of the Anthropomorphites at great length, and abundantly refuted it," in accordance with the Origenian tenet of the exclusively spiritual nature of God. This letter, as Cassian informs, was received with bitterness by most of the monks residing in Egypt, due to "their simplicity and error," meaning precisely the error of anthropomorphism. The consequence of such embitterment was

> that the greater part of the Elders decreed that on the contrary bishop Theophilus ought to be abhorred by the whole body of the brothers as tainted with heresy of the worst kind, because he seemed to impugn the teaching of the holy Scripture by the denial that the Almighty God was formed in the fashion of a human figure, though Scripture teaches with perfect clearness that Adam was created in His image. (Cass. *Con.* 10.2.2)

Finally, Theophilus' letter was rejected also by the monks who were living in the desert of Scete and who are said by Cassian to have surpassed all those who were in the monasteries of Egypt, in perfection and in knowledge. The consequence of this general reaction was that,

> except Abbot Paphnutius, the presbyter of our congregation, not one of the other presbyters, who presided over the other three churches in the same desert, would suffer Theophilus' letter to be even read or repeated at all in their meetings. (Cass. *Con.* 10.2.2)

The anthropomorphite monks were rejecting the festal letter of their bishop.

Cassian then focuses on what he calls the heresy of anthropomorphism. He devotes section 3 to Abbot Sarapion and "the heresy of the Anthropomorphites, into which he fell in the error of simplicity" (on Sarapion, see DelCogliano, 2003). Among those who embraced anthropomorphism in Egypt in the time of Theophilus, there was Sarapion, an ascetic, described by Cassian as perfect in discipline, but ignorant in theology. Sarapion could not be persuaded to abandon anthropomorphism by many exhortations of Presbyter Paphnutius, "because this view seemed to him a novelty, and one that was not ever known to or handed down by his predecessors." But a very learned → deacon from Cappadocia, Photinus, who relied on the Origenian theology absorbed by the Cappadocians and by Evagrius himself, arrived in the Egyptian desert and was warmly welcomed by Paphnutius. The latter confirmed the anti-anthropomorphite doctrine of Theophilus' letter, placed Photinus in the midst and

> asked him before all the brothers how the Catholic Churches throughout the East interpreted the passage in Genesis where it says "Let us make man after our image and likeness" [Gen 1:26]. And when he explained that the image and likeness of God was taken by all the leaders of the churches not according to the base sound of the letters, but spiritually, and supported this very fully and by many passages of Scripture, and showed that nothing of this sort could happen to that infinite and incomprehensible and invisible glory, so that it could be comprised in a human form and likeness, since its nature is incorporeal and uncompounded and simple, and what can neither be apprehended by the eyes nor conceived by the mind, which is the exposition of Origen's theology, then Abbot Sarapion "was shaken by the numerous and very weighty assertions of this most learned man, and was drawn to the faith of the Catholic tradition." (Cass. *Con.* 10.2.3)

Cassian tells that Abbot Paphnutius and all of the monks rejoiced greatly at Abbot Sarapion's abandoning of the anthropomorphite heresy, since he thereby crowned a life full of virtues with "the right faith." Everybody prayed in thanksgiving, and Abbot Sarapion also prayed, but

> was so bewildered in mind during his prayer because he felt that *the anthropomorphic image of the Godhead which he used to set before himself*

in prayer, was banished from his heart, that on a sudden he burst into a flood of bitter tears and continual sobs, and cast himself down on the ground and exclaimed with strong groaning: "Alas! wretched man that I am! they have taken away my God from me, and I have now none to lay hold of; and whom to worship and address I know not." (Cass. *Con.* 10.2.3)

From this it emerges that, as P.A. Patterson has suggested (see above), the anthropomorphites cherished having a mental image of the divinity especially in the time of prayer. This, in my view, illuminates the insistence of Evagrius – the heir of Origen and the Cappadocians, particularly of Gregory of Nyssa (Ramelli, 2013a; 2015) – on the importance of imageless prayer (on which see Stewart, 2001). I suspect this is a polemic against anthropomorphite tendencies among Egyptian monks, Evagrius' milieu. Indeed, Evagrius sided with the Origenian and anti-anthropomorphite monks, the Tall Brothers, and died just before the precipitation of the anthropomorphite incident with Theophilus in 399 CE, as a result of which the Origenian monks were chased out of Egypt.

In section 4 Cassian goes on to report how, after the episode with Abbot Sarapion, he and the other monks returned to the wise Abbot Isaac and asked him about the anthropomorphite heresy, which the monks deemed conceived by the craft of demons (→ Demonology/Demons), because

> it is no small despair by which we are cast down when we consider that through the fault of this ignorance [i.e. anthropomorphism] Abbot Sarapion has not only utterly lost all those labors which he has performed in so praiseworthy a manner for 50 years in this desert, but has also incurred the risk of death in the aeon to come. (Cass. *Con.* 10.2.4)

So the monks asked Abbot Isaac why Abbot Sarapion was so deceived, and how one can arrive at imageless prayer – precisely the ideal of Evagrius. The answer by Abba Isaac is reported in section 5. He argued that it was not surprising that a really simple man, who had never received any instruction on the substance and nature of the Godhead, could be entangled and deceived by an error of simplicity and the habit of a longstanding mistake, or better could continue in the ancient error that was being brought about, not – as Cassian and his fellow monks supposed – by a new illusion of the demons, but by the ignorance typical of the ancient pagan world. For the pagans – Isaac remarks, along with many ancient Christian apologists – used to worship idols that were actually demons, and these were shaped in the figure of human beings. So, owing to this deception, the simple minded even among the Christians were still thinking that the incomprehensible and ineffable glory of the true deity had to be worshipped under the limitations of some figure or shape. For they believed that they could grasp and hold nothing if they had not some image set before them, which they could continually address while they were praying, and which they could "carry around in their mind and have always fixed before their eyes." Against this mistake, Isaac invoked Paul's charge against the Gentiles in Rom 1:23: "And they changed the glory of the incorruptible God into the likeness of the image of corruptible man." Isaac also quoted Jer 2:11: "My people have changed their glory for an idol."

Now, Isaac noted, this error, which was typical of pagans, was shared also by some simple and ignorant Christians, due to their wrong exegesis of Gen 1:26: "Let us make the human being in our image and after our likeness" (this point is common to all heresiological accounts of anthropomorphism). From this interpretation Isaac traces the origin of

> a heresy called that of the Anthropomorphites, which maintains with obstinate perverseness that the infinite and simple substance of the Godhead is fashioned in our lineaments and human configuration. (Cass. *Con.* 10.2.4)

The orthodox Christians, instead, according to Isaac, had to abhor anthropomorphism as heathenish blasphemy, and therefore

> arrive at that perfectly pure condition in prayer which will not only not connect with its prayers any figure of the Godhead or bodily lineaments – which it is a sin even to speak of – but will not allow in itself even the memory of a name, or the appearance of an action, or an outline of any character. (Cass. *Con.* 10.2.4)

Isaac's representation of pure, imageless prayer, as formulated by Cassian, is the expression of Evagrius'

ideal of prayer, which in turn probably developed as a reaction to Egyptian anthropomorphite monks. In his *Chapters on Prayer*, Evagrius shows how, in rising through the diverse contemplations of all of creation to the simplest knowledge of God the Creator, the intellect has to ascend from multiplicity to unity (see Ramelli, 2013b) and from images to imagelessness. This is the state of perfect prayer, which for Evagrius is also perfect theology. In *Orat.* 55, Evagrius hammered home the necessity of liberating oneself from mental concepts and images to attain perfection in prayer:

> The person who has attained impassivity has not already found true prayer as well, for one can be among simple intellections and be distracted by the information they provide, and so be far from God.

Apatheia is necessary, but not sufficient for perfect prayer: this must be free from all mental concepts and images – those so cherished by the anthropomorphite monks.

In *Orat.* 56 Evagrius further details that, even when the intellect does not linger among the simple intellections of objects, it has not yet attained true prayer, because it can

> remain in the contemplation of objects and be engaged in meditation on their *logoi*, which, even though they involve simple expressions, nevertheless, insofar as they are contemplations of objects, leave their impression and form on the intellect and lead it far from God.

All intellections, even the most simple and unified, imply a duality between knower and known that must be done away with, if one aims at achieving perfect prayer in union with God. In *Orat.* 57 Evagrius explains that not only the contemplation of corporeal nature, but also the knowledge of intelligible objects and their multiplicity, must be left aside for the attainment of true prayer. This is because, contrary to what the anthropomorphite monks thought, but consistently with what Origen taught, God is formless, simple, immaterial, and spiritual. And the intellect, being the image of God, is also formless, simple, immaterial, and spiritual; after the fall, the intellect has acquired form, multiplicity, and corporeality, but to revert and be restored to God – ultimately eschatologically, but in prayer by anticipation of the *eschaton* – the intellect must give up all multiplicity and thus all intellections.

This is why Evagrius, with a clearly anti-anthropomorphite move, in *Orat.* 66 recommended,

> When you pray, *do not form images of the divine within yourself*, nor allow your intellect to be impressed with any form, but approach the Immaterial immaterially and you will come to understanding.

In *Skem.* 21 Evagrius explains likewise that in order to reach the peak of prayer, that is, imageless prayer, the intellect must be in formlessness:

> When the intellect is in πρακτική [i.e. asceticism], it is in the intellections of this world. When it is in gnosis, it passes its time in contemplation. Having come to be in prayer, it is in formlessness, which is called the "place of God."

M. Tobon insightfully relates imageless prayer with the apophatic theology of Evagrius as expressed in the "missing chapters" of his *Kephalaia Gnostika* or *Chapters on Knowledge*. Evagrius' aversion for anthropomorphism and anthropomorphite prayer (i.e. non-imageless prayer) is clear. And Cassian was the direct heir of Evagrius also in his polemic against the Egyptian anthropomorphite monks and their imperfect prayer.

Historiography

Anthropomorphisms and their criticism in ancient philosophy have been studied in Xenophanes and Stoic allegoresis by several historians of ancient philosophy (systematically by Ramelli, 2004; 2007a; 2022), and their presence and interpretation in the Bible have been studied in scholarship on Jewish Hellenistic and ancient Christian exegesis of Scripture, with reference especially to Philo, Aristobulus, and the Origenian line of allegoresis of Scripture (Simonetti, 2004, Ramelli, 2008; 2011; 2014). I. Ramelli (2007; 2013, 81–87) has analyzed anthropomorphisms applied to animals in early Christian literature.

The specific controversy involving the ancient Christian Anthropomorphites at the time of Theophilus of Antioch (on which see below in this entry), has been examined by P.A. Patterson (2012) and I. Ramelli (2013, within the Origenistic controversy).

Evagrius' imageless prayer (Stewart, 2001) can be considered a response to anthropomorphism, as suggested by I. Ramelli (2013a; 2013b; 2015), and Cassian's involvement in the controversy has been hypothesized by M. DelCogliano (2003).

Bibliography

DelCogliano, M., "Situating Sarapion's Sorrow: The Anthropomorphite Controversy as the Historical and Theological Context of Cassian's Tenth Conference on Pure Prayer," *CistSQ* 38, 2003, 377–421.

DePalma Digeser, E., H. Marx & I.L.E. Ramelli, eds., *Problems in Ancient Biography: The Construction of professional Identities in Late Antiquity*, Cambridge MA, 2024.

Giulea, D.A., "Simpliciores, Eruditi, and the Noetic Form of God," *HThR* 108, 2015, 263–288.

Griffin, C.W., & D.N. Paulsen, "Augustine and the Corporeality of God," *HThR* 95, 2002, 97–118.

Patterson, P.A., *Visions of Christ: The Anthropomorphite Controversy of 399 CE*, Tübingen, 2012.

Ramelli, I., *Allegoria*, vol. I: *L'età classica*, Milan, 2004.

Ramelli, I., "Mansuetudine, grazia e salvezza negli *Acta Philippi*," *IL* 29, 2007a 215–228.

Ramelli, I., *Allegoristi dell'età classica*, Milan, 2007b.

Ramelli, I., "Philosophical Allegoresis of Scripture in Philo and Its Legacy in Gregory Nyssen," *SPhA* 20, 2008, 55–99.

Ramelli, I., "The Philosophical Stance of Allegory in Stoicism and its Reception in Platonism," *IJCT* 18, 2011, 335–371.

Ramelli, I., "Dieu et la philosophie: Le discours de Paul à Athènes dans trois 'actes apocryphes' et dans la philosophie patristique," *Greg* 93, 2012, 75–91.

Ramelli, I., *The Christian Doctrine of Apokatastasis: A Critical Assessment From the New Testament to Eriugena*, Leiden, 2013.

Ramelli, I., "Evagrius and Gregory: Nazianzen or Nyssen? A Remarkable Issue that Bears on the Cappadocian (and Origenian) Influence on Evagrius," *GRBS* 53, 2013a, 117–137.

Ramelli, I., "Harmony between *arkhē* and *telos* in Patristic Platonism," *IJPlT* 7, 2013b, 1–49.

Ramelli, I., "Valuing Antiquity in Antiquity by Means of Allegoresis," in: J. Ker & C. Pieper, eds., *Valuing the Past in the Greco-Roman World*, Leiden, 2014, 485–507.

Ramelli, I., "The Divine as Inaccessible Object of Knowledge in Ancient Platonism: A Common Philosophical Pattern across Religious Traditions," *JHI* 75, 2014a, 167–188.

Ramelli, I., *Evagrius Ponticus' Kephalaia Gnostika: Propositions on Knowledge*, Leiden, 2015.

Ramelli, I., "Gregory Nyssen's and Evagrius's Biographical and Theological Relations: Origen's Heritage and Neoplatonism," in: I. Ramelli, ed., *Evagrius Between Origen, the Cappadocians, and Neoplatonism*, Louvain, 2017,

165–231; in collaboration with K. Corrigan, G. Maspero & M. Tobon.

Ramelli, I., "Epicureanism and Early Christianity," in: Ph. Mitsis, ed., *Oxford Handbook to Epicurus and Epicureanism*, Oxford, 2020, 582–612.

Ramelli, I., "Gregory and Evagrius," *SP* 101, 2021, 177–206.

Ramelli, I., "Evagrius' Kephalaia Gnostika: Novel Research into Its Literary Structure and Philosophical Theology and A Look at Its Heritage," *Scr.&e-Scr.* 22, 2022, 73–98.

Ramelli, I., "Allegorizing and Philosophizing," in: R.S. Smith & S.M. Trzaskoma, eds., *Oxford Handbook of Greek and Roman Mythography*, Oxford, 2022, 331–348.

Simonetti, M., *Origene esegeta e la sua tradizione*, Brescia, 2004.

Stewart, C., "Imageless Prayer and the Theological Vision of Evagrius Ponticus,"*JECS* 9, 2001, 173–204.

Tobon, M., "A Word spoken in Silence: The 'Missing Chapters of Evagrius' *Kephalaia Gnostika*," *SP* 72, 2014, 197–210.

Tzamalikos, P., *The Real Cassian Revisited: Monastic Life, Greek Paideia, and Origenism in the Sixth Century*, Leiden, 2012a.

Tzamalikos, P., *A Newly Discovered Greek Father: Cassian the Sabaite Eclipsed by John Cassian of Marseilles*, Leiden, 2012b.

ILARIA L.E. RAMELLI

Antichrist

In the patristic period, the figure of antichrist becomes the eschatological archenemy of Jesus Christ, whose advent is expected to precede the → *parousia*. The belief in this figure emerged as part of a gradual process in which various earlier ideas on eschatological opponents merged into one, more or less coherent, scenario (→ Apocalypse).

1. Jewish Antecedents

Early Jewish writings contain various traditions on the final stage of history, such as the climax of → evil that was expected to take place preceding God's ultimate intervention in history, the expected appearance of false prophets, the advent of an eschatological tyrant, the final battle with Belial/Beliar and his ultimate defeat, the defeat of the chaos monsters (Leviathan and Behemoth), the tradition of the final assault of Gentile nations, and the legend of *Nero redivivus*. The period immediately preceding God's ultimate intervention in history is consistently described as a time of upheaval in which

the order of creation will be disturbed. In general, this disturbance takes the form of a climax of evil. Descriptions of this kind are found in Dan 7–8 and 11–12; *Jub.* 23:13–21; *1 En.* 80:2–7; 91:6–7; 91:11; 93:9–10; 99:4–8; 100:1–4; *As. Mos.* 7–8; *4 Ezra* 5:1–12; 6:18–24; 8:49–50; 9:3–6; 14:16–18; *2 Bar.* 48:26–41; 70:2–71:11; 89:9–21; and *Sib. Or.* 3:635–651, 796–806; 4:152–161. In many of these descriptions, the influence of the idea of a periodization of history – such as that found in especially Daniel (esp. 7:8, 20–27; 8:9–12, 23–25; 11:21–45) – is evident. A variety of figures is expected to appear in this chaotic time (see *As. Mos.* 8:1–3; *4 Ezra* 5:6; 11:29–35; 12:23–31; *2 Bar.* 36:7–11; 40:1–3; *Sib. Or.* 3:75–92, 611–615). Various texts speak about Belial – or the Greek form, Beliar – as the chief angelic figure who instigates many forms of evil. In the writings of Qumran, Belial functions like Satan or the → devil does in other texts. He is the head of the forces of the "Sons of Light" (1QM) and will rule until God finally intervenes in history (e.g. 1QM 14.8–10; 1QS 4.18–23). This particular idea of Belial has strongly influenced the Christian *Testaments of the Twelve Patriarchs*, which describes Beliar in a similar fashion (see e.g. *T. Benj.* 3:8; *T. Dan* 5:10–11; *T. Jud.* 25:3; *T. Levi* 3:3; 18:12; *T. Zeb.* 9:8). Occasionally, an eschatological advent of Belial is described (see CD 8.2; *Sib. Or.* 2:154–173; 3:63–74). The two chaos monsters that are thought to be kept by God until their final defeat are Leviathan and Behemoth (see *1 En.* 60:7–8, 24–25; *4 Ezra* 6:49–52; *2 Bar.* 29:4). Another prominent element in many descriptions of the final battle of history entails an assault on Jerusalem and Palestine by the nations (see *Jub.* 23:22–25; *1 En.* 56:5–8; 90:13–19; 4Q246; *4 Ezra* 13:5–38; *Sib. Or.* 3:657–668; see the interpretation of Ps 2 in 4Q174). In *Sib. Or.* 3:63–74; 4:119–224, 137–139; 5:28–34, 137–151, 214–227, and 361–371, the legend of the return of Emperor Nero has left its traces: here, the expected eschatological tyrant is modeled after his example. Among the Qumran scrolls (→ Dead Sea Scrolls), evidence is found on a pair of eschatological figures that shares traces of the later Christ/antichrist antagonism. This pair is described as Melchizedek and Melchiresha (11QMelch; 4QAmram; 4Q280), and while the latter is in charge of the forces of evil, the former is seen as a positive figure. In sum, in early Jewish sources, we find a variety of expectations concerning the ultimate intervention of God in history. A comparable variety is traceable with regard to the positive figures who are thought to intervene on behalf of God, and where emerging Christianity focuses on Jesus Christ as the one and only positive divine eschatological agent, his counterpart antichrist was modeled out of his many examples in much the same way.

2. Eschatological Opponents in the Earliest Christian Texts

The figure of antichrist is mentioned for the first time in the Johannine Epistles (1 John 2:18–22; 4:1–6; 2 John 7) and by → Polycarp of Smyrna (*Phil.* 7:1). The term can denote either an "anti-messiah" or a "false messiah," and the ambivalence in the term always remained throughout the history of its use. 1 John 2:18 refers to the tradition of antichrist as a familiar idea for his readership ("as you have heard that antichrist is coming") and applies this apparently traditional motif to the situation in the congregation that is addressed by the letter: the rise of opponents who reject the advent of Christ "in the flesh" is interpreted as evidence of the arrival of "many antichrists." It is clear that the main characteristic of antichrist as perceived in the Johannine Epistles is his attempt to lead believers astray. In 1 John 4:1–6, the deceitful preachers who deny Jesus' appearance in the flesh are described as ruled by the spirit of antichrist and are identified as "false prophets" (ψευδοπροφῆται), and in 2 John 7, the term "antichrist" is equated with "deceiver" (πλάνος).

Closely connected to the tradition of antichrist are several figures in early Christian documents who function as "false prophets." Jesus himself warns against false messiahs and false prophets in Mark 13:22 (and Matt. 24:24; see *Apoc. Pet.* 2:7–13), and the term "false prophet" is also used in the book of Revelation as a description of the second Beast of Rev 13:11–18 (see Rev 16:13; 19:20; 20:10). A second motif that is often found in early Christian writings is the idea of eschatological deceit: at the end of history, deceivers will appear to lead the believers astray, and this activity is caused by an important characteristic of the devil. The prominent fear of, and resistance against, false teachings expressed by the stress on false prophets/messiahs and the deceit motif is a typical characteristic of early Christian literature. This is an indication that, already in the formative period of early Christianity, emphasis was placed on ideas and knowledge as crucial to the identity of the developing Christian movement.

Two sources that have greatly contributed to the formation of a single antichrist legend in later Christian sources are 2 Thessalonians and the book of Revelation. The book of 2 Thessalonians, a deutero-pauline epistle that was probably written in the late 1st or early 2nd century CE, describes a scenario in terms of the early Jewish tradition of an evil eschatological tyrant. Based on 2 Thess 2:2 (μήτε δι' ἐπιστολῆς ὡς δι' ἡμῶν), it is highly probable that 2 Thessalonians intends to replace 1 Thessalonians with its expectation of the imminent *parousia* (2 Thess 4:11–18). In order to do so, its author describes the "man of lawlessness" as a blaspheming tyrant who will not be able to appear anytime soon, until an enigmatic restraining force (τὸ κατέχον, 2 Thess 2:6) or person (ὁ κατέχων, 2 Thess 2:7) is removed. The obfuscating terms in which this scenario is described have given rise to many interpretations as to the identity of this restraining power. Rhetorically, though, the effect of its mention is that the letter points out that the advent of the eschatological tyrant is an event of the distant future. Since in the scenario of 2 Thess 2 the *parousia* of Christ cannot take place until after the lawless one has been defeated, the description as a whole intends to point out that God's final intervention in history should be seen as an event of the distant rather than the near future. The lawless one of 2 Thess 2 is not only depicted as an eschatological tyrant, though. An important detail that brings him in close proximity with the figure of antichrist is the fact that he will act "in the working of Satan, who uses all power, signs, lying wonders, and every kind of wicked deception for those who are perishing" (2 Thess 2:910).

The book of Revelation contains a description of Satan and his two helpers, the Beast from the Sea (Rev 13:1–10) and the Beast from the Land (Rev 13:11–18) as the ultimate eschatological opponents of Jesus Christ. In Revelation, the term "antichrist" does not occur. As indicated above, the second Beast is referred to in later chapters as "the False Prophet." It is especially the first Beast that is interpreted by later authors as a description of antichrist. This is not strange, given the fact that the seer John models this particular beast (Rev 13:1–3) after the example of the lamb mentioned earlier in the book (Rev 5:6). In the symbolic language of Revelation, the devil and his two companions function as counterparts to God, Christ, and the seven Spirits of God described in Rev 4–5. The scenario of chapters 19–20 describes how the devil and his companions will be defeated by Christ. The Beast and the False Prophet will be cast into a lake of fire (Rev 19:20), but the devil will be incarcerated for a 1,000 years to be unleashed afterward (Rev 20:1–3). During this 1,000-year period (→ Chiliasm), Christ will rule with his "saints." At the end of this period of messianic reign, Satan will be unleashed again, only to be destroyed immediately (Rev 20:7–10). After that, the Last Judgment will be held, at which the final decision on the life and death of human beings is proclaimed (Rev 20:11–15).

3. 2nd-Century CE Sources

In a number of early extracanonical writings, eschatological opponents are described in terms similar to the ones used in the writings discussed above. Three figures worth mentioning in this respect are the "deceiver of the world" of *Did.* 16, the eschatological tyrant described in Danielic terms in *Barn.* 4, and the figure of Beliar as featuring in *Ascen. Isa.* 4.

In his *Dialogue with Trypho*, → Justin Martyr speaks about the "two advents" of Christ: the first one is an event in the past and refers to Jesus' ministry before his crucifixion, whereas the second advent is what Paul (→ Paul the Apostle) describes as the *parousia* (see Just. *Dial.* 32). In chapter 110 Justin seems to betray knowledge of the scenario of 2 Thess 2: he describes the "man of apostasy" (→ Apostasy/Apostates) in terms that strongly remind the reader of this deuteropauline depiction.

In the writings of → Irenaeus of Lyon and → Tertullian, the process moves one step further, and the scenario of 2 Thess 2 is combined with the term "antichrist" and other eschatological prophecies. In *Haer.* 3.6, Irenaeus explicitly quotes 2 Thess 2:4 and states that its description refers to "antichrist" (see also Iren. *Haer.* 3.7; 4.29). The analysis of the final stage of history in *Haer.* 5.25–36 combines the term "antichrist" with 2 Thess 2, a reading of Daniel, the book of Revelation, and various other eschatological

descriptions in prophetic and apostolic writings. Thus, Irenaeus' work is indicative of the process of the 2nd century CE: the variety of ideas found in writings that were regarded as authoritative had to be analyzed and brought into a more or less coherent scenario.

The same development can be discerned in Tertullian. In his *Res.* 24–27, Tertullian describes the future resurrection of the dead (→ Resurrection) on the basis of the letters of Paul. Here, Tertullian interprets 2 Thess 2 as a description of the activities of antichrist, and he continues by interpreting the prophecies of the book of Revelation as also referring to the same antagonist. In *Marc.* 1.22.1, Tertullian uses the name "antichrist" as a reference to → Marcion, who – in his eyes – had attacked Christ by a false theology (see also Tert. *Marc.* 3.8.2). In *Marc.* 5.16.4, Tertullian briefly states his position on antichrist: regarding the description of the man of lawlessness of 2 Thess 2, Tertullian argues that "According to our view, he is antichrist; as is taught us in both the ancient and the new prophecies and especially by the apostle John [...]" (trans. *ANF*, vol. III, 464). Tertullian here juxtaposes his own interpretation of 2 Thessalonians over against Marcion's. The latter seriously considers identifying the man of lawlessness as "the Creator's Christ" (trans. *ANF*, vol. III, 464).

4. Late Patristic Sources

Of later authors, especially Hippolytus of Rome has become highly influential. He devotes a large section of his commentary on Daniel to antichrist (*Commentarium in Danielem*) and writes a treatise in which he focuses especially on the antagonism between Christ and antichrist (*De Christo et Antichristo*). In these texts Hippolytus moves beyond the position of Tertullian and Irenaeus by giving a systematic and more or less coherent scenario for the appearance of antichrist.

The Coptic *Apoc. El.* 3 gives a description of the physical appearance of antichrist in the style of physiognomy. It is clear that this 3rd-century CE Egyptian writing was familiar with the figure of antichrist as the one and ultimate eschatological opponent of Jesus Christ. From this period onward, descriptions of antichrist combine elements from various sources and traditions into a single scenario in which the arrival of antichrist will precede the second coming of Jesus Christ. Usually antichrist is depicted as a deceiver who claims to be Christ himself and tries to lead the believers astray while at the same time inaugurating a tyrannical and oppressive rule. A similar picture is painted in the later, perhaps even 9th-century CE, Greek *Apocalypse of Daniel*.

5. The Reception of Antichrist

In the course of the development depicted above, the figure of antichrist has increasingly become an anti-Jewish symbol. The development started in the 2nd century CE, when Irenaeus (*Haer.* 5.30.2) brought the figure of antichrist in contact with the tribe of Dan. Antichrist as a Jewish figure from the tribe of Dan has given rise to many treatises, sermons, and expositions on the advent of antichrist and the threat he poses.

Various later authors describe antichrist or a similar figure in terms derived from the sources discussed above. → Ephrem the Syrian, Pseudo-Hippolytus (*Treatise on the End of the World*), the later pseudepigraphic *Apocalypse of John*, → Cyril of Jerusalem, and other authors all point back at the initial development described above (see Bousset, 1895; ET: 1999). In yet later ages, the antichrist legend inspired authors like Beda Venerabilis, Godfrey of Viterbo, Adso of Melk, and the unknown author of the *Ludus de Antichristo* to describe his advent in colorful detail. In the Reformation period, antichrist discourse came to dominate the discussion between the early Reformers and the Vatican. And in even more recent times, antichrist has remained a prominent figure in the eschatological hopes and especially fears of more fundamentalist Christian groups.

Historiography

The modern study of antichrist was inaugurated by W. Bousset (1895; ET: 1999). According to him, the variety of ideas found in the earliest sources should be seen as reflecting one coherent, esoteric oral tradition on the final eschatological opponent. W. Bousset's view has influenced scholars throughout the 20th century (see e.g. Friedländer, 1901; Charles, 1920). Only at a relatively late moment did scholars

start to note the variety in the texts they studied (see Ernst, 1967; Jenks, 1991; Hill, 1995; Lietaert Peerbolte, 1996; 1999; 2010). Though some would still argue in favor of a pre-Christian tradition on antichrist (see esp. Lorein, 2003; and more subtly Horbury, 2003), the majority of scholars seems to agree that this tradition is the result of a Christian reinterpretation of various pre-Christian, Jewish sources that were considered authoritative in the early church. It is this Christian reinterpretation of Jewish materials that is still influential in various Christian circles.

Bibliography

Almond, P., *The Antichrist: A New Biography*, Cambridge, 2020.

Bousset, W., *Der Antichrist in der Überlieferung des Judentums, des Neuen Testaments und der alten Kirche*, Göttingen, 1895; ET: A.H. Keane, *The Antichrist Legend: A Chapter in Christian and Jewish Folklore*, AARTTS 24, Atlanta, 1999.

Bousset, W., "Antichrist," in: J. Hastings, ed., *ERE*, vol. I, New York, 1924, 578–581.

Charles, R.H., *A Critical and Exegetical Commentary on the Revelation of St. John*, vol. II, ICC, Edinburgh, 1920.

Ernst, J., *Die eschatologischen Gegenspieler in den Schriften des Neuen Testaments*, BU 3, Regensburg, 1967.

Friedländer, M., *Der Antichrist in den vorchristlichen jüdischen Quellen*, Göttingen, 1901.

Hill, C.E., "Antichrist from the Tribe of Dan," *JThS* n.s. 46, 1995, 99–117.

Horbury, W., "Antichrist among Jews and Gentiles," in: M. Goodman, ed., *Jews in a Graeco-Roman World*, Oxford, 1998, 113–133; also in: W. Horbury, *Messianism among Jews and Christians: Twelve Biblical and Historical Studies*, London, 2003, 329–350.

Jenks, G.C., *The Origins and Early Development of the Antichrist Myth*, BZNW 59, Berlin, 1991.

Kusio, M., *The Antichrist Tradition in Antiquity: Antimessianism in Second Temple and Early Christian Literature*, WUNT II/352, Tübingen, 2020.

Lietaert Peerbolte, L.J., *The Antecedents of Antichrist: A Traditio-Historical Study of the Earliest Christian Views on Eschatological Opponents*, JSJ.S 49, Leiden, 1996.

Lietaert Peerbolte, L.J., "Antichrist," in: K. van der Toorn, B. Becking & P.W. van der Horst, eds., *DDD*, Leiden, [2]1999, 62–64.

Lietaert Peerbolte, L.J., "Antichrist," in: J.J. Collins & D.C. Harlow, eds., *EDEJ*, Grand Rapids, 2010, 333–334.

Lorein, G.W., *The Antichrist Theme in the Intertestamental Period*, JSP.S 44, London, 2003.

McGinn, B., *Antichrist: Two Thousand Years of the Human Fascination with Evil*, San Francisco, 1994.

BERT JAN LIETAERT PEERBOLTE

Antidicomarianites

The term "Antidicomarianites" is a label first formulated by → Epiphanius of Salamis to describe, denounce, and refute various persons and groups of the second half of the 4th century CE as one autonomous sect from Arabia, who claimed – mainly based on their exegesis of the Canonical Gospels – that Mary had normal marital relations to and sexual intercourse with Joseph after the birth of Christ. Therefore, these persons rejected the concept of Mary's *virginitas post partum* (enduring virginity after Christ's birth) and the perpetual virginity of Mary altogether, in support of a general equality of marriage and celibacy.

1. The Antiheretical Terminology and its Problems

Ἀντιδικομαριαμῖται or Ἀντιδικομαριανῖται derives from ἀντίδικος (adversary) and Μαρία, hence meaning "Adversaries of Mary." It is first to be found in the works of Epiphanius of Salamis and was later inherited by → Augustine of Hippo and others in their antiheretical or historiographical writings.

It can be taken for granted that the term "Antidicomarianites" was not used as a self-description of a Christian group, for the representatives of such positions mentioned by Epiphanius did not oppose Mary in general, but tried to fight against the drastic emergence of Mary's over-idealization in favor of virginity (→ Virgin/Virginity) and celibacy to the detriment of → marriage. There are examples for exonyms, which later on were adapted and used by persons or groups to describe themselves. But this is unlikely the case with the term "Antidicomarianites" – there are simply no known sources in which someone labels himself as such. Hence, it is reasonable to assume that either Epiphanius or one of his correspondents invented this term in the traditional antiheretical style and thus subsumed various persons under this single label (see Shoemaker, 2008, 376).

2. Patristic Sources

The main source on the so-called Antidicomarianites is Epiphanius' central heresiological work, the Πανάριον (medicine chest, or Lat. *Adversus haereses*),

which was finished in 376/377 CE. The Antidicomarianites are mentioned by Epiphanius in *Pan.* 78 after his extensive description of the Apollinarists (Epiph. *Pan.* 77) and are followed by the Kollyridians (*Pan.* 79), which are pictured as the opposite extreme view on Mary, named after their rite of giving breadlike offerings (κολλυρίς; "roll/loaf of bread") to → Mary, whom they adored like a goddess according to Epiphanius.

Pan. 78 consists of a brief frame by Epiphanius (*Pan.* 78.1.1–1.4; 24.7), encompassing the detailed quotation of an earlier letter by Epiphanius, presumably written in 370 CE (see Kösters, 2003, 37–41) and addressed to fellow Christian clerics and laymen in Arabia (Epiphanius, *Epistula ad Arabes* = *Pan.* 78.2.1–24.6). Epiphanius' knowledge is solemnly based on hearsay, without giving away any names of the sources or accused.

The Antidicomarianites are also mentioned in other parts of the *Panarion* (preface 1.4.2; 1.5.9; and 77.36.2–4). There is a short note on them in his dogmatic work *Ancoratus* (*The Anchored*), written in 374 CE prior to the *Panarion* (Epiph. *Anc.* 13.8) and in the *Anacephalaiosis*, which is a brief summary of the *Panarion* (see *Anac. ad Tom.* 7.2 ["Summary/'Recapitulation' of/on Book VII"]). All these notes give no new insights and are therefore to be neglected.

Other heresiological authors strictly rely on Epiphanius and show no knowledge of other sources or own experiences on this alleged sect. Augustine, depending mostly on the *Anacephalaiosis*, gives short notes of them in Aug. *Haer.* 56 and 84. However, unlike Epiphanius, he links them in the latter chapter to the Helvidians, certainly due to the close relation or even congruence of their teachings. Other authors offer no new information by repeating the *Anacephalaiosis*' brief account (e.g. Dam. *Haer.* 78).

3. Historical Background

Arguments against and for the perpetual virginity and the *virginitas post partum* based on the exegesis of the New Testament writings stand in a long tradition from the 2nd century CE onward (see e.g. *Prot. Jas.* 9:1–2; for an overview on these different opinions and their history, see Campenhausen, 1979). They culminate in Mariological controversies during the late second half of the 4th century CE in both the eastern and – slightly delayed – western part of the Roman Empire (Campenhausen, 1979, 135–136, sees the construction of the Antidicomarianites by Epiphanius as the climax of these developments). As to the point of Epiphanius mentioning those so-called Antidicomarianites by name, no council judgments or condemnations against them were declared, and no dogma on Mary's *virginitas post partum* and ἀειπαρθενία (perpetual virginity) was formulated.

According to Epiphanius the positions proclaimed by those Antidicomarianites arose especially in *Arabia* (see *Pan.* 78.1.1), which equals modern Transjordan. It can be derived from the assumed dating of his letter to Arabia that the positions spread by those labeled "Antidicomarianites" came up about the year 370 CE. On the genealogy of the Antidicomarianites, Epiphanius furthermore mentions a notion that sees the central element of their teaching – that Mary had sexual intercourse with Joseph after she gave birth to Christ – to be claimed by Apollinaris himself or some of his pupils and followers, thus constructing Apollinaris as the ancestor of the Antidicomarianites. Epiphanius remains doubtful about this genealogy – with a tendency to reject it – and does not give it any further thought (see *Pan.* 78.1.4); with a lack of concrete evidence, this theory can be neither proven nor fully rejected.

Other theological thinkers formulated positions similar or even identical to those of the Antidicomarianites, especially in the last two decades of the 4th century CE. First to be mentioned is → Helvidius, author of an exposition written around 380 CE against the radical ascetic view of a monk known as Carterius and his concept of the perpetual virginity of Mary. → Jerome refuted this work by Helvidius in his treatise *Adversus Helvidium de Mariae virginitate perpetua* three years later. Both authors strongly depended on exegesis of the Gospels in their argumentation. Helvidius claims that the brothers of Christ mentioned in the Scriptures indicate a sexual relation between Mary and Joseph after his birth (see Jer. *Helv.* 17), whereas Jerome replied that those brothers were children of Elizabeth, Mary's sister and the mother of → John the Baptist, thus cousins of Christ (see *Helv.* 11–17). Jerome here faces the same arguments and questions in Rome as Epiphanius about ten years earlier in the East (for a comparative study on Jerome's *Adversus Helvidium* and Epiphanius' *Panarion*, see Karmann, 2013, 120–136).

Similar "antidicomarianitian" views were also taught by Jovinian in the late 4th century CE, who proclaimed the equal status of marriage and celibacy against the concept of the perpetual virginity and who was refuted by Jerome too (see Jerome's *Adversus Jovinianum libri II*). → Bonosus, former bishop of Sardica during the late 4th century CE, likewise argued that Mary gave birth to further children after Christ's birth. Others ascribed to proclaim related opinions are the Arian (→ Arianism) theologians → Eudoxius of Antioch (d. c. 370 CE) and → Eunomius of Cyzicus (d. c. 393 CE).

Closely related to the question of the virginal state of the mother of Christ is the vital and contemporary aspect of equality of marriage and celibacy (see e.g. Karmann, 2013, 118–120; and Hunter, 2007, 187, who sees "the zeal for ascetic renunciation" in the last decades of the 4th century CE fuel a "new enthusiasm for the doctrine of [Mary's] virginitas post partum"). This is most obvious in Jerome's conflict with Helvidius and Jovinian, who were arguing against the concept of Mary's perpetual virginity – and therefore against her as the role model of a chaste and stainless lifestyle – in support of the equal status of both the marital and opposite lifestyle, whereas Jerome strongly supports asceticism, virginity, and abstinence. This heavily debated topic is also reflected in Epiphanius refutation: in *Pan.* 78.16.1 Epiphanius asks several rhetorical questions about the status of marriage in general, reacting to the issue raised by those he called Antidicomarianites, who too considered the status of marriage endangered.

Just like Helvidius, the Antidicomarianites refuted by Epiphanius built their argumentation against the *virginitas post partum* on their exegesis of the New Testament writings, especially the Gospels. Epiphanius rejects their literal reading of the Scripture early on in his *Panarion* as "ignorance of persons who do not know the sacred Scriptures well" (*Pan.* 78.7.1). According to Epiphanius the Antidicomarianites claimed to know how "to distinguish between the senses of the Scriptures" (*Pan.* 78.17.3), but fail to get the true meaning, unlike Epiphanius, who boast himself on knowing the Scripture's right sense due to his close studies (*Pan.* 78.9.3–4).

4. Positions of the Antidicomarianites and Their Refutation by Epiphanius

One central position of the so-called Antidicomarianites is that Mary had a normal marriage with Joseph, and consequently she had a sexual relationship with her husband after she bore Christ, and gave birth to several more children (see *Pan.* 78.1.3; 78.7.1; 78.23.2). This is derived from and supported by their reading of Matt 1:18 ("Mary was found with child of the holy ghost before they came together") and 1:25 ("he knew her not until she had brought forth her son, the firstborn" [both readings by Epiphanius]). These passages were seen as statements that referred to sexual intercourse by the use of the verbs συνέρχομαι (to come together) and γινώσκειν (to get to know), which could be understood in this meaning. Likewise, the temporal prepositions πρίν (before) and ἕως (until) were interpreted as sure indications for a physical relationship *after* Christ's birth. The Antidicomarianites also understood Christ's depiction τὸν πρωτότοκον (the firstborn) as him being the first of several children of Mary.

Epiphanius replies in opposition to this reading of Matt 1:18 that Mary and Joseph were *expected* to come together (see *Pan.* 78.17.1), but actually it did not happen (see *Pan.* 78.20.2; 78.20.4; 78.21.1). In his interpretation of Matt 1:25, he avoids a sexual connotation of γινώσκειν by taking it in a strictly literal sense (see *Pan.* 78.20.1). Epiphanius even uses εἰδέναι (to know; see *Pan.* 78.17.7–9) in support of his reading instead of the biblical γινώσκειν: "He did not know [ἤδει] her, then, until he had seen the wonder; he did not know [ἤδει] how wondrous she was until he had seen 'that which was born of her'" (*Pan.* 78.17.9; this and all subsequent translations by Williams, 2013). By understanding "to know her" in a nonsexual way, he also circumvents the problem of interpreting ἕως. According to Epiphanius, Christ is only called firstborn in Matt 1:25 because he is the "firstborn of all creation" (see Col 1:15), which Epiphanius interprets as Christ being born of Mary's flesh (= *her* son), but not in the meaning of the first of several children of her (*the* firstborn, not *her* firstborn;

see *Pan.* 78.17.4–7; 21.2–4). Other arguments in favor of Mary's perpetual virginity are rather farfetched: at the very beginning of his *Epistula ad Arabes* ("Letter to the Arabs"), Epiphanius states that Mary has always been called a virgin and that the title was given to her by God, just like Jacob received the name "Israel" (see *Pan.* 78.6.1–2); also Mary has to be seen as a prophetess, and as such, she remained sexually abstinent (*Pan.* 78.16.1–8). Epiphanius even tries to defend Mary's *virginitas post partum* by comparing her to a lioness, since she gave birth to Christ, who must be called a lion, as Epiphanius argues in reference to Christologically interpreted passages on King → David taken from the Hebrew Bible. He builds this on the antique zoological belief (e.g. Hdt. 3.108), that a lioness only gives birth once, as its womb is supposedly destroyed by the birth of its cub (see *Pan.* 78.12.1–7); for this reason Mary cannot conceive again and remains a virgin.

Two secondary arguments taken from the Scriptures support the main Antidicomarianitian claim, structured

1. around Joseph as Mary's *husband*, and;
2. around the *brothers* of Christ (on theories on Christ's brothers, see Blinzler, 1967, 136–144).

Obviously, both terms were taken in a literal sense, understanding marriage as including the sexual act.

One of Epiphanius' arguments against the understanding of Joseph as Mary's husband is that Joseph was a widower, titled Mary's husband because of the Jewish law only, and that Mary was entrusted to him not for marriage, but to protect her virginity and to be a witness of her glory (see *Pan.* 78.7.2–4; 78.8.4; 78.15.1–3). In addition, Joseph was supposedly too old to take a virgin for a wife and lost his first wife many years prior (see *Pan.* 78.7.5; 78.8.1–2; 78.8.4). Two more statements in support of Epiphanius' view are taken from his exegesis of Matt 1:18f. First, he states in reference to Matt 1:18 that Mary was called his "*espoused* wife" not "*married* wife" (see *Pan.* 78.8.2, italics mine). Second, Joseph was described as just (see Matt 1:19), therefore "he would not dare to keep wanting her" after he "had heard that that which was in her was 'of the Holy Spirit'" (*Pan.* 78.8.4; see also 78.8.5; 78.14.1–3; → Holy Spirit).

The second group of Antidicomarianitian subsidiary arguments against the *virginitas post partum* is based on the account of the brothers of Christ in such passages as Matt 12:47 and Gal 1:19. Epiphanius takes the brothers mentioned in Matt 12:47 for sons of Joseph's first marriage (see *Pan.* 78.9.5) and continues by raising the question of why Christ entrusted Mary to John and John to Mary if Mary had children and her husband was alive to protect her (see John 19:26–27). He deduces that she was entrusted to John since she was a virgin and had no sons to protect her after Joseph's death (see *Pan.* 78.10.9–10; 10.13). Mary was not his mother by nature, Christ only said so "to show that [as] the originator of virginity she was his mother, since the life began with her" (*Pan.* 78.10.11).

The so-called Antidicomarianites also mentioned James specifically as Christ's brother by nature in support of their line of argument against the perpetual virginity of Mary in reference to Gal 1:19. Epiphanius vehemently refutes this, stating that James was the firstborn son of Joseph by an earlier marriage (*Pan.* 78.7.6–7) and was entitled "the Lord's brother not by nature, but by grace, because of being brought up with him" (*Pan.* 78.7.9).

5. Reception

The Antidicomarianites were condemned by name on the Third Council of Constantinople in 680/681 CE. Earlier Jovinian and his teachings had to face condemnation by councils in 390 CE (Rome and Milan), Bonosus likewise in Capua 391 CE – both under the involvement of Bishop Siricus I of Rome.

From the Reformation onward, the term "Antidicomarianites" was used by Protestant and particularly Roman Catholic Church historians to label all historical and contemporary Christian groups or positions against Mary's perpetual virginity as Antidicomarianites. Moreover it was utilized in polemics against Protestants, who did not see a need for Mary's *virginitas post partum* in their concept of faith and could not find proof for it based on the Scriptures. Consequently, most Protestant theologians from the 17th century onward refused to consider the Antidicomarianites' positions as heretical.

Historiography

Due to the limited number of sources and lack of new finds – or even personal testimonials of Antidicomarianites – which would support Epiphanius'

claim to see them as an autonomous sect, modern scholarship practically ceased following this trail. It now focusses on basically two aspects. Firstly, the Antidicomarianites are viewed as an example for constructed → heresy (see e.g. Pourkier, 1992, 39, 113, 486–487); this research furthermore supports the assumption that there was not one clearly shaped sect that defined itself by its negative Mariology, but rather several different Christian groups and single persons who uttered such views and could be labeled as Antidicomarianites in a far broader sense, if one wants to use Epiphanius' biased terminology. Closely connected to this insight is, secondly, that Epiphanius' refutation of the so-called Antidicomarianites is now primarily viewed in the context of asceticism, celibacy, and marriage during the late 4th century CE, giving those groups and persons of "Antidicomarianitian" positions a proper cause for their views, which lies not in an undefined grudge against Mary in general, but in their fear of Mary becoming the central role model of ascetic life and celibacy, leading to a degradation of marriage (see e.g. Karmann, 2013).

Bibliography

Bauckham, R., "The Brothers and Sisters of Jesus: An Epiphanian Response to J.P. Meier," *CBQ* 56, 1994, 686–700.

Bauckham, R., *Jude and the Relatives of Jesus in the Early Church*, London, 2004.

Bienert, W.A., & P. Gemeinhardt, "Jesu Verwandtschaft," in: C. Markschies, J. Schröter & A. Heiser, eds., *Antike christliche Apokryphen in deutscher Übersetzung*, vol. I/1: *Evangelien und Verwandtes*, Tübingen, 2012, 280–298.

Blinzler, J., *Die Brüder und Schwestern Jesu*, SBS 21, Stuttgart, 1967.

Campenhausen, H. von, "Die Jungfrauengeburt in der Theologie der alten Kirche," in: H. von Campenhausen, *Urchristliches und Altkirchliches: Vorträge und Aufsätze*, Tübingen, 1979, 63–161.

Fernández, D., *De mariologia sancti Epiphanii*, Rome, 1968.

Holl, K., & J. Dummer, eds., *Epiphanius*, vol. III: *Panarion haer. 65–80: De Fide*, GCS 37, Berlin, ²1985, 452–475.

Hörmann, J., *Des heiligen Epiphanius von Salamis Erzbischofs und Kirchenlehrers ausgewählte Schriften*, BKV 38, Munich, 1919.

Hunter, D.G., *Marriage, Celibacy, and Heresy in Ancient Christianity: The Jovianist Controversy*, Oxford, 2007.

Karmann, T.R., "'Er erkannte sie aber nicht, …' Maria, das Virginitätsideal und Mt 1,18–25 im späten 4. Jahrhundert," in: H.-U. Weidemann, ed., *Asceticism and Exegesis in Early Christianity: The Reception of New Testament Texts in Ancient Ascetic Discourses*, NTOA 101, Göttingen, 2013, 118–147.

Koch, H., *Adhuc virgo: Mariens Jungfrauenschaft und Ehe in der altkirchlichen Überlieferung bis zum Ende des 4. Jahrhunderts*, BHTh 2, Tübingen, 1929.

Koch, H., *Virgo Eva – Virgo Maria: Neue Untersuchungen über die Lehre von der Jungfrauenschaft und Ehe Mariens in der ältesten Kirche*, AKG 25, Berlin, 1937.

Kösters, O., *Die Trinitätslehre des Epiphanius: Ein Kommentar zum Ancoratus*, FKDG 86, Göttingen, 2003.

Pourkier, A., *L'hérésiologie chez Épiphane de Salamine*, CHRA 4, Paris, 1992.

Pratscher, W., *Der Herrenbruder Jakobus und die Jakobustradition*, FRLANT 139, Tübingen, 1987.

Shoemaker, S.J., "Epiphanius of Salamis, the Kollyridians, and the Early Dormition Narratives: The Cult of the Virgin in the Fourth Century," *JECS* 16/3, 2008, 371–401.

Williams, F., ed. & trans., *The Panarion of Epiphanius of Salamis*, Books 2–3: *De Fide*, NHMS 79, Leiden, [2]2013.

MARC BERGERMANN

Anti-Judaism

Anti-Judaism and anti-Semitism are sometimes used interchangeably. In America, anti-Semitism is used more frequently than in Europe, where often a distinction is made between the religious attitude of anti-Judaism and a social or racial attitude of anti-Semitism. Making a distinction between anti-Judaism and anti-Semitism may, however, lead to an apologetic use of anti-Judaism, as if religious anti-Jewish stereotypes are less harmful than anti-Semitic stereotypes and as if there is no connection at all between both. Still, one should distinguish between the religious polemic of early Christianity and Second Temple Judaism and outright anti-Semitism. Apparently, religious groups competed with one another to be the legitimate heir to biblical tradition. The expression of this cannot be identified with anti-Judaism, as some of these groups were Jewish themselves. We define anti-Judaism as a religiously motivated prejudice and hatred against Jews, whereas anti-Semitism denotes a broader phenomenon in which social and religious elements coincide with an attitude of stereotyping and discrimination.

First, we will deal with pagan anti-Semitism, and then with early Christian attitudes toward Judaism insofar as these are Christian anti-Judaism.

1. Pagan Anti-Semitism

Two elements form the key to pagan anti-Semitism: the supposed xenophobia of → Judaism and the refusal to acknowledge the religion of the state, including the veneration of the Roman gods and the veneration of the → emperor. By paying tribute, one acknowledged both political and religious orders. The rejection of the state cult aroused the curiosity of Roman writers as to why the God of the Jews could not be integrated into the pantheon. This may account for the strange fact that Jews were accused of venerating the head of a donkey, a kind of calumnious counterhistory of the Exodus, which circulated in Egypt and the Roman world. According to this, the Israelites were expelled from Egypt because of their leprosy. A donkey showed them where there was water (Plut. *Quaest. conv.* 4.5). The dietary rules of the ancient Jews aroused antagonism, and it did not help that the Jews were perceived as attacking the gods of the ancient Egyptians. Tacitus writes that they sacrifice a ram to denigrate Ammon and an ox to deride the Egyptian god Apis (Tac. *Hist.* 5.3.4).

The Jews usually chose to live somewhat separated from other citizens in a town to avoid idolatry and to be near a river for the ritual bath. In spite of their having objectively valid reasons for their separation, Greek and Latin authors accused Jews of xenophobia and unwillingness to mingle with others. Thus, the counterstory of the Exodus as told by the Egyptian Manetho (3rd cent. BCE) explained the supposed xenophobia of the Jews as part of an oath the Jews swore to → Moses to kill all sacred Egyptian animals and to connect only to their own people (*ap.* Jos. *Apion.* I.31). → Tacitus speaks about the Jewish loyalty to one another and of their hatred of humanity, "odium humani generis" (Tac. *Hist.* 5.5.2). Charges against Judaism contain a mixture of xenophobic projections and a misunderstanding of Jewish rituals. This resulted in sporadic accusations of ritual murder. The highly anti-Semitic pagan writer Apion (1st cent. CE) relates how Antiochus IV Epiphanes discovered a fat Greek in the Jerusalem Temple (→ Temple, Jerusalem) who was to be ritually slaughtered.

As to the Romans, their anti-Judaism was primarily based upon the Jewish refusal to venerate the emperor and to fulfill one's obligations, which was equated with disloyalty to the emperor and with → atheism. Hence the Jews could be accused of atheism or of *asebeia* ("lack of piety"), in spite of their cult of the invisible God, which was somehow known to the Roman writers. The dietary laws were another proof of misanthropy, insofar as the food regulations and sacrifices were explained as directed against the Egyptian gods or as a later *superstitio* added to the religion.

Some motifs of pagan anti-Semitism could be transferred to Christians such as the anti-Christian graffiti of Alexamenos venerating a crucified donkey (Tert. *Apol.* 16.1–3).

2. Christian Anti-Judaism in the New Testament

The expression "True Israel" does not feature in the New Testament. Paul emphasizes that God has never rejected his people Israel: "I ask, then, has God rejected his people? By no means!" (Rom 11:1). The Gospel uses the expression the "new covenant" (Luke 22:20), clearly derived from Jer 31:31. The *Letter to the Hebrews* points to the heavenly temple service with Christ as high priest, a service vastly superior to the earthly service in the Jewish Temple, although heavily influenced by the latter. The claim of a heavenly Jerusalem replacing, at least for the moment, the → of Matthew (→ Matthew, Gospel of), generally Temple in Jerusalem, has been detected in the Qumran scrolls (→ Dead Sea Scrolls) as well (CD 6.19). Hence, antagonism against Jerusalem and the Temple service is not only a Gentile-Christian phenomenon but may have also existed in certain branches of ancient Judaism. In addition, Gentile Christianity is not by definition more aggressive against Judaism than Jewish Christianity: the Gospel of Matthew (→ Matthew the Apostle), generally considered Jewish-Christian, is sometimes embittered against Judaism, whereas Luke seems to be more moderate, perhaps because of a greater distance from the Jewish mainstream.

Another way of looking at the New Testament is wondering whether some sweeping statements may stem from pagan anti-Semitism. Whereas the Gospel of Matthew targets the Pharisees, the Gospel of John (→ John the Apostle) speaks quite often categorically about the Jews, although some scholars claim that

this means "Judaeans." An extremely harsh statement can be found in John 8:44: "You Jews have the devil as father." In *b. Yebam.* 16a, the expression "first-born of the devil" is applied to a → rabbi belonging to the school of Shammai and differing in halakhic decisions from the others (Dahl, 1964). In view of this, the harsh statement in the Gospel of John might be understood as an internal Jewish debate. The Gospel creates a massive dichotomy between Jesus and the Jews, as if Jesus himself does not belong to the Jews. This is, however, a far cry from the attempts to present Jesus as not Jewish at all, as has been advocated by the influential German theologian W. Grundmann (1906–1976), whose anti-Semitism as a member of the Nazi party is beyond doubt. The tone of John's Gospel when it comes to the Jews has sometimes been compared to that of a rejected lover in its bitterness. The Gospel refers to early followers of Jesus being rejected from the → synagogue (John 12:42; 16:2), while maintaining that "salvation is from the Jews" (John 4:22), which can be seen as a symptom of "rejected love."

Another sweeping statement against Judaism can be found in 1 Thess 2:14–16:

> For you suffered the same things from your own countrymen as they (namely the churches in Judea) did from the Jews, who killed both the Lord Jesus and the prophets, and drove us out, and displease God and oppose all men by hindering us from speaking to the Gentiles that they may be saved – so as always to fill up the measure of their sins. But God's wrath has come upon them at last!

It may well be that violence of Judaism against the early Christian community lies at the origin of this bitter statement. Nevertheless, the accusation contains two topics that are part and parcel of anti-Judaism: the Christian accusation that the Jews have killed Jesus and the prophets, and the (pagan) accusation that Jews are enemies of humankind. As to the first, the killing of the prophets is a *topos* that accompanies the prophetic rebuke of Israel and warning to repent. Historically, not many prophets were killed, but this *topos* received surprising emphasis in postbiblical Jewish literature. Although this *topos* has its origin in Judaism (Steck, 1967; Murmelstein, 1936), it can still be transformed into anti-Jewish invective. The meaning of the accusation to have killed the prophets changes dramatically if applied not as an inner-Jewish prophetic criticism, but as an accusation from outside to seal Israel's divine rejection.

This accusation goes together in 1 Thess 2:14–16 with the accusation that the Jews killed Jesus. From a historical point of view, although involvement by the Sadducees and the priests cannot be excluded, it is certain that the Pharisees were not involved in the execution of Jesus. In addition, crucifixion (→ Cross/Crucifixion) was a Roman method of execution, which Jesus shared with thousands of Jews. The (categorical) prophetic call to repentance from *within* Judaism is here transformed into a massive condemnation of Judaism from *outside*. Hence 1 Thess 2:14 may be understood as a mixture of an inner-Jewish polemic and a condemnation of Judaism from the outside, the latter reinforced by adducing as a second accusation of Jews being "enemies of humankind." This second accusation can be explained as anti-Semitic prejudice about the *odium humani generis*, from pagan provenance, adopted here by early Christianity to give vent to embitterment against Judaism.

3. Paul

Until some decades ago, the general conviction was that Paul (→ Paul the Apostle) had announced the end of Jewish observance of the law. Jewish scholars reacted by drawing a demarcation line between Jesus and Paul, claiming Jesus for Judaism and Paul representing a serious distortion of it. A newer view of Paul distinguishes between the observance of the Law for Jews and for non-Jews. Non-Jews/Gentiles who wish to observe the law in order to become genuine followers of Jesus are sternly rebuked by Paul. They create fragmentation between Christians and thus make the union in Christ void. "By circumcising themselves they cut themselves off from Christ" (Gal 5:2). In addition, these Judaizing Christians should not select a few commandments, but should fulfill all of them. If this new picture of Paul is correct, we can conclude that most of the church fathers have not properly understood Paul. The burden of anti-Judaism should then be sought in postbiblical developments. Even when biblical quotations are adduced, their original meaning has been transformed into anti-Jewish invectives in which the inner-Jewish polemics have gradually disappeared.

In spite of the hardening of accusations against Judaism, real encounters between Jews and Christians remained possible. → Origen (184–253 CE), who uttered the anti-Jewish statement of Jews as allies of Judas and relegated both to hell (PG 12.1468), continued to exchange views about the Hebrew Bible with rabbis in Caesarea. In order to understand the patristic attitudes toward Judaism, we should realize that there were also other opponents of the church fathers. This explains the conflicting attitudes toward Judaism as well as the sometimes surprisingly positive statements about Jews. In the case of Origen, he defends Judaism against the accusation of the (pagan) → Celsus that Jews were originally lepers in Egypt and hate humankind (Or. *Cels.* 4.32; 5.43). Origen in turn praises the law of the Jews and their philosophical status. He does so to rebut opponents who maintain the opposite and, by doing so, want to denigrate Christianity as well.

4. The Church Fathers and the Jewish Law

→ Marcion (85–160 CE) had argued that the whole of the Hebrew Bible had been revealed by an inferior god, whose domain was justice, but not love, as offered by the Father of Jesus Christ. Marcion's well-known antitheses contrasted greed for luxury with New Testament asceticism, Moses' and Joshua's warfare with the pacifism of the Sermon on the Mount. Marcion advocated a metaphysical split between the god of the Hebrew Bible and the Father of Christ, hereby severing the Hebrew Bible from the New Testament. Some of Marcion's tenets are related to Gnosticism (→ Gnosis/Gnosticism), especially the metaphysical split and the aversion to the law. Because of his extreme Christocentrism, Marcion rejects any authentic revelation before Christ. The early church had to defend itself against Marcion by saving the authenticity of the law as revealed by the one God, Creator, Lawgiver, and Father of Jesus Christ.

Obviously, both Marcionite, gnostic, and pagan criticisms of the Hebrew Bible had to be rejected by the church fathers. This did not mean, however, that the church fathers avoided anti-Judaism. Marcion's approach was metaphysical but refrained from speculations about the nature of Judaism. The church fathers, who had to explain the revelation of all the ceremonial commandments that according to them became obsolete after Christ, pointed to the low moral level of the Israelites after they went out of Egypt. The Golden Calf had been the clear manifestation of that, and hence a strong antidote against the "poison" of idolatry was needed: the ceremonial and dietary laws (Poorthuis, 2014). Hence, the inferiority of the laws should not be explained from a metaphysical perspective but out of the inferior nature of the Jewish people as prone to idolatry. The first set of commandments given to → Moses contained only the ethical laws that remained in force after Christ. The second set of tables of the commandments, after the incident of the Golden Calf, was supposed to contain all the additional ceremonial and dietary laws, valid until Christ, but abolished by him. Judaism, by continuing the whole of the law, not only rejected Christ but also continued their idolatrous nature. Hence, opposition against Marcion could go together with anti-Judaism.

The *Epistle of Barnabas* (c. 98 CE; → Barnabas) toys with the idea that the law or at least circumcision had been revealed by a wicked angel (*Barn.* 9:4), an idea far too close to Gnosticism and Marcionite to be acceptable to later church fathers. The letter rejects circumcision and the physical Temple service without properly explaining their prominent position in the Hebrew Bible. Barnabas does not go as far as to deny revelation in the Hebrew Bible, but he reserves all the promises for the church and the curses for Judaism (*Barn.* 5:2). Barnabas emphasizes the Golden Calf as the ultimate sin of Israel in such a way that the covenant had been abolished even before it had been contracted! Later church fathers, such as Origen, refined this idea by resorting to rampant allegorization, which resulted in a double advantage: the unity between Hebrew Bible and New Testament was affirmed against Marcion, and the "real" significance of the Hebrew Bible was affirmed against the Jews. Another train of thought, especially in the *Didascalia* (→ *Didascalia Apostolorum*), emphasized the reality of the commandments without resorting to allegory, but limited its validity to the period until the coming of Christ.

The Epistle to Diognetus (2nd cent. CE; → *Diognetus, Epistle to*) admits that the Christian rejection of idolatry and the veneration of the one invisible God parallels Judaism. However, bringing bloody sacrifices and keeping the → Sabbath and observing → circumcision is superstitious, the author maintains. When he describes the Christian way of life, he subtly continues his polemic against Judaism, perhaps averting similar criticism of Christianity by shifting the onus to Judaism:

> For the Christians are distinguished from other men neither by country, nor language, nor the customs which they observe. For they neither inhabit cities of their own, nor employ a peculiar form of speech, nor lead a life which is marked out by any singularity. (*Diogn.* 5:1)

One may read this as an implicit reproach to Judaism, which is supposed to do all that Christianity does not do. Judaism, it is implied, distinguishes itself by speech and customs and by living apart from others. Perhaps the implicit rhetoric aims at legitimizing Christian religion in the Roman empire, vis-à-vis the existing legitimacy of a xenophobic Judaism.

5. Melito of Sardis (d. 180 CE) and His Anti-Jewish Easter Sermon

Proof that closeness to Judaism does not automatically imply a pro-Jewish attitude is the Easter sermon of → Melito of Sardis, the first Christian writer to introduce the idea of deicide and attributes the death of Jesus to the Jews alone, absolving the Romans. He celebrated → Easter on the 14th of Nissan, as was tradition in Asia Minor. He is well informed about the Jewish Passover celebration, as is attested in his sermon *Peri Pascha*. However, Melito is convinced that the true meaning of Passover is Jesus as the Paschal lamb.

Melito values the ceremonial laws regulating the temple cult and the life of the people as precious gifts of God, but these had lost their value from the moment Christ as the Paschal Lamb appeared (Mel. *Pascha* 297–298).

When Melito starts to describe the suffering of Christ, he contrasts God's goodness with the disloyalty of Israel, as in the reproaches of God in Mic

6:1–4, clearly alluding to the Jewish celebration of Passover, including the sequence of wine and bread and reclining:

> You had wine to drink and bread to eat,
> He had vinegar and gall [...]
> You were reclining on a soft couch,
> he in grave and coffin. (Mel. *Pascha* 566–581)

Further on, Melito refers to the bitter herbs of Pesach as an indication of the bitter fate of Israel, which no longer deserves that name. This strong anti-Jewish polemic cannot be explained by pagan anti-Semitism and should be seen as theological in nature. Similar sharp polemics against Judaism can be found in Syriac-speaking Christianity, especially in the writings of → Ephrem the Syrian, who were acquainted with Jewish traditions, but this did not guarantee a peaceful coexistence. These anti-Jewish invectives were not directed against Jews, but against Christians who were attracted to Jewish feasts and customs.

6. John Chrysostom

From 380 CE onward, anti-Judaism developed from verbal abuse into physical threat and discriminatory measures against Jews. → John Chrysostom's vehement anti-Jewish preaching still remained verbal and took place during Jewish festivals and was meant to deter Christians from joining the Jews in the synagogue (see his *Eight Sermons against the Jews*; PG 48.843–942; see Wilken 2004). Christians had preferred Jewish blessings to Christian ones because of their venerated antiquity and mysterious aura. Chrysostom rebukes a Christian woman who had gone to the synagogue to pledge a vow there. When Chrysostom preached and wrote, around 400 CE, it was a time of transition in which Christianity began to gradually use state power to suppress Judaism.

Antioch in Chrysostom's time still reflects a religious pluralistic society. His sermons are marked by a theological anti-Judaism: the Israelites behaved shamefully against Moses, and the prophets and killed Jesus. The present plight of the Jews should be explained as a divine punishment for this crime. While forgiveness might suit Christianity, from a theological perspective Israel has been rejected, and

wherever Paul speaks about the lasting promise to the Jews, he means Jewish-Christians. The cultic element in Judaism becomes a special target of Chrysostom's invectives, and he identifies the synagogue with a theater and a brothel (Chrys. *Jud.* 1–3). He tries to invalidate the Jewish feasts because there is no Temple. Chrysostom's real target remains non-Jews – probably full Christians who want to celebrate Jewish feasts, observe the Sabbath, and even sleep in a synagogue to receive revelations, as a kind of incubation. There is an element of paranoia in his invectives: "If the Jewish cult would be significant and honorable, then ours can contain nothing but lies and fraud." Christians who Judaize put the true claims of Christianity at risk! Judaizing is no less than a disease, Chrysostom exclaims. For Chrysostom, not Jews as such, but Christian Judaizers are the real target of his anti-Jewish invectives. Christians and Jews shared a heritage of the rejection of idolatry. Judaism, because of its greater antiquity, earned the respect of the Christian believers, especially of the newly converted who sought for arguments to supersede the Roman past. Moses and the patriarchs served that goal. All this was a source of worry for the church fathers who sought to prevent fraternization, and it aroused anti-Jewish feelings, of Chrysostom and of earlier church fathers. Thus → Eusebius of Caesarea (236–339 CE) tried to refute Judaism by arguing that the biblical patriarchs were *Christian* ancestors, and Christianity had a history going back to Adam (→ Adam and Eve) himself as the first Christian (Eus. *Hist. eccl.* 2.6). Chrysostom did not appeal to civil authorities to act against Judaism, but the ominous transition from verbal abuse to physical aggression took place in the same period. → Ambrose of Milan (340–397 CE) was the first to incite violence against Jews, as is testified in his 40th letter from 388 CE. He persuaded → Theodosius I not to intervene on behalf of Jews whose synagogue in Callinicum on the Euphrates had been destroyed by Christians. By rhetorically blaming himself for the fire, Ambrose prevents the emperor from punishing the guilty perpetrators. Incidentally, Ambrose complains about churches being destroyed by Jews during the reign of the emperor → Julian the Apostate, a period of insecurity for Christians. The letter proves that the general Roman policy was to protect religious minorities and that neither Chrysostom nor Ambrose was in a position to command the emperor. Nevertheless, it is an example of how Christianity gradually began to use state power to discriminate against Judaism, and it marks the beginning of a heinous anti-Jewish policy in which church and state power increasingly coincided.

Conclusions

At first, Judaism occupied a legitimate position denied to a persecuted Christianity, which may have fueled bitterness at the Christian side leading to anti-Judaism. Christian apologies to the Roman rulers emphasize that Christianity deserves to be tolerated, even more than Judaism, which distances itself from the Christians in order not to lose the privilege of *religio licita*.

Some pagan anti-Semitic clichés were reused by Christian writers about Judaism, although many of those clichés concerned Christianity as well. A process of mutual accusation between Jews and Christians may have been the result. However, Christian writers firmly took a stand against pagan and gnostic tendencies to denigrate the Hebrew Bible as an inferior document. Christology as such cannot be made responsible for anti-Judaism, as is proven by Paul's theology, which should be understood within Judaism. The church fathers, however, did not view the execution of Jesus in the perspective of Roman execution of Jews, which would connect the passion of Jesus with that of many Jewish martyrs, but shifted the passion to a Jewish execution of Jesus, by transforming prophetic challenge into condemnation. This accusation of being the murderers of Christ, brought forward by Melito and with far more influence by Chrysostom, became in the mind of Christians a permanent and categorical divine curse on the head of Judaism. This formed the foundation of Christian anti-Judaism, which cannot be explained as a mere extrapolation of pagan anti-Semitism. The next step, which would take nearly another century, was to use state power to marginalize the Jews is a decisive transition from theological dissension to the execution of violence against the Jews.

Historiography

The modern study of Christian anti-Judaism began with M. Simon's *Verus Israel* (1948). Jewish scholars (Stern, 1967; Isaac, 1962) are inclined to consider pagan anti-Semitism as less massive than Christian anti-Semitism. J.N. Sevenster (1975) claims the opposite. M. Simon rejects the use of the word anti-Semitism for the period of the early church, by pointing out that the racial connotations of 19th-century anti-Semitism are foreign to the first centuries of our era. The tendency from the 1960s onward among historians and exegetes to search for the origin of Christian anti-Semitism in the New Testament itself was a result of the Holocaust (Schreckenberg, 1982). M. Simon's *Verus Israel* suggests that the claim to be the true Israel lies at the heart of Christian anti-Judaism, but this may reflect an inner-Jewish debate. M. Simon's suggestion of an active Jewish proselytizing has been criticized (Baumgarten, 1999) and may not have been the principal reason for animosity. In both Melito and in Chrysostom (Wilken, 2004), proselytes were not the main issue, but the attraction for Christians of Jewish ceremonies. M. Simon's main point, however, is that Judaism remained a powerful factor in society in the first five centuries of the Common Era, a fact that has often been ignored by Christian scholars.

Bibliography

Baumgarten, A., "Marcel Simon's *Verus Israel* as a Contribution to Jewish History," *HThR* 92/4, 1999, 465–478.

Bickermann, E., "Ritualmord und Eselskult," *MGWJ* 71, 1927, 171ff., 255ff.

Binder, S., *Tertullian, on Idolatry and Mishnah 'Avodah zarah: Questioning the Parting of the Ways between Christians and Jews in Late Antiquity*, Leiden, 2012.

Carleton Paget, J., "Barnabas 9:4: A Peculiar Verse on Circumcision," *VigChr* 45/3, 1991, 242–254.

Dahl, N., "Der Erstgeborene Satans und der Vater des Teufels (Polykarpus 7:1 und John 8:44)," in: E. Haenchen, W. Eltester & F.H. Kettler, eds., *Apophoreta: FS für Ernst Hänchen*, Berlin, 1964, 70–84.

Fischel, H.A., "Martyr and Prophet," *JQR* 37, 1946–1947, 265–280.

Gager, J., *The Origins of Antisemitism*, Oxford, 1983.

Hall, S.G., *Melito: "On Pascha" and Fragments*, Oxford, 1979.

Hengel, M., *Judentum und Hellenismus*, Tübingen, 1969.

Isaac, J., *L'Enseignement du mépris: Vérité historique et mythes théologiques*, Paris, 1962.

Lange, N. de, *Origen and the Jews*, Cambridge UK, 1976.

Limor, O., & G. Stroumsa, eds., *Contra Iudaeos: Ancient and Medieval Polemics between Christians and Jews*, Tübingen, 1986.

Lindner, A., *The Jews in Roman Imperial legislation*, Jerusalem, 1987.

Lovsky, F., *Antisemitisme et mystère d'Israel*, Paris, 1955.

Meeks, W., & R. Wilken, *Jews and Christians in Antioch in the First Four Centuries of the Common Era*, Missoula, 1978.

Millar, F., "Jews of the Graeco-Roman Diaspora between Paganism and Christianity AD 312–438," in: J. Lieu et al., eds., *The Jews among Pagans and Christians in the Roman Empire*, London, 1992.

Murmelstein, B., "The Agada on the Blood of Zecharia (hebr.)," in: J. Klausner, ed., *Sefer Ha-Jovel Samuel Krauss*, Jerusalem, 1936.

Poorthuis, M., "The Improperia and Judaism," *QLP* 72/1, 1991, 1–24.

Poorthuis, M., "Mani, Augustinus en de Kabbala over eten en sex: Een vergelijking," in: P. van Geest & H. van Oort, eds., *Augustiniana Neerlandica*, Louvain, 2005, 257–285 (Dutch).

Poorthuis, M., "Sacrifice as Concession in Christian and Jewish Sources: The Didascalia Apostolorum and Rabbinic Literature," in: A. Houtman, M. Poorthuis, J. Schwartz & Y. Turner, eds., *The Actuality of Sacrifice: Past and Present*, Leiden, 2014.

Schreckenberg, H., *Die Adversus-Iudaeos texte in ihr literarisches und historisches Umfelt (1.11. Jh.)*, Bern, 1982.

Setzer, C., *Jewish Responses to Early Christianity: History and Polemic 30–150 CE*, Minneapolis, 1994.

Sevenster, J.N., *The Roots of Pagan anti-Semitism in the Ancient World*, Leiden, 1975.

Shukster, M., & P. Richardson, "Temple and *Bet Hamidrash* in the Epistle of Barnabas," in: S. Wilson, ed., *Anti-Judaism in Early Christianity*, vol. II: *Separation and Polemic*, Waterloo, 1986, 17–31.

Simon, M., *Verus Israel: Étude sur les relations entre les chrétiens et juifs dans l'empire romain (135–425)*, Paris, 1983.

Steck, O.H., *Israel und das gewaltsame Geschick der Propheten*, WMANT 23, Neukirchen, 1967.

Stern, M., *Greek and Latin Writers on Jews and Judaism*, 3 vols., Jerusalem, 1967.

Wilken, R., *John Chrysostom and the Jews, Rhetoric and Reality in the Late Fourth Century*, Stock, 2004.

Wilson, S., "Melito and Israel," in: S. Wilson, ed., *Anti-Judaism in Early Christianity*, vol. II: *Separation and Polemic*, Waterloo, 1986, 181–102.

M.J.H.M. POORTHUIS

Antioch, Councils of

Antioch, among the oldest of Christian centers, was a powerful metropolitan see and an important place of learning in the 3rd and 4th centuries CE. Its bishops were some of the most influential, and the councils that took place in the city regularly gathered clerics from across the province of Syria and farther afield in the eastern Roman Empire, dealing with matters of pressing urgency to the development of doctrine and church polity.

While the theological and practical concerns of each council varied, an overview of this period identifies repeated themes, as well as developments in conciliar approach and episcopal politics. We see the diminishing role of the laity, → deacons, and presbyters (→ Priest/Presbyter) in councils (compare the council in 268 CE with most in the 4th cent. CE). We also see the increasing need of bishops to seek imperial favor (note the influence of Jovian on the council of 363 CE and events surrounding it), matched by increasing interventions of emperors in the church's work (note Constantius' rejection of the council of 357/358 CE and the exiles that followed). The Antiochene councils also demonstrate changing attitudes in the East toward the relative authority of episcopal councils and the appellate jurisdiction of Rome (note the marked difference between the canons of Antioch in 338 CE and the council of 379 CE). On these broader subjects and on the development of conciliar form as demonstrated in the councils listed below, see particularly J. Gaudemet (1979), H.J. Sieben (1979), and H. Hess (2002).

1. 264, 268, 269? CE

In 261 CE, Paul (commonly "of Samosata") was elected bishop of Antioch (→ Paul of Samosata). He functioned as a charismatic church leader and powerful civic figure under the patronage of Zenobia, queen of an autonomous kingdom based at Palmyra in the Syrian desert, which existed until its recapture by Rome under Aurelian. Paul was popular locally but was treated with caution by neighboring bishops because of his style of leadership and his theological teachings. By 264 CE, opposition was sufficiently roused that a council was held in Antioch to consider his position, attended by a large number of local bishops and clergy (Eus. *Hist. eccl.* 7.27–28). Sufficient assurances were made by Paul to calm the bishops' fears, but he failed to adhere to them and a further council was held in 268 CE. The second council is widely believed to have deposed Paul, although it has been argued that the ancient sources are confused and that a further council took place in 269 CE, which finally achieved his deposition (Hefele, 1894, 125).

Eusebius of Caesarea recounts the actions of the deposing council and records parts of its synodical letter (Eus. *Hist. eccl.* 7.29–30; → Eusebius of Caesarea). Paul was accused of being a worldly figure, busy with secular interests and concerned with the privileges of high office. His immorality included close relationships with women and the exploitation of the poor. His increasing self-aggrandizement within the church meant those who did not cheer his words were persecuted and, during worship, Psalms were exchanged for hymns to Paul himself.

In contrast with most councils later in this period, the main work of this council was done by a presbyter, Malchion, not a bishop. Malchion, head of a school of → rhetoric in Antioch, successfully challenged Paul's theological teachings as heretical (*Hist. eccl.* 7.29). Modern interpretations of Paul's heresy characterize him as an → adoptionist who denied the ontological union of Father and Son, believing the man Jesus to have been united with the divine *logos*, which was not a separate person but merely an expression or virtue of the divine Father (see Kelly, 1977, 116–119; Hanson, 2005, 70–72, 193–195). However, much of the theological content of the synodical letter is missing in Eusebius' account, save that Paul denied that the Son of God was from heaven and believed that Christ was not divine. Regular attacks on Paul were made in later years, which generally characterized him as denying that Jesus was more than simply a man.

Allusions to the acts of the 268 CE council have been identified in wider sources (Mansi, vol. I, 1102; see Loofs, 1924; Riedmatten, 1952). Two creeds were attributed to the council in anti-Nestorian documents of the Council of → Ephesus (Mansi, vol. IV. 1010; vol. V, 175; Kinzig, 2017, 256–265), but the association is not widely accepted as authentic. Significantly, however, there is sufficient evidence to conclude that the council condemned the use of the word ὁμοούσιος (Athan. *Syn.* 43–45; Hil. Poit. *Syn.* 81–88; Bas. *Ep.* 52.1; Epiph. *Pan.* 73.12.3). The intention of the council in doing this remains unclear, as does Paul's own approach to the word (see Stead, 1977, 216–217; Hanson, 2005, 194–195; Edwards, 2009, 85–86). However, this specific condemnation and Paul's continued association with Arius (→ Arianism), Sabellius (→ Sabellians), and → Marcellus of Ancyra are helpful in explaining continuing resistance in the East to the use of ὁμοούσιος, even after its adoption by the Council of Nicaea in 325 CE.

The council of 268 CE enacted the first deposition of a major prelate by bishops gathered from neighboring provinces in council. Its power, however, was limited. The bishops who deposed Paul elected Domnus his successor and, in a sign of the increasing claims of the Roman see, Felix of Rome took it upon himself to communicate with Maximus of Alexandria to continue the defense of the faith against Paul's teachings (Mansi, vol. I, 1114). However, Paul remained in the episcopal palace under the protection of Zenobia until her defeat in 272 CE. He finally was forced to leave the city after the appeal of the bishops to Aurelian for assistance in his removal (Eus. *Hist. eccl.* 7.30). Despite this, support for Paul continued, to the extent that the 19th canon of Nicaea addressed the matter of his followers returning to the orthodox faith.

2. 324/325 CE

Modern knowledge about a council in Antioch shortly preceding the Council of Nicaea emerged in the early 20th century, with the publication by E. Schwartz (1905) of a letter written by the council, recorded in a Syriac manuscript (the Cod. Par. Syr. 62). E. Schwartz published a retroversion into Greek, later improved by L. Abramowski (1975) and published in English (Cross, 1939; a recent translation also drawing on L. Abramowski's work is in Kinzig, 2017, 277–279). The authenticity of the letter was debated after its original publication, but alternative manuscript copies of the letter were later published (Nau, 1909; Chadwick, 1948). It is generally now viewed as a legitimate pre-Nicene document, although not by all (notably Holland, 1970, 163–181; Strutwolf, 1999).

The synodical letter identifies 59 bishops present from eastern provinces, a number of whom also attended the Council of Nicaea. Originally believed to have been led by a Eusebius, the council was probably chaired by Ossius of Cordova (Chadwick, 1948; 1958). It is most commonly assumed, following the analysis of the origins of the Arian crisis by H.-G. Opitz (1934), that the council took place early in 325 CE (see Kelly, 1972; Williams, 2001; Chadwick, 2001; Hanson, 2005). However, variations in the chronology surrounding the death of Eustathius' predecessor, Philogonius, and subsequent disputes over his replacement have caused others to challenge this and propose a date late in 324 CE (see Burgess, 1999).

The synodical letter indicates that this council was held in a period of disorder in the city and was most likely called primarily to appoint Eustathius as bishop of Antioch (Soz. *Hist. Eccl.* 1.2 states that the appointment was made at Nicaea, but this was convincingly refuted by Schwartz, 1905; Chadwick, 1958). The letter also speaks of bishops caught up in the theological dispute between Arius, the famed heretic presbyter, and Alexander of Alexandria. It demonstrates a firm loyalty to Alexander, labeling Arius a heretic, and the council's creed is couched in the theology of Alexander's work opposing Arius (see Hall, 1991; Hanson, 2005; Parvis, 2006). It is a long, formal creed, the first of this kind to have been written by a council of bishops. Strongly anti-Arian, it declares that the Son was begotten from the Father in a mysterious and unknown way, not like the rest of creation, and not from nothing; that there was not a time when the Son did not exist; and that the Son is immutable and unalterable. It defines the Son as image of the Father's hypostasis, drawing on traditional eastern use of image Christology that reflected biblical language (Heb 1:3), and which featured in later Antiochene creeds.

The council is important for demonstrating the complex and varied history of the use of οὐσία to denote the divine substance. While sharing anti-"Arian" sentiment with the Council of Nicaea, the Antiochene creed did not affirm that the Son was from the Father's οὐσία (as would be stated

at Nicaea), nor did it use the famed ὁμοούσιος, the centerpiece of the Nicene Creed (for precedents, see Edwards, 2009, 76, 115–116). H.-G. Opitz (1934) also located at this council a debate between Narcissus of Neronias and Ossius about how many οὐσίαι were contained in the Godhead (Eus. *Marc.* 1.4.39; 1.4.53–54), showing fundamental differences among theologian bishops about the interpretation of the word οὐσία in Trinitarian language (→ Trinity).

This was the first ecclesiastical council to anathematize particular theological statements as heterodox, condemning those who stated that the Son was a creature or was made, that there was a time when he was not, that he was immutable by an exercise of his will rather than by his nature, and that he came out of nothing: firmly anti-Arian condemnations. All the bishops present subscribed to the creed and anathemas, except three: Theodotus of Laodicea, Narcissus of Neronias, and Eusebius of Caesarea. Along with Arius, these bishops were excommunicated, although their cases were referred to the upcoming Council of → Ancyra (Nicaea) for examination.

3. 327, 328 CE (Variously 326–331 CE)

At least three important councils took place in Antioch between 327 and 331 CE, probably dated to 327–328 CE. The first, in 327 CE, deposed Eustathius of Antioch and appointed Paulinus in his place, after which Eustathius was exiled by Constantine to Illyricum (Eus. *Vita Const.* 3.59; Athan. *Hist. Ar.* 4.1; Thdt. *Hist. eccl.* 1.21). Paulinus died after six months as bishop, and a second council (in 327/328 CE) elected Eulalius (Eus. *Marc.* 1.4.2; Philost. *Hist. eccl.* 3.15; Thdt. *Hist. eccl.* 1.22.1).

Disputes between Eustathius' supporters and opponents led to violence on the streets of Antioch. Constantine sent representatives to urge peace, reiterating Eustathius' deposition (Eus. *Vita Const.* 3.59). Correspondence between local bishops, Eusebius of Caesarea, and Constantine shows that a further council, possibly two, met to appoint a successor to Eulalius, most likely in 328 CE (Eus. *Vita Const.* 3.60–62). Bishops meeting in Antioch tried to elect Eusebius, who refused on the grounds of canon law that prohibited episcopal translation (Nicaea, c. 15). Constantine supported his decision but urged Eusebius to assist, recommending two suitable candidates, including Euphronius, who was elected (Eus. *Vita Const.* 3.62).

The causes of Eustathius' deposition were variously described in the sources as his Sabellianism (Socr. *Hist. eccl.* 1.24), sexual and moral immorality (Thdt. *Hist. eccl.* 1.21; Soz. *Hist. eccl.* 2.19; Jer. *Ruf.* 3.42), and insulting the emperor's mother (Athan. *Hist. Ar.* 4). It is widely assumed that the council that deposed Eustathius also deposed Asclepas of Gaza (on unknown charges), along with further bishops known to have lost their sees during Constantine's reign: Euphration of Balanea, Cyrus of Beroea, Cymatius of Paltos, Cymatius of Gabala, and Carterius of Antarados (Athan. *Apol. sec.* 45; *Fug.* 3.3; *Hist. Ar.* 5.2; see Barnes, 1981, 228). Following the assessment of the early historians (Soz. *Hist. eccl.* 2.19; Thdt. *Hist. eccl.* 1.21), scholars have traditionally presented the deposition of Eustathius as part of an Arian purge of pro-Nicene bishops (Barnes, 1981; Hanson, 2005; Parvis, 2006). However, the Arian-Nicene polarization during this period is increasingly shown to be a false construct requiring reconsideration (see Gwynn, 2007; Stephens, 2015).

The assumption that Eustathius was deposed at the same council as Asclepas has inspired considerable debate about the date of their depositions. The letter of the western Council of Serdica stated that Asclepas was deposed 17 years previously. Following → Socrates Scholasticus' 347 CE date for the Council of Serdica, the Antioch council was traditionally dated to 330–331 CE, after the return of Eusebius of Nicomedia from exile (supported most recently by Hanson, 1984). Dating Serdica to 342 CE and associating the deposition of Eustathius with Helena's tour of the Holy Land after the deaths of Crispus and Fausta, H. Chadwick (1948) built on the work of E. Schwartz (1911a) to date the Council of Antioch instead to 326 CE, before the restoration of Eusebius. H. Chadwick's general narrative is now widely accepted, although a date of 327 CE is most commonly offered for the council in Antioch, following the acceptance of 343 CE as the date of the Council of Serdica (Simonetti, 1975; Barnes, 1978; Williams, 2001; Parvis, 2006). R.W. Burgess (2000) drew on additional sources to adjust the date of the deposition to 328 CE, but the same sources have been used

subsequently to affirm the 327 CE date (Parvis, 2006, 102–103; Gwynn, 2007, 141).

The Council of Antioch in 328 CE, which appointed Euphronius, is believed by many to have written the 25 canons of Antioch traditionally associated with the so-called Dedication Council of 341 CE (see Hess, 1958, 145–150). However, the weight of evidence indicates that they belong instead to a Council of Antioch in 338 CE (Stephens, 2015).

These Antiochene councils created an opportunity for Arius and the bishops exiled by the Council of Nicaea to return and seek restoration by Constantine, further causing divisions among the bishops and encouraging the continuation of a Eustathian party, which remained active in Antioch for many years. A Council of Alexandria was called in 362 CE to attempt to deal with the resulting division in the city (Athan. *Tom.* 3–7).

4. 337–342 CE, "The Dedication Council"

Early in Constantius II's rule, a celebration was held to dedicate the great Golden Church in Antioch, which provided opportunity for 90 (Socr. *Hist. eccl.* 2.8) or 97 (Soz. *Hist. eccl.* 3.5) eastern bishops to meet in what became known as the Dedication Council, the oldest accounts of which are provided by → Athanasius of Alexandria (*Syn.* 22–25) and → Hilary of Poitiers (*Syn.* 28–33). The Dedication Council is most commonly dated to 341 CE, either in the summer (following Schwartz, 1911b, 497, 503–505) or at the feast of the → Epiphany (following Eltester, 1937, 254–256). S. Parvis (2006, 160–162) argues that the council began late in 340 CE.

Athanasius (*Syn.* 21; 22–25; 26) attributes to the council three theological creeds, and to its bishops a fourth, written shortly after the council (Kinzig, 2017, 341–348). A Dedication Council that produced four creeds featured in scholarship for many centuries and continues to be assumed in some more recent accounts (Hall, 1991, 140–142; Parvis, 2006, 115). However, that assumption has not been widely followed, even by the earliest historians, who separated the production of the first from the second and third creeds, and who placed the fourth at a significantly later council in Antioch (Socr. *Hist. eccl.* 2.8–18). It is most commonly now assumed that the council in

341 CE produced the first two creeds of Athanasius' account and received the third from Theophronius of Tyana in defense against accusations of Sabellianism, but that the fourth was the product of an Antiochene council in 342 CE (Barnes, 1993; Hanson, 2005; Gwynn, 2007).

Much more was done by councils in Antioch during the period 337–343 CE, most likely at the provincial meetings that met in the city regularly, as instructed by canon 15 of Nicaea. Such was the frequency of important synodical action in Antioch that this period has been seen as an early example of a "Permanent Synod" (see Hefele, 1876, 56–58; Hajjar, 1998, 207–215; Stephens, 2015, 90–95). This synodical activity largely constituted opposition to the returns of Athanasius of Alexandria, Marcellus of Ancyra, and Asclepas of Gaza from exile in 337 CE and resistance to the support those figures found in the West. The most likely sequence of events is as follows.

In 337–338 CE, a council in Antioch reiterated Athanasius' deposition and elected Pistus bishop of Alexandria, causing a rival council to be held in Alexandria in 338 CE (Athan. *Ep. encycl.* 6; *Apol. sec.* 3–19; 24). In 338 CE, a further council in Antioch wrote 25 canon laws (for the text and on their contested authorship, see Stephens, 2015), which reaffirmed the validity of the deposition. This led to successive councils at Antioch in 338–339 CE, which first proposed Eusebius of Emesa as bishop of Alexandria, and then appointed Gregory (Socr. *Hist. eccl.* 2.9–10). The council that elected Gregory most likely issued what was to become known as the first of the Dedication Council creeds (Stephens, 2015, 38–49) and led to the ejection of Athanasius from Alexandria by Gregory's supporters in 339 CE (Athan. *Ep. encycl.* 5).

The eastern bishops refused to attend a summons from Julius of Rome, who convened a council at Rome in 340 CE that defended Athanasius and Marcellus and rebuked their opponents (Soz. *Hist. eccl.* 3.8 – for the contested date of this council, see Stephens, 2015, 44n109). In response, the Dedication Council of 341 CE, which composed the "Dedication Creed" (the second attributed to the council by Athanasius), reiterated the exiles' deposition. In 342 CE, a smaller council produced the fourth creed, taken by eastern bishops to the Emperor Constans in Gaul. This was perhaps an attempt at reconciliation (Kelly, 1972, 272), but effectively became the prelude to the divided Council of Serdica in 343 CE.

The four Antioch creeds from this period do not use the Nicene ὁμοούσιος, and Athanasius describes the Dedication Council as part of a movement in the East obsessed with overturning the theological decisions of Nicaea. His account, reiterated by the early historians, is echoed in modern scholarship, much of which defines the creeds as having Arian or anti-Nicene intent (Hess, 2002, 100ff.; Hanson, 2005, 284–291; Parvis, 2006, 162–178). Recent reconsiderations of this period show the polemic of Athanasius to have had undue influence on this narrative, shaping the false idea of a theologically Arian party battling a Nicene party (Gwynn, 2007; Edwards, 2009; 2013). The theology espoused in the Antiochene creeds of this period – particularly the description of the Son as the image or perfect image of the Father – can indeed be shown to be both non-Nicene and also as reflecting traditional orthodoxy.

The canon law issued at Antioch in 338 CE demonstrates that defining episcopal and conciliar authority was of crucial importance to eastern bishops. The canons affirmed the supreme power of the episcopal synod in decision making, above that of any individual. They fought against the interventions of western bishops in affairs of the eastern church, and particularly the notion that the bishop of Rome had a special juridical authority. With the western Serdican canons, these laws illustrate a major rift between East and West about the nature and location of authority in the church, which dominated the concerns of bishops in the years that followed.

5. 344 CE

Following the divided Council of Serdica in 343 CE, attempts were made toward reconciliation between East and West, one of which involved a visit to Antioch from Euphrates of Cologne and Vincentius of Capua. While there, Stephanus of Antioch was exposed as attempting to discredit the visitors, falsely, as fornicators, which led to his being deposed and replaced by Leontius at a council in Antioch (Athan. *Hist. Ar.* 2.20 and Thdt. *Hist. eccl.* 2.9–10). This is now commonly assumed to be the same council that was called in 344 CE and which wrote the *Ecthesis Macrostichos*: the "Macrostich" or Long-Lined Creed, described by Socrates (*Hist. eccl.* 2.19) and Athanasius (*Syn.* 26) and summarized by → Sozomen (*Hist. eccl.* 3.11; for the text, see Kinzig, 2017, 362–369).

The formula takes up the fourth creed traditionally associated with the Dedication Council but in fact written in 342 CE, reiterated at the eastern Serdican council in 343 CE. It adds to it some anathemas and provides a long explanation of the bishops' theological position, apparently for the purposes of demonstrating to western bishops the orthodoxy of the eastern traditional view. The theological content is widely interpreted as an attempt to appease opponents of the leading eastern bishops (Kelly, 1972, 279–281; Brennecke, 1984, 53–56; Hanson, 2005, 309–312). The use of οὐσία in Trinitarian language is avoided in the creed, and the unity of the Godhead is emphasized greatly, separation being described in terms of πρόσωπα (persons). The bishops were particularly concerned to condemn Marcellus of Ancyra and Photinus of Sirmium, and their creed has been described as a veiled rebuke of western Sabellian sympathizers (Beckwith, 2008, 32–33).

A small group of bishops took the creed of this council to the West with the aim of explaining their theological position to the western bishops (Athan. *Syn.* 26; Hilary of Poitiers, *Collectanea Antiariana Parisina* (*Fragmenta historica*), ed. Feder, 1916, series B.2.4–6), the response to which came from a council in Milan. In the following decade, this creed held great significance in the East, becoming both a text against which Athanasius was particularly keen to argue and also one which Constantius used as central to an agenda for unity in the church (on this see Kopecek, 1979, 116–120; Beckwith, 2008, 52).

6. 349/351/352 CE

Sozomen (*Hist. eccl.* 4.8.3–4) describes a meeting of around 35 bishops in Antioch, which reiterated the deposition of Athanasius, declaring his return to Alexandria without proper synodical restoration to have been against the laws of the church, and which wrote widely to fellow bishops to instruct them not to communicate with him. T.D. Barnes (1993, 98–100, 194–195; followed by Ayres, 2004, 144; Parvis, 2006, 42; Gwynn, 2007, 17) believes that the letter to which

Sozomen had access was that of a formal council in Antioch that took place in 349 CE and argues that the *Apologia Contra Arianos* was shaped into its final form by Athanasius to be taken by envoys to defend him at this council. R.P.C. Hanson (2005, 325, 338) dates the council instead to 351/352 CE and argues that it also appointed George as bishop in Alexandria.

7. 357/358 CE

Eudoxius of Antioch called a council shortly after succeeding Leontius as bishop, which issued a letter of thanks to Valens of Musra, Ursacius of Singidunum, and Germinius of Sirmium for bringing the West back to the true faith (Soz. *Hist. eccl.* 4.12–15) and affirming what is commonly labeled the second creed of → Sirmium: a theological tract written in the autumn of 357 CE (Kinzig, 2017, 404–408).

This reaffirmation of what Hilary had quickly condemned as the blasphemy of Sirmium (Hil. Poit. *Syn.* 3; 10–11; 27; 63) marked a further rejection of the use of the word οὐσία (and so ὁμοούσιος and also ὁμοιούσιος) when describing the relationship of Father and Son in the Trinity. This has been described variously as an early step toward a radical neo-Arianism (Hanson, 2005, 348), the rise of the Homoian movement (Ayres, 2004, 138–139), and the surrender of Antioch to the Anomoeans (Hefele, 1876, 228).

The council, attended by Acacius of Caesarea and Uranius of Tyre, was not representative of a dominant theological position. Responding to it, a council was held in 358 CE at Ancyra, led by Basil of Ancyra, Marcellus' successor. The council issued a creed and anathemas (Kinzig, 2017, 408–411) and established the *homoiousian* position. Constantius welcomed this and rejected the statement issued in Antioch, condemning and exiling Eudoxius and others associated with it (Soz. *Hist. eccl.* 4.13–14).

8. 360–361, 362? CE

The divided church in Antioch was brought into further chaos during 360–361 CE by the appointment and speedy exile of Meletius of Antioch, during which time synodical meetings certainly took place in the city, but the details of which are not clear (for general accounts of these events, see Socr. *Hist. eccl.* 2.44; Soz. *Hist. eccl.* 4.28. See also Gwatkin, 1900, 186–188; Chadwick, 2001, 292–294; Hanson, 2005, 382–384).

In 361 CE, following the election of Euzoius as bishop and before the death of Constantius in November of that year, a council was held in Antioch (Athan. *Syn.* 31; Socr. *Hist. eccl.* 2.45; Soz. *Hist. eccl.* 4.29). The council, populated by what Socrates describes as followers of Acacius of Caesarea and of the influential theologian Aetius, attempted to revise the theological position established at Niké in 359 CE and by the Council of Constantinople in 360 CE (Kinzig, 2017, 420–425). The instigators of this move argued that the Son is unlike the Father in substance (οὐσία) and will and that he was made from nothing. They were therefore labeled *Anomoeans* and *Exoucontians* by their pro-*homoousian* opponents. Members of this group have been characterized as marginal and extreme heretics, not necessarily aligned theologically with Acacius or even Aetius (Hanson, 2005, 573, 580–581). They were unable to defend their position properly at the council in Antioch, and their revisions were rejected.

Philostorgius (*Hist. eccl.* 7.5) mentions further synods in Antioch prior to the death of Constantius, which restored Aetius from his deposition by the Council of → Constantinople in 360 CE, and which elected him as a bishop. However, we know that Aetius was recalled from exile after → Julian the Apostate became emperor (Jul. *Ep.* 79), and so, if one or more councils did take place in Antioch for these purposes (deemed unlikely by Hanson, 2005, 614–615), they must have taken place during or after 362 CE.

9. 363 CE

The accession of Jovian after the death of Julian in June 363 CE encouraged a range of clerics to approach the new emperor seeking favor for themselves and their theological positions (Socr. *Hist. eccl.* 3.24; Soz. *Hist. eccl.* 6.5; Thdt. *Hist. eccl.* 4.2; Philost. *Hist. eccl.* 8.6–7).

Among this flurry of activity, Meletius called a council in Antioch, formed of his supporters and those of Acacius of Caesarea (on the appearance of

Acacius at the council and on its specific date, see Brenneke, 1988, 174–176; Zachhuber, 2004, 84–85). Accounts of the council are provided by Sozomen (*Hist. eccl.* 6.4) and Socrates (*Hist. eccl.* 3.25), who includes the full text of a letter to Jovian, signed by 29 clerics including Meletius, Eusebius of Samosata, and Pelagius of Laodicea. Socrates tells us that the letter had been preserved by Sabinus.

The bishops in Antioch, many of whom had previously subscribed to the homoian creed of the Council of Constantinople in 360 CE, professed that the Nicene Creed should be the focus of unity in the church. They addressed the problematic tradition surrounding the use of ὁμοούσιος, offering their support for it both as the means by which those at Nicaea had intended to discredit the Arian view that the Son was created out of nothing and also as a defense against the present-day *Anhomoians*, who threatened church unity. The letter specifically defined the Nicene ὁμοούσιος as meaning the Son was born from the οὐσία of the Father, that he was therefore like the Father in οὐσία, so equating ὁμοούσιος with ὅμοιος κατ᾽ οὐσίαν (like according to substance). The bishops stated that using οὐσία did not imply that a πάθος (process) occurred in the generation of the Son, nor did it have any association with its use in pagan traditions.

The council in 363 CE has been described as marking the beginnings of a Neo-Niceneism (Zachhuber, 2004, 92) and as producing the most important theological document of Jovian's reign (Gwatkin, 1900, 230–231). However, Socrates believed the council to be the work of sycophants, always seeking favor from the greatest secular authority (*Hist. eccl.* 3.25), a view echoed by → Epiphanius of Salamis (*Pan.* 7.23). → Apollinarius of Laodicea described the council as an anti-Nicene deception (Bas. *Ep.* 364, on which see Zachhuber, 2004, 96–97), and it has indeed been characterized in later scholarship as encouraging a weakening of the Nicene formula with an Arian slant (Hefele, 1876, 283).

Despite their common profession of allegiance to the Nicene Creed, Athanasius and Meletius did not reconcile at this time, and both bishops found themselves exiled by Valens after the death of Jovian in February 364 CE.

10. 379 CE

The Council of Antioch in 379 CE, called by Meletius (after returning from his final period of exile and most likely as part of efforts to secure his position against Paulinus), was a significant event. It has been described as supporting the move toward consensus in doctrine across the empire and reconciliation in the church (King, 1961, 25–26; Hanson, 2005, 802–805), although the achievements of the council itself in securing that consensus have been questioned (e.g. Ayres, 2004, 242–243).

Information about the council is fragmented, and our knowledge of its work is limited (on the sources, see particularly Bardy, 1933; Schwartz, 1935, 198–200; 1936, 19–23; Simonetti, 1975, 446–447). With the possible exception of a confused account by Theodoret of Cyrrhus (*Hist. eccl.* 4.8–9), the council is not described by the early ecclesiastical historians. → Gregory of Nyssa indicated that he attended the council (*Vita Sanctae Macrinae*), and the synodical letter of the Council of Constantinople in 382 CE mentions it (Thdt. *Hist. eccl.* 5.9), from which we learn that the Antiochene meeting produced a theological statement (τόμος). More directly, the Codex Verona LX(58) contains a text signed by over 150 bishops identified with this council, led by Meletius and Eusebius of Samosata and offering universal support for a collection of documents sent to the East from Rome (for the text, see Schwartz, 1936, 19–23; Telfer, 1943). The content of those documents has been associated with letters from a council held under → Damasus at Rome, recorded by Sozomen (*Hist. eccl.* 6.23) and Theodoret (*Hist. eccl.* 2.17), and the Antiochene council is therefore believed to have condemned the followers of Apollinarius of Laodicea amongst a range of other heretics (King, 1961, 25; Kelly, 1972, 335; Simonetti, 1975, 447).

The detail of the council's theological τόμος is unclear, although W. Telfer (1943, 196–197) argued that a document attributed to the Council of Serdica in the Verona Codex should be identified with this Antiochene council. Whatever its exact content, the pro-Nicene position of the τόμος is certain. The council affirmed the position of Damasus of Rome and most likely wrote to Theodosius following an early public indication of his own doctrinal sympathies (Cod. Theod. 16.5.5). The bishops in Antioch were later described by the Council of Constantinople in 382 CE as part of their theological tradition (Thdt. *Hist. eccl.* 5.9).

11. 380 CE

The death of → Valens led to the restoration from exile of clerics (Socr. *Hist. eccl.* 5.2), including Eunomius, who had been exiled to Naxos (Philost. *Hist. eccl.* 9.11). Philostorgius mentions a meeting in Antioch gathered by Eunomius for the purposes of arranging matters among his supporters elsewhere in the East (*Hist. eccl.* 9.18). The meeting, most likely held in 380 CE, is characterized by M. Simonetti (1975, 453–454) as a council of radical Arians.

12. 383? CE

The Messalinans (or Euchites) were a pietistic, mendicant group of ascetics, opposed greatly by Flavian of Antioch (Thdt. *Hist. eccl.* 4.11). Photius (*Bibl.* codex 52) describes a council, supported by three further bishops and 30 priests and deacons, which met in Antioch to affirm the decisions of a larger Council of Sida in Pamphylia, which had condemned the Messalians. The evidence for both councils has been doubted (Hefele, 1876, 389–390).

13. 388/389 CE

Theodoret mentions a Council of Antioch in 388/389 CE, which dealt with the aftermath of violence associated with the destruction of pagan shrines (Thdt. *Hist. eccl.* 7.15). Marcellus of Apamea had been instructed by Theodosius to destroy a number of local temples, the events surrounding which are described by Theodoret (*Hist. eccl.* 5.21). In carrying this out, Marcellus was killed by pagans. His sons sought revenge against those responsible, but the council in Antioch forbade this and instead proposed that the death of Marcellus should be celebrated as martyrdom.

Historiography

The synodical meetings in Antioch during this period have not been studied comprehensively in any one work since the (still useful) histories of the early ecclesiastical councils written in the 19th century (see Hefele, 1876; 1894). Most commonly, individual councils or focused groups of councils across shorter periods have received attention because of particular decisions they made, some debates about which have extended across generations of scholars (e.g. the dates of the depositions of Eustathius of Antioch and Asclepas of Gaza mentioned above). Even within this literature, longer historical and theological works have not focused exclusively on councils in Antioch, but instead discuss them alongside wider conciliar action across the church.

Amongst the Antiochene councils described here, those which took place after 325 CE feature most prominently in theological scholarship relating to the so-called Arian crisis. The earliest historians presented a more nuanced view of their creeds (Hil. Poit. Syn. 28–33), but centuries of modern scholarship have presented the councils as those of heretic bishops, determined to undermine the creed established at the Council of Nicaea. Influential writers sustaining this view include J.N.D. Kelly (1977), W.H.C. Frend (2003) and R.P.C. Hanson (2005). However, a revisionist opinion has emerged in recent decades, which reinterprets the role of key individuals on either side of this apparent theological divide (see Gwynn, 2007; Edwards, 2009) and offers a more complex and sympathetic analysis of the Antiochene councils' theological work.

Interest in the regulatory work of the early councils in general has declined in the past century (compare Turner, 1936, 178–182 with Scheibelreiter, 2005, 695–696). However, debates about the content and origin of canon law written by a council or councils in Antioch in the 4th century CE have been a feature of sustained scholarly interest (Schwartz, 1911a; Chadwick, 1948; Hess, 1958; Stephens, 2015). Studying these laws allows the councils in Antioch to be seen as important for the development of ideas about conciliar power, episcopal authority, and the nature and efficacy of canon law in the church.

Bibliography

Abramowski, L., "Die Synode von Antiochien 324/325 und ihr Symbol," *ZKG* 86, 1975, 356–366.

Ayres, L., *Nicaea and Its Legacy: An Approach to Fourth-Century Trinitarian Theology*, Oxford, 2004.

Bardy, G., "Le Concile d'Antioche (379)," *Rben* 45, 1933, 196–213.

Barnes, T.D., "Emperor and Bishops, AD 324–344: Some Problems," *AmJAH* 3, 1978, 53–75.

Barnes, T.D., *Constantine and Eusebius*, London, 1981.

Barnes, T.D., *Athanasius and Constantius: Theology and Politics in the Constantinian Empire*, London, 1993.

Beckwith, C.L., *Hilary of Poitiers on the Trinity: From* De Fide *to* De Trinitate, Oxford, 2008.

Brennecke, H.C., *Hilarius von Poitiers und die Bischofsopposition gegen Konstantius*, vol. II: *Untersuchungen zur dritten Pase des arianischen Streites (337–361)*, Berlin, 1984.

Burgess, R.W., *Studies in Eusebian and Post-Eusebian Chronography*, Stuttgart, 1999.

Burgess, R.W., "The Date of the Deposition of Eustathius of Antioch," *JThS* n.s. 51/1, 2000, 150–160.

Chadwick, H., "The Fall of Eustathius of Antioch," *JThS* 49, 1948, 27–35.

Chadwick, H., "Ossius of Cordova and the Presidency of the Council of Antioch, 325," *JThS* n.s. 9, 1958, 292–304.

Chadwick, H., *The Church in Ancient Society: From Galilee to Gregory the Great*, Oxford, 2001.

Cross, F.L., "The Council of Antioch in 325 AD," *CQR* 128, 1939, 49–76.

Edwards, M.J., *Catholicity and Heresy in the Early Church*, Farnham, 2009.

Edwards, M.J., *Image, Word and God in the Early Christian Centuries*, Farnham, 2013.

Eltester, W., "Die Kirchen Antiochias im IV. Jahrhundert," *ZNW* 36, 1937, 251–286.

Feder, A.L., ed., *S. Hilarii episcopi Pictaviensis Opera: Pars quarta*, CSEL 65, Vienna, 1916.

Frend, W.H.C., *The Early Church: From the Beginnings to 461*, London, 2003.

Gaudemet, J., *La formation du droit séculier et du droit de l'Église aux IVe et Ve siècles*, Paris, 1979.

Gwatkin, H.M., *Studies of Arianism*, Cambridge UK, 1900.

Gwynn, D.M., *The Eusebians: The Polemic of Athanasius of Alexandria and the Construction of the "Arian Controversy"*, Oxford, 2007.

Hajjar, J., *Antioche entre Rome, Byzance et la Mecque*, vol. I, Beyrouth, 1998.

Hall, S.G., *Doctrine and Practice in the Early Church*, London, 1991.

Hanson, R.P.C., "The Fate of Eustathius of Antioch," *ZKG* 95, 1984, 171–179.

Hanson, R.P.C., *The Search for the Christian Doctrine of God: The Arian Controversy, 318–381*, Grand Rapids, 2005.

Hefele, K.J. von, *A History of the Councils of the Church from the Original Documents*, vol. II, Edinburgh, 1876.

Hefele, K.J. von, *A History of the Councils of the Church from the Original Documents*, vol. I, Edinburgh, 1894.

Hess, H., *The Canons of the Council of Sardica AD 343: A Landmark in the Early Development of Canon Law*, Oxford, 1958.

Hess, H., *The Early Development of Canon Law and the Council of Serdica*, Oxford, 2002.

Holland, D.L., "Die *Synode von Antiochien* (324/325) und ihre Bedeutung für Eusebius *von* Caesarea und das Konzil *von* Nizäa," *ZKG* 81, 1970, 163–181.

Kelly, J.N.D., *Early Christian Creeds*, London, 1972.

Kelly, J.N.D., *Early Christian Doctrines*, London, 1977.

King, N.Q., *The Emperor Theodosius and the Establishment of Christianity*, London, 1961.

Kinzig, W., *Faith in Formulae: A Collection of Early Christian Creeds and Creed-Related Texts*, vol. I, Oxford, 2017.

Kopecek, T.A., *A History of Neo-Arianism*, Cambridge MA, 1979.

Loofs, F., *Paulus von Samosata: Eine Untersuchung zur altkirchlichen Literatur- und Dogmengeschichte*, Leipzig, 1924.

Nau, F., "Littérature canonique syriaque inédite," *ROC* 14, 1909, 1–31.

Opitz, H.-G., "Die Zeitfolge des arianischen Streites von den Anfängen bis zum Jahr 328," *ZNW* 33, 1934, 131–159.

Parvis, S., *Marcellus of Ancyra and the Lost Years of the Arian Controversy 325–345*, Oxford, 2006.

Riedmatten, H. de, *Les actes du procès de Paul de Samosate: Étude sur la christologie du IIIe au IVe siècle*, Fribourg, 1952.

Scheibelreiter, G., "Church Structure and Organisation," in: P. Fouracre, ed., *NCMH*, vol. 1, Cambridge UK, 2005, 675–709.

Schwartz, E., *Zur Geschichte des Athanasius*, sixth paper, NAWG.PH, 1905, 257–299.

Schwartz, E., *Zur Geschichte des Athanasius*, eighth paper, NAWG.PH, 1911a, 188–264.

Schwartz, E., *Zur Geschichte des Athanasius*, ninth paper, NAWG.PH, 1911b, 469–552.

Schwartz, E., "Zur Kirchengeschichte des vierten Jahrhunderts," *ZNW* 34, 1935, 129–213.

Schwartz, E., "Über die Sammlung des Cod. Veronensis LX," *ZNW* 35, 1936, 1–23.

Sieben, H.J., *Die Konzilsidee der Alten Kirche*, Paderborn, 1979.

Simonetti, M., *La crisi ariana nel IV secolo*, Rome, 1975.

Stead, G.C., *Divine Substance*, Oxford, 1977.

Stephens, C.W.B., *Canon Law and Episcopal Authority: The Canons of Antioch and Serdica*, Oxford, 2015.

Strutwolf, H., *Die Trinitätstheologie und Christologie des Euseb von Caesarea: Eine dogmengeschichtliche Untersuchung seiner Platonismusrezeption und Wirkungsgeschichte*, FKDG 72, Göttingen, 1999.

Telfer, W., "The Codex Verona LX(58)," *HThR* 36/3, 1943, 169–246.

Turner, C.H., "The Organisation of the Church," in: *CMH*, vol. I, Cambridge UK, 1936, 143–82.

Williams, R.D., *Arius: Heresy and Tradition*, London, 2001.

Zachhuber, J., "The Antiochene Synod of AD 363 and the Beginnings of Neo-Nicenism," *ZAC* 4/1, 2004, 83–101.

CHRISTOPHER W.B. STEPHENS

Antioch of Caria, Synods of

Antioch-upon-Maeander, a city of the province of Caria (metropolitan see: Aphrodisias), in the civil diocese of Asia, hosted two Homoiousians synods in 366 and 378 CE.

In Spring 366 CE, a group of Oriental bishops gathered at the Synod of Tyana in Caria (Soz. *Hist. eccl.* 6.12.2–3). Prompted by a letter from Liberius of Rome (→ Liberius [Bishop of Rome]), they decided to subscribe the Creed of → Nicaea (325 CE) and adopt its controverted adjective ὁμοούσιος/*homoousios* ("consubstantial"). → Sozomen relates that 34 unnamed Asian bishops, gathered at "Antioch of Caria," refused to rally the group and reiterated their subscription to the formula of the Synod of → Antioch of 341 CE (*Hist. eccl.* 6.12.4). Actually, the subscription to this formula was, since 358 CE, the distinguishing mark of the partisans of the Christological formula ὅμοιος κατ' οὐσίαν/*homoios kat' ousian* ("similar according to the substance"). These Homoiousians, which Sozomen also calls Macedonians because of their proximity with now dead Makedonios of Constantinople, are probably the same that gathered again at Cyzicus in 376 CE around Eleusios of Cyzicus and Eustathius of Sebaste (Bas. *Ep.* 244, 5–9).

Socrates Scholasticus (*Hist. eccl.* 5.4.1, followed by Soz. *Hist. eccl.* 7.2.2–4; → Socrates Scholasticus) mentions another synod of the same group at "Antioch of Caria" (following the Armenian version of Socrates and Sozomen, rather than "Antioch of Syria"), which adopted the same decisions. The gathering is dated just after the death of Emperor → Valens (Aug 9, 378 CE) and the publication of a law by Gratian (also mentioned in Cod. Theod. 165.5 of Aug 3, 379 CE) allowing exiled Nicaean bishops to recover their sees.

The group maintained its stance and sent 36 Asian bishops, mainly from the Hellespont, led by Eleusios of Cyzicus and Markianos of Lampsacus, to the second ecumenical council in Constantinople in 381 CE (Socr. *Hist. eccl.* 5.8.5). The bishops were denied the right to sit with the others and their doctrine was condemned.

Historiography

K.J. von Hefele (1873, 735, followed by Ritter, 1965) wrongly dates the Synod of Lampsacus in 365 CE and, consequently, the Synods of Tyana and Antioch of Caria in 367 CE (Hefele, 1873, 738). T.D. Barnes dates the Synod of Lampsacus in 364 CE (Barnes, 1993, 161) and Tyana and Antioch of Caria in 365 CE (Barnes, 1993, 291n65). Dates in W.-D. Hauschild (1967, 10n1, 226) are inconsistent. A proposed dating, 366 CE, takes into account the time necessary for the journey of the Oriental delegates in Occident, sent after the imperial decree of May, 365 CE (*Hist. Aceph.* 5.1) and before the death of Liberius of Rome on Sep 24, 366 CE.

Bibliography

Barnes, T.D., *Athanasius and Constantius: Theology and Politics in the Constantinian Empire*, Cambridge MA, 1993, 162; 1st synod.

Hauschild, W.-D., *Die Pneumatomachen: Ein Untersuchung zur Dogmengeschichte der vierten Jahrhunderts*, Hamburg, 1967.

Haykin, M.A.G., *The Spirit of God: The Exegesis of 1 and 2 Corinthians in the Pneumatomachian Controversy of the Fourth Century*, Leiden, 1994, 178; 2nd synod.

Hefele, K.J. von, *Conciliengeschichte*, Fribourg, ²1873, § 88, 738 & § 91, 743.

Meinhold, P., *Pneumatomachoi*, RECA.S, vol. XXI/1, Stuttgart, 1951, 1066–1101.

Pietri, C., "Le débat pneumatologique à la veille du Concile de Constantinople (358–381)," in: J. Saraiva Martins, ed., *Credo in Spiritum Sanctum*, vol. I, Vatican City, 1983, 55–87; 2nd synod.

Ritter, A.M., *Das Konzil von Konstantinopel und sein Symbol: Studien zur Geschichte und Theologie des II: Ökumenischen Konzils*, Göttingen, 1965, 71; 1st synod; 75–76; 2nd synod.

XAVIER MORALES

Antony the Great

Antony (or Anthony; d. 356 CE) was an Egyptian ascetic, desert monk, and monastic teacher. He is considered the first hermit and the father of monasticism (→ Monasticism). The most important – but also problematic – source on Antony is his *Vita* written shortly after his death by Bishop → Athanasius of Alexandria (d. 373 CE).

Antony needs to be described from three different perspectives:

1. as historical figure who was probably the author of a series of letters that are preserved under his name;
2. as textual creation in Athanasius' *Vita Antonii* and other sources, particularly the collections of *Apophthegmata patrum*, Jerome's hagiographical works, and the monastic *Historiae*;
3. as late antique and medieval imagination: the first monk and Egyptian founding father of eremitic monasticism, a new type of saint for whom ascetic discipline takes the place of martyrdom, and a model for ascetic life.

1. The Historical Antony

According to Athanasius, Antony was born to a wealthy family in Middle Egypt, possibly in the village of Koma (today Qîmân al-Ariâs) close to Herakleopolis (according to Soz. *Hist. eccl.* 1.13). After his parents' death, Antony decided to give up his possessions and his social position in order to live a life of ἄσκησις, emulating and surpassing the model of other ascetics in his surroundings. He first lived in a dwelling close to his home village, then in a tomb, where he allegedly fought a fierce battle against demons. Later, he withdrew into an abandoned military barrack, where he, as Athanasius tells, spent 20 years as a recluse. In order to escape a growing crowd of disciples and people searching for help and advice, he moved into the desert. He established first a dwelling at Mount Pispir (Dayr al-Maymūn, c. 75 km south of Memphis) and later another one at Mount Galala near the Red Sea (today Dêr Mar Antonios). For the rest of his life, he moved back and forth between these two places, alternating between a public life as teacher, healer, exorcist, and mediator and an eremitical life, surrounded only by a small number of disciples.

Athanasius reports that Antony left the desert twice. In 311 CE he traveled to Alexandria in order to tend to Christians imprisoned during the persecution of Maximinus Daia, and to seek martyrdom (→ Martyrs) himself (Athan. *Vit. Ant.* 46). In 338 CE he came to support the clergy of Alexandria in their fight against Arius (*Vit. Ant.* 69–71). At this journey he may have encountered Athanasius, who would later become his hagiographer.

Antony died in 356 CE at an advanced age (according to his own saying, he was 105 years old) after having arranged to be buried at an undisclosed place lest his body be mummified and turned into an object of veneration (*Vit. Ant.* 89–92). His disciples founded a monastery at his dwelling at Mount Galala, which still exists today (Meinardus, 1961, 31–88). Legendary tradition claims that his grave was miraculously discovered in 561 CE. The physical remains found there were brought to Alexandria; later they came to Constantinople and moved from there to the Church of La-Motte-Saint-Didier close to Vienne, where the hospitaller order of the Brothers of Saint Antony was founded in 1095 CE (Noordeloos, 1942; Bertrand, 2005, 15–16). The Church of Saint-Trophime in Arles claims to own his skull and one of his leg bones.

According to Athanasius, Antony consciously decided not to receive any formal education and to remain illiterate. He spoke Coptic, interacted with his Greek-speaking interlocutors through interpreters, and did not write any theological works (*Vit. Ant.* 1; 16; 66; 72–74; 93; Jer. *Vit. Hil.* 30; Pall. *Hist. Laus.* 21.15). Athanasius probably strongly exaggerates Antony's lack of learning in order to contrast his wisdom, which he received from God through strict discipline, with the inane learnedness of philosophers and pagans whom he put to shame with his simple reasoning (*Vit. Ant.* 72–80; Rousseau, 2000). Antony's supposed illiteracy and his lack of education and access to Greek learning conflict with his profound familiarity with biblical texts and theological and philosophical concepts as they appear in the three lengthy speeches Athanasius inserted in his *Vita*, which cover almost a half of the text (on demons, *Vit. Ant.* 16–43; on perseverance and ascetic life, *Vit. Ant.* 55–56; against the pagans, *Vit. Ant.* 74–76). His involvement in the debates between Arians (→ Arianism) and Athanasians (*Vit. Ant.* 68–70; 82), several references to Antony as letter writer (e.g. *Vit. Ant.* 81; 86; *Apophth. Patr. (coll. alph.)* 31; Soz. *Hist. eccl.* 2.31; Jer. *Vit. Hil.* 24), and the fact that he recommended that his monks to write down their sins and thoughts on wax tablets (*Vit. Ant.* 55) also speak against his illiteracy. Yet Athanasius suppressed any information about Antony's training, aside from vague references to him emulating the ascetic practices of other ascetics in his village (*Vit. Ant.* 3–4). S. Rubenson (1995, 95–99) argues that

a Coptic-speaking well-to-do Egyptian in the 4th century CE could have obtained the theological and philosophical knowledge Antony displayed.

Antony was, as S. Rubenson (1995, 35–47) convincingly points out, the author of a series of seven letters written in Coptic, which are mentioned by → Jerome (*Vir. ill.* 88). These letters, which were written roughly between 340 and 350 CE, are, aside from a Coptic fragment, preserved only in translations: a Georgian and a late medieval Latin translation of a lost Greek version, and an Arabic translation and a Syriac fragment based on the Coptic original text (Rubenson, 1995, 15–34). A monastic rule ascribed to Antony that had been preserved in an Arabic version (Lat. trans., PG 40.1065–1074) is most likely not original, but may have been written by his pupils.

In order to grasp the "historical" Antony beyond the scarce and not necessarily reliably biographical information provided in the *Vita Antonii*, it is necessary to situate him in the socioeconomic, political, and theological context of 3rd- and 4th-century CE Egypt. S. Rubenson (1995, 89–95) links Antony's conversion to ascetic life to the hardships caused by Roman taxation, which often resulted in a not necessarily religiously motivated ἀναχώρησις that caused a severe economic crisis. J.E. Goehring (1999, 20–26, 73–88) contrasts the geographic and social realities of 3rd-century CE monasticism with the textual representation of the desert. P. Brown (2016, 71–108) compares the sedentary, self-supporting, and socially integrated ascetic ideal of 3rd-century CE Egypt with Syriac radical migrant asceticism. All three authors emphasize that Antony was by no means the first monk or hermit but rather – predominantly thanks to Athanasius – the most prominent and influential representative of a broader ascetic phenomenon.

2. Antony as a Textual Construct

The *Vita Antonii*, the scattered references to Antony in other sources (esp. the → *Apophthegmata patrum*, in the monastic *Historiae*, and in Jerome's entirely fictitious *Vita Pauli* and *Vita Hilarionis*), and Antony's own letters seem to refer to three different personae, or at least three very different representations of the same historical Antony (Goehring, 1999, 18–26; Dörries, 1966).

Athanasius' *Vita Antonii* is in itself a rather heterogeneous work that is inspired by different Christian and non-Christian biographic traditions, particularly the *Life of Pythagoras* (Bertrand, 2005, 20–22; Rubenson, 2013). It shaped the nascent genre of → hagiography, even though it may not have been Athanasius' intention to produce a text that would be read as a saint's Life. Underneath a vaguely chronological order, the text is mostly structured around specific themes. It expresses – as most scholars agree – rather Athanasius' own theological viewpoints and political agendas than those of Antony (Brakke, 1995, 201–265). Athanasius admits in the prologue of his *Vita* that he reports only a fraction of what there is to tell about Antony but claims nevertheless a discursive monopoly on him. His work begins with Antony's conversion to monastic life, providing a catalogue of ascetic practices and virtues, which include poverty, fasting, sexual abstinence, vigils, constant prayer, rejection of bodily pleasure, and a gradual withdrawal from social structures. This ascetic catalogue had a strong impact on eastern and western monastic ideals (Diem, 2019). Antony's asceticism– unlike that of Syrian ascetics (as described e.g. in → Theodoret of Cyrrhus' *Historia religiosa*) – does not emphasize bodily mortification and self-inflicted punishment, but aims at gaining control over one's body and thoughts, achieving full dedication to God, and fighting vices and temptations (*Vit. Ant.* 44–45). It is, however, described as a worthy alternative to martyrdom (*Vit. Ant.* 47).

A central theme of Athanasius' work is the fight against demons (→ Demonology/Demons) that take various shapes and attack Antony both physically, and through temptations, illusions, and "thoughts" (λογισμοί; *cogitationes*). Athanasius uses Antony's battle against demons as a stepping stone for an extensive reflection on the nature of demons, which defines ascetic life to a large extent as a battle against demonic → temptation. This reflection is presented in the form of a speech of Antony to his disciples that covers almost a third of the entire *Vita* (on Athanasius' demonology: Brakke, 2006, 23–47). The second half of the *Vita Antonii* describes Antony's interaction with his surrounding world. He becomes a charismatic monastic teacher of an increasing number of disciples; he presents a monastic program based on his own ascetic practices; he fights against

heretics, converts pagans, and ensnarls philosophers in theological discussions in which they have to surrender to his simple arguments; and he gains widespread fame (which even reaches the imperial court, *Vit. Ant.* 81) as a miracle worker and exorcist (*Vit. Ant.* 54–62) and as an advisor of judges, mediator in conflicts, and spokesman of the poor and persecuted (*Vit. Ant.* 81–82, 84–88). As such he displays the key traits of the late antique "holy man" as described by P. Brown (1971, 89–95).

Athanasius turns Antony into a vigorous spokesman of his own theological agenda, into a champion in his fight against Arianism (refuting attempts of Arians to claim Antony for themselves), and into a superior alternative to ascetically inclined philosophers, particularly of the Neo-Pythagorean tradition (Rubenson, 2013). More importantly, however, his *Vita* transforms a representative of a potentially subversive ascetic movement into a model for a socially compatible asceticism that avoids excess and by no means undermines ecclesiastical authority (*Vit. Ant.* 4; 67) or questions the legitimacy of non-ascetic Christian life. Moreover, Athanasius' textual creation of Antony proposes a monastic ideal that unfolds itself in the "desert," thus at a safe distance from to world of villages and cities (*Vit. Ant.* 84–85, see also Goehring, 1999, 73–133). As Athanasius' creation, Antony can indeed be called the first monk – whose ascetic repertoire is moderate enough to form a model of emulation, whose teaching is philosophical enough to shame traditional philosophers, but simple enough not to challenge theologically trained bishops. His natural habitat is the desert, not the civilized world; his enemies are demons and heretics rather than lukewarm Christians or unworthy priests. Athanasius himself and after him → Gregory of Nazianzus (d. 390 CE) emphasize that the *Vita Antonii* should be read as a monastic rule (*Vit. Ant.* prologue 3; 94; Greg. Naz. *Or.* 21.5), arguing that for monks the *Life of Antony* is a sufficient pattern of discipline (van Geest, 2010).

It is in this context important to notice that Athanasius' Antony is not presented as a saint. He is never called ἅγιος (*sanctus*) and only at two occasions μακάριος (*beatus*). The critical apparatus of P. Bertrand's edition of → Evagrius of Antioch's Latin translation shows, however, that the epithet *sanctus* got woven into later textual traditions of the

Vita Antonii at least thirteen times. Antony *became* a saint, thanks to the *Vita Antonii*, even though the text uses ἅγιος (*sanctus*) only in the context of martyrs and biblical figures – possibly because the notion that ascetics could be considered saints had not been fully established at that point. Athanasius' persistent claim that not Antony but God caused all the → miracles ascribed to Antony (*Vit. Ant.* 48; 56–58; 71; 80; 83–84) may have been not only an attempt of "theological correctness," but also of turning Antony into a model of a perfect monk and the embodiment of a monastic rule, rather than fueling Antony's reputation as a holy man whose holiness might overshadow ecclesiastical authority. Jerome shares Athanasius' reluctance to call Antony *sanctus*, though he occasionally uses the epithet *beatus*. In the *Apophthegmata patrum* Antony is usually called *Abbas Antonius*. The → *Historia monachorum* and the Greek *Historica Lausiaca* finally transform Antony into Saint Antony by calling him consistently ἅγιος Ἀντώνιος (*sanctus Antonius*), μακάριος Ἀντώνιος (*beatus Antonius*) and μέγας Ἀντώνιος (*magnus Antonius*).

The role Antony plays in sources other than the *Vita Antonii* is slightly different from that envisioned by Athanasius. In the *Apophthegmata Patrum*, the *Historia monachorum*, the *Historia Lausiaca* and John Cassian's work (esp. *Apophth. Patr.* (*coll. alph.*) 1–38; Ruf. *Hist. mon.* 31; Pall. *Hist. Laus.* 21–22; Cass. *Con.* 2.2; 8.18–19; 18.6; 24.11), Antony appears not so much as public persona, but as a hermit who praises the withdrawal from the civilized world. He receives visits from other monks asking him for words of wisdom, and gathers around him a select circle of disciples (see esp. *Hist. mon.* 13.2; 25.5; 26.6; 28.1; 31.1). Antony responds to those who approach him with simple ascetic advice on the necessity of renunciation, the fight against temptations, and on chastity humility, discretion, brotherly love, moderation, prayer, simplicity, silence, and poverty. This image of Athanasius as a serene hermit who seeks solitude and provides plain wisdom, rather than deep theological reflections, aligns with Athanasius' claim of his simplicity (*Vit. Ant.* 55–56), but not really with his role as an avid preacher, fierce fighter against paganism and heresy, and public persona.

His collection letters reveal traits of Antony that had been suppressed in all the narrative sources.

Here he appears as a teacher of a refined ascetic theology who addresses his disciples through texts that self-confidently emulate the style of the Pauline Epistles. The theological program of Antony's letters is significantly different from that represented in the *Vita Antonii* and strongly rooted both in Neoplatonic philosophical traditions and in Origenist and Valentinian theology (→ Origen; → Valentinus/Valentinians). Since most of the letters contain recurring phrases and ideas, S. Rubenson (1995, 46–47) assumes that they addressed various monastic communities. I would suggest a different reading, regarding the entire corpus as *one* work in which the author lays out a number of core themes, which he applies in each letter to a different aspect of ascetical life. Almost all of his letters elaborate on the Platonic notion of a dichotomy of → body and → soul along with a division of the soul between an immortal essence that forms a unity with God, and the mind. The → fall is understood as withdrawal from this immortal essence into passions and irrationality. It is a disease of the soul that cannot be repaired by natural law (he calls it the "law of promise") or the written law given by → Moses, but only by Christ, the physician who heals the wound caused by the disruption from the immortal essence. Asceticism is, in Antony's letters, predominantly a strife for knowledge, self-knowledge, and knowledge of God that allows to regain access to one's immortal essence, to restore unity, and to bridge the rupture caused by the fall. Each letter elaborates within this framework on a number of different themes: asceticism as form of repentance and purification of the mind, body, and speech (*Ep.* 1); the role of Christ as the savior and physician and on the necessity of discernment and constant preparation (*Ep.* 2); eternal truth, the transitory nature of the earthly existence and the necessity of perseverance (*Ep.* 3); restraining one's passions, self-knowledge, and the unforgivable wickedness of Arius (*Ep.* 4); the necessity of incessant → prayer and of renunciation of the world (*Ep.* 5); the nature of demons (*Ep.* 6); the promise of freedom and salvation and the coming of Christ, and the necessity of mutual love (*Ep.* 7). *Ep.* 6, by far the longest, develops a theory of demons that is strikingly different from the demonology that Antony (or maybe rather Athanasius) laid out in the *Vita Antonii*. In Athanasius' work, demons are predominantly tempters, cause despair, claim and defend space, attack mind and body, and take on corporeal shapes (animals, women, a black boy, pagan gods etc.). They are eventually utterly powerless and can be defeated through ascetic discipline. The demons evoked in *Ep.* 6 are noncorporeal. As an effect of the fall, they have become even more remote from the unity with God than humans, and their aim is to increase confusion through instilling thoughts and causing diversification in order to draw humans further away from the oneness with God. Instead of taking a bodily shape, they manifest themselves in the thoughts they instill, become visible in the person they attack, and reveal themselves in his or her deeds. D. Brakke summarizes the demonology of Antony's letter. as follows:

> Because Antony considers the monk's life to be a process of return to an original undifferentiated unity, the demons represent the tendency toward separation, division, and individuality. (Brakke, 2006, 21)

3. The Afterlife of Antony

Athhanasius' letters, aside from one parallel in the *Apophthegmata Patrum* (*Apophth. Patr.* (*coll. alph.*) 22 paraphrasing Ant. Gr. *Ep.* 1.35–42 on the "movements of the flesh," probably spontaneous erections), left no identifiable traces of reception and, even though they were mentioned by Jerome, did not impact how Antony was imagined in later history. The late antique and medieval image of Antony was created to a large extent on the basis of the *Vita Antonii*, which was soon translated into Latin twice, but also into Coptic and Syriac (on the translations, Bartelink, 1994, 96–101; Vivian & Athanassaki, 2003, provide a translation of the Coptic and the Greek text). According to J. Goehring the

> image of Antony as the father of Christian monasticism is dependent less on the historical undertaking of Antony than on the literary success of the *Life of Antony*. (Goehring, 1999, 19)

More than 165 manuscripts with the Greek original version are preserved (Bartelink, 1994, 77–95), and P. Bertrand (2005, 445–451) counted almost 400 manuscripts containing second Latin translation by Evagrius of Antioch's (d. c. 393 CE).

One of the earliest, and certainly most famous, traces of reception of the *Vita Antonii* can be found in → Augustine of Hippo's *Confessions*. Augustine tells here how two of his friends read the *Vita Antonii* in Trier and how the text had convinced them (and eventually also Augustine) to abandon their careers and to live a life of chastity (Aug. *Conf.* 8.6–7).

Throughout its reception history, the *Vita Antonii* had been read selectively. Authors focused on specific aspects of the text while entirely ignoring others. A case in point is → Sozomen's (or Sozomenos; d. 450 CE) *Historia ecclesiastica*. Sozomenos provides a summary of Athanasius' narrative that leaves out all the theological statements, his demonology, and the miracles, but emphasizes his poverty, ascetic achievements, illiteracy, ascetic teaching, and his role as a mediator in secular matters (Soz. *Hist. eccl.* 1.13).

Evagrius' Latin translation of the *Vita Antonii* usually appears in manuscript form in hagiographic compendia that include (among other texts) Jerome's hagiographic works, the Latin translation of the *Historia Lausiaca*, the *Historia monachorum*, and Latin translations of the *Apophthegmata patrum* (Bertrand, 2005, 453–504). Along with → John Cassian's works, these compendia created the still-prevailing notion that monasticism originated in the Egyptian desert and that Antony played a crucial role in its emergence and spread through and beyond the Roman Empire.

Antony and the *Vita Antonii* manifest themselves in medieval hagiographic texts on three different levels. Several *vitae* explicitly refer to the *Vita Antonii* as a literary model (e.g. Dion. Ex. *Vita Pac.* 1; Jonas of Bobbio, *Vita Columbani* preface; *Pass. Praei.* prologue); others refer to Antony as a model for ascetical practice (e.g. *Vita Pach. Iun.* 7; *Vita Patr. Iur.* 12; 52–58; 128; Braul. *Vita Aemil.* 12; Bede *Vita Cuth.* 19). The prevalent and probably most determining form of reception of the *Vita Antonii* consists, however, of using the text as a quarry of clearly recognizable narrative motives and allusions. An educated audience should recognize traits of Antony in the protagonist of the saint's life they hear or read. P. Bertrand (2005, 40–60) documents numerous allusions to the *Vita Antonii* in Latin hagiographic works and discusses particularly its impact on the *Vita Martini*, the *Vita patrum Iurensium*, the *Dialogi* of → Gregory the Great, and the hagiographic works of Jonas of Bobbio. J. Leclercq (1956) documents the role of Antony as a role model for eremitic life and for monastic reform in the High and Late Middle Ages.

The most dramatic part of the *Vita Antonii*, Antony's fierce battle against demons (*Vit. Ant.* 8–10), has an afterlife in art and literature that reaches beyond the Middle Ages. Well known are Hieronymus Bosch's and Matthias Grünewald's depictions of the temptation of Antony, G. Flaubert's *La Tentation de Saint Antoine* (completed 1874), and B. Johnson Reagon's opera from 2003. P. Gemeinhardt (2013, 154–196) provides more examples of modern literary and artistic representations of the tempted Antony.

Historiography

The most important contributions to scholarship on the *Vita Antonii* are the studies of S. Rubenson (1995; 2013) who argues for the authenticity of the letters ascribed to Antony but expresses doubts about whether the *Vita Antonii* was indeed the work of Athanasius. The reference work on Athanasius is D. Brakke (1995). For the broader historical context of Egyptian desert monasticism, see J.E. Goehring (1999) and P. Brown (1971; 2016). P. Bertrand (2000) provides a detailed analysis of the text, textual transmission and reception history of the *Vita Antonii*. A critical edition of both Latin versions of the *Vita Antonii* by P. Bertrand and L. Gandt has recently been published as CChr.SL 170.

Bibliography

Agaiby, E., & T. Vivian, *Door of the Wilderness: The Greek, Coptic, and Copto-Arabic Sayings of St. Antony of Egypt: An English Translation, with Introductions and Notes*, Leiden, 2022.

Bartelink, G.J.M., *Athanase d'Alexandrie: Vie d'Antoine*, SC 400, Paris, 1994, crit. ed. & Fr. trans. of the Gk.

Bertrand, P., "Die Evagriusübersetzung der Vita Antonii: Rezeption-Überlieferung-Edition: Unter besonderer Berücksichtigung der Vitas patrum-Tradition," diss., Utrecht, 2005; http://dspace.library.uu.nl/handle/1874/7821.

Bertrand, P., & L. Gandt, eds., *Athanasius Alexandrinus, Evagrius Antiochenus, Anonymus Vitae Antonii Versiones latinae Vita beati Antonii abbatis Evagrio interprete: Versio uetustissima*, CChr.SL 170, Turnhout, 2019.

Brakke, D., *Athanasius and the Politics of Ascetism*, Oxford, 1995.

Brakke, D., *Demons and the Making of the Monk: Spiritual Combat in Early Christianity*, Cambridge MA, 2006.

Brown, P., "The Rise and the Function of the Holy Man," *JRS* 61, 1971, 80–101.

Brown, P., *Treasure in Heaven: The Holy Poor in Early Christianity*, Charlottesville, 2016.

Cartwright, S., "Athanasius's Vita Antonii as Political Theology: The Call of Heavenly Citizenship," *JEH* 67/2, 2016, 241–264.

Diem, A., "The Limitations of Asceticism," *MeWO* 9, 2019, 112–138.

Dörries, H., "Die Vita Antonii als Geschichtsquelle," in: H. Dörries, *Wort und Stunde*, vol. I: *Gesammelte Studien zur Kirchengeschichte des vierten Jahrhunderts*, Göttingen, 1966, 145–224.

Geest, P. van, "Athanasius as Mystagogue in his *Vita Antonii*," in: P. van Geest, ed., *Athanasius of Alexandria: New Perspectives on his Theology and Asceticism*, CHRC 90, Leiden, 2010, 199–221; special issue.

Gemeinhardt, P., *Antonius: Der erste Mönch: Leben, Lehre, Legende*, Munich, 2013.

Gemeinhardt, P., *Vita Antonii – Leben des Antonius*, Darmstadt, 2018.

Goehring, J.E., *Ascetics, Society, and the Desert: Studies in Early Egyptian Monasticism*, Harrisburg, 1999.

Hoppenbrouwers, H.W.F., *La plus ancienne version latine de la vie de S. Antoine par S. Athanase*, Nijmegen, 1960.

Leclercq, J., "Saint Antoine dans la tradition monastique médiévale," in: B. Steidle, ed., *Antonius Magnus Eremita 356–1956: Studia ad antiquum monachismum spectantia*, Rome, 1956, 229–247.

Lorié, L.T.A., *Spiritual Terminology in the Latin Translation of the Vita Antonii*, Nijmegen, 1955.

Meinardus, O.F.A., *Monks and Monasteries of the Egyptian Deserts*, Cairo, 1961.

Noordeloos, P., "La translation de Saint Antoine en Dauphiné," *AnBoll* 60, 1942, 68–81.

Prädicow, S.-T., *Intertextualität in den Mönchsviten des Athanasios und des Hieronymus: Eremiten zum Dialog bestellt*, Berlin, 2020.

Rousseau, P., "Antony as Teacher in the Greek *Life*," in: T. Hägg, P. Rousseau & C. Høgel, eds., *Christian Greek Biography and Panegyrics in Late Antiquity*, Berkeley, 2000, 89–109.

Rubenson, S., *The Letters of St. Antony: Monasticism and the Making of a Saint*, Minneapolis, 1995.

Rubenson, S., "Apologetics of Asceticism: The Life of Antony and its Political Context," in: B. Leyerle & R.D. Young, eds., *Ascetic Culture: Essays in Honor of Philip Rousseau*, Chicago, 2013, 75–96.

Vivian, T., & A.N. Athanassakis, *The Life of Antony: The Coptic Life and the Greek Life*, Kalamazoo, 2003.

ALBRECHT DIEM

Apatheia

Ἀπάθεια, sometimes translated "impassivity" or "impassibility," means the absence of passions or bad emotions, πάθη, as opposed to good emotions or εὐπάθειαι. Thus, it is not the absence of emotions tout court (see Graver, 2007; Ramelli, 2008), as it is sometimes misrepresented. Apatheia was a core ethical ideal in Stoicism and in most of Platonism, including Middle Platonism and Neoplatonism. Porphyry of Tyre, for example, stated that the → soul is joined to the → body when it converts to the passions that originate from the body, but apatheia frees the soul (Porph. *Sent.* 7). The ideal of apatheia was taken over by Christian Platonists such as Clement of Alexandria, Origen, Gregory of Nyssa, and Evagrius of Pontus, as well as by others, including the Christian compiler of the *Sentences of Sextus*. But also reflection on the emotions of Jesus, rooted in the New Testament (although these do not figure very prominently there: Warfield, 1950; Voorwinde, 2005; Quispel, 2008a; Barbaglio, 2009), made the object of of the reflection of philosophically minded church fathers (Layton, 2000; Barton, 2011).

Clement insisted that apatheia is a characteristic of the perfect Christian or gnostic (Clem. *Strom.* 7.84.2; see 7.13.3). Indeed, like → Philo of Alexandria, with whose writings he was well acquainted, → Clement of Alexandria maintained that a lesser degree of perfection is characterized by metriopatheia or moderation of passions, the ethical ideal for Aristotelianism, but the highest degree by apatheia or eradication of passions (on Clement's doctrine of apatheia, with overview of previous scholarship, see Kovacs, 2012). → Origen and → Gregory of Nyssa also posited apatheia, and not simply the limitation of passions, as the highest ethical ideal. Virginity itself was conceived very broadly by ascetics such as Origen, Methodius of Olympus, and Gregory of Nyssa, to the point of embracing the whole of the self-discipline that aimed at apatheia, the eradication of passions from one's soul with a view to purification as the first stage in the ascent to contemplation (for Methodius and Origen, see Ramelli, 2016, 20–21, 235; for Gregory of Nyssa, see Boersma, 2013, 117–128).

Evagrius developed a refined doctrine of apatheia, making it the center of asceticism (→ Evagrius of Pontus). He followed Origen in regarding the soul as an intellect that, because of carelessness, has fallen down from unity (initially the intellect was undivided) and, due to its lack of vigilance, has descended to the order of the πρακτική, being now a soul that needs ascetic training against passions (Eva. Pon. *KG* 3.28). Each intellectual creature initially enjoyed spiritual contemplation, but after the → fall it became divided into intellect, soul, and body. The intellect has now descended to practical life – the level of the soul – which needs ascesis and the search for virtue and liberation from passions. Πρακτική indicates moral life and moral development, aimed at the attainment of apatheia through ascetic discipline and the obedience to commandments. For the glory and light of the intellect is knowledge, whereas the glory and light of the soul is apatheia (*KG* 1.81). Absence of passions is the goal of ethics, specifically of ascetic training, that is, πρακτική in Evagrius' terminology; knowledge is the end of intellectual activity, but it can be attained only through the purification provided by πρακτική. In *KG* 1.70 Evagrius outlines a descending hierarchy:

1. the one who knows the Trinity;
2. the one who contemplates the intellections of intelligible beings;
3. the one who contemplates the incorporeal realities;
4. the one who knows the contemplation of the aeons;
5. the one who possesses the apatheia of the soul.

This hierarchy in knowledge reflects an ontological hierarchy: God (the → Trinity), the intelligible beings or Ideas, the incorporeal realities, and the worlds or eons, which are the theatre of the transformations of matter. Under these degrees of contemplation (θεωρία), the ethical ideal of the apatheia of the soul is placed, which is the domain of the πρακτική. Therefore, as in *KG* 1.67, Evagrius posits ascesis, purification from passions, and the attainment of virtue as indispensable steps towards the acquisition of knowledge.

Evagrius describes the return of rational creatures to God in terms of five subsequent transformations into a better state, in an ascending hierarchy that begins with purification from → evil and passions, and therefore the attainment of apatheia – which is coextensive with virtue – and passes on to knowledge, first of the world and then of rational creatures, and finally that of the Trinity, which will eventually be reached by all (*KG* 2.4, text according to the edition of and relevant commentary in Ramelli, 2015). Knowledge, indeed, is the reward for those ascetic souls that have reached apatheia (*KG* 2.6). Apatheia is the goal of the πρακτική, which is ascetic life; knowledge follows it and cannot be independent of it, since knowledge – according to Evagrius just as to most Neoplatonists – cannot dwell in a soul full of passions. Evagrius opposes physical sense perception, which is a pathos depending on impressions, and intellectual knowledge, which is not a pathos but a state of impassivity or apatheia of the → *nous*, the intellectual or rational faculty in the soul. This state is not natural, but is produced by divine grace (*KG* 1.37). Apatheia consists primarily in the eradication of passions that besiege the inferior faculties of the soul (desiring or appetitive, and irascible, according to Plato's tripartition, which Evagrius follows). The link between asceticism (πρακτική) and apatheia, as well as knowledge, is clear in a number of passages from Evagrius' works, such as Eva. Pon. *Skem.* 16: "The ascetic intellect is the one that always receives the intellections in a manner free from the passions [ἀπαθῶς] of this world." In *Prak.* 67 Evagrius explains that the soul possesses apatheia not when it is not affected by things, but rather when it remains untroubled by things and even their memories. The impassive person is for Evagrius, as for the Stoics, a serene person, and not a stone.

Evagrius associates apatheia with the inferior faculties of the soul (e.g. in Eva. Pon. *Gnos.* 2), with the soul in general (e.g. in *KG* 1.81), with the heart, and also with the intellect or the rational faculty of the soul, for example in *KG* 1.37 and *Skem.* 3: "Apatheia is the tranquil state of the rational soul, which consists in mildness and temperance," where mildness is the impassive state of the irascible faculty and temperance the impassive state of the desiring/appetitive faculty. Moreover, apatheia is cocxtensive with charity-love: in Eva. Pon. *Eul.* 21.23, love is described as "the elimination of passions." Bodily passions are overcome by continence; those of the soul are overcome by spiritual love (ἀγάπη πνευματική, *Eul.* 35). Reciprocally, apatheia brings about charity-love (ἀγάπη "is the product of apatheia," *Prak.* 81), and love is the door to knowledge of nature, which leads to theology and the supreme blessedness (Eva. Pon.

An. 8). Evagrius delineates an ascending path from faith to apatheia to love to gnosis, the highest peak of which is the knowledge of God. The same progression, from faith to charity-love to knowledge of God, is delineated in Eva. Pon. *Mon.* 3: "Faith is the principle/beginning of charity-love [ἀγάπη], and the end/aim of charity-love is the knowledge of God." In *KG* 1.86 love and knowledge of God are inseparable:

> Love is the perfect state of the rational soul, a state in which the soul cannot love anything which is among corruptible beings more than the knowledge of God.

Gregory of Nyssa very probably inspired Evagrius with the notion of the inseparability of knowledge of God and love. For Gregory in Greg. Nyss. *Anim. et res.* 96C places knowledge and love together at the highest level, within the divine life:

> The life of the divine nature is love, since Beauty/ Goodness is absolutely loveable to those who know it. Now the divine knows itself, and this knowledge [γνῶσις] becomes love [ἀγάπη].

For Evagrius, as for Gregory, ἀγάπη is not a pathos, but impassivity: "Ἀγάπη is the bond of impassivity and the expunging of passions [...] ἀγάπη possesses nothing of its own apart from God, for God is ἀγάπη itself" (Eva. Pon. *Eul.* 22). Precisely because ἀγάπη is not a pathos, this is why it will abide in the end: ἀγάπη is the life of God, who is supremely free from passions and is perfect knowledge. The link between apatheia and ἀγάπη is also stressed in Eva. Pon. *Prak.* 8: "Ἀγάπη is the progeny of impassivity."

Apatheia is, as mentioned, the goal of πρακτική. Πρακτική, πρακτικός, and related terms are also attested in pagan Neoplatonism in the sense of "ethics" (Olymp. Y. *Proleg. Arist. Cat.* 8). Evagrius offers his definition in *Prak.* 78: "Πρακτική is the spiritual method for purifying the part of the soul subject to passions," its aim being apatheia (on apatheia in Evagrius see Suzuki, 2009, and now Tobon, diss, 2010, publ. forthcoming). The ascetic (πρακτικός) is one who is concerned solely with the achievement of apatheia in the portion of the soul that is liable to passions; the gnostic (i.e. the perfect Christian, perfected in knowledge) has the function of salt for the impure and light for the pure (Eva. Pon. *Gnos.* 2–3). Πρακτική is deemed by Evagrius the first component of the Christian doctrine, which is inseparable from the highest component, theology (Eva. Pon. *Prak.* 1).

Virtue is attached to πρακτική and knowledge to theology, but I. Ramelli (2014 and 2015) has highlighted how for Evagrius virtue and knowledge go hand in hand. The close connection between πρακτική, aiming at apatheia as the compendium of all virtues, and knowledge is stressed in *Prak.* 2–3: "The Kingdom of Heavens is apatheia in the soul, along with the true knowledge of beings. The kingdom of God is the knowledge of the Holy Trinity." Evagrius, as indicated above, calls the perfect Christian gnostic, like Clement, and apatheia is closely related to knowledge for Evagrius: as virtue and knowledge are entirely interdependent, so are apatheia and knowledge, since virtue is freedom from passions and the very goal of πρακτική. The close connection between apatheia and knowledge is clear for example in *Prak.* 56 and 67. Apatheia is the perfection of the soul liable to passions, knowledge is that of the intellect (Eva. Pon. *KG* 6.55). The relation between apatheia and knowledge is made clear especially by *KG* 4.70: freedom from passions allows for contemplation. The intellect approaches intelligible realities when it does not unite itself any longer to λογισμοί arising from the inferior soul liable to passions (*KG* 1.81). The intellect possesses a creative power when it is free from passions, and intellectual knowledge becomes completely independent of sense-perception (*KG* 5.12).

That virtues and apatheia, the domain of πρακτική, are the prerequisite of knowledge is pithily confirmed by Evagrius in *Schol. in Prov.* 258: the soul, in the sense of the soul subject to passions, is "the mother of the intellect" because "by means of virtues it brings the intellect to light." This, again, is from the viewpoint of the present life, since from the protological and ontological viewpoint, the intellect was before the soul, and eschatologically the soul will be elevated to the rank of intellect. To Evagrius' mind, just as to Gregory of Nyssa's, the ideal of apatheia is related to the conception of passions as adventitious in rational creatures and against nature. Evagrius argues that, since all the faculties that humans share with animals belong to the corporeal nature, then the irascible and desiring/greedy/appetitive faculties were not created together with the rational nature before the movement of

will that determined the fall (*KG* 6.85). This means that they are adventitious, not belonging to the authentic human nature, which is the prelapsarian nature of rational creatures. Evagrius in *KG* 6.83 squarely declares the irascible and desiring/greedy/appetitive parts of the soul to be "against nature." Their major fault is that they produce tempting thoughts (λογισμοί) that prevent the intellect from knowing God. Intellects were created by God that they might know God; this is their nature. The faculties of the inferior soul that create an obstacle to this knowledge are against nature. This is why, since passions were not at the beginning – being not included in God's plan for rational creatures – they will not endure in the end. However, in *KG* 3.59 Evagrius warns that what is really against nature are not the inferior faculties of the soul per se, but their bad use, that is, again, their use against nature, since it is from this that evilness or vice derives, through passions.

Consistently, in *KG* 5.22 Evagrius describes the resurrection of the soul (→ Resurrection) as its return from the condition of vulnerability to passions to apatheia. This is not a passage but a return: the reference is to Origen's and Gregory of Nyssa's conception of resurrection as → *apokatastasis*, the restoration to the original state (Ramelli, 2013), in which the soul was not liable to passions. This is also the way Maximus the Confessor maintained that resurrection should be understood in Gregory of Nyssa's writings. Faithful to his ideal of apatheia, Evagrius insists that passions must be completely eradicated once and for all, and not fought all the time by the rational faculty of the soul (*KG* 5.36). Following the precepts of the moral law, the commandments, which aim at apatheia, is the way of πρακτική, which "fights in view of apatheia" (*KG* 5.38). The soul that has attained apatheia – the soul of the ascetic, the πρακτικός – is detached, so it sees in itself the intellections of things on earth, but is unsullied by them (*KG* 5.64). The soul's apatheia is described as an "intelligible wall," a protection against the attacks of demons (*KG* 5.82), since demons (→ Demonology/Demons) try to elicit passions in a soul. Especially monks should aim at apatheia and the knowledge of God, and not to worldly honors, power, and money (*KG* 5.86). Even the person who has attained apatheia is still tempted by λογισμοί or tempting thoughts, but these cannot arouse passions in her and cannot cause her to sin, thanks to her purity of heart, that is, apatheia (in *Eva. Pon. Schol. in Prov.* 199 on Prov 19:17 Evagrius identifies purity of heart with apatheia).

Also in the *Sentences of Sextus* (→ *Sextus, Sentences of*), a 2nd-century CE collection of originally pagan Pythagorean sentences on moral philosophy compiled by a Christian (Pevarello, 2013), apatheia, the goal of asceticism, features prominently and is represented as going hand in hand with benefiting all humans and avoiding mistreating them (*Sent. Sextus* 209–212). These *Sentences* draw a connection between lack of possessions and passions and self-sufficiency, and also link lack of possessions to moral freedom, which Sextus, like the Stoics, has depend on apatheia and opposes to a passion, greed for possessions (*Sent. Sextus* 274–275). Indeed, Sextus opposes the possession of wealth, which is better to lose, to true freedom, that of the philosopher, which is never lost (*Sent. Sextus* 17; 275). In *Sent. Sextus* 263–264b, life according to self-sufficiency implies leaving one's possessions to follow the right *logos* – for Sextus, Christ-*logos*, and for "pagan" philosophers the philosophical *logos*; thus, one will be free. And *Sent. Sextus* 76, like *Pyth. Sent.* 110c, denounces love of money (φιλοχρηματία) as a symptom of love of the body (φιλοσωματία), seen as negative in an ascetic perspective in that it facilitates passions (see Ramelli, 2016, 14–19). So, apatheia is constitutively connected with freedom: from passions, from enslavement to the body, and from enslavement to material possessions. It is meaningful that the Origenian ascetic and monk Rufinus, the friend of the Origenian ascetics Melania and Evagrius, saw such a continuity between the ascetic ideas expressed in these *Sentences* and the Christian ideals of asceticism and monasticism as to ascribe this collection of Christianized Pythagorean wisdom to Pope Sixtus II, martyred under Valerian and a younger contemporary of Origen. Since this attribution is also found in the independent Syriac translation of our *Sentences*, it is probable that Rufinus received it from an earlier tradition. Rufinus was aware that Origen knew this collection and attributed it to a Christian philosopher. In *Hom. Ezech.* 1 Origen quoted *Sent. Sextus* 352 and ascribed it to a wise Christian. Jerome, another monk who once was a friend of Rufinus, in Jer. *Ep.* 133, written after his U-turn against Origen, denounced this cultural operation by

claiming that the author of the *Sentences* was Sextus, a pagan Pythagorean. Jerome was wrong, since the *Sentences of Sextus* were already Christianized, and cast light onto early Christian asceticism prior to the formal establishment of monasticism. Now, in the monastic tradition, as is clear especially from Evagrius, apatheia was the primal ethical ideal.

Historiography

The study of apatheia is part and parcel of ancient philosophy and ancient asceticism, Christian, Jewish, and pagan. From both sides, the study of apatheia has advanced, and the relation between early Christian apatheia and pagan philosophical apatheia has been, and still has to be, explored. From the philosophical viewpoint M. Graver (2007) and I. Ramelli (2008) have investigated the concept of apatheia especially in Stoicism, highlighting that this is not absence of emotions tout court, but absence of bad emotions. This aspect was taken over by early Christian thinkers. The Christianized Pythagorean *Sentences of Sextus*, well known to Origen and Jerome, promoted this ideal (Ramelli, 2016, 14–19). Clement of Alexandria's doctrine of apatheia has been studied by J. Kovacs (2012) and Origen's and Gregory of Nyssa's lofty and all-encompassing notion of apatheia has been explored by I. Ramelli (2016, 20–21, 235) and H. Boersma (2013, 117–128). Evagrius' central notion of apatheia within his theological and ascetic system is analyzed by J. Driscoll (1999), J. Suzuki (2009), K. Corrigan (2009), M. Tobon (diss., 2010, publ. forthcoming) and I. Ramelli (2014; 2015; 2017). The development of passions, pre-passions, εὐπάθειαι and ἀπάθεια from Stoicism to Christian late antiquity is the focus of R. Sorabji (2000), I. Ramelli (2003), D. Konstan and I. Ramelli (2010), and research into apatheia after Evagrius as well as in western patristics needs to be developed further (→ Stoicism and the Fathers and the relevant historiography).

Bibliography

Barbaglio, G., *Emozioni e sentimenti di Gesù*, Bologna, 2009.

Barton, S., "Eschatology and the Emotions in Early Christianity," *JBL* 130/3, 2011, 571–591.

Bobonich, C., & P. Destrée, eds., *Akrasia in Greek Philosophy: From Socrates to Plotinus*, Leiden, 2007.

Boersma, H., *Embodiment and Virtue in Gregory of Nyssa*, Oxford, 2013.

Clark, S., "Evagrius, Nous, and the Noonday Demon," in: I. Ramelli et al., eds., *Human and Divine Nous from Ancient to Renaissance Philosophy and Religion*, forthcoming.

Corrigan, K., *Evagrius and Gregory: Mind, Soul and Body in the Fourth Century*, Burlington, 2009.

Driscoll, J., "Apatheia and Purity of Heart in Evagrius," in: H.A. Luckman & L. Kulzer, eds., *Purity of Heart in Early Ascetic and Monastic Literature*, Collegeville, 1999, 141–159.

Graver, M., *Stoicism and Emotion*, Chicago, 2007.

Konstan, D., & I. Ramelli, "The Use of XAPA in the New Testament and its Background in Hellenistic Moral Philosophy," *ExCl* 14, 2010, 185–204.

Kovacs, J., "Saint Paul as Apostle of apatheia," in: M. Havrda et al., *The Seventh Book of the Stromateis*, Leiden, 2012, 199–216.

Layton, R., "Propatheia: Origen and Didymus on the Origin of the Passions," *VigChr* 54/3, 2000, 262–282.

Mirguet, F., *An Early History of Compassion: Emotion and Imagination in Hellenistic Judaism*, Cambridge MA, 2017.

Nguyen, J., *Apatheia in the Christian Tradition: An Ancient Spirituality and Its Contemporary Relevance*, Eugene, 2018.

Pevarello, D., *The Sentences of Sextus and the Origins of Christian Asceticism*, Tübingen, 2013.

Quispel, G., "Eros and Agape in the Gospel of John," in: J. van Oort, ed., *Gnostica, Judaica, Catholica: Collected Essays of Gilles Quispel*, Leiden, 2008a, 695–698.

Quispel, G., "God is Love," in: J. van Oort, ed., *Gnostica, Judaica, Catholica: Collected Essays of Gilles Quispel*, Leiden, 2008a, 715–737.

Ramelli, I., "Stoic and Christian Passions," *Aevum* 77, 2003, 217–221.

Ramelli, I., *Stoici Romani Minori*, Milan, 2008.

Ramelli, I., "Tears of Pathos, Repentance, and Bliss," in: T. Fögen, ed., *Tears in the Graeco-Roman World*, Berlin, 2009, 367–396.

Ramelli, I., "Harmony between *arkhē* and *telos* in Patristic Platonism," *IJPlT* 7, 2013a, 1–49.

Ramelli, I., *The Christian Doctrine of Apokatastasis*, Leiden, 2013b.

Ramelli, I., "Evagrius Ponticus, the Origenian Ascetic (and not the Origenistic 'Heretic')," in: J.A. McGuckin, ed., *Orthodox Monasticism, Past and Present*, New York, 2014, 147–205.

Ramelli, I., *Evagrius Ponticus' Kephalaia Gnostika*, Leiden, 2015.

Ramelli, I., *Social Justice and the Legitimacy of Slavery*, Oxford, 2016.

Ramelli, I., "Gregory Nyssen's and Evagrius's Biographical and Theological Relations: Origen's Heritage and Neoplatonism," in: I. Ramelli, ed. in collaboration with

K. Corrigan, G. Maspero & M. Tobon. *Evagrius between Origen, the Cappadocians, and Neoplatonism*, Louvain, 2017, 165–231.

Ramelli, I., "The Soul-Body Relation in Origen of Alexandria: Ensomatosis vs. Metensomatosis," in: P. van Geest & N. Vos, eds., *Early Christian Mystagogy and the Body*, Louvain, 2022, 97–119.

Ramelli. I., "Slavery and Religion in Late Antiquity: Their Relation to Asceticism and Justice," in: C.L. De Wet, M. Kahlos & V. Vuolanto, eds., *Slavery in the Late Antique World, 150–700 CE*, Cambridge UK, 2022a, 43–65.

Ramelli, I., "The Legacy of Origen in Gregory of Nyssa's Theology of Freedom," *MoTh* 38/2, 2022b, 363–388.

Ramelli, I., "The Life of Macrina and The Life of Evagrius: Erotic Motifs and Ascesis," in: K. De Temmerman, ed., *Novel Saints: Stories of Erotic Love and Desire in Late Antique and Early Medieval Hagiography*, Turnhout, 2023.

Sorabji, R., *Emotion and Peace of Mind: From Stoic Agitation to Christian Temptation*, Oxford, 2000.

Suzuki, J., "The Evagrian Concept of Apatheia and its Origenism," in: G. Heidl & R. Somos, eds., *Origeniana IX*, Louvain, 2009, 605–611.

Tobon, M., "Apatheia in the Teachings of Evagrius Ponticus: The Health of the Soul," diss., London, 2010; publ. London, 2023.

Voorwinde, S., *Jesus' Emotions in the Fourth Gospel: Human or Divine?* London, 2005.

Warfield, B.B., "The Emotional Life of Our Lord," in: S.G. Craig, ed., *The Person and Work of Christ*, Philadelphia, 1950, 93–145.

ILARIA L.E. RAMELLI

Apelles

Apelles, who died after 180 CE, was the most prominent disciple of Marcion, as well as a Christian teacher and headmaster of a school. He taught in Rome, where he engaged in philosophical and religious disputes (e.g. with Rhodon, a student of Tatian). → Tertullian's remark that Apelles became familiar with Platonic philosophy in Alexandria (Tert. *Praesc.* 30.5–6) is probably a polemical device, like the claim that Apelles abandoned Marcionitism by rejecting radical Marcionite asceticism and "falling into women" (Tert. *Carn. chr.* 6.1).

Apelles was the author of at least two works no longer extant: *Revelations* (Φανερώσεις), which was based on the views of the prophetess Philumene, and *Syllogisms* (Συλλογισμοί), which used syllogistic methods to demonstrate that the myth which

→ Moses told concerning God was completely false (Ps.-Tert. *Haer.* 6.6). His connection with contemporary gnostic thinking is not easy to evaluate and is a matter of constant dispute (Harnack, 1924; May, 2005).

1. The Historical Transmission

We learn of Apelles' works and doctrine from the most important accounts of Rhodon in → Eusebius of Caesarea (*Hist. eccl.* 5.13) and from Tertullian, who was a fierce opponent of all Marcionites (→ Marcion/Marcionites/Marcionism). Tertullian's first treatise against them, now lost, was probably named *Adversus Apelleiacos.* Hippolytus of Rome, → Origen, Pseudo-Tertullian, → Epiphanius of Salamis and Filastrius also knew and rejected Apelles. In his *De Paradiso,* → Ambrose of Milan cited some of *Syllogism.* → Jerome claimed that Apelles composed his own gospel (Jer. *Comm. Matt.* Praefatio). E. Junod (1992) believed this to be true because Jerome depended on Origen. But no other source hints in this direction. Maybe Apelles simply modified the Marcionite gospel.

According to Rhodon, who wrote several books against the Marcionites, they were divided into three different groups adhering to different opinions concerning the number of principles:

> Therefore also they disagree among themselves, maintaining an inconsistent opinion. For Apelles, one of the herd, priding himself on his manner of life and his age, acknowledges one principle [...] (Eus. *Hist. eccl.* 5.13.2)

Others were closer to their master Marcion's two principles, while another group claimed there were three. Rhodon's aim was to demonstrate their inconsistency and the fact that they were unable to give any good reasons for their teachings. A teacher who cannot prove his own opinions is nothing but ridiculous. For this reason, he reported a direct disputation between Apelles and himself:

> When I said to him, Tell me how you know this or how can you assert that there is one principle, he replied that the prophecies refuted themselves, because they have said nothing

true, for they are inconsistent, and false, and self-contradictory. (Eus. *Hist. eccl.* 5.13.6)

But Apelles was far from being an incompetent teacher; he asserted for his part that Jewish Scripture has nothing to say about the one and only principle, the good God.

2. The Syllogisms

Apelles composed at least 38 books of syllogisms (Ambr. *Parad.* 5.28), an impressive collection of critical arguments dressed in school logic to deduce absurd consequences from the texts (Junod). There was, for example, a detailed criticism of the story of Noah's ark: if we take the scriptural dimensions seriously, the ark could hardly have accommodated four elephants, and there would have been no space left for all the other animals of every species. At the end of each syllogism, according to Origen, Apelles added the conclusion: "The story is therefore false; the Scripture therefore does not come from God" (Or. *Hom. Gen.* 2.2). Possibly Apelles felt entitled to evaluate the truth of these stories by the famous agraphon: "Be approved money-changers," which he read in his gospel (Epiph. *Pan.* 44.2.6). Several syllogisms deal with the way God created the imperfect Adam (→ Adam and Eve). Taking Genesis literally, and without using any allegorical exegesis (→ Allegory), Apelles asked many painful questions, such as,

> Did God know Adam would transgress his commandment or did he not? If he did not know, there is no assertion of divine power. But if he did know and yet gave orders that inevitably were neglected it is not godlike to give a superfluous precept. But he gave an order to that first-formed Adam which he knew he would in no way keep. God does nothing superfluous; therefore the writing is not of God. (Ambr. *Parad.* 8.38; see Greschat, 2000, 50–72, for all known syllogisms)

Despite the polemic of Rhodon and Tertullian that Apelles was no longer a true Marcionite, we see him developing Marcion's *Antitheseis* (Ἀντιθέσεις) in a strikingly logical fashion (Grant, 1993, 77).

3. Cosmological and Christological Thinking

Accepting only one eternal principle, Apelles had to modify the cosmological ideas of his teacher. But instead of believing in the Genesis story of a good God as Creator of the universe and of humanity, he taught that this good God generated two angelic beings: a demiurge, an *angelus inclitus* or *angelus gloriosus* (Tert. *Praescr.* 34.4; *Carn. chr.* 8.2), and the fiery angel of the Jewish Scriptures who was the origin of Mosaic → law and sinful human flesh (Tert. *An.* 23.3). The demiurge (→ Gnosis/Gnosticism) tried to form the terrestrial world to be like the perfect celestial world, but he failed, and the world turned out to be an imperfect copy, wherefore the angel was penitent. Some typical gnostics shared Apelles' assumption of some aspects of platonic cosmogony and agreed with him in understanding the → parable of the lost sheep (Luke 15) in terms of a lapsed spiritual being (i.e. the Valentinians). So God sent his own son, Christ, to correct the work of the demiurge and to release heavenly souls from the second angel's enslavement through the law and the flesh. It was this wicked and fiery angel who lured souls down to earth by preparing delicious food to snare them (Tert. *An.* 23.3).

Apelles followed his teacher in believing that Christ possessed a real body, not like our carnal ones born by women but one of angelic substance. Apparently Apelles wanted to go further in giving a comprehensible explanation for the provenance of Christ's material condition, which he cast aside after his resurrection, because there is no resurrection of the body (→ Resurrection). Tertullian tells us that Apelles was led by the apostle Paul's saying "The first man is of the earth, the second man is the Lord from heaven" (1 Cor. 15:47; Tert. *Carn. chr.* 8.5) to assume that Christ "borrowed [...] his flesh from the stars, and from the substances of the higher world" (*Carn. chr.* 6.2). Similar to the platonic idea of the soul's astral body, Christ, descending from heaven to earth, formed his body from the matter of the heavenly bodies and dissolved it during his ascent into the heavenly realms (Ps.-Tert. *Haer.* 6.5). Hippolytus, Epiphanius, and Filastrius give us a different view and submit that the Apelleian Christ

"formed his body by taking portions of it from the substance of the universe: that is, hot and cold, moist and dry" (Hipp. *Haer.* 7.38.3–5). It is impossible to decide which of these two accounts is the most reliable.

4. The Revelations

Rejecting the authenticity of Jewish Scripture, Apelles appealed to the authority of the prophetic utterances of Philumene and wrote down her *Revelations*. Tertullian was foremost in denouncing her as a female seducer and an illegitimate, highly dangerous spiritual factor responsible for turning Apelles away from his master Marcion (Hanig, 1999). This is merely the polemic of a Christian teacher who dedicated himself to the new prophecy (→ Montanism/Montanists)! Due to this difficult situation, it is virtually impossible to say anything about the structure or contents of Apelles' book of *Revelations*.

The Marcionite Apelles attested to the vitality of the Marcionite Church in his time. One can imagine how educated contemporaries were drawn toward his teachings as an attractive form of Christian apologetics. Nevertheless, the fragmentary records of his antagonists do not always allow us to fill in all the gaps, and the further impact of his doctrines remains unclear.

Historiography

In 1874 A. von Harnack wrote his postdoctoral thesis on Apelles based on all known sources of this time. But he was more interested in Marcion and characterized Apelles in his famous book on Marcion as a Marcionite with gnostic tendencies. Most scholars in the 20th century affirm or negate A. von Harnack's position but G. May (2005) and K. Greschat (2000) situate Apelles within the theological developments of the 2nd century CE.

Bibliography

Grant, R., "The Syllogistic Exegesis of Apelles," in: R. Grant, *Heresy and Criticism: The Search for Authenticity in Early Christian Literature*, Louisville, 1993, 75–88.

Greschat, K., *Apelles und Hermogenes: Zwei christliche Lehrer des zweiten Jahrhunderts*, SVigChr 48, Leiden, 2000.

Hanig, R., "Der Beitrag der Philumene zur Theologie der Apelleianer," *ZAC* 3, 1999, 241–277.

Harnack, A. von, *Marcion: Das Evangelium vom fremden Gott: Eine Monographie zur Grundlegung der katholischen Kirche*, Leipzig, ²1924.

Junod, E., "Les attitudes d'Apelles, disciple de Marcion, à l'égard de l'Ancien Testament," *Aug.* 22, 1992, 113–133.

May, G., "Apelles und die Entwicklung der markionitischen Theologie," in: K. Greschat & M. Meiser, eds., *Markion: Gesammelte Aufsätze*, Mainz, 2005, 93–110.

KATHARINA GRESCHAT

Aphrahat

Aphrahat (c. 270–c. 345 CE), "the Persian sage," was a Christian ascetic and author who lived in Adiabene (northern Mesopotamia), within the Persian Empire. His very name, Aphrahat, seems to be the Syriacized version of a Persian name, but when he entered the Christian, or the monastic, life, he took on the Jewish-Christian name Jacob. He wrote in Syriac, likely between 337 and 344 CE, 23 *Demonstrations*, or *Expositions*, for his fellow ascetics, the "children [i.e. members] of the covenant." Aphr. *Dem.* 1, for instance, is on faith, *Dem.* 2 on charity, *Dem.* 3 on fasting, *Dem.* 4 on prayer, *Dem.* 8 on the resurrection, *Dem.* 18 on virginity, and *Dem.* 20 on almsgiving. Doubts have been raised about the authenticity of *Dem.* 14, but it is probable that this too is by Aphrahat. Here he seems to write on behalf of a synod to the clergy of Seleucia-Ctesiphon, the Persian capital city. This is also why it has been hypothesized that Aphrahat was a bishop, but this is uncertain. The first 22 *Demonstrations* begin each with a letter of the Syriac alphabet, in alphabetical order. *Dem.* 23, the last extant, was possibly meant to be the beginning of a new series, which seems to have never been composed, or, at any rate, is not extant.

As an ascetic, Aphrahat elected poverty (→ Wealth) and virginity (→ Virgin/Virginity), like all his fellow ascetics, women and men, who owned no slaves either. In *Dem.* 6, devoted to recommendations to these ascetics, Aphrahat warns them to beware of deriders, who, because of their greed for money, despise and ridicule the ascetics. He also quotes Luke 16:14 in this connection, a verse that comes immediately after Jesus' teaching, "you cannot serve God and money (mammon) at the same time." In

Dem. 14, Aphrahat associates the "children of the covenant" with the poor and the innocent (§7). Aphrahat is attacking corrupt chiefs who oppressed the poor and the ascetics who elected a voluntary poverty: these leaders are iniquitous and usurers; they

> falsify judgment and are respecters of persons, absolve the guilty and declare guilty the innocent. They love the rich and hate the poor [...] they love bribes and reject the truth [...] The judge judges according to bribes; they despise the needy and exterminate the poor from the earth: they bite them with their teeth. (§3)

These people do the opposite of what is recommended by God through Isa 1:17, quoted in §4.

In *Dem.* 22 Aphrahat meditates on death and the worldly divisions that it will eliminate, such as those between men and women (§12), between rich and poor, and between masters and slaves (§§7–8). He associates the institution of slavery with social injustices leading to excessive wealth and poverty. In death there will be neither concupiscence nor greed for riches (§12). The ascetic life of the "children of the covenant" endeavored to anticipate on earth that eschatological condition by means of celibacy and voluntary poverty. Consistently with this, Aphrahat exhorts the rich to remember death, which will make them unable to enjoy wealth (§6). Aphrahat, like → Origen, → Gregory of Nyssa, Evagrius Ponticus, and other ascetics, seems to draw the equation between wealth and theft as a sinful state (Ramelli, 2017). For he addresses thieves and oppressors of fellow humans as sinners on the path to hell (→ Hades):

> O hardened thieves, oppressors, deceivers of your fellow humans, remember death and do not multiply your sins! For sinners will not be allowed any more to convert down there.

Likewise, in §14 Aphrahat warns again those who have acquired wealth iniquitously and all oppressors, whose deeds are denounced harshly (§§8.10). This is why, according to Aphrahat, the anticipation of the eschatological state) lies in asceticism, with the renunciation of possessions as well as of oppression of other humans.

Aphrahat devoted *Dem.* 20 to the care of the poor. Straight from the beginning, he exhorts his readers to give to the poor, but warns that one whose money comes from the oppression of other people cannot give alms that are acceptable to God: one should give "the fruit of the work of one's hands, not money coming from robbing other people" (§1). Rich readers are warned by Aphrahat that they should correct their sins with care of the poor. In §5 Aphrahat bases himself on Matt 25:34–45, where Christ identifies himself with the poor, and states that the final judgment will bear on each one's behavior toward the poor. The works that one should do for the poor, detailed in Matt 25, were already indicated in Isa 58:6–7, which Aphrahat quotes in §1–2 with Deut 24:19–22 and Exod 23:10–11. → Death "is what happens to the man who accumulates wealth for himself and does not become rich before God" (§6). Aphrahat identifies again Christ with the poor in the parable of Dives and Lazarus, representing Lazarus as a figure of Christ (§§8–11). Against any unjust or underpaid treatment of workers, Aphrahat cites Deut 24:14–15 in §3. Aphrahat puts forward King → David as an example, with reference to 1 Chr 27:25–31, where David is declared to have taken care of the poor, the unfortunate, and orphans and widows, and to have established people responsible for providing food and assistance to the poor (§4). Aphrahat offers a selection of passages from Psalms, traditionally ascribed to David, and Proverbs, which show concern for the poor and present this concern as welcome to God. The notion that wealth is tantamount to theft is found again in Aphrahat at §5, where the rich are said to rob the poor. Likewise Aphrahat in §13 quotes Amos 5:11 about trampling upon the poor, afflicting the righteous, and turning aside the needy (vv. 11–12). The sin of Sodom is identified by Aphrahat as a sin against the poor, because its inhabitants were rich, but they did not help the needy.

Aphrahat concludes that God takes care of the poor (§14), and with Jesus exhorts his readers to give one's riches, which in themselves are iniquitous, to the poor, that the latter may become a support for the rich in the other world (he quotes Luke 16:9 in §16). The poor themselves thus become one's treasure in heaven. Aphrahat's and his ascetics' asceticism and love for the poor were grounded in Jesus' own prescription to sell all that one possessed and give the revenue to the poor, so as to acquire a treasure in heaven, and thus follow Jesus. It will be hard for a rich man to enter the kingdom of Heaven (Matt 19:21–24, cited in §18). Aphrahat overtly denounces rich people's greed for money, which he associates with injustice and the tendency to oppress other people and behave with iniquity, and strongly advocates care of the poor, as an image of Christ.

Aphrahat's creed, albeit stemming from around 340 CE, displays remarkable simplicity and archaic features. The main source of Aphrahat's theology is certainly the Bible, not only the New Testament but, prominently, also the Hebrew Bible, although his theology is often labeled as supersessionist, since Aprahat sees Christianity as the true fulfilment of, and therefore substitution for, Judaism (esp. in *Dem.* 11, 12, and 13, respectively, on circumcision, the Passover, and the Sabbath). For the Gospels, Aphrahat seems to have used Tatian's *Diatessaron*, but apparently also the *Vetus Syra* or Old Syriac version, where the four Gospels were separated and not harmonized as in Tatian. Moreover, Aphrahat refers to some books that eventually did not make their way into the canon, such as *3 Corinthians*. Aphrahat quoted this pseudepigraphon, considered it to be a letter by Paul (→ Paul the Apostle), and drew from it important motifs (Walters, 2013).

The *Demonstrations* of Aphrahat attest to a profound knowledge of Scripture, but are generally considered to be rather isolated within patristic literature. They reveal no trace of the lively theological debates of Aphrahat's day, as his creed also confirms. However, despite Aphrahat's general lack of interest in philosophy, I. Ramelli (2015) noticed that some of his *Demonstrations* show impressive similarities with the letter of the Stoicizing Mara Bar Serapion and with the ideas of the Christian philosopher and theologian Bardaisan of Edessa, both those expressed in the *Book of the Laws of Countries* and those found in other works, such as his notions of the resurrection, of spiritual death, and of the mystery of the cross. Aphrahat also seems to have against Bardaisan at least a couple of points.

Mara's *Letter to His Son* is extant in Syriac and was probably composed by an upper-class Stoic from Commagene who was a prisoner of the Romans in the 70s of the 1st century CE after these had captured Samosata. This letter was interesting for Christian authors because of its mention of Jesus Christ, "the wise king of the Jews," together with Socrates and Pythagoras as an example of a philosopher unjustly persecuted but later rewarded by God (Ramelli, 2005; 2008; 2012). Aphrahat, however, does not limit his echoes of Mara's letter to this single element, but includes others from other parts of the letter, making it very probable that this document was available to him in its entirety. Only partially can the similarities between Mara's letter and Aphrahat's *Demonstrations* be traced back to a common wisdom tradition. Even when the parallels thematically pertain to wisdom tradition, the correspondences between Mara and Aphrahat indicated by I. Ramelli (2014; 2015) are so close, even in the precise choice of wording and examples, as to suggest some direct or indirect dependence between these two texts, probably of Aphrahat on Mara's Letter, if the latter – as is probable – is earlier than Aphrahat.

In *Dem.* 14, in which possible echoes from Mara's letter can be detected concerning Jesus the just killed unjustly, whose elimination determined the removal of the kingdom from the Jews, Aphrahat seems to be not only alluding, but also explicitly responding, to an argument put forward by Bardaisan in the *Book of the Laws of Countries*. According to → Bardaisan, animals, as well as elements, are prisoners of their nature, as Aphrahat's adversary in *Dem.* 14 maintains. Aphrahat himself, instead, seems to intend to correct Bardaisan's thesis: he maintains that elements and animals are not governed by nature, as Bardaisan taught, but directly by the will of God. It is human beings who, unlike other creatures, often disobey God. In *Dem.* 13, however, which is devoted to the Sabbath, at section 2 Aphrahat shares with Bardaisan the conviction that animals, although they do the will of God, are not endowed with free will, and therefore they have no moral law and no sin, unlike humans. In this respect Aphrahat agrees with Bardaisan.

Another extremely interesting convergence between Aphrahat and Bardaisan emerges from *Dem.* 4. At sections 5–6 Aphrahat employs twice the very same Syriac expression that was used by Bardaisan in reference to the cross of Christ: "The Mystery [*razā*] of the Cross." Moreover, in *Dem.* 8 Aphrahat very probably rejects Bardaisan's and his followers' notion of the resurrected body as a spiritual body. Aphrahat refutes some Christians whom he does not identify and who maintained that the risen body will be heavenly and spiritual. Now the ideas of these adversaries, as represented by Aphrahat himself, correspond very closely to Bardaisan's notion of the resurrection as reconstructed by I. Ramelli (2009) on the basis of a critical analysis of all the available evidence.

Also, in *Dem.* 8.17–18 Aphrahat clearly accepts, and expands upon, the notion of spiritual death, in other words death to God caused by sin, as the real death, with the related paradox that one can be dead spiritually even when still alive physically. This idea of spiritual death was shared by Bardaisan, as well as by Origen, and earlier by Philo of Alexandria and some Platonists and Stoics; it is also present in the New Testament. Even Aphrahat's interpretation of Adam's death as spiritual death, which is evident in *Dem.* 8.17, seems to be susceptible of being put in conversation with Bardaisan's interpretation of Adam's death, the way this idea is reflected in Ephrem.

Both Mara's *Letter to His Son* and the *Book of the Laws of Countries* from Bardaisan's school were transmitted in the same manuscript in the 7th century CE; it is possible that they were already transmitted together in the 4th century CE, when Aphrahat read both and alluded to both, often in the same *Demonstration*. The same ideas of Bardaisan with which Aphrahat seems acquainted were also known to Ephrem, who likewise polemicized against them in certain respects. Even if Ephrem lived slightly later than Aphrahat and was active in Edessa and Nisibis, and not in Adiabene, it is conceivable that the same means that conveyed Bardaisan's ideas to Ephrem could also convey them to Aphrahat. In conclusion, the most recent research argues that Aphrahat's sources are not limited to Scripture and that he was not so totally isolated from the broader intellectual environment of early Christianity. Rather, he did engage in some conversation with a Christian philosopher-theologian such as Bardaisan and with a pagan Stoicizing popular philosopher such as Mara, whose letter in Aphrahat's time was already probably transmitted together with Christian philosophical texts on account of its mention of Jesus as a philosopher.

Historiography

The work of Aphrahat has recently received special attention, also as a result of recent editions, translations, and commentaries, such as M.-J. Pierre (1988–1989), P. Bruns (1991–1992), A. Lehto (2010), and G. Lenzi (2012). A revisitation of the influence of 3 Corinthians on Aphrahat has been provided by J.E. Walters (2013). I. Ramelli (2015) has argued that Aphrahat is not so isolated from the philosophico-theological debates of his time, as has often been represented, but seems to have been acquainted with the Christian philosophical works of Mara Bar Serapion (a Stoicizing thinker) and Bardaisan (a Middle Platonist, as shown in I. Ramelli (2009; and elsewhere). His attitude towards poverty and slavery has also been investigated recently (Ramelli, 2017).

Bibliography

Bruns, P., ed., *Aphrahat: Unterweisungen*, Freiburg, 1991–1992.

Lehto, A., ed., *The Demonstrations of Aphrahat, the Persian Sage*, Piscataway, 2010.

Lenzi, G., ed., *Afraate: Le esposizioni*, 2 vols., Brescia, 2012.

Pierre, M.-J., ed., *Aphraate le sage person: Les exposés*, Paris, 1988–1989.

Ramelli, I., "Gesù tra i sapienti greci perseguitati ingiustamente in un antico documento filosofico pagano di lingua siriaca," *RFNS* 97, 2005, 545–570.

Ramelli, I., *Stoici romani minori*, Milan, 2008, 2555–2598.

Ramelli, I., *Bardaisan of Edessa: A Reassessment of the Evidence and a New Interpretation: Also in the Light of Origen and the Original Fragments from* De India, Piscataway, 2009; Berlin 2019.

Ramelli, I., "Mara Bar Sarapion's Letter: Comments on the Syriac Edition, Translation, and Notes by David Rensberger," in: A. Merz & T. Tieleman, eds., *The Letter of Mara bar Serapion in Context*, Leiden, 2012, 205–231.

Ramelli, I., "Review of Lenzi, 2012," *HJSS* 17, 2014, 153–160.

Ramelli, I., "Revisiting Aphrahat's Sources: Beyond Scripture?" in: *Mélanges offerts à l'Abbé Élie Khalifé-Hachem = ParOr* 41, 2015, 367–397.

Ramelli, I., *Social Justice and the Legitimacy of Slavery: The Role of Philosophical Asceticism from Ancient Judaism to Late Antiquity*, Oxford, 2017.

Ramelli, I., "Bardaisan of Edessa, Origen, and Imperial Philosophy: A Middle Platonic Context?" *ARAM* 30, 2018, 337–53.

Ramelli, I., "Sources and Reception of Dynamic Unity in Middle and Neoplatonism," *JBRec* 7, 2020, 31–66.

Ramelli, I., "Theodicy in the Letter of Mara Bar Serapion," in: B.B. Ashkelony, M. Hjalm & R. Kitchen, eds., *The Syriac Lung: New Trajectories in Syriac Studies: FS Sebastian Brock*, Louvain, 2022.

Ramelli, I., "Christian Slavery in Theology and Practice: Its Relation to God, Sin, and Justice," in: *CHAC*, Cambridge UK, forthcoming.

Walters, J.E., "Evidence for Citations of 3 Corinthians and Their Influence in the *Demonstrations* of Aphrahat," *VigChr* 67, 2013, 248–262.

ILARIA L.E. RAMELLI

Apocalypse/Apocalypticism/ Eschatology

This article will discuss several themes that emerge from the reception history of Jewish apocalypticism in the early church, both in terms of the production of new apocalypses, the integration of an apocalyptic worldview and the development of early patristic eschatology.

One overarching theme is the on-even history of the canonization of the book of Revelation in the early church. Another theme is how the church fathers reflected theologically on the book of Revelation, in addition to the book of → Daniel, and how they connected it to the broader, mostly Jewish but also Greco-Roman, apocalyptic, and eschatological speculations of the days. A third theme is how this relates to the production of the many new Christian apocalypses which often actualized previous and older Jewish apocalypses.

Some of the texts discussed will be from the church fathers and their comments on the book of Revelation or reflections on apocalyptic topics important for the early church, namely (in Greek) from Irenaeus of Lyon, Hippolytus of Rome, Origen, Eusebius of Caesarea, Basil of Caesarea, and Cyril of Alexandria, and (in Latin) from Tertullian, Victorin, Lactantius, and Augustine of Hippo. Some of the antique and late antique apocalypses here are the ones attributed to Adam, Baruch, Elijah, Ezra, James, Mary, Paul, Peter, and Thomas, but especially to Daniel.

1. A Definition of Apocalypse, Apocalypticism, and Eschatology

There exist several ways to define the terms "apocalypse" and "apocalypticism." One can approach an apocalypse as a literary genre and describe apocalypticism as a worldview. One can ask the question, whether apocalypticism is a typical (ancient) Jewish, Christian, or universal phenomenon, and one may also want to differentiate apocalypticism from a definition of eschatology. The latter is mostly used to describe a set of beliefs about the end of days, with or without an apocalyptic worldview, going back to the biblical prophets and culminating in a church "doctrine about the last things."

As a genre, scholarship has adopted the definition of J.J. Collins and his mostly North American colleagues by describing an apocalypse in J.J. Collins' well-known volume: *Apocalypse: The Morphology of a Genre* as follows:

> A genre of revelatory literature with a narrative framework, in which a revelation is mediated by an otherworldly being to a human recipient, disclosing a transcendent reality which is both temporal, insofar as it envisages eschatological salvation, and spatial insofar as it involves another, supernatural world. (Collins, 1979, 9)

With this definition, the well-known and so-called "intertestamental" apocalypses can be divided into two (or four) groups, namely:

1. historical apocalypses without heavenly journeys:
    1.1. apocalypses with a cosmic or political eschatology
    1.2. apocalypses with a personal eschatology
2. historical apocalypses with a heavenly journey:
    2.1. heavenly journeys with a cosmic or political eschatology
    2.2. heavenly journeys with a personal eschatology

As a worldview, one can point at the following characteristics, although they are not found all together in a single apocalypse or a writing with apocalyptic contents. Instead, they are often found individually and spread out over a broader collection of literature:

a myth of origin, and the search for the origin of evil in fallen demons;

an ethical and cosmological dualism between good and evil;

which can also be personalized in God and Satan, Christ and antichrist, angels, and demons;

a periodized and eschatological understanding of time;

mankind's time on earth being limited between creation and eschaton;

from which the understanding of the eschaton as a new creation arises;

in addition to concepts like a messianic age, Golden Age;

namely mostly but not exclusively in the postexilic prophets and apocalyptic authors from Hellenistic and Roman period;

however, before this a catastrophic end precedes the new world;

a catastrophe, which is humanly and/or divinely induced, and which exact time can be calculated;

with the end or latter-day turn-around coming with the help of a messianic savior figure, human, or cosmic;

and an emphasis on human sin, caused by fallen angels/demons, who are responsible for the evil in the world throughout history;

with good and bad times interchanging in a periodized history dependent on whether people repent and improve their behavior;

with the possibility of repentance as found in prophetic literature being less dominant in apocalyptic literature, in which the end is more seen as catastrophic and unavoidable;

resulting in the observation that the apocalyptic worldview is much more deterministic and pessimistic and often has more detailed doomsday scenarios than other worldviews.

One derives these characteristics from an analysis of the multiple examples of the genre "apocalypse," mainly from antiquity, as they have influenced the later Judeo-Christian tradition. At the same time, one assumes that they also reflect elements of a wider ancient apocalyptic worldview, witnessed in other apocalypses, from Greek and Roman to Iranian and Egyptian ones, and even beyond.

2. Historiography/Bibliography: Apocalypse

After a first wave of interest in apocalyptic literature in the 19th century, which was limited to the books of Daniel and Revelation, important collections of apocalyptic writings and translations began to appear, of which the collection of Old Testament apocrypha and pseudepigrapha (→ Bible), which included the important book of *1 Enoch*, by R.H. Charles in 1913 was a first hallmark. Notwithstanding important publications in other languages, such as German, French, and Italian, at the end of the 20th century R.H. Charles' edition was followed by another important and authoritative collection edited by J.R. Charlesworth in 1983, containing many more apocalyptic writings than before and expanding the limits of the Greco-Roman period. In the 1970s scholars like K. Koch (1970), K. Berger (1976), and J.J. Collins (1979) proposed literary and historical criteria of the genre "apocalypse" to systematically study this specific form of literature. With their studies they paved the way for many new venues of research, as well as new overviews and translations, a phase of research, which since the 2000s only seems to have been growing and is covering a constantly expanding range of topics.

a. Collections

Charles, R.H., *The Apocrypha and Pseudepigrapha of the Old Testament*, Oxford, 1913.
Charlesworth, J.H., ed., *The Old Testament Pseudepigrapha*, vol. I: *Apocalyptic Literature and Testaments*, New York, 1983.
Criteria
Berger, K., *Die griechische Daniel-Diegese: Eine altkirchliche Apokalypse: Text, Übersetzung und Kommentar*, Leiden, 1976.
Collins, J.J., ed., *Apocalypse: The Morphology of a Genre*, Missoula, 1979.

b. Overviews

Collins, J.J., ed., *The Oxford Handbook of Apocalyptic Literature*, Oxford, 2014.
Hanson, P.D, "Apocalyptic Literature," in: A.K. Douglas &G.M. Tucker, eds., *The Hebrew Bible and Its Modern Interpreters*, Atlanta, 3rd ed., 1985, 1993, 465–488.
Oegema, G.S., *Zwischen Hoffnung und Gericht: Untersuchungen zur Rezeption der Apokalyptik im frühen Christentum und Judentum*, Neukirchen-Vluyn, 1999.
Oegema, G.S., *Apokalypsen*, JSHRZ.S., vol. VI/1.5, Gütersloh, 2001.

c. Studies

Henze, M., "Apocalypse and Torah in Ancient Judaism," in: J.J. Collins, ed., *The Oxford Handbook of Apocalyptic Literature*, Oxford, 2014, 312–325.
Jassen, A.P., "Scriptural Interpretation in Early Jewish Apocalypses," in: J.J. Collins, ed., *The Oxford Handbook of Apocalyptic Literature*, Oxford, 2014, 69–84.
Martin Hogan, K., *Theologies in Conflict in 4 Ezra: Wisdom Debate and Apocalyptic Solution*, Leiden, 2008.
Najman, H., "The Inheritance of Prophecy in Apocalypse," in: J.J. Collins, ed., *The Oxford Handbook of Apocalyptic Literature*, Oxford, 2014, 36–51.
Oegema, G.S., "Kanon und Apokalyptik: Der Einfluß der Johannesoffenbarung auf die Kanonisierung der christlichen Bibel," in: *Proceedings of the International Symposium "The Interpretation of the Bible" in Ljubljana, September 1996*, Ljubljana 1998, 277–296.
Sheinfeld, S., "2 Esdras," in: G.S. Oegema, ed., *Oxford Handbook of the Apocrypha*, Oxford, 253–270.

3. Historical Background: Jewish Apocalypticism in the Greco-Roman World

For a history and discussion about the beginnings of apocalypticism, which possibly goes back to ancient Persia and from there has entered early → Judaism during the 3rd/2nd century BCE, culminating into *1 Enoch* and the book of Daniel and some of the → Dead Sea Scrolls, the reader is referred to other literature. It suffices here to say that Jewish apocalypticism during the Greco-Roman period has greatly influenced early Christianity, more so than the sporadic apocalyptic thoughts we find in other religions of the Greco-Roman world. It is only open to scholarly debate, how widespread and deep apocalypticism has influenced early Christianity, especially when looking at the theology and worldview of the historical Jesus (→ Christ) and the apostle Paul (→ Paul the Apostle). Although a decisive answer cannot be given here, in the following some broader developments and trends in the early church will be discussed.

4. Apocalypses in Early Christianity

Early Christianity produced several new apocalypses and at the same time adopted or Christianized several Jewish apocalypses. Among the former we count the Revelation of John and the *Apocalypse of Peter* (→ Peter the Apostle), the *Apocalypse of Paul* (→ Paul the Apostle), and the *Apocalypse of Mary*, as well as the *Shepherd of Hermas* (→ Hermas), whereas among the latter ones we list the books of *4 Ezra* and *2 Baruch*, the *Apocalypse of Abraham*, and others. One can even say that there was a widespread and growing popularity of Christianized Jewish and newly written Christian apocalypses during much of late antiquity in many branches of Christianity. The authorship of these apocalypses was often associated with biblical authors (Adam, Abraham, Baruch, Daniel, Elijah, Ezra, Isaiah, Moses, Sedrach, but also James, John, Mary, Paul, Peter, Thomas, etc.), whereas the production, translation and dissemination took place in many different languages (Greek, Latin, Syriac, Coptic, Ethiopic, Arabic, etc.).

Among the growing number of new and Christianized older apocalypses, several stand out, namely Daniel, Revelation of John, *4 Ezra*, *2 Baruch*, the *Apocalypse of Paul*, the *Apocalypse of Peter* and the *Ascension of Isaiah* (→ Isaiah), offering either a more historical-eschatological contents or contents with an ascent and descent into and scenes of heaven and hell. When looking at the use and interpretation of apocalypses by the church fathers as well as the various canon decisions, we can observe a widespread use of the book of Daniel, the book of Revelation, and the *Apocalypse of Peter* in the early church. These writings play both a crucial role as part of the canon of a Christian Bible and as basis for the development of Christian thought about the end of days, specifically about the when and how of the second coming of Christ, the required Christian moral behavior, but also about the Christian attitude towards the Roman Empire and other empires.

5. The Influence of the Book of Revelation on the Canonization of the New Testament

As for the canon of the early church, the apocalyptic worldview would play an important role in it, as the early church did not start with a fixed New Testament canon. Instead, the canonization of the book of Revelation and that of the *Apocalypse of Peter* took several centuries to be finalized. In addition, also the *Shepherd of Hermas* and the *Apocalypse of Paul* were for a while still kept in high esteem by some, even if in the end they would not be added to the canon. Furthermore, the Christian church already held a higher number of biblical books for canonical than those in the Masoretic Text, as it had accepted the Septuagint (→ Bible) as its Hebrew Bible canon. This Christian canon had been expanded in the Latin translation of the Vulgate with the *Prayer of Manasseh* and the *3 Ezrah* and *4 Ezrah*, in the last case, therefore, with an additional apocalypse. Finally, the first lists of the New Testament writings found in the works of Justin Martyr, Irenaeus, → Papias of Hierapolis, and the *Canon Muratori*, written around 200 CE mention – beside the New Testament writings known to us – as noncanonical books the *Shepherd of Hermas* and the *Apocalypse of Peter*.

Especially in the East the canonicity of the book of Revelation was questioned repeatedly; in the 4th and 5th century CE it was still refused by → John Chrysostom, → Theodoret of Cyrrhus, → Basil of Caesarea, → Gregory of Nyssa, and → Gregory of Nazianzus. In the West the New Testament canon was closed with → Athanasius of Alexandria (367 CE) as well as on the Synods of → Hippo Regius (393 CE) and → Carthage (397 & 419 CE;), even if the canonicity of the letter to the Hebrews was discussed over and over again. In the Peshitta of the Syrian Church 1 John, 1 Peter, and James, are absent and so is the book of Revelation. What can we make of these observations?

a. The Statements of the Church Fathers About the Canonicity of the Apocalypses

In the following, we want to ask the most important Greek and Latin authors (Fathers of the church and theologians) about their position on the canonicity of the aforementioned apocalypses. Our aim is to get an impression, how exactly the canon history of the book of Revelation the *Apocalypse of Peter*, the *Shepherd of Hermas*, and the *Apocalypse of Paul* has developed.

b. The Greek Authors

Irenaeus of Lyon (c. 130/140–200 CE) counts two apocalypses to the New Testament canon, the book of Revelation and the *Shepherd of Hermas*.

Hippolytus of Rome (1st half of 3rd cent. CE) considers the letter to the Hebrews as noncanonical, however, he defends the canonicity of the book of Revelation energetically. He knew the → Apostolic Fathers as well as the *Shepherd of Hermas*, the *Apocalypse of Peter*, and other New Testament pseudepigrapha (→ Pseudepigraphy).

Origen's (c. 185–253/253 CE) New Testament consisted of four Gospels, the Acts of the Apostles, the book of Revelation, the Letters of Paul, 1 Peter, 1 John, the letter to the Hebrews, and the letter of Jude. He also knew and cited the Apostolic Fathers, the apocryphal gospels and other apocrypha like the *Shepherd of Hermas*. He reports that some doubted about the canonicity of 2 Peter, 3 John, and James until the beginning of the 3rd century CE

Eusebius of Caesarea (c. 265–340 CE) differentiates in his *De ecclesiastica theologica*, as far as the New Testament canon is concerned, and in his *Historia ecclesiastica*, between

1. those books of which all churches and authors agree that they belong to the canon;
2. those books which are rejected by everybody;
3. those books, about which different opinions exist.

Four Gospels and the Acts of the Apostles, the Letters of Paul, 1 Peter, and 1 John as well as the book of Revelation about which different opinions exist belong to the first category. The *Acts of Paul* (→ Paul the Apostle), the *Shepherd of Hermas*, the *Apocalypse of Peter*, the *Letter of Barnabas* (→ Barnabas), and many others belong to the second category, as well as the book of Revelation, about which different opinions exist, whereas to the third category belong James, Jude, 2 Peter, and 2 and 3 John. In other words, the book of Revelation belongs as much to the canon

as at the same time there are differences about its canonicity in the churches as well as with the different authors whom he has questioned. Here speak both the historian Eusebius observing a current practice in the church (the apocalypse is adopted), as well as the theologian Eusebius believing that the apocalypse is problematic just because it was misused by Montanists (→ Montanism/Montanists) and other millenarists, as he reports elsewhere.

It is also of interest that two of the oldest and complete New Testament manuscripts preserved until this day originate from the same period in which Eusebius worked, namely the Codex Sinaiticus and the Codex Vaticanus. The Codex Sinaiticus includes as New Testament writings: four Gospels, 14 Letters of Paul, the Acts of the Apostles, seven Catholic letters, the book of Revelation as well as the *Letter of Barnabas* and the *Shepherd of Hermas* (*Mand.* 4. 3.6).

Concluding we can say that the canon of the New Testament, as far as the Greek church fathers are concerned, at the beginning of the 4th century CE had not yet completely been closed, and that there were at that time still different opinions about the book of Revelation, the *Apocalypse of Peter*, and the *Shepherd of Hermas*.

c. The Latin Authors

For → Tertullian (c. 150/160–c. 220 CE) Montanism has been of great importance. This influence also arises from the fact that in the course of his theological development he has thought differently about the *Shepherd of Hermas*. In his early writings he judges the *Shepherd* still positively, but during his Montanistic years he values the writing of Hermas as a purely apocryphal one. The book of Revelation he values again continuously as firmly belonging to the New Testament canon.

Jerome (c. 347–419 CE) has revised the different Latin translations of the New Testament. This translation, known as the Vulgate, contains the New Testament books as one knows them in the West until today. Merely about the Catholic letters, the letter to the Hebrews and the book Revelation, Jerome reports elsewhere, that the different churches had again and again doubted their canonicity, but that during his days it was already custom to include them in the canon. Furthermore, for him the *Letter of Barnabas* and the *Shepherd of Hermas* are almost on the same level as the New Testament writings.

Augustine of Hippo (354–430 CE; → Augustine of Hippo) describes in his (387–396 CE written and) in 426 CE published work *De doctrina Christiana* the canon of the New Testament as follows It contains the following 27 writings: 4 Gospels, 14 Letters of Paul, 1 and 2 Peter, 1, 2 and 3 John, Jude, James, the Acts of the Apostles, and the book of Revelation. At least in the West, the canon was now finally closed, as this was confirmed by the Fathers of the church of Hippo (393 CE) and Carthage (397 and 419 CE).

d. Question: The Canonization of the (New Testament) Apocalypses

As far as the canon history of the New Testament is concerned, the book of Revelation, the *Apocalypse of Peter* and the *Apocalypse of Paul* as well as the *Shepherd of Hermas* pose to us the following two questions:

1. Why were these writings until the 5th century CE considered to be canonical (at least in certain circles of the Christian world).
2. Why was in most churches afterwards only the book of Revelation seen as canonical?

We can discern three main moments in the process of canonization of the apocalypses in the New Testament apocalypses (in the West):

Around 160–200 CE the → *Canon Muratori* – a text translated into barbarian Latin, based on a lost Greek original – mentions the book of Revelation, the *Apocalypse of Peter* and the *Shepherd of Hermas*. Of these writings it is said that the book of Revelation and the *Apocalypse of Peter* may be read in the church, although some say they do not want to read them, but of the *Shepherd of Hermas* it is said, it may be read, but not before the people:

[*Can. Mur.* 71] We receive only the apocalypses of John and Peter, [*Can. Mur.* 72] though some of us are not willing that the latter be read in church. [*Can. Mur.* 73] But Hermas wrote the *Shepherd* [*Can. Mur.* 74] very recently, in our times, in the city of Rome, [*Can. Mur.* 75] while Bishop Pius, his brother, was occupying the [episcopal] chair [*Can. Mur.* 76] of the church of the city of Rome [*Can. Mur.* 77]. And therefore, it ought indeed to be read; but [*Can. Mur.*

78] it cannot be read publicly to the people in church either among [*Can. Mur.* 79] the Prophets, whose number is complete, or among [*Can. Mur.* 80] the apostles, for it is after [their] time.

From the *Canon Muratori*, and therefore from the period up to the end of 2nd century CE, we can conclude that apocalypses were both read and written at that time and that they could be read either in the church or by theologians to the people or also privately. In the latter case one can differentiate between "canonical" and "useful" (i.e. as educational and/or devotional literature). We can furthermore observe that revelation or the gift of → prophecy was still considered to be present in the church (at least in the case of the apocalypses), but this is not said of the writings of the apostles. Also, the meaning of a writing as educational or private devotional literature has a lot of weight, because the *Shepherd of Hermas* is mentioned after the book of Revelation and the *Apocalypse of Peter* specifically with this qualification (*Can. Mur.* 37). The *Canon Muratori* mentions the following criteria for canonicity of a writing: it is of prophetic or apostolic origin and the authority of the church stands behind it. Besides, one needs to pay attention to the fact that the decision about the canonicity of a writing is unalterable "until the end of the times."

Around 300 CE Eusebius makes a distinction between the book of Revelation of which all churches and authors say that it belongs to the canon, although some reject it, and the *Shepherd of Hermas* as well as the *Apocalypse of Peter*, which all rejected.

Around 400 CE the canon consists only of the book of Revelation, as we can conclude from the writings of Augustine's and the council acts of Hippo and Carthage. Hence, we may state that between the 3rd and 4th century CE a change has taken place: during and up to 3rd century CE apocalypses were written and could be added to the canon or were seen as an apocryphal, educational, and devotional literature, but from the 4th century CE on all apocalypses were rejected, with the exception of the book of Revelation. One of the reasons of this change, which took place in two opposite directions (origin of new apocalypses versus exclusion of older apocalypses) may have been the fact, that up to the end of 3rd century CE many new apocalypses were written or, if they had originated as Jewish apocalypses, were reworked with a Christian framework.

We can therefore formulate the following thesis: the history of apocalypticism and its integration in Christian theology is at the same time the history of the exclusion of several apocalypses and is a process that took place from the 3rd to the 4th century CE. Two examples may elucidate this process: on the one hand the route of the *Apocalypse of Peter* and on the other side the role of the book of Revelation in the process of canonization of the Christian Bible.

6. The Use of the Book of Revelation in Early Patristic Eschatology

The use and function of eschatology in the early church can easily be exemplified with the reception of the book of Revelation in early patristic eschatology. Given the prominence of the book of Revelation, tied together with that of Daniel, it can be shown how the church fathers were able to actualize and adapt the future expectations of the past, as preserved in Revelation and other biblical books, with a clear eye on their own situation.

7. The Reception of the Book of Revelation by the Church Fathers

a. Irenaeus of Lyon

The first author of the early church who dealt with the book of Revelation was → Irenaeus of Lyon. In his most important work, written in Greek in the 80s of the 2nd century CE and widely known under the title *Adversus Haereses*, he clearly expresses his anti-gnostic views. After a detailed interpretation of the paradise narrative in *Haer.* 5.22–24 (Gen 2 is explained with John 8:44), in *Haer.* 5.24.1 he concludes his salvation-historical line of thought by saying:

> Like he [i.e. the devil] has lied in the beginning he also has done so at the end by falsely stating: "This all has been given to me, and I will give it to those, whom I choose to give it to." (Luke 4:6)

Irenaeus then elaborates that the worldly power and the dominion of kings can only lie in the hand of God, after which in *Haer.*5.24.2–3 there follows an excursus on earthly power: it is not a tool of the → devil but has been created by God as a "means to limit evil." Against the background of this example of salvation history there seems to lie apocalyptic thinking, according to which the good and evil powers have dominated mankind since the days of creation.

Following this, he deals with the *topoi* "antichrist" (→ Antichrist) and "1000-year reign." As it was prophesied at the beginning of the world (Gen 3:15) and is indicated in the narrative about the temptation of Jesus (Matt 4:1–11), at the end of days Christ will besiege the great Seducer and finally destroy him. This then becomes the main theme in *Haer.* 5.25.1–30.4. He begins to discuss the theme of the antichrist in detail, which until then had been only briefly touched, in *Haer.*5.25f. In this section he mostly refers to the key passages of Dan 2 and 7–9, Matt 24, 2 Thess 2, and Rev 13 and 17.

Whereas the expression "antichrist" is Christian, the image of an anti-divine ruler is much older and is already found in the Hebrew Bible and in the Jewish apocalypses of the Second Temple period. Besides Dan 7 and 9:11, *As. Mos.* 8; *4 Ezra* 11–12, and *2 Bar.* 39, one should think of 1 John 2:18; 2:22; 4:3; 2 John 7; 2 Thess 2:3–12; John 5:43; Rev 13; 17; Bar (1) 4:1–5; *Ascen. Isa.* 4; *Sib. Or.* 8.88f.; 139–159; as well as Just. *Dial.* 31.2–32.4; 110.2. From these passages one can conclude that the image of an anti-divine ruler in the 2nd century CE is still quite diverse and certainly not unified. This antichrist figure could either be identified with a political figure (Antiochus IV Epiphanes in Dan 7–9 and 11, the last Roman emperor in *4 Ezra* 11–12, *Nero Redivivus* in Rev 13 and *Ascen. Isa.* 4) – or be associated with expressions like "son of destruction," "Satan," and "antichrist," as well as "false prophet" and "pseudo-anointed."

Irenaeus, therefore, stands at the beginning of the development of a more and more consistent "antichrist theology" – in which a cosmic battle between the antichrist and the Messiah/Christ is seen behind the struggle between Israel/the church and the world powers, starting already at the time of creation. He then gives a detailed account of the expected sequence of events during the coming of the antichrist in *Haer.* 5.25.1.

b. Hippolytus of Rome

Hippolytus of Rome (first half of the 3rd cent. CE [?]; about whose life little is known), who according to Eusebius was a → bishop, possibly in Palestine or surrounding area, was

> a churchman who disdained profane science in order to cultivate the Scriptures. His works are essentially commentaries on sacred texts and nearly always on the Old Testament, interpreted by a typological exegesis, which he applies to Christ and the church. (Nautin, 1992, 384)

His *Commentarium in Danielem* preserved in Greek – one of the first Christian Bible commentaries – is of great importance for our topic. A work that is also relevant is the older treatise *De Antichristo*, a florilegium of apocalyptic passages from the Hebrew Bible and the New Testament. Hippolytus expects the antichrist (chs. 6; 49), who will rebuild Jerusalem (ch. 6), but will be subordinated to the power of Rome, the "new Babylon" (chs. 30–36). The antichrist will seduce mankind (chs. 54–58) and persecute the church (chs. 59–63). At the end of days, John and → Elijah (ch. 64; see also chs. 44ff.) and, afterwards, Christ himself (ch. 64) will come. Christ will execute the judgement, after which the righteous will inherit → paradise, and the wicked ones will be punished in hell (ch. 65).

In Hippolytus' *Commentary on Daniel*, Book IV is particularly important, as it offers an interpretation of Daniel's vision of the four animals (Dan 7), which is then actualized from the perspective of the book of Revelation and the later historical situation, namely the early church found itself in. It refers to

1. the empire of the Medes, Assyrians, and Babylonians;
2. the empire of the Persians;
3. the empire of the Macedonians, Hellenes, or Greeks (Hipp. *Comm. Dan.* 4.3–4);
4. the presently ruling empire of the Romans (Hipp. *Comm. Dan.* 4.5).

At the end of this he clearly identifies the situation during his own time:

> However, the now ruling animal is not one nation, but it is a collection of all languages and generations of mankind and is prepared to be a multitude of warriors, who are all called Romans, but do not originate from one country. (Hipp. *Comm. Dan.* 4.8)

At the end of the four empires according to Dan 7:17–18 the heavenly reign will start (*Comm. Dan.* 4.10).

But also here Hippolytus interprets the text of Daniel from a later Christological perspective. Christ is the firstborn, the Son of God, to whom everything on earth and in heaven has been subordinated, the firstborn "before the angels" and the first born "from the dead" (*Comm. Dan.* 4.11). Hippolytus answers the question of when "the Seducer" will come and on which day the *parousia* of the Lord will be (*Comm. Dan.* 4.16), with a peculiar calculation. The age of the world has been set at 6000 years, and as Christ was born 5500 years after the creation, the end of days will take place 500 years after that (*Comm. Dan.* 4.23). The calculation of the age of the world is found (as can be found in earlier interpretations) on the basis of verses like Gen 2:3; Ps 90:4 (= LXX Ps 89:4), and 2 Pet 3:8. Afterwards Hippolytus interprets in in *Comm. Dan.* 4.35 Dan 9:25–27 as referring to the second coming of Christ and the time of the → resurrection of the dead as follows. After the 62 weeks have passed and Christ has returned, and the gospel has been preached everywhere in this world and the time has passed, there is one week left, in which Elijah and Enoch will come, and in their midst appears the abomination of the antichrist, who will announce destruction to the world. Afterwards he will abolish the sacrifice (Dan 9:27), which has been sacrificed at every place and by every nation to God.

Then in *Comm. Dan.* 4.49f., Hippolytus gives an even more vivid description of the antichrist, about which "all scriptures, both the Prophets" speak, "as well as the Lord has given testimony of, and the Apostles taught about, [and] his name was secretly revealed by John in the book of Revelation." The text of Dan 9:26–27, which in earlier times had been linked to Antiochus IV Epiphanes, Hippolytus now applies to the antichrist and makes him – in connection with the Synoptic apocalypse (Mark 13 par.) and the book of Revelation –central to his detailed description of the end of days (see *Comm. Dan.* 4.5ff.). In summary we can say that Hippolytus expected the coming of the antichrist, who would rebuild Jerusalem; the coming of Elijah and Enoch; and the return of Christ, who would capture the antichrist, after which there would follow the resurrection and the final judgement. Hippolytus bases his interpretation on Gen 1 (the six days of creation) and Rev 20 (the capture of Satan and the 1000-year reign), which he, with the help of Ps 90:4 and 2 Pet 3:8, joins to an all-embracing view of history.

c. Origen

Origen (c. 185–253/254 CE; → Origen), who was born in Alexandria and worked in Caesarea, was according to B.J. Daley (2002) one of the "most important Greek church fathers" and at the same time "without doubt the most controversial figure in the development of early Christian eschatology." He was a student of the Neoplatonic → Ammonius Saccas and possibly of → Clement of Alexandria and was well versed in Hebrew Bible interpretations. He is the author/editor of the so-called Hexapla (→ Bible), the Bible edition in Hebrew, Hebrew in Greek transcript, as well as in the Greek translations of a recension of the Septuagint and those of Aquila, Symmachus, and Theodotion.

In his *Commentary on Matthew* (*Commentarium in Evangelium Matthaei* XXXII–LIX), Origen deals with the Synoptic apocalypse (according to Matt 24:3–44). In it he treats the following thematic topics: the "announcement of the destruction of the Temple" (chs. 29–31), the "beginning of the time of distress" (chs. 32–39), the "culmination of the time of distress" (chs. 40–47), the "coming of the Son of Man" (chs. 48–52), and the "warnings for the end of days" (chs. 53–59). Here it will be of interest to refer to his interpretation of Dan 9:24–27 (about the 70 weeks and the "abomination"), in which he explains the characteristics of Christian Bible interpretation and refers, for example, to the destruction of Jerusalem: only those inspired by the → Holy Spirit can truly understand Scripture, especially the book of Revelation, and they will recognize that the prophet has foresaid that the destruction of the → Temple and Jerusalem will last until the end of days, in other words, the fulfillment of the world.

d. Eusebius of Caesarea

Eusebius of Caesarea (→ Eusebius of Caesarea [Palestine]) was since 313 CE bishop of Caesarea and was influenced by Origen, whose library he inherited, as well as by one of Origen's students, whose name (Pamphilus) he adopted. The diligently historical and exegetical Eusebius became mainly known through his *Historia ecclesiastica*. From his writing *Life of Constantine*, a panegyric on the first "Christian" emperor → Constantine I in four books, whom he compares favorably with Cyrus, Alexander, and → Moses, the final passage is worth citing here:

> He alone of all the Roman emperors has honored God the All-sovereign with exceeding godly piety; he alone has publicly proclaimed to all the word of Christ; he alone has honored his church as no other since time began; he alone has destroyed all polytheistic error and exposed every kind of idolatry [...] (Eus. *Vit. Const.* 75)

e. Jerome

Jerome was born in 347 CE in Dalmatia, studied in Rome, and lived from 386 to his death in 419 CE in Bethlehem. He revised the various Latin translations of the New Testament, and this translation, known as the Vulgate, contains all the books of the New Testament as we know it today in the West. → Jerome's eschatology is intrinsically connected with his knowledge of the Bible, his former admiration of Origen, his other personal contacts, and the many events in his long and ascetic life as a scholar. In the context of his spiritual-personal, allegorical exegesis, he would interpret the apocalyptic future expectations mostly as a confrontation of the individual with death. However, later in his life he would also take the apocalyptic tradition increasingly literally: so, his *Commentary on Daniel* (written in 399 CE, to refute → Porphyry of Tyre's historicizing explanation of that book) interprets the antichrist as a human figure, a Jew of humble origin, who will soon overthrow the Roman Empire and rule the world (Jer. *Comm. Dan.* 2.7.7f.; 2.7.11; 4.11.21).

Also, his commentaries on → Isaiah, written between 408 and 410 CE (Jer. *Comm. Isa.* 6.14.1; 14.51.6; 16.59.14; 18.65.17f.), and → Ezekiel, written after 411 CE (Jer. *Comm. Ezech.* 11.36.38), express his latter-day expectations, which may have been influenced by the attack of the → barbarians at the beginning of the 5th century CE: the Roman Empire will soon fall, the antichrist is near, and the appearance of heretics (→ Heresy) within the church is a sign of the coming end. Finally in his commentary on Daniel (*Explanatio in Danielem*) it becomes obvious that he does not look upon the biblical books from a historical distance, as is the case with Neoplatonic Porphyry, but the book of Revelation is for the time in which Jerome lived, still very relevant. When the western → Goths attacked Rome in the year 408 CE, Jerome thought this to be a sign of the end of days, but after the city had been taken and the end did not come, he softened this acute expectation of the end.

8. Concluding Observations

As far as Jewish apocalypticism is concerned, these few examples will suffice to illuminate the reception history of the book of Revelation in the early church, and specifically how close the interpretation of the book of Revelation is tied into the interpretation of the book of Daniel. In addition, also other biblical passages considered to be eschatological as well as the broader Christological perspective on both world history and its imminent end are part of this reception. In this process, the church fathers understood the struggle between the church and the Roman Empire as a cosmic battle between the antichrist and Christ. This not only goes back to the book of Revelation, but even further back in history to the books of Genesis and Daniel, a theology which the church fathers could now fully understand through the Holy Spirit. The main elements of apocalyptic thinking are thus found in the influence on mankind of good and evil or personified of that of the antichrist and the Messiah/Christ since the creation, as well as the calculation of the exact time of the end of days. Examples of eschatology are especially found in the scheme of salvation history and the apocalyptic survey of history by using Daniel's scheme of the seventy weeks, whereas cosmogonic and sapiential motives are mostly connected with the creation narrative. For the church fathers, however, these genres were mere means to interpret the past in order to know more about the future. We can furthermore make the important observation that in the period from the 2nd to the 5th century CE there is a shift away from focusing on the antichrist and the Fourth Empire of the book of Revelation as represented by the Roman Empire to a more friendly approach to the Roman Empire. This empire would then at the end of the 4th century CE – in other words, after Constantine the Great and the success of the Christian mission – be understood in a Christian way, now endangered by evil powers from outside (the barbarian invasion), or, as an alternative, was seen as the Fifth Empire replacing the four previous ones. In all of this for the church fathers it didn't matter, whether their political interpretation was typical cosmogonic, sapiential, eschatological, or apocalyptic exegesis, as long as it was Christological, although they knew the many rhetorical advantages of these and other genres, as they were able to use and adapt them for their own specific purposes.

9. Historiography/Bibliography: Apocalypticism

The study of apocalypticism, whether as something more specifically found in the ancient Jewish and Christian tradition, or more generally as a worldview typical of the ancient world, or even a universal mindset, began with the question by K. Koch in 1970, what to do with apocalypticism, and was followed by a history of research of the study of the books of Daniel and Revelation in the 19th and early 20th century by J. Schmidt (1976). Other studies expanded the horizon, notably the ones collected by P.D. Hanson (1979) and D. Hellholm (1983). Overviews by C. Rowland (1982), J. VanderKam and W. Adler (1996), J.J. Collins, B. McGinn and J.S. Stein (1999), and L. DiTommaso (2021) followed.

a. The Question

Hanson, P.D. *The Dawn of Apocalyptic: The Historical and Sociological Roots of Jewish Apocalyptic Eschatology*, rev. ed., Philadelphia, 1979.

Hellholm, D., *Apocalypticism in the Mediterranean World and in the Near East*, 2nd ed., Tübingen 1983; 1989.

Koch, K., *Ratlos vor der Apokalyptik: Eine Streitschrift über ein vernachlässigtes Gebiet der Bibelwissenschaft und die schädlichen Auswirkungen auf Theologie und Philosophie*, Gütersloh, 1970.

Schmidt, J.J., *Die jüdische Apokalyptik: Die Geschichte ihrer Erforschung von den Anfangen bis zu den Textfunden von Qumran*, 2nd ed., Neukirchen-Vluyn, 1976.

b. Overviews

Beker, J.C., *Paul the Apostle: The Triumph of God in Life and Thought*, Philadelphia, 1990.

Collins, J.J., B. McGinn & J.S. Stein, eds., *The Encylopedia of Apocalypticism*, vol. I: *The Origins of Apocalypticism in Judaism and Christianity*, ed. J.J. Collins, New York, 1999.

Cook, S.L., *Prophecy and Apocalypticism: The Postexilic Setting*, Minneapolis, 1995.

Cook, S.L., "Apocalyptic Prophecy," in: J.J. Collins, ed., *The Oxford Handbook of Apocalyptic Literature*, Oxford, 2014, 19–35.

DiTommaso, Lorenzo, "The Apocrypha and Apocalypticism," in: G.S. Oegema, *Oxford Handbook of the Apocrypha*, Oxford, 2021, 219–252.

García Martínez, F., *Qumran and Apocalypticism: Studies on the Aramaic Texts from Qumran*, Leiden, 1992.

García Martínez, F., ed., *Wisdom and Apocalypticism in the Dead Sea Scrolls and in the Biblical Tradition*, Louvain, 2003.

Grabbe, L.L., "Prophetic and Apocalyptic: Time for New Definitions–and New Thinking," in: L.L. Grabbe & R.D. Haak, eds., *Knowing the End from the Beginning: The Prophetic, Apocalyptic and Their Relationships*, JSP.S 46, London, 2003, 106–133.

Nautin, P., "Hippolytus," in: A. Di Berardino, ed., *EEC*, Cambridge UK, 1992, 383–385,

Oegema, G.S., "Was the Maccabean Revolt a Prophetic, Apocalyptic or other Movement?" in: L.L. Grabbe, ed., *The Seleucid and Hasmonean Periods and the Apocalyptic Worldview*, London, 2016, 69–87.

Portier-Young, A., *Apocalypse Against Empire: Theologies of Resistance in Early Judaism*, Grand Rapids, 2011.

Rowland, C., *The Open Heaven: A Study of Apocalyptic in Judaism and Early Christianity*, New York, 1982.

c. Studies

VanderKam, J.C., & W. Adler, *The Jewish Apocalyptic Heritage in Early Christianity*, Assen, 1996.

Wassén, C., & T. Hågerland, eds., *Jesus the Apocalyptic Prophet*, New York, 2021.

10. Eschatology

The question of how to speak about the eschatology of the early church in light of the historical developments of biblical and early Jewish apocalypticism in antiquity and its influence on the concepts and worldviews of early Christianity, is a theological one and touches upon the much-debated relation between history of religion and theology. The first author, who systematically categorized the eschatological beliefs of the 3(4) Jewish sects of his days, the Sadducees, Pharisees, Essenes, and Zealots, was actually → Flavius Josephus (37–100 CE), namely in his *Jewish Antiquities* (18.11–17), compare his *Jewish War* (2. 8.2–13). He writes about the Pharisees:

> They [...] believe that souls have an immortal rigor in them, and that under the earth there will be rewards or punishments, according as they have lived virtuously or viciously in this life; and the latter are to be detained in an everlasting prison, but that the former shall have power to revive and live again. (Jos. *Ant.* 18.11–17)

Both the → Essenes and → Zealots had similar beliefs with some differences, but the Sadducees did not.

As such, eschatology has a long tradition in Christian theology and the history of church doctrine and constitutes a central element in it. Although we already find a more systematic discussion of Christian eschatology in the works of Ignatius of Antioch (37–107 CE; → Ignatius, Epistles of), → Justin Martyr (100–165 CE), Tertullian and Origin, the term eschatology is used first only by Abraham Calovius (1612–1686) and becomes most popular since the 18th century. For the first centuries CE, its religion-historical background plays a much more important role. However, when speaking of eschatology as an area of theology concerned with the last things, one normally follows a more systematic path, while at the same time one acknowledges that the various key themes have been interpreted differently in later periods and by later authors and groups.

The central themes of Christian eschatology are: some or all biblical prophecies have been fulfilled. Connected with this are different understandings of history and especially salvation history (preterist, historicist, and futurist) as well as different forms of biblical interpretation. We find this already in the New Testament, especially in the Synoptic Gospels of Mathew, Mark, and Luke, but also in the Epistles of Paul and the letter to the Hebrews. Central to it is the concept of realized eschatology, namely that some or more of the future expectations have happened. It is one of the defining characteristics of early Christian hermeneutics and centers around the experience of and reflection on the death and → resurrection of Jesus Christ. It will be followed in the future by his second coming, which is preceded by apocalyptic events marking the end of days and the final judgment. There is both tension and overlap between realized and futuristic eschatology in such a way that the events predicted for the future have already started in the presence or even in the past. These future events are outlined in the Synoptic apocalypse Mark 13 and parallels, Paul's First Epistle to the Thessalonians and especially in great detail in the book of Revelation, from which most eschatological concepts have been derived. However, as such this goes back to many biblical and prophetic books, especially the book of Daniel. Christian eschatology is therefore mostly based on these two books, Daniel and Revelation. Finally, one should also differentiate between personal and collective eschatology, as some texts deal specifically with the fate after death of the individual and others with whole groups, nations and even the universe.

Most key themes, eschatological concepts and images are derived from the book of Revelation. They are: the 144,000 saved (Rev 6:17), a demonic host released at the end of days (Rev 9), a large army from the Euphrates (Rev 9:13–16), the Two Witnesses (Rev 11:1–12), the 1260 Days (Rev 11:3), the Woman and the Dragon (Rev 12:1–6), the Beast of the Sea (Rev 13:1–8), the Beast of the Earth (Rev 13:11–18), the False Prophet (Rev 13:11–18), the Number of the Beast being 666 (Rev 13:18), Armageddon (Rev 16:16), Babylon the Great Harlot (Rev 17:1–5), the Seven Heads and the Ten Horns (Rev 17:9–11), the Thousand Years (Rev 20:1–3), the Rapture (Rev 19:17–19), the Marriage of the Lamb (Rev 19:6–8), the Great Tribulation (Rev 4:1), the Abomination that causes Desolation (Rev 13:5–8 going back to Matt 24 and Dan 7), the invasion of Gog and Magog (Rev 20:8 going back to Ezek 38), and the Last Judgment (Rev 20:10).

There exist other ways of systematically list the key themes, which allows them to be placed in a broader religion-comparative scheme, as many eschatological concepts are also found in other religions, both ancient and modern, namely as follows:

a. Death and Afterlife

Belief in → afterlife (with an intermediate state and/or purgatory) in Judaism begins in Dan 12:2 and 2 Macc 7 with some earlier texts hinting at it as well, such as Gen 5:24, 2 Kgs 2:11, Isa 26:19, Ezek 37:1. But only after the Maccabean Revolt in 167–164 BCE, eschatological ideas would start to develop, mostly among the Pharisees (see the text of Josephus), influence Jesus, → John the Baptist, and most of the books of the New Testament. Crucial for the Christian faith is the belief in the resurrection of Jesus, through which everyone else, who believes in him will also take part in the bodily resurrection. Contrary to this, the belief in the immortality of the → soul goes back to the Greek religion and can also be found in the Egyptian and other religions. This belief has important implications for the relation between body and soul.

b. The Great Tribulation

The time of Great Tribulation (unexpected, with abomination of desolation, and prophecy of 70 weeks) is a time expected for the future, when natural and man-made disasters are on a bigger scale than there has ever been in the history of mankind (Matt 24:21–22). Whereas it's exact time of arrival is unknown, it will precede the coming of the Messiah or the second coming of Christ. It will also be a time of the abomination of desolation, a time of great sacrilege, which is associated with the desecration of the Temple and goes back to the time of the Maccabean Revolt (→ Maccabees) and the book of Daniel (Matt 24:15–26). This time of tribulation will last according to some seven years, a belief that goes back to the "seventy weeks" in Dan 9:26–27, in the middle of which there will be the rebuilding of the Temple and the reinstitution of the sacrifice (see also 2 Thess 2:3–4).

c. Rapture

This (→ Rapture) is the belief that some believers, both the living and the dead, will rise into heaven and join Christ before all the others; this goes back to 1 Thess 4:17, after which Christ's second coming will be and his 1000-year kingdom will commence, according to Matt 24, 1 Cor 15, and Rev 20–22 (see below). This also implies that there will be two timely separated resurrections and has led to the question whether the resurrections will be bodily or not. According to Matt 22:30 and 1 Cor 15:42–44 the resurrected body will be a spiritual one.

d. The Second Coming (*Parousia*)

This belief (→ *Parousia*) is based upon the Synoptic apocalypse Mark 13, specifically on Matt 24:27–31, as well as on 1 Thess 4:15–17, which offers a kind of brief summary of the end-time events:

> For this we declare to you by the word of the Lord, that we who are alive, who are left until the coming of the Lord, will by no means precede those who have died. For the Lord himself, with a cry of command, with the archangel's call and with the sound of God's trumpet, will descend from heaven, and the dead in Christ will rise first. Then we who are alive, who are left, will be caught up in the clouds together with them to meet the Lord in the air, and so we will be with the Lord forever.

e. Millennium (1000-Year Reign)

This concept is based on Rev 20–22, specifically on Rev 20:2–6. It will be preceded by the first resurrection (see "Rapture" above) and followed by the second universal resurrection.

f. The End of the World

At the end of days this world, which was created 6000 years ago, will be destroyed by war and natural disasters, Satan will be released, → Gog and Magog will fight, and Armageddon will take place.

g. Last Judgment

After the end of the world there will be the final judgment executed by the One, who sits on a Throne (Rev 20:11–15), Satan will be chained and thrown into the abyss forever, and death will be no more.

h. New Heaven and New Earth

God will then create a New Heaven and a New Earth (with New Jerusalem and Tree of Life), rebuild Jerusalem more beautiful than before and begin his eternal reign. Some of these ideas and beliefs go back to the prophet Isaiah (esp. chs. 65–66) and Rev 20–22.

11. Concluding Observations

As way of summary, we can state that the main eschatological beliefs of the Greek and Latin church fathers are unified in three things. First, all eschatology begins and ends with Christ's first and second coming and is therefore Christological in nature. Second, all eschatology is biblical in that it interprets biblical passages, especially verses, chapters, and thoughts from the Prophets, in light of its Christologically centered eschatology. Third, early patristic eschatology is ecclesiastical in that it gives a central place to the church in its eschatology that spans and transforms world history and time itself.

12. Historiography/Bibliography: Eschatology

With eschatology as such being a broad term, traditionally it has been applied to both the eschatological beliefs of the Hebrew Bible prophets, the variety of eschatological concepts during the Second Temple period as well as the eschatology of the early church.

a. Prophetic Literature

Barton, J., *Oracles of God: Perceptions of Ancient Prophecy in Israel After the Exile*, London, 1986.

Boccaccini, G., & J.J. Collins, eds., *The Early Enoch Literature*, Leiden, 2007.

Brueggemann, W., *A Commentary on Jeremiah: Exile and Homecoming*, Grand Rapids, 1998.

Charles, R.H., *A Critical History of the Doctrine of a Future Life, in Israel, in Judaism, and in Christianity, or, Hebrew, Jewish, and Christian Eschatology from Pre-Prophetic Times till the Close of the New Testament Canon*, 2nd ed., London, 1913.

Grabbe, L.L., *Priests, Prophets, Diviners, Sages: A Socio-Historical Study of Religious Specialists in Ancient Israel*, Valley Forge, 1995.

Grabbe, LL., "Prophetic and Apocalyptic: Time for New Definitions–and New Thinking," in: L.L. Grabbe & R.D. Haak, eds., *Knowing the End from the Beginning: The Prophetic, Apocalyptic and Their Relationships*, JSP.S 46, London, 2003, 106–133, esp. 109–114.

Grabbe LL., & R.D. Haak, eds., *Knowing the End from the Beginning: The Prophetic, Apocalyptic and Their Relationships*, JSP.S 46, London, 2003.

Heschel, A.J., *The Prophets*, New York, 1969–1975.

Hogeterp, A.L.A., *Expectations of the End: A Comparative Traditio-Historical Study of Eschatological, Apocalyptic and Messianic Ideas in the Dead Sea Scrolls and the New Testament*, Leiden, 2008.

Macaskill, G., *Revealed Wisdom and Inaugurated Eschatology in Ancient Judaism and Early Christianity*, Leiden, 2007.

Mowinckel, S., *The Spirit and the Word: Prophecy and Tradition in Ancient Israel*, Minneapolis, 2002.

Oegema, G.S., *The Anointed and His People: Messianic Expectations from the Maccabees to Bar Kochba*, JSP.S, vol. XXVII, Sheffield, 1998.

Reuss, E., *Die Propheten*, Braunschweig, 1892.

Tucker, G.M., "Prophecy and the Prophetic Literature," in: D.A. Knight & G.M. Tucker, eds., *The Hebrew Bible and Its Modern Interpreters*, 3rd ed., Atlanta, 1985, 1993, 325–368.

Wilson, R.R., *Prophecy and Society in Ancient Israel*, Philadelphia, 1980.

Yoshiko Reed, A., *Fallen Angels and the History of Judaism and Christianity: The Reception of Enochic Literature*, New York, 2005.

b. Early Church

Ehrman, B.D., *Jesus: Apocalyptic Prophet of the New Millenium*, Oxford, 2001.

Oegema, G.S., "Back to the Future in the Early Church: The Use of the Book of Daniel in Early Patristic Eschatology," in: P. Kirkpatrick et al., eds., *The Function of Ancient Historiography*, Edinburgh, 2008, 186–198.

Oegema, G.S., *The Heritage of Jewish Apocalypticism in Late-Antique and Early Medieval Judaism, Christianity and Islam*, in: R. Wisnovsky et al., eds., *Vehicles of Transmission, Translation, and Transformation in Medieval Cultures*, CuMU, vol. IV, Turnhout, 2012, 103–129.

GERBERN S. OEGEMA

Apocrisarius

The apocrisiarius or apocrisarius (lit. "answerer") was the point of contact among the four patriarchates of Rome, Jerusalem, Antioch, and Alexandria, and the headquarters of the imperial church in Constantinople. Extant from the 5th century CE, the office was institutionalized in law under Justinian I (527–565 CE). The apocrisiarius could be a cleric functioning as the diplomatic representative or legate of a bishop of the patriarch to the Byzantine imperial court, or his permanent representative resident in another see (Neil & Allen, 2014, 223). While papal apocrisaries have been the focus of most recent scholarship (e.g. Rennie, 2013), the eastern ones should not be forgotten. Even though the evidence is sketchy and piecemeal, acts of church councils and episcopal letters allow the tentative reconstruction of the office of apocrisiarius and its scope presented here. It is compared with two other offices, the legate and the papal vicar.

Pope → Leo I (440–461 CE) appointed the first recorded papal apocrisiarius. Bishop Julian of Cos was sent to the court of Marcian (450–457 CE) and represented the apostolic see at the Council of → Chalcedon (451 CE) in the midst of the Christological controversy over the natures of Christ (Leo M. *Ep.* 9; PL 54.1251B – *Actio XVI Chalcedonensis*). In two earlier letters to Julian from Leo (*Ep.* 34 and *Ep.* 35; PL 54.801–810) of Jun 13, 449, Leo discusses the appointment of three legates *a latere* (from his side) to the Second Council of Ephesus (449 CE): Bishop Julius, the priest Renatus, and the deacon Hilary. (Hilary later became Leo's successor as bishop of Rome.) From Leo's correspondence, we can deduce that the failure of these three legates to persuade the patriarchs of Jerusalem, Antioch, Alexandria, and Constantinople to the Roman point of view at the "Robber Synod" necessitated the use of stronger representation the next time around. Although it is not made explicit, it seems likely that Julian spent a considerable period of time in Constantinople. This may have been the distinguishing feature of the apocrisiarius as opposed to the more temporary legate.

Papal deacons were generally preferred for the role of apocrisiarius in Constantinople. For example, the future pope Gregory I served as apocrisary there for Pelagius II for six or seven years in from 579 CE, before his appointment as bishop of Rome (590–604 CE). Knowledge of Greek was an asset; thus, Roman apocrisaries were often not Roman themselves. An example is Maximus the Confessor's companion, the priest Anastasius (d. 668 CE), apocrisiarius for Popes Theodore (642–649 CE) and Martin I (649–654 CE), who, like the latter pope, died in exile (*Hypomn.* 6; Allen & Neil, 2002, 156). Knowledge of Greek was not, however, an absolute prerequisite – → Gregory the Great professed an inadequate knowledge of the language (Neil, 2015, 242), and the papal apocrisiarius and deacon Martin of Tuder (modern Todi) seems not have known much Greek at all (Neil, 2006, 199n92).

In the Roman church, two offices operated alongside the apocrisiarius: the apostolic vicar (*apostolicus vicarius*) and the legates (*legatus ad causam*). The apostolic vicar helped the popes to govern the churches under Roman jurisdiction from a distance. His duties included convening and presiding over local councils, which helped to expedite local and regional cases and to free the pope from being inundated by trivial requests (Rennie, 2013, 123), although appeals could always be made. The earliest apostolic vicar was appointed by Pope → Damasus in 380 CE, the bishop of Thessalonica (Illyricum). In the 5th century CE, Pope → Innocent I also appointed an apostolic vicar in Thessalonica, as did Leo and → Gelasius I. Pope Symmachus appointed the bishop of Arles to this post in Gaul in 514 CE (Rennie, 2013, 41–55). Later, western vicars were established in Spain and Sicily.

The temporary legate (*legatus ad causam*) did not have to be a cleric. He functioned as an arbiter of cases outside Rome on behalf of Peter (Rennie, 2013, 153). The legate could also play a role in doctrinal controversies by presenting one patriarchate's orthodoxy to another. For instance, Faustus the *magister* was sent as Gelasius' legate to Constantinople during the → Acacian schism, as we know from Gelasius' letter of instruction to him (Gelas. *Ep.* 10; Neil & Allen, 2014, 109–115).

K.R. Rennie plausibly maintains that, under Pope Leo I, the office of papal legate had obtained a degree of specialization in both administrative and legal terms, with an emerging classification system of temporary legates, vicars, and permanent legates (Rennie, 2013, 128). Papal legates successfully represented Roman interests at the Council of → Sardica (modern Sofia), convened in 343 CE under Constans II (Rennie, 2013, 134–135). Papal legations, however, did not always go so well, as for instance in 483 CE, at the beginning of the Acacian schism, when

Felix III's legates Tutus and Misenus were turned to the Constantinopolitan point of view, under duress (*Ep.* 30, Neil & Allen, 2014, 128–138). Another failure of Roman legates to prevail occurred at the Council of → Carthage in 419 CE (Rennie, 2013, 138–140). Their success was wholly dependent on the willingness of the host to receive the delegation's point of view. Even the aforementioned legation that Leo I sent to the Second Council of Ephesus failed to have his *Tome to Flavian* (*Ep.* 28) read out aloud there.

Gregory I frequently refers to papal envoys (*responsales*) in his letters, 854 of which are preserved in a single *Register* (Jasper, 2001, 70–81). Under Gregory,

> the apocrisiarius relayed messages to Rome on behalf of the imperial chancery; operated as a military judge; handled religious matters; was sent as an envoy from the patriarchal sees of Antioch, Jerusalem, or Alexandria; and maintained political communications between the Byzantine emperor and Rome. (Eichbauer, 2015)

The apocrisiarius was obliged to follow papal mandates, set out in often lengthy letters known as *commonitoria* (Rennie, 2013, 108–110), which reminded the legate of the basis of his authority, the Petrine commission (Matt 16:18–19). An example is found in Gelasius' *Commonitorium* to the legate Faustus, mentioned above (Gelas. *Ep.* 10.9; Neil & Allen, 2014, 114). Their activity in civic affairs was naturally subject to imperial law (Rennie, 2013, 64).

The apocrisiarius was a role not without danger to the incumbent. Apocrisaries in Constantinople could be expelled, confined in custody, sent into exile, or whipped ("Martinus papa," Duchesne & Vogel, vol. I, 1955–1957, 338). This is evident from the career of Martin, apocrisiarius to Constantinople under Pope Theodore. Martin was expelled from the city before he became pope in 649 CE and later arrested in Rome and brought back to Constantinople for trial (Duchesne & Vogel, vol. I, 1955–1957, 338) during the doctrinal controversy over the number of wills in Christ.

The office of apocrisiarius ceased to operate between Rome and Constantinople between the mid-8th and early 9th centuries CE, being replaced by the more flexible office of the *legatus ad causam*, which by then included messengers with financial powers and the power to arrange alliances (*nuncii*) and church defenders (*defensores ecclesiae*; Rennie, 2013, 66).

Historiography

Modern attention to this office has been scarce, due to the lack of clarity in the early medieval sources. According to K.R. Rennie, by the late 6th and turn of the 7th centuries CE, the *defensores ecclesiae* formed a diplomatic corps acting as "the pope's eyes and ears" while administering regional papal landholdings (Rennie, 2013, 72–79). This view supports T.F.X. Noble's claim that the papal apocrisiarii resident in the imperial capital from the 5th century to the 730s CE were not ambassadors, as previously thought, but remained "essentially messengers" without plenipotentiary powers until the 12th century CE (Noble, 1984, 239). All diplomatic exchanges between the eastern and western churches were impacted by the iconoclast controversy from 743 CE. Papal claims to primacy, which expanded to claims of temporal authority over the disputed territories of Illyricum, also contributed to a breakdown in relations and the suspension of the office.

Bibliography

Duchesne, L., & C. Vogel, eds., *Le Liber Pontificalis*, 3 vols., Paris, 1955–1957².

Eichbauer, M., Review of K.R. Rennie, *The Foundations of Medieval Papal Legation*, London, 2013, *MeRe*; put online 2015.

Jasper, D., "The Beginning of the Decretal Tradition," in: D. Jasper & J. Fuhrmann, *Papal Letters in the Early Middle Ages*, HMCL, Washington DC, 2001, 3–133.

Martyn, J.R.C., trans., *The Letters of Gregory the Great*, 3 vols., MSiT 40, Toronto, 2004.

Migne, J.-P., ed., PL 54, Paris, 1881.

Neil, B., *Seventh-Century Popes and Martyrs: The Political Hagiography of Anastasius Bibliothecarius*, SAAu 2, Sydney, 2006.

Neil, B., "Gregory the Great," in: K. Parry, ed., *The Wiley-Blackwell Companion to Patristics*, Oxford, 2015, 238–249.

Neil. B, & P. Allen, eds. & trans., *Maximus the Confessor and His Companions: Documents from Exile*, OECT, Oxford, 2002, 149–171.

Neil, B., & P. Allen, trans., *The Letters of Gelasius I (492–496): Pastor and Micro-Manager of the Church of Rome*, Adnot. 1, Turnhout, 2014.

Neil, B., & P. Allen, *Conflict and Negotiation in the Early Church: Letters from Late Antiquity, Translated from the Greek, Latin and Syriac*, Washington DC, 2020.

Noble, T.F.X., *The Republic of St Peter: The Birth of the Papal State 680–825*, Philadelphia, 1984.

Norberg, D., ed., CCSL 140 & 140A, 2 vols., Turnout, 1982.

Rennie, K.R., *The Foundations of Medieval Papal Legation*, London, 2013.

Salzman, M.R. "Lay Aristocrats and Ecclesiastical Politics: A New View of the Papacy of Felix III (483–492 CE) and the Acacian Schism," *JECS* 27, 2019, 465–489.

BRONWEN NEIL

Apocriticus

A certain Macarius Magnes, or "Makarios the Magnesian," compiled a work known under the title "A.". It is one of three surviving comparable apologies dealing with and quoting extensively from pagan intellectual attacks on Christianity. However, the A. has received less interest than → Origen's *Contra Celsum* or → Cyril of Alexandria's *Contra Julianum* by modern scholarship so far (see Volp, 2013b, ix–xxxii). Dating and localizing the A. is still a matter of controversy (see below). The meaning and implications of the full title Μακαρίου Μάγνητος Ἀποκριτικὸς ἢ Μονογενής πρὸς Ἕλληνας ("A. or Monogenes by Macarius Magnes to the Greeks"), are also debated (ibid.). The Christological term Μονογενής ("only-begotten") is used 17 times in the surviving portions of the A. Instead of A., John Malalas and John Carpathius know of the term ἀπόκρισις (an answering). The A., as the term implies, is divided into *Quaestiones* and *Solutiones* ("Questions and Solutions") as was typical for a classic Erotapokrisis (see Papadoyannakis, 2006) although those of the A. are longer and less stereotypical than one would normally expect. A. is perhaps a secondary title (see Goulet, 2003, 44). However, the work also lacks the degree of interaction normally present in a dialogue, although its author introduces some dramatic elements into the pagan-Christian exchange which he claims to have recorded for a certain Theostenes (see the preface to Book 3 and 4). The second title, πρὸς Ἕλληνας ("to the Greeks"), is a more common title of Christian apologetic literature, mostly written by converts who had been asked to write a testimony of their new Christian faith (see Kinzig, 2000). Hence, it seems to belong to a tradition with similar texts by Justin Martyr, Tatian, Apollinaris, Pseudo-Justin Martyr (*CPG* 1082), and Tertullian. The A. was perhaps not intended for publication which would explain its numerous repetitions and prolixity. The title πρὸς Ἕλληνας may also have been chosen in order to signal that it represented a philosophical ἔλεγχος ("refutation") rather than an instructional work from an academic or missionary context for which προτρεπτικός ("exhortation") would have been used. This would also justify the format of the text, and the use of rhetorical "weapons" from the pagan tradition, allowing for an aggressive tone and a certain freedom in dealing with the *Quaestiones*: the ἔλεγχος traditionally permits the disclosure of its own arguments, which do not respond directly to the attacks of the enemy, but may significantly stray from it. Even though the A. is hardly the transcript of a slanging match between a Christian and a pagan opponent, it is characterized by an atmosphere of harassment, threat and perhaps prosecution which may contribute to fixing a plausible date of its composition (see below).

The main source for the surviving text is C. Blondel's transcription (see Blondel, 1876) of the Codex Atheniensis which was discovered in 1867, but was subsequently lost. It contained a portion from the middle of the second to the middle of the fourth book. The Codex Vaticanus Graecus 1650, folio 187, contains tables of contents of Books 1–3 which were first published by G. Mercati (1941). Further fragments survive in Nic. *Epik.* 12.37–51, because the A. was quoted from during the Byzantine iconoclasm debate in the 9th century CE (see Featherstone, 2002). The Jesuit scholar Turrianus used the A. as an authority against the Lutherans in the 16th century. They both provide some more text, some of it in Latin translation, and from different manuscripts (see Goulet, 2003, and Volp, 2013b, for all of these fragments).

1. Authorship and Date

The A. consists of a series of anti-Christian *Quaestiones* by a "Greek" (ὁ Ἕλλην) who had a profound knowledge of Christian doctrine and the biblical books, especially the Gospels and the epistles of Paul (→ Paul the Apostle). The *Quaestiones* are provided together with *Solutiones* by a Christian (Macarius?)

that refute them. The authorship of these texts is still controversial. In the 18th century, M. Le Quien identified Macarius with a → bishop from Magnesia who, according to Phot. *Bibl.* 59, appeared before the Synod ad Quercum (403 CE) as a prosecutor against Heraclides, bishop of Ephesus. A. von Harnack (1911, 16), and R. Goulet (1977, 45), agreed with M. Le Quien – without this theory, however, being generally accepted as a result. The text is probably the result of the work of two or even three authors (Goulet suspected editorial layers), because the texts differ in style and vocabulary. *Quaestiones* and *Solutiones* quote from different editions of the Bible, and the type of argument changes quite markedly: strictly exegetical observations are used alongside arguments from popular philosophical teachings, a stringent and focused reasoning is followed by poetic (referring to the tragedians, Homer and Hesiod) and linguistically overloaded passages. There have been a number of suggestions as to the authorship of the *Quaestiones*: an anonymous 2nd-century CE writer (Turrianus), → Porphyry of Tyre (Crusius, 1857; Harnack, 1916; Hoffmann, 1944; Rinaldi, 1989), the Roman emperor → Julian the Apostate (Frassinetti, 1949), and Sossianus Hierocles (Duchesne, 1877; Crafer, 1907; Depalma Digeser, 2002; see Goulet, 2003, 14–40).

The text itself provides no evidence for an episcopal office having been held by its author. However, a certain bishop Macarius of Magnesia played a key role in the victory over the Origenists at the Synod ad Quercum (403 CE), which is hard to reconcile with the Origenism of the *Solutiones*. Their Trinitarian terminology include οὐσία ("being"; the "Cappadocian" formula τρεῖς ὑποστάσεις ἐν οὐσίᾳ μιᾷ ["three substances in one being"] in A. 4.25 may be an interpolation, however), presupposing the Nicene controversies of the 4th century CE. The A. identifies several regions which the gospel had not yet reached (4.13), but which had in fact been Christianized at least since the middle of the 4th century CE. Paul is said to have been dead for about 300 years (4.2, but the correct reading of this passage is still being debated, see the different possible readings in U. Volp [2013b, 316]). The general atmosphere of persecution against the Christians described above may be an argument against too late a dating after about 380 CE. E. Depalma Digeser assumes that the "last

Christian persecution ends in 313" (2002, 485). However, later situations also posed a threat to Christian believers, for example in the uncertain years during and after the reign of Emperor Julian (361–363). The situation seemed for many to be finally decided only after Theodosius rose to power in 379 CE. Arians (→ Arianism) – who are not openly considered to be heretical in the A. – were also finally condemned only then. Such a dating of the A. to the second half of the 4th century CE, but before the reign of Theodosius was first suggested by C. Blondel end P.F. Foucart (1876) and recently argued for by U. Volp (2011; 2013b).

2. Content

The fictional setting of the A. is a five day rhetorical dispute, reported in five books, of which only one has survived in its entirety. The pagan opponent always begins with a series of seven to ten objections which are then responded to by the Christian, before the pagan resumes the discussion with new *Quaestiones*. Whether it really is a transcript (see Crafer, 1907; Depalma Digeser, 2002), an excerpt of another work (Harnack, 1911) or a free compilation of similarly structured pagan attacks on Christianity is, for the reasons given above, controversial. It lacks a stringent final editing as well as a focus on a particular readership, so it may not have been intended for publication at all. The A. also does not follow a unifying systematic structure, but the order of the *Quaestiones* at least in part results from the sequence of the biblical texts discussed.

The *Quaestiones* criticize the behavior of Jesus in the New Testament writings which reveal him to be an ordinary man with weaknesses and inconsistencies (e.g. 3.19). From the middle of the 3rd book onwards, Peter (→ Peter the Apostle) and then Paul (→ Paul the Apostle) are portrayed as cowardly, devious and contradictory. Towards the end of the 3rd book fundamental issues come into view such as the Pauline ethics, then, in the 4th book, cosmology and eschatology with reference to Paul and the *Apocalypse of Peter* (→ Peter the Apostle), the irrationality of the Christian doctrine of → baptism and → monotheism or polytheism with the superiority of the temples and statues, the → incarnation and

the → resurrection. The main target of criticism is the person of the Son of God himself, whose revelation in secret and in the company of unworthy and insignificant people is anything but worthy of a God (2.14) – not to mention the humiliation of the Passion (3.1f.; see the similar criticism in Or. *Cels.* 2.24, 35). The author is an outspoken polytheist who strongly opposes the idea of a universe created by one God (2.15; see Volp, 2013a). Pagan philosophy, on the other hand, believes in an eternal, hierarchically ordered universe (4.1) directed by a universal providence (3.32) which ensures the proper functioning of the whole. The Christian idea of angels is also regarded as supporting polytheistic and anthropomorphic teachings of God (4.21; → Anthropomorphism). The Christian doctrine of the resurrection of the → body and the destruction of the heavenly bodies, the idea of an end of all times contradict this view of the world in an unreasonable manner (4.1–7). The idea of a bodily resurrection of an already decayed body defies any logic to which God must also be subject to (4.24). The A.'s criticism of Christianity centers further on the criticism of Christian ethics (e.g. 3.5 and 4.8; see Volp, 2009). Matt 10:24 is criticized in the (non-surviving) chapter 2.7 as inhumane, as the harsh conduct of Jesus illustrates (2.10 with reference to Matt 17:17) or indeed his disregard for the lives of defenseless animals (3.4 with reference to Mark 5:13). Peter (3.22) and Paul (3.30–36) are described as fickle, contradictory and mercenary. Finally, the pagan author criticizes the literary approach of the evangelists (see Porphyry according to Eus. *Hist. eccl.* 6.19.2, and Hierocles according to Eus. *Hier.* 2): John and Matthew are seen as storytellers, not historians, since they had become entangled in contradictions and reported very conflicting versions of Jesus' death which is why they should not be trusted in other respects.

The unsystematic responses of Makarios follow the order of the *Quaestiones*, without always focusing on the exact line of thought of the *Quaestiones*. Despite the absence of a systematically structured theological concept, his idea of the divine plan of salvation dominates all other subjects (see Waelkens, 1974), including the important doctrine of God as Creator, sin, ethics and eschatology. The Christian's other, main ambition, however, seems to show a rhetorical mastery that outguns the pagan's literal abilities. The *Solutiones*' linguistic creativity and tireless efforts to pile up words and arguments against the more concise pagan *Quaestiones*, however, impeded modern reception – and translation – for a long time.

3. Importance

The A.'s importance arises not from the originality and singularity of its argument. *Quaestiones* and *Solutiones* are prime examples of a well testified tradition of pagan criticism of Christianity and its Christian rebuttal. Outstanding, however, is the scope and extent of the pagan-Christian *Doppeltext* preserved in the A. with only Origen's *Contra Celsum* and Cyril of Alexandria's *Contra Iulianum* as rivals. The great anti-Christian writings of Porphyry and Hierocles and many others were destroyed by Christians. The A. is therefore a rare piece of evidence of a literal struggle between pagan philosophy and Christianity without which the literary and intellectual history of late antiquity cannot be adequately understood.

Bibliography

Barnes, T.D., "Porphyry Against the Christians: Date and Attribution of Fragments," *JThS* n.s. 24, 1973, 424–442.

Berchman, R.M., *Porphyry Against the Christians*, AMMTC 1, Leiden, 2005; ET of "Porphyrian" frgms. from A., 192–218.

Blondel, C., & P.F. Foucart, eds., *Makariou Magnetos Apokritikos e monogenes: Macarii Magnetis quae supersunt*, Paris, 1876.

Cook, J.G., *The Interpretation of the New Testament in Greco-Roman Paganism*, STAC 3, Tübingen, 2000, 168–249.

Corsaro, F., "L'Apocritico di Macario di Magnesia e le sacre scritture," *NUDI* 7, 1957, 1–24.

Corsaro, F., *La dottrina eucaristica di Macario di Magnesia*, CODO, 1959, 69–86.

Corsaro, F., *Le quaestiones nell'Apocritico di Macario di Magnesia: Testo con traduzione e introduzione critica*, Catania, 1968; *Quaestiones* only, text & Ital. trans.

Corsaro, F., "La reazione pagane nel iv secolo e l'Apocritico di Macario di Magnesia," *QCSCM* 6, 1984, 173–195.

Crafer, T.W., "Macarius Magnes: A Neglected Apologist," *JThS* 8, 1907, 401–426, 546–571.

Crafer, T.W., "The Work of Porphyry against the Christians, and its Reconstruction," *JThS* n.s. 15, 1914, 360–395, 481–512.

Crafer, T.W., *The Apocriticus of Macarius Magnes*, TCoL. GK, London, 1919; ET and summary of selected passages.

Crusius, M., "Macarius Magnes: Dissertatio historico-theologica," PG 10, Paris, 1857, 1343–1406.

Depalma Digeser, E., "Porphyry, Julian, or Hierokles? The Anonymous Hellene in Makarios Magnēs' Apokritikos," *JThS* 53, 2002, 466–502.

Duchesne, L., *De Macario Magnete et scriptis eius*, Paris, 1877.

Featherstone, J.M., "Opening Scenes of the Second Iconoclasm: Nicephorus's Critique of the Citations from Macarius Magnes," *REByz* 60, 2002, 65–112.

Frassinetti, P., "Sull'autore delle questioni pagane conservate nell'Apokritico di Macario di Magnesia," *NUDI* 3, 1949, 41–56.

Goulet, R., "La théologie de Macarios Magnès," *MSR* 34, 1977, 45–69, 145–180.

Goulet, R., "Porphyre et Macaire de Magnésie," *StPatr* 15, Oxford, 1984, 448–452.

Goulet, R., *Macarios Magnès: Apocriticus: Introduction générale, édition critique*, TeT 7, Paris, 2003; *Quaestiones* and *Solutiones*, crit. text, Fr. trans. & Comm.

Harnack, A. von, *Kritik des Neuen Testaments von einem griechischen Philosophen des 3. Jahrhunderts: Die im Apocriticus des Macarius Magnes enthaltene Streitschrift*, TU 37/3, Berlin, 1911; *Quaestiones* only, text and Ger. trans.

Harnack, A. von, *Porphyrius, Gegen die Christen: 15 Bücher: Zeugnisse, Fragmente und Referate*, APAW.PH, Berlin, 1916; selected *Quaestiones* attributed to Porphyry: vol. I, 5, 5; vol. II, 13, 15f., 18 (Turrianus), 23–36; vol. III, 48–55, 57–64, 67–69, 71f.; vol. IV, 74–78, 87–90a; 94; vol. V, 95f.

Hoffmann, R.J., *Against the Christians: The Extracts of Macarius Magnes*, Amhurst, 1994; *Quaestiones* only, ET.

Kinzig, W., "Überlegungen zum Sitz im Leben der Gattung Πρὸς Ἕλληνας/Ad nationes," in: R. von Haehling, ed., *Rom und das himmlische Jerusalem: Die frühen Christen zwischen Anpassung und Ablehnung*, Darmstadt, 2000, 152–183.

Magny, A., "Porphyry in Fragments: Jerome, Harnack, and the Problem of Reconstruction," *JECS* 18, 2010, 515–555.

Mercati, G., *Per l'Apocritico di Macario Magnete*, StT 95, Vatican City, 1941, 49–74; frgms. from *Vaticanus Graecus*, 1650.

Palm, J., "Textkritisches zum Apokritikos des Macarius Magnes," *ScMi* 4, Lund, 1961.

Papadoyannakis, Y., "Instruction by Question and Answer: The Case of Late Antique and Byzantine Erotapokriseis," in: S.F. Johnson, ed., *Greek Literature in Late Antiquity: Dynamism, Didacticism, Classicism*, Aldershot, 2006, 91–106.

Rinaldi, G., *Biblia gentium: Primo contributo per un indice delle citazioni, dei riferimenti e delle allusioni alla bibbia negli autri pagani, Greci e Latini, di età imperial*, Rome, 1989.

Volp, U., Beobachtungen zur antiken Kritik an den Begründungszusammenhängen christlicher Ethik, in: F.W. Horn & R. Zimmermann, eds., *Jenseits von Indikativ und Imperativ: Kontexte und Normen neutestamentli-*

cher Ethik/Contexts and Norms of New Testament Ethics, vol. I, WUNT 238, Tübingen, 2009, 347–365.

Volp, U., "'... for the fashion of this world passeth away': The Apokritikos by Makarios Magnes – an Origenist's Defense of Christian Eschatology?" in: S. Kaczmarek & H. Pietras, eds., *Origeniana Decima: Origen as Writer*, BEThL 244, Louvain, 2011, 873–889.

Volp, U., "Der Schöpfergott und die Ambivalenzen seiner Welt: Das Bild vom Schöpfergott als ethisches Leitbild im frühen Christentum in seiner Auseinandersetzung mit der philosophischen Kritik," in: H.-G. Nesselrath & F. Wilk, eds., *Gut und Böse in Mensch und Welt: Philosophische und religiöse Konzeptionen vom Alten Orient bis zum frühen Islam*, ORA 10, Tübingen, 2013a, 143–159.

Volp, U., *Makarios Magnes: Apokritikos: Kritische Ausgabe mit deutscher Übersetzung*, TU 169, Berlin, 2013b; *Quaestiones* and *solutiones*, crit. text & Ger. trans.

Wagenmann, J.A., "Porphyrius und die Fragmente eines Ungenannten in der athenischen Makariushandschrift," *JDT* 23, Gotha, 1878, 269–314; *Quaestiones* only, Ger. trans.

Schalkhausser, G., *Zu den Schriften des Makarius von Magnesia*, TU 37/4, Berlin, 1907.

Waelkens, R., *L'economie, thème apologetique et principe hermeneutique dans l'Apocritique de Macarios Magnes*, Louvain, 1974.

ULRICH VOLP

Apocrypha → Bible: III. Apocrypha and Pseudepigrapha

Apokatastasis

The notion of *apokatastasis* (ἀποκατάστασις) is that of restoration or restitution to an original state, from ἀποκαθίστημι, "I restore, reconstitute, return."

In Greek the term *apokatastasis* had a variety of applications, from the medical field (somebody's restoration to health from illness; a displaced limb's restoration to its proper place) to the military or political (somebody's restoration to one's military unit or homeland after expulsion or exile) and especially the astronomical (the return of a heavenly body to its original place after a revolution, or of all heavenly bodies to their original positions after a whole cosmic cycle). The cosmological meaning was prominent in Stoicism, where the doctrine of *apokatastasis* implied the cyclical repetition of cosmic ages or eons (→ Aeon), in each of which the same people live, making always the same choices, and all events are repeated, identical or almost identical every eon. The sequence of eons was considered infinite, since the universe itself has neither beginning nor end.

The Christian doctrine of *apokatastasis*, that is, the restoration of all rational creatures, or the whole cosmos, or all human beings to God – the good – in the end, took a number of forms in the many theologians who supported it. But it differs from the Stoic *apokatastasis* theory essentially in two respects:

1. The sequence of eons or ages is not infinite, but it had a beginning with creation and will have an end with *apokatastasis* itself.
2. Each aeon is different from the others because it results from rational creatures' freewill and not necessity.

These two elements of differentiation from Stoic *apokatastasis* are especially clear in → Origen of Alexandria, the first Christian major supporter of this doctrine. However, Origen is not the inventor of this doctrine. → Bardaisan already supported it, and → Clement of Alexandria presented it in a seminal form (Ramelli, 2009; 2012b). Ancient Christian pseudepigrapha, too, suggested it, such as the *Apocalypse of Peter* (→ Peter the Apostle), which Clement knew and deemed inspired like the rest of what became the New Testament. There, the damned are said to be removed by Jesus from the otherworldly "river of fire" to a place of blessedness thanks to the intercession of the just. In Gnosticism (→ Gnosis/Gnosticism), too, the notion of *apokatastasis* emerges with a certain prominence, but in general not as universal – "hylic" or material people are excluded therefrom – and not joined to the resurrection of the body (Ramelli, 2012a; → Resurrection).

The *apokatastasis* doctrine spread in Greek and Latin patristics (→ Patrology/Patristics), until Eriugena. The principal supporters then were → Origen, Didymus the Blind, → Eusebius of Caesarea, → Macrina Junior, → Gregory of Nyssa, → Evagrius of Pontus, and the theologians of the Antiochene school, → Diodore of Tarsus and → Theodore of Mopsuestia. The last two based their *apokatastasis* doctrine especially on the argument of the commensurability between sins (finite) and punishment (which cannot be eternal) and on the consideration that the resurrection must be a good and not an evil, as it would be for those who will rise to eternal damnation. Sin is limited; Origen, Methodius of Olympus, Gregory of Nyssa, and others deemed physical death providential, in that it puts a limit to sin and reveals the finitude of → evil, thus eliminating an eternity of evil and an eternity of condemnation. Origen and Gregory of Nyssa based their *apokatastasis* doctrine on the ontological nonsubsistence of evil – which will vanish in the end just as it did not exist in the beginning – God's goodness, rational creatures' freewill, and scriptural passages such as 1 Cor 15:28 (after the elimination of evil and death and the submission of all enemies to Christ, which Origen and Gregory of Nyssa deemed voluntary, "God will be all in all") and Acts 3:21 (the return of Christ will be at "the time of the restoration of all," ἀποκατάστασις πάντων). Evil, which is a lack of good, will vanish, "returning to its original nature": nonbeing. For no one will choose it anymore.

In the Latin world, Rufinus, the early → Jerome, and the early → Augustine of Hippo (Ramelli, 2013b, 2013c) all upheld *apokatastasis*. In *mor.* 2.7.9 Augustine declared: "God's goodness [*Dei bonitas*] [...] orders all creatures [*omnia*] that have fallen [...] until they return to the original state from which they fell." In Syriac patristics, Isaac of Nineveh is the most fascinating supporter, but by no means the only one. This line continued in the Middle Ages, with Julian of Norwich (to whom Jesus reveals: "All shall be well," "I shall make all things well," "I shall make well all that is less," and "the Trinity shall make well all that is not well"), in the Renaissance with the rediscovery of Origen, the Cambridge Platonists, J. Lead(e), and the modern age up to recent and contemporary theology (H.U. von Balthasar, K. Rahner, J. Moltmann, J. Hick, T. Talbott, D.B. Hart, etc.). Each of these has produced his or her own arguments.

But the main arguments were put forward already in the patristic age (analyzed critically in Ramelli, 2013b). Before Christianity, no religion or philosophy had maintained universal restoration, not even Plato. Origen indeed corrected Plato's statement that some persons are too deeply plunged into evil to be curable: Origen rather declared that nothing is impossible for the omnipotent, no being is incurable for Christ *logos* who created it, echoing Matt 19:26;

Mark 10:27; and Luke 18:27 ("impossible to humans, but nothing is impossible to God"). Neoplatonists such as Macrobius and Proclus seem to have maintained it, but then pagan → Neoplatonism cannot be deemed absolutely impermeable to Christianity. In any case Neoplatonic *apokatastasis* differs from the patristic doctrine, for example in that it excludes the resurrection of the body (Ramelli, 2017). Patristic *apokatastasis* is also christocentric, especially in Bardaisan, Origen, Gregory of Nyssa, Evagrius, and Eriugena. It is based on Christ's → incarnation, death, and → resurrection, and on God's being the supreme good. It is grounded in God's grace and the divine will "that all humans be saved and reach the knowledge of Truth" (1 Tim 2:4). The *apokatastasis* doctrine is embedded in a broad tradition, rooted in the New Testament and Jewish universalistic expectations.

Origen and Gregory of Nyssa also founded their *apokatastasis* theory on ethical intellectualism, in line with Socrates and Plato: what one chooses depends on what one knows; the choice for evil cannot be free. It comes from an ill or obfuscated mind, which has to be cured and illuminated by Christ *logos*. In addition, many church fathers realized that the understanding of αἰώνιος as "eternal" in scriptural references to otherworldly → fire, punishment, and → death is linguistically untenable (Ramelli & Konstan, 2007). Universal *apokatastasis* is compatible with free will, of which Origen was one of the strongest assertors, since all will adhere to the good, God, voluntarily in the end. And this will be better than the beginning, in that in the end the good will be chosen voluntarily and will not be just given from the outside. The final unity in *apokatastasis*, in Origen's view, will be a unity of will more than of substances, a unity of love and participation in God, who represents all possible goods. Thus, God will be "all in all." Within their christocentric and theocentric concept of *apokatastasis*, Origen, Gregory of Nyssa, → Gregory of Nazianzus, Rufinus, and (initially) Augustine employed a specifically theological argument in support of the *apokatastasis* theory: the eternal damnation of human beings or rational creatures is unworthy of God.

Basil of Caesarea, Theophilus of Alexandria, Augustine, and others indicate that up to the end of the 4th century CE, many Christians adhered to the *apokatastasis* doctrine (→ Basil of Caesarea; → Theophilus of Alexandria). Origen and Gregory of Nyssa supported it in defense of Christian orthodoxy: Origen against "Gnosticism" and Marcionism, and Gregory against → Arianism (Ramelli, 2013ab). All patristic supporters of *apokatastasis* were faithful to the Christian church; among them are many saints, such as Pamphilus of Caesarea, Gregory of Nyssa, Macrina, Gregory of Nazianzus, Evagrius, Isaac of Nineveh, Maximus the Confessor, and many others, including Jerome and Augustine for a certain time (Ramelli, 2013c). For Gregory of Nyssa, the eventual *apokatastasis* will be both the οἰκείωσις ("becoming familiar with") of all creatures to God, who is their πρῶτον οἰκεῖον (the primary most familiar thing), but also and especially the godhead's own definitive act of οἰκείωσις or reappropriation of what belongs to it, in other words all of its creatures, which were alienated by evil. In *In Illud: Tunc et Ipse Filius*, Gregory depicts the final march of the good, which conquers all evil, from the slightest to the worst. Destruction of evil coincides with the transformation of all sinners and their return to the good/God.

Historiography

Interest in the doctrine of *apokatastasis* has been alive from the Renaissance onwards, and many pamphlets and popular publications have been produced, or partial studies (such as Ludlow, 2000, on Gregory of Nyssa). But the first scientific, comprehensive, and detailed study of *apokatastasis* in all of Patristics (1st to 9th cents. CE) has been provided by I. Ramelli (2013b). This monograph, along with other articles, has demonstrated the biblical and philosophical foundations of the doctrine of *apokatastasis* in ancient Christianity, its Christological gist and close relation to the defense of orthodoxy, and its widespread diffusion. Further work is needed, and underway, on the rejection of the doctrine of *apokatastasis* by the "Church of the Empire," under the influence of Justinian in the East and Augustine in the West. Another line of investigation, which is being pursued, concerns a comparison between the patristic doctrine of *apokatastasis* and pagan philosophical doctrines of *apokatastasis*, from the pre-Socratics to late Neoplatonism (Proclus, Damascius).

Bibliography

Hart, D.B., *That All Shall Be Saved: Heaven, Hell, and Universal Salvation*, New Haven, 2019.

Ludlow, M., *Universal Salvation: Eschatology in the Thought of Gregory of Nyssa and Karl Rahner*, Oxford, 2000.

Ramelli, I., "Christian Soteriology and Christian Platonism: Origen, Gregory of Nyssa, and the Biblical and Philosophical Basis of the Doctrine of Apokatastasis," *VigChr* 61, 2007, 313–356.

Ramelli, I., "Origen, Bardaisan, and the Origin of Universal Salvation," *HThR* 10, 2009, 135–168.

Ramelli, I., "Origen and Apokatastasis: A Reassessment," in: S. Kaczmarek & H. Pietras, eds., *Origeniana Decima*, Louvain, 2011a, 649–670.

Ramelli, I., "Gregory of Nyssa's Trinitarian Theology in *In Illud: Tunc et ipse Filius*," in: V.H. Drecoll & M. Berghaus, eds., *Gregory of Nyssa: The Minor Treatises on Trinitarian Theology and Apollinarism*, Leiden, 2011b, 445–478.

Ramelli, I., "Apokatastasis in Coptic Gnostic Texts from Nag Hammadi," *JCST* 14, 2012a, 33–45.

Ramelli, I., "*Stromateis* VII and Clement's Hints of the Theory of Apokatastasis," in: M. Havrda et al., eds., *The Seventh Book of the Stromateis*, Leiden, 2012b, 239–257.

Ramelli, I., "Harmony between *arkhē* and *telos* in Patristic Platonism and the Imagery of Astronomical Harmony Applied to the Apokatastasis Theory," *IJPLT* 7, 2013a, 1–49.

Ramelli, I., *The Christian Doctrine of Apokatastasis: A Critical Assessment from the New Testament to Eriugena*, Leiden, 2013b.

Ramelli, I., "Origen and Augustine: A Paradoxical Reception," *Numen* 60, 2013c, 280–307.

Ramelli, I., "Basil and Apokatastasis: New Findings," *JECH* 4.2, 2014, 116–136.

Ramelli, I., "Proclus of Constantinople and Apokatastasis," in: D. Butorac and D. Layne, *Proclus and His Legacy*, Berlin, 2017, 95–122.

Ramelli, I., "From God to God: Eriugena's Protology and Eschatology Against the Backdrop of His Patristic Sources," in: I. Ramelli, ed., *Eriugena's Christian Neoplatonism and its Sources in Patristic and Ancient Philosophy*, Louvain, 2021, 99–123.

Ramelli, I., "Origen, Evagrius, and Dionysius," in: M. Edwards, D. Pallis & G. Steiris, eds., *Oxford Handbook of Dionysius the Areopagite*, Oxford, 2022, 94–108.

Ramelli, I., "Christology and Universal Salvation (Apokatastasis)," in: J. Barter, ed., *Encyclopaedia of Christian Theology, Christology*, London, 2023.

Ramelli, I., & D. Konstan, *Terms for Eternity: Aionios and Aidios in Classical and Christian Authors*, Piscataway, 2007, ²2011.

ILARIA L.E. RAMELLI

Apollinarian Forgeries
→ Anonymous Appolinarist/
Apollinarian Forgeries

Apollinaris of Hierapolis

Claudius Apollinaris, bishop of Hierapolis, was an early Christian apologist who flourished in the 2nd century CE during the reign of Emperor Marcus Aurelius. He wrote a number of texts referred to by early Christian historians; he focused on attacking the Phrygian heresy (→ Montanism/Montanists) and → Marcion. Unfortunately some of the evidence about this is erroneous; → Eusebius of Caesarea (*Hist. eccl.* 5.16–18) contradicts himself in the details he provides. In common with many of the heretics whose works were refuted by apologists, virtually none of Apollinaris' writings has survived, but this has not been confirmed by modern scholars and no critical editions exist.

1. Dates and Identity

Apollinaris is listed among the Greek apologists alongside → Melito of Sardis, who was writing after → Justin Martyr. He lived at the same time as the historian → Hegesippus, who also wrote refutations against → heresy (*Hist. eccl.* 4.21, 26), in five volumes of memoirs on his return from Rome. Apollinaris' see was in the city Phrygia on the river Maeander (modern-day Pamukkale in Turkey), and he was appointed during the reign of Marcus Aurelius (161–180 CE). His feast day is Jan 8. He may have associated with Polycrates and was perhaps known to the influential martyred bishop → Polycarp of Smyrna and influenced by him: → Irenaeus of Lyon was another of Polycarp's pupils, which adds credence to the suggestion that Apollinaris was part of a circle of apologists as he, too, was an inveterate writer against heresy. The date of his death cannot be determined. Some of the references by Eusebius suggest that Montanism was, "as it were, beginning to sprout, while Montanus with his false prophecies

was making the beginnings of the error" (*Hist. eccl.* 4.27), but elsewhere in his very long citations from the text he refers to "the false prophecies of Maximilla," who he states as having died nearly 14 years previously, which places it outside the lifetime of Apollinaris (*Hist. eccl.* 5.16f.). The references here to peacetime help with a dating of this episode to before the wars of Septimus Severus. He probably died before Marcus Aurelius, in 180 CE. There is no evidence of a cult to Apollinaris having begun immediately after his death, but he was added to the Roman martyrology by Baronius in 1586.

2. Christian Apologetics in the 2nd Century CE

Christian → apologetics flourished as a genre of writing in the 2nd century CE, when no more apostles with firsthand knowledge of Christ's teachings remained alive and a new criterion of authenticity evolved, often allied to martyrdom (→ Martyrs). The refutations of heresies contained in these texts paved the way for the doctrinal statements issued by ecumenical councils from the 4th century CE onward, by beginning to draw boundaries around what was acceptable Christian teaching, with heterodox teachings being condemned as heresy, their promulgators anathematized and sympathizers excommunicated. "Apologies," being the reverse of what their name suggests in common parlance, might be addressed to new converts, Jews, philosophers, and heretics. From the second quarter of the 2nd century CE, apologetics became one of the most dominant forms of Christian witness and often expressed critique of both religious and political practices. They were sometimes dedicated to emperors in the hope that they would promote the Christian message and gain socially influential converts to the faith. In the case of Marcus Aurelius, this aim was only partially achieved. → Persecutions of Christians and others continued apace, however, until the Edict of Milan in 313 CE, when all religions became subject to imperial toleration and fewer instances of persecution took place.

3. Main Works of Apollinaris of Hierapolis

The writings attributed to Apollinaris include a long *Defence of the Faith* dedicated to Emperor Marcus Aurellius in 172 CE (referred to and extensively cited by Eus. *Hist. eccl.* 5.16), five treatises *Against the Pagans* and two each on *Truth* and *Against the Jews* (*Hist. eccl.* 4.27). In the 7th century CE, the unknown author of the *Chronicon Pascale* cites two fragments from a text on → Easter, attributing them to Apollinaris, but this is unconfirmed. In the 9th century CE, Photius added to this collection of writings by Apollinaris a treatise *On Piety*. Jerome *Ep. 70 ad Magnus IV* (PL 23) suggests that Apollinaris, along with Eusebius, Methodius, and → Origen, wrote against → Celsus, suggesting a copious number of tracts.

In his apology Apollinaris reminded Marcus Aurelius that the victorious 12th legion of the Roman army had been largely composed of Christians. Among other miracles invoked by these soldiers was a miraculous shower that provided them with desperately needed drinking water during a battle and an accompanying tempest with lightning so dramatic it blinded the enemy; this, Apollinaris allegedly wrote, caused the legion to be known as "the Thundering Legion" on account of their extraordinary ability to invoke natural phenomena to aid their success. Compelling though this story is, it is sadly an enthusiastic and anachronistic interpretation by Eusebius; the so-called *Legio duodecima Fulminata* (legion armed with lightning) had been raised by Julius Caesar in 58 BCE, though the name was later changed to *Legio Fulminatrix* (*Hist. eccl.* 5.18). Marcus Aurelius was seen by some as a champion of Christian orthodoxy in the face of gnostic heresy (→ Gnosis/Gnosticism); equally he was determined not to allow the state pagan religion to be undermined by other cults, and this included Christianity. Eusebius records severe persecutions under this emperor in Lyon and Vienne.

4. Reception of Apollinaris' Works

There are references to Apollinaris' Apologetics in several sources, including Eusebius of Caesarea, → Jerome, and → Theodoret of Cyrrhus, that confirm his status as a defender of orthodox teaching. By some he was even compared to Justin Martyr, who had been put to death in 165 CE.

Christian apologetics formed part of a fierce dialogue with the heresiarchs it attacked. Claim and counterclaim bounce off each other, and both sides attracted large followings. This means it was possible for either side to suppress the manuscripts; it is rare for either the apologetic material or what it attacks to survive. In Eusebius' account Serapion of Antioch refers to a letter by "the late most blessed bishop at Hierapolis in Asia" against the "lying organization called the new Prophecy" (Montanism; *Hist. eccl.* 5.19), but as there were many writers of anti-Montanist apolegetics, so it cannot be proven that our Apollinaris was the author of this tract.

Bibliography

Altaner, B., *Patrologie: Leben, Schriften und Lehre der Kirchenväter*, Freiburg, 1978, 109–110.

Bareille, G., "Apollinaris," in: A. Vacant, ed., *DThC*, vol. I, Paris, 1923, 1407–1408.

Day, E., "Apollinaris of Hierapolis," in: T. Carson & J. Cerrito, eds., *NCE*, vol. I, Washington DC, 2003, 560.

Doyle, P., ed., *Butler's Lives of the Saints*, 12 vols., Chicago, 1999.

Dulles, A., *A History of Apologetics*, Eugene, 1999.

Edwards, M., *Catholicity and Heresy in the Early Church*, Farnham, 2009.

Farmer, D.H., "Apollinaris the Apologist," in: *ODS*, Oxford, 1978.

Ferguson, E., "Apollinaris of Hierapolis," in: *EOEC*, New York, 1997.

Frend, W.H.C., *The Archaeology of Early Christianity: A History*, London, 1996.

Grant, R.M., *Greek Apologists of the Second Century*, Philadelphia, 1988.

Labriolle, P. de, "Apollinaris of Hierapolis," in: A. Baudrillart, ed., *DHGE*, vol. III, Paris, 1912, 959–960.

Lightfoot, J.B., *Apostolic Fathers*, 3 vols., London, 1885.

Otto, J.C.T., *Corpus Apologetarum Christianorum*, vol. IX, Jenae, 1872, 479–495.

Quasten, J., *Apollinaris of Hierapolis*, Patr., vol. I, Utrecht, 1975, 228–229.

Quispel, G., "Valentinus and the Gnostikoi," *VigChr* 50, 1996, 1–4.

Rahner, H., "Claudius Apollinaris," in: *LThK*, vol. I, ed. J. Hofer & K. Rahner, Freiburg, 1957–1965, 713–714.

Routh, M.J., *Reliquiae Sacrae*, vol. I, Oxford, 1846, 155–174.

Walsh, M., ed., "Claudius Apollinaris, (St.), Bishop of Hierapolis," in: *DCB*, New York, 2001.

HANNAH HUNT

Apollinaris of Laodicea

A dichotomous view of Apollinarius of Laodicea (c. 315–c. 390 CE) prevailed throughout antiquity. On the one hand, he was the poet, the commentator on biblical works, the contemporary of Basil of Caesarea and Gregory of Nazianzus (Philost. *Hist. eccl.* 8.13), the teacher and exponent of Nicene orthodoxy. On the other hand, he was the source of a → heresy, and his followers were condemned from 377 CE onward at various synods, the first in Rome, and then from 383 CE on through imperial edicts. It was clearly proving increasingly difficult to maintain a uniform perspective on his character (Andrist, 2014).

The earliest reports are from Laodicea, where he and his father, of the same name, were clerics and both had received a literary education as teachers of grammar and → rhetoric, respectively (Soz. *Hist. eccl.* 6.25.9–11; Socr. *Hist. eccl.* 3.16.2). In his history of the church, → Sozomen first mentions Apollinarius in connection with the reign of → Julian the Apostate (361–363 CE). Julian had forbidden Christians from attending schools and from handling ancient poetry as teachers. Apollinarius, himself a teacher and gifted in every genre of literature, helped remedy the situation, as Sozomen (*Hist. eccl.* 5.18.2–4; see *Suda*) approvingly relates, providing, with his history of Israel up to the time of → David, cast into hexameter, an alternative to Homer as the textual basis for instruction. Gregory of Nazianzus (*Ep.* 101.73) speaks of a new psalter, while → Socrates Scholasticus divides the biblical texts between father and son. Sozomen (*Hist. eccl.* 5.18.6) also mentions an apologetic text, Ὑπὲρ ἀληθείας ("On behalf of the truth"). → Jerome (*Vir. ill.* 104) highlights Apollinarius' 30 books against Porphyry as one of his best works, but no fragments survived. On top of his literary and rhetorical talents, Apollinarius had received an excellent philosophical education, of which nothing more specific is known (Epiph. *Pan.* 7.24.8). Like many other heretics, Apollinarius was ascribed a certain knowledge of Aristotle. In any case, his use of methods of logic is plainly apparent in the surviving fragments of his work.

In the sixth book of his history of the church, while treating the reign of → Valens, Sozomen again includes a lengthy passage on Apollinarius, this time on Apollinarius the heretic: "During this period Apollinarius openly expounded the heresy named for him, separating many people from the church and collecting them to himself." Here again Sozomen alludes to Apollinarius' poetic gifts, mentioning that the new church employed his hymns to promote its message:

> His melodies are sung by men feasting and working and by women at the loom. For times both serious and restful, for festivals and other occasions, whatever fit the prevailing mood, he composed idylls, all serving to glorify God. (Soz. *Hist. eccl.* 6)

Sozomen inquires into the genesis of the new heresy and church and collates what is known of Apollinarius from earlier times. This includes Apollinarius' encounter with → Athanasius of Alexandria (Soz. *Hist. eccl.* 6.25.6–8). After his banishment was rescinded in 346 CE, Sozomen reports, Athanasius passed through Laodicea on his way to Alexandria, met there with Apollinarius, and became his friend. As consequence, according to Sozomen, Apollinarius was expelled from the church by George, bishop of Laodicea. This brief report tempts us to consider Apollinarius in parallel to the early Nicene Eustathius and Paulinus in Antioch, and to view him as a marginalized → Nicaea in Laodicea, perhaps associated with an early Nicene community there. But there is no evidence of this. Even Sozomen himself goes on to say that Apollinarius requested on several occasions that the homoean George rescind his excommunication, but the latter refused to do so (Soz. *Hist. eccl.* 6.26.13). It is reasonable to assume that there was a conflict between Apollinarius and George of Laodicea. But we can determine nothing specific about it. Altogether, the Athanasius episode is not suited as a source of information on Apollinarius' early years (Spoerl, 2014).

Sources on Apollinarius first appear in the early 360s CE. It is generally assumed that Apollinarius became bishop around 360 CE. Reference to monks serving under Apollinarius in the *Tomus ad Antiochenos* is often taken as evidence of this, though this appears only in the long version of the tomus. There are three texts by Apollinarius from the early 60s in which the doctrine of the → Trinity occupies a central position: Apollinarius' letter to → Basil of Caesarea, his letter to Jovian, and *Kata meros pistis*.

H. Lietzmann included *Kata meros pistis* in his collection of fragments, and the predominant practice is to view this detailed confession of faith as having been written by Apollinarius between 360 and 363 CE. *Kata meros pistis* is attributed in the manuscript to → Gregory Thaumaturgus, though Theodoret and later Leontius of Byzantium already quote from this text as a work of Apollinarius. The quotations, however, deviate significantly from the text edited by H. Lietzmann. He believes that the excerpts in Leontius are quotations from a completely reworked version of the text (Lietzmann, 1904, 132). The text by Apollinarius is, however, clearly evident in these quotations (a different view is taken by Mühlenberg, 1969, 100–104).

There is consensus that the correspondence between Basil and Apollinarius is genuine (Bas. *Ep.* 361–364). Basil (*Ep.* 361) asks Apollinarius for an explanation of the term ὁμοούσιος in view of the prohibition on using the term substance. Basil is thus referring to the Homoean creeds of 359/360 CE (fourth formula of Sirmium, 359 CE [Thdt. *Hist. eccl.* 21; Athan. *Syn.* 30], repeated in Constantinople 360 CE) and favors a Homoeousian explanation of the doctrine of the Trinity. Apollinarius is determined to uphold the Nicene ὁμοούσιος (Bas. *Ep.* 364). In his response to Basil (Bas. *Ep.* 362), he defines the consubstantiality of Father and Son with reference to relations of descent (Zachhuber, 2014). Just as every father passes on his nature to his son, the Son is the one God through descent from the one God. The Father is the origin (ἀρχή) of the Son, who (φυσικῶς ["by nature"]) possesses the paternal divinity. As the Son he is subordinate to the Father. In contradistinction to the Arians (→ Arianism), however, for Apollinarius the subordinate position of the Son remains within the doctrine of God's one substance. In *Kata meros pistis* Apollinarius begins with an anti-Arian stance and counters the Arian theory of God by stating that its subordination of the Son necessarily implies a division of the godhead through the coexistence of different parts. At the same time, he rejects any position that fails to conceive of the three Trinitarian persons as individuated (Apol. *Kat.* 2.167.18–168.4; Lietzmann, 1904). Apollinarius rejects the ἀνυπόστατον πρόσωπον (*Kat.* 13 [171.22; Lietzmann, 1904]; see *Kat.* 15 [172.10f.; Lietzmann, 1904]), but this does not lead him to apply the notion of hypostasis to the Trinitarian persons. He identifies the one substance of God primarily with the Father, which results in Son and Spirit occupying a subordinate position, but at the same time he was reluctant to apply the concept of hypostasis to Son and → Holy Spirit. This led to a discussion of whether Apollinarius deviates from the doctrine of the one hypostasis (Gemeinhardt, 2006; Spoerl, 2001).

Analysis of *Ad Iovianum* (Drecoll, 2014) shows that Apollinarius was in search of common ground with exponents of the intermediate Eusebian (anti-Marcellian) position and was looking to appeal to those potentially willing to embrace the Nicene ὁμοούσιος. It is in this light that we must interpret Bas. *Ep.* 362 to Basil. Apollinarius sought to win Basil over to the concept of ὁμοούσιος and provided him with ideas for his doctrine of the Trinity. So it was not just Basil and Athanasius, as evident in the *Tomus ad Antiochenos*, who sought to unite the Nicene Christians, but Apollinarius as well. This explains why he was remembered as a Nicene partisan. *Kata meros pistis* and Bas. *Ep.* 362, however, reflect the doctrine of the Trinity around 360 CE. Nothing is known concerning the later development of Apollinarius' views on the Trinity. It is reported that Apollinarius, like Basil, composed a text against Eunomius (Phot. *Lex.* 8.12; Jer. *Vir. ill.* 120).

Gregory of Nazianzus (*Ep.* 101.66f.) was the first to criticize Apollinarius' Trinitarian doctrine because, he asserts, Apollinarius assumes the existence of ranks within God and is thus teaching the subordination of Son and Spirit. → Theodoret of Cyrrhus makes a similar criticism. For him, Apollinarius' Trinitarian doctrine no longer met the requirements of an orthodox, 5th-century CE Nicene conception of the Trinity. In the late 6th and early 7th centuries CE, Theodoret was followed by Timotheus Constantinopolitanus, Georgius Monachus, and the author of *De sectis*, all of whom identify Apollinarius' Trinitarian doctrine as one of his heretical teachings. Recently, the text *Pseudo-Basilius, Contra Eunomium IV–V*, has been attributed to Apollinarius (Risch, 1992). Common features present in a number of texts that go beyond the usual Neo-Nicene commonalities play a key role in the attribution to Apollinarius or the Apollinarians of texts on the doctrine of Trinity.

Apollinarius' teachings are shaped in significant part by his desire to link the doctrine of the Trinity and Christology. The → incarnation of God, according to Apollinarius, has brought humanity salvation. But only God can bring salvation, which according to Apollinarius cannot be conceived as originating from outside of the Trinity, but only from within the divine subject. Corporeality thus cannot be separated from the triune God, and this finds expression in the formula of the one nature of the incarnate God. "His body and God, whose body he is, are one and the same." Apollinarius explains this unity by asserting that the Son of God assumed a human → body without a rational → soul, and in this incarnate form human reason was replaced by divine reason. In the early 60s, Apollinarius had yet to develop the Christological hallmarks later associated with his name. In *Ad Iovianum* we find the earliest evidence of the phrase μία φύσις τοῦ θεοῦ λόγου σεσαρκωμένη ("one incarnate nature of the word of god"), though there is no attestation in this text of the Christology that would later become so characteristic of Apollinarius (for a different view, see Lietzmann, 1904, 11; Karmann, 2009, 255). In *Ad Iovianum* the "two sons" doctrine is rejected. A distinction is made between the perspectives κατὰ πνεῦμα ("according to the spirit") and κατὰ σάρκα ("according to the flesh"). Apollinarius underlines that the one born of the *Theotokos* ("Mother of God, God-bearer") → Mary is the true God in his very nature and not through grace or participation (χάριτι καὶ μετουσίᾳ ["through grace or participation"]). This may betoken a conflict with Diodorus, who was also active in Antioch at the time. The clash between Diodorus and Apollinarius manifested itself in a number of texts (Apollinarius of Laodicea, *Contra Diodorum ad Heraclium* and *Ad Diodorum*, Πρὸς Διόδωρον ἢ Τὸ κεφάλειον βιβλίον; Lietzmann, 1904, frgms. 117–139; Diodorus of Tarsus, *Contra Synousiastas*) and was continued by → Theodore of Mopsuestia.

In *Ad Iovianum* the question of the soul remains unaddressed. But it is taken up in Athan. *Tom.* 7 (362 CE), which recounts the attempt by Athanasius to reconcile two Nicene groups, which possibly can be identified as the Paulinians and Meletians in Antioch, with the doctrine of the Trinity being the object of the conflict between them. In paragraph 7, however, reference is also made to a Christological dispute, and the consensus view is affirmed that "the Savior did not have a body without a soul,

incapable of perception and irrational." In the later 370th CE Apollinarius quotes these words, however, integrated and explained within his own concept (*Epistula ad Diocaesareenses*, Lietzmann, 1904, 256, ll. 7f).

In *Tom.* 7 the locution "body without a soul" appears in connection with an Antiochian dispute. One may assume that there had been a debate on the soul of Christ in Antioch involving Origenist ideas. Diodorus developed a Christology in which Jesus the man and therefore Jesus' soul plays a significant role, while he rejected the preexistence of this soul (on the fragments in the *Vatopedi-Florileg*, see Heimgartner, 2014) and defended himself against claims that he himself espoused Origenist notions. By disputing that Jesus possessed a soul or more precisely a rational soul, Apollinarius adopts a markedly anti-Origenist position. Starting in the mid-80s at the latest, Arius and Eunomius, and the Arians and Eunomians, were considered Apollinarius' forerunners with respect to the doctrine of a soulless Christ, as is evidenced in the work of → Gregory of Nyssa (*Antirrheticus adversus Apollinarium*). H.C. Brennecke (2014), however, has shown that there was no Arian Christology before the 70s. The question of the human soul played no role in the dispute with Arianism until → Epiphanius of Salamis. Only Eustathius of Antioch reproaches the Arians for teaching a Χριστὸς ἄψυχος (soulless Christ). This fragment is not sufficient evidence of an Arian doctrine of a soulless Christ (Uthemann, 2007). What it does demonstrate is the occurrence of an Antiochian debate in which Apollinarius was involved, and that exercised a significant influence on him, perhaps an even greater influence than Athanasius.

Writings of Apollinarius were already being spuriously attributed to Athanasius in connection with the Christological dispute in the 5th century CE. Yet there are in fact few points of contact between the two. Sozomen reports a positive statement by Apollinarius on Athanasius' election as bishop (Soz. *Hist. eccl.* 2.17.2–3, see *Epistula ad Diocaesareenses*; Lietzmann, 1904, 255, ll. 21–24). There is a note from the 6th century CE stating that Apollinarius' follower Timotheus went to Rome with a letter of recommendation from Athanasius requesting support for Apollinarius. Christology is not central to Athanasius' work. This has become particularly clear since

Contra Arianos IV is no longer attributed to Athanasius. Athanasius' silence on the topic of Christ's soul should not be interpreted as a position foreshadowing that of Apollinarius. Christ's soul was not (yet) a subject of debate for Athanasius. Only late on, in around 370 CE, in his letter to Epictetus, does Athanasius turn to opponents potentially from the same camp as Apollinarius. At issue here is the consubstantiality of the body with the divinity of the Son, a consequence of the idea that the Son or *logos*, through his own body, does not introduce a foreign element into the Trinity. Epiphanius of Salamis (*Pan.* 7.3–13) already cites the *Epistula ad Epictetum* in connection with the dispute with Apollinarius.

In Antioch in the early 70s, Apollinarius is caught up in the clash between Paulinus, recognized as bishop by Rome and favored by Athanasius, and Meletius, the bishop supported by Basil of Caesarea. Epiphanius went to Antioch to mediate between Vitalis, follower of Apollinarius, a bishop by this point, and Paulinus, also a bishop. Epiphanius distinguishes among followers of Apollinarius, who diverged significantly from one another in their convictions, Vitalis, and Apollinarius himself. Epiphanius rejects Vitalis' teaching that, in the incarnation, the Son of God had assumed a human body without a rational soul. In 375 CE (before the episcopal consecration and thus before Epiphanius' visit according to Cavarella and Mühlenberg), Vitalis traveled to Rome and presented a creed to Damasus that the latter temporarily acknowledged (Greg. Naz. *Ep.* 102). In 377 CE Timotheus, a follower of Apollinarius, again sought to gain recognition for the latter in Rome. Now, however, Apollinarius and his adherents were condemned there for heresy (Thdt. *Hist. eccl.* 5.10; Pseudo-Leontius, *Adversus fraudes Apollinistarum* ("Against the Frauds of the Apollinarists"); PG 86.1976.A). Basil tried but failed to achieve recognition for Meletius on this occasion. Rome continued to recognize Paulinus as bishop of Antioch.

During this period Apollinarius was still active in Antioch. Jerome continued to listen to his exegetical lectures (Jer. *Ep.* 84.3) without impairment. The tide turned when Meletius returned to Antioch (379 CE) following Gratian's accession to power and convened a major synod shortly afterward (Greg. Nyss. *Vita Mac.* 15). How this synod affected the Apollinarians cannot be determined. When the general Sapor arrived in Antioch, chiefly in order to regulate the property of the churches, three congregations put forward claims: those of Paulinus, Meletius, and Apollinarius. Apollinarius' congregation, Theodoret reports (*Hist. eccl.* 5.3), was not granted a church. It would soon fall foul of new heresy laws. The first of these was promulgated in Constantinople on Dec 3, 383 CE (Cod. Theod. 16.5.12). Like other heretics, Apollinarians are forbidden to gather in public or private in city or country, and they must not practice their religion or develop a clergy. Houses in which gatherings take place in contravention of the ban are passed to the *fiscus* ("state"). Adherents are to be sought out, and if not from Constantinople they are to be sent back home. The second edict of Jan 21, 384 CE (Cod. Theod. 16.5.13) is specifically concerned with the clergy. A third edict of Mar 10, 388 CE, repeats the prohibition on assembly and forbids Apollinarians from bearing the title of bishop (Cod. Theod. 16.5.13). The subsequent edict (Cod. Theod. 16.5.14), published on Jun 14, 388 CE, again threatened punishment. These laws and the gradual process of criminalization they entail did not prevent the spread of the Apollinarian church (see Soz. *Hist. eccl.* 7.12.11f.). This is can be seen from the fact that ten years later, on Apr 1, 397 CE, Apollinarian teachers are again expelled from Constantinople, and there is a repeat of the threat that houses in which gatherings take place will be passed to the *fiscus* (Cod. Theod. 16.5.33). In 428 CE a portion of the Apollinarians in Antioch merged with the recognized church (Thdt. *Hist. eccl.* 5.38.2). The same year saw a reaffirmation of the ban on Apollinarian churches in all cities; they were, however, spared the full consequences of infamy status (Cod. Theod. 16.5.65).

In the 380s CE → Gregory of Nazianzus wrote *Ep.* 202, in which he exhorts Nectarius, his successor as bishop of Constantinople, not to underestimate the Apollinarians and to move more forcefully against them (*Ep.* 202.7). Gregory himself had seen how Apollinarians in Nazianzus had built up a congregation and won numerous adherents. The letters to Cledonius (*Ep.* 101 and 102) indicate the basic themes of the arguments put forward by the Apollinarians in Nazianzus. Gregory was accused of teaching the existence of two sons, one human and one divine, and it was claimed that his defective concept of God/human unity made his followers "worshippers of human beings." Given that only the Trinity is a fit subject for worship, but the flesh and body of Jesus are worshipped, Apollinarius concludes that the flesh and body are not alien to the Trinity (Apol. *Fid.* 4f.; Lietzmann, 1904, 195.5–12.22–25). In *Ep.* 101.30 Gregory refers to the "flesh come down from heaven," though this likely represents an exaggeration of Apollinarius' ideas rather than anything he himself expressed. The concept of the soulless Christ is also fundamental in the account of Apollinarius' stance by Gregory of Nazianzus. There is also mention of a debate on Mary as God bearer (Greg. Naz. *Ep.* 101.16; see Theodor of Mopsuestia, *De incarnatione*, ACO 4.1.80.2–20; Jansen, 2009, 258f.).

Between 384 and 386 CE, in the *Antirrheticus adversus Apolinarium*, Gregory of Nyssa composes a refutation of Apollinarius' *Demonstratio de diuina incarnatione ad similitudinem hominis*. While Gregory of Nyssa has a tendency to overstate Apollinarius' views and to highlight consequences of his statements not articulated by Apollinarius himself, and while it is difficult to determine the boundaries of quotations, we can nevertheless discern the overall structure of Apollinarius' text, making the fragments recorded by Gregory an important source for Apollinarius' Christology. The shorter writings *De unione corporis et diuinitatis in Christo* (Lietzmann, 1904, 186–192) and *Epistula ad Dionysium I* (Lietzmann, 1904, 256–262) are also indispensable in reconstructing Apollinarius' Christology. Also worthy of note are the excerpts from Apollinarius' biblical commentaries found in the catenas (Mühlenberg, 1978).

Historiography

I.A. Dorner (1851), who values the achievements of Apollinarios highly, sees in his ideas the turning point in the history of dogma, shifting from the struggle over the doctrine of Trinity to its continuation into Christology. For I.A. Dorner the central point in Apollinarios is that he raised the question if Christ's humanity should be conceived personal or not.

Most important for modern research was, following work of G. Voisin, the edition of the fragments of Apollinarios by H. Lietzmann (1904). Since H. Lietzmann, the attribution of fragments and anonymously transmitted writings to Apollinarios has been an ongoing discussion (Hübner, 1989; Risch, 1992).

Apollinarius' Christology was outlined by G. Voisin (1901), C.E. Raven (1923), H. de Riedmatten (1948), R.A. Norris (1963), E. Mühlenberg (1969), A. Grillmeier (1979). Various points of contact to anthropology and philosophy were invoked as explanation. Since antiquity Apollinarios has been identified with his specific doctrine of Christology. That his ideas must be understood on the basis of the Nicene dogma has already been pointed out by C.E. Raven (1923). That our picture of Apollinarios have to be freed from the hindsight view and from the Chalcedonian orthodoxy has been demonstrated (Brennecke, 2014). The focus shifted towards Apollinarios' specific form of the dogma of Trinity and towards his writing *Kata Meros Pistis* (Gemeinhardt, 2006; Spoerl, 2001; 2015). H.J. Vogt (1995) drew attention to the exchange of letters with Basil of Caesarea. More recently the contextualization of Apollinarius in the city of Antioch, and the reception of and later views on Apollinarios in the following centuries (Andrist, 2005; 2014) are in the foreground.

Bibliography

Andrist, P., "Les protagonistes égyptiens du débat apollinariste," *REAugP* 34, 2005, 285–306.

Andrist, P., "The Two Faces of Apollinarius: A Glimpse into the Complex Reception of an Uncommon Heretic in Byzantium," in: S.-P. Bergjan, M. Heimgartner & B. Gleede, eds., *Apollinarius und seine Folgen*, STAC, Tübingen, 2014.

Bergjan, S.-P., "Anti-arianische Argumente gegen Apollinarios: Gregor von Nyssa in der Auseinandersetzung mit Apollinarios," in: V.H. Drecoll & M. Berghaus, eds., *Gregory of Nyssa: The Minor Treatises on Trinitarian Theology and Apollinarism*, SVigChr 106, Leiden, 2011, 481–499.

Bergjan, S.-P., "Theodoret von Cyrus, Apollinarius und die Apollinaristen in Antiochien: Zur Interpretation der Schrift 'Eranistes'," in: S.P. Bergjan, M. Heimgartner & B. Gleede, eds., *Apollinarius und seine Folgen*, STAC, Tübingen, 2014.

Bergjan, S.-P., "Konkurrenz unter den Nizänern: Die Christen Antiochiens im 4. Jahrhundert," in: S.-P. Bergjan & S. Elm, eds., *Antioch: The Many Faces of Antioch: Intellectual Exchange and Religious Diversity, CE 350–450*, Tübingen, 2018, 391–428.

Brennecke, H.C., "'Apollinaristischer Arianismus' oder 'arianischer Apollinarismus': Ein dogmengeschichtliches Konstrukt?" in: S.-P. Bergjan, M. Heimgartner & B. Gleede, eds., *Apollinarius und seine Folgen*, STAC, Tübingen, 2014, 73–91.

Drecoll, V.H, "Apollinarius, Ad Iovianum: Analyse und Bedeutung für die Apollinariuschronologie," in: S.-P. Bergjan, M. Heimgartner & B. Gleede, eds., *Apollinarius und seine Folgen*, STAC, Tübingen, 2014, 35–37.

Dorner, I.A., *Entwicklungsgeschichte der Lehre von der Person Christi*, vol. I, *Die Lehre von der Person Christi in den ersten vier Jahrhunderten*, Berlin, 1851, 975–1036.

Gemeinhardt, P., "Apollinaris von Laodicea: A Neglected Link of Trinitarian Theology between East and West?" *ZAC* 10, 2006, 286–301.

Grillmeier, A., *Jesus der Christus im Glauben der Kirche*, vol. I: *Von der Apostolischen Zeit bis zum Konzil von Chalcedon*, Freiburg, 1979, 480–493.

Heimgartner, M., "Neue Fragmente Diodors von Tarsus aus den Schriften 'Gegen Apollinarius', 'Gegen die Manichäer' und 'Über den heiligen Geist'," in: S.-P. Bergjan, M. Heimgartner & B. Gleede, eds., *Apollinarius und seine Folgen*, STAC, Tübingen, 2014, 185–203.

Hübner, R., *Die Schrift des Apolinarius von Laodecea gegen Photin (Ps.-Athanasius, Contra Sabellianos) und Basilius von Caesarea*, Berlin, 1989.

Jansen, T., *Theodor von Mopsuestia: De incarnatione*, PTS 65, Berlin, 2009.

Karmann, T.R., *Meletius von Antiochien: Studien zur Geschichte des trinitätstheologischen Streits in den Jahren 360–364 n. Chr.*, RSTh 68, Frankfurt am Main, 2009.

Lietzmann, H., *Apollinaris von Laodicaea und seine Schule*, Tübingen, 1904.

Mühlenberg, E., *Apollinaris von Laodicea*, FKDG 23, Göttingen, 1969.

Mühlenberg, E., "Apollinaris von Laodicea," in: *TRE*, vol. III, Berlin, 1978, 262–271.

Norris, R.A., *Manhood and Christ: A Study in the Christology of Theodore of Mopsuestia*, Oxford, 1963.

Raven, C.E., *Apollinarianism: An Essay on the Christology of the Early Church*, Cambridge UK, 1923.

Riedmatten, H. de, "Some Neglected Aspects of Apollinarist Christology," *DoSt* 1, 1948, 239–260.

Risch, F.X., *Pseudo-Basilius, Adversus Eunomium IV–V: Einleitung, Übersetzung, Kommentar*, SVigChr 16, Leiden, 1992.

Spoerl, K. McCarthy, "Apollinarius on the Holy Spririt," *SP*, vol. XXXVII, 2001, 571–592.

Spoerl, K. McCarthy, "The Circumstances of Apollinarius' Election in Laodicea?" in: S.-P. Bergjan, M. Heimgartner & B. Gleede, eds., *Apollinarius und seine Folgen*, STAC, Tübingen, 2015, 19–33.

Uthemann, K.-H., "Eustathios von Antiochien wider den seelenlosen Christus der Arianer," *ZAC* 10, 2007, 472–521.

Vogt, H.J., "Zum Briefwechsel zwischen Basilius und Apollinaris," *ThQ* 175, 1995, 46–60.

Voisin, G., *L'Apollinarisme: Etude historique, littéraire et dogmatique sur le début des controverse christologiques au IVe siècle*, Louvain, 1901.

Zachhuber, J., "Derivative Genera in Apollinarius of Laodicea: Some Remarks on the Philosophical Coherence of his Thought," in: S.-P. Bergjan, M. Heimgartner & B. Gleede, eds., *Apollinarius und seine Folgen*, STAC, Tübingen, 2014, 93–113.

SILKE-PETRA BERGJAN

Apollinaris of Valence

Apollinaris (c. 450/460–c. 520/524 CE) was bishop of Valentia (present-day Valence), a suffragan diocese of Vienne in the Burgundian kingdom. He is among the first identifiable bishops of Valence (Duchesne, 1907, 223), in office well before 517 CE, probably already in the 490s CE (or even earlier, if we can believe the figure of 34 years in office from the *Vita*; a bishops' list from Valence states that he was installed by his brother Alcimus Avitus "in the reign of Zeno," emperor from 474 till 491 CE; see Duchesne, 1907, 217). He was probably born sometime during the 450s CE, as was his (probably elder) brother (Hecquet-Noti, 1999, 24). The date of his birth, which is persistently given as "circa 453 CE," suggests greater exactitude than is actually attainable; it is in fact due to a fanciful calculation by the Bollandist editor (*AASS* Oct 3d.5.45–65). A plausible *terminus ante quem* for his death is the Council of → Arles, held in June 524 CE, on whose attendance list he no longer figures (Clercq, 1963, 42–46). Apollinaris was remembered for his adherence to anti-Arian measures as well as to strict → marriage norms. Revered as a saint, locally as Saint Aplonay, his feast day is Oct 5 (*Mart. Hier.* fol. 122b in *AASS* Nov 2.1.129); the town's cathedral is dedicated to him.

A member of the ramified and interrelated aristocratic families of the Aviti and the Apollinares, he was the son of Hesychius, bishop of Vienne, and of Audentia, who could have been a sister of → Sidonius Apollinaris (Mathisen, 1981, 100). His brother Alcimus Avitus succeeded their father in the see of Vienne before 494/496 CE. As was characteristic of aristocratic families, their sister Fuscina entered the monastic life. Avitus wrote a poem in praise of chastity for her, which features a cover letter to Apollinaris (after c. 506/507; Shanzer & Wood, 2002, 262). Likewise, Avitus' bible epic *De spiritalis historiae gestis* (*The Spiritual History of Mankind*) is dedicated to his brother (c. 497–500 CE; Hecquet-Noti, 1999, 33).

The direct sources for his life are few. Including these two cover letters, the correspondence that has come down to us as part of the corpus of Avitus' oeuvre numbers ten items, two of them written by Apollinaris, eight addressed to him by Avitus. In all of these letters, the greeting formulas mention Apollinaris as bishop. All in all, they point to a time in office in the 500s and 510s CE, while not excluding an earlier start. In letter 13, Apollinaris confesses to having forgotten to commemorate Fuscina's death; hence, it cannot be earlier than 506/507 CE. Among Avitus' letters, numbers 87 and 88 stand out. The former alludes to the Visigothic defeat in the Battle of Vouillé in 507 CE and seems to suggest an economic cause for this war; it is also of art-historical interest, since it contains instructions for a ring which Avitus wants Apollinaris to have made for him (Shanzer & Wood, 2002, 251–253). Letter 88 seems to imply that Avitus is on his deathbed (he died on Feb 5, 518 CE), as he asks Apollinaris to see to the selection of a successor   which is as uncanonical as it is informative about Gallican episcopal succession.

Further sources include the attendance lists of councils and his hagiography. In the list of subscribers of the canons enacted by the Burgundian Council of Epaone (September 517 CE; Clercq, 1963, 20–37), Apollinaris ranks fifth, which marks him out as a senior member. The list is headed by the initiators, his brother Avitus and Viventiolus of Lyon. The year 517 CE is the only precise date in Apollinaris' biography. In 516 CE, the Arian king Gundobad had been succeeded by his orthodox son Sigismund. Despite heavy pressure on Gundobad, Avitus had not been successful in converting the monarch to orthodox Catholicism. Now, he and the other bishops were quick to tip the scales away from diversity in the traditionally tolerant kingdom. The council ruled on conversion, the proper behavior of the clergy, and the alienation of church property. Among other issues, a strict ruling on incestuous marriages touched upon a topical problem. As the king himself attempted to bypass this ruling and to condone a case in point involving his treasurer Stephanus, the

bishops convened twice in Lyon. The minutes of the second meeting, held sometime between 518 and 523 CE, have come down to us (Clercq, 1963, 38–41). Apollinaris is third in the order of subscribers and, according to the *Vitae*, played a prominent role in the decision process as well as in the enforcement of Stephanus' excommunication by means of a walkout directed against the king (compare Shanzer & Wood, 2002, 20–24).

There are two lives, the *Vita Aviti* and the *Vita Apollinaris*. The greater part of the *Vita Aviti*, identical to one of two main sections of the *Vita Apollinaris*, is devoted to Apollinaris' perseverance in this episcopal strike. After Sigismund had forced the other bishops to go back to work, Apollinaris remained in exile. When the heat made the water of the Rhône undrinkable, he uncovered a miraculous well. Then the king fell ill. The queen begged Apollinaris to give up his cloak for the king to use as a blanket. As soon as the cloak touched him, the king recovered. Crying with remorse, he kissed Apollinaris' feet. The other section of the *Vita Apollinaris*, told by a self-styled eyewitness in the 34th year of Apollinaris' episcopate and thus immediately before his death, is devoted to a boat journey by Apollinaris, equally interspersed with → miracles, to visit his relatives in Avignon, Arles, and Marseilles. Pious local tradition indeed remembered Apollinaris for having been a miracle worker, in contrast to his eloquent brother (see Ado's chronicle, PL 123.105D, and his martyrology, PL 123.374D; from there in the *Martyrium Romanum*; see also Hofmeister, 1934).

According to R. Peiper in the foreword of his edition (1883, xx–xxiii), the *Vita Aviti* is contemporary with → Gregory of Tours (538/539–594 CE) and slightly later than the *Vita Apollinaris*, from which it has copied the ill-matching section on Stephanus. B. Krusch (1896, 195–196), however, argued that the *Vita Apollinaris* is Carolingian (9th cent. CE) and that the author of the *Vita Aviti* awkwardly combined the episode from the *Vita Apollinaris* with information from Ado of Vienne's (c. 800–875 CE) chronicle (accepted by Stroheker, 1948, 146). Nowadays, his arguments are not considered conclusive, and there is no compelling reason for not regarding the *Vita Apollinaris* as the work of a contemporary (Beck, 1950, xxxiii; Heinzelmann, 1982, 557), while the *Vita Aviti* may still be late (Shanzer & Wood, 2002, 10).

Historiography

The date of the *Vitae* has been an object of discussion, whether they are contemporary 6th century CE or Carolingian 9th century CE. The *Vita Apollinaris*, at least, could be early (Peiper, 1883; Beck, 1950; Heinzelmann, 1982, *contra* Krusch, 1896, and Stroheker, 1948).

Bibliography

Ado Viennensis, "Opera," PL, vol. CXXIII, Paris, 1852, cols. 9–444.

Beck, H.G.J., *The Pastoral Care of Souls in South-East France during the Sixth Century*, Rome, 1950.

Clercq, C. de, *Concilia Galliae A. 511–A. 695*, CCSL 148A, Turnhout, 1963, 20–46.

Duchesne, L., *Fastes épiscopaux de l'ancienne Gaule*, vol. I, Paris, 1907.

Hecquet-Noti, N., *Avit de Vienne, Histoire spirituelle*, vol. I, SC 444, Paris, 1999.

Heinzelmann, M., "Apollinaris 6," in: "Gallische Prosopographie 260–527," *Francia* 10, 1982, 531–718, esp. 556–557.

Heinzelmann, M., "Apollinaris," in: *LThK*, vol. I, Freiburg, 1993, col. 829.

Hofmeister, A., ed., *Miracula S. Apollinaris episcopi Valentinensis*, MGH.SS, vol. XXX/2, Leipzig, 1934, 1343–1346.

Jones, A.H.M., "Apollinaris 5," in: *PLRE*, vol. II, Cambridge UK, 1980, 115.

Krusch, B., ed., *Vita Apollinaris*, MGH.SRM, vol. III, Hannover, 1896, 194–203.

Mathisen, R.W., "Epistolography, Literary Circles and Family Ties in Late Roman Gaul," *TAPhA* 111, 1981, 95–109.

Peiper, R., ed., *Vita Aviti*, MGH.AA, vol. VI/2, Berlin, 1883, 177–181, introduction on xx–xxiii.

Peiper, R., ed., *Alcimi Ecdicii Aviti Viennensis episcopi opera quae supersunt*, MGH.AA, vol. VI/2, Berlin, 1883, 46–47 (Letters 13 Apollinaris to Avitus, and 14 Avitus to Apollinaris), 57–58, 87 (27 and 61 Avitus to Apollinaris), 90 (71 Apollinaris to Avitus), 90, 96–97 (72, 87 and 88 Avitus to Apollinaris), 201–202, 274–275 (dedicatory letters to Apollinaris for *De spiritalis historiae gestis* and *De consolatoria castitatis laude*).

Shanzer, D., & I. Wood, *Avitus of Vienne: Letters and Selected Prose*, TTH 38, Liverpool, 2002.

Stroheker, K.F., "Apollinaris," in: K.F. Stroheker, *Der senatorische Adel im spätantiken Gallien*, Reutlingen, 1948, repr. Darmstadt, 1970, 146, no. 23.

JOOP VAN WAARDEN

Apollonius of Tyana

As far as can be seen from scanty historical evidence, Apollonius of Tyana was a Neo-Pythagorean philosopher and wandering wonderworker of the 1st century CE. He was born shortly after the turn of the century and likely died in the reign of Nerva (96–98 CE). While the historical Apollonius remains a sketchy and shadowy figure, the literary Apollonius is anything but. Apollonius "the legend" was created by Philostratus, and then took on a life of its own, independent of the historical figure. This Apollonius, in its turn, slightly less than a 100 years after Philostratus, was exalted as a superior rival to Christ by Sossianus Hierocles in his *Lover of Truth* (φιλαληθεῖς) at the end of the 3rd century CE. With this, the murky imposter of the 1st century CE ends up a pagan saint. The purpose of this article is to acquaint the reader with the figure of Apollonius, the distinction between his historical identity and the image later created of him, and the associated scholarly issues.

The most information about Apollonius is contained in the problematic *Life of Apollonius* written by Philostratus around 217 CE, more than a 100 years after its subject's death. Outside Philostratus, and sources dependent upon him, all traditions agree that Apollonius was a prophet and wonderworker, but most hold a contemptuous opinion of him. Slightly earlier than Philostratus, Lucian of Samosata (c. 120–c.180 CE) dismissed Apollonius as a mere showman (Luc. *Alex.* 5). Philostratus' contemporary Dio describes him as both a γόης ("imposter") and skillful magician (Dio. *Hist. rom.* 77.18.4). In the early 3rd century CE, → Origen asserts that a now lost biography of Apollonius by one Moiragenes, prior to Philostratus, stated that Apollonius initially took in serious philosophers through his magic tricks (μαγείας), though they later regarded him as a γόης (Or. *Cels.* 6.41).

Only one species of evidence may have come from Apollonius' own lifetime, indeed may even have been written by Apollonius himself. This is a set of letters of Apollonius, edited and translated by R.J. Penalla (1979) and subsequently by C.P. Jones (2006). It is interesting to note that in these, Apollonius defends himself against the accusation of → magic (μαγεία) by asserting that the term μάγος in its origins was a term for a godly and just man (*Epp. Apoll.* 16 & 17). He expresses no surprise in there being contrary opinions of him, since all eminent sages shared a similar conflicting reputation (*Epp. Apoll.* 48.2). Philostratus quotes the letters in his work in Books 4 through 8, particularly focusing on Apollonius' explanation and defense of his integrity and manner of life. The authenticity of these letters is debated – Philostratus states that collections of forged letters circulated in Apollonius's own lifetime (Philostr. *Vita ap.* 7.3.5) – as is what "authenticity" should mean in this regard. The frequently apologetic tone of many of the letters suggests posthumous authorship. R.J. Penella (1979), the first editor of the corpus of the letters, found the letters concordant with the *Life of Apollonius* and discrepancies explicable, though he was largely noncommittal regarding authorship. E.L. Bowie (1978) argued they were either collected or fabricated in Athens circa 140 CE and formed part of the work of Moiragenes. The most recent editor of the letters, C.P. Jones (2006), avoids general statements, other than that the letters are not one authorially edited collection, and that different writers had different sets of letters available to them. Ultimately he counsels that the best procedure is to judge each letter on its own merits.

Lastly, mention should be made of a work Philostratus states was written by Apollonius himself (Philostr. *Vita ap.* 3.41), *On Sacrifices* (περὶ θυσιῶν), which → Eusebius of Caesarea claims to quote in *Praep* 4.13 (150b). The passage in Eusebius states that sacrifice is an inappropriate form of worship for the highest deity, obviously useful in Christian apologetic (→ Apologetics) and in attacking pagan practice. *Epp. Apoll.* 26 and 27 express the same sentiment, as does → Porphyry of Tyre in *Abst.* 2.94, and the objection to sacrifice goes back as far as the pre-Socratics in the 6th century BCE. Philostratus, however, also says something very peculiar about the work: ἄν τις ἑρμηνεύοι αὐτό, which has been translated "if someone could translate [ἑρμηνεύοι] it." This makes little sense, since Apollonius, who was so proud of his flawless Attic dialect (Philostr. *Vita ap.* 1.7), would hardly have written it in a language other than the universally accessible Greek. C.P Jones (2005) renders the sense as "how could anyone characterize it [...]" My own preference would be "if anyone could

interpret it," meaning that the work discussed such abstract and arcane concepts that an expert was required to put it in layman's terms. Whatever the case, such a small passage of such a commonplace idea in a Christian author does not tell us much about Apollonius.

1. Philostratus and the *Life of Apollonius*

What is conventionally called the *Life of Apollonius of Tyana* was likely titled by Philostratus something akin to "Things Pertaining to Apollonius of Tyana"; the precise ancient title has not come down to us. By the standards of ancient literary lives, the work is a behemoth: eight books taking up two entire Loeb Library volumes. It is, in fact, far too long and too wide ranging to fit into the genre of ancient → biography. What exactly its genre is has been a matter of largely fruitless debate. Scholars have endeavored to classify it as a miracle tale, a Hellenistic novel, a *Reiseroman*, a pagan hagiography, and the prototypical holy-man legend (see Francis 1995, 118–125, esp. nn117–119). The *Life of Apollonius* has characteristics of all these, but refuses to fit into any one genre definitively; it seems best to simply categorize it as sui generis.

The overall framework of the *Life of Apollonius* follows the travel and adventures of the sage from his birth to death, but with a depth of detail and frequency of digression uncharacteristic of biography, and with an absence of the character analysis that forms the core of the writing of lives in antiquity. Philostratus begins the work discussing not Apollonius but Pythagoras and introduces his hero as greater than the canonical Greek sage. Not being content with a mortal comparison, Philostratus further relates the story that the god Proteus appeared to Apollonius' mother announcing that she will give birth to the god himself (1.4). The *Life of Apollonius* moves through Apollonius' education, first cure as a youth, devotion to religion and asceticism, discipline of five years of silence, and first services to cities (1.7–17). From the start, as Apollonius moves through the Greek world, he educates cities, temples, and priests on religion and corrects and restores religious practices. Throughout the *Life of Apollonius*, his divine wisdom is coupled with expert religious knowledge. Book 1 ends with his journey eastward into Mesopotamia, Babylon, and modern-day Afghanistan.

Books 2 and 3 are devoted to his travel to and adventures in India. The first of these books contains a lengthy discussion of the natural history along the route. Book 3 continues in this vein until Apollonius encounters the Brahmans, the ultimate goal of his journey (3.15). These original masters of the true and ancient wisdom welcome Apollonius as one like themselves. The purpose appears to be to show Apollonius as a "super philosopher," one who has not only mastered but also transcended the Greek philosophical tradition, and drunk from an even older and more hallowed font of wisdom. At the same time, it must be said that Apollonius' "philosophy" as delineated in the *Life of Apollonius* is not particularly profound or intellectually rigorous. It consists in preaching traditional Greek civic virtues; abstinence from animal products and animal → sacrifice, a feature of Pythagoreanism; a devoted, fastidious religiosity; and a sort of homespun common sense.

Book 4 sees the sage return to Greece. All Ephesus turns out to welcome him. The gods themselves laud him in messages from their oracles and sanctuaries. Cities dispatch embassies awarding him the status of ξένος and adviser in correct manners of life and religion. Throughout he preaches the study of → philosophy, which for the ordinary run of humanity mainly involves right living and civic and religious piety. In Ephesus, Apollonius preaches the virtue of κοινωνία ("commonweal"), while at Smyrna his theme is φιλοτιμία ("competition in civic benefaction," 4.3, 8). This tour is punctuated by several wonders and miracles, for example, averting plague (4.4); curing plagues through exorcism (4.10); prophecy (4.18); exorcising a dissolute, impious youth (4.20); and raising a girl from the dead (4.45). These sorts of miracles have invited comparison with those of Jesus in the Gospels (see below on Hierocles) and presage later Christian → hagiography, especially such works as the *Life of Antony*. Toward the end of the book, Apollonius journeys westward and arrives at Rome during the reign of Nero (54–68 CE). This affords him his first opportunity to denounce tyranny and depravity and serves as the prelude to his climactic confrontation with Domitian later in the *Life of Apollonius*.

Books 5 and 6 continue Apollonius' journey west, all the way to the Pillars of Hercules (Gibraltar).

As with the Indian journey in Book 3, this episode is heavy on natural history and mythological geography. After reaching Spain, the sage heads back east through the Mediterranean – Sicily, Athens, and Rhodes – completing his world tour in the one significant region remaining: Egypt. Unlike other parts of Apollonius' journey, the sojourn in Egypt is prompted by a specific event of landmark importance, the presence of the Roman general Vespasian in Alexandria. Having left the siege of Jerusalem to his son Titus, Vespasian is poised to advance on Rome to depose the third successor to Nero, Vitellius, and take the throne. Notables across the empire flock to his side, giving their counsel to the soon-to-be emperor. Apollonius speaks in favor of monarchy (5.27–41). Because he lives as a subject of the gods, he is indifferent to constitutions, but since one man of outstanding virtue can change a democracy into the rule of one best man, so the rule of one man who seeks the common good changes a monarchy into a democracy. Vespasian should shoulder the responsibility his virtue places upon him and rule as emperor (5.35). After the episode with Vespasian, Apollonius goes down into Egypt to visit another group of philosophers older than the sages of Greece, the Gymnosophists (6.5). Unlike the Brahmans, the Gymnosophists are suspicious of Apollonius, in part out of "professional jealousy" of both the Brahmans and the Greeks. As would be expected, Apollonius defends both these groups, and the Gymnosophists come off rather badly, but the episode allows Philostratus to reprise the Indian episode and again highlight Apollonius' claim to the loftiest and most ancient wisdom.

Books 7 and 8 provide the climax to the *Life of Apollonius*, bringing Apollonius into a final face-to-face confrontation with a tyrant, this time Domitian (81–96 CE), and the work ends with wondrous stories about the death of the sage. Philostratus begins Book 7 by stating that their behavior under tyranny is the best test of philosophers, and Apollonius will pass this test in a most unusual way. Through his divine foreknowledge, the sage knew that Nerva would succeed after Domitian's assassination. He made a statement before a statue of Domitian that tyrants were not above fate, and that the emperor would fail in his attempts to kill the man who would succeed him (7.9). Apollonius was arrested. His journey to Rome and subsequent imprisonment afford the opportunity of having Apollonius deliver extended dialogues on the philosophical life, painting Domitian, along with Nero and all other tyrants, as enemies of philosophy and Apollonius as a willing martyr to it. But the sage is master of his own life and death and his own freedom, demonstrating this dramatically by simply removing his leg shackle in his prison cell and putting it back on again (7.38.2), a scene reminiscent of Peter's imprisonment in Acts 12:5–10.

Apollonius' trial before Domitian begins with Book 8. The four specific charges that concern the emperor, and Apollonius' responses, synopsize the negative view of the historical figure and Philostratus' strategy for rehabilitating him (8.5.1–3). The first is why Apollonius wears such peculiar clothing. It should first be noted that philosophers in the period are generally distinguished by a threadbare "cloak" (*tribon*), "walking staff" (*baculum*), and "wallet" (*pera*), signs of ascetic renunciation and otherworldliness. This "habit" was especially characteristic of Cynic philosophers who, like Apollonius, wandered from city to city denouncing wrongdoing, preaching the value of a "philosophical" life, and generally rabblerousing. Such philosophers were regularly perceived as enemies to the Roman authorities, and this charge appears to reflect suspicions regarding the historical Apollonius. Philostratus does not confront this accusation but rather mitigates it; Apollonius responds assuming that the peculiarity of his dress lies in its being made from not animal but plant material. As such, he simply states that he is clothed by the earth without disturbing the animals, a Pythagorean sentiment. The next accusation is that people call Apollonius a god. Some sort of claim to divine power or status (so also did the mob denounce Jesus to → Pontius Pilate [→ Pilate]) is a typical feature of the γόης, and once again the accusation fits historically. The sage's response is that good men should rightly be honored with this title. The third accusation concerns how Apollonius knew beforehand that a plague would strike Ephesus, which suggests the practice of magic. The sage's explanation is utterly mundane: because he eats a light, abstemious, vegetarian diet, his senses are keener and so he perceives things before others

do. No magic; just good health. The fourth accusation, Philostratus says, took everyone by surprise and concerns the sacrifice of an Arcadian boy (see 7.11.3; 7.20.1). The accusation is intended to connect Apollonius with Nerva and others plotting against the emperor, since the sacrifice was allegedly performed for Nerva to ascertain his chances of success in toppling Domitian. Such a sacrifice would also suggest "black magic" and chthonic rites, hence treason, magic, and perverse religion are all wrapped up in the charge. The emperor's accusation appears so ludicrous that the court applauds Apollonius' simple "how dare you" reply. Frustrated, Domitian exonerates the sage on all counts, but announces he wishes to speak with him further. Apollonius replies that he will not stay in the midst of evil men, and that the emperor cannot hold him since he is not destined to die (some translate "since I am not mortal," ἐπεὶ οὔτοι μόρσιμός εἰμι, 8.5.3; see 8.8). With that, the sage simply vanishes from sight "in a supernatural way, not easy to describe" (8.8; see 8.5.4).

After this, Philostratus moves to close the *Life of Apollonius*. After disappearing from Rome, Apollonius reappears in Greece and again makes a round of Greek cities, teaching and performing wonders. The Greeks now generally, though not unanimously, accept that his nature is divine. He gains approval from temples and oracles, the gods themselves proclaiming his wisdom as their own. When Domitian finally meets his end, Apollonius is capable of seeing the event in Greece as if he were an eyewitness in Rome (8.26–27). Philostratus states that there are many varying accounts of Apollonius' death – if, indeed, he did actually die (8.29). The final scene of the *Life of Apollonius* relates the story of a young philosopher from Tyana itself who could not bring himself to believe in the immortality of the → soul. He prayed to Apollonius for nine months that he would appear to him and reveal the truth; four days later Apollonius appeared to him while he slept, and the young man believed. The former suspicious γόης is now prayed to and appears miraculously, and in the last sentence of the *Life of Apollonius*, Philostratus speaks of the shrine the emperors built to him at Tyana. He has become a pagan saint.

2. Literary and Historical Significance of Philostratus' Apollonius

Philostratus is believed to have been born circa 170 CE and died sometime during the reign of Philip the Arab (244–249 CE). His reputation as a man of letters brought him to the attention of the empress Julia Domna, wife of Septimius Severus (193–211 CE). Known for her literary and cultural interests, according to the *Life of Apollonius*, she asked Philostratus to compose an account of Apollonius using the memoirs she had received from the family of the sage's constant companion Damis, a Syrian from Hieropolis (1.3). That the *Life of Apollonius* was "commissioned" by the empress but not dedicated to her has been taken to suggest that the work was published after Julian Domna's death in 217. Philostratus states that the memoirs of Damis, along with the letters attributed to Apollonius, a memento by Maximus of Aegeae, and Apollonius' own will and testament make up his sources. He also mentions a work on Apollonius in four books written by Moiragenes, which he dismisses as unreliable; this is the work mentioned by Origen (*Cels.* 6.41) mentioned above, which may have painted an unfavorable picture of Apollonius. Scholars have in the past fought over the reliability and historicity of Damis, but more recently Damis and his memoirs have been seen as a "self-authenticating" literary device (Jones, 2005, vol. I, 3) or fictional strategy (Francis, 1998) invented by Philostratus himself. Certainly, the *Life of Apollonius* possesses a highly complex, at times bewildering, narrative structure with first-person narration by both Philostratus and "Damis," quotations, digressions, documents, and hearsay.

The uniqueness and intricacy of the *Life of Apollonius* is indicative of another important characteristic of the work; it is part of the literary and cultural movement known as the Second Sophistic, a term coined by Philostratus himself (Philostr. *Vitae soph.* 481). This movement sought a revival and renewal of Greek culture and letters, and its members both regarded rhetoric and the refined accomplishments of παιδεία as the acme of learning and culture, while at the same time engaging in literary experimentation and the creation of new forms in which to transmit the received culture of Hellenism. The *Life*

of Apollonius is one such experiment. Furthermore, the character of Apollonius himself can be seen to embody the values and goals of the Second Sophistic. He is an expert on Greek values and chides whole cities to return to correct behavior and traditional ideals, even in opposition to Roman power and cultural influences (Philostr. *Vita ap.* 4.5; 5.36, 41; *Epp. Apoll.* 30; 42f–h; 54; 71; 72). Like the "new sophists" themselves, he lays claim to universal expertise and serves as an adviser to cities, provinces, and emperors.

More importantly in terms of early Christianity, the *Life of Apollonius* reflects a world where street-corner philosophers, miracle mongers, and wandering magicians and prophets are common – the historical reality found in other writers of the period such as Lucian, Aelius Aristides, Dio of Prusa, and → Celsus. And as with Apollonius, the distinctions between philosopher and magician, prophet and imposter, are often blurred. The popularity of these figures, despite their being derided by the educated and cultured classes, attests to their power and attraction. The *Life of Apollonius* harnesses this appeal and its connection to otherworldly power and brings it under the umbrella and into the service of proper behavior and belief. Whether all this is evidence of a broader existential anxiety, quest for salvation, or other kind of metaphysical inquietude in the 2nd and 3rd centuries CE cannot be discussed here. What can be said is that, whether deliberately or not, Philostratus made the figure of the "divine" or "holy man" (θεῖος ἀνήρ) respectable to the elite classes of the empire.

3. Reprise and Afterward

An important inscription, likely from the 3rd-century CE Cilicia and first published in 1978, appears to speak of Apollonius as a savior figure. Though the text remains, in part, disputed (see Dzielska, 1983, 64–71, 160–162, for a synopsis of the variants proposed and discussion), it is clear that Philostratus' characterization of Apollonius as the model of a divine man became the predominant view (see also the later *Testimonia* compiled in Jones, 2006, 83–143). A key text in this regard is Sossianus Hierocles' *Lover of Truth* (φιλαληθεῖς). This work, written at the end of the 3rd century CE by one of the leading lights in the persecutions of Diocletian and Galerius, was apparently a broad attack on Christianity in which the comparison of Apollonius to Jesus Christ formed only a part. Hierocles' text is not extant and is known only from the reply written to it by Eusebius of Caesarea (c. 260–c. 340 CE). It is, in fact, Eusebius who focuses solely on Apollonius (Eus. *Hier.* 1–7). Though the English title is rendered *Against Hierocles*, from the conventional Latin *Contra Hieroclem*, Eusebius' Greek title makes this clear: πρὸς τὰ ὑπὸ Φιλοστράτου εἰς Ἀπολλώνιον διὰ τὴν Ἱεροκλεῖ παραλειφθεῖσαν αὐτοῦ τε καὶ τοῦ Χριστοῦ σύγκρισιν (*Against the Work of Philostratus About Apollonius Handed Down Through Hierocles About Comparing Him and Christ*). Eusebius spends little time addressing Hierocles, and the bulk of the work (*Hier.* 7–44) is devoted to a book-by-book refutation of the *Life of Apollonius*. When Eusebius does take on Hierocles at the beginning of the work, we see that the latter's arguments for Apollonius and against Christ parallel the accusations and apologetics found in the *Life of Apollonius*. Apollonius performs his wonders through wisdom, not γοητεία; it is Jesus who is the γόης (2.1). The slanders brought against Apollonius by his opponents are here leveled against Christ, and it is interesting to note how these characterizations remain constant in both pagan and Christian contexts. Eusebius, for his part, calls Apollonius a wandering sophist begging from city to city, that is, a Cynic philosopher or γόης (5). Thus in the period of "the rise of the holy man," to use P. Brown's landmark expression, from Lucian's satires such as the *Death of Peregrinus* and *Alexander the False Prophet* and Celsus' anti-Christian polemic *True Doctrine* toward the end of the 2nd century CE, through the *Life of Apollonius* in the early 3rd century CE to Hierocles and Eusebius in the late 3rd century CE, the features of the negative characterization of the divine man figure remain constant. The contribution of Philostratus in the *Life of Apollonius* lies in enunciating the criteria and characteristics for the respectable holy man and embodying them into an iconic figure: Apollonius of Tyana. Thus, moving into the Christian era, the divine or holy man must be not only a wonderworker with a special relationship to the divine, but also an ascetic, a social benefactor, a defender of true religion, and fearless in the face of evil.

Apollonius himself also lives on. Though notoriously unreliable as an historical source, the 3rd- or 4th-century CE *Historia Augusta* relates two stories pertaining to Apollonius as god or saint. The first concerns the lararium of the emperor → Alexander Severus (208–235 CE), grand nephew of Julia Domna, supposedly containing images of deified "good" emperors, as well as statues of Orpheus, Abraham, Christ, and Apollonius (SHA *Alex. Sev.* 29.2). In another passage, Emperor Aurelian (214–275 CE) considers sacking the city of Tyana when Apollonius appears before him and, speaking in Latin, dissuades him from attacking his birthplace. The emperor recognized the sage from the many statues he has seen of him in temples (SHA *Aurel.* 24.2–9; on surviving representations of Apollonius, see R. Smith, 143 and n42). In 5th-century CE Gaul, the Christian → Sidonius Apollinaris writes approvingly of him (Sid. *Ep.* 8.3.5), and he appears in various medieval Islamic works. In more recent times, Apollonius figures prominently in a number of Theosophical writings and remains a favorite of various esoteric and spitiualist groups, as well as of various "debunkers" of Christianity (on the nachleben of Apollonius and the *Vita apollonii*, see Dzielska, 1983, 153–183, 193–211; Jones, 2005, vol. I. 17–21; Jones, 2006).

Historiography

The most recent text and English translation of Philostratus's *Life of Apollonius* is C.P. Jones (2005), based on a revised version of C.L. Keyser's Greek text of 1844. C.P. Jones' edition also contains the Letters of Apollonius and Hierocles' *Lover of Truth*, and a thorough and concise presentation on Apollonius, his *nachleben*, and history of scholarship. Modern scholarship on Apollonius begins in the context of early 20th century biblical studies and the search for parallels to the gospels: R. Reitzenstein (1906) and E. Meyer (1917). F. Grosso ((1954) argued for the historicity of Philostratus's account. This prompted a lengthy and enlightening chain of research: E.L. Bowie (1978); G. Anderson (1986); M. Dzielska (1986); and J.A. Francis (1998). Most recently see: K. Demoen and D. Praet (2009) and S. Panayotakis, G. Schmeling and M. Paschalis (2015).

Bibliography

Anderson, G., *Philostratus: Biography and Belles-Lettres in the Third Century AD*, London, 1986.

Anderson, G., *Saint, Sage, and Sophist: Holy Man and Their Associates in the Early Roman Empire*, London, 1994.

Barnes, T.D., "Sossianus Hierocles and the Antecedents of the Great Persecution," *HSCP* 80, 1976, 239–252.

Boter, G., "The Title of Philostratus' *Life of Apollonius of Tyana*," *JHS* 135, 2015, 1–7.

Bowie, E.L., "Apollonius of Tyana: Tradition and Reality," in: *ANRW*, vol. II/16/2, Berlin, 1978, 1652–1699.

Bowie, E.L., "Philostratos: Writer of Fiction," in: J.R. Morgan & R. Stoneman, eds., *Greek Fiction: The Greek Novel in Context*, London, 1994, 181–199.

Bowie, E.L., & J. Elsner, eds., *Philostratus*, Cambridge UK, 2009.

Brown, P.R.L., "The Rise and Function of the Holy Man in Late Antiquity," *JRS* 61, 1971, 80–101 = *Society and the Holy in Late Antiquity*, Berkeley, 1982, 103–152.

Brown, P.R.L., "The Saint as Exemplar in Late Antiquity," *Repr.* 1, 1983, 1–26.

Cangh, J.M. van, "Santé et salut dans les miracles d'Épidaure, d'Apollonius de Tyane et du Nouveau Testament," in: J. Reis et al., eds., *Gnosticisme et monde hellénistique: Actes du Colloque de Louvain-la-Neuve (Mar 11–14, 1980)*, Louvain, 1982, 263–277.

Cox, P., *Biography in Late Antiquity: A Quest for the Holy Man*, Berkeley, 1983.

Demoen, K., & D. Praet, eds., *Theios Sophistes: Essays on Flavius Philostratus' Vita Apollonii*, Leiden, 2009.

Dzielska, M., *Appoloniusz z Tiany: Legenda i rzeczywistosc*, Rozprawy habilitacyjne Uniwersytet Jagiellonski 78, Krakow (Habil.), 1983; ET: P. Pienkowski, *Apollonius of Tyana in Legend and History*, PRSA 10, Rome, 1986.

Elsner, J., "Hagiographic Geography: Travel and Allegory in the Life of Apollonius of Tyana," *JHS* 117, 1997, 22–38.

Flintermann, J.-J., *Power, Paideia, and Pythagoreanism*, Amsterdam, 1995.

Forrat, M., *Contre Hiéroclès*, Gk text ed. E. des Places, SC 333, Paris, 1986.

Fowden, G., "The Pagan Holy Man in Late Antique Society," *JHS* 102, 1982, 33–59.

Francis, J.A., *Subversive Virtue: Asceticism and Authority in the Second-Century Pagan World*, University Park, 1995; esp. 83–130, where the *Vita apollonii* and the Letters of Apollonius are discussed synoptically.

Francis, J.A., "Truthful Fiction: New Questions to Old Answers on Philostratus' Life of Apollonius," *AJP* 119, 1998, 419–441.

Grosso, F., "La 'Vita di Apollonio di Tiana' come fonte storica," *Acme* 7, 1954, 333–352

Hägg, T., "Hierocles the Lover of Truth and Eusebius the Sophist," *SO* 67, 1992, 138–150.

Jones, C.P., "An Epigram on Apollonius of Tyana," *JHS* 100, 1980, 190–194.

Jones, C.P., "A Martyria for Apollonius of Tyana," *Chiron* 12, 1982, 137–144.

Jones, C.P., "Apollonius of Tyana's Passage to India," *GRBS* 42, 2001, 185–199.

Jones, C.P., *Philostratus: The Life of Apollonius of Tyana*, 2 vols., LCL 16–17, Cambridge MA, 2005.

Jones, C.P., *Philostratus: Apollonius of Tyana, Letters of Apollonius, Ancient Testimonia, Eusebius's Reply to Hierocles*, LCL 458, Cambridge MA, 2006.

Jones, C.P., "Apollonius of Tyana in Late Antiquity," in: S.F. Johnson, ed., *Greek Literature in Late Antiquity: Dynamism, Didacticism, Classicism*, Aldershot, 2006, 49–64.

Junod, E., "Polémique chrétienne contre Apollonius de Tyane," *RThPh* 120, 1988, 475–482.

Meyer, E., "Apollonius von Tyana und die Biographie des Philostratos," *Hermes* 52, 1917, 371–424 (= *Kleine Schriften* 2, Halle, 131–191, 1924).

Miles, G., *Philostratus: Interpreters and Interpretation: Image, Text and Culture in Classical Antiquity*, London, 2018.

Panayotakis, S., G. Schmeling & M. Paschalis, eds., *Holy Men and Charlatans in the Ancient Novel*, ANS 19, Groningen, 2015.

Penella, R.J., *The Letters of Apollonius of Tyana: A Critical Text with Prolegomena, Translation and Commentary*, Mn.S. 56, Leiden, 1979.

Petzke, G., *Die Traditionen über Apollonius von Tyana und das Neue Testament*, SCHNT 1, Leiden, 1970.

Praet, D., "Death and the Maiden in Philostratus, About Apollonius of Tyana 4.45: Miracle, Mystery or Philosophical Skepticism?" *Mn.* 75, 2022, 169–206.

Raynor, D.H., "Moeragenes and Philostratus: Two Views of Apollonius of Tyana," *CQ* n.s. 34, 1984, 222–226.

Reitzenstein, R., *Hellenistische Wundererzählungen*, Leipzig, 1906.

Smith, M., "Prolegomena to a Discussion of Aretalogies, Divine Men, the Gospels and Jesus." *JBL* 90, 1971, 174–199.

Smith, M., "On the History of the Divine Man," in: A. Benoit, M. Philonenko & C. Vogel, eds., *Paganisme, Judaïsme, Christianisme: Influences et affrontements dans le monde antique: Mélanges offerts à Marcel Simon*, Paris, 1978, 335–345.

Smith, R.R.R., "Late Roman Philosopher Portraits from Aphrodisias," *JRS* 80, 1990, 127–155.

Speyer, W., "Zum Bild des Apollonius von Tyana bei Heiden und Christen," *JbAC* 1, 1974, 47–63.

JAMES A. FRANCIS

Apologetics

In Greek an ἀπολογία is a speech for the defense, but thanks to the compositions of Plato and Xenophon on behalf of their master Socrates, the term passed into philosophy without losing its forensic associations. Eusebius of Caesarea was the first to apply the term "apologetic" to Christian literature (Eus. *Hist. eccl.* 4.3; 4.13 etc.), but the works that are commonly brought under this rubric by modern scholars fall into four overlapping categories:

1. *vindicatory* writings, which expose the falsity of pagan charges;
2. *polemical* assaults on Judaism, Greek philosophy, or Roman religion;
3. *controversial* responses to named detractors of Christianity;
4. *constructive* expositions of the faith that offer not only defense but instruction to the church.

1. Vindications

The writings of this class, most or all of which fall between 120 and 220 CE, are the *Apology* of → Aristides of Athens, the *Letter to Diognetus*, the *First* and *Second Apologies* of Justin Martyr, the *Embassy* of Athenagoras, and the *Apology* of Tertullian and his treatise *To the Nations*, together with his shorter works *To Scapula* and *On the Shows*. To this list we may one day hope to add the lost effusions of Quadratus, Apollinaris, and Melito of Sardis. All are, at least ostensibly, the bitter fruits of Greek persiflage and Roman persecution. In literary as in political circles, Christianity was regarded as a foreign superstition whose adherents were poor, illiterate, and seditious. In its defense the apologists

1. assert the innocence of Christians;
2. display their education;
3. demand the esteem accorded to philosophers;
4. contest the superiority of Greek culture;
5. unmask the origins of pagan cult.

a. Assert the Innocence of Christians

The apologists of this period unanimously declare that Christians violate no law except the law against being a Christian. → Tertullian protests that Christians pray for the emperor, and scoffs that, in their case only, the aim of torture is to elicit denial rather than confession. He and Justin quote imperial rescripts deprecating excessive zeal in search and trial. Both allude to charges of "Oedipodal conjugations and Thyestean banquets" that are also known to Athenagoras. These have been explained as true accounts of gnostic rituals, as distorted representations of the → Eucharist and the holy → kiss, and as

fanciful applications of the principle that anyone who publicly eschews what the world deems lawful will be secretly practicing what the world forbids (see Tac. *Hist.* 5.5; Edwards, 1992).

b. Display their Education

In contrast to the authors of our New Testament, all the Greek apologists affect a polished style, their grammar and vocabulary being for the most part classical though not Attic. In Latin the extravagances of Tertullian clearly bespeak an excess, not a deficit, of rhetorical education (Sider, 1971). Titles such as *Embassy* and *Apology* suggest particular addressees and occasions of delivery. Indeed, they represent the three acknowledged branches of oratory:

1. the deliberative, which addresses political questions;
2. the forensic, which is suited to legal advocacy;
3. the epideictic, whose purpose is not so much to instruct or persuade as to exhibit the speaker's talents.

None of our surviving texts falls wholly into one category, for all have the professed aim of defending the faith against its calumniators, but all move rapidly into the deliberative mode as they exhort the pagans to turn from their idols and embrace the truth. Some or all may deserve to be classified as epideictic, insofar as none is known to have been delivered to an audience, or even perused by its nominal addressee.

c. Demand the Esteem Accorded to Philosophers

Aristides and → Athenagoras style themselves philosophers, while Justin proudly flaunts the philosopher's cloak. In adopting this posture, Christians were not so much conforming to the ambient culture as claiming the right to differ with legal impunity. Tertullian, notwithstanding his infamous question "What has Athens to do with Jerusalem?" (Tert. *Praesc.* 7), is able to quote the Stoics in his arguments for the corporeality of the soul. Justin and Athenagoras favor Plato, whose teachings on creation and the afterlife approximated more closely to biblical teaching than those of any other school. For all that, Justin is far from being a Platonist: the superficial agreements that he finds between Platonic and biblical doctrines are attributed in every case to plagiarism rather than to direct inspiration (Just. 1 *Apol.* 44; 59; 60). Only the prophets, Hystaspes and the Sibyl, enjoyed any direct communication of truth (1 *Apol.* 44.12). There were indeed philosophers who discerned the futility of pagan religion by the unaided exercise of *logos* or reason (1 *Apol.* 46.3); but Socrates, Heraclitus, and Musonius are not credited with any accurate knowledge of → God, → creation, or the → afterlife.

d. Contest the Superiority of Greek Culture

The pretensions of the Greeks are repeatedly held up to derision (Nasrallah, 2005). Justin, a Samarian if not a Samaritan, asserts that among the barbarians – that is, the Hebrews – the philosophers were Christians while the Greeks still labored in darkness. Just as Manetho, Berossus, → Flavius Josephus, and Philo of Byblos endeavored to prove the superior antiquity of their own peoples, so Tertullian demonstrates that → Moses was older than Homer (Tert. *Apol.* 19.2; see further Droge, 1989). In thus refuting the charge of innovation, he also implies that the church deserves the legal immunities that had been granted to the Jews. Some apologists introduce new ethnographies, in which to be Greek is simply to occupy one category of false belief. The designation "third race," stemming perhaps from Matt 21:43, is attested by Tertullian (*Nat.* 1.8–11) and perhaps echoed in the *Letter to Diognetus* (5.4–5; → *Diognetus, Epistle to*), which insists that Christians, as the soul of the world, are not set apart by dress or diet (see Gruen, 2017). The Greek version of the *Apology* of Aristides divides the world by religion into Christians, Jews and polytheists, while the Syriac further divides the polytheists into barbarians and Greeks (Geffcken, 1907).

e. Unmask the Origins of Pagan Cult

Building on Paul's (→ Paul the Apostle) admonition that the pagan gods are demons, the apologists devised their own genealogy of religion. According to Justin (2 *Apol.* 5), idolatry is the cult of the dead, promoted by fallen angels who wish to involve humanity in their ruin. Athenagoras adds that the devil, as prince of matter, brings souls into subjection by persuading them to worship wood and stone

(Ath. *Leg.* 24–27). The whole of Roman society, says Tertullian, is a pageant of the → devil (Tert. *Spect.* 12.5). No Christian writer, however, anticipates → Porphyry of Tyre in making demons responsible for earthquakes, and all the apologists hold that matter itself, though now corrupt, is a work of God that will be redeemed through the new creation.

Apart from Tertullian, all the apologists are sparse in their quotations of identifiable passages from the New Testament. It is possible that Justin was unacquainted with the Gospels as we know them, for the source of his own allusions is named only as the "memoirs of the apostles" (Just. 1 *Apol.* 66.3; 67.3; see Shotwell, 1965). On the other hand, it is possible that some at least elected not to quote books to which no authority would be attached by a pagan audience. Fear of incomprehension, or perhaps of betraying mysteries, will account for the absence of any account of the → incarnation in Athenagoras or Diognetus. Athenagoras at least is no mere catechumen, for he can distinguish the begetting of the Son from the contingent origin of other beings. Justin not only bears witness to the worship of Father, Son, and → Holy Spirit, but is the first author to give a detailed account of eucharistic and baptismal practice (1 *Apol.* 61–66). His aim, no doubt, is to deflect false suspicions, but his co-religionists seem to have pursued the same end by reticence, or as we now say, "reserve."

2. Polemic

Under this rubric we may collect the literature that denounces a class of adversaries without a named interlocutor, and without citing persecution as the principal motive for writing. Christian polemic has three objects:

1. the Jews;
2. the philosophers;
3. civic religion.

a. Jews

Melito's homily *On Pascha* (→ Melito of Sardis), which proclaims Christ as the *Logos* (or → Word) whose passion fulfills and abrogates the nomos or law, is the earliest specimen of unilateral preaching against the Jews. The first work to be entitled *Against the Jews* is a short tract by Tertullian, which asserts that, as in the Gospel, so in paradise the whole of the law was to love God and one's neighbor. After the → fall God subjected his chosen nation to positive ordinances, yet even in the prophets we learn that God does not care for → Sabbaths or sacrifices, that the true circumcision is that of the heart, that the Temple made by human hands will perish, and that those outside Israel will recognize their savior in the child of a virgin womb. In an anonymous treatise, *On Mounts Sinai and Zion*, the two peaks symbolize the law and the Gospel, hence the → synagogue and the church. The superiority of the Christian polity is proved in part by numerological reasoning, but primarily by the argument that Christ alone possessed the clean hands and heart that are required of those who are to ascend the hill of Zion.

Cyprian of Carthage, to whom this text was falsely attributed, produced his own compilation of *Testimonia Against the Jews* in three books (→ Cyprian of Carthage). The first, commencing with the visitation of God's wrath upon the Jews in the Roman era, maintains that both the sins of the people and the abrogation of the law were already prefigured in their own Scriptures. It adds that these Scriptures foretold the supersession of Moses by a greater prophet, and the second book assembles texts that, when collated with the known facts of Christ's ministry, bear witness to his divinity, his sinlessness, his messianic character, the necessity and efficacy of his death on the → cross, and his future coming in judgment. The third book discovers presages in the law of the higher morality of the Gospel, which includes the unconditional love of God, the willing practice of virginity, the observance of the Eucharist and for some the consummation of martyrdom. → Augustine of Hippo borrows the title *Against the Jews* for a shorter work, which at the end adds to this vein of literature by praying that the Jews will allow themselves to be redeemed by the passover of Calvary.

b. Philosophers

Tatian, a disciple of Justin, imitates the scurrility of the Cynics in his *Oration to the Greeks* (→ Tatian). Making only incidental reference to charges against the Christians, this is an indiscriminate satire on the folly and foppery of the Greek philosophers, their unacknowledged dependence on the wisdom of barbarians, the artificiality of Attic prose, the subjection of the pagan world to demons, and the ubiquitous cult of matter. A self-professed barbarian who can nonetheless use the works of Greek chronographers to his advantage, Tatian alludes to the prophets and has a rudimentary doctrine of the *logos*, though he ignores the incarnation. We might describe his work as a combination of Cynic diatribe with the characteristic traits of the vindicatory literature. More urbane, and apparently more learned (Papadogiannakis, 2013, 2–13), is the 5th-century CE compilation of → Theodoret of Cyrrhus, the *Cure for Greek Distempers*, which collates the erroneous teachings of the philosophers, together with their occasional approximations to truth as the church receives it. The subjects of its 12 books are successively faith, the first principle, the angels, matter, human nature, providence, the cult of martyrs, sacrifice, law, oracles, the last assize, and practical virtue. The excerpts and paraphrases agree so often with those of Eusebius or the doxographic tradition as to leave us doubting whether Theodoret knew any of his sources – even Plato, whom he cites copiously – at first hand. Christian traditions, of course, he knows well, and in the closing books episodes from history proclaim the irreversible defeat of polytheism.

c. Civic Religion

Clement of Alexandria's *Protrepticus*, or *Exhortation*, urges that ancestral precedent cannot justify the worship of wood and stone, let alone the widespread custom of human sacrifice. He is one of our chief informants regarding the mysteries, whose execrable rites he professes to know at first hand (→ Clement of Alexandria). Even the philosophers, he avers, have taken their notion of the divine from barbarous and idolatrous nations, except when they were shrewd enough to steal from the Hebrew prophets, of whom we also hear occasional echoes in the poets. Clement, however, cannot match the vehemence of → Firmicus Maternus, whose treatise *On the Error of Pagan Religions* represents the pagan cults as demonic parodies of the sacraments, and exhorts the sons of → Constantine I to suppress them. Firmicus allots to each of the barbarous nations the worship of one element: the Egyptian Osiris is thus a personification of water (Firm. *Err. prof. rel.* 2), the Phrygian Attis of earth (*Err. prof. rel.* 3), the Syrian goddess of air (*Err. prof. rel.* 4), and the Persian Mithras of fire (*Err. prof. rel.* 5). The abominations of which he accuses Greek adepts of Dionysius (*Err. prof. rel.* 6) would not surprise any Roman who was familiar with Livy's account of the Senate's proscription of this cult in 186 BCE; the Romans themselves, however, are accused by Firmicus of failing to understand that the serpent whom they venerate is an ectype of the devil (*Err. prof. rel.* 26). Where Firmicus is the sole witness to a phenomenon – for example the resurrection of Attis after his lugubrious rites of burial (*Err. prof. rel.* 8) – it is possible that he has witnessed a development in religious practice under Christian influence, but equally possible that he is exaggerating the likeness between the caricature and its Christian prototype.

The seven books of → Arnobius of Sicca's *Against the Nations*, an epideictic exercise according to → Jerome, profess to be written in answer to the pagan complaint that the gods have withdrawn their favor because their altars are neglected, and make occasional reference to the punitive measures taken against the church in the name of these gods between 303 and 311 CE. Nevertheless, the argument is in substance polemical rather than vindicatory, its point being that Rome herself habitually practices the religious innovation that she adduces as a pretext for the execution of Christians. Even her methods of torture are new; no wonder then that she embraces the cult of every conquered people, while the philosophers most in vogue are *novi viri* ("new men"), though the elements of their thought are both eclectic and antiquated (Simmons, 1995, 156–163). If these are disciples of Porphyry, they may also have furnished Arnobius with a number of his arguments against the inhumanity and futility of sacrifice in Book 7. Of Christ he says little except in the closing chapters of Book 1, which may have been written, as Jerome indicates, as late as 325 CE (Edwards, 2016). At that time Christians still feared a return of persecution; 50 years later Ambrosiaster can only pour bewildered execrations on those pagans who refuse to acknowledge the truth of the Gospel, the triumph of Christianity, the purity and antiquity of its doctrines, or its power to shape not merely the philosophy of its converts but their lives.

3. Controversial Literature

Controversial writing against a named opponent naturally takes the form of dialogue. In the *Octavius* of → Minucius Felix, it is the eponymous Christian speaker who initiates the quarrel when he chides his friend Caecilian for doing homage to an icon. Caecilian replies with the Ciceronian argument that we know nothing of the gods except what is handed down from our forefathers; he denounces in turn the ignorance and depravity of the Christians, quoting Fronto, his fellow-African and tutor to Marcus Aurelius, as a reliable witness to their rites of cannibalism and incest. In response Octavius, without naming Christ, imputes the foundation of pagan cults to demons and employs conventional arguments for the unity and incorporeality of God. It thus presents a contrast to the *Dialogue with Trypho* by → Justin Martyr, a work of the mid-2nd century CE, in which the Jew and the Christian exchange interpretations of the messianic texts in the Septuagint. For Justin this alone is the word of God, not only an inspired translation but a treasury of passages that have been cunningly expunged from the Jewish version. In his proof that Jesus fulfilled the other prophecies Justin quotes from no known gospel, though we are often reminded of Matthew (→ Matthew the Apostle). It has been surmised that Trypho was a real personage, not only because his name resembles that of the rabbi Tarfon, but because it seems that Justin cannot always answer his challenge to prove that promises given to Israel were intended for the church (Horner, 2001).

In his work *Against Celsus*, written about 248 CE, → Origen takes as his interlocutor a man who had written against the church some 70 years before (see Reemts, 1998). The first book justifies the adhesion of Christians to the barbarous philosophy of Moses and their claims regarding the Savior's marvelous birth. The second explains why the resurrected Christ (→ Resurrection) was visible only to his disciples, and refutes the charge (put into the mouth of a Jew) that the church is an renegade sect of → Judaism. The third book contends that → Celsus is wrong to argue that the → miracles of Christ and the church are equaled or surpassed in other traditions, while the fourth, contrasting Hesiod and Plato with the Bible, concludes that the sacred texts of the Greeks are not only more obscene on the surface but less amenable to a figurative interpretation. The fifth responds to the argument that gods do not appear on earth in person but only through their intermediaries and discusses the relation between the universal law of God and the laws by which he sanctified the Jews. The sixth book maintains that, far from having plagiarized the doctrines of Plato without understanding them, Christians possess writings that are older than Plato and more authoritative: recounting humanity's fall from the knowledge of God, he warns his adversary that he cannot fathom the mystery so long as he confounds Christians with heretics and approaches the → anthropomorphisms of Scripture without a hermeneutic key. In the seventh book Origen argues that, as we cannot know God without his own revelation, the wisdom of the prophets is more profound than all the philosophy of the Greeks, including Plato. The eighth book meets the argument that Christians, being atheists, are bad citizens, by denying that the demons have any mandate from the supreme God or that refusal to worship those who have drunk the blood of one's co-religionists is evidence of disloyalty to Rome.

We may assign to this category the letter of Cyprian to Demetrianus (post-250 CE), which answers the charge that natural disasters had become more frequent because the gods resented the desertion of their altars. Without questioning the phenomenon, Cyprian ascribes it to the ageing of the earth (see Daniélou, 1977, 251–260) and adds, foreshadowing Arnobius, that the cruelty of torture has also increased. In the course of Diocletian's persecution 50 years later, the sophist Hierocles ridiculed Christ, pronouncing his feats inferior to those of the Pythagorean ascetic → Apollonius of Tyana; the retaliatory tract *Against Hierocles*, which argues that either Apollonius or his biographer was a charlatan, is attributed to Eusebius, though its style has an elegance that he lacks elsewhere (Hägg, 1992). The most dramatic setting is the one devised by Macarius Magnes for his *Apocriticus*, a stilted exercise even by the canons that prevailed in the late 4th century CE. The villain is an unnamed Hellene, whose grimaces and frowns become increasingly comic as each of his criticisms on the New Testament is exploded by the narrator and his allies. A. von Harnack (1916) proposed that Porphyry was the true author of these knowledgeable strictures, while it

has been suggested in recent years that Hierocles or → Julian the Apostate was his model (Digeser, 2002); but of course it is equally possible that Macarius has drawn both the Hellene's sneers and his own replies from a cluster of sources, not excluding his own imagination. Julian's treatise *Against the Galileans* was among the most resented of his insults to Christianity: why, he demanded, had Greeks who numbered Plato among their countrymen taken up the barbarous idiom of the Jews with its attendant superstitions? → Cyril of Alexandria (d. 444 CE) undertook a posthumous refutation, defending both the antiquity of Moses and his moral superiority to Hesiod, while at the same time asserting that it was only Christians who understood him. As for Plato, he too has the moral and intellectual advantage of all the other Greek philosophers, but he is equal to Moses only in what he steals.

The best of these performances is the last, the treatise of John Philoponus' *On the Eternity of the World Against Proclus*. While all Christians held, in defiance of Aristotle, that the physical world has a finite history, Philoponus was the first to maintain that Aristotle's own principles entail this, since they would not allow him to hold that the number of human beings who have lived is already infinite, as it must be if the world has existed forever. He goes on to maintain that as the world is spatially finite, so it has only finite power, and hence not the power to persist eternally; indeed we perceive that, being composed of matter, it is destructible, and only that which is generated is subject to destruction. To those who object that the act of creating the world would entail a change in God, he replies that to will a change is not the same thing as to change one's will. If these are familiar arguments to philosophers and historians of philosophy, it is because Philoponus has made them so (Sorabji, 1983, 214–223, 241).

4. Constructive Literature

From early times, not all apologists were content to act as counsel for the defense by demonstrating the antiquity or innocence of Christian beliefs. Two treatises, one ascribed to Athenagoras and the other (quite impossibly) to Justin, undertake to show that the resurrection of the body is perfectly consonant with the natural order in which death and life succeed each other in cyclic alternation. Justin is also the putative author of an *Address to the Greeks, an Exhortation to the Greeks* and a declamation *On Monarchy*, which assemble pagan testimonies to the unity of God. Orphic verses (no doubt as genuine as any others) sit cheek by jowl in these compositions with patent forgeries, often attributed to the comic poets because they were famous purveyors of edifying maxims. The three books of Theophilus to his pagan friend Autolycus reach a higher level of erudition and literary craft. The first book – allegedly prompted, like the others, by the doubts of the silent addressee – combines a brief sketch of the attributes of God with the usual jeremiads against idolatry and polytheism. The constructive enterprise begins in the second book, which may have sued Jewish sources for its allegorical reading of the first chapter of Genesis, together with an explanation of God's design in fashioning → Adam and Eve as infants (νήπιοι) in → paradise (Gen 2:15), with a free choice between the way of → death and way of → immortality (Zeegers, 1998, 142–151). The third book, an exposition of Christian ethics, is methodical but purposely devoid of originality.

No Christian author before → Nicaea can vie in erudition (or in prolixity) with Clement, whose *Stromateis* (or *Miscellanies*, after Plutarch) is addressed simultaneously to Greek philosophers who have never heard of Moses and to Christians who regard philosophy as the devil's scripture. Gnosis or knowledge for Clement is not the preserve of the so-called Gnostics, whose enormities he rehearses at length in the third book, but of the perfect of faith and therefore of obedience (Ashwin-Siejkowski, 2008, 104–144; Osborn, 1994). Just as his fellow-Alexandrian Philo had commended the "encyclopaedic" disciplines as a preparation for biblical study, so Clement makes "eclectic" drafts on Greek discoveries in the arts of life and natural sciences (Clem. *Strom.* 1.37.6). Better versed in Plato than Justin, he finds a homology between the world of ideas and the *logos*, whom he extols as the δύναμις or power of God in the formation, governance, and salvation of the created order (*Strom.* 7.2.7). At the same time, he does not grant the philosophers a share in the direct revelation that God vouchsafed to the Sibyl and Hystaspes (*Strom.* 6.42–43), and he maintains at length in his

fifth book that the Greeks owe whatever they know of God to plagiarism from the Hebrew prophets (*Strom.* 5.89.2–141.4). He is not ashamed, however, to cite Pythagorean usage as a precedent for his allegorical reading of cryptic passages in the Scriptures (*Strom.* 5.28), and he demonstrates his proficiency in logic in the fragmentary eighth book.

Eusebius treats the philosophers with more charity, so long as they offer no excuse for popular superstitions (→ Eusebius of Caesarea). In the first three books of his *Preparation for the Gospel*, he argues, quoting liberally from Porphyry's treatise *On Statues*, that the myths of polytheism do not lend themselves to physical or theological allegory; in Books 4–6 he proves from Porphyry and the Cynic Oenomaus that philosophers are aware of the presence of demons in every shrine of the pagan world. Books 7–9 recount the history of the Hebrew patriarchs and the miraculous origins of the Septuagint, whose authors are widely agreed to inculcate a higher standard of rectitude. In the last six books, a sustained comparison of Plato and Moses is prefaced by examples of Greek plagiarism (again derived from Porphyry). It is no surprise therefore to find that, while Plato always falls short of Moses, there are passages in which he is able to mimic his sublimity. The Platonist Numenius, who adumbrates his own doctrine of the → Trinity, confesses that his master is merely an "Atticizing Moses" (Eus. *Praep.* 10.11.14; see Ridings, 1995). Other Platonists illustrate the divisions within the school and its occasional acts of homage to the Gospel. Thus, the ground is cleared for the *Demonstration of the Gospel*, of which ten books survive from the original 20. The first two reinforce the thesis of Book 7 of the *Preparation*, that Christianity is the religion of the Hebrew patriarchs. The third maintains that the life of Christ, while leaving no doubt of his being fully human, also manifests his divinity; Books 4 and 5 construct the first systematic account of the attributes of this "second god" from the Psalms and prophecies of the elder Scriptures. The last five books give evidence in detail of the fulfillment of these prophecies in Christ's ministry, culminating in his passion. A fragment of Book 15 appears to be part of defense of the book of → Daniel against Porphyry, who is also said to have been the object of a whole dissertation in 20 books.

While this work *Against Porphyry* is lost (see Kofsky, 2002, 71–73), we possess a Syriac translation of the *Theophany* in five books. Book 1 contends that the harmony of the world attests the universal government of the *logos* and hence the preeminence of humanity as the one species endowed with reason; the corruption of religion, rehearsed at length in Book 2, has found its antidote in Christianity, the spread of which, according to Book 3, has been providentially assisted by the ascendancy of Rome. The fourth book urges that we cannot deny the incarnation of God the Word when we read the Gospel, and the fifth that we cannot doubt the truth of the Gospel when we reflect on the striking marriage of simplicity and fortitude in its authors. Some of this argumentation reappears (notwithstanding their theological differences) in the diptych of → Athanasius of Alexandria's *Against the Nations* and *On the incarnation*. The former treatise inveighs against idolatry as a failure to grasp the incorporeal nature of the → soul, and against the cult of many gods as a failure to grasp that even superhuman δυνάμεις or powers in the physical realm are the products and instruments of the one uncreated power. In the latter treatise, Athanasius argues that, as God was bound to punish the transgression of the first humans but did not wish to destroy them, the only expedient was that the Word through whom we had been created should become a man himself, not only to guide us by his teaching and example, but to subsume us in his death so that when he rose again (as, being God, he was bound to do), we too should be taken up with him into everlasting life. While its ostensible adversaries are Platonists, it was probably written during the Arian controversy (→ Arianism), which Athanasius addresses by presenting his own Christology as the uncontested teaching of the church (Anatolios, 1998, 28–30).

Porphyry may be one of the philosophers whom → Lactantius denounced as a toady of Diocletian in Book 5 of *his Divine Institutes* (Digeser, 1999). His declared aim is to give instruction to Christians (Lact. *Inst.* 5.1), though it is only in the fourth book, where he vindicates the divinity of Christ and his messianic claims, that he deploys the customary arguments from Scripture. Elsewhere, whether he is tracing pagan religion to the worship of dead impostors in his first book, setting out the principles of true religion in the third, or denying that justice is compatible with social inequality in the fifth, his method is to argue in a Ciceronian style, and from the classics of pagan literature, that the virtues to which the Romans aspire cannot be realized without faith in Christ. Even the premonitions of divine wrath in Book 7 are underwritten by the Sibyl (→ Oracles). The work left its mark on Constantine's *Oration to the Saints*, which, while it manifests very little originality of thought, is the earliest writing to bring apologetic tropes into a personal confession of belief.

If Constantine quarried Lactantius, Augustine imitated and thereby eclipsed him in his monumental *City of God*. Ostensibly a rebuttal of the charge that Rome's desertion of her gods exposed her to the gothic sack of 409 CE, it exemplifies all four of our categories in its 22 books. The first, vindicatory book maintains that the churches afforded a refuge for the victims of the sack; the next seven argue polemically that Rome mistakes the vices of empire for heroic virtues, and that her celebrated piety consists in the observation of false niceties toward fictitious gods. The controversial mode supervenes in Books 8–10, where Augustine confutes the teaching of the Platonists on the necessary eternity of the world and the instrumentality of demons (as he calls them) in the exercise of providence and the answering of prayer. The constructive project commences in Book 11 with the creation, and Augustine pursues the course of history through the fall and the Flood to the age of the patriarchs in order to prove his thesis that God has secretly been populating an eternal city while human polities have risen and passed away. In the 19th book, he contends that there is no city of God on earth, where even a Christian magistrate cannot live by the principles of the Gospel. The supersession of all earthly kingdoms by the Last Judgment (→ Judgment, Biblical Concept) in Book 20 is followed in Books 21 and 22 by meditations on the eternity of punishment in hell and of bliss in heaven. This work is the theological, if not the chronological, peroration of apologetic literature in late antiquity.

Historiography

In his *Lehrburch der Dogmengeschichte* (1888), A. von Harnack presents apologetic as a philosophical enterprise, not warranted by the New testament, which promoted the Hellenization of Christianity. J. Geffcken (1907) argued that the first Greek apologists built upon the engagement of Hellenized Jews with pagan culture, and this thesis was sustained by E.R. Goodenough (1923). J. Daniélou (1961) widened the study of early Christian commerce with Greek culture and brought the same erudition to the neglected Latin apologists in his *Les origines du christianisme latin* (1964; ET: 1977). The arguments for the antiquity of the Christian faith were examined at length by A. Droge (1989) and D. Ridings (1995), while R. Grant (1988) considers apologetic both as a mode of theology and as a means of "coming to terms" with the ambient culture. Pagan, Jewish and Christian strands of thought are brought together by M.J. Edwards, S.R F. Price and M.D. Goodman (1999), just as by B. Pouderon and J. Doré (1998). Recent Anglophone writing on 4th-century CE apologetic has discussed the effects of Porphyry's polemics against Christianity: see M. Simmons (1995), E. De Palma Digeser (2000), and A. Kofsky (2000). Twenty-first century studies of apologetic in its imperial context include those of S. and P. Parvis (2007), E. Osborn (2009), and B. Colot (2016).

Bibliography

Ashwin-Siejkowski, P., *Clement of Alexandria: A Project of Christian Perfection*, London, 2008.

Anatolios, K., *Athanasius: The Coherence of his Thought*, London, 1998.

Colot, B., *Lactance, penser la conversion de Rome au temps de Constantin*, Florence, 2016.

Daniélou, J., *Message évangélique et culture hellénistique*, Paris, 1961.

Daniélou, J., *The Origins of Latin Christianity*, trans. J.A. Baker, 1977.

Digeser, E.D., *The Making of a Christian Empire: Lactantius and Rome*, Ithaca, 1999.

Digeser, E.D., "Porphyry, Julian or Hierokles? The Anonymous Hellene in Macarius Magnes' *Apokritikos*," *JHS* 53, 2002, 466–502.

Droge, A., *Homer or Moses? Early Christian Interpretations of the History of Culture*, Tübingen, 1989.

Edwards, M.J., "Some Early Christian Immoralities," *AncSoc* 23, 1992, 71–82.

Edwards, M.J., "Some Theories on the Dating of Arnobius," *EThL* 92, 2016, 671–684.

Edwards, M.J., S.R.F. Price & M.D. Goodman, eds., *Apologetics in the Roman World*, Oxford, 1999.

Geffcken, J., *Zwei griechischen Apologeten*, Leipzig, 1907.

Goodenough, E.R, *The Theology of Justin Martyr*, Jena, 1923.

Grant, R., *Greek Apologists of the Second Century*, London, 1988.

Gruen, E., "Christianity as a 'Third Race': Is Ethnicity an Issue?" in: J. Carleton Paget & J. Lieu, eds., *Christianity in the Second Century*, Cambridge UK, 2017.

Hägg, T., "Hierocles the Lover of Truth and Eusebius the Sophist," *SO* 67, 1992, 138–150.

Harnack, A. von, *Lehrburch der Dogmengeschichte*, Freiburg 1888.

Harnack, A. von, *Porphyrius: Gegen die Christen*, Berlin, 1916.

Horner, T., *Listening to Trypho*, Louvain, 2001.

Kofsky, A., *Eusebius of Caesarea against Paganism*, Leiden, 2002.

Nasrallah, L., "Mapping the World: Justin, Tatian, Lucian and the Second Sophistic," *HThR* 98, 2005, 283–314.

Osborn, E., "Arguments for Faith in Clement of Alexandria," *VigChr* 48, 1994, 1–24.

Osborn, E., *Clement of Alexandria*, Cambridge MA, 2009.

Papadogiannakis, I., *Christianity and Hellenism in the Fifth-Century East*, Washington DC, 2013.

Parvin, S., & P. Parvis, eds., *Justin Martyr and his Worlds*, Minneapolis, 2007.

Pouderon, B., & J. Doré, eds., *Les apologistes chrétiens et la culture grecque*, Paris, 1998.

Reemts, C., *Vernunftgemässer Glaube*, Bonn, 1998.

Ridings, D., *The Attic Moses: The Dependency Theme in Some Early Christian Writers*, Goteborg, 1995.

Shotwell, W., *The Biblical Exegesis of Justin Martyr*, London, 1965.

Sider, R.D., *Ancient Rhetoric and the Art of Tertullian*, Oxford, 1971.

Simmons, M.B., *Arnobius of Sicca*, Oxford, 1995.

Sorabji, R., *Time, Creation and the Continuum*, London, 1983.

Waszink, J.H., *Septimi Florentis Tertulliani De Anima*, Amsterdam, 1946.

Zeegers, N., "Les trois cultures de Théophile d'Antioche," in: B. Pouderon & J. Doré, eds., *Les apologistes chrétiens et la culture grecque*, Paris, 1998, 137–176.

MARK EDWARDS

Aponius

Almost all that can be said about Aponius (often Apponius) comes from the voluminous commentary on the Song of Songs that bears his name. The editors of the 1986 critical edition (B. de Vregille & L. Neyrand) argued for a dating in the first decade of the 5th century CE and the location as most likely northern Italy. By the time of their annotated translation some two decades later, they had revised their estimate of its dating to between 420 and 430 CE. One reason for this was that the author knew → Augustine of Hippo's *City of God* – yet it has to be said that any knowledge of Augustine is superficial at best. It is clear that he knew and used the (Ps.)-Pelagian *De induratione cordis pharaonis*. This reinforces a hypothesis of an Italian monastic setting. In the last decade, P. Hamblenne has wanted to date him much later, as someone working in the library of the monastery of Corbie in still barbarian Gaul, around 680 CE. P. Hamblenne sees allusions to → Cassiodorus, → Isidore of Seville, and even → Gregory the Great in the commentary (Hamblenne, 2001, 452) and claims that Aponius' ignorance of the Roman classical tradition means that he cannot have been an Italian or Irish monk. Bede the Venerable, who used the commentary, is a clear terminus.

Military invasions seem part of the background (see Book 12; CCSL 19.227–236), as does western → Origenism. These features do little for close dating, but they do perhaps help explain how the Song of Songs came to be read as an allegory that reflected the turbulent history of the people of God under great pressure. There is a salvation-historical approach to the Song of Songs, rare for its time, yet perhaps with precedent in the Targum, which had interpreted it as running from deliverance from Egypt through exile (→ Deportation/Exile) into messianic times. For Aponius, the time line is less clear, but certainly the starting place seems to be the early Jewish church and the end point the conversion of the Jews. The high point comes with the Christological mysteries and especially the betrothed and beloved soul of Christ. It might not quite be the case that the betrothal is interpreted as "the moment of crucifixion" (Studer, 2014), but Song 6:8–11 is clearly central as concerning the incarnate union. He was playing with the idea of the preexistence of the soul, but with conceptual connections to → Gregory of Nyssa and → Theodore of Mopsuestia, yet gives these a western spin, toward a proto-Anselmian soteriology, in terms of the salvific contribution of the

perfect humanity (Grillmeier, 1975, 384–388). It is perhaps pushing things too far to think that the Song of Songs is made to tell the story of humanity on its way to God (Barry, 1997). In any case its Christological contribution found no keen response in the centuries that followed. The commentary seems to have fallen victim to the post-patristic-era love of excerpting. Only with Erasmus, then the 1548 Freiburg edition, was there a new appreciation of its worth. The edition by J. Martini of 1843 stood outside the "canon" of foremost patristic writers represented by J.-P. Migne's Patrologiae cursus completus.

Historiography

The publication of the *Commentarius in Canticum Canticorum* in the Patrologia Latina Supplementum in 1967 had at least the effect of facilitating A. Grillmeier (1975) to devote a section of his history of Christology to Aponius. The 1986 critical edition of B. de Vregille and L. Neyrand, on which the Sources Chrétiennes edition and translation was based, also inspired the annotated translation and dissertation by H. König (1992), emphasising what A. Grillmeier had pointed to – the theology of the human soul of Christ. B. Stubenrauch's work (1991) was largely exegetical and descriptive. Despite B. Studer's regarding the provenance to be less important than the staurological theology of the work, P. Hamblenne's arguments (1991) suggest that the dating by the editors did not convince everyone. Recently L. Crociani (1991), has offered a form of *Sachkritik* in the light of Mariology. The mysterious message of the text is rivalled only by the continuing uncertainties concerning authorship.

Bibliography

Barry, C., "Review of Vregille and Neyrand," *ScEs* 49, 1997, 368–369.

Crociani, L., "Il recupero di alcune lezioni del testo delle Explanationes in Canticum Canticorum di Apponio der la ricostruzione della sua dottrina sulla Madre di Dio," in: *Virgo liber Verbi*, Rome, 1991, 133–171.

Didone, M., "L'*Explanatio di Apponio* in relazione all'Expositio *di* Beda ed alle Enarrationes in Cantica *di* Angelomus," *CClCr* 7, 1986, 77–119.

Elliott, M.W., *The Song of Songs and Christology*, Tübingen, 2000, 381–451.

Grillmeier, A., *Christ in Christian Tradition: From the Apostolic Age to Chalcedon (451)*, Atlanta, 1975, 384–388.

Hamblenne, P., "Deux métaphores apponiennes (In Cant., III,l. 92 s. et IX, l. 110–112)," *SE* 39, 2000, 21–35.

Hamblenne, P., "Apponius: Le moment, une patrie," *Aug.* 41, 2001, 425–464.

König, H., *Apponius: Die Auslegung zum Lied der Lieder: Die einführenden Bücher I–III und das christologisch bedeutsame Buch IX*, AGLB 21, Freiburg, 1992.

Stubenrauch, B., *Der Heilige Geist bei Apponius: Zum theologischen Gehalt einer spätantiken Hoheliedauslegung*, Freiburg, 1991.

Studer, B., "Aponius," in: *EAC*, Downers' Grove, 2014.

Vregille, B. de, & L. Neyrand, eds., *Apponius in Canticum Canticorum*, CCSL 19, Turnhout, 1986; text with notes and introduction in SC 420, 421, 430, Paris, 1997, 1998.

MARK W. ELLIOTT

Apophthegmata Patrum

The *Apophthegmata Patrum*, often referred to as *Adhortationes Patrum* or *Verba Seniorum* in Latin and *Gerontikon* in Greek, and generally designated *The Sayings of the Desert Fathers* in English, are among the most copied and used collections of early Christian literature. The *Apophthegmata Patrum* are not one specific collection of texts but refer to a large number of collections of sayings and short anecdotes emerging from or related to the early monastic tradition. Numerous sayings or *exempla* in the collections, moreover, do not belong to the classical genre of apophthegmata in a strict sense, but are excerpts from homilies, letters, legends and *Vitae*. Sayings in the *Apophthegmata Patrum* thus often also occur outside of the sayings collections.

Due to the adaptability of the individual sayings, as well as the collections of sayings, to the circumstances of their transmission, they are typical for what is termed a fluid text transmission; in other words, the texts have undergone constant revision based on the interests and resources of the transmitters. The revisions have mainly concerned the arrangement and selection of sayings included, but often also the attribution and the text itself. Multiple translations and repeated revisions of these in the various languages, sometimes based on a selective use of models, together with repeated addition of new material manifest in many collections preclude the establishment of an original date, extent or text for the *Apophthegmata Patrum* (Rubenson, 2013).

Even though the precise origin of the sayings tradition as a whole as well as of individual sayings remains unknown, all evidence indicate that the tradition began in the monastic settlements of lower Egypt and was developed and organized in Palestine (Guy, 1993, 79–84; Regnault, 1981; Harmless, 2000). The core of the tradition has a strong focus on the settlements of Kellia, Nitria and Scetis in the desert area south and southeast of Alexandria. The earliest attestations of monastic sayings are found in the writings of → Evagrius of Pontus at the end of the 4th century CE and his disciple → John Cassian in the early 5th century CE. A large number of sayings also appear in the ascetic collection attributed to Isaiah of Gaza in the latter part of the 5th century CE.

In contrast to older studies regarding the sayings as originating in an oral culture of uneducated desert monks, recent studies have demonstrated a clear continuity between the early monastic tradition in Egypt and classical paideia (Larsen, 2006; 2013; Rubenson, 2012).

Although the sayings were originally composed in Greek, our earliest evidence for the collections of them, and thus for the *Apophthegmata Patrum* as such, are the collections translated into Syriac and attested in manuscripts dated to the 530's CE (Holmberg, 2013). Since these collections are organized neither alphabetically nor thematically, they most probably predate the organization of the Greek material into collections organized either according to the names of the monastic figures or according to pedagogical lists of virtues and vices. This organization of the material must have been made before the 540's CE when a thematic collection was translated into Latin, most probably in Constantinople (Guy, 1993, 80). A thematic collection was also soon translated into Coptic and Palestinian Aramaic. Collections of sayings were in subsequent centuries translated into Sogdian, Armenian, Georgian, Arabic, Ethiopic and Old Slavonic, and from the beginning of the 13th century into the various vernacular languages of medieval Europe.

Since the individual sayings (*apohthegmata*) lack an immediate relation to one another it has been easy throughout the process of transmission to make selections and rearrangements according to the specific needs and interests of the users, creating a situation where collections differ widely and few (if any) manuscripts have exactly the same content and arrangement. We thus find manuscripts with short collections of only some dozen sayings, as well as manuscripts with several thousand sayings, manuscripts with sayings organized alphabetically, thematically or in mixed combinations, but also without any obvious structure. In contrast to the structures and contents of the collections, the transmission of the text of individual sayings, at least in the Greek and Latin versions, seems to be fairly stable and varying mainly in introductory formula and attribution (Faraggiana di Sarzana, 1997; Rubenson, 2013).

In addition to the bewildering variety of collections in a large number of languages, a major problem for research on the *Apophthegmata Patrum* is that collections of sayings are often combined with, or even intertwined with, other material from the early monastic tradition, in particular shorter hagiographic accounts, but also excerpts from sermons, letters and treatises, thus making it hard to define the borders of the tradition (Faraggiana di Sarzana, 1997; Rapp, 2010; Dahlman, 2013). Although a large part of the material has its origin before the mid-6th century CE, units were also most probably composed and added later, in particular in the non-Greek versions.

1. The Greek Tradition

Within the Greek transmission the organization of the sayings in an alphabetic (in which anonymous sayings are included at the end) or in a thematic order has dominated. As shown by J.-C. Guy in his detailed discussion of the Greek collections, the two types to a large degree contain the same material and clearly relate to one another in the order of the units, but do not seem to be directly dependent one of the other (Guy, 1984, 182). A number of Greek manuscripts do, moreover, present the *Apophthegmata Patrum* according to slightly different patterns that sometimes combine features from the alphabetic-anonymous and the thematic orders.

The alphabetic part of the alphabetic-anonymous type of collection, known as *G*, was edited by J.B. Cotelier in 1677 and reprinted by J.-P. Migne in

Patrologia Graeca (65). This edition was, according to J.B. Cotelier's preface, based on the manuscript Codex regius 2466 (= Paris BN grec 1599), a manuscript that has later been shown to differ considerably from a majority of the most important manuscripts (Guy, 1984, 37). The anonymous part of the alphabetic-anonymous collection, designated *GN*, was partly edited by F. Nau in a series of articles in 1905–1913 on the basis of the manuscript Paris BN Coislin 126. A new and complete edition by J. Wortley was published in 2013 based on two other manuscripts, Sinai Saint Catherine 448 and Vatican Gr. 1599. As for the transmission of the alphabetic-anonymous type of collection J.-C. Guy was unable to distinguish clear stages. The 12 manuscripts used for the alphabetic part proved to differ considerably from one another. Based on the assumption that the manuscripts that had a considerably shorter series of sayings represented abridged versions, he dismissed the manuscript Paris BN grec 1596, which, together with manuscript Vatican Gr. 2592 and Venezia Marciana graeca 2.70, according to C. Faraggiana di Sarzana, constitute the oldest stage in the development of the alphabetic part of this type. According to her this early alphabetic-anonymous collection was the principal source of the first Greek systematic collection (Faraggiana di Sarzana, 1993; 1997, 455–460). An edition of the earliest alphabetic collection is being prepared by C. Faraggiana di Sarzana.

The transmission of the sayings in chapters according to monastic themes, traditionally referred to as the Greek systematic collection (designated as *GS*) was divided by J.-C. Guy into three stages (with some substages) on the basis of inclusions and order of material from other sources (Guy, 1984, 187). The only manuscript known that may represent the first stage in full is Paris BN grec 2474. J.-C. Guy identifies the second stage by its use of material from the corpus attributed to Isaiah of Gaza. He divided this stage into three groups represented by a number of manuscripts, among those the most important are Athos Protaton 86 and Paris BN grec 917. The third expanded stage is attested by two manuscripts (Guy, 1984, 182–190).

A few fragments of earlier codices from Egypt, the earliest dating back to the 6th century CE, have been identified, but they only contain singular sayings (Gallazzi, 1990; Bagnall & Gonis, 2003; Stroppa, 2016).

An edition of the Greek systematic collection was prepared by J.-C. Guy, but only published posthumously (Guy, 3 vols., 1993; 2003; 2015). Unfortunately, the edition does not make use of Paris BN grec 2474, and, in an attempt to be comprehensive, does not clearly distinguish the specific stages or variants within the tradition, but presents an accumulated collection that is not represented by any manuscript. It even includes the Latin text for sayings for which no Greek evidence had been found in the manuscripts of the systematical collection. An edition made by B. Dahlman of some of the chapters of the two most important manuscripts is published in the book series Paradiset: volume IV (Par. gr. 2474) and volumes V–IX (Athos Protaton 86; Dahlman & Rönnegård, 2012–2016).

Three other Greek types of collections have been briefly discussed in previous scholarship. The first two were regarded by J.-C. Guy as being derived from the standard alphabetic-anonymous and systematic collections and thus termed "derivées," a conclusion that has later been criticized (Dahlman, 2013). The first type has the probably largest number of sayings in any Greek manuscript, a total of 1883 in the important manuscript Paris Coislin 127. It was compiled from manuscripts both of the alphabetic-anonymous and of the systematic types, and was organized thematically, resulting in numerous doublets. This type of collection was edited by the Greek convent "To Genesion tes Theotokou" in the 1990s (*To Mega Gerontikon*, 1994–1999). J.-C. Guy regarded the second type as a systematic collection that had simply been reorganized alphabetically and enlarged by extracts from other monastic writings (Guy, 1984, 212–214). This type is primarily represented by the manuscripts Escorial R-II-1 and Paris BN grec 919, which also contain a small collection of old independent hagiographic and apophthegmatic material making them valuable text witnesses of an old textual tradition contrary to J.-C. Guy's conclusions (Dahlman, 2013). The third type, termed "Sabaitic" by J.-C. Guy on account of the fact that the oldest manuscript representing the type was written at the Monastery of Saint Sabas (Paris BN grec 1598), is also organized alphabetically, in this case with anonymous sayings at the end of each letter heading. On account of the numerous extracts from other monastic writings it is seen as a monastic compilation

rather than as a collection of sayings (Guy, 1984, 221–230). However, it has been demonstrated that many of the nominal sayings have been transmitted in a very old textual tradition sharing many features with the earliest known Syriac collections (Dahlman, 2012).

2. Latin

The Latin transmission of the *Apophthegmata Patrum* is known in a number of different, largely overlapping collections, all translated from Greek. The most widely diffused is known as the *PJ* collection, named after the two translators, mentioned in the manuscripts, Pelagius and John. The first translator is probably to be identified as Pope → Pelagius I, who lived in Constantinople from 536 to 543 CE, while the second translator is often identified as, but less likely to be, his papal successor John III. The translation was most probably made or at least begun in Constantinople during Pelagius' stay in the city. The collection is a translation of the Greek thematic collection represented by the manuscript Paris BN grec 2474. The collection was edited by H. Rosweyde in 1615 on the basis of 24 manuscripts, out of which six have been identified (Wilmart, 1922) and among which the oldest and most important is Brussels BR 9850–52 from circa 700 CE. The last chapter of the second and third stages of the Greek systematic collection is missing in H. Rosweyde's edition as well as in most Latin manuscripts, although present in a number of early manuscripts such as Milan, Ambrosianus F 84 sup. from the early 8th century CE and Paris BN latin 5387 from the end of the 9th century CE. This chapter was edited by A. Wilmart in 1922 on the basis of these two, as well as two later, manuscripts. Some 20 sayings preserved in several Latin manuscripts of the systematic collection, including Brussels BR 9850–52, were, moreover, omitted from H. Rosweyde's edition. They were edited by P.V. Nikitin, who also made emendations of many of the other sayings. The same 20 sayings were later edited once again by C. Batlle, who was not aware of P.V. Nikitin's previous edition (Nikitin, 1915–1916; Batlle, 1971).

Three other Latin collections were also part of H. Rosweyde's edition. The probably oldest of these, designated as *MD*, is attributed to Martin, bishop of Braga (c. 520–580 CE; → Martin of Braga). It consists of a series of 110 sayings without any apparent order. A critical edition of the collection was made by C. Barlow in 1950 on the basis of a number of manuscripts, the oldest and most important being Bruxelles BN 3595 (today Bruxelles KBR 8216–18) dated 819 CE, a manuscript also used by H. Rosweyde (Barlow, 1950). The collection is of great interest since it has numerous sayings not attested in the *PJ* collection or any other edited Latin collection. Many of these sayings are found in the Greek alphabetic-anonymous collection of which no Latin version is known, but others are only found in Syriac or in no other known collection.

The second and largest of the additional collections, designated as *PA*, is attributed to Paschasius, the → deacon of Martin of Braga, in which the sayings are organized in 101 short chapters based on virtues and vices. This collection was edited by J.G. Freire in 1971 on the basis of six manuscripts, the oldest being Madrid, Academia Regia Historica 80 of the 9th century CE (Freire, 1971). The collection is more closely related to the thematic *PJ* collection than *MD*, but it also includes numerous sayings that are neither a part of *PJ* nor of the oldest known layer of the Greek alphabetic collection. It is thus an important witness to the early existence of collections of sayings that were not made part of the early alphabetic or thematic collections.

The third collection was by H. Rosweyde erroneously attributed to → Rufinus of Aquileia. It constitutes a combination of a collection not included in H. Rosweyde's edition, the so called *Commonitiones Sanctorum Patrum*, designated as *CSP*, followed by the *PA* collection with only minor omissions.

The *Commonitiones Sanctorum Patrum* consists of 61 sayings and was first edited by J.G. Freire in 1974 based primarily on the manuscript Österreichische Nationalbibliothek cod. 433. His analysis shows it to be independent of *PJ*, *MD* and *PA* (Freire, 1974). It contains sayings clearly representing augmented versions with additional introductions, explanations, and biblical quotations. However, it also contains sayings transmitted in an old textual tradition most likely preserving original features lost in Greek (Faraggiana, 1997; Gould, 2001). Since the collection differs considerably in both text and structure from the known alphabetic and systematic collections, it is not likely to be derived from either of them. As with the *PA* collection, it is thus an important witness to an early independent collection presumably deriving from a now lost Greek *Vorlage*.

3. Coptic

Although originating in Egypt the *Apophthegmata Patrum* do not seem to have been widely used in the Coptic tradition. In Sahidic only three codices are known, all preserving a thematic collection closely related to the Latin and Greek thematic collections but with a series of sayings unattested in these. From two of these codices only minor fragments have hitherto come to light. A few leaves of a papyrus codex dated to the 7th century CE were edited by P.E. Kahle (1954, vol. I, 416–423) and fragments of a parchment codex, University of Pennsylvania Museum, E 16395, were published by A. Suciu (2012). The best manuscript of the Sahidic text is a codex from the White Monastery, designated as MONB.EG. Like many other Coptic manuscripts, this parchment manuscript was dismembered and only parts of it have yet been identified. Folios from a large number of dispersed folios were edited by M. Chaine in 1960 and some folios kept in Moscow were edited in 1994 by A. Elanskaya (Chaine, 1960; Elanskaya, 1994). Some additional fragments of the same manuscript were edited by E. Lucchesi (2004) and a photo of one page of the same manuscript found in the Thomas Fisher Rare Book Library, University of Toronto, was published by A. Alcock (2015). The Bohairic tradition has received much less attention. Two collections of sayings, one attributed to Saint Antony and another to Saint Macarius, were edited by É. Amélineau (1895).

4. Syriac

The *Apophthegmata Patrum* were very early translated into Syriac as is evident from the existence of large collections in a number of Syriac manuscripts dated to the first half of the 6th century CE. The oldest two manuscripts are London, BL Add. 17176 dated 532 CE and Sinai Syriac 46, dated 534 CE. Since the two manuscripts are clearly independent of one another in content and sequence, but share the same translation of some individual sayings, they must depend on earlier collections in Syriac. Since their series of sayings are neither ordered alphabetically, nor thematically, they are most likely translated from Greek collections predating the organization of the Greek material in themes and/or sequences (Holmberg, 2013). None of these earlier manuscripts have yet been published, but a transcript of the Sinai manuscript has been made by B. Holmberg for Monastica (monastica.ht.lu.se).

A later Syriac compilation including huge collections of sayings was first edited by P. Bedjan (1897). The edition is based on five manuscripts all preserving a collection originally made by the east Syriac scholar Enanisho in the 7th century CE. An almost identical text was published by E.A.W. Budge in 1904, who also published an English translation (Budge, 1907). This later Syriac collection has a clear relation to the collections of the early manuscripts but rearranged the material in thematic chapters and added numerous sayings not found in the early manuscripts. In spite of the fact that the sayings generally overlap with those in the Greek and Latin thematic collections and that the equivalent chapter titles are used, there is no correlation between the contents of the chapters.

The popularity of the sayings in Syriac is not only demonstrated by the numbers of preserved manuscripts ranging from the 6th to the 19th century, but also by a popular commentary on the *Apophthegmata Patrum* by the east Syrian author Dadisho Qatraya, a commentary later attributed to Philoxenus of Mabboug and translated both into Arabic and Ethiopic (Sims-Williams, 1994; Kitchen, 2006; Witakowski, 2006; Phillips, 2012).

5. Sogdian

A number of sayings from the *Apophthegmata Patrum* are also known in Sogdian versions preserved among the Turfan texts, more precisely in the manuscripts designated as C2 and C67 (Sims-Williams, 1985). They most probably all derive from Syriac sources. Some of those attested by the manuscript C2 are literal translations of texts included in the *Paradise of the Fathers* by Enanisho, the most important collection of apophthegmata in Syriac. Those known from the manuscript C67 agree in substance but not in wording with stories found in Enanisho's *Paradise*, while two further anecdotes occurring in C2 form part of a work by Macarius.

6. Arabic

In Arabic there are a large number of different collections and recensions of the *Apophthegmata Patrum* preserved in numerous manuscripts, of which only a few have been studied in detail. What is likely to be the oldest Arabic version is represented by one manuscript, Strasbourg Oriental 4225, dated to 901 CE. The manuscript was analyzed and transcribed in an unpublished dissertation by J. Mansour (1972). J. Mansour's text has been revised by J. Zaborowski for Monastica. J.-M. Sauget has shown that the *Apophthegmata Patrum* collection of this manuscript, which is also found in several other manuscripts, represents a translation made from a Greek thematic version done in the 9th century CE, most probably at the Monastery of Saint Catherine in Sinai. Some of the Greek manuscripts of this recension have been identified by C. Faraggiana di Sarzana (2002).

A second Arabic collection also related to the Monastery of Sinai, and probably made in the 10th century CE is represented in an 11th-century manuscript, Paris Arabe 276. The manuscript gives us the Arabic translation of the anonymous section of the Greek alphabetic-anonymous collection.

A third Arabic collection, represented by the manuscript Paris Arabe 253, is an extraordinary example of how new collections were made on the basis of earlier models. The Arabic text which is arranged alphabetically ultimately derives from a Syriac thematic version of the same type as the one edited by E.A.W. Budge. In the process of translating it the units have been rearranged into an alphabetic order on the basis of a Greek manuscript of the alphabetic-anonymous type (Sauget, 1987).

The Arabic version is of particular interest when studying how a translation across a cultural and linguistic border influences the work. The different Arabic versions use different strategies in adapting the text to the Islamic environment thus demonstrating different attitudes (Zaborowski, 2018).

7. Ethiopic

Among the least studied versions of the *Apophthegmata Patrum* are the Ethiopic (Witakowski, 2006; Bausi, 2007). Although the number of manuscripts in which collections of sayings have been identified is rather limited, there is a rich variety of content and order. Moreover, most probably several manuscripts have not yet identified series of apophthegmata. Four different Ethiopian collections were edited by V. Arras, all on the basis of a few manuscripts. Most likely all four collections represent translations done from Arabic sources. The first collection designated as *Collectio Monastica* and published in 1963 is based on two manuscripts, BL Oriental 764 and BV Cerulli 220 (Arras, 1963). The collection consists of some 500 units in which only minor sections follow any of the other edited versions. Only 20–25% of the material is found in the large edited Greek, Syriac and Armenian collections and only circa 10% of their material is represented in the Ethiopic. The second collection, designated as *Patericon Aethiopicae*, was published in 1967 on the basis of seven manuscripts. The collection comprises circa 540 units and is clearly related to the Greek thematic tradition with which it shares circa 50% of its units. It is clearly based on an Arabic version. The third collection designated as *Asceticon* is based on a single manuscript, BL Orient 768 (Arras, 1984). Its circa 350 units are mainly excerpts from other monastic writings among which a few sayings can be found. The fourth collection designated as *Geronticon* is based on two manuscripts. It contains more than 800 units out of which half are found in the large Greek manuscript, Paris Cosilin 127 (Arras, 1986). Much of the rest are excerpts from other monastic writings such as the *Pratum Spirituale* of John Moschos and the *Narrationes* of Anastasius Sinaita. A small independent collection was edited by J.-M. Sauget (1973–1977).

8. Armenian

Among major versions of the *Apophthegmata Patrum* collections that date back to early medieval times, the Armenian is the least studied. A large Armenian thematic collection was edited by the famous patriarch of Jerusalem, Grigor the Chainbearer, and a certain Yohannis of Constantinople and printed in Istanbul in 1720 (repr. 2012). The collection is closely related to the Greek collection of the thematic type represented by the large Greek manuscript Paris Coislin 127. In 1855, the Mechitarist scholar N. Sarkissian edited two other Armenian collections on the basis of a number of Armenian manuscripts in the Mechitarist libraray in Venice (Sarkissian, 1855). The edition of N. Sarkissian was subsequently translated very literally into Latin by L. Leloir in order to give scholars without knowledge of Armenian access to the material (Leloir, 1974–1976).

The shorter of the two collections, designated as *A*, represents an older translation into Armenian and the longer, designated as *B*, a more recent translation that presents the same material as *A* as well as a large number of additional texts. In order to simplify comparisons between the two translations of the same paragraphs N. Sarkissian, followed by L. Leloir, reorganized the *B* collection. For each paragraph he placed the equivalent from *B* together with the text of *A*, irrespective of the sequence of the *B* collection, placing the units not found in *A* as appendices at the end of each chapter. Neither the edition nor the translation by L. Leloir does thus reveal the sequence of the sayings in *B*. A comparison of the appendices with the 1720 edition shows, however, that the manuscripts used by Grigor and Yohannis and those used by N. Sarkissian for his *B* text must have been closely related to one another and based on the same Greek collection. However, the sequence of the *A* text as compared with the 1720 edition shows that although the chapters are basically the same, the content and sequence within the chapters vary significantly which indicates that the Armenian *A* collection is probably based on an earlier, not yet identified Greek collection.

Unfortunately neither the first nor the second edition account for the manuscripts used. Ongoing research by Anahit Avagyan into the Armenian manuscripts shows that there are a large number of Armenian medieval manuscripts in the Matendaran library in Yerevan as well as in Jerusalem, Venice and other places. Some of these, such as the 13th century manuscript MM 787, contain Armenian collections that seem to be quite independent of those edited.

The importance of the Armenian was observed already by W. Bousset, who noticed that there were significant relations between the Armenian, Syriac and the minor Latin versions independent of any known Greek text (Bousset, 1923).

9. Georgian

The Greek alphabetic-anonymous as well as a Greek systematic tradition are both represented in Georgian translations.

An early translation of an alphabetic-anonymous collection is represented by the manuscript Sinaiticus ibericus 35, copied in the Monastery of Saint Sabas in the Jordan valley in 907 CE. On the basis of its linguistic features the translation is dated to the late 8th or early 9th century CE (Outtier, 1980, 10). The collection was edited in 1974 on the basis of this and two other manuscripts, Athos Iviron 12 and Sinaiticus ibericus 8 (Dvali, 1974).

A Georgian thematic collection was edited in 1966 by M. Dvali on the basis of the manuscript Tbilisi A-35 (Dvali, 1966). The manuscript is from the 10th century CE and transmits a translation by Euthymios of Iviron (d. 1028 CE). Another manuscript, Tbilis A-1105 represents another translation of the same Greek tradition but in a more extensive version closely related to the Armenian edited thematic collection. The Greek tradition translated is of the same type as the one represented by the manuscript Parisinus Coislin 127 (Esbroeck, 1975, 382; Outtier, 1977). A different Georgian thematic collection is represented by the manuscript Athos Iviron 17 (Dvali, 1981).

10. Medieval Reception in the Vernaculars

Due to their popularity in Latin as well as their adaptability, the *Apophthegmata Patrum* were among the first texts to be translated from Latin into the spoken languages of Western Europe. This was usually done together with *Vitae*, legends and early accounts, all part of Latin collections designated as *Vitas Patrum*. The earliest translations known to us were done in verse. An Anglo-Norman verse version from the end of the 12th century is mentioned by U. Williams (1997, 1767) and the Old French verse translation of the 13th century has been edited by E. Pinto-Mathieu (2009). The first German version

is a verse adaptation known under the title *Der Veter Buoch*, dating back to the 13th century, and the earliest known collection of texts in German (Reissenberger, 1914).

During the 14th and 15th century six different German prose translations of material from the *Vitas Patrum* were produced, one of which was a translation of a collection of sayings (*verba seniorum*) edited by U. Williams (1996) on the basis of 70 manuscripts and 12 early printings. Four further translations, the Bavarian *Verba Seniorum*, produced around 1400, the Melker *Verba Seniorum* from the first half of the 15th century, as well as two translations only preserved in single manuscripts (Willliams, 1996, 7–8). Of these only the so-called Olmützer *Verba Seniorum* has been edited (Schütz-Buckl, 1991).

An early Dutch translation, in which the sayings are called *Der vader collacien*, is dated circa 1360 and attributed to Peter Naghel, known as the "Bijbelvertaler." A second Dutch translation was made in the early 15th century (Williams, 1996, 8). The early printed Dutch text made by Pieter van Os in Zwolle at the end of the 15th century is based on the Alemannic corpus printed in Strasbourg circa 1480 (Studer, 2012, 3). In French five different prose translations of texts from the *Vitas Patrum* are known, the earliest of which was made by Wauchier de Denain before 1212 (Studer, 2012, 3). A second independent translation was made for Blanca of Navarra before 1229, introduced by a prologue in rhyme. The first Middle English translation was made by William Caxton on the basis of a French text and printed in 1495 (Williams, 1997, 1767).

Historiography

Modern scholarship on the *Apophthegmata Patrum* began with T. Hopfner (1918) and W. Bousset, whose monumental work *Apophthegmata* (1923) remains an unmatched standard. Their attempts at comprehensive analyses of all versions was followed by detailed work on the manuscripts of different versions, primarily the Greek by J.-C. Guy (1962) and the Latin by C. Batlle (1971), as well as by editions of Latin, Greek as well as Georgian and Ethiopic versions (Rubenson, 2013). The reliability of the sayings as historical sources based on an original oral transmission was taken for granted by W. Bousset and J.-C. Guy, as well as in the historical works on early monasticism by Heussi (1936) and Dörries (1949), and first questioned by S. Rubenson (1990) and Goehring (1993). Recent scholarship has demonstrated the literary and educational character of the sayings (McVey, 1998; Larsen, 2006; 2017). The study of the various versions of the sayings and their relations is made available through Monastica, a dynamic library and research tool provided by Lund University (https://monastica.ht.lu.se).

Bibliography

Alcock, A., "English Translation of the Coptic Sahidic version of the Apophthegmata Patrum," 2015, https://alinsuciu.com/2015/01/09/guest-post-anthony-alcock-english-translation-of-the-coptic-sahidic-version-of-the-apophthegmata-patrum/.

Amélineau, E., ed., *Monuments pour servir à l'histoire de l'Égypte chrétienne aux IVe et Ve siècles*, MMAFC, vol IV/2, Paris, 1895.

Arras, V., *Collectio Monastica*, CSCO 238–239, Louvain, 1963.

Arras, V., *Patericon Aethiopice*, CSCO 177–178, Louvain, 1967.

Arras, V., *Ascetikon*, CSCO 458–459, Louvain, 1984.

Arras, V., *Geronticon*, CSCO 476–477, Louvain, 1986.

Bagnall R., & N. Gonis, "An Early Fragment of the Greek Apophthegmata Patrum," *ARG* 5, 2003, 260–278.

Barlow, C., *Martini Episcopi Bracarensis Opera Omnia*, New Haven, 1950.

Batlle, C., "'Vetera Nova' Vorläufige kritische Ausgabe bei Rosweyde fehlender Vätersprüche," in: J. Autenrieth & F. Brunhölzl, eds., *FS Bernhard Bischoff zu seinem 65. Geburtstag*, Stuttgart, 1971, 32–42.

Bausi, A., "Monastic Literature," in: S. Uhlig & B. Yimam, eds., *Encyclopaedia Aethiopica*, . vol. III: *He-N*, Wiesbaden, 2007, 993–999.

Bedjan, P., *Acta martyrum et sanctorum Syriace*, vol. VII, Paris, 1897.

Bousset, W., *Apophthegmata: Studien zur Geschichte des ältesten Mönchtums*, Tübingen, 1923.

Budge, E.A.W., The Paradise or Garden of the Holy Fathers, Being Histories of the Anchorites, Recluses, Monks, Coenobites and Ascetic Fathers of the Deserts of Egypt, London, 1907.

Chaine, M., *Le manuscrit de la version copte en dialecte sahidique des "Apophthegmata Patrum"*, BEC 6, Cairo, 1960.

Cotelier, J.B., ed., *Ecclesiae Graecae monumenta*, vol. I. Paris, 1677, 338–712; repr. in J.-P. Migne, ed., PG 65, Paris, 1858, 71–440.

Dahlman, B., "The Sabaitic Collection of the Apophthegmata Patrum," in: D. Searby, E. Balicka Witakowska

& J. Heldt, eds., *ΔΩΡΟΝ ΡΟΔΟΠΟΙΚΙΛΟΝ: Studies in Honour of Jan Olof Rosenqvist*, AUU.SBU 12, Uppsala, 2012, 133–146.

Dahlman, B., 2013, "The Collectio Scorialensis Parva: An Alphabetical Collection of Old Apophthegmatic and Hagiographic Material," in: *StPatr*, vol. LV ed. M. Vinzent; vol. III: *Early Monasticism and Classical Paideia* ed. S. Rubenson, Louvain, 23–33.

Dahlman, B., & P. Rönnegård, eds., *Paradiset: Ökenfädernas tänkespråk, den systematiska samlingen*, vols. IV–VII, SiAp 4–8, Bjärka-Säby, 2012–2016.

Dörries, H., Die Vita Antonii als Geschichtsquelle, 1949, Göttingen.

Dvali, M., *Sua saukunet'a novelebis jveli k'art'uli t'argmanebi*, vol. I, Tbilisi, 1966.

Dvali, M., *Sua saukunet'a novelebis jveli k'art'uli t'argmanebi*, vol. II, Tbilisi, 1974.

Dvali, M., "Types of Georgian Manuscripts of the Apophthegmata Patrum," *PoKn* 4, 1981, 19–25.

Elanskaya A., *The Literary Coptic Manuscripts in the A.S. Pushkin State Fine Arts Museum in Moscow*, SVigChr, vol. XVIII, Leiden, 1994.

Esbroeck, M. van, "Les Apophthegmes dans les versions orientales," *AnBoll* 93, 1975, 381–389.

Faraggiana di Sarzana, C., "Il paterikon Vat. gr. 2592, già di Mezzoiuso, e il suo rapporto testuale con lo Hieros. S. Sepulchri gr. 113," *BBGG* 47, 1993, 79–96.

Faraggiana di Sarzana, C., *Apophthegmata Patrum: Some Crucial Points of Their Textual Transmission and the Problem of a Critical Edition*, Louvain, 1997, 455–467.

Faraggiana di Sarzana, C., "Nota sul rapporto fra l'Ambr. L. 120 Sup. e la più antica tradizione dei detti dei padri del deserto," *RSBN* 39 n.s., 2002, 55–57.

Freire, J.G., *A versão latina por Pascásio de Dume dos Apophthegmata Patrum*, vols. I–II, Coimbra, 1971.

Freire, J.G., *Commonitiones sanctorum patrum: uma nova collecção de apotegmas, estudo filológico*, texto crítico, Coimbra, 1974.

Gallazzi, C., "P. Cair. SR 3726: Frammento degli Apophthegmata Patrum," *ZPE* 84, 1990, 53–56.

Goehring, J., "The Encroaching Desert: Literary Production and Ascetic Space in Early Christian Egypt," *JECS* 1, 1993, 281–296.

Gould, G., *Some Authentic Material in a Latin Collection of Apophthegmata Patrum*, Louvain, 2001, 81–89.

Guy, J.-C., *Recherches sur la tradition grecque des Apophthegmata Patrum*, SHG 36, Brussels, 1962.

Guy, J.-C., *Recherches sur la tradition grecque des Apophthegmata Patrum*, SHG 36, 2nd ed. & suppls., Brussels, 1984.

Guy, J.-C., ed., *Les Apophtegmes des Pères: Collection systématique*, 3 vols., SC 387 (vol. I–IX); 474 (vols. X–XVI); 498 (vols. XVII–XXI), Paris, 1993, 2003, 2005.

Harmless, W., "Remembering Poemen Remembering: The Desert Fathers and the Spirituality of Memory," *ChH* 69, 2000, 483–518.

Heussi, K., *Der Ursprung des Mönchtums*, Tübingen, 1936.

Holmberg, B., "The Syriac Collection of *Apophthegmata Patrum* in MS Sin. syr. 46," in: S. Rubenson, *Early Monasticism and Classical Paideia*, 2013, 35–57.

Hopfner, T., *Über die koptisch-sa'idischen Apophthegmata Patrum Aegyptiorum und verwandte griechische, lateinische, koptisch-bohairische und syrische Sammlungen*, KAWW.PH.D 61.2, Vienna, 1918.

Kahle, P., *Bala'izah: Coptic Texts from Deir el-Bala'izah in Upper Egypt*, vol. I, London, 1954, 416–423.

Kitchen, R., *Dadisho Qatraya's Commentary on Abba Isaiah: The Apophthemata Patrum Connection*, Louvain, 2006, 35–50.

Larsen, L.I, "The *Apophthegmata Patrum* and the Classical Rhetorical Tradition," in: F. Young, M. Edwards & P. Parvis, eds., *Historica, Biblica, Ascetica et Hagiographica*, Louvain, 2006, 409–415.

Larsen, L.I. "Re-drawing the Interpretive Map: Monastic Education as Civic Formation in the *Apophthegmata Patrum*," *Cop.* 12, 2013, 1–34.

Larsen, L.I., "Monastic Paideia: Textual Fluidity in the Classroom," in: L.I. Lied & H. Lundhaug, eds., *Snapshots of Evolving Traditions: Jewish and Christian Manuscript Culture, Textual Fluidity and New Philology*, Berlin, 2017, 146–177.

Leloir, L., *Paterica armeniaca a P.P. Mechitaristis edita (1855) nunc latine reddita*, vols. I–IV, CSCO 353, 361, 371, 379, Louvain, 1974–1976.

Lucchesi, E., "Un petit complément au manuscrit de la version copte en dialect sahidique des *Apophthegmata Patrum*," in: *Aegyptus Christiana: Mélanges d'hagiographie égyptienne et orientale dédiér à la mémoir du P. Paul Devos Bollandiste*, Genève, 2004.

Mansour, J., "Homélies et légendes religieuses: Un florilège arabe chrétien du xe siècle (Manuscrit Strasbourg 4225)," unpubl. diss., Strasbourg, 1972.

McVey, K., "Chreia in the Desert: Rhetoric and the Bible in the Apophthegmata Patrum," in: A.J. Malherbe et al., eds., *The Early Church in its Context. Essays in Honour of Everett Ferguson*, NT.S 90, London, 1998, 245–255.

Monastica: A Dynamic Library and Research Tool 1, 2016, http://www.monastica.ht.lu.se.

Nikitin, P.V., "Grečeskij Skitksij Paterik i ego drevnij latinskij perevod," *ViVr* 22, 1915–1916, 127–171.

Outtier, B., "Le modèle grec de la traduction georgienne des Apophtegmes par Euthyme," *AnBoll* 95, 1977, 119–131.

Outtier, B., "La plus ancienne traduction géorgienne des apophtegmes: son étendue et son origine," *Mrav.* 7, 1980, 7–17.

Phillips, D., "The Syriac Commentary of Dadisho' Qatraya on the Paradise of the Fathers: Towards a Critical Edition," *BABELAO* 1, 2012, 1–23.

Pinto-Mathieu, E., *La vie des pères: Genèse de contes religieux du XIIIe siècle*, NBMA 91, Paris, 2009.

Rapp, C., "The Origins of Hagiography and the Literature of Early Monasticism: Purpose and Genre Between Tradition and Innovation," in: C. Kelly, R. Flower & M. Stuart Williams, eds., *Unclassical Traditions*, vol. I: *Alternatives to the Classical Past in Late Antiquity*, PCPS.S 34, 2010, 119–130.

Regnault, L.,"Les Apophtegmes des pères en Palestine aux Vè–VIè siècles," *Irén.* 54, 1981, 320–330.

Reissenberger, K., ed., *Das Väterbuch*, Berlin, 1914; repr. Dublin, 1967.

Rosweyde, H., ed., *Vitae Patrum*, vols. III, V–VII, Antwerp, 1615; repr. in J.-P. Migne, ed., PL 73, Paris, 1849, 739–810, 851–1062.

Rubenson, S., *The Letters of St. Antony: Origenist Theology, Monastic Tradition and the Making of a Saint*, Lund, 1990.

Rubenson, S., "The Apophthegmata Patrum in Syriac, Arabic, and Ethiopic: Status Questionis," *PO* 36, 2011, 305–313.

Rubenson, S., "Monasticism and the Philosophical Heritage," in: S.F. Johnson, ed., *OHLA*, Oxford, 2012, 487–512.

Rubenson, S., "The Formation and Re-Formations of the Sayings of the Desert Fathers," in: S. Rubenson, ed., *Early Monasticism and Classical Paideia*, Louvain, 2013, 3–22.

Sarkissian, N., *Vies et pratiques des saints pères selon la double traduction des anciens*, Venice, 1855.

Sauget, J.-M., "La courte série d'*Apophtegmata Patrum* du manuscrit Vatican Ethiopien 33," *RSE* 26, 1973–1977, 44–46.

Sauget, J.-M., *Une traduction arabe de la collection d'apophtegmata patrum de 'Enânîshô*, CSCO 495, Louvain, 1987.

Schütz-Buckl, C., "Die Olmützer Verba seniorum: Untersuchung und Edition," *StoRu* 28, 1991, 57–123.

Sims-Williams, N., *The Christian Sogdian Manuscript C2*, SGKAO, vol. XII, Berlin, 1985.

Sims-Williams, N., "Dādišo' Qatrāyā's Commentary on the Paradise of the Fathers," *AnBoll* 112, 1994, 33–64.

Stroppa, M., "*Apophthegmata Patrum (coll. syst.) 6.15 e 17–19 (?, Sec VI d.C.)*," in: A. Casanova, G. Messerie & R. Pintaudi, eds., *Sì d'amici pieno: Omaggio di studiosi italiani a Guido Bastianini per il suo settantesimo compleanno*, Florence, 2016, 27–31.

Studer, M., "Vitas Patrum: A Short Summary' Online Publication," 2012, http://www.opvs.fr/?q=fr/VuePresentationProjet.

Suciu, A., "A New Fragment from the Sayings of the Desert Fathers: The University of Pennsylvania Coptic Fragment E 16395," 2012, https://alinsuciu.com/2012/05/17/a-new-fragment-from-the-sayings-of-the-desert-fathers-the-university-of-pennsylvania-coptic-fragment-e-16395/.

To mega gerontikon ed. To Genesion tes Theotokou, vols. I–IV, Thessaloniki, 1994–1999, [2]2009–2014.

Williams, U., ed., *Die Alemannischen Vitaspatrum: Untersuchungen und Edition*, TeTe 45, Tübingen, 1996.

Williams, U., "Vitas patrum," in: *LMA*, vol. VIII, Munich, 1997, 1765–1768.

Wilmart, A., "Le recueil latin des Apophthegmata Patrum," *Rben* 34, 1922, 175–184.

Witakowski, W., "'Filekseyus', The Ethiopic Version of the Syriac Dadisho Qatraya's 'Commentary on the Paradise of the Fathers'," in: W. Witakowski & L. Lykowska, eds., *Wälättä Yohanna: Ethiopian Studies in Honour of Joanna Mantel-Niecko on the Occasion of the 50th Year of Her Work at the Institute of Oriental Studies*, RoOr 59, Warsaw, 2006, 281–296.

Wortley, J., *The Anonymous Sayings of the Desert Fathers: A Select Edition and Complete English Translation*, Cambridge UK, 2013.

Zaborowski, J., "Greek Thought, Arabic Culture: Approaching Arabic Recensions of the Apophthegmata Patrum," in: L. Larsen & S. Rubenson, eds., *Monastic Education in Late Antiquity: The Transformation of Classical Paideia*, Cambridge UK, 2018, 326–342.

SAMUEL RUBENSON

Apostasy/Apostates

Apostasy, derived from Greek ἀποστασία or Latin *apostasia*, is the technical term for the renunciation of faith. Based on the Greek etymology of the word, late antiquity considers that a person who "turns away" or "backs away" from God has abandoned the faith (see Clem. *Strom.* 2.15.68.1; Greg. Nyss. *Eun.* 3 3.10.16; Hornung, 2016, 13). Often used in a broad sense in literary texts, the concept of apostasy is given a narrower definition in church discipline and state legislation: an apostate, or renegade, is he who commits idolatry as a Christian, that is:

1. by taking part in the pagan cult;
2. by converting to Judaism, or also;
3. by adhering to heresies (see Greg. Nyss. *Ep. can.* 1f.; Cod. Theod. 16.7.3).

As opposed to → heresy and → schism, apostasy is a broad generic term and refers to any form of renunciation in a nonspecific way. In addition to apostasy/apostate, Greek and Latin dispose of many other expressions and paraphrases to describe the renunciation of faith or the renegade (e.g. ἀποτρέπειν, καταλείπειν; *avertere*, *deviare*; ἄρνησις, πτῶσις; *abscessio*, *lapsus*; see Hornung, 2016, 20–26, for further examples).

1. Greco-Roman

"Renunciation" and "defection" are not a specifically Christian phenomenon but are also found in the environment of ancient Christianity. Especially in the ancient schools of medicine and philosophy, one comes across forms of defection that were interpreted as apostasies (see Burkert, 1982, 18). Ancient sources record that various physicians studied medicine under more than one teacher. Philinus of Cos (3rd cent. BCE), for instance, is said to have emancipated himself from his teacher and to have founded an empirical school (see Staden, 1982, 78); Agathinus of Sparta (1st cent. CE) also established a school of his own, through which he distinguished himself from the methodology of his teacher (see Wellmann, 1895, 11f.). The different approaches led to animosities and conflicts between the schools. → Iamblichus of Chalcis attests to the expulsion of novices among the Pythagoreans (Iamb. *Vita Pyth.* 17.73). In this example, the outward form of the expulsion is only the expression of the candidate's inner aversion, who is henceforth the subject of lifelong contempt (*Vita Pyth.* 17.73). A particularly strict organizational structure is attested for the *Kepos* (see De Witt, 1936, 205–211). The school remained firmly committed to the teachings of → Epicurus long after his death; the method of instruction consisted largely in the memorization and repetition of Epicurean doctrines (see Erler, 1993, 285). Whoever deviated from the right doctrine was considered a patricide (Phil. *Rhet.* 1, col. 7, 18–29). Despite attempts to permanently bind students to a philosophical orientation, the biographies of philosophers demonstrate that it was quite common to switch schools (see Hornung, 2016, 43f.). A well-known example is that of Dionysius of Heraclea (4th cent. BCE), also known under the byname ὁ μεταθέμενος, "the Renegade" (D.L. 7.166; see Arnim, 1903, 973f.). He had initially been a disciple of Zeno of Citium before leaving his teacher on account of a different assessment of pain (Cic. *Tusc.* 2.25.60). Dionysius became an Epicurean. In the polemical depiction of Diogenes Laertius, he is now presented as a licentious man who indulges in the passions. His suicide appears as the logical consequence of his dissolute lifestyle (D.L. 7.167). At the same time, the switch from one philosophical school to another is not generally viewed negatively, as one can gather from Diogenes Laertius' depiction of Dionysius. Only when the schools exhibit more fixed structures and make a claim to exclusivity is deviance depicted in a negative manner and condemned (e.g. Pythagoreans or Epicureans).

2. Jewish

Jewish conceptions have undoubtedly influenced the Christian views on apostasy. In the Hebrew Bible, a lapse in faith is thus characterized much in the same way as in the Christian definitions from late antiquity, namely as a "forsaking of God" (see Deut 28:20; Jer 2:19). The forsaking of God is regularly associated with the worship of foreign gods (Deut 29:25f.). This context becomes evident when God prophesies to → Moses that the Israelites will forsake him after the latter's death (Deut 31:16): "This people will rise and whore after the foreign gods among them in the land that they are entering, and they will forsake me and break my covenant that I have made with them." The visible sign of this defection is the worship of foreign gods, that is, idolatry (Judg 2:12f.; Isa 65:11); in a broader understanding, any transgression of a divine prohibition can also appear as a breach of the covenant and as a forsaking of God (Hornung, 2016, 50f.). Punishments for apostasy are the ban or even death (Exod 22:20; Deut 13:1–11; 17:2–7); divine wrath can strike individuals or Israel as a whole (Lohfink, 2000, 246ff.). In Hellenistic → Judaism, the category of apostasy gains increasing importance. Diaspora Jews are in constant danger of abandoning the ancestral laws and customs and of gradually adapting themselves to "Greek ways of life." The Jewish dietary rules acquire particular importance. Being an identity marker, their violation appears as an outward indicator of apostasy (Philo *Virt.* 182; Cohen, 1993, 26; Rajak, 2001, 344f.). The apostasy of Tiberius Julius Alexander, who pursued an administrative and military career in the Egyptian city of Alexandria in the 1st century CE and even rose to the rank of praetorian prefect in Rome, is particularly prominent. → Flavius Josephus accuses him of not having retained the ancestral customs (Jos. *Ant.* 20.100); → Philo of Alexandria has Julius Alexander appear as a discussion partner in two dialogues (*De providentia*; *De animalibus*) in which the latter professes a cosmology centered on the human being (see Turner, 1954, 54–64). The image of Julius Alexander conveyed therein is that of a typical apostate who shows a tendency to abandon Jewish doctrines and customs through the exercise of public functions in the → Diaspora. In such cases, the renunciation does not occur suddenly and abruptly but gradually over a longer period of time. That a non-Jewish context, particularly in the Diaspora, increases the danger of apostasy is also alluded to by Philo *Virt.* 182 (see Wilson, 2004, 36). Legal definitions of the apostate and corresponding attempts at demarcation can be discerned in rabbinic Judaism. *Sifre Deut.* 148 on Deut 17:2 calls the renegade "evil, breaker of the covenant, blasphemer, angerer, and rebel." The precise demarcation of apostates from other groups (heretics, denouncers, and *apikorsim*) is difficult. The characteristic feature of the renegade is that he violates the Jewish laws. In the Babylonian → Talmud, moreover, a distinction can be made between a "general" and a "limited apostasy" (*b. ʿErub.* 69b); consideration is also given to the motivation (greed or defiance) that leads to the violation of a law (*b. ʿAbod. Zar.* 26b; see Hornung, 2016, 72–76). Individual provisions address concrete aspects of the conduct of life: the consumption of suet and carrion as well as the drinking of libation wine are prohibited as idolatrous practices, as is the wearing of mixed fabrics with reference to Lev 19:19 (*b. Hor.* 11a). The just punishment for the apostate is death. He is likewise guilty of five offenses: he defiles the Temple, desecrates the *Haschem*, the "Name (of God)," causes the presence of God (*Shekhinah*) to depart, causes Israel to be defeated by the sword, and brings about its exile (*Sifre Deut.* 148 on Deut 17:2). His punishments will last forever (*b. Roš Haš.* 17a). Due to his forsaking of Judaism, Elisha ben Abuyah became the most noted apostate in rabbinic tradition (2nd cent. CE). Having belonged to the circle of Rabbi Akiva for a time, his alienation from the rabbis probably led to his fundamental separation from Judaism (see Hornung, 2016, 80f.).

3. New Testament

The act of personally turning away from Jesus is the salient characteristic of apostasy in the Gospels of the New Testament (Rese, 2009): upon the arrest of Jesus in the Garden of Gethsemane, the disciples abandon Jesus and flee (Matt 26:56; see also John 6:53f.). The separation can be accompanied by the denial of the discipleship. A prominent example is that of Peter (→ Peter the Apostle), who, following the arrest of Jesus, denies three times that he had been his disciple (Mark 14:66–72 parr. Matt 26:69–75; Luke 22:54–62; John 18:17, 25–27. Just as the phrase "to be with him" (μετ᾽ αὐτοῦ εἶναι) can technically denote the discipleship (Mark 3:14; 5:18), so does the abandonment of the latter stands for the renunciation of faith (see Brown, 1969, 56, 88). In the New Testament Scriptures that do not belong to the Gospels, moreover, the meaning of apostasy undergoes a change: here, the renunciation of the faith means to renounce the faith in Jesus Christ and is linked to idolatry. In the Epistle to the Galatians (1:6), Paul writes: "I am astonished that you are so quickly deserting the one who called you to live in the grace of Christ and are turning to a different Gospel." ([…] ὅτι οὕτος ταχέως μετατίθεσθε […] εἰς ἕτερον εὐαγγέλιον)

Apparently, several congregations in Galatia had turned away from the message of Jesus and placed their faith in a new gospel (see also 1 Tim 4:1f.). In addition, the New Testament also preserves the stories of apostasies by individuals or, as in the case of the Galatians, of entire communities. All of the sevangelists view Judas Iscariot as a renegade on account of his betrayal of Jesus, albeit with different emphases: in Mark 14:17–21, Judas illustrates the danger of apostasy that threatens every Christian. Matt 26:25 heightens the negative depiction of the figure of Judas and turns him into an instrument of → evil. In Luke 22:3, he is also the instrument of Satan in which the eschatological struggle between God and the devil is carried out. In the Fourth Gospel, the demonization of the renegade is even set at the beginning: in John 6:70f. Judas himself becomes the devil. → Ananias and Sapphira symbolize the danger of apostasy in the early church (Acts 5:1–11). After the couple has sold a plot of land, they do not bequeath all the proceeds to the community but keep a portion for themselves. The very fact that they choose to lie when asked whether the donated sum represents the entire proceeds of the sale has the effect of doubling the offense (see Brown, 1969, 98–109; Weiser, 1979, 157). Forms of a general renunciation of faith are linked to the eschaton and described in colorful terms that partly make use of extreme imagery (see 2 Thess 2:3; 1 Tim 4:1; Rev 13).

4. Early Christianity

The testimony of the Gospels and the Pauline epistles reveal that apostasy already constituted a permanent threat in the first Christian congregations. Further evidence from the church in East and West generally confirms this for the first three centuries CE: external threats and periods of persecution, issues of social prestige and economic advancement, as well as a still problematic demarcation from Judaism, which had yet to be systematically achieved in certain areas, were fundamentally favorable to apostasy (Wilson, 2004, 77). The Roman Christian → Hermas, in his work *The Shepherd* (written around 140 CE), addresses the topic of apostates in several passages (Herm. *Sim.* 9.19.1–3). In his view, they should be denied the possibility of repentance; the only appropriate punishment for them is death. Times of → persecution are possibly an underlying motive, while the economic aspect may also lead to a renunciation of the faith (Herm. *Vis.* 3.6.5; Wilson, 2004, 77). Cases of apostasy in the narrower sense occur in the events in Lyon and Vienne, which are reported by → Eusebius of Caesarea. In the year 177 CE, both Gallic cities witnessed pogrom-like riots against Christians, during which parts of the congregations renounced the faith out of fear of death (see Eus. *Hist. eccl.* 5.1.11; 5.25; 5.32–35; 5.45–48). Eusebius' account reveals that the congregations apparently encompassed different groups with a varying degree of closeness to the Christian faith. While some were prepared to confess their faith and suffer martyrdom, others lacked the willingness and the strength to do so (*Hist. eccl.* 5.1.11). Pliny the Younger's letter on the persecutions of Christians documents the fact that as early as the beginning of the 2nd century CE, Christians in Asia Minor repeatedly renounced the faith and did so over a longer period of time. Writing to Emperor → Trajan in Rome, Pliny informs him that he has identified different groups among those who have been denounced to him as Christians: along with staunch confessors and deniers, he mentions a third group of people who stated that they had once been Christian: "Some [of them] three years ago, others several years ago, and still others even twenty years ago." (Quidem ante triennium, quidem ante plures annos, non nemo etiam ante viginti; Plin. Y. Ep. Tra. 10.96.6)

Scholars have made various attempts to assign the described apostasies to different periods of persecution (*inter alios* Domitian), although their arguments ultimately fail to convince (see Freudenberger, 1967, 157). It is more probable that Pliny indirectly points out the weaknesses of the Christian mission and that Christians abandoned the church without external coercion (see Reichert, 2002, 227–250; Schöllgen, 2016, 977–988). The relationship to Judaism remained close even in the 2nd century CE. Judaizing tendencies and apostasies are frequently attested. The *Epistle of Barnabas* (→ Barnabas) reveals that the Judaizers among the Christians were inclined to follow Jewish customs (*Barn.* 5.4; 16.7). Just. *Dial.* 47.4 also attests to the existence of gentile Christians who converted to Judaism and subsequently denied Christ. For the 3rd century CE, numerous apostasies from the time of the Decian → persecution (in the years 249–251 CE) are documented (see Vogt, 1954, 1183–1187; Moreau, 1961, 85–87). The first empire-wide persecutions, carried out under the Roman emperor Decius on the basis of general edicts, caused numerous clerics and laypeople to renounce the faith, offer the required sacrifice, or at least to obtain a certificate confirming that they had done so (Cyp. *Ep.* 59.10; 65.1; 67). → Cyprian of Carthage presents a particularly vivid testimony for North Africa. Having himself gone into hiding during the persecutions, he devoted an entire tractate to the problem of how to deal with apostates: *De lapsis*, "On the Fallen." He distinguishes between different groups of apostates:

1. those who actually offered sacrifice during the persecutions (*sacrificati*; Cyp. *Laps.* 22f.);
2. those who obtained certificates but did not sacrifice themselves (*libellicati*; *Laps.* 27), and finally;
3. those who had (even if only once) contemplated offering sacrifice but had not actually done it (*Laps.* 28).

Cyprian stipulates that the individual *lapsi* can only be readmitted to the church after undergoing a period of penance, the length of which is to be commensurate with the gravity of the offense (Burns, 2002, 25–50). With regard to himself, the tractate serves as a form of apology (→ Apologetics) by which he seeks to justify his flight during the persecution and to stabilize his – accordingly shaken – authority as bishop of Carthage (*Laps.* 3).

5. Late Antiquity

The Diocletianic persecution of the early 4th century CE marked the last time that Christians were subjected to empire-wide persecutions. These were particularly intensive in the eastern provinces of the Roman Empire, and the Christian congregations were hard-pressed. Eusebius emphasizes the Christians' readiness to suffer martyrdom and their steadfastness (see below). In spite of the sketchy state of the documentation and of a tendency of the existing sources to pass occurrences of apostasy under silence, lapses of faith are attested on various occasions: in the writings of Eusebius, the apostates serve as a negative background against which the author seeks to contrast the accomplishments of the → martyrs (Eus. *Mart. Pal.* 1.1). A reference to the apostasy of clerics, probably of bishops, is found in Eus. *Hist. eccl.* 8.3.1: "Countless others, however, were paralyzed in spirit by fear and succumbed instantly at the first onslaught." In the *Africa proconsularis*, the Christians of a country estate, laypeople as well as clerics, renounced the faith in the face of threatening torment; only two women, Maxima and Donatilla, resisted the general urge to apostatize (see *Mart. S. Crisp.* 1; 3). The imperial Edict of Toleration from the year 311 CE also indicates that numerous Christians renounced the faith during the Diocletianic persecutions (Eus. *Hist. eccl.* 8.17.8). With the so-called Constantinian Shift and the increasing privileging of Christianity, the persecutions of Christians in the Roman Empire came to an end (from 324 CE at the latest in the East, following Constantine's victory over Licinius). Apostasies under external coercion and under threat to life and limb now ceased. Nonetheless, renunciations of the faith are still attested in certain forms in post-Constantinian times. Christians turn their backs on their confession, take part in Jewish or pagan celebrations, and consult magicians or even perform magical practices themselves, apparently because Christianity's claim to exclusivity is not clear to them (see Bas. *Hom.* 18.3 [in *Gordium martyrem*]; PG 31.496f.). Various forms of apostasy in times of peace, from the 4th century CE onward, will be discussed below from the perspectives of theological reflection, church discipline, and pastoral care.

6. Theology

In the early church, apostasy is almost unanimously traced back to the → devil. Most early Christian authors view him as the first apostate from whom the general motivation to renounce the faith once came. Ἀποστάτης or *apostata* therefore became typical designations of the devil (see Hornung, 2016, 152). Furthermore, the devil's apostasy is linked to salvation history and set at its beginning: the devil's rebellion comes first and is followed by the fall of the spirit-beings or angels (see Aug. *Gen. lit.* 11.13). According to → Origen, a spiritual creation precedes the earthly one. In the former, the spirit-beings rebel against God, thus prompting him to create the earthly world, which is to serve as their abode (Or. *Princ.* 2.9.2). The devil's apostasy is followed by that of the human being; it takes place as the → fall of Man in → paradise (see Gen 3). The human being is tempted by the serpent, who is partly interpreted as an instrument and partly also as the devil himself (see Chrys. *Hom. Gen.* 16.2; Aug. *Gen. Man.* 2.14.20; Kelly, 1997, 119–124; Mann, 2001, 40–48). The serpent is envious of the human being's status in paradise and therefore lures him into the fall himself (Chrys. *Hom. Gen.* 22.2; Aug. *Gen. lit.* 11.14; Caesar. *Serm.* 179.2). The human being becomes guilty of sin for having yielded to the → temptations of the devil. He is unsteady and weak by nature, and capable of both sin and virtuous behavior (Ambr. *Enarrat. Ps.* 47.8). The reason for the human fall is seen in his penchant for "pride" (*superbia*). With recourse to biblical prototypes (Ezek 28:17; Isa 14:12–22; esp. Sir 10:14f.: "The beginning of human pride is the forsaking of God [...] The beginning of every sin is pride"), *superbia* becomes the cardinal sin and the typical reason for the human fall (see Procopé, 1991, 844). In the perception of the church authors, the further course of history was characterized by a steady descent into sin until the coming of Christ. The devil and the demons (→ Demonology/Demons) attempted to lead the human being further and further away from God, and thus to increase the amount of sin

and apostasy. Only through Christ was the absolute power of the devil broken and initially suspended (Chrys. *Exp. Ps.* 44.4; 44.6; Ambr. *Exc.* 2.6). The time until the anticipated return of Jesus is interpreted as a time of testing. The human being still lives in constant battle with the demons, through which he can attain heaven (Or. *Hom. Num.* 14.2). In this way, the church authors are able to extract a positive meaning from the immediate present. By and large, apostasy in late antiquity is linked to the course of salvation history and broken down into 5 phases:

1. the rebellion of the devil and of some of the angels;
2. the Fall of Man in paradise;
3. the accumulation of sin and apostasy over the course of history;
4. the coming of Christ and the termination of the devil's absolute power;
5. the testing of the believers during the course of history until the *parousia* (Hornung, 2016, 155).

In theological reflection, individual apostasy is thus associated with the fall of the devil and of the demons. It is viewed as part of a divine salvation plan and as inherent to history. Historiography, diabolology, and demonology thus build a framework into which the phenomenon of apostasy is integrated. At the same time, the renunciation of faith is fundamentally given a broad definition and placed in proximity to every type of sin.

7. Discipline

Church discipline mostly addressed the topic of apostasy at synods held from the 4th century CE onward. The conditions of apostasy are believed to be met when a person commits idolatry. The focus of discipline lies on the everyday relations and actions of Christians. To an increasing degree, the public as well the private sphere came under the scrutiny of church discipline; transgressions were subjected to harsh punishments (excommunication for laypeople, dismissal for clerics). The corresponding requirements fall into different categories:

1. conduct of life;
2. relations with Jews;
3. various other categories (see Hornung, 2016, 256).

The category of the conduct of life is treated in a particularly differentiated manner in church discipline. In addition to the prohibition of pagan sacrifice, it includes the attendance at theater and festival events, oaths, magic, and divination. *Did. Syr.* 13 and Concilium Trullanum anno 691/692 CE, cc. 51; 71, for instance, take steps against theatergoing; the attending of pagan festivals is opposed by *Did. Syr.* 4; Basilius Caesariensis, c. 81; Concilium Autissiodorense anno 561/605 CE, c. 1, and Concilium Trullanum anno 691/692 CE, cc. 62; 65. Especially the participation in pagan celebrations is a clear sign that Christians were still integrated into the non-Christian environment and continued to take part in its events; efforts to establish a demarcation were apparently only progressing at a slow pace. Various councils and church disciplinary texts also prohibited oath taking (Basilius Caesariensis, c. 81; Concilium Trullanum anno 691/692 CE, c. 94). The background of the Christian prohibition appears to have been Jesus' ban on swearing oaths (Matt 5:34). Concilium Aurelianense anno 541 CE, c. 16 shows that oath taking was frequently viewed as a pagan relic and accordingly interpreted as a dangerous form of apostasy. This was even more so in the case of → magic and → divination (see Frenschkowski, 2016, 285–287, 293–295). The numerous provisions against magical and divinatory practices display close similarities and indicate that such practices were wholly condemned by church discipline. Magical traditions were repeatedly characterized as pagan and therefore forbidden to Christians (see Concilium Ancyranum anno 314 CE, c. 24; Concilium Laodicense c. 36; Concilium Agathense anno 506 CE, c. 42; Harmening, 1979; Hornung, 2016, 258). With regard to Judaism, the policy of church discipline was one of general separation. The danger of apostasy appears to have been particularly high here. Christians were not allowed to attend Jewish banquets (Concilium Agathense anno 506, c. 40), and a Jewish proselytism was forbidden (Concilium Aurelianense anno 541 CE, c. 31; Concilium Toletanum anno 633 CE, c. 59; Boddens Hosang, 2010, 161–163). As late as the 7th century CE, a Toledan council had to take steps against reversions to Judaism by issuing two canons to this effect (Concilium Toletanum anno 633 CE, c. 59; 64). Interestingly, it did not call for the exclusion of the apostates but for their reintegration into the church:

> Such apostates [*transgressores*] should, after having been reprimanded by the episcopal authority, be called back to the Christian religion, so that those whose own will does not amend may be chastened by the bishop's rebuke. (Concilium Toletanum anno 633 CE, c. 59; Katz, 1937, 50)

Further provisions contain measures against those who fail to attend church services (Concilium Arelatense anno 314 CE, c. 22), while also prohibiting idolatry (Sir. *Ep.* 1.3.4) and the veneration of angels (Concilium Laodicense c. 35; Boddens Hosang, 2010, 103–105). Any form of apostasy was generally made a punishable offense by Concilium Nicaenum anno 325 CE, c. 11. The various provisions indicate that church discipline had established a differentiated system of punishments in order to minimize lapses in faith and the fundamental threat of their occurrence. For this purpose, everyday Christian life and its realities were described in an increasingly comprehensive manner. From the late 4th century CE onward, church discipline was supplemented by state legislation, which made apostasy a punishable offense comparable to heresy and threatened renegades with succession constraints, confiscations, residential and professional limitations, as well as capital punishments (Cod. Theod. 16.7; Cod. Justin. 1.7; Baccari, 1981, 538–581; Karabélias, 1994, 483–524; Cococcia, 2008, 457–466).

8. Pastoral Ministry

Along with the individual provisions, church discipline also elaborated a differentiated system of punishments in order to pass sentences on apostasies. Individual transgressions were described in detail and subjected to specific punishments. In the context of the congregational pastoral ministry, one cannot help noticing that the individual provisions were apparently only enforced to a very limited extent (see Hornung, 2016, 304–362). Against this background, the corpuses of the sermons delivered by → John Chrysostom and Caesarius of Arles afford an exemplary insight into the situation of the congregations of Syria and Gaul in late antiquity. In the city of Antioch, according to the testimony provided by Chrysostom, Christians were in close contact with non-Christians, Jews, or even pagans (Sandwell, 2007). Christians frequently attended pagan festivals (Chrys. *Kal.* 2), wore amulets (Chrys. *Hom. Col.* 8.5) and went to pagan theater performances (Chrys. *Laz.* 7.1). They cultivated close ties with their Jewish neighbors, took part in their celebrations, and fasted with them (Chrys. *Jud.* 1.1). Judaizing Christians who professed Christianity and nonetheless attended Jewish worship services were numerous (see Brändle, 1987, 142–160). According to church discipline, such a close proximity of Christians to their non-Christian neighbors could be interpreted as apostasy. In his sermons, Chrysostom nevertheless refrained from invoking the provisions of church discipline and merely enjoined the faithful to pursue a specific and distinctly Christian way of life (see Maxwell, 2006, 119; Hornung, 2016, 328–334). The evidence pertaining to the Gallic city of Arles essentially confirms the aforementioned testimony for Syrian Antioch. In his own sermons, Caesarius also describes a conspicuous proximity between Christians and non-Christians but nevertheless refrains from applying the legislation on apostasy to counter the syncretistic tendencies in his congregation. Instead, Caesarius prefers to rely on processes of depaganization (repression of pagan cult traditions) and Christianization (instilling of Christian doctrine and rites). The latter included the renaming of the weekdays (Caes. *Serm.* 193.4; Klingshirn, 1994, 234), the replacing of pagan feasts by Christian ones (Caes. *Serm.* 33.4), and the requirement that the believers learn the fundamental Christian texts by heart (Caes. *Serm.* 6.3). Caesarius trusts in regular instruction during the sermon and makes use of paraenesis (see Harmening, 1979, 58f.; Klingshirn, 1994, 158f.); at the same time, far less emphasis is placed on the enforcement of church discipline. In the light of the insights gained from the collected sermons of Chrysostom and Caesarius, it becomes clear that the concrete implementation of the church discipline regarding apostasy must be viewed with caution; to all appearances, there was a diastasis between the abstract legal formulation and its practical application in the pastoral ministry. A pastoral strategy of depaganization and Christianization was adopted on the congregational level in an attempt to at least minimize the dangers of apostasy.

9. Reception

The confrontation with various forms of apostasy played a crucial role until well into late antiquity. Even after the persecutions of Christians had ended, the believers were still liable to turn away from Christianity and renounce the faith. Against this background, church discipline produced numerous definitions of what a specifically Christian lifestyle should entail; various forms of deviance, even unconscious ones, were regarded as punishable lapses in faith. The category of apostasy thus assumed an important identity-defining function alongside heresy and schism (Hornung, 2016, 365f.).

Historiography

Studies on apostasy in ancient Christianity were long restricted to the first three centuries CE; the focus lay on the persecutions of Christians, not on the renunciation of faith (see Alföldi, 1938, 323–348; Moreau, 1961; Stöver, 1982). S.G. Wilson's study showed a new interest in apostasy as a specific phenomenon; his investigation of the renunciation of faith in Christianity was expanded to include Judaism and parallel phenomena in the Greco-Roman environment (Wilson, 2004). The focus of C. Hornung's research lay on apostasy in post-Constantinian times (Hornung, 2016). At the same time, studies on apostasy are increasingly being linked to the identity discourse in ancient studies, just as the functional significance of the category "apostasy" is being recognized along with that of heresy and schism (see Piepenbrink, 2005; Kahlos, 2007; Rebillard, 2012; Hornung, 2017).

Bibliography

Alföldi, A., "Zu den Christenverfolgungen in der Mitte des 3. Jahrhunderts," *Klio* 31, 1938, 323–348.
Arnim, H. von, "Dionysios nr. 119," in: *PRE*, vol. V/1, Stuttgart, 1903, 973f.
Baccari, M.P., "Notae gli apostati nel Codice Teodosiano," *Apoll.* 54, 1981, 538–581.

Boddens Hosang, F.J.E., *Establishing Boundaries: Christian-Jewish Relations in Early Council Texts and the Writings of Church Fathers*, JCPS 19, Leiden, 2010.

Brändle, R., "Christen und Juden in Antiochien in den Jahren 386/87: Ein Beitrag zur Geschichte altkirchlicher Judenfeindschaft," *Jud.* 43, 1987, 142–160.

Brown, S., *Apostasy and Perseverance in the Theology of Luke*, AnBib 36, Rome, 1969.

Burkert, W., "Craft versus Sect: The Problem of Orphics and Pythagoreans," in: B.F. Meyer et al., eds., *Jewish and Christian Self-Definition*, vol. III: *Self-Definition in the Greco-Roman World*, Philadelphia, 1982, 1–22, 183–189.

Burns, J.P., *Cyprian the Bishop*, New York, 2002.

Cococcia, A., "La législation sur l'apostasie dans le Code Théodosien," in: J.N. Guinot et al., eds., *Empire chrétien et église aux IVe et Ve siècles: Intégration ou "concordat"? Le témoinage du Code Théodosien: Actes du colloque international, Lyon, 6, 7 & 8 Oct 2005*, Paris, 2008, 457–466.

Cohen, S.J.D., "Those Who Say They Are Jews and Are Not: How Do You Know a Jew In Antiquity When You See One?" in: S.J.D. Cohen & E.S. Frerichs, eds., *Diasporas in Antiquity*, BJS 288, Atlanta, 1993, 1–45.

De Witt, N.W., "Organization and Procedure in Epicurean Groups," *CP* 31, 1936, 205–211.

Erler, M., "Philologia medicans: Wie die Epikureer die Texte ihres Meisters lasen," in: W. Kullmann et al., eds., *Vermittlung und Tradierung von Wissen in der griechischen Kultur*, ScOr 61, Tübingen, 1993, 281–303.

Frenschkowski, M., *Magie im antiken Christentum: Eine Studie zur Alten Kirche und ihrem Umfeld*, StAnCh 7, Stuttgart, 2016.

Freudenberger, R., *Das Verhalten der römischen Behörden gegen die Christen im 2. Jahrhundert dargestellt am Brief des Plinius an Trajan und den Reskripten*, MBPR 52, Munich, 1967.

Harmening, D., *Superstitio: Überlieferungs- und theoriegeschichtliche Untersuchungen zur kirchlich-theologischen Aberglaubensliteratur des Mittelalters*, Berlin, 1979.

Hornung, C., *Apostasie im antiken Christentum: Studien zum Glaubensabfall in altkirchlicher Theologie, Disziplin und Pastoral (4.–7. Jahrhundert n.Chr.)*, SVigChr 138, Leiden, 2016.

Hornung, C., "Die Konstruktion christlicher Identität: Funktion und Bedeutung der Apostasie im antiken Christentum," *SP* 92, 2017, 431–440.

Kahlos, M., *Debate and Dialogue: Christian and Pagan Cultures c. 360/430*, Aldershot, 2007.

Karabélias, E., "L'apostasie à Byzance selon le droit imperial du VIe siècle et la discipline ecclésiastique," *Il diritto Romano canonico quale diritto proprio delle comunità Cristiane dell'oriente mediterraneo: IX colloquio internazionale Romanistico canonistico*, Vatican City, 1994, 483–524.

Katz, S., *The Jews in the Visigothic and Frankish Kingdoms of Spain and Gaul*, MMAA 12, Cambridge MA, 1937.

Kelly, H.A., "The Devil in Augustine's Genesis Commentaries," *SP* 33, 1997, 119–124.

Klingshirn, W.E., *Caesarius of Arles: The Making of a Christian Community in Late Antique Gaul*, CSMLT 22, Cambridge MA, 1994.

Lohfink, N., "Der Zorn Gottes und das Exil: Beobachtungen am deuteronomistischen Geschichtswerk," in: R.G. Kratz & H. Spieckermann, eds., *Liebe und Gebot: Studien zum Deuteronomium: FS L. Perlitt*, FRLANT 190, Göttingen, 2000, 137–155.

Mann, W.E., "Augustine on Evil and Original Sin," in: E. Stump et al., eds., *CAA*, Cambridge UK, 2001, 40–48.

Maxwell, J.L., *Christianization and Communication in Late Antiquity: John Chrysostom and His Congregation in Antioch*, Cambridge MA, 2006.

Moreau, J., *Die Christenverfolgung im römischen Reich*, AWR 2, Berlin, 1961.

Piepenbrink, K., *Christliche Identität und Assimilation in der Spätantike: Probleme des Christseins in der Reflexion der Zeitgenossen*, SAG 3, Frankfurt am Main, 2005.

Procopé, J., "Hochmut," in: *RAC*, vol. XV, Stuttgart, 1991, 795–858.

Rajak, T., "The Jewish Community and Its Boundaries," in: T. Rajak, ed., *The Jewish Dialogue with Greece and Rome: Studies in Cultural and Social Interaction*, AGJU 48, Leiden, 2001, 335–354.

Rebillard, É., *Christians and Their Many Identities in Late Antiquity: North Africa 200/450 CE*, Ithaca, 2012.

Reichert, A., "Durchdachte Konfusion: Plinius, Trajan und das Christentum," *ZNW* 93, 2002, 227–250.

Rese, M., "Apostasy," in: *EBR*, vol. II, Berlin, 2009, 460–466.

Sandwell, I., *Religious Identity in Late Antiquity: Greeks, Jews and Christians in Antioch*, Cambridge UK, 2007.

Schöllgen, G., "Plinius der Jüngere," in: *RAC*, vol. XXVII, Stuttgart, 2016, 277–288.

Staden, H. von, "Hairesis and Heresy: The Case of haireseis iatrikai," in: B.F. Meyer et al., eds., *Jewish and Christian Self-Definition*, vol. III: *Self-Definition in the Greco-Roman World*, Philadelphia, 1982, 76–100, 199–206.

Stöver, H.-D., *Christenverfolgung im Römischen Reich: Ihre Hintergründe und Folgen*, Düsseldorf, 1982.

Turner, E.G., "Tiberius Iulius Alexander," *JRS* 44, 1954, 54–64.

Vogt, J., "Christenverfolgung I (historisch)," in: *RAC*, vol. II, Stuttgart, 1954, 1159–1208.

Weiser, A., "Das Gottesurteil über Hananias und Saphira Apg 5, 1–11," *ThGl* 69, 1979, 148–158.

Wellmann, M., *Die pneumatische Schule bis auf Archigenes in ihrer Entwicklung dargestellt*, Berlin, 1895.

Wilson, S.G., *Leaving the Fold: Apostates and Defectors in Antiquity*, Minneapolis, 2004.

CHRISTIAN HORNUNG

Apostle(s)

I. Apostle/Disciple ◆ II. Apostles, Apocryphal Acts of the
◆ III. Apostles' Creed ◆ IV. *Apostles, Epistle of the*

I. Apostle/Disciple

Ἀπόστολος is a term not much used in Greek literature, meaning "messenger, ambassador, or envoy," a natural derivation from the verb ἀποστέλλειν, "to send off" (*Liddell/Scott*, s.v). It occurs only once in the Septuagint (3 Kings 14:6) in the sense of "one sent" with a message. Its 80-fold usage in the New Testament would therefore be somewhat surprising to the initial listeners to and readers of the New Testament documents. In the New Testament, the term is predominantly used in the Pauline letters (34) and in Acts (28), with the other New Testament literature yielding only one or two cases, apart from Luke (6) and Revelation (3).

1. Did Jesus Use the Term?

In only one case does the term appear in words attributed to Jesus: "Therefore also the Wisdom of God said, 'I will send them prophets and apostles, some of whom they will kill and persecute'" (Luke 11:49). However, the Q parallel (Matt 23:34) reads somewhat differently – "Therefore I send you prophets, sages and scribes, some of whom you will kill and crucify." It is certainly possible that the Lukan version retains an early sense of ἀπόστολος as "emissary." But a more decisive consideration is that Luke's version reflects the (by his time) more established sense of "apostle," as evident in his other uses of "apostle" in Luke and Acts, "apostle" as the new covenant equivalent of the old covenant's prophets. In other words, it remains at least doubtful whether Jesus himself ever used the word "apostle" in reference to his disciples.

2. The Gospels

The scarce use of the term in three of the canonical gospels strengthens the suggestion that "apostle" was not recalled as frequently used in passing on the Jesus tradition. John (→ John the Apostle), for example, only uses the term once in the customary sense of "one sent" in contrast to the one sending (John 13:16). And Matthew (→ Matthew the Apostle) also uses it only once, in quoting, as it would appear, "the names of the twelve apostles" (Matt 10:2). Both cases are interesting since Matthew and John have clear ideas of Jesus' disciples being "sent out" by Jesus (Matt 10:5, 16; John 17:18; 20:21), but in both cases the primary focus is on Jesus as the one sent (Matt 15:24; 21:37; regularly in John, e.g. John 17:3, 8). But both refrain from using the term "apostle" as a regular descriptor of Jesus' disciples. In John at least, the focus is almost exclusively on Jesus as the one "sent."

Only Luke (→ Luke, Gospel of) uses the term in describing Jesus' appointment of the twelve disciples "whom he named apostles" (Luke 6:13), though the same phrase may have been an early addition to Mark's (→ Mark, Gospel of) account of the commissioning of the twelve (Mark 3:14). In fact, Mark's only (other) usage is his description of how "the apostles gathered around Jesus" (Mark 6:30, followed by Luke 9:10) on their return from the mission on which Jesus had sent them out "two by two" (Mark 6:7, where the term "apostle" is not used). This latter usage (6:30) suggests that Mark was familiar with the more specialized sense of "apostle," as disciples of Jesus appointed by him to be sent out. But nevertheless it is striking that the dominant descriptor in each evangelist is "disciple" (μαθητής) It was evidently more important that the close followers of Jesus were there to learn from him rather than to be sent out as his ambassadors.

Luke was more familiar with the Christian adoption of the term "apostle" as a definitional descriptor of Jesus' close disciples. This is implicit in Luke 11:49 with its quotation from "the Wisdom of God": "I will send them prophets and apostles" – the ἀπόστολος as a special messenger from God, to be ranked with the prophets. Luke's latter references to Jesus' disciples simply as "the apostles" (Luke 17:5; 22:14; 24:10) doubtless foreshadows his dominant usage in Acts. But it also reflects the fact that their apostolic status was not primarily a reflection of their subsequent missionary work but primarily a consequence of their appointment by Jesus, their time with Jesus, and their teaching from Jesus. Nor should Luke's further note be missed that the women's report of the empty tomb and of the angelic announcement of Jesus' → resurrection "seemed to them (just referred to as "the apostles") an idle tale, and they did not believe them" (Luke 24:11). In Luke's account of the beginnings of Christianity, "the apostles" were important as close disciples of Jesus, and not yet as figures of authority.

3. Acts

The situation and status of Jesus' disciples as "apostles" changes almost immediately with the beginning of Luke's second volume. In the opening sentence of Acts (→ Acts, Book of), the account of Jesus' → ascension is delayed until "after he had given instructions through the → Holy Spirit to the apostles whom he had chosen" (Acts 1:1–2). And the chapter initially focuses on their commission – when their apostolic role is set out by the risen Christ (Acts 1:8). This will be when they really become "apostles" – the empowering by the Spirit, which will drive forward the rest of the narrative, the establishment of the earliest Christian mission, and the foundation of the first churches. Since this promise is followed immediately by Jesus' ascension, it is clear that Luke intended this commissioning of the apostles to be the principal feature of the opening of his second volume. The rest of the chapter is given to the renaming of the 11 apostles (Acts 1:13), the account of the death of the twelfth (Judas; Acts 1:16–20), and the account of his replacement by the choice of Matthias to be "added to the 11 apostles" (Acts 1:26).

The term does not appear again until well through Acts 2, but the reestablished twelve apostles are clearly the focus group on the day of → Pentecost, when "all of them were filled with the Holy Spirit" (Acts 2:4). And when Peter preaches the first Christian sermon, he does so "standing with the 11" (Acts 2:14), that is, as spokesman for the apostles. This is confirmed by Luke's account of the crowd's response to Peter's sermon, when people respond "to Peter and to the other apostles" (Acts 2:37). The 3,000, converted and baptized, "devoted themselves to the apostles' teaching and fellowship, to the breaking of bread and the prayers" (Acts 2:42). Clearly Luke presents Peter as spokesman of the twelve as a whole; the teaching to which the new converts devoted themselves was the teaching of all the apostles. And the awe-filled impact on the whole community was made by the "many wonders and signs done by the apostles" as a whole (Acts 2:43).

Equally significant is the summary account of the first believing community in Acts 4:32–37. The powerful "testimony to the resurrection of the Lord Jesus" is attributed to "the apostles," "and great grace was upon them all" (Acts 4:33). The money raised by the sale of believers' property is "laid at the apostles' feet" and distributed (presumably at their behest and with their guidance) to each as any had need (Acts 4:35). According to Luke, their acknowledged leadership of the new community is attested by their giving a new name (→ Barnabas) to Joseph of Cyprus, who had sold a field and laid the proceeds at the feet of the apostles (Acts 4:36–37).

In the final chapter of the initial account of the new Jerusalem community of believers in Jesus as the Christ, the apostles are referred to regularly – as a kind of ruling directors of the community. The proceeds of property sold are laid at their feet (Acts 5:2). "Many signs and wonders were done among the people through the apostles" (Acts 5:12). "The apostles" as a body are arrested at the behest of the high priest and put in prison (Acts 5:18), only for them to be released by an angel and sent forth to preach and teach in the Temple (Acts 5: 20–21, 25). When brought before the Sanhedrin and questioned as to why they continued to preach in the name of Jesus, the refusal to desist is attributed to "Peter and the apostles" (Acts 5:29). As a result, the apostles (as a whole) are called in, flogged, ordered not to speak in the name of Jesus, and released (Acts 5:40). But they simply rejoiced and every day continued to teach and proclaim Jesus as the Messiah (Acts 5:41–42).

Thereafter "the apostles" appear to function primarily as the established leadership of the Jerusalem community of believers. The seven men chosen "to wait at tables" in diaconal ministry are presented "before the apostles, who prayed and laid their hands on them" (Acts 6:6). When a severe persecution is set in train "against the church in Jerusalem" following the martyrdom of Stephen, all are scattered throughout Judea and Samaria, apart from, no surprise, "the apostles" (Acts 8:1). This is all the odder, since it is those who were thus scattered who "went from place to place, proclaiming the word" (Acts 8:4). Moreover, the first place mentioned, where the word was thus proclaimed, is Samaria – the territory that the apostles were explicitly commissioned to evangelize in Acts 1:8. But the evangelist is Philip, one of the seven chosen for diaconal ministry in Acts 6:5. "The apostles" only appear again in Acts 8:14, significantly referred to as "the apostles in Jerusalem," where Luke seems to take the opportunity to underline their rootedness in Jerusalem. To be sure, Peter and John are sent out to Samaria to make good flaws in Philip's ministry, and it is through the laying on of their hands that the Spirit is given to the Samaritan believers (Acts 8:18). This is doubly curious: that it is through the apostles' hands that the Spirit is given; yet the apostles as a body remain rooted in Jerusalem.

Somewhat curious also is the fact that in the description of Saul's/Paul's conversion, in the following chapter, the word "apostle" is never used, nor does Luke even talk of Paul being "sent out." It is only when Saul/Paul has returned to Jerusalem that Barnabas takes him to the (doubting) "apostles" and describes how Saul has been converted and become a bold preacher "in the name of the Lord" (Acts 9:27). Similarly curious is the account of Peter's breakthrough in taking the gospel to the Roman centurion, Cornelius (→ Cornelius [Centurion]), where the word "apostle" never appears until used to narrate how the good news came to the apostles (still in Jerusalem) and the brothers who were in Judea (Acts 11:1).

Only in chapter 14, early in Paul's mission, do we find a somewhat different use of the term "apostle." Paul and Barnabas, in their mission through southern (modern) Turkey, are referred to simply as "the apostles": when their preaching provoked controversy stirred by "the unbelieving Jews," some of the residents of Iconium sided "with the Jews, and some with the apostles" (Acts 14:4). And again in Lystra, when "the apostles Barnabas and Paul" (Acts 14:4) were being hailed as gods, they could barely restrain the crowd (Acts 14:18). Since this usage is unusual in Acts, it suggests that Luke has drawn his account from Paul's own recollection of the events.

The six remaining references to "apostles" in Acts all have the double phrase "the apostles and elders/ presbyters," and all, significantly, are in reference to the leadership of the Jerusalem community. When it comes to the issue whether the new Gentile converts should be circumcised, Paul and Barnabas go to Jerusalem "to discuss the question with the apostles and elders" (Acts 15:2). When they arrive in Jerusalem, they " were welcomed by the church and the apostles and the elders" (Acts 15:4). "The apostles and the elders met together to consider the matter" (Acts 15:6). After the discussion and decision, "the apostles and the elders, with the consent of the whole church," decided to send news of the decision to the headquarters of the mission of Paul and Barnabas (Syrian Antioch; Acts 15:22). Their message begins, "The apostles and the elders, brothers, to the Gentile brothers in Antioch, Syria and Cilicia" (Acts 15:23). And the final reference is of the same character: as Paul and Barnabas "went from town to town, they delivered to them [...] the decisions which had been reached by the apostles and elders who were in Jerusalem" (Acts 16:4).

This reversion to the understanding of "the apostles" as rooted in Jerusalem, now joined in an established structure of "apostles and elders," is very striking. Luke goes on to devote the rest of his history of Christianity's beginnings to Paul's mission, in Asia Minor, Greece, and then to Rome, after his imprisonment and trials in Jerusalem. But never does he use the term "apostle" again. This, no doubt, is because the Jerusalem leadership of the Christian movement does not reappear; so far as Luke's account is concerned, it is they, the Jerusalem leadership, who were "the apostles." Nevertheless, it is striking that he withholds the term from any of his descriptions of Paul's latter missionary work or in reference to Paul himself as an apostle.

It was clearly, then, Luke's intention to depict the close disciples of Jesus as not only empowered to be witnesses by the Spirit at Pentecost, but also authorized thereby to function as leaders of the resulting community of believers in Jerusalem. This is all slightly curious, since the word "apostle" itself indicates someone "sent out," and, as already noted, the Spirit's coming upon them at Pentecost is explicitly to equip Jesus' immediate disciples as witnesses, not only in Jerusalem but also "in all Judea and Samaria, and to the ends of the earth" (Acts 1:8). Yet "the apostles" seem to remain more or less fixed in Jerusalem, with only occasional usage in reference to mission apart from Jerusalem. Given what will become evident in consideration of Paul's own use of the term, it looks very much as though Luke's account reflects a later and what might be described as an establishment understanding of "the apostles" as a centralized structure in Jerusalem holding together the rapidly expanding Christian movement.

4. Paul

When one turns to the letters of Paul (→ Paul the Apostle), the feature that immediately catches attention is his regular introduction of himself in the letter opening as "Paul, slave of Christ Jesus, called to be an apostle" (Rom 1:1), "Paul, called to be an apostle of Christ Jesus" (1 Cor 1:1), and "Paul, apostle of Christ Jesus" (2 Cor 1:1). The later letters fall into the regular self-introduction – "Paul, apostle of Christ Jesus" (Eph 1:1; Col 1:1; 1 Tim 1:1; 2 Tim 1:1; Tit 1:1). More regular is the addition "apostle of Christ Jesus by the will of God" (1 Cor 1:1; 2 Cor 1:1; Eph 1:1; Col 1:1; 2 Tim 1:1). The variations are interesting but not very significant – "set apart for the gospel of God" (Rom 1:1), "by the command of God our Savior and of Christ Jesus our hope" (1 Tim 1:1), "for the sake of the faith of God's elect and the knowledge of the truth which accords with godliness" (Tit 1:1). Of the later Pauline letters, only in Philippians and Philemon does Paul refrain from brandishing his apostolic title, presumably because both letters are primarily expressions of friendship and appeals on the basis of friendship than occasions to exercise his apostolic authority.

What is more interesting is the fact that in neither of the two letters to the Thessalonians is Paul's regular practice of introducing himself as "apostle" not followed – the opening words being simply, "Paul, Silvanus and Timothy, to the church of the Thessalonians" (1 Thess 1:1; 2 Thess 1:1). In sharp contrast, the letter to the Galatians begins with an emphatic insistence on Paul's apostolic status – "Paul, an apostle, not from men nor through men but through Jesus Christ and God the Father who raised him from the dead" (Gal 1:1) – before something like the usual greeting. Since 1 Thessalonians is usually reckoned to be the first of Paul's letters, it would appear that something must have happened after he wrote to the Thessalonians, which stirred Paul to assert his status as an "apostle." What this could have been is clearly hinted at in Galatians and elaborated in 1 Corinthians.

What emerges in Galatians is that Paul was concerned not primarily for his status as an apostle. In the only other occurrences of the term, in Gal 1:17 and 19, it refers to the Jerusalem apostles, including James, the Lord's brother. Paul refers to them as "those who were apostles before me" (Gal 1:17), the "before me" indicating that Paul had no doubts as to his own apostleship. But his principal concern was to insist on his having been commissioned directly by God to proclaim his Son among the Gentiles (Gal 1:15–16). His commission to the Gentiles was no different from Peter's apostolic commission to the circumcised (Gal 2:8). It was this commission and its successful outcome that Paul was concerned to defend in the face of attempts to promote and proclaim the gospel as a means to Judaize Gentiles (Gal 2:14–16). Galatians, then, is one of the clearest indicators of what Paul saw an apostle to be – as again in his opening salvo, "apostle not from men nor through men but through Jesus Christ" (Gal 1:1). It was that commissioning, rather than any status or title, on which he focused his self-defense – "God set me apart from my mother's womb and called me through his grace to reveal his Son in me, in order that I might proclaim him among the Gentiles" (Gal 1:15–16).

That Paul did not push the title "apostle" at this point in the face of his readers, and in the face by inference of his critics, suggests that the meaning of the term "apostle" was not yet clearly defined. Paul takes it for granted that the Jerusalem leadership, including James, were apostles (Gal 1:17, 19). But the fact that in the letter in which Paul first insisted on his apostleship (Gal 1:1) the only other two "apostle" references are to the Jerusalem apostles suggests that the idea so prominent in Acts, that "the apostles" were rooted in Jerusalem, was already well established. It is Paul, then, who in effect insisted that an apostle was indeed one who had been "sent out," that the good news of Jesus Christ was not just for Jews but for Gentiles as well – an insistence that gave rise to the furor addressed in Galatians.

What is probably the next Pauline letter, his first to the Corinthians, suggests that Paul soon became accustomed to talking about himself as an apostle, and, in effect, to insisting on what it meant to be an apostle. His first use of the term follows the letter's introduction where he depicts apostles as "last of all, as though sentenced to death, because we have become a spectacle to the world, to angels and to humankind" (1 Cor 4:9). Paul evidently had no qualms in portraying apostles not as figures of authority but as prominent in confronting, or victims of the world's power and greed.

But in his next use of the term (1 Cor 9:1–2), we have one of the clearest insights into what for Paul constituted an "apostle." The first defining feature was that an apostle had seen Christ, that is, as will become clear in chapter 15, an apostle is one who had been personally commissioned by the risen Christ. The second defining feature is that an apostle was instrumental in converting individuals and establishing churches, that is, gatherings of those converted for worship and instruction. This was precisely why Paul could claim and seek to exert such authority as he does in his letters. Implicit is the limited authority of the apostle as so envisaged. Paul accepted that he might not be recognized as bearing apostolic authority by others, by other churches, other communities of believers, including the Jerusalem church(?), but he had no qualms about claiming apostolic authority in relation to the churches that had come into being through his own ministry.

This foundational role of apostles, for Paul, is made even clearer in the way Paul sketches out how the community of believers should operate together as a church (chs. 12–14). In the list of gifts and ministries (1 Cor 12:4–6), through which a church functions as the body of Christ, apostles have the front rank. In Paul's mind, no doubt, this will be because apostles had established the church. But Paul also saw the relation of an apostle and a church founded by the apostle as ongoing. From Paul's own history as a missionary, that did not mean an apostle had to settle down to remain with the church he had founded. But it explains why Paul strongly felt that he had a continuing obligation and ministry to churches he had founded even after he had moved on to establish other churches. It is because of this vision of (his) apostleship that he continued to care for his churches and wrote to them even when he had moved on elsewhere. It is this sense of what

an apostle does and what an apostle is responsible for – in converting individuals to establish churches, and in maintaining pastoral oversight for these churches – which makes Paul's concept of apostleship so distinctive and so enduring.

Only in 1 Cor 15 does Paul's sensitivity over his claim to be an apostle come to full light. He fully acknowledged a degree of precedence in the case of Jesus' own disciples and of those who became disciples before him – Cephas, the twelve, more than 500, and James. To them the risen Christ had appeared first and well before him (1 Cor 15:5–7). Fifth in the list is Jesus' appearance to "all the apostles," where it is clearly implied that the number of apostles, those sent out by the risen Jesus in mission, was larger than "the twelve," that is, a circle much wider than the circle of Jesus' own disciples. This must mean that Paul knew of and acknowledged the church-founding missionary work of many of those who had been evangelizing before he himself became engaged in mission. But his concern was primarily to ensure that his readers and audience understood Paul himself to have been included in the number of apostles appointed by the risen Christ (1 Cor 15:8–9).

In this chapter it is especially clear that for Paul an "apostle" is one who had been commissioned by the risen Christ to proclaim Christ, to win converts, and thus to establish churches. Probably significant is the fact that in this key passage in 1 Cor 15, while Paul freely acknowledges the primacy of Cephas and "the twelve," he reserves the title "apostle" for a much larger group of (more than 500?) and hastens to add his own title as "apostle" (by implication a member of that group), as one who saw apostleship as a commission to preach well beyond the bounds of Jerusalem and Judea.

2 Corinthians gives further indication of how sensitive Paul was on the whole question of apostleship. He fully recognizes that the term may be used in the less technical sense of "messengers" commissioned by the churches (2 Cor 8:23). These "apostles" represented their churches, but had not been commissioned by Christ and did not have authority over their churches, such as Paul sought to exercise in relation to the churches he founded. But in the added material of chapters 10–13, we meet another type of apostle – "super-apostles" (2 Cor 11:5; 12:11). Were these members of the 500 (1 Cor 15:6), or those

claiming a commission from Christ that Paul did not recognize? The term "super" certainly indicates a dismissive attitude on Paul's part, though it may also indicate exalted claims made by the persons involved. They certainly claimed an authority that exceeded that of Paul, as indicated not least by their fluency of speech (2 Cor 11:6). But his indignant dismissal of them as "false apostles, deceitful workers, disguising themselves as apostles of Christ," indeed "servants of Satan [...] disguised as servants of righteousness" (2 Cor 11:13–15), evidences a degree of rancor in the earliest Christian mission for which Acts had not prepared us. In response Paul had no qualms in claiming that his apostolic authority was in no way inferior to that of the "super-apostles," and that the proof of his apostleship ("the signs of the apostle") was evident in the "signs and wonders and mighty works" he had performed among them (2 Cor 12:11–12). There are no more disturbing features of the earliest history of Christianity than in these chapters.

The other two references in Romans have particular significance. In a letter where Paul had to do much to introduce himself, it is striking that he did so by referring to himself as "an apostle to the Gentiles." The important fact, however, is that he saw his Gentile mission as a means to stirring his own people to respond positively to his gospel (Rom 11:13) – his answer, no doubt, to the criticism that he expected to be common among his fellow Jews in Rome. The other reference comes in the greetings appended at the end of the letter, where Paul asks for greetings to be passed on to Andronicus and Junia, "my fellow prisoners, who were eminent among the apostles, and who were in Christ before me" (Rom 16:7). This all-too-brief reference is presumably to two of "all the apostles" mentioned in 1 Cor 15:7, and confirms that these apostles traveled well beyond Judea. That one of them was a woman (Junia) should not escape notice.

The other "apostle" references in the Pauline letters add little to the total picture. Probably the earliest reference in Paul's letters is 1 Thess 2:7: "Though we might have made demands on you as apostles of Christ, we were gentle among you, like a nurse tenderly caring for her own children." Implicit in this earliest reference is Paul's assumption that apostles had been directly appointed by Christ. But equally significant is Paul's claim that he had exercised that authority in a sensitive way – though some in his churches would probably have questioned that! Probably in accordance with his unwillingness to assert his apostleship/apostolic authority to the Philippians, the only use of the term in the letter is the grateful reference to Epaphroditus as not only "my brother, and co-worker and fellow-soldier," but also as "your apostle and minister to my need" (Phil 2:25). Here again, the basic sense of "apostle" as commissioned to be sent on a particular mission is clear. Again it is striking that Paul refrains from using the more technical term (apostle of Christ) with the heavy weight of authority implicitly attached to it.

In the later Pauline letters, Ephesians has the most interesting uses of the term. The (probably) later perspective is indicated by the reference to "the apostles and prophets" as "foundation" of the church, "with Christ Jesus himself as the cornerstone" (Eph 2:20). The foundational character of the apostles is further signified by reference to the core revelation made "to the holy apostles and prophets by the Spirit" – the core revelation being, in true Pauline terms, that the Gentiles are to be full sharers in the gospel (Eph 3:5–6). And the same emphasis is reinforced in the final reference in elaboration of Paul's earlier vision of the church as the body of Christ: the gifts given by the ascended Christ are first of all apostles, then prophets, evangelists, pastors, and teachers, charged to equip the saints for the work of ministry, for building up the body of Christ (Eph 4:11–12).

The only other references in the Pastoral Epistles reinforce the emphasis within the Pauline tradition that Paul's apostolic status and authority were unquestioned among his followers and churches. To proclaim the one God and Christ Jesus was Paul's commission as "a herald and an apostle [...] a teacher of the Gentiles in faith and truth" (1 Tim 2:7). Paul had been "appointed a herald and an apostle and a teacher" of the gospel of God's grace "given to us in Christ Jesus," nothing to be ashamed of even though it brought so much suffering on Paul (2 Tim 1:11–12). These two references quite effectively sum up the distinctive use of the term "apostle," which Paul stamped upon it by his mission and in his letters. The lasting impression Paul leaves on the word is of outgoing mission and of the authority in reference to gospel and churches central to the enduring success of that mission.

5. The Rest of the New Testament

The sole Hebrews reference, Heb 3:1, is unique in describing Jesus as "the apostle and high priest of our confession." Jesus as "high priest" is central to and distinctive of Hebrews, and this conjunction of "apostle" with it gives the latter a unique Christological sense and raises the status of the concept. By implication, the apostles are primarily representatives of the one sent by God to mediate his people's reconciliation with God.

The two letters of Peter (→ Peter the Apostle) both introduce themselves with the words "Peter, [...] an apostle of Jesus Christ" (1 Pet 1:1; 2 Pet 1:1). Clearly, by the time they were written, the term "apostle" had become well established as a, or rather the, title for Jesus' close disciples. The other 2 Peter reference – "you should remember the words spoken in the past by the holy prophets, and the commandment of the Lord and Savior spoken through your apostles" (2 Pet 3:2) – confirms that apostles were regarded as mouthpieces of the exalted Lord, ranked alongside and in effect playing the same role as prophets of old (2 Pet 1:19–21). The reference to them as "your apostles" suggests a sense of close relation to these authoritative spokesmen of the faith, probably to help counter any sense in this last of the New Testament documents of increasing distance from these founding fathers. The sole reference in Jude – reminding the readers of "the predictions of the apostles of our Lord Jesus Christ" concerning worldly "scoffers" (Jude 17) – has the same implication that "the apostles" had first proclaimed and defined their faith.

The three references in Revelation equally confirm the status that "apostles" had late in the 1st century. Rev 18:20 calls on "you saints and apostles and prophets" to rejoice over the fall of Babylon. Once again the collocation of "apostles and prophets" suggests that apostles played a similar role to that of prophets in the previous dispensation. And that "apostles" can be distinguished from "saints" no doubt reflects the status of the most immediate followers of Jesus and of those commissioned to preach the Christian message. Rev 21:14 confirms the fundamental status and role of "the apostles" – in the vision of the new Jerusalem, "the wall of the city has 12 foundations, and on them the 12 names of the twelve apostles of the Lamb". Here it is striking that the tradition of the twelve disciples appointed by Jesus is retained, even though one (Judas) had presumably been discounted, to be replaced by whom (Matthias, Acts 1:26; Paul, 1 Cor 15:8–10)? Most interesting, though somewhat surprising in view of these later references in Revelation, is 2:2, with the note that the Church of Ephesus had "tested those who claim to be apostles but are not, and have found them to be false."

6. Closing Reflection

What emerges from this study is the way in which the term "apostle" became more formalized. It seems to have been introduced in the earliest days of Christian mission, in itself probably an early expression of the first Christians' conviction that they were commissioned to proclaim the good news of Jesus. It is dubious as to whether Jesus himself so spoke of his disciples. And Paul himself does not seem to have introduced the term. But the clear implication of his usage is that it came into common Christian currency because it gave expression to the earliest sense of being commissioned to spread the gospel focused on Jesus. It was certainly this sense that Paul inherited and to which he gave fresh and vigorous expression. He did not forget the sense of "emissary," but his conviction as to his own commission gave the term its classic Christian sense: the double sense of specially commissioned directly by (the risen) Christ, commissioned to preach Christ well beyond the bounds of Judea, and commissioned to establish and maintain communities (churches) of believers in Jesus.

The subsequent use of the term understandably read it back to some degree into reminiscences of Jesus' own mission. But the principal tendency, as particularly evident in Acts, was to focus the term, one might say, almost bureaucratically – that is, on a ruling body, centrally located in Jerusalem, and having oversight over the church and mission from that central location. The uncomfortable question remains, whether that shift in focus – from outgoing missionary to established authority – was an entirely positive and healthy development for Christianity.

Bibliography

Ashton, J., *The Religion of Paul the Apostle*, New Haven, 2000.

Baur, F.C., *Paul: The Apostle of Jesus Christ*, 2 vols., London, 1873, 1875.

Becker, J., *Paul: Apostle to the Gentiles*, Louisville, 1993.

Bruce, F.F., *Paul: Apostle of the Free Spirit*, Exeter, 1977.

Chae, D.J.-S., *Paul as Apostle to the Gentiles: His Apostolic Self-awareness and its Influence on the Soteriological Argument in Romans*, Carlisle, 1997.

Clark, A.C., "The Role of the Apostles," in: I.H. Marshall & D. Peterson, eds., *Witness to the Gospel: The Theology of Acts*, Grand Rapids, 1998, 169–190.

Cullmann, O., *Peter: Disciple, Apostle, Martyr*, London, 1962.

Dunn, J.D.G., "Paul: Apostate or Apostle of Israel?" *ZNW* 89, 1998, 256–271.

Epp, E.J., *Junia: The First Woman Apostle*, Minneapolis, 2005.

Fridrichsen, A., *The Apostle and his Message*, Uppsala, 1947.

Lüdemann, G., *Paul, Apostle to the Gentiles: Studies in Chronology*, Philadelphia, 1984.

Mitchell, M.W., "Reexamining the 'Aborted Apostle': An Exploration of Paul's Self-Description in 1 Corinthians 15.8," *JSNT* 25, 2003, 469–485.

Perkins, P., *Peter: Apostle for the Whole Church*, Minneapolis, 1994, 2000.

JAMES D.G. DUNN (†)

II. Apostles, Apocryphal Acts of the

The Apocryphal Acts of the Apostles are noncanonical narratives describing the travels and activities of apostles, which generally include the performance of miracles, the promotion of sexual abstinence, conversion of prominent individuals (frequently women), and conflicts with government officials (often related to the conversion of prominent women). These acts end with the death of the apostle, typically by public execution. Five works – the *Acts of John* (→ John the Apostle), *Acts of Andrew* (→ Andrew the Apostle), *Acts of Peter* (→ Peter the Apostle), *Acts of Paul* (→ Paul the Apostle), and *Acts of Thomas* (→ Thomas the Apostle) – are generally referred to as the "major apocryphal acts" or the "early apocryphal acts," these five having likely been produced between the mid-2nd and mid-3rd centuries CE. But Christians continued to write, read, edit,

and circulate narratives concerning the apostles well beyond this period. The category "apocryphal acts" also includes the *Acts of Philip*, the *Acts of Peter and the Twelve Apostles* (→ Peter the Apostle), the *Acts of Andrew and Matthias in the City of the Cannibals*, the *Acts of Andrew and Bartholomew*, and a host of other narratives composed in the 3rd, 4th, and 5th centuries CE and beyond. M. Geerard includes 109 distinct acts in his *Clavis Apocryphorum Novi Testamenti* (Geerard, 1992), and this list could be expanded even further. The Pseudo-Clementines (→ Clementine Literature, Pseudo-), which describe the life and experiences of Clement as a disciple of Peter, may also belong in this category.

1. Language

Of the five early apocryphal acts, only Thomas seems to have been composed in Syriac (though, of the extant versions, the Greek text frequently presents the more ancient tradition; Klijn, 2003). The other four were composed in Greek, though the bulk of the *Acts of Peter* is only extant in a single Latin manuscript (on which see Thomas, 2003 & Baldwin, 2005). Nor was Latin by any means the only language into which these texts were translated: apocryphal acts (in full or fragmentary form) are extant in a wide variety of languages, including Syriac, Coptic, Armenian, Georgian, Arabic, Slavonic, Ethiopic, Irish, and other European vernaculars.

2. Corpus

The notion that the *Acts of John*, *Acts of Andrew*, *Acts of Peter*, *Acts of Paul*, and *Acts of Thomas* form a corpus has its roots in the probable use of a collection of these five texts by Manicheans (→ Mani/Manichaeism) in the 4th century CE, as evidenced above all in the Manichean Psalm-book (Schäferdiek, 1992; but see Kaestli, 1977). Further evidence is Filastrius of Brescia's reference to the Manicheans' *Acts of Andrew, John, Peter*, and *Paul*, with specific reference to talking animals (a phenomenon that occurs in the *Acts of Peter*, *Acts of Paul*, and the (unmentioned) *Acts of Thomas* (Filas. *Haer.* 88.6). → Augustine of Hippo also provides evidence of a collection in his quotation of the Manichaean Faustus of Milevis, who describes the apostles Peter, Andrew, Thomas,

John, and Paul (with specific reference to Thecla) as commending celibacy to young men and women (Aug. *Faust.* 30.4).

Some four and a half centuries later, Photius reports reading one book comprising the *Acts of Peter, John, Andrew, Thomas,* and *Paul,* to which he gives the title "The Circuits of the Apostles" (τῶν ἀποστόλων περίοδοι), naming a certain "Leucius Charinus" as author. Photius is by no means neutral as to the value of this book. He concludes that

> in a word, this book encompasses myriad childish, unbelievable, ill-conceived, false, stupid, self-contradictory, impious and godless things; one would not stray far from the truth in calling it the font and mother of every heresy. (Phot. *Bibl.* 114)

Despite his negative assessment, the details he provides make it clear that he was reading some version of the five early acts as we know them. While Photius is the only author to include "Charinus" as surname, the name "Leucius" is attached to one or more apocryphal acts by Augustine, Evodius, Innocent I, Turribius of Astorga, and others; elsewhere, the name is associated with a disciple of the apostle John (e.g. by → Epiphanius of Salamis in *Pan.* 2.6.9; for a collection of the relevant passages, see Zahn, 1880, 195–218). In the 5th century CE, *Transitus Mariae* of Pseudo-Melito of Sardis (→ Melito of Sardis), the two streams of "Leucius" tradition (i.e. as the author of apocryphal texts and as a companion of John) come together: the prologue of the text refers to a "certain Leucius" who had been a companion of the apostles, but, having been led astray, wrote in his books about their great deeds, but "lied a great deal about their teaching." Because both → Innocent I and Turribius attach the name Leucius only to the *Acts of John* and without reference to a corpus of texts, it seems likely that the name was first attached to that text (perhaps even by the author in the lost beginning of the text) and only later was attached to the other four (see Schäferdiek, 1992).

The reception of these texts among Manicheans (and the not unrelated rejection of them by other Christian authors) aside, it must be emphasized that the five texts do not, in fact, form a corpus. Though there seems to be some literary relationship among them, there is no reason to think that a single author

wrote more than one, though M.R. James at one point argued that the *Acts of Peter* and *Acts of John* were the product of one author (James, 1897). In fact, while they certainly have common generic features and share an interest in issues of sexual asceticism and self-control, each has its own particular theological outlook, and no two are the same in this regard.

3. Date

While most contemporary scholars are agreed that the five early apocryphal acts were composed between the mid-2nd and mid-3rd centuries CE and are similarly unanimous in placing the *Acts of Thomas* in the first half of the 3rd century CE, there is little agreement on the more specific dating of the other four texts within this hundred-year window. To offer just three examples, H.J. Klauck (2008) proposes the following order:

1. *Acts of John* (c. 150–160 CE);
2. *Acts of Paul* (c. 170–180 CE);
3. *Acts of Peter* (c. 190–200 CE);
4. *Acts of Andrew* (c. 200–210 CE);
5. *Acts of Thomas* (c. 220–240 CE).

R. Pervo (2015; with J.K. Elliott, 1993, agreeing on order) suggests the following:

1. *Acts of Paul* (c. 175 CE);
2. *Acts of Peter* (c. 185 CE);
3. *Acts of John* (c. 200 CE);
4. *Acts of Andrew* (c. 215 CE);
5. *Acts of Thomas* (c. 225 CE).

P. Foster (2015) proposes:

1. *Acts of Andrew* (c. 150);
2. *Acts of Peter* (c. 180–190);
3. *Acts of Paul* (c. 185–195);
4. *Acts of John* (c. 200–250);
5. *Acts of Thomas* (c. 200–250).

Much of the variation results from different conclusions regarding the interrelation of these texts, particularly the *Acts of Peter, Acts of Paul,* and *Acts of John.* Some have argued that the *Acts of John* are dependent on the *Acts of Paul* (Jones, 1993; MacDonald, 1997); others argue the other way around (Lalleman, 1998; Klauck, 2008, 50). Similarly, many scholars have argued that the *Acts of Peter* are dependent on the *Acts of Paul* (MacDonald, 1997), while others place Peter before Paul (Spittler, 2008, 146–147). The firmest piece of evidence as to date – upon which most other arguments for date are ultimately based – is → Tertullian's mention of the *Acts of Paul* in Tert. *Bapt.* 17.5; this mention provides a *terminus ante quem* for the composition of the *Acts of Paul* at circa 200 CE. Estimations of the interval of time between composition and reception by Tertullian (which range from five to 30 years) seem to be related to one's conclusions regarding dependence.

4. Genre: Ancient Novel?

Generic similarities between the Apocryphal Acts of the Apostles and the ancient novel have been noted and studied for more than a century (Dobschütz, 1902, being perhaps the first to publish on the topic, though James, 1897, was already referring to apocryphal acts as "romances" and "novels"). In 1932, R. Söder published a highly influential monograph, in which she details five primary elements of novelistic Greek literature:

1. the motif of wandering;
2. the aretalogical element;
3. the teratological element;
4. the tendentious (whether religious or ethical) element;
5. the erotic element.

She finds each of these at play in – and indeed central to – both ancient novels and the apocryphal acts, though the erotic element is inverted in the apocryphal acts (in the prevention of marriages and the chaste relationships between converted woman and apostle, as opposed to the more typical love stories depicted in the non-Christian narratives). R. Söder's work is particularly important inasmuch as she expands the boundaries of what should be considered an ancient "novel" (Ger. *Roman*) or "novelistic literature," particularly when drawing comparisons with Christian literature. Whereas E. von Dobschütz, following E. Rohde, restricted the designation to the sophistic erotic novels (i.e. those, such as Chariton's, that narrate the adventures of star-crossed lovers), R. Söder argues for the inclusion of historical novels (e.g. *Alexander Romance*), philosophical biographies (e.g. → Porphyry of Tyre's and → Iamblichus of Chalcis' lives of Pythagoras and Philostratus' *Life of Apollonius of Tyana*), and comic adventure novels (e.g. [Ps.-] Lucian's *Onos* and Apuleius' *Metamorphoses*; Söder, 1932).

While R. Söder's work has been the object of criticisms (some more justified than others; see Thomas, 2003, 4–5), the basic notion that the apocryphal acts are in some sense a Christian variety of ancient novelistic literature is widely accepted. Some have argued that the canonical Gospels – as opposed to the canonical Acts – are the nearest antecedent to the apocryphal acts (Bovon, 1981), but this observation has little bearing on the issue of genre, since the genre of the canonical Gospels (and their own relation to novelistic literature) is itself very much an open question. In fact, many discussions of the genre of the apocryphal acts – and early Christian narrative more broadly – have been severely hampered by an overemphasis on the canonical and noncanonical status of texts. Thus, the canonical Acts has typically been compared with ancient historiography, while apocryphal acts are compared with fiction; the canonical Acts is supposed to have a "theological programme," while the apocryphal acts are regarded as telling miraculous stories "for their own sake"; the canonical Acts is characterized as having a "restrained spirituality," while the apocryphal acts are described as "crudely sensational" (see discussion in Spittler, 2019). Exceptions to this tendency are R. Pervo and C. Thomas, both of whom ultimately argue for the great value of studying apocryphal acts (which both authors characterize as historical novels) in achieving a better understanding of the composition, development, and function of canonical narratives (Pervo, 1986; Thomas, 2003; see also Charlesworth, 1987, 2–3, for clear statement of the problem with respect to the study of canonical and noncanonical texts in general).

Historiography

In 1987, J.M. Charlesworth divided the history of the study of apocryphal Christian literature into four phases (Charlesworth, 1987). The first, running from the middle ages through the 18th century, was, according to Charlesworth, characterized by three tendencies:

1. the assessment of apocryphal literature "in light of the superiority of the canon";
2. "the preoccupation with dogma";
3. the judgment that *some* apocryphal texts are authentic.

The most important publication of this era was J.A. Fabricius' *Codex Apocryphus Novi Testamenti* (1703), a two-volume collection of apocryphal texts, including apocryphal acts and testimonia. Charlesworth's second phase encompasses the 19th century, during which time the first two tendencies continued, though the third faded in the light of progress in historical criticism. Key publications for the study of apocryphal acts were C. Tischendorf's *Acta Apostolorum Apocrypha* in 1851 and R.A. Lipsius and M. Bonnet's updated and expanded editions in three volumes (publ. 1891, 1898, and 1903), which retained C. Tischendorf's title. The third phase, which Charlesworth places in the first two-thirds of the 20th century, is marked by the publication of translations (above all, Hennecke, 1904, *Neutestamentliche Apokryphen*, expanded to two volumes in the 1959 and 1964 editions of W. Schneemelcher, and M.R. James' *The Apocryphal New Testament*). In addition to the production of these translations, which made the texts accessible to a wider variety of scholars, 20th-century scholarship was driven by new discoveries – among papyri caches but also (and more importantly for apocryphal acts) among the thousands of manuscripts housed in European libraries (see e.g. Bovon, Bouvier & Amsler, 1999).

These two fonts (new texts and new translations) fueled a surge in scholarship that would play out in Charlesworth's fourth phase, that is, the remaining decades of the 20th century (from which he was writing). The key moment in this era was the founding in 1981 of the *L'Association pour l'étude de la littérature apocryphe chrétienne* with the express goal of producing critical editions, translations, and commentaries of apocryphal texts for the Corpus Christianorum Series Apocryphorum (which to date numbers 19 vols., treating nine apocryphal texts and one collection of texts). Beyond fostering the production of editions and translations, the *L'Association pour l'étude de la littérature apocryphe chrétienne* represented a new approach to apocryphal literature in general, one that broke with traditional classification and definition of apocryphal texts with respect to canonical texts – as is evident in their preference for "apocryphal Christian literature" as opposed to "New Testament apocrypha" as a general designation for noncanonical texts (Junod, 1983).

Of particular note amid the plethora of scholarship on apocryphal acts in the last decades of the 20th century (and these early years of the 21st cent.) is work informed by feminism and gender studies. The figure of → Thecla – a young woman who, according to the *Acts of Paul* (and *Acts of Paul and Thecla*) became a follower of Paul against the wishes of her family, faced and survived multiple attempts at public execution, baptized herself in a pool of vicious seals, and ultimately preached the word of God to others – understandably attracted the attention of historians of women and gender in early Christianity (as did Mygdonia in the *Acts of Thomas*, Drusiana in the *Acts of John*, etc.). Three monographs of the 1980s (Davies, 1980; MacDonald, 1983; Burrus, 1987) presented various readings of apocryphal acts each suggesting that the texts represent (or were, indeed, composed within) women-centered communities of early Christians. Their arguments have been individually (and often collectively) critiqued from various quarters, but they sparked an important discussion concerning our ability to reconstruct historical early Christian women on the basis of the representation of women in apocryphal acts. Particularly important is the intra-feminist critique of K. Cooper, who reads in these texts not evidence of the roles of historical women but evidence of early Christian rhetoric and apologetics (Cooper, 1996). Ultimately, these arguments have underscored the political nature of all historiography (ancient and contemporary), making this an instance where apocryphal acts scholarship has had wide and enduring impact on the broader field (Matthews, 2001).

Bibliography

Baldwin, M., *Whose Acts of Peter?* WUNT 196, 2nd series, Tübingen, 2005.

Bovon, F., "La vie des apôtres: Traditions bibliques et narrations apocryphes," in: F. Bovon et al., eds., *Les actes apocryphes des apôtres: Christiansme et monde païen*, Genève, 1981.

Bovon, F., B. Bouvier & F. Amsler, *Acta Philippi*, CChr.SA 11 & 12, Turnhout, 1999.

Burke, T., "Entering the Mainstream: Twenty-five Years of Research on the Christian Apocrypha," in: P. Piovanelli & T. Burke, eds., *Rediscovering the Apocryphal Continent: New Perspectives on Early Christian and Late Antique Apocryphal Texts and Traditions*, WUNT 349, Tübingen, 2015.

Burrus, V., *Chastity as Autonomy*, Lewiston, 1987.

Charlesworth, J.M., *The New Testament Apocrypha and Pseudepigrapha: A Guide to Publications, with Excurses on Apocalypses*, ATLA.BS 17, Metuchen, 1987.

Cooper, K., *The Virgin and the Bride: Idealized Womanhood in Late Antiquity*, Cambridge MA, 1996.

Davies, S., *The Revolt of the Widows: The Social World of the Apocryphal Acts*, Carbondale, 1980.

Dobschütz, E. von, "Der Roman in der altchristlichen Literatur," *DeRu* 111, 1902, 87–106.

Elliott, J.K., *The Apocryphal New Testament*, Oxford, 1993.

Foster, P., "Christology and Soteriology in Apocryphal Acts and Apocalypses," in: A. Gregory & C. Tuckett, eds., *OHECA*, Oxford, 2015, 213–232.

Geerard, M., *Clavis Apocryphorum Novi Testamenti*, Turnhout, 1992.

James, M.R., *Apocrypha Anecdota: Second Series*, Cambridge UK, 1897.

Jones, F.S., "Principal Orientations on the Relations between the Apocryphal Acts (*Acts of Paul* and *Acts of John, Acts of Peter* and *Acts of John*)," in: E.H. Lovering, ed., SBL.SP, Atlanta, 1993, 485–505.

Junod, E., "Apocryphes du NT ou Apocryphes Chrétiens Anciens?" *ETR* 3, 1983, 409–421.

Kaestli, J.D., "L'utilisation des actes apocryphe des apôtres dans le Manichéisme," in: M. Krause, ed., *Gnosis and Gnosticism: Papers Read at the Seventh International Conference on Patristic Studies*, NHS 8, Leiden, 1977, 107, 116.

Klauck, H.J., *The Apocryphal Acts of the Apostles: An Introduction*, Waco, 2008.

Klijn, A.F.J., *The Acts of Thomas: Introduction, Text, and Commentary*, 2nd rev. ed., Leiden, 2003.

Lalleman, P., *The Acts of John: A Two-Stage Initiation into Johannine Gnosticism*, SAAA 4, Louvain, 1998.

MacDonald, D.R., *The Legend and the Apostle: The Battle for Paul in Story and Canon*, Philadelphia, 1983.

MacDonald, D.R., "Which Came First? Intertextual Relationships among the Apocryphal Acts of the Apostles," *Semeia* 80, 1997, 11–42.

Matthews, S., "Thinking of Thecla: Issues in Feminist Historiography," *JFSR* 17/2, 2001, 39–55.

Pervo, R., *Profit with Delight*, Philadelphia, 1986.

Pervo, R., "Early Christian Fiction," in: J.R. Morgan & R. Stoneman, eds., *Greek Fiction: The Greek Novel in Context*, New York, 1994.

Pervo, R., "The Role of the Apostles," in: A. Gregory & C. Tuckett, eds., *OHECA*, Oxford, 2015, 306–318.

Plümacher, E., "Apokryphe Apostelakten," in: *RE*, suppl. vol. XV, Munich, 1978, 11–70.

Ramelli, I., *I romanzi antichi e il cristianesimo: Contesti e contatti*, GREC 6, Madrid, 2001.

Santos Otero, A. "Later Acts of the Apostles," in: W. Schneelmelcher, ed., *New Testament Apocrypha*, vol. II, Louisville, 1992, 426–482; trans. R.McL. Wilson.

Schäferdiek, K., "The Manichean Collection of Apocryphal Acts Ascribed to Leucius Charinus," in: W. Schneelmelcher, ed., *New Testament Apocrypha*, vol. II, Louisville, 1992, 87–100; trans. R.McL. Wilson.

Söder, R., *Die apokryphen Apostelgeschichten und die romanhafte Literatur der Antike*, Stuttgart, 1932.

Spittler, J.E., *Animals in the Apocryphal Acts of the Apostles: The Wild Kingdom of Early Christianity*, WUNT 247, 2nd series, Tübingen, 2008.

Spittler, J.E., "The Development of Miracle Traditions in the Apocryphal Acts of the Apostles," in: C. Clivaz, J. Frey & T. Nicklas, eds., *Between Canonical and Apocryphal Texts*, Tübingen, 2019.

Thomas, C., *The Acts of Peter, Gospel Literature, and the Ancient Novel: Rewriting the Past*, Oxford, 2003.

Zahn, T., *Acta Joannis*, Erlangen, 1880.

JANET E. SPITTLER

III. Apostles' Creed

The "Apostles' Creed" is the → creed best known in western Christianity, and the most unknown one in eastern Christianity. → Hilary of Poitiers, in the years 358/359 CE, reports to his western colleagues with astonishment from the East that controversies here "had led to the *creation* of creeds as written documents, a literary genre which so far had been unknown in the West" (Kinzig, 2017a, vol. I, 11). Belief was a conviction "abundant in the Spirit" which needed not "the letter," hence the ignorance of "written creeds" (*conscriptas fides*), as Hilary writes in *De synodis* (63). This discrepancy between West and East alone should make one thinking about the origin of creeds in general and more particularly about that of the Apostles' Creed, its reception and its place in the history of Christianity.

In a centenary article of 1999, responding by the same title ("Recent Research on the Origin of the Creed") to the opening article of the first issue of the *Journal of Theological Studies* from 1899, the origin of the Apostles' Creed was placed into a new framework of credal developments in early Christianity. Much research had been done on this topic and research had amounted to a "new consensus," developed in the years before by scholars like H. von Campenhausen (1972) and A.M. Ritter (1984). This consensus stated that declaratory creeds, such as the Apostles' Creed, "was not a celebration of baptism" (→ Baptism) and that "we do not even know of *any* declaratory confession before the first half of the

4th century" (Kinzig & Vinzent, 1999, 539). Concerning the Apostles' Creed, it was taken as going back to "its original version, the Roman Creed, which itself occurs for the first time in the middle of the 4th century" (Kinzig & Vinzent, 1999, 539). In turn, the Roman Creed as the *Vorlage* of the Apostles' Creed, seemed to have been influenced by earlier baptismal interrogations and rules of faith created mostly ad hoc by individual theologians of the 3d and 4th centuries CE. More recently, however, W. Kinzig made a case that not only these questions and rules of faith existed, but also an early form of a Roman Creed, the "only possible way to explain [...] the great similarities between Tertullian's Christ summary and the summary of the Roman Creed" (Kinzig, 2017b, 287). This explanation, however, contrasts already with his own statement in the same study, that → Tertullian in his fight against Praxeas enlarged the second article (Kinzig, 2017b, 286) on the basis of "Northern African and not Roman influences," admitting that a similar Christ summary is unknown from Rome (Kinzig, 2017b, 290). There are, indeed, no witnesses for a Roman Creed prior to Marcellus of Ancyra. Especially Tertullian is a good proof for the absence of a fixed, written creed at this time in the Latin speaking West. Tert. *Virg.* 1.4 and *Prax.* 2.1 provides two rules of faith that differ markedly. In the first of these, he speaks about the "birth of the virgin Mary" (→ Mary), and that "Jesus Christ [...] was crucified under Pontius Pilate," in the second, he states instead that Christ "was send by the Father into the virgin," while → Pilate remains unmentioned, instead, Tertullians writes: "This one suffered, this one died and was buried according to the Scriptures." The reference to the Scriptures – not to the Roman Creed – is a correct lead to his source (so also Tert. *Carn. chr.* 20). Already the theological differences between rules of faith of one and the same author (see also Tert. *Apol.* 17; 18; *Praesc.* 13; 20; 21; 23; 36; 37; *Carn. chr.* 5; 20; *Prax.* 2; 4; 30; see Kinzig, 2017a, vol. I, 222–233), make the existence of a reference formula on which he relied, unlikely (see also Kinzig, 2017a, ch. 9, vol. I, 293–310, 304–305; and compare all other authors of the 3rd cent. CE. in Kinzig, 2017a, vol. I, 165–268).

The first written summaries that seem to have had some sort of a fixed text and which existed during the 3rd century CE were baptismal questions. These, however, were rather short and did not ask for more than what the *Old Gelasian Sacramentary* (→ *Sacramentarium Gelasianum*) lists:

> Do you believe in the Father, almighty?
> He answers: I believe.
> Do you believe in Jesus Christ, his son, our sole Lord, who was born and had suffered?
> He answers: I believe.
> Do you also believe in the Holy Spirit, the Holy Church, the forgiveness of sins, the resurrection of the flesh?
> He answers: I believe. (Kinzig, 1999, 141–142; trans. author)

Hence, the second question, for example, with regard the belief in Jesus Christ is asking for no more than him being the single son of our Lord, who was born and had suffered. No indication, therefore is given to the more extended text of the second article that we find in both the Apostles' Creed and its *Vorlage*, the Roman Creed:

> I believe [...] in Christ Jesus his only begotten son, our Lord, who was born from the Holy Spirit and the Virgin Mary, who was crucified under Pontius Pilate and buried and on the third day rose from the dead, ascended into the heavens, and is sitting at the right hand of the Father, from whence he is coming to judge the living and dead (Marcellus of Ancyra, "Epistula ad Iulium," in Epiph. *Haer.* 72.2.6–3.4; Vinzent, 1993, 126–128, 128).

The question, as indicated, has troubled scholarship, how this first formulation, given by → Marcellus of Ancyra, of an extended second article came about, and whether Marcellus borrowed from an already existing Roman Creed that later influenced the Apostles' Creed, or whether it was the other way around, that Marcellus first formulated his individual creed which subsequently influenced the Roman Church and through it made its way to become reformulated as the creed which became later known as the Apostle's own creed. All we know is that, as mentioned, prior to 358 CE no formal written creed existed in the mind of Hilary and his addressees, while around the same time, in the year

356/357 CE in the description of the baptism of → Marius Victorinus at Rome, → Augustine of Hippo indicates that a fixed texts might have been in use. It has been suggested (Heil, 2009), that the Roman Creed had been formulated at a Roman synod in 340 CE, before Marcellus put down the text in his letter to the Roman bishop Julius, written during his exile at Rome in the year 340 CE, leading up to this Roman synod, the Synod of → Antioch (341 CE), and the synod following it, the Synod of Serdica (342/343 CE). Yet, the surviving documents by Julius of Rome and → Athanasius of Alexandria, who report about the Synod of Rome, highlight that Marcellus had an active role at this synod and that he put down his personal creed, after he had explained himself at the synod and after being "asked by the bishops, handed over his creed in written form" (Athan. *Hist. Ar.* 6; see Vinzent, 1997, lxxxvi). The very special occasion of this creed explains, why, despite being formulated in Rome, one of the important ecclesial centers, it remained for some time the sole exception of a written creed in the West until sometime later and remained completely unknown then and hundreds of years later in the Greek East. For it is a common explanation that Christian traditions that are known and sometimes accepted or even disputed in West and East derive from times before the great break between the western and eastern bishops at Serdica and between the drifting apart of their theological and liturgical developments (Vinzent, 2006, 321). With the Apostles' Creed (as with the Roman Creed), it is likely that it falls into the same pattern – being a post-Serdica development, exclusively bound to the West. What about, however, the hypothesis that Marcellus picked up a novel Roman creed, formulated at a Roman synod? A first question arises – if setting down creeds in written form was something alien to the West, why would a western synod move away from its tradition which was hailed as typical of a spirit lead community in the West even 20 years later by Hilary of Poitiers? It seems more likely that it was in line with the eastern tradition that a bishop from the East, Marcellus of Ancyra, did, what the eastern bishops did since → Nicaea, putting down their personal and institutional creeds into writing and transmitting

it to colleagues, as Marcellus does in his letter to Julius.

Except for Marcellus' letter (and the mentioned indication by Augustine, though without giving the wording of what was recited) and three witnesses, all from Rome, who attest to knowing his creed from this letter (Liberius of Rome, a Roman synod under Auxentius of 369/371 CE, Damasus of Rome; Vinzent, 2006, 325–328), we have no earlier text surviving from the Apostles' Creed than what we can extract from the commentary of the creed by → Rufinus of Aquileia in the beginning of the 5th century CE (Simonetti, 1961). This commentary gives us not only access to the Roman Creed's wording, but also further background to answer the question, how this creed made its way into the western churches to also reach Aquileia.

In the opening of his commentary, Rufinus admits that despite all his efforts, he was unable to locate any other earlier commentary on the Roman Creed than that of a heretic, Photinus. → Photinus was bishop of the border town of Sirmium in Roman Pannonia, today Serbia. Prior to this appointment, he was the secretary of Marcellus, the bishop of Ancyra, mentioned above as the earliest source of the text of the Romanum (Vinzent, 2006, 334–335; Hübner, 1989, 187–191). If his commentary on this creed was the only one that Rufinus could reach out to, on which he had to rely and which he integrated into his own commentary, it moves the text that has been commented upon even closer to Marcellus, not to the Roman synod of 340 CE that was claimed as the place where it was formulated. Or why would the bishop's secretary write on a fragment of one of his lord's letters a commentary – the sole person to do this in the 4th century CE – if it were not the words of his master, but a snippet, taken from an otherwise unknown Roman Creed, that he would comment upon? It is more likely that after the Roman synod of 340 CE, where Marcellus' belief was discussed, accepted and he himself reinstated in his authority, Marcellus sat down and pinned the letter, rehearsed his belief with references to earlier Roman baptismal questions and traditional orthodox material from earlier authorities (like → Justin Martyr, → Irenaeus of Lyon, Tertullian, and others) with the help of his bilingual secretary. And it was this secretary, Photinus, who singled out one part of his bishop's letter which suited his own theology best – namely the part of the creed that had only a short reference to believe "in God, almighty, and in Christ Jesus, his only begotten son, our Lord, who was born [...]," hence, without mention of Christ's pre-existence, but solely concentrating on his → incarnation (Vinzent, 2006. 334–335). The commentary of this creed that was endorsed by the Roman synod summarized Photinus' belief. In it Rufinus read not only what he believed was the unaltered creed of the Roman Church, but because of being the creed of the city of Peter (→ Peter the Apostle), he also stylized it as the creed of the apostles. This, he does, by claiming that what Photinus had written down had not "the objective of explaining the meaning of the [credal] text to his readers, but of wresting things simply and truthfully said in support of his own dogma" (Ruf. *Exp. symb. Apost.* 1). Rufinus then admits that the creed is a "short word, as we have called it," perhaps missing much of what other creeds like the Nicene or some other credal statements had to say about the pre-incarnational Son and Logos, and then he lays down the way this creed "came to be given to the Churches." If this creed had been known to have been derived from the Roman Church, this would have been the place to explain it. Rufin does not. He develops what later became known as the foundational legend by which this creed made its way into the western world: Rufinus refers to his "forefathers" in the most unspecific way, hence does not mention bishops or the bishop of Rome, not a synod,

> who have handed down to us the tradition, that, after the Lord's ascension, when, through the coming of the Holy Spirit, tongues of flame had settled upon each of the Apostles [...], they composed, as we have said, this brief formulary of their future preaching, each contributing his several sentences to one common summary: and they ordained that the rule thus framed should be given to those who believe. (Ruf. *Exp. symb. Apost.* 2)

As can be seen from his legendary narrative, the origin of this creed is traced down to the first → Pentecost and to the apostles. There is no single word of it being a creation of bishops, gathered at Rome.

The only claim with regards to Rome, he adds, is that "in the Church of the city of Rome" no additions to the wordings of the apostles can be found, an even strong rejection of the idea that the Roman Church had anything to do with the origin of this creed (*Exp. symb. Apost.* 3). It seems, therefore, that the trajectory of Marcellus as the one who had written down this text as part of his larger creed, where, first, indeed, the pre-incarnational life of the Son Logos "who ever exists with the Father" is expounded (Marcellus of Ancyra, *Epistula ad Iulium*), and of Photinus, who had shortened this text according to his own views, commented upon it, a commentary that was grasped by Rufinus, paved the way for this creed moving from being the creed of an individual to becoming that of the apostles (Vinzent, 2006, 359–360).

It is also more than likely that Rufinus had come across this creed as part of the acts of the Synod of Rome (340 CE) or of Serdica (342/343 CE) which were copied and send around to the western churches. This would explain the enormous distribution of the text of this creed in numerous churches in Northern Italy, like Aquileia, southern France and further away in the West. It has been shown by L.H Westra and more recently again by W. Kinzig, the almost exclusive presence of this credal text or variations of it across the Latin western churches from the 5th century CE onwards far into the Middle Ages (Westra, 2002; Kinzig, 2017), but not before this time.

Going back to Tertullian's *De virginibus velandis* (1.4; *The Veiling of Virgins*) and the parallels to the Christ summary of Marcellus' letter, we might get an indication, of the relation between western and eastern tradition. → Eusebius of Caesarea, the theological opponent of Marcellus, knew Tertullian and seems to have read him in Greek, even Jerome wrote about Tertullian. Tertullian himself does not refer to the rules of faith as his own, neither does Marcellus. Authorship in such texts is different from how we understand the concept today. They formulated their belief trusting that they conveyed tradition. This, they were able to do, using different wordings and expressions, precisely, because no fix reference text existed. And yet, they borrowed from each other, even, as shown (Vinzent, 1999), especially when they were competitors, if not opponents. Not before the unfolding of the Trinitarian belief happened during the long debates during the 4th century CE and the Christological formulae created at various synods and councils during the 5th century CE and later, creeds became foundational and reference points for Christian authors, bishops and even emperors, it was the beginning of such creeds also entering the liturgies of baptism, the catechetical rehearsal of the creed (i.e. *redditio symboli*), the Mass. The Apostles' Creed is one of these formulae which in different Latin western churches became a nucleus, the "short word" that was acceptable to both Arians (→ Arianism) and Catholics and, even though it seems to have derived from precisely those debates during the early 4th century CE allowed for a minimal consensus.

Historiography

As shown in the historiographical survey of M. Vinzent (2006), the critical study of the Apostles' Creed begins with Laurentius Valla (1406–1457) and Reginald Pavo (1393–1461). Laurentius Valla pointed out that the Nicene Creed (325 CE) was known as the oldest creed, so, suggested that the Apostles' Creed could not be derived from the apostles. Reginald Pavo noticed that elements of this creed like the descent to hell were not part of the original text, however, he lost his bishopric as a result of his views in 1458 (Vinzent, 2006, 31–35). Modern and contemporary studies of the Apostles' Creed (see e.g. Kelly, 1950; Westra, 2002) frequently refer to the *opus magnum* by F. Kattenbusch (1894; 1900) und the study by J. de Ghellinck (1949), both tendentious (Kattenbusch from a Protestant, J. de Ghellinck from a Catholic perspective), while the more solid study of the historiography of the Apostles' Creed by (the Catholic) B. Dörholt (1898) has been largely overlooked. Today's general opinion that baptismal questions, known from the 3rd century CE resemble the Apostles' Creed and seem to be its precursors (Nautin, 1947) holds, while the relation between the two have been further nuanced, particularly by comparing the western with the eastern traditions and the development of creeds during the 4th and 5th centuries CE (Hägglund, 1958; Smulders, 1970; 1971; Campenhausen, 1972; Hanson, 1975; Tetz, 1984; Ritter, 1984; Westra, 2002; Kinzig, 1979; 2017; Vinzent, 1999; 2006).

Bibliography

Campenhausen, H. Freiherr von, "Das Bekenntnis im Urchristentum," *ZNW* 63, 1972, 210–253.

Dörholt, B., *Das Taufsymbol der alten Kirche nach Ursprung und Entwicklung*, Paderborn, 1898.

Ghellinck, J. de, *Les recherches sur les origines du Symbole des Apôtres*, Gembloux, 1949.

Hägglund, B., "Die Bedeutung der 'regula fidei' als Grundlage theologischer Aussagen," *StTh* 12, 1958, 1–44.

Hanson, R.P.C., "Dogma and Formula in the Fathers," *SP* 13/2, Berlin, 1975, 169–184.

Heil, U., "Markell von Ancyra und das Romanum," in: A. v. Stockhausen & H.C. Brennecke, eds., *Von Arius zum Athanasianum: Studien zur Edition der "Athanasius Werke"*, Berlin, 2009, 85–104.

Holl, K., & J. Dummer, eds., *Epiphanius III: Panarion haer. 65–80, De fide*, GCS, Berlin, 1985.

Hübner, R.M., *Die Schrift des Apolinarius von Laodicea gegen Photin (Pseudo-Athanasius, contra Sabellianos) und Basilius von Cäsarea*, PTS 30, Berlin, 1989.

Kattenbusch, F., *Das apostolische Symbol: Seine Entstehung, sein geschichtlicher Sinn, seine ursprüngliche Stellung im Kultus und in der Theologie der Kirche: Ein Beitrag zur Symbolik und Dogmengeschichte*, 2 vols., Leipzig, 1894; 1900.

Kelly, J.N.D., *Early Christian Creeds*, London, 1950.

Kinzig, W., "'[...] natum et passum etc.' Zur Geschichte der Tauffragen in der lateinischen Kirche bis zu Luther," in: W. Kinzig, C. Markschies & M. Vinzent, *Tauffragen und Bekenntnis: Studien zur sogenannten "Traditio Apostolica", zu den "Interrogationes de fide" und zum "Römischen Glaubensbekenntnis"*, AKG 74, Berlin, 1999, 73–183.

Kinzig, W., ed., *Faith in Formulae: A Collection of Early Christian Creeds and Creed-Related Texts*, 4 vols., vols. I–II, Oxford, 2017a.

Kinzig, W., *Neue Texte und Studien zu den antiken und frühmittelalterlichen Glaubensbekenntnissen*, AKG 132, Berlin, 2017b.

Kinzig, W., & M. Vinzent, "Recent Research on the Origin of the Creed," *JThS* n.s. 50/2, 1999, 535–559.

Klostermann, E., & G.C. Hansen, eds., *Eusebius Werke*, vol. IV, GCS, Berlin, 1972.

Nautin, P., "Je crois à l'Esprit Saint dans la sainte église pour la résurrection de la chair: Étude sur l'histoire et la théologie du symbole, UnSa 17, Paris, 1947.

Opitz, H.-G. et al., eds., "Athanasius Werke," in: A. von Stockhausen et al, eds., *DGAS*, vol. III, Berlin, 1934ff.

Ritter, A.M., "Art. Glaubensbekenntnis(se)," in: G. Krause & G. Müller, eds., *TRE*, vol. XIII, Berlin, 1984, 399–412.

Simonetti, M., ed., *Tyranni Rufini Opera*, CChr.SL 20, Turnhout 1961.

Smulders, P., "Some Riddles in the Apostles' Creed," *Bijdr.* 31, 1970, 234–260.

Smulders, P., "Some Riddles in the Apostles' Creed II: Creeds and Rules of Faith," *Bijdr.* 32, 1971, 350–366.

Spoerl, K.M., & M. Vinzent, trans., *Eusebius of Caesarea: Against Marcellus and On Ecclesiastical Theology*, FaCh 135, Washington DC, 2017.

Tetz, M., "Zum altrömischen Bekenntnis: Ein Beitrag des Marcellus von Ancyra," *ZNW* 75, 1984, 107–127.

Vinzent, M., ed. & trans., *Asterius von Kappadokien: Die theologischen Fragmente: Einleitung, kritischer Text, Übersetzung und Kommentar*, SVigChr 20, Leiden, 1993.

Vinzent, M., ed. & trans., *Markell von Ankyra: Die Fragmente und der Brief an Julius von Rom*, SVigChr 39, Leiden, 1997.

Vinzent, M., "Die Entstehung des 'Römischen Glaubensbekenntnisses'," in W. Kinzig, C. Markschies & M. Vinzent, *Tauffragen und Bekenntnis: Studien zur sogenannten "Traditio Apostolica", zu den "Interrogationes de fide" und zum "Römischen Glaubensbekenntnis"*, AKG 74, Berlin, 1999, 185–409.

Vinzent, M., *Der Ursprung des Apostolikums im Urteil der kritischen Forschung*, FKDG 89, Göttingen, 2006.

Vogt, H.J., "Gab es eigentlich in Caesarea in Palästina ein Glaubensbekenntnis?" *AHC* 38, 2006, 1–34.

Vokes, F.E., "Apostolisches Glaubensbekenntnis I. Alte Kirche und Mittelalter," in: G. Krause & G. Muller, eds., *TRE*, vol. III, Berlin, 1978, 528–554.

Westra, L.H., *The Apostles' Creed: Origin, History, and some Early Christian Commentaries*, IPM 43, Turnhout, 2002.

MARKUS VINZENT

IV. *Apostles, Epistle of the*

Epistula Apostolorum (*Epistle of the Apostles*) is the title of a gospel-like text dating from the second half of the 2nd century CE in which epistolary and narrative frames enclose a dialogue between Jesus and his male disciples on Easter morning, in the interval of just three hours between his rising from the dead (*Ep. Apos.* 9:2–10:2) and his → ascension into heaven (*Ep. Apos.* 51:1–4). The dialogue occupies the long central section of this work (*Ep. Apos.* 12:1–50:11) and it takes the form of a series of questions and answers intended to equip the disciples for the worldwide mission that they have been commanded to undertake (see *Ep. Apos.* 30:1–5).

The *Epistula Apostolorum* was originally written in Greek but is preserved in full only in Ethiopic (Ge'ez) translation. A Coptic translation is extant in a single damaged manuscript from the 4th century CE, in which 30 of the original 68 pages are missing (Watson, 2020, 42). Missing sections include chapters 1–6, although surviving pagination makes it highly

likely that these chapters were originally included. There are multiple small-scale textual variants both between the Coptic and Ethiopic translations and within the Ethiopic textual tradition, but there is no evidence of separate recensions.

The epistolary frame is established at the outset by the double opening in which the 11 apostolic authors first speak of their purpose in writing (*Ep. Apos.* 1:1–5) and only subsequently identify themselves and their addressees in the conventional way (*Ep. Apos.* 2:1–3). While the apostolic authors immediately warn their readers against the heretical "venom" of the false apostles Simon and Cerinthus (*Ep. Apos.* 1:1–3; see 7:1–4), there is little trace of a polemical agenda in the main body of the work, which focuses on communicating "what Jesus Christ revealed to his disciples," that is, "what we have heard and remembered" (*Ep. Apos.* 1:1; 1:4), especially "after he rose from the dead, when he revealed to us what is great and wonderful and true" (*Ep. Apos.* 2:3). The epistolary opening is followed by a confession of faith that ascribes to "our Lord and Savior Jesus Christ" (*Ep. Apos.* 3:1) the creation of heaven and earth (*Ep. Apos.* 3:5–9) and of "humankind in his image and likeness" (*Ep. Apos.* 3:10), before acknowledging him as "the Word who became flesh of Mary, carried in her womb by the Holy Spirit" and so born "not by the desire of the flesh but by the will of God" (*Ep. Apos.* 3:13–14; see John 1.13–14). At this point the confession expands into a cycle of miracle stories that appear to follow the chronological order of the confession, beginning with the occasion when the child Jesus exposes his teacher's ignorance of the true meaning of the alphabet (*Ep. Apos.* 4:1–2; see Iren. *Haer.* 1.20.1; *Inf. Gos. Thom.* 6:9) and continuing with the wedding at Cana (*Ep. Apos.* 5:1; see John 2:1–11) and a selection of miracle stories familiar from the Synoptic Gospels – the hemorrhaging woman (*Ep. Apos.* 5:3–8), the demon legion (*Ep. Apos.* 5:10–12), the walking on the water (*Ep. Apos.* 5:13) the fish with a coin in its mouth (*Ep. Apos.* 5:14–16), and the feeding of the 5,000 (*Ep. Apos.* 6:17–21). After an unexpected recapitulation and expansion of the opening explanation of the reasons for writing (*Ep. Apos.* 6:1–8.2; see 1:1–4), the confession is briefly resumed as the apostolic authors acknowledge "that the Lord was crucified by Pontius Pilate and Archelaus between the two thieves and he was buried in a place called 'The Skull'" (*Ep. Apos.* 9:1). Here too confession develops into narrative, which now remains uninterrupted till the end of the text. The central dialogue (*Ep. Apos.* 12:3–50:11) is bracketed by the encounters between the risen Jesus and female then male disciples on the one hand (*Ep. Apos.* 9:2–12:1) and the ascension on the other hand (*Ep. Apos.* 51:1–4). Further narrative elements occur within the dialogue as Jesus recounts his incarnational descent in the form of the angel Gabriel (*Ep. Apos.* 13:1–14:8), his descent into hell (*Ep. Apos.* 27:1–2), and – in the future tense – the angelic release of an unnamed disciple from prison in order to celebrate Pascha/Easter (*Ep. Apos.* 15:1–7) and the conversion of Saul/Paul (*Ep. Apos.* 31:1–33:9). Major topics discussed between Jesus and his disciples include mission and ministry (*Ep. Apos.* 19:1–7; 29:5–30:5; 40:5–42:9), the resurrection of the flesh (*Ep. Apos.* 19:17–26:6), the coming time of trial (*Ep. Apos.* 34:1–38:7), divine justice (*Ep. Apos.* 39:1–40:4; 43:1–45:8), and communal discipline (*Ep. Apos.* 46:1–50:11).

While the *Epistula Apostolorum* shows some knowledge of at least three of the canonical Gospels (Hannah, 2008), it treats them with considerable freedom (compare *Ep. Apos.* 11:7–12:2 with John 20:24–29; *Ep. Apos.* 14:1–7 with Luke 1:26–38; *Ep. Apos.* 41:1–42:4 with Matt 23:8–10). In presenting itself as a communication from the entire group of 11 apostles to the universal church of the east and the west, the north and the south (*Ep. Apos.* 2:2), the *Epistula Apostolorum* appears to claim a higher status for itself than earlier texts ascribed to individual apostles or their followers.

1. Context and Date

The nonstandard list of the fictive apostolic authors of this text may provide a clue as to its place of origin. The first five names are John, Thomas, Peter, Andrew, and James (*Ep. Apos.* 2:1), in contrast to the sequence of Peter, Andrew, James, and John (Matt 10:2/Luke 6:14), or Peter, James, John, and Andrew (Mark 3:16–18). While the Matthean and Lukan sequence preserves the relationship between

two pairs of brothers and the Markan one prioritizes the inner circle of three disciples (see Mark 5:37; 9:2, 14:33), the primacy of Peter is taken for granted in all three cases. A geographical factor seems the most likely explanation for the transfer of primacy to John in the *Epistula Apostolorum*. John's association with Asia is already attested in the messages to the seven churches in the book of Revelation (2–3; given the assumption that the John who authored this text was the apostle), and a link specifically to Ephesus is confirmed by authors writing in the later decades of the 2nd century CE and cited by → Eusebius of Caesarea (Irenaeus of Lyon and Clement of Alexandria, Eus *Hist. eccl.* 3.23; Polycrates and Gaius, *Hist. eccl.* 3.31). An Asian origin for the *Epistula Apostolorum* therefore seems plausible (Hill, 1999).

The clearest evidence for the dating of this text occurs after Jesus has announced his → *parousia*, when he will "come like the rising sun, shining seven times more than it," descending to earth to "judge the living and the dead" (*Ep. Apos.* 16:3; 16:5). In response to the disciples' question, "Lord, after how many years will these things be?" (*Ep. Apos.* 17:1), Jesus states that the *parousia* will occur "when the 120th year is completed [...]" (Coptic) or "when the 150th year is completed [...]" (Ethiopic), adding a still more precise though confusing reference to the time of year: "[...] between → Pentecost and the Feast of Unleavened Bread" (*Ep. Apos.* 17:2). The difference between the 120 or 150 years is one of the few substantive variants between the Coptic and the Ethiopic texts, and, if we could assume reasonably accurate chronological knowledge, these figures would imply dates for the text prior to circa 150 or 180 CE, respectively. Yet, chronological precision is not to be expected from this author, who believes that Pentecost occurs 50 days before not after the Feast of Unleavened Bread and who associates the crucifixion (→ Cross/Crucifixion) with the rule of Archelaus (*Ep. Apos.* 9.1). A date of circa 170 CE is suggested by the unusual focus on plague or pandemic as a key sign of the imminent end (*Ep. Apos.* 34.7–14; 36.3; 36:7; 36:9) – a possible reference to the devastating Antonine plague of this period (Watson, 2020, 8–11; Duncan-Jones, 1996).

Historiography

The *Epistula Apostolorum* was composed in Greek, and the many Greek loanwords in the Coptic translation most likely preserve the vocabulary of the original composition. The single Coptic manuscript may date from the 4th century CE and translates the text into the sub-Akhmimic or Lycopolitan dialect. The only extant evidence of ongoing Coptic reception is the reuse in the gnostic → *Pistis Sophia* of the distinctive motif of Jesus's incarnational descent in the form of the angel Gabriel (*Ep. Apos.* 13:2–14:5; *Pist. Soph.* 1.17.12; Schmidt & McDermott, 1978). There is evidence of a Latin translation, parts of which are preserved in a palimpsest in which it accompanies an *Apocalypse of Thomas* (→ Thomas the Apostle; Bick, 1908; Hauler, 1908; Schmidt, 1908). In contrast, there are multiple extant manuscripts of this text in Ethiopic (Ge'ez), although none of them is likely to be older than the 15th century. Like the Coptic, the Ge'ez text was translated directly from Greek; the earlier assumption of a transmission through an Arabic version has been discredited (Hannah, 2021). In its Ethiopic guise, the *Epistula Apostolorum* becomes an appendix to a later and longer text, the → *Testamentum Domini* Nostri Iesu Christi, in which the risen Jesus provides his disciples with detailed instructions relating primarily to church order (Rahmani, 1899; Cooper & McLean, 1902; Beylot, 1984). The link is not accidental, for the opening scene of the *Testamentum Domini Nostri Iesu Christi* shows the influence of *Epistula Apostolorum*'s account of Jesus's reunion with his disciples on Easter morning (Watson, 2020, 269). In the Ethiopic manuscript tradition *Epistula Apostolorum* is also provided with a new introduction, set in Galilee, and serving to link it to the *Testamentum Domini Nostri Iesu Christi* by drawing material from both texts (Watson, 2020, 267–277). The transmission of *Epistula Apostolorum* in at least four languages (Greek, Latin, Coptic, Ge'ez) is testimony to its widespread popularity among Christian reading communities. Most early readers may have taken at face value its claim to be an authentic Catholic letter from the entire apostolic group to the worldwide church.

Although the existence of the incomplete Coptic version of the *Epistula Apostolorum* was first made known to western scholars in 1895 (Schmidt, 1895), its publication was delayed for a further quarter-century due largely to the independent identification and publication of the full text in Ge'ez (Guerrier, 1907; 1912; James, 1910). In the *editio princeps* (Schmidt, 1919), all extant material in Coptic, Ge'ez, and Latin is presented in poorly coordinated form, giving rise to the tradition of presenting the two versions synoptically in parallel columns (Duensing, 1925; Hennecke & Schneemelcher, 1990; Elliott, 1999; Hills, 2009, Markschies & Schröter, 2012). This tradition has been criticized on the grounds that the many small-scale variants between the versions – and within the Ethiopic manuscript tradition – are best presented in a textual apparatus, attached to a single translation usually based on the Coptic where it is extant and on the Ge'ez where it is not (Watson, 2020). Verse enumeration added to C. Schmidt's section divisions (Hills, 2009; Watson, 2020) also serves to make the text more accessible. Issues of interest to the few scholars who have so far engaged seriously with this important and neglected text include its relation to so-called gnostic gospels featuring a dialogue between the Savior and his disciples shortly before his departure (Hornschuh, 1965; Hartenstein, 2000; Parkhouse, 2019), its dependence or otherwise on canonical Gospels (Hannah, 2008; Watson, 2018), and its compositional techniques (Hills, 2008).

Bibliography

Beylot, R., *Testamentum Domini éthiopien: Édition et traduction*, Louvain, 1984.

Bick, J., *Wiener Palimpseste*, part 1: *Codex Palat. Vindobonensis 16 olim Bobbiensis*, SAWW.PH 159, Vienna. 1908, 90–99.

Cooper, J., & A.J. Maclean, *The Testament of Our Lord: Translated into English from the Syriac with Introduction and Notes*, Edinburgh, 1902.

Duensing, H., *Epistula Apostolorum nach dem äthiopischen und koptischen Texte herausgegeben*, Bonn, 1925.

Duncan-Jones, R.D., "The Impact of the Antonine Plague," *JRAr* 9, 1996, 108–136.

Elliott, J.K., *The Apocryphal New Testament: A Collection of Apocryphal Christian Literature in an English Translation Based on M.R. James*, Oxford, ²1999.

Guerrier, L., "Un 'Testament (éthiopien) de Notre-Seigneur et Sauveur Jésus-Christ' en Galilée," *ROC* 12, 1907, 1–8.

Guerrier, L., *Le Testament en Galilée de Notre-Seigneur Jésus-Christ*, Paris, 1912; repr. 2003.

Hannah, D., "The Four-Gospel 'Canon' in the *Epistula Apostolorum*," *JThS* 59, 2008, 598–633.

Hannah, D., "The of the Ethiopic Version of the : Greek or Arabic?" in: M.T. Gebreananaye, L. Williams & F. Watson, eds., *Beyond Canon: Early Christianity and the Ethiopic Textual Tradition* LNTS 643, London, 2021, 97–115.

Hartenstein, J., *Die zweite Lehre: Erscheinungen des Auferstandenen als Rahmenerzählungen frühchristlicher Dialoge*, TU 146, Berlin, 2000.

Hauler, E., "Zu den neuen lateinischen Bruchstücken der Thomasapokalypse und eines apostolischen Sendschreibens im Codex Vind. Nt. 16," *WSt* 30, 1908, 308–340.

Hennecke, E., & W. Schneemelcher, *neutestamentlichen Apokryphen in deutscher Übersetzung*, vol. I: *Evangelien*, Tübingen, ⁶1990.

Hill, C.E., "The Epistula Apostolorum: An Asian Tract from the Time of Polycarp," *JECS* 7, 1999, 1–53.

Hills, J.V., *Tradition and Composition in the Epistula Apostolorum*, 2nd ed., Cambridge MA, 2008.

Hills, J.V., *The Epistle of the Apostles*, ECAp, Santa Rosa, 2009.

Hornschuh, M., *Studien zur Epistula Apostolorum*, PTS 5. Berlin, 1965.

James, M.R., "The Epistola Apostolorum in A New Text," *JThS* 12, 1910, 55–56.

James, M.R., *The Apocryphal New Testament*, Oxford, 1924.

Markschies, C., & J. Schröter, eds., *Antike christliche Apokryphen in deutscher Übersetzung*, vol. I: *Evangelien*, Tübingen, 2012.

Parkhouse, S., *Eschatology and the Saviour: The Gospel of Mary Among Early Christian Dialogue Gospels*, SNTSMS 176, Cambridge UK, 2019.

Rahmani, Patriarch Ignatius Ephraem II, *Testamentum Domini Nostri Iesu Christi*, Mainz, 1899; repr. 1968.

Schmidt, C., "Eine bisher unbekannte christliche Schrift in koptischer Sprache," SPAW, Berlin, 1895, 705–711.

Schmidt, C., *Eine Epistola apostolorum in koptischer und lateinischer Überlieferung*, SPAW, Berlin, 1908, 1047–1056.

Schmidt, C., *Gespräche Jesu mit seinen Jüngern: Ein katholisch-apostolisches Sendschreiben des 2. Jahrhunderts*, Leipzig, 1919, repr. 1967.

Schmidt, C., & V. McDermott, *Pistis Sophia*, NHS, vol. IX, Leiden, 1978.

Watson, F., "A Gospel of the Eleven: The Epistula Apostolorum and the Johannine Tradition," in: F. Watson & S. Parkhouse, eds., *Connecting Gospels: Beyond the Canonical/Non-Canonical Divide*, Oxford, 2018, 189–215.

Watson, F., *An Apostolic Gospel: The "Epistula Apostolorum" in Literary Context*, SNTSMS 179, Cambridge UK, 2020.

FRANCIS WATSON

Apostolic Canons

The so-called *Apostolic Canons* are 85 in number. They made up the final part of the *Apostolic Constitutions of Clement*, a great canonical-liturgical work which was composed in eight books at the end of the 4th century CE. The literary creation, a common occurrence in that genre of literature, attests of itself an apostolic origin, but the text was transmitted by means of Clement. Many anonymous ancient texts pretended to have a Clementine origin. The length of each individual book of the *Apostolic Constitutions* was unequal. Their author or redactor had utilized preexisting texts: the → *Didache* (*Can. ap.* 7.1–32), the → *Apostolic Tradition* (*Diataxeis*; 7.39–45) for Christian initiation, but in particular the *Didascalia of the Apostles* (→ *Didascalia Apostolorum*) for Books 1–6. These texts were adapted to the localities and to the changes that had taken place in the meanwhile, and they were enriched with biblical citations. The eighth book makes use of the *Apostolic Tradition* (8.3–46) and enlarges it; thence, from chapter 47, the *Apostolic Canons* follow. The *Apostolic Constitutions* remade themselves, too, along the lines of the Pseudo-Clementine works (the *Homilies* and the *Recognitions*; → Clementine Literature, Pseudo-), on the model of the *Epistle to the Corinthians* by Clement of Rome, and after the manner of various apocryphal texts. There has been discussion regarding the identity of the author of the *Apostolic Constitutions*. Various scholars, especially P. Nautin, thought of and opted for a certain Julianus, an Arian, and the author of a *Commentary on Job* (*NDPAC*, vol. I, 848). Concerning the place, there is the general supposition that it was a large city, due to the way in which the liturgy is described therein, and as a region of Syria, so as to conclude that the city was Antioch, around the year 380 CE, at the time of the Council of → Constantinople (381 CE). The compilation begins with the following affirmation: "The apostles and the presbyters, to all of those who are of pagan origin and have believed in the Lord Jesus Christ." The apostolic origin is repeated, too, in other places, as if by ordinances that have been given: "by the apostles and the elders to all the believers, spread about in the different nations" (*Can. ap.* 8.4.1) and transmitted by Clement (6.18.11; 8.46.13; 47.85).

The final part of the eighth book contains the 85 *Apostolic Canons*. Its redactor made use of and reelaborated a letter by Clement to James and some conciliar texts: Ancyra (314? CE), → Nicaea (325 CE), → Neocaesarea (319 CE), → Antioch (around 330 CE), and → Laodicea (between 343 and 381 CE). The canons were mentioned by the Council of Constantinople in 394 CE, over which Nectarius presided, and they were already called the *Apostolic Canons* (Mansi, vol. III, 853). Is it, however, making reference to our collection? This must be asked because in the ancient texts the phrase "apostolic canons" is very often used to refer to prescriptions that would date back to the apostles (or were of the tradition), but not to any precise collection (*DDC*, vol. II, 1290).

On account of a series of internal indications and of parallels in both form and content, the redactor was the same for the entire work. There are no arguments that can sustain the claim that these have a different source. The *Canons of the Apostles*, in some manuscripts, although not always, are joined to the *Apostolic Constitutions*. Yet, they also had a life of their own, especially after the council in Trullo (Quinisextus: 691/692 CE). This council condemned the *Apostolic Constitutions*, because

> in them, even from long ago, there have been insertions by the heretics – to the ruin of the church – false teachings and those which are foreign to piety, which have rendered darker and cloudier for us the elegant beauty of the divine instructions, we therefore have opportunely refused such constitutions, for the edification and the security of the flock – so devoted to Christ – by absolutely not allowing the productions of the heretics lies nor inserting them into the pure and perfect teaching of the apostles. (c. 2)

The same council, on the other hand, accepted the canons with these words:

> This holy synod has furthermore established, as a very great and most important decree that henceforth they must remain stable and settled, for the salvation of souls and the healing of the passions, the 85 canons gathered and confirmed by the holy and blessed fathers who have preceded us, and which canons have been passed down to us under the name of the holy and glorious apostles. (c. 2)

With the acceptance of the ancient texts that had a juridical character, these canons are placed before

the Council of Nicaea in 325 CE, because there was a very favorable tradition. In fact, John Scholasticus places them at the beginning of the *Synagoghé*, and Justinian accepts them and recognizes them (Novella 6 and 137). It was not so much the presumed apostolic origin of the canons that pushed the council toward a full acceptance of them, rather it was because the "canons [were] received and confirmed by the holy and blessed fathers." John Damascene also accepted them (Dam. *Fid.* 4.18). The approbation of the council favored, too, the circulation of these canons separately from the entire work, of which they made up a part.

The 85 canons were also translated into the eastern languages. In the West, on the other hand, they were refused – the refusal is not present in all of the manuscripts – by the so-called → *Decretum Gelasianum* (5th cent., beginning of the 6th cent. CE), which considered them to be apocryphal, calling them *Liber qui appellatur Canones Apostolorum*. For in some prescriptions they differed from the Roman tradition; for example, in canons 46 and 47 the deposition of the → bishop and of the → priest is asked for, if they recognized the → baptism and the → Eucharist of the heretics. Now, western theology, after the great debates against › Donatism, absolutely did not admit nor permit rebaptism. Canon 64 was the prohibition against → fasting on Saturday, with the subsequent deposition of a cleric and the excommunication of a layman, while at Rome and in the African church one did fast (on Saturday). Canon 68 proscribed the reordination of clerics ordained in heresy (in a heretical group); the canon concluded with these words: "for those who have been baptized or ordained by the heretic it is not possible that they be either the faithful or clerics." Two biblical books were not included in the canon (book of Judith and the Apocalypse) in canon 85, which also added

> two (letters) of Clement. Moreover the ordinances given and directed to you bishops, by me, Clement, in eight books, which ought not to be read in public because of the secrets which they contain, furthermore the Acts of Us Apostles.

It seems that the author wished to confer canonicity upon the entire work.

In *Decretum Gelasianum*, the title, *Liber qui appellatur Canones Apostolorum*, suggests two things: that a Latin translation of only a collection of the canons existed, which was circulating already disattached from the entire work, and had been completed prior to the time of → Dionysius Exiguus. The *Collectio Veronensis* is a witness of this primitive translation and of the independent circulation of the 85 canons (see Metzger, *SC*, vol. CCCXX, 73). Dionysius had foreseen a new translation only of the first 50 canons (only the beginning of this canon), placing them at the beginning of his collection. Following that, he did not include them in his successive collection (Mansi, vol. I, 50–57; see Turner, E.O.M.I.A, 1899, vol. I, 1–32; *DDC*, vol. II, 1920). He himself was not convinced of their apostolic origin, since he qualified them as *canones qui apostolorum dicuntur*, and he added that many did not easily give them any credence. He recognized, however, that many bishops made use of them in order to establish discipline (*Epistle ad Stephanum:* PL 67, 141–142; Mansi, vol. I, 3), and even the Roman Pontiffs had used them. Thus, if a preexisting translation existed, why did Dionysius translate them again? Notwithstanding the prohibition of the *Decretum Gelasianum*, just as the first translation by Dionysius was still circulating, these had enjoyed a certain circulation in the Middle Ages. They had been used by Pseudo-Isidore. Humbertus of Silva Candida, the legate of Pope John VIII (d. 882 CE), considered the Pseudo-Clementine texts to be apocryphal, and therefore also the *canones apostolorum*, wherefore they were repudiated by the fathers, but he accepted the first 50 (PL 143.990A). His discourse was for refuting those who refused the fasting on Saturdays. They were known to Leo IX (d. 1049 CE) and to the medieval canonists, such as Gratian, who utilized the first 50 (Hefele & Leclercq, *Histoire des conciles*, vol. II, 1206).

Canon 50, in its explanation of the formula and of the rite of baptism, presents two redactions: one that is shorter and one that is longer. The longer redaction, which represents the original version, offers explanations concerning → Trinity – which the majority of the manuscripts exclude (Turner, 524–530) – and it has a Pneumatomachian (→ Pneumatomachi) tendency. The briefer version is a posterior redaction

that was composed according to orthodox theology, after the affirmation of the divinity of the → Holy Spirit at the Council of → Chalcedon in 381 CE, by applying to the Spirit, too, the adjective ὁμοούσιος. For its imprecise theology, Dionysius Exiguus did not continue the translation, halting it before that point. John the Scholastic reworked the canon.

The arguments in the canons are treated without any specific order: ecclesiastical discipline, the ordinations of ministers and the impediments connected thereto, the celebration of the Eucharist, the marriages of the clergy, Easter, the ecclesiastical hierarchy, simony, the canonical books, fasting, the prohibition to read apocryphal books in church, and so on.

There is a practical note: the enumeration of the canons differs in the various editions. Today we normally follow the edition compiled by Joannou, which is also the one used in my volume that reprints his critical text. Joannou, furthermore, also brings forward in the first part the Latin translation by Dionysius Exiguus and for the second part the text of the *Collectio Veronensis*. In some ancient editions sometimes the number 84 is given instead of 85. That depends on the division for which one opts. Beyond the Latin version, there are Syriac, Coptic, Ethiopian (three recensions), and Arabic versions. The canons are also used by the Nestorians (→ Nestorianism/ Nestorius) and by the Monophysites (→ Miaphysites/ Miaphysitism).

Bibliography

Berardino, A. di, ed., *I concili della chiesa antica*, vol. I: *I concili greci*, trans. C. Noce, C. Dell'Osso & D. Ceccarelli Morolli, Rome, 2006.

Boxler, F., *Die sogenannten Apostolischen Constitutionen und Canones*, BKV, Kempten, 1874.

Donaldson, J. "The Constitutions of the Holy Apostles," *ANF*, Edinburgh, 1867, 385–505.

Enermalm-Ogawa, A., *Un langage de prière juif en grec: Le témoignage des deux premiers livres des Maccabées*, Stockholm, 1987.

Fiensy, D.A., *Prayers Alleged to be Jewish: An Examination of the Constitutiones Apostolorum*, Chico, 1985.

Funk, F.X., *Die apostolischen Konstitutionen*, Rottenburg, 1891.

Funk, F.X., ed., *Didascalia et Constitutiones apostolorum*, 2 vols., Paderborn, 1905; Torino, 1962.

Hagedorn, D., *Der Hiobcommentar*, Berlin, 1973.

Kopecek, T., "Neo-Arian Religion: The Evidence of the Apostolic Constitution," in: R.C. Gregg, *Arianism: Historical and Theological Reassessments*, Philadelphia, 1985, 153–179.

Lanne, E., "Les ordinations dans le rite copte: Leurs relations avec les Constitutions Apostoliques et la tradition de saint Hippolyte," *OrSyr* 5, 1960, 81–106.

Magne, J., *Tradition Apostolique sur les charismes et Diatexeis des saints Apôtres*, Paris, 1975.

Mansi, vol. I, Paris, 1899ff., 29–48.

Metzger, M., *Les Constitutions Apostoliques*, SC 320, 1985, 1986, 1987.

Metzger, M., "Le mariage dans les communautés et l'euchologe des témoignage de Constitutions Apostoliques," in: *Le mariage: Conférence Saint-Serge*, Rome, 1994, 223–238.

Mueller, J.G., *L'Ancien Testament dans l'ecclésiologie des Pères: Une lecture des Constitutions apostoliques*, Turnhout, 2004.

Sigal, P., "Early Christian and Rabbinic Liturgical Affinities: Exploring Liturgical Acculturation," *NTS* 30, 1984, 63–90.

Spada, D., & D. Salachas, *Costituzioni dei Santi Apostoli per mano di Clemente*, Rome, 2001.

Steimer, B., *Vertex traditionis: Die Gattung der altchristlichen Kirchenordnungen*, Berlin, 1992, 114–133.

Synek, E.M., *"Dieses Gesetz ist gut, heilig, es zwingt nicht ..." Zum Gesetzesbegriff der Apostolischen Konstitutionen*, Vienna, 1997.

ANGELO DI BERARDINO

Apostolic Church Order

The *Apostolic Church Order* (Ger. *Apostolische Kirchenordnung*; Fr. *Canons ecclésiastiques des apôtres*) is a text describing a fictive apostolic council, at which 11 apostles are present. Kephas and Peter are counted as separate apostles, as are Nathanael and Bartholomew. Opening chapters set the agenda, by which the apostles are to determine the organizational arrangements for the church following the instructions left by Jesus. Each then speaks in turn.

After the introduction, introducing the presence of the apostles in a manner which in time would become common in the church order tradition, the content first turns to the two ways which is divided between the various apostles (*Apos. Ch. Ord.* 4–13). This version is close to that found in the → *Didache*, though not identical, as it expands the common material on occasion, and significantly

omits not only the *sectio evangelica* of *Did.* 1.3–6 but also the *Haustafel* of *Did.* 4.9–11. An eschatological conclusion to the two ways with similarities to that found at the conclusion of the two ways in Barnabas (*Apos. Ch. Ord.* 14) concludes the section. The apostles then turn to the appointment and duties of a → bishop (*Apos. Ch. Ord.* 16), presbyters (*Apos. Ch. Ord.* 17–18), a reader (*Apos. Ch. Ord.* 19; who is appointed on the understanding that the bishop need not be literate), widows (*Apos. Ch. Ord.* 21), and deacons (*Apos. Ch. Ord.* 20; 22), as well as paying attention to the duties of the laity (*Apos. Ch. Ord.* 23). The presbyters (→ Priest/Presbyter) are clearly ascetics; although the directions regarding the election of a bishop simply suggest a quorum of 12 men it seems that by the time of redaction these are the presbyters, who are thus both candidates and electoral college. The deacons appear to be the active ministers of the community, and exercise an economic ministry of collecting funds, whereas goods are distributed by the presbyters. The widows are to number three, one of whom is to have revelations, thus hinting at a common cultural milieu with the new prophecy. The layman is to keep to his place.

The focus then turns to ministries for women (*Apos. Ch. Ord.* 24–28) in which, on the basis that the women were not permitted to stand with the apostles at the Last Supper, it is concluded that the only appropriate ministry for women is to support women in need. This discussion refers to a series of agrapha relating to Martha and → Mary; it is not clear whether the text indicates that these figures were actually present at the Last Supper (as argued by Kateusz, 2019, 131–149), but agreed that this indicates some issue regarding female presidency at the → Eucharist. It is on this basis that A.C. Stewart (2006) had suggested a 3rd-century CE date. However, as A.M. Ernst (2009, 235–241) points out, the question posed in the *Apostolic Church Order* is whether women should stand with the men. Hence women, states a fictive Kephas, should not pray standing but seated, and a fictive James thus deduces that female ministry should be restricted to care for needy women. Thus A.C. Stewart, in his second edition, concludes that this relates to a practice akin to that of the → *Testamentum Domini*, where widows have an honored position among the clergy at the Eucharist. Thus, he suggests that although the original material related to female presidency, the final redaction re-uses the material to refer to the practice of a community which is otherwise ideationally close to that of the *Apostolic Church Order*. It is also, possibly, geographically close. Since A.C. Stewart had already argued that the *Testamentum* is Cappadocian, he is clearer than before in assigning an Asian provenance to the final product, as well as to the sources.

The document concludes with an → agraphon concerning sharing (*Apos. Ch. Ord.* 29), and a warning, with links to the two-ways tradition, not to add to or to subtract from the commandments (*Apos. Ch. Ord.* 30).

The controversy over female ministry is a clear point of recent interest (thus Ernst, 2009; Kateusz, 2019), which is serving to rescue the text from its former obscurity. However, the work is also valuable for its evidence regarding the development of ministry more generally, as for the *Wirkungsgeschichte* of the two-ways material, both in its sources and in the use to which the redactor puts them.

Historiography

The text was first published in Ethiopic by J. Leutholf (1691, 304–314), and subsequently discovered in Greek by J.W. Bickell (1843, 107–132) who edited the text from a single Viennese manuscript. J.W. Bickell referred to it as a *Kirchenordnung* since he saw it as like the reformation church orders with which he was familiar. As other documents of a similar regulatory purpose were discovered throughout the 19th century, so the term became generically applied to them all.

Subsequent to J.W. Bickell's publication further editions from the Greek were made (Lagarde, 1856, 74–79; Pitra, 1864, 77–88; Harnack, 1886a; Funk, 1887, 50–73), and versions in Coptic (Lagarde, 1883, 239–248), Syriac (Arendzen, 1901), Arabic (Horner, 1904, 89–95), and a substantial fragment in Latin (Hauler, 1900, 91–101; subsequently re-edited by Tidner, 1963, 105–113) were discovered. In addition several ancient epitomes of the two-ways section of the text are extant (see Schermann, 1903; Gebhardt, 1878, XXIX–XXXI; Lincicum, 2018), which extends the textual

basis of the document (although it is possible that these epitomes are not derived from the *Apostolic Church Order* itself, but from one of its sources.) However, this document was eclipsed in scholarly attention by the discovery of the *Didache*. It was in his monograph on the *Didache* that A. von Harnack (1886a) determined that the *Apostolic Church Order* was a late and secondary work, the product of Egypt in the 4th century CE and, although he recognized that ancient sources lay behind the church order material (Harnack, 1886b), it is his conclusion on date and provenance which is remembered. Although the document received occasional attention in the 20th century (notably Bartlet, 1943; Faivre, 1981; 1992; Lemoine, 1999) it was only in the early 21st century that the text was re-edited with proper attention to the value of the versions in reconstructing the corrupt Greek text (Stewart, 2006).

In the study accompanying his text A.C. Stewart argued for a 3rd-century CE date and an Asian, or Syrian, provenance. Thus although, according to A. von Harnack (1886a, 217), the duplication of Peter and Kephas points to an Alexandrian origin, as the same peculiarity is found in Clement of Alexandria (cited in Eus. *Hist. eccl.* 1.12), C. Schmidt (1919, 242–243) suggests that the list is far closer to that of *Ep. Apos.* 2. Both are lists of eleven apostles and both locate the gathering of the disciples after the resurrection (→ Resurrection). It is this which leads to an identification of the sources, and ultimately the redaction, of the *Apostolic Church Order* as Asian. A.C. Stewart then observed significant parallels between the discussion of women's ministry in the final section and the *Acta Philippi*, and indications that gnostic and Montanist groups might be within the purview of the redactor of the work. On this basis he assigned a 3rd-century CE date. He has now revised his opinions, partly under the influence of A.M. Ernst (2009), and suggests that, although the sources all date from the 3rd century CE or earlier (on the basis of his earlier argument), the assemblage is the work of a 4th-century CE redactor, possibly contemporary with the *Testamentum Domini* and possibly deriving from a comparable ascetic circle (Stewart, forthcoming).

Bibliography

Arendzen, J.P., "An Entire Syriac Text of the 'Apostolic Church Order'," *JThS* 3, 1901, 59–80.

Bartlet, J.V., *Church-Life and Church-Order During the First Four Centuries*, Oxford, 1943.

Bickell, J.W., *Geschichte des Kirchenrechts*, vol. I, Giessen, 1843.

Ernst, A.M., *Martha from the Margins: The Authority of Martha in Early Christian Tradition*, Leiden, 2009.

Faivre, A., "Le texte grec de la constitution ecclésiastique des apôtres 16–20 et ses sources," *RevSR* 55, 1981, 31–42.

Faivre, A., "Apostolicité et pseudo-apostolicité dans la 'constitution ecclésiastique des apôtres': L'Art de faire parler les origines," *RevSR* 66, 1992, 19–67.

Funk, F.X., *Doctrina duodecim apostolorum*, Tübingen, 1887.

Gebhardt, O. et al., *Patrum Apostolicorum Opera*, vol. I/2, Leipzig, 1878.

Harnack, A. von, *Die Lehre der zwölf Apostel nebst Untersuchungen zur ältesten Geschichte der Kirchenverfassung und des Kirchenrechts*, TU, vol. II/1, Leipzig, 1886a.

Harnack, A. von, *Die Quellen der sogenannten apostolischen Kirchenordnung, nebst einer Untersuchung über den Ursprung des Lectorats und der anderen niederen Weihen*, TU, vol. II/5, Leipzig, 1886b.

Hauler, E., *Didascaliae apostolorum fragmenta ueronensia Latina: Accedunt canonum qui dicuntur apostolorum et Aegyptiorum reliquies*, Leipzig, 1900.

Horner, G., *The Statutes of the Apostles or Canones Ecclesiastici*, London, 1904.

Kateusz, A., *Mary and Early Christian Women: Hidden Leadership*, Cham, 2019.

Lagarde, P. de, *Reliquiae iuris ecclesiastici antiquissimae*, Leipzig, 1856.

Lagarde, P. de, *Aegyptiaca*, Göttingen, 1883.

Lemoine, B., "Étude de la notice sur l'évêque dans la 'constitution ecclésiastique des apôtres (C.E.A.)'," *QuLi* 80, 1999, 5–23.

Leutholf, J., *Iobi Ludolfi alias Leutholf dicti ad suam Historiam Aethiopicam antehac commentarius*, Frankfurt am Main, 1691.

Lincicum, D., "An Excerpt from the Apostolic Church Order (CPG 1739)," *SE* 57, 2018, 439–444.

Pitra, J.B., *Iuris ecclesiastici Graecorum historia et monumenta*, vol. I, Rome, 1864.

Schermann, T., *Eine Elfapostelmoral oder die x-Rezension der "beiden Wege"*, VKSM vol. II 2/2Munich, 1903.

Schmidt, C., *Gespräche Jesu mit seinen Jüngern nach der Auferstehung*, TU 43, Leipzig, 1919.

Stewart, A.C., *The Apostolic Church Order: The Greek Text with an Introduction, Translation and Annotation*, ECSt 10, Sydney, 2006; 2nd ed. Sydney, 2021.

Tidner, E., *Didascaliae apostolorum, canonum ecclesiasticorum, traditionis apostolicae versiones Latinae*, TU 75; Berlin, 1963.

ALISTAIR C. STEWART

Apostolic Constitutions

The *Apostolic Constitutions* (*Constitutiones apostolorum*) is one of a number of early Christian texts known collectively to modern scholars as ancient church orders (Bradshaw, 2015), in this case containing extensively reworked and expanded versions of three others – the *Didascalia apostolorum* (forming Books 1–6 of the work), the *Didache* (in Book 7), and the *Apostolic Tradition* (in Book 8) – together with some other material in Books 7–8. It claimed to embody the teaching of the apostles mediated through Clement of Rome (*Const. ap.* 6.18.11; 8.46.13; 8.47.85). In its current form, the writing should be dated to c. 375–380 (see below, Historiography).

1. Contents

As noted above, Books 1–6 are an expansion and reworking of → *Didascalia apostolorum*. The moral teaching of its source was extended and references to liturgical practices brought up to date. So, for example, where the *Didascalia* had directed that a visiting bishop should "say the words over the cup," the compiler, apparently not understanding this obsolete practice, substituted "give the blessing to the people" (*Const. ap.* 2.58.3). Similarly, a post-immersion anointing, which had recently been adopted in West Syria, was added to the directions about → baptism from the *Didascalia* (see Bradshaw, 2015, 48–50).

Book 7.1–32 similarly contains a revised version of the → *Didache*, chapters 33–38 a collection of prayers that have similarities to Jewish prayers, and chapters 39–49 other texts and prayers that have not been studied closely (but see Chazon, 2004). This contrasts with the eucharistic prayers in Book 7.25–26 revised from the meal prayers in *Did.* 9–10, which have received more attention: see, for example, M. Metzger (1971), E. Mazza (1979), and A. Verheul (1980) The two prayers from chapter 9 were joined into one, with the bread before the cup, and references to Christ's → incarnation, passion, and → resurrection inserted. The only slight allusion to the Last Supper was the addition of the words "as he himself has ordered us, to show forth his death." The prayer from chapter 10 became a post-communion thanksgiving. With regard to the "Jewish" prayers in chapters 33–38, the consensus of earlier scholars, both Jewish and Christian, was that not only these but also certain other prayers in Books 7 and 8 were originally synagogue prayers taken over and adapted by Christians (Horst, 2008, 9–15). D.A. Fiensy (1985) reexamined the matter rigorously. He argued that Jewish roots could only be ascribed with certainty to the six prayers in Book 7.33–38, and he concluded that they arose out of an early oral Hebrew version of the Jewish Seven Benedictions (as some previous scholars had also suggested) that were translated into Greek in Syrian diaspora synagogues and adopted from there by Christians circa 300 CE.

Book 8.1–2 seems to extract from an otherwise unknown treatise on charisms; chapters 3–46 are based on the → Apostolic Tradition but greatly expanded with material from other sources and with the various parts being said to be spoken by individual apostles; and the final chapter 47 is known as the "Canons of the Apostles."

The instructions and texts for celebrating the ordination Eucharist of a bishop in Book 8.3–15, though drawing in small part on the Apostolic Tradition, have a strong resemblance to the late-4th-century CE Antiochene rite, but with some features that seem to reflect the particular views of the compiler. This was often called "the Clementine Liturgy" (after Clement of Rome) by earlier generations of scholars, and has been much studied, especially its eucharistic prayer: see, for example, M. Metzger (1971) and A. Verheul (1980). The first section of the prayer is chiefly concerned with the nature of God. At the end of the third paragraph, it has every appearance of leading into the → Sanctus, that is the chant, "Holy, Holy, Holy," and so on, but instead embarks on the theme of creation in great detail, starting with the heavenly bodies and continuing with the four elements of air, fire, earth, and water. Next come humankind; the story of the → fall; and a summary of the Hebrew Bible as far as the fall of Jericho. Eventually, the Sanctus is reached, followed by a section on the birth, ministry, and death of Christ, where clearer quotations from the prayer in the Apostolic Tradition begin to appear. It continues with the institution narrative, an anamnesis ("Remembering, therefore [...]"), and a consecratory epiclesis (an invocation of the Holy Spirit on the bread and wine). The final part of this enormously long prayer is a comparatively short series of intercessions.

A long succession of scholars sought to find Jewish roots to this prayer, like those in Book 7.33–38, until corrected by D.A. Fiensy (1985). In addition to the eucharistic prayer of Apostolic Tradition, other scholars have looked to contemporary eastern eucharistic prayers as source material. W.E. Pitt (1958) conjectured that these were the prayers used in Jerusalem, along with another prayer that he did not identify; W.H. Bates (1975) found similarities with the homilies of → John Chrysostom and the → anaphoras (eucharistic prayers) of Saint Basil and Saint James; and J.R.K. Fenwick (1989) suggested that the prayer had been constructed on the foundation of an old Antiochene eucharistic prayer that was the common ancestor of the anaphora of John Chrysostom and of the Syriac anaphora of the twelve apostles. The most recent study, by R. Graves (1997), concluded that, although some elements in the prayer showed parallels with the anaphora of Saint Basil and there were two points of contact with the anaphora of Chrysostom, the majority of the prayer had close similarities to other prayers and passages in the Apostolic Constitutions, thus implying that it was chiefly the compiler's own composition.

The 85 "Canons of the Apostles" in chapter 47 may have had an independent existence prior to their attachment to this church order, but not many years before as they include 20 canons from the Council of Antioch in 341 CE, while some scholars regard them as a later addition to the church order. They certainly existed independently later in various languages and were given official recognition in the East by the Trullan Synod, even though the rest of the church order was not. The western church only recognized the first 50 canons. The final canon (85) lists all the books of the Hebrew Bible that the alleged apostolic authors recognize, as well as all the New Testament books that they claim to have written (with the absence of the Book of Revelation and the inclusion of the two Epistles of Clement and of "the Constitutions of me Clement, addressed to you bishops, in eight books, which are not to be published to all on account of the mystical things in them").

Although not an integral part of the *Apostolic Constitutions*, what is known as the "Epitome of the Eighth Book of the *Apostolic Constitutions*" is a series of five extracts from it, each with its own subheading (*Const. ap.* 8:1–2; 4–5; 16–28; 30–34; 42–46; text in Funk, vol. II, 1905, 72–96), that for the second extract being the "Constitutions of the Holy Apostles concerning ordination through Hippolytus," which has sometimes been applied as an alternative title of the whole work (without the words "concerning ordination"). However, at two points – in the prayer for the ordination of a bishop and in the instructions for appointing a reader – its text is closer to what it appears to have been the original Greek of the *Apostolic Tradition* rather than the expanded form in the *Apostolic Constitutions*. In addition, one manuscript alone has, for some reason, a similar version of *Apostolic Tradition* (23). Thus, whether in origin this was a first draft of the *Apostolic Constitutions* (8) or – as seems more likely – a later condensation of it, its editor appears also to have had access to a text of the *Apostolic Tradition* itself, although C. Markschies (1999, 15–19) contended that this was not the original Greek text of that church order as such but a version of it that had already undergone some modification.

2. Purpose

Scholars have long debated the purpose of the composition of the *Apostolic Constitutions*. Early opinion was commonly that its aim was to propagate particular doctrines. F.X. Funk (1891, 356–361) rejected this, claiming that its intention was to rescue ancient documents from oblivion. Similar views have been expressed by more recent scholars (Metzger, 1985, 49; Grisbrooke, 1990, 6). However, the process might be better described as "preserving the imagined past" because of the large number of interpolations and modifications made by the compiler to the sources used, presumably in the belief that they too stemmed from the apostolic age.

Other proposals have also been made. E. M. Synek (1998) viewed the *Apostolic Constitutions* as a Christian → Talmud. This seems unwarranted because "in spite of the parallels of both a structural and conceptual nature that can be pointed out, the differences

between the two corpora remain too great to justify such a designation" (Horst, 2008, 6).

Nevertheless, building on E.M. Synek's work, J.G. Mueller (2004, 120–126) proposed that the *Apostolic Constitutions* reflected an anti-imperial and anti-Nicene stance and that it had adapted traditional techniques of Hebrew Bible exegesis to fit 4th-century CE ecclesiological contexts. He later went further and argued (Mueller, 2007) that the compilers of all the church orders employed interpretations of Hebrew Bible material that adopted hermeneutical techniques used by Jews in the first few centuries, a mix of → halakhah and haggadah. To describe them as exegesis of Scripture, however, misrepresents them. When the Hebrew Bible is cited in the church orders, it is in support of the teaching that is given: the teaching is not derived from it. And unlike the Mishnah, for example, alternative opinions of authorities are not offered.

One thing we can be certain about. The *Apostolic Constitutions* was never intended as a practical manual for liturgical use. The directions in Books 1–6, which were already too immersed in surrounding commentary in the *Didascalia* to be of practical use, were made even less so by the expansion here. Moreover, it seems highly improbable that a late-4th-century CE Christian community would actually have used both of the two very different eucharistic prayers in Books 7 and 8. That in Book 7 is much more archaic in style and theology than that in Book 8 and has the appearance of an artificial construction; and the excessive length of the prayer in Book 8 makes it highly improbable that it was ever the regular diet of any congregation. In any case, its theological formulations would have rendered it unacceptable in orthodox circles after the Trinitarian doctrinal decisions of the Council of → Constantinople in 381 CE.

Historiography

The first of the church orders to become known in modern times, its Greek text was published in full in 1563 by the Spanish Jesuit Francisco Torres (reproduced in PG 1.509–1156). It was translated into English by W. Whiston (1711), and it was regarded by some scholars throughout the 18th century as of genuine apostolic origin, while others quickly judged its final form to belong instead to the second half of the 4th century CE, although retaining some much older material. Today, it is generally agreed that it was composed in Syria, and probably in Antioch, between 375 and 380 CE. It is unlikely to be much earlier than that, because it includes a reference to the feast of → Christmas, which was only just beginning to make an appearance in eastern churches, and it is unlikely to be much later, because its doctrine of the → Holy Spirit is incompatible with the definition agreed at the Council of Constantinople in 381 CE.

On the other hand, the identity and theological stance of the compiler have long been a matter of debate. Indeed, the orthodoxy of the document became suspect at an early date, and it was decided by the Trullan Synod (691–692 CE) that heretics must have falsified the original apostolic work. Photius, patriarch of Constantinople (d. 891 CE), criticized the whole compilation for its → Arianism, although subsequently opinion was divided over this question. Among modern scholars, F.X. Funk in his edition of the text (Funk, 1905), which was generally treated as definitive, tended to play down the heterodoxy of the work by preferring orthodox variant readings wherever possible and by claiming that any suspect formulae came from the compiler's source and thus antedated the Arian controversy. C.H. Turner (1913; 1914; 1920) criticized F.X. Funk's textual methods and argued strongly for an Arian compiler, and B. Capelle (1949) later showed that the text of *Gloria in excelsis* in the *Apostolic Constitutions* (7.47) was not the original form of the hymn, as had been thought, but that the compiler had changed a hymn addressed to Christ into one addressed to the Father.

As early as the 17th century James Ussher, archbishop of Armagh, had proposed that the *Apostolic Constitutions* was the work of the same person responsible for creating the longer recension of the letters of Ignatius of Antioch because of similarities of language, a conclusion generally accepted by scholars today. Recent contributions to the authorship debate are by G. Wagner (1972), who drew linguistic parallels with the writings of Eunomius, by D. Hagedorn (1973), who attributed the composition to a certain bishop named Julian, and by M. Metzger

(1983), who built upon D. Hagedorn's suggestion. M. Metzger concluded that, although Julian's commentary on Job was much more explicitly Arian than the more moderate subordinationism of the *Apostolic Constitutions*, this difference could be explained by the fact that the latter was partly a liturgical work and so drew upon traditional material. He did not think, however, that its compiler could be considered a strict Arian. M. Metzger also published a new edition of the text (Metzger, 1985–1987), making use of a wider range of manuscripts and free from the orthodox bias of F.X. Funk's edition.

Bibliography

Bates, W.H., "The Composition of the Anaphora of Apostolic Constitutions VIII," *StPatr* 13, Oxford, 1975, 343–355.

Bradshaw, P.F., *Ancient Church Orders*, JLS 80, Norwich, 2015.

Capelle, B., "Le texte du 'Gloria in exclesis Deo,'" *RHE* 44, 1949, 439–457.

Chazon, E.G., "A 'Prayer Alleged to Be Jewish' in the *Apostolic Constitutions*," in: E.G. Chazon et al., eds., *Things Revealed: Studies in Early Jewish and Christian Literature in Honor of Michael E. Stone*, Leiden, 2004, 261–277.

Donaldson, J., *Constitutions of the Holy Apostles*, Edinburgh, 1867 .

Fenwick, J.R.K., *The Missing Oblation: The Contents of the Early Antiochene Anaphora*, JLS 11, Nottingham, 1989.

Fiensy, D.A., *Prayers Alleged to be Jewish: An Examination of the Constitutiones Apostolorum*, BJS 65, Chico, 1985.

Funk, F.X., *Die apostolischen Konstitutionen: Eine litterar-historische Untersuchung*, Rottenburg, 1891; repr. Frankfurt, 1970.

Funk, F.X., *Didascalia et Constitutiones Apostolorum*, Paderborn, 1905; repr. Turin, 1979.

Graves, R., "The Anaphora of the Eighth Book of the *Apostolic Constitutions*," in: P.F. Bradshaw, ed., *Essays in Early Eastern Eucharistic Prayers*, Collegeville, 1997, 173–194.

Grisbrooke, W.J., *The Liturgical Portions of the Apostolic Constitutions: A Text for Students*, JLS 13–14, Nottingham, 1990.

Hagedorn, D., *Der Hiobkommentar des Arianers Julian*, Berlin, 1973, XXXIV–LVII.

Horst, P.W. van der, "The Hellenistic Synagogal Prayers in the *Apostolic Constitutions*," in: P.W. van der Horst & J. Newman, eds., *Early Jewish Prayers in Greek*, Berlin, 2008, 1–94.

Kopecek, T.A., "Neo-Arian Religion: The Evidence of the *Apostolic Constitutions*," in: R.C. Gregg, ed., *Arianism: Historical and Theological Reassessments*, Philadelphia, 1985; repr. Eugene, 2006, 153–180.

Markschies, C., "Wer schrieb die sogenannte Traditio Apostolica? Neue Beobachtungen und Hypothesen zu einer kaum lösbaren Frage aus der altkirchen Literaturgeschichte," in: W.Kinzig, C. Markschies & M. Vinzent, eds., *Tauffragen und Bekenntnis*, AKG 74, Berlin, 1999, 8–43.

Mazza, E., "La 'gratiarum actio mystica' del libro VII delle Constituzioni Apostoliche: Una tappa nella storia della anafora eucaristica," *EL* 93, 1979, 123–137.

Metzger, M., "Les deux prières eucharistiques des Constitutions apostoliques," *RevSR* 45, 1971, 52–77.

Metzger, M., "La théologie des Constitutions apostoliques par Clement," *RevSR* 57, 1983, 29–49, 112–122, 169–194, 273–294.

Metzger, M., *Les Constitutions apostoliques*, SC 320, 329, 336, Paris, 1985–1987.

Mueller, J.G., *L'Ancien Testament dans l'ecclésiologie des Pères: Une lecture des Constitutions Apostoliques*, IPM 41, Turnhout, 2004.

Mueller, J.G., "The Ancient Church Order Literature: Genre or Tradition?" *JECS* 15, 2007, 337–380.

Pitt, W.E., "The Anamnesis and Institution Narrative in the Liturgy of Apostolic Constitutions Book VIII," *JEH* 9, 1958, 1–7.

Synek, E.M., "Die Apostolischen Konstitutionen–ein 'christlicher Talmud' aus dem 4. Jh.," *Bib.* 79, 1998, 27–56.

Turner, C.H., "A Primitive Edition of the Apostolic Constitutions and Canons," *JThS* 15, 1913, 53–65.

Turner, C.H., "Notes on the Apostolic Constitutions," *JThS* 16, 1914, 54–61, 523–538; 21, 1920, 160–168.

Verheul, A., "Les prières eucharistiques dans les 'Constitutiones Apostolorum,'" *QuLi* 61, 1980, 129–143.

Wagner, G., "Zur Herfunkt der apostolischen Konstitutionen," in: *Mélanges liturgiques offerts au R. P. Dom Bernard Botte OSB*, Louvain, 1972, 525–537.

Whiston, W., *Primitive Christianity Reviv'd*, vol. II: *The Constitutions of the Holy Apostles by Clement in Greek and English*, London, 1711.

PAUL F. BRADSHAW

Apostolic Fathers

"Apostolic Fathers" is the name given to the Christian writings that have been preserved from the early decades of the 2nd century CE, regarded and revered as associates or disciples of the apostles to whom the New Testament writings themselves were attributed. The most famous study of the texts involved has been by J.B. Lightfoot, *Apostolic Fathers*, part I: *S. Clement of Rome*, 1890, 2 vols., and part II: *S. Ignatius, S. Polycarp*, 1885, 3 vols. The collection was first made in 1672 by J.B. Cotelier (details in Lightfoot, 1890, vol. I, 3).

Some of the texts were sometimes bound up with the New Testament writings themselves. The most famous and striking example are the 4th-century CE Codex Sinaiticus, which contains the *Epistle of Barnabas* and part of the *Shepherd of Hermas*, and the somewhat later Codex Alexandrinus, which contains large sections of *1* and *2 Clement*. This attests the esteem in which they were held and the instability of the New Testament canon in the 4th century CE. Initially only the letters of Clement, Ignatius, Polycarp, and Barnabas with the → *Shepherd of Hermas* were counted as Apostolic Fathers, with Diognetus and Papias later added, as also *Didache*, following its discovery in 1873. For a survey of literature on the Apostolic Fathers up to the 1980s, see W.R. Schoedel (1989, 457–498). The writings will be examined here only briefly in what is the most probable chronological sequence. For more information on the individual texts, see the separate entries.

1. *1 Clement*

The premier member of the Apostolic Fathers is undoubtedly *1 Clement* (→ Clement), primarily because it/he was almost certainly the earliest of the Apostolic Fathers, and because it was attributed to Clement, subsequently designated as bishop of Rome, more or less from the beginning. This and the opening of the letter itself provide almost all that can be known in terms of author, origin, occasion and recipients, and date.

According to the letter's introduction, it was written from "the church of God that temporarily resides in Rome to the church of God that temporarily resides in Corinth." The reason seems clear also: the writer was concerned to have learned that there was factionalism in the Corinthian church; evidently younger members were rebelling against the leadership of the senior members (presbyters; 3:3), failing to give them the respect due to their seniority (1:3; 21:6), and causing strife and schism (2:6; 46:5, 9; 54:2; see Welborn, 1992; Horrell, 1996, 244–250). Clement writes to ensure and exhort due respect for the established leadership. It is somewhat ironic that the 1st-century CE church into which we have most insight (→ Corinth) occasioned the letters that provide that information (1 & 2 Corinthians; *1 Clement*) because of its factiousness.

The letter was obviously written by a leading member of the Church of Rome, who could write with the authority of the church in the empire's capital, making in effect a claim to some authority over a provincial church. The references to bishops (42:4–5; 44:1, 4), and the authority exercised in the letter itself, could suggest that the writer was someone who claimed episcopal authority, echoing the exhortation and authority of "the epistle of that blessed apostle, Paul" (47:1; 58:2; 63:2–4; 65:1), though whether a monarchical episcopacy was established in Rome quite so early is open to question (Richardson, 1953, 36–37; Ehrman, 2003, vol. I, 21–23). There never seems to have been any doubt in the patristic period that the author was Clement, venerated as the third (or second) bishop of the Church of Rome (Iren. *Haer.* 3.3.1; Eus. *Hist. eccl.* 3.4.21; 4.23.11). The earliest supporting evidence may be provided by Hermas, who was instructed to write two little books and to send one to Clement (the same Clement?) who had the responsibility (and authority) to forward it to other centers (Herm. *Vis.* 8.3). And later in the 2nd century CE (before 170 CE), Dionysius of Corinth refers to a letter "sent to us through Clement," which was still being read in the Corinthian church for its admonition (*Hist. eccl.* 4.23.11). → Hegesippus similarly refers to the epistle of Clement to the Corinthians (*Hist. eccl.* 4.22.1); J.B. Lightfoot provides a thorough examination of all possible references to or echoes of *1 Clement*, from Barnabas onward (Lightfoot, 1890, vol. I, 148–200). The subscription added later at the end of the letter, "The First Epistle of Clement to the Corinthians," simply reflects the unanimous opinion of the early church.

a. Date

As to date, the most striking indication is the reference in chapter 5 to Peter (→ Peter the Apostle) and Paul (→ Paul the Apostle) as "noble examples of our own generation," and the clear implication of chapter 44 is that those appointed by the apostles should not be removed from their ministry and therefore were still in post. So the traditional view, that

1 Clement was written at the end of Domitian's reign, that is, 95 CE or 96 CE, appears to be well founded (Lightfoot, 1890, vol. I, 346–358; Horrell, 1996, 239–242; Lona, 1998, 75–78; Ehrman, 2003, vol. I, 23–25). C.N. Jefford prefers a date before 70 CE; but reference to the Jerusalem Temple as though still active does not necessarily imply that the Temple was still active. On the other hand, L.L. Welborn is too skeptical in concluding that there can be no greater confidence than between 80 and 140 CE (Welborn, 1992, 1060), though Clement's allusion to "sudden and repeated misfortunes and setbacks we have experienced" (1:1) hardly sounds like a reference to a persecution by Domitian (*pace* Barnard, 1966, 5–15). If the dominant opinion is accepted, it should not escape notice that *1 Clement* was almost certainly earlier than some of the writings that were (finally) included within the New Testament. Had it not been for the fact that Clement so clearly distinguished himself from the apostles (4:1; 5:3; 42:1–2; 47:1–4), *1 Clement* might well have been a strong candidate to be included in the New Testament canon.

It is notable that *1 Clement* draws more extensively on the Scriptures (OT) than any earlier Christian document. Clement assumes as completely self-evident that there is a direct continuum from the history of Israel's good and bad examples to that of the Christians in Rome and Corinth; it was their history too. In some ways most significant for the Christianity he sought to inculcate, Clement drew his ecclesiology from Israel's priestly orders and sacrificial ritual (40–41), assuming too that the continuum with Israel included Christian ministry as the continuation of Israel's priestly cult.

In short, *1 Clement* is more aware of the Jewishness of Christianity than almost any other writer from the period – both of Christianity's deep roots in Israel's history, and of Israel's Scriptures as a/the primary resource for Christian exhortation and discipline.

Of particular interest is the knowledge of Jesus' teaching that *1 Clement* demonstrates in 13:2 and 46, each quoting a sequence of Jesus' words: "Remember the words of the Lord Jesus, for he said [...]" However, the variation of wording from the New Testament Gospels makes it less likely that Clement was quoting any written gospel as such (Koester, 1957, 23). But it is equally clear that the Jesus tradition, as attested in the Synoptic tradition, was well known in different groupings and valued as integral to Christian → catechesis and paraenesis. Clement regarded Paul very highly *1 Clem.* 5:5–7 reflects a clear impression of Paul toward the end of the 1st century CE, in Rome, an impression based on some knowledge of Paul's teachings and of his life as a missionary and his death. *1 Clem.* 47:1–3 certainly indicates knowledge of 1 Cor 1–4 and *1 Clem.* 47:3 certainly draws on 1 Cor 1:12. But his conservative → ecclesiology is evident in his depiction of the apostles as appointing "the first fruits of their ministries as bishops and deacons" (42:1–5), in reverting to distinctions between priest and laity and in depicting the bishop as a sacrifice-offering priest (40–41; 44:1–4). Insofar as there was influence from Paul, therefore, this was Paul or the Pauline heritage being conformed to the pattern of religion as it was normally understood, organized, and practiced (see Lindemann, 1979, 199).

2. Ignatius of Antioch

The letters of Ignatius of Antioch (→ Ignatius, Epistles of) provide one of the most vivid depictions of Christianity in Asia Minor in the early decades of the 2nd century CE. Ignatius had evidently been arrested during some persecution or unrest in Antioch (Schoedel, 1985, 10–11; Ehrmann, 2003, vol. I, 208–209) and was being led under military escort, "night and day, bound to ten leopards, which is a company of soldiers" (Ign. *Rom.* 5.1), on his way to face the wild beasts in the arena in Rome (Ign. *Eph.* 1.2). It was a martyrdom that he gladly anticipated, and in the only letter he wrote to churches ahead of him, to Rome where he was destined for execution, he urged them not to intervene on his behalf (*Rom.* 1–2; 4–7).

The author of the epistles introduces himself in the opening of each of the letters as "Ignatius, who is also called God-bearer." In *Rom.* 2.2 he refers to himself as "the bishop of Syria," and he closes each letter with a request that the letter recipients pray for the church in Syria (Ign. *Eph.* 21.2; *Magn.* 14.1; *Trall.* 13.1; *Rom.* 9.1), or expresses gratitude for their prayer for the church at Antioch in Syria (Ign. *Phld.* 10.1; *Smyrn.* 11.1; *Pol.* 7.1). He was evidently feted by the Asia Minor believers, and his letters were written probably to churches in cities his escort did not pass through. His aim in writing seems to have

been primarily political, in that he used the opportunity to enhance the importance of each community's bishop (*Eph.* 1, 2, 3, 4, 5–6; *Magn.* 2–4, 6–7, 13; *Trall.* 2–3, 7, 13.2; *Phld.* inscrip. 1.3–4, 7–8; *Smyrn.* 8–9; *Pol.* 5–6; *Romans* is a striking exception).

The date of Ignatius' journey to martyrdom through Asia Minor, during which the letters were written is unclear. All we learn from patristic sources is that Ignatius was bishop of Antioch during the reign of → Trajan (98–117 CE; Eus. *Hist. eccl.* 3.22, 36.2). A date in the late 100s or early 110s CE seems early (surprisingly early for some), but there is nothing in the letters, in terms of their antagonism to Judaism, or their opposition to docetic views, or their Christology – Ignatius regularly refers to Jesus as God, "our God," "God come in the flesh," and so on (*Eph.* inscrip. 1.1; 7.2; 15.3; 18.2; 19.3; *Trall.* 7.1; *Rom.* inscrip. 3.3; 6.3; *Smyrn.* 1.1; 10.1; *Pol.* 8.3) – or promotion of monoepiscopacy, or emphasis on the → Eucharist, which rules out such an early date (Lightfoot, 1885, vol. I, 30; Jefford, 2006, 12). It is equally as probable, or more so, that Ignatius provides evidence of how early were the issues, and the attitudes expressed on these issues, within 2nd-century CE Christianity. The more important question, in fact, is how representative was Ignatius in the views he expressed, and how typical were the developments within Christian thought and organization to which he attests. Or is he more to be regarded as the most effective spokesman for a particular faction within developing Christianity?

Ignatius knew the forms of Jesus tradition that are recorded in Matthew (→ Matthew the Apostle) and Luke (→ Luke, Gospel of) in particular (*Eph.* 5.2/Matt 18:19–20; *Smyrn.* 1.1/Matt 3:13–15; *Smyrn.* 3.2–3/Luke 24:39, 42–43; *Smyrn.* 6.1/Matt 19:12; *Pol.* 2.1/Luke 6.32; *Pol.* 2.2/Matt 10:16). It is also clear that Ignatius venerated the apostle Paul (*Eph.* 12.2; *Rom.* 4.3) and was familiar with a number of his letters, particularly Romans and 1 Corinthians – see *Eph.* 8.2 (Rom. 8:5, 8; 1 Cor 3:1–3); *Eph.* 18.1–2 (Rom. 1:3–4; 1 Cor 1:18, 20, 23); *Rom.* 5.1, 9.2 (1 Cor 4:4; 15:8–9).

3. Polycarp of Smyrna

Polycarp was bishop of Smyrna (→ Polycarp of Smyrna), where Ignatius lodged for some days during his traverse across Asia province, where they commaned together. It was to Polycarp that Ignatius wrote what was probably his last letter. Polycarp is still better known as a martyr, the account of whose martyrdom is an early Christian classic. And according to → Irenaeus of Lyon, Polycarp himself provided a firsthand link back to the apostle John, and a bridge between the apostles and Irenaeus, enabling Irenaeus to depict himself as only two generations distant from the disciples of the Lord (Eus. *Hist. eccl.* 5.20.5–8); in the epilogue added to the *Martyrdom of Polycarp*, Irenaeus is also referred to as a disciple of Polycarp (*Mart. Pol.* 22:2). If his martyrdom can be dated to 155 CE, and he was 86 when he died (*Mart. Pol.* 9:3 – or 86 years since his conversion?), then he must have been born around 70 CE and must have met and supported Ignatius when he was about 40 and already a bishop (Ehrman, 2003, vol. I, 362; Jefford, 2006, 13–14).

Polycarp's letter to the Philippians has more the character of a general exhortation, not so political or polemical as Ignatius' letter, but fitting naturally with Ignatius' letters as a kind of addendum to them. For Polycarp makes it clear that he wrote in response to Ignatius' request. Pol. *Phil.* 9.1–2 is usually taken to imply that Ignatius had already been martyred, though it is quite possible that what the Philippians saw was someone doomed to death and already being savagely treated. But if 9.1–2 does imply Ignatius' martyrdom, then, taken with 13.2, we would have to envisage some months elapsing between Ignatius passing through Philippi and his death – time for him to reach Rome, for his sentence to be executed, and for the news to reach back to Polycarp. Even so, Polycarp's letter to the *Philippians* quite likely followed Ignatius' letters only a few months later – that is, still in the 110s CE (Schoedel, 1967, 37–38; Holmes, 1989, 120–121).

Polycarp evidently was familiar with the Jesus tradition; indeed, what appears to be the same or a very similar collection of Jesus' teaching (*Phil.* 2.3) as in *1 Clem.* 13:2 and *Phil.* 6.2 and 7.2 probably echo the Lord's Prayer. And he likewise venerated Paul (*Phil.* 3.2). The probable echoes of Paul's Letters – 1.3 (Eph 2:5, 8–9), 4.1 (1 Tim 6:7, 10), 5.1 (Gal 6:7), 5.3 (1 Cor 6:9–10), 11.2 (1 Cor 6:2), 12.1 (Eph 4:26) – are instructive on the extent to which the Pauline corpus was already revered.

The *Martyrdom of Polycarp* has the form of a letter written by someone called Marcion (*Mart. Pol.* 20:1), from the church in Smyrna to the church in Philomelium (in Phrygia) and for wider distribution (prescript). It is a vivid and moving account of Polycarp's execution. The *Martyrdom* recounts how Polycarp was caught up in a persecution of Christians by local Roman authorities, in which several were persuaded to "take the oath and offer a sacrifice" (4). The date of Polycarp's martyrdom is usually taken to be 155 CE (Schoedel, 1967, 78–79). The account claims to have been written by an eyewitness (15:1).

4. *Didache*

Didache or the *Teaching of the Twelve Apostles* (→ *Didache*) is one of the most fascinating members of the Apostolic Fathers. Although mentioned by → Eusebius of Caesarea (*Hist. eccl.* 3.25.4), it was not known until a complete text was discovered by P. Bryennios in Constantinople in 1873 which revolutionized the study of early Christianity.

This was because each of the main sections of the *Didache* seems to provide highly valuable insights into early Christianity's development: the section on "the two ways" (chs. 1–6) confirmed the importance of this Jewish paraenetic tradition in Christian catechesis; the treatment of → baptism and Eucharist (chs. 7–10) sheds fascinating light on the liturgical developments of the early 2nd century CE; particularly intriguing is the prominence given to the ministry of itinerant apostles (missionaries), prophets, and teachers (chs. 11–13), alongside that of the locally appointed bishops (plural) and deacons (ch. 15), which indicated that the early modes of church ministry and governance were more diverse than what could be deduced from the Pastoral and Ignatian Epistles (Harnack, 1992, 334–354); and chapter 16 indicated the continuing of apocalyptic expectation.

As to date, the influence of distinctively Matthean features suggests a *terminus a quo* of the mid-80s CE (Audet, 1958, 192, 210, disputes Matthean influence and argues for an earlier, even pre-70 CE date). But the partial development of the final ascription of the → Lord's Prayer ("For the power and the glory are yours forever" – 8:2), the fact that the Eucharist is still a meal (10:1), and the prominence given to itinerant missionaries and prophets (11–13) suggest an early stage in liturgical and ecclesiastical development, and a *terminus ad quem* not far into the 2nd century CE. A date in the period between 100 and 120 CE seems as good a fit with that sequence of data as any other (Niederwimmer, 1993, 79; Ehrman, 2003, vol. I, 411).

Among its several interesting features, the exposition and contrast of the "two ways" (1:2–6) draw heavily on the material underlying Matthew's Sermon on the Mount, and the section on baptism, → fasting, the Lord's prayer, and the Eucharist also reflects influence from Matthew – *Did.* 7:2–3 (Matt 28:19); 8:1–2 (Matt 6:2, 5, 9–13, 16). Other echoes of Matthew confirm that the tradition on which Matthew drew was widely known and used – *Did.* 9:5 (Matt 7:6); 11:1–4 (Matt 10:40–41); 11:7 (Matt 12:31); 13:2 (Matt 10:0); and *Did.* 16 seems to draw repeatedly on Matthew's version of the apocalyptic discourse (Matt 23).

5. *Epistle of Barnabas*

A complete text of *Barnabas* (→ Barnabas) was unknown until the discovery of Codex Sinaiticus (1859) and Codex Hierosolymitanus (1873). The text itself is anonymous. Attribution to Barnabas is already taken for granted by Clement of Alexandria (*Strom.* 2.6.31; 2.7.35; 2.20.116) – but is now almost universally doubted, not least because of the likely date of the letter. However, the letter is written in first-person terms, as a personal address, and despite the author's disclaimers in 1:8 and 4:9, it is more than likely that he regarded himself as a teacher (1:5–6), as his command of Scripture also suggests (Kraft, 1965, 44; Hvalvik, 1996, 46–52; Prostmeier, 1999, 141). The letter's perspective on the Jewish law is more that of an outsider: he talks of the "us" who are to "their law" as "latecomers" (*epēlytoi* – 3:6), of "their covenant," and "the circumcision in which they trusted" (9:4, 6); and he speaks as representative of converted Gentiles (16:7; Wilson, 1995, 128–129; Hvalvik, 1996, 43–44; Prostmeier, 1999, 132).

Barnabas has traditionally been thought to have originated in Alexandria. → Clement of Alexandria not only knew *Barnabas*, but evidently found its thought conducive (see esp. Kraft, 1965, 45–56), implying his appreciation of a similar cast of mind. This is strengthened by the fact that the closest

parallels to *Barnabas'* interpretation of various Torah passages and rituals are to be found in Alexandrian literature. There is broad agreement that the letter has to be dated after the destruction of the Jerusalem Temple (16:4); the majority of scholarship tends to favor 96–100 (Jefford, 2006, 33–34, but see Shukster & Richardson 1983 and Horbury 1996, 319–321).

Barnabas has a few references to the Jesus tradition; most striking is *Barn.* 4:14 (Matt 22:14). Though the epistle has many quotations from the Hebrew Bible (with extensive use of typology in 7:3–8:1 and 12), the attitude toward Israel is much darker than in other early 2nd-century CE Christian writings (particularly 4:6–8, 14; 9:1, 4, 9; 14:1–7). This more negative attitude toward Israel may explain why Paul, even though apostle of the Gentiles, is almost entirely ignored.

6. *Shepherd of Hermas*

Shepherd of Hermas (→ Hermas) contains a lengthy series of five visions, 12 commandments, and ten parables, most of them explained to Hermas by an angel, particularly with reference to the problem of postbaptismal sin. It is one of the most intriguing Christian writings to have emerged from the early 2nd century CE – intriguing because it operates at a rather naive level, and yet proved to be very popular, included even with *Barnabas* in the Codex Sinaiticus together with the New Testament writings (Ehrman, 2003, vol. II, 162; details in Osiek, 1999, 4–7). It presumably, therefore, indicates the level of intellectual engagement and ethical discipleship that typified the main body of Christians during these decades.

Although the book's three sections suggest the possibility of multiple authors, most believe it to have a single authorship, though perhaps composed at different times (Snyder, 1968, 23–24; Osiek, 1999, 8–10; Ehrman, 2003, vol. II, 165–166; Jefford, 2006, 25–28). The only indication of the author's identity is his opening self-identification as a slave of a certain woman named Rhoda, in Rome (Herm. *Vis.* 1.1.1) – presumably able now to write as a freedman (Lampe, 2003, 218–220, and further 220–224). And he regularly identifies himself as "Hermas" (*Vis.* 1.1.4; 1.2.2–4; 1.4.3; 2.2.2; 2.3.1; 3.1.6, 9; 3.8.11; 4.1.4, 7). The identification, initially by → Origen, of Hermas with the Hermas of Rom 16:14 (Eus. *Hist. eccl.*

3.3.6) is at best fanciful. He makes no claim to have any leadership position in the Church of Rome, nor does he identify himself as a prophet or teacher.

The origin of the book in Rome is rarely questioned (Schoedel, 1989, 471).

The date, however, is more disputed. The most obvious dating is suggested by the Muratorian Fragment, which notes that Hermas wrote "very recently" while his brother Pius was the bishop of Rome (73–76 CE). Since Pius I was bishop of Rome (142–157 CE), this would suggest a date between about 145 and 155 CE. However, the date of the Muratorian Fragment is itself disputed (see the brief review, with substantial bibliography, in Gamble, 2002, 269–270). If the testimony of the Muratorian Fragment is discounted, or the historical association with Pius regarded as questionable, or the result of some confusion, then the only remaining clue is probably the mention of "elders" (*Vis.* 2:4.2–3; 3:1.8) and "bishops" (*Vis.* 3:5.1; *Sim.* 9:27.2), which implies a stage of ecclesiology prior to the establishment of a single bishop. How much weight can be placed on this and the other clues is still debated.

Although probably one of the latest of the Apostolic Fathers, when one or more of the New Testament Gospels would certainly have been becoming better and more widely known, Hermas makes no explicit quotation of or allusion to any New Testament Gospel (or to Paul's Letters). And though one might have expected greater scope for echoes of the Jesus tradition, in fact they are few and far between.

7. *2 Clement*

2 Clement (→ Clement) is a homily that was probably written to be read out in a Christian gathering for worship (as implied in *2 Clem.* 19:1). Its author and place of composition are unknown, and there are no real clues on either point within the document itself (see also Ehrman, 2003, vol. I, 157–158). The best clue is probably to be found in Eusebius' reference to a letter of Dionysius (bishop of Corinth, c. 170 CE; Eus. *Hist. eccl.* 4.23.9). In that letter, Dionysius seems to be referring to two letters attributed to Clement (see further Richardson, 1953, 185–186). If so, it means that *2 Clement* was known and designated as such (to have been written by Clement), around 170 CE, and

understood to have been written also from Rome to Corinth, like *1 Clement*. Different places of origin have been suggested: Corinth (Lightfoot, 1890, vol. II, 199), Alexandria (Richardson, 1953, 186–187), Egypt (Koester, 1957, vol. II, 234–236; Pratscher 2007, 659–661).

A further implication is probably that it was the church in Corinth that preserved both *1 Clement* and *2 Clement*, together with copies of the several letters written by Dionysius, to which Eusebius refers (*Hist. eccl.* 4.23.9–13). So perhaps we should simply infer that *2 Clement* became associated with *1 Clement* either because both were read every so often in the Corinthian church assemblies, and/or were stored together in the archive of the church in Corinth, with the result that when *2 Clement* began to become better known (as *1 Clement* always had been), it was assumed to be a second letter of Clement to Corinth (thus, Lightfoot, 1890, vol. II, 197–198; Harnack, cited by Lake, 1912, vol. I, 126). In the end, the issue remains at best confused.

The date of *2 Clement* is equally obscure. The fact that only "elders" are mentioned (17:3, 5) is more or less all that we have to go on, the implication being, that, with no bishop(s) being mentioned, the document was composed before the more widespread establishment of monoepiscopacy. The fact that *2 Clem.* 12:2 quotes a saying of Jesus, which was almost certainly part of the elaboration of the early Jesus tradition, as evidenced by the *Gos. Thom.* 22:1–5 and Clem. *Strom.* 3.13, also suggests a date some way into the 2nd century CE. Thus date around 140 CE is probably the best that we can guess.

Clement regularly draws in quotations from (Israel's) Scripture with introductory phrases like, "The Scripture says," "the Lord says." The Jesus tradition is quoted quite often, the three most interesting quotations being *2 Clem.* 2:4 (Mark 2:17 parr. referred to as "another Scripture"); 8:5 (Luke 16:10, referred to as "the gospel"); and 13:4 (Luke 6:32–34, introduced as "God says"). Intriguingly *Clement* also includes quotations with the same introductory formula from sources unknown to us: 4:5; 5:4; and 14:3.

8. Papias of Hierapolis

Papias (→ Papias of Hierapolis) is included here since, although his five-volume work entitled *Expositions of* the *Sayings of the Lord* is not extant, the quotations from it, particularly in Eusebius but also in various others, provide fascinating information especially about transmission of the Jesus tradition and the composition of some of the New Testament Gospels (for the range of fragments of Papias variously drawn on, see Holmes, 1989, 308, 312). According to church tradition (Eus. *Hist. eccl.* 2.15.2; 3.36.2), Papias was the bishop of Hierapolis (one of the Lycus Valley cities, not far from Colossae and Laodicea). Irenaeus knew him as "the hearer of John and a companion of Polycarp" (Iren. *Haer.* 5.33.4; Eus. *Hist. eccl.* 3.39.1), though the reference to "John" revives the discussion as to whether the apostle or the elder John was in view, and Eusebius adds that Papias himself in the preface of his writings "makes plain that he had in no way been a hearer and eyewitness of the holy apostles" (Eus. 3.39.2; discussion in Schoedel, 1967, 89–90). If this information is trustworthy, these two figures (John and Polycarp) provide a frame within which Papias must have flourished, that is, between circa 90 and 135 CE. And if we assume that it was when he was bishop that he wrote his magnum opus, that would push us to about 130 CE for the date when he wrote – though W.R. Schoedel is willing to date Papias' writing as early as 110 CE (Schoedel, 1967, 92), and presumably in Hierapolis.

9. *The Epistle to Diognetus*

The Epistle to Diognetus (→ *Diognetus, Epistle to*) is more naturally ranked with the apologists in date and character, but is usually included with the Apostolic Fathers. It is one of the most polished pieces of early Christian writing, of a markedly higher rhetorical quality than its predecessors. It is most famous for its characterization of Christians as in the world what the soul is in the body, a theme beautifully elaborated in chapter 6. Equally impressive is the rhetorical elaboration of the Pauline understanding of the Gospel in terms of the righteous one given for the unrighteous (ch. 9).

The author of chapters 11 and 12 describes himself as "a disciple of the apostles" (*Diogn.* 11:1) – which is probably why Diognetus was included in the Apostolic Fathers – but otherwise is unknown. In any event, the *Epistle* indicates a growing desire to distance Christianity from Judaism and no real

willingness to acknowledge Christianity's origins within early Judaism and its Jewish character.

Bibliography

Audet, J.-P., *La Didache*, EtB, Paris, 1958.

Barnard, L.W., *Studies in the Apostolic Fathers and their Background*, Oxford, 1966.

Ehrman, B.D., *The Apostolic Fathers*, 2 vols., LCL, Cambridge MA, 2003.

Gamble, H.Y., "The New Testament Canon: Recent Research and the Status Quaestionis," in: L.M. McDonald & J.A. Sanders, eds., *The Canon Debate*, Peabody, 2002, 267–294.

Harnack, A. von, *The Mission and Expansion of Christianity in the First Three Centuries*, New York, 1962; ET: 1908.

Holmes, M.W., *The Apostolic Fathers*, Grand Rapids, 1989.

Horbury, W., "Jewish-Christian Relations in Barnabas and Justin Martyr," in: J.D.G. Dunn, ed., *Jews and Christians*, Tübingen, 1992, 315–345.

Horrell, D.G., *The Social Ethos of the Corinthian Correspondence*, Edinburgh, 1996.

Hvalvik, R., *The Struggle for Scripture and Covenant: The Purpose of the Epistle of Barnabas and Jewish-Christian Competition in the Second Century*, WUNT, 2nd series, 82, Tübingen, 1996.

Jefford, C.N., *The Apostolic Fathers and the New Testament*, Peabody, 2006.

Koester, H., *Synoptische Überlieferung bei den apostolischen Vätern*, Berlin, 1957.

Kraft, R.A., "Barnabas and the Didache," in: R.M. Grant, ed., *The Apostolic Fathers*, vol. III, London, 1965.

Lake, K., *The Apostolic Fathers*, LCL, 2 vols., London, 1912, 1913.

Lampe, P., *From Paul to Valentinus: Christians in Rome in the First Two Centuries*, Minneapolis, 2003.

Lightfoot, J.B., *Apostolic Fathers*, part I: *S. Clement of Rome*, London, ²1890; part II: *S. Ignatius, S. Polycarp*, 3 vols., London, 1885.

Lindemann, A., *Paulus im ältesten Christentum*, Tübingen, 1979.

Lona, H.E., *Der erste Clemensbrief*, KAV 2, Göttingen, 1998.

Niederwimmer, K., *Die Didache*, KAV 1, Göttingen, ²1993.

Osiek, C., *The Shepherd of Hermas*, Hermeneia, Minneapolis, 1999.

Pratscher, W., *Der zweite Clemensbrief*, KAV 3, Göttingen, 2007.

Prostmeier, F.R., *Der Barnabasbrief*, KAV 8, Göttingen, 1999.

Richardson, C.C., *Early Christian Fathers*, London, 1953.

Schoedel, W.R., *The Apostolic Fathers*, vol. V: *Polycarp, Martyrdom of Polycarp, Fragments of Papias*, London, 1967.

Schoedel, W.R., *Ignatius of Antioch*, Hermeneia, Philadelphia, 1985.

Schoedel, W.R., "The Apostolic Fathers," in: E.J. Epp & G.W. MacRae, eds., *The New Testament and Its Modern Interpreters*, Atlanta, 1989.

Shukster, M.B., & P. Richardson, "Barnabas, Nerva and the Yavhean Rabbis," *JThS* 33, 1983.

Snyder, G.F., "The Shepherd of Hermas," in: R.M. Grant, ed., *The Apostolic Fathers*, vol. VI, London, 1968.

Welborn, L.L., "Clement, First Epistle of," in: *ABD*, vol. I, New York, 1992, 1058–1059.

Wilson, S.G., *Related Strangers: Jews and Christians 70–170 CE*, Minneapolis, 1995.

James D.G. Dunn (†)

Apostolic History → **Arator**

Apostolic Tradition

Apostolic Tradition is the name that was eventually given to an anonymous and untitled ancient church order, first published by H. Tattam (1848) in a manuscript translated into the Bohairic dialect of Coptic as recently as 1804, which also contained two other previously discovered church orders – the *Apostolic Church Order* and a recension of *Const. ap.* 8. For want of a better title, it was first designated as the "Egyptian Church Order." In subsequent years, versions of it in the Sahidic dialect, Latin, Arabic, and Ethiopic also came to light, and E. von der Goltz (1906) suggested that they might really be translations of a Greek work from the early 3rd century CE by Hippolytus of Rome, *Traditio Apostolica*, that had been thought to have been lost. His theory was taken up and elaborated by E. Schwartz (1910) and then quite independently and much more fully by R.H. Connolly (1916).

1. Contents

After a very brief prologue, it gives directions for the ordinations of a → bishop, presbyter (→ Priest/Presbyter), and → deacon and provides ordination prayers to be used for each one. In the case of the bishop's ordination, it also sets out a specimen form of eucharistic prayer for him to use, although permitting the substitution of his own words if he wishes. It then proceeds to the simpler process of the appointment of widows, readers, virgins, subdeacons, and those with the gift of healing. Lengthy instructions follow concerning the process of Christian initiation, beginning with the procedure for admission to the catechumenate, which required sponsors to vouch for the good character of the applicants, together with a list of occupations forbidden to prospective Christians. After regular instruction in the faith normally lasting three years, candidates were admitted to the final stage of preparation for → baptism, provided that their sponsors again attested to their virtuous behavior while catechumens. During this time, they were to hear "the gospel" and be exorcised daily. The baptismal rite itself was intended for both adults and children and began with a renunciation of Satan (→ Devil) and a pre-baptismal exorcism with oil, followed by a threefold profession of faith accompanying a triple immersion in the water. A post-baptismal anointing of the body and prayer with imposition of hands by the bishop, together with another anointing (this time of the head), then followed. After the exchange of a kiss and prayer shared with the faithful for the first time, the → Eucharist with the first communion of the neophytes concluded the rite. The final part of the work deals with other liturgical matters, chief among them the conduct of a community supper, the observance of a two-day fast before Easter, the times of daily prayer and instruction in the word, and the use of the sign of the cross.

2. Historiography

Although the conclusions reached by E. Schwartz (1910) and R.H. Connolly (1916) won general acceptance in the first half of the 20th century, a few voices were raised to challenge the consensus, most notably R. Lorenz (1929) and H. Engberding (1948), but their views were subjected to heavy criticism by other scholars. In 1950, E.C. Ratcliff asserted that its eucharistic prayer had been extensively reworked in the 4th century CE, and in 1964, he extended this argument to encompass the whole work, but this seemingly radical proposal was largely ignored. The same fate befell the claims made by A. Salles (1955), who questioned the Roman character of its baptismal rite, by J.M. Hanssens (1959), who argued at great length that the whole work had originated in Alexandria, and by J. Magne (1965; 1975), who asserted that its true title was the *Diataxeis tôn hagiôn apostolôn* and that because of its lack of unity, its doublets, and its contradictions, it had been compiled of elements from different places and time periods. Unfortunately, J. Magne's further explanation for it – that an unknown church order had been fused with a passage from a genuine "Tradition apostolique sur les charismes" of Hippolytus – was too unconvincing for his theory to win any serious consideration from others.

It was not, therefore, until M. Metzger published a series of articles (1988; 1992a; 1992b) developing the idea advanced by J. Magne and also briefly by A. Faivre (1980, 286) – that not only was this church order not the *Apostolic Tradition* of Hippolytus, but it was not the work of any single author at all but rather a piece of "living literature" – that scholars began to give the notion proper attention. Like J. Magne, M. Metzger argued that its lack of unity or logical progression, its frequent incoherences, doublets, and contradictions, all pointed away from the existence of a single editorial hand. Instead, it had all the characteristics of a composite work, a collection of community rules from quite disparate traditions.

C. Markschies (1999) added to the doubts about its traditional attribution. He pointed out that the sole evidence for a connection with Hippolytus was in two other church orders thought to be derived from this one – the title of the *Canons of Hippolytus* and the reference to him in the second subheading of the *Epitome* of *Const. ap.* 8 – and that these were not added to those works until the late 4th or early 5th century CE, and thus much too late to credit them with any historical reliability. Furthermore, the mention of "apostolic tradition" in the prologue and conclusion of the document had been misinterpreted by other scholars and could not allude to the title of the work.

In any case, the tendency to associate documents with apostolic figures or with those believed to have close connections to such persons so as to enhance their authority is very common in the ancient Christian world, and there are certainly other works that are known to have been falsely attributed to Hippolytus. Even the very existence of a document entitled *Apostolic Tradition* by Hippolytus of Rome is not above suspicion. The title is found among an anonymous list of works on the right-hand side of the base of a statue of a seated male figure discovered in Rome in 1551, and as some of these were known works attributed to Hippolytus, the rest were assumed to be also. But this list does not correlate exactly with the works of Hippolytus that are catalogued both by → Eusebius of Caesarea and → Jerome. Very surprisingly, it omits those that are most strongly attested as genuinely his, including the commentary on Daniel, and this has led some scholars to propose the existence of two authors or even a school of authors as responsible for the works on the list.

J.A. Cerrato (2002) made an important contribution to the debate by arguing that because Hippolytus was a common name in the ancient world, the various works may be the creations of quite different and unrelated authors from diverse places and that at least some of the works attributed to Hippolytus belonged to an eastern figure of that name rather than a Roman one. In a final bizarre twist to the tale, archeological research has revealed that the statue itself was in origin not a representation of Hippolytus at all but of a female figure, which was restored in the 16th century as a male bishop because of the list of works inscribed on its base, using parts taken from other statues.

M. Metzger's verdict has been endorsed and developed by a growing number of scholars, who hence refer to the work as "the so-called *Apostolic Tradition*." However, A. Stewart-Sykes (2001) has clung to a modified version of the original attribution and, building on a theory put forward by A. Brent (1995) that there was an Hippolytean school of writers at Rome, argued that it was the work of members of this school over the period from the late 2nd century to the mid-3rd century CE, and this accounted for the disunity of the text. However, this solution does not address other questions surrounding the work. In particular, it does not explain why some practices specified within it reflect West Syrian rather than Roman liturgical traditions, and why, although some elements do appear to date from the mid-2nd century CE, if not earlier, others have no parallel before the mid-4th century CE. All this suggests a geographically wider range of sources and a much longer period of aggregation.

3. The Text

Because the original Greek no longer exists (except for a very few small fragments), the text has to be reconstructed from the various ancient translations that were mentioned earlier, but it should also be noted that a different version of the Ethiopic, in all probability derived directly from Greek and known to the translator of the other Ethiopic version, has been published by A. Bausi (2011). Some assistance in that reconstruction is also provided by the adaptations that were made of the work in other church orders – the *Canons of Hippolytus*, the → *Testamentum Domini*, and the → *Apostolic Constitutions*. As all these translations and versions often differ significantly from one another in many places, there has been a tendency to treat the Latin translation as the most reliable because the palimpsest on which it is written dates only from the 5th century CE, with the actual translation having been made perhaps about half a century before that. The other witnesses have then been used to supplement or correct its reading where it was deficient or judged to have been amended. This principle was adopted by those who published editions and translations of the text, most notably G. Dix (1937) and B. Botte (1963).

However, now that there is growing acceptance that the *Apostolic Tradition* was not the work of a single hand in one time period, this method will not suffice. In this multilayered work, we need instead to consider the era and if possible, the geographical area in which each of its constituent parts originated. We need to acknowledge that all the linguistic strands, including the Latin, have undergone alteration and expansion in the course of their transmission and that the oldest reading may sometimes have been preserved in places in a late translation or a heavily modified version while it has been written out of the others. And we also need to recognize that at least some liturgical units within the text, such as ordination and baptism, appear themselves to be composite, artificial literary creations made by combining different local traditions from different time periods rather than comprising a single authentic rite that was celebrated in that particular form anywhere in the ancient world. These are the principles followed in the commentary on the church order by P.F. Bradshaw, M.E. Johnson, and L.E. Phillips (2002).

At the same time, it is important to note that just because something is regarded as a later addition to the text does not necessarily mean that it is a later composition. In many cases, this may be so, but in others, the material may be as old as the core itself, but only added to it at a later date. This seems to be true in particular with regard to the eucharistic prayer in the *Apostolic Tradition*. There is growing acceptance that this was a later interpolation into the ordination of a bishop and that the supper material toward the end of the church order was originally understood as eucharistic. Yet the prayer reveals some language that has affinities with the 2nd century CE as well as elements that are not otherwise attested before the 4th century CE, suggesting that it too derives from an early time and was later "modernized," either before or after it was added to this church order. A recent study by M. Smyth (2007) points to its essentially West Syrian rather than Roman character.

Although it is difficult to be precise about where the core material of the document might begin and end and the extent to which it has been redacted by later hands, it appears that it may have been formed of three parts, or alternatively three smaller collections of material were combined together:

- Directives about appointments to various ministries, to which ordination prayers and other related material were added later, perhaps at different times, and then, the eucharistic prayer and prayers for oil, cheese, and olives were interpolated.
- Directives about the initiation of new converts without any indication of roles assigned to specific ministers, to which were added later explicit statements about the actions of the bishop and then later still a third layer of more detailed ritual instructions that referred to presbyters and deacons.
- Directives about community meals and prayer practices, which were subsequently greatly expanded by several hands.

In some cases, the additions seem to have been drawing on preexistent written texts; in others, they appear as short interpolations amplifying, clarifying, or correcting the core material. These many emendations do not readily fall into groups of common concerns that might have suggested a small number of specific hands at work but rather point to an extended process of piecemeal revision and updating of the contents. While some of the elements in the core strongly imply a North African or Roman origin, much of the later material is paralleled in West Syrian practice instead.

Conclusion

When what was thought to be the early 3rd-century CE *Apostolic Tradition* of Hippolytus became known in the 20th century, it created great excitement among liturgical historians because it seemed to reveal the oldest extant forms of the liturgical rites of the church at Rome, and indeed of Christianity anywhere, which bore resemblance to practices otherwise known only from the late 4th century CE onward. But interest in this church order did not remain a merely academic matter. In the process of liturgical revision and renewal that swept through the major western churches in the 1960s and 1970s, because of its supposed antiquity and actual use in the Roman Church, its eucharistic prayer was widely adopted as the foundation for modern compositions, and in some cases, its ordination prayer for a bishop and its initiation rite also had an influence on contemporary practice. Now that its true origin and character are being revealed, future processes of liturgical revision in the churches may wish to lean less heavily on this church order as a fundamental archetype and instead draw on a wider range of ancient sources for inspiration.

Bibliography

Bausi, A., "La nuova versione Etiopica della Traditio Apostolica: Edizione e traduzione preliminare," in: P. Buzi & A. Camplani, eds., *Christianity in Egypt: Literary Production and Intellectual Trends*, SEAug 125, Rome, 2011, 19–69.

Botte, B., *La tradition apostolique de saint Hippolyte: Essai de reconstitution*, LQF 39, Münster, 1963, ⁵1989.

Bradshaw, P.F., "Who Wrote the Apostolic Tradition? A Response to Alistair Stewart-Sykes," *SVTQ* 48, 2004, 195–206.

Bradshaw, P.F., "Conclusions Shaping Evidence: An Examination of the Scholarship Surrounding the Supposed Apostolic Tradition of Hippolytus," in: P. van Geest, M. Poorthuis & E. Rose, eds., *Sanctifying Texts, Transforming Rituals: Encounters in Liturgical Studies*, Leiden, 2017, 13–30.

Bradshaw, P.F., *The Apostolic Tradition: A Text for Students*, JLS 91, Norwich, 2021.

Bradshaw, P.F., M.E. Johnson & L.E. Phillips, *The Apostolic Tradition: A Commentary*, Minneapolis, 2002.

Brent, A., *Hippolytus and the Roman Church in the Third Century: Communities in Tension before the Emergence of a Monarch-Bishop*, SVigChr 31, Leiden, 1995.

Cerrato, J.A., *Hippolytus between East and West: The Commentaries and the Provenance of the Corpus*, Oxford, 2002.

Cerrato, J.A., "The Association of the Name Hippolytus with a Church Order, Now Known as the Apostolic Tradition," *SVTQ* 48, 2004, 179–194.

Connolly, R.H., *The So-Called Egyptian Church Order and Derived Documents*, Cambridge UK, 1916.

Dix, G., *The Treatise on the Apostolic Tradition of St Hippolytus*, London, 1937, ²1968.

Engberding, H., "Das angebliche Dokument römische Liturgie aus dem Beginn des dritten Jahrhunderts," in: *Miscellanea liturgica in honorem L. Cuniberti Mohlberg*, vol. I, Rome, 1948, 47–71.

Faivre, A., "La documentation canonico-liturgique de l'église ancienne," *RevSR* 54, 1980, 273–297.

Goltz, E. von der, "Unbekannte Fragmente altchristlicher Gemeindeordnungen," *SPAW*, 1906, 141–157.

Hanssens, J.M., *La Liturgie d'Hippolyte: Ses documents, son titulaire, ses origines et son charactère*, vol. I, OCA 155, Rome, 1959, ²1965, vol. II, Rome, 1970.

Lorenz, R., *De egyptische Kerkordening en Hippolytus van Rome*, Haarlem, 1929.

Magne, J., "La prétendue Tradition apostolique de Hippolyte de Rome s'appelait-elle *Ai diataxeis tôn hagiôn apostolôn*, 'Les statuts des saints Apôtres'?" *OS* 14, 1965, 35–67.

Magne, J., *Tradition apostolique sur les charismes et Diataxeis des saints Apôtres*, Paris, 1975.

Magne, J., "En finir avec la 'Tradition' d'Hippolyte!" *BLE* 89, 1988, 5–22.

Markschies, C., "Wer schrieb die sogenannte Traditio Apostolica? Neue Beobachtungen und Hypothesen zu einer kaum lösbaren Frage aus der altkirchen Literaturgeschichte," in: W. Kinzig, C. Markschies & M. Vinzent, eds., *Tauffragen und Bekenntnis*, AKG 74, Berlin, 1999, 8–43.

Metzger, M., "Nouvelles perspectives pour la prétendue Tradition apostolique," *EO* 5, 1988, 241–259.

Metzger, M., "Enquêtes autour de la prétendue Tradition apostolique," *EO* 9, 1992a, 7–36.

Metzger, M., "À propos des règlements écclesiastiques et de la prétendue Tradition apostolique," *RevSR* 66, 1992b, 249–261.

Ratcliff, E.C., "The Sanctus and the Pattern of the Early Anaphora," *JEH* 1, 1950, 29–36, 125–134.

Ratcliff, E.C., "Review of Botte, *La tradition apostolique*," *JThS* 15, 1964, 405.

Ratcliff, E.C., "Apostolic Tradition: Questions Concerning the Appointment of the Bishop," *SP* 8, 1966, 266–270.

Salles, A., "La 'Tradition apostolique' est-elle un témoin de la liturgie romaine?" *RHR* 148, 1955, 181–213.

Schwartz, E., *Über die pseudoapostolischen Kirchenordnungen*, Strasbourg, 1910.

Smyth, M., "L'anaphore de la prétendue 'tradition apostolique et la prière eucharistique romaine," *RevSR* 81, 2007, 95–118; "The Anaphora of the So-Called 'Apostolic Tradition' and the Roman Eucharistic Prayer," in: M.E. Johnson, ed., *Issues in Eucharistic Praying in East and West*, Collegeville, 2011, 71–97.

Stewart-Sykes, A., *Hippolytus: On the Apostolic Tradition*, Crestwood, 2001, ²2015.

Stewart-Sykes, A., "Traditio Apostolica, the Liturgy of Third-Century Rome and the Hippolytean School or Quomodo historia liturgica conscribenda sit," *SVTQ* 48, 2004, 233–248.

Tattam, H., *The Apostolical Constitutions or the Canons of the Apostles in Coptic with an English Translation*, London, 1848.

Walls, A.F., "The Latin Version of Hippolytus' Apostolic Tradition," *SP 3*, 1961, 155–162.

PAUL F. BRADSHAW

Apostolicity

The role of apostolicity in the early church was extremely important. Apostolicity is the belief that something, usually a writing or ecclesiastical office, was produced by or connected to a person from the historical Jesus' (→ Christ) most inner circle. If a writing were believed to come from the hand of one of Jesus' apostles – persons such as Matthew, Simon Peter, James the son of Zebedee, John the brother of James, Andrew, Philip, Bartholomew, Thomas, James the son of Alphaeus, Thaddaeus, Simon the Zealot, and Judas the son of James – it had authority: it could be trusted. Christianity was diverse in belief and practice. Therefore, it was important to know which interpretation of Jesus was correct.

As a diversity of irreconcilable Christian beliefs flourished – such as those held by Ebionites (→ Ebionites/Ebionitism), gnostics (→ Gnosis/Gnosticism), → adoptionists, Marcionites (→ Marcion/Marcionites/Marcionism), Montanists (→ Montanism/Montanists), and those who have come to be called proto-orthodox – apostolic succession was employed by Irenaeus of Lyon (e.g. *Haer.* 3.3.1–3.3.4), Tertullian (e.g. *Praesc.* 32), and even → Eusebius of Caesarea (e.g. *Hist. eccl.* 4.1.1–2) to weed out false doctrine. They claimed that they could, for example, trace the lineage of the then-current bishop of Rome back to an apostle such as Peter who, of course, knew Jesus himself. This is how the proto-orthodox knew that their narrative of Christianity, complete with Jesus' virgin birth as well as his death and → resurrection from the dead, was the correct narrative. And apostolic succession declared competing narratives false. These competing narratives suggested, for example, that Jesus only appeared to be human, or that Jesus was born of male and female sexual union just as anyone else, or that Jesus prayed to a god different from the God presented in the Hebrew Bible. It is important to note here that some who embraced these competing narratives *also* claimed apostolic succession for *their* own beliefs as is evidenced in the gnostic Ptolemy's letter to Flora. This letter is preserved in → Epiphanius of Salamis' *Panarion* (33.3.1–33.7.10).

In the paragraphs to come, the importance of apostolicity in early Christianity will be illustrated via four domains: the 4th-century CE document *Apostolic Constitutions*, the early 4th-century CE bishop and author Eusebius of Caesarea, the 2nd-century CE document the *Acts of Paul and Thecla*, and the mostly 1st-century CE "New Testament documents."

1. *Apostolic Constitutions*

The → *Apostolic Constitutions* is a lengthy document, consisting of eight books, which contains first-person narration from some of Jesus' apostles themselves. For example, statements such as "I Matthew" or "I Peter" are found throughout. Furthermore, these first-person accounts of the teachings of Jesus' apostles claim to have been collected and written down by Clement. It is not known exactly who the Clement is supposed to be, perhaps the Clement mentioned by Paul in Phil 4:3. The document contains teaching, supposedly from the apostles, relevant to topics traditionally found in church orders such as baptism, communion, instructions for catechumens, proper gender relations, and the ordination of bishops and priests.

The scholarly consensus today is that the *Apostolic Constitutions* is, indeed, a collection of various church orders from the 2nd century CE forward. In fact, is has been proven that Books 1–6 contain parts of the 3rd-century CE → *Didascalia Apostolorum*, Book 7 holds portions of the 2nd-century CE → *Didache*, and Book 8 consists of the → *Apostolic Tradition*. Someone then has put these documents together and added first-person apostolic references as well as other editorial additions with the hopes of passing them off as truly apostolic. Scholars generally agree, due to anachronisms found throughout, that the editor performed his task sometime in the mid- to late 4th century CE. It is often thought that the same person responsible for this forged adaptation of early church manuals is the same hand that performed the same task with the Ignatian long recension.

Whatever the exact scenario, we see here the importance of apostolicity. For those readers, small in number, who have deemed the *Apostolic Constitutions* authentic, such as W. Whiston (1711–1712), the *Apostolic Constitutions* serve as blueprint to church governance much as the Pentateuch served as a blueprint to governance for the ancient Israelites. And thus, this document, if apostolic, would have the power to unite the many different strands of Christianity in existence.

2. Eusebius of Caesarea

Eusebius, 4th-century CE writer and church leader, demonstrates the importance of apostolicity in his *Ecclesiastical History* as he explains the conditions under which documents were accepted into the New Testament (→ Eusebius of Caesarea). In *Hist. eccl.* 5.8.1, Eusebius acknowledges that earlier in his work, he promised "to quote from time to time" the statements of earlier church leaders about the "canonical Scriptures" (ἐνδιάθηκον γράφων). Eusebius then quotes from Irenaeus, bishop of Lyon (→ Irenaeus of Lyon) from 177 CE until his death. Irenaeus' major work is *Against Heresies*. Scholars date it to around 180 CE. Eusebius quotes from Book 3. Here Irenaeus says that Matthew published his Gospel among the Hebrews, Peter and Paul were in Rome starting the church there, Mark's Gospel consists of Peter's preaching, Luke's Gospel consists of Paul's preaching, and John (a disciple of the Lord) wrote his Gospel while living in Asia. Note that Eusebius relies on Irenaeus' confirmation that Matthew and John were written by Jesus' disciples – they are eyewitness accounts. Mark and Luke were not eyewitnesses of Jesus' ministry. However, Irenaeus (and others) report that when Mark was in Rome he heard Peter's preaching. Therefore, Mark's Gospel contains the preaching of Peter – another eyewitness to the life of Jesus. As for Luke, the traveling companion of Paul, Irenaeus says that his Gospel contains the preaching of Paul. Paul did not encounter the earthly Jesus. However, he did have an encounter with the resurrected Jesus on the road to Damascus. Therefore, Paul had apostolic authority.

Furthermore, Eusebius makes known the debates in the early church over Hebrews and Revelation due to uncertainty over the authorship of these documents. For example, even though Eusebius is persuaded that Paul wrote Hebrews, he makes his readers aware that Hebrews was rejected by the church in Rome because it was not believed to be from the apostle Paul (*Hist. eccl.* 3.1.4). In fact, Eusebius refers to a Roman intellectual Gaius, who lived when Zephyrinus was bishop of Rome (bishop c. 198–217 CE). Gaius referred to only 13 epistles of Paul – excluding Hebrews (*Hist. eccl.* 6.20.3).

When we turn to Revelation, we find once again that the authorship of the document was an unsettling matter for early Christians. Eusebius mentions Revelation on nine occasions in his *Ecclesiastical History* (3.18.1; 3.25.3; 3.39.6; 4.18.8; 4.24.1; 5.8.5; 5.18.14; 6.25.10; 7.25). The most detailed treatment of Revelation is found in *Hist. eccl.*7.25. Here Eusebius quotes the opinions of Dionysius of Alexandria on Revelation. Dionysius was bishop of Alexandria from 247 to 265 CE. In Book 2 of his *On Promises*, Dionysius states that some people reject Revelation because it is difficult to understand. In fact, some early Christians believed that Revelation was a forgery composed by the gnostic Cerinthus. Dionysius, however, says that the difficulty in understanding Revelation is no reason to reject it. Even so, Dionysius concludes that John the elder, not John the apostle, wrote Revelation.

3. *The Acts of Paul and Thecla*

We know that some early Christians made up stories about apostles in order to give the teaching found in these fictitious stories necessary authority for widespread acceptance within the Christian community. One reason we know this is because we have an actual confession. → Tertullian records this confession in his *On Baptism* written sometime in the early 3rd century CE. He wrote *On Baptism* because a woman representing the Cainite version of Gnosticism taught that → baptism was not necessary. Apparently, her efforts were met with significant success, if Tertullian's angry tone is any indicator. Toward the end of his treatise, Tertullian says that it is fine for laypeople to administer baptism if they have permission from the bishop or priest and they are not female (Tert. *Bapt.* ch. 17).

The *Acts of Paul and Thecla* was in circulation when Tertullian wrote *On Baptism*. In this writing, → Thecla, a woman engaged to man named Thamyris, hears Paul's discourse on virginity. She then decides to break off her engagement and follow Paul. The part of the story that Tertullian wishes to combat is Thecla's practice of teaching and baptizing. To confute this teaching of female ecclesiastical liberty, Tertullian says that these writings, which falsely carry the name of Paul upon them, were forged by a presbyter (→ Priest/Presbyter) in Asia. When this presbyter was caught, he admitted his deed and said that he had done it due to his love for the apostle Paul. Of course, such statements must be examined with a critical eye as they originate in service to polemics.

4. The New Testament

It is well known that the New Testament Gospels – Matthew, Mark, Luke, and John (→ Matthew the Apostle; → Mark, Gospel of; → Luke, Gospel of; → John the Apostle) – are anonymous. In other words, none of these works claims to have been written by Matthew, Mark, Luke, or John. Yet without apostolic authority behind them, they would likely never have made it into the New Testament canon. As discussed above concerning Eusebius of Caesarea, early church traditions gave these documents the needed apostolic credentials.

When we turn to other New Testament documents we again encounter the importance of apostolicity to gain a hearing in early Christianity. There are 13 New Testament letters that bear Paul's name. Of those 13, seven are considered undisputed – 1 Thessalonians, 1 Corinthians, 2 Corinthians, Galatians,

Romans, Philemon, and Philippians. The overwhelming consensus among scholars is that these letters are in fact what they claim to be – letters written by Paul. The other six letters are debated – 2 Thessalonians, Colossians, Ephesians, 1 Timothy, 2 Timothy, and Titus. Some scholars believe that some (or all) of these letters are in fact by Paul; other scholars are of the opinion that some (or all) of these letters are forgeries. In other words, they are plagiarism, as we think of plagiarism today, in reverse. They were written by someone whose identity we will never know. And this unknown person signed the letters with Paul's name to give the instruction found in them apostolic authority. There are questions as to the Pauline authenticity of these letters because the characteristic vocabulary is different from the undisputed seven, and there are reflections of a time period found in these letters that appear to emerge after the lifetime of the apostle Paul.

Scholars can identify a handful of reasons why early Christians participated in what seems to us today to be dishonest activity. As demonstrated above, via Tertullian's record of the Asian presbyter's forgery of the *Acts of Paul and Thecla*, one motivation for forgery in the early Christian world was deceit according to the proto-orthodox. We also know, however, that in the ancient world disciples of wellknown persons often wrote in that person's name after that person's death to carry on their teacher's instruction. For example, students of the Pythagorean school attributed their writings to Pythagoras. Also, Tertullian is helpful once again. In his *Against Marcion*, he states the opinion that Luke's Gospel is dependent on Paul (Tert. *Marc.* 4.5). Therefore, "And it may well be that the works which disciples publish belong to their masters" (translation taken from *ANF* 3). To our knowledge, Luke's Gospel never circulated under Paul's name. However, it appears for Tertullian that when we read what Luke wrote, we are exposed to what Paul thought.

Conclusion

Clearly the issue of authority was important in the early church. Considering the diversity of early Christian interpretations of Jesus and his message, there was significant anxiety over which interpretation was closest to correct. It was a game changer if a writing could carry the claim to apostolicity. Thus, some Christians, who were confident in their understanding of Christianity, had no difficulty affixing the name of an apostle to something they produced. The irony is that it is difficult to know if we have any Christian remains that actually emerged from the hands of an apostle with the exception of Paul; and by his own admission, he was an apostle "untimely born."

Historiography

One landmark study that is relevant to apostolicity is W. Bauer's *Orthodoxy and Heresy in Earliest Christianity* (1971). His book was first published in 1934 as *Rechtgläubigkeit und Ketzerei im ältesten Christentum*. In this work, W. Bauer challenges the classical understanding of → heresy as found in proto-orthodox writes such as Irenaeus of Lyon, Tertullian, and Eusebius of Caesarea discussed above in the main entry. The proto-orthodox suggest that Christianity began unified and orthodox – that is proto-orthodox orthodoxy of course. From this original purity, error crept in and spread, due to the heretic's desire for faction and/or an insatiable appetite for the pursuit of new ideas, so that there existed contradictory Christian beliefs and practices. W. Bauer makes a cogent argument that reveres the proto-orthodox understanding. He contends that Christianity was diverse from its very beginnings. Furthermore, in some geographical locations, the first forms of Christianity were not proto-orthodox. Instead, they were forms of Christianity that would later be labeled heterodox. W. Bauer's historical reconstruction of early Christianity's development was so disturbing to some that H. Turner responded to W. Bauer with a scholarly defense of the classical proto-orthodox view in his 1954 Bampton Lectures at Oxford University. He entitled his lectures, "The Pattern of Christian Truth: A Study in the Relations Between Orthodoxy and Heresy in the Early Church." These lectures were published later in the same year under the same title.

Bibliography

Achtemeier, P.J., *1 Peter: A Commentary on First Peter*, Hermeneia, Minneapolis, 1996, 39–40.

Bauckham, R., *Jesus and the Eyewitnesses: The Gospels as Eyewitness Testimony*, Grand Rapids, [2]2017.

Bauer, W., *Orthodoxy and Heresy in Earliest Christianity*, Philadelphia, 1971.

Bradshaw, P.F., *The Search for the Origins of Christian Worship: Sources and Methods for the Study of Early Liturgy*, New York, [2]2002.

Bradshaw, P.F., *Reconstructing Early Christian Worship*, Collegeville, 2009.

Bradshaw, P.F., M.E. Johnson, & L.E. Phillips, *The Apostolic Tradition: A Commentary*, Hermeneia, Minneapolis, 2002.

Brox, N., *Falsche Verfasserangaben: Zur Erkärung der frühchristlichen Pseudepigraphia*, Stuttgart, 1975.

Carriker, A.J., *The Library of Eusebius of Caesarea*, SVigChr 67, Leiden, 2003.

Clarke, K.D., "The Problem of Pseudonymity in Biblical Literature and Its Implications for Cannon Formation," in: L.M. McDonald & J.A. Sanders, eds., *The Canon Debate*, Peabody, 2002, 440–468.

Davids, A., "The Era of the Apostles According to Eusebius' History of the Church," in: A. Hilhorst, ed., *The Apostolic Age in Patristic Thought*, SVigChr 70, Leiden, 2004, 194–203.

Ehrman, B.D., *Lost Scriptures: Books that Did Not Make It into the New Testament*, New York, 2005.

Ehrman, B.D., *Forgery and Counterforgery: The Use of Literary Deceit in Early Christian Polemics*, New York, 2012.

Gilliam III, P.R., "William Whiston: No Longer an Arian," *JEH* 66/4, 2015, 755–771.

Gilliam III, P.R., *Ignatius of Antioch and the Arian Controversy*, SVigChr 140, Leiden, 2017, 50–55.

Gilliam III, P.R., *William Whiston and the Apostolic Constitutions: Completing the Reformation*, SPS 11, 2022.

Johnson, S.F., *The Life and Miracles of Thekla: A Literary Study*, HeSts 13, Cambridge MA, 2006.

Manor, T.S., "Papias, Origen and Eusebius: The Criticisms and Defense of the Gospel of John," *VigiChr* 67/1, 2013, 1–21.

Manor, T.S., *Epiphanius' Alogi and the Johannine Controversy: A Reassessment of Early Ecclesial Opposition to the Johannine Corpus*, SVigChr 135, Leiden, 2016.

Meier, J.P., "The Circle of the Twelve: Did It Exist during Jesus' Public Ministry?" *JBL* 116/4, 1997, 635–672.

Metzger, M., *Les Constitutions Apostoliques*, SC, 3 vols., Paris, 1985.

O'Leary, De L., *The Apostolic Constitutions and Cognate Documents, with Special Reference to their Liturgical Elements*, London, 1906.

Turner, H., *The Pattern of Christian Truth: A Study in the Relations Between Orthodoxy and Heresy in the Early Church*, Eugene, 2004.

Whiston, W., *Primitive Christianity Reviv'd*, 5 vols., London, 1711–1712.

PAUL R. GILLIAM III

Apothetic Theology → Negative Theology

Arabic Bible → Bible: XVI. Arabic Versions

Arator

Arator (fl. 544 CE) composed an impassioned and highly rhetorical hexameter epic on the Acts of the Apostles (→ Acts, Book of), known from the manuscripts as *Historia Apostolica*, which was recited in Rome, in the Church of Saint Peter ad Vincula, in the year 544 CE. Born into a noble family in the late 5th century CE, in Liguria, he received his early education in Milan. Some years later he moved to Ravenna, where he tells us that he read the "histories" of Julius Caesar (i.e. *The Gallic War*) as well as secular or non-Christian poems – works in which he recognized "sweet charm" but also "deceitful artistry" and "proud display" – and "truthful," that is, Christian, works, in classical meters. He was a keen writer of verse from boyhood, but turned his back on this "frivolous" work and was urged to attend to the praise of God. Besides the *Historia Apostolica*, there are three letters in verse written in his maturity, which shed various light on his life and friends. Formerly the seat of the Roman emperors, Ravenna was now occupied by the → Goths; Arator turned to the Gothic court for his career, and flourished. Soon becoming an advocate, he made a good impression for his role in an embassy to the Gothic king, Theoderic. His subsequent departure for Rome, at an uncertain date, may have been the result of régime change in Ravenna, or the threat of invasion by Belisarius on behalf of the eastern emperor → Justinian; this actually happened in 540 CE. He exchanged the Gothic court for the Roman church, expressing great gratitude to Pope Vigilius, to whom the *Historia Apostolica* is dedicated. He describes this new home as "the untroubled sheepfolds of Peter," but Rome was besieged by the Gothic king Vitigis in 537–538 CE and would be besieged again in 546 CE. His epic was written in volatile and troubled times,

perhaps indeed in an atmosphere of constant crisis. Whether Arator survived even to 550 CE is uncertain.

Arator may have thought of writing a poem on Hebrew Bible material, but there is no sign of one. It is fairly clear why he chose Acts; not because it had not hitherto been rendered in verse (as is no doubt the case), and had been rarely commented on in any form, but because of its importance as a narrative of Peter's apostleship (→ Peter the Apostle) and its relevance to the present situation. Arator recasts Acts as two books of epic length, each over a 1,000 lines. The first book follows Acts from the description of → Pentecost to the heightened treatment of Peter's escape from prison, in which there is a climactic reference to the chains now displayed in the church that, as Arator makes clear, guarantee Rome's safety. No doubt there was especially great rejoicing and applause at this point, the end of Book 1 (an extant record of the event shows that the recitation of the *Historia Apostolica* needed to be prolonged over five days). The second book, like Acts, is dominated by the works and journeys of Paul (→ Peter the Apostle), but Peter is not neglected, for it was he who sanctified Paul for his mission, and he, Peter, is presented as the only speaker in the pivotal debate at Jerusalem on the propriety of admitting the Gentiles. The poem's carefully crafted ending jubilantly describes Paul's arrival in Rome and then presents Peter and Paul together as "lights of the world," and foreshadows their martyrdoms. The primacy of Peter is unobtrusively presented and an allusion made to Peter's rise to prominence early in Acts.

For his reenactment of Acts, Arator selected almost 50 particular episodes and, allowing for various other omissions, has been estimated to have used some two-thirds of its material (Schwind, 1990, 39). There is no single discernible reason for the omissions, whether of episodes or of verses (examined by Green, 2006, 277–282). In most editions each episode is preceded by a short digest in prose. Some manuscripts have this feature, others do not; for various compelling reasons they are best treated as subsequent additions to clarify the poem (Green, 2006, 270–273). Arator's poetic paraphrase is made with a broad brush, often departing somewhat from the original, and is certainly not word for word. Some features of the narrative are developed at length, with minor details omitted. Typically half an episode consists of exegesis, often delivered in a richly rhetorical, indeed declamatory, manner. The style is certainly Arator's own complicated style rather than the Bible's, but there are many examples of material taken from popular preaching, much of it ultimately based on → Origen (Schwind, 1990, 343–345). Favored methods of drawing out spiritual significance are typology and the explanation of *figurae* (figures), digressions to bring in related biblical passages, etymologies of names, and numerology (the number three is especially prominent, mainly because it points to the Trinity). There are frequent attacks on → Arianism (Rome's Gothic foes were Arians, and such verbal attacks served to confirm Roman confidence and identity), and denunciations of the Jews.

In the exegetical additions, there is, not surprisingly, little that shows the influence of epic, or aspirations to its language or style; but throughout the narratives and in many of the speeches included within them, there is frequent allusion not only to → Virgil but also to Lucan, author of the epic *The Civil War*. Virgil is often seen as the supreme example of epic in late antiquity, but Lucan also was much read at the time, and Arator's use of him in various ways in the poem may be seen from the outset (Green, 2006, 321–324). When applying the notion of hero to *Historia Apostolica*, Virgil is often seen as the salient model (Deproost, 1990, 307–312; Bureau, 1997, 102–109), but the structural contribution from Lucan, which often presents itself by inversion or reversal, or by other means of contrast, may be a more helpful guide (Green, 2006, 327–329). In the protagonists Caesar and Pompey, Lucan has two heroes (Virgil has but one, and his Aeneas was never strongly embraced by Christian writers), both of whom are devoted to warfare and destruction, and both of whom leave behind the city of Rome, which is thus peripheral to the narrative; contrastingly, Arator's two heroes or leaders are devoted to peace and edification, to giving life and not dealing out death, and they come together, without friction, in Rome, which was pagan in their time but is now Christian.

This last point has an important bearing on some of the criticism that Arator is not really epic (Hillier, 1993, 15). It is true that the heroes are unlike Aeneas, who is, in R. Hillier's words, "impelled by divine destiny" and (one might add) not always pleased with it, but the recipe for a hero in classical antiquity is not static, as the poem of Lucan, when compared with its predecessors, reveals. J. Schwind (1990, 46–49) has also questioned whether there is really a continuous narrative, because of the frequent lack of details of time and place; to some extent Lucan, with his desultory transitions from episode to episode before he comes to his climax, offers an explanation and justification for the episodic nature of Arator. It is also true that, as M. Roberts (1985, 180–181) points out, much poetic writing in late antiquity was episodic.

Historiography

Arator's work quickly became popular and remained popular until at least the early 15th century. In the generation after him, Arator is present in the list of Christian poetic precursors praised by → Venantius Fortunatus, another poet from Ravenna, but now in Gaul. He mentions Arator's "flowing eloquence" and makes the ubiquitous pun on his name (it is also Latin for "ploughman"). In the following century, Arator is very important to the English scholar The Venerable Bede, who cites Arator as one of the authorities for his commentary on Acts, and also quotes him verbatim, in his versified *Life of St. Cuthbert*. Arator is also well known to the English scholars Aldhelm and Alcuin (7th and early 8th cents. CE), and to pupils of Alcuin, such as Rabanus Maurus. Plentiful manuscript evidence shows that, especially in England, Arator had become and continued to be one of the most valued school texts. In the later Middle Ages, the reading of the famous classical epics is sometimes seen as ancillary to the reading of Christian epics, and they are often recommended as a replacement or antidote for pagan tales, which is how some saw classical literature. In the early Renaissance, Arator was valued by Petrarch and is included in the long catalogue of poets and other writers in his tenth Eclogue, again with the pun on his name. In England, it seems that early interest in Arator flagged as the 16th century wore on; but not so in Spain, where Arator (perhaps because he imitated the Spanish-born Lucan), was studied by A. de Nebrija and A. Barbosa, both of whom wrote commentaries on the *Historia Apostolica*.

Arator was one of the Christian poets printed by A. Manutius (1501–1504), and Arator acquired quick popularity, especially in Spain with the commentary of A. Barbosa (1516). But the only significant work from the next two or three centuries was that of H. Arntzenius (1769), reprinted in J.-P. Migne (1847); Arator had fallen from favor, whether under the weight of his own incessant rhetoric or because of general disinterest in the 6th century CE. The edition in J.-P. Migne (PL 68) is that of J. Arntzen. There are now modern editions replete with information by A.P. McKinlay (1951) and A.P. Orbán (2006). An edition of his text in the Corpus Scriptorum Ecclesiasticorum series came out as late as 1951; in its introduction this provided copious medieval testimonies to his life and his skill, an enumeration of orthographical variants, and a large list of manuscripts which, however, were put to little critical use in establishing the text. J. Schwind (1990) itself is a work of great thoroughness and consummate scholarship, systematically discussing the presentation of the work, its use of allegory, its patristic models, and the poet's aims. J. Schwind does not run away from the rhetoric but takes it in his stride. There is an adequate translation, perhaps the first in English, in R.J. Schrader (1987). M. Roberts (1985) and R.P.H. Green (2006) are essential, and works of high literary interest have appeared by B. Bureau (1997) and P.-A. Deproost (1997), to mention but a few of their studies.

Bibliography

Arntzenius, H., ed., *Arator, S. Ecclesiae Romanae Subdiaconus de actibus Apostolorum libri duo, et epistolae tres ad Florianum, Vigilium, et Parthenium*, Zutphen, 1769; repr. J.-P. Migne, PL 68. 45–252, Paris, 1847.

Barbosa, A., *Aratoris Cardinalis Historia Apostolica cum commentariis*, Salamanca, 1516.

Bureau, B., *Lettre et sens mystique dans l'Historia Apostolica d'Arator: Exégèse et épopée*, EAA 153, Paris, 1997.

Deproost, P.-A., *L'Apôtre Pierre dans une épopée du vie siècle: L'historia apostolica d'Arator*, EAA 126, Paris, 1990.

Deproost, P.-A., "L'Épopée biblique en langue latine: Essai de définition d'un genre littéraire," *Latomus* 56, 1997, 14–39.

Green, R.P.H., *Latin Epics of the New Testament: Juvencus, Sedulius, Arator*, Oxford, 2006.

Hillier, R., *Arator on the Acts of the Apostles: A Baptismal Commentary*, Oxford, 1993.

Manutius, A., *Aratoris Cardinalis Historiae Apostolicae Libri duo*, Venice, 1501–1504.

McKinlay, A.P., ed., *Aratoris subdiaconi De Actibus Apostolorum*, CSEL, vol. LXXII, Vienna, 1951.

Orbán, A.P., ed., *Aratoris subdiaconi Historia Apostolica*, CCSL 130, Turnhout, 2006.

Roberts, M., *Biblical Epic and Rhetorical Paraphrase in Late Antiquity*, Liverpool, 1985.

Schrader, R.J., ed., *Arator's On the Acts of the Apostles (De Actibus Apostolorum)*, CRS 6, Atlanta, 1987.

Schwind, J., *Arator-Studien*, Hyp. 94, Göttingen, 1990.

ROGER GREEN

Arbogast

Nothing is known about the early career of Arbogast until 380 CE, when he is assistant of Gratian's *magister equitum* Bauto, sent to help → Theodosius I against the → Goths in the Balkans (Zos. *Hist.* 4.33.1–2; Eun. *Frgm.* 53). The written sources emphasize, however, on his Frankish origin (Eun. *Frgm.* 53; John Ant. *Frgm.* 187; Philost. *Hist. eccl.* 11.2) and that he was beyond corruption or avarice, a prudent and brave soldier (Zos. *Hist.* 4.53.1). He had been expelled from his homeland (Claud. *Pan. Tertio* 66; *Pan. Quarto* 74) and joined the Roman army, where, due to military skills and talent as well as his relation as nephew of Frankish general Richomer, advanced rapidly and became lieutenant of Bauto. His close relation with the latter reflects in the statement that Arbogast was wrongly called Bauto's son (John Ant. *Frgm.* 187). He was probably at that time *comes domesticorum* (Seeck, 1895, 415–416), but it is unclear if he had *comes rei militaris* (?) of Gratian (*PLRE*, vol. I, 95).

It was not until Theodosius' campaign that Arbogast was promoted to *magister militum*. Indeed, after Bauto's death around 385–386 CE, he received that title through *acclamation* of the *troops* (Zos. *Hist.* 4.53.1; John Ant. *Frgm.* 187), but it was only when Theodosius decided to cope with Maximus Magnus, that he recognized Arbogast's *magister militum* (Zos. *Hist.* 4.47.1, 4.53.1; Burns, 1994, 98 – *magister peditum*). The Frankish general played an important role in the civil war and neutralized Flavius Victor (Magnus Maximus' son) (Oros. *Adv. pag.* 7.35.12; Philost. *Hist. eccl.* 10.8; Greg. T. *Hist. Fr.* 2.9; *Hist.* 4.47.1; Ps.-Aur. Vict. *Epit. Caes.* 48.6; *Cons. Const.* s.a. 388 CE; *Cons. Ital.* s.a.388 CE; Hyd. *Con. ch.* 17). After

Theodosius leaves in 391 CE, he was left as protector of the reinstated Valentinian II and in fact real governor of the western part of the empire (Greg. T. *Hist. Fr.* 2.9; John Ant. *Frgm.* 187). Arbogast's domination and arrogance made Valentinian II complain to Theodosius, but in vain (Zos. *Hist.* 4. 53. 4; John Ant. *Frgm.* 187). The general even slew one of Valentinian's counselors seeking protection under the emperor's cloak.

In order to secure the Roman order, Arbogast revealed himself as military leader and politician. He gradually filled the important positions of the administration with trustful persons, most of them of Frankish origin, which allowed him to get full control over the administration. When necessary, Arbogast launched military campaigns on countrymen (P.Deac. *Vita Ambr.* 30; Greg. T. *Hist. Fr.* 2.9). He conciliated with the pagan Senate in Rome and he was a friend of → Ambrose of Milan (*Vita Ambr.* 30) at the same time.

Valentinian II tried to dismiss Arbogast, and the arrogant reaction of the general, tearing up the dismissal notice and roaring that he would be dismissed only by those who installed him (Zos. *Hist.* 4.53.3; John Ant. *Frgm.* 187; see P.Deac. *Vita Ambr.* 30; Eun. *Frgms.* 9.58.2.22–29; 9.58.2.29–38; Sulpicius Alexander *ap.* Greg. T. *Hist. Fr.* 2.9), shows that he was too powerful and as such might be a threat for Theodosius. It seems that this was realized in Constantinople; Theodosius had not needed another usurper. Initially, he made no any step, but eventually he decided to reduce Arbogast's influence.

In 392 CE barbarian troops reached demilitarized Italy. Ambrose appealed for military help led by Valentinian II, which he accepted (Ambr. *Ob. Val.* 2.23–24). By this Valentinian seeks for his freedom and limitation of Arbogast's influence. This initiative displeased both Arbogast and Theodosius (Ambr. *Ob. Val.* 2.23–24) and was not allowed. This additionally humiliated and depressed the young emperor so much that on May 15, 392 CE, he was found hanged in his residence in Vienna (Matthews, 1975, 238–239). None of the contemporaries blamed Arbogast for this (Ruf. *Hist. eccl.* 11.31), as Ambrose at first thought that the emperor was murdered (Ambr. *Ob. Val.* 33) but later reconsidered (Ambr. *Ob. Theo.* 39–40). The well-known hostility between Arbogast and Valentinian II, and the not Roman origin of he

former, which makes him suspicious in Roman eyes, however, allowed another contrary version appeared and spread (Zos. *Hist.* 4.53.3; John Ant. *Frgm.* 187; Philost. *Hist. eccl.* 11.1), which in fact became the official version (Claud. *Pan. Quarto* 75; 93), and "Theodosian's one" (Croke, 1976, 239–243). Arbogast sent an embassy to Constantinople to reassure his loyalty to Theodosius and claimed suicide of the emperor (Ruf. *Hist. eccl.* 2.31), but in vain. The general, however, did not act like a usurper; he promoted recognition of Arcadius by striking a large number of coins for him (Carson, Humphrey, Sutherland, Mattingly & Pearce, 1997, xxiv; Bland, 2010) and waited for Theodosius' further instructions. In the meantime, he launched the last Roman successful military expedition on the other side of the Rhine (Greg. T. *Hist. Fr.* 2.9). In fact, he would not gain any benefit from murdering the emperor, as he already held all power in the west, including over the emperor. Killing the emperor who was under his full control to secure the throne for someone else (Zos. *Hist.* 5.54.3) seems very implausible and unnecessary for Arbogast. Indeed, the new emperor would also be easily manipulated in military matters, but not as completely as Valentinian II had been. Theodosius, however, took advantage of the situation and decided to get rid of Arbogast, spreading the rumor that he was actually Valentinian's killer. He maintained silence for at least two months, but made crucial changes when removing from the office the praetorian prefect of Rome Nicomachus Flavianus, a friend of Arbogast (*PLRE*, vol. I, 348). This made Arbogast feel unsecure, and on Aug 22, 392 CE, he proclaimed Flavius Eugenius, the *magister* of *scrinium* (Socr. *Hist. eccl.* 5.25. 1; rhetoric: Zos. *Hist.* 4.54.1), as the new emperor in the west (Zos. *Hist.* 4.53.4f, John Ant. *Frgm.* 187; Oros. *Adv. pag.* 7.35.10–11; Socr. *Hist. eccl.* 5.25; Soz. *Hist. eccl.* 7.22;; Philost. *Hist. eccl.* 11.1;). This rebellion was not on religious grounds (McEvoy, 2013) as Arbogast's army included many Christians, and was not prompted by dissatisfaction with the dynastic succession as suggested (Salzmann, 2010). Theodosius raised his son Honorius as the ruler of west in 393 CE (*PLRE*, vol. I, 442) and in 394 CE appeared as Valentinian's avenger, declaring the civil war as "holy." On Sep 5/6, 394 CE, at the battle at the River Frigidus, the western troops were defeated, Eugenius was murdered, and Arbogast fled. On Sep 8, he committed suicide, not accepting the emperor's *clementia* (Claud. *Pan. Tertio* 102f.; *Pan. Quarto*, 91f.; Zos. *Hist.* 4.58.6; Ridley, 1982, 98). With his death, however, his family did not cease and his grandson, also named Arbogast, was even *comes Treverorum* (*PLRE*, vol. II, 128–129).

Arbogast's career is comparable with that of the other non-Roman leaders in Roman army. He kept his loyalty to Theodosius with concentration of great power in his hands, while he acted as an experienced soldier-politician. His career is an important example of a barbarian leader who governed the western part of the empire and followed in the footsteps of his ancestors (Maver, 2016).

Historiography

The most comprehensive modern study on Arbogast's activity remains O. Seeck (1895, 415–419) and *The Prosopography of the Later Roman Empire* (vol. I, 95–97). His military career and actions are discussed in J. O'Flynn (1983, 7–13), T.S. Burns (1994), and A. Maver (2016), where his career is explained as a result of rising the importance of the barbarians in the Roman army. His domination over his nominal sovereign Valentinian II is presented in almost all studies, but most recently in M. McEvoy (2013), while the nature of his rebellion with the enthronization of Eugenius was studied in religious (Salzmann, 2010) and aristocratic context (Matthews, 1975). B. Croke's study (1976) reveals the machinations about Valentinian's death that eventually led to Arbogast's fail, despite his loyalty to Theodosius and the imperial family, as the coins reveal (Carson, Humphrey, Sutherland, Mattingly & Pearce, 1997, xxiv; Bland, 2010, 205–214; see also Szidat, 2012).

Bibliography

Bland, R., "Anonymous Half-Siliquae of the Late 4th Century AD," *NumCe* 170, 2010, 205–214.
Burns, T.S., *Barbarians within the Gates of Rome: A Study of Roman Military Policy and the Barbarians, ca. 375–425 AD*, Bloomington, 1994.
Carson, R.A.G, C. Humphrey, V. Sutherland, H. Mattingly & J.W.E. Pearce, *RIC*, vol. IX, London, 1997, XXIV.
Croke, B., "Arbogast and the Death of Valentinian II," *Hist.* 25/2, 1976, 235–244.
Matthews, J., *Western Aristocracies and Imperial Court AD 364–425*, Oxford, 1975.

Maver, A., "Arbogastova 'germanska' kariera," *AcHi* 24/3, 2016, 561–572.
McEvoy, M., *Child-Emperor Rule in the Late Imperial West, AD 367–455*, Oxford, 2013.
O'Flynn, J., *Generalissimos of the Western Roman Empire*, Edmonton, 1983.
Ridley, R.T., *Zosimus: New History: A Translation with Commentary by Ronald. T. Ridley, Australian Association for Byzantine Studies*, ByAu 2, Canberra, 1982.
Salzmann, M., "Ambrose and the Usurpation of Arbogastes and Eugenius: Reflections on Pagan-Christian Conflict Narratives," *JECS* 18/2, 2010, 191–223.
Seeck, O., "Arbogast," in: *RE*, Gotha, 1895.
Szidat, J., "Historische Fiktion bei Zosimus: der Tod Valentinians II. Überlegungen zu Zos. 4,54, 3/4 und seinen Quellen," *Hist.* 61/3, 2012, 368–382.

IVO TOPALILOV

Archaeus

As H. Jordan has tried to prove (see Jordan, 1912), Archaeus (fl. c. 190 CE?), bishop of Leptis Magna (today Lebda/Libya) in the late 2nd century CE, may owe his existence to scribal inaccuracies and their misinterpretation in modern scholarship. J.-B. Pitra's (1884, vol. VII) mention of Archaeus as one of those early church fathers whose works are lost for us today is based on the Latin translation (Mai, 1840, 707; see also PG, vol. V, 1489f.) of a small Arabic fragment on the dating of → Easter. The translation of the fragment bears the following heading: *Archaei qui post discipulos Domini episcopus fuit leptinanae urbis in Africa* ("From Archaeus who was bishop of the city Leptis [Magna] in Africa after the disciples of the Lord"). The fragment itself is preserved in Codex Arabicus Vaticanus 101 and argues that Easter is to be celebrated on a Sunday. The fragment is not contained in Codex Vaticanus Reginae Suecicae 130 as given by A. Audollent (1924, 1528, following Harnack, 1958, 776, who admitted his mistake to Jordan, 1912, 15/III). Therefore its historical context is the Easter controversy that hit its peak during the reign of Pope Victor I (c. 189–199 CE; see Eus. *Hist. eccl.* 5.23–25).

However, the fragment attributed to Archaeus bears very close parallels to a fragment of → Irenaeus of Lyon (being part of Severus of Antioch's *Contra Additiones Iuliani*, now edited in Hespel, 1968) which was edited by W.W. Harvey (1857, 456, frgm. 27) from Codex addidit 12158 in the British Library (late 6th cent., Egypt; see Wright, 1871, 555–557; Pock, 2012, 25). Hence, H. Jordan concluded that Vaticanus arabicus 101 and British Museum addidit 12158 witness the same fragment of a letter (Hamm, 2003, 353) written by Irenaeus to an inhabitant of Alexandria ("writing to a certain Alexandrian man," trans. Harvey, 1857, 456n1).

In H. Jordan's view, "Archaeus" might have been created relatively early in the transmission of the text by a scribe who took an expression like ἀρχαῖος ἐπίσκοπος ("old bishop") as a reference to a bishop *named* Archaeus. Even if this is the case, the mention of Leptis Magna remains puzzling. In addition to the possible explanations discussed by H. Jordan (1912, 158–160), it may be noted that some (later) traditions connect none other than Victor I, who is called an African by the → *Liber pontificalis* (see Duchesne, 1886, 137), with the city of Leptis Magna (see Oden, 2011, 107–112). An argument for connecting Victor to the expression "archaios episkopos" would require a lengthy and detailed examination of the evidence, so for now it remains an open question.

Hence, there are still some challenging riddles creeping around the (fictitious?) figure and legacy of Archaeus.

Bibliography

Audollent, A., "Archaeus," in: A. Baudrillart, ed., *DHGE*, vol. III, Paris, 1924, 1527–1531.
Duchesne, L., *Le Liber pontificalis*, vol. I, Paris, 1886.
Hamm, U., "Irenäus von Lyon," in: S. Döpp & W. Geerlings, eds., *LACL*, Freiburg, ³2002, 351–355.
Harnack, A. von., *Geschichte der altchristlichen Literatur bis Eusebius*, vol. I/2, Leipzig, ²1958.
Harvey, W.W., *Sancti Irenaei episcopi Lugdunensis libros quinque adversus haereses*, vol. II, Cambridge UK, 1857.
Hespel, R., *Sévère de Antioche: La polémique antijulianiste*, vol. II/A: *Contra Additiones Juliani*, CSCO 295/296, Louvain, 1968.
Höffner, R., "Archaeus," in: S. Döpp & W. Geerlings, eds., *LACL*, Freiburg, ³2002, 57.
Jordan, H., "Wer war Archaeus?" *ZNW* 13, 1912, 157–160.
Mai, A., *Spicilegium Romanum*, vol. III, Rome, 1840.
Oden, T.C., *Early Libyan Christianity: Uncovering a North African Tradition*, Downers Grove, 2011.
Pitra, J.B., *Analecta sacra Spicilegio Solesmensi parata*, vol. II, Paris, 1884.

Pock, S.P., "A Tentative Checklist to Dated Syriac Manuscripts up to 1300," *HJSS*. 15, 2012, 21–48.
Wright, W., *Catalogue of Syriac Manuscripts of the British Museum Acquired since the Year 1838*, vol. II, London, 1871.

WOLFGANG GRÜNSTÄUDL

Archbishop

The earliest use of this title (ἀρχιεπίσκοπος) probably referred to the senior → bishop of an ecclesiastical province that included other metropolitan churches. The first known text in which the title appears is the *Breviarium Meletii*, where it is used to refer to Alexander of Alexandria (Athan. *Apol. sec.* 71, in: Opitz, 1935, vol. II/151, 30–31). → Epiphanius of Salamis assigned it to Peter of Alexandria and to Meletius of Lycopolis, who had tried to extend his authority over the Thebaid to the detriment of the Alexandrian see (Epiph. *Haer.* 68–69; GCS 141.11; 143.8; 154.24). During the same time, two presbyters (→ Priest/Presbyter) – who supported Ursinus' faction – ironically designated Damasus of Rome as archbishop (*Lib. prec.* 22; PL 13.98). In the 5th century CE, this title was assigned to the protagonists of the Christological dispute: → Cyril of Alexandria, John and Domnos of Antioch, Nestorius, Maximilian, Proclus and Flavian of Constantinople, and Menno of Ephesus. → Sozomen defined Simon of Seleucia-Ctesiphon as an archbishop, probably because he was the head of all Christians in the Sasanian Empire (Soz. *Hist. eccl.* 2.9; GCS 61.26). At the Council of → Chalcedon (451 CE), Leo the Great, Anatolius of Constantinople, Dioscurus of Alexandria, Maximus of Antioch, and Juvenal of Jerusalem were referred to as archbishops, although this also applied to Thalassius of Ceasarea, Eusebius of Ancyra, Julian of Cos, Eunomius of Nicomedia, Stephen of Ephesus, and Dionysus of Cyzicus. Maximus of Antioch also addressed the papal legates to the council as archbishops.

In the East, during the 5th and 6th centuries CE, this title was used exceedingly frequently, referring not only to titulars of churches with supra-metropolitan authority (for whom the title of patriarch was beginning to be used) but also to metropolitans. In the West, the title was still rarely used. A canon of the Council of Carthage of 393 CE perhaps referred to the title of archbishop, without formally testifying to the aforementioned usage, but rather stating that the title of *primae sedis episcopus* can only designate primates of ecclesiastical regions (*Breuiarium Hipponense*, CChr.SL 149.40; 150–152). Some 150 years later, Liberatus of Carthage used the title of archbishop for → Capreolus of Carthage. Liberatus' text, however, reflects the way the term was used in the West during the mid-6th century CE, and not the 5th century CE. In the case of Rufus of Thessaloniki and others bishops, furthermore, the term "archbishop" seems to have been retroactively applied by Liberatus (ACO 2.5; 103.22), although Rufus, through his apostolic vicariate, was truly endowed with supra-metropolitan powers over the bishopric of Illyricum. This term was used more appropriately by Liberatus when he referred to patriarchs. In the East, metropolitans were the heads of ecclesiastical provinces, ranking below patriarchs (eparchies). In the 5th century CE, a → metropolitan would occasionally be called an archbishop, as was the case in Athens, but this would obviously not be the same as the archbishop of Constantinople. The autocephalous archbishop was a special case.

Originally, the metropolitan see used to be the main city in a civil province, but if the government decided to divide the province and grant the same status to another city, then its bishop would want to be considered a metropolitan as well. This would be opposed by the existing metropolitan of the original province, and a solution would then be found by giving the newly created metropolitan a purely honorary rank, as an independent or autocephalous archbishop standing directly under the patriarch's authority, without any suffragans. These latter archbishops are found throughout the Middle Ages and differ from other archbishops, such as the autonomous archbishop of Cyprus, who had suffragans and, since 431 CE, was independent from the patriarch of Antioch (Hussey, 1986, 325). When Cyprus of Seville subdivided the *ordo episcoporum* into four categories (patriarchs, archbishops, metropolitans, and bishops), the title of archbishop was being extensively used in the West as well. An archbishop was described as *princeps episcoporum sicut metropolitanus a mensura ciuitatum* (Isid. *Etym.* 7.12.10); therefore, he was *summus episcoporum, tenet enim uicem*

apostolicam, et praesidet tam metropolitanis quam episcopis ceteris (Isid. *Etym.* 7.12.6). Isidore linked this title to a special apostolic authority.

However, it is difficult to determine whether this was actually the case. It is true that the bishops of Arles – who used to be apostolic vicars for Gaul during the 5th and 6th centuries CE – never used this title. Augustine of Canterbury did not use it, although Gregory had subjected all British bishops to his authority (*Brittaniarum uero omnes episcopos tuae fraternitati committimus*; Bede *Hist. eccl.* 1.27.6), not even after the establishment of the metropolitan see of York, when the only difference between the two metropolitan sees was a *distinctio honoris*: [...] *inter Lundoniae et Eburacae ciuitatis episcopos in posterum honoris ista distinctio* (Bede *Hist. eccl.* 1.29). Augustine was ordained *archiepiscopus genti Anglorum*, alternatively referred to as *Brittaniarum archiepiscopus* by Etherius of Arles, although the use of the title should in this case be attributed to Bede (*Hist. eccl.* 1.27; 2.3). → Gregory the Great, in the letters mentioned by Bede, always defined him only as *episcopus* (Bede *Hist. eccl.* 1.27.6; 29; 30; 32). The attribution of this title to Willibrord is more realistic, since he was defined by Bede as *Fresonum archiepiscopum* (Bede *Hist. eccl.* 3.13). In Bede's time, the title was usually applied to metropolitan bishops. The pallium was frequently associated with apostolic authority, which was exercised on the Roman pontiff's behalf, but this did not necessarily imply the use of the title of archbishop (Gregory the Great in Bede *Hist. eccl.* 1.27.7; 29; in Gaul, the pallium was also worn by other bishops who held no supra-metropolitan authority). Gregory, in his letters, attributed the title to several bishops of sees revolving around the Byzantine area, albeit not consistently or exclusively, for instance Cagliari, Corinth, Salona, and Thessaloniki. Gregory never used it for John of Ravenna, whereas Marianianus of Ravenna was called archbishop (CChr.SL 140A; 1096.6–1097.10). In *Ep.* 13.50, Gregory was merely quoting the *Novella* of the *Code of Justinian* 123.13 (CChr.SL 140A; 1061.73) when he referred to a number of trials about which archbishops had to decide. According to the custom of the Constantinopolitan chancery, it was the emperor who installed Gregory as archbishop and patriarch (Greg. M. *Ep.* 1.16b; MGH 1, 22). In Gregory's epistolary, there is a letter to the bishops of Istria who attributed this title to Severus of Aquileia (Greg. M. *Ep.* 1.16.a; MGH 1; 19.2).

Starting from the 8th century, the title was used with increasing frequency in the West as well. Sometimes, it did not even refer to any supra-metropolitan responsibility, as was the case in Spain and Italy. In England, according to Bede, Augustine's successors in Canterbury held a broader authority than that described by Gregory in his letters, and they used the title of archbishop: Wigheard of Canterbury, had he not died prematurely, *accepto ipse gradu archiepiscopatus*, could have ordained all the bishops of Britannia (Bede *Hist. eccl.* 3.29; 4.1); his immediate successor, Theodore of Tarsus, was the first *in archiepiscopis* to receive obedience from all the churches of the Angles (Bede *Hist. eccl.* 4.2; 6). At the council of 742, which was attended by Boniface and six other bishops – including the bishops of Würzburg, Cologne, Bamberg, Eichstätt, and Strasbourg – Carloman elevated *super eos archiepiscopum Bonifacium* and defined him *missus sancti Petri*, thus reviving the Isidorian bond between archbishop and apostolic vicar (MGH.Conc *Karolini aevi* 1.3 [year 742]; see also MGH.L *Sectio* 2, *Capitularia regum Francorum* 1.1; 25.5). In France, during the 8th century, new archbishops were created in Reims and Sens (MGH.Conc *Karolini aevi* 1.34).

Starting from the Carolingian age, all metropolitans would gradually be designated as archbishops, as was the case with those of Rouen, Metz, Mainz, and Bourges. Leo III (795–816 CE) called Metropolitan Arno of Salzburg *archiepiscopum Baiowariorum* (*Ep.* 3; MGH.Ep *Karolini aevi* 3.59.5) and defined his prerogatives over Bavarian bishops as: *in eorum diocesibus archiepiscopatus iura* [...] *habere* (*Ep.* 4; MGH.Ep *Karolini aevi* 3.60.7–8). In the West, the term *archiepiscopatum* was used to indicate the ecclesiastical province (*Archiepiscopatum totius Beneuenti*, Erch. *Hist. Langob. Benev.*36). In the East, canon 19 of the Council of Constantinople of 869 CE still differentiated between archbishops and metropolitans, and this distinction was also reflected in the *subscriptiones*: following a hierarchical order, the first signatories would be the Roman representatives, followed by patriarchs or their representatives, emperors, and then 18 archbishops, metropolitans, and, lastly, bishops without any recognizable order (c. 19; PL 129; 158C–D). Generally speaking, the main

privileges of an archbishop were to ordain all metropolitans in the diocese, their own ordination having been received by a diocesan synod; to convene diocesan synods and to preside over them; to receive appeals from metropolitans and from metropolitan synods; and to censure metropolitans and their suffragans.

See the bibliography for sources and studies of a more specialized nature and historiography on the theme.

Bibliography

Amanieu, A., "Archevêque," in: *DDC*, vol. I, Paris, 927–934.

Butler, D., "Archbishop," in: W. Smith & S. Cheetham, eds., *ADCA*, vol. I, Hartford, 1880, 135.

Chénon, E., "L'apparition du mot archiepiscopus dans les texts franks," *BSNAF*, 1916, 150–159.

Crysos, E., "Zur Entstehung der Institution der autokephalen Erzbistümer," *ByZ* 62, 1969, 263–286.

Grotz, H., *Die Hauptkirchen des Ostens von den Anfängen bis zum Konzil von Nikaia (325)*, OCA 169, Rome, 1964.

Herman, E., "Appunti sul diritto metropolitico nella Chiesa bizantina," *OCP* 13, 1947, 522–550.

Hussey, J.M., *The Orthodox Church in the Byzantine Empire*, Oxford, 1986.

Leclercq, H., "Archevêque," in: *DACL*, vol. I/2, Paris, 1924, 2732–2733.

Leclercq, H., "Pallium," in: *DACL*, vol. XIII/1, Paris, 1937, 931–940.

Orioli, G., "Gli arcivescovi maggiori, origine ed evoluzione storica fino al secolo settimo," *Apoll.* 58, 1985, 615–627.

Örsy, L., "The Development of the Concept of 'Protos' in the Ancient Church," *Kanon* 9, 1989, 83–97.

Popek, A.S., *The Rights and Obligations of Metropolitans*, CLSt 260, Washington DC, 1947.

Tomadakis, N., "I titoli 'vescovo, arcivescovo e proedro' della Chiesa Apostolica Cretese nei testi agiografici," *OCP* 21, 1955, 321–326.

Turner, C.H., *Metropolitans and Their Jurisdiction in Primitive Canon Law*, SECH, Oxford, 1912, 71–96.

ROCCO RONZANI

Archelaus, Acts of

The *Acts of Archelaus*, attributed to an otherwise unknown writer named Hegemonius (the name is found in both the Latin manuscript tradition and in Photius, *Bibl.* cod. 85), is a polemical work against Manichaeism composed in the early 4th century CE (first attested by Cyril of Jerusalem), which proved to be highly influential in subsequent orthodox Christian anti-Manichaean works (Scopello, 2000). It purports to give an account of debates between Mani, the Babylonian founder of Manichaeism, and representatives of orthodox Christianity on the Roman side of the frontier. In actuality, it appears to have been compiled from a variety of Manichaean and other sources to create a fictitious scenario in order to refute arguments of the Manichaean mission to the West. It quickly became the standard reference for biographical details about Mani in Christian literature, beginning with Cyril of Jerusalem (*Cat.* 6), followed by Epiphanius (*Pan.* 3.66), Philastrius (*Div. haer.* 33), Socrates (*Hist. eccl.* 1.22.1–15), Theodoret (*Haer. fab.* 1.26), and a wide array of later Greek, Latin, and Coptic writers (Lieu, 2001, 10–13). Even though the narrative and its setting are undoubtedly fictitious, the *Acts of Archelaus* nonetheless provides important information about the confrontation of nascent orthodox and Manichaean interpretations of Christianity with one another in the late 3rd and early 4th centuries CE, including possibly accurate and authentic Manichaean sources.

Jerome (*Vir. ill.* 72) claims the *Acts of Archelaus* was originally composed in Syriac, and K. Kessler (1889, 87–157) sought to prove this. It is unlikely, however, given the portrayal of Mani as the speaker of an exotic foreign language, and the evident Greek medium through which some of its contents have been accessed by later Syriac writers (Lieu, 1994, 46). The *Acts of Archelaus* survives complete only in a Latin version that, as K. Kessler (1889, 166–171) and L. Traube (1903) have demonstrated, shows signs of significant redaction in comparison to both the order and details of content found in citations of the Greek version in Epiphanius (*Pan.* 3.66.6.1–11, 7.5, and 25.2–31.8), Cyril of Jerusalem (*Cat.* 6.20–35), and Photius (*Bibl.* cod. 85). Likewise, the 10th century CE writer Severus of Asmonina includes narrative details missing from the Latin version, and seems not to know any of the content of the *Acts of Archelaus* following the first debate between Archelaus and Mani. Other Coptic sources also show familiarity with content from the *Acts of Archelaus* (Crum, 1907; Bilabel, 1924; Polotsky, 1932; Klein, 1992).

1. Structure and Content

The *Acts of Archelaus* consists of four more or less distinct parts. Part I is a literary frame, including (a) the introduction of the esteemed layman Marcellus (1–3), (b) Mani's letter to him and his to Mani (4–6), and (c) a summary of Manichaean cosmogony provided by the messenger Turbo (7–13). Part II presents the first encounter and debate between Archelaus and Mani (14–43.2). Part III covers (a) Mani's flight to the village Diodoris (43.3–5), (b) the letter of the local priest (Diodorus in the Latin version, but Tryphon in the Greek) to Archelaus and Archelaus' to him (44–51), and (c) the confrontation between Mani and the priest (52), all as the preamble to (d) Mani's second debate with Archelaus (53–60). Part IV is a closing frame awkwardly appended directly to the second debate, consisting of (a) Archelaus' presentation of Mani's unseemly past (61–65), (b) Mani's flight, capture, and death at the hands of the Persian king (66), and (c) a comparison of Mani's views with those of other heretics (67–68). The Latin manuscript Monacensis adds further heresiological comments after the main text's conclusion (Beeson, 1906, 98 line 18–100, line 13; Vermes, 2001, 151–153), which should not be considered part of the original *Acts of Archelaus*.

Mani's letter to Marcellus (*Acts of Archelaus* 5) highlights two topics: dualism and Christology, and these become the respective subjects of the first (*Acts of Archelaus* 14–43.2) and second (*Acts of Archelaus* 53–60) debates with Archelaus. Mani's argument in both debates is heavily laced with biblical citations from the New Testament. By contrast, the summary of Mani's teachings by Turbo (*Acts of Archelaus* 7–13) makes no reference to biblical proof-texts. This juxtaposition corresponds with the author's desire to portray Mani as the originator of a system wholly alien to Christianity, who superficially added Christian elements as a promotional tactic (*Acts of Archelaus* 65). In between the two debates, Mani is reported raising issues not anticipated in his letter to Marcellus, specifically the contrast between the teachings of the Hebrew Bible and New Testament in the tradition of Marcionite antitheses (*Acts of Archelaus* 44–45). There is good reason to think that some of these complexities in the *Acts of*

Archelaus reflect regional developments of the Manichaean mission in its close encounter with other forms of Christianity in the west, superimposed on the character of Mani within the narrative.

Historiography

The *editio princeps* of the Latin text of the *Acts of Archelaus* was made on the basis of the manuscript Montecassino 371 by L.A. Zacagni (1689, reproduced in Migne, Patrologia Graeca, vol. X, cols. 1405–1528); then with some improvements by M.J. Routh (1848), on which basis S.D.F. Salmond (1871) produced the first English translation. L. Traube's (1903) discovery of the more complete Latin manuscript Monacensis enabled C.H. Beeson (1906) to produce a critical edition (with manuscripts from the 6th to the 12th century CE), which formed the basis for the English translation of M. Vermes (2001).

A substantial amount of the history of scholarship on the *Acts of Archelaus* entails investigation of its historical value, either on the specific events at the center of the story or on the life of Mani more generally (Lieu, 1988 and 1994). Place names given in the text – such as Kaschar/Carchar, Castellum Arabionis, and Stranga – have prompted speculative identifications, while claims made in the text about Mani's origins and his ultimate fate have been compared to other available testimony, at first in Arabic sources and later in recovered Manichaean accounts (Flügel, 1862; Kessler, 1889; Klíma, 1962; Gardner, 2015). The narrative of a series of debates between Mani and Archelaus has been generally understood to be the fictitious creation of the author, and today has no defenders as historical. The *Acts of Archelaus'* biographical notices about Mani's life before and after the fictitious debates with Archelaus, on the other hand, although clearly shaped by polemical purposes (Scopello, 1989 and 1995; Coyle, 2007a and 2007b), have been scrutinized as possibly preserving distorted permutations of information found independently in Manichaean sources (see esp. Gardner, 2020).

A distinct line of research has delved into the possible sources the author may have used in constructing the *Acts of Archelaus*. H. von Zittwitz (1873) proposed that the author utilized an extract from an original letter of Mani, and constructed Mani's side of the debates from the latter's original writings. His suggestions have been explored and developed by I. Gardner (2007) and J. BeDuhn (2007a). Zittwitz similarly, followed by A. Oblasinski (1874) and E. Rochat (1897), considered the summary of Manichaean doctrine found in the discourse of Turbo (*Acts of Archelaus* 7–11) a genuine Manichaean text. More recently, M. Scopello (2000, 542–543) and T. Sala (2007) have further supported its earnest, non-polemical character, although it may derive from a non-Manichaean doxographical report (BeDuhn & Mirecki, 2007, 17–19). Attention has also been given to the author's non-Manichaean sources, including his biblical text (Harnack, 1893; Hansen, 1966). J.L. Jacobi (1877, 493–497) scrutinized the account of Basilides appended to the end of the work, as has B. Bennett (2007), while J. BeDuhn (2007b) identified a Marcionite source embedded in *Acts of Archelaus* 44–45.

Other studies have focused on the *Acts of Archelaus* as an example of polemical literature, examining the author's rhetorical construction of orthodoxy and heresy in comparison with other works from the same period, as well as situating the author's own theological affinities (Lof, 1974; Klein, 1991; Coyle, 2007a and 2007b).

Bibliography

BeDuhn, J., "A War of Words: Intertextuality and the Struggle over the Legacy of Christ in the *Acta Archelai*," in: J. BeDuhn & P. Mirecki, eds., *Frontiers of Faith: The Christian Encounter with Manichaeism in the Acts of Archelaus*, Leiden, 2007a, 77–102.

BeDuhn, J., "Biblical Antitheses, Adda, and the *Acts of Archelaus*," in: J. BeDuhn & P. Mirecki, eds., *Frontiers of Faith: The Christian Encounter with Manichaeism in the Acts of Archelaus*, Leiden, 2007b, 131–148.

BeDuhn, J., & P. Mirecki, "Placing the Acts of Archelaus," in: J. BeDuhn & P. Mirecki, eds., *Frontiers of Faith: The Christian Encounter with Manichaeism in the Acts of Archelaus*, Leiden, 2007, 1–22.

Beeson, C.H., *Hegemonius, Acta Archelai*, GCS 16, Leipzig, 1906.

Bennett, B., "Basilides' 'Barbarian Cosmogony': Its Nature and Function within the *Acta Archelai*," in: J. BeDuhn & P. Mirecki, eds., *Frontiers of Faith: The Christian Encounter with Manichaeism in the Acts of Archelaus*, Leiden, 2007, 157–166.

Bilabel, F., *Ein Koptisches Fragment über die Begründer des Manichäismus*, Heidelberg, 1924.

Coyle, J.K., "Hesitant and Ignorant: The Portrayal of Mani in the *Acts of Archelaus*," in: J. BeDuhn & P. Mirecki, eds., *Frontiers of Faith: The Christian Encounter with Manichaeism in the Acts of Archelaus*, Leiden, 2007a, 23–32.

Coyle, J.K., "A Clash of Portraits: Contrasts between Archelaus and Mani in the *Acta Archelai*," in: J. BeDuhn & P. Mirecki, eds., *Frontiers of Faith: The Christian Encounter with Manichaeism in the Acts of Archelaus*, Leiden, 2007b, 67–76.

Crum, W.E., "Eusebius and the Coptic Church Historians," in: *Proceedings of the Society of Biblical Archaeology*, 1907, 76–77.

Flügel, G., *Mani, seine Lehre und seine Schriften*, Leipzig, 1862.

Gardner, I., "Mani's Letter to Marcellus: Fact and Fiction in the *Acta* Archelai Revisited," in: J. BeDuhn & P. Mirecki, eds., *Frontiers of Faith: The Christian Encounter with Manichaeism in the Acts of Archelaus*, Leiden, 2007, 33–48.

Gardner, I., "Mani's Last Days," in: I. Gardner, J. BeDuhn & P. Dilley, *Mani at the Court of the Persian Kings: Studies in the Chester Beatty* Kephalaia *Codex*, Leiden, 2015, 159–208.

Gardner, I., *The Founder of Manichaeism: Rethinking the Life of Mani*, Cambridge UK, 2020.

Hansen, G.C., "Zu den Evangelienzitaten in den 'Acta Archelai'," in: *StPatr* 7, Texte und Untersuchungen 92, 1966, 473–485.

Harnack, A. von, "Die Acta Archelai und das Diatessaron Tatians," in: *Texte und Untersuchungen* 1, 1893, 137–153.

Jacobi, J.L., "Das ursprüngliche basilidianische System," *ZKG* 1, 1877, 481–544.

Kessler, K., *Mani. Forschungen über die manichäische Religion*, Berlin, 1889.

Klein, W., *Die Argumentation in den griechisch-christlichen Antimanichaica*, Wiesbaden, 1991.

Klein, W., "Ein koptisches Antimanichaikon von Schenute von Atripe," in: G. Wießner & H.J. Klimkeit, eds., *Studia Manichaica, II. Internationaler Kongreß zum Manichäismus*, Wiesbaden, 1992, 367–379.

Klíma, O., *Manis Zeit und Leben*, Prague, 1962.

Lieu, S.N.C., "Fact and Fiction in the *Acta Archelai*," in: P. Bryder, ed., *Manichaean Studies: Proceedings of the First International Conference on Manichaeism, August 5–9, 1987*, Lund, 1988, 69–88; reprinted in: S.N.C. Lieu, *Manichaeism in Mesopotamia and the Roman East*, Leiden, 1994, 132–152.

Lieu, S.N.C., "Introduction," in: M. Vermes, *Hegemonius, Acta Archelai (Acts of Archelaus)*, Turnhout, 2001, 1–34.

Oblasinski, A., *Acta disputationis Archelai et Manetis, Ein Abschnitt au seiner Darstellung und Kritik der Quellen zur Geschichte des Manichäismus*, Leipzig, 1874.

Polotsky, H.J., "Koptische Zitate aus den *Acta Archelai*," *Muséon* 45, 1932, 18–20.

Rochat, E., *Essai sur Mani et sa doctrine*, Geneva, 1897.

Routh, M.J., *Reliquiae sacrae*, vol. IV, Oxford, ¹1818, 119–282; vol. V, Oxford, ²1848, 1–206.

Sala, T., "Narrative Options in Manichaean Eschatology," in: J. BeDuhn & P. Mirecki, eds., *Frontiers of Faith: The Christian Encounter with Manichaeism in the Acts of Archelaus*, Leiden, 2007, 49–66.

Salmond, S.D.F., "Acts of Archelaus," in: A. Roberts & J. Donaldson, eds., *Ante-Nicene Christian Library*, vol. XX, Edinburgh, 1871, 267–419.

Scopello, M., "Simon le Mage, prototype de Mani dans les Acta Archelai," *Revue de la Société Ernest-Renan* 37, 1989, 67–79

Scopello, M., "Vérités et contr-vérités: La vie de Mani selon les *Acta Archelai*," *Apocrypha* 6, 1995, 203–234.

Scopello, M., "Hégémonius, Les *Acta Archelai* et l'histoire de la controverse anti-manichéenne," in: R.E. Emmerick, W. Sundermann & P. Zieme, eds., *Studia Manichaica: IV. Internationaler Kongreß zum Manichäismus, Berlin, 14–18. Juli 1997*, Berlin, 2000, 528–545.

Traube, L., "Acta Archelai, Vorbemerkung zu einer neuen Ausgabe," in:*Sitzungsbericht der kaiserlich Bayrischen Akad. Der Wissensch., phil.-hist. Kl.*, Munich, 1903, 533–549.

Lof, L.J. van der, "Mani as the Danger from Persia in the Roman Empire," *Augustiniana* 24, 1974, 75–84.

Vermes, M., *Hegemonius, Acta Archelai (The Acts of Archelaus)*, Turnhout, 2001.

Zacagni, L.A., *Collectanea monumentorum veterum*, vol. I, Rome, 1689, xii–xvii, 1–105.

Zittwitz, H. von, "Acta disputationis Archelai et Manetis, nach ihrem Umfang, ihren Quellen und ihrem Werthe Untersucht," *Zeitschrift für die historische Theologie* 43, 1873, 467–528.

JASON D. BEDUHN

Archimandrite

The word "archimandrite" derives from the Greek term *archimandrites*, signifying "head (*archos*) of the sheepfold (*mandra*)," and it describes the ecclesiastical office, in the eastern Christian churches, of a senior monastic clergyman (higher in rank than an ordinary *hieromonk*, or ordained monastic). It is usually a priest who is so designated, but in some notable cases in the 5th century CE, the office holder was a monk in → deacon's orders (*hierodiakonos*; Thalassius of Constantinople, *Libellus ad Theodosium*, PG 91.1472; Cyr.Alex. *Ep.* 69), and the *Acts of the Council of Chalcedon* mention an archimandrite who was an unordained monastic. → Cyril of Alexandria's *Letters* speak of the archimandrite Dalmatius, who was a notable leader of the monks of the capital (described as "archimandrite and blessed exarch of the royal monasteries") whose support the → archbishop was anxious to secure in the time of the early 5th-century CE Nestorian controversy (Cyr.Alex. *Ep.* 23). There are a few instances of the title used also for female heads of monastic houses (*archimandríte, archimandrítissa; Vita Dan.* 7; *Vita Eup.* 17), but not for any female monastic office holder of more than purely local remit.

The term is found in use from the mid-4th century CE onward, to designate a monastic superior of a house. It was used first in the Antiochene patriarchal monasteries as the title of the head of the monastic brotherhood in a single house, the western equivalent of abbot. From its original use in Antiochene-Mesopotamian ascetical polity, the use of the term spread to Constantinople. The latter city was originally an obscure part of the broader Syro-Antiochene ecclesial hinterland, following Antiochene liturgical and monastic customs, but it soon emerged as a new ecclesiastical "proving ground" as it quickly became the internationally ascendant imperial capital: an ecclesial advancement that can be discerned at the Council of → Constantinople in 381 CE, but which is especially noted by the early 5th century CE. From this time onward, Constantinople claimed a role of governance over the adjacent churches, taking large parts of the older Syrian and Asia Minor canonical ecclesial territories to itself. At the same time, monasticism developed greatly in the capital at Constantinople, fusing ancient traditions of monastic life and patterns inherited from Syria, Palestine, and Egypt, to make of them the new and energized synthesis of "Byzantine" monasticism – which at the capital itself became a unique "city monachism" as religious houses originally in the suburbs were progressively swallowed up in the rapid urban extension witnessed there. It was at Constantinople that the original concept of archimandrite became redundant when the word *higoumenos* replaced it as the normative term for a monastic superior of a local house. The title archimandrite thus began to assume more of the character of a higher honorific for monastic leaders. In the time of the emperor → Justinian in the 6th century CE (Justin. *Nov.* 5.7.133.4), it emerged as a title equivalent to *exarch* in monastic contexts – that is, a superintendent of monasteries of a large area, reporting to the hierarchical synod. In 7th-century CE Palestine, the term is used in this sense, but with

slight variations, to designate the superior monastic leader of a cluster of houses (Cyr.Scyt. *Vita Sab.* 30). So, for example, there was, under the patriarchate of Jerusalem at this time, one archimandrite appointed to supervise all the cenobitic monasteries and have a leadership role over the *higumens* of the various houses, and another to perform the same office for all eremitical establishments. In later Byzantine usage, the great *sakellarios* at the capital took over the role of the supervision of the city monasteries on behalf of the patriarch, and then the term "archimandrite" began to be applied increasingly as an honorific, for the heads of great monastic establishments, or for exceptionally revered monastic leaders. That Constantinopolitan practice was the chief agency in popularizing the term (Palladius of Helenopolis' *Lausiac History* attributes it freely to the Egyptian monks, esp. Pachomios of Tabennese) is perhaps witnessed today from the fact that this monastic title is not currently applied in the Armenian, Syrian, Chaldaean, Coptic, or Ethiopic church (→ Orthodoxy). This honorific usage among the Byzantines has continued to the present in the eastern orthodox church, while the structural office of superintendency has lapsed in most cases. The office of supervision is now most commonly fulfilled in the eastern churches by the archdiocesan *protosinghel* (from *protosyncellos:* first of the cell companions of the bishop), a priest of monastic order who fulfils the role of the hierarch's chancellor. In later orthodox ecclesiastical usage (esp. among the Greeks), the title of archimandrite came generally to designate a mark of episcopal honor for a senior monastic priest, usually one who does not hold any particular office of governance but who is respected because of his superior education. The title is now widely applied as an honorific for monastic clergy of several years' standing. All archimandrites now have to be monastics in holy orders. The highest rank an orthodox married priest can assume is archpriest or protopresbyter. Slavic orthodox usage currently retains more of the sense of the practice of the Middle Byzantine era, and the title archimandrite is more rarely awarded and still designates a very senior monastic cleric (always a priest today). After 1764 the monasteries of Russia were extensively rearranged into three classes. The title of archimandrite was only permitted for the leaders of the first two classes of monastic establishment, while the heads of the third class were to be styled *higumen*. In Russian liturgical services, the archimandrite who rules a monastery wears a miter (without a **cross** on the top of it, which is reserved for bishops), a monastic mantle with embroidered texts, and carries a staff of office. In other eastern churches influenced by Slavic practice, the title of archimandrite is customarily awarded to those who are shortly to be elevated to the episcopate and announced as an elevation at the same time as the news of their episcopal selection by the local synod.

Bibliography

Anonymous, *Vita Danieli*, ed. L. Clygnet, *ROC*, vol. V, Paris, 1900, 87–96.
Anonymous, *Vita Eupraxiae*, ActaSS, Brussels, 1634–.
Marin, E., *Les moines de Constantinople*, Paris, 1897.
Meester, P. de, *De monachico statu iuxta disciplinam byzantinam*, Rome, 1942.
Pargoire, J., "Archimandrite," in: F. Cabrol & H. Leclercq, eds., *DACL*, vol. I, Paris, 1907, cols. 2739–2761.

JOHN A. MCGUCKIN

Archpriest

The origin of the office of archpriest is unclear. After the permanent establishment of the distinction between bishops and priests, it appears that senior presbyters had certain recognized rights by virtue of their seniority; but there is no evidence of them having been called by a specific name until the late 4th century CE. In individual churches, "archpriest" is applied to the same person in the corresponding passage by Socrates (see below); in later times, the archpriest used to be the oldest presbyter (→ Priest/Presbyter), therefore the most authoritative one. We learn from → Jerome that there was only one archpriest for every episcopal church (Jer. *Ep.* 125.15; CSEL 56, 133). Jerome referred to a figure that was similar to a local clergy official who, as time went by and the presbyterium grew in size, became the head of the presbyterium. He could replace the → bishop in ordinary pastoral activities when the latter was absent, in the same way as the archdeacon would do in administrative and financial matters. Evidence shows that there was competition between archpriests and archdeacons for some time, perhaps with priority initially being given to archdeacons, as can be inferred from the documentation provided by the *Decretals* (the letters containing pontifical decision; *Ut archidiaconus post episcopum sciat se vicarium esse in omnibus, decretall* vol. I, *tit.* 23, *de officio archidiaconi*, 149–150). Regarding the archpriest's responsibilities, disputes were also reported among the local clergy, as in the case which Leo the Great was asked to settle in 448 CE following a request from the priest Paul of Benevento. It involved a newly ordained presbyter named Epicarpius, who, with the agreement of the *primus* and *secundus presbyter*, had been promoted to the head of the Beneventan *presbyterium* by Bishop Dorus. Leo urged the bishop of Benevento to safeguard Paul's rights – which had obviously been infringed by the newcomer – and to abide by the rule of ordination seniority (Leo M. *Ep.* 19; PL 54.709–714).

In the acts of the Roman synod of 499 CE, immediately after the signatures of attending bishops, we find the signatures of Roman priests, headed by Caelius Laurentius, archpriest of Saint Prassede (MGH.AA 12.411). In his letters, → Gregory the Great often mentions the Sardinian presbyter Epiphanius, who was charged with several crimes but always acquitted, and ultimately promoted to archpriest (Greg. M. *Ep.* 3.36; 4.24; 9.198; 14.2). Later, the names of other Roman and Italian archpriests appear in epigraphs (ILCV 1.1123, 1124, 1125; 2.3765) and in the → *Liber pontificalis*. In the *Life of Cono* (686–687 CE), the archpriests of the Roman Church, Peter and Theodore, are mentioned; from the *Life of Sergius I* (687–701 CE), we learn that Theodore was elected pope by a segment of the Romans. In the *Life of Hadrian*, reference is made to the archpriest Peter, who was sent to Constantinople with Peter, abbot of Saint Saba. Both Eugene II (824–827 CE) and Sergius II (844–847 CE) had been archpriests of the Roman church prior to becoming bishops (*LP* 1.368; 371; 511). At the Roman synods of 743 CE and 745 CE, John of Saint Susan placed his signature as archpriest *sanctae Romanae ecclesiae*; in 761 CE, Gregory of Saint Balbina and others are also documented (MGH. Conc *Aevi Karolini* 1.1.25; 38; 40; 44.9; 70.18).

Later, the title of archpriest was gradually applied to the holders of the highest rank in the presbyteral order of the college of cardinals. In the East, the title of archpriest was attributed to a priest, Peter, who was expelled from Alexandria by Bishop Theophilus (see Socr. *Hist. eccl.* 6.9.3; GCS 326.14; Soz. *Hist. eccl.* 8.12; GCS 56.133; → Theophilus of Alexandria). Arsacius (d. 405 CE), who replaced → John Chrysostom as bishop of Constantinople, was referred to as archpriest before his consecration (Phot. *Bibl.* 59; PG 103.112C). Protherius of Alexandria (451–457 CE), who replaced the deposed Dioscurus, had been appointed archpriest by his predecessor (LibCar. *Brev.* 14; ACO 2.5; 125.31). The *Statuta Ecclesiae Antiquae*, a canonical collection from 5th-century CE Gallo-Roman churches, noted the bishops' responsibility to take care of widows, children, and pilgrims through archpriests and archdeacons (c. 7; CChr.SL 148; 167.15–18). In his writings, → Gregory of Tours mentioned a number of archpriests. Their duties may be inferred from various canons of Gallican and Spanish councils. In Merovingian Gaul, an → archpriest could be deposed by bishops with the consent of other presbyters and abbots (CChr. SL 148A; 178). A synod summoned by Aunacharius of Auxerre (561–605 CE) established that archpriests were to watch over the clergy's sexual conduct and give their opinion to secular authorities when action had to be taken against priests under their authority; furthermore, archpriests also seemed to wield a broad authority over the laity in their jurisdiction (CChr.SL 148A; 267–268; 270).

The reform Council of Clichy (626–627 CE), summoned by Chlothar II (584–629 CE), established that *in parrociis*, no layperson could be promoted to the rank of archpriest; instead, the eldest member of the clergy should be appointed (CChr.SL 148A; 295). This provision shows that in some cases, laypeople would have been appointed archpriests, in a way similar to the lay patrons of monasteries. However, a lay archpriesthood never actually came to pass. The Synod of Chalon-sur-Saône (647–653 CE) revoked visiting rights for *iudices publici* to parishes and monasteries, unless these visits were requested by monastery abbots or parish archpriests (CChr.SL 148A; 305). The Synod of Losne (673–675 CE) reiterated the ban on the appointment of laypeople as archpriests (CChr. SL 148A; 316). Canon 20 of the Council of Tours (567 CE) deserves particular attention, because it proves the existence of *archipresbyteri vicani*. In addition to urban archpriests, there is also evidence of rural archpriests who held responsibility over a parish (where a baptismal font was located).

During the Carolingian age, their responsibility extended to broader areas of pastoral care (diaconates), and they were also in charge of the clergy's pastoral activities and conduct (*vicani* presbyters, deacons, and subdeacons). Furthermore, the presence of an archpriest as the first of the royal chaplains or head of the royal chapel is also attested (archpriest in 768 CE: *Fulradus capellanus noster siue archipresbyter*, MGH.D 1, 27). To describe the archpriest's functions, the terms *archipresbyteratus* and *archipresbyteria* were used. In Visigothic Spain, the title of archpriest was used only for urban clerics who took care of the clergy and oversaw the administration of a part of the church's assets that were used for worship (see Vives, 1963). In the *Euchologium sive ritualem Graecorum*, many references to the archpriest's responsibilities can be found, as they developed over time.

See the bibliography for sources and studies of a more specialized nature and historiography on the theme.

Bibliography

Amanieu, A., "Archidiacre," in: *DDC*, vol. I, Paris, 1935, 948–1004.

Amanieu, A., "Archiprêtre," in: *DDC*, vol. I, Paris, 1935, 1004–1026.

"Archipresbyter," in: J.F. Niermayer, C. van de Kieft & J.W.J. Burgers, eds., *MLLM*, Leiden, 2002, 76.

Faure, J., *L'archiprêtre, des origines au droit décretalién*, Grenoble, 1911.

Goar, J., ed., *Euchologium sive rituale Graecorum*, Venice, 1730.

Griffe, É., "Les origines de l'archiprêtre de district," in: *RHEF* 13, 1927, 16–50.

Griffe, É., *Les paroisses rurales de la Gaule*, MD 36, Paris, 1953, 33–62.

Hatch, E., "Archipresbyter," in: W. Smith & S. Cheetham, eds., *ADCA*, Hartford, 1880, 139.

Huard, G., "Considérations sur l'histoire de la paroisse rurale, des origines à la fin du Moyen Âge," *RHEF* 24/102, 1938, 5–22.

Leclercq, H., "Archiprêtre," in: *DACL*, vol. I/2, Paris, 1924, 2761–2763.

Martigny, M., "Archiprêtre," in: *DAC*, Paris, 1877, 59.

Pietri, L., "Archiprêtre," in: *DAn*, Paris, 2005, 197–198.

Sägmüller, J.B., *Die Entwicklung des Archipresbyterats und Dekanats bis zum Ende der Karolingerreiches*, Tübingen, 1898.

Vives, J., ed., *Concilios Visigóticos e hispano-romanos*, Barcelona, 1963.

ROCCO RONZANI

Arian Sermons

Although Arian (non-Nicene; → Arianism) communities were numerous in late antiquity, information about their liturgy and preaching is scarce. The few Latin preserved sermons are thus precious witnesses and require further study.

1. The Verona Collection

The most important collection of sermons is preserved in manuscript LI (49) of the Biblioteca Capitolare in Verona (to which must be added the folio R7v held in Venice in the Giustiniani Recatani Collection). Although not all the texts in this manuscript are Arian, the 15 festal sermons (fols. 1rv + 40r–77v) have been clearly written by a non-Nicene preacher, who was irenic, well-trained and had access to a well-furnished library – notably, the preacher borrow from the works of → Cyprian of Carthage frequently. The collection contains several duplicates, and some of the sermons looks like centos.

In 1922, B. Capelle attributed the writings preserved in the Verona manuscript to the Arian bishop Maximinus (who traveled to Africa in 427 CE, where he had a public debate with → Augustine of Hippo). But 60 years later, R. Gryson convincingly refuted this hypothesis. He argued that the Verona manuscript was copied by a non-Nicene community that did not consider itself persecuted, sometime between 350 and 500 CE. This manuscript may have been produced during the domination of Theodoric (493–533 CE). The geographic origin of these writings is not clear: the manuscript was likely copied in northern Italy (in Verona itself?), but some of the texts it contains could have a non-Italian origin.

The first seven festal sermons are dedicated to the Nativity of the Lord (1), Epiphany (2), Easter (3), Ascension (4, 5, 6), Pentecost (7). Eight hagiographical sermons follow: the Birth of Children (i.e. the Holy Innocents), the Birth of Jean the Baptist (9), the Birth of Saint Stephen (10), the Passion of Saint Peter and Saint Paul (11), the Birth of Saint Cyprian (12), the Birth of Martyrs (13), the Birth of All Martyrs (14–15).

R. Gryson published a semi-diplomatic edition of all these sermons in 1982, and a word index. They remain, however, poorly studied. The study of M. Meslin is an exception. This scholar showed that the festal sermons of Verona combined eastern and western liturgical practices.

2. The Munich Collection

R. Etaix discovered another collection of non-Nicene sermons in manuscript Munich, Bayerische Staatsbibliothek, Codex latinus monacensis 6329. They are distributed discontinuously in a heterogeneous collection of 28 sermons (fols. 120v–136v, 139v–147v, 156v–162v, 166r–173r). Unfortunately, the sermons are difficult to understand, as either the copyist was working poorly or his model was of very low quality. R. Etaix tried to reconstruct the text of these homilies, which may contain some lacunae; his careful conjectures were discussed by R. Gryson in 1993. A new edition of these texts that corrects the few transcription errors and takes into account the conjectures of R. Gryson is needed.

Four sermons on the birth of the Lord (7–10), three sermons on Epiphany (12–14), one on Lent (18), one *In diebus Ieiuniorum* (19), two on Judas (21–22), and one on the betrayal of the Lord (23) are preserved. R. Etaix argued that all these homilies were written by a single preacher. This conclusion was accepted by R. Gryson in 1993. He noted that this preacher knew a Greek version of the Scriptures and was also familiar with the Gothic translation of the Gospels (5th cent. CE). This polyglot preacher may have been Gothic – and may have lived in the eastern part of Illyricum sometime between 350 CE and 450 CE. He was an activist non-Nicene preacher who was willing to warn his audience against deviating from the true faith.

Bibliography

Capelle, B., "Un homéliaire de l'évêque arien Maximin," *Rben* 34, 1922, 81–108.

Etaix, R., "Sermons ariens inédits," *REAugP* 26, 1992, 143–179.

Gounelle, R., "The Arian Sermons (Pseudo-Maximinus)," in: A. Dupont & J. Leemans et al., eds., *Preaching in the Latin Patristic Era*, Leiden, 2008, 168–176.

Gryson, R., "Les citations scripturaires des œuvres attribuées à l'évêque arien Maximinus," *Rben* 88, 1978, 48–80.

Gryson, R., *Littérature arienne latine: Concordance et index*, vols. I–III, digitized and studies of texts 11.1–3, Louvain-la-Neuve, 1980–1983.

Gryson, R., *Le recueil arien de Vérone (Ms. LI de la bibliothèque capitulaire et feuillets inédits de la collection Giustiniani Rescati): Etude codicologique et paléographique*, IP 13, Steenbrugge, 1982a.

Gryson, R., *Scripta Arriana Latina*, vol. I: *Collectio Veronensi: Scholia in Concilium Aquiliense: Fragmenta in Lucam rescripta: Fragmenta theologica rescripta*, CChr. SL 87, Turnhout, 1982b, 47–92.

Gryson, R., "Les sermons ariens latins du *Codex latinus monacensis 6329*: Etude critique," *REAug* 39, 1993, 334–339.

Meslin, M., *Les ariens d'Occident (335–430)*, PaBi 8, Paris, 1967.

RÉMI GOUNELLE

Arianism

In the literary tradition of late antiquity, there is only a single piece of evidence for the word Ἀρειανισμός, in → Gregory of Nazianzus (*Or.* 21.22). The derivative neo-Latin term "Arianism" was constructed during the early modern period and subsequently adopted in the modern European languages (Fr. *Arianisme*; Ital. *Arianesimo*; Ger. *Arianismus*).

Arianism, in its proper sense, both in the history of theology and in the history of dogma, refers to the theological positions or teachings of the Alexandrian presbyter Arius (Ἄρειος), which brought him into conflict with his bishop Alexander. This conflict – initially limited to the Christian community in the city of Alexandria – triggered the so-called Arian controversy in the early 4th century CE, several years before Constantine became sole emperor in 324 CE. From Egypt, the conflict spread to the East, and by the mid-4th century CE it had encompassed the Christian Church of the entire Roman Empire, as a fundamental controversy about a Trinitarian understanding of God. The conflict lasted for decades, until Emperor → Theodosius I assembled the Second Ecumenical Council of → Constantinople in 381 CE, which resulted in an authoritative formulation of the Christian doctrine concerning the → Trinity, any departure from which would be considered heresy (Cod. Theod. 16.1.3; the Creed of Constantinople was perhaps formulated later in connection with the 383 CE Council of Constantinople).

The history of the Arian controversy is inextricably linked to the so-called Constantinian shift. In the course of the Christianization of the Roman Empire, the conflict that had initially been a purely theological debate within the church gained considerable political relevance.

The concept of Ἀρειανισμός employed by Gregory of Nazianzus should be considered primarily as theological polemics. It is indeed debatable whether the polemical notion of Arianism has much to do with its namesake, the Alexandrian presbyter Arius and with his teachings. To be associated with Arius – who had been condemned at the First Ecumenical Council of Nicaea in 325 CE – meant, since that time, that one would be viewed by worldly powers as a heretic to be persecuted.

1. Sources and Transmissions

The Arian controversy, up to the Council of Constantinople in 381 CE, is arguably one of the most well-documented conflicts of the late antiquity. After Arianism was branded as → heresy, however, this record was largely discontinued. In particular, as regards the Arian Churches of the Germanic kingdoms, their structure and their organization, we have to rely on scant source material.

It is particularly important to note that the institution of the synod – which was initially a purely ecclesial assembly – developed, during the course of the conflict of the 4th century CE, into an institutional link between the emperor and the episcopate. In a historical reconstruction of this period, it is therefore necessary to consult the great quantity of documents that emerged from the activities of the synods.

The countless synods of the 4th century CE pose considerable problems for historical research. No records of these assemblies have been transmitted, and historians have to rely on secondary sources, such as later reports or collections that related and preserved a selection of the synods' individual documents. Several reports on the synods' proceedings exist, although only few of them were written by participants. The majority were composed by late antique church historians, whose sources are rarely known.

These reports, naturally, are not neutral, but rather interpret and take positions. As the distance from the reported events grew, however, the accounts began to show more and more traces of legendary and hagiographic influences, particularly when dealing with the later, so-called ecumenical synods (see the late 5th-cent. CE church history of Pseudo-Gelasius Cyzicenus).

In addition, there is an abundance of primary documents related to the synods and transmitted in wholly other contexts. The synods communicate their decisions – which were binding for the entire church – through letters, which provide an important corpus of sources. Imperial letters instructing the bishops have been preserved (esp. instructions issued by Constantine and Constantius II). Most important are the synodal letters themselves, addressed to the whole church, to the emperor, and to local churches particularly affected by the decisions, as well as to individuals. The lists of signatories attached to these letters have been poorly transmitted. Since the circular letters of the synod were often very extensive, church historians tended to provide only regesta or excerpts. In cases where the complete letter is not known, this practice can lead to significant problems of interpretation.

The theological declarations of the synods, usually known by the rather inaccurate term "creed," form a special category of texts. Among these "creeds," the Nicene declaration and the profession of Constantinople in 381 CE (probably finalized in 383 CE?), which was later included in the liturgy as the "symbolum Nicenum," proved to be most influential. A great number of these statements of theological standpoints are directly connected to the dogmatic disputes of the 4th century CE concerning the Trinity. They provided the synods with normative criteria to distinguish true belief from heresy. The oldest preserved synodal confession (which is known only in a Syriac translation) was formulated at an Antiochean synod shortly before the Council of Nicaea (doc. 20). In the case of some synods, we know of individuals

who had to profess such declarations, to prove their adherence to the true faith (Eusebius of Caesarea at the Synod of Nicaea, doc. 24; at the Synod of → Antioch in 341 CE a certain Theophronius of Tyana, doc. 41.3; at the Synod of Seleucia in 359 CE Hilary of Poitiers, doc. 61).

Epiphanius of Salamis recorded a theological debate between two disputants at the Synod of → Sirmium in 351 CE (doc. 47.2), which does not provide an authentic account of the discussion. But this problematic text shows that professional scribes were taking down a protocol of such discussions (→ Epiphanius of Salamis).

The *canones* of a synod, short, thesis-like sentences that clarified disputed questions, especially those related to the order of the church, pose particular problems, because they have their own tradition in collections often dissolved from other documents of a synod.

Documents that were composed in the synodal context prove to be a highly problematic corpus of sources. The reports of the synodal dealings held in connection with the Arian controversy were not handed down. It was only later that these reports were assembled, apparently from church archives, sometimes with a completely different emphasis. Many of these documents were also included in the collections of canon law that began to be assembled in the 5th century CE. It is unknown, however, how the many letters addressed to the bishops were preserved at the episcopal seats. In any case, they were produced in cases of necessity, and cited. Again, the original wording of these letters has not been preserved.

As indicated above, the later church historians included synodal documents in their accounts – in many cases, however, only in the form of regesta – where they were meant to support the authors' opinion. Occasionally, this entailed omissions of passages that did not quite suit the authors' purposes.

A typical trait of the Arian controversy is the transmission of synodal documents in the writings of bishops who were immediately and actively involved in the disputes. This includes, most importantly, the works of → Athanasius of Alexandria, who added whole collections of reports to his own work, or embedded them in his own portrayal of events. In addition to his *De decretis Nicaenae synodi* and his

Apologia secunda, his work *De synodis*, an annotated collection of synodal documents pertaining to the Arian controversy and meant to be used as a preparation for a specific later synod, needs to be taken into consideration. In Alexandria, Athanasius could apparently rely on an excellent archive.

During his exile in Asia Minor in the mid-4th century CE (c. 357 CE), the Gallic bishop → Hilary of Poitiers created a similar annotated collection of synodal documents translated into Latin, to inform his Gallic brothers about the Arian controversy. Unfortunately, Hilary's compilation survives only in a very poor 9th-century CE manuscript that distorted the text to a considerable degree. Nevertheless, it remains the only available source for a great number of synodal documents. A second annotated collection of documents, which Hilary compiled in preparation for the great Imperial Synod of Rimini and Seleucia, again for the benefit of his brothers in Gaul, has been better preserved (*Liber de synodis seu de fide Orientalium*). The sources from which Hilary, as an exile from Gaul, obtained these documents are unknown.

Sabinus, the bishop of Heraklea in the 360s CE, prepared a similar annotated compilation of synodal documents, in this case, however, from the perspective of the critics of the decisions of Nicaea. The text is, unfortunately, wholly lost to us, but it can be partially reconstructed through its use by later church historians.

Another document of key importance for the synods connected to the Arian controversy is a poorly preserved collection of Latin translations of Greek synodal documents, which exists only in a single Veronese manuscript from the 7th century CE (Cod. Ver. 60) and was linked to other similar compilations. Thus, a large part of these synodal documents is no longer in the original language, but rather in translations dating from the late antique period.

Hilary translated from Greek into Latin, but also used, in part, originals that were themselves translations, from Latin into Greek. This means that some of the documents on the Arian controversy have undergone a double process of translation – from Latin to Greek and then back to Latin – which, in certain cases, led to serious distortions of the text. In many documents one cannot even determine the original language with certainty; in some cases one

has to conclude that the text was meant to be bilingual in the first place.

A significant number of synodal documents exists only in Syriac translation, in the late classical Syriac collections of canon law, for example the confession of an Antiochean synod shortly before Nicaea, or – in fragmented form – Constantine's letter of invitation to the Synod of Nicaea (doc. 22). Thus, since we lack a coherent transmission of synodal texts, we are forced to reconstruct them from the very different types of sources available to us.

The confession of the Synod of Nicaea, for example, is first found in a letter by → Eusebius of Caesarea sent from the synod to his brother bishops in Palestine. It was included by Athanasius among the documents he attached to his own writing on the Council of Nicaea. Two Latin versions of this confession (not wholly identical) were cited by Hilary in both of his compilations of synodal texts.

The transmission of documents from the disastrous Synod of Serdica (Sofia) is especially complicated; from the very beginning, the synod had divided into two partial synods (East and West), which mutually excommunicated each other. The church historians offer thorough but conflicting reports on these events. Even the exact date of the synod raises problems, as does the list of participants. The 11 known documents relating to these two divided synods have been preserved in wholly different contexts; some of them have passed through several rounds of translation. In some cases we are lucky enough that a document is available in several versions; in contrast, special problems are created by documents that are, for example, only known through the Verona manuscript or the collections of Hilary or Epiphanius, in highly distorted form. It is important to note that the documents available to us are those composed by the Nicene faction, which, in the long run, prevailed due to the support of Theodosius. We have to assume that the documents of the opposition, those theologians who, after 381 CE, were labeled as Arians, have not been preserved in noteworthy numbers. In this case, the source material is particularly fragmentary.

Because of the extremely complicated state of the many 4th-century CE documents that relate to the Arian controversy, E. Schwartz (1959)proposed in his *Athanasiusstudien* (1904–1911) that a critical edition be made of these sources, which come to us in very different secondary contexts.

2. Arius of Alexandria

The conflict over the description of the relationship between God the Father and God the Son (λόγος) broke out between Arius and his bishop Alexander around the year 315 CE, during the reign of Licinius. Arius was presbyter (→ Priest/Presbyter) at the Baukalis Church in Alexandria (Epiph. *Haer.* 69.1.2). Alexander had been appointed bishop of the Egyptian metropolis in 313 CE, after the short episcopate of Achilles, who, in 311 CE, had succeeded Petrus, a martyr during the new flare-up of the Diocletian → persecution in the East under Maximinus Daia. Arius, who was from Libya (Epiph. *Haer.* 69.1.2), by the time the controversy with his bishop began, was already described as γέρων ("old man").

Very little has been preserved of Arius' own writings. He was quoted by Alexander and his successor Athanasius of Alexandria, but these citations must not be seen as unambiguous evidence of Arius' teachings, since neither Alexander nor Athanasius distinguished between Arius' actual statements and the theological consequences that, in their opinion, resulted from these statements. The only two sources useable for a reconstruction of his views are:
a. the theological declaration that Arius and his supporters read during an Alexandrian council, in order to justify their theological position (doc. 1), and
b. a letter that Arius wrote to Eusebius, the bishop at the Imperial residence in Nicomedia (doc. 15).
Both Arius and his bishop Alexander apparently stood in the Alexandrian tradition of the theology of the *logos* of → Origen. The legacy of Origen was somewhat ambiguous: it allowed different possibilities for interpreting the relationship between God the Father and the *logos*. Arius wanted to emphasize the transcendence and sole divinity of God as opposed to Alexander, who argued for a co-eternal state shared by God and the *logos*. God alone is, for Arius, without beginning, unbegotten, and eternal. In the terminology of negative theology, Arius stresses monotheism with ever-renewed attempts. God can only be understood as Creator. He denies the co-eternal state of the *logos* with God, since

otherwise God would be stripped of his absolute uniqueness. God alone is ἄναρχος (without beginning), and thus he was not always Father. Before all time, and before the creation of the world, God called the Son into being ἐξ οὐκ ὄντων ("out of nothing"). Following Prov 8:22–25, Arius is able to argue that the Son was created. For Arius the *logos* belongs wholly on the side of the divine, but he is markedly subordinate to God.

Arius does oppose the school of theology common in Egypt and in Libya that identifies God the Father and God the Son with one another (→ Modalism), since such a view negates the transcendence of God. In his radical emphasis on God as Creator, he also repudiates the Manichaean belief (→ Mani/Manichaeism) in emanation. Striving to maintain and emphasize the uniqueness of God, Arius formulates a drastic separation between the Father and the Son/*logos* that seems unacceptable to his bishop, who reacts with a stern rebuke.

Alexander and his successor Athanasius, who, at the beginning of the controversy, serves as deacon in Alexandria, essentially confirm these statements of Arius, but they also sharpen them and draw from them what they consider to be their theological consequences. According to Alexander, Arius has assigned the *logos* a place among created beings (which Arius explicitly denies); from that, he draws the conclusion that the Son/*logos* of Arius is merely a man. In this polemic, Arius appears as a representative of a Judaizing theology of adoption, in line with → Paul of Samosata.

In order to understand the virulence of the conflict in Alexandria, one ought not to neglect the fact that Arius, who had found considerable support in Alexandria, had in essence refused to show his bishop obedience. Within the ancient church, this act alone had to be considered heresy.

During an Egyptian synod called by Alexander, Arius and some of his followers in the Alexandrian clergy were deposed, excommunicated, and apparently even driven from the city (doc. 15). In many circles of eastern bishops, the harsh actions of Alexander against his own clerics were criticized. Arius found support among several prominent bishops of the East, including Eusebius of Caesarea, Eusebius of Nicomedia, Paulinus of Tyrus, and others.

A Bithynian and a Palestinian synod expressed their explicit solidarity (doc. 3; doc. 8).

The strong support that Arius received outside of the Egyptian metropolis, and from a whole series of prominent bishops, proves that in this historical situation, the theological ideas of Arius were not especially unusual. Similar statements can be found half a century earlier in the works of Dionysius of Alexandria; both Eusebius of Nicomedia and his far better-known namesake from Caesarea, as well as many others, considered the statements of Arius to be at least conceivable even if they would not subscribe to his opinion. And the two Eusebiuses were authoritative teachers.

Therefore, the conflict that arose from a theological disagreement between the bishop of Alexandria and one of his presbyters began to affect the whole church within the eastern half of the Roman Empire, just as Constantine became the sole ruler after his victory over Licinius.

It could not have taken long until Constantine heard about this conflict dividing the church in the East and sought to mediate. His theological advisor Ossius of Cordoba delivered an Imperial letter to Alexandria, which showed how intensively the emperor had read up on the controversy (doc. 19), even if he did not fully grasp the momentousness of this theological conflict. Constantine perceived it as a rather marginal debate on the interpretation of a particular verse of Scripture (Prov 8:22–25). The whole mission turned out to be a total failure. On his journey, however, the emperor's theological advisor convened a synod in Antioch that condemned Arius and his sympathizers (including the well-known Eusebius of Caesarea), subject to the judgment of a larger synod; this synod also ordained Eustathius as bishop of Antioch, who was known as an outspoken opponent of Origenist theology. Here, it becomes apparent how the character of the controversy began to shift – from a dispute among the adherents of the Origenist tradition to a conflict between the heirs of Origen and their theological opponents.

3. The Council of Nicaea (325 CE)

In order to solve this question, as well as others, Constantine invited the bishops early in 325 CE to a council in his residence at Nicaea, where more than

250 bishops assembled. This council would later be considered as the first ecumenical council. His right to do so was, incidentally, uncontested. With the help of the emperor, a strict anti-Arian majority was able to prevail and to formulate a theological declaration, which, in opposition to the Origenist theological heritage, removed the differentiation between the Father and the Son to a great degree, describing the Son as ὁμοούσιος (one-in-essence) with the Father and emphasizing the co-eternity of the Son and the Father (doc. 26). Eusebius of Caesarea signaled his agreement in a rather convoluted statement, but one can deduce that he was not particularly happy about the decision.

Previously, ὁμοούσιος had not been a term commonly applied to the Trinity. Eusebius asserted that it was introduced by the emperor himself, but this claim is problematic. It seems more likely that the word ὁμοούσιος was used just because Arius had polemically branded it as "Manichaean." According to custom, the conclusions of the synod were declared law, and Arius and a few followers were sent into exile.

After the Synod of Nicaea, Arius himself disappeared from the theological discussion, but the debates continued.

Arius himself recanted after two years and was rehabilitated by a small synod assembled at the command of the emperor (doc. 34). Alexander was reluctant, however, to allow him to return to Alexandria. It seems most probable that Arius died shortly thereafter. The idea of a second condemnation at the beginning of the 330s CE is, most likely, a modern construction caused by the lack of reliable sources for this period, which create more problems than they solve (doc. 27–28; see Brennecke, Heil, Stockhausen & Wintjes, 2007, XXXVI–XXXVIII).

The interpretation that perceives Arius in the context of Origenist Alexandrine teachings about the *logos* was developed by scholars no earlier than the second half of the 20th century. Before that, researchers tended to adhere to the polemical image of Arius framed by his contemporary opponents, like Alexander of Alexandria and especially Athanasius, from whom we have a rich and full corpus of texts. In dogmatic history, it was customary to portray the conflict between Arius and his bishop as a conflict between the Alexandrian and the Antiochean theological traditions. Researchers, following the polemic of Alexander and Athanasius until well into the 20th century, assumed that Arius' beliefs had been shaped by the adoptionism of Paul of Samosata, which emphasized only the humanity of Jesus. Thus, not only Arius himself, but also all those eastern theologians from the Origenist tradition, who had been polemically grouped by Athanasius and others under the name Arians, were considered to be representatives of a theology that saw Christ as a created being, one who was incarnated only in the sense that he was a man adopted by God.

4. After Nicaea

After the Synod of Nicaea, the debate shifted and became a debate over unity and trinity in the Trinitarian notion of God. A large number of the eastern theologians positioned themselves theologically in the diverse Origenist tradition, which stressed the threefold nature of God and spoke of three distinct divine hypostases. In opposition to these beliefs, groups formed who, in criticism of Origen, emphasized the unity of God more strongly and spoke only of one divine hypostasis. This anti-Origenist faction was by no means a monolithic bloc, and we can find significant differences of opinion (e.g. Eustathius of Antioch, Marcellus of Ancyra, or Photinus).

Only after researchers began to position Arius within the Origenist tradition did it become possible to see that the development after Nicaea was not a conflict between Nicenes and Arians, but rather a debate on the nature of divine hypostasis – in particular, on the question whether it was appropriate to speak of one single or three distinct hypostases. The text of the declaration of Nicaea and its definition of the relation between God and the *logos*/Son as ὁμοούσιος, which was apparently problematic for all participants, disappeared from the debates for almost 30 years. The representatives of a position that strongly emphasizes the unity of God, that is to say a single-hypostasis theology, denounced the triple-hypostasis doctrine as Arian (an accusation regularly used by Athanasius of Alexandria, among others) – in other words, as fundamentally heretical. Conversely, the adherents of the triple-hypostasis theory characterized their opponents who argued for a single divine hypostasis or οὐσία as Sabellians – in other words, as followers of that repeatedly rejected theology of identification, which identifies God and Christ (→ Sabellians).

The emperor Constantine formally adhered to the decisions of Nicaea until the end of his life. Eusebius of Nicomedia, however, who had intervened on the side of Arius, became the most important theological advisor to the emperor after 326 CE and acted as spokesman for a triple-hypostasis theology. Due to his important role, the representatives of this theory, who were critical of the conclusions of Nicaea, were often labeled as "Eusebians" (οἱ περὶ Εὐσέβιον) in contemporary polemics.

Athanasius of Alexandria became the most important protagonist of the single-hypostasis theology and he was almost exclusively concerned with his struggle against Arianism. He consistently and categorically denounced all of his opponents (Melitians, Eusebians and all supporters of triple-hypostases theology) as Arians, and the church historians of the 5th century CE followed him.

It was only after Constantine's death in 337 CE that the Latin West was confronted with this conflict. In many cases, the Latin tradition failed to grasp the theological problem with which the Greeks were wrestling. In the West, a theology of the *logos* had been developed by 3rd-century CE writers such as → Tertullian, Hippolytus of Rome (who wrote in Greek), and → Novatian, but the heritage of Origen, which so strongly influenced the East, had hardly any impact on western Christianity. There, theologians were usually content with simple proclamations of the unity of God. After 340 CE, the West, guided by the exiles Marcellus and Athanasius, sided entirely with the single-hypostasis theologians. Thus, by the 340s CE, West and East were opposed to each other not only in ecclesiastic politics, but also with regard to theology.

The political developments after the death of Constantine in 337 CE, when the empire was ruled first by three, and then by two, emperors, had a profound influence on church politics. In their rivalries, the emperors did not hesitate to exploit ecclesiastical conflicts to further their own agenda. Emperor Constans supported "his" church in the West, and his brother Constantius did the same in the East. Thus, the theological antagonism gained a stronger political component and developed into a conflict between the two parts of the empire.

The eastern representatives of the triple-hypostasis theory had defined their theological position at a synod on the occasion of the dedication of the great Church of Antioch (doc. 41). They rejected the charge of Arianism with indignation. In their theological declaration (doc. 41.4, the so-called Second Antiochian Formula), they emphasized their agreement with the apostolic tradition, distanced themselves clearly from Arius, and confessed the co-eternity of the Father and the Son, but in the sense of a theology of three divine hypostases: one ought to bear witness to the Trinity in three hypostases, which with regard to the συμφωνία ("harmony") are one.

The Synod of Serdica (doc. 43), convened by both emperors to settle the grievances between the theological factions and to solve problems regarding the appointment of church dignitaries, turned out to be a disaster. Right from the beginning, the assembly split into an eastern and a western synod, both of which excommunicated each other. The result of this synod was a schism, which nearly led to war between the two brother emperors. The following years were marked by various interesting efforts to reach a reconciliation, both in theological matters and in the sphere of ecclesiastic politics.

In 350 CE, Emperor Constans was murdered by the usurper Magnentius. After a difficult war, Constantius was able to defeat the murderer of his brother and after 353 CE became sole ruler for almost a decade, like his father before him. Theologically, it is significant that the declaration of Nicaea now became important for the single-hypostasis theologians, especially for the western representatives of this position.

The triple-hypostasis theologians, on the other hand, searched for ways to emphasize the unity of the divine Trinity, while still preserving the three divine hypostases. This development was triggered by the theology of Eunomius, who strictly divided the *logos*/Son from God. This theology, misleadingly labelled neo-Arianism, had absolutely nothing to do with Arius. In several very interesting texts dating from the 350s CE, which are, unfortunately, poorly transmitted, there are various theologically complex attempts to describe the divine hypostases in a different form as "alike" (ὅμοιος). In this period, an astounding differentiation occurred among Greek theologians in the East, centered on the possible definitions of the likeness between these hypostases. The differentiation between Homoeousians and Homoians turned out to be crucial. These two groups are then named for the theological words they used in order to describe the relationship between God and his *logos*/Son. These designations originate from the modern scholarship. In contemporary texts, the groups are always personalized and named for important actors: Macedonians, Acacians, and so on. In this context it is important to note that the question of the role of the → Holy Spirit within the Trinity became more and more critical. Emperor Constantius supported the Homoians.

Immediately after the death of Constantius in 361 CE and Julian's failed attempt at an enforced restoration of paganism (→ Pagan/Paganism), we can observe a theological development that did not aim to establish a compromise, but a true solution for the conflict between single- and triple-hypostasis theories: the so-called neo-Nicene theology. This solution was made possible by a differentiation of philosophical terminology that distinguished between οὐσία and ὑπόστασις and expressed the unity of God through οὐσία and the Trinity through the ὑποστάσεις: God is one οὐσία in three ὑποστάσεις. This is a distinction drawn by the Cappadocian Fathers (→ Cappadocians). Representatives of this solution came, interestingly enough, from all different theological schools. This solution, which also included the Holy Spirit, was adopted in the confession probably of the Second Ecumenical Council in 381 CE (or later) and has been regarded as a basic statement of faith by almost all Christian churches, up to the present day. Nevertheless, at first, the other theological camps persisted, both the strict single-hypostasis theologians (the Antiochian schism) and also the different variations of the triple-hypostasis theology, who refused to accept this new solution.

It appears critically important to note that the name Arians remains in the ancient debbate, but only as a designator for the group of the Homoians (Cod. Theod. 16.1.3). It remains uncertain why the name Arians was applied only to this one group. The Homoians did play a leading role in the Imperial church during the reign Valentinians and Valens, after the death of Emperor Constantius. Nevertheless, the great range of theological and ecclesiopolitical positions does not allow one to speak of one theological or ecclesiopolitical party. The term "Homoians" can, in a very general way, be applied to the theologians and church leaders who brought about the confessions of Rimini (doc. 59.11) and Constantinople (doc. 62.5) in 359 CE.

The reversal to Nicene orthodoxy under Emperor Theodosius I marks a deep caesura. Up to the Council of Constantinople and the Synod of Aquileia in 381 CE, the Homoians were a heterogeneous group within the one Imperial Church, based on the confessions of Rimini and Constantinople, and rather active in church politics. Within this group, a broad spectrum of theological opinions existed that were difficult to reconcile with one another. At the Constantinopolitan Council of 381 CE, however, the Homoians were branded as Arians and thus declared to be heretics. Along with the other opponents of the conclusions of Nicaea, they were expelled from the church (c. 1 of the Council of Constantinople in 381 CE).

Nevertheless, the laws of heresy after the Council of Constantinople distinguish terminologically with precision between Arians and other anti-Nicene groups, all of which Athanasius had lumped together as Arians (Cod. Theod. 16.5.6). Only now, after they had been outlawed, did the loose community of Homoians, who had previously formed one group within the church, organize their own Arian Church. After 381 CE, Arians (Ἀρειανοί, Lat. *Arriani*) therefore are no longer a theological group, but rather a juridical term for a church deemed to be heretical and therefore illegal under Imperial law. This Arian Church was based on the declarations of Rimini and Constantinople (359 CE), which had nothing to do with the theology and the theological concerns of Arius and his teaching. At the Constantinople Synod of 359 CE, which had formulated the confession of this so-called Arianism, the Gothic bishop Wulfila had also been present as a participant. Homoian Arianism later became the confession of the Goths and, through the Goths, of most Germanic gentes later pouring into the empire.

As foederati (bound by treaty to Rome or to the emperor), they were not subject to the Imperial religious laws (see c. 2 of the Council of Constantinople) and held fast to this form of Christian belief for over 200 years, until – after the military destruction of the Ostrogothic and Vandal kingdoms – they gradually converted to Catholicism, a process that lasted up to the early 7th century CE. In the East, no traces of this Arianism have been recorded after the time of Justinian.

Historiography

The apologetic writings of Athanasius of Alexandria, Hilarius of Poitiers, the catalogue of heretics of Epiphanius (*Pan.* 69), the ancient church historians → Socrates Scholasticus, → Sozomen, → Theodoret of Cyrrhus (in the West in their Latin translation of *Historia tripartita* of Cassiodor/Epiphanius) and Rufin influenced the image of Arianism until modern times. Research on Arianism in the West only began in modern times in connection with the editions of patristic texts, especially by the Mauristes in the 17th and 18th centuries.

Since the 17th century, the first interpretations of Arianism (Maimbourgh, 1673; Tillemont, 1732; Walch, 1764) were also published, but they were also influenced by the confessional controversies of the early modern period.

The actual study of Arianism only begins with the critical history of the church and dogmas of the 19th century.

In 1840 G. Waitz published a text by Auxentius of Durostorum about the life of the Gothic bishop Wulfila, poorly preserved only in the margin notes of a Paris manuscript, with a homoian confession of Wulfila, which he had to present to Emperor Theodosius shortly before his death. In the nationalism of the late 19th and early 20th centuries, (homoian) Arianism, as witnessed by → Wulfila, was then seen above all in nationalist journalism as the form of Christian faith appropriate to the Germanic peoples. This view of Germanic Arianism was then propagated in National Socialism. This interpretation of Arianism, which basically came from the ancient polemics of Athanasius and claimed that only the historical Jesus was important for the Arianism of the Germanic peoples, must now be regarded as refuted.

Since the anti-Arian polemics of Athanasius and Alexander of Alexandria in particular had associated Arianism with almost all heresies of the ancient church, Jewish and paganism, pagan philosophy and heretical gnosis, the theological backgrounds of Arius were already controversially discussed in the early modern period.

It was important that Alexander of Alexandria brought Arius back to a heretical genealogy about Lucian of Antioch, Paul of Samosata to Artemon and Ebion. Thus Arius was considered a Jewish-influenced theologian in an Antiochenian adoptive tradition of Paul of Samosata, with whom he was connected via Lucian of Antioch (*Urkunde* 14; see Opitz, 1934–1935), for whom Jesus was not divine but only a man.

Thus J.H. Newman (2001; [1]1833) interpreted Arius from an Antiochian Jewish background, while H.M. Gwatkin (1900) saw Arius as influenced by pagan philosophy. For Münscher Arius stood in the tradition of the subordinatian theology of the apologists. Already in the 19th century the question of a theological dependence of Arius on Origen was discussed (e.g. Neander, 1830). In his *Lehrbuch der Dogmengeschichte* (published in several editions and various translations), which was important not only in Germany and shaped generations, A. von Harnack had seen Arius as being influenced by the adoptive theology of Paul of Samosata and Lucian of Antioch, whom he interpreted as an Origenist. Arius was for him a representative of a special Antiochian tradition that combined Adoptianism and Origenism.

Up to the 20th century this interpretation of A. von Harnack (with minor corrections of Loofs and others) remained predominant. In the interpretation of Arianism as Adoptianism, the historical Jesus was important, but it never played a role for Arius and his followers. Research here basically continued the polemics of Alexander and Athanasius. Since the end of the 19th century, the theological developments have been more clearly seen in the groups that had previously been generally called Arians, above all the differentiation of Homoeousians, Homoians and Eunomians, as well as the emergence of Neo-Nicenism.

From the second half of the 20th century a new debate arose about the theological origin of Arianism. T.E. Pollard (1970) had basically argued for the thesis of A. von Harnack in various studies until 1970. He was particularly opposed by M. Simonetti (1975), C. Stead (1994), L.W. Barnard (1970; 1972), and

E. Boularand (1972, who still adopted Antiochene and Alexandrian traditions at Arius). Since these investigations it is clear and meanwhile also *opinio communis* that Arius' theology can be completely explained by the theological and philosophical tradition of Alexandria (Middle Platonism). Thus, since the 1970s, the later course of the Arian controversy could become clearer as a conflict between one- and three-hypostases theology and no longer simply as a conflict between Nicenes and Arians, Since T. Zahn (1867) the definition of the Son of God as ὁμοούσιον τῷ πατρί in Nicaea was regarded as a western tradition (Tertullian), which must now also be regarded as refuted (Stead, 1994). Since then, research on Arianism has concentrated more on Christology, soteriology (Gregg & Groh, 1981) and pneumatology, which, as is well known, was only discussed in the Arian dispute since the late fifties of the 4th century CE.

Since Epiphanius there was the assumption that the Arians, like Apollinarius of Laodicea, denied a human soul of Christ. This view, which Augustine then made known and popular in the Latin West, probably dates back to Eustathius of Aniochia, but had played no discernible role in the conflicts of the Arian dispute itself. Since the 1970s R. Lorenz (1980; 1983) and A. Grillmeier (1979) have emphasized the denial of the human soul of Christ as the real theological concern of Arianism.

Due to the intensive discussions about Arianism since the middle of the last century, the controversies about Arianism were the outstanding topic of the Oxford Conference on Patristic Studies in 1983 (see Ritter, 1990).

In addition to questions of the theological background, questions of historical events and thus of the chronology of the documents handed down have played an important role since L. de Tillemont's (1732) historical investigations. After H.M. Gwatkin's (1900) first modern presentation of the Arian controversy, E. Schwartz (1959) in particular presented studies on the historical reconstruction of the Arian controversy. The authenticity of a letter discovered by E. Schwartz and transmitted only in Syriac from an Antioch synod immediately before the Council of Nicaea, which allowed the prehistory of the Council of Nicaea to be seen anew in many respects, led to a controversy between E. Schwartz and A. von

Harnack which has been repeatedly discussed in the last 100 years but can now be considered settled in favor of the authenticity of this Antioch synod.

The chronology of the documents handed down up to the Council of Nicaea has also been controversially judged. As preparatory work for a collection of the traditional documents requested by E. Schwartz, H.-G. Opitz presented a chronology of the Arian dispute up to 328 in 1934, which could then be considerably improved by W. Schneemelcher (1954), R. Williams (2001), and H.C. Brennecke, U. Heil, A. von Stockhausen & A. Wintjes (2007).

H.-G. Opitz then began in 1934/1935 to collect the documents on the history of the Arian controversy; this project was interrupted by the Second World War and only continued in a modified form in recent years.

In 1988, R.C.P. Hanson published a summary basic monograph, which ends with the Second Ecumenical Council of 381 CE.

Since R.C.P. Hanson's work is in the center of the research the later phases of the Arian controversy, above all the theological and church-political differentiations in Greek theology, the development of Neo-Nicenism, Latin Neo-Nicenism since Ambrosius (Ulrich, 1994; Markschies, 1995; 2000) as well as the homoian kingdoms on the soil of the Western Roman Empire (Berndt & Steinacher, 2014) and the transitions of these kingdoms from the homoian confession of the Synod of Rimini to the Nicene Catholicism.

Bibliography

Anatolios, K., *Retrieving Nicea: The Development and Meaning of Trinitarian Doctrine*, Grand Rapids, 2011.

Ayres, L., *Nicea and its Legacy: An Approach to Fourth-Century Trinitarian Theology*, Oxford, 2006.

Bardy, G., *Recherches sur Saint Lucien d'Antioche*, Paris, 1936.

Barnard, L.W., "The Antecedents of Arius," *VigChr* 24, 1970, 172–188.

Barnard, L.W., "What was Arius' Philosophy?" *ThZ* 28, 1972, 110–117.

Barnes, M.R., & H.H. Williams, eds., *Arianism after Arius: Essays in the Development of the Fourth-Century Trinitarian Conflict*, Edinburgh, 1993.

Barnes, T.D., *The New Empire of Diocletian and Constantine*, Cambridge MA, 1982.

Barnes, T.D., *Athanasius and Constantius: Theology and Politics in the Constantinian Empire*, Cambridge MA, 1993.

Berndt, G.M., & R. Steinacher, eds. *Arianism: Roman Heresy and Barbarian Creed*, Farnham, 2014.

Boularand, E., *L'héresie d'Arius et la Foi de Nicée*, Paris, 1972.

Brennecke, H.C., *Hilarius von Poitiers und die Bischofsopposition gegen Konstantius II.*, PTS 26, Berlin, 1984.

Brennecke, H.C., *Studien zur Geschichte der Homöer: Der Osten bis zum Ende der homöischen Reichskirche*, BHTh 73, Tübingen, 1988.

Brennecke, H.C., "Homéens," in: *DHGE*, vol. XXIV, Paris, 1993, cols. 932–960.

Brennecke, H.C., "Nicäa I. Ökumenische Synode von 325," in: *TRE*, vol. XXIV, Berlin, 1994, 429–441.

Brennecke, H.C., "Lateinischer oder germanischer 'Arianismus'?" in: H. Müller, D. Webe & C. Weimann, eds., *Collatio Augustini cum Pascentio, Einleitung, Text, Übersetzung*, SÖAW 779, Vienna, 2008, 125–144.

Brennecke, H.C., U. Heil, A. von Stockhausen & A. Wintjes, *Dokumente zur Geschichte des arianischen Streites*, fasc. 3: *Bis zur Ekthesis makrostichos* (Athanasius, Werke, vol. III/1), Berlin, 2007.

Brennecke, H.C., A. von Stockhausen, C. Müller, U. Heil & A. Wintjes, *Dokumente zur Geschichte des arianischen Streites*, fasc. 4: *Bis zur Synode von Alexandrien 362*, Athanasius Werke, vol. III/1, Berlin, 2014.

Cavallera, F., *Le schisme d'Antioche*, Paris, 1905.

Gemeinhardt, P., ed., *Athanasius Handbuch*, Tübingen, 2011.

Gregg, R.C., ed., *Arianism: Historical and Theological Reassessments*, Cambridge MA, [2]2006.

Gregg, R.C., & D.E. Groh, *Early Arianism: A View of Salvation*, London, 1981.

Gummerus, J., *Die homöusianische Partei bis zum Tode des Konstantius*, Leipzig, 1900.

Grillmeier, A., *Jesus der Christus im Glauben der Kirche*, vol. I: *Von der apostolischen Zeit bis zum Konzil von Chalkedon*, Freiburg, [1]1979.

Gwatkin, H.M., *Studies of Arianism*, Cambridge UK, [2]1900.

Gwynn, D.M., *The Eusebians: The Polemic of Athanasius of Alexandria and the Construction of the "Arian Controversy"*, Oxford, 2007.

Gwynn, D.M., "Archeology and the 'Arian Controversy' in the Fourth Century," in: D.M. Gwynn & S. Bangert, eds., *Religous Diversity in Late Antiquity*, Leiden, 2010, 229–263.

Gwynn, D.M., *Athanasius of Alexandria: Bishop, Theologian, Ascetic, Father*, Oxford, 2012.

Hanson, R.P.C., *The Search for the Christian Doctrine of God: The Arian Controversy 318–381*, Edinburgh, 1988.

Heil, U., *Avitus von Vienne und die homöische Kirche der Burgunder*, PTS 66, Berlin, 2011.

Kannengiesser, C., *Arius and Athanasius: Two Alexandrien Theologians*, Hampshire, 1991.

Karmann, T.K., *Meletius von Antiochien: Studien zur Geschichte des Ttrinitätstheologischen Streits in den Jahren 360–364 n.Chr.*, RSTh 68, Frankfurt, 2009.

Kopecek, T.A., *A History of Neo-Arianism*, 2 vols., PatMS 8, Cambridge MA, 1979.

Lienhard, J.T., "The 'Arian' Controversy: Some Categories Reconsidered," *TS* 48, 1987, 415–437.

Löhr, W.A., *Die Entstehung der homöischen und homöusianischen Kirchenparteien: Studien zur Synodalgeschichte des 4. Jahrhunderts*, Bonn, 1986.

Löhr, W.A., "Arius Reconsidered," *ZAC* 9, 2005, 524–560; 10, 2006, 121–157.

Loofs, F., "Arianismus," in: *Realencyklopädie für protestantische Theologie und Kirche*, vol. II, Leipzig, 1897, 6–45.

Lorenz, R., *Arius judaizans? Untersuchungen zur dogmengeschichtlichen Einordnung des Arius*, FKDG 31, Göttingen, 1980.

Lorenz, R., "Die Christusseele im arianischen Streit," *ZKG* 94, 1983, 1–51.

Luibhéid, C., *Eusebius of Caesarea and the Arian Crisis*, Dublin, 1981.

Lyman, R., "Arius and the Arians," in: S. Ashbrook Harvey & D.G. Hunter, eds., *OHECS*, Oxford 2008, 237–257.

Maimbourgh, L., *Histoire de l'arianisme depuis sa naissance jusqu'à sa fin, avec l'origine et le progrès de l'hérésie des sociniens*, Paris, 1673.

Markschies, C., *Ambrosius von Mailand und die Trinitätstheologie*, BHTh 90, Tübingen, 1995.

Markschies, C., *Alta Trinità beata: Gesammelte Studien zur altkirchlichen Trinitätslehre*, Tübingen, 2000.

Meslin, M., *Les Ariens d'Occident 335–430*, PatSor 8, Paris, 1967.

Münscher, W., *Handbuch der christlichen Dogmengeschichte*, vol. III, Marburg, 1802.

Neander, A., *Allgemeine Geschichte der christlichen Religion und Kirche*, vol. II/2, Hamburg, 1830.

Newman, J.H., *The Arians of the Fourth Century with an Introduction and Notes by Rowan Williams*, Notre Dame, 2001, [1]1833.

Opitz, H.-G., "Die Zeitfolge des arianischen Streites von den Anfängen bis zum Jahr 328," *ZNW* 33, 1934, 131–159.

Opitz, H.-G., ed., *Urkunden zur Geschichte des arianischen Streites*, fasc. 1–2, (Athanasius, *Werke*, vol. III/1), Berlin, 1934–1935.

Parvis, S., *Marcellus of Ancyra and the Lost Years of the Arian Controversy 325–345*, Oxford, 2006.

Pollard, T.E., *Johannine Christology in the Early Church*, Cambridge MA, 1970.

Ritter, A.M., *Das Konzil von Konstantinopel und sein Symbol*, FKDG 15, Göttingen, 1965.

Ritter, A.M., "Arianismus," in: *TRE*, vol. III, Berlin, 1978, 692–719.

Ritter, A.M., "Arius redivivus?" *ThR* 55, 1990, 153–187.

Schneemelcher, W., "Zur Chronologie des arianischen Streites," *ThLZ* 79, 1954, 393–400.

Schwartz, E., *Zur Geschichte des Athanasius: Gesammelte Schriften*, vol. III, ed. W. Eltester & H.D. Altendorf, Berlin, 1959.

Simonetti, M., *La crisi ariana nel IV seculo*, Rome, 1975.

Stead, G.C., "Homoousios," in: *RAC*, vol. XVI, Stuttgart, 1994, cols. 364–433.

Stockhausen, A. von, & H.C. Brennecke, eds., *Von Arius zum Athanasianum: Studien zur Edition der "Athanasius Werke"*, TU 164, Berlin, 2010.

Tetz, M., *Athanasiana: Zu Leben und Lehre des Athanasius*, ed. W. Geerlings & D. Wyrwa, BZNW 78, Berlin, 1995.

Tillemont, L. de, *Mémoires pour servir à l'histoire ecclésiastiques des six premiers siècles*, vol. VI, Venedig, 1732.

Ulrich, J., *Die Anfänge der abendländischen Rezeption des Nizänums*, PTS 39, Berlin, 1994.

Vaggione, R.P., *Eunomius of Cyzicus and the Nicene Revolution*, Oxford, 2000.

Waitz, G., *Über das Leben und die Lehre des Ulfila: Bruchstücke eines ungedruckten Werkes aus dem Ende des 4. Jahrhunderts*, Hannover, 1840.

Walch, F.G., *Entwurf einer vollständigen Historie der Ketzereien*, vol. II, Leipzig, 1764.

Williams, R., *Arius-Heresy and Tradition*, London, [2]2001.

Zahn, T., *Marcellus von Ancyra*, Gotha, 1867.

HANNS CHRISTOF BRENNECKE

Ariminian Churches in the Germanic Kingdoms

Traditionally the non-Nicene Churches in the Germanic kingdoms have been called Arian (→ Arianism). Scholars, however, have established for some time now that Arianism after the death of Arius (336 CE) was largely an invention by → Athanasius of Alexandria. The misnomer Arian is particularly objectionable for the churches in the Germanic kingdoms which were established during the 5th century CE.

Groups of → Goths within the borders of the Roman Empire had been converted to Christianity in the second half of the 4th century CE; they were baptized in the creed and taught in the doctrinal understanding that predominated at that time. This was not the Trinitarian Creed of the Council of → Nicaea (325 CE) which is regarded today as the first ecumenical council, but the creed that had been accepted at the Councils of Ariminum (today: Rimini/Italy) and Seleucia (today: Silifke/Turkey) in 359 CE and confirmed at the Council of → Constantinople in 360 CE. The Gothic bishop Ulfila (d. 383 CE), who has been considered a preeminent missionary to the Germanic tribes at the time (but might have been only one among a number of missionaries), was present at the latter council and subscribed to its formula of faith. The creed explicitly refused the term *homoousios* ("of one substance," which the Creed of Nicaea used to describe Christ) as non-scriptural, and it therefore did not regard the son to be of the same "substance" (→ *ousia*) as the Father. Instead, it saw the son as "like" (*homoios*) the Father "according to the Scriptures," and can therefore be called a Homoean creed.

However, it makes more sense to speak of "Ariminian" than Homoean Christians, as late antique Christians would define their orthodoxy by listing the ecumenical councils to which they agreed (and also modern scholarship usually speaks of Nicene, not Homoousian Christianity). During late antiquity, the Council of Nicaea became the gold standard of orthodoxy for mainstream Christianity, but imperial legislation considered the Council of Ariminum as an acceptable counter-council: an imperial law of 386 CE decreed that those who followed the doctrine established at the Council of Ariminum (*Ariminensi concilio*) should have the right of assembly (Cod. Theod. 16.1.4). In the Latin West, it was always the Council of Ariminum that stood for Homoean Christianity while the Councils of Seleucia and Constantinople are usually not mentioned (see Ambr. *Epist.* 21; Ruf. *Hist. eccl.* 10.22; Aug. *Coll. Max.* 2; Vic. Vit. *Hist.* 3.5 names Ariminum together with Seleucia). Nicene sources narrating the religious history in the Germanic kingdoms define their Arian opponents as adherents to the Council of Ariminum in 359 CE – up to the Third Council of → Toledo in 589 CE, which ruled in its 17th anathema: "Whoever has not wholeheartedly rejected and condemned the Council of Ariminum (*Ariminense Concilium*), shall be anathema" (Diez & Rodríguez, 1992, 83). Therefore, it is accurate to call the non-Nicene Churches in the Germanic kingdoms Ariminian Churches – not Arian Churches.

1. The Genesis of the Ariminian Churches

The Christian Church(es) developed a threefold ecclesiastical hierarchy during the first centuries of its existence, and in late antiquity, the deaconate (→ Deacon/Deaconess), presbyterate (→ Priest/Presbyter), and episcopate (→ Bishop [Episcopos]) were firmly established (with further differentiations and a few lower offices). Church legislation also ruled that clergy were ordained (→ Ordination) for a specific altar or – in the case of a bishop – for a specific city and diocese. This general rule of territorial episcopal sees was modified when bishops were ordained "for the barbarian peoples" (*in barbaricis gentibus*; → Barbarians) in the 4th century CE (Mathisen, 1997). Here, beyond the border of the Roman Empire, bishops could not be ordained for cities but were ordained for a *gens*. This might have been regarded as temporary solution, but it probably continued to play a role in the churches in post-Roman successor states. Ariminian bishops in the post-Roman Germanic kingdoms have been regarded as "nearly always 'bishops without portfolio'" (Mathisen, 2014, 171). This hypothesis has been criticized, particularly for the Vandal kingdom (→ Vandals; Whelan, 2017, 41–46; see also Heil, 2011, 109), but as sources are almost exclusively Nicene and not concerned with the characteristics and features of the Ariminian Churches, definite answers even to such basic questions as ecclesiastical infrastructure, church life, liturgy, and so forth are lacking.

2. Common Characteristics of the Ariminian Churches in the Germanic Kingdoms

More than 15 years ago, T. Brown noted that the "role of the Arian Church has been one of the most obscure and tendentious aspects of the history of the Ostrogothic kingdom" (Brown, 2007, 417). His judgement is true also for the Ariminian Churches of other Germanic kingdoms, although Ariminianism played a different role in the various Germanic post-Roman successor states (Heil, 2018, 24–25). One issue, however, is true for all Ariminian Churches: no attempt is known to unite the regional churches in the Germanic successor states and establish any kind of superstructure beyond and on top of the regional ecclesiastical infrastructures. No ecclesiology was developed of integrating the various Ariminian Churches within one universal church (but see below for patriarchs in Vandal North Africa). This, however, did not stop Vandal and Ostrogothic kings from lobbying in Constantinople for Ariminian faithful throughout the eastern Roman Empire. All Ariminian Churches probably claimed to be orthodox or catholic to some extent (→ Orthodoxy); however, in the Visigothic and Ostrogothic kingdoms, no condemnation of the *alter communio* ("another communion," a phrase used by Pope → Gelasius I (492–496) to designate a *comes* as belonging to the Ariminian Church; Bronwen & Allen, 2014, 183) occurred in the early decades, and the Visigothic king Leovigild (568–586 CE) differentiated between *religio romana* of the Nicenes and *catholica fides* of the Ariminian Church, only after 580 CE. In contrast, in the Vandal kingdom, discriminations and persecutions of Nicene Christians started early on after the Vandalic conquest in the 430s CE.

Vandal North Africa is also unique, as its Ariminian ecclesiastical hierarchy knew patriarchs (Vic. Vit. *Hist.* 2.13 and 2.54); for instance, Patriarch Jucundus (c. 467–481? CE), formerly house priest of Theuderich, the son of King Gaiseric (428–477 CE) and his successor Cyrila (c. 481?–after 484 CE) who presided over the conference with the Nicene bishops in Carthage in 484 CE, are known by name. It can be assumed that these patriarchs were the leaders of the Ariminian Church in Vandal North Africa, but the use of the term *patriarcha* might indicate that they perhaps intended to establish themselves as the head of all Ariminian Christians. The manifest protests by the Nicene bishops against (the usurpation of) this title shows the impact of the patriarchal claim; it can hardly have been an imitation of the Nicene Church hierarchy for which this designation became common only in the 6th century CE (Norton, 2015). The title of patriarch, however, does not prove any independence of the Ariminian Church from the Vandal court and king. On the contrary, one of the two known patriarchs, Jucundus, was even burned alive on order of King Huneric (477–484 CE) for political reasons.

The Germanic kings were patrons of the Ariminian Churches in their kingdoms. This is particularly notable in the Ostrogothic capital → Ravenna: textual evidence (Agnel. *LPR* 70 and 86) informs us that six Ariminian churches (with baptisteries and episcopal palace) existed in and around Ravenna during the reign of King Theoderic (493–526 CE) and the (former Ariminian) Churches of Santo Spirito and Sant'Apollinare Nuovo, as well as the so-called "Arian Baptistery," are still standing today (Heil, 2018, 26–27). In Rome, Sant'Agata dei Goti, an Ariminian

church (*Arianorum ecclesia*) from the 5th century CE, has partially survived. It is scholarly consensus that Ariminian church building and iconography were not substantially different from their Nicene counterparts (Bockmann, 2014). The Codex Argenteus, the remnants of a magnificent gospel manuscript in Gothic translation (and the main textual witness of Gothic), written with silver (and gold) script on purple-dyed parchment, might have been commissioned by King Theodoric and produced in Ravenna (Munkhammar, 2011, 22; 57–64; Schäferdiek, 2009, 227–230; see Streitberg, 2000, for the Gothic Bible). No comparable material evidence has survived from any of the other Germanic kingdom, but it should be assumed that also the other kings promoted the(ir) Ariminian Churches and built (or appropriated) church buildings particularly in the royal capitals like Toledo in Visigothic Spain and Carthage in Vandal North Africa (see Bockmann, 2014, 203–206, for the latter).

More than just patrons, the Germanic kings might also have been involved in the appointment of bishops and ecclesiastical affairs of the Ariminian Churches. In Visigothic Merida, a dispute between the Nicene bishop Masona of Merida (c. 573–605 CE) and the Ariminian bishop Sunna was decided by an ecclesiastical council instituted by Leovigild (Menze, 2024). Maybe councils instituted by the kings were a common tool for the governance of the (Ariminian) Churches in the Germanic kingdoms, but no information survives. There is no scholarly agreement if the infrastructures and the ecclesiastical hierarchies of the Ariminian Churches were roughly the same as their Nicene counterparts or strikingly different. R.W. Mathisen (2014) notes differences in the terminology of the ecclesiastical hierarchy, and his bishops "without portfolio" paint the image of churches without territorially defined dioceses. No definite → metropolitan orders are known for any Ariminian Church, but it seems that in Visigothic Spain, King Leovigild attempted to install a territorially Ariminian Church only after the Ariminian Council of → Toledo in 580 CE (Menze, 2024).

If true, the lack of territorially organized dioceses would be in stark contrast to Nicene Churches but it befitted churches which primarily served Germanic *gentes* who conquered the respective kingdoms. → Victor of Vita (*Hist.* 1.2) speaks of 80,000 Vandals who must have ruled a few million inhabitants in Roman North Africa, and Victor attempted to categorize all Vandals as Arian heretics (and persecutors). However, the alignment of ethnic identity with religious affiliation has long been questioned in scholarship because the late antique reality was more nuanced. In the first decades of Ostrogothic Italy, *Gothi* were not equated with *Arriani* (Cohen, 2016), and religious boundaries were permeable as the Romano-Nicene bishop Revocatus who converted to Ariminianism under King Huneric in Vandal North Africa, and Masona as Nicene bishop of Merida with Visigothic origin prove. Nevertheless, ethnic affiliation played a role to some extent in the Ariminian Churches: in a papyrus (PItal 34) from Ravenna, dated to 551 CE, Gothic clerics of Sancta Anastasia (today Santo Spirito; see above) identified themselves as members of the "Church of the Gothic Confession" (*eclesie legis Gothorum*: Tjäder, 1982, 102 [who translates *lex* with "law," but see *lex catholica* in Nicetius of Trier's *Letter to Clothsind*, and Greg. T. *Hist.* 5.38; 5.43; Schäferdiek, 2009]). Similarly, at the Third Council of → Toledo in 589 CE, King Reccared (586–601 CE) converted with the *omnis gens Gotorum* ("the whole people of the Goths") to Catholicism (Diez & Rodríguez, 1992, 56–58).

It is notable that the Ariminian Churches never held any councils (but see Heil, 2011, 80–85) before 580 CE when Leovigild summoned a Visigothic-Ariminian Council in his capital Toledo. This speaks for an underdeveloped ecclesiastical life, as church councils played a major role in mainstream Christianity not only concerning theological issues and doctrinal controversies but also for ecclesiastical legislation and governance. Apparently, no theological controversies broke forth within the Ariminian Churches, and hardly any new Ariminian theological trends can be detected for the time period of the post-Roman successor states, although a few Ariminian texts, particularly sermons, have survived from the 5th century CE (→ Arian Sermons; Gounelle, 2018; Szada, 2020, 560–564). Next to nothing can be said about the liturgies in the Ariminian Churches, but all converts to Ariminiansm needed to be rebaptized until the Ariminian Council of → Toledo in 580 CE stopped this custom in Visigothic Spain. The Ariminian doxology of the *Gloria Patri per Filium in Spiritu Sancto* was slightly different from the Nicene

(Heil, 2011, 204–209). A Gothic fragment of an Ariminian liturgical calendar with feasts of → martyrs and saints, presenting a translation of a 4th-century CE Greek martyrology from Constantinople, has survived. The translation of biblical texts known from the Codex Argenteus and the tiny surviving Vandal fragment "'Froia arme' quod interpretatur 'Domine miserere'" (*Collatio Augustini cum Pascentio* 15; Müller, Weber & Weidmann, 2008, 202–203) indicate that specific Gothic(-Vandal) liturgies should be considered a possibility. Similar to the Nicene Churches, the Ariminian Churches took care of the poor as Victor of Vita reports for Vandal North Africa (*Hist.* 3.14).

No educational center for Ariminian clerics has been identified; the papyrus PItal 34 from Ravenna (see above) noted two *bokareis* ("scribes") who might have been part of an Ariminian book production workshop. When Ariminian clerics converted to the Nicene Church, they needed to be re-ordained which could indicate that Ariminian clerics were not regarded as qualified (Council of Orléans, 511 CE, and Council of Zaragoza, 592 CE). No Ariminian monks or monasteries are known from any post-Roman Germanic kingdom, but the papyrus PItal 34 includes also church members designated as *spodei*, that is, "zealous," probably referring to a semi-monastic community in Ravenna (Schäferdiek, 2009, 223–225). The complete disappearance of Ariminian Churches quickly after the fall of the *regna* (in case of the Vandal or Ostrogothic kingdoms) or the conversion of the *gens* (in the case of the Visigoths) speaks against dedicated Ariminian clergy defending their tradition in times of persecutions; however, the lack of any evidence for an underground church might be deceptive.

Historiography

A comprehensive study comparing the Ariminian Churches in the Germanic kingdoms is missing, but U. Heil (2018) offers an excellent introductory overview. U. Heil and C. Scheerer (2022) collect the source material for the Ariminian-Nicene controversy in the post-Roman successor states with up-to-date introduction, translation, and critical commentary. D. König's published PhD-thesis (2008) presents a thorough study of the motifs why the Germanic peoples converted to Christianity. R.W. Mathisen (2014) offers a compelling study on Germanic-Ariminian clergy, in which he questions the territoriality of the Ariminian churches. R. Whelan (2017), focusing on the Ariminan-Nicene quarrels in the Vandal state, gives an in-depth treatment of the controversy in North Africa and argues for structurally similar churches and considers the Ariminian Church to be on equal terms with the Nicene Church. K. Schäferdiek (1967) is a dated but still very valuable study for the ecclesiastical life in the Visigothic and Suebian kingdoms. V. Menze (2024) offers new introductory notes on the infrastructure of the Visigothic-Ariminian Church and its ecclesiology. For the church(es) in the Burgundian kingdom U. Heil's book on Avitus of Vienne is foundational (Heil, 2011).

The most debated issues in scholarship remain questions of ethnicity, but this discussion is not necessarily tied to ecclesiastical affiliation; strictly ecclesiastical are the questions of territoriality of the Ariminian Churches and if they have similar or different structures to the Nicene Churches; related to this is also the question of (relative) tolerance in most Germanic kingdoms with the Vandal kingdom being the notable exception. It might be that the post-Augustinian Nicene Church, battle seasoned by fighting the Donatists (→ Donatism/Donatists), opposed more keenly the new Ariminian overlords than the Nicenes in other Germanic kingdoms and thereby caused stern Vandal repercussions. A new comparative study might lead to a better understanding of the Ariminian Churches.

Main Editions and Translations

Bronwen, N., & P. Allen, *The Letters of Gelasius I (492–496): Pastor and Micro-Manager of the Church of Rome: Introduction, Translation and Notes*, Turnhout, 2014.

Diez, G.M., & F. Rodríguez, eds., *La Coleccion Canonica Hispana: Concilios Hispanos: Segunda Parte*, vol. V, MHS 5, Madrid, 1992.

Heil, U., & C. Scheerer, eds., *Athanasius Werke*, vol. III/2: *Die Entwicklung in den Nachfolgestaaten des römischen Reiches bis zum Symbolum Quicumque*, Berlin, 2022.

Lancel, S., ed. & trans., *Victor de Vita: Histoire de la persécution Vandale en Afrique suivie de La Passion des Sept Martyrs register des provinces et des cités d'Afrique*, Paris, 2002.

Müller, H., D. Weber & C. Weidmann, eds., *Collatio Augustini cum Pascentio: Einleitung, Text, Übersetzung: Mit Beiträgen von H.C. Brennecke, H. Reichert und K. Vössing*, Vienna, 2008.

Nauerth, C., ed. & trans., *Agnellus von Ravenna: Liber Pontificalis: Bischofsbuch*, 2 vols., Freiburg, 1996.

Tjäder, J.-O., *Die nichtliterarischen lateinischen Papyri Italiens aus der Zeit 445–700, Papyri 29–59*, vol. II, Stockholm, 1982.

Bibliography

Bockmann, R., "The Non-Archaeology of Arianism–What Comparing Cases in Carthage, Haïdra and Ravenna Can Tell Us About 'Arian' Churches," in: G.M. Berndt & R. Steinacher, eds., *Arianism: Roman Heresy and Barbarian Creed*, Farnham, 2014, 201–218.

Brown, T.S., "The Role of Arianism in Ostrogothic Italy: The Evidence from Ravenna," in: S.J. Barnish & F. Marazzi, eds., *The Ostrogoths from the Migration Period to the Sixth Century: An Ethnographic Perspective*, Woodbridge, 2007, 417–441.

Cohen, S., "Religious Diversity," in: J. Arnold, S. Bjornlie & K. Sessa, eds., *A Companion to Ostrogothic Italy*, Leiden, 2016, 503–532.

Gounelle, R., "Les sermons Ariens (Pseudo-Maximinus)," in: A. Dupont, S. Boodts, G. Partoens & J. Leemans, eds., *Preaching in the Patristic Era: Sermons, Preachers, and Audiences in the Latin West*, Leiden, 2018, 168–176.

Heil, U., *Avitus von Vienne und die homöische Kirche der Burgunder*, Berlin, 2011.

Heil, U., "Arianismus als theologisches und soziales Problem," in: W. Spickermann, ed., *Frühes Christentum im Ostalpenraum: Beiträge der internationalen Tagung "Frühes Christentum im Ostalpenraum" in Graz vom 1.–3. Juni 2016*, Graz, 2018, 17–37.

König, D., *Bekehrungsmotive: Untersuchungen zum Christianisierungsprozess im römischen Westreich und seinen romanisch-germanischen Nachfolgern (4.–8. Jahrhundert)*, Husum, 2008.

Mathisen, R.W., "Barbarian Bishops and the Churches 'in barbaricis gentibus' during Late Antiquity," *Spec.* 72, 1997, 664–695.

Mathisen, R.W., "Barbarian 'Arian' Clergy, Church Organization, and Church Practices," in: G.M. Berndt & R. Steinacher, eds., *Arianism: Roman Heresy and Barbarian Creed*, Farnham, 2014, 145–191.

Menze, V., "The Quest for an Ecclesiology: The Ariminian-Visigothic Church in Sixth-Century Spain," in: S. Panzram, ed., *How to Govern in the Long Late Antiquity? Institutions, Administration and Legal Structures on the Iberian Peninsula and in North Africa*, Leiden, 2024.

Munkhammar, L., *The Silver Bible: Origins and History of the Codex Argenteus*, Uppsala, 2011.

Norton, P., "Patriarch," in: T. Klauser, ed., *RAC*, vol. XXVI, Stuttgart, 2015, 1091–1109.

Schäferdiek, K., *Die Kirche in den Reichen der Westgoten und Suewen bis zur Errichtung der westgotischen katholischen Staatskirche*, Berlin, 1967.

Schäferdiek, K., "Die Ravennater Papyrusurkunde Tjäder 34, der *Codex Argenteus* und die ostgotische arianische Kirche," *ZKG* 120, 2009, 215–231.

Streitberg, W., *Die gotische Bibel*, vol. I: *Der gotische Text und seine griechische Vorlage*, Heidelberg, [7]2000.

Szada, M., "The Missing Link: The Homoian Church in the Danubian Provinces and Its Role in the Conversion of the Goths," *ZAC* 24, 2020, 549–584.

Whelan, R., *Being Christian in Vandal Africa: The Politics of Orthodoxy in the Post-Imperial West*, Oakland, 2017.

VOLKER MENZE

Aristides of Athens

Aristides of Athens (2nd cent. CE) belongs to the generation of Christian writers known as the Apologists (→ Apologetics). Throughout the 2nd century CE, they worked for the defense of their coreligionists and of their religion during a period in which they perceived Christianity to be quite misunderstood by the civil authorities and the pagan masses. For a long time, Aristides' name was known only through the testimony of → Eusebius of Caesarea (*Hist. eccl.* 4.3.3; *Chron. ad annum* 124–125 ed. Karst, *ad annum* 125 ed. Helm), and hence through Jerome and the martyrologies. In Eusebius' writings, we only learn that Aristides addressed (ἐπιφωνήσας) or delivered (*dedere*) an *apology* to Hadrian on behalf of the Christians at roughly the same time as Quadratus, "a disciple of the apostles," composed his own; he relates it to the emperor Hadrian's initiation into the mysteries of Eleusis during one of his voyages to the East (Autumn 124 CE) and also to → Hadrian's Rescript to Minucius Fundanus, which set the official state policy with regard to the Christians.

In the late 19th century, however, the successive discovery and publication of an Armenian text fragment written by "Aristides, philosopher of Athens" to Hadrian (Aristid. *Apol.* 1–2) as well as that of a complete Syrian text of an "apology" authored by "the philosopher of Athens Marcianus Aristides" and addressed to *Titus Hadrianus Antoninus*, that is, Antoninus Pius, allowed the identification of a Greek version of the *Apology* in the *Book of Barlaam* (pp. 239–255, ed. Boissonade), traditionally attributed to John Damascene. Following this, two Greek papyrus fragments were identified as being part of this *Apology* – which has proved to be an extremely precious tool for judging the liberties taken with the original text by the Syriac and Armenian translators and by the Greek metaphrast. It is thus that the identity of Aristides begins to take shape: he was a "philosopher" – that is, an intellectual by profession – from Athens who bore the Latin *nomen* (name) Marcianus and the Greek *cognomen* (surname) Aristides, and who addressed an apologetic work to one of the two Antonini on behalf of his community.

However, there remained one unknown fact of central importance: For which emperor was the *Apology* intended and, as a consequence, during which period was it written? Was it for Hadrian (P. Aelius Hadrianus), during one of his two stays in Attica, either between 124 CE and 125 CE or during the three winters of 128 CE to 134 CE? Or was it for Antoninus (T. Aelius Hadrianus Antoninus Pius)? The similarity of the titles has, without a doubt, created a great deal of confusion between the two Aelii Hadriani. However, the consistency between Eusebius' indications and the manner in which the Armenian version is addressed allows us to rule clearly in favor of Hadrian.

Whatever the case may be, the evidence provided by the Syriac version cannot be ignored. The strange formulation of the address ("to the almighty Caesar Titus Hadrianus Antoninus") and the use of the Syriac plural for the rest of the imperial titles ("august and merciful") have given birth to two hypotheses. The first posits that the work could have been addressed to the two "emperors" Hadrian and Antoninus during their joint reign following Antoninus' adoption and appointment as Caesar by Hadrian around 138 CE. The other surmises that although the work may have originally been destined for Hadrian, it was finally addressed to Antoninus Pius, either due to the death of Hadrian or to Aristides' need to revise his work in response to changing circumstances. This would also help explain the daring, or simply tactless, condemnation of homosexuality in a work destined for the emperor whose male lover, the young Antinoüs, had drowned in 130 CE. This last hypothesis does not, however, completely rule out an earlier dating of the original text, which, written around 124/125 CE, would be rather similar to the current preserved version.

The problems posed by the existence of different versions are not limited to dating; there is also a discrepancy between the ways in which the races are classified in the prologue and, consequently, in the whole work. The prologue of both versions contains one of the first known examples of the division of the races according to their manner of worship, placing the Jews and Christians into two distinct categories. But this classification differs in each version: while the Syriac text distinguishes between four human "races" (γένη), classified two by two (the barbarians and the Greeks, the Jews and the Christians), the metaphrast of the *Barlaam* distinguishes only three races – the adorers of false gods, further divided into Chaldeans, Greeks and Egyptians, and then the Jews and the Christians. Indeed, it is well known that the presence of the Chaldeans is peculiar to the *Story of Barlaam* – which clearly disqualifies it, in this respect, from being an accurate example of the original *Apology*. Therefore, it is in the Syriac text that we must look for the original outline of the *Apology*.

At any rate, the comparison of the different versions (the Greek text of the *Barlaam*, the Syriac text, the Armenian text, and the papyrus fragments) confirms beyond doubt that the Syriac text is superior to the Greek. The possible liberties taken with the original text appear to be fewer and quite unlike those taken by the Greek metaphrast, who simply omitted a lot.

A final philological difficulty is the presence or the absence, in the original text, of a very harsh passage dealing with the pious practices of the Jews. This rather violent critique is, in effect, only found in the Greek text of the *Barlaam* (Aristid. *Apol.* 14.2 Greek, borrowed from *Barlaam* p. 252, ed. Boisonnade, discourse of Nachor), and not in the Syriac one. It is important to dwell on this possible condemnation so as to be able to judge the relationship between the Jews and the Christians at such an early period of Christian history. We have already shown that, inasmuch as this passage is also present in an earlier paraphrase of the *Apology* integrated into the *Barlaam* (pp. 53–54, ed. Boissonade, discourse of Barlaam), though certainly in a more modest and much freer way than the later one, it is highly likely that the author of the *Barlaam* borrowed it from a previous document, that is, Aristides' *Apology*, and that he did not merely plagiarize himself (from

a few attacks integrated into the discourse of the holy hermit Barlaam, where they are given a much longer development and placed in the mouth of the pagan hermit Nachor). It is therefore necessary to restore this passage to the original *Apology*, despite its harshness.

The structure and purpose of the *Apology* are very simple: to demonstrate the superiority of Christian doctrine over Jewish piety and the practices of idolaters. In a long prologue (*Apol.* 1), Aristides supports his case for the existence of an uncreated God by contrasting God with matter and the created world as well as with the creatures that inhabit it. This is followed by his famous classification of the four human "races" (γένη; barbarians, Greeks, Jews, and Christians) and what he considers to be their origin (Kronos [undoubtedly a Greek interpretation of the Babylonian god Baal], Hellen, Abraham, and Jesus Christ, respectively); these subdivisions are also seen as an introduction to the rest of his work (*Apol.* 2 Syriac).

The opening chapters of the work's corpus (*Apol.* 3–7) are then set aside for the discussion of the barbarians, those who adore the corruptible elements. One naturally thinks of the Chaldeans, held in esteem during the High Empire: the Chaldeans were worshippers of fire and of the stars, which were frequently grouped together with the "elements" of the world. This is certainly how the author of the *Barlaam* understood it, since he uses the word Χαλδαῖοι in place of the probably original βάρβαροι, which never appears in the *Barlaam*. The worship of the different elements is then listed: earth, water, fire, wind (i.e. air), followed by the sun, the moon, and the stars. Oddly, Aristides then examines the worship of humans from old times who have been divinized, becoming simply "dead images," in accordance with the euhemerist theory of deification. Next, he discusses the Greeks and their anthropomorphic gods, who are subject to all the human passions (*Apol.* 8–13). He mentions Kronos (under the name of the Semitic god Kewan in the Syriac version), his son Zeus, then their descendants, including Hephaistos, Hermes, Asclepios, Ares, Dionysos, Heracles, Apollo and Artemis, Aphrodite and Adonis (under the name of the Babylonian god Tammuz in the Syriac version), Rhea, the mother of the gods and lover of Attis, possibly confused with Demeter, and finally Kore. In the middle of these chapters, Aristides includes a digression on the zoomorphic deities of the Egyptians as well as their anthropomorphic gods, such as Isis, Osiris, and Horus (*Apol.* 12). The following chapter (*Apol.* 13) returns to the Greek "poets and philosophers," whose errors and contradictions are denounced, in particular their allegorical exegesis. This approach is considered to have been an effort by the Greeks to preserve the dignity of their myths and of the divinities involved, although it actually denies them of any sacred nature.

The 14th chapter of the *Apology* is devoted to the Jews. It consists of two parts. One treats their moral life, which the author praises, and the other their theology and worship. While praising their → monotheism, he harshly rebukes them for their ritual practices, coming to a rather harsh conclusion: the Jews believe that they know God, whereas in reality they ignore him (*Apol.* 14.3–4; very similar to frgm. 4 of the *Kerygma of Peter*) and have shown him the greatest ingratitude, having gone as far as to put to death the Son he had sent them (*Apol.* 14.2 Greek, missing in the Syriac, except a short passage in *Apol.* 2.4 Syriac, hard to situate in the original text).

The three final chapters (*Apol.* 15–17) are devoted to the Christians, the only γένος to have found the truth. It is essentially their manner of living that he explains: the purity of their morals, their charity toward their neighbors, their faithfulness to God alone, and so on. It is worth noting that this description is essentially a replica of the passage devoted to Jewish morals in the preceding chapter (*Apol.* 14.3 Syriac), even if it is far more developed here. This undoubtedly explains why G.C. O'Ceallaigh (1958) believed that the *Apology* was a Judeo-Hellenistic document that had been superficially Christianized at a later date. Nevertheless, there does remain the fact that it contains veiled references to the evangelical tradition, and that various theological notes are present in the text. One can even identify formulae borrowed from an early creed (in *Apol.* 15.1 Greek or 2.4 Syriac), though it does not seem possible to identify exactly where these formulae stood in the original *Apology*. The conclusion of the work invites to tolerance and discreetly calls for conversion in the form of a peroration (*Apol.* 17.3 Syriac).

The genre of the work is difficult to define. Despite being addressed to the emperor and containing several apostrophes, it does not have the character of an official petition (*libellus*). Rather, it would seem to resemble an informal open letter, an ambassadorial address (πρεσβευτικὸς λόγος), or a hortatory discourse (προτρεπτικὸς λόγος) – which would explain why it was reused as a speech in the *Book of Barlaam*. However, it is much closer in style to a written treatise than to an oratorical work, having much in common with a diatribe (in the modern sense of the term). The probable reworking, for reasons of publication, of what should have been a work of circumstance hinders a precise definition of the original text's purpose and genre. Eusebius later placed it in the polymorphous category of the "apology."

Aristides shows little originality, despite the fact that → Jerome credits him with much eloquence in *De viris illustribus* (20). Two of the most remarkable passages of his *Apology* are borrowed from other writings. The first of these is the prologue (*Apol.* 1), in which God is defined as a perfectly transcendent being, according to the criteria and the terminology of → Middle Platonism. He is described as an unmoved mover, incomprehensible, uncreated, impassive, with neither beginning nor end, without needs, and so on. R. van den Broek (1988) has very convincingly demonstrated that the prologue of the *Apology* is drawn from the same source text as three gnostic writings found at → Nag Hammadi (that is to say → *Eugnostos the Blessed* [NHC III,3 and V,1], the *Wisdom of Jesus Christ* [NHC III,4], and the → *Tripartite Tractate* [NHC I,5]), which was quite probably a Jewish treatise founded on one or several other Middle-Platonic documents).

This, however, does not appear to be the only Jewish source used in the *Apology*. In all likelihood, *Apol* 14.3 Syriac is inspired by one or several other Jewish documents with regard to its positive description of Jewish cultural practice and worship. Some of these possible source documents include an apologetic work praising the πολιτεία of the Jews and another (or perhaps the same) work listing the prayer formulae of *Shemone Esre* and *Shema Israel*.

There are also numerous similarities with contemporary or earlier Christian texts. Thus, it has long been established that there are relatively clear parallels between the *Kerygma of Peter* and the *Apology;* they both define God as a transcendental being, both distinguish between the Christian γένος and that of the Jews, and both contain an exposition on the Jewish understanding and misunderstanding of God, and so on. Again, Aristides' treatment of the Christian way of life (*Apol.* 15–16) seems to have borrowed extensively from a manual on the Christian life, on which the → *Didache* and the *Epistle of Barnabas* (→ Barnabas) also drew a lot of material. Even in the clearly later *Epistle to Diognetus* (→ *Diognetus, Epistle to*) one can see the links between the various texts.

However, the *Apology* also borrows from works other than those previously mentioned. The apologist develops a rather interesting theology in his text. The entirety of his exposition (futility of pagan worship, superiority of Christian truth) is based on a principle, taken from Platonist thought, that is clearly laid out from the prologue onward. God is located in a purely transcendental sphere and is distinguished through his own nature from the materially based gods (i.e. the elements and inanimate idols), in the same way as the uncreated is distinguished from the created, the impassible from the passible, the invisible from the visible, the unlimited from the limited. He is also a cosmic God who moves the world, in accordance with Aristotle's doctrine. According to Stoic principles, it is the beauty of the cosmos that proves his existence. But he is no less the God of Abraham, Isaac, and Jacob, who features prominently in the writings of → Justin Martyr, as the God of the Gospels, which are clearly referenced in the *Apology* (*Apol.* 2.4 Syriac = 15.1 Greek). Thus, the God of Aristides is distinguished from the God of the philosophers. Through his dispensation, he demonstrates his love for mankind, going as far as to send them his only Son. The Son is at the same time described as their "Christ" and the "Son of God"; only a lone passage in the Syriac text (*Apol.* 2.4 Syriac, missing in the corresponding Armenian fragment) describes him as being God himself. What is more, the parallels established between the founders of different religions tend to put him on the same level as Abraham or even Kronos and Hellen. He is undoubtedly a divine man, perhaps God, but not the incarnate *Logos*, coeternal with God, as he appears in Justin's works. The → Holy Spirit is absent in the Syriac version, although he is present in the text of *Barlaam* and also in the Armenian fragment, being simply the agent of the → incarnation. This reservation in affirming the Son's complete divinity is undoubtedly explained by the intended audience, either the imperial authorities who would receive the *libellus* or the pagan population at large, for which the final publication was intended. Only the formulae of an early creed link the author to the Great Church, which indisputably identifies the work as an ecclesiastical text. Incidentally, the reference to salvation ("the door of light," *Apol.* 17.3 Syriac) does not seem to be linked to the passion of Christ. Rather, Aristides sees it as the reward of a holy life, lived in charity and purity, which will be given to the deserving in the world to come, after the final judgement pronounced by Christ.

Despite its apparent weaknesses, the *Apology* of Aristides had a wide distribution. This is attested by the fact that it could be found in many ancient communities (according to Eus. *Hist. eccl.* 4.3.3) and that it was translated into several languages, including Syriac and Armenian, and finally included both in the corpus of the *Book of Barlaam* and in diverse Georgian martyrologies. Without a doubt, the *Apology* was considered to be a venerable masterpiece and thus worthy of the highest consideration.

Historiography

Scholarly research on the *Apology of Aristides* has long been limited to the establishment of his text, either through the separate or consecutive rendering of the various preserved versions (Syr., Gk, Armen., papyrus frgms.: Harris & Robinson, 1891; Outtier, Pierre & Pouderon, 2003) or through attempts to reconstruct the original text (Geffcken, 1907; Alpigiano, 1988), as well as to its commentary (Geffcken, 1907; Pouderon, 2003). However, other avenues have also been explored: the dating of the *Apology* (Grant, 1955), the sources of the *Apology* and of its prologue (O'Ceallaigh, 1958; Lazzati, 1938; Broek, 1988), its structure (Pouderon, 2015), its classification of the races (Pouderon, 2003), its depiction of → Judaism (Pouderon, 2001; Rutherford, 2003), its description of Christianity (Lattke, 2018, preliminary studies for a commentary).

Bibliography

Alpigiano, C., *Aristide di Atene: Apologia*, BPat, Florence, 1988.

Broek, R. van den, "Eugnostus and Aristides on the ineffable God," in: R. van den Broek, ed., *Knowledge of God in the Greco-Roman World*, Leiden, 1988, 202–218.

Geffcken, J., *Zwei griechische Apologeten*, Leipzig, 1907.

Harris, J.R., & J.A. Robinson, *The Apology of Aristides on behalf of the Christians*, Texts and Studies 1/1, Cambridge UK, ¹1891.

Lattke, M., trans, *Aristides: Apologie, Kommentar zu frühchristlichen Apologeten*, vol. II, Basel, 2018.

Lazzati, G., "Ellenismo e cristianesimo: Il primo capitolo dell' Apologia di Aristide," *ScC* 66, 1938, 35–51.

O'Ceallaigh, G.C., "Marcianus Aristides on the Worship of God," *HThR* 51, 1958, 227–254.

Outtier, B., M.-J. Pierre & B. Pouderon, eds., *Texte syriaque, texte grec, fragments arméniens et traductions françaises données à la suite les uns des autres: Introduction et commentaire*, SC 470, Paris, 2003.

Pouderon, B., "Aristide et les juifs: Sur l'authenticité d'*Apol.* 14,2 Ba," *SP* 36, 2001, 76–86.

Pouderon, B., *Les apologistes grecs du IIe siècle*, Paris, 2005, 121–130.

Pouderon B., "La structure de l'Apologie d'Aristide et son chapitre sur les juifs," *JaAj* 3, 2015, 253–282.

Rutherford, W.C., "Reinscribing the Jews: The Story of Aristides' *Apology* 2.2–4 and 14.1b–15.2," *HThR* 106, 2003, 61–91.

BERNARD POUDERON

Aristo of Pella

Aristo of Pella, in Jordan (at one time the capital of Alexander the Great), flourished somewhere between 135 and 178 CE and was a Greek writer of Christian → apologetics. The chief text attributed to him is a record of a dispute; this text, entitled *The Dialogue between Jason and Papiscus*, claims to be the exchange between (the Christian) Jason and (the Jew) Papiscus, and it is regarded as the first piece of Christian writing directed against the Jews and encouraging their conversion to Christianity. Modern scholarship has failed to resolve the issue of whether Aristo was the author of this influential tract. As with very many early Christian sources, the manuscript tradition is sparse, and indeed no complete manuscript has yet been discovered, although various fragments have been preserved. Suggestions by → Clement of Alexandria (in his now lost *Hypotyposeis*) that the author of this dialogue may have been Luke the evangelist are dismissed as "fanstastic" by scholars from the Enlightenment onward (Tolley, 2012, 523).

1. Christian Apologetics in the 2nd Century CE

Aristo's reputation rests on his contribution to the genre of Christian apologetics, which flourished in the 2nd century CE, when no more apostles with firsthand knowledge of Christ's teachings remained alive and a new criterion of authenticity evolved, often allied to martyrdom. The refutations of → heresies contained in these texts paved the way for the doctrinal statements issued by ecumenical councils from the 4th century CE onward, by beginning to draw boundaries round what was acceptable Christian teaching, with heterodox teachings being condemned as heresy, their promulgators anathematized, and sympathizers excommunicated. "Apologies," being the reverse of what their name suggests in common parlance, might be addressed to new converts, Jews, philosophers, and heretics. Aristo's *Dialogue*, purporting to treat the conversion of Jews, was therefore a significant contribution to the literature. From the second quarter of the 2nd century CE, apologetics became one of the most dominant forms of Christian witness, and they often expressed critique of both religious and political practices. They were sometimes dedicated to emperors or others in authority in the hope that they would promote the Christian message and gain socially and politically influential converts to the faith. → Persecutions of Christians and others continued apace, however, until the Edict of Milan in 313 CE, when all religions became subject to imperial toleration and fewer instances of persecution took place. At this stage, although exegesis of the Hebrew Scriptures was taking place, the Jewish faith was not acknowledged as forming a building block for Christianity, but was seen rather as apostasy or heresy, and some Christian apologetics appear anti-semitic today. The Jews were blamed for murdering Christ as well as being resistant to the idea that Christian exegesis reads the Hebrew Bible as prefiguring the New Testament.

2. Historical Context

Eusebius of Caesarea provides useful background to interfaith relations at the time, both those between Jews and Christians and the dominant claims of Roman pagan religion supported by imperial policy (→ Eusebius of Caesarea). He mentions Aristo when he sets the context to the uprising of the Jews that was suppressed by the Roman emperor Hadrian, the so-called Bar Kochba revolt, which took place between 132 and 136 CE and resulted in Hadrian renaming the province Syria "Palaestina" (Eus. *Praep.* 9.21.7; Jacobson, 2001, 45). Eusebius explains how Hadrian forbad the Jews even seeing from afar their ancestral home; "Such is the account given by Aristo of Pella" (Eus. *Hist. eccl.* 4.6).

3. *The Dialogue Between Jason and Papiscus*

The dialogue attributed to Aristo is variously described as a "memorable and glorious" discussion after which Papiscus is converted by Jason to Christ as the true messiah and savior, and he begs Jason to baptize him. → Origen records → Celsus as having seized on it, pilloried it in his *True Account*, saying that it was "fitted to excite pity and hatred instead of laughter" (Or. *Cels.* 4.51–52). Celsus' ridicule seems based on the use of the allegorical interpretation of the Hebrew Scriptures in the recasting of the opening of Genesis as relating to Jesus Christ. Origen defends the disputation (without attributing it to anyone in particular) on account of its honesty and sincerity and in so doing defends the allegorical method itself. Allegory was an evolving means of exegeting Christian teaching, commonly adopted by the theologians from Alexandria such as Origen.

4. Reception of the Text

The reception of the text rapidly acquired legendary status. → Tertullian (*Prax.* 5) and → Hilary of Poitiers' *Commentary on Psalm 2* both refer to it when exegeting the opening verses of Genesis. Origen, → Cyprian of Carthage, Eusebius, and → Jerome refer to the disputation, but all without connecting it directly to Aristo of Pella. Jerome refers directly to the dispute in the start of his commentary *Hebrew Questions on Genesis* when discussing the phrase "In the beginning, God made the heaven and the earth" (Jer. *Qu. hebr. Gen.* 1.1). He argues for a Christological interpretation of this opening phrase of the Bible, in accordance with the Septuagint translation. He does not, however, pass any comment on who the author of the dispute might be, though he juxtaposes it to Tertullian's polemic against Praxeas. The content of the disputation fits with this North African context; Jason, a Hebrew-born Christian (Williams, 1935, 28), is arguing with a Jew from Papiscus in Alexandria about whether prophecies concerning the Christ can be attributed to Jesus rather than the Jewish messiah who is yet to come. Jerome refers to this again in his commentary on Galatians (Jer. *Comm. Gal.* 2.3).

Reference to the dispute in the *Chronicon Pascale*, a 7th-century CE Greek Christian history of the universe, merely replicates what is in Eusebius and has gained no more credibility in the transmission. This disputation was first attributed to Aristo by Maximus the Confessor in the 7th century CE, where a reference to it appears in the Scholia to the *Mystical Theology* of Dionysius the Areopagite (Maximus the Confessor, *Scholia in opera S. Dionysii Areopagitae*; PG 4). John of Scythopolis, in *his* paraphrase of Dionysius the Areopagite, attributes the disputation to Aristo. A later author named Celsus, known as Celsus the African to distinguish him from the heretic attacked by Origen, translated it into Latin. He adds the detail that Jason was by origin himself a Hebrew Christian and his disputant an Alexandrian Jew. Cyprian, bishop of Carthage (c. 200–258 CE), includes Celsus' translation in a long letter addressed to Bishop Vigilius (to be found in PL 6.49–58). The Latin fragment was falsely attributed to Cyprian under the title *Ad Vigilium episcopum de judaica incredulitate*, but this is in fact merely the preface to the text (Quasten, 1975, 195).

Historiography

Contemporary scholars have failed to resolve the issue of authorship. A. von Harnack at one stage thought he had found the entire text in the *Altercation of Simon the Jew and Theophilus the Christian* attributed to Evagrius (PL 20.1165–1182, and see also PG 5.1277–1286), but he later withdrew this assertion, having realized that Celsus the African was not writing in the 5th century CE but at the end of the third. J. Quasten writes confidently of Aristo having been the author even though the text is no longer extant, and he believes it to have been written around 140 CE. As noted above, only fragments remain of the text; recently a further fragment was discovered by J.M. Duffy inside a text by Sophronius, during research into texts at Saint Catherine's monastery on Mount Sinai. To date there is no critical edition of the fragments.

Bibliography

Altaner, B., *Patrologie: Leben, Schriften und Lehre der Kirchenväter*, Freiburg, 1978.

Bardenhewer, I., *Geschichte der altkirchlichen literature*, ²1913, 202–206.

Bovon, F., & J.M. Duffy, "A New Greek Fragment from Ariston of Pella's Dialogue of Jason and Papiscus," *HThR*, 105, 2012, 457–465.

Cross, F.L., & E. Livingstone, *ODCC*, Oxford, 2005.

Dulles, A., *A History of Apologetics*, Eugene, 1999.

Edwards, M., *Catholicity and Heresy in the Early Church*, Farnham, 2009.

Ferguson, E., *EOEC*, New York, 1997.

Frend, W.H.C., *The Archaeology of Early Christianity: A History*, London, 1996.

Geerard, M., & F. Gloire, eds., *CPG*, vol. I., Turnhout, 1983–1998, 43.

Grant, R.M., *Greek Apologists of the Second Century*, Philadelphia, 1988.

Jacobson, D., "When Palestine Meant Israel," *BAR*, 27/3, 2001, 42–47.

Harnack, A. von, *Die Überlieferung der griechischen Apologeten des Zweiten Jahrhunderts in der alten Kirche und im Mittelalter*, TU, vol. I, Leipzig, 1882, 1–11, 115–130.

Klauser, T., *RAC*, Stuttgart, 1941–1950.

Labriolle, P. de, "Ariston de Pella," in: A. Baudrillart, ed., *DHGE*, Paris, 1930, vol. IV, 201–202.

Otranto, G., "La disputa tra Giasone et Papisco sul Christo falsamente attribuita ad Aristone de Pella," *VetChr* 33, 1996, 337–351.

Otto, J.C.T., ed., *Corpus Apologetarum*, vol. IX, Jena, 1972–1974.

Peterson, E., "Aristo of Pella," in: *EC*, vol. I, Vatican City, 1948, 1911.

Quasten, J., "Aristo of Pella," in: *Patr.*, vol. I, Utrecht, 1975, 195–196.

Routh, M.J., ed., *Reliquae Sacrae*, vol. I, Oxford, 1846.

Schürer, E., F. Millar & G. Vermes, *The History of the Jewish People in the Age of Jesus Christ (175 BC–AD 135)*, Edinburgh, 1973, 37–40.

Tolley, H., "Clement of Alexandria's Reference to Luke the Evangelist as Author of Jason and Papiscus," *JThS* 63/2, 2012, 523–532.

Walsh, M., ed., *DCB*, New York, 2001.

Williams, A.L., *Aversus Judaeos: A Bird's Eye View of Christian Apologiae until the Renaissance*, Cambridge UK, 1935.

HANNAH HUNT

Aristotelianism

Aristotle was rarely a major focus of interest among early Christian authors. Allusions to him in patristic writings are often brief and dismissive, criticizing him particularly for his inadequate theology and ethics and his rejection of the immortality of the soul. Aristotelian logic was widely seen as a tool of heretics, particularly in the 4th century CE, when it was associated with Aetius of Antioch and Eunomius of Cyzicus. The only lengthy discussions of Aristotelian philosophy in the patristic era, those of Hippolytus of Rome and Eusebius of Caesarea, are also highly critical.

Yet this negative record is far from the whole story. Christian authors did occasionally invoke Aristotle with approval, particularly in the 5th century CE and later, as pagan philosophy gradually ceased to be seen as a serious rival to the faith. More importantly, they freely made use of Aristotelian ideas without attribution. Some of the most interesting cases of Aristotelian influence were in fact probably not recognized as Aristotelian at all, as we shall see below.

The following discussion will proceed through the various areas of Aristotle's philosophy to which Christian authors offered substantive reaction: theology, ethics, psychology, and logic (including the account of substance in the *Categories*). It will conclude with some examples of more diffuse, and probably unrecognized, Aristotelian influence.

1. Theology

The most frequent complaint lodged by Christian authors against Aristotle was that he denied the operation of divine providence below the sphere of the moon. The attribution of this view to Aristotle, often as an illustration of the shortcomings of his philosophy as a whole, is a patristic commonplace (Tat. *Orat.* 2; Ath. *Leg.* 25; Clem. *Protr.* 5; *Strom.* 5.14; Hipp. *Haer.* 7.19; Or. *Cels.* 1.21; 3.75; Eus. *Praep.* 15.5, 12;

Greg. Naz. *Or.* 14.32; 27.10; Nem. *Nat. hom.* 43; Ambr. *Off.* 1.13; Cyr.Alex. *C. Jul.* 2.15; Thdt. *Affect* 5.47; 6.6). The Fathers saw such a view as both unworthy of God and an invitation to immorality. Their criticisms on this score echoed those of Stoics and Platonists such as the 2nd-century CE Platonist Atticus, whose writings against Aristotle are quoted at length by → Eusebius of Caesarea (*Praep* 15.4–9, 12–13). Interestingly, → Clement of Alexandria supposes that Aristotle was led to his view by a misinterpretation of Ps 36:5, "Your steadfast love, O Lord, extends to the heavens, your faithfulness to the clouds" (Clem. *Strom.* 5.14). Clement offers this example to illustrate his general theory that Greek philosophy was plagiarized from the Hebrew Bible. It is repeated in the commentaries on the Psalms of → Origen, Didymus the Blind, and Cyril of Alexandria (Runia, 1989, 15).

A modern reader is likely to find the attribution of this view of providence to Aristotle puzzling. Aristotle's surviving works scarcely mention providence (πρόνοια), and it would seem to be a fair inference from the theology of the Prime Mover that Aristotle did not believe in providence of *any* kind, whether in the heavens or on earth. Nonetheless, the ancient doxographers agree with Christian authors in attributing a doctrine of solely supralunary providence to Aristotle (Aet. *Plac.* 2.3; D.L. 5.32). Scholars have offered various explanations for this situation. A.J. Festugière suggested that the source for the attribution was the Pseudo-Aristotelian *De Mundo*, which was generally accepted as authentic in antiquity (Festugière, 1932, 226–31). E. Bignone, J. Pépin, and others argued that one ought instead to look to the so-called cosmic theology of Aristotle's lost dialogue, *On Philosophy* (Bignone, 1936; Lazzati, 1938; Guthrie, 1933; Pépin, 1964; according to the reconstruction of these scholars, Aristotle's "cosmic theology" identified God with the ether, the element of the celestial bodies.) More recently, A.P. Bos has argued that the attribution of such a theology to *On Philosophy* is mistaken and that the *De Mundo* is, after all, the most likely source (Bos, 1989; 1993).

The subject is complicated by the variety and obscurity of patristic testimonia regarding Aristotle's theology beyond the subject of providence. Athenagoras reports that Aristotle believes that God possesses a → soul and → body, the body consisting of the ethereal regions and the soul of the reason (λόγος) that moves them (Ath. *Leg.* 6). Clement likewise says that Aristotle believes that God is the soul of the cosmos, although he finds this view inconsistent with the denial of sublunar providence (Clem. *Protr.* 5). Hippolytus states that Aristotle believed in the world soul (Hipp. *Haer.* 1.20) and adverts briefly to his "definition" (actually a description) of God as self-thinking thought (*Haer.* 7.19). → Minucius Felix reports that Aristotle sometimes identifies God with mind (*mens*) or the cosmos and sometimes sets him above the world altogether (Min.Fel. *Oct.* 19). Pseudo-Justin Martyr attributes to Aristotle a belief that God exists "in some kind of aetherial and unchangeable body," although he adds that he also places after the first God certain "intelligible gods" (Ps.-Just. *Exh.* 5–6). Pseudo-Clement of Rome offers a strange report that Aristotle introduced a fifth element, which he calls nameless, "without doubt indicating him who made the world by joining four elements into one" (*Ps.-Clem. R* 8.15). Lactantius remarks that on the subject of God, Aristotle is "at variance with himself […] yet on the whole bears witness that one Mind presides over the universe" (Lact. *Inst.* 1.5). (This report and that of Minucius Felix may well derive from a famous passage of Cicero, which similarly complains of Aristotle's inconsistency: Cic. *Nat. d.* 1.13.) → Ambrose of Milan states that Aristotle recognized two first principles, matter and form, along with a third that he (Aristotle) calls "active" (*operatorium*) and that is sufficient to bring things into existence (Ambr. *Hex.* 1.1). Eusebius quotes the report of Pseudo-Plutarch that Aristotle believes the highest God to be a separate form "riding upon" the celestial sphere, while each of the lower spheres is a living being governed by its own soul (Eus. *Praep.* 14.16). → Cyril of Alexandria repeats the description of God as a separate form, but adds that Aristotle *denies* that the cosmos has soul or reason (Cyr.Alex. *C. Jul.* 1.39; 2.36).

This is not the place to attempt to reconcile these various reports, an effort that in any case would also require taking into account the surviving fragments and non-Christian testimonia. (See the works cited earlier by Pépin, Bos, and others for some representative attempts.) For the most part, Christian authors had little interest in Aristotle's theology for its own sake. They cited it primarily when doing so suited their polemical aims, either in support of monotheism or in the course of arguing that differences among the philosophers discredited pagan philosophy as a whole.

In view of their general hostility, it is surprising that they did not say more about an aspect of Aristotle's theology that Christians of later eras would find highly objectionable: his belief that the cosmos is uncreated and eternal. These points are mentioned only occasionally and without much attention (Hipp. *Haer.* 1.20; 7.19; Eus. *Praep.* 15.6; Lact. *Inst.* 2.10; 7.1). It seems unlikely that this aspect of Aristotle's teaching was not widely known, for it is mentioned explicitly by Cicero (*Acad. post.* 2.38) and → Philo of Alexandria (*Aet.* 3). The first Christian works to give it focused attention were the *Theophrastos* of Aeneas of Gaza and the *Ammonios* of Zacharias of Mytilene, along with the *Refutation of Certain Aristotelian Doctrines* by Pseudo-Justin Martyr, all dating from the late 5th century CE (see Champion, 2014; Martin, 1989).

2. Ethics

Apart from his denial of providence, the other teaching of Aristotle that Christian authors most frequently criticized was his belief that happiness requires not only virtue but also bodily and external goods. The fundamental objection was stated by → Tatian: on this view "those who have neither beauty, nor wealth, nor bodily strength, nor high birth, have no happiness" (Tat. *Orat.* 2). Clement similarly complains that, according to Aristotle, the poor, diseased, and slaves cannot achieve happiness (Clem. *Strom.* 2.21), and similar criticisms are made by Eusebius (*Praep.* 11.4; 15.3–4) and → Theodoret of Cyrrhus (*Affect.* 11.13–14). → Gregory of Nazianzus probably has this aspect of Aristotle's teaching in mind in referring dismissively to its merely human character (τὸ ἀνθρωπικὸν τῶν δογμάτων; Greg. Naz. *Or.* 27.10).

It is likely that these authors were reacting to Aristotle's views as presented in the doxographical tradition, or perhaps in works now lost, rather than to the currently surviving ethical works. Diogenes Laertius gives a highly compressed account of Aristotle's ethics that says little more than that Aristotle held all three types of goods to be necessary for happiness

(D.L. 5.30). The view expressed in the *Nicomachean Ethics* is considerably more complex. It is true that Aristotle there concedes that bodily and external goods are necessary for happiness, but only as an "accessory" required to perform certain kinds of virtuous acts, not as intrinsic to the nature of happiness as such (Arist. *Eth. Nic.* 1.8, 10). It might be possible to reconcile this view with the concern expressed by Tatian and Clement by emphasizing the sorts of virtuous acts of which even the poor, sick, and enslaved are capable, but there is no sign that Christian authors were interested in such a possibility.

Despite their professed hostility, Christian authors did draw upon Aristotelian ideas in articulating their own ethical vision. Clement derives from Aristotle (probably as mediated by doxography) the identification of contemplation as the end of human life, the distinction of the three types of friendship, and the description of a virtuous friend as "another self" (Clem. *Strom.* 1.25; 2.9, 19; see Clark, 1977, 27–44). He also makes selective use of Aristotle's discussion of the conditions of moral responsibility, particularly in identifying the various ways in which ignorance can render an act involuntary (Clem. *Strom.* 2.14; see Arist. *Eth. Nic.* 3.1; and Clark, 1977, 45–66). → Gregory of Nyssa repeats frequently, although without attribution, the Aristotelian doctrine that every virtue is a mean between two vices (e.g. Greg. Nyss. *Virg.* 7; *Hom. Eccl.* 6; *Icc.* 9). Jerome draws from a lost work of Aristotle on marriage for exempla in his defense of virginity (Jer. *Jov.* 1.41–49; see Courcelle, 1969, 71–72). Augustine was converted to the philosophical life by reading Cicero's *Hortensius*, a work that was modeled on Aristotle's *Protrepticus* and that set forth in an introductory way Aristotle's position that wisdom is the highest good (Aug. *Conf.* 3.4; see Tkacz, 2012). → Nemesius of Emesa – who clearly read the *Nicomachean Ethics* directly – refers with approval to Aristotle's doctrines that pleasure is a kind of activity and that the virtues are acquired through practice (Nem. *Nat. hom.* 18, 39). He also offers a detailed description of the relationship among wish (βούλησις), choice (προαίρεσις), and deliberation (βούλευσις), and the conditions under which an act is "up to us" (ἐφ' ἡμῖν), all drawn primarily (although without attribution) from Aristotle (Nem. *Nat. hom.* 33–34, 39–40). Through his mediation these distinctions eventually entered the mainstream of medieval

3. Psychology

Another frequent object of attack was Aristotle's doctrine of the soul. Pseudo-Justin lists as one of several points on which Plato and Aristotle disagree – thus discrediting them both – Aristotle's teaching that the soul is actuality (ἐντελέχεια), immovable, and mortal (Ps.-Just. *Coh.* 6). Eusebius quotes at length the criticism by Atticus of Aristotle's view that the soul is immovable and that only the mind (νοῦς) is divine and imperishable (Eus. *Praep* 15.9). He also quotes criticisms by → Plotinus and → Porphyry of Tyre of the doctrine that the soul is the form of a naturally organized body, remarking, in his own words, that such is "the impious doctrine of impious men" (*Praep* 15.10–11). Gregory of Nazianzus lists among the false teachings of Aristotle his "mortal reasonings" about the soul (Greg. Naz *Or.* 27.10). Theodoret elaborates the disagreements of the philosophers about the soul, Aristotle among them, concluding much as does Pseudo-Justin that their disagreements discredit them all (Thdt. *Affect.* 5.16–48). The author who offers the most penetrating and original engagement with Aristotle's psychology is unquestionably Nemesius of Emesa. He includes Aristotle among those whose views are to be rejected because they hold that the soul is not a substance. His complex criticisms of Aristotle's view include that the soul is receptive of opposites such as goodness and badness, and so must be substance rather than merely form, and that Aristotle has failed to offer an adequate account of how the soul can move the body as an unmoved mover (Nem. *Nat. hom.* 2).

Most of these reports seem to derive from doxography rather than from an actual engagement with Aristotle's text. Aetius mentions Aristotle's definition of the soul as the first actuality of a body potentially having life (Aet. *Plac.* 4.2.6), as well as noting that Aristotle held the soul to be immovable and mortal (4.6.2; 5.1.2), and no doubt other sources now lost included further information. Such reports evidently derive from the *De Anima* rather than from Aristotle's lost *Eudemus*, which *did* hold the soul to be immortal (→ Immortality), so to that extent the version of Aristotle's views under discussion was the same as that familiar today. Nemesius' complaint that Aristotle did not regard the soul as substance may seem odd in light of the clear statement of Arist. *De an.* 2.1 that the soul is substance in the sense of form. However, Nemesius was working with an understanding of substance as that which exists in its own right rather than as present in a substrate, a definition that owes more to the *Categories* than to the *De Anima* and that reflects centuries of Platonic and Neoplatonic critique of the peripatetic position (see the notes to the translation of Nemesius by Sharples & Eijk, 2008).

As in other areas, critique of Aristotle did not prevent a selective appropriation of his thought. Gregory of Nyssa adopts the Aristotelian division of soul into vegetative (or nutritive), animal (or sensitive), and rational parts (Greg. Nyss. *Hom. opif.* 8). He adds that in human beings the "true and perfect" soul is the rational part (*Hom. opif.* 14), a view with affinities to Aristotle's teaching that the true self is the intellect (Arist. *Eth. Nic.* 9.8; 10.7). Gregory also observes that we know of the existence (although not the nature) of mind and soul through their activities (ἐνέργειαι), echoing an important methodological passage of the *De Anima* (Greg. Nyss. *Hom. opif.* 29; *De anima et resurrectione*; PG 46.40.C; Arist. *De an.* 2.4.415b14–19). Nemesius of Emesa, despite his criticism of Aristotle's definition of soul, presents without demurral the more elaborate Aristotelian division of the soul into five parts – vegetative, sensitive, locomotive, appetitive, and rational – as well as that in the *Ethics* among the rational, the nonrational that can listen to reason, and the nonrational that does not listen to reason (Nem. *Nat. hom.* 15). In the West, Augustine may have been indebted to the *De Anima* for his description of sensation as involving the reception of the form of the object by the sense (Aug. *Trin.* 9.11; 11.2; *Gen. lit.* 12.11; 16, 23) – although, since there was no Latin translation of this work, these ideas presumably reached him through some Middle Platonic or Neoplatonic intermediary.

4. Logic

Logic was another area in which Aristotle had a largely negative reputation, evident particularly in the association of Aristotelian logic with → heresy. As early as → Irenaeus of Lyon, one finds the accusation that the Valentinians (→ Valentinus/Valentinians) derived their "subtlety and overly precise speech" from Aristotle (Iren. *Haer.* 2.14.5). → Tertullian likewise blames the Valentinians for using the art of dialectic invented by the "wretched Aristotle" (Tert. *Praesc.* 7). Eusebius observes that the followers of Artemon and → Paul of Samosata "strain every nerve to find a syllogistic figure to bolster their godlessness" and "treat Aristotle and Theophrastus with reverent awe" (Eus. *Hist. eccl.* 5.28). A particularly surprising version of the association between Aristotle and heresy occurs in Hippolytus of Rome. In keeping with his general thesis that the heretics borrowed their key ideas from Greek philosophy, Hippolytus identifies Aristotle's division of substance into genus, species, and the individual in the *Categories* as the inspiration for the Gnosticism (→ Gnosis/Gnosticism) of → Basilides. According to Hippolytus, Aristotle holds that the subsistence (ὑπόστασις) of each more particular level derives from the one that is prior to it; since the genus itself is nothing, however, this means that the subsistence of all things derives from nonbeing (ἐξ οὐκ ὄντων; Hipp. *Haer.* 7.16–17). Fanciful though it may be as an account of Aristotelian ontology, this reading has some parallels in the arguments of the ancient skeptics against the reality of universals and may reflect skeptical critiques of Aristotle that were current at the time (C. Osborne, 1987, 35–67; Mueller, 1994).

The association of Aristotle with heresy reached its height in the 4th century CE with the rise of the neo-Arianism of Aetius and Eunomius. Aetius was well known for having mastered the *Categories* – or at least for purporting to have done so – and imparting this knowledge to his disciple → Eunomius of Cyzicus (Socr. *Hist. eccl* 2.35; 4.7; 5.24; Soz. *Hist. eccl.* 3.15; 6.26). The reliance of the neo-Arians on Aristotelian logic was a prominent theme in the critique of their views by the orthodox. Basil of Caesarea accuses Eunomius of following the *Categories* on the question of the meaning of privative terms, thus adhering to "the wisdom of the rulers of this age" rather than the teaching of the → Holy Spirit (Bas. *Eun.* 1.9). Gregory of Nyssa reports that Aetius derived his heresy from Aristotle's "evil art" (κακοτεχνία), a term that apparently includes the use of syllogism as well as the adoption of specific

teachings from the *Organon* (Greg. Nyss. *Eun.* 1.55; see also 1.46; 2.410; 2.620; Basil *Hom.* 16.4; Greg. Naz. *Or.* 32.25). By the late 4th and early 5th centuries CE, the accusation that Aetius and Eunomius relied excessively on Aristotelian dialectic was a commonplace, repeated by among others Didymus the Blind (*Trin.* 2.3), Epiphanius (*Pan.* 69.71; 76.2, 23, 26, 37), and Severian of Gabala (*Joh. 1:13 hom.* 3). Latin authors also associated Aristotle with heresy: → Jerome states that → Arianism "borrows its streams of argument from the fountain of Aristotle" (*Lucif.* 11), Faustinus calls Aristotle "the bishop of the Arians" (Faust. *Trin.* 12), and Augustine repeatedly accuses Julian of Eclanum of relying upon Aristotle's *Categories* without having understood it (Aug. *C. Jul.* 1.4.12; 2.10.37; 3.2.7; 5.14.51; *C. Jul. op. imp.* 2.51).

As Augustine's charge indicates, the predominant objection was to the abuse of Aristotelian logic, accompanied sometimes by a naive attempt to apply to God doctrines that properly hold only for creatures, rather than to logic as such. Well before the 4th century CE, Clement of Alexandria had already provided a lengthy summary of key teachings from the *Organon* (although without mentioning their source), including the nature of induction, definition via genus and difference, the relation of names to concepts and things, the ten categories, and the definition of synonym, homonym, and paronym (Clem. *Strom.* 8.6, 8). The very criticisms offered by Basil and Gregory of the alleged logical lapses of the neo-Arians indicate a considerable acquaintance with Aristotelian technical terminology, whether derived by direct reading or from handbooks (Frede, 2005, 148–157). Didymus the Blind evidently possessed a remarkable knowledge of the *Organon*, for on several occasions he quotes it from memory in order to amplify points of scriptural exegesis (Runia, 1989, 14–15; Frede, 2005, 145–147). Cyril of Alexandria also displays an impressive acquaintance with Aristotelian logical terminology, although he does not refer to Aristotle directly (Siddals, 1987). Among the Latin fathers, Jerome claims to have studied the *Organon* with the logical commentaries of → Alexander of Aphrodisias (Jer. *Ep.* 50.1), and Augustine studied the *Categories* closely, as will be noted below. The main propagator of Aristotelian logic, however, was → Marius Victorinus, who translated Porphyry's *Isagoge* and is reported by → Cassiodorus to have translated the *Categories* and *De Interpretatione*, and who may also be the author of a paraphrase of the former work entitled *Decem Categoriae* (Kenny, 2008).

Christian authors also drew freely from the *Organon* in contexts having nothing particular to do with logic. Clement cites with approval a saying he attributes to Aristotle, that "the judgment which follows knowledge, affirming a thing is in truth, is faith," as part of his argument that faith (πίστις) is necessary to knowledge (Clem. *Strom.* 2.4). Theodoret cites a similar saying, "faith is the criterion of knowledge," also with approval (Thdt. *Affect.* 1.90). Neither saying appears in Aristotle's surviving works or elsewhere within surviving doxography. If an Aristotelian source is to be found, the most plausible would appear to be the doctrine of the *Posterior Analytics* that one must believe more firmly (μᾶλλον πιστεύειν) the premises of a syllogism than the conclusion in order for the conclusion to count as knowledge (Arist. *An. post.* 1.2; see various other proposals in Wolfson, 1956, 112–115; Lilla, 1971, 132–135; Clark, 1977, 21–23, and E. Osborne, 2005, 193–195). Another teaching deriving from the *Organon* that seems to have been well known was the doctrine of *De Interpretatione* (2) that names are significant by convention rather than by nature. Origen cites this as the view of Aristotle, rejecting it because it would imply that names have no magical efficacy (Or. *Cels.* 1.24; 5.45). Despite his opposition, it eventually became the predominant view thanks to its adoption and defense at some length (though without attribution to Aristotle) by the Cappadocians (Bas. *Eun.* 2.4; Greg. Nyss. *Eun.* 2.197–293).

By far the most important influence of the *Organon*, however, was in the area of Trinitarian theology. The Cappadocians appear to have modeled the distinction between the common divine essence (οὐσία) and three divine persons (πρόσωπα or ὑποστάσεις) largely on that between primary and secondary substance in the *Categories*. The most developed explanation of this distinction, Basil's *Ep.* 38 (which may be by his brother, Gregory of Nyssa), uses the telltale Aristotelian formula "definition of essence" (λόγος τῆς οὐσίας) in describing what beings of the same essence have in common (Bas. *Ep.* 38.2; see also λόγος τοῦ εἶναι ("definition of being") in Bas. *Eun.* 1.19). When Basil wishes to summarize the distinction

between οὐσία and ὑπόστασις, he states simply that it is that between "the general and the particular, such as the animal and the particular man" (*Ep.* 236.6), a statement that could equally apply to secondary and primary substance in the *Categories*. Gregory of Nyssa chides Eunomius for his apparent ignorance of the doctrine of the *Categories* that οὐσία does not admit of degree (Greg. Nyss. *Eun.* 1.180–181). Of course, there is also much in the Cappadocians' distinction that is not Aristotelian, including the term ὑπόστασις itself, as well as the notion that hypostases are distinguished by a unique set of individuating properties (ἰδιότητες or ἰδιώματα) – albeit the latter probably derives from an Aristotelian commentary, Porphyry's *Isagoge*, and so belongs to Aristotelian logic in a broad sense.

The Trinitarian theology of Augustine also makes use of the *Categories*. Augustine recounts with some pride his mastery of this work as a young man, although he says that it initially led him astray into thinking of God as a subject with attributes (Aug. *Conf.* 4.16). In the *De Trinitate* he elaborates this idea, arguing that because God is not a subject with attributes, he is not properly substance (*substantia*) but should rather be called essence (*essentia*; Aug. *Trin.* 7.5). Nonetheless, the categories do apply to God in the limited sense that some predicates are said of God "according to" (i.e. in the category of) substance – such as "God," "great," "good," and so on – whereas others, such as "Father," "Son," and "Holy Spirit," are said according to relation (*Trin.* 5.3–8). There is also a further type of relation that applies to God, that of "relative accidents" such as becoming lord of man when man is created (*Trin.* 5.16). Apart from the categories of substance and relation, however, Augustine rejects the application of the categories to God in any save a metaphorical sense, since he sees them as implying change or corporeality (*Trin.* 5.4–5).

5. Some Further Forms of Influence

Although the areas just surveyed include the most significant explicit discussions of Aristotle by early Christian authors, they by no means exhaust the full range of his influence. Aristotle was widely recognized as an authority on scientific matters, and Christian authors freely drew on him when they found it helpful, sometimes with attribution but more often without. Basil, for example, gives a respectful description of the theory of the natural places of the elements taught by "some physicists," as also of the ether, although he ultimately dismisses both as of little importance (Bas. *Hex.* 1.10–11; see other examples cited by Wallace-Hadrill, 1968). Sometimes it is hard to tell whether an idea is due to indirect Aristotelian influence or has been arrived at independently. Basil again provides some interesting examples. His argument that there was no first moment of time (*Hex.* 1.6) *may* owe something to the similar argument of Aristotle that there can be no first moment of a change (Arist. *Phys.* 6.6), but he may equally have arrived at it independently. Likewise Basil's observation that when all qualities are removed from an object "the substratum will be nothing" seems to echo a famous discussion in Aristotle's *Metaphysics*, although the similarity may be coincidental (Bas. *Hex.* 1.8; Arist. *Metaph.* 7.3).

Rather than focusing only on the influence of specific passages or doctrines, it is important also to note the ways in which Aristotelian concepts entered pervasively, although generally with significant alteration, into Christian discourse. The very pervasiveness of the concepts involved meant that they were not recognized as distinctively Aristotelian, although from our own standpoint, Aristotle's role in their formation appears crucial. The remainder of this article will point to three such cases of broad but diffuse influence.

First is the analysis of created beings into matter and form. By the early Christian era, such analysis had become part of the common stock of ideas shared by the educated. Tatian, for example, asserts that God is the creator of both matter and form, a formula that became a common way of affirming creation *ex nihilo* (Tat. *Orat.* 4–5; Iren. *Haer.* 2.10; 16.3; 4.20.1; Or. *Princ.* 2.1.4; Bas. *Hex.* 2.2; Aug. *Fid. Symb.* 2; *Conf.* 12.4–8). Christian authors generally assumed, in common with the learned culture of the time, that matter is necessary for both change and numerical diversity. Bringing this premise to bear on their belief in the soul and in angels, both of which undergo change and are numerically diverse, led to a theory sometimes called "pneumatic hylomorphism." This is the view that all creatures, including angels and souls, are composites of form and matter,

although obviously the matter of angels and souls is highly refined in comparison to that of sensible bodies. As John Damascene would later put it, the angels are "incorporeal and immaterial" in relation to human beings but "dense and material" in relation to God (Dam. *Fid.* 17). Pneumatic hylomorphism seems to have been more or less universally held in the early church, particularly since it meshed well with biblical passages such as the parable of → Lazarus and the various appearances of angels (e.g. Just. *Dial.* 5; Tat. *Orat.* 4; 12–13; Iren. *Haer.* 2.34; Athan. *Vit. Ant.* 31; Tert. *An.* 7; *Carn.chr.* 11; *Res.* 17; Basi. *Ep.* 8 [probably by Evagrius]; Greg. Naz. *Or.* 28.31; 38.9). Augustine is a partial exception, since he affirms that angels possess spiritual bodies (Aug. *Gen. lit.* 6.19, 24) but argues at length for the incorporeality of the soul (e.g. Aug. *Quant. an.* passim). Even he, however, ultimately concedes that although the soul is not a body, it may well be made of "spiritual matter" (*Gen. lit.* 7.27–28).

Another important strand of Aristotelian influence – although in this case one that is not solely Aristotelian, but includes Platonic and even Pre-Socratic elements – is the patristic understanding of → *nous*. This is a term most frequently translated "mind" or "intellect," although depending on the context it can also mean reason, understanding, thought, judgment, resolve, or disposition. It appears in Greek philosophy in two closely linked contexts. On the one hand, *nous* is present within each human being as that which thinks, or, more specifically, that which apprehends intelligible reality. It is thus the highest faculty of the soul, one that has an innate affinity with divinity. Although this distinctive role of *nous* was adumbrated by Plato, it was defined most fully by Aristotle, who identifies *nous* as the faculty that apprehends the first principles that are the basis of all subsequent knowledge (Arist. *An. post.* 2.19; *Eth. Nic.* 6.6). He adds that *nous* is for each of us our truest and highest self (*Eth. Nic.* 9.8; 10.7). On the other hand, Plato and Aristotle also give *nous* a cosmic role. In Plato *nous* is the demiurge who created the world by imposing form upon the receptacle of becoming; in Aristotle it is the Prime Mover, which exists eternally at the highest level of actuality and by its "self-thinking thought" gives order to the cosmos. Each of the two aspects of *nous*, human and cosmic, enhances the importance of the other. In effect Plato and Aristotle posit that at the deepest core of the human being lies something divine, a capacity to apprehend and in some sense to share in the Mind that is the source of all things.

It is not surprising that Christian authors found this vision appealing; it has obvious affinities, not only with the Christian belief in the creator, but also with that in humanity as made in the image and likeness of God. Even so it could hardly be adopted wholesale, for in identifying each person's truest self with intellect, it ignores the human person's psychosomatic complexity, and in identifying this intellect as a kind of participation in God, it blurs the line between creature and creator. The full story of how Christian thought appropriated the classical concept of *nous* cannot be told here (see Bradshaw, 2009). Suffice to say that, although the Greek fathers readily incorporated *nous* within their → anthropology, they did so as only one pole of a complex unity. The other pole was the heart, understood in a way inspired less by philosophy than by the Bible. *Nous* remains, on this view, the innate capacity to apprehend spiritual and transcendent reality; in our fallen state, however, this capacity needs to be restored and refocused within the heart, which (following passages such as 2 Cor 1:22 and Gal 4:6) Christian authors viewed as the locus of divine grace. To "draw the mind into the heart" through prayer and ascetic discipline thus became a major goal of monastic practice, particularly within the eastern Christian tradition (Hausherr, 1978).

This complex legacy also explains a peculiarity of much Greek patristic exegetical and liturgical writing, namely the concept of the "noetic" (νοητός). The noetic is simply that which is apprehended by *nous*. But, of course, what this means changes with the concept of *nous* itself. Whereas νοητός in classical Greek means intelligible as opposed to sensible, in Christian writing it came to mean that which is apprehended spiritually in light of the entire teaching of the church. Often this concept was used to make a typological or poetic identification: Satan (→ Devil) is the noetic pharaoh, Christ is the noetic lamb, the → Eucharist is the noetic pearl, the demons are noetic roaring lions, and so on (see Lampe, 1961, s.v. νοητός). In such contexts "noetic" could almost be

translated as "true or real," in that it is that which is perceived by a mind properly attuned to reality.

A final example of broad but diffuse Aristotelian influence is the concept of divine energy. This concept in its ultimate form is certainly not to be found in Aristotle, but its origins lie partly with him, and there is a clear trajectory leading from his works to its final flowering in the Greek fathers. The trajectory begins with Aristotle's coining of the term ἐνέργεια to indicate the active use of a faculty, as opposed to its mere possession. From this point the term came to bear in Aristotle's mature works two distinct but related meanings, those of "activity" and "actuality." (The former is predominant in the ethical and rhetorical works, the latter in the *Metaphysics* and *De Anima*.) These meanings reconverge in Arist. *Metaph.* 12. The Prime Mover as described there is a being that is pure ἐνέργεια in two distinct but related senses:

a. (it has no unrealized capacities to act or be acted upon; in other words, it is pure actuality;

b. it is identical with its own independent and self-subsistent activity of thought (νόησις).

From these premises one may infer that the Prime Mover's activity of thought embraces all possible intelligible content, for otherwise there would be a kind of thinking in which it could engage but does not, and it would fail in that respect to be fully actual. The intelligible content of a thing is simply its form, that which makes it what it is. So the Prime Mover may fairly be said to embrace, in its single eternal act of thought, the forms of all things. However, it does more than merely think them, for Aristotle also holds that thought at the highest level of actuality is *identical* with its object. This means that the Prime Mover not only thinks the forms of all things; in some sense it *is* those forms, existing eternally and in full actuality as an integral whole. In other words, the fully actual and eternal activity that is the Prime Mover does not remain isolated from the rest of the cosmos, but is actively present in all things, constituting them as what they are. This conclusion was not drawn explicitly by Aristotle, but it was by his first great commentator, Alexander of Aphrodisias, and it is integral to the Neoplatonic understanding of *Nous* (Intellect) as the second hypostasis (Bradshaw, 2004, 24–44, 68–72).

Obviously not all aspects of this complex philosophical legacy were known to, or would have been endorsed by, the church fathers. Its importance lies rather in the semantic richness it gave to ἐνέργεια and cognate terms, such as the verb ἐνεργεῖν. Unlike other word groups that are superficially similar (e.g. δρᾶμα/δρᾶν, ποίησις/ποιεῖν), ἐνέργεια and its cognates always indicated a kind of activity that can, in the right circumstances, enter into and be shared by another. This means not simply that the two agents share the same activity, but that that of the agent who is the source of the ἐνέργεια vivifies and informs the recipient, while at the same time enabling the recipient to act authentically on his or her own behalf. Such a meaning is already evident when Paul speaks of the divine ἐνέργεια that is being realized or made effective (ἐνεργουμένην) in him (Col 1:29; see further examples and discussion in Bradshaw, 2006). It was primarily thanks to the influence of Paul that this meaning soon became established in the church fathers, particularly in contexts dealing with demonic possession or human–divine interaction (Bradshaw, 2004, 123–127, 153–172).

These examples by no means exhaust the Aristotelian legacy in early Christian thought. They should suffice to illustrate, however, the extent to which Aristotle remained continuously present, even when his presence was not fully recognized.

Historiography

The modern study of the presence of Aristotle within patristic literature began with attention to his influence on the hexaemeral writings (Müllenhoff, 1867; Plass, 1905). A.J. Festugière in a pioneering study took a more comprehensive approach, although still focused on certain selected themes and topics (Festugière, 1932). Attention then shifted to the question of what can be gleaned from patristic writings about Aristotle's lost works (Guthrie, 1934; Bignone, 1936; Lazzati, 1938; Waszink, 1947; Alfonsi, 1948; 1953; Pépin, 1964; Bos, 1989; 1993). Drawing partly on this work, D.T. Runia returned to the comprehensive approach of A.J. Festugière, providing a comprehensive list and analysis of all the explicit references to Aristotle in patristic works (Runia, 1989). Meanwhile more focused studies continued apace of both Aristotle's influence on particular Fathers (Lilla,

1971; Clark, 1977; Martin, 1989; Mueller, 1994; Tkacz, 2012) and the influence of particular Aristotelian works (Frede, 2005; Kenny, 2008). Most recently S. Lilla and G. Karamanolis have provided comprehensive summaries of the state of research (Lilla, 2014; Karamanolis, 2016). The approach taken here differs from theirs in being organized thematically rather than chronologically and in greater attention to the pervasive (but largely unattributed) role of certain fundamental Aristotelian ideas.

Bibliography

Alfonsi, L., "Traces de jeune Aristote dans la Cohortatio ad gentiles faussement attribuée à Justin," *VigChr* 2, 1948, 65–88.

Alfonsi, L., "Motivi tradizionali del giovane Aristotele in Clemente Alessandrino e in Atenagora," *VigChr* 7, 1953, 129–142.

Bignone, E., *L'Aristotele perduto e la formazione filosofica di Epicuro*, Florence, 1936.

Bos, A.P., *Cosmic and Meta-Cosmic Theology in Aristotle's Lost Dialogues*, Leiden, 1989.

Bos, A.P., "Clement of Alexandria on Aristotle's (Cosmo-) Theology (Clem. Protrept. 5.66.4)," *CQ* 43, 1993, 177–188.

Bradshaw, D., *Aristotle East and West: Metaphysics and the Division of Christendom*, Cambridge UK, 2004.

Bradshaw, D., "The Divine Energies in the New Testament," *SVTQ* 50, 2006, 189–223.

Bradshaw, D., "The Mind and the Heart in the Christian East and West," *FaPh* 26, 2009, 576–598.

Champion, M.C., *Explaining the Cosmos: Creation and Cultural Interaction in Late-Antique Gaza*, Oxford, 2014.

Clark, E.A., *Clement's Use of Aristotle: The Aristotelian Contribution to Clement of Alexandria's Refutation of Gnosticism*, New York, 1977.

Courcelle, P., *Late Latin Writers and Their Greek Sources*, Cambridge MA, 1969.

Festugière, A.J., "Aristote dans la literature grecque chrétienne jusqu'a Théodoret," in: A.J. Festugière, *L'idéal religieux des grecs et l'évangile*, Paris, 1932, 221–263.

Frede, M., "Les Catégories d'Aristote et les pères de l'église grecs," in: O. Bruun & L. Corti, eds., *Les Catégories et leur histoire*, Paris, 2005, 135–173.

Gauthier, R.A., "Saint Maxime le Confesseur et la psychologie de l'acte humain," *RThAM* 21, 1954, 51–100.

Guthrie, W.K.C., "The Development of Aristotle's Theology," *CQ* 27, 1933, 162–172; 28, 1934, 90–98.

Hausherr, I., *The Name of Jesus*, Kalamazoo, 1978.

Karamanolis, G., "Early Christian Philosophers on Aristotle," in: A. Falcon, ed., *Brill's Companion to the Reception of Aristotle in Antiquity*, Leiden, 2016, 460–479.

Kenny, A., "Aristotle's Categories in the Latin Fathers," in: A. Kenny, ed., *From Empedocles to Wittgenstein: Historical Essays in Philosophy*, Oxford, 2008, 62–73.

Lampe, G.W.H., *PGL*, Oxford, 1961.

Lazzati, G., *L'Aristotele perduto e gli scrittori cristiani*, Rome, 1938.

Lilla, S., *Clement of Alexandria: A Study in Christian Platonism and Gnosticism*, Oxford, 1971.

Lilla, S., "Aristotelianism," in: A. di Berardino et al., eds., *EAC*, Downer Grove, vol. I, 2014, 228–235.

Martin, J.P., "El Pseudo-Justino en la historia del Aristotelismo," *PaMe* 10, 1989, 3–19.

Mueller, I., "Hippolytus, Aristotle, Basilides," in: L.P. Schrenk, ed., *Aristotle in Late Antiquity*, Washington DC, 1994, 143–157.

Müllenhoff, K., "Aristoteles bei Basilius von Caesarea," *Hermes* 2, 1867, 252–258.

Osborne, C., *Rethinking Early Greek Philosophy*, Ithaca, 1987.

Osborne, E., *Clement of Alexandria*, Cambridge UK, 2005.

Pépin, J., *Théologie cosmique et théologie chrétienne: Ambroise Exam. I, 1–4*, Paris, 1964.

Plass, P., *De Basilii et Ambrosii excerptis ad historiam animalium pertinentibus*, Marburg, 1905.

Runia, D.T., "Festugière Revisited: Aristotle in the Greek Patres," *VigChr* 43, 1989, 1–34.

Sharples, R.W., & P.J. van der Eijk, trans., *Nemesius of Emesa: On the Nature of Man*, Liverpool, 2008.

Siddals, R., "Logic and Christology in Cyril of Alexandria," *JThS* 38, 1987, 341–367.

Tkacz, M., "St. Augustine's Appropriation and Transformation of Aristotelian *Eudaimonia*," in: J. Miller, ed., *The Reception of Aristotle's Ethics*, Cambridge UK, 2012, 67–84.

Wallace-Hadrill, D.S., *The Greek Patristic View of Nature*, Manchester, 1968.

Waszink, J.H., "Traces of Aristotle's Lost Dialogues in Tertullian," *VigChr* 1, 1947, 137–149.

Watts, E., "An Alexandrian Christian Response to Fifth-Century Neoplatonic Influence," in: A. Smith, ed., *The Philosopher and Society in Late Antiquity*, Swansea, 2005, 215–229.

Wolfson, H.A., *The Philosophy of the Church Fathers*, vol. I: *Faith, Trinity, and Incarnation*, Harvard, 1956.

DAVID BRADSHAW

Arius → Arianism

Arles

Roman Arles was designated as a colony for veterans in 46 BCE and eventually received the name Colonia Julia Paterna Arelate Sextanorum (Klingshirn, 1994, 36–37). The site derived its importance from its location on the Rhône river at a key access point to the Mediterranean on the one hand, and the Gallic hinterland on the other, and it had long been inhabited by both Gauls and Greeks (Heijmans, 2004, 7–10). By the late 1st century BCE Arles began to accumulate its Roman urban infrastructure and impressive monuments, many of which are still visible today: a grid street plan, forum, theater, amphitheater, baths, and aqueducts (Heijmans, 2004, 10–20). The remaining traces of the circus, and of a recently discovered basilica that may have served as an audience hall, hint at how much more there once was (Esmonde Cleary, 2013, 210–211). Arles was an imperial city. In 313 CE it gained the imperial mint; around 395 CE it became the seat of the praetorian prefecture, and it was also an occasional residence of emperors (Benoît, 1954, 15–21). It was a center for trade, commerce, and for movement between the Mediterranean and the interior of Gaul (Loseby, 1996, 46). This importance brought at least some of its inhabitants great wealth: the Trinquetaille region features remains of some ornate villas, and Arles is noted for its large number of expensively decorated → sarcophagi (Heijmans, Roquette & Sintès, 2006, 43; Benoît, 1954, 2).

The nodal position of Arles within Roman transport networks kept the money flowing in and the goods flowing through in late antiquity (Klingshirn, 1994, 54–56). Ausonius of Bordeaux in his *Ordo urbium nobilium* (*The Order of Famous Cities*) claimed that Arles "gathers the merchandise of the Roman world, and scatters it, enriching other peoples and the towns which Gaul and Aquitaine treasure in their wide bosoms" (Aus. *Urb. nob.* 10). Furthermore, as a city with important imperial connections, Arles remained linked to relatively wide-ranging networks (Esmonde Cleary, 2013, 143). Although some peripheral housing areas were abandoned in the 3rd century CE, there are no long-term signs of economic contraction until the late 5th and 6th centuries CE, suggesting that Arles fared better in late antiquity than a number of its neighbors (Sintès, 1992, 141–146; Esmonde Cleary, 2013, 408).

Nonetheless, there were a number of signs that by late antiquity, the relationship of Arles' inhabitants to their urban spaces was changing. By the early 5th century CE the forum was being cannibalized for building materials and housing was being built into the walls of some public buildings (Sintès,

1994). S.T. Loseby (1996, 55; 2006, 80–82) argues that this indicates an increasingly pragmatic attitude to urban monuments and a shift in the style of elite display, away from public space. There remains an interesting gap between the city's position in the mentality of its inhabitants and the archaeological story. In the 460s CE, → Sidonius Apollinaris wrote that during a visit to Arles he walked down to the forum (Sid. *Ep.* 1.11.7), and a forum is also mentioned in the 6th-century CE *Vita Caesarii* (2.30; *Life of Caesarius*), yet archaeologists assure us that there was no longer a forum to speak of in Arles by the mid-5th century CE (Gauthier, 1999, 204; Sintès, 1994, 191; Esmonde Cleary, 2013, 405). The "image" of the imperial city may have outlasted its physical form.

1. Christianity

Arles' secular importance was paralleled by a religious role – it was the site of an important church council in 314 CE, and in 417 CE Pope Zosimus (→ Zosimus [Bishop of Rome]) granted Patroclus, bishop of Arles, metropolitan rights over many of the bishoprics of southern Gaul (Klingshirn, 1994, 57, 66). Arles had a number of prominent and active bishops, including → Hilary of Arles (429–449 CE) and Caesarius of Arles (502–542 CE), each of whom left a significant stamp on Gallic Christianity and its institutions.

Christianity also made an early and important impression upon the urban landscape of Arles. The site of the first cathedral was prominent – just inside the city walls, close to one of the main gates, on a raised area, looking down over the city (Gauthier & Picard, 1986, 80). Excavations have uncovered an enormous basilica in this area, which may be the remains of this original church (Heijmans, 2005; 2009). A church was also built in the center of the city, near the forum, perhaps in the 5th century CE (Benoît, 1954, 18; Février, 1978, 133). This would eventually become the cathedral, although the timing of that transition is unclear. Arles boasted a number of other Christian sites. There were smaller churches, a baptistery, a clerical house, a residence for the sick, a monastery for men built before the end of the 5th century CE, and a monastery for women built by Caesarius on the site of the former cathedral in the early 6th century CE (Griffe, 1965; Gauthier & Picard,

1986, 81–84; Hubert, 1947; Viellard-Troiekouroff, 1976, 37–40). More peripheral areas of the city were marked by spaces deemed sacred to Saint Genesius, a local martyr (Cavallin, 1945; Pietri, 1991, 357–378). Genesius was buried in the Alyscamps cemetery, on the south bank of the river, beyond the city's walls and he eventually received a church over his tomb, dedicated to his memory. The site of his martyrdom, however, was on the north bank, and this too became a venerated sacred site (Hubert, 1947, 17). A number of late antique writers commented on the fact that Arles was divided by the river which also brought it its wealth – Ausonius called it *duplex Arelate*, "divided by the streams of headlong Rhône" (*Urb. nob.* 10). The annual pilgrimage between the two sites sacred to Genesius, however, linked the divided city. The author of a sermon on Genesius, most likely Hilary of Arles (Bailey, 2010, 33), matched it all up, calling Genesius' two sites a "two-fold honor" for a two-fold city. "The saint sanctifies that bank with his triumph, this with his tomb; he illuminates that with his blood, this with his body" (Euseb. Gall. 56.6). The importance of religion to the lay people of Arles can be seen in the scriptural images which decorated their sarcophagi (Benoît, 1954, 2). Many of these were discovered near the site of Genesius' tomb, which may indicate *ad sanctos* burial and popular enthusiasm for his cult (Heijmans, Rouquette & Sintès, 2006, 45).

Historiography

The archaeology of Roman Arles is amply documented in a number of publications, ranging from the early and foundational work of F. Benoît (1954), then P.-A. Février (1978), through to the more recent analyses and excavation reports by C. Sintès (1992; 1994) and M. Heijmans (1999; 2004; 2005; 2009). S. Esmonde Cleary (2013) and S.T. Loseby (1996; 2006) include Arles in their important discussions of urban culture in Roman Gaul, with an especial focus on the late Roman period. The Christian history of Arles has drawn considerable attention – it was a central element to the work of É. Griffe (1965) and N. Gauthier (1999). B. Beaujard (1991), S. Cavallin (1945), and L. Pietri (1991) discuss the development of saints' cults in Arles, while the Christian topography of the city is detailed in N. Gauthier & J.-C. Picard

(1986), J. Hubert (1947), and M. Viellard-Troiekouroff (1976).W. Klingshirn (1994) includes extensive material on the history of Arles and its religious communities in his work on its bishop, Caesarius.

Bibliography

Bailey, L.K., *Christianity's Quiet Success: The Eusebius Gallicanus Sermon Collection and the Power of the Church in Late Antique Gaul*, Notre Dame, 2010.

Beaujard, B., "Cités, évêques et martyrs en Gaule à la fin de l'époque romaine," in: *Les fonctions des Saints dans le monde occidental (IIIe–XIIIe siècle)*, Rome, 1991, 175–191.

Benoît, F., "Arles," in: F. Benoît, P.-A. Février, J. Formigé & H. Rolland, eds., *Villes épiscopales de Provence: Aix, Arles, Fréjus, Marseilles et Riez de l'époque Gallo-Romaine au Moyen Age*, Paris, 1954, 15–21.

Benoît, F., *Sarcophages paléochrétiens d'Arles et de Marseilles*, Paris, 1954, 2.

Cavallin, S., "Saint Genès le notaire," *Eranos* 43, 1945, 150–175.

Esmonde Cleary, S., *The Roman West, AD 200–500: An Archaeological Study*, Cambridge UK, 2013.

Février, P.-A., "Arles aux IVe et Ve siècles, ville impériale et capitale régionale," in: *XXV corso di cultura sull'arte ravennate e bizantina*, Ravenna, 1978, 127–158.

Gauthier, N., "La topographie chrétienne entre idéologie et pragmatisme," in: G.P. Brogiolo & B. Ward-Perkins, eds., *The Idea and Ideal of the Town between Late Antiquity and the Early Middle Ages*, Leiden, 1999, 195–209.

Gauthier, N., & J.-C. Picard, *Topographie chrétienne des cités de la Gaule des origines au milieu du VIIIe siècle*, vol. III: *Provinces ecclésiastiques de Vienne et d'Arles (Viennensis et Alpes Graiae et Poeninae)*, Paris, 1986.

Griffe, É., *La Gaule chrétienne a l'époque romaine*, vol. III: *La cité chrétienne*, Paris, 1965.

Heijmans, M., "La topographie de la ville d'Arles durant l'antiquité tardive," *JRAr* 12, 1999, 143–167.

Heijmans, M., *Arles durant l'antiquité tardive: De la "duplex Arelas" à l'"Urbs Genesii"*, Rome, 2004.

Heijmans, M., "L'église paléochrétienne de l'enclos Saint-Césaire, à Arles," in: X. Delestre, ed., *15 ans d'archéologie en Provence-Alpes-Côte d'Azur*, Aix-en-Provence, 2005, 212–213.

Heijmans, M., "Les fouilles de l'enclos Saint-Césaire la decouverte d'une des plus grande églises paleochrétiennes," *BAAT* 18, 2009, 27–29.

Heijmans, M., J.-M. Rouquette & C. Sintès, *Arles antique: Guides archéologiques de la France*, Paris, 2006.

Hubert, J., "La topographie religieuse d'Arles au VIe siècle," *CAr* 2 1947, 17–27.

Klingshirn, W., *Caesarius of Arles: The Making of a Christian Community in Late Antique Gaul*, Cambridge UK, 1994.

Loseby, S.T., "Arles in Late Antiquity: *Gallula Roma Arelas* and *Urbs Genesii*," in: N. Christie & S.T. Loseby, eds., *Towns in Transition: Urban Evolution from Late Antiquity to the Early Middle Ages*, Aldershot, 1996, 45–70.

Loseby, S.T., "Decline and Change in the Cities of Late Antique Gaul," in: J.-U. Krause & C. Witschel, eds., *Die Stadt in der Spätantike – Niedergang oder Wandel?* Stuttgart, 2006, 67–103.

Pietri, L., "Culte des saints et religiosité politique dans la Gaule du Ve et du VIe siècle," in: *Les fonctions des saints dans le monde occidental (IIIe–XIIIe siècle)*, Rome, 1991, 353–369.

Sintès, C., "L'évolution topographique de l'Arles du haut-empire à la lumière des fouilles récentes," *JRAr* 5, 1992, 130–147.

Sintès, C., "La reutilisation des espaces publics a Arles: Un témoinage de la fin de l'antiquité," *AnTa* 2, 1994, 181–192.

Viellard-Troiekouroff, M., *Les monuments religieux de la Gaule d'après les oeuvres de Grégoire de Tours*, Paris, 1976.

LISA KAAREN BAILEY

Armageddon

Armageddon is mentioned in Rev 16:16 (→ Revelation, Book of) as the place where the kings of the world are gathered for the battle against God and his people.

1. Armageddon in the Context of Revelation

Armageddon is part of the pouring of the sixth bowl (Rev 16:12–16), which is an element in the septet of the pouring of the bowls (Rev 16:1–21). The pouring of the bowls is the third septet, following the opening of the seals (Rev 6:1–8:9) and the seven trumpets (Rev 8:6–11:19).

The pouring of the sixth bowl causes the Euphrates to dry up, a reference to the Exodus and later judgment texts (Exod 14:21–22; Isa 11:15; 44:27; Jer 50:38 MT). The Euphrates, serving as a border of the Roman Empire, enables the "kings from the east" to invade. John then sees the dragon (Satan; → Devil), the beast (the Roman political system), and the false prophet (the Roman religious system, esp. the imperial cult; Rev 19:20; 20:10) bringing forth "three unclean spirits like frogs," an image of idolatrous seducing powers linked with Babylon (Rev 17:4; 18:2). The signs they perform, relating them to the beast (Rev 13:13–14), persuade the political powers of the world to fight for the satanic trio (Rev 19:19; 20:8). The believers are warned that Jesus will come suddenly, as a thief (Matt 24:43–44; Rev 3:2–3), and they must be prepared and clothed in the new life of Christ (Rev 3:4; 6:11). The place of the gathering of verse 14 is then revealed in verse 16 as being Armageddon. What becomes apparent in this scene is that God is in control and brings out these kings to destroy Babylon and its power.

The battlefield is displayed in the seventh bowl (Rev 16:17–21), a further elaboration of this battle can be found in Rev 17–18 and 19:11–21. Babylon, being the dominant force in the world, is brought down and destroyed in the divine judgment on the Day of the Lord (Joel 2:11; 2:31; Zeph 1:14).

2. The Etymology of Armageddon

There has been much discussion about the etymology of the name Armageddon. John explicitly mentions that the name Armageddon is "in Hebrew" (Ἑβραϊστί/*Ebraïstí*; Rev 16:16).

The textual tradition of Rev 16:16 does not provide us with any clarity. Armageddon is written as Ἀρμεγηδών/*Armegedón*, Ἀρμεγεδδών/*Armegeddón*, Ἀρμεγεδων/*Armegedón*, Ἀρμαγεδῶ/*Armagedô*, Ἀρμαγεδον/*Armagedon*, and Ἀρμαγεδωμ/*Armagedóm*, but also as Μαγεδδών/*Mageddón*, Μαγεδών/*Magedón*, Μαγεδωδ/*Magedód*, Μαγιδων/*Magidón*, and Μακκεδων/*Makkedón*. The Novum Testamentum Graece (Nestle-Aland, 28th ed.) reads Ἀρμαγεδών/*Harmagedón*, the most probable and substantiated reading.

The majority position is that Armageddon can be read as a Greek transcription of *har měgiddôn*, "the mountain of Megiddo." Megiddo is a well-known tell in the Hebrew Bible (Josh 12:21; 17:11; Judg 1:27; 1 Kgs 4:12; 2 Kgs 9:27; 1 Chr 7:29) that also served as a battlefield in several instances (Judg 5:19; 2 Kgs 23:29–30; 2 Chr 35:22; Aune, 1998, 898; Ussishkin, 2018). Archaeologists have shown that Megiddo was an inhabited city until the Persian times (Ussishkin, 2018). In Roman times, the city was probably a Roman camp called *Legio* (Ussishkin, 2018, 22).

This specific grammatical form of Megiddo, *měgiddôn*, seems to refer to Zech 12:11 (MT), a text that speaks about "the valley of Megiddo" (*b^ebiq^cat*

měgiddôn). J. Day (1994) has argued for this verse from the Masoretic Text as the precise background of Armageddon in Rev 16:16. His five arguments are:

1. Zech 12:11 is the only text prior to Rev 16:16 that places Megiddo in an apocalyptic context.
2. It is the only text that spells *měgiddôn*, with a paragogical *nun*, instead of the conventional *měgiddô*. There are some instances in the Septuagint in which this form is used (Judg 1:27 LXX A; 2 Chr 35:22), but J. Day points towards the identification of Armageddon by John as "in Hebrew" (Day, 1994, 320). Thus, only Zech 12:11 (MT) qualifies.
3. The book of Zechariah has a major influence on Revelation (Jauhiainen, 2005a), as can be seen in the multiple allusions and citations of Zechariah in the text (Zech 12:11 in Rev 1:7; Zech 6 in Rev 6:2–8; Zech 4 in Rev 11:4; Zech 14 in Rev 21:25 and 22:3).
4. Some note a contrast between the valley of Megiddo in Zechariah and the mountain of Megiddo in Revelation. This discrepancy can easily be solved by assuming that a valley may presuppose the presence of a mountain. Others have pointed out that Megiddo is in the vicinity of Mount Carmel, the mountain on which Elijah defeated the priests of Baal (1 Kgs 18; Shea, 1980).
5. The term "mountain" (*har*) cannot be found in Zech 12:11 (MT), because it refers to the end-time battle of Gog and Magog (Ezek 38:8; 39:2; 39:4; 39:17). John uses this image also in Rev 19:17–21 and 20:7–10 to narrate the final eschatological battle.

There are some flaws in this argumentation (see also Jauhiainen, 2005b). The first argument of J. Day is circular reasoning, because one has to first accept the reading *har měgiddôn* before one can locate Megiddo in the apocalyptic context of Zech 12. Second, the book of Zechariah has influenced Revelation, just as other Hebrew Bible books like Daniel (Beale, 1984) and Isaiah (Fekkes, 1994). Third, a *har* in Hebrew qualifies as a real mountain, while a tell like Megiddo is usually described as *gib^câ*. Archaeological evidence does not suggest that there was a mountain in this part of the Jezreel valley. The Septuagint translates "the valley" in Zech 12:11 as "leveled place, plain" (πεδίον/*pedíon*) instead of "valley, ravine" (φάραγξ/*pháranx*) or "deep valley" (κοιλάς/*koilás*), the latter words suggesting that the valley may contain a mountain.

The majority reading of Armageddon as "the mountain of Megiddo" thus is reasonable, but not conclusive. Other alternatives for the etymology of Armageddon have been mentioned in research. Some scholars read *har môʿĕd*, "mountain of assembly" (Hommel, 1890, 406–407n3; Jeremias, 1932; Torrey, 1938; Loasby, 1989). The Hebrew Bible text which is referred to in this reading is Isa 14:13, a prophetic taunt of the haughtiness of the Babylonians who tried to equate themselves with YHWH. The sentence *har môʿĕd* can be transliterated to Ἀρ-Μωγέδ, later assimilated to Armageddon (Beale, 1999, 839). The γ is then a transliteration of the ʿ, a phenomenon found in several other languages too (Violet, 1932; Day, 1994, 316–317; Oberweis, 1995, 316–317).

There are some problems with the reading *har môʿĕd* though. First, the reading *har môʿĕd* and its transliteration Ἀρ-Μωγέδ require a significant redaction to become Ἀρμαγεδών. This redactional process is not uncovered in contributions of proponents and no one has provided a sufficient explanation how Ἀρ-Μωγέδ became Ἀρμαγεδών. J. Day (1994, 317) states: "*Har môʿĕd* is too remote in form to be a credible source of the name Armageddon." Second, this reading redundantly repeats information. That the kings are gathered (συναγαγεῖν/*sunagagein*) at a specific place, is already mentioned in Rev 16:14 and 16:16.

Some take this reading further and equate *har môʿĕd* with → Jerusalem, specifically Mount Zion (Torrey, 1938; Kline, 1996). The same conclusion is drawn by other scholars, only then with a different reading of Armageddon. Thus, R.H. Charles reads Ἀρμαγεδών as a textual corruption of *har migdô*, "his fruitful mountain" (Charles, 1920, 50). Another possibility R.H. Charles offers is the reading ʿar ḥemdâ, "the desirable city" (Charles, 1920, 50). The problem with the latter reading is that this expression is never used for a city and the word ʿar as a replacement for ʿir is only used in the place name ʿar, the Moabite city mentioned in several Hebrew Bible texts (Num 21:15; Deut 2:9). The problem with the first reading of R.H. Charles is almost the same as the latter: this expression is never employed for a mountain or city (Day, 1994, 317).

The equation of *har môʿĕd* with Jerusalem coheres with the identification of the apostate city Babylon as Jerusalem (Kline, 1996). Apocalyptic literature (→ Apocalypse) which can be dated roughly contemporary of Revelation use the image of Babylon as a description of Rome though (*4 Ezra* 3:1–2; *2 Bar.* 10:1–3; *Sib. Or.* 5:143; Beale, 1999, 20–21). The final battle of history indeed takes place within the vicinity of Jerusalem and Mount Zion, yet Armageddon is connected to the defeat of Babylon (Rome) in Rev 16. The description of Babylon in Rev 17–18, as an economic superpower who suppresses and seduces the addressees, makes no sense when it refers to Jerusalem. Thus, the image of Armageddon evokes Hebrew Bible imagery of the end-time battle in the vicinity of Jerusalem (Beale, 1999, 840), but the context of the Babylon-imagery makes clear that Armageddon itself cannot be equated with Jerusalem or any adjacent place.

Another dominant reading of Ἀρμαγεδών uses Zech 12:11 (LXX) as the precise background of Armageddon. The Septuagint (→ Bible) of Zech 12:11 has transliterated *bᵉbiqʿat mĕgidôn* ("in the valley of Megiddo") as ἐν πεδίῳ ἐκκοπτομένου (*en pedíôi ekkoptoménou*; "in the valley of being cut down"). This reading thus has understood its Hebrew *Vorlage* in a symbolic way, reading *mĕgiddôn* not as a place name, but as deriving from the root *gdd* I ("to cut off"; Koehler-Baumgartner: 2001, 177). Most scholars favoring this reading read Ἀρμαγεδών as "mountain of the cut down" (LaRondelle, 1989) or "mountain of slaughter" (Jauhiainen, 2005b, 392). This position is substantiated with comments from early commentators: the 6th-century CE writers Oecumenius and Andreas of Caesarea argue that Ἀρμαγεδών means "mountain of slaughter" and that at Armageddon the kings are destined to be destroyed (Hoskier, 1928, 179–180; Schmid, 1955, 175).

R.D. Bauckham (2009) wants to combine the latter reading with the meaning of the reading *har môʿĕd*, only deriving *môʿĕd* not from *ydd* ("to collect"), but from *gdd* II ("to band together"; Ps 56:7; 59:4; 94:21). He argues that Armageddon both entails the notion of slaughter from *gdd* I and the gathering of troops from *gdd* II, combined with the allusion to the end-time character of *har* in Ezek 38–39.

The reading "mountain of slaughter" seems plausible, yet there are some problems. First, the destruction of Babylon can be found in the seventh bowl, not yet in the sixth bowl. The kings are gathered at Armageddon (Rev 16:14), but there is no fighting yet. Second, *gdd* I and II with the participial prefix *me-* can only be found in the hitpolēl-stem in the Hebrew Bible (Deut 14:1; 1 Kgs 18:28; Jer 30:23). This stem shapes the verb *gdd* in such a way that it does not resemble the *mĕgiddôn* or Μαγεδών reading of Revelation. The verb *gdd* would be *migĕtdôdêd* in the hitpolēl-stem. This observation also brings to the third objection against this reading: the vocalization pattern of this particular stem does not match the vocalization pattern *mĕgiddôn* in Rev 16:16. Alternative stems, such as the Hif'il or Hof'al, also provide a different vocalization pattern, while the Pi'el conjugation of *gdd* with this specific vocalization pattern is non-existent in the Hebrew Bible texts. The suffix *-ôn* is also remarkable in this reading and cannot be explained sufficiently. The Hebrew grammar thus seems to deny the possibility of such a reading.

Several other, less supported, readings can be mentioned. H. Gunkel has stated that John derived Ἀρμαγεδών from an unknown apocalyptic tradition, perhaps parallel to *1 En.* 6:6 (Gunkel, 1895, 263–266). H. Zimmern, in a note added to H. Gunkel's book, has argued that Ἀρμαγεδών has a background in Babylon mythology and must be read as a form of Ὑεσεμιγαδων/*Uesemigadôn*, the name of the husband of the Babylonian goddess of the underworld (Gunkel, 1895, 389n2). R.H. Charles mentions the reading of D. Völter: *ʾaraʿmĕggidôn* ("the land of Megiddo"; Charles, 1920, 50). A. van den Born (1954) argues for the reading *ʾrṣ hmgg* ("mount of the Macedonians"). M. Oberweis (1995) reads *nôd ʿămrâh* ("Nod and Gomorrah"), referring to the murder of Abel in Gen 4:14 at Nod and the destruction of Gomorrah in Gen 19. All these proposals can be deemed far-fetched and speculative, conjectures without textual basis and not making sense in the context of Rev 16:16.

R.H. Charles states in his commentary from 1920: "No convincing interpretation has as yet been given of this phrase" (Charles, 1920, 50). The same is said by J. Jeremias 12 years later: "The riddle of Ἀρμαγεδών still awaits solution" (Jeremias, 1932, 77). We still have not reached a conclusive reading of Ἀρμαγεδών

almost 100 years later. It is better to understand Armageddon as "a purely literary space, built from references contained in memories and texts" (Burnet & Detal, 2023, 5).

3. Armageddon in the Early Church

R. Burnet and P.E. Detal (2023) provide an overview of the reception of Armageddon in the early church. They note that the first interpreters of Revelation are not that much interested in elucidating the meaning of Armageddon. → Tyconius simply states in his *Expositio Apocalypseos* (5.44; 7.24) that it is a place of gathering, an opinion shared by Primasius of Hadrumetus in his *Commentarius in Apocalypsin* (4.16). The aforementioned Oecumenius and Andreas of Caesarea are examples of later interpretation of Armageddon in the East: Armageddon is a place of slaughter (διακοπή/*diakopē*; διακοπτομένη/ *diakoptomênê*), referring to Zech 12:11 (LXX).

Jerome provides an explanation from the West: "Armageddon means the raising of the roof, or the raising at first, but better the mount of robbers or the globular mount" (*Armageddon consurrectio tecti sive consurrectio in priora. Sed melius mons a latrunculis vel mons globosus*; Jer. *Nom. hebr.* 117; see also Aug. *Civ.* 20.11). → Jerome bases this interpretation on a saying of Pseudo-Origen: "Armageddon is the roof of the house or the raising at first" (Ἀρμαγεδών ἐξέργεσις τοῦ δώματος ἢ εἰς τὰ ἐμπροσθεν ἐξέγερσις/*Armagedôn exégersis tou dômatos ě eis tà emprosthen exégersis*; De Lagarde, 1897, 187). R. Burnet and P.E. Detal explain that the first part of Jerome's explanation, the raising of the roof, depends on two paronyms or homophones: *gd* is read as *gg*, thus Gog and Magog meaning "roof" (*gĕg*). The mount of brigands can also be explained using Pseudo-Origen's exegesis, understanding *gôd* as "to be a pirate, a bandit" (πειρατεύειν/*peirateúein*). The globulous mount is derived from the exegesis of *gād*, "small ball."

R. Burnet and P.E. Detal (2023) show that reading the name of Armageddon symbolically was done extensively in the early church. The majority position, reading Ἀρμαγεδών as "the mountain of Megiddo," has become dominant since the 16th century (Burnet & Detal, 2023, 9–14).

The idea of a place of gathering before the end-time battle is attested in several early Christian sources, both apocalyptic and non-apocalyptic (DiTommaso, 2009). Armageddon is for → Augustine of Hippo not a literal place, but a symbolic eschatological place of resistance against the worldwide Church of Christ (Aug. *Civ.* 20.11). → Lactantius reads the episode from Rev 16 as a literal battle between Christ and the demonic forces (Lact. *Inst.* 7.17–19). Early Christian authors understand the end-time battle, including Armageddon, either in the line of Augustine's symbolic interpretation or in Lactantius' literal exegesis.

Historiography

The most elaborated contribution on the reading "the mountain of Megiddo" is J. Day (1994). Contributions arguing for the reading *har mô'ĕd* are F. Hommel (1890), J. Jeremias (1932), C.C. Torrey (1938), R.E. Loasby (1989), and M.G. Kline (1996). The reading "place of slaughter" is supported by H.K. LaRondelle (1985; 1989). Other articles on the subject of Armageddon are W.H. Shea (1980), M. Oberweis (1995), M. Jauhiainen (2005b), and R.D. Bauckham (2009). A reception history of Armageddon is provided by R. Burnet and P.E. Detal (2023) and in a lesser degree by L. DiTommaso (2009).

Bibliography

Adams, A.D., ed., *Primasius Hadrumetinus: Commentarius in Apocalypsin*, CCSL 92, Turnhout, 1985.

Aune, D.E., *Revelation 6–16*, WBC 52b, Nashville, 1998.

Bauckham, R.D., "Armageddon I. New Testament," in: S.L. McKenzie et al., eds., *EBR*, vol. II: *Anim–Atheism*, Berlin, 2009, 769–772.

Beale, G.K., *The Use of Daniel in Jewish Apocalyptic Literature and in the Revelation of St. John*, Lanham, 1984.

Beale, G.K., *The Book of Revelation*, NIGTC, Grand Rapids, 1999.

Born, A. van den, "Études sur quelques toponymes bibliques," *OTS* 10, 1954, 197–201.

Burnet, R., & P.E. Detal, "Armageddon: A History of the Location of the End of Time," *JBRec* 10/2, 2023, 1–27.

Charles, R.H.,*A Critical and Exegetical Commentary on the Revelation of St. John*, vol. II, ICC, Edinburgh, 1920.

Day, J., "The Origin of Armageddon: Revelation 16:16 as an Interpretation of Zechariah 12:11," in: S.E. Porter, P. Joyce & D.E. Orton, eds., *Crossing the Boundaries: FS M.D. Goulder*, Bib.Int.S 8, Leiden, 1994, 315–326.

De Lagarde, P., *Onomastica Sacra*, Göttingen, 1897.

DiTommaso, L., "Armageddon III.A. Patristic and Medieval Times," in: S.L. McKenzie et al., eds., *EBR*, vol. II: *Anim–Atheism*, Berlin, 2009, 777–779.

Fekkes, J., *Isaiah and Prophetic Traditions in the Book of Revelation: Visionary Antecedents and their Development*, JSNT.S 93, Sheffield, 1994.

Gryson, R., ed., *Tyconius Afer: Expositio Apocalypseos (Textus Reconstructus)*, CCSL 107A, Turnhout, 2011.

Gunkel, H., *Schöpfung und Chaos in Urzeit und Endzeit*, Göttingen, 1895.

Hommel, F., "Inschriftliche Glossen und Exkurse zur Genesis und zu den Propheten," *NKZ* 1, 1890, 393–412.

Hoskier, H.C., ed., *The Complete Commentary of Oecumenius on the Apocalypse: Now Printed for the First Time from Manuscripts at Messina, Rome, Salonika, and Athos*, UMS.H 23, Ann Arbor, 1928.

Jauhiainen, M., *The Use of Zechariah in Revelation*, WUNT 199, 2nd series, Tübingen, 2005a.

Jauhiainen, M., "The OT Background to *Armageddon* (Rev. 16:16) Revisited," *NT* 47, 2005b, 381–393.

Jeremias, J., "Har Magedon (Apc 16 16)," *ZNW* 31, 1932, 73–77.

Kline, M.G., "Har Magedon: The End of the Millenium," *JETS* 39, 1996, 207–222.

Koehler, L., & A. Baumgartner, *The Hebrew and Aramaic Lexicon of the Hebrew Bible: Study Edition*, vol. I: א-ע, Leiden, 2001; trans. & ed. M.E.J. Richardson.

LaRondelle, H.K., "The Biblical Concept of Armageddon," *JETS* 28, 1985, 21–31.

LaRondelle, H.K., "The Etymology of Har-Magedon (Rev. 16:16)," *AUSS* 27, 1989, 69–73.

Loasby, R.E., "'Har-Magedon' According to the Hebrew in the Setting of the Seven Last Plagues of Revelation 16," *AUSS* 27, 1989, 129–132.

Migne, J.P., ed., *S. Eusebii Hieronymi Opera Omnia*, PL 23, Turnhout, 1997.

Oberweis, M., "Erwägungen zur apokalyptischen Ortsbezeichnung 'Harmagedon'," *Bib.* 76, 1995, 305–324.

Schmid, J., *Studien zur Geschichte des griechischen Apokalypse-Textes*, part 1: *Der Apokalypse-Kommentar des Andreas von Kaisarea*, Munich, 1955.

Shea, W.H., "The Location and Significance of Armageddon in Rev 16:16," *AUSS* 18, 1980, 157–162.

Torrey, C.C., "Armageddon," *HThR* 31, 1938, 237–248.

Ussishkin, D., *Megiddo-Armageddon: The Story of the Canaanite and Israelite City*, Jerusalem, 2018.

Violet, B., "Har Magedon," *ZNW* 31, 1932, 205–206.

ARJAN VAN DEN OS

Armenium Bible → Bible: XIV. Armenian

Arnobius of Sicca

One of the least understood Christian authors of the pre-Constantinian period, Arnobius was a rhetor from Sicca Veneria (Le Kef, Tunisia), in the Roman province of *Africa Proconsularia*, and Lactantius was his pupil (Jer. *Ep.* 70; *Vir. ill.* 80). His *Adversus nationes* in seven books was first published in Rome in 1542 by Franciscus Sabaeus, curator of the Vatican Library, and since that time more than 30 editions of the Latin text have appeared. A. Reifferscheid's edition, published as volume IV of the *Corpus scriptorum ecclesiasticorum latinorum* (1875), superseded all previous editions until C. Marchesi's 1934 publication in volume LXII of the *Corpus scriptorum latinorum Paravianum*. In recent years editions of various books of the *Adversus nationes* have appeared in the Budé series. Two manuscripts preserve the original Latin text: the *Parisinus Latinus* 1661 (P) at the Bibliothèque Nationale and the *Bruxellensis Latinus* 10847 (B) at the Bibliothèque Royale de Bruxelles. Both contain the *Octavius* of Minucius Felix as the eighth book. → Jerome, the sole source of information about Arnobius from antiquity, offers intriguing biographical data about him in his *Chronicon*:

> Arnobius enjoys great repute as a rhetorician in Africa. While he was giving instruction in oratory to the youth of Sicca and was yet a pagan, he was drawn as the result of dreams to belief in Christianity. Failing, however, to obtain from the bishop acceptance into the faith which he had hitherto always attacked, he gave all his efforts to the composition of most splendid books against his former religion, and with these as so many pledges of his loyalty, he at last obtained the desired affiliation. (Jer. *Chron.* 326–327 CE; Simmons, 1995, 94–130, analyzes Jerome's remarks about Arnobius)

The contents of the *Adversus nationes* and the incipit of Book 5, which states *Arnobius orator*, indisputably support the remark that Arnobius was a rhetor (→ Rhetoric). References to the cult of Saturn, Moorish deities, the Psylli, Garamentes, Gaetuli and Zeugitani, and ethnic customs, as well as possible allusions to the marble quarries at Simitthu (Chemtou) and the testimonial about pagan practices before his conversion to Christ, betray an African background for the author (Simmons, 1995, 8, 16; and Arn. *Adv. nat.* 1.16; 1.36; 1.39; 2.32; 2.40; 2.68, 70, 71; 3.6–29; 4.9; 4.14, 20, 22, 24, 26; 5.3; 6.5; 6.12, 25). Personal devotion to a deity as the result of dreams is also deeply imbedded in the religious culture of Roman North Africa, and it is not something that Jerome himself fabricated. M.B. Simmons has shown that Books 1–2 represent a revocation of the criticisms of Porphyry of Tyre derived from his anti-Christian works, which Arnobius used when he himself had attacked Christianity. Books 3–7 reveal that the author used the same method, literary retorsion, against paganism (→ Pagan/Paganism), that Porphyry used against Christian beliefs and practices. When Arnobius had proved to the bishop that he had revoked his formerly held Porphyrian criticisms and used Porphyry's method against paganism, he was admitted into membership in the church at Sicca (Masterson, 2014, 373–398, 387).

The *Chronicon* passage gives the dates of 326–327 CE for Arnobius, which disagrees with two passages from *De viris illustribus* placing him in the reign of → Diocletian. Most scholars reject the later chronology as erroneous, explaining the conflict of dates as resulting from confusing the *Vicennalia* of Diocletian with those of Constantine (see Bryce & Campbell, 1975, 406; McCracken, 1949, vol. I, 7–12; Bonniec, 1982, 33; Simmons, 1995, 6f.; Fragu, 2010, xxi–xxii; and Masterson, 2014, 375n6), and in any event the contents of the *Adversus nationes* provide strong evidence that it was written during the Great Persecution (→ Persecution of Christians). In *Adv. nat.* 4.36 Arnobius asks why Christian Scriptures have been given to the flames and places of worship have been violently torn down, a clear reference to the first edict against the Christians promulgated on Feb 24, 303 CE. References to contemporary persecutions occur in all seven books of the work. Roman officials despoil Christians of their goods and inflict capital punishment on them (*Adv. nat.* 1.26). Arnobius alludes to Apollo's oracle at Didyma consulted before the persecution (*Adv. nat.* 1.25–26). Christian executions result from unjust hatred (*Adv. nat.* 1.35, 55, 64). All kinds of morbid tortures are mentioned

(*Adv. nat.* 2.5, 77, 78). Christians are being burned alive, thrown to wild beasts (*Adv. nat.* 3.36), and exiled (*Adv. nat.* 5.29). The "new penalties" of *Adv. nat.* 6.11 (see *Adv. nat.* 6.27) allude to Diocletian's second and third edicts, and most of Book 7 attacks animal sacrifices, which were universally required of the empire's subjects by the fourth edict. Conversely, there is no mention in the work of any of the post-311 CE events favoring the Christians, which attracted the keen interest of contemporary apologists (→ Eusebius of Caesarea and → Lactantius), for example Galerius' Edict of Toleration (Apr 30, 311), the "Edict of Milan," Constantine's vision before the battle of the Milvian Bridge and his subsequent conversion, his massive church-building program, the Council of → Nicaea, nor any of the pro-Christian policies that positively impacted Roman North Africa and the other provinces of the empire. G.E. McCracken is therefore correct to conclude that 311 CE should be taken as an absolute terminus ante quem for dating the *Adversus nationes*, and most scholars have agreed with M.B. Simmons, who posits 302–305 CE.

1. Structure and Style

Of the seven books of the *Adversus nationes*, the first two contain retractations of Porphyrian criticisms of Christianity that Arnobius had formerly used against the Christian religion before his conversion (Edwards, 1999, 200n14: "A very cogent case."). Books 5–7 represent a sustained attack upon pagan beliefs and practices. Due to a deficient knowledge of the Bible and Christian doctrine, Arnobius is more effective in his attack upon paganism than in his defense of Christianity. Strategically interwoven in the work are seven résumés (*Adv. nat.* 1.18; 3.12–13; 4.28; 6.2; 7.4–5; 7.35–36) that recapitulate the argument that the gods are not immortal, retorting, for example, Porphyry's Hecatean oracle that proclaimed Christ to be only a good mortal being (Aug. *Civ.* 19.23). Each book develops an appropriate polemical theme in conjunction with this literary infrastructure. Book 1 responds to the pagan accusations blaming all the evils occurring in the empire upon the Christians and that the gods are angry at their impiety due to worshipping a mere man, and are thus punishing the Roman Empire. A digression from the main theme,

Book 2 is an intriguing critique of philosophical doctrines in which Arnobius develops his notion of the nature and destiny of the → soul, which is granted immortality only by Christ. Book 3 attacks the anthropomorphic depiction of the gods that has resulted from the erroneous and contradictory views of pagan theologians. It is therefore the pagans who should be blamed for the gods' anger toward humanity. The immoral nature and behavior of the gods are addressed in Book 4. Applying a method of literary retorsion, Book 5 calumniates the mystery cults and pagan mythology, which are described as pure literary fiction. Pagan temples and images (Book 6) and animal sacrifice (Book 7) terminate one of the best polemical arguments against paganism in the ante-Nicene period. Since Book 7 breaks off abruptly and betrays the need of editorial revision, Arnobius might have planned a final eighth book that was never realized due most probably to his death circa 305 CE of unknown causes.

The great erudition represented by a vast knowledge of Greek and Latin works is evident throughout the work. Arnobius certainly knew Greek, and of the 51 Greek authors named, Plato, mentioned 14 times, exerted the greatest influence upon his thought, though many others are cited including Aristotle, Sophocles, Epictetus, Hesiod, Homer, Numenius, Plutarch, and Pythagoras. Latin sources include Cicero, Q. Fabius Pictor, and Verrius Flaccus, among many others, with Varro and Lucretius heading the list of the most frequently cited. Jerome's pejorative assessment of Arnobius' style as "uneven and prolix and without clear divisions in his work, resulting in confusion" (Jer. *Ep.* 58.10) has been challenged and modified by modern scholarship. H. Bryce and H. Campbell (1975) note the abundance of solecisms and barbarisms, while at times Arnobius rises to genuine eloquence. H le Bonniec (1982) observes his penchant for abstraction, a tendency toward archaic words in imitation of Cicero, and the employment of poetic language. G.E. McCracken (1949) partly agrees with Jerome while noting the organic unity of the work and rightly attributes any stylistic deficiencies to the author's rhetorical device. In making his point, Arnobius is often repetitive. B. Fragu (2010) and others have shown his mastery of irony and a sardonic wit reminiscent of Tertullian articulated with a rich vocabulary, neologisms, and a complex word order preserved by a Latinity that has been described as between classical metrical and medieval rhythmic prose.

2. Knowledge of Christianity

As a recent convert to Christ and not yet under catechetical instruction as he wrote the *Adversus nationes*, Arnobius did not have a sound knowledge of Scripture, the sacrament, or basic teaching of the church, nor does his concept of God cohere with evolving orthodox views. Described as the Father of all things and high king to whom Christians pray daily, God is the creator of the universe, but not of human beings, who were created by an inferior demiurgic figure (*Adv. nat.* 2.45–48). Conceived as highly transcendent and understood apophatically (*Adv. nat.* 3.19), the supreme being is the first god without form who does not possess anthropomorphic characteristics (*Adv. nat.* 1.31) and cannot express anger (*Adv. nat.* 6.2; 7.35). Omnipotent and omnipresent, God does not remove evil from the world (*Adv. nat.* 2.54–65) even though he is aware of its existence. Christ is repeatedly described as God, and not a human being as the pagans claim. He is more powerful than the fates and has liberated his disciples from the error of polytheism (*Adv. nat.* 1.38). Christ's miracles included healing the sick and exorcising demons (→ Demonology/Demons) and prove his deity, though the miracle of glossolalia recorded in Acts 2 is incorrectly attributed to Christ. Christians worship him daily as a divine being (*pro numine*), but the relation between the Father and the Son is unclear, and Arnobius does not offer a theological exposition of the doctrines of the → incarnation, crucifixion (→ Cross/Crucifixion), and → resurrection. Christ came to earth in human form to reveal knowledge of the supreme God and to confer immortality upon human souls. There is no mention of the → Holy Spirit in the work.

Arnobius does not exhibit knowledge of the doctrine of original sin (arguably, there is no *doctrine* of the original sin yet). The soul possesses an intermediate character between life and death (*Adv. nat.* 2.35–36) and sins due to a natural weakness, not free will or choice. Wretched and unhappy, it is totally blind and ignorant (*Adv. nat.* 1.49) but can be delivered from death to life by Christ's teachings. At death

souls without knowledge of God will experience torments (*Adv. nat.* 2.14). Arnobius shows no familiarity with the Hebrew Bible and makes only a few allusions to the New Testament, though he has a basic knowledge of Christ's miracles. The only Christian predecessor cited is Simon Peter, who is depicted as destroying the arch heretic → Simon Magus. This implies an influence from the cult of Peter observed in the North African provinces of the period. → Clement of Alexandria, → Tertullian, → Cyprian of Carthage, and → Minucius Felix represent the principal Christian sources used by Arnobius.

3. Arnobius and Porphyry

Since the publication of M.B. Simmons' book (1995), there has been a growing scholarly consensus that the principal adversary of Arnobius was his contemporary → Porphyry of Tyre, the author of the *Contra Christianos* and *De philosophia ex oraculis*, which contained a number of anti-Christian oracles published before the launching of the Great Persecution. At the beginning of the *Adversus nationes*, Arnobius alludes to pagans speaking against Christianity in oracular fashion, which is a response to the *De philosophia ex oraculis* of Porphyry. After his conversion Arnobius used the same methods against Prophyry: by means of literary retorsion, he argues that the pagan myths are ridiculous and contradictory (e.g. *Adv. nat.* 5.2–4), a good example of the kind of method Porphyry used in criticizing Christian Scripture (Champeaux, 2007, xxvi note 51; and Fragu, 2010, xxv). The *New Men* (*viri noui*) of *Adv. nat.* 2.15 have been identified as Porphyry and his followers. In the work Arnobius develops a sustained attack upon major Porphyrian themes (e.g.): Christianity is antisalvific (*Adv. nat.* 1.3), theurgical rituals (*Adv. nat.* 2.13), souls are sent to earth to learn evil and receive their wings at death (*Adv. nat.* 2.33–42), temples and images (Book 6), the true nature of a god (Book 7), and the belief that Aesculapius cured Rome of the plaque, which Arnobius denies (*Adv. nat.* 7.47f.), retorting Porphyry's claims that since Christ began to be worshipped Asclepius and the other gods have not blessed the eternal city.

Arnobius also responds to the attacks that Porphyry made directly upon Christ and the apostles by defending the criticism that Christian faith cannot prove that what it claims is true (*Adv. nat.* 1.4; 2.8–10); Christ was a mere man (*Adv. nat.* 1.36f.), the disciples were entangled in error and did not acquire knowledge of God (*Adv. nat.* 1.38f.), Christ died an ignominious death by crucifixion (*Adv. nat.* 1.41), the disciples were rustic and uneducated men (*Adv. nat.* 1.50–59) who fabricated lies about Christ (*Adv. nat.* 1.57), Christianity is a new religion (*Adv. nat.* 1.57), the advent of Christ is recent (*Adv. nat.* 2.74), the disciples were fated not to receive salvation from the gods (*Adv. nat.* 1.47; 2.2; 2.14), Christians have abandoned ancestral religious customs (*Adv. nat.* 2.67), and Christianity does not offer the *via salutis universalis animae liberandae* (*Adv. nat.* 2.64–74). Arnobius responds to the latter, mentioned by Augustine of Hippo in Book 10 of *De civitate dei*, throughout the *Adversus nationes*, but especially in Book 2, by showing that Christ is the only way to the salvation of the soul, and this gift is conferred on anyone who asks, resulting in the soul's immortality and bliss with God in the afterlife (*Adv. nat.* 2.60–65).

4. Significance for Early Christianity

The 6th-century CE *Decretum de libris recipiendis et non recipiendis* formerly ascribed to Pope Gelasius, which included the *Adversus nationes* among the apocrypha *a catholicis vitanda*, can help to explain the reason for the work's neglect until the post-Enlightenment period. Although still one of the most highly ignored Christian writers of late antiquity, Arnobius is increasingly gaining the attention he deserves from ancient historians and patristic scholars as an important source for Greco-Roman religion and philosophy due to the fact that the *Adversus nationes* offers a goldmine of information on pagan beliefs and practices. It also provides invaluable insight for an understanding of the pagan/Christian conflict during the age of Diocletian, and specifically the intellectual background to the Great Persecution of 303–305 CE. Recent scholarship has shown how the works of Arnobius, Lactantius, and Eusebius studied together can shed light on the composite picture of Christian apologetics in the period leading up to the conversion of Constantine.

Historiography

Critical editions of the *Adversus nationes*, often accompanied by commentaries (e.g. Marchesi, 1953; Laurenti, 1962; Bonniec, 1982, Book 1; Gierlich, 1985; Champeaux, 2007, Book 3; Amata, 2007; Fragu, 2010, Books 6–7; see Bryce & Campbell, 1975; Duval, 1986) appeared after the two-volume study published in 1949 by G.E. McCracken. Contextual studies of the 20th century aimed at offering a better understanding of Arnobius' social, literary, philosophical, and religious background (Courcelle, 1955; Swift, 1965; Vogt, 1968; Dillon, 1973; Gareau, 1980; Laurenti, 1981; Gigon, 1982). C. Marchesi (1930), M.B. Simmons (1995; 1997; 2012; 2015), M.J. Edwards (1999), E. Otón Sobrino (2001), and A.R. Birley (2005), have analyzed the major apologetical argument of *Adversus nationes*. Beginning with the ground-breaking monograph by E.R. Micka in 1943 which critically examined the notion of divine anger in the works of Arnobius and Lactantius, there have been subsequent studies of the Christian views of Arnobius (Guglielmino, 1947; Scheidweiler, 1955; Sirna, 1964; McDonald, 1966; Jufresa, 1973; Madden, 1981; Schmid, 1984; Amata, 1984; 1986; 1989; Bodelón, 1998–1999).

The seminal work on Arnobius in English for the late 20th and continuing into the 21st century is M.B. Simmons (1995). O. Nicholson (1984), M.B. Simmons (1995; 2015), M.J. Edwards (2004), C.M. Lucarini (2005), and M. Masterson (2014) have proposed various dates for the *Adversus nationes*. In recent decades a growing number of works have focused on Arnobius' relation to Graeco-Roman culture (Putten, 1971; Bonniec, 1974; Beatrice, 1988; Podemann Sorensen, 1989; Heim, 1992; Blomart, 1993; Mora, 1994; Simmons, 1995; 1997; 2012; 2015; North, 2007; Quinn, 2010; Masterson, 2014; Kaabia, 2015); literary style of *Adversus nationes* (e.g. Gabarrou, 1921b; Hagendahl, 1936; 1983; Marin, 2008; Santorelli, 2012); Roman North African *Sitz im Leben* (e.g. Places, 1972; Fasce, 1980; Simmons, 1995; 2015; Lipinski, 2005; Guédon, 2011–2012); and the identification of the *viri novi* (*new men*) polemically addressed in *Adv. nat.* 2.15 (Festugière, 1940; Courcelle, 1953; Mazza, 1963; Fortin, 1973; Simmons, 1995, 2012, 2015). Finally, major monographs on various aspects of *Arnobiana* include those of C. Stange (1893), F. Gabarrou (1921a), H. Hagendahl (1936), E. Rapisarda (1939),

L. Berkowitz (1967), A. Sitte (1970), C. Burger (1971), B. Amata (1984), F. Mora (1994), M.B. Simmons (1995), and N.L. Thomas (2011).

This article is dedicated to the author's granddaughter: Ava Grace Wildermuth (born Sept. 18, 2009).

Bibliography

Amata, B., *Problemi di antropologia Arnobiana*, Rome, 1984.

Amata, B., "Destino finale dell'uomo nell'opera di Arnobio di Sicca (III–IV sec. d. C.)," in: S. Felici, ed., *Morte e immortalità: Nella catechesi dei padri del iii–iv secolo: Convegno, Fac. Di Lett. Cristiane e classiche, Roma, 16–18 mars 1984*, Rome, 1985, 47–62.

Amata, B., "Dubbio e certezza in Arnobio di Sicca," *SP* 21, 1989, 217–245.

Amata, B., *Arnobii Siccensis Adversus nationes L.VII*, Rome, 2007.

Beatrice, P.F., "Un oracle antichrétien chez Arnobe," in: Y de Andia et al., eds., *Memorial Dom Jean Gribomont*, Rome, 1988, 107–129.

Berkowitz, L., *Index Arnobianus*, Hildesheim, 1967.

Birley, A.R., "Attitudes to the State in the Latin Apologists," in: A. Wlosok et al., eds., *L'apologétique chrétienne gréco-latine à l'époque prénicénienne: Vandoeuvres-Genève, 13–17 septembre: Sept exposés suivis de discussions*, Genève-Vandoueuvres, 2005, 249–277.

Blomart, A., "Frugifer: Une divinité mithriaque léontocéphale décrite par Arnobe," *RHR* 210, 1993, 5–25.

Bodelón, S., "Arnobio y el problema del alma racional," *MHA* 19–20, 1998–1999, 62–79.

Bonniec, H. le, "Tradition de la culture classique: Arnobe témoin et juge des cultes païens," *BAGB*, 1974, 201–222.

Bonniec, H. le, *Arnobe: Contre les gentils: Livre I*, Paris, 1982.

Bryce, H., & H. Campbell, "Arnobius," in: A. Roberts & J. Donaldson, eds., *The Ante-Nicene Fathers*, vol. VI, Grand Rapids; repr. 1975, 405–543.

Burger, C., *Die theologische Position des älteren Arnobius*, Heidelberg, 1971.

Champeaux, J., *Arnobe: Contre les gentils: Livre III*, Paris, 2007.

Colombo, S., "Arnobio Afro e I suoi sette libri *Adversus nationes*," *Didas.* 5, 1930, 1–124.

Courcelle, P., "Les sages de Porphyre et les 'uiri noui' d'Arnobe," *REL* 31, 1953, 257–271.

Courcelle, P., "La polémique antichrétienne au début du IVe siècle: Qui sont lest adversaires païens d'Arnobe?" *RHR* 147, 1955, 122–123.

Dillon, J., "The Concept of Two Intellects: A Footnote to the History of Platonism," *Phron.* 18, 1973, 176–185.

Duval, Y.-M., "Sur la biographie et les manucrits d'Arnobe de Sicca: Les informations de Jérome, leur sens et leurs sources possibles," *Latomus*, 1986, 69–99.

Edwards, M.J., "The Flowering of Latin Apologetics," in: M.J Edwards, M. Goodman & S. Price, eds., *Apologetics in the Roman Empire*, Oxford, 1999, 197–221.

Edwards, M.J., "Dating Arnobius: Why Discount the Evidence of Jerome?" *AnTa* 12, 2004, 263–271.

Fasce, S., "Paganesimo africano in Arnobio," *Vich.* 9, 1980, 173–180.

Festugière, A.-J., "La doctrine des *noui uiri* chez Arnobe 11, 16 sqq.," *Cinquantenaire de l'école biblique et archéologique frqnçaise de Jérusalem (15 novembre 1890–15 novembre 1940): Mémorial Lagrange*, Paris, 1940, 97–132.

Festugière, A.-J., "Arnobiana," *VigChr* 6, 1952, 208–254.

Festugière, A.-J., *Hermétisme et mystique païenne*, Paris, 1967.

Fortin, E.L., "The 'Viri Novi' of Arnobius and the Conflict Between Faith and Reason in the Early Christian Centuries," in D. Neiman & M. Shatkin, eds., *The Heritage of the Early Church*, Rome, 1973, 197–226.

Fragu, B., *Arnobe: Contre les gentils: Livres VI–VII*, Paris, 2010.

Gabarrou, F., *Arnobe: Son œuvre*, Paris, 1921a.

Gabarrou, F., *Le latin d'Arnobe*, Paris, 1921b.

Gareau, E., "Le fondement de la vraie religion d'après Arnobe," *CEtA* 11, 1980, 13–23.

Gierlich, G., *Arnobius von Sicca: Kommentar zu den ersten beiden Büchern seines Werkes Adversus nationes*, Aachen, 1985.

Gigon, O, "Arnobio: Cristianesimo e mondo romano," in: *Mondo classico e cristianesimo*, BiIC 7, Rome, 1982, 87–100.

Guédon, S., "Les confins des espaces civiques dans l'Afrique romaine: Quelques éléments de réflexion," *Caes.* 45–46, 2011–2012, 597–614.

Guglielmino, C., "La dottrina di Arnobio," *NUDI* 1, 1947, 99.

Hagendahl, H., *La prose métrique d'Arnobe*, Göteborg, 1936.

Hagendahl, H., *Von Tertullian zu Cassiodor: Die profane literarische Tradition in dem lateinischen christlichen Schriftum*, Göteborg, 1983.

Heim, F., "L'animation des statues d'après les apologistes du IIIe siècle," *Latomus* 70, 1992, 22–23.

Jufresa, M., "La divinidad y lo divino en Arnobio," *BIEH* 7, 1973, 61–64.

Kaabia, R., "Arnobe de 'Sicca' du paganism au christianisme: L'evolution cultuelle d'un lettré romanoafricain," in: P. Ruggieri & M. Bastiana Cocco, eds., *L'Africa romana: Momenti di continuità e rottura: Bilancio di trent'anni di convegni 'L'Africa romana' atti del Convegno internazionale di studi, Alghero-Porto Conte Ricerche, 26–29 settembre 2013*, 3 vols., Rome, 2015, vol. II, 1217–1228.

Kroll, W., "Arnobiusstudien," *RMP* 72, 1917, 62–112.

Laurenti, R., ed., *I sette libri contro i pagani*, Turin, 1962.

Laurenti, R., "Il platonismo di Arnobio," *StFi* 4, 1981, 3–54.

Lipinski, E., "Bonchor de Béja," *Latomus* 64/2, 2005, 404–408.

Löfstedt, *Arnobiana*, Lund, 1917.

Lorenz, T. *De clausibus Arnobianis*, Breslau, 1910.

Lucarini, C.M., "Questioni arnobiane," *MDATC* 54, 2005, 123–164.

Madden, J.D., "Jesus as Epicurus: Arnobius of Sicca's borrowings from Lucretius," *CClCr* 2, 1981, 215–222.

Marchesi, C., "Il pessimismo di un apologetta cristiano," *Pègaso* 2, 1930, 536–550.

Marchesi, C., *Arnobii Adversus Nationes Libri VII*, 2nd ed., Turin, 1953.

Marin, M., "Reflessioni intorno alla retorica della verità nella cristianità antica," in: S. Nienhaus, ed., *L'attualità della retorica: Atti del convegno internazionale di Foggia: 18–19 maggio 2006*, Bari, 2008, 121–139.

Masterson, M., "Authoritative Obscenity in Iamblichus and Arnobius," *JECS* 22/3, 2014, 373–398.

Mazza, M., "Studi Arnobiani I: La dottrina del *vir novi* nel secondo linro dell'*Adversus nationes* di Arnobio," *Helikon* 2, 1963, 111–169.

McCracken, G.E., "Arnobius of Sicca: The Case Against the Pagans," 2 vols., in: J. Quasten & J.C. Plumpe, eds., *ACW*, New York, 1949.

McDonald, H.D., "The Doctrine of God in Arnobius, *Adversus Gentes*," *SP* 9/3, 1966, 75–81.

Micka, E.R., *The Problem of Divine Anger in Arnobius and Lactantius*, Washington DC, 1943.

Mora, F., *Arnobio e i culti di misterio: Analisi storico-religiosa del V libro dell'Adversus nationes*, Rome, 1994.

Mora, F., "La critica del sacrificio nel VII libro di Arnobio," *Cass.* 5, 1999, 203–224.

Nicholson, O., "The Date of Arnobius' *Adversus gentes*," *SP* 15, 1984, 100–107.

North, J.A., "Arnobius on Sacrifice," in: J.F. Drinkwater & R.W. Benet, eds., *Wolf Libeschuetz Reflected: Essays Presented by Colleagues, Friends & Pupils*, London, 2007, 27–36.

Opelt, I., "Schimpfwörter bei Arnobius dem Älteren," *WSt* 9, 1975, 161–173.

Otón Sobrino, E., "La polémica de Arnobio y Lactancio en torno a la 'ira Dei'," in: A. González et al., eds, *Actas del congreso internacional "cristianismo y tradición latina", Málaga, 25 a 28 de abril de 2000*, Madrid, 2001, 85–101.

Places, É. des, "Les oracles chaldaïques dans la tradition patristique africaine," *SP* 11, 1972, 27–41.

Podemann Sorensen, J., "The Myth of Attis: Structure and Myesteriosophy," in: J. Podemann Sorensen, ed., *Rethinking Religion: Studies in the Hellenistic Process*, Copenhagen, 1989, 23–29.

Putten, J.M.P.B. van der, "Arnobe croyait-il à l'existence des dieux païens?" *VigChr* 24, 1971, 52–55.

Quinn, D.P., "Roman Household Deities in the Latin Christian Writers," *SP* 44, 2010, 71–75.

Rapisarda, E., *Clemente fonte di Arnobio*, Turin, 1939.

Santorelli, P., "Un dio da distruggere: Modalità del discorso polemico in Arnobio," in A. Capone, ed., *Lessico, argomentazioni e struture retoriche nella polemica di età cristiana (III–V sec.)*, Turnhout, 2012, 189–214.

Scheidweiler, F., "Arnobius und der Marcionitismus," *ZNW* 45, 1955, 42–67.

Schmid, W.P., "Christus als Naturphilosoph bei Arnobius," in: W.P. Schmid, ed., *Ausgewählte philologische Schriften*, Berlin, 1984, 562–583.

Simmons, M.B., *Arnobius of Sicca*, Oxford, 1995.

Simmons, M.B., *Universal Salvation: Porphyry of Tyre and the Pagan-Christian Debate in Late Antiquity*, Oxford, 2015.

Simmons, M.B., "The Function of Oracles in the Pagan-Christian Conflict during the Age of Diocletian: The Case of Arnobius and Porphyry," *SP* 31, 1997, 49–56.

Simmons, M.B., Review of B. Fragu, "Arnobe: Contre les gentils: Livres VI–VII," *BMCR* 2012.08.36.

Sirna, F.G., "Arnobio e l'eresia marcionita di Patrizio," *VigChr* 18, 1964, 37–50.

Sitte, A., *Mythologische Quellen des Arnobius*, Vienna, 1970.

Stange, C. *De Arnobii oration*, Saargemünd, 1893.

Swift, L.J., "Arnobius and Lactantius: Two Views of the Pagan Poets," *TPAPA* 96, 1965, 439–448.

Thomas, N.L., *Defending Christ: The Latin Apologists Before Augustine*, Turnhout, 2011.

Vogt, J., "Toleranz und Intoleranz im constantinischen Zeitalter: Der Weg der lateinische Apologtik," *Saec.* 19, 1968, 344–361.

MICHAEL BLAND SIMMONS

Asarbus

Asarbus (Asariuus) was one of → Priscillian's of Avila lay disciples and probably joined his ascetic community at an early stage. He is mentioned in Priscillian's first tractate and is indicated as the co-author of a Priscillianist libellus, together with Tiberianus and others:

> although we condemned the doctrines of all the heretics by declaring our faith in numerous writings, and by the book of our brothers Tiberianus, Asarbus, and all the others, with whom we share a single faith and a single opinion. (Prisc. *Tract.* 1.4–7; see Conti, 2009)

Unfortunately, the libellus of which Asarbus (Asariuus) is said to have been one of the authors is lost, so that it is impossible to reconstruct its contents. However, since Priscillian's first tractate is a detailed defense of Priscillianist orthodoxy, which he was forced to write because the libellus by Asarbus, Tiberianus, and others did not satisfy the opponents of → Priscillianism, we can suppose that the libellus was similar in content and scope to the first tractate, but less extensive and exhaustive.

After Priscillian's execution in Trier in 385 CE, Emperor Maximus, who had advocated Priscillian's condemnation, sent tribunes to Spain in order to seek out Priscillian's supporters there. As a consequence, new executions were carried out, including that of Asarbus (Asariuus): see Sul. *Dial.* 3.11 (CSEL 1.208–10); *Chron.* 2.51.2 (CSEL 1.104; SC 441.344).

Bibliography

Burrus, V., *The Making of a Heretic: Gender, Authority, and the Priscillianist Controversy*, Berkeley, 1995.
Chadwick, H., *Priscillian of Avila: The Occult and the Charismatic in the Early Church*, Oxford, 1976.
Conti, M., *Priscillian: Complete Works*, Oxford, 2009.

MARCO CONTI

Ascension of Jesus Christ

According to the longer ending of Mark 16:19, Luke 24:51, and Acts 1:9–11, Jesus was carried up to heaven after having appeared on earth for a certain length of time after his resurrection (Acts alone specifies 40 days). Acts, which offers the most detailed narrative, describes Jesus rising and disappearing in a cloud and the appearance of two men in white who ask the apostles why they are gazing up into heaven. Acts 1:12 implies that the ascension took place on the Mount of Olives, consistent with Luke's locating it at Bethany, which is on the Mount's southwestern slope. Acts does not explicitly include the Virgin Mary at the ascension, but church tradition has interpreted Acts 1:14 as evidence that she was present. The Gospel of Matthew (→ Matthew the Apostle) is silent on the subject of the ascension, although it seems implicit in John 3:13, John 6:62, and John 20:17. Of the New Testament epistles, only Ephesians unequivocally refers to the ascension (Eph 4:7–14), although other references to Christ's being taken up to heaven, exalted, and enthroned at the right hand of God have been interpreted as alluding to it (e.g. Rom 8:34; 10:6–7; Phil 2:9; Col 3:1; 1 Tim 3:16; Heb 2:9; and 1 Pet 3:21–22).

A narrative of the ascension also appears in the *Apocryphon of James* (→ James the Apostle: VII. *James, Secret Book of*), in which Peter and James, whom Christ specially chooses, witness his ascension, accompanied by the sound of battle, trumpets, and general chaos.

As a dogmatic assertion, the ascension occurs as an article of faith in one of the earliest Christian summaries of kerygma (*ascendit in caelos*), the Old Roman Creed, often dated (in its Greek version) to the early 3rd century CE but translated and transmitted in the Latin Church only in the 4th century CE. → Irenaeus of Lyon includes the ascension in his rule of the faith (Iren. *Haer.* 1.10.1).

The ascension was not a major subject of theological discussion in the first three centuries CE, although Christian writers typically linked the ascension with the incarnation as proof of Christ's divinity (descent from heaven) and his identity as the true Messiah and Lord of Hosts (e.g. Just. 1 *Apol.* 50; *Dial.* 36; Nov. *Trin.* 11; 13–14; 17). Irenaeus uses the ascension as proof against the gnostics (→ Gnosis/Gnosticism), that Christ's descent and ascent were both bodily (Iren. *Epid.* 86) and links the ascension with the text from Ps 110:1 to confirm the prophet's words that the Father invites the Son to sit at his right hand in heaven (Iren. *Haer* 3.10.5; *Epid.* 85–86). Irenaeus also gives the ascension as an instance of Christ's recapitulation of Adam (→ Adam and Eve) and the prototype for human resurrection (→ Resurrection) from death (*Haer.* 5.21.1). In contrast to Irenaeus, Origen links the ascension with the resurrection but resists understanding it either in a physical or spatial sense as he maintains that God cannot be circumscribed in time or space. Thus, according to → Origen, Christ ascended after his earthly body was purified and transformed (Or. *Comm. Jo.* 6.37.292). → Tertullian, like Irenaeus, however, uses the event of the ascension against gnostics and followers of → Marcion to stress Christ's bodily reality and exaltation in heaven (Tert. *Res.* 22, 51). In his treatise *Against Praxeas*, Tertullian uses the ascension to emphasize the distinction between Father and Son (Tert. *Prax.* 30).

In the 4th century CE, the ascension became more central in the debates between Nicenes and Arians (→ Arianism) over whether the Son was fully god. This is evident in → Basil of Caesarea's writings (Bas. *Ep.* 8.3) and in → Ambrose of Milan's treatise *On the Faith*, in which the bishop of Milan uses the ascension to refute Arian claims that the Son was subordinate to the Father (Ambr. *Fid.* 1.10.63; 2.8.60). In that same treatise, Ambrose describes Christ as a conqueror, coming to heaven's gates with the spoils of his triumph (the cross). He contrasts Christ with Enoch and Elijah who were taken up, but had not descended nor, like Christ, died and been resurrected (*Fid.* 4.1.8).

Although → John Chrysostom was among the first to preach an exegetical discourse on the ascension (Chrys. *Ascens.*), the most extensive set of patristic homilies on the ascension comes from → Augustine of Hippo, who preached more than a dozen sermons on the occasion of the feast from around 396 to 420 CE. He used his pulpit to emphasize Christ's simultaneous existence on earth and in heaven (see John 3:13) and encouraged his flock to understand themselves as ascending with Christ in spirit insofar as the church constitutes the members of Christ's ecclesial body even while he remains their head. Although Christ is physically absent in his individual body (now glorified and exalted), he remains spiritually present in and operative in his earthly followers (see Aug. *Serm.* 263A). Another common theme in Augustine's ascension sermons is the link between Christ's ascension and his second coming in which he returns to the text of Acts (1:11), in which the two men in white assure the apostles that Christ will return in the same way that they saw him ascend.

1. Feast of the Ascension

The feast of the ascension was evidently commemorated in the early centuries of Christianity, although not on its own date but coinciding with either → Easter or → Pentecost. Celebration according to the Lukan chronology of 40 days after Easter seems to be consistent only in the Latin Church from the 5th century CE on. Tertullian, for example, maintains that Pentecost is an auspicious day for baptism because it incorporates the joy of both Christ's → resurrection and ascension (Tert. *Bapt.* 19). → Eusebius of Caesarea, for example, specifies that the ascension was commemorated on the 50th day or at the same time as Pentecost, and as such marked the end of the Easter season (Eus. *Vita Const.* 4.64.1). This was also true in the (probably) 3rd-century CE document, the Syriac → *Didascalia Apostolorum*, which commends

a celebration of the ascension at the completion of 50 days following Easter (*Did. Apost.* 19.9). The 4th-century CE → *Apostolic Constitutions*, however, notes a distinct feast for the ascension on the 40th day after Easter (*Const. ap.* 5.19; 8.33). The 43rd canon of the Council of Elvira (c. 300–310 CE) refers to the "fortieth day" but does not explicitly name it as the Ascension Day. Similarly, the ninth canon of the Council of → Nicaea ordered a provincial meeting on the "fortieth day" but does not specify any relationship to Easter.

A more certain 4th-century CE witness to the feast comes from Bishop → Chromatius of Aquileia (388–407 CE), who preached a sermon on the ascension for the 40th day (Chrom. *Serm.* 8.1). From this point onward, the celebration on the 40th day after Easter appears to have become established, as is evident from the sermons of Augustine and Leo the Great (→ Leo I [Bishop of Rome]) on the occasion. Augustine, in particular, mentions the 40-day interval between the resurrection and the ascension, noting that its duration corresponds to the length of Jesus' fasting in the wilderness, the length of the flood, and in itself a highly symbolic number (Aug. *Serm.* 263A.4; 264.5; 265B.1). Leo's sermons, preached on the mid-5th century CE, attend to the faith-confirming aspect of the ascension, noting that the apostles' seeing Christ ascend erased all doubts about his divinity (Leo M. *Serm.* 74; 74).

2. Shrine of the Ascension

Pilgrims to the Holy Land testify to the existence of a shrine on the Mount of Olives, dedicated to the ascension. This may have been the one that Eusebius attributes to Helena's foundation (Eus. *Vita Const.* 3.25–41) or the shrine said to have been built by the Roman noble woman, Poemenia, as described in Palladius of Helenopolis' *Life of John of Lycopolis* (Pall. *Hist. Laus.* 35.14). → Jerome remarks that → Paula observed a glistening cross on spot where Christ ascended (Jer. *Ep.* 108.12). Whatever structure existed on the site in the early 4th century CE was destroyed by the Persians in 614 CE and rebuilt by the patriarch Modestus sometime in the 620s CE and again by the crusaders in the 1150s.

3. Ascension of Christ in Art

The earliest surviving iconographic depictions of Jesus' ascension date to the late 4th century CE. One of the oldest, an ivory panel now in the Bayerisches Nationalmuseum in Munich appears to conflate the story of the resurrection with the ascension. On the right, a beardless and nimbed Jesus climbs up to heaven upon a bank of clouds. God's right hand reaches down from another cloud to grasp Christ's right hand, as if to assist him up the slope. In his left hand, Christ grasps a scroll. Just below Christ, two disciples crouch, one with his hands over his face as if fearing to gaze upon the scene; the other looks up with a gesture of awe. These might be Peter and James, especially chosen by Christ to witness his ascension as told in the *Apocryphon of James* (*NTApoc* 1:296). On the left is a small square brick structure topped by a domed, cylindrical, and colonnaded cupola, that may have been meant to evoke the aedicule at the Holy Sepulcher or, alternatively, the small shrine erected in the late 4th century CE at the site of the ascension at the Mount of Olives. Behind the building rises an olive tree in which two birds perch and peck at the fruit. Two soldiers stand to the side, one burying his head in his sleeve, the other stoically observing at the events before him. Three women approach (probably the two Marys and Salome according to Mark 16:1). They form a solemn procession moving from the lower right of the composition toward the building. They do not carry any jars of spices, but they are greeted by a wingless angel, thus confirming that these are meant to depict the women arriving at the empty tomb.

A few other 4th-century CE depictions of the ascension show similar composition to the Munich ivory. Two Gallican sarcophagus fragments, one from Arles and another from the Cathedral of Clermont-Ferrand, show Christ in profile, climbing up to heaven and grasping God's hand in his right.

A similar, but more simplified, image appears on a small marble relief from the Church of San Giovanni Battista in Ravenna, that was likely part of a marble casket, the so-called reliquary of Santi Julitta and Quiricus. Likely originating from northern Italy, it is dated to the early 5th century CE. Here two (not three) women kneel before Christ as he mounts a small step, presumably into heaven. Christ grasps a

Fig. 1: Ascension of Jesus Christ, ivory panel (c. 400 CE; Bavarian National Museum, Munich).

cross staff and an unfurled scroll in his right hand and with his left grasps the hand of God, which reaches down to aid his ascent. A rectangular structure with an arched door and crenellated rampart presumably represents the empty tomb. Here again the iconography joins depictions of the resurrection with the ascension. The two women are probably intended to refer to the two in Matthew who greet Jesus as they meet him on the road (Matt 28:9).

A completely different representation of the ascension appears on a small wooden panel found on the door of Rome's Basilica of Santa Sabina. Dated to the early 5th century CE, it depicts three angels evidently guiding Jesus upward. No divine hand reaches down to assist. Below are four figures. One sits with his head in his hands, gazing rather thoughtfully; the other three look up as if in astonishment.

Other images of the ascension occur on pottery lamps, many of them from North Africa, generally dated to the 4th and 5th centuries CE. In the center of these lamps' top surfaces (between the handle and the spout) are depictions of the ascension that show Christ standing, facing forward, with a cross over his right shoulder. Beneath his feet are two angels who appear to be carrying him upward toward heaven. In the upper section of the spout are two men; their faces turned upward and their hands making a gesture of acclamation (the two men in white?).

Depictions of the ascension from the 6th and 7th centuries CE are different from either of these compositions and reflect a gradually standardized composition. A prototypical example, found in the Syriac *Gospel of Rabbula* (c. 586 CE), shows Jesus standing within a dark blue areole (mandorla), making the gesture of blessing with his right hand and holding an unfurled scroll in his left. The aureole (*mandorla*)is being borne to heaven by → Ezekiel's four living creatures with wheels beneath them and eyes on their wings (Ezek 1:15–21, see Rev 4:7–8). The divine hand here reaches down from the cherubic chariot. To the left and right, angels hold out crowns or appear to guide the mandora as it moves upward. The sun and moon peek out of left and right corners.

Below, in front of a mountainous landscape, intended, no doubt, to represent the Mount of Olives, the Virgin → Mary and the twelve apostles are joined by two winged and nimbed men in white. These figures direct the apostles' gaze up to the ascending Christ. Mary, by contrast, stands in the center, calmly facing forward, her hands in the prayer posture. She wears a deep blue *maphorion* and, like Christ, the two men in white, and the angels, she also has a halo.

This composition is echoed in a late 5th- or early 6th-century CE icon from the Monastery of Saint Catherine in Sinai, in which Paul is prominently included in the group of apostles and on Mary's immediate right hand. It also appears on a reliquary box containing stones gathered from various pilgrimage sites in the Holy Land and now in the Vatican Museum.

This composition also has parallels on Byzantine rings and 6th-century CE pilgrimage ampullae from the Holy Land, in which Christ rises within a mandorla supported by angels. In the lower register, the twelve apostles stand to either side of the Virgin Mary. She faces forward with her hands outstretched in the prayer posture. The apostles make a variety of gestures indicating their surprise and awe. On some of these ampullae, the hand of God and the dove of

the Holy Spirit descend from above top, thereby linking the ascension to the event of Pentecost.

This basic composition – Jesus being borne to heaven in a mandorla supported by angels and cherubim above the twelve awe-struck apostles, two men in white, and the centrally positioned and front-facing Virgin – is more or less repeated in eastern Christian art through the centuries.

In some variants Christ is enthroned instead of standing. Occasionally, the Virgin appears in profile rather than facing forward. Later western compositions are often influenced by this Byzantine type but include some imaginative adaptations. The Drogo Sacramentary (8th cent. CE) depicts Christ as in the Munich ivory, climbing up a cloud bank and grasping God's hand, a motif repeated in an 11th-century ivory from Cologne; others show Jesus rising on a cloud platform without the assistance of angels. By the high middle ages in the West, many representations include only Christ's feet, rising out of the picture space, with the viewers watch them disappear.

Scholars have compared early depictions of Jesus' ascension to depictions of imperial apotheoses as well as images of → Elijah being taken up (2 Kgs 2:11). Although Jesus is not shown as rising in a chariot, the imagery has certain similarities, especially a posthumous coin of the emperor Constantine, which shows the hand of God coming down to guide the ruler up to heaven.

Historiography

One of the most influential works on the ascension is that of J.G. Davies (1958). J.G. Davies' work includes a helpful summary of biblical and patristic texts on the subject. Following J.G. Davies and sometimes challenging his conclusions on interpreting certain New Testament texts (e.g. Mark 9:38 and 14:62) are the works of G. Lohfink (1972) and A.W. Zwiep (1997) who both summarize prior scholarship on the question of how to interpret Gospel texts that appear to allude to the ascension but may have had the same intention as the texts from Luke–Acts. A more recent work by J. Kramer (2016), has a very useful early chapter on biblical sources and patristic writings on ascension theology.

The subject of the ascension in early Christian art has been less studied than the iconography of the resurrection. Among the most useful studies are by S.H. Gutberlet (1934), who considers the influence of Ezekiel's vision on the early Christian depictions, and the essay by A. van den Hoek and J. Herrmann (2003), which considers variations in the theme with special attention to North African artifacts.

Bibliography

Danielou, J.,"Grégoire de Nysse et l'origine de la fête de l'ascension," in: P. Grangield & J.A. Jungmann, eds., *Kyriakon: FS Johannes Quasten*, 2 vols.,vol. II, Münster, 1970, 663–666.

Davies, J.G., *He Ascended into Heaven*, New York, 1958.

Deshman, R., "Another Look at the Disappearing Christ," *ArtB* 79, 1997, 518–546.

Dewald, E.T., "The Iconography of the Ascension," *AJA* 19, 2nd series, 1915, 277–319.

Engemann, J., "A Modern Myth": The Sixth-Century Starting Date of the 'Eastern' Representation of Christ's Ascension," in: A.C. Olovsdotter, ed., *Envisioning Worlds in Late Antique Art*, Berlin, 2018, 199–207.

Farrow, D., *Ascension and Ecclesia*, Grand Rapids, 1990.

Gutberlet, H., *Die Himmelfahrt Christi in der bildenden Kunst von den Anfängen bis ins hohe Mittelalter*, Strasburg, 1934.

Hoek, A. van den, & J. Herrmann, "Two Men in White: Observations on an Early Christian Lamp from North Africa with the Ascension of Christ," in: D. Warren et al., eds., *Early Christian Voices in Texts, Traditions, and Symbols: FS François Bovon*, Leiden, 2003, 293–318.

Kramer, J., *Between Heaven and Earth: Liminality and the Ascension of Christ in Anglo-Saxon Literature*, Manchester, 2016.

Lohfink, G., *Die Himmelfahrt Jesu: Erfindung oder Erfahrung*, KRB 18, Stuttgart, 1972.

Marrevee, W.H., *The Ascension of Christ in the Works of St. Augustine*, Ottawa, 1967.

Mihoc, J., "The Ascension of Jesus Christ: A Critical and Exegetical Study of the Ascension in Luke–Acts and in the Jewish and Christian Contexts," Master's thesis, Durham, 2010.

Schapiro, M., "The Disappearing Christ: The Ascension in English Art around the Year 1000," *GBA* 23, series 6, 1943, 133–152.

Schmid, A.A., "Himmelfahrt Christi," in: E. Kirschbaum et al., eds., *LCI*, vol. II, Rome, 1976, 269–276, 273.

Schrade, H., *Zur Ikonographie der Himmelfahrt Christi*, Leipzig, 1930.

Zwiep, A.W., *The Ascension of the Messiah in Lukan Christology*, NovTSup 87, Leiden, 1997.

ROBIN M. JENSEN

Asceticism

The word "asceticism" is a neologism based on the Greek ἄσκησις/*askēsis* ("exercise," "discipline," or "study") The root sense in Greek was athletic training, but the word was also used for philosophical discipline. In Christian usage, *askesis* denoted an array of physical and intellectual practices designed to hone spiritual receptivity. These practices included fasting, almsgiving, denial of sleep, prayer, the reading of the Bible, and direction from an experienced guide. Sexual renunciation was a common element of Christian asceticism, whether virginity, abstinence after marriage, or not remarrying when widowed. Despite its ambiguity, the term has become the generic label for ways of life characterized by emphasis on those disciplines, including the later monastic form of asceticism (Diem, 2019).

The study of early Christian asceticism is hindered by the lack of comprehensive evidence owing to the dominance of monastic asceticism from the mid-4th century CE onwards. As earlier models of ascetic life were subsumed or rendered obsolete, their texts were less frequently copied, replaced by translations of Egyptian monastic literature and new compositions inspired by that tradition (→ Monasticism). The partial recovery of earlier forms has been a major element of 19th- and 20th-century scholarship on early Christianity.

1. Origins of Christian Asceticism

The theory and practice of specifically Christian asceticism arose from three sources: the sectarian Jewish movements in Palestine such as those represented in the → Dead Sea Scrolls; the foundational Christian writings that formed the New Testament (→ Bible); and the intellectual and physical disciplines used by certain Greek/Hellenistic philosophical schools.

The Hebrew Bible elaborates cultic practices to be done by the Temple priesthood as well as ritual and dietary practices to be done in the context of household and family. Warriors and prophets were the ascetic elite, and theirs were not lifelong commitments. The eccentric lifestyles of certain prophets later became types for Christian monks, particularly that of Elijah, whose retreat into the desert, preaching of repentance, and dependence on God's providence made him, as → Antony the Great said in the 4th century CE, "the mirror of monks" (Athan. *Vit. Ant.* 7). In the Hebrew Bible, however, the prophets are hardly patterns for imitation.

At the time of Jesus there were ascetic groups among the Jews of Palestine. They responded to the attempted Hellenization of their culture and the subsequent Roman occupation with an apocalyptic and eschatological (→ Apocalypse) perspective elaborated in writings similar to the later portions of the book of Daniel (Dan 7–12). These texts typically feature an ultimate judgment of sinners by a heavenly figure and the vindication of those who remain faithful to the law. Many of these "intertestamental" writings survived into the early Christian period, notably the Enoch literature and the "testaments" of biblical patriarchs, and were sometimes included in Christian biblical manuscripts (Collins, 2016; Charlesworth, 1983, vol. I).

The → Essenes mentioned by → Philo of Alexandria, → Flavius Josephus, and Pliny the Elder were one such ascetic movement (Simon, 1985; Boccaccini, 1998, 21–49; Mason, 2011). The non-biblical texts found among the Dead Sea Scrolls such as the *Community Rule* and *Damascus Document* – whether written by Essenes or not – reveal the strongly sectarian worldview of a community that saw itself as a faithful remnant persecuted by a corrupt Temple priesthood. While the four canonical Gospels often mention Pharisees, scribes, and Sadducees, they never allude to the Essenes or other ascetic groups. This is perhaps explicable by the affinity of the preaching of → John the Baptist and Jesus with the themes of eschatological judgment and messianic vindication found in the apocalyptic tradition. When viewed in the context of Essenes and other sectarians, John the Baptist appears neither novel nor exceptional, but exemplary of a well-established current of Jewish thought and practice in Palestine.

The Jesus of the Gospels, though unmarried and seemingly unencumbered with possessions, was more a wandering preacher than a sectarian ascetic. He fasted and prayed as expected of faithful Jews, and his teaching about the eschatological coming

of a → Son of Man (e.g. Matt 24:30; see Dan 7:13–14) echoes the intertestamental and sectarian writings, but he is not portrayed as insistent upon perfect observance of the law (→ Law/Decalogue/Torah). He did, however, call for renunciation of family, property, and even self for the sake of discipleship: "If you wish to be perfect, go, sell your possessions, and give the money to the poor, and you will have treasure in heaven; then come, follow me" (Matt 19:21; also 6:24; 8:21–22; Matt 10:37/Luke 14:26; Matt 19:21; 19:28–29). His cryptic sayings about those "who have made themselves eunuchs for the sake of the kingdom of heaven" (Matt 19:12) and "in the resurrection they neither marry nor are given in marriage, but are like angels in heaven" (Matt 22:30) would later be understood as a warrant for celibacy, though the apostles themselves – with the exception of Paul – were married men (1 Cor 9:5).

2. Earliest Christianity

Paul (→ Paul the Apostle) and the authors of the four canonical Gospels wrote in Greek, a language replete with vocabulary for emotions, ethics, and metaphysics. Long before Paul, the Septuagint translation (→ Bible) of the Hebrew Bible and the composition by Jews of works in Greek such as the Wisdom of Solomon had brought this vocabulary into → Judaism. The combination of Stoic ethics and Platonic metaphysics that would shape the development of early Christian theology was already at work among Hellenized Jews such as Philo of Alexandria and others of that school (Collins, 1997; Spanneut, 1957; Rasimus et al., 2010). Paul's ethical instructions relied on language and content of Stoic origin. The concepts of ἄσκησις/*askēsis* ("discipline," "training") and ἐγκράτεια/*enkrateia* ("self-restraint") found in Christian texts had deep philosophical roots. The philosophical inheritance was developed further in analyses of human psychology by → Clement of Alexandria, → Origen, and → Evagrius of Pontus (Camelot, 1969; Hadot, 1987; Stewart, 2005).

In the first decades after the death of Jesus, Christians in Palestine and in the communities of the Pauline mission continued the disciplines of prayer, fasting, and almsgiving received from Judaism. Their initiatory rite of → baptism and the ritual remembrance of the Last Supper both had Jewish antecedents. The Acts of the Apostles (→ Acts, Book of) depicts a community in Jerusalem in which the believers held their goods in common and gathered regularly for prayers, instruction, and the "breaking of the bread" (Acts 2:42–47; 4:32–37). This idealized portrait of the earliest followers of Jesus would later have a great influence on ascetic self-understanding, particularly as communities of ascetics sought a biblical warrant for their way of life.

It was the task of Paul and his successors to hold together a Christian community that consisted for the most part of traditional households yet also included members drawn to a more radical way of awaiting the return of Jesus. Paul's famous instruction about virginity and marriage in 1 Cor 7 shows an early phase of this tension. Though he affirms that "it is well for a man not to touch a woman" (1 Cor 7:1) during what was expected to be a brief period before the → parousia, the return of Christ, Paul advises → marriage for most people lest they be overwhelmed by sexual desire. The argument is tortuous, and the chapter is as much a defense of his married followers as it is praise for the unmarried state. But it was the latter that would be remembered, becoming a key justification for Christian celibacy:

> The unmarried man is anxious about the affairs of the Lord, how to please the Lord; but the married man is anxious about the affairs of the world, how to please his wife, and his interests are divided. And the unmarried woman and the virgin are anxious about the affairs of the Lord, so that they may be holy in body and spirit; but the married woman is anxious about the affairs of the world, how to please her husband. (1 Cor 7:32–34)

3. Into the 2nd Century CE

The tensions over celibacy glimpsed in 1 Cor 7 endured. Both Clement of Rome (c. 35–99 CE) and Ignatius of Antioch (fl. early 2nd cent. CE; → Ignatius, Epistles of) caution those who have remained "pure in the flesh" not to boast about their achievement (1

Clem. 38.2; Ign. Pol. 5.2). In the Pastoral Epistles (1–2 Timothy; Titus), written in Paul's name but dating from the early 2nd century CE, there is a clear preference against remarriage for those who have been widowed (unless they are young female widows, who are suspected of frivolity, 1 Tim 5:9–16). Even so, this is strictly held only for → bishops and → deacons, lest there be any confusion in the community with "the hypocrisy of liars [...] [who] forbid marriage and demand abstinence from foods, which God created to be received with thanksgiving by those who believe and know the truth" (1 Tim 4:2–3). Here we see an early hint of the long-running controversy over the Encratites (from ἐγκράτεια/enkrateia, "self-restraint"), who were alleged to oppose any marriage as well as the consumption of meat and drinking of wine (Chadwick, 1962). As with many early Christian controversies, it is difficult to identify a specific group or individual holding such views, though the theologian → Tatian (c. 120–c. 180 CE) has been associated with them (Hunt, 2003). Throughout the literary record of what was later regarded as the "orthodox" current of Christianity runs a thread of anxiety about the potentially destabilizing effects of elitist, sectarian groups.

In the mid-2nd century CE, the era of the apologists (→ Apologetics) such as → Justin Martyr, references to dedicated virginity or celibacy begin to multiply (Solignac, 1994). Justin claims that the strict sexual morality of Christians was a proof of their superior virtue, and he writes of the "many" men and women in their 60s and 70s who remained "uncorrupted" since childhood (Just. 1 Apol. 15). Even the pagan physician → Galen noted that Christian sexual renunciation and self-control with respect to food and drink rivalled that of the philosophers (Walzer, 1951, 99).

By the later 2nd century CE, there were many Christian writings in circulation with a dualistic – or seemingly dualistic – worldview. Some, like the Gospel of Thomas (→ Thomas the Apostle), were not far removed in content and tone from the canonical Gospels, especially that of John. Others were sharper in their distinction between matter and spirit, the divine and the human. → Marcion (c. 85–c. 160 CE) based his rejection of the Hebrew Bible and much of the New Testament on their alleged confusion between the material creation and the realm of the spiritual and divine (Harnack, 1924; Lieu, 2015). The Marcionite church was a significant presence well into the 5th century CE. In the mid-3rd century CE, the Mesopotamian ascetic Mani (c. 216–c. 275 CE; → Mani/Manichaeism), who styled himself "apostle of Jesus Christ," drew on such writings as he elaborated a new religion based on a sharply dualistic cosmology. Mani devised an ecclesiastical structure with an ascetic elite, the "Elect," who were believed to have privileged access to a spiritual realm of light. We know more about the Manichaeans than the Marcionites, though both seem to have restricted full membership to the celibate ascetics. The Manichaean Elect played a crucial role in the religious economy of the movement. In a ritual meal analogous to the Christian Eucharist, the catechumens ("householders") offered food to the Elect in return for spiritual benefits (Tardieu, 1997; Pettipiece, 2015).

4. Dedicated Virginity

In addition to the acts of the famous virgin martyrs such as Agnes, Cecilia, Agatha, and Lucy, there was a growing literature extolling virgins and the virginal state (→ Virgin/Virginity; → Martyrs). The most famous was the story of → Thecla, known from the mid-2nd century CE *Acts of Paul* (→ Paul the Apostle). In this strongly ascetic work, Paul teaches "the word of God concerning *enkrateia* and resurrection," including a version of the Beatitudes:

Blessed are those who keep the flesh undefiled [ἀγνός/*agnos*], for they shall be a temple of God;
Blessed are the abstinent [ἐγκρατεῖς/*enkrateis*], for God will speak to them;
Blessed are those who renounce this world, for they shall be pleasing to God [...]
Blessed are the bodies of the virgins, for they shall be pleasing to God and they shall not lose the reward of their chastity [ἀγνεία/*agneia*] (*Acts Paul* 5–6)

Overhearing Paul's instructions, the young Thecla is moved to follow him, breaking with mother and fiancé to do so. The story is remarkable for its emphasis on Thecla's agency, not only in leaving family and intended marriage, but also defending herself before

officials condemning for her Christian faith, eluding the wild beasts meant to carry out the sentence of death, and baptizing herself (*Acts Paul* 34).

Another work, the *Symposium* of Methodius of Olympus (late 3rd cent. CE), loosely based on the Platonic dialogue of the same name, features an all-female cast of virgins (Bracht, 2017). Gathered at a banquet hosted by *Arētē* ("Virtue"), the daughter of Philosophia, the symposiasts are called upon to speak about the excellence of virginity. One of them explains why virginity figures little in the Hebrew Bible, for "it was reserved to the Lord alone to impart this knowledge [...] [and to] be hailed as the first among virgins" (Meth. *Symp.* 1.4[23]). The winning speaker is a virgin named Thecla.

Such literature relied heavily on the Christian Platonist metaphysics and spiritual interpretation of the Bible associated most famously with Origen (e.g. *Homiliae in Canticum*; *Commentarius in Canticum*). In this view, the spiritual, eternal realm looms much larger than the transitory experience of sexual desire in this life, and the virginal body mirrors that vaster reality (Brown, 2008, 160–177). The Song of Songs and the parable of the wise virgins (Matt 25:1–13) provided imagery for praise of female virginity, while the males were generally left with exempla of heroic biblical figure and "those who have made themselves eunuchs for the sake of the kingdom of heaven" (Matt 19:12). The emphasis on female virgins also reflects traditional obsessions with purity and virginal physical intactness (Kelto Lillis, 2023). Only after the 5th century CE did the Virgin Mary become a particular exemplar for virgins.

Some treatises on virginity were addressed to both male and female virgins. An example from perhaps the 3rd century CE, the Pseudo-Clementine *Letters* (→ Clementine Literature, Pseudo-), contains a general encomium to virginity in its first part, but the second section is entirely devoted to the itinerant life of the male ascetics, who exercised an apostolic ministry of preaching (Lightfoot, 1890, 407–414; Harnack, 1891). More typical was the expectation that virgins – whether female or male – would remain in the family home, supervised, and protected by parents (Camelot, 1952). A treatise attributed to → Basil of Caesarea but likely from the early 4th century CE, addressed parents of both female and male virgins (Pseudo-Basil, *Homilia ad Virgines*) The parents of female virgins are to be vigilant concerning any contact of their daughter with men, even those professing virginity (*Hom. virg.* 33). Fathers are to take a particular concern for their ascetic sons lest they become lazy and dissipated (*Hom. virg.* 60,63). A theme repeated here and in similar writings is the philosophical trope of the "deleterious effects of marriage" (*molestiae nuptiarum*), which not only distracts from any higher purpose but also brings woes of its own (*Hom. virg.* 60). As Eusebius of Emesa (mid-4th cent. CE) observed, "marriage is the root of virginity, but the root is for the sake of the fruit" (Eus.Em. *Hom. Mart.* 6.6.155). In other words, the highest achievement of marriage was the production of virgins.

During the 3rd and 4th centuries CE, the dedication to lifelong virginity was becoming a public act, with virgins recognized as an "order" in the church (Elm, 1994). The early 3rd century CE North African theologians → Tertullian and → Cyprian of Carthage promoted virginity and the controversial conferral upon virgins of the veil normally worn by married women (Hunter, 1999; Dunn, 2003). The practice came later to Italy, introduced in Rome by Popes → Liberius and → Damasus in the mid-4th century CE, and then in Milan by Ambrose (→ Ambrose of Milan), who made it a central theme of his episcopate (Brown, 2008, 341–365).

By the early 4th century CE, ecclesiastical councils from Spain to Asia Minor were drafting legislation to regulate and protect the status of dedicated virgins, just as they had for clergy and married people (Magnani, 2020). Apart from the numerous condemnations of cohabitation by ascetic men and women, the legislation focuses almost entirely on female virgins. The earliest is from the Council of Elvira in Spain (305/306 CE), which laid down penalties for breaking the "covenant" of virginity (c. 13). The mid-4th century CE *De vera virginitate* (*On True Chastity in Virginity*) by Basil of Ancyra (d. 362 CE), a priest and physician, describes dedicated virginity as having the canonical status of marriage and comparable penalties for breaking the vow (Bas. Anc. *Virg.* 37–42; see 61; Shaw, 1998; Burgsmüller, 2005). Basil is refreshingly less concerned with bodily intactness than with spiritual integrity, arguing that virginity could be restored through asceticism (*Virg.* 49–50).

5. Ascetic Community

For many virgins, living in the family home was not always an option or an attractive one. The simplest, but most controversial, form of ascetic community was the cohabitation of male and female ascetics. An array of ecclesiastical canons beginning in the late 3rd century CE denounce the practice as dangerous and potentially scandalous. The pejorative term for women in such relationships, συνείσακτοι/ *syneisaktoi* ("introduced ones"; Lat. *subintroductae*), suggested concubinage rather than spiritual friendship (Achelis, 1902; Clark, 1977; Leyerle, 2001). Canon 3 of the Council of → Nicaea forbade clerics to have any "introduced" woman living with them apart from blood relatives.

There were other forms of ascetic community. According to → Athanasius of Alexandria's *Vita Antonii*, in the late 3rd century CE Antony left his sister at a παρθενών/*parthenōn*, that is a house of Christian virgins, when he set off to become an ascetic. Other evidence suggests communities of ascetic women in Alexandria in the first half of the 4th century CE (Elm, 1994, 331–372; Brakke, 1995,17–79). → Martin of Tours created a community of hermit scribes at Marmoutier in the later 4th century CE (→ Sulpicius Severus, *Vita sancti Martini*; *Dialogi*), and at the very end of the same century, → Augustine of Hippo established communities for both men and women in the region of Hippo, writing for them the *Praeceptum*, the first Latin "rule" (Lawless, 1987). Notably, he does not allude to Egyptian monasticism as any kind of inspiration, though the Latin translation of the *Vita Antonii* had played a key role in his own conversion (Aug. *Conf.* 8.6[15]) and he was aware of the practice of brief and intense prayers by Egyptian monks (Aug. *Ep.* 130.20).

6. Syriac and Cappadocian Asceticism

The Syriac Christian tradition of Mesopotamia had a markedly ascetic orientation (Murray, 2004, 3–38). The reasons for this emphasis are unclear. By the early 4th century CE there was a recognized ascetic order in the church known as the *qyāmā* (from *qwm*, meaning "to stand" or "to rise"). The origin of this and similar Syriac ascetic groups is unknown (Bumazhnov, 2011). After a century-long lacuna in the extant literary tradition, they appear fully formed in the early 4th-century CE writings of → Aphrahat (c. 280–c. 345 CE) and → Ephrem the Syrian (c. 306–373 CE). Often translated as "covenant," the *qyāmā* included both male and female virgins (*bnay* and *bnat qyāmā*, "sons and daughters of the covenant"), and others who were widowed or separated from their spouses (Griffith, 1995; Pierre, 2010). They lived in towns and villages, serving the church liturgically and in charitable works. The theologian and poet Ephrem used a choir of *bnāt qyāmā* to sing his hymns. The prominence of the *qyāmā* is demonstrated by the lists and legends of Christian martyrs in the Persian Empire, where the *bnay* and *bnat qyāmā* are indicated as a distinct order in the church, alongside bishops, priests, deacons, and "those in the world." Members of the *qyāmā* were also called *īḥīdāyē* ("single ones"), which was later the common Syriac term for monks.

The Syriac → *Book of Steps* describes a similar group of ascetics as "perfect ones" (Syr. *gmīrē*) living within the larger Christian community of householders (Syr. *kēnē*, the "just" or "righteous" ones). The *Book of Steps* describes the *gmīrē* as walking the earth while their minds dwell in heaven. They have received the full presence of the Paraclete, while the *kēnē* receive only the "pledge" of the spirit (Syr. *'ūrbānā*, see 2 Cor 1:22 and 5:5; Eph 1:14; Stewart, 1991, 199–203).

The asceticism of the Marcionites and Manichaeans shadowed – and may have influenced – the development of the *qyāmā*. According to Ephrem and other writers, even those belonging to Nicene communities like theirs were edified by the ascetic accomplishments of Marcionites and Manichaeans and were easily seduced into thinking of them as authentically Christian:

> For their works resemble our works, as their fast resembles our fast, but their faith does not resemble our faith. Rather than being known by the fruit of their works, they are best recognized by the fruit of their words. (Ephr. *Ref.* 5.184.28–39)

It is possible that the *qyāmā* played a role in the development of an ascetic movement to the northwest of Mesopotamia in the region of Sebasteia (modern Sivas in Turkey), and thereby on the ascetic communities of men and women in Cappadocia guided by Basil the Great. Eustathius of Sebasteia (c. 300–c. 377 CE) studied in Alexandria and traveled widely, including Syria and Mesopotamia. Controversial in his youth for ascetic zeal and sectarian tendencies of the kind described in the canons of the Council of → Gangra (mid-4th cent. CE), he eventually found acceptance for his model of ascetic communities serving the church and was made bishop of Sebasteia (Elm, 1996, 184–223; Silvas, 2005, 486–494). Though he had direct experience of Egyptian asceticism, he never invokes it as a model for his own efforts, which were closer in form to the *qyāmā*.

Eustathius was close to Basil's ascetically inclined family and a frequent visitor to their home. Basil's *Askētikon*, a manual for ascetic communities in his diocese of Cappadocian Caesarea, follows Eustathius' model but with a particular emphasis on close ties with the hierarchical church and avoidance of any suggestion of sectarian elitism. He therefore shuns technical ascetic vocabulary such as "monk" or "monastery," speaking rather of a "life of piety" devoted to the practice of the commandments. Eustathius' influence on Basil's ascetic views was largely effaced in the historical record owing to a later conflict over interpretation of Nicene Christology. Basil was a hardline *homoousian*, Eustathius an advocate of the more irenic *homoiousian* perspective. Ironically, Eustathian asceticism in its Basilian guise would become paradigmatic for Byzantine cenobitic monasticism, and Basil would be the only ascetic authority mentioned by name in the *Regula Benedicti* (73.5).

We can detect other pathways of Syriac influence on asceticism in Greek-speaking churches. Beginning in the late 4th century CE in Syriac sources and shortly thereafter in Greek ones, there are condemnations of those called → Messalians, so-called from the Syriac *mṣalyānē*, meaning "those who pray." Like the Encratites (→ Encratism/Encratites), these ascetics were named pejoratively for their alleged excesses rather than after a founder; in both cases it is impossible to determine whether there was an actual group or simply a tendency that attracted attention. The condemnations are of their supposed devotion to prayer to the exclusion of work, an emphasis on spiritual experience rather than sacramental practice, and optimism that sin could be completely uprooted from the soul (Stewart, 1991; Fitschen, 1998).

Associated with the Messalians were writings variously attributed to a Symeon of Mesopotamia or to a certain Macarius, later wrongly assumed to be Macarius the Great (→ Desert Fathers) of Egypt. These parenetic texts, composed in Greek, used experiential metaphors of light, warmth, and assurance/fulfilment, and proved to be very important for the development of Byzantine spirituality (Hausherr, 1935). The vivid language of the Pseudo-Macarian corpus has strong affinities with imagery common in Syriac literature (Stewart, 1991). A Syriac translation of the Pseudo-Macarian writings had a great influence on Isaac the Syrian, and in turn the Greek version of Isaac's treatises became a mainstay of Byzantine devotional reading. The association with the Messalians went unnoticed until modern studies identified the Pseudo-Macarian writings as the source of condemned Messalian propositions preserved by → Theodoret of Cyrrhus and later authors (Stewart, 1991, 241–281). A further complication was the recognition that → Gregory of Nyssa had adapted the *Epistola Magna* (*Great Letter*) of Pseudo-Macarius in his *De instituto christiano* (Staats, 1984).

7. Trajectories

In the 4th century CE a "new" ascetic paradigm, monasticism, emerged as an ecclesiastically promoted form of asceticism that eventually succeeded or incorporated earlier ascetic ways of life. As more and more bishops were drawn from monasteries, there was an asceticizing of the episcopate and the growing expectation that bishops would be celibate (→ Celibacy of Clergy). The influence of ascetic views of sexuality meant that even in the lower ranks of clergy there was an increasing belief that marital intercourse was inappropriate the night before celebration of the Eucharist.

Historiography

Before the modern era, early Christian asceticism was generally viewed as a precursor or preliminary stage in the development of monasticism. The element of sexual renunciation was a topic of polemics in the west from the Reformation era.

The 19th century saw a revival in the study of eastern Christianity thanks to the arrival in Europe of manuscripts from libraries in the Middle East. The early Syriac ascetic traditions were discovered by western scholars in the very early manuscripts from Deir al-Suryani in Egypt, preserved by the desert climate from decay. Large collections ended up at the Vatican and the British Museum and were the basis for reference works and catalogs by J. Assemani (1687–1768) for the Vatican (Assemani, 1719–1728; 1758–1759) and W. Wright for the manuscripts in London (Wright, 1870–1872). Their work recovered writings by Aphrahat, Ephrem, and other early Syriac ascetic authors that ceased to be copied by later scribes. These texts tended to be interpreted in monastic terms.

By the later 20th century, the study of asceticism was no longer dominated by clergy or members of religious orders interested in the origins of monasticism. It was also increasingly influenced by literary theory and the "cultural turn." The work of A. Rousselle (1983) and M. Foucault on sexual asceticism (Foucault, vol. III, 1976–1984), and of P. Brown on the social role of ascetics (Brown, 1971) as well as changing understandings of sexual renunciation in early Christianity (Brown, 2008) generated a wealth of scholarship. Numerous publications focused particularly on asceticism as a rare opportunity for agency and self-determination by early Christian women (Cooper, 1996; Martin & Cox Miller, 2005).

Bibliography

Achelis, H., *Virgines subintroductae: Ein Beitrag zum VII. Kapitel des I. Korintherbriefs*, Leipzig, 1902.

Amand, D., & M.C. Moons, "Une curieuse homélie grecque," *RBen* 63, 1953, 211–238.

Assemani, J., *Bibliotheca Orientalis*, 4 vols., Rome, 1719–1728.

Assemani, J., *Bibliothecae Apostolicae Vaticanae codicum manuscriptorum catalogus, in tres partes distributus, in quarum prima Orientales, in altera Graeci, in tertia Latini, Italici aliorumque Europaeorum idiomatum codices*, Rome, 1758–1759.

Bianchi, U., ed., *La tradizione dell'enkrateia: Motivazioni ontologiche e protologiche: Atti del colloquio internazionale, Milano, 20–23 Aprile 1982*, Rome, 1985.

Boccaccini, G., *Beyond the Essene Hypothesis: The Parting of the Ways Between Qumran and Enochic Judaism*, Grand Rapids, 1998.

Bracht, K., ed. *Methodius of Olympus: State of the Art and New Perspectives*, TU 178, Berlin, 2017.

Brakke, D., *Athanasius and the Politics of Asceticism*, Oxford, 1995.

Brown, P., "The Rise and Function of the Holy Man in Late Antiquity," *JRS* 61, 1971, 80–101.

Brown, P., *The Body and Society: Men, Women, and Sexual Renunciation in Early Christianity*, New York, ²2008.

Bumazhnov, D.F., "Some Ecclesiological Patterns of the Early Christian Period and Their Implications for the History of the Term ΜΟΝΑΧΟΣ (Monk)," in: A.A. Alexeev et al., eds., *Einheit der Kirche im Neuen Testament: Dritte europäische orthodox-westliche Exegetenkonferenz in Sankt Petersburg 24–31. August 2005*, Tübingen, 2008.

Bumazhnov, D.F., "Qyāmā Before Aphrahat: The Development of the Idea of Covenant in Some Early Syriac Documents," in: D.F. Bumazhnov & H.R. Seeliger, eds., *Syrien im 1.–7. Jahrhundert nach Christus*, Tübingen, 2011, 65–81, 251–264.

Burgsmüller, A., *Die Askeseschrift des Pseudo-Basilius: Untersuchungen zum Brief "Über die wahre Reinheit in der Jungfräulichkeit"*, STAC 28, Tübingen, 2005.

Burrus, V., *The Making of a Heretic: Gender, Authority, and the Priscillianist Controversy*, Berkeley, 1995.

Camelot, P.T., "Les traités '*De virginitate*' au IVe siècle," in: D. de Brouwer, *Mystique et continence*, CEC, Bruges, 1952, 273–292.

Camelot, P.T., "Héllenisme (et spiritualité patristique)," *DSp* 7, 1969, 145–164.

Chadwick, H., "Enkrateia," in: T. Klauser et al., eds., *RAC*, vol. V, Stuttgart, 1962, 343–365.

Charlesworth, J.H., & G.W. MacRae, *The Old Testament Pseudepigrapha*, vol. I: *Apocalyptic Literature and Testaments*, Garden City, 1983.

Clark, E.A., "John Chrysostom and the 'Subintroductae'," *ChH* 46, 1977, 177–185.

Clark, E.A., *The Origenist Controversy: The Cultural Construction of an Early Christian Debate*, Princeton, 1992.

Collins, J., *Jewish Wisdom in the Hellenistic Age*, Louisville, 1997.

Collins, J., *The Apocalyptic Imagination: An Introduction to Jewish Apocalyptic Literature*, Grand Rapids, 2016.

Cooper, K., *The Virgin and the Bride: Idealized Womanhood in Late Antiquity*, Cambridge MA, 1996.

Diem, A., *The Limitations of Asceticism*, in: W. Pohl & I. Hartl, eds., "Monasteries and Sacred Landscapes & Byzantine Connections," *MeWo* 9, 2019, 112–138.

Dunn, G., "Infected Sheep and Diseased Cattle, or the Pure and Holy Flock: Cyprian's Pastoral Care of Virgins," *JECS* 11, 2003, 1–20.

Elm, S., *"Virgins of God": The Making of Asceticism in Late Antiquity*, Oxford, 1994.

Fiey, J.M., "Aonès, Awun et Awgin," *AnBoll* 80, 1962, 52–81.

Fitschen, K., *Messalianismus und Antimessalianismus: Ein Beispiel ostkirchlicher Ketzergeschichte*, FKDG 71, Göttingen, 1998.

Foucault, M., *Histoire de la sexualité*, 4 vols., vol. III: *Le souci de soi*, Paris, 1976–1984.

Griffith S., "'Singles' in God's Service: Thoughts on the Ihidaye from the Works of Aphrahat and Ephraem the Syrian," *Harp* 4, 1991, 145–159.

Griffith S., "Julian Saba, 'Father of the Monks' of Syria," *JECS* 2, 1994, 185–216.

Griffith S., "Asceticism in the Church of Syria: The Hermeneutics of Early Syrian Asceticism," in: V.L. Wimbush & R. Valantasis, *Asceticism*, New York, 1995, 220–245.

Hadot, P., *Exercices spirituels et philosophie antique*, Paris, ²1987.

Harnack, A. von, "Die pseudoclementinischen Briefe de virginitate und die Entstehung des Mönchtums," *SPAW*, 1891/1, 361–385.

Harnack, A. von, *Markion: Das Evangelium vom fremden Gott*, Leipzig, ²1924.

Hausherr, I., "Les grands courants de la spiritualité orientale," *OCP* 1, 1935, 114–138.

Hunt, E., *Christianity in the Second Century: The Case of Tatian*, London, 2003.

Hunter, D.G., "Clerical Celibacy and the Veiling of Virgins," in: W.E. Klingshirn & M. Vessey, *The Limits of Ancient Christianity: Essays on Late Antique Thought and Culture in Honor of Robert A. Markus*, Ann Arbor, 1999, 139–152.

Hunter, D.G., *Marriage, Celibacy, and Heresy in Ancient Christianity: The Jovinianist Controversy*, Oxford, 2007.

Kelto Lillis, J., *Virgin Territory: Configuring Female Virginity in Early Christianity*, Oakland, 2023.

Lawless, G., *Augustine of Hippo and His Monastic Rule*, Oxford, 1987.

Leyerle, B., *Theatrical Shows and Ascetic Lives: John Chrysostom's Attack on Spiritual Marriage*, Berkeley, 2001.

Lieu, J., *Marcion and the Making of a Heretic: God and Scripture in the Second Century*, Cambridge UK, 2015.

Lightfoot, J.B., *The Apostolic Fathers*, part 1: *S. Clement of Rome*, London, 1890.

Magnani, E., "Female Ascetics from the Fourth to the Twelfth Century," in: A.I. Beach & I. Cochelin, eds., *The Cambridge History of Medieval Monasticism in the Latin West*, vol. I, Cambridge UK, 2020, 213–231.

Martin, D.B., & P. Cox Miller, *The Cultural Turn in Late Ancient Studies: Gender, Asceticism, and Historiography*, Durham, 2005.

Mason, S., "The Historical Problem of the Essenes," in: P.W. Flint et al., *Celebrating the Dead Sea Scrolls: A Canadian Collection*, SBL.EJL 30, Atlanta, 2011, 201–250.

Mendieta, D.A. de, "La virginité chez Eusèbe d'Émèse et l'ascétisme familial dans la première moitié du IVe siècle," *RHE* 50, 1955, 777–820.

Murray, R.M., *Symbols of Church and Kingdom: A Study in Early Syriac Tradition*, Piscataway, ²2004.

Pettipiece, T., "Manichaeism at the Crossroads of Jewish, Christian, and Muslim Traditions," in: B. Bitton-

Ashkelony et al., eds., *Patristic Studies in the Twenty-First Century: Proceedings of an International Conference to Mark the 50th Anniversary of the International Association of Patristic Studies*, Turnhout, 2015, 299–313.

Pierre, M.J., "Les 'membres de l'ordre', d'Aphraate au Liber Graduum," in: F. Jullien, ed., *Le monachisme syriaque*, EtSy 7, Paris, 2010, 11–35.

Quispel, G., "The Study of Encratism: A Historical Survey," in: U. Bianchi, ed., *La tradizione dell'enkrateia: Motivazioni ontologiche e protologiche: Atti del colloquio internazionale, Milano, 20–23 Aprile 1982*, Rome, 1985, 35–82.

Rasimus, T. et al., *Stoicism in Early Christianity*, Peabody, 2010.

Rousselle, A., *Porneia: De la maîtrise du corps à la privation sensorielle, IIe–IVe siècles de l'ère chrétienne*, Paris, 1983; ET: F. Pheasant, *Porneia: On Desire and the Body in Antiquity*, Oxford, 1988.

Shaw, T., "Askesis and the Appearance of Holiness," *JECS* 6, 1998, 485–499.

Silvas, A., *The Asketikon of St Basil the Great*, Oxford, 2005.

Simon, M., "L'ascétisme dans les sects juives," in: U. Bianchi, ed., *La tradizione dell'enkrateia: Motivazioni ontologiche e protologiche: Atti del colloquio internazionale, Milano, 20–23 Aprile 1982*, Rome, 1985, 393–431.

Solignac, A., "Virginité chrétienne," *DSp* 16, 1994, 924–949.

Spanneut, M., *Le stoïcisme des pères de l'église, de Clément de Rome à Clément d'Alexandrie*, PatSor 1, Paris, 1957.

Staats, R., *Makarios-Symeon, Epistola Magna: Eine Messalianische Mönchsregel und ihre Umschrift in Gregors Von Nyssa "De Instituto Christiano"*, AAWG 134, Göttingen, 1984.

Stewart, C., *"Working the Earth of the Heart": The Messalian Controversy in History, Texts, and Language to AD 431*, Oxford, 1991.

Stewart, C., "Evagrius Ponticus and the 'Eight Generic Logismoi'," in: R. Newhauser, ed., *In the Garden of Evil: The Vices and Culture in the Middle Ages*, Toronto, 2005, 3–34.

Stewart, C., "The Ascetic Taxonomy of Antioch and Edessa at the Emergence of Monasticism," *Adamantius* 19, 2013, 207–221.

Tardieu, M., *Le manichéisme*, Paris, ²1997; ET: M.B. DeBevoise, *Manichaeism*, Urbana, 2008.

Walzer, R., *Plato Arabus*, vol. I: *Galeni Compendium Timaei Platonis: Aliorumque Dialogorum Synopsis Quae Extant Fragmenta*, CPMA, London, 1951.

Wimbush, V.L., *Ascetic Behavior in Greco-Roman Antiquity: A Sourcebook*, Minneapolis, 1990.

Wimbush, V.L., & R. Valantasis, *Asceticism*, New York, 1995.

Wright, W., *Catalogue of Syriac Manuscripts in the British Museum Acquired Since 1838*, 3 vols., London, 1870–1872.

COLUMBA STEWART

Ascitae

The word *Ascitae* ("heresy") is derived from the Greek word meaning "wine skin" or "leather bottle" (ἀσκός) and refers to a → heresy described as a group of individuals who, while intoxicated, would dance around an inflated wine skin or leather bottle "claiming to be what the gospel refers to as new wine skins filled with new wine" (Aug. *Haer.* 62). → Augustine of Hippo uses the term *Ascitae* (*Haer.* 62) in his *De haeresibus* written in 427 or 428 CE. His knowledge of this heresy is based on the *Diversarum hereseon liber* (c. 384 CE), written by Filastrius, bishop of Brescia. Augustine discloses in *De haeresibus* that he had in fact met Filastrius but also uses *Diversarum hereseon liber* to give a detailed account of heresies that he himself had not encountered. Filastrius describes the same heresy but uses the name *Ascodrugitae* (Filas. *Haer.* 75) and states that this was a heresy from the region known as Galatia: *Alii sunt iterum Ascodrugitae in Galatia*. Augustine does not include this information in his brief description. It is not clear why Augustine truncated the name used by Filastrius. One theory is that he abbreviated the term Filastrius used in order to get rid of "the unintelligible second element" (*DCB*, 176). Another theory regarding heresy sees a similarity or perhaps a confusion with the *Ascodrugitae* and the heresy that → Epiphanius of Salamis (*Haer.* 416) refers to as the *Tascodrugitae* (Τασκός) or *Passalorhynchites* (see *DCB*, 175). The connection is grounded in the similarity of the Greek spelling of the words (Τασκός) *Tascodrugitae* and (ἀσκός) *Ascitae*, which Epiphanius and Filastrius both claim were heresies situated in Galatia. Augustine, however, having based his writing of *De haeresibus* on the writings of both Epiphanius and Filastrius, as well as others, did not include the *Ascitae* in the section derived from the writing of Epiphanius. It is interesting to note that Augustine also names *Passalorhynchitae* (Aug. *Haer.* 63) as a separate heresy, directly following his writing on the *Ascitae* and describing the *Passalorhynchitae* in the same manner as Filastrius demonstrating his claim that he would present the heresies that Filastrius gives, but that are not found in Epiphanius (Aug. *Haer.* 57). There is some question as to whether Augustine used the *Anacephaleosis* whose authorship is questionable or the *Panarion*, which is considered to be an authentic work of Epiphanius (see Muller, 1956, 22–33; Sadowski, 2015, 467). A connection is also drawn between the *Ascodrugitae* used by Filastrius and the heresy → Jerome refers to as *Ascodrobi* (see *DCB*, 175). The connection between the two is that they both were found in Galatia, and the other two heresies Jerome cites (*Passalorhynchites* and *Artotyrites*) precede and follow the *Ascodrobi*. This is similar to Filastrius, who places the *Artotyrites* prior to the *Ascodrugitae* and the *Passalorhynchite* directly after that entry. Here, again, this assumption is difficult as there seems nothing else to connect the heresies other than location.

What is known or written about the *Ascitae* or *Ascodrugitae* by both Filastrius and Augustine is simply that they would dance around an inflated wine skin or leather bottle in Bacchian *bacchantes* or drunken manner. Both refer to drunkenness, dancing, and the inflated wine skin or leather bottle.

Bibliography

Sancti Aurelii Augustini: De Haeresibus as Quoduultdeum liber unus, in: R. Vander Plaetse & C. Beukers, eds., CCSL 46, Turnhout, 1979, 286–345.

Herbermann, C. et al., eds., *ThCE*, New York, 1911.

Muller, L., *The De Haeresibus of Saint Augustine: A Translation with and Introduction and Commentary*, Washington DC, 1956.

Sadowski, S., "A Critical Look and Evaluation of Augustine's *de haeresibus*," *Aug.* 55, 2015.

Sancti Filastrii Episcopi Brixiensi: Diversarum Hereseon Liber, CSEL, Friderici Marx, 1898.

Smith, W., & H. Wace, eds., *DCB*, 1877.

SYDNEY SADOWSKI

Asia, Central

The geographic landscape of Central Asia stretches from east Iran to western → China and from the south of Lake Balkhash in the north to Afghanistan in the south. The early Christian communities in Central Asia in the pre-Islamic period were established mainly in the historical region of Khorasan, which extended from the Caspian Sea to the Oxus River (Amu Darya) and from central Iranian deserts to the mountains of central Afghanistan. From Khorasan, Christianity spread eastward to China. This vast area connecting the Far East with the eastern Mediterranean through the historical Silk Road was mainly inhabited by Iranian, Hunnic, and Turkic peoples before the Arab conquest in the middle of the 7th century CE. Early Christians in Central Asia belonged mainly to the Church of the East ("Nestorian"), although traces of West Syrian ("Jacobites") and Melkite Christians can also be found in written records.

1. Sources

Primary sources concerning the history of Christianity in pre-Islamic Central Asia are scarce and fragmentary. The earliest reference to Christians in this area comes from the Syriac writer → Bardaisan (154–222/223 CE), who mentioned, in circa 196 CE in the *Book of the Laws of Countries* (Drijvers, 2006, 60), Christians in Gilan in the southwest of the Caspian Sea and in the realm of the Kushan Empire (1st–4th cents. CE). Later, the Latin writer → Jerome (c. 347–420 CE), in his letter to Laeta dated 403 CE (Migne, 1841–1849, xxii, 870), described some Christian elements among the → Huns and the seminomadic Scythians in Central Asia: *Hunni discunt Psalterium, Scythiae frigora fervent calore* (The Huns learn the Psalter and the chilly Scythians are warmed with the glow of the faith).

Most of the reliable though not elaborate information on the Church of the East dioceses in Central Asia is found in *Synodicon Orientale* (Chabot, 1902, with Fr. trans.; Ger. trans. O. Braun, 1975), a collection of the synod records of the Church of the East from 410 to 775 CE, compiled in Syriac at the end of the 8th century CE. These synod records list the names of bishops and metropolitans from several East Syrian dioceses in Central Asia, who signed the acts of the synods. Canon 21 of the Synod of Isaac in 410 CE states that the bishops including the one from the area of Abrshahr (Nishapur in Khorasan) must accept the definition of the council at a later date (Chabot, 1902, 273, Braun, 1975, 32–33). By implication, the area of Abrshahr had such sizable Christian communities that a diocese could be created. Fourteen years later, more bishops from Central Asia attended the Synod of Dadisho. Among the signatories were Bishops Bar Shabba of Merw,

Yazdoi of Herat, Aphrid of Segestan, and David of Abrshahr (Braun, 1975, 46; Chabot, 1902, Fr. 285, Syr. 43). The bishops of Abrshahr in the west of Khorasan were present at the synods of 410, 420, and 424 CE. Thus, another diocese northeast of Abrshahr also had a bishop in 421 CE, who gained permission from the Sasanian king Bahram V (r. 420–438 CE) to vote for an East Syrian patriarch (Fiey, 1973, 88). Herat, located in the northwestern part of today's Afghanistan, was the interior of the historical region of Khorasan, and its Christian population in the 5th century CE appeared to be of Iranian-speaking peoples, and the bishops there had also Iranian names (Fiey, 1973, 89). In Segestan (Sistan), a historical region extending over present-day east Iran, southern Afghanistan, and western Pakistan, one bishopric in Zarang is attested from the 5th to the 6th century CE.

The names of bishops from dioceses in Central Asia, as listed in *Synodicon Orientale*, suggest that from early 5th century to late 6th century CE, East Syrian dioceses underwent merging and disintegration in terms of church administration. On the one hand, some early dioceses such as Abrshahr and Tus were no longer mentioned in the synod records of the 6th century CE, which may suggest that these two dioceses might have been integrated into the metropolitanate of Merw; on the other hand, in the area farther northeast of Abrshahr and Tus, new bishoprics of Abiward Shahr Peroz and Merw-i-Rud were created, whose bishops were listed at the Synod of Joseph in 554 CE (Hunter, 1992, 364). The Christian population in Central Asia must have grown so rapidly that by the middle of the 6th century CE, Merw and Herat had been elevated as metropolitanates.

2. Merw as a Missionary Center

Merw (near present-day Mary in Turkmenistan), an oasis city in Central Asia, was a strategic station of the historical Silk Road. It was the intersection of the northern and southern trade routes from China to Asia Minor. From Merw a southward route led to the Iranian realm and a westward route via Tabriz went farther, to Trabzon on the Black Sea or via Anatolia to Constantinople. From the 1st to the 7th century CE, Merw came under the rule of the Kushans, the Parthians, and the Sasanians and was invaded by the Hephthalites and Turkic tribes. Therefore, the oasis

city became a multicultural center with east Iranian (such as the Sogdians), Greek, Turkic, and Hephthalite inhabitants. During the Sasanian period, Merw developed into a major administrative, military, and trading center. According to Chinese dynasty history *Liang Shu* (*Book of Liang*) compiled around 636 CE, Merw, known as Mo Guo (country of Mo) to the Chinese, was bordered in the north with the land of the Dingling (a Turkic tribe), in the west with Persia, and in the east with Baiti, that is, the White Huns or the Hephthalites (*Liangshu*, vol. LIV). The Hephthalites ruled Central Asia from the mid-5th to the mid-6th century CE. From the Chinese record, one can draw a political map of Merw with its environs and can catch a glimpse of the cultural diversity of the city during the period of the Chinese Liang Dynasty (502–557 CE). Being an intersection along the Silk Road, Merw emerged as a multicultural and multireligious center. Buddhist and Manichean missionaries in Central Asia began their China mission from Merw. By the same token, from the 5th century CE onward, Merw served also as the headquarters of Christian missions in Central Asia. East Syrian Christians began their missions in Merw and later in Transoxiana among the Persian, Sogdian, Turkic, and Hephthalite peoples. From Merw, Christian missionaries and merchants traveled farther east into China and settled in the main cities of Turfan, Dunhuang, Xi'an, and Luoyang, where Syriac Christianity in medieval times is better documented through the Christian Manuscripts discovered in Turfan and Dunhuang and the inscriptions unearthed in Xi'an and Luoyang.

Sources on early Christian communities in Merw were not plentiful. Yet, recently, archaeological excavations in Merw have unearthed some Christian artifacts in the area of the citadel, such as some metal "Greek crosses" and a small metal mold for a cross from the late Sasanian period (Simpson, 2014, 20). However, at this stage, the available literary and archaeological information cannot fully reflect the Christian demography in Merw in the pre-Islamic period. At the synods of 424, 486, and 497 CE, the delegates from Merw signed themselves as bishops. Although the 10th-century CE anonymous history *Chronicle of Seert* mentions that the metropolitan David of Merw helped to precipitate the schism of Narsai and Elisha by consecrating the latter in Seleucia-Ctesiphon in 524 CE (Scher, 1911, 149), it was only at the Synod of Mar Aba in 544 CE that a metropolitan of Merw was listed. The first bishopric in Merw mentioned in *Synodicon Orientale* was represented by Bishop Bar Shabba at the Synod of Dadisho in 424 CE. The Syriac name Bar Shabba, meaning "Son of the Deportation" may indicate that some of the first Christians in Merw were those deported from Roman territories (Fiey, 1973, 76) by Shapur I (r. c. 240–272 CE). Bar Shabba is venerated in East Syrian, West Syrian, and Melkite churches. His *Vita* is found in the *Chronicle of Se'ert*, the Turfan Bulayïq Syriac (shelf mark TIIB 9, no.3) and Sogdian fragments (shelf mark TIIB 52), and a 12th-century West Syrian Manuscript from Tur 'Abdin (Brock, 1995, 195–198). The Turfan Bar Shabba fragments may well indicate a shared tradition between the Christian communities in Merw and Turfan.

By the year 554 CE, the Christian population must have grown so rapidly in Merw that the city already had a metropolitan named David who attended the Synod of Joseph (Braun, 1975, 162). Even though the number of Christians or Christian communities under the ecclesiastical administration of the metropolitanate is not clear, the metropolitan province of Merw ranked the seventh in precedence at the Synod of Joseph in 554 CE.

Christian missionaries and merchants used the trade routes that linked Persia with Central Asia to reach the Sogdians and various Turkic and Hunnic tribes in Transoxiana on the other side of the Oxus. The *Chronicle of Seert*, written in Arabic, contains a passage on the Sasanian king Kawad I (r. 488–531 CE) encountering Turkic Christians in the territory of the Hephthalites. According to the *Chronicle*, in 498 CE, Kawad, who was driven from his throne, sought refuge from the Hephtalites. He escaped to the country of the Turks, who rendered military assistance to him and helped him to return to his reign. The *Chronicle* describes that a certain Turkic Christian helped Kawad on his way to the Turkic king, who together with his people dwelt in the land of the Hephthalites (Scher, 1911, 128). After Kawad returned to the throne in Persia, he was benevolent toward Christians since some of them had helped him during his refuge in the land of the Hephthalites (Scher, 1911, 128). The Syriac biographical *History*

of Mar Aba describes that in 549 CE, the Haptraye (Syriac for Hephthalites) in the region of Bactria and Transoxiana asked the East Syrian patriarch Mar Aba I to send them a bishop (Bedjan, 1895, 266–269).

Christianity had spread among the Turkic peoples in Transoxiana by 591 CE. After Khosrau II (r. 591–628 CE) put down the rebellion of the Persian general Bahram with the help of the Roman army, he killed all prisoners of Bahram's army except the Turks who were Christians and sent them to Emperor Maurice. The Turks explained that an epidemic had struck their land in east Sogdiana and some Christians there had told them to tattoo a cross on their foreheads to keep safe (Chavannes, 1900, 245).

The names of the bishops who were present at the Church of the East synods from the 5th to the 6th century CE give an impression that the missionary center was shifted northeast to the Merw environs with a number of satellite dioceses such as Abiward and Merw-i-Rud. The East Syrian diocese of Merw as a hub of Syriac Christianity certainly played a key role in missionary expansions to Bukhara and Samarkand on the other side of the Oxus and farther east into China. Due to the paucity of records, how Christianity spread in Central Asia, especially among the Sogdians and the Turkic tribes, remains unknown to us.

In the middle of the 7th century CE, shortly before the Muslim conquest of Persia, Christian missionary activities led by Eliya, metropolitan of Merw, were carried out in Transoxiana, the land of Sogdians and Turkic tribes. The anonymous *Chronica Minora*, whose compilation was completed in 680 CE, attributes the conversion of Turkic tribes near the Oxus River to Eliya, metropolitan of Merw. It illustrates an event around 644 CE, when Eliya, through performing miracles, converted a large number of Turkic people near the borderline of Merw. The metropolitan led them to a river, baptizing all of them and appointing among them priests and deacons (Nöldeke, 1893, 39; Guidi, 1903, 34–37). Additionally, a 14th-century Chinese local chronicle, the *Annals of Zhenjiang of the Zhishun Period* (1330–1333), also refers to a certain Mar Eliya, who was the spiritual master of the church in Samarkand. According to this reference, the 14th-century Syriac Christian heritage in Zhenjiang traced back to Samarkand, where Mar Yeliya (Eliya) was the founding master of the church communities there a few hundred years earlier (*Annals of Zhenjiang*, 365). This Mar Eliya corresponds, most likely, to Eliya, metropolitan of Merw, who evangelized the Turkic tribes in Central Asia.

3. West Syrians and Byzantine Melkites

The Syriac Orthodox historian Bar Hebraeus (1226–1286) wrote in his *Ecclesiastical History* that in the second part of the 7th century CE there were Orthodox (West Syrian) Christians living in Segestan and Khorasan, who had been deported from Edessa. These Christians requested the Orthodox Maphrian Marutha to send them bishops (Abbeloos & Lamy 1877, cols. 125–127). The Syriac Orthodox Christians (known as the Jacobites) in Segestan and Herat traveled eastward into Chinese Central Asia, where they survived up to the 13th century, when Marco Polo visited their places. Marco Polo's travelogue mentions that he encountered some "Jacobite Christians" in the province of Yarcan or Yarkand (trans. Moule & Pelliot, 1938, 145) in today's Shache area in Xinjiang, China.

The Sasanian king Shapur I (r. 240–270 CE), after defeating the Roman emperor Valerian (r. 253–260 CE), deported Roman captives including many Melkite Christians to Persis and other places where the Sasanians and their ancestors had royal estates. The Greek crosses of circa 6th century CE unearthed in Merw were parallel to the crosses found in the Byzantine world (Hermann & Kurbansakhatov, 1994, 68). This may well testify to the existence of Melkite Christians in Central Asia during the Sasanian period. Meanwhile, fragments from a Melkite book of Psalms with Greek lines (Sims-Williams, 2004, 623–631) discovered in Turfan also confirm that Melkite Christians went eastward and settled down in Chinese Central Asia.

4. Christianity in a Multicultural and Multireligious Context

Before the Islamic conquest, the inhabitants of Khorasan practiced Zoroastrianism, Buddhism, Manichaeism, Shamanism, some form of Hinduism, and Christianity. The main challenge to Christians in Persia and Central Asia came from Zoroastrian magi and rulers. Since East Syrian missionaries, especially

monks, won many new converts among Persian Zoroastrians, persecutions from the magi and from several Sasanian kings befell Christians from time to time. Persian Christians who abandoned their Zoroastrian religion often suffered martyrdom. The Church of the East has many celebrated martyrs and saints, many of them being Persian converts. Some of the characteristics of Christianity in pre-Islamic Central Asia were reflected in Christians being caught in the storms of the political conflicts between the Persian and the Roman Empires, the Christological controversies of the early church, and the split that they must have gone through after the Council of → Chalcedon in 451 CE. In the meantime, Christians in remote dioceses of Central Asia encountered in daily life challenges from a multireligious and sometimes hostile environment. Despite the difficulties, the Syriac Church expanded and won converts from among many Zoroastrian and Shamanist believers. Persians, Sogdians, and various Turkic peoples formed the first Christian diaspora in Central Asia.

The adaptation of the Syriac alphabet for writing by the Sogdians, Manicheans, and even at a later period by the Uighurs and the Mongols, as attested in the Turfan Christian fragments and medieval Christian epitaphs, evidences a strong cultural influence of Syriac Christians across Central Asia. Christian monks, diplomats, artisans, and merchants played an indispensable role in spreading Christianity along the Silk Road from Persia, to Central Asia and China.

Historiography

The modern study on Christianity in pre-Islamic Central Asia was pioneered by a number of European scholars in the 20th century, who conducted their studies in various European languages, such as W. Barthold in Russian (Ger. trans. Stübe, 1901), F. Nau (1913) in French, E. Sachau (1919) in German and A. Mingana (1925) in English, J. Dauvillier (1956) in French. Due to the limited sources available during that time, the studies on the early church history in Central Asia depended mostly on two main sources: the Church of the East synod records from 410 to 775 CE composed in Syriac during the 8th century CE and the 6th-century CE *History of Mĕšīḥā-Zĕḵā* later known as *The Chronicle of Arbela* edited by A. Mingana himself (1907), the historical reliability of the latter being doubted by some scholars of today. The critical edition of the synod records together with its French translation by J.B. Chabot (1902) under the title *Synodicon Orientale* paved the way for the studies on the early history of the Church of the East, as the records give indications of various church dioceses in Central Asia up to the year 775 CE. A German translation of *Synodicon Orientale* by O. Braun was published in 1975 but without the original Syriac text. A more extensive and detailed investigation on East Syrian dioceses in Central Asia was published in French by J.M. Fiey (1973). Fiey gave detailed descriptions about each individual Syriac Christian community in Khorasan and Segestan with mapped locations. Since the end of the 20th century, new studies on Christianity in Central Asia have focused largely on the medieval period but with introductions to the pre-Islamic period, such as studies done by E.C.D. Hunter (1992) and M. Dickens (2018).

The canonical records of the Church of the East provide less information on the mission of the church, except for mentioning the names of the bishoprics. The main area of church expansion in pre-Islamic Central Asia was the historical region of Khorasan. Recent studies also take into account new archaeological discoveries in the region. One of the characteristics of early Central Asia was its ethnic diversity. Therefore, studies on early Syriac Christianity in Central Asia tend to focus on the conversion of peoples of Turkic, Hunnic, Iranian and other ethnic heritage.

Bibliography

Abbeloos, J.-B., & T.J. Lamy, eds., *Gregrorii Barhebraei Chronicon Ecclesiasticum*, vol. III, Paris, 1897.

Barthold, W., *Zur Geschichte des Christentums in Mittel-Asien bis zur mongolischen Eroberung: Berichtigte und vermehrte deutsche Bearbeitung nach dem russischen Original von R. Stübe*, Tübingen, 1901.

Bedjan, P., *Histoire de Mar Jab-alaha, de trois autres patriarches, d'un prêtre et de deux laiques, nestoriennes*, Leipzig, 1895.

Braun, O., *Das Buch der Synhados oder Synodicon Orientale*, Amsterdam, 1975.

Brock, S.P., "Bar Shabba/Mar Shabbay, First Bishop of Merv," in: M. Tamcke, W. Schwaigert & E. Schlarb, eds., *Syrisches Christentum weltweit: Studien zur syrischen*

Kirchengeschichte: FS Prof. Hage, SOK 1, Münster, 1995, 190–201.

Chabot, J.-B., ed. & trans., *Synodicon orientale ou receuil synodes nestoriens*, Paris, 1902.

Chavannes, E., *Documents sur les Tou-Kiue (Turcs) occidentaux*, Paris, 1900.

Dauvillier, J., "L'Expansion de l'église syrienne en Asie Centrale et en Extrême-Orient," *OrSyr* 1, 1956, 76–87.

Dickens, M., "Syriac Christianity in Central Asia," in: D. King, ed., *The Syriac World*, London, 2018, 583–624.

Drijvers, H.J.W., *The Book of the Laws of Countries: Dialogue on Fate of Bardaisan of Edessa: New Introduction by Jan Willem Drijvers*, Piscataway, 2006.

Fiey, J.M., "Chrétiens syriques du Horasan e du Ségestan," *Muséon* 86/1–2, 1973, 75–104.

Gillman, I., & H.-J. Klimkeit, *Christians in Asia Before 1500*, London, 1999.

Guidi, I., ed., *Corpus Scriptorum Christianorum Orientalium: Scriptores Syri: Textus Series Tertia Tomus IV: Chronica Minora*, Leipzig, 1903.

Hermann, G., & K. Kurbansakhatov, "The International Merv Project Preliminary Report on the Second Season (1993)," *Iran*, vol. XXXII, 1994, 53–75.

Hunter, E.C.D., "Syriac Christianity in Central Asia," *ZRGG* 44, 1992, 362–368.

Hunter, E.C.D, "The Church of the East in Central Asia," *BJRL* 88/3, 1996, 129–142.

Migne, J.-P., "Hieronymus Epistola CVII," in: J-P. Migne, ed., *Patrologia Latina*, vol. XXII, Paris, 1841–1849.

Mingana, A., "The Early Spread of Christianity in Central Asia and the Far East: A New Document," *BJRL* 9, 1925, 297–366.

Moule, A.C., & P. Pelliot, trans., *Marco Polo: The Description of the World*, London, 1938.

Nau, F., "L'Expansion nestorienne en Asie," in: *Annales du Musée Guimet, Bibliothèque de Vulgarisation*, vol. XL, Paris, 1913.

Nöldeke, T., trans., *Die von Guidi herausgegebene syrische Chronik*, SAWW.PH 128/9, 1893, 1–48.

Sachau, E., "Zur Ausbreitung des Christentums in Asien," *APAW* 1, 1919.

Scher, A., trans. "Histoire nestorienne inédite: Chronique de Se'ert," *PO* 7, 1911.

Simpson, S.J., "Merv, an Archaeological Case-Study from the Northeastern Frontier of the Sasanian Empire," *JAH* 2, 2014, 1–28.

Sims-Williams, N., "A Greek-Sogdian Bilingual from Bulayïq," in: *La Persia e Bisanzio: Atti del Convegno dei Lincei*, Rome, 2004, 623–631.

Wilmshurst, D., *The Martyred Church: A History of the Church of the East*, London, 2011.

Yao, Silian, *Liang Shu*, Shanghai, 1916; ET: *Book of Liang*.

Yu, Xilu, ed., *Zhishun Zhenjiang Zhi*, Nanjing, 1999; ET: *Annals of Zhenjiang of the Zhishun Period*.

Li Tang

Assembly/Meeting

Christianity was from its very beginnings a communitarian religion. By being baptized, Christians became members of a "church" (ἐκκλησία), which itself consisted of local "churches" (congregations) but at the same constituted one community. Already in the New Testament, the unity of both the entire Christian community and the local congregations were expressed by the key concept of κοινωνία and by various metaphors, such as "body" (of Christ; Rom 12:5; 1 Cor 12:12–30; Eph 4:4–16; Col 1:18, 24) and temple as a building (Eph 2:20–22), city (of God; Heb 12:22). The communitarian aspect of Christianity and the unity of the church also formed a central theme in the later patristic literature and were strongly emphasized by the church fathers, especially when in their eyes this unity was under threat.

The communitarian character of early Christianity becomes most clearly visible in the assemblies, the gatherings that from the very beginning were held at a regular basis and played a pivotal role in the formation of the identity(/ies) of the early Christian congregations. The mere choice of the word ἐκκλησία as a designation for the early Christian communities is revelatory: in profane Greek it referred to an "assembly" of citizens that was convened to take (political) decisions that were of great importance for the entire community, and, even more importantly, in the Septuagint (→ Bible) it is frequently employed to designate the fact of assembling people (usually the entire Jewish people), specifically a community that has been assembled (it is mostly used to translate the Hebrew word *qahal*, which has basically the same meaning; see Burtchaell, 1992, 209–215).

1. Pre-Christian Forerunners of Early Christian Assemblies

Although the word most frequently used for early Christian communities evoked the connotation of "assembly," it is noteworthy that it is not used in early Christian literature to designate *gatherings* the (see for the Greek and Latin terms used in the sources: Metzger, 2015, 298–299). This linguistic fact in itself leads one to suspect that there is no direct historical link between the Greek and Jewish assemblies designated by this term and the meetings of the first Christians. A comparison between the early Christian gatherings and the assemblies mentioned and also a study of the available sources just confirms this presumption: the character of the early Christian assemblies and the reasons for which they were convened differed basically from the profane Greek and Hebrew Bible ones, and the direct historical roots of the Christian gatherings have to be sought elsewhere.

Two types of meetings can be considered as the immediate forerunners of the Christian assemblies:

a. banquets (symposia) and
b. the meetings in the Jewish "synagogues" (the meaning of which is: [place of] "gathering," "assembly").

The questions of which of these traditions was most influential in the development of early Christian assemblies and to what extent this was the case remain a matter of debate, but there is strong evidence that both traditions played an important role in the formation and the development of the early Christian gatherings.

Banquets were a very common phenomenon in the entire Greco-Roman world – including Judaism – and were held at various occasions by social groups that were bound by kinship or by professional, religious, or social ties. They were celebrated in the evening and consisted of a meal proper that was followed by a *symposion* (lit. "drinking party") during which wine was drunk. Banquets had a more or less formalized character and included ritual elements such as the singing of hymns and libations (ritual pouring of wine), and in the case of Jewish symposia specific prayers that had the character of blessings. Most time there were also certain rules that were related to the social status of the participants and gender roles. Depending on the group, the after-dinner drinking course could involve (philosophical) conversation or entertainment. The communal dimension of banquets was very important. They played a central role in strengthening the bonds between the members of the social groups celebrating these meals (Smith, 2002; McGowan, 2014, 20–25).

The origins and the early development of the synagogue in the period before and after the destruction of the Second Temple continue to give rise to many unsolved questions and remain disputed (Levine, 2000). Most probably, the → synagogue originated in the → Diaspora, where, from the outset, alternatives for the Temple cult were an indispensable necessity, even before its destruction. Synagogues were community centers that were used for diverse liturgical and nonliturgical purposes. It is certain that even before the emergence of Christianity, Jews came together on the Sabbath in the synagogue to read, study, and discuss parts of the Torah (→ Law/Decalogue/Torah), that is, the first five books of → Moses, perhaps already in combination with selected passages from the Prophets as was the case in later synagogue practice. It was probably only after the destruction of the Temple that the communal recitation of the statutory prayers, such as the 18 benedictions, became an integral part of the (liturgical) gatherings in the synagogue. Another striking characteristic of the meetings in the synagogue was their democratic character: each synagogue had an "archisynagogos" (a synagogue leader), but his role was just that of a chairman/supervisor: the prayers and portions of the Torah and the Prophets were recited by the (male) members of the congregations.

2. Early Christian Communal Meals

As was the case in many other associations and groups that existed in the Greco-Roman world, communal meals held a central place in early Christian communities (McGowan, 2014, 25–57). In the first two centuries CE, they were celebrated at the usual time, namely in the evening or night, most probably in the evening or night after the → Sabbath, which was part of the first day of the week (later also called "Sunday"). It emerges from the earliest descriptions of these meals that they had many elements in common with the banquets that were held by Jews and pagans. One recognizes many customs that were typical of Greco-Roman symposia in Paul's discussion of the meal practices of the Christians of Corinth (1 Cor 11:17–34), in → Tertullian's description of the Christian love meal (Tert. *Apol.* 39), and in the communal meals mentioned in the document that is known as the → *Apostolic Tradition* (ch. 26–30). The eucharistic meals underlying *Did.* 9 and 10 betray influences from a Jewish variety of the banquet tradition (see

for the Jewish connection of the prayer texts said during these meals: Bradshaw, 2004, 32–35).

Although the basic patterns of the earliest Christian banquets were derived from Greek, Roman, and sometimes from Jewish meal customs, the earliest Christian banquets exhibited peculiar features that were related to the specific character of early Christian communities and to the religious convictions their members shared. What distinguished the Christian banquets from Jewish and pagan ones was first of all the belief in Jesus as the Lord and Messiah, and the fact that his words were transmitted and that the major events of his life, death, and → resurrection were commemorated during the assemblies. These traditions as well as the expectation of his return in the nearby future colored and determined the character of the rituals and prayers that accompanied the meals.

In the 3rd and 4th centuries CE, the early Christian meals underwent several changes that impacted on both their ritual form and their religious meaning (Bradshaw & Johnson, 2012, 25–59). It was at least in part due to the growth of the communities that the significance of the evening banquets declined, and instead a small quantity of bread and wine was distributed during liturgical meetings that took place no longer in the evening but in the morning. In the same period, one also discerns an increasing tendency to emphasize the links between these eucharistic meals and the Last Supper described in the Synoptic Gospels. The Last Supper became more and more explicitly considered as the foundation of the early Christian meals, and its shape began to serve as the model for the ritual pattern of these meals. This process eventually led to the incorporation of the institution narrative into the eucharistic prayer (probably from the mid-3rd cent. CE). Owing to these developments, the character of the meals changed considerably. Commensality, sharing, and consuming food and drink by the members of the community remained an important aspect of communal meals other than eucharistic celebrations, but in the latter emphasis was increasingly placed on the communion with the body and blood of Christ and the commemoration of his sacrificial death. Thus the (ritualized) banquets eventually evolved into sacramental meals in which the eating and drinking had a merely spiritual meaning and no longer served for the satisfaction of physical hunger and thirst (see McGowan, 2014, 47–52).

3. Assemblies for the Word

The reading of authoritative texts and forms of preaching very soon became a central part of early Christian assemblies, but it remains difficult to reconstruct their beginnings and further development (see McGowan, 2014, 65–110). It is generally agreed that Christians of Jewish provenance continued the practice of reading from the Torah (and the Prophets) on Sabbath, but we know nothing about the impact which the fact that they believed in Jesus had on the ways they read and interpreted these texts. Even less can be said with certainty about the role authoritative texts and preaching played in Gentile Christian communities. It is at least certain that Paul's letters were read in the communities that had been founded by him and equally that stories about Jesus and sayings and words ascribed to him were handed on in early Christian assemblies. It is however not clear how and when this happened, whether they were for instance read during the communal meals or in separate meetings. Another unsolved question relates to the reading and explanation of the Hebrew Bible (see Rouwhorst, 2002, 318–330). There is strong evidence that the pattern and character of Gentile Christian assemblies were different from the meetings in the Jewish synagogues. Does this, however, mean that in the beginning the Hebrew Bible was not read at all? Finally, it may be asked what role prophecy and other charismatic phenomena played in the gatherings. To what degree was the situation described – and criticized – by Paul representative of many other assemblies or was it rather exceptional? There cannot be any doubt about at least one thing: the existence of a great variety of forms.

From at least the mid-2nd century CE, there is unambiguous evidence of the existence and development of two types of assemblies in which the reading of the Bible – the New Testament but frequently also the Old Testament – played a central role. → Justin Martyr is the first known author who proves to be familiar with a bipartite assembly consisting of a liturgy of the word – which comprised a reading from the Scriptures, a sermon, and prayers – and

next an → anaphora (eucharistic prayer) followed by the distribution of bread and wine (Just. 1 *Apol.* 65–67). We do not know how widespread this type of assembly was in the time of Justin, but it found general acceptance from the second part of the 3rd century CE at the latest and formed the basis for the early Christian → Eucharist as celebrated especially on → Sundays, but also on other weekdays and other occasions.

Besides the reading of Scripture in the first part of the Eucharist, also separate services of the word existed that were exclusively devoted to the reading and explanation of the Bible. For instance, a large part of → Origen's homilies on various books of the Hebrew Bible were delivered during this type of services of the word (Rouwhorst, 2002, 323–324; 2013a, 832).

The reading of the Bible provided these assemblies for the word with a didactic character, which became stronger to the degree that more emphasis was laid upon the interpretation of the texts that were read. Here one may note a remarkable similarity and also at least some sort of historical relationship with the reading and explanation of the Torah and the Prophets in the Jewish synagogue.

4. Assemblies for Communal Prayer

Like Jews, Christians prayed (→ Prayer) at set times during the day and often also during the night. In the first three centuries CE, these prayers, whether done alone or with others, were usually said in the domestic setting of private homes. During the 3rd and 4th centuries CE, this custom developed into the formation of special prayer services that were held in church buildings and lay at the basis of what later was called the divine office or liturgy of the hours (Bradshaw, 1981; McGowan, 2014, 183–215). The oldest nucleus was formed by the so-called cathedral office, which basically consisted of communal morning and evening prayers that were attended by members of the laity and the clergy. The basic elements of these services consisted of prayer and a small number of selected psalms. Originally, these assemblies as a rule did not involve the reading of biblical passages other than psalms (insofar as other biblical lections appear in later services, it is usually the result of a fusion with other types of liturgical meetings). After the rise of monasticism, this "cathedral" practice was increasingly affected by monastic traditions. This led to an increase in the number of services during the day and the night and moreover to a considerable expansion of their length. Even more important was the impact of monastic spirituality, which placed a strong emphasis upon the penitential aspect and upon personal growth and salvation by means of a life of ceaseless prayer. This implied that the focus became increasingly on the individual rather than on the corporation dimension of these assemblies (see Bradshaw, 2009, 108–113).

5. Alternative Assemblies: Jewish Christians and Gnostics

Most of the earliest data concerning early Christian assemblies relate to communities that can be qualified as proto-orthodox, the forerunners of Orthodox Christianity that later would obtain a predominant position. However, in the first three centuries CE, Christianity was characterized by a great diversity of groups. Besides proto-orthodox churches, a great variety of (mainly) Jewish Christian and gnostic communities flourished. The theological views and sociological structures peculiar to each of these groups were naturally reflected in their assemblies.

Little precise information is available about the character of the assemblies of Jewish Christian groups that consisted of ethnic Jews who maintained Jewish practices that were not observed by most Gentile congregations. There is at least strong evidence that they continued meeting at the Sabbath for a regular reading of the Torah (and the Prophets).

Most of the gnostic movements were critical about the assemblies and the rituals of the (proto-) orthodox) Christians. One of the clearest examples is the fierce attack of the Eucharist found in the *Gospel of Judas* (see for this question Rouwhorst, 2011; → *Judas, Gospel of*). However, gnostic groups had their own rituals that often were very similar to those of the Orthodox Christians. A clear case in point are the Valentinians (→ Valentinus/Valentinians), whose meetings, probably held on Sundays, showed a certain familiarity with Christian Sunday worship as described by Justin (see further),

consisting of baptism, preaching, and a eucharistic meal. A remarkable prominence was, however, given to communal singing and prophecy, and the assemblies were understood from a specifically Valentinian perspective, emphasis being laid upon the attainment of gnosis and the communion of the Valentinian ἐκκλησία with the divine realm, the → *pleroma* (Thomassen, 2013).

6. The Communal Dimension: Unity of the Congregation

One of the most striking features of early Christian communities, as presented by most early Christian sources, was their strong inner cohesion in combination with a high degree of exclusiveness. These sources place a strong emphasis upon group solidarity and depict Christian congregations as holy communities, which distinguished themselves from their non-Christian surroundings – that is, Greco-Roman religion and society as well as → Judaism and other Christian groups viewed as heterodox or interpreting Christianity in a wrong manner. Even if social reality will have been more complicated, the existence of a high degree of cohesiveness and exclusiveness are undeniable. They were strongest in the first generations (Meeks, 1983, 84–107), but remained also characteristic of Christian communities in later periods, even in the 4th and 5th centuries CE.

The emphasis upon unity and cohesion becomes most clearly manifest during the communal meals which served to strengthen the identity and unity of the congregations. This emphasis was most conspicuous in the period of the beginnings, when the number of Christians was relatively small and the meals were held in private houses. Telling are the emphasis laid on the breaking of the (one) bread that symbolized the unity of the Christian congregations and also the fact that participants were drinking wine from the same cup (see esp. 1 Cor 10:16–17), which in general was not customary in antiquity. The closed character of the gatherings also appears from the fact that only (baptized) members could take part in the communal meals (see e.g. *Did.* 10:5 and Just. 1 *Apol.* 65 and 67). The concern with the unity of the Christians participating in the communal meals was not unique to the earliest periods but also played a prominent role in the eucharistic celebrations of the 4th and 5th centuries CE. Receiving the consecrated bread and wine during the Eucharist meant having communion not only with Christ but also with the entire body of which he was the head, the church. This idea appears in the writings of most church fathers (Lubac, 2006, 4–6), but is most emphatically developed by → Augustine of Hippo, especially in passages where he elaborates on the theme of the one bread used in the Eucharist as symbolizing the unity of the church (see esp. Aug. *Serm.* 272; *Guel.* 7.1–2).

Although the communal dimension of the early Christian congregations was most clearly visible in the communal meals and in the Eucharist, it also played a prominent role in other types of assemblies. It found a particularly clear expression in the festivals that were held during the year (Holy Week and → Easter, → Christmas and → Epiphany, anniversaries of the death of → martyrs) and besides eucharistic celebrations included other types of meetings and rituals such as vigils, and processions that attracted large crowds of people, being more popular than the weekly recurring Sunday Eucharist (Cassingena-Trévedy, 2009, 186–242).

While being assembled for the celebration of the Eucharist – or for another ritual or festival – early Christians felt united not only with a community that was much larger and included other Orthodox Christian congregations, but also with the angels celebrating their celestial liturgy. The latter element finds its clearest expression in the sanctus, the "thrice holy" (of Isa 6:3), which from the 4th century CE is an integral part of all eastern and western eucharistic prayers (see Spinks, 1991). The theme of the communion with the angels is in particular – frequently and extensively – developed in the writings of Greek church fathers (Cassingena-Trévedy, 2009, 80–92).

7. Differentiation and Stratification

The inner cohesiveness of the earliest Christian communities, their emphasis on the unity of the congregations and the awareness of being different from the surrounding environment, left little or no room for distinguishing different categories or classes of Christians, making for instance a distinction between more and less initiated ones. Such distinctions were made in various gnostic movements, but not in the proto-orthodox communities.

Two factors, however, contributed to a differentiation among different types of believers that directly affected the character of the (proto-)orthodox assemblies (Rouwhorst, 2008, 118–120). At the latest in the course of the 2nd or 3rd centuries CE, a period of preparation for baptism, the catechumenate (→ Catechesis), came into existence, which had as a result the emergence of a specific category of candidate Christians: the catechumens. Another specific group, in certain respects comparable to them, was constituted by the penitents who had been baptized but had nonetheless committed a grave sin and had to do public penance (→ Penitence/Penance), which meant that they were temporarily excluded from full community with the other Christians and were during a certain period regressed to the status of the catechumens. The special position these two groups held within the Christian communities became clearly visible in the liturgical assemblies, which included a (eucharistic) meal. In chapters 26 and 27 of the *Apostolic Tradition*, which probably describes a Christian banquet, the catechumens do not sit together with the faithful, and receive special (exorcized) bread (see Bradshaw & Johnson, 2012; Philips, 2002, 142–145). From the end of the 3rd century CE, it became common practice to dismiss in the bipartite Eucharist – which had become current at that time – the (often large groups of) catechumens and equally the penitents after the service of the word with the result that only the baptized participated in the second part of the celebration.

The architectural plans of church buildings of several regions betray a further gender-related (→ Gender) compartmentalization of the congregations: in northern Syria separate spaces are reserved for men and women, men staying in the more eastern part, and the women in the more western part, that is the farthest from the liturgical center (*Did. Apost.* 12 = *Apos. Con.* 2.57.4). Separate spaces and entrances for men and women are also attested by the *Apos. Con.* 2.57.4; *T. Dom.* 1.19 and equally appear to have existed in Antioch (Chrys. *Hom. Matt.* 73.3 = PG 58.677; see also Sodini, 2006, 231–233). It emerges from Augustine's *De civitate dei* (2.28) that a separation of the sexes during the services also existed in North Africa.

8. Leadership and Ministries

It emerges from the earliest Christian sources available that the Christian assemblies involved from the very start forms of leadership roles and a division of services and tasks that were geared to the specific character of the Christian assemblies (even if they mostly present parallels with and often find their origin in pre-Christian, Jewish, or Greco-Roman leadership roles and functions; see Metzger, 2015, 507–660). In the beginning, we find a great variety of offices and functions, most of which could probably be fulfilled by both men and women: householders and patrons who hosted community dining at their homes, itinerant apostles and (charismatic) prophets, appointed local officers leaders such as elders (presbyters) and overseers (ἐπίσκοποι), and deacons. The roles of these various officers, their position within the communities, and the tasks they fulfilled during the assemblies were not clearly defined, and considerable differences existed among the various local communities (see for an overview of the various reconstructions of the development of these offices: Burtchaell, 1992, 61–179). However, from at least the 2nd century CE, a process of institutionalization started in the [proto-]orthodox communities; see K. Torjesen (2008), which was severely criticized by Montanist and several gnostic groups. The role of charismatic prophets and female leaders during the assemblies was reduced, the tasks and the competences of the appointed leaders were more clearly defined and the authority of the overseer increased. This resulted in the formation of a tripartite ministry that is first unambiguously attested by writings that can be dated to the 3rd century CE such as the → *Didascalia Apostolorum* (Schöllgen, 1998) and *Apostolic Tradition* and included a bishop being at the head of the community, one or more deacons, and several presbyters, each of which fulfilled specific tasks during the assemblies. Some tasks that were not reserved for the tripartite clergy were allotted to holders of specific minor offices, in particular specialized "readers" (McGowan, 2014, 92–93) and singers and choirs (McGowan, 2014, 117–119). These developments involved a reduction of the role of the laypeople. More in particular, because women were excluded from the major ministries and offices, these developments also contributed to a further minimizing of the role of women during the assemblies. This, however, was not everywhere the case with all offices and tasks. In several regions, certain liturgical tasks were fulfilled by female deacons, and in Syriac churches hymns (*madrashe* = lit. teaching songs), which played a central role in liturgical assemblies, were performed by women's choirs probably made up of female ascetics (Ashbrook Harvey, 2012).

From the end of the 3rd century CE and especially in the 4th and 5th centuries CE, several factors that are partly interconnected reinforced the tendency to specify and to fix the roles of the clergy in the assemblies while at the same time demarcating the boundaries between clergy and laity:

1. the rapidly increasing size of the assemblies, which made a further developed organization and stratification necessary;
2. the progressive ritualizing of the most important liturgical celebrations, especially the Eucharist, which involved a further structuring of the assemblies;
3. the construction of church buildings in which special spaces and seats were reserved in the area around the cathedra and the altar (choir) for the members of the clergy with the laypeople staying in the nave;
4. the use of priestly terminology for the liturgical presidency and the performance of liturgical actions by the bishop (and later also of the priests), especially his role during the Eucharist;
5. the use of Neoplatonic concepts and terminology, providing a cosmological foundation for the ordered structure of the assemblies and relating the hierarchical divisions that are considered to be an inherent part of that order to the celestial hierarchies of the angels (see esp. Dionysius the Pseudo-Areopagite's *Ecclesiastical Hierarchy*).

9. The Participation of the Faithful

Although early Christian communities were from the very beginning familiar with at least some sort of division of tasks and roles, and even if gradually – especially in the mainstream churches – a further differentiation and fixation of liturgical offices and ministries took place, the assemblies of these communities were characterized by various forms of participation of all the baptized Christians, including the "lay" people who did not hold special offices, and, in spite of certain centrifugal tendencies (see further), this remained the case during the entire early Christian era.

In the early communal meals and in the eucharistic celebrations of the later period, the major form of participation consisted of the consuming of food and drink, especially eating the bread and drinking from the cup (which usually contained wine mixed with water and in some cases only water). Taking part in these meals, consuming the bread and the wine, was reserved for the baptized Christian and therefore also a sign of full membership. At least until the mid-4th century, it was common practice that all the Christians present at the moment of the recitation of the eucharistic prayers received both the bread and the cup. A form of participation that appears to have only existed in western Christianity consisted of the offering of bread and wine (and other gifts) by the faithful – before the beginning of the eucharistic prayer – that were either collected or brought forward in a procession (Rouwhorst, 2013b, 65–73).

In the services for the word, the principal activity of the faithful consisted of listening to the lectures and the homilies. To enter in contact with their audience and to capture the attention of the people, the homilists made use of the rhetorical devices that were practiced in classical rhetoric. Famous examples are the homilies of → Melito of Sardis (*On Passover*), → John Chrysostom, Augustine, and many other church fathers.

A form of participation encountered in all types of early Christian assemblies consisted of singing (McGowan, 2014, 111–128). Evidence of it is already found in the letters to the Colossians (3:16) and Ephesians (5:18–20), which encourage the singing of "psalms, hymns and spiritual songs." The singing of various types of nonbiblical poetic songs   commonly designated by the term "hymns" – is attested by various sources. It held a very central place, especially in the assemblies of the Syriac-speaking churches (*Odes of Solomon* [→ *Solomon, Odes of*]; *madrashe*/teaching songs of → Ephrem the Syrian; see Ashbrook Harvey, 2012) but also in gnostic communities, for instance in Valentinian churches (Thomassen, 2013). Biblical psalms appear to have

first played a rather minor role in the assemblies, but they obtained an increasingly prominent place from the second half of the 4th century CE in both eastern and western Christianity (McKinnon, 1998, 98). If the faithful were familiar with the texts and the melodies, the songs were performed in unison by the entire congregation. However, if the believers did not know the texts by heart and if more sophisticated melodies were used, the performance of the songs required a division of roles which meant that the most complicated parts were sung by a choir, soloist, or worship leader. In that case, however, the congregation could take part in the singing by means of refrains, responds, or antiphons. Whatever the precise division of the roles, communal singing was viewed as the expression of the unity of the assembly.

A very common way for the congregations to express their communal agreement and involvement with what was said or done during the assembly was the saying or singing of acclamations that had their origin in profane meetings, for instance, the inauguration of emperors, speeches of orators, or theater spectacles (Klauser, 1950). These acclamations consisted of very few words, sometimes even of one word. They could be more or less spontaneous expressions of approval (e.g. with the content of a sermon), but very often fixed formulas were used. Examples of the latter category were Amen, → *Kyrie Eleison*, Allelluja, anathema (an expression of exclusion and excommunication), and Hagios (list in Klauser, 1950, 227–231). The term "acclamation" is also frequently used for the parts of the eucharistic prayer that are said or sung by the congregation, such as the response of the introductory dialogue at the beginning, the → *Sanctus*, the Amen at the end, and many other texts that were inserted in the various anaphoras (Schneiders, 1990).

The building of large churches (esp. basilicas) in the 4th and the 5th centuries CE and the fact that the Christian liturgy took on a public character, especially also the development of a stational liturgy in big cities like Jerusalem, Rome, and Constantinople (Baldovin, 1987), made a new form of participation by the faithful possible, namely the procession (→ Processions). The members of the community moved in procession through the church buildings, but also through the cities walking from one sanctuary, holy place, or church to the other (esp. in the pilgrimage liturgy of Jerusalem and its surroundings, but also in Rome and Constantinople).

Members of the congregations finally participated in the liturgical celebrations by bodily postures and gestures, such as standing, facing east, kneeling, rising, bowing, and offering gifts (see Sheerin, 2008, 717–718). Compared to textual elements, relatively little mention is made of these forms of physical participation in the sources and even less so in the secondary literature. They formed, however, an essential part of communal worship.

10. Centrifugal Tendencies

Although the sources give clear evidence of the participation of entire congregations in the liturgical celebrations, and although early Christian authors emphasize the importance of the unity of the assembly, this does not mean that all the members of the congregations participated in the meetings with the same intensity and conviction.

From the second part of the 4th century CE, one finds clear traces of a decline of the frequency of reception of communion, that is, baptized Christians attended the eucharistic liturgy, but only rarely received communion (see e.g. Chrys. *Hom. Eph.* 3.4; *Hom. 1 Tim 5*.3; *Hom. Heb.* 17.4; Ambr. *Sacr.* 5.25; see Sheerin, 2008, 720). This phenomenon may have been caused by religious awe of the consecrated bread and wine, but perhaps even more by the high ethical demands that bishops made on Christians who went to communion.

Sources of the same period also complain about and thereby also give evidence of the fact that many Christians do not regularly attend the "ordinary" assemblies on the Sundays during the year, but only go to church on the big festivals (this topic frequently recurs in the works, esp. the homilies of → John Chrysostom; see Cassingena-Trévedy, 2009, 48–53).

Centrifugal tendencies, however, also existed among Christians who regularly and with much devotion attended the entire celebrations from the beginning until the end. It could take the form of an inner distancing of the individual believer, who was primarily looking for spiritual development, from the community and the communal rituals.

This tendency existed in gnostic groups that minimized the importance of the rituals and placed a strong emphasis on the development of personal spiritual knowledge (Rouwhorst, 2006, 116–118), but also in monastic milieus (Bradshaw, 2009, 108–113; see also above) and circles that, inspired by Neoplatonic philosophy (→ Neoplatonism), strived for mystical communion of the soul with "the One" (see esp. the very influential writings of Dionysius the Pseudo-Areapogite). There was a continuing tension between the corporate, ecclesial dimension of the assemblies and the spiritual life of their individual members.

Bibliography

Ashbrook Harvey, S., "Performance as Exegesis: Women's Liturgical Choirs in Syriac Tradition," in: B. Goen, S. Hawkes-Teeples & S. Alexopoulos, *Inquiries into Eastern Christian Worship*, ECS 9, Louvain, 2012, 47–64.

L'Assemblée liturgique et les différents rôles dans l'assemblée: Conférences Saint-Serge: XXIIIe semaine d'études liturgiques 1976, BELS 9, Rome, 1997.

Baldovin, J., *The Urban Character of Christian Worship: The Origins, Development, and Meaning of Stational Liturgy*, OCA 228, Rome, 1987.

Bradshaw, P., *Daily Prayer in the Early Church*, London, 1981.

Bradshaw, P., *Eucharistic Origins*, Oxford, 2004.

Bradshaw, P., *Reconstructing Early Christian Worship*, London, 2009.

Bradshaw. P., & M.E. Johnson, *The Eucharistic Liturgies: Their Evolution and Interpretation*, Minnesota, 2012.

Bradshaw P., M.E. Johnson & E.P. Philips, *The Apostolic Traditon*, Minneapolis, 2002.

Burtchaell, J., *From Synagogue to Church: Public Services and Offices in the Earliest Christian Communities*, Cambridge UK, 1992

Cassingena-Trévedy, F., *Les pères de l'église et la liturgie*, Paris, 2009.

Klauser, T., "Akklamationen," in: *RAC*, vol. I, Stuttgart, 1950, 216–233.

Levine, L., *The Ancient Synagogue: The First Thousand Years*, New Haven, 2000.

Lubac, H. de, *Corpus Mysticum: The Eucharist and the Church in the Middle Ages*, London, 2006 (orig. Fr. ed.: *Corpus mysticum: L'eucharistie et l'église aus moyen âge*, 2nd ed., Paris, 1949).

McGowan, A., *Ancient Christian Worship: Early Christian Practices in Social, Historical and Theological Perspective*, Grand Rapids, 2014.

McKinnon, J., "The Fourth Century Origin of the Gradual," *EMH* 7, 1987, 91–106, repr. in: J. McKinnon, *The Temple, the Church Fathers and Early Western Chant*, Aldershot, 1998.

Meeks, W., *The First Urban Christians*, New Haven, 1983.

Metzger, M., *L'Église dans l'empire romain: Le culte*, vol. I: *Les institutions*, StAns 163, Rome, 2015.

Rouwhorst, G., "The Reading of Scripture in Early Christian Liturgy," in: L. Rutgers, ed., *What Athens Has To Do with Jerusalem: Essays on Classical, Jewish, and Early Christian Art and Archaeology in Honor of Gideon Foerster*, ISACR 1, Louvain, 2002, 305–331.

Rouwhorst, G., "Christian Initiation in Early Christianity," *QuLi* 87, 2006, 100–119.

Rouwhorst, G., "The Gospel of Judas and Early Christian Eucharist," in: J. van den Berg, A. Kotzé, T. Nicklas & M. Scopello, *"In Search of Truth": Augustine, Manichaeism and other Gnosticism: Studies for Johannes van Oort at Sixty*, NHMS 74, Leiden, 2011.

Rouwhorst, G., "The Bible in Liturgy," in: J. Carleton Paget & J. Schaper, *The New Cambridge History of the Bible*, vol. I: *The Bible from the Beginnings to 600*, Cambridge UK, 2013a, 822–842.

Rouwhorst, G., "Oblationen II (Sachen)," in: *RAC*, vol. XXVI, Stuttgart, 2013b, 47–74.

Schneiders, M., "Acclamations in the Eucharistic Prayer," in: C. Caspers & M. Schneiders, eds., *Omnes circumadstantes: Contributions Towards a History of the Role of the People in the Liturgy: Presented to Herman Wegman*, Kampen, 1990, 78–100.

Schöllgen, G., *Die Anfänge der Professionalisierung des Klerus und das kirchliche Amt in der syrischen Didaskalia*, JbAC.S., vol. XXVI, Münster, 1998.

Sheerin, D., "Eucharistic Liturgy," in: S. Ashbrook Harvey & D. Hunter, eds., *OHECS*, Oxford, 2008, 711–743.

Smith, D.E., *From Symposium to Eucharist: The Banquet in the Early Christian World*, Minneapolis, 2002.

Spinks, B., *The Sanctus in the Eucharistic Prayer*, Cambridge UK, 1991.

Sodini, J.-P., "Archéologie des églises et organisation spatiale de la liturgie," in: F. Cassingena-Trévedy & J. Jurasz, eds., *Les liturgies syriaques*, EtSy 3, Paris, 2006, 229–266.

Thomassen, E., "Going to Church with the Valentinians" in: A. DeConick, G. Shaw & J. Turner, eds., *Practicing Gnosis: Ritual, Magic, Theurgy and Liturgy in Nag Hammadi, Manichaean and Other Ancient Literature: Essays in Honor of Birger A. Pearson*, NHMS 85, Leiden, 2013, 183–198.

Torjesen, K., "Clergy and Laity," in: S. Ashbrook Harvey & D. Hunter, *OHECS*, Oxford, 2008, 389–405.

GERARD ROUWHORST

Asterius the Sophist

Asterius of Cappadocia (b. between 260 and 280 CE, Cappadocia, d. after 341 CE) had become a Christian before the year 303 CE, as he recanted during the → persecution under Emperor Maximian. He had received a training in the arts (esp. in rhetoric), was inspired by Philo of Alexandria and → Origen, and shows Middle Platonic influences. → Epiphanius of Salamis and Philostorgius identify him as a pupil of Lucian of Antioch (Epiph. *Haer.* 76.3, see Holl & Dummer, 1985; Philost. *Hist. eccl.* 2.14 [Bidez & Winkelmann, 25]). In contrast, Marcellus does not mention Lucian, but twice claims Paulinus of Tyre to have been the "father" of Asterius (Marcellus, frgm. 18; Vinzent, 1993, 122). Because of Asterius having sacrificed during the persecution, he remained a lay person during his life, although he may have shown some interest in a career as a → bishop. As secretary of the bishop Dianius of Cappadocia, however, not only did he become influential on the Eusebians, but he was also seen as a key defender of Eusebius of Nicomedia, fighting off Alexander of Alexandria's accusations, apparently in a private letter that was addressed to Paulinus. In it he had voiced views that must have become public (Marcellus, frgm. 18; Vinzent, 1993, 18). In support of Eusebius, Asterius travelled around Syria in the spring and summer of 329 CE giving readings from his συνταγμάτιον. If we can trust → Athanasius of Alexandria, Asterius must have been one of the prime inspirations for the Eusebians, and particularly for Arius. Athanasius mentions that "Arius transcribes" what "Asterius has written" (Athan. *Decr.* 8.1) and that "Arius learned from him [Asterius]" (*Decr.* 20.2; see also Athan. *Syn.* 18.2).

The only works we know of and of which only fragments have come down to us are Asterius' Συνταγμάτιον and his defense of Eusebius.

Like other → Eusebians (and Arius, → Arianism), Asterius believed in two or three hypostases of Father, Son, and Spirit. Asterius used the Porphyrian example of a human father and son to explain the generation of the divine Son from God. Even before the father actually becomes a father, so Asterius with Porphyrius, the Father always had the potential to become a father, but once the father had generated a son, this son was a different being or hypostasis from his father (Asterius, frgm. 52 and also frgms. 22, 54, 75; Eus. *Eccl. theol.* 2.19.21; Marcellus, frgm. 85; Vinzent, 1993, 74). To Asterius the relation between the Word and the Father, therefore, was one of harmony of words and deeds (Asterius, frgms. 39–40; Eus. *Marc.* 2.2.15–25; Marcellus, frgms. 73 and 74; Vinzent, 1993,

62–64), not one of identity. And yet he believed (as did Philo *Opif.* 8–9, 100; *Mut.* 259–264) that God was eternal intellect and had in himself a *logos* and a wisdom that were ingenerate, were always together with God, and identical with him (Asterius, frgms. 64–73). To safeguard both the transcendence of the divine principle of everything generated and created, but also the creatures who, as in Philo *Mut.* 27–29; *Spec.* 1.60, could not encounter and bear God directly, he conceptualized the Son as the medium between God and world. The Son exerted this mediatory role by being a creature essentially like those creatures to whom he mediated God's gifts, even if he was the first of them and the only one who came into being without mediation. As God had chosen a man, → Moses, to pass on his law to Moses' fellow people, so the Son as first creature passed on God's salvation to the other creatures, in order that "through the similar the similar beings" would be able to receive God's gifts (i.e. "through Jesus the normal beings would be able to [...]" Asterius, frgm. 47). Asterius differentiates primarily between God's essential characteristics that define who he is from those essential characteristics that are proper to him, but which he can share with whom and what he generates and creates (Vinzent, 1993, 41–48). The prime distinction is not between God and creation or between Father and Son, but between the utterly transcendent divine essence and everything else. The divine essence itself is characterized by only two incommunicable essential characteristics, namely, the state of being "ingenerate" and "eternal," a Middle Platonic pair of concepts that we can already find in → Philo of Alexandria (*Opif.* 171). That God also is without beginning, is invisible, creates out of himself, and that he is origin, God, generator, Father, power, *logos*, wisdom, Lord, king, teacher, being, savior, light, and so forth – and that he is one, the one alone, perfect, and true – are all implications of his ingenerate and eternal essence; all those implications are not exclusive to him, contrary to his designation as "ingenerate" and "eternal." Except for the two characteristics of being "ingenerate" and "eternal," all others can be communicated. Oneness, therefore, does not mark God's non-communicable characteristic, as in Arius, but is counted among those qualities that God is able to share even with his creatures. Or, as Asterius says, "See, there is even

only one single Sun, and one Earth" (Asterius, frgm. 24). Yet, solely "ingenerate" and "eternal" denote God alone.

In stating his belief in three hypostases, he asserted, "to think that the Father is truly Father and that the Son is truly Son and likewise [regarding] the Holy Spirit" (Asterius, frgm. 60; Marcellus, frgm. 1; Vinzent, 1993, 4; see Eusebius of Nicomedia, *Epistula ad Paulinum from Tyre* [= *Urkunde* 8 in Opitz, 1934, 15–17]). The "likewise" indicates that Asterius did not understand the procession of the Spirit in the same anthropological way as he saw the generation of the Son by the Father, although he regarded the Spirit – like the Son – derived and generated by the Father, in a similar way as he saw the entire creation derived and generated by the Father through the Son. The Spirit (→ Holy Spirit), therefore, is not the Son, but a third hypostasis that has come into being. As the Son is mediator of the Father, the Son also mediates the procession of the Spirit. It is part of any Platonic mediation scheme that mediation means a reduction in being. Hence, the Son is less than the Father, and the Spirit is even lesser than the Son or the Father. This Platonic reductionist scheme Asterius must have read in Luke 1:35, where it is said that the Spirit "overshadowed" Mary (see Marcellus, frgm. 61; Vinzent, 1993, 54; Eus. *Marc.* 2.2.4; Klostermann & Hansen, 1972, 35, ll. 21–25; *Eccl. theol.* 2.1.1; Klostermann & Hansen, 1972, 99, ll. 17–21) and, therefore, could not be equated with the divine light of the Father. This "reductionist," or in Asterius' eyes protective, scheme of creation and salvation that shields the creatures from an overpowering and potentially deadly pure hand of God is made explicit with regard to the Son. According to Asterius, the Son was light and shone above all things in the noetic world, himself being one of the noetic beings (like the Sun that is shining on everything by being one of those created elements that receive its sunshine; Asterius, frgm. 23). Thus the Son made the divine light of the Father bearable to the creation, because "the God of the universe, when he decided to make the created nature, recognized that it could not stand the nonweakened hand of God" (Asterius, frgm. 26). As the Son was both less divine than the Father and at the same time protected creation from the overpowering pure nature of God, so did the Spirit further reduce the otherwise threatening divine power. Mary was not touched by the direct, full divine light of the Father, but the Son was engendered in her by the shadow of the Spirit whose divinity was proportionate to her. On this understanding of the incarnation, one can see the need for Asterius' clear distinction of the three hypostases of the Father, Son, and Spirit.

His teachings were opposed by → Marcellus of Ancyra in a book against Asterius (the title of which is not known, but may have been *Against Asterius*), but defended in repeated attacks of Marcellus' book by → Eusebius of Caesarea in his two books *Against Marcellus* and the three books *On Church Theology*. A middle position between Asterius, Marcellus, and Eusebius is then taken by → Apollinaris of Laodicea, who in his first known work (Pseudo-Athanasius, *Oratio IV Against the Arians*) is critical of all three positions and makes a case for a Nicene homoousion theology that later influenced Athanasius of Alexandria, especially in his *Three Orations Against the Arians*.

Bibliography

Bidez, J., & F. Winkelmann, eds., *Philostorgius, Kirchengeschichte: Mit dem Leben des Lucian von Antiochien und den Fragmenten eines arianischen Historiographen*, GCS, Berlin, 1981.

Holl, K., & J. Dummer, eds. *Epiphanius III: Panarion haer. 65–80, De fide*, GCS, Berlin, ²1985.

Kinzig, W., *In Search of Asterius: Studies on the Authorship of the Homilies on the Psalms*, FKDG 47, Göttingen, 1990.

Klostermann, E., & G.C. Hansen, eds., *Eusebius Werke*, vol. IV, GCS, Berlin, 1972.

Opitz, H.-G., et al., eds., "Athanasius Werke," in: *DGAS*, vol. III, Berlin, 1934ff.

Spoerl, K.M., & M. Vinzent, trans., *Eusebius of Caesarea. Against Marcellus and On Ecclesiastical Theology*, FaCh 135, Washington, 2017.

Vinzent, M., ed. & trans., *Asterius von Kappadokien: Die theologischen Fragmente: Einleitung, kritischer Text, Übersetzung und Kommentar von Markus Vinzent*, SVigChr 20, Leiden, 1993.

Vinzent, M., ed. & trans., *Markell von Ankyra: Die Fragmente und der Brief an Julius von Rom*, SVigChr 39 Leiden, 1997.

MARKUS VINZENT

Asterius Turcius Rufus

Turcius Rufius Apronianus Asterius (consul in 494 CE) was one of the Roman elites of late antiquity whose names appear in subscriptions to manuscripts of Latin authors such as Apuleius, Caesar, Cicero, Fronto, Horace, and Livy. The name of this scion of the famous 4th-century CE Turcii Aproniani is found in a subscription to the Codex Mediceus, containing the works of Virgil (Florence, Biblioteca Laurenziana, MS Laur. 39.1, f. 8r; following the Eclogues, possibly an autograph). Asterius declares that he "read and punctuated the codex" (*legi et distincxi codicem*) and gives credit to God for his accomplishments (*non mei fiducia set eius, cuius et ad omnia sum devotus arbitrio*). In an elegiac poem that appears in the same codex, Asterius claims to have spent a lot of time and energy editing the work despite the necessity of having to put on consular games: *operi sedulus incubui* ("I labored over the work diligently"; *Anth. Lat.* 3.1–2; Lunelli, 2006, 176).

Unlike members of patrician families such as the Symmachi and Nicomachi, whose names appear in subscriptions to the works of pagan Latin authors, it appears that Asterius was a Christian. The implicit reference to a single deity in the Virgilian subscription suggests as much, but the consul's religious affinities become clearer when his editorial involvement in the production of another poem is taken into account: the *Paschale carmen* of → Sedulius (fl. 425–450 CE). According to a notice preserved in the oldest complete manuscript of the poem (*Taur.* E.4.42; like the Codex Mediceus, from Bobbio), this "sacred work" was found by Turcius Rufius Asterius among the "scattered papers" that Sedulius left behind and that the ex-consul collected and organized:

> Incipit sacrum opus, id est ex vetere testamento liber primus, et ex novo quattuor, quod Sedulius inter cartulas suas sparsas reliquit, et recollecti adunatique sunt a Turcio Rufio Asterio. (Springer, 1995, 17)

In his dedicatory poem to the *Paschale carmen*, Asterius makes his Christian faith explicit (*gratia Christi*). Unfortunately, we do not know the identity of the "holy" personage to whom Asterius is referring (*sacer meritis*) in the first line:

Sume, sacer meritis, ueracis dicta poetae,
Quae sine figmenti condita sunt uitio,
Quo caret alma fides, quo sancti gratia Christi,
Per quam iustus ait talia Sedulius.
Asteriique tui semper meminisse iubeto,
Cuius ope et cura edita sunt populis.
Quem quamuis summi celebrent per saecula fastus,
Plus tamen ad meritum est, si uiget ore tuo.

You who are sanctified by your virtues, accept the verses of a truthful poet, / Composed without falling into the sin of falsehood, / A fault absent from the faith that sustains us and the grace of our holy Christ, / Thanks to which, righteous Sedulius composed this work. / And bid your Asterius be always remembered, / By whose aid and diligence this work was given to the people. / Even if lists of highest office-holders should record his memory through the ages, / Nonetheless it is more to his credit if he thrives because of your words. (*Anth. Lat.* 491; Springer, 2013, 229)

J. Huemer (1878, 36) suggests that Asterius is addressing Pope → Gelasius I (492–496 CE) and with this dedicatory epigram hopes to ensure the poem's inclusion in the Gelasian Decree's listing of approved readings, as it eventually was: *Item venerabilis Sedulii paschale opus, quod heroicis descripsit versibus, insigni laude praeferimus* ("Likewise the paschal work of the venerable Sedulius, which he composed in heroic verse, we esteem with high praise"). But it is unlikely that Gelasius is the dedicatee since it is not at all clear that he was himself responsible for the so-called Gelasian Decree, now most often dated to the early 6th century CE.

Given the garbling of the consul's name in the Sedulian manuscript tradition, it has been suggested that the Sedulian subscription may refer to another consul with a similar name, such as Flavius Astyrius, consul in 449 CE, although most scholars have not accepted this identification. If the adjective *sedulus* in the second line of Asterius' poem in the Codex Mediceus is a pun on the name of Sedulius, the identification of the ex-consul in the *Taurinensis* subscription as the consul of 494 CE would be surer. Even if, as the pun suggests, Asterius had Sedulius in mind in 494 CE when the Codex Mediceus was published, he did not publish his work on the Christian poem until 495 CE or later when he was an "ex-consul" (see *Taur.* E.4.42).

What exactly might Asterius' editorial assignments have entailed? As A. Cameron (e.g. 2011, 421–497) has repeatedly cautioned, the time and effort devoted to editorial "drudgery" by Asterius and other elites whose names appear in subscriptions like these may be exaggerated. → Virgil's poetic corpus already had enjoyed a long tradition of use in schools and was the subject of frequent commentary in the centuries between Virgil's death in 19 BCE and 494 CE. Asterius' own contributions to a new "edition" of the poet's works may have been minimal. In the case of the poetry of Sedulius, however, who most probably lived and wrote just a generation or two before Asterius, the ex-consul may have played a more decisive editorial role. In fact, one later version (Vienna, Österreichische Nationalbibliothek, 85) of the notice found in *Taur.* E.4.42 suggests that Asterius actually had to complete Sedulius' work, because the poet died leaving it unfinished (*moriens ergo indigestum dereliquit hoc opus in cartulis scriptum*). The fact that Sedulius' own prose paraphrase of the *Paschale carmen*, written after he composed the poem, survives intact, however, militates strongly against the idea that the author himself did not finish and organize the poetic work that served as the basis for the prose paraphrase. If the *Paschale carmen* originally circulated in four or five separate books in scroll form, it is possible that Asterius' editorial work (perhaps delegated to others) involved little more than collecting individual book scrolls (*recollecti*) and converting them into a single codex (*adunati*). On the other hand, the task of editing Sedulius could have been more demanding if the poem was widely read and copied in the second half of the 5th century CE (echoes have been found in the works of → Paulinus of Pella and Paulinus of Périgueux, both of whom postdate Sedulius). If so, Asterius (or his assistants) may have actually had to reconcile divergent readings and correct false ones in order to produce a single, new text.

If it is important not to overstate the nature and extent of Asterius' editorial work, it should also not be dismissed as altogether without significance. It is possible, as M. Roberts (1985, 78) suggests, that these two codices "represent a conscious programme by

Asterius to produce reliable texts of the chief pagan and chief Christian poet of his day." Certainly, Asterius was not the only consul whose name appears in a subscription to an edition of a Christian as well as a pagan Latin poet (on Vettius Agorius Basilius Mavortius, consul in 527 CE, and his "editions" of Prudentius and Horace, see Springer, 1988, 82). And there is a strong connection between Virgil and Sedulius. The Christian poet draws heavily on Virgil's diction (sometimes borrowing entire lines). If the *Aeneid* was the preeminent Latin epic during the Middle Ages, Sedulius' "biblical epic" enjoyed something of the same sort of high regard in the centuries that followed its composition. The *Paschale carmen* was copied in scriptoria (hundreds of manuscripts containing some or all of Sedulius' works still survive), read in schools, and cited in theological controversies, and some passages were even included in the church's liturgy. The two poets are featured prominently in a 9th-century CE guide to the liberal arts now in the Bibliothèque municipale in Laon (ms. 468). That Virgil comes first in a list of pagan poets compiled by Ermoldus Nigellus for Louis the Pious, son of Charlemagne, while Sedulius is listed first among the Christian poets is surely no accident (Springer, 1988, 133).

Asterius was apparently willing to use the prestige of his consular status to further the preservation and continued popularity of these two poets. He may have realized that in so doing he would ensure that the memory of his own name as a patron of the literary arts would endure long after the expensive but ephemeral public games that he sponsored had been forgotten. It is a tribute to the consul's critical discernment that he picked two literary authors upon whom to concentrate his editorial efforts, such as they were, whose long-lived popularity would guarantee his own associated fame.

Historiography

Scholarship devoted to Asterius may be said to begin to with the work of O. Jahn, whose fundamental study of subscriptions by Roman aristocrats in manuscripts of late antiquity was published in 1851. Since then there have been a number of considerations of Asterius from a prosopographical perspective (there is considerable disagreement, for instance, as to

what his full name might have been), but the most important issue has been how best to understand his involvement in editing the works of Virgil (and Sedulius). A. Cameron (2011) and others have sensibly cautioned against taking the consul's editorial claims too seriously. M. Roberts (1985) was one of the first to inquire into the significance of Asterius' choice of ancient authors, Virgil and Sedulius, in which to take such interest, suggesting that already at the end of the 5th CE century Sedulius was being taken seriously as a kind of Christian alternative to Virgil.

Bibliography

Cameron, A., *The Last Pagans of Rome*, Oxford, 2011.

Huemer, J., *De Sedulii poetae vita et scriptis commentatio*, Vienna, 1878.

Jahn, O., "Über die Subscriptionen in den Handschriften römischer Classiker," *BVSAW* 3, 1851, 327–72.

Lunelli, A., "Filologia e archeologia: Sull'epigramma virgiliano di Aproniano Asterio," *PAR* 61, 2006, 176–184.

Matthews, J., *Western Aristocracies and Imperial Court AD 364–425*, Oxford, 1975.

Martindale, J.R., *The Prosopography of the Later Roman Empire*, vol. II: *AD 395–527*, Cambridge UK, 1980.

Reynolds, L.D., & N.G. Wilson, *Scribes and Scholars: A Guide to the Transmission of Greek and Latin Literature*, Oxford, ³1991.

Roberts, M., *Biblical Epic and Rhetorical Paraphrase in Late Antiquity*, Liverpool, 1985.

Springer, C., *The Gospel as Epic in Late Antiquity: Sedulius' Paschale Carmen*, Leiden, 1988.

Springer, C., *The Manuscripts of Sedulius: A Provisional Handlist*, Philadelphia, 1995.

Springer, C., *Sedulius: The Paschal Song and Hymns*, Atlanta, 2013.

CARL SPRINGER

Astrology

Astrology is the study of the positions and movements of stars and planets in relation to their presumed capacity of providing information on future events. As part of magical practices, teaching and use of astrology were relatively common in antiquity. While most ancient scholars had a clear-cut notion with which to separate scientific knowledge, such as astronomy, from its derivative astrology, which was generally thought to be morally inferior, much of the ancient evidence for astrology is from polemical contexts, and as such the difference between the two is tenuous. Roman emperors frequently sought to prohibit the practice of astrology since it not only threatened the imperial monopoly on interpreting public religious affairs but also could occasion seditious rumors on the fate of the government and on the well-being of the emperor and his family. In the polemical language of Christian authors and in religious legislation of late antiquity, as well as in law enforcement, the term "astrology" was normally used as a derogatory label with which to denounce certain schools of knowledge as contrary to the canonical Bible truth for similar reasons. Christian authors and ecclesiastical and Roman authorities alike thought it was important to assign prophetical properties exclusively to the Bible, as a means either of demonstrating that Christianity is the true religion or of exerting social control.

1. Mesopotamian and Egyptian Backgrounds

Human beings have often felt the need to interpret the visible signs of the sky, particularly everything noteworthy and difficult to comprehend, as possible indicators of future events. There is documentary evidence to suggest that Babylonian astrologers observed connections between celestial positions and human affairs, such as wars, rebellions, and crops, and were employed as such to give advice to the authorities beginning in the 2nd millennium BCE. By the mid-1st millennium BCE, their tasks included writing up individual horoscopes that contained information about the prospects of an individual's life, based on birthdate.

The art of astrology came to the world of the Greeks from Babylonia via Egypt as part of the cultural assimilation process during the age of Hellenism. Knowledge exchange between the East and the West is evident in the scientific works of Hipparchus, in the mid-2nd century BCE, who owed much to Babylonian mathematical astronomy. Although most Christian authors came to attribute the invention of astrology to the Persian prophet Zoroaster, there was disagreement in antiquity over the origin of astrology, whether it came from Babylon in Mesopotamia or from Egypt. Greek and Roman authors,

such as Diodorus Siculus (*Bib. hist.* 2.31.8), Cicero (*Div.* 1.19; 2.46), and Pliny the Elder (*Nat.* 7.193) maintained that the Chaldeans had originally practiced astrology, although all of these authors are skeptical of the claim that they had done so for hundreds of thousands of years, something that was probably advertised by those who practiced astrology at that time. Diodorus (*Bib. hist.* 1.81) knows of a very old tradition of astrological studies practiced in Egypt, which he describes as the homeland of Hellenistic astrology. Several Egyptian ostraca, the earliest dating from around 250 BCE (Neugebauer, 1943, 121), verifies the existence of astrology, but tells us little about its origins.

Hesiod's poem *Work and Days* (written around 700 BCE) is the first Greek-language piece to indicate interest in star constellations as well as their impact on the farmer's year. Since their work is generally lost, there is only scant evidence that pre-Socratic philosophers, such as Thales of Miletus or Pythagoras and his disciples, were directly interested in astrological interpretations of the world. While it does appear certain that there was a strong cosmological interest at their time of writing, Christian authors later attempted to discredit these authors as closely related to Chaldean practices. Some ancient historians and authors of the Roman imperial period (Jos. *Apion.* 1.129; Vitr. *Arch.* 9.2; 9.6.3; *FGH* 680) attest that a man called Berossus (who they thought was a Babylonian priest who settled on Cos) was the first to transmit the knowledge of Chaldean astrology to the Greek world, but this claim cannot be corroborated.

Clement of Alexandria (*Strom.* 6.4.35–37; → Clement of Alexandria) is the first to mention a number of texts, 42 books in total, attributed to the god → Hermes Trismegistus, suggesting that a corpus of "Hermetic" treatises circulated by that time. The Nag Hammadi library (→ Nag Hammadi Writings) contains a collection of mainly gnostic texts (→ Gnosis/Gnosticism) and among them some Hermetic texts written in Coptic, an Egyptian language written in letters based on the Greek alphabet, indicating the confluence of Egyptian and Greek traditions within these texts. While none of these Hermetic texts has been handed down to us, ancient references indicate that this corpus of texts included philosophical as well as magical and astrological treatises. Chief among them are astrological works attributed to

Petosiris and Nechepso, who were probably not historical persons, but who were nevertheless cited as founders and authorities of Egyptian astrology. The extant fragments have been edited by E. Riess (1892).

2. Greek and Roman Worlds: Criticism and Attempts to Curb Astrology

As with many other aspects of Greek learning that came to flood Rome during the expansion of the 2nd century CE, upper-class Roman conservatives viewed Hellenistic astrology with suspicion. The earliest reference is by Cato the Elder, a representative of this early view, who warned that the manager of an estate (*vilicus*, i.e., a freedmen or slave in charge of overseeing the slaves employed on the farm) should consult neither traditional Roman fortune tellers nor "Chaldean" astrologers (Cat. *Agr.* 5.4), apparently in order to avoid any semblance of insubordination. Latin authors of the late republican and early imperial periods, too, associated astrologers and the consultation of astrologers with the lower classes (Cic. *Div.* 1.132; Juv. *Sat.* 6.582–588).

While fortune telling was traditional to Etruscan and Roman religions, the advent of a specific Hellenistic/Babylonian mode of predicting future events by observing the positions of celestial objects was part of a wider turn toward Hellenistic philosophies, which became increasingly popular among all echelons of society in Italy and Rome from the 2nd century BCE onward. Chief among them were the Stoics and Epicureans (→ Epicurus/Epicureans). The Stoics in particular believed in fate, while Epicurean philosophers thought that the movements of the stars and planets were due to natural forces of a "self-moving" universe and therefore predetermined. Cicero's treatise *On Divination*, our main source of knowledge on the relationship between astrology and philosophy, attests that several Greek philosophers, many of whom flourished in Rome, discussed the extents to which the future can be made known in advance by observations in nature.

Accordingly, some of the political strongmen of the late Roman republic were keen on taking advantage of astrological fortune telling in order to gauge the political mood, personal fate, and overall state of the republic (Plut. *Mar.* 42.4–5; *Sull.* 37.1; Cic. *Div.* 2.47.99). Caesar, who was himself an Epicurean and therefore denied any link among the divine, the natural phenomena of the material world, and human affairs, famously disregarded divinatory advice on his own assassination on the Ides of March. This episode shows that it was a matter of life and death for future emperors to curb the circulation of rumors and predictions – astrological or not – on their own well-being or that of their families, and indeed any unaccredited prediction generally and on political events in particular. Augustus did this, for example, by burning the non-canonical Sibylline books, keeping only an accredited selection (Suet. *Aug.* 31.1). A manifest symbol of this policy, of monopolizing the traditional religious realm of divination, is the *solarium Augusti*, a giant astronomical sundial that placed Augustus' birthdate in the center of Roman politics since its shadow pointed to the *ara pacis* on that day.

Julio-Claudian emperors took various measures to banish unaccredited astrological advice. The precedent was again set by Augustus and his ally Agrippa, who in 33 BCE expelled foreign astrologers and magicians (→ Magic) from the city of Rome (Dio. *Hist. rom.* 49.43.5), presumably because of rumors circulating in advance of the impending Battle of Actium against Mark Antony and Cleopatra. This was only the second time in Rome's history that astrologers were expelled. The only such incident during the Roman Republic was a praetorian edict of the year 139 BCE that ordered the "Chaldeans" to leave Rome and Italy within ten days for no apparent reason other than that a number of scholars from the Hellenistic East moved to Italy during the expansion of the 2nd century CE (Val. Max. 1.3.3). Any rise in expulsions of astrologers went hand in hand with rising numbers of *maiestas* trials, in which senators were forced into suicide for actual or alleged involvement in conspiracies against the emperor or his family. Tiberius expelled astrologers from Italy, whereas he personally consulted astrologers for advice on politics and his own fate (Tac. *An.* 2.32.3; Suet. *Tib.* 36; Dio. *Hist. rom.* 57.15.7–9; Ulp. *Off. pro.* 7= *CLMR* 15.2.1; Tac. *An.* 4.17). Claudius did the same in 52 CE (Tac. *An.* 12.52.3; Dio. *Hist. rom.* 61.33.3b). Both emperors immediately reacted to conspiracies.

Subsequent emperors occasionally banished astrologers for similar reasons, and sometimes even philosophical schools that were widely seen as training grounds for divinatory practices. Vitellius, one of the short-lived successors of the emperor Nero in the turbulent Year of the Four Emperors, expelled astrologers from Italy and Rome (Tac. *Hist.* 2.62.2; Suet. *Vit.* 14.4; Dio. *Hist. rom.* 64.1.4). Emperor → Vespasian, who immediately succeeded him, renewed this edict when rumors circulated that his own reign was going to be as short as that of his predecessor (*Hist. rom.* 65.9.2). The first emperor to have ordered the expulsion of philosophers, and indeed the only one for a long time to come, was the last Flavian emperor Domitian in 93 CE just a few years before he was eventually assassinated in 96 CE (Tac. *Agr.* 2; Suet. *Dom.* 10.3; Plin. Y. *Ep.* 3.11; Philostr. *Apoll.* 7.3; Dio. *Hist. rom.* 67.13.2–3; Gell. *Noct. att.* 15.11.4–5; Luc. *Peregr.* 18). Senators hostile to the emperor identified themselves as part of the Stoic opposition. As such, it can be presumed that they not only ostentatiously shunned death in view of the tyrannical emperor in order to display the attitudes of the ideal Stoic philosophers, but also discussed Stoic ideas of predestination, something that could be seen as an illegal act of divination. Later Christian authors, however, are wrong to allege that Domitian expelled astrologers along with philosophers (Jer. *Chron.* s.a. 90 and 94 CE; PL 27.459; Sync. *Chron.* P.343D = Dindorf, vol. I, 650; *Suda*, D.1352). These Christian accounts clearly reflect the discourses and practices of their own time period. Nevertheless, the emperors themselves, like Caracalla (188–217 CE), who consulted astrologers throughout the Roman Empire (Her. *Marci* 4.12.3), were very keen on learning about their own fate.

Probably as a result of general bans of astrological writings, few comprehensive texts from antiquity are extant today. Of those that do survive in whole or in part, most are from the 2nd century CE, suggesting not necessarily that astrology was particularly popular at that time, but rather that its practice and the circulation of related writings were more tolerated than in other centuries. Like most of Hellenistic literature, astrological texts survive only in fragments. The Latin author Marcus Manilius wrote a didactic poem *Astronomica* in the early 1st century CE, which is the earliest astrological work to survive in a manuscript tradition, although not in full. Poggio discovered this work in 1417. All medieval copies are dependent on this 10th-century CE manuscript, which is lost today. A 1st-century CE Greek poem by Dorotheus of Sidon is known only in its Arabic translation. The famous 2nd-century CE astronomer Ptolemy wrote the *Tetrabiblos*, which is the earliest surviving prose work on, and the most scientific treatment of, astrology. Ptolemy (*Tetr.* 1.1) himself sees this work as a continuation of his *Almagest*, widely regarded as authoritative for its geocentric worldview throughout the Middle Ages, suggesting that many ancient scholars regarded astronomical and astrological questions as nearly identical subject matters. The *Anthology* of Vettius Valens is a slightly later work and, like the *Tetrabiblos*, of Alexandrian origin. Convinced that human life is predetermined, Vettius Valens tells us a great deal about the practical application of astrology and includes a number of horoscopes. No manuscript survives from before 1300 CE (Vaticanus Graecus 191 CE, Marcianus Graecus 314 CE), but the 5th-century CE archetype was known to Byzantine astrologers from the 10th to 12th centuries.

Subsequent surviving texts already date from late antiquity. → Firmicus Maternus was a pagan scholar who converted to Christianity and became one of its leading apologists (→ Apologetics). His astrological treatise *Mathesis* was written between 334 and 337 CE. Later astrological authors (probably of the late 4th cent. CE) include Hephaistion of Thebes, Paulus of Alexandria, and the anonymous author of *The Treatise on the Bright Fixed Stars*. Greek astrological manuscripts, often containing short treatises, notes, or comments, are listed in the *Catalogus Codicum Astrologorum Graecorum*. This catalogue indicates ongoing interest into astrology among medieval Christian scholars. Astrological papyri from Oxyrhynchus have been edited and translated by A. Jones (1999), horoscopes from papyrological and literary sources by O. Neugebauer and H.B. van Hoesen (1959).

As with magical and other arcane practices, pagan authors of antiquity were often critical of astrology. In addition to Cicero's *De Divinatione*, Pliny the Elder, for example, tends to describe popular astrology as risible and treacherous (Plin. *Nat.* 2.5.20; 2.5.23; 2.6.28), although he does consider some degree of divine influence on the world as likely, in accordance with the Stoic philosophy of his day and age. The skeptical philosopher Sextus Empiricus (around 200 CE) is generally critical, in his work *Against the Mathematicians*, of the possibility that human beings can attain real knowledge in various academic disciplines. In his taxonomy, astrology could be synonymous to the "mathematical art" (μαθηματική) as a whole, including its subfields arithmetic and geometry. He understands "Chaldeans" as astrologers in a negative sense, while acknowledging that this group identified itself as "mathematicians" (Sex.Emp. *Math.* 5.1–2). Firmicus Maternus gave the advice not to predict illegal future events, such as the fate of the emperor, suggesting that personal astrological consultations, even in public, were reasonably safe up to the early 4th century CE (Firm. *Math.* 2.30). The general picture is that ancient authors did not generally frown upon astrology as a subject of knowledge, but that they used terms like "astrology" and "Chaldean" in a derogatory sense in the same way that they use terms like "magic" to describe negative aspects of scientific knowledge. In a legal sense, astrology could be seen as potentially harmful in its capacity of predicting another person's fate, specifically with a view to the imperial family.

3. Astrology in the New Testament

Despite harsh attitudes of Christian authors toward astrology, astrological practices are present in the canon of biblical books, most prominently the interpretation of the stars and the prediction of Christ's birth (→ Christ) by the → Magi in the Gospel of Matthew (2:1–12). This episode prompted a number of responses in ancient Christian literature, with several authors arguing that the star was an angel sent by God rather than an astrological sign as such. To → John Chrysostom, for example, the star really was a divine illumination (Chrys. *Hom. 6 in Matt* 2–3; PG 57.64–65), and to Prudentius a winged messenger (Prud. *Apoth.* 611–612). Some Christian authors interpreted the victory of the new star in this episode as representative for the victory of Christ over human fate, that is, for the very end of traditional astrology (e.g. Prud. *Cath.* 12–5–32; Clem. *Exc.* 74.2; see Hegedus, 2007, 206–211). The Book of Revelation contains some allusions to ancient astrological theories. The Four Living Creatures (Rev 4:7), for example, an

imagery that is itself modeled on Ezek 1:5–14, corresponds to four heavenly constellations, and the beginning of Rev 12 recalls the 12 signs of the zodiac. While the author of Revelation neither endorses nor condemns astrology, he was clearly informed by astrological theories and therefore did not share the hostile attitudes of later Christian authors.

On the other hand, astrology is seen as particularly hostile to the Christian way of life, as an immediate counterworld to the hope of salvation, in the Pauline writings. According to the Epistle to the Galatians (→ Paul the Apostle), "when we were children, we were enslaved to the elements of the world" (Gal 4:3). In a similar vein, the Epistle to the Colossians says that Christians should "beware lest any man spoil you through philosophy and vain deceit, after the tradition of men, after the elements of the world, and not after Christ" (Col 2:8). Both lines indicate that Christ has rescued from a predetermined fate those who believe in him and have therefore grown up to become adults. Much controversy surrounds the exact interpretation of the phrase "elements of the world" in its 1st-century CE context (see DeMaris, 1994, 18–40, on different views). It is clear, however, as has been argued by D.E.H. Whiteley (1974, 23–25) and T. Hegedus (2007, 224–226), that the Pauline letters see some connection between celestial powers and the fate of human beings. Although Epicurean philosophy strongly denied that there is any interference of the divine in the material world, an important later Christian author such as → Augustine of Hippo, writing at a time when philosophies like these were no longer actively cultivated, understood that "elements of the world" stands for pre-Socratic and Epicurean theories of ancient atomism. Augustine's argument is that, while followers of materialist philosophies such as Epicureanism believed that the human soul consists of atoms and will therefore die along with the → body, Christ had overcome the death barrier and so rescued humankind from being caught in the cycle of life and death (Aug. *Civ.* 8.10; 22.5). Augustine nevertheless advised others to exercise similar caution against astrologers (*mathematici*: Aug. *Gen. lit.* 2.17), suggesting that he too regarded both groups, astrologers and certain philosophers, as interrelated.

4. Early Christian Authors

Early Christian authors generally condemned the art and practice of astrology as part of a demonical counterworld. In so doing, they adopted earlier philosophical counterarguments concerning determinism, fate, and celestial signs. Some Christian authors, like the authors of biblical books, were nevertheless themselves interested in the astrological knowledge of their day and age. They at any rate appropriated this knowledge for their own Christian worldview. In that case early Christian authors did not regularly associate this knowledge with pagan astrology and its related taxonomy. They instead developed a number of strategies with which to exempt themselves from participating in these shunned aspects of pagan culture, in a similar way that pagan authors, as well as Christian authors labeled as heretical, avoided describing themselves as "astrologers" or in similar related terms.

Polemical heresiological catalogues normally include astrological groups, which the authors of these catalogues ascribe to the realm of false knowledge. → Irenaeus of Lyon's work *Against Heresies* (c. 180 CE) already denounces Christian groups, such as the Marcosian gnostics, as infected by pagan, magical, and astrological practices, which are all deeply related to one another (Iren. *Haer.* 1.15.6). In the *Refutation of All Heresies*, an early 3rd-century CE work attributed to Hippolytus of Rome, both "astrologers" and "Chaldeans" (Babylonian or Egyptian specialist astrologers) feature prominently among the groups of false teachers in Book 4, along with practitioners of the magical arts. It is worth noting that these astrological and magical groups are themselves preceded by a catalogue of Greek philosophers in the preceding books (of which the first book is the only one extant) and that the astrologers are finally, at the end of Book 4, linked to Christian gnostic authors such as Valentinus the Gnostic (→ Valentinus/Valentinians) and the biblical figure → Simon Magus, who was generally seen as the precursor of all Christian → heresies in antiquity. Books 4 and 9 draw similar comparisons. Astrological and astronomical theories are indiscriminately ranked next to each other, for example, in chapters 8 to 12 of Book 4, which intend to refute calculations of the distances of stars and planets proposed by such imminent

ancient scientists as Archimedes and Aristarchus of Samos. Therefore, there is little evidence to suggest that Christian heresiologists viewed astrology as fundamentally different from other aspects of Greco-Roman or Christian heretical teachings.

Apologetic-polemical authors likewise attributed the existence of astrological knowledge, like other parts of pagan culture, to the time before the advent of Christ whom they saw as a manifest sign that any previous false knowledge had now been replaced with divine revelation. In the early 3rd century CE, → Tertullian thought about the problem of why the Gospel of Matthew mentions astrologers from the East successfully predicting the birth of Christ (Tert. *Idol.* 9). He concluded that divine providence had allowed this area of knowledge, along with all other subjects of pagan antiquity, to flourish and so prepared humankind for the advent of Christ through a number of predictions that have come true because they were divinely inspired. Applying a great deal of wishful thinking, Tertullian goes on to assert that "after the Gospel, you will nowhere find either sophists, Chaldeans, enchanters, diviners, or magicians, except as openly punished" (*Idol.* 9.7). Apparently, he takes his earlier point that astrologers are expelled from Rome and Italy (generally valid, but not ascertained for the time of writing) to prove that all pagan knowledge had been replaced by the Gospel and that Christianity is therefore the one and true religion, juxtaposing the banishing of astrologers with the occasional banishing of philosophers in the early imperial period.

Any time that Christian authors spoke of astrology in a positive way, they regarded its knowledge as originating from the Abrahamic tradition and interpreted this as the correct reading of how God had arranged the stars and planets. The Pseudo-Clementine *Recognitions* (1.28.1–2; → Clementine Literature, Pseudo-) asserts that the work of God's creation included signs of things to come, which are however recognizable only to the selected few, not the many. Statements like these reconfirm the general view that astrology is a crime if practiced by non-Christians. → Eusebius of Caesarea, on the other hand, attests that according to a Jewish tradition, → Abraham was in fact the inventor of astrology, which was therefore only later abused by the Egyptians (Eus. *Praep.* 9.18). This view was probably supported by Gen 15:5, where God asks Abraham to count all the stars of heaven if he is able to do so. → Origen likewise held the opinion that pagan predictions of future events are not so much wrong as they are damning exactly because these predictions are inspired by demons (→ Demonology/Demons), but that God too was able to speak to his believers in terms of heavenly signs and that the angels are able to understand these signs (Or. *Cels.* 1.36; 1.58–59; *Philoc.* 23). These generally agreed-upon positions indicate that Christian authors, as with many other aspects of the knowledge of their day and age, did not generally refuse to believe in astrology, but only when it was cloaked in a pagan garment. They nevertheless used the term of astrology polemically as a tool with which to discredit views and ideas in conflict with the Bible.

5. Christian Authors of Late Antiquity

Orthodox authors of late antiquity built on the views of their predecessors of the 1st centuries CE, but they did so safe in the knowledge that the tables had turned and that previous laws and political safeguards against astrology and magic now served as the backdrop against which paganism was officially banned in imperial legislation. Christian polemical attacks against astrology were therefore often driven by a desire to persuade their audiences of the need to act harshly against such vulnerable aspects of a pagan culture in retreat. → Gregory of Nazianzus linked to astrologers those philosophers who had advised the late pagan emperor → Julian the Apostate to act against Christians by banning Christians from teaching pagan material in schools in the teacher edict from 362 CE (Cod. Theod. 13.5.5; Greg. Naz. *Or.* 4.31). Writing at a time when Christians could not entirely be convinced that paganism was in a terminal decline, polemical attacks such as these underline the shift from defending biblical views on astrology to discrediting the views of political or intellectual enemies.

Instrumental in their aim to discredit pagan philosophy as demonical was an increasingly blurred terminology of the astrological art and related disciplines throughout late antiquity. This is because the term μαθηματικός/*mathematicus* in both Greek and Latin could mean either an astrologer or general

scholar, scientist or philosopher, and the related adjective the subject taught or practiced by these groups. As we have already seen, for example, Christian historians from the 4th century CE and later commonly understood that Emperor Domitian (81–96 CE) expelled astrologers (*mathematici*) alongside philosophers, even though their sources from the early and high imperial periods know only of the expulsions of philosophers, suggesting that the two terms had roughly the same meaning. In the 2nd century CE, Aulus Gellius (*Noct. att.* 1.9.6–7) is very clear that "the common people" call *mathematici* those who are in reality astrologers ("Chaldeans"), even though the true meaning of the word is that of practitioners of higher learning, and that there was now little terminological difference between astrologers and "natural philosophers" (φυσικοί). Writing at the end of the 4th century CE, → Ammianus Marcellinus likewise attests that the understanding of the term *mathematicus* among common people was different from his own and that his own understanding was that *mathematici* were in fact scholars investigating questions like the physical shape of the universe rather than astrologers (Am. 15.1.4; 29.2.6). The overall picture therefore is that there was little semantic difference between "astrology" and wider areas of learning, at any rate characterized as pagan, and that the charge of astrological leanings was used to discredit religious or scientific "otherness."

Christian ecclesiastical authors reinforce the overall impression that the borderline between astrological and general pagan knowledge was elusive. Rather than shunning astrology as such, they labeled a specifically pagan learning as astrological or magical in order to align it with forbidden, illegal practices. Augustine mentions the case of an actual *mathematicus* who had recently burned his books to demonstrate to the congregation that he had truly become a Christian and so had forsaken his own sinful past, apparently driven by the hope that he will in turn be rewarded with a career within the clergy. Augustine primarily narrates this event as a general conversion from paganism rather than specifically from pagan astrology (Aug. *Enarrat. Ps.* 61.23; and see also Aug. *Tract. Ev. Jo.* 8.5–11). This episode is therefore remindful of Augustine's own conversion from Manichaeism (→ Mani/Manichaeism) to Christianity (Aug. *Conf.* 5.7.12). The conversion of Firmicus

Maternus mirrors the conversion narrated by Augustine. Known as the author of an astrological treatise, the *Mathesis*, he went on to write a polemical work against paganism (→ Pagan/Paganism), *De errore profanarum religionum*, following his conversion. A similar case is preserved in the conversion narrative of Cyprian of Antioch, a pagan scholar with astrological leanings who eventually became bishop and martyr (*CSP* 18 = *ActaSS Sep* 7.235).

Writing in the early 5th century CE, both → Cyril of Alexandria (378–444 CE) and → Theodoret of Cyrrhus, the last authors of polemical works against paganism in the Roman Empire, separate pagan "mathematicians" from Christian "true philosophers," arguing that the former are in reality practitioners of the minor arts (music, astronomy, geometry) and that they should have no place in a Christian society as they are not concerned with finding the truth (Cyr.Alex. *C. Jul.* 5.38; PG 76.773.D–776.A; Thdt. *Affect.* 1.33). They both borrow this verdict from Plato's *Republic*, who does not, however, mention the term mathematician/astrologer at all in this context (Plato *Rep.* 5.475e). Nor do earlier Christian authors use that term when they quote this passage from Plato (Clem. *Strom.* 1.19.93.3; Eus. *Praep.* 2.7.4–7; 13.3.3–6), suggesting that a terminological shift had occurred in late antiquity. Cyril of Alexandria therefore went as far as to link the beginning of pagan μαθήματα, the art practiced by *mathematici*, to original sin and the temptation of the serpent in paradise (Cyr.Alex. *C. Jul.* 3.26; PG 76.640.B–C). In so doing, he provides an explanation for the frequent use of the serpent metaphor to discredit pagan or heretical knowledge.

Astrology, philosophy, and wider areas of pagan knowledge were seen as interwoven with one another in late antiquity because these subject areas bordered on questions of fate, determinism, and human free will. In late antique Christianity, there was general agreement that although God had created the world and continued to govern it with divine providence, nevertheless all human beings were free to choose their actions wisely since otherwise there was no human responsibility and no place for penance or reward or punishment in the afterlife. Classical authors such as Cicero in his treatise *De divinatione* (who was himself relying on earlier authors such as Carneades) had long since discussed questions like these and particularly the deductions from determinism inherent to Stoic philosophy. Drawing on a moral line of argument, Christian authors therefore reasoned that astrology denies freedom of will, undermines morality and justice, and renders religion and prayer useless (see Amand, 1945). They were opposed to astrology because, as with several other areas of pagan knowledge and particularly with all modes of pagan divination, its origin was devilish and demonic. The 2nd-century CE writer Tatian, for example, asserted that demons had deliberately taught "the signs of the constellations" to human beings to make them subject to demonical worship (Tat. *Orat.* 8.1–2). Statements like these were, however, part of a larger condemnation of pagan culture. Cyril of Alexandria therefore linked Greek philosophy, that is, those parts of philosophy that were in opposition to Christianity, to divination (Cyr.Alex. *Isa.* 4.1; PG 70.893.D–896.A). Epicurean philosophy, even though its students were convinced that the divine is entirely detached from the natural world and its material phenomena, came to be seen, in late antiquity, not only as the origin of false heretical teaching but also as largely identical with astrological knowledge. This is evident in the Marcianus entry in *Suda* where Epicurean philosophy, that is, research on the evolution of the universe, is synonymous with astrological inquiries into the fate of the emperor and his family (*Suda*, M.209 Adler). The overall picture is that Christian authors were not generally hostile against astrology but rather that they took advantage of a public hostility against astrology in order to discredit as such those parts of pagan culture that they disliked.

6. Persecution of Astrology and Wider Impact

Although many emperors strongly rejected astrological inquiries because they were concerned about attacks against their own lives and those of their families, any sanctions against astrologers were regionally and temporally limited before the emperors became Christians, as has been argued in greater detail by F.H. Cramer (1954, 247–248). Neither magical nor astrological books were ordered to be burned by imperial or senatorial decree before late antiquity. This fundamentally changed when emperors started to privilege Christianity and gradually, while adopting ecclesiastical law (e.g. Concilium Ancyranum, c. 23, Mansi, vol. II, 534), to outlaw the most conspicuous aspects of paganism, causing its eventual demise. Trying to deal with the instability of the 3rd-century CE crisis and the many assassinations of emperors that came with it, the emperors Diocletian and Maximian (286–305 CE) banished astrology empire-wide, but they also made it clear at that occasion that "the art of geometry is to the public interest" (Cod. Justin. 9.18.2), suggesting that there was a long-standing debate on the extent and meaning of that term. This first empire-wide ban is included in the → Codex Justinianus, apparently because it served as a precedent for the harsh persecutions of astrologers and pagans in the age of → Justinian (527–565 CE). None of the subsequent laws, signed off by Christian emperors, made such a distinction. This shows that the battle against astrology was meant to be a wider ban of pagan culture.

Laws against astrology are therefore among the earliest with which to crack down on suspicious pagan activity. A law by Emperor Constantius from 357 CE outlawed consultations of astrologers and other groups involved in divination (Cod. Theod. 9.16.4). Writing to Modestus, praetorian prefect of the East, Emperor Valens again banned astrology in Constantinople in 370 CE (Cod. Theod. 9.16.8). Modestus (PLRE, vol. I, Modestus 2, 605–608) went on to chair a commission to judge the subsequent magic trials that started in Antioch in the early 370s CE. The immediate cause for these magic trials was an attempt by a group of pagan philosophers and scholars to learn about the death and succession of the Christian emperor through → divination (Am. 29.1.25–40; Soz. Hist. eccl. 6.35.1–2; Zos. Hist. 4.14.2–15.3). This situation soon spiraled out of control as a great many books were initially burned, including general-knowledge books, and people throughout the eastern provinces burned their private libraries to avoid prosecution (Am. 29.1.40–41; 29.2.4; Chrys. Hom. 38 in Act. 5; PG 60.274–275). The emperors Honorius and Theodosius II ordered in 409 CE that astrologers be expelled "not only from the city of Rome but from all cities" unless they burned their books and converted (Cod. Theod. 9.16.12). Augustine attests that clerics actively enforced this law and burned books in North Africa (Aug. Tract.

Ev. Jo. 8.10), while Prudentius alludes to the expulsion of "enemies" from the city of Rome probably in 409 CE or shortly before (Prud. Sym. 1.529–537; see Rohmann, 2016, 73–76, 258). The normal term for astrology in late antiquity was mathematicus. As has been argued by L. Desanti (1995), the meaning of mathematici was not limited to "astrologers," but did encompass a wider group of "enemies of the church," such as heretics and learned pagans in disagreement with Christianity (see also Rohmann, 2016, 77–85). Thus also, for example, the famous philosopher Hypatia, being herself a "mathematician," was killed in a way similar to the punishment prescribed in a 4th-century CE law (Cod. Theod. 9.16.6), and this had perhaps to do with her astronomical knowledge, as the Neoplatonic philosopher Damascius claims (Damasc. Isid. frgm. 163–164, see Zintze, 1967). Astrology continued to be persecuted in the age of Zeno (e.g. Zachariah Rhetor, Vita Severi, see Kugener, 1907, 66–67) and in the age of Justinian. The anonymous Life of Simeon Stylites the Younger speaks of systematic inquiries, public book-burnings, and punishment of book owners "involved in paganism, Manichaeism, astrology, automatism, and other gruesome heresies" in Antioch and in the entire East (Vita Sym. Styl Iun. 161, see Ven, 1962). Other sources confirm that Justinian punished astrologers as part of an overall effort to clamp down on paganism and heterodoxy (Pro. Anec. 11.31; 11.37; 18.34; Malalas Chron. 18.42–43; 18.136; Theoph. Conf. AM 6022).

Historiography

The subject of Greek and Roman astrology has received a great deal of attention in modern scholarship. An early and detailed work is the landmark study by A. Bouché-Leclercq (1899). Following this, scholars such as F. Cumont and F.J. Boll contributed a lot to making astrological texts accessible to modern researchers, including their initiative in editing the Catalogus Codicum Astrologorum Graecorum (Cumont et. al., 1898–1924). Subsequent scholarship often focused on the history of astrology. To name but a few authors, O. Neugebauer's work (1943) was instrumental in rescuing ancient astrology from the odium of superstition attached to it and in aligning it to ancient scientific knowledge, while scholars such as F. Cramer (1954) and M.T. Fögen (1993) studied the extents to which astrology was controlled and banned in various periods. In the late 20h century a controversy emerged on whether the scientific advancement of astrology was owed to the Greek study of astrology in the Hellenistic period or can already be traced back to Mesopotamian astronomy, with D. Pingree (1992) turning out to be one of the fiercest adversaries of the Hellenophile strand of scholarship. Jewish and Christian reception of astrology in antiquity has received comparatively little consideration, perhaps because these two groups were long thought to be in outright opposition to ancient astrology, with K. von Stuckard's monograph (2000a) still representing the most detailed discussion in this area.

Bibliography

Amand, D.D., *Fatalisme et liberté dans l'antiquité grecque*, Louvain, 1945.

Barton, T., *Ancient Astrology*, London, 1994a.

Barton, T., *Power and Knowledge: Astrology, Physiognomics, and Medicine under the Roman Empire*, Ann Arbor, 1994b.

Beck, R., *A Brief History of Ancient Astrology*, Malden, 2007.

Bouché-Leclercq, A., *L'Astrologie grecque*, Paris, 1899.

Caseau, B., "Firmicus Maternus, un astrologue converti au christianisme, ou la rhétorique du reject sans appel," in: D. Tollet, ed., *La religion que j'ai quittée*, Paris, 2007, 39–63.

Cramer, F.H., *Astrology in Roman Law and Politics*, Philadelphia, 1954.

Cumont, F. et al., eds., *Catalogus Codicum Astrologorum Graecorum*, 12 vols., Brussels, 1898–1924.

DeMaris, R.E., *The Colossian Controversy*, Sheffield, 1994.

Desanti, L., "Astrologi: eretici o pagani? Un problema esegetico," *AARC* 10, 1995, 687–696.

Fögen, M.T., *Die Enteignung der Wahrsager: Studien zum kaiserlichen Wissensmonopol in der Spätantike*, Frankfurt, 1993.

Hegedus, T., *Early Christianity and Ancient Astrology*, New York, 2007.

Jones, A., ed., *Astronomical Papyri from Oxyrhynchus (P. Oxy. 4133–4300a)*, 2 vols., Philadelphia, 1999.

Kugener, M.-A., ed., *Zacharias: Vita Severi*, PO 2, vol. I, Paris, 1907.

Neugebauer, O., "Demotic Horoscopes," *JAOS* 63, 1943, 115–127.

Neugebauer, O., & H.B. Van Hoesen, *Greek Horoscopes*, Philadelphia, 1959.

Pingree, D., "Hellenophilia versus the History of Science," *Isis* 83, 1992, 554–563.

Riedinger, U., *Die Heilige Schrift im Kampf der griechischen Kirche gegen die Astrologie: Von Origenes bis Johannes von Damaskos*, Innsbruck, 1956.

Riess, E., *Nechepsonis et Petosiridis fragmenta magica*, Göttingen, 1892.

Rohmann, D., "Book Burning as Conflict Management in the Roman Empire (213 BCE–200 CE)," *AncSoc* 43, 2013, 115–149.

Rohmann, D., *Christianity, Book-Burning and Censorship in Late Antiquity: Studies in Text Transmission*, Berlin, 2016; Waco, 2017.

Stuckrad, K. von, *Das Ringen um die Astrologie: Jüdische und christliche Beiträge zum antiken Zeitverständnis*, Berlin, 2000a.

Stuckrad, K. von, "Jewish and Christian Astrology in Late Antiquity – A New Approach," *Numen* 47, 2000b, 1–40.

Ven, P. van den, ed., *Vita Symeonis Stylitae Iunioris*, Brussels, 1962.

Volk, K., "Astrology," in: M. Gagarin & E. Fantham, eds., *OEAGR*, vol. I, Oxford, 2010, 285–287.

Whiteley, D.E.H., *The Theology of St. Paul*, Oxford, 1974.

Zintzen, C., ed., *Damascius: Vitae Isidori reliquiae*, Hildesheim, 1967.

DIRK ROHMANN

Asylum

The term "asylum" in the ancient world is generally synonymous with the granting of refuge, protection, or sanctuary, to an individual or a group of individuals who are in the midst of being persecuted or pursued for a crime or misdemeanor. Asylum ensured inviolability for a period of time under certain conditions.

Early Christian asylum evolved from a long tradition, as attested by ancient Hebrew, Greek, and Roman sources. References to asylum in classical and early Christian literature may be plentiful, yet they tend to be brief and occur in a broad array of contexts and literary genres (see e.g. Rigsby's collection of epigraphic evidence of asylum from the Hellenistic era; Rigsby, 1996). Reconstructing this phenomenon in a particular historical period or geographical region involves collating this highly variegated material. The latter can be sketchy, eliciting much speculative interpretation.

1. Pre-Christian Literary Sources

a. The Hebrew Bible

The Hebrew Bible is a rich source of the ancient practices of asylum, providing narratives of Israelites and non-Israelites fleeing from their homes to a place of refuge. The most large-scale example is the story of the Hebrews' flight from Egypt to Palestine led by → Moses (Exod 12–13). Following the revelation of the Ten Commandments to Moses, more divine instructions were administered (Exod 20–21), such as the right to asylum for persons committing involuntary manslaughter at an altar or a specific place of refuge (Exod 21:12–14). The latter alludes to the six "Cities of Refuge," which are identified in Josh 20. These cities, Kedesh, Shechem, Hebron, Bezer, Ramot-Gilead and Golan, were located evenly throughout ancient Israel; three on each side of the Jordan river. Persons who had committed an involuntary act of homicide were able to find safety in one of these cities and be rendered free from harm from private vengeance (see also Num 35:9–16; Deut 4:41–43; 19:1–13). Additionally, Moses exhorts the Israelites to care for sojourners and provide for them: they are to be treated well and not oppressed, as their own bitter experiences from the past should inform them (Lev 19:33). Concern for the sojourner was part of a wider ethical vision that also embraced widows, fatherless children, the poor, and others in need (Exod 22:20).

b. Ancient Greece and Rome

The Greek term ἀσυλία literally means "not plundering" or the condition of not being abducted. It is more accurately defined as the inviolability of a place bearing sacred significance. Originally, the place of refuge was a temple or shrine, which ensured security from assault in the presence of consecrated altars, statues, or other religious objects. The asylum seeker clasped onto these objects. A counterpart of the concept of *asylía* was ἱκεσία, denoting "supplication." *Hikesía* involved a recognized ritual or gesture by the person in danger, such as touching the chin, grasping the knees, or seizing the hands of a protector as a demonstration of submission. Protection could thus be obtained from an influential person, a god, or a community (e.g. Hdt. 1.157–159). Scenes of supplication occur, for example, in both the Homeric poems (e.g. Hom. *Od.* 14.257–284), Greek tragedies (e.g. Euripid. *Ion* 1.1250–1260) or depicted occasionally in art work or coins.

In ancient Greece, a broad array of needy individuals could claim asylum: orphans, abandoned children, adolescent girls escaping an arranged marriage, runaway slaves, criminals, those unjustly accused of a crime, as well as long-distance travelers on the road or at sea. The belief that the gods took vengeance upon those who mistreated suppliants was widespread (e.g. Hdt. 6.75; Thuc. *Hist.* 1.128.1–2; Paus. *Descr.* 7.25.1). Greek temples were to be immune to war and acts of violence. Infringements of sacred asylum were however not uncommon. Suppliants were sometimes dragged away from the temple or altar; or guilty offenders attempted to exploit it (e.g. Thuc. *Hist.* 4.97–98). From the early 5th century CE onward, the idea began to prevail that divine protection could not be offered automatically and invariably to criminals (Chaniotis, 1996, 65–72, 83–86; 2007, 236).

In some city-states such as Athens, communal law imposed restrictions on particular categories of persons who would be denied asylum, such as: murderers, felons, those defiled by pollution (*miasma*) through birth, marriage, or death, or those deprived of civic rights (e.g. Dem. *Or.* 59.86). Greek states apparently did not issue legislation regarding asylum or supplication. What we see instead are laws which addressed other matters which affected these practices (Chaniotis, 2007, 240–244).

In the Hellenistic Period, or perhaps somewhat earlier, the inviolability of designated holy places was recognized as a legal right (e.g. Serv. *Verg.* 2.761; 8.342). Approximately 16 prominent Greek *poleis* were honored as "sacred and inviolable," legitimized by the epiphanies of Apollo and their prestigious temples (e.g. Tac. *An.* 3.60–63). In Ptolemaic Egypt, the right to asylum was also guaranteed by the state, but only at specific temples (OGIS 761).

Under Roman administration, Greek temples regularly acquired sanctuary privileges by the imperial court. Although Roman penal law generally respected the ancient Greek supplication traditions, it did not automatically grant protection to persons who sought refuge in temples and consequently, it limited asylum to specific temples as well (Tac. *An.* 3.60–63). The Roman tradition acknowledged *asylum* for fugitive slaves who had the right to seek respite from their masters. In the imperial era, asylum could be obtained at a statue of the emperor (Gai. *Inst.* 1.53). As late as 386 CE (under Christian administration), this ancient rule was reinstated (Justin. *Inst.* 1.8.2). Other forms of asylum in the ancient Roman world included: fleeing to an influential person and pleading mercy (*ad patrocinium confugere*; e.g. Dio. *Hist. rom.* 48.19) or to the military (*ad militiam confugere*).

c. The New Testament

Although there is little historical documentation from the first centuries CE of the practice of Christian asylum, stories in the New Testament of persons seeking respite from dire need are plentiful. The most celebrated is the portrayal of Jesus and his family as refugees, forced to flee for their safety (Matt 2:13–15). Although Jesus' teachings did not directly address sanctuary seekers, many aspects of his preaching and the stories of his life could have been upheld by early Christians as models of exemplary behavior, which in turn stimulated the practice of church asylum. For example, the accounts of the holy family escaping cruel governmental decrees could have reinforced the belief that Jesus empathized with the sufferings of refugees. Other examples include: Christ's assertion that he had come to the world to save the destitute, the oppressed, and the broken-hearted (e.g. Luke 4:18); and the commandment to love one's neighbor, understood as a way of life and to be put into action, exemplified in the → parable of the Good Samaritan (Luke 10:25–37).

d. The Early Church

Following the legalization of Christianity in 313 CE by → Constantine I, imperial measures were undertaken to close pagan temples. The prohibition against entry automatically diminished their capacity to receive suppliants. Once churches had begun to be built, Christians began to assume the sanctuary custom from pagan temples, yet in a distinctly different manner.

The term *asylum* was rarely used in Latin; the phenomenon was more often referred to as "fleeing to a church" (*ad ecclesiam confugere*). The oldest literary statements on church asylum date from the 4th century CE. These sources disclose that tax debtors, criminals, oath breakers, slaves, and whoever was oppressed by the more powerful were able to take refuge in church buildings in order to avoid severe or capital punishment. The practice of church asylum could have been a response to traditional Roman legislation which at times issued harsh penalties or unfair tax laws. Similar to the Greek and Roman traditions, consecrated church buildings protected fugitives against their pursuers; the latter were not allowed to chase the asylum seeker out of the building or drag him/her out. The ecclesiastical authorities would then take the refugee under their wing and intercede with the secular authorities.

Descriptions of asylum incidents in churches occur in the writings of Roman historians (e.g. Am. 15.5.31; 15.26.3.3; Zos. *Hist.* 4.40.5; 5.8.2; 5.18.1; 5.19.4), and hagiographies of contemporary Christian leaders (e.g. of Basil the Great by Gregory of Nazianzus; see *Or.* 43.56; and of → Ambrose of Milan by Paulinus of Milan; see *Vita Ambr.* 34). Remarkable episodes of asylum involving prominent public officials, such as Eutropius, were reported by → John Chrysostom (*Eutrop.* 2–7; *Hom. Eutrop. Div. Van.* 1–6). Although these accounts of asylum usually involved notable or affluent persons, fleeing to a church was open to all economic levels of society.

Church fathers, such as Ambrose and → Augustine of Hippo, actively supported the right of sanctuary in defense of persons accused or convicted of crimes (Paul. Mil. *Vita Ambr.* 34; see e.g. Aug. *Ep.* 268.1). The works of Augustine, in particular, provide profuse accounts of church asylum and its underlying theology (see Dodaro, 1999).

2. Roman Imperial and Ecclesiastical Legislation of Church Asylum

The first official recognition of asylum by ecclesiastical authorities was in 343 CE at the Council of Serdica. Canon 8 (or 7 in the Gk version) established that persons suffering injustice, having been banned or condemned for some crime, could appeal to the church for help. Assistance (even shelter) should not be refused and *intercessio* should be made.

Christian intercession or "intervention" was characteristically a pastoral activity which strived to reform sinners. It included saving criminals from the death penalty, enabling them to repent, do penance, turn over a new leaf, and eventually attain eternal salvation. The sources reveal a broad spectrum of intervention possibilities. Bishops and clerics (those holding ecclesiastical privileges) could utilize their personal influence to the greatest extent possible, even going so far as paying a fugitive's debts, as Augustine himself reports to have done (e.g. Aug. *Ep.* 268). Refugees could acquire church privileges if ordained as priest or presbyter (→ Priest/Presbyter) or admitted to a cloister. Sometimes runaway slaves were taken in, in defiance of church regulation (→ Gangra). However, intercession for debtors and other offenders was not intended to obstruct secular justice, nor promote immunity from punishment.

Augustine's correspondence with the Catholic vicar Macedonius, although it is from a much later date (413–414 CE), spotlights the underlying idealism of Christian asylum intervention. The vicar had written to the bishop to object to his interceding for criminals condemned to be executed. In Augustine's response (Aug. *Ep.* 153), he explicated not only his refusal but also his criteria for the treatment of lawbreakers which should characterize the Christian approach to justice. Criminals should be loved and pitied. Judges and public officials, like bishops, were bound to offenders in a human fellowship. Society ought, therefore, to seek their reform, not their destruction.

Christian emperors from the late 4th to the middle 5th century CE initiated a series of mandates, alluding to frequent occurrences of abuse of asylum which necessitated restrictions. In 392 CE, a mandate by Valentinian II, → Theodosius I, and Arcadius (Cod. Theod. 9.40.15) prohibited in the eastern Roman Empire anyone – namely clerics and vicars – to assist convicted criminals in evading their sentences. Legislation followed, now specifically addressing ecclesiastical sanctuary, imposing restrictions in matters which threatened to undermine the interests of the imperial government. Between 392 and 398 CE, Emperors Arcadius and Honorius decreed three constitutions entitled *De his qui ad*

ecclesiam confugiunt. The first, Cod. Theod. 9.45.1 (in 392 CE), commanded the surrender of debtors to the imperial treasury. The second, Cod. Theod. 9.45.2 (from 397 CE), refused the right of asylum to certain categories of persons, such as Jews. It specified that they should be expelled and accepted for asylum only after they had paid all their debts and their innocence proved. The third was Cod. Theod. 9.45.3 (in 398 CE) which denied church asylum to slaves, debtors, and decurions who had neglected specific public duties. These persons were required to be returned to the courts.

An imperial instruction Jul 27, 398 CE, reinstated that those who lent help to convicted criminals would be harshly penalized (Cod. Theod. 9.40.16). Evidently clerics were still initiating activities to spare condemned offenders of severe or unjust penalties. Canon 56 from the Council of → Carthage in 399 CE appears to have been a response to the above, prescribing (in a request to Emperor Arcadius) that no one should be expelled from a church, regardless of the offense committed. In 409 CE, Honorius and Theodosius II apparently reversed the imperial course, declaring that no one, whether guilty or innocent, fleeing to a church for refuge should be dragged away from the premises (Cod. Theod. 16.8.19). Encroachment upon asylum would be regarded as an act of treason, a capital crime. This mandate is often cited as having established the first legal basis for church asylum, guaranteed by the emperor.

Two additional constitutions likewise confirmed the inviolable right of churches, specifying the areas where it was to be observed:

1. by Emperors Honorius and Theodosius II, dated Dec 21, 419 CE (*ConSir* 13), and;
2. by Emperors Theodosius II and Valentinian III of Mar 23, 431 CE (Cod. Theod. 9.45.4 and Mansi, vol. V 437–445).

The former declared the space of 50 paces from the doors of the building as inviolable; the latter extended it to the adjacent church property, such as houses, gardens, baths, squares, and porches. The earlier restrictions from the 390s CE against exceptional categories of persons (debtors of the treasury, Jews, public officers, etc.) were, however, repeated. The injunction included that if the asylum seeker was carrying weapons, he could be evicted by imperial authorities only after the bishop had been consulted.

From 431 CE onward, imperial regulations and statutes stipulated more extensively the measures to be taken by clergy (e.g. in 437–445 CE, Cod. Theod. 9.45.5 = Cod. Justin. 1.12.4). The first canonic law explicitly spelling out the provisions of intercession was no. 5 of the Council of → Orange from 441 CE (*Decr. Grat.* 87.5–6). More directives followed, reiterating the matter of asylum or imposing limitations (e.g. by Pope Leo I for the East in 466 CE; see Cod. Justin. 1.12.6; and at the Council of Orléans in 511 CE; and Lérida; c. 8 in 546 CE). These pronouncements determined to a large extent the framework of asylum in the Roman canonical tradition for the next millennium. The transmission of sanctuary law into early medieval legal codes allowed the practice to become deeply rooted in European legal traditions and flourish until the 16th century, when it was abolished.

Historiography

In the 16th and 17th centuries, studies on the practice of asylum in late antiquity surged in European intellectual circles and were used as the basis of argument for debates on church and state relations (see Shoemaker, 2011, for the complete historiography; also Hallebeek, 2005). Many questions raised then are still being addressed now, such as: to what extent early Christian asylum evolved from pre-existing, social pagan practices and customs, or had been promulgated by secular legal codes (Hallebeek, 2015; Traulsen, 2004; Shoemaker, 2011; Ducloux, 1994)? In fact, there is much evidence to support each position.

Up until recently, it was assumed that Roman penal systems had a long-standing tradition of opposition toward the practice of asylum, regarding it as an obstruction of justice and shielding wrongdoers. Some scholars held that imperial courts periodically attempted to eliminate it altogether. This resulted in the view that imperial sanctuary laws in the Christian era gradually but reluctantly conceded to the phenomenon and intended it as a "privilege," wrested by an increasingly powerful church. Researchers now perceive more acutely the challenges involved in interpreting antiquated

constitutions and the disparate literary accounts of asylum. Yet even so, it appears that legal scholars still occasionally lose sight of the difficulty – if not the impossibility – of assessing the effectiveness or impact of ancient Roman imperial edicts.

In all the studies on asylum included in this bibliography, there is an inclination to interpret the sources in terms of conflict or friction between the secular state and religious institutions, even though these two factors throughout antiquity were closely intertwined. Investigations of ancient Greek asylum wrestle to minimalize this interpretative dichotomy (Chaniotis, 2007; Dietrich, 2007; Garland, 2014). A welcome supplementation to the strictly political or legal context in the study of ancient Christian asylum is the utilization of patristic sources. The perspective is enhanced tremendously when adequate consideration is given to the theological basis underpinning Christian *intercessio* and *asylum*, as well as to the generally close collaboration between governmental and ecclesiastical authorities during this era (Dodaro, 1999; Shoemaker, 2011). The recent renewed interest in historical asylum today can be attributed to the global refugee crisis which has persisted since the latter half of the 20th century.

Bibliography

Chaniotis, A., "Conflicting Authorities: *Asylia* between Secular and Divine Law in the Classical and Hellenistic *Poleis*," *Kernos* 9, 1996; online.

Chaniotis, A., "Die Entwicklung der griechischen *Asylie*: Ritualdynamik und die Grenzen des Rechtsvergleichs," in: L. Burckhardt, K. Seybold & J. von Ungern-Sternberg, eds., *Gesetzgebung in antiken Gesellschaften: Israel, Griechenland, Rom*, Berlin, 2007, 233–246.

Coleman-Norton, P.R., ed., *Roman State and Christian Church: A Collection of Legal Documents to AD 535*, 3 vols., London, 1966.

Dietrich, C., "Asylgesetzgebung in antiken Gesellschaften," in: L. Burckhardt, K. Seybold, & J. von Ungern-Sternberg, eds., *Gesetzgebung in antiken Gesellschaften: Israel, Griechenland, Rom*, Berlin, 2007, 193–220.

Dodaro, R., "Church and State," in: A. Fitzgerald et al., eds., *Augustine Through the Ages*, Grand Rapids, 1999, 176–184.

Dodaro, R., "Between Two Cities: Political Action in Augustine of Hippo," in: J. Doody, K. Pfaffenroth, & K. Hughes, eds., *Augustine and Politics*, Lexington, 2005, 99–115.

Ducloux, A., *Ad ecclesiam confugere: Naissance du droit d'asile dans les églises (IV e–milieu du Ve s.)*, Paris, 1994.

Garland, R., *Wandering Greeks: The Ancient Greek Diaspora from the Age of Homer to the Death of Alexander the Great*, Princeton, 2014, 114–130.

Hallebeek, J., "Church Asylum in Late Antiquity, Concession by the Emperor or Competence of the Church?" in: E.C. Coppens, ed., *Secundum Ius: Opstellen aangeboden aan prof. mr. P.L. Nève*, Nijmegen, 2005, 163–182; Rechtshistorische reeks van het Gerard Noodt Instituut, no. 49.

Houston, F.S., *You Shall Love the Stranger as Yourself: The Bible, Refugees, and Asylum*, New York, 2015.

Marfleet, P., "Understanding 'Sanctuary': Faith and Traditions of Asylum," *JRSt* 24/3, 2011, 440–455.

Rigsby, K.J., *Asylia: Territorial Inviolability in the Hellenistic World*, Berkeley, 1996.

Shoemaker, K., *Sanctuary and Crime in the Middle Ages, 400–150*, New York, 2011, 9–46.

Traulsen, C., *Das sakrale Asyl in der Alten Welt: Zur Schutzfunktion des Heiligen von König Salomo bis zum Codex Theodosianus, Jus Ecclesiasticum*, vol. LXXII, Tübingen, 2004.

LAELA ZWOLLO

Asylum, Right of

The concept of → asylum (from ἄσυλος, "inviolable"), a place that is recognized as a person's refuge in the case of necessity, was born of a system of values and religion. This system included the right to immunity for the one seeking refuge, if he or she was being sought by the authorities for some crime; and the right to receive and to protect someone in a place held to be sacred, for it was the special quality of the place which guaranteed that whoever made use of it should remain inviolable. Yet, because there was this special quality of inviobility that came to be respected by the civil or military authorities, this had to be acknowledged by the conscience of the persons involved – that their transgression entailed consequences – as, for example, the fear of committing a sacrilege on account of the sacredness of the place. The term "asylum" (ἄσυλον) was traditional in a pagan environment and was used by the pagan historian Zosimus (→ Zosimus [Historian]). It was used very rarely by the Christians, who preferred the expression *ad ecclesiam confugere* ("refuge into the church") or other such similar expressions (*DACL*, vol. IV, 1556; *ad domum ipsius fidei confugerant* – "they take refuge in the house of faith"; Aug. *Ep.* [*Div.*] 1.3; *adiutorium in ipsa domo fidei requirebant*; Aug.

Ep. 250.1). In Jewish (the Temple; a city of refuge), Greek, Egyptian, and Roman areas, some sanctuaries enjoyed the right of refuge, but there were other means of obtaining protection, such as touching the knees of a particular person, the altars dedicated to certain divinities, or the statues of the emperor. In this case the sacredness and the protection came from the statue, which represented the grandeur of the emperor. → Tacitus speaks of a woman who had an image of Tiberius in her hand, which allowed her to hurl insults, since the one being insulted did not intervene lest he commit a sacrilege of *laesa maiestas* (the crime of "high treason"; Tac. *An* 3.36). Only with Theodosius I was the value of asylum near statues recognized with the concession of ten days of immunity, which was then abolished under → Justinian (Cod. Theod. 9.44.1 of 386 CE = Cod. Justin. 1.25.1).

Closely connected with asylum was the practice of *intercessio*, which consisted of an intervention before the authorities on the part of the → bishops for the sake of the person who found him- or herself in difficulty (it was not a simple recommendation, which itself also happened often). *Intercessio* came from the Christian concept of forgiveness with a view to the amendment of the culpable person. *Intercessio* and asylum were distinct practices, but often they were connected, for asylum normally entailed an *intercessio*, with the authorities in favor of the refugee.

In Christian contexts, the first known case of asylum concerns Felix of Cirta (Numidia), who sought refuge with Bishop Mensurius while sought by the imperial authorities for writting a book against the Emperor Maxentius, (before 312 CE; see Duval, 1995). The second regards → Martin of Tours around the year 326 CE (Sul. *Vita Mart.* 2.1; 2; 3). At the the Council of Serdica in 343 CE, bishops in canon 7 discussed *intercessio* and sought to regulate the practice of asylum:

> It often occurs that some people who are worthy of mercy take refuge in church, they who are condemned for their guilt either to prison or to exile on an island, or they are punished for some other reason, one must not deny them aid, but their pardon must be sought from the civil authorities without delay and without hesitation.

The person who sought refuge in a church also could have been innocent. In those cases the time of protection was useful in order to prove the person's innocence. The first official request of which we have knowledge dates to the Council of → Carthage, held on April 27, 399 CE, in which two bishops, Epigonius and Vincentius, were charged with going to the court in order to obtain a law by which no one would dare to remove anyone who had sought refuge in a church (*confugientes ad ecclesiam*/who take refuge into church; CCL 149, 194–194). The intervention of the council, which wanted to regulate a *de facto* practice of seeking refuge in churches (*saepe contingit* – "often it happens"), signals that this had already arisen and there was an intervention so as to obligate the bishops to take to heart the lot of those seeking refuge.

The church, as an edifice of Christian worship, which for Christians was invested with a sacred character already, was beginning to acquire a sacred mark and notion in the common mentality, which was also respected by the civil and military authorities. The text of the council does not specify whether the refugees were Christians or pagans; all were able to seek recourse there. The nature of the sacredness of the buildings only came to be recognized by the imperial authorities in 395 CE (Cod. Theod. 16.2.29; see 16.2.31). Legally the churches could have been violated, because no law of protection existed, and sometimes they were indeed violated: what is more, we know of many cases of violation. Therefore, the churches did not offer an absolute guarantee (see Am. 26.3.3: the *auriga*/charioteer Hilarinus, who took refuge at the *ritus Christiani sacrarium* – "building of Christian worship", was taken and decapitated; Am. 15.5: the usurper Silvanus had taken refuge in a church, yet he was captured and killed). In the sources asylum is referred to in order to narrate episodes of its violation (Stilicho, who ordered Cresconius apprehended from a church; Paul. Mil. *Vita Ambr.* 34). During the sack of Rome in 410 CE, → Alaric I respected the right to asylum – even for the pagans – who had sought refuge in the Roman churches (Aug. *Civ.* 1.7; Oros. *Adv. pag.* 7.39.10). The insistence of → Augustine of Hippo that the act of seeking refuge in a church was accepted and respected by Romans and by the barbarians indicates a change in the mentality.

In 392 CE → Theodosius I intervened on several occasions to limit *intercessio* and asylum. According to Cod. Theod. 9.40.15 (Mar 13), it was forbidden that ecclesiastics might impede the fulfillment of sentences with an appeal or by the removal of the condemned; Cod. Theod. 11.36.31 (Apr 9): neither was the *intercessio* of the clergy permitted on behalf of a condemned or of a guilty party that had confessed; Cod. Theod. 9.45.1 (Oct 18): asylum in churches was not conceded to public debtors or, that is, that their debts be paid by the bishops (the first law regulates this matter); Cod. Theod. 9.45.2 (Jun 17, 397 CE): it was also prohibited to the Jews who pretended to convert in order to make use of asylum; Cod. Theod. 9.45.3 (Jun 27, 398 CE): the slaves and private debtors were deprived of the right of asylum, or rather, their debts were paid by the church; Cod. Theod. 9.45.2 (Jun 17, 397 CE): through the influence of Eutropius, asylum was not granted for the crime of *laesa maiestas* (high treason), which could have been understood in a broad sense (see Cod. Theod. 9.14.3.2; Sep 4, 397 CE). Yet, it was precisely Eutropius, in the following year, who took refuge in a church, and the intervention of → John Chrysostom did not save him from → death.

The first formal recognition of asylum in the churches comes from the year 419 CE (*ConSir* 13). An allusion to this law can be found in Augustine (*Ep.* [*Div.*] 22.3 from 420 CE), who makes the observation that – all things considered – this privilege favors few people: "Thus it came about that we, in the best case scenario, may be able to come to the aid and to defend very few of those who seek refuge in the church." The right of asylum became better regulated in its particulars with the law of Mar 23, 431 CE (Cod. Theod. 9.45.1) and with that of 432 CE (Cod. Theod. 9.45.5). The → Codex Theodosianus brings forth only a portion of the law from 431 CE, which is preserved integrally in another source (Mansi, vol. V, 437–445). Around Christian buildings, sometimes, they noted the confines within which asylum would work (see *DACL*, vol. IV, 1555f.). The Council of Orange in 441 CE legislated some norms that concerned asylum in the churches (cc. 5 and 6); in the East the emperor Leo intervened (Cod. Justin. 1.12.6 from 466 CE). At Constantinople Justinian constituted a college that had to evaluate the position of those who took refuge at the Hagia

Sophia for asylum (slaves, debtors, those accused of homicide).

Bibliography

Baccini, T., "Una nuova bulla del collegio degli ekklesiekdikoi di S. Sofia," *Byz.* 71, 2001, 263–266.

Dreher, M., "Das Asyl in der Antike von seinen griechischen Ursprüngen bis zur christlichen Spätantike," *Tyche* 11, 1996, 79–96.

Ducloux, A., *Ad ecclesiam confugere: Naissance du droit d'asile dans les églises (IVe-milieu du Ve s)*, Paris, 1994.

Duval, Y., "Les gesta apud Zenonophilum et la 'paix de Maxence' (Gesta f° 22b)," *AnTa* 3, 1995, 55–63.

Freyburger, G., "Le droit d'asile à Rome," *EtCl* 60, 1992, 139–151.

Gamau, R., *Ad statuam licet confugere: Untersuchungen zum Asylrecht im römischen Prinzipat*, Frankfurt, 1999; see *IURA* 50, 1999, 251–265.

Giordano, L., "Gregorio Magno e il diritto di asilo," *VetChr* 37, 2000, 391–406.

Görisch, G., *Kirchenasyl und staatliches Recht*, Berlin, 2000.

Manfredini, A.D., "'Ad ecclesiam confugere,' 'ad statuas conferre,' nell'età di Teodosio I," *AARC* 6, 1986, 39–58.

Rigsby, K.J., *Asylia: Territorial Inviolability in the Hellenistic World*, Berkeley 1997.

Wenger, L., "Asylrecht," in: *RAC*, vol. I, Stuttgart, 1950, 836–844.

Angelo Di Berardino

Ataraxia

The word ἀταραξία means imperturbability, that is, the lack of disturbance (privative α + ταραχή = disturbance) in the soul. This term has its roots in ancient Greek pagan thought and indicates an utmost good that is utterly crucial for obtaining the kind of happiness to which the continuous exercise of philosophy must lead. It is above all in the field of Hellenistic philosophy (→ Hellenism and Christianity), and especially in Epicureanism, that the term ataraxia plays a significant role, since here it coincides with the ultimate goal of philosophy. In the field of Christianity, this word has not been frequently used. Based on its occurrences in some Christian sources, we learn that Christians essentially accepted the original pagan meaning of the word and in most cases considered ataraxia a "virtue" that the Christian believer must pursue. It is also significant that ataraxia is considered not only a virtue for believers (i.e. human beings), but also a divine attribute, a meaning already basically implied in Epicureanism (see Epic. *Her.* 82; *Pyt.* 85; 96; *Men.* 128; esp. 135).

1. Democritus and Pyrrho of Elis

Through a passage from Stobaeus (*Ecl.* 2.7.3.i, vol. II, p. 52, 13 Wachsmuth, 1884 = 68 A 167 Diels & Kranz, 1903 = VII 27 D231 Laks & Most, 2016), which in turn transmits a doxographical extract by Arius Didymus, we know that already Democritus called happiness (εὐδαιμονίη) by various different names, including ataraxia. It is not possible to determine whether Democritus made regular use of this term; but it seems that the philosopher preferred to make greater use of words such as "well-being" (εὐεστώ), "tranquility or balance of mind" (εὐθυμία), and "absence of fear" (ἀθαμβία) in order to define happiness (see Cic. *Fin.* 5.8.23 = 68 A 169 Diels & Kranz, 1903 = VII 27 D230 Laks & Most, 2016). It is highly likely that, before the Hellenistic age, ataraxia was already a technical term in Pyrrho's philosophy. According to a passage from Posidonius reported by Diogenes Laertius (D.L. 9.68 = *Posid.* F 287 Edelstein & Kidd, 1989 = *Pyrrho* 17 A Decleva Caizzi, 1981/2020), Pyrrho believed that the wise man must remain in a state of imperturbability in the face of the uncontrollable vicissitudes of fate. Aristocles of Messene (*ap.* Eus. *Praep.* 14.18.1–4 = *Aristocl.* F 4 Chiesara, 2001 = *Pyrrho* 53 Decleva Caizzi, 1981/2020) reports that according to Pyrrho all things are equally without distinction, without stability, and indiscriminate; therefore, one should hold no opinions on anything. For this reason (according to Aristocles' passages just quoted), Timon of Phlius, Pyrrho's disciple and follower and the "heir" to his philosophy, argues that whoever possesses this disposition will attain first ἀφασία and then ataraxia (see also Agath. *Hist.* 2.29 = *Pyrrho* 91 Decleva Caizzi, 1981/2020).

2. Plato and Aristotle

In Plato and Aristotle, the word ataraxia does not acquire a technical meaning, unlike in the case of Pyrrho and later in the field of Hellenistic philosophy.

In Plato the term ataraxia does not appear at all, in fact, for it does not represent the ultimate goal of philosophy. Plato, however, uses the word ταραχή, or "disturbance," in a very generic sense. It is noteworthy that the most revealing occurrences of this term come from the *Phaedo*, where Plato repeatedly presents disturbance as an erroneous and negative state caused by the → body (Plato *Phaed.* 66a.5; 66d.6; 79c.8). In the *Republic*, however, ταραχή is used to describe the confused state of a soul whose different parts are not in harmony with one another (see Plato *Rep.* 4.444b.6; 9.577e.1; 10.602d.1). As far as Aristotle is concerned, significant occurrences of ἀτάραχος are to be found in the *Nicomachean Ethics*, where this adjective essentially indicates the quality of the virtuous person. The braver a person is, the more imperturbable he or she will be in the face of sudden or expected dangers (Arist. *Eth. Nic.* 3.11.1117a.19) and frightening events (*Eth. Nic.* 3.12.1117a.31; the relationship between courage/fortitude and ataraxia is also detectable in Cyril of Alexandria: see below). The same applies to those who are mild: for they wish to remain imperturbable and not be overwhelmed by passion (*Eth. Nic.* 4.11.1125b34). The idea of a link between meekness and ataraxia is also attested in Origen (*Sel. Ps.* 12.1649.36).

3. Neo-Pyrrhonian Skepticism

It has already been pointed out that Pyrrho – who is (perhaps wrongly) considered the founder of Neo-Pyrrhonian skepticism (one of the two 'skeptical' currents in ancient philosophy, the other being the so-called "skeptical" academy of Arcesilaus) – had used the term ataraxia to describe the condition of imperturbability characterizing the sage. As the latter knows that all things are inherently unstable and indiscriminate, he or she will not formulate any opinions on them. Diogenes Laertius (D.L. 9.107 = *Aenesidemus* B 21B Polito, 2014) reports that according to skeptics such as Timon (the aforementioned disciple of Pyrrho's) and Aenesidemus (another Neo-Pyrrhonian skeptical philosopher) and their followers, the aim (τέλος) of philosophy is the suspension of judgment (ἐποχή), which is followed like a shadow by ataraxia. In order to grasp the notion of ataraxia

in Neo-Pyrrhonian skepticism, it is necessary first of all to turn to the works of Sextus Empiricus. Sextus (*Pyr.* 1.25) argues that the purpose of skepticism is ataraxia with respect to things that are subject to opinion (ἐν τοῖς κατὰ δόξαν) and the moderation of necessarily occurring affections (μετριοπάθεια). The skeptic, according to Sextus Empiricus, by failing to settle the disagreement arising from the equipollence (ἰσοσθένεια) of the arguments raised by dogmatists, suspends his judgment; and this suspension, as if by chance (τυχικῶς), is followed by ataraxia (see *Pyr.* 1.26). This clarification is crucial: since skeptics do not dogmatize, they cannot dogmatically assert that ataraxia necessarily arises from the suspension of judgment; all they can say is that imperturbability fortuitously follows the suspension of judgment. In addition to the more "theoretical" and "intellectual" definition of ataraxia as imperturbability in the field of opinions (*Pyr.* 1.25; 30), Sextus provides a further but more "practical" definition, in which it is possible perhaps to detect a significant Epicurean influence. For the skeptic (*Pyr.* 1.10) ataraxia is freedom from disturbance and calmness of soul (ψυχῆς ἀοχλησία καὶ γαληνότης; the term ἀοχλησία is significant in Stilpo's moral philosophy (see Alex. Aphrod. *De an. lib. mantissa* 150, 34–35 Bruns = *SSR* II O 34), in Speusippus' ethics – see Clem. *Strom.* 2.22.133.4 = *Speusippus* 101 Isnardi Parente, 1980 = F 77 Tarán, 1981 – and is attested in Epic. *Men.* 127 too). It is important to point out that Sextus uses the word γαληνότης here, which literally describes the stillness of the sea – the *maris tranquillitas*, as Cicero puts it (*Tusc.* 5.6.16). It is a word that Epicurus uses as well (see Epic. *Her.* 83) and that we already find in Timon of Phlius, where it is employed to describe the happiness of the person who lives without disturbances (see Sex. Emp. *Math.* 11.141 [*Timon* 63–64 Diels, 1901] = *Pyrrho* 59 Decleva Caizzi, 1981/2020). It is certainly striking that this association between ataraxia and the stillness of the sea was later taken up by Christian authors, such as → Origen (*Fr. Ps.* 75.3.17), → Gregory of Nyssa (*ICc* [*Homiliae* 15] 6.103.4), → Eusebius of Caesarea (*Comm. Ps.* 23.880.30; 1225.9), → Basil of Caesarea (*Ca.* 31.1324.40), → John Chrysostom (*Hom. Jo.* 59.333.59), and → Cyril of Alexandria in his *Expositio in Psalmos* (69.961.56–964.1).

4. Epicurus

Ancient Stoics preferred to talk about ἀπάθεια to characterize the impassivity of the sage (see D.L. 7.117 = *SVF* 3.448), although the possibility cannot be ruled out that they may have used the term ataraxia to indicate the imperturbability of the soul, without any reference to the pleasures of the senses (see Por. *Hor.* 2.4.1 = *SVF* 3.449). After Pyrrho and before Epictetus (see esp. Epict. *Diatr.* 2.1.22; 2.2; and *Ench.* 12.2), it is mainly with → Epicurus that the term ataraxia takes on a specific technical meaning, perfectly suited to the Epicurean philosophical system. Epicurus (see Epic. *Men.* 131, and D.L. 10.136 = *Epic.* 2 Usener, 1966 = [7] Arrighetti, 1973) believes that happiness coincides with the lack of disturbance in the soul (ataraxia) and of pain in the body (ἀπονία). Ataraxia must not be understood merely as a state of mind: in order to achieve it, one must adopt forms of behavior and perform actions that promote a truly happy life (namely, by following Epicurus' philosophy). According to Epicurus, philosophy is divided into three parts: canonics, the science of nature, and ethics (see D.L. 10.29–30). These parts are "ordered," meaning that philosophy necessarily begins from canonics (i.e. the epistemological part of the system), which provides the tools to learn about nature. The knowledge of nature, finally, allows one to understand ethical precepts and to practically apply them in daily life. Consequently, ethics is not "independent": its contents are justified by the science of nature, which can be studied using the tools (or "canons") provided by canonics. If Epicurus' system is an ordered one, this means that ethics represents the culmination of philosophy as a whole (see Epic. *Rat.* 11–12). A person does not engage in philosophy, therefore, in order to increase his or her theoretical knowledge, but to be really happy within the chronological and spatial horizon of his or her life. For this reason, even in the investigation of nature, as for example of celestial phenomena, the only aim is ataraxia (see Epic. *Pyt.* 85; 96), namely the condition of imperturbability. This may be attained either by eliminating those fears that seriously hinder a person's happiness (esp. the fear of the gods and of death: see Epic. *Rat.* 1–2; *Men.* 123–126), or by the uninterrupted recollection (μνήμη) of the basic doctrines of Epicurus' philosophy (see Epic. *Her.* 82 and the Epicurean Diogenes of Oinoanda 3.I.11 Smith). In the *Letter to Menoeceus* (128), which is entirely devoted to ethics, Epicurus clearly states that our every act of choice or refusal should be directed to the health of the body (ἐπὶ τὴν τοῦ σώματος ὑγίειαν) and the imperturbability of the soul (τὴν τῆς ψυχῆς ἀταραξίαν): for this is the aim of the blessed life (τοῦτο τοῦ μακαρίως ζῆν ἐστι τέλος) – the very life enjoyed by the gods, who possess the attributes of incorruptibility (ἀφθαρσία) and beatitude (μακαριότης: see Epic. *Men.* 123). Diogenes Laertius (D.L. 10.136 = *Epic.* 2 Usener, 1966/[7] Arrighetti, 1973) fortunately has preserved a fragment of Epicurus' work *On Choices* (Περὶ αἱρέσεων), where the philosopher claims that ataraxia, or the lack of disturbance in the soul, and ἀπονία, or the absence of pain in the body, are static pleasures (καταστηματικαὶ ἡδοναί). Tradition credits Epicurus with the distinction between static pleasures, or pleasures at rest, and kinetic pleasures, or pleasures in motion (ἐν κινήσει), perhaps in order to distinguish his position from that of the Cyrenaics (see D.L. 10.136). According to Epicurus (*Men.* 131), pleasure is a "negative concept": it coincides with the absence of pain in the body (τὸ μήτε ἀλγεῖν κατὰ σῶμα) and the lack of disturbance in the soul (μήτε ταράττεσθαι κατὰ ψυχήν). This notion of pleasure has no licentious or hedonistic undertones: it is the beginning and end of the blessed life (see Epic. *Men.* 128 and *Gnomologium Vaticanum* 33). Beatitude is not only a condition of the gods (who in addition are marked by the physical incorruptibility of the body, which, unlike other atomic compounds, always regenerates itself), for it is also open to human beings, who can achieve happiness by embracing the Epicurean doctrine and become gods among humans (see Epic. *Men.* 135). Static pleasures, therefore, are higher pleasures because they are able to eliminate the disturbance of the soul and bodily pain. Those who live blissfully (gods and humans) have fully achieved ataraxia, a condition "beyond all comparison with success in some great command" (see Plut. *Adv. Col.* 31 1125C = *Epic.* 556 Usener, 1966; trans. Einarson & De Lacy, 1967). In coinciding with happiness, ataraxia thus represents the ultimate aim to which Epicurus' philosophy leads.

5. Christian Reception

Although ataraxia was a pagan and pre-Christian ideal, it was not seen to differ substantially in meaning from the concept of impassibility or ἀπάθεια; like many other ancient notions, therefore, it was soon adopted by Christians. In the Septuagint the term is present only in the book of *4 Maccabees* (8:26.3), an appendix to the Greek Bible, but here it does not seem to take on any particular meaning. With his solid knowledge of Greek thought (esp. of Platonic and Stoic philosophy), → Clement of Alexandria (*Strom.* 4.7.55.4) is well aware that ataraxia and the impassibility of the soul (ἀπάθεια ψυχῆς) are ancient ideals, pursued by the ancient righteous (οἱ παλαιοὶ δίκαιοι) – a probable reference to the Epicureans (for ataraxia) and Stoics (for ἀπάθεια). Clement also transmits a fragment of Epicurus on ataraxia, where we read that, according to the Greek philosopher, the best fruit of justice (δικαιοσύνη) is ataraxia (Clem. *Strom.* 4.2.24.10 = *Epic.* 519 Usener, 1966). According to Clement, the Christian God is without passions (ἀπαθής): for this reason, fear toward him should be equally passionless, and assimilation (ὁμοίωσις) to God can be seen as a way of attaining ἀπάθεια (see *Strom.* 2.20.103.1). In *Paedagogus* (2.7.58.3) Clement clearly argues that the aim Christians must pursue is ataraxia (τέλος ἡμῖν ἡ ἀταραξία), which essentially coincides with peace (εἰρήνη; see also Jos. *Ant.* 8.433.4). Furthermore, the expression "peace be with you" (which recalls the greeting of the risen Jesus: e.g. John 20:19) is a wish to be free from perturbation (we observe the same position in Cyril of Alexandria: see below). The idea of ataraxia as a virtue is closely connected to that of moderation in a letter written by → Gregory of Nazianzus (*Ep.* 244.9.2), where the author urges his addressee to harmonize and give order to his way of live through ataraxia ('Ρύθμιζε [...] τὸ δὲ ἦθος ἀταραξίᾳ). The early Christian writers primarily considered ataraxia to be a state of the soul (see e.g. Chrys. *Virg.* 68.5; *Natal.* 49.362.26), as is suggested by their (already mentioned) frequent association of ataraxia with the stillness of the sea (γαληνότης or γαλήνη), as a way of describing the calm and peace of the soul. Ataraxia, however, is also a state of mind, and this is confirmed by a passage in the *Life of Antony* (36.3), where → Athanasius of Alexandria describes the irruption of evil spirits. The presence of these violent spirits frightens and disturbs the soul and causes the scattering of thoughts (*Vit. Ant.* 36.2: ἀταξία λογισμῶν); it throws the soul into an utter confusion of mind. When there is a holy vision, the fear is transformed into joy, and the ἀταξία λογισμῶν converts itself into λογισμῶν ἀταραξία, in other words the imperturbability of thoughts, which coincides with mental order and clarity. In another section of the same work (*Vit. Ant.* 43.3), Athanasius invites his readers not to be afraid of the → devil and, in the case of a diabolic vision, to expose the adversary by boldly questioning him. Asking "Who are you and where are you from?" is already a sign of imperturbability (ἀταραξίας [...] τεκμήριον) and, consequently, of lucidity. The relationship between ataraxia and the mind is detectable in Cyril of Alexandria's *Exposition in Psalmos* (69.928.32). In Cyril's *Commentarii in Joannem* (2.511.14), moreover, we can find an interesting connection between ataraxia and courage or fortitude (ἀνδρεία): the Spirit is sufficient to allay all tumult of the mind, and Christ promises to give us what is needed to maintain our courage and ataraxia by saying that he leaves his peace to us (John 14:27). Ataraxia does not merely describe a condition of the soul or the mind, but is a state to be achieved even in prayer; as such, it is also related to solitude (see *Catena in Matthaeum* [cod. Paris. Coislin. gr. 23] p. 117 14: ἡ μόνωσις [...] ἀταραξίας ἐστὶ μήτηρ). All this would sound absurd to an Epicurean philosopher: for according to the Epicureans, the attaining of ataraxia also requires a philosophical community of friends and the presence of the "Master" (Epicurus) or – at any rate – of a paradigmatic and charismatic figure capable of encouraging or admonishing his or her disciples. John Chrysostom (*Hom. Matt.* 58.504.46), in his commentary on Matt. 14:23–24, urges the reader to seek ataraxia in prayer (θηράσθαι ἐν ταῖς εὐχαῖς ἀταραξίαν), in other words that imperturbability that constitutes freedom from distraction. Finally, it is very important to note that in the Christian context ataraxia is not only a characteristic of the believer or a condition to which the worshipper must aspire, but also an attribute of God. A papyrus now in Vienna (P.Vindob./P.Rain. Inv. 19896 = Van Haelst 1012 = Trismegistos 63044 = LDAB 4240; ed. C. Wessely, 1924, *Les plus anciens monuments du christianisme* 2 [PO 18.3] p. 445–449) records a Christian prayer or hymn (dated to anywhere between

100 and 640 CE) in which the author (*verso*; l. 24) offers praises to the Lord, his powers (δυνάμεις), his splendor (φέγγη), and his "imperturbabilities" (ἀταραξίας). In the context of Epicureanism, by contrast, the attribution of ataraxia to divine beings is not explicit but only implicit (also for the great scarcity of sources): the Epicurean god is imperturbable because of his beatitude. Epicurus regarded ataraxia as a typically human condition, and not as a specifically divine state. Although ἀπάθεια is the quality most commonly assigned to divine beings, the attribution of ataraxia to God seems to be a specifically Christian feature, which remained only implicit in Epicurus' philosophy. Consequently, just as ἀπάθεια can be either divine or human, in the same way the early Christian writers developed a notion of ataraxia that applies not just to humans but also (and esp.) to God.

Historiography

Unfortunately, a volume completely devoted to the Christian appropriation of the ancient Greek notion of ataraxia does not exist. While in the Christian field this issue was scarcely studied, we find several articles and volumes on ataraxia in ancient Greek philosophy. M. Spanneut's articles (1990; 1994; 2002) provide very meticulous studies about the Christian use and reception of the Greek pagan notions of ataraxia and apatheia. It is important to underline that M. Spanneut's studies focused especially on the Christian appropriation of the Stoic notion of apatheia. The term ataraxia specifically belongs to the ancient philosophical Greek tradition and, more precisely, to Epicurus' philosophy. It is mandatory to indicate the two standard and more recent monographies about this concept: J. Warren (2002) and K. Held (2007). The latter extensively concerns the close relationship between pleasure and ataraxia in Epicurus' philosophy; the former is a very significant contribution about the "archaeology" of this concept. J. Warren, indeed, particularly deals with Democritus' ethics (and Pyrrho of Elis' moral position too) considered as an important philosophical antecedent of Epicurus' conception of ataraxia and happiness.

Bibliography

Arrighetti, G., *Epicuro: Opere*, Turin, 1960, ²1973.

Bett, R., *Pyrrho, His Antecedents, and His Legacy*, Oxford, 2000.

Chiesara, M.L., *Aristocles of Messene: Testimonia and Fragments*, Oxford, 2001.

Decleva Caizzi, F., *Pirrone: Testimonianze*, Naples, 1981 (New Edition: F. Decleva Caizzi, *Pirroniana*, Milan, 2020).

Diels, H., *Poetarum Philosophorum Fragmenta*, Berlin, 1901.

Diels, H., & W. Kranz, *Die Fragmente der Vorsokratiker: Griechisch und Deutsch*, 8th ed., print of the 3rd ed., with suppls., vol. I–II ed. H. Diels; vol. III ed. W. Kranz & H. Diels, Berlin, 1903, ²1956.

Edelstein, L., & I.G. Kidd, *Posidonius*, vol. I: *The Fragments*, Cambridge UK, 1972, ²1989.

Einarson, B. & P.H. De Lacy, *Plutarch's Moralia*, vol. XIV, Cambridge MA, 1967.

Held, K., *Hēdonē und Ataraxia bei Epikur*, Paderborn, 2007.

Heßler, J.E., *Epikur, Brief an Menoikeus: Edition, Übersetzung, Einleitung und Kommentar*, Basel 2014.

Hossenfelder, M., "Ataraxie," in: H. Cancik & H. Scheider, eds., *DNP*, vol. II, Stuttgart, 1997, cols. 146–147.

Isnardi Parente, M., *Speusippo: Frammenti*, Precedono testimonianze sull'Academia scelte e ordinate da M. Gigante, Naples, 1980.

Laks, A., & G.W. Most, *Early Greek Philosophy*, vol. VII: *Later Ionian and Athenian Thinkers*, part 2, Cambridge MA, 2016.

Machuca, D., "The Pyrrhonist's ἀταραξία and φιλανθρωπία," *AP* 26, 2006, 111–139.

Polito, R., *Aenesidemus of Cnossus: Testimonia*, Cambridge UK, 2014.

Schmid, W., "Epikur," in: T. Klauser, ed., *RAC*, vol. V, Stuttgart, 1961, cols. 681–819.

Smith, M.F., *Diogenes of Oinoanda: The Epicurean Inscription*, Naples, 1993.

Spanneut, M., "L'impact de l'apatheia stoïcienne sur la pensée chrétienne jusqu'à Saint Augustin," *CATIR* 7, 1990, 39–52.

Spanneut, M., "L'apatheia ancienne," in: *ANRW*, vol. II/36/7, Berlin, 1994, 4641–4717.

Spanneut, M., "L'apatheia chrétienne aux quatre premiers siècles," *POC* 52, 2002, 165–302.

Svavarsson, S.H., "Two Kinds of Tranquility: Sextus Empiricus on Ataraxia," in: D.E. Machuca, ed., *Pyrrhonism in Ancient, Modern, and Contemporary Philosophy*, Dordrecht, 2011, 19–32.

Svavarsson S.H., "Tranquility: Democritus and Pyrrho," in: S. Marchand & F. Verde, eds., *Épicurisme et scepticisme*, Rome, 2013, 3–23.

Striker, G., "Ataraxia: Happiness as Tranquillity," in: G. Striker, *Essays on Hellenistic Epistemology and Ethics*, Cambridge UK, 1996, 183–195.

Tarán, L., *Speusippus of Athens: A Critical Study with a Collection of the Related Texts and Commentary*, Leiden, 1981.

Usener, H., *Epicurea*, Leipzig, 1887; repr. Rome, 1963; Stuttgart, 1966.

Verde, F., "La polemica sulla natura del saggio tra Epicuro e Stilpone e in Colote," *Antiquorum Philosophia* 16, 2022, 73–92.

Wachsmuth, C., *Ioannis Stobaei Anthologii libri duo priores, qui inscribi solent Eclogae physicae et ethicae*, vol. II, Berolini (Berlin), 1884.

Warren, J., *Epicurus and Democritean Ethics: An Archaeology of Ataraxia*, Cambridge UK, 2002.

Warren, J., *The Pleasures of Reason in Plato, Aristotle, and the Hellenistic Hedonists*, Cambridge UK, 2014

Wolfsdorf, D., *Pleasure in Ancient Greek Philosophy*, Cambridge UK, 2013.

FRANCESCO VERDE

Athanasius of Alexandria

When Athanasius was elected bishop of Alexandria, the metropolis of Egypt, he succeeded a line of great bishops: from Demetrius, at the end of the 2nd century CE, Dionysius in the middle of the 3rd century CE, Peter at the beginning of the 4th century CE, one of the last martyrs of the Great Persecution of Diocletian (→ Persecution of Christians), who died on Nov 25, 311 CE, and finally, Alexander, who was elected in 313 CE (→ Alexander I of Alexandria). The bishop of Alexandria, since Demetrius, ordained bishops for Egypt, the Thebaid and the two Libyas, who formed, at the time of Alexander, a college of a 100 suffragans responsible for ordaining their → metropolitan. If one adds that the bishop of Alexandria was at the head of more than 40 priests for Alexandria and the Mareotis, and of about 50 deacons, one understands the extent of his task: to organize a church in full development.

When Alexander died on Apr 17, 328 CE, Athanasius was the designated successor: while still a young deacon, "he was with Bishop Alexander most of the time and the latter held him in high esteem," to the point of taking him with him to the Ecumenical Synod of → Nicaea in 325 CE, where he "spoke out openly against the impiety of the followers of Arius' madness" (Athan. *Apol. sec.* 6,2). Following A. Möhler (1827) and G.C. Stead (1988), he may be assumed to have drafted the 324 CE encyclical letter

Henos Sōmatos, by which Alexander of Alexandria renews the condemnation of Arius and warns the eastern bishops against the Arians' petitions for support (→ Arianism).

However, the election of Athanasius was not without problems. First, he was a → deacon, whereas the bishop of Alexandria was traditionally chosen among the → priests of the city. Second, he was very young, whereas the canonical age was 30. Third, he was absent from Alexandria at the time of Alexander's death. Fourthly and above all, the Egyptian bishops were divided, since, during the → persecution of Diocletian, in 304 CE, Melitius, bishop of Lykopolis, had ordained priests and deacons for dioceses other than his own, without the permission of either the imprisoned ordinaries or the bishop of Alexandria, Peter. Now Athanasius, the *protégé* of Alexander, was the candidate of the bishops opposed to the integration of the Melitian hierarchy programmed at the Council of Nicaea, and, by that very fact, undesirable to the Melitian bishops. His election, on Jun 8, 328 CE, was probably the result of a coup: throughout all his life, Athanasius would show that he is "a man of power, prompt to use violent means" (Camplani, 2003, 219).

The Melitians then turned to the emperor. Their leader, → John Arkaph, was received in audience by → Constantine I thanks to Eusebius of Nicomedia and accused Athanasius of obstruction and violence against the Melitians. There followed a series of letters between the emperor and the young bishop, who finally had to answer a summons to the imperial court at the end of 331 CE. At Psamathia, near Nicomedia, Athanasius appeared before Constantine, and returned to Alexandria in the middle of the fast (→ Fasting/Abstinence) preparatory for the feast of → Easter 332 CE, bearing an imperial letter that acquitted him.

Aware of the fragility of his authority, Athanasius spent the first years of his episcopate visiting the vast territory that was subject to him: the Thebaid in 330 CE; the Libyan Pentapolis and the Ammoniaca in 331–332 CE; the Delta in 333–334 CE. Throughout his career, the bishop would tour Egypt, particularly attentive to attracting the good graces of the monastic milieu, then in full development: → Antony the Great and → Pachomius of Tabennese would offer him their support.

The adversaries of Athanasius did not stand down. In 333–334 CE, he was summoned to the Synod of Caesarea (Palestine), before which he refused to appear. Finally, the emperor himself summoned him to appear before the Synod of Tyre, in Jul 335 CE, which placed him under arrest while it dispatched a commission of inquiry in the Mareotis. Athanasius fled and arrived at Constantinople on Oct 29 to plead his cause before the emperor. Constantine, who had just recommended to the bishops of the Synod of Tyre to receive in their communion Arius and his followers, exiled Athanasius, who left for Trier on Nov 7.

In response to his condemnation, Athanasius was going to bind his cause to that of the Council of → Nicaea: while his adversaries wanted to condemn him for apparently disciplinary reasons, it was actually because they wanted to undo the theological decisions of Nicaea against Arius' Christology. Indeed, they had already condemned the other great bishops of the council, Eustathius of Antioch and → Marcellus of Ancyra, and had just received the partisans of Arius at the Synod of Jerusalem of September 335 CE. According to Athanasius, the whole affair was simply a new attempt to impose Arianism on the churches. In fact, after the death of Constantine (May 22, 337 CE) and the return of Athanasius to Alexandria (Nov 23, 337 CE), the bishop signed his first anti-Arian work: the tenth festal letter, announcing the date of Easter for 338 CE. At the synod which he organized that year in Alexandria, Athanasius denounced a collusion between the Melitians and the Arians. The eastern bishops opposed to Athanasius then named Gregory of Cappadocia bishop of Alexandria, which made his entry in Alexandria in spring 339 CE, with the support of the prefect of Egypt. Athanasius escaped an attempted arrest during the Easter vigil and left Alexandria on Apr 16, 339 CE, to take refuge in Rome. There, together with Marcellus of Ancyra, he enjoyed the support of bishop Julius, who convened a synod in March 341 CE to overturn the decisions of Tyre. This second exile was probably the occasion of the drafting of the important *Discourses against the Arians*. Athanasius also succeeded in conciliating the western emperor, Constans, who pressured his brother → Constantius II to let Athanasius return to Alexandria in 346 CE, after the death of his competitor Gregory.

After the death of Constans in 350 CE, the emperor Constantius, ever more powerful, managed to have Athanasius condemned in → Arles in 353 CE and in → Milan in 355 CE, while exiling recalcitrant western bishops like → Eusebius of Vercelli, Dionysius of Milan, or Lucifer of Cagliari (→ Luciferians) and, in 356 CE, → Hilary of Poitiers. Finally, Athanasius was forced by public force to flee in February 356 CE, leaving the place to a new competitor, George of Cappadocia, while remaining in hiding in Egypt.

The following years were marked by profound transformations in the theological horizon, because of the emergence of a new theological proposal, that of Aëtius and → Eunomius of Cyzicus: anomoeism. Athanasius took up the pen again and brandished the Nicene symbol (*De decretis Nicaenae synodi* [*On the Decisions of the Council of Nicaea*]; *De sententia Dionysii* [*On the Opinion of Dionysius*]) against the majority known as homoean who had been victorious at the Synod of → Sirmium (357 CE) and at the synods of the end of 359 CE, and attempted an alliance with the homoeusians gathered around Basil of Ancyra (*De synodis* [*On the Councils of Rimini and Seleucia*]). He took advantage of the death of Constantius II (Nov 3, 361 CE) and the lynching of his adversary George (Dec 24, 361 CE) to return to Alexandria (February 362 CE). Again, as in 338 CE and in 346 CE, Athanasius gathered his Egyptian and Libyan suffragans in synod to recompose the unity. This synod of the Lent 362 CE was also the occasion, for Athanasius, to extend his policy of ecclesiastical unification (*Epistula ad Rufinianum* [*Letter to Rufinianus*]) around the Nicene formula beyond his own territory: the Alexandrian, at the conclusion of the synod, addressed a letter to the Antiochians (*Tomus ad Antiochenos* [*Tome to the People of Antioch*]) who remained faithful to the Nicene positions of Eustathius of Antioch, who had been deposed of his seat at the end of the years 320 CE, and were opposed to the partisans of Meletius, bishop of Antioch since spring 360 CE. He analyzed the theological positions of the two camps, proving their compatibility, and proposed a reconciliation based on his own interpretation of the Nicene formula. This solution would be gradually adopted in the following two decades.

After a fourth exile decided by the emperor → Julian the Apostate in October 362 CE, Athanasius gained the favor of the new emperor Jovian (*Epistula ad Jovianum* [*Letter to Jovian*], autumn 363), and returned to Alexandria. Exiled one last time by the emperor → Valens, he remained hidden in the city between May 365 and February 366 CE. In his last years, he was an authority in the party of those who, like the young bishop of Caesarea of Cappadocia, Basil, militated in favor of the faith of Nicaea (→ Basil of Caesarea). However, it was around Meletius of Antioch that the new Nicene majority would be constituted, with the support of the theology of Basil and his friend → Gregory of Nazianzus. It finally triumphed at the Synod of Constantinople of 380 CE, seven years after the death of Athanasius on May 2, 373 CE.

1. Works

With the exception of the double apologetic treatise *Against the Pagans* (*Contra gentes*, CPG 2090; → Apologetics) and *On the Incarnation of the Word* (*De incarnatione*, CPG 2091), considered to be an early work, Athanasius' written work is primarily occasional: in addition to the *Festal Letters* (*Epistulae festales*, CPG 2102), annual letters in which the bishop of Alexandria announced the date of the feast of Easter, encouraging the faithful to conversion and penance (→ Penitence/Penance) and informing of new episcopal ordinations in his territory, the majority of his writings adopt the epistolary form and polemical tone. The main purpose of these letters was the defense of the legitimacy of Athanasius' episcopate against those who sought to depose him. The strategy applied by Athanasius from 338 CE onwards consisted in moving from the canonical and ecclesiastical field to the theological field, thanks to the reductive amalgamation of all his opponents, in particular, the Egyptian Christians under the Melitian movement and the eastern bishops dominated by Eusebius of Nicomedia who, in the years following the Synod of Nicaea, obtained the disgrace of the victors of 325 CE.

A first group of polemical works offers a narrative and documentary treatment of Athanasius' setbacks: after the expulsion of 339 CE, the *Encyclical Letter* (*Epistula encyclica*, CPG 2124) first tells the bishops of the world about the heavy-handed replacement of Athanasius by Gregory of Cappadocia. The *Letter to the Monks* (*H. Ar. ep.*, CPG 2126) once believed to

be joined to the *History of the Arians* and the *Letter to Serapion on the Death of Arius* (*Epistula ad Serapionem de more Arii*, CPG 2125) probably date from the same period. Two letters sent from the Synod of Sardica (343 CE) have been preserved in Latin translation: a *Letter to the Presbyterate of Alexandria and Parembole* (*Ep. Al. Par.*, CPG 2111) and a *Letter to the Church of Mareotis* (*Ep. Mar.*, CPG 2112).

After the expulsion of 356 CE, Athanasius composed several writings to defend himself: the *Letter to the Bishops of Egypt and Libya* (*Epistula ad episcopos Aegypti et Libyae*, CPG 2092), written between Jun 15, 356, and Feb 24, 357 CE, the *Apology to Constantius* (*Apologia ad Constantium*, CPG 2129), which may have been begun in the mid-350s CE, to be published in the summer of 357 CE, and the *Apology on His Flight* (*Apologia de fuga sua*, CPG 2122), which must be contemporary with, or slightly later than, the *Apology to Constantius*.

The *Apology Against the Arians*, also known as the *Second Apology* (*Apologia secunda*, CPG 2123), published at the same time, was probably composed over time. It is a vast collection of pieces for the prosecution (against the Arians) or for the defense (in favor of Athanasius), supposed to instruct the tribunal of Athanasius' rehabilitation. The *History of the Arians* (*Historia Arianorum ad monachos*, CPG 2127), the beginning of which seems to have been lost, is a more ambitious text: it is no longer a compilation of documents, but a continuous account of events from the Synod of Tyre (335 CE) to Athanasius' third exile.

A second group of works defend not so much Athanasius himself as the faith he championed: the first two *Discourses against the Arians* (*Orationes contra Arianos*, CPG 2093), probably composed during his Roman sojourn in the early 340s CE, refute a collection of Arian fragments, slogans, and scriptural interpretations. The third *Discourse*, a continuation of the first two, begins by refuting a new set of Arian scriptural interpretations. The remainder of the discourse deepens Athanasian Christology, reflecting on the weaknesses of Christ's human nature, which suggests a later date of composition. The fourth *Discourse* is not authentic.

The letter *On the Decisions of the Council of Nicaea* (*De decretis Nicaenae synodi*, CPG 2120), or more exactly: "That the Synod of Nicaea, having detected the trickery of the Eusebians, set forth in a manner appropriate and in conformity with piety the decisions taken against the Arian heresy" is a direct response to the Synod of Sirmium of 357 CE, whose formula of faith implicitly condemns that of Nicaea. The later works in which Athanasius would interpret and defend the Nicene formula all take up the arguments of this initial letter, which also includes an appendix with various documents, in particular the letter that → Eusebius of Caesarea wrote from the Council of Nicaea in 325 CE. The letter *On the Opinion of Dionysius* (*De sententia Dionysii*, CPG 2121) returns to one of the ancient authors invoked in the controversy, Dionysius of Alexandria, showing that his letter of *Defense and Apology* does not reject, but on the contrary, accepts the use of the term "consubstantial" to qualify the relationship between the Father and the Son.

The *Letter on the Synods of Rimini and Seleucia of Isauria* (*De synodis*, CPG 2128), composed between the end of 359 and December 361 CE, intends to reveal the true intention of the two synods, that is, to reaffirm the exclusive validity of the Nicene formula, and to prove the falsity of those who ultimately imposed a homoean formula of faith, while reaching out to Basil of Ancyra and his allies, the homoeusians. The inclusion of a collection of fragments of Arius and his followers and of formulae of faith written by a dozen synods between 335 and 361 CE makes the letter an essential historical document.

On his return from exile in 362 CE, Athanasius defined his theological position in several essential documents, already mentioned above: the *Tome to the Antiochians* (*Tomus ad Antiochenos*, CPG 2134), the *Letter to Rufinianus of Thessalonica* (*Epistula ad Rufinianum*, CPG 2107) and the *Letter to Jovian* (*Epistula ad Jovianum*, CPG 2135). The *Catholic Letter* (*Ep. cath.*, CPG 2241), dating from the same period, is pseudepigraphic. The *Letter to the Africans* (*Epistula ad Afros episcopos*, CPG 2133), written in the name of the provincial synod of autumn 371 CE, reminds the addressees of this theological position: the faith of the Catholic church is summarized in the Nicene formula, and not in that which the emperor Constantius II sought to impose on the two synods of the end of 359 CE.

The four *Letters to Serapion* (*Epistulae ad Serapionem*, CPG 2094), probably written during the third

exile (357–362 CE), open a new theological field: that of the ontological status of the Holy Spirit. The letters *to Epictetus, Bishop of Corinth* (*Epistula ad Epictetum*, CPG 2095), *to Adelphios, Bishop of Onuphis* (*Epistula ad Adelphium*, CPG 2098) and *to Maximos the Philosopher* (*Epistula ad Maximum*, CPG 2100) date from the last years of Athanasius' life and refute various Christological positions, in particular those soon to be attributed to → Apollinaris of Laodicea.

In addition to the festal letters, already mentioned, various particular letters are preserved: there remains a fragment in Latin of a *Letter to Potamios of Lisbon* (CPG 2109), one of the participants of the Synod of Sirmium of 357 CE. The letter will bear fruit since Potamius will write to Athanasius to implicitly condemn the formula of the synod in which he had participated. Two *Letters to Lucifer of Cagliari* preserved in Latin (CPG 2232) must belong to the same context of the late 350s CE. Lucifer, who had opposed the condemnation of Athanasius at the Council of Milan in 355 CE, was sent into exile in the East, and resided in the Thebaid. Athanasius asks Lucifer for a copy of his treatise *Quia absentem nemo debet iudicare nec damnare siue de Athanasio* (CPL 114), and then thanks him for sending it. In the short *Letter to the Monks* (*Epistula ad monachos*, CPG 2108), preserved in a Latin version and Greek fragments, Athanasius warns his correspondents against Arian or crypto-Arian visitors. The beginning of a *Letter to Diodoros of Tyre* (CPG 2164) is quoted in Latin by Facundus of Hermiane (Fac. *Def.* 4.2.10–11). In it, Athanasius approves the election of the recipient, ordained by Paulinus of Antioch between 362 and 365 CE. The letters *to John and Antiochos* (*Epistula ad Joannem et Antiochum presbyteros*, CPG 2130), and *to the Cappadocian Palladios* (*Epistula ad Palladium*, CPG 2131) document the relationship between Athanasius and Basil, bishop of Caesarea since 370 CE: they show that Athanasius recognizes the authority of the young bishop, to whom he refers his correspondents.

The ascetical texts (→ Asceticism) include what is perhaps the jewel in the crown of Athanasius' work: his *Life of Antony* (*Vita Antonii*, CPG 2101), composed shortly after the death of the Egyptian anchorite, in January 356 CE, at a very advanced age, immediately became a bestseller and a literary model for the whole later hagiographic tradition (→ Hagiography).

There is still a long *Letter to the Virgins* in Coptic translation (*CPG* 2147), and the fragment in Arabic translation of another *Letter to the Virgins* (*CPG* 2154); still in Coptic, *Instructions and Precepts for Virgins* (*CPG* 2149) and various other fragments (*CPG* 2150) whose authenticity is difficult to corroborate; in Syriac, a *Letter to Virgins Who Had Gone to Pray in Jerusalem* (*CPG* 2146), and a *Treatise on Virginity* (*CPG* 2145); finally, in Greek, the fragment of a *Letter of Consolation* (*CPG* 2162) addressed to the virgins molested in the spring of 356 CE for their fidelity to Athanasius (→ Virgin/Virginity).

The authenticity of the *Letter on Charity and Temperance* (*CPG* 2151), because of its resemblance to the Pacomachean *Catechesis to a Resentful Monk* (CSCO 159, 14–24), is dubious. Other fragments in Coptic concern more generally the ascetic life, such as those of a homiletic style writing *On Penance* (*CPG* 2152) or various other fragments (*CPG* 2153), to which one must add a fragment in Greek taken from a *Letter on Illness and Health* (*CPG* 2160).

The *Letter to Amun* (*Epistula ad Amun*, *CPG* 2106), preserved in its entirety and in Greek, dated perhaps before February 356 CE, has a rather circumstantial theme: Athanasius answers a question about the moral value of sperm ejaculations during sleep. The *Letter to Dracontios* (*Epistula ad Dracontium*, *CPG* 2132) is addressed, in 353 CE, to a monk who refused his election to the episcopal see of Hermopolis. A fragment of letter (*Epistula ad Orsisium I, CPG* 2103) as well as a letter (*Epistula ad Orsisium II, CPG* 2104) are addressed to Horsiesos, the disciple of Pachomius, in 368 CE. These letters testify to Athanasius' attention to monastic communities, not only for spiritual reasons, but also for reasons of ecclesiastical government. The *Letter to Marcellinus* (*Epistula ad Marcellinum*, *CPG* 2097), in which Athanasius instructs his correspondent to use the psalter in his daily life, is the only exegetical work of Athanasius with undeniable authenticity. The commentary on the Psalms attributed to him is not authentic.

2. Theology

If one accepts the hypothesis of an early dating for the double treatise *Against the Pagans* and *On the Incarnation of the Word*, and that of an intervention of Athanasius in the drafting of the encyclical of Alexander of Alexandria renewing the condemnation of Arius in 324 CE, one can situate the young bishop Athanasius within the framework of post-Origenian Alexandrian theology (→ Origenism/Origenist Controversy). The reference to Origen is explicit (Athan. *Decr.* 27.1; *Ep. Serap.* 4.5.1), and Athanasius' preoccupation with the free will of the human being in the treatise *Against the Pagans* is a clear legacy of the great Alexandrian. However, Origen's theology was subject to criticism and reinterpretation in the second half of the 3rd and early 4th centuries CE. Athanasius therefore receives it through their filter.

a. Christology

The closest influence on the young Athanasius was probably Alexander of Alexandria (→ Christology). Of particular note is the manner in which Alexander emphasizes the difference between the → Word and the creatures, asserting that the Word is the "authentic" (Gk γνήσιος/ *gnēsios*) and "proper" (Gk ἴδιος/ *idios*) Son of the Father (Alex. Alex. *Urk.* 14.32). The adjective ἴδιος ("proper"), an allusion to Rom 8:32, would become an Athanasian watchword. Different from creatures, the Son is "one" with the Father (John 10:30). This unity is interpreted by Alexander as a "similitude" of "the indistinguishable image of the Father" (Alex. Alex. *Urk.* 14.38). Athanasius uses this expression in his early works (Athan. C. *Gent.* 41.1; 46.8; *Ar.* 1.26.4; 2.33.3; 3.5.3; 3.11), as an interpretation of the controversial Greek adjective ὁμοούσιος/*homoousios* ("consubstantial") of the Nicene formula, which was seldom used by the bishop before 357 CE (Athan. *Ar.* 1.9.2): the similitude must be considered at the level of the "substance" itself (Gk οὐσία/*ousia*; → Ousia), not of the will (Athan. *Ar.* 1.20.1; 1.21.2; 3.26.1). Yet, when the group of bishops led by Basil of Ancyra at the Synod of → Ancyra in 358 CE brandishes the Greek expression ὅμοιος κατ' οὐσίαν ("similar according to substance") as an alternative to ὁμοούσιος, Athanasius considers this interpretation insufficient and goes so far as to speak of an identity (Athan. *Decr.* 20.3; *Syn.* 53.2); however, he never interprets this identity as a unicity of substance. In Athanasius' interpretation, ὁμοούσιος does not apply to the Trinity as a whole, namely as a "Trinity which is one οὐσία" (Ps.-Athan. *Ep. cath.* 7; Didy. *Comm. Zach.* 3.261; see also Pseudo-Serapion of Thmuis *Ep.*

mon. 11; Ps.-Bas. *Eun.* 5., PG 29, 712), but to the relation between the Son and the Father, that is, the generation, as a relation of origin and similitude at the level of the very being of the two terms of the relation.

The consubstantiality of the Son with the Father allows to cut off any ambiguity about his begetting: the Son is "begotten" (Gk γεννητός), not "come into being" (Gk γενητός, Athan. *Ar.* 1.31.4) in line with the Nicene formula: "begotten, not made." The combination of this definition of the Son as begotten and his consubstantiality offers what can be considered Athanasius' Christological slogan: the Word is "the own begotten entity of the substance of the Father" (Gk *idion tēs ousias tou Patros gennēma*, Athan. *Ar.* 1.9.2).

The Logos-Christology inherited from Origen presented a consequence: the mediating status of the Word tended to reduce him to a "servant to the creator" (Or. *Comm. Jo.* 2.104), a mere "instrument" (Gk ὄργανον) in the hands of God (Eus. *Dem. ev.* 4.4.2). In this context, it is difficult to maintain at the same time an ontological equality between God and his Word. Therefore, Athanasius rejects the notion of a "subordinate servant" (Athan. *Ar.* 2.24.2–31) and reserves the application of the concept of "instrument" to the human body assumed by the Word (Athan. *Inc.* 8.3; 9.2; 42.6–7; 43.6; 44.2–3; 45.1; *Ar.* 3.31.1; 35.1; 53.3). As a result, the Word is not defined by its mediating function in the coming into being of the world, but as a Son in eternal relationship with a Father, issuing from him in a procession *sui generis*. This idea opens the way to the definition of the persons in the Trinity through the key concept of relation (Gk πρός τι), as Arius had reluctantly noticed (Opitz, 1934–1935, 6.4). Indeed, for Athanasius, "Father," "Son," and "Spirit," as relative names, are the only proper and exclusive names of each of the three persons of the Trinity: "Absolutely all that one can find said about the Father, one can find it said also about the Son, except being Father" (Athan. *Syn.* 49.5); "applied to the divinity, and only in this case, the Father is properly Father, and the Son is properly Son" (Athan. *Ar.* 1.21.10). The concept of an immanent Trinity begins to emerge.

b. Trinity

In spite of his insistence on the unity of the → Trinity, Athanasius never speaks of a single οὐσία. Actually, for him, οὐσία means "being," "existence," "subsistence," and is synonymous with hypostasis (ὑπόστασις; Athan. *Ep. Afr.* 4.3). Therefore, it is uncountable, and whether there is one or three *ousiai* (οὐσίαι) or *hypostaseis* (ὑποστάσεις) in the Trinity is not a relevant question. In the *Tome to the Antiochians* in 362 CE, Athanasius recognized that the formulae "one *hypostasis*" and "three ὑποστάσεις/*hypostaseis*" are compatible, as long as they serve to express "the identity of nature" (Athan. *Tom.* 6.1–2), and the real existence of the Son and the Holy Spirit (*Tom.* 5.3–4), while Athanasius prefers the formula: "one divinity in a Trinity" (Athan. *Ar.* 1.18.1; 3.15.15; *Ep. Serap.* 1.2.3 passim; *Ep. Jov.* 4.2).

c. Pneumatology

In the *Letters to Serapion*, Athanasius extends the demonstration of the consubstantiality between the Father and the Son to the → Holy Spirit, through a transitive reasoning: "the Son is 'image of the invisible Father' (Col 1:15), and the Spirit is image of the Son" (Athan. *Ep. Serap.* 3.3.3):

> If the Son, since he is of the Father, is the proper Son of his substance, the Spirit, since he is said to be "of God" (1 Cor 2:12), is necessarily the proper Spirit of the Son according to substance. (Athan. *Ep. Serap.* 1.5.2)

This transitivity of reasoning prevents Athanasius from conceiving the procession of the Holy Spirit in its specificity. Athanasius never uses the word and concept of "procession" (Gk ἐκπόρευσις), as Gregory of Nazianzus soon will (Greg. Naz. *Or.* 31.8). This understanding might have led him to emphasize the Father as the direct origin of the Spirit. Instead, Athanasius always expresses the procession of the Spirit in relation to that of the Son, in propositions that will be interpreted retrospectively as supporting the *Filioque*. The Holy Spirit "shines forth, is sent and given by the Word who is confessed to come from the Father" (*Ep. Serap.* 1.20.4).

d. Incarnation

In the *Tome to the Antiochians*, Athanasius describes a Christological conflict that arose in Antioch at the time of the Synod of Nicaea and will be the focus of the next 100 years of theological debate: that of the integrity of Christ's humanity and its relationship with his divinity. The question was that of the mutability and passibility ascribed to Christ in the Scripture. Athanasius maintains that this passibility is to be referred to the human nature of Christ, which includes a (human) soul, and not to his divine nature (Athan. *Decr.* 8–9; *Ar.* 3.26–58). The argument is soteriological. Whereas only a god can really save humankind from its fall in death and corruptibility and restore the divine image according to which it was created in the beginning (Athan. *Inc.* 7.4; *Ar.* 2.69–70; *Ep. Adelph.* 8), nonetheless, only by making his own (Gk ἰδιοποεῖν) a body similar to ours (*Inc.* 8.2–3; *Ar.* 3.31–32), that is, including a human soul and intellect (Athan. *Tom.* 7.2; *Ep. Epict.* 7.1), can the Word of God really save mankind. However, this distinction between the two natures is balanced by a prefiguration of the Chalcedonian definition: "the same" acts "humanly and divinely" (*Tom.* 7.3).

3. Soteriology and Anthropology

Athanasius fundamentally conceives salvation as a new creation (Athan. *Ar.* 2.65). Consequently, humanity can only be recreated by that which created them. Nevertheless, this new creation is not simply a restoration of the primary status of mankind. It goes beyond:

> Mankind was perfected in the Word and restored, as it had come into being in the beginning, and rather with a major grace, since, resurrected from the dead, we do not fear death anymore. (Athan. *Ar.* 2.67.3)

Adam, before the → fall, had received grace as something that could be lost (→ Adam and Eve). The incarnation of the Word fixed grace in human nature, so that "grace should become inalienable and be kept stable for men" (*Ar.* 2.68.4). In this context, the new creation of humanity means their participation in the divine nature, their "deification" (Gk θεοποίησις/*theopoiēsis*; *Ar.* 2.70; Hess, 1996). Athanasius' formulae of exchange, possibly inherited from → Irenaeus of Lyon, are famous: the Word himself "became man, in order that we ourselves should be deified" (Athan. *Inc.* 54.3; *Ar.* 1.39.1; 3.34.6; 3.38.1; *Ep. Adelph.* 4; → Soteriology; → Anthropology).

4. Posterity

Athanasius' defense of the Nicene formula made him the authoritative figure of the new theological trend that gradually emerged during the 360s CE, based on the acceptance of this formula. But at the same time, the conceptual distinction between *ousia* and *hypostasis*, elaborated by the Cappadocian theologians (→ Cappadocians), eclipsed Athanasius' Trinitarian propositions.

Athanasius' literary influence during his lifetime came mainly from his ascetical writings. Eventually, his biography of Antony became a bestseller: it was translated into Latin almost as soon as published. Augustine describes its spiritual impact on his friend Pontitianus in a famous page of his *Confessions* (Aug. *Conf.* 8.6.15).

Nevertheless, Athanasius' Christological reflections gained importance at the occasion of the Council of → Ephesus (431 CE). The party of Cyril of Alexandria included a citation of the third *Discourse Against the Arians* and one of the *Letter to Epictetus* in the patristic (→ Patrology/Patristics) anthology they presented during the council, and the *Letter to Epictetus* was alleged by John of Antioch and his party as an authority to be added to the formula of Nicaea in their successive proposals of reconciliation with Cyril after the council. Athanasius became a touchstone in the subsequent debates on the relation between the human and the divine nature in the incarnate Word. In the same period, the three great historians of the church, → Socrates Scholasticus, Sozomen, and → Theodoret of Cyrrhus, used Athanasius' apologetical writings as a source of documentation for their works, transmitting to posterity the biased account of the champion of Nicaea.

Historiography

The main source of historical information on Athanasius is Athanasius himself. His very apologetic point of view was taken up by the three great historians of the beginning of the 5th century CE, Socrates, Sozomen, and Theodoret of Cyrrhus, and already by Gregory of Nazianzus in the panegyric delivered in Constantinople on May 2, 380 CE: Athanasius is one of "those who fought for the truth" (Greg. Naz. *Or.* 21.37), "the stele of the church" (*Or.* 21.26) who defended the Trinity against those, Arians and → Pneumatomachi, who tried to divide it. The decrees of deposition by various synods of eastern bishops, the edicts of exile promulgated by the emperors, were not brought against his own person but against the Trinity (*Or.* 21.27).

The attribution to Athanasius of the symbol of faith *Quicumque*, which is proclaimed daily in many western liturgical traditions, ensured the transmission of this interpretation throughout the Middle Ages. On the threshold of the modern era, J. Gerhardt, in his *Patrologia*, still presents Athanasius as *Arianorum hostis acerrimus* (Gerhardt, 1653, 204).

On the other hand, in an unpublished study from the early 1690s, I. Newton radically criticizes the Athanasian version of the Arian controversy, questioning its veracity.

The monograph of the Tübingen theologian A. Möhler on Athanasius (1827) opened a new period of scholarly research on Athanasius, marked by J.H. Newman's study *The Arians of the Fourth Century* (1833), followed by J.H. Newman's English translation of much of Athanasius' work (1842–1844). The studies of E. Schwartz, published between 1904 and 1911, paved the way for the great work of critical editing by H.G. Opitz, published between 1934 and 1941, and continued from the 1990s by a team of German scholars led by M. Tetz and H.C. Brennecke.

The publication of Papyrus London 6.1914 (https://papyri.info/ddbdp/p.lond;6;1914) by H.I. Bell in 1924, which seems to sketch the portrait of an intolerant and violent, calculating, and manipulative bishop (see the nuanced interpretation of Hauben, 2012), directs attention to Athanasius' role as a religious leader (see Schneemelcher, 1951–1952; Barnes, 1993).

J. Roldanus' monograph (Roldanus, 1968) on Athanasius' anthropology is one of the few exceptions among this line of investigation, as is C. Kannengiesser's straightforward theological interest (Kannengiesser, 1990).

In 1996, A. Martin's dissertation, *Athanasius of Alexandria and the Church of Egypt*, abandoning the question of "whether Athanasius was 'a gangster' or 'a saint,'" focuses on Athanasius' "relationship to the Church of Alexandria and Egypt" (Martin, 1996, 2), while D.M. Gwynn's monograph (Gwynn, 2006), refines the critique of the Athanasian interpretation of the dogmatic evolution of the years 320–370 CE. D. Brakke (1995), carefully studying Athanasius' ascetical corpus and assessing its authenticity, shows the close relationship Athanasius succeeded in forging with the monastic communities in Egypt.

In this new historiographical framework, Athanasius' theology is reassessed as a contribution, in polemical dialogue with others, to the elaboration of a theoretical model to describe the relationship between the Father, the Son and the Holy Spirit (Anatolios, 1998; Ayres, 2004; Morales, 2006).

Main Editions and Translations

B. Athanasii archiepiscopi Alexandrini Opera quae reperiuntur omnia [...], *ex officina commeliniana*, 2 vols., Heidelberg, 1601.

Camplani, A., *Atanasio di Alessandria, Lettere festali: Anonimo, Indice delle Lettere festali*, Milan, 2003. ET: *Select Writings and Letters of Athanasius, Bishop of Alexandria*, ed. & trans. A. Robertson, NPNF, vol. II/4, Oxford, 1892; repr., Grand Rapids, 1991.

Migne, J.P., ed., *Patrologie grecque* 25–28, Paris, 1884–1887.

Athanasius Werke, Berlin, 1934–2016; for the description of the contents of each volume, see https://www.degruyter.com/view/serial/16029.

Athanasius werke, III/1.1–2, *Urkunden zur Geschichte des arianischen Streites 318–328*, H.G. Opitz, ed., Berlin, 1934–1935.

Montfaucon, B. de, & J. Lopin, *Sancti Patris nostri Athanasii archiep. Alexandrini Opera omnia quae exstant*, 3 vols., Paris, 1698.

Bibliography

Anatolios, K., *Athanasius: The Coherence of His Thought*, London, 1998.

Ayres, L., *Nicaea and Its Legacy: An Approach to Fourth Century Trinitarian Theology*, Oxford, 2004.

Barnes, T.D., *Athanasius and Constantius: Theology and Politics in the Constantinian Empire*, Cambridge MA, 1993.

Brakke, D., *Athanasius and Asceticism*, Baltimore, 1995.

Bell, H. I., *Jews and Christians in Egypt: The Jewish Troubles in Alexandria and the Athanasian Controversy*, London British Museum, 1924.

Butterweck, C., *Athanasius von Alexandrien: Bibliographie*, Westhofen, 1995.

Gemeinhardt, P., ed., *Athanasius Handbuch*, Tübingen, 2011.

Gerhardt, J., *Patrologia sive de primitivae ecclesiae christianae doctorum vita et lucubrationibus opus posthumum*, Jena, 1653.

Gwynn, D.M., *The Eusebians: The Polemic of Athanasius of Alexandria and the Construction of the 'Arian Controversy,'* Oxford, 2006.

Gwynn, D.M., *Athanasius of Alexandria: Bishop, Theologian, Ascetic, Father*, Oxford, 2012.

Hauben, H., "The Papyrus London VI (P. Jews) 1914 in Its Historical Context (May 335)," in: P. van Nuffelen, ed., *Studies on the Meletian Schism in Egypt (AD 306–335)*, Farnham, 2012.

Hess, H., "The Place of Divinization in Athanasian Soteriology," *StPatr* 26, 1996, 369–374.

Kannengiesser, C., *Le Verbe de Dieu selon Athanase d'Alexandrie*, Tournai, 1990.

Leemans, J., "Thirteen Years of Athanasius Research (1985–1998): A Survey and Bibliography," *SE* 39, 2000, 105–217.

Martin, A., *Athanase d'Alexandrie et l'église d'Egypte au ive siècle (328–373)*, Rome, 1996.

Möhler, A., *Athanasius der Grosse und die Kirche seiner Zeit besonders im Kampfe mit dem Arianismus*, Mainz, 1827.

Morales, X., *La théologie trinitaire d'Athanase d'Alexandrie*, Paris, 2006.

Müller, G., *Lexicon Athanasianum*, Berlin, 1952.

Newman, J.H., *The Arians of the Fourth Century: Their Doctrine, Temper, and Conduct, Chiefly as Exhibited in the Councils of the Church, Between AD 325, and AD 381*, London, 1833.

Newman, J.H., *Select Treatises of St. Athanasius in Controversy with the Arians*, 2 vols., Oxford, 1842 & 1844.

Newton, I., *Paradoxical Questions Concerning the Morals and Actions of Athanasius and his Followers;* https://www.newtonproject.ox.ac.uk/view/texts/normalized/THEM00117 and https://www.newtonproject.ox.ac.uk/view/texts/diplomatic/THEM00010; consulted Dec 21, 2022.

Roldanus, J., *Le Christ et l'homme dans la théologie d'Athanase d'Alexandrie: Étude de la conjonction de sa conception de l'homme avec sa christologie*, Leiden, 1968.

Schneemelcher, W., "Athanasius von Alexandrien als Theologe und als Kirchenpolitiker," *ZNW* 43, 1951–1952, 242–256.

Schwartz, E., ed., *Gesammelte Schriften*, vol. III: *Zur Geschichte des Athanasius*, Berlin, 1959.

Stead, G.C., "Athanasius' Earliest Written Work," *JThS* 39, 1988, 76–91.

Tetz, M., *Athanasiana. Zu Leben und Lehre des Athanasius*, Berlin, 1995.

Online up-to-date bibliography at:

http://www.athanasius.theologie.uni-erlangen.de/bibliographie.html.

XAVIER MORALES

Atheism/Atheist

The word "atheist" comes from the Greek adjective ἄθεος/*atheos* which originally meant "godless." This meaning of the word persisted, but in the 4th century BCE it also took on the additional sense of disbelief in the existence of the gods. Atheism of this sort is hard to detect in antiquity, with limited evidence for anyone voicing openly atheistic statements. Atheism nonetheless played a role in philosophical and religious debates, including those involving Christians and Jews. Christians were accused of being atheists and they in turn leveled the same accusations against Jews, pagans, and other Christians they deemed heretics. In almost all cases, the people accused of being atheists disputed this charge vigorously.

1. Atheism in Classical and Hellenistic Greece

In the Greco-Roman world, atheism reached its apogee in Athens during the late 5th and early 4th centuries BCE (Sedley, 2013). Intellectuals in this city built on earlier developments of Ionian philosophy and the skepticism its proponents displayed toward the anthropomorphic depictions of the gods in Homer and Hesiod (e.g. Xenoph. *Frgms.* 29–33; Graham, 2010). Skepticism of this sort took on fuller form in the work of Protagoras of Abdera, an intellectual star who made a great impact in Athens as an associate of Pericles. Protagoras' *On the Gods* expressed uncertainty about whether the gods existed, a view that may have gone beyond simple agnosticism and reached outright atheism (Prot. *Frgms.* 29–31; Graham, 2010).

Controversy about all these ideas resulted, and charges were made against intellectuals for holding impious or atheistic views. A seer named Diopeithes was apparently responsible for a decree directed against the intellectual associates of Pericles who held skeptical, if not atheistic, views about the gods (Plut. *Per.* 32.2). The decree focused on ἀσέβεια/ *asebeia* ("impiety"), a word that could be applied in flexible ways against any form of religious nonconformity. Two of the first intellectuals to be tried for impiety were Anaxagoras, who was singled out for his connections to Pericles (Diod. Sic. *Bib.* 12.39.2; D.L. 2.12), and the poet Diagoras of Melos, whose critique of the → Eleusinian Mysteries made him a target (Winiarczyk, 2016). Late in the 4th century BCE, the philosopher Theodorus of Cyrene was also tried for *asebeia* (Philo *Prob.* 127). Theodorus may have expressed atheistic views, publishing a work *On the Gods* that likely followed in the tradition of Protagoras (D.L. 2.97).

These accusations provide context for the works of Plato and his account of the death of Socrates. Socrates' trial in 399 BCE was based on the decree of Diopeithes about *asebeia*. At the trial, Socrates claimed that he was not *atheos* (Plato *Apol.* 26c), in the process revealing that the word had by this time gained the sense of disbelief in the gods. Plato's account of Socrates' trial helps to demonstrate that atheism in a modern sense was at that time generally recognized.

As we move into the Hellenistic period, accusations of atheism persisted. These focused especially on the philosophical school founded by → Epicurus, though he was himself critical of others charged with atheism, including Diagoras (Phil. *Piet.* 19.519–41). The author Euhemerus was also called an atheist for his suggestion that the beings worshipped as gods were originally human kings (Winiarczyk, 2013).

The Hellenistic period's major contribution to subsequent ideas about atheism was the development of doxographical lists of atheists. The most influential of these lists seems to have been made in the 2nd century BCE by the Skeptic philosopher Clitomachus of Carthage (Winiarczyk, 1976). Subsequent discussions of the history of atheism drew from Clitomachus' list of atheists, which included Diagoras of Melos, Theodorus of Cyrene, Euhemerus, Protagoras, Epicurus, and others (Sex.Emp. *Math.* 9.50–8; Cic. *Nat. d.* 1.1.63). This list of reputed atheists reappeared in the doxographical collections used by scholars in the Roman Empire (Ps.-Plut.

Plac. philos. 880d–882a; Runia, 1996). Together with Plato's works, the doxographical collections were fundamental to subsequent discussions of atheism.

2. Atheism in the Roman Empire

Open professions of atheism are lacking in the extant epigraphic, literary, and papyrological evidence from the Roman Empire. A lack of evidence, however, provides only an argument from silence in support of the claim that atheistic beliefs were rare or nonexistent (Whitmarsh, 2015, 216). As it is, extant literary sources provide many signs of skeptical or irreverent attitudes about the gods, notably in the works of the satirist Lucian of Samosata (e.g. *Diologi mortuorum – Dialogues of the Dead*). The Roman Empire also provides much evidence indicative of continuing controversy about atheism, and accusations of atheistic beliefs made against members of rival religious or philosophical groups. This includes charges about the supposedly atheistic views of the Epicurean school of philosophy (e.g. Diog. Oen. *Frgm.* 16; Smith, 1993).

a. Judaism

Judaism was another target for charges about atheism. Much of the evidence for these charges comes from the works of Jewish authors, but atheism does seem to have been one area of criticism made against → Judaism by Greeks and Romans. During the reign of Domitian, some Romans of senatorial rank were tried on charges of atheism in connection with their interests in Judaism, leading to the execution of the consul Flavius Clemens (Dio. *Hist. rom.* 67.14.1–3). From roughly the same period, Pliny the Elder remarked on the "insolence" (*contumelia*) of Jews toward the gods, hinting at an accusation of atheism (Plin. *Nat.* 13.46). → Flavius Josephus suggests that this was a charge explicitly brought against Jews by Apollonius Molon, a teacher of oratory in the 1st century BCE (Jos. *Apion.* 2.148). A similar charge may also have been made by the grammarian and poet Apion, again reported by Josephus (*Apion.* 2.65).

Philo of Alexandria reveals that Jews could also make accusations about atheism against their rivals. Atheism served for → Philo of Alexandria as a flexible label that could be applied to anything he deemed a challenge to the unique authority of God (Reynard, 2002). Polytheism of any sort consequently qualified as atheistic for Philo, on the grounds that it introduced rival and illegitimate gods (Philo *Praem.* 162; *Migr.* 69; *Fug.* 114). The animal worship practiced by Egyptians was especially atheistic on these grounds (e.g. Philo *Ebr.* 109–110), as was the effort of Caligula to declare himself a god (Philo *Legat.* 77). Philo even applied the same principle in his discussion of philosophical schools, labeling Epicureans, Stoics, and atomists as atheists (Philo *Aet.* 10). But, as a counterpoint to these critiques of philosophers, Philo found reason to praise the reputed atheist Theodorus of Cyrene, arguing that he was denying the Athenian gods, rather than God (Philo *Prob.* 130). Atheists from the classical period of Greece could consequently be redeployed as allies of monotheists (→ Monotheism) against polytheism, a pattern that continued for subsequent critics.

b. Early Christianity

Like Philo, early Christian authors drew heavily on the context of the Roman Empire and its fascination with the Greek past when they engaged with atheism. Little explicit guidance was provided to them about atheism from the New Testament, which only uses the word *atheos* once, and this in a context where it must mean "godless" or "without God," rather than disbelief in the existence of gods (Eph 2:12; Harnack, 1905, 3). The word *atheos* likewise makes no appearance in the Septuagint translation of the Hebrew Bible, which only hints briefly at people who may deny the existence of God (Ps 9 β [10]:4, 13[14]:1). A similar pattern continued in Christian works of the apostolic period, where the word *atheos* only appears once (Ign. *Trall.* 10.1). As such, when Christians began engaging more with the concept of atheism in the second half of the 2nd century CE, they turned to other sources, drawing liberally from treatments of the subject in doxographic collections (e.g. Min.Fel. *Oct.* 8.2–3). The engagement of Christian authors with atheism reflected their deep involvement with the intellectual and philosophical culture of the Roman Empire.

Charges that Christians were atheists first become noticeable in our evidence around 150 CE, coinciding with the period when Christians began to make themselves better known in the Roman Empire (Walsh, 1991). There is some evidence for charges of this sort outside of Christian sources (e.g. Luc. *Alex.* 25.38; Iamb. *Myst.* 3.31; Beatrice, 2004, 137). But Christian apologists likely chose to emphasize the charge of atheism however much or little it was made against them (Whitmarsh, 2017), recognizing that this effort linked them with Socrates and other philosophers who had been similarly accused (Just. 1 *Apol.* 5.3; Ath. *Leg.* 31.2; Luc. *Peregr.* 12). In this sense, offering a defense against the charge of atheism functioned as a way for Christian apologists (→ Apologetics) to present themselves as legitimate philosophers and intellectuals (Secord, 2020).

Justin Martyr led the way for Christian discussions of atheism, revealing the range of approaches later Christians would take. → Justin Martyr demonstrates how easily the accusation of atheism could be cast back and forth by intellectuals in the Roman Empire. He alleges that he was called an atheist by his rival, the Stoic philosopher Crescens (Just. 2 *Apol.* 8.2). According to Justin, Christians were also called atheists by Jews (Just. *Dial.* 17.1; 108.2). In return, Justin throws this accusation back at Jews (*Dial.* 47.5; 92.4; 120.2), while at the same time alleging that Christians he deemed heretics were also atheists (*Dial.* 35.4–6; 80.3; 82.3; 1 *Apol.* 58.2). Justin places all of this in the context of doxographical traditions on atheism, identifying Socrates and other philosophers charged with being atheists as Christians *avant la lettre* (1 *Apol.* 4.9; 5.3; 46.3). In effect, Justin claimed the word *atheos* for Christian use, defining it in a way that made an atheist of anyone who was not an orthodox Christian.

Other apologists continued what Justin started, using similar conceptions of atheism and basing arguments on doxographic lists of famous atheists. Justin's engagement with the doxographic tradition on atheism was eccentric, leading him to identify Heraclitus as an atheist while omitting more obvious candidates (1 *Apol.* 46.3; Winiarczyk, 1984, 172). → Athenagoras far surpassed Justin in this respect, introducing his discussion of atheism with reference to Diagoras of Melos (Ath. *Leg.* 4.1) and concluding with Euhemerist theories about the human origins of the pagan gods (*Leg.* 28.1–10). → Tatian followed a similar pattern, claiming that atheists such as

Diagoras were still respected by Greeks, even as they objected to similar critiques of polytheism made by Christians (Tat. *Orat.* 27.2). Tatian also cited the Euhemerist ideas of Leon of Pella that explored the human origins of the Egyptian gods (*Orat.* 27.3; Djurslev, 2020, 62–70). Theophilus of Antioch, meanwhile, took a different approach, offering a list of atheists as an example of the inconsistent and erroneous beliefs of Greeks (Theophil. *Autol.* 3.6–7). Epicurus, Clitomachus, and other reputed atheists were not allies for Theophilus, but they still provided evidence for his defense of Christianity.

In Alexandria, Clement and → Origen built on the significant role that atheism had gained in Christian apologetics while also moving beyond the limits of the doxographical tradition. Both authors reveal the influence that Philo's conception of atheism had on them, citing him by name, unlike earlier Christian authors who likely read Philo but never mentioned him (Runia, 1993; Alexandre, 1998). Like Philo, Clement and Origen emphasized that polytheists were atheists because they denied or ignored the existence of God (Clem. *Protr.* 2.23.1; Or. *Mart.* 32; *Cels.* 1.1). → Clement of Alexandria also followed Philo in praising a group of atheists, including Diagoras, Euhemerus, and Theodorus, for their acuity in recognizing errors associated with polytheistic belief (*Protr.* 2.24.2). Clement likewise displays a pattern familiar from the works of both Philo (*Deus* 163–164; *Spec.* 4.147) and Plutarch (*Superst.* 171e–f) whereby true piety is reached by finding a middle path between the two extremes of superstition and atheism (Clem. *Protr.* 2.25.1). The label of "atheist" still has some of the same force for Clement as it does for the earlier apologists. He applies it indiscriminately to Christians he deemed heretical, including Tatian (Clem. *Strom.* 3.12.81), something that Origen also does (Or. *Or.* 24). But both authors demonstrate greater sophistication than the earlier apologists in their references to atheism, revealing their familiarity with philosophical conceptions of piety in the Roman Empire.

Apart from apologetics, atheism also plays a role in heresiology and martyrology, where rivals inside and outside of Christianity were labeled atheists. This was an older pattern in Christian discourse, to judge by Ignatius of Antioch's (→ Ignatius, Epistles of) suggestion that his docetic (→ Docetism) rivals were atheists (Ign. *Trall.* 10.1). Justin Martyr's lost work of heresiology most likely used the same technique (Just 1 *Apol.* 26.8), given his liberal application of this charge in his extant works. Irenaeus (e.g. *Haer.* 1.6.4) and Pseudo-Hippolytus (e.g. *Haer.* 1, preface 1) followed this example, as did → Tertullian in Latin, conveying the force of the Greek word *atheos* with the Latin *impius* (e.g. Tert. *Marc.* 1.23.8). Atheism also functioned as a basic charge thrown back and forth in accounts of Christian martyrdom (e.g. Eus. *Hist. eccl.* 5.1.9). In the famous account of his martyrdom, → Polycarp of Smyrna is asked to repudiate his fellow Christians as atheists (*Mart. Pol.* 3.2). He repeats the words that he was ordered to say, but the text makes clear that he was directing them at the non-Christians gathered to watch his death, rather than his fellow Christians (*Mart. Pol.* 9.2). In this sense, Polycarp's character redefines the word *atheos*, using it in a Christian way, as did apologists and heresiologists.

Atheism continued to be a theme referenced in Christian works of late antiquity, following on the examples of earlier writers. The standard lists of atheists from doxographical collection were still known to Christian writers of the 3rd century CE and later (Lact. *Inst.* 1.2.2; *Ir.* 9; Eus. *Praep.* 14.16.1; Thdt. *Affect.* 3.4; 6.6). Christian authors likewise referred to the ideas of Euhemerus, finding in these a way to combat polytheistic views (Lact. *Inst.* 1.11.33; Aug. *Civ.* 6.7; 7.27). Latin and Greek writers also claimed that Christians were still being called *atheoi* by their rivals (Arn. *Adv. nat.* 1.29; 3.28; 5.30; 6.27; Eus. *Praep.* 1.2.2). Proof that this was happening comes from the works of the emperor → Julian the Apostate (e.g. *Deo.* 180b; *Gal.* 43b; 238b). As such, the idea of atheism continued to resonate for Christians, though evidence for nonbelievers in gods or God is difficult to find in late antiquity (Edwards, 2013).

Historiography

Atheism in antiquity has traditionally received little attention. Older studies of atheism were dismissive of the phenomenon and based on outdated assumptions about the inferiority of polytheism (e.g. Drachmann, 1922). Over the last several decades, the work of M. Winiarczyk has provided a more secure foundation for the study of ancient atheism, collecting and testing evidence with a rigorous philological approach (Winiarczyk, 1976; 1984; 2013; 2016). New evidence relating to ancient atheism has also been discovered, particularly in the works of the Epicurean philosophers Philodemus and Diogenes of Oenoanda (Obbink, 1989; Smith, 1993). Recent work on atheism now hinges on the question of whether the lack of explicit evidence for atheism should be interpreted as a sign that there were few atheists in the Greco-Roman world (Bremmer, 2007; Edwards, 2013), or as an indication that atheists found it safer to keep silent about their disbelief, given the condemnation that might result (Sedley, 2013; Whitmarsh, 2015). Early Christianity has received relatively little mention in recent research on ancient atheism. More sustained attention on early Christianity and atheism has come in the forms of scattered articles and chapters (Walsh, 1991; Beatrice, 2004; Whitmarsh, 2017). A full monograph on atheism and early Christianity is a desideratum, expanding on the foundational but dated treatment of the subject by A. von Harnack (1905). Especially welcome would be more attention to atheism in late antiquity, collecting and studying the frequent use of the word *atheos* by Christian writers.

Bibliography

Alexandre, M., "Apologétique judéo-hellénistique et premières apologies chrétiennes," in: B. Pouderon & J. Doré, eds., *Les apologistes chrétiens et la culture grecque*, TH 105, Paris, 1998, 1–40.

Beatrice, P.F., "L'accusation d'athéisme contre les chrétiens," in: M. Narcy & É. Rebillard, eds., *Hellénisme et christianisme*, Villeneuve-d'Ascq, 2004, 133–152.

Bremmer, J., "Atheism in Antiquity," in: M. Martin, ed., *CCAthe*, Cambridge UK, 2007, 11–26.

Djurslev, C.T., *Alexander the Great in the Early Christian Tradition: Classical Reception and Patristic Literature*, BSCR, New York, 2020.

Drachmann, A.B., *Atheism in Pagan Antiquity*, London, 1922.

Edwards, M., "The First Millennium," in: S. Bullivant & M. Ruse, eds., *OHAthe*, Oxford, 2013, 152–163.

Graham, D.W., *The Texts of Early Greek Philosophy: The Complete Fragments and Selected Testimonies of the Major Presocratics*, 2 vols., Cambridge UK, 2010.

Harnack, A. von, *Der Vorwurf des Atheismus in den drei ersten Jahrhunderten*, TU 28/4, Leipzig, 1905.

Obbink, D., "The Atheism of Epicurus," *GRBS* 30/2, 1989, 187–223.

Reynard, J., "La notion d'athéisme dans l'œuvre de Philon d'Alexandrie," in: G. Dorival & D. Pralon, eds., *Nier les dieux, nier Dieu*, TDMAM, Aix-en-Provence, 2002, 211–221.

Runia, D.T., *Philo in Early Christian Literature: A Survey*, Assen, 1993.

Runia, D.T., "Atheists in Aëtius: Text, Translation and Comments on *De Placitis* 1.7.1–10," *Mn.* 49/5, 1996, 542–576.

Secord, J., *Christian Intellectuals and the Roman Empire: From Justin Martyr to Origen*, InChr, College Park, 2020.

Sedley, D., "The Atheist Underground," in: V. Harte & M. Lane, eds., *Politeia in Greek and Roman Philosophy*, Cambridge UK, 2013, 329–348.

Smith, M.F., *Diogenes of Oinoanda: The Epicurean Inscription*, SdiE.S 1, Napoli, 1993.

Walsh, J.J., "On Christian Atheism," *VigChr* 45/3, 1991, 255–277.

Whitmarsh, T., *Battling the Gods: Atheism in the Ancient World*, New York, 2015.

Whitmarsh, T., "'Away with the Atheists!' Christianity and Militant Atheism in the Early Empire," in: J.C. Paget & J. Lieu, eds., *Christianity in the Second Century: Themes and Developments*, Cambridge UK, 2017, 281–293.

Winiarczyk, M., "Der erste Atheistenkatalog des Kleitomachos," *Ph.* 120, 1976, 32–46.

Winiarczyk, M., "Wer galt im Altertum als Atheist?" *Ph.* 128/2, 1984, 157–183.

Winiarczyk, M., *The "Sacred History" of Euhemerus of Messene*, BzA 312, Berlin, 2013; ET: W. Zbirohowski-Kościa.

Winiarczyk, M., *Diagoras of Melos: A Contribution to the History of Ancient Atheism*, BzA 350, Berlin, 2016; ET: W. Zbirohowski-Kościa.

JARED SECORD

Athenagoras

Athenagoras (2nd cent. CE, year of birth and death unknown; see Jacobsen, 2014) was one of the earliest Christian apologists (→ Apologetics). The oldest manuscript containing his writings, Codex Parisinus Graecus 451 dating from 914 CE, introduces Athenagoras as an "Athenian, Philosopher, and Christian." Unfortunately, this is all we know of him. A later manuscript, Codex Bodleianus Baroccianus (p. 142, col. 216) from the 14th century, quotes the historian Philip from Side that Athenagoras was the first leader of the catechetical school in Alexandria (→ Alexandria). That he at some point lived in Egypt might then be added to our limited knowledge of Athenagoras – however, Philip from Side is often an unreliable source (Rankin, 2009, 5–6).

Despite the characterization of Athenagoras in Codex Parisinus Graecus 451, scholars do not agree on his philosophical skills and education – thus, some have argued that Athenagoras was simply familiar with a few philosophical compendia (Barnard, 1972a; Malherbe, 1969, convincingly argues that Athenagoras' *Legatio pro Christianis* has the same three-part structure as the Middle Platonic philosopher Albinus' *Didaskalikos*; see also pp. 6–12 for Athenagoras' use of Plato's *Timaeus*; concerning Athenagoras' relation to the Platonic milieu in Athens, see Rankin, 2009, 6–10). Nonetheless, *Legatio* shows clear signs of the author's relatively high level of education. He reveals close familiarity with classical philosophy, especially the Platonic tradition. This is evident, for example in the way he uses Greek philosophical literature in connection with his arguments for monotheism, especially Plato's *Timaeus* (see Ath. *Leg.* 4.2 and chs. 5–6 referring to Plato *Tim.* 27 and 28; see also *Leg.* 15.1–4 and 19.2). His familiarity with Greek traditions also suggests that he was a Christian convert. It is striking that Athenagoras rarely quotes or makes references to the biblical texts, as if he did not feel quite at home in the Christian Scriptures. However, Athenagoras' very limited direct use of the biblical texts may not be due to little knowledge of them, but rather to his apologetic purpose and intended readership (Barnard, 1972a, 12–13).

1. Athenagoras' Writings

Two theological treatises are connected to Athenagoras: *Legatio pro Christianis* and *De resurrectione*. Both writings are included in Codex Parisinus Graecus 451. Scholars generally agree that Athenagoras is the author of *Legatio*, but his authorship of *De resurrectione* is disputed. R.M. Grant (1954) was the first to question Athenagoras' authorship of *De resurrectione*, while scholars such as L.W. Barnard (1972b; 1984), B. Pouderon (1986; 1989), and, more moderately, D. Rankin (2009, 11) claim that Athenagoras is indeed its author. N. Zeegers-Vander Vorst (1992) argues that Athenagoras did not write *De resurrectione* by going through and rejecting B. Pouderon's arguments one by one (see also Rankin, 2009, 19–23; Lona, 1988, similarly rejects Athenagoras as author of *De resurrectione*, e.g. by showing that the use and

meaning of the word "flesh" [*sarx*] is very different in the two treatises).

The doubts about Athenagoras' authorship of *De resurrectione* stem, firstly, from the fact that the two treatises differ hugely in style and vocabulary, pointing to different authors. This may, however, be due to the very different themes handled in the treatises. Yet, *De resurrectione*'s arguments in favor of → resurrection also seem to depend on (among others) → Origen from Alexandria (185–254 CE), suggesting that the text is later than Origen (see Grant, 1954, 123–124; Schoedel, 1972, xxv–xxxiv Consequently, only *Legatio* can be assigned to Athenagoras with any kind of certainty.

2. The Dating of *Legatio*

Legatio was probably written between 176 and 178 CE. It is addressed to the coruling caesars Marcus Aurelius and Commodus, and they only shared imperial power between 176 CE, when Commodus became coregent, and 180 CE, when Marcus Aurelius died. Furthermore, if one takes the comment about a "deep peace" reigning in the empire (*Leg.* 1.2) at face value, Athenagoras wrote *Legatio* prior to 178 CE, when war was resumed with the Germans. Furthermore, if we assume that *Legatio* was delivered or read to the emperors during their visit to Athens, the work may be dated precisely to 176 CE (for dating, see Schoedel, 1972, xi).

3. *Legatio*'s Genre and Readership

Legatio bears many similarities to other early apologetic works (the traditional category "apology," which tended to be understood as a literary genre, has been problematized during the last decades: see Edwards et al., 1999; Jacobsen, 2009; Young, 1999; Cameron, 2002; Petersen, 2009). This is the case with the apologetic strategies that Athenagoras uses in order to create strategic alliances with various involved parties, but also in the text's arguments and intended readers – pagans, Jews, and Christians alike. *Legatio* nevertheless presents itself as a petition to the Roman emperors, not as an apology. In fact, *Legatio* is so named because the oldest manuscript calls the treatise a *presbeia*, or in Latin *legatio* – "petition" or "embassy." As some scholars believe, including W.R.

Schoedel (1989), Athenagoras presented his petition to the caesars personally when Marcus Aurelius and Commodus traveled to Greece and farther east in September 176 CE (Barnes, 1975, 114, proposed this theory). Based on similarities with other petitions, W.R. Schoedel concludes – despite *Legatio*'s deviations from the usual petition genre – that Athenagoras' text combines two literary genres: petition and apology (Schoedel, 1989, 70–78; see also Barnes, 1975, 111; Grant, 1988, 100). However, other scholars insist that *Legatio* was simply an apology presented only in the form of a petition (much of this debate is based on Millar, 1977, esp. 564–565; see also Rankin, 2009, 25). Thus, P.L. Buck considers *Legatio*'s deviations from the petition genre to be so significant that it cannot in fact be considered a petition. He therefore concludes that Athenagoras styled his apology in the form of a petition for rhetorical reasons and sought simply to draw attention to it by addressing it to Marcus Aurelius and Commodus.

This brings us to the question of the intended readership. According to P.L. Buck (1996, 11), the emperors were not the intended recipients, but rather Jews, pagans, and other Christians. Many 2nd-century CE Christians – both educated and uneducated – were not very well grounded in the theoretical basis of Christianity. Hence, they needed to be provided with cohesive arguments justifying Christianity and showing its philosophical and moral superiority. It may therefore well have been Athenagoras' intention that Christians, and not the emperors, should read his *Legatio*.

Additionally, *Legatio* is presented as a defense against charges put forward by people who persecute Christians "using slander and lies" (*Leg.* 1.3; regarding this charge, see Rankin, 2009, 101–127) – a regular trait of apologies aimed at hostile pagans. The people raising these charges might have had several motives for doing so. According to Roman legal practice, the person who raised a charge was able to share in the property of the accused in certain cases if the accused was condemned. In other words, there may have been economic motives for raising charges against Christians (I thank my colleague J. Engberg for this information on the Roman legal practice and his reference to Steven; see esp. Jacobsen, 2014, 35–44).

However, Athenagoras' claim of false charges also indirectly accuses the Roman authorities of not handling the charges raised against Christians thoroughly enough. If they did, it would be revealed that the charges were false (*Leg.* 1.3). This suggests that the intended readership could have been pagans in administrative positions. But this does not exclude the possibility that if the emperor was a real addressee, he would be persuaded to put his officials in the right place. In conclusion, the two views about *Legatio*'s recipients and genre outlined above are not necessarily conflicting but supplement each other – *Legatio* is probably both an apology and a petition.

4. Main Themes in *Legatio*

Athenagoras responds to three main charges against Christians, the first of which he considers to be the most important:

1. atheism;
2. incest and promiscuity;
3. cannibalism (see *Leg.* 1.3).

The first major theme Athenagoras takes up is the issue of the difference between → atheism and → monotheism (*Leg.* 3.1). According to Athenagoras, Christians were accused of being atheists – a serious charge. Being an atheist in the Roman Empire in the 2nd century CE was viewed as detrimental to society because the correct worship of the gods was essential for the survival of the Roman state; thus Christians were simultaneously accused of being antisocial. However, so many different gods were worshipped within the Roman Empire that, according to Athenagoras, this fact alone makes it meaningless to charge Christians with atheism (*Leg.* 14). In *Leg.* 2–12, Athenagoras argues that Christians are not *atheists*, but *monotheists* – there is only one God, who has created everything, but was not himself created. Christians reject the notion that anything created can be divine, but not the existence of a divine creator standing above the created. Athenagoras refers to Plato's *Timaeus*, which, he argues, also distinguishes between the created and the creator. The reason why Athenagoras refers to *Timaeus* and not to the Hebrew Bible is probably due both to his apologetic strategy – seeking points of overlap between Christianity and the traditions of the non-Christian critics – and to the fact that Athenagoras was most likely more familiar with Plato than with → Moses. This distinction between the created and the uncreated was reinforced in early Christianity because Christians argued within the framework of the dominant Platonic philosophy of the time – → Middle Platonism – which emphasizes the transcendence of the divine above anything else, including the material world (see e.g. Alb. *Epit.* 10, and Dillon's comments on the chapter, 1993, 100–111). He follows this strategy again in *Leg.* 5–12, where he attempts to demonstrate that the Christian monotheistic conception of God has long been partially acknowledged among educated pagan philosophers and poets (e.g. *Leg.* 7.1–10.1). Athenagoras asks his readers why Christians should be punished (regarding the legislation of the Roman authorities against Christians, see the section on this topic in Ulrich, 2014) for advancing a conception of the divine that was promoted and well known among the poets and philosophers esteemed at the time, and to which the emperors themselves adhered (*Leg.* 5.1; 7.1). He further argues that Christians as people who believe in a positive, creating, nurturing, and controlling power can make a positive contribution to maintaining and developing society through the practice of their religion.

Athenagoras then explains the impacts of Christian monotheism on their participation in other religious activities, in particular the official cults of the empire. He wants to justify the fact that Christians do not sacrifice to or worship idols and in doing so considers theoretical aspects of the nature of idols at length.

One of Athenagoras' basic arguments is that those who criticize and persecute Christians do not possess any form of theological awareness. Rather, they measure piety based on the quantity of sacrifices – a mistake because the only true God is not interested in bloody sacrifices, only in people knowing the creator and his will (*Leg.* 13.1–4). Being monotheists, Christians claimed that all other "gods" than the Christian god are either make-believe gods or something other than gods. Hence, they do not sacrifice to or worship idols. However, Athenagoras does not completely reject the possibility that there were realities behind the idols and statues. They could represent demonic powers, something that Athenagoras sees as a reality, in line with his contemporaries (*Leg.* 23.1; see

Rankin, 2009, 63–66). He believes that the demonic powers, which have taken over certain statues, are not divine but created powers that are in opposition to God (*Leg.* 23.1–2). Athenagoras explains this by referring to the legends about fallen angels who violated the daughters of men, giving rise to the birth of "giants" (Gen 6:1–4). Demons (→ Demonology/ Demons) are the souls of these giants, which wander the earth (*Leg.* 25.1). Athenagoras' description of the origins and nature of these demons is thus dependent on Jewish, Christian, and Greek traditions (in → Philo of Alexandria's treatise *Gig.* 6 and 16, the relationship among demons, angels, and souls is defined in the same way as by Athenagoras; however, in Alb. *Epit.* 15–16, demons are not necessarily negative beings, but can be intermediaries between God and the created; regarding teachings on angels and demonology in general in Athenagoras, see Andres, 1914, 66–96). These demons possess the statues and lead weak people to believe that the movements demons create in the souls of the weak are an expression of the divinity and power of the statues (*Leg.* 26–27).

In *Leg.* 31–36, Athenagoras defends Christians against the charges of → cannibalism and sexual promiscuity – particularly incest. There was something both alluring and repulsive about the Christian fellowship and gatherings, of which most people only had superficial knowledge. This lack of knowledge may have been due in part to the fact that the eucharistic element of Christian services was not accessible to everyone, not even to the catechumens (→ Catechesis) who were receiving teaching on → baptism. On this background, rumors may easily have arisen about the "flesh" and "blood," which participants partake of in this ceremony. Athenagoras also suggests that the greeting in the form of a kiss on the cheek, associated with the services, had raised concern among outsiders. He thus insists that the Christians intervene if someone kisses the same person twice during the services. The first argument Athenagoras presents against the charge of immorality rests on the Christian concept of judgment and resurrection. Since Christians know that their afterlife – in eternal bliss or torment – depends on their actions in this world, it is unthinkable that they would do → evil and thereby surrender themselves to the coming punishment, according to Athenagoras

(*Leg.* 31.3–4; 36). In *Leg.* 31.3, Athenagoras assumes that the emperors are familiar with the Christian concept of judgment and are therefore able to easily follow his argument. However, this is unlikely to have been the case.

In *Leg.* 32–35, Athenagoras continues his argument against the charge of immorality. As the apologists often do, he now turns the accusations against the accusers. The Greeks have no right criticizing Christians for immorality because they and their gods are highly immoral themselves. Zeus had children by both his mother and his daughter and was married to his sister. Nor do the Greeks refrain from promiscuous sexuality. They earn money running brothels and do not even refrain from male prostitution. When they criticize the Christians' sexual morality, it is therefore as if a prostitute admonishes the chaste (*Leg.* 32.1; 34.1–2). Moreover, Christians have laws that prohibit them from even looking lustfully at women. According to Athenagoras, sexuality is not the only area in which Christian morality surpasses that of non-Christians. Christians also refrain from watching executions and attending gladiator battles. They see these activities as participation in murder. Nor are Christians permitted to undergo abortion or abandon newborn children (*Leg.* 35.4–6).

None of Athenagoras' arguments were apparently known in broad circles. The sparse tradition of quoting his treatise makes it clear that Athenagoras influenced the formation of Christianity only to a very limited degree in the centuries after his death. It is difficult to say why. Perhaps *Legatio* simply has too little to say about Christ's life and work. Further, the concept of God, which Athenagoras develops in the treatise, depends heavily on the political context of his time, and therefore may not have caught the attention of the following generations. However, as is obvious in the increasing number of scholarly articles on Athenagoras during recent decades, he and his treatise as well as other early Christian apologetics have again become an important theme in the study of early Christianity.

Historiography

In the text above the discussions about Athenagoras' education and authorship of *De resurrectione* have already been summarized. E. Schwartz published a critical edition of Athenagoras' works in 1891 titled *Athenagoras libellus pro Christianis: Oratio De resurrectione*. This edition became the basis for modern scholarship on Athenagoras. Other editions and translations were published in the second half of the 20th century. Of these some are especially noteworthy, for example the publications of J.H. Chehan's (1955), M. Marcovich (1990), W.R. Schoedel (1972), and B. Pouderon (1992).

The mentioned editions except M. Marcovich's include two works: *Legatio* and *De Resurrectione*. The tradition has attributed both texts to Athenagoras, but most modern scholars claim that *De Resurrectione* was not written by Athenagoras. However, a recent major work from N. Kiel (2016) claims that Athenagoras was also the author of *De resurrection*. The scholarship on Athenagoras has concentrated on this question including the dating of the two texts (see Kiel, 2016) and on Athenagoras' identity (see above), his philosophical background (see above), and the genre and addressee of *Legatio* (see above).

Bibliography

Andres, F., *Die Engellehre der griechischen Apologeten des zweiten Jahrhunderts und ihr Verhältnis zur griechisch-römischen Dämonologie*, Paderborn, 1914.

Barnard, L.W., "The Philosophical and Biblical Background of Athenagoras," in: J. Fontaine & C. Kannengiesser, eds., *Epektasis: Mélanges patristiques offertes au cardinal Jean Daniélou*, Paris, 1972a, 3–16.

Barnard, L.W., *Athenagoras: A Study in Second Century Christian Apologetic*, Paris, 1972b.

Barnard, L.W., "The Authenticity of Athenagoras' *De Resurrectio*," *SP* 15, 1984, 39–49.

Barnes, T.D., "The Embassy of Athenagoras," *JThS* 26, 1975, 111–114.

Buck, P.L., "Athenagoras's *Embassy*: A Literary Fiction," *HThR* 89, 1996, 209–226.

Cameron, A., "Apologetics in the Roman Empire: A Genre of Intolerance," in: J.-M. Carrié & R.L. Testa, eds., *"Humana Sapit": Études d'antiquité tardieve offertes à Lellia Cracco Ruggini*, Turnhout 2002, 219–227.

Chehan, J.H., *Athenagoras: Embassy for the Christian: The Resurrection of the Dead*, ACW 23, New York, 1955.

Dillon, J., *Alcinous: The Handbook of Platonism: Translated with an Introduction and Commentary*, Oxford, 1993.

Edwards, M. et al., eds., *Apologetics in the Roman Empire*, Oxford, 1999, 1–13.

Grant, R.M., "Athenagoras or Pseudo-Athenagoras," *HThR* 47, 1954, 123–124.

Grant, R.M., *Greek Apologists of the Second Century*, Philadelphia, 1988.

Jacobsen, A.-C., "Apologetics and Apologies–Some Definitions," in: J. Ulrich, A.C. Jacobsen & M. Kahlos, eds., *Continuity and Discontinuity in Early Christian Apologetics*, ECCA 5, Frankfurt am Main, 2009, 9-21.

Jacobsen, A.-C., "Athenagoras," in: J. Engberg, A.-C. Jacobsen & J. Ulrich, eds., *In Defense of Christianity: Early Christian Apologists*, ECCA 15, Frankfurt am Main, 2014, 81–100.

Kiel, N., *Ps-Athenagoras De Resurrectione: Datierung und Kontextualisierung der dem Apologeten Athenagoras zugeschriebenen Auferstehungsschrift*, Leiden, 2016.

Lona, H.E., "Bemerkungen zu Athenagoras und Pseudo-Athenagoras," *VigChr* 42, 1988, 352–363.

Malherbe, A.J., "The Structure of Athenagoras' *Supplicatio pro Christiani*," *VigChr* 23, 1969, 1–20.

Marcovich, M., ed., *Athenagoras: Legatio pro Christianis*, PTS 31, Berlin, 1990.

Millar, F., *The Emperor in the Roman World 31 BC–AD 337*, London, 1977.

Petersen, A.K., "The Diversity of Apologetics: From Genre to Mode of Thinking," in: A.C. Jacobsen, J. Ulrich & D. Brakke, eds., *Critique and Apologetics: Jews, Christians and Pagans in Antiquity*, ECCA 4, Frankfurt am Main, 2009, 15-41.

Pouderon, B., "L'Authenticité du traité sur la résurrection attribué à l'apologiste Athénagore," *VigChr* 40, 1986, 226–244.

Pouderon, B., *Athénagore d'Athènes: Philosophe chrétien*, Paris, 1989.

Pouderon, B., *Supplique au sujet des chrétiens et Sur la résurrection des morts*, SC 379, Parijs, 1992.

Rankin, D., *Athenagoras: Philosopher and Theologian*, Ashgate, 2009.

Schoedel, W.R., ed., *Athenagoras' Legatio and De Resurrectione*, OECT, Oxford, 1972.

Schoedel, W.R., "Apologetic Literature and Ambassadorial Activities," *HThR* 82, 1989, 55–78.

Steven, H., *Imperial Inquisitions: Persecutors and Informants from Tiberius to Domitian*, Florence, 2001.

Ulrich, J., "Apologists and Apologetics in the Second Century," in: J. Engberg, A.-C. Jacobsen & J. Ulrich, eds., *In Defense of Christianity: Early Christian Apologists*, ECCA 15, Frankfurt am Main, 2014, 1-32.

Young, F., "Greek Apologists of the Second Century," in: M. Edwards et al., eds., *Apologetics in the Roman Empire*, Oxford, 1999, 82–92.

Zeegers-Vander Vorst, N., "La paternité athénagorienne du *De Resurrectione*," *RHE* 87, 1992, 337–374.

ANDERS-CHRISTIAN JACOBSEN

Athens

Athens is almost the only Greek site to show continuous occupation from its very beginnings in the Mycenaean age (Osborne, 1989, 397). It showed early signs of cultural dominance in its production of Protogeometric pottery, found with the cremated remains of the dead in burial sites from circa 1030 to 900 BCE. The city-state of Athens was established in the 7th century BCE but took its classical form in the mid-5th century BCE during the time of Pericles, the Athenian statesman who designed many of the buildings of the Acropolis, the fortified citadel and religious center overlooking the city. The city was named for Athena, the virgin goddess of war and wisdom. Her temple, the Parthenon, still stands among the remains of a massive complex of buildings that celebrated Athens's many deities and one of the most famous and recognizable buildings in the world. It is a witness to the lasting legacy of the ancient Greeks and their architectural ingenuity. It has been seen as central to the history of western civilization, and a lasting symbol of democracy.

Democracy or rule by the people was introduced by Cleisthenes at the end of the 6th century BCE. The greatest challenge to Athenian hegemony came from Persia in the 5th century BCE, with a series of wars over 50 years from 499 BCE. The Persian sack of Athens in 480 BCE was a low point of this period in its history. In 479 BCE, the statesman Themistocles established a wall around the city with several gates, one providing access to the harbor at Piraeus (Theocharaki, 2011, 73–74). Athens finally emerged the victor in 448 BCE, initiating a period of peace and a golden age for philosophy and culture that lasted until the Peloponnesian wars. In the 440s and 420s BCE, the Long Walls were built to provide protected access from the city to its twin harbors of Piraeus and Phaleron. Plato, whose legacy was to last well into the early Christian period, was born in 428–427 BCE to a noble family and died in 348–347 BCE. After a protracted war against Sparta and its allies in the Peloponnesian league from 431 BCE, culminating in the Spartan victory with Persian aid at the Battle of Aegospotami (405 BCE), Athens was briefly ruled by the Thirty Tyrants, a puppet regime controlled by Sparta. When this regime was overthrown in 404 BCE, Athens was left depleted but regained some of its strength after a second defeat by Sparta, again with Persian help, in the Corinthian War (395–386 BCE).

1. The Hellenistic Period

To the north, the Macedonian dynasty rose to power over all of Greece under Philip II (r. 359–336 BCE). Athens declared war against this powerful foe in 330 BCE. Two years after, defeating Athenian forces in 338 BCE, Philip was assassinated, and power passed to his son Alexander (r. 336–323 BCE), whose military campaigns in Egypt, Persia, and India increased Greek power and influence further than ever before. Alexander was tutored by the Athenian philosopher Aristotle. The three centuries from Alexander's untimely death in 323 BCE until the beginning of Roman rule over the Greek Empire are known as the Hellenistic period. This was marked by a flourishing of Greek ideas and culture across the empire, and especially in Alexandria.

The Hellenistic period saw Athens' power diminish as Alexandria and Hellenistic Egypt rose in cultural influence. The stability of Athenian democracy continued to be challenged by tyrannical rule. Around 296–295 BCE, Lachares, a native citizen of Athens, stripped the Parthenon's massive gold-and-ivory statue of Athena Parthenos of her ornaments to pay his troops. To combat such abuses, Athenians employed a system of banishment from the city, for up to ten years, for officials who seemed to be exceeding the limits of their positions. Public involvement in the political process of ostracism is evidenced by "shards of small clay voting tablets" (*ostraka*) from 490 BCE onward (Kosmin, 2015).

2. The Roman Period

The Roman general Sulla captured the city in 86 BCE. Athens was the source of many institutions that were adopted by the Romans in their foundation of an empire which stretched from North Africa to Germany, and from Spain in the west to Syria in the east. Under the eastern Romans or Byzantines, the boundaries of the Greco-Roman empire were extended much further. Julius Caesar and his successor the emperor → Augustus funded the building of a new marketplace in Athens for olive oil and other goods, east of the ancient agora. The Roman emperor Augustus was honored with a small circular temple dedicated to him and the goddess Roma towards the end of the 1st century BCE, the only major addition

to the Acropolis after the 5th and 4th centuries BCE (Spawforth, 2006, 144). The new temple perhaps signaled Athenian acceptance of, or at least resignation to, Roman rule under Augustus, and associated the imperial cult with that of Athena. However, the lingua franca of the first two centuries CE continued to be Greek, not Latin, even in Rome.

In the first 200 years of their rule, Roman emperors undertook a building and restoration program in the ancient Greek capital. Emperor Hadrian (117–138 CE) brought to completion the massive Temple of Olympians Zeus just inside the walls in the southeastern quarter of the city. The temple was dedicated in 132 CE, around 650 years after it had been begun by the sons of the tyrant Peisistratus. Pausanias describes the massive structure as it was in the 2nd century CE, and the enormous statue of Zeus made of ivory and gold at its entrance (Paus. *Descr.* 1.18.6–9). Other improvements to the city under Hadrian included an aqueduct, which brought fresh water to the city from the mountains to the north. A gymnasium, a pantheon or temple to all the gods, a monumental arch, and a library further improved life for the inhabitants of the city under Hadrian. The Olympeion precinct became the focus of the Roman imperial cult in the Greek-speaking East, starting with Hadrian who was celebrated by many large statues in the precinct.

3. The Early Christian Period

When the apostle Paul of Tarsus (→ Paul the Apostle) visited Athens in 51 CE, as part of his proselytizing tour of the Mediterranean, he was reportedly troubled by the number of idols he found in the city, including an altar dedicated to "the Unknown God" (Acts 17:16–34; NIV). First, he addressed the Jews and "God-fearing Greeks" in the synagogue and the Athenian people in the agora. The author of Acts (→ Acts, Book of) gives some idea of the intellectual foment of the city at that time: "All the Athenians and the foreigners who lived there spent their time doing nothing but talking about and listening to the latest ideas" (Acts 17:21; NIV). Paul's pastoral letters to Corinth, Philippi, Colossi, and Thessaloniki reveal the issues faced by other nascent center of Christianity on mainland Greece at this time, which would also have challenged Athenian Christians. These problems included persecution by Roman emperors, most famously Nero, and infighting between Christian factions. On the one hand were the Jerusalemites, who accepted the ongoing validity of Jewish law and rituals in their liturgical practice. On the other were those who – like the ex-Jew Paul and many others in Greece, Alexandria, Antioch, and Asia Minor – adopted a Hellenized form of Christianity, based loosely on the moral precepts of Stoicism and the dualism of body and soul that was characteristic of Platonism.

In Athens, a group of Epicureans (→ Epicurus/Epicureans) and Stoics invited Paul to present his radical ideas in a public debate with the archons, members of the city council, on the Areopagus hill. As a result of Paul's defense of Christian doctrines, including the resurrection of the dead, the archon Dionysius (known as the Areopagite) converted to Christianity and others, including a woman named Damaris, followed, leading to the establishment of a small church there. It was not as well established as the Church of Corinth, on the Peloponnese peninsula, however, some 100 km away. In the early Christian period, Athens was the home of Christian apologists (→ Apologetics) such as → Athenagoras (133–190 CE), a former Platonist who defended Christianity as superior on moral and philosophical grounds, but it proved a difficult place for the new religion to take hold. Athenagoras penned two extant works, an apology for Christians from 176–177 CE (Athenagoras, *Legatio pro Christianis*), and a later treatise defending the doctrines of Christ' physical → resurrection, the immortality of the → soul, and the bodily resurrection of believers after death (Athenagoras, *De resurrectione mortuorum*; Rankin, 2009).

Engagement with the dualism of Plato, the dialectic method of Aristotle, Stoic ethics and cosmology (→ Cosmos/Cosmology), and the Epicureans, whose values were centered on this life and not the next, continued to exercise Latin- and Greek-speaking Christians in late antiquity. → Tertullian, writing from the North African city of Carthage at the beginning of the 3rd century CE, railed against the Athenian philosophers. In his work, *The Prescription of Heresies*, he asserted that, when Paul

was in Athens, the apostle became acquainted with human wisdom, which only pretends to know the truth and is divided into many → heresies (Tert. *Praesc.* 7). Tertullian explicitly contrasted the "love of wisdom" (*philosophia*) of the Greeks with that of the Jews: "What indeed has Athens to do with Jerusalem? What harmony is there between the Academy and the Church? What between heretics and Christians? Our instruction comes from "the porch of Solomon," (Acts 5:12)," who taught that "the Lord should be sought in simplicity of heart (Wis 1:1)" (Tert. *Praesc.* 7). Tertullian's defense of the apparent irrationality of religion against the demands of reason, and his appeal to the Book of Wisdom, attributed to Solomon, against the wisdom of Plato, Aristotle, Zeno, Valentinus, and other Greek philosophers, sums up the early Christian ambivalence towards Athens and the traditions of secular learning that it represented. It also ignores the great debt to Athenian intellectual culture that influenced the formation of Hellenistic Jewish scholars like Paul and later → Philo of Alexandria (c. 20 BCE–c. 50). Philo's reinterpretation of Platonism to accommodate his belief in a single Creator God was to shape generations of Christian Neoplatonists from → Clement of Alexandria and → Origen, through → Evagrius of Pontus, to the Cappadocian Fathers (→ Cappadocians) and Maximus the Confessor, among others.

In 267 CE, the Germanic tribe of the Heruli breached the city walls and sacked many buildings in the lower city, including the agora. The Temple of Zeus was destroyed and fell into disuse. The Acropolis seems to have survived these attacks without much damage. The restoration of new city walls within the outer circuit began under Emperor Probus (276–282 CE), using as building materials the rubble left after the destruction of the lower town. The philosopher → Iamblichus of Chalcis, a benefactor of the city who lived there between 362 and 391 CE, undertook serious repairs to curtain walls and towers (Theocharaki, 2011, 134–135). The curtain walls were nonstructural and a cheap way to keep the weather out and the occupants safe within the city.

4. Byzantine Rule

The early Byzantine centuries saw something of a revival, to judge by the rebuilding of the original outer walls of the city and the evidence of historical sources. After the official adoption of Christianity as the sole religion and the consequent abolition of pagan worship, churches began to be built on the model of basilicas, the long rectangular halls built of stone with wooden roofs supported by two rows of internal columns stretching the length of the building. From the 6th or 7th century CE, the Parthenon served as an orthodox church dedicated to another virgin, → Mary the Mother of God, and served as a locus of pilgrimage until 1453 (Kaldellis, 2009). Other ancient temples converted to Christian worship and still standing in Athens include the marble Temple of Hephaistos, to the west of the ancient agora, and the Erechtheion, a temple dedicated to Athena and Poseidon, god of the sea. Around 22 churches are known to have existed in this period of repurposing classical buildings for Christian usage.

Athens remained the educational and intellectual center of the Greek-speaking world until the 6th century CE. Many great thinkers received at least part of their education there, including the apostate emperor Julian (→ Julian the Apostate), → Basil of Caesarea and → Gregory of Nyssa who became two of the most famous bishops of Cappadocia, and their contemporary, the rhetorician Libanius of Antioch, who studied there between 336 and 340 CE. The Platonic Academy of Athens was closed by → Justinian in 529 CE, after which Athens' reputation for scholarship declined and its status and population was reduced to that of a provincial town. The traditional explanation of this closure refers to Justinian's wish to abolish the study of pagan philosophy. How far the Academy of Athens still represented the tradition of Plato by the 6th century CE is debated. Justinian seems to have been more focused on destroying Christian heretics than Neoplatonists.

In 582 CE, Athens was attacked by the Slavs. With the Persian and Muslim wars of the 7th century CE, Athens' fortunes continued to decline. It is rarely mentioned in the historical sources of the 7th to 10th centuries CE, apart from occasional mentions in chronicles and saints' lives, and archaeological evidence is scarce. However, the visit of Emperor Constans II in 662–663 CE is testimony to the ongoing strategic importance of the city in the campaign against the Slavs to the north. By the 8th century CE, the Church of the Theotokos in the converted Parthenon had become for eastern Christian pilgrims the fourth major destination after Constantinople, Jerusalem, and Thessaloniki in northern Greece.

The golden age of church-building in Athens was inspired by the military successes of Emperor Basil II Nikephoros (976–1025 CE), known as the "Bulgar-Slayer" for his victories in the Balkans. Several cruciform, domed Byzantine churches were built from marble, brick, and stone during the 11th and 12th centuries. Four surviving examples from the restoration period are the Church of the Holy Theodori, the Church of the Holy Apostles or Holy Apostles of Solaki, located on the site of the ancient agora, the Church of Panagia Kapnikarea in Monastiraki, and the Church of Panagia Georgoupekous, built when Michael Choniates was bishop of Athens (1180–1204). In the 12th century, the Parthenon was rededicated to "Theotokos Atheniotissa" and was celebrated throughout eastern Christendom as a place of pilgrimage, a dedication which extended beyond Athens to churches as far away as Constantinople (Kaldellis, 2009).

5. Latin Rule

An unthinkable disaster befell Athens during the Fourth Crusade, due to an invincible combination of crusaders and Venetian forces. The Third Crusade had ended in 1192 with the Treaty of Jaffa, after western forces failed in their combined attempts to take back parts of the Middle East from the Arab conqueror Saladin. In 1204, Frankish knights and Venetian soldiers looted and destroyed Athens on their way to dislodge Emperor Alexios Comnenos from the throne in Constantinople. The Parthenon was converted to a Roman Catholic church and received the addition of a bell tower. Baldwin of Flanders became Baldwin I of Constantinople in the largest church of that city, Hagia Sophia. Athens remained in Frankish hands for the next 250 years, although Constantinople was restored to the Byzantines in 1261 with a greatly reduced territorial scope.

Historiography

R. Osborne (1989) makes art history central to his interpretation of the archaeological evidence for the Athenian settlement of Attica in the 7th century BCE. Many scholars have traced the origins of modern European and New World institutions to classical Athens in the areas of law, defense, agriculture, architecture, philosophy, education, and politics. Paul's speech on the Areopagus hill (Acts 17:16–34) was a pivotal moment in New Testament history and has been regarded as the starting point of Christian missiology (Flemming, 2002). For some ancient apologists, like Athenagoras, it symbolized the end of enslavement to the many gods of Hellenic state religion, and the freedom of belief in and devotion to one God and Savior, Jesus (Rankin, 2009). For other commentators, such as Pausanias, the shift from democracy to autocracy under the Roman emperor Augustus was not necessarily a move in the right direction (Hutton, 2008). Historical theologians like J. Pelikan (1997) have emphasized the debt of many Greek-speaking, early Christian thinkers to the groundbreaking work of Plato, particularly in the areas of cosmology, anthropology, and educational ethics. A. Cameron (2016, 205–246) presents a reinterpretation of the familiar story of Justin's closure of the schools of Athens, suggesting that the training in Platonic philosophy and rhetoric once offered in Athens to elite males, Christian and non-Christian alike, seems to have fallen into abeyance well before 539 CE. Recent studies of Athens in the early to middle Byzantine periods have shown that traditional accounts of the city's decline in the so-called "dark ages," from the 7th to 10th centuries CE, have been exaggerated. Recently, A. Grenda (2020) reappraised the archaeological and architectural evidence for the built environment of Athens in the 7th century CE, concluding that it was a vibrant and fully functioning urban center that embarked on a major building campaign for the visit of Constans II and his army in the winter of 662–663 CE. The city's ongoing historical significance as a pilgrimage center is evident in the program of church-building that was executed in the 11th and 12th centuries, and especially in the long-lasting success of the cult of the Virgin, "Theotokos Atheniotissa" (Kaldellis, 2009).

Bibliography

Cameron, A., *Wandering Poets and Other Essays on Late Greek Literature and Philosophy*, Oxford, 2016.

Flemming, D., "Contextualizing the Gospel in Athens: Paul's Areopagus Address as a Paradigm for Missionary Communication," *Miss* 30/2, 2002, 199–214.

Grenda, A., "'Dark Age' Re-Enlightened: A Reassessment of the Archaeological and Architectural Evidence of Seventh-Century CE Athens," diss., Davis, 2020.

Hutton, W., "The Disaster of Roman Rule: Pausanias 8.27.1," *CQ* 58/2, 2008, 622–637.

Kaldellis, A., *The Christian Parthenon: Classicism and Pilgrimage in Medieval Athens*, Cambridge UK, 2009.

Kosmin, P.J., "A Phenomenology of Democracy: Ostracism as Political Ritual," *ClAn* 34/1, 2015, 121–162.

Osborne, R., "A Crisis in Archaeological History? The Seventh Century BC in Attica," *ABSAth* 84, 1989, 297–322.

Pelikan, J., *What Has Athens to Do with Jerusalem? Timaeus and Genesis in Counterpoint*, Jerome Lectures 21, Ann Arbor, 1997.

Rankin, D., *Athenagoras: Philosopher and Theologian*, Farnham, 2009.

Spawforth, T., *The Complete Greek Temples*, London, 2006.

Theocharaki, A.M., "The Ancient Circuit Wall of Athens: Its Changing Course and the Phases of Construction," *Hesp.* 80/1, 2011, 71–156.

BRONWEN NEIL

Atonement

As its etymology implies, the term "atonement" (at-one-ment) denotes the restored state of fellowship between God and humanity – God and humanity being "at one." In the early church, a variety of categories – such as redemption, forgiveness, revealed knowledge, purification or expiation, and propitiation – contribute to making "atonement." The word is, therefore, used here with two caveats. First, while the term itself was unavailable to early Christians, the idea that, because of Jesus, God and humanity can dwell together in harmony and close proximity is central to early Christianity. The notion is so ubiquitous and fundamental that the survey here can only trace major contours and note illustrative examples. Second, while the various concepts noted above can be explored in a given ancient text independently of one another, they could equally intermingle and/or be treated as concurrent. This study identifies distinct categories, but it would be a mistake to assume that any given author or text necessarily conceived of one category as mutually exclusive of others. Often one finds multiple conceptions in play. Importantly, the various concepts invoked largely depend upon the human problems that Jesus solves (see Tuckett, 1992, 518). To speak about atonement in early Christianity is, therefore, to speak about the variety of ways that various early Christians conceived of Jesus and his work as negotiating the variety of problems that prevent humanity from being "at one" with God. We here examine four major categories of problem and their corresponding solutions: sin, enslavement to → death and the → devil, the fallen human condition, and false knowledge. Amidst the diversity, it is clear that in the patristic era both the divinity and the humanity of Jesus were viewed as making essential contributions to atonement.

1. Sin and Atonement

One of the most pervasive problems that early Christians envisioned Jesus solving was that of → sin. Interest in sin flowed directly from the movement's Jewish and biblical taproot, which provided many of the metaphors for conceiving of the problem and its solutions. Four of the most significant metaphors are sin as impurity/stain, sin as offense, sin as weight/burden, and sin as debt/enslavement. Each of these has a corresponding solution. Impurity needs to be purged by rituals such as washing and/or blood sacrifice. Restitution, repentance, and sacrifice can deal with an offense and its corresponding guilt. The burden needs to be lifted or carried away, as in the so-called scapegoat ritual of the Day of Atonement (→ Atonement, Day of). Debt requires payment in appropriate currency. All of these conceptions of sin and their solutions are directly related to Jesus' person and work by early Christians.

The biblical and Jewish practices of particular sacrificial and washing rituals, as well as confession and expressions of genuine repentance, were central to obtaining purification and for maintaining peace with God. Links between these practices and Jesus are already evident in the earliest Christian texts collected in the New Testament (e.g. Matt 26:28; Luke 24:47; John 1:29; Acts 2:38; 3:19; 22:16; Rom 3:25; Col 1:20–22; Heb 1:3; 2:17; 9:26; Jas 5:16; 1 John 1:9;

2:2), but they find substantial development in the patristic era.

A diverse number of ritual ideas are applied to Jesus to show how he solves the problem of sin. Christian → baptism is viewed as a means of washing away or forgiving sins (*Barn.* 11.1–11; Just. 1 *Apol.* 61; *Dial.* 14.1; Iren. *Epid.* 3). The notion that Jesus died as the sacrificial victim of a sin offering/"for sins" is ubiquitous. Ignatius of Antioch (→ Ignatius, Epistles of), while not explicitly calling Jesus' death a sacrifice, appears to assume this notion when conceiving of his own death sacrificially (Ign. *Rom.* 4–6; Daly, 1978b, 320). *1 Clement* (→ Clement) speaks of the pouring out of Jesus' blood as enabling repentance (*1 Clem.* 6.4; 12.7). *1 Clement* further highlights the importance of repentance for cleansing the stain of sin (*1 Clem.* 7.5–8.5; see also 2 *Clem.* 8). *Barn.* 5.1 links Jesus' sprinkled blood with → forgiveness of sin (similarly *Barn.* 7.3; 12.1). Other 2nd-century CE sources connect Jesus' death and awaited return with the two goats of the Day of Atonement (*Barn.* 7.3–11; Just. *Dial.* 40.4; Tert. *Marc.* 3.7.7–8). The idea that Jesus' blood purifies believers is clearly attested (Just. *Dial.* 54.1; Iren. *Epid.* 57). Jesus' blood also rescues people from the power of death like the blood of the → Passover lambs (Just. *Dial.* 40.1; 111.3–4; Iren. *Epid.* 25; Tert. *Marc.* 4.40; 5.7; Mel. *Pascha* 31–32; 67). → Origen argues that Jesus' flesh was sacrificed for sin. Thus Jesus' death enabled the purification and destruction of sin because sin, which Jesus bore in his body, was condemned in the death of his flesh (Or. *Comm. Rom.* 6.12). → Ephrem the Syrian likens the → cross to a censer on which Jesus, like incense, was offered to God (Ephr. *Hom. Lord* 9.2). Notably, too, the suffering and death of Jesus, as well as his burial and → resurrection (Iren. *Epid.* 72), could be identified as the means of bringing God and humanity together without ritual ideas being explicitly invoked. Ignatius identifies the cross as the central mechanism that carries humanity up to God (Ign. *Eph.* 9.1; similarly, Iren. *Epid.* 45). Such reflection on the sacrificial significance of Jesus' death only continues to develop in later centuries.

Another link between Jesus' atoning work and Jewish sacrificial concepts lies in the identification of Jesus as both the great high priest and the → sacrifice offered to God. When reflecting on Jesus' high priesthood, special attention is often directed to the particular contribution that Jesus' humanity makes toward effecting atonement (see Moffitt, 2017). → Justin Martyr points to Jesus' high-priestly service as the means for removing the stain of sin and providing forgiveness (Just. *Dial.* 116.1–3). → Irenaeus of Lyon implies that Jesus' ascension marked the presentation of his humanity as a sacrificial offering to God (Iren. *Haer.* 3.19.3; see *Haer.* 3.17.3). The ascended Jesus now intercedes for his people and thereby redeems them (Iren. *Epid.* 88). He also describes Jesus' high-priestly work in terms of propitiating God and releasing exiled humanity from condemnation to regain their inheritance without fear (Iren. *Haer.* 4.8.2). Origen holds that Jesus' blood was sprinkled "for sins" on earth when he died in Jerusalem. He also argues that, because of Jesus' → resurrection and ascension, Jesus serves as the high priest who sprinkled his blood as a spiritual offering at the altar in heaven (Or. *Hom. Lev.* 1.3.19–33; 7.1.110–118; 7.2.37–57). Through this dual-sacrificial activity, Jesus made peace on earth by defeating the evil powers, and in heaven by bringing humanity in his own person back into God's presence (Young, 1979, 175–179). Expanding on the latter point, Origen makes an analogy to the high priest's actions on the Jewish Day of Atonement (see Lev 16), especially as interpreted in the Epistle to the Hebrews. Just as the earthly high priests entered the holy of holies once a year to intercede for the people while offering the sacrificial blood for forgiveness and purification, so Jesus rose from the dead and ascended into heaven there to offer himself once to God to make propitiation and to intercede continually for his people at the heavenly altar (Or. *Hom. Lev.* 7.2.37–57; 9.5.51–112).

The idea that Jesus presented himself – that is, his resurrected humanity – to God in heaven as a sacrificial offering continued to be influential, especially in the East (though see also Hipp. *Noet.* 4). → Gregory of Nazianzus speaks of the "sacrifice of the resurrection" (Greg. Naz. *Ep.* 171). → Theodoret of Cyrrhus, commenting on Heb 8:1–4, argues that Jesus assumed human nature in order to offer that nature to God on behalf of the rest of humanity when he ascended into heaven (Theodoret of Cyrrhus, *Commentarii in omnes Pauli Epistulas*; PG 82.736). Regarding Heb 9:24–26 he claims that Jesus, as the great high priest, appeared as a human being before God in the tabernacle of heaven to present himself as a sacrifice, his perfected humanity dealing decisively with sin (PG 82.745). → Narsai speaks of Jesus' ascension with his resurrected body of dust as his entry into the holy of holies to serve as high priest. There he appeared before God to make atonement by offering the sacrifice of himself (Narsai, *Hom. Ascen.* 81–84; 200–210).

The idea that the burden of sin was removed by Jesus' suffering and death is also prominent. The so-called servant songs of Isaiah are important in this regard (*1 Clem.* 16.4, 12, 14; Pol. *Phil.* 8.1; Or. *Comm. Rom.* 6.12). Explicit comparisons between Jesus and the scapegoat ritual further develop this idea. Origen identifies Jesus as the one who led the "lot of the scapegoat," that is, the powers of the devil, sin, and death, off into the wilderness of hell when he died (Or. *Hom. Lev.* 9.5.26–33, 42–50). Somewhat differently, → Cyril of Alexandria argues that Jesus bore sins away like the scapegoat when, after his resurrection, he carried them off to heaven as part of his offering to the Father (Cyril of Alexandria, *Glaphyra on Leviticus*; PG 69.588–589).

The notions that Jesus is the redeemer who pays off the debt owed by sinners, or who offers himself in place of those who are rightfully held in bondage because of their sin, are also common (see further "Enslavement and Atonement" below). Jesus' own life and/or suffering can be seen as given in exchange for others (*1 Clem.* 49.6; 55.1–2; Pol. *Phil.* 9.2; *Diogn.* 9.2–6; Iren. *Haer.* 5.1.1; Cyr.Alex. *Ep.*41; see Lyonnet & Sabourin, 1970, 197–198). Irenaeus, among others (Williams, 2011) envisions Jesus' suffering as taking away the punishment rightly due to sinners (Iren. *Epid.* 69). He also identifies the sacrifice of Isaac as pointing to the sacrifice of Jesus for → redemption (Iren. *Haer.* 4.5.4). He argues as well that Jesus' suffering provided merit or credit that can be used to pay off the debts of sinners (*Haer.* 5.17.3; see also Anderson, 2009, 121–132). Even the individual Christian can make a contribution. The work of one's hands, suffering for "the name," and almsgiving are among the activities explicitly identified as paying or ransoming for one's sin (*2 Clem.* 16.4; *Did.* 4.5–8; *Barn.* 19.10–11; Pol. *Phil.* 10.2; Herm. *Sim.* 9.28.3–7; see Garrison, 1993, 76–142; Anderson, 2009, 152–188; Downs, 2016).

2. Enslavement and Atonement

While related to the problem of sin, especially conceived of as debt, reflection on how Jesus provides the solution to humanity's enslavement to death and the devil tends to focus on the way that Jesus frees humanity from these powers in order to restore their fellowship with God. Here, too, both Jesus' divinity and humanity are essential. Jesus' redeeming work is viewed in terms of his leading humanity out of slavery to death and the devil (*Barn.* 14.5–6; 16.9). Jesus' birth is identified by Justin as liberating humanity from demonic power (*Dial.* 78.9). On the basis of texts such as Eph 6:12 and Col 2:14–15, many thought in terms of Jesus' death serving as payment or satisfaction for the legal claim of the powers of sin, death, and the devil. This so-called ransom theory is already present in the 2nd century CE. Irenaeus explains that humanity fell into debt to death and into the power of the devil when → Adam and Eve disobeyed. Because the → Word of God was immortal, he had to become human, for only as a human being could he bind the strong man, defeat death, and rise again to free the rest of humanity from sin and death and restore union with God (Iren. *Haer.* 3.18.6–7; 3.5.21–23; *Epid.* 31, 37–39). → Tertullian clearly speaks about Jesus' death and blood as payment for humanity's debt. Because of Jesus' death, hell (→ Hades) and the evil angels had to give up their rightful claim on humanity (Tert. *Fug.* 12). → Athanasius of Alexandria also argues that the → incarnation of the immortal Word of God was necessary to free humanity because only as a human being could the Word die, void death's legal claim on humanity, and free humanity to the life of resurrection (Athan. *Inc.* 6–10). These ideas are expanded to include notions of the humanity of the Word serving as bait. The devil thought he could defeat Jesus by killing his humanity, but was tricked and "hooked" since Jesus' divinity ensured that his humanity would not remain subject to death (Greg. Nyss. *Or. catech. magna* 22–24, 26). Jesus' humanity is also portrayed as concealing the divinity of the Word of God like a medicine. Death unwittingly consumed the medicine, which induced the vomiting out of those whom it had previously devoured (Ephr. *Hom. Lord* 3.1–4).

3. The Human Condition and Atonement

The "recapitulation theory," prominent in Irenaeus, highlights the need for every phase of human existence to be restored in order for God and humanity to dwell together. Again, both the divinity and humanity of Jesus contribute to this restoration. The entire sweep of the incarnation, from Jesus' conception in → Mary's womb to his heavenly ascension and session, is seen as the means of gathering humanity together for redemption, as well as of healing every stage of fallen human existence. Irenaeus identifies the totality of the incarnation as solving the conjoined problems of sin, mortality, and the corruption of the human body. In the incarnation the Word passed through every period of human life in order to defeat death and restore fellowship between God and humanity (Iren. *Haer.* 3.18.7). In this way Jesus returned the image of God, which Adam had lost, to humanity and advanced humanity to perfection, making the human body immortal and incorruptible (*Haer.* 3.18.1, 7; 3.19.1, 3; 4.38.1–4; 5.1.3; *Epid.* 31; Daly, 1978a, 93–94). The idea that the Word of God became a human in order that humanity might become like the Word of God anticipates the later doctrine of deification (Russell, 2004, 105–110).

4. Knowledge and Atonement

Another major category of problem that separates God and humanity is that of ignorance or false knowledge, particularly as these are a significant source of disobedience. In arguing with the gnostics, it becomes clear for the proto-orthodox that the solution to the problem of false knowledge rests in the contributions of both Jesus' humanity and divinity. Jesus brings to humanity right knowledge in his teaching, as well as, by virtue of his divinity, making God and his ways visible in his human body. Texts such as Matt 11:27 and John's Gospel, especially the depiction of Jesus as the *logos* and the light shining in the darkness, are particularly influential in this regard. Ignatius identifies the birth of Jesus as an event that destroyed ignorance, freeing humanity from the grip of magic and the bondage of evil. The manifestation of God in a human manner threw the realm of death into chaos (Ign. *Eph.* 19). Even those who criticized the gnostics thought that true knowledge was essential for restored fellowship with God. For Irenaeus, sin stains the flesh, while false knowledge and teaching stain the soul. Both keep humanity away from God and lead to death (Iren. *Epid.* 2). Right teaching illuminates the path the believer should walk to have union with God (*Epid.* 1). He identifies the cross as the tree that destroys the knowledge of evil while revealing the knowledge of good (*Epid.* 34). The incarnation provides salvation by making knowledge of the invisible God known to humanity in the visible Jesus (Iren. *Haer.* 4.7.1–7). For → Clement of Alexandria, Christ, whom he calls the "Pedagogue" (Clem. *Paed.* 1.1), imparts the true knowledge that leads humanity to God. As God, the Word forgives our sin. As the human being Jesus, the Word trains us not to sin (*Paed.* 1.3). Only the Christian is truly able to follow Socrates' advice to "know thyself," and knowledge of God even enables deification (*Paed.* 3.1; see also Hipp. *Haer.* 10.30). → Tatian the Syrian identifies the acquisition of the knowledge of God as the way in which the → soul, illumined by the *logos*, becomes immortal, is united with the Spirit of God, and is enabled to be united with God (Tat. *Orat.* 13, 15).

Historiography

Numerous studies on or relating to some aspect of atonement in the patristic era have appeared in the last 100 years (e.g. Rashdall, 1919; Lyonnet & Sabourin, 1970; Daly, 1978b; Young, 1979; Anderson, 2009; Downs, 2016). J. Johnson offers a helpful discussion of key patristic figures and ideas, along with an annotated biography of selected secondary texts (Johnson, 2016). Several useful short essays addressing atonement in certain patristic figures can be found in the *T&T Clark Companion to Atonement* (Johnson, 2017). While dated, G. Aulén's *Christus Victor* (1931) stands among the most influential modern contributions. G. Aulén challenged the "Latin idea" of atonement (esp. as exemplified by Anselm) and its suggestion that Jesus' sacrifice effected atonement as an offering from humanity to God. He argued that God's victory over the opposing powers through the death and resurrection of Christ was entirely God's own work, and that this was the dominant "classic idea" of the atonement in the patristic era. G. Aulén helpfully brought an undervalued or demythologized aspect of the atonement in early Christianity back into view. His recovery of the theme of Christ's victory over evil has been taken up in developments of liberation and feminist theologies (e.g. Ray, 1998). Nevertheless, his attempt to remove from early Christianity the idea that Jesus' humanity contributed to effecting atonement is reductive and does not fit all the evidence. Early Christian conceptions of Jesus as the high priest in heaven, for example, particularly highlight the essential contribution of his humanity in procuring atonement (see Moffitt, 2017). The recent work of D.J. Downs refocuses attention on the importance of acts of charity and alms giving in patristic discussions of atonement, something not deemed to conflict with the essential salvific work of Jesus (Downs, 2016).

Bibliography

Anderson, G.A., *Sin: A History*, New Haven, 2009.

Aulén, G., *Christus Victor: An Historical Study of the Three Main Types of the Idea of Atonement*, trans. A.G. Herbert, London, 1931.

Daly, R.J., *The Origins of the Christian Doctrine of Sacrifice*, Philadelphia, 1978a.

Daly, R.J., *Christian Sacrifice: The Judaeo-Christian Background Before Origen*, SCA 18, Washington DC, 1978b.

Downs, D.J., *Alms: Charity, Reward, and Atonement in Early Christianity*, Waco, 2016.

Garrison, R., *Redemptive Almsgiving in Early Christianity*, JSNT.S 77, Sheffield, 1993.

Johnson, A.J., ed., *T&T Clark Companion to Atonement*, London, 2017.

Johnson, J., *Patristic and Medieval Atonement Theory: A Guide to Research*, Illum., London, 2016.

Lyonnet, S., & L. Sabourin, *Sin, Redemption, and Sacrifice: A Biblical and Patristic Study*, AnBib 48, Rome, 1970.

Moffitt, D.M., "Jesus' Heavenly Sacrifice in Early Christian Reception of Hebrews: A Survey." *JThS* 68, 2017, 46–71.

Rashdall, H., *The Idea of Atonement in Christian Theology*, BaLe 1915, London, 1919.

Ray, D.K., *Deceiving the Devil: Atonement, Abuse, and Ransom*, Cleveland, 1998.

Russell, N., *The Doctrine of Deification in the Greek Patristic Tradition*, OECS, Oxford, 2004.

Tuckett, C.M., "Atonement in the New Testament," in: D.N. Freedmen, ed., *ABD*, vol. I, New York, 1992, 518–522.

Williams, G.J. "Penal Substitutionary Atonement in the Church Fathers," *EvQ* 83, 2011, 195–216.

Young, F.M., *The Use of Sacrificial Ideas in Greek Christian Writers from the New Testament to John Chrysostom*, PatMS 5, Philadelphia, 1979.

David M. Moffitt

Atonement, Day of

Celebrated in autumn on the tenth day of the seventh month (10 Tishri), the atoning rituals of the annual Day of Atonement, or Yom Kippur, were central to the maintenance of the covenant relationship between the God of Israel and his people. These rituals provided important categories for early Christians as they reflected on Jesus and the salvific work he performed. While virtually every detail of the day's rite was open to examination, two aspects in particular exercised widespread and enduring influence on Christological, soteriological, ethical, and apologetic reflection:

1. the presentation of the two goats, one to be slaughtered and one to be sent away;
2. the distinctive annual entry of the high priest into the holy of holies to sprinkle the sacrificial blood there.

The latter element provided a pattern whereby Jesus' death, → resurrection, and → ascension were explained in terms of the ultimate, heavenly Day of Atonement. This correlated with the development of the Christian spiritual cult. The former aspect came to serve as an influential Hebrew Bible type prefiguring Jesus' divine and human nature.

1. Conceptual and Ritual Background

The primary biblical instructions for the Day of Atonement are found in Lev 16, Lev 23:26–32, and Num 29:7–11. According to Lev 16, the "anointed priest" (later called the "high priest") must bathe and put on holy linen garments (Lev 16:4). Lev 16 indicates that a bull, two goats (one chosen by lot for the Lord and the other chosen by lot for Azazel; Lev 16:7–10), and two rams were offered (a third goat is also offered according to Num 29:7–11). The anointed priest first took incense and blood from the bull and went behind the veil into the inner sanctuary (later called the "holy of holies"). There he sprinkled some of the blood on the lid of the Ark of the Covenant (the ἱλαστήριον, LXX) and in front of it. He then repeated this process with blood from the goat chosen by lot for the Lord (Lev 16:14–15). After this he placed his hands upon the goat designated for Azazel (the so-called scapegoat), confessed the sins of the people, and sent it away alive. A "prepared

man" led the goat into the wilderness and released it (Lev 16:20–22). Additionally, the people were obligated to refrain from work and afflict themselves (Lev 16:29–31; 23:26–32; Num 29:7).

During the Second Temple period, fasting and confession were understood to satisfy the vague command to "afflict" oneself. The holiday even came to be identified as the "day of the fast" (e.g. 1QpHab 11.7–8; CD 6.19; Philo *Spec.* 2.200) or simply "the fast" (e.g. Jos. *Ant.* 18.95; Philo *Spec.* 1.186; Acts 27:9; see also 11QT 25.11–12; Schiffman, 1998; Jos. *Bell.* 5.236–37). The traditions of wrapping scarlet wool around the scapegoat's head, abusing it, and killing it by taking it into the wilderness and pushing it down a steep hill also appear to be practiced during this period, though the evidence is late (*m. Yoma* 6.4–6; see also *Barn.* 7.7–8; Just. *Dial.* 40.4; Tert. *Marc.* 3.7.7–8). The notion that Azazel was a demon may underlie the depiction in *1 En.* 10.4–6 of the demon Asael being bound, thrown down into Doudael in the wilderness upon sharp stones, and covered with darkness to await the final judgment. This is suggestive of the tradition of leading the goat for Azazel into the wilderness and throwing it down a precipice (Stökl Ben Ezra, 2003, 85–88).

2. Use in the Earliest Christian Sources

Paul's depictions

1. of God putting Christ forward as the ἱλαστήριον (Rom 3:25);
2. of Jesus, perhaps like the high priest in the holy of holies, interceding for believers in God's very presence (Rom 8:34);
3. of Jesus, perhaps like the scapegoat, becoming a curse (Gal 3:13) or being made sin (2 Cor 5:21; Rom 8:3) hint at the influence of the Day of Atonement in his thinking (Finlan, 2004).

More explicit are the references to Jesus as a propitiation (ἱλασμός) for sins in 1 John 2:2 and 4:10, particularly in light of the themes of purification, confession, and Jesus' heavenly intercession in the near context (Stökl Ben Ezra, 2003, 205–206). Yom Kippur may also underlie the Markan and Matthean accounts of Barabbas being set free while Jesus is condemned to death (so Berenson Maclean, 2007; Stökl Ben Ezra, 2012, 179–184). The Epistle to the Hebrews, however, is unique in the New Testament in drawing sustained connections between Jesus and the holiday. Hebrews links the death, resurrection, ascension, and heavenly session of Jesus with the high priest's act of sprinkling blood in the holy of holies. Jesus is presented as the great high priest who ascended through the heavens (Heb 4:14; 7:26), entered the heavenly sanctuary (Heb 8:1–2), and approached God in order to present his redemptive offering (Heb 9:11–14, 24–28). By appealing to the process of the blood rituals on Yom Kippur, the author develops a Christology and corresponding soteriology that understand Jesus' death, resurrection, and ascension in terms of the high-priestly activity in the earthly holy of holies (Moffitt, 2011, 43, 297–303). The linkage of this sequence of events with the process of the Yom Kippur rituals becomes determinative for early Christian reflection on Lev 16.

3. Developments in the 2nd through 4th Centuries

Much of the 2nd-century Christian literature that explicitly refers to some facet of the Day of Atonement does so to apologize for Christian claims about Jesus and to polemicize against Jews. The *Epistle of Barnabas* (7.3–11; → Barnabas), → Justin Martyr's *Dialogue with Trypho* (*Dial.* 40.4), and → Tertullian's *Against Marcion* (*Marc.* 3.7.7–8) and *Against the Jews* (*Adv. Jud.* 14.9) all contain similar appeals to Yom Kippur. Each refers to the holiday in terms of its fast (*Barn.* 7.3; *Dial.* 40.4–5; *Adv. Jud.* 14.9). Curiously, while Lev 16:27 prohibits eating any of the goat for the Lord (see also Heb 13:10), both *Barnabas* and Tertullian claim that a goat was to be eaten by the priests while everyone else was to fast (*Barn.* 7.4; *Marc.* 3.7.7; *Adv. Jud.* 14.9). The solution may be to identify this goat with the additional goat offered for sins according to Num 29:11 (so Stökl Ben Ezra, 2003, 150). According to *Barnabas*, the priests were to eat the entrails of this goat with vinegar (*Barn.* 7.4). This prefigured Jesus being given vinegar and gall on the → cross. The fasting and mourning to be observed by everyone else prefigured Jesus' suffering (*Barn.* 7.5). Tertullian states that the priests in the → Temple were to eat the goat itself while the people outside fasted. This symbolized Jesus' glorious return when the church will feast on the Lord's grace while those

who are outside will fast from salvation (*Marc.* 3.7.7; *Adv. Jud.* 14.9).

The presumed likeness between the two goats distinguished by lots was linked to Jesus' two advents. Barnabas connects the scapegoat being cursed and abused, having red wool wrapped around its head, and being cast into the desert with the treatment of Jesus during his passion (*Barn.* 7.7–9). When Jesus returns crowned and wearing a scarlet robe, the Jews will recognize him as the very one whom they mocked, abused, and crucified (*Barn.* 7.9–10). Here Barnabas invokes the likeness of the goats, though he does not clearly explain how Jesus' return resembles the goat offered to the Lord (see Carleton Paget, 1994, 137–138). Justin and Tertullian more explicitly develop this point. Both claim that the scapegoat prefigured his first advent. Thus, he was abused and killed/sent away. In his glorious return he will be recognized as the slaughtered goat whose blood has dealt with the sins of those who belong to him.

Origen, following Hebrews' lead, offers sustained reflection on the Day of Atonement in his *Homilies on Leviticus*. In homily nine he explores the ways Jesus is like the individuals who handle the two goats – the high priest, who offers the blood sacrifice, and the "prepared man," who leads the scapegoat into the wilderness. The earthly holy of holies represents the heavenly space where God dwells most fully. Thus, the entry of the high priest into that earthly space points forward to the time when the incarnate Son would enter the heavenly reality. The latter event occurred when the resurrected Jesus ascended into heaven dressed, like the Levitical high priest, in the holy garments of his resurrected body (Or. *Hom. Lev.* 9.2.26–32). → Origen points to the singular nature of the annual blood offering as a figure for the duration of the present age during which Christians await Jesus' return. The blood rituals on the Day of Atonement provided a key for interpreting the temporal space between Jesus' ascension and his return. Just as the people waited for the high priest who left them once a year to enter God's presence in the holy of holies, so Jesus, after his time among the people, left them and went once into heaven (*Hom. Lev.* 9.2.22–25; 5.85–98). There he now ministers for his people before the heavenly altar, in the very presence of the Father. The end of this "true Day of Atonement" (*verus dies propitiatonis*; *Hom. Lev.* 9.5.54) will occur when Jesus returns. This will mark the completion of his atoning work and the end of the present age (*Hom. Lev.* 9.5.107–112).

When Origen turns his attention to the "prepared man" who led the scapegoat away, he reflects on Jesus' crucifixion and descent into hell (→ Christ). Drawing on Col 2:14–15 and Eph 6:12, Origen identifies the cross as the place where Jesus triumphed over the powers and principalities of this world, whom Origen dubs "the lot of the scapegoat." In his death he led these malevolent forces away into the ultimate wilderness of hell (*Hom. Lev.* 9.5.26–33, 42–50). Returning from that wilderness, his earthly work completed, he rose from the dead and ascended to the heavenly altar to perform his high-priestly work (*Hom. Lev.* 9.5.51–54). Thus Jesus' blood has made peace for things in heaven and things on earth (Col 1:20; see *Hom. Lev.* 1.3–4 for a slightly different account). While now dated, G. Aulén's well-known claim that the "classic Christian idea of the Atonement" in the fathers holds incarnation and redemption firmly together particularly by highlighting the victory of Jesus over the evil powers in his death and in his resurrection (Aulén, 1931; similarly Young, 1979) captures an essential aspect of Origen's use of the Day of Atonement.

Origen's claims about the heavenly offering of Jesus directly relate to his understanding of the universal priesthood of believers and the spiritual sacrifices Christians are to offer. Because Jesus now serves as the great high priest in heaven, Christians can participate in the spiritual cult. The practice of Christian virtues in every church becomes the incense that fills Jesus' hand and that he offers in the heavenly holy of holies (*Hom. Lev.* 9.8). Deeds such as martyrdom, love of others, and mortification of the flesh all become spiritual sacrifices offered by every individual upon the outer altar of the church only then to be taken behind the veil and offered by Jesus in heaven (*Hom. Lev.* 9.9; see also Daly, 1982, 875–876).

Origen's tenth homily chastises Christians who observe Yom Kippur by fasting together with the Jews (see also Or. *Hom. Jer.* 12.13). The homily presupposes continuing observance of at least some Jewish holidays and practices by at least some Christians (see Stökl Ben Ezra, 2003, 74–75, 273–283). Unlike homily nine, Origen here compares Jesus to the goat chosen by lot for the Lord and offered on account

of sins. Barabbas, he suggests, is akin to the goat that was sent into the desert. Pilate is likened to the prepared man who first washed his hands to purify/prepare himself and then released Barabbas (*Hom. Lev.* 10.2.24–44). Christians ought to eschew the Jewish fast observing instead the fasts that please God – abstaining from sins (similarly, see Just. *Dial.* 15.1–7; 40.4). His reflection on the Day of Atonement, and indeed on Leviticus in general, helps solidify the role of cultic categories for Christian ethical and moral discourse (Wilken, 1995, 90).

A somewhat different approach may be seen in → Cyril of Alexandria. Cyril looks to the goats offered on the Day of Atonement as types of Jesus' salvific death, resurrection, and ascension, as well as of his divine and human natures (see his 41st letter [PG 77] and his *Glaphyra on Leviticus* [PG 69]). He is concerned to demonstrate that the scapegoat had no connection with a demon (PG 69, 585, 588; 77, 204–205, 208). Whereas interpretation in the 2nd and 3rd centuries CE tended to reverse the order of the events detailed in Lev 16 (connecting the expulsion of the scapegoat with the initial event of Jesus' crucifixion and the offering of the slaughtered goat with the subsequent events of Jesus' resurrection, ascension, heavenly session, and return), Cyril finds significance in the order of the rituals as given in Lev 16. The crucifixion was the moment when Jesus, like the first goat, died as the sin offering. As such, he was a sinless substitute for sinners who took God's condemnation upon himself (PG 77, 209, 212). The second goat prefigured Jesus' subsequent resurrection and ascension since it was sent away alive. Like the scapegoat, Jesus also bore away sins when he ascended to the Father's presence (PG 69, 589; 77, 212–213, 216). There he intercedes for his people. Clearly, then, the scapegoat was not offered to a demon, for Jesus ascended as an offering to the Father, a place that was previously inaccessible to humanity and so like a wilderness (PG 69, 588–589). Thus two successive goats were required in order to represent the full scope of Jesus' → sacrifice precisely because Jesus' sacrifice involved not only his death, but also his resurrection and ascension (PG 69, 588–589; 77, 208, 220; see Lyonnet & Sabourin, 1970, 276). Cyril further sees Jesus' two natures prefigured in the two goats. Jesus' passible humanity is evident in the goat that dies, while his impassable divinity as the → Word is prefigured in the goat sent away alive (PG 77, 212, 217). Cyril's linkage of the scapegoat with the resurrection and ascension of Jesus and his discussion of the two goats in terms of Jesus' two natures exercised significant influence on later tradition (Lyonnet & Sabourin, 1970, 279). Interpreters such as the commentary on Leviticus attributed to Hesychius of Jerusalem (PG 93, esp. 991–992; Lyonnet & Sabourin, 1970, 277), Procopius of Gaza (PG 87, 747–749; Elliott, 2012, 161), and → Theodoret of Cyrrhus (*Quaest. Lev.* 22; PG 80, 328–333) all take similar approaches when reflecting on Yom Kippur's two goats.

4. Modern Study of the Day of Atonement in Early Christianity

The discovery of the → Dead Sea Scrolls and the realization that the so-called parting of the ways occurred later than generally assumed have helped kindle renewed interest in the Jewish context of early Christianity. Within these larger trends has come new work on the influence of the Day of Atonement. Of particular note in this regard are the studies of D. Stökl Ben Ezra (1999; 2003) on the significance of Yom Kippur for multiple aspects of early Christian belief and practice. The importance, as noted above, of the high priest's entry into the holy of holies as a paradigm for interpreting Jesus' ascension and current absence from his people in terms of his ongoing high-priestly ministry only becomes clearer in the light D. Stökl Ben Ezra's work.

Bibliography

Aulén, G., *Christus Victor: An Historical Study of the Three Main Types of the Idea of Atonement*, London, 1931, trans. A.G. Herbert.

Berenson Maclean, J.K., "Barabbas, the Scapegoat Ritual, and the Development of the Passion Narrative," *HThR* 100, 2007, 309–334.

Carleton Paget, J., *The Epistle of Barnabas: Outlook and Background*, WUNT 64, 2nd series, Tübingen, 1994.

Daly, R.J., "Sacrificial Soteriology in Origen's Homilies on Leviticus," *StPatr* 17/2, 1982, 872–878.

Elliott, M.W., *Engaging Leviticus: Reading Leviticus Theologically with Its Past Interpreters*, Eugene, 2012.

Finlan, S., *The Background and Content of Paul's Cultic Atonement Metaphors*, ACBI 19, Atlanta, 2004.

Moffitt, D.M., *Atonement and the Logic of Resurrection in the Epistle to the Hebrews*, NT.S 141, Leiden, 2011.

Lyonnet, S., & L. Sabourin, *Sin, Redemption, and Sacrifice: A Biblical and Patrisitic Study*, AnBib 48, Rome, 1970.

Stökl Ben Ezra, D., "Yom Kippur in the Apocalyptic Imaginaire and the Roots of Jesus' High Priesthood: Yom Kippur in Zechariah 3, 1 Enoch 10, 11QMelchizedek, Hebrews and the Apocalypse of Abraham 13," in: J. Assmann & G.G. Stroumsa, eds., *Transformations of the Inner Self in Ancient Religions*, SHR 83, Leiden, 1999, 349–366.

Stökl Ben Ezra, D., *The Impact of Yom Kippur on Early Christianity: The Day of Atonement from Second Temple Judaism to the Fifth Century*, WUNT 163, Tübingen, 2003.

Stökl Ben Ezra, D., "Fasting with Jews, Thinking with Scapegoats: Some Remarks on Yom Kippur in Early Judaism and Christianity, in Particular 4Q541, Barnabas 7, Matthew 27 and Acts 27," in: T. Heike & T. Nicklas, eds., *The Day of Atonement: Its Interpretation in Early Jewish and Christian Traditions*, TBN 15, Leiden, 2012, 165–187.

Schiffman, L.H., "The Case of the Day of Atonement Ritual," in M.E. Stone & E.G. Chazon, eds., *Biblical Perspectives: Early Use and Interpretation of the Bible in Light of the Dead Sea Scrolls*, STDJ 28, Leiden, 1998, 181–188.

Wilken, R.L., "Origen's Homilies on Leviticus and Vayikra Rabbah," in: G. Dorival & A. Le Boullucc, eds., *Origeniana Sexta: Origène et la Bible*, Louvain, 1995, 81–91.

Young, F.M., *The Use of Sacrificial Ideas in Greek Christian Writers from the New Testament to John Chrysostom*, PatMS 5, Philadelphia, 1979.

DAVID M. MOFFITT

Atticus

Socrates Scholasticus informs us that Atticus came from Sivas (ancient Sebastea in the province of Armenia Prima in the civil diocese of Pontus) on the Kızılırmak (also called Halys) River. He had been ascetical from a young age, and → Socrates Scholasticus remarks on his learning and prudence (Socr. *Hist. eccl.* 6.20). As a bishop, Atticus was known for effective pastoral leadership (flourishing churches, a balanced treatment of heretics in that he could be both harsh and clemeent, and his ease in the company of others), his dedication to study so as to be able to combat philosophers and sophists, and his preaching (which changed from committing homilies to memory to an extemporaneous and eloquent style, which Socrates says came from application and confidence), but although his discourses were eloquent, they were not well received or deemed worthy of being recorded (*Hist. eccl.* 7.2).

Sozomen adds to this that Atticus' asceticism had come from the monks who followed Macedonius, a former bishop of Constantinople, who denied the divinity of the → Holy Spirit and was deposed for the second time in 360 CE. These monks, highly trained in philosophy, were organized by Eustathius, bishop of Sivas, whose theological position on → Arianism seems to have oscillated wildly. As an adult, Atticus joined Catholicism and became a presbyter in Constantinople. → Sozomen also states that he was good at intrigues, hid what knowledge he had lest his lack of knowledge become exposed, and was a formidable debater (Soz. *Hist. eccl.* 8.27).

1. Second Exile of John Chrysostom

Atticus is best known for his involvement in the second exile of → John Chrysostom, bishop of Constantinople from 397 to 404 CE, and his subsequent election as one of John's successors in 406 CE. John attracted enemies, who were responsible for his first exile after the Synod of the Oak in 403 CE and again for his final exile at Pentecost in 404 CE. Eudoxia, wife of Emperor Arcadius, is blamed as being John's chief antagonist, who succeeded in getting her husband to use first → Theophilus, bishop of Alexandria, to lead charges against him in 403 CE and then other bishops to condemn him in 404 CE (Pseudo-Martyrius; Socr. *Hist. eccl.* 6.15 and 18; Soz. *Hist. eccl.* 8.16 and 20). This has been accepted by some (Kelly, 1995, 211, 212; Brändle, 2004, 82–86) and challenged by others (Holum, 1982, 48–78; Liebeschuetz, 1985; Mayer, 2006). The latter argue convincingly that Theophilus did not need to be manipulated by Eudoxia. Even Socrates (*Hist. eccl.* 6.9-12) and Sozomen (*Hist. eccl.* 8.2) detail long-standing antagonism between Theophilus and John. Further, while Palladius, bishop of Hersek (ancient Helenopolis in the province of Bithynia in the civil diocese of Pontus), certainly attributes John's first exile to Theophilus, who influenced the empress (Pall. *Dial.* 1, 5, and 7–9) (and includes a letter from John to Innocent I, bishop of Rome [*Dial.* 2] to the same effect), he also believed that local bishops, jealous of John's position, conspired against him (*Dial.* 2, 3, 6, 9, and 10). Sozomen too reports on hostile local bishops (Soz. *Hist. eccl.* 8.10).

After John's final exile in the middle of 404 CE, the elderly and lackluster Arsacius, brother of John's predecessor, Nectarius, was elected as bishop of Constantinople and was succeeded, four months after his death, by Atticus in March 406 CE (Pall. *Dial.* 11; Socr. *Hist. eccl.* 6.20; Soz. *Hist. eccl.* 8.27). Palladius portrays Atticus as the chief ringleader against John and as someone who took active steps to force opponents of himself, Theophilus, and Porphyry of Antioch to submit. John denounced him in *Liber ad eos qui scandalizati sunt.* Heavy recriminations continued against his supporters for some time after John's death in exile in September 407 CE (Pall. *Dial.* 20; Socr. *Hist. eccl.* 7.36; Thdt. *Hist. eccl.* 5.34), including, it would seem, the relocation of a number of bishops. The pressure from the excommunication of Constantinople, Alexandria, and Antioch by Innocent I of Rome eventually led to reconciliation, with Atticus receiving John's name back into the liturgical diptychs and urging → Cyril of Alexandria to do the same (Nic.Cal. *Hist. eccl.* 14.26; Dunn, 2005; 2012).

2. Atticus as Bishop

Not a great deal is known about the rest of Atticus' time as bishop until his death in 425 CE (Socr. *Hist. eccl.* 7.25). → Theodoret of Cyrrhus quotes approvingly from one of Atticus' letters on the Christological controversy over the two natures of Christ, which would become a major theological issue under Nestorius, successor of Atticus' successor Sisinnius I, who held the see for just under two years (Thdt. *Eran.* 2, later cited in the address to Marcian appended to the *acta* of the Council of → Chalcedon). Emperor Arcadius' daughters received a work from Atticus in which the later Christology of Nestorius was anticipated and denounced (Gennad. *Vir. ill.* 53; Marcel. *Chron.* a 416). Sisinnius is desccribed as a friend of Atticus and enemy of John (Socr. *Hist. eccl.* 6.22).

Theodoret regarded both John Chrysostom and Atticus as heralds of the truth (Thdt. *Ep.* 145 and 151). Socrates contains glowing reports of ecclesiastical achievements under Atticus, including his negotiations with the Persians, and his charity toward the poor and the Novatianists (Socr. *Hist. eccl.* 7.4, 18, 25). His severity against heretics, such as the → Messalians and → Pelagians, earned him later praise (Phot. *Bibl.* 52; Celes. *Ep.* 1–3; Merc. Com. *Coel.* 1).

3. Constantinople and the Translation of Perigenes

Atticus was dragged into the dispute over the translation of Perigenes as bishop of Corinth. Dissatisfied with the support given to Perigenes by Rufus of Thessaloniki and Boniface I of Rome, who traditionally supervised ecclesiastical affairs in Corinth, a number of local bishops appealed to Atticus, the nearest major bishop (and one who had the ear of an emperor). Although Constantinople did not have a recognized authority over other regional bishops (which does not appear until 451 CE, in canon 28 of the Council of Chalcedon), the church of the eastern capital had been aiming for increased authority for some time.

Atticus responded favorably when approached by disgruntled bishops and seems to have succeeded since Theodosius II issued a law in 421 CE asserting that the bishop of Constantinople had long held supervision over the churches of Illyricum (Cod. Theod. 16.2.45). The claim was false. It is true that much of the Balkans had passed from the political jurisdiction of the West to the East and that, in imitation, ecclesiastical supervision ought to have passed from Rome to elsewhere, but the letters of the *Collectio Thessalonicensis* reveal that Rome held onto that role through the bishop of Thessaloniki as their delegate. Boniface resisted this law, and five of his letters (Bon. *Ep.* 5, 4, and 13–15) detail his actions, which seems to have included getting Honorius in Ravenna to make his nephew, Theodosius, repeal it. Boniface was never directly critical of Atticus, instead targeting the local disgruntled bishops (Dunn, 2017). Perigenes remained bishop of Corinth for more than a decade.

Historiography

Atticus does not feature as the object of scholarly attention, except insofar as he is mentioned in discussion about the aftermath of the exiles of John Chrysostom. It is only recently that attention has been turned to his role in the translation of Perigenes.

Bibliography

Brändle, R., *John Chrysostom: Bishop–Reformer–Martyr*, trans. J. Cawte & S. Trzcionka, ECSt 8, Strathfield, 2004.

Dunn, G.D., "The Date of Innocent I's *Epistula* 12 and the Second Exile of John Chrysostom," *GRBS* 45, 2005, 155–170.

Dunn, G.D., "The Roman Response to the Ecclesiastical Crises in the Antiochene Church in the Late-Fourth and Early-Fifth Centuries," in: D. Sim & P. Allen, eds., *Ancient Jewish and Christian Texts as Crisis Management Literature: Thematic Studies from the Centre for Early Christian Studies*, LNTS 445, London, 2012, 112–128.

Dunn, G.D., "Boniface I and Roman Ecclesiastical Supervision of the Churches of *Illyricum Orientale*: The Evidence of *Retro maioribus* to Rufus of Thessaloniki," in: *Costellazioni geo-ecclesiali da Costantino a Giustiniano: dalla chiese 'principali' alle chiese patriarcali* (XLIII Incontro di studiosi dell'antichità cristiana, Roma 7–9 maggio 2015), SEAug 149, Roma, 2017, 221–235.

Holum, K., *Theodosian Empresses*, Berkeley, 1982.

Kelly, J.N.D., *Golden Mouth: The Story of John Chrysostom, Ascetic, Preacher, Bishop*, Ithaca, 1995.

Liebeschuetz, J.H.W.G., "The Fall of John Chrysostom," *NMS* 29, 1985, 1–31.

Mayer, W., "Doing Violence to the Image of an Empress: The Destruction of Eudoxia's Reputation," in: H.A. Drake, ed., *Violence in Late Antiquity: Perceptions and Practices*, Aldershot, 2006, 205–213.

GEOFFREY D. DUNN

Attila

The Hunnic ruler Attila is by far the most epochal figure of the 5th century CE. From his accession in the mid-430s to his death in 453 CE, he succeeded in briefly creating a realm in Central Europe powerful enough to repeatedly humiliate the eastern Roman court, and devastate various cities in the Balkans and Italy. His main significance in the history of early Christianity lies in the later reception of his meeting with the bishop of Rome, Leo I, in 452 CE.

1. Background

Attila was the son of Mundiuc, who in turn was the brother of the Hunnic diarchs Octar and Rua (Jor. *Get.* 180). We do not know when Attila was born, though a date in the early 5th century CE seems plausible. By 400 CE, the → Huns were a relatively new established presence in continental Europe.

They first appeared north of the Black Sea in the 370s CE, where they shattered established polities of Alans and → Goths (Am. 31.2–3). However, the Huns were not a unified force, and instead a variety of smaller pastoral nomad groups are attested the next 20 years in raids as far and wide as Raetia and Syria. It is only at the very end of the 4th century CE that we hear of an established Hunnic presence with named leaders north of the Danube. Attila's uncle Rua was the first Hunnic ruler to unite the various smaller European groups under the joint rule of him and Octar. This "tribal empire" was able to lord over a wide variety of previously established groups in *Barbaricum* north of the Danube and the Black Sea, such as Gepids, Rugians, Scirians, or the various Goths who later formed the basis for the new entity of the Ostrogoths. These communities provided the brunt of Hunnic forces. After Octar (d. 430 CE) and Rua (d. 435 CE) had died, they were succeeded by the brothers Attila and Bleda (Priscus, *Frgm.* 2).

2. Accession and Wars with Theodosius II

Attila's first recorded public feat is the negotiation of a treaty with the eastern Roman court at the Danubian city of Margus. In previous decades, the Huns had acted as mercenaries for both the western and eastern imperial governments, though they also had a propensity to raid frontier provinces. The result of this meeting was the doubling of eastern Roman tribute to a total of 700 pounds of gold per annum, to avert Hunnic aggression (Priscus, *Frgm.* 2). By 440 CE, however, it became clear that Constantinople had failed to keep up its side of the pact to deliver the agreed sums. In retaliation, Attila and Bleda crossed the Danube with their forces and sacked Illyrian garrison cities such as Viminacium, Singidunum, and Naissus (Priscus, *Frgm.* 6.1–2). The latter was especially alarming, since Naissus been the birth city of Constantine I, and no barbarian army had previously possessed the necessary siege technology to storm and sack Imperial cities. The Huns were aided in this campaign, however, by the fact that eastern Roman armies were committed at this time to operations in Sicily against the → Vandals, and on the Levantine frontier against the Persians. For the moment, the emperor Theodosius II (408–450 CE)

agreed to double the amount of tribute, yet also took the opportunity to reorganize the defense of his Danubian frontier the following years. By the mid-440s CE, Bleda had probably died at the hands of Attila, as various sources claim, and now went on to hold sole rule over the Huns (Pros. *Epit. chron.* s.a. 444 CE; Mar. Com. *Chron.* s.a. 445 CE; Jor. *Get.* 181). In 447 CE, Attila went to war again with Theodosius, over renewed friction regarding late payments. He unleashed his armies as far and wide as the Thracian Chersonese and Thermopylae, even defeating eastern field armies in pitched battle. There was a brief moment of panic in Constantinople when an earthquake destroyed a section of the fortified walls and no less than 57 towers (Mar. Com. *Chron.* s.a. 447.1 CE). These were hurriedly patched up before the arrival of Attila's armies. Nevertheless, Theodosius' government was still forced to pay back arrears running up to 6,000 pounds of gold and increase the annual tribute to a staggering 2,100 pounds of gold per annum (Priscus, *Frgm.* 9.3). Even more alarming, Attila demanded the creation of a wide no-mans-land immediately south of the Danube. The court was so desperate at this point, that it even attempted to organize an undercover assassination of the Hunnic leader, as part of a diplomatic mission to Attila's own court in 449 CE. This turned into a fiasco as immortalized in the fragmentarily preserved history of Priscus of Panion, who was a member of the embassy and eyewitness to the botched operation (Priscus, *Frgms.* 11–15). Priscus' report of Attila and his court is rare among 5th-century CE sources for its autopsy, complexity, and care for great detail, showing a ruler who was incredibly adroit at power politics, ruthless against enemies and traitors, yet also surprisingly modest in his lifestyle, generous to his allies, and a loving father to his sons.

3. Invading Gaul

Surprisingly, Attila did not pounce on this fiasco to settle scores with the Roman East yet instead diverted his gaze to the West. Three reasons probably stand behind this: First, there was the fact that even the Huns did not possess the resources and technology to storm Constantinople, whose recently reinforced triple walls made it the most daunting bastion of ancient and medieval Europe. Second, by 450 CE Theodosius II had fatally succumbed to a hunting accident and was succeeded by Marcian (450–457 CE), who immediately annulled all tribute to the Huns (Lyd. *Mag.* 3.42). This was probably a gamble based on the estimation that the eastern Roman Balkans had already been thoroughly depleted, and that Attila would be unable to take his forces beyond Constantinople. Third, Attila had received an unexpected invitation from the western princess Honoria to marry her, as a means to rescuing her from her brother, the emperor Valentinian III (425–455 CE). Outlandish as it sounds, there may have been some truth to the matter (Meier, 2019). Valentinian had kept Honoria from marrying even when she was in her 30s and had executed her steward after discovering he was having an affair with his sister (John Ant. *Frgm.* 199.2). Honoria quickly disappears from the historical record after Attila took up the invitation and invaded Gaul with his armies. One suspects she may have paid a lethal price for her damning proposal. In the late spring of 451 CE, Attila and his troops crossed the Rhine, and launched a series of devastating raids across northern Gaul. Prior to the invasion, Attila had hoped to facilitate his advance by sowing dissent among the western Roman government and the various polities in Gaul. Rather than achieving this goal, the Aquitanian Goths, Alans, Burgundians, and a part of the Franks joined the western Roman commander Flavius → Aëtius (d. 454 CE) with their forces. There is a certain irony here, considering Aëtius had risen to power on the back of Hunnic support (425 CE and again in 433 CE), and had used Hunnic mercenaries in his fights against the various aforementioned polities in Gaul (425–439 CE) (Wijnendaele, 2017). The narrative tradition holds that Attila was on the verge of capturing the city of Orléans, until the allied-imperial army arrived and forced him to retreat. The two sides eventually met at the so-called Catalaunian Fields, a site located between Châlons-en-Champagne and Troyes. They clashed in the greatest land battle of the century, which pitched opponents as far removed as Aquitania and Crimea against one another (Jor. *Get.* 178–218). The result was a stalemate, yet Attila did retreat beyond the Rhine in the aftermath. This was the very first and only time he had been halted in battle.

4. Invading Italy and Death

One year later, in 452 CE, Attila struck back with vengeance and invaded Italy. The contemporary chronicler Prosper of Aquitaine, based in Rome, claims that Aëtius had failed to properly garrison the Alpine passes, and even contemplated abandoning the plight of Italy (Pros. *Epit. chron.* s.a. 452 CE). The reality on the ground may have been far more complex, with the western army still licking its wounds from the Gallic war, and not being able to call upon its allies thence. Attila probably caught Italy off-guard. His army stumbled upon stiff resistance at the city of Aquileia, on the eastern gateway into the peninsula. Yet once the city fell after a long siege, the Po valley lay wide open (Pro. *Bel.* 3.4.29–34). Cities such as Padua and even Milan, a former imperial residence, were taken and pillaged (*Suda* M.405). It is at this juncture that Attila received an imperial delegation consisting of high-ranking dignitaries and → Leo I, bishop of Rome. Prosper, who had served at the behest of Leo, claimed Attila was so delighted meeting the bishop that he immediately turned back home (Pros. *Epit. chron.* s.a. 452 CE). However, as J. Bury already wrote a century ago: "It is unreasonable to suppose that this heathen king would have cared for the thunders or persuasions of the Church." (Bury, 1923, 295) The contemporary Christian chronicler Hydatius is probably correct when he states that Attila was compelled to retreat, since his army was suffering from famine and disease (Hyd. *Chron.* 146[154]). It also seems that Marcian had taken the opportunity to harass Hunnic territories north of the Danube. These factors warranted a speedy return. By 453 CE, both the eastern and western courts will have held their breath to see what Attila's next move might be. Rather surprisingly, Attila succumbed to death on his wedding night that year. The various tributary peoples previously under Hunnic rule took the opportunity to rise in 454 CE and shatter the Hunnic realm (Jor. *Get.* 259–263).

5. Legacy in Christian Memory

Attila's famous epithet of *Flagellum Dei* ("scourge of God"), as visible on the 19th-century Certosa di Pavia medallion bearing a stylized reproduction of his image, is not a product of contemporary sources.

While → Augustine of Hippo (d. 430 CE) already used the expression generically in his *De civitate Dei* (Aug. *Civ.* 1.8), we have to wait until the *Vita* of Lupus of Troyes (d. 478 CE) to see an author attributing the title to the Hunnic monarch, during an alleged meeting with the saint (*Vita Lup.* 5). The date of this *Vita* has been disputed, ranging from a near-contemporary production to a Carolingian one, though recent scholarship is willing to see it as a 6th-century CE creation (see the database *The Cult of Saints in Late Antiquity*: http://csla.history.ox.ac .uk/record.php?recid=E00673). Yet contemporary authors took a far more sober view. Leo I himself did not exploit his meeting with Attila in his writings; in fact, he never mentioned it at all. Prosper made sure to also include the names of the senators Avienus and Trygetius as members of the imperial embassy of 452 CE (Pros. *Epit. chron.* s.a. 452 CE). Even the later → *Liber pontificalis*' biography of Leo I devotes only a single line to the meeting but does attribute sole responsibility to the bishop for having cast out Attila (*LP*, vol. XLVII, 7). Local Gallic saints' lives, however, do mention how their respective bishops or holy men and women (e.g. Lupus of Troyes, Genevieve of Paris) helped save their cities during the Hunnic invasion of Gaul, sometimes during direct verbal confrontations with Attila, or became martyrs in the attempt (e.g. Nicasius of Reims) (Barnish, 1992). Mutatis mutandis, Christianity is altogether a negligible feature in Attila's own story. We hear of the bishop of Margus selling out his community to the Huns (Priscus, *Frgm.* 6.1), and we know that Marcian organized the great Ecumenical Council of → Chalcedon in the same year Attila invaded Gaul. Yet at far as Attila was concerned, these were trivial affairs. Christianity certainly was not a reason for exclusion at his multi-ethnic court, as evidenced by his Roman secretary Orestes (whose widow later sponsored an important monastery near Naples). By the time of → Isidore of Seville (d. 636 CE), Attila's legend was fully integrated in the Christian imagination (Isid. *Chron. Mai.* 279). The fame of his meeting with Leo I has been further immortalized by Raphael in the *Stanza di Eliodoro* of the Apostolic Palace of the Vatican, and he stands behind the character of Etzel in the *Nibelungen* saga.

Historiography

As stated earlier, Attila takes a rather marginal position in the history of early Christianity. The same cannot be said, however, about how he has been viewed in the secular history of this era. Scholarship has long been divided over the question whether we should see the Huns as a prime element in the volatile cocktail formerly known as "The Fall of Rome" (restated as recently as e.g. Heather, 2005) or not (e.g. Kulikowski, 2019). This is also noticeable in how we approach Attila's reign. For E.A. Thompson (1948) Attila was neither an inspiring general nor diplomatic genius, but merely a predatory ruler who made the most use of the unifying initiatives of his predecessors. More recently, H.J. Kim (2013) has made the most vigorous case for viewing as an empire the realm Attila governed and expanded, with a long-lasting impact on the cultures and development of Western-European societies. In between these oft-times diametrically opposed views, it is possible to approach Attila as a cunning leader who was able to inflict severe damage on both halves of the Roman Empire at a critical moment in their history (e.g. Kelly, 2008).

Bibliography

Barnish, S.J.B., "Old Kaspars: Attila's Invasion of Gaul in the Literary Sources," in: J. Drinkwater & H. Elton, eds., *Fifth-Century Gaul: A Crisis of Identity?* Cambridge MA, 1992, 38–47.

Boná, I., *Les Huns: Le grand empire barbare d'Europe*, Paris, 2002.

Bury, J.B., *A History of the Later Roman Empire from the Death of Theodosius I to the Death of Justinian*, vol. I, London, 1923.

Heather, P., *The Fall of the Roman Empire: A New History of Rome and the Barbarians*, Oxford, 2005.

Kelly, C., *Attila the Hun: Barbarian Terror and the Fall of the Roman Empire*, London, 2008.

Kim, H.J., *The Huns, Rome, and the Birth of Europe*, Cambridge MA, 2013.

Kulikowski, M., *Imperial Tragedy: From Constantine's Empire to the Destruction of Roman Italy, AD 363–568*, Harvard, 2019.

Maenchen-Helfen, J.O., *The World of the Huns*, Berkeley, 1973.

Meier, M., "A Contest of Interpretation: Roman Policy Toward the Huns as Reflected in the 'Honoria Affair' (448/450)," *JLAn* 10/1, 2019, 42–61.

Rosen, K., *Attila: Der Schrecken der Welt*, Munich, 2016.

Thompson, E.A., *A History of Attila and the Huns*, Oxford, 1948.

Wijnendaele, J.W.P., "The Early Career of Aëtius and the Murder of Felix," *Hist.* 66/4, 2017, 468–482.

Jeroen W.P. Wijnendaele

Audentius

Audentius was bishop of Toledo in the 4th century CE (c. 385–395 CE). According to Ildefonsus (*Vir. Ill.* 2; PL 96.199), he succeeded to the episcopal seat of Toledo. H. Chadwick (1976) sees an onomastic correlation between the Audentius (mentioned by → Gennadius of Marseilles) and one of the 12 bishops who attended the Council of Saragossa (379 CE) under the name Auxentius (or Augentius).

Gennadius of Marseilles (late 5th cent. CE) writes the following:

> Audentius, bishop in Spain, wrote a book entitled *On the Faith against Heretics* against the Manicheans, the Sabellians, the Arians, and, with particular design, against the Photinians, who are now called Bonosiacs. Therein, he shows that the Son of God is as old as the Father and co-eternal with him; that he did not begin to receive the godhead from the Father at the time when he, by divine agency (*Deo fabricante*), was conceived in the womb of the Virgin Mary and came into the world. (Gennad. *Vir. ill.* 14)

At the height of → Priscillianism, Audentius spoke out against the ideas of the movement, which was not yet known by the name of its founder (*priscillianistae*). The Council of Saragossa does not mention the group or its founder. This is the age of Filastrius of Brescia (who calls them *Abstinentes*); Emperor Maximus names them *manichaei*, while the *Indiculus de haeresibus* speaks of *gnostici alii* (Sanchez, 2012). Throughout the standard heresiological accusations, there is a strong stigmatization of dualistic tendencies (→ Mani/Manichaeism), of unitarian or Monarchian Trinitarianism (→ Sabellians), and of deviant theology (as in the case of → Arianism, albeit for other reasons). The mention of Photinians (from Photinus, a disciple of → Marcellus of Ancyra), renamed Bonosiacs in the 4th century CE (from Bonosus, bishop of Sardica, who taught that the Virgin → Mary was no longer such after giving birth), places the heresiological focus on the Priscillianist tendency to stress the unity of the three persons of the → Trinity. Priscillian's archaic theology was very soon suspected of being heretical, as the movement did not express itself in the clear language of the Council of → Nicaea (325 CE) but with the help of pre-Nicene terms (*forma* instead of *persona*). Moreover, it insisted on the unity of the three persons in order to better demarcate itself from Arianism, which, conversely, was theologically adamant that each hypostasis should be clearly distinguished.

A.C. Vega (1972) identifies Audentius' book against all heresies with Sermon 233 of the apocryphal homilies attributed to → Augustine of Hippo in the Maurist edition. U. Dominguez del Val (1997) contradicts this argumentation.

(As the sources are limited, a historiography is not applicable.)

Bibliography

Chadwick, H., *Priscillian of Avila: The Occult and the Charismatic in the Early Church*, vol. XIV, Oxford, 1976, 13, 172, 220.

Domínguez del Val, U., "Audencio," in: *DHEE*, vol. I, Madrid, 1972, 152–153.

Domínguez del Val, U., "Audencio," in: U. Domínguez del Val, *Historia de la antigua literatura latina hispanocristiana*, CPHi 5, Madrid, 1997, vol. II: *Siglos IV–VI*, 25.

Sanchez, S.J.G., "Les priscillianistes ou 'les autres gnostiques'," *Emerita* 80/1, 2012, 125–148.

Vega, A.C., "De patrología española: ¿Ha perecido el Liber adversus omnes haereticos de Audencio, obispo de Toledo (mort en 395)?" *BRAH* 169, 1972, 263–325.

Sylvain J.G. Sanchez

Augustine of Hippo

Throughout history, Augustine of Hippo had an immense influence on the way people thought about humans and their abilities, about God and his omnipotence and grace, and about the order underlying creation and society. A philosophical Augustinianism emerged in which reason, together with faith and love, were at the service of the search for truth, and love was opposed to the alleged egoism and isolation of the Cartesian subject (Geerlings, 2010) In medieval political Augustinianism, the two opposing cities described by Augustine in *De civitate Dei* (*The City of God*, 413–427 CE) were seen as representing church and state (Dodaro, 2004). A theological Augustinianism was present in the debates on the definition of (the efficacy of) grace and the position of post-fall human nature in relation to divine grace, as conducted for hundreds of years. Augustine's work was the *Fundgrube* ("rich source") for M. Luther (1483–1536), J. Calvin (1509–1564) and Jansenists like A. Arnauld, who conceived of grace and election not as gifts but as favors, granted by a sovereign God to sinful man regardless of his good works; M. Luther and J. Calvin assumed faith as essential for this. L. de Molina (1536–1600) was less pessimistic about human abilities on the basis of Augustine. The influence of these forms of Augustinianism on the religious, political, scientific identity of Europe was enormous.

1. Biography

In his works, Augustine brings together the building blocks for his own → biography with the aim of convincing his audience that the Christian view of the world, the human being, and God was the most fulfilling (Brown, 2000; Fuhrer, 2004, Catapano, 2010; Lancel, 1999, Matthews, 2005; Van der Meer, 1947, O'Donnell, 2005, Hollingworth) About one of the most profound experiences in his life, the death of his son Adeodatus, he barely speaks. Autobiographical remarks serve as protreptrics and paraenesis: Augustine tries to convince "unbelievers" respectively that his view of humanity and God is the best and to confirm his own faithful in this view.

Aurelius Augustine was born at Thagaste (North Africa) on Nov 13, 354 CE, the son of a non-Christian and much absent father, Patricius – Roman and belonging to the small rural nobility – and a Christian mother of Berber descent, Monica. He had at least one brother and sister. Thanks to the support of Romanianus – probably family – he was able to complete his rhetorical studies in Madaura and Carthage. With ambitious friends, he left for Carthage around 370 CE, described by him as both a fascinating and horrifying "boiling cauldron" (*Conf.* 3.1) During this

period, he started the relationship with his concubine, to whom he would remain faithful for 15 years and who gave birth to Adeodatus in 372 CE., Augustine's desire for truth and wisdom then was ignited especially through reading Cicero's *Hortensius* in 373 CE, Aristotle and the Neoplatonists (*Conf.* 3.7; see 4.28; 7.13). Also because of their network, Augustine joined the Manicheans around 373 CE as an *auditor* (the third class). Like them, at that time he reduced suffering to the existence of bad matter and an evil creator; not so much to human initiatives as to a dramatic cosmic catastrophe, by which the light of the supreme God had become trapped in matter. His being and efficacy, however, became noticeable in Christ as teacher and sufferer, "crucified in the visible universe." In Christ, then, a different God from the evil God in the Hebrew Bible (→ Bible) revealed himself.

Until 383 CE, Augustine taught → rhetoric at Thagaste and Carthage. After frustrating experiences with inattentive and non-paying students and an illness in Rome, he obtained in 384 CE an appointment as professor of rhetoric in Milan, the center of power, with the help of the senator and city prefect of Rome Symmachus. At this point Augustine's concubine was sent back to Africa because top Roman officials were not supposed to have concubines. Meanwhile, Monica, who had travelled after her son to Italy to find him a wife of equal standing, arranged for Augustine to marry a young heiress who was still several years short of marriageable age.

In Milan, Ambrose made him grasp the value of → Neoplatonism (see Marrou, 1983; Madec, 1996; → Ambrose of Milan): the depiction of God as immaterial and the repentance and intellectual ascent as the way to truth brought him liberation (*Conf.* 7.1–2; 7.16), just as Ambrose's allegorical reading (→ Allegory) helped him better understand the words about God's essence and efficacy in Scripture. Around 386 CE, by reading Paul's Letters, he became familiar with the insight that "escaping" the ephemeral, changeable world did not come about thanks to one's own efforts alone but also through the power of God's Spirit. Also, Paul's assumption that all humans are under divine condemnation (Rom 5:12; 5:18–19) and are unable to avoid sin, (Rom 3:20; 7:7–11) would henceforth shape his thinking.

Physically weakened, Augustine resigned his office of state rhetor in 386 CE to dialogue, at Cassiciacum with friends, his son, and his mother on the problem of skepticism, happiness, and order in creation. He describes Monica as a wine drinker and important philosopher; emancipatory qualifications because women in the Roman Empire were forbidden by law to drink and philosophize (see *Ord.* 1.31–32; 2.45). On the Easter Vigil of 387 CE, Augustine, his son, and some friends were baptized by Ambrose in Milan. Augustine, however, did not marry the wealthy bride his mother had handpicked. After Monica's death in Ostia – the place where the group embarked to return to Africa – he led a life as a "lay monk" (*servus dei*) in the parental home in Thagaste with friends.

With the consent of the people, Augustine was tearfully ordained a → priest at Hippo in 391 CE. Bishop Valerius was assured of an erudite priest. In the bishop's garden at Hippo, Augustine founded his second community of male laymen. After Valerius' death in 395 CE, he became the second bishop of Hippo. His third community also served a strategic purpose. It was at the same time a training institute for the priesthood and episcopacy; several members became bishops. Augustine left a great mark on the church in Africa (see Hermanowicz, 2008).

Although he considered God's grace relevant as a gift, until 395 CE he held the view that the human will was free and strong enough to resist ingrained bad habits and come to faith (see *Exp. quaest. Rom.* 37.52; 54–56). A question from Simplicianus brought him the insight that the human will was only able to be good by God's prevenient grace. The consequence of the breakthrough of this insight was that human beings depend on God's favor to be saved (*Div. quaest. Simpl.* 1.2.1–1.2.2; 1.2.20), though Augustine did note after Paul that God's hatred cannot be directed at his own creature but "only" at his sins (*Div. quaest. Simpl.* 1.2.18; see Patout Burns, 1980; Hombert, 1996, Drecoll, 1999; 2004). He would be reproached during his lifetime that he downplayed human autonomy and some claimed that his thinking about human determinacy because of God was reducible to his indebtedness to the Manichean view of the human condition on earth because of an evil God and evil matter.

Preaching was a core task of the → bishop in early Christianity. The roughly 1,000 sermons known of Augustine probably constitute only seven or eight percent of those he preached. Because he regarded Scripture as a sacrament, the sermon formed a duality with the Eucharist, and Augustine was of the opinion that God himself taught in the sermon. On Sundays and daily during → Lent and → Easter, from 391 until his death in 430 CE, he expounded Scripture and his insights fought in the writing room.

A second constant in Augustine's life as a bishop was justice. In the *secretarium* of his episcopal church, he ruled almost every morning on issues of property rights, inheritances, or contracts. He was also in charge in cases of slavery, asylum, or adultery. Augustine himself indicates that someone who administers justice must be considered capable of sharply judging one's own actions and motives and treating a defendant empathetically. He characterizes his work as a judge as that of a doctor: the pain caused by a sharp inquisitor is like an incision: both serve the healing of the patient, which is brought about in gratitude for the judge's lenient judgement (*Ep.* 133.2; *Serm.* 278.3.3–5.5; 286.4.4).

The third constant in Augustine's life is controversy: for the sake of church unity and purity of doctrine he argued especially with Donatists (391–411 CE) and Pelagians (412–430 CE); for the sake of the credibility of Christianity he engaged with non-Christians in *De civitate Dei*.

Reading both Donatist and anti-Donatist tracts led him as early as around 391 CE to realize that the Donatist Church was too regionally oriented to guarantee the universality of the church (*Enarrat. Ps.* 149.7; 104.8). He also contested their view of holiness. Almost all Donatist theologians believed that holiness was a quality achieved by virtue of rituals and required no moral effort (*Parm.* 2.4.8). Augustine saw holiness as a moral command (*Bapt.* 3.15.20; *Ep.*93.10.43; *Parm.* 3.1.1; *C. litt. Petil.* 3.52.64) and argued that in both the Donatist and the Catholic Churches – the city of God on earth – there is a *commixtio malorum cum bonis*, that is, mixing of bad people with good ones (*Cath. fr.* 48; 55; see *Cresc.* 4.26). The church is a threshing floor, where chaff and wheat have not yet been separated in the Last Judgement (*Ep.* 108.3.11, *Cresc.* 2.26; 2.27; 2.4). But the church should not be abandoned because bad people are present in it (*Cresc.* 2.43; 2.44; Hove, 2020).

In his disputes with the Donatists, Augustine was initially process-oriented. To the Donatist bishops Maximinus and Proculeianus and a group of Donatist laymen he proposed in 391–397 CE a set of rules for dialogue (*Ep.* 23.6; 33.1–2; 33.5–6; 34.5; 35.1; 44.14). When the unification of the churches failed, he opted for a strategy, which can be traced to his vision of Christ as physician and the judge as doctor. In 399 CE, he subjected the Donatist bishop Crispinus to sharp questioning and declared that he would accept state intervention to force the Donatists into dialogue (*Ep.* 51.3; 66; see 51.2; 51.5). He conceived coercion as painful medicine to make the body of Christ whole (see *Enarrat. Ps.* 46.31; *Ep.* 93.1.1; 93.1.3; 93.1.4; 93.2.4). But he argued that coercion should be followed by instruction (see *Ep.* 93.1.3; see *Serm.* 112.8; *Enarrat. Ps.* 118; *Serm.* 17.2) and legitimized only insofar as aimed at establishing unity (*Ep.* 185.2.8; 185.3.13). At the Council of → Carthage in 411 CE, the power of the Donatists was broken (see *Breviculus collationis cum Donatistis*).

The reason for his struggle for the credibility of Christianity was the destruction of the city of Rome in 410 CE by the Visigoths (→ Goths) and the subsequent accusation by the literate pagans that this decline was due to the influence of the Christians and their belief in a crucified God. He also wanted to address the highly educated Roman aristocrats in Carthage who found the idea unreasonable that God had lowered himself by becoming human. For them he wrote his monumental *De civitate Dei*, partly to show that the earthly city manifests itself in human history even in the most glorious civilizations when people are haughty or possessed by lust for power (see below Works and the Developments in Augustine's Thought). Augustine's struggle with the Pelagians had a great impact in Africa (Brown, 1972) and on the history of the Occident (see Bonner, 2002; Dupont, 2013; Elm & Blunda, 2021) In the first phase, from 412 CE onwards, he emphasized that human nature remained infected by original sin, that grace is not just an external force working through in the law or Christ, and that infant baptism is essential to wash away the guilt of original sin; humans remain weakened, however, and therefore capable of nothing good on their own strength, and thus doomed

without the help of God's grace (*De natura et gratia*). Initially rehabilitated on the basis of his *Libellus fidei* by Pope Zosimus (→ Zosimus [Bishop of Rome]) in 417 CE, Pelagius was condemned, along with the like-minded Caelestius, the following year at the instigation of Augustine (Rees, 1998; Egmond, 2013).

Augustine's disputes with → Julian of Eclanum, who was also excommunicated (→ Excommunication), constituted the second phase (Lössl, 2001; Lamberigts, 2017). This young and self-conscious bishop interpreted Augustine's idea that humans were too weakened by the consequences of original sin as a form of gnostic dualism (→ Gnosis/Gnosticism), because humans, rendered unfree by the weakening and dependent on God's grace to do good, could not be held responsible for their actions. In response, Augustine argued that "free will" (*liberum arbitrium*) belongs to our human nature (*C. Jul. op. imp.* 6.11) but is subject to limitations. The *libertas*, that is, the freedom not to sin, has been lost since the fall (*C. Jul. op. imp.* 1.100; 1.103; 5.38; *C. du. ep. Pelag.* 1.5). Despite the gloominess of this message, he describes God as providing the *initium caritatis* ("beginning of love") and uses affective terms to signify the relationship of God and man (*C. Jul. op. imp* 1.131; *C. du. ep. Pelag.* 2.21; 4.11; *C. Jul.* 5.9; Lamberigts, 2005).

The third phase was initiated around 426 CE by questions from monks in Hadrumetum and Marseilles, including those about the necessity of exhortation if God still predestines people regardless of their efforts or ascetic form of life (see e.g. *Ep.* 214–215; → Asceticism). Augustine answered them that admonitions remain necessary, but he continued to emphasize that God will justify people not according to the principles of justice but out of pure mercy (Augustine of Hippo, *De correptione et gratia*, passim; Augustine of Hippo, *De praedestinatione sanctorum*, passim).

On Sep 26, 426 CE, Augustine transferred his responsibility for the diocese of Hippo to Eraclius. After this he worked on his annotated bibliography, the *Retractationum libri II* (*Retractations*, 426/427 CE), his survey of heresies in *De haeresibus* (*On Heresies*, 427 CE) and his *Speculum de scriptura sancta* (*The Mirror*, 427 CE), a synthesis of commandments from Scripture for the purpose of self-evaluation (*Spec.* preface). His concern for his own reputation, for orthodoxy and for the integrity of his clergy remained undiminished at the end of his life. The *De haeresibus* and *Retractationes* remained unfinished as did his last work against Julian. In 428 CE, the → Vandals, who were Arians, reached Africa. During the siege of Hippo, Augustine died on Aug 28, 430 CE; his library was spared. His first biographer → Possidius of Calama mentions that he drew comfort from words about commonness of dying a "wise man" (Pos. *Vita Aug.* 28.11); words borrowed from Plotinus' *Enneads* (1.4.7.23–25). Possidius also noted that it was impossible to read all Augustine's works. Augustine's body rests in Pavia, Italy.

2. Works and the Developments in Augustine's Thought

To trace the developments in Augustine's thinking on God, creation, and humankind, we have chosen to organize his works by genre and then discuss them in chronological order. However, dividing lines between genres are wafer-thin. *Enarrationes*, for instance, sometimes resemble sermons, letters have the character of a tractate or apologetic writing; the last books of the "autobiographical" *Confessiones* are the prelude to the "dogmatic" *De Trinitate*.

3. Philosophical Writings

Around 380 CE, Augustine wrote the lost *De pulchro et apto* (*On the Beautiful and the Fitting*), in which he described beauty as the essential of material things and harmony as the essential of spiritual things and relates virtue to this harmony and the good (see *Conf.* 4.24). Unfinished were his introductions to certain disciplines *De grammatica*, *De arithmetica*, *De dialectica*, *De geometrica*, *De philosophia* and *De rhetorica* (387 CE). In Thagaste, he completed only *De musica* in which he wrote about meter and number symbolism (387–389 CE).

The Cassiciacum dialogues led to *Contra academicos* (*Against the Academics*, 386 CE), *De ordine* (*On Order*, 386 CE), *De vita beata* (*The Happy Life*, 386 CE), and *Soliloquiorum libri II* (*Soliloquies*, 386/387 CE). The question of happiness is central to these works. In the first work, Augustine speaks of despair when it cannot be proved, as the sceptics believed, that truth knowledge and wisdom

are attainable (*Acad.* 1.6.18ff; 2.1.1–2.3.9; 3.15.34; see *Retract.* 1.1.1). He also speaks of the role of the authority of Scripture and the creed on the one hand and reason on the other in the search for wisdom (*Acad.* 3.43; see *Conf.* 7.13) and of the role of fortune in this (*Acad.* 2.5.13; 3.2.3). In *De vita beata*, he describes happiness as "having God" (*Beat.* 11) and confesses the Triune God as Truth and Supreme Measure (*Beat.* 4.34; 4.35), to which man becomes receptive by keeping the right measure (*Beat.* 4.25; 4.35). Later, he will define happiness as "enjoying God" (*Civ.* 8.8; *Trin.* 3.10). In *De ordine*, Augustine reflects on the order in the (Neoplatonic) *mundus intelligibilis* ("world of intelligible realities") which is simultaneously knowable and incomprehensible (*Ord.* 2.51). Again, he emphasizes that a good order of life leads to God (*Ord.* 2.54). In this period, his interest in the soul culminates in a trilogy. In the aforementioned *Soliloquia*, he articulates the desire to know God and soul (*Solil.* 1.2.7); for the purified minds, the intellect turns out to be the path to wisdom; for the simple-minded, it is the authority of the church (*Solil.* 1.13.23; see Bochet, 1982). In *De immortalitate animae* (*The Immortality of the Soul*, 386/387 CE), he describes the connections between eternity, truth, the soul, substance, the human mind, corporeality, and mutability (*Immort. an.* 1.1.; 6.11; 16.24); the → body "subsists through the soul" (*Immort. an.* 1.1; 14.24). *De quantitate animae* (*The Magnitude of the Soul*, 388 CE) deals with the origin and size of the soul created by God (*Quant. an.* 2–3), the consequences of the union and separation of body and soul (*Quant. an.* 3.4; 25.48). Augustine argues, in Neoplatonic fashion, that the "greatness" of the soul does not refer to spatial vastness, but to its rational and contemplative faculties, described as immaterial, through which man can attune to God (*Quant. an.* 3–36, esp. 22; 70–76). After Plato, he defines the soul as "a rational substance capable of ruling over a body" (*Quant. an.* 22) For the first time, Augustine speaks of the resurrection (*Quant. an.* 33.76). *De magistro* (*The Teacher*, 389 CE) can also be counted among the early philosophical dialogues, because here Augustine and Adeodatus discuss the relation of signs to reality, and Augustine following Plato explains a priori knowledge through the image of the inner teacher, Christ, in the soul, implying the presence of inner norms. (*Mag.* 37–38;

Fuhrer, 2004). This image is also discussed in *De vera religione* (*True Religion*, 390 CE). Here Augustine emphasizes that Platonists can easily be Christians (*Ver. rel.* 3.5.; 4.7) and that mercy is the expression of true religion (*Ver. rel.* 23.40–45). He would remain throughout his life indebted to Neoplatonic notions (Harrison, 2006). *De libero arbitrio* (*On Free will*, 388–395 CE) is discussed below.

4. Exegetical Works

The study of Scripture, a constant in Augustine's life as priest and bishop, led to a tremendous series of biblical commentaries. As early as 389 CE, in *De Genesi contra Manichaeos* (*On Genesis Against the Manicheans*, 389 CE), on the basis of the creation narratives in Gen 1:1–2:3 and Gen 2:4–3:24 he contests the Manichean idea that evil would be coeternal to God and not reducible to choices of man. Creation is an expression of God's love. He restates these thoughts in 393 CE in an unfinished commentary on Genesis, *De Genesi ad litteram liber imperfectus* that finally takes shape in *De Genesi ad litteram liber* (399–415 CE). The moralistic and anagogical hermeneutics in *De Genesi contra Manichaeos* he also applies here in his often question-worded explanation of the creation by the Triune God in six stages (Books 1–5), the interpretation of events such as the fall (Books 6–11) and the description of → paradise (Book 13, based on 2 Cor 12:2–4). But he also pays attention to the proper meaning of the events (see *Gen. lit.* 1.1.1; incidentally, *Conf.* 11–12 and *Civ.* 11 contain Augustine's fourth and fifth commentaries on Genesis).

In his *De sermone Domini in monte* (*Sermon on the Mount*, 393 CE), Augustine depicts the → Sermon on the Mount as a synthesis of Christ's ethics; in the first book he emphasizes the need for mercy and in the second that of the purification of the heart based on Mat 5:1–48 and 6:1–7:28, respectively. His fascination with Paul (→ Paul the Apostle) led in 394–395 CE to the *Epistula ad Romanos inchoata expositio* (*Beginning of a Commentary on the Epistle to the Romans*), an unfinished exposition on Paul's salutation in the Letter to the Romans and the issue of sin against the Holy Spirit, and the *Expositio quarumdam quaestionum in epistula ad Romanos* (*Commentary on Statements in the Letter of Paul to the Romans*), in which he describes the four stages in salvation history while conceiving of them as stages in the individual process of a person willing and able to do good: "before the law" (*ante legem*), "under the law" (*sub lege*), "under grace" (*sub gratia*), "at peace" (*in pace*; *Exp. quaest. Rom.* 13–18). As in his *Expositio ad Galatas* (*Commentary on the Letter to the Galatians*, 394/395 CE), here he still emphasizes free choice as crucial to come to believe in Christ as mediator and receive his help in the form of grace (*Exp. quaest. Rom.* 44.3; 62.9). He also does this to counter the Manichean view that the will is bound: man can freely decide to ask God for help, which because of faith is also given (*Exp. Gal.* 1; 15; 18; 32; 44; 46; *Exp. quaest. Rom.* 16; *Exp. quaest. Rom.* 62).

Besides his commentaries on Paul, Augustine writes in these years his unfinished and lost *Expositio epistulae Jacobi* (*Commentary on the Letter to James*, 394 CE), makes notes on the book of Job in which Job is presented as the prototype of human misery (*Adnotationes in Job*, 399 CE). His *Quaestiones Evangeliorum* (*Questions on the Gospels*, 397–400 CE) consist of 47 short commentaries on passages from the Gospel of Matthew and 51 from Luke; his *Quaestiones XVI in Matthaeum* (400–411 CE) of 16 questions on Matthew. *De consensu evangelistarum* (*Harmony of the Gospels*, 404 CE) includes an introduction to the structure of the four Gospels, an explanation of the purpose of each evangelist and a study of the parallel texts on the passion and resurrection to demonstrate the harmony between the evangelists, especially between Mark, Luke, and John. Augustine also addresses the divinity of Christ.

Augustine's commentary on the First Letter of John, *In epistulam Johannis ad Parthos tractatus* (*Tractates on the First Epistle of John*, 407 CE) consists of ten discourses in which love appears to be a multi-layered concept (Canning, 1993; Bavel, 1987; Schrama, 2002). In its highest form, love is God himself (*Tract. ep. Jo.* 1.11; 8.5–8.7), but it is also a force, a fundamental attitude and a way of life in human beings through which they can love neighbors and in this, love the love that enables human beings to love: God Himself (*Tract. ep. Jo.* 9.10; see 1.9; 5.2; 6.4; 9.1.; 10.4; 10.5, mostly with reference to Rom 13:10; *Tract. ep. Jo.* 6.10; 7.5; 7.6; see 1 John 4:7–8). He thus appears to rebuke the ritual holiness view of the Donatist also in his scriptural commentaries.

Between 408 and 420 CE he prepares his *In Evangelium Johannis tractatus* (*Tractates on the Gospel of John*), divided into 24 tractates. In a lively style and with a pastoral purpose, he comments on all the verses in this Gospel. Reflecting on the → Word made flesh, he calls this the mystery of God's humility (*Tract. Ev. Jo.* 45.13). He considers it necessary for those who want to grasp God to imitate God in God's humility (*Tract. Ev. Jo.* 45.5) and to act out of love of justice (*Tract. Ev. Jo.* 41.10) in order to share in his → resurrection (*Tract. Ev. Jo.* 9.9–10.13). In addition to these treatises, Augustine also wrote *Enarrationes in Psalmos* (*Enarrations on the Psalms*, 392–418 CE): "expositions" on the Psalms, which, like the commentaries on John, differ from his sermons in that Augustine's explicit aim in writing or dictating the *tractatus* and *enarrationes* was to provide a continuous verse-by-verse commentary. Often pictorially, Augustine emphasizes that passages in the psalms are sometimes obscure, and the letter of the psalm serves to access the mystery of God. → Anthropomorphisms are not to be taken literally (*per litteram scrutari mysteriam*; *Enarrat. Ps.* 131.2; see 28.9; 34.2.5; 98.1; 127.2). He especially identifies Christ, who is love, as hidden and at the center of the psalms (*Enarrat. Ps.* 4.1; 36.3.3; 98.1; 140.2). In early *Enarrationes*, he argues, in Neoplatonic fashion, that people can ascend to this love (*Enarrat. Ps.* 4.1. 103.1.9; O'Daly, 2001; Zwollo, 2018).

At the time of the Donatist struggle, he again emphasizes that Christ is the head of his church, which together with his body, the church, constitutes the "whole Christ" (*totus Christus*; *Enarrat. Ps.* 37.6).

Later, Augustine prepared *De octo quaestionibus ex Veteri Testamento* (*Eight Questions from the Old Testament*, 419 CE?), enlightening eight problems on the Hebrew Bible's notion of justice, and finally the *Quaestiones in Heptateuchum* (*Questions on the Heptateuch*, 419 CE), a commentary on the first seven books of the Bible. Together with his much shorter Locutionum in Heptateuchum (*Sayings in the Heptateuch*) in which he addresses the translation issues concerning these books, he wrote this work in Carthage for a council of African bishops; it also served as a preliminary study for Books 15 and 16 of *De civitate Dei*. Around 425 CE, he answers questions to Dulcitius (*De octo Dulcitii quaestionibus/The Eight*

Questions of Dulcitius) on the situation of baptized sinners in hell (→ Hades) and on the connection between the last judgement and the Lord's return. Augustine here draws heavily on his own work. More exegetical is the question of whether the Spirit of God who hovered over the waters during the days of creation was the → Holy Spirit (*Dulc.* 8.2., see *Gen. lit.* 1.11–13). For his commentaries, Augustine studied the works of → Jerome, → Eusebius of Caesarea, → Origen, → Tyconius, Ambrose of Milan, → Gregory of Nyssa, among others.

Finally, in 426 CE, he completed his handbook of exegesis, hermeneutical approaches, and homiletics: *De Doctrina Christiana* (*Christian Instruction*). For Augustine, love of God and neighbor turns out to be the criterion for exegetical adequacy (Pollmann, 1996); words in Scripture are outward signs that must lead to this love only to discover that on earth God transcends all language and thought. Crucial in this context is Augustine's elaboration of the distinction between "enjoyment" (*frui*) and "use" (*uti*; *Doctr. chr.* 1.4). Immorality he reduces to the inversion of use and enjoyment. Those who wish to enjoy wealth as their highest goal or deify themselves "enjoy" what they should see as instruments; only God as their highest goal applies to enjoyment. His *Speculum de scriptura sancta* is not actually a scriptural commentary but a sequence of Scriptures, with which Augustine aims to confront his reader with himself without too many hermeneutical translations.

5. Sermons

As mentioned, there is a connection between the *Tractatus* and *Enarrationes* and Augustine's *Sermones ad populum* (*Sermons to the People*). Stenographers, in the churches where Augustine preached, wrote down verbatim what Augustine, impromptu, preached in concise and expressive sentences, sometimes not devoid of humor or irony, and using examples from everyday life. He often employed the *dialecticon*: a dialogue with a fictitious partner – Christ, apostles, fictitious opponents – to whom he posed questions directly. He also fired rhetorical questions at his audience to foment a lively, casual dialogue with them. The sermons include catechetical, exegetical, exhortatory sermons on texts of the Hebrew Bible and the New Testament, major liturgical feasts, on saints, and many other topics (Dolbeau, 2005; Patout Burns, 2022) Unique are the two sermons in which he confesses and justifies the offence against the communion of goods in his own community (*Serm.* 354–355; Partoens, Boodts, Partoens & Leemans, 2018). He often valorizes insights discovered in the study on Trinity or on the errors in → heresies. This makes their dating easier. Augustine must have held around 7,000 sermons (Dolbeau, 2005). He was unable to implement the intention, stated in the *Retractationes* (2.67) to organize them.

6. Works on Christian Doctrine of Faith

In *De utilitate credendi* (*The Usefulness of Believing*, 391 CE) Augustine first makes his *uti-frui*-distinction and explains his literal/historical, etiological, analogical, allegorical modes of reading (*Util. cred.* 3.5). He assumes faith as prior to reason, and he denies as later in *De civitate Dei* that people on earth can become happy because they already see God here (*Util. cred.* 11.25). *De fide et symbolo* (*Faith and the Creed*, 393 CE) is a sermon on the creed for the bishops in North Africa in which he describes, against the Manicheans, the *creatio ex nihilo* (*Fid. symb.* 2.2–3), the Son's divinity and consubstantiality with the Father and the Holy Spirit (*Fid. symb.* 3.4; 9.17–18). *De agone christiano* (*Christian Combat*, 396–397 CE), a small manual, describes the Christian life as a struggle against lusts and the (demonic) forces, which prevent people from following God's commandments (*Agon.* 1–6). Christ, however, shows that healing is possible through justice and service (*Agon.* 7–11). *De catechizandis rudibus* (*Catechizing the Uninstructed*, 399–405 CE) is a manual for catechists, in which he defines the Hebrew Bible and the New Testament as well as the history of the church (*Cat. rud.* 3.5) as catechetical material and depicts Christ as the center of this *objectum materiale* ("material object"). Man is conceived as having a double will (*Cat. rud.* 18.31). In *De fide rerum quae non videntur* (*Faith in Things Unseen*, 400 CE) he rejects the idea that Christian faith is opposed to reason because it presupposes faith in invisible things. *De divinitate daemonum* (*The Divination of Demons*, 407 CE; → Demonology/Demons) is a treatise on God's omnipotence, to which, in the end, demonic powers are shown to be subordinate (*Div.* 2.5; see

7.11–10.24); *De videndo Deo* (*On seeing God*, 413 CE) a letter to Paulina on the capacity of the body after the → resurrection (see *Civ.* 22); *De praesentia Dei* (*On the Presence of God*, 417 CE) a letter on God's omnipresence in creation and Christ's omnipresence as God on earth, in hell and in heaven (*Praes.* 187.7–11). Omnipresence implies that God works through in people who do not know God (*Praes.* 187.36). At the same time, Augustine emphasizes the necessity of → baptism (*Praes.* 187.25; 187.33). The creedal commentaries, which he unfolded in *De fide et symbolo*, in *Sermones* (212–215), *De symbolo ad catechumenos* (*The Creed: For Catechumens*, 400 CE), culminate in his *Enchiridion de fide, spe, et caritate* (*Enchiridion on Faith, Hope, and Love*, 421–423 CE). Here he argues that wisdom lies in *pietas* ("worship of God") which presupposes knowledge of faith as well as a good way of life, in which hope (*Enchir.* 114–116), love (*Enchir.* 117–121) but above all faith (*Enchir.* 9–113) are driving forces (*Enchir.* 3). Incidentally, in his *Quaestiones expositae contra paganos numero sex* (*Six Questions Against Pagans*, 406–411 CE), he answers six questions, for non-Christians, on such topics as the Requiem, the difference in Christian and pagan sacrifice and King Solomon's understanding of the Son of God. Augustine's masterpiece on a crucial aspect of the doctrine of faith is *De Trinitate* (*The Trinity*, 396–420 CE; → Trinity). He considers it appropriate only for those with a keen intellect, which caused him to delay finishing it (*Trin.* 7.9.10). In the first books, he describes the atemporal way in which God the Father begets the Son; as a Person, the Holy Spirit is their bond of love; the three persons are one in essence. Augustine, like the Latin fathers, uses *substantia* (Gk *ousia*, the philosophical term for an independent entity), but also *essentia* to denote this unity (*Trin.* 5.8–9) and "persona" to describe God as relationship (*Trin.* 5.9.10; 7.9.10). The Son is the incarnation of the eternal Word, mediator, inner teacher; the incarnate Christ indicates the divine Logos as referred to a concept in a word (*Trin.* 15.20; see *Doctr. chr.* 1.12). The Holy Spirit represents divine love and will as gift to the world. In the last six of the 15 books, he unfolds his psychological Trinity doctrine. "Love" (*amor*), the "human mind" (*mens*), and "knowledge" (*notitia*; *Trin.* 9.4.4) are three substances that are one and as such *imago trinitatis*, just as "memory" (*memoria*), "understanding" (*intelligentia*), and "will" (*voluntas*) are three and one (*Trin.* 10. passim), but due to the weakness of the will do not make a perfect Trinity (*Trin.* 12.9.14; 12.10.15). Such an analysis of the human mind was unparalleled in antiquity (Smalbrugge, 1988; Brachtendorf, 2000).

7. Works on Christian Virtue Practice

In *De utilitate jejunii* (*The Usefulness of Fasting*, 411–412 CE), Augustine defines fasting (→ Fasting/Abstinence) as a prelude to the practice of mercy and justice; against the Donatists he also links it to unity in the church. *De continentia* (*Continence*, 418–420 CE) involves an anti-Pelagian reflection on the immense power of the concupiscence of the flesh, which is neutralized by abstinence that is supplied by grace (*Contin.* 2.3–5). In *De fide et operibus* (*Faith and Works*, 413 CE), he emphasizes that justification by faith does not imply that well-educated Christians (*Fid. op.* 13.9; 27.49) need not do good works; without good works there is no salvation (*Fid. op.* 14.21–22). In *De patientia* (*Patience*, 415–417 CE) Augustine distinguishes spurious patience from the genuine one that endures evil out of love for God and is primarily reducible to God's wisdom and grace (*Pat.* 15). In his two tracts on → lying, *De mendacio* (*On Lying*, 394 CE) and *Contra mendacium* (*Against Lying*, 420 CE), Augustine differentiates many forms of lies. In both works he points out that even white lies are not permissible because whoever "has one thing in his mind but expresses something else" (*De mend.* 3), will not meet the Truth (see *C. mend.* 40). In *De cura pro mortuis gerenda* (*The Care to Be Taken for the Dead*, 422 CE) he describes that care for the dead as expression of human piety and faith in the resurrection is meaningful without affecting God (*Cur.* 3.5; 18.22). *De disciplina christiana* (*Christian Discipline*, undated) contains a sermon on the love of self, neighbor and God in which the negative consequences of the former as an end in themselves are broadly discussed (*Disc.* 2–11).

8. Works on the Christian States of Life

Prompted by circumstances, Augustine, especially between 397 and 405 CE, contemplated the various Christian states of life. For the members of his second community of life, he wrote the *Praeceptum* (*Rule*) in 397 CE, in which he postulated communion of goods, (common) prayer, fasting, transparency, leadership, and mutual correction as requirements for unity of heart and soul (*Reg.* 3.1; 8). The guidelines were modeled on principles from *De vita beata* and had repercussions in Augustine's reflections on *disciplina* ("discipline"") and *concordia* ("harmony") for the sake of social order in *De civitate Dei*. Incidentally, his lost *Versus in mensa* (*A Table Verse* after 411 CE) is a verse to combat gossiping at the table.

To defend the alternation of prayer and manual labor against the → Messalians who only intended spiritual work on the basis of Matt 6:23–35, he wrote *De opere monachorum* (*The Works of Monks*, 400 CE; see Grote, 2001). To ensure the balance between prayer and work and to suggest to monks that for the sake of their autonomy and credibility they should earn their own living, he invoked 2 Thess 3:10 (*Op. mon.* 40). In his *Epistula ad Probam de orando deo* on → prayer, the guidelines on prayer times, fasting, communal living in the service of the desire for God of the *Praeceptum* echo (*Prob.* 9.18; 10-.19; 16.31; 9.18; *Reg.* 3.1–3; 8). Maintaining the middle ground between Jerome, who despised marriage (see Jer. *Jov.* 1.47) and Jovinian, who equated all states of life, Augustine in *De bono conjugali* (*The Good of Marriage*, 400 CE) calls → marriage "good" because conceiving and caring for children in a marriage is a good, that is, the "good of offspring" (*bonum prolis*; *Bon. conj.* 13.15; 17.19; 29.32); partners, through mutual sexual fidelity, perpetuate the spiritual bond and "love" (*caritas*), which is a second good, the "good of fidelity" (*bonum fidei*; *Bon. conj.* 4.4); the indissolubility of the marriage bond reflects the bond between Christ and his church, which is the third good, the "good of the sacrament" (*bonum sacramenti*). That he conceives of abstinence as a higher good is evident in *De sancta virginitate* (*Holy Virginity*, 401 CE); the openly made vow out of love of God includes the foreshadowing of eternal life. (Elm, 1994; Hunter, 2007).

It must not, however, lead to arrogance (*Virginit.* 31–57). In *De bono viduitatis* (*The Excellence of Widowhood*, 414 CE) he summarizes his view of the various states of life and the necessary fidelity to them; against the Pelagians, he formulates abstinence as a virtue, in which grace precedes the will (*Vid.* 3.4–6.9; 8.11; 17.21; 18.22). In *De adulterinis coniugiis* (*On Adulterous Marriages*, 419–421 CE), he emphasizes that abstinence in marriage need not always be a good: the bond of communion takes precedence; the pursuit of a higher good by one, without the consent of the other, must never lead to disruption of the marriage (*Adult. coniug.* 1.7.7). Augustine denounces men because their sense of superiority prevents forgiveness in adultery and they often have double standards (*Adult. coniug.* 2.8.7)

9. Apologetic Works

a. Anti-Manichean Writings

To emphasize the superiority of Catholic asceticism (*Mor. manich*, 1.30–62–1.35.80), after making *De Genesi contra Manichaeos*, Augustine, in *De moribus Manichaeorum* (*The Way of Life of the Manichaeans*, 389 CE), defines temperance, courage, justice and prudence as variants of love of God and of human beings (*Mor. manich.* 1.15.46–1.29–61; see 1.3.4–1.14.24; Eguiarte Bendímez, 2017; → Mani/Manichaeism). In *De duabus animabus* (*Two Souls*, 391–before 395 CE), he challenges the Manichean view that humans have received a good soul from God and an evil one from the power of darkness, which means that humans cannot be held responsible for evil (*Duab.* 15). *De libero arbitrio* is also an anti-Manichean work because Augustine traces the origin of → evil to free will, which is good when people choose good (*Lib.* 1.25–29) but is also susceptible to evil and thus can be the source of it (*Lib.* 2.47–53). In this early work, Augustine already supposes that it was solely Adam's wrong choice of will (→ Adam and Eve), and not God, that weakened the nature of his descendants; a view he would elaborate in detail in his battle with the Pelagians (*Lib.* 3.3.52; 3.19.54). In *Contra Adimantum* (*Against Adimantus*, 394 CE), as in the *Acta contra Fortunatum Manicheum* (*Debate with Fortunatus, a Manichean*), the verbatim record of a fierce discussion with Manichean Fortunatus on Aug 28 and 20, 395 CE, he would defend the unity of the Hebrew Bible and the New Testament by identifying the contradictions therein as complementary. *Contra epistulam Manichaei quam vocant Fundamenti* (*Against the Letter of the Manichaeans That They Call "The Basics"*, 396/397 CE) includes an account of his transition to Catholicism, criticism of Mani's

title "Paraclete" – and of the Manichean idea of two eternal substances (*Fund.* 13–15; 20–24; 26–29). *Contra Faustum Manicheum* (*Against Faustus the Manichean*, 398–400 CE), is Augustine's most complete refutation – 33 books – of the Manichean view of the authority of the law and the prophets, the God of Israel, the → incarnation, and the value of the New Testament. *Contra Felicem Manichaeum* (*Against Felix the Manichean*, 398 CE), contains an account of two-day dispute in which Augustine turns his thoughts on free will in relation to evil (*Fel.* 2.8), God's good nature, and his incarnation (*Fel.* 2.9–1) into a threat of legal condemnation of Felix, who then renounces Mani's teachings in a declaration (*Fel.* 2.22). *De natura boni contra Manichaeos* (*On the Nature of the Good*, 404 CE?) Augustine again disputes the Manichean two-principle-doctrine (*Nat. bon.* 44) by describing God as supreme good and the order in nature and in living beings as good; evil he reduces to man's striving to occupy a higher place in the order (*Nat. bon.* 1–40, esp. 16; Bouton-Touboulic, 2004) Also, in *Contra Secundinum Manichaeum* (*Against Secundinus the Manichean*, 404 CE), he emphasizes the goodness of God and his creation (*Secund.* 10–20) to exclude bad matter as the cause of evil (*Secund.* 21–23). Augustine described this work as the last of his anti-Manichean treatises (*Retract.* 2.10). But nothing could be further from the truth. Also, in *De continentia* he still disputes the idea that man consists of two antagonistic substances and in *Contra adversarium legis et prophetarum* (*Against the Opponent of the Law and the Prophets*, 420–421 CE) he refutes the idea that God did not give the law to Moses. Also, in *De haeresibus* (46) he devotes another agitated discourse to Manicheism, which has thus always preoccupied him.

b. Anti-Donatist Works

Many works from this period have been lost, such as *Contra epistulam Donati haeretici* (393–394 CE), *Contra partem Donati* (397 CE), *Contra quod adtulit Centurius a Donatistis; Contra epistulam Donati heretici; Contra nescio quem Donatistam; Contra partem Donati* and his *Probationum et testimoniorum contra Donatistas*: often responses to concrete reproaches by Donatists (→ Donatism/Donatists).

Possibly in response to slogans by the Donatist bishop Parmenian, Augustine wrote a satirical poem with 12-line stanzas and a refrain, the *Psalmus contra partem Donati* (*Psalm Against the Donatists*, 393–394 CE; see the also lost *Versus de S. Nabore*, a verse against the Donatists on Nabor). In his response to the letters of Donatist bishop Petilian, *Contra litteras Petiliani* (*Against the Book of Petilian*, 400–404 CE), he points out the lack of evidence for the accusation that Catholics sprang from the *traditores*, disputes for the first time the Donatist's ritualistic view of holiness, and refutes the idea that the Donatist Church is the true church by pointing to the universality of the *catholica* (Book 1). He refutes Petilian's conviction – supported by a literal interpretation of certain passages of Scripture – that sinners must be physically separated from the church by interpreting it allegorically: one must endure the sinner, but not assent to his actions (Book 2). In *Contra epistulam Parmeniani* (*Against the Letter of Parmenian*, 400 CE), Augustine outlines the injustices committed against Catholics, speaks of the possibility for Christian rulers to exert pressure on heretics and schismatics, and points out inconsistencies in the Donatist (re)baptismal practice: some were re-baptized, and others were not. He again rules out that the regional Donatist Church embodies the universal church as a bond of love, emphasizing that the church is a place of mutual correction and errors should not lead to schism.

In *De baptismo contra Donatistas* (*On Baptism Against the Donatists*, 400–401 CE), in seven books, he further completes his criticism of the practice of rebaptism by heretics or schismatics and refutes the Donatist interpretation of → Cyprian of Carthage's view in this regard. As in the second book against Petilian, he emphasizes that the sins of the minister of the sacrament do not affect the validity of baptism because Christ is the *auctor* of the sacrament. The lost *Contra quod attulit Centurius a Donatistis* (*Against that Which Centurius Brought Forth*, 400 CE) was followed in 401 CE by *Ad catholicos fratres* (i.e. *De unitate ecclesiae*/*The Unity of the Church*, 401 CE): a compendium for Catholic bishops in which he explains the universality of the (Catholic) church as a condition of veracity and, thus undermining the schism by the Donatists, and asserts that the separation of good and evil people takes place only at the end of time. In the four books of *Contra Cresconium grammaticum* (*et*) *Donatistam libri quatuor* (*Against Cresconius, a Donatist grammarian*, 405 CE), he explicates the dialectical method by which he disputes the Donatists, points out, more fiercely than before, the invalidity of their rebaptism, and describes the separation of the Maximinianists from the Donatists as undermining their claim to be the true church (see also his lost *Admonitio Donatistarum de Maximinianistis*, an admonition to the Donatists about the Maximinianists). Remarkably, in *De unico baptismo* (*Single Baptism*, 410 CE) he emphasizes, in addition to the universality of the church, that the good can also be found outside the church and is not reserved for a sect (*Unic. bapt.* 5.7). Augustine's *Breviculus collationis cum Donatistis* (*Summary of the Proceedings of the Conference with the Donatists*, 411 CE) and the *Contra donatistas post conlationem* (*Against the Donatists After the Conference*, 411 CE) make it clear that around 411 CE the two sides were still accusing each other of acts of violence to undermine each other's claim to be the true church. (cf. Shaw, 2011). This can also be inferred from Augustine's *Sermo ad Caesariensis ecclesiae* (*Sermon to the Church of Caesarea*), delivered in 418 CE before the Donatists at Caesarea (Mauretania), and the *Gesta cum Emerito* (*Proceedings with Emeritus*, 418 CE). The sermon included a peaceful appeal to the Donatists to rejoin the Catholics; the *Gesta* offered a criticism of the Maximinianists' readmission to the Donatist Church without rebaptism based on the Donatists' own principle that traitors contaminated the church community with whom they interacted (Maximinianist Schism). That Augustine, in *De correctione Donatistarum* (*Ep.* 185; *On the Correction of Donatists*) and *Contra Gaudentium Donatistarum episcopum* (*Against Gaudentius the Donatist Bishop*, 420 CE), still legitimizes the (threat of) violence as a prelude to formation and for justice's sake, indicates that unity was still imperfect at the time of the Pelagian struggle.

c. Anti-Pelagian Works

Augustine laid the basis for his view, carried through to extreme details and consequences, of the weakness of human nature since Adam, original sin and the primordiality of God's grace for the development of a good will and justification in the aforementioned *De diversis quaestionibus ad Simplicianum* (*Various Questions for Simplicianus*, 396 CE). In his early exegesis of Rom 9, Augustine argued, as was customary in Catholic exegesis at the time, that Paul did not abolish free will (*Exp. quaest. Rom.* 13–18). Reading 1 Cor 4:7 made him realize that grace must precede even good will (*Div. quaest. Simpl.* 1.2). In addition, he argued, as did the North Africans → Tertullian and Cyprian, that original sin is a personally culpable guilt associated with disordered, destructive tendencies in humans, results in physical death and justifies human damnation (*Div. quaest. Simpl.* 1.2.20). Like the good will, he reduced faith to God's prevenient, and not merely assisting-enlightening grace after man had first made a good choice all by himself (*Div. quaest. Simpl.* 1.2.7). It is not out of justice but out of mercy that God chooses some out of dysfunctional humanity who will be saved. That many are called but few chosen relates to the incongruity of the calling and the state of man (*Div. quaest. Simpl.* 1.2.10–14; see Matt 22:14; see *Spir. et litt.* 29.50–34.60).

Especially in the disputes with the Pelagians (→ Pelagians/Pelagianism), Augustine emphasized that original → sin transformed the ability not to sin into an inability not to sin; only grace can recreate the affected faculties into inability to sin in the next life (see *Nat. grat.* 61–67; *Nupt.* 1.35) and be of help to humans (*Nat. grat.* 3–4). At this time, Augustine also emphasizes that grace as a gift (*donum*) works the remission of sins (*Nat. grat.* 29; *Corrept.* 43) and, as in 396 CE, bears witness especially to God's undeserved mercy (*Grat.* 21) and love (*caritas, dilectio; Gest. Pelag.* 34; see Rom 5:12–19). Thanks to the sacrifice and mediation of Christ (*Nat. grat.* 3.51) and the Holy Spirit (*gr. et pecc.* or 1,37), grace frees man from sin (*Nat. grat.* 46; 48; *Nupt.* 1.33; 2.5; 2.8; *C. du. ep. Pelag.* 1.21; 1.23–24; *Corrept.* 29–30).

As in the Donatist struggle, Augustine's tone is initially mild. In *De Gratia Novi Testamenti* (*Ep.* 140; *On the Grace of the New Testament*, 412 CE), he replies to Honoratus that he appreciates the Pelagians for their high morality but warns them like the virgins (→ Virgin/Virginity) in 401 CE against pride, which Christ, as humble, can nevertheless cure (*Grat. N. Test.* 22.52; 28.68). In *De peccatorum meritis et remissione et de baptismo parvulorum* (*On the Merits of Forgiveness*

of Sins and on Infant Baptism, 411–412 CE), however, he already elaborates the North African idea that unbaptized children bear the guilt of original sin although their damnation is mild (*pecc. mer.* 1.16.21; 3.4.7). Similarly, in *De peccatorum meritis et remissione peccatorum et de baptismo parvulorum* (411–412 CE) and *De perfectione justititiae hominis* (*On the Perfection of Human Righteousness*, 414/415 CE), he arrives at a condemnation of Pelagius' (antitraducian) thought that the will is still free enough after the fall not to sin again (*perf. iust.* 11.23– 19.42).

He repeats these thoughts in *De spiritu et littera* (*The Spirit and the Letter*, 412 CE) to substantiate the necessity of the indwelling of the Holy Spirit for the strengthening of the will (*Spir. et litt.* 3.5). Pelagius is accused in his *De natura et gratia* (*Nature and Grace*, 413–415 CE) of disregarding the difference in the nature of Adam and his descendants before and after the → fall and thereby downplaying the necessity of grace for the weakened nature after the fall (*Nat. grat.* 67.80–81) to an extent that nature and the grace of Christ almost coincide (*Nat. grat.* 44.52, 59.69). That Pelagius' anthropological optimism ran counter to Augustine's most deeply experienced and thoughtful conviction is the explanation for Augustine's "harsh" description of humanity as *massa damnata* if God were not merciful (*Nat. grat.* 3.3–5.5) and would not administer restorative grace (*Nat. grat.* 53.62; see Lössl, 2001, 2–8; Drecoll 2007, 488–497 CE). In *De gestis Pelagii* (*Proceedings of Pelagius*, 415 CE; written after acquittal of Pelagius by the Synod of Diospolis; see *Gest. Pelag.* 23.47–24.48) and *De gratia Christi, et de peccato originali* (*The Grace of Christ and Original Sin*, 418 CE; written after his subsequent condemnation) Augustine vehemently and repeatedly emphasizes the necessity of prevenient grace to maintain commandments (*Grat. Chr.* 1.3.4.; 1.44–48– 1.44–58) as well as the necessity of baptism because grace withdraws a child from the *massa perditionis* (*Grat. Chr.* 2. 31.36). In his *De origine animae* (415 CE) on the origin of the soul and the relation of the soul to the power of original sin he even disavows the notion he developed in the Donatist struggle: that of the baptism of desire (see *Bapt.* 4.22.29). Much more than in *De bono conjugali* and even *De gratia et peccati originali* (2.34. 38–39), he describes in *De nuptiis et concupiscentia ad Valerium comitem* (*Marriage and Concupiscence*,

420 CE) the intrinsic connectedness of the sexual act and concupiscence, which infected humanity after original sin and continues to weaken it despite the washing away of guilt in baptism (*Nupt.* 1.1.1; 1.32.37; 1.35.59). In *Contra Iulianum* (*Against Julian*, c. 421 CE) Augustine most comprehensively explains the consequences of Adam's choice (Book 3) and original sin (Books 1–2) for the deterioration of human nature, the connection between original sin and baptism (Book 4) and the relationship between predestined and condemned (Book 5). As in *Contra duas epistulas pelagianorum* (*Against Two Letters of the Pelagians*, 419/420–421 CE), in Book 6 he refutes Julian's idea that the transmission of original sin does not occur and argues that *libido* is the consequence of the fall (*C. du. ep. Pelag.* 3.16.30). *Contra secundam Juliani responsionem imperfectum opus* (*Unfinished Work Against Julian*, 428–430 CE) involves a sometimes hastily worded explanation of how children can be charged with sin if God is just, how the will can be free if nature determines man negatively (*C. Jul. op. imp.* 1.78; 2.39), and how concupiscence after the fall cannot possibly be a healthy appetite, as → Julian the Apostate believed (*C. Jul. op. imp.* 4.48–54; see 1.47; 5.28; 5.40–42, etc.). In *De anima et eius origine* (*On the Soul and its Origin*, 419/420 CE) Augustine refuted the idea that man cannot be afflicted with original sin because each soul was created separately (*an. et or.* 4.11.16). The aforementioned monks at Hadrumetum and Marseilles forced him to safeguard himself from the suspicion of fatalism. Therefore, in *De Gratia et libero arbitrio* (*Grace and Free Will*, 426–427 CE) he emphasizes that grace and free will choice are, on the contrary, mutually reinforcing, (*Grat.* 4.7; 6.13) and in *De correptione et gratia* (*Admonition and Grace*, 426–427 CE) he points out the usefulness of fraternal correction (*Corrept.* 9.25; 15.46); Christians should act as if they were chosen (*Corrept.* 15.46; see 10.280). In *De dono perseverantia* (*The Gift of Perseverance*, 428 CE) and *De praedestinatione sanctorum* (*The Predestination of the Saints*, 428–429 CE), he defines predestination for the monks as God's atemporal preparation of the gifts of grace (*Praed.* 10.19; *Persev.* 14.35; 16.41–17.42; see Eph 1:4). Even though he carries the logic of grace to its extreme consequences in the Pelagian controversy, he speaks not only of the *iustitia dei* ("justice of God") but also of the *ordo caritatis* ("order of love") and of God as mysterious and hidden equity.

d. Other Apologetic Works

In *De Trinitate*, certain passages in *In Evangelium Johannis tractatus*, as well as in *Quaestio* 16, 23, 37, 50, 60, and 69 of his *De diversis quaestionibus LXXXIII* (*Eighty-Three Different Questions*, 388–397 CE) – a work on numerous diverse ecclesiastical and theological questions – Augustine contests the inequality of being between Father and Son as Arians advocated (→ Arianism). He does this most vehemently in *Contra sermonem Arianorum* (*Against a Sermon of the Arians*, 418 CE); though less vehemently in the *Collatio cum Maximino Arianorum episcopo* (*Debate with Maximinus, Bishop of the Arians*, 427–428 CE) and *Contra Maximinum* (*Against Maximinus*, 428 CE). In *Serm.* 117 (418 CE) he even argues that Arians and orthodox would do better together to remain silent before God than to speak of God's very essence. In *Ad Orosium contra Priscillianistas et Origenistas* (*To Orosius Against the Priscillianists and the Origenists*, 415 CE; → Priscillianism; → Origenism/Origenist Controversy) he refutes their idea that the soul is divine, and that even the devil will be saved; hell he considers eternal. Finally, in his *Retractationes*, he retraces his own work to save himself from any reproach of unorthodoxy. *Tractatus adversus Judaeos* (*In Answer to the Jews*, 426–430 CE) involves an equipping in dealing with the Jews and a plea for a spiritual interpretation of the Torah (→ Law/Decalogue/Torah). The *De haeresibus ad Quodvultdeum* (428 CE) is an account of 88 heresies based on → Epiphanius of Salamis' *Panarion*, Filastrius of Brescia's *Diversarum haereseon* liber, and his own findings with Manicheans, Donatists and Pelagians. Life practices also prove heretical.

e. Letters

Until 1981, 276 letters by Augustine were known. In that year, J. Divjak discovered 31 additional ones. Augustine dictated them and interpreted them as conversation (*Ep.* (*Div.*) 138.1). Besides being a source of information on theological, political, and domestic issues, they also give insight into Augustine's daily concerns, his health, his joys, and sorrows about ecclesiastical and social developments. Unsparingly, he makes mention of clerical abuse, sexual, financial, political (*Ep.* 1*; 7*; 8*; 13*; 22*; 23*; 23*A; *Ep.* 54–55; 77–78). *Ad Inquisitiones Ianuarii* (*Responses to Januarius*, year of writing unknown) and the lost *Contra Hilarum de cantico ad altare* (*Against Hilarus on the Song on the Entrance to the Altar*) concern liturgical issues. Worth mentioning is his correspondence with Jerome on matters of Bible interpretation (*Ep.* 40; 72; 73; 75; 82, etc.). His letters in particular show that he always saw Donatists as brothers (*Ep.* 23; 33); to Tribune Marcellinus he wrote not to put condemned Donatists to death. It was to remain with mild punishments and threats (*Ep.* 133).

f. The Monuments

To absolve himself from criticism of his Manichean past, to show non-Christians the beauty of Christian worldview, image of humankind and of God, and to convince fellow Catholics that the human will is subject to many limitations, he wrote the *Confessionum libri XIII* (*Confessions*, 397–401 CE) in beautiful Latin around 397 CE (Simonetti, 1992–1997; O'Donnell, 1992). He gave it the form of an autographic prayer in which recognition of one's own guilt and imperfection (Books 1–9) forms the prelude to praise to the Triune God, who created all and everything (Books 10–13). *Confiteri* ("confession," *Conf.* 1.1.) encompasses this recognition and this praise simultaneously. Although he accuses the Platonists of arrogance because, as he will argue more explicitly later, they think they can achieve happiness through their own virtue (see *Civ.* 12.14; 19.4), he does embrace the Neoplatonic notion of intellectual-spiritual ascent that presupposes introspection and ascension by focusing primarily on the intellectually perceptible in order to "experience" God as higher than the highest and deeper than the deepest "I" (*Conf.* 3.11; Kenney, 2005). Knowledge of Christ he carefully formulates in the spirit of philosophical therapeutic tradition as a healing process in which he addresses God as inner healer (Claes, 2011). Later he would present Christ in sermons as a physician (*Christus medicus*), who must inflict pain on man in order to free him from the tumor of pride (Eijkenboom, 1960). What Augustine pursues as a judge in his judgments, he pursues as a protreptic

in the *Confessions*: the painful recognition of one's own imperfection in the first nine books becomes embedded in the healing power of gratitude for the sake of human faculties-memory above all (Book 10), creation, time, Christ as mediating inner teacher (Book 11, esp. *Conf.* 11.2–9) and the goodness of God, who created the world even though God himself needed no creature (Book 12).

After Augustine had already preached about the destruction of Rome in *De excidio urbis Romae* (*The Destruction of the City of Rome*, 411 CE), he also wrote in reaction to this from 413–427 CE his *De civitate Dei*: a mirror in which he reflects history and salvation history in order to confront his reader with the consequences of misdirected, prideful, "love of self" (*cupiditas*, see *De nuptiis et concupiscentia*) and virtuous because orderly love (*caritas*) for God (*Civ.* 14.7; 14.28; 15.22; O'Daly, 1999; Kaiser, 2023). The citizenship of the earthly city or the city of the devil is the result of the first choice; that of the Christ-founded city of God the result of the second (*Civ.* 1, prologue; 11.1; see Ps 86:3). The history of the two cities begins immediately after creation through the fall of the devil and the sin of Adam and Eve (Books 11–14); in the history of Israel, it becomes clear that this people is the first earthly representative of the city of God; after the coming of Christ, this is the church, whose history unfolds into that of the world (which Augustine also depicts extensively in Books 15–18). The final destination of the two cities appears to be eternal damnation or eternal bliss (Books 19–22; O'Daly, 1999). The highest good can already be known to some extent on earth when ordered tranquility and peace reign on the personal and collective levels (Book 19). The last judgment, theories of and criticisms of punishment for the damned and eternal reward are discussed in Books 20–22, respectively. Constantly resonating is the idea that the Roman people and their philosophers knew what virtue was, yet their history was marked by pride: the very cause of civilization's decline. Political criticism with Augustine is moral criticism of the Roman ruling class and their lack of self-criticism (*Civ.*5.12. see Dodaro, 1994). In his discussion of Varro, Augustine further argues that classical philosophers did not know how to deal with the tragic nature of society (see Markus, 1970; Müller, 1993), in which contention defines the sphere of life; an insight that was much echoed in Augustine's stance during the Pelagian disputes.

10. Synthesis

Possibly thanks to the Neoplatonic therapeutic tradition, Augustine, around 386 CE, developed an unprecedented ability to evaluate in detail his words, thoughts, acts, and omissions; initially in the light of God as Supreme Measure and Supreme Order, later in the light of the *Logos*, who became man and, practicing humility, was humanity's physician and teacher. No one before him, apart from the description of the strength and weakness of human faculties, also expressed the duality in human drives as succinctly as he did; not only in his *Confessiones* but also in many of his sermons or in works on the Christian order of life and states of life. His self-analytical ability was accompanied by an extremely sharp power of observation and an exceptional talent to describe with painful clarity the ambivalence and tragedy in the world as well as to reduce it exclusively to the aforementioned duplicity, weakness and the selfish pride of individuals, who pass on to each other what they received from their ancestors: a human condition determined by the opposite of the Goodness, later described as Love, which was at the root of the order of creation. The unambiguity of this Goodness, God, and that of God-created nature, Augustine seeks to secure throughout his life.

Augustine's ultra realist view of history, the weakened phenomenon of man, the dynamics in networks and the logic of sin in it, along with his enduring high regard for Paul, may have been the reason why he was so vehemently opposed to the – in his eyes possibly naive – assumption that a person can be healed and justified in his own strength. Human beings constantly need a physician. The terms justification and healing sometimes have the same connotation. But in his refutation of Manichaeans and Pelagians, he refuses to characterize the sick person as morally non-autonomous. Moderation, radical honesty, inner peace and, in connection with it, social peace are ways in which people become receptive to the Highest Measure and Truth (*De vita beata*; *De mendacio*; *Civ.* 19, table of peace) and begin to experience the order in themselves and themselves in the divine order, despite the chronic

and indispensable need for help, because the hereditary condition is of such a nature that although it does not eliminate freedom, it limits it. And along with the outrageous realism about the tragedy in the world – which he articulates more starkly as opponents emphasize man's good will and nature – he formulates God's grace and election not in terms of arbitrariness but of love and mercy, though the message about the *conditio humana* is harsh (Wetzel, 2000). He remains reticent in his judgments about humans, about social relationships and about God, though this reticence does not dominate every discourse. Knowing the power of his own desires, fears and questions, Augustine concludes that he has become himself a question (*Conf.* 4.8.9.). Paradoxically, the restraint in his judgment works inclusiveness: because people do not know who among them is bad or good – appearances can be deceiving – one must tolerate one another and order life together in church and society in such a way that the longing for the spiritual beauty that is Christ (*Reg.3.* 8) increases. Sectarianism does not help in this. And despite the firmness with which Augustine highlights the necessity of baptism, the indispensability of grace and aspects of God's being and activity in his exegesis: in his work he continues to interweave passages, the essence of which he pithily summarizes in his *Serm.* 117: "If you can comprehend it, it isn't God" (*si comprehendis non est deus*; Van Geest, 2011). But this did not take away from the fact that thanks to Christ much was known about God.

Historiography

The "Bulletin Augustinien" section of the *Revue des études augustiniennes* publishes the bibliography of the immense research on the life and work of Augustine since 1955. This journal is issued by the Institut des Études Augustiniennes in Paris. *Augustiniana*, published by the Augustinian Historical Institute of the Catholic University Leuven, includes an extensive section with reviews on recent publications. The *Corpus Augustinianum Gissense a Cornelio Muyer editum*, third edition, is not only a database of Augustine's complete works in Latin, based on the most recent editions of his works, but also contains a bibliographical database with over 50,000 articles. In the "Literatur-Portal" under the responsibility of the Zentrum für Augustinusforschung, University of Würzburg, this database of Augustine literature is complemented.

In the predecessor of the *Revue des études augustiniennes*, the journal, *Année théologique (Augustinienne)*, bibliographical surveys were published from 1940–1954. The literature included in bibliographical records was processed per work of Augustine in A. Trapè, *Nuova biblioteca agostiniana opere di sant' Agostino* (Institutum Patristicum Roma).

For the purpose of publishing Augustinian research, the following journals have been established over time: *Analecta augustiniana* (1905, Institutum Historicum Augustinianum); *Augustiniana* (1951, Augustijns Historisch Instituut, Katholieke Universiteit Leuven); *Augustinianum* (1961, Institutum Patristicum Augustinianum); *Augustinian Studies* (1970, Augustinian Institute Villanova University); *Augustinus* (1956, Agostinianos recoletos); *La ciudad de dios* (1881– Real Monasterio El Escorial; for a broad audience); *Revista Agustiniana* (1960– Editorial revista agustiniana); *Revue des études Augustiniennes* (1955, Institut des Études augustininiennes); The *Revue bénédictine* (Abbaye de Maredsous) is of importance for numerous publications on Augustine and for text-critical editions of discovered sermons or letters.

The following lexicons consistently reflect the state of Augustinian research. The *Augustinus Lexikon* (1986–) published by the Zentrum für Augustinus Forschung, is exhaustive. See furthermore A. Fitzgerald, ed., *Augustine Through the Ages: An Encyclopedia*, Grand Rapids, 1999 (Fr. *Saint Augustin: La Méditerranée et l'Europe, IVe–XXIe siècle*, Paris, 2005; Ital. *Agostino: Dizionario enciclopedico*, Rome, 2007); D. Meconi and E. Stump, eds., *The Cambridge Companion to Augustine*, Cambridge UK, ²2014; M. Vessey, ed., *A Companion to Augustine*, Chichester, 2012; T. Toom, ed. *Cambridge Companion to Augustine's* Confessions, Cambridge UK, 2020.

The influence of Augustine's thought in the history of politics, religion, culture, philosophy, theology, and art spiritual is exhaustively described in the articles on relevant persons, works, and themes in: K. Pollmann, ed., *The Oxford Guide to the Historical Reception of Augustine*, 3 vols., Oxford, 2013.

Bibliography

Bavel, T. van, "The Double Face of Love in Augustine," *LouvSt* 12, 1987, 116–130.

Bochet, I., *Saint Augustin et le désir de Dieu*, Paris, 1982.

Bonner, G., *St Augustine of Hippo: Life and Controversies*, 3rd ed., Norwich, 2002.

Bouton-Touboulic, A.-I., *L'Ordre caché: La notion d'ordre chez saint Augustin*, Paris, 2004.

Brachtendorf, J.J., *Die Struktur des menschlichen Geistes nach Augustinus: Selbstreflexion und Erkenntnis Gottes in De Trinitate*, Hamburg, 2000.

Brown, P., *Augustine of Hippo: A Biography: A New Edition with an Epilogue*, London, 2000; 1st ed. 1967.

Brown, P., *Religion and Society in the Age of Saint Augustine*, Londen, 1972.

Canning, R., *The Unity of Love for God and Neighbour in St. Augustine*, Heverlee, 1993.

Catapano, G., *Agostino*, 2010.

Claes, M., "Exercitatio mentis als casus: Een onderzoek naar Augustinus als pedagoog," diss., Almere, 2011 (Dutch).

Connolly, W.F., *The Augustinian Imperative: A Reflection on the Politics of Morality*, Newbury Park, 1993.

Djuth, M., "Augustine on Necessity," *AugS* 31, 2000, 195–210.

Dodaro, R., "Eloquent Lies, Just Wars and the Politics of Persuasion: Reading Augustine's 'City of God' in a 'Postmodern" World'," *AugS* 25, 1994, 77–137.

Dodaro, R., *Christ and the Just Society in the Thought of Augustine*, Cambridge UK, 2004.

Dolbeau, F., *Augustin et la prédication en Afrique: Recherches sur divers sermons authentiques, apocryphes ou anonymes*, Paris, 2005.

Drecoll, V.-H., *Die Entstehung der Gnadenlehre Augustinus*, Tübingen, 1999.

Drecoll, V.-H., "Gratia," in: C. Mayer, ed., *AugL*, vol. IV, Basel, 2004, 182–242.

Drecoll, V.-H., ed., *Augustin Handbuch*, Tübingen, 2007.

Dupont, A., *Gratia in Augustine's Sermones ad populum During the Pelagian Controversy: Do Different Contexts Furnish Different Insights?* Leiden, 2013.

Egmond, P. van, *"A Confession Without a Pretence": Text, Context of Pelagius' Defence of 417 AD*, Amsterdam, 2013.

Eguiarte Bendímez, E.A., "La santidad en 'De moribus Ecclesiæ catholicæ' y en los primeros escritos de san Agustín: Continuidad sin fractura ni futuros perdido," *Augustinus* 62, 2017, 27–78.

Eijkenboom, P.C.J., *Het Christus-medicusmotief in de preken van Sint Augustinus*, Assen, 1960 (Dutch).

Elm, S., *"Virgins of God": The Making of Asceticism in Late Antiquity*, Oxford, 1994.

Elm, S., & C.M. Blunda, eds., *The Late (Wild) Augustine*, Leiden, 2021.

Fitzgerald, A.D., ed., *Augustine Through the Ages: An Encyclopedia*, Grand Rapids, 1999; Fr. *Saint Augustin: La Méditerranée et l'Europe, IVe–XXIe siècle*, Paris, 2005; Ital. *Agostino: Dizionario enciclopedico*, Rome, 2007.

Fuhrer, T., *Augustinus*, Darmstadt, 2004.

Geerlings, W., *Fußnoten zu Augustinus: Gesammelte Schriften Wilhelm Geerlings*, Turnhout, 2010; ed. G. Röwekamp.

Grote, A., *Anachorese und Zönobium: Der Rekurs des frühen westlichen Mönchtums auf monastische Konzepte des Ostens*, Stuttgart, 2001.

Harrison, C., *Rethinking Augustine's Early Theology: An Argument for Continuity*, Oxford, 2006.

Hermanowicz, E.T., *Possidius of Calama: A Study of the North African Episcopate in the Age of Augustine*, Oxford, 2008.

Hombert, P.-M., *Gloria Gratiae: Se glorifier en Dieu, principe et fin de la théologie augustinienne de la grace*, Paris, 1996.

Hove, B. ten, *Koren en kaf op de dorsvloer: De kerk in het licht van het laatste oordeel: Een onderzoek naar de betekenis van de area als metafoor voor de ecclesia bij Augustinus,*" Apeldoorn, 2020 (Dutch).

Hunter, D.G., *Marriage, Celibacy, and Heresy in Ancient Christianity: The Jovinianist Controversy*, Oxford, 2007.

Kaiser, H., *In ordinata concordia: Het subsidiariteitsbeginsel en de geordende eendracht in de politieke economie*, Tilburg, 2023 (Dutch).

Kenney, J.P., *The Mysticism of Saint Augustine: Rereading the Confessions*, New York, 2005.

Lamberigts, M., "Julian and Augustine on Jesus Christ," *AugS* 36, 2005, 159–194.

Lamberigts, M., "Julian of Eclanum," in: H.-J. Klauck et al., eds., *EBR*, vol. IV, Berlin, 2017.

Lancel, S., *Saint Augustin*, Paris, 1999.

Lössl, J., *Julian von Aeclanum: Studien zu seinem Leben, seinem Werk, seiner Lehre und ihrer Überlieferung*, Leiden, 2001.

Madec, G., *Saint Saint Augustin et la philosophie: Notes critiques*, Paris, 1996.

Markus, R.A., *Saeculum: History and Society in the Theology of St Augustine*, Cambridge UK, 1970.

Marrou, H.I., *Saint Augustin et le fin de la culture antique*, Paris, ²1983.

Matthews, G.B., *Augustine*, Malden, 2005.

Mayer, C., ed., *Augustinus-Lexikon*, Basel, 1986–.

Meconi, D., & E. Stump, eds., *The Cambridge Companion to Augustine*, Cambridge UK, ²2014.

Meer, F. van der, *Augustinus de zielzorger: Een studie over de praktijk van een kerkvader*, Brussels, 1947 (Dutch).

Müller, C., *Geschichtsbewußtsein bei Augustinus: Ontologische, anthropologische und universalgeschichtlich/heilsgeschichtliche Elemente einer augustinischen "Geschichtstheorie"*, Würzburg, 1993.

O'Daly, G.J.P., *Augustine's "City of God": A Reader's Guide*, Oxford, 1999.

O'Daly, G.J.P., *Platonism Pagan and Christian: Studies in Plotinus and Augustine*, 2001.

O'Donnell, J.J., *Augustine: Confessions*, 3 vols., Oxford, 1992.

O'Donnell, J.J., *Augustine: A New Biography*, New York, 2005.

Partoens, G., S. Boodts, G. Partoens & J Leemans, eds., *Preaching in the Patristic Era: Sermons, Preachers, and Audiences in the Latin West*, Leiden, 2018, 177–197.

Patout Burns, J., *The Development of Augustine's Doctrine of Operative Grace*, Paris, 1980.

Patout Burns, J., *Augustine's Preached Theology: Living as the Body of Christ*, Grand Rapids, 2022.

Pollman, K., *Doctrina Christiana: Untersuchungen zu den Anfängen der christlichen Hermeneutik unter besonderer Berücksichtigung von Augustinus, De doctrina christiana*, Freiburg, 1996.

Pollmann, K., & W. Otten, eds., *The Oxford Guide to the Historical Reception of Augustine*, 3 vols., Oxford, 2013.

Rees B.R., *Pelagius: Life and Letters*, Woodbridge, 1998.

Rist, J., *Augustine: Ancient Thought Baptized*, Cambridge UK, 1994.

Schrama, M. *Augustinus: De binnenkant van zijn denken*, Zoetermeer, 2002 (Dutch).

Shaw, B., *Sacred Violence: African Christians and Sectarian Hatred in the Age of Augustine*, Cambridge UK, 2011.

Simonetti, M. et al., eds., *Sant'Agostino: Confessioni*. 5 vols., Milan, 1992–1997.

Smalbrugge, M., *La nature trinitaire de l'intelligence augustinienne de la foi*, Amsterdam, 1988.

Toom, T., ed. *Cambridge Companion to Augustine's Confessions*, Cambridge UK, 2020.

Van Geest, P., *The Incomprehensibility of God: Augustine as a Negative Theologian*, Louvain, 2011.

Vessey, M., ed., *A Companion to Augustine*, Chichester, 2012.

Wetzel, J., *Snares of Truth: Augustine on Free Will and Predestination*, London, 2000.

Zwollo, L., *St. Augustine and Plotinus: The Human Mind as Image of the Divine*, Leiden, 2018.

PAUL VAN GEEST

Augustus

Gaius Octavianus was born on the Palatine in Rome Sep 23, 63 BCE (d. Aug 19, 14 CE), to Gaius Octavius, a *homo novus* of Velitrae and governor of Macedonia, and Atia, the niece of Julius Caesar (Suet. *Aug.* 3–4; Tac. *An.* 1.9–10). Octavian's father died in 59 BCE, and he was reared by his maternal grandmother, Julia Caesaris, for whom he gave a funeral oration in 51 BCE (Suet. *Aug.* 8). His stepfather, Lucius Marcius Philippus, introduced him to political life, and he fought with Caesar against Pompeian forces in Spain (45 BCE). Shortly thereafter he was designated Caesar's adoptive son and the principal heir to his vast fortune. When the dictator was assassinated on the Ides of March (44 BCE), Octavian left Apollonia,

Macedonia, and returned to Rome to obtain his inheritance. The political situation was delicate because the Romans were divided about whether Mark Antony should succeed Caesar while some senators supported Cassius and Brutus. Cicero's *Philippics* expressed the growing sentiment in Rome that Antony was a threat to the Republic, and the great orator obtained for Octavian propraetorian power in January 43 BCE. Octavian accompanied the consuls Hirtius and Pansa to Mutina in north Italy, where Antony and his forces were defeated and the consuls died during the battle (Suet. *Aug.* 9). Octavian marched to Rome with 18 legions who acclaimed him *imperator*, and he was elected consul (*Res gest.* divi Aug. 1). On November 43 BCE at Bologna, Octavian, Antony, and Lepidus created the Second Triumvirate. The proscriptions that ensued resulted in the execution of many Romans and the confiscation of their property (Dio. *Hist. rom.* 46.55.4–5). When the Senate deified Julius Caesar (January 42 BCE), Octavian as his adopted son became *Divi filius*, and by autumn of the same year, Antony and Octavian avenged the dictator's murder by defeating Brutus and Cassius at the Battle of Philippi (Dio. *Hist. rom.* 47.37–49; *Res gest. divi Aug.* 2; Suet. *Aug.* 9–11).

Territorial divisions of the triumvirs were established by the Treaty of Brundisium: Octavian ruled the provinces of Gaul, Hispania, and Italia; Anthony controlled the East; and Lepidus governed Africa (Dio. *Hist. rom.* 48.27–31; 48.36–38, adds that Sextus Pompeius was given Sicily). The crushing of the rebellion of Lucius Antonius and Fulvia at Perugia (40 BCE), the defeat of the fleet of Sextus Pompeius at Naulochus by Marcus Vipsanius Agrippa (36 BCE; Suet. *Aug.* 16; Dio. *Hist. rom.* 49.1–18; *Res gest. divi Aug.* 25; see Dio. *Hist. rom.* 48.36 for the conference at Misenum in 39 BCE, which ensured Sextus' governorship in Sicily, Sardinia, and Achaia for five years and his commitment to lift the blockade that had been set up and provide grain for Rome), and the forced resignation of Lepidus from the Triumvirate (36 BCE) were the principal causes of Octavian's becoming the dominant *imperator* of the West (Suet. *Aug.* 14–16; Dio. *Hist. rom.* 48.1–15; for the Treaty of Tarentum, which renewed the Triumvirate for another five years, see Plut. *Vita Ant.* 35; App. *Bell. civ.* 5.93–94; Dio. *Hist. rom.* 48.54). The Senate

conferred on him the inviolability (*sancrosanctitas*) of a tribune (*Res gest. divi Aug.* 10), and he now had command of 45 legions and a fleet of 600 ships. Relations between the two remaining triumvirs became strained when Antony separated from Octavian's sister Octavia and married Cleopatra VII, the queen of Egypt, with whom he had three children. The donations of Alexandria that conferred titles on Antony, Cleopatra, and their children were perceived to be a threat to the Republic and caused a permanent rift in Antony's relations with Rome (Plut. *Vita Ant.* 50). After Octavian acquired Antony's will from the Vestal Virgins in Rome, and it was discovered that his children by Cleopatra were named his heirs, Italy and the western provinces swore an oath of loyalty to him, and the Senate declared war on Cleopatra (Suet. *Aug.* 17; Dio. *Hist. rom.* 50.3.1–5; 50.6.1; *Res gest. divi Aug.* 25). With the assistance of Agrippa, who served as the admiral of his fleet, Octavian won a decisive victory at the Battle of Actium off the Adriatic coast of Greece (31 BCE). By August 30 BCE, Antony and Cleopatra, who had fled to Egypt, committed suicide after Octavian invaded Alexandria (Suet. *Aug.* 17; Dio. *Hist. rom.* 51.10–14). Having restored the Republic, he was now the uncontested master of the Roman world. Octavian returned to Rome and closed the gates of the Temple of Janus, which symbolized the cessation of the civil wars and the beginning of the *Pax romana* (*Res gest. divi Aug.* 13; Suet. *Aug.* 22; Dio. *Hist. rom.* 51.20.4) and celebrated a triple triumph for his victories in Dalmatia, Actium, and Egypt (*Res gest. divi Aug.* 6; Dio. *Hist. rom.* 51.19.102; Suet. *Aug.* 27).

1. The Principate

The political ingenuity of Octavian manifests itself in the creation of the Principate, which brought about revolutionary changes to republican structures without a revolution, culminating in the incremental transference of executive authority (*imperium*) to the *Princeps* in the aftermath of Julius Caesar's unsuccessful dictatorship (Tac. *An.* 1.1.1; 1.9.3). Autocratic ambitions were often concealed by proactive manipulative constitutional reforms made possible by the enormous wealth inherited from his great uncle and being the commander of an extremely powerful army. The first phase in the evolution of the Principate occurred in January 27 BCE, when the Roman Senate conferred on Octavian the title Augustus (Dio. *Hist. rom.* 53.16.6–8; *Res gest. divi Aug.* 34). A golden shield was hung in the Curia inscribed with the four cardinal Roman virtues (bravery, clemency, justice, piety: *Res gest. divi Aug.* 35), which exemplified the achievements of *Imperator Caesar Divi filius Augustus*. He was granted Proconsular imperium for ten years, which was renewed each decade until his death. A *concilium principis* or emperor's council was formed that consisted of the consuls, 15 senators, and various magistrates. Augustus' command of the imperial provinces in such areas as Gaul, Spain, Syria, and Egypt gave him control over most of the legions and guaranteed his "absolute control of all matters for all time" (Dio. *Hist. rom.* 53.16.1). The second phase, which occurred in 23 BCE, solidified Augustus' new regime on the basis of *imperium*, *tribunicia potestas*, and *auctoritas* ("imperial power, tribunician power and authority") by initially surrendering his position of consul and obtaining an *imperium maius*, which extended over the whole empire. The tribunician power was for life and allowed him to convene the Senate, propose laws, veto decisions, preside over elections, help citizens in need (*ius auxilii*), and have the right to first speech. He was granted a special privilege that allowed him to cross the *pomerium* without losing his *imperium* or having to renew it. He now had authority over all political institutions of the *res publica restituta* and was in full control of most of its legions. Beginning in late 23 BCE, Augustus made a tour of the eastern provinces and returned to Rome in 19 BCE, where he embarked upon further social, political, and religious reforms (see below). Lepidus' death in 12 BCE made it possible for the *Princeps* to be elected as the → *Ponti Maximus*, the most prominent religious office in Rome. The final addition to his powers occurred in 2 BCE, when the Senate and the people acknowledged him as *Pater patriae* or father of his country (Suet. *Aug.* 58; *Res gest. divi Aug.* 35). The first emperor of Rome died Aug 19, 14 BCE, at Nola in Campania in his 76th year.

2. Imperial Policies

The policies that Augustus set forth helped to make the Principate successful and laid the political and social foundations of the Roman Empire for the next 300 years. He created an imperial civil administration, reorganized the equestrian order, and revised the role of the senators (*Res gest. divi Aug.* 8) who arose from the municipal leaders of Italy. Freemen were given greater economic and social mobility. The *Princeps* controlled foreign and military policies and by means of the *nomination*, and *commendation* controlled the elections of magistrates. A permanent standing army was created, and approximately 300,000 veterans after the civil war were settled in colonies in Italy, Spain, or Gaul (*Res gest. divi Aug.* 3; Suet. *Aug.* 13). Legionaries swore an oath (*sacramentum*) to the emperor, and every triumph belonged to him alone. In 6 CE the *aerarium militare* was created, which provided pensions to soldiers honorably discharged (*Res gest. divi Aug.* 16f.). Nine praetorian cohorts served as the emperor's military escort, and three urban cohorts maintained order in Rome. The new naval bases at Misenum and Ravenna possessed permanent fleets under the command of a prefect from the equestrian order (Suet. *Aug.* 49). The greatest military disaster under Augustus was the loss of three legions under Varus in 9 CE to German forces in the Teutoberg Forest. Augustus' moral reform included new laws against excessive expenditure, adultery, the regulation of marriages, and the promotion of chastity (Suet. *Aug.* 34). The emancipation of slaves and the granting of citizenship to foreigners were restricted. Laws enacted in 18 BCE encouraged procreation among the upper classes and penalized families without children. Territorial expansion doubled the size of the new empire. Egypt was annexed in 30 BCE, Tiberius Nero subjugated the Pannonian tribes, Illyricum was extended to the Danube, and the Dacians were subjected (*Res gest. divi Aug.* 30). Royal embassies from India often visited Rome, and Armenia became a client state (*Res gest. divi Aug.* 27; 31). Galatia became a province in 25 BCE, and a part of Judaea was annexed to Syria in 6 CE. The Iberian Peninsula was divided into three provinces. New territories were acquired in the area of the Alps, Raetia, Noricum, Germania, and Moesia (*Res gest. divi Aug.* 26). Military expeditions took place in south Egypt around the first cataract, the Red Sea and Arabia, North Africa, and northern Europe. Public games and festivals consisting of gladiatorial and athletic shows and many hunting spectacles helped to endear the masses to the new regime and made the new leader very popular (*Res gest. divi Aug.* 22; Suet. *Aug.* 43). But it was the secular games (*ludi saeculares*) celebrated in 17 BCE that symbolized the end of the *Res publica* and the dawning of a golden age under the protection of Apollo (Hor. *Saec.* 50). Popular public entertainments also included chariot races (*ludi circenses*) and theatrical performances (*ludi scaenici*). In the city of Rome, Augustus provided subsidized grain and large sums of money for the plebs (*Res gest. divi Aug.* 5; 15). His vast building projects included the Senate House, the Temple of Apollo on the Palatine, and many other temples dedicated to various deities (Dio. *Hist. rom.* 53.1.3; *Res gest. divi Aug.* 19; Suet. *Aug.* 29). In 7 BCE he divided Rome into 14 districts; established police and fire departments; built new roads, bridges, and aqueducts; and created an imperial postal service. The city of Rome was under the authority of the *praefectus urbi* of senatorial rank.

3. Religious Reforms

Augustus reformed Roman ritual religion according to the ancestral customs of the *res republica*, boasting in the *Res gestae divi Augusti* (7) that he was *Pontifex Maximus*, an augur, a fetial, and a member of the College of Fifteen, College of Seven, the Arval Brothers, and the *Titii Sodales* (see Scheid, 2005, 175–193, p. 177, who argues convincingly that Augustus brought about a real reform of Roman ritual religion). Suetonius states that he reinstituted many ancient rituals that had fallen into disuse (Suet. *Aug.* 31). A total of 82 Roman temples were repaired (*Res gest. divi Aug.* 20), and in 29 BCE, the Temple of the Divine Julius was dedicated in the Forum. In the same year the Senate arranged that Augustus' name be included in hymns along with those of the gods (Dio. *Hist. rom.* 51.20.1). He gave many splendid gifts on behalf of Roman religion, including 16,000 pounds of gold to the Temple of Capitoline Jupiter (Suet. *Aug.* 30). Grain distributions were associated with the cults of Ops and Ceres. Symbolizing the *Pax romana* established by Augustus, the Senate decreed the construction of an altar of peace (*Ara Pacis Augustae*) in 13 BCE (*Res gest. divi Aug.* 11), and the first public altar dedicated to the numen of the emperor (→ Emperor/ Imperial Cult) in the West was built in 9 CE on the

Iberian Peninsula. Before then, however, the foundations for the imperial cult in the East had already been laid. Although according to Roman mythology Romulus became a deity and Julius Caesar was deified by the Senate shortly after his assassination, the historical roots of the imperial cult go back to the worship of the pharaohs in Egypt and Alexander the Great's ruler cult established by eastern monarchs during the Hellenistic Age (323–30 BCE). After the Battle of Actium, Octavian took part in the mysteries of Demeter and Kore and instituted the quadrennial *Aetia*, which included musical and gymnastic contests and horse racing (Dio. *Hist. rom.* 51.1.2–3; 4.1), and as early as 29 BCE the cult of Roma and Augustus was instituted in Pergamum followed by Thyatira, Philadelphia, Mytilene, and other cities of Asia Minor (Tac. *An.* 4.37; Dio. *Hist. rom.* 51.20.6–9). Horace's *Odes* reinforced this imperial religious propaganda by depicting Augustus as a deity descended from heaven.

4. Legacy and Significance for Early Christianity

Augustus was cut from the same mold as his uncle Julius Caesar, driven by the same lust for power, and as determined to possess the same kind of unprecedented civil and military power that led to the assassination of his great uncle. Keenly aware of the latter's disrespect of the Senate and the sacred *mos maiorum* it was expected to preserve, Augustus manipulated the ruling classes of Rome by a shrewd employment of "reverse psychology" that had the pretense of not having the power-hungry ambitions of Caesar yet ultimately obtaining more civil and military power than Caesar was ever able to acquire. Augustus was successful due to his puritanical moral principles, respect for Rome's ancient traditions, manipulation of public sentiment by "bread and games," enormous wealth that was used to placate powerful politicians, the command of a large army, the provision of veteran benefits, presenting Antony and Cleopatra as a serious threat to Roman civilization, and having the ability to surround himself with capable magistrates and generals. He is one of the few great leaders of ancient history who orchestrated revolutionary changes without a revolution, terminating the long period of civil wars, and ushering in the golden age of the *Pax romana*, a period of peace and prosperity that extended from the British Isles to Africa, Greece, and the Middle East. Jesus of Nazareth was born during the Principate, and the early church eventually designed a centralized government controlled by bishops who presided over dioceses patterned after the imperial system. Latin remained the principal language of the Western Church throughout the Medieval period in Europe. The imperial cult often conflicted with the Christian claims that only in Christ could there be found the real universal savior for all people (Simmons, 2015, 187–209). The empire that Augustus initiated created an ambience compatible with the propagation of the gospel, the geographical dissemination of Christianity, the institutional growth of the church, the inevitable conflict with paganism, and the eventual triumph of the religion that began in an obscure corner of the Roman world.

Historiography

A selective list of the extensive bibliography of modern works on Augustus and his age would include biographies (Baldwin, 1980; Bengtson, 1981; Bleicken, 1998; Carter, 1970; Earl, 1968.; Eck, 2007; Everitt, 2007; Galinsky, 2012; Goldsworthy, 2014; Grant, 1978; Jones, 1970; Kienast, 1982; Massie, 1983; Millar, 1977; Richardson, 2012; Shotter, 2005; Simmons, 2004; Southern, 1998; Stahlmann, 1998), with A. Goldsworthy's monograph (2014) being the most recent comprehensive analysis of the life and career of the first Roman emperor. D. Fishwick (2002), K. Galinsky (2005), J. Scheid (2005; 2007), and P. Zanker (1988) offer fresh appraisals of the imperial cult initiated during the reign of Augustus. Volume X of *The Cambridge Ancient History* (2nd ed.) provides detailed analysis of every aspect of the Augustan Age. J.M. Carter (1970) and R.A. Gurval (1998) analyze the historical, social, and political significance of the Battle of Actium, a turning point in the career of Octavian. R. Syme's (1939) seminal study of Augustus in the context of revolutionary changes at the end of the Roman Republic has impacted modern historians' understanding of Roman constitutional development.

The contextualization of the Augustan *Principate* with respect to its unique social, political, military, and cultural features is analyzed by A. Alföldi (1971), C. Ando (2000), T.D. Barnes (1974), G.W. Bowersock (1990), P.A. Brunt (1984), K. Chisholm and J. Ferguson (1981), V. Ehrenberg and A.H.M. Jones (1976), K. Galinsky (1998), M. Grant (1978), M. Hammond (1968), B.M. Levick (1983), R. MacMullen (2000), F. Millar (1986), F. Millar and E. Segal (1984), K.A. Raaflaub and M. Toher (1990), H.H. Scullard (1982), and R. Wallace (2000). The first court of appeal for numismatic evidence during the reign of Augustus is C.H.V. Sutherland (1984). Epigraphical studies of the period can be found in P.A. Brunt and J.M. Moore (1988) and V. Ehrenberg and A.H.M. Jones (1976).

This article is dedicated to the author's great-grandson: Marshall Ezra Thrasher (b. Sep 20, 2021).

Bibliography

Alföldi, A., *Der Vater des Vaterlandes im römischen Denken*, Darmstadt, 1971.

Ando, C., *Imperial Ideology and Provincial Loyalty in the Roman Empire*, Los Angeles, 2000.

Barnes, T.D., "The Victories of Augustus," *JRS* 64, 1974, 21–26.

Baldwin, B., *The Roman Emperors*, Montreal, 1980.

Bengtson, H., Kaiser Augustus: Sein Leben und seine Zeit, Munich, 1981.

Béranger, J., *Principatus: Études de notions et d'histoire politiques dans l'antiquité greco-romaine*, Geneva, 1973.

Bleicken, J., *Augustus: Eine Biographie*, Berlin, 1998.

Bowersock, G.W., "The Pontificate of Augustus," in: K.A. Raaflaub & M. Toher, eds., *Between Republic and Empire: Interpretations of Augustus and His Principate*, Berkeley, 1990.

Brunt, P.A., "The Role of the Senate in the Augustan Regime," *CQ* 3, 1984, 424–444.

Brunt, P. A., & J.M. Moore, eds., *Res Gestae Divi Augusti: The Achievements of the Divine Augustus*, Oxford, 1967, repr. 1988.

Carter, J.M., *The Battle of Actium: The Rise & Triumph of Augustus Caesar*, New York, 1970.

Chisholm, K., & J. Ferguson, eds., *Rome, the Augustan Age*, Oxford, 1981.

Earl, D., *The Age of Augustus*, New York, 1968.

Eck, W., "Augustus und die Großprovinz Germanien," *KöJa* 37, 2006, 11–20.

Eck, W., *The Age of Augustus*, 2nd ed., Oxford, 2007.

Edmondson, J., ed., *Augustus*, Edinburgh, 2009.

Ehrenberg, V., & A.H.M. Jones, eds., *Documents Illustrating the Reigns of Augustus & Tiberius*, 2nd ed., Oxford, 1976.

Everitt, A., *The First Emperor: Caesar Augustus and the Triumph of Rome*, London, 2007.

Fishwick, D., *The Imperial Cult in the Latin West: Studies in the Ruler Cult of the Western Roman Empire*, vol. III, Leiden, 2002.

Galinsky, K., *Augustan Culture*, Princeton, 1998.

Galinsky, K., ed., *The Cambridge Companion to the Age of Augustus*, Cambridge UK, 2005.

Galinsky, K., *Augustus: Introduction to the Life of an Emperor*, Cambridge UK, 2012.

Goldsworthy, A., *Augustus: First Emperor of Rome*, New Haven, 2014.

Grant, M., *History of Rome*, New York, 1978.

Griffin, J., "Augustan Poetry and Augustanism," in: K. Galinsky, ed., *The Cambridge Companion to the Age of Augustus*, Cambridge UK, 2005, 306–320.

Gurval, R.A., *Actium and Augustus*, Ann Arbor, 1998.

Hallett, J.P., "*Perusinae glandes* and the Changing Image of Augustus," *AmJAH* 2, 1977, 151–171.

Hammond, M., *The Augustan Principate in Theory and Practice During the Julio-Claudian Period*, New York, 1968.

Jones, A.H.M., "The Imperium of Augustus," *JRS*, vol. XLI, parts 1 and 2, 1951, 112–119.

Jones, A.H.M., *Augustus*, London, 1970.

Kienast, D., Augustus, Prinzeps und Monarch, Darmstadt, 1982.

Levick, B.M., "The *Senatus Consultum* from Larinum," *JRS* 73, 1983, 97–115.

MacMullen, R., *Romanization in the Time of Augustus*, New Haven, 2000.

Massie, A., *The Caesars*, London, 1983.

Millar, F., *The Emperor in the Roman World*, London, 1977.

Millar, F., *The Augustan Aristocracy*, Oxford, 1986.

Millar, F., & E. Segal, eds., *Caesar Augustus: Seven Aspects*, Oxford, 1984.

Raaflaub, K.A., & M. Toher, eds., *Between Republic and Empire: Interpretations of Augustus and His Principate*, Berkeley, 1990.

Richardson, J.S., *Augustan Rome 44 BC to AD 14*, Edinburgh, 2012.

Scheid, J., "Augustus and Roman Religion: Continuity, Conservatism, and Innovation," in: K. Galinsky, ed., *The Cambridge Companion to the Age of Augustus*, Cambridge UK, 2005, 175–193.

Scheid, J., *Res Gestae Divi Augusti: Hauts faits du divin Auguste*, Paris, 2007.

Schnurbein, S. von, "Augustus in Germania and His New 'Town' at Waldgirmes East of the Rhine," *JRAr* 16, 2003, 93–107.

Scullard, H.H., *From the Gracchi to Nero: A History of Rome from 133 BC to AD 68*, 5th ed., London, 1982.

Shotter, D., *Augustus Caesar*, 2nd ed., London, 2005.

Simmons, M.B., "Augustus," in: P.G. Jestice, ed., *Holy People of the World*, vol. I, Santa Barbara, 2004, 83–84.

Simmons, M.B., *Universal Salvation in Late Antiquity: Porphyry of Tyre and the Pagan-Christian Debate*, OSLA, Oxford, 2015.

Southern, P., *Augustus*, London, 1998.

Spawforth, A.J.S., *Greece and the Augustan Cultural Revolution*, Cambridge UK, 2012.

Stahlmann, I., *Imperator Caesar Augustus*, Darmstadt, 1988.

Sutherland, C.H.V., *The Roman Imperial Coinage*, vol. I, London, 1984.

Syme, R., *The Roman Revolution*, Oxford, 1939.

Talbert, R.J.A., *The Senate of Imperial Rome*, Princeton, 1984.

Wallace, R., *Res gestae divi Augusti: Texts with Notes*, Wauconda, 2000.

Wallace-Hadrill, A., "Image and Authority in the Coinage of Augustus," *JRS* 76, 1986, 66–87.

Zanker, P., *The Power of Images in the Age of Augustus*, Ann Arbor, 1988.

MICHAEL BLAND SIMMONS

Ausonius of Bordeaux

Ausonius (c. 310–c. 395 CE) was a Roman poet and professor of rhetoric from Burdigala (modern Bordeaux in France). His learned works, firmly rooted in pagan Greco-Roman culture, also show various traces of Christian concepts. However, there is discussion about the extent and depth of his Christian beliefs. By all means, Ausonius is a representative of the Roman cultural elite in the age between the Edict of Milan (313 CE) and the reign of → Theodosius I (379–395 CE).

1. Biography

Ausonius' life is relatively well known, mostly on account of his works, of which many have been transmitted (Latin texts with commentary: Green, 1991; with English translation: Evelyn White, 1919–1921; with German translation and commentary: Dräger, 2011–2015).

His name has traditionally been referred to as Decimus Magnus Ausonius, but recent research has called this into question, arguing that his first name must have been Decimius (Salomies, 2016). Ausonius was born about 310 CE in Burdigala (Bordeaux) in Aquitania, in southwestern f bishop of Nola and an important Gaul. He was the son of Julius Ausonius of Bazas, a country physician from low birth (possibly even a former slave: Green, 1991, xxv), and Julia Aeonia, who stemmed from a family of high status. His parents had four children (two boys, two girls), two of whom died early; only Ausonius and his sister Dryadia reached maturity.

Young Ausonius went to Toulouse (after 320 CE), where he was educated by his uncle Arborius. On his return to Bordeaux, he married Sabina, the daughter of Lucanus Talisius, who belonged to the local aristocracy. Having given birth to three children (one of whom died early), she died at the age of 28. For some 30 years, Ausonius was a professional teacher in his native city, first as a *grammaticus*, later as a *rhetor*, and he led a mostly quiet, uneventful life. The most famous of his pupils was Paulinus of Bordeaux, who later became bishop of Nola and an important author. During his early years in Bordeaux, Ausonius as a poet produced merely occasional poems for private use.

Probably on account of his excellent reputation as a teacher, he was invited by the emperor Valentinian I (emperor from 364 to 375 CE) to Trier, where he was to devote himself to the education of his eldest son, Gratian (the later emperor of the West from 367 to 383 CE). This crucial change in Ausonius' life took place in the mid-360s CE, probably about 365 CE.

In Trier, he met all the important men of the age, among whom the orator Quintus Aurelius Symmachus, and it was here that he composed his most important poems, such as the famous *Mosella*, a small epic poem on the river Moselle. For about 20 years he lived and worked at the imperial court in Trier, where he was highly esteemed by both Valentinian and Gratian. He was even granted the prestigious titles *comes* and *quaestor sacri palatii*, and obtained the rank of *quaestor*. After Valentinian's death in 375 CE, Ausonius' influence grew even further, as the new emperor, his former pupil Gratian, promoted the career of both Ausonius and of his family members. In 379 CE Ausonius even became consul, the highest political honor. However, in 383 CE Gratian was killed by the usurper Magnus Maximus, and Ausonius was forced into the background, although he was compelled to stay in Trier for some years. In the mid-380s CE (perhaps as late as 388 CE) he was finally allowed to retire to his native Bordeaux, where he devoted his remaining time and energy to studying and writing poetry (many of his poetical works date from this period). His last work is a poetical correspondence with his former pupil → Paulinus of Nola (390–394 CE), who,

unlike Ausonius, had adopted an ascetic Christian lifestyle. Shortly afterwards, Ausonius died at the advanced age of about 85 (for Ausonius' life and career: see Green, 1991, xxiv–xxxii; see further e.g. Dräger, 2002, 251–254; a broader study is the monography of Sivan, 1993).

2. Works

The standard critical edition of Ausonius counts no fewer than 27 authentic poetical works of various length (Green, 1991; for the manuscript tradition see Green, 1991, xli–xlix). These may be divided into various subcategories.

P. Dräger (2002, 254–258) conveniently distinguishes "personal and family poems," among which the *Ephemeris* or "diary" (see below), from "scholastic and historical poetry," such as the *Commemoratio professorum Burdigalensium*, a series of poetical portraits of rhetoric teachers from Bordeaux. A third main category is constituted by what is called "Kunstdichtung," poems of a highly artificial nature showing great literary expertise and erudition. To this category belong the *Cento Nuptialis* (a wedding poem of 131 hexameters entirely assembled from lines and half-lines from Virgil), the *Griphus ternarii numeri* (a literary feat of 90 lines celebrating the number three), the *Mosella*, and *Bissula* (four erotic poems about a young German slave girl whom the poet had obtained as a gift from the emperor after a successful campaign in Germany).

3. Christian Elements

Ausonius did not stem from a manifestly Christian family. It is not known whether his parents were Christian or not. However, there were some devoted Christians in Ausonius' wider circle: two of his aunts apparently adopted a monastic life (see Aus. *Parent.* 6 and 26), and his sister Dryadia is credited with a sole concern "to know God" (*unaque cura/nosse Deum*; *Parent.* 12.7–8), which possibly alludes to her Christian faith. As for Ausonius himself, we have to rely on specific passages in his poetry.

The large majority of Ausonius' works may be called "traditionally pagan". Most of them are steeped in Greco-Roman history and literature, mythology and culture, and do not show any trace of Christianity. There are even texts which may be considered as pagan prayers (see the *Precationes Variae*, three poems addressed to divinities such as Phoebus, Janus, and Sol). However, a number of his works, mostly in the first and third categories mentioned above, do contain explicit references to Christianity, Christ, and the → Trinity, as well as allusions to other Christian notions and ideas. The most important passages are the following.

In the *Ephemeris* ("The daily round"), an (incomplete) cycle of eight poems picturing the poet's day from dawn till nightfall, a Christian morning prayer is given much prominence. First it is announced in the short poem Aus. *Ephem.* 2.7–14 and briefly alluded to in *Ephem.* 1.15–21, most notably in *Ephem.* 1.15–18: *Deus precandus est mihi/ac filius summi dei,/ maiestas unius modi,/sociata sacro spiritu* ("I have to pray to God and to the Son of the only God, the majesty of one nature, in fellowship with the Holy Spirit"). Phrased in traditional language without a specifically Christian color, the lines nonetheless present an orthodox view of the Holy Trinity.

Next, *Ephem.* 3, a long poem of 85 hexameters, offers a full prayer text. It is, in fact, one of the earliest non-liturgical prayer texts in Christian Latin (see Green, 1991, 250; for French translation and commentary of the poem: Martin, 1971; further analysis in e.g. Langlois, 1991; Green, 1995). It is directed to "the Almighty One" (*Omnipotens*), who is described and praised in the first section (*Ephem.* 1.1–26) as the Maker and Cause of everything in the world. Distinctly Christian elements are not obvious to the general reader, except for references to "the Word" (*ipse dei verbum, verbum deus* – "himself the Word of God, the Word which is God"; *Ephem.* 1.9) and to his bearing the sins of man and suffering ignominious death (*Ephem.* 1.21–22). A second, short section (*Ephem.* 1.27–30) addresses the Son of the highest Father, who is requested to bring the poet's prayers to his father. The central part of the poem (*Ephem.* 1.23–79) consists of a number of requests: the poet prays that he may remain firm against → evil and → sin, ascend from the → body, see the eternal light, be granted pardon, live a peaceful and quiet life, and expect → death without fear. Most of it could well have been written by any 4th-century CE Latin poet. It is merely the names of → Adam and Eve (*Ephem.* 1.33–34), Elias and Enoch (*Ephem.* 1.42), or

easy allusions to famous Bible texts, such as a reference to Father, Son, and → Holy Spirit "who floated over the waves of the sea" (*qui super aequoreas volitabat spiritus undas*; *Ephem.* 1.48) which mark the prayer as Christian. In the closing lines (*Ephem.* 1.79–85), the Son is asked to transmit the poet's prayers to his Father. Again, Christian notions are present, but rather unobtrusively, for example, *filius, ex vero verus, de lumine lumen/aeterno cum patre manens, in saecula regnans* ("the Son, True God of True God, Light of Light, who remains with the eternal Father, reigning unto the ages"; *Ephem.* 1.82–83) or the final word *amen* (*Ephem.* 1.85). Again, the poet seems keen to pay tribute to orthodox formulae as fixed in the Nicene Creed of 325 CE, amended in 381 CE at Constantinople (for a comprehensive list of verbal echoes: Martin, 1971, 376). It may be relevant to note that *Ephem.* 3 may be dated to 381 CE (Polymerakis, 2011, 48; see for another view e.g. Sivan, 1993, 163).

Rather surprisingly, the next little poem, *Ephem.* 4 opens with the line *satis precum datum deo* [...] ("enough prayers have been given to God," a rather harsh statement slightly softened in the following two lines), and the remaining parts of the cycle do not refer to religion or Christian teaching again, but rather concentrate on daily routines, such as lunch and conversation with friends (*Lucifer* in *Ephem.* 8.39 appears to refer to the rising sun rather than to the → devil; there may be just a hint to the Gospel story about Jesus "walking on the water" in *Ephem.* 8.8–9; see Green, 1991, 264). It is, perhaps, the absence of further religious elements in the poetical description of the poet's day that seems surprising.

A rather more overtly Christian poem are the so called *Versus Paschales*, dating from 371 to 375 CE and probably written on the occasion of a baptism in the imperial family of Valentinian (Green, 1991, 269). It is a piece of 31 hexameters, that shows remarkably little that refers to → Easter. Most of the poem is taken by an elaborate address of the Supreme God, hailed as Father of all things, bringer of the law and the prophets, and of "your Word, who is the Son and God, in all things like You and equal to You" (Aus. *Pasch.* 1.16–17). Again, trinitarian doctrine is underscored: *Trina fides auctore uno, spes certa salutis* ("Threefold object of faith, from a single source, certain hope of salvation"; *Pasch.* 1.22), before the closing eight lines offer a surprise: they draw a parallel between the Trinity and the imperial family, with the emperor (Valentinian) as the father of twin Augusti (Gratian and Valentinian II), sharing his power with both his son (Gratian) and his brother (Valens) "without dividing it." The three closely connected "rulers on earth and servants of heaven" are then commended to Christ, who is to claim them with his Father. The evidently political image at the end, rather strained as it is, seems to be the real purpose of the poet, apart from his emphasizing contemporary doctrine concerning the Trinity.

A poem of similar length, the *Oratio consulis Ausonii versibus rhopalibus*, often included in Ausonius' works, is now generally considered to be spurious (Green, 1991, 667). It is a metrical showpiece (*versus rhopales* contain words of an increasing number of syllable, e.g. the opening line *spes, deus, aeternae stationis conciliator* – "hope, God, granter of an eternal abode"), which as such could be Ausonian, but shows too many shortcomings as well as particularities of idiom to count as authentic.

In addition to these Christian prayer poems, there are some shorter references to Christianity scattered through Ausonius' works. The prose preface of the *Epicedion in patrem* opens with the words *post deum semper patrem colui* ("after God I always revered my father"), which can be (but do not necessarily have to be) taken in a Christian sense.

The curious poem *Griphus ternarii numeri* is a learned, poetical showpiece, listing various elements in nature or culture dominated by "three." Starting with "drinking thrice" and passing through numerous mythological tales involving three figures (the three Muses among them), the three Punic wars, scientific elements, and much more, it effectively ends in the following line: *Ter bibe; tris numerus super omnia, tris deus unus* ("Drink thrice, the number three [is] above all, three [is] one God"), followed by two closing lines that make the point the whole poem consists of three times 30 lines. The casual reference to the Trinity, as which *tris deus unus* is commonly interpreted, may seem awkward to modern readers. However, as R.P.H. Green (1991, 445) rightly remarks, it is "not mocking or blasphemous, but typical of the author's broad-minded urbanity."

Inevitably, scholars have tried to find further, more implicit signs of Christianity in Ausonius' works

(for some examples: see Polymerakis, 2011, 49–50; to which may be added Aus. *Ep.* 23.32–38, with Skeb, 2000, 345). However, it seems fair to say that his poetical oeuvre is more conspicuous in showing a consistent lack of openly Christian elements wherever these might have been expected. Neither the numerous portraits in the *Commemoratio professorum Burdigalensium* nor the brilliant *Mosella* present anything Christian. In the *Eclogae* we find several pieces (2, 3, and 4) offering ethical advice from the tradition of Pythagoras, and Ausonius even composed a poem about *Cupido cruciatus* (with the Christian keyword *cruciatus* meaning merely "in torment"; see also Polymerakis, 2011, 62).

To sum up: Ausonius' works definitely show Christian elements and a certain degree of familiarity with Christian teaching, particularly concerning the Trinity. However, they mostly remain firmly rooted in the pagan tradition of classical mythology and culture, as exemplified by Homer and Virgil, and often seem remarkable for the absence of Christian elements.

4. Synthesis

Given the evidence provided by Ausonius' works, it is impossible either to claim that he did not feel any sympathy toward Christianity, or to maintain that he was a deeply convinced adherent of the Christian religion, let alone a fanatic believer. Ausonius seems to be, so to speak, somewhere in between. Whether he personally adopted the new religion and was baptized, cannot be ascertained, but he at least formally acknowledged its basic doctrines, most of all as expressed in the Nicene Creed. The fact that Emperor Valentinian had adopted Christianity as his religion may well have been the decisive factor here. It seems that Ausonius conformed to the dominant doctrine of his time, while staying away from religious fanaticism and intolerance (Polymerakis, 2011, 53). It is, perhaps, significant, that there are no references to Christianity in Ausonius' latest works, written in his final years in Bordeaux, after his return from the imperial court in Trier.

Historiography

The evidently Christian elements in some of Ausonius' undisputedly authentic pagan works easily caught the attention of classical scholars, even at an early stage, and were found to be difficult to accept as such.

Broadly speaking, earlier scholarship on Ausonius until 1900 showed a tendency to play down Christian elements in Ausonius' works, assuming them to be no more than lip service to the new religion. Ausonius, then, was considered to be not a proper Christian, or put differently: an essentially pagan author (for examples: Skeb, 2000, 327). Traces of this approach remain visible in scholarly literature; for example, the influential textbook by M. von Albrecht (1997) in his useful survey of Ausonius' life and works (Albrecht, 1997, 1320–1330) fails to mention the question, consistently placing Ausonius in the tradition of Catullus and Horace and other classical Roman poets (Albrecht, 1997, 1323), without even considering any Christian influence.

By contrast, in the 20th century, scholars took to the other extreme, claiming that Ausonius, for all his pagan poetical language and themes, had in fact become a truly Christian believer and author. The eminent Ausonius expert R.P.H. Green exemplifies the latter attitude, suggesting in his standard edition that Ausonius may well have been a lifelong Christian, as he was born after the Edict of Milan, and was not likely to be chosen by Valentinian as the teacher of his son unless he were a Christian in the first place. R.P.H. Green even suggests, even more speculatively, that the poet may have belonged to a Christian faction at the university of Bordeaux (Green, 1991, xxvii–xxviii; see also Green, 1995, 342–342: "Ausonius is [...] a committed Christian secure in the teaching of the Church and wishing to live an acceptable life within it"). For earlier appraisals of Ausonius as a Christian, see, for example, M.J. Pattist (1925) and A. Stanislaus (1944). According to M.J. Pattist, Ausonius did accept the Christian faith, but was "spiritually not profound enough to accept the Christian life as well" (Pattist, 1925, 92), while A. Stanislaus concludes that "Ausonius was Christian in his prayers and pagan in his classroom" (Stanislaus, 1944, 157).

Only recently, scholars started to reopen the debate, without resorting to speculation in either direction, not based on a preconceived image of the poet, whether merely pagan or merely Christian. A fair appraisal of the various elements to be detected in Ausonius' texts produces a rather more blurred and mixed image: Ausonius obviously belongs "to both worlds," that of Christianity and of pagan culture, two worlds which in the 4th century CE probably were not yet as distinctly divided as later centuries would sometimes have it. Indeed, some have argued that the entire question whether or not Ausonius was a Christian is wrong, given the "intellectual syncretism" typical for so many authors of Ausonius' days (Gasti, 2013, 83), or even the "verinnerlichte Frömmigkeit eines Intellektuellen für den sich die Alternative 'Heide oder Christ' so wenig stellte wie für viele seiner Zeitgenossen" ("the internalized piety of an intellectual for whom the alternative of 'pagan or Christian' was as unimportant as it was for many of his contemporaries"; Skeb, 2000, 352).

The 21st-century western world, in which Christianity has ceased to be the unquestionable, dominant religion, and in which Christian voices may be heard among many other, often contrasting, ones, may well be more suited to appreciate a religiously multiform poet such as Ausonius.

Bibliography

Albrecht, M. von, *A History of Roman Literature: From Livius Andronicus to Boethius: With Special Regard to Its Influence on World Literature*, rev. G. Schmeling & M. von Albrecht, trans. with the assistance of F. & K. Newman, Leiden, 1997.

Dräger, P., *D. Magnus Ausonius, Mosella, Bissula: Briefwechsel mit Paulinus Nolanus: Herausgegeben und übersetzt*, SaTu, Düsseldorf, 2002.

Dräger, P., *Decimus Magnus Ausonius, Sämtliche Werke*, 3 vols., Trier, 2011–2015.

Evelyn White, H.G., *Ausonius with an English Translation*, LCL 96 & 115, Cambridge MA, 1919–1921.

Gasti, F., *Profilo storico della letteratura tardolatina*, Pavia, 2013, 75–84.

Green, R.P.H., *The Works of Ausonius: Edited with Introduction and Commentary*, Oxford, 1991.

Green, R.P.H., "The Christianity of Ausonius," *SP* 28, 1993, 39.

Green, R.P.H., "Ausonius at Prayer," in: L. Ayres, ed., *The Passionate Intellect: Essays on the Transformation of*

Classical Traditions: FS for Professor I.G. Kidd, RUSCH VII, New Brunswick, 1995, 333–343.

Langlois, P., "Die christlichen Gedichte und das Christentum des Ausonius," in: M.J. Lossau, ed., *Ausonius*, WdF 652, Darmstadt, 1991, 55–80; Ger. trans. of Fr. paper from 1969.

Martin, J., "La prière d'Ausone: Texte, essai de traduction, esquisse de commentaire," *BAGB* 30, 1971, 369–382.

Pattist, M.J., "Ausonius als Christen," diss., Amsterdam, 1925.

Polymerakis, F., "Θρησκευτικές αντιλήψεις του Δέκιμου Μάγνου Αυσόνιου: χριστιανός ή εθνικός," *MedChr* 1, 2011, 45–71; consulted in ET produced through https://www.deepl.com.

Salomies, O., "The Nomenclature of the Poet Ausonius," *Arctos* 50, 2016, 133–142.

Sivan, H., *Ausonius of Bordeaux: Genesis of a Gallic Aristocracy*, London, 1993.

Skeb, M., "Subjektivität und Gottesbild: Die religiöse Mentalität des Decimus Magnus Ausonius," *Hermes* 128, 2000, 327–352.

Stanislaus, A., "The Christian Ausonius," *ClWe* 37, 1944, 156–157.

VINCENT HUNINK

Auspicius of Toul

Auspicius (c. 390/400?–475/480? CE) was bishop of Tullum Leucorum (present-day Toul) in the former Roman province of Belgica Prima (capital Trier), then Frankish territory. He is traditionally the fifth in succession, and the first to be historically tangible (Duchesne, 1915, 62). The noble Gallo-Roman family of the Auspicii can be traced from the 3rd to the 7th century CE (Brandes, 1905, 13–14; *TLL*, vol. II, 1549, 46–58; *PLRE*, vol. I, 141; vol. II, 203). Presumably educated in the classical fashion, well connected, and comfortable, Auspicius would have fitted into the characteristic Gallic pattern of the aristocratic bishop (see Stroheker, 1970). In the sources (see below), he is visible to us in the 470s CE, and emerges as one of Gaul's most distinguished senior bishops. Endowed with theological and administrative authority and involved in networks of patronage, he was also a poet, having authored a verse letter that is among the first nonmetrical poems to have come down to us from antiquity. He therefore plays a crucial role in the study of the development from ancient metrical to medieval rhythmical prosody.

The sources allow us to roughly approximate the years of his birth and death. He is mentioned by → Sidonius Apollinaris in a letter written after 470 CE (Loyen, 1970, 253: c. 471; *PLRE*, vol. II, 128: c. 477) and addressed to Arbogastes, at the time *comes* of Trier (Sid. *Ep.* 4.17.3). Arbogastes had asked Sidonius for a biblical commentary. Sidonius respectfully refused and suggested that Arbogastes would do better to consult either his own bishop or local specialists such as Lupus of Troyes or Auspicius, to whom, on top of their seniority, he ascribed a special status among the Gallican bishops (*incliti Galliarum patres et protomystae*, "illustrious fathers and foremost initiates of Gaul"). Lupus was indeed the doyen of Gaul, having been born around 383 CE, and in office since c. 426 CE. Accordingly, Auspicius may have had a similar, though somewhat shorter tenure in office, which would place his birth somewhere in the last decade of the 4th century CE. A further terminus post quem for his death is provided by a letter dating from 471/474 CE and sent to him by Sidonius (*Ep.* 7.11), who solicited Auspicius' patronage for its bearer.

By chance, one letter from Auspicius' own hand has survived, a poetical tribute and admonition to the same Arbogastes. It has been preserved in the 9th-century CE Codex Vaticano-Palatinus 869, which contains the so-called *Litterae Austrasicae*. It is number 23 in this collection of 48 letters (two of which are in verse) by worldly and spiritual dignitaries. The collection was probably compiled in the late 6th century CE in King Childebert's II chancellery in Metz to serve as a model of letter writing (Gundlach, 1892; Brandes, 1905, 3). Of these letters, the one by Auspicius is the oldest. Auspicius congratulates the city of Trier on its eminent leader (ll. 49–52 *congratulandum tibi est,/o Trevirorum civitas,/quae tali viro regeris,/antiquis comparabili* – "you are to be congratulated, city of Trier, on being governed by such a man, who is comparable to the ancients") and credits him with the merit of being a true Christian (ll. 63–64 *Christi nomen invocat/religioni deditus* – "he invokes Christ's name, dedicated to faith"), but then warns him at length against the temptations of "greed" (*cupiditas*) to which he is exposed. Finally, Auspicius says that he considers him as "already prefigured for the office of bishop" (ll. 151–52 *iam sacerdotio/praefiguratum*), which would oblige him, among other things, to honor his local bishop Jamblichus.

The text constitution is problematic as the only manuscript, in its first hand, is corrupt, and has been freely corrected by a second hand (11th/12th cent.). W. Gundlach (1892) retains a lot of the original jumble, considering it to be the Merovingian original, but W. Brandes (1905) has shown that his reasoning is flawed, and provides an emended text, in which he is followed by K. Strecker (1923).

This verse epistle is the first datable rhythmical poem in nonmetrical iambic dimeters; it is also the only rhythmical poem that dates with certainty from the 5th century CE. It is remarkable for being in hymn form despite the fact that it was meant to be read and not sung. W. Brandes (1905 and later) was the first to print it as a sequence of 41 strophes of four verses each, each verse counting eight syllables. He interpreted this as the direct transposition of the metrical, Ambrosian, model to a popular, accentuated form with alternating rhythm. W. Meyer (1906 and later) pointed out that there is no regular alternation of unaccentuated and accentuated syllables and proposed a much more complicated scheme: essentially, each verse begins as prose and ends in an iambic cadence. According to D.L. Norberg (2004, 100–103), however, the epistle does imitate the metric dimeter of classic hymns; more precisely, it imitates its distribution of words and its word accents, without attention to quantity ("imitation de la structure"), which entails the complete loss of the metrical ictus. P. Klopsch (1972, 13–16 and table p. 11; 1991, 104–106) argues that quantitative versification and the sense of a verse ictus were still very much alive at the time, and consequently opts for a system of "floating emphasis" (Klopsch, 1972, 15).

The scholarly debate has concentrated on the striking rhythmical form of this poem, but an analysis of its contents and its historical setting could also enhance our understanding of Auspicius. Arbogastes was a descendant of the famous *magister militum* Arbogastes (*PLRE*, vol. I, 95–97), and does not fail to mention this (ll. 53–60). He must have had a more or less traditional Roman education, for Sidonius praises his literary skill (*Quirinalis impletus fonte facundiae* –"having been filled from the spring of Roman eloquence") and professes confidence that Latin culture will survive in the barbarian kingdoms

while Arbogastes lives (Sid. *Ep.* 4.17.1–2). He seems to have been a regional ruler who tried to keep apart from the → Franks. If he is the same as the Arbogastes who was bishop of Chartres in the 480s CE, he was later to retire from, or to be driven out of, Trier (MacGeorge, 2002, 75).

Auspicius' aims in this situation would have been the following:

1. to reinforce his influence on Arbogastes by sending him a "mirror of princes" (Nürnberg, 1993);
2. to tie him in with the local episcopate and boost regional cohesion, in line with Sidonius' advice and as against Arbogastes' ambition to court more distant alliances; and
3. in so doing, to further a policy that kept its distance to the "barbarians," perhaps politically, but in any case culturally and ecclesiastically. Against this "old-school" backdrop in one of the last tenuous pockets of Roman culture (Riché, 1962, 255), the poem to Arbogastes has a striking novelty about it: it is consciously modern in order to perpetuate traditional values in new circumstances. The very fact that it is a poem rather than one of the usual prose letters creates a sense of intimacy through the then fashionable poetic exchange in the Gallic upper class and heightens the sense of a common cause.

Historiography

W. Gundlach's Monumenta Germaniae historica Epistolae edition (1892), although reprinted in Corpus Christianorum: Series latina (1957), is inadequate and has been superseded by W. Brandes (1905) and K. Strecker (1923).

Auspicius' letter to Arbogastes was first recognized for being rhythmical (accentual, non-metrical) poetry by W. Brandes (1905). It is the first example to have come down to us from antiquity. The precise nature of its rhythm is debated: while W. Brandes identifies lines of eight syllables with alternating rhythm recalling Ambrose, W. Meyer (1906) argues that only the verse endings are rhythmical, and P. Klopsch (1972) sees a floating emphasis; D.L. Norberg (2004), however, comes close to W. Brandes in pointing out the accentual imitation of hymnal versification.

As to the poem's message, R. Nürnberg (1993) sees a "mirror of princes." It could do, however, with further analysis, for which an outline has been sketched in the above.

Bibliography

Brandes, W., *Des Auspicius von Toul rhythmische Epistel an Arbogastes van Trier*, WBJG, Wolfenbüttel, 1905.

Duchesne, L., *Fastes épiscopaux de l'ancienne Gaule*, vol. III, Paris, 1915.

Gruber, J., "Auspicius of Toul," in: *DNP*, vol. II, Stuttgart, 1997, cols. 335–336; also *BNP*, Brill Online.

Gundlach, W., MGH.Ep. 3.135–137, Berlin, 1892; repr. in CCSL 117.442–447, Turnhout, 1957.

Jülicher, A., "Auspicius," *PRE*, vol. I, Stuttgart, 1896, cols. 2587–2588.

Klopsch, P., *Einführung in die mittellateinische Verslehre*, Darmstadt, 1972.

Klopsch, P., "Der Übergang von quantitierender zu akzentuierender lateinischer Dichtung," in: H.L.C. Tristram, *Metrik und Medienwechsel = Metrics and Media*, Tübingen, 1991, 95–106.

Loyen, A., *Sidoine Apollinaire*, vol. II: *Lettres livres 1–5*, Paris, 1970.

MacGeorge, P., *Late Roman Warlords*, Oxford, 2002.

Mathisen, R.W., "*P.L.R.E.* II: Suggested Addenda and Corrigenda," *Hist.* 31, 1982, 364–386, esp. 367–368.

Meyer, W., *Die rhythmischen Iamben des Auspicius*, AGWG. PH, Göttingen, 1906, 192–229, in: W. Meyer, *Gesammelte Abhandlungen zur mittellateinischen Rhythmik*, vol. III, ed. W. Bulst, Berlin, 1936, 1–41, Hildesheim, 1970.

Norberg, D.L., *An Introduction to the Study of Medieval Latin Versification*, trans. G.C. Roti & J. de La Chapelle Skubly, ed. & introd. J. Ziółkowski, Washington DC, 2004; Fr. orig.: *Introduction à l'étude de la versification latine médiévale*, Stockholm, 1958.

Nürnberg, R., "Auspicius," in: *LThK*, vol. I, Freiburg, 1993, cols. 1268–1269.

Prelog, J., "Auspicius," in: *LMA*, vol. I, Stuttgart, 1980, col. 1249.

Riché, P., *Éducation et culture dans l'occident barbare: VIe–VIIIe siècles*, Paris, 1962.

Sauser, E., "Auspicius," in: *BBKL*, vol. XXI, Nordhausen, 2003, col. 44.

Schanz, M., et al., *Die Literatur des fünften und sechsten Jahrhunderts*, vol. IV/2 of M. Schanz & C. Hosius, *Geschichte der römischen Literatur bis zum Gesetzgebungswerk des Kaisers Justinian*, Munich, 1920, repr. 1971.

Strecker, K., in MGH.PL 4.2.614–617, Berlin, 1923.

Stroheker, K.F., *Der senatorische Adel im spätantiken Gallien*, Tübingen, 1948, repr. Darmstadt, 1970.

JOOP VAN WAARDEN

Autobiography

The notion of *autobiography* in antiquity is far from evident. In modern times, autobiography is generally understood as the concept of a book written with the sole object to give a portrait of the author him- or herself. The author is the one who is writing, but at the same time, he or she is the one who is being portrayed. Finally, he or she is the narrator. Therefore, what we have in a modern autobiography is the identity of three persons at the same time: the author, the narrator, and the character. Besides, there are other formal elements. Looking at the genre of the autobiography, we come across the element of a play with reality and truth that is so often associated with an autobiography (Popkin, 2005). An autobiography will produce a sense of reality on the reader. The reader is not occupied by mere fiction but by facts. At least, that is what he thinks. In his view, the eyes of the beholder, the author strives to describe the bare reality of his life and is aiming at writing the truth. Even if the reader is aware of the fact that any author will make his own selection as to the elements he incorporates in his autobiography. A selection justified by motives of self-justification or other reasons like flattery or secrets. Think for example of the *Apologia pro vita sua* by Cardinal Newman. Hence, what the reader assumes, is that the elements of truth and autobiography are strongly related one to another. This then is also the main difference with the other genre resembling to that of the autobiography: the memoirs. Memoirs intend to describe a certain history in which the writer was closely involved. Yet, they do not claim to be autobiographical nor to be entirely trustworthy. See the famous *Mémoires* from Saint-Simon. No one expects to find in these *Mémoires* a detailed portrait of Saint-Simon himself, or only perhaps in an implicit way. Nor do we expect to have a story entirely true. What we do expect however, is a lively picture of life at the court of Louis XIV. Hence memoirs can be defined as testimonies of a certain history, written by one of the actors in this history, yet not focusing on the person of author himself. Therefore memoirs do not confront us with the problematic triangle of the complete identity of the writer, the person about whom the author is writing and the narrator. They try to cope with the triangle between author, his environment, and the story relating the first element to the second. They don't deal with the identity of the writer himself.

This identity is the eminently philosophical problem autobiography is dealing with. Can these three persons – the author, the narrator, and the character – be one at the same time? Apparently, the problem can only be solved by constantly developing new forms of autobiography, going along with the development of → philosophy. Books like *A Portrait of the Artist as a Young Man*, from J. Joyce, but also of *À la recherche du temps perdu* of M. Proust, can't be compared to the *Confessions*. Philosophical reflection about the identity and subject has radically changed since the 4th century CE.

1. Autobiography in Antiquity

Yet, it is in antiquity that we can find the roots of even modern autobiography, though certainly we do not need to focus in the first place on the *Confessions* of Augustine of Hippo (Thompson, 2006; Lancel, 1999; Brown, 2000, 152; O'Donnel, 2005; Brachtendorf, 2005; Lössl, 201; Anderson, 2001).

Research has shown us that autobiography has its roots in the old discipline of → rhetoric. What a philosopher needed and what therefore a rhetorician needed was to convince his audience. In order to do so, he had to prove to be trustworthy. This can only be done by telling about oneself. Therefore, the first origins of the autobiography do not lie in a discovery of the interior person, but in the need to convince others. Early "autobiography" was not directed at the subject of the writer but at the reader. Its outlook was not the study of the soul of the author, but the mind of his audience and his readers (Lyons, 1995; Pellung, 2009, 41–64). It was not a turn inward, but a turn outwards. In this sense, autobiography was part of the *demonstrativum* genre (the art of speaking in an honorable way) amidst the three genres in rhetorical oratory (the other two being the *genus iudiciale*, showing the right structure, and the *genus deliberativum*, the political structure). It was meant to prove something. Yet, moral and social guidelines had to be observed. Aristotle already mentioned striving for compliments wasn't acceptable. Therefore, proving one's qualities had sharply to be distinguished from boasting of oneself. Theoretically, the distinction between these two elements was clear, yet not easy to be respected. Could modesty be integrated in one's oratorical skills without undermining the power of the demonstration, aiming at convincing the audience?

At least, the distinction showed that from the very beginning of autobiography, the genre was heavily influenced by morals. The beginning of autobiography was not situated in the search of truth, but in the search of virtue. The orator had to prove that his examples and convictions were worth to be taken seriously, which would only be the case of they were situated within the limits of moral conventions. One of the best examples of this approach is certainly Marcus Aurelius' *Meditationes* (Hadot, 1997). What the author intends, is giving us the example of wise behavior, going completely along with the social and moral standards of his time. Fiction therefore is not an element that can easily enter in such an autobiography. This doesn't imply however that fiction is entirely excluded in these oldest autobiographies. Lives have to be reshaped in order to become instructive examples and from that moment on fiction enters into the story. Style, structure and forms prevail and do create a new reality, allowing a story to become history. A good example of such a plan may be the *Apologiae* and the *Dialogus cum Tryphone* of → Justin Martyr, which seemingly do contain some autobiographical elements, but which in fact are writings aimed at showing the high moral standards of Christians. Classical autobiography therefore is first of all an example of virtue and only in that sense it intends to speak about the author. Personal lifetimes are meant to point at this virtue and hence function as an exhortation, as we find it in the later autobiographies of → Ambrose of Milan (his funeral discourse at the death of his brother) and Augustine. They contain a strongly protreptic element (Kotzé, 2004).

Thus emerging from within the rhetoric, the first autobiographies are mainly occupied with giving a reliable and trustworthy image of the author, in order that it might serve as example. Therefore, they are not only exhortations, but tend also to be apologies of one's life. → Flavius Josephus might be an excellent example of this stance (Mader, 2000). His career, as a member of the Jewish nobility, led him to the rank of a general, who shifted nevertheless his allegiance. Emphasizing that he was a member of the highest nobility, he thus tries to insist on his "inborn" reliability. At the same time explaining and defending the choices he made, his *Vita* remains a mixture of virtue and self-justification.

To sum up, classical autobiography – though the word remains an anachronism – found its origin in rhetoric, had a strong moral character, and was intended not to explore the inner life of the author, but to give a trustworthy example of how life is to be lived. Implying at the same time that autobiography wasn't meant to represent a form of history. Not even in the case of Flavius Josephus. He aims at a trustful rendering of his own life and doesn't intend to write down the history of the Jewish insurrection. In that sense, there is already a sort of difference between the "objective" historiography of antiquity (*sine ira et studio* – "without anger and zealousness") and the personal "subjective" story that always was the autobiography. Yet, we have to keep in mind that there is not yet a reflection on what the subject of the author exactly is (Popkin, 2005).

2. The Arrival of Christianity

Though personal stories, these classical "autobiographies" do not appear as a clearly defined genre. They figure in different genres, like the *apologiae* (Plato, *Apologia*), the letters (Cicero, *Ad Atticum*), the funeral speeches and biographies (Ambrose of Milan, *De excessu fratris*; Plutarch, *Vitae*). The arrival of Christianity does not radically change this pattern and it would certainly be incorrect to suppose that the autobiography was born within this new religion: it was not. Not even the *Confessions*, so often considered as the first autobiography, was meant to be an autobiography in the modern sense (Nalbantian, 2001, 3; Brown, 2000, 160; Sturrock, 1993, 20; Lancel, 1999; Brachtendorf, 2005; O'Donnell, 2005). It starts with a prayer and ends with a prayer, and though the initial prayer might be considered a *captatio benevolentiae* (phrases meant to capture the benevolence of the audience), we have to take this religious element seriously. It was meant to be a prayer, though other motives are not to be excluded. Yet, we must realize that all that Augustine says about himself is not principally introspection, but first of all a comment on his life before God. He has "become a big

question to himself" (Aug. *Conf.* 4.4.10), but not to God. He does not know how to know himself: God does (Marion, 2005, 1–24; 2008). Therefore, it is God who traces the patterns of his life, and what seems to be an autobiography is in fact an acknowledgment of the fact that it is God who guides his life. It intended to praise God by showing how his life was guided by him. The rendering of his life in the *Confessions* is not an autobiography: it is a biography written by God. As he puts it in his *Revisions* (Aug. *Retract.* 2.6.1: *Confessionummearum libri tredecim, et de malis et de bonis meis Deum laudant iustum et bonum* – "the thirteen books of my *Confessions* praise the just and good God in my good and my bad things") Again, the classical pattern has not changed. Augustine presents his life in order to set an example. He wants to be a convincing author, one whose first aim is not to write an exciting tale about his own life, but to convert his readers to the God. The work can therefore be considered to be principally a protreptic book).

However, though the classical pattern was not broken by the arrival of Christianity, things nevertheless slightly changed. Christian times brought about at least another way of proving that an author is a convincing and trustworthy writer. Yet, it took a long time. Christian writers advanced their arguments in more or less the same way as their pagan contemporaries. We can find some fine examples of these Christian "autobiographies" in Christian funeral speeches. In this genre, the eulogy, the first elements of these changes can be detected. When the eulogy concerns one of the authors relatives, we also witness elements of the history of the authors family. We are confronted with sparkles of the author's life, at least when he is speaking, for example, about the deceased's parents as equally his own parents. So in these works, fragments can be found of autobiographical sketches. However, in most cases these elements still aim at showing how great an example the deceased relative was. Implying that the discourse only tries to be convincing as a eulogy, its purpose is to place the autobiographical elements in the bigger scheme of an oration that must be trustworthy. Once again, the protrepic motive. A specific sample of this kind of speech is Gregory of Nazianzus' discourse held at the occasion of the death of his sister Gorgonia, which is of course also a kind of autobiography, given the fact that he relates the life of his sister, a life closely interwoven with his own. His oration does not change the classical scheme of autobiography, but still intends to convince us of the perfect image of what might be Christian life. It focusses again on *virtus*. So when Gregory touches on the theme of his parents, he merely points out how pious they were and how they represent in a perfect way the virtuous life that classical times valued so much (Greg. Naz. *Or.* 8.5). Then, continuing about his sister, he explains that she excelled no less in virtue, prudence, modesty, humility, and spiritual beauty – of course, only because she is the daughter of such outstanding parents. Gorgonia, child of these admirable parents, is capable of combining the best of two worlds, the spiritual and the carnal one. She remains the classical ideal of *virtus*. Even her death was a moment of exceptional behavior. Being completely calm, the last words she spoke were a quotation of Ps 4:9, "I will lay me down in peace and take my rest" (*Or.* 22, trans. www.ccel.org). So this "autobiographical" eulogy does not show us any change compared with the classical autobiography. What matters is to be convincing, and thus Gregory wrote a classical work, as he also did when writing the eulogy for Basil, his dearest friend, and on Caesarius, his beloved brother. All these works were classical forms of the eulogy, and though they may contain autobiographical elements, their intention was to show us convincing and inspiring examples of holy and virtuous life (Brown, 1982) that we might want to imitate.

The same way of writing and thinking can be found in Ambrose when he speaks at the death of his beloved brother Satyrus in his *De excessu fratris*. What we observe is a man who has lost his brother Satyrus, a person who indeed was a great support to Ambrose, and the bishop of Milan is eager therefore to show his audience that this brother was a man who fully devoted himself to the case of the church. But there is more. In this speech, Ambrose transforms his brother's life into an argument in favor of his own position, as both of them have been devoted defenders of the church (McLynn, 1994). He clearly encourages people to help him in the same way his brother did. Hence, he doesn't go into the details of his personal life, nor that of his brother. In this respect, the *De excessu fratris* is still a classical monument (Biermann, 1995) of funeral discourse,

and it could have been written a century earlier without changing the modes and aims the author displays. However, if we compare it with the funeral discourse Gregory held, we encounter much more personal aspects. Especially the fact that Ambrose is confronting his readers with his own emotions. Which has to be considered to be something new, certainly compared to the funeral discourse Gregory held. Ambrose amply describes his grief, telling us about a life he entirely shared with his brother. Which was not untrue. Once Ambrose was ordinated → bishop, Satyrus, gave up his own profession (he was a lawyer), and helped Ambrose as much as he could, arranging Ambrose's affairs and being in fact the one who was responsible of their common fortune. But besides showing us his emotions, Ambrose points out that Satyrus is now living another life. It is this very belief in the → afterlife that allows Ambrose to turn his discourse into a sermon on the → resurrection, a theme he will speak on in the second part of this book. Showing thus that the convincing part of the autobiography had to concern this time the resurrection. Yet, following the classical examples, Ambrose also takes care to describe his brother as a real paragon of virtue, a moral example. Again, he remains the classical rhetorician, occupied in revealing a brilliant specimen of an extremely virtuous life. The life of his brother, but no less in fact his own life! That is where rhetoric serves a two folded goal. Hence we find in the discourse some old and new elements. We see a man sharing his inner feelings with us – things are changing indeed – but who at the same time introduces the theme of the resurrection in an autobiography, Despite these small changes, he keeps repeating the old lessons of a morally high-standing life. Implying that he indirectly is speaking about himself. However, though there may be more personal elements in this oration, it is still far from the modern autobiography, the autobiography that represents the journey to one's inner life and that tries to explore the different thoughts, moods, and times.

3. The Changes Christianity Brought About: Gregory of Nazianzus

Was it Augustine who invented modern autobiography? Definitely, we have to emphasize that the

Confessions are not to be considered a modern auto-biography. Yet, they represent a genre that appears to be a first step in the direction of the modern autobiography, though Augustine was perhaps not the first to set these steps. Our starting point was the observation of the difference between the classical autobiography, focusing on virtue and conviction, and the modern autobiography, mainly interested in the identity of the author and the development of this identity. What both types do have in common, is the wish to construct a narrative showing in some way or another the identity of the author, either in his moral outlook or in his inner developments (Eakin, 2008; Brockmeier & Carbaugh, 2001). Yet, it is not very likely to presume that it was only the genius of Augustine that created this genre; rather it was the genius of Christianity that paved the way to introspection and subjectivity. Christianity insisting on the importance of adopting a new personality. A striking example of this autobiography as the act of looking back on the "old man" (Rom 6:6) might be found, once again, in → Gregory of Nazianzus, a very talented poet who was forced to become bishop. He wrote an autobiography that is no less shocking in its modernity than the *Confessions* of Augustine, though less famous. His *De vita sua* (*peri ton eautou bion*) is a real autobiography in the modern sense in which he tries to be clear not only about his feelings but also about his the contradictions he sees in his own life. At the beginning, he explains his readers that his mother wanted so early to become pregnant that "she promised to give the gift she hoped to receive" (Greg. Naz. *Vita* 71–73; White, 2005). But he also speaks of his father. This time however, the tone of voice is strikingly different. He describes his father as a tyrant, someone who forced him to accept priesthood, though Gregory himself absolutely did not want it. In his own words,

> For although my father was well aware of my views, he forced me to accept a place, inferior only to the bishop's throne – I don't know why. Maybe he was motivated by fatherly love [for terrible is the love which is combined with power] and wished to bind me with the shackles of the spirit and honor me with the best of what he had. I suffered such pain as the result of this tyrannical behavior [for I cannot call it by any other name; may the Holy Spirit forgive

me for feeling thus]. (Greg. Naz. *Vita* 338–348; White, 2005)

Afterward he continues in the same way, stressing that he feared his father's love, "running back into the abyss" as he was afraid that this love might turn into a curse if he didn't obey. Later, his father conspired with Basil the Great (→ Basil of Caesarea) in order to have Gregory appointed as a bishop: "He and my father tricked me twice over" (*Vita* 425; White, 2005). These lines, well written in the delicate language of classical poetry, show us the inner life of a man who tries to understand why he did what he did and what were the origins and the consequences of what he did (McGuckin, 2001a; 2001b; Daley, 2006; Eftymiadis, 2006; Beeley, 2008).

This is what we might call the beginning of an autobiography in the modern sense. However, the same questions arise again as in the case of Augustine: was it the mere talent of Gregory that led to the invention of this genre? Probably not. What we are looking at, is an author who still wants to be trust-worthy. Therefore, the part of fiction is a limited one. In that sense, the modern autobiography is still not there. But it slowly comes nearer. We have in front of us a man who is already conscious of the fact that the subject he is writing on is a divided person. What he senses is that he "reveres the altar, but as one who stands at a distance" (*Vita* 330; White, 2005). So he believes and he rightly wants to uphold his faith. But at the same time, he is unable to identify himself with the altar. There is always someone else inside the person he is, and this second person will always accompany him. He is the man who frequently speaks about himself, but who always shows us he wants to be elsewhere. He is constantly is aware of the divided subject he is, but he is not yet able to see that the split in his personality will be visible in his autobiography and that rightly the autobiography will allow him to obtain some kind of unity. In that sense, the idea of imagination and fiction being part of autobiographies does not occur to him. Hence, it doesn't occur to him that an autobiography is always the portrait the author wants to depict of himself, creating in fact his own "reception." On the contrary, Gregory still wants to show how trustwor-thy he is and how his life is only an illustration of the point he is making: the fact that God leads our lives (*Vita* 103–106). In that sense, autobiography still remains within the borders of the traditional framework of an autobiography: virtue and piety are central elements. However, his desire to be elsewhere, implies a certain, though unconscious, role of fiction and imagination. This imagination is attributed to God, the one who chooses Gregory's destiny. For when Gregory wants to be elsewhere, he wants to be in God: "Not merely to seem to be training for the highest form of life, but to be, rather than seem, the friend of God" (*Vita* 322–323; White, 2005). What he wants is to be faithful to God, hence showing his readers that his self-portraiture is a reliable one. The fact however that even in rendering the truth as he sees it, he has to rely on imagination, on fiction, implies a change in the genre.

4. The Changes Christianity Brought About: Augustine of Hippo

The next step in this process of modifying the autobiography will be taken by → Augustine of Hippo, who wrote not only his famous *Confessions*, but also other quasi-autobiographical works, such as the *Soliloquia*. These *Soliloquia* are the rendering of an inner dialogue, in which Augustine speaks with himself. It is has been written as a discussion between Augustine's intellect (*ratio*) and the author himself. Considering these two writings as a form of an autobiography, is there a difference with the work of Gregory? In a certain way, there is. Augustine is firmly convinced of the fact that there is no self-portrait possible without mentioning the presence of God in human life. Put otherwise, he is only able to talk about himself by referring to God. The self-portraiture is at the same time the portrait of his God, and these two elements cannot be separated. There is no knowledge of oneself that can be realized without knowledge of God. Knowing yourself, is knowing how God made you live your life. In order to be trustworthy, you have to point to God. There is no self without God, and whatever we want to demonstrate, we cannot do it without showing that what we do is what God wants us to do. As he puts it: "Give what you command and command what you will" (Aug. *Conf.* 10.29.40: *da quod iubes et iube quod vis*). However, this approach also confronts us with certain boundaries. If we cannot give an image of ourselves without referring to God, wouldn't it be correct then to state we're also giving an image of God? Put in other words, should we not say that the image of God we are giving is the part of fiction introduced in the autobiography? This at least is what one might think of Augustine's approach, which in fact is a rhetorical subterfuge. Though the reader may be convinced to be confronted with the inner self of Augustine, Augustine knew that what he was writing was destined to be published. He made his choices, but we don't know what these choices were. Augustine thus consciously introduced – on account of his great belief – the element of fiction and imagination in the autobiography: faith, the image of God, as imagination. Autobiography now becomes a genre that also intends to create a certain image of the author, an image that to a certain extent is a constructed one, an image made up by fiction. Considered that way, the *Retractationes* are part of Augustine's desire to frame his own reception, to create his own image. He wanted only a certain image of himself to be handed down to the next generations and thus was strongly occupied in creating this reception.

What Augustine does therefore is widening the notion of the image and imagination. There is no real proof of it, but is it a mere coincidence that both Gregory and Augustine were the great theologians who reflected intensely on the → Trinity, the doctrine in which the notion of image is a central one? And not only the notion of image, but also the Neoplatonic notions of ἔξοδος and ἐπιστροφή, *aversio* and *conversio* (projection and return), implying that the triangle of author, character, and narrator are one and the same, but at the same time clearly distinguished. One might venture the thesis that it is this Trinitarian doctrine that has contributed to the existence of the modern autobiography. Rightly because, within the Trinity, truth and imagination, cannot be separated. As wrote Augustine in his *Soliloquia*, when an actor plays the role of Hector, he can only do so in a truly convincing manner being a false Hector. Truth in this sense can be shown by falsehood (Aug. *Solil.* 2.10.18). Given the development of the Trinitarian doctrine and the influence Neoplatonic thought had on it, we might suggest that the notion of the image that goes out from the godhead and turns back to him may have influenced the birth of modern autobiography in which truth and imagination are simply intertwined in such a way that they contribute to the identity of the writer (Reichel, 2005; Folkenflik, 1993; Schäfer, 2001). What happens in the autobiography is that the story becomes part of the identity. There is no truth without imagining it.

Historiography

Studies on ego-documents in late antiquity, have often focused on Augustine and his *Confessions* as the introduction of a new genre, namely the "autobiography" (Brown, 2000; Lancel, 1999; Brachtendorf, 2005; Schäfer, 2001; Frederiksen, 2012). More recently, autobiography in late antiquity is no longer considered to be the introduction of a new genre, but as one of the variants of narrative techniques, used for different aims, such as self-justification, political aims and spiritual exhortation (Maraso, 2011; Botha, 1997; Kotzé, 2004). Moreover, the study of autobiography, in particular the Augustinian approach, has very much been influenced by the debate on the narrative nature of historiography (Scordilis Brownlee, 1982; Spiegel, 2005; Popkin, 2005; Elbaz, 1987; Brockmeier & Carbaugh, 2001). The current debate on the very nature of autobiography as historiography is an ongoing one (Assmann, 2006; Rowlands, 2016).

Bibliography

Anderson, L., *Autobiography*, London, 2001.

Assmann, J., "Remembering in Order to Belong: Writing, Memory, and Identity," in: J. Assmann, *Religion and Cultural Memory*, Stanford, 2006, 81–100.

Beeley, C., *Gregory of Nazianzus on the Trinity and the Knowledge of God: In Your Light We Shall See Light*, Oxford, 2008.

Biermann, M., *Die Leichreden des Ambrosius van Mailand*, Stuttgart, 1995.

Botha, P., "History, Rhetoric and the Writings of Josephus," *Neotest.* 31, 1997, 1–20.

Brachtendorf, J., *Augustins "Confessiones"*, Darmstadt, 2005.

Brockmeier, J., & D. Carbaugh, *Narrative and Identity: Studies in Autobiography, Self and Culture*, Amsterdam, 2001.

Brown, P., *Society and the Holy in Late Antiquity*, London, 1982

Brown, P., *Augustine of Hippo: A Biography*, new ed., London, 2000, 152.

Daley, B.E., *Gregory of Nazianzus*, London, 2006.

Eakin, P.J., *Living Autobiographically: How We Can Create Identity In Narrative*, Ithaca, 2008.

Eftymiadis, S., "Two Gregories and Three Genres: Autobiography, Autohagiography and Hagiography," in: J. Børtnes & T. Hägg, *Gregory of Nazianzus: Images and Reflections*, Copenhagen, 2006, 239–256.

Elbaz, R., *The Changing Nature Of The Self: A Critical Study of the Autobiographic Discourse*, Iowa, 1987.

Folkenflik, R., ed., *The Culture of Autobiography: Constructions of Self-Representation*, Stanford, 1993.

Frederiksen, P., "The Confessions as Autobiography," in: M. Vessey, ed., *A Companion to Augustine*, Oxford, 2012, 87–98

Hadot, P., *Introduction aux "Pensées" de Marc Aurèle: La citadelle intérieure*, Paris, 1997.

Lancel, S., *Saint Augustin*, Paris, 1999.

Kotzé, A, *Augustine's Confessions: Communicative Purpose and Audience*, Leiden, 2004.

Lössl, J., "Augustine's Confessions as a Consolation of Philosophy," in: J.A. van den Berg et al., eds., *In Search of Truth: Augustine, Manichaeism and other Gnosticism: Studies for Johannes van Oort at Sixty*, Leiden, 2011, 47–73.

Lyons, G., *Pauline Autobiography: Toward a New Understanding*, Atlanta, 1995.

O'Donnel, J.J., *Augustine: A New Biography*, New York, 2005.

Pelling, C., "Was There an Ancient Genre of Autobiography? Or, Did Augustus Know What He Was Doing?" in: C. Smith & A. Powell, eds., *The Lost Memoirs of Augustus and the Development of Roman Autobiography*, Oxford, 2009, 41–64.

Popkin, J.J., *History, Historians and Autobiography*, Chicago, 2005.

Mader, G., *Josephus and the Politics of Historiography: Apologetic and Impression Management in the "Bellum Judaicum"*, Leiden, 2000.

Marasco, G., *Political Autobiographies and Memoirs in Antiquity*, Leiden, 2011.

Marion, J.-L., "Mihi magna quaestio factus sum: The Privilege of Unknowing," *JR* 85, 2005, 1–24.

Marion, J.-L., *Au lieu de soi: L'approche de Saint Augustin*, Paris, 2008.

Thompson, S., "The Confessions of Saint Augustine: Accessory to Grace," in: T. Mathien & D.G. Wright, eds., *Autobiography as Philosophy: The Philosophical Uses of Self-Presentation*, Oxon, 2006, 31–63.

McGuckin, J.A., *St. Gregory of Nazianzus: An Intellectual Biography*, New York, 2001a.

McGuckin, J.A., "Autobiography as Apologia in St. Gregory of Nazianzus," *StPatr* 37, 2001b, 160–177.

McLynn, N.B., *Ambrose of Milan: Church and Court in a Christian Capital*, Berkeley, 1994.

Nalbantian, S., *Aesthetic Autobiography: From Life to Art in Marcel Proust, James Joyce, Virginia Woolf and Anaïs Nin*, New York, 2001.

Popkin, J.D., "Narrative Theory, History and Autobiography," in: J.D. Popkin, *History, Historians & Autobiography*, Chicago, 2005, 33–56 (as well as the next chapter: *Historians as Autobiographers*, 57–91).

Reichel, M., ed., *Antike Autobiographien: Werke-Epochen-Gattungen*, Cologne, 2005.

Rowlands, M., "The Metaphysical and the Autobiographical Self," in: M. Rowlands, *Memory and the Self: Phenomenology, Science and Autobiography*, Oxford, 2016, 75–92.

Schäfer, C., "Aqua Haeret: A View on Augustine's Technique of Biographical Self-Observation in De Ordine," *Aug(L)* 51, 2001, 65–75.

Scordilis Brownlee, M., "Autobiography as Self-(Re)presentation: The Augustinian Paradigm and Juan Ruiz's Theory of Reading," in: J.D. Lyons & S.G Nichols Jr., *Mimesis: From Mirror to Method, Augustine To Descartes*, Hannover, 1982, 71–82.

Spiegel, G.M., ed., *Practising History: New Directions in Historical Writing After the Linguistic Turn*, New York, 2005.

Sturrock, J., *The Language of Autobiography: Studies in The First Person Singular*, Cambridge MA, 1993.

White, C., trans., *Gregory of Nazianzus: Autobiographical Poems*, Cambridge MA, 2005.

MATTHIAS SMALBRUGGE

Auxentius of Milan

Auxentius (320?–374 CE), bishop of Milan, should not be confused with Auxentius of Durostorum, who was another eastern cleric who supported Homoian theology and operated sometime after 384 CE in Milan. An early 5th-century CE Arian scholium, written in the margins of → Ambrose of Milan's *De fide* (Codex Parisinus ms. Lat. 8907), establishes their separate identities: "For although you remember both of the Auxentii, you do not indicate of which you speak, whether the one now alive, that is, of Durostorum, or of Milan." When Dionysius of Milan was deposed in 355 CE by a council held in that city, a Greek-speaking easterner named Auxentius was installed (Hil. Poit. *CAP* 1.9.3), likely because of his anti-Athanasian convictions. Since Dionysius died in exile, there was no later contestation for the Milanese episcopacy as there were in other sees (e.g. Rome).

Unfortunately, Auxentius seems to have left nothing in writing, and nearly all contemporary sources that provide information about him (i.e. Athanasius of Alexandria, Hilary of Poitiers) are hostile. Nonetheless, Auxentius made no secret about his ecclesiastical and theological allegiances. There is no doubt that Auxentius was a stalwart supporter of the Homoian formula ("Father is like the Son") as agreed upon by the Council of Ariminum (359 CE) and ratified in Constantinople a year later as the official position of orthodox Catholicism. This statement became infamous for having included a condemnation of any creedal language that used οὐσία (substance) such as the Nicene Creed (325 CE). Although the extant documentation from the Ariminum council reveals the majority of bishops affirmed that no other statement of faith than the Nicene should be received, imperial pressure to find unanimity compelled the majority eventually to embrace a Homoian creed on the ground that it was less controversial than → Nicaea and that its most vocal advocates, including Auxentius, assured everyone that it was not an Arian (→ Arianism) formula.

Ecclesiastical matters quickly changed with Emperor Constantius' death in 361 CE. A neo-Nicene movement began to sweep through the West, initiated by the return of western bishops who had been exiled to the East under Constantius. By 363 CE, hundreds of bishops had abjured their subscription to the Ariminum profession on the grounds that they had been deceived about its meaning. In northern Italy and Gaul, Eusebius of Vercelli and Hilary of Poitiers began consolidating a neo-Nicene platform to which most western bishops now turned. The Council of Paris (361 CE) represented the growing surge of the neo-Nicene campaigns. At this council, Auxentius of Milan was condemned in the strongest terms, along with several others, as "apostate priests" and for endorsing the exile of innocent bishops (like Dionysius). By the mid-360s CE, → Athanasius of Alexandria reported in his letter to the bishop of Corinth that synods in Gaul, Spain, and Italy had unanimously anathematized Auxentius and the heretical Illyrian bishops (Athan. *Ep.* . 1), though these condemnations had no noticeable impact on Auxentius' hold on the church in Milan.

The absence of imperial recognition of any one religious persuasion over all others effectively expropriated the power of several attempts to depose any proponents of Ariminum. Policies of religious non-involvement under Valentinian I (d. 375 CE) served as an effective cloak for preserving pro-Homoian bishops in their sees. It was nearly impossible to condemn a → bishop on doctrinal grounds only. But the political situation did not prevent several attempts to remove Auxentius. Of these, the best documented is the occasion when → Hilary of Poitiers came to Milan and asked for a formal hearing of Auxentius on the grounds of → heresy. Hilary says he appealed to the "king," Valentinian I, who was residing at the imperial residence in Milan from late October to early December 364 CE. In a method reminiscent of the proceedings at Ariminum under Constantius, Valentinian appointed two imperial officials to hear the case, while ten bishops acted as theological advisors. Some record of events was kept since Auxentius' oral testimony was used by Hilary to contradict Auxentius' later written statement of faith. In response, Auxentius sought to disqualify his accuser by questioning Hilary's authority as a bishop since he had once been condemned (at Béziers in 356 CE). Hilary (and → Eusebius of Vercelli) was then accused of trying to create a schism in Milanese church, which would have been perceived as inciting a riot. Hilary was compelled to leave Milan as a disturber of the peace. Soon after his departure, Hilary wrote an open letter, *Contra Auxentium*, to all fellow bishops in Gaul and Italy who had repudiated Homoian theology. In it, Hilary accuses Auxentius of duplicity in his teaching one true God as the Father, but not the Son.

There were other efforts to thwart Auxentius, none of which were successful. An otherwise unattested Italian synod, held in Rome around 368 CE, sent the results of its decisions to pro-Nicene bishops in Illyricum publicly condemning Auxentius and all supporters of Ariminum (Soz. *Hist. eccl.* 6.23.7–15; Thdt. *Hist. eccl.* 2.22). Around this same time, an itinerant apologist for the Nicene faith named Filastrius came to Milan, where he is said to have resisted the Arian Auxentius. According to his biographer Gaudentius, Filastrius made some kind of an attempt to organize dissident Catholics in Milan in order to rise up against their bishop. He too was driven out of the city. Yet another council held in Rome around 370/371 CE condemned Auxentius. This event seems to have been sparked by a Milanese deacon, Sabinus, who abandoned the church and the city because of his pro-Nicene sympathies. We cannot say exactly when this took place or whether it had any relation to Filastrius' campaign, but Sabinus was in attendance and presumably gave testimony concerning Auxentius' Arian theology.

It can be reasonably said that Auxentius was not an Arian in the sense that he did not subscribe to the theology of the historical Arius or Eusebius of Nicomedia. Auxentius himself declared that "I never knew Arius [...] nor acknowledged his teaching" (Hil. Poit. *Contra Aux.* 14), which is a surprising remark for one who (according to Hilary) once served as a presbyter (→ Priest/Presbyter) in Alexandria under George who replaced Athanasius in 357 CE. Even so, it was not uncommon for easterners to disavow any connection with Arius. As a bishop in the West, Auxentius claimed to believe in "one only true God the Father" and in Jesus Christ "true God the Son from true God the Father." The Son was indeed God, but "our Lord and God, the Savior," distinguished from the divinity of the Father. Auxentius also makes plain that he acknowledged the creed of Ariminum as the Catholic faith. Indeed, the Ariminum and Nicene Creeds (→ Creeds) competed for the West's allegiance well into the 5th century CE.

The degree of acceptance that Auxentius shared with his Milanese clergy and congregation is difficult to gauge. Sabinus notwithstanding, the bishop must have had sufficient support to account for the fact that at Auxentius' death the church was locked in near riotous conflict in 374 CE over the choice of a successor. That Auxentius was proscribed by a number of councils in Italy and Gaul insinuates that his influence on the region was not minimal. At one point in the *Contra Auxentium*, Hilary expressed apprehension that Auxentius was able to take retribution upon him even as far away as central Gaul. → Jerome's exaggerated statement, "After the long-awaited death of Auxentius of Milan, Ambrose was made bishop and he converted all of Italy to a sound faith" (Jer. *Chron.* 374) says as much about Auxentius as it does about Ambrose. There is no doubt that Auxentius was politically savvy and well connected enough to remain as bishop of the most powerful see in the West (next to Rome) for 19 years and the reigns of four emperors.

Bibliography

Brennecke, H.C., *Studien zur Geschichte der Homöer: Der Osten bis zum Ende der homöischen Reichskirche*, Tübingen, 1988.

Duval, Y.-M., "Vrais et faux problemes concernant le retour d'exil d'Hilaire de Poitiers et son action en Italie en 360–363," *Ath.* 48, 1970, 251–275.

Hanson, R.P.C., *The Search for the Christian Doctrine of God: The Arian Controversy 318–381*, Edinburgh, 1988.

Kaufman, P., "Diehard Homoians and the Election of Ambrose," *JECS* 5/3, 1997, 421–440.

Meslin, M., *Les Ariens d'occident 335–430*, Paris, 1967.

Williams, D.H., "The Anti-Arian Campaigns of Hilary of Poitiers and the 'Liber Contra Auxentium'," *ChH* 61, 1992, 7–22.

Williams, D.H., *Ambrose of Milan and the End of the Nicene-Arian Conflicts*, Oxford, 1995.

D.H. Williams

Axiopolis

Axiopolis was founded as a port by the Greeks of Tomis in the 4th century CE upon a hill along the left bank of the River Axius on the right shore of the Danube, almost at their meeting point, near the little isle of Hinog, about 50 km from Tomis. Previously it was called Heracleia. It was a port and a fortress, where one could station the fleet; in Roman times it was the seat of the *Collegium nautae universi Danubii*. It was there that the *Legio II Herculea* stationed itself, created around 285 CE. Today the ancient remains are less than 3 km to the south of the head of Cernavoda's railway bridge. It was located along the way between Sacidava (a village of Mîrleanu, about 25 km to the south, along the Danube) and Calidava (26 km to the north). The last fortification dates back to the time of → Justinian. In the 7th century CE it was captured by the Bulgarians, and it then became their religious capital in the 10th century CE, as the Christian patriarch's residence. The archaeological research brought to light the walls of three fortresses (one Hellenistic, one Roman, and one feudal), and some edifices, among which are the remains of two churches. In 1947 a Greek inscription was discovered, dating to the beginning of the 4th century CE, and dedicated to three Christian → martyrs: Cyrillus, Kyndeas (Chindeus), and Tasius (Dasius); their bodies were not found, yet they were perhaps located in the cemetery church where the inscription was found. The inscription is now located at the museum in Bucharest.

Another inscription recalled "Anthusa, the daughter of the great *comes* Gibastes." The ancient martyrologies (Syr. *Hieronymianum*, and Greek) relate the names of the martyrs of Axiopolis at the time of Diocletian. Cyril was greatly venerated; in the Syriac martyrology he was venerated alone on May 12 and together with Kyndeas on Mar 9; in the → *Martyrologium Hieronymianum* on Apr 26 (Codex Epatcensisis) and in a codex at Bern on May 9 together with Quindeas and Zenon; and on May 10, in the same codex, together with Quindeas (Kyndeas), Zenon, Dio(n) Acacius, and Crispus. Cyril may have died on Apr 26. The most well known and venerated of them was Cyril, who – according to Procopius – had honored Axiopolis (Pro. *De aedif.* 4.7). A manuscript of the *Martyrologium Hieronymianum* indicates that Cyril was a → bishop, but that does not seem likely. Kyndeas (Chindeus) is remembered on different days in the various martyrologies; the Syriac martyrology observes him alone on Jan 20. There is a special story regarding Dasius. The cited inscription places him at Axiopolis, perhaps because he was martyred there. According to the other martyrologies, however, he was killed at Durostorum. He was considered a native of Durostorum (Silistra, Bulgaria), which is located 60 km to the south, where the Legio XI Claudia was stationed. The martyrologies place him on different dates: on Nov 20; the *Hieronymianum* on Aug 5 (in Axiopoli Hirenei, Eraclii, Dasii). He was a Christian soldier, killed there, perhaps because he was in service at Axiopolis, during the festival of the Saturnalia. His body was carried to Durostorum. Or, he may have been killed at Durostorum and later the body was transferred to Axiopolis. Probably during the invasions of the Avars and the Slavs he would have been brought to Ancona (Italy). It is also possible that his body was taken to Ancona at the time of the Gothic (→ Goths) invasions. A Greek inscription on his sarcophagus reads, "the Holy martyr Dasius taken by Dorostolon." His Greek *passio* was posterior, because it contained some anachronisms; it may be based on a more ancient Latin text. The marble sarcophagus (→ Sarcophagi, Christian) is currently located in the diocesan Museum of Ancona, beside the Cathedral of Saint Cyriacus; the bones, on the other hand, are found underneath the main altar. Cumont thinks that the letters could not be dated before the 6th century CE.

Nearly in the center of the fortification of Axiopolis, from the excavations of 1899, there was a small building with a cruciform basin, believed to be a baptistery. Other objects, too (lanterns, amphoras, etc.) were marked with the sign of the cross. In recent years a tomb has been discovered that seems to have held the entire family, as two men, two women, and a child are buried therein. The tomb, which has diverse Christian signs (colored crosses, a golden cross, letters), dates back to the 5th/6th century CE.

Bibliography

Barnea, I., *Les monuments paléochrétiens de Roumanie*, Vatican City, 1977.

Barnea, I., *Christian art in Romania*, vol. I, Bucharest, 1979.

Barnea, I., "Inscripţia martirilor de la Axiopolis: Noi observaţii," *Pontica* 30, 1997, 199–203.

Chera, C., & V. Lungu, "Römische Wandmalereien in neugefundenen Gräbern aus den Nekropolen der Dobrogea," in: R. Pillinger, A. Pülz & H. Vetters, eds., *Die Schwarzmeerküste in der Spätantike und im frühes Mittelalter*, Vienna, 1992, 93–96.

Gabrielli, G.M., *I sarcofagi paleocristiani e altomedievali delle Marche*, Bologna, 1961.

*LThK*³, vol. III, 31.

Năsturel, P.Ş., "Un mot de plus sur l'inscription chrétienne de Axiopolis (IVe siècle)," in: V. Ciorbea, ed., *Dobrogea 1878–2008: Orizonturi deschise de mandatul european*, Constanţa, 2008, 104–108.

Netzhammer, R., *Die christlichen Altertümer der Dobrudscha*, Bucharest 1918.

Parvan, V., "Municipium Aurelium Durostorum," *RFIC* 2, 1924, 3–36.

Pillinger, R., ed. & trans., *Das Martyrium des Heiligen Dasius*, Vienna, 1988.

Poenaru Bordea, V., R. Ocheşeanu & E. Nicolae, "Axiopolis aux IIIe–VIIe siècles de notre ère à la lumière des découvertes monétaires," *SCN* 9, 1989, 53–73.

Popescu, E., *Inscriptiile grecesti si latine din secolele IV–XIII descoperite in România*, Bucharest, 1976.

Prescendi, F., "Le sacrifice humain: Une affaire des autres! A propos du martyre de saint Dasius," in: F. Prescendi & Y. Volokhine, eds., *Dans le laboratoire de l'historien des religions: Mélanges offerts à Philippe Borgeaud*; issue 24 of *Religions en perspective* 24, 2011, 345–357.

"Province Romane: Scythia Minor," in: *EAA*, 2nd suppl., Rome, 1994.

Rădulescu, A., & V. Lungu, "Le christianisme en Scythie Mineure à la lumière des dernières découvertes archéologiques," in: *Actes du XIe Congrès International d'Archéologie Chrétienne*, vol. III, Rome, 1989, 2561–2615.

Suceveanu, A., & I. Barnea, "Contributions à l'histoire des villes romaines de la Dobroudja," *Dacia* n.s. 37, 1993, 159–179.

Angelo Di Berardino

B

Baetica

Among the Hispanic provinces resulting from the various Roman administrative reforms, Baetica is certainly the wealthiest, not only in terms of historical and archaeological evidence, but also with regard to the early proofs of its Christianization. The abundance of natural resources, and a rich and diverse orography, with fertile plains, mountains, and several kilometers of coastline – which allowed the intensive exploitation of agriculture, livestock, and fisheries – along with the wealth of mineral resources explain the concentration of settlements and the interest of different passing civilizations in taking over such a fertile territory. Its main river, the Baetis (Guadalquivir) flowed through the territory from east to west and gave its name to the Roman province. Roughly speaking, ancient Baetica coincides with three-quarters of current Andalusia and a small part of Extremadura.

The Rock of Gibraltar, located in Baetican territory and known in ancient times as Mons Calpe, was considered by mythology to be one of the two Pillars of Hercules – the other was already located on African soil – marking the western boundary of the known world.

1. Romanization and Early Christianity

The Muslim conquest, which began when Berber troops crossed the Strait of Gibraltar in 711 CE, marks the end of the Christian hegemony in the region. It was not fully restored until the Christian conquest of Granada in 1492. Nevertheless, it is obvious that the late antique Christianity that had taken root in Baetica did not disappear overnight, surviving in several well-organized communities – called "Mozarabic" – with Eulogius and Alvaro of Cordoba (9th cent. CE) as prominent spiritual leaders.

The arrival of General Scipio in the northeast of the Iberian Peninsula in 218 BCE was intended to stop the actions of Hannibal and to deprive him of his reserves, both human and material, in the south of Iberia. The peninsular Roman conquests were then divided into Hispania Ulterior (southern half) and Hispania Citerior (northern half). By 13 BCE, the Roman administration split off a portion of the Ulterior, thereby creating Baetica, the boundaries of which were not affected by Diocletian's provincial reforms. From the very beginning, Baetican territory had permanent military contingents, whose soldiers eventually settled as agricultural settlers/colonizers once they had completed their military service, which would explain the early Romanization of the province in relation to other territories of Hispania. The oldest Roman colonies of the Iberian Peninsula are documented in the southern part of the peninsula: Corduba, established in 152 BCE, and Italica, birthplace of → Trajan and Hadrian, founded at the end of the Second Punic War. During the High Empire, Baetica's large concentration of towns in relation to the other western provinces was a factor in its success, as was its intense trade with Rome. All these factors, along with its close proximity to North Africa, influenced in a remarkable way the occurrence of an early and deep Christianity.

The legendary medieval stories recount the passage of James and Paul through Baetica, and the first evangelization of the territory by the so-called seven apostolic men. What is actually verified is that Jewish colonies proliferated, more than in any other Hispanic province, as a result of the Diaspora that followed on the Bar Kochba revolt of 135 CE – colonies that are well documented, especially from the 4th century CE, but that were already present in the previous centuries. Their existence would have eased the work of evangelization in coastal and trading towns in pre-Constantinian times, although the influences on the genesis of Baetican Christianity should be sought especially in the African, Italic, and Hellenic orbit. Despite the fact that no Baetican see is mentioned in the first historical Christian document concerning *Hispania* – Epistle 67 of → Cyprian of Carthage to the churches of Mérida and Astorga-Leon, 254/255 CE – the wording allows us to assume that the Baetican churches and Christian communities had a degree of organization similar to that of the churches mentioned in the letter. From the mid-3rd century CE, there was a significant presence of Christians in the area, favored by the "little Peace of the Church," which occurred between the general persecutions of Decius and those undertaken during the Tetrarchy – the martyrs of which were sung only a few generations later (404/405 CE) by Prudentius (*Peri.* 4.19–20): Acisclus, Zoilus, and "three more crowns" identified by other sources as Faustus, Januarius, and Martial, all of them from Corduba. The later *passiones*, which have an apologetic-legendary character, but are often based on earlier historical documents (*acta*), confirm the characters already known to Prudentius and complete the cast of early Baetican martyrs through the inclusion of Justa and Rufina, who reached the crown in the amphitheater of *Hispalis*, as well as of Servandus and Germanus, both martyred on a rural property in the *territorium* of Gades, and of someone called Victoria, who supposedly accompanied Acisclus in his Cordoban martyrdom, though this latter *passio*, written in the 10th century CE, is of very little historical credibility.

The first documented episcopal sees would be those appearing in the controversial proceedings of the Illiberris council, traditionally dated to 300/305 CE: Acci (Guadix), Corduba (Cordova), Epagra (Aguilar de la Frontera), Hispalis (Sevilla), Illiberris (Granada), Malaca (Málaga), Tucci (Martos), and Urci (Villaricos). Judging from the Baetican

provenances of some of the priests who undersigned these proceedings, the following may also have been episcopal sees: Acinipo (Ronda la Vieja), Aiune (Arjona?), Alauro (Alora), Astigi (Écija, certain see in 590 CE), Ategua (Espejo), Barbi (El Castillón) Carbula (Almodóvar del Río), Drona (Brona or Brana?), Egabrum (Cabra, certain see in 589 CE), Epora (Montoro), Iliturgi (Mengíbar), Ossigi (Mancha Real?), Segalbinia (Salobreña), Solia (Alcaracejos?), Ulia (Montemayor), and Urso (Osuna). Other sees documented in later times were Ilipla (Niebla, 589 CE), Italica (Santiponce, 589 CE), and Assidona (Medina Sidonia, 619 CE).

Though the metropolitan system was implemented in Baetica before the irruption of the barbarians in Hispania, the → metropolitan see was not permanently established in the provincial capital of Corduba, as was generally determined at the Council of → Nicaea, nor in Illiberris, headquarters of Ossius, who most likely exerted the provincial primacy in the early 4th century CE. The see was established in Hispalis, the imperial vicar's residence from the 4th century CE and a city that attained prominence during the 5th century CE, as the province was troubled by great political instability and barbarian migrations, which, for some scholars, would explain the difficult consolidation of a metropolitan who could exercise his authority throughout the territory (see Ubric, 2004, 117–121). The political events of the time also affected Hispalis and its bishop Sabinus, who, in 441 CE, was expelled from the city by the Suabians and reinstated by the Visigoths when they took control of the province some years later. His successor in the miter, Zeno, was appointed by Pope Simplicius to be apostolic vicar in Hispania between 468 and 483 CE. In spite all indications, however, the final confirmation of the metropolitan status of Hispalis did not come until the period of Visigothic rule.

The most prominent exponent of early Baetican Christianity is certainly Ossius (256–357 CE), bishop of his hometown (Corduba), counselor of Constantine I, litigator against → Donatism, opponent of Arius, president of the Council of Nicaea (325 CE), and drafter of the Nicene Creed (→ Nicaea) resulting from that council. He was also appointed by the imperial authorities to preside over the Council of Sardica (343 CE), in which the condemnation of → Arianism was reaffirmed. Unverified sources claim that he converted to this → heresy at the end of his long life. Indeed, the leading issues of the 4th century CE were the heterodoxies that occurred within Christianity itself, which were obviously connected with the political conflicts of the time and had deep socioeconomic causes. Particularly → Priscillianism and Arianism, but also Donatism and Luciferianism influenced the future of a Baetican Christianity which, according to the available documentation, mostly remained close to Catholic → orthodoxy. Compared to other western provinces, Priscillianism had a minor impact on Baetica. Yet, some of the main actors involved in the conflict were Baetican, as for instance Bishop Hyginus of Corduba, who initially denounced this heresy but eventually joined it, thus leading to his excommunication and exile. Gregory, ordained bishop of Illiberris (Granada) before 359 CE, was a prominent opponent of the Arian postulates. In the mid-4th century CE, the priest Vincent of Corduba aligned himself with Luciferianism and was denouced, along with his congregation, before the consular governor of Baetica. A reference to → Nestorianism, which barely impacted the Hispanic provinces, is documented in a letter that some alleged supporters of the doctrine – Vital and Constantius, possibly from Baetica or from the Levante – sent to Capreolus of Carthage in the third decade of the 5th century CE.

Together with the literary evidence, mostly related to urban life, and more specifically to the episcopates, archaeological studies spanning the last Roman centuries (4th–5th cents. CE) show how some of the old Baetican *villae* from the High Empire period survived into late antiquity, transformed into large economic and religious centers with oratories and basilicas that constituted the material reflection of the new Christian mentality of the landed aristocracy. It is on one of these estates that the Christian couple Lucino and Theodora may have lived, a late 4th-century CE couple that exchanged letters with → Jerome in order to perfect its ascetic life through the most common practices of the day: continence, fasting, and charity; thanks to these letters, we also have a record of the sending of vast riches from Baetica to distant churches such as Jerusalem and Alexandria. Other secular potentates of the province, such as the *uir clarissimus* Terentianus, travelled to Rome between 483 and 492 CE to meet the pope.

2. Visigothic Period

The Muslim conquest, which began when Berber troops crossed the Strait of Gibraltar in 711 CE, marks the end of the Christian hegemony in the region. It was not fully restored until the Christian conquest of Granada in 1492. Nevertheless, it is obvious that the late antique Christianity that had taken root in Baetica did not disappear overnight, surviving in several well-organized communities – called "Mozarabic" – with Eulogius and Alvaro of Cordoba (9th cent. CE) as prominent spiritual leaders.

As the first waves of barbarians reached Hispania during the 5th century CE, and in the context of the struggle for imperial power, pretenders to the throne and usurpers made a pact for the settlement of certain groups in some of the Iberian provinces in exchange for military aid. The Siling Vandals initially established themselves in Baetica (411/412 CE), but Honorius regained his Hispanic possessions soon afterward (416 CE) with the aid of the Visigoths of Valia. However, the → Vandals soon returned to Baetica, subsequently plundering and imposing their supremacy over several Hispanic provinces before moving on to North Africa in 429 CE. Following their departure, the Suabians imposed their authority on the provinces of Lusitania, Carthaginensis, and Baetica, and it was their Catholic king Rechiario (448–456 CE) who forged an alliance with the Visigoths by his marriage to a daughter of Theodoric I. The alliance was very short-lived, as Theodoric II faced and defeated Rechiario in 456 CE, seizing the Hispanic territories under Suabian control. These turbulent events were a reflection of a weak Roman power unable to maintain its hegemony, and it affected the expectations of the Romano-Hispanic aristocratic class, which developed various strategies to hold on to its supremacy, one of which was to join the church hierarchy. All off this – added to the fact that this aristocracy did not disappear with the fall of the empire, but rather retained its social and economic power until the Third Council of → Toledo (589 CE) replaced it with a Gothic aristocracy – explains the overall flourishing of the Hispanic Catholic Church and its Baetican sees during the Visigothic centuries. The leading ecclesiastical representatives of this period are the church fathers Isidore (by the quantity and influence of his writings, and through his political role in the creation of the Visigoth kingdom of Toledo), his brother Leander, and Bracarius, all of them metropolitans in Hispalis.

The confessional unification of Reccared proclaimed at the Third Council of → Toledo meant the definitive disappearance of the Arianism prevalent among the Visigoths, some of whose kings had attempted to establish a state hegemony under this creed. A few years earlier, Hermenegild, son of King Leovigild and brother of the future king Reccared, had been appointed governor of Baetica, where he converted to Catholicism, sparking an armed conflict (581–584 CE) that some modern historians regard as a simple rebellion of Hermenegild against his father, for which the religion would rather be the excuse and not the cause. In any case, and despite the failure and death of the rebel, Catholicism ended up prevailing a few years later, leading to Hermenegild's canonization by the Catholic Church in the 16th century. We do not know what impact the Byzantine occupation had on Baetican Christianity. Beginning in the mid-6th century CE, it was confined to the southern part of the Baetica and lasted for less than a century.

The Muslim conquest, which began when Berber troops crossed the Strait of Gibraltar in 711 CE, marks the end of the Christian hegemony in the region. It was not fully restored until the Christian conquest of Granada in 1492. Nevertheless, it is obvious that the late antique Christianity that had taken root in Baetica did not disappear overnight, surviving in several well-organized communities – called "Mozarabic" – with Eulogius and Alvaro of Cordoba (9th cent. CE) as prominent spiritual leaders.

3. Christian Archaeology and Topography

Archaeological remains from ancient Baetican Christianity are plentiful. For the 4th century CE, they basically consist of inscriptions and early Christian funerary artworks such as sarcophagi – notably that of Berja as well as the columned sarcophagus of Cordoba, with scenes from the Hebrew Bible and New Testament – mosaics, and objects of personal attire. They also include the sculpture of the good shepherd from the House of Pilate in Seville, most likely of Italic origin and one of the very few freestanding sculptures of early Christian times found in *Hispania*.

The late 4th century CE and the Visigothic era witnessed intensive building activity. Paradigmatic cases include the remains of the Cathedral of Saint Vincent, located under the Great Mosque of Cordoba, and the rural basilicas with baptistery and necropolis in San Pedro de Alcántara (La Vega del Mar, Málaga) and Gerena (Seville), among the oldest. The churches of El Germo (Espiel, Cordova), the one in Burguillos, and that of Morón de la Frontera (Seville) are from a later period.

Typical of Baetica are the so called in-mold decorated bricks that exhibit Christian iconography and inscriptions – often with personal names – and have been linked to the decoration of basilicas and tombs. The paradigm of movable Baetican sacred art is the Visigothic treasure of Torredonjimeno (Jaén), a set of gold and goldsmithed votive crosses and crowns offered to a church dedicated to the Saints Justa and Rufina – most likely the one attested in Hispalis. The treasure, found far from the place where it was originally displayed, was probably hidden due to the imminent arrival of the Muslims in 711 CE.

Among the novelties of recent years, it is worth mentioning the research conducted in the Alcázar of Seville, and above all the discovery and partial excavation of the Cordovan site of Cercadilla, an imposing palatial complex with Christian buildings that was constructed from late 3rd century CE onward and that has been identified, according to some proposals, as the Maximianus Herculean palace and even as Ossius' residence. Again in Cordoba, the Christianization of its amphitheater in the late 4th century CE has recently been proposed.

The constant references to other basilicas (the Holy Jerusalem and the one of Justa and Rufina in Seville or that of Felix in Cordova) and to monasteries (Fructuosus of Braga founded the monasteries of Nonus and Benedicta by the mid-7th cent. CE) in written sources, along with the epigraphic testimonies of buildings, consecrations, and restorations – including three basilicas dedicated by Pimenius, bishop of Assidona, in Vejer de la Miel, Alcalá de los Gazules, and Salpensa (see Vives, 1969; Salvador & Jesús, 2001) – round off a geographical and topographical landscape that was already deeply Christianized before the arrival of Muslims.

4. Councils

Today, it can no longer be stated that the oldest surviving proceedings of a council, which had for centuries been dated to the early 4th century CE, correspond to a council held in Baetica – specifically in Illiberris. Following the path opened by other authors such as M. Meigne, recent analytical studies have clearly shown that the canons attributed to a "Council of Illiberris" are, in fact, a series of canons composed of texts that have diverse backgrounds and chronologies, and, moreover, that they were amended on several occasions before they were included in Hispanic canonical collections in the second half of the 6th century CE. Furthermore, these pseudo-Iliberritan canons present discontinuities in relation to their preface in the *Hispanic Canonical Collection*, which contains a list of bishops and, in some manuscripts, also a series of priests who cannot be linked with such canons (see Vilella & Barreda, 2013). Invalidating the chronology and homogeneity of these canons is not a minor issue, because, until recent times, they were used as the quintessential source for the knowledge and study of Baetican Christianity immediately before the Constantinian era.

After the Council of Illiberris, further documented councils include the Council of Cordova, organized by Ossius in mid-4th century CE, the First Council of Seville (590 CE), and the Second Council of Seville (610 CE). The participation of Baetican bishops in the successive Councils of → Toledo was constant and plentiful; Isidore, for example, presided over and wrote the acts of the Fourth Council of Toledo (633 CE).

Historiography

There are numerous *cronicones* from the 16th and 17th centuries recounting the Christianization of *Baetica* in a fictitious and fantastical manner. A proper history of Christianity would have to wait until the 18th century, with Father Enrique Flórez's work concerning *Baetica* in his towering *España Sagrada*. Another source that greatly contributed to our understanding of Christianity in *Baetica* was the rise of specific studies, such as epigraphy, between the late 19th and the first half of the 20th centuries,

for example *Inscriptiones Hispaniae Cristianae* (Hübner, 1871) or *Inscripciones cristianas de la España romana y visigoda* (Vives, 1942).

In Spain, the work of the German Archaeological Institute (*Instituto Arqueológico Alemán*) pioneered a detailed and critical systematization of archaeological remains in the Iberian Peninsula in the monograph *Die Denkmaler der frühchristlichen und westgotischen Zeit* (1978), with a noteworthy chapter on the many scattered archaeological remains of *Baetica*. The recent and outstanding research undertaken by M. Sotomayor has dealt with all aspects of this Christian *provintia*, from a complete study of the Council of *Iliberris* (undoubtedly *the* main source of our understanding of primitive Christianity in Andalusia) to a keen interest in archaeological discoveries, as well as a veritable plethora of sources and Christian authors of the time.

Bibliography

Fernández Ubiña, J., "Aristocracia provincial y cristianismo en la Bética del siglo IV," in: C. González Román, ed., *La Bética en su problemática histórica*, Granada, 1991, 31–62.

García Moreno, J.L., "Transformaciones de la Bética durante la Tardoantigüedad," *Main.* 29, 2007, 433–471.

González, J., & P. Pavón, eds., *Andalucía romana y visigoda, ordenación y vertebración del territorio*, Rome, 2009.

Palol Salellas, P., *Arqueología cristiana de la España romana (siglos IV–VI)*, Madrid, 1967.

Perea Caveda, A., ed., *El tesoro visigodo de Torredonjimeno*, Madrid, 2009.

Salvador Ventura, F., *Prosopografía de Hispania meridional: III Antigüedad Tardía (300–711)*, Granada, 1998.

Salvador Ventura, F., & A. Jesús Cobo, "Propuesta de topografía monástica meridional en época hispano-visigoda," *Flor.* 12, 2001, 351–363.

Sánchez Velasco, J., "Christianization and Religious Violence in Baetica: Three Case-Studies of Destruction of Pagan and Mythological Sculpture Around the Theodosian Age," in: R. García-Gasco, S. González Sánchez & D. Hernández de la Fuente, eds., *The Theodosian Age (AD 379–455): Power, Place, Belief and Learning at the End of the Western Empire*, Oxford, 2013, 45–51.

Ubric Rabaneda, P., *La iglesia en la Hispania del siglo V*, Granada, 2004.

Vilella Masana, J., "Las iglesias y las cristiandades hispanas: Panorama prosopográfico," in: R. Teja Casuso, ed., *La Hispania del siglo IV: Administración, economía, sociedad, cristianización*, Bari, 2002, 117–159.

Vilella Masana, J., & P.E. Barreda Edo, "Un decenio de investigación en torno a los cánones pseudoiliberritanos: Nueva respuesta a la crítica unitaria," *RHE* 108/1, 2013, 300–336.

Vives Gatell, J., *Inscripciones cristianas de la España romana y visigoda*, Barcelona, 1969.

JORDINA SALES-CARBONELL

Balai

Balai (fl. early 5th cent. CE) was a Syriac poet and chorepiscopus in Roman Syria renowned to later generations for his compositions in five-syllable meter, of which he was (incorrectly) thought to be the originator. A large number of supplicatory hymns (*ba'awata*) as well as other works in this meter are attributed to Balai in the West Syrian tradition, though titling does not always distinguish between works authored by him and those simply in his characteristic meter (Zetterstéen, 1902, 4). Of undisputed authenticity is a hymn (*madrasha*) on the dedication of a church at Chalcis ad Belum (Syr. *Qenneshrin*) near Aleppo (*Hymn on the Dedication of the Church in Qenneshrin*) and five hymns on a recently deceased bishop of Aleppo, Acacius of Beroea (d. c. 433 CE; *Hymns on Acacius*). These hymns provide our limited data about Balai; the meager biography found in later chroniclers cannot be relied upon.

The *Hymn on the Dedication of the Church in Qenneshrin* is the earliest extant hymn composed for the dedication of a church. Balai teaches, a novelty for the time, that on earth God inhabits not only the human mind and heart, but also his sacred earthly precinct, and there elevates humankind to the heavenly dwelling it mirrors through his eucharistic and incarnational presence. In its anagogical reasoning, the *Hymn on the Dedication of the Church in Qenneshrin* represents an important precursor to mystical commentary on church architecture ("architectural *theoria*") found in later dedicatory hymns (McVey, 1993). The *Hymns on Acacius* is a serialized eulogy for Acacius that celebrates him as a model of piety and athlete of the monastic virtues, while ignoring his fame as an ecclesiastical controversialist. The final hymn, strikingly lyric, is cast in the voice of Acacius himself, in which he celebrates at the moment of

→ death that he has stayed the course and that the grave now seals up his righteous deeds as an earnest of heavenly glory.

Almost all other works attributed to Balai are found only in later manuscripts (post-9th cent. CE) and await critical examination of authorship. Exceptional is an early cycle of 12 metrical homilies (*memre*) on the patriarch Joseph. Though not composed in Balai's signature meter, he is named as the author in the earliest manuscript to contain any part of the cycle (BL Add. 12,166; 6th cent. CE); later tradition uniformly, but dubiously, assigns them to → Ephrem the Syrian. R.R. Phenix has argued for Balai as author, but more prevalent is the view that they must be regarded as anonymous.

Historiography

The primary focus of scholarship to date has been on editing, translating, and establishing the authenticity of works attributed to Balai, with particular scrutiny of the disputed Joseph cycle (Näf, 1923; Heal, 2008; Phenix, 2008). Of Balai's undisputed works, only the *Hymn on the Dedication of the Church in Qenneshrin* has received any notable attention from scholars (Graffin, 1981–1982; McVey, 1983; 1993; 2010; Vergani, 2002).

Bibliography

Graffin, F., "Poème de Mar Balaï pour la dédicace de l'église de Qennešrin," *ParOr* 10, 1981–1982, 103–121; Fr. trans. of *Hymn on the Dedication of the Church in Qenneshrin*.

Heal, K.S., "Tradition and Transformation: Genesis 37 and 39 in Early Syriac Sources," diss., University of Birmingham, 2008.

Landersdorfer, S., *Ausgewählte Schriften der syrischen Dichter: Cyrillonas, Baläus, Isaak von Antiochien und Jakob von Sarug*, BKV 6, Kempten, 1913; Ger. trans. of *Hymn on the Dedication of the Church in Qenneshrin* and *Hymns on Acacius*.

McVey, K.E., "The Domed Church as Microcosm: Literary Roots of an Architectural Symbol," *DOP* 37, 1983, 91–121.

McVey, K.E., "The Sogitha on the Church of Edessa in the Context of Other Early Greek and Syriac Hymns for the Consecration of Church Buildings," *ARAM* 5, 1993, 329–370; ET of *Hymn on the Dedication of the Church in Qenneshrin*.

McVey, K.E., "Spirit Embodied: The Emergence of Symbolic Interpretations of Early Christian and Byzantine

Architecture," in: S. Ćurčić & E. Hadjitryphonos, eds., *Architecture as Icon: Perception and Representation of Architecture in Byzantine Art*, Princeton, 2010, 38–71.

Näf, H., *Syrische Josef-Gedichte, mit Übersetzung des Gedichts von Narsai und Proben aus Balai und Jaqob von Sarug*, Zürich, 1923.

Phenix, R.R., *The Sermons on Joseph of Balai of Qenneshrin: Rhetoric and Interpretation in Fifth–Century Syriac Literature*, STAC 50, Tübingen, 2008.

Vergani, E., "*Isaia 6* nella letteratura siriaca: Due autori del V secolo: Balai e Giovanni il Solitario," *ASR* 7, 2002, 169–192.

Zetterstéen, K.V., *Beiträge zur Kenntnis der religiösen Dichtung Balai's nach den syrischen Handschriften des Britischen Museums, der Bibliothèque Nationale zu Paris und der Königlichen Bibliothek zu Berlin*, Leipzig, 1902.

CARL GRIFFIN

Baleares

Before falling under Roman control, the Balearic archipelago was divided into two parts: on the one hand the Pytiussae (Ibiza and Formentera), which belonged to the Phoenician-Punic κοινή, and on the other the Baliares (Majorca, Minorca, and the tiny Cabrera). The so-called Talayotic culture flourished on the latter during the prehistoric period. Located halfway between the Iberian Peninsula, North Africa, and the islands of Corsica and Sardinia, the Balearic Islands occupied a strategic position on the Mediterranean shipping routes, something that did not go unnoticed by the Romans and explains its commercial vitality during the centuries in which early Christianity developed.

1. Roman Administration and Early Christianity

On the pretext of ridding them of pirates and by order of the Senate of Rome, the consul Quintus Caecilius Metellus conquered the Balearic Islands, which thus joined the Roman orbit in 123 BCE, being attached to the Hispania Citerior province. As a result of the reorganization of Augustus, they became part of the provincia Tarraconensis, but were joined to the Carthaginensis in the wake of Diocletian's rearrangement of the provinces, until Theodosius finally created a new district in the late 4th century (c. 385 CE): the provincia Insulae

Balearis (Pol. Silv. *Chron.* 4.7). The islands were home to an important industry for the extraction of murex tincture, used for the production of purple, and this led to the installation of the headquarters of one of the nine *procuratores bafii* of the Western Roman Empire on the Balearic Islands (*Not. Dign.* 11.71). In the early days of Balearic Christianity, Paul (→ Paul the Apostle) may have landed on the islands during his promised, though still unconfirmed journey to Hispania. What did play a decisive role in the introduction of Christianity was the commercial nature of the islands, with frequent arrivals of traders and slaves and regular contacts with North Africa. However, the first certain evidence of Christians' presence is post-Constantinian, consisting of funerary inscriptions from the mid- to late 4th century CE (see Gómez Pallarés, 2002, 62).

The Jewish element of the Balearics, documented prior to the Christian one, not only has a late appearance in the form of a generic class of merchants and traders – as in other territories of the Roman Empire – but is also represented by landowners and slaveholders: Theodore, the head of the synagogue, also presided over the curia of Magona in the early 5th century CE, having gone through all municipal posts, while Caecilianus, also a Jew, was elected *defensor civitatis* of this same locality in 418 CE, and Litorius, another powerful Jew, held the position of *praeses insularum Balearum*. It is well known that legislative pressure tended to forbid Jews from holding public office, especially after → Theodosius I had issued laws in favor of the exclusivity of Christian orthodoxy, so that it cannot be excluded that the islands' Phoenician-Punic background had encouraged the early settlement of numerous Jews, which would have led to the formation of oligarchies in certain localities. In fact, the coexistence of Jews and Christians on the islands appears to have been friendly until the early 5th century CE, when tensions are documented for the first time: Paulus Orosius (c. 383–c. 420 CE), a priest native to Gallaecia, was returning from a trip to Palestine, where he had "found" and brought the relics of the first martyr Stephen, when his ship laid over in Magona (Maó, Minorca) in the autumn of 417 CE. A few months later, having enlisted the help of Severus, the island's newly appointed → bishop, and of a Christian layman named Consentius, he undertook a vigorous campaign to convert the Jews to the only religion permitted and imposed by Theodosius only a few years before. Severus of Minorca is also the author of the *Epistula de conuersione Iudaeorum apud Minorcam insulam meritis sancti Stephani facta*, a text commonly known as the *Circular letter of Severus*, which is the most important document of early Balearic Christianity and constitutes the primary source of information for the forced conversion that took place in Minorca early February 418 CE – a conversion attributed by the bishop to the miraculous action of → Stephen the Martyr's relics, which, according to the text, were placed in a basilica outside the walls of Magona. The letter is rich in characters, geographies, colorful details, and events of all kinds. Jewish matrons are described as the most reluctant during the inexorable conversion of the Balearic Jewish aristocracy, while the text also notes the presence of an enigmatic group of monks, probably local, who sang Psalms in the culminating moments and served as the primary agents of the plan to convert the Jews. The letter may also have been coauthored by the aforementioned Consentius, a wealthy layman native to the Tarraconensis who had moved to Minorca, perhaps fleeing from the barbarians, and who had become a correspondent of → Augustine of Hippo. Consentius sent him a series of letters containing information about Balearic Christianity. In fact, the African even dedicated his book *Contra mendacium* to Consentius in response to one of his letters. Thus, the letter 12* furnished additional details of the events described in the circular of Severus, and letter 11* records that between the years 418 CE and 419 CE, a monk named Fronton had come to the islands from Arles with reports of an anti-Priscillianist campaign that was taking place in Hispania and Gallia, a fight which Consentius himself had led from his Balearic residence. Another bishop named Agapius – from Tarraconensis(?) – also visited Consentius at this time, having been tasked with delivering some correspondence to Fronton.

The documented Balearic episcopal sees are not known by the name of a city, but by the name of the respective island, which has been interpreted as a sign that no insular → metropolitan see had become firmly established, and that episcopal cities were not very large (see Amengual, 1991–1992, 413–438). These venues are Minorica (Minorca, 418 CE), Maiorica (Majorca, 483 CE), and Ebusus (Ibiza, 483 CE), and they correspond to the three largest islands.

Literature and hagiographic traditions have not reported any Balearic martyr, so it is considered likely that the persecutions had little or no impact on the archipelago.

2. Vandal Domination and Byzantine "Reconquest"

In 455 CE, the political power in the islands passed to the Vandal kingdom of Carthage under the rule of King Genseric, who gained control with a limited military contingent. For the majority of the population, the conquest brought little change to their way of life compared to the Roman period. In many ways, the Balearic Islands did play more than a peripheral role in the Vandal conquests. The → Vandals followed the Arian creed (→ Arianism), so that King Hunneric's persecution against Catholics, undertaken in 484 CE from North Africa, reached the three Balearic episcopates appearing in the list of those attending the Conference of Carthage (see below). The king had ordered the general confiscation of the *homousiani* – Catholic – churches, which were subjected to the same legislation that the Roman emperors had decreed against heretics (Vic. Vit. *Hist.* 3.2), forbidding the Catholic clergy to celebrate liturgical acts or ordinations and ordering their expulsion from their villages, the burning of their books, and their condemnation to hard labor. However, the consequences and the exact scope of these provisions for Balearic Christianity remain unknown. Apart from these specific political events, it becomes clear, at least for the 79 years of Vandal domination over the Balearic territory, that the catastrophes traditionally ascribed to the Vandal invasion are a modern historiographical invention and have no archaeological or literary basis. Good evidence in support of this are the numerous basilicas built during this period.

Justinian's campaigns for the sake of the "restoration" of the empire included the conquest of the Balearic Islands by Apollinarius in 534 CE and, most likely, the allocation of the islands to the province of Mauritania II, whose capital was Septem (Ceuta; → Justinian). At the ecclesiastical level, the Balearics strengthened their links to the churches of southern and western Hispania, territories that had also been occupied by the Byzantines. A sample of these closer ties between churches was the resolution, around the year 595 CE, of a theological conflict caused by Vincentius, a naive bishop of Ibiza who was convinced that he had received a letter from heaven signed by Jesus himself, in which the latter ordered → Sunday rest – in reality a ploy by certain Judaizing circles wishing to mimic the Jewish → Sabbath. It was Licinianus, the bishop of Cartago Spartaria, who eventually exposed the fraud on the basis of theological and literary arguments (Lic. Car. *Ep.* 3). Stronger links were also established with Rome, and it was probably the papacy that exercised ecclesiastical authority over the Balearic venues at that time, as evidenced by some letters of Pope Gregory I (→ Gregory the Great), and also as suggested by the fact that a man named Bassus, who died and was buried in Majorca, turns out to have been a priest of the Church of Rome, as specified by his tombstone found in the Basilica of Son Peretó (Manacor). During the Byzantine occupation, the imperial authorities increasingly used the Balearic Islands as a place of exile, to which such illustrious dissenters as the chronicler and African bishop Victor of Tunna were banished, the latter in 555 CE (Victor Tonnensis, *Chronica*, year 555.2).

In the late 8th century CE, Muslims who had settled in Tortosa carried out violent raids against the islands, forcing Balearic Christians – referred to by Arab sources as *rum* – to ask Charlemagne for help. From 848 CE, the islands began feeling the pressure of the Caliphate of Córdoba; in early 10th century CE, the Islamic conquest was already a fact. After a dark period, which included plundering by the Normans, the Balearics did not recover their Christian hegemony until the conquest undertaken by the kingdom of Aragon in the 13th century.

3. Christian Archaeology and Topography

The presence of a significant Jewish population led to the construction of synagogues, some of which were converted into Christian basilicas: the above-mentioned circular of Severus speaks of the new basilica that supplanted Magona's synagogue within the walls, which implies that a number of other Balearic basilicas from the early 5th century CE may have similar substrates. Likewise, Severus'

circular indicates that Magona's primitive basilica was located outside the city walls, while the conversion of the synagogue, located within the walls, involved the construction of the second basilica. To the present day, however, there is no archaeological confirmation of this literary information. Similarly, there is no direct archaeological data on the buildings belonging to the episcopates: as regards Minorica, the circular specifies that its bishop Severus resided in Iamona (Ciutadella), where the episcopal complex should be located, at least early 5th century CE. For Maiorica, the physical location of the bishop was in Palma (Palma), a Roman *colonia* and the leading city of the island. As for Ebusus, two areas of a late antique necropolis that yielded lamps and pottery decorated with Christian iconography are documented in the city of the same name, where the island's new cathedral was also built over the earlier main mosque in the Middle Ages, a significant phenomenon of religious continuity that also occurred in Iamona and in Palma – where the major mosques of the respective islands were located – and that can be traced to a religious leadership that sought its roots in late antiquity. Other Roman nuclei of Christianization were Pollentia (Alcúdia, Majorca), where the presence of late antique tombs is attested in the area of the forum and in the theater, and Sanisera (Sanitja, Minorca), where a late antique necropolis has also been found, with liturgical furniture and architectural elements that are most likely related to a basilica.

The most prominent feature in Balearic Christian archaeology is the presence of numerous rural basilicas, many of them with baptistery, dating from the mid-5th century CE and whose precise dating is still being discussed: in Majorca, those of Son Peretó and Sa Carrotja (Manacor), that of Son Fadrinet (Campos), and that of Cas Frares (Santa Maria del Camí); in Minorca, Fornàs de Torelló (Maó), Son Bou (Alaior), and Cap des Port (Fornells); and probably those of S'Almudaina (Alaior), Ses Canèssies (Binipati), and Es Trabucs (Ciutadella). Mention should also be made of those on Illa del Rei and Illa d'en Colom, two islets very close to Minorca whose geographical isolation, along with the presence of built-up areas surrounding the first construction of the basilicas, could indicate their eremitical-monastic usage. In Ibiza, the identification of the potential basilicas of Ses Figueretes and S'Hort des Palmer awaits archaeological confirmation. The rich floor mosaics associated with this Christian architecture, with biblical themes, eucharistic readings, eschatological allusions, and Jewish cultural references, represent later additions from Byzantine times and were executed by African artisans, notably those of Fornàs de Torelló, Illa del Rei, Son Fadrinet, Cas Frares – now disappeared – and Son Peretó. The latter site has also the sepulchral mosaic of Baleria, dated to the second half of the 6th century CE. Another noteworthy sepulchral mosaic is that found in Sa Carrotja.

The wild and barren island of Cabrera was first occupied by a Christian monastery located in Clot des Guix, where a number of structures delimit a large enclosure around a basilica. Unlike the hypothetical cases of Illa del Rei and Illa d'en Colom, the monastic nature of this island is known because of a reference from the Byzantine period, being mentioned in an epistle of Pope Gregory I – written in August 603 CE (*Registrum* book 13 *ep.* 48) – as the place where a monastic community suffered some discipline problems, whose resolution the *pontifex* entrusted to *defensor* Johannes. The *defensor* eventually went to the island to investigate the monks' way of life and to rebuke and correct their attitude. The Balearic Capraria should not be confused with the island of the same name in the Adriatic Sea, mentioned in letter 48 of Augustine addressed to abbot Eudoxius. The rural Basilica of Torelló d'Es Fornás (Maó), built according to a design of probably eastern origin, may also belong to a monastic establishment (see Gurt & Buxeda, 1996, 155).

Among the movable objects of Balearic Christian art, particular mention should be made of the bronze censer of Aubenya (Majorca, 6th cent. CE), of the cross and the gem with the Agnus Dei representation from Cap des Port, and of the liturgical jar of Coptic origin from Son Peretó, dated to the second half of the 7th century CE.

4. Councils

There are no documents regarding the convening of any ecclesiastical council in the Balearics. Nor is there evidence of the presence of its bishops at the peninsular councils, a fact that has been attributed to the Vandal occupation, which would have led to the organizational and material separation of Balearic Christianity from the Hispanics. Balearic bishops may nevertheless have attended African councils, considering the ties of cultural and commercial nature that may have been the cause of the earliest Christian presence on the islands. In any case, a single notice can be inferred on this issue in the preserved documentation: the almost certainly Balearic bishops Helias of Maiorica, Macarius of Minorica, and Opilio of Ebuso participated in the conference of Carthage in 484 CE, since they appear in the list of Catholic bishops who were summoned by the Vandal king Huneric to attend the meeting in the African capital. This list was drawn up a year before the conference convened (see Vilella, 2002, 460–467) and was included in the *Notitia prouinciarum et ciuitatum Africae*. The three bishops are included among the eight bishops of the island of Sardinia – *nomina episcoporum insulae Sardiniae* – from which we may infer that the Balearic Islands formed part of the ecclesiastical province of Sardinia at this time.

Historiography

A considerable wake-up call for the study of primitive Christianity in the Balearic Islands was the discovery and subsequent publication by J. Divjak (1970–1980) of a series of letters sent by a certain Consentius to Augustine of Hippo, which are thematically and chronologically related to Severus of Minorca's circular letter, our main historical source which also bears Consentius' authorship.

A string of interventions in various late antiquity necropolis, which were sponsored by local scientific societies in the late 19th and early 20th centuries, as well as one-off excavations undertaken in the mid-20th century in the basilica of Son Bou (Mallorca) by the bishopric and the systematic investigations of paleochristian basilicas in Mallorca and Minorca by Pere de Palol between the 1950s and 1980s (some of which had been unearthed as recently as the 19th century), contributed to the rise of scientific Christian archaeology in the Balearic Islands. Corresponding findings have been duly published in the Reuniones de Arqueología Cristiana Hispánica and a range of international gatherings.

Bibliography

Amengual Batlle, J., *Orígens del cristianisme a les Balears i el seu desenvolupament fins a l'època musulmana*, 2 vols., Palma de Majorca, 1991–1992.

Amengual Batlle, J., "Les seus episcopals de les Illes Balears: La manca de correspondència entre els testimonis literaris i els arqueològics," in: *VI Reunió d'arqueologia cristiana hispana: Les ciutats tardoantigues d'Hispania: Cristianització i topografia*, Barcelona, 2005, 189–194.

Amengual Batlle, J., & M.A. Cau Ontiveros, "Antigüedad Tardía en las Illes Balears," in: F. Tugores Trunyol, ed., *El mundo romano en las Illes Balears*, Barcelona, 2005, 130–138.

Buenacasa Perez, C., & J. Sales Carbonell, "Baleari," in: A. Di Berardino, ed., *NDPAC*, vol. I: *A–E*, 2006, Genova, cols. 689–692.

Duval, N., "La place des églises des Baléares dans l'archéologie chrétienne de la méditerranée occidentale," in: *III Reunió d'arqueologia cristiana hispana*, Barcelona, 1994, 203–211.

Gómez Pallarés, J., *Epigrafía cristiana sobre mosaico de Hispania*, OPEP 9, Rome, 2002.

Gurt Esparreguera, J.M., & J. Buxeda Garrigós, "Metrologia, composició modular i proporcions de les basíliques cristianes," in: *Spania: Estudis de l'antiguitat Tardana oferts en homenatge al professor Pere de Palol i Salellas*, Barcelona, 1996, 137–155.

Palol Salellas, P., *Arqueología cristiana de la España romana (siglos IV–VI)*, Madrid, 1967.

Palol Salellas, P., "Història i arqueologia cristiana a les Balears," in: *Les Illes Balears en temps cristians fins als àrabs*, Maó, 1988, 9–14.

Riera Rullan, M., ed. *Investigaciones arqueológicas sobre el monasterio de época bizantina del archipiélago de Cabrera (siglos V al VII d.C.)*, Madrid, 2009.

Sánchez León, M.L., ed. *Les Balears romanes: Nous estudis*, Palma, 2012.

Vilella Masana, J., "Relacions comercials de les Balears des de Baix Imperi fins als àrabs," in: *Les Illes Balears en temps cristians fins als àrabs*, Maó, 1988, 51–58.

Vilella Masana, J., "Las relaciones eclesiásticas de Hispania con África en época vándala," *Aug.* 42/2, 2002, 445–468.

Zucca, R., "Il Cristianesimo primitivo nelle *Insulae Baliares*," in: P.G. Spanu, ed., *Insulae Christi: Il cristianesimo primitivo in Sardegna, Corsica e Baleari*, Oristano, 2002, 539–552.

Jordina Sales-Carbonell

Baptism

Baptism is a central rite of entrance into the Christian church, normally in the early centuries CE observed as an immersion in water accompanied by a confession of faith in Christ.

The application of water (by sprinkling, pouring, or dipping) for the purpose of ceremonial purity was common in ancient Mediterranean religions. Jewish practice according to rabbinic literature was a full bath, self-administered and frequently performed. Archaeological discoveries of *mikvaoth* (immersion pools) confirm the practice by law-observant Jews, including the Qumran community, in the period before the destruction of the Jerusalem temple in 70 CE. Sometime soon after 70 CE, a self-immersion was formalized as part of the conversion process of Gentiles (proselyte baptism) to Judaism.

John the Baptist (Mark 1:4–5; Matt 3:1–6; Luke 3:1–9; → John the Baptist) came as an innovator, performing a one-time administered immersion, not just for outward purity but for → forgiveness of sins, and calling on Jews to repent in preparation for the coming → kingdom of God. Jesus was among those who came to John for baptism, but his baptism had the unique aspect of inaugurating his ministry as the Messiah. Nevertheless, it had features with a formal similarity to later Christian baptism: an association with forgiveness of sins (implicit in John's reluctance to baptize him – Matt 3:13–15), the coming of the → Holy Spirit, and acknowledgement as Son of God (Matt 3:16–17; Mark 1:10–11; Luke 3:21–22).

Christians saw their baptism as based on the command of the resurrected Jesus for his followers to make disciples of all the nations; to baptize them in the name of Father, Son, and Holy Spirit; and to teach obedience to all Jesus commanded (Matt 28:18–20). If the background of the phrase "in" or "into the name" is Hebrew, the idea was "with reference to" or even "in worship of"; if Greek, the idea was "into possession of."

1. Development of the Practice

According to the Acts of the Apostles, baptism was administered from the beginning of the church (Acts 2), and such would be consistent with John's report of a baptizing ministry by Jesus and his disciples in continuity with the practice of John the Baptist (John 3:22, 26; 4:1–2).

The writings of the New Testament indicate that the practice was immersion.

1. Such is the meaning of βαπτίζω (baptize). Its two most frequent uses in classical literature are for the sinking of ships and the drowning of persons, both rather thorough submersions, and these usages continued in the Jewish author Flavius Josephus (*Bell.* 3.423; *Ant.* 15.55).
2. Jewish ritual washings for purification were a complete submersion of the body in water.
3. Only one action makes sense of the circumstantial accounts of baptism: John baptized in the Jordan River and at Aenon because "water was abundant there" (John 3:23), Jesus after his baptism "came up from the water" (Matt 3:16), and Philip and the Ethiopian treasurer "went down into the water" and "came up out of the water" (Acts 8:38–39).
4. The symbolism of baptism as death and resurrection is suggested by the burial in water (Rom 6:3–4; Col 2:12).
5. The evidence from early church history indicates that the normal action was immersion.

Although the most common usage of βαπτίζω was for dipping in water, water does not inhere in the word. Christian baptism was water baptism, as in the above accounts and in other references (Acts 10:47, in distinction from the preceding baptism in the Holy Spirit – see 11:15 in reference to 2:2; Eph 5:26, explaining the "one baptism" of 4:4; and 1 Pet 3:20–21). Baptism in the Holy Spirit, as in the Acts passages, was given to a few persons in special circumstances, was not commanded, and was not the baptism for all nations. Nor was baptism "into Christ Jesus" (Rom 6:3; Gal 3:27) a baptism into his personality as if he were the element, but water baptism was the means of baptism into him.

The recipients of baptism were those who were taught (Acts 8:35; 16:32), who believed and confessed their faith (Acts 18:8; 22:16, "calling on his name"), and who repented of their sins (Acts 2:38). The distinguishing mark of Christian baptism was its relation to Jesus Christ (Acts 2:38; 19:5). The phrase "name of Christ" may refer to calling on him in confession or pronouncing his name by the administrator. The household baptisms in the New Testament are often cited as supporting infant baptism, but in nearly all cases, something is said about the households that

is not applicable to children (Acts 11:14, a message by which the household is saved; 16:15–16, listening eagerly; 16:31–34, believing and rejoicing; 18:8, believing; 1 Cor 1:16; 16:15, serving the saints).

Different authors in the New Testament give different statements of the blessings associated with baptism: Luke, forgiveness of sins and gift of the Holy Spirit (Acts 2:38; 22:16); John, birth from above (John 3:3, 5); Paul, a burial of the old self and resurrection to new life (Rom. 6:3–4), entrance into Christ (Gal 3:27), and initiation into the church (1 Cor 12:13); Peter, salvation (1 Pet 3:20–21).

Did. 7 provides the earliest noncanonical description of baptism. Baptism followed a period of instruction and a fast of one to two days. It was administered using the same Trinitarian formula as Matt 28:19. Jewish influence is evident in the preference for running water. In its absence, the baptism was to be administered in cold water (a natural pool), or in its absence in warm water (an artificial pool). As a last resort, water could be poured three times over the head, an exception not repeated in subsequent transmission of the text.

Justin Martyr (mid-2nd cent. CE; → Justin) gave a circumstantial account of Christian baptism as part of his defense to Roman authorities of the innocence of Christians (Just. 1 *Apol.* 61; 65). Converts were instructed to fast and pray and then were taken to where there was water. For his non-Christian readers, Justin uses the words "bath" and "wash" instead of "baptism." He twice says that those who received baptism were those who believed ("persuaded and believe the things taught by us," "persuaded and give their consent") and repented ("promise to be able to live" according to Christian teaching, "repent of sins"). The baptism was in the Trinitarian name. Justin describes the washing as bringing forgiveness of sins; his favorite terminology is regeneration (ἀναγέννησις, paraphrasing John 3:5) and enlightenment (φωτισμός). He imaginatively describes salvation, on the analogy of Noah, as coming from the water, faith, and wood (cross – Just. *Dial.* 138).

Tertullian provides the first Latin witness to Christian practice and the earliest surviving treatise *On Baptism.* Unlike the → Didache, → Tertullian affirmed that "all waters, when God is invoked, acquire sacred significance," and the Holy Spirit comes down to sanctify them (Tert. *Bapt.* 4.3–4). He affirmed that the most solemn time for baptism was the Pasch (Easter), since baptism is into the Lord's passion (*Bapt.* 19.1); next in appropriateness was → Pentecost; nevertheless, every day is suitable (*Bapt.* 19.2–3).

Tertullian is the first to testify to a practice of triple immersion, "making a somewhat ampler pledge than the Lord has appointed in the gospel" (Tert. *Cor.* 3), words that alternatively may refer to the threefold confession of faith accompanying the threefold immersion. He is also the first to give explicit testimony to infant baptism, a practice he opposed (*Bapt.* 18). The likely origin of infant baptism, as indicated by funerary inscriptions, was with children (of whatever age) who were on the point of death, for there was a feeling that they would not enter the kingdom of heaven if they died unbaptized.

Tertullian, in explaining the postbaptismal rites of anointing in the sign of the cross and laying on of hands, ascribed the imparting of the Holy Spirit to these actions and so separated the coming of the Spirit on the one baptized from the water rite, which brought → forgiveness of sins and so purified the → soul for the coming of the Spirit (*Bapt.* 7–8; Tert. *Res.* 8). The giving of a separate significance to the accompanying postbaptismal actions established a doctrinal basis for the later development of confirmation as a separate sacrament in the medieval western church.

The most commonly mentioned prerequisites for baptism were repentance of sins and faith in Christ. These came to be verbalized in the liturgy as a renunciation of Satan and a profession of faith (either as a positive confession, an affirmative response to questions, or sometimes both).

The 3rd and 4th centuries CE saw a considerable elaboration in the liturgy of baptism, marking baptism as the high point of Christian experience. The → *Apostolic Tradition* is representative of the development. It contains elements that likely go back to the 2nd century as well as 4th-century CE features but may be substantially from those of the 3rd century CE. A three-year period of instruction preceded the ceremonies in the week before → Sunday, during which time the candidates were examined about their manner of life, prayed, fasted, and received exorcisms. Prayer was said over the water. The candidates made a renunciation of "Satan, with all your service and all your works" (Hipp. *Trad. ap.* 21.9). There was an anointing of the candidates with oil

of exorcism (indicating that the candidate was still in the realm of Satan prior to the baptism). The candidates were nude and were baptized in the order children, men, and women (*Trad. ap.* 21.3–5). With the administrator's hand on the head of each in turn, the candidate was asked three questions concerning faith in God the Father, then Christ, and then the Holy Spirit, and with each affirmative answer, the person's head was dipped under the water (*Trad. ap.* 21.15–18). There followed an anointing with the oil of thanksgiving. The newly baptized dressed and entered the church, where the → bishop laid his hand on them, invoking God to send grace on them; anointed the head of each; and signed the forehead (*Trad. ap.* 21.20–24). They then joined the faithful in prayer, the exchange of the kiss of peace, and the → Eucharist (*Trad. ap.* 21.25–40).

Syrian sources from the 3rd and 4th centuries CE indicate that the primary anointing was prebaptismal, not postbaptismal as in other regions, and it received a significance rivalling the water rite (*Did. Apost.* 16; *AXP* 2; *JSZ* 15; 19–21; 26; 54–61).

Baptismal practice in the late 4th century CE may be illustrated for the Greek East and Latin West from the lectures that → Cyril of Jerusalem and → Ambrose of Milan gave to the newly baptized about the significance of the baptismal ceremony. Cyril lectured on the creed in the weeks preceding baptism (Cyril of Jerusalem, *Catechetical Lectures/Catecheses ad illuminandos*). The *Mystagogical Lectures*, dated to the 380s CE, include in the pre-immersion rites a renunciation of Satan and a profession of faith in Father, Son, and Holy Spirit. The candidates removed their clothes and were anointed with the oil of exorcism. In the baptismal pool, the candidates responded to three questions about their faith (an interrogatory confession) accompanying a triple immersion, related to the three days Jesus' body was in the heart of the earth (Cyr.Jer. *Cat. Myst.* 1–2). The postbaptismal unction with μύρον (a perfumed oil) conferred the name "Christian," as anointed ones, and symbolized the anointing by the Holy Spirit (*Cat. Myst.* 3).

Ambrose's *On the Sacraments* and *On the Mysteries* were delivered around 390 CE. During Lent Ambrose gave moral and spiritual teaching to those enrolled for baptism (*competentes*, the petitioners for baptism). Scrutinies and exorcisms determined the fitness of the candidates for baptism, and on the Sunday before → Easter, the creed was delivered (*traditio symboli*) for the candidates to memorize. On Holy Saturday night, the bishop touched the ears and nose of the baptizand with the words "Be opened" (*ephphatha*, Mark 7:34) so that each would understand what was being said and done (Ambr. *Sacr.* 1.1.2–3). The candidates entered the baptistery, were anointed, and renounced the devil (*Sacr.* 1.2.5). The water of the font had been previously consecrated by an invocation of the Trinity (*Sacr.* 1.5.18; 2.5.14). They descended into the pool and received a triple immersion accompanying a triple interrogatory confession (*Sacr.* 2.7.20). The bishop then anointed the head with μύρον (*Sacr.* 2.7.24). The distinctly different element in Milan's ceremony was a foot washing accompanied by the reading of John 13, which was given a sacramental interpretation (*Sacr.* 3.1.4–7).

2. The Fathers

The writings of the church fathers elaborate on the theology of baptism. → Clement of Alexandria listed the names for baptism:

This work [having been regenerated; ἀναγεννηθέντες] is variously called a grace gift [χάρισμα], illumination [φώτισμα], perfection [τέλειον], and bath [λουτρόν]. (Clem. *Paed.* 1.6.26.2)

Gregory of Nazianzus gave a similar list (→ Gregory of Nazianzus):

We call it gift, grace, baptism, illumination, anointing, clothing of immortality, bath of regeneration [Titus 3:5], seal, everything honorable. (Greg. Naz. *Or.* 40.4)

Basil of Caesarea gave an impressive list of the blessings associated with baptism (→ Basil of Caesarea):

Baptism is a ransom to captives, a forgiveness of debts, the death of sin, regeneration [παλιγγενεσία] of the soul, a shining garment, an unassailable seal, a chariot to heaven, the agent of the kingdom, the gift of adoption. (Bas. *Hom. ex. Bapt.* 5)

Gregory of Nazianzus outdoes him:

Enlightenment is the splendor of souls, the conversion of life, the pledge of the conscience

to God. It is the aid to our weakness, the renunciation of the flesh, the following of the Spirit, the fellowship of the Word, the improvement of the creature, the overwhelming of sin, the participation of light, the dissolution of darkness. It is the carriage to God, the dying with Christ, the perfecting of the mind, the bulwark of faith, the key of the kingdom of heaven, the change of life, the removal of slavery, the loosing of chains, the remodeling of the whole person. (Greg. Naz. *Or.* 40.3)

The terminology and motifs of four influential 4th-century CE authors from different regions will illustrate common features and distinctive emphases.

Ephrem the Syrian's (c. 296–373 CE; → Ephrem the Syrian) poetic imagination found in the law of → Moses three principal types of baptism – circumcision, ceremonial ablutions, and sprinkling of blood and water with hyssop. Christian baptism is a circumcision, by which "the hidden mark of the Spirit is imprinted by the oil on bodies anointed in baptism and sealed in the dipping" (Ephr. *Hym. Vir.* 7.6). This statement accords with the Syrian order of the unction preceding the immersion and the emphasis on the association of the Spirit with the unction. Christ's baptism put an end to the Hebrew Bible bathings and sprinklings (*Hym. Vir.* 8.10). Ephrem identified the institution of baptism with the baptism of Christ and with the water and blood from his side on the → cross (John 19:34 – *Hym. Vir.* 15.3; Ephr. *Nis. Hym.* 39.7). Baptism is meaningless without faith, but faith is without efficacy if not sealed by baptism (Ephr. *Hym. Fid.* 13.3). Ephraim understood baptism as conferring principally forgiveness of sins and the gift of the Holy Spirit (e.g. Ephr. *Comm. Rom.* 7.13; *Nis. Hym.* 46.84). Both gifts were sometimes associated with the anointing (*Hym. Vir.* 4.9, 11; 7.6–7), but the statements can be reconciled because the ceremony was considered as a whole and its benefits sometimes ascribed to one part and at another time to another part.

John Chrysostom's homiletic mind found images of the significance of baptism in → marriage (Chrys. *Bapt. Instr.* 1.1, 11–15; → John Chrysostom), in military enlistment to fight against the → devil (*Bapt. Instr.* 1.1, 5; 12.30–32), and in a contract (*Bapt. Instr.* 1.33; 4.31). He frequently uses the word "grace" for the divine activity in baptism, to which one responds in faith and repentance (*Bapt. Instr.* 2.9; 11.12–14; 12.22). Quite prominent in Chrysostom's teaching is the identification of the one being baptized with the death, burial, and → resurrection of Jesus Christ (*Bapt. Instr.* 2.25; Chrys. *Hom. Rom.* 10 on Rom 6:3–4; 11 on Rom 6:5). Baptism is a new creation (*Bapt. Instr.* 4.12–16; 7:14) in which regeneration occurs (*Hom. Rom.*16 on Rom 9:9). Forgiveness of sins is received in baptism (Chrys. *Hom. Eph.* 11 on Eph 4:4–7), but Chrysostom defended infant baptism, even though the infant has no sins, on the basis of other gifts conferred in baptism (*Bapt. Instr.* 3.6). The Holy Spirit descends on the person at baptism (Chrys. *Hom. Matt.* 12.3 on Matt 3:16). In baptism one is sealed and circumcised (Chrys. *Hom. Heb.* 13.9; *Bapt. Instr.* 9.12), but the → circumcision is not baptism itself but what the Spirit does in baptism (Chrys. *Hom. Col.* 6.2 on Col 2:11). Chrysostom names baptism enlightenment (*Bapt. Instr.* 9.12) and describes it as being clothed with Christ (*Bapt. Instr.* 2.11; 5.18). In his baptismal instructions, Chrysostom was especially concerned to bring out baptism's moral consequences.

Gregory of Nyssa's favorite names for baptism were "bath" or "washing" (from Tit 3:5) and "regeneration" (ἀναγέννησις and παλιγγενεσία, apparently used interchangeably; → Gregory of Nyssa). Because of what Christ did, "baptism is a purification of sins, a forgiveness of trespasses, a cause of renewal and regeneration" (Greg. Nyss. *Lum.*, *GNO*, vol. IX, 224, ll.14–16). Baptism is an identification with the death, burial, and resurrection of Christ (Greg. Nyss. *Or. catech. magna* 35; *Lum.*, *GNO*, vol. IX, 228, ll. 13–26). Associated with the washing in water was the idea of cleansing (*Or. catech. magna* 36). Those not purified in water now will be purified in fire at the resurrection (*Or. catech. magna* 35). The renewal and cleansing of baptism are not effected by the water itself but by the activity of the Holy Spirit (*Lum.*, *GNO* vol. IX, 227, ll. 5–7). If there is no resultant change of life, "the water is water, since the gift of the Holy Spirit is in no way manifest in what occurred" (*Or. catech. magna* 40; *GNO* vol. III/1, 105, 19 to 106, l. 11). Enlightenment is another key element of Gregory's baptismal theology (*De iis qui baptismum differunt*; PG 46.432.A). The words "grace" and "gift" appear frequently in his treatise *Against Those Who Defer Baptism*. Among other common motifs are "seal" (*De instituto Christiano*; *GNO*, vol. VIII/1, 58, ll. 12–13),

clothing with immortality (Greg. Nyss. *Icc.* 11 on Song 5:3), and escape from the devil (*Lum.*, *GNO* vol. IX, 233, ll. 9–14). He occasionally uses the word "mystery" in reference to baptism and other sacred acts (*Or. catech. magna* 35), a usage that prepared the way for "mystery" to become the word in the Greek church roughly equivalent to "sacrament" in the Latin church. When properly received and with the proper results, baptism for Gregory is necessary for salvation (*Or. catech. magna* 35.)

Hilary of Poitiers (bishop 353–367 CE; → Hilary of Poitiers) does not give an extended discussion of baptism but mentions it rather frequently. In commenting on Col 2:11–12, Hilary identifies baptism as the occasion of receiving the "circumcision of Christ" through death to the old self and being born again to the new life of the resurrection (Hil. Poit. *Trin.* 9.9; 1.13). Regeneration (*Trin.* 6.36; 12.57) and the burial and resurrection with Christ (Hil. Poit. *Trin.* 1.13; *Tract.* 118 15.13) are important themes often linked together for him. Baptism is also an illumination of the soul (*Tract.* 118, preface 4; 3.9). Baptism in the Holy Spirit awaits Christians in cleansing fire either in martyrdom or after death (Hil. Poit. *Comm. Ps.* 135.3; 137.2–3). The most frequently mentioned blessings associated with baptism were the forgiveness of sins and the gift of the Holy Spirit.

The high doctrine of baptism expressed by the church fathers has been called baptismal regeneration. More accurately it was regeneration in baptism. When the Fathers were careful about their statement, they ascribed the regeneration not to the water nor to the act of immersion but to the working of the Godhead either in the water or as accompanying the act of baptism. Gregory of Nyssa affirmed:

> The water does not grant the benefit [of regeneration] [...] but the ordinance of God and the intervention of the Spirit coming mystically to set us free. But the water serves to exhibit the cleansing." (Greg. Nyss. *Lum.*, *GNO* vol. IX, 224, ll. 17–24)

John Chrysostom explained that the priest pronounced the formula, "So-and-so is baptized in the name of the Father, and of the Son, and of the Holy Spirit"; he did not say, "I baptize so-and-so," showing that "in this way that it is not he who baptizes but those whose names have been invoked" (Chrys.

Bapt. Instr. 11.14), for the priest is "only the minister of grace," and it is the undivided Trinity that fulfills all things (*Bapt. Instr.* 2.26).

3. Iconography and Archaeology

Perhaps the earliest depiction of baptism is a fresco in the Catacomb of Callistus, in the crypt of Lucina (beginning of 3rd cent. CE?). It shows an adult, nude Jesus ascending from the water (Matt 3:16) and being received by John the Baptist standing on the shore. A dove descends toward the head of Jesus, and water is sketched in broad strokes around his body.

The image that became standard, in both catacomb paintings and sculpture on sarcophagi, showed a full-sized John placing his hand on the head of a small nude Jesus. An imposition of hands occurred at various points in the baptismal liturgy, but the two most likely events, as indicated in the literary sources, were the administrator's laying on of hands at the confession of faith accompanying the immersions (Hipp. *Trad. ap.* 21.14–18) or after the baptism invoking God's grace (*Trad. ap.* 21.21). Or, there may be a composite picture. The smaller size of the one baptized was not an allusion to infant baptism but followed the artistic convention of showing the lesser figure as smaller, and thus in this case alluding to the humility of Jesus in assuming the human condition. The nudity probably represented the motif of new birth. Among the scenes representing the standard iconography are a picture in the "Chapel of the Sacraments" (A 3, dated 220–230 CE) in the Catacomb of Callistus, where a spray of water surrounds the body of the baptizand as well as being painted at his feet, and another of the same date in room 21 of the Catacomb of Callistus, showing the body of the baptizand leaning forward, which if not the result of the artist's lack of skill may represent the usual practice of bending the body forward in an immersion.

One scene often claimed to depict an aspersion is in room 43 of the 4th-century CE Catacomb of Peter and Marcelinus. It shows eight rays descending from a dove and surrounding Jesus. In spite of the damage to the picture, the hand of the administrator is clearly on the head of Jesus and not pouring out something. Rather than water, the rays from the dove may represent the oil of the Holy Spirit, the Holy Spirit himself, or light. If the rays represent water,

the allusion may be to running water rather than a baptismal pouring. A similar scene occurs inscribed on a gravestone from Aquileia, representing the baptism of a young girl who stands in a shallow basin. From a circle, in which is pictured a dove, there descend streams, either of water, oil, or light. Once more the baptizer has his hand on the head of the one baptized.

Perhaps the earliest representation of a baptism on a sarcophagus (from the last third of the 3rd cent. CE; → Sarcophagi, Christian) is found in the Church of Santa Maria Antiqua on the Roman Forum. A small nude Jesus stands in water to his ankles, a large dove approaches, and John dressed as a Cynic philosopher lays his hand on the head of Jesus. The shallow water is allusive, for it is at the same height as the water in which the sea monster swims, and on which floats the ship from which → Jonah is thrown overboard. From near the same time is a sarcophagus from the Via della Lungara in Rome, now in the Museo Nazionale delle Terme. The baptizer holds an open scroll in his left hand (representing the instruction accompanying baptism) and places his right on the head of the smaller baptizand, who stands in water to his knees. A live tree and a dead tree flank the baptism, alluding either to John's preaching (Matt 3:8–10), to Ps 1:3–4, or to the convert's passing from death to life.

Accompanying the baptismal scenes in the catacombs are pictures of other items associated with baptism: a paralytic carrying his bed (either John 5:2–9, pool of Bethzatha, or Mark 2:2–12, "your sins are forgiven"), a fisherman (Matt 4:9, disciples as "fishers of men"), Samaritan woman at the well (John 4:5–30). The sarcophagi include, in addition to these, with some frequency the cycle of Jonah (notably the sarcophagus from Santa Maria Antiqua and the "Jonah Sarcophagus" in the Vatican's Museo Pio Cristiano) and water from the rock when struck by Moses or Peter (e.g. the "Jonah Sarcophagus" and the right end of a sarcophagus in Musée de l'Arles Antique).

Depictions of baptism in the 5th and 6th centuries CE become more "historical" and less allusive. Two spectacular mosaics are found in Ravenna. In both, a fully grown nude Jesus stands in water to his waist. Both introduce a third figure, a personification of the river god, who reverently acknowledges

Jesus. Both mosaics are in the dome of baptisteries, directly above the baptismal font. The earlier, the Baptistery of the Orthodox by Bishop Neon from the mid-5th century CE, has what might be the earliest representation of John pouring water on Jesus; but this part of the mosaic is clearly a restoration and represents later practice. What the original mosaic pictured is shown by the mosaic in the Baptistery of the Arians from the late 5th century CE, clearly modeled on the earlier baptistery. It follows the traditional iconography with John's right hand resting on Jesus' head.

A miniature illustration in the 6th-century CE Syriac Rabbula gospels (fol. 4b) has the Trinitarian (→ Trinity) feature of the hand of God, the dove of the Holy Spirit, and Christ, who is in water above his waist. John's hand is on Christ's head. A new feature is a flame of fire on the water, indicating a theophany. Justin Martyr in the 2nd century CE had already recorded the tradition that at Jesus' baptism a fire was kindled in the Jordan (Just. *Dial.* 88.2–4).

The earliest securely dated baptistery was found at → Dura-Europos in eastern Syria (240s CE). Christians remodeled a house for their community use and installed a font at one end of one of the rooms. The font's dimensions were 1.63 m in length, a width of 0.948 m on one side and 1.065 m on the other, and a depth of 0.955 m. Immediately behind the font was a picture of a good shepherd carrying a large ram on his shoulders, and at the bottom left of the picture, a later artist added a small → Adam and Eve, serpent, and tree. On the walls were biblical scenes – Samaritan woman at the well, Jesus saving Peter from unsuccessfully walking on water, and the paralytic carrying his bed. Quite prominent is a procession of women, either the virgins of the parable in Matt 25:1–12 or the women approaching the tomb on the morning of Jesus' resurrection (Luke 24:10).

The octagonal Lateran Baptistery in Rome was influential on the architecture of baptisteries, especially in the West. It was constructed under Constantine and in its second phase had a circular baptismal pool. Pope Sixtus III (432–440 CE) gave the baptismal pool its present octagonal shape, 8.5 m in diameter and so designed for multiple immersions.

Impressive ruins remain of the baptistery of the Church of Saint Mary in Ephesus. Its first phase is perhaps from the late 4th century CE. Eight niches give an octagonal appearance to the baptistery. The centralized pool is round with extensions of four steps each on the east and west ends and a depth of 1.15 m.

Baptismal pools come in many shapes – rectangular, round, cruciform, hexagonal, octagonal – each with a possible symbolic meaning (tomb, womb or eternity, cross, death or creation, resurrection and eternal life, respectively), but in many cases practical requirements or local styles may have been determinative.

The trend in the 5th and 6th centuries CE was to constructing smaller fonts, remodeling older fonts to a smaller size, or adding a second smaller font. The baptismal pools in North Africa are an exception. This trend may reflect the increasing practice of baby baptism, but the smaller fonts may have had another purpose, such as foot washing or holding oil.

The authors of comprehensive regional surveys of baptismal pools – M. Ben-Pechat (1985) for Israel, I.H. Volanakis for Greece (1976), and to a lesser extent J.-C. Picard (1989; working mainly with literary texts but correlated with archaeological discoveries) for southern France and northern Italy – conclude that the pools were sufficient for immersion as the normal practice.

4. Controversies

The major controversy involving baptism in the pre-Nicene period concerned the acceptance of baptism performed by heretics or schismatics. → Cyprian of Carthage (bishop 248–258 CE), took the position that since there is one baptism in the one holy church, the Holy Spirit could be imparted only by a baptism performed by a minister of this one church (Cyp. *Ep.* 69). He declared, "If one is to have God for Father, he must first have the church for mother" (*Ep.* 74.7.2). Cyprian had the support of his fellow North African bishops (*Judgments of the Eighty-Seven Bishops*) and Firmilian, bishop of Caesarea in Cappadocia (*Ep.* 75). He was opposed by Stephen, bishop of Rome (254–257 CE), who took his stand on the custom of the Roman church and his authority as a successor of Peter to receive those baptized by heretics or schismatics as penitents without requiring a "rebaptism." The anonymous author of a treatise *On Rebaptism* rejected Cyprian's position, claiming that the name of Christ gave baptism its effectiveness regardless of who administered the baptism; the Holy Spirit is imparted by the postbaptismal imposition of hands, which is given on a person's coming from the heretical or schismatic body to the catholic church. In subsequent decades the position of Stephen came to prevail, for one's salvation could not be made dependent on the status of the baptizer. When the Donatists (→ Donatism/Donatists) in North Africa maintained the position of Cyprian, the Council of Arles (314 CE) ruled that a heretic baptized in the name of Father, Son, and Holy Spirit was to be received by imposition of hands, but one who did not give the Trinity as his faith was to be (re)baptized (c. 9). Basil of Caesarea represented the position of the Greek church that rejected baptism by heretics but accepted that by schismatics (Cyp. *Ep.* 188, c. 1).

There was discussion but no real controversy over sickbed or emergency baptism. The schism led by → Novatian in Rome (beginning in 251 CE) entered into the rebaptism controversy, for he rejected baptism by an administrator of doubtful moral character or who compromised the faith in persecution. Novatian's own baptism was under a cloud, for he had received baptism by pouring on his sickbed and then recovered. When later he was proposed as a presbyter, many objected that it was not lawful for someone who received sickbed baptism to become a clergyman (Eus. *Hist. eccl.* 6.43.14–17). It is not clear to what extent the objection in this case was due to the pouring instead of immersion, the delay of baptism until the approach of death calling into question the depth of his conviction, or the fact that his baptism was not completed by a bishop's sealing. Cyprian, although he opposed Novatian's schism, defended the validity of pouring as an abridgement of immersion in cases of emergency against those who expressed doubts about it (Cyp. *Ep.* 69.12).

Baptism entered into the Messalian controversy of the 4th and 5th centuries CE. A later compilation of the errors with which the ascetic movement designated by the name → Messalians (or Euchites, "Those Who Pray") were charged included that baptism does not make one perfect, for only prayer cleanses the soul; that one remains in sin even after baptism; and that one obtains freedom from the passions and partakes of the Holy Spirit by the sensation of full assurance (Dam. *Haer.* 80).

Diadochus, bishop of Photice in the later 5th century CE, was under the influence of Messalians but opposed its extremes. He explained that "before baptism grace exhorts the soul to the good from the outside, but Satan hides in the depth of the soul," but after the regeneration of baptism, "the demon passes to the outside and grace is inside" (Diad. *Spir. per.* 76–77). Mark the Monk, of uncertain date, was a strong anti-Messalian voice. He faced the dilemma posed by the experience of persons who sinned after baptism, which supposedly destroyed sin. He replied that those who asserted the need for ascetic works to eliminate sin replaced grace with works (PG 65.988.A). He was not opposed to works, however, for "faith is not only to be baptized into Christ but also to do his commands" (PG 65.985.D).

Baptism provided a key argument for → Augustine of Hippo in his controversy with → Pelagians on original sin. Both sides acknowledged that baptism was for the forgiveness of sins and accepted infant baptism. Since infants had not committed any sins of their own, the custom of infant baptism and the church's doctrine of baptism provided Augustine with a decisive argument for original sin.

> [T]hose people [Pelagians] grant that little ones should be baptized, because they cannot stand up against the authority, which was beyond any doubt, given to the whole church through the Lord and apostles. They should, then, also grant that they need these benefits of the mediator so that, washed by the sacrament, [...] they might be reconciled to God. Thus they would become in him living, saved, set free, redeemed, and enlightened. From what, save from death, [...] guilt, [...] and darkness of sins? And since they committed at that age no sin in their own life, there remains only original sin. (Aug. *Pecc. merit.* 1.26.39)

Augustine argued from the practice of infant baptism to the doctrine of original sin. After his viewpoint prevailed in the Latin church, original sin became the doctrinal basis for infant baptism.

The fact that controversies on other subjects – the unity and holiness of the church, the place of ascetic works, and original sin – were argued in terms of baptism shows the importance of baptism for early Christians.

Historiography

Two works in French set forth comprehensive coverage of baptism: J. Corblett (1881) and T. Maertens (1962). L. Heiser (1987) concentrates on the Greek fathers. Two works in English give briefer, but comprehensive surveys: M.E. Johnson (1999) and B.D. Spinks (2006). The liturgy of baptism is especially the theme of A. Stenzel (1958) and G. Kretschmar (1964–1966). V. Saxer (1988) is interested in initiation as a whole, not just its separate parts. Topical studies of note are J. Ysebaert (1962) and D. Wright's articles on infant baptism (2007).

Three works that appeared near the same time give the current state of the study of baptism: E. Ferguson (2009); D. Hellholm, T. Vegge, O. Norderval and C. Hellholm (2011); and R. Jensen (2012).

Bibliography

Ben-Pechat, M., *L'architecture baptismale de la terre sainte du IVème au VIIème siècle: Étude historique, archéologique et liturgique*, 3 vols., Paris, 1985.

Corblett, J., *Histoire dogmatique, liturgique, et archeologique du sacrement de baptême*, Paris, 1881.

Fausone, A.M., *Die Taufe in der frühchristlichen Sepulkralkunst*, Vatican City, 1982.

Ferguson, E., *Baptism in the Early Church: History, Theology, and Liturgy in the First Five Centuries*, Grand Rapids, 2009.

Heiser, L., Die Taufe in der orthodoxen Kirche: Geschichte, Spendung, un Symbolik nach der Lehre der Vater, Basel, 1987.

Helholm, D., T. Vegge, O. Norderval & C. Hellholm, eds., *Ablution, Initiation, and Baptism: Late Antiquity, Early Judaism, and Early Christianity*, 3 vols., Berlin, 2011.

Jensen, R.M., *Living Water: Images, Symbols, and Settings of Early Christian Baptism*, Leiden, 2011.

Jensen, R.M., *Baptismal Imagery in Early Christianity: Ritual, Visual, and Theological Dimensions*, Grand Rapids, 2012.

Johnson, M.E., *The Rites of Christian Initiation: Their Evolution and Interpretation*, Collegeville, 1999.

Kretschmar, G., "Die Geschichte des Taufgottesdienstes in der alten Kirche," in: *Leit.*, vol. V, Kassel, 1964–1966, 31–35.

Maertens, T., *Histoire et pastorale du rituel du catéchuménat et du baptême*, Bruges, 1962

Picard, J.-C., "Ce que les textes nous aprennent sur les équpements et le mobilier liturgiques nécessaires pour le baptême dans le sud de la Gaul et l'Italie du Nord," in: *Actes du XIe Congrès International d'Archéologie Chré-*

tienne, Lyone, Vienne, Grenoble, Genève et Aoste, Vatican City, 1989, vol. II, 1451–1468.

Ristow, S., *Frühchristliche Baptisterien*, JbAC.S. 27, Münster, 1998.

Saxer, V., *Les rites de l'initiation chretienne du IIe au VIe siecle*, Spoleto, 1988.

Spinks, B.D., *Early and Medieval Rituals and Theologies of Baptism*, Aldershot, 2006.

Stenzel, A., *Die Taufe: Eine Genetische Erklarung der Taufliturgie*, Innsbruck, 1958.

Volanakis, I.H., Τα παλαιοχριστιανικά Βαπτιστήρια της Ελλάδος, Athens, 1976.

Wright, D.F., *Infant Baptism in Historical Perspective: Collected Studies*, Carlisle, 2007.

Ysebaert, J., Greek Baptismal Terminology: Its Origins and Early Development, Nijmegen, 1962.

EVERETT FERGUSON

Barbarians

The Greek and Roman concept of the barbarian (βάρβαρος) designates the foreigner in terms of language and origin, thus also denoting his or her linguistic and cultural otherness. From archaic times to late antiquity, the concept underwent characteristic changes and was eventually also employed by Christian authors in the construction of identities and alterities.

1. The Greek Concept

The ancient Greek noun βάρβαρος (along with the less frequently attested adjective βάρβαρος, the derivatives βαρβαρικός "barbaric, non-Greek"], βαρβαρίζω ["to behave" or "speak like a barbarian"], and βαρβαρισμός ["barbarism"], as well as composites such as βαρβαροφωνέω ["to speak Greek barbarously"], βαρβαρότης ["nature" or "conduct of a barbarian"], and the like) has Indo-Germanic roots (for its semantics and etymology, see *TLG*, s.v. "βαρβᾰρίζω, βάρβᾰρος, βαρβᾰροστομία"; *DGE*, s.v. "βάρβᾰρος"; Chantraine, 1968, s.v. "βάρβαρος"; Frisk, 1960, s.v. "βάρβαρος"; Broisacq, 1916, s.v. "βαβαί, βαρβαρόφωνος"); its originally nonjudgmental, onomatopoetic meaning (in the sense of "stammering unintelligibly") is still detectable in the Greek context (Hom. *Il.* 2.867 refers to the Carians as βαρβαρόφωνος [see Brügger et al., 2003, 284f.]; see also Hdt. 8.20; 9.43; Aesch. *Sept.* 463; Aristoph. *Av.* 1512; Sex.Emp. *Pyr.* 1.74). In the wake of colonization, but especially as a consequence of the Persian wars, the term acquired a pejorative sense and was now mostly used disparagingly in reference to the cultural, religious, and moral traits of the foreigner (Aristoph. *Nub.* 492; Dem. *Or.* 21.150; 26.17; Men. *Epitr.* 898; Arist. *Frag.* 658 R[3]; comp. Arist. *Pol.* 1.2 [1252a24ff.]; 3.14 [1285a20ff.]; *Eth. Nic.* 5.1 [1145a29ff.]; see also Buchner, 1954).

This development marked the rise of the highly momentous antithesis Hellenes/barbarians (see Jüthner, 1923, 1–22): from then on, the term "barbarian" was usually applied to the reputedly uneducated, unrefined, and morally inferior person of foreign extraction, who might be partially integrated into the Greek world (e.g. as a slave or metic) or socially completely excluded from it (e.g. through exclusion from the Olympic Games and the Eleusinian Mysteries). Via the concept μηδισμός (i.e. association with Persians), the allegation of collaboration with the (primarily Near Eastern) barbarians became a political battle slogan (Thuc. *Hist.* 1.95.128–134; see Gillis, 1979; Graf, 1984). However, occasionally the value-neutral meaning of barbarian was still used (*Hist.* 1.1), and from the late 4th century BCE onward (Alexander's wars of conquest, the integration of the eastern elites, the growing influence of Hellenized *literati* of non-Greek extraction, the advent of Hellenism), cosmopolitan approaches are increasingly encountered in the works of Stoics and Cynics, and later also of Neo-Pythagoreans and Neoplatonists (they followed, among others, Hom. *Il.* 13.1–9; Aesch. *Pers.*; 696b; Xen. *Cyr.*; Plato *Leg.* 3.693d–696b; Isoc. *Or.* 9.37f.), partially in conjunction with the notion that Greek philosophy could be traced back to the pristine wisdom of eastern barbarians (for the late classical and early Hellenistic eras, see the works of Ephorus, Onesicritus, Hecataeus of Abdera, Dicaearchus; for the Hellenistic period: Demetrius of Callatis, Artapanus, Eupolemus; for the Roman Imperial period: → Justin Martyr, → Tatian, → Clement of Alexandria, → Origen, → Porphyry of Tyre, → Eusebius of Caesarea, → Augustine of Hippo). In the course of this development, the aspect of Greek literacy acquired greater weight with respect to the factor of geographic or ethnic origin (on the Greek perception of foreign people, see Harrison, 2022).

2. The Roman Concept

With the intensification of cultural contacts between Romans and Greeks, the concept was carried over into Latin (as the noun *barbarus*, along with adjective *barbarus* and the derivatives *barbaricus* [foreign, strange], *barbarismus* [barbarism], *barbaria/barbaries/barbaricum* [foreign land]; for the corresponding semantics and etymologies, see *TLL*, s.v. "barbaria, barbaricus, barbarismus, barbarus"; *OLD*, s.v. "barbaria, barbaricus, barbarus"; Walde, 1938, s.v. "balbus"), and the concept was also used by Romans in reference to their own language, at first in the initial neutral meaning of "non-Greek" (thus e.g. in Plaut. *Asin.* prologue 10; *Curc.* 150; *Mil. glor.* 211; *Most.* 828; *Stic.* 193; see also Festus, *De Verborum significatione* s.v. "Barbari"; Livy 31.29.15; Cic. *De or.* 48 [160]). With Rome's rise to political and military supremacy in the Mediterranean world, its appropriation of Greek culture, and the accompanying transformation of Roman self-perception, the established dichotomy of Hellenes/barbarians was expanded into the triad Hellenes/Romans/barbarians (Cic. *Fin.* 2.49; *Div.* 1.84; *Quint. fratr.* 5.10.24; Juv. *Sat.* 10.138; Dio *Hist.* 44.2.2; 56.7.5; Ael. Arist. *Or.* 14; Or. Cels. 8.37; Eus. *Vita Const.* 4.75; see also Jüthner, 1923, 60–87). From the Greek perspective as well, the Romans were soon clearly distinguished from the other non-Greeks and no longer referred to as βάρβαροι but as Ῥωμαῖοι (*Romans*) by the Greeks, who came to view the Romans as equal or even as superior to themselves (thus e.g. in the historical works of Polybius and Dionysius of Halicarnassus or in Plutarch's *Parallel Lives*). The fulfillment of this decisive conceptual precondition meant that with the integration of the Greek-speaking cultural sphere into the Roman Empire, the new formula Romans/non-Romans (programmatically formulated e.g. in Ael. Arist. *Or.* 14) came to the fore. At the same time, the semantics of the concept "barbarian" witnessed a significant shift. The citizen status, which was increasingly used as an instrument of integration, now became the central politico-legal reference point of Roman identity, while Hellenic/Roman culture constituted the leading paradigm of cultural self-understanding (see Sherwin-White, 1973). The term *barbarus* was henceforth primarily used in reference to persons without Roman citizenship or to individuals of non-Roman extraction with their own linguistic and cultural characteristics. The concept could now be applied to the members of tribes or nations beyond the borders of the Roman Empire (e.g. Gauls, Germanic peoples, Scythians, Persians, Syrians, etc.; see e.g. Cic. *Verr.* 4.77; 5.150; Caes. *Bell. gall.* 1.31.5; 4.22.1; 5.54.4; Tac. *An.* 2.16; Pliny Y. *Pan.* 56.4; Am. 20.4.4; on the archaeological evidence, see Wells, 1999) the settlement areas that lay beyond the limits of the Roman Empire were then conceived of as *barbaricum* (see Cod. Justin. 4.63.2 [374 CE]; Eut. *Brev.* 7.9; 9.4; Am. 17.12.21; 18.2.14; 27.5.6; *Not. Dign. Occ.* 32f.; Ambr. *Fid.* 2.16.140; Oros. *Adv. pag.* 1.2.54). But the notion could also be applied to persons within the Roman social order when they were of foreign birth or descent, in which case the concept displays various shades of meaning.

Barbarians might serve in the Roman army, initially as mercenaries, then increasingly in auxiliary units or as *foederati*. Through their honorable discharge (*honesta missio*) or on account of their special merits, barbarian soldiers could obtain Roman citizenship for themselves and their descendants. The importance of the army for the conferral of citizenship rights led to a steady increase in the number of barbarian soldiers, so that "barbarian" eventually became synonymous with "soldier" (e.g. *GPBM*, vol. II, 298, no. 410). The military thus acquired a particular significance in the forming of barbarian identities and alterities within the empire (Stickler, 2007). Moreover, barbarian soldiers of late antiquity also became important supporters of Christianization (Liebeschuetz, 1990). As shown by recent scholarship, however, the literary sources pertaining to the barbarian *habitus* of the soldiers (e.g. the writings of → Claudian, → Synesius of Cyrene, and → John Chrysostom) are characterized by topical images of the barbarian and can only conditionally be drawn upon for the interpretation of archaeological findings (Rummel, 2007). Legal status could in any case outweigh a person's cultural origins – an important precondition for the citizenship policy of Emperor Caracalla (*Constitutio Antoniniana*; see Ando, 2016), through which the primacy of the legal aspect was cemented in the early 3rd century CE. By the 4th century CE at the latest, various ethnic groups within the Roman Empire were no longer regularly addressed as barbarians but as Romans (see Them. *Or.* 16.211c–d). Citizenship entailed equal rights and duties for its bearers and may literally be seen as a "universal citizenship" on account of its claim to universal validity (Mathisen, 2006).

The Latin semantic field also exhibits the characteristic ambivalence between the pejorative connotations of the concept "barbarian" and an occasional usage in a value-neutral or even positive sense (for appreciation of barbarians, see e.g. Sal. *Gub.* 5.5.21; for their negative appraisal, Sid. *Ep.* 7.14.10). In the field of Roman imperial discourses, the barbarians regularly served as a projection screen, especially in the context of Roman triumphal ideology. Until well into late antiquity, the emperor's *fortitudo* and *providentia* were exemplarily manifested in the struggle against barbarian tribes and nations. The parading of captured barbarians in triumphal processions or their spectacular slaughtering in the circus was equally welcome (Engemann, 2016). Imperial victory titles such as *germanicus maximus*, *sarmaticus maximus*, or *persicus maximus* (→ Julian the Apostate was even called *barbarorum extinctor*: Conti, 2004, no. 17f.) served to communicate the military successes of the emperor, whose merits were measured against the ideal of *propagatio imperii*. From the 3rd and 4th centuries CE onward, however, the emperor's salvific actions on the outer borders were less and less expressed in bellicose terms and increasingly shifted to the field of diplomacy, affording the late antique/early Byzantine emperors alternative courses of action beyond the military struggle against the barbarians (Maier, 2019; on borders and foreign relations, see also Whittaker, 2004; Becker, 2013; Nechaeva, 2014). In the eastern Roman Empire, these traditions can be traced far into Byzantine times; the relationship between Romans and barbarians in the cultures of the western Mediterranean world, on the other hand, underwent radical transformations in the course of the "barbarian migration" and the end of the western Roman Empire (Heather, 1991; Arnold, 2014; Meier, 2019) in current scholarly research, this development is no longer primarily subsumed under the concept of ethnogenesis but understood as a process of integration and identity formation (Gillett, 2002; Pohl, 2002; Kulikowski, 2012).

3. The Christian Concept

The early Christians were classified as barbarians (Eus. *Praep.* 11.19.1 and 2; Libian. *Or.* 18.158; Porph. *Abst.* 1.42), and they even adopted the term in reference to themselves, as did the later Christian apologists (Tat. *Orat.* 42.1; Clem. *Strom.* 6.2.4), while the New Testament writings were criticized as exhibiting stylistic barbarism (Isid. Pelus. *Ep.* 4.28; Thdt. *Affect.* prologue 1 and 1.18). The use of the concept of the barbarian in the books of the New Testament is ambivalent: both the classical concept as well as criticism of the notion appear in the texts (1 Cor 14:11; Acts 28:2, 4). Innovations are mostly encountered in the writings of Paul (→ Paul the Apostle), who initially still adhered to the classical dichotomy Hellenes/barbarians in Rom 1:14 but subsequently put the concept of the barbarian into perspective (1 Cor 14:11: "If then I do not know the meaning of a sound, I will be a foreigner to the speaker and the speaker a foreigner to me"), finally expanding the contrasting pair by adding the Christians (as converted Jews and pagans) as a third element (1 Cor 1:22–24; thus also later in Aristid. *Apol.* 2.2; for explicit references to a τρίτον γένος or *tertium genus*, see Clem. *Strom.* 6.5.41 and Tert. *Nat.* 1.8). Consequentially, Paul views the difference as overcome with the confession of faith in Jesus (Col 3:11; compare 1 Tim 2:4) – a crucial premise that enabled the contrasting pair Hellenes/Christians (in the sense of polytheists versus monotheists) to gain acceptance. The church fathers mostly adopted the conceptual relativization developed by Paul; in those cases where the unbelievers are conceived of as barbarians, biblical-apocalyptic concepts were also employed (Humphries, 2010).

A new momentum emerged from the Christianization of the Roman monarchy. Triumphal rulership was still phrased in terms of a struggle against the barbarians (even if civil wars gained increasing importance in late antiquity), but anti-barbarian ideology began to be questioned as early as the reign of Constantine, when Christian protagonists formulated their reservations in direct interaction with the emperor: in his laudatory speech on the occasion of → Constantine I's *tricennalia*, Eusebius ostentatiously avoided attaching importance to the imperial struggle against "the visible barbarians" (οἱ ὁρατοὶ βάρβαροι), focusing instead on the battle against demons, whom he explicitly described as "another kind of barbarians" (ἄλλων τουτωνὶ βαρβάρων; Eus. *Laud. Const.* 7.2, 6.21; see also Wienand, 2012, 444–448). In this manner, piety (*pietas*/εὐσέβεια) became the new measure of an emperor's acceptability – a virtue he was expected to demonstrate in his commitment even to those Christians who lived beyond the imperial borders. Constantine reacted to these demands with his letter to Shapur II and demonstratively championed the cause of Christians in the Persian Empire (Eus. *Vita Const.* 4.9–13): an important factor of late antique foreign diplomacy was thus prefigured (Blockley, 1992; Goffart, 1980), and the imperial encouragement of a Christian "mission to the barbarians" can be interpreted along the same lines (Mathisen, 1997). Christian religion played an important role also in the integration of those barbarians who were settled on Roman soil. Especially during the 4th and 5th centuries CE (a phase of intensified intellectual dispute between pagans and Christians), Christian apologists were frequently at a loss to explain why Roman emperors had suffered military defeats against barbarians in spite of the support afforded by their new tutelary deity (as becomes particularly clear with the sack of Rome by → Alaric I in the year 410 CE). It was not least in order to introduce a conceptual distinction between the imperial fortunes in the struggle against the barbarians and the notion of divine goodwill that Augustine authored *De civitate Dei*.

Bibliography

Ando, C., *Citizenship and Empire in Europe 200–1900: The Antonine Constitution after 1800 Years*, Stuttgart, 2016.

Arnold, J.J., *Theoderic and the Roman Imperial Restoration*, Cambridge MA, 2014.

Becker, A., *Les relations diplomatiques romano-barbares en Occident au Ve siècle: Acteurs, fonctions, modalités*, Paris, 2013.

Blockley, R.C., *East Roman Foreign Policy: Formation and Conduct from Diocletian to Anastasius*, Leeds, 1992.

Broisacq, É., *Dictionnaire étymologique de la langue grecque*, Heidelberg, 1916.

Brügger, C., M. Stoevesandt & E. Visser, *Homers Ilias: Gesamtkommentar*, vol. II: *Zweiter Gesang (B)*, part 2: *Kommentar*, Munich, 2003.

Buchner, E., "Zwei Gutachten für die Behandlung der Barbaren durch Alexander den Großen," *Hermes* 82, 1954, 378–384.

Chantraine, P., *Dictionnaire étymologique de la langue grecque, A–D*, Paris, 1968.

Conti, S., *Die Inschriften Kaiser Julians*, Stuttgart, 2004.

Engemann, J., "'Dich aber, Konstantin, sollen die Feinde hassen!' Konstantin und die Barbaren," in: A. Demandt & J. Engemann, *Konstantin der Große*, Trier, 2016, 173–187.

Frisk, H., *Griechisches etymologisches Wörterbuch*, vol. I: *A–Ko*, Heidelberg, 1960.

Gillett, A., ed., *On Barbarian Identity: Critical Approaches to Ethnicity in the Early Middle Ages*, Turnhout, 2002.

Gillis, D., *Collaboration with the Persians*, 1979.

Goffart, W.A., *Barbarians and Romans, A.D. 418–584*, Princeton, 1980.

Graf, D.F., "Medism: The Origin and Significance of the Term," *JHS* 104, 1984, 15–30.

Harrison, T., *Greeks and Barbarians*, Edinburgh, 2022.

Heather, P.J., *Goths and Romans (332–489)*, Oxford, 1991.

Humphries, M., "'Gog Is the Goth': Biblical Barbarians in Ambrose of Milan's De fide," in: R.A. Flower, C.M. Kelly & M.S. Williams, eds., *Unclassical Traditions: Alternatives to the Classical Past in Late Antiquity*, Cambridge UK, 2010, 44–57.

Jüthner, J., *Hellenen und Barbaren: Aus der Geschichte des Nationalbewußtseins*, Leipzig, 1923.

Kulikowski, M., "Barbarische Identität: Aktuelle Forschungen und neue Interpretationsansätze," in: M. Konrad & C. Witschel, eds., *Römische Legionslager in den Rhein- und Donauprovinzen – Nuclei spätantik-frühmittelalterlichen Lebens?* Munich, 2012, 103–111.

Liebeschuetz, J.H.W.G., *Barbarians and Bishops: Army, Church, and State in the Age of Arcadius and Chrysostom*, Oxford, 1990.

Maier, F.K., *Palastrevolution: Der Weg zum hauptstädtischen Kaisertum im Römischen Reich des vierten Jahrhunderts*, Paderborn, 2019.

Mathisen, R.W., "Barbarian Bishops and the Churches 'in barbaricis gentibus' during Late Antiquity," *Spec.* 72, 1997, 664–697.

Mathisen, R.W., "Peregrini, Barbari, and Cives Romani: Concepts of Citizenship and the Legal Identity of Barbarians in the Later Roman Empire," *AHR* 111, 2006, 1011–1040.

Meier, M., *Geschichte der Völkerwanderung: Europa, Asien und Afrika vom 3. bis zum 8. Jahrhundert n.Chr.*, Munich, 2019.

Nechaeva, E., *Embassies – Negotiations – Gifts: Systems of East Roman Diplomacy in Late Antiquity*, Stuttgart, 2014.

Pohl, W., *Die Völkerwanderung: Eroberung und Integration*, Stuttgart, 2002.

Rummel, P. von, *Habitus barbarus: Kleidung und Repräsentation spätantiker Eliten im 4. und 5. Jahrhundert*, Berlin, 2007.

Sherwin-White, A.N., *The Roman Citizenship*, Oxford, ²1973.

Stickler, T., "The Foederati," in: P. Erdkamp, ed., *A Companion to the Roman Army*, Malden, 2007, 495–514.

Walde, A., *Lateinisches Etymologisches Wörterbuch*, vol. I: *A–L*, Heidelberg, ³1938

Wells, P.S., *The Barbarians Speak: How the Conquered Peoples Shaped Roman Europe*, Princeton, 1999.

Whittaker, C.R., *Rome and its Frontiers: The Dynamics of Empire*, London, 2004.

Wienand, J., *Der Kaiser als Sieger: Metamorphosen triumphaler Herrschaft unter Constantin I.*, Berlin, 2012.

JOHANNES WIENAND

Barbarus Scaligeri → *Excerpta Latina Barbari*

Barbelo

Barbelo (Gk Βαρβηλώ) is a name of an entity who in several texts attributed to gnostics is described as the first emanation of the androgynous God. Barbelo is not created by God but comes forth from him. Some narratives describe how she emerges from God's overflowing thoughts (see *the Apocryphon of John*; → John the Apostle: IV. *John, Secret Revelation of*) or that she is the reflection of God in the primal waters that became a separate being (Codex Berolinensis 8502: *Apocryphon of John*). She thus occupies the second place in the divine realm and is the source of all further existence. Part of her → aeon is the triad of subaeons consisting of Kalyptos (meaning *hidden*), Protophanes (describing the initial manifestation), and Autogenes (i.e. self-begotten) which have come forth from her as perfect images and in turn produce more beings (NHC XI,*3* 51; compare also Burns, 2014, 70–71). The figure of Barbelo is difficult to pin down as she has multiple alternative names, occupies many roles, and has various "avatars" that function as her projections beyond her own aeon (Turner, 2001, 553).

1. Gender

In the Coptic Nag Hammadi Codices (→ Nag Hammadi Writings), Barbelo, whom B. Layton describes as a "stock character" of the gnostic creation myth (Layton, 1987, 15; → Gnosis/Gnosticism), is referred to with the feminine article and pronouns. However, in these treatises Barbelo is not only feminine but includes masculine aspects as well, which is illustrated by her epithets (e.g. "Mother-Father," "First Man," "Triple Male" [II,*1*, 5, 7–8], and "Male Virgin" [XIII,*1* 46, 22]. This might tie into the gnostic idea that androgyny is the archetypical state (Rudolph, 1977, 80; Turner, 2001, 174). The association of the feminine principle with the dyad, however, goes back to Platonic metaphysics (Kalvesmaki, 2013, 57; Turner, 2001, 193). At an early point in the tradition, Barbelo was conceived as both female and male (sometimes having the cognomen "Triple Male Child," for the development of this, see Turner, 2001, 547–548). These characteristics were then developed into two distinct entities, that is, into the Mother, Barbelo, and the Son, Autogenes (Turner, 2001, 174–175). It appears as if the conception of the triad as Father, Mother, and Child underwent changes in the Platonizing Sethian (→ Sethians) treatises, which shift the focus to Barbelo not as mother but as the Intellect (Turner, 2001, 193, 296–297). Presumably under Christian influence, Barbelo and the Father was identified with Christ (e.g. *The Gospel of the Egyptians* and also Irenaeus of Lyon's account). Barbelo is also equated with Ennoia or Protonoia. Sometimes, for example, in the *Eugnostos* (→ *Eugnostos the Blessed*), she is identified with Sophia in her divine state (as opposed to her fallen state; Arthur, 1984, 64–65; Sieber, 1978, vol. II, 788–795). One of the proposed etymologies for the name is "Barba-Elo" (= "The Deity in Four") by W. Harvey, as Barbelo is related to the four principles of intellect, prescience, incorruptibility, and eternal life (Harvey's edition, 1857, of Irenaeus' *Adversus omnes haereses*, 221n02).

2. Barbelo in the Nag Hammadi Codices

Barbelo figures prominently in the *Apocryphon of John* (NHC II,*1*; III,*1*; IV, *1*; BG 8502.2). It contains the Sethian creation myth in which Barbelo is described as the first power and the forethought of the All. The first principle, the Father, contemplates himself so that his Thought in his image comes forth from him. This is the Barbelo who now functions as the Father's female consort. She sets off creation by requesting foreknowledge, indestructibility, and eternal life from the invisible spirit who makes them come forth.

She then conceives Christ, the self-begotten one (= Autogenes), who existed as a divine being before his incarnation (compare NHC II,*1* 4–7). This account is close to the one in the version of the *Apocryphon of John* found in the Coptic Codex Berolinensis 8502 (see for a comparison King, 1988, 161–162).

Barbelo is also mentioned in other Nag Hammadi texts, such as *Allogenes* (→ *Allogenes, Book of*), the *Gospel of the Egyptians*, the *Three Steles of Seth* (→ *Seth, Three Steles of*), *Marsanes*, *Melchizedek*, *Zostrianos*, and once in *Trimorphic Protennoia* (NHC XIII,*1* 38). In *Allogenes* (NHC XI,*3*), Barbelo also has a soteriological aspect as she grants access to salvation through the Thrice-Male child (NHC XI*3* 51; see also Burns, 2014, 92). On his ascent toward the contemplation of the highest levels of existence, the visionary in *Allogenes* passes through the aeon of Barbelo (NHC XI,*3*, 58–59; see also Arthur, 1984, 172; Brakke, 2010, 78–79).

She is also central to the *Gospel of the Egyptians* (NHC III,*2*; IV,*2*). This text describes how the first heavenly beings, Father, Mother Barbelo, and Son, emanate from the Invisible Spirit (NHC III,*2* 41). The second of the *Three Steles of Seth* (NHC VII,*5*) emphasizes her relationship with the highest power opening with the following words: "Great is the first aeon, the male virginal Barbelo, the first glory of the invisible Father, she who is called 'perfect'" (NHC VII,*5* 121, trans. Robinson in the NHLE pp. 398–399). *Marsanes* and *Melchizedek* (NHC X,*4*; IX,*1* 16) mention Barbelo in conjunction with other heavenly beings. She also appears many times in *Zostrianos* (e.g. NHC VIII,*1* 36). The *Thunder* (NHC VI,*2*) refers to Epinoia who also has a soteriological task and is described in a similar language so that T.B. Halvgaard regards her as a different aspect of the same divine entity to which Barbelo also belongs (Halvgaard, 2014, 119–120).

3. Barbelo in Patristic Sources

In patristic texts, she is described by the heresiologist → Irenaeus of Lyon as a never-aging aeon in a virginal spirit to whom, according to the gnostics, the Father manifested himself, creating four beings coming forth from him while she gave birth to three (or four) other beings (Iren. *Haer.* 1.29.1). → Epiphanius of Salamis mentions (Epiph. *Haer.* 25.2–3) that

Barbelo lives in the eighth heaven, was put forth by the Father, and was the mother of Yaldabaoth who considered himself to be the only God, to the dismay of his mother. There might also have been communities specifically devoted to Barbelo. Irenaeus mentions a group he calls the Barbelo Gnostics (Iren. *Haer.* 1.29.1–4) while Epiphanius speaks of the "Barbeliots" or "Borborians" (→ Borboriani) and describes them as worshipping Barbelo but also belonging to a libertine gnostic current (βόρβορος = "filthy one"; Epiph. *Haer.* 25.2–3; 26). These communities were, according to J.D. Turner, at first distinct from Sethianism, but later integrated into it so that extant Sethian texts usually include Barbeloite features as well (Turner, 2001, 257).

Historiography

While there is as of yet no systematic study of Barbelo alone, there are several studies about the female principle in gnostic thought (e.g Arthur, 1984; King, 1988; Halvgaard, 2017). J.H. Sieber studied the specific relationship between Barbelo and Sophia in gnostic texts (e.g. Sieber, 1978). A main source for general information about Barbelo remains J.D. Turner (2001) who devotes large parts of his book to the Barbeloites and the role their teachings played in the development of gnostic Sethianism. In the course of this study, he describes the realm or aeon of Barbelo and the positions Barbelo holds in the divine world according to various treatises.

Bibliography

Arthur, R.H., *The Wisdom Goddess: Feminine Motifs in Eight Nag Hammadi Documents*, Lanham, 1984.
Bergermann, M., & C.F. Collatz, *Epiphanius I: Ancoratus und Panarion Haer*, Berlin, 2013, 1–33.
Brakke, D., *The Gnostics: Myth, Ritual, and Diversity in Early Christianity*, Cambridge MA, 2010.
Burns, D.M., *Apocalypse of the Alien God: Platonism and the Exile of Sethian Gnosticism*, Philadelphia, 2014.
Halvgaard, T.B., *Linguistic Manifestations in the 'Trimorphic Protennoia' and the 'Thunder: Perfect Mind': Analysed Against the Background of Platonic and Stoic Dialectics*. NHMS 91, Leiden, 2014.
Halvgaard, T.B., "Life, Knowledge, and Language in Classic Gnostic Literature: Reconsidering the Role of the Female Spiritual Principle and Epinoia," in: U. Tervahauta, I. Miroshnikov, O. Lehtipuu & I. Dunderberg,

eds., *Women and Knowledge in Early Christianity: FS Antti Marjanen*, Leiden, 2017, 237–252.
Kalvesmaki, J., *The Theology of Arithmetic: Number Symbolism in Platonism and Early Christianity*, Washington DC, 2013.
King, K.L., ed., *Images of the Feminine in Gnosticism*, Philadelphia, 1988.
Layton, B., *The Gnostic Scriptures: A New Translation with Annotations and Introductions*, New York, 1987.
Members of the Coptic Gnostic Library Project of the Institute for Antiquity and Christianity, *The Nag Hammadi Library in English*, San Francisco, 1977.
Rudolph, K., *Gnosis: The Nature and History of Gnosticism*, San Francisco, 1977; ET ed. R.McLachlan Wilson.
Sieber, J.H., "The Barbelo Aeon as Sophia in Zostrianos and Related Tractates," in: B. Layton, ed., *The Rediscovery of Gnosticism*, vol. II, Leiden, 1978, 788–795.
Turner, J.D., & A. McGuire, eds., *The Nag Hammadi Library After Fifty Years: Proceedings of the 1995 Society of Biblical Literature Commemoration*, NHMS 44, Leiden, 1997; esp. M. Waldstein, "The Primal Triad in the Apocryphon of John," 154–187.
Turner, J.D., *Sethian Gnosticism and the Platonic Tradition*. BCNH.É 6, Louvain, 2001.
Wigan Harvey, W., ed., *Irenaeus: Adversus Omnes Haereses*, Cantabrigiae, 1857.

RAMONA TEEPE

Barcelona

Barcino, modern-day Barcelona (Spain), lay on the Mediterranean coast in the northeast of the Iberian Peninsula, between the mouths of the rivers Llobregat and Besòs. There, the Romans founded a small colony with little more than 19 km^2 of urban area, its walls surrounding the gentle hill named Mons Taber (16.9 m above sea level), where there had previously been an Iberian settlement built by the Laietani. There is no agreement on the etymology of the name Barcino, but it is documented on Iberian coins.

1. Romanization and Early Christianity

As part of a major administrative reorganization carried out in the northeast of the Iberian Peninsula, the Colonia Iulia Augusta Faventia Paterna Barcino was founded by → Augustus (c. 15 BCE) to distribute land among some of his veterans. Its creation led to the construction of a new branch of the Via Augusta. In late antiquity, the city walls were refortified, and the city became an episcopal see.

Prudentius (*Peri.* 4.33–34) mentions the veneration of Cucuphas, who was probably martyred in Barcelona in 303/304 CE; according to a 7th-century CE *passio*, he was a native of Scillium (*Pass. Cucuf.* 2.7). Far less reliable are the late translations referring to the martyrs Severus and Eulalia. The latter, possibly the same person as Eulalia of Mérida, was already being venerated in the city in the 7th century CE: a surviving *passio* and an anonymous hymn ("Hymnus de sancta Eulalia") mention that Bishop Quiricus of Barcelona built a monastery next to the martyr's tomb (Fábrega, 1958).

From the 3rd century CE onward, Barcino grew in geopolitical importance, a position it subsequently maintained. Attested since 343 CE, its episcopal see may have already existed for several decades beforehand. In that year, Bishop Praetextatus attended the Council of → Sardica (or Serdica, modern Sofia). The next → bishop mentioned in the city is Pacian, a *clarissimus* (most famous man) with a solid rhetorical and literary education who converted to Christianity as an adult. His son Nummius Aemilianus Dexter held a high office in the eastern administration of the Roman Empire. It is not certain when Pacian was consecrated as a bishop, but, according to → Jerome (*Vir. ill.* 106), he wrote several treatises during his bishopric, one of which, entitled *Cervulus* (now lost), was a homily against the irreverent pagan new year celebrations, in which people dressed up and engaged in debauchery. His surviving works refer to sin and how to combat it: a sermon on baptism, three letters (the third is really a treatise) from his correspondence with the Novatianist Sympronianus, and an exhortation (another homily) to penance (*Paraenesis ad paenitentiam*). Pacian reveals his knowledge of both pagan and Christian authors, and, naturally, also of biblical texts (used in versions that predate the Vulgate). His *Sermo de baptismo* spells out the evil passed on to the sons of Adam (→ Adam and Eve) and the salvation offered by regenerative baptism; its description of fallen man coincides remarkably with the theology of original sin later developed by → Augustine of Hippo. Jerome says that Pacian died as an old man under → Theodosius I. His death can therefore be dated between 379 CE (the start of the Hispanic emperor's reign) and 392 CE, when the catalogue of Jerome's work was published.

Lampius, who attended the First Council of → Toledo (400 CE), is already recorded as the bishop of Barcelona on Dec 25, 393 CE: on this very → Christmas day, and at the behest of the crowd, he ordained Meropius Pontius Paulinus, who agreed to be ordained a presbyter on the condition that he would not be linked to the church of Barcelona; he later became bishop of Nola. Paulinus and his wife, Therasia, probably travelled to Italy in the company of Vigilantius, a native of Comminges who was presbyter of a church in Barcelona. As a *clientulus* of Paulinus, Vigilantius was entrusted with a letter for Jerome and with a panegyric composed by Paulinus in honor of Theodosius I, as well as with the task of handing out donations from his *patroni* in Jerusalem. There is no record of the name of the Catholic bishop of Barcino at the time of Sigesarius, the Arian Goth bishop who had baptized the usurper Priscus Attalus (409 CE) and accompanied Ataulf's army and Aelia Galla Placidia during their arrival and short-lived stay in the city (414/415 CE). There, Sigesarius tutored Ataulf's three children from his first wife. The next recorded bishop of Barcino is Nundinarius, who, at some time before November 19, 465 CE, and with the consent of → Metropolitan Ascanius and other bishops from his province, ordained Irenaeus a bishop in a municipality (in all probability Egara) that had always been a diocese of Barcino. He also left instructions that Irenaeus was to succeed him in the see of Barcino. After receiving varying advice from Tarraconensis (Tarragona), Pope Hilary opposed this succession and ordered Irenaeus to leave Barcino and return to his original see; if he refused, he would be deposed (Vilella, 2002b, 338–344).

2. Roman Decline and Visigothic Centuries

Barcino probably became the capital of the usurper Maximus between 410 CE and 411 CE (Gurt & Godoy, 2000, 436–439). Some years later in Narbonne, Ataulf, now king of the Visigoths, married Aelia Galla Placidia (daughter of Roman emperor Theodosius I), who had been taken as a hostage by → Alaric I during the siege of Rome (410 CE). After being expelled from Narbonne by troops loyal to Honorius, Ataulf, accompanied by his wife, was forced to retreat southward and set up base in Barcino in 414/415 CE. During Ataulf and Placidia's brief stay in the city, their only child died and the king was murdered (Olymp. *Frag.* 26).

During the Arian Visigothic period (which ended with the Third Council of Toledo, in 589 CE), Catholic and Arian ecclesiastics coexisted side by side in Barcino (where King Amalaric perished at the hands of the Franks inside a church). Agricius subscribed to both the Council of Tarragona (Nov 6, 516 CE) and the Council of Gerona (Jun 8, 517 CE). Nibridius attended the First Council of Barcelona (held at some time before 546 CE). Paternus subscribed to the Council of Lérida (Aug 6, 546 CE). We only have records of one Arian bishop of Barcino, Ugnas: having become a Catholic, he subscribed to the Third Council of Toledo and the Second Council of Barcelona, in 599 CE. Barcino might not have had a Catholic bishop in Ugnas' time, a possibility supported by the fact that the Third Council of Toledo was not attended by any Catholic bishop of Barcino (whereas it was attended by two bishops of Tortosa, one Arian and one Catholic), but also by the fact that Liuvigild banished John of Bíclaro to Barcelona for refusing to profess the Arian creed and that the Catholic councils were discontinued before 589 CE.

We have somewhat more detailed records of bishops of Barcelona from the Catholic Visigoth kingdom. Emila subscribed to Gundemar's decree in 610 CE and, four years later, the Council of Egara. Severus (who was appointed by King Sisebut to oversee the Barcelona see) was represented by his presbyter Iohannes at the Fourth Council of Toledo (633 CE). Oya subscribed to the following two Councils of Toledo (636 CE and 638 CE). Quiricus attended the Tenth Council of Toledo (656 CE); he sent his friend Taius of Zaragoza an epistle successfully urging him to publish his *Sententiae* and also wrote letters to Ildefonsus of Toledo to thank him for sending him a copy of *De virginitate perpetua beatae Mariae*, dedicated to Quiricus, and to urge him to comment on biblical books. Idalius was represented at the 13th Council of Toledo (683 CE) by his deacon Laulfus and attended the 15th Council of Toledo (688 CE) in person; he was on friendly terms with Julian of Toledo (who dedicated his *Prognosticum futuri saeculi* to him) and Suniefredus, metropolitan

of Narbonne. Laulfus (probably Idalius' representative at the 13th Council of Toledo) subscribed to the 16th Council of Toledo (693 CE). Barcino was conquered by the Muslims in 714 CE and reconquered in 801 CE by Louis the Pious, who established a line of Carolingian bishops who gradually replaced the old Visigothic rites with Latin ones.

3. Christian Archaeology and Topography

From the Christian Roman Empire onward, and with the progressive Christianization of society, time, and space, and the subsequent new urban monumentalization (phenomena that outlived imperial decline), the bishop became not only the main figure of reference in religious matters, but also the chief civil authority. The bishops of Barcino managed to raise the city to the status of one of the leading metropolises on the eastern Iberian Peninsula, as made clear by the range and spectacular nature of the remains of the episcopal complex from late antiquity (a good example of what has been called "the architecture of power"), above all if we compare them with the meager, fragile civil architecture in the city during the same period.

As the chief example of Christian architecture in the city, this episcopal complex within the city walls features a collection of structures dating from the 4th century CE and expanded throughout late antiquity. The main remains include a baptistery with an octagonal floor plan, a cruciform chapel, a reception hall, the episcopal *palatium*, and private baths (Beltrán de Heredia, 2013, 30–41). However, the cathedral church has yet to be found; it probably lies beneath the current cathedral, the same site (turned into a mosque during the Muslim occupation) as the Romanesque cathedral.

Also within the walls, recently excavated remains beneath the Church of Saint Justus and Saint Pastor have been attributed to a basilica and a baptismal pool dating from the 6th century CE, which have been interpreted (relying strictly on the described data) as forming part of a second episcopal complex created as a result of the Catholic bishop's "movement" by the Arian bishop (Beltrán de Heredia, 2013, 26–27). The Church of Saint Michael (dating back to the 5th cent. CE, but today lost), finally, was built by reusing parts of the city's public baths (Sales, 2011a, 33).

Outside the walls, Barcino housed the tomb of Cucuphas, almost certainly on the enclosed site where the Church of Sant Cugat del Rec has been recorded since the 10th century. Here and in the surrounding area lies a very extensive necropolis from late antiquity that should be set in the context of the martyr's more primitive funerary church erected in honor of the local saint.

In addition to the archaeological remains linked to the martyrdom of Saint Cucuphas, but not continuous with them, there are also other funerary structures of a Christian nature outside the walls, specifically at the Mercat de Santa Caterina and the Plaça d'Antoni Maura. These include a suburban basilica, containing a splendid Christian funerary mosaic dated to the early 5th century CE: it boasts a large central monogram of Christ of extraordinary artistic quality, dominated by the color purple. This remarkable tombstone has been linked to the tomb of a martyr or a local bishop, or even to the episode in Olympiodorus of Thebes' *Fragmenta* that speaks of the huge funeral for Ataulf and Placidia's son in a church outside the city walls (Sales, 2011a, 34–36).

There is also evidence of other suburban basilicas. There might have been one in the ground beneath Santa Maria del Mar, where, according to the "Hymnus de sancta Eulalia," Bishop Quiricus built a monastery next to the saint's tomb. On this spot (where an extensive necropolis [4th–7th cents. CE] has been found), there was probably an amphitheater during the Roman Empire (Sales, 2011b, 61–74). There might have been another basilica on the grounds of the medieval Monastery of Sant Pau del Camp, where a Christianized Roman villa is recorded. Santa Maria del Pi (at one of the main thoroughfares out of the city) might also have been the site of a funerary basilica.

This archaeological data, added to the information supplied by written sources, makes it possible to say that Barcino (at least from the mid-4th cent. CE) had an outstanding Christian civic structure in place, along with a skyline that began to take shape in the 5th century CE and developed quite remarkably in the 6th and 7th centuries CE (Sales, 2014). Furthermore, it is important to note the coexistence of Catholic and Arian basilicas in the 5th and, above all, in the 6th century CE.

4. Councils

At least two councils were held in the city, both provincial in scope. The minutes of the First Council of Barcelona are not included in the Colección Canónica Hispana, only in the Codex Aemilianensis and the Epítome Hispano, and these reviews do not give the date on which they were held. As a result, they can only be vaguely dated by comparing the names of the bishops who attended them with those who subscribed to the Council of Lérida, dated to Aug 6, 546 CE. Based on this comparison, and bearing in mind the order in which the names appear at both councils, the First Council of Barcelona seems to have taken place some years before the Council of Lérida, although it is impossible to be more precise: the date traditionally attached to this episcopal assembly (540 CE) is only hypothetical. Meeting under the presidency of Metropolitan Sergius of Tarragona, assisted by seven prelates, its ten canons dealt with aspects linked to reciting the 50th psalm, blessing the faithful at matins, clerics' hair and beards, the → deacon's position before the presbyter (→ Priest/Presbyter), presbyters' prayers before the bishop, penitents (→ Penitence/Penance), administering the viaticum, and monks' observance of the provisions of the Council of → Chalcedon.

Recorded only in the Codex Aemilianensis, the Second Council of Barcelona, also provincial in scope, was held at the Church of the Holy Cross on Nov 1, 599 CE, under the presidency of Asiaticus of Tarragona assisted by 12 bishops, including the host, the former Arian Ugnas. In addition to passing rules against simoniacal practices and forbidding marriage between penitents and virgins, this synod also legislated on matters related to the appointment of bishops, by requiring the times stipulated by ecclesiastical law to be respected. Likewise, it reveals the promotion of bishops *per sacra regalia*, a procedure that had not been previously recorded on the Iberian Peninsula. This form was maintained: a letter from Sisebut to Eusebius of Tarragona (Asiaticus' successor) urged the metropolitan to give his canonical consent to the ordination of the monarch's candidate at the see of Barcino.

Following the Third Council of Toledo, regular annual Catholic synods were once again held in the provinces of the Visigothic kingdom, after being interrupted during the period preceding the great religious-political unification. As stipulated in canon 18, these councils were also to be attended by tax authorities, so that, in accordance with and under the control of the bishops, they could set the corresponding tax rates for the year and district in question, thus consolidating the understanding reached between the Catholic Church and the Visigothic monarchy. This is made clear in the *Epistula de fisco Barcinonensi*, a document written seven years before the Second Council of Barcelona and aimed at the *numerarii* of Barcino, in which the bishops gave their consent to a certain tax and banned any attempt to increase it. Dated three days after the start of the Second Council of Zaragoza (Nov 1, 592 CE), also provincial in scope, this epistle was signed by the bishops of Tarraconensis whose dioceses answered to the treasury of Barcino when it came to tax matters pertaining to the eastern or coastal part of this province.

Historiography

The earliest indications of Christian archaeology in Barcelona date back to the 16th century, in particular to the attempted finding of the body of Saint Pacian, second documented bishop of Barcelona in the late 4th century CE. The subsoil of the Church of Saints Justus and Pastor was excavated in 1590 – a pioneering but ultimately fruitless task. These early studies in Christian archaeology also focused on the legends of Eulalia of Barcelona – following an *inventio* of the saint's body in the 9th century CE, the actual authenticity of a Barcelona-Roman martyr was much debated until the works of À. Fàbrega Grau in the middle 20th century proved that it was, in fact, a splitting of Eulalia of Mérida, who in any event was also worshipped in late antiquity Barcelona (as evidenced by the 7th century CE hymn "Fulget hic honor sepulchri," signed by Bishop Quiricus).

During the first half and late quarter of the 20th centuries, the pioneering archaeological efforts of A. Duran i Sanpere in Roman *Barcino* gave way to a modern Christian archaeology of the city. In recent decades, the team of the Museu d'Història de la Ciutat has led excavations and investigations in the earliest Christian *Barcinona*. This was followed by a much credited summary work in 2001, which shed a light on the birth and evolution of Barcelona's ancient episcopal group (Beltrán de Heredia, 2001). New data constantly arises along with urban construction, which awaits systematization and a corresponding update within a single volume.

Bibliography

Beltrán de Heredia, J., *De Barcino a Barcinona (siglos I–VII): Los restos arqueológicos de la plaza del Rey de Barcelona*, Barcelona, 2001.

Beltrán de Heredia, J., "Barcino, de colònia romana a sede regia visigoda, medina islàmica i ciutat comtal: Una urbs en transformació," *QAHB* 9, 2013, 17–118.

Bonnet, C., & J. Beltrán de Heredia, "Nouveau regard sur le groupe épiscopal de Barcelone," *RivAC* 80, 2004, 137–158.

Fábrega Grau, Á., *Santa Eulalia de Barcelona: Revisión de un problema histórico*, Rome, 1958.

Granado, C., *Pacien de Barcelone: Écrits: Introduction, texte critique, commentaire et index*, SC 410, Paris, 1995.

Gurt Esparreguera, J.M., & C. Godoy Fernández, "Barcino, de sede imperial a urbs regia en época visigoda," in: G. Ripoll López & J.M. Gurt Esparreguera, eds., *Sedes regiae (ann. 400–800)*, Barcelona, 2000, 425–466.

Mundó Marcet, A.M., "El fisc reial a Barcelona al final del segle VI," in: A.M. Mundó, *Obre completes*, Barcelona, 1998, 54–56.

Sales Carbonell, J., *Arqueologia de les seus episcopals tardoantigues al territori català (259–713)*, Barcelona, 2011a.

Sales Carbonell, J., "Santa María de las Arenas, Santa María del Mar y el anfiteatro romano de Barcelona," *RAP* 21, 2011b, 61–74.

Sales Carbonell, J., "El skyline cristiano de Barcino en el siglo VI," in: *Bárbaros en la ciudad tardoantigua: Presencias y ausencias en los espacios públicos y privados: Romania Gothica IV (Barcelona, November 2010)*, Bologna, 2014.

Vilella Masana, J., "Las iglesias y las cristiandades hispanas: Panorama prosopográfico," in: R. Teja, ed., *La Hispania del siglo IV: Administración, economía, sociedad, cristianización*, Bari, 2002a, 117–159.

Vilella Masana, J., "Los concilios eclesiásticos de la Tarraconensis durante el siglo V," *Flor.* 13, 2002b, 327–344.

Vilella Masana, J., "Los concilios eclesiásticos hispanos del período visigodo-arriano: Análisis histórico-prosopográfico," *MP* 25, 2008, 1–47.

Vilella Masana, J., "Introduzione," in: F. Gori, *I canoni dei concili della chiesa antica*, vol. II: *I concili latini*, part 3: *I concili spagnoli*, Rome, 2013, 7–31 (= SEAug 137).

JORDINA SALES-CARBONELL
JOSEP VILELLA MASANA

Bardaisan

Bardaisan (154–222 CE) was a Christian philosopher and theologian. His interests embraced astronomy, archery, ethnography, geography, music, history, literature (including Christian "apocrypha"), poetry, and allegoresis. He was a friend of Abgar the Great (king of Edessa; → Abgarids), with whom he had been educated in the Greco-Roman *paideia*, and a dignitary at his court. According to → Eusebius of Caesarea (*Hist. eccl.* 4.30), Bardaisan's work *Against Fate* was dedicated to a Roman emperor, "Antoninus." Julius Africanus, the Christian chronographer who corresponded with → Origen, witnessed his prowess as an archer (Afric. *Kes.* 1.20). A Christian church existed in Edessa at that time, and according to the *Book of the Laws of Countries* stemming from Bardaisan's school, Abgar himself was a Christian (Ramelli, 1999a; 1999b; 2004).

Ancient heresiologists labeled Bardaisan a heretic, associating him with Valentinianism (→ Valentinus/Valentinians), Marcionism (→ Marcion/Marcionites/Marcionism), and Manichaeism (→ Mani/Manichaeism). However, he opposed Marcionism, while Manichaeism only spread after his lifetime; he was no "gnostic" either (Ramelli, 2009a; 2021a). That he was indeed a Christian is demonstrated by the use of "us Christians" in *BLC* 15, in quotations from the New Testament in the *Book of the Laws of Countries* and elsewhere, and in authentic fragments preserved by → Porphyry of Tyre, → Ephrem the Syrian, and the "cosmological traditions" that highlight the role of Christ-*logos* as creator and savior with his cross. Bardaisan's thought was based on biblical exegesis in the light of Greek philosophy, especially → Middle Platonism. This had already been done by → Philo of Alexandria, and later by Origen, Bardaisan's semi-contemporary, who displays impressive similarities with Bardaisan's thought (Ramelli, 2009, 135–168; 2009a passim; 2015, chs. 3–4; 2018). Along with → Clement of Alexandria and Origen, Bardaisan produced one of the first syntheses of Greek philosophical traditions and Christianity. Bardaisan, like Origen, played a key role in lending Christianity a philosophical and cultural credibility (Ramelli, 2015a). As Christian philosophers, they were both theologians and philosophers – Bardaisan a "Middle Platonist," Origen a Middle/Neoplatonist; both were also influenced by Stoicism.

Bardaisan and his disciples knew Greek and Syriac; according to Eusebius, the latter translated his works from Syriac into Greek. Bardaisan's school in Edessa was a Christian philosophical and theological – possibly also exegetical and scientific – "school" that was independent of ecclesiastical institutions. Similar schools were those of Justin in Rome (whose disciple Tatian, the author of the *Diatessaron*, was probably known to Bardaisan), Pantaenus and Clement (and possibly Ammonius Saccas) in Alexandria, and Origen in Alexandria and Caesarea.

The *Book of the Laws of Countries* reflects Bardaisan's ideas and likely his work *Against Fate* (Drijvers, 1966–2014; Ramelli, 2009a, 70–107; forthcoming, introduction). The *Book of the Laws of Countries* is modeled after Plato's dialogues, even with precise verbal echoes, and its protagonists, Bardaisan's disciples, are Christians, apart perhaps from Awida, Bardaisan's critical interlocutor, who might be a pagan or a Marcionite. Anti-Gnosticism, anti-Marcionism, and the concern for theodicy are paramount in Bardaisan's thought and manifest in the *Book of the Laws of Countries*. The latter can be methodically compared with two fragments preserved by Porphyry (*Frgm.* 376; Smith, 1993; literal quotations from Bardaisan's *On India* with Christological, cosmological, anthropological, and metaphysical doctrines) and other nominal quotations in Ephrem and the cosmological traditions, and Eusebius' literal quotations from Bardaisan's *Against Fate* in *Praeparatio Evangelica*. I. Ramelli (2009a, 70–107 passim) demonstrates that this comparison points to the trustworthiness of the *Book of the Laws of Countries* for the reconstruction of Bardaisan's ideas. Moreover, if the *Book of the Laws of Countries* were – as G. Levi (1921) and T. Jansma (1969) supposed – a mitigation of Bardaisan's heretical doctrines aimed at construing him as orthodox, then fate would have been entirely eliminated from it. But fate is kept there, albeit as subject to God. Thus, → Diodore of Tarsus criticized Bardaisan for maintaining fate, instead of removing it even in name. I. Ramelli (2009a; 2009b; 2015) contributes to the critical evaluation of the reliability of the sources on Bardaisan, their comparative analysis, the assessment of the convergences which she points out between Bardaisan and Origen, the importance of Bardaisan's fragments preserved by Porphyry, and Platonic, Middle Platonic, and Stoic elements in Bardaisan's thought (there was reciprocal influence between Stoicism and Middle Platonism, and both systems are reflected in Jewish and Christian authors such as Philo, Clement, Origen, and Bardaisan).

At the end of the *Book of the Laws of Countries* (section 16, Ramelli, 2009b), Bardaisan, like Origen at many points in his oeuvre, supports the doctrine of apocatastasis or restoration of all rational creatures to God, the "good," after their fall and detachment from the good, by means of purification, instruction, persuasion, and conversion (Ramelli, 2009, 135–168; 2015; endorsed by Crone, 2012). Bardaisan and Origen are the first explicit supporters of this doctrine. → *Apokatastasis* is enabled by the eradication of → evil – a state of weakness and nonbeing in which no creature can remain forever – and the triumph of God's providence, which respects rational creatures' free will but brings them to salvation. Both Bardaisan and Origen connected their defense of free will and their polemic against the separation of God's justice and goodness with the eventual apocatastasis (Ramelli, 2001; 2009). Indeed, they both grounded apocatastasis in their anti-gnostic, anti-astrological, and anti-Marcionite theory of free will. Bardaisan, in the *Book of the Laws of Countries* (section 16, Ramelli, 2009b), theorizes on apocatastasis just after refuting Marcionism, Valentinian predestinationism, and astrological determinism, and after arguing that God is both good and just and has gifted rational creatures with a free will. The same line of reasoning, from the refutation of Marcionism and gnostic determinism to the theorization of apocatastasis, is clear in Origen, especially in Or. *Princ.* 3 (Ramelli, 2013, 110–119, 137–215). Both Origen and Bardaisan consider apocatastasis to depend on Christ; they also shared a lack of enthusiasm for apocalypticism (→ Apocalypse), precisely because they embraced universal restoration (Ramelli, 2009).

Bardaisan and Origen shared many ideas and unfounded accusations (such as those of being gnostics and denying the resurrection). Many sources concerning Bardaisan describe him as a heretic, but,

interestingly, the most favorable and best informed stem from Origenian authors (Ramelli, 2009a, 46–62, 131–138, 164–172, 262–266, 379–381). Bardaisan and Origen shared metaphysical monism and the ontological non-subsistence of evil; both were inclined to Socratic-Platonic and Stoic ethical intellectualism; both built upon the notions of Christ-*logos*/wisdom/power; both shared the "theology of the image" and a good deal of → anthropology, → protology, and eschatology (→ Apocalypse); and both privileged the allegorical exegesis of Scripture and its interpretation in the light of philosophy. There may have been a relationship between Bardaisan and Origen, and/or their schools.

In his *Book of Domnus*, Bardaisan probably referred to Middle Platonic ideas (Ramelli, 2009a, 32–38). Among creatures, there is nothing incorporeal (only God is, as Origen also thought); human ideas are abstractions and can be deemed audible words, unlike God's Ideas, which have ontological consistency in God's mind, that is, Christ-*logos*-wisdom (Ramelli, 2021c; forthcoming, ch. 4). Middle Platonism also lurks in Bardaisan's cosmological fragments (one preserved word for word by Porph. *Frgm.* 376; Smith, 1993) and literal quotes in the so-called cosmological traditions, later Syriac or Arabic quotations or paraphrases of Bardaisan's cosmological doctrines, all analyzed by I. Ramelli (2009a, 314–355). The ontological non-subsistence of evil entails not only its eviction at apocatastasis, but also its negative nature and accidental origin, as is clear from the "cosmological traditions": an initial "incident" or "accidental happening" brought about disorder among the existing "beings" (creatures of God) and determined their invasion by darkness-evil. Hence their appeal to God and the intervention of Christ-*logos* who arranged the beings, saved them from darkness, and created this world.

Both Bardaisan and Origen drew inspiration from Plato's *Timaeus*, both posited creatures prior to the creation of this world, and both Christianized fate as the expression of God's providence administered by stars, which may signify but do not determine anything. Both upheld the intellect/soul/body tripartition. Like Origen, Bardaisan studied, and probably taught, Greek culture and philosophy besides theology, but in the service of Christian faith. He deemed faith necessary for knowledge. Their theology of Christ-*logos* (the "Word of thought"), the cosmic Christ, and the mystery of the → cross are similar. Both valued instruction over constriction (Ramelli, forthcoming, ch. 3). Bardaisan and Origen regarded Christ-*logos*-wisdom as the seat of the ideas or *logoi*, the "archetypes" of beings, and the agent of creation. Bardaisan's image of decorations representing, as paradigms, all creatures on the body of Christ-*logos* has a perfect parallel in Origen's conception of the paradigms of creatures that were found at the beginning as decorations on the body of Christ-*logos*-wisdom. For both Bardaisan and Origen, Christ has two functions in creation: efficient and noetic cause.

Historiography

After the edition by F. Nau and T. Nöldeke (1907) and the Italian translation and study by G. Levi della Vida (1921), a great impulse to the study of Bardaisan was given by H.J.W. Drijvers with the first scientific, and quite balanced, English monograph and a translation (1965; 1966, with the important and updated new edition, 2014). T. Jansma (1969), like G. Levi della Vida (1921), deemed the *Book of the Laws of Countries* a mitigation of Bardaisan's heretical doctrines aimed at construing him as orthodox. I. Ramelli (1999b; 2001; 2009a; 2009b; 2018; 2021; 2022a; forthcoming) has contributed to the critical evaluation of the reliability of the sources on Bardaisan, their comparative analysis, the assessment of the convergences she points out between Bardaisan and Origen, the importance of Bardaisan's fragments preserved by Porphyry, and Platonic, Middle Platonic, and Stoic elements in Bardaisan's thought.

P. Crone (2012) and many other scholars accepted I. Ramelli's perspective. Recently, Bardaisan has also been assessed as one of the first supporters of the doctrine of apocatastasis (Ramelli, 2009; 2013; 2018), what had escaped scholars so far. All Middle Platonists, pagans and Christians (including Clement and Origen), as well as Jewish (Philo), absorbed much of Stoicism, especially on the ethical plane. They indeed display Platonic metaphysics and Stoicizing ethics. So, it is not surprising to find Stoic ethical elements in Bardaisan, especially in the *Book of the Laws of Countries* (elements highlighted by Robertson, 2017), which reflects Bardaisan's

anti-deterministic arguments, the same that were supported by Origen and the Origenian tradition.

Bibliography

Crone, P., "Daysanis," in: *EncIS*, Leiden, [3]2012, 116–118.

Drijvers, H.J.W., ed., The *Book of the Laws of Countries*, Assen, 1965, [2]2006.

Drijvers, H.J.W., *Bardaiṣan of Edessa*, Assen, 1966; new ed. introd. J.W. Drijvers, Piscataway, 2014

Jansma, T., *Natuur, lot en vrijheid*, Wageningen, 1969 (Dutch).

Levi della Vida, G., *Il dialogo delle leggi dei paesi*, Rome, 1921.

Nau, F., & T. Nöldeke, eds., *Bardesanes: Liber Legum Regionum*, Paris, 1907.

Ramelli, I., "Edessa e i Romani tra Augusto e i Severi," *Aevum* 73, 1999a, 107–143.

Ramelli, I., "Linee generali per una presentazione e un commento del *Liber legum regionum*," *RIL* 133, 1999b, 311–355.

Ramelli, I., "Bardesane e la sua scuola tra la cultura occidentale e quella orientale: Il lessico della libertà nel *Liber legum regionum*," in: R.B. Finazzi & A. Valvo, eds., *Pensiero e istituzioni del mondo classico nelle culture del vicino oriente*, Alessandria, 2001, 237–255.

Ramelli, I., "Abgar Ukkama e Abgar il Grande alla luce di recenti apporti storiografici," *Aevum* 78, 2004, 103–108.

Ramelli, I., "Origen, Bardaisan, and the Origin of Universal Salvation," *HThR* 102, 2009, 135–168.

Ramelli, I., *Bardaisan of Edessa: A Reassessment of the Evidence and a New Interpretation, Also in the Light of Origen and the Original Fragments from De India*, Piscataway, 2009a; Berlin, 2019.

Ramelli, I., *Bardesane di Edessa contro il Fato, Κατὰ Εἱμαρμένης/Liber legum regionum*, Rome, 2009b.

Ramelli, I., *The Christian Doctrine of Apokatastasis: A Critical Assessment from the New Testament to Eriugena*, Leiden, 2013.

Ramelli, I., "Ethos and Logos: A Second-Century Apologetical Debate between 'Pagan' and Christian Philosophers," *VigChr* 69, 2015, 123–156.

Ramelli, I., "Bardaisan of Edessa, Origen, and Imperial Philosophy: A Middle Platonic Context?" *ARAM* 30, 2018, 1–30.

Ramelli, I., "The Logos/Nous One-Many Between 'Pagan' and Christian Platonism: Bardaisan, Clement, Origen, Plotinus, and Nyssen," *SP* 102, 2021, 11–44.

Ramelli, I., "Bardaisan: A Gnostic or a Polemicist Against Gnostic Tenets?" *ARAM* 33, 2021a, 1–25.

Ramelli, I., "The Reception of Paul's Nous in the Christian Platonism of Bardaisan, Origen and Evagrius," in: J. Frey & M. Nägele, eds., *Der νοῦς bei Paulus im Horizont griechischer und hellenistisch-jüdischer Anthropologie*, Tübingen, 2021b, 279–316.

Ramelli, I., "The Body of Christ as Imperishable Wood: Hippolytus and Bardaisan of Edessa's Complex Christology," in: E. Vergani, ed., *12th Symposium Syriacum 2016*, Rome, 2022a, 1–33.

Ramelli, I., "Fate and Freewill in Bardaisan of Edessa as a Background to Muslim Debates: Theodore Abu Qurra," in: P. Tarras & F. Jaecker, eds., *Free Will in Christian Arabic Thought*, Leiden 2022b.

Ramelli, I., ed., *Bardaisan on Free Will, Fate, and Human Nature: The Book of the Laws of Countries*, Tübingen, forthcoming.

Robertson, P., "Greco-Roman Ethical-Philosophical Influences in Bardaisan's *Book of the Laws of Countries*," *VigChr* 71, 2017, 511–540.

Smith, A., *Porphyrii philosophi fragmenta*, Stuttgart, 1993.

ILARIA L.E. RAMELLI

Barnabas

I. Barnabas ♦ II. *Barnabas, Epistle of*

I. Barnabas

One of the prominent leaders of the first community in Jerusalem, Barnabas was overshadowed by his second-in-command Paul and by the overwhelming figure of Peter. But eventually, his homeland, Cyprus, enabled him to regain prominence.

1. Notable in the First Community of Jerusalem

Barnabas makes his first appearance in the Acts of the Apostles when he gives the proceeds of the sale of a field to the apostles. Acts 4:36–37 provides further explanations: he has a double name, Joseph and Barnabas; he is a Levite; he is a Cypriote. If Joseph was one of the most frequent Jewish names at that point – we know of 523 people named Joseph in antiquity (Ilan, Ziem & Hünefeld, 2002–2010) – Barnabas is a little mystery (Öhler, 2003, 139–167). The author of Acts provides a wrong etymology to his reader: one should read Barnabas as "the son of encouragement," whereas the only nearest Aramaic word is *nebuha*, "prophecy." Is his true name Βαρνεβοῦς, "the Son of Nabu" from a Palmyrenian God? Has the author confused him with another disciple, Manaen, a name that also means

"encouragement"? Did he ironically suggest that the given money was an encouragement for the apostles? In any event, obviously Barnabas comes from a wealthy Levite family that emigrated to Cyprus like many Jews (Mitford, 1980). His selling of the field complies with the communitarian program of property sharing. And he serves as a model of the servant benefactor, in opposition to the countermodel of Ananias and Saphira (Acts 5:1–11).

After this coup d'éclat, Barnabas begins to wield influence on the early communities of Jerusalem and Antioch. In Acts 9:27 Barnabas seizes Paul (→ Paul the Apostle) to lead him to the apostles. In their presence, he has enough prominence to go beyond the prejudices aroused by Paul's past and defend him. His prestige is great enough to be the legate of the Jerusalem Church during the formation of the community of Antioch (Acts 11:19–24). And his Cypriot origin approves him as an emissary besides his stature, as Luke records: he is a man of weight "full of the Holy Spirit," a label already given to Stephen.

Afterward, Barnabas stands tall among the leaders at Antioch. Not only does Barnabas regain his role as mentor to Paul, but he also assumes credit for the success of Antioch's preaching. Barnabas and Saul are sent as ambassadors to Jerusalem, in charge of bringing the subsidies of the community of Antioch (Acts 11:29). Barnabas, already a model of generosity in the Church of Jerusalem, confirms his status. A few years later, he is dispatched to strengthen the ties between Antioch and his home island, Cyprus. This trip is often presented as Paul's "first missionary journey," but the precise reading shows that Barnabas is actually the leader of the small group since he is first named by the Holy Spirit (Acts 13:2).

2. Disappearance of Barnabas

If the "Cyprus operation" marks the peak of Barnabas' influence, it also begins its decline. Two explanations demonstrate this.

The reader realizes first a change in leadership. The trial before Sergius Paulus becomes favorable to Paul and damaging to Elymas but also, to some extent, to Barnabas (Acts 13:6–12). The proconsul's conversion gives Paul a distinct advantage and a new status that Luke (→ Luke, Gospel of) expresses through the systematic use of the name of Paul, and above all from now on Luke quotes Paul first. This new leadership effects first extension of the mission. Inexplicably, the two friends leave for Pamphylia. Little by little relations reverse. It is now Paul who guides the mission: he makes important speeches at Antioch of Pisidia (Acts 13:16–41), cures the infirm of Lystres (Acts 14: 8–11), gains missionary stature, and increases his personal charisma. Besides, Paul could have enjoyed the support of the powerful Sergius Paulus (Pervo, 2009, 324–325). The change of his name might suggest that Paul would have placed himself under his protection.

The departure for Pamphylia from the orb of Antioch marks changes in the hierarchical relationship, at least in the Lukan narrative. In other words, Paul's decision to leave the Antiochian network gives him the stature of an prominent apostle, more important than Barnabas his mentor.

The second explanation for the loss of authority granted to Barnabas may be the difficulty he experienced to preserve his position at Antioch. The Antiochian community in these years has a new leader, Peter (→ Peter the Apostle). Not only the liturgical feast in his honor (the chair of Peter at Antioch) but also the historical reception of the figure Peter in the Syrian regions (Bockmühl, 2003) confirm his prominence. Until now, Barnabas remained a bridge between Jerusalem and Antioch; between the Judean tendency of James close to the Temple and a diasporic party, prone to free the access of the non-Jews to the community. But with the presence of Peter – whose legitimacy was established during the lifetime of Jesus, the posture of Barnabas was no longer of any interest.

In Luke's account, not only Barnabas but also Peter himself disappears. This double disappearance affronts the historian with a question: is it only the result of Luke's ideological choice, and who takes Paul's side? Does it hint at a broader upheaval leading to the end of the middle position carried by the first community and progressively marginalize Christianity's Jewish origin (Robinson, 2009; Zetterholm, 2001; 2005)?

The reception history of the figure of Barnabas in the Syro-Alexandrian region confirms this memory of a middle way. The *Epistle of Barnabas* contains polemics against a group promoting a restrictive interpretation of the law (perhaps close to a Judean milieu), turning the law into an idol (Hvalvik, 1996). It is no surprise that some church fathers (→ Origen, → Jerome, and above all → Clement of Alexandria) and some excellent manuscripts assigned this position to the apostle. In a collective memory, Barnabas remained the representative of this position of equilibrium.

Varied versions of the Pseudo-Clementine novel (→ Clementine Literature, Pseudo-) allude to Barnabas. These writings came originally from the Syrian region and connect to the reception history of the figure of Barnabas in his church of origin, Antioch. The memory of his eminent role has not disappeared: in this violent anti-Pauline writing, the apostle fights for the truth. The *Recognitions* preserve his role as a bridge between two worlds. As a *natione hebræus*, he was the first Christian to meet the hero of the book, Clement, in Rome (*Ps.-Clem. R* 1.6–10). Barnabas is the first to preach the gospel in the city, and the first to fascinate Clement, who recognizes in him an example of simplicity of good quality (*Ps.-Clem. R* 1.7.15). Barnabas presented him afterward to Peter. The Pseudo-Clementine novel recombines the characters of primitive Christianity and rewrites a story in which Paul has no place (Burnet, 2008). Barnabas thus receives some of Paul's features, for instance the power to resist the confrontation with the intelligentsia (see Acts 17:22–34) or to oppose the pagans (see Acts 17:19). But at the same time, Barnabas remains Barnabas: the one who introduces the disciples to Jerusalem (Acts 9:27). The *Homilies*, another version of the text, are more discreet about the apostle. They do not name the preacher whom Clement meets in Rome, nor mention the great gathering in Jerusalem. Barnabas confined himself to his role of a go-between: he meets him in Alexandria and keeps the role of introducer of Clement to Peter, who always referred to him as "the herald of the Truth" (*Ps.-Clem. H* 1.16). The liturgical sources in the East preserve this notable tradition of Barnabas' evangelization of Alexandria, and the menology of Basil II proves it.

3. The Apostle of Cyprus

The Acts of the Apostles left Barnabas on his way to the island of Cyprus, and thus the resulting claim of the Cypriotes to their native apostle is no surprise. It happened somewhat late, during the quarrels with

Antioch about the autocephaly of the Island. A council in Constantinople settled the question, perhaps in 488 CE. While on their departure to sail to the metropole of Syria, the bishops of the island discovered the body of Barnabas bearing the Gospel of Matthew on his chest. Thanks to this "timely" invention of relics, Anthemius, the bishop of Cyprus, could take the precious corpse to Constantinople and proclaim the autocephaly of his church because of its apostolic foundation. This episode shows that Barnabas held enough authority in the 5th century CE to legitimize the independence of a local church.

Two books justify this apostolic tradition: the *Acts of Barnabas* (*BHG* 225) and the *Eulogy of Barnabas* of the monk Alexander (*BHG* 226 = *CPG* 7.400). The two of them differ about the destiny of the apostle's body. For *Acts*, Barnabas was cremated and only a box remained, while for the *Laudatio*, his whole body was found. This difference can be explained in two ways. First, the writing of the *Acts of Barnabas* precedes the discovery (and, so to speak, perhaps gave the idea of "inventing" Barnabas) meaning that it dates before 488 CE. Second, there could be two discoveries (an ashes box with the Gospel and a body), and the writing of *Acts of Barnabas* predates the official version of 530 CE.

The *Acts of Barnabas* (Lipsius, 1883, 292–302 for the text) presents itself as a text written by John Mark in two parts. The first one (chs. 1–9) tries to explain the dispute that led Paul and Barnabas to separate. A psychological reason explains all: Paul is ill and moody. He reacts strongly to John Mark losing parchments in Pamphylia (a motif borrowed from 2 Tim 4:13). The second part recounts a repetitive journey, during which John Mark and Barnabas visit all the main cities of the island except Paphos and Amathous, whose entry is forbidden by a certain Bar-Jesus. This Bar-Jesus fearing the arrival of a powerful person spells the end of the apostle. These Acts are popular literature, without much interest in theology or in biblical accounts. Their two real heroes are the island of Cyprus and its church. The lengthy description of the island (chs. 15–22) refers even the smallest villages like Lampadistos, Palai-Paphos, Kourion, and Amathous. They intend to make Cyprus a holy land, consecrated by the visit of the apostolic group to its tiniest places.

Thus, Barnabas is an absolutely flat character, led by the necessities of the path, contrary to John Mark, the narrator, and to Paul, the ill-tempered apostle. Barnabas is only a name, a pure abstraction. The astonishing preeminence of Mark could reflect the figure of the apostle of Alexandria. Did the author intend to associate the island with the Egyptian metropolis by promoting the person of its mythical first bishop?

The *Laudatio of Alexander the Monk*: placed under the name of Alexander the monk, a porter of the convent built on the tomb of the saint, the *Laudatio Barnabae* does not seek to compose a full figure of an apostle. The praise of Barnabas is rather the story of the discovery of the relics and the proof of the autocephaly the Church of Cyprus. The prologue is full of praiseworthy epithets for the apostle. The first part paraphrases the Acts of the Apostles. It comments further on coming to Jerusalem to follow the teachings of Gamaliel as a parallel to Paul, on early conversion, and on imposing the name of Barnabas by Peter. The second part describes a colorless mission in Cyprus, without specific episodes or naming places. Here, Barnabas baptizes, instructs his brothers, celebrates Mass, and dies. The third part narrates the ways of Peter the Fuller, who annexes the Church of Antioch in its movement. Finally, the fourth part describes the discovery of the relics and confirms the autocephaly. Hence, the memory of Barnabas is of less concern to the author than his name, his funeral, and his relics. The aim is rather to legitimize the Cypriot claims: Barnabas is no more than a vector of authority.

4. Barnabas in Milan

From the 7th century CE onward, a new tradition based on the legend of Barnabas' apostolate in Rome made him the founder of the Milan Church. The roots of this tradition do not predate the apostolic lists, in particular the one credited to → Epiphanius of Salamis (*BHG* 150–150m). The legend culminates in the *De situ ciuitatis Mediolani*, also known as *Datiana historia* (since it was attributed to Datius, the bishop of Milan, who died in 552 CE), an anonymous chronicle of the bishops of Milan modeled on the Roman → *Liber pontificalis* (Duchesne, 1892). Compiled under Arnulf II (998–1018 CE), it assigns

Milan to Barnabas as a field of evangelization. The note on Barnabas in chapter 3 reveals the real purpose of the call to the apostle: the true hero is not Barnabas, but Anathlon or Anatole, the first bishop, also known from a notice from the *De ordine episcoporum Metensium* of Paul the Deacon. The strict purpose of Barnabas' appearance is to name him as a *coapostolus* ("co-apostle") and to ordain him as a bishop of Milan and Brescia.

This tradition of an apostolic foundation of Milan was slow to prevail. In his sermon of 1059, Pierre Damien can still cite the history of the diocese of Milan without mentioning Barnabas. The Ambrosian sacramentary does not include the name of Barnabas in the *Nobis quoque*. The bishop's catalogues do not mention the apostle before the 13th century.

5. Barnabas at the Renaissance

The memories of Barnabas made a last appearance in the famous *Gospel of Barnabas*, preserved in two manuscripts: an Italian translation given in 1709 to Prince Eugene and a less complete version in Spanish. It triggered speculation because it makes Muhammad the true prophet and claims that Jesus, who is not the true Son of God, would have pretended to die on the → cross. This text unsurprisingly serves a certain Islamist propaganda (Leirvik, 2002).

A bundle of proofs suggests Moorish origin. It could be the work of one Mudejar converted by force to Christianity, who wrote a work of combat, in a controversy. The work is similar to Dante in expression. A systematic comparison of the two versions shows that the Spanish version was a translation of an Italian original. Its use of a harmonized popular version of the gospels that goes back to the Vetus Latina supports a draft in Italy (Joosten, 2010).

The attribution to Barnabas is more than evanescent. If the apostle replaces Thomas in the list of the Twelve (ch. 14) it is mainly because he opposed Paul and is accused of renouncing circumcision, abandoning the rules of *kashru* ("the Jewish dietary rules"), and preaching Jesus as God. Therefore, it has more to do with the opposition between the two apostles and less with any tradition that the text was attributed to Barnabas.

Historiography

After the seminal work of R.A. Lipsius (1883), the interest in the acts or stories of the apostles was very rare, and Barnabas made no exception to the rule. The apostles were considered as fictional characters of minor interest in a historical perspective: a "modernist" historian as L. Duchesne (1892) expresses deeper irony and even a certain sneer. With the growing interest in apocryphal studies (Verheyden, 2008; Starowieyski, 2008) and a better understanding of Christian memory formation (Bockmühl, 2003), the reception of the apostle in Christian literature became a topic in itself (Öhler, 2003; Burnet, 2013).

Bibliography

Bockmühl, M., "Syrian Memories of Peter: Ignatius, Justin and Serapion," in: P.J. Tompson & D. Lambers-Petry, eds.,*The Image of the Judaeo-Christians in Ancient Jewish and Christian Literature*, WUNT 158, Tübingen, 2003, 124–148.

Burnet, R., "Les Reconnaissances et leur intrigue," in: F. Amsler, A. Frey & C. Touati, eds., *Nouvelles intrigues pseudo-clementines*, PIRSB 6, Lausanne, 2008, 177–182.

Burnet, R., "Barnabé et les processus de construction de la légitimité apostolique," *RHE* 108, 2013, 595–625.

Duchesne, L., "Saint Barnabé," in: J.-B. de Rossi, ed., *Mélange*, Paris, 1892, 41–71.

Hvalvik, R., *The Struggle for Scripture and Covenant: The Purpose of the Epistle of Barnabas and Jewish-Christian Competition in the Second Century*, WUNT 82, 2nd series, Tübingen, 1996.

Ilan, T.A., T. Ziem & K. Hünefeld, in: *LJNLA*, 4 vols., TSAJ 91, 92, 126, 141, Tübingen, 2002–2010.

Joosten, J., "The Date and Provenance of the Gospel of Barnabas," *JThS* 61, 2010, 200–215.

Kollmann, B., *Joseph Barnabas: His Life and Legacy*, Collegeville, 2004.

Leirvik, O., "History as a Literary Weapon: The Gospel of Barnabas in Muslim-Christian Polemics," *StTh* 56, 2002, 4–26.

Lipsius, R.A., *Die apokryphen Apostelgeschichten und Apostellegenden: Ein Beitrag zur altchristlichen Literaturgeschichte*, vol. II/2, Braunschweig, 1883.

Mitford, T.B., "Roman Cyprus," in: H. Temporini, ed., *ANRW*, vol. II/7/2, Berlin, 1980, 1285–1384.

Öhler, M., *Barnabas die historische Person und ihre Rezeption in der Apostelgeschichte*, WUNT 153, Tübingen, 2003.

Pervo, R.I., *Acts*, Hermeneia, Minneapolis, 2009.

Robinson, T.A., *Ignatius of Antioch and the Parting of the Ways: Early Jewish-Christian Relations*, Peabody, 2009.

Starowieyski, M., "Datation des Actes (Voyages) de S. Barnabé (*BHG* 225; ClAp 285) et du Panégyrique de S. Barnabé par Alexandre le Moine (*BHG* 226; CPG 7400; ClAp 286)," in: A. Schoors & P. van Deun, eds., *Philohistôr: Miscellanea in Honorem Caroli Laga septuagenarii*, OLA 60, Louvain, 1994, 193–198.

Starowieyski, M., "La légende de Saint Barnabé," in: F. Amsler, A. Frey & C. Touati, eds., *Nouvelles intrigues pseudo-clementines*, PIRSB 6, Lausanne, 2008, 135–148.

Verheyden, J., "Presenting Minor Characters in the Pseudo-Clementine Novel: The Case of Barnabas," in: F. Amsler, A. Frey & C. Touati, eds., *Nouvelles intrigues pseudo-clementines*, PIRSB 6, Lausanne, 2008, 249–257.

Zetterholm, M., *Synagogue and Separation: A Social-Scientific Approach to the Formation of Christianity in Antioch*, Lund, 2001.

Zetterholm, M., *The Formation of Christianity in Antioch: A Social-Scientific Approach to the Separation between Judaism and Christianity*, RECM, London, 2005.

RÉGIS BURNET

II. *Barnabas, Epistle of*

The *Epistle of Barnabas* is an early Christian tractate that evinces concern for a community to distance and differentiate itself from non-Christian Jews, to appropriate Jewish Scriptures as their own, and to live an ethical lifestyle. The details of its authorship, date, intention, and situation must be deduced from the text itself, and so competing hypotheses about these matters attend the *Epistle*.

1. Manuscripts, Editions, and Translations

Barnabas survives in full in two Greek manuscripts, both rediscovered in the 19th century: Codex Sinaiticus, in a hand assigned to Scribe A (fols. 334r–340v), and Codex Hierosolymitanus (fols. 39r–51v), which also contains the sole complete manuscript of the → *Didache*. Previously, it was known through a deficient Greek text that only included *Barn*. 5:7–21:9 following directly from Pol. *Phil*. 1.1–9.2: the 11th-century Codex Vaticanus graecus 859 and 12 manuscripts descended from it (Funk, 1880; Prostmeier, 1994). A papyrus fragment assignable to the 4th century CE contains a fragmentary text of 9:1a–6 (PSI 7.757; Vitelli, 1925, no. 757; Kraft, 1967; Wayment, 2013, 37–39), with affinities to the textual tradition

represented by the Vatican manuscript family. A yet-unpublished papyrus fragment from Oxyrhynchus is also known to exist. A Latin translation of 1:1–17:2, possibly made as early as the 3rd century CE, is preserved in a single manuscript preserved in the Russian National Library Codex Petropolitanus (call number Bibl. Publ. Q. v. I. 39), fols. VIII–XX (Heer, 1908). There is also extant a single fragment in Syriac containing 19:1, 2, 8, and 20:1 (Codex Cantabrigiensis Univ. Add. 2033, fol. 61v; Wright, 1901, 600–628; Baumstark, 1912), a quotation of 6:11–13 and 6:17–18 in a 4th-century CE Coptic work, P. Berolinensis 20915, probably made "on the fly" rather than indicating a complete lost translation into Coptic (Schenke, 1995; Schenke-Robinson, 2004), and a lost Armenian translation noted in the codicil to Codex Vaticanus graecus 859 (Prostmeier, 1994; 1999).

The *editio princeps* of *Barnabas* was prepared by Archbishop Ussher in 1642 (Backhouse, 1883), drawing on the Latin manuscript to fill the gap in then-known Greek manuscripts of 1:1–5:6. *Barnabas* then featured in the collections of apostolic fathers by J.B Cotelier (1672) and W. Wake (1693; though not Ittig) later in the 17th century and has been a regular feature of such collections since. The most authoritative edition is that by P. Prigent and R.A. Kraft (1971), but the older editions (esp. Hilgenfeld, 1877) are still worth consulting. P. Prigent's notes (1971) and F.R. Prostmeier's exhaustive commentary (1999) supply excellent guides to the treatise, and once again older works by R.A. Kraft (1965) and H. Windisch (1920) still repay careful reading. Convenient facing-page English translations with Greek editions are available in M. Holmes (2007, 370–441) and B. Ehrman (2003, vol. II, 3–83).

2. Title and Early Reception

Although the tractate is formally anonymous, with no authorial claim internal to the document (and so, contra Drobner, 2007, 36–37, cannot be deemed pseudonymous), it comes early to be ascribed to Barnabas. From early on, the letter was ascribed to the same Barnabas mentioned with some regularity in the New Testament (Acts 4:36; 9:27; 11:22, 30; 12:25; 13:1; 13.2; 13:7; 13:43; 13:46; 13:50; 14:12; 14:14; 14:20; 15:2; 15:12; 15:22; 15:25; 15:35; 15:36; 15:37; 15:39; 1 Cor 9:6; Gal 2:1; 2:9; 2:13; Col 4:10). For example, → Jerome writes,

Barnabas from Cyprus, surnamed Joseph the Levite, ordained apostle to the Gentiles with Paul, wrote one *Epistle*, valuable for the edification of the church, which is reckoned among the apocryphal writings. Afterwards he separated from Paul on account of John, a disciple also called Mark, but nonetheless exercised the work of preaching the Gospel laid upon him. (Jer. *Vir. ill.* 6.1–2; Halton, 1999, 15)

Earlier, → Clement of Alexandria, who treats the text as authoritative, calls Barnabas "one of the 70 and a co-worker of Paul" (Clem. *Strom.* 2.20.116; see Clement in Eus. *Hist. eccl.* 2.1.4–5; 6.13.6; 6.14.1), and elsewhere he simply refers to him as "the apostle Barnabas" (ὁ ἀπόστολος Βαρνάβας; Clem. *Strom.* 2.6.31; see 2.7.35). Origen (*Cels.* 1.63) refers to what is written in the Catholic *Epistle of Barnabas* (ἐν τῇ Βαρνάβα καθολικῇ ἐπιστολῇ). Eus. *Hist. eccl.* 3.25.4 places it among the spurious books, as the "Epistle of Barnabas" (Βαρναβᾶ ἐπιστολὴ). Didymus the Blind mentions it by name several times (Didy. *Comm. Zach.* 3.196; 4.312; *Comm. Ps.* 37:5; 41:5; see Koch, 2003). Codex Sinaiticus seems to treat it as part of the canon of Scripture, while the stichometry of Nicephorus mentions it among the disputed books of the New Testament (together with the *Apocalypse of John*, the *Apocalypse of Peter*, and the Gospel according to the Hebrews), rather than among the "apocrypha" (ἀπόκρυφα). And in the so-called List of the 60 Books, *Barnabas* is listed among the apocryphal books in the 7th century CE (Markschies, 2012, 143–146). It is also mentioned as spurious in the 14th-century Nicephorus Callistus Xanthopolus' *Historia ecclesiastica* (2.46.73), who was probably dependent on → Eusebius of Caesarea. In Codex Claromontanus, we find listed "Barnabae Epist. Ver. DCCCL," that is, "*Epistle of Barnabas*, 850 (lines)," although the codex itself does not contain the book (Andry, 1951). In the Latin tradition, Barnabas is sometimes taken to be the *auctor ad hebraeos*, and this has sometimes led to confusion about which *epistle* of Barnabas is in view (e.g. Tert. *Pud.* 20, on which see Boer, 2014, although elsewhere → Tertullian knows the *Epistle*: e.g. Tert. *Marc.* 3.7.7; 3.18; see Jer. *Dard.* no. 1293). But it seems as though the figure of Barnabas comes to be differentiated in some measure from the tractate. There is a 5th-century CE *Vita* of Barnabas and a 6th-century CE *Laudatio sancti Barnabae*, but neither

mentions the *Epistle*, and while one may trace various echoes or allusions to *Barnabas*, on the whole the western tradition seems more reticent than the eastern to cite the tractate (Dekkers, 1996).

At any rate, it is clear that the authorship of the *Epistle* can hardly be laid at the feet of the Jewish Christian Barnabas, known from the New Testament. The anti-Jewish elements of the tractate (on which see below) loom too large to render such an ascription plausible, particularly in the absence of internal evidence. Therefore, it seems that the ascription arose as a result of early Christian desire to banish anonymity and attach authoritative names to authoritative texts.

3. Content

Although *Barnabas* is known early as an "epistle," its genre is mixed. It retains certain elements of epistolarity, for example, a greeting in *Barn.* 1:1 and 21:9, reference to "sending" in 1:5, and mention of "writing" in 4:9, 6:5, and 21:9. But the epistolary frame seems largely to be a literary device (so Holmes, 2007, 370) and *Barnabas* is best described as a tract or essay in epistolary guise. Although some have wished to see *Barnabas* as a written homily (Barnard, 1961), such a concrete setting is difficult to ascertain. While the anonymous author suggests he does not fancy himself a "teacher" (1:8; 4:9), he uses pedagogical language throughout (e.g. the repeatedly punctuated command, "Learn!" in 5:6; 6:9; 9:7; 14:4; 16:2; 16:7; 16:8) and implies his habitual teaching in 9:9. The author appears to know the recipients or audience, casting them as "sons and daughters" (1:1) or "brothers" (2:10; 3:6; 6:10), whom he longs to see (1:3), since he is "one who is one of you and loves all of you in a special way more than my own soul" (4:6). He also describes himself as a "servant" (4:9; 6:5) and calls the recipients "children of joy" (7:1), "children of love" (9:7), "children of love and peace" (21:9), or simply "children" (15:4).

After an initial greeting and thanksgiving (1:1–5), *Barnabas* falls into two major parts: a long polemical attempt to dissuade the audience from Judaizing practices and persuade them to an allegorical understanding of Scripture (1:6–17:2), and a concluding ethical section consisting of "two ways" material, with much in common with the *Didache* (chs. 18–20), before closing with a final exhortation and greeting (ch. 21). Although the *Epistle* mentions in its opening three basic doctrines, the hope of life, righteousness, and a glad and rejoicing love (1:6), these do not feature prominently in the structuring of subsequent content. In the long central section, *Barnabas* writes of sacrifices that God "has nullified these things" (ταῦτα οὖν κατήργησεν; 2:6) and goes on to speak of a "new law" (καινὸς νόμος) of our Lord Jesus Christ, without the yoke of necessity – see τὸν λαὸν τὸν καινὸν in 5:7. Likewise, he criticizes literal understandings of sacrifices (ch. 2), fasting (ch. 3), circumcision (9:6), dietary laws (ch. 10), the Sabbath (ch. 15), and the Temple (ch. 16). On the other hand, *Barnabas* wants to avoid "lawlessness" (ἀνομία; 4:1, 10) and urges close attention to the "righteous requirements of the Lord" (τὰ δικαιώματα κυρίου; 2:1; 4:11). There will be a judgment according to works (4:12; see 21:1), the result of which – rather than the basis – will be justification for the righteous (4:10). Moreover, he upholds the goodness of the Torah: "Observe how well Moses legislated!" (βλέπετε πῶς ἐνομοθέτησεν Μωϋσῆς καλῶς; 10:11).

Like the 3rd-century CE *Didascalia* (Unnik, 1983), Barnabas achieves interpretive mileage from the golden calf episode. He argues that → Israel "lost [the covenant] completely" (4:6) at the episode of the golden calf. When → Moses descended, he "hurled the two tablets from his hands, and their covenant was shattered, in order that the covenant of the beloved Jesus might be sealed in our heart" (4:8). When *Barnabas* wants to investigate "whether this people or the former people is the heir, and whether the covenant is theirs or ours" (13:1), the reversal of the right of primogeniture that he finds in Genesis serves his supersessionist purposes well. Had not God sworn to give the covenant to the patriarchs? According to *Barnabas*, he did in fact give it, but Israel could not receive it because of their sins (14:1–4). Therefore true Christian belief and praxis should be oriented to a symbolic understanding of the Torah (→ Law/Decalogue/Torah), rather than what *Barnabas* characterizes as Jewish literalism.

The so-called two-ways section (chs. 18–20) comprises material with significant verbal overlap with *Did.* 1–6. A flurry of publications sought to assess the relationship between *Barnabas* and *Didache* after the latter's initial publication in the 1880s, but a relatively stable consensus has emerged that both draw on a common source, with Jewish roots (Stewart, 2011, who also supplies useful synopses). That *Barnabas* polemicizes against the *Didache* community in its appropriation of the two-ways material seems difficult to sustain (contra Draper, 1995), although the material clearly seems to function in a less nomistic way in *Barnabas*. Despite the fact that the Latin version lacks the two-ways tradition, the material seems original to *Barnabas* and is anticipated earlier in the tractate: "The works of the evil way" in 4:10 and the two ways in 5:4 both seem to have chapters 18–20 already in view (Rhodes, 2011). The paraenetic material in the two-ways section arguably functions in some way as a replacement for the ethical void left by the allegorizing of the law.

4. Location, Date, and Situation

The composition of *Barnabas* has been most regularly located in Alexandria (e.g. Carleton Paget, 1994, 30–42; Loman, 2005) because of its shared interest in allegorical interpretive strategies with the *Letter of Aristeas*, → Philo of Alexandria, and possibly the radical allegorizers whom Philo mentions (Philo *Migr.* 89–93); its early reception there in Clement and → Origen; and perhaps one or two incidental details in the text that might place it in Egypt (Harris, 1890). Alexandria, however, had no monopoly on allegorical reading (consider Melito of Sardis, Justin Martyr, Irenaeus of Lyon, and Tertullian), and the early reception of the Roman *Shepherd of Hermas* (→ Hermas) in Egypt sounds a note of caution for the argument from reception. Consequently some prefer to see *Barnabas* as composed in Rome, in Syria-Palestine (Prigent & Kraft, 1971, 23–24), or in Asia Minor, where perhaps the Ignatian correspondence (esp. Ign. *Phld.* 8.2) attests similar Judaizing currents (Wengst, 1984, 115–118). The situation it envisages could have arisen at various points around the eastern Mediterranean in the early 2nd century CE, and given the tendency of interpretive traditions, apocalyptic motifs, and texts themselves to circulate, it is inadvisable to tie one's interpretation of *Barnabas* too closely to any one putative place of origin, even if on balance the Alexandrian claims are stronger than competing options.

The date of *Barnabas* is likewise possible to fix only in probabilities. It clearly mentions the destruction of the Temple (*Barn.* 16:2–3) and so must postdate 70 CE, and Clement of Alexandria's use of the text supplies a firm terminus ante quem. Most date the letter between 70 and 132 CE, with majority opinions clustering around the reigns of Nerva (96–98 CE; Richardson & Shukster, 1983; Carleton Paget, 1994) or Hadrian (130–132 CE; Prostmeier, 1999). The internal evidence turns on the identity of the ten kingdoms in 4:4, and the possible attempt to rebuild the Temple mentioned in 16:3–4, 10. Those who identify the tenth kingdom (*varia lectio* "king") with Vespasian date *Barnabas* in the mid-70s CE (e.g. Lightfoot, 1890, 505–512; Robinson, 1976, 313–319); those who see the tenth kingdom as a reference to the Flavian dynasty, in the late 90s CE (Williams, 1933; Carleton Paget, 1994). If, however, *Barnabas* has made use of an apocalyptic source or borrowed traditional imagery, it may be inadvisable to press for a firm identification of the kingdoms with known emperors (Wengst, 1984, 114; Hvalvik, 1996). If there is an actual program of rebuilding the Temple reflected in chapter 16, it is difficult to identify this with any known historical circumstance. Some have seen here a reflection of Nerva's reversal of Flavian policies toward the Jews, which in turn might have inculcated hopes for restoration of the Temple and induced sympathetic Gentiles to consider full proselytism (a situation against which *Barnabas* would then be reacting; e.g. Goodman, 1989; 2007, pointing to coinage of Nerva that states, a "false accusation [against] the Jews has been wiped away" [for the coin, see *RIC*, vol. II, 227, no 58; 228, nos. 72 and 82]), while others consider that the reference to rebuilding may arise from Hadrian's reconstructive building program of Jerusalem as Aelia Capitolina, in the years immediately preceding the Second Jewish Revolt, circa 130–132 CE (Hvalvik, 1996, 17–34; Prostmeier, 1999, 111–119; 2010, 33).

The general situation envisaged by the *Epistle*, one in which the author's audience is envisioned as contemplating a turn (or possibly return) to → Judaism, fits well the lively period of self-definition and counterdefinition on the part of both emergent Judaism and Christianity in the first half of the 2nd century CE. The precise occasion for *Barnabas'* anti-Judaism has been a matter of some debate (Prostmeier, 2002). Does the author concern himself about proselytes who found themselves inclined to (re-)turn to Judaism, only envisage the possibility of such a temptation, or seek to strengthen the self-identity of the community by railing against a merely "symbolic" Judaism? To ascertain certainty about the community's situation "on the ground" is difficult, but the author clearly writes of what he perceives to be a threat, and urges "that we might not shipwreck ourselves as proselytes to their law" (3:6), and the concrete rhetoric certainly seems to favor one of the former two options (Carleton Paget, 2015). To see the *Epistle* as reflecting a discrete liturgical occasion, for example a paschal feast, is to press the evidence too far (contra Barnard, 1961).

5. Theological Themes

Barnabas offers as one of its most distinctive contributions a novel attempt to appropriate Jewish Scripture as Christian resource in a thoroughgoing way. It presents itself as offering an approach to *gnosis* and uses the language of knowledge and its cognates with some frequency (e.g. 1:7; 2:3; 5:3; 6:9; 18:1; 19:1), as well as the theme of revelation (e.g. 3:6; 6:7; 7:1; see Kraft 1965, 24; Draper 1995, 95). *Gnosis* is, in part at least, the proper understanding of Scripture. *Barnabas* expresses the idea in this way in 5:2: "For what is written about him has to do partly with Israel, partly with us." Note that some Scriptures are said in *Barnabas'* introductory formulas to be addressed "to them" (2:7; 3:1; 5:2; 6:8; 9:5a; 10:2; 12:7) while others are to or for "us" (2:4; 2:10; 3:3; 5:2; see 6:13a; 9:13; see Hvalvik, 1996, 113). Most striking is 3:1–2, which bifurcates Isa 58, with verses 4–5 spoken "to them" and verses 6–10 to "us" (see Rom 10:18–19). In this way, *Barnabas* attempts to offer a comprehensive hermeneutical strategy for disappropriating Israel of her Scriptures. *Barnabas* contains dozens of quotations, including several from unknown or non-extant sources (2:10; 4:3; 4:4; 7:8; 7:11; 10:5; 11:9; 11:10; 12:1). It also echoes synoptic tradition at a couple of points (4:14; 5:9) and describes Abraham as "father of the uncircumcised" in 13:7 in a way that recalls Rom 4:11; 4:17, but it is unclear whether *Barnabas* knows any of our New Testament texts directly, knows intermediary sources, or simply relies on oral (or secondary oral) tradition (Carleton Paget, 1996;

2005). Its purpose would not lead one to expect to see the writings that became the New Testament cited explicitly, so the implications of this evidence should not be pressed.

With reference to contemporary non-Christian Judaism, *Barnabas* evinces a "unique radicalism" with "almost no counterpart in all patristic literature" (Lowy, 1960, 1). In contrast to Paul's assertion in Rom 11:1, *Barnabas* argues that Israel was "forsaken" (4:14). Curiously, this anti-Judaism is mingled with knowledge and use of Jewish exegetical tradition, an "outlook which, despite anti-Judaism, is formed by Jewish culture and influenced by Jewish public opinion" (Horbury, 1998, 130). Later authors, beginning with → Justin Martyr in the *Dialogue with Trypho* and → Irenaeus of Lyon in his *Adversus Haereses*, will be more reserved in their criticism of the Jewish law, not least in light of the problems for understanding divine goodness and providence *Barnabas*' approach engenders.

The starkness of *Barnabas*' approach to Israel has led to the question of whether the treatise evinces a one-covenant or two-covenant approach to salvation history – indeed, whether it is proper to speak of salvation history at all with respect to Israel. Most interpreters see *Barnabas* as operating with a concept of a single covenant, originally given to Israel but then suspended until it could be restored in Christ, with the entire stretch of Israel's history from the golden calf to the coming of Jesus one long misstep, marked by literalism and hard-hearted rejection of the divine purpose. As K. Backhaus puts it, for *Barnabas*, "[d]er 'erste Bund' war allenfalls ein heilsgeschichtlicher Fehlversuch" (the "first covenant" was at most a failed experiment in salvation history; Backhaus, 2009, 166). This involves *Barnabas* in some inconsistency, since, for example, he quotes the prophets as true representatives of God. J.N. Rhodes' attempt (2004b) to see the *Epistle* as employing the Deuteronomic tradition rather than the more robustly critical stance seen by most commentators sounds a helpful caution, but does not entirely succeed in establishing a two-covenant approach in *Barnabas*. One key statement in the letter, at 4:6b, forms a textual crux (see Rhodes, 2004a, whose proposed emendation, adopted by Holmes, 2007, is attractive, even if ultimately unconvincing in light of the Latin reading that makes good sense

and is adopted by Prigent & Kraft, 1971), but any reading of the variant will need to be assimilated to a broader reading of the *Epistle*'s themes.

Moreover, the threat *Barnabas* senses is not simply reducible to Judaism, but also includes the perilous situation of the present evil age: the "days are evil and the one who is at work is in power" (2:1); the audience must beware of the "evil one" (2:10) who could cause some error to imperil salvation. 4:1–5 speaks of the "deception of the present age," while *Barnabas* offers moral imperatives for living "in the last days" (4:9b–14; see 19:11; 20:1). The presence of → evil is also registered backward in time, and (confusingly, given that *Barnabas* elsewhere ascribes this to divine agency), at 9:4 it is said that an "evil angel" enlightened them, that is, Israel. But the community should take heart, since the day is near when everything will perish, together with the evil sone (21:3).

Barnabas most often refers to Jesus as "the Lord" (the term occurs well over 75 times, in reference to either Jesus or God, often in Septuagintal quotations), but also as Jesus (16x), Beloved (3:6; see 4:8), Son of God (e.g. 5:9; 5:11), servant of the Lord (6:1; see 9:2), the righteous one (6:7), king (11:5), Messiah/Christ (12:10; 12:11), and Son of David (12:10). The divine is most often referred to as "God" or Lord, but also occasionally as our/the Father (2:9; 12:8; 14:6), and in some references it is difficult to tell whether Jesus or God is intended (e.g. "master" in 1:7; 4:3), a testament to *Barnabas*' high if relatively undeveloped Christology. The Spirit (or "Spirit of the Lord") features as well, even if somewhat less prominently (e.g. 1:3; 9:7; 11:9).

The author is aware of Jewish tradition throughout and draws on it, as noted above, even in the course of its anti-Jewish treatment (Barnard, 1959). For example, in chapters 5 and 7, Jesus is presented as the fulfillment of the day-of-atonement ritual. In 7:8, 11, *Barnabas* writes of scarlet thread, something not mentioned in the biblical account in Lev 16, but widely reflected in Jewish tradition and later early Christian echoes of that tradition (e.g. *m. Yoma* 6.7; Tert. *Adv. Jud.* 14.9; see Ayali-Darshan, 2013). Or again, the allegorical interpretation of the food laws in chapter 10 recall the allegorical interpretations, sometimes very similar, in the *Letter of Aristeas*. All this suggests that *Barnabas* reflects a close contact with Jewish thought, taking elements of it for granted while problematizing its broader significance.

Finally, the hermeneutic *Barnabas* uses for discovering Jesus in the Hebrew Bible continuously finds Jesus figured in advance there, whether by prophetic claim, or by a "type" (7:7; 7:10; 7:11; 12:5; 12:6; see 8:1). In one striking instance, *Barnabas* has rewritten Isa 45:1 as an address not to Cyrus (τῷ χριστῷ μου Κύρῳ) but to my Lord (τῷ χριστῷ μου κυρίῳ) – an instance of scribalism that could result from inserting an additional iota, reading a manuscript with a *nomen sacrum* through Christian eyes, or even an independent, tendentious rendering of the unpointed Hebrew (although it should be admitted that *Barnabas* shows little independent evidence for knowledge of Hebrew, and his quotations of the Septuagint, even where various, make most sense as inter-Greek phenomena). Many of its well over 100 citations and major allusions are traditional in nature, and the author has probably made use of earlier Christian sources and *testimonia* collections in constructing its sustained argument against Jewish proselytism.

Historiography

In the decades after the Second World War, scholarship on *Barnabas* concerned itself with the detection and elucidation of sources and preexisting traditions, seeing the *Epistle* rightly as an instance of "evolved literature" that nevertheless had its own (variously stressed) theological perspective (most importantly: Prigent, 1961; Kraft, 1961; Wengst, 1971). J. Carleton Paget (1994) offers an important critical survey of research and proposes that *Barnabas* be seen as an Alexandrian composition in Nerva's reign that incorporated sources in the formation of its distinctive theological outlook. R. Hvalvik (1996) provides sustained consideration of the anti-Jewish elements of *Barnabas* and contextualizes these within early Christianity, while J.N. Rhodes (2004) usefully compares the *Epistle* with the Deuteronomic tradition, suggesting that the tendentious telling of salvation history is not solely focused on the golden calf episode but equally includes in its purview the death of Jesus. F.R. Prostmeier's commentary (1999) offers the fullest treatment of *Barnabas* to date and

is unlikely to be surpassed in depth of analysis and erudition. Several editions, commentaries, and monographs on the *Epistle* are currently in progress, and a full-scale study of the *Epistle*'s textual *Vorlagen* that takes advantage of recent gains in Septuagintal scholarship remains a desideratum.

Bibliography

Andry, C.F., "Barnabae Epist Ver DCCCL," *JBL* 70, 1951, 233–238.

Ayali-Darshan, N., "The Origin and Meaning of the Crimson Thread in the Mishnaic Scapegoat Ritual in Light of an Ancient Syro-Anatolian Custom," *JSJ* 44, 2013, 530–552.

Backhaus, K., "Das Bundesmotiv in der frühkirchlichen Schwellenzeit: Hebräerbrief, Barnabasbrief, Dialogus cum Tryphone," in: K. Backhaus, *Der sprechende Gott: Gesammelte Studien zum Hebräerbrief*, WUNT 240, Tübingen, 2009, 153–173.

Backhouse, J.H., *The Editio Princeps of the Epistle of Barnabas by Archbishop Ussher, as Printed at Oxford, AD 1642, and Preserved in an Imperfect Form in the Bodleian Library; with a Dissertation*, Oxford, 1883.

Barnard, L.W., "The Epistle of Barnabas and the Tannaitic Catechism," *ATR* 41, 1959, 177–190.

Barnard, L.W., "The Epistle of Barnabas – A Paschal Homily?" *VigChr* 15, 1961, 8–22.

Baumstark, A., "Der Barnabasbrief bei den Syrern," *OrChr* 2, 1912, 235–240.

Bihlmeyer, K., *Die Apostolischen Väter, Neubearbeitung der Funkschen Ausgabe, Sammlung ausgewählter kirchenund dogmengeschichtlicher Quellenschriften*, 2nd ed., 2nd series, vol. I/1, Tübingen, 1956.

Boer, E. de, "Tertullian on 'Barnabas' Letter to the Hebrews' in *De pudicitia* 20.1–5," *VigChr* 68, 2014, 243–263.

Carleton Paget, J., *The Epistle of Barnabas: Outlook and Background*, WUNT 64, 2nd series, Tübingen, 1994.

Carleton Paget, J., "Paul and the Epistle of Barnabas," *NT* 38, 1996, 359–381.

Carleton Paget, J., "The *Epistle of Barnabas* and the Writings that Later Formed the New Testament," in: A. Gregory & C. Tuckett, eds., *The Reception of the New Testament in the Apostolic Fathers*, Oxford, 2005, 229–249.

Carleton Paget, J., "Barnabas and the Outsiders: Jews and Their World in the *Epistle of Barnabas*," in: M. Grundeken & J. Verheyden, eds., *Early Christian Communities Between Ideal and Reality*, WUNT 342, Tübingen, 2015, 177–202.

Cotelier, J.B., *SS. Patrum qui temporibus apostolicis floruereunt*, Paris, 1672.

Dekkers, E., "Saint Barnabé dans la tradition médiolatine," in: R. Nip, ed., *Media latinitas: A Collection of Essays to Mark the Occasion of the Retirement of L.J. Engels*, Turnhout, 1996, 199–203.

Draper, J.A., "Barnabas and the Riddle of the Didache Revisited," *JSNT* 58, 1995, 89–113.

Drobner, H., *The Fathers of the Church: A Comprehensive Introduction*, Grand Rapids, 2007; ET: S. Schatzmann.

Edwards, J.C., *The Gospel According to the Epistle of Barnabas: Jesus Traditions in an Early Christian Polemic*, WUNT 503, 2nd series, Tübingen, 2019.

Ehrman, B., *The Apostolic Fathers*, 2 vols., LCL, Cambridge MA, 2003.

Funk, F.X., "Der Codex Vaticanus gr. 859 und seine Descendenten," *ThQ* 62, 1880, 629–637.

Funk, F.X., *Patres Apostolici*, vol. I, Tübingen, ²1901.

Gebhardt, O. von, & A. Harnack, *Barnabae Epistula*, Leipzig, ²1878.

Goodman, M., "Nerva, the *fiscus Judaicus* and Jewish Identity," *JRS* 79, 1989, 40–44.

Goodman, M., "The Meaning of 'Fisci Judaici Calumnia Sublata' on the Coinage of Nerva," in: S.J.D. Cohen & J.J. Schwartz, eds., *Studies in Josephus and the Varieties of Ancient Judaism: Louis H. Feldman Jubilee Volume*, AGJU 67, Leiden, 2007, 81–89.

Halton, T.P., *St. Jerome, On Illustrious Men*, FaCh 100, Washington DC, 1999.

Harris, J.R., "On the Locality of Pseudo-Barnabas," *JBL* 9, 1890, 60–70.

Heer, J.M., *Die Versio Latina des Barnabasbriefes und ihr Verhältnis zur altlateinischen Bibel*, Freiburg im Breisgau, 1908.

Hilgenfeld, A., *Barnabae Epistula*, Leipzig, ²1877.

Holmes, M., *The Apostolic Fathers: Greek Texts and English Translations*, 3rd ed., Grand Rapids, 2007.

Horbury, W., "Jewish-Christian Relations in Barnabas and Justin Martyr," in: W. Horbury, *Jews and Christians in Contact and Controversy*, Edinburgh, 1998, 127–161.

Hvalvik, R., "Barnabas 9:7–9 and the Author's Supposed Use of Gematria," *NTS* 33, 1987, 276–282.

Hvalvik, R., *The Struggle for Scripture and Covenant*, WUNT 82, 2nd series, Tübingen, 1996.

Ittig, T., *Bibliotheca Patrum Apostolicorum Graeco-Latina*, Leipzig, 1699.

Koch, D.-A., "Textkritik in frühchristlicher Literatur außerhalb des Neuen Testaments: Barn 1,6 als Beispiel," in: W.J.C. Weren & D.-A. Koch, eds., *Recent Developments in Textual Criticism: New Testament, Other Early Christian and Jewish Literature*, Assen, 2003, 145–163.

Kraft, R.A., "The Epistle of Barnabas, its Quotations and their Sources," diss., Cambridge MA, 1961.

Kraft, R.A., *The Apostolic Fathers: A New Translation and Commentary*, vol. III: *Barnabas and the Didache*, New York, 1965.

Kraft, R.A., "Unnoticed Papyrus Fragment of Barnabas," *VigChr* 21/3, 1967, 150–163.

Lightfoot, J.B., *The Apostolic Fathers: Clement, Ignatius, and Polycarp: Revised Texts with Introductions, Notes, Dissertations, and Translations*, vol. I/2, London, 1890.

Loman, J., "The Letter of Barnabas in Early Second-Century Egypt," in: A. Hilhorst & G.H. van Kooten, eds., *The Wisdom of Egypt: Jewish, Early Christian, and Gnos-tic Essays in Honour of Gerard P. Luttikhuizen*, Leiden, 2005, 247–265.

Lowy, S., "The Confutation of Judaism in the Epistle of Barnabas," *JJS* 11, 1960, 1–33.

Markschies, C., "Haupteinleitung," in: C. Markschies & J. Schröter, with A. Heiser, eds., *Antike christliche Apokryphen in deutscher Übersetzung*, vol. I: *Evangelien und Verwandtes*, Tübingen, 2012, 1–180.

Prigent, P., *Les Testimonia dans le christianisme primitif: L'Epître de Barnabé 1–16 et ses sources*, Paris, 1961.

Prigent, P., & R.A. Kraft, *Épître de Barnabé*, SC 172, Paris, 1971.

Prostmeier, F.R., "Zur handschriftlichen Überlieferung des Polykarp- und des Barnabasbriefes: Zwei nicht beachtete Deszendenten des Cod. Vat Gr. 859," *VigChr* 48, 1994, 48–64.

Prostmeier, F.R., *Der Barnabasbrief*, KAV 8, Göttingen, 1999.

Prostmeier, F.R., "Antijudaismus im Rahmen christlicher Hermeneutik: Zum Streit über christliche Identität in der Alten Kirche Notizen zum Barnabasbrief," *ZAC* 6, 2002, 38–58.

Prostmeier, F.R., "The Epistle of Barnabas," in: W. Pratscher, ed., *The Apostolic Fathers: An Introduction*, Waco, 2010, 27–45.

Prostmeier, F., *Epistola Barnabae/Barnabasbrief – Ad Diognetum/An Diognet: Griechisch–Deutsch*, FChr 5, Freiburg im Breisgau, 2018.

Rhodes, J.N., "Barnabas 4.6b: The Exegetical Implications of a Textual Problem," *VigChr* 58, 2004a, 365–392.

Rhodes, J.N., *The Epistle of Barnabas and the Deuteronomic Tradition*, WUNT 188, 2nd series, Tübingen, 2004b.

Rhodes, J.N., "The Two Ways Tradition in the Epistle of Barnabas: Revisiting an Old Question," *CBQ* 73, 2011, 797–816.

Richardson, P., & M.B. Shukster, "Barnabas, Nerva, and the Yavnean Rabbis," *JThS* 34, 1983, 31–55.

Robinson, J.A.T., *Redating the New Testament*, London, 1976.

Rodenbiker, K., "The Claromontanus Stichometry and Its Canonical Implications," *JSNT* 44/2, 2021, 240–253.

Schenke, H.-M., "Der Barnabasbrief im Berliner 'Koptischen Buch' (Pap. Berolinensis 20915)," *Enchoria* 25, 1999, 53–75.

Schenke-Robinson, G., *Das Berliner "Koptische Buch": Eine wiederhergestellte frühchristlich-theologische Abhandlung*, CSCO 610–611, CSCO.C 49–50, Turnhout, 2004.

Scorza Barcellona, F., *Epistola di Barnaba*, CPS 1, Turin, 1975.

Stewart-Sykes, A., ed., *On the Two Ways: Life or Death, Light or Darkness: Foundational Texts in the Tradition*, PPS 41, Yonkers, 2011.

Unnik, W.C. van, "The Significance of Moses' Law for the Church of Christ According to the Syriac Didascalia," in: W.C. van Unnik, *Sparsa Collecta*, vol. III, Leiden, 1983, 7–39.

Vitelli, G., ed., *Papiri greci e latini VII (731–870)*, PSIRPE, Florence, 1925, 40–43, no. 757.

Wake, W., *The Genuine Epistles of the Apostolical Fathers*, London, 1693.

Wayment, T., *The Text of the New Testament Apocrypha (100–400 CE)*, London, 2013.

Wengst, K., *Tradition und Theologie des Barnabasbriefes*, AKG 42, Berlin, 1971.

Wengst, K., *Didache (Apostellehre), Barnabasbrief, Zweiter Klemensbrief, Schrift an Diognet*, Munich, 1984.

Williams, A.L., "The Date of the Epistle of Barnabas," *JThS* 34, 1933, 337–346.

Windisch, H., *Der Barnabasbrief*, HNT, suppl. vol.: *Die Apostolischen Väter III*, Tübingen, 1920.

Wright, W., *A Catalogue of the Syriac Manuscripts Preserved in the Library of the University of Cambridge*, Cambridge UK, 1901, vol. II, 600–628.

DAVID LINCICUM

Bartholomew the Apostle

I. Bartholomew (Apostle) ♦ II. *Bartholomew, Questions of*

I. Bartholomew (Apostle)

While lists of the twelve apostles (Mark 3:16–19; Matt 10:2–4; Luke 6:14–16; Acts 1:13) always mention Bartholomew, there is no mention of him in the canonical texts, thus allowing a number of appropriations of his character. Bartholomew is one of the apostles who has known various receptions, depending on the communities and interests that took possession of him.

1. An Unknown Apostle

"Saint Bartholomew was a Galilean, as well as all the other apostles among whom he was placed by Jesus Christ, and that is all the Gospel tells us" (Le Nain de Tillemont, 1693, 381). Already in the 17th century, that is how L.-S. Le Nain de Tillemont concluded his record of Bartholomew. More than 300 years later, we are still at the same point. The fact that he is one of the twelve is guaranteed by his presence in the four lists, sometimes in sixth and sometimes in seventh position. His name comes from bar-Tolmai, a proper name found in Josh 15:14, in 2 Sam 13:37, or in → Flavius Josephus (*Ant.* 20.1.1). This name may come from the Hebrew transliteration of the name

of Ptolemy. It has been claimed that he was a Greek and, according to some ancient authors, a person of royal descent (Baronius, 1598, 383). That is the long and short of it.

2. Was Bartholomew Nathanael?

To give a little more depth to the character, Bartholomew has often been identified with Nathanael on the basis of an argument summarized by Rupert of Deutz (Rup. *Com. Ion.* 2.118): Nathanael is called by Philip in John, but is not present in the Synoptics, which usually associate Philip and Bartholomew in their lists. Nathanael may therefore be Bartholomew's other name. This assimilation, traditional since at least the 9th century CE, was challenged in the 16th century by Baronius (1864, 67; 1598, 383) and remained the subject of fierce debate until the 18th century (Nahr, 1740). In fact, Philip is rather associated with Andrew in the apostolic lists, and the oldest traditions privilege instead an assimilation between Nathanael and James, son of Alphaeus (*Epistula Apostolorum* 2). In addition, identifying the son by the father's name was customary when the name was common (Bauckham, 2006, 103), but since Nathanael is not a frequent name, why would the name bar-Tolmai be selected if "Nathanael" was sufficient to distinguish the two apostles?

3. The Starting Point for the Tradition on Bartholomew: Eusebius and Rufinus of Aquileia

a. The Traditions of Eusebius of Caesarea and Rufinus of Aquileia

Eusebius' information about Bartholomew can be found in a statement regarding Pantaenus of Caesarea (Eus. *Hist. eccl.* 5.10; → Eusebius of Caesarea). Pantaenus, who founded the Didascalia in Alexandria – a highly questionable piece of information in itself, as B. Pouderon has demonstrated (Pouderon, 1994) – became the herald of the gospel "unto the land of India." Once there, he discovered that he had been preceded by the Gospel of Matthew (→ Matthew the Apostle), already known to some natives of the country: Bartholomew had already preached to them and had left with them the book of Matthew in Hebrew characters.

Rufinus confirms this Indian journey in his *Ecclesiastical History* (Ruf. *Hist.* 10.9; → Rufinus of Aquileia), and this tradition was taken up by → Socrates Scholasticus (*Hist. eccl.* 1.19) and → Sozomen (*Hist. eccl.* 2.24.1). Rufinus relates how destiny allotted Parthia to Thomas, Ethiopia to Matthew, and "contiguous Citerior India to Bartholomew" (*adhærens citerior India Bartholomæo*). Conscious that this geographical precision may be ambiguous, Rufinus specifies that this *India citerior* is not the *India ulterior*, which was only Christianized under Constantine. It is precisely at that time, he goes on, that Edesius and Frumentius brought Christianity to the kingdom.

b. Evaluation of the Two Traditions

Given the geographical inaccuracy that lasted until the Byzantine period, the record of the two historians raises the question of location. In the minds of the ancients, Africa was connected to the Indian subcontinent by a strip of land. India could therefore refer to the inner regions of Africa (Ethiopia and South India) as well as to the coastal area of the Arabian Peninsula, or to Gangetic India (Dihle, 1964). From the story of Rufinus, we understand that ulterior India is probably the kingdom of Axum, the Christianization of which under Ezana II is well documented (Thelamon, 1981, 37–83). Citerior India could then be Gangetic India or South India.

Until the 19th century, scholars bravely endorsed the Indian route, including hagiographers (Stilting, 1741, 25E) and "official" historians of the Raj (Hunter, 1886, 235). They shift Bartholomew's mission to Bactria, the current Afghanistan (Milne Rae, 1892, 62–75), on the pretext that India was unknown to the ancients. In fact, literary evidence about India and trade routes to the subcontinent through the Red Sea show that such a trip does not seem totally unrealistic (Dihle, 1984, 69): South India's counters overflowed, attended to by Egyptians and Greeks. The fact that there is no evidence related to/attesting to Bartholomew's presence in India may be explained by the disappearance of Egyptian trade to South India with a later resumption of missions, this time headed by Syria (Vadakkekara, 2007, 168): Bartholomew vanished in favor of the patron of

the Syriac church, Thomas (→ Thomas the Apostle). An onomastic confusion may have fostered his disappearance: Bar Tholomai may simply have been understood to be Mar Thomas, Saint Thomas (Jullien, 2002, 51).

4. From India to the Lipari Islands: Bartholomew's Routes from the 4th to the 6th Century CE

Subsequent legends about Bartholomew's missions all derive from the tradition of the Indian route.

a. From India to Colchis (5th–6th cents. CE)

In the 5th century CE, the writings of → Eucherius of Lyon (*Instructionum ad Salonium*) and → Venantius Fortunatus (*Car.* 8.3) took up the Indian journey based on Eusebius' data. The first apostle lists also mention the Ἰνδοὶ εὐδαίμονες (the "happy Indies" in imitation of the *Arabia felix* [Schermann, 1907, 270]). But from the 6th century CE onward, the *Passion of Bartholomew* (*CANT* 259 = *BHL* 1002; Lat. text in: Bonnet, 1898, 128–150; Eng. summary in: Elliott, 2005, 518–520; Fr. trans. in: Alibert et al., 2005, 791–810), which belongs to the collection of Pseudo-Abdias, shifted Bartholomew's apostolic activity from an India that cannot be precisely located to a rather fantastic area that can be identified with Colchis. Indeed, the text incorporates the mission to India, but says

> That there are three Indies, this is what historians provide. The first one is the India extending to Ethiopia, the second one going up to the Medes, the third one that constitutes the border. Indeed, at one side it touches the region of darkness, on the other side, the Ocean. In this India, the Apostle Bartholomew entered. (Lipsius & Bonnet, 1898)

If the "first India" refers to southern Arabia (now Yemen), and the "second India" refers rather to Persia, then the third is utterly imaginary since it touches non-localizable areas such as the "region of darkness" or the "Ocean." To address his lack of knowledge, the author drags Bartholomew from India to the Pontus. Indeed, he calls Polymius the "good king" of this region, converted by Bartholomew.

This name refers to Caius Julius Polemon II (10/15–64 CE), the king of Pontus whom Caligula appointed ruler of Colchis.

The passion narrative is quite simple. In India, the demon Astaroth, who can be identified with the belligerent Phoenician Astarte (Lipsius, 1883, 71), kept the people under his control by his artifices (1–5). Bartholomew arrived opportunely and began healing those possessed by the → devil (6–13). Pleading his case before the king, he obtained the devil's confession, destroyed the temple, and converted Polymius (14–21). This last act excited the jealousy of the king's brother, Astriges, who put the apostle (22–25) to death.

Despite its apparent simplicity, this text is actually a treatise on → demonology and an insightful reflection on idolatry. It makes Bartholomew a champion in the fight against idols. The old gods live on: they are demons who inhabit the effigies. Indeed, the text undertakes an accurate description of the mechanism of idolatry represented as a hoax: the devil sends his people calamities he can heal, making them disappear in exchange for devotion. In reality, he cures nothing: he only takes away what he has previously created himself. This enables him to play the saving god, although he is actually just a troublemaker. This demonstration of idolatrous deceit goes hand in hand with great optimism regarding the power of the Christian religion. The text assures its readers that the devil is inherently weak. Let the apostle accompanied by angels of the Lord appear, and his temple is destroyed. Since the core of the devil's mock power remains in the idol, the text advocates aniconism and commands that any figurative representation should be destroyed.

The role of Bartholomew is simple: to expel demons and (what amounts to the same) destroy statues. He exerts this apostolic action on the demons inhabiting the people: the passion recounts two stories of healing that are, in fact, exorcisms. He was also capable of expelling demons from the temples: the heart of the text is the destruction of the great temple of Astaroth. He is eventually able to thwart the demonic machinations: all the speeches he gives reveal the derisory mechanism behind the influence of false gods.

From the passion of Bartholomew comes a description of the peculiar death suffered by Bartholomew:

flaying. That kind of death may have been inspired by the martyrdom which one tradition attributes to Mani; in the *Acta Archelai* of Hegemon, the heretic was condemned to be flayed by reeds (Marquart, 1896, 232–235).

5. Bartholomew in Armenia (6th–8th Centuries CE)

If the passion explicitly mentioned India, it remained elusive about the precise location of the country, which gradually tended to move toward the Caucasian region and in particular toward Armenia. The basis of this shift was laid by lists of apostles identifying the city of Bartholomew's death with an Armenian city, Albanopolis. No such identification predates the early 6th century CE and the *De Ortu et Obitu prophetarum* (Schermann, 1907, 270; Dolbeau, 1994, 106). Pseudo-Hippolytus, in turn, joined the Indian tradition with the Armenian one, and was followed in this by all subsequent apostolic lists. The Armenian location, even if it does not seem to have originated in Armenia, was widely adopted in the country thanks to a worship tradition that was considerably expanded from the 8th century CE onward (Esbroeck, 1983).

Armenian tradition led to the writing of a martyrdom story (*BHO* 156) that is known in three versions (text and Fr. trans. in: Leloir, 1992; another trans. in: Calzolari, 2011). All three have the same structure: after a drawing of lots in Jerusalem, Bartholomew leaves for Edem in India. There, he performs various miracles: he dries up a spring that had been the object of a cult to demons, casts out the aforementioned demons and carries out healings, and makes water gush forth from a rock, enabling him to baptize believers. He then rides to Babylonia and preaches to the Medes and Elamites, but his message is not well received. Moving on to Coele-Syria, he raises the son of Andronikos and preaches the Gospel of Matthew. He subsequently visits the Germaniceans, before returning to the Parthians, Medes, and Elamites, always teaching them the Gospel of Matthew. He finally reaches the Armenian province of Golthn, where he replaces Thaddeus. At Artashu, he meets Jude, and both of them eventually ride to Urbianos (Albanos/Albanopolis). There, he converts Ogohi, niece of King Abgar and sister of Sanatrouk:

her brother flies into a terrible rage and puts his own sister and the apostle to death.

A last text, a story on the invention of relics by the Syrian Marutha, allows us to combine the western and eastern traditions (Calzolari, 2011). In 399 CE, Bishop Marutha, known otherwise from two Greek lives (*BHG* 2265 and 2266), obtained permission from the Sassanid king Yazdegert I to collect the remains of the → martyrs of the persecution conducted by Yazdegert's predecessor Shapur II and to deposit them in the capital Maiperqat (now Silvan in Turkey), which quickly became known as Martyropolis. Of course, none of these precious relics belonged to Bartholomew, but one life of Marutha insists that the holy bishop subsequently obtained consent to search the entire Sassanid Empire for other relics. At a later date, this tradition is reworked in a text, the *Discovery of the Holy Apostle Bartholomew* (*BHO* 159). The text relates how Marutha, after gathering the relics of Martyropolis, went to Barm (maybe Ourbanopolis) to discover the remains of Bartholomew. They were stored in an inaccessible place. Fortunately, a celestial event occurred: an earthquake quite opportunely opened their resting place, allowing the fearless Marutha to recover a good part of them while leaving the rest behind. According to this story, the remains of Bartholomew arrived at Sophene, a western province of Greater Armenia, and became incorporated into the foundation of the Armenian church.

6. The Lipari Legend (6th Century CE)

After these eastern adventures, it comes as no surprise that the West should claim its share. In the *Glory of the Martyrs*, which may be dated to around 580 CE, → Gregory of Tours' account signals a new turn of events in the legend of the remains of Bartholomew. According to him, while Christians were being persecuted anew, the gentiles saw them rushing to the apostle's tomb for regular prayers and incense burning. Inflamed with hatred, the gentiles carried off the holy corpse. Placing it in a lead coffin, they threw it into the sea, saying, "No longer will you be able to entice our people." The coffin was brought to the Lipari Islands, where Bartholomew continued to perform miracles (Greg. T. *Glor. Mart.* 34).

In this story, we are confronted with a classic example of the invention of relics whose origin is justified *post eventum*. This legend is inserted into Bede's, Usuard's, and Roman martyrologies; from the 7th century CE onward, they constitute sufficient evidence of an important worship of Bartholomew, also noticeable in liturgical sources and references to him (Rose, 2009, 80–81). The body of Bartholomew was revered in the Lipari Islands until the 9th century CE, when the Arab invasion ravaged the island and the apostle's tomb was broken open. Opportunely, a monk gathered up the relics and entrusted them to the Lombards, who placed them under an altar in the Cathedral of Benevento in 839 CE (Stilting, 1741, 39–108). This translation of relics is celebrated on Aug 25, even in the Greek Church, and is widely echoed by Jacobus of Voragine in the *Golden Legend*.

This same Jacobus of Voragine is nonetheless quite uncomfortable in describing the type of martyrdom undergone by Bartholomew. Indeed, as we have seen, the traditions differ. The Dominican quotes Pseudo-Dorotheus, who speaks of crucifixion; Theodore Studite, who mentions flaying; and others, who refer to decapitation. He finally concludes:

> We can resolve this contradiction by saying that they beat and crucified him first, and before he died, he was descended from the cross, and to add to his ordeal, was flayed and finally beheaded. (Jacobus of Voragine, *Legenda aurea*, ch. 123)

7. The Particular Case of Coptic Legends (5th–6th Centuries CE)

The collection known as the *Contendings of the Apostles*, only acknowledged in the Coptic world, supplies additional information specific to the Egyptian Church. They are also preserved in Arabic and Ethiopian (trans. 6th–13th cents.). They seem quite *sui generis* and not to have been subject to any external influence. Three texts involve Bartholomew: the *Preaching of Bartholomew in the Oasis*, *The Martyrdom of Bartholomew*, and the *Acts of Saint Andrew and Bartholomew among the Parthians*.

8. The Preaching of Bartholomew in the Oasis and The Martyrdom of Bartholomew

The *Preaching of Bartholomew in the Oasis* (*CANT* 261) is known in Coptic (*BHO* 154, 155; ed. and Eng. or Ger. trans. in: Crum, 1905, 126–127; Lemm, 1890, 509–680; White & Gerard, 1926, 43–45), Arabic (*BHO* 152; ed. in: Smith-Lewis, 1904a, 58–64; ET in: Smith-Lewis, 1904b, 69–75), and Ethiopian (*BHO* 153; ed. in: Budge & Wallis, 1901, 83–94; ET in: Budge & Wallis, 1901b, 76–86; Fr. trans. in: Bausi, 2005, 881–893). *The Martyrdom of Bartholomew* (*CANT* 260) is known only through small fragments in Coptic (Bausi, 2005, 878), but is well preserved in Arabic (*BHO* 157; ed. in: Smith-Lewis, 1904a, 64–66; ET in: Smith-Lewis, 1904b, 76–79) and Ethiopian (*BHO* 158; ed. in: Budge & Wallis, 1901, 93–100; ET in: Budge & Wallis, 1901b, 87–92; Fr. trans. in: Bausi, 2005, 894–899). One text seems to follow the other, forming a unit. They describe how Bartholomew managed to enter the city of Oasis, how he performed miracles, and finally how he died. These two texts lack originality and seem to borrow heavily on their ancient novelistic/narrative precedents. We can distinguish two key elements.

1. *The renewal of the "ascetic triangle" common to apocryphal acts.* As for instance in the *Acts of Thomas*, the text plays on the famous "love triangle" of the Greek novel and theater to produce what might be called the "ascetic triangle": the apostle who preaches abstinence is seen as a rival by the husband whose wife has become a Christian. In a kind of ascetic remake of *Lysistrata*, the apostolic tour triggers a kind of "sex strike" which, in turn, triggers male hostility toward the apostles. To counteract this resentment, Bartholomew, who proves to be as skilful as "the wily Odysseus of many tricks and turns returning to Ithaca," adopts one of the most popular topoi of the novel: disguise. He plays Joseph sold by his brothers, but a consenting Joseph sold by his brother Peter to the inhabitants of the city for 30 staters. Since Joseph was sold for 20 pieces of silver, there may be an allusion to the 30 pieces of Judas.

Thus incognito, Bartholomew can convert the city of Oasis, found a church, and proclaim his message. The question of asceticism is not mentioned (proof that it was a novelistic technique) before his appearance before the king of the country, Aqrepos. His trial mimics the *Acts of Peter* (→ Peter the Apostle) even in the ruler's name (Aqrepos reminding us of Agrippa). Jealous of the apostle, the king wants to kill him. The kind of death he commands is especially atrocious: Bartholomew is to be placed in a bag of sand and cast into the sea.

2. *The miracle creates faith.* The second distinctive feature of these two texts is the accumulation of miracles: Bartholomew raises camels in the desert (48–54), gives sight to a blind man (55–61), grows the fruit of the vine (62–83), and raises a magistrate (84–107).

During his appearance before Aqrepos, he heals yet another blind man. These miracles somehow represent the narrative framework of the story, to such an extent that it is almost inappropriate to speak of a preaching Bartholomew; the apostle is rather shown as a thaumaturge. The use of the miracle itself is repetitive: invariably, it serves to create a wonder that leads to faith. These features are characteristic of the text's popular origin and disclose the ordinary Egyptian people's veneration of Bartholomew.

9. The *Acts of Andrew and Bartholomew* among the Parthians: Companionship with Andrew

These Coptic Acts (*BHG* 2056 = *CANT* 238), only known through fragments published by E. Lucchesi and J.-M. Prieur (Prieur & Lucchesi, 1978, 349–350), are preserved in Arabic (*BHO* 55; text and ET in: Budge & Wallis, 1901, 183–214) and Ethiopian (*BHO* 56; text and ET in: Smith-Lewis, 1904, 58–64). They seem to draw on details from the ministry of Andrew among the Parthians. It is obviously a popular story, replete with a wittiness that borrows heavily from older models.

The story begins with a vision of Bartholomew. The apostle, who is staying in Makatran, in the country of Azreyanos (maybe the Siwa Oasis), is called upon to evangelize the barbarous nations. The vision is unappealing; the worst tortures await the apostle: stake, crucifixion, drowning. Meanwhile, the apostle Andrew is called in a similar way. Accompanied by his two disciples, the apostle is on the shore wondering how to join Bartholomew. In the Arabic text, a heavenly boat picks him up while asleep, whereas the Ethiopian text repeats Jonah's experience: leaving for the wilderness (which is called the land of Barbarians), Andrew is swallowed by a big fish. The two apostles finally meet.

They take a boat whose captain is actually the Christ. They begin by chasing demons from the wife of the governor of Macedonia, subsequently arriving in the famous land of barbarians.

The rest of the story tells of the barbarian city's evangelization. They make a first attempt. Despite the intervention of the Christ-captain, who makes himself known to them, they are not successful. The two apostles are driven out of town and have to take refuge in the desert.

The second attempt is more successful. Providentially, they are supported by a powerful ally: the man with a dog's head. Both apostles encounter a "dog-headed man." He is actually a former dog who was summoned by an angel who hunted his animal nature through a kind of spiritual baptism. The text clearly plays on the name "Lycaonia." Because the cynocephali have, since Ctesias (5th cent. BCE), symbolized people living in the wilderness on the margins of the world, the text simultaneously expresses the belief that the apostles brought the gospel to the ends of the earth. With this powerful ally as companion, they return to the city, have close shaves with death, and are saved by the dog-headed man, who impresses the barbarians, who are converted and baptized in the heart of the city, thanks to a fountain that the apostles miraculously cause to spring forth from a pillar.

This simple summary may suffice to characterize the text. It is a piece of popular origin, multiplying wondrous elements with some fairly banal pieces of preaching embedded in it. It is not even a cautionary tale, but an exciting story in which the pleasure of the narrative wins out.

These stories are specific to the Coptic church and have enjoyed a long history in Egypt, as evidenced by the Jacobite synaxary, which provides a synthesis of these narratives on the 1st of Tout (Aug 29).

10. The Visionary

While various churches put the figure of Bartholomew to good use by presenting him as a model missionary, some communities appropriated the apostle in a manner that raised him to visionary status. The visionary nature granted to him is probably due to assimilation with Nathanael, of whom it is said in John 1:51 (Kaestli & Cheirix, 1993, 15): "Verily, verily, I say unto you, you will see the sky opened and the angels of God ascending and descending upon the Son of man." This text makes Nathanael a symbol of the true Israel, ready to welcome Jesus: he is a doctor of the law, called a "true Israelite" by Jesus (Léon-Dufour, 1988, 195). With that promise, Nathanael becomes a sort of new Jacob seeing a new ladder. He is, by prolepsis, the representative of the fulfillment announced in John 1:31. As M.-J. Lagrange remarked, "here is the program of the divine manifestation that will accomplish" (Lagrange, 1925, 51). Unfortunately, tracing this visionary tradition, which is preserved in the *Questions of Bartholomew* and the *Book of the Resurrection of Jesus Christ by Bartholomew*, is extremely problematical due to the difficulty of relating the texts to a specific historical context.

Neither text has a direct literary dependence, even if they seem to belong to a common tradition (Kaestli, 1988). We know that the → *Decretum Gelasianum* and Jerome's list both speak of a *Gospel of Bartholomew*. Is this text the same as the one which Pseudo-Dionysius quotes, "It is in this sense that the divine Bartholomew said that theology is both developed and concise, the gospel spacious and great, yet concise" (Dion. Ar. *Myst.* 3)? It is impossible to say with certainty whether any of these texts have something to do with our gospel.

The *Book of the Resurrection of Jesus* in its current form dates to the 5th or 6th century CE. It is very difficult to date the *Questions of Bartholomew*, which may go back to a very old tradition (2nd cent. CE) but contains some 6th-century CE features, such as a version of the Descent into Hell, which seems older than the one in the *Gospel of Nicodemus*. On the other hand, the text borrows some elements of the *Protoevangelium of James*, dating from the 3rd century CE, and shows an older Mariology than that of the Council of → Ephesus.

11. *Questions of Bartholomew*

The *Questions of Bartholomew* (*CANT* 63 = *BHG* 228; Fr. trans. in Kaestli, 1997a) consists of various parts compiled in two Greek versions (P. Vindobonensis hist. gr. 67, 13th cent., fols. 9–15ᵛ; P. Saint Sabas, Jérusalem, 13, 10th–11th cents., fols. 114ᵛ–116ᵛ), two Latin versions (Vat. Reg. 1050, 9th–10th cents. CE, fol. 4; Biblioteca Casanatense 1880, 11th cent., fols. 161ᵛ–169), and five Slavonic versions, with significant differences. The text is divided into several distinct episodes:

1. crucifixion and descent into hell,
2. a question about the virginal conception of Jesus by Mary,
3. a question about Belial, the opponent, and finally
4. Bartholomew's prayer for sinners.

Bartholomew plays a highly influential role in this book and is a true competitor of the other apostles, especially Peter (→ Peter the Apostle). Bartholomew appears as an important member of the apostolic community, playing the role of the beloved disciple. Jesus repeatedly accords him this title, reminiscent of the anonymous Johannine character. Bartholomew, and not the beloved disciple, follows Jesus from afar during his arrest: "While all the apostles went away, I have followed you" (1:6). Bartholomew is also the one who hears the voice in the abyss, triggering the story of the descent into hell. "*He can still see [...]*" the body of Jesus hanging on the → cross and watch "the angels ascending before Adam" (1:23 see 1:6) as fulfillment of the promise made to Nathanael. The answer to all of Bartholomew's visions follows immediately. Jesus pronounces a series of beatitudes such as "Blessed art thou, Bartholomew my beloved" (1:8, 26), confirming the apostle's status as the favored recipient of divine visions.

In the *Questions of Bartholomew*, the leadership, traditionally given to Peter, is entrusted to the apostle. Indeed, → Mary is present at the meeting and Bartholomew requests his colleagues to ask her questions, but the apostles hesitate. Bartholomew even has to exhort Peter, "Father Peter, since you are the head, approach you and ask her" (2:3). Peter offloads onto John. Finally, Bartholomew must question Mary himself and even has to cajole Peter into taking charge of prayer (2:7). Throughout this episode with Mary, Bartholomew reveals himself as the true rock: "You Bartholomew place your knees firmly against my shoulders and grip them well: I don't want my bones to disintegrate when I start talking," she says (2:14); to resist the emotion grasping her during the story she is about to tell, Mary finds a powerful aid in Bartholomew.

Indeed, throughout these *Questions*, Bartholomew appears as the mighty apostle par excellence, able to play all the roles. He first becomes the privileged interlocutor of Mary and her son, subsequently proving his worth in dispute with Belial, being able to crush his neck (4:22) and to push Belial's face "into the earth to the ears." He is also the beloved one. At the end of the text, he adopts two new roles: intercessor for humanity (4:61) and scribe for what he has heard (4:69).

In the *Questions of Bartholomew*, the apostle thus established himself as the best interlocutor for matters regarding mysteries of the afterlife. His name is attached to revelations of what happens after death. This text confirms the veneration some communities had for Bartholomew, assimilating him to the seer Nathanael. Needing to legitimize their esoteric teaching, they naturally turned to the apostle whom they considered the best visionary.

12. The *Book of the Resurrection of Jesus*

The *Book of the Resurrection of Jesus* (*CANT* 80–82; text and ET in: Budge & Wallis, 1913; Fr. trans. in: Kaestli, 1997b), only known in Coptic, may date back from the 5th century CE (Gardner & Johnston, 2010). It entrusts quite a prominent role to Bartholomew. The apostle is utterly absent from the first chapters, but from 10:3 on, he is found right behind the gardener Philogenes, who assists at the → resurrection. He even becomes a gardener himself (17:3), perhaps in remembrance of the fact that Nathanael was called under a fig tree. From this privileged position, he can contemplate the divine liturgy of the seventh heaven and become its scribe (14:2; 27:1), transcribing the heavenly hymns heard in chapters 12–16.

From chapter 21 onward, however, he loses some of his importance as the action focuses on Thomas and his disciple Siophanes. The latter tells at length how he has come back from the dead (evidence of the influence of the *Acts of Thomas* on the text; → Thomas the Apostle). Bartholomew then leaves center stage and reappears for a minor exhortation to Thomas (23:8).

Conclusion

If Bartholomew enjoyed a lavish reception in some eastern churches, its extension was short-lived. Bartholomew is typical of those "small" apostles who did not leave profound marks on the communities: this ignorance makes all appropriations possible, mainly by local churches or communities on the margins. One might think of Simon, "captured" by Persia, the successive annexations of Jude, or the various places of martyrdom assigned to James the Less (Burnet, 2014; → James the Apostle). These appropriations, however, are rarely incorporated into the common tradition of the churches. The most common iconography of Bartholomew describes the position he occupies perfectly: the whole legend boils down to his martyrdom. At first represented only with a knife, he is subsequently often shown during his execution. The flaying he suffered often found expression in striking visions of *écorchés* and dreadfully skinned bodies, taking inspiration from the iconography of Marsyas, a victim of Apollo's jealousy. The apostle is sometimes wrapped in his skin (statue of Marco d'Agrate in the Duomo Cathedral of Milan, 1562), sometimes holding it in his hand. This stripping was a source of pure fascination – we are reminded of Michelangelo's extraordinary frescoes in the Sistine Chapel – most often found in Counter-Reformation paintings, especially in 17th-century Spain, which was particularly fond of horror, as seen in the works of Ribera (Réau, 1958, 183).

Historiography

The history of the view of the figure of Bartholomew follows that of every ancient saint. Objects of worship were first the subject of more or less gullible hagiographical accounts that were "criticized" in several stages. Contrary to common belief, the *Golden Legend* of Jacques de Voragine was one of these stages, which was followed by the works of modern times: L.-S. Le Nain de Tillemont (1693) and the Bollandist J. Stilting (1741) are good representatives of this new approach. The 19th century and

its historical-critical perspective only deepened the results of the 17th century. The difference is that they considered the hagiographical accounts as legends: this is what the synthesis of R.A. Lipsius (1883) does, which makes extensive use of apocryphal texts. Since this book, no great synthesis has been dedicated to the apostle, who is, admittedly, a minor figure of Christianity. The interest of researchers for the apostle is occasionally aroused by their interest in certain corpuses such as Syriac texts (Budge, 1901a; 1901b; Smith Lewis, 1904a; 1904b), Armenian texts (Esbroek, 1983; Calzolari Bouvier, 2011), or the cycle of the descent to hell (Kaestli, 1988). The role that Bartholomew is supposed to play in the evangelization of India focused attention on him during the establishment of the Raj (Hunter, 1886; Milne Rae 1892) and still explains his popularity among Indian Christians (Vadakkekara, 2007).

Bibliography

Alibert, D., G. Besson, M. Brossard Dandré & S.C. Mimouni, "Passion de Barthélemy," in: P. Geoltrain & J.-D. Kaestli, eds., *Écrits apocryphes chrétiens*, vol. II, BiPl, Paris, 2005, 791–810.

Baronius, C., *Annales Ecclesiastici*, vol. I, Barri-Ducis (Bar-le-Duc), 1864.

Baronius, C., *Martyrologium Romanum ad Novam Kalendarii Rationem et Ecclesiasticæ Historiæ Veritate Vestitutum*, Rome, 1598.

Bauckham, R., *Jesus and the Eyewitnesses: The Gospels as Eyewitness Testimony*, Grand Rapids, 2006.

Bausi, A., "Prédication et Martyre de Barthélemy," in: P. Geoltrain & J.-D. Kaestli, eds., *Écrits apocryphes chrétiens*, vol. II, BiPl, Paris, 2005, 875–900.

Budge, E., & A. Wallis, *The Contendings of the Apostles: Being the Histories of the Lives and Martyrdoms and Deaths of the Twelve Apostles and Evangelists: The Ethiopic Texts*, London, 1901a.

Budge, E., & A. Wallis, *The Contendings of the Apostles: Being the Histories of the Lives and Martyrdoms and Deaths of the Twelve Apostles and Evangelists: The English Translation*, London, 1901b.

Budge, E., & A. Wallis, *Coptic Apocrypha in the Dialect of Upper Egypt*, London, 1913.

Burnet, R., *Les douze apôtres*, JAOC, Turnhout, 2014.

Calzolari Bouvier, V., *Les apôtres Thaddée et Barthélemy aux origines du christianisme arménien*, Apocryphes, Turnhout, 2011.

Crum, W.E., *Catalogue of the Coptic Manuscripts in the British Museum*, London, 1905.

Dihle, A., *Antike Und Orient Gesammelte Aufsätze*, AWH. PH, Heidelberg, 1984.

Dihle, A., "The Conception of India in Hellenistic and Roman Literature," *CCJ* 10, 1964, 15–23.

Dolbeau, F., "Nouvelles recherches sur le De Ortu et Orbitu Prophetarum et Apostolorum," *Aug.* 34/1, 1994, 91–107.

Elliott, J.K., *The Apocryphal New Testament: A Collection of Apocryphal Christian Literature in an English Translation*, Oxford, 2005.

Esbroeck, M. van, "La naissance du culte de Saint Barthélémy en Arménie," *REArm* 17, Paris, 1983, 171–195.

Gardner, I., & J. Johnston, "The Liber Bartholomaei on the Ascension: Edition of Bibliothèque Nationale Copte 1321 F. 37," *VigChr* 64/1, 2010, 74–86.

Hunter, W.W., *The Indian Empire: Its People, History and Products*, London, 1886.

Jullien, C., & F. Jullien, *Apôtres des confins, processus missionnaires chrétiens dans l'empire iranien*, RO, Louvain, 2002.

Kaestli, J.-D., "Où en est l'étude de l'évangile de Barthélemy?" *RB* 95, 1988, 5–33.

Kaestli, J.-D., "Questions de Barthélemy," in: F. Bovon & P. Geoltrain, eds., *Écrits apocryphes chrétiens*, vol. I, BiPl, Paris, 1997a, 257–297.

Kaestli, J.-D., "Livre de la résurrection de Jésus-Christ par l'apôtre Barthélemy," in: F. Bovon & P. Geoltrain, eds., *Écrits apocryphes chrétiens*, vol. I, BiPl, Paris, 1997b, 299–357.

Kaestli, J.-D., & P. Cherix. *L'évangile de Barthélemy d'après deux écrits apocryphes*, Apocryphes, Paris, 1993.

Lagrange, M.-J., *Évangile selon Saint Jean*, EtB, Paris, 1925.

Leloir, L., *Écrits apocryphes sur les apôtres*, CChr.SA, Turnhout, 1992.

Lemm, O. von, "Koptische apokryphe Apostelacten," *BASS* 33, 1890, 509–581.

Le Nain de Tillemont, L.-S., *Mémoires pour servir à l'histoire ecclésiastique des six premiers siècles: Justifiez par les citations des auteurs originaux*, Paris, 1693.

Léon-Dufour, X., *Lecture de l'évangile selon Jean*, ParD, Paris, 1988.

Lipsius, R.A., *Die apokryphen Apostelgeschichten und Apostellegenden: Ein Beitrag zur altchristlichen Literaturgeschichte*, vol. II/2, Braunschweig, 1883.

Lipsius, R.A., & M. Bonnet, *Acta Apostolorum Apocrypha 2.1*, Leipzig, 1898, 127

Lucchesi, E., & J.-M. Prieur, "Fragments Coptes des Actes d'André et Matthias et d'André et Barthélemy," *AnBoll* 9/3–4, Brussels, 1978, 339–350.

Marquart, J., *Untersuchungen Zur Geschichte von Eran*, Göttingen, 1896.

Milne Rae, G., *The Syrian Church in India*, Edinburgh, 1892.

Nahr, I.N., *Nathanaelem Apostolum a Bartholomaeo Non Diversum*, Lipsiae (Leipzig), 1740.

Pouderon, B., "Le témoignage du Codex Baroccianus 142 sur Athénagore et les origines du Didaskaleion d'Alexandrie," in: G. Argoud, ed., *Science et vie intellectuelle à Alexandrie (Ier–IIIe siècle après J.-C.)*, MCJP, Saint-Étienne, 1994, 163–224.

Réau, L., *Iconographie des Saints*, vol. III, Paris, 1958.

Rose, E., *Ritual Memory the Apocryphal Acts and Liturgical Commemoration in the Early Medieval West (c. 500–1215)*, MITS, Leiden, 2009.

Schermann, T., *Propheten- und Apostellegenden: Nebst Jüngerkatalogen des Dorotheus und verwandter Texte*, TU 31, Leipzig, 1907.

Smith Lewis, A., *Acta Mythologica Apostolorum*, HSem, London, 1904a.

Smith Lewis, A., *The Mythological Acts of Apostles*, HSem, London, 1904b.

Stilting, J., "De Bartholomaeo Apostolo," in: *Acta Sanctorum Augusti*, Antwerp, 1741, 7–108.

Thelamon, F., *Païens et chrétiens au IVe siècle: L'apport de l'histoire ecclésiastique de Rufin d'Aquilée*, Paris, Éaug, 1981.

Vadakkekara, B., *Origin of Christianity in India: A Historiographical Critique*, Delhi, 2007.

White, E., & H. Gerard, *The Monasteries of the Wadi'n Natrûn I: The Metropolitan Museum of Art, Egypt Exploration*, New York, 1926.

RÉGIS BURNET

II. *Bartholomew, Questions of*

The (*Apocryphal*) *Questions of Bartholomew* (*BHG* 228; *CANT* 63) is a Christian text, of a possible Egyptian provenance and originally written in Greek. The text was later translated into Latin and Old Church Slavonic. The relationship between these various versions has not yet been fully explored. The text survives in three Greek, two Latin, and six Slavonic manuscripts, which are mostly incomplete. The most ancient witness is attested in a fragmentary Latin manuscript dated to the 9th/10th century CE (Vat. Reg. 1050).

The date of the work remains uncertain. More recent scholarship has dated the text to the late 3rd or 4th century CE, although later dates have been suggested as well.

The text is related to apocryphal revelation dialogues of the resurrected Jesus with his disciples (→ Resurrection). The figure of the apostle Bartholomew as a recipient of heavenly revelations is well attested in early Christianity. The title "Questions of Bartholomew" is witnessed in three of the manuscripts and corresponds to the content and the literary genre of the work. In the Slavonic context the title "Bartholomew's Questions to Mary" appears as well (Chromá, 2019, 9).

There are hardly any direct references to this work in early Christian literature. A writing under the title *Gospel of Bartholomew* is mentioned by → Jerome (Prologue, *Commentary on Matthew*; CChr.SL 77, 1.7f.). *Gospels of Bartholomew* are listed in the Gelasian Decree (→ *Decretum Gelasianum*) among the "apocryphal books" (*Decr. Gel.* 4.4). The relation of these references to our text remains speculative.

A possible reference to the text is preserved in an 8th-century CE writing, *De vita sanctissimae Deiparae* (25), by the Byzantine author, Epiphanius the Monk (PG 120.214C), whereas a quotation seems to survive in a 7th/8th-century CE Latin sermon (Pelle, 2014). In addition, a probable reference appears to be included in a 14th-century Ethiopic work, *The Book of the Mysteries of Heaven and Earth* (2.7); PO 6.3(1911).404, as well as in the Ethiopic *Homily on the Annunciation of Gabriel to Mary* (Piovanelli, 2013, 102).

There is no evidence for a direct relation of the text to the so-called Bartholomew literature that is mainly transmitted in Coptic, such as the *Book of Bartholomew* (or *Book of the Resurrection of Christ*; *CANT* 80). However, the text demonstrates literary affinities to Christian pseudepigrapha, such as the *Questions of James to John* (*CANT* 279), the *Dialogue Between Jesus and the Devil* (*CANT* 84), and the *Gospel of Nicodemus* (→ Pilate: *Pilate, Acts of*; *CANT* 62).

The *Questions of Bartholomew* contains important para-biblical, angelological, and demonological information. Possible "gnosticizing" features of the text as well as traces of monophysitism and doceticism have been suggested but are debated (Baeston, 1974; Markschies, 2012, 701; Chromá, 2019, 12–13).

The text is composed as a post-resurrection revelatory discourse by Jesus to his gathered disciples, placed in the narrative frame of the "questions and answers" literary genre (Gk *erotapokriseis*). Scholars have stressed the apocalyptic character of certain parts of the text (Kaestli, 1988, 10). The narrative unfolds in five scenes of various length and themes.

Jesus elucidates questions posed mainly by the apostle Bartholomew on a variety of "apocryphal" or "secret" subjects, the knowledge of which is even considered to be perilous for the spiritually immature apostles except for Bartholomew, who was granted a vision during Jesus' crucifixion. The major questions discussed refer to heavenly secrets, the number of souls in heaven, the "hidden" events during Jesus' crucifixion, including the "harrowing of hell," as well as conversations between the → devil and a personified → Hades. The Virgin → Mary tentatively answers questions about Jesus' conception but is prevented by Jesus from revealing this "awesome mystery." The text includes interesting apocalyptic elements, such as the revelation of the apocalyptic abyss, which is briefly uncovered by the angels on Jesus' command, but the apostles cannot bear the sight of it. The Virgin Mary also explains the theological importance of her rendering Eve's (→ Adam and Eve) transgression ineffective. The Slavonic manuscripts end with the description of the tremendous and frightful appearance of the chained Beliar (also → antichrist or devil). The Greek and Latin recensions include questions about Beliar's name, his fall, and his angels. Questions about the number, nature, and ranks of the angels including interesting cosmological associations are also addressed. Certain recensions relate the devil's ways to deceive humanity and describe the categories of sinners and hell torments. Finally, in a concluding part largely preserved in one Latin manuscript, and probably a later redactional addition, Jesus answers questions about the various sins of humanity and their respective severity.

Historiography

The text was (re-)discovered by modern scholarship through editions of Church Slavonic (Pypin, 1862; Tichonravov, 1863) and Greek (Vassiliev, 1893) manuscript witnesses as well as translations into modern languages in the second half of the 19th century (Bonwetsch, 1897). Early scholarship speculated about the relationship of the *Questions of Bartholomew* with the *Gospel of Batholomew* mentioned in early Christian literature (see above) and suggested – even if with some caution – that the *Questions of Bartholomew* at least relates to the *Gospel* (Wilmart & Tisserant, 1913). More recent scholarship has maintained the independent literary character of the *Questions of Bartholomew* with regard to other works that circulated under the name of the apostle Bartholomew (Kaestli, 1988; Kaestli & Cherix, 1993; Markschies, 2012).

Manuscripts and Editions

Bonwetsch, N., "Die Apokryphen Fragen des Bartholomäus," *NAWG*, 1897, 1–42.

Chromá, M., *Apocryphal Questions of Bartholomew in the Slavonic Tradition*, Prague, 2019.

Kaestli, J.-D., "Questions de Barthélemy," in: F. Bovon & P. Geoltrain, eds., *Écrits apocryphes chrétiens*, vol. I, Paris, 1997, 257–295.

Kaestli, J.-D., & P. Cherix, *L'évangile de Barthélemy: D'après deux écrits apocryphes*, Apocryphes 3, Turnhout, 1993.

Markschies, C., "Die Fragen des Bartholomaeus," in: C. Markschies & J. Schröter, eds., *Antike christliche Apokryphen in deutscher Übersetzung*, vol. I/2, Tübingen, 2012, 702–850.

Moricca, U., "Un nuovo testo dell 'Evangelo di Bartolemeo'," *RivBib* n.s. 18 (= 30), 1921, 481–516; n.s 19 (= 31), 1922, 20–30.

Pypin, A.N., Ložnyia I otrečennyja knigi russkoj stariny, Graf Gr. Kušelev-Bezborodko, ed. Vyp. 3, Saint Petersburg, 1862, 109–112.

Tichonravov, N., "Varpholomeevy voprosy Bogoroditse," in: *Pamjatniki otrechennoj russkoj literatury*, vol. II, Saint Petersburg, 1863, 18–22.

Vassiliev, A., *Anecdota graeco-byzantina*, Moscow, 1893, 10–22.

Wilmart, A., & E. Tisserant, "Fragments grecs et latins de l'évangile de Barthélemy," *RB* 10, 1913, 161–190, 321–368.

Bibliography

Beeston, A.F.L., "The Quaestiones Bartholomae," *JThS* 25, 1974, 124–127.

Kaestli, J.-D., "Où en est l'étude de 'l'évangile de Barthélemy'?" *RB* 95, 1988, 5–33.

Pelle, S., "A Quotation from the Questions of Bartholomew in an Early Medieval Latin Sermon," *Apocrypha* 25, 2014, 133–149.

Piovanelli, P., "Rewriting: The Path from Apocryphal to Heretical," in: W. Mayer & B. Neil, eds., *Religious Conflict from Early Christianity to the Rise of Islam*, Boston, 2013, 87–108.

EMMANOUELA GRYPEOU

Basil of Caesarea

Basil of Caesarea (c. 330–379 CE) belonged to a distinguished Christian family from the Roman province of Pontus, north of Cappadocia, in modern-day Turkey. Gregory of Nazianzus, his contemporary and dear friend, testifies that Basil's ancestors on his father's side had suffered as confessors in the Great Persecution (303–313 CE; → Persecution of Christians) under Emperor Maximinus (Greg. Naz. *Or.* 43.3; 43.5). → Gregory of Nyssa, one of Basil's younger brothers, adds the detail that their paternal grandmother, Macrina, for whom Basil's older sister Macrina was named, was among these confessors (Greg. Nyss. *Vita Mac.* 2). Basil's parents, Basil and Emmelia, lived a devout Christian life marked by generosity to the poor, hospitality, and self-discipline → Gregory of Nazianzus notes that they had dedicated a portion of their property to God (Greg. Naz. *Or.* 43.9). Basil's mother had at first chosen not to marry, but reconsidered in the face of the risk that she would be forced against her will by the violence of some suitors (Greg. Nyss. *Vita Mac.* 2). Macrina, the oldest child in the family, essentially had the Psalter memorized and recited it at the proper times of the day. At the age of 13 or so, she decided also to live as a consecrated virgin in their home, performing the tasks of the slaves – for those who embraced the ascetic life, at least in the East, left behind the class distinctions, such as master and slave, that exist only in this fallen world and no longer exist in heaven.

It is clear enough that not all the members of the family lived life as Macrina (→ Macrina, the Elder and the Younger) in these early years, but it would be safe to say, given all the evidence, that the whole family took the obligations of the Christian life seriously. It does not take too much imagination to see in these early years the roots of the ascetic practice that Basil will develop later in life. Indeed, eventually the entire family followed Macrina's lead, and their home became a domestic monastery of sorts (Silvas, 2013, 71–75).

Basil's father gave him his first education in Pontus, and after this moved on to Caesarea where he either finished his education in grammar or began the second stage of ancient education, that of → rhetoric. He certainly was educated in rhetoric when he studied in Athens in the home of Prohaeresius (in Athens teachers taught students in their homes; see Watts, 2012, 471). Prohaeresius himself had come from Basil's region and, therefore, would develop a following among students from there (Watts, 2006, 63n67). Although Prohaeresius was a Christian, he would have taught the standard curriculum in rhetoric, which took about three years, just as the pagan teachers did, and probably himself had pagan students, as the Christians Basil and Gregory seem to have been in the distinct minority in attending church regularly (Watts, 2006, 63). Basil's rhetorical education would have picked up with exercises where the grammarian left off and progressed to the point of deeper literary and moral analysis from the rhetor together with the mastery of rhetoric demonstrated in their own writing in the various rhetorical genres (Watts, 2006, 4). After a course in rhetoric some students went on to study philosophy. In the school of the philosopher, students "would listen to what amounted to line-by-line discussions of philosophical texts and their meaning" (Watts, 2006, 4). Presumably it is this philosophical education that Gregory of Nazianzus pursued in Alexandria once he and Basil finished their course of rhetoric in Athens.

From Athens, Basil returned home. A. Silvas has offered the intriguing suggestion that he returned home at this point because of a tragedy in the family (Silvas, 2005, 68). His brother Naucratius had died in a hunting accident that shook the whole family. At this point, Basil's life took an unexpected turn. The usual course would have been to become a rhetor, and, perhaps to follow in his father's footsteps, but Basil took a different line: he became an ascetic and underwent baptism. Gregory of Nyssa presents this as a significant moral transformation inspired by Macrina. He tells us that Basil came home from school (around 355–356 CE) puffed-up and conceited (Greg. Nyss. *Vita Mac.* 6). He himself admits that he had labored on the path to worldly success: he aspired to be a rhetor, that most prestigious and respected position in ancient society. In retrospect, however, Basil saw his intense study of rhetoric as time lavished on vanity and futility. He writes:

> I occupied myself with the acquirement of the precepts of that wisdom made foolish by God [and] one day arising as from a deep sleep I looked out upon the marvelous light of the truth of the gospel, and beheld the uselessness of the wisdom "of the princes of this world that come to nought" [1 Cor 2:6]. (Bas. *Ep.* 223.2)

We should balance this, perhaps too harsh, self-criticism with Basil's qualified but positive estimation of the study of pagan literature in his *To Young Men.* Nevertheless, Gregory of Nyssa writes that Macrina won Basil

> so swiftly [...] to the ideal of philosophy that he renounced worldly appearance, showed contempt for the admiration of rhetorical ability and went over of his own accord to this active life of manual labor, preparing for himself, by means of his complete poverty, a way of life which would tend without impediment towards virtue. (Greg. Nyss. *Vita Mac.* 5)

Basil sought a mentor on this new path, Eustathius of Sebaste, an ascetic and then bishop, who eventually broke friendship with Basil over a disagreement about the divinity of the Holy Spirit (Bas. *Ep.* 1). Eustathius may well have been familiar to Basil from childhood, a friend of the family and admired man of God (Silvas, 2005, 56; Bas. *Ep.* 244). After travelling around in search of Eustathius, Basil returned home, determined to live a rustic life of withdrawal (*Ep.* 14). It is at this time that he was baptized. With this decision, Basil set in motion a spiritual force that ultimately would lead to a fully articulated and highly complex ascetic life. It began with a simple desire to live the gospel with friends, set apart from the business of the world. Basil had encouraged Gregory of Nazianzus to join him in the effort, and Gregory did visit him, but was unable to stay, as his own obligations to his parents drew him back to Nazianzus (Greg. Naz. *Or.* 43.25). While they were together, however, they put together a set of New Testament texts by which they could live their lives. One of Basil's early ascetic works, the *Morals*, is a witness to this collection of texts.

So, Basil had retired to Pontus in 358 CE or so to live a life according to the Gospel, but not long after he got his first entry into ecclesiastical affairs. In the company of Eustathius of Sebaste and Basil of Ancyra he attended the Synod of → Constantinople in 359 CE. At this time, the Christian world had been torn asunder by the dispute over the teaching of Arius (→ Arianism) that the Son of God was a uniquely created God, and this synod in Constantinople was one in a long line of imperial attempts to bring unity, even if at the cost of doctrinal precision. Basil's first taste of this side of life in the church was bitter. Apparently, he was to engage in debate with Aëtius of Antioch, the founder of a new sect of radical Arians who claimed that the Son was unlike the Father in substance, among other things. In fact, as → Eunomius of Cyzicus, the chief disciple of Aëtius has it, Basil fled the council altogether (Greg. Nyss. *C.Eun.* 1.9). Basil was also distressed that the bishop of Caesarea who had baptized him and ordained him a lector, Dianius, had signed an Arianizing creed. So, he withdrew to Pontus to continue there the ascetic life that the councils had interrupted. This experience in Constantinople forms the backdrop for one of Basil's earliest works, his *Against Eunomius.*

In 362 CE, Basil brought his ascetic life to the city and the institutional church. He had left his monastic retreat to return to Caesarea and be reconciled to Bishop Dianius. After Dianius' death, Basil stayed in Caesarea, and under the new bishop, Eusebius, Basil was ordained a presbyter (→ Priest/Presbyter) and continued to live the monastic life, but in a different form. Division arose and Basil again withdrew to Pontus, whence he wrote *Ep.* 22 to the ascetics he had left behind (Greg. Naz. *Or.* 43.28). This letter marks important developments in Basil's understanding of the ascetic life: a complex and structured social life centered on love of the other. It was also at this time in Pontus that Basil wrote his *Morals* and his *Against Eunomius.* In 365 CE, however, Basil returned to Caesarea and reconciled with Eusebius.

In the late 360s CE, Cappadocia was struck by a severe famine, and this was the occasion for Basil to write some searing sermons against the rich and to organize a set of charitable activities that became institutionalized in a sort of Christian social order that culminated in the *Basileiados,* a series of buildings which Gregory of Nazianzus termed the "new city" where the poor and ill were cared for and fed (*Or.* 43.35). The *Basileiados* was also a sort of monastic center, for many of those who cared for the poor and sick were Basil's brothers and sisters in the ascetic life. Hence, it served as a point of interface between monastery and secular world, a point wherein ordinary Christians could be exposed to the monastic life and from which they could be drawn into it (Rousseau, 1994, 143–144).

Eusebius died in 370 CE, and after a controverted election, Basil became the bishop of Caesarea late in 370 CE. As a late antique bishop, Basil had two overarching sets of obligations: one religious, the other, civic. Above all he was the leader of a Christian community, all about the business of celebrating the liturgy, especially baptisms and Eucharists (→ Eucharist), the administration of penance (→ Penitence/Penance), preaching, and the dispensation of charity. But on the civic side, the late antique bishop became eventually the central figure in civic administration and a source of wealth and patronage (Rapp, 2005, 290). One can see these various roles in Basil's many letters: he was expected and obliged to intercede for his flock with various secular authorities to secure justice for them in matters of inheritance and taxation (Bas. *Ep.* 72–73; 83–84; 94; 107–109).

The course of Basil's episcopate can be understood as both the unwinding and the development of relationships. The best example of the former is the ruin of his friendship with Eustathius of Sebaste, while the best example of the latter is his successful mentorship of Amphilochius of Iconium. Several of Basil's most important works emerge out of this context: his *On the Holy Spirit,* dedicated to Amphilochius and written against the Eustathians; his "canonical letters" written to Amphilochius, which give us fantastic insight into Basil's regulation of the penitential discipline of his flock; his dogmatic letters, several written to Amphilochius, wherein one can trace his significant theological contributions, such as the incomprehensibility of → God, the distinction between essence and energies, and the distinction between "substance" (→ *ousia*) and "persons" (*hypostases*) in the Trinity (Bas. *Ep.* 9; 125; 214; 236, as example of dogmatic letters; the canonical letters are *Ep.* 188; 199; 217). Just before his death in 379 CE, Basil wrote one of his most enduring works, a set of sermons on the six days of creation, his *Hexaemeron.*

1. Significant Themes

Basil was not an ivory-tower bishop-theologian. He did not retire from the issues and controversies of his time and make his contributions to Christian thought by taking up questions in a systematic way and spinning out a theoretical vision; but he made a profound contribution nonetheless, and his contribution in so many ways was the flowering of the seeds of devotion that were planted in Basil's childhood and grew, when he was a young man, into the intense desire to live the commandments, to lead a life conformed to the gospel. What, then, were the issues and controversies that provided Basil the opportunity to make so profound a contribution to Christian life? If we put them in the form of a list, they would be: the controversy over how to interpret the creation narrative; the secularization of the church in general (provoking questions about the moral standard that Christian were called to live and about the place of the ascetic life) and the corruption of church leadership in particular (provoking questions about what sort of man should become a bishop); the dispute over the status of the Son and the Spirit (Arianism and its progeny, one of which was Pneumatomachianism; → Pneumatomachi).

a. Scripture

While the so-called "Origenist Controversy" (→ Origenism/Origenist Controversy) did not begin until shortly after Basil's death, Origen's allegorical method (→ Allegory), especially applied to the → creation narrative, had already become a subject of dispute in Basil's lifetime. It is in this context that Basil offered his own interpretation of the creation narrative. Basil's *Hexaemeron* – and I would add his two sermons on the creation of man – was the crowning achievement of his episcopal career and one of his most influential works. In spite of several anti-allegorical passages, it would be wrong to think of the *Hexaemeron* as a work devoted to the rejection of allegorical method – in fact Basil himself used this method both in his *Homilies on the Psalms* and in the *Hexaemeron* itself. Rather, what Basil is about here is that same thing that Origen was about. Christians, especially educated ones, had to show their pagan contemporaries and themselves that the scriptural account of the origin of the world made better sense than the pagan accounts.

Basil calls the created world a book, but he calls it also a "school for rational souls and a place for instruction in the knowledge of God" (Bas. *Hex.* 1.6). Indeed, the created world is designed by God with this specific purpose. Moreover, it is not simply to the knowledge of God that the world will bring us, but to the worship of him: "Let us glorify," Basil urges, "the best Artisan for what has been wisely and skillfully made" (*Hex.* 1.11; see 3.1).

Especially in the *Hexaemeron*, but also in his other sermons, Basil displays a vast knowledge of ancient natural science and of the behavior and character of all sorts of plants and animals. He is quite familiar with the positions of different natural philosophers, and current with the disputed questions of natural science and uses what he has learned from pagans to show his audience both the folly of human wisdom and the sagacity of Scripture. He uses his knowledge of natural science both to praise God and to put reason in its proper place (*Hex.* 1.10). The *Hexaemeron* is, essentially, a close reading of Gen 1:1–25, where Basil explains the biblical text verse by verse, sometimes word by word, engaging (sometimes refuting) pagan thought along the way and making moral applications to Christian life.

It is in the course of carrying out this larger task, that Basil opposes the excesses of allegorical interpretation, but he still uses it (see *Hex.* 9.1; 2.5; for the anti-allegorical texts see *Hex.* 3.9). His exegetical method did not radically change in the years during which he wrote homilies on the Psalms and creation: he never let go of a theological reading of the Hebrew Bible (→ Bible) and never restricted God's communication to historical narrative, though it is true that he became far more sensitive to the abuses of the allegorical method that one could see in gnostic interpretations as well as Origen's. The controversy over allegorical interpretation turns more fundamentally, then, on deeper theological questions. Basil remains throughout committed to the unity of the Hebrew Bible and the New Testament (→ Bible) and to the freedom of God to communicate truths about Christ and the life of Christians through the texts of the Hebrew Bible: these things are the immediate and obvious consequences of the text's divine authorship.

b. The Moral and Acetic Life

Basil's own life was a turning away from a secular career and toward a life of devotion to the commandments of the Lord. But he drew many others into this movement – first Gregory of Nazianzus, then his ascetic followers in Caesarea, then the countless number of ascetics who read his ascetic works translated into Latin by → Rufinus of Aquileia and studied them at the behest of → Benedict of Nursia, who commanded that all the followers of his rule read fathers such as Basil (Ben. *Reg.* 73). Basil's desire to keep the commandments and to help others to do so led him to commit to writing and to develop over time a mature and complicated vision for the ascetic life. These ascetic works are letters (e.g. Bas. *Ep.* 1; 2; 4; 14; 22), sermons, and, above all, the *Great Asceticon* and the *Small Asceticon*, which is extant only in the Latin translation of Rufinus, a younger snapshot, so to speak, of the more mature *Great Asceticon*. And the *Small* and *Great Asceticon* are a series of questions and answers that bear on just about every conceivable aspect of the monastic life.

Basil's life of Christian mindfulness involved forgetting the things of this word; it involved, to be sure prayer and Scripture study, but also sacramental participation; and it was a calling that resulted in ever more formal ascetic practice. As Basil sees it, if we would let the Lord's grace have its way with us, if we would follow our baptism to its end and keep all the commandments; we would end up in the monastic life. Indeed, Basil's word (*eisagomenoi*; "inductee") for candidates seeking to enter the monastic community is also the word for catechumens (→ Catechesis), indicating a "link between the ascetic life and baptism" (Holmes, 2000, 196). Basil's "monks" – as they would later be called and as we call them – "were simply," R. Taft writes, "Christians taking the whole business seriously" (Taft, 1986, 84).

Basil's understanding of this monastic life has certain salient features. The necessary condition for any sort of organized monastic life is the state of being set apart and withdrawn from ordinary intercourse in the world and even among ordinary Christians. But to live apart is not necessarily to live alone. Indeed, Basil's ascetic theology is justly famous for his insistence upon the necessity of life in common. So, one must live secluded, apart from the world, but in community with others who are likewise withdrawn from the world. He thought the common life superior to the hermetic life because the provision of bodily needs requires the former, as does the commandment to love, and the opportunity for fraternal correction. Perhaps most significantly, only the community as a whole can keep all the commandments, something impossible for a single individual (Bas. *Reg. Long.* 7.1–2).

Even though the monastic life is at its best a common life, this common life itself was highly structured. Candidates for the community, for example, were separate for a time from the fully- fledged members; adults lived apart from children, men from women, boys from girls, guests and the sick from members of the community. Moreover, the members of Basil's community enjoyed a common life that was structured around a single basic relationship: the seniors or elders and, for lack of a better word, the subordinates. The point is really a very simple one, though it gets worked out in myriad concrete and complex ways: those more experienced in the spiritual life, those further on the path to holiness, must lead the less experienced into deeper communion with God. The primary way, moreover, whereby the senior ascetics fulfill this obligation and need is through the giving of counsel, what Basil so often calls the "charism of the word" from 1 Cor 12.

The basic relationship of authority created by God's gift of a word explains the very existence of the *Small* and *Great Asceticon*. Basil is the experienced Christian whose advice in matters of holiness, virtue, sin, and the interpretation of Scripture is sought out by others, who confess their own struggles and obey the advice given in response. Indeed, we can think of the *Small* and *Great Asceticon* as nothing but a collection of such questions and Basil's answers to them, a collection of "words" on the various questions that arose in the ascetic life: practical questions like those which surround admission, dress, diet and so on; theological or scriptural questions; and spiritual questions about how to progress in the life of holiness. While the practice of confession and the social structures that make it possible give the monastic community its basic form, the stuff of everyday life for the monks was work (e.g. weaving, leatherwork, building, carpentry, copper-work, and farming) and prayer (Bas. *Reg. Long.* 38). The community came together for prayer seven or eight times a day to sing psalms and read Scripture (see *Reg. Long.* 37.3–5; Taft, 1986, 86)

c. God-Father, Son, and Holy Spirit

The ascetic context gave rise not only to myriad practical, moral, and spiritual questions, but also to questions about the nature of the Christian God and the best way to think of and speak of God. What would be more appropriate than these monks engaging in discussion about the object of their longing? Indeed, this ascetic context lay behind Basil's two great polemical and doctrinal works: *Against Eunomius*, written at the behest of Eustathius, and *On the Holy Spirit*, written against Eunomius and to Amphilochius. The former emerges out of monastic conferences involving Basil and Eustathius, while the latter is best thought of as a conference from a distance, wherein Basil offers a response to Amphilochius' questions about the → Holy Spirit.

In the controversy over the → Trinity, the basic question was not whether the Son is divine. Everyone, no matter where he stood in the controversy, confessed that the Son was God, for this is the plain and repeated teaching of the New Testament. Rather, the real question was: are the Son and the Spirit God in the same way that the Father is? Are Father, Son, and Holy Spirit on one side of the gap between creator and creature? Or is the Father on the one side, and the Son and the Holy Spirit ranked among the creatures, created Gods of a sort? The answers are not obvious in Scripture.

How one answers these questions depends on a prior question. On both sides of the issue there was the realization that there had to be posited a "break," a gap, or *diastēma*, in the line of beings from God the Father to lowest creature,

> for unlike their pagan contemporaries these otherwise divided Christians were convinced that there was no continuum, no unbroken chain linking final shade to ultimate source. The opening words of Scripture had created a gap in the chain of being which no mere creature could cross. (Vaggione, 2002, 123)

So, if all agree that there must be a gap or break, the question is where to put it. In short, in the non-Nicene framework – and Eunomius and Eustathius are subscribers to this – the gap is between the Father and the Son, and in the Nicene framework, it is between the Trinity and everything else (→ Nicaea).

The Nicenes and Basil, even before he would have called himself a Nicene, put the break between the Father, Son, and Holy Spirit on the one hand, and creatures on the other. A couple of examples that span Basil's theological career will suffice. In the third book of *Against Eunomius*, Basil's first theological work, he writes:

> If we speak of two kinds of things – the Godhead and creation, the power to rule and slavery, the power to make holy and being made holy, having virtue by nature and being made upright by choice – on which side will we place the Spirit? (Bas. *Eun.* 3.2)

Of course, Basil answers that the Spirit, as well as the Son, belongs on the side of divinity. From the mid- to late 370s CE we have the fantastic text *On the Holy Spirit*. Basil here refutes the idea that the Spirit occupies a middle position between God and creature. The Spirit-fighters say that he is neither slave nor master but freeman (Bas. *Spir.* 20.51). Basil responds that these men, the Spirit-fighters, have thought of God in too human a way, as if the differences of rank that obtain among men will obtain also with "the divine and unspeakable nature" (*Spir.* 20.51). This middle rank that they propose for the Spirit does not exist, so that if the Spirit "is created, he is clearly a slave along with everything else [...] but if he is above creation, he participates in the kingship" (Bas. *Spir.* 20.51).

Along with this conception of a radical break between God and creation comes the distinction between "theology" and "economy." Scripture testifies not only to theology, the relationship among Father, Son, and Holy Spirit in themselves, the life of God apart from creation, but also to the work of the Son and Spirit in the economy of salvation. For Basil (and the other Nicenes), it is very important to discern which scriptural texts refer to the Son and Spirit theologically and which, economically. For example, when Peter in Acts 2:36, said, "let all the house of Israel therefore know assuredly that God has made him both Lord and Christ, this Jesus whom you crucified," it was not his intention, Basil explains, "to communicate to us the subsistence [*hypostasis*] of the Only-Begotten before the ages"; Peter was not

> talking about the very substance of God the Word, who *was in the beginning with God* [John

1:2], but about the one who *emptied himself in the form of a slave* [Phil 2:7], became *similar in form to the body of our lowliness* [Phil 3:21], and *was crucified through weakness* [2 Cor 13:4]. (Bas. *Eun.* 2.3)

Basil goes on to say that Peter obviously does not intend to "teach us in the mode of theology, but hints at the reasons of the economy" (Bas. *Eun.* 2.3; see also 2.14).

While biblical texts that speak of or about the Spirit cannot be handled in just the same way as those regarding the Son, because the Spirit was not incarnate, Basil does find it very useful to employ the distinction between theology and economy in *On the Holy Spirit*. Some texts are theological and so refer to the Spirit's eternal relationship with the Father and the Son, while others are economic and denote, as Basil says, "the grace given to us" (Bas. *Spir.* 27.68). For example, Basil uses the distinction between theology and economy to defend his doxology: "Glory to the Father, with the Son, together with the Holy Spirit." "Why," Basil reports the question of his opponents,

> why, [...] if the word 'in' is peculiarly suitable for the Spirit and is quite enough for our every thought about him – why, then, do you introduce this new word by saying "with the Holy Spirit" instead of "in the Holy Spirit"? (Bas. *Spir.* 26.65)

Basil responds that each phrase "contributes to true religion": "in," Basil offers, describes well "what concerns us," "the grace given to us," (*Spir.* 27.68) and "the grace that works in those who share it" (*Spir.* 25.63); "with" describes "the Spirit's communion with God," his dignity (*Spir.* 27.68), "his pre-temporal existence," and "his unceasing abiding with the Father and the Son" in eternal union (*Spir.* 25.63). This is the distinction between theology and economy applied to the Spirit.

Thus is Basil's main response to the Eunomians (→ Eunomianism) and the Eustathians. It is nothing short of a radically different vision of God and his relationship to the world, and a correspondingly different way of reading God's self-revelation in Scripture. His chief objection to their respective views is that they compromise our access to God the Father and so ruin our very salvation. They have no

"theology" – or only an impoverished one of the Father alone, cut off from the Son and the Spirit. For them, there is no one to bridge the gap, while for Basil, this is precisely the work of the economy.

Historiography

The study of the works of Basil has a long history, beginning before his death. Several of his works were translated into Latin within his own lifetime and exercised an influence especially in the monastic (*Small Asceticon*) and dogmatic (*On the Holy Spirit*) traditions of the church.

The first printed editions of Basil's works began to appear in the 16th century, and during the Renaissance, Basil's *To Young Men*, a defense of the study of Greek pagan literature, received much attention. The Benedictines of Saint Maur brought a new sense of history and critical inquiry to the study of Basil, his life, and his writings: Julien Garnier and Prudentius Maran Garnier published a critical edition with introductions and commentary in three volumes between 1721 and 1730. Their textual work remains influential, and, in many respects unsurpassed, and many of their historical judgments (e.g. the broad outlines of the chronology of Basil's life) have stood the test of time.

The studies of Basil in our time can be placed in one of two broad camps, with many points of commonality and intersection: the study of late antiquity and that of early Christianity. The difference between them is one of starting point as well as scope. The study of early Christianity often begins from a place of faith and is more narrowly focused. Here Basil is studied as a witness in the much larger Christian tradition and a source of theological understanding and ecclesial life (the works of A. Silvas would be good examples). Scholars of late antiquity take a more secular – no pejorative connotations are intended here – starting point and are interested in Basil not so much as an influential member of a confessional tradition but as a representative of ancient society and culture, of course, worthy of study in their own right (the works of R. van Dam would be good examples).

While a theological stance marks a clear difference between the study of late antiquity and that of early Christianity, the disciplines remain intertwined especially because they have so many objects of study in common and because their respective findings are of mutual influence and interest.

Bibliography

Ayres, L., *Nicaea and Its Legacy: An Approach to Fourth-Century Trinitarian Theology*, Oxford, 2004.

Behr, John., *The Nicene Faith*, FCT 2, Crestview, 2004.

Hanson, R.P.C. *The Search for the Christian Doctrine of God: The Arian Controversy 318–381*, Edinburgh, 1988; repr. Grand Rapids, 2006.

Hildebrand, S.M., *Basil of Caesarea*, FTECS, Grand Rapids, 2014.

Holmes, A., *A Life Pleasing to God: The Spirituality of the Rules of St. Basil*, London, 2000.

Rapp, C., *Holy Bishops in Late Antiquity: The Nature of Christian Leadership in an Age of Transition*, Berkeley, 2005.

Radde-Gallwitz, A., *Basil of Caesarea, Gregory of Nyssa, and the Transformation of Divine Simplicity*, OECS, New York, 2009.

Rousseau, P., *Basil of Caesarea*, Berkeley, 1994.

Silvas, A., *The Asketikon of St. Basil the Great*, OECS, New York, 2005.

Taft, R., *The Liturgy of the Hours in East and West: The Origins of the Divine Office and Its Meaning for Today*, Collegeville, 1986.

Vaggione, R.P., *Eunomius of Cyzicus and the Nicene Revolution*, New York, 2002.

Watts, E., *City and School in Late Antique Athens and Alexandria*, Berkeley, 2006.

Watts, E., "Education: Thinking, Speaking, and Socializing," in: S.F. Johnson, ed., *OHLA*, New York, 2012, 467–486

STEPHEN M. HILDEBRAND

Basileiad

Basil, bishop of Cappadocia from 370 to 379 CE, built a "new city," as it was called by → Gregory of Nazianzus (*Or.* 43; 63), which, in honor of its founder, was then called "Basileiad" (see Soz. *Hist. eccl.* 6.34.9: "Basileiad, a famous hospice for the poor which was founded by Basil, bishop of Caesarea (→ Basil of Caesarea), from which at the beginning it took the name it keeps today" around 450 CE; Firm. Caes. *Ep.* 43 speaks of "the poor who live in Basileiad"): it had been created for the needs of the weak and destitute, to heal the sick and to give shelter to the poor

and to pilgrims (see Giet, 1941, 419–423; Vischer, 1953; Gain, 1985, 277–287).

1. The Ideas That Inspired It

It was above all an act of Christian charity that places love and the sharing of possessions with those in need that needs to be carried out in a concrete way (see the various *Homiliae* of Basil above all those about poverty and wealth: Pizzolato, 2013); the idea of interdependence between the rich man and the poor man and social solidarity (see Bas. *Reg. Fus.* 3.1; 7.1, see also Bas. *Hex.* 8.4); the dignity of human beings (see Bas. *Hom.* Ps 48:8; *Hom.* 3 *in illud attende tibi* 3 and 6); the hospitality given to male and female orphans or presented by relations to be educated in monastic communities (see Bas. *Reg. Fus.* 15;). The basis of this social solidarity lies in religious and ethical reasons that originate from the gospels (see Bas. *Ep.* 203).

Basil's family was also engaged in charity work (see Rousseau, 1994, 1–126): Emelia, his mother, fed the poor and showed → hospitality to strangers (see Greg. Naz. *Or.* 43.9; *Ep.* 5,4), and likewise Naucratius, Basil's brother, cared for poor people and went hunting to provide them with food (Greg. Nyss. *Vita Mac.* 26). His sister Macrina and his brother Peter during the famine of 368–369 CE helped the needy (see Greg. Nyss. *Vita Mac.* 12). Macrina took in little girls who had been abandoned to wander around the streets. She both fed and educated them (see Greg. Nyss. *Vita Mac.* 26). Basil also wrote about this famine, Bas. *Ep.* 27 and 31; Greg. Naz. *Or.* 43, 34–36; Greg. Nyss. *Bas.* 17).

There was also the εὐεργέτης, the benefactor, a wealthy man who awarded benefits to the city. He thus assumed the role of master and benefactor of the citizens as he bestowed his gifts on them. The Christians contributed to the building of churches, hospices for the sick and the poor, centers of assistance and so on: "Generosity was the ancient characteristic quality of sovereigns and the aristocracy" (see Bernardi, 1968, 332).

Further there was also the cooperation between the state and the church to relieve the conditions of the poor in the aftermath of wars and economic disaster (see Bas. *Ep.* 94 and *Ep.* 142; 143; 144).

Apparently the emperor → Valens, when he visited Caesarea, donated a piece of land belonging to the state (see Thdt. *Hist. eccl.* 4.19.13).

Basil did not oppose the state but "proposed to all the heads of the people [...] compassion and generosity" toward the needy (Greg. Naz. *Or.* 43; 63).

2. Basileiad: An Institution

The "new city" was built outside the walls of the ancient city of Caesarea in the years between 372 and 374 CE, with the aid of imperial subsidies, the generosity of wealthy people, and the wealth of Basil's own family. It was a well-organized town with many social services. It was a charitable institution that included a church (or a "memorial" on account of the presence of relics of martyrs: see Bas. *Ep.*150.3) and buildings for the clergy and civil servants; lodging for the clergy, doctors, nurses, and artisans who worked in the city; hospices for the sick with various parts in order to avoid any contagion, even a part for lepers since lepers were abandoned by everyone; shelters for the homeless and strangers; workshops that provided the necessities for the life of the community; schools for instruction and learning a trade; and stalls for the animals used for transport (see Daley, 1999; see also Mazza, 1983; Scicolone, 1982; Rousseau, 1994, 139–144; Holman, 2001, 74–76; Pizzolato, 2013, 125–130).

Basileiad was therefore an institution that was intended to fulfil the needs of the various forms of poverty, ranging from the lack of good health to social unease, that existed in the area. In this context it assumed the function of storing and distributing necessities such as food, clothing, shelter, of treating various illnesses, and of training people for work and producing an economy in contrast to the evil of moneylending.

Basil wrote in 372 CE to Elia, the governor of the province, to declare:

We are building hospices for strangers, for temporary pilgrims and for those sick people who are in need of care. We give them what they need to in order to be comforted: nurses, doctors, beasts of burden and their drivers. (Bas. *Ep.* 94; see also *Ep.* 176, in which Basil invites Amphilochius, bishop of Iconius, to the " hospice for the poor" πτωχοτροφεῖον for the feast

of the Sep 5; see also Bas. *Ep.* 142–143, in which he begs for aid for the "hospice for the poor." See also *Ep.* 150.3 when Heraclides, a friend of Amphilochius, remembers how he stayed in the πτωχοτροφεῖον built by Basil near to the city of Caesarea)

Gregory of Nyssa also praises this charitable institution by saying (→ Gregory of Nyssa):

What a tabernacle of testimony he, that is Basil, has built on the outskirts of the city rendering, by his good teaching, the materially poor, poor in spirit with the result that poverty has become a blessing and has procured for them the grace of the true Kingdom. (Greg. Nyss. *Bas.* 21)

Basil also cares for the lepers" in imitation of Christ, who did not heal the lepers just with words but really healed them (Greg. Naz. *Or.* 43; 63).

Basil also elaborated some projects for building hospices for the poor in the countryside, which, although functional, were on more modest scale than those of Basileiad. He entrusted them to the care of his fellow bishops (Bas. *Ep.* 142–145; see Salamito, 2000).

Basileiad became so important that the inhabitants of the old city gradually moved into it with the result that the new one substituted the old city. In the 6th century CE, → Justinian built new walls around it but not around the old city of Caesarea (Daley, 1999, 458–459). The present Turkish city of Kaisery was built upon the site of Basileiad and not on that of the old city (Patitsas, 2008, 270).

3. The Running of Basileiad

Basileiad was "the first regular and permanent organization of assistance in the East which was directed by monks and the church" (Scicolone, 1982, 357). It was administrated by χωρεπίσκοποι, and monks served in the hospice (see Bas. *Reg. Brev.* 155; 160.292) and to the sick, just as in the hospice built by Eustathius of Sebaste. The personnel belonged to the monastic community. The monks of the rule of Basil tried to meet the needs of the weakest members of society. Basil not only urged the monks to pray and to achieve spiritual perfection but also to dedicate themselves to service of the poor and the education of young people (see Bas. *Reg. Brev.* 155; 160.292). A fundamental aspect of Basilian coenobitism was its social function. For this reason, the monasteries had to be near urban settlements. Basil, together with his monks and helpers, took an active part in the life of the community. In reply to the accusations that were leveled against Basil and were certainly made by his Arian adversaries (→ Arianism), that he used his work of assistance as a political instrument and that he was opposed to the civil authorities, Basil replied that the state was not damaged by his charitable activities (Bas. *Ep.* 94.25), and that on the contrary, it ought to be something of which the governor should be proud (*Ep.* 94.43). It was an expression of cooperation between the church and the state. In other letters he asked for the hospice to be exempted from taxation for humanitarian reasons (Bas. *Ep.* 142; 143; 144).

Basileiad therefore represents an original, fecund, and realistic answer to social problems and poverty of the ancient world, particularly in the 4th and 5th centuries CE.

Bibliography

Bernardi, J., *La prédication des pères cappadociens: Le prédicateur et son auditoire*, Paris 1968.

Bianco, M.G., "Basiliade," in: *NDPAC*, Genoa, 2006, 720–721.

Cracco Ruggini, L., "I vescovi e il dinamismo sociale nel mondo cittadino di Basilio di Cesarea," in: *Basilio di Cesarea: La sua età la sua opera e il basilianesimo in Sicilia: Atti del congresso internazionale (Messina 3–6 XII 1979)*, Messina, 1983, 97–124.

Daley, B.E., "Building the New City: The Cappadocian Fathers and the Rhetoric of Philanthropy," *JECS* 7, 1999, 431–461.

Fox, M.M., *The Life and Time of St. Basil the Great as Revealed in His Works*, Washington DC, 1939.

Gain, B., *L'Église de Cappadoce au IVe siècle d'après la correspondance de Basile de Césarée (330–378)*, OCA 225, Rome, 1985, 277–289.

Giet, S., *Les idées et l'action sociale de saint Basile*, Paris, 1941.

Giet, S., "Saint Basile et l'assistance aux malheureux," in: H.C. Desroches et al., *Inspiration religieuse et structures temporelles*, Paris, 1948, 107–137.

Holman, S.R., *The Hungry are Dying: Beggars and Bishops in Roman Cappadocia*, OSHT, Oxford, 2001, 74–76.

Holman, S.R., *Wealth and Poverty in Early Church and Society*, HCSPTH, Grand Rapids, 2008, 268–270, 282–285.

Karayannopoulos, I., "St. Basil Social Activity: Principles and Praxis," in: P.J. Fedwick, ed., *Basil of Caesarea:*

Christian, Humanist, Ascetic: A Sixteen-Hundredth Anniversary Symposium, vol. I, Toronto, 1981, 375–391.

Lunardi, G., "Il lavoro in Basilio il Grande," *VetChr* 21, 1984, 313–326.

Mazza, M., "Monachesimo basiliano: Modelli spirituali e tendenze economico-sociali nell'impero del IV secolo," in: *Basilio di Cesarea: La sua età la sua opera e il basilianesimo in Sicilia: Atti del congresso internazionale (Messina 3–6 XII 1979)*, Messina, 1983, 55–96.

Mille, T., *The Birth of the Hospital in the Byzantine Empire*, Baltimore, ²1997, 85–88.

Patitsas, T., "St. Basil's Philanthropic Program and Modern Microlending Strategies for Economic Self-Actualization," in: S.R. Holman, ed., *Wealth and Poverty in Early Church and Society*, HCSPTH, Grand Rapids, 2008, 268–270.

Salamito J.-M., "Cristianizzazione e vita sociale," in: L. Pietri & C. Pietri, eds., *La nascita di una cristianità*, Rome, 2000, esp. 646–658.

Pizzolato, L.F., ed., *Basilio di Cesarea: La cura del povero e l'onere della ricchezza: Testi dalle Regole e dalle Omelie*, Milan, 2013, esp. 125–130: *L'impresa di Basiliade*.

Rousseau, P., *Basil of Caesarea*, Berkeley, 1994, 139–144.

Rousselle, A., *Aspects sociaux du recrutement ecclésiastique au IVe siècle*, MEFR.A 89, Rome, 1977.

Scicolone, S., "Basilio e la sua organizzazione dell'attività assistenziale a Cesarea," *CClCr* 3, 1982, 353–372.

Vischer L., *Basilius der Grosse: Untersuchungen zu einem Kirchenvater des vierten Jahrhunderts*, Basel, 1953, 140–144.

MARIO MARITANO

Basilides

Basilides was a Christian teacher in Alexandria during the time of Hadrian (Clem. *Strom.* 7.106.4). → Irenaeus of Lyon claims that Basilides was inspired by → Simon Magus and a certain Menander (Iren. *Haer.* 1.24.1). However, since Irenaeus credits Basilides with a doctrine that probably reflects the views of later Basilideans (see below), his doxographical construction is very doubtful. We know very little about the life of Basilides or his school: he had a son and pupil called Isidore (*Strom.* 2.113.3).

Eus. *Hist. eccl.* 4.7.5–8 cites a certain Agrippa Castor with additional information about Basilides. According to → Eusebius of Caesarea, Agrippa was a contemporary of Basilides and wrote a treatise against him (Löhr, 1996, 5–14; Willing, 2008, 144–147). It is, however, possible that Agrippa Castor lived and wrote after Irenaeus and that portions of his heresiological portrait were drawn from the heresiography of the bishop of Lyon (Löhr, 1996, 9–11): Agrippa related that Basilides had written 24 books "on the gospel" and had referred to various prophets, among them two named Barkoph and Barkabbas. Moreover, as Agrippa claimed, Basilides had taught that to partake of the meat of idols is a thing of indifference and that it is permitted to deny the faith in times of persecution; all those wishing to join the Basilideans have to observe complete silence for a period of five years. The information about the commentary on the/a gospel in 24 books and the recourse to esoteric prophetic wisdom is probably trustworthy (see below). It is, however, doubtful whether Basilideans recommended denying the faith in times of persecution. The five-year period of silence assimilates the Basilideans to Pythagorean groups. We have little or no knowledge of Basilideans in the 3rd and following centuries (see Löhr, 1996, 36–37.40–41).

Clement of Alexandria and the *Acta Archelai* have preserved fragments from the 13th and the 23rd book of Basilides' commentary on the gospel (*pace* Kelhofer 2005: It is unclear which gospel Basilides commented upon, but there are indications that it may have been the Gospel of Luke (→ Luke, Gospel of) or a version thereof. As regards Isidore, → Clement of Alexandria also mentions, and quotes from, three of his writings: *Ethica*, *About the Attached Soul*, and *Interpretations of the Prophet Parchor* (in at least two books; Clem. *Strom.* 6.53.2–5). He further preserves a number of notices in indirect speech that report opinions or definitions of Basilides or Basilideans. It is unclear whether in these cases, too, Clement draws on those Basilidean writings from which he quotes.

The extant quotations and notices in Clement of Alexandria, the *Acta Archelai*, and → Origen do not offer a coherent picture of a Basilidean doctrine or system. In his commentary, Basilides discusses not only the origin of → evil (from the 13th book: Acta Archelai 67.4–12; Löhr 1996, 219–249; Bennett, 2007) but also the question of whether the justice and goodness of God can be maintained despite the sufferings of the Christian martyrs. Basilides claims that God's justice can be defended throughout: even if the Christian → martyrs had not in fact committed a sin, they still were inclined to sin, a weakness that

is attached to every human being and that merits divine punishment – the view of Origen seems to be anticipated here (Löhr, 1996, 133–136). In any case, Basilides avers, "I will say anything rather than call providence evil" (from the 23rd book: Clem. *Strom.* 4.81–83.1). Pain and terror affect God's creatures like rust corrodes iron (*Strom.* 4.88.5). The simile is Platonic (Plato *Rep.* 609A), and the parallels in other writers (*Corp. herm.* 14.7 ed. Festugière-Nock; Plot. *Enn.* 4.7.10) seem to suggest that here Basilides denies divine responsibility for the suffering of the martyrs, preferring to view it as an inevitable and natural consequence of human existence. As an appropriate response, moreover, Basilides recommends to love all creatures as part of an encompassing order, and neither to desire nor to hate anything (*Strom.* 4.86.1). Basilides also seems to have accepted the migration of souls (Or. *Comm. ser. 38 Matt.*). Origen quotes a Basilidean exegesis of Rom 7:9, according to which life without law is to be applied to the soul that lived in an animal body before its entry into a human body (Or. *Comm. Rom.* 5.1). This interpretation seems to evoke an ancient view according to which animal cannibalism proves that → animals live without law (Hes. *Op.* 277–279; Plut. *Mor.* 964B; Löhr, 1996, 215). Since Clement quotes Basilidean teachings out of context, some of them remain enigmatic: in *Strom.* 4.162.1, it is said that Basilides maintained that justice and her daughter, peace, remain supports of the Ogdoas. The allusion to the language of the Greek psalter (Pss 84:11; 88:15; 96:2; LXX) seems to be clear enough. But which Ogdoas is meant? Likewise, in *Strom.* 5.74.3, it is said that according to Basilides, Moses did not permit altars and shrines to be set up in various places, but by erecting a single temple of God, he proclaimed a singular cosmos. To attribute the building of the Temple in Jerusalem to → Moses (if that is what is meant here) is rare: Hekataios of Abdera provides a parallel (Diod. Sic. *Bib. hist.* 40.3). The phrase "singular cosmos" (μονογενὴς κόσμος) possibly alludes to Plato *Tim.* 31AB. The passage may point to a qualified affirmation of this world which, however, maintains that the God of Moses is not the true and highest God.

Isidore, in his *Ethica*, discusses the question of whether to marry by interpreting first Matt 19:11f. (Clem. *Strom.* 3.1.1–4): employing the key terms φύσις, ἀνάγκη, and λόγος, he distinguishes between three kinds of eunuchs:

1. the eunuchs from birth, in other words those who have natural aversion [φυσικὴ ἀποστροφή] against women;
2. the eunuchs out of necessity [ἀνάγκη], in other words theatrical eunuchs and those who have been castrated by misfortune;
3. the eunuchs for the sake of the kingdom of God, in other words those who live continently out of rational considerations [κατὰ λόγον].

Whereas the "theatrical" eunuchs are probably actors, particularly singers, who in antiquity were often advised to live continently for the sake of their art (Juv. *Sat.* 6.48; Martial *Epigr.* 7.82; 11.75), the second group of eunuchs "out of necessity" may have been slaves or persons who were castrated as a punishment. The third group, eunuchs who live continently by rational choice, are those who fear the lack of leisure that comes with the husband's duty to provide for his wife and children. Here, Isidore rehearses a standard argument of the discussion about whether the truly wise man should marry (Löhr, 1996, 110–111). Isidore pursues the argument with an interpretation of 1 Cor 7:9 (Clem. *Strom.* 3.2.1–3.2). He advises against too much resistance to sexual desire: a soul that is totally focused on preserving its continence separates itself from Christian → hope. The prayer of "thanksgiving" (εὐχαριστία) degenerates into a request that asks not to yield to temptation rather than to accomplish good works. In this case, marriage is advisable. If, however, the unchaste Christian is too young or too poor to marry, he should not separate from his Christian brothers. He should remind himself of his baptism (saying to himself, "I have entered the holy; nothing can happen to me!") and should ask his Christian brother for a blessing. Ultimately, Isidore explains – reminding his readers of an Epicurean maxim – for human beings there are some things that are both necessary and natural, such as clothing. There are, however, some others that are merely natural, such as sex (Löhr, 1996, 118–119). These fragments from Isidore's *Ethica*, then, offer a glimpse of the care of souls as practiced in the school of Basilides. In this respect, the Basilideans are comparable to other ancient schools of philosophy that married theory and practice, intellectual endeavor and the care of souls (Hadot, 1995). In *Strom.* 2.112.1–114.2, Clement of Alexandria summarizes and quotes another writing of Isidore entitled *About the Attached Soul*: Isidore claims that the irrational passions of the soul are certain spirits that have attached themselves to the rational soul "according to an original disturbance and confusion." A second kind of spirit, illegitimate and of a different nature, has also grown upon the soul: they have the nature of animals, for example of a wolf, monkey, or lion. They try to shape the desires of the soul by presenting certain fantasies to it. In this way, the soul can acquire animal passions. Isidore discusses objections against his doctrine of the soul: does it not provide bad people with a wonderful excuse for doing bad things? They may claim that they have been overpowered by the force of the attached spirits! But Isidore does not accept this objection: bad people are still responsible for what they do if they do not resist the force of the attachments: "We must be superior with the rational part of our soul and must show that we rule over the lower creation within ourselves." Here, Isidore effects an interesting combination of Platonic and Christian anthropology: the lower part of the soul (Plato *Rep.* 519A–B; 611C–D; *Tim.* 42A; 69C–D; Alb. *Epit.* 16), which is somehow influenced by unruly matter (Plato *Tim.* 30A; 52D–53A; *Leg.* 896E; 897D; Plut. *Mor.* 1014C), is equated with the animal creation that humans are called upon to dominate (Gen 1:28; Philo *Quaest. Gen.* 2.56). No complete eradication of the passions seems to be envisaged, and Isidore prefers moderate μετριοπάθεια to the Stoic ideal of ἀπάθεια. In *Strom.* 6.53.2–5, Clement quotes one fragment from the first book of the *Interpretations of the Prophet Parchor* and two fragments from the second book of the same work in support of his claim that Greek philosophy was built on purloined wisdom. In the first fragment, Isidore discusses the circumstances and conditions of prophecy and mentions in this context the δαιμόνιον of Socrates and the opinion of Aristotle, according to whom all men use demons that accompany them during life in the body. According to modern scholarship, Isidore is quoting here directly or indirectly from Aristotle's *On the Pythagoreans*. In that case, the quoted opinion may in fact have been a piece of Pythagorean doctrine (Löhr, 1996, 202). Isidore claims that Aristotle did not mention from which source he had stolen it. In the second fragment, Isidore declares that the intellectual property of the "elect" (probably the Basilidean Christians; see Clem. *Strom.* 2.10.1–11.2; 4.165.3) is not to be considered the invention (εὕρεμα) of some philosophers. Rather, the philosophers stole it from some prophets. In the third fragment, Isidore offers another example: Pherecydes of Syros had taken the essence of his allegorical theology – the "winged oak" and the "vestment spread over it" – from the prophecy of Cham. This remark seems to apologetically counter the recourse to early pagan wisdom – Celsus had reckoned Pherekydes among the sages of primeval time (Or. *Cels.*1.16) – by citing an even earlier biblical prophet: Cham, the son of Noah, who was the ancestor of the Phoenicians (Gen 10:6f.) to whom Pherekydes had been apprenticed, according to Greek tradition (Löhr, 1996, 205n51). These fragments present Isidore as an informed and adroit participant in the contemporary debates of 2nd-century CE "post-Hellenistic" philosophy about ancient wisdom and the legitimacy, or otherwise, of Platonic and Christian claims to its legacy (Boys-Stones, 2001).

"Faith" (πίστις) is a key term: the Basilideans defined it (in a Stoic manner) as an "assent" (συγκατάθεσις) of the soul to those things that do not affect perception because they are not present (Clem. *Strom.* 2.27.2) or – as Basilides himself probably put it – (in a more Platonic manner) as a "special kind of knowledge" (νόησις ἐξαιρετός), a kingdom and a creation of good things that is worthy to exist close to the creator (*Strom.* 5.3.2). There seem to be degrees of faith that correspond to the different degrees of knowledge among the elect (*Strom.* 2.10.1). Clement also paraphrases and quotes a Basilidean exegesis of Prov 1:7 according to which the Archon, when he heard the utterance of the "serving spirit" (διαχονούμενον πνεῦμα), was shattered because he had received the gospel quite unexpectedly. And the consternation (ἔκπληξις) was called fear (φόβος, see D.I. 7.112), and this fear became the beginning of a wisdom that selects, distinguishes, perfects, and brings everything to its proper place (Clem. *Strom.* 2.36.1). A comparison with Clem. *Exc.* 16 reveals that the "serving spirit" is most likely the dove that descended on Jesus during his baptism in the River Jordan. Consequently, the Archon is symbolized by → John the Baptist, who is surprised by the apparition (compare the similar

exegesis of the Valentinian Herakleon in Or. *Comm. Jo.* 6.39).

Iren. *Haer.* 1.24.3–7 presents a heresiological notice attributing a doctrine to Basilides/the Basilideans that is largely incompatible with the information provided by Clement, Origen, and the *Acta Archelai*. The notice, however, seems to be based on authentic material (such as a gnostic revelation discourse or dialogue) that may have been produced by later Basilideans. It is this notice that has largely fixed the image of the Basilidians as transmitted by the heresiological tradition. According to this report, Basilides taught that from the unborn Father, there emanated Nous, Logos, and Phronêsis; from Phronêsis, there derived Sophia and Dynamis. From this last pair, the rulers and angels who created the first heaven took their origin. From these first rulers, other rulers and angels derived, who created further heavens. In this way, 365 heavens came into existence. The angels of the last heaven, the heaven of our world, distributed the earth among themselves and their nations. One of these angels is the God of the Jews. Because he tried to subjugate the other nations to the Jews, the other angels fought against him, as did the other nations against the Jews. The highest God and Father, seeing the war among the angels of the last heaven, sent his only begotten Intellect (Nous) in order to liberate humankind from the power of the angels. The Nous appeared on earth and performed miracles. When the angels plotted to crucify him, he quickly changed his outward appearance to that of Simon of Cyrene. He mocked the angels and escaped from them. The ignorant angels crucified Simon of Cyrene in his stead (compare Nag Hammadi Library, Codex VII,2 56.5ff.; VII,3 81.15ff.; → Nag Hammadi Writings). The Nous, a bodiless power, ascended to the Father, rendering himself invisible by assimilating himself. All those who know this mystery are liberated from the power of the angels and know the order of salvation (οἰκονομία) of the highest God. Those, however, who confess the crucified one are still under the power of the angels (Iren. *Haer.* 1.24.4). Moreover, Irenaeus relates, only the soul will be saved according to Basilides , whereas the body will perish. The creator angels are behind the prophecies, whereas the first among them, the God of the Jews, has given the law. To partake of meat for idols is an indifferent action, as is every kind of debauchery.

The Basilideans practice magic and assign a name to each and every angel and ruler of the 365 heavens. The name of the savior during his descent into, and his ascent from, this world is "Caulacau" (*Haer.* 1.24.5; Saudelli, 2013). Whoever has learned the names of all the angels becomes invisible for them, as the savior Caulacau has done. Their motto is: "You may know everything, but you may remain unknown to all." The Basilideans avoid martyrdom, and only very few people, they allege, have a knowledge that is similar to theirs. They are no longer Jews, but not yet Christians. Their mysteries should not be made public (*Haer.* 1.24.6). They calculate the positions of their 365 heavens. The ruler of the heavens is called Abrasax because its name has the number value of 365 (*Haer.* 1.24.7). The notice of Irenaeus is centered around the salvific action of the Nous of the unborn Father (Löhr, 2012, 368–373): adapting Aristotle's much discussed doctrine of the soul (Arist. *De an.* 3.5), Christ is conceptualized here as the Agent Intellect who knows every form by becoming every form (= changing his outward appearance) and thus escapes the shameful death prepared for him by the angels. The triumphant Nous mocks death like a true philosopher should (see Or. *Cels.* 2.33–34; 6.53; Löhr, 2013, 591). The Basilidean Christians are called upon to imitate the Nous by knowing everything while staying unknown to all.

Hipp. *Haer.* 7.20–27 and 10.14 present a second Basilidean system that is also largely incompatible with the information provided by the other sources (including Irenaeus). However, it formulates a rather interesting version of negative theology: in the beginning, there was the absolute nothing, a nothing that is not even "ineffable" (ἄρρητος). Apparently, the ineffable nothing is identical to the nonexistent God. This nonexistent God wills to create – although "willing" cannot be used here in a proper manner – the world, in other words, the seed of the world (σπέρμα τοῦ κόσμου) that contains the complete world in an undeveloped state. This is the creation from nothing (i.e. from the nonexistent God) that can neither be conceptualized as a process of emanation nor as a (Platonic) demiurgical shaping of preexistent matter. Everything develops from the seed: in it, there is a tripartite sonship that is consubstantial with the nonexistent God. The three parts of the sonship are differentiated by their degree of refinedness: the first, most refined, and light part ascends with the sowing of the world seed straightaway into the realm of the nonexistent god; it is erotically attracted by the beauty of the nonexistent God. The second part, whose substance was coarser, had more difficulty rising to this height: it was helped in its ascent by a wing, which is the → Holy Spirit. However, once it came near the nonexistent God, it left behind the wing of the Holy Spirit, which was consubstantial with neither the nonexistent God nor its sonship. Meanwhile, the third part of the tripartite sonship remains in the world seed: these are the pneumatic Christians. There is now a hypercosmic realm, the cosmos, and, as the firmament and boundary between the two, the Holy Spirit. From the world seed there originated two archons. The archon of the Ogdoas created for himself a Son – who is superior to him and sits at his right hand, and who created and ruled the heavenly realm from the firmament down to the moon. The second archon, who likewise creates a son who is superior to him, rules over the Hebdomas. He reveals himself to Moses (Exod 6:3), and he speaks through the prophets who lived before the savior. Through the mediation of the two sons of the two archons, the gospel that starts from the transcendent sonship beyond the boundary of the Holy Spirit reaches the lowest part of the cosmos, where the third part of the tripartite sonship still remains. This gospel/light finally illuminated Jesus, the Son of Mary. The world will not end before the remaining part of the sonship (i.e. the pneumatic Christians) will have been purified and will have followed Jesus into the hypercosmic realm. Once the whole tripartite sonship is established in the realm beyond this world, God will cast a great "ignorance" (ἄγνοια) over the world: none of the souls of this world will yearn to rise to the world beyond. All desire and with it all death and corruption will ultimately cease, and everything will inhabit its natural position and in this way be immortal. The Basilidean system as reported by Hippolytus, with its bold negative theology and its implicit criticism and correction of Platonic and gnostic theologie, may be the creation of later Basilideans who took their cue from a selective reading of the Basilidean material in Clement of Alexandria and Irenaeus of Lyon. However, at the present state of research into the sources of the

Refutatio of Hippolytus of Rome, nothing definitive can be established (Löhr, 1996, 313–323).

Bibliography

Bennett, B., "Basilides' 'Barbarian Cosmogony': Its Nature and Function in the Acta Archelai," in: J. Beduhn & P. Mirecki, eds., *The Frontiers of Faith: The Christian Encounter with Manichaeism in the Acts of Archelaus*, Leiden, 2007, 157–166.

Boys-Stones, G.R., *Post-Hellenistic Philosophy*, Oxford, 2001.

Hadot, P., *Qu'est-ce que la philosophie antique?*, Paris, 1995.

Jurasz, I., "Ce que les gnostiques ont fait du principe du bien: Le cas de Basilide," *Chôra* 15, 2017, 487–514.

Kelhofer, J.A., "Basilides's Gospel and Exegetica (Treatises)," *VigChr* 59, 2005, 115–134.

Löhr, W., *Basilides und seine Schule*, Tübingen, 1996.

Löhr, W., "Christian Gnostics and Greek Philosophy in the Second Century," *EChr* 3, 2012, 349–379.

Löhr, W., "Gnostic and Manichean Interpretation," in: J. Carleton-Paget & J. Schaper, eds., *NCHB*, vol. I: *From the Beginnings to 600*, Cambridge UK, 2013, 584–604.

Löhr, W., "A Variety of Docetisms: Valentin, Basilides and Their Disciples," in: J. Verheyden, ed., *Docetism in the Early Church*, Tübingen 2018, 231–260.

Saudelli, L., "Le nom barbare Kaulakau selon l'hérésiologie chrétienne," in: M. Tardieu, A. van den Kerchove & M. Zago, eds., *Noms Barbares I: Formes et contextes d'une pratique magique*, Turnhout, 2013, 287–299.

Schibli, H.S., *Pherekydes of Syros*, Oxford, 1990.

Tardieu, M., "Basilide, 'prédicateur chez les Perses': Problèmes du fragment 19," in: F. Ruani & M. Timus, *Quand les dualistes polemiquaient: Zoroastriens et Manichéens*, Louvain, 2020, 179–197.

Willing, M., *Eusebius von Cäsarea als Häresiograph*, Berlin, 2008.

WINRICH LÖHR

Basiliscus

Basiliscus was an eastern Roman emperor from January 475 to August 476 CE. Basiliscus rose to prominence as a soldier in the 460s CE, aided by the influence of his sister Verina, the wife of Emperor Leo I (457–474 CE). In 465 CE he held the consulship, and in 468 CE he was given command as *magister militum* over the great expedition to retake North Africa from the → Vandals. The expedition was a catastrophe, the fleet destroyed with enormous loss of life (Pro. *Bel.* 3.6). There were accusations of treachery and corruption, that Basiliscus had taken bribes from the Vandal king Gaiseric, and on his return to Constantinople Basiliscus took sanctuary in Hagia Sophia until Verina secured his pardon.

Leo I died in 474 CE, as did his young son Leo II. Power passed to the Isaurian general Zeno (emperor 474–475 and 476–491 CE), but he had reigned for less than a year when he was driven from Constantinople in a palace coup. Zeno fled into exile, and Basiliscus seized the throne. Our sources for Basiliscus' short reign are universally hostile, and his political and religious motives are still debated. Anti-Isaurian feeling against Zeno had contributed to the latter's fall, but to legitimize his usurpation Basiliscus needed wider support. He therefore became involved in the theological disputes that already divided the eastern churches.

The doctrines of the Council of → Chalcedon (451 CE) had remained imperial orthodoxy under Leo I, yet many eastern Christians opposed the council and its definition of the two natures of Christ. Shortly after Basiliscus' coup, an embassy came to Constantinople from Alexandria. The embassy had been intended for Zeno, but they now appealed to Basiliscus to restore Timothy Aelurus ("the cat" or "the weasel"), the Miaphysite bishop of Alexandria (Zach. Rhet. *Hist. eccl.* 5.1; Eva. Schol. *Hist. eccl.* 3.4). Basiliscus granted their request, allowing Timothy to return from Cherson in the Crimea. Possibly influenced by Timothy, Basiliscus then issued an encyclical to the eastern churches. The text survives in slightly different forms in Zach. Rhet. *Hist. eccl.* 5.2 and Eva. Schol. *Hist. eccl.* 3.4.

Like earlier emperors, Basiliscus hailed the importance of piety and devotion to Christ for the salvation of the empire. The encyclical proclaims that the only safeguard of the true faith is the original Nicene Creed of 325 CE, "the basis and confirmation of human prosperity." This creed had been reaffirmed at the Council of → Constantinople in 381 CE and again at Ephesus against Nestorius and his followers (the text of the encyclical given by Zachariah explicitly upholds both Councils of → Ephesus, the controversial Second Council of 449 CE as well as the council that condemned Nestorius in 431 CE, but the version preserved by Evagrius does not). In contrast to this proclamation of the Nicene faith (→ Nicaea), the *Tome* of Leo and the Chalcedonian Definition are both condemned.

> That which overthrew the unity and good order of the holy churches of God and the peace of the whole universe, namely the so-called *Tome* of Leo and all that was said and transacted at Chalcedon in definition of faith or in exposition of the creed, or of interpretation, or of instruction, or of discussion, for innovation contrary to the aforementioned holy creed of the 318 holy fathers, we decree that these be anathematized both here and everywhere in every church.

The encyclical repeatedly denounces any innovation on Nicaea as the root of the current turmoil. There is little theological precision, with no reference to the human and divine natures of Christ, and while Eutychian views are condemned, → Eutyches himself is never named. All eastern bishops were required to sign the encyclical, and those who continued to teach "the innovation which was made at Chalcedon" were threatened with deposition and legal sanctions.

When the encyclical was proclaimed in April 475 CE, it received significant eastern support. Along with Timothy Aelurus of Alexandria, the exiled anti-Chalcedonian bishop of Antioch Peter the Fuller had also been recalled. At a council held in Ephesus, Timothy and Peter then appointed Paul as the bishop of that city (Zach. Rhet. *Hist. eccl.* 5.3–4; Eva. Schol. *Hist. eccl.* 3.5–6), in direct contradiction of the Chalcedonian canon, which gave the see of Constantinople the authority to select the bishop of Ephesus. Anastasius of Jerusalem shared the same convictions, and the strength of anti-Chalcedonian feeling in the East is reflected in the claim that either 700 (Zach. Rhet. *Hist. eccl.* 5.2) or 500 (Eva. Schol. *Hist. eccl.* 3.5) eastern bishops obeyed Basiliscus' command and signed the encyclical.

Opposition to Basiliscus came above all from the imperial city of Constantinople itself. Acacius, the bishop of Constantinople (→ Acacius of Constantinople), was threatened by the reinstatement of Timothy and Peter and regarded their election of Paul of Ephesus as an open attack on the authority of his see. Whether he disputed the theological arguments of the encyclical is less certain, and he would later come into conflict with Rome over his support for the Henotikon of Zeno. But in 475 CE he

rejected Basiliscus' encyclical and appealed to Rome, where Bishop Simplicius wrote to the emperor and the Constantinopolitan church praising Acacius' resistance and condemning Timothy Aelurus (*Ep. Avell.* 56–57; 59). The monks and the population of Constantinople supported Acacius (Eva. Schol. *Hist. eccl.* 3.7), led (according to the saint's *Vita*) by the famous stylite Daniel, whose pillar stood just north of the city.

The *Life of Daniel* is vehement in its condemnation of Basiliscus unlike the relatively mild Evagrius, who makes no mention of the saint or his reported role. According to the *Life*, Basiliscus initially sent an envoy asking Daniel to pray for him, but his plea was dismissed and Daniel denounced Basiliscus for adopting Jewish ideas and denying Christ's → incarnation (*Vita Dan.* 71). Acacius in turn then sought Daniel's aid, and in a dramatic gesture Daniel descended from his pillar and came to Hagia Sophia to rally resistance against Basiliscus, whom he described as "a second Diocletian" (*Vita Dan.* 72–73).

Whether due chiefly to the efforts of Acacius (Zach. Rhet. *Hist. eccl.* 5.5; Eva. Schol. *Hist. eccl.* 3.7) or of Daniel (*Vita Dan.* 83–84), the opposition cowed Basiliscus and forced him into a retraction. In 476 CE he issued a counter-encyclical (quoted in Eva. Schol. *Hist. eccl.* 3.7, who observes that the Miaphysite Zachariah Rhetor omitted this decree) revoking his previous edict.

> We enjoin that whatever has occurred during our reign, whether as encyclicals or in other forms, or indeed anything else whatsoever connected with faith and ecclesiastical organization, be null and void, while we anathematize Nestorius and Eutyches, and every other heresy, and all who hold the same opinions; and that there will be no synod or other investigation concerning this subject, but these matters will remain unbroken and unshaken; and that the provinces, whose ordination the see of this imperial and glorious city controlled, should be returned to the most devout and most holy patriarch and archbishop, Acacius.

Contrary to Evagrius, the counter-encyclical did not directly commend Chalcedon but merely withdrew the previous attack upon the council. But the rights of Acacius and the see of Constantinople were fully restored.

These tensions over religion weakened Basiliscus' already precarious position. His short reign also saw a major fire, which destroyed many books and art treasures in Constantinople (Mal. *Frgm.* 11), a disaster seen by some as evidence of divine wrath, while high taxes further aroused resentment (Mal. *Frgm.* 9.3). The shifting tide of popular opinion provided Zeno with the opportunity to win back the support of the army and return to the imperial city. Basiliscus took refuge in the baptistery of Hagia Sophia, but surrendered on the promise that he would not be executed. Together with his wife and son, he was taken to the fortress of Limnae in Cappadocia, where they were sealed inside a tower and left to die of hunger and cold (Pro. *Bel.* 3.7.22–25; Malalas *Chron.* 379–380).

Zeno immediately rescinded Basiliscus' edicts (Eva. Schol. *Hist. eccl.* 3.8). Peter the Fuller of Antioch and Paul of Ephesus were exiled, and a similar sentence was dispatched to Alexandria, but Timothy Aelurus died before it could be carried out. Yet the tensions dividing the eastern Christians remained, and Basiliscus' encyclical and counter-encyclical set a precedent for imperial intervention that would be followed by Zeno himself in the Henotikon and by → Justinian.

(A historiography for this topic is not applicable.)

Bibliography

"Basiliscus 2," in: J.R. Martindale, ed., *PLRE*, vol. II, , Cambridge UK, 1980.

Brandes, W., "Familienbände? Odoaker, Basiliskos und Harmatios," *Klio* 75, 1993, 407–437.

Frend, W.H.C., *The Rise of the Monophysite Movement: Chapters in the History of the Church in the Fifth and Sixth Centuries*, Cambridge UK, 1972.

Gray, P.T.R., *The Defence of Chalcedon in the East (451–533)*, Leiden, 1979.

Grillmeier, A., *Christ in Christian Tradition*, 2 vols., revised ed., London, 2013.

Meyendorff, J., *Imperial Unity and Christian Divisions: The Church 450–680 AD*, New York, 1989.

Redies, M., "Die Usurpation des Basiliskos (475–476) im Kontext der aufsteigenden monophysitischen Kirche," *AnTa* 5, 1997, 211–221.

David M. Gwynn

Bath/Mikveh

"Mikveh" (pl. *mikva'ot*), literally referring to a "gathering" as in a "gathering of water" (*mikveh mayim*; Lev 11:36), is today commonly used to designate a humanmade deep, stepped pool that is being used for ritual immersion and purification from the state of impurity caused, for instance, by contact with sexual fluids or diseases. Archaeological excavations and surveys have uncovered hundreds of such water installations in the southern Levant, mainly in modern Israel but also in the West Bank, southern Lebanon, and western Jordan.

1. Textual Sources

The Hebrew Bible records that "bathing" in water (→ Water, in the Bible) was necessary for purification from the state of ritual impurity (Lev 11–15; Num 19). This could be obtained through various means, such as contact with carrion, childbirth, skin diseases, and bodily discharges (e.g. seminal, menstrual, illness-related). Such impurity affected not only humans, but also clothing, vessels, and other objects.

As testified by the accounts of → Flavius Josephus and → Philo of Alexandria, as well as in the → Dead Sea Scrolls, the act of ritual bathing – and, with it, a focus on ritual impurity – received more interest during the 2nd century BCE to 1st century CE. While these later accounts referred to ritual washing as described in the Hebrew Bible, they tended to gloss over the various details of purification, as if all were handled similarly (e.g. Jos. *Ant.* 3.261–265, 269; Philo *Spec.* 1.261–262). At the same time, they also introduced ritual uses of washing that are not mentioned in earlier texts, such as hand washing (*Let. Aris.* 305–306; Jos. *Ant.* 12.106; Philo *Cont.* 66, 89), washing in preparation for prayer (Jdt 12:7–9; Jos. *Bell.* 2.128–129), and washing after defecation (*Bell.* 2.149). The wider range of practices during this period associated with ritual washing suggests a greater diversity and innovation than before, but also hints at the greater significance of this practice during this period.

It is difficult to deduce from these texts how ritual bathing was practiced. Josephus (*Bell.* 2.161) notes that → Essenes remained clothed for washing, while the Dead Sea Scrolls offer some information on how ritual bathing was carried out (see Lawrence, 2006, 141–149). What is clear is that these later accounts emphasize full immersion with respect to ritual bathing (e.g. Jos. *Ant.* 3.263; CD 10.10–13; Mark 7:3–4; Luke 11:38), as well as the amount and nature of water in which one immersed (CD 10.10–12; 4Q270.6.4.21). The use of "living water," such as that of rivers, lakes and springs, as well as rain water, was regarded as most important for ritual-purification washing (e.g. Lev 14:5, 50–52; 15:13; 4Q213[a].1.1.6–10; 11QT[a].45.15–17), something also emphasized in later rabbinic traditions (see below).

The first discussion of a human made installation that was used for ritual immersion and purification is found in the rabbinic literature only. Both the Mishnah (redacted c. 200–225 CE) and the Tosefta (redacted c. 3rd cent. CE) offer an entire tractate, entitled *Miqwa'ot*, to situations that would validate or invalidate the water of such ritual-immersion baths. The Mishnah is also the first textual source to give this installation a specific name: "bet tevilah" ("house of immersion"; e.g. *m. Parah* 3.7; *Yoma* 3.2–3) or, more commonly, "mikveh" ("gathering"; e.g. *m. Miqw.* 1.1). A mikveh was not necessarily a human-made installation, but was also used by the → rabbis for natural sources of water that were considered ritually pure such as lakes and springs (*m. Miqw.* 1.1, 4–8).

The rabbinic discussions on the validity of water for ritual purification specified what needed to be considered in the construction of a mikveh. For instance, rain or spring water (i.e. living water) had to be channelled directly into the installation (*m. Miqw.* 2.3–9), and the installation had to contain at least 40 *se'ah* of water (often considered equal to approx. 500 litres, though precise volume remains debated; *m. Miqw.* 1.7). Notwithstanding the specifications being given, the rabbinic literature provides no fixed conception of what a humanmade mikveh looked like (see Miller, 2015, 32–103).

2. Structural Characteristics

If one were to describe a mikveh, probably the most characteristic definition would be a rectangular pool, sometimes roofed, that is hewn into the bedrock and coated with hydraulic plaster, with a

Fig. 1: *mikveh* in a residential area in Sepphoris, Israel (photo by Rick Bonnie).

flight of steps spanning its full width, and which is fed (either directly or indirectly through a connected cistern or reservoir) by rainwater that was collected and channeled from a building's rooftop (fig 1.).

However, since the term "mikveh" is a functional rather than a structural description, neither ancient texts nor modern scholars provide a common standard for its material components, construction methods, and ultimate design. There are some defining elements, though, that scholars nowadays use to identify a mikveh in the archaeological record.

As with other installations that are used to hold water (e.g. cisterns, aqueducts, pools), in order for water not to leak directly into the ground, mikva'ot are almost always found coated with hydraulic lime plaster. Exceptions to this are few. Four recently exposed mikva'ot at Magdala/Taricheae, a site located on the northwestern shore of the Sea of Galilee (northern Israel), were built in alluvial clay and thus were fed by groundwater seeping through its stone masonry walls (Reich & Zapata Meza, 2014).

Another notable feature – often deemed a mikveh's most iconic feature – is the presence of a flight of steps leading from the rim of the pool to the floor. Mikva'ot therefore often also go by the (structural) name "stepped pools." Usually these steps span the pool's entire width, though in some examples the steps form a narrow staircase abutting one of the pool's inner walls – sometimes descending in a straight direction, sometimes taking a bend. In the latter cases, such baths bear a striking resemblance to – and, as a result, have sometimes been confused with – wine vats from the late Roman or

Byzantine period that have been exposed in the region.

Mikva'ot were usually carved out of the bedrock. In some cases, they had ceilings, either made of bedrock or vaulted humanmade constructions, while in other cases the steps and pool area were simply kept unroofed. There are rare instances in which the installation was not hewn into bedrock at all, but constructed entirely of stone masonry and plaster. The pools also come in different shapes and sizes. Most are trapezoidal or rectangular, but round and ovoid examples are known as well. Similarly, while some pools are barely able to fit one individual, the largest known pools are able to fit several individuals easily.

Some mikva'ot have a low partition running down the middle of the steps or a double entrance into the pool, essentially dividing the staircase into two. It is generally suggested, often through reference to textual accounts (*Let. Aris.* 105–106; *m. Šeqal.* 8.2; P.Oxy. 840; see Miller, 2015, 56–62, 104–152, for discussion), that such partitions and double entrances acted as a "divider" between those going into the pool and those coming out of it, in order to avoid physical contact and contamination.

3. Physical Functioning

It is commonly understood that, as indicated by textual sources (see above), miqva'ot had to be fed directly by "living" water. With the exception of the recent discovery of groundwater-filled pools at Magdala/Taricheae, this means in most cases that rainwater was collected on (part of) a building's roof from where it was distributed through vertical pipes and rock-hewn channels directly into the stepped pool, or, alternatively, first into a cistern or reservoir that was connected to such a pool. However, because only the lower courses of a house usually preserve in the archaeological record, there is for the vast majority of pools little to no evidence of how water was collected and distributed to them.

Moreover, as none of the found pools show evidence of an outlet from which used water could be discharged, little is known about the frequency and methods by which these pools were eventually emptied and cleaned (on the sensorial experiences of ritual bathing, see Bonnie, 2021). Possibly this was done manually. This makes changing the water and cleaning the mikva'ot a more challenging task that may have not been carried out frequently. A related concern is that, if not frequently changed, the stagnant water in these open pools posed a likely hygienic risk for its surroundings. For example, aside from other health risks, these pools probably were attractive breeding grounds for various mosquito species responsible for malaria (see Kligler, 1930, 41, for an early modern example). However, it is unclear how used water could have been regularly changed in these pools during the long and dry summer in the semi-arid region of the southern Levant. On the other hand, in the absence of water outlets in these pools, it is equally unclear in the majority of cases how these pools coped with the discharge of superfluous rainwater in the event of heavy rainfalls during winter.

Finally, little has been done so far about the effect of climate change on the collection and usage of water in these pools in this semi-arid region, although paleo-climatic proxy data and archaeological evidence from the region show that the heyday of construction and usage of mikva'ot was an extremely humid and rainy period with high lake water levels (e.g. Dubowski, Erez & Stiller, 2003). The fact that this in the centuries that followed (starting c. 2nd–3rd cents. CE) changed to a drier climate with reduced rainfall may be one explanation for the decline in usage of earlier mikva'ot and the severely reduced construction rate of new ones around this time (for a hydrological analysis, see Aarnio 2021; for other explanations, see below).

4. Archaeological Context

The majority of mikva'ot are found in domestic contexts, on the ground floor or basement level. They appear both in elite urban mansions as well as in smaller farmstead houses. In the Hasmonean and Herodian palaces, they usually are located in its private bathing facility, where they functioned as a plunge pool in the *frigidarium* (e.g. Jericho, Herodium). In most cases, however, the specifics regarding their location within houses remains not well understood. Some pools apparently had a public, communal function, such as those located near some of the 1st-century CE synagogues (e.g. Gamla).

No such communal mikva'ot have been found near any of the late Roman and Byzantine synagogues. In Jerusalem, a large number of mikva'ot are found near entrances to the Temple, such as the Huldah Gates, the Robinson Arch, and the Wilson Arch, where they were probably used by Jewish pilgrims.

A number of mikva'ot have also been found near winepresses and oil presses, where peasants apparently used them to ensure the ritual purity of the wine and oil produced there. The Mishnah alludes to the presence of mikva'ot near such installations (*m. Miqw.* 7.3) and describes the necessity of winemakers and olive-press workers to immerse (*m. Ṭehar* 10.3). Finally, some mikva'ot have been attested near catacombs and other burial sites, presumably to be used by those who had contracted corpse impurity through indirect contact. While the Priestly Code (Num 19:11–19) instructs a process of purification of seven days for those who had direct contact with a corpse, one who only had indirect contact was considered impure only until that evening (*m. 'Ohal.* 1.1). The latter was a less severe form of impurity for which bathing alone would suffice.

5. Chronological and Geographical Distribution

The earliest found mikva'ot date to the Hasmonean period and were constructed around the late 2nd or early 1st century BCE. Stepped, plastered pools from this early period have been exposed in Jerusalem, Jericho, and Khirbet Qumran, as well as farther north in Gamla. However, in Marissa, a large Hellenistic town in Idumea (southern Israel), comparable installations were already found in use during the 3rd and 2nd centuries BCE, before the arrival of the Hasmoneans there in 112/111 BCE. This may testify to (perhaps similar ritual) bathing practices among Marissa's earlier Idumean population.

From around the time of Herod the Great onward, but especially during the 1st century CE, mikva'ot were in use throughout the Herodian kingdom: from Galilee in the north to Idumea in the south, as well as on the eastern banks of the Jordan River. There are, however, conspicuous geographical blanks in the distribution of these pools, with relatively few of them found in settlements in the coastal plain, in the Golan (except Gamla), and in the West Bank

(ancient Samaria). The precise reasons for this are still unclear, but may have something to do with the regions' particular geology (solid basalt underground in Golan), history of research (a lack of excavations and a poor state of reporting on excavations in the West Bank), or population at that time (little is known about whether and how Samaritans would have practiced ritual purification).

The largest concentration of these baths is found in and around Herodian Jerusalem, where they served the large local population of the town as well as Jewish pilgrims. Another large concentration of mikva'ot has been found in and around the Western Quarter of Sepphoris (northern Israel). However, after exploration and identification of mikva'ot surged in the 1990s, hundreds of stepped pools have turned up in (rescue) excavations in rural areas of Idumea, Judea, and Galilee as well. The number of mikva'ot found in these villages or farmsteads varies significantly. At some sites, such as in the town of Gamla, the low number of mikva'ot suggests that at least some of them may have had a communal function.

Moving outside the southern Levant, into the setting of the Jewish → Diaspora, material remnants of mikva'ot in the archaeological record become conspicuously absent (Rutgers, 1998, 105). The identification of a bell-shaped cistern that was found near a Hellenistic-period building (the alleged "synagogue") at Delos as a mikveh is highly doubtful, nor is the identification of a late antique water basin that was recently found at Limyra (southwest Turkey) as a mikveh in any way secure. Later mikva'ot do appear from the late 6th or 7th century CE onward in the Mediterranean region, such as one in Syracuse (southern Italy). Yet, no comprehensive study of these late antique mikva'ot has so far appeared, leaving us without any details of the structures and their precise regional distribution (for an overview, see Harck, 2014).

The main majority of the hundreds of found mikva'ot in Judea, Idumea, and Galilee went out of use in the later 1st or in the first half of the 2nd century CE. Sometimes they simply were built over by new structures without mikva'ot, in other cases these stepped pools were given different functions, such as storage chambers, glass refuse pits, or pottery dumps. The reasons for why these pools were no longer used for ritual purification are not clear. R. Reich

(2013) suggested that the decline was a direct result of the cessation of the Temple cult in 70 CE, a theory still followed by many. Recently, Y. Adler (2017) has suggested, however, that many, if not most, mikva'ot continued in use after 70 CE and may have only fallen out of use after the later Bar Kochba revolt (132–135 CE). One reason for this decline around this time, though speculative as such, may be the fact that Jews no longer understood the Pentateuchal laws as prescriptive but rather as descriptive, and hence saw no practical purpose for ritual purity any longer.

Stepped, plastered pools that were built or continued in use as mikva'ot postdating 70 CE and the Bar Kochba revolt are far fewer in number, not more perhaps than several dozen or so. They mostly are found in Galilee and in the southern Hebron hills, mainly in large concentrations in the towns of Sepphoris and Susiya, respectively. In the case of Sepphoris, however, it remains unclear how many precisely continued in use as mikva'ot after the 2nd century CE and how significant they still were for its population. The continued significance of these pools to its population is often merely presumed (e.g. Miller, 2015, 185–197). In fact, it is noteworthy that during the new construction spree in Sepphoris during the 2nd-3rd centuries CE, most notably on its acropolis and on the lower plateau to the east, no efforts were made to include mikva'ot in any of the new houses (see Bonnie, 2019, 287–304).

Historiography

For a long time, mikva'ot were not given much consideration in the study of early and rabbinic → Judaism. In his three-volume study *Talmudische Archäologie*, S. Krauss (1910, vol. II, 219) discusses them merely in passing and mentions the term "mikveh" only once. This changed when excavations led by Y. Yadin at Masada in 1963–1964 exposed a stepped, plastered installation attributed to the Sicarii defenders there (66–73/74 CE). The installation, found in the southern casemate wall, was connected to an adjacent plastered pool via a pipe in its wall. Y. Yadin and others thought that the exposed installation pool bore strong structural similarities with modern mikva'ot, where the immersion pool is usually connected to an adjacent reservoir (*ōṣār*), and hence suggested

a similar functionality. The *ōṣār* would have been filled with rainwater, which could make any drawn water in the stepped pools suitable upon contact by opening the pipe between these installations. Thus, though similar installations were already known from Beth She'arim and Khirbet Qumran, Y. Yadin for the first time identified a stepped installation as a mikveh.

Large-scale excavations in the late 1960s and 1970s in Jerusalem's Old City exposed dozens of these stepped, plastered pools. R. Reich, who worked in the Jewish Quarter excavations, identified these as ritual-purification baths and indicated that the presence of an adjoining *ōṣār* was not necessarily required for the pools to be suitable for ritual immersion. His subsequent 1990 dissertation (published in updated form as Reich, 2013), in which he surveyed and examined over 300 stepped pools in the southern Levant, lay the groundwork for the archaeological study of mikva'ot. Since then, Y. Adler (2011) has updated this picture and identifies in his dissertation over 850 stepped pools as mikva'ot.

With a large number of stepped pools across Israel identified as mikva'ot, scholars of New Testament and early Christianity, among others, began to consider this evidence of purity observance among Jews in early Roman Judea. Disagreement, however, surged concerning how to interpret the spread and variety of pools in terms of religious observance of people. Some, notwithstanding the noted variety in design and context of these pools (see below), have viewed the spread of mikva'ot as a general acceptance of ritual-purity laws among the Jewish population at large (Sanders, 1992, 223; Hengel & Deines, 1995). Others take a more minimalist stance in which mikva'ot are understood as a heightened concern with personal purity only where such installations have been found (Regev, 2000).

Over the last two decades, however, more critical attitudes have been fostered toward joining textual and material sources for our understanding of mikva'ot and associated bathing practices. B. Wright (1997) was one of the first to caution on using (later rabbinic) texts to identify earlier-dated stepped pools as functioning primarily for ritual purification, as rabbinic mikva'ot. This caution of reading too much into our textual sources for understanding the usage of excavated stepped pools led to a stronger emphasis on the archaeological context and material aspects of these pools (Galor, 2003; 2007; Berlin, 2005, 451–453; Adler, 2011). Simultaneously, it has led to a more cautionary study of the textual sources on ritual bathing practices. This has led to a "softer" understanding of the potential usage of these pools, which could have had other functions alongside ritual bathing (Miller, 2015). Moreover, this more critical reading also has shown that the adjacent reservoirs that previously were understood as an *'ôsār* were in fact not used as such. As Y. Adler (2014) has shown, the *'ôsār* is not discussed as a device in any ancient source but was a much later innovation of the 19th century.

Bibliography

Aarnio, N., "Hydrological Analysis of Stepped Pools in Roman Palestine," master's thesis, Helsinki, 2021.

Adler, Y., "The Archaeology of Purity: Archaeological Evidence for the Observance of Ritual Purity in Erez-Israel from the Hasmonean Period until the End of the Talmudic Era (164 BCE–400 CE)," diss., Ramat-Gan, 2011; Heb.

Adler, Y., "The Myth of the *'ôsār* in Second Temple-Period Ritual Baths: An Anachronistic Interpretation of a Modern-Era Innovation," *JJS* 65, 2014, 263–283.

Adler, Y., "The Decline of Jewish Ritual Purity Observance in Roman Palaestina: An Archaeological Perspective on Chronology and Historical Context," in: Z. Weiss & O. Tal, eds., *Expressions of Cult in the Southern Levant in the Greco-Roman Period: Manifestations in Text and Material Culture*, Turnhout, 2017.

Berlin, A.M., "Jewish Life before the Revolt: The Archaeological Evidence," *JSJ* 36, 2005, 417–470.

Bonnie, R., *Being Jewish in Galilee, 100–200 CE*, Turnhout, 2019.

Bonnie, R., "Pure Stale Water: Experiencing Jewish Purifications Rituals in Early Roman Palestine," in: K. Neumann & A. Thomason, eds., *The Routledge Handbook of the Senses in the Ancient Near East*, London, 2021, 234–253.

Dubowski, Y., J. Erez & M. Stiller, "Isotopic Paleolimnology of Lake Kinneret," *LaO* 48, 2003, 68–78.

Galor, K., "Plastered Pools: A New Perspective," in: J.-B. Humbert & J. Gunneweg, eds., *Khirbet Qumrân et 'Aïn Feshkha*, Göttingen, 2003, 291–320.

Galor, K., "The Stepped Water Installations of the Sepphoris Acropolis," in: D. Edwards & C.T. McCollough, *The Archaeology of Difference: Gender, Ethnicity, Class and the "Other" in Antiquity: Studies in Honor of Eric M. Meyers*, Boston, 2007, 201–213.

Harck, O., *Archäologische Studien zum Judentum in der europäischen Antike und dem zentraleuropäischen Mittelalter*, Petersberg, 2014.

Hengel, M., & R. Deines, "E.P. Sanders' 'Common Judaism', Jesus, and the Pharisees," *JThS* 46, 1995, 1–70.

Kligler, I.J., *The Epidemiology and Control of Malaria in Palestine*, Chicago, 1930.

Krauss, S., *Talmudische Archäologie*, 3 vols., Leipzig, 1910.

Lawrence, J.D., *Washing in Water: Trajectories of Ritual Bathing in the Hebrew Bible and Second Temple Literature*, Atlanta, 2006.

Miller, S.S., *At the Intersection of Texts and Material Finds: Stepped Pools, Stone Vessels, and Ritual Purity Among the Jews of Roman Galilee*, JAJ.S 16, Göttingen, 2015.

Regev, E., "Pure Individualism: the Idea of Non-Priestly Purity in Ancient Judaism," *JSJ* 31, 2000, 176–202.

Reich, R., *Jewish Ritual Baths in the Second Temple, Mishnaic, and Talmudic Periods*, Jerusalem, 2013, Heb.

Reich, R., & M. Zapata Meza, "A Preliminary Report on the Miqwa'ot of Migdal," *IEJ* 64, 2014, 63–71.

Rutgers, L.V., *The Hidden Heritage of Diaspora Judaism*, CBET 20, Louvain, 1998.

Sanders, E.P., *Judaism: Practice & Belief, 63 BCE–66 CE*, London, 1992.

Wright, B.G., "Jewish Ritual Baths – Interpreting the Digs and the Texts: Some Issues in the Social History of Second Temple Judaism," in: N.A. Silberman & D.B. Small, eds., *The Archaeology of Israel: Constructing the Past, Interpreting the Present*, Sheffield, 1997, 190–214.

RICK BONNIE

Beatitudes

It is hard to overestimate the importance of the Beatitudes to early Christianity. This is especially true of Matthew's version (Matt 5:3–12), which received comparatively greater attention than Luke's version (Luke 6:20–26). Early Christians saw the Beatitudes, in Augustine of Hippo's words, as *perfectum vitae christianae modum* ("the perfect mode of the Christian life"; Aug. *Serm. Dom.* 1.1.1). The Beatitudes shaped – and were shaped by – Christian understandings of virtue, theōsis, and the eschaton. Over time, the Beatitudes became a cornerstone in Christian attitudes toward prayer, holiness, sin, and salvation.

Despite the differences in the two evangelists' accounts, early Christians assumed that the two versions were in essential harmony. Occasionally, an early Christian writer would propose that Matthew's version was more complete or perfect. The earliest text to take this path appears to be the 5th-century CE *Opus Imperfectum in Matthaeum* (*Incomplete Commentary on Matthew*), which judges that Luke partially set out the Beatitudes, while Matthew's are more perfect. The author deduces this in part from the respective contexts: Luke's Beatitudes were spoken to ordinary people on a plain, whereas Matthew's were given to the apostles on a mountain, which represents the height of virtue (*Op. Imp. Matt. Homily* 9; *Homily* 21).

This view became far more common in the medieval era when the split between laypeople and those in holy orders became wider. Most early Christians, however, believed that the Matthean and Lukan Beatitudes preserved the same essential teaching, and that both versions were intended as a way of life for all Christians.

1. The Beatitudes and the Hebrew Bible

A few early church writers focused on demonstrating the connections between the Beatitudes and the Hebrew Bible. Although these writers were not the dominant voices, they were influential, including among their ranks Tertullian (155–240 CE), Jerome (c. 342–420 CE), and Chromatius of Aquileia (d. 407 CE). → Tertullian wielded the Beatitudes against → Marcion of Sinope, who famously used a truncated version of Luke's Gospel as part of his anti-Jewish Christian canon. It is no mistake, then, that Tertullian turned to Luke's version of the Beatitudes to undermine Marcion, by demonstrating the thorough grounding of Luke's Beatitudes in Isa 61:1–3 (Tert. *Marc.* 4.14). In all the Beatitudes, Tertullian observed, Christ simply renews principles already laid down by the Creator (*Marc.* 4.15). Just as the God of Israel "loved, consoled, protected and avenged the beggar, and the poor, and the humble, and the widow, and the orphan," so Christ displays these same divine attributes in his Beatitudes (*Marc.* 4.14; trans. in *ANF*, vol. III, 365).

Likewise, → Jerome interpreted the Beatitudes against Isaiah's backdrop. In his commentary on Isaiah, Jerome repeatedly quoted the → blessing on the meek (along with one reference to the poor in spirit) as a fulfillment of promises made throughout the book of Isaiah (Jer. *Comm. Isa.* 1.26; 6.21; 16.10; 18.32;

unfortunately, Jerome frequently paired this fulfillment rhetoric with anti-Jewish sentiment, writing that Jews were only able to interpret the Scriptures carnally and not spiritually).

Around the same time that Jerome was writing his commentary, → Chromatius of Aquileia was exploring the Beatitudes in relation to the Mosaic covenant. Chromatius described → Moses and Christ as lawgivers who ascended a mountain to give God's law (Exod 19:20; Matt 5:1). He quoted from a Psalm (84:7) and the prophet Jeremiah (31:31–33) to argue that Christ was "proving himself to be the author of both laws" – the old and the new (→ Law/Decalogue/Torah) – when he ascended the mountain and blessed his apostles with the Beatitudes (Chrom. *Tract. Matt.* 17.1.3). Throughout his exposition of the Beatitudes, Chromatius repeatedly observed how the Beatitudes confirm Hebrew Bible teachings, especially the Psalms and Isaiah; and he points to David, Moses, Jeremiah, and Daniel as exemplars of various Beatitudes (*Tract. Matt.* 17.2.5–6; 17.32–5; 17.4.2–3; 17.6.3–6; 17.7.2.4–6).

2. Asceticism

Another early thread reads the Beatitudes in light of ascetic ideals. Several Beatitudes became associated with ascetic practices, especially the blessing on the poor with voluntary poverty; the blessing on those who hunger with fasting; and the blessing on the pure of heart with celibacy. The latter received special attention.

As early as the 2nd century CE, sexual purity, especially virginity (→ Virgin/Virginity), became closely associated with purity of heart (Matt 5:8). In the *Acts of Paul and Thecla* (c. 160 CE; → *Paul and Thecla, Acts of*), the apostle Paul (→ Paul the Apostle) preaches an extended version of the blessing on the pure of heart: "Blessed are they that have kept the flesh chaste, for they shall become a temple of God [...] blessed are the bodies of the virgins, for they shall be well pleasing to God, and shall not lose the reward of their chastity" (*Act. Paul. Thec.* 3; trans. in *ANF*, vol. VIII, 487).

Some writers viewed the Beatitudes as a whole through an ascetic lens. → Clement of Alexandria (c. 150–c. 215 CE) understood all the Beatitudes as training and "discipline" (*askēsis*) for the soul. Drawing on principles from Platonic thought (e.g. Plato *Phaed.* 67c–d; 80e), Clement wrote that "the Lord's discipline," as represented in the Beatitudes, "draws the soul gladly away from the body" and its sinful desires (Clem. *Strom.* 4.6; trans. in *ANF*, vol. II, 413–414).

This emphasis flowers in later eastern thought, especially in meditations on the pure of heart (Matt 5:8) in relation to → *apatheia* ("freedom from the passions") and the mystical contemplation of God. It also overlaps in part with the thought of the many theologians who viewed the Beatitudes as training in virtue, leading to ever greater godlikeness.

3. Virtues and Steps of Ascent Toward God

Three late 4th-century CE theologians together laid a trajectory that dominated interpretation of the Beatitudes for the rest of the early church period and into the medieval era. Gregory of Nyssa (c. 335–c. 395 CE), Ambrose of Milan (c. 340–397 CE), and John Chrysostom (c. 347–407 CE) understood the Beatitudes as virtues that progressively cleanse the soul and draw the Christian into union with God. While Chrysostom and Ambrose explored the Beatitudes as virtues more broadly, Ambrose focused on the Lukan Beatitudes and the four cardinal virtues (justice, prudence, temperance, and fortitude).

Ambrose wrote that Luke chose four Beatitudes "in honour of the four cardinal virtues," whereas Matthew chose the mystical number eight because of the phrase "for the octave" found at the head of many Psalms (→ Ambrose of Milan). The octave "denotes the completion and fulfillment of our hopes; the octave is, also, the sum of all the virtues" (Ambr. *Exp. Luc.* 5.49; trans. Ní Riain, 2001, 133). Matthew's eight are contained in Luke's four; thus, all eight ultimately flow from the four cardinal virtues. The blessing on the poor (Matt 5:3; Luke 6:20) represents the virtue of temperance, which implies also purity of heart (Matt 5:8). Those who hunger (Matt 5:6; Luke 6:21a) signify the virtue of justice, which implies mercy (Matt 5:7); those who weep (Matt 5:4; Luke 6:21b) indicate the virtue of prudence, which implies peace (Matt 5:9); and the persecuted (Matt 5:10–12; Luke 6:22–23) display the virtue of fortitude, which implies gentleness (Matt 5:5).

John Chrysostom connected the Beatitudes to the virtues through the metaphor of the salt of the earth (Matt 5:13; → John Chrysostom). In order to preserve people from returning to their sins once they had been set free by Christ, the disciples would need to be virtuous; and they would become virtuous by conforming to the Beatitudes. The meek, merciful, and righteous person "shuts not up his good deeds unto himself only, but also provides that these good fountains should run over for the benefit of others" (Chrys. *Hom. Matt.* 15.10; trans. in *NPNF¹*, vol. X, 97).

Ambrose's contemporary → Gregory of Nyssa linked the Beatitudes not to the four cardinal virtues but to the broader concept of beatitude (a state of blessedness) and to the role of virtues in paving the way toward beatitude. Gregory defined blessedness, or beatitude, as "a possession of all things held to be good," and since "the one thing truly blessed is the Divinity Itself," then Godself is beatitude (Greg. Nyss. *Beat. Homily* 1; trans. Graef, 1954, 87). Inasmuch as the end of the Beatitudes is blessedness, the end of the Beatitudes is God (*Beat. Homily* 4).

For Gregory, then, the end is virtue not for virtue's sake, but for the sake of taking on God's (virtuous) character, since the end of a life of virtue is to become ἡ πρὸς τὸ Θεῖον ὁμοίωσις ("like to God"; *Beat. Homily* 1; trans. Graef, 1954, 89). Participating in the virtues of the Beatitudes assists in the process of making human beings like God, by restoring God's image in them. Through the virtues of the Beatitudes, God washes away "the filth of sin" that has disfigured the beauty of the original image of God in humanity (*Beat. Homily* 5; trans. Graef, 1954, 148). Augustine echoes a similar theme when he describes the blessing on the peacemakers as the final step of the Beatitudes and therefore as "wisdom itself, that is, contemplation of the truth, bringing peace to the whole man and effecting a likeness to God" (Aug. *Serm. Dom.* 1.3.10).

For each of these thinkers, the order of the Beatitudes is not incidental. Instead, Christ gave the Beatitudes in a certain order for a reason. As Chrysostom wrote:

> [...] in each instance, by the former precept making way for the following one, [Christ] hath woven a sort of golden chain for us. Thus, first,

he that is "humble," will surely also "mourn" for his own sins: he that so "mourns," will be both "meek," and "righteous" [...] (Chrys. *Hom. Matt.* 15.9; trans. *NPNF¹*, vol. X, 96)

They did not always agree on *how* the order matters. They generally agreed that → humility (poverty of spirit) was first because it combats the vice of pride, the root of all → evil. From there, reflections on the order diverge. Interpreters did not always agree even on the order itself, since they used two different manuscript traditions. Some patristic interpreters, like Ephrem the Syrian, had access to the western manuscript tradition (followed by the Latin Vulgate), which presents "blessed are the meek" as the second Beatitude and "blessed are those who mourn" as the third. Many other interpreters, however, including Gregory of Nyssa, John Chrysostom, Ambrose, Augustine, and Jerome, read manuscripts in which the mourners are blessed before the meek (an order followed by most English translations today).

The transposition of Matt 5:4 and Matt 5:5 could lead to variations in application. → Ephrem the Syrian, for example, wrote in his commentary on the *Diatessaron* that the blessing on the meek or lowly follows the blessing on the poor for a specific reason: "Lest they become exalted by this poverty, [Jesus] said, 'Blessed are the lowly' [Matt 5:5]" (Ephr. *Comm. Diat.* 6.1a; trans. McCarthy, 1993, 108). Compare this with Chrysostom, who explained: "First, he that is 'humble,' will surely also 'mourn' for his own sins: he that so 'mourns,' will be both 'meek,' and 'righteous' [...]" (Chrys. *Hom. Matt.* 15.9; trans. in *NPNF¹*, vol. X, 96).

While Chrysostom imagined the Beatitudes as a chain, Ambrose and Gregory imagined them as a ladder. For these two thinkers, not only is the order significant, so that one follows them in a logical and connected sequence, but they are an ascending set of steps that draws one higher and higher toward God. They are, in Ambrose's words: "The steps that form the ladder of virtue" (Ambr. *Exp. Luc.* 5.52, 5.60; trans. Ní Riain, 2001, 134, 137). Likewise, Gregory of Nyssa wrote that the Beatitudes were given to assist in an ascent "from superficial and ignoble thoughts to the spiritual mountain of sublime contemplation" (Greg. Nyss. *Beat. Homily* 1; trans. Graef, 1954, 85). Echoing Ambrose, he mused: "It seems to me that the Beatitudes are arranged in order like so

many steps, so as to facilitate the ascent from one to the other" (Greg. Nyss. *Beat. Homily* 2; trans. Graef, 1954, 97).

It is difficult to judge which one came to the idea first; some scholars propose it was Ambrose whereas others argue for Gregory. Either way, both theologians firmly embedded this view of the Beatitudes into Christian thought from this point forward. But neither of them was the great innovator of Beatitude interpretation in the late 4th century CE. Instead, that mantle belongs to their near-contemporary, Augustine (354–430 CE).

4. Petitions and Gifts: Augustine of Hippo

Like Gregory and Ambrose, the North African theologian → Augustine of Hippo described the Beatitudes as a series of steps undertaken by the soul (Aug. *Serm. Dom.* 1.3.10). Unusually, Augustine counted the Beatitudes using the number seven, rather than the number eight. He did so because the first and the eighth Beatitudes have the same reward ("for theirs is the kingdom of heaven"). Thus, for Augustine the eighth Beatitude circles back to, and recapitulates, the first (*Serm. Dom.* 1.3.10).

Augustine then used the number seven to link the Beatitudes to two other sets of seven: the seven gifts of the → Holy Spirit in Isa 11:2 (in the Old Latin translation), and the seven petitions of the Lord's Prayer in Matt 6:9–13 (*Serm. Dom.* 1.4.11; 2.11.38). To match the three sets, Augustine inverted the order of the spiritual gifts from Isaiah, appealing to Ecclesiastes as authorization: "The fear of the Lord" (the last gift in Isaiah's list) "is the *beginning* of wisdom" (Eccl 1:16, emphasis added; *Serm. Dom.* 1.4.11–12; 2.11.38).

After Augustine, it became remarkably common for Christians to interpret the Beatitudes in relation to the gifts of the Holy Spirit and the petitions of the Lord's Prayer. The virtues of the Beatitudes thus became closely associated with prayer and with the power of the Holy Spirit. This association permeates other aspects of Augustine's influential teaching. For example, in *De doctrina Christiana* (*Christian Instruction*), he used the gifts and Beatitudes, in sequential order, as the necessary stages for a student of the divine Scriptures to learn to read and understand them properly (Aug. *Doctr. chr.* 2.7.9–11).

5. Eschatological Context

Although early Christians used different numbers to count the Beatitudes, the two predominant numbers (seven and eight) had something important in common: their eschatological overtones. Both numbers in their own way pointed forward to the eschaton – the new creation, God's new age.

Seven, of course, is a number that symbolizes perfection or completion. Yet for Augustine, the Beatitudes were not merely seven; they were seven plus one, with the eighth hidden in the first. Likewise, Jesus was raised on the first day of the week – that is, on an eighth day, or seven plus one. Just as Jesus' → resurrection heralded the dawning of the eschaton and the arrival of God's new creation, so the eight (or seven) Beatitudes also herald and usher in the eschaton. For early Christians, all the promises of the Beatitudes flow from the promise of the first and the eighth: "For theirs is the kingdom of heaven" (Matt 5:3; 5:10), which means that each promised reward (mercy, seeing God, being filled) is about inheriting the kingdom of God.

For Gregory of Nyssa (as for Ambrose), the eighth day or octave is another term for the next age. Like other patristic writers, Gregory connected the number eight to the rite of → circumcision (which occurs on the eighth day after birth) and to the resurrection (which occurs on an eighth day, i.e. seven plus one; Greg. Nyss. *Beat. Homily* 8). As the "summit of all the Beatitudes," the eighth Beatitude "contains the re-instatement in heaven of those who had fallen into servitude, and who are now from their slavery recalled to the Kingdom" (*Beat. Homily* 8; trans. Graef, 1954, 166). For Gregory, ascending the ladder of the Beatitudes progressively reverses the damage done by the fall and restores the image of God to its full glory.

For these reasons, the early Christians typically saw all the Beatitudes as eschatological promises. They are fulfilled partially or proleptically in this life ("through a glass, darkly") and completely and perfectly in the next life or in the new age ("but then face to face"; 1 Cor 13:12; KJV).

Historiography

Although J. Dupont was not the first to study the Beatitudes from a historical perspective, his three-volume work *Les Béatitudes* (Dupont, 1958; 1969; 1973) remains the most thorough historical-critical study, and all subsequent scholarly work remains in his debt. J. Dupont's first volume explored the relationship of the two versions of the Beatitudes in Matthew and Luke (Dupont, 1958); the second argued that four Beatitudes (the poor, hungry, weeping, and hated) were authentic teachings of Jesus (Dupont, 1969); and the third laid out how Matthew and Luke shaped the Beatitudes for their respective audiences (Dupont, 1973). Another influential study appeared in H.D. Betz's Hermeneia commentary *The Sermon on the Mount* (Betz, 1995), although not all scholars accept H.D. Betz's views of the origin and sources of the Sermon (for one critique, see Snodgrass, 1991).

Most modern scholars typically follow two paths when discussing the Beatitudes: they view Luke's version as more authentic while they see Matthew's as a "spiritualized" version of Jesus' teaching; and they debate whether the Beatitudes are eschatological blessings or "entrance requirements" to the kingdom, using a phrase coined by H. Windisch (1937) and popularized by R. Guelich (1976). D. Allison offers important and sophisticated correctives to both tendencies (Allison, 1999; 2005). The volume of work on the Beatitudes makes a comprehensive bibliographic list impossibly long, but two additional studies worth noting are those by H.B. Green (2001) and J. Pennington (2017).

Bibliography

Allison, D., *The Sermon on the Mount: Inspiring the Moral Imagination*, New York, 1999.

Allison, D., *Studies in Matthew: Interpretation Past and Present*, Grand Rapids, 2005.

Betz, H.D., *The Sermon on the Mount*, Hermeneia, Minneapolis, 1995.

Coxe, A.C., trans., *Clement of Alexandria: Stromata*, PG, vol. VIII, Paris, 1857ff., 685–1382; ET: "Stromata," in: A. Roberts & J. Donaldson, eds., *ANF*, vol. II, New York, 1885–1887, 299–556.

Dupont, J., *Le problème littéraire – Les deux versions du Sermon sur la montagne et des Béatitudes*, vol. I of *Les Béatitudes*, Bruges, 1958.

Dupont, J., *La Bonne Nouvelle*, vol. II of *Les Béatitudes*, Paris, 1969.

Dupont, J., *Les Évangélistes*, vol. III of *Les Béatitudes*, Paris, 1973.

Eklund, R., "Blessed Are the Image-Bearers: Gregory of Nyssa and the Beatitudes," *ATR* 99/4, 2017, 729–740.

Graef, H.C., trans., *Gregory of Nyssa: De Beatitudinibus*, PG, vol. XLIV, Paris, 1857ff., 1193–1302; ET: *The Lord's Prayer; The Beatitudes*, ACW 18, Mahwah, 1954.

Green, H.B., *Matthew, Poet of the Beatitudes*, Sheffield, 2001.

Guelich, R., "The Matthean Beatitudes: 'Entrance Requirements' or Eschatological Blessing?" *JBL* 95, 1976, 415–34.

Green, R.P.H., *Augustine: De doctrina christiana*, PL vol. XXXIV, Paris, 1841ff., 15–122; ET: *On Christian Teaching*, Oxford, 1997.

Holmes, P., trans., *Tertullian: Adversus Marcionem*, CCL 14, Turnhout, 1953ff.; ET: "Against Marcion," in: A. Roberts & J. Donaldson, eds., *ANF*, vol. III, New York, 1885–1887, 271–423.

Jepson, J.J., trans., *Augustine: De sermone Domini in monti*, PL, vol. XXXIV, Paris, 1841ff., 1229–1308; ET: *The Lord's Sermon on the Mount*, ACW 5, Mahwah, 1948.

Kellerman, J.A., trans., T.C. Oden, ed., *Opus Imperfectum in Matthaeum*, PG, vol. LVI, Paris, 1857ff., 611–946; ET: *Incomplete Commentary on Matthew*, Downers Grove, 2010.

McCambley, C., "On the Sixth Psalm, Concerning the Octave by Saint Gregory of Nyssa," *GOTR* 32/1, 1987, 39–50.

McCarthy, C., trans., *St. Ephrem's Commentary on Tatian's Diatessaron*, Oxford, 1993.

Ní Riain, Í.M., trans., *Ambrose of Milan: Expositio Evangelii secundum Lucam*, PL vol. XV, Paris, 1841ff., 1327–1830; ET: *Commentary of Saint Ambrose on the Gospel According to Saint Luke*, Dublin, 2001.

Pennington, J.T., *The Sermon on the Mount and Human Flourishing: A Theological Commentary*, Grand Rapids, 2017.

Prevost, G., trans., *John Chrysostom: Homiliae in Matthaeum*, PG, vol. LVII, Paris, 1857ff., 21–472; ET: "Homilies on the Gospel of Saint Matthew," in: P. Schaff, ed., *NPNF1*, vol. X, Buffalo, 1886–1889; repr. 1994.

Scheck, T.P., trans., *Jerome: Commentariorum in Isaim Prophetam*, PL, vol. XXIV, Paris, 1841ff., 17–678B; ET: *Commentary on Isaiah; St. Jerome's Translation of Origen's Homilies 1–9 on Isaiah*, ACW 68, Mahwah, 2015.

Scheck, T.P., trans., *Chromatius of Aquileia: Tractatus 17 in Evangelium S. Matthaei*, PL, vol. XX, Paris, 1841ff., 327–368; ET: *Sermons and Tractates on Matthew*, ACW 75, New York, 2018.

Snodgrass, K., "A Response to Hans Dieter Betz on the Sermon on the Mount," *BR* 36, 1991, 88–94.

Walker, A., trans., "Acts of Paul and Thecla," in: A. Roberts & J. Donaldson, eds., *ANF*, vol. VIII, New York, 1885–1887, 487–492; repr. 1994.

Windisch, H., *Der Sinn der Bergpredigt*, Berlin, 1937.

REBEKAH EKLUND

Belisarius (Scholasticus)

Belisarius (5th cent. CE; *Bellesarius* in most mss.), called *Scholasticus* or rhetorician to distinguish him from the homonymous general who lived under Emperor → Justinian (d. 565 CE), was a Christian Latin intellectual from the late 5th century CE. We know practically nothing about his life and career. His name, Belisarius, was originally a Thracian name; it was used in Visigothic Iberia and in the Italic kingdom of the Longobards (Wagner, 1984).

He is the author of an acrostic in praise of → Sedulius' poetry, placed by the manuscript tradition at the end of Sedulius' works (CPL 1451; Riese's [1906] *Anthologia Latina* §492; reproduced in Panagl's [2007], and Springer's [2013], editions, respectively, on pp. 307–310 and 230–231). Sedulius himself was a 5th-century CE Christian poet, perhaps a presbyter (→ Priest/Presbyter), whose Latin biblical epic, *Carmen Paschale* or *Easter Song*, and hymns became enormously popular during the Middle Ages and the early modern period (Nicola, 2006). The acrostic that Belisarius composed in honor of Sedulius is the second acrostic appended to Sedulius' works in the manuscripts, the first being an acrostic by the poet Liberius or Liberatus Scholasticus. However, both acrostics may stem from the same author, Belisarius, since the manuscript tradition is divided between the attribution of this acrostic to Liberius/Liberatus or Belisarius. Both acrostics consist of 16 Vergilian hexameters. The initial and final verses of the two small poems (acrostics and telestics) use the designation *Sedulius antistes* or "Sedulius the priest/teacher."

The acrostic that is unanimously ascribed to Belisarius extols Sedulius because he described the → miracles of Christ in his verses. In particular, Belisarius singles out the miracle of the multiplication of bread and fish and insists on the simplicity of the food mentioned by Sedulius; he hopes that Sedulius' poetry, like the bread and fish of the miracle, can fulfil the reader's need for spiritual food.

On Belisarius there is virtually no historiography; the little existent falls under Sedulius.

Bibliography

Green, R., *Latin Epics of the New Testament: Juvencus, Sedulius, Arator*, Oxford, 2008.

Nicola, A. de, "Belisario Scolastico," in: A. Di Berardino, ed., *NDPAC*, Genoa, 2006, 759–760.

Panagl, V., ed., *Sedulius: Opera Omnia, Ex Recensione Iohannis Huemer*, CSEL 10, Vienna, 2007.

Ramelli, I.L.E., "Generic Innovation and Diversity," in: G. Kelly & A. Pelttari, eds., *CHLLL*, Cambridge UK, 2023.

Riese, E., *Anthologia Latina*, vol. I/2, Leipzig, 1906.

Springer, C., trans., *Sedulius: Paschal Song and Hymns*, WGRW, Atlanta, 2013.

Wagner, N., "Belisarius," *ZVS* 97, 1984, 123–129.

ILARIA L.E. RAMELLI

Benedict I

Born in Rome as the son of Boniface, Benedict was the bishop of Rome for only four years (575–579 CE). During his brief papacy, he witnessed great hardships and afflictions (*LP*, vol. I, 308) following the Lombard conquest of Italy and the ensuing famine. The invasion led to an interruption of regular contacts with Constantinople, and Benedict was consecrated only when the emperor's permission was received on Jun 2, 575 CE, 11 months after his predecessor's death. The abbot of the Monastery of Saint Mark in Spoleto appealed to Benedict to obtain the return of some lands the monastery owned near Minturno, which shows that relations with the conquerors had improved, at least with Duke Faroaldus I of Spoleto (d. 590 CE). In the meantime, hunger had already forced several Byzantine troops to surrender, and Benedict, fearing for Rome's fate, made sure that the city could rely on sufficient supplies, which were provided by ships loaded with wheat from Egypt, sent by Emperor → Justin II (d. 578 CE).

A famous reliquary cross donated to Benedict, which is preserved in the Vatican basilica, was probably a gift from Justin II. In the midst of all the sorrow and difficulties, Benedict was able to exercise his ecclesiastical rule and consecrated 21

bishops, probably in the sees of Byzantine Italy and → Ravenna, where he certainly sent Bishop John III (607–625 CE), as we learn from Agnellus (c. 800–850 CE) in the *Liber pontificalis ecclesiae Ravennatis* (98). John, in a letter he sent to → Gregory the Great (590–604 CE) in 593 CE, actually recalled that he had been formed in the womb of the Roman Church (CChr.SL 140A; 1098.18). Rome's intervention in the episcopal succession of the exarchal capital city was quite remarkable and must have been connected to the battle waged by the bishops of Rome against Ravenna's ambitions of autonomy and the enduring schism of the Three Chapters in northeast Italy. Benedict died on Jul 30, 579 CE, during the Lombard siege of Rome and was buried in the *secretarium* (sacristy) of Saint Peter's Basilica. Nothing remains of his epitaph.

See the bibliography for sources and studies of a more specialized nature and historiography on the theme.

Bibliography

Baix, F., "Benoît I," in: *DHGE*, vol. XIII, Paris, 1935, 7–9.

Bertolini, O., *Roma di fronte a Bisanzio e ai Longobardi*, Bologna, 1941.

Bertolini, O., "Benedetto I," in: *EdP*, vol. I, Rome, 2000, 539–541.

Caspar, E., *Geschichte des Papsttums*, vol. I, Tübingen, 1930.

Gregorovius, F., *Storia della città di Roma nel medio evo*, vol. I, Rome, 1900.

Grisar, H., *Roma alla fine del mondo antico*, vol. II, Rome, 1930.

Hartmann, L.M., *Geschichte Italiens im Mittelalter*, vol. II/1, Gotha, 1900.

Seppelt, F.X., *Geschichte der Päpste*, vol. I, Munich, ²1954.

ROCCO RONZANI

Benedict of Nursia

The second volume of → Gregory the Great's *Dialogi* is practically the only source we have about Benedict's life (480/490–547 CE), whereas only very limited information can be gleaned from later texts such as Mark's *Versus in Benedicti laudem* and an 11th-century hagiographical text from Cassino. Gregory's broad biographical sketch has an openly hagiographical character, considering this work's avowed aim, which mainly was to narrate the miracles performed by Italian saints. Hence, there have been doubts regarding its reliability. However, the number of specific and detailed facts reported is so high that we can assume that Gregory had access to first-hand testimonies, particularly those provided by four of the saint's disciples, one of whom was the abbot of the Lateran monastery in Rome.

Benedict was born around 480/490 CE in Nursia, where he lived throughout his childhood. Gregory states that Benedict came from a prominent local family, but there is no real evidence to prove that he belonged to the *gens Anicia* (the Roman Anicia family). Around 497 CE, he moved to Rome to pursue further education. However, preferring a solitary life, he left Rome for the Simbruini mountains, part of Latium's Apennine foothills. First, he found refuge in the village of Enfide (Affile, about 60 km from Rome) and later, after performing a miracle that attracted the attention of the local population, he went to the rocky and wild ravines of the Aniene valley, near Nero's villa *ad Simbruina stagna* in Subiaco. There, in this solitary place, Benedict met the monk Romanus of Roso (see Greg. M. *Dial.* 2.1.3–4), who lived in a nearby monastery. About three years later, some monks who lived in Vicovaro, a village between Subiaco and Tivoli, asked Benedict to give up his eremitic life. Benedict accepted, but after risking poisoning by the monks, he returned to his eremitical life. Benedict's reputation started to attract many people from neighboring areas, some of whom started living with him as his disciples. Two Roman aristocrats, Equitius and Tertullus, also decided to entrust Benedict with their children's education (Maurus and Placidus). Probably viewed as a competitor by the local clergy, especially by the presbyter Florentius, Benedict was forced to leave Subiaco and reached the hill overlooking ancient Casinum along the Via Latina (Cassino, 140 km south of Rome). Around 529 CE, Benedict reused the remains of an ancient pagan temple located on the hilltop, building a church dedicated to Martin, a chapel dedicated to → John the Baptist (where he would eventually be buried), and a monastery which, despite many vicissitudes, demolitions, and rebuildings, would later become one of the most important symbols of medieval Christianity. Benedict would never leave the monastery again, not even to visit Terracina, where he sent several monks (Greg. M. *Dial.* 2.22; SC 260.200–204). In Cassino, he received several pilgrims on their way to Rome, followers, would-be monks, and also prominent visitors such as King Totila (d. 552 CE). Some facts narrated by Gregory in the *Life of Benedict* can be dated: the famine of 537–538 CE, Germanus of Capua's death in 541 CE (*Dial.* 2.35.3–4; SC 260.239), Totila's visit in 546 CE (*Dial.* 2.14–15; SC 260.180–184), and the Goth Zalla, who flourished between 542 and 552 CE (*Dial.* 2.31; SC 260.222–226). Mar 21, 547 CE, is given as the date of Benedict's death. Both this dating and the hypothesis that would postpone it somewhere between 555 and 560 CE are consistent with the chronological data provided by the *Dialogi*. His body was laid to rest in the same tomb as that of his sister Scholastica, the protagonist of one of the best-known pages from Benedict's Gregorian biography (*Dial.* 2.33; 34.2; SC 260.231–234).

1. Rule

Gregory considered Benedict's monastic rule to be excellent in its judgment and enlightening in its discourse (Greg. M. *Dial.* 36; SC 260.242). It has been effectively summarized in the motto *ora et labora* (pray and work), which is not explicitly written in the rule. A. Vogüé believes that it should be stated as follows: *ora, labora, lege, meditare* (pray, work, read the Bible, and meditate; SC 86a.339). But the traditional formulation includes such actions as well, since *labora* encompasses both manual work and study, as → Augustine of Hippo would also argue, whereas *ora* includes communal prayer, meditation, and contemplation. The history concerning the text's transmission has produced its own legend. Apparently, there were two *specimina* of the rule written by Benedict himself: one was given by the saint to his disciple Maurus for him to carry to France; the other one was carried to Rome after Montecassino's destruction by the Lombards (577 CE) and taken back to the monastery during Zachary's papacy (750 CE), after the reconstruction carried out by Abbot Petronax (670–747 CE). Later, the manuscript was lost when the monks had to move to Teano and Capua after the monastery had been destroyed yet again by the Saracens (883–896 CE). Prior to its destruction, the text was supposedly used by Abbot Theodomar (d. 798 CE) to copy the codex that was sent to Charlemagne (742–814 CE) and used by Benedict of Aniane (d. 821 CE) to reform Carolingian monasticism. It seems that an apograph of this copy still exists in the Codex Sangallese 914 – drafted by two monks of Reichenau for the monastery of Inda and then brought to Sankt Gall by Abbot Grimald (841–872 CE) – and in other 9th-century codices (Drobner, 1998, 462). The textus receptus is not a literal transcription of Benedict's text – spred mainly through Charlemagne's Aachener Normal Codex after 787 CE – but comes from a 9th-century version. This text normalized Benedict's Latin, while shortening the prologue and other passages, and added a number of notes. Apparently, the rule was not written with a specific intention in mind, but primarily reflects Montecassino's monastic life. Often rewritten over time, the rule might have been composed toward the end of Benedict's life, as the final chapters 67–73 seem to date back to those years. The text reflects both eastern and Latin monastic traditions; the influence of → Pachomius of Tabennese (d. 348 CE), → Basil of Caesarea (329/330–379 CE), Augustine of Hippo (354–430 CE), → John Cassian (360–435 CE), and the *Vitae Patrum* is quite clear. The structure and one-third of the text are shared with the *Regula Magistri* (Prologue 1.2.4–7), a circumstance that led to a long debate about which text was written first. So far, A. Genestout's (1940) assertion that the *Regula Magistri* came first has gained greater acceptance. Both texts were probably inspired by the same source, which could be the rule of → Eugippius (465–533 CE), dating back to the first half of the 6th century (534 CE). In the rule, Benedict achieved a new synthesis of numerous different elements found in monastic literature: a deeply christocentric synthesis. Its popularity was due to Benedict's critically pondered knowledge and experience, which made the text sensible, benevolent, and flexible (Drobner, 1998, 641). Furthermore, Benedict of Aniane's role in disseminating the rule should not be forgotten (817 CE), nor should the great popularity it attained thanks to Charlemagne and his successors, as a result of which Benedict's rule was applied in practically all European monasteries between the 9th and 11th centuries.

See the bibliography for sources and studies of a more specialized nature and historiography on the theme.

Bibliography

Arnaldi, G., "San Benedetto guadagnato alla storia (in margine a una nuova edizione della Regola)," in: *Studi sul Medioevo cristiano offerti a R. Morghen*, Rome, 1974, 1–27.

Boesh Gajano, S., "Narratio e expositio nei Dialoghi di Gregorio Magno," *BISI* 88, 1979, 1–33.

Cracco, G., "Gregorio I," in: *EdP*, vol. II, Rome, 2000, 546–574.

Drobner, H.R., "Benedetto da Norcia," in: H.R. Drobner, *Patrologia*, Casale Monferrato, 1998, 637–645.

Dunn, M., "Mastering Benedict: Monastic Rules and their Authors in the Early Medieval West," *EHR* 105, 1990, 567–594.

Ermini, F., *Benedetto da Norcia*, Rome, 1929.

Francheschini, E., "La questione della Regola di S. Benedetto," in: *Il monachesimo nell'alto medioevo e la formazione della civiltà occidentale*, SdS 4, Spoleto, 1957, 221–256.

Genestout, A., "La Règle du Maître et la Règle de S. Benoît," *RAM* 21, 1940, 51–112.

Grégoire, R., "La Regula Magistri tra san Benedetto e Cassiodoro," *InFr* 37, 1987, 71–104.

Gribomont, J., ed., *Commentaria in Regulam*, vol. I, StAns 84, Rome, 1982.

Jaspert, B., *Die Regula Magistri - Regula Benedicti Kontroverse*, RBS.S 3, Hildesheim, 1975.

Manning, E., "Problèmes du monachisme bénédictin primitif," *RHS* 48, 1972, 113–114.

Maréchaux, B., *Saint Benoît: Sa vie, sa règle, sa doctrine spirituelle*, Paris, 1911.

Meyveart, P., "Problems concerning the 'Autograph' Manuscript of St. Benedict's Rule," *RBen* 69, 1959, 3–21.

Meyveart, P., "Towards a History of the Textual Transmission of the Regula S. Benedicti," *Script.* 17, 1963, 83–110.

Morin, G., *Regulae Sancti Benedicti traditio codicum manuscriptorum cassinensium*, Montecassino, 1900.

Mohrmann, C., "La latinité de S. Benoît: Étude linguistique sur la tradition manuscrite de la Règle," *RBen* 62, 1952, 108–139.

Mohrmann, C., "La langue de S. Benoît," in: P. Schmit, ed., *S. Benedicti regula monachorum*, Maredsous, ²1974, 9–39.

Penco, G., *Storia del monachesimo in Italia dalle origini alla fine del Medio Evo*, Rome, 1961, 47–135.

Pricoco, S., "Benedetto da Norcia, santo," in: G. Cremascoli & A. Degl'Innocenti, eds., *Enciclopedia Gregoriana: La vita, l'opera e la fortuna di Gregorio Magno*, AG 15, Florence, 2008, 26–28.

San Benedetto e il suo tempo (Norcia, Subiaco, Cassino, Montecassino, Sep 29–Oct 5, 1980): *Atti del VII Congresso internazionale di studi sull'Alto Medioevo*, Spoleto, 1982.

Tosti, L., *Della vita di S. Benedetto*, Montecassino, 1892.

Traube, L., *Textgeschichte der Regula S. Benedicti*, ed. H. Plenkers, Munich, 1898, ²1910.

Turbessi, G., *Ascetismo e monachesimo in Benedetto*, Rome, 1965.

Vandenbroucke, F., "Sur les sources de la règle bénédictine et de la Regula Magistri," *RBen* 62, 1952, 216–273.

Vogüé, A. de, "Benoît modèle de vie spirituelle d'après le deuxième livre des Dialogues de saint Grégoire," *CC* 38, 1976, 147–157.

Vogüé, A. de, "Les recherches de Fr. Masai sur le Maître et s. Benoît," *StMon* 24, 1982, 7–42, 271–301.

Vogüé, A. de, *Le Maître, Eugippe et S. Benoît: Recueil des articles*, RBS.S 17, Hildesheim, 1984.

Vogüé, A. de, "The Master and S. Benedict: A Reply to Marilyn Dunn," *EHR* 197, 1992, 95–103.

Vogüé, A. de, "La Maîtrise littéraire du Maître d'après une étude récente," *CC* 58, 1996, 149–160.

Zelser, K., "Regulae monachorum," in: P. Chiesa & L. Castaldi, eds., *La trasmissione dei testi latini del medioevo: Medieval Latin Text and their Transmission*, vol. I, Florence, 2004, 364–389.

Zelzer, M., "Gregory's Life of Benedict: Its Historico-Literary Field," *CistSQ* 43, 2008, 327–328.

Zelzer, M., "Gregory's Life of Benedict and the Bible: The Decoding of an Exegetical Program," *CistSQ* 44, 2009, 82–102.

ROCCO RONZANI

Bethany

Bethany (*Bethania*) is identified with the town of Al-Azariya in the West Bank, on the southeastern slope of the Mount of Olives, and to the east of Jerusalem. The place-name might be derived from *Beth Ananiah*, a site mentioned in Neh 11:32 and located between Anatoth and Nob to the east of Jerusalem (Murphy-O'Connor, 2013, 86) or from *beth 'ani* in Hebrew or *beth'anya* in Aramaic, meaning "house of the poor." The latter etymology could indicate that Bethany was the site of an almshouse (Capper, 2006, 496–502). The Arabic means "place of Lazarus" (see below).

1. One Bethany or Two?

The Gospel of John (→ John the Apostle) mentions two places named Bethany. The first one was on the other side or beyond the Jordan River (πέραν τοῦ Ἰορδάνου; John 1:28), and the second was 15 stadia (3 km) from Jerusalem (John 11:18). We refer first to the second one. This Bethany is located "at the Mount of Olives" (πρὸς τὸ ὄρος τὸ καλούμενον Ἐλαιῶν; Luke 19:29, mentioned with Bethphage) and to the east of Jerusalem. Bethany beyond the Jordan, where → John the Baptist baptized Jesus (John 1:28–31), is identified with Al-Maghtas in Wadi Al-Kharar near the southern end of the Jordan River, across from Jericho and 9 km north of the Dead Sea. The two sites are not to be confused (Murphy-O'Connor, 2013, 90–98). → Origen read *Bēthabará* ("house of passing" = "place of crossing") instead of Bethania in John 1:28. This reading, though, may be descriptive and not be a place name (Hutton, 2008). Others have suggested that Bethany in John 1:28 referred to Batanaea east of the Sea of Galilee (Riesner, 2002). The present entry deals with Bethany near Jerusalem.

2. Jesus in Bethany

John 11:1–44 describes a man named → Lazarus who lived at Bethany together with his sisters Martha and Mary. Lazarus fell ill and his sisters sent a message to Jesus who had sought refuge across the Jordan. Although Jesus loved them, he waited for two days. Upon his return, he found that Lazarus was dead and had been buried in his tomb for four days. Martha met Jesus who then went to call her sister Mary. They went to the tomb of Lazarus in a burial cave, removed the stone at the entrance, and Lazarus came forth in his shrouds resuscitated. While the Lazarus tradition has elicited literary and theological interest (e.g. Burkett, 1994; Lang, 2016), little of this has been concerned with Bethany.

Mark 11:1 (Luke 19:29) has Jesus approaching Jerusalem from the direction of Bethphage and Bethany. Bethphage is identified with et Tur on the Mount of Olives and thus Jesus would have first passed through Bethany, further away and not Bethphage. The account in Matt 21:1 mentions only Bethphage. After going up to the → Temple, Jesus returned to Bethany where he lodged (Mark 11:11–12; Matt 21:17). On the following day, after they had left Bethany, Jesus passed by a fig tree and wished to eat a fig. The tree had no figs and Jesus cursed it (Mark 11:12–24; Matt 21:18–22).

When in Jerusalem, Jesus lodged at two houses in Bethany, as it was cheaper to lodge in a nearby village like Bethany than to stay in Jerusalem itself (Murphy-O'Connor, 2013, 86). The first was the house of Martha, Mary, and Lazarus and Jesus arrived there six days before Passover. At a supper held in his honor, Mary brought out pure nard oil, an expensive perfume, and anointed the feet of Jesus and wiped them with her hair (John 12:1–8; Coakley, 1988). A similar version of the story appears in Mark 14:3–9 (Matt 26:6–13). Jesus lodged at Bethany in the house of Simon the Leper, and an unnamed woman poured nard over his head. This version may reflect the view that Bethany was or was near one of the dwelling places allotted to lepers "east of the city" according to the *Temple Scroll* of the Dead Sea Sect (col. 46, 16–18; → Dead Sea Scrolls). This might also reflect Essene activity (→ Essenes) in Bethany (Capper, 2006, 496–502). The story appears a third time in Luke 7:36–50. In this account, Simon is a Pharisee, but Bethany is not mentioned, nor is the woman's name mentioned. She is, though, described as a "sinner" (ἁμαρτωλός). Mary of Bethany has been conflated in tradition and sometimes in scholarship with Mary Magdalene. Both Marys were, in turn, conflated with the anonymous sinner of Luke (Beavis, 2012).

The last mention of Bethany is in Luke 24:50–53 when Jesus leads the 11 disciples to Bethany and instructs them to remain in Jerusalem until the coming of the → Holy Spirit. The → ascension of Jesus Christ took place from the Mount of Olives s(Acts 1:12) nearby.

3. Bethany Venerated

The empty tomb of Lazarus in Bethany was known to the Christian community and venerated. There was no church there in the early 4th century CE, since → Eusebius of Caesarea calls it "the Place of Lazarus" (Eus. *Onom.* 58.15) and the Bordeaux Pilgrim pointed out only Lazarus' tomb cave (*Itin. Burd.* 596.1). → Jerome, however, in his translation of the *Onomasticon* in the late 4th century CE mentions a church in proximity to the tomb. The late 4th-century CE pilgrim → Egeria describes the celebrations at this church in Bethany and calls it the Lazarium (Eger. *It.* 29.5). The excavations at the church (see

below) have shown that the church and the tomb were linked as sources stated. Egeria mentions a second church by the road, about half a mile before the Lazarium and at the purported spot where Jesus met Mary (John 11:29; Eger. *It.* 29.4). This church has not been uncovered. Jerome mentions that the pilgrim → Paula visited the "guest room" (*Hospitium*) of Martha and Mary (Jer. *Ep.* 108.12), perhaps considered the room in which Jesus stayed when he resided in Bethany (see above) which had been turned into a pilgrim cave chapel. The *Hospitium* has been identified with the cave discovered in the property of the Sisters of Charity in Bethany (Taylor, 1987).

4. Archaeology

Archaeological excavations took place at Bethany between 1949 and 1953 and were directed by the Franciscan Father S.J. Saller (1957). The excavations showed that the ancient site was occupied from 6th–5th (5th–4th cents.) centuries BCE to the 12th century CE, although from the 2nd century until the 4th century CE, the settlement dwindled. In the Byzantine period, its pilgrim-site status revived it.

The excavations extended to two areas. The first was the area of the Lazarium near the road to Jericho. These excavations uncovered several superimposed churches in proximity to the tomb, which were once connected. The earliest church dates to the 4th century CE and was destroyed in an earthquake. The second church, constructed over this, is dated to the 5th–6th centuries CE. Nearby, the Crusader period monastery was built.

The second area of excavations was to the west of the Lazarium excavations there uncovered parts of the ancient settlement such as rooms or parts of houses, granaries, rock-hewn cisterns, columbaria, or dovecotes, a quarry, agricultural terraces. The large number of ritual baths discovered there as well as the large number of stone vessels, both common ethnic markers of Jewish settlement and additional Jewish markers such as *kokhim* and stone ossuaries in the burial caves on the outskirts of the village, prove that the village was Jewish. It is impossible to know if the ritual baths were for local use, for pilgrims on the way to Jerusalem, or both. The latest indication of a Jewish presence is from the beginning of the 2nd century CE.

A small pagan settlement existed there afterward until Byzantine times when the village flourished once again, this time as a Christian pilgrim site.

5. Rabbinic Literature

There are few mentions of Bethany in rabbinic literature yet even when seemingly mentioned, the reading Bethany is often problematical or not clear. One may eat figs in the sabbatical year (→ Sabbath/ Sabbatical Year) until the (unripe) figs (*pagi*) of Beth Vani are finished (*t. Šeb.* 7.14). This place-name seemingly has nothing to do with Bethany. However, other readings of the place name are Bethy'ni, Beth 'Oni, and Betyyny. All these readings are somewhat similar to Bethany and the parallel tradition in *b. Pesaḥ.* 53a reads Beth Hini (i.e.Bethany), as does a tradition in *b. Ḥul.* 53a on a bathhouse in Beth Hini in which a ewe-lamb was clawed by a fox. *B. Meṣiʿa* 88a mentions the stores of Beth Hini (or Hino) destroyed during the War of Destruction.

Under the best of circumstances, none of the traditions are historical, although the figs or *pagi* of Beth Hini may reflect nearby Bethphage, if the name of that site does derive from figs and perhaps the New Testament fig-tree tradition (above) in the Bethany-Bethphage region. Some scholars identified the site of all these traditions with Beth Yannai (see the reading Betyyny above) which is near Caesarea and not Jerusalem. This identification would vitiate all relevance of these sources for Bethany (Klein, 1910). Other scholars are of the opinion that Bethphage and Bethany were considered by the → rabbis to be one village and that the many rabbinic traditions on Bethphage connecting the site to Jerusalem and the Temple could reflect also on Bethany (Shahar, 2004).

Historiography

Scholarship on Bethany revolves around three axes:
1. Theology;
2. Archaeology;
3. Geography.

Theological studies concentrate on the resurrection of Lazarus and the anointing by Mary of Bethany (e.g. Coakley, 1988; Burkett, 1994; Beavis, 2012; Lang, 2016). The major study on the archaeology of

Bethany is still the excavation report by S.J. Saller (1957). The scholarship on the geography and historical-geography of Bethany pertains for the most part to the issue of the two Bethanys (Reisner, 2002; Hutton, 2008; Murphy-O'Connor, 2013).

Bibliography

Beavis, M.A., "Reconsidering Mary of Bethany," *CBQ* 74/2, 2012, 281–297.
Burkett, D., "Two Accounts of Lazarus' Resurrection in John 11," *NT* 36/3, 1994, 209–232.
Capper, B.J., "Essene Community Houses and Jesus' Early Community," in: J.H. Charlesworth, ed., *Jesus and Archaeology*, Grand Rapids, 2006, 472–502.
Coakley, J.F., "The Anointing at Bethany and the Priority of John," *JBL* 107/2, 1988, 241–256.
Hutton, J.M., "'Bethany beyond the Jordan' in Text, Tradition, and Historical Geography," *Bib.* 89/3, 2008, 305–328.
Klein, S., "Bemerkungen zur Geographie des alten Palästina," *MGWJ* 54, 1910, 18–22.
Lang, B., "The Baptismal Raising of Lazarus: A New Interpretation of John 11," *NT* 58/3, 2016, 301–317.
Murphy-O' Connor, J., "Place-Names in the Fourth Gospel (II): Bethany (JN1:28; 11:18) and Ephraim (JN 11:54)," *RB* 120/1, 2013, 85–98.
Riesner, R., *Bethanien jenseits des Jordan. Topografie und Theologie im Johannes Evangelium*, Gießen, 2002.
Saller, S.J., *Excavations at Bethany (1949–1953)*, Jerusalem, 1957.
Shahar, Y., "Bethphage, Bethany, and the Environs between Them-On the Clarifications of Theological Toponomy," *NStJ* 10, 2004, 119–136.
Taylor, J., "The Cave at Bethany," *RB* 94/1, 1987, 120–123.

JOSHUA SCHWARTZ

Bethlehem

Bethlehem is a small city in the West Bank, 9 km south of Jerusalem, on the road to Hebron, at the northernmost tip of the Hebron Mountains and on the border of the Judean Desert. It lacks springs or other perennial surface water sources and until late Hellenistic or early Roman times, depended on cisterns. The Hebrew name is Beth Leḥem ("House of Bread"), the Arabic is Bayta Laḥm ("House of Meat"), both names reflecting the fertile nature of its farmland and pastureland in contrast to the nearby desert. Some scholars speculated that Beth Leḥem originally referred to a Canaanite fertility deity, cognate with the Akkadian deity Laḥmu. Medieval Jewish kabbalistic tradition saw the name as being derived from *lhm*, "battle" or "war" ("House of Battle"). In the Hebrew Bible it is also called Bethlehem Ephrathah (Mic 5:1[2]) or just Ephrath (Ephrathah; Gen 35:16), and Bethlehem Judah (1 Sam 17:12). There was also a Bethlehem in the Galilee in the northern Jezreel Valley (Josh 19:15). This entry relates mostly to the Bethlehem in Judah.

1. Ancient Bethlehem

The first settlements of ancient Bethlehem were on the low ground to the east of the modern-day city, near present-day Bait Sahur and its wadis and fertile fields. Remains from the Neolithic, Chalcolithic, and Early Bronze periods have been found there. A Middle Bronze necropolis was discovered at Khalet al-Jam'a, 2.2 km southeast of the Basilica of the Nativity. In the Iron Age, Bethlehem was a stronghold or small town. As the use of cisterns became widespread, the settlement moved westward to the top of the Bethlehem ridge, with Iron Age remains found in the vicinity of the Basilica of the Nativity (Prag, 2000; Nigro, 2015).

Some scholars identified "Beth Laḥmi" mentioned in the Amarna Letters, the diplomatic correspondence of Egypt with its representatives in → Canaan (14th cent. BCE), with Bethlehem, but this is unlikely (Nigro, 2015, 6). Bethlehem appears first in the Hebrew Bible in connection with Rachel who died near there (Gen 35:19). It is the setting for the book of Ruth and was the birthplace and home of Ruth's descendant → David. David was later anointed king there by Samuel (1 Sam 16:1–13). The Hebrew Bible refers to a cistern or well by the city gate when Bethlehem was garrisoned by the Philistines in the time of David (2 Sam 23:15–17; 1 Chr 11:18). Bethlehem was fortified by Rehoboam, David's grandson, after the division of the monarchy between Israel and Judah (2 Chr 11:6–12). Fortifications were found near Manger Square which some attempted to identify with these fortifications (Nigro, 2015, 8). Mic 5:1[2] associates Bethlehem with the future messianic ruler over Israel (see Matt 2:1; Luke 2:4–6). A recent 7th-century BCE *bulla* ("seal") found in Jerusalem mentions Beth Leḥem, indicating that it was part of the royal administrative system (Nigro, 2015, 9). It was resettled in the period of the Restoration of → Zion (Ezra 2:21), but is not mentioned in later Hellenistic-period sources. The Lower Aqueduct to Jerusalem, dating from the Hasmonean period, and beginning at Solomon's Pools near Bethlehem, ran beneath Bethlehem through a tunnel mostly blocked today. The Aqueduct eventually arrived at the Temple Mount.

2. New Testament Bethlehem

Bethlehem is not mentioned often in the New Testament, but plays an important role. Matt 2:1 states that Jesus was born at Bethlehem in Judaea during the reign of → Herod. After his birth, wise men (→ Magi [Kings]) from the East arrived in Jerusalem asking: "Where is the one who has been born king of the Jews?" (Matt 2:2). Herod was perturbed by this and asked the chief priests and teachers in Jerusalem where the Messiah was to be born. They replied that he was to be born in Bethlehem citing Mic 5:1[2] (Matt 2:5–6):

> But you, Bethlehem Ephrathah, though you are small among the clans of Judah, out of you will come for me one who will be ruler over Israel, whose origins are from of old, from ancient times.

Herod sent them to Bethlehem asking that when they had found the child that they return and report to him (Matt 7–12). They did not return, and the family of Jesus fled to Egypt (Matt 2:13–15). When Herod realized that he had been tricked, he ordered the massacre of all children in Bethlehem and its environs under the age of two (Matt 2:16–18). Matthew cites Jer 31:15, which has Rachel "weeping for her children," implying that Rachel's Tomb was in Bethlehem, perhaps at its present-day location at the entrance to the city (Shragai, 2005). Fourth-century CE Christian tradition places it to the south of Jerusalem (Wilkinson, 2002, 340). After the death of Herod, the family returns to → Nazareth and not to Bethlehem (Matt 2:19–23).

Luke 2:1–5 mentions a Roman general census during the reign of Augustus, right before the birth of Jesus (→ Quirinius). It was because of this census that Joseph and → Mary journeyed to Bethlehem. When they arrived there, she gave birth to Jesus and placed him in a manger because there was no guest room available (Luke 2:4–7). At the same time, shepherds in a field nearby had a vision of an angel who informed them of what had taken place in Bethlehem. After hearing the heavenly choir sing of "Glory to God in the highest heaven" (Luke 2:14), the shepherds hurried off to Bethlehem to find Mary, Joseph, and the baby (Luke 2:8–20).

John 7:42 is aware that "the Messiah will come from David's descendants and from Bethlehem, the town where David lived." Mark does not refer to Bethlehem at all and relates to Nazareth as Jesus' earliest hometown. The focus of Jesus' activities will be → Galilee and thus Jesus, while born according to the nativity traditions in Bethlehem, returns with his family to Galilee to their hometown of Nazareth.

3. Which Bethlehem?

Some have contested identifying the site of Jesus' birth with Bethlehem in Judaea because the identification is dependent on the prophecy in Mic 5:1[2]. Others stress the Galilean background of Jesus and the fact that a Galilean birth would be more appropriate. Some are in favor of Nazareth as the birthplace of Jesus and others favored Bethlehem in the Galilee (see above), in spite of the Judaean setting of the birth narratives (Matt 2:1; Wansbrough, 2009, 4–22). Bethlehem in the Galilee had clear evidence of a Jewish settlement in the time of Jesus and the area had a large Christian population in the Byzantine period. However, by the 2nd century CE, the Bethlehem in Judaea identification was firm as both the *Protoevangelium of James* (→ *Protevangelium Jacobi*) and → Justin Martyr speak of an actual cave in which Jesus was born and Origen in the mid-3rd century CE puts the cave and the manger in Bethlehem (Or. *Cels.* 51; Wilkinson, 2002, 286). It is hard to know, though, how this can be squared with the statement of → Jerome that after the Second Jewish Revolt (136 CE), Hadrian established a shrine with a sacred grove of trees to the cult of Adonis over the same cave where Jesus was born (Jer. *Ep.* 58.3). The pagan shrine at the spot would most likely have destroyed or dimmed the memory of the cave

and Jesus. However, some have claimed that local Jewish-Christians maintained the memory of the identification of the cave, even in the face of pagan adversity, although the role of Jewish-Christians here has been questioned (Bacci, Bianchi, Campana & Fichera, 2012, e6).

4. Holy Sites

Places mentioned in the Nativity story were soon located at specific spots in Bethlehem. It was the cave, however, and not the church erected by → Constantine I that continued to be the main pilgrim focus in Bethlehems, facilitating worship of the visual and spatial mementoes of the birth of Jesus. Nearby grottoes and some specific spots in the basilica were identified with events in the story, such as the Slaughter of the Holy innocents. Various parts of the church complex began over time to be connected to the presence and activities of important personalities of the time. Jerome, for instance, had a two-room cave "study" or grotto under the church (Bacci, Bianchi, Campana & Fichera, 2012, e6).

According to → Eusebius of Caesarea, the Basilica of the Nativity was constructed by Constantine to mark the site of Christ's birth and dedicated in the presence of the empress Helena on May 31, 329 CE (Eus. *Vita Const.* 3.43). The Bordeaux Pilgrim (598.5) visited the basilica in 333 CE. According to tradition, the church was re-built in the 6th century CE at the expense of → Justinian, even though Bethlehem is not mentioned by → Procopius of Caesarea in his *On Buildings* (Bacci, Bianchi, Campana & Fichera, 2012, e7). Recent archaeological work and analysis has shown that the basilica is the result of a single, unitary construction process, although there is still discussion as to whether this has its roots in a Constantinian construction process. This has also shown that the rebuilding probably began in the last years of Justinian's reign and continued for a number of decades afterward (Bacci, Bianchi, Campana & Fichera, 2012, e24–25). The new rebuilt Justinian structure was a large-scale basilica which made the underground grottoes accessible, both those with theological significance as well those connected with a monastic presence (Bacci, Bianchi, Campana & Fichera, e25). Most of the celebrated art in the church, however, dates to the Crusader period or the Middle Ages and is outside the purview of this entry (Bacci, Bianchi, Campana & Fichera, e25).

Apart from the basilica and church, an early memory celebrated in Bethlehem before the 4th century CE was the tomb of David shown in different places in Bethlehem as well as David's family home (Wilkinson, 2002, 286). This tomb was perhaps meant to compete with the Jewish tomb of David located in Jerusalem (see Acts 2:29).

5. Surrounding Holy Sites

The environs of Bethlehem mentioned in the Gospels were identified and included in visits to Bethlehem. Shepherd's Field, in which the angels sang of the glory of God, was identified with Kenīset er-Ru'wāt, a cave with a Christian mosaic dating to the 4th century CE. During the 5th century CE, a large ecclesiastical building was constructed at the site of the cave (De Cree, 1999, 76). Another identification for Shepherd's Field is nearby Khirbet Siyar el Ghanem, which also has a cave and a Byzantine period monastery (Corbo, 1955). In the 5th century CE, on the road from Jerusalem to Bethlehem, the Kathisma ("place of sitting") church was built to commemorate the spot in which Mary rested before arriving in Bethlehem (Wilkinson, 2002, 323).

Historiography

Most interest in Bethlehem relates to the New Testament Nativity traditions. The history and archaeology of the site (Prag, 2000; Nigro, 2015) and its environs (De Cree, 1999) are the backdrop for a better understanding of the New Testament tradition. This tradition, however, ultimately faces challenges to the historicity of the Bethlehem location for the birth of Jesus (Wansbrough, 2009). Another popular field of study is the history and archaeology of the Basilica of the Nativity (Bacci, Bianchi, Campana & Fichera, 2012) as well attempting to identify the sites mentioned in the pilgrim traditions both in Bethlehem and in its environs (Wilkinson, 2002). Jewish interest revolves around Rachel's Tomb (Shragai, 2005).

Bibliography

Bacci, M., G. Bianchi, S. Campana & G. Fichera, "Historical and Archaeological Analysis of the Church of the Nativity," *JCH* 13, 2012, e5–e26.

Corbo, V.C., *Gli scavi di Kh. Siyar el-Ghanam (Campo dei Pastori) e i monasteri dei dintorni*, Jerusalem, 1955.

De Cree, F., "History and Archaeology of the BētSāḥur Region: A Preparatory Study for a Regional Survey (The Bethlehem Archaeology Project)," *ZDPV* 115, 1999, 59–84.

Nigro, L., "Bethlehem in the Bronze and Iron Ages in the Light of Recent Discoveries by the Palestinian Mota-Dach," *ViOr* 19, 2015, 1–24.

Prag, K., "Bethlehem: A Site Assessment," *PEQ* 132, 2000, 169–181.

Shragai, N., *The Story of Rachel's Tomb*, Jerusalem, 2005 (Heb.).

Wansbrough, H., "The Infancy Stories of the Gospels Since Raymond Brown," in: J. Corley, ed., *New Perspectives on the Nativity*, London, 2009, 4–22.

Wilkinson, J., *Jerusalem Pilgrims before the Crusades*, Warminster, 2002, 286–288.

JOSHUA SCHWARTZ

Bethphage

Bethpage is a village on the Mount of Olives and means "house of the un-ripe fig," recalling that there Jesus cursed a fig tree with leaves and no fruit (see Mark 11:12), although → Jerome offers a different etymology, "house of the jawbone" (Jer. *Ep.* 108.12; CSEL 55.320; Jer. *Tract. Marc.* 11.1–10; CCSL 78.485; Jer. *Comm. Matt.* 3; CCSL 77.182).

Bethphage appears three times in the New Testament (Matt 21:1; Mark 11:1; Luke 19:29). It was from that place that the disciples brought the donkey on which Jesus rode triumphantly into Jerusalem.

The village is mentioned by → Eusebius of Caesarea, though it seems that he was unable to identify the place (Eus. *Onom.* 58.13 [CGS 11.1.58–59]). Bethphage does not appear on the itinerary of → Egeria's *Travels*, although she mentions the place (*Per. Eg.* 29.4) when describing the memory of Jesus' triumphal entrance into Jerusalem. Theodosius, the author of *De situ terrae sanctae*, early 6th century CE, mentions a church at Bethphage that apparently claimed to possess relics of Thecla (*De situ terrae sanctae* 21; CSEL 39.146).

At Bethphage on the Mount of Olives, there was a Galilean settlement, as indicated by the discovery of a 1st-century CE ossuary with the name "Galileans" in 1923. It bears an inscription of 27 short lines, incised in cursive Jewish script in two columns, along one short edge of the inner surface. This inscribed ossuary lid was among 11 ossuaries found in a three-chambered, rock-hewn burial complex with loculi in Bethphage near the Franciscan church (*CII* 1.1, 681–686).

Bibliography

Brownrigg, R., *Who's Who in the New Testament*, New York, 1993.

Cotton, H.M., L. di Segni & W. Eck, eds., *Corpus Inscriptionum Iudaeae: Palestinae*, vol. I: *Jerusalem*, part 1, Berlin, 2010.

Davis, S.J., *Cult of Saint Thecla: A Tradition of Women's Piety in Late Antiquity*, Oxford, 2008.

Green, R.P.H., *Latin Epics of the New Testament: Juvencus, Sedulius, Arator*, Oxford, 2006.

JUAN ANTONIO CABRERA MONTERO

Bethsaida

Bethsaida (βηθσαϊδά; βηθσαϊδάν, in Mark), "House of the Fisherman" (or Hunter), is best known from the New Testament Gospels as a primary venue for the activities of Jesus of Nazareth and the home of his first disciples. Several miracles are attributed to Jesus in and around Bethsaida, as well as an ominous pronouncement against its inhabitants for failing to repent in light of these extraordinary deeds. The village is mentioned in both rabbinic literature and medieval Christian pilgrimage accounts, the latter preserving an ancient legend based on Jesus' words of condemnation that the → antichrist would arise from there (Roddy, 2004). Cursed or not, Bethsaida was abandoned in or around the 3rd century CE, disappearing from history until its recent identification with et-Tell, a sizeable mound located near the northern shore of the biblical Sea of Galilee. Beneath the ruins of Hellenistic-Roman Bethsaida, excavators are uncovering an impressive monumental city rooted in the mid-10th century BCE, which they identify as the capital of the biblical kingdom of Geshur.

1. Bethsaida in Ancient Sources

The New Testament provides the earliest attestation of Bethsaida, which it identifies as a fishing village near the shore of the freshwater Sea of Galilee. Textual variations aside, there are seven references to Bethsaida, and only Jerusalem and Capernaum are mentioned more frequently. It is from here that Jesus enlists the first members of his inner circle: Andrew (→ Andrew the Apostle); his brother, Simon Peter (→ Peter the Apostle); and Philip (→ Philip the Apostle; John 1:44; 12:21) – fishermen by trade, summoned to become fishers of people (Mark 1:17; Matt 4:19). A later tradition, known to → John Chrysostom (PG 59.30–31) and likely derived from Mark 1:16–20 and Matt 4:18–22, adds the disciples James and John, sons of Zebedee, to the list of Bethsaida fishermen.

The village and its environs provide the arena for much of Jesus' activity in the → Galilee, including his putative "deeds of power" (δυνάμεις). Although the details are impossible to reconcile, all four Gospels implicate Bethsaida and its surrounding open areas (ἔρημος τόπος, "deserted place") with the feeding of multitudes (Mark 6:30–45; 8:1–11; Matt 14:13–21; 15:32–39; Luke 9:10–17; John 6:1–13). Bethsaida is also identified as the location for Jesus' walk upon the water (Mark 6:45–48) and the healing of a blind man (Mark 8:22–26). Finally, Matthew and Luke preserve a saying from Q (10:13–15) that ascribes to Jesus a prophetic judgment against the cities of Bethsaida, Chorazin, and → Capernaum for failing to repent in light of the mighty works performed in their midst (Matt 11:20–24; Luke 10:13–15). Although this condemnation may reflect the Q community's own frustrations over rejection, multiple attestations of Jesus' presence in and around Bethsaida witness to its significance for the origins of his Galilean Jewish movement, reinforced by Matthew's resurrection account, which posits an unnamed mountain in Galilee as the place where the disciples are commissioned as apostles (Matt 28:16–20).

Flavius Josephus mentions the site several times in his writings, but almost without exception refers to Bethsaida as Julias, reflecting Philip Herod's expansion and reconstitution of the village as a polis (c. 30 CE) renamed in honor of the deified wife of Caesar → Augustus (Jos. *Bell.* 2.168; *Ant.* 18.28). → Flavius Josephus also recounts his own leadership in a battle with the Roman general Sulla that took place in the marshy plain near Bethsaida (66 CE), during which time he fell from his horse and injured his wrist (Jos. *Vita* 398–406). Other Roman-period sources include Pliny the Elder, who refers to Julias as one of four pleasant cities (along with Taricheae, Tiberias, and Hippos) located around the great lake Genesarea (Plin. *Nat.* 5.15), and Claudius Ptolemaeus, who lists Julias as a city in the Galilee (Ptol. *Geo.* 5.16.4).

According to R. Freund (1995), Bethsaida may also be present in rabbinic literature. Several rabbinic stories begin with *Maaseh beTzaidan*, "it happened in Tzaidan," which may indicate a complex morphological process by which a fuller reference to Bethsaida (or Bethsaidan, as in Mark), a town lying on the northern frontier of the land of Israel, may have been collapsed by medieval scribes and commentators no longer cognizant of an early Roman-period border town by this name. Not always aware of what they were copying, these scribes latched on to the better-known name of the Phoenician coastal city of Sidon, which in Hebrew shares the same basic meaning, spelling, and vocalization save for lack of a *yodh* and the particle *beth*, which were likely abandoned for the apparent past redundancy in the phrase *maaseh beBethsaida* (Freund, 1995, 274). If so, texts in the Mishnah, Tosefta, and Midrashim posit Bethsaida as a place where rabbinic legal rulings occasionally found precedent.

By the 4th century CE, a viable Bethsaida seems to fade altogether from Jewish and Christian sources. → Eusebius of Caesarea mentions Bethsaida in several of his works; but in light of his seemingly wholesale reliance upon information from the Gospels, the village seems hardly more than a regional memory. It is perhaps telling that Bethsaida is not mentioned at all in his *Ecclesiastical History*, nor does it appear in his *Martyrs of Palestine*. Byzantine sources simply follow suit in echoing biblical references.

In the centuries that followed, the fact that no one seemed to know Bethsaida's actual location did little to impede the imagination of medieval pilgrims and map makers. A few pilgrimage accounts, not always penned by actual pilgrims, seem only to copy Willibald's 8th-century CE witness to the presence of a church at Bethsaida, purportedly constructed by Helen, mother of Constantine, which he himself claims to have visited. However, any Byzantine-period church Willibald would have visited would have to have been situated somewhere else, perhaps at nearby Capernaum, Heptapegon (Tabgha), Magdala, or el-Araj. Finally, a few pilgrimage accounts transmit a legend that the antichrist would be born and raised at Bethsaida, the origin of which appears to be the late 7th-century CE Syriac text *Apocalypse of Pseudo-Methodius*.

2. The Archaeology of Bethsaida

In 1838, American biblical scholar E. Robinson explored northern Palestine and identified biblical Bethsaida with et-Tell, a mound located just over circa 1,4 km north of the great lake. Exactly 50 years later, German explorer G. Schumacher surveyed the region and refuted E. Robinson's claim on the basis of his opinion that the site was located too far from the lake to be the fishing village described in the Gospels. Instead, G. Schumacher suggested that one of two smaller sites located nearby and closer to the shore, namely el-Araj and el-Mesadiyeh, were better candidates; however, in recent years various probes and the application of ground-penetrating technologies have revealed a lack of habitation at either of these sites before the Byzantine period.

Besides its considerable distance from the water and other related geological factors, Bethsaida's identification with et-Tell has been questioned on the basis of a few ancient texts. Because John 12:21 mentions "Bethsaida of Galilee," a few have suggested that there were in fact two villages called Bethsaida, with John's Bethsaida situated west of the Jordan River, and Bethsaida-Julias, perched on the eastern bank, technically Roman Gaulanitis (hence the term Golan). Others have challenged the identification of Bethsaida on the grounds that Flavius Josephus describes Bethsaida-Julias as a polis, while features of a classical Greco-Roman polis have yet to be found at et-Tell.

The first set of challenges is addressed by citing other sources contemporary with the Gospels that also include areas north of the lake and east of the Jordan in the Galilee. Moreover, the existence of another site sharing the name – name that would not be all that uncommon in places where fishing or hunting took place – not really pose problems for the identification of Bethsaida with et-Tell. The latter argument, based on Josephus (Jos. *Bell.* 2.168; *Ant.* 18.28) and stating that et-Tell lacks the institutions of a classical polis, is also countered on the basis of Josephus, who clearly places Bethsaida-Julias on the eastern side of the Jordan River, where the river empties into the great lake (*Ant.* 18.28; *Bell.* 2.168) near a marshy plain (Jos. *Vita* 402). Thus, the more one insists that Josephus be taken at his word, the more et-Tell emerges as the only viable candidate for the site in the region. It seems more reasonable to reconsider Josephus' description of Bethsaida-Julias in light of the modest nature of Philip Herod's renovations and not with the model of a classical polis in mind.

Fig. 1: Iron Age four-chambered gate and paved entrance into the city (photo by author).

The problem of Bethsaida's distance from the lake was addressed by various geomorphic studies that indicated seismic activity along the Jordan rift that had dammed and released large volumes of water, creating an alluvial plain and pushing the water farther away from the tell. Other evidence that Bethsaida once looked out upon the lake include the remains of lake-dwelling organisms at the base of the tell and the wealth of fishing equipment recovered from one of its courtyard-style house structures, dubbed by excavators the Fisherman's House, including large basalt anchors weighing over 20 kg each.

Systematic excavations at et-Tell began in 1987, under the direction of chief archaeologist R. Arav and sponsored by the Golan Research Institute and the University of Haifa. In 1991, the Consortium of the Bethsaida Excavations Project was formed. Coordinated by the University of Nebraska at Omaha, Bethsaida Archaeology continues under the direction of Dr. Arav to the present day. Before excavations began, this roughly 80 m² site stood about 30 m above its surroundings, hiding the remains of roughly 13 centuries of human activity under its surface. In all, six levels and several phases of occupation have since been identified, sometime around the mid-10th century BCE, to its eventual abandonment in the late Roman period.

On the basis its impressive monumental architecture and location, excavators have identified Bethsaida's Iron Age II city as the capital of the ancient biblical kingdom of Geshur, which may have been called Zer (or Zed; Josh 19:35). According to the Bible, King David cemented a protective royal alliance with Talmai, the Geshurite king, by marrying his daughter, Maacah, from which union Absalom and Tamar were born (2 Sam 3:3; 13:1). Excavations have revealed two phases of an impressive city (Level 6) protected by extraordinarily thick stone walls measuring upwards of 8 m in width. A *bit hilāni*-style palace, 30 m × 15 m in size, was also discovered just inside the eastern wall (Area B). The city was approached by a paved road measuring roughly 4 m wide, which runs upward along the eastern edge of the city before making a sharp right-hand turn through a massive four-chambered gate. These chambers measure roughly 3 x 10 m in size and, on the basis of the material record, appear to have served different civil, military, and/or cultic functions. In 1997, this writer's excavation team uncovered Bethsaida's iconic bull's head stela near a stepped high place (*bamah*) just outside Chamber 4. Dedicated to a Mesopotamian moon god, its destruction into several large pieces witnesses to the Assyrian conquest of the latter phase of the Level 6 city by Tiglath Pileser III (bibl. Pul) in 732 BCE, after which the palace was structurally reconfigured.

A relative paucity of material remains following the Assyrian destruction attests to a significant disruption of the settlement in the region extending throughout the Persian period. At Bethsaida, only scant indications of human presence are in evidence for these centuries. The paucity of finds – Phoenician, but including also an Achaemenid "court-style" cylinder seal with apparent Persian and Phoenician motifs – plus the fact that the mound lies along natural east-west and north-south travel routes, suggests that the site may have served as some sort of imperial outpost within a Phoenician cultural orbit.

The Hellenistic-Roman period (Level 2) witnesses to a sudden significant increase in ceramic finds and Ptolemaic coinage, and the construction of a number of large courtyard houses, best represented at the northern end (Area C). Unique designations for some of the dwellings have derived from the types of small finds recovered in or near them. These include Fisherman's House, based on the large number of basalt anchors and fishing implements found inside; the Vintner's House, so named on the basis of pruning implements, as well as the discovery of several large wine amphorae, found in situ in a cellar directly beneath the structure; and the Clinic, based on the number of tiny ceramic vessels (*unguentaria*) and delicate, surgical-type instruments found inside. A large paved road was recently uncovered, which runs eastward from these houses, widening to what appears to be a large public area, perhaps the local marketplace.

In 1988, excavations at the southern apex of the mound revealed a rectangular structure measuring roughly 20 × 7 m in size, identified in the reports as a temple of the imperial cult. This structure, along with nearby later-phased Level 2 walls and terraces, would appear to support Josephus' testimony that Philip Herod had converted Bethsaida into a polis (Jos. *Bell.* 168; *Ant.* 18.28). The modest nature of these finds does not support a polis of classical proportions, but suggests that one should not overestimate the tetrarch's resources, or perhaps his regard for Rome. Although Josephus reports that Philip is buried at Bethsaida (*Ant.* 18.108), on the basis of the material record, it appears that Caesarea Philippi received far more attention during the course of its namesake's life.

Dr. C. Savage, assistant director of excavations from Drew University, has devoted a significant amount of research aimed at recovering the sociocultural make-up of Hellenistic-Roman Bethsaida. Although it is clear that Bethsaida remained largely within a Phoenician cultural orbit throughout much of the Persian and Hellenistic periods, C. Savage has noted a significant increase in Judean cultural and religious indicators in the ceramic, zoological, and numismatic records for the decades leading up to the turn of the Common Era and peaking in the

1st century CE. The coin record reflects changes in political power over time and evidences ongoing commercial ties with Tyre and Akko-Ptolemais well into the Roman period. During the Hasmonean and Herodian periods, Jewish coins are found at the site, but Roman imperial coins are also well represented until late in the 3rd century CE. Thus, C. Savage's evidence for a predominately Jewish Bethsaida in the 1st century CE is compelling.

Bethsaida's appearance in rabbinic sources indicates a continued Jewish presence prior to the beginning of the Byzantine period; however, the material record does not provide an accurate picture of the ethnic makeup of the settlement beyond the 1st century. At any rate, socioeconomic factors exacerbated by a series of significant regional earthquakes documented for the years 115 CE and 306 CE may have helped bring about Bethsaida's final surrender to the dust of time.

Based on the coin and ceramic records, a Mamluk phase of occupation at et-Tell is in evidence around the 12th century. During the latter part of the Ottoman period (17th–20th cents.), et-Tell provided a burial center for the el-Talawiyeh Bedouin tribe. Prior to the Six-Day War, et-Tell was part of modern Syria. As a result, mid-20th-century military entrenchments, including several concrete bunkers, scar the mound in several places, disrupting ancient architecture and contaminating the stratigraphy.

Despite regional tensions, regular excavations continue at the site under the direction of Dr. Arav, coordinated by the University of Nebraska at Omaha and joined by a global consortium of institutions. With the help of advanced technologies like Ground Penetrating Radar and Electrical Resistivity Tomography, many new discoveries are expected to be made.

Bibliography

Arav, R., "Et-Tell and el-Araj," *IEJ* 38/3, 1988, 87–88.
Arav, R.,"Et-Tell," *IEJ* 39/1–2, 1989, 99–100.
Arav, R., & R. Freund, eds. *Bethsaida: A City by the North Shore of the Sea of Galilee*, 4 vols., Kirksville, 1995–2009.
Bernett, M., & O. Keel, *Mond, Stier und Kult am Stadttor: Die Stele von Bethsaida (et-Tell)*, OBO 161, Göttingen, 1998.
Freund, R., "The Search for Bethsaida in Rabbinic Sources," in: R. Arav & R. Freund, eds., *Bethsaida: A City by the*

North Shore of the Sea of Galilee, vol. I, Kirksville, 1995, 267–311.

Kuhn, H.-W., *Betsaida/Bethsaida-Julias (et-Tell): Die ersten 25 Jahre der Ausgrabung (1987–2011)/The First Twenty-Five Years of Excavation (1987–2011)*, NTOA.SA, Göttingen 2015.

Roddy, N., "Antichrist at Bethsaida," in: R. Arav & R. Freund, eds., *Bethsaida: A City by the North Shore of the Sea of Galilee*, vol. III, Kirksville, 2004, 273–294.

Savage, C.E., *Biblical Bethsaida: An Archaeological Study of the First Century*, Lanham, 2011.

Schipper, F., & A. Rottloff, "Archäologische Forschungen auf et-Tell: Späthellenistisch-frühromische Befunde und die Frage nach der Identifizierung der Stätte mit Bethsaida/Iulias," *WJT* 5, 2004. 345–373.

Skupinska-Løvset, I., *The Temple Area of Bethsaida: Polish Excavations on et-Tell in the Years 1998–2000*, Lódz, 2006.

Strickert, F., *Philip's City: From Bethsaida to Julias*, Collegeville, 2011.

NICOLAE RODDY

Bibiana

The most ancient mention of Bibiana/Viviana's cult dates back to the late 5th century CE. It occurs in *The Book of the Popes* (→ *Liber pontificalis*), where we read that Pope Simplicius (468–483 CE) "dedicated [...] another basilica to the blessed martyr Bibiana within the city of Rome, near the Licinian palace, where her body rests" (*LP*, vol. I, 249). The author refers to the basilica, which still exists today, situated on the Esquiline Hill in Rome, in the area once occupied by the *Horti Liciniani*, the gardens of the *gens Licinia*. There is no evidence of the historical existence of Bibiana, but we possess a well-attested hagiographic tradition, starting from the *Passio S. Bibianae*, also known as the *Passio S. Pimenii/Pygmenii*. We know two redactions of it (6th–7th cents. CE), which are similar for the essential elements of the story:

1. *BHL* 1322 (with some variants: *BHL Novum Supplementum* 1322a e 1322c.);
2. *BHL* 1323. Somehow comparable to *BHL* 1322 is the *Passio S. Pimenii*, also called *S. Bibianae* (*BHL* 6849), edited by H. Delehaye (1936, 259–263).

The first redaction of the *Passio* (listed as *BHL* 1322) tells the events occurred to priest Pimenius, the tutor of the emperor → Julian the Apostate (361–363 CE), and to urban prefect Flavianus and his family: his wife Dafrosa; their two daughters, Demetria and Bibiana; and a pagan relative, Faustus. Flavianus is sent into exile and dies *ad aquas Taurinas* (perhaps the small town today called Montefiascone; see Fedini, 1627, 23). His wife, Dafrosa, converts Faustus, who dies after receiving baptism, in the presence of Julian. The emperor then orders his body to be left unburied, but Dafrosa inhumes it "in his house, close to the house of the Saints John and Paul." Then she comes back to Flavianus' house, where she dies (a natural death, five days later) and is buried. Julian sends for her daughters, but Demetria dies of fright, while Bibiana is turned over to a woman, named Rufina, who tries to persuade her to sacrifice to idols and to renounce her chastity. But the girl remains firm to her purpose and is condemned by the emperor to be beaten with scourges and laden with lead plummets. Four days later, she dies from injuries, and her body is left unburied by order of Julian *in forum tauri* (the Forum Boarium, in Rome;

Fig. 1: Saint Bibiana by Gian Lorenzo Bernini, Santa Bibiana, Rome.

see Nibby, 1820, 257). Two days after her death, a priest named John (a figure often present in Roman *Passiones* as a gravedigger of holy bodies) buries Bibiana near her mother and sister in her home, "near to the Licinian palace." After Julian's death, the house where the three women were inhumed was turned into a church, thanks to a noble kinsman, Olympina (or Olympia). She built a basilica, to which a monastery was attached.

The second redaction (*BHL* 1323) only tells Bibiana and her family's story, without mentioning Pimenius.

Perhaps another redaction existed, which is not listed in *BHL* though. It might have been merged into the popular *Vita di S. Bibiana, vergine e martire romana* (*Life of S. Bibiana, Roman Virgin and Martyr*) by Domenico Fedini (1575–1629). The *Life* was written in 1627, during the restoration of the Church of Saint Bibiana, on the road connecting the main pilgrimage stations of the Basilica of Saint Lawrence outside the Walls and Saint Mary Major. Domenico Fedini's *Life* is longer and more articulate in comparison to late antique *Passio*. Many pages of the book are devoted to describing Emperor Julian's life and character, but he however has no role, directly, in Bibiana's story, but is replaced by the cruel Apronianus. This probably was an attempt by the author, a learned man of the 16th–17th century, to correct the mistake of Julian's presence, who never was in Rome as an emperor. Moreover, in Domenico Fedini's *Life*, Dafrosa does not die a natural death like she does in the *Passio*, but is beheaded.

In its original form, the tradition about Bibiana is linked to a complex hagiographical cycle, with many interpolations; it contains a remarkable number of supposed Roman martyrs of the age of Julian (Franchi de' Cavalieri, 1915, 43–48; Delehaye, 1936, 124–143; Gaiffier, 1956, 27–38; Drijvers, 2007, 9–12; Lanéry, 2010, 204–215, 289). The cycle, named "of the Saints John, Paul and Pimenius" (Gaiffier, 1956, 27), also includes the *Acts of Saint Gallicanus* (Lanéry, 2010, 208–209). It was probably drafted in Rome, between the 6th and 7th centuries CE, with the aim of explaining the origins of some *tituli* (buildings of cult) that were under the direction of a permanently appointed presbyter. Among them was the *titulus* of Bibiana (Dufourcq, 1900, 123; Delehaye, 1936, 135).

We do not find Bibiana in the → *Martyrologium Hieronymianum* (*Martyrology of Jerome*), while she is remembered on Dec 2, the day of her burial, in the martyrology of Ado (9th cent. CE); her father's name is Faustus, not Flavianus, either by mistake or because Ado read another version of the *Passio*. The martyr is remembered on the same date in Caesar Baronius' *Martyrologium Romanum*.

A special mention should be made of the Basilica of Saint Bibiana, known since the 5th century CE. It is one of the few martyrial sanctuaries *intra moenia* in Rome (Krautheimer, 1937, 94; Claussen, 2002, 178–185; Schirò, 2012, 175–177). Archaeological surveys do not clarify whether it was raised on a martyrial grave placed in a cemetery area before the building of the Aurelian walls or was connected to the cult of relics put in a private household, as suggested by the *Passio* (Fiocchi Nicolai, 2008, 316–317; Spera, 2010, 274). However, we know that, at the end of the 7th century CE, in response to Lombard raids, Pope Leo II (682–683 CE) transferred the relics of a number of martyrs from their catacombs to churches inside the city walls. The relics of Simplicius, Faustinus, and Beatrix were removed from the catacombs in *Via Portuense* and carried to a church "near the Church of Saint Bibiana" (*LP*, vol. I, 360), thus increasing the devotional function of the sanctuarial complex (Schirò, 2012, 175–176). The basilica was mentioned in the *Itinerarium* of Einsiedeln (Valentini & Zucchetti, 1942, 189, 194) between the end of 8th century and the beginning of 9th century CE; in the same period Pope Leo III (795–816 CE) gave donations to the annexed monastery (*LP*, vol. II, 24), and later, in 1224, Pope Honorius III (1216–1227) rebuilt the church and "solemnly consecrated" it (Fedini, 1627, 59, 77). In the 17th century, Gian Lorenzo Bernini's reconstruction of the church, commissioned by Pope Urban VIII (1623–1644), gave the building its present appearance. During the church restoration, three bodies were found and identified as the bodies of the mother, Dafrosa, and her two daughters, Demetria and Bibiana. The bodies were laid in an ancient alabaster urn of good quality found in the same place, that still today, under the major altar, serves as their sarcophagus. Bibiana's head, instead, was already kept in Saint Mary Major; it was usually exposed on her feast day and during the Easter cycle (Fedini, 1627, 19).

Domenico Fedini (1575–1629), the author of the *Life of Saint Bibiana*, was just a canon of Saint Mary Major. In his hagiographical work, he tells the story of the Basilica of Saint Bibiana, from its foundation, which, on the basis of the *Passio*, he attributes to Olympina, up to the restoration ordered by Urban VIII, who was a devotee of the saint. He also writes that the pope had commissioned a cycle of frescoes on the life and martyrdom of Bibiana and the members of her family (Fedini, 1627, 76–77). The cycle was indeed realized, between 1624 and 1626, by painters Pietro da Cortona (1596–1669) and Agostino Ciampelli (1565–1630).

Even today, the flogging column is preserved in the Basilica of Saint Bibiana. In the past pilgrims and devotees used to scratch it in order to obtain a powder, which was dissolved in water for the treatment of a disease. Even "Saint Bibiana 's grass" (*Eupatorium cannabinum*), so commonly called because it was widespread in the garden beside the church, was widely used in the pharmacopoeia, for it was believed to heal numerous diseases.

Bibiana is portrayed as a young girl with the palm of martyrdom; she is often bound to a column; another common element is a bunch of grass in her hand or at her feet.

Bibliography

Amore, A., *I martiri di Roma*, Rome, 1975.

BHL 1322, text: CatBrux, vol. I/1, Brussels, 1886, 161–164; *BiblCas*, vol. III: *Florilegium*, Montecassino, 1887, 191–193.

BHL 1323, text: Mombritius, B., *Sanctuarium*, Milan, 1477[?], vol. I, 274.

Claussen, C.P., *Die Kirchen der Stadt Rom im Mittelalter 1050–1300*, vol. I: *A-F*, Stuttgart, 2002, 178–185.

Delehaye, H., *Étude sur le légendier romain: Les saints de novembre et de décembre*, Brussels, 1936, 124–143, 259–263.

Donckel, E., "Studien über den Kultus der hl. Bibiana," *RQ* 43/1–2, 1935, 23–33.

Donckel, E., "Der Kultus der hl. Bibiana in Rom," in: *RAC*, vol. XIV/1–2, Stuttgart, 1937, 125–135.

Drijvers, J.W., "Julian the Apostate and the City of Rome: Pagan-Christian Polemics in the Syriac Julian Romance," in: W.J. van Bekkum, J.W. Drijvers & A.C. Klugkist, eds., *Syriac Polemics: Studies in Honour of Gerrit Jan Reinink*, Louvain, 2007, 1–20.

Dufourcq, A., *Étude sur les Gesta Martyrum romains*, vol. I, Paris, 1900.

Fedini, D., *La vita di S. Bibiana vergine e martire romana*, Rome, 1627.

Fiocchi Nicolai, V., "Sviluppi funzionali e trasformazioni monumentali dei santuari martiriali a Roma nella tarda antichità e nell'alto medioevo," in: S. Boesch Gajano & F. Scorza Barcellona, eds., *Lo spazio del santuario: Un osservatorio per la storia di Roma e del Lazio*, Rome, 2008, 313–334.

Franchi de' Cavalieri, P., "Del testo della *Passio SS. Iohannis et Pauli*," in: P. Franchi de' Cavalieri, *Note agiografiche*, vol. V, Rome, 1915, 41–62.

Gaiffier, B. de, "'Sub Iuliano Apostata' dans le martyrologe romain," *AnBoll* 74, 1956/1, 5–49.

Krautheimer, R., *Corpus Basilicarum Christanarum Romae: Le basiliche paleocristiane di Roma (sec IV–IX)*, vol. I, Vatican City, 1937.

Lanéry, C., "Hagiographie d'Italie (300–550): I. Les passions latines composée en Italie," in: G. Philippart, ed., *Hagiographies: Histoire internationale de la littérature hagiographique latine et vernaculaire en Occident des origines à 1550*, vol. V, Turnhout, 2010, 15–369.

Leyser, C., "'A Church in the House of the Saints': Property and Power in the Passion of John and Paul," in: K. Cooper & J. Hillner, eds., *Religion, Dynasty, and Patronage in Early Christian Rome, 300–900*, Cambridge UK, 2007, 140–162.

Nibby, A., *Roma antica di Famiano Nardini riscontrata ed accresciuta delle ultime scoperte, con note ed osservazioni critico antiquarie*, vol. IV, Rome, 1820.

Schirò, G., "Santa Bibiana," in: S. Boesch Gajano, T. Caliò, F. Scorza Barcellona & L. Spera, eds., *Santuari d'Italia: Roma*, Rome, 2012, 175–178.

Spera, L., "Le forme del culto e della devozione negli spazi intramuranei," in: A. Coscarella & P. De Santis, eds., *Martiri, Santi, Patroni: Per una archeologia della devozione: Atti del X congresso nazionale di archeologia cristiana*, Arcavacata di Rende, 2012, 265–298.

Valentini, R., & G. Zucchetti, eds., *CTCR*, vol. II, Rome, 1942.

VINCENZA MILAZZO